Glencoe
World Geography

Features and Benefits

Dynamic Instructional Strategies

. . . present a clear and comprehensive coverage of geography.
- Engaging section introductions include Consider What You Know, Reading Strategy, Read to Find Out, and A Geographic View from National Geographic.
- Viewpoint Case Studies, by the National Geographic Society, provide opportunities for students to discuss the environmental challenges facing the world's regions.
- Summary and Study Guide features offer a concise summary of important chapter topics and can be used to preview, review, or summarize chapter content.

A Strong Reading Strand

. . . encourages active reading and learning for students of all reading levels.
- Geography Skills for Life questions ask students to interpret a visual.
- World Culture features highlight interesting information to engage students.
- Reading Checks help students check their reading comprehension.

Differentiated Instruction

. . . makes *Glencoe World Geography* accessible to students of all learning levels.
- Differentiated Instruction activities and strategies are designed for students of differing abilities and learning challenges.
- Reading for Information teaches students how to approach the text to retain course information and get the most value out of the Student Edition.

Standardized Test Preparation

. . . gives students the opportunity to practice for state and national exams.
- Chapter assessments and Standardized Test Practice Workbook provide a variety of standardized test practice, including Multiple Choice, Open-ended Short Response, and Open-ended Extended Response.
- Test-Taking Tip helps students learn how to successfully approach test questions.

A Variety of Geography Activities and Features

. . . are essential for student success and get students excited about geography.
- Geography Handbook shows students how to use essential tools, such as globes, maps, and graphs.
- Geography and History shows students how geography has affected historical events in various regions of the world.
- Geography Lab Activities help students apply what they have learned as they complete a range of classroom-tested experiments.

Teacher Resources

. . . provide convenient strategies to help new and experienced teachers.
- The Planning Guide in each unit provides background information to help you prepare for each unit.
- Fast File™ unit resources contain important reproducible masters.
- Foldables help students organize and process key concepts as they read.

Technology

. . . provides time-saving software products to help creatively engage students and reduce prep time.
- National Geographic Video Programs
- Glencoe Skillbuilder Interactive Workbook, Level 2
- NGS Online provides lesson plans, atlas updates, cartographic activities with interactive maps, an online map store, and links to boundless subjects of maps and geography.
- Geography Online, **www.geography.glencoe.com**, provides resources and activities designed for your book.

Improving Active Reading and Study Skills

Dinah Zike's

FOLDABLES™

Foldables are easy-to-make, three-dimensional, interactive graphic organizers that students create out of simple sheets of paper. The Teacher Classroom Resources includes *Dinah Zike's High School World Geography Reading and Study Skills.* This booklet provides you with step-by-step instructions for using Foldables in your classroom. Each Foldable is designed to be used as a study guide for the main ideas and key points presented in a chapter. Foldables can also be used for a more in-depth investigation of a concept, idea, opinion, event, or a person or place studied in a chapter. These unique hands-on tools for studying and reviewing were created exclusively for Glencoe by education specialist Dinah Zike.

Why Use Foldables in Social Studies?

Because they:

- organize, display, and arrange information, making it easier for students to grasp social studies concepts, theories, facts, opinions, questions, research, and ideas.

- are student-made study guides that are compiled as students listen for main ideas, read key points, or conduct research.

- provide a multitude of creative formats in which students can present projects, research, interviews, and inquiry-based reports.

- replace teacher-generated writing or photocopied sheets with student-generated print.

- incorporate the use of such skills as comparing and contrasting, recognizing cause and effect, and finding similarities and differences.

- continue to "immerse" students in previously learned vocabulary, concepts, information, generalizations, ideas, and theories, providing them with a strong foundation that they can build upon with new observations, concepts, and knowledge.

- can be used by students or teachers to easily communicate data through graphs, tables, charts, models, and diagrams, including Venn diagrams.

- allow students to make their own journals for recording observations, research information, primary and secondary source data, surveys, and so on.

- can be used as alternative assessment tools by teachers to evaluate student progress or by students to evaluate their own progress.

- integrate language arts, the sciences, and mathematics into the study of social studies.

- provide a sense of student ownership or investiture in the social studies curriculum.

Teacher Wraparound Edition

Glencoe

World Geography

Senior Author

Richard G. Boehm, Ph.D.

NATIONAL GEOGRAPHIC

McGraw Hill **Glencoe**

New York, New York   Columbus, Ohio   Chicago, Illinois   Peoria, Illinois   Woodland Hills, California

About the Authors

Senior Author
RICHARD G. BOEHM

Richard G. Boehm, Ph.D., was one of seven authors of *Geography for Life*, national standards in geography, prepared under Goals 2000: Educate America Act. He was also one of the authors of the *Guidelines for Geographic Education*, in which the five themes of geography were first articulated. In 1990, Dr. Boehm was designated "Distinguished Geography Educator" by the National Geographic Society. In 1991 he received the George J. Miller award from the National Council for Geographic Education (NCGE) for distinguished service to geographic education. He was President of the NCGE and has twice won the *Journal of Geography* award for best article. He has received the NCGE's "Distinguished Teaching Achievement" award and presently holds the Jesse H. Jones Distinguished Chair in Geographic Education at Southwest Texas State University in San Marcos, Texas.

NATIONAL GEOGRAPHIC SOCIETY

The National Geographic Society, founded in 1888 for the increase and diffusion of geographic knowledge, is the world's largest nonprofit scientific and educational organization. Since its earliest days, the Society has used sophisticated communication technologies, from color photography to holography, to convey geographic knowledge to a worldwide membership. The School Publishing Division supports the Society's mission by developing innovative educational programs—ranging from traditional print materials to multimedia programs including CD-ROMs, videos, and software.

Contributing Writer

Bob Haddad, ethnomusicologist, developed the World Music features in the Student and Teacher Wraparound editions of *Glencoe World Geography*. He also chose the music selections for Glencoe's *World Music: A Cultural Legacy* program and authored the accompanying teacher guide. Mr. Haddad is founder of Music of the World and president of Owl's Head Music.

Glencoe

The McGraw·Hill Companies

Send all inquiries to:
Glencoe/McGraw-Hill
8787 Orion Place
Columbus, Ohio 43240-4027

ISBN 0-07-860699-3 (Student Edition)   ISBN 0-07-860700-0 (Teacher Wraparound Edition)

Printed in the United States of America

1 2 3 4 5 6 7 8   071/043   09 08 07 06 05 04

Consultants

General Content Consultant
KAY E. WELLER, Ph.D.
Associate Professor of Geography
University of Northern Iowa
Cedar Falls, Iowa

Geography Consultant
SARI J. BENNETT, Ph.D.
Director of Geographic Education
University of Maryland, Baltimore County
Baltimore, Maryland

Cultural Consultant
JOSEPH P. STOLTMAN, Ph.D.
Professor of Geography
Western Michigan University
Kalamazoo, Michigan

Religion Consultants
CHARLES H. LONG, Ph.D.
Professor of Religion (Retired)
University of California
Santa Barbara, California

BLUMA ZUCKERBROT-FINKELSTEIN
Instructor, University of Memphis
Memphis, Tennessee

SHABBIR MANSURI
Founding Director

SUSAN L. DOUGLASS
Affiliated Scholar
Council on Islamic Education
Fountain Valley, California

Introduction to Geography
BURRELL E. MONTZ, Ph.D.
Professor of Geography and Environmental
   Studies
Binghamton University
Binghamton, New York

United States and Canada
JOSEPH D. ENEDY, Ph.D.
Professor of Geography
James Madison University
Harrisonburg, Virginia

Latin America
CYRUS B. DAWSEY, Ph.D.
Professor of Geography
Auburn University
Auburn, Alabama

Europe
FIONA M. DAVIDSON, Ph.D.
Associate Professor of Geography
University of Arkansas
Fayetteville, Arkansas

DOUGLAS C. WILMS, Ph.D.
Professor Emeritus of Geography
East Carolina University
Greenville, North Carolina

Russia
GARY J. HAUSLADEN, Ph.D.
Professor of Geography
University of Nevada
Reno, Nevada

OLGA MEDVEDKOV, Ph.D.
Professor of Geography
Wittenberg University
Springfield, Ohio

**North Africa, Southwest Asia, and
Central Asia**
NORMAN BETTIS, Ph.D.
Professor Emeritus of Education
Illinois State University
Normal, Illinois

MOUNIR A. FARAH, Ph.D.
Associate Director of Middle Eastern
   Studies
University of Arkansas
Fayetteville, Arkansas

JOSEPH HOBBS, Ph.D.
Professor of Geography
University of Missouri
Columbia, Missouri

Africa South of the Sahara
EZEKIAL KALIPENI, Ph.D.
Associate Professor of Geography
University of Illinois
Urbana, Illinois

GARTH A. MYERS, Ph.D.
Assistant Professor of African & African-
   American Studies, and Geography
University of Kansas
Lawrence, Kansas

South Asia
WILLIAM R. STRONG, Ph.D.
Professor of Geography
University of North Alabama
Florence, Alabama

East Asia
KENJI K. OSHIRO, Ph.D.
Professor of Urban Affairs and Geography
Wright State University
Dayton, Ohio

SUSAN M. WALCOTT, Ph.D.
Associate Professor of Anthropology and
   Geography
Georgia State University
Atlanta, Georgia

Southeast Asia
JON D. GOSS, Ph.D.
Professor of Geography
University of Hawaii
Honolulu, Hawaii

RALPH LENZ, Ph.D.
Professor of Geography
Wittenberg University
Springfield, Ohio

Australia, Oceania, and Antarctica
ALYSON L. GREINER, Ph.D.
Associate Professor of Geography
Oklahoma State University
Stillwater, Oklahoma

LAURIE MOLINA, Ph.D.
Program Director, Geography Education
   and Technology
Florida State University
Tallahassee, Florida

Teacher Reviewers

ROBERT M. ASHLEY
Red Bud High School
Red Bud, Illinois

NATE COLLINS
Buffalo Gap High School
Swoope, Virginia

PAUL T. GRAY, JR.
Russellville High School
Russellville, Arkansas

DANIEL J. LANGEN
Oak Hills High School
Cincinnati, Ohio

DONNA MERLAU
Onondaga Central Junior-Senior
   High School
Nedrow, New York

KAY MORGAN
Central High School
Carrollton, Georgia

BETTY SCOOPMIRE
J.H. High School
Greenville, North Carolina

CHERIE VELA
ABC Secondary School
Cerritos, California

FRED WALK
Normal Community High School
Normal, Illinois

BARBARA S. WILLIAMS
Buena High School
Sierra Vista, Arizona

AMY ZORN
Anna High School
Anna, Ohio

Contents

NATIONAL GEOGRAPHIC

REFERENCE ATLAS

NATIONAL GEOGRAPHIC

GEOGRAPHY SKILLS HANDBOOK 1

Unit 1

The World 16

Contents

Contents

Unit 4

Unit 5

Contents

Contents

Contents

Features

GLOBAL CONNECTION

GEOGRAPHY AND HISTORY

Viewpoint

CASE STUDY on the Environment

SKILLBUILDER

MAP & GRAPH SKILLBUILDER

CRITICAL THINKING SKILLBUILDER

TECHNOLOGY SKILLBUILDER

STUDY & WRITING SKILLBUILDER

Geography Lab Activities

WORLD CULTURE

Maps

Reference Atlas

Geography Skills Handbook

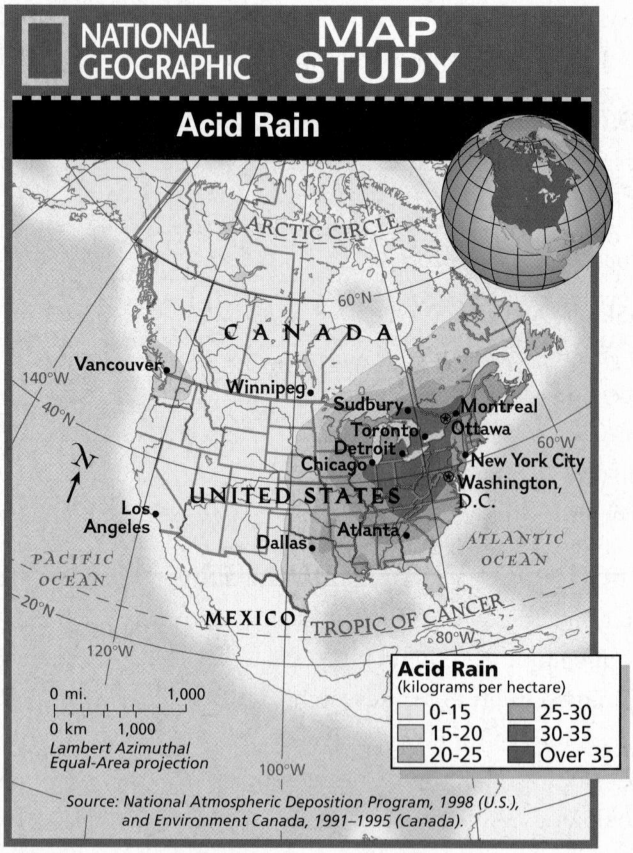

NATIONAL GEOGRAPHIC
MAP STUDY
Acid Rain
ARCTIC CIRCLE
60°N
CANADA
Vancouver
Winnipeg
Sudbury
Montreal
Ottawa
Toronto
Detroit
Chicago
New York City
Washington, D.C.
UNITED STATES
Los Angeles
Atlanta
Dallas
140°W
40°N
60°W
PACIFIC OCEAN
ATLANTIC OCEAN
20°N
MEXICO
TROPIC OF CANCER
80°W
120°W
100°W
0 mi. 1,000
0 km 1,000
Lambert Azimuthal Equal-Area projection
Acid Rain
(kilograms per hectare)
0-15
15-20
20-25
25-30
30-35
Over 35
Source: National Atmospheric Deposition Program, 1998 (U.S.), and Environment Canada, 1991–1995 (Canada).

UNIT 1

The World

UNIT 2
The United States and Canada

UNIT 3
Latin America

UNIT 4
Europe

UNIT 5
Russia

Graphs, Charts and Diagrams

NATIONAL GEOGRAPHIC GRAPH STUDY

World Trade

■ $billion GDP   ■ $billion Trade

World GDP

World Trade

Gross domestic product (GDP) is the value of goods and services produced within a country in a year.

Source: World Trade Organization

NATIONAL GEOGRAPHIC DIAGRAM STUDY

Inside the Earth

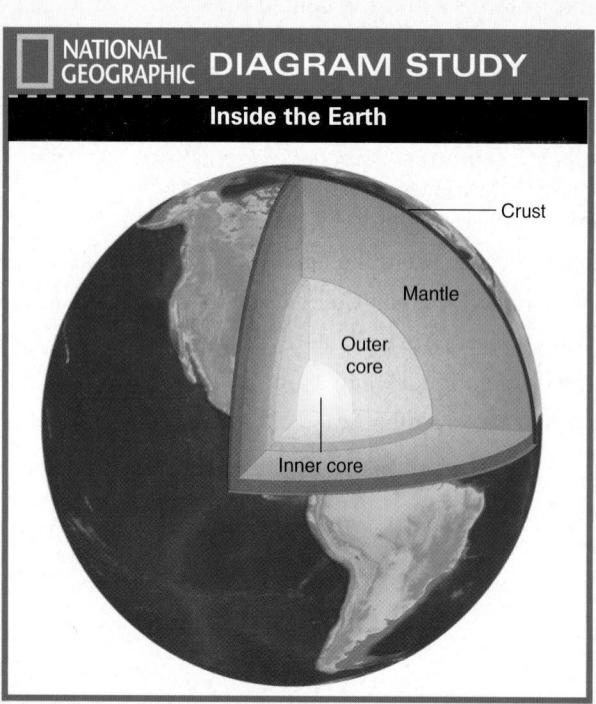

Crust

Mantle

Outer core

Inner core

NATIONAL GEOGRAPHIC CHART STUDY

Jobs in Geography

Geography Field	Description	Applications/Careers
Physical Geographer	Studies Earth's features and the geographic forces shaping them	Forecasting weather, tracing causes and effects of pollution, conserving wilderness areas
Human Geographer	Analyzes human aspects of culture—population, language, ethnicity, religion, government	Developing cultural policies for international organizations, such as the United Nations
Economic Geographer	Examines human economic activities and their relationship to the environment	Urban planning, focusing on the location of industries or transportation routes
Regional Geographer	Studies geographic features of a particular place or region	Assisting government and business in making decisions related to a region
Environmental Specialist	Focuses on all aspects of the environment	Advising government and business on ways of protecting the environment
Geographic Educator	Teaches about geography	Teaching geography at all educational levels; serving as consultant to business and government

Primary Sources

NG = National Geographic

Project CRISS

How Can I Teach My Students How to Learn Social Studies?

by Carol M. Santa, Ph.D

We all know that teaching social studies involves far more than teaching just course content. We understand that students need to become engaged, confident learners. Achieving that goal means helping them to understand, organize, and retain information.

Teaching Both Content and Skills

In other words, we want our students to have the skills and confidence to be life-long learners. With its rich content, social studies offer an ideal arena for teaching both content and skills.

✔ **A Dual Responsibility** Let's take a moment to consider why the dual responsibility of teaching both content and skills is so important. Think back to your own middle and high school years. What do you remember about the content

you learned? If I recall my experiences, I find I remember remarkably little content. What did I learn in biology or history? What did my textbooks look like? As the years go by, I don't even remember the names of most of my teachers.

✔ **An Inspiring Teacher** Yet I have vivid memories of my eighth-grade social studies teacher, who came out of retirement to fill in for a history teacher who left on maternity leave. I remember how fascinated I became with ancient history; I recall giving oral reports and how she helped me become comfortable speaking before a group. In fact, I remember more from her class than any other I took during high school.

✔ **Teach How to Learn** More important, I now understand that she taught me how to learn to learn. She showed me how to underline, how to organize information using different note-taking formats, and how to write coherent

answers on essay tests. She taught me the need to test myself on what I knew. And during that vulnerable, adolescent year, I went from being a mediocre student to being an excellent one.

This inspirational teacher did something else for me. At some point during that eighth-grade year, I decided to become a teacher. Later I realized that she had launched me on my professional mission—to spread her wisdom to others. Eventually this led to Project CRISS.

What is CRISS?

CRISS stands for **CR**eating **I**ndependence through **S**tudent-owned **S**trategies. It is a staff development program that I created in collaboration with middle and high school teachers in Kalispell, Montana.

✔ **Origin of CRISS** CRISS had its start 20 years ago in a lunchtime conversation in a teacher's lounge. One of the social studies teachers said, "My students aren't doing a good job of answering chapter questions. In fact, I don't think they even read my assignments. My reading assignments are becoming a waste of time!" His words struck a chord. "My students don't have a clue about how to study, and they don't write very well either," another teacher lamented.

✔ **Evolving Strategies** Supported by a state grant, we started working together to find practical ways to help students read, write, and learn content. We met in teams, read professional literature, and designed studies to test classroom strategies. From these efforts, we evolved a project to help students become better readers, writers, and

Tom & DeeAnn McCarthy/CORBIS STOCK MARKET

learners. Once the project took shape, we shared our discoveries with other teachers by offering a two- or three-day CRISS workshop to schools and districts in the state.

✔ **Constant Growth** Over the last two decades, Project CRISS has spread from teacher to teacher across this country, into Canada, and to several European countries. The project seems to sell itself. Teachers who use CRISS principles and strategies find that their students attain a deeper understanding of course content and become better readers, writers, and learners at the same time. In fact, data from numerous quantitative studies shows that using CRISS strategies improves student learning. (For the most recent data and for information on CRISS workshops, see www.projectcriss.com.)

CRISS Strategies in the Teacher Edition

When the editors of Glencoe/McGraw-Hill asked me and my colleagues to help them integrate CRISS strategies into their social studies texts, we welcomed the opportunity. In this teacher wraparound edition, we offer many references to CRISS strategies. We have packed the pages with strategies that help students gain a deeper understanding of specific content.

CRISS Training

We have one word of caution, however: the integration of CRISS strategies within this teacher wraparound edition does not take the place of a Project CRISS workshop, which provides an in-depth knowledge of CRISS. So, if you haven't yet participated in a CRISS workshop, we encourage you to do so. During a workshop, CRISS trainers take you step-by-step through the philosophy and instructional strategies. Participants are actively involved in all aspects of the program—practicing, adapting, and applying strategies to meet teaching needs.

Long-lasting change occurs when teachers and administrators work together to share, extend ideas, and problem solve. The most effective implementations occur when the initial workshop is supported by follow-up sessions, including a specific follow-up day. At this session, teachers bring examples of strategies they have used since the initial training. Part of this time may be spent in review and in learning new strategies. The rest of the time is for sharing applications. Additional on-going support can occur in teacher planning periods.

In any case, for those of you unfamiliar with Project CRISS, let's begin with a little background knowledge. In this way you will have some context for the various activities suggested throughout the teacher wraparound edition.

The CRISS Philosophy

The first thing to know is that Project CRISS is more than a collection of learning strategies. Its underlying power rests not on the individual strategies but on the teaching philosophy behind them. This philosophy integrates work from cognitive psychology, social learning theory, and neurological research about how the brain learns. It includes these overlapping principles:

✔ background knowledge and purposeful reading
✔ author's craft
✔ active involvement
✔ discussion
✔ organization
✔ writing
✔ teacher modeling

Let's look at each of these principles in more detail, along with examples of instructional strategies that illustrate them.

Background knowledge and purposeful reading are powerful determinants of reading comprehension.

Teachers involved in Project CRISS often talk about the importance of background knowledge. Readers are

(Continued on next page)

Using CRISS to Set a Purpose

Advice from Malla S. Kolhoff
Palm Harbor University High School
International Baccalaureate Program
Palm Harbor, Florida

As educators, it is our responsibility to set a purpose for historical reading. Students often must struggle to connect history with their own lives. To compare and contrast, establish cause and effect, and sequence events in chronological order presents a challenge for even the best reader. CRISS strategies allow students to move beyond words to the real significance for their society. With CRISS, my students are able to become engaged in the learning process through:

a. background knowledge
b. active reading, listening, and learning
c. discussion

d. metacognition
e. writing
f. organization
g. understanding

I have found that these strategies help my students attain a higher level of historical thinking and understanding.

Project CRISS

far more likely to learn new information when they have some previous knowledge and have a purpose in mind before they read or listen.

✔ **More Than Simply Reading** We warn students not to simply begin reading. We ask them, *"What might you already know about the topic? What questions do you have about the topic?"* We also remind them to preview the assignment and think about their goals for reading. We often have to be very explicit about the goals. For example, we might tell students, *"After reading this selection, you should be able to . . . ,"* or, *"After viewing the video, you should be able to identify. . . ."*

✔ **KWLH** In the teaching strategies included for each chapter in this book, we offer ideas for helping students tap into their background knowledge. For example, we suggest that students preview their reading assignment and consider what they already know about a topic. Or, we might develop a whole class **KWLH** chart (**K**now, **W**ant to learn, **L**earned, **H**ow to learn more), where students work on this task together. They can generate questions about what they want to learn, and then, after completing the assignment, they can list the new information they have learned and how they can learn more.

K	W	L	H
What I **Know**	What I **Want** to Find Out	What I **Learned**	**How** I Can Learn More

✔ **Reading Goals** We also suggest ways to make sure your students have clear goals for their reading. Each section opener lists reading strategies and

main ideas that outline reading goals. Most students will skip over this material and simply start reading. Teachers need to help students understand that the reading goals are important tools for understanding. We tell students, *"Don't ignore your purposes for reading. Take time to think about them before delving into your reading."* Project CRISS also provides hints about how to get students to use these purpose statements to evaluate whether they have understood their reading.

Good readers have an intuitive understanding of the author's craft.

When students know how authors craft their writing, they can more readily understand and remember what they read.

✔ **Pay Attention** Good readers and writers know that paying attention to how text is organized—its headings and paragraphs, for example—makes it easier to comprehend its content. Good readers will analyze the author's style of presentation as they read. They might ask themselves, *"What is this author doing to help me learn key concepts? How does the writer lead me from one idea to the next?"* When students become aware of what the author is doing to impart content, they have a clearer idea of what the author is saying.

✔ **The Walk Through** In the sample lesson on pages T26–T27, we offer advice about "walking through" the text to discover the author's style of presentation. Our suggestions go beyond examining the surface structure (headings, bold print, color coding of topical headings, italicized words) to analyzing how the author elaborates on key topics.

Effective learners are actively involved when they listen and read.
We learn best when we act on the information presented. We can do this by using a variety of organizing activities that require us to write, talk, and transform the information we are absorbing. None of us learns much from reading alone—it's far too passive.

CRISS strategies encourage active engagement in learning. We might ask students to read a section and describe what they are learning to a partner, or we might be more elaborate and have students develop concept maps or write summaries.

Students need many opportunities to talk with one another about what they are learning.
Discussion is critical to learning. The discussions we advocate are different from those in which the teacher remains the authority figure, with students simply reciting answers to

(Continued on next page)

Jose L. Pelaez/CORBIS STOCK MARKET

questions. If discussion becomes mere recitation and there is little interaction among students, little learning occurs. Thus we focus on how to get students to lead their own discussions about a topic. We want them to understand that it is their discussing, their oral grappling with meaning—not ours—that leads to deeper understanding.

Competent readers know several ways to organize information for learning.

Learning depends on organization. We show students different ways to organize information. They can take notes, underline selectively, develop concept maps, and summarize ideas in charts. Once we have taught students these techniques, we tell them, *"You have to do more than just read this assignment. How are you going to organize the information from this assignment? You have to change it, to transform it so that it becomes your own."*

For each chapter of this text, we offer ideas for assisting students in organizing information. Once students have learned a variety of organizing systems, we suggest ways to help them apply these structures independently.

Students deserve opportunities to write about what they are learning.

Writing is an integral part of the CRISS project. Writing lets us figure out what we know and what we still need to know. We cannot write about something we do not understand. While we teach students how to write expository papers and essay exams, we also encourage students to write more informally by questioning, speculating, and writing explanations in learning logs. We make sure that students are writing continually about what they are learning.

For each chapter of this text, we offer ideas for assisting students in organizing information. Once students have learned a variety of organizing systems, we suggest ways to help them apply these structures independently.

Teaching involves explanation and modeling.

Our final principle has to do with our own teaching. Students learn to think strategically when we use these processes as part of our instruction. Our demonstrations are especially critical for struggling readers. Most have never been taught how to learn.

We have to show them how.

✔ **Take Center Stage** When you introduce a new strategy, you should take the center stage: showing, telling, modeling, demonstrating, and explaining not only the content but the process of active reading. As students learn, gradually release responsibility to them. Strategy instruction involves two overlapping steps. First we explain what the strategy is and why students should use it. If students do not know why they are performing an activity, they will rarely use the activity on their own. Next, we demonstrate and talk about procedures for carrying out the strategy. We discuss, demonstrate, and think aloud while modeling. Then, students practice under our guidance and feedback.

✔ **A Systematic Approach** Project CRISS is a valuable basis for instruction. It provides a systematic approach for using what we now know about teaching and learning. The following chart lists questions we need to continually ask ourselves while we are teaching. Use this chart to monitor your efforts to incorporate CRISS principles into your teaching.

CRISS Principles	The CRISS Philosophy	Yes	No	Somewhat
Background knowledge:	Did I assist students in thinking about what they already knew about the topic before beginning the unit? Did I develop necessary concepts before students read?			
Purpose setting:	Did my students have a clear purpose about what they were going to learn before beginning the lesson?			
Author's craft:	Can my students use the author's style of presentation to facilitate their understanding?			
Active involvement:	Were my students engaged in the topic? Did I help students become actively involved in their learning?			
Discussion:	Did my students have opportunities to talk about what they were learning?			
Organization:	Did my students organize information in a variety of ways?			
Writing:	Did my students write about what they were learning?			
Teacher modeling:	Did I do enough teacher modeling of learning strategies so that students could begin doing them on their own?			

Project CRISS

How Do I Use Project CRISS to Teach Glencoe World Geography?

When students know how authors structure their writing, they can better understand and remember what they read. For the first several chapters of this book, show students how to analyze the author's craft by "walking through" the chapter. Then show students how to use the author's organization to develop two-column notes.

To demonstrate these strategies, make transparencies of the first several pages of Chapter 1, *How Geographers Look at the World.* Then organize students into small groups to complete the following activities.

Chapter Introduction:

Place a transparency of pages 18–19 on the overhead and begin modeling:

Tell students: *"Before reading a text, I take time to figure out how the author has presented the information. If I understand the author's craft, I can do a better job of reading and learning. The authors of this book have a consistent organization plan for presenting information. Let's discover what they do."*
Ask students to turn to pages 4–5.
Then say: *"In your small groups, read through these two pages and discuss the following questions:*
✔ *What type of information has the author included?*
✔ *How might you use this information* (Photograph, Geography Online, Guide to Reading,

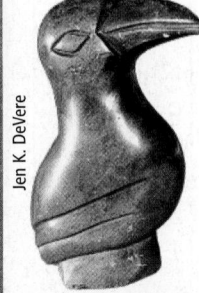

Jen K. DeVere

A Geographic View) *to understand the content of this chapter?*
✔ *How might you use the reference to Geography Online to expand your understanding of the chapter content?"* Ask one or more students to explore what is available online for this chapter and report to the class on ways that this information could be used.

SECTION 1: Exploring Geography

Guide to Reading

Direct students to page 19. *"Notice how this page is organized. It begins with a Guide to Reading that includes: Consider What You Know, Read to Find Out, Terms to Know and Places to Locate. Let's take a moment and talk about how these features might help you."*

Consider What You Know:

"What is the author's purpose in asking these questions?" (To help us think about what we already know. Helps us consider how geography might influence our own lives.)

Read to Find Out:

"Why has the author included these questions?" (To help readers set goals or purposes for reading the chapter.) *"Keep these questions in mind as you read. After reading, see if you can answer them. The author has provided us with a way to check our comprehension."*

Terms to Know:

"Now look at the list of key terms (state, nation, etc.) and skim the first several pages of the chapter. What do you notice about how the key terms are sequenced

and highlighted in this chapter?" (The key terms are highlighted in blue and presented in the same order in the chapter as listed here.)

Places to Locate:

"Why has the author listed these places before you read about them?" (To help us think about what we already know.)

A Geographic View

Ask students to read this excerpt. *"Why has the author included this selection at the beginning of each section?"* (To provide background knowledge, generating interest in reading the chapter.)

Walking through the Narrative

As you talk aloud note features on chapter transparencies of pages 19–22. *"Now let's see how the authors have helped us figure out the main topics covered in this chapter. Notice the bold print heading. The main topics are printed in larger red print and the subtopics are printed in smaller green print. Vocabulary words are printed in smaller blue type. This organization and color coding should help me figure out what is important.*

At the end of each section, I notice an Assessment. I should read through these questions before I begin reading. This way, I will know what I am supposed to get out of this section.

As I continue my walk-through of the chapter, I also notice the Diagram Studies. I realize these visuals contain important information for understanding the content. I should never just skip over them."

Reading the Chapter

Assign students to read silently pages 19–22, paying close attention to the bold print topics and vocabulary words.

Main Idea–Detail Notes

Ask students to divide their notebook paper into two columns. Explain that you will be showing them how to use the author's craft to take notes over the first section of this chapter. They will record key points in the left-hand column and details explaining the key points in the right-hand column. Main points can be questions or key words. Students then use their notes as a study guide. They cover the information on the right and use the key words or question to quiz themselves.

Teacher Modeling

Demonstrate how to use the author's clues (headings, bold print vocabulary) to develop main idea-detail notes. On a blank transparency develop two-column notes over the first section of the chapter while students take notes at their desks. Model how to include main topics and vocabulary terms essential to understanding the content in the left column. On the right record details that elaborate on the main points. Talk about being brief and using your own words. Explain why making the author's message your own insures better comprehension and retention.

✔ Continue modeling notes over the rest of this section. Then ask students to work in pairs or small groups to develop two-column notes over the rest of the chapter. Ask students to share their notes in a whole class discussion.

✔ Demonstrate how to use the notes to test themselves. Show students how you cover the right-hand column with a sheet of paper and recite what you can remember. Talk about why self-testing is so important for learning. *"You are the only one who knows if you know. Self-testing is an excellent way to learn and to check your understanding."*

✔ Take time for reflection. After students have completed their notes, allow time for discussion about reading and learning strategies. Ask students to write and then to talk about how analyzing the author's craft and developing two-column notes helped them read and learn content. How might they use these strategies in the future?

Dr. John Reinhard/NGIC

SAMPLE ORGANIZER

Elements of Geography

1. World in spatial terms	
Absolute location	Exact location on globe using network of imaginary lines: 1. Equator—divides world into Northern and Southern Hemispheres 2. Prime Meridian—divides world into Eastern and Western Hemispheres 3. Grid system—located by lines of longitude and latitude Absolute location given in degrees N or S of Equator and E or W of Prime Meridian
Relative location	Locate places in relation to one another—example—New Orleans at mouth of Mississippi River
2. Places and regions	
Place	particular place with unique characteristics—determined by environment and/or people
Region	places grouped together based on common human or physical factors—corn belt, metropolitan areas, "heartland"
3. Physical systems	physical features (volcanoes, mountain areas, ecosystems)
4. Human systems	how people shape the world
5. Environment and society	ways people use the environment
6. Uses of geography	information for planning, decision making, building highways, malls

Reading in the Content Areas

How Can I Use Jamestown Education Products to Help Struggling Readers?

For over 30 years, Jamestown Education has made its primary focus helping older readers become better readers. The Jamestown products shown on this page support the basic elements of reading cited by the National Reading Panel. Each of them can help your struggling readers become better readers.

Timed Readings Plus in Social Studies

✔ **Reading Levels:** 4-13+

✔ **Benefits:**

This ten-book series will help your students increase both reading rate and comprehension. The nonfiction passages cover current social studies topics and are similar to those found on both state and national tests. Each of the two-part lessons focuses on reading rate, factual recall, comprehension strategies, and higher-level critical thinking skills.

Reading in the Content Areas: Social Studies

✔ **Reading Levels:** 4-12+

✔ **Benefits:**

This book concentrates on six essential reading skills that will help your students better comprehend what they read. Seventy-five high-interest nonfiction passages written at increasing levels of difficulty, followed by consistent, targeted skills, teach the techniques needed to organize, understand, and apply information.

Reading Fluency

✔ **Reading Levels:** 1-10

✔ **Benefits:**

This seven-book series will help your students read smoothly, accurately and expressively. Students work in pairs to provide immediate feedback and self-assessment. Author Camille Blachowicz states that "the ability to read fluently is highly correlated with many other measures of reading competence."

Jamestown's Reading Improvement

✔ **Reading Levels** 4-10

✔ **Benefits:**

Authored by renowned reading expert Edward Fry, this eight-book series focuses on helping build your students' comprehension, vocabulary, and skimming and scanning skills. Repeated practice with targeted exercises ensures mastery of valuable reading skills.

Critical Reading Series

✔ **Reading Levels:** 2–8

✔ **Benefits:**

This twenty-four book high-interest series, written at three reading spans, encourages your reluctant readers to build a love for nonfiction while focusing on critical reading skills. Topics ranging from Fateful Journeys to Weird Science to Heroes draw students in, while giving students ample opportunities to master important skills found on both state and national tests.

To order Jamestown products, call 1-800-334-7344

In addition to the Project CRISS Reading Strategies, you may find it effective to implement some of the following instructional methods. They help *your* struggling students take increasing ownership of the reading process.

Reciprocal Teaching

Reciprocal teaching is characterized by a dialogue between you and your student, and ultimately among students in a group, in which students take the role of dialogue reader. Construction of meaning is built upon four reading strategies:

✔ **Summarizing** Readers identify the most important information in a segment of text and state that information in their own words. Summarizing involves students in recognizing and communicating the significant ideas in a text.

✔ **Questioning** Readers ask themselves questions about the text segment. Self-questioning aids comprehension by helping students identify where their understanding of the text has broken down and what they still need to know in order to understand what they have read.

✔ **Clarifying** Readers try to find answers to the question they have raised and to make sense of parts of the text that have caused confusion. They seek clarification by rereading, reading ahead or by seeking outside help, such as through a peer or a reference source.

✔ **Predicting** Readers tell what they think will happen next, basing their predictions on evidence from the text they have already read.

Modeling

An important element of strategic instruction is teacher modeling. As a part of the modeling process, think aloud as you apply a strategy to solve a reading problem, putting words to the inner voice that successful readers have with text and demonstrating the strategy used for understanding. To construct a "think-aloud," read aloud a passage, stopping at pertinent points to talk about what you are thinking. A think-aloud demonstrates the cognitive process and allows students to observe how a proficient reader approaches a problem with reading.

"Fix-Up" Strategies

Explain that readers perform certain tasks. Guide them through these following steps:

✔ **Stop** Tell students to stop and fix the problem when they do not understand.

✔ **Identify the Problem** Have students ask themselves when they stopped understanding and what they don't understand.

✔ **Apply a Fix-up Strategy** Encourage students to try these strategies:

✔ **Reread**

✔ **Read ahead**

✔ **Alter** the pace or voice

✔ **Ask** for help

CRISS and the Jamestown Reader

Advice from Dr. Sara Wartenberg
Palm Harbor University High School
International Baccalaureate Program
Palm Harbor, Florida

Help your students achieve testing success by combining CRISS strategies with the Jamestown Readers. The stories appeal to students of all reading levels. The stories are interesting and informative for students and teachers alike. Implementing CRISS strategies as students read the selections will help them respond with greater success to the questions that accompany each selection. Students will gain confidence and thus work for greater skill in reading comprehension and critical thinking.

Test-Taking Strategies
How Can I Help My Students Succeed on Tests?

It's not enough for students to learn social studies facts and concepts—they must be able to show what they know in a variety of test-taking situations.

How Can I Help My Students Do Well On Objective Tests?

Objective tests may include multiple choice, true/false, and matching questions. Applying the following strategies can help students do their best on objective tests.

Multiple Choice Questions

✔ Students should read the directions carefully to learn what answer the test requires—the best answer or the right answer. This is especially important when answer choices include "all of the above" or "none of the above."

✔ Advise students to watch for negative words in the questions, such as *not, except, unless, never,* and so forth. If the question contains a negative, the correct answer choice is the one that does not fit.

✔ Students should try to mentally answer the question before reading the answer choices.

✔ Students should read all the answer choices and cross out those that are obviously wrong. Then they should choose an answer from those that remain.

True/False Questions

✔ It is important that students read the entire question before answering. For an answer to be true, the entire statement must be true. If one part of a statement is false, the answer should be marked *False*.

✔ Remind students to watch for words like *all, never, every,* and *always*. Statements containing these words are often false.

Matching Questions

✔ Students should read through both lists before they mark any answers.

✔ Unless an answer can be used more than once, students should cross out each choice as they use it.

✔ Using what they know about grammar can help students find the right answer. For instance, when matching a word with its definition, the definition is often the same part of speech (noun, verb, adjective, and so forth) as the word.

How Can I Help My Students Do Well On Essay Tests?

Essay tests require students to provide thorough and well-organized written responses, in addition to telling what they know. Help students use the following strategies on essay tests.

Analyze:	To **analyze** means to systematically and critically examine all parts of an issue or event.
Classify or Categorize:	To **classify** or **categorize** means to put people, things, or ideas into groups, based on a common set of characteristics.
Compare and Contrast:	To **compare** is to show how things are similar, or alike. To **contrast** is to show how things are different.
Describe:	To **describe** means to present a sketch or impression. Rich details, especially details that appeal to the senses, flesh out a description.
Discuss:	To **discuss** means to systematically write about all sides of an issue or event.
Evaluate:	To **evaluate** means to make a judgment and support it with evidence.
Explain:	To **explain** means to clarify or make plain.
Illustrate:	To **illustrate** means to provide examples or to show with a picture or other graphic.
Infer:	To **infer** means to read between the lines or to use knowledge and experience to draw conclusions, make a generalization, or form a prediction.
Justify:	To **justify** means to prove or to support a position with specific facts and reasons.
Predict:	To **predict** means to tell what will happen in the future, based on an understanding of prior events and behaviors.
State:	To **state** means to briefly and concisely present information.
Summarize:	To **summarize** means to give a brief overview of the main points of an issue or event.
Trace:	To **trace** means to present the steps or stages in a process or event in sequential or chronological order.

Read the Question

The key to writing successful essay responses lies in reading and interpreting questions correctly. Teach students to identify and underline key words in the questions, and to use these words to guide them in understanding what the question asks. Help students understand the meaning of some of the most common key words, listed in the chart on page T24.

Plan and Write the Essay

After students understand the question, they should follow the writing process to develop their answer. Encourage students to follow the steps below to plan and write their essays.

1. Map out an answer. Make lists, webs, or an outline to plan the response.

2. Decide on an order in which to present the main points.

3. Write an opening statement that directly responds to the essay question.

4. Write the essay. Expand on the opening statement. Support key points with specific facts, details, and reasons.

5. Write a closing statement that brings the main points together.

6. Proofread to check for spelling, grammar, and punctuation.

How Can I Help My Students Prepare for Standardized Tests?

Students can follow the steps below to prepare for a test.

Jose L. Pelaez/CORBIS STOCK MARKET

✔ **Read About the Test** Students can familiarize themselves with the format of the test, the types of questions that will be asked, and the amount of time they will have to complete the test.

✔ **Review the Content** Consistent study throughout the school year will help students build social studies knowledge and understanding. If there are specific objectives or standards that are tested on the exam, help students review these facts or skills to be sure they are proficient.

✔ **Practice** Provide practice, ideally with real released tests, to build students' familiarity with the content, format, and timing of the real exam. Students should practice all the types of questions they will encounter on the test—multiple choice, short answer, and extended response.

✔ **Analyze Practice Results** Help students improve test-taking performance by analyzing their test-taking strengths and weaknesses. Spend time discussing students' completed practice tests, explaining why particular answers are right or wrong. Help students identify what kinds of questions they had the most difficulty with. Look for patterns in errors and then tailor instruction to review the appropriate test-taking skills or social studies content. ✦

Help Students Learn by Reviewing Graded Tests

Advice from Tara Musslewhite
Humble Independent School District
Humble, Texas

Frequently reviewing graded tests is a great way for students to assess their test-taking skills. It also gives teachers the opportunity to teach test-taking strategies and review content. As the class re-reads each test question, guide students to think logically about their answer choices. Show students how to:

1. Read each question carefully to determine its meaning.
2. Look for key words in the question to support their answers.
3. Recognize synonyms in the answer choices that may match phrases in the question.
4. Narrow down answer choices by eliminating ones that don't make sense.
5. Anticipate the answer before looking at the answer choices.
6. Circle questions of which they are unsure and go back to them later. Sometimes a clue will be found in another question on the test.

Alternative Assessment Strategies

How Can I Go Beyond Tests to Assess Students' Understanding of Social Studies Facts and Concepts?

In response to the growing demand for accountability in the classroom, educators must use multiple assessment measures to accurately gauge student performance. In addition to quizzes, tests, essay exams, and standardized tests, assessment today incorporates a variety of performance-based measures and portfolio opportunities.

What Are Some Typical Performance-Based Assessments?

There are many kinds of performance-based assessments. They all share one common characteristic—they challenge students to create products that demonstrate what they know. One good way to present a performance assessment is in the form of an open-ended question.

Writing

Performance-based writing assessments challenge students to apply their knowledge of social studies concepts and information in a variety of written ways. Writing activities are most often completed by one student, rather than by a group.

✔ **Journals** Students write from the perspective of a historical character or a citizen of a particular historical era.

✔ **Letters** Students write a letter from one historical figure to another or from a historical figure to a family member or other audience.

✔ **Position Paper or Editorial** Students explain a controversial issue and present their own opinion and recommendations, supported with strong evidence and convincing reasons.

✔ **Newspaper** Students write a variety of stories from the perspective of a reporter living in a particular historical time period.

✔ **Biographies and Autobiographies** Students write about historical figures either from the third person point of view (biography) or from the first person (autobiography).

✔ **Creative Stories** Students integrate historical events into a piece of fiction, incorporating the customs, language, and geography of the period.

✔ **Poems and Songs** Students follow the conventions of a particular type of song or poem as they tell about a historical event or person.

✔ **Research Reports** Students synthesize information from a variety of sources into a well-developed research report.

Oral Presentations

Oral presentations allow students to demonstrate their social studies literacy before an audience. Oral presentations are often group efforts, although this need not be the case.

✔ **Simulations** Students hold simulations, or reenactments, of actual events, such as trials, acts of civil disobedience, battles, speeches, and so forth.

✔ **Debates** Students debate two or more sides to a historical policy or issue. Students can debate from a contemporary perspective or in a role play in which they assume a viewpoint held by a historical character.

✔ **Interview** Students conduct a mock interview of an historical character or bystander.

✔ **Oral Reports** Students present the results of research efforts in a lively oral report.

✔ **Skits and Plays** Students use historical events as the basis for a play or skit. Details should accurately reflect customs, language, and the setting of the period.

Visual Presentations

Visual presentations allow students to demonstrate their social studies understandings in a variety of visual formats. Visual presentations can be either group or individual projects.

✔ **Model** Students make a model to demonstrate or represent a process, place, event, battle, artifact, or custom.

✔ **Museum Exhibit** Students create a rich display of materials around a topic. Typical displays might include models, illustrations, photographs, videos, writings, and audiotaped explanations.

✔ **Graph or Chart** Students analyze and represent historical data in a line graph, bar graph, table, or other chart format.

✔ **Drawing** Students represent or interpret a historical event or period through illustration, including political cartoons.

✔ **Posters and Murals** Posters and murals may include maps, time lines, diagrams, illustrations, photographs, and written explanations that reflect students' understandings of historical information.

- ✔ **Quilt** Students sew or draw a design for a patchwork quilt that shows a variety of perspectives, events, or issues related to a key topic.
- ✔ **Videotapes** Students film a video to show historical fiction or to preserve a simulation of a historical event.
- ✔ **Multimedia Presentation or Slide Show** Students create a computer-generated multimedia presentation containing historical information and analysis.

How Are Performance Assessments Scored?

There are a variety of means used to evaluate performance tasks. Some or all of the following methods may be used.

- ✔ **Scoring Rubrics** A scoring rubric is a set of guidelines for assessing the quality of a process and/or product. It sets out criteria used to distinguish acceptable responses from unacceptable ones, generally along a scale from excellent to poor.
- ✔ **Models of Excellent Work** Teacher-selected models of excellent work concretely illustrate expectations and help students set goals for their own projects.
- ✔ **Student Self-Assessment** Common methods of self-assessment include ranking work in relation to the model, using a scoring rubric, and writing their own goals and then evaluating how well they have met the goals they set for themselves. Regardless of which method or methods students use, they should be encouraged to evaluate their behaviors and processes, as well as the finished product.

- ✔ **Peer or Audience Assessment** Many of the performance tasks target an audience other than the classroom teacher. If possible, the audience of peers should give the student feedback. Have the class create rubrics for specific projects together.

- ✔ **Observation** As students carry out their performance tasks, you may want to formally observe students at work. Start by developing a checklist, identifying all the specific behaviors and understandings you expect students to demonstrate. Then observe students as they carry out performance tasks and check off the behaviors as you observe them.
- ✔ **Interviews** As a form of ongoing assessment, you may want to conduct interviews with students, asking them to analyze, explain, and assess their participation in performance tasks. When projects take place over an extended period of time, you can hold periodic interviews as well as exit interviews. In this way the interview process allows you to gauge the status of the project and to guide students' efforts along the way.◆

Targeting Multiple Intelligences

Advice from John Cartaina
Consultant, New Jersey Council of Social Studies

Authentic performance assessment provides students with different learning styles opportunities to demonstrate their successful learning. The table below list types of learning styles.

Learning Style	Characteristics of Students
Linguistic	Read regularly, write clearly, and easily understand the written word
Logical-Mathematical	Use numbers, logic, and critical thinking skills
Visual-Spatial	Think in terms of pictures and images
Auditory-Musical	Remember spoken words and produce rhythms and melodies
Kinesthetic	Learn from touch, movement, and manipulating objects
Interpersonal	Understand and work well with other people
Intrapersonal	Have a realistic understanding of their strengths and weaknesses
Naturalist	Can distinguish among, classify, and use features of the environment

You may want to assign activities to students that accommodate their strongest learning styles, but frequently ask them to use their weakest learning styles.

Primary Source Strategies
How Do I Use Primary Sources in My Classroom?

A primary source is direct evidence of an event, idea, period, or development. It is an oral or written account obtained from actual participants in an event. Examples of primary sources include the following:

✔ official documents (records, statistics)
✔ political declarations, laws, and rules for governance
✔ speeches and interviews
✔ diaries, memoirs, and oral histories
✔ autobiographies
✔ recipes and cookbooks
✔ advertisements and posters
✔ letters

Physical objects, such as tools and dishes, can be primary sources; so can visual evidence in the form of fine art, photographs, maps, films, and videotapes. Primary sources can also include songs and audio recordings.

Why Use Primary Sources in Your Classroom?

Using primary sources to teach transforms the study of social studies from a passive process to an active one. Students become investigators—finding clues, formulating hypotheses and drawing inferences, making judgments, and reaching conclusions. Bringing primary sources into the classroom stimulates students to think critically about events, issues, and concepts rather than just memorizing dates, names, and generalizations reached by others.

Choosing Primary Sources

✔ Provide exposure to a variety of source types, including historic photographs, folk or popular music, financial records or household accounts, as well as letters, journals, and historic documents.
✔ When choosing print sources, consider the interests and reading levels of your students. Many texts contain challenging vocabulary and unfamiliar sentence structure. You may need to create a reader's guide that defines key vocabulary and paraphrases the main points of the reading.
✔ Some documents may be too long. Decide whether using an excerpt will provide enough information for students to draw conclusions.
✔ Depending upon the topic and your instructional objectives, you may need to provide several different primary sources to expose students to a variety of perspectives.
✔ Decide how students will access the primary sources: through the Internet, the library, a museum, or other print resources. Consider the possibility of an Internet virtual field trip for students. Moving from URL to URL, students can visit museum sites and other Web pages to view artifacts; interpret economic or census data; and read journals, letters, and official documents.

How Do I Introduce Students to Primary Sources?

Carefully explain the nature of primary sources when you introduce them to students. Although primary sources contain valuable clues, be sure to alert students that primary sources contain biases and prejudices, and must be approached with caution. Every primary source reflects the creator's point of view to some degree.

Using Primary Sources in the Classroom

Primary sources provide a rich source of inspiration for a variety of instructional strategies. They can be used to spark interest in a new topic, foster deeper exploration into a historical era, or assess students' understanding of social studies concepts and facts.

✔ **Pre-Reading Activities** Present a primary source for students to study at the beginning of a new chapter or topic. Have students analyze the source, using the questions and guidelines presented on the next page. Then have students make

Interpreting a Primary Source

Before students interpret a primary source, they need to know the context into which the source fits. Then they can use questions and guidelines, such as those below, to help them analyze and interpret the primary source.

Print Sources

- Who created the source, and what was the purpose for doing so?
- Did the writer personally experience or witness the event(s)?
- At what point did the writer record the information—as it happened or afterward? How long after?
- Who was the intended audience?
- Was the writer trying to record facts, express an opinion, or persuade others to take action?
- What is the author's main message?
- What values does the document convey?
- What bias does it reflect?
- What information about the topic can you gather from this document?
- Compare this document with what you know about the topic. Does it confirm those ideas or introduce a new perspective?
- How might other accounts about this topic support or modify the message this source delivers?

Visual Sources

- Who created the source, and what was the purpose for doing so?
- What does the image show?
- What mood does the image convey?
- Who or what dominates the image or catches your eye?
- How does the view impact the message?
- What details can you learn from the image?
- What is excluded from view?
- What bias does the visual reflect?
- What information about the topic can you gather from this visual?
- How might other visuals about this topic support or modify the message this one delivers?

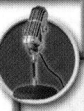

Audio Sources

- Who created the source? What was the purpose for creating this source?
- What is the main idea of the audio?
- What mood does the recorder's voice convey?
- What bias does the audio text reflect?
- What information about the topic can you gather from this audio source?
- Compare the information in this source with what you already know about the topic. Does it confirm those ideas or introduce a new perspective?
- How might other sources about this topic support or modify the message that this one delivers?

predictions about what they might learn in the upcoming lessons.

✔ **Exploring Information** Provide a variety of primary sources related to a topic or time period. Have students use their journals to compare and contrast the items, analyzing the information, making inferences, and drawing conclusions about the period.

✔ **Evaluation Activities** Have students evaluate a primary source and tell how it supports or refutes what they learned in the textbook or have students read a primary source document that provides one perspective on a topic, and have students write their own account, presenting another perspective or opinion.◆

How to Use the Declaration of Independence in Your Classroom

Advice from Susan Hirsch
East Wake High School
Wendell, North Carolina

Divide students into groups of three or four. Tell students that it is 1777, and one member of their group has been arrested for joining the revolutionary struggle against Great Britain. This person will be sent to London to be tried on charges of treason. Hanging is the punishment for those found guilty of treason. Each group must prepare a defense using only one source—the Declaration of Independence. One person from each group will speak to the class, acting as either the defendant or the defendant's attorney. After all the presentations, the class will vote to determine which person did the best job of defending himself or herself or the client.

Addressing the Needs of Special Students

How Can I Help ALL my Students Learn Social Studies?

Today's classroom contains students from a variety of backgrounds and with a variety of learning styles, strengths, and challenges. With careful planning, you can address the needs of all students in the social studies classroom. The following tips for instruction can assist your efforts to help all students reach their maximum potential.

✔ Survey students to discover their individual differences. Use interest inventories of their unique talents so you can encourage contributions in the classroom.

✔ Model respect of others. Adolescents crave social acceptance. The student with learning differences is especially sensitive to correction and criticism—particularly when it comes from a teacher. Your behavior will set the tone for how students treat one another.

✔ Expand opportunities for success. Provide a variety of instructional activities that reinforce skills and concepts.

✔ Establish measurable objectives and decide how you can best help students meet them.

✔ Celebrate successes and praise "work in progress."

✔ Keep it simple. Point out problem areas—if doing so can help a student affect change. Avoid overwhelming students with too many goals at one time.

✔ Assign cooperative group projects that challenge all students to contribute to solving a problem or creating a product.

How Do I Reach Students with Learning Disabilities?

✔ Provide support and structure. Clearly specify rules, assignments, and responsibilities.

✔ Practice skills frequently. Use games and drills to help maintain student interest.

✔ Incorporate many modalities into the learning process. Provide opportunities to say, hear, write, read, and act out important concepts and information.

✔ Link new skills and concepts to those already mastered.

✔ Allow students to record answers on audiotape.

✔ Allow extra time to complete tests and assignments.

✔ Let students demonstrate proficiency with alternative presentations, including oral reports, role plays, art projects, and with music.

✔ Provide outlines, notes, or tape recordings of lecture material.

✔ Pair students with peer helpers, and provide class time for pair interaction.

How Do I Reach Students with Behavioral Disorders?

✔ Provide a structured environment with clear-cut schedules, rules, seat assignments, and safety procedures.

✔ Reinforce appropriate behavior and model it for students.

✔ Cue distracted students back to the task through verbal signals and teacher proximity.

✔ Set very small goals that can be achieved in the short term. Work for long-term improvement in the big areas.

How Do I Reach Students with Physical Challenges?

✔ Openly discuss with the student any uncertainties you have about when to offer aid.

✔ Ask parents or therapists and students what special devices or procedures are needed, and whether any special safety precautions need to be taken.

✔ Welcome students with physical challenges into all activities, including field trips, special events, and projects.

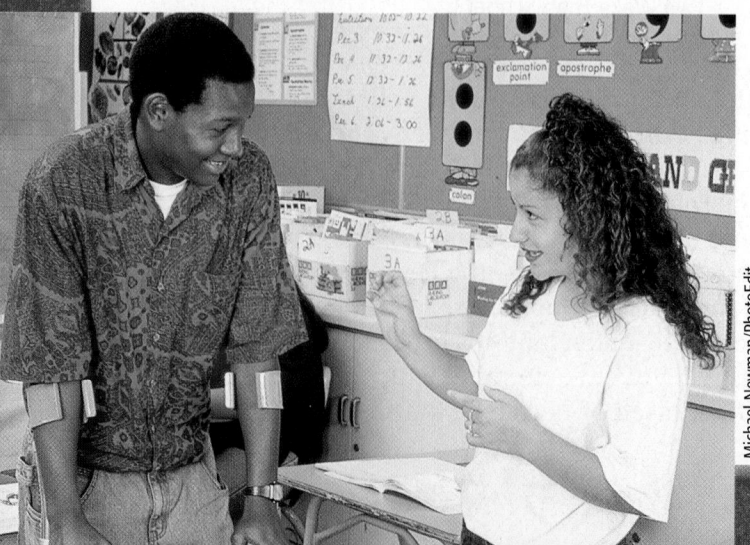

Michael Newman/PhotoEdit

✔ Try to incorporate the students' cultural experience into your instruction. The help of a bilingual aide may be effective.
✔ Avoid cultural stereotypes.
✔ Pre-teach important vocabulary and concepts.
✔ Encourage students to preview text before they begin reading, noting headings, graphic organizers, photographs, and maps.

How Do I Reach Gifted Students?

✔ Make arrangements for students to take selected subjects early and to work on independent projects.
✔ Ask "what if" questions to develop high-level thinking skills. Establish an environment safe for risk taking.
✔ Emphasize concepts, theories, ideas, relationships, and generalizations.
✔ Promote interest in the past by inviting students to make connections to the present.
✔ Let students express themselves in alternate ways, such as journal or creative writing, acting, debate, simulations, drawing, or music.
✔ Provide students with a catalog of helpful resources, listing such things as agencies that provide free and inexpensive materials, appropriate community services and programs, and community experts.
✔ Assign extension projects that allow students to solve real-life problems related to their communities.✦

✔ Provide information to help able-bodied students and adults understand other students' physical challenges.

How Do I Reach Students with Visual Impairments?

✔ Facilitate independence. Modify assignments as needed.
✔ Teach classmates how and when to serve as guides.
✔ Limit unnecessary noise in the classroom, if it distracts the student with visual impairments.
✔ Provide tactile models whenever possible.
✔ Foster a spirit of inclusion. Describe people and events as they occur in the classroom. Remind classmates that the student with visual impairments cannot interpret gestures and other forms of nonverbal communication.
✔ Provide taped lectures and reading assignments.
✔ Team the student with a sighted peer for written work.

How Do I Reach Students with Hearing Impairments?

✔ Seat students where they can see your lip movements easily and where they can avoid visual distractions.

✔ Avoid standing with your back to the window or light source.
✔ Use an overhead projector to maintain eye contact while writing.
✔ Seat students where they can see speakers.
✔ Write all assignments on the board, or hand out written instructions.
✔ If the student has a manual interpreter, allow both student and interpreter to select the most favorable seating arrangements.
✔ Teach students to look directly at each other when they speak.

How Do I Reach English Language Learners?

✔ Remember, students' ability to speak English does not reflect their academic abilities.

Customize Your Classroom!

Advice from Marilyn Gerken
Pickerington Local Schools
Pickerington, Ohio

Provide individualized activities and assignments for a variety of student ability levels. Develop learning packets for chapters and units of study with varying formats, levels, and types of assignments. Assign points and contract students based on their selection of activities to be completed. The activities in the Student Edition can be used for many of the learning activities and assignments.

Alternate Course Outlines

Glencoe World Geography may be used in a variety of courses.
Listed below are five examples.

OUTLINE 1

Emphasizes Physical Geography

UNIT 1   The World ....Chapters 1, 2, 3
UNIT 2   The United States and Canada ....Chapter 5
UNIT 3   Latin America ....Chapter 8
UNIT 4   Europe ....Chapter 11
UNIT 5   Russia ....Chapter 14
UNIT 6   North Africa, Southwest Asia,
          and Central Asia ....Chapter 17
UNIT 7   Africa South of the Sahara.......................Chapter 20
UNIT 8   South Asia..Chapter 23
UNIT 9   East Asia ....Chapter 26
UNIT 10 Southeast Asia..Chapter 29
UNIT 11 Australia, Oceania, and Antarctica..........Chapter 32

OUTLINE 2

Emphasizes Cultural Geography

UNIT 1   The World ....Chapter 4
UNIT 2   The United States and Canada ....Chapter 6
UNIT 3   Latin America ....Chapter 9
UNIT 4   Europe ....Chapter 12
UNIT 5   Russia ....Chapter 15
UNIT 6   North Africa, Southwest Asia,
          and Central Asia ....Chapter 18
UNIT 7   Africa South of the Sahara.......................Chapter 21
UNIT 8   South Asia..Chapter 24
UNIT 9   East Asia ....Chapter 27
UNIT 10 Southeast Asia..Chapter 30
UNIT 11 Australia, Oceania, and Antarctica..........Chapter 33

From Geography Themes

In the past decade, instruction in geography has been organized around the five themes of geography: location, place, human-environment interaction, movement, and regions. The popularity of these content organizers set the stage for the development of two additional, more comprehensive instructional frameworks: the "Six Essential Elements" and the "Eighteen Geography Standards" within the elements. These two interlocking frameworks provide the structure of the publication *Geography for Life: National Geography Standards 1994.*

6 ESSENTIAL ELEMENTS AND

 1 The World in Spatial Terms

Geography studies the relationships between people, places, and environments by mapping information about them into a spatial context.

The geographically informed person knows and understands:

1. How to use maps and other geographic representations, tools, and technologies to acquire, process, and report information from a spatial perspective
2. How to use mental maps to organize information about people, places, and environments in a spatial context
3. How to analyze the spatial organization of people, places, and environments on Earth's surface

 2 Places and Regions

The identities and lives of individuals and peoples are rooted in particular places and in those human constructs called regions.

The geographically informed person knows and understands:

4. The physical and human characteristics of places
5. That people create regions to interpret Earth's complexity
6. How culture and experience influence people's perception of places and regions

 3 Physical Systems

Physical processes shape Earth's surface and interact with plant and animal life to create, sustain, and modify ecosystems.

The geographically informed person knows and understands:

7. The physical processes that shape the patterns of Earth's surface
8. The characteristics and spatial distribution of ecosystems on Earth's surface

to Geography Standards

How Themes and Standards Compare

It is important to keep in mind that the five themes and the standards look at the same geographic universe. The themes represent an instructional approach; they allow a particular focus to be given to the lesson of the moment. The standards comprise the geographic subject matter, skills, and perspectives of geography. The 5 themes flow through all the 18 geography standards and can be used in the instruction of all of them, at any grade level.

The chart below explains the 6 essential elements and lists the standards within each. The chart on pages T42–T49 provides:

- An explanation of the 18 standards
- Which of the five themes relate most closely to each standard
- Page numbers in the student and teacher editions of *Glencoe World Geography* that utilize each standard

18 GEOGRAPHY STANDARDS

 4 Human Systems

People are central to geography in that human activities help shape Earth's surface, human settlements and structures are part of Earth's surface, and humans compete for control of Earth's surface.

The geographically informed person knows and understands:

9. The characteristics, distribution, and migration of human populations on Earth's surface
10. The characteristics, distribution, and complexity of Earth's cultural mosaics
11. The patterns and networks of economic interdependence on Earth's surface
12. The processes, patterns, and functions of human settlement
13. How the forces of cooperation and conflict among people influence the division and control of Earth's surface

 5 Environment and Society

The physical environment is modified by human activities, largely as a consequence of the ways in which human societies value and use Earth's natural resources, and human activities are also influenced by Earth's physical features and processes.

The geographically informed person knows and understands:

14. How human actions modify the physical environment
15. How physical systems affect human systems
16. The changes that occur in the meaning, use, distribution, and importance of resources

 6 The Uses of Geography

Knowledge of geography enables people to develop an understanding of the relationships between people, places, and environments over time—that is, of Earth as it was, is, and might be.

The geographically informed person knows and understands:

17. How to apply geography to interpret the past
18. How to apply geography to interpret the present and plan for the future

Correlation of *Glencoe World Geography* to the National Geography Standards

National Geography Standards & Related Themes	Student Edition Page	Teacher Edition Page
🌐 STANDARD 1 **How to use maps and other geographic representations, tools, and technologies to acquire, process, and report information from a spatial perspective** Maps are the most commonly used representations of detailed geographic information on features or places. Along with other tools such as globes, aerial photographs, satellite images, and statistical databases, they bring the whole world into focus. Maps range from simple sketch maps to complex Geographic Information Systems (GIS) analysis. **Related themes: Location, Place**	24, 30, 84-85, 90, 92, 95, 98, 107-109, 118-120, 122-123, 139, 125-126, 128-129, 137, 141, 145, 151, 152, 154-155, 164, 166, 169, 171, 174-175, 183, 185, 195, 198, 200, 203, 206-209, 212, 216-217, 221-222, 225, 232, 234-235, 243, 247, 252-253, 261, 263, 272, 276, 278-279, 281, 284, 291, 295, 299-300, 302, 307, 310-311, 316, 319, 325, 330, 413, 423-424, 426, 428-429, 431-432, 434-435, 443, 447, 449, 451-452, 460, 468, 470-471, 473, 478, 501, 504, 506-507, 509-510, 512-513, 518, 520-524, 529, 534-535, 544, 547, 549, 552-553, 571, 574, 576, 578-580, 582, 585, 591, 595, 597, 601-602, 608-609, 639, 647, 650, 652-653, 655, 658, 665, 669, 671-672, 680, 682, 690-691, 696-697, 702, 711, 713, 721, 724, 726-727, 729, 732-733, 739, 742, 744-745, 749, 753, 765, 777, 785, 787, 795, 798, 800, 803, 806, 809, 815, 818, 821, 827, 830, 835, 837, 841, 846	16, 20, 25, 32, 93, 100, 106, 116, 153, 176, 182, 202, 254, 260, 261, 272, 332, 339, 404, 412-413, 480, 516, 554, 560, 571, 630, 636, 637, 638, 647, 663, 721, 727, 728, 796, 813
🌐 STANDARD 2 **How to use mental maps to organize information about people, places, and environments in a spatial context** A mental map exists only in the mind's eye. It represents each individual's knowledge of the location of geographic features such as countries, cities, seas, mountain ranges, and rivers. A mental map is also made up of approximate size dimensions and cultural characteristics. In scale, it may include our route to a local store or theater, or it may serve as the framework for the location of the Khyber Pass, Brasília, or the Yangtze Gorges. This map grows in complexity as experience, study, and the media bring us new geographic information. **Related themes: Location, Place, Regions**	21-22, 43, 60, 66-67, 69, 78-79, 81-85, 90, 92, 95, 108-109, 119-120, 122-123, 125, 129, 137, 145, 155, 164, 166, 169, 171, 175, 185, 200, 203, 207, 209, 212, 216-217, 221-222, 225, 231-232, 235, 243, 253, 263, 278, 281, 291, 295, 299-300, 307, 355, 431, 429, 431-432, 434, 443, 447, 449, 451-452, 468, 470-471, 473, 476, 478, 506-507, 509-510, 518, 520-524, 529, 544, 547, 574, 576, 578, 591, 595, 597, 601-602, 639, 650, 652-653, 655, 669, 671-672, 680, 690-691, 696-697, 713, 726, 727, 729, 733, 742, 749, 753, 765, 787, 800, 803, 809, 815, 818, 835, 837	18, 561, 721, 796

National Geography Standards & Related Themes	Student Edition Page	Teacher Edition Page
STANDARD 3 **How to analyze the spatial organization of people, places, and environments on Earth's surface** Human structures organize space. Pattern, regularity, and reason are inherent in the locations of cities, factories, malls, cemeteries, and other human landscape creations. To understand the spatial patterns and processes that organize Earth's surface, it is essential to know concepts such as distance, direction, location, connections, and association. Understanding these concepts enables one to say what factors influence a locational decision for a hospital, a county seat, a sanitary landfill, or a regional shopping center. **Related themes: Place, Human-Environment Interaction**	27, 31, 45, 92-93, 95, 99, 137, 139, 155, 161, 164, 175, 198, 206-207, 209, 217, 219, 241, 252-253, 284, 331, 341, 359, 429, 431, 435, 470, 478, 520, 531, 535, 539, 549, 552, 574, 578, 583, 585, 617, 655, 729, 733, 742, 765, 795, 798, 809, 814, 823	17, 88, 200, 338, 636-638, 663, 763
STANDARD 4 **The physical and human characteristics of places** Places may be distinguished by their physical and human characteristics. Physical characteristics include landforms, climate, soils, hydrology, vegetation, and animal life. Human characteristics include language, religion, political and economic systems, population, and quality of life. Places change over time as new technologies, resources, knowledge, and ideologies are introduced and become part of a place's geography. Such change leads to the rise and fall of empires, may derive from shifts in climate or other physical systems, or may be generated by population expansion. **Related themes: Place, Human-Environment Interaction**	84-85, 120, 142, 145, 151, 169, 203, 212, 217, 219, 231, 234-235, 276, 291, 293, 299, 306, 310, 319, 330, 426, 434, 443, 447, 449, 451-452, 473, 475, 504, 509, 523, 571, 574, 591, 608-609, 647, 667, 672, 683, 724, 729, 732-733, 739, 742, 745, 749, 753, 756, 830, 843	74, 97, 101-103, 108, 114, 117, 127, 132, 135, 173, 178-179, 185, 196, 205, 244, 256-257, 270, 272, 306, 309, 337, 344, 357, 362, 370, 378, 386, 406, 409, 417, 420, 428, 433, 438, 470, 477, 480-482, 485-486, 490, 492-493, 498, 511, 514, 541, 568, 570, 576-577, 586, 594, 610, 619, 627, 631-633, 635-636, 638, 640, 646-648, 657, 675, 690, 722, 727, 758, 761, 764, 792, 801, 826, 842, 845

National Geography Standards & Related Themes	Student Edition Page	Teacher Edition Page
STANDARD 5 **That people create regions to interpret Earth's complexity** Regions are defined as having one or more common characteristics that give them a measure of unity and make them distinct from surrounding areas. As worlds within worlds, regions simplify geographic analysis by organizing a specific area into a unit of explicit physical and human elements. The criteria in the definition of a region can be as precise as coastline or political boundaries, or as arbitrary as the general location of people loyal to a specific athletic team. Regions are human constructs, created to facilitate the understanding of a large, varied, complex, and changing world. **Related themes: Regions, Human-Environment Interaction**	43, 69, 79, 84-85, 92-93, 95, 98-99, 109, 117-120, 125, 135, 141, 143-145, 151, 154-155, 161-162, 164, 174, 196, 172, 174, 196, 198, 200-203, 207, 212, 217, 219, 221-222, 225, 227, 230-231, 234-235, 239, 247, 252, 272, 278-281, 284-285, 291, 293, 297, 300, 306-307, 310-311, 315-316, 319, 323-325, 327, 330-331, 350, 355, 373, 379, 381, 384, 399, 413, 423-426, 428-432, 434-435, 440, 442-443, 445, 447, 449, 451-452, 456-457, 460-461, 464-465, 467-468, 470-473, 475-476, 478, 501-504, 506-508, 510, 513, 517-518, 520-524, 526-527, 529, 534-535, 538-539, 541-542, 544-545, 547, 549-550, 552-553, 571, 574, 576-580, 582-583, 589-591, 594-597, 599-603, 605, 608-609, 639, 646-647, 649-650, 652-655, 658-659, 662, 664-665, 667, 669-672, 674, 676, 679, 682-683, 687-688, 690-691, 693-695, 697, 702-703, 720-724, 726-729, 732-733, 736, 738-739, 742-745, 749, 751-753, 756-757, 760-765, 767, 769-771, 773, 776-777, 794-798, 801-803, 806, 813-815, 818, 820, 825-827, 830-831, 834-837, 839, 841, 843, 846-847	21, 273, 279, 424, 467, 576, 630, 636, 800
STANDARD 6 **How culture and experience influence people's perception of places and regions** Perception of all places and regions depends upon personal experience, culture, age, gender, and other factors. It is sometimes said that there is no reality, only perception. In geography there is always a mixture of both. For example, a wilderness can be attractive to a camper, a source of anxiety for a child, and a nuisance to a pioneering farmer. **Related themes: Regions, Place, Movement**	22, 82, 85, 98, 113, 143, 155, 230-231, 252-253, 288, 293, 298-300, 303, 310-311, 443, 451-452, 457, 460, 522-524, 529, 552, 591, 599, 672, 682, 745, 756, 815, 830, 841	74, 110, 158, 177, 192, 256, 309, 335, 342, 344, 380, 386, 390, 405, 407, 418, 462, 557, 565, 627, 641, 644, 653, 797, 810, 819, 832, 836

National Geography Standards & Related Themes	Student Edition Page	Teacher Edition Page
STANDARD 7 **The physical processes that shape the patterns of Earth's surface** Physical processes create natural landscapes and environments arrayed across Earth's surface in spatial patterns. Understanding these forces is indispensable in daily decision-making, e.g., evaluating homesites in earthquake zones or floodplains, or building a highway along the ocean coastline. There is a systematic order in this continual remaking of Earth's surface. The geographically informed person understands the interplay of systems, forces, boundaries, thresholds, and equilibrium as they influence patterns on Earth's surface. **Related themes: Place, Regions**	36, 38-39, 47, 49, 52, 56, 61, 63-64, 66, 69, 72-73, 117, 120, 122-125, 128-129, 131, 155, 158, 172, 196, 198, 200-203, 206-207, 276, 278-281, 284-285, 319, 425-426, 428-429, 432, 434, 436, 478, 503, 506, 509, 512-513, 534, 545, 574, 576, 578-579, 582-583, 646-647, 650, 652, 655, 658-659, 696, 699, 702, 721, 724, 726-729, 732-733, 798, 801-803, 806, 823, 843	38-39, 41, 42, 51, 54, 114, 272, 334, 362, 410, 423, 425, 501, 507, 573, 581, 632, 644, 652, 696, 795, 842
STANDARD 8 **The characteristics and spatial distribution of ecosystems on Earth's surface** Ecosystems are communities of living things—plants and animals—interacting with each other and with the physical environment. Ecosystems are dynamic and ever changing. They are self-regulating,open systems that maintain flows of energy and matter that naturally move toward maturity, stability, and balance. By understanding how these systems and processes work in shaping the physical environment, students will be better able to comprehend the basic principles that guide environmental management. Such knowledge will enable them to anticipate the consequences of ongoing human effort to transform Earth's landscapes. **Related themes: Location, Place, Regions**	45, 49, 58, 67-69, 72, 92, 120, 123, 125, 128, 131, 155, 158, 171, 197-198, 200, 203, 206, 217, 235, 241, 249, 279, 281, 284-285, 311, 319, 395, 429-432, 434-435, 470, 478, 508-509, 512-513, 534, 542, 545, 549, 552, 574, 576, 582, 647, 655, 658, 729, 732, 773	35, 66, 67, 71, 114, 116, 122, 168, 170, 201, 248, 267, 323, 347, 353, 411, 430, 456, 483, 536, 544, 581, 619, 646, 744, 761, 764, 772, 802, 840
STANDARD 9 **The characteristics, distribution, and migration of human populations on Earth's surface** The characteristics and distribution of human populations are never static. Factors such as natural increase, war, famine, disease, and rate of urbanization play decisive roles in where people live. At any one time, some populations are bound to be migrating—leaving one place, striking out for a second, possibly settling in a third. The factors that give definition to a country's population profile, patterns of growth or decline, and inclinations toward migration combine to be significant geographic information. **Related themes: Human-Environment Interaction, Movement, Regions**	98, 136-137, 143, 145, 150, 154-155, 164, 169, 212-213, 215-217, 227, 231, 234-235, 239, 291, 293, 297-300, 306-307, 310-311, 319, 330, 418, 434, 443, 451-452, 478, 496, 504, 509, 518, 521-522, 524, 535, 545, 552, 590-591, 597, 599, 601, 609, 665, 667, 682-683, 739, 747, 753, 756-757, 763, 813, 815, 821, 830	76, 77, 81, 163, 184, 189, 215, 275, 286, 289, 299, 344, 414, 441-442, 447-451, 488, 496, 516-517, 562, 589, 633-634, 637, 663-664, 738, 813

National Geography Standards & Related Themes	Student Edition Page	Teacher Edition Page
STANDARD 10 **The characteristics, distribution, and complexity of Earth's cultural mosaics** Culture defines each group's unique view of itself and others, and includes the material goods, skills, and social behavior transmitted to successive generations. It is expressed through art, language, beliefs and institutions, the built environment, and numerous other features. Cultural patterns are never static. They change in response to human migration, diffusion, and the steady introduction of new and competing cultural traits. **Related themes: Location, Regions, Place**	85, 93, 98, 113, 139, 148, 150, 154, 190, 212-213, 227, 231, 234-235, 293, 298-300, 307, 310, 319, 418, 443, 451, 460, 468, 496, 521-524, 529, 531, 534, 566-567, 597, 601, 609, 667, 682, 745, 756-757, 821, 827, 830	60, 82-83, 97, 104, 107, 113, 142, 148-150, 180-181, 183, 187-188, 191, 210, 212-213, 222-223, 227-230, 233, 236, 258-259, 265-266, 269, 336, 340, 343, 346, 408, 419, 484, 487, 495, 497, 286, 292, 295, 303, 305, 309, 312, 365, 377-378, 441-442, 448, 450-451, 454, 459, 527-528, 530, 533, 555, 558-559, 566, 588, 593, 595, 601-602, 604, 607, 610, 615, 627, 631, 633-634, 637, 640, 653, 663, 671, 675-678, 688-689, 734, 750, 752, 762, 769-770, 814, 826
STANDARD 11 **The patterns and networks of economic interdependence on Earth's surface** The goods that we need daily to make life work have sources all over the world. Economic networks at all scales, from local to global, have been developed to promote the efficient interchange of goods. Linkages of transportation, communication, language, currency, and custom have been fashioned out of the human desire to have more than what is available locally. For United States citizens, learning about the nature and significance of global interdependence is an essential aspect of being geographically well informed. **Related themes: Movement, Regions, Human-Environment Interaction, Location**	89-90, 93, 95, 98, 113, 120, 139, 155, 164, 190, 198, 206, 216, 219, 225, 239, 241, 249, 252, 300, 307, 310-311, 330-331, 395, 426, 434-435, 443, 465, 468, 479, 504, 512-513, 522, 534, 547, 552, 566, 642, 667, 672, 682, 691, 697, 702, 739, 742, 821	63, 89, 92, 124, 156, 160, 162, 186, 214, 240, 264, 317, 344, 374, 389, 391, 401, 416, 466, 477, 489, 491, 521, 538, 590, 612, 616, 639, 642-643, 649, 666, 670, 687, 762, 796, 835, 845
STANDARD 12 **The processes, patterns, and functions of human settlement** Settlement is one of the most basic human responses to the environment. As social animals, humans achieve proximity, shared environments, and the opportunity to engage in effective economic and social interaction through settlement. Nearly half the human population has opted for city residence. However, there is a vast variety of cultural landscapes in urban settings, just as there is in village and town settings for most of the rest of the population. In all varieties of settlements, cultural landscapes reflect local resources and human preferences. **Related themes: Place, Regions, Movement**	79, 85, 98, 109, 135, 137, 145, 154-155, 214, 217, 234-235, 247, 249, 291, 297-299, 306, 310-311, 319, 443, 451, 496, 518, 534-535, 583, 590-591, 597, 599, 601, 665, 667, 682-683, 736, 738-739, 756-757, 763, 813, 815, 821, 830	87, 97, 109, 173, 215, 221, 262, 268-269, 295, 298, 329, 333, 415, 441-442, 448, 450-451, 454, 481, 657, 663, 738, 836, 845

National Geography Standards & Related Themes	Student Edition Page	Teacher Edition Page
STANDARD 13 **How the forces of cooperation and conflict among people influence the division and control of Earth's surface** The tendency to divide space into segments that provide identity and a sense of security is universal. This human drive covers all scales, from individual homesteads through neighborhood and city limits to state and national boundaries. We have long declared borders, built walls, demarcated rivers and mountain ridges, and had arbitrary lines mapped across deserts. This trait relates to a wish to enclose that which we desire or perhaps exclude that which is feared. Multinational alliances as well as community interest groups are all motivated by the human capacity for expression of cooperation and conflict in the control of Earth's surface. **Related themes: Regions, Movement, Human-Environment Interaction**	85, 87, 95, 98, 120, 139, 212–213, 217, 219, 225, 249, 252, 293, 298–300, 307, 319, 395, 418, 443, 452, 475, 522–524, 531, 552, 574, 597, 599, 667, 671–672, 682, 747, 757, 763, 821, 835	88, 92, 111, 143–144, 224, 246, 290, 297, 304, 329, 370, 372, 392, 449, 450–451, 466, 522, 523, 530, 588, 595, 598, 622, 666, 670, 671, 742–743, 746, 769, 818–819
STANDARD 14 **How human actions modify the physical environment** When humans first occupied the environment, levels of technology were low enough that modifications of the physical setting were generally simple, although significant over time. However, as we have developed more powerful technology to assist us in such modification, we have made hot areas cool, cold areas warm, dry areas gardenlike, and wet areas habitable. Changing the landscape has become a signature of human use of Earth, and will be a significant theme as we see just what we have gained (and lost) in such transformations. **Related themes: Human–Environment Interaction, Place, Regions**	45, 49, 53, 58, 69, 72–73, 95, 124–125, 128, 131, 139, 155, 167–169, 171, 174, 207, 219, 235, 241, 243, 247, 249, 252, 276, 284–285, 291, 322–325, 330–331, 348, 350, 355, 375, 395, 397–399, 402, 426, 431, 434, 437, 445, 473, 475, 478–479, 509, 513, 518, 545, 549, 552–553, 574, 583, 585, 650, 659, 694–695, 697, 699, 702, 747, 767, 770–771, 773, 776, 807, 815, 836–837, 840–841, 846–847	44, 57, 68, 119, 130, 138, 141, 159, 161, 167, 170–171, 173, 197, 218, 245, 249, 296, 318, 322, 326–327, 329, 397, 436, 471, 475, 502, 508, 539, 546, 549, 572, 614, 621, 694–695, 699, 718, 723, 751, 808, 843

National Geography Standards & Related Themes	Student Edition Page	Teacher Edition Page
STANDARD 15 **How physical systems affect human systems** Expanding settlement of floodplains, coastal margins, and seismic zones has brought us face-to-face with striking evidence of ways in which physical systems have profound effects on human systems. Less dramatic—but ultimately more significant—aspects of the effect of physical systems on human systems are such issues as freshwater use, ozone depletion, global warming, and soil loss. Knowledge of Earth's physical systems will be critical to the human use of Earth in the years to come and is central to Geography for Life. **Related themes: Place, Regions, Human-Environment Interaction**	41, 43, 45, 49, 52–53, 73, 79, 95, 113, 120, 124, 131, 139, 167, 169, 171, 174, 190, 207, 219, 235, 243, 247, 249, 252, 272, 285, 291, 323, 325, 330, 350, 434, 437, 442, 445, 472–473, 475, 478, 504, 509, 535, 545, 552–553, 574, 583, 585, 650, 655, 659, 694–695, 697, 699, 702, 724, 768–769, 771, 776, 801, 823, 836–837, 841, 843, 847	40, 61, 112, 118, 123, 138, 141, 173, 184, 190, 216, 218, 239, 274, 280, 283, 306, 324, 349, 429, 465–466, 471–472, 508, 545, 548, 556, 639, 654, 768, 801–802, 822, 842
STANDARD 16 **The changes that occur in the meaning, use, distribution, and importance of resources** We extract, process, market, and consume those things we value in the environment. The activity related to putting values on resources, and the subsequent demands on the environment, establish patterns of economic, political, and cultural interaction. Some natural resources we require: air, water, vegetation—and space. Others commonly used, such as oil, tin, diamonds, bananas, and coffee, have gained their value by human decisions that generally relate to levels of technology and economic development. A geographer must understand what makes an item a resource, and what the subsequent geographic implications of such as appraisal might be. **Related themes: Human-Environment Interaction, Place, Regions**	53, 73, 79, 113, 131, 139, 171, 190, 247, 285, 330–331, 348, 435, 445, 452, 479, 513, 524, 547, 552–553, 559, 566, 642, 659, 697, 702, 776–777, 837, 847	48, 94, 118, 138, 195, 201, 263, 298, 314–315, 348, 369, 394, 397–398, 444, 465–466, 471–472, 503, 563, 613, 620, 624, 639, 649, 737, 820, 845

National Geography Standards & Related Themes	Student Edition Page	Teacher Edition Page
STANDARD 17 **How to apply geography to interpret the past** An understanding of spatial and environmental perspectives leads to a fuller appreciation of the human use of Earth in the past. By determining how people have assessed their own settings, and gaining understanding of why they used their settings as they did—or changed them the way they did—we can see the role that geography has played in our histories. **Related themes: Human-Environment Interaction, Movement, Regions**	84-85, 92, 94-95, 120, 125, 141-143, 145, 154-155, 209, 213, 219, 225, 231, 246, 293, 297–300, 307, 310, 350, 355, 377, 402, 418, 443, 445, 450-452, 460, 496, 504, 518, 522–524, 545, 549, 552, 566, 583, 599, 642, 667, 699, 756, 809	84, 136, 208, 371, 383, 448, 596, 738, 743, 808, 819–820, 822
STANDARD 18 **How to apply geography to interpret the present and plan for the future** Geography leads people to think about spatial patterns, connections between places, integration of local to global scales, diversity, and systems. With such a scope, it is easy to see how completely geography influences the present, and how it can be significant in achieving effective planning for the future. Issues that range from resources to population to paths of movement all relate to the essence of geography. Being able to put this breadth of impact to work in planning for the future is one of the benefits of being geographically well-informed. **Related themes: Regions, Human-Environment Interaction, Place**	45, 53, 73, 75, 113, 190, 209, 225, 241, 253, 361, 325, 327, 331, 375, 395, 418, 435, 437, 445, 464, 473, 475, 479, 513, 518, 535, 542, 547, 553, 566, 574, 578, 599, 605, 609, 654, 667, 683, 691, 697, 699, 703, 733, 757, 771, 803, 807, 809, 823, 831, 843, 847	24, 26, 29, 34, 45, 47, 56, 62, 76, 78, 251, 316, 354, 360, 379, 383, 395, 470, 474, 494, 540, 551, 564, 578, 584, 689, 609, 625, 699, 738, 772, 808, 814, 842–843

Geography Skills for Life

If you think that geography means memorizing a list of states and their capitals, think again. Geography is a broad and ever-changing subject. It includes the study of Earth's physical features, as well as the countless and fascinating ways that humans, animals, and plants interact with the world around them.

To understand how our world is connected, some geographers have broken down the study of geography into five themes. The Five Themes of Geography are (1) location, (2) place, (3) human-environment interaction, (4) movement, and (5) regions.

Most recently, geographers have begun to look at geography in a different way. Geography educators have created a set of eighteen learning standards called *Geography for Life.* Each of these eighteen standards is organized into six essential elements, which are explained for you below. Being aware of these elements will help you sort out what you are learning about geography.

1 The World in Spatial Terms

Each time you tell a classmate how to get to your home or give directions to a school visitor, you use geography. You are thinking about places in terms of their location in space. Knowing how to read maps, give directions, and create your own mental maps of spaces around you will help you throughout life as you travel down new paths and into unfamiliar locations.

◀ Street signs on Monhegan Island, Maine, U.S.

2 Places and Regions

Are you a Texan? How about a city dweller, a beachcomber, or a Midwesterner? Places and regions exert such a powerful force in our lives that many people define themselves in terms of a specific place or region. Places and regions impact how people live, their career choices, culture, language, and even their view of the world. Learning more about places and regions will build your understanding and respect for the similarities and differences among the world's people.

▼ Woman weaving decorative cloth, Antigua, Guatemala

▲ Satellite photo of tropical storm Irene, south of Cuba

③ Physical Systems

When a skateboarder checks the weather forecast before heading outside for the nearest hill, she uses geographic information. Earth's physical processes, including climate, erosion, and earthquakes, shape the pattern of Earth's surface. Understanding the past and future effects of Earth's forces may someday guide your choice of where and how to live.

▼ Curbside recycling in Palm Springs, California, U.S.

④ Human Systems

Do you use a cell phone or a pager? Communications systems like these rely on geographic information to send and receive signals. How humans settle Earth, use resources, and build the transportation, communications, and economic systems that keep life going are part of the geography of modern society. As you become a contributing member of the workforce, you will help to shape this network of economic interdependence on Earth's surface.

▲ Passenger train in Leipzig, Germany

⑤ Environment and Society

Separating recyclables from the rest of your trash requires that you apply geographic perspectives in everyday life. As a responsible citizen of Earth, you will continually be called upon to weigh human needs against the limitations of the physical world. You will use geographic perspectives to make informed decisions about how best to protect Earth's physical environment.

⑥ The Uses of Geography

In school you practice core geography skills as you study the history of Earth, read maps, and interpret historical events with respect to location. Your future use of geography may be less direct, but far more important. Applying geographic principles and perspectives will help you build a better future for the world's people and safeguard the best interests of our planet.

▲ Tourists in Tiananmen Square, Beijing, China

Reading
for
Information

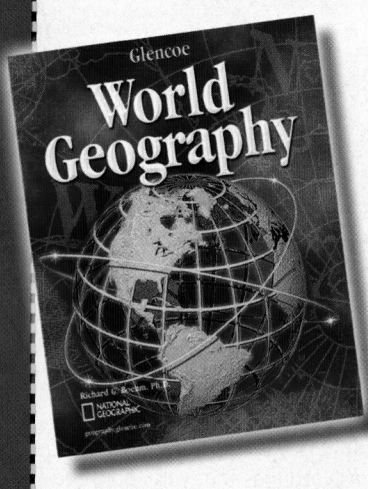

Think about your textbook as a tool that helps you learn more about the world around you. It is an example of nonfiction writing—it describes real-life events, people, ideas, and places. Here is a menu of reading strategies that will help you become a better textbook reader. As you come to passages in your textbook that you don't understand, refer to these reading strategies for help.

Before You Read

Set a Purpose
- Why are you reading the textbook?
- How does the subject relate to your life?
- How might you be able to use what you learn in your own life?

Preview
- Read the chapter title to find what the topic will be.
- Read the subtitles to see what you will learn about the topic.
- Skim the photos, charts, graphs, or maps. How do they support the topic?
- Look for vocabulary words that are boldfaced. How are they defined?

Draw From Your Own Background
- What have you read or heard about concerning new information on the topic?
- How is the new information different from what you already know?
- How will the information that you already know help you understand the new information?

As You Read

Question

- What is the main idea?
- How do the photos, charts, graphs, and maps support the main idea?

Connect

- Think about people, places, and events in your own life. Are there any similarities with those in your textbook?
- Can you relate the textbook information to other areas of your life?

Predict

- Predict events or outcomes by using clues and information that you already know.
- Change your predictions as you read and gather new information.

Visualize

- Pay careful attention to details and descriptions.
- Create graphic organizers to show relationships that you find in the information.

After You Read

Summarize

- Describe the main idea and how the details support it.
- Use your own words to explain what you have read.

Assess

- What was the main idea?
- Did the text clearly support the main idea?
- Did you learn anything new from the material?
- Can you use this new information in other school subjects or at home?
- What other sources could you use to find more information about the topic?

Look for Clues As You Read

- **Comparison-and-Contrast Sentences:**

  Look for clue words and phrases that signal comparison, such as *similarly, just as, both, in common, also,* and *too.*

  Look for clue words and phrases that signal contrast, such as *on the other hand, in contrast to, however, different, instead of, rather than, but,* and *unlike.*

- **Cause-and-Effect Sentences:**

  Look for clue words and phrases such as *because, as a result, therefore, that is why, since, so, for this reason,* and *consequently.*

- **Chronological Sentences:**

  Look for clue words and phrases such as *after, before, first, next, last, during, finally, earlier, later, since,* and *then.*

REFERENCE ATLAS

NATIONAL GEOGRAPHIC

ATLAS KEY

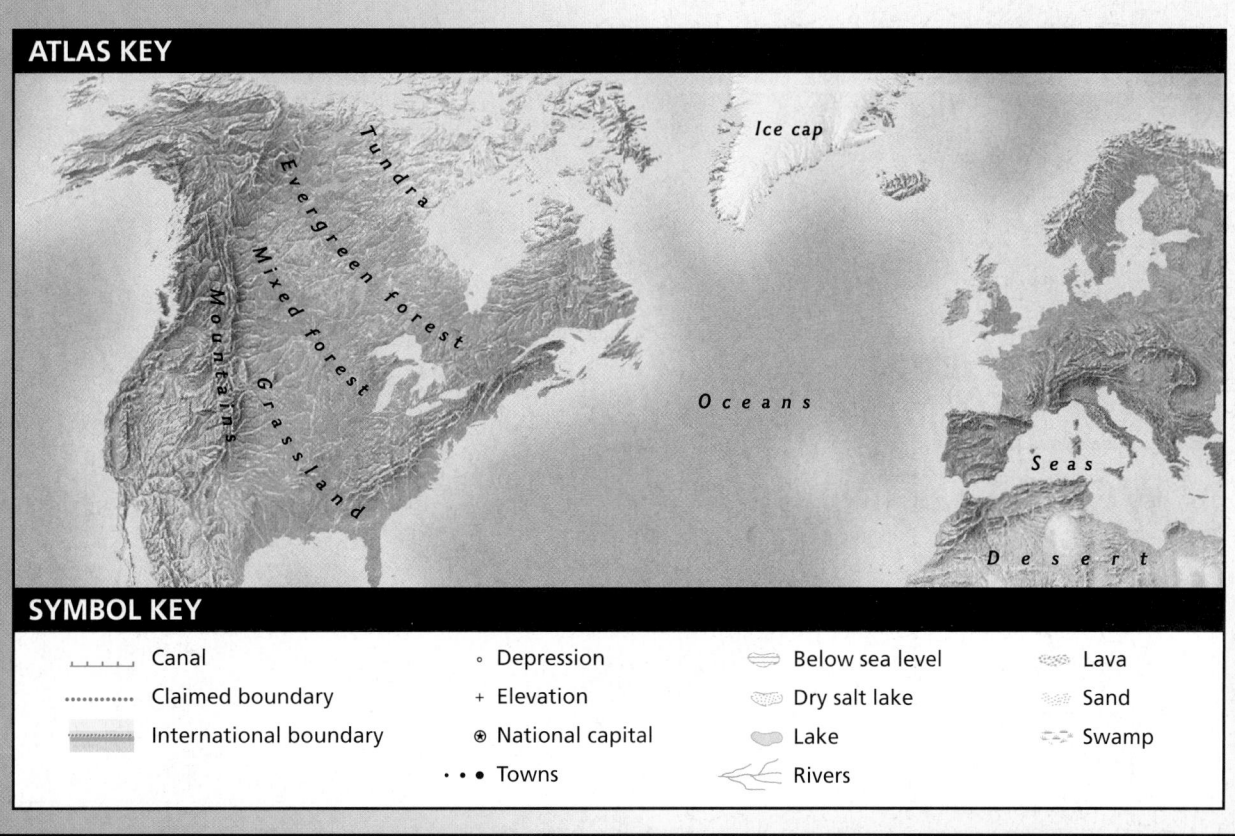

SYMBOL KEY

⊥⊥⊥	Canal	○	Depression	➾	Below sea level	⬤	Lava
··········	Claimed boundary	+	Elevation	➾	Dry salt lake	⬤	Sand
▨▨▨	International boundary	⊛	National capital	➾	Lake	➾	Swamp
		• • •	Towns	⪕	Rivers		

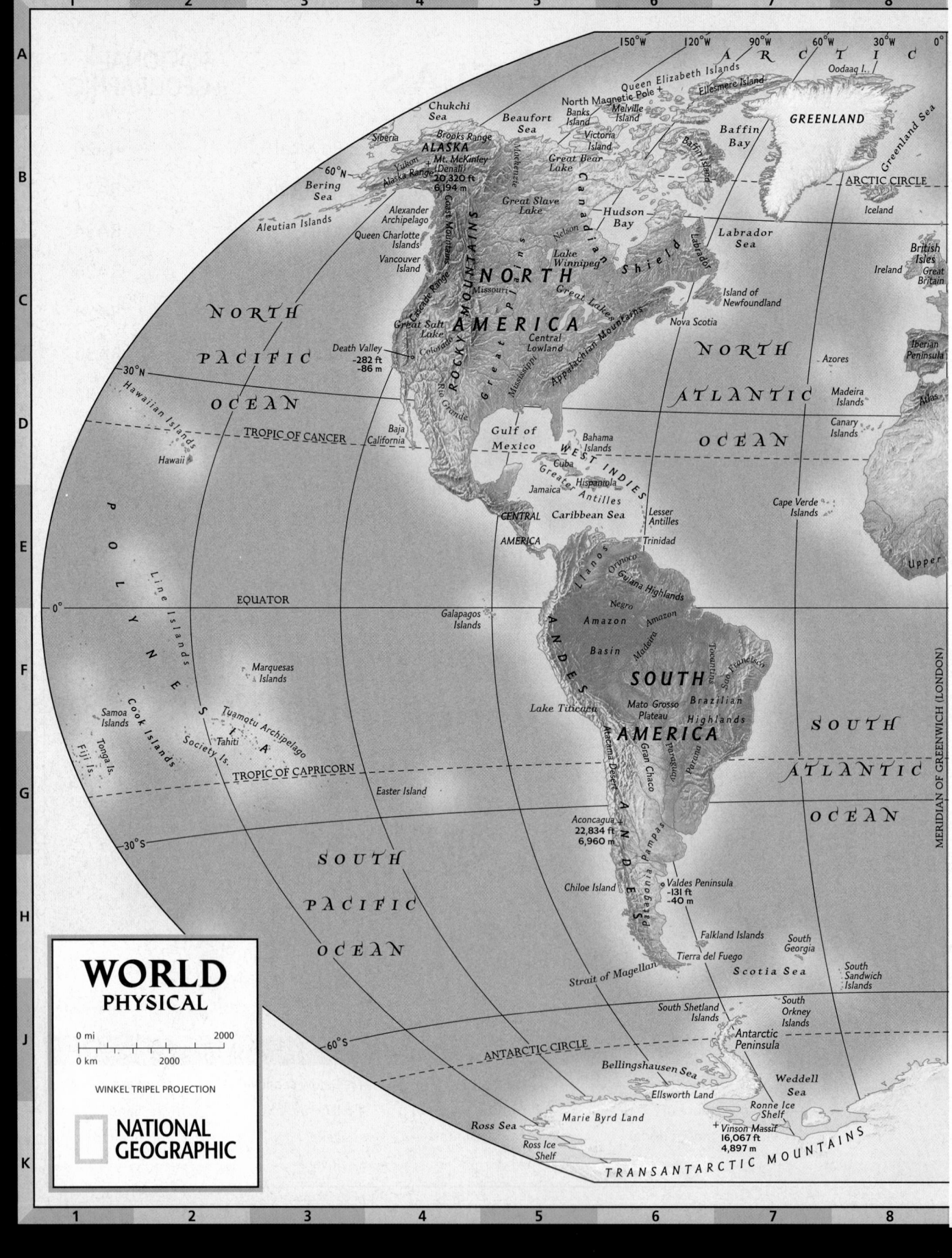

WORLD
PHYSICAL

0 mi — 2000
0 km — 2000

WINKEL TRIPEL PROJECTION

NATIONAL GEOGRAPHIC

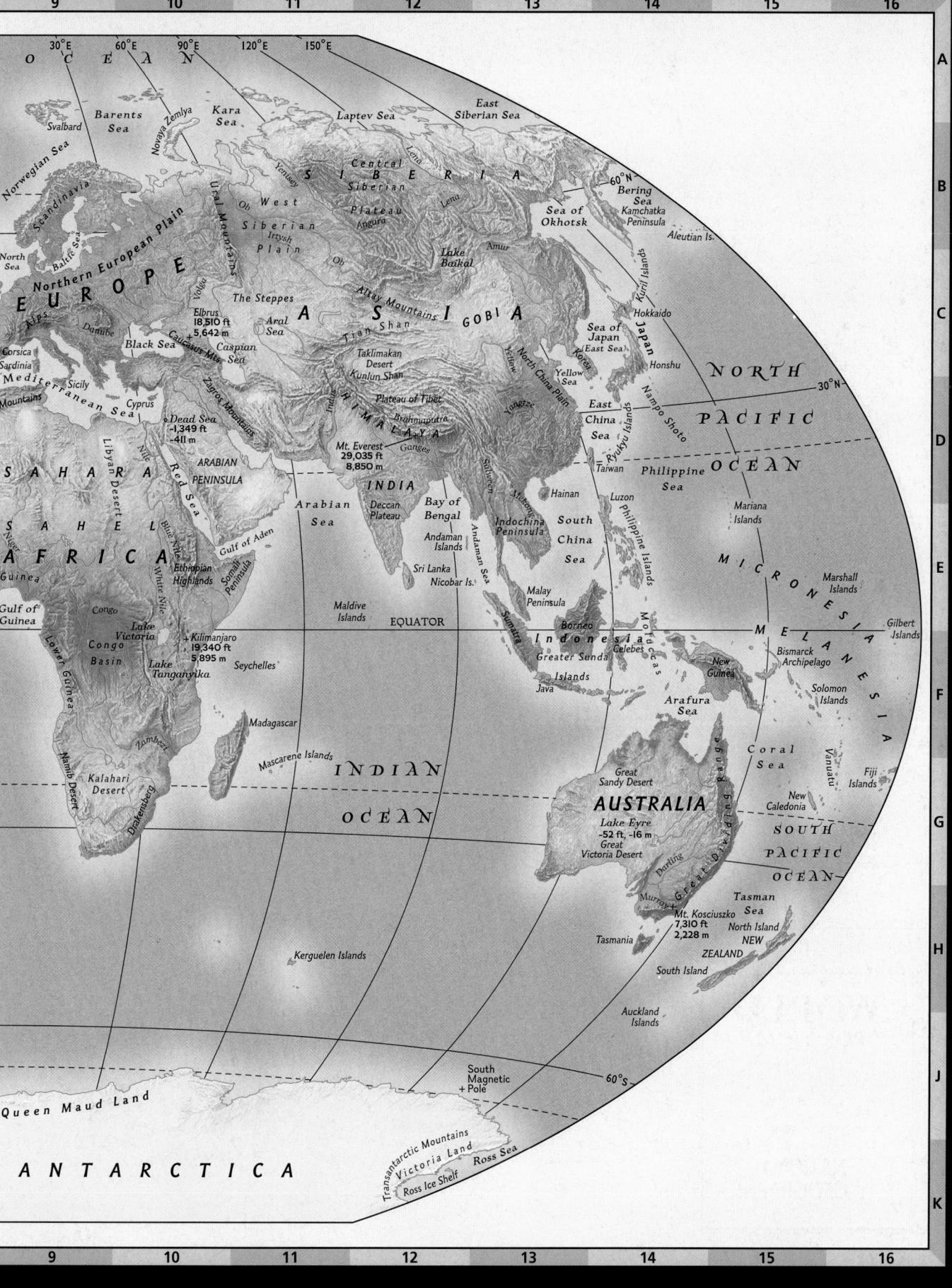

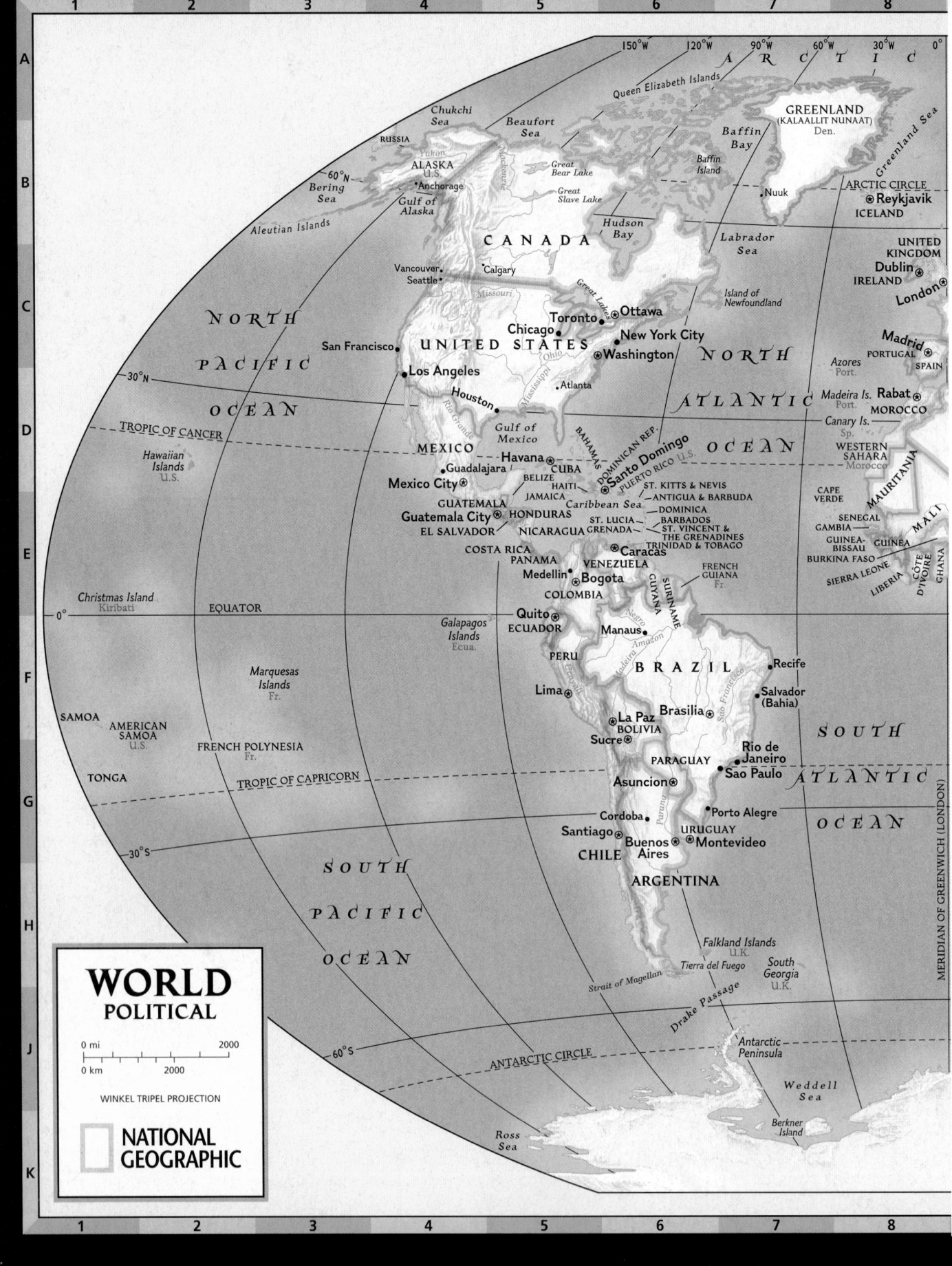

WORLD
POLITICAL

0 mi   2000

0 km   2000

WINKEL TRIPEL PROJECTION

NATIONAL
GEOGRAPHIC

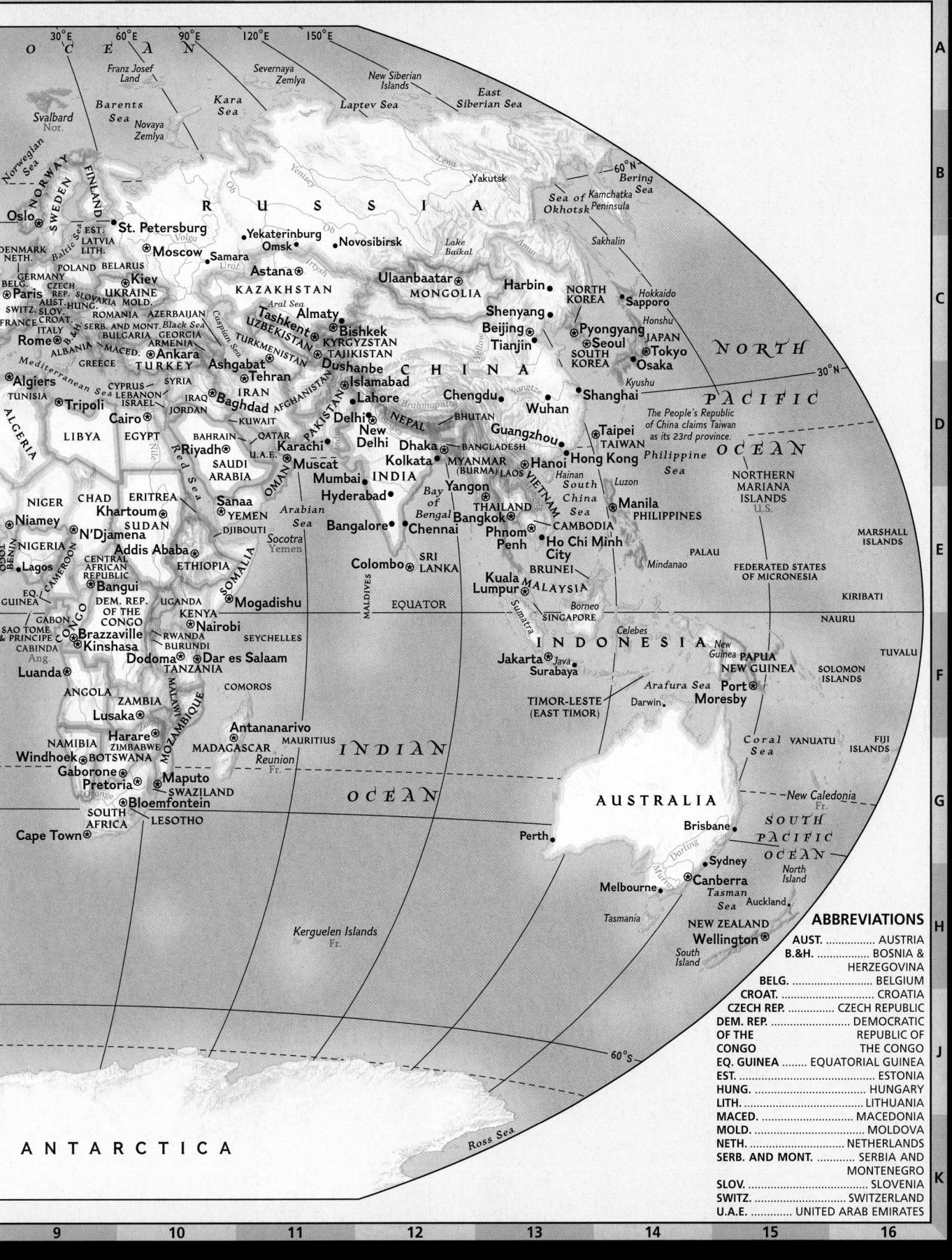

ABBREVIATIONS

AUST.	AUSTRIA
B.&H.	BOSNIA & HERZEGOVINA
BELG.	BELGIUM
CROAT.	CROATIA
CZECH REP.	CZECH REPUBLIC
DEM. REP. OF THE CONGO	DEMOCRATIC REPUBLIC OF THE CONGO
EQ. GUINEA	EQUATORIAL GUINEA
EST.	ESTONIA
HUNG.	HUNGARY
LITH.	LITHUANIA
MACED.	MACEDONIA
MOLD.	MOLDOVA
NETH.	NETHERLANDS
SERB. AND MONT.	SERBIA AND MONTENEGRO
SLOV.	SLOVENIA
SWITZ.	SWITZERLAND
U.A.E.	UNITED ARAB EMIRATES

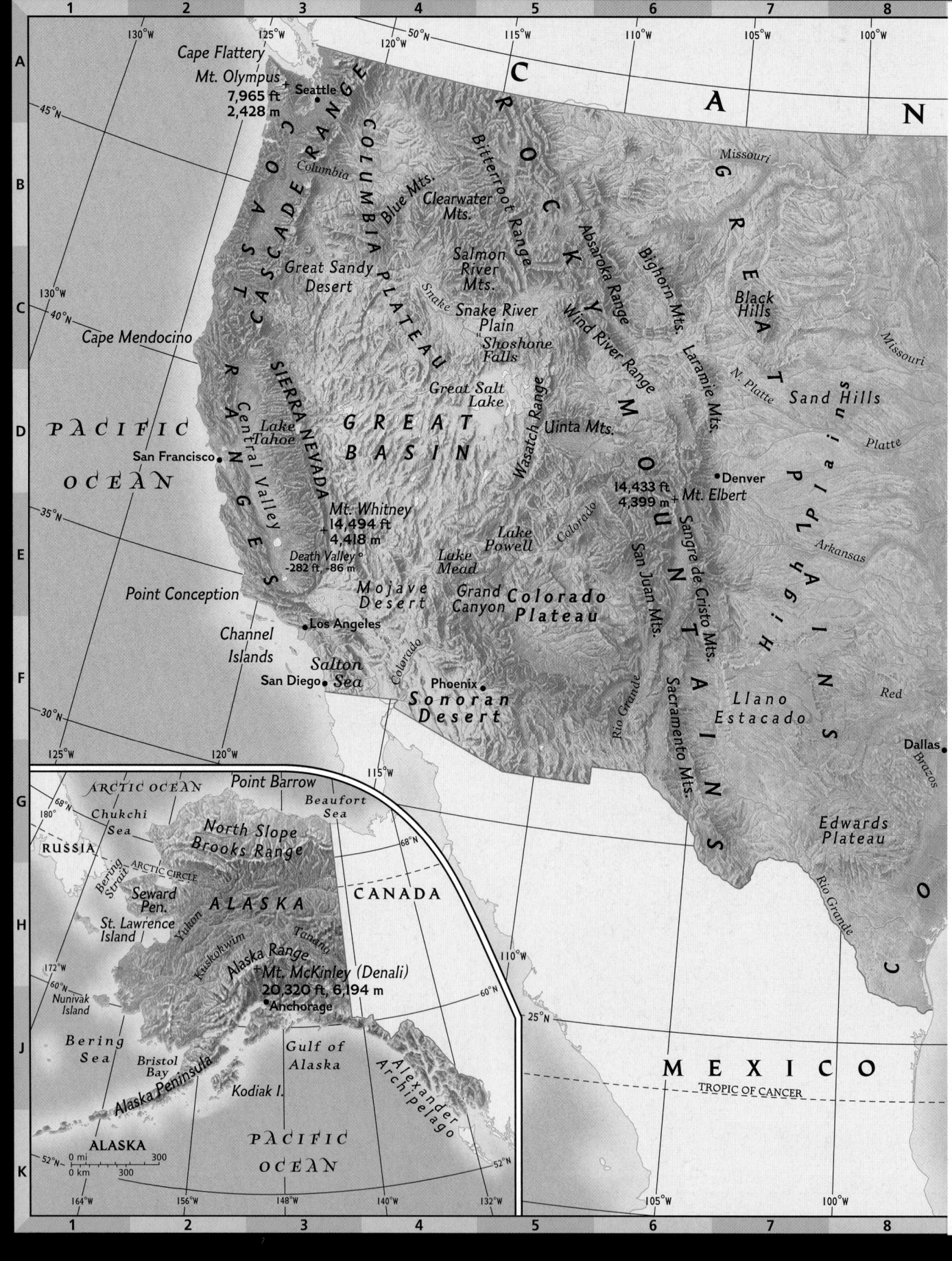

CANADA

1   2   3   4   5   6   7   8

A
Cape Flattery
Mt. Olympus
7,965 ft
2,428 m   • Seattle
45°N

C A N A D A

Missouri

B
Columbia

C A S C A D E   R A N G E
COLUMBIA PLATEAU

Blue Mts.
Clearwater Mts.
Bitterroot Range
Salmon River Mts.
Great Sandy Desert

R O C K Y

G R E A T

C
130°W
40°N
Cape Mendocino

Snake
Snake River Plain
Shoshone Falls

Absaroka Range
Bighorn Mts.
Laramie Mts.
Wind River Range

Black Hills

Missouri

N. Platte

D
PACIFIC
OCEAN
San Francisco •
Central Valley
Lake Tahoe
SIERRA NEVADA

GREAT BASIN

Great Salt Lake

Wasatch Range
Uinta Mts.

M O U N T A I N S

14,433 ft
4,399 m + Mt. Elbert
• Denver

Sand Hills
Platte

E
35°N
Point Conception

Mt. Whitney
14,494 ft
4,418 m
Death Valley °
-282 ft, -86 m

Lake Mead

Lake Powell

Colorado

San Juan Mts.

Sangre de Cristo Mts.

H I G H   P L A I N S

Arkansas

F
30°N
Channel Islands
San Diego •   Salton Sea
• Los Angeles

Mojave Desert

Grand Canyon

Colorado Plateau

Colorado

Rio Grande

Sacramento Mts.

Llano Estacado

Red

Dallas •
Brazos

Sonoran Desert
Phoenix •

125°W   120°W   115°W

G
180°   68°N
ARCTIC OCEAN
Chukchi Sea
RUSSIA
Point Barrow
Beaufort Sea
North Slope
Brooks Range

68°N

Edwards Plateau

C O

H
172°W
60°N
Bering Strait
ARCTIC CIRCLE
Seward Pen.
St. Lawrence Island
Nunivak Island

ALASKA

Yukon
Kuskokwim
Tanana
Alaska Range
+ Mt. McKinley (Denali)
20,320 ft, 6,194 m
• Anchorage

CANADA

110°W

Rio Grande

J
Bering Sea
Bristol Bay
Alaska Peninsula
Kodiak I.
Gulf of Alaska
Alexander Archipelago

60°N

25°N

M E X I C O

TROPIC OF CANCER

K
52°N   ALASKA   300
0 mi
0 km   300

PACIFIC OCEAN

52°N

164°W   156°W   148°W   140°W   132°W   105°W   100°W

1   2   3   4   5   6   7   8

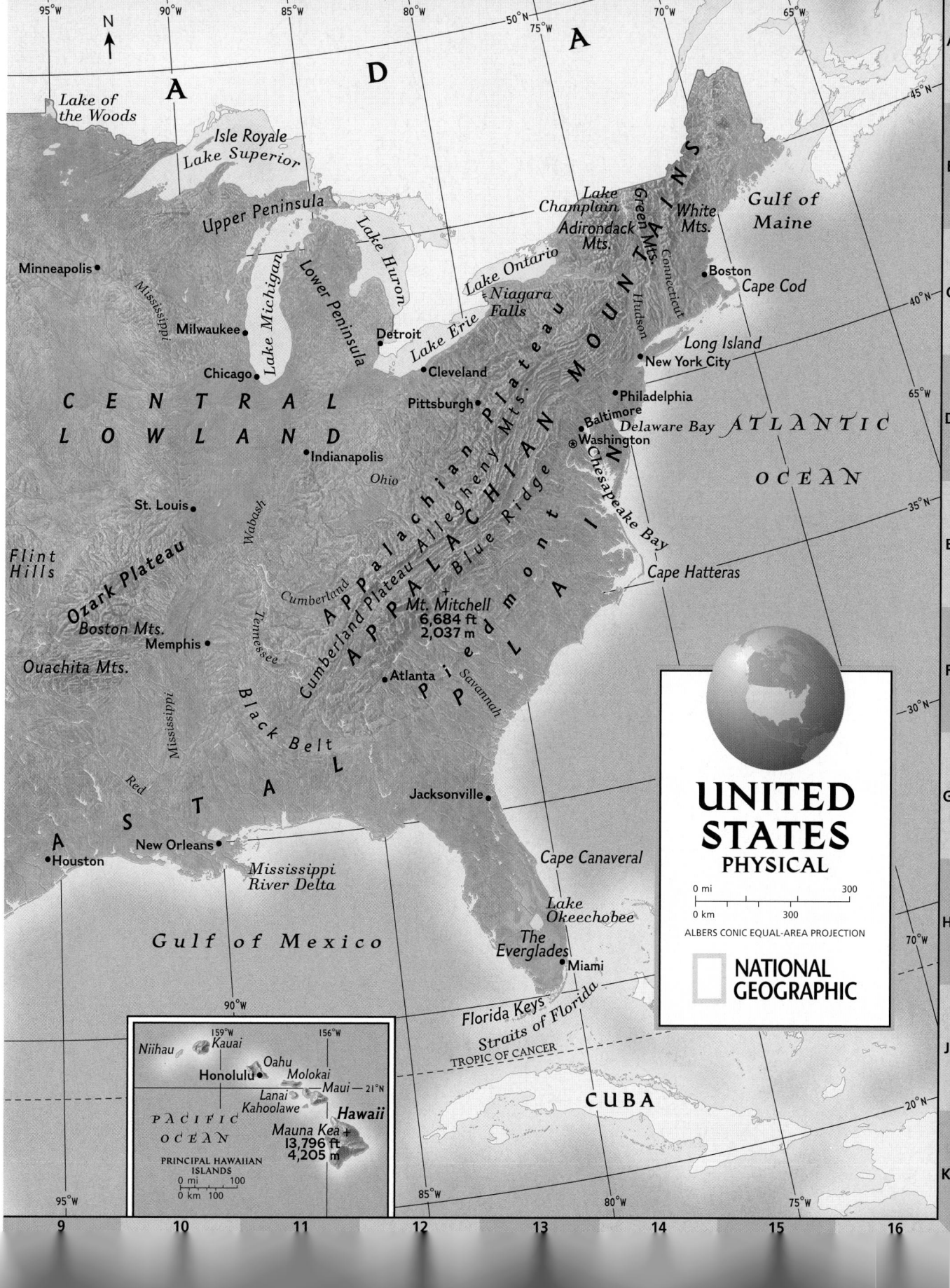

UNITED STATES

PHYSICAL

0 mi   300

0 km   300

ALBERS CONIC EQUAL-AREA PROJECTION

NATIONAL GEOGRAPHIC

CANADA

Lake of the Woods

Isle Royale
Lake Superior

Upper Peninsula

Lower Peninsula

Lake Huron

Lake Michigan

Lake Ontario

Lake Erie

Niagara Falls

Lake Champlain

Adirondack Mts.

Green Mts.

White Mts.

Gulf of Maine

Connecticut

Hudson

Boston

Cape Cod

Long Island

New York City

Philadelphia

Baltimore

Delaware Bay

Washington

Chesapeake Bay

ATLANTIC OCEAN

Cape Hatteras

Minneapolis

Milwaukee

Chicago

Detroit

Cleveland

Pittsburgh

Indianapolis

Mississippi

CENTRAL LOWLAND

Ohio

St. Louis

Wabash

Flint Hills

Ozark Plateau

Boston Mts.

Memphis

Ouachita Mts.

Tennessee

Mississippi

Red

Black Belt

Appalachian Plateau

Allegheny Mts.

APPALACHIAN MOUNTAINS

Cumberland Plateau

Cumberland

Blue Ridge

Mt. Mitchell
6,684 ft
2,037 m

APPALACHIAN

Piedmont

Atlanta

Savannah

C O A S T A L

Houston

New Orleans

Mississippi River Delta

Jacksonville

Cape Canaveral

Lake Okeechobee

The Everglades

Miami

Gulf of Mexico

Florida Keys

Straits of Florida

TROPIC OF CANCER

CUBA

PRINCIPAL HAWAIIAN ISLANDS

Niihau

Kauai

159°W

Oahu

Honolulu

Molokai

Lanai

Kahoolawe

Maui — 21°N

156°W

Hawaii

Mauna Kea
13,796 ft
4,205 m

PACIFIC OCEAN

0 mi   100

0 km   100

N

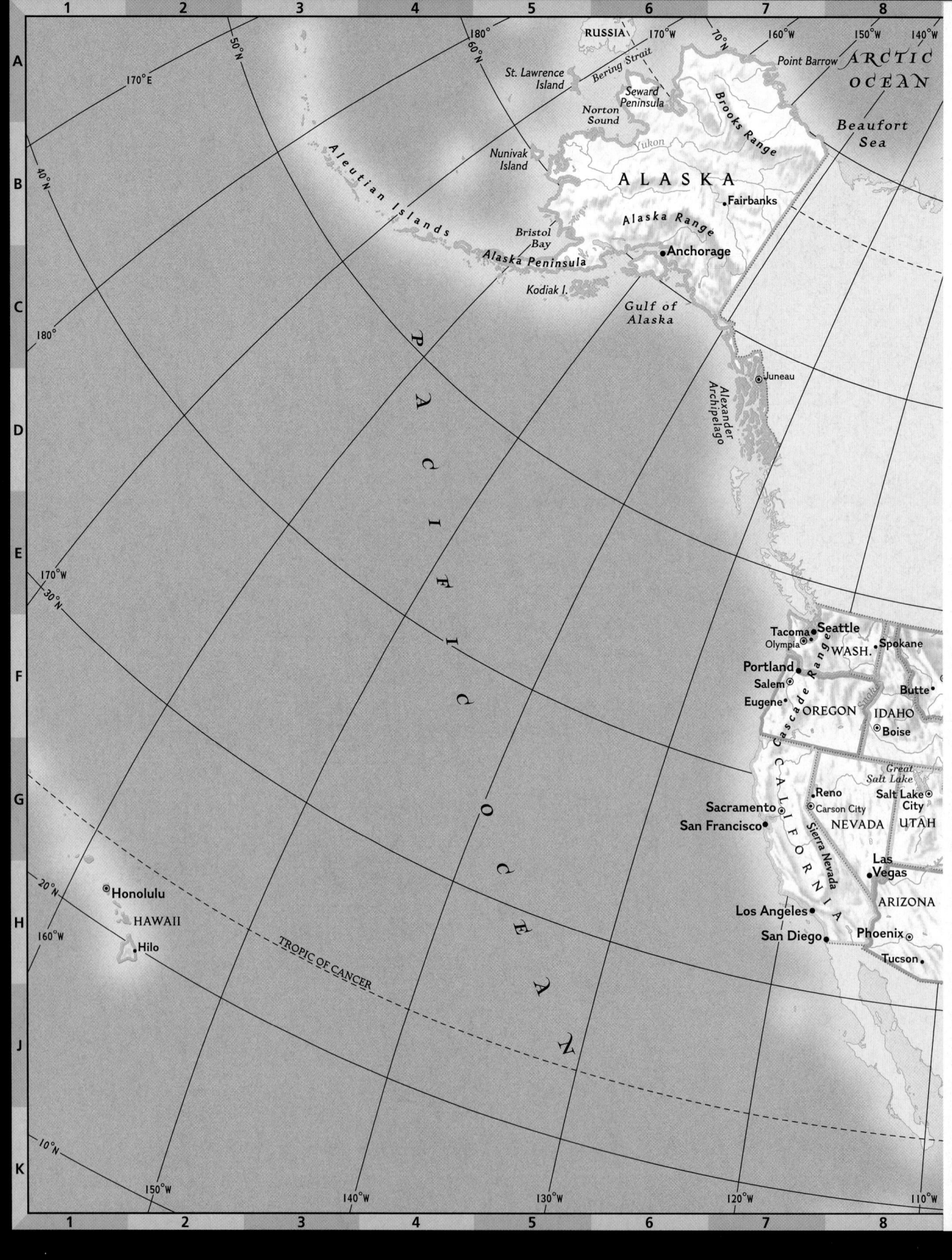

UNITED
STATES
POLITICAL

0 mi   600
0 km   600

OBLIQUE AZIMUTHAL EQUIDISTANT PROJECTION

NATIONAL
GEOGRAPHIC

GREENLAND
(KALAALLIT NUNAAT)
Den.

ARCTIC CIRCLE

C A N A D A

MONTANA
Helena
Billings

NORTH
DAKOTA
Bismarck

MINNESOTA

Lake Superior

MICHIGAN

MAINE
Augusta

Montpelier
Portland
Concord, N.H.

NEW
YORK
Albany
Boston, MASS.
Providence, R.I.
Hartford, CONN.

SOUTH
DAKOTA
Pierre

Minneapolis
St. Paul
WISCONSIN
Milwaukee
Madison
Lansing

L. Michigan

Lake Huron

Detroit
Cleveland PA.
L. Erie
Buffalo

New York City
Trenton, N.J.
Philadelphia

WYOMING
Casper
Cheyenne

Sioux City
IOWA
Des Moines

Chicago

Toledo
IND.
OHIO
Columbus
Pittsburgh

Harrisburg

Dover, DEL.
Annapolis, MD.
Washington, D.C.

Denver

NEBRASKA
Lincoln
Omaha

Indianapolis

Dayton W. VA.
Cincinnati

Charleston
Richmond
Virginia Beach

COLORADO

Kansas City
MISSOURI
Topeka
Jefferson City

Springfield
St. Louis
Frankfort
Louisville
KENTUCKY

VIRGINIA

KANSAS

Raleigh
NORTH CAROLINA
Charlotte
SOUTH
CAROLINA
Columbia

Bermuda Is.
U.K.

Santa Fe
Albuquerque

Tulsa
Nashville
TENNESSEE

Oklahoma City
OKLAHOMA

ARKANSAS
Memphis
Little Rock

Atlanta
GEORGIA

Charleston

NEW
MEXICO
El Paso

Birmingham
MISS.
ALABAMA
Jackson
Montgomery

Savannah

Fort
Worth
Dallas

LOUISIANA

TEXAS

Tallahassee

Jacksonville

Austin

Baton Rouge

FLORIDA

San Antonio

Houston

New Orleans

Tampa

Gulf of
Mexico

Miami

BAHAMAS

M E X I C O

Rio Grande

Straits of Florida

ANTIGUA
& BARBUDA
ST. KITTS
& NEVIS

CUBA

Caribbean

Sea

JAMAICA

HAITI
DOMINICAN
REPUBLIC

San Juan
PUERTO
RICO
U.S.

DOMINICA

ATLANTIC OCEAN

APPALACHIAN MTS.

Lake
Ontario

Pierre

Pittsburgh

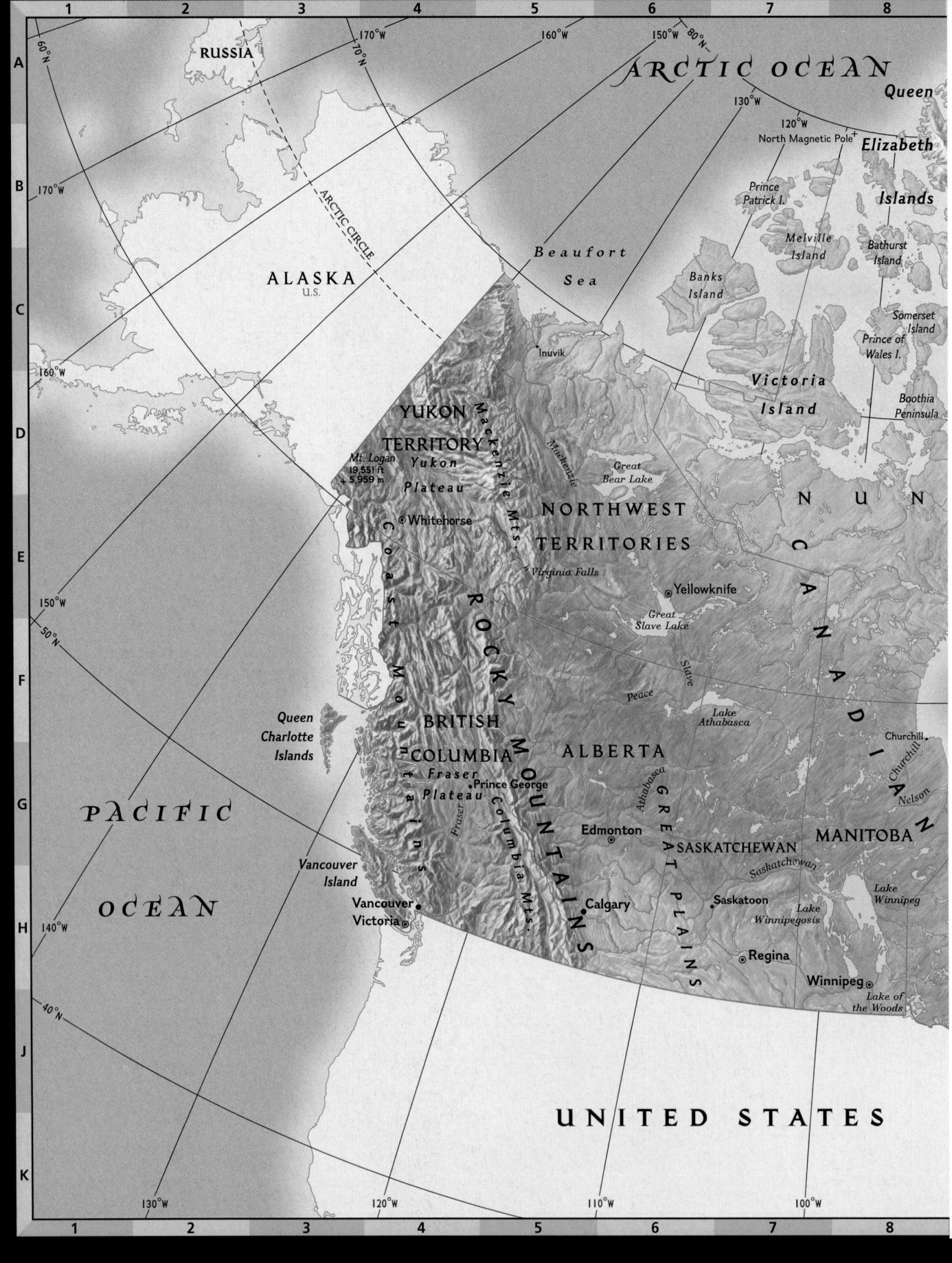

CANADA
PHYSICAL/POLITICAL

0 mi   400
0 km   400

AZIMUTHAL EQUIDISTANT PROJECTION

NATIONAL GEOGRAPHIC

N

Ellesmere
Island

Devon Island

GREENLAND
(KALAALLIT NUNAAT)
Den.

ICELAND

Baffin
Bay

Baffin Island

Davis Strait

Melville
Peninsula
Foxe
Basin

A V U T

Southampton
Island

Iqaluit

Hudson Strait

Labrador
Sea

Ungava
Bay

Hudson

Bay

Belcher
Islands

James Bay

QUEBEC

Schefferville

Smallwood
Reservoir

Happy Valley-
Goose Bay
Churchill Falls

Cartwright

NEWFOUNDLAND
AND LABRADOR

Island of
Newfoundland

St. John's
Avalon
Peninsula

St.-Pierre & Miquelon
Fr.

S H I E L D

ONTARIO

Lake
Nipigon

Thunder
Bay
Lake
Superior

Sudbury

Rouyn-Noranda

Chicoutimi

Quebec
City

Manicouagan
Reservoir
Sept-Iles

Gaspe
Pen.

Anticosti I.

Gulf of
St. Lawrence

PRINCE
EDWARD
ISLAND

Cape Breton I.

Charlottetown

NOVA
SCOTIA

ATLANTIC

NEW
BRUNSWICK

Fredericton
Saint John

Halifax

St. Lawrence

Bay of Fundy

OCEAN

Montreal
Ottawa

Lake
Huron

Lake Michigan

Toronto

Niagara Falls
London

L. Ontario

L. Erie

MIDDLE
AMERICA
PHYSICAL/POLITICAL

0 mi   400
0 km   400

AZIMUTHAL EQUIDISTANT PROJECTION

NATIONAL
GEOGRAPHIC

UNITED STATES

N

Tijuana
Mexicali
Sonoran Desert
30°N
BAJA CALIFORNIA
Gulf of California
Baja California
Ciudad Juarez
SONORA
CHIHUAHUA
Chihuahua
Rio Grande
COAHUILA
M E X I C O
Sierra Madre Occidental
Sierra Madre Oriental
BAJA CALIFORNIA SUR
DURANGO
Nuevo Laredo
SINALOA
La Paz
False Cape
Mazatlan
ZACATECAS
Monterrey
NUEVO LEON
Matamoros
TAMAULIPAS
Gulf of Mexico
20°N
SAN LUIS POTOSI
NAYARIT
Ciudad Madero
Tampico
AGUASCALIENTES
Guadalajara
San Luis Potosi
QUERETARO
Revillagigedo Islands
Mex.
JALISCO
Leon
VERACRUZ
HIDALGO
TLAXCALA
Merida
YUCATAN
Coz
Isla
Yucatan
GUANAJUATO
Mexico City
Orizaba
18,855 ft
+5,747 m
Bay of Campeche
Yucatan Peninsula
QUINTANA ROO
COLIMA
MICHOACAN
Popocatepetl
17,802 ft
5,426 m
PUEBLA
Veracruz
CAMPECHE
DISTRITO FEDERAL
Sierra Madre del Sur
TABASCO
Belize City
MEXICO
Belmopan
GUERRERO
OAXACA
CHIAPAS
BELIZE
Gulf of Honduras
MORELOS
Acapulco
Gulf of Tehuantepec
Isthmus of Tehuantepec
Sierra Madre
HON
GUATEMALA
Tegucigalpa
10°N
Guatemala City
EL SALVADOR
San Salvador
Leon
CENTRAL
AMERICA
PACIFIC
OCEAN
Cocos Island
C.R.
0°
110°W
100°W
90°W

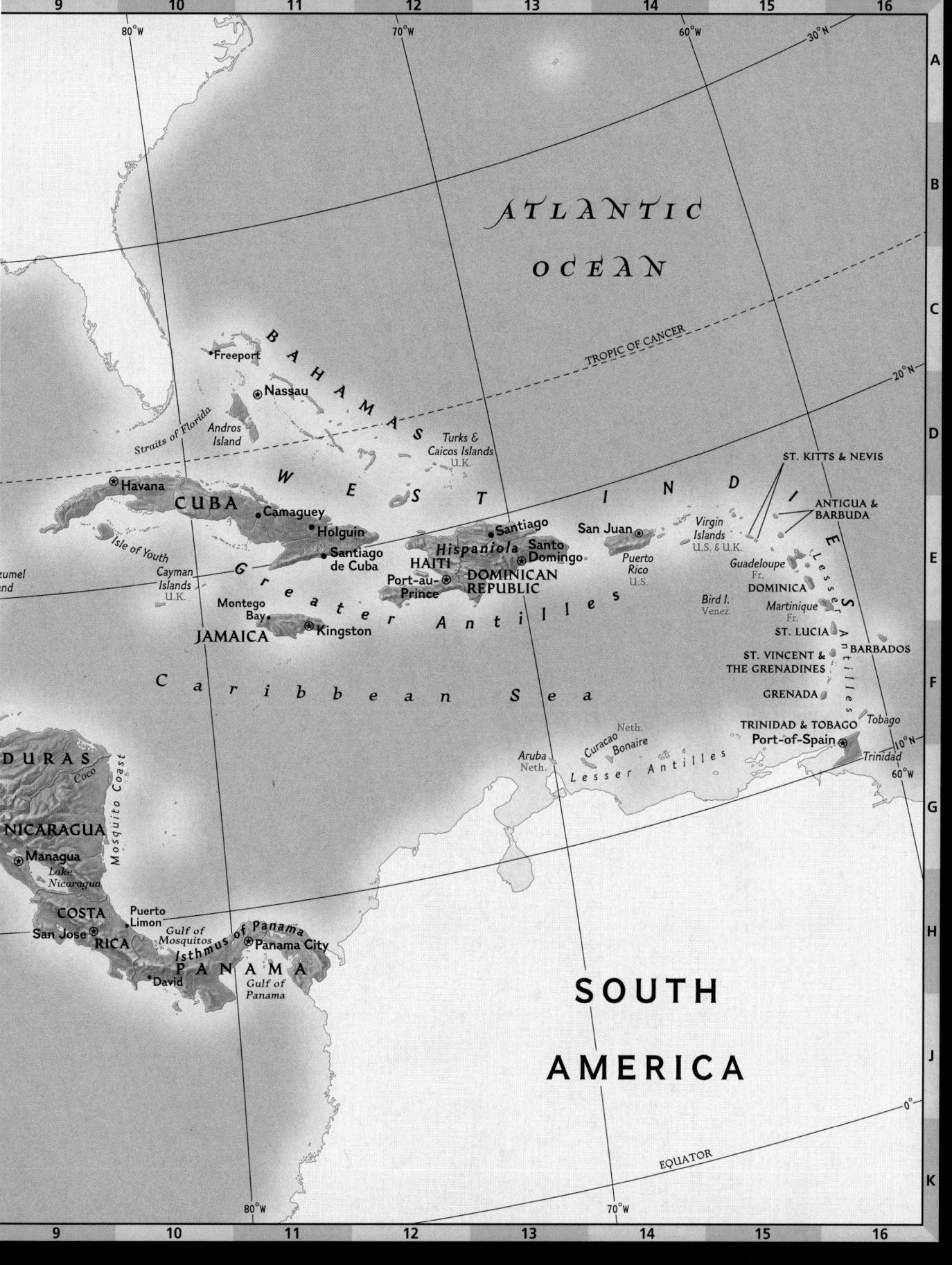

ATLANTIC

OCEAN

TROPIC OF CANCER

BAHAMAS

•Freeport

⊛ Nassau

Straits of Florida

Andros
Island

Turks &
Caicos Islands
U.K.

ST. KITTS & NEVIS

W E S T

⊛ Havana

CUBA

• Camaguey

I N D I E S

Virgin
Islands
U.S. & U.K.

ANTIGUA &
BARBUDA

• Holguin

Santiago
Hispaniola

San Juan ⊛

Guadeloupe
Fr.

Isle of Youth

• Santiago
de Cuba

Santo
⊛ Domingo

Lesser

Cayman
Islands
U.K.

HAITI

Puerto
Rico
U.S.

DOMINICA

Cozumel
sland

G

e

Port-au-
Prince ⊛

DOMINICAN
REPUBLIC

Bird I.
Venez.

Martinique
Fr.

Montego
Bay •

ST. LUCIA

BARBADOS

JAMAICA

⊛ Kingston

r   e   a   t   e   r

A n t i l l e s

ST. VINCENT &
THE GRENADINES

GRENADA

Antilles

C   a   r   i   b   b   e   a   n   S   e   a

TRINIDAD & TOBAGO

Tobago

Port-of-Spain ⊛

Curacao Neth.
Bonaire

Trinidad

DURAS

Coco

Mosquito Coast

Aruba
Neth.

Lesser Antilles

NICARAGUA

⊛ Managua

Lake
Nicaragua

Puerto
• Limon

Gulf of
Mosquitos

Isthmus of Panama

COSTA

San Jose ⊛

RICA

⊛ Panama City

SOUTH

P A N A M A

• David

Gulf of
Panama

AMERICA

EQUATOR

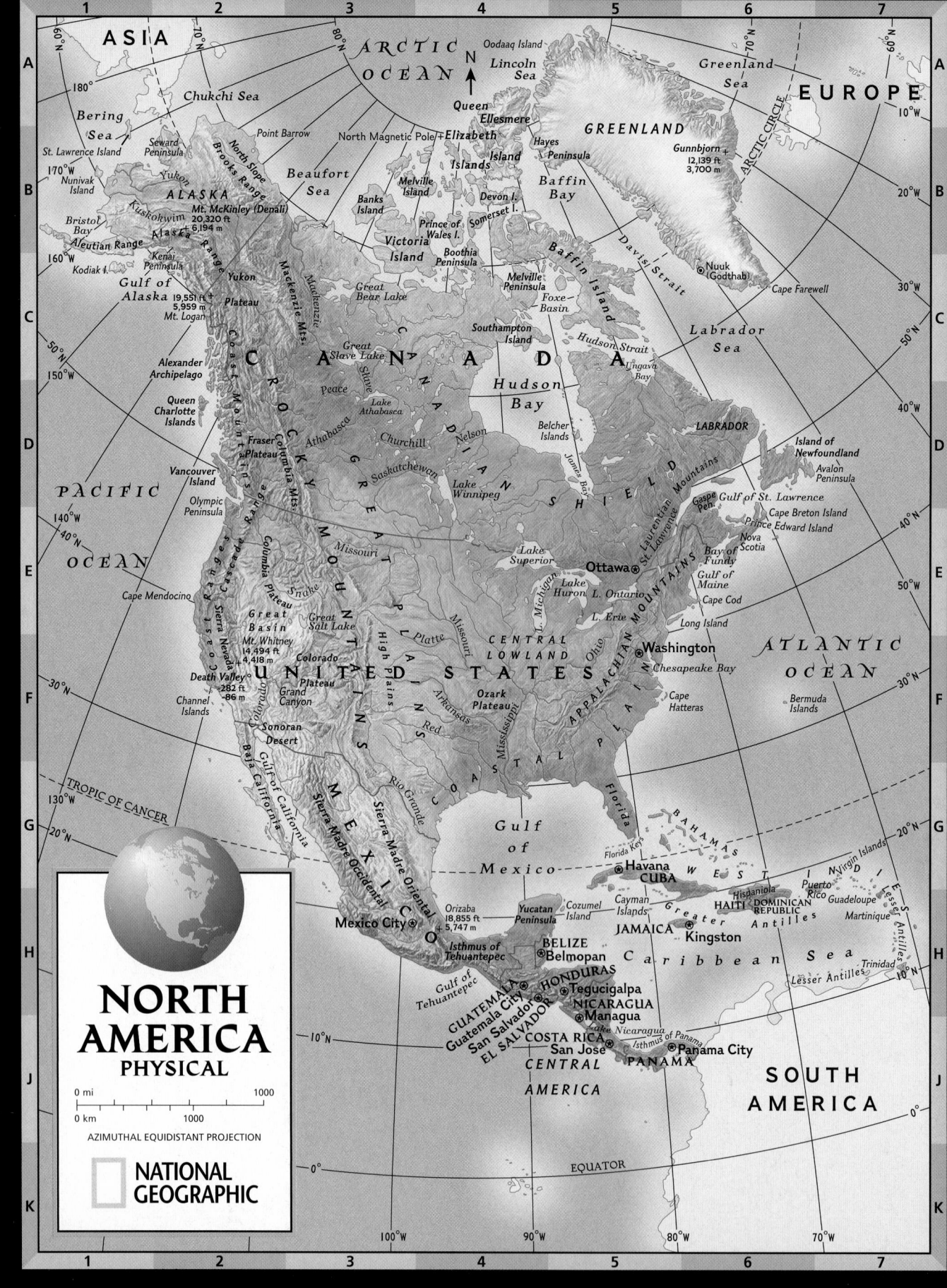

NORTH AMERICA
PHYSICAL

0 mi 1000

0 km 1000

AZIMUTHAL EQUIDISTANT PROJECTION

NATIONAL GEOGRAPHIC

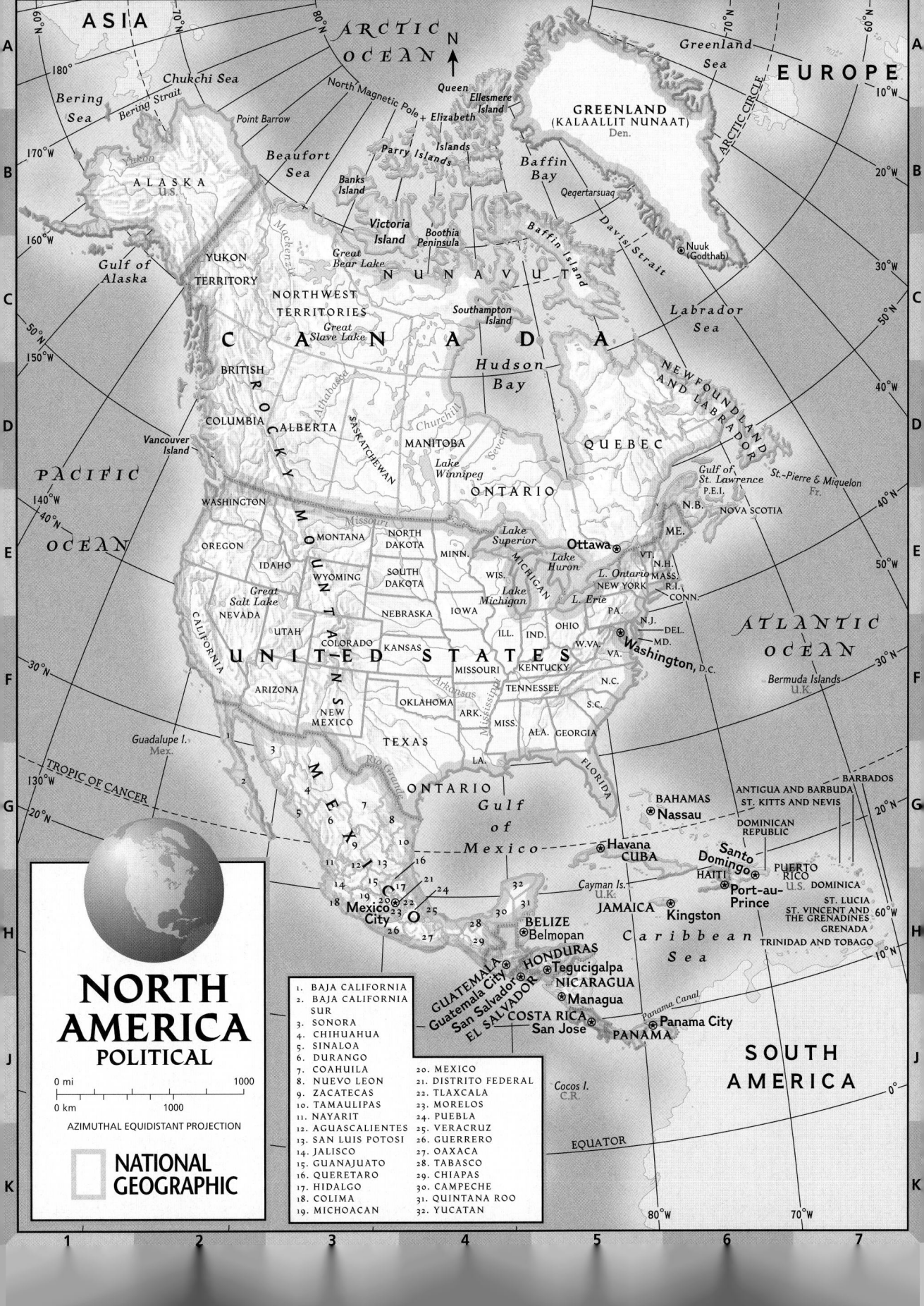

NORTH AMERICA
POLITICAL

0 mi — 1000
0 km — 1000

AZIMUTHAL EQUIDISTANT PROJECTION

NATIONAL GEOGRAPHIC

1. BAJA CALIFORNIA
2. BAJA CALIFORNIA SUR
3. SONORA
4. CHIHUAHUA
5. SINALOA
6. DURANGO
7. COAHUILA
8. NUEVO LEON
9. ZACATECAS
10. TAMAULIPAS
11. NAYARIT
12. AGUASCALIENTES
13. SAN LUIS POTOSI
14. JALISCO
15. GUANAJUATO
16. QUERETARO
17. HIDALGO
18. COLIMA
19. MICHOACAN
20. MEXICO
21. DISTRITO FEDERAL
22. TLAXCALA
23. MORELOS
24. PUEBLA
25. VERACRUZ
26. GUERRERO
27. OAXACA
28. TABASCO
29. CHIAPAS
30. CAMPECHE
31. QUINTANA ROO
32. YUCATAN

A map of South America (Physical), labeled with a grid of numbers 1–7 horizontally and letters A–K vertically.

Caribbean Sea

N

Lake Maracaibo

Caracas

VENEZUELA

Orinoco

GUYANA
Georgetown

LLANOS

SURINAME
Paramaribo

Malpelo I.

Bogota

COLOMBIA

Angel Falls
Total drop
3,212 ft 979 m

GUIANA HIGHLANDS

Cayenne
FRENCH
GUIANA

ATLANTIC
OCEAN

Boundary claimed
by Suriname

Quito
ECUADOR

Negro

Amazon

Marajo
Island

EQUATOR

A
M
A
Z
O
N

Amazon

Madeira

Tapajos

Xingu

Selvas

Purus

Teles Pires

Tocantins

BASIN

São Francisco

P
E
R
U

Ucayali

BRAZIL

Lima

Machu Picchu

Lake Titicaca

BOLIVIA
La Paz

MATO GROSSO

PLATEAU

BRAZILIAN

Brasilia

Sucre

HIGHLANDS

Altiplano

Salar
de Uyuni

PARAGUAY

GRAN CHACO

Paraguay

Iguazu
Falls

TROPIC OF CAPRICORN

San Felix I.   San Ambrosio I.

A
N
D
E
S

Asuncion

Parana

Uruguay

Aconcagua 22,834 ft
6,960 m

Juan Fernandez Is.

Santiago

Buenos
Aires

URUGUAY
Montevideo

Rio de la Plata

A
R
G
E
N
T
I
N
A

P
A
M
P
A
S

Negro

Chiloe Island

-131 ft
-40 m Valdes Peninsula

PATAGONIA

Taitao
Peninsula

Gulf of
San Jorge

PACIFIC
OCEAN

Wellington I.

Falkland Islands
(Islas Malvinas)

Stanley

Strait of Magellan
Tierra del Fuego

Cape Horn

South Georgia I.

80°W   60°W   50°W   40°W

10°N

0°

10°S

20°S

30°S

40°S

50°S

100°W   90°W   80°W   70°W   60°W   50°W   40°W   30°W   20°W

**SOUTH
AMERICA
PHYSICAL**

0 mi — 800
0 km — 800

AZIMUTHAL EQUIDISTANT PROJECTION

**NATIONAL
GEOGRAPHIC**

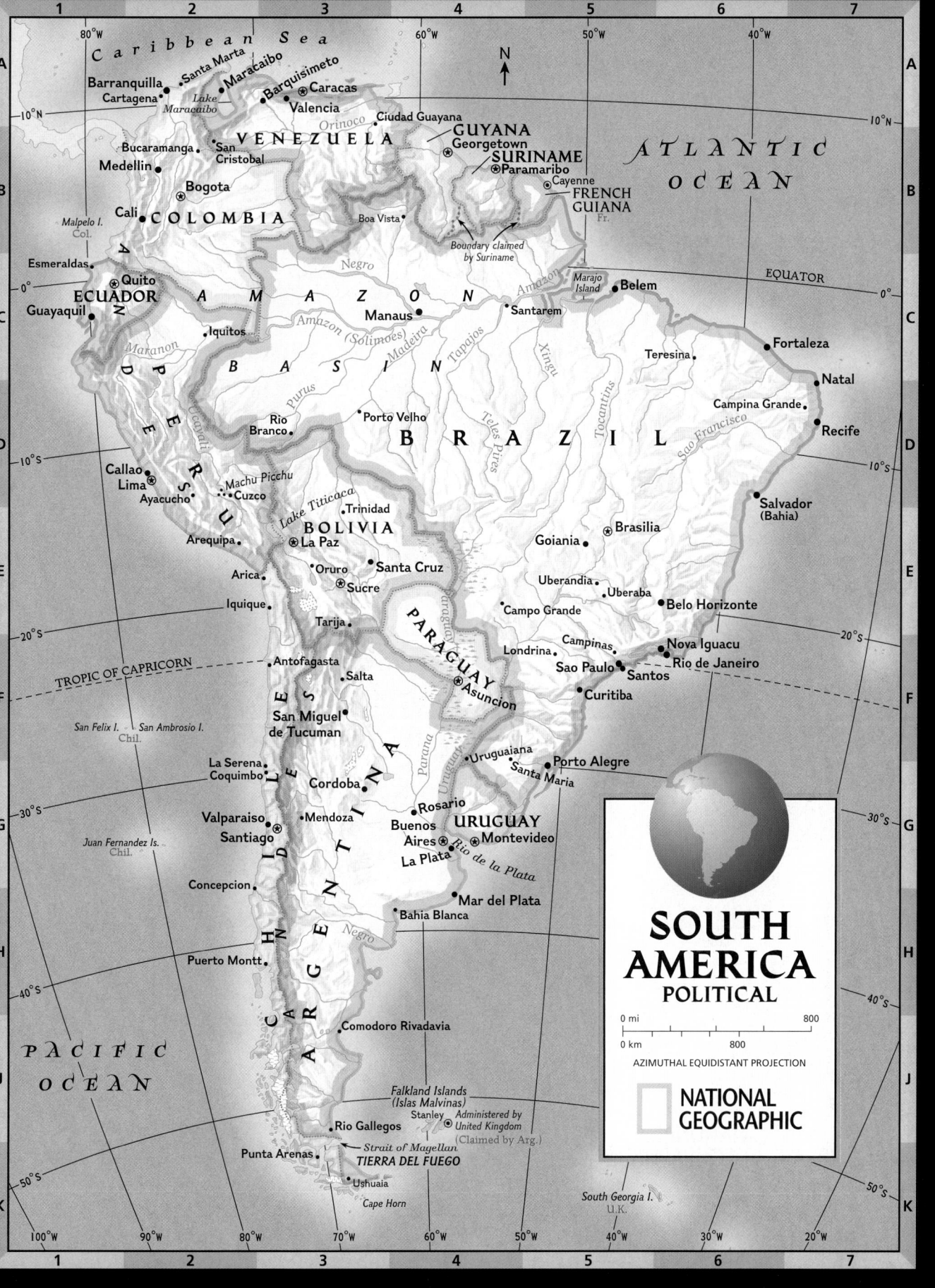

South America Political map

Grid coordinates: columns 1-7 (top and bottom), rows A-K (left and right)

Caribbean Sea

Longitude lines: 80°W, 60°W, 50°W, 40°W

Barranquilla
Santa Marta
Cartagena
Maracaibo
Barquisimeto
Caracas
Valencia
Lake Maracaibo
10°N

VENEZUELA
Ciudad Guayana
GUYANA
Georgetown
SURINAME
Paramaribo
Cayenne
FRENCH GUIANA Fr.

Bucaramanga
San Cristobal
Medellin
Bogota
COLOMBIA
Cali
Malpelo I. Col.
Boa Vista

Boundary claimed by Suriname

ATLANTIC OCEAN

Esmeraldas
Quito
ECUADOR
Guayaquil
EQUATOR
0°

Orinoco
Negro
Amazon
Marajo Island
Belem

Manaus
Santarem

A M A Z O N B A S I N

Amazon (Solimões)
Madeira
Tapajos
Xingu
Tocantins

Iquitos
Maranon
Ucayali
Purus

Teresina
Fortaleza
10°S
Natal
Campina Grande
Recife

P E R U
Rio Branco
Porto Velho
Teles Pires

B R A Z I L

Sao Francisco

Callao
Lima
Ayacucho
Cuzco
Machu Picchu
Trinidad
Lake Titicaca
BOLIVIA
La Paz
Arequipa
Oruro
Santa Cruz
Sucre
Arica
Iquique
Tarija

Salvador (Bahia)
10°S

Goiania
Brasilia
Uberlandia
Uberaba
Campo Grande
Belo Horizonte
20°S

A N D E S

TROPIC OF CAPRICORN
Antofagasta
Salta

PARAGUAY
Asuncion
Paraguay River

Londrina
Campinas
Sao Paulo
Santos
Nova Iguacu
Rio de Janeiro
Curitiba

San Felix I. — San Ambrosio I. Chil.

San Miguel de Tucuman

La Serena
Coquimbo
Cordoba
Mendoza
Rosario
Buenos Aires
La Plata
URUGUAY
Montevideo
Rio de la Plata
Parana
Uruguay
Uruguaiana
Santa Maria
Porto Alegre
30°S

Valparaiso
Santiago
Juan Fernandez Is. Chil.

Concepcion

A R G E N T I N A

Negro
Mar del Plata
Bahia Blanca
40°S

PACIFIC OCEAN

Puerto Montt

Comodoro Rivadavia

Falkland Islands (Islas Malvinas)
Stanley Administered by United Kingdom (Claimed by Arg.)

Rio Gallegos
Strait of Magellan
Punta Arenas
TIERRA DEL FUEGO
Ushuaia
Cape Horn

South Georgia I. U.K.
50°S

SOUTH AMERICA POLITICAL

0 mi 800
0 km 800

AZIMUTHAL EQUIDISTANT PROJECTION

NATIONAL GEOGRAPHIC

Longitude lines (bottom): 100°W, 90°W, 80°W, 70°W, 60°W, 50°W, 40°W, 30°W, 20°W

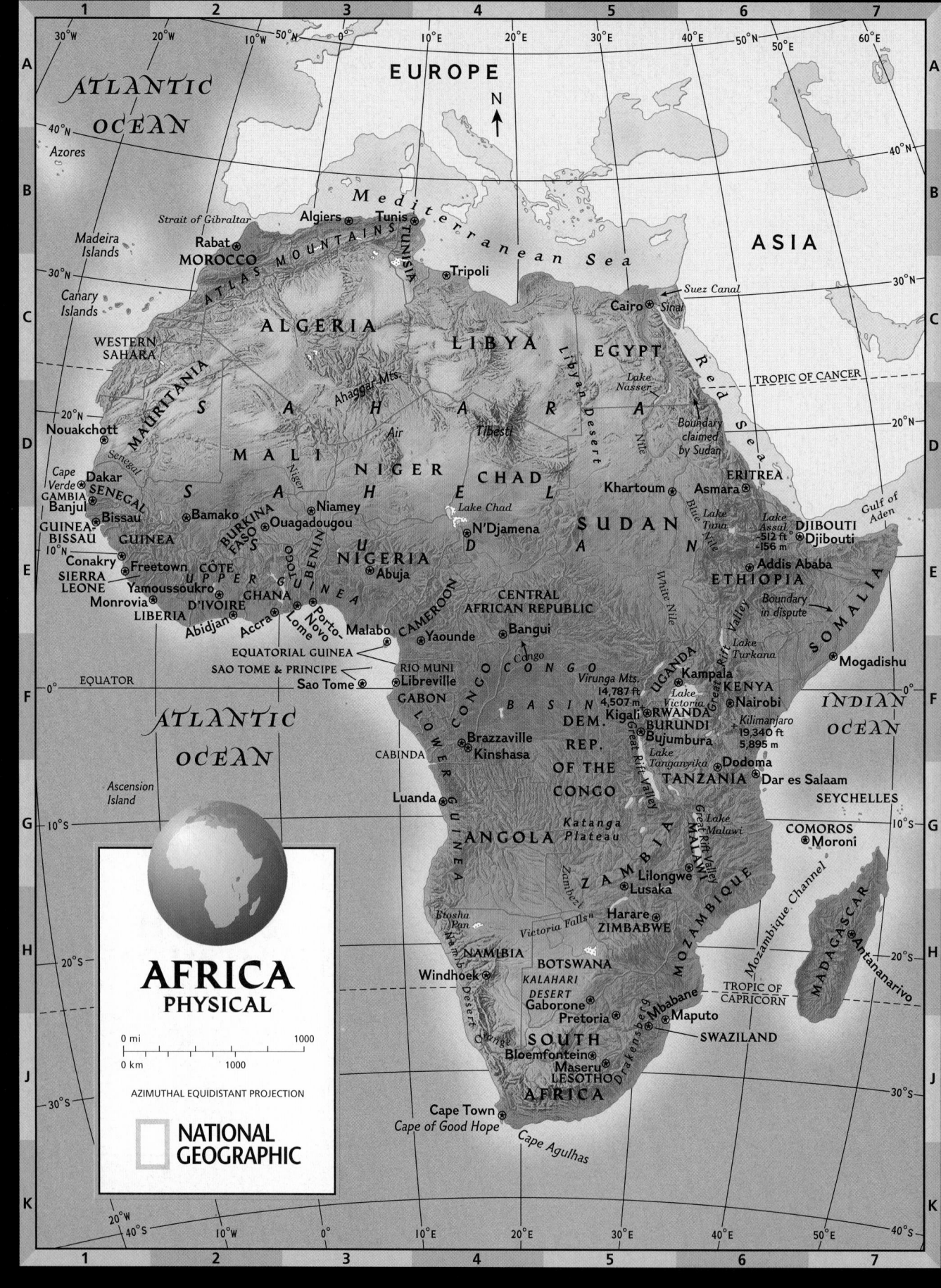

AFRICA
PHYSICAL

0 mi 1000
0 km 1000

AZIMUTHAL EQUIDISTANT PROJECTION

NATIONAL GEOGRAPHIC

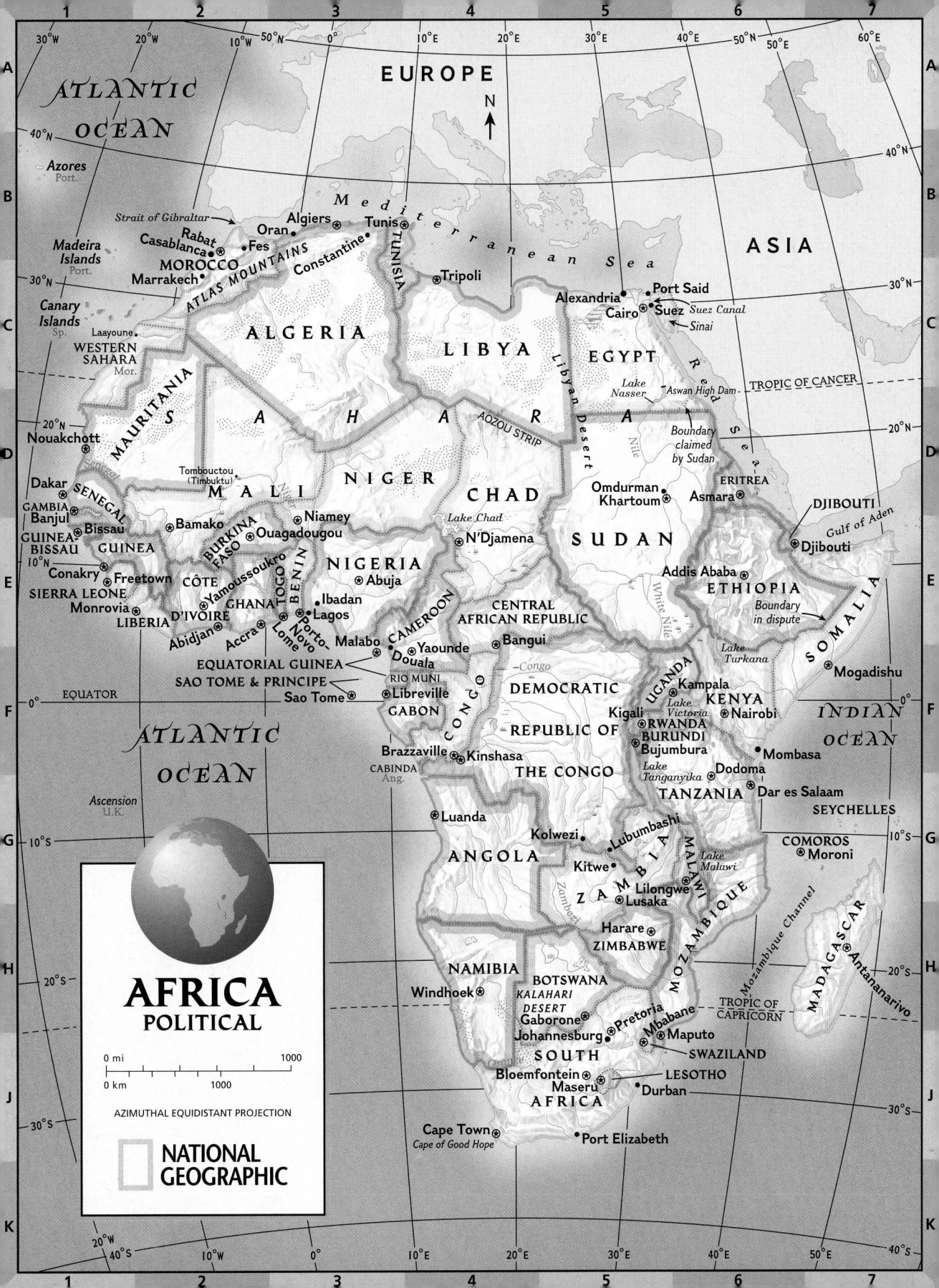

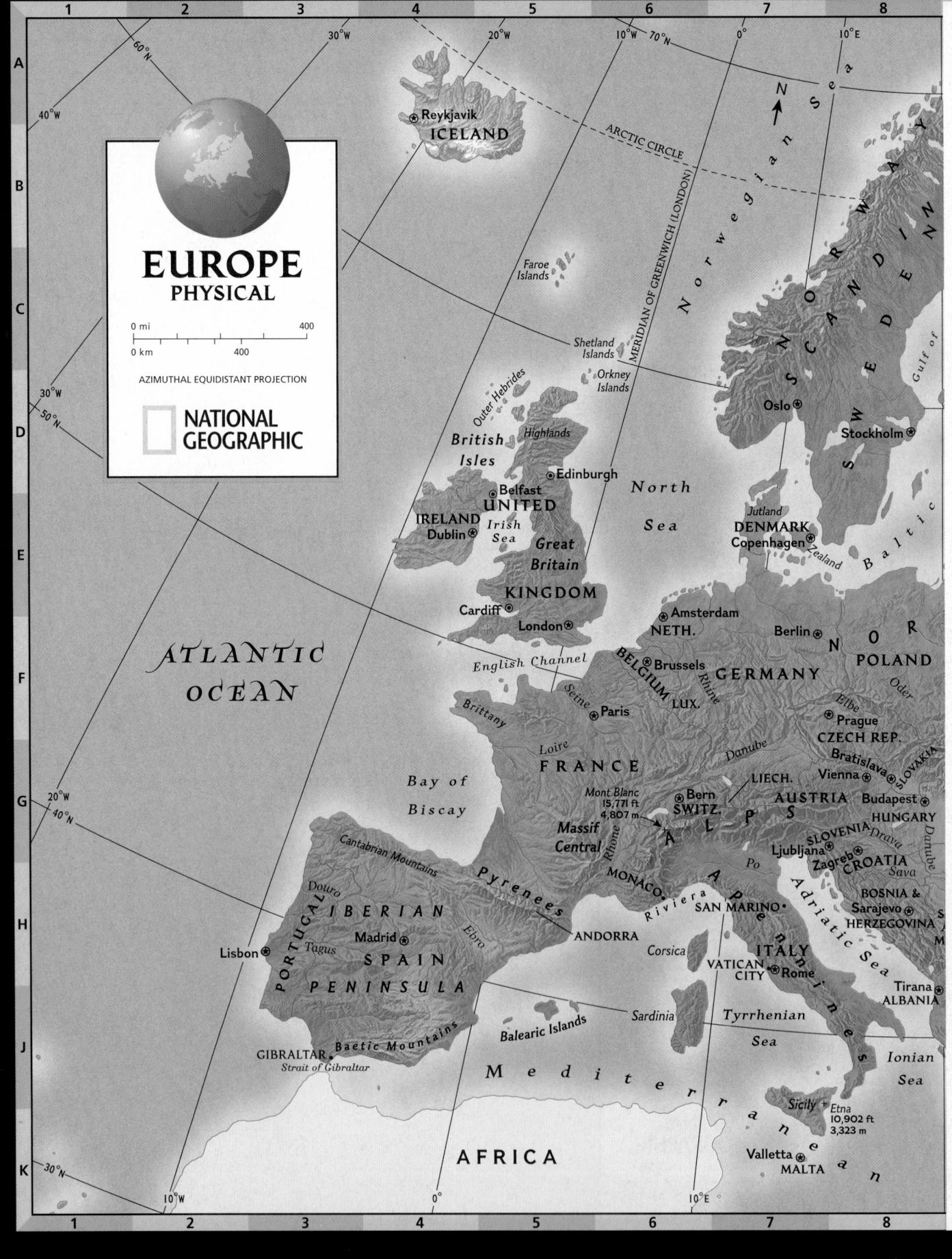

EUROPE
PHYSICAL

0 mi   400
0 km   400

AZIMUTHAL EQUIDISTANT PROJECTION

NATIONAL GEOGRAPHIC

ICELAND
Reykjavik

ARCTIC CIRCLE

Faroe Islands

Shetland Islands
Orkney Islands

Outer Hebrides
Highlands
British Isles
Edinburgh
Belfast
UNITED
IRELAND
Dublin
Irish Sea
Great Britain
KINGDOM
Cardiff
London

North Sea

Jutland
DENMARK
Copenhagen
Zealand

Oslo
Stockholm

SWEDEN

Baltic

Gulf of

SCANDINAVIA

Norwegian Sea

MERIDIAN OF GREENWICH (LONDON)

N O R

Berlin
POLAND

Amsterdam
NETH.
BELGIUM
Brussels
LUX.
GERMANY
Rhine
Elbe
Prague
CZECH REP.
Bratislava
SLOVAKIA
Vienna

Oder

English Channel
Seine
Paris
Brittany
Loire
FRANCE

Danube

LIECH.
Bern
SWITZ.
AUSTRIA
Budapest
HUNGARY

A L P S
SLOVENIA
Drava
Ljubljana
Zagreb
CROATIA
Sava
Danube

ATLANTIC
OCEAN

Bay of
Biscay

Cantabrian Mountains
Douro

Pyrenees

Mont Blanc
15,771 ft
4,807 m
Massif
Central
Rhone

MONACO
Riviera
Po
SAN MARINO
BOSNIA &
Sarajevo
HERZEGOVINA

Adriatic Sea

IBERIAN
Madrid
SPAIN
PENINSULA
Tagus
Ebro
PORTUGAL
Lisbon

ANDORRA
Corsica
VATICAN CITY
ITALY
Rome

Apennines

Tirana
ALBANIA

GIBRALTAR
Baetic Mountains
Strait of Gibraltar

Balearic Islands

Sardinia

Tyrrhenian
Sea

Ionian
Sea

AFRICA

M e d i t e r r a n e a n

Sicily
Etna
10,902 ft
3,323 m

Valletta
MALTA

60°N
40°W
30°W
50°N
20°W
40°N
30°N
10°W
0°
10°E
20°W
30°W
20°N
70°N
10°W
0°
10°E

N

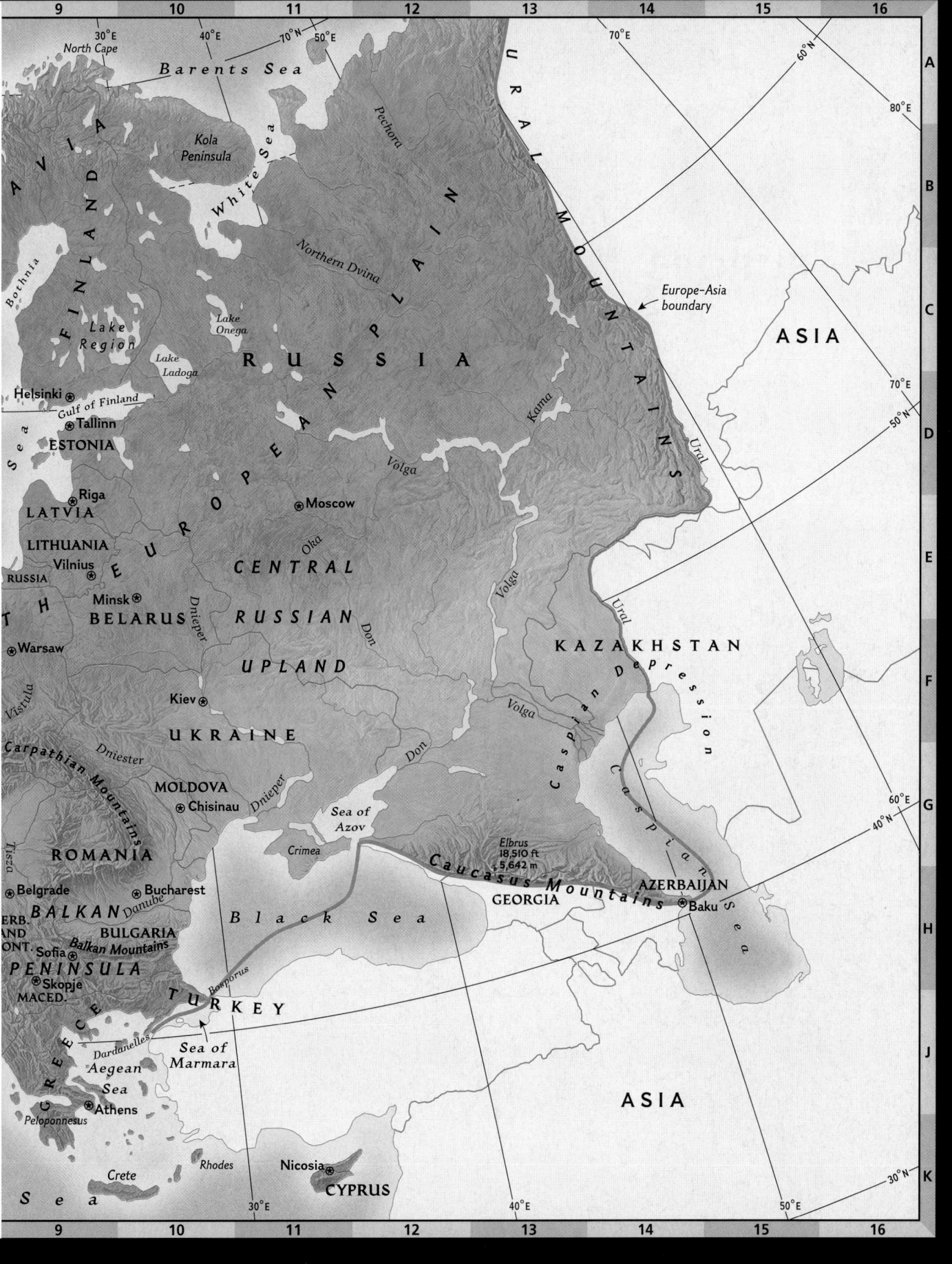

9   10   11   12   13   14   15   16

30°E   40°E   70°N   50°E   70°E   60°N

North Cape

Barents Sea

A

80°E

Kola
Peninsula

Pechora

White Sea

B

URAL MOUNTAINS

Northern Dvina

Europe-Asia
boundary

ASIA

C

Lake
Onega

70°E

Kama

50°N

Lake
Region

R U S S I A

E U R O P E A N   P L A I N

Ural

D

Lake
Ladoga

Volga

Helsinki

Gulf of Finland

Tallinn

ESTONIA

Moscow

Oka

Ural

C E N T R A L

E

Riga

LATVIA

LITHUANIA

Vilnius

Volga

R U S S I A N

Caspian Depression

KAZAKHSTAN

RUSSIA

Dnieper

Minsk

BELARUS

Don

U P L A N D

F

60°E

Warsaw

Vistula

Kiev

U K R A I N E

Volga

40°N

G

Carpathian Mountains

Dniester

MOLDOVA

Chisinau

Dnieper

Sea of
Azov

Don

Caspian Sea

Tisza

ROMANIA

Crimea

Elbrus
18,510 ft
5,642 m

Caucasus   Mountains

AZERBAIJAN

H

Belgrade

Bucharest

GEORGIA

Baku

BALKAN

Danube

Black   Sea

ERB.
AND
ONT.   Sofia

BULGARIA

Balkan Mountains

PENINSULA

Skopje

MACED.

Bosporus

T U R K E Y

J

Dardanelles

*Sea of
Marmara*

GREECE

*Aegean
Sea*

A S I A

Athens

Peloponnesus

K

30°N

Sea

Crete

Rhodes

Nicosia

CYPRUS

30°E   40°E   50°E

9   10   11   12   13   14   15   16

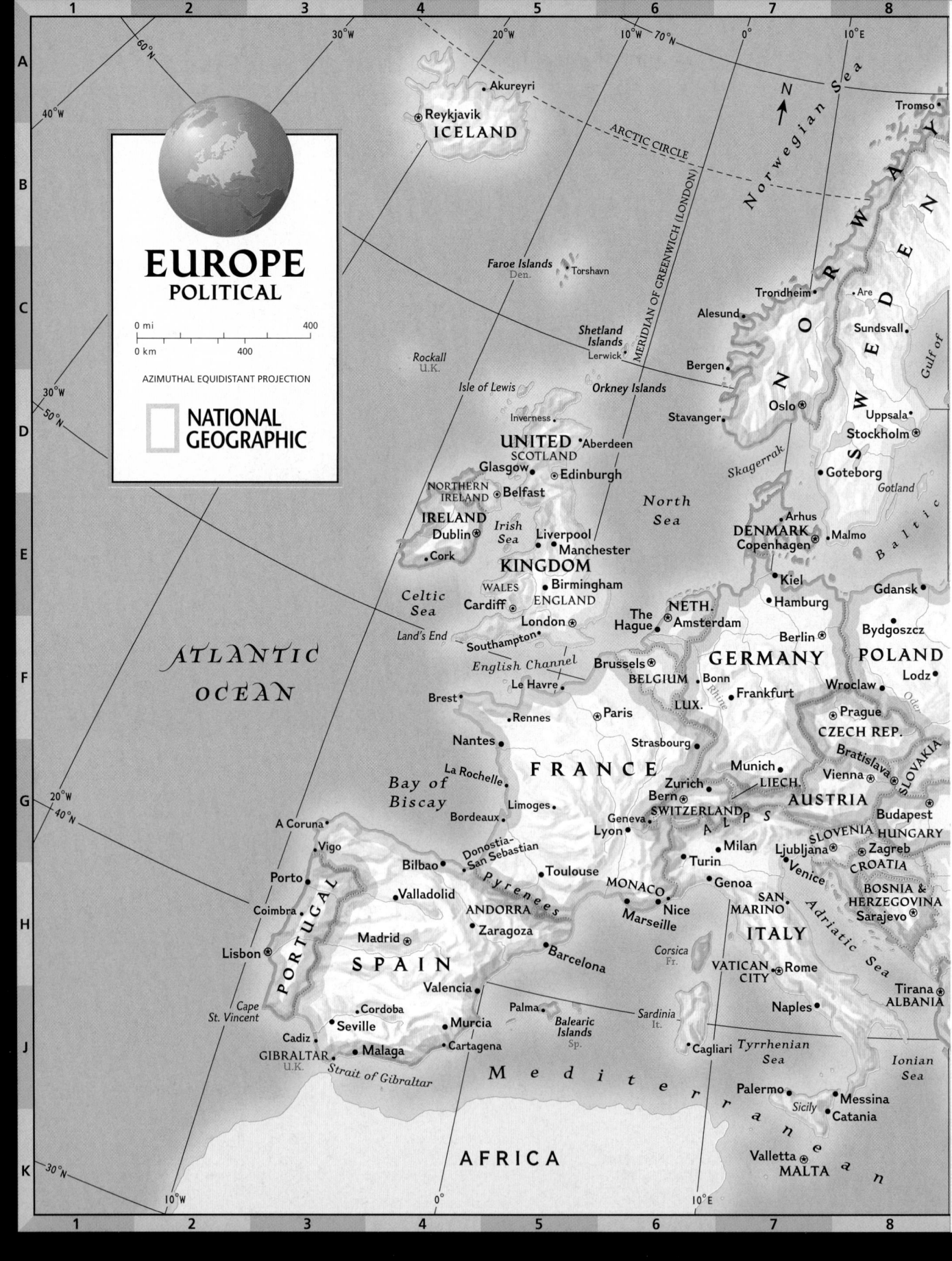

EUROPE
POLITICAL

0 mi   400
0 km   400

AZIMUTHAL EQUIDISTANT PROJECTION

NATIONAL
GEOGRAPHIC

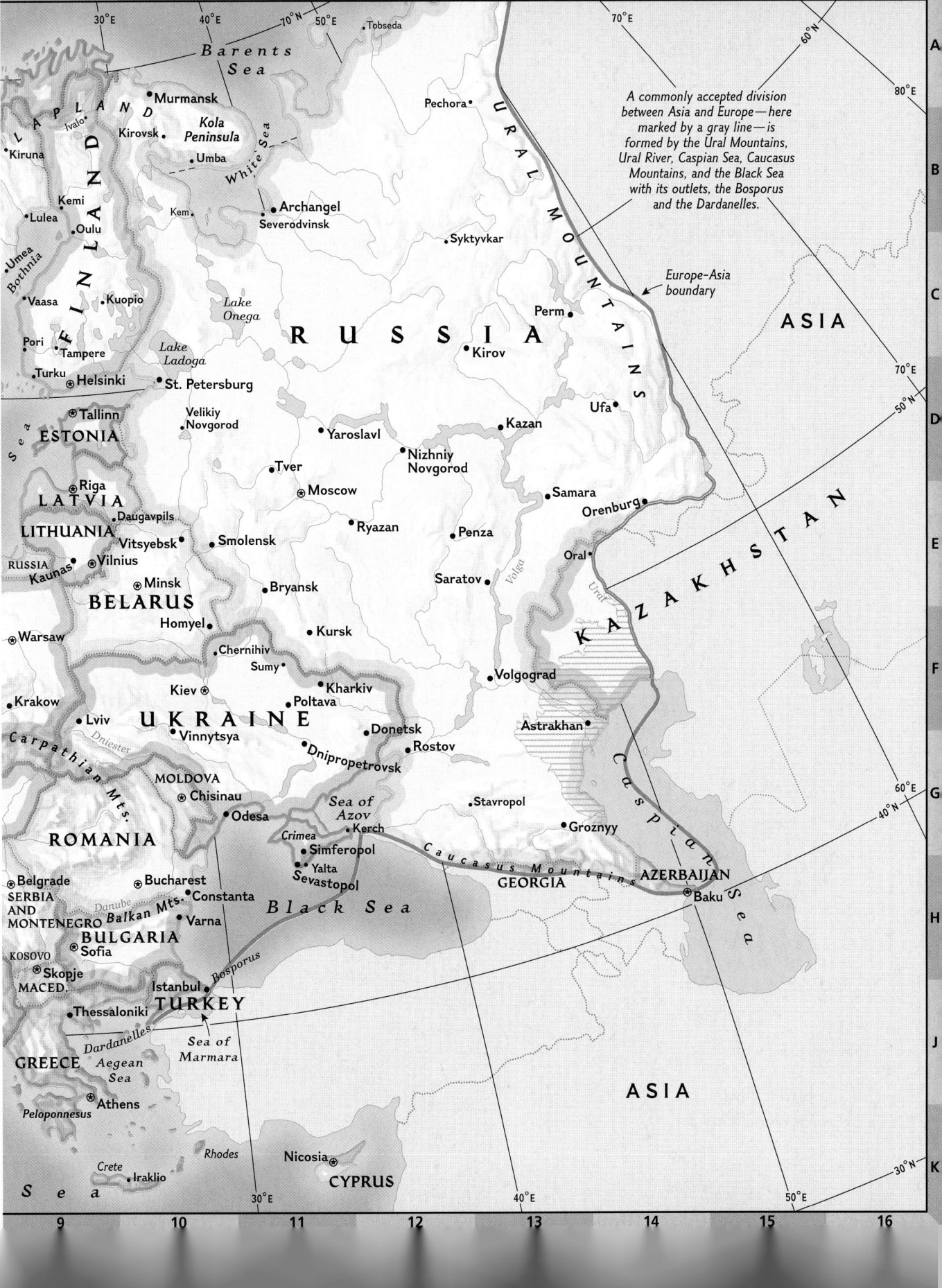

A commonly accepted division between Asia and Europe—here marked by a gray line—is formed by the Ural Mountains, Ural River, Caspian Sea, Caucasus Mountains, and the Black Sea with its outlets, the Bosporus and the Dardanelles.

Europe-Asia boundary

ASIA

RUSSIA

KAZAKHSTAN

UKRAINE

BELARUS

FINLAND

LATVIA

LITHUANIA

ESTONIA

ROMANIA

BULGARIA

TURKEY

GREECE

CYPRUS

SERBIA AND MONTENEGRO

MOLDOVA

GEORGIA

AZERBAIJAN

ASIA

Barents Sea

Kola Peninsula

White Sea

Ural Mountains

Caspian Sea

Black Sea

Sea of Azov

Caucasus Mountains

Sea of Marmara

Aegean Sea

Sea

Crimea

Lake Onega

Lake Ladoga

Volga

Ural

Dniester

Danube

Carpathian Mts.

Balkan Mts.

Bosporus

Dardanelles

Bothnia

LAPLAND

KOSOVO

MACED.

Peloponnesus

Crete

Rhodes

Murmansk
Kirovsk
Kiruna
Ivalo
Kemi
Lulea
Oulu
Umea
Vaasa
Kuopio
Pori
Tampere
Turku
Helsinki
Tallinn
Riga
Daugavpils
Vitsyebsk
Vilnius
Kaunas
Warsaw
Minsk
Homyel
Krakow
Lviv
Vinnytsya
Chisinau
Odesa
Belgrade
Bucharest
Constanta
Varna
Sofia
Skopje
Thessaloniki
Athens
Nicosia
Iraklio
Istanbul
Kerch
Simferopol
Yalta
Sevastopol
Kiev
Poltava
Kharkiv
Sumy
Chernihiv
Bryansk
Kursk
Smolensk
Ryazan
Moscow
Tver
Yaroslavl
Velikiy Novgorod
St. Petersburg
Archangel
Severodvinsk
Umba
Kem
Syktyvkar
Pechora
Tobseda
Perm
Kirov
Ufa
Kazan
Nizhniy Novgorod
Samara
Orenburg
Oral
Penza
Saratov
Volgograd
Astrakhan
Dnipropetrovsk
Donetsk
Rostov
Stavropol
Groznyy
Baku
Dniester
RUSSIA

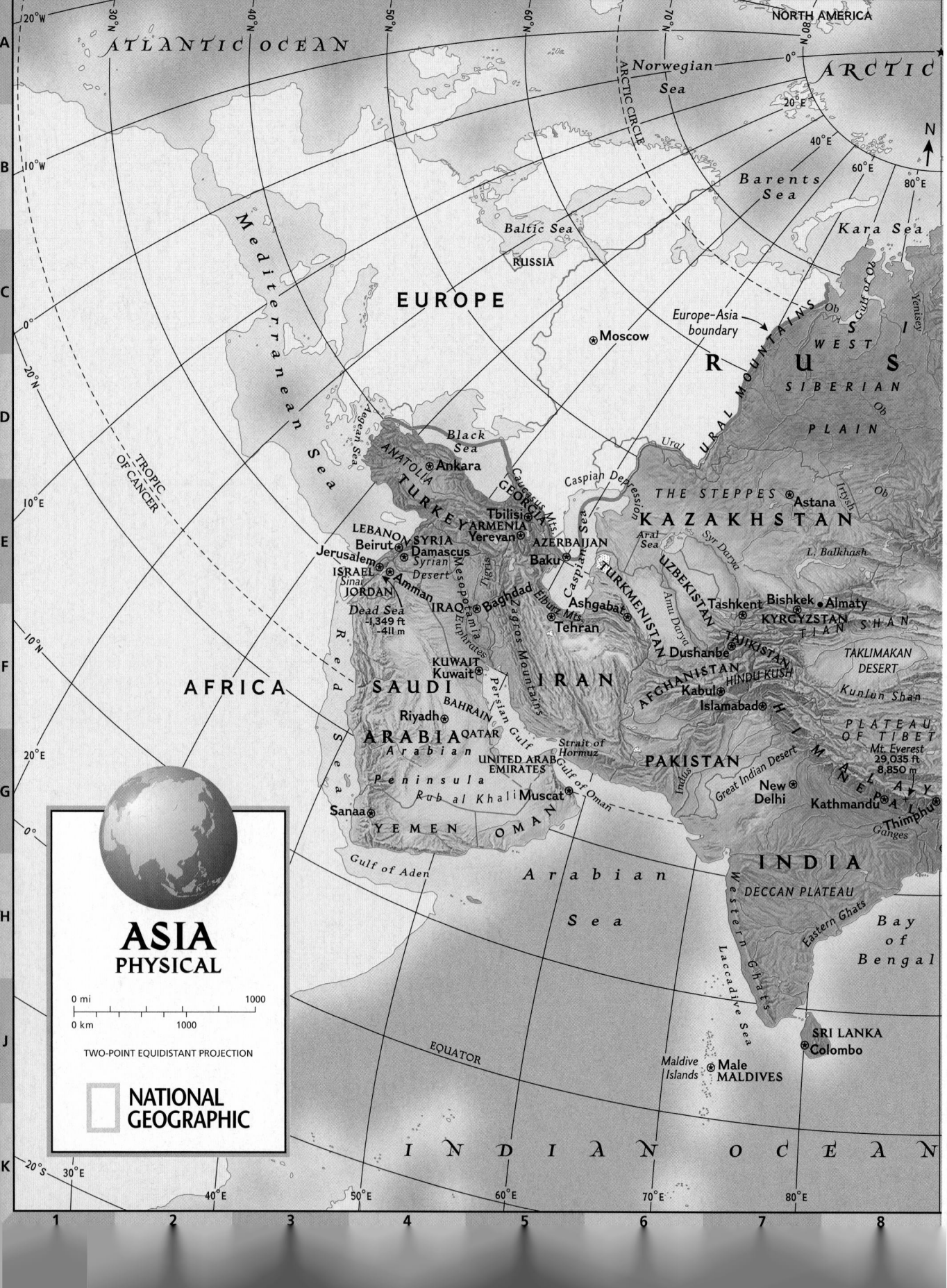

ASIA
PHYSICAL

0 mi   1000
0 km   1000

TWO-POINT EQUIDISTANT PROJECTION

NATIONAL
GEOGRAPHIC

ATLANTIC OCEAN

NORTH AMERICA

ARCTIC

N

Norwegian
Sea

ARCTIC CIRCLE

Barents
Sea

Kara Sea

Baltic Sea

RUSSIA

EUROPE

Moscow

Europe-Asia
boundary

URAL MOUNTAINS

WEST

S I B I R

Ob

Gulf of Ob

Yenisey

WEST

SIBERIAN

PLAIN

Ob

Irtysh

Mediterranean Sea

Aegean Sea

ANATOLIA

Ankara

TURKEY

Black
Sea

Caucasus Mts.

GEORGIA

Tbilisi

ARMENIA

Yerevan

AZERBAIJAN

Baku

Ural

Caspian Depression

Caspian Sea

THE STEPPES

Astana

KAZAKHSTAN

Aral
Sea

Syr Darya

L. Balkhash

TROPIC
OF CANCER

LEBANON

Beirut

Jerusalem

ISRAEL

JORDAN

SYRIA

Damascus

Syrian
Desert

Amman

Sinai

Dead Sea
-1,349 ft
-411 m

Mesopotamia

Tigris

Euphrates

IRAQ

Baghdad

Zagros Mountains

TURKMENISTAN

Ashgabat

Elburz Mts.

Tehran

UZBEKISTAN

Amu Darya

Tashkent

Bishkek

Almaty

KYRGYZSTAN

TIAN SHAN

Dushanbe

TAJIKISTAN

TAKLIMAKAN
DESERT

AFRICA

Red Sea

SAUDI

Riyadh

KUWAIT

Kuwait

BAHRAIN

QATAR

ARABIA

Arabian

Peninsula

Rub al Khali

Sanaa

YEMEN

Persian Gulf

IRAN

Strait of
Hormuz

UNITED ARAB
EMIRATES

Gulf of Oman

Muscat

OMAN

AFGHANISTAN

Kabul

HINDU KUSH

Islamabad

PAKISTAN

Indus

Kunlun Shan

PLATEAU
OF TIBET

Mt. Everest
29,035 ft
8,850 m

Great Indian Desert

New
Delhi

Kathmandu

Thimphu

Ganges

H I M A L A Y A

INDIA

DECCAN PLATEAU

Western Ghats

Eastern Ghats

Bay
of
Bengal

Gulf of Aden

Arabian
Sea

Lacadive Sea

SRI LANKA

Colombo

Maldive
Islands

Male
MALDIVES

EQUATOR

INDIAN OCEAN

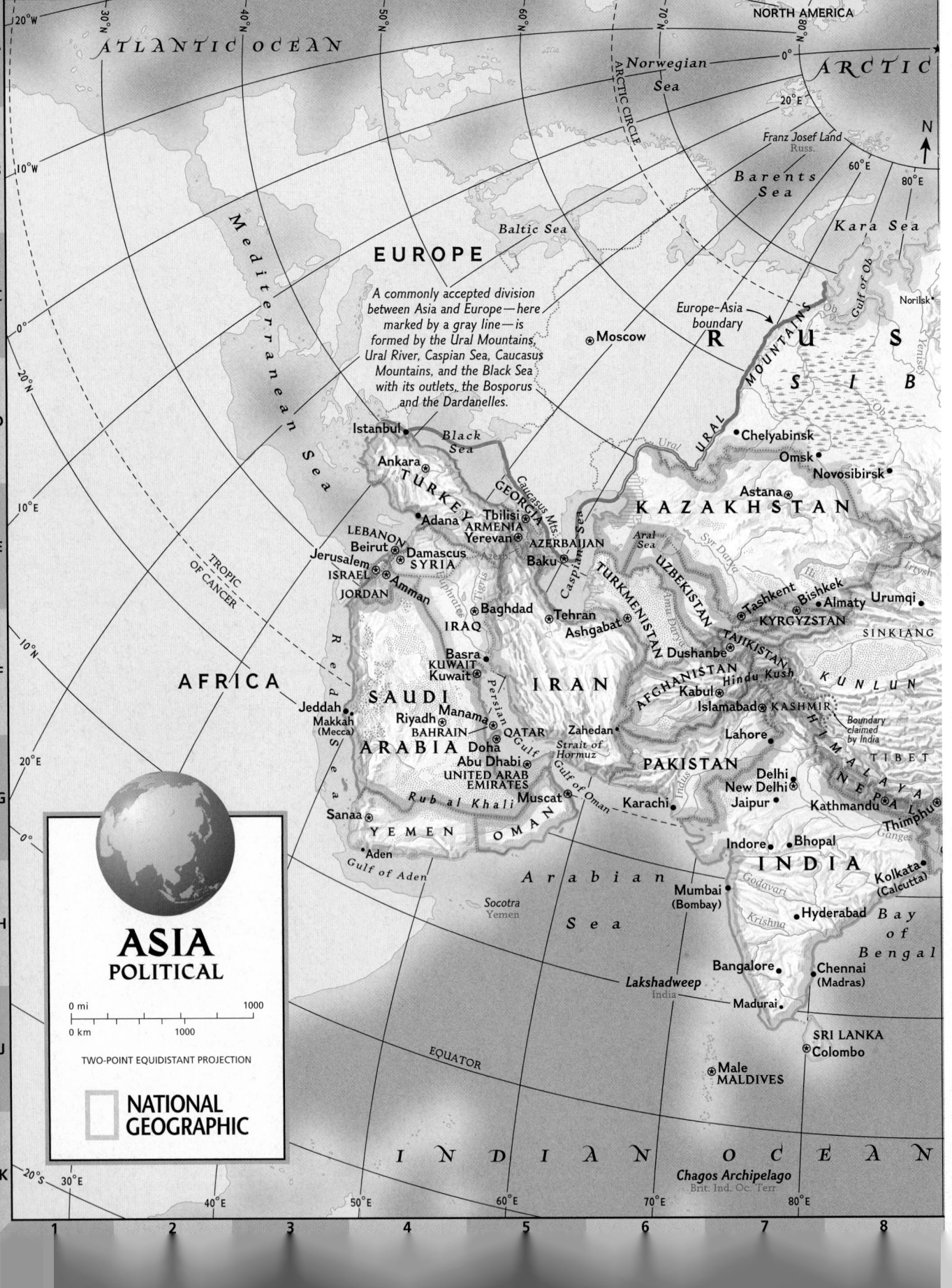

ATLANTIC OCEAN

ARCTIC

NORTH AMERICA

Norwegian Sea

ARCTIC CIRCLE

Franz Josef Land
Russ.

Barents Sea

Kara Sea

Norilsk

Baltic Sea

EUROPE

Mediterranean Sea

A commonly accepted division
between Asia and Europe—here
marked by a gray line—is
formed by the Ural Mountains,
Ural River, Caspian Sea, Caucasus
Mountains, and the Black Sea
with its outlets, the Bosporus
and the Dardanelles.

Moscow

Europe-Asia
boundary

R U S S I B

Chelyabinsk
Omsk
Novosibirsk

Istanbul
Black Sea
Ankara
TURKEY
GEORGIA
Tbilisi
Adana
ARMENIA
Yerevan
AZERBAIJAN
Baku
Caucasus Mts.
Caspian Sea
Ural

KAZAKHSTAN

Astana

Aral Sea
Syr Darya

Il
Irtysh

TROPIC OF CANCER

LEBANON
Beirut
Damascus
Jerusalem
SYRIA
ISRAEL
Amman
JORDAN

Euphrates
Tigris

Baghdad
IRAQ

Tehran
Ashgabat
TURKMENISTAN

UZBEKISTAN
Tashkent
Bishkek
Almaty
KYRGYZSTAN

Urumqi

SINKIANG

AFRICA

Red Sea

SAUDI

Basra
KUWAIT
Kuwait

Riyadh
BAHRAIN
Manama
QATAR
Doha
Abu Dhabi
UNITED ARAB
EMIRATES

Persian Gulf

IRAN

Zahedan

Dushanbe
TAJIKISTAN
AFGHANISTAN
Hindu Kush
Kabul
Islamabad
KASHMIR

KUNLUN

Boundary
claimed
by India

TIBET

Jeddah
Makkah
(Mecca)

ARABIA

Strait of
Hormuz

Lahore

PAKISTAN

Karachi
Indus

Delhi
New Delhi
Jaipur

Kathmandu
NEPAL
Thimphu
BHUTAN

HIMALAYA

Sanaa
YEMEN

Rub al Khali

Muscat
OMAN
Gulf of Oman

Indore
Bhopal

INDIA

Ganges

Aden
Gulf of Aden

Arabian

Socotra
Yemen

Sea

Mumbai
(Bombay)

Godavari
Krishna

Hyderabad

Bay
of
Bengal

ASIA
POLITICAL

0 mi   1000

0 km   1000

TWO-POINT EQUIDISTANT PROJECTION

NATIONAL
GEOGRAPHIC

Lakshadweep
India

Bangalore
Chennai
(Madras)

Madurai

SRI LANKA
Colombo

EQUATOR

Male
MALDIVES

I N D I A N   O C E A N

Chagos Archipelago
Brit. Ind. Oc. Terr.

NORTH AMERICA

Bering Strait

North Pole

OCEAN

*Chukchi
Sea*

Wrangel I.

Gulf of
Anadyr

Anadyr

Bering
Sea

Commander Is.

North
Land

*East
Siberian
Sea*

*New Siberian
Islands*

*Laptev
Sea*

*Kamchatka
Peninsula*

Cherskiy Range

Verkhoyansk Range

Magadan

Kolyma Range

S I B E R I A

Yakutsk

Sea of
Okhotsk

Lena

Aldan

Irkutsk

Lake
Baikal

Sakhalin

Kuril Islands

Hokkaido

Sapporo

Yenisey

Ulaanbaatar

MONGOLIA

ALTAY MTS.

Herlen

GOBI

MANCHURIA

Vladivostok

Changchun

Shenyang

*Sea of
Japan
(East Sea)*

JAPAN

Tokyo

Honshu

Kyoto

Marcus I.
Jap.

TROPIC
OF CANCER

PACIFIC   OCEAN

NORTH
KOREA

Pyongyang

Beijing

Seoul
SOUTH
KOREA

Osaka

Hiroshima

Kyushu

SHAN

Lanzhou

Shijiazhuang

Qingdao

Yellow

Xuzhou

Sea

Bonin Is.
Jap.

C H I N A

Xian

Nanjing

Shanghai

*East
China*

Volcano Is.
Jap.

Yangtze

Chengdu

Nanchang

Fuzhou

Sea

Ryukyu Islands

Okinawa

Changsha

Guiyang

Taipei

TAIWAN

Parece Vela
Jap.

*Boundary
claimed
by China*

Kunming

Guangzhou

Hong Kong

Macau

The People's Republic of China claims
Taiwan as its 23rd province.

BHUTAN

BANGLADESH

Dhaka

Irrawaddy

MYANMAR
(BURMA)

Hanoi

Haiphong

South

Hainan

China

Philippine

Luzon

Quezon City

Manila

Samar

PHILIPPINES

Sea

Yangon
(Rangoon)

Vientiane

LAOS

Da Nang

Mindoro

Panay

Negros

Leyte

Andaman
Islands
India

THAILAND

Bangkok

CAMBODIA

VIETNAM

Phnom Penh

Ho Chi Minh City

Sea

Palawan

*Andaman
Sea*

Nicobar
Islands
India

Kuala Lumpur

Medan

SINGAPORE

MALAYSIA

Bandar Seri
Begawan
BRUNEI

SABAH

SARAWAK

Borneo

Gulf of Thailand

Mindanao

Moluccas

Morotai

Halmahera

Biak

Jayapura

New Guinea

Kepi

Merauke

Aru
Is.

Dolak

EQUATOR

I N D O N E S I A

Celebes

Buru

Ceram

*Tanimbar
Is.*

Sumatra

G R E A T E R

Jambi

S U N D A   I S L A N D S

Java Sea

Dili
TIMOR-LESTE
(EAST TIMOR)

Kupang

Timor

Sea

AUSTRALIA

Mentawai
Islands

Jakarta

Java

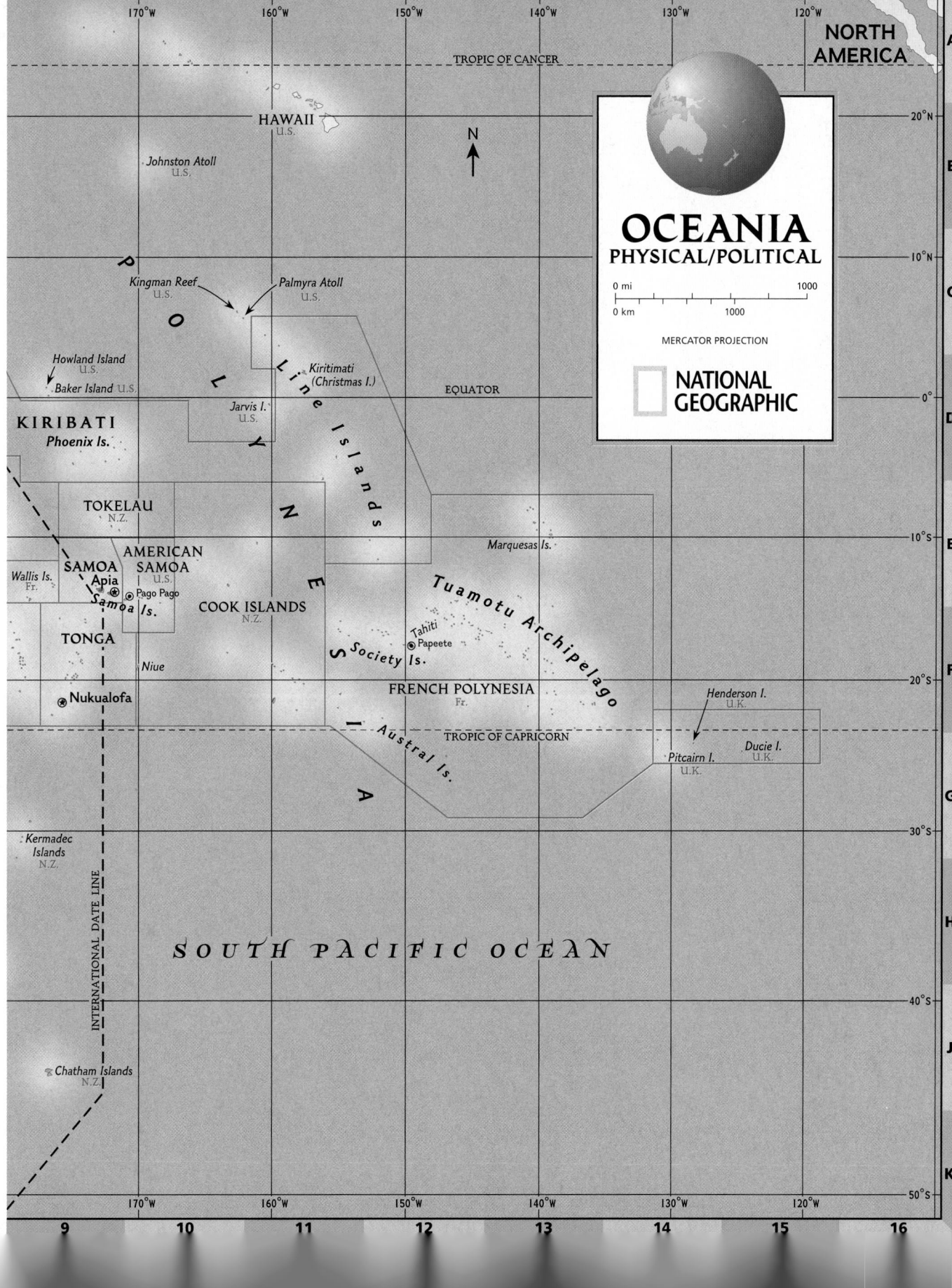

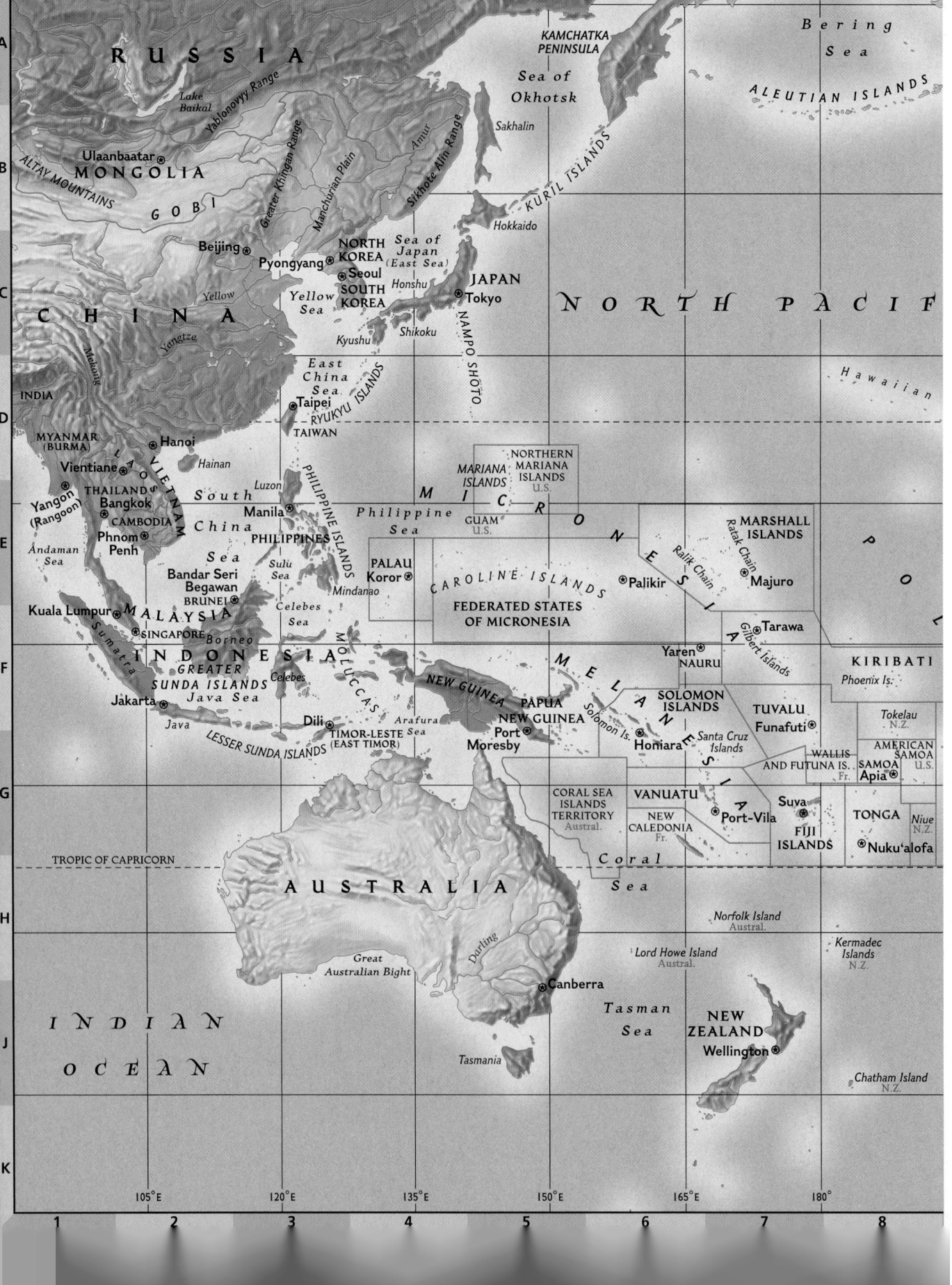

Gulf of
Alaska
Kodiak I.
Alexander
Archipelago
Queen
Charlotte
Islands
Vancouver
Island

Gulf of Mexico

Hudson
Bay

ROCKY MOUNTAINS

Coast Mountains

Cascade Range

CANADA

GREAT

CANADIAN SHIELD

Ottawa ⊛
Great Lakes

GREAT PLAINS

CENTRAL
LOWLAND

UNITED STATES

Missouri

Mississippi

APPALACHIAN MTS.

⊛ Washington

COASTAL PLAIN

ATLANTIC
OCEAN

IC OCEAN

45°N

30°N

Baja California

Gulf of California

Sierra Madre Occidental

MEXICO

Sierra Madre Oriental

TROPIC OF CANCER

Gulf of
Mexico

Nassau ⊛

Havana ⊛ CUBA

BAHAMAS

DOMINICAN
REPUBLIC

D

Islands
HAWAII
U.S.

15°N

Mexico
City ⊛

BELIZE
GUATEMALA
HONDURAS
GUATEMALA ⊛ Tegucigalpa
Guatemala City ⊛
San Salvador ⊛ NICARAGUA
EL SALVADOR Managua ⊛

JAMAICA HAITI

Santo
Domingo

Caribbean
Sea

Caracas

Line Islands

Kiritimati

EQUATOR

0°

San Jose ⊛
COSTA RICA

Panama City
PANAMA ⊛

LLANOS

VENEZ.

Bogota ⊛
COLOMBIA

Galapagos
Islands
Ecua.

Quito ⊛
ECUADOR

AMAZON
BASIN

BRAZIL

Y
N
E
S
I
A

Marquesas Is.

15°S

Tuamotu Archipelago

PERU

Lima ⊛

COOK
ISLANDS
N.Z.

Society Is.

FRENCH POLYNESIA
Fr.

Austral Is.

Pitcairn Island U.K.

La Paz ⊛ BOLIVIA

30°S

SOUTH

PACIFIC

OCEAN

45°S

PACIFIC
RIM
PHYSICAL/POLITICAL

0 mi   1500

0 km   1500
MILLER CYLINDRICAL PROJECTION

NATIONAL
GEOGRAPHIC

Santiago ⊛

Chiloe
Island

ANDES

ARGENTINA

PATAGONIA

165°W   150°W   135°W   120°W   105°W   90°W   75°W

9   10   11   12   13   14   15   16

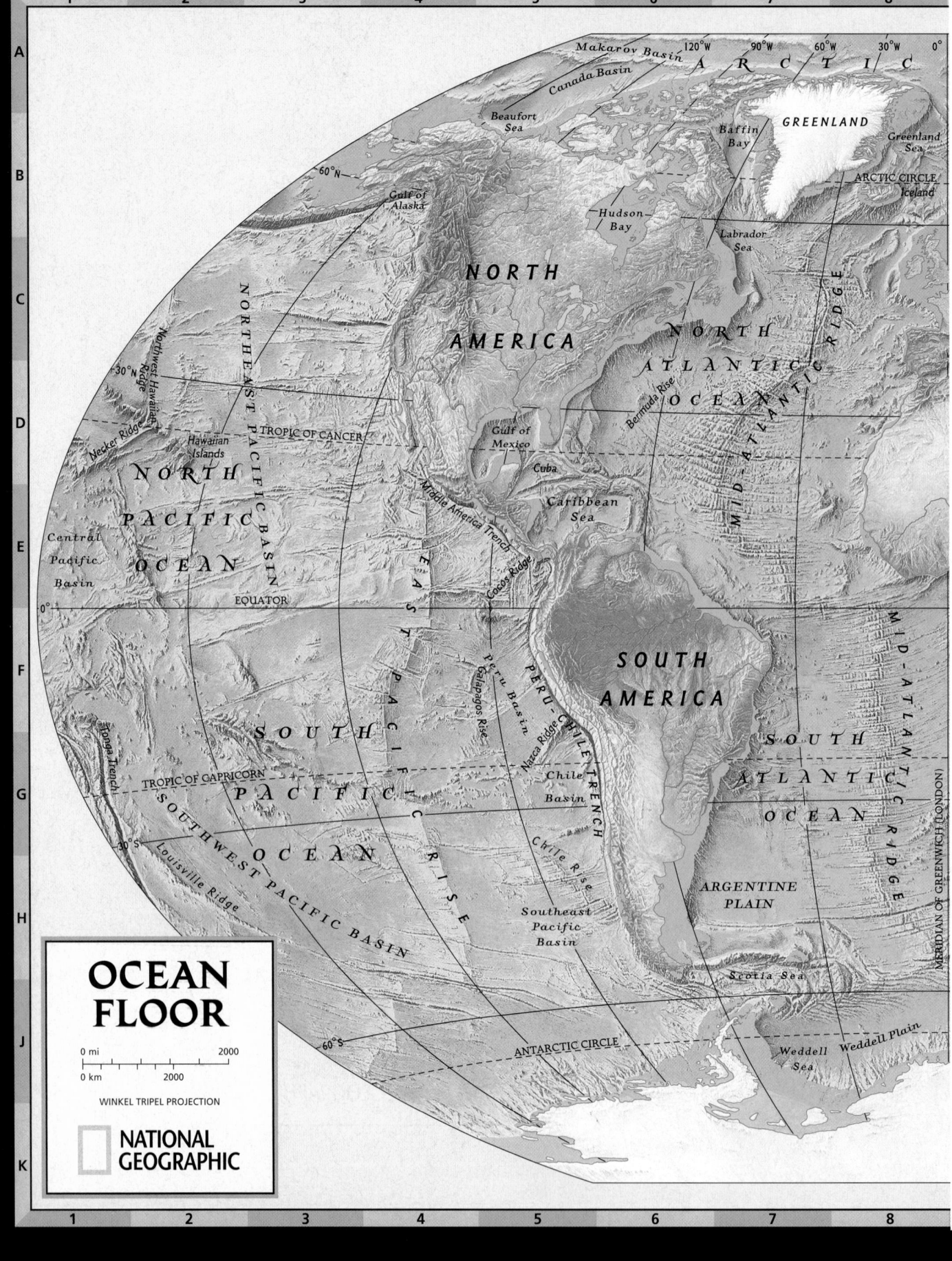

OCEAN FLOOR

0 mi ⊢———————————⊣ 2000

0 km ⊢———————————⊣ 2000

WINKEL TRIPEL PROJECTION

NATIONAL GEOGRAPHIC

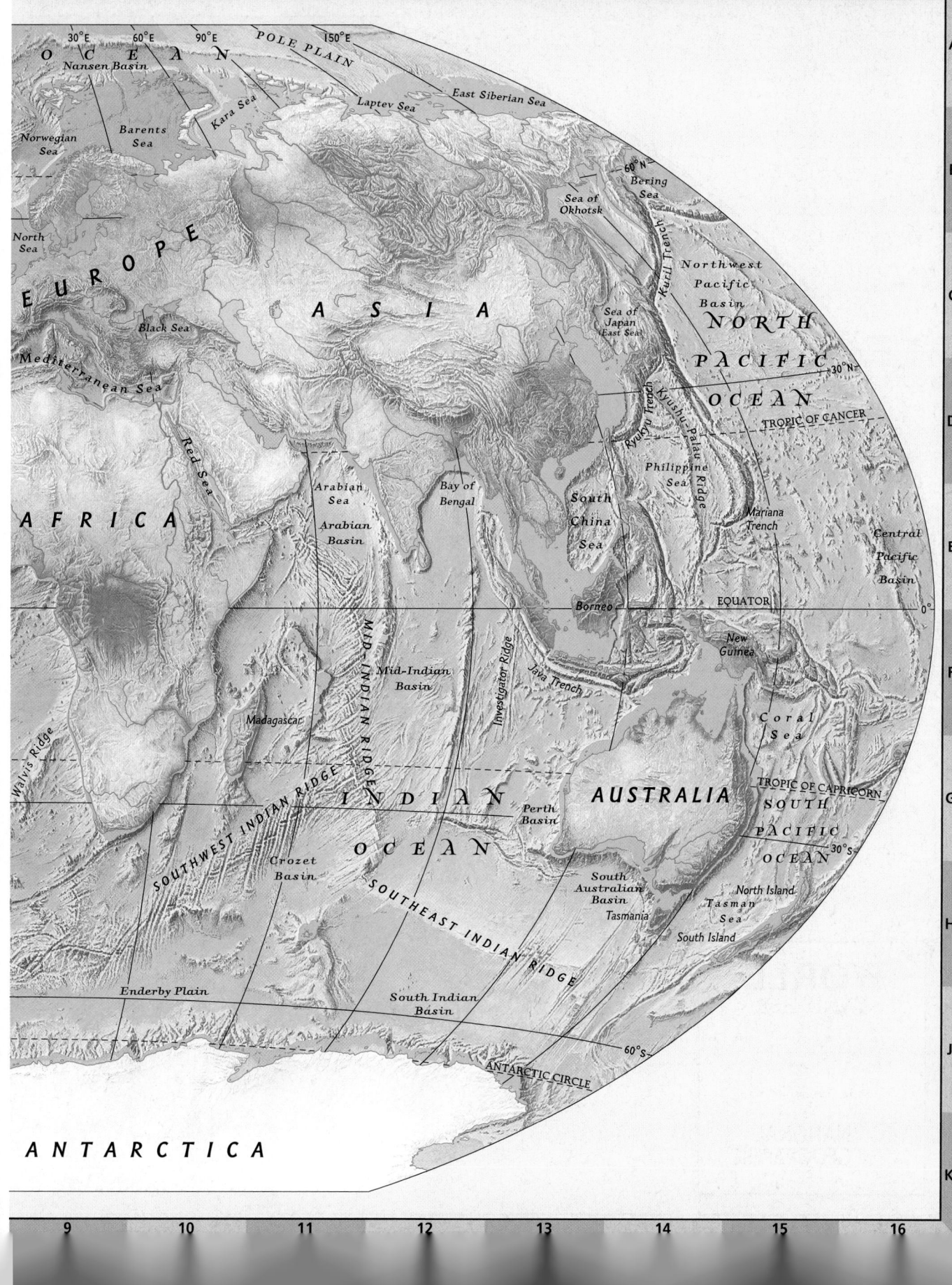

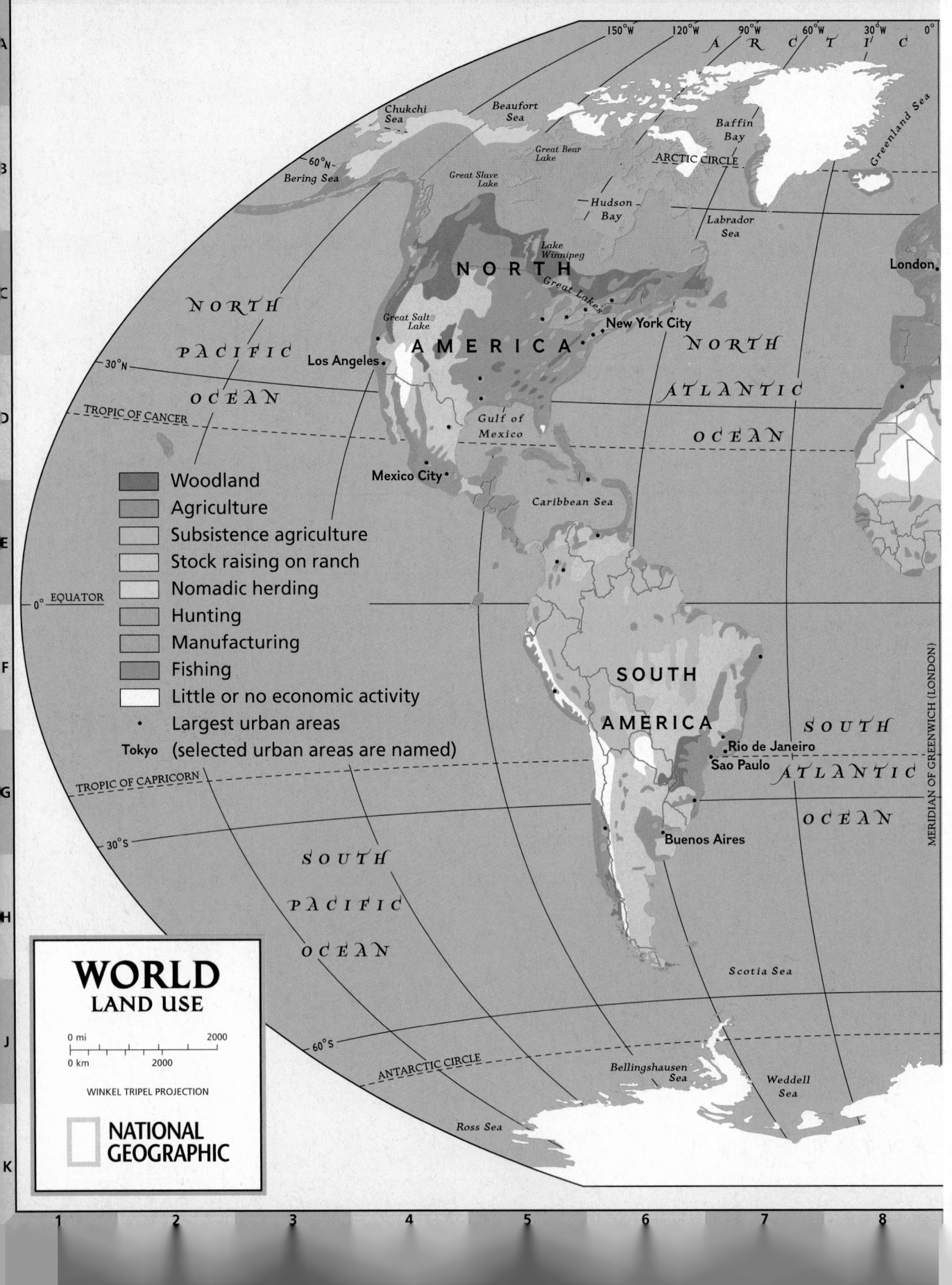

WORLD
LAND USE

Legend:
- Woodland
- Agriculture
- Subsistence agriculture
- Stock raising on ranch
- Nomadic herding
- Hunting
- Manufacturing
- Fishing
- Little or no economic activity
- • Largest urban areas
- Tokyo (selected urban areas are named)

0 mi — 2000
0 km — 2000

WINKEL TRIPEL PROJECTION

NATIONAL GEOGRAPHIC

Map labels:

A R C T I C

Chukchi Sea

Beaufort Sea

Great Bear Lake

Baffin Bay

Greenland Sea

60°N — Bering Sea

Great Slave Lake

ARCTIC CIRCLE

Hudson Bay

Labrador Sea

Lake Winnipeg

N O R T H

London

NORTH PACIFIC OCEAN

Great Lakes

Great Salt Lake

A M E R I C A

New York City

NORTH ATLANTIC

30°N

Los Angeles

OCEAN

TROPIC OF CANCER

Gulf of Mexico

OCEAN

Mexico City

Caribbean Sea

0° EQUATOR

SOUTH AMERICA

SOUTH ATLANTIC

Rio de Janeiro

Sao Paulo

TROPIC OF CAPRICORN

OCEAN

30°S

SOUTH PACIFIC OCEAN

Buenos Aires

MERIDIAN OF GREENWICH (LONDON)

Scotia Sea

60°S

ANTARCTIC CIRCLE

Bellingshausen Sea

Weddell Sea

Ross Sea

150°W 120°W 90°W 60°W 30°W 0°

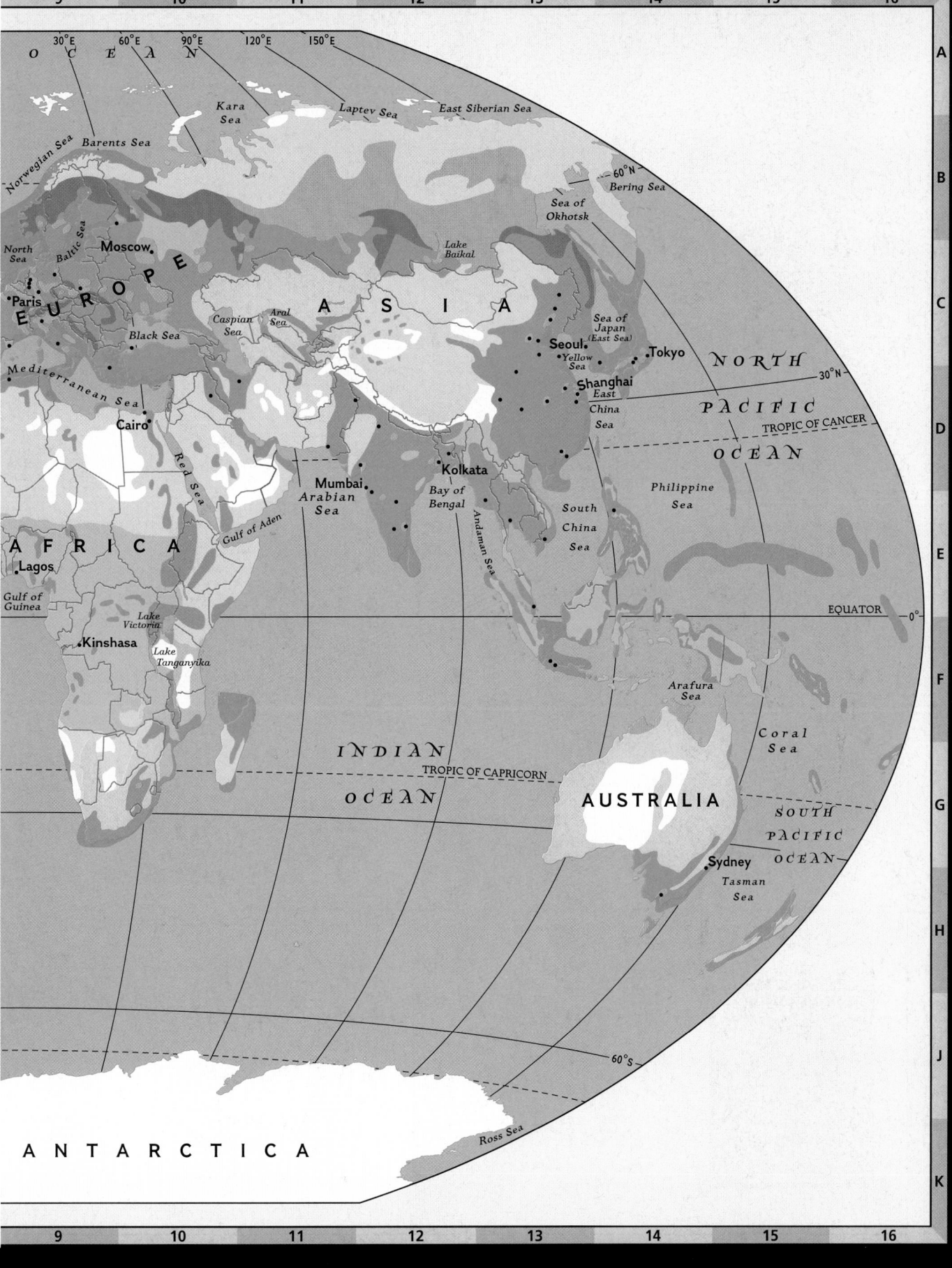

OCEAN

30°E 60°E 90°E 120°E 150°E

Norwegian Sea
Barents Sea
Kara Sea
Laptev Sea
East Siberian Sea

60°N Bering Sea

Sea of Okhotsk

North Sea
Baltic Sea
Moscow

Lake Baikal

Paris
EUROPE
Black Sea
Caspian Sea
Aral Sea
A S I A

Sea of Japan (East Sea)

Mediterranean Sea
Seoul
Yellow Sea
Tokyo
NORTH

Cairo
Shanghai
East China Sea
PACIFIC
30°N

Red Sea
TROPIC OF CANCER
OCEAN

AFRICA
Gulf of Aden
Kolkata
Philippine Sea

Lagos
Mumbai
Arabian Sea
Bay of Bengal
Andaman Sea
South China Sea

Gulf of Guinea
Lake Victoria
Kinshasa
Lake Tanganyika

EQUATOR 0°

Arafura Sea

INDIAN
Coral Sea

TROPIC OF CAPRICORN

OCEAN
AUSTRALIA
SOUTH

PACIFIC
G

Sydney
OCEAN
Tasman Sea

60°S

ANTARCTICA

Ross Sea

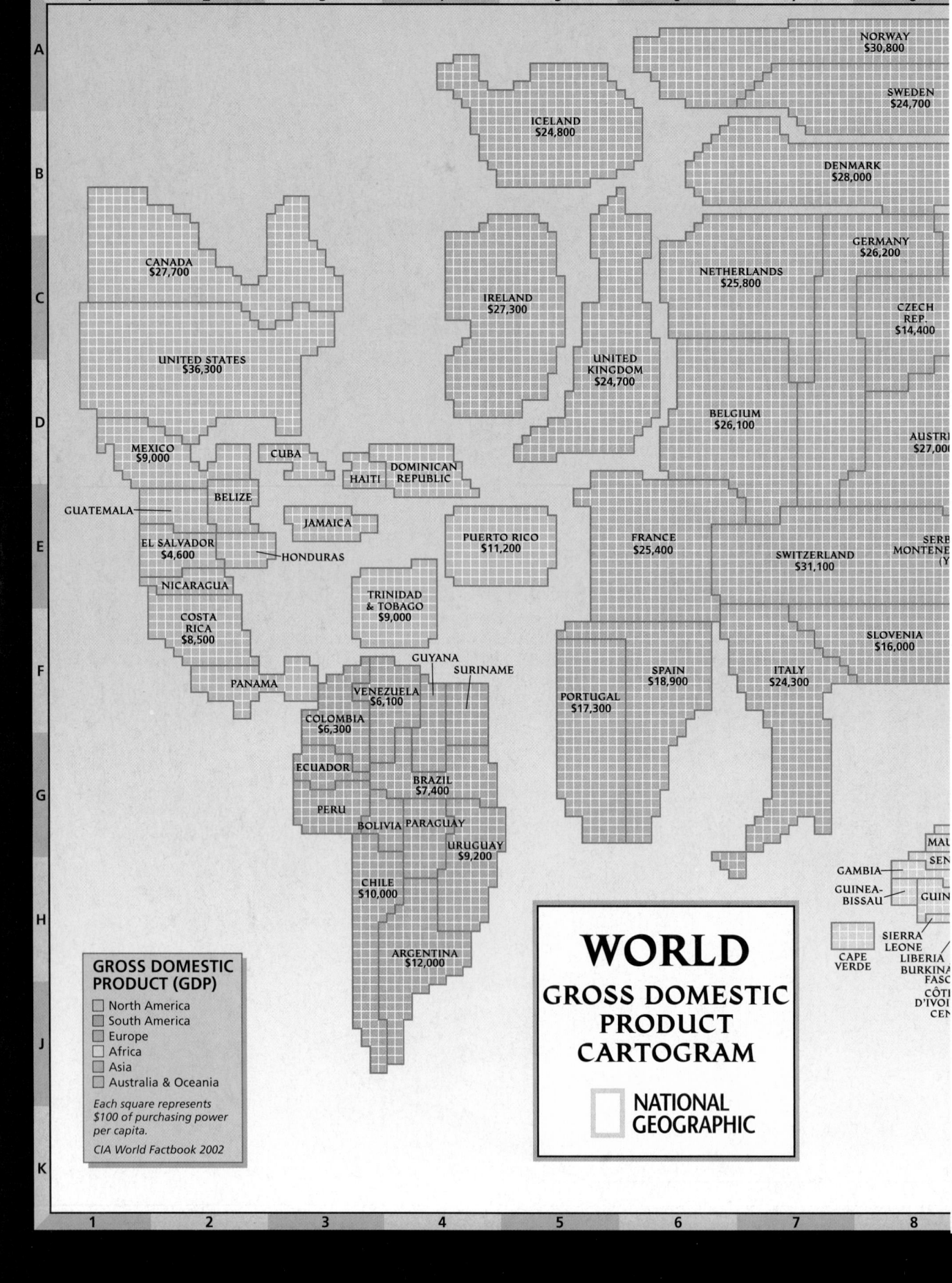

GROSS DOMESTIC PRODUCT (GDP)

- North America
- South America
- Europe
- Africa
- Asia
- Australia & Oceania

Each square represents $100 of purchasing power per capita.

CIA World Factbook 2002

WORLD
GROSS DOMESTIC PRODUCT CARTOGRAM

NATIONAL GEOGRAPHIC

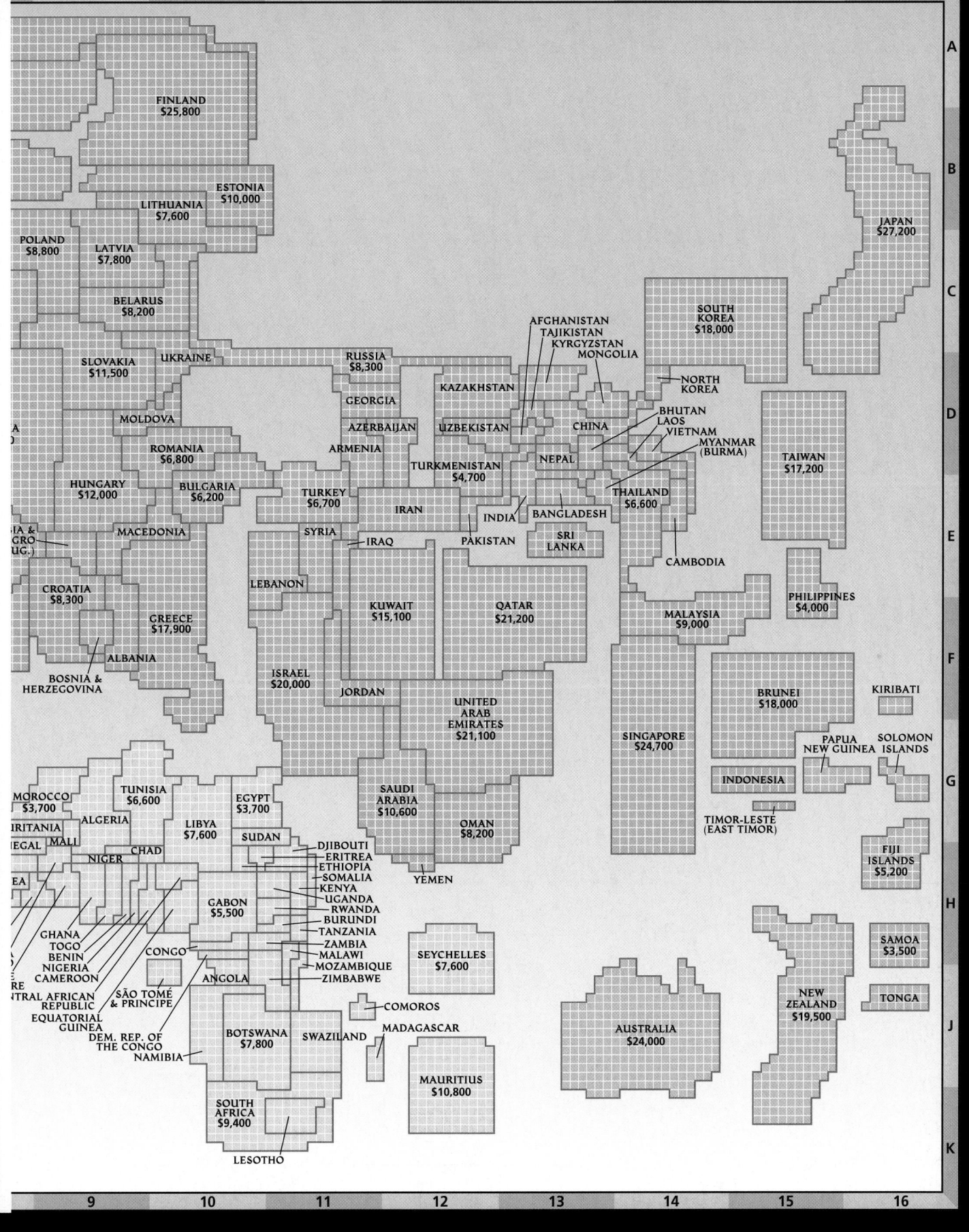

FINLAND
$25,800

ESTONIA
$10,000

LITHUANIA
$7,600

POLAND
$8,800

LATVIA
$7,800

BELARUS
$8,200

JAPAN
$27,200

SLOVAKIA
$11,500

UKRAINE

RUSSIA
$8,300

SOUTH
KOREA
$18,000

AFGHANISTAN
TAJIKISTAN
KYRGYZSTAN
MONGOLIA

NORTH
KOREA

MOLDOVA

GEORGIA

KAZAKHSTAN

ROMANIA
$6,800

AZERBAIJAN

UZBEKISTAN

CHINA

BHUTAN
LAOS
VIETNAM
MYANMAR
(BURMA)

TAIWAN
$17,200

HUNGARY
$12,000

ARMENIA

NEPAL

BULGARIA
$6,200

TURKMENISTAN
$4,700

THAILAND
$6,600

TURKEY
$6,700

MACEDONIA

IRAN

INDIA

BANGLADESH

IA &
GRO
UG.)

SYRIA

IRAQ

PAKISTAN

SRI
LANKA

CAMBODIA

CROATIA
$8,300

LEBANON

GREECE
$17,900

KUWAIT
$15,100

QATAR
$21,200

MALAYSIA
$9,000

PHILIPPINES
$4,000

ALBANIA

BOSNIA &
HERZEGOVINA

ISRAEL
$20,000

JORDAN

UNITED
ARAB
EMIRATES
$21,100

KIRIBATI

BRUNEI
$18,000

SINGAPORE
$24,700

PAPUA
NEW GUINEA

SOLOMON
ISLANDS

MOROCCO
$3,700

TUNISIA
$6,600

EGYPT
$3,700

INDONESIA

RITANIA

ALGERIA

LIBYA
$7,600

SAUDI
ARABIA
$10,600

TIMOR-LESTE
(EAST TIMOR)

FIJI
ISLANDS
$5,200

EGAL

MALI

SUDAN

NIGER

CHAD

OMAN
$8,200

DJIBOUTI
ERITREA
ETHIOPIA
SOMALIA
KENYA
UGANDA
RWANDA
BURUNDI
TANZANIA

YEMEN

GABON
$5,500

SAMOA
$3,500

GHANA
TOGO
BENIN
NIGERIA
CAMEROON

CONGO

ZAMBIA
MALAWI
MOZAMBIQUE
ZIMBABWE

SEYCHELLES
$7,600

ANGOLA

RE

TRAL AFRICAN
REPUBLIC
EQUATORIAL
GUINEA
DEM. REP. OF
THE CONGO
NAMIBIA

SÃO TOMÉ
& PRINCIPE

COMOROS

TONGA

BOTSWANA
$7,800

SWAZILAND

MADAGASCAR

AUSTRALIA
$24,000

NEW
ZEALAND
$19,500

MAURITIUS
$10,800

SOUTH
AFRICA
$9,400

LESOTHO

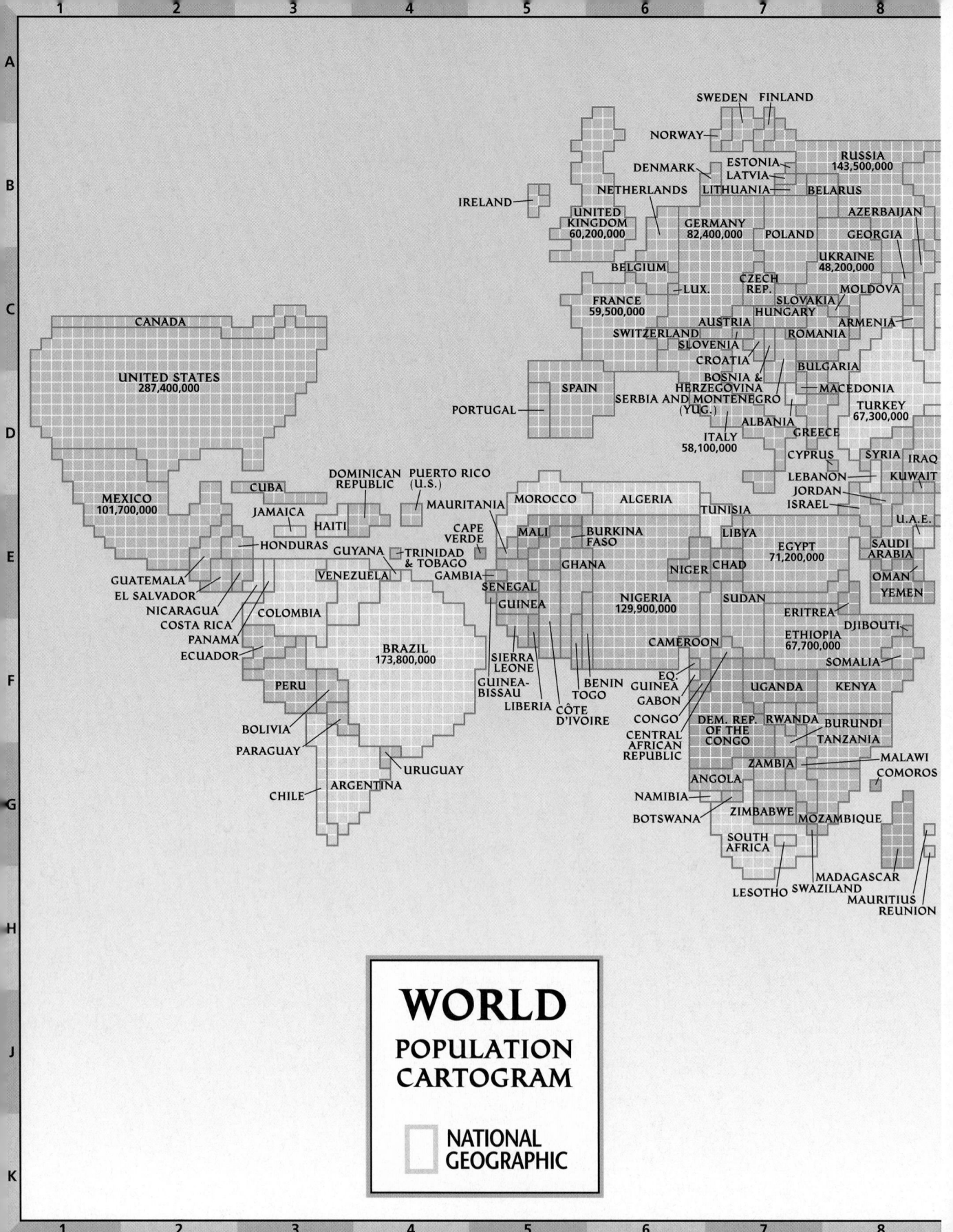

WORLD
POPULATION
CARTOGRAM

NATIONAL
GEOGRAPHIC

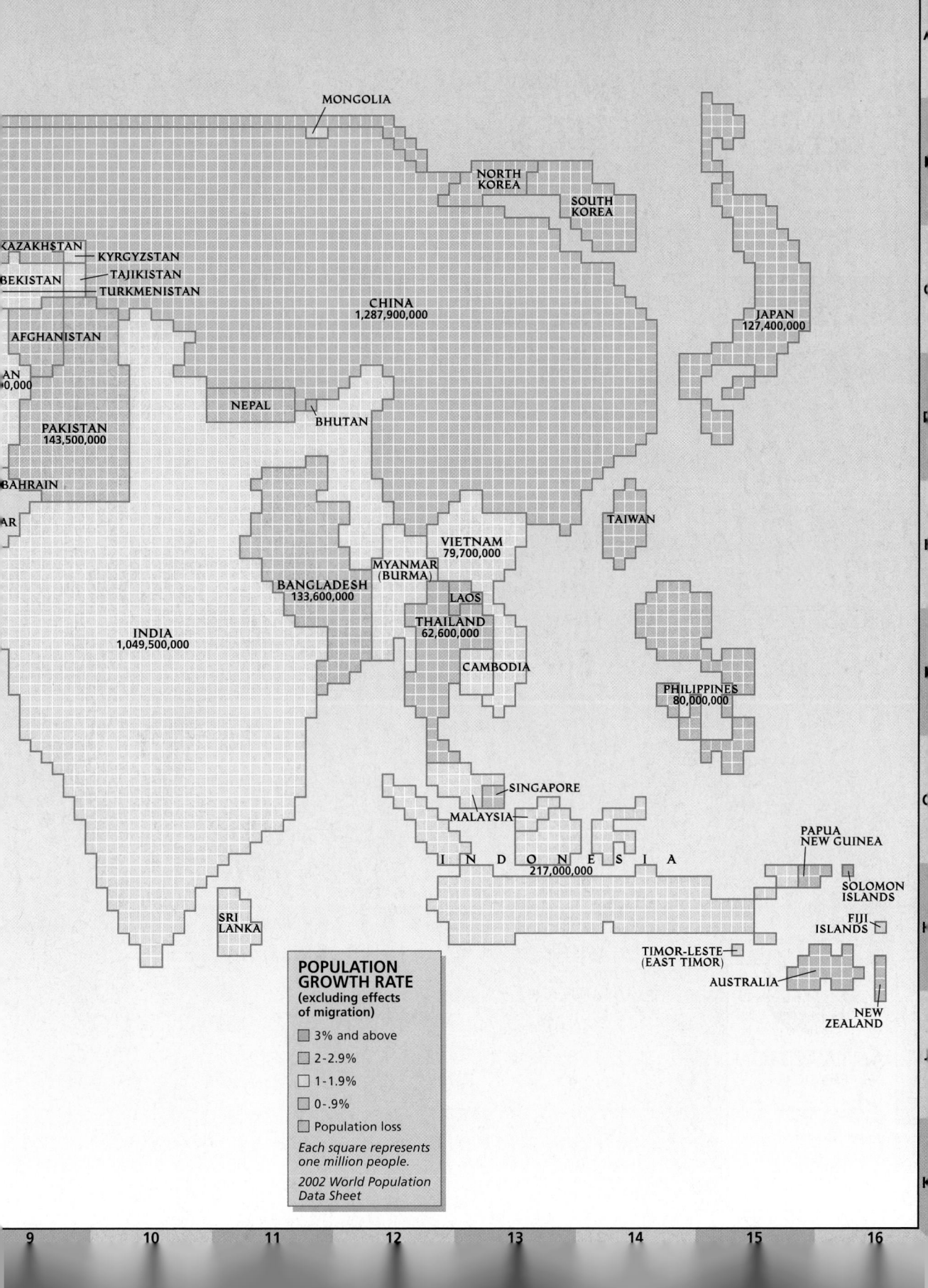

MONGOLIA

NORTH
KOREA

SOUTH
KOREA

JAPAN
127,400,000

KAZAKHSTAN

KYRGYZSTAN

BEKISTAN

TAJIKISTAN

TURKMENISTAN

CHINA
1,287,900,000

AFGHANISTAN

AN
0,000

NEPAL

BHUTAN

PAKISTAN
143,500,000

BAHRAIN

AR

TAIWAN

VIETNAM
79,700,000

BANGLADESH
133,600,000

MYANMAR
(BURMA)

LAOS

THAILAND
62,600,000

INDIA
1,049,500,000

CAMBODIA

PHILIPPINES
80,000,000

SINGAPORE

MALAYSIA

PAPUA
NEW GUINEA

I N D O N E S I A
217,000,000

SOLOMON
ISLANDS

SRI
LANKA

FIJI
ISLANDS

TIMOR-LESTE
(EAST TIMOR)

AUSTRALIA

NEW
ZEALAND

POPULATION
GROWTH RATE
(excluding effects
of migration)

☐ 3% and above

☐ 2-2.9%

☐ 1-1.9%

☐ 0-.9%

☐ Population loss

*Each square represents
one million people.*

*2002 World Population
Data Sheet*

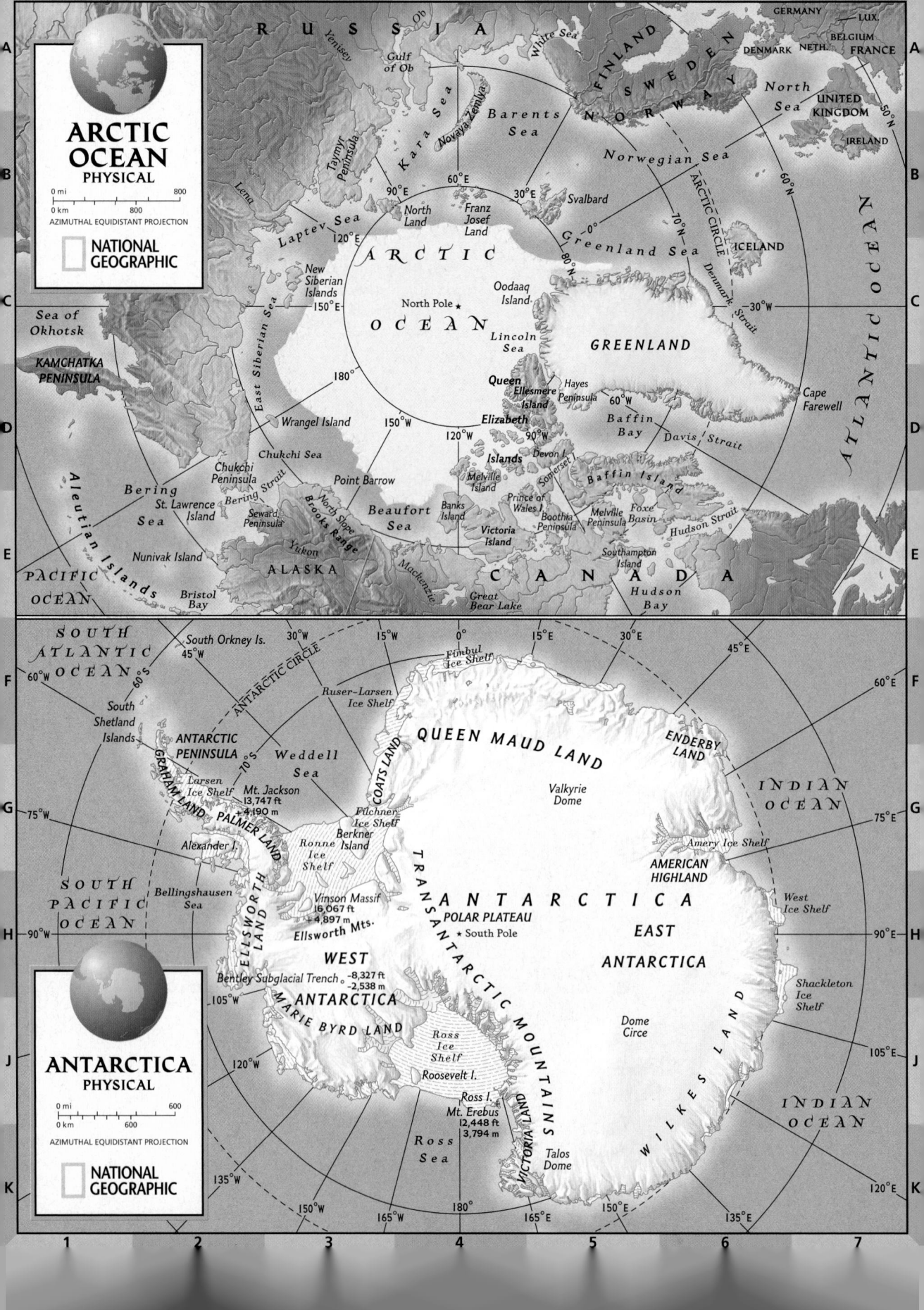

ARCTIC OCEAN PHYSICAL

0 mi 800
0 km 800
AZIMUTHAL EQUIDISTANT PROJECTION

NATIONAL GEOGRAPHIC

RUSSIA
GERMANY
LUX.
BELGIUM
DENMARK NETH. FRANCE

Ob
Yenisey
Gulf of Ob
White Sea
FINLAND
SWEDEN
NORWAY
DENMARK
North Sea
UNITED KINGDOM
IRELAND
50°N

Taymyr Peninsula
Kara Sea
Novaya Zemlya
Barents Sea
Norwegian Sea
ARCTIC CIRCLE
60°N

Lena
90°E
60°E
30°E
Svalbard
Greenland Sea
ICELAND
ATLANTIC OCEAN

North Land
Franz Josef Land
0°
70°N
80°N

Laptev Sea
120°E

ARCTIC
New Siberian Islands
150°E
Oodaaq Island
GREENLAND
30°W

OCEAN
North Pole ★
Lincoln Sea

East Siberian Sea
180°
Queen
Ellesmere Island
Hayes Peninsula
60°W
Cape Farewell

Sea of Okhotsk
Wrangel Island
150°W
Elizabeth
Devon I.
Baffin Bay
Davis Strait

KAMCHATKA PENINSULA
Chukchi Sea
120°W
90°W
Islands
Melville Island
Somerset I.
Baffin Island

Chukchi Peninsula
Point Barrow
Banks Island
Prince of Wales I.
Boothia Peninsula
Melville Peninsula
Foxe Basin
Hudson Strait

Bering Sea
St. Lawrence Island
Bering Strait
North Slope
Brooks Range
Beaufort Sea
Victoria Island
CANADA

Seward Peninsula
Aleutian Islands
Nunivak Island
Yukon
ALASKA
Mackenzie
Southampton Island
Hudson Bay

PACIFIC OCEAN
Bristol Bay
Great Bear Lake

ANTARCTICA PHYSICAL

0 mi 600
0 km 600
AZIMUTHAL EQUIDISTANT PROJECTION

NATIONAL GEOGRAPHIC

SOUTH ATLANTIC OCEAN
South Orkney Is.
45°W
30°W
15°W
0°
15°E
30°E
45°E

60°W
60°S
ANTARCTIC CIRCLE
Fimbul Ice Shelf
60°E

South Shetland Islands
Ruser-Larsen Ice Shelf

ANTARCTIC PENINSULA
70°S
Weddell Sea
QUEEN MAUD LAND
ENDERBY LAND

GRAHAM LAND
Larsen Ice Shelf
Mt. Jackson 13,747 ft +4,190 m
Filchner Ice Shelf
COATS LAND
Valkyrie Dome
INDIAN OCEAN

75°W
PALMER LAND
Berkner Island
Amery Ice Shelf
75°E

Alexander I.
Ronne Ice Shelf
AMERICAN HIGHLAND

SOUTH PACIFIC OCEAN
Bellingshausen Sea
ELLSWORTH LAND
Vinson Massif 16,067 ft +4,897 m
ANTARCTICA
West Ice Shelf

90°W
Ellsworth Mts.
POLAR PLATEAU
South Pole ★
EAST ANTARCTICA
90°E

WEST
-8,327 ft -2,538 m
ANTARCTICA

105°W
Bentley Subglacial Trench
TRANSANTARCTIC MOUNTAINS
Shackleton Ice Shelf

MARIE BYRD LAND
120°W
Ross Ice Shelf
Roosevelt I.
Dome Circe
WILKES LAND
105°E

135°W
Ross I.
Mt. Erebus 12,448 ft 3,794 m
VICTORIA LAND
INDIAN OCEAN
120°E

150°W
Ross Sea
Talos Dome

165°W
180°
165°E
150°E
135°E

NATIONAL GEOGRAPHIC

Geography Skills Handbook

Geography skills provide the tools and methods for us to understand the relationships between people, places, and environments. We use geographic skills when we make daily personal decisions—where to buy a home; where to get a job; how to get to the shopping mall; where to go on vacation. Community decisions, such as where to locate a new school or how to solve problems of air and water pollution, also require the skillful use of geographic information.

This **Geography Skills Handbook** introduces you to the basic geographic tools—globes, maps, graphs—and explains how to use them. From this foundation, you will gain more reinforcement and practice in the **SkillBuilder** features located throughout the textbook. These resources will help you get the most out of your geography course—and provide you with skills you will use for the rest of your life.

Contents

GEOGRAPHY SKILLS HANDBOOK ACTIVITY

Planning a Trip Have students use atlases and other resources to plan a cross-country trip through the United States. Direct them to choose a definite starting point and destination and plot the route between the two points. Have them calculate the approximate distance of the journey, how long the journey might take, and to list points of interest along the way. Allow time for students to share their itineraries.

EE1 The World in Spatial Terms: Standard 3

1

Meeting National Standards

Geography for Life
See National Geography Standards in front of book for more information about the National Standards in Geography and how they are integrated with the five themes as a basis for teaching geography skills and content.

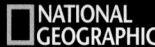

INTERDISCIPLINARY connection

LITERATURE Anthony Trollope, Thomas Hardy, Sinclair Lewis, and Robert Louis Stevenson all drew maps to help readers picture characters in their literary landscapes.

Thinking Like a Geographer

Geographers use a wide array of tools and technologies—from basic globes to high-tech global positioning systems—to understand the earth. These help them collect and analyze a great deal of information. However, the study of geography is more than knowing a lot of facts about places. Rather, it has more do with asking questions about the earth, pursuing their answers, and solving problems. Thus, one of the most important geographic tools is inside your head: the ability to think geographically.

Skills for Learning Geography

Geography educators have identified a set of five skills that are key to geographic understanding. These skills, highlighted in the *Geography for Life* national geography standards, are listed in the chart below. Maps, globes, charts, graphs, satellite photos, global positioning systems, geographic information systems, library materials, the Internet, and this textbook are some of the resources available to help you in your study of geography.

Skill	Examples	Tool and Technologies
Asking Geographic Questions involves posing questions about your surroundings.	• Ask questions about why traffic has increased along a particular road. • Determine what factors should be considered in order to build a new community sports facility.	• Maps • Globes • Internet • Remote sensing • News media
Acquiring Geographic Information helps you answer geographic questions.	• Compare aerial photographs of a region taken over time. • Design a survey to determine who might use a community facility.	• Field observation • Interviews • GPS • Reference works • Satellite imagery • Historical records
Organizing Geographic Information helps you analyze and interpret the information you have collected.	• Compile a map that shows the spread of housing development over a period of time. • Summarize information obtained from interviews.	• Field maps • Databases • Statistical tables • Graphs • Diagrams • Summaries
Analyzing Geographic Information involves looking for patterns, relationships, and connections.	• Draw conclusions about the effects of road construction on traffic patterns. • Compare the information from different maps that show available land and zoning districts.	• Maps • Charts • Graphs • GIS • Spreadsheets
Answering Geographic Questions involves applying the information to real-life situations and problem-solving.	• Present a report that conveys the results of a case study. • Suggest locations for a new facility based on the geographic and community data gathered.	• Sketch maps • Reports • Research papers • Oral or multimedia presentations

GEOGRAPHY SKILLS HANDBOOK ACTIVITY

Using Maps Copy and distribute the political map of the United States in the *Outline Map Resource Book.* Have students color-code the state in which they live. Then have them color-code the states they have visited or passed through. Provide students with an adhesive label to put in the corner of their maps. Ask them to draw a key on the label that explains the meanings of the colors used on their maps. ELL

EE1 The World in Spatial Terms: Standard 1

Latitude, Longitude, and Location

Geography is often said to begin with the question: *Where?* The answer can be described in many ways, including direction, distance, country, or region. However, the basic tool for answering the question is **location.** Lines on globes and maps provide information that can help you locate places. These lines cross one another, forming a pattern called a **grid system.** This system helps you find exact places on the earth's surface.

Latitude

Lines of **latitude,** or **parallels,** circle the earth parallel to the Equator and measure the distance north or south of the Equator in degrees. The Equator is measured at 0° latitude, while the Poles lie at latitudes 90° N (north) and 90° S (south). Parallels north of the Equator are called **north latitude,** and parallels south of the Equator are called **south latitude.**

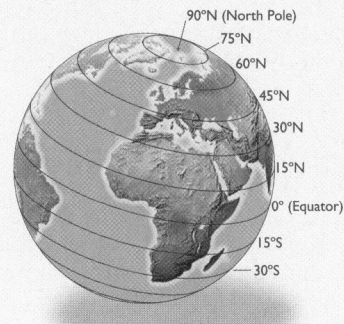

Longitude

Lines of **longitude,** or **meridians,** circle the earth from Pole to Pole. These lines measure distances east or west of the starting line, which lies at 0° longitude and is called the **Prime Meridian.** By international agreement, the Prime Meridian is the line of longitude that runs through the Royal Observatory in Greenwich, England. Places east of the Prime Meridian are known as **east longitude,** and places west of the Prime Meridian are known as **west longitude.**

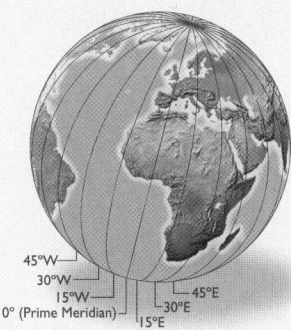

The Global Grid

Every place has a global address, also called its absolute location (see page 9). You can identify the absolute location of a place by naming the longitude and latitude lines that cross exactly at that place. For example, the city of Tokyo, Japan, is located at 36°N latitude and 140°E longitude. For more precise readings, each degree of latitude and longitude is subdivided into 60 units called minutes.

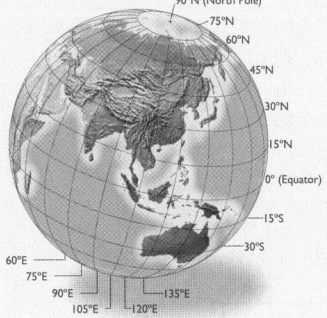

Geography Skills Handbook 3

☐ NATIONAL GEOGRAPHIC **GEOFACT**

The National Geographic Society Cartographic Division prefers to label the Prime Meridian as the Meridian of Greenwich (London).

Absolute Location There is a place with no latitude and longitude. The absolute location where the Prime Meridian and the Equator intersect is 0°N-S, 0°E-W.

DIFFERENTIATED INSTRUCTION

At-Risk Students The grid system is a prerequisite to understanding other aspects of geography, so ensure that all students grasp it at this point. To help students who are having difficulty understanding the grid system, draw a simplified grid of three horizontal lines labeled A, B, and C, and three vertical lines labeled 1, 2, and 3. Have students practice naming locations with this simple grid system. When they are comfortable with the basic concept, draw a more complex grid of 10 horizontal and 3 vertical lines labeled with degrees. Finally, have students practice on a globe. **ELL**

🌐 **EE1 The World in Spatial Terms: Standards 1, 3**

Longitude Until the 1700s, sailors seldom knew exactly where they were because they had only lines of latitude to guide them. John Harrison, an English instrument maker, created longitude by inventing a clock that could keep accurate time at sea. A navigator can determine the longitude by figuring the difference between Greenwich Mean Time (GMT), the exact time at the Prime Meridian, and the time where the ship is.

□ NATIONAL GEOGRAPHIC **GEOFACT**

▶ **Early Arab mapmakers placed north at the bottom rather than at the top of maps. Marco Polo used one of these early Arab maps on his journey to East Asia.**

From Globes to Maps

A **globe** is a scale model of the earth. Because the earth is round, a globe presents the most accurate depiction of geographic information such as area, distance, and direction. However, globes show little close-up detail.

A printed **map** is a symbolic representation of all or part of the planet on a flat piece of paper. Unlike globes, maps can show small areas in great detail. Another advantage of printed maps is that they can be folded, stored, and easily carried from place to place.

From 3-D to 2-D

Think about the surface of the earth as the peel of an orange. To flatten the peel, you might have to cut it like the globe shown here. To create maps that are not interrupted, mapmakers, or **cartographers,** use mathematical formulas to transfer information from the three-dimensional globe to a two-dimensional map. However, when the curves of a globe become straight lines on a map, distortion of size, shape, distance, or area occurs. The purpose of the map usually dictates which projection is used.

How Map Projections Work

To create maps, cartographers project the round earth onto a flat surface—making a **map projection.** There are more than a hundred kinds of map projections, some with general names and some named for the cartographers who developed them. Three basic categories of map projections are shown here: **planar, cylindrical,** and **conic.**

Planar Projection

A planar projection shows the earth centered in such a way that a straight line coming from the center to any other point represents the shortest distance. Also known as an azimuthal projection, it is most accurate at its center. As a result, it is often used for maps of the Poles.

CRITICAL THINKING ACTIVITY

Synthesizing Information Challenge students to make their own "map projections" by trying to depict a curved surface on a flat map. Have each student draw several imaginary countries on a balloon. Then tell students to measure the length and width of their countries and the distances between them on the balloon. Ask students to try to reproduce the same measurements on a flat sheet of paper. Have them analyze differences between the countries on the balloon and those on the map. *(The shapes of the countries on the map may be distorted.)* **ELL** ⊕ **EE1 The World in Spatial Terms: Standard 1**

Great Circle Routes

A straight line of true direction—one that runs directly from west to east, for example—is not always the shortest distance between two points on Earth. This is due to the curvature of the earth. To find the shortest distance between any two places, stretch a piece of string around a globe from one point to the other. The string will form part of a *great circle*, or imaginary line that follows the curve of the earth. Traveling along a great circle is called following a **great circle route.** Ship captains and airline pilots use great circle routes to reduce travel time and save fuel.

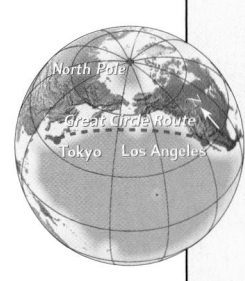

The idea of a great circle shows one important difference between globes and maps. Because a globe is round, it accurately shows great circle routes, as indicated on the partial globe shown (top). However, on a flat map, such as the Mercator projection (right), the great circle distance (dotted line) between Tokyo and Los Angeles appears to be far longer than the true direction distance (solid line). In fact, the great circle distance is 345 miles (555 km) shorter.

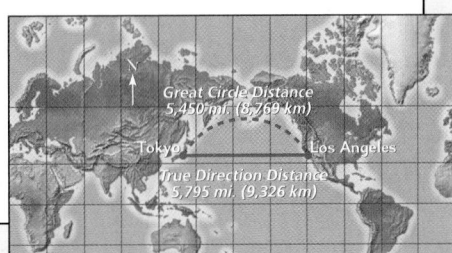

Cylindrical Projection

A cylindrical projection is based on the projection of the globe onto a cylinder. This projection is most accurate near the Equator, but shapes and distances are distorted near the Poles.

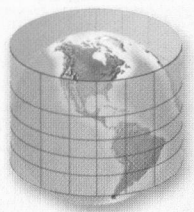
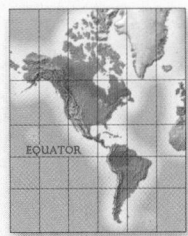

Conic Projection

A conic projection comes from placing a cone over part of a globe. Conic projections are best suited for showing limited east–west areas that are not too far from the Equator. For these uses, a conic projection can indicate distances and directions fairly accurately.

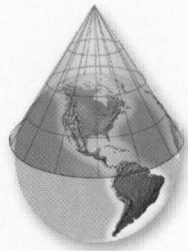
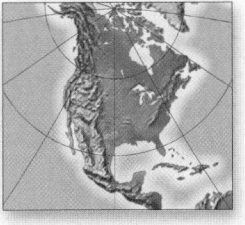

NATIONAL GEOGRAPHIC **MAP STUDY**

Map Skills Practice
Movement If an airplane averages 500 miles per hour on the journey between Los Angeles and Tokyo, how much time does it save by taking the great circle route? *(about 40 minutes)*

Culture NOTE

The Arctic The early Inuit labeled distances on their maps with the time they took to travel rather than with miles. A map would show the distance between what is now Nome and Point Barrow as 10 days rather than 525 miles (845 km).

EXTENDING THE CONTENT

Great Circle Air Routes Have students use commercial and economic atlases as well as other reference books to locate great circle air routes between the Western and Eastern hemispheres and between North America and Europe. Ask students to compare distances and flight times between two points by polar and non-polar routes. **ELL**

EE1 The World in Spatial Terms: Standard 1

INTERDISCIPLINARY
connection

COMPUTER LITERACY
Computers have revolutionized cartography. They reduce distortions and calculate changes at incredible speeds. They gather, process, and store data about contour reliefs, ethnicities, economics, waterways, and much more. They even produce animated "flow maps," such as those that show storm movement.

Common Map Projections

The curved surface of the earth cannot be shown accurately on a flat map. Every map projection stretches or breaks the curved surface of the planet in some way as it is flattened. Distance, direction, shape, or area may be distorted.

Cartographers have developed many map projections, each with some advantages and some degree of inaccuracy. Four of the most popular map projections, named for the cartographers who developed them, are shown on these pages.

Winkel Tripel Projection

Most general reference world maps use the Winkel Tripel projection. Adopted by the National Geographic Society in 1998 for use in most maps, the Winkel Tripel projection provides a good balance between the size and shape of land areas as they are shown on the map. Even the polar areas are depicted with little distortion of size and shape.

Robinson Projection

The Robinson projection has minor distortions. The sizes and shapes near the eastern and western edges of the map are accurate, and the outlines of the continents appear much as they do on the globe. However, the shapes of the polar areas appear somewhat distorted.

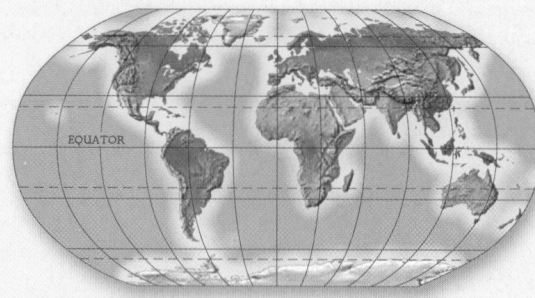

CRITICAL THINKING ACTIVITY

Classifying Information Draw a grid on the board. Across the top, write the headings "True Size," "True Shape," and "True Distance." To the left of the grid, list the map projections discussed in the lesson. Then ask students to place checks next to each projection under the headings that apply to that projection. **ELL**
⊕ **EE1 The World in Spatial Terms: Standard 1**

Goode's Interrupted Equal-Area Projection

An **interrupted projection** map looks something like a globe that has been cut apart and laid flat. Goode's Interrupted Equal-Area projection shows the true size and shape of the earth's landmasses, but distances are generally distorted.

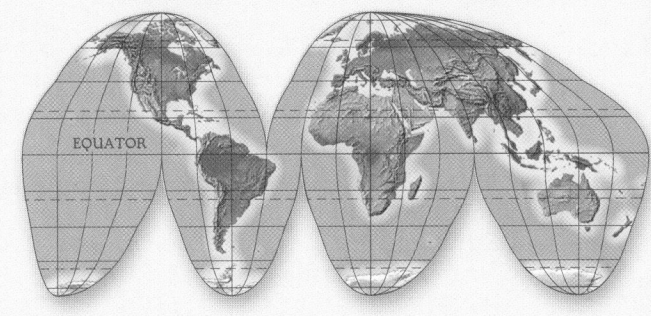

INTERDISCIPLINARY
connection

HISTORY The Mercator projection map has been favored by sailors for more than 400 years. It is ideal for sea navigation for three reasons: (1) it shows true directions; (2) parallels and meridians are straight, not curved; and (3) parallels and meridians intersect at right angles. Thus, navigators can simply plot direct compass courses on the map and follow them at sea.

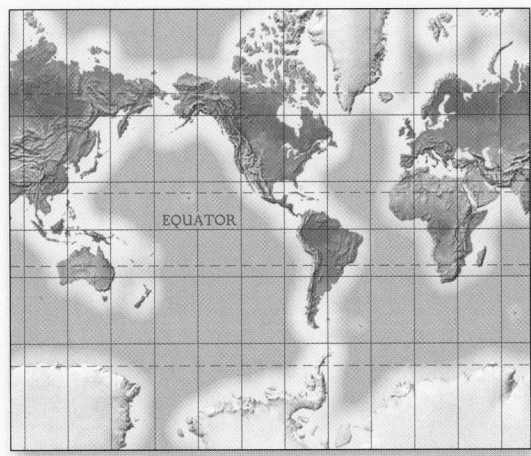

Mercator Projection

The Mercator projection, once the most commonly used projection, increasingly distorts size and distance as it moves away from the Equator. This makes areas such as Greenland and Antarctica look much larger than they would appear on a globe. However, Mercator projections do accurately show true directions and the shapes of landmasses, making these maps useful for sea travel.

A cartographer uses GIS to make a map.

Geographic Information Systems

Modern technology has changed the way maps are made. Most cartographers use computers with software programs called **geographic information systems (GIS).** A GIS is designed to accept data from many different sources, including maps, satellite images, and printed text and statistics. The GIS converts the data into a digital code, which arranges it in a database. Cartographers then program the GIS to process the data and produce the maps they need. With GIS, each kind of information on a map is saved as a separate electronic "layer" in the map's computer files. Because of this modern technology, cartographers are able to make maps—and change them—quickly and easily.

CRITICAL THINKING ACTIVITY

Evaluating Information Ask students to draw a grid similar to the one in the last activity, except across the top they will list the purposes for the maps. Refer them to *Why in the World: Adventures in Geography* by George J. Demko for examples. The names of map projections will again be listed on the left. Under each purpose, have students rank that projection's usefulness, using a scale from 1 (not useful) to 4 (most useful). Ask students to select the map projection they prefer and explain why. **ELL**

🌐 **EE1 The World in Spatial Terms: Standard 1**

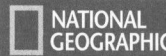

NATIONAL GEOGRAPHIC Geography Skills Handbook

NATIONAL GEOGRAPHIC **GEOFACT**

The Chinese invented the compass and applied it to navigation about A.D. 1000.

NATIONAL GEOGRAPHIC **MAP STUDY**

Map Skills Practice

Location Study the boundaries of France shown on the map of pre-World War I Europe. What large nation was located northeast of France? *(Germany)*

Reading a Map

In addition to scale and the lines of latitude and longitude, maps feature other important tools to help you interpret the information they contain. Learning to use these map tools will help you read the symbolic language of maps more easily.

Key

Cartographers use a variety of symbols to represent map information. Graphic symbols are easily understood by people around the world. To be sure that the symbols are clear, however, every map contains a **key**—a list that explains what the symbols stand for. This key shows symbols commonly used on a political map.

Compass Rose

N
W
E
S

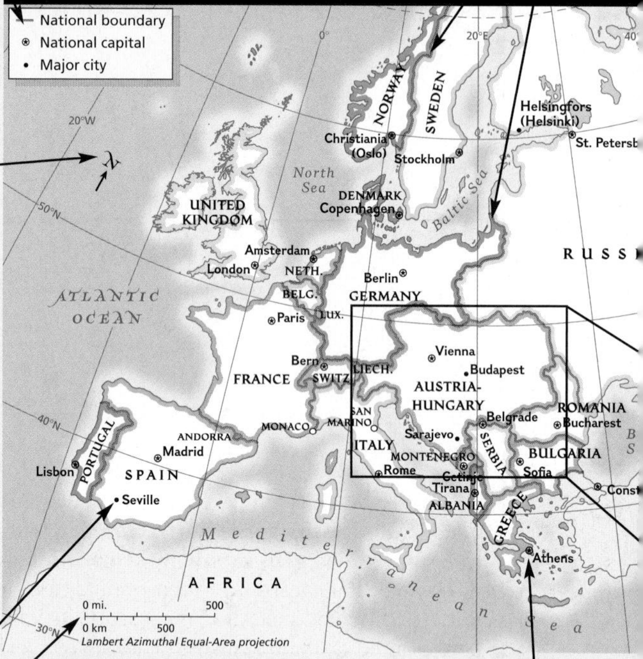

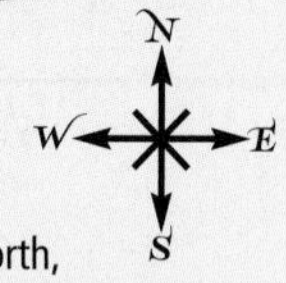

Most maps feature a **compass rose,** a marker that indicates directions. The four **cardinal directions**—north, south, east, and west—are usually indicated with arrows or points of a star. The **intermediate directions**—northeast, northwest, southeast, southwest—may also be shown, usually with smaller arrows or star points.

Sometimes a compass rose may point in only one direction because the other directions can be determined in relation to the given direction. The compass rose on this map indicates north only.

Cities

Cities are represented by a dot. Sometimes the relative sizes of cities are shown using dots of different sizes.

Boundary Lines

On political maps of large areas, boundary lines highlight the borders between different countries, states, or counties.

Europe Before World War I

National boundary
National capital
Major city
20°W
0°
20°E
N
NORWAY
SWEDEN
Christiania (Oslo)
Stockholm
Helsingfors (Helsinki)
St. Petersb
North Sea
Baltic Sea
DENMARK
Copenhagen
UNITED KINGDOM
London
Amsterdam
NETH.
BELG.
LUX.
Berlin
GERMANY
RUSS
50°N
ATLANTIC OCEAN
Paris
FRANCE
Bern
SWITZ.
LIECH.
Vienna
Budapest
AUSTRIA-HUNGARY
ROMANIA
Bucharest
Belgrade
SERBIA
Sarajevo
MONTENEGRO
Cetinje
BULGARIA
Sofia
SAN MARINO
MONACO
ITALY
Rome
Tirana
ALBANIA
GREECE
Athens
Const
40°N
PORTUGAL
Lisbon
ANDORRA
Madrid
SPAIN
Seville
Mediterranean Sea
AFRICA
30°N
0 mi. 500
0 km 500
Lambert Azimuthal Equal-Area projection

Scale Bar

The **scale bar** shows the relationship between map measurements and actual distances. By laying a ruler along the scale bar, you can calculate how many miles or kilometers are represented per inch or centimeter.

Capitals

National capitals are often represented by a star within a circle.

COOPERATIVE LEARNING ACTIVITY

Making Maps Organize students into several groups to work as cartographers. Assign each group a particular map—a map of the classroom, the school grounds, or another small area, for example. Different group members should be responsible for the following tasks: measuring and making a scale, using a compass to determine direction and make a compass rose, creating a map key, and drawing the map itself. Group members should cooperate to coordinate their work and to display their maps. ELL

EE1 The World in Spatial Terms: Standard 1

Using Scale

All maps are drawn to a certain scale. **Scale** is a consistent, proportional relationship between the measurement shown on the map and the measurement of the earth's surface. The scale of a map varies with the size of the area shown.

Use the scale bar to find actual distances on a map. The **scale bar** gives the relationship between map measurements and actual distances. Most scale bars are graphic representations, allowing you to use a ruler to calculate actual distances.

Small-Scale Maps

A small-scale map, like this political map of Mexico, can show a large area but little detail. Note that the scale bar for this map indicates that about ½ of an inch is equal to 300 miles and a little more than ½ of a centimeter is equal to 300 kilometers.

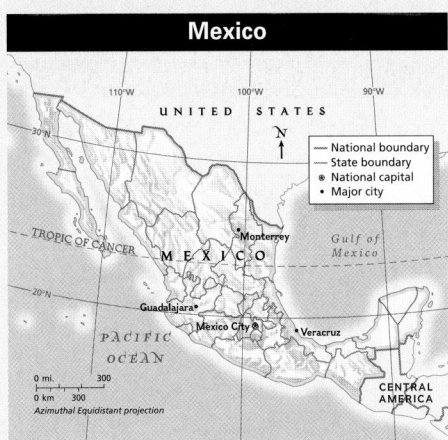

Large-Scale Maps

A large-scale map, like this map of Mexico City, can show a small area on the earth's surface with a great amount of detail. Study the scale bar. Note that the map measurements correspond to much smaller distances than on a small-scale map.

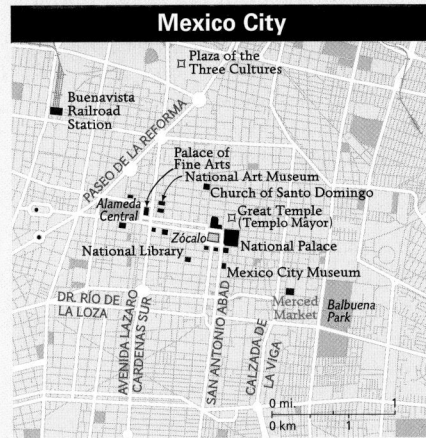

Absolute and Relative Location

As you learned on page 3, a place's **absolute location** is found at the precise point where one line of latitude crosses a line of longitude. Another way that people indicate location is

by relative location. You may be told, for example, to look for a street that is "two blocks north" of another street. **Relative location** is the location of one place in relation to another place.

To find relative location, find a reference point—a location you already know—on a map. Then look in the appropriate direction for the new location. For example, locate Vienna (your reference point) on this map. The relative location of Budapest can be described as southeast of Vienna.

COOPERATIVE LEARNING ACTIVITY

Class Challenge Organize the class into teams. Have each team record the absolute location (in degrees of latitude and longitude) of 20 named places on the globe (cities, natural features, and so on). Then pit teams against each other in a round-robin Absolute Location Tournament. In each round, one team will state the latitude and longitude of five places and time the other team as they locate the places on a globe. The teams will then switch roles. The team with the better time wins the round. **ELL**

EE1 The World in Spatial Terms: Standards 1,3

Airspace National boundaries run to the center of the earth and to the top of the atmosphere. Airplanes need a country's permission to fly into its airspace.

Types of Maps

Maps are prepared for many uses. The use for which a map is intended determines the kinds of information it contains. Learning to recognize a map's purpose will help you make the best use of its content.

General-Purpose Maps

Maps that show a wide range of information about an area are called **general-purpose maps.** General-purpose maps are typically used for reference, education, and travel. Two common forms of general-purpose maps are **physical maps** and **political maps.**

Physical Maps

A physical map shows the location and the **topography,** or shape, of the earth's physical features. Physical maps use colors or patterns to indicate **relief**—the differences in **elevation,** or height, of landforms. Some physical maps have **contour lines** that connect all points of land of equal elevation. Physical maps may show mountains as barriers to transportation. Rivers and streams may be shown as routes into the interior of a country. These physical features often help to explain the historical development of a country.

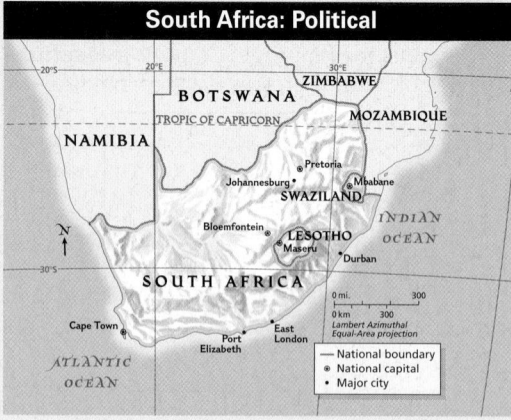

Political Maps

A political map shows the boundaries between countries. Smaller internal divisions, such as states or counties, may also be indicated by different symbols. Political maps often show human-made features such as capitals, cities, roads, highways, and railroads.

Special-Purpose Maps

Maps that emphasize a single idea or a particular kind of information about an area are called **special-purpose maps.** There are many kinds of special-purpose maps, each designed to serve a different need. You can learn more about several types of special-purpose maps in the SkillBuilder features in this textbook: relief maps (page 126), climate maps (page 172), population density maps (page 232), vegetation maps (page 432), elevation profiles (page 580), economic activity maps (page 680), and cartograms (page 754).

Some special-purpose maps—such as economic activity maps and natural resource maps—show the distribution of particular activities, resources, or products in a given area. Colors and symbols represent the location or distribution of activities and resources.

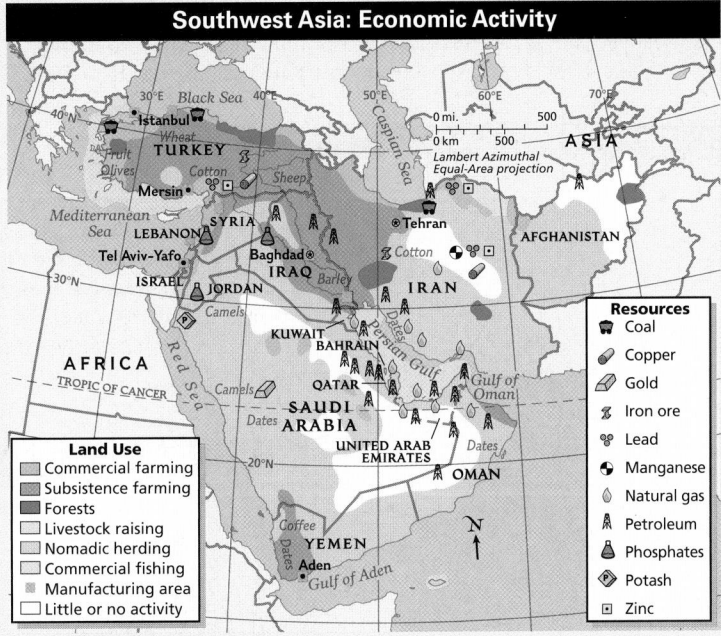

An Economic Activity Map

The special-purpose map above shows the distribution of land use and natural resources in Southwest Asia. Geographers use maps like this one to study the distribution of natural resources. Governments and industry leaders use land use maps and natural resource maps to monitor the economic activities of countries and regions.

NATIONAL GEOGRAPHIC **MAP STUDY**

Map Skills Practice
Region Mineral resources, such as petroleum, bring wealth to certain areas of Southwest Asia. According to the economic activities map, which area in the region has the largest concentration of petroleum and natural gas? *(the Persian Gulf area)*

Cartography Among the variety of special-purpose maps are hydrographic charts. They cover the surfaces of large bodies of water and are used for the navigation of ships. On a hydrographic chart, depths are given at frequent intervals by printing the number of fathoms of water at low tide. Shoal areas, channel boundaries, and the types of underwater bottoms, such as sand or rock, are also indicated. Hydrographic charts display coastal features, such as lighthouses and other prominent landmarks that can aid in navigation.

CRITICAL THINKING ACTIVITY

Special-Purpose Maps Have students bring special-purpose maps to class. Special-purpose subjects include bicycle routes, the path of killer bees, ocean currents, energy use, and pizza delivery routes. Even the treasure map that opens Robert Louis Stevenson's classic adventure story, *Treasure Island*, is a special-purpose map. Have each student write a brief paragraph explaining why his or her map is a special-purpose map. ELL
🌐 EE1 The World in Spatial Terms: Standard 1

NATIONAL GEOGRAPHIC   GRAPH STUDY

Skills Practice

Region Study the line graph of U.S. population growth. What was the population of the United States in 1900? In 1930? *(75 million, 125 million)*

INTERDISCIPLINARY
connection

HISTORY The U.S. Census, or the official population count by the federal government, is used to determine not only the size of the U.S. population but also the characteristics of its people, such as their age, gender, ethnic background, and income. Held every 10 years, the first U.S. Census took place in 1790. It counted the U.S. population at 3.9 million. Enslaved people were counted as three-fifths of a person, while Native Americans were excluded.

NATIONAL GEOGRAPHIC   GRAPH STUDY

Skills Practice

Region Look at the bar graph on page 12 and list the countries that have the largest and the smallest lumber production. *(United States, China)*

Graphs, Charts, and Diagrams

In addition to globes and maps, geographers use other visual representations to display and interpret data. Graphs, charts, and diagrams provide valuable information in forms that are well organized and easy to read.

Graphs

A **graph** is a visual presentation of information. There are many kinds of graphs, each suitable for certain purposes. Most graphs show two sets of data, one displayed along the vertical axis and the other displayed along the horizontal axis. Labels on these axes identify the data being displayed.

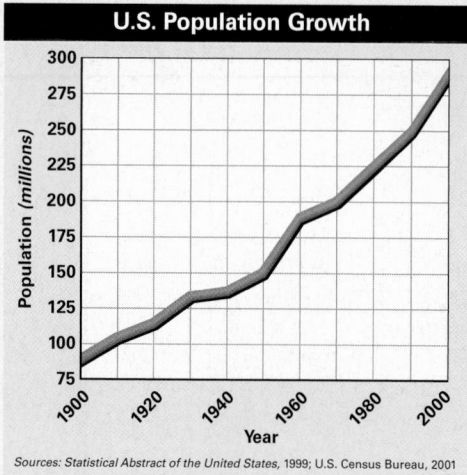

U.S. Population Growth

Sources: Statistical Abstract of the United States, 1999; U.S. Census Bureau, 2001

◄ Line Graphs

A **line graph** shows changes in two variables, or changing sets of circumstances over periods of time. To analyze data on a line graph, study the changes and trends as shown by the line. Then draw conclusions based on the information. This line graph shows U.S. population growth between 1900 and 2000. The vertical axis lists population, and the horizontal axis indicates the passage of time.

Bar Graphs ►

A **bar graph** shows comparisons. To analyze a bar graph, note the differences in quantities. Then make generalizations or draw conclusions based on the data. This bar graph shows lumber production among the top five lumber-producing countries in the world. The vertical axis shows the amount of lumber produced.

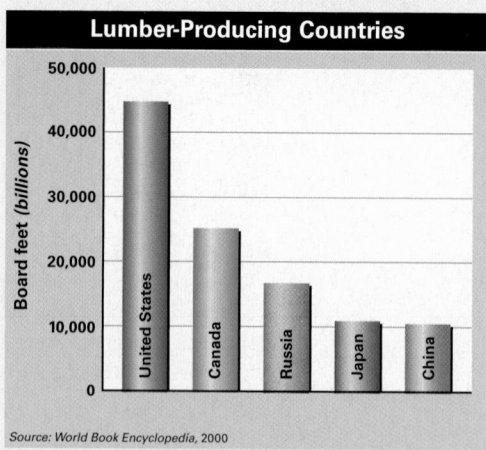

Lumber-Producing Countries

Source: World Book Encyclopedia, 2000

CRITICAL THINKING ACTIVITY

Population Change Have students research the 2000 U.S. Census. Suggest that they look for answers to questions such as these: *How is the population distributed throughout the United States?; Where are particular ethnic groups concentrated?; Which states have lost population since 1990, and which states have gained population?; How do the census results affect the U.S. House of Representatives?* Have students report their answers to these questions in the form of bar graphs. For instance, a student might make a bar graph comparing the number of congressional representatives from different states. **ELL**

🌐 **EE1 The World in Spatial Terms: Standard 1**

World Land Areas

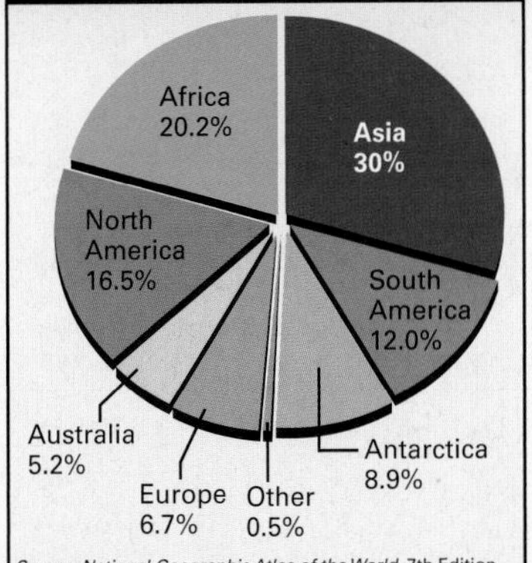

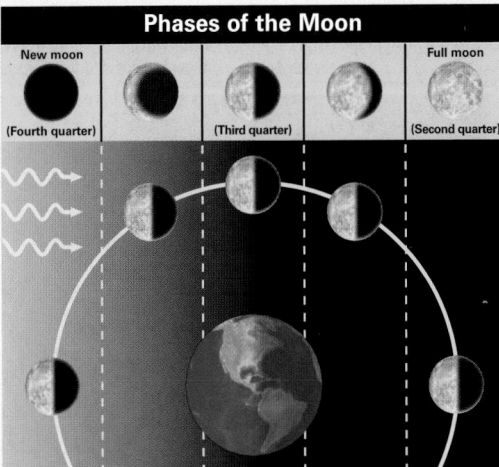

World Land Areas

- Africa 20.2%
- Asia 30%
- North America 16.5%
- South America 12.0%
- Antarctica 8.9%
- Australia 5.2%
- Europe 6.7%
- Other 0.5%

Source: National Geographic Atlas of the World, 7th Edition

◄ Circle Graphs

A **circle graph,** or **pie graph,** shows the relationship of parts to a whole. Percentages are indicated by relative size and sometimes by color. To analyze a circle graph, study the relationships of areas to one another and to the whole. This circle graph shows the land areas of the world's continents and other landmasses, such as islands, expressed as percentages of Earth's total landmass.

Charts and Tables

Data are arranged in columns and rows in a **chart** or **table.** Charts and tables display facts in an organized manner and make comparisons easy. To find key information in a chart or table, look for the intersections of columns and rows.

The table at right displays information about the population and land area of the world's continents.

Continents of the World

Continent	Population	Land Area
Africa	818,000,000	11,698,111 sq. mi. 30,298,107 sq. km
Antarctica	No permanent inhabitants	5,500,000 sq. mi. 13,209,000 sq. km
Asia	3,720,000,000	12,262,691 sq. mi. 31,760,369 sq. km
Australia	19,400,000	2,988,888 sq. mi. 7,741,220 sq. km
Europe	727,000,000	8,875,867 sq. mi. 22,988,495 sq. km
North America	491,000,000	8,747,613 sq. mi. 22,656,317 sq. km
South America	350,000,000	6,898,579 sq. mi. 17,867,319 sq. km

Source: World Population Data Sheet, 2001

Phases of the Moon

Phases of the Moon

New moon — (Fourth quarter) — (Third quarter) — (Second quarter) — Full moon

Diagrams

A **diagram** is a drawing that shows what something is or how something is done. Many diagrams feature several drawings or sections that show the steps in a process.

The diagram at left shows the way the moon seems to change shape as it goes through its phases each month. Note that as the moon revolves around the earth, it goes from the new moon phase, when it is almost invisible, to the full moon phase, when it appears as a giant globe.

NATIONAL GEOGRAPHIC — GRAPH STUDY

Skills Practice

Region Study the circle graph on world land areas. What percentage of the earth's land area is occupied by Africa? *(20.2 percent)*

□ NATIONAL GEOGRAPHIC GEOFACT

► **Most growth in world population has been recent. Ninety percent of all the people who ever lived are alive today.**

NATIONAL GEOGRAPHIC — CHART STUDY

Skills Practice

Region Study the chart on the world's continents and name the continent that has the largest population. *(Asia)*

NATIONAL GEOGRAPHIC — DIAGRAM STUDY

Skills Practice

Region Study the diagram "Phases of the Moon." When is the moon not seen from the earth? *(the fourth quarter)*

EXTENDING THE CONTENT

Determining Population Density Point out that the numbers on the chart of the world's continents can be used to produce other information. Demonstrate how to calculate population density by dividing the population by the square miles or square kilometers. Ask students to determine which populated continent has the lowest population density *(Australia)* and which has the highest *(Asia).* **ELL**

🌐 **EE1 The World in Spatial Terms: Standard 1**

Culture NOTE

The Geographer's Language
The terms that geographers use to describe the earth come from many different languages. The term *tsunami* is a Japanese word meaning "overflowing wave." *Mesa* is a Spanish word meaning "table." *Fjord* is a Norwegian word meaning "long, narrow bay."

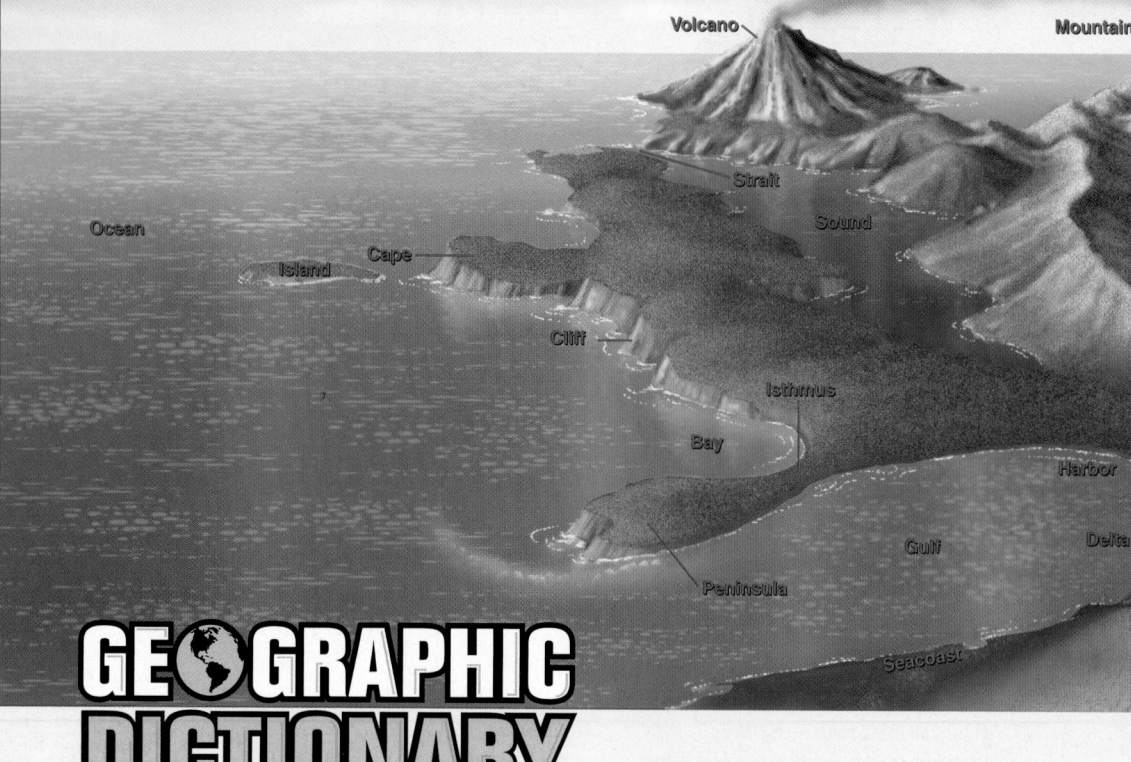

GEOGRAPHIC DICTIONARY

As you read about the world's geography, you will encounter the terms listed below. Many of the terms are pictured in the diagram.

absolute location exact location of a place on the earth described by global coordinates

basin area of land drained by a given river and its branches; area of land surrounded by lands of higher elevations

bay part of a large body of water that extends into a shoreline, generally smaller than a gulf

canyon deep and narrow valley with steep walls

cape point of land that extends into a river, lake, or ocean

channel wide strait or waterway between two landmasses that lie close to each other; deep part of a river or other waterway

cliff steep, high wall of rock, earth, or ice

continent one of the seven large landmasses on the earth

delta flat, low-lying land built up from soil carried downstream by a river and deposited at its mouth

divide stretch of high land that separates river systems

downstream direction in which a river or stream flows from its source to its mouth

elevation height of land above sea level

Equator imaginary line that runs around the earth halfway between the North and South Poles; used as the starting point to measure degrees of north and south latitude

glacier large, thick body of slowly moving ice

gulf part of a large body of water that extends into a shoreline, generally larger and more deeply indented than a bay

harbor a sheltered place along a shoreline where ships can anchor safely

highland elevated land area such as a hill, mountain, or plateau

hill elevated land with sloping sides and rounded summit; generally smaller than a mountain

island land area, smaller than a continent, completely surrounded by water

isthmus narrow stretch of land connecting two larger land areas

lake a sizable inland body of water

latitude distance north or south of the Equator, measured in degrees

longitude distance east or west of the Prime Meridian, measured in degrees

lowland land, usually level, at a low elevation

CRITICAL THINKING ACTIVITY

Determining Relative Location Have students identify at least 10 ways to describe the school's relative location. Have them list these ways and then have them use a map of the state or a city map that identifies latitude and longitude to find the school's absolute location. ELL ⊛ EE1 The World in Spatial Terms: Standard 1

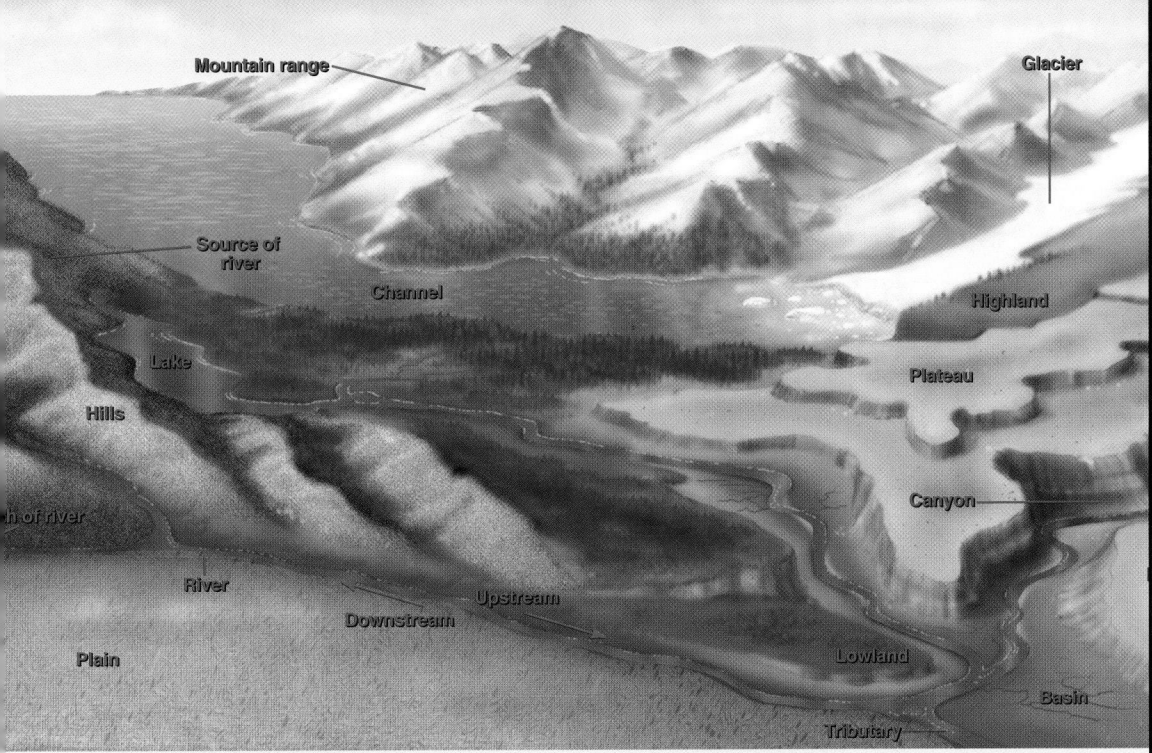

Mountain range

Glacier

Source of river

Channel

Highland

Lake

Plateau

Hills

h of river

Canyon

River

Upstream

Downstream

Plain

Lowland

Basin

Tributary

map drawing of the earth shown on a flat surface

meridian one of many lines on the global grid running from the North Pole to the South Pole; used to measure degrees of longitude

mesa broad, flat-topped landform with steep sides; smaller than a plateau

mountain land with steep sides that rises sharply (1,000 feet or more) from surrounding land; generally larger and more rugged than a hill

mountain peak pointed top of a mountain

mountain range a series of connected mountains

mouth (of a river) place where a stream or river flows into a larger body of water

ocean one of the four major bodies of salt water that surround the continents

ocean current stream of either cold or warm water that moves in a definite direction through an ocean

parallel one of many lines on the global grid that circles the earth north or south of the Equator; used to measure degrees of latitude

peninsula body of land jutting into a lake or ocean, surrounded on three sides by water

physical feature characteristic of a place occurring naturally, such as a landform, body of water, climate pattern, or resource

plain area of level land, usually at low elevation and often covered with grasses

plateau area of flat or rolling land at a high elevation, about 300 to 3,000 feet (90 to 900 m) high

Prime Meridian line of the global grid running from the North Pole to the South Pole at Greenwich, England; starting point for measuring degrees of east and west longitude

relief changes in elevation over a given area of land

river large natural stream of water that runs through the land

sea large body of water completely or partly surrounded by land

seacoast land lying next to a sea or an ocean

sound broad inland body of water, often between a coastline and one or more islands off the coast

source (of a river) place where a river or stream begins, often in highlands

strait narrow stretch of water joining two larger bodies of water

tributary small river or stream that flows into a large river or stream; a branch of the river

upstream direction opposite the flow of a river; toward the source of a river or stream

valley area of low land usually between hills or mountains

volcano mountain or hill created as liquid rock and ash erupt from inside the earth

COOPERATIVE LEARNING ACTIVITY

Map Quiz Organize the class into two teams. Provide one team with a map of their county and the other team with a map of their state. Assign each team the following task: Locate every major body of water in your assigned area. Record your findings, including (1) the name of each major body of water; (2) what type of water body it is—lake, river, bay, and so on; and (3) its relative and/or absolute location. When each team has completed its task, have them create a map quiz based on their work. Have teams trade maps and challenge each other with their quizzes. 🌐 **EE1 The World in Spatial Terms: Standard 3**

TEACHING TRANSPARENCIES

L2 Unit 1 Map Overlay Transparencies

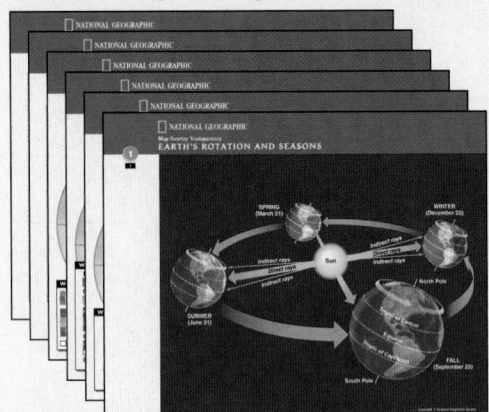

L2 Political Map Transparency 1

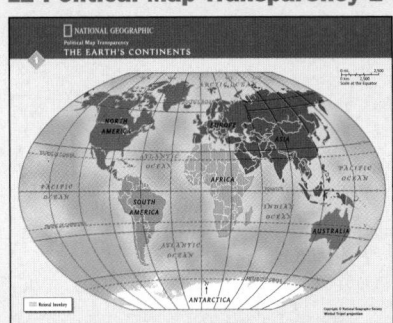

APPLICATION AND ENRICHMENT

L2 Location Activity 1

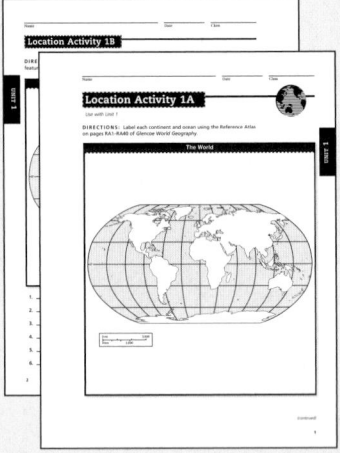

L2 Real-Life Applications and Problem-Solving Activity 1

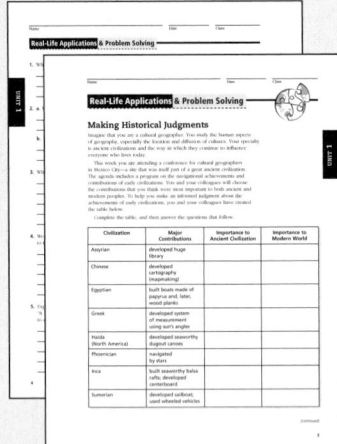

L2 GeoLab Activity 1

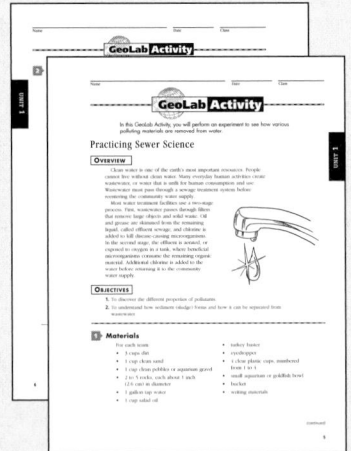

L2 Environmental Issues Case Study 1

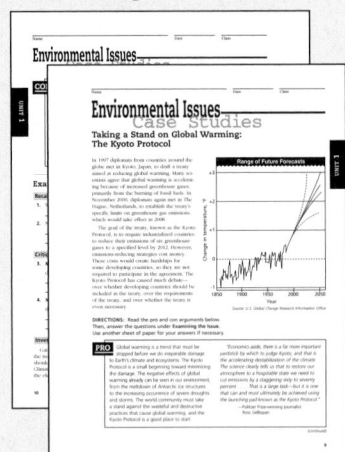

GEOGRAPHIC LITERACY

Focus on Geography Literacy

Building Geography Skills for Life

ASSESSMENT

ASSESSMENT

Use the following to easily assess student learning in a variety of ways:

· Performance Assessment Activities and Rubrics
· Section Quizzes
· Chapter and Unit Tests
· Interactive Tutor Self-Assessment CD-ROM
· ExamView® Pro Testmaker
· MindJogger Videoquiz
· geography.glencoe.com
· Standardized Test Practice Workbook
· SAT I/II Test Practice

L2 Unit 1 Pretest and Tests

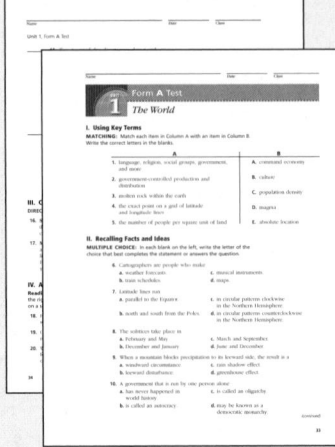

INTERDISCIPLINARY CONNECTIONS

L2 World Literature:
Contemporary Selection 1

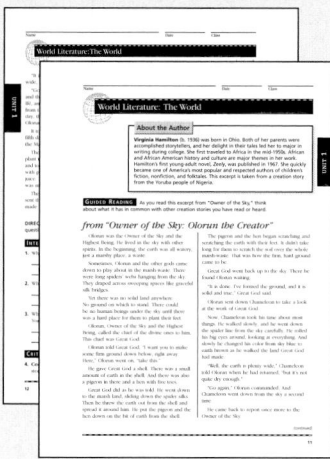

Foods Around the World

Multimedia

- World Art and Architecture Transparencies
- World Art Prints
- World Music: A Cultural Legacy
- World History Primary Source Document Library

BIBLIOGRAPHY

Readings for the Student

Don't Know Much About Geography, by Kenneth C. Davis. New York, NY: Avon Books, 1999.

The Illustrated Longitude, by Dava Soble. New York, NY: Walker & Co., 1998.

Readings for the Teacher

The Globalization Reader, edited by Frank Lechner and John Boli. Malden, MA: Blackwell Publishing, 1999.

Infinite Perspectives: Two Thousand Years of Three-Dimensional Mapmaking, by Brian M. Ambroziak and Jeffrey R. Ambroziak. Princeton, NJ: Princeton Architectural Press, 1999.

Multimedia Resources

GIS for Everyone. Redlands, CA: Environmental Systems Research, 1999. CD-ROM with book.

The Greatest Places (IMAX). Chatsworth, CA: Image Entertainment, 1999. DVD or videocassette, 50 minutes.

READING SUPPORT FROM JAMESTOWN EDUCATION

- *Timed Readings Plus in Social Studies* help students increase their reading rate and fluency while maintaining comprehension. The 400-word passages are similar to those found on state and national assessments.

- *Reading in the Content Area: Social Studies* concentrates on six essential reading skills that help students better comprehend what they read. The book includes 75 high-interest nonfiction passages written at increasing levels of difficulty.

- *Reading Fluency* helps students read smoothly, accurately, and expressively.

- *Jamestown's Reading Improvement,* by renowned reading expert Edward Fry, focuses on helping build your students' comprehension, vocabulary, and skimming and scanning skills.

- *Critical Reading Series* provides high-interest books, each written at three reading levels.

For more information about these products, see the Jamestown Education materials in the Classroom Solutions in the front of this Teacher Wraparound Edition.
To order these products, call Glencoe at 1-800-334-7344.

Background Information

CHAPTER 1 (pp. 18–31)

How Geographers Look at the World

"As the world grows smaller and more interdependent daily," said Gilbert M. Grosvenor, chairman of the National Geographic Society, "our country's future absolutely depends on our ability to see the connections between ourselves and our global neighbors." Geography is the science concerned with the environment of the earth's surface and the relationship of humans to this environment. As a result, it is an important means of understanding the many connections among the world's peoples.

The Study of Geography

Modern geographic study has its origins in the work of early nineteenth-century scientists, such Germany's Alexander von Humboldt, often called the "father of modern geography." Humboldt and other pioneers began to describe, classify, measure, and compare geographic features and to study the interrelationship of humans and the environment. Since then, geographers have extended the frontiers of geographic knowledge by collecting vast amounts of data, analyzing the information, and recording their results in charts, graphs, maps, and text.

During the 1900s, geographers made increasing use of quantitative methods in their work. Computers now have become an important factor in geographic analyses. Geographic Information Systems (GIS), for example, create two- or three-dimensional models of global areas for study, and also process massive amounts of geographic data speedily and accurately.

Geographers at Work

Geographers today work as urban planners, meteorologists, surveyors, educators, and consultants to government and industry. They also are involved in the exploration of uncharted territory— whether in distant space or deep beneath the oceans. To carry out these tasks, geographers rely on a variety of techniques, from personal observation in the field to the most sophisticated satellite and computer technologies.

In recent years, increasing stress has been placed on geographic education among the population at large, and national standards have been developed to promote students' geographic literacy. Students use geographic data and tools, such as maps, charts, and computer technology, to analyze location and spatial relationships, places and regions, and the dynamic interactions between humans and the physical environment.

CHAPTER 2 (pp. 32–53)

The Earth

Geographic study focuses on Earth, the third planet in distance outward from the sun. Earth orbits the sun at a speed of about 18.5 miles (29.8 km) per second, completing one revolution in 365.25 days. As it revolves around the sun, the earth spins on its axis and rotates completely once every 23 hours 56 minutes and 4 seconds.

The outward-moving force of Earth's rotation makes the planet bulge at the Equator. As a result, Earth's shape is flatter near the Poles than near the Equator. The fifth largest planet of the solar system, Earth is small in size compared, for example, with Jupiter. Yet it is the only planet in the solar system that has conditions suitable for life, as we know it. The earth's atmosphere consists of a mixture of gases, including 78 percent nitrogen and 21 percent oxygen. The only planet known to have liquid water, Earth has a hydrosphere consisting of seawater, freshwater, and ice.

A Dynamic Planet

Earth is constantly changing, shaped by internal forces—volcanic eruptions and earthquakes, for example—and external forces, such as erosion and weathering. The planet is surrounded by a region of strong magnetic forces extending upward from about 90 miles (about 140 km) in the upper atmosphere.

In this region, Earth's magnetic field traps charged particles—most of which come from the sun—and creates a shield that protects life on the planet's surface. Scientists believe that the magnetic field is caused by the flow of electric charges in the fluid molten metal of Earth's interior outer core.

CHAPTER 3 (pp. 54–73)

Climates of the Earth

Climate is the long-term effect of the sun's radiation on the rotating earth's diverse surface and atmosphere. Weather, however, refers to day-to-day variations. Both climate and weather can be understood in terms of precipitation and temperature.

The word *climate* comes from the Greek term *klima*, referring to the sun's inclination. In studying the climate of a given place, scientists consider latitude (or the sun's inclination), terrain, distance from the ocean, and relationship to mountains and inland bodies of water. They also study the impact of dynamic natural forces, such as air pressure and wind and ocean currents on the earth's surface. Wide-ranging climate patterns in various parts of the world are described in terms of climate regions, or zones, which are traced between the Equator and each Pole. Each region has a unique combination of climate factors that characterize it and distinguish it from other climate regions.

Climatic Causes and Effects

Climate has a profound effect on vegetation, animal life, and humans—sometimes a matter of life and death. For example, in low-lying Bangladesh, heavy monsoon rains and flooding may destroy homes and kill thousands of people. Humans, in turn, can affect climate by introducing pollutants into the atmosphere. New scientific and technological developments, such as developing better storm warning systems, have helped people better cope with the destructive aspects of climate and weather.

CHAPTER 4 (pp. 74–99)

The Human World

Human, or cultural, geography looks at all aspects of human activity in relation to the physical environment. It includes analyses of human-constructed geographic features, such as settlements and political entities, and lines of communication and transportation. Cultural geographers investigate how human population growth, distribution, and density affect Earth's physical and human systems. They also research human cultural features, such as languages and social groupings, as well as economic activities. Industries, for example, rely on cultural geographic studies for data concerning the uses of raw materials, the recruitment of labor, and marketing of products. The building of transportation facilities, highways, and resorts also depends to some extent on the findings of cultural geography.

A World of Connections

Advances in communications, transportation, and education have reduced the distances and overcome the obstacles that once divided countries and peoples. Issues of trade, environmental protection, and human migration transcend national boundaries, making various parts of the world interdependent. One of the geographer's greatest challenges is to explore how the planet's limited resources might best be managed and distributed. Studying global regions will help students understand their connections to the physical and human world.

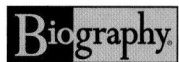

`00:00` **OUT OF TIME?**

If time does not permit teaching each chapter in this unit, you may want to use the **Reading Essentials and Study Guide** summaries.

Unit Launch Activity

Ask: How would you describe the earth to a visitor from another galaxy? Have students brainstorm the facts and impressions about planet Earth that they might want to communicate. Prompt students to describe physical features, location in space, and inhabitants of the planet (including human systems). Have volunteers list responses on the board. Ask another volunteer to transfer the list to a poster. Display the list as you work through this unit, and ask students to revise inaccurate statements and add new information as you go along.

GLENCOE
TECHNOLOGY

☐ NATIONAL GEOGRAPHIC

WORLD REGIONS
VIDEO PROGRAM

Unit 1, The World
The following segments enhance the study of this unit:

- **Ocean Journey**
- **Homo Sapiens Sapiens**
- **Goodwill Games**

 Available in DVD and VHS

The World

WHY IT'S IMPORTANT—

Entering the twenty-first century, the world is a much smaller place than it was at the time of your great-grandparents a hundred years ago. Advances in technology, communication, and transportation are responsible for much of this change. They have narrowed vast distances and made neighbors of the world's people. The Internet, for example, now puts you in immediate touch with people in other parts of the world. In the years to come, you and your generation—here and elsewhere—will be challenged to work together to use this and other technology to make the world a better place for everyone.

World Regions Video
To learn more about the physical and human geography of the world, view the *World Regions* video "Looking at the World."

16   Unit 1

🌐 GETTING TO KNOW THE WORLD

Map Activity Display Political Map Transparency 1 and **Ask:** What are the names of the continents? *(North America, South America, Europe, Africa, Asia, Australia, Antarctica)* What is the largest landmass on Earth that is not a continent? *(the island of Greenland, politically part of Denmark)* What is the largest body of water on Earth? *(the Pacific Ocean)* Which continents are located entirely above the Equator? *(North America, Europe)* Which large bodies of water border Asia? *(Pacific Ocean, Indian Ocean, Arctic Ocean)* On which continent is Mexico located? *(North America)* 🔲 EE1 The World in Spatial Terms: Standard 1

NATIONAL GEOGRAPHIC

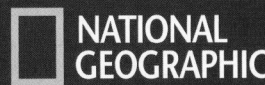

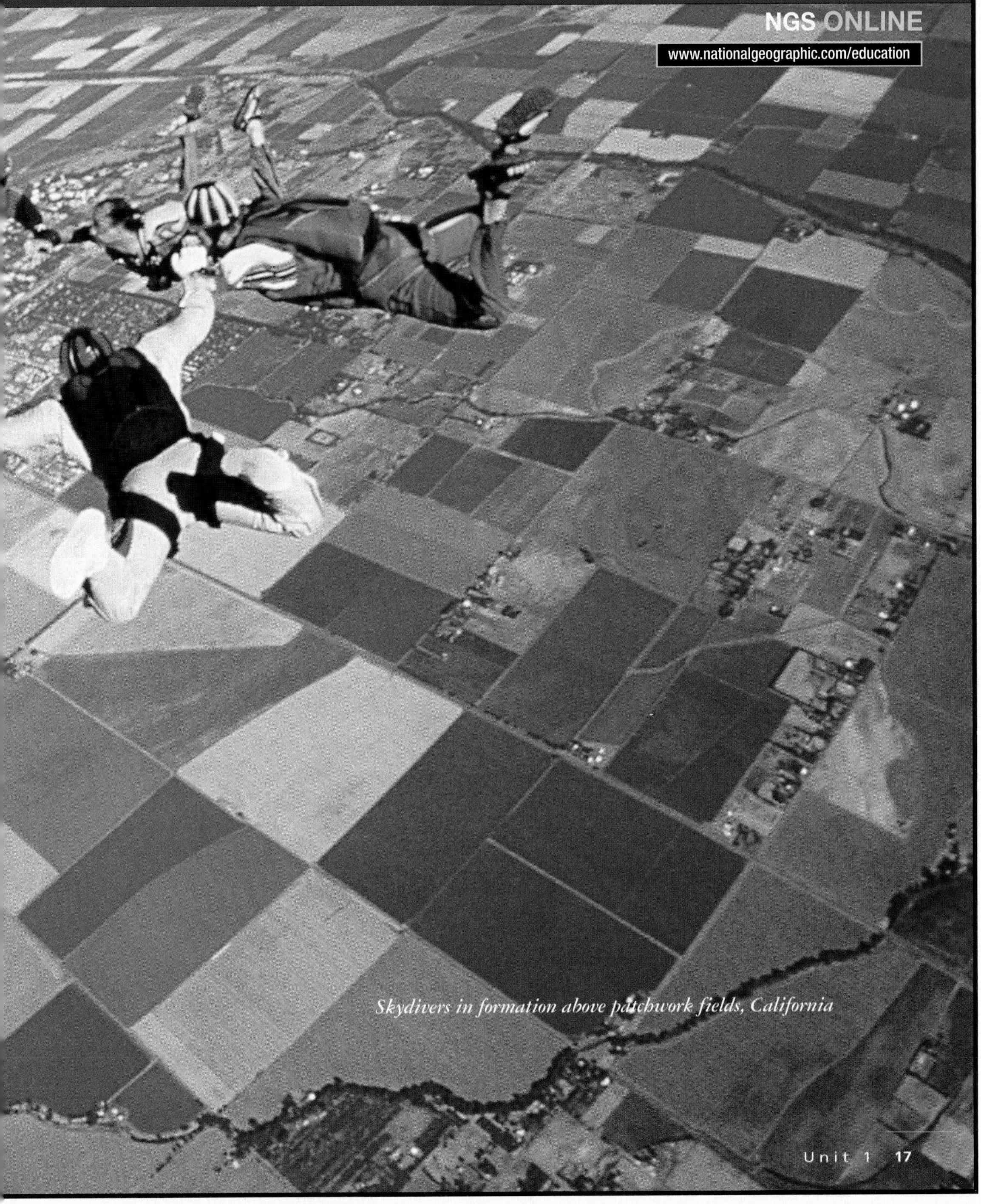

Skydivers in formation above patchwork fields, California

Unit 1 17

NGS ONLINE
www.nationalgeographic.com/education

This online resource, brought to you by the National Geographic Society, provides lesson plans, atlas updates, cartographic activities with interactive maps, an online map store, and links to the boundless subjects of maps and geography.

Unit Overview

This unit introduces students to the physical and cultural geography of the earth as well as to its peoples. The first chapter helps students see the world as geographers do. Point out that the following global issues are of special concern to geographers:

- climate patterns and the ability to predict weather
- issues of population growth and density
- the impact of human activity on the environment and of physical geography on human systems
- the location, distribution, development, and conservation of the planet's resources

ABOUT THE PHOTO

Visual Instruction This photograph, taken from an airplane, symbolizes the overview of world geography that Unit 1 provides. The aerial perspective is a reminder of the enhanced technologies—satellite imaging, computer mapping, GIS, and global positioning systems—that geographers use to study the planet. The patchwork pattern of the fields echoes the diversity of Earth's physical and human systems and the human need to organize this diversity into meaningful patterns. **Ask:** **What does this photograph tell you about the structure of the earth?** *(The earth is roughly spherical. The curve of the horizon is visible in the photograph, as is the layer of visible haze that marks the lowest reaches of Earth's atmosphere.)*
EE1 The World in Spatial Terms: Standard 3

PLANNING GUIDE

NOTE: The following materials may be used when teaching Chapter 1. Section-level support materials are shown at point-of-use in the margins of the Teacher Wraparound Edition.

TEACHING TRANSPARENCIES

L2 Unit 1 Map Overlay Transparencies

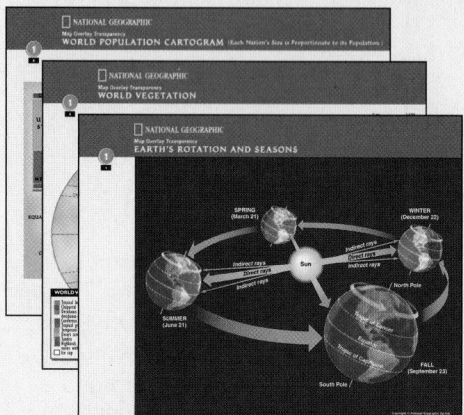

L2 Political Map Transparency 1

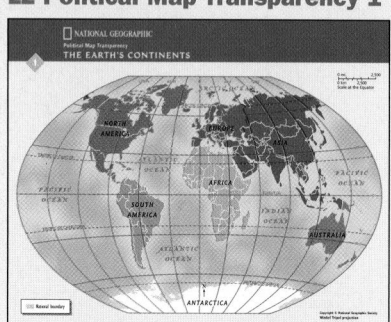

GEOGRAPHIC LITERACY

Focus on Geography Literacy

APPLICATION AND ENRICHMENT

L3 Enrichment Activity 1

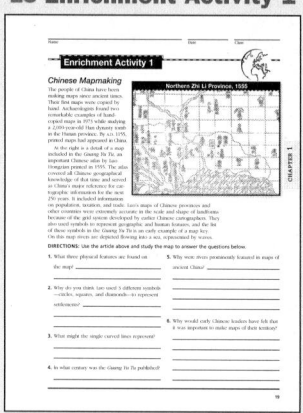

REVIEW AND REINFORCEMENT

L1 Vocabulary Activity 1   L1 Reinforcing Skills Activity 1   L1 Reteaching Activity 1

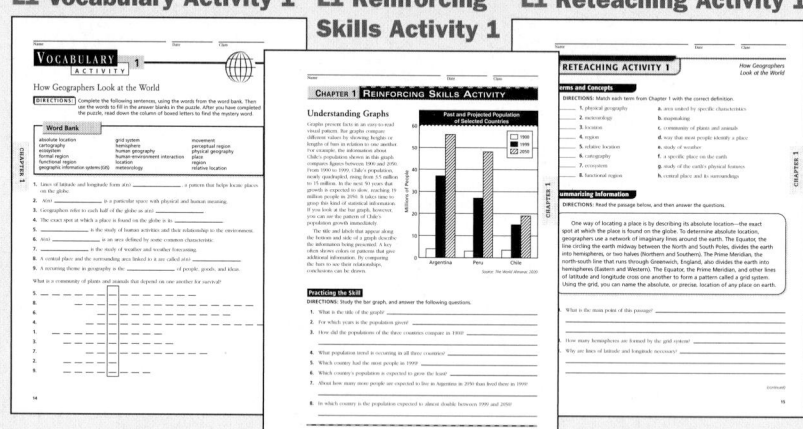

ASSESSMENT

L2 Chapter 1 Test Form A

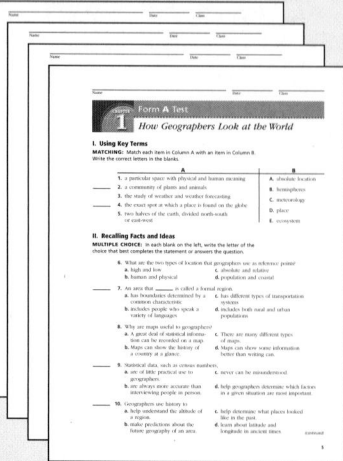

L2 Chapter 1 Test Form B

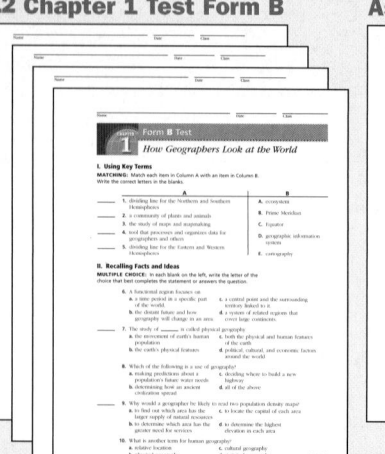

L1/ELL Performance Assessment Activity 1

ExamView® Pro Testmaker

The following Spanish language materials are available in the Spanish Resources binder:

- 📁 Spanish Vocabulary Activities
- 📁 Spanish Guided Reading Activities
- 📁 Spanish Reteaching Activities
- 📁 Spanish Summaries
- 📁 Spanish Quizzes and Tests
- 📁 Spanish Reading Essentials and Study Guide

- 📼 World Regions Video
- 📼 MindJogger Videoquiz
- 💿 Vocabulary PuzzleMaker CD-ROM
- 💿 Interactive Tutor Self-Assessment CD-ROM
- 💿 ExamView® Pro Testmaker CD-ROM
- 💿 Audio Program
- 💿 TeacherWorks CD-ROM
- 💿 Interactive Student Edition CD-ROM
- 💿 Glencoe Skillbuilder Interactive Workbook CD-ROM, Level 2
- 💿 Presentation Plus! CD-ROM

Timesaving Tools

TeacherWorks™ All-In-One Planner and Resource Center

- **Interactive Teacher Edition** Access your Teacher Wraparound Edition and your classroom resources with a few easy clicks.
- **Interactive Lesson Planner** Planning has never been easier! Organize your week, month, semester, or year with all the lesson helps you need to make teaching creative, timely, and relevant.

Use Glencoe's **Presentation Plus!** multimedia teacher tool to easily present dynamic lessons that visually excite your students. Using Microsoft PowerPoint® you can customize the presentations to create your own personalized lessons.

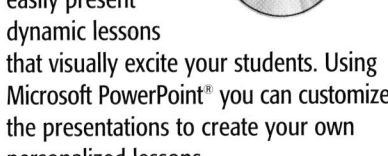

GEOGRAPHY *Online*

Use our Web site for additional resources. All essential content is covered in the Student Edition.

You and your students can visit geography.glencoe.com, the Web site companion to *Glencoe World Geography*. This innovative integration of electronic and print media offers your students a wealth of opportunities. The student text directs students to the Web site for the following options:

- **Chapter Overviews**
- **Student Activities**
- **Self-Check Quizzes**
- **Textbook Updates**

Answers are provided for you in the "Web Activity Lesson Plan." Additional Web resources and Interactive Tutor puzzles are also available.

▶ **Additional Glencoe Teacher Support**

- Teaching Strategies for the Geography Classroom (including Block Scheduling Pacing Guides)
- Graphic Organizer Transparencies Strategies and Activities
- Outline Map Resource Book
- Reading in the Content Area

PLANNING GUIDE

SECTION RESOURCES

Daily Objectives	Reproducible Resources	Multimedia Resources

SECTION 1 Exploring Geography

1. Describe the physical and human features that geographers study.
2. Explain how geographers describe the earth's features and their patterns.
3. Discuss how geography is used.

Reproducible Lesson Plan 1-1
Daily Lecture Notes 1-1
Guided Reading Activity 1-1*
Reading Essentials and Study Guide 1-1*
Section Quiz 1-1*

Daily Focus Skills Transparency 1-1
Political Map Transparency 1
Unit 1 Map Overlay Transparencies
Interactive Tutor Self-Assessment CD-ROM
ExamView® Pro Testmaker CD-ROM*
Presentation Plus! CD-ROM

SECTION 2 The Geographer's Craft

1. Identify the major branches of geography and the topics each branch studies.
2. Describe the research methods geographers use.
3. Discuss the relationship of geography to other subject areas.
4. List the kinds of geographic careers that are available today.

Reproducible Lesson Plan 1-2
Vocabulary Activity 1*
Daily Lecture Notes 1-2
Guided Reading Activity 1-2*
Reading Essentials and Study Guide 1-2*
Reteaching Activity 1*
Reinforcing Skills Activity 1
Section Quiz 1-2*

Daily Focus Skills Transparency 1-2
Unit 1 Map Overlay Transparencies
Vocabulary PuzzleMaker CD-ROM
Interactive Tutor Self-Assessment CD-ROM
ExamView® Pro Testmaker CD-ROM*
Presentation Plus! CD-ROM

Blackline Master

Transparency

Software

CD-ROM

Videocassette

DVD

Also available in Spanish

00:00 OUT OF TIME? Assign the Chapter 1 **Reading Essentials and Study Guide.**

Block Schedule

Activities that are particularly suited to use within the block scheduling framework are identified throughout this chapter by the following designation:

KEY TO ABILITY LEVELS

Teaching strategies have been coded for various learning styles and abilities.

L1   **BASIC** activities for all students

L2   **AVERAGE** activities for average to above-average students

L3   **CHALLENGING** activities for above-average students

ELL   **ENGLISH LANGUAGE LEARNER** activities

Teacher to Teacher

Tom Ehrhart
St. Peter-Marian
High School
Worcester, MA

Introducing Location

This activity introduces students to the concept of absolute location and works well as an icebreaker at the beginning of the school year.

On the first day, introduce the study of geography. While discussing location, explain the use of the grid and help students figure out the cardinal directions in the classroom. On the second day, each student receives a sheet of paper as he or she enters the room. On each paper is written the name of a place—a city, a physical feature, a state, or a country—and its absolute location in degrees of latitude and longitude. Have the long rows of seats labeled as specific degrees of longitude and the shorter side-to-side rows labeled as degrees of latitude. Students must find their assigned absolute locations among the rows of seats. Students become acquainted as they interact with each other to find these absolute locations. Check their locations with a master list. This activity can be applied to various regions of the world by changing the labels for degrees of latitude and longitude in the grid.

 **NATIONAL GEOGRAPHIC** **TEACHER'S CORNER**

Index to National Geographic Magazine:

The following articles may be used for research relating to this chapter:

- *Physical World*, a National Geographic Special Edition, May 1998.
- "Revolutions in Mapping," by John Noble Wilford, February 1998.
- "Blueprints for Victory," by John F. Shupe, May 1995.

National Geographic Society Products:

To order the following products for use with this chapter, call National Geographic Society at 1-800-368-2728.

- *Latitude and Longitude* (Video)
- *Physical Geography of the Continents Series* (Videos)
- *Physical Earth* (Map)
- *National Geographic Desk Reference* (Book)
- *National Geographic Atlas of the World, Seventh Edition* (Book)
- *Tool Kit for Teaching Geography* (Geography Lesson Kit)

NGS ONLINE

Access National Geographic's Web site for current events, activities, links, interactive features, and archives.
www.nationalgeographic.com

 ## Meeting National Standards

Geography For Life

The following standards are highlighted in Chapter 1:

Section 1   EE1 The World in Spatial Terms:
Standards 1, 2
EE2 Places and Regions:
Standard 5

Section 2   EE1 The World in Spatial Terms:
Standards 1
EE6 The Uses of Geography:
Standard 18

Local Objectives

_____

_____

MEETING SPECIAL NEEDS

In addition to the Differentiated Instruction strategies found in each section, the following resources are also suitable for your special needs students:

- *ExamView® Pro Testmaker CD-ROM* allows teachers to tailor tests by reducing answer choices.
- The *Audio Program* includes the entire narrative of the student edition so that less-proficient readers can listen to the words as they read them.
- The *Reading Essentials and Study Guide* provides the same content as the student edition but is written two grade levels below the textbook.
- *Guided Reading Activities* give less-proficient readers point-by-point instructions to increase comprehension as they read each textbook section.
- *Enrichment Activities* include a stimulating collection of readings and activities for gifted and talented students.

Chapter Objectives

1. Describe the elements of geography and the topics geographers study.

2. Identify the tools and applications of geography and its relationship to other fields of study.

GLENCOE TECHNOLOGY

Use *MindJogger Videoquiz* to preview the Chapter 1 content.

GeoJournal

For access to additional information on geography skills, tools, and careers go to www.nationalgeographic.com (See Teacher pages in front for strategies for using journals in the geography classroom.)

GEOGRAPHY Online

Introduce students to chapter content and key terms by having them access **Chapter Overview 1** at geography.glencoe.com

FOLDABLES™
Study Organizer

Dinah Zike's Foldables are three-dimensional, interactive graphic organizers that help students practice basic writing skills, review key vocabulary terms, and identify main ideas. Have students complete the Foldable activity in the **Dinah Zike's Reading and Study Skills Foldables** booklet.

CHAPTER 1

How Geographers Look at the World

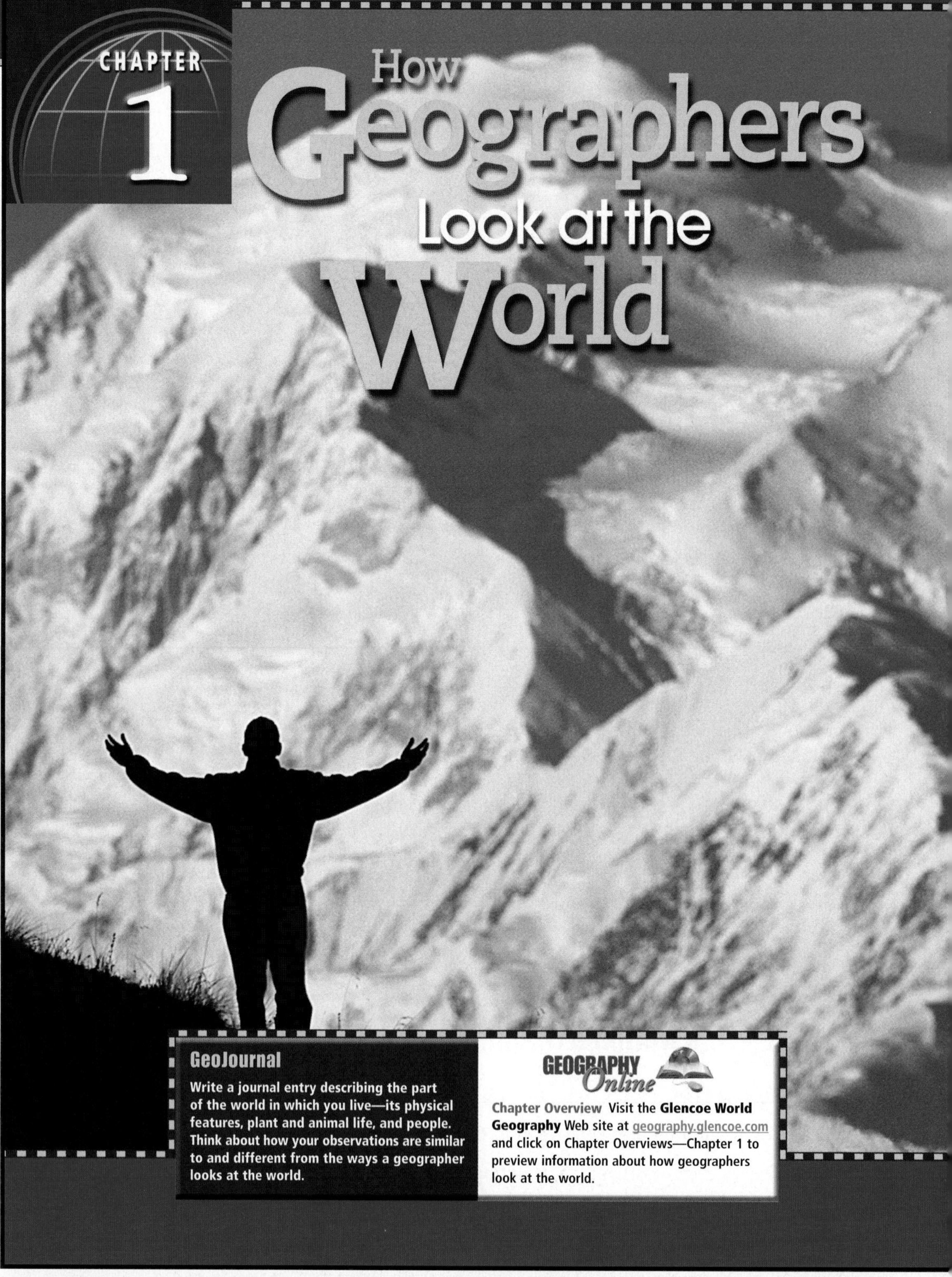

GeoJournal

Write a journal entry describing the part of the world in which you live—its physical features, plant and animal life, and people. Think about how your observations are similar to and different from the ways a geographer looks at the world.

GEOGRAPHY Online

Chapter Overview Visit the **Glencoe World Geography** Web site at geography.glencoe.com and click on Chapter Overviews—Chapter 1 to preview information about how geographers look at the world.

ABOUT THE PHOTO

Visual Instruction The above photograph shows a hiker silhouetted against the peak of Mt. McKinley in the Alaska Range. At 20,320 feet (6,194 m), the South Peak of Mt. McKinley is the highest point on the North American continent as well as the highest peak in the United States. Known to the Athabaskan people of Alaska as Denali, or "the great one," the mountain received its English name in honor of U.S. President William McKinley.
Ask: How do you think Mt. McKinley compares in elevation with the world's highest peaks? *(Mt. McKinley actually ranks 109th, below the towering peaks of South Asia's Himalaya and South America's Andes.)* Visit the National Geographic Society web site to view topographic maps of the United States and the Alaska Range. ▓ EE1 The World in Spatial Terms: Standard 2

Guide to Reading

Consider What You Know

Think about where your school is located and the ways in which a place's location can be described. How many different ways can you think of to describe your school's location to another person?

Reading Strategy

Organizing As you read about places on Earth, create a web diagram similar to the one below by listing three types of regions.

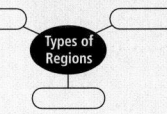

Types of Regions

Read to Find Out

- What are the physical and human features geographers study?
- How do geographers describe the earth's features and their patterns?
- How is geography used?

Terms to Know

- location
- absolute location
- hemisphere
- grid system
- relative location
- place
- region
- formal region
- functional region
- perceptual region
- ecosystem
- movement
- human-environment interaction

Places to Locate

- Equator
- North Pole
- South Pole
- Prime Meridian

◀ *Mt. McKinley, Alaska, United States*

Exploring Geography

NATIONAL GEOGRAPHIC

A Geographic View

Earth's Variety

A small planet in a modest solar system, a tumbling pebble in the cosmic stream, and yet . . . [t]his home is built of many mansions, carved by wind and the fall of water, lush with living things beyond number, perfumed by salt spray and blossoms. Here cool in a cloak of mist or there steaming under a brazen sun, Earth's variety excites the senses and exalts the soul.

—Stuart Franklin, "Celebrations of Earth," National Geographic, January 2000

Labrador coast, Canada

How would you describe the world around you? Would it be in terms of people, places, things, or all of these? Geography is the study of the earth's physical features and the living things—humans, animals, and plants—that inhabit the planet. Geography looks at where all of these elements are located and how they relate to one another. In this section you will gain an understanding of what geography is and why it is important to study it.

The Elements of Geography

The root of the word *geography* is an ancient Greek word meaning "earth description." Geographers are specialists who describe the earth's physical and human features and the interactions of people, places, and environments. They not only describe but also search for patterns in these features and interactions, seeking to explain how and why they exist or occur. For example, geographers may study volcanoes and why they erupt, or they may analyze a city's location

Chapter 1 19

FOCUS

Section Overview

This section discusses the essential elements of geography—how geographers look at the world, what they study, and why they study it.

BELLRINGER
Skillbuilder Activity

- Project transparency and have students answer questions.
- Available as blackline master.

Daily Focus Skills Transparency 1-1

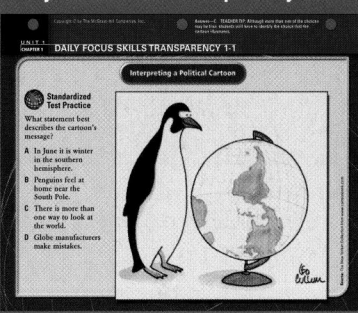

Guide to Reading

Consider What You Know
Answer *List responses on the board. Prompt students to describe the location in relation to other places.*

Reading Strategy
Answer *Types of Regions: formal region, functional region, perceptual region*

Preteaching Vocabulary
Write the following Greek and Latin roots on the board: *locus* (place); *hemi* (half); *sphere* (globe); and *eco* (environment). As students read, have them use the roots to predict the definitions of new terms.

RESOURCE MANAGER

📁 Reproducible Masters
- Reproducible Lesson Plan 1-1
- Daily Lecture Notes 1-1
- Guided Reading Activity 1-1
- Reading Essentials and Study Guide 1-1
- Section Quiz 1-1

🖥 Transparencies
- Daily Focus Skills Transparency 1-1
- Political Map Transparency 1
- Unit 1 Map Overlay Transparencies

Multimedia
- 💿 Interactive Tutor Self-Assessment CD-ROM
- 💿 ExamView® Pro Testmaker CD-ROM
- 💿 Presentation Plus! CD-ROM

TEACH

L1 Identify

Have students form two teams. Each team takes a turn naming an element of geography, and the other team must name an example of that element.

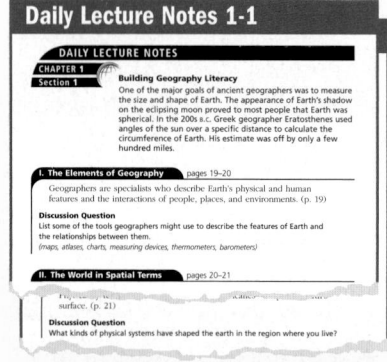

Daily Lecture Notes 1-1

NATIONAL GEOGRAPHIC DIAGRAM STUDY

Answers

1. *Equator, Prime Meridian*

2. *Northern, Western*

Skills Practice

Location In which hemispheres is most of South America located? *(Southern, Western)*

L1/ELL

Guided Reading Activity 1-1

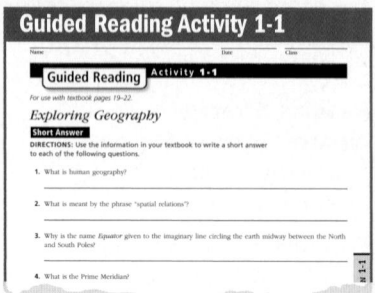

---

in relation to climate, landscape, and available transportation. In their work, geographers consider:

- *The world in spatial terms (location)*
- *Places and regions*
- *Physical systems*
- *Human systems*
- *Environment and society*
- *The uses of geography*

The World in Spatial Terms

Spatial relations refer to the links that places and people have to one another because of their locations. For geographers, location, or a specific place on the earth, is a reference point in the same way that dates are reference points for historians.

Absolute Location

One way of locating a place is by describing its absolute location—the exact spot at which the place is found on the globe. To determine absolute location, geographers use a network of imaginary lines around the earth. The **Equator**, the line circling the earth midway between the **North** and **South Poles**, divides the earth into hemispheres, or two halves (Northern and Southern). The **Prime Meridian**, the 0° north-south line that runs through Greenwich, England, and the 180° north-south line running through the mid-Pacific Ocean also divide the earth into hemispheres (Eastern and Western).

The Equator, the Prime Meridian (also called the Meridian of Greenwich), and other lines of latitude and longitude cross one another to form a pattern called a grid system. Using the grid, you can name the absolute, or precise, location of any place on Earth. This location is generally stated in terms of *latitude*, degrees north or south of the Equator, and *longitude*, degrees east or west of the Prime Meridian. For example, Dallas, Texas, is located at latitude 32°N (north) and longitude 96°W (west).

Relative Location

Although absolute location is useful, most people locate a place in relation to other places, or by its relative location. For example, New Orleans is located near the mouth of the Mississippi River. Knowing the relative location of a place helps you orient yourself in space and develop an awareness of the world around you.

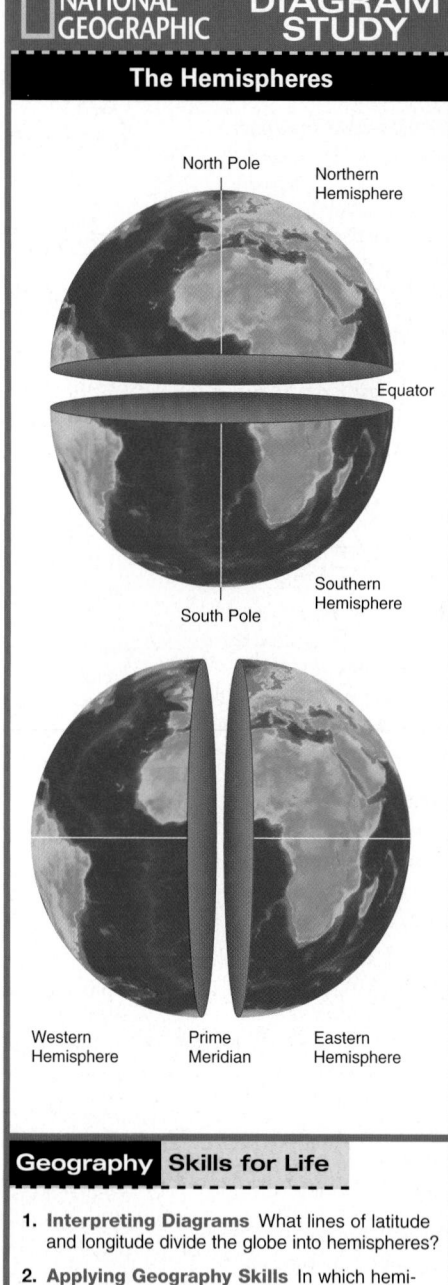

NATIONAL GEOGRAPHIC DIAGRAM STUDY

The Hemispheres

North Pole

Northern Hemisphere

Equator

South Pole

Southern Hemisphere

Western Hemisphere

Prime Meridian

Eastern Hemisphere

Geography Skills for Life

1. **Interpreting Diagrams** What lines of latitude and longitude divide the globe into hemispheres?

2. **Applying Geography Skills** In which hemispheres do you live?

DIFFERENTIATED INSTRUCTION

Visual/Spatial Use three-dimensional visual aids to help students gain mastery of the geographic terms and concepts of hemisphere, latitude, and longitude. In addition to traditional world globes, you may wish to use inflatable beach balls, plastic foam balls, oranges, or other spherical objects. Demonstrate hemispheres and latitude/longitude segments by carefully slicing fruit or plastic foam balls into appropriate sections. Students may experiment by using dental floss or thread to slice clay globes into appropriate segments.

🌐 **EE1 The World in Spatial Terms: Standard 1**

📂 Refer to *Inclusion for the Social Studies Classroom Strategies and Activities.*

NATIONAL GEOGRAPHIC — DIAGRAM STUDY

The Global Grid

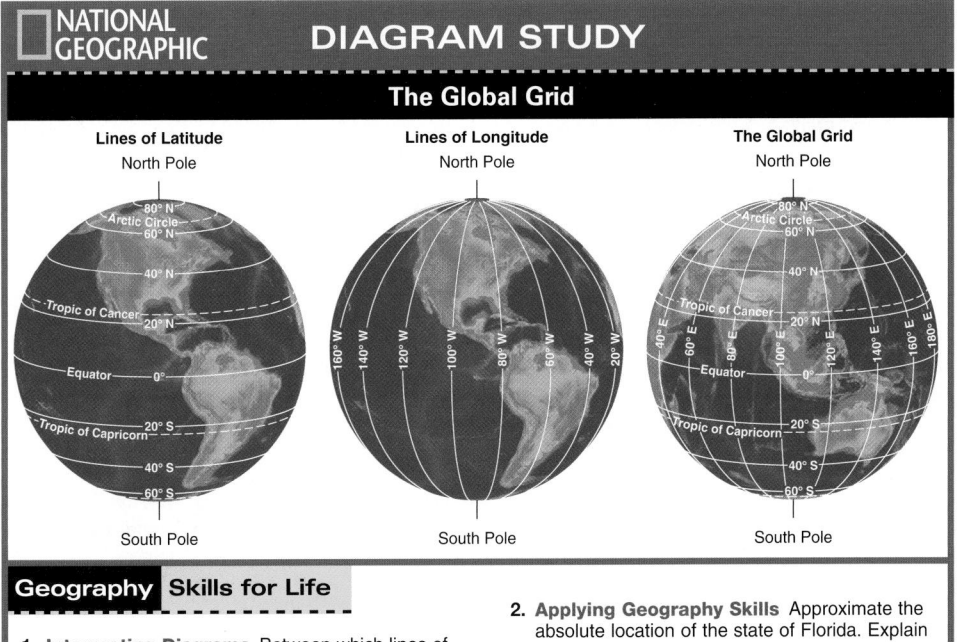

Lines of Latitude
North Pole
South Pole

Lines of Longitude
North Pole
South Pole

The Global Grid
North Pole
South Pole

Geography | Skills for Life

1. **Interpreting Diagrams** Between which lines of latitude is the Arctic Circle located?

2. **Applying Geography Skills** Approximate the absolute location of the state of Florida. Explain how you determined the answer.

Places and Regions

A **place** is a particular space with physical and human meaning. Every place on Earth has its own unique characteristics, determined by the surrounding environment and the people who live there. One task of geographers is to understand and explain how places are similar to and different from one another. To interpret the earth's complexity, geographers often group places into **regions**, or areas united by specific factors. The defining factors of a region may be physical, such as soil type, vegetation, river systems, and climate. A region may also have human factors that help define it. These may include language, religion, cultural traditions, forms of government, and trade networks.

Geographers identify three types of regions: formal, functional, and perceptual. A **formal**, or uniform, **region** is defined by a common characteristic, such as a product produced there. The Corn Belt—the Iowa-Illinois area in the United States—is a formal region because corn is its major crop. A

functional region is a central place and the surrounding area linked to it, for example, by a highway system. Metropolitan areas such as Los Angeles and Tokyo are functional regions. A **perceptual region** is defined by popular feelings and images rather than by objective data. For, example, the term "heartland" refers to a central area in which traditional values are believed to predominate.

Physical Systems

In their work geographers analyze how certain natural phenomena, such as volcanoes, hurricanes, and floods, shape the earth's surface. The earth's systems are endlessly fascinating.

> " Every astronaut loves to take pictures of the Earth. To me, that's the best part of flying in space. "
> Rick Searfoss, quoted in "Geographica," *National Geographic*, November 1996

NATIONAL GEOGRAPHIC — DIAGRAM STUDY

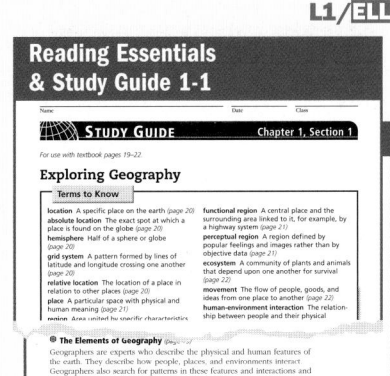

Answers
1. *60°N and 80°N*
2. *about 30°N, 80°W*

Skills Practice
Place What is the name of the line of latitude at 23 1/2°S? *(Tropic of Capricorn)*

L1/ELL

Reading Essentials & Study Guide 1-1

③ ASSESS

Assign Section 1 Assessment as homework or as an in-class activity.

⬥ Have students use **Interactive Tutor Self-Assessment CD-ROM**.

L2

Section Quiz 1-1

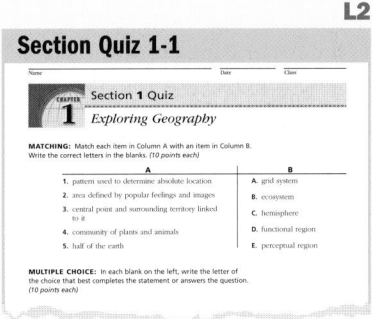

COOPERATIVE LEARNING ACTIVITY

Regions Have students research the regions in which your school is located. Organize the class into three groups. Assign one type of region to each group. Have each group use research tools (reference books, maps, and the Internet) to identify at least three examples of its assigned type of region that encompasses the school. Each group should collect as much information as possible on its type of region. Groups should then exchange the results of their research and generate simple regional maps. Each map should show the school in relation to a particular region and should indicate visually whether the region is formal, functional, or perceptual. ▦ **EE2 Places and Regions: Standard 5**

Saving Ecosystems with Maps
Scientists show habitat loss and endangered species on color-coded maps that can be used to convince individuals, corporations, and politicians to support conservation and preservation efforts.

Reteach

Have students reread the section and outline the key points, using the text subheads as organizers. Tell them to list key terms under the appropriate points.

Enrich

Have students work in small groups to brainstorm lists of geography themes, topics, and questions they are interested in investigating. Keep a class list, or have students list their interests in their GeoJournals.

4 CLOSE

Have students write a paragraph to introduce geography to younger students. Have students reread "A Geographic View" on page 19 as a model for descriptive language that sparks interest.

Geographers look at how physical features interact with plant and animal life to create, support, or change ecosystems. An **ecosystem** is a community of plants and animals that depend upon one another, and their surroundings, for survival.

Human Systems

Geographers also examine how people shape the world—how they settle the earth, form societies, and create permanent features. A recurring theme in geography is the ongoing **movement** of people, goods, and ideas. For example, migrants entering a long-established society usually bring different ideas and practices that may transform that society's traditional culture. In studying human systems, geographers also look at how people compete or cooperate to change or control aspects of the earth to meet their needs.

Environment and Society

Human-environment interaction, or the study of the interrelationship between people and their physical environment, is another theme of geography. Geographers examine the ways people use their environment, how and why they have changed it, and what consequences result from these changes. In some cases the physical environment affects human activities. For example, mountains and deserts often pose barriers to human movement. In other instances human activities, such as building a dam, cause changes in the physical environment. By understanding how the earth's physical features and processes shape and are shaped by human activity, geographers help societies make informed decisions.

The Uses of Geography

Geography can provide insight into how physical features and living things developed in the past. It can also interpret present-day trends to plan for future needs. Governments, businesses, and individuals use geographic information in planning and decision making. Data on physical features and processes can determine whether a site is suitable for human habitation or has resources worth developing. Geographic information on human activities, such as population trends, can help planners decide whether to build new schools or highways in a particular place. Geographic information helps determine where to locate fire stations and shopping malls. As geographers learn more about the relationships among people, places, and the environment, their knowledge can help us plan and build a better future.

SECTION 1 ASSESSMENT

Checking for Understanding

1. **Define** location, absolute location, hemisphere, grid system, relative location, place, region, formal region, functional region, perceptual region, ecosystem, movement, human-environment interaction.

2. **Main Ideas** In a web diagram, list six elements in the study of geography (hint: use the headings in this section). Then explain how each is applied.

Elements of Geography

Critical Thinking

3. **Categorizing Information** Consider the physical and human factors that constitute a region. Identify the differences among formal, functional, and perceptual regions.

4. **Drawing Conclusions** How might geographers' knowledge of human systems benefit people?

5. **Making Generalizations** Explain how knowing about the geography of a particular city might influence your decision to move there.

Analyzing Diagrams

6. **Location** Study the diagram of the hemispheres on page 20. In which hemispheres is Africa located?

Applying Geography

7. **Relative Location** Write a paragraph that describes the relative location of your school in at least five ways. In what instances might relative location be more useful than absolute location? In what instances might absolute location be more useful?

SECTION 1 ASSESSMENT ANSWERS

1. All vocabulary terms are defined in the text.

2. the world in spatial terms, places and regions, physical systems, human systems, environment and society, and the uses of geography

3. Formal: common feature; functional: central place and surroundings; perceptual: defined by image

4. developing resources, locating structures

5. climate, landforms, population, or culture

6. Africa extends into all four hemispheres: Northern, Southern, Eastern, and Western.

7. **Applying Geography** Relative location involves using familiar places; absolute location is important for navigation at sea. Students should use standard grammar, correct spelling, sentence structure, and punctuation.

Guide to Reading

Consider What You Know

People use different types of maps when they need to move from place to place or learn where something is located. What kinds of maps have you used and for what purposes?

Reading Strategy

Organizing As you read about the work of geographers, complete a graphic organizer similar to the one below by listing the specialized research methods geographers use.

Research Methods

Read to Find Out

• What are the major branches of geography and the topics each branch studies?

• What research methods do geographers use at work?

• How is geography related to other subject areas?

• What kinds of geographic careers are available today?

Terms to Know

• physical geography
• human geography
• meteorology
• cartography
• geographic information systems (GIS)

The Geographer's Craft

NATIONAL GEOGRAPHIC

A Geographic View

The Power of Maps

Guyana [in 1966] . . . agreed to give Indians title to lands traditionally recognized as theirs. But in 1982 a tally of "village lands" using out-of-date maps reduced Indian holdings to a few fragments. . . . Local Earth Observation turned Indian villagers into digital mappers. Armed with handheld [GPS] . . . units that determine location using satellites, villagers named and located more than 4,000 . . . territorial landmarks. The data they collected were combined with drainage patterns to produce a large-scale map. . . . [T]he power of maps that merge ancient knowledge and modern technology has vastly strengthened their case.

—Allen Carroll, "CartoGraphic," National Geographic, *March 2000*

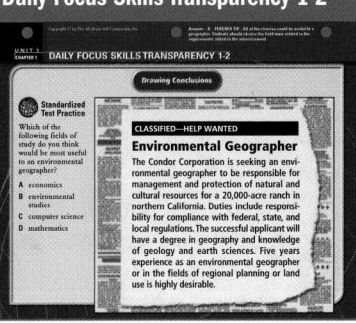
Mapping Guyana with GPS

Geography is more than just learning place names. It also has practical uses—in the example above, using a global positioning system, or GPS, to settle a land dispute. In this section you will explore the ways in which geographic information applies to real-life situations and learn how different types of geographers study the earth.

Branches of Geography

Geography is a discipline that covers a broad range of topics. To make their work easier, geographers divide their subject area into different branches. Two major branches are physical geography and human

1 FOCUS

Section Overview

This section discusses the branches of geography, the tools and techniques used by geographers, related fields of study, and careers in geography.

BELLRINGER
Skillbuilder Activity

Project transparency and have students answer questions.

Available as blackline master.

Daily Focus Skills Transparency 1-2

Guide to Reading

Consider What You Know
Answer *Answer may include road maps, hiking or biking trail maps, bus route maps, theme park maps, and shopping mall directories.*

Reading Strategy
Answer Research Methods: *direct observation, mapping, interviewing, statistics, technology*

Preteaching Vocabulary
Use the **Vocabulary Puzzle-Maker CD-ROM** to create crossword and word-search puzzles.

RESOURCE MANAGER

Reproducible Masters

• Reproducible Lesson Plan 1-2
• Vocabulary Activity 1
• Daily Lecture Notes 1-2
• Guided Reading Activity 1-2
• Reading Essentials and Study Guide 1-2
• Reinforcing Skills Activity 1
• Reteaching Activity 1
• Section Quiz 1-2

Transparencies

• Daily Focus Skills Transparency 1-2
• Unit 1 Map Overlay Transparencies

Multimedia

Vocabulary PuzzleMaker CD-ROM
Interactive Tutor Self-Assessment CD-ROM
ExamView® Pro Testmaker CD-ROM
Presentation Plus! CD-ROM

② TEACH

L1 Direct Observation

Have students take notes about the classroom environment, using direct observation. Invite volunteers to share what they learned.

NATIONAL GEOGRAPHIC **World Explorer**

Answer
It is a large city beside a river.

More About the Photo
New Orleans is called the "Crescent City" because it was first settled along a curve of the Mississippi River. The city's busy harbor is the basis of its economy.

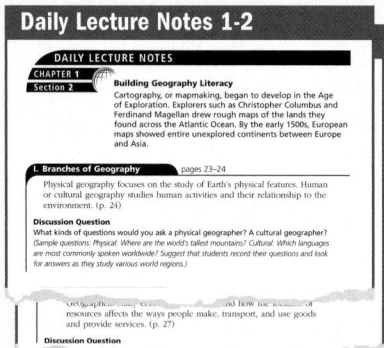

Daily Lecture Notes 1-2

DAILY LECTURE NOTES

CHAPTER 1
Section 2

Building Geography Literacy
Cartography, or mapmaking, began to develop in the Age of Exploration. Explorers such as Christopher Columbus and Ferdinand Magellan drew rough maps of the lands they found across the Atlantic Ocean. By the early 1500s, European maps showed entire unexplored continents between Europe and Asia.

I. Branches of Geography   pages 23–24

Physical geography focuses on the study of Earth's physical features. Human or cultural geography studies human activities and their relationship to the environment. (p. 24)

Discussion Question
What kinds of questions would you ask a physical geographer? A cultural geographer? (Sample questions: Physical: Where are the world's tallest mountains? Cultural: Which languages are most commonly spoken worldwide? Suggest that students record their questions and look for answers as they study various world regions.)

Geographers ... and how the location of resources affects the ways people make, transport, and use goods and provide services. (p. 27)

Discussion Question

☐ NATIONAL GEOGRAPHIC **GEOFACT**

▶ **Nighttime photographs taken from space capture population patterns by showing blazes of light where people live.**

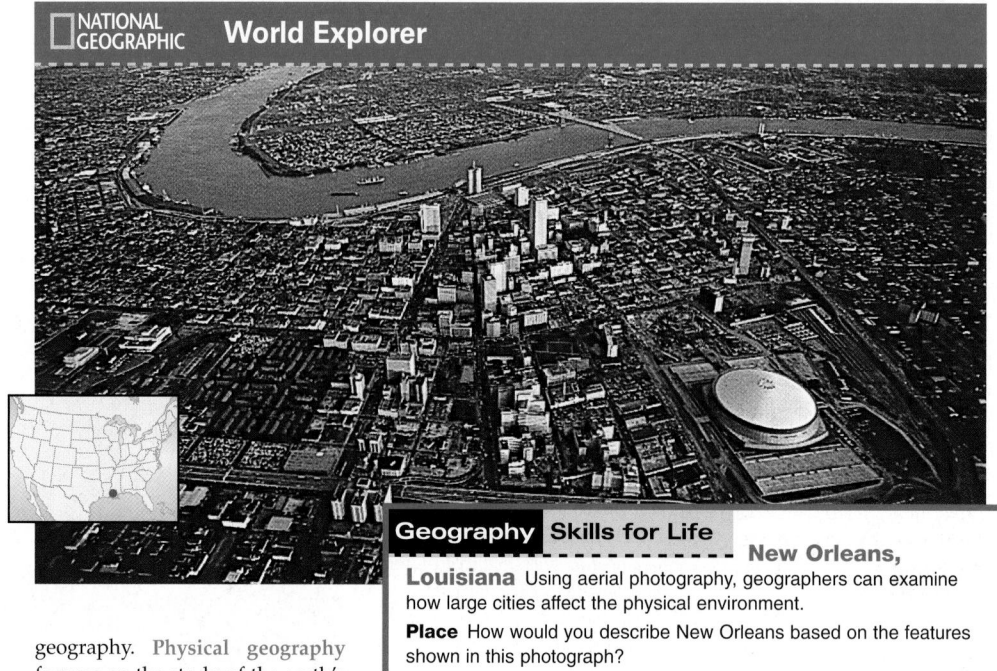

NATIONAL GEOGRAPHIC **World Explorer**

Geography | Skills for Life

New Orleans, Louisiana Using aerial photography, geographers can examine how large cities affect the physical environment.
Place How would you describe New Orleans based on the features shown in this photograph?

geography. **Physical geography** focuses on the study of the earth's physical features. It looks at climate, land, water, plants, and animal life in terms of their relationships to one another and to humans. **Human geography**, or cultural geography, is the study of human activities and their relationship to the cultural and physical environments. It concentrates on political, economic, and cultural factors, such as population density, urban development, economic production, and ethnicity.

Physical geography and human geography are further divided into smaller subject areas. Examples are **meteorology**, the study of weather and weather forecasting, and historical geography, the study of places and human activities over time and the various geographic factors that have shaped them.

Geographers at Work

Geographers use specialized research methods in their work. These methods include direct observation, mapping, interviewing, statistics, and the use of technology.

Direct Observation

Geographers use direct observation in studying the earth and the patterns of human activities that take place on its surface. They will often visit a region to gather specific information about the region and its geographic features. Geographers also employ remote sensing to study the earth, using aerial photographs and satellite images. For example, geographers may use aerial photographs or satellite images to locate mineral deposits or to determine the size of freshwater sources. They also might observe a forest that has been damaged by air pollution.

Mapping

Making and using maps are basic activities of geographers. Geographic specialists who make and design maps are known as cartographers; their area of work, known as **cartography**, involves studying and making maps.

Many geographic research findings can be shown on maps better than they can be explained

---

DIFFERENTIATED INSTRUCTION

Reading Support For students who have trouble with reasoning, this section's concept load can present challenges. Remind students to use the subheads as guides. Direct them to the "Guide to Reading" on page 23, which sums up key concepts and terms. Students may wish to make verbal or visual flashcards to help them organize the branches of geography, specialized research methods used by geographers, related disciplines, and geography careers. 🌐 **EE6 The Uses of Geography: Standard 18**

📁 Refer to *Inclusion for the Social Studies Classroom Strategies and Activities.*

in written text. Cartographers select complicated pieces of information about an area and present them in a more understandable form on a map. In this way they easily can show the location, features, patterns, and relationships of people, places, and things. In addition, maps allow a visual comparison between places and regions. For example, a geographer might compare population density maps of two counties in order to determine where to build new schools.

Interviewing

To answer a geographic question, geographers often must go beyond mere observation. In many cases geographers want to find out how people think or feel about certain places. They also may want to examine the ways in which people's beliefs and attitudes have led to changes in the physical environment. This kind of information is obtained by interviewing. Geographers choose a particular group of people for study. Instead of contacting everyone in that group, however, geographers talk to a carefully chosen sample whose answers represent the whole group.

Statistics

Some of the information that geographers use is numerical. Temperature and rainfall data point to a region's climate, for example. Geographers use computers to organize this information and present it in clear, understandable ways. They also analyze the data to find patterns and trends. For example, census data can be studied to learn about rates of population growth; the age, ethnic, and gender makeup of the population; and income levels. After identifying these patterns and trends, geographers use statistical tests to see whether their ideas are valid.

Technology

Geographers often use scientific instruments in their work. They especially depend on advanced technological tools, such as satellites and computers. Satellites orbiting the earth carry remote sensors, high-tech cameras, and radar that gather data and images related to the earth's environment, weather, human settlement patterns, and vegetation. Geographic information systems (GIS) are computer tools that process and organize data and

satellite images with other pieces of information gathered by geographers and other scientists. GIS technology is valuable to urban planners, retailers, and local government officials who use this technology to help them determine where to build roads, stores, and parks.

The development of computer technology has also transformed the process of mapmaking. Allen Carroll, chief cartographer of the National Geographic Society, describes the changes in cartography as "revolutions in mapping." Technology has created

> " ... computers that store vast archives of map data and render lines with superhuman precision, software programs that turn maps into analytical tools, satellite imagery that combines photographic beauty with cartographic precision, global electronic networks that enable maps to stream across our ever shrinking globe. "
>
> Allen Carroll, *National Geographic Atlas of the World*, 1999

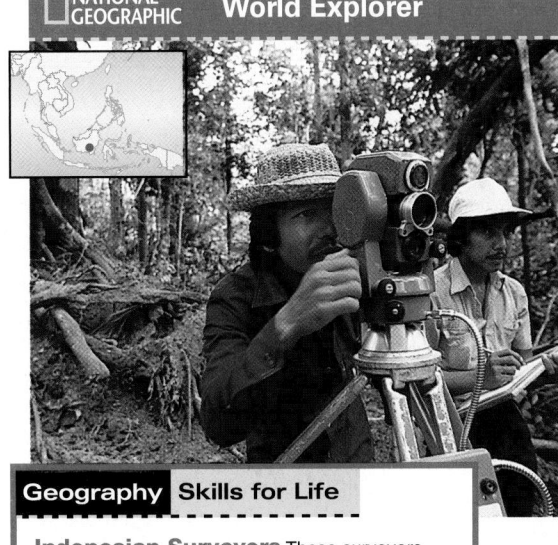

NATIONAL GEOGRAPHIC **World Explorer**

Geography Skills for Life

Indonesian Surveyors These surveyors are helping plan a road in Borneo, Indonesia.
Human-Environment Interaction How do geographers play a part in our everyday lives?

L3 Human-Environment Interaction

Ask students for examples of the geographic information needed from satellites or GIS technology to choose a new highway route.

L1/ELL

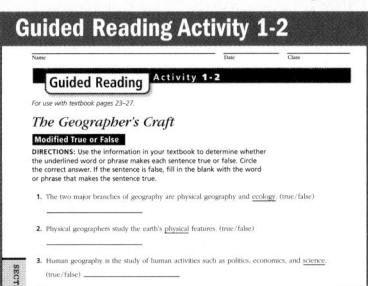

NATIONAL GEOGRAPHIC **World Explorer**

Answer
help people develop resources, overcome geographic obstacles, plan, and build

More About the Photo
Borneo's rain forest presents obstacles to transportation. New surveying technologies make it possible to clear land and build roads with less environmental damage.

L1/ELL

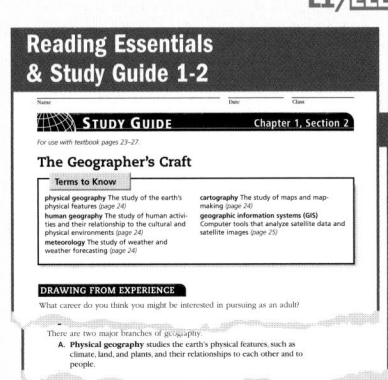

COOPERATIVE LEARNING ACTIVITY

Geography Research Methods Organize the class into five groups. Assign each group one of the specialized research methods used by geographers: direct observation, mapping, interviewing, statistics, and technology. Give each group the same assignment: to gather geographic information about the neighborhood in which your school is located. Each group should use only its assigned research method. Have each group report its findings. **Ask:** How does each research method contribute to an overall understanding of the geography of the neighborhood? Which group obtained information most easily? Which group faced the greatest challenge? 📦 🌐 EE1 The World in Spatial Terms: Standard 1

NATIONAL GEOGRAPHIC — CHART STUDY

Answers

1. *population, language, ethnicity, religion, government*

2. *interviews, statistics, satellite images*

Skills Practice
Human-Environment Interaction

How does each geography field and career deal with human-environment interaction?

(Answers should show an understanding of how humans interact with the physical world.)

 **ASSESS**

Assign Section 2 Assessment as homework or as an in-class activity.

⊕ Have students use **Interactive Tutor Self-Assessment CD-ROM** to review Section 2.

L2

Section Quiz 1-2

Name _____ Date _____ Class _____

CHAPTER 1 | Section 2 Quiz
The Geographer's Craft

MATCHING: Match each item in Column A with an item in Column B. Write the correct letters in the blanks. *(10 points each)*

A	B
1. the study of maps and mapmaking	A. satellites and computers
2. method geographers use to find out how people think or feel	B. cartography
3. scientific instruments used by geographers	C. cultures
4. human social structures	D. interviewing
5. the study of the earth's physical features	E. physical geography

MULTIPLE CHOICE: In each blank on the left, write the letter of the choice that best completes the statement or answers the question. *(10 points each)*

Today, most cartographers rely on computers and computer software to make maps. Each type of data on a map is kept as a separate "layer" in the map's digital files. This method allows cartographers to make and change maps more quickly and easily.

Geography and Other Disciplines

Geographers study both the physical and human features of the earth and also analyze the patterns and relationships among geography and other disciplines. Studying subjects such as history, government, sociology, and economics helps geographers to understand how each of these subjects affects and is affected by geography.

History and Government

Geographers use history to help them understand what places looked like in the past. For example, geographers might want to know how Boston, Massachusetts, looked during the colonial years. They might also wish to look at the changes that have occurred in Boston over the past two centuries. Geographers may begin by gathering information about time periods in the city's history. This information could be used to answer such geographic questions as: How have human activities changed the natural vegetation in the area? Are the waterways different than they were in the past? Answers to these questions can help people make better decisions and plans for the future.

NATIONAL GEOGRAPHIC — CHART STUDY

Jobs in Geography

Geography Field	Description	Applications/Careers
Physical Geographer	Studies Earth's features and the geographic forces shaping them	Forecasting weather, tracing causes and effects of pollution, conserving wilderness areas
Human Geographer	Analyzes human aspects of culture—population, language, ethnicity, religion, government	Developing cultural policies for international organizations, such as the United Nations
Economic Geographer	Examines human economic activities and their relationship to the environment	Urban planning, focusing on the location of industries or transportation routes
Regional Geographer	Studies geographic features of a particular place or region	Assisting government and business in making decisions related to a region
Environmental Specialist	Focuses on the two-way interaction between humans and the physical environment	Advising government and business on ways of protecting the environment
Geographic Educator	Teaches about geography	Teaching geography at all educational levels; serving as consultant to business and government

Geography Skills for Life

1. **Interpreting Charts** What does a human geographer study?

2. **Applying Geography Skills** How might human geographers studying the effects of population growth gather information for their research?

Geographers study political science to help them see how people in different places are governed. They look at how political boundaries have formed and how they have been changed. Geographers are interested in how the natural environment has influenced political decisions and how governments change natural environments. For example, the Egyptian government, helped by financing from abroad, built the massive

---

CRITICAL THINKING ACTIVITY

Determining Relevance Have students work in small groups to generate lists of everyday situations and challenges in communities or businesses that might benefit from geographic knowledge and skills. Encourage students to think in practical terms and to list common situations. Have groups exchange lists and suggest specific ways in which a geographer could assist in each situation or challenge. Ask a volunteer from each group to report on its work, or display the annotated lists.

🌐 **EE6 The Uses of Geography: Standard 18**

Aswan High Dam on the Nile River. The dam altered the surface of the earth in profound ways and so has had an impact on the region's people.

Culture

Human geographers use the tools of sociology and anthropology to understand the culture of societies throughout the world. They study the relationships between the physical environment and social structures. They examine people's ways of life in different parts of the world. Human geographers also seek to understand how the activities of different groups affect their physical environments and how the environment affects culture groups differently.

Economics

Geographers use economics to help them understand how the locations of resources affect the ways people make, transport, and use goods, and how and where services are provided.

Student Web Activity Visit the **Glencoe World Geography** Web site at geography.glencoe.com and click on Student Web Activities—Chapter 1 for an activity about careers in geography.

Geographers are interested in how locations are chosen for various economic activities, such as farming, mining, manufacturing, and selling. A desirable location usually includes plentiful resources and good transportation routes. Geographers are also interested in the interdependence of people's economic activities throughout the world. New developments in communications and transportation make the movement of information and goods faster and more efficient than ever before. A business can operate globally without depending on any one specific place to fill all of its needs.

Geography as a Career

Although people trained in geography are in great demand in the workforce, many of them do not have *geographer* as a job title. Geography skills are useful in so many different situations that geographers have more than a hundred different job titles. Geographers often combine the study of geography with other areas of study. For example, a salesperson must know the geographic characteristics of the region in which he or she is selling products. Also, a travel agent must have some knowledge of other places in order to plan trips for clients. Still, as the chart on page 26 shows, because geography itself has many specialized fields, there are many different kinds of geographers.

SECTION 2 ASSESSMENT

Checking for Understanding

1. **Define** physical geography, human geography, meteorology, cartography, geographic information systems (GIS).

2. **Main Ideas** Copy the table below on your paper, and fill in the ways geographers study the earth and use geography.

Geography Branches	
Geography Methods	
Other Disciplines	
Jobs in Geography	

Critical Thinking

3. **Predicting Consequences** What might happen if an economic geographer did not interview citizens when preparing a city transportation plan?

4. **Making Inferences** What kinds of geographers might be employed by a manufacturing company?

5. **Making Generalizations** How does the study of other disciplines help geographers in their work as countries become increasingly interdependent?

Analyzing Maps

6. **Place** Study the map of the United States in the Reference Atlas on pages RA6–RA7. What kinds of information can you learn from this map? How does the information on this map differ from the map on pages RA8–RA9?

Applying Geography

7. **Research Methods** As a geographer working on a plan for a new community center, what research methods would you use? Explain your choices in a paragraph.

SECTION 2 ASSESSMENT ANSWERS

1. All vocabulary terms are defined in the text.

2. Students should organize appropriate information under the section subheads.

3. The plan may not reflect the needs and travel patterns of the citizens and may be unsuccessful.

4. economic geographers, environmental specialists

5. Using many disciplines helps geographers contribute effective solutions.

6. Students should demonstrate key differences between physical and political maps.

7. **Applying Geography** Answers will vary; students should be able to defend their choices.

Global Culture Music, food, and entertainment are crossing traditional boundaries. "World Music" is a growing musical category, and new "fusion" cuisines blend foods from different countries.

Objectives, goals, and answers to the student activity can be found in the Web Activity Lesson Plan feature at geography.glencoe.com

Reteach

Have students reread the section. Ask volunteers to summarize each subhead, including key terms.

Enrich

Read aloud a portion of an article suggested in "Index to *National Geographic* Magazine" on page 18D. Ask students to speculate about what tools and techniques the author used to gain information for the article.

Have each student write an employment ad describing his or her dream job in the field of geography.

Teaching the Skill

On the board, copy the following information on U.S. cities:

City	2000 Population
Baton Rouge, LA	227,818
Chicago, IL	2,896,016
Houston, TX	1,953,631
Kansas City, MO	441,545
Los Angeles, CA	3,694,820
New York, NY	8,008,278

Ask: Which type of graph might be best to display this information? *(bar graph)* How could this information be arranged on a bar graph? *(by largest to smallest city or by smallest to largest)* Why would a line graph or a circle graph be inappropriate? *(the information does not show changes over time or percentages of a whole)*

Additional Practice
L1

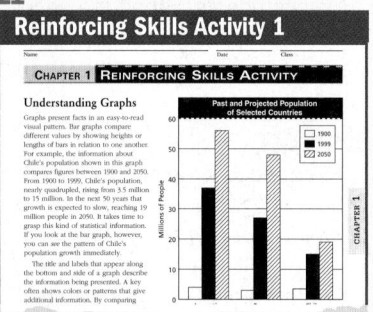

Reinforcing Skills Activity 1

GLENCOE
TECHNOLOGY

Glencoe Skillbuilder Interactive Workbook, Level 2

Understanding Graphs

Graphs are visual representations of statistical data. Large amounts of information can be condensed when presented in graphs. Studying graphs allows readers to see relationships clearly.

Learning the Skill

The three main types of graphs present numerical information. **Line graphs** record changes in data over time. The vertical axis (*y*-axis) shows units of measurement, and the horizontal axis (*x*-axis) shows intervals of time. **Bar graphs** use bars of different lengths to compare different quantities. **Circle graphs** show the relationship of parts to a whole as percentages. To understand a graph:

- **Read the graph title to identify the subject.**
- **Study the labels to understand the numerical information presented.**
- **Study the information presented and the use of colors and patterns.**
- **Compare the lines, bars, or segments, and look for relationships in order to draw conclusions.**

Practicing the Skill

Study the graphs to answer these questions.

1. **Line graph** What is the difference in population between the low and high projections?
2. **Bar graph** In which decade did migration cause the least change in population?
3. **Circle graph** What percent of immigrants to the United States in the 1990s came from Europe?
4. What general population trends do the three graphs show?

Applying the Skill

Take a poll of your classmates about a geographical topic. Design and draw a graph using the data. Consider geographic features, distributions, and relationships.

Go To The Glencoe Skillbuilder Interactive Workbook, Level 2 provides instruction and practice in key social studies skills.

World Population Projections

Source: United Nations Population Division, 2000

U. S. Population Change Due to Migration

Source: U.S. Census Bureau, 2000

U.S. Immigrants by Region of Origin (%)

1960-1969: Other 11%, Latin America 38%, Europe 40%, Asia 11%

1990-1997: Other 5%, Europe 13%, Latin America 52%, Asia 30%

Source: U.S. Immigration and Naturalization Service, 1999

ANSWERS TO PRACTICING THE SKILL

1. 3
2. 1930s
3. 13 percent
4. increase in world population, growing effect of migration on population change, growing numbers of Asian and Latin American immigrants to the United States

CHAPTER 1 — SUMMARY & STUDY GUIDE

SECTION 1 — Exploring Geography (pp. 19–22)

Terms to Know
- location
- absolute location
- hemisphere
- grid system
- relative location
- place
- region
- formal region
- functional region
- perceptual region
- ecosystem
- movement
- human-environment interaction

Key Points
- Geographers study the earth's physical and human features and their interrelationships.
- Geographers use absolute and relative locations as reference points.
- Geographers identify three types of regions—formal, functional, and perceptual.
- Geography contributes knowledge about the relationships among human activities, the earth's physical systems, and the environment in order to develop a better future.

Organizing Your Notes
Create an outline using the format below to help you organize information about how geographers study the earth.

> **Exploring Geography**
>
> I. Elements of Geography
>   A. World in spatial terms
>   1. Absolute location

SECTION 2 — The Geographer's Craft (pp. 23–27)

Terms to Know
- physical geography
- human geography
- meteorology
- cartography
- geographic information systems (GIS)

Key Points
- Geographers use special research skills, such as direct observation, mapping, interviewing, statistics, and technology.
- Studying other social sciences helps geographers analyze the patterns and relationships among these different fields.
- Geographers can specialize and may work in government, business, science, planning, or education.

Organizing Your Notes
Use a graphic organizer like the one below to help you organize your notes for this section.

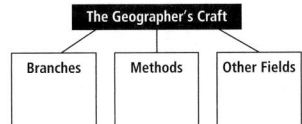

The Geographer's Craft — Branches | Methods | Other Fields

▲ A scientist uses a global positioning system.

CHAPTER 1
Summary & Study Guide

Using the Chapter 1 Summary & Study Guide

Use the Chapter 1 Summary & Study Guide to preview, review, condense, or reteach the chapter.

Preview/Review

🔘 **Vocabulary PuzzleMaker CD-ROM** reinforces "Terms to Know."

🔘 **Interactive Tutor Self-Assessment CD-ROM** provides a review of Chapter 1 content.

Condense

Have students read the Chapter 1 Summary & Study Guide.

🔘 Chapter 1 Audio Program

🗂 Chapter 1 Guided Reading Activities

Reteach

🗂 Chapter 1 Reteaching Activities (Spanish also available)

🗂 Chapter 1 Reading Essentials and Study Guides

GLENCOE TECHNOLOGY

🔲 NATIONAL GEOGRAPHIC

WORLD REGIONS VIDEO PROGRAM

Unit 1, The World
The following segments enhance the study of this unit:
- **Ocean Journey**
- **Homo Sapiens Sapiens**
- **Goodwill Games**

CHAPTER CULMINATING ACTIVITY

Synthesizing Information Ask: Based on what you have learned about how a geographer looks at the world, what do you think your study of world geography will involve? Have students reflect on their notes from this chapter and write a course description for the rest of the text. The course description should include students' predictions about the topics they will study, the skills they will practice, and the tools they will use.

🔲 EE6 The Uses of Geography: Standard 18

NOTE: This activity may be completed separately, or you may wish students to incorporate it in their GeoJournals.

GEOGRAPHY Online

Have students visit the Web site at geography.glencoe.com to review Chapter 1 and take the **Self-Check Quiz.**

GLENCOE TECHNOLOGY

Use *MindJogger Videoquiz* to review the Chapter 1 content.

Reviewing Key Terms

1. ecosystem
2. grid system, absolute location
3. Human geography
4. formal region
5. cartography
6. Relative location
7. geographic information systems (GIS)
8. Physical geography

Reviewing Facts

SECTION 1

1. using the latitude/longitude grid or locating places in relation to other places
2. formal, functional, and perceptual regions
3. to understand how the earth affects and is affected by human activity so that informed decisions can be made

SECTION 2

4. Physical geography is the study of the earth's physical features. Human geography focuses on human activities in relation to the physical world.
5. direct observation, mapping, interviewing, statistics, technology
6. history and government, culture, and economics

Reviewing Key Terms

Write the key term that best completes each of the following sentences. Refer to the Terms to Know in the Summary & Study Guide on page 29.

1. Plants and animals depend on one another in a(n) _____.
2. Geographers use a(n) _____ formed by lines of latitude and longitude to determine _____.
3. _____ is the study of the human aspects of geography.
4. A(n) _____ has boundaries determined by a common characteristic.
5. Another name for mapmaking is _____.
6. _____ is expressed in relation to other places.
7. Computer tools that process data and satellite images with other pieces of geographic information are called _____.
8. _____ focuses on the study of the earth's physical features.

Reviewing Facts

SECTION 1

1. How do geographers determine the locations of places?
2. What are the three types of regions identified by geographers?
3. Why do geographers study human systems and human-environment relationships?
4. What are two ways that every place on the earth can be located?

SECTION 2

5. How do physical and human geography differ?
6. What research methods do geographers use?
7. What other subjects do geographers study?

Critical Thinking

1. **Summarizing the Main Idea** How do geographers use the elements of geography to study the earth?
2. **Making Inferences** What subjects might you study in order to become an urban planner? Explain.
3. **Predicting Consequences** Consider the many ways that technology has affected the way people live and work. Then imagine that you have become a geographer of the future. How do you think technology will change the way you work?
4. **Categorizing Information** Use a web diagram like the one below to show five methods of geographic research.

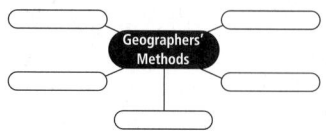

Geographers' Methods

NATIONAL GEOGRAPHIC — Locating Places
The World: Physical Geography

Match the letters on the map with the places and physical features of the earth. Write your answers on a sheet of paper.

1. North America
2. South America
3. Africa
4. Asia
5. Europe
6. Antarctica
7. Australia
8. Atlantic Ocean
9. Indian Ocean
10. Pacific Ocean

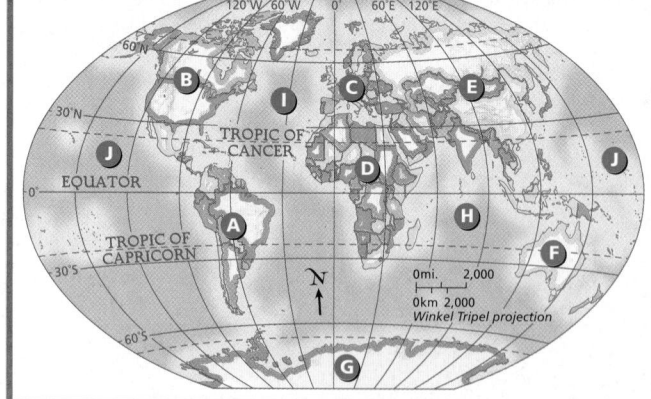

Critical Thinking

1. The elements of geography help geographers organize information about the earth and learn about geographic events and patterns.
2. Answers may include geography, statistics, economics, architecture, and urban design.
3. Answers should demonstrate knowledge of appropriate geographic tools.
4. Webs should show appropriate examples of direct observation, mapping, interviewing, statistics, and technology.

NATIONAL GEOGRAPHIC — Locating Places

| 1. B | 3. D | 5. C | 7. F | 9. H |
| 2. A | 4. E | 6. G | 8. I | 10. J |

Thinking Like a Geographer

Data: number of families with school-age children, presence of possible hazards (polluting industries, busy highways), existing schools, present school enrollment. Methods: direct

Thinking Like a Geographer

Imagine that you are an urban planner. What kinds of data might you want to assemble in order to plan a location for a new school? What methods would you use to collect the data? How would you use the data to determine the location for the school?

Problem-Solving Activity

Contemporary Issues Case Study Look at newspapers and magazines to identify one of the following issues:

- a local issue that involves land use.
- a local issue that involves economic development.
- a national issue that involves water resources.

Choose one issue, and research to learn more about its history, the various points of view surrounding the issue, and the final outcome. Use this information to prepare an outline. Then write an essay describing the influence of physical and human geography on the issue.

GeoJournal

Descriptive Writing Refer to the entry you wrote in your GeoJournal and the information in this chapter. Then imagine you are a physical geographer and write a paragraph describing another part of the earth's surface. For example, if you live in a plains area, describe how the geography of the mountains or the seashore would be different from your location. Include as many concrete details as you can to describe the physical and human geography of the place you chose.

Technology Activity

Using the Internet for Research Search the Internet for Web sites that provide information about geography to the public. Sponsors may include government agencies, scientific organizations, or special-interest magazines. Prepare a list of the five best sites, write a brief description of the kinds of information each one contains, and explain why you included it.

Standardized Test Practice

Use the circle graph below and your knowledge of geography to answer questions 1 and 2.

EARTH'S LAND AND WATER

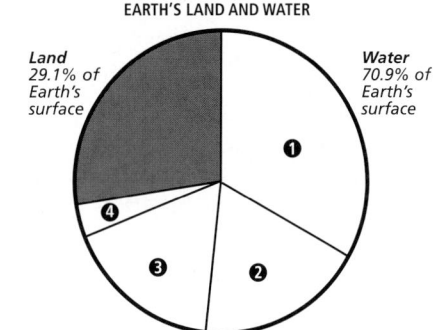

Land 29.1% of Earth's surface

Water 70.9% of Earth's surface

❶ Pacific Ocean 64,169,000 sq. mi. (166,241,000 sq. km)
❷ Atlantic Ocean 33,411,00 sq. mi. (86,557,000 sq. km)
❸ Indian Ocean 28,342,800 sq. mi. (73,427,000 sq. km)
❹ Arctic Ocean 3,661,200 sq. mi. (9,485,000 sq. km)

1. **Which ocean covers the smallest area of the earth's surface?**

   A Atlantic   C Pacific
   B Indian   D Arctic

2. **Which ocean covers about as much of the earth's surface as land does?**

   F Indian   H Arctic
   G Pacific   J Atlantic

Test-Taking Tip Study the information shown on the circle graph for the areas of the earth covered by land and by oceans. Then compare the relative sizes of the different graph segments. By comparing the segments you will be able to determine the correct answers.

Standardized Test Practice

1. D
2. G

Tested Objectives: analyzing information interpreting graphs

Additional Practice and Test-Taking Tips

Standardized Test Practice Workbook

❓ CHAPTER BONUS TEST QUESTION

Why are international time zones determined from the time at the Royal Naval Observatory at Greenwich, England (Greenwich Mean Time)? *(because the Prime Meridian passes through Greenwich)*

---

observation, interviewing, statistics, GIS technology. Use: compare data to find where a school is most needed and the safest location.

Problem-Solving Activity

You may wish to assign this case study as a cooperative learning activity, with group members assuming various tasks (topic selection, print research, Internet research, outlining, essay, supportive documentation). Allow time for group presentations, or display students' work.

GeoJournal

If necessary, direct students to appropriate Internet research sites. You may wish to recommend findings from the "Technology Activity" below. Students should use standard grammar, correct spelling, sentence structure, and punctuation in paragraphs.

Technology Activity

You may wish to have students collect their findings in a class Internet guide.

PLANNING GUIDE

NOTE: The following materials may be used when teaching Chapter 2. Section-level support materials are shown at point-of-use in the margins of the Teacher Wraparound Edition.

TEACHING TRANSPARENCIES

L2 Unit 1 Map Overlay Transparencies

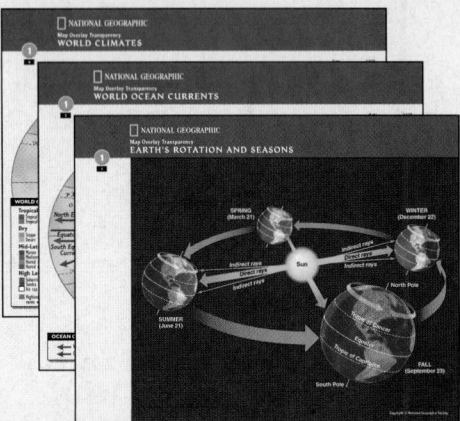

L2 Political Map Transparency 1

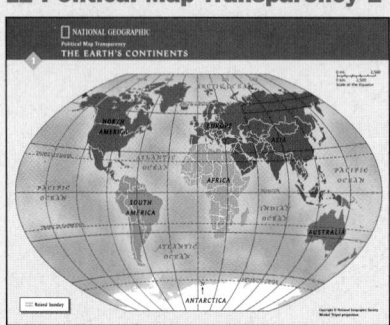

GEOGRAPHIC LITERACY

Focus on Geography Literacy

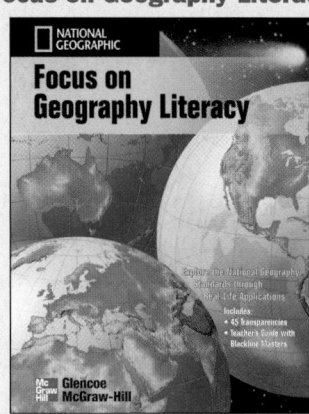

APPLICATION AND ENRICHMENT

L3 Enrichment Activity 2

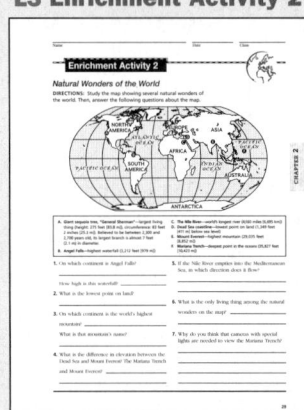

REVIEW AND REINFORCEMENT

L1 Vocabulary Activity 2   L1 Reinforcing Skills Activity 2   L1 Reteaching Activity 2

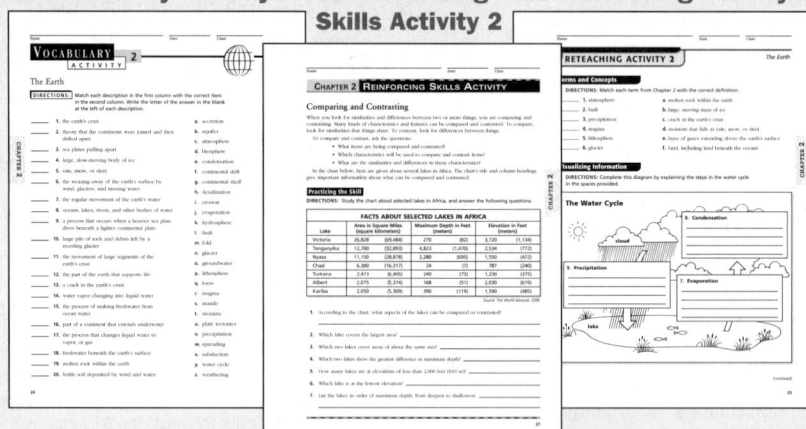

ASSESSMENT

L2 Chapter 2 Test Form A

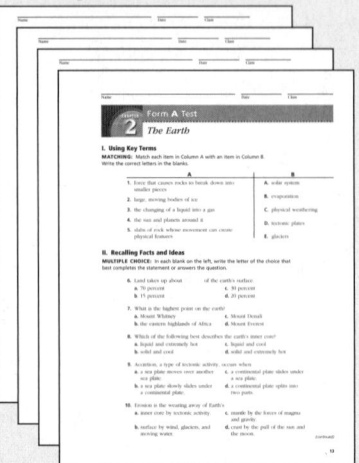

L2 Chapter 2 Test Form B

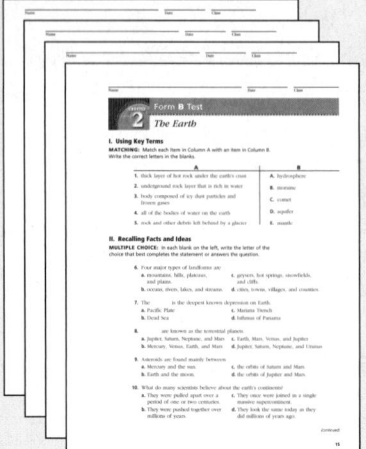

L1/ELL Performance Assessment Activity 2

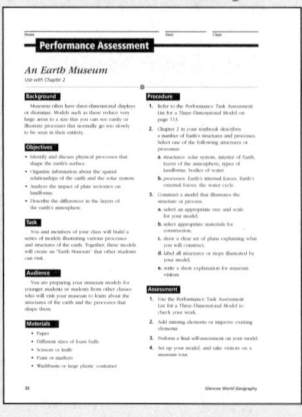

ExamView® Pro Testmaker

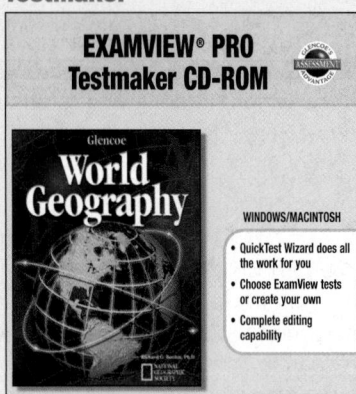

EXAMVIEW® PRO Testmaker CD-ROM

Glencoe
World Geography

WINDOWS/MACINTOSH

- QuickTest Wizard does all the work for you
- Choose ExamView tests or create your own
- Complete editing capability

SPANISH RESOURCES

The following Spanish language materials are available in the Spanish Resources binder:

- 📁 Spanish Vocabulary Activities
- 📁 Spanish Guided Reading Activities
- 📁 Spanish Reteaching Activities
- 📁 Spanish Summaries
- 📁 Spanish Quizzes and Tests
- 📁 Spanish Reading Essentials and Study Guide

MULTIMEDIA

- 📼 World Regions Video
- 📼 MindJogger Videoquiz
- 💿 Vocabulary PuzzleMaker CD-ROM
- 💿 Interactive Tutor Self-Assessment CD-ROM
- 💿 ExamView® Pro Testmaker CD-ROM
- 💿 Audio Program
- 💿 TeacherWorks CD-ROM
- 💿 Interactive Student Edition CD-ROM
- 💿 Glencoe Skillbuilder Interactive Workbook CD-ROM, Level 2
- 💿 Presentation Plus! CD-ROM

Timesaving Tools

TeacherWorks™ **All-In-One Planner and Resource Center**

- **Interactive Teacher Edition** Access your Teacher Wraparound Edition and your classroom resources with a few easy clicks.
- **Interactive Lesson Planner** Planning has never been easier! Organize your week, month, semester, or year with all the lesson helps you need to make teaching creative, timely, and relevant.

Use Glencoe's **Presentation Plus!** multimedia teacher tool to easily present dynamic lessons that visually excite your students. Using Microsoft PowerPoint® you can customize the presentations to create your own personalized lessons.

GEOGRAPHY Online

Use our Web site for additional resources. All essential content is covered in the Student Edition.

You and your students can visit geography.glencoe.com, the Web site companion to *Glencoe World Geography*. This innovative integration of electronic and print media offers your students a wealth of opportunities. The student text directs students to the Web site for the following options:

- **Chapter Overviews**
- **Self-Check Quizzes**
- **Student Activities**
- **Textbook Updates**

Answers are provided for you in the "Web Activity Lesson Plan." Additional Web resources and Interactive Tutor puzzles are also available.

▶ Additional Glencoe Teacher Support

- ■ **Teaching Strategies for the Geography Classroom (including Block Scheduling Pacing Guides)**
- ■ **Graphic Organizer Transparencies Strategies and Activities**
- ■ **Outline Map Resource Book**
- ■ **Reading in the Content Area**

PLANNING GUIDE

SECTION RESOURCES

Daily Objectives	Reproducible Resources	Multimedia Resources

SECTION 1 Planet Earth

1. Describe the solar system and Earth's location in it.
2. Identify Earth's shape.
3. Discuss Earth's structure.
4. List Earth's landforms.

Reproducible Lesson Plan 2-1
Daily Lecture Notes 2-1
Guided Reading Activity 2-1*
Reading Essentials and Study Guide 2-1*
Section Quiz 2-1*

Daily Focus Skills Transparency 2-1
Political Map Transparency 1
Unit 1 Map Overlay Transparencies
Interactive Tutor Self-Assessment CD-ROM
ExamView® Pro Testmaker CD-ROM*
Presentation Plus! CD-ROM

SECTION 2 Forces of Change

1. Explain how Earth's layers contribute to the planet's physical characteristics.
2. Describe the internal forces of change that affect Earth's surface.
3. Describe the external forces that affect Earth's surface.

Reproducible Lesson Plan 2-2
Daily Lecture Notes 2-2
Guided Reading Activity 2-2*
Reading Essentials and Study Guide 2-2*
Section Quiz 2-2*

Daily Focus Skills Transparency 2-2
Unit 1 Map Overlay Transparencies
Interactive Tutor Self-Assessment CD-ROM
ExamView® Pro Testmaker CD-ROM*
Presentation Plus! CD-ROM

SECTION 3 Earth's Water

1. Explain how the amount of water on Earth remains fairly constant.
2. Discuss the distribution of the water that makes up 70 percent of Earth's surface.
3. Describe why freshwater is important to humans.

Reproducible Lesson Plan 2-3
Vocabulary Activity 2*
Daily Lecture Notes 2-3
Guided Reading Activity 2-3*
Reading Essentials and Study Guide 2-3*
Reteaching Activity 2*
Reinforcing Skills Activity 2
Section Quiz 2-3*

Daily Focus Skills Transparency 2-3
Unit 1 Map Overlay Transparencies
Vocabulary PuzzleMaker CD-ROM
Interactive Tutor Self-Assessment CD-ROM
ExamView® Pro Testmaker CD-ROM*
Presentation Plus! CD-ROM

Blackline Master
Transparency
Software
CD-ROM
Videocassette
DVD

Also available in Spanish

00:00 OUT OF TIME? Assign the Chapter 2 **Reading Essentials and Study Guide.**

 **Block Schedule**

Activities that are particularly suited to use within the block scheduling framework are identified throughout this chapter by the following designation:

KEY TO ABILITY LEVELS

Teaching strategies have been coded for various learning styles and abilities.

L1   BASIC activities for all students

L2   AVERAGE activities for average to above-average students

L3   CHALLENGING activities for above-average students

ELL   ENGLISH LANGUAGE LEARNER activities

Teacher to Teacher

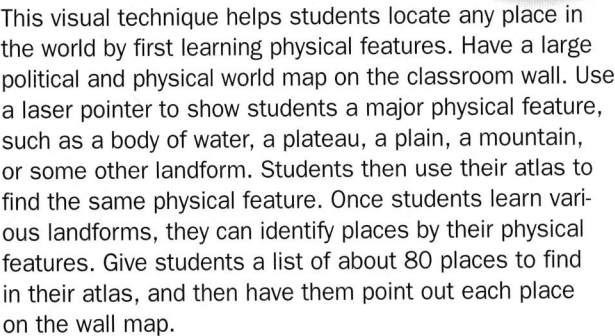

Lou Camilotto
McCutcheon High School
Lafayette, IN

Locating Physical Features

This visual technique helps students locate any place in the world by first learning physical features. Have a large political and physical world map on the classroom wall. Use a laser pointer to show students a major physical feature, such as a body of water, a plateau, a plain, a mountain, or some other landform. Students then use their atlas to find the same physical feature. Once students learn various landforms, they can identify places by their physical features. Give students a list of about 80 places to find in their atlas, and then have them point out each place on the wall map.

Students can take turns locating places, or they can turn the activity into a game by creating teams and having the teacher point to various physical features. Teams can take turns identifying a feature and earn a point for each correct answer. If the team member gives an incorrect answer, they forfeit their turn to the other team. The game continues until all the physical features have been located. Students enjoy the laser pointer technique and the game is a high-interest way to involve students in learning about physical features.

Meeting National Standards

Geography For Life

The following standards are highlighted in Chapter 2:

Section 1   EE1 The World in Spatial Terms: Standard 1
EE3 Physical Systems: Standard 8
EE6 The Uses of Geography: Standard 18

Section 2   EE3 Physical Systems: Standard 7
EE5 Environment and Society: Standards 14, 15

Section 3   EE5 Environment and Society Standard 16
EE6 The Uses of Geography: Standard 18

Local Objectives

_____

_____

TEACHER'S CORNER

Index to National Geographic Magazine:

The following articles may be used for research relating to this chapter:

- "John Glenn: Man With a Mission," by William R. Newcott, June 1999.
- "Living with Natural Hazards," by Michael Parfit, July 1998.
- "Landsat's Views of a Changing Earth," by Boris Weintraub, November 1997.

National Geographic Society Products:

To order the following products for use with this chapter, call National Geographic Society at 1-800-368-2728.

- *PicturePack: World Geography Library* (Transparencies)
- *Physical Geography of the Continents Series* (Videos)
- *Physical Earth* (Map)

NGS ONLINE

Access National Geographic's Web site for current events, activities, links, interactive features, and archives.
www.nationalgeographic.com

MEETING SPECIAL NEEDS

In addition to the Differentiated Instruction strategies found in each section, the following resources are also suitable for your special needs students:

- *ExamView® Pro Testmaker CD-ROM* allows teachers to tailor tests by reducing answer choices.
- The *Audio Program* includes the entire narrative of the student edition so that less-proficient readers can listen to the words as they read them.
- The *Reading Essentials and Study Guide* provides the same content as the student edition but is written two grade levels below the textbook.
- *Guided Reading Activities* give less-proficient readers point-by-point instructions to increase comprehension as they read each textbook section.
- *Enrichment Activities* include a stimulating collection of readings and activities for gifted and talented students.

Chapter Objectives

1. Describe Earth's location and structure.
2. Identify the forces that shape Earth's surface.
3. Discuss the water cycle.

GLENCOE TECHNOLOGY

Use *MindJogger Videoquiz* to preview the Chapter 2 content.

GeoJournal

For access to additional information on the physical geography of the earth, go to www.nationalgeographic.com **(See Teacher pages in front for strategies for using journals in the geography classroom.)**

GEOGRAPHY Online

Introduce students to chapter content and key terms by having them access Chapter Overview 2 at geography.glencoe.com

FOLDABLES™ Study Organizer

Dinah Zike's Foldables are three-dimensional, interactive graphic organizers that help students practice basic writing skills, review key vocabulary terms, and identify main ideas. Have students complete the Foldable activity in the **Dinah Zike's Reading and Study Skills Foldables** booklet.

CHAPTER 2

The Earth

GeoJournal

As you read this chapter, use your journal to note facts about our planet. Include descriptive details about Earth's physical features, its structure, and the forces of change that shape its surface.

GEOGRAPHY Online

Chapter Overview Visit the **Glencoe World Geography** Web site at geography.glencoe.com and click on Chapter Overviews—Chapter 2 to preview information about Planet Earth.

ABOUT THE PHOTO

Visual Instruction When the Apollo 17 crew traveled to the moon, they were able to photograph a large portion of the earth from the spacecraft. Here, the photo shows the area from the Mediterranean Sea to Antarctica's ice cap. **Ask: What part of Africa can you see?** *(almost all of the coastline and the Arabian Peninsula)* **Where is the Asian mainland?** *(on the horizon, toward the northeast)* 🌐 **EE1 The World in Spatial Terms: Standard 1**

Guide to Reading

Consider What You Know

What do you know about Planet Earth? How does it compare to other planets and to other objects, such as stars and moons? How would you describe the surface of the earth?

Reading Strategy

Categorizing As you read about Earth, complete a graphic organizer similar to the one below by describing the four components of Earth.

Component	Description
Hydrosphere	
Lithosphere	
Atmosphere	
Biosphere	

Read to Find Out

- Where is Earth located in our solar system?
- How is Earth shaped?
- What is Earth's structure?
- What types of landforms are found on Earth?

Terms to Know

- hydrosphere
- lithosphere
- atmosphere
- biosphere
- continental shelf

Places to Locate

- Australia
- South America
- Antarctica
- Africa
- Europe
- Mount Everest
- Asia
- Dead Sea
- North America
- Mariana Trench

◀ *Earth viewed from space*

Planet Earth

NATIONAL GEOGRAPHIC

A Geographic View

Patterns of Life

As we fly over the Sahara, we all strain to see Lake Chad, which is between the northern deserts and the green portion of equatorial Africa. Its level is a good indicator of how wet or dry this boundary region, called the Sahel, has been. It was mostly cloudy during my first flight: a good sign for those living below. On my second flight, 17 months later, we could see that the level had risen: The drought in the Sahel had abated [ended] for the moment.

Lake Chad, northern Africa

—*Jay Apt, "Orbit: The Astronauts' View of Home,"* National Geographic, *November 1996*

An astronaut, seeing Earth from the blackness of space, described it as "piercingly beautiful." From the vantage point of space, the earth's great beauty resembles a blue and white marble, with contrasts of water and land beneath huge swirls of white clouds. Together these features form the physical environment of the earth. In this section you will discover what humans know about the physical nature of our planet, Earth.

Our Solar System

Earth is part of our solar system, which is made up of the sun and all of the countless objects that revolve around it. At our solar system's center is the sun—a star, or ball of burning gases. About 109 times wider than Earth, the sun's enormous mass—the amount of matter it contains—creates a strong pull of gravity. This basic physical force keeps the earth and the other objects revolving around the sun.

Chapter 2 🌐 33

FOCUS

Section Overview

This section discusses the location of Earth in the solar system and the planet's basic features.

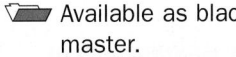

BELLRINGER
Skillbuilder Activity

📇 Project transparency and have students answer questions.

📂 Available as blackline master.

Daily Focus Skills Transparency 2-1

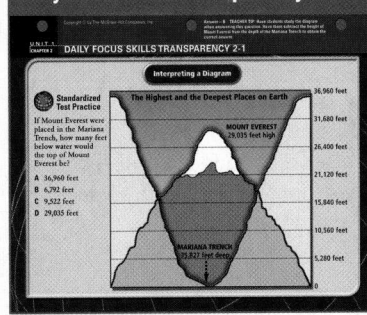

Guide to Reading

Consider What You Know
Answers *Earth is smaller and cooler than stars. It orbits the sun and is larger than most moons. Earth's surface is an uneven mixture of land and water, heights and depths.*

Reading Strategy
Answer hydrosphere: *all bodies of water;* lithosphere: *the earth's crust, all land, including land beneath oceans;* atmosphere: *the layer of gases extending about 6,000 miles above the earth's surface;* biosphere: *all people, animals, and plants that live on the earth's surface and in the atmosphere*

Preteaching Vocabulary
Write on the board the Greek prefixes *hydro-* (water), *litho-* (stone), *atmo-* (vapor), and *bio-* (life) with their English translations. Tell students to keep this information in mind as they discuss the earth's features.

RESOURCE MANAGER

📖 **Reproducible Masters**
- Reproducible Lesson Plan 2-1
- Daily Lecture Notes 2-1
- Guided Reading Activity 2-1
- Reading Essentials and Study Guide 2-1
- Section Quiz 2-1

📠 **Transparencies**
- Daily Focus Skills Transparency 2-1
- Political Map Transparency 1
- Unit 1 Map Overlay Transparencies

Multimedia
- 💿 Interactive Tutor Self-Assessment CD-ROM
- 💿 ExamView® Pro Testmaker CD-ROM
- 💿 Presentation Plus! CD-ROM

2 TEACH

NATIONAL GEOGRAPHIC **DIAGRAM STUDY**

Answers

1. *Mercury, Venus, Earth, Mars*

2. *inner planets—solid, rocky crusts; outer planets (except Pluto)—large diameter, less dense, gaseous structures, distant from the sun*

Skills Practice

Location Where is the Asteroid Belt? *(between the orbits of Mars and Jupiter)*

L1 Location

Ask students to identify the continents on a world map or globe, or refer them to the Reference Atlas on pages RA2–RA3.

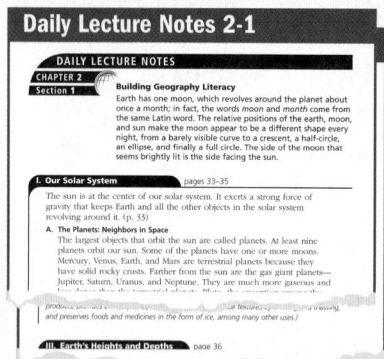

Daily Lecture Notes 2-1

L2 Evaluating Information

Explain that scientists are debating Pluto's status as a planet. Have students research this debate, evaluate the information, and decide how they would vote.

NATIONAL GEOGRAPHIC **DIAGRAM STUDY**

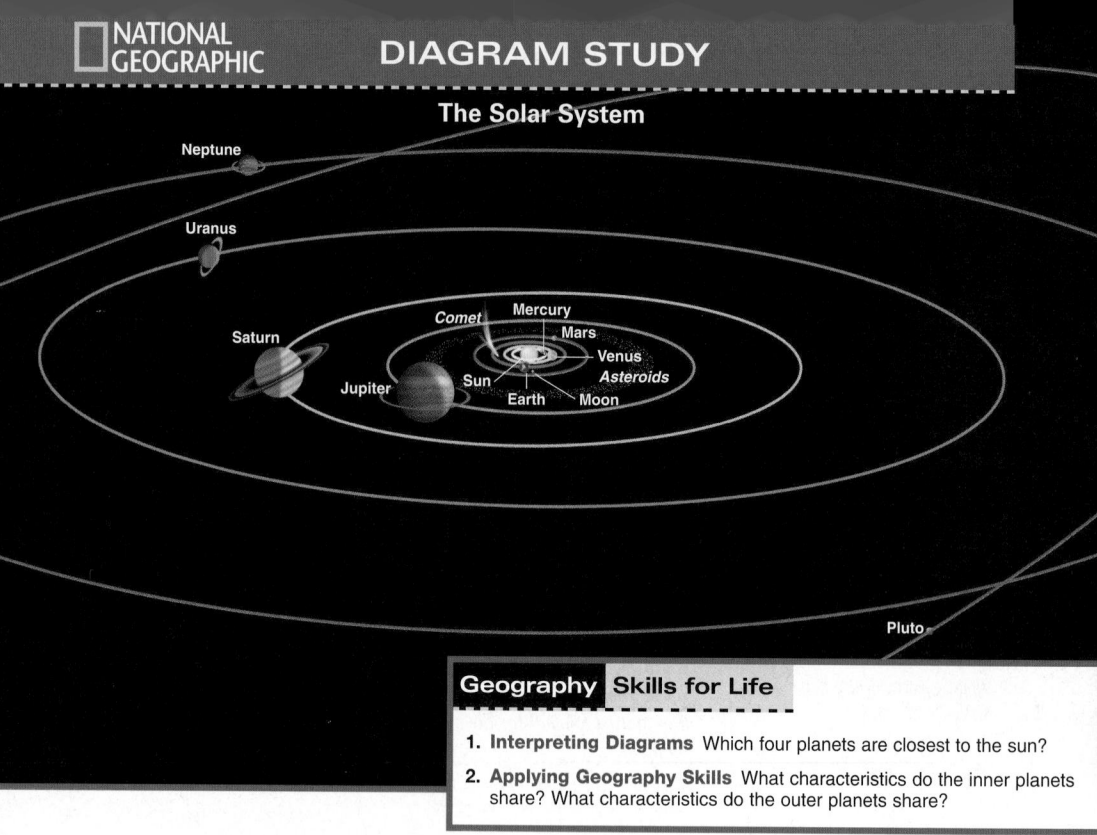

The Solar System

Geography **Skills for Life**

1. **Interpreting Diagrams** Which four planets are closest to the sun?

2. **Applying Geography Skills** What characteristics do the inner planets share? What characteristics do the outer planets share?

The Planets: Neighbors in Space

Except for the sun, spheres called planets are the largest objects in our solar system. At least nine planets exist, and each is in its own orbit around the sun. The diagram above shows that the planets vary in distance from the sun. Mercury, Venus, Earth, and Mars are the inner planets, or those nearest the sun. Earth, the third planet from the sun, is about 93 million miles (about 150 million km) away. Farthest from the sun are the outer planets—Jupiter, Saturn, Uranus, Neptune, and Pluto.

The planets vary in size. Jupiter is the largest. Earth ranks fifth in size among the planets, and distant Pluto is the smallest. All of the planets except Mercury and Venus have moons, smaller spheres or satellites that orbit them. The number of

moons each planet has also differs. Earth has 1 moon, and Saturn has at least 18 moons.

All of the planets except Pluto are grouped into two types—terrestrial planets and gas giant planets. Mercury, Venus, Earth, and Mars are called *terrestrial planets* because they have solid, rocky crusts. Mercury and Venus are scalding hot, and Mars is a cold, barren desert. Only Earth has liquid water at the surface and can support varieties of life.

Farther from the sun are the *gas giant planets*— Jupiter, Saturn, Uranus, and Neptune. They are much more gaseous and less dense than the terrestrial planets, even though they are larger in diameter. Each gas giant planet is itself like a miniature solar system, with orbiting moons and thin, encircling rings. Only

---

DIFFERENTIATED INSTRUCTION

English Learners This chapter contains many scientific terms that may be difficult for English language learners. Ask students to keep lists of unfamiliar vocabulary. Allow time for them to practice pronunciation with partners proficient in English. Ask students to watch for terms (such as some planet names) that may have roots or equivalents in their primary languages. Invite English language learners to share with the rest of the class the names given to the planets in their primary language. **ELL**

EE6 The Uses of Geography: Standard 18

Refer to *Inclusion for the Social Studies Classroom Strategies and Activities.*

Saturn's rings, however, are easily seen from Earth by telescope. Pluto, the exception among the planets, is a ball of ice and rock.

Asteroids, Comets, and Meteoroids

In addition to the planets, thousands of smaller objects, including asteroids, comets, and meteoroids, revolve around the sun. Asteroids are small, irregularly shaped, planetlike objects. They are found mainly between the orbits of Mars and Jupiter in a region called the *asteroid belt*. A few asteroids follow paths that cross the earth's orbit.

Comets, made of icy dust particles and frozen gases, look like bright balls with long, feathery tails. Their orbits are inclined at every possible angle to the earth's orbit. They may approach from any direction.

Meteoroids are pieces of space debris—chunks of rock and iron. When they occasionally enter Earth's gravitational field, friction usually burns them up before they reach the earth's surface. Those that collide with Earth are called meteorites. Meteorite strikes, though rare, can significantly affect the landscape, leaving craters and causing other devastation. In 1908 a huge area of forest in the remote Russian region of Siberia was flattened and burned by a "mysterious fireball." Scientists theorize it was a meteorite or comet. As a writer describes the effects:

> " *The heat incinerated herds of reindeer and charred tens of thousands of evergreens across hundreds of square miles. For days, and for thousands of miles around, the sky remained bright with an eerie orange glow—as far away as western Europe people were able to read newspapers at night without a lamp.* "
>
> Richard Stone, "The Last Great Impact on Earth," *Discover*, September 1996

Getting to Know Earth

Although globes show our planet as a perfect sphere, the earth is really a rounded object wider around the center than from top to bottom. Earth has a larger diameter at the Equator—about 7,930 miles (12,760 km)—than from Pole to Pole, but the

difference is less than 1 percent. With a circumference of about 24,900 miles (40,070 km), Earth is the largest of the inner planets.

Water, Land, and Air

The surface of the earth is made up of water and land. About 70 percent of our planet's surface is water, which gives the planet the deep blue appearance that astronauts see from space. Oceans, lakes, rivers, and other bodies of water make up a part of the earth called the **hydrosphere.**

About 30 percent of the earth's surface is land, including continents and islands. Land makes up a part of the earth called the **lithosphere,** the earth's crust. The lithosphere also includes the ocean basins, or the land beneath the oceans.

The air we breathe is part of Earth's **atmosphere,** a layer of gases extending about 6,000 miles (9,700 km) above the planet's surface. The atmosphere is composed of 78 percent nitrogen, 21 percent oxygen, and small amounts of argon and other gases.

All people, animals, and plants live on the earth's surface, close to the earth's surface, or in the atmosphere. The part of the earth that supports life is the **biosphere.** Life outside the biosphere, such as on a space station orbiting Earth, exists only with the assistance of mechanical life-support systems.

Landforms

Landforms are the natural features of the earth's surface. The diagram on pages 14–15 shows many of the earth's landforms, made up of physical features with a particular shape or elevation. Four major landforms are mountains, hills, plateaus, and plains. Others include valleys, canyons, and basins. Landforms often contain rivers, lakes, and streams.

Underwater landforms are as diverse as those found on dry land. In some places the ocean floor is a flat plain. Other parts of the seabed feature mountain ranges, cliffs, valleys, and deep trenches.

Seen from space, Earth's most visible landforms, however, are the seven large landmasses called continents. Two continents, **Australia** and **Antarctica,** stand alone, while the others are joined in some way. **Europe** and **Asia** are actually parts of one huge landmass called Eurasia. A narrow neck of land called the Isthmus of Panama links **North America** and **South America.** At the Sinai

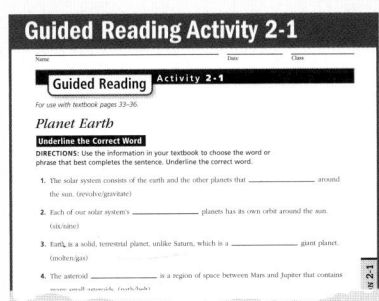

L1/ELL

Guided Reading Activity 2-1

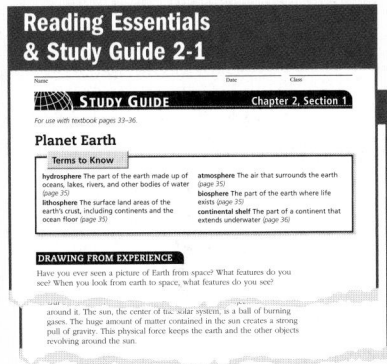

L1/ELL

Reading Essentials & Study Guide 2-1

ASSESS

Assign Section 1 Assessment as homework or as an in-class activity.

Have students use **Interactive Tutor Self-Assessment CD-ROM.**

L2

Section Quiz 2-1

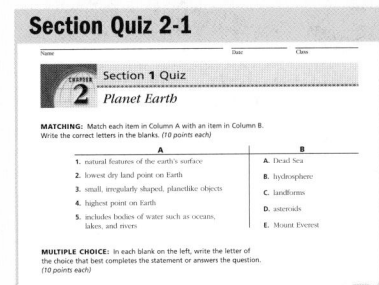

COOPERATIVE LEARNING ACTIVITY

The Biosphere Have students work in small groups to develop a graphic display showing Earth's biosphere. Assign each group a level—atmosphere, hydrosphere, lithosphere on the surface (including how the earth's crust appears on dry land), and lithosphere under the surface (including representatives of the earth's crust beneath the sea)—to research. Groups should find examples of life forms that their assigned area supports. Have the groups work together to make a graphic display of their information as either a three-dimensional model or a cross-section illustration on poster board.

🌐 **EE3 Physical Systems: Standard 8**

Reteach

Ask students to review the section, summarizing the material under each subhead and providing examples.

Enrich

Have students work in groups to look through back issues of *National Geographic* magazine or illustrated travel magazines. Ask them to point out photographs that depict the solar system, various layers of the biosphere, or landforms and other physical features of the earth.

④ CLOSE

Have students imagine they are visiting Earth from another part of the solar system. Ask them to write postcards describing what they see. If time allows, have students illustrate their postcards with drawings or photos from magazines.

NATIONAL GEOGRAPHIC World Explorer

Geography Skills for Life

Planet Earth Parts of the atmosphere (left), lithosphere (center), and hydrosphere (right) form the biosphere, the part of the Earth where life exists.

Human-Environment Interaction How does human activity impact the biosphere?

Peninsula, the human-made Suez Canal separates **Africa** and **Asia**.

The part of a continent that extends underwater is called a continental shelf. Continental shelves are narrow in some places and wide in others. They slope out from land for as much as 800 miles (1,287 km) and descend gradually to a depth of about 660 feet (200 m) where a sharp drop marks the beginning of the continental slope. This area drops more sharply to the ocean floor.

Earth's Heights and Depths

Great contrasts exist in the heights and depths of the earth's surface. The highest point on Earth is in South Asia at the top of **Mount Everest**, which is 29,035 feet (8,852 m) above sea level. The lowest dry land point, at 1,349 feet (411 m) below sea level, is the shore of the **Dead Sea** in Southwest Asia. Earth's deepest known depression lies under the Pacific Ocean southwest of Guam in the **Mariana Trench**, a long, narrow, underwater canyon about 35,827 feet (10,923 m) deep. These and other natural features have developed as the earth has changed over millions of years. In the next section you will learn about the forces of change that have shaped the earth.

SECTION 1 ASSESSMENT

Checking for Understanding

1. **Define** hydrosphere, lithosphere, atmosphere, biosphere, continental shelf.

2. **Main Ideas** Copy the diagram below on your paper, filling in information about the structures of the solar system and the earth.

Structures

| Solar System | Earth |

Planets

Critical Thinking

3. **Drawing Conclusions** Recently NASA has launched space probes to explore Mars. Why might Mars have been chosen for these explorations?

4. **Making Inferences** Think about Earth's surface and list conditions that must be present in a space station in order to support life.

5. **Comparing and Contrasting** How do the inner planets differ from the outer planets?

Analyzing Diagrams

6. **Location** Study the diagram of the solar system on page 34. How is the size of a planet's orbit influenced by its distance from the sun?

Applying Geography

7. **A Delicate Balance** Think about the ratio of water and land on Earth. Write a description of how Earth's physical features would be different if the proportions were reversed.

SECTION 1 ASSESSMENT ANSWERS

1. All vocabulary terms are defined in the text.

2. Diagrams should include information about planets, asteroids, comets, and meteoroids as well as Earth's land, water, air, landforms, heights, and depths.

3. Mars is close to Earth, is a terrestrial planet like Earth, and is cooler than other nearby planets.

4. breathable air, freshwater, soil or other material to support agriculture, artificial sunlight

5. Inner planets are smaller and more solid than the larger, gaseous outer planets.

6. Orbits are larger as the distance from the sun increases.

7. **Applying Geography** much larger landmasses; fewer large bodies of water; fewer glaciers; planet would appear brownish-green from space

Guide to Reading

Consider What You Know

Through observation you are familiar with some features of the earth's surface. These features have been shaped by forces above and beneath the earth's surface. How many of these forces can you name?

Reading Strategy

Taking Notes As you read about the forces that change the earth, use the major headings of the section to create an outline similar to the one below.

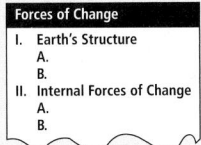

Forces of Change

I. Earth's Structure
   A.
   B.
II. Internal Forces of Change
   A.
   B.

Read to Find Out

- How do Earth's layers contribute to the planet's physical characteristics?
- What internal forces operate to affect Earth's surface, the setting for human life?
- What external forces affect Earth's surface?

Terms to Know

- mantle
- continental drift
- magma
- plate tectonics
- subduction
- accretion
- spreading
- fold
- fault
- weathering
- erosion
- loess
- glacier
- moraine

Places to Locate

- San Andreas Fault
- Ring of Fire

Forces of Change

NATIONAL GEOGRAPHIC

A Geographic View

A Planet in Motion

Scientists now know that the earth is dynamic and enormously complex. At the [earth's] surface ride more than a dozen huge, stiff fragments, or plates. They move at a slower-than-snail's pace— only inches a year—but cover thousands of miles over millions of years. As they collide and separate, they change the face of the globe by deforming and rearranging its features. The engine that propels [these] plates lies below: hot inner layers that churn like thick soup simmering in very slow motion.

San Andreas Fault, California

—Keay Davidson and A.R. Williams, "Under Our Skin: Hot Theories on the Center of the Earth," National Geographic, January 1996

Although we cannot look into the center of the earth, scientists have concluded from available evidence that it is a dynamic interior of intense heat and pressure. Movements deep within the earth drive numerous changes that renew and enrich the earth's surface. In this section you will learn about the earth's structure and the natural forces that continually act upon our planet.

Earth's Structure

For hundreds of millions of years, the surface of the earth has been in slow but constant motion. Some forces that change the earth, such as wind and water, occur on the earth's surface. Others, such as volcanic eruptions and earthquakes, originate deep in the earth's interior.

Chapter 2 37

① FOCUS

① FOCUS

Section Overview

This section discusses the earth's inner composition as well as the internal and external forces that shape the planet's surface.

BELLRINGER
Skillbuilder Activity

 Project transparency and have students answer questions.

 Available as blackline master.

Daily Focus Skills Transparency 2-2

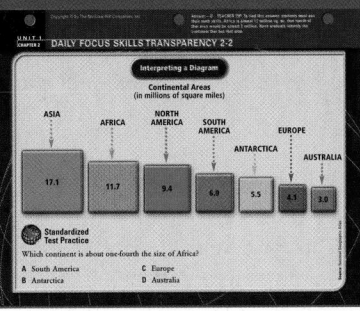

Guide to Reading

Consider What You Know
Answers *volcanic activity, weathering, erosion, plate movement, folding, faulting*

Reading Strategy
Answer Students should complete the outline by including all heads in the section.

Preteaching Vocabulary
Have students list the terms and predict whether each is a force or a feature. *(forces: continental drift, plate tectonics, subduction, accretion, spreading, weathering, erosion; features: mantle, magma, fold, fault, loess, glacier, moraine)*

RESOURCE MANAGER

📁 **Reproducible Masters**
- Reproducible Lesson Plan 2-2
- Daily Lecture Notes 2-2
- Guided Reading Activity 2-2
- Reading Essentials and Study Guide 2-2
- Section Quiz 2-2

📠 **Transparencies**
- Daily Focus Skills Transparency 2-2
- Unit 1 Map Overlay Transparencies

Multimedia
- 💿 Interactive Tutor Self-Assessment CD-ROM
- 💿 ExamView® Pro Testmaker CD-ROM
- 💿 Presentation Plus! CD-ROM

TEACH

DIAGRAM STUDY

Answers

1. *mantle*

2. *push up mountains, create volcanoes, earthquakes, ridges, and trenches*

Skills Practice

Location Which of Earth's layers is part of the biosphere? *(crust)*

L1 Vocabulary

To guide students in reading this section, review the pronunciation of the terms *silicon*, *aluminum*, *magnesium*, *oxygen*, and *tectonics*. **ELL**

L1 Demonstrate

Have students demonstrate the effects of chemical weathering by immersing a seashell in a container of lemon juice or white vinegar for a period of time. Ask volunteers to report the changes.

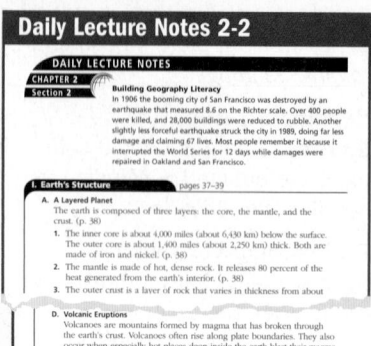

Daily Lecture Notes 2-2

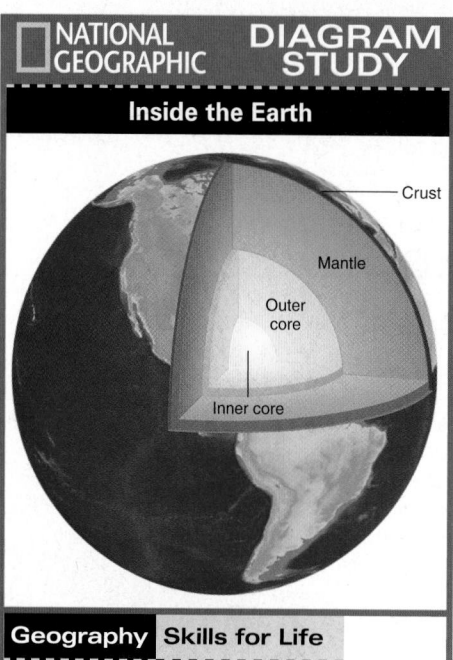

NATIONAL GEOGRAPHIC DIAGRAM STUDY

Inside the Earth

Crust

Mantle

Outer core

Inner core

Geography **Skills for Life**

1. **Interpreting Diagrams** Which of Earth's layers is between the crust and the outer core?

2. **Applying Geography Skills** How do the plates of the earth's crust shape the physical landscape?

A Layered Planet

As you see in the diagram above, the earth is composed of three layers—the core, the mantle, and the crust. At the very center of the planet is a super-hot but solid inner core. It lies about 4,000 miles (6,430 km) below the surface of the earth. Scientists believe that the inner core is made up of iron and nickel under enormous pressure.

Surrounding the inner core is a liquid outer core, about 1,400 miles (2,250 km) thick. A band of melted iron and nickel, the outer core begins about 1,800 miles (2,900 km) below the surface of the earth. Temperatures there reach a scalding 8,500°F (about 4,700°C).

Next to the outer core is a thick layer of hot, dense rock called the mantle. The mantle consists of silicon, aluminum, iron, magnesium, oxygen, and other elements. This mixture continually rises,

cools, sinks, warms up, and rises again, releasing 80 percent of the heat generated from the earth's interior.

The outer layer is the crust, a rocky shell forming the earth's surface. This relatively thin layer of rock ranges from about 2 miles (3.2 km) thick under oceans to about 75 miles (121 km) thick under mountains. The crust is broken into more than a dozen great slabs of rock called plates that rest—or more accurately, float—on a partially melted layer in the upper mantle. The plates carry the earth's oceans and continents. The map on page 39 shows the boundaries of the various plates.

Plate Movement

If you had seen the earth from space 500 million years ago, the planet probably would not have looked at all like it does today. Many scientists believe that most of the landmasses forming our present-day continents were once part of one gigantic supercontinent called *Pangaea* (pan•JEE•uh). Over millions of years, this supercontinent has broken apart into smaller continents. These continents in turn have drifted and, in some places, recombined. The theory that the continents were once joined and then slowly drifted apart is called continental drift.

Many scientists theorize that plates moving slowly around the globe have produced Earth's largest features—not only continents, but also oceans and mountain ranges. Most of the time, plate movement is so gradual—only about 4 inches (10 cm) a year—that it cannot be felt. As they move, the plates may crash into each other, pull apart, or grind and slide past each other. Whatever their actions, plates are constantly changing the face of the planet. They push up mountains, create volcanoes, and produce earthquakes. When the plates spread apart, magma, or molten rock, is pushed up from the mantle and ridges are formed. When the plates bump together, one may slide under another, forming a trench.

Scientists use the term plate tectonics to refer to all of these activities, which create many of the earth's physical features. Many scientists estimate that plate tectonics have been shaping the earth's surface for 2.5 to 4 billion years. According to some scientists, plate tectonics will have sculpted a whole new look for our planet millions of years from now.

DIFFERENTIATED INSTRUCTION

Kinesthetic Help students simulate physical forces with the following demonstrations: (1) To demonstrate folding of the earth's crust, have students lay a sheet of paper on a flat surface and slowly push opposite edges of the paper toward its center. (2) To demonstrate the two kinds of energy waves (fast P waves and slow S waves) generated by earthquakes, have students stretch a metal spring and then abruptly let it go (fast waves) and snap a rope to make ripples (slow waves).

EE3 Physical Systems: Standard 7

Refer to *Inclusion for the Social Studies Classroom Strategies and Activities.*

Scientists, however, have not yet determined exactly what causes plate tectonics. They theorize that heat rising from the earth's core may create slow-moving currents within the mantle. Over millions of years, these currents of molten rock may shift the plates around, but the movements are extremely slow and difficult to detect.

Internal Forces of Change

The surface of the earth has changed greatly over time. Scientists believe that some of these changes come from internal forces associated with plate tectonics. One of these internal forces relates to the slow movement of magma within the earth. Other internal forces involve movements that can fold, lift, bend, or break the rock along the earth's crust.

Colliding and Spreading Plates

Mountains are formed in areas where giant continental plates collide. For example, the Himalaya ranges in South Asia were thrust upward when the Indian landmass rammed into Eurasia. Himalayan peaks are still getting higher as the Indian landmass continues to push against them.

Mountains also are created when a sea plate collides with a continental plate. In a process called subduction (suhb•DUHK•shuhn), the heavier sea plate dives beneath the lighter continental plate. Plunging into the earth's interior, the sea plate becomes molten material. Then, as magma, it bursts through the crust to form volcanic mountains. The Andes, for example, were formed over millions of years as a result of the process of subduction.

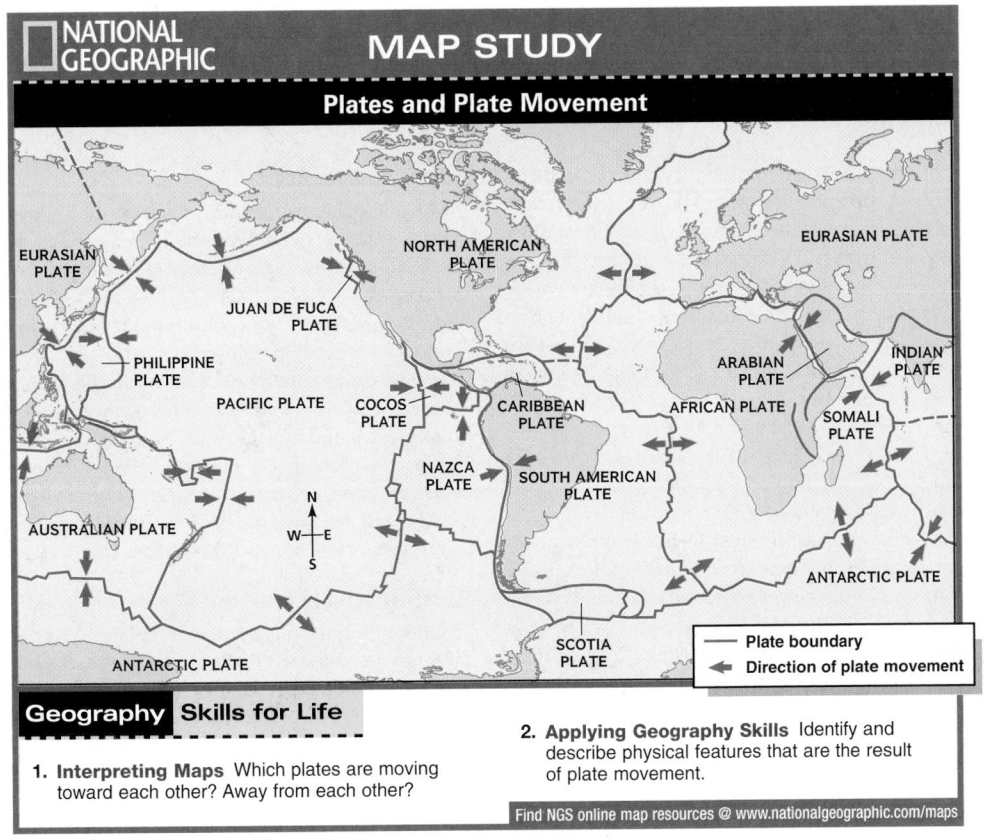

NATIONAL GEOGRAPHIC

MAP STUDY

Plates and Plate Movement

Plate boundary
Direction of plate movement

Geography Skills for Life

1. **Interpreting Maps** Which plates are moving toward each other? Away from each other?

2. **Applying Geography Skills** Identify and describe physical features that are the result of plate movement.

Find NGS online map resources @ www.nationalgeographic.com/maps

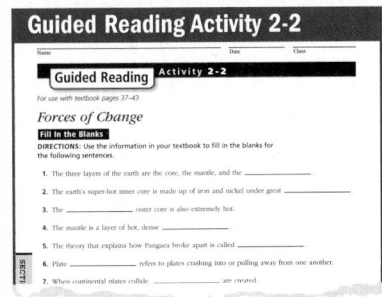

L1/ELL

Guided Reading Activity 2-2

Name _____ Date _____ Class _____

Guided Reading Activity 2-2

For use with textbook pages 37–43

Forces of Change

Fill in the Blanks

DIRECTIONS: Use the information in your textbook to fill in the blanks for the following sentences.

1. The three layers of the earth are the core, the mantle, and the _____
2. The earth's super-hot inner core is made up of iron and nickel under great _____
3. The _____ outer core is also extremely hot.
4. The mantle is a layer of hot, dense _____
5. The theory that explains how Pangaea broke apart is called _____
6. Plate _____ refers to plates crashing into or pulling away from one another.
7. When continental plates collide, _____ are created.

L2 Personal Narratives

Ask students if they or their family members have ever experienced an earthquake or been in the vicinity of a volcanic eruption. Have students share their impressions of these experiences.

NATIONAL GEOGRAPHIC **MAP STUDY**

Answers

1. toward: *North American and Juan de Fuca; Pacific and Cocos, Australian, Philippine, Eurasian; Indian and Somali; Arabian and African; Nazca and South American, Cocos* away: *North American and Eurasian; African and North American, South American, Antarctic; Pacific and Antarctic*

2. *mountains, volcanoes, ridges, trenches*

Map Skills Practice
Location On which plate is the state of Hawaii located? *(Pacific Plate)*

COOPERATIVE LEARNING ACTIVITY

Mountain Ranges Have students work in three groups to develop a chart of the physical activity that gave rise to Earth's major mountain ranges. Have one group list and identify the locations of 10 large mountain ranges; have another group research the forces that formed the ranges (including the movement of specific plates, if applicable), and have the third group prepare a graphic display of the information.
⊕ **EE3 Physical Systems: Standard 7**

L1/ELL

Reading Essentials & Study Guide 2-2

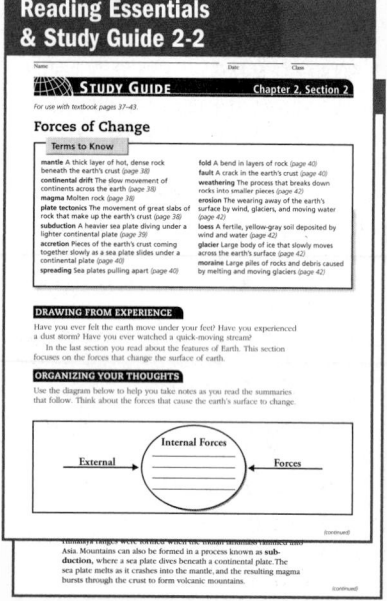

L2 Model

Direct students to find a relief map of your state or local area. Have them use clay to create a model of the landscape and its major physical features. Suggest that they mark main cities. **Ask: How have the area's physical features affected settlement patterns?**

□ NATIONAL GEOGRAPHIC **DIAGRAM STUDY**

Forces of Change

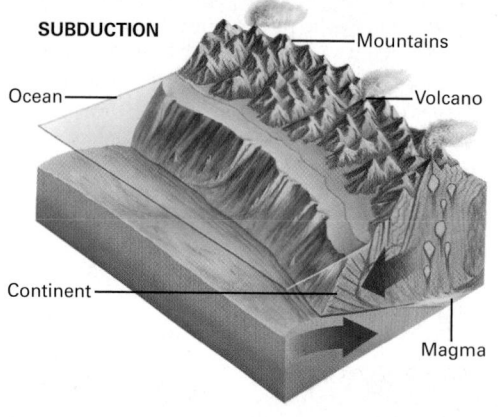

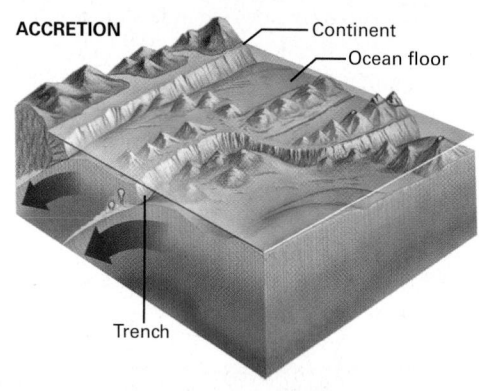

In other cases where continental and sea plates meet, a different process, known as accretion, occurs. During accretion (uh•KREE•shuhn), pieces of the earth's crust come together slowly as the sea plate slides under the continental plate. This plate movement levels off seamounts, underwater mountains with steep sides and sharp peaks, and piles up the resulting debris in trenches. Such a buildup can cause continents to grow outward. Most scientists believe that much of western North America expanded outward over more than 200 million years as a result of the process of accretion.

New land is also created where two sea plates converge. In this process one plate moves under the other, often forming an island chain at the boundary. Sea plates also can pull apart in a process known as spreading. The resulting rift, or deep crack, allows magma from within the earth to well up between the plates. The magma hardens to build undersea volcanic mountains or ridges. This spreading activity occurs down the middle of the Atlantic Ocean's floor, pushing Europe and North America away from each other.

Folds and Faults

Moving plates sometimes squeeze the earth's surface until it buckles. This activity forms folds, or bends, in layers of rock. In other cases plates may grind or slide past each other, creating cracks in the earth's crust called faults. One famous fault is the **San Andreas Fault** in California.

The process of faulting occurs when the folded land cannot be bent any further. Then the earth's crust cracks and breaks into huge blocks. The blocks move along the faults in different directions, grinding against each other. The resulting tension may release a series of small jumps, felt as minor tremors on the earth's surface.

Earthquakes

Sudden, violent movements of plates along a fault line are known as earthquakes. These shaking activities dramatically change the surface of the land and the floor of the ocean. For example, during a severe earthquake in Alaska in 1964, a portion of the ground lurched upward 38 feet (11.6 m).

Earthquakes often occur where different plates meet one another. Tension builds up along fault

---

CRITICAL THINKING ACTIVITY

Identifying Alternatives Organize the class into three groups. Have the groups research the damage caused by recent earthquakes (magnitude 8 or above) in three different areas of the world. Have group members identify the causes of damage and recommend alternative methods of construction, retrofitting (bringing old buildings up to current standards), and emergency preparedness for the area in the future. Allow time for groups to share and compare information. **Ask: Do proposed alternatives apply equally well to all three areas, or should different methods be used in different parts of the world?** 📦 🖥 EE5 Environment and Society: Standard 15

SPREADING

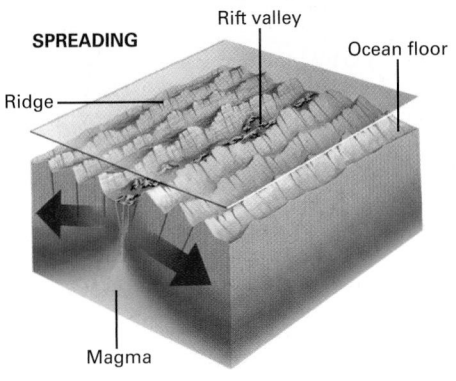

Rift valley
Ocean floor
Ridge
Magma

FAULTING

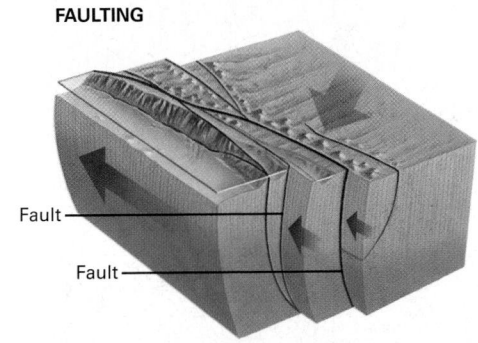

Fault
Fault

Geography Skills for Life

1. **Interpreting Diagrams** How does the process of accretion create deep trenches in the earth's surface?

2. **Applying Geography Skills** How do you think human settlement is affected by the process of faulting?

---

lines as the plates stick. The strain eventually becomes so intense that the rocks suddenly snap and shift. This movement releases stored-up energy along the fault. The ground then trembles as shock waves surge through it away from the area where the rocks snapped apart.

In recent years disastrous earthquakes have occurred in Kobe, Japan, and in Los Angeles and San Francisco, California. These cities are located along the **Ring of Fire**, one of the most earthquake-prone areas on the planet. The Ring of Fire is a zone of earthquake and volcanic activity surrounding the Pacific Ocean. It marks the boundary where the plates that cradle the Pacific meet the plates that hold the continents surrounding the Pacific.

Volcanic Eruptions

Volcanoes are mountains formed by lava or by magma that breaks through the earth's crust. Volcanoes often rise along plate boundaries where one plate plunges beneath another. This kind of volcanic formation occurs, for example, along the Ring of Fire. In such a process the rocky plate melts as it dives downward into the hot mantle. If the molten rock is too thick, its flow is blocked and pressure builds. A cloud of ash and gas may then spew forth, creating a funnel through which the red-hot magma rushes to the surface. There the lava flow may eventually form a large volcanic cone topped by a crater, a bowl-shaped depression at a volcano's mouth.

Volcanoes also arise in areas away from plate boundaries. Some areas deep in the earth are hotter than others, and magma often blasts through the surface as volcanoes. As a moving plate passes over these hot spots, molten rock flowing out of the earth's surface may create volcanic island chains. An example of this type of formation is the Hawaiian Islands in the Pacific Ocean. At various hot spots, molten rock may also heat underground water, causing hot springs or geysers. Yellowstone National Park in Wyoming has many spectacular geysers formed by this process, such as Old Faithful, which regularly sends water and steam into the air.

Krakatau In 1883 an explosive volcanic eruption on the Indonesian island of Krakatau created a tsunami (giant tidal wave) that washed over nearby islands and eventually reached the coast of England. More than 36,000 people were killed by the explosion and the tsunami. Ash clouds colored sunsets around the world for two years.

TEAM-TEACHING ACTIVITY: SCIENCE

Compare Types of Rocks Have students work with a science teacher to identify and compare the three main types of rock (igneous, metamorphic, and sedimentary). Have students review the earth's internal and external forces of change and determine which are responsible for the formation of each type of rock. If time allows, have students analyze samples of rocks found in your area to determine their types and the forces responsible for their formation. ⊛ **EE3 Physical Systems: Standard 7**

L2 Place

Have students refer to the world map on pages RA2–RA3 of the Reference Atlas. Have students locate Greenland and Antarctica. **Ask:** Why are these places covered by glaciers? (Climate at far northern and southern latitudes is too cold to allow ice to melt.) Which other parts of the world might be covered with glaciers? (Students should name other places located in extreme northern or southern latitudes.)

③ ASSESS

Assign Section 2 Assessment as homework or as an in-class activity.

Have students use **Interactive Tutor Self-Assessment CD-ROM** to review Section 2.

L2

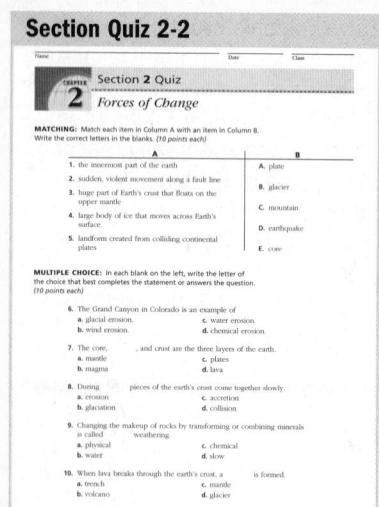

Section Quiz 2-2

▲ *Water erosion in the Grand Canyon*

External Forces of Change

External forces, such as wind and water, also change the earth's surface. They have transformed the planet's appearance over millions of years and continue to do so today. Wind and water movements involve two processes: weathering and erosion. **Weathering** is the process that breaks down rocks on the earth's surface into smaller pieces. **Erosion** is the wearing away of the earth's surface by wind, glaciers, and moving water.

Weathering

The earth is changed by two basic kinds of weathering—physical weathering and chemical weathering. Physical weathering occurs when large masses of rock are physically broken down into smaller pieces. For example, water seeps into the cracks in a rock and freezes, then expands and causes the rock to split.

The process of chemical weathering changes the chemical makeup of rocks, transforming their

minerals or combining them with new elements. For example, water mixed with carbon dioxide from the air easily dissolves certain rocks, such as limestone. Many of the world's caves have been and continue to be formed by this process.

Wind Erosion

Wind erosion involves the movement of dust, sand, and soil from one place to another. Plants help protect the land from wind erosion; however, in dry places where people have cut down trees and plants, winds pick up large amounts of soil and blow it away. Serious wind erosion devastated the Great Plains in the central United States during the 1930s. Fierce winds swept up dry, overworked soil from exposed farmland and carried it away in dust storms.

Wind erosion, however, also provides benefits. The dust carried by wind often forms large deposits of mineral-rich soil. These deposits provide fertile farmland in various parts of the world. China's Yellow River basin, for example, is thickly covered with **loess** (LEHS), a fertile, yellow-gray soil deposited by wind.

Glacial Erosion

Another cause of erosion is **glaciers**, or large bodies of ice that slowly move across the earth's surface. Glaciers form over a long period of time as layers of snow press together and turn to ice. Their great weight causes them to move slowly downhill or spread outward. As they move, glaciers pick up rocks and soil in their paths. Glacial movements change the landscape, destroying forests, carving out valleys, altering the courses of rivers, and wearing down mountaintops.

When glaciers melt and recede, in some places they leave behind large piles of rocks and debris called **moraines**. Some moraines form long ridges of land, while others form dams that hold water back and create glacial lakes.

There are two types of glaciers—sheet glaciers and mountain glaciers. Sheet glaciers are flat, broad sheets of ice. Today sheet glaciers cover most of Greenland and all of Antarctica. They advance a few feet each winter and recede during the summer. Large blocks of ice often break off from the coastal edges of sheet glaciers to become icebergs floating in the ocean.

EXTENDING THE CONTENT

Weathering The process of weathering is affected by climate, soil and rock types, and vegetation. Although weathering happens all over the world, geologists have found a link between certain kinds of climates and certain patterns of weathering. In dry areas located near large bodies of water, for example, salt crystals build up as moisture evaporates. In the United States, the land around Utah's Great Salt Lake and the region surrounding the Colorado River are subject to weathering through salt-crystal buildup.
🌐 EE3 Physical Systems: Standard 7

Mountain glaciers are more common than sheet glaciers. They are located in high mountain valleys where the climate is cold, such as in the Rocky Mountains and Cascade Range of North America. As they move downhill, mountain glaciers gouge out round, U-shaped valleys. As these glaciers melt, rock and soil are deposited in new locations.

Water Erosion

Fast-moving water—rain, rivers, streams, and oceans—is the most significant cause of erosion. Water erosion begins when springwater and rainwater flow off the land downhill in streams. As the water flows, it cuts into the land, wearing away the soil and rock. The resulting sediment—small particles of soil, sand, and gravel—acts like sandpaper, grinding away the surface of rocks along the stream's path. Over time, the eroding action of water forms first a gully and then a V-shaped valley. Sometimes valleys are eroded even further to form valleys with high, steep walls, called canyons. The Grand Canyon of the Colorado River is a good example of the eroding power of water. Peter Miller describes the canyon's various layers as he hiked from the canyon rim to its floor:

> " [A]s we hiked down the twisting Kaibab Trail to the Colorado River at the bottom of the canyon, we were hoping . . . to share a . . . great adventure. The canyon opened up before us with all the drama we had imagined. After we dropped below the ponderosa pine forests of the South Rim, we descended narrow ridgelines past crumbling cliffs of white sandstone, red limestone, chocolate sandstone, and maroon shale, descending 4,700 feet to the river. "
>
> Peter Miller, "John Wesley Powell: Vision for the West," *National Geographic*, April 1994

In addition to streams and rivers, oceans play an important role in water erosion. Pounding waves continually erode coastal cliffs, wear rocks into sandy beaches, and move sand away to other coastal areas. Violent storms speed up this process. In the next section, you will learn about the oceans and other water features of our planet and how they affect the earth's surface.

SECTION 2 ASSESSMENT

Checking for Understanding

1. **Define** mantle, continental drift, magma, plate tectonics, subduction, accretion, spreading, fold, fault, weathering, erosion, loess, glacier, moraine.

2. **Main Ideas** Copy the organizer below, and fill in information about forces that shape Earth's features. Then choose one force that shapes the earth's surface and explain this process.

Forces of Change	
Composition (layers)	
Internal forces	
External forces	

Critical Thinking

3. **Predicting Consequences** Based on your understanding of plate tectonics, what changes would you predict to the earth's appearance millions of years from now?

4. **Making Inferences** Think about water erosion associated with rivers and streams. Based on that information, what would you expect the areas where rivers empty into the oceans to be like? Explain.

5. **Drawing Conclusions** In what ways can erosion be both beneficial and harmful to agricultural communities?

Analyzing Maps

6. **Region** Study the map of plates and plate movement on page 39. Which plates are responsible for the earthquakes that have occurred in California in the United States?

Applying Geography

7. **Consequences of Earth's Forces** Review how internal forces shape the surface of the earth. Now imagine that the mantle ceased to circulate molten rock. Write a description of how land formation on the surface of the earth would be different.

L3 Creative Writing

Have students read or view a film version of Jules Verne's *Journey to the Center of the Earth*. Have students write about a journey to the earth's core based on current scientific knowledge.

Reteach

Refer students to their lists of vocabulary terms labeled as *forces* or *features*. Have students make any necessary corrections in their predictions.

Enrich

Play portions of Grofé's *Grand Canyon Suite*, and have students imagine the music as a soundtrack to the forces shaping the earth's surface. Ask students to write about or draw their impressions.

4 CLOSE

Ask students to describe the processes (weather, tectonic forces, wave action, freezing and thawing, gravity, and soil-building) that have shaped the earth's surface in your state.

SECTION 2 ASSESSMENT ANSWERS

1. All vocabulary terms are defined in the text.
2. Charts and descriptions should include information about Earth's layers and internal and external forces of change.
3. North America will be farther from Eurasia and South America farther from Africa; new mountain ranges will emerge where plates collide; boundaries of landmasses will be substantially different.

4. Rivers erode soil, carry it downstream, and deposit it where they empty into oceans, forming an extension of the land, or delta.
5. benefits: breaks up large rocks into finer soil; harms: washes away good topsoil, carries polluted runoff, floods
6. Pacific, North American

7. **Applying Geography** Plates would no longer move; magma would not rise; no earthquakes or volcanoes; most landforms would wear away through weathering/erosion and not be replaced by new mountain ranges.

① FOCUS

Put the following headings on the board, and ask students to list items for each category:

· *plants native to our area*
· *plants introduced into our area*
· *animals native to our area*
· *animals introduced into our area*

Be prepared to suggest examples of native and alien species. **Ask: Have any introduced plants or animals become pests or environmental challenges?**

② TEACH

Have students list causes for the global challenge of invasive species. **Ask: Why is this issue more of a problem today than in the past?** *(Advances in transportation and trade enable species to move across great distances.)* Identify the origins of local invasive species.

Biological Hitchhikers Studies indicate that windblown dust clouds traveling from Africa to the United States and the Caribbean may cause increases in respiratory ailments, such as asthma. The dust clouds may also carry bacteria, viruses, and dangerous chemical pollutants, such as mercury.

Viewpoint
CASE STUDY on the Environment

A Global Concern: Invasive Species

Until a few centuries ago, plants and animals living in one part of the world rarely mixed with those on other continents. This changed, however, as new ways of transport allowed more and more people to travel the planet. A turning point was the Columbian Exchange, the transfer of plants, animals, and diseases between Europe and the Americas that began with the voyages of Columbus. Since then, the biological exchange has become global. As a result, thousands of "alien" plants and animals have been introduced into areas where the species do not occur naturally. Some introduced species are beneficial, while others are invasive and pose environmental threats.

44   Unit 1

LOOKING TO THE FUTURE

The Hawaiian Dilemma The Hawaiian Islands, with their small land area and limited food webs, are an ideal laboratory for studying the effects of invasive species. In the years since 1778, when Captain James Cook visited the islands, almost 4,000 species of plants and animals have been introduced into the Hawaiian ecosystem, with many disastrous results. More than half of Hawaii's native bird species—including the state bird, the *nene* goose—and 20 percent of native plant species are threatened with extinction. As the world becomes "smaller" through global connections, the challenges to Hawaii's biodiversity may offer lessons for ecosystems elsewhere.
🌐 **EE5 Environment and Society: Standard 14**

If you live near a wetland, you've probably seen the purple or pinkish flowers of the purple loosestrife (left). Native to Europe, purple loosestrife was brought to the United States as a garden plant. It soon spread to wetlands, where it now threatens native plants. Invasive species such as purple loosestrife are a global problem.

Sometimes invasive species arrive in new environments by accident—as seeds or as eggs or tiny insects hidden in packing materials, in food or soil, or in the ballast water of visiting ships. Without natural predators in their new habitats, alien species can multiply at alarming rates and crowd out native species. These invaders also can cause widespread environmental damage. The gypsy moth, for example, was accidentally introduced to the United States in the late 1800s. The insect, during its caterpillar stage, feeds on the leaves of several kinds of trees. Gypsy moth caterpillars have destroyed huge swaths of American forests.

Workers (below) cut invasive water hyacinths clogging waters in India. Yet some imported plants are beneficial. In Turkey (right), women harvest wheat to feed their families. ▼

Plants and animals are also introduced into new environments intentionally. For example, an insect might be imported to combat a crop pest. Some introduced species have turned out to be great successes. Wheat, for example, originated in the Middle East and is now grown on almost every continent. Spanish explorers brought horses to the Americas.

Yet for every helpful introduction, there have been many destructive ones. In 1859 British settlers released two dozen rabbits in Australia. Now millions of rabbits roam the continent. They devour crops and grasslands, creating deserts in the hot, dry climate. Water hyacinth, another invasive species, went from South America to Africa for use in ornamental ponds. The fast-growing plant soon spread to lakes and rivers, forming dense mats that interfere with boating and fishing.

Some scientists argue that alien species are serious threats to biodiversity. These people want laws to limit trade and to

◄ A gypsy moth caterpillar kills trees by eating their leaves.

halt the spread of plants and animals from place to place. Many biologists think using foreign species to control pests is too risky. Scientists cite numerous examples of introduced species that have damaged their new environments.

Some farmers and economists point out that in a world where trade and transportation bring countries together, a global redistribution of species is inevitable. Such people, fearing financial losses, oppose laws that limit trade. Farmers generally support importing foreign species to control pests. These biological controls cause less environmental damage than the use of pesticides.

What's Your Point of View?
Should international trade be restricted to limit the risks of spreading invasive species around the world?

3 ASSESS

Have students answer the **What's Your Point of View?** question on page 45. Encourage students to support their arguments with facts.

4 CLOSE

Problem Solving Have students work in small groups to suggest solutions other than trade restrictions to the challenges of invasive species. Ask the groups to list their options and discuss them with the rest of the class.

Meeting National Standards

Geography for Life
The following standards are met in the Student Edition feature:

EE1 The World in Spatial Terms:
   Standard 3
EE3 Physical Systems:
   Standard 8
EE5 Environment and Society:
   Standards 14, 15
EE6 The Uses of Geography:
   Standard 18

WHAT CAN YOU DO?

- Contact regional or state agricultural authorities to find out which introduced plant species or insects pose threats to your area. Prepare an informational brochure for gardeners, landscapers, or farmers.
- Use the Internet to learn more about plans to conserve biodiversity around the world. Support organizations working for

biodiversity by raising money or disseminating information.
- Design a garden using only plant species native to your area.
- Look for news stories about this issue. Write an editorial expressing your position.

 EE6 The Uses of Geography: Standard 18

Section Overview

This section discusses Earth's water resources and the water cycle that maintains them.

BELLRINGER
Skillbuilder Activity

 Project transparency and have students answer questions.

 Available as blackline master.

Daily Focus Skills Transparency 2-3

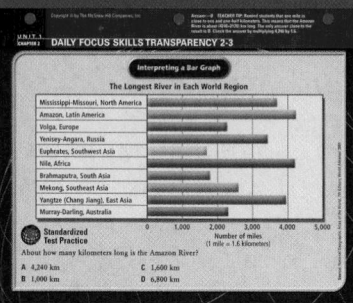

Guide to Reading

Consider What You Know
Answers *Have students brainstorm a list of water uses. Help them trace the source of the water as far as they can. Students should support their opinions about water availability.*

Reading Strategy
Answers *evaporation, condensation, precipitation*

Preteaching Vocabulary
⬤ Use the **Vocabulary Puzzle-Maker CD-ROM** to create crossword and word-search puzzles.

Guide to Reading

Consider What You Know

Think of the ways you use water every day. Where does that water come from? Do you think it will always be available?

Reading Strategy

Organizing As you read about the water cycle, complete a graphic organizer similar to the one below by listing the processes that contribute to the water cycle.

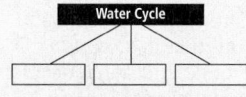

Read to Find Out

• How does the amount of water on Earth remain fairly constant?

• How is the water that makes up 70 percent of Earth's surface distributed?

• Why is freshwater important to humans?

Terms to Know

• water cycle
• evaporation
• condensation
• precipitation
• desalination
• groundwater
• aquifer

Places to Locate

• Pacific Ocean
• Atlantic Ocean
• Indian Ocean
• Arctic Ocean

Earth's Water

NATIONAL GEOGRAPHIC

A Geographic View

Under the Arctic Ocean

In a world that's been almost completely mapped, it's easy to forget why cartographers used to put monsters in the blank spots. Today we got a reminder. The submarine captain had warned us that we were in uncharted waters. . . . Yet the first days of our cruise through this ice-covered ocean, Earth's least explored frontier, were . . . smooth. . . . Even when we passed over a mile-high mountain that no one on the planet knew existed, the reaction was one of quiet enthusiasm—"Neat."

—Glenn Hodges, "The New Cold War: Stalking Arctic Climate Change by Submarine," National Geographic, *March 2000*

Navy submarine in the Arctic

A submarine crew investigating the Arctic Ocean can still experience the thrill of exploring uncharted territory—one of Earth's last frontiers. Although humans live mostly on land, water is important to our lives, and all living things need water to survive. Rivers, lakes, and oceans contain water in liquid form. The atmosphere holds water vapor, or water in the form of a gas. Glaciers and ice sheets are water in solid form. In this section you will learn about Earth's water and its importance to human life.

The Water Cycle

As you recall, oceans, lakes, rivers, and other bodies of water make up a part of the earth called the hydrosphere. Almost all of the hydrosphere is salt water found in the oceans, seas, and a few large saltwater lakes. The remainder is freshwater found in lakes, rivers, and springs.

 RESOURCE MANAGER

Reproducible Masters
• Reproducible Lesson Plan 2-3
• Vocabulary Activity 2
• Daily Lecture Notes 2-3
• Guided Reading Activity 2-3
• Reading Essentials and Study Guide 2-3
• Reteaching Activity 2
• Reinforcing Skills Activity 2
• Section Quiz 2-3

Transparencies
• Daily Focus Skills Transparency 2-3
• Unit 1 Map Overlay Transparencies

Multimedia
⬤ Vocabulary PuzzleMaker CD-ROM
⬤ Interactive Tutor Self-Assessment CD-ROM
⬤ ExamView® Pro Testmaker CD-ROM
⬤ Presentation Plus! CD-ROM

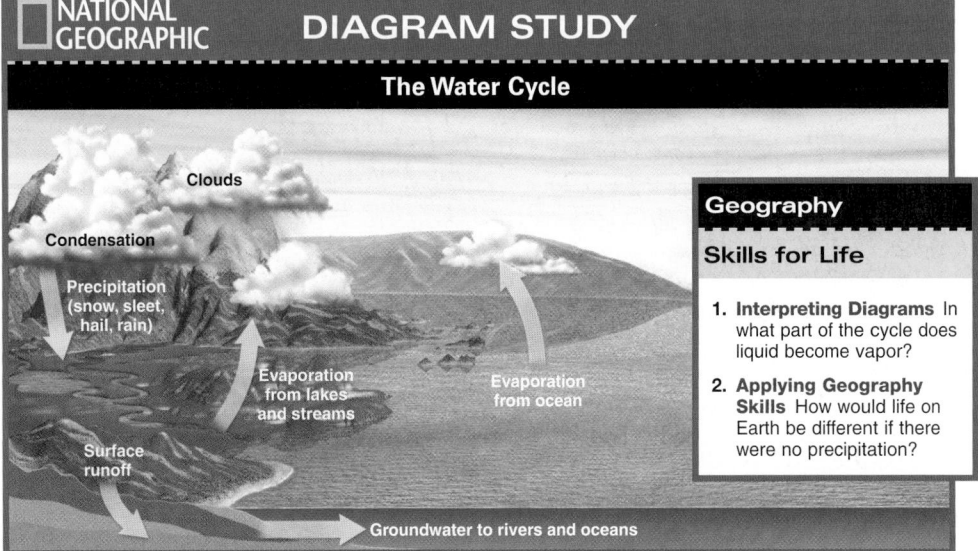

NATIONAL GEOGRAPHIC — DIAGRAM STUDY

The Water Cycle

Clouds

Condensation

Precipitation (snow, sleet, hail, rain)

Evaporation from lakes and streams

Evaporation from ocean

Surface runoff

Groundwater to rivers and oceans

Geography

Skills for Life

1. **Interpreting Diagrams** In what part of the cycle does liquid become vapor?

2. **Applying Geography Skills** How would life on Earth be different if there were no precipitation?

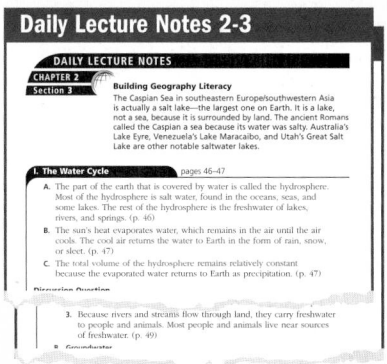

The total amount of water on the earth does not change, but the earth's water is constantly moving—from the oceans to the air to the ground and finally back to the oceans. The *water cycle* is the name given to this regular movement of water. The diagram above shows the major parts of the water cycle.

The sun drives the cycle by evaporating water from the surfaces of oceans, lakes, and streams. *Evaporation* is the changing of liquid water into vapor, or gas. The sun's heat causes evaporation. Water vapor rising from the oceans, other bodies of water, and plants is gathered in the air. The amount of water vapor the air holds depends on its temperature. Warm, less dense air holds more water vapor than does cool air.

When warm air cools, it cannot retain all of its water vapor, so the excess water vapor changes into liquid water—a process called *condensation*. Tiny droplets of water come together to form clouds. When clouds gather more water than they can hold, they release moisture, which falls to the earth as *precipitation*—rain, snow, or sleet, depending on the air temperature and wind conditions. This precipitation sinks into the ground and collects in streams and lakes to return to the

oceans. Soon most of it evaporates, and the cycle begins again.

The amount of water that evaporates is approximately the same amount that falls back to the earth. This amount varies little from year to year. Thus, the total volume of water in the water cycle is more or less constant.

Bodies of Salt Water

Seen from space, the earth's oceans and seas are more prominent than the landmasses. As mentioned earlier, about 70 percent of the earth's surface is water, but almost all of it is salt water. Freshwater makes up only a small percentage of Earth's water.

Oceans

About 97 percent of the earth's water consists of a huge, continuous body of water that circles the planet. Geographers divide this enormous expanse into four oceans: the **Pacific**, the **Atlantic**, the **Indian**, and the **Arctic**. The Pacific, the largest of the oceans, covers more area than all the earth's land combined. The Pacific Ocean is also deep enough in some places to cover Mount Everest, the world's highest mountain, with more than 1 mile (1.6 km) to

---

2 TEACH

Daily Lecture Notes 2-3

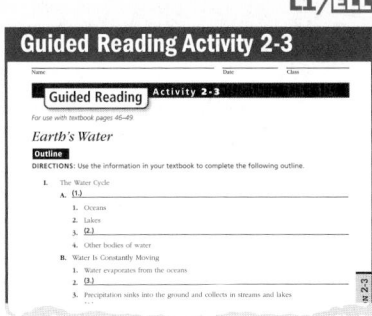

NATIONAL GEOGRAPHIC — DIAGRAM STUDY

Answers

1. *evaporation*

2. *Groundwater and oceans would not be replenished, plants would die, and life would end.*

L2 Drawing Conclusions

Have students list the forms of precipitation common in your area. **Ask: What influences the type and amount of precipitation we have?** *(climate, landforms, location)*

L1/ELL

Guided Reading Activity 2-3

DIFFERENTIATED INSTRUCTION

Gifted and Talented Have students gather and label samples from local water sources: home taps, ponds, rivers or streams, wells, ocean beaches, rain or snow collectors, and so on. (Safety note: Students should avoid contaminated or possibly contaminated sources, wear protective gloves when collecting samples, and never drink water from untreated sources.) Have students note any visible differences among the samples and speculate on the reasons for the differences.

EE6 The Uses of Geography: Standard 18

   Refer to ***Inclusion for the Social Studies Classroom Strategies and Activities.***

L1/ELL

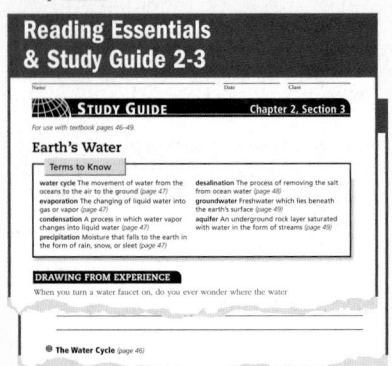

Answer

Freshwater resources are limited and unevenly distributed; much freshwater is locked in ice.

More About the Photo The towers contain chambers in which the desalinated water is stored.

Objectives, goals, and answers to the student activity can be found in the Web Activity Lesson Plan feature at geography.glencoe.com

3 ASSESS

Assign Section 3 Assessment as homework or as an in-class activity.

Have students use **Interactive Tutor Self-Assessment CD-ROM**.

---

spare. The immense size of Earth's oceans continues to inspire awe and fascination in humans.

> *It is useless to speculate at great length about why the sea has such a hold on us. Its mystery, its seeming infinity must be part of the reason. . . . And along with its vastness comes a visible, enduring wildness. We can raze the Amazonian rain forest if we like; we can settle the Alaskan tundra or the Arabian desert given the right economic incentives. We cannot, to the same extent, tame the ocean. . . .*
>
> Robert Kunzig, *The Restless Sea: Exploring the World Beneath the Waves,* 1999

Seas, Gulfs, and Bays

Seas, gulfs, and bays are bodies of salt water smaller than oceans. These bodies of water are often partially enclosed by land. The Mediterranean Sea, one of the world's largest seas, is almost entirely encircled by southern Europe, northern Africa, and southwestern Asia. The Gulf of Mexico is nearly encircled by the coasts of the United States and Mexico. Scientists have identified 66 separate seas, gulfs, and bays, and many smaller divisions.

Economics

Ocean Water to Drinking Water

Although 97 percent of the world's water is found in oceans, the water is too salty for drinking, farming, or manufacturing. Today efforts focus on ways to meet the world's increasing need for freshwater, such as turning ocean water into freshwater by removing the salt. This process, known as desalination, is still in the early stages of development. Because desalination is expensive, only a small amount of freshwater is obtained this way. Even so, certain countries in

Student Web Activity Visit the **Glencoe World Geography** Web site at geography.glencoe.com and click on Student Web Activities—Chapter 2 for an activity about the earth's oceans.

NATIONAL GEOGRAPHIC World Explorer

Geography Skills for Life

Kuwait Towers These towers—Kuwait's most famous landmark—have restaurants, an observation deck, and reservoirs storing 2 million gallons (7.6 million l) of desalinated water.

Human-Environment Interaction Why are scientists looking for ways to increase the amount of freshwater?

Southwest Asia and North Africa use desalination because other freshwater sources are scarce.

Bodies of Freshwater

Only about 3 percent of the earth's total water supply is freshwater, and most is not available for human consumption. More than 2 percent of Earth's total water supply is frozen in glaciers and ice caps. The Antarctic ice cap, for example, contains more freshwater than the rest of the world's regions combined. Another 0.5 percent is found beneath the earth's surface. Lakes, streams, and rivers contain far less than 1 percent of the earth's water.

COOPERATIVE LEARNING ACTIVITY

Observation Have students observe the water cycle in action over a period of time. Ask some students to choose an observation site, such as a local pond or a rain gauge. Other students should outline an observation process and pose questions for observers. A third group should carry out the observations and answer the questions. All groups should work together to share and summarize information gathered from the process.
EE5 Environment and Society: Standard 16

Lakes, Streams, and Rivers

A lake is a body of water completely surrounded by land. Most lakes contain freshwater, although some, such as Southwest Asia's Dead Sea and Utah's Great Salt Lake, are saltwater remnants of ancient seas. Most lakes are found where glacial movement has cut deep valleys and built up dams of glacial soil and rock that held back melting ice-water. North America has thousands of glacial lakes.

Flowing water forms streams and rivers. Melt-water, an overflowing lake, or a spring may be the source, or beginning, of a stream. Streams may combine to form a river, a larger stream of higher volume that follows a channel along a particular course. When rivers join, the major river systems that result may flow for thousands of miles. Rain, runoff, and water from tributaries or branches swell rivers as they flow toward a lake, gulf, sea, or ocean. The place where the river empties into another body of water is its mouth.

Although lakes, streams, and rivers hold only a small part of the earth's water, they meet important needs. Most large urban areas began as settlements along the shores of lakes and rivers, where people would have a constant supply of water.

Groundwater

Groundwater, freshwater which lies beneath the earth's surface, comes from rain and melted snow that filter through the soil and from water that seeps into the ground from lakes and rivers. Wells and springs tap into groundwater and are important sources of freshwater for people in many rural areas and in some cities. An underground porous rock layer often saturated with water in the form of streams is called an aquifer (A•kwuh•fuhr). Aquifers and groundwater are important sources of freshwater.

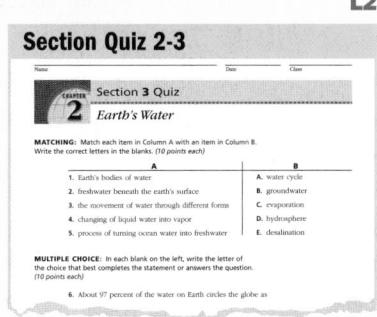

NATIONAL GEOGRAPHIC World Explorer

Geography Skills for Life

Freshwater The Snake River in southern Idaho provides vital freshwater for agriculture.
Human-Environment Interaction How have freshwater sources affected the development of human settlements?

SECTION 3 ASSESSMENT

Checking for Understanding

1. **Define** water cycle, evaporation, condensation, precipitation, desalination, groundwater, aquifer.

2. **Main Ideas** Use a web like the one below to organize information about Earth's water features.

Earth's Water Features

Critical Thinking

3. **Drawing Conclusions** Use your knowledge of the water cycle to explain how droughts might occur.

4. **Making Inferences** Why might salt water someday provide water for drinking, farming, and manufacturing?

5. **Identifying Cause and Effect** How is drinking water contaminated by hazardous substances released on land or into rivers and lakes?

Analyzing Diagrams

6. **Physical Geography** Look at the diagram of the water cycle on page 47. What source of water supplies wells and springs?

Applying Geography

7. **Importance of Rivers** Many large urban areas developed in river basins. Write a description of how a river or rivers contributed to your community's development.

SECTION 3 ASSESSMENT ANSWERS

1. All vocabulary terms are defined in the text.

2. Webs should include information on oceans, lakes, rivers and streams, and groundwater.

3. Warm air might not cool down enough to form clouds and release moisture, or wind patterns or physical features might block rainfall.

4. Earth's limited freshwater resources make desalination of seawater an important future source of freshwater.

5. Hazardous substances may filter into groundwater, polluting wells and aquifers, or enter water systems through rivers and lakes that collect in reservoirs.

6. groundwater

7. **Applying Geography** If students have trouble associating a river with your community, point out indirect connections, such as seacoast or lakeside locations. In irrigated areas, such as Southern California, help students connect their community to its possibly distant water source.

Section Quiz 2-3

Section 3 Quiz
Earth's Water

MATCHING: Match each item in Column A with an item in Column B. Write the correct letters in the blanks. *(10 points each)*

A	B
1. Earth's bodies of water	A. water cycle
2. freshwater beneath the earth's surface	B. groundwater
3. the movement of water through different forms	C. evaporation
4. changing of liquid water into vapor	D. hydrosphere
5. process of turning ocean water into freshwater	E. desalination

MULTIPLE CHOICE: In each blank on the left, write the letter of the choice that best completes the statement or answers the question. *(10 points each)*

6. About 97 percent of the water on Earth circles the globe as

---

NATIONAL GEOGRAPHIC World Explorer

Answer
People need a dependable water supply, so they usually settle near freshwater sources.

More About the Photo
The Snake River originates in the Rocky Mountains. It flows through the deepest river gorge in North America, a chasm that is 1 mile (1.6 km) deep.

Reteach
Have students develop a presentation that explains the water cycle.

Enrich
Have students create travel posters for the world's great bodies of water.

 **CLOSE**

Have students list items that they recycle at home/school, and have them describe how the items are processed and reused. Tell students to compare the recycling process with the water cycle.

Teaching the Skill

Place several objects on a desk or table, and have students compare and contrast them. **Ask: How are these objects alike? In what ways do they differ from one another?** Invite volunteers to suggest categories into which the objects might be organized. Brainstorm a list of characteristics (such as size, color, and so on) that could be used as a basis for comparing and contrasting the objects.

Additional Practice
L1

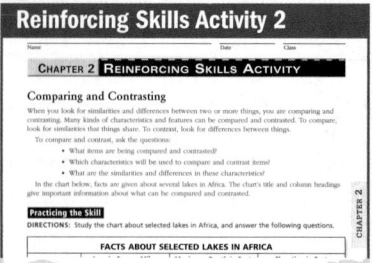

Reinforcing Skills Activity 2

GLENCOE
TECHNOLOGY

Glencoe Skillbuilder Interactive Workbook, Level 2

This interactive CD-ROM reinforces student mastery of essential social studies skills.

CRITICAL THINKING

SkillBuilder

Comparing and Contrasting

Do you have a friend or relative who lives in a different state? You may have talked about the similarities and differences in the places where you each live. If so, you have compared and contrasted those states.

Learning the Skill

Comparing and contrasting help you identify similarities and differences between two or more things. Understanding similarities and differences can help you make better judgments about those things. When you compare, you look for similarities. Things that share at least one common quality can be compared. When you contrast, you look for differences. Things that differ from one another in at least one way can be contrasted.

To compare and contrast, apply the following steps:

- **Decide which items you will compare and contrast.** In the example above, you might compare and contrast the states' populations or their climates.

- **Determine which characteristics you will use to compare and contrast items.** In the example, you might decide to focus on the population sizes or the average temperatures of the two states.

- **Identify the similarities and differences in these characteristics.** In the example, you might compare populations and contrast climates.

- **If possible, identify causes for the similarities and differences.** For example, a state may have a larger population because it has a warmer climate.

Country	Languages	2003 Population (millions)	Government
Argentina	Spanish	36.9	Republic
Australia	English	19.9	Parliamentary democracy
Canada	English, French	31.6	Parliamentary democracy
France	French	59.8	Republic
Japan	Japanese	127.5	Constitutional monarchy
Kenya	English, Swahili	31.6	Republic

Source: 2003 World Population Data Sheet

Practicing the Skill

Study the chart above to answer the following questions.

1. What characteristics are used to compare and contrast the countries in the chart?

2. Which are the two smallest countries in population size? Which country is the largest?

3. How do Argentina and Japan differ in their population sizes? How do they differ in their governments?

4. How are Kenya, Canada, and Australia similar in the languages spoken?

5. Which two countries can you infer probably share similar cultural characteristics? Explain your answer.

Applying the Skill

With a partner, select four U.S. cities to research. Decide on at least three characteristics, such as population or land area, to compare and contrast. Collect the information for each of the three characteristics for each city. Design and draw a chart using your information. Develop three questions based on the chart. Exchange your work with another pair of students to answer the questions.

Go To The Glencoe Skillbuilder Interactive Workbook, Level 2 provides instruction and practice in key social studies skills.

ANSWERS TO PRACTICING THE SKILL

1. language, 2003 population, government
2. Australia and Kenya and Canada (tie); Japan
3. Japan has 90.6 million more people than Argentina. Argentina's government is a republic; Japan's is a constitutional monarchy.

4. English is spoken in all three countries.
5. Australia and Canada share a language and the same form of government; students may infer that both countries had a similar history as British colonies.

CHAPTER 2 SUMMARY & STUDY GUIDE

SECTION 1 — Planet Earth (pp. 33–36)

Terms to Know
- hydrosphere
- lithosphere
- atmosphere
- biosphere
- continental shelf

Key Points
- Planet Earth is located in our solar system.
- The hydrosphere (water), lithosphere (land), and atmosphere (air) make Earth's biosphere suitable for plant and animal life.
- Great contrasts exist in the heights and depths of the earth's surface.

Organizing Your Notes
Use a web like the one below to help you organize information about Planet Earth.

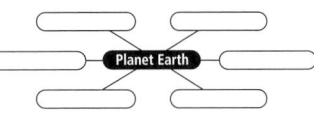
Planet Earth

SECTION 2 — Forces of Change (pp. 37–43)

Terms to Know
- mantle
- continental drift
- magma
- plate tectonics
- subduction
- accretion
- spreading
- fold
- fault
- weathering
- erosion
- loess
- glacier
- moraine

Key Points
- Planet Earth is composed of three layers—the core, the mantle, and the crust.
- Plates that move slowly around the globe produced Earth's largest features—continents, oceans, and mountain ranges.
- Mountains and islands are created by internal forces called subduction and accretion.
- Internal forces, such as earthquakes and volcanoes, also shape the surface of the earth.
- External forces, such as weathering and wind, glacial, and water erosion, also shape the surface of the earth.

Organizing Your Notes
Create a series of flowcharts like the ones below to show which forces or physical processes shape Earth's various and distinctive landforms.

Effects of Earth's Forces

Landform		Shaped by Force(s)
	→	
	→	
	→	
	→	

SECTION 3 — Earth's Water (pp. 46–49)

Terms to Know
- water cycle
- evaporation
- condensation
- precipitation
- desalination
- groundwater
- aquifer

Key Points
- The amount of water on Earth remains fairly constant and moves in the water cycle.
- Water makes up 70 percent of the earth's surface.
- Earth's water features are classified as salt water or freshwater.
- Freshwater is necessary to sustain human life.

Organizing Your Notes
Create an outline using the format below to organize this section's notes.

Earth's Water
I. The Water Cycle
   A. Evaporation
      1.
      2.

Using the Chapter 2 Summary & Study Guide

Use the Chapter 2 Summary & Study Guide to preview, review, condense, or reteach the chapter.

Preview/Review

Vocabulary PuzzleMaker CD-ROM reinforces "Terms to Know."

Interactive Tutor Self-Assessment CD-ROM provides a review of Chapter 2 content.

Condense

Have students read the Chapter 2 Summary & Study Guide.

Chapter 2 Audio Program

Chapter 2 Guided Reading Activities

Reteach

Chapter 2 Reteaching Activities (Spanish also available)

Chapter 2 Reading Essentials and Study Guides

GLENCOE TECHNOLOGY

NATIONAL GEOGRAPHIC
WORLD REGIONS
VIDEO PROGRAM

Unit 1, The World
The following segments enhance the study of this unit:

- **Ocean Journey**
- **Homo Sapiens Sapiens**
- **Goodwill Games**

CHAPTER CULMINATING ACTIVITY

Design an Exhibit Have students work together to create a natural history museum exhibit about the earth's physical features and processes. Displays might include a mobile of the solar system, a model of the earth's structure, an illustration of Earth's internal and external forces of change, or a diagram of the water cycle. Students may work in small groups to develop displays. Encourage students to be accurate and creative and to use a variety of media. An alternative would be to have each student design and make notes for a display. **EE3 Physical Systems: Standard 7**

GLENCOE
TECHNOLOGY

Use *MindJogger Videoquiz* to review the Chapter 2 content.

Reviewing Key Terms

1. atmosphere, lithosphere, hydrosphere, biosphere
2. accretion
3. continental drift
4. aquifer
5. fold
6. condensation
7. Magma
8. precipitation
9. fault
10. plate tectonics
11. evaporation
12. Erosion

Reviewing Facts

SECTION 1

1. terrestrial, gas giants
2. mountains, hills, plateaus, plains

SECTION 2

3. inner core, outer core, mantle, crust
4. movement of plates

SECTION 3

5. water cycle
6. liquid, vapor, clouds, precipitation, surface runoff

Critical Thinking

1. Internal forces cause rising of landforms and can be dramatic and sudden; external forces usually wear away landforms and are usually slow.

Reviewing Key Terms

Write the key term that best completes each of the following sentences. Refer to the Terms to Know in the Summary & Study Guide on page 51.

1. Four parts of the earth's surface are _____, _____, _____, and _____.
2. Underwater trenches are created through the process of _____.
3. The theory that continents are slowly moving is called _____.
4. An _____ is an underground porous rock layer often saturated with water.
5. A _____ is a bend in layers of rock.
6. Water vapor changes into liquid through _____.
7. _____ is molten rock within the earth.
8. Moisture that falls from the clouds is _____.
9. A _____ is a break in the earth's crust.
10. The activity of the earth's moving plates is called _____.
11. Liquid water changes into water vapor through the process of _____.
12. _____ wears away the earth's surface.

Reviewing Facts

SECTION 1

1. What are two types of planets?
2. What are the four major types of landforms found on Earth?

SECTION 2

3. Describe the earth's layers.
4. What produced some of Earth's largest landforms?

SECTION 3

5. What process keeps the amount of Earth's water constant?

6. Describe the forms that water takes throughout the water cycle.

Critical Thinking

1. **Comparing and Contrasting** How do internal and external forces of change affect Earth's surface differently?
2. **Making Inferences** How might the relationship among climate, vegetation, soil, and geology affect distribution of plants and animals in different regions?
3. **Finding and Summarizing the Main Idea** Copy the graphic organizer below, and write the main idea of each section in the outer ovals and the main idea of the chapter in the center oval. Write a summary using appropriate vocabulary.

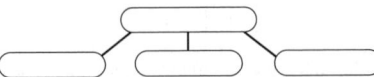

Locating Places
The Earth: Physical Geography

Match the letters on the map with the physical features of Earth. Write your answers on a sheet of paper.

1. Rocky Mountains
2. Isthmus of Panama
3. Gulf of Mexico
4. Andes
5. Himalaya
6. Ural Mountains
7. Arctic Ocean
8. Mediterranean Sea
9. Bay of Bengal
10. Europe

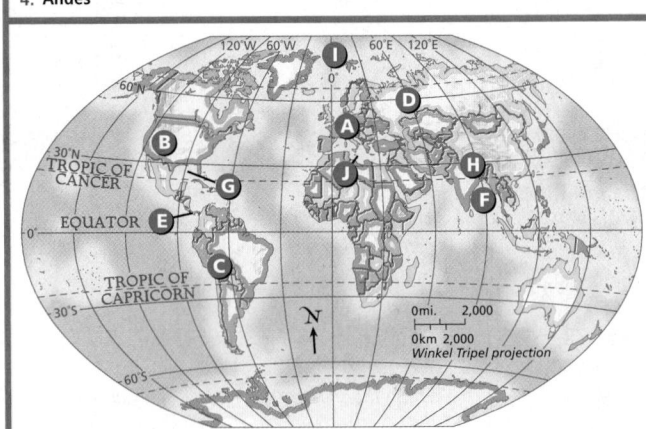

2. Plants and animals tend to be found where freshwater is abundant, soils are fertile, temperatures are moderate or warm, and the landscape is not too rugged or high in elevation.

3. Diagrams should show appropriate terms under the topics: planet Earth, forces of change, and water.

NATIONAL GEOGRAPHIC   **Locating Places**

1. B	3. G	5. H	7. I	9. F
2. E	4. C	6. D	8. J	10. A

52

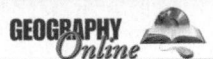

GEOGRAPHY Online

Self-Check Quiz Visit the **Glencoe World Geography** Web site at geography.glencoe.com and click on Self-Check Quizzes—Chapter 2 to prepare for the Chapter Test.

Thinking Like a Geographer

Think about the ways in which geographers classify the earth's physical features. As a geographer, in what other ways might you classify those features? What would your reasons be for classifying features differently? Identify different classification systems that may be helpful to geographers.

Problem-Solving Activity

Problem-Solution Proposal Using the Internet and library resources, learn more about a specific location where freshwater is scarce and the reasons for the scarcity. Then write a proposal identifying the problem and explaining possible solutions for the scarcity. Choose one solution, and give reasons why you think it is the best alternative. Include charts, graphs, or other data that will help readers understand the basis for your conclusions.

GeoJournal

Descriptive Writing Use the journal entries you wrote in your GeoJournal as you read this chapter. Pick one feature, structure, or force of change, and write an expanded description of it. Paint a word picture using concrete, specific details. Consider sights, sounds, smells, and textures associated with the feature. Be sure to organize your description in an order that guides your reader through your composition.

Technology Activity

Using the Internet for Research Choose one of the earth's features, such as mountains, lakes, or rivers. Use the Internet to find specific examples of that feature in different parts of the world. Note the measurement for each and the continent where it is located. Organize your findings in a chart. If, for example, you choose rivers as a feature to research, you might include headings such as longest river, widest river, swiftest river, highest volume river, and so on. Then write a summary, ranking the continents by the sizes of their features.

Standardized Test Practice

Use the information in the chart below to answer the questions. If you have trouble answering the questions, use the process of elimination to narrow your choices.

Notable Volcanic Eruptions

Year	Volcano	Location	Deaths (est.)
1631	Mt. Vesuvius	Italy	4,000
1783	Laki	Iceland	9,350
1883	Krakatau	Indonesia	36,000
1902	Mt. Pelée	Martinique	28,000
1980	Mt. St. Helens	United States	57
1991	Mt. Pinatubo	Philippines	800

1. Based on the information shown in the chart, in which century did the deadliest eruption occur?

A seventeenth
B eighteenth
C nineteenth
D twentieth

2. The chart probably contains data from the past 300+ years because

F more volcanoes erupted then.
G more information is available.
H no volcanoes erupted before 1631.
J eruptions are getting closer together.

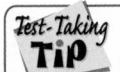

Test-Taking Tip Look at the chart title to see what kind of information is presented. For question 1, find out what categories are being compared. Identify which eruption caused the greatest number of deaths. Then, identify in which century it occurred. Question 2 asks you to infer causes. Note the chart's title, which gives a clue to the answer.

Standardized Test Practice

1. C
2. G

Tested Objectives: analyzing information, making inferences

Additional Practice and Test-Taking Tips

Standardized Test Practice Workbook

CHAPTER BONUS TEST QUESTION

How might space exploration benefit the quality of life on Earth? *(Possible answers: greater knowledge of geologic processes on other planets and moons could help scientists understand the forces that shape Earth; valuable resources may be developed on other planets; observation of Earth from space helps scientists understand processes such as global warming; satellite technology helps predict weather.)*

Thinking Like a Geographer

All suggested classifications should be supported by logical reasons. Students should be able to identify specific ways that classification systems are useful.

Problem-Solving Activity

Proposals should be well organized, demonstrate thorough research and analysis, and include supporting visual aids. Students should make a logical choice of recommended action from among their possible solutions.

GeoJournal

Students' descriptions should provide a vivid picture and follow a logical order.

Technology Activity

Information in the charts should be organized under headings appropriate to the chosen feature. Students' summaries should use sizes of the feature to rank continents.

CHAPTER 3

PLANNING GUIDE

NOTE: The following materials may be used when teaching Chapter 3. Section-level support materials are shown at point-of-use in the margins of the Teacher Wraparound Edition.

TEACHING TRANSPARENCIES

L2 Unit 1 Map Overlay Transparencies

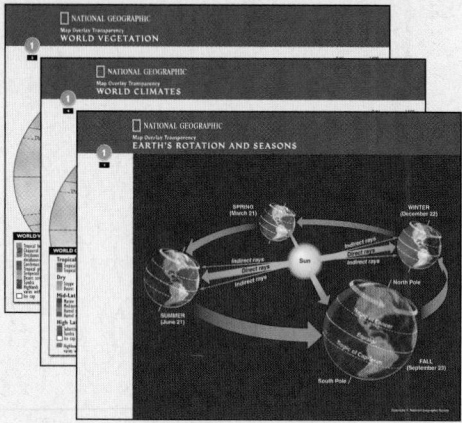

L2 Political Map Transparency 1

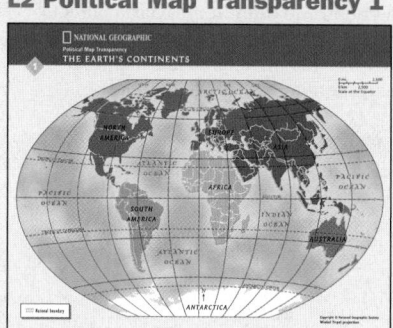

GEOGRAPHIC LITERACY

Focus on Geography Literacy

APPLICATION AND ENRICHMENT

L3 Enrichment Activity 3

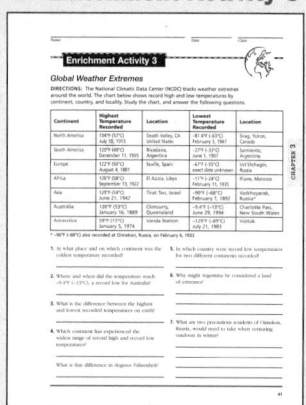

REVIEW AND REINFORCEMENT

L1 Vocabulary Activity 3 L1 Reinforcing Skills Activity 3 L1 Reteaching Activity 3

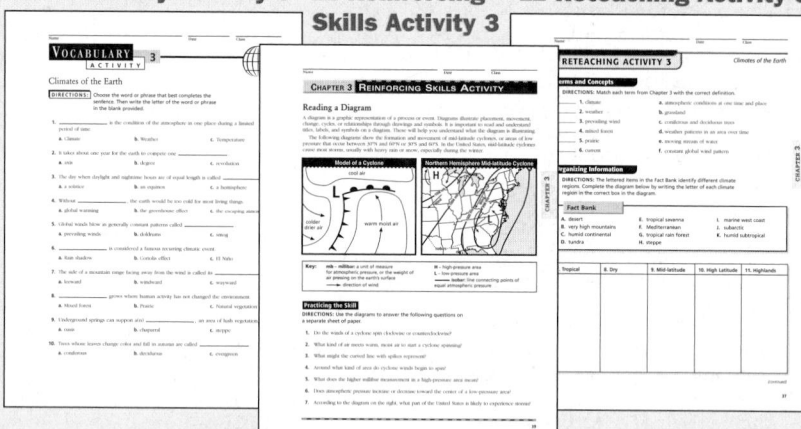

ASSESSMENT

L2 Chapter 3 Test Form A

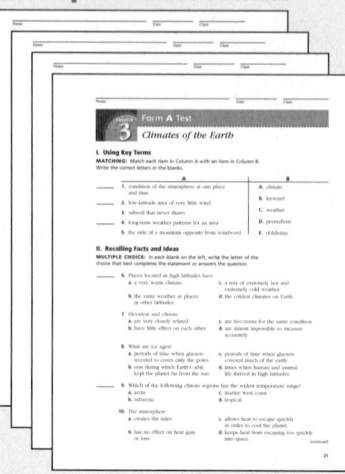

L2 Chapter 3 Test Form B

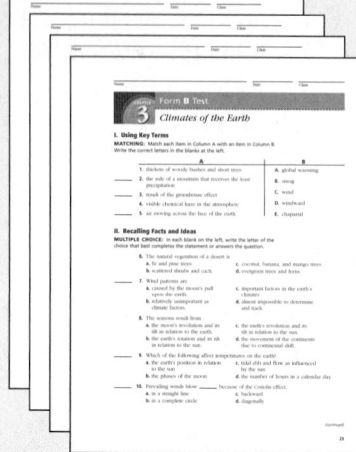

L1/ELL Performance Assessment Activity 3

ExamView® Pro Testmaker

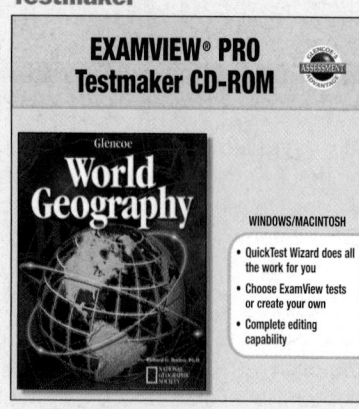

EXAMVIEW® PRO
Testmaker CD-ROM

Glencoe
World Geography

WINDOWS/MACINTOSH

- QuickTest Wizard does all the work for you
- Choose ExamView tests or create your own
- Complete editing capability

SPANISH RESOURCES

The following Spanish language materials are available in the Spanish Resources binder:

- 📁 Spanish Vocabulary Activities
- 📁 Spanish Guided Reading Activities
- 📁 Spanish Reteaching Activities
- 📁 Spanish Summaries
- 📁 Spanish Quizzes and Tests
- 📁 Spanish Reading Essentials and Study Guide

MULTIMEDIA

- World Regions Video
- MindJogger Videoquiz
- Vocabulary PuzzleMaker CD-ROM
- Interactive Tutor Self-Assessment CD-ROM
- ExamView® Pro Testmaker CD-ROM
- Audio Program
- TeacherWorks CD-ROM
- Interactive Student Edition CD-ROM
- Glencoe Skillbuilder Interactive Workbook CD-ROM, Level 2
- Presentation Plus! CD-ROM

Timesaving Tools

TeacherWorks™   All-In-One Planner and Resource Center

- **Interactive Teacher Edition** Access your Teacher Wraparound Edition and your classroom resources with a few easy clicks.

- **Interactive Lesson Planner** Planning has never been easier! Organize your week, month, semester, or year with all the lesson helps you need to make teaching creative, timely, and relevant.

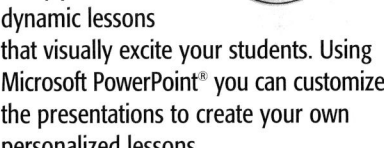

Use Glencoe's **Presentation Plus!** multimedia teacher tool to easily present dynamic lessons that visually excite your students. Using Microsoft PowerPoint® you can customize the presentations to create your own personalized lessons.

GEOGRAPHY Online

Use our Web site for additional resources. All essential content is covered in the Student Edition.

You and your students can visit geography.glencoe.com, the Web site companion to *Glencoe World Geography*. This innovative integration of electronic and print media offers your students a wealth of opportunities. The student text directs students to the Web site for the following options:

- **Chapter Overviews**
- **Student Activities**
- **Self-Check Quizzes**
- **Textbook Updates**

Answers are provided for you in the "Web Activity Lesson Plan." Additional Web resources and Interactive Tutor puzzles are also available.

▶ Additional Glencoe Teacher Support

- Teaching Strategies for the Geography Classroom (including Block Scheduling Pacing Guides)
- Graphic Organizer Transparencies Strategies and Activities
- Outline Map Resource Book
- Reading in the Content Area

PLANNING GUIDE

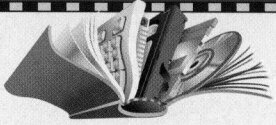

SECTION RESOURCES

Daily Objectives	Reproducible Resources	Multimedia Resources

SECTION 1 Earth-Sun Relationships

1. Describe how Earth's position in relation to the sun affects temperatures on Earth.
2. Explain how Earth's rotation causes day and night.
3. Discuss the relationship of Earth to the sun during each season.
4. Identify how global warming might affect Earth's air, land, and water.

- Reproducible Lesson Plan 3-1
- Daily Lecture Notes 3-1
- Guided Reading Activity 3-1*
- Reading Essentials and Study Guide 3-1*
- Section Quiz 3-1*

- Daily Focus Skills Transparency 3-1
- Political Map Transparency 1
- Unit 1 Map Overlay Transparencies
- Interactive Tutor Self-Assessment CD-ROM
- ExamView® Pro Testmaker CD-ROM*
- Presentation Plus! CD-ROM

SECTION 2 Factors Affecting Climate

1. Discuss how latitude and elevation affect climate.
2. Describe the role wind patterns and ocean currents play in Earth's climates.
3. Explain how landforms and climate patterns influence each other.

- Reproducible Lesson Plan 3-2
- Daily Lecture Notes 3-2
- Guided Reading Activity 3-2*
- Reading Essentials and Study Guide 3-2*
- Section Quiz 3-2*

- Daily Focus Skills Transparency 3-2
- Unit 1 Map Overlay Transparencies
- Interactive Tutor Self-Assessment CD-ROM
- ExamView® Pro Testmaker CD-ROM*
- Presentation Plus! CD-ROM

SECTION 3 World Climate Patterns

1. Identify the climate regions of the world.
2. Describe each climate region's characteristic vegetation.
3. Examine how recurring phenomena influence climate patterns.

- Reproducible Lesson Plan 3-3
- Vocabulary Activity 3*
- Daily Lecture Notes 3-3
- Guided Reading Activity 3-3*
- Reading Essentials and Study Guide 3-3*
- Reteaching Activity 3*
- Reinforcing Skills Activity 3
- Section Quiz 3-3*

- Daily Focus Skills Transparency 3-3
- Unit 1 Map Overlay Transparencies
- Vocabulary PuzzleMaker CD-ROM
- Interactive Tutor Self-Assessment CD-ROM
- ExamView® Pro Testmaker CD–ROM*
- Presentation Plus! CD-ROM

Blackline Master   Software   Videocassette   *Also available in Spanish*

Transparency   CD-ROM   DVD

00:00 OUT OF TIME? Assign the Chapter 3 **Reading Essentials and Study Guide.**

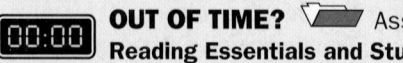

Block Schedule

Activities that are particularly suited to use within the block scheduling framework are identified throughout this chapter by the following designation:

KEY TO ABILITY LEVELS

Teaching strategies have been coded for various learning styles and abilities.

L1   **BASIC** activities for all students

L2   **AVERAGE** activities for average to above-average students

L3   **CHALLENGING** activities for above-average students

ELL   **ENGLISH LANGUAGE LEARNER** activities

Teacher to Teacher

Roger Liska
Stagg High School
Palos Hills, IL

Exploring Climate Patterns

To give students a better understanding of the factors affecting climate, have them research and compare the climates of specific locations. Each student first chooses one location anywhere in the world. Using the Internet, students research the location's climate, noting temperatures, precipitation, and vegetation. They also gather as much information as possible on the factors—latitude, elevation, wind patterns, ocean currents, landforms— that affect the location's climate.

Then ask them to choose a location in a different country, which shares the same latitude or the same elevation as the first location. Students complete the same climate research on the second location, noting any similarities and differences between the two places. Students then write a paragraph comparing and contrasting the climates as well as describing the factors which cause the differences.

NATIONAL GEOGRAPHIC — TEACHER'S CORNER

Index to National Geographic Magazine:

The following articles may be used for research relating to this chapter:

- "Arctic Submarine," by Glenn Hodges, March 2000.
- "El Niño/La Niña," by Curt Suplee, March 1999.

National Geographic Society Products:

To order the following products for use with this chapter, call National Geographic Society at 1-800-368-2728.

- *Old-Growth Forest: An Ecosystem* (Video)
- *A Swamp Ecosystem* (Video)
- *Weather: Come Rain, Come Shine* (Video)
- *Physical Geography of the Continents Series* (Video)
- *Ancient Forests* (Video)
- *Physical Earth* (Map)

NGS ONLINE

Access National Geographic's Web site for current events, activities, links, interactive features, and archives.
www.nationalgeographic.com

Meeting National Standards

Geography For Life

The following standards are highlighted in Chapter 3:

Section 1   EE2 Places and Regions: Standard 4
EE3 Physical Systems: Standard 7
EE5 Environment and Society: Standard 14
EE6 The Uses of Geography: Standard 18

Section 2   EE4 Human Systems: Standards 10, 11
EE5 Environment and Society: Standard 15
EE6 The Uses of Geography: Standard 18

Section 3   EE3 Physical Systems: Standard 8
EE5 Environment and Society: Standard 14

Local Objectives

_____

_____

MEETING SPECIAL NEEDS

In addition to the Differentiated Instruction strategies found in each section, the following resources are also suitable for your special needs students:

- *ExamView® Pro Testmaker CD-ROM* allows teachers to tailor tests by reducing answer choices.
- The *Audio Program* includes the entire narrative of the student edition so that less-proficient readers can listen to the words as they read them.
- The *Reading Essentials and Study Guide* provides the same content as the student edition but is written two grade levels below the textbook.
- *Guided Reading Activities* give less-proficient readers point-by-point instructions to increase comprehension as they read each textbook section.
- *Enrichment Activities* include a stimulating collection of readings and activities for gifted and talented students.

Chapter Objectives

1. Explain the effects of the Earth-sun relationship on life on Earth.

2. Identify the factors that contribute to Earth's climates.

3. Describe the major climate patterns found on Earth.

GLENCOE TECHNOLOGY

Use *MindJogger Videoquiz* to preview the Chapter 3 content.

GeoJournal

For access to additional information on the climates of the earth, go to www.nationalgeographic.com (See Teacher pages in front for strategies for using journals in the geography classroom.)

GEOGRAPHY Online

Introduce students to chapter content and key terms by having them access **Chapter Overview 3** at geography.glencoe.com

FOLDABLES
Study Organizer

Dinah Zike's Foldables are three-dimensional, interactive graphic organizers that help students practice basic writing skills, review key vocabulary terms, and identify main ideas. Have students complete the Foldable activity in the **Dinah Zike's Reading and Study Skills Foldables** booklet.

CHAPTER 3
Climates of the Earth

GeoJournal

As you read this chapter, note factors that affect climate. Then write a description of the climate in your community. List three factors that contribute to climate, and sketch a landscape showing one kind of common weather in this climate.

GEOGRAPHY Online

Chapter Overview Visit the **Glencoe World Geography** Web site at geography.glencoe.com and click on Chapter Overviews—Chapter 3 to preview information about Earth's climates.

ABOUT THE PHOTO

Visual Instruction Deserts in Namibia, the Namib and the Kalahari, are often what people think of as true deserts—expanses of sand, whipped into towering dunes by desert winds. Often photographed at sunset when the dunes vary from pale apricot to vivid red and orange, the dunes in the *Sossusviei* area, for example, provide a rich backdrop for the horizontal oases typical in this region. During rainy seasons, horizontal oases are created by rivers that flow into pans where the water slowly evaporates. Few rivers in Namibia ever reach the sea. **EE2 Places and Regions: Standard 4** **EE3 Physical Systems: Standard 7**

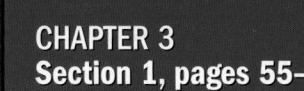
Guide to Reading

Consider What You Know

News reports sometimes feature unusual events such as solar eclipses or solar flares, intense bursts of energy from the sun's surface. In what ways does the sun affect human activities?

Reading Strategy

Categorizing Complete a graphic organizer similar to the one below by listing the major characteristics of the summer and winter solstices.

Northern Hemisphere

Summer Solstice	Winter Solstice
•	•
•	•
•	•

Read to Find Out

• How does Earth's position in relation to the sun affect temperatures on Earth?

• How does Earth's rotation cause day and night?

• What is Earth's position in relation to the sun during each season?

• How might global warming affect Earth's air, land, and water?

Terms to Know

• weather
• climate
• axis
• temperature
• revolution
• equinox
• solstice
• greenhouse effect
• global warming

Places to Locate

• Tropic of Cancer
• Tropic of Capricorn

◀ *Flamingoes enjoy an oasis at the foot of sand dunes in Namibia.*

Earth-Sun Relationships

NATIONAL GEOGRAPHIC

A Geographic View

Our Home Star

Through a small occulting telescope [equipped to block the sun's surface from view] . . . I stared at the dark-ened face of the sun, ringed by its glowing, gauzy corona. From that blazing disk high in the Hawaiian sky comes the endless power that drives and rules all life on earth: its plant growth and the food chains of all its creatures; the winds, rains, and churning weather of the planet; the ocean currents, forests, prairies, and deserts.

Sunset at the beach

—Samuel W. Matthews, "Under the Sun: Is Our World Warming?"
National Geographic, *October 1990*

From atop the Mauna Loa Observatory on the island of Hawaii, scientists gather data about changes in the earth's atmosphere. Their research reveals information about the dynamic rela-tionships between the earth and the sun, which influence all life on Earth. In this section you will explore how earth-sun relationships affect climate.

Climate and Weather

Climate is often confused with weather, which is a short-term aspect of climate. **Weather** is the condition of the atmosphere in one place during a limited period of time. When people look out the window or watch the news to see whether they need umbrellas or sunscreen, they are checking the weather. **Climate** is the term for the weather patterns that an area typically experiences over a long period of time. People who live in Seattle, Washington, for example, frequently use umbrellas

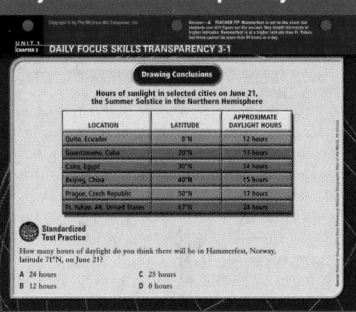

① FOCUS

Section Overview

This section discusses the relationship between Earth and the sun, and the ways in which that relationship affects Earth's days, seasons, and climates.

BELLRINGER
Skillbuilder Activity

🖐 Project transparency and have students answer questions.

🗂 Available as blackline master.

Daily Focus Skills Transparency 3-1

Guide to Reading

Consider What You Know
Answers *Answers may include providing daylight and affecting temperature and seasons.*

Reading Strategy
Answers summer solstice: *summer in Northern Hemisphere, direct sun rays along Tropic of Cancer, approximately June 21, longest day of sunlight;* winter solstice: *winter in Northern Hemisphere, direct sun rays along Tropic of Capricorn, approximately December 22, shortest day of sunlight*

Preteaching Vocabulary
Direct students to find the mean-ings of *equinox* and *solstice* in a dictionary. Ask them how these meanings relate to the meanings of the Latin root words.

RESOURCE MANAGER

🗂 **Reproducible Masters**
• Reproducible Lesson Plan 3-1
• Daily Lecture Notes 3-1
• Guided Reading Activity 3-1
• Reading Essentials and Study Guide 3-1
• Section Quiz 3-1

✒ **Transparencies**
• Daily Focus Skills Transparency 3-1
• Political Map Transparency 1
• Unit 1 Map Overlay Transparencies

Multimedia
💿 Interactive Tutor Self-Assessment CD-ROM
💿 ExamView® Pro Testmaker CD-ROM
💿 Presentation Plus! CD-ROM

② TEACH

NATIONAL GEOGRAPHIC World Explorer

Answer
Time: weather is short term; climate occurs over long periods of time.

More About the Photo
Lightning is an exchange of electrons between clouds or between a cloud and the earth. The electrons' path is about an inch wide, giving lightning its "bolt" shape.

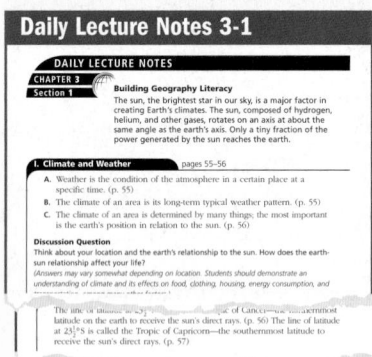

Daily Lecture Notes 3-1

L1/ELL

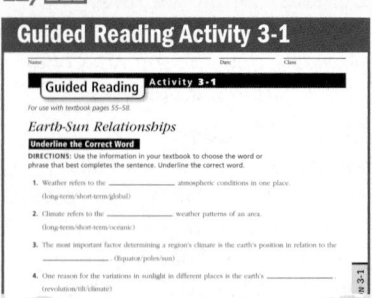

Guided Reading Activity 3-1

---

because of the rainy, wet climate. In contrast, people who live in the dry, desert climate of Arizona must protect themselves from the sun.

Whether the climate in a particular region is cool and wet or hot and dry is determined by many factors, the most important of which is the earth's position in relation to the sun.

The sun's heat and light reach the earth as warmth and sunlight, but they do not reach all parts of the earth at the same time or with the same intensity.

Earth's Tilt and Rotation

Earth's tilt is one reason for variations in sunlight. The earth's **axis**—an imaginary line running from the North Pole to the South Pole through the planet's center—is currently tilted at an angle of about $23\frac{1}{2}°$. Because of the tilt of this axis, not all places on the planet receive the same amount of direct sunlight at the same time.

For this reason the angle of tilt affects the **temperature**—the measure of how hot or cold a place is. Areas that receive a large amount of direct sunlight have warmer temperatures than places that receive little direct sunlight. Temperature is usually measured in degrees on a set scale. The most common scales for measuring air temperature are Fahrenheit (°F) and Celsius (°C).

Whether or not a particular place on Earth receives light also depends on the side of the planet that is facing the sun. Earth rotates on its axis, making one complete rotation every 24 hours. Rotating from west to east, the earth turns first one hemisphere and then the other toward the sun, alternating between the light of day and the darkness of night.

Earth's Revolution

While planet Earth is rotating on its axis, it also is traveling in an orbit around the sun, our nearest star. It takes the earth a few hours more than 365 days—1 year—to complete one **revolution**, or trip around the sun.

NATIONAL GEOGRAPHIC World Explorer

Geography Skills for Life
- - - - - - - - - - - **Arizona Lightning**
Lightning and thunder are related weather events that result from the powerful air currents of thunderstorms during the warm-weather months.
Place What factor distinguishes weather from climate?

The earth's revolution and its tilt cause changes in the angle and amount of sunlight that reach different locations on the planet. These changes follow a regular progression known as the seasons. During the course of a year, people on most parts of the earth experience distinct differences in the length of days and the daily temperature as the seasons change.

The seasons are reversed north and south of the Equator. When it is spring in the Northern Hemisphere, it is fall in the Southern Hemisphere. When it is winter in the Southern Hemisphere, it is summer in the Northern Hemisphere. Around March 21, the sun's rays fall directly on the Equator. This day is called an **equinox** (meaning "equal night") because daylight and nighttime hours are equal. In the Northern Hemisphere, the day on which this equinox falls marks the beginning of spring.

The Tropics of Cancer and Capricorn

As the earth continues its revolution around the sun, it moves so that eventually the sun's rays directly strike the latitude $23\frac{1}{2}°$N. This latitude is known as the **Tropic of Cancer**—the northernmost point on the earth to receive the direct rays of the sun. These direct rays reach the Tropic of Cancer about June 21, bringing the Northern Hemisphere

---

DIFFERENTIATED INSTRUCTION

At-Risk Students For students with attention deficit disorder, it is helpful to divide content into manageable segments. Set limited goals for each subsection of the text to help students focus their reading and stay on task. For example, have students find the highlighted key terms in each section and restate the definitions in their own words.
🌐 EE6 The Uses of Geography: Standard 18
📂 Refer to *Inclusion for the Social Studies Classroom Strategies and Activities.*

its longest day of sunlight. This date, known as the summer solstice, marks the beginning of summer in the Northern Hemisphere.

By about September 23, the earth has moved so that the sun's rays directly strike the Equator again. This equinox marks the beginning of fall in the Northern Hemisphere. Gradually the sun's direct rays strike farther south, reaching their southernmost latitude—$23\frac{1}{2}°$S, or the **Tropic of Capricorn**—about December 22. The winter solstice is the day of shortest daylight in the Northern Hemisphere, beginning the season of winter. This cycle repeats itself each year as the earth revolves around the sun.

The Poles

The amount of sunlight at the Poles varies most dramatically as the earth's revolution and tilt cause the changing seasons. For six months of the year, one Pole is tilted toward the sun and receives continuous sunlight, while the other Pole is tilted away from the sun and receives little to no sunlight. An Arctic explorer describes the surreal quality of the winter day:

> 66 *The winter sun had completely disappeared below the horizon, and the 'days' were now only a few hours long. . . . I saw the Arctic in a whole new way, with its twilight days and auroral nights.* 99
> Keith Nyitray, "Alone Across the Arctic Crown," *National Geographic*, April 1993

At the North Pole, the sun never sets from about March 20 to September 23. At the South Pole, continuous daylight lasts from about September 23 to March 20. The tilt of the earth's axis as it revolves around the sun causes this natural phenomenon, known as the midnight sun. The occurrence of the

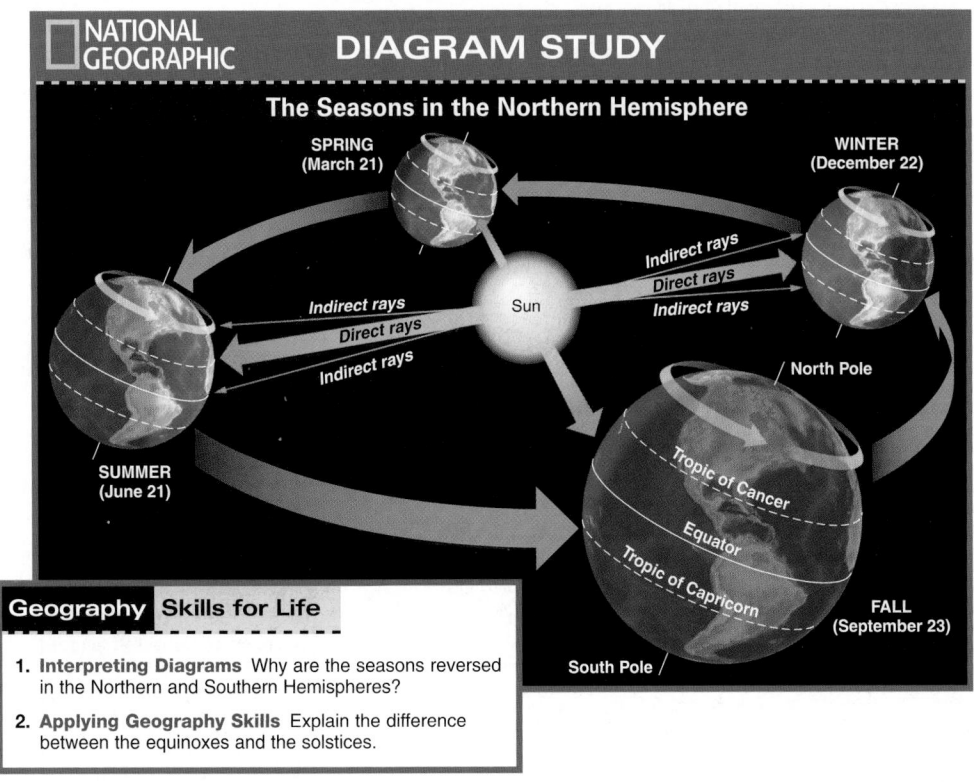

NATIONAL GEOGRAPHIC **DIAGRAM STUDY**

The Seasons in the Northern Hemisphere

SPRING (March 21)

WINTER (December 22)

Indirect rays
Direct rays
Indirect rays

Indirect rays
Direct rays
Indirect rays

Sun

North Pole

SUMMER (June 21)

Tropic of Cancer
Equator
Tropic of Capricorn

FALL (September 23)

South Pole

Geography Skills for Life

1. **Interpreting Diagrams** Why are the seasons reversed in the Northern and Southern Hemispheres?

2. **Applying Geography Skills** Explain the difference between the equinoxes and the solstices.

L1/ELL

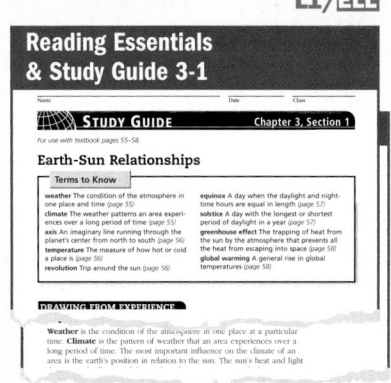

Reading Essentials & Study Guide 3-1

Name _____ Date _____ Class _____

🌐 **STUDY GUIDE** Chapter 3, Section 1

For use with textbook pages 55–58

Earth-Sun Relationships

Terms to Know

weather The condition of the atmosphere in one place and time *(page 55)*
climate The weather patterns an area experiences over a long period of time *(page 55)*
axis An imaginary line running through the planet's center from north to south *(page 56)*
temperature The measure of how hot or cold a place is *(page 56)*
revolution Trip around the sun *(page 56)*

equinox A day when the daylight and night-time hours are equal in length *(page 57)*
solstice A day with the longest or shortest period of daylight in a year *(page 57)*
greenhouse effect The trapping of heat from the sun by the atmosphere that prevents all the heat from escaping into space *(page 58)*
global warming A general rise in global temperatures *(page 58)*

DRAWING FROM EXPERIENCE

Weather is the condition of the atmosphere in one place at a particular time. **Climate** is the pattern of weather that an area experiences over a long period of time. The most important influence on the climate of an area is the earth's position in relation to the sun. The sun's heat and light

NATIONAL GEOGRAPHIC **DIAGRAM STUDY**

Answers

1. *Because of Earth's tilt, the sun's rays strike these hemispheres at different times of the year.*

2. *At the equinoxes, the sun's rays directly strike the Equator; at the solstices, the sun's rays directly strike the Tropic of Cancer or the Tropic of Capricorn.*

Skills Practice

Location What keeps the sun's rays from striking the Poles directly? *(Earth's tilt and orbit keep the Poles from receiving direct sunlight.)*

**ASSESS**

Assign Section 1 Assessment as homework or as an in-class activity.

⊕ Have students use **Interactive Tutor Self-Assessment CD-ROM**.

COOPERATIVE LEARNING ACTIVITY

Model the Greenhouse Effect Have students work in groups to design mini-greenhouses. Provide materials such as egg cartons, plastic wrap, clear plastic boxes, wooden pallets, and sheets of glass, but allow each group to design and construct its own greenhouse. Students may research greenhouses in gardening books or on the Internet. Have each group fill its completed greenhouse with potting soil and plant lima beans, place their greenhouses in direct sunlight and monitor the progress of their plants. After a designated time, have the class evaluate the success of each greenhouse design. 📦

🌐 **EE5 Environment and Society: Standard 14**

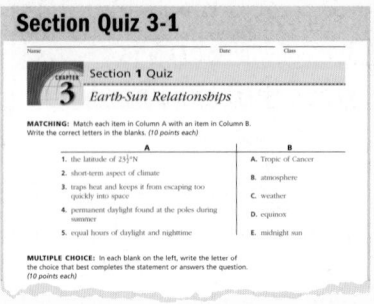

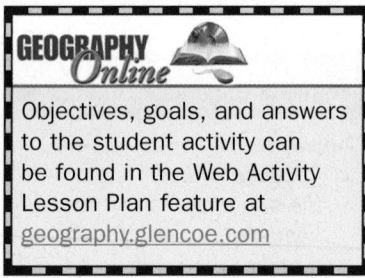

Objectives, goals, and answers to the student activity can be found in the Web Activity Lesson Plan feature at geography.glencoe.com

Reteach

Read the section subheads aloud, and have students name two key facts or important details for each.

Enrich

Play portions of Vivaldi's *Four Seasons* for students, and have them draw or write about their impressions.

4 CLOSE

Ask students to imagine they are scientists presenting papers on Earth-sun relationships. Have them write short essays or Geo-Journal entries about how annual changes in Earth-sun relationships affect weather phenomena and climate.

---

midnight sun goes almost unnoticed in sparsely populated Antarctica. Parts of northern North America (including Alaska) and northern Europe in the Arctic, however, have become popular tourist destinations as "lands of the midnight sun."

The Greenhouse Effect

Even on the sunniest days in the warmest climates, only part of the sun's radiation passes through the earth's atmosphere. The atmosphere reflects some radiation back into space. Enough radiation, however, reaches the earth to warm the air, land, and water.

Because the atmosphere traps some heat and keeps it from escaping back into space too quickly, Earth's atmosphere is like the glass in a greenhouse—it traps the sun's warmth for growing plants even in cold weather. Without this greenhouse effect, the earth would be too cold for most living things. The diagram on page 70 shows the greenhouse effect.

In order to support plant growth, conditions in a greenhouse must be regulated. If too much heat escapes, the plants will freeze. If too much heat is trapped, the plants will wilt or dry out.

The greenhouse effect of Earth's atmosphere follows some of the same general rules. Normally, the atmosphere provides just the right amount of insulation to promote life on the planet. The 50 percent of the sun's radiation that reaches the earth is converted into infrared radiation, or heat. Clouds and greenhouse gases—atmospheric components such as water vapor and carbon dioxide (CO_2)—absorb the heat reflected by the earth and radiate it back again so that a balance is created.

Many scientists, however, claim that in recent decades a rise in atmospheric CO_2 levels has coincided with a general rise in global temperatures. This trend—known as global warming—is believed to be caused in part by human activities, such as the burning of coal, oil, and natural gas. As more fossil fuels are burned, greenhouse gases enter the atmosphere and trap more heat.

Using computer models, some scientists predict that global warming will make weather patterns more extreme. Water, for example, will evaporate more rapidly from oceans, increasing humidity and rainfall generally. Rapid water evaporation from soil, however, will cause land to dry out more quickly between rains. Some areas may even become drier than before.

Scientists do not all agree on the nature of global warming and its effects. Some claim that a natural cycle, not human activity, is causing rising temperatures. Others claim that the evidence for global warming is inconclusive and that it is too early to forecast future effects.

Student Web Activity Visit the **Glencoe World Geography** Web site at geography.glencoe.com and click on Student Web Activities—Chapter 3 for an activity about global warming.

SECTION 1 ASSESSMENT

Checking for Understanding

1. **Define** weather, climate, axis, temperature, revolution, equinox, solstice, greenhouse effect, global warming.

2. **Main Ideas** On a chart, list characteristics of the earth-sun relationship and describe their effects on climate.

Earth-Sun Relationships	Effects on Climate

Critical Thinking

3. **Comparing and Contrasting** What differences in the weather would you expect in Alaska and in Florida? Explain.

4. **Drawing Conclusions** What effects does the earth's tilt on its axis have on your daily life?

5. **Analyzing Information** What would you pack if you were visiting Argentina in December?

Analyzing Diagrams

6. **Location** Study the diagram of the seasons on page 57. In what months do the sun's rays strike the Equator directly? The Tropics of Cancer and Capricorn?

Applying Geography

7. **Effects of Global Warming** Review the text in Section 1 about global warming. In what ways might agriculture be affected? Explain.

SECTION 1 ASSESSMENT ANSWERS

1. All vocabulary terms are defined in the text.

2. Entries should include the effects of Earth's tilt, rotation, and revolution, and of the greenhouse effect.

3. Alaska—mostly cold, snowy; Florida—mostly warm, humid; differences caused primarily by location (latitude)

4. The tilt causes temperature variations and affects any daily activities that are dependent on weather or temperature (choice of clothing, outdoor activities, indoor heating or cooling, and so on).

5. clothing for warm weather (in low elevations), warm clothing for mountains or extreme southern latitudes

6. March and September; December or June

7. **Applying Geography** agriculture possible in some places where climate does not now permit it; flooding of coastal agricultural lands; drought caused by higher temperatures

Guide to Reading

Consider What You Know

You are familiar with the climate of the area where you live, such as the usual weather and temperature range for each season. What geographic factors do you think affect your climate?

Reading Strategy

Organizing As you read about factors that affect Earth's climate, create a web diagram similar to the one below by listing factors that cause both winds and ocean currents.

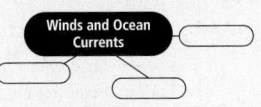

Read to Find Out

- How do latitude and elevation affect climate?
- What role do wind patterns and ocean currents play in Earth's climates?
- How do landforms and climate patterns influence each other?

Terms to Know

- prevailing wind
- Coriolis effect
- doldrums
- current
- El Niño
- windward
- leeward
- rain shadow

Places to Locate

- low latitudes
- high latitudes
- Arctic Circle
- Antarctic Circle
- mid-latitudes

Factors Affecting Climate

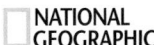

NATIONAL GEOGRAPHIC

A Geographic View

The Stormy Sea

As I survey the wreckage [from my yacht]—broken steering wheel, patched sails, ruined winches, life rails ripped away by bounding seas . . . I can see it's been a harrowing 4,600 miles since the start [of this leg of the Whitbread race] in Cape Town, South Africa. For eight of the twelve men aboard, including Paul Cayard, the skipper, the run east has been their first encounter with the ocean latitudes known as the roaring forties and furious fifties, where gales blow year-round and seas build to towering peaks, "the liquid Himalayas," as one Kiwi [New Zealand] broadcaster calls them.

—*Angus Phillips, "The Whitbread—Race Into Danger,"* National Geographic, *May 1998*

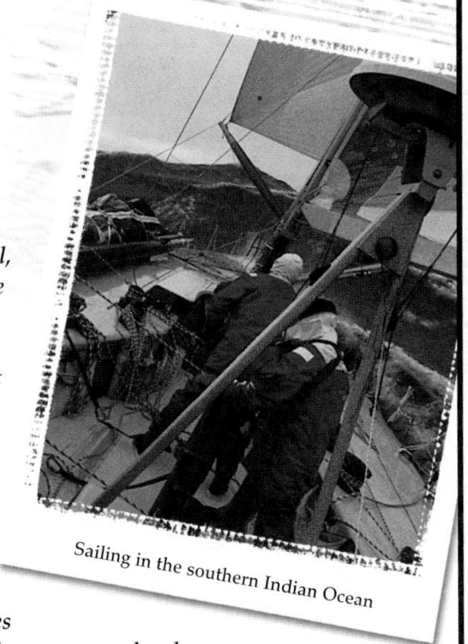

Sailing in the southern Indian Ocean

Sailing in the Whitbread race can be frightening. The part of this journey from South Africa to Australia is dangerous because of high winds and strong ocean currents at these latitudes. In this section you will learn how latitude, wind and water patterns, and landforms combine with the earth-sun relationship to influence Earth's climates.

Latitude and Climate

The influence of latitude on climate is part of the earth-sun relationship. During the earth's annual revolution around the sun, the sun's direct rays fall upon the planet in a regular pattern. This pattern can be

1 FOCUS

Section Overview

This section discusses the factors that affect Earth's climates: latitude, elevation, wind patterns, ocean currents, and landforms.

BELLRINGER
Skillbuilder Activity

Project transparency and have students answer questions.

Available as blackline master.

Daily Focus Skills Transparency 3-2

Guide to Reading

Consider What You Know

Answers *Answers may include location, landforms, wind, and water.*

Reading Strategy

Answers *changes in air pressure, differences in water temperature, Earth's rotation*

Preteaching Vocabulary

Have students make vocabulary flashcards, predicting each term's definition. Have students revise definitions as they read.

RESOURCE MANAGER

Reproducible Masters

- Reproducible Lesson Plan 3-2
- Daily Lecture Notes 3-2
- Guided Reading Activity 3-2
- Reading Essentials and Study Guide 3-2
- Section Quiz 3-2

Transparencies

- Daily Focus Skills Transparency 3-2
- Unit 1 Map Overlay Transparencies

Multimedia

- Interactive Tutor Self-Assessment CD-ROM
- ExamView® Pro Testmaker CD-ROM
- Presentation Plus! CD-ROM

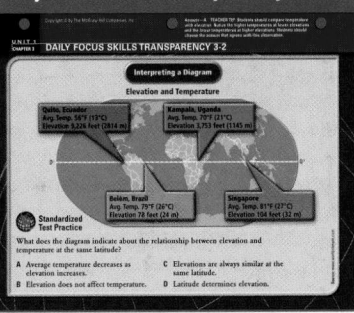

TEACH

L2 Climate Riddles

Ask: Where do I live if my home is near the Equator but covered with ice and snow year-round? *(on top of a high mountain)* Challenge students to come up with similar climate riddles.

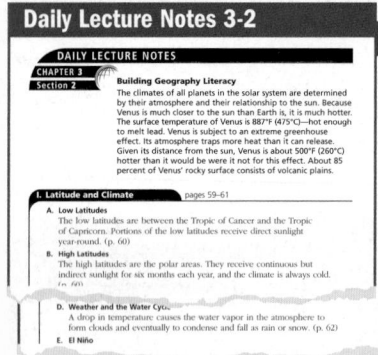

Daily Lecture Notes 3-2

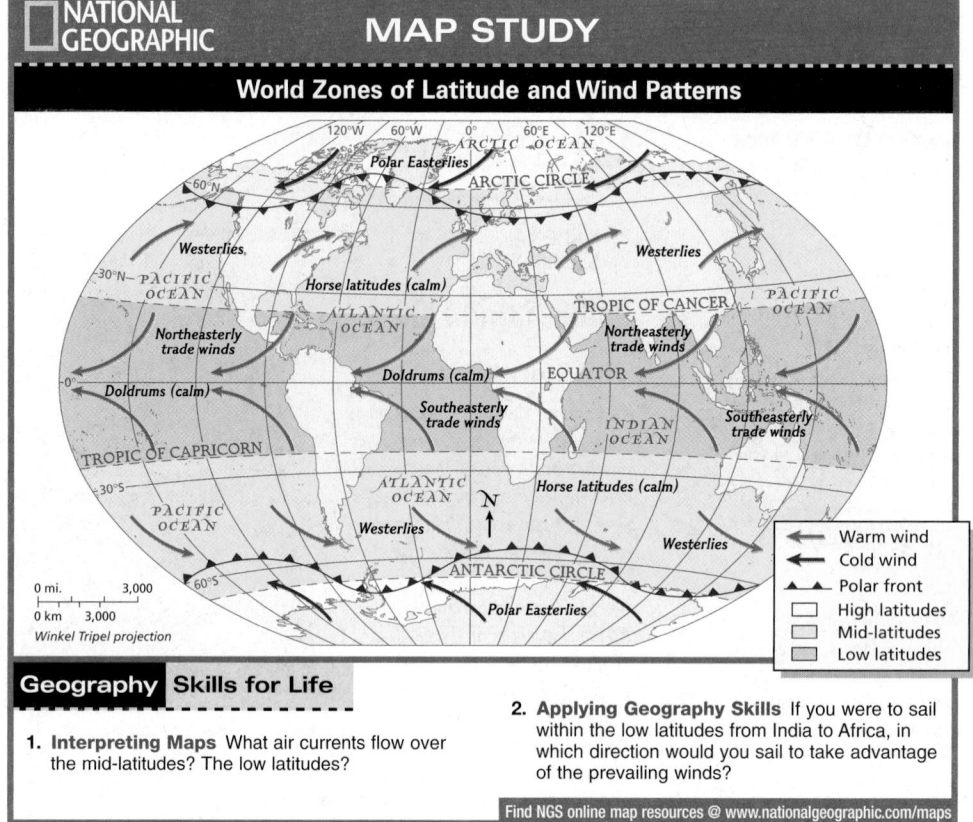

NATIONAL GEOGRAPHIC — **MAP STUDY**

World Zones of Latitude and Wind Patterns

Winkel Tripel projection

Legend:
- Warm wind
- Cold wind
- Polar front
- High latitudes
- Mid-latitudes
- Low latitudes

Geography | Skills for Life

1. Interpreting Maps What air currents flow over the mid-latitudes? The low latitudes?

2. Applying Geography Skills If you were to sail within the low latitudes from India to Africa, in which direction would you sail to take advantage of the prevailing winds?

Find NGS online map resources @ www.nationalgeographic.com/maps

---

correlated with bands, or zones, of latitude to describe climate regions. Within each latitude zone, the climate follows general patterns.

Low Latitudes

Between the Tropic of Cancer and the Tropic of Capricorn is a zone known as the **low latitudes**. This zone includes the Equator. Portions of the low latitudes receive the direct rays of the sun year-round. Places located in the low latitudes have warm to hot climates. Because of the latitudes that form its boundaries, this zone is called the Tropics.

High Latitudes

The earth's polar areas are called the **high latitudes**. When either the Northern or the Southern Hemisphere is tilted toward the sun, its polar area receives continuous, but indirect, sunlight. From about March 20 to about September 23, the polar area north of the **Arctic Circle** (latitude 66°N) experiences continuous daylight or twilight. The polar area south of the **Antarctic Circle** (latitude 66°S) experiences continuous daylight or twilight for the other six months of the year.

Mid-Latitudes

The most variable weather on Earth is found in the **mid-latitudes** between the Tropic of Cancer and the Arctic Circle in the Northern Hemisphere and between the Tropic of Capricorn and the Antarctic Circle in the Southern Hemisphere. In summer the mid-latitudes receive warm masses of air from the Tropics. In winter, cold masses of air move into the mid-latitudes from the high latitudes. The

---

DIFFERENTIATED INSTRUCTION

Auditory/Musical Have students create wind chimes. Students may work independently or in groups to research the kinds of material and forms of construction used around the world to make wind chimes. Have students hang their completed wind chimes outdoors and listen for the differences in tone that accompany various wind speeds and patterns.

🌐 **EE4 Human Systems: Standard 10**

📁 Refer to *Inclusion for the Social Studies Classroom Strategies and Activities.*

NATIONAL GEOGRAPHIC — MAP STUDY

World Ocean Currents

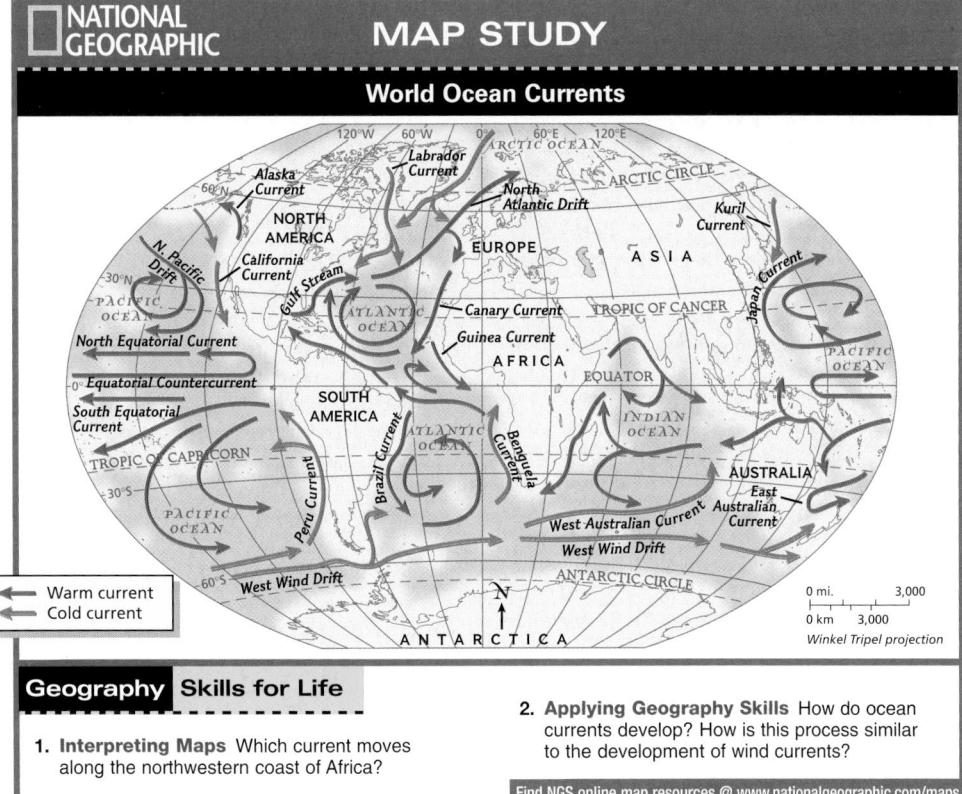

Warm current
Cold current

Geography Skills for Life

1. **Interpreting Maps** Which current moves along the northwestern coast of Africa?

2. **Applying Geography Skills** How do ocean currents develop? How is this process similar to the development of wind currents?

Find NGS online map resources @ www.nationalgeographic.com/maps

---

NATIONAL GEOGRAPHIC — MAP STUDY

Answers

1. *Canary Current*

2. *Both are caused by the earth's rotation, changes in air pressure, and water temperature differences; both are influenced by the Coriolis effect.*

Map Skills Practice

Place Which current brings warm water from the Caribbean up the Atlantic coast of North America? *(Gulf Stream)*

L1/ELL

Guided Reading Activity 3-2

Guided Reading Activity 3-2

For use with textbook pages 59–64

Factors Affecting Climate

Fill in the Blanks

DIRECTIONS: Use the information in your textbook to fill in the blanks for the following sentences.

1. Climate follows general patterns between each _____ zone.
2. The zone between the Tropic of Cancer and the Tropic of Capricorn is called the _____.
3. Mid-latitudes get the most _____ weather on the planet.
4. At any latitude, the higher the _____ the colder the temperature.
5. Winds occur because the sun heats the earth's _____.
6. The _____ effect causes prevailing winds to blow diagonally rather than along

The Tropics of Cancer and Capricorn are named for the constellations through which the sun appears to be traveling when its rays strike these lines of latitude directly.

---

mid-latitudes generally have a temperate climate—one that ranges from fairly hot to fairly cold—with dramatic seasonal weather changes.

Elevation and Climate

At all latitudes elevation influences climate because of the relationship between the elevation of a place and its temperature. The earth's atmosphere thins as altitude increases. Thinner air retains less heat. As elevation increases, temperatures decrease by about 3.5°F (1.9°C) for each 1,000 feet (305 m). This effect occurs at all latitudes. For example, in Ecuador, the city of Quito (KEE•toh) is nearly on the Equator. However, Quito lies in the Andes at an elevation of more than 9,000 feet (2,743 m), so average temperatures are about 32°F (17°C) cooler than in the nearby lowlands.

Sunlight is bright in Quito and other places with high elevation because the thinner atmosphere filters fewer rays of the sun. Even in bright sunlight, the world's highest mountains are cold, snowy places year-round.

Wind and Ocean Currents

Wind and water combine with the effects of the sun to influence Earth's weather and climate. Air moving across the face of the earth is called wind. Winds occur because the sun heats up the earth's atmosphere and surface unevenly. Rising warm air creates areas of low pressure, and falling cool air causes areas of high pressure. The cool air then flows in to replace the warm rising air. These movements over the earth's surface cause winds, which distribute the sun's heat around the planet.

Chapter 3 🌐 61

COOPERATIVE LEARNING ACTIVITY

World Wardrobes Organize the class into three groups, and assign each group a latitude region: high latitudes, mid-latitudes, and low latitudes. Have each group plan a year-round wardrobe for people living in its region. If necessary, suggest examples such as insulated gloves for people in high latitudes. After each group has made its list, have the class compare wardrobes and determine which area requires the greatest variety of clothing.
🌐 EE5 Environment and Society: Standard 15

L3 Analyze Information

Have students collect news reports of weather events around the world, such as cold snaps or monsoon flooding. Have them analyze the reports to determine whether each weather event is characteristic or uncharacteristic of the climate region in which it occurred.

The Maelstrom is a swift current in the Arctic Ocean off the coast of Norway. Strong winds cause this dangerous current to form huge whirlpools that can destroy small ships. After American author Edgar Allan Poe wrote about the Maelstrom, its name came to mean any whirlpool or any kind of severe turmoil.

L1/ELL

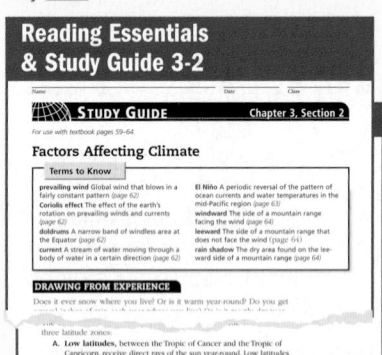

Wind Patterns

Global winds blow in fairly constant patterns called prevailing winds, shown on the map on page 60. The direction of prevailing winds is determined by latitude and is affected by the earth's movement. Because Earth rotates to the east, the global winds are displaced clockwise in the Northern Hemisphere and counterclockwise in the Southern Hemisphere. This phenomenon, called the Coriolis effect, causes prevailing winds to blow diagonally rather than along strict north-south or east-west lines.

Winds are often named for the direction from which they blow, but they sometimes were given names from the early days of sailing. Named for their ability to move trading ships through the region, the prevailing winds of the low latitudes are called *trade winds*. They blow from the northeast toward the Equator from about latitude 30°N and from the southeast toward the Equator from about latitude 30°S. *Westerlies* are the prevailing winds in the mid-latitudes, blowing diagonally west to east between about 30°N and 60°N and between about 30°S and 60°S. In the high latitudes, the *polar easterlies* blow diagonally east to west, pushing cold air toward the mid-latitudes.

History
The Horse Latitudes

At the Equator, global winds are diverted north and south, leaving a narrow, generally windless band called the doldrums. Two other narrow bands of calm air encircle the globe just north of the Tropic of Cancer and just south of the Tropic of Capricorn. In the days of wind-powered sailing ships, crews feared being stranded in these windless areas. With no moving air to lift the sails, ships were stranded for weeks in the hot, still weather. Meanwhile, food supplies dwindled, and perishable cargoes spoiled as the ships sat. The English poet Samuel Taylor Coleridge described this frightening experience:

> ❝ *Day after day, day after day*
> *We struck, nor breath nor motion;*
> *As idle as a painted ship*
> *Upon a painted ocean.* ❞
>
> Samuel Taylor Coleridge, *The Rime of the Ancient Mariner*, 1798

To lighten the load so the ships could take advantage of the slightest breeze, sailors would toss excess cargo and supplies overboard, including livestock being carried to colonial settlements. This practice gave rise to the name by which the calm areas at the edges of the Tropics are known—the *horse latitudes*.

Ocean Currents

Just as winds move in patterns, cold and warm streams of water, known as currents, move through the oceans. Ocean currents are caused by many of the same factors that cause winds, including the earth's rotation, changes in air pressure, and differences in water temperature. The Coriolis effect is observed in ocean currents, too, causing them to move in clockwise circles in the Northern Hemisphere and counterclockwise circles in the Southern Hemisphere.

As ocean currents circulate, cold water from the polar areas moves slowly toward the Equator, warming as it moves through the Tropics. This water forms the warm ocean currents. The warm water, in turn, moves away from the Equator, cooling to become a cold ocean current.

Ocean currents affect climate in the coastal lands along which they flow. Cold ocean currents cool the lands they pass. Warm ocean currents bring warmer temperatures. For example, the North Atlantic Drift, a warm-water extension of the Gulf Stream current, flows near western Europe. This current gives western Europe a relatively mild climate in spite of its northern latitude.

Weather and the Water Cycle

Wind and water work together to affect weather in another important way. Driven by temperature, condensation creates precipitation, moisture falling to the earth in the form of rain, sleet, hail, or snow. The sudden cloudburst that cools a steamy summer day is an example of how precipitation both affects and is affected by temperature. Water vapor forms in the atmosphere from evaporated surface water. As colder temperatures cool the rising moist air, the vapor condenses into liquid droplets, forming clouds. Further cooling causes rain to fall, which can help lower the temperature on warm days.

CRITICAL THINKING ACTIVITY

Predicting Consequences Explain to students that most of the world's commercial fishing grounds are located in the ocean over continental shelves where upwelling—the stirring up of cold waters to the surface by seasonal winds—occurs. These ocean fisheries are found primarily off the coasts of Peru, western North America, northwest and southwest Africa, Somalia, the Arabian Peninsula, and Antarctica. Have students work in small groups to research these fisheries. Ask students to predict the consequences for commercial fishing if upwelling were affected by changes in ocean levels and seasonal wind patterns caused by global warming. 🎲 🌐 **EE6 The Uses of Geography: Standard 18**

El Niño

Climate is also affected by recurring phenomena, or events, that alter weather patterns. The most famous of these recurring climatic events is the El Niño (ehl NEE•nyoh) phenomenon. El Niño is a periodic change in the pattern of ocean currents and water temperatures in the mid-Pacific region.

El Niño does not occur every year, but its frequency appears to have increased in the latter half of the 1900s. In an El Niño year, the normally low atmospheric pressure over the western Pacific rises, and the normally high pressure over the eastern Pacific drops. This reversal causes the trade winds to diminish or even to reverse direction. The change in wind pattern reverses the equatorial ocean currents, drawing warm water from near Indonesia east to Ecuador, where it spreads along the South American coast.

The changed air pressures resulting from El Niño influence climates around the world in a kind of domino effect. Precipitation increases along the coasts of North and South America, warming winters and increasing the risk of floods. Hawaii experiences reduced winds like those in the doldrums, and also drier weather. In Southeast Asia and Australia, drought and occasional massive forest fires occur.

Scientists are not sure what causes El Niño or why it appears to be occurring more frequently. Preliminary studies have linked this climatic event to global warming. The costs in human and economic terms of the weather catastrophes associated with El Niño make learning more about this climatic event vitally important.

Landforms and Climate

The surface features of the earth, such as bodies of water and mountains, also can affect and be affected by climate. The climates of places located at the same latitude can be very different, depending on the presence or absence of certain landforms.

Large bodies of water, for example, are slower to heat and to cool than land. As a result, water temperatures are more uniform and constant than land temperatures. Coastal lands receive the benefit of this moderating influence and experience less changeable weather than do inland areas. Large lakes, such as the Great Lakes in the United States and Canada, also create this effect.

NATIONAL GEOGRAPHIC — DIAGRAM STUDY

El Niño

NORMAL CONDITIONS

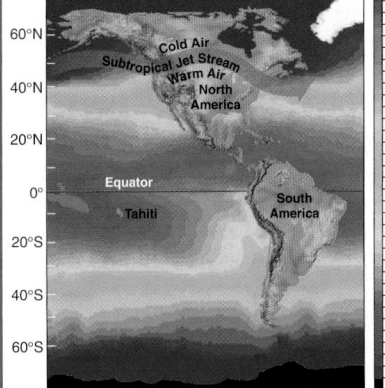

EL NIÑO CONDITIONS

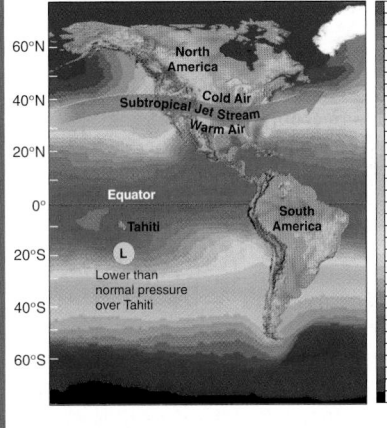

*Sea surface temperature data taken at one-degree intervals.

Geography Skills for Life

1. **Interpreting Diagrams** At what latitude does the subtropical jet stream flow under normal conditions?

2. **Applying Geography Skills** Describe the impact of El Niño on the lives of people in different parts of the world.

The El Niño phenomenon generally occurs during December or January, around the Christmas season, so Peruvian sailors nicknamed the event after the Christ Child—*el niño santo*, "the holy little boy" in Spanish.

NATIONAL GEOGRAPHIC — DIAGRAM STUDY

Answers

1. *about 50°N*

2. *changes in precipitation, warmer winters, reduced winds, drought or floods*

Skills Practice
Movement What happens to the subtropical jet stream during El Niño? (*It is pushed south.*)

❸ ASSESS

Assign Section 2 Assessment as homework or as an in-class activity.

Have students use **Interactive Tutor Self-Assessment CD-ROM**.
L2

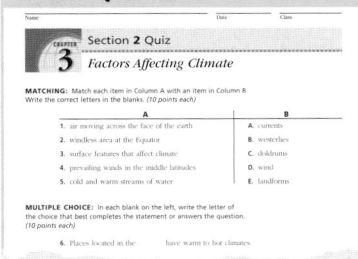

Section Quiz 3-2

TEAM-TEACHING ACTIVITY: ECONOMICS

The Costs of El Niño Have students work with an economics teacher to research the global economic effects of the most recent El Niño events. Have students work together to graph their findings and make predictions about the economic consequences of future El Niño events. 📦 🌐 **EE4 Human Systems: Standard 11**

Answers

1. *windward*

2. *Winds from oceans are pushed upward by mountain ranges; the rising air cools and precipitation is released; wind then becomes warmer and drier, creating area of little precipitation (rain shadow).*

Skills Practice

Place What kinds of climates would you expect to find in rain shadows? *(dry climates such as desert or steppe)*

Reteach

Have students review section content using their vocabulary flash cards. Organize students in pairs, and have partners take turns showing the terms and telling the definitions.

Enrich

Invite students to bring to class poems or songs that deal with wind, rain, or the ocean. Organize students in small groups, and ask them to share what they have brought.

Have students describe the location of their ideal vacation and identify the latitudes at which these places are found.

Mountain ranges also influence precipitation and affect climate. Winds that blow over an ocean are pushed upward when they meet a mountain range. The rising air cools and releases most of its moisture in the form of precipitation on the windward side—the side of the mountain range facing the wind. After the precipitation is released, winds become warmer and drier as they descend on the opposite, or leeward, side of the mountains. The hot, dry air produces little precipitation in an effect known as a rain shadow. The rain shadow effect often causes dry areas—and even deserts—to develop on the leeward sides of mountain ranges.

From the interaction of landforms, wind and water currents, latitude, and elevation arise a remarkable variety of climates. In the next section, you will learn about the earth's climate regions and the kinds of natural vegetation that grows in each climate region. You will also learn about the ways that climates have changed over millions of years and explore the many natural causes of climate change. As you explore the ways that human activities may cause climate change, you will also learn about ways that humans can protect their environment.

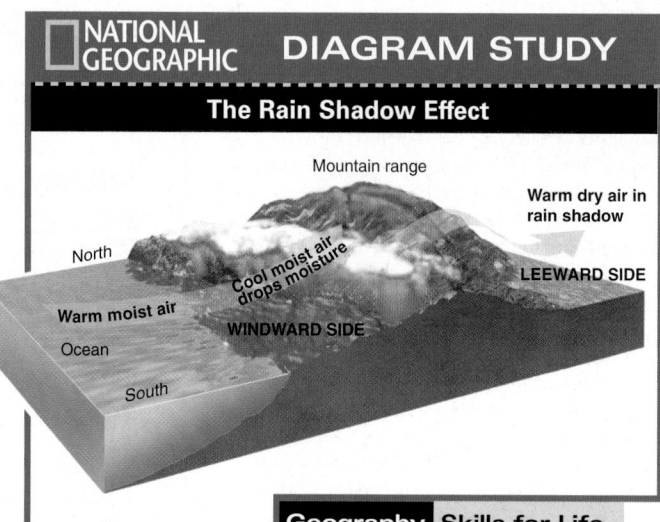

NATIONAL GEOGRAPHIC DIAGRAM STUDY

The Rain Shadow Effect

Mountain range

Warm dry air in rain shadow

North

Cool moist air drops moisture

LEEWARD SIDE

Warm moist air

WINDWARD SIDE

Ocean

South

Geography Skills for Life

1. **Interpreting Diagrams** On which side of a mountain does precipitation fall?

2. **Applying Geography Skills** How do landforms cause the formation of a rain shadow?

SECTION 2 ASSESSMENT

Checking for Understanding

1. **Define** prevailing wind, Coriolis effect, doldrums, current, El Niño, windward, leeward, rain shadow.

2. **Main Ideas** On a web diagram, fill in information about each of the factors affecting climate. Indicate whether these factors affect the climate where you live.

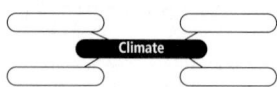

Climate

Critical Thinking

3. **Comparing and Contrasting** Describe the general differences in climate between the low latitudes and the mid-latitudes.

4. **Predicting Consequences** Without the Coriolis effect, how might the earth's climates be different?

5. **Identifying Cause-and-Effect Relationships** How does the presence of mountain ranges influence climate?

Analyzing Maps

6. **Location** Study the map of wind patterns on page 60. Where are the high latitudes located?

Applying Geography

7. **Movement of Ocean Currents** Study the map on page 61. If your ship were drifting from west to east in the Equatorial Countercurrent, what might happen as you drifted past longitude 120°W?

64 ⊕ Unit 1

SECTION 2 ASSESSMENT ANSWERS

1. All vocabulary terms are defined in the text.

2. Webs should include latitude, elevation, wind and ocean currents, and landforms.

3. Low latitude climates are warm to hot year-round; mid-latitude climates have hot and cold extremes and seasonal changes.

4. Climates would be more extreme, or not as mild.

5. Mountain ranges create rain shadows, affecting precipitation levels (moist on windward, arid on leeward).

6. polar areas

7. **Applying Geography** The ship would reverse its direction and drift from east to west with the North Equatorial Current.

Guide to Reading

Consider What You Know
Think about the types of vegetation that grow in the region where you live. What does the vegetation reveal about the regional climate there?

Reading Strategy
Organizing Complete a graphic organizer similar to the one below by filling in a brief description of each climate region.

Climate	Description
Tropical	
Dry	
Mid-Latitude	
High Latitude	
Highlands	

Read to Find Out
- How do geographers classify the climate regions of the world?
- Which kinds of vegetation are characteristic of each climate region?
- How do recurring phenomena influence climate patterns?

Terms to Know
- natural vegetation
- oasis
- coniferous
- deciduous
- mixed forest
- chaparral
- prairie
- permafrost
- hypothesis
- smog

Places to Locate
- Tropics
- Sahara
- Mediterranean Sea

World Climate Patterns

NATIONAL GEOGRAPHIC

A Geographic View

Damage from El Niño

From South America, cradle of El Niño, came reports of appalling flood damage. I headed south, past drought-stricken Mexico, and alighted on the soggy soil of Guayaquil, Ecuador. Three months before Christmas a colossal slab of warm water 450 feet thick had arrived off Ecuador and Peru, smothering the cool ocean surface. Coastal fishing ceased, and the simmering sea brought rains that threatened to wash Ecuador into the sea. "Areas that normally measure precipitation in inches have had ten feet," said Jimmy Aycart, . . . director of emergency relief for the Guayaquil area.

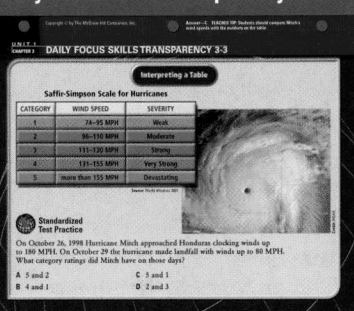
Flooding in Ecuador caused by El Niño

—Thomas Y. Canby, "El Niño's Ill Wind," National Geographic, February 1984

The effects of El Niño are felt around the world. It has triggered floods in southern California and droughts in Africa. However, even ordinary climate patterns vary from region to region, depending on the climate factors present. In this section you will learn how geographers classify the world's climates and how climate change occurs.

Climate Regions

Geographers often divide the earth into climate regions—tropical, dry, mid-latitude, high latitude, and highlands. Because climates vary within these broad regions, geographers further divide the major regions into smaller ones. Each of these divisions has its own

① FOCUS

Section Overview
This section discusses the climate patterns and types of vegetation around the world.

BELLRINGER
Skillbuilder Activity

- Project transparency and have students answer questions.
- Available as blackline master.

Daily Focus Skills Transparency 3-3

Guide to Reading

Consider What You Know
Answers *Students should make connections between local vegetation types and climate factors.*

Reading Strategy
Answer tropical: *tropical rainforest and tropical savanna are the most widespread;* dry: *either desert with sparse plant life and little rainfall or steppe with dry, largely treeless grasslands;* mid-latitude: *variable weather patterns and seasonal changes create a variety of vegetation;* high latitude: *limited variety and amount of vegetation, freezing temperatures much of the year;* highlands: *similar vegetation regardless of latitude, vegetation varies as elevation increases and air becomes cooler and thinner*

Preteaching Vocabulary
Use the **Vocabulary Puzzle-Maker CD-ROM** to create crossword and word-search puzzles.

② TEACH

L1 Categorize

Ask students to list as many television shows, movies, books, and plays as they can that are set in each major climate region.

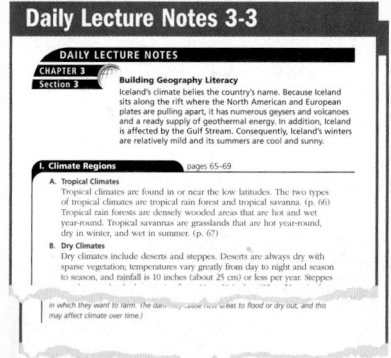

Daily Lecture Notes 3-3

DAILY LECTURE NOTES

CHAPTER 3
Section 3

Building Geography Literacy
Iceland's climate belies the country's name. Because Iceland sits along the rift where the North American and European plates are pulling apart, it has numerous geysers and volcanoes and a ready supply of geothermal energy. In addition, Iceland is affected by the Gulf Stream. Consequently, Iceland's winters are relatively mild and its summers are cool and sunny.

I. Climate Regions pages 65–69

A. Tropical Climates
Tropical climates are found in or near the low latitudes. The two types of tropical climates are tropical rain forest and tropical savanna. (p. 66) Tropical rain forests are densely wooded areas that are hot and wet year-round. Tropical savannas are grasslands that are hot and wet in summer. (p. 67)

B. Dry Climates
Dry climates include deserts and steppes. Deserts are always dry with sparse vegetation; temperatures vary greatly from day to night and season to season, and rainfall is 10 inches (about 25 cm) or less per year. Steppes

in which they want to farm. The dams may cause new areas to flood or dry out, and this may affect climate over time.

NATIONAL GEOGRAPHIC — MAP STUDY

Answers
1. *in or near low latitudes (between Tropics of Cancer and Capricorn)*

2. *The water circulates in warm or cold currents and either warms or cools coastal lands.*

L1/ELL

Guided Reading Activity 3-3

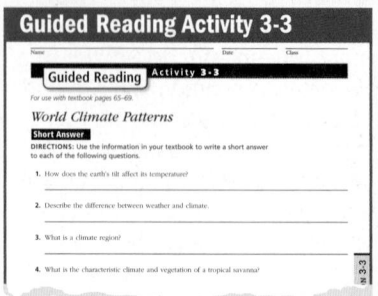

Name _____ Date _____ Class _____

Guided Reading Activity 3-3

For use with textbook pages 65-69.

World Climate Patterns

Short Answer
DIRECTIONS: Use the information in your textbook to write a short answer to each of the following questions.

1. How does the earth's tilt affect its temperature?

2. Describe the difference between weather and climate.

3. What is a climate region?

4. What is the characteristic climate and vegetation of a tropical savanna?

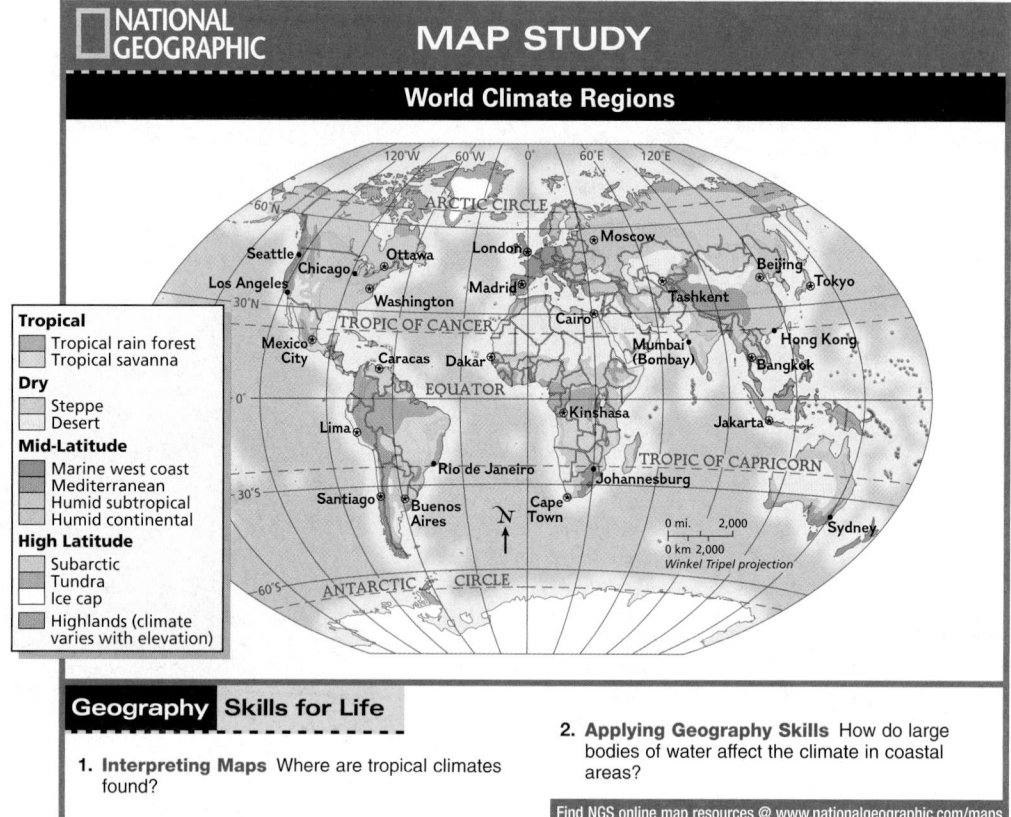

NATIONAL GEOGRAPHIC — MAP STUDY

World Climate Regions

Tropical
- Tropical rain forest
- Tropical savanna

Dry
- Steppe
- Desert

Mid-Latitude
- Marine west coast
- Mediterranean
- Humid subtropical
- Humid continental

High Latitude
- Subarctic
- Tundra
- Ice cap
- Highlands (climate varies with elevation)

0 mi. 2,000
0 km 2,000
Winkel Tripel projection

Geography Skills for Life

1. **Interpreting Maps** Where are tropical climates found?

2. **Applying Geography Skills** How do large bodies of water affect the climate in coastal areas?

Find NGS online map resources @ www.nationalgeographic.com/maps

characteristic soils and *natural vegetation*—the plant life that grows in an area where the natural environment is unchanged by human activity.

Tropical Climates

Tropical climates are found in or near the low latitudes—the **Tropics**. The two most widespread kinds of tropical climate regions are tropical rain forest and tropical savanna.

Hot and wet throughout the year, *tropical rain forest* climates have an average temperature of 80°F (27°C). The warm, humid air is saturated with moisture, producing rain almost daily. Yearly rainfall averages about 80 inches (203 cm). Lush vegetation is common in tropical climates, although the continual rain tends to leach, or draw out, nutrients from the soil in these climates. Wildlife is also abundant.

> *Like an undiscovered continent encircling the globe, tropical rain forests shelter an astonishing abundance of organisms—probably more than half the Earth's plant and animal species.*
>
> Edward O. Wilson, "Rain Forest Canopy: The High Frontier," *National Geographic*, December 1991

Tropical rain forest vegetation grows thickly in layers. Tall teak or mahogany trees form a canopy over shorter trees and bushes. Vines and shade-loving plants grow on the forest floor. The world's largest tropical rain forest is in South America's Amazon River basin. Similar climate and vegetation exist in other parts of South America, in the Caribbean area, and Asia and Africa.

66 🌐 Unit 1

DIFFERENTIATED INSTRUCTION

English Learners Ask students to think about the types of vegetation common to the countries from which they or their families originally came. Have students list the names of several common plants or trees in their primary language. Have students work with partners proficient in English to determine which plant names are also used in English, and to find English-language equivalents for others. Some kinds of plants are unique to specific areas and may not have English equivalents. **ELL**

🌐 EE3 Physical Systems: Standard 8

Refer to *Inclusion for the Social Studies Classroom Strategies and Activities.*

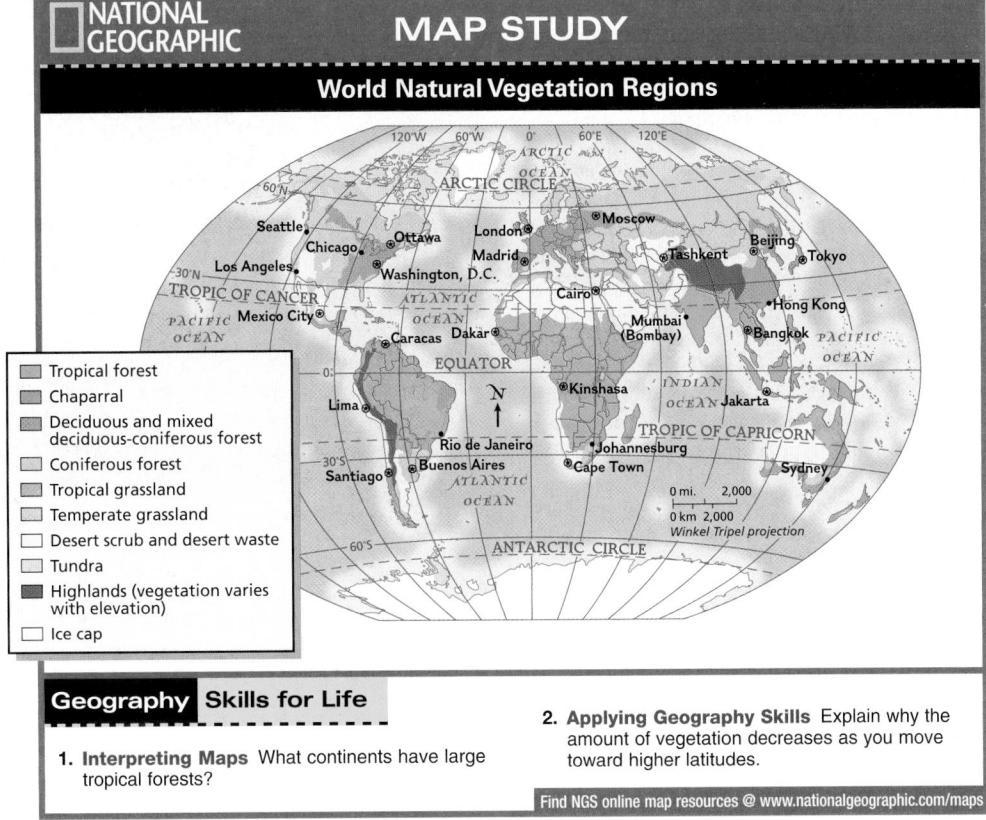

NATIONAL GEOGRAPHIC — MAP STUDY

World Natural Vegetation Regions

Legend:
- Tropical forest
- Chaparral
- Deciduous and mixed deciduous-coniferous forest
- Coniferous forest
- Tropical grassland
- Temperate grassland
- Desert scrub and desert waste
- Tundra
- Highlands (vegetation varies with elevation)
- Ice cap

Geography Skills for Life

1. **Interpreting Maps** What continents have large tropical forests?

2. **Applying Geography Skills** Explain why the amount of vegetation decreases as you move toward higher latitudes.

Find NGS online map resources @ www.nationalgeographic.com/maps

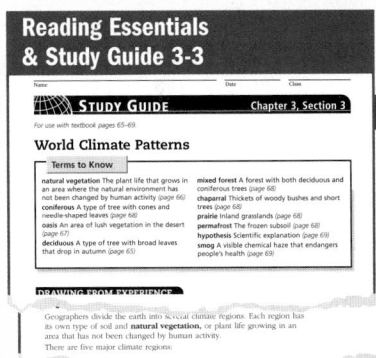

NATIONAL GEOGRAPHIC — MAP STUDY

Answers

1. *Asia, Africa, South America*
2. *lack of direct sunlight, cold temperatures*

Map Skills Practice

Place What landform accounts for the highlands climate of western South America? *(high mountains—Andes)*

L1/ELL

Reading Essentials & Study Guide 3-3

STUDY GUIDE — Chapter 3, Section 3

For use with textbook pages 65-69

World Climate Patterns

Terms to Know

natural vegetation The plant life that grows in an area where the natural environment has not been changed by human activity *(page 66)*
coniferous A type of tree with cones and needle-shaped leaves *(page 66)*
oasis An area of lush vegetation in the desert *(page 67)*
deciduous A type of tree with broad leaves that drop in autumn *(page 66)*

mixed forest A forest with both deciduous and coniferous trees *(page 66)*
chaparral Thickets of woody bushes and short trees *(page 68)*
prairie Inland grasslands *(page 68)*
permafrost The frozen subsoil *(page 68)*
hypothesis Scientific explanation *(page 69)*
smog A visible chemical haze that endangers people's health *(page 69)*

DRAWING FROM EXPERIENCE

Geographers divide the earth into several climate regions. Each region has its own type of soil and **natural vegetation**, or plant life growing in an area that has not been changed by human activity.

There are five major climate regions.

INTERDISCIPLINARY connection

HEALTH Scientists have noted rising rates of diseases that may stem from environmental hazards. Skin cancer, triggered by exposure to the sun's ultraviolet rays, is rising as the atmosphere's protective ozone layer thins.

Tropical savanna climates have dry winters and wet summers, accompanied by high year-round temperatures. In the dry season, the ground is covered with clumps of coarse grass. Fewer trees exist in savanna regions than in the rain forests. Tropical savannas are found in Africa, Central and South America, Asia, and Australia.

Dry Climates

Geographers have identified two types of dry climates, based on the vegetation in each. Both *desert* and *steppe* climates occur in many parts of the world.

Dry areas with sparse plant life are called deserts. Yearly rainfall in deserts seldom exceeds 10 inches (about 25 cm), and temperatures vary widely from the heat of day to the cool of night and from season to season. Desert climates occur in just under one-third of the earth's total land area. The **Sahara** alone extends over almost the entire northern one-third of the African continent.

The natural vegetation of deserts consists of scattered scrub and cactus, plants that tolerate low humidity and wide temperature ranges. In some desert areas, underground springs may support an oasis, an area of lush vegetation. Some deserts have dunes or rocky surfaces, and others have fertile soil that can yield crops through irrigation.

Often bordering deserts are dry, largely treeless grasslands called steppes. Yearly rainfall in steppe areas averages 10 to 20 inches (25 to 51 cm). The world's largest steppe stretches across eastern Europe and western and central Asia. Steppes are also found in North America, South America, Africa, and Australia.

COOPERATIVE LEARNING ACTIVITY

The World Café Have students form five groups, and assign a major climate region to each group. Have each group compile a list of dishes made from plant products (fruits, vegetables, nuts, grains, and so on) common to its climate region. Students may use encyclopedias, cookbooks, or Internet resources for research. Then have all the groups create the menu for a world cafe that includes dishes from each climate region.

🌐 **EE3 Physical Systems: Standard 8**

Answer

grasses in humid subtropical; evergreen and deciduous trees in both

More About the Photo

Chaparral grows in the regions with hot, dry summers and mild, wet winters, such as the Southwest region of the United States, the area around the Mediterranean Sea, at the southern tip of Africa, southwestern Australia, and central South America.

③ASSESS

Assign Section 3 Assessment as homework or as an in-class activity.

🌐 Have students use **Interactive Tutor Self-Assessment CD-ROM** to review Section 3.

L2

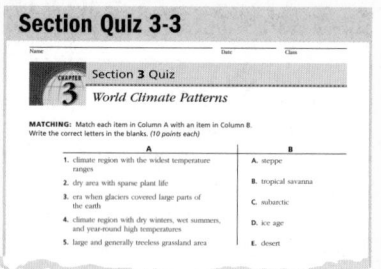

Mid-Latitude Climates

The world's mid-latitudes include four temperate climate regions. Mid-latitude climates experience variable weather patterns and seasonal changes that give rise to a variety of natural vegetation.

Along western coastlines, between the latitudes of 30° and 60° north and south, are regions with a *marine west coast* climate. The Pacific coast of North America, much of Europe, and parts of South America, Africa, Australia, and New Zealand have marine west coast climates. In these areas ocean winds bring cool summers and damp winters. Abundant rainfall supports the growth of both coniferous and deciduous trees. Coniferous trees, most of which are evergreens, have cones. Deciduous trees, most of which have broad leaves, change color and drop their leaves in autumn. Typical of marine west coast climates are mixed forests with both kinds of trees.

Lands surrounding the **Mediterranean Sea** have mild, rainy winters and hot, sunny summers. The natural vegetation includes chaparral (SHA•puh•RAL), thickets of woody bushes and short trees. Geographers classify as *Mediterranean* any coastal mid-latitude areas with similar climate and vegetation. Such areas also include Southern California and parts of southern Australia.

In the southeastern United States and in southeastern parts of South America and Asia, a *humid subtropical* climate brings short, mild winters and nearly year-round rain. The wind patterns and high pressure related to nearby oceans keep humidity levels high in these areas. Vegetation consists of prairies, or inland grasslands, and forests of evergreen and deciduous trees.

In some mid-latitude regions of the Northern Hemisphere, such as southern Canada, western Russia, and northeastern China, landforms influence climate more than winds, precipitation, or ocean temperatures do. These *humid continental* climate regions do not experience the moderating effect of ocean winds because of their northerly continental, or inland, locations. The farther north one travels in these humid continental areas, the longer and more severe are the snowy winters and the shorter and cooler are the summers. Vegetation in humid continental regions is similar to that found in marine west coast areas, with evergreens outnumbering deciduous trees in the northernmost areas of the region.

NATIONAL GEOGRAPHIC World Explorer

Geography Skills for Life

Mid-latitude Vegetation Chaparral, which includes shrubs and olive trees, grows in Mediterranean climate zones.

Region What kind of vegetation grows in humid subtropical climate zones? Humid continental?

High Latitude Climates

In high latitude climates, freezing temperatures are common throughout much of the year because of the lack of direct sunlight. As a result, the amount and variety of vegetation is limited.

Just south of the Arctic Circle lie the *subarctic* climate regions. Winters here are bitterly cold, and summers are short and cool. Subarctic regions have the world's widest temperature ranges, varying from winter to summer by as much as 120°F (49°C). In parts of the subarctic, only a thin layer of surface soil thaws each summer. Below it is permanently frozen subsoil, or permafrost. Brief summer growing seasons may support needled evergreens.

Closer to the polar regions, *tundra* climate regions are very cold. Here the winter darkness and bitter cold last for half the year, and the sun's indirect rays bring constant summer light but little heat. In tundra regions, most of which lie in the far north of the Northern Hemisphere, the layer of thawed soil is even thinner than in the subarctic.

CRITICAL THINKING ACTIVITY

Analyzing Information Have students research the acidity levels at which acid precipitation begins to affect the environment. Have students collect samples of local rain or snow and use litmus strips to determine acid levels. Invite students to make predictions about the effects of acid precipitation on the local environment based on their findings.
📀 **EE5 Environment and Society: Standard 14**

Trees cannot establish roots on these frigid plains, so tundra vegetation is limited to low bushes, very short grasses, mosses, and lichens (LY•kuhns).

Snow and ice, often more than 2 miles (3 km) thick, constantly cover the surfaces of *ice cap* regions. Lichens are the only form of vegetation that can survive in these areas, where monthly temperatures average below freezing. Earth's largest polar ice cap covers almost all of Antarctica. Greenland's interior also has an ice cap climate.

Highlands Climates

Elevation can determine a climate region, regardless of latitude. High mountain areas, even along the Equator, share some of the same characteristics of high latitude climates because of the thinning of the atmosphere at high altitudes. The higher the elevation, the cooler the temperatures. The natural vegetation of highlands climates also varies with elevation. Mixed forests generally lie at the bases of mountain ranges. Higher up, meadows with small trees, shrubs, and wildflowers line the mountainsides.

Climatic Changes

Climates change gradually over time, although the causes of these changes are unclear. Scientists search for answers by studying the interrelationships among ocean temperatures, greenhouse gases, wind patterns, and cloud cover.

During the last 1 to 2 million years, for example, the earth passed through four ice ages, eras when glaciers covered large areas of the planet's surface. One hypothesis, or scientific explanation, for these ice ages is that the earth absorbed less solar energy because of variations in the sun's output of energy or because of variations in the earth's orbit. Another hypothesis suggests that dust clouds from volcanic activity reflected sunlight back into space, cooling the atmosphere and lowering surface temperatures.

Human interaction with the environment also affects climate. Burning fossil fuels releases gases that mix with water in the air, forming acids that fall in rain and snow. Acid rain can destroy forests. Fewer forests may result in climatic change. The exhaust released from burning fossil fuels in automobile engines and factories is heated in the atmosphere by the sun's ultraviolet rays, forming smog, a visible chemical haze in the atmosphere that endangers people's health. Other human-driven changes result from dams and river diversions. These projects, intended to supply water to dry areas, may cause new areas to flood or to dry out and may affect climate over time.

Reteach

Have students form teams and take turns challenging one another by describing a type of vegetation and having the other team name the appropriate climate region.

Enrich

Have students research selected animals from different world regions and write an essay that explains their distribution in terms of climate, vegetation, soil, and geology.

4 CLOSE

Have students look through their textbooks (not limited to this chapter) and find at least two photographs of places in each major climate region.

SECTION 3 ASSESSMENT

Checking for Understanding

1. **Define** natural vegetation, oasis, coniferous, deciduous, mixed forest, chaparral, prairie, permafrost, hypothesis, smog.

2. **Main Ideas** Create a table like the one below, adding information and a brief description about each of the world's climate regions.

Earth's Climates	
Climate Region	**Features**

Critical Thinking

3. **Analyzing Information** What patterns of vegetation are typical of tropical climates? Explain.

4. **Comparing and Contrasting** What factors account for the similarities and differences between the sub-divisions in tropical climate zones?

5. **Categorizing Information** How are the five major climate regions related to the three zones of latitude?

6. **Drawing Conclusions** What are the two main categories of factors causing climate change?

Analyzing Maps

7. **Region** Study the map of world natural vegetation regions on page 67. What vegetation type dominates Europe? Canada and the United States?

Applying Geography

8. **Climate and Settlement Patterns** On the map of world climate regions on page 66, locate the climate regions for Tashkent, Cape Town, Lima, Chicago, London, and Jakarta. What can you conclude about the relationship between climate and settlement?

SECTION 3 ASSESSMENT ANSWERS

1. All vocabulary terms are defined in the text.
2. Chart information should reflect features of the five climate regions.
3. Lush rain forest vegetation exists in areas of high temperatures and heavy rainfall, and grasses with fewer trees grow in areas with dry winters and wet summers.
4. Both subdivisions have high year-round temperatures, but they differ in rainfall. Tropical rain forest climate has rain year-round, but tropical

savanna climate has dry winters and wet summers.

5. Tropical climate is found in low latitudes; mid-latitude, in the middle latitudes; high latitude in the high latitudes; dry and highlands climates may occur in more than one zone of latitude.
6. variations in the earth-sun relationship; human activity
7. Europe: deciduous and mixed deciduous-coniferous forests; United States and Canada:

deciduous and mixed deciduous-coniferous forests as well as coniferous forests; large area of U.S. temperate grassland

8. **Applying Geography** dry: Tashkent, Cape Town, Lima; mid-latitude: Chicago, London; tropical: Jakarta; Major population centers are found in a variety of climates except high latitude.

Teaching the Skill

Write the following list of activities on the board:

- *programming an electronic device*
- *assembling a bicycle*
- *changing a printer cartridge*
- *preparing to execute a soccer, basketball, or hockey play*
- *using a public copy machine*
- *playing a video game*

Ask: What do all these activities have in common? *(They all involve reading, referring to, or following a diagram.)* Invite students to name other activities that involve the use of diagrams.

Additional Practice
L1

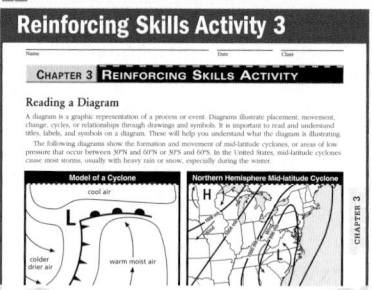

Reinforcing Skills Activity 3

CHAPTER 3 REINFORCING SKILLS ACTIVITY

Reading a Diagram

GLENCOE
TECHNOLOGY

Glencoe Skillbuilder Interactive Workbook, Level 2

This interactive CD-ROM reinforces student mastery of essential social studies skills.

Reading a Diagram

Have you ever assembled a model airplane or car? Kits and how-to books give detailed instructions that often include diagrams. Because they present information visually, diagrams can help explain ideas and processes easily.

Learning the Skill

A diagram is a graphic design that shows a process or event. Diagrams are extremely useful in communicating information clearly and quickly. A diagram can show placement, relationships, cycles, and movement, using symbols and drawn objects. Diagrams can be very useful for showing changes over time or for comparing two or more actions or relationships. Presenting information visually can make complex events or ideas more understandable.

Newspapers, magazines, and the Internet use diagrams to supplement written information. Geographers use diagrams to explain complex processes such as climate and weather phenomena. A diagram can be a very effective way of communicating an idea.

Follow these steps to understand a diagram:

- **Note its title, caption, and labels.** These features provide information that is important for understanding the diagram.
- **Study carefully the objects and symbols used.** Sometimes a diagram includes a key to the symbols.
- **Look at the relationships or actions shown.** If the diagram compares two or more things, look for details that show how the relationship

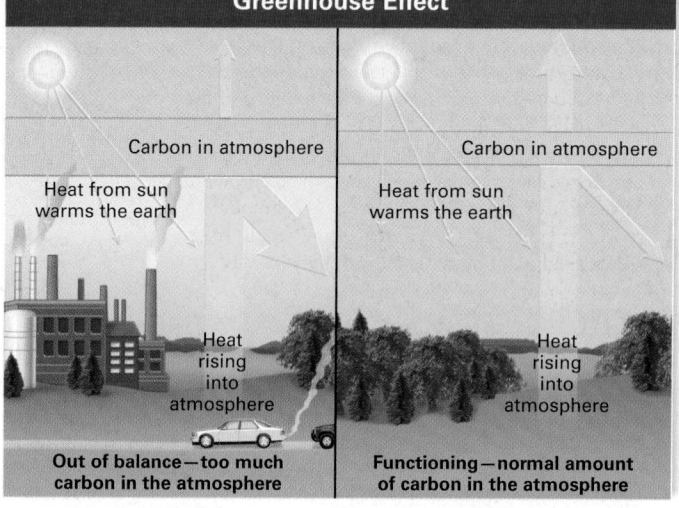

Greenhouse Effect

Carbon in atmosphere

Heat from sun warms the earth

Heat rising into atmosphere

Out of balance—too much carbon in the atmosphere

Carbon in atmosphere

Heat from sun warms the earth

Heat rising into atmosphere

Functioning—normal amount of carbon in the atmosphere

or action changes under different circumstances.

Practicing the Skill

The diagrams above explain and compare two aspects of the greenhouse effect. Use the diagrams to answer the following questions.

1. Describe the two aspects of the greenhouse effect shown above.

2. How is plant life different in the two diagrams?

3. What objects are shown contributing more carbon to the atmosphere?

4. How is the amount of heat retained in the Earth's atmosphere related to the amount of carbon in the atmosphere?

Applying
the Skill

Design and draw a diagram that explains a natural process. Look through newspapers or magazines for ideas relating to geography. In the diagram, include drawn objects, symbols, a title, and labels.

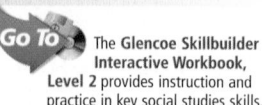

Go To The Glencoe Skillbuilder Interactive Workbook, **Level 2** provides instruction and practice in key social studies skills.

ANSWERS TO PRACTICING THE SKILL

1. out-of-balance and functioning
2. out-of-balance: little plant life; functioning: lots of plant life
3. cars (exhaust from internal-combustion engines) and factory smokestacks
4. The more carbon in the atmosphere, the more heat is retained.

SECTION 1 — Earth-Sun Relationships (pp. 55–58)

Terms to Know
- weather
- climate
- axis
- temperature
- revolution
- equinox
- solstice
- greenhouse effect
- global warming

Key Points
- The earth's position in relation to the sun affects temperatures on Earth.
- The rotation of the earth causes day and night.
- The earth's revolution and its tilt in relation to the sun produce the seasons.
- Global temperatures may be increasing as a result of human activity.

Organizing Your Notes
Use a graphic organizer like the one below to help you organize your notes for this section.

Earth-Sun Relationship
- Earth's Tilt and Rotation
- Earth's Revolution
- Greenhouse Effect

SECTION 2 — Factors Affecting Climate (pp. 59–64)

Terms to Know
- prevailing wind
- Coriolis effect
- doldrums
- current
- El Niño
- windward
- leeward
- rain shadow

Key Points
- Latitude and elevation affect climate.
- Wind patterns and ocean currents play a key role in the earth's climates.
- Climate is affected by recurring phenomena such as El Niño.
- Landforms shape and are shaped by climate patterns.

Organizing Your Notes
Use a table like the one below to help you organize information about climate.

Climate Factors	
Location	
Currents	
Surface Features	

SECTION 3 — World Climate Patterns (pp. 65–69)

Terms to Know
- natural vegetation
- oasis
- coniferous
- deciduous
- mixed forest
- chaparral
- prairie
- permafrost
- hypothesis
- smog

Key Points
- Geographers divide the world into major climate regions.
- Each climate region has its own characteristic natural vegetation.
- Climate patterns change over time as a result of both natural processes and human activity.

Organizing Your Notes
Use an outline like the one below to help you organize your notes for this section.

Climate Patterns
I. Tropical climates
A. Tropical rain forest
1. High temperatures
2. Rain all year
B.

Using the Chapter 3 Summary & Study Guide

Use the Chapter 3 Summary & Study Guide to preview, review, condense, or reteach the chapter.

Preview/Review

Vocabulary PuzzleMaker CD-ROM reinforces "Terms to Know."

Interactive Tutor Self-Assessment CD-ROM provides a review of Chapter 3 content.

Condense

Have students read the Chapter 3 Summary & Study Guide.

Chapter 3 Audio Program

Chapter 3 Guided Reading Activities

Reteach

Chapter 3 Reteaching Activities (Spanish also available)

Chapter 3 Reading Essentials and Study Guides

GLENCOE TECHNOLOGY

NATIONAL GEOGRAPHIC
WORLD REGIONS
VIDEO PROGRAM

Unit 1, The World
The following segments enhance the study of this unit:
- **Ocean Journey**
- **Homo Sapiens Sapiens**
- **Goodwill Games**

CHAPTER CULMINATING ACTIVITY

Global Gardens Organize the class into five groups, one for each of the world's major climate regions. Ask each group to design a garden or nature center featuring typical vegetation of its region. Subdivisions within each region should have their own subsections of the garden or nature center. Groups should research specific plants to include, and should create graphic displays in the form of illustrated landscape plans or annotated garden maps. Display finished work. **EE3 Physical Systems: Standard 8**

ASSESSMENT & ACTIVITIES

CHAPTER 3

Have students visit the Web site at geography.glencoe.com to review Chapter 3 and take the **Self-Check Quiz.**

GLENCOE TECHNOLOGY

Use *MindJogger Videoquiz* to review the Chapter 3 content.

Reviewing Key Terms

earth-sun relationships: equinox, revolution, solstice, axis

climate factors: greenhouse effect, Coriolis effect, temperature, prevailing wind, doldrums, rain shadow, El Niño, current

climate patterns: mixed forest, deciduous, chaparral, permafrost, oasis, prairie

Reviewing Facts

SECTION 1

1. All cause changes in the way the sun's rays strike the earth, leading to day-night, seasons, and climate variations.

2. Tropic of Cancer receives direct sunlight in June; Tropic of Capricorn receives direct sunlight in December; Poles never receive direct sunlight.

3. Carbon dioxide traps heat in the atmosphere.

SECTION 2

4. latitude, air and ocean currents, landforms

5. trade winds; westerlies

6. Large bodies of water bring cool or warm currents that cool or warm land; mountains cause rain shadows with heavy precipitation on the windward side and arid climates on the leeward side.

Reviewing Key Terms

On a sheet of paper, classify these key terms under the correct heading: earth-sun relationship, climate factors, or climate patterns.

greenhouse effect	temperature	El Niño
mixed forest	prevailing wind	oasis
equinox	chaparral	prairie
revolution	doldrums	current
deciduous	permafrost	solstice
Coriolis effect	rain shadow	axis

Reviewing Facts

SECTION 1

1. What are the effects of the earth's tilt, rotation, and revolution?

2. What are the differences in sunlight at the Tropic of Cancer, the Tropic of Capricorn, and the Poles?

3. How is CO_2 related to the greenhouse effect?

SECTION 2

4. List three key factors that affect climate.

5. Describe the changes in air pressure that occur during an El Niño year. How do these changes affect wind patterns?

6. How do large bodies of water and mountains affect climate?

SECTION 3

7. What are the major climate regions into which geographers divide the earth?

8. What main types of vegetation grow in the earth's major climate regions?

9. In what ways might the burning of fossil fuels affect a region's vegetation?

Critical Thinking

1. Predicting Consequences How might increased global warming affect the earth's climates? Give examples to support your answer.

2. Making Generalizations Why do the mid-latitudes have a temperate climate?

3. Categorizing Information Create a web diagram like the one below. Connect the items with a line to show that they are related. Describe the geographical events and phenomena associated with each category.

Factors Affecting Climate

Earth-Sun Relationship — Types of Climate

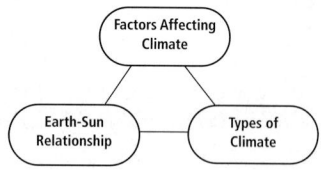

Locating Places
The World: Physical Geography

Match the letters on the map with the appropriate places and physical features. Write your answers on a separate sheet of paper.

1. Equator
2. Arctic Circle
3. Tropic of Capricorn
4. Warm current, Atlantic
5. Tropic of Cancer
6. Antarctic Circle
7. Cold current, Pacific

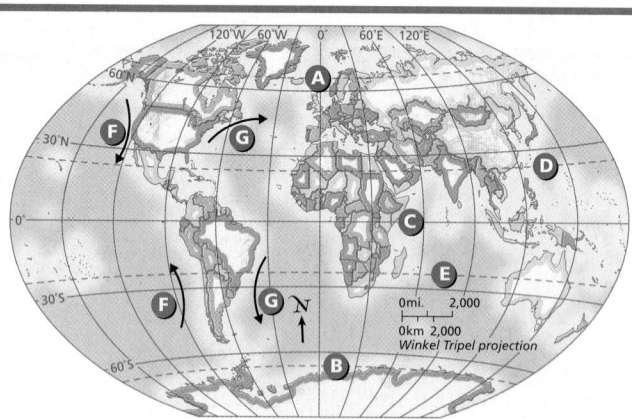

SECTION 3

7. tropical, dry, mid-latitude, high latitude, highlands

8. tropical: rain forest or savanna grass; dry: scrub or treeless grasslands; mid-latitude: various trees, shrubs, prairie grasses; high latitude: needled evergreens, short grasses, mosses, and lichens; highlands: varies with elevation

9. Emissions can harm vegetation through smog, acid rain, and global warming.

NATIONAL GEOGRAPHIC Locating Places

1. C	**3.** E	**5.** D	**7.** F
2. A	**4.** G	**6.** B	

Critical Thinking

1. higher temperatures would melt polar ice, raise sea levels; disrupt ocean currents

2. Ocean winds moderate the temperatures.

3. Webs should reflect text information and logical connections.

Thinking Like a Geographer

Imagine that you have been asked to speak about global warming to a group in your community. Your goal is to persuade the audience to take steps to reduce global warming. Write an outline of the remarks you will make to the group, and use visuals to support your arguments.

Problem-Solving Activity

Problem-Solution Proposal Research and analyze the effects of a physical geographic pattern, such as El Niño, on world economies. What actions did countries take in response? Determine what preparations might lessen the impact of this pattern in the future. Write a proposal in which you outline the problem, present several possible solutions, and recommend a course of action. Include diagrams, charts, maps, and other visual elements.

GeoJournal

Cause and Effect Review your journal entries about factors affecting climate. Write a story that takes place in the future. The climate in your community has changed. Include details about how this change occurred and how it has affected vegetation, economic activities, and human and animal populations. Use specific examples as well as illustrations and concrete language to make your story interesting and engaging.

Technology Activity

Using the Internet for Research Work with a team to search the Internet for information about the climate in your community. Include information such as climate region, local factors that influence climate, seasonal changes, and any unusual climatic events. Then choose one aspect of your area's climate and write a paragraph explaining its effect on people in your community. For example, if your community has experienced a weather-related disaster, such as a hurricane or tornado, what effects did the event have on your community?

Standardized Test Practice

Use the graph below and your knowledge of geography to answer the question. If you have trouble answering the question, use the process of elimination to narrow your choices.

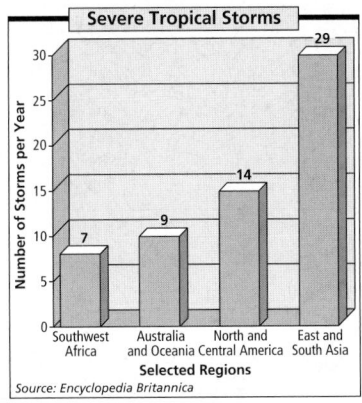

Severe Tropical Storms

Number of Storms per Year

Southwest Africa	Australia and Oceania	North and Central America	East and South Asia
7	9	14	29

Selected Regions

Source: Encyclopedia Britannica

1. Which of the following statements can be inferred from the graph?

   F Severe tropical storms are rare in Oceania.

   G East and South Asia have about four times as many severe tropical storms as Southwest Africa.

   H North and Central America never go through a month without a storm.

   J South America does not have tropical storms.

 **Test-Taking Tip** Read the title and labels on the graph carefully to determine what is being presented. For example, the label on the bottom of the graph tells you that only selected regions are shown. The label on the left indicates the number of storms per year, but not the month in which they occur.

Standardized Test Practice

1. G

Tested Objectives:
interpret graphs

Additional Practice and Test-Taking Tips

📁 Standardized Test Practice Workbook

❓ CHAPTER BONUS TEST QUESTION

Why is a straight line not always the "fastest route between two points" when sailing over long distances? *(The Coriolis effect causes wind patterns and ocean currents to move diagonally. Sailors may make better use of prevailing winds and currents by plotting courses that follow these variations.)*

Thinking Like a Geographer

Outlines should include actions that may reduce global warming as well as persuasive reasons for taking the actions. Students' visuals may vary but their content should clearly relate to the recommended actions or persuasive reasons.

Problem-Solving Activity

Proposals should be well organized, demonstrate thorough research and analysis, and include supporting visual aids. Students should make a logical choice of recommended action from among their possible solutions.

GeoJournal

Students' stories will vary but should show an understanding of climate factors and climate change.

Technology Activity

Paragraphs should demonstrate knowledge of the influence of climate on human activities.

CHAPTER 4 PLANNING GUIDE

NOTE: The following materials may be used when teaching Chapter 4. Section-level support materials are shown at point-of-use in the margins of the Teacher Wraparound Edition.

TEACHING TRANSPARENCIES

L2 Unit 1 Map Overlay Transparencies

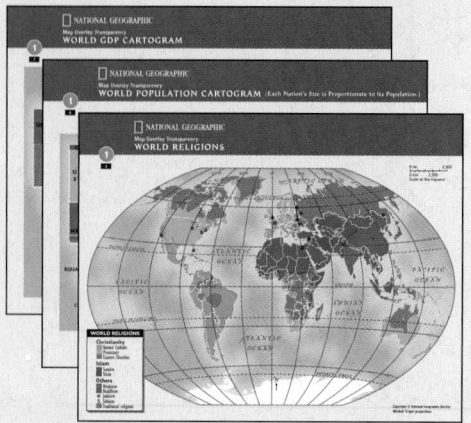

L2 Political Map Transparency 1

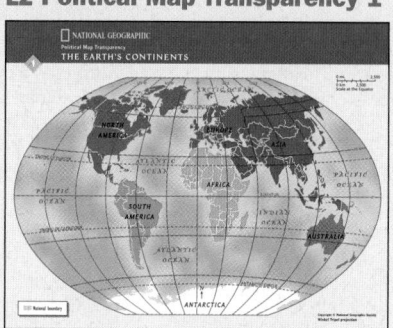

GEOGRAPHIC LITERACY

Focus on Geography Literacy

APPLICATION AND ENRICHMENT

L3 Enrichment Activity 4

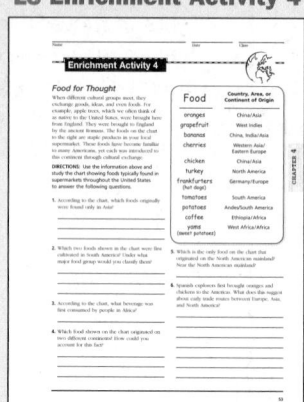

REVIEW AND REINFORCEMENT

L1 Vocabulary Activity 4   **L1 Reinforcing Skills Activity 4**   **L1 Reteaching Activity 4**

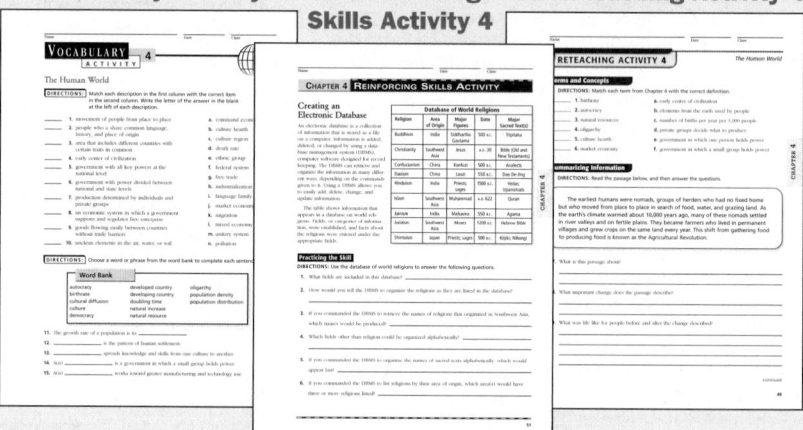

ASSESSMENT

L2 Chapter 4 Test Form A

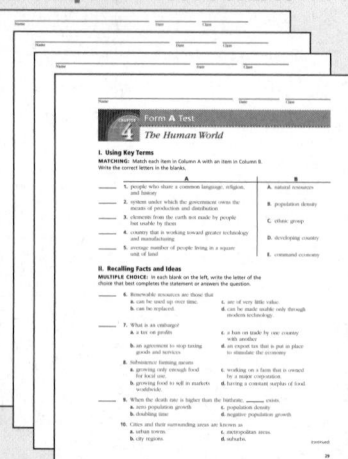

L2 Chapter 4 Test Form B

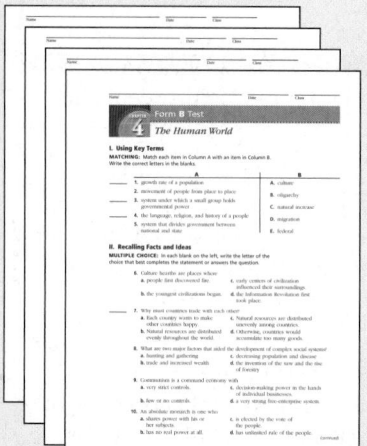

L1/ELL Performance Assessment Activity 4

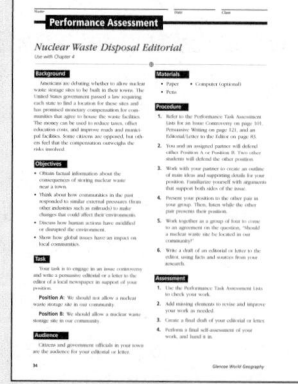

ExamView® Pro Testmaker

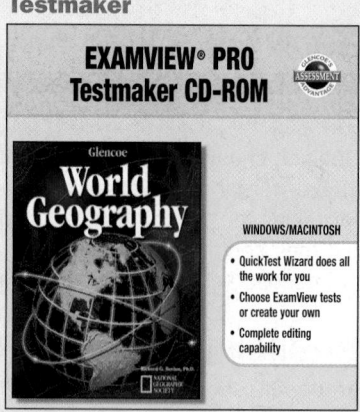

The following Spanish language materials are available in the Spanish Resources binder:

- Spanish Vocabulary Activities
- Spanish Guided Reading Activities
- Spanish Reteaching Activities
- Spanish Summaries
- Spanish Quizzes and Tests
- Spanish Reading Essentials and Study Guide

- World Regions Video
- MindJogger Videoquiz
- Vocabulary PuzzleMaker CD-ROM
- Interactive Tutor Self-Assessment CD-ROM
- ExamView® Pro Testmaker CD-ROM
- Audio Program
- TeacherWorks CD-ROM
- Interactive Student Edition CD-ROM
- Glencoe Skillbuilder Interactive Workbook CD-ROM, Level 2
- Presentation Plus! CD-ROM

Timesaving Tools

TeacherWorks™ All-In-One Planner and Resource Center

- **Interactive Teacher Edition** Access your Teacher Wraparound Edition and your classroom resources with a few easy clicks.

- **Interactive Lesson Planner** Planning has never been easier! Organize your week, month, semester, or year with all the lesson helps you need to make teaching creative, timely, and relevant.

Use Glencoe's **Presentation Plus!** multimedia teacher tool to easily present dynamic lessons that visually excite your students. Using Microsoft PowerPoint® you can customize the presentations to create your own personalized lessons.

GEOGRAPHY Online

Use our Web site for additional resources. All essential content is covered in the Student Edition.

You and your students can visit geography.glencoe.com, the Web site companion to *Glencoe World Geography*. This innovative integration of electronic and print media offers your students a wealth of opportunities. The student text directs students to the Web site for the following options:

- Chapter Overviews
- Self-Check Quizzes
- Student Activities
- Textbook Updates

Answers are provided for you in the "Web Activity Lesson Plan." Additional Web resources and Interactive Tutor puzzles are also available.

Additional Glencoe Teacher Support

- Teaching Strategies for the Geography Classroom (including Block Scheduling Pacing Guides)
- Graphic Organizer Transparencies Strategies and Activities
- Outline Map Resource Book
- Reading in the Content Area

PLANNING GUIDE

SECTION RESOURCES

Daily Objectives	Reproducible Resources	Multimedia Resources

SECTION 1   World Population

1. List the factors that influence population growth.
2. Identify the challenges that population growth poses for the planet.
3. Explain why the world's population is unevenly distributed.

 Reproducible Lesson Plan 4-1
 Daily Lecture Notes 4-1
 Guided Reading Activity 4-1*
 Reading Essentials and Study Guide 4-1*
 Section Quiz 4-1*

- Daily Focus Skills Transparency 4-1
- Political Map Transparency 1
- Unit 1 Map Overlay Transparencies
- Interactive Tutor Self-Assessment CD-ROM
- ExamView® Pro Testmaker CD-ROM*
- Presentation Plus! CD-ROM

SECTION 2   Global Cultures

1. Identify the factors that define a culture.
2. Describe the major culture regions of the world.
3. Discuss the developments that have affected interaction between cultures in recent years.

 Reproducible Lesson Plan 4-2
 Daily Lecture Notes 4-2
 Guided Reading Activity 4-2*
 Reading Essentials and Study Guide 4-2*
Section Quiz 4-2*

- Daily Focus Skills Transparency 4-2
- Unit 1 Map Overlay Transparencies
- Interactive Tutor Self-Assessment CD-ROM
- ExamView® Pro Testmaker CD-ROM*
- Presentation Plus! CD-ROM

SECTION 3   Political and Economic Systems

1. Identify the levels of government.
2. Describe the major types of governments in the world today.
3. Discuss the major types of economic systems in the world.

 Reproducible Lesson Plan 4-3
 Daily Lecture Notes 4-3
 Guided Reading Activity 4-3*
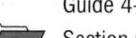 Reading Essentials and Study Guide 4-3*
 Section Quiz 4-3*

- Daily Focus Skills Transparency 4-3
- Unit 1 Map Overlay Transparencies
- Interactive Tutor Self-Assessment CD-ROM
- ExamView® Pro Testmaker CD-ROM*
- Presentation Plus! CD-ROM

SECTION 4   Resources, Trade, and the Environment

1. Describe the types of energy most likely to be used in the future.
2. Identify the factors that determine a country's economic development and trade relationships.
3. Discuss how human economic activities affect the environment.

 Reproducible Lesson Plan 4-4
 Vocabulary Activity 4*
Daily Lecture Notes 4-4
 Guided Reading Activity 4-4*
 Reading Essentials and Study Guide 4-4*
 Reteaching Activity 4*
 Reinforcing Skills Activity 4
 Section Quiz 4-4*

- Daily Focus Skills Transparency 4-4
- Unit 1 Map Overlay Transparencies
- Vocabulary PuzzleMaker CD-ROM
- Interactive Tutor Self-Assessment CD-ROM
- ExamView® Pro Testmaker CD-ROM*
- Presentation Plus! CD-ROM

Blackline Master	Software	Videocassette	*Also available in Spanish*
Transparency	CD-ROM	DVD	

OUT OF TIME? Assign the Chapter 4 **Reading Essentials and Study Guide.**

 **Block Schedule**

Activities that are particularly suited to use within the block scheduling framework are identified throughout this chapter by the following designation:

KEY TO ABILITY LEVELS

Teaching strategies have been coded for various learning styles and abilities.

L1   BASIC activities for all students

L2   AVERAGE activities for average to above-average students

L3   CHALLENGING activities for above-average students

ELL   ENGLISH LANGUAGE LEARNER activities

Teacher to Teacher

Barbara J. Royce
Monson Jr/Sr High School
Monson, MA

Local Geography

This activity helps students learn about their community and locate appropriate research sources. It also acquaints students with geographic factors that may affect their community.

Our community publishes a report that contains information about its history, government, public services, and other items of interest to residents. Using the report as a starting point, I write 25 questions for students to answer and give them two weeks to turn in their written responses. The questions cover topics such as location, climate, government, demographics, history, culture, and general information. In order to answer them, students must read the community report, use a historical atlas, contact local government offices, and practice library skills. Although our community has a Web site, I require students to use methods other than Internet research to find the answers in order to strengthen their library research skills.

NATIONAL GEOGRAPHIC — TEACHER'S CORNER

Index to National Geographic Magazine:

The following articles may be used for research relating to this chapter:

- "People Like Us," by Rick Gore, July 2000.
- "Celebrations of Earth," by Stuart Franklin, January 2000.
- *Global Culture*, a National Geographic Special Edition, August 1999.
- *Population*, a National Geographic Special Edition, October 1998.

National Geographic Society Products:

To order the following products for use with this chapter, call National Geographic Society at 1-800-368-2728.

- *Physical Geography of the Continents Series* (Videos)
- *Healing the Earth* (Video)
- *Pollution: World at Risk* (Video)
- *Recycling: The Endless Circle* (Video)

NGS ONLINE

Access National Geographic's Web site for current events, activities, links, interactive features, and archives.
www.nationalgeographic.com

Meeting National Standards

Geography For Life

The following standards are highlighted in Chapter 4:

Section 1   EE2 Places and Regions: Standards 4, 6
EE4 Human Systems: Standard 9
EE6 The Uses of Geography: Standard 18

Section 2   EE4 Human Systems: Standards 9, 10
EE6 The Uses of Geography: Standard 17

Section 3   EE1 The World in Spatial Terms: Standard 1
EE4 Human Systems: Standards 11, 13
EE5 Environment and Society: Standard 16

Local Objectives

_____

_____

MEETING SPECIAL NEEDS

In addition to the Differentiated Instruction strategies found in each section, the following resources are also suitable for your special needs students:

- *ExamView® Pro Testmaker CD-ROM* allows teachers to tailor tests by reducing answer choices.
- The *Audio Program* includes the entire narrative of the student edition so that less-proficient readers can listen to the words as they read them.
- The *Reading Essentials and Study Guide* provides the same content as the student edition but is written two grade levels below the textbook.
- *Guided Reading Activities* give less-proficient readers point-by-point instructions to increase comprehension as they read each textbook section.
- *Enrichment Activities* include a stimulating collection of readings and activities for gifted and talented students.

Chapter Objectives

1. Discuss global population densities and distributions.

2. Describe the culture regions into which geographers classify the world.

3. Identify various forms of government found around the world.

4. Explain how the distribution of natural resources influences trade.

GLENCOE TECHNOLOGY

Use *MindJogger Videoquiz* to preview the Chapter 4 content.

GeoJournal

For access to additional information on world population and other relevant information, go to www.nationalgeographic.com (See Teacher pages in front for strategies for using journals in the geography classroom.)

GEOGRAPHY Online

Introduce students to chapter content and key terms by having them access **Chapter Overview 4** at geography.glencoe.com

Study Organizer

Dinah Zike's Foldables are three-dimensional, interactive graphic organizers that help students practice basic writing skills, review key vocabulary terms, and identify main ideas. Have students complete the Foldable activity in the *Dinah Zike's Reading and Study Skills Foldables* booklet.

CHAPTER 4

The Human World

GeoJournal

As you read this chapter, use your journal to record information about aspects of the human world. Include details that show how geographers describe population, culture, government, resources, and the environment.

GEOGRAPHY Online

Chapter Overview Visit the **Glencoe World Geography** Web site at geography.glencoe.com and click on Chapter Overviews—Chapter 4 to preview information about the human world.

ABOUT THE PHOTO

Visual Instruction Located in west-central Bolivia, the city of Oruro, like many cities in Latin America and around the world, celebrates All-Saint's Day on November 1. This holiday celebration may have originated when Pope Gregory III dedicated a chapel in St. Peter's, Rome, to honor all the saints. Pope Gregory IV, however, made it an official holiday. Oruro, which became an important silver mining center during the Spanish colonial period, adapted many religious festivals from the Roman Catholic religion practiced by Spanish colonizers. **EE2 Places and Regions: Standards 4, 6**

Guide to Reading

Consider What You Know
The world's largest cities are often in the news. Think about where these cities are located and what their locations have in common. Why do you think people have settled in these places?

Reading Strategy
Organizing As you read about changes in world population, create a web diagram like the one below by listing the challenges created by population growth.

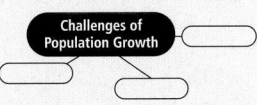

Read to Find Out
- What factors affect a country's population growth rate?
- What challenges does population growth pose for the planet?
- Why is the world's population unevenly distributed?

Terms to Know
- death rate
- birthrate
- natural increase
- doubling time
- population distribution
- population density
- migration

Places to Locate
- Nile Delta
- Hungary
- Germany
- Canada
- Bangladesh
- Mexico City

◄ *Young and old flock to a carnival in Oruro, Bolivia.*

World Population

NATIONAL GEOGRAPHIC

A Geographic View

Nile Delta in Peril
The black soil of the Nile Delta has made it the foundation stone of seven millennia of human history.... Today Egypt's battle is to preserve the soil and water that have always given life to the delta. One hundred fifty years ago this nation had five million acres of farmland and five million citizens; now it has seven million acres of farmland and 60 million citizens. And every nine months there are nearly a million more Egyptians to feed.... The Nile Delta ... has survived many challenges from without. Now the challenges it must survive come from its own population....

—Peter Theroux, "The Imperiled Nile Delta," National Geographic, January 1997

Farmland in the Nile Delta

The effects of rapid population growth on Egypt's fertile **Nile Delta** reflect the global challenge humans face today. How can people maintain conditions favorable to human life without endangering those very conditions through overpopulation? In this section you will learn about the earth's human population—how it changes and how geographers measure these changes.

Population Growth
About 6.2 billion people now live on Earth, inhabiting about 30 percent of the planet's land. Global population is growing rapidly and is expected to reach about 7.8 billion by the year 2025. Such rapid growth was not always the case. The graph of population growth on page 76 shows that from the year 1000 until 1800, the world's population

Chapter 4 ● 75

CHAPTER 4
Section 1, pages 75-79

① FOCUS

Section Overview
This section discusses the factors that influence worldwide population density and distribution, and it examines the consequences of rising global population rates.

BELLRINGER
Skillbuilder Activity
- Project transparency and have students answer questions.
- Available as blackline master.

Daily Focus Skills Transparency 4-1

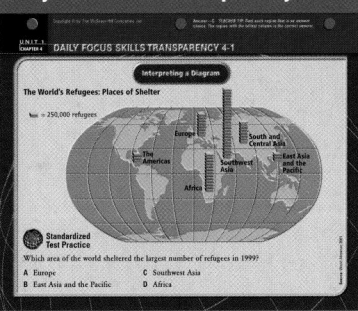

Guide to Reading

Consider What You Know
Answers *favorable climate, presence of natural resources, access to freshwater, geography favorable to transportation and trade*

Reading Strategy
Answers *adequate food production, uneven age distribution, increased use of resources*

Preteaching Vocabulary
Have students review the list of "Terms to Know." **Ask:** What quality do most of these terms have in common? (*They deal with mathematical concepts.*)

RESOURCE MANAGER

Reproducible Masters
- Reproducible Lesson Plan 4-1
- Daily Lecture Notes 4-1
- Guided Reading Activity 4-1
- Reading Essentials and Study Guide 4-1
- Section Quiz 4-1

Transparencies
- Daily Focus Skills Transparency 4-1
- Political Map Transparency 1
- Unit 1 Map Overlay Transparencies

Multimedia
- Interactive Tutor Self-Assessment CD-ROM
- ExamView® Pro Testmaker CD-ROM
- Presentation Plus! CD-ROM

L3 Place

Ask volunteers to research the birthrate and death rate for your local county or similar administrative area. Have students calculate the rate of population increase and the projected date when the population will double if the rate remains constant.

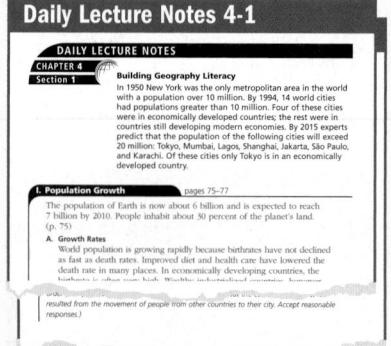

NATIONAL GEOGRAPHIC **GRAPH STUDY**

Answers

1. *about 1 billion*

2. *about 1900; steep increase due to better nutrition and sanitation, advances in health care and technology, high birthrates*

Skills Practice

What generalization can you make about population growth from 1000 to 1700? *(Almost no growth occurred.)*

---

increased slowly. Then the number of people on Earth more than doubled between 1800 and 1950. By 2000 the world's population had soared to more than 6 billion. If the population continues to grow at its current rate, it will pass 9 billion by the year 2050.

Growth Rates

Global population is growing rapidly because birthrates have not declined as fast as death rates. The death rate is the number of deaths per year for every 1,000 people. The birthrate is the number of births per year for every 1,000 people. Scientists in the field of *demography*, the study of populations, calculate the natural increase, or growth rate, of a population as the difference between an area's birthrate and its death rate.

Population growth occurs at different rates in various parts of the world. Over the past 200 years,

death rates have gone down in many places as a result of improved health care, more abundant food supplies, advances in technology, and better living conditions. In many wealthy industrialized countries, a declining death rate has been accompanied by a low birthrate. These countries have reached what is known as *zero population growth*, in which the birthrate and death rate are equal. When this balance occurs, a country's population does not grow.

In many countries in Asia, Africa, and Latin America, however, the birthrate is high. Families in these regions traditionally are large because of cultural beliefs about marriage, family, and the value of children. For example, a husband and wife in a rural agricultural area may choose to have several children who will help farm the land. A high number of births combine with low death rates to greatly increase population growth in these areas. As a result, the doubling time, or the number of years it takes a population to double in size, has been reduced to only 25 years in some parts of Asia, Africa, and Latin America. In contrast, the average doubling time of a wealthy, industrialized country can be more than 300 years.

Challenges of Population Growth

Rapid population growth presents many challenges to the global community. As the number of people increases, so does the difficulty of producing enough food to feed them. Fortunately, since 1950 world food production has risen on all continents except Africa. Because so many people in various parts of Africa need food, warfare or severe weather conditions that ruin crops can bring widespread famine.

In addition, populations that grow rapidly use resources more quickly than populations that do not grow as rapidly. Some countries face shortages of water, housing, and clothing, for example. Rapid population growth strains these limited resources. Another concern is that the world's population is unevenly distributed by age, with the majority of some countries' populations being infants and young children who cannot contribute to food production.

While some experts are pessimistic about the long-term effects of rapid population growth, others are optimistic that, as the number of humans increases, the levels of technology and creativity also will rise. For example, scientists

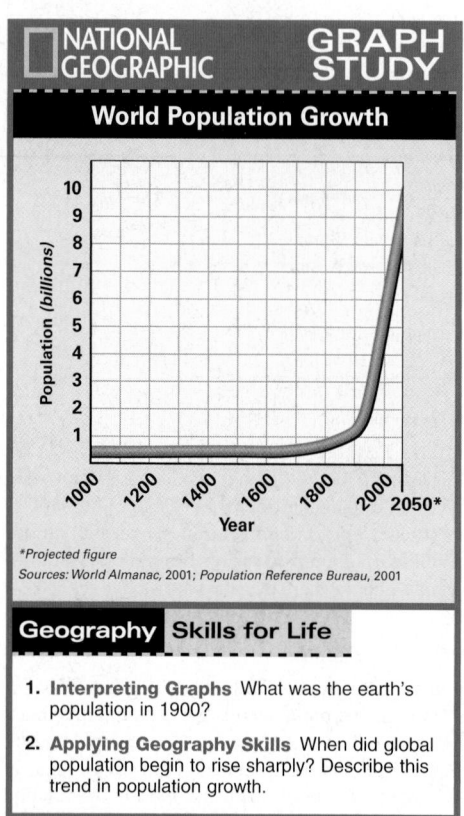

NATIONAL GEOGRAPHIC **GRAPH STUDY**

World Population Growth

*Projected figure
Sources: World Almanac, 2001; Population Reference Bureau, 2001

Geography **Skills for Life**

1. **Interpreting Graphs** What was the earth's population in 1900?

2. **Applying Geography Skills** When did global population begin to rise sharply? Describe this trend in population growth.

DIFFERENTIATED INSTRUCTION

Reading Support Have students skim this section and list the ways in which geographers use mathematical concepts and skills to analyze population change. Ask students to write a brief essay or speech describing these uses and explain how mathematics might contribute to an understanding of global population trends.
🌐 **EE4 Human Systems: Standard 9;** 🌐 **EE6 The Uses of Geography: Standard 18**

📁 Refer to *Inclusion for the Social Studies Classroom Strategies and Activities.*

continue to study and develop ways to boost agricultural productivity. Fertilizers can improve crop yields. Irrigation systems can help increase the amount of land available for farming. New varieties of plants such as wheat and rice have been created to withstand severe conditions and yield more food.

Economics
Negative Population Growth

In the late 1900s, some countries in Europe began to experience negative population growth, in which the annual death rate exceeds the annual birthrate. **Hungary** and **Germany**, for example, show growth rates of –0.4 and –0.1, respectively. This situation has economic consequences different from, but just as serious as, those caused by high growth rates. In countries with negative population growth, it is difficult to find enough workers to keep the economy going. Labor must be recruited from other countries, often by encouraging immigration or granting temporary work permits. Although the use of foreign labor has helped countries with negative growth rates maintain their levels of economic activity, it also has created tensions between the "host" population and the communities of newcomers.

Population Distribution

Not only do population growth rates vary among the earth's regions, but the planet's population distribution, or the pattern of human settlement, is uneven as well. Population distribution is related to the earth's geography. Only about 30 percent of the earth's surface is made up of land, and much of that land is inhospitable. High mountain peaks, barren deserts, and frozen tundra make human activity very difficult. As the population density map on page 78 shows, almost everyone on Earth lives on a relatively small portion of the planet's land—a little less than one-third. Most people live where fertile soil, available water, and a climate without harsh extremes make human life sustainable.

Geography **Skills for Life**

War Refugees War can cause population shifts by forcing refugees to flee to safety in other countries.

Movement How might population growth rates affect a country's economy?

Of all the continents, Europe and Asia are the most densely populated. Asia alone contains more than 60 percent of the world's people. Throughout the world, where populations are highly concentrated many people live in *metropolitan areas*—cities and their surrounding urbanized areas. Today most people in Europe, North America, and Australia live in or around urban areas.

Population Density

Geographers determine how crowded a country or region is by measuring population density—the average number of people living on a square mile or square kilometer of land. To determine population density in a country, geographers divide the total population of the country by its total land area.

GEOGRAPHY *Online*

Student Web Activity Visit the **Glencoe World Geography** Web site at geography.glencoe.com and click on Student Web Activities—Chapter 4 for an activity on world population.

L1/ELL

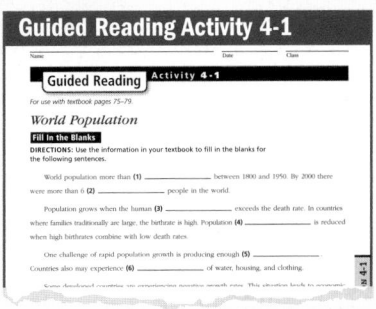

Guided Reading Activity 4-1

Guided Reading Activity 4-1

For use with textbook pages 75–79.

World Population

Fill in the Blanks

DIRECTIONS: Use the information in your textbook to fill in the blanks for the following sentences.

World population more than (1) _____ between 1800 and 1950. By 2000 there were more than 6 (2) _____ people in the world.

Population grows when the human (3) _____ exceeds the death rate. In countries where families traditionally are large, the birthrate is high. Population (4) _____ is reduced when high birthrates combine with low death rates.

One challenge of rapid population growth is producing enough (5) _____. Countries also may experience (6) _____ of water, housing, and clothing.

World Explorer

Answers

rapid growth: strain on food supply, job shortages, higher cost for public services; negative growth: worker shortages, cultural conflict due to imported labor

More About the Photo

Although a truce was signed in July 1999, civil war skirmishes continue to plague the Democratic Republic of the Congo. The conflict began when refugees from Rwanda and Burundi flocked into the country.

GEOGRAPHY *Online*

Objectives, goals, and answers to the student activity can be found in the Web Activity Lesson Plan feature at geography.glencoe.com

COOPERATIVE LEARNING ACTIVITY

Population Densities Have students choose partners. Assign each pair the name of a country. (Do not assign large countries with population densities in the thousands per square mile/km.) Have pairs use almanacs or Internet resources to find the population density of their assigned countries. Give each pair a floor tile or cardboard 12 inches square and a sack of dry beans. Tell students that each tile represents one square mile and each dry bean represents 10 people. Have pairs glue dry beans to their tiles to represent the population densities of their assigned countries. Have students label and display their completed tiles. 🌐 **EE4 Human Systems: Standard 9**

MAP STUDY

Answers

1. *South Asia, East Asia, Europe*

2. *physical features not conducive to human settlement in sparsely populated interior*

Map Skills Practice

Place Which areas of the Southern Hemisphere are uninhabited? Why?

(Antarctica, inland southern Africa, Australian inland; harsh climates)

L1/ELL

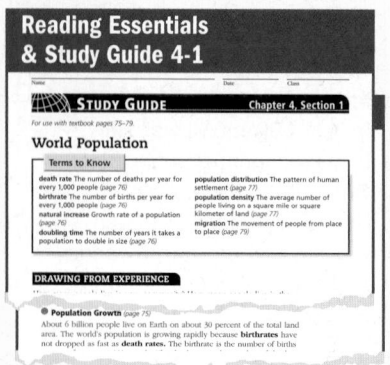

Reading Essentials
& Study Guide 4-1

ASSESS

Assign Section 1 Assessment as homework or as an in-class activity.

Have students use **Interactive Tutor Self-Assessment CD-ROM** to review Section 1.

NATIONAL GEOGRAPHIC — MAP STUDY

World Population Density

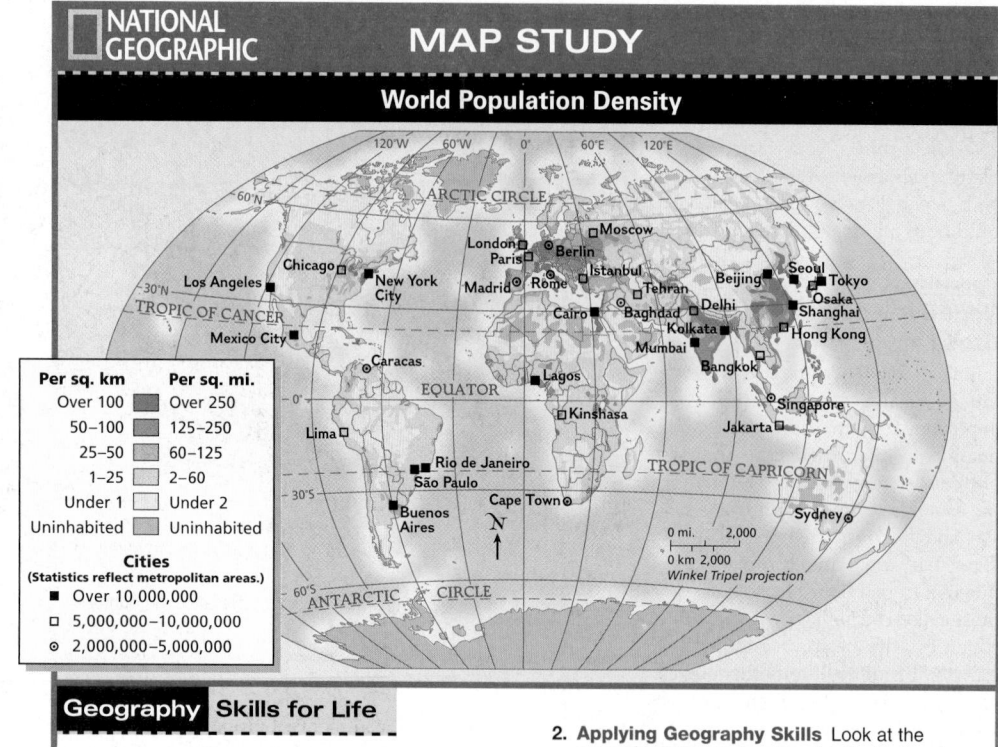

Geography | **Skills for Life**

1. **Interpreting Maps** Which areas of the Northern Hemisphere are most densely populated?

2. **Applying Geography Skills** Look at the general population densities for South America. What conclusions can you draw about the continent's physical geography?

Find NGS online map resources @ www.nationalgeographic.com/maps

---

Population density varies widely from country to country. **Canada**, with a low population density of about 8 people per square mile (3 people per sq. km), offers wide-open spaces and the opportunity to choose between living in thriving cities or quiet rural areas. The country of **Bangladesh**, at the other extreme, has one of the highest population densities in the world—about 2,639 people per square mile (1,019 people per sq. km). In tiny Bangladesh even the rural areas are more crowded than many of the world's cities.

Countries that have populations of nearly the same size do not necessarily have similar population densities. For example, Zambia and Belgium have about the same number of people, roughly 10.4 million. With a smaller land area, Belgium has 881 people per square mile (340 people per sq. km).

However, Zambia has an average of only 37 people per square mile (14 people per sq. km). Belgium, then, is more densely populated than Zambia.

Because population density is an average, it does not account for uneven population distribution within a country—a common occurrence. In Egypt, for example, overall population density is 186 people per square mile (72 people per sq. km). In reality, about 99 percent of Egypt's people live within 20 miles of the Nile River. The rest of Egypt is desert. Thus, some geographers prefer to describe a country's population density in terms of land that can be used to support the population rather than total land area. When Egypt's population density is measured this way, it equals about 5,807 people per square mile (2,242 people per sq. km)!

CRITICAL THINKING ACTIVITY

Distinguishing Fact from Opinion Have students collect articles about global population issues from print media and Internet news sites. Have them work in small groups to categorize the information in the articles as fact or opinion. Write *Fact* and *Opinion* on the board, and have each group list the titles of their articles under the appropriate headings. Choose two or three sample articles, and have the class work together to evaluate the accuracy of the categorizations. **Ask:** Why is it important to distinguish fact from opinion when addressing global issues? *(solutions should be based on accurate information rather than opinion)* ▣ EE6 The Uses of Geography: Standard 18

Population Movement

Migration is the movement of people from place to place. The earth's human population is moving in great numbers. Some people are moving from city to city or from suburb to suburb. Large numbers of people are migrating from rural villages to cities.

> *Migration is the dynamic undertow of population change. . . . It is, as it has always been, the great adventure of human life. Migration helped create humans, drove us to conquer the planet, shaped our societies, and promises to reshape them again.*
>
> Michael Parfit, "Human Migration," *National Geographic*, October 1998

The resulting growth of city populations brought about by migration and the changes that come with this increase in population are called *urbanization*. Urbanization has many causes. The primary cause is the desire of rural people to find jobs and a better life in more prosperous urban areas. Rural populations certainly have grown, but the amount of land that can be farmed has not

increased to meet the growing number of people who need to work and to eat. As a result, many rural migrants find urban jobs in manufacturing or in service industries, such as tourism.

About half of the world's people live in cities—a far higher percentage than ever before. Between 1960 and 2000, the population of metropolitan **Mexico City** rose from about 5 million to about 18 million. Other cities in Latin America, as well as cities in Asia and Africa, have seen similar growth. Some of these cities contain a large part of their country's entire population. For example, about one-third of Argentina's people live in the city of Buenos Aires.

Population movement also occurs between countries. Some people emigrate from the country of their birth and move to another. They are known as emigrants in their homeland and are called immigrants in their new country. In the past 40 years, millions of people have left Africa, Asia, and Latin America to find jobs in the wealthier countries of Europe, North America, and Australia. Some people were forced to flee their country because of wars, food shortages, or other problems. They are *refugees*, or people who flee to another country to escape persecution or disaster. In the next section, you will learn how the movement of peoples has influenced the development of cultures.

SECTION 1 ASSESSMENT

Checking for Understanding

1. **Define** death rate, birthrate, natural increase, doubling time, population distribution, population density, migration.

2. **Main Ideas** On a table like the one below, fill in the main points about population growth and population distribution from this section.

Population Growth	Population Distribution
•	•
•	•
•	•

Critical Thinking

3. **Comparing and Contrasting** How do the effects of zero population growth and negative population growth differ? How are they similar?

4. **Drawing Conclusions** How might the population growth rates of developing countries be affected as they become increasingly industrialized?

5. **Predicting Consequences** What will happen to the standard of living in cities as urbanization increases? How might the standard of living differ between cities in the developing world and cities in the developed world?

Analyzing Maps

6. **Human-Environment Interaction** Look at the population density map on page 78. Identify three of the most densely populated areas on Earth. What physical features do they have in common?

Applying Geography

7. **Influences of Physical Geography** What geographic features might be present in countries that have large numbers of people concentrated in relatively small areas? Write a paragraph with supporting details to explain your answer.

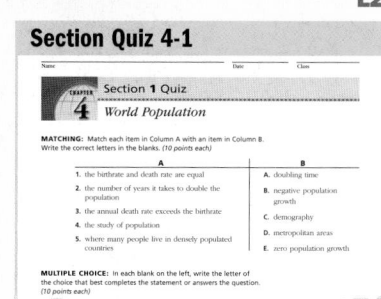

Section Quiz 4-1

Section 1 Quiz
World Population

MATCHING: Match each item in Column A with an item in Column B. Write the correct letters in the blanks. *(10 points each)*

	A		B
1.	the birthrate and death rate are equal	A.	doubling time
2.	the number of years it takes to double the population	B.	negative population growth
3.	the annual death rate exceeds the birthrate	C.	demography
4.	the study of population	D.	metropolitan areas
5.	where many people live in densely populated countries	E.	zero population growth

MULTIPLE CHOICE: In each blank on the left, write the letter of the choice that best completes the statement or answers the question. *(10 points each)*

Reteach

On the board, list *Population Growth*, *Population Distribution*, and *Population Challenges*. Have students list as many facts as possible under each heading.

Enrich

Share with students the *National Geographic* Map Supplement "Refugees" (2/2000), tracing movement of displaced peoples.

4 CLOSE

Have students research trends in past world population growth and distribution. Then ask them to develop and defend a hypothesis on likely population patterns for the future.

SECTION 1 ASSESSMENT ANSWERS

1. All vocabulary terms are defined in the text.

2. Tables should reflect key points in the text.

3. Answers might include that both allow effective use of resources; negative population growth can cause economic and social hardships by reducing the labor force, causing dependence on imported workers.

4. Growth rates may decrease as fewer children

are needed to maintain subsistence agriculture, lowering birthrates; growth rates may increase as better health care allows more people to live past infancy, lowering death rates.

5. Quality of life will decline as higher populations put stress on urban resources. The stress will be greater (and the quality of life lower) in developing countries which already have limited

economic resources and social services.

6. access to bodies of water and other natural resources; fertile and accessible land capable of sustaining agriculture

7. **Applying Geography** smaller overall land area, sparsely populated desert, mountains; densely populated river valleys

① FOCUS

Section Overview

This section discusses the factors that define a culture, the major culture regions of the world, and the effects of interaction among cultures.

BELLRINGER
Skillbuilder Activity

 Project transparency and have students answer questions.

 Available as blackline master.

Daily Focus Skills Transparency 4-2

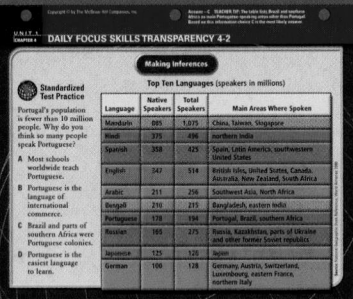

Guide to Reading

Consider What You Know

Answers *Students may mention ethnicity, country of origin, language, religion, or social group.*

Reading Strategy

Answer *United States and Canada; Latin America; Europe; Russia; North Africa, Southwest Asia, and Central Asia; Africa South of the Sahara; South Asia; East Asia; Southeast Asia; Australia, Oceania, and Antarctica*

Preteaching Vocabulary

Invite a volunteer to define the term *hearth*. *(a fireplace, the symbolic gathering place of a family in a home)* Ask students to predict the definition of the term *culture hearth* based on this information.

Guide to Reading

Consider What You Know

You probably know that, as a country of immigrants, the United States includes people from a great variety of cultural backgrounds. How do you define your own cultural background?

Reading Strategy

Organizing As you read about the cultures of the world, complete a graphic organizer similar to the one below by listing the world culture regions.

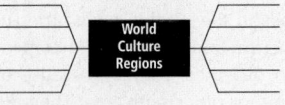

Read to Find Out

- What factors define a culture?
- What are the major culture regions of the world?
- What developments have affected interaction between cultures in recent years?

Terms to Know

- culture
- language family
- ethnic group
- culture region
- cultural diffusion
- culture hearth

Places to Locate

- Egypt
- Iraq
- Pakistan
- China
- Mexico

Global Cultures

NATIONAL GEOGRAPHIC

A Geographic View

Beijing Construction Boom

[T]oday's Beijing is awash with change, where the old Confucian ideals of personal cultivation and family values clash with a new emphasis on money and the market, . . . where a construction boom is reshaping Beijing's low-slung profile and cramped alleys with soaring skyscrapers of glass and steel, where car traffic clogs streets that once rang with bicycle bells. . . . Over the centuries the people of Beijing have become expert at adjusting. Like the willows planted around the capital, people have survived by being flexible, yielding to strong winds, then springing back as stillness returns.

Beijing, China

—Todd Carrel, "Beijing: New Face for the Ancient Capital," National Geographic, *March 2000*

The Chinese people have shown a remarkable ability to adapt to changes over time. The evidence of change in Chinese and other societies is apparent in such areas as architecture, family customs, and economic activities. These factors and many others express the values that a group of people share and pass down from one generation to another. In this section you will read about how the world's people organize communities, develop their ways of life, and cope with their differences and similarities.

Elements of Culture

In addition to population trends, geographers study culture, the way of life of a group of people who share similar beliefs and customs. A particular culture can be understood by looking at various elements: what languages the people speak, what religions they

---

RESOURCE MANAGER

📁 Reproducible Masters
- Reproducible Lesson Plan 4-2
- Daily Lecture Notes 4-2
- Guided Reading Activity 4-2
- Reading Essentials and Study Guide 4-2
- Section Quiz 4-2

🎬 Transparencies
- Daily Focus Skills Transparency 4-2
- Unit 1 Map Overlay Transparencies

Multimedia
- 💿 Interactive Tutor Self-Assessment CD-ROM
- 💿 ExamView® Pro Testmaker CD-ROM
- 💿 Presentation Plus! CD-ROM

follow, and what smaller groups form as parts of their society. The study of a culture also includes examining people's daily lives. Still other factors are the history the people have shared and the art forms they have created. Finally, culture includes how people govern their society and how they make a living.

Language

Language is a key element in a culture's development. Through language, people communicate information and experiences and pass on cultural values and traditions. Sharing a language is one of the strongest unifying forces for a culture. Even within a culture, however, there are language differences. Some people may speak a dialect, or a local form of a language that differs from the main language. These differences may include variations in pronunciation and the meaning of words.

Linguists, scientists who study languages, organize the world's languages into language families—large groups of languages having similar roots. Seemingly diverse languages may belong to the same language family. For example, English, Spanish, Russian, and Hindi (spoken in India) are all members of the Indo-European language family. The world map below shows where languages from the different language families are spoken.

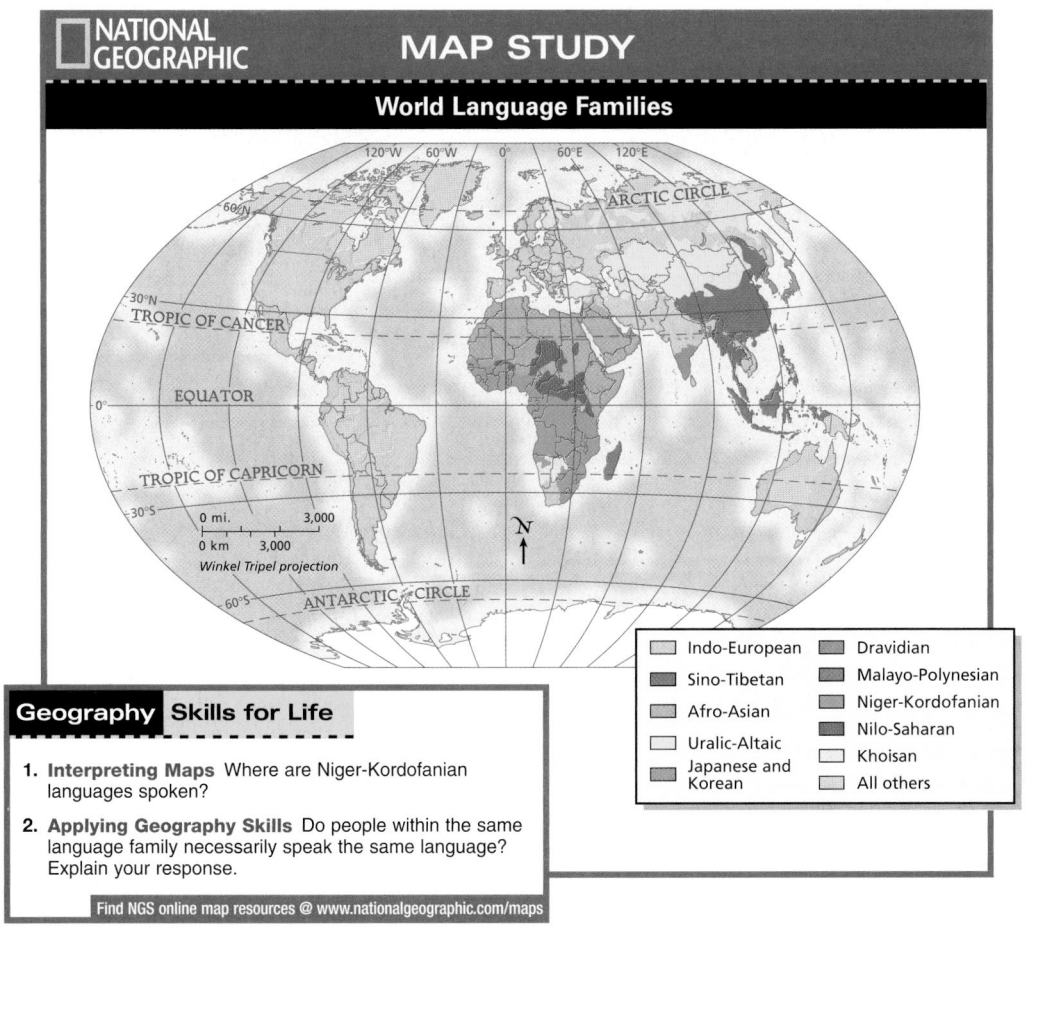

NATIONAL GEOGRAPHIC — MAP STUDY

World Language Families

Legend:
- Indo-European
- Sino-Tibetan
- Afro-Asian
- Uralic-Altaic
- Japanese and Korean
- Dravidian
- Malayo-Polynesian
- Niger-Kordofanian
- Nilo-Saharan
- Khoisan
- All others

Winkel Tripel projection
0 mi. 3,000
0 km 3,000

Geography Skills for Life

1. **Interpreting Maps** Where are Niger-Kordofanian languages spoken?
2. **Applying Geography Skills** Do people within the same language family necessarily speak the same language? Explain your response.

Find NGS online map resources @ www.nationalgeographic.com/maps

② TEACH

L1 Movement

Have students interview family members to find out where they or their ancestors came from. Display a large outline map of the world, and have students place colored dot stickers on their families' places of origin.

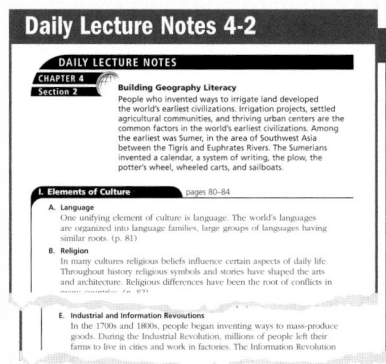

Daily Lecture Notes 4-2

DAILY LECTURE NOTES

CHAPTER 4
Section 2

Building Geography Literacy
People who invented ways to irrigate land developed the world's earliest civilizations. Irrigation projects, settled agricultural communities, and thriving urban centers are the common factors in the world's earliest civilizations. Among the earliest was Sumer, in the area of Southwest Asia between the Tigris and Euphrates Rivers. The Sumerians invented a calendar, a system of writing, the plow, the potter's wheel, wheeled carts, and sailboats.

I. Elements of Culture   pages 80–84

A. Language
One unifying element of culture is language. The world's languages are organized into language families, large groups of languages having similar roots. (p. 81)

B. Religion
In many cultures religious beliefs influence certain aspects of daily life. Throughout history religious symbols and stories have shaped the arts and architecture. Religious differences have been the root of conflicts in many countries. (p. 82)

E. Industrial and Information Revolutions
In the 1700s and 1800s, people began inventing ways to mass-produce goods. During the Industrial Revolution, millions of people left their farms to live in cities and work in factories. The Information Revolution

NATIONAL GEOGRAPHIC — MAP STUDY

Answers

1. *Africa, from south of the Sahara to about the Tropic of Capricorn*

2. *No; a language family includes many languages that may vary greatly but which have the same roots.*

Map Skills Practice
Place From which language family do the languages spoken in North Africa and Southwest Asia come? South America? *(Afro-Asian; Indo-European, others)*

DIFFERENTIATED INSTRUCTION

English Learners Have students identify the language family to which their primary language belongs. Then have students work together to make a sign for the classroom. The sign should read *English spoken here* as well as the equivalent in the primary language of each English language learner in class. **ELL**

⊕ **EE4 Human Systems: Standard 9**

📁 Refer to *Inclusion for the Social Studies Classroom Strategies and Activities.*

MAP STUDY

Answers
1. *North America, northern Europe, South Africa, Australia*
2. *Religious subjects or styles occur in music, art, food, or holidays.*

Map Skills Practice
Movement Islam originated in Southwest Asia. In what other parts of the world has Islam become predominant? *(North Africa, Central Asia, Southeast Asia)*

L1/ELL

Guided Reading Activity 4-2

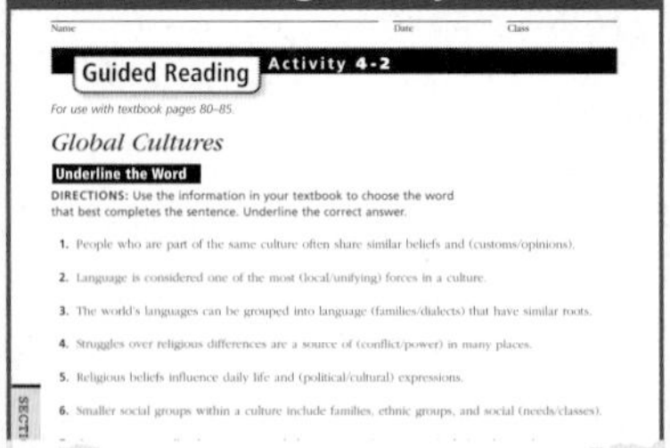

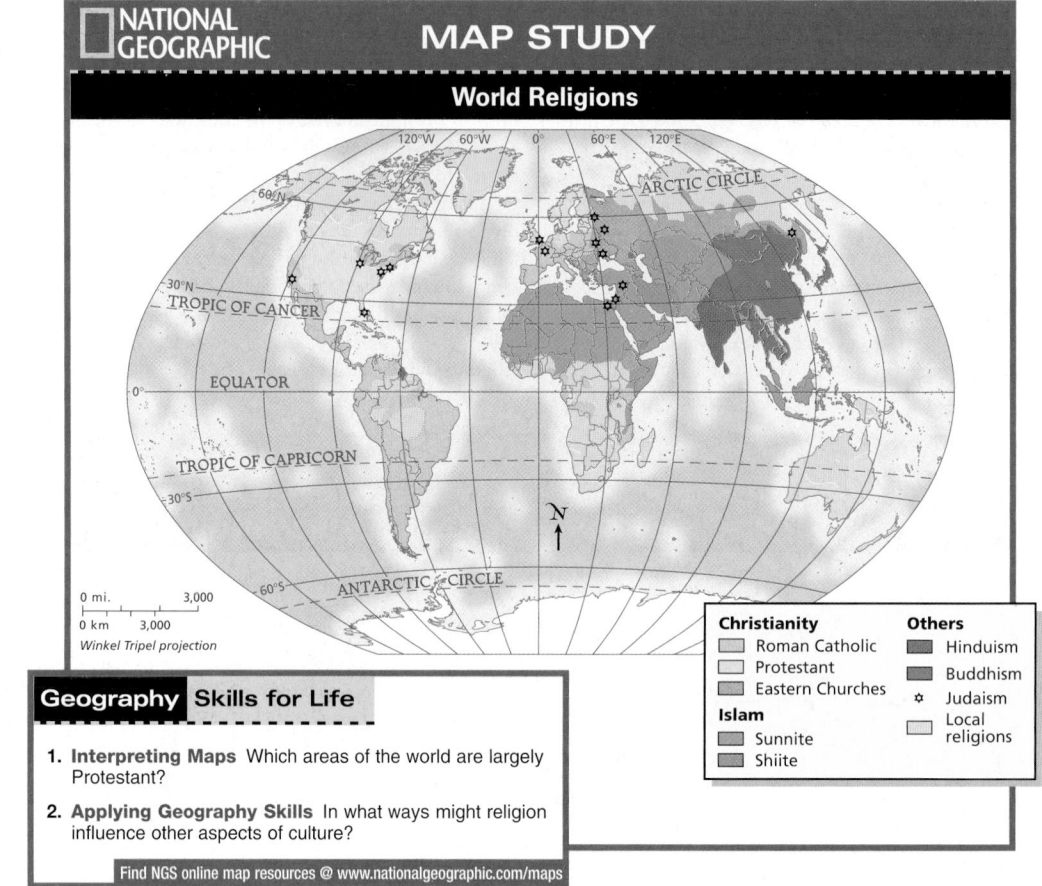

NATIONAL GEOGRAPHIC MAP STUDY

World Religions

Winkel Tripel projection

0 mi. 3,000
0 km 3,000

Christianity
- Roman Catholic
- Protestant
- Eastern Churches

Islam
- Sunnite
- Shiite

Others
- Hinduism
- Buddhism
- Judaism
- Local religions

Geography Skills for Life

1. **Interpreting Maps** Which areas of the world are largely Protestant?
2. **Applying Geography Skills** In what ways might religion influence other aspects of culture?

Find NGS online map resources @ www.nationalgeographic.com/maps

Culture NOTE

Language Loss As many as half of the world's 3,000–6,500 known languages are expected to disappear by 2100. As global communications increase, the need for languages that are widely spoken becomes greater. Today children learn languages such as English, Spanish, or Arabic.

Religion

Another important part of culture is religion. Religious beliefs vary significantly around the world, and struggles over religious differences are a source of conflict in many countries. In many cultures, however, religion enables people to find a sense of identity. It also influences aspects of daily life, from the practice of moral values to the celebration of holidays and festivals. Throughout history, religious symbols and stories have shaped cultural expressions such as painting, sculpture, architecture, music, and dance. Some of the major world religions are Hinduism, Buddhism, Judaism, Christianity, and Islam. The map above shows the areas of the world where these religions are practiced.

Social Groups

Every culture includes a social system in which the members of the society fall into various smaller groups. A social system develops to help the members of a culture work together to meet basic needs. In all cultures the family is the most important group, although family structures vary somewhat from culture to culture. Most cultures are also made up of social classes, groups of people ranked according to ancestry, wealth, education, or other criteria. Moreover, cultures may include people who belong to different ethnic groups. An ethnic group is made up of people who share a common language, history, place of origin, or a combination of these elements.

82 ⊕ Unit 1

COOPERATIVE LEARNING ACTIVITY

Charting Languages Have students form nine groups. Assign each group one of the world's major language families—other than "Indo-European" and "All others"—listed on the map on page 81. Have each group research its language family and prepare a table listing the most common languages within the family, the places where these languages are spoken, and the numbers of speakers. As a class, students should rank language families by numbers of speakers or numbers of individual languages.
🗺 **EE4 Human Systems: Standard 10**

Government

A society's government reflects the uniqueness of its culture. Despite differences, governments of the world share certain features. Each government, for example, maintains order within the country, provides protection from outside dangers, and supplies other services to its people. Governments are organized according to levels of power—national, regional, and local—and by type of authority—a single ruler, a small group of leaders, or a body of citizens or their representatives.

Economic Activities

People in every kind of culture must make a living, whether in farming or in industry or by providing services such as preparing food or designing Web pages. In examining cultures, geographers look at economic activities. They study how a culture utilizes its natural resources to meet such human needs as food and shelter. They also analyze the ways in which people produce, obtain, use, and sell goods and services.

Culture Regions

To organize their understanding of cultural development, geographers divide the earth into specific areas called culture regions. Each culture region includes many different countries that have certain traits in common. They may share similar economic systems, forms of government, and social groups. Their histories, religions, and art forms may share similar influences. The food,

L1 Classify

Have students refer to the world map on which they displayed information about family origins.
Ask: Into which world culture region do geographers classify your family's place of origin? Poll students to determine which culture region contributed the most students to the class.

L1/ELL

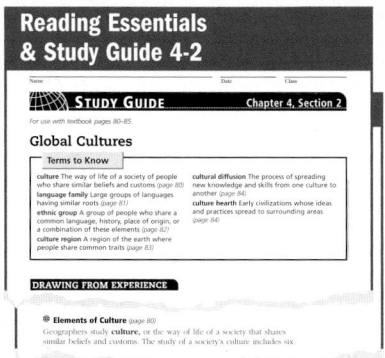

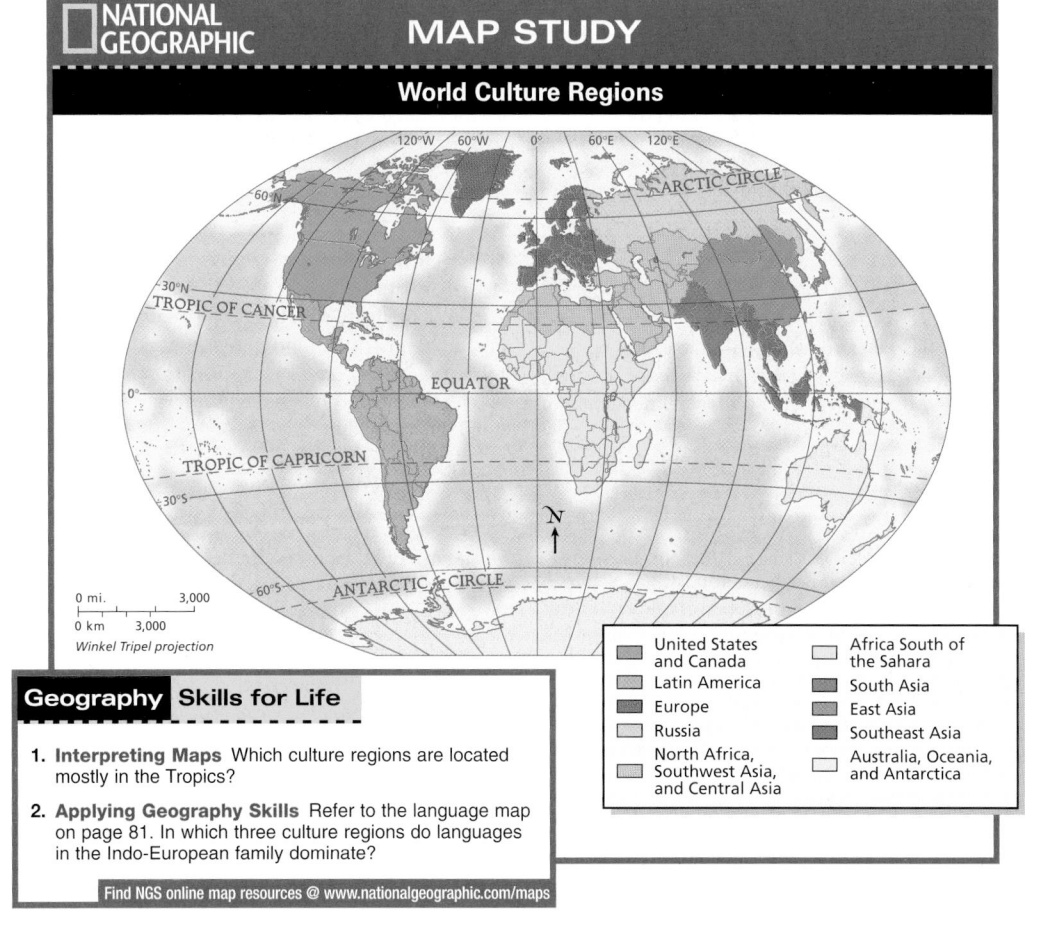

MAP STUDY

World Culture Regions

120°W   60°W   0°   60°E   120°E

ARCTIC CIRCLE

60°N

30°N

TROPIC OF CANCER

0°   EQUATOR

TROPIC OF CAPRICORN

30°S

N

0 mi.   3,000
0 km   3,000
Winkel Tripel projection

60°S   ANTARCTIC CIRCLE

■ United States and Canada	■ Africa South of the Sahara
■ Latin America	■ South Asia
■ Europe	■ East Asia
■ Russia	■ Southeast Asia
■ North Africa, Southwest Asia, and Central Asia	■ Australia, Oceania, and Antarctica

Geography Skills for Life

1. **Interpreting Maps** Which culture regions are located mostly in the Tropics?

2. **Applying Geography Skills** Refer to the language map on page 81. In which three culture regions do languages in the Indo-European family dominate?

Find NGS online map resources @ www.nationalgeographic.com/maps

NATIONAL GEOGRAPHIC   **MAP STUDY**

Answers
1. *Latin America, Africa South of the Sahara, Southeast Asia (also parts of Southwest Asia, South Asia, Australia)*

2. *United States and Canada, Latin America, Europe*

Map Skills Practice
Region Which culture regions include a continent with no permanent population? (*Australia, Antarctica, and Oceania*)

CRITICAL THINKING ACTIVITY

Synthesizing Information Have students survey family members and friends to find out which of the elements of human civilization they think are most important. Have them ask: If you were going to establish a human colony on a distant planet, what would you bring to the colony? Have students work together to report the results of their survey, grouping responses under the five characteristics of culture regions: *language, religion, social groups, government,* and *economic activities.* 🔲 🌐 **EE4 Human Systems: Standard 10**

MAP STUDY

Answers

1. *Indus Valley, Yellow River valley, Mesopotamia*
2. *rivers*

Map Skills Practice
Location In which zones of latitude are culture hearths located? *(the Tropics and mid-latitudes)* What characteristic do these latitudes share? *(mild climates capable of supporting agriculture and human settlement near a source of water)*

GEOGRAPHY AND THE HUMANITIES

 World Music:
A Cultural Legacy

 World Art and Architecture
Transparencies

 World Art Prints

**ASSESS**

Assign Section 2 Assessment as homework or as an in-class activity.

◉ Have students use **Interactive Tutor Self-Assessment CD-ROM** to review Section 2.

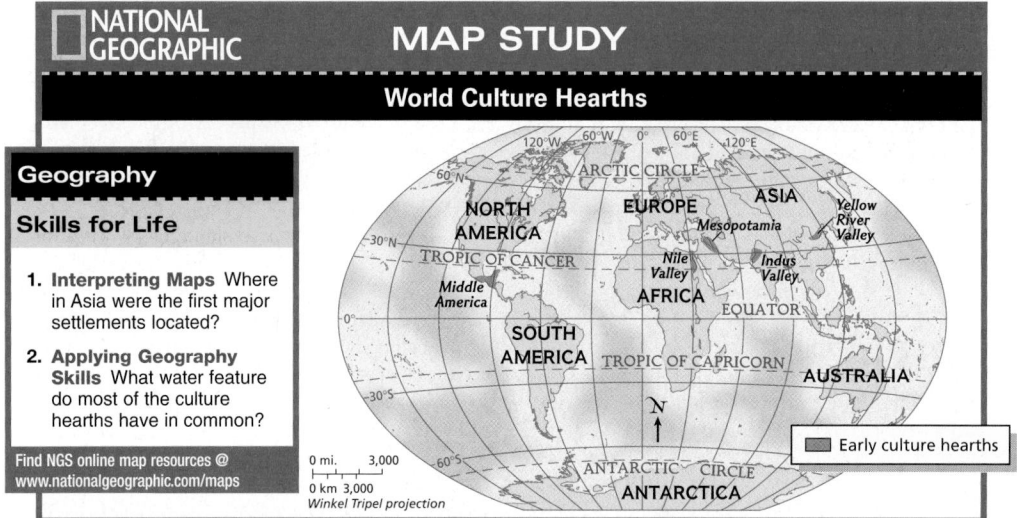

NATIONAL GEOGRAPHIC **MAP STUDY**

World Culture Hearths

Geography

Skills for Life

1. **Interpreting Maps** Where in Asia were the first major settlements located?

2. **Applying Geography Skills** What water feature do most of the culture hearths have in common?

Find NGS online map resources @
www.nationalgeographic.com/maps

0 mi. 3,000
0 km 3,000
Winkel Tripel projection

Early culture hearths

---

clothing, and housing of people in these countries may all have common characteristics as well. The map on page 83 shows the various culture regions that you will study in this textbook.

Cultural Change

No culture remains the same over the course of time. Internal factors—new ideas, lifestyles, and inventions—create change within cultures.

Change can also come to a culture through spatial interaction, such as trade, the movement of people, and war. The process of spreading new knowledge and skills from one culture to another is called cultural diffusion.

The Agricultural Revolution

Cultural diffusion has been a major factor in cultural development since the dawn of human history. The earliest humans were nomads, groups of herders who had no fixed home but who moved from place to place in search of food, water, and grazing land. As the earth's climate warmed about 10,000 years ago, many of these nomads settled in river valleys and on fertile plains. They became farmers who lived in permanent villages and grew crops on the same land every year. This shift from gathering food to producing food is known as the Agricultural Revolution.

By about 3500 B.C. some of these early farming villages had evolved into *civilizations*, highly organized, city-based societies with an advanced knowledge of farming, trade, government, art, and science.

Culture Hearths

The world's first civilizations arose in what are known as culture hearths, early centers of civilization whose ideas and practices spread to surrounding areas. As you can see from the map above, the most influential culture hearths developed in areas that now make up the modern countries of **Egypt**, **Iraq**, **Pakistan**, **China**, and **Mexico**. In Mexico the Olmec culture

❝ . . . *flourished along Mexico's Gulf Coast between 1200 and 400 B.C. . . . Because of early achievements in art, politics, religion, and economics, the Olmec stand for many as a kind of 'mother culture' to all the civilizations that came after, including the Maya and the Aztec.* ❞

George E. Stuart, "New Light on the Olmec," *National Geographic*, November 1993

TEAM-TEACHING ACTIVITY: WORLD HISTORY, ART

Cultural Contributions Have students work with world history and art teachers to develop a visual display of the key cultural contributions of each of the world's major culture hearths. Have students include examples of physical and cultural patterns associated with each hearth, and write a description of how these patterns influenced the development of innovations that later spread to other world regions. Students might focus on cultural developments or technologies that are still identifiable in American culture today. Students may work in small groups, with each group concentrating on a culture hearth. Then, combine their completed work into a class display. 📦 🌐 **EE6 The Uses of Geography: Standard 17**

These five culture hearths had certain geographic features in common. They all emerged from farming settlements in areas with a mild climate and fertile land and were located near a major river or source of water. The peoples of the culture hearths made use of these favorable environments. They dug canals and ditches in order to use the rivers to irrigate the land. All of these factors enabled people to grow surplus crops.

Economics
Specialization and Civilization

Surplus food set the stage for the rise of cities and civilizations. With more food available, there was less need for everyone in a settlement to farm the land. People were able to develop other ways of making a living. They created new technology and carried out specialized economic activities, such as metalworking and shipbuilding, that spurred the development of long-distance trade.

In turn, the increased wealth from trade led to the rise of cities and complex social systems. The ruler of a city needed a well-organized government to coordinate harvests, plan building projects, and manage an army for defense. Perhaps most importantly, officials and merchants created writing systems that made it possible to record and transmit information.

Cultural Contacts

Cultural contact among different civilizations promoted cultural change as ideas and practices spread through trade and travel. Permanent migration, in which people leave one land to seek a new life in another, also has fostered cultural diffusion. People migrate to avoid harsh governments, wars, persecution, and famines. In some cases, such as that of enslaved Africans brought to the Americas, mass migrations have been forced. Conversely, positive factors—a favorable climate, better economic opportunities, and religious or political freedoms—may draw people from one place to another. Migrants carry their cultures with them, and their ideas and practices often blend with those of the people already living in the migrants' adopted countries.

Industrial and Information Revolutions

Cultural diffusion has increased rapidly during the last 250 years. In the 1700s and 1800s, some countries began to industrialize, using power-driven machines and factories to mass-produce goods. New production methods dramatically changed these countries' economies, since goods could be produced quickly and cheaply. This development, known as the Industrial Revolution, also led to social changes. As people left farms for jobs in factories and mills, cities grew larger. Harsh working and living conditions at the outset of the Industrial Revolution eventually improved.

At the end of the 1900s, the world experienced a new turning point—the Information Revolution. Computers now make it possible to store huge amounts of information and to send information all over the world in an instant, thus linking the cultures of the world more closely than ever before.

SECTION 2 ASSESSMENT

Checking for Understanding

1. **Define** culture, language family, ethnic group, culture region, cultural diffusion, culture hearth.

2. **Main Ideas** Fill in the main features of global cultures on a web diagram like the one below.

Global Cultures
Elements of Culture Cultural Change

Critical Thinking

3. **Making Generalizations** Explain the factors that influence a country's power to control territory.

4. **Identifying Cause and Effect** What cultural changes have resulted from the Information Revolution?

5. **Analyzing Information** How do factors, such as trade, war, migration, and inventions, affect cultural change?

Analyzing Maps

6. **Place** Study the map of world religions on page 82. What factors are related to the diffusion of world religions?

Applying Geography

7. **Culture and Environment** Research the Internet to make a list of examples in which varying cultures view particular places or features differently.

Chapter 4 🌐 85

L2

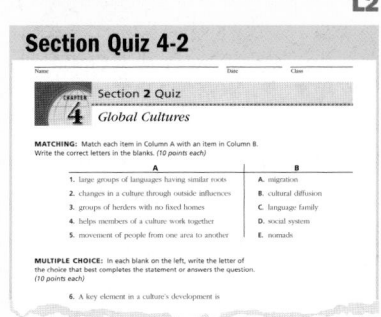
Reteach
Name the five characteristics geographers use to identify culture regions—language, religion, social groups, government, and economic systems. Have students provide examples.

Enrich
Have students draw a map that shows the spatial diffusion of a language, belief, commodity, or disease (such as the bubonic plague). Then, ask them to write a description of the phenomenon's effects on regions of contact.

 CLOSE

Invite students to create a dinner menu that includes one food item from each culture region of the world.

SECTION 2 ASSESSMENT ANSWERS

1. All vocabulary terms are defined in the text.

2. Webs should reflect pertinent details of the text.

3. Cultural, economic, religious, and political achievements; powerful military forces; access to trade routes and natural resources.

4. Geographically separated cultures have been brought into close contact through telecommunications and the Internet; businesses can locate anywhere in the world.

5. Factors, such as trade, war, migrations, and inventions help bring people into contact with each other. These encounters lead to a blend or clash of cultures, and the exchange of ideas, practices, and products.

6. World religions that originated in culture hearths spread via trade, conquest, missionary activity, and migration.

7. **Applying Geography** Students' work should demonstrate an understanding of how people view the same phenomenon differently as a result of their varying cultural experiences.

FOCUS

Section Overview

This section discusses the major political and economic systems found in the world today.

BELLRINGER
Skillbuilder Activity

 Project transparency and have students answer questions.

 Available as blackline master.

Daily Focus Skills Transparency 4-3

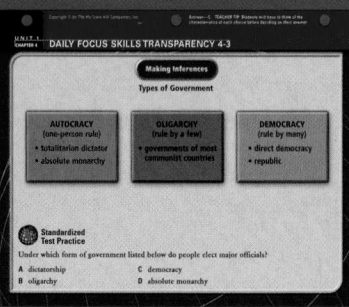

Guide to Reading

Consider What You Know
Answer *Students should identify their local and state political systems as well as the economic system of the United States.*

Reading Strategy
Answer Students should complete the outline by including all heads in the section.

Preteaching Vocabulary
Have students use dictionaries to determine the meaning of the following prefixes and suffixes: *uni-, auto-, eco-, olig-, demo-, -cracy, -nomy, -archy.* Have them then make predictions about the meaning of this section's key terms.

Guide to Reading

Consider What You Know
Political and economic systems help define a people's culture, or way of life. Think about the political and economic systems in your own region. How do they impact your culture?

Reading Strategy
Taking Notes Use the major headings of the section to create an outline similar to the one below.

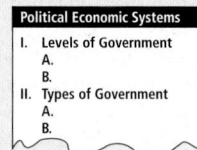

Political Economic Systems
I. Levels of Government
   A.
   B.
II. Types of Government
   A.
   B.

Read to Find Out
- What are the various levels of government?
- What are the major types of governments in the world today?
- What are the major types of economic systems in the world?

Terms to Know
- unitary system
- federal system
- autocracy
- oligarchy
- democracy
- traditional economy
- market economy
- mixed economy
- command economy

Places to Locate
- United States
- Saudi Arabia
- United Kingdom
- China
- Vietnam

SECTION 3

Political and Economic Systems

NATIONAL GEOGRAPHIC
A Geographic View

Global Connections

Geographic location of resources, labor, and capital means less as scattered countries use information technologies to work together. Many cars have parts made in a half dozen countries; stores sell look-alike clothes sewn on four continents. . . . Money moves most easily. Stocks, currency, and bonds traded on worldwide electronic markets amount to an estimated three trillion dollars each day, twice the annual U.S. budget.

—*Joel L. Swerdlow, "Information Revolution,"* National Geographic, *October 1995*

Mercantile Exchange, Chicago

As information technology continues to link the world's cultures, the governments and economies of countries around the globe become increasingly interconnected. Government is the institution through which a society maintains social order, provides public services, ensures national security, and supports its economic well-being. An economy is the way a society produces, distributes, and uses goods and services. In this section you will study the major political and economic systems found in the world today.

Features of Government

Today the world is made up of nearly 200 independent countries that vary in size, military might, natural resources, and world influence. Each country is defined by characteristics such as its territory, its population, and its sovereignty, or freedom from outside control. All of these elements are brought together under a government. In carrying out its tasks, a government must make and enforce policies and laws that are binding on all people living within its territory.

RESOURCE MANAGER

📁 Reproducible Masters
- Reproducible Lesson Plan 4-3
- Daily Lecture Notes 4-3
- Guided Reading Activity 4-3
- Reading Essentials and Study Guide 4-3
- Section Quiz 4-3

🖥 Transparencies
- Daily Focus Skills Transparency 4-3
- Unit 1 Map Overlay Transparencies

Multimedia
- 💿 Interactive Tutor Self-Assessment CD-ROM
- 💿 ExamView® Pro Testmaker CD-ROM
- 💿 Presentation Plus! CD-ROM

Levels of Government

The government of each country has unique characteristics that relate to that country's historical development. To carry out their functions, governments have been organized in a variety of ways. Most large countries have several different levels of government. These usually include a national or central government, as well as the governments of smaller internal divisions such as provinces, states, counties, cities, towns, and villages.

Unitary System

A unitary system of government gives all key powers to the national or central government. This structure does not mean that only one level of government exists. Rather, it means that the central government creates state, provincial, or other local governments and gives them limited sovereignty. The United Kingdom and France both developed unitary governments as they gradually emerged from smaller territories during the late Middle Ages and early modern times.

Federal System

A federal system of government divides the powers of government between the national government and state or provincial governments. Each level of government has sovereignty in some areas. The **United States** developed a federal system after the thirteen colonies became independent.

Another similar type of government structure is a confederation, a loose union of independent territories. The United States at first formed a confederation, but this type of political arrangement failed to provide an effective national government. As a result, the U.S. Constitution made the national government supreme, while preserving some state government powers. Today other countries with federal or confederal systems include Canada, Switzerland, Mexico, Brazil, Australia, and India.

Geography Skills for Life

Ultimate Authority Though an absolute monarch, King Fahd of Saudi Arabia is assisted by a cabinet, or group of advisers.

Place Describe the powers of an absolute monarch.

Types of Governments

The governments of the world's countries also differ in the way they exercise authority. Governments can be classified by asking the question: "Who governs the state?" Under this classification system, all governments belong to one of the three major groups: (1) autocracy—rule by one person; (2) oligarchy—rule by a few people; or (3) democracy—rule by many people.

Autocracy

Any system of government in which the power and authority to rule belong to a single individual is an autocracy (aw•TAH•kruh•see). Autocracies are the oldest and one of the most common forms of government. Most autocrats achieve and maintain their position of authority through inheritance or by the ruthless use of military or police power.

Several forms of autocracy exist. One is an absolute or totalitarian dictatorship. In a totalitarian dictatorship, the decisions of a single leader determine government policies. The government under such a system can come to power through revolution or an election. The totalitarian dictator seeks to control all aspects of social and economic life. Examples of totalitarian dictatorships include Adolf Hitler's government in Nazi Germany (from 1933 to 1945), Benito Mussolini's rule in Italy (from 1922 to 1943),

NATIONAL GEOGRAPHIC World Explorer

② TEACH

L1 Discuss
Invite students to identify and discuss the forms of government they experience every day. **Ask:** What is the structure of government at school? In clubs or organizations? On sports teams? In your local community? Have students identify similar forms of government in other parts of the world.

NATIONAL GEOGRAPHIC World Explorer

Answer
An absolute monarch is not subject to laws or limits.

More About the Photo
Since Saudi Arabia's founding as an Islamic kingdom, its kings have all been the sons of one man—Abdul Aziz ibn Saud, who gave his family name to the country.

Daily Lecture Notes 4-3

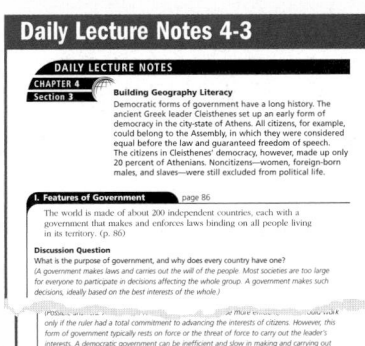

DAILY LECTURE NOTES

CHAPTER 4 Section 3

Building Geography Literacy

Democratic forms of government have a long history. The ancient Greek leader Cleisthenes set up an early form of democracy in the city-state of Athens. All citizens, for example, could belong to the Assembly, in which they were considered equal before the law and guaranteed freedom of speech. The citizens in Cleisthenes' democracy, however, made up only 20 percent of Athenians. Noncitizens—women, foreign-born males, and slaves—were still excluded from political life.

I. Features of Government *page 86*

The world is made of about 200 independent countries, each with a government that makes and enforces laws binding on all people living in its territory. (p. 86)

Discussion Question
What is the purpose of government, and why does every country have one?
(A government makes laws and carries out the will of the people. Most societies are too large for everyone to participate in decisions affecting the whole group. A government makes such decisions, ideally based on the best interests of the whole.)

DIFFERENTIATED INSTRUCTION

At-Risk Students For students who have problems with speaking, provide tape recorders and suggest that students role-play as radio news reporters covering a change in one of the world's governments (a military coup, a revolution, an election or the coronation of a monarch, for example). Have students develop simple scripts, emphasizing logical structure, and practice reading or reciting them on tape until they are satisfied with the pace, clarity, and confidence of their delivery. ⬤ **EE4 Human Systems: Standard 12**

📂 Refer to *Inclusion for the Social Studies Classroom Strategies and Activities.*

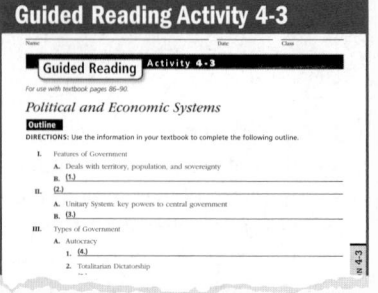
L2 Government

Ask: Should students your age be allowed to vote? Encourage students to provide arguments for their positions.

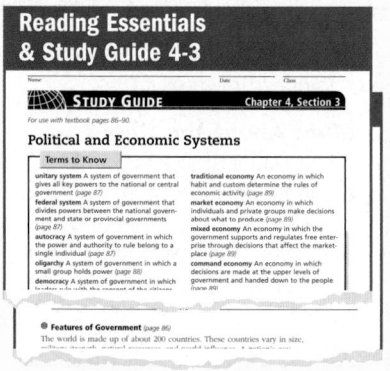
NATIONAL GEOGRAPHIC **World Explorer**

Answer
Direct: citizens meet to decide on issues; representative: citizens elect representatives to govern.

More About the Photo
Amendments to the U.S. Constitution have granted the vote to formerly enslaved peoples, women, and young adults ages 18–21.

---

and Joseph Stalin's regime in the Soviet Union (from 1924 to 1953). In such dictatorships, the government is not responsible to the people, and the people have no power to limit their rulers' actions.

Monarchy (MAH•nuhr•kee) is another form of autocratic government. In a monarchy, a king or queen exercises the supreme powers of government. Monarchs usually inherit their positions. Absolute monarchs have complete and unlimited power to rule their people. The king of **Saudi Arabia**, for example, is an absolute monarch. Absolute monarchs are rare today, but from the 1400s to the 1700s kings or queens with absolute powers ruled most of Western Europe.

Today some countries, such as the United Kingdom, Sweden, Japan, Jordan, and Thailand, have constitutional monarchies. Their monarchs share governmental powers with elected legislatures or serve as ceremonial leaders.

Oligarchy

An **oligarchy** (AH•luh•GAHR•kee) is any system of government in which a small group holds power. The group derives its power from wealth, military power, social position, or a combination of these elements. Sometimes religion is the source of power. Today the governments of communist countries, such as China, are mostly oligarchies. In such countries, leaders in the Communist Party and the armed forces control the government.

Both dictatorships and oligarchies sometimes claim they rule for the people. Such governments may try to give the appearance of control by the people. For example, they might hold elections but offer only one candidate or control the election results in other ways. Such governments may also have some type of legislature or national assembly elected by or representing the people. These legislatures, however, only approve policies

and decisions already made by the leaders. As in a dictatorship, oligarchies usually suppress all political opposition—sometimes ruthlessly.

Democracy

A **democracy** is any system of government in which leaders rule with the consent of the citizens. The term *democracy* comes from the Greek *demos* (meaning "the people") and *kratia* (meaning "rule"). The ancient Greeks used the word *democracy* to mean government by the many in contrast to government by the few. The key idea of democracy is that people hold sovereign power.

Direct democracy, in which citizens themselves decide on issues, exists in some places at local levels of government. No country today has a national government based on direct democracy. Instead, democratic countries have representative democracies, in which the people elect representatives with the responsibility and power to make laws and conduct government. An assembly of the people's representatives may be called a council, a legislature, a congress, or a parliament.

Many democratic countries, such as the United States and France, are republics. In a republic, voters elect all major officials, who are responsible to the people. The head of state—or head of government—is usually a president elected for a specific term. Not every democracy is a republic. The **United**

NATIONAL GEOGRAPHIC **World Explorer**

Geography **Skills for Life**
The Right to Vote In the United States, voters such as this man in Mississippi elect their officials.
Place How do direct democracies and representative democracies differ?

COOPERATIVE LEARNING ACTIVITY

Make a Circle Graph Have students work together to make a circle graph of the types of government practiced by the countries of the world. Students may work in pairs or in small groups to carry out the following tasks: (1) Use almanacs and other reference sources to determine the type of government practiced in each country. (2) Classify these types under general headings, such as *constitutional monarchies* or *federal republics*. (3) Determine what proportion of the total of the world's countries each category represents. (4) Display information as a circle graph. **EE1 The World in Spatial Terms: Standard 3; EE4 Human Systems: Standard 13**

Kingdom, for example, is a democracy with a monarch as head of state. This monarch's role is ceremonial, and elected officials hold the power to rule.

Economic Systems

Governments around the world deal with many kinds of economic systems. All economic systems, however, must make three basic economic decisions: (1) what and how many goods and services should be produced, (2) how they should be produced, (3) who gets the goods and services that are produced. The three major types of these economic systems—traditional, market, and command—make decisions differently.

Traditional Economy

In a traditional economy, habit and custom determine the rules for all economic activity. Individuals are not free to make decisions based on what they would like to have. Instead their behavior is defined by the customs of their elders and ancestors. For example, it was a tradition in the Inuit society of northern Canada that a successful hunter would share the spoils of the hunt with the other families in the village. This custom allowed the Inuit to survive the Arctic climate for thousands of years. Today, traditional economic systems exist in very limited parts of the world.

Market Economy

In a market economy, individuals and private groups make decisions about what to produce. People, as shoppers, choose what products they will or will not buy, and businesses make more of what they believe consumers want. A market economy is based on *free enterprise*, the idea that private individuals or groups have the right to own property or businesses and make a profit with only limited government interference. In a free enterprise

NATIONAL GEOGRAPHIC World Explorer

Geography Skills for Life
California Entrepreneur
The owner of a bicycle shop uses a telephone and laptop computer to conduct business.
Region How does a market economy affect the economic activities in a region?

system, people are free to choose what jobs they will do and for whom they will work. Another term for an economic system organized in this way is *capitalism*.

No country in the world, however, has a pure market economy system. Today the U.S. economy and others like it are described as mixed economies. A mixed economy is one in which the government supports and regulates free enterprise through decisions that affect the marketplace. In this arrangement the government's main economic task is to preserve the free market by keeping competition free and fair and by supporting the public interest. Governments in modern mixed economies also influence their economies by spending tax revenues to support social services such as health care, education, and housing.

Command Economy

In a command economy, the government owns or directs the means of production—land, labor, capital (machinery, factories), and business managers—and controls the distribution

---

CRITICAL THINKING ACTIVITY

Identifying Cause and Effect Lead a discussion in which students analyze the causes and effects of the shift from command economies to market economies. **Ask:** What causes a command economy to stagnate or decline? *(Businesses have no incentive to be creative or efficient; consumers may not want the available products.)* What are the expected effects of changing to a market economy? *(Businesses will grow in the long run because they are free to produce more of what consumers will buy.)*
🌐 **EE4 Human Systems: Standard 11**

NATIONAL GEOGRAPHIC World Explorer

Answer
A market economy promotes free enterprise and diverse economic activities.

More About the Photo
An *entrepreneur* is a person who starts his or her own business. A high rate of entrepreneurship is one of the indicators of a strong market economy.

**ASSESS**

Assign Section 3 Assessment as homework or as an in-class activity.

🔵 Have students use **Interactive Tutor Self-Assessment CD-ROM.**

L2

Section Quiz 4-3

Name	Date	Class

CHAPTER 4 Section **3** Quiz
Political and Economic Systems

MATCHING: Match each item in Column A with an item in Column B. Write the correct letters in the blanks. *(10 points each)*

A		B
1. command economy with strict governmental control		A. oligarchy
2. a small group holds power		B. confederation
3. a king or queen shares power with elected representatives		C. constitutional monarchy
4. loose union of independent territories		D. market economy
5. businesses make what they believe consumers want		E. communism

MULTIPLE CHOICE: In each blank on the left, write the letter of the choice that best completes the statement or answers the question.

Reteach

Have students write paragraphs summarizing the section content. Have them incorporate all of the "Terms to Know" from page 86 in their summaries.

Enrich

Have students research the foreign policy positions of selected nations, such as the United States, Japan, Israel, and the United Kingdom regarding the government of Iraq. What geographic factors might shape the positions taken by these countries on this issue?

 CLOSE

Have students use atlases and almanacs to prepare outline maps of a specific world region or continent. They should label the countries and next to each, write down its form of government.

---

of goods. Believing that such economic decision making benefits all of society and not just a few people, countries with command economies try to distribute goods and services equally among all citizens. Public taxes, for example, are used to support social services, such as housing and health care, for all citizens. However, citizens have no voice in how this tax money is spent.

Government
Socialism and Communism

A command economy is called either socialism or communism, depending on how much the government is involved. In theory, communism requires strict government control of almost the entire society, including its economy. The government decides how much to produce, what to produce, and how to distribute the goods and services produced. One political party—the Communist Party—makes decisions and may even use various forms of coercion to ensure that the decisions are carried out at lower political and economic levels.

Supporters of the market system claim, however, that without free decision making and incentives, businesses will not innovate or produce products that people want. Customers will be limited in their choices and economies will stagnate. As a result of these problems, command economies often decline. An example is the former Soviet Union, as described by a Russian observer.

> *In 1961 the [Communist] party predicted ... that the Soviet Union would have the world's highest living standard by 1980.... But when that year came and went, the Soviet Union still limped along, burdened by ... a stagnant economy.*
>
> Dusko Doder, "The Bolshevik Revolution," *National Geographic*, October 1992

By 2000, Russia and the other countries that were once part of the Soviet Union were developing market economies. **China** and **Vietnam** have allowed some free enterprise to promote economic growth, although their governments tightly control political affairs.

An economic system called socialism allows an even wider range of free enterprise alongside government-run activities. Socialism has three main goals: (1) the equal distribution of wealth and economic opportunity; (2) society's control, through its government, of all major decisions about production; and (3) public ownership of most land, factories, and other means of production. Politically, some socialist countries, especially those in western Europe, are democracies. Under democratic socialism, people have basic human rights and elect their political leaders, even though the government controls certain industries.

SECTION 3 ASSESSMENT

Checking for Understanding

1. **Define** unitary system, federal system, autocracy, oligarchy, democracy, traditional economy, market economy, mixed economy, command economy.

2. **Main Ideas** Copy the outline below, and complete it with information from the section.

   Political and Economic Systems
   I. Levels of Government
      A. Unitary System
         1.

Critical Thinking

3. **Comparing and Contrasting** What different roles might local citizens have in government decision making under a unitary system, a federal system, and a confederation?

4. **Making Generalizations** What functions do all types of governments carry out?

5. **Categorizing Information** Describe the characteristics of traditional, command, and market economies.

Analyzing Maps

6. **Region** Study the map of world religions on page 82. Then write two generalizations about the distribution of the world's religions.

   Applying Geography

   7. **Political Systems** Research political systems and geography. What geographic factors influence a country's foreign policy? Use Iraq, Israel, Japan, and the United Kingdom as examples.

SECTION 3 ASSESSMENT ANSWERS

1. All vocabulary terms are defined in the text.

2. Outlines should reflect key concepts.

3. unitary: local citizens have little say in national government; federal: local citizens have direct input on local level, indirect (representative) input on national level; confederation: local citizens have substantial influence

4. All governments maintain social order, provide public services, ensure national security, and support economic well-being.

5. Traditional: based on custom and habit, no individual decision-making; command: government ownership, control, and decision-making aimed at promoting social equality; market: private or group ownership and decision-making about what to produce and buy; profits made with only limited government interference

6. Possible answers include that Christianity is practiced throughout North and South America and Europe. Buddhism occurs mainly in East

Asia. Islam is practiced mainly in a large area spanning Africa and Asia.

7. **Applying Geography** Essays should consider a country's location, resources, history and culture, and form of government. Iraq: dictatorship, oil; Israel: historic claims, conflict with Arabs; Japan: limited resources, trading economy; U.K: imperial power to European partner.

Guide to Reading

Consider What You Know

People are dependent on the world's resources for survival. Yet you may have heard that certain economic activities threaten humans' future access to these resources. What are some actions people can take to preserve the world's natural treasures?

Reading Strategy

Organizing As you read about natural resources, complete a web diagram similar to the one below by listing types of renewable energy resources.

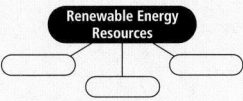

Read to Find Out

- What types of energy most likely will be used in societies in the future?
- What factors determine a country's economic development and trade relationships?
- How do human economic activities affect the environment?

Terms to Know

- natural resource
- developed country
- developing country
- industrialization
- free trade
- pollution

Places to Locate

- Malaysia
- European Union

Resources, Trade, and the Environment

NATIONAL GEOGRAPHIC

A Geographic View

Globalization in High Gear

Humans have been weaving commercial and cultural connections since before the first camel caravan ventured afield. In the 19th century the postal service, newspapers, transcontinental railroads, and great steam-powered ships [brought about] fundamental changes. . . . Now computers, the Internet, cellular phones, cable TV, and cheaper jet transportation have accelerated and complicated these connections. Still, the basic dynamic remains the same: Goods move. People move. Ideas move. And cultures change. The difference now is the speed and scope of these changes.

—Erla Zwingle, "A World Together," National Geographic, August 1999

Buddhist monks in California restaurant

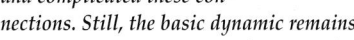

At the start of the twenty-first century, technological advances such as the Internet were connecting people around the globe. These connections continue to make the world's peoples increasingly interdependent, or reliant on each other. In this section you will learn about the growth of a global economy and the ways in which the world's peoples use—and misuse—natural resources.

Resources

Earth provides all the elements necessary to sustain life. The elements from the earth that are not made by people but can be used by them for food, fuel, or other necessities are called natural resources. People can use some natural resources as much as they want. These

Chapter 4   91

RESOURCE MANAGER

Reproducible Masters
- Reproducible Lesson Plan 4-4
- Vocabulary Activity 4
- Daily Lecture Notes 4-4
- Guided Reading Activity 4-4
- Reading Essentials and Study Guide 4-4
- Reinforcing Skills Activity 4
- Reteaching Activity 4
- Section Quiz 4-4

Transparencies
- Daily Focus Skills Transparency 4-4
- Unit 1 Map Overlay Transparencies

Multimedia
- Vocabulary PuzzleMaker CD-ROM
- Interactive Tutor Self-Assessment CD-ROM
- ExamView® Pro Testmaker CD-ROM
- Presentation Plus! CD-ROM

FOCUS

Section Overview

This section discusses the world's resources, the connection between trade and economic development, and the impact of human economic activity on the environment.

BELLRINGER
Skillbuilder Activity

- Project transparency and have students answer questions.
- Available as blackline master.

Daily Focus Skills Transparency 4-4

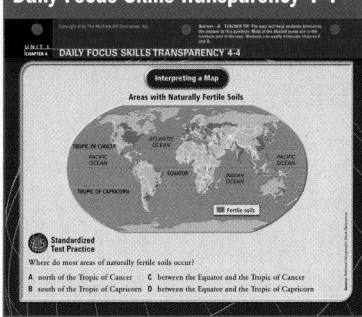

Guide to Reading

Consider What You Know

Answers *Possible answers may include conserve, reuse, recycle, develop renewable alternatives, change patterns of consumption.*

Reading Strategy

Answers *hydroelectric power, nuclear energy, solar energy*

Preteaching Vocabulary

Use the **Vocabulary Puzzle-Maker CD-ROM** to create crossword and word-search puzzles.

② TEACH

L1 Classify

Display a variety of items. Have students determine the natural resources from which they were made and classify each resource as renewable or nonrenewable.

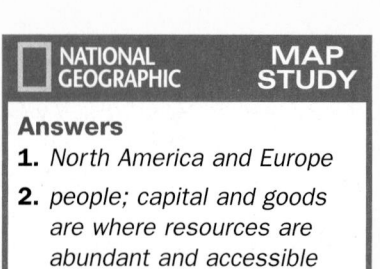

NATIONAL GEOGRAPHIC · MAP STUDY

Answers

1. *North America and Europe*
2. *people; capital and goods are where resources are abundant and accessible*

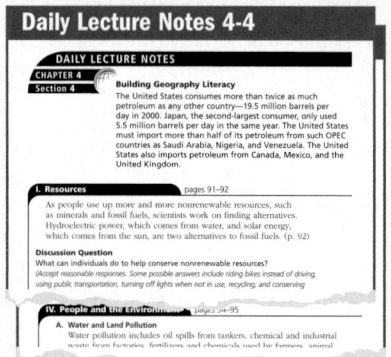

Daily Lecture Notes 4-4

World Bank Statistics show that one-sixth of the world's people produce 78 percent of the world's products and services and earn 78 percent of its income. Three-fifths of the world's people in the 61 poorest countries earn only 6 percent of the world's income.

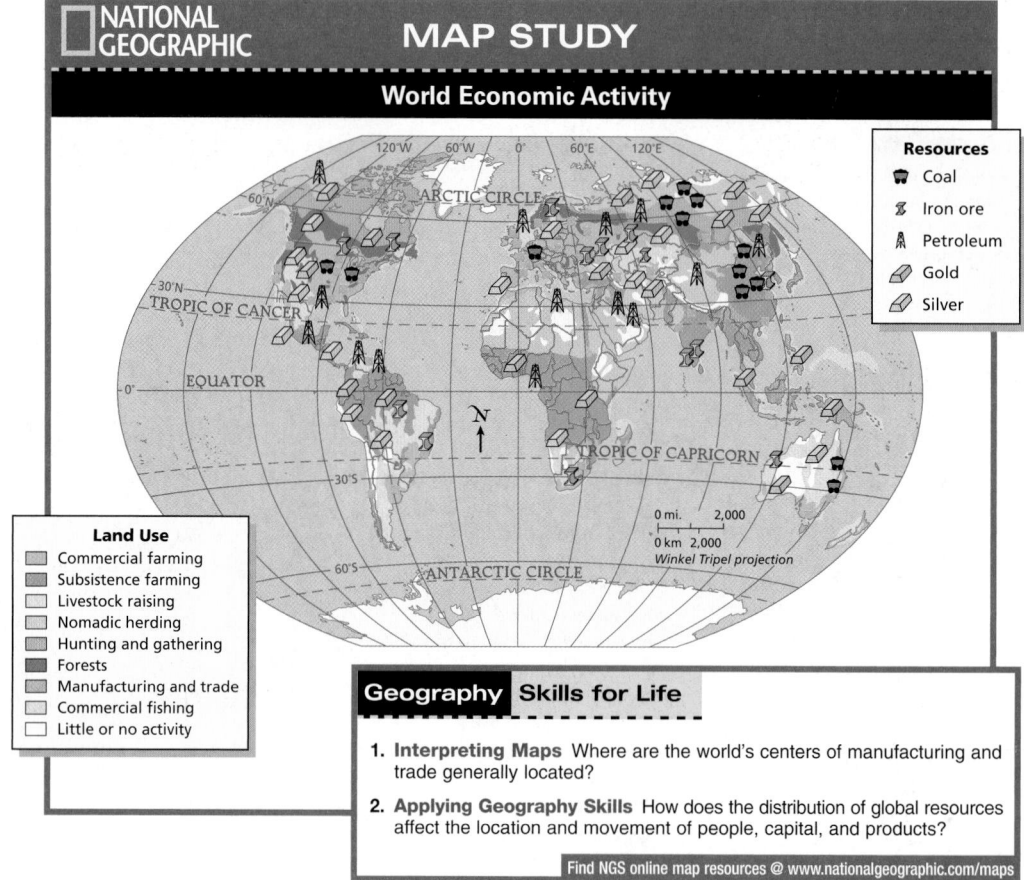

NATIONAL GEOGRAPHIC · MAP STUDY

World Economic Activity

Land Use
- Commercial farming
- Subsistence farming
- Livestock raising
- Nomadic herding
- Hunting and gathering
- Forests
- Manufacturing and trade
- Commercial fishing
- Little or no activity

Resources
- Coal
- Iron ore
- Petroleum
- Gold
- Silver

0 mi. 2,000
0 km 2,000
Winkel Tripel projection

Geography Skills for Life

1. **Interpreting Maps** Where are the world's centers of manufacturing and trade generally located?
2. **Applying Geography Skills** How does the distribution of global resources affect the location and movement of people, capital, and products?

Find NGS online map resources @ www.nationalgeographic.com/maps

renewable resources cannot be used up or can be replaced naturally or grown again in a relatively short amount of time. Wind, sun, water, forests, and animal life are examples of renewable resources. The earth's crust, however, contains many *nonrenewable resources* that cannot be replaced, such as minerals and fossil fuels.

Resource Management

Because fossil fuels, like coal and oil, and other nonrenewable resources cannot be replaced, they must be conserved. The immediate goal of conservation is to manage vital resources carefully so that people's present needs are met. An equally important long-term goal is to ensure that the needs of future generations are met.

With these future needs in mind, environmental experts have encouraged people to replace their dependence on fossil fuels with the use of renewable energy sources. Many countries, for example, already produce hydroelectric power—a renewable energy source generated from falling water. Another renewable energy source is solar energy—power produced by the sun's heat. Unfortunately, harnessing solar energy requires large, expensive equipment, so it is not yet an economical alternative to other energy sources.

Still another renewable source is electricity created by nuclear energy, the power made by creating a controlled atomic reaction. Many concerns, however, surround the use of nuclear power because of the dangerous waste products it produces.

DIFFERENTIATED INSTRUCTION

Gifted and Talented Encourage students to look at issues of world trade as interpersonal relationships played out on a global scale, with a similar need to pay attention to issues of communication and respect. Have students role-play a trade negotiation between two countries in the form of a two-person conversation.

🌐 **EE4 Human Systems: Standards 11, 13**

📂 Refer to *Inclusion for the Social Studies Classroom Strategies and Activities.*

Economic Development

Most natural resources are not evenly distributed throughout the earth. This uneven distribution affects the global economy, as you see from the economic activities map on page 92. As a result, countries specialize in the economic activities best suited to their resources. Geographers and economists classify all of the world's economic activities into four types:

- *Primary economic activities* involve taking or using natural resources directly from the earth. They include farming, grazing, fishing, forestry, and mining. Primary economic activities take place near the natural resources that are being gathered or used. For example, coal mining occurs at the site of a coal deposit.

- *Secondary economic activities* use raw materials to produce something new and more valuable. Examples of secondary economic activities include manufacturing automobiles, assembling electronic goods, producing electric power, or making pottery. These activities occur close to the resource or close to the market for the finished good.

- *Tertiary economic activities* do not involve directly acquiring and remaking natural resources. Instead they are activities that provide services to people and businesses. Doctors, teachers, lawyers, truckers, and store clerks all provide professional, wholesale, or retail services.

- *Quaternary economic activities* are concerned with the processing, management and distribution of information. They are vitally important to modern economies that have been transformed in recent years by the computer revolution. People performing these activities include "white collar" professionals working in education, government, business, information processing, and research.

Economic activities help influence a country's level of development. Those countries having much technology and manufacturing, such as the United States, are called developed countries. There, most people work in manufacturing or service industries and enjoy a high standard of living. Farmers in developed countries engage in commercial farming, raising crops and livestock to sell in the market. Because of modern techniques, only a small percentage of these countries' workers is needed to grow food to feed entire populations. Those countries working toward greater manufacturing and technology use are called developing countries. In many developing countries, which are mainly in Africa, Asia, and Latin America, agriculture remains dominant. Despite much commercial farming, most farmers in these countries engage in subsistence farming, growing only enough food for family needs. As a result, most people in developing countries remain poor. Industrialization, or the spread of industry, however, has transformed once largely agricultural countries, such as China and Malaysia.

Despite advances, the global influence of developed countries has sparked resentment in some developing countries. Feeding on this discontent, militant groups have tried to strike back by engaging in terrorism, or the use of violence to create fear in a given population. Small in size and often limited in resources, these groups seek to use the fear unleashed by violence to heighten their influence to promote change.

World Trade

The unequal distribution of natural resources promotes a complex network of trade among countries. Countries export their specialized products, trading them to other countries that cannot produce those goods. When countries cannot produce as much as they need of a good, they import it, or buy it from another country. That country, in turn, may buy the first country's products, making the two countries trading partners.

A major stimulus to world trade has come from multinational companies. A multinational company is a firm that does business in many places throughout the world. Multinationals are usually headquartered in a developed country and often locate their manufacturing or assembly operations in developing countries with low labor costs. In recent decades many developing countries have allowed multinationals to buy property and build factories or form partnerships with local companies.

Chapter 4 ⊕ 93

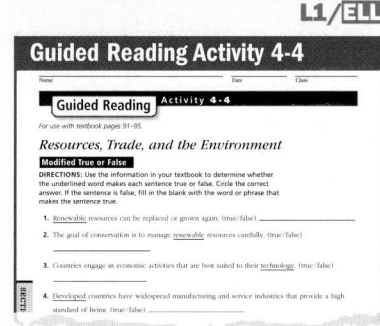

L1/ELL

Guided Reading Activity 4-4

Guided Reading Activity 4-4

For use with textbook pages 91–95

Resources, Trade, and the Environment

Modified True or False

DIRECTIONS: Use the information in your textbook to determine whether the underlined word makes each sentence true or false. Circle the correct answer. If the sentence is false, fill in the blank with the word or phrase that makes the sentence true.

1. Renewable resources can be replaced or grown again. (true/false) _____

2. The goal of conservation is to manage renewable resources carefully. (true/false) _____

3. Countries engage in economic activities that are best suited to their technology. (true/false) _____

4. Developed countries have widespread manufacturing and service industries that provide a high standard of living. (true/false) _____

L2 World Trade

Have students research atlases to sketch maps showing global trade patterns at different periods of time. Ask them to develop hypotheses to explain changes in world trade and the effects of these changes.

L1/ELL

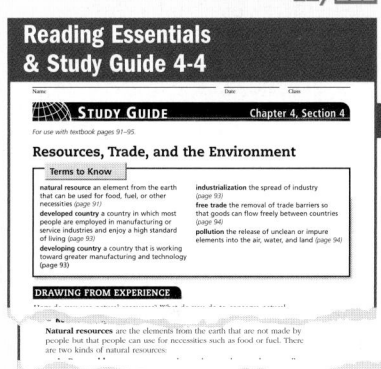

Reading Essentials & Study Guide 4-4

STUDY GUIDE — Chapter 4, Section 4

For use with textbook pages 91–95

Resources, Trade, and the Environment

Terms to Know

natural resource an element from the earth that can be used for food, fuel, or other necessities (page 91)

developed country a country in which most people are employed in manufacturing or service industries and enjoy a high standard of living (page 93)

developing country a country that is working toward greater manufacturing and technology (page 93)

industrialization the spread of industry (page 93)

free trade the removal of trade barriers so that goods can flow freely between countries (page 94)

pollution the release of unclean or impure elements into the air, water, and land (page 94)

DRAWING FROM EXPERIENCE

Natural resources are the elements from the earth that are not made by people but that people can use for necessities such as food or fuel. There are two kinds of natural resources:

COOPERATIVE LEARNING ACTIVITY

Make Economic Activity Maps Have students work together to make maps that show key natural resources and economic activities of your local community and your state. You may divide the tasks (resources research, economic activities, and preparation of the map display based on the data) among three groups. Then, have students use their community and state economic activity maps, the economic activity map of the United States and Canada on page 109, and the world economic activity map on page 92 to compare and contrast the ways humans depend on, adapt to, or modify the physical environment at each of these levels. 🌐 **EE1 The World in Spatial Terms: Standard 1**

NATIONAL GEOGRAPHIC **GRAPH STUDY**

Answers

1. *by about $3,800 billion; freer trade; technological innovation*

2. *Increasing GDP tends to increase trade; decreasing GDP tends to decrease trade. Free trade agreements make more of each country's goods and services available on world markets, thus increasing the proportion of world GDP that is sold abroad.*

Skills Practice

Movement What is the relationship between economic performance and global trade? *(Economic growth boosts exports and global trade.)*

ASSESS

Assign Section 4 Assessment as homework or as an in-class activity.

Have students use **Interactive Tutor Self-Assessment CD-ROM.**

L2

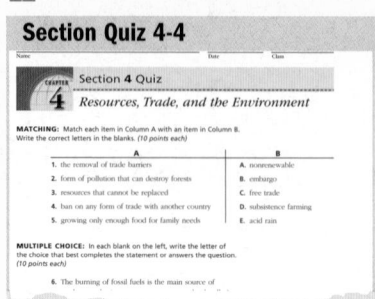

Section Quiz 4-4

Section 4 Quiz
Resources, Trade, and the Environment

MATCHING: Match each item in Column A with an item in Column B. Write the correct letters in the blanks. *(10 points each)*

A	B
1. the removal of trade barriers	A. nonrenewable
2. form of pollution that can destroy forests	B. embargo
3. resources that cannot be replaced	C. free trade
4. ban on any form of trade with another country	D. subsistence farming
5. growing only enough food for family needs	E. acid rain

MULTIPLE CHOICE: In each blank on the left, write the letter of the choice that best completes the statement or answers the question. *(10 points each)*

6. The burning of fossil fuels is the main source of

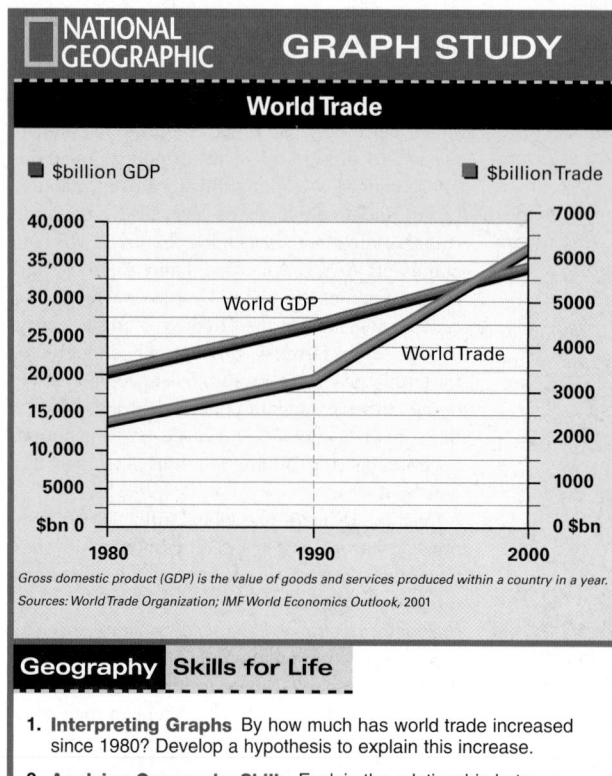

NATIONAL GEOGRAPHIC **GRAPH STUDY**

World Trade

■ $billion GDP	■ $billion Trade

World GDP

World Trade

Gross domestic product (GDP) is the value of goods and services produced within a country in a year.

Sources: World Trade Organization; IMF World Economics Outlook, 2001

Geography Skills for Life

1. **Interpreting Graphs** By how much has world trade increased since 1980? Develop a hypothesis to explain this increase.

2. **Applying Geography Skills** Explain the relationship between world trade and world GDP.

Economics
Barriers to Trade

A government tries to manage its country's trade to benefit its own economy. Some governments add a tariff, or a tax, to the price of goods that are imported. Because tariffs make imported goods more costly, governments often use them to influence people to buy products made in their home country instead of imported goods.

Governments sometimes create other barriers to trade. They might put a strict quota, or number limit, on the quantity of a particular product that can be imported from a particular country. A government may even impose an embargo, banning trade with another country altogether as a way to punish that country for political or economic differences.

Free Trade

In recent years governments around the world have moved toward free trade, the removal of trade barriers so that goods can flow freely among countries. The General Agreement on Tariffs and Trade (GATT) was the first international agreement to promote free trade. In 1995 GATT became the World Trade Organization (WTO), to which most countries now belong.

In various parts of the world, several countries have joined together to create regional free trade agreements. For example, the United States, Mexico, and Canada have set up the North American Free Trade Agreement (NAFTA) to eliminate all trade barriers to one another's goods. The **European Union** (EU), the largest trading bloc, includes many of the countries of Europe. Many members of the European Union have adopted a regional currency, the euro, to extend their cooperative efforts. Referring to decreasing trade restrictions, a U.S. trade official observed that

❝ . . . an opening world economy has allowed trade to expand fifteen-fold, sparking a six-fold increase in world economic production and a three-fold increase in global per capita incomes. ❞
Charlene Barshefsky, *remarks on trade policy at the National Press Club,* Washington, D.C., October 19, 2000

People and the Environment

In recent decades human economic activities have drastically affected the environment. A major environmental challenge today is pollution—the release of unclean or impure elements into the air, water, and land.

CRITICAL THINKING ACTIVITY

Analyzing Information Have students research, identify and give examples of different points of view on an environmental issue, such as pollution, global warming, or fuel consumption. The issue may be important on local, state, national, or international levels. Write statements of the points of view related to the issue on the blackboard. Have students choose the statement that best expresses their point of view and use it as the topic sentence of a paragraph defending that position. Remind students to reread this section and include supporting details based on information in the text.

EE5 Environment and Society: Standard 16

Water and Land Pollution

Earth's bodies of water are normally renewable, purifying themselves over time, but this natural cycle can be interrupted by human activity. Tankers and offshore rigs can cause oil spills and industries may dump chemical waste that enters and pollutes the water supply. Fertilizers and pesticides from farms can seep into groundwater and cause harm, as can animal waste and untreated sewage.

Land pollution occurs where chemical waste poisons fertile topsoil or solid waste is dumped in landfills. Radioactive waste from nuclear power plants and toxic runoff from chemical processing plants can also leak into the soil and cause contamination.

Air Pollution

The main source of air pollution is the burning of fossil fuels by industries and vehicles. Burning fuel gives off poisonous gases that can seriously damage people's health. Acidic chemicals in air pollution also combine with precipitation to form acid rain. Acid rain eats away at the surfaces of buildings, kills fish, and can even destroy entire forests.

Forests provide animal habitats, prevent soil erosion, and conduct photosynthesis (FOH•toh•SIHN•thuh•suhs)—the process by which plants take in carbon dioxide and, in the presence of sunlight, produce carbohydrates. The oxygen released during photosynthesis is vital for human and animal survival. Decreasing acid rain will help preserve a region's environmental balance.

Some scientists believe that rising levels of pollutants in the atmosphere are contributing to a general increase in the earth's temperatures, a trend they call global warming. Although not all experts agree that global warming is occurring, scientists who study it warn that the increase in temperature may have disastrous effects, causing glaciers and ice caps to melt and raising the level of the world's oceans. Higher water levels in oceans, they claim, could flood coastal cities and submerge smaller islands.

The Fragile Ecosystem

As humans expand their communities, they threaten natural ecosystems, places where the plants and animals are dependent upon one another and their environment for survival. Ecosystems can be found in every climate and vegetation region of the world. Because the earth's land, air, and water are interrelated, what harms one part of the system harms all the other parts—including humans and other living things. As people become more aware of how their actions affect this delicate balance of life, they are starting to manage resources more wisely, by improving water treatment, preserving wilderness areas, and developing alternatives to fossil fuels.

☐ NATIONAL GEOGRAPHIC **GEOFACT**

▶ Of about 3,000 minerals, around 100—including iron and aluminum—are widely available and are used in large quantities. Other minerals, such as titanium, are scarce or difficult to obtain, and command high prices.

Reteach

Have students generate two questions from each subsection of the text with which to quiz one another.

Enrich

Read aloud a selection from *Water*, a National Geographic Special Edition (November 1993). Discuss with students the importance of water resources to a country's economy.

4 CLOSE

Ask students to look through their backpacks and other personal possessions and list where each item was manufactured. Mark these countries with colored tacks or stickers on a large world map. Give a prize to the student who has the object manufactured in the part of the world farthest from where you live.

SECTION 4 ASSESSMENT

Checking for Understanding

1. **Define** natural resource, developed country, developing country, industrialization, free trade, pollution.

2. **Main Ideas** Copy the chart below onto a sheet of paper. Fill in the challenges that each category presents to the world's countries.

Economic World			
Resources	Development	Trade	Environment

Critical Thinking

3. **Evaluating Information** Evaluate the impact of innovations, such as fire, steam power, diesel machinery, and electricity, on the environment.

4. **Making Inferences** What might be the advantages and disadvantages to a developing country of joining a free trade agreement?

5. **Making Comparisons** Research and compare two countries in the ways they depend on the environment for products that they export.

Analyzing Maps

6. **Region** Look at the world economic activity map on page 92. What regions of the world produce the most oil? The most coal?

Applying Geography

7. **Effects of Trade Policies** Think about the reasons countries use quotas and embargoes. How are quotas and embargoes different? What unintended consequence do you think quotas and embargoes might have on a country's economy?

SECTION 4 ASSESSMENT ANSWERS

1. All vocabulary terms are defined in the text.

2. Chart entries should reflect logical inferences based on text material.

3. Students should focus on both positive and negative aspects of technological change on the environment.

4. advantages: increased flow of investment capital into the country, wider markets for exports, jobs; disadvantages: overdependence on developed countries, environmental damage from uncontrolled industrialization

5. Students should select two countries that have some differences as well as similarities.

6. oil: Southwest Asia, Europe; coal: Russia, East Asia

7. **Applying Geography** Quotas limit the quantity of imports; embargoes ban trade altogether. Both can cause other countries to respond by establishing tariffs and embargoes of their own, negatively impacting a country's economy.

Teaching the Skill

On the board, copy this excerpt from a database on the various percentages of a country's labor force employed in segments of its economy.

COUNTRY	SERVICES, GOVERNMENT	INDUSTRY, MINING
Brazil	51%	23%
Canada	74%	22%
France	71%	25%
Israel	79%	19%
Japan	63%	32%
Saudi Arabia	69%	26%

Source: The Economist Pocket World in Figures, 2001

Ask students what fields are used in the database. *(country; services, government; industry, mining)* Ask how the data is organized. *(alphabetically by country)* Have students name other ways to organize the data. *(by ascending or descending percentage order of either economic heading)*

Additional Practice
L1

Reinforcing Skills Activity 4

CHAPTER 4 **REINFORCING SKILLS ACTIVITY**

Creating an Electronic Database

TECHNOLOGY
SkillBuilder

Creating an Electronic Database

A computerized database program can help you organize and manage a large amount of information. Once you enter data in a database, you can quickly locate a record according to key information.

Learning the Skill

An electronic database is a collection of facts that are stored in a file on the computer. The information is organized into different fields. The table, for example, contains three fields: *Language, Speakers (in millions),* and *Main Areas Where Spoken.*

A database can be organized and reorganized in any way that is useful to you. By using special software developed for record keeping—a database management system (DBMS)—you can easily add, delete, change, or update information. You give commands to the computer that tell it what to do with the information, and it follows your commands. When you want to retrieve information, the computer searches through the files, finds the information, and displays it on the screen.

Follow these steps to create a database:

- **Determine what facts you want to include in your database.**
- **Follow the instructions in the DBMS you are using to set up fields.**
- **Determine how you want to organize the facts in the database—alphabetically, chronologically, or numerically.**

Language	Speakers (in millions)	Main Areas Where Spoken
Han Chinese (Mandarin)	874	China, Taiwan, Singapore
Hindi	366	Northern India
Spanish	358	Spain, Latin America, southwestern United States
English	341	British Isles, Anglo-America, Australia, New Zealand, South Africa, former British colonies in tropical Asia and Africa, Philippines
Bengali	207	Bangladesh, eastern India
Arabic	206	Southwest Asia, North Africa
Portuguese	176	Portugal, Brazil, southern Africa
Russian	167	Russia, Kazakhstan, parts of Ukraine and other former Soviet republics
Japanese	125	Japan
German	100	Germany, Austria, Switzerland, Luxembourg, eastern France, northern Italy

Source: National Geographic Desk Reference

- **Follow the instructions in the DBMS to sort the information in order of importance.**

Practicing the Skill

Enter the data in the table above into an electronic database. Then use the DBMS commands to answer the following questions.

1. In what order is the information in the table displayed?
2. Sort the data alphabetically by language. Which record appears first?
3. Request the database to display only those languages with more than 200 million speakers. Which records will *not* appear?
4. Sort your records using Africa as the main area where spoken. How many languages appear? What are they?

Applying the Skill

Study the world religion and world cultures maps on pages 82 and 83. Combine the information into an electronic database showing which religions are practiced in the world's culture regions. Write three questions that require sorting these records.

ANSWERS TO PRACTICING THE SKILL

1. in order of largest to smallest number of speakers
2. Arabic
3. Portuguese, Russian, Japanese, German
4. three: English, Arabic, Portuguese

SUMMARY & STUDY GUIDE

CHAPTER 4

SECTION 1 — World Population (pp. 75–79)

Terms to Know
- death rate
- birthrate
- natural increase
- doubling time
- population distribution
- population density
- migration

Key Points
- Population growth rates vary, posing different problems for different countries.
- The world's population is unevenly distributed.
- Large numbers of people are migrating from rural villages to cities.
- People emigrate because of wars, food shortages, persecution, lack of jobs, or other problems.

Organizing Your Notes
Use a graphic organizer like the one below to help you organize your notes for this section.

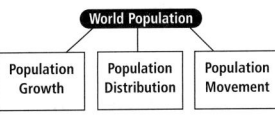

World Population
- Population Growth
- Population Distribution
- Population Movement

SECTION 2 — Global Cultures (pp. 80–85)

Terms to Know
- culture
- language family
- ethnic group
- culture region
- cultural diffusion
- culture hearth

Key Points
- Language, religion, social groups, government, and economic activities define cultures.
- Geographers divide the earth into specific culture regions.
- Trade, migration, and war change cultures.
- The world's first civilizations arose in culture hearths.

Organizing Your Notes
Create an outline using the format below to organize your notes.

Global Cultures
I. Elements of Culture
   A. Language
      1.

SECTION 3 — Political and Economic Systems (pp. 86–90)

Terms to Know
- unitary system
- federal system
- autocracy
- oligarchy
- democracy
- traditional economy
- market economy
- mixed economy
- command economy

Key Points
- A country's different levels of government may be organized as a unitary system, a federal system, or a confederation.
- An autocracy, an oligarchy, and a democracy differ in the way they exercise authority.
- The three major economic systems are traditional economy, market economy, and command economy.

Organizing Your Notes
Create a chart like the one below to organize your notes for this section.

Political and Economic Systems	Characteristics
Features of Government	

SECTION 4 — Resources, Trade, and the Environment (pp. 91–95)

Terms to Know
- natural resource
- developed country
- developing country
- industrialization
- free trade
- pollution

Key Points
- Peoples are increasingly interdependent.
- Because natural resources are not evenly distributed, countries must trade.
- Governments can create or eliminate trade barriers.
- Human economic activities have led to pollution.

Organizing Your Notes
Create a chart like the one below to organize your notes.

Trade	Resources	Development	Environment

Using the Chapter 4 Summary & Study Guide

Use the Chapter 4 Summary & Study Guide to preview, review, condense, or reteach the chapter.

Preview/Review

Vocabulary PuzzleMaker CD-ROM reinforces "Terms to Know."

Interactive Tutor Self-Assessment CD-ROM provides a review of Chapter 4 content.

Condense

Have students read the Chapter 4 Summary & Study Guide.

Chapter 4 Audio Program

Chapter 4 Guided Reading Activities

Reteach

Chapter 4 Reteaching Activities (Spanish also available)

Chapter 4 Reading Essentials and Study Guides

GLENCOE TECHNOLOGY

NATIONAL GEOGRAPHIC
WORLD REGIONS
VIDEO PROGRAM

Unit 1, The World
The following segments enhance the study of this unit:
- **Ocean Journey**
- **Homo Sapiens Sapiens**
- **Goodwill Games**

CHAPTER CULMINATING ACTIVITY

Defining a Culture Region Tell students that they are geographers who have discovered a new culture region. As a class, brainstorm a description of the new region's physical features. Organize students in five groups to script a TV documentary on this new culture region. Assign each group the responsibility to focus on one element of culture: language, religion, social groups, government, or economic activities. Each element should reflect the influence of the region's physical geography. Have the groups come together to present their show. **EE2 Places and Regions: Standard 4**
EE4 Human Systems: Standards 10, 12

CHAPTER 4

ASSESSMENT & ACTIVITIES

GLENCOE TECHNOLOGY

Use *MindJogger Videoquiz* to review the Chapter 4 content.

Reviewing Key Terms
Population: a, c, p
Cultures: b, e, f, h, k
Political and Economic Systems: g, j, l, m, n
Resources, Trade, and Environment: d, i, o

Reviewing Facts
SECTION 1
1. Population growth increases demands on resources and the environment.
2. greater economic opportunity

SECTION 2
3. language, religion, social groups, government, economy
4. internal; new ideas, lifestyles, inventions; external: trade, migration, war

SECTION 3
5. totalitarian dictatorship, absolute monarchy
6. market economy: freedom of choice in buying and selling, right to make and keep profits; command economy: social security, equal access to resources and services

SECTION 4
7. Renewable resources can be replaced; nonrenewable cannot.
8. advances in technology, transportation, communications; freedom of trade; need to manage resources; environmental concerns

Reviewing Key Terms
On a sheet of paper, classify each of the terms below into one of the following categories:

- **Population**
- **Political and Economic Systems**
- **Cultures**
- **Resources, Trade, and Environment**

a. death rate
b. culture
c. population distribution
d. free trade
e. language family
f. culture region
g. democracy
h. culture hearth
i. developed country
j. autocracy
k. cultural diffusion
l. market economy
m. mixed economy
n. federal system
o. developing country
p. birthrate

Reviewing Facts
SECTION 1
1. How does population growth affect the global community?
2. Why are large numbers of people moving to cities?

SECTION 2
3. What are the elements of a culture?
4. What influences may change a culture?

SECTION 3
5. Name two forms of autocratic government.
6. What kinds of benefits do people receive in a market economy system? In a command economy system?

SECTION 4
7. What is the difference between a renewable and a nonrenewable resource?
8. What factors make the world's countries increasingly interdependent?

Critical Thinking
1. **Analyzing Information** Explain the operation of a traditional economy, using Canada's Inuit as an example.
2. **Making Inferences** Why do you think geographers find it useful to divide the world into culture regions? Identify the human factors that constitute a region.
3. **Predicting Consequences** On a sheet of paper, create a graphic organizer like the one below to list the possible challenges faced by the citizens of a country whose government has changed from an autocracy to a democracy. Then suggest ways that people might address these challenges.

Autocracy to Democracy	
Challenges	Ways to Address Them
•	•
•	•
•	•
•	•

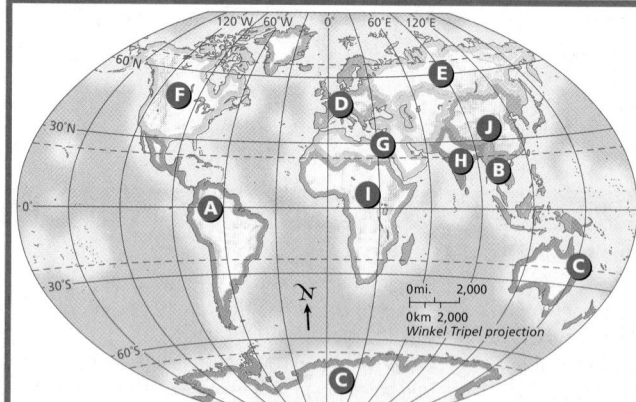

NATIONAL GEOGRAPHIC **Locating Places**
The World: Cultural Geography
Match the letters on the map with the appropriate world culture regions. Write your answers on a sheet of paper.

1. United States and Canada
2. Latin America
3. Europe
4. Russia
5. North Africa, Southwest Asia, and Central Asia
6. Africa South of the Sahara
7. South Asia
8. East Asia
9. Southeast Asia
10. Australia, Oceania, and Antarctica

Critical Thinking
1. The hunting and sharing of food rested on ancestral tradition.
2. Regions make it easier to study and compare cultural developments; human factors include language, government, economic activities, social groups, and religion.
3. Students should demonstrate an understanding of the increased responsibilities placed on individual citizens.

NATIONAL GEOGRAPHIC **Locating Places**

1. F	**3.** D	**5.** G	**7.** H	**9.** B
2. A	**4.** E	**6.** I	**8.** J	**10.** C

Thinking Like a Geographer

Based on what you know about cultural diffusion, research the role that diseases such as the bubonic plague have played in this process over the course of time. Create a map that traces the disease's spread from its point of origin to other areas. Write a paragraph that describes the disease's effects on regions of contact.

Problem-Solving Activity

Group Research Project Work with a group to find out more about the North American Free Trade Agreement (NAFTA). Research the important elements of the agreement, the supporting and opposing opinions, and the costs and benefits to participating countries. Decide whether NAFTA might be used as a model agreement for other regions, and present your decision and supporting reasons as a letter to a national news magazine. Include charts, graphs, or tables to support your ideas.

GeoJournal

Creative Writing Choose one of the world's culture regions. Use the notes in your GeoJournal and other sources to research and analyze the effects of human geographic patterns on the region's environment. Write a description of specific human activities that have positively or negatively changed physical features and natural resouces there.

Technology Activity

Creating an Electronic Database Choose several developed and developing countries and create a database of their trading activities. Include data about products they import and export and the amount of income each country earns from trade. Then write a paragraph explaining what the data show about developed and developing countries. Consider the differences among countries related to the kinds of products each category of country produces and the amount of income each kind produces. What accounts for the differences?

Standardized Test Practice

Choose the best answer for the following multiple-choice questions. If you have trouble answering the questions, use the process of elimination to narrow your choices.

1. **Which of the following is a challenge that rapid population growth presents to the global community?**

   A Shortages of metropolitan areas
   B Shortages of housing
   C Low population density
   D Disloyal military forces

2. **What is the most accurate description of an autocratic government?**

   F Power is divided among the national government and state or provincial governments.
   G A small group of people have the power to govern, often because of wealth, military power, or social position.
   H Leaders rule with the consent of the citizens.
   J One person holds the power to rule and may use military or police power to maintain authority.

 **Test-Taking Tip** Read the questions carefully to determine what is being asked. Look for the key words and phrases that will help you identify the correct answer, such as the phrase *rapid population growth* in question 1 and the word *autocratic* in question 2. Sometimes more than one answer choice seems correct. You must find the answer choice that is the *best*.

Technology Activity

Students should draw accurate conclusions from the data and provide a reasonable explanation for differences. Students should use standard grammar, correct spelling, sentence structure, and punctuation in paragraphs.

Standardized Test Practice

1. B
2. J

Tested Objectives:
categorize data
analyze information

Additional Practice and Test-Taking Tips

 Standardized Test Practice Workbook

CHAPTER BONUS TEST QUESTION

What cultural traits do the United States and Canada share with Australia, New Zealand, and South Africa? *(Because all were British colonies, they share a common language—English.)*

Thinking Like a Geographer

Students should consider physical factors (mountains, bodies of water) that helped or hindered the spread of disease as well as human factors (migrations, population characteristics, cross-cultural exchanges).

Problem-Solving Activity

Students' letters should reflect an understanding of the elements of NAFTA and how they apply to another region's economic characteristics and needs, include well-considered reasons, and be accompanied by at least one visual aid.

GeoJournal

Information in the paragraph should reflect an accurate understanding of the culture region and include specific ways its people are affected.

TEACHING TRANSPARENCIES

L2 Unit 2 Map Overlay Transparencies

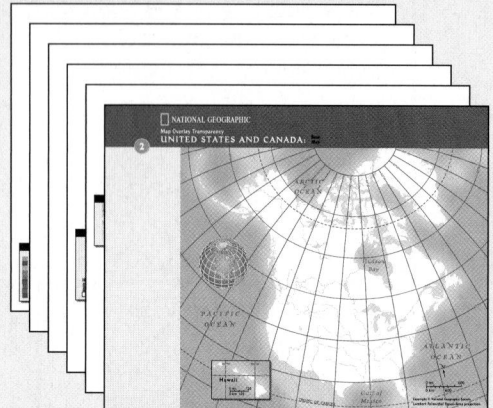

L2 Political Map Transparency 2

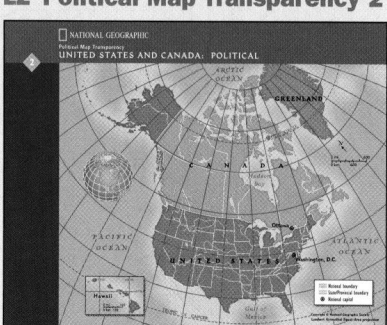

L2 World Cultures Transparencies 1, 2

APPLICATION AND ENRICHMENT

L2 Location Activity 2

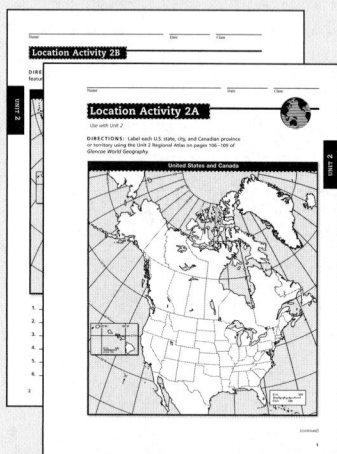

L2 Real-Life Applications and Problem-Solving Activity 2

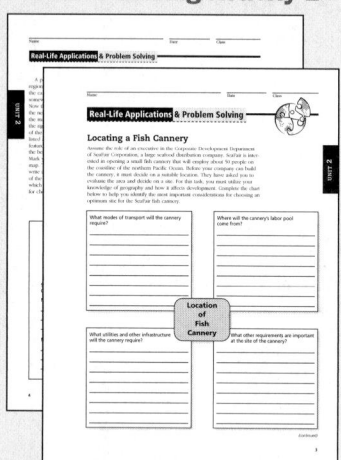

L2 GeoLab Activity 2

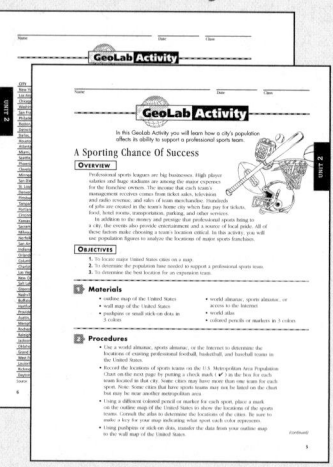

L2 Environmental Issues Case Study 2

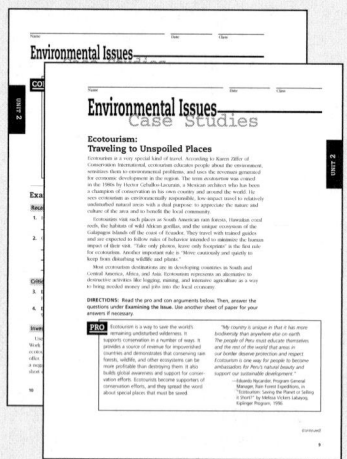

GEOGRAPHIC LITERACY

Focus on Geography Literacy

Building Geography Skills for Life

ASSESSMENT

GLENCOE'S ASSESSMENT ADVANTAGE

Use the following to easily assess student learning in a variety of ways:
- Performance Assessment Activities and Rubrics
- Section Quizzes
- Chapter and Unit Tests
- Interactive Tutor Self-Assessment CD-ROM
- ExamView® Pro Testmaker
- MindJogger Videoquiz
- geography.glencoe.com
- Standardized Test Practice Workbook
- SAT I/II Test Practice

L2 Unit 2 Pretest and Tests

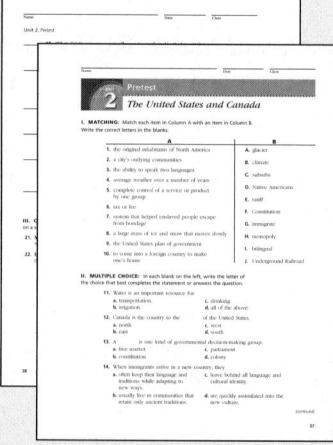

INTERDISCIPLINARY CONNECTIONS

L2 World Literature:
Contemporary Selection 2

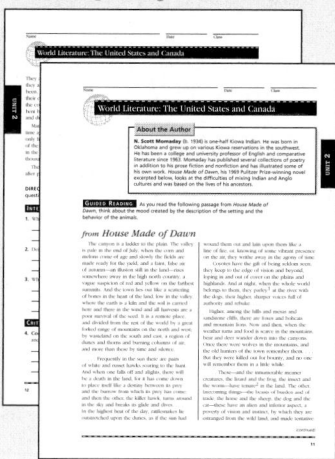

Foods Around the World

Multimedia

- **World Art and Architecture Transparencies**
- **World Art Prints**
- **World Music: A Cultural Legacy**
- **World History Primary Source Document Library**

BIBLIOGRAPHY

Readings for the Student
Remix: Conversations with Immigrant Teenagers. Henry Holt & Co. Inc., New York, NY, 1999.

A Brief History of Canada. Facts on File, 2000.

Readings for the Teacher
Iroquois Culture & Commentary. Clear Light Publishers, Santa Fe, NM, 2000.

From Ellis Island to JFK. Yale University Press, New Haven, CT, 2000.

Multimedia Resources
Hawaii Paradise Preserved. Questar Video, Inc. 1997. Videocassette, Chicago, IL, New York, NY, and Los Angeles, CA, 52 minutes.

Grand Canyon: Its Beauty, History, and Native People. Questar Video, Inc. 1997. Videocassette, Chicago, IL, New York, NY, and Los Angeles, CA, 60 minutes.

READING SUPPORT FROM JAMESTOWN EDUCATION

- *Timed Readings Plus in Social Studies* help students increase their reading rate and fluency while maintaining comprehension. The 400-word passages are similar to those found on state and national assessments.

- *Reading in the Content Area: Social Studies* concentrates on six essential reading skills that help students better comprehend what they read. The book includes 75 high-interest nonfiction passages written at increasing levels of difficulty.

- *Reading Fluency* helps students read smoothly, accurately, and expressively.

- *Jamestown's Reading Improvement,* by renowned reading expert Edward Fry, focuses on helping build your students' comprehension, vocabulary, and skimming and scanning skills.

- *Critical Reading Series* provides high-interest books, each written at three reading levels.

For more information about these products, see the Jamestown Education materials in the Classroom Solutions in the front of this Teacher Wraparound Edition.
To order these products, call Glencoe at 1-800-334-7344.

Background Information

CHAPTER 5 (pp. 114–131)

The Physical Geography of the United States and Canada

The United States and Canada share the largest part of North America, which also includes Mexico, Central America, and the Caribbean Islands. The United States is the world's fourth largest country, and Canada is the second largest after Russia. Canada extends southward from the North Pole to the U.S. border. From east to west, Canada extends over six time zones. The United States and Canada share a 5,523-mile (8,893-km) undefended border (including Alaska) and similar topography.

Climate and Natural Resources

Climate zones in the United States vary from tundra to tropical rain forest and tropical savanna. Although many people think of Canada's climate as subarctic, much of the country is temperate. Canada's southernmost point, Pelee Island, at the tip of the peninsula of southern Ontario, is located south of 11 U.S. states. Both countries have abundant natural resources, including rivers and other waterways, forests, minerals, and oil and natural gas. Only about 5 percent of Canada's land is arable; the United States has about 20 percent arable land. Because Canada has a strategic global position along the great circle routes between the United States and Europe, many commercial airlines fly over Canada.

CHAPTER 6 (pp. 132–155)

The Cultural Geography of the United States and Canada

At the end of the 1900s, archaeologists were forced to rethink the conventional theory that North America was populated by nomads who crossed a land bridge from Asia. Archaeological discoveries suggest that humans may have lived in parts of North America long before the end of the last Ice Age. Native American oral histories explain tribal origins, and linguistic and physical evidence uncovered by archaeologists appears to support these oral traditions. The Mohawk, for example, say that their tribe originally came from the American Southwest near where the Hopi lived. Gradually, they dispersed throughout the Great Plains and into the northeastern part of the North American continent.

Cultural Traits

The cultures of the United States and Canada are similar in language, religion, and the use of technology. Yet Canadians have certain values and traditions that distinguish them from their southern neighbors. Historically, Canadians did not support the United States's fight for independence in 1776 and only gradually broke away from British rule. While Americans believe in "life, liberty, and the pursuit of happiness," Canadians adhere to the principles of "peace, order and good government."

Population and Migration

Both the United States and Canada are peopled predominantly by immigrants and their descendants. Diverse populations were attracted to the region for many reasons—religious, political, and economic—a trend that continues today for many of the same reasons.

Today the United States and Canada have a combined population that is about 5 percent of the world's population. About 90 percent of Canada's population lives near the U.S. border on about 10 percent of the country's total land area. In the United States, the Sunbelt—states in the South and West—had greater population gains than the Northeast and the Midwest. More than 75 percent of Canada's population is urbanized, which is similar to the percentage for the United States.

Demographic issues challenge both countries. The United States will soon have almost 30 percent of its population—baby boomers born between 1946 and 1964—retiring and beginning to collect Social Security benefits. Continued immigration to both countries will result in ethnic shifts from Anglo European dominance to a greater proportion of Asians in Canada and Hispanics and African Americans in the United States. Hispanic immigrants, who once lived mostly in the U.S. Southwest, are moving into states such as Arkansas, North Carolina, and Nebraska, often filling low paying or dangerous jobs in industries such as meat packing.

Mexican Americans

Mexican Americans will soon become the largest minority group in the United States. Mexican foods, music, and language are becoming increasingly important threads in the cultural fabric of the United States.

CHAPTER 7 (pp. 156–175)

The United States and Canada Today

Both the United States and Canada have diversified economies, in part because of their abundant natural resources. Both countries are among the most highly developed countries in the world. Agriculture, mining, forestry, and industry play an important part in their economies. Industries in the United States produced about 40 percent of the total output of goods worldwide by the middle of the 1900s, even though U.S. population is only around 5 percent of the world's total. The immense wealth of the United States and Canada is coupled with a lifestyle characterized by convenience and abundance. Although the United States has a

small percentage of the world's population, its citizens consume more of the earth's resources than those of any other country. The region also produces more greenhouse gases than any other country. Globally, as more people seek to adopt the American lifestyle, pressure on the earth's finite resources increases. Water limits already challenge the U.S. Southwest. Too much diversion into dams and aqueducts for irrigation and other uses has caused the Colorado River to run out before it reaches its traditional destination of the Sea of Cortez.

Regional and Global Challenges

Many scientists believe that the rise of greenhouse gases released by human activity is helping quicken the pace of global warming. Measurements taken at various places around the world indicate that not only are glaciers retreating but that they are rapidly thinning as well. Canada especially will feel the impact in its polar region. On average, the Arctic ice cap has thinned 42 percent since the 1950s. Scientists predict that, by mid-century, the ice which covers the Arctic Ocean could melt every summer, which would open the Arctic Ocean to commercial navigation. That event could have significant environmental and economic consequences for this region. Rising sea levels related to thawing ice caps would impact low-lying areas in both countries.

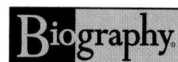

00:00 OUT OF TIME?

If time does not permit teaching each chapter in this unit, you may want to use the **Reading Essentials and Study Guide** summaries.

Unit Launch Activity

Ask: What do the United States and Canada have in common in terms of geographical, historical, cultural, and political ties? Tell students to make four columns on a sheet of paper and label them *Geographical*, *Historical*, *Cultural*, and *Political*. Give students a few minutes to list their responses. Make the same four columns on the board. As students volunteer their answers, write them on the board. Have students add to their lists as they listen to the responses.

GLENCOE TECHNOLOGY

NATIONAL GEOGRAPHIC
WORLD REGIONS
VIDEO PROGRAM

Unit 2, The United States and Canada
The following segments enhance the study of this unit:

- **Preserving Wilderness**
- **Land of Immigrants**
- **Brass Bands**

Available in DVD and VHS

UNIT 2

The United States and Canada

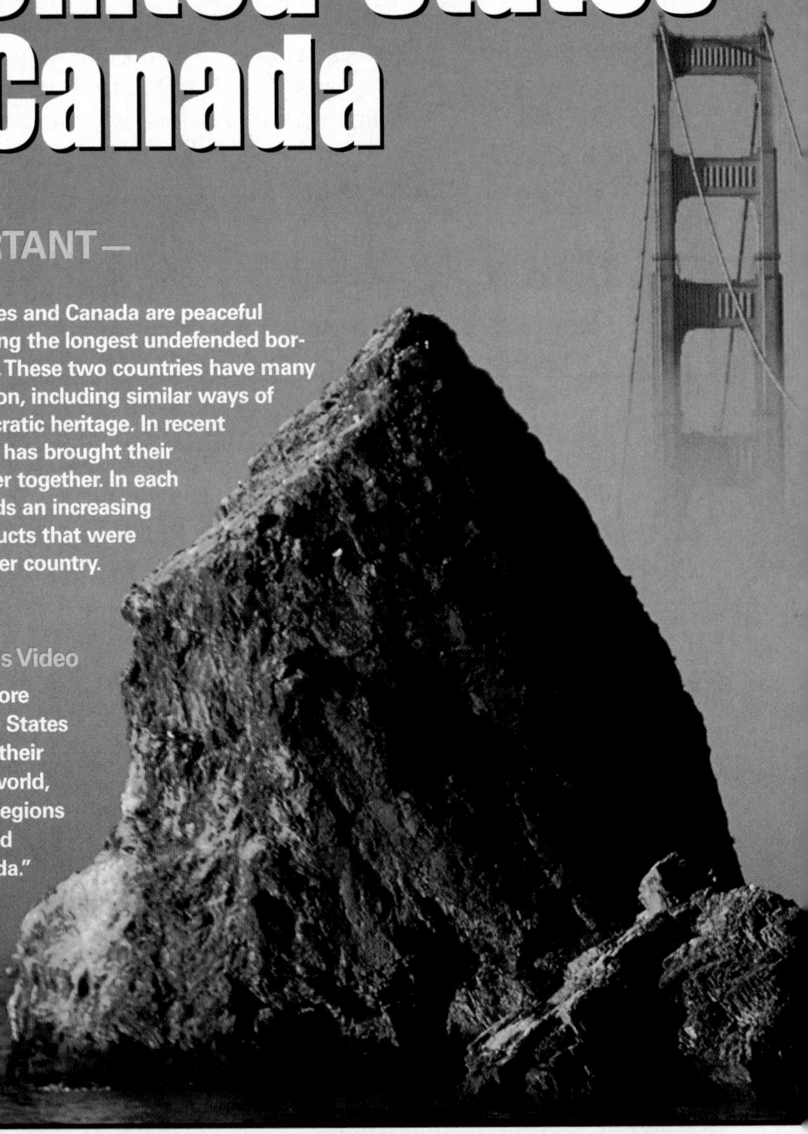

WHY IT'S IMPORTANT—

The United States and Canada are peaceful neighbors, sharing the longest undefended border in the world. These two countries have many things in common, including similar ways of life and a democratic heritage. In recent years, free trade has brought their economies closer together. In each country, one finds an increasing number of products that were made in the other country.

World Regions Video To learn more about the United States and Canada and their impact on your world, view the World Regions video "The United States and Canada."

GETTING TO KNOW THE REGION

Map Activity Have students look at the maps on pages RA2 and RA4 of their texts. **Ask: On what continent are Canada and the United States?** *(North America)* **What body of water separates the continent from Europe?** *(Atlantic Ocean)* **Asia?** *(Pacific Ocean)* **In what hemispheres do the two countries lie?** *(northern, western)* **What continent lies south of the United States?** *(South America)* **Where is the United States in relation to Canada?** *(south)* **What direction would you fly traveling from Canada to Africa?** *(southeast)* **In what direction would you sail to get from the United States to Australia?** *(southwest)*

EE1 The World in Spatial Terms: Standard 1

NGS ONLINE
www.nationalgeographic.com/education

Golden Gate Bridge across the entrance to San Francisco Bay

Unit 2   101

This online resource, brought to you by the National Geographic Society, provides lesson plans, atlas updates, cartographic activities with interactive maps, an online map store, and links to the boundless subjects of maps and geography.

Unit Overview

The three chapters that comprise this unit introduce students to the physical and cultural geography of the United States and Canada, and the peoples of that region. Point out that although the United States and Canada have many things in common, such as similar landscapes, buildings, and dress, some features distinguish the two countries:

- Canada's languages and education systems are influenced by French and English forebears as well as by Canada's proximity to the United States.
- The Canadian government, political organization, and judiciary resemble British institutions more than those of the United States.

ABOUT THE PHOTO

Visual Instruction Construction of the Golden Gate Bridge was difficult because of frequent storms, swiftly moving tides, and the challenge of blasting rock in deep water to anchor earthquake-proof foundations. Thick fog caused a cargo vessel to collide with and damage one of the bridge's trestles during construction. The Golden Gate Bridge was completed in 1937. It was the world's longest suspension bridge with a span of 4,200 feet (1,280 m) until the Verrazano-Narrows Bridge was built at the entrance to New York Harbor in 1964. **Ask:** *Why do you suppose the Golden Gate Bridge is San Francisco's most famous landmark? (Answers may include that the bridge has a construction that is not very common throughout the country, so it is eye-catching.)* ⌖ **EE2 Places and Regions: Standard 4**

UNIT **2** REGIONAL ATLAS

① FOCUS

These features and activities may be used as an introduction to the unit or as teaching tools throughout the course of the unit.

L1 Using Flash Cards Activity

Before beginning the study of this unit, use the **Countries of the World Flash Cards** to preview students' knowledge of Canada and the United States. Have students write two facts about each country and about each U.S. state. Before showing students the flash cards, ask them to name each country's capital, and the capitals of U.S. states.

L2 Photo Description Activity

Have students study the photos on pages 102–105. Have students describe the photos in the style often used on postcards. Then have them write a postcard message to a friend as though they were visiting that place or participating in that activity.

INTERDISCIPLINARY
connection

HISTORY The Prairie Provinces of Canada have long been a magnet for immigrants. By World War I, half the people in these inland provinces were of foreign birth. Increasingly, immigrants today come from places like India, Korea, and China.

What Makes the United States and Canada a Region?

T he United States and Canada span most of North America, stretching from the Pacific Ocean to the Atlantic. These two huge countries share many physical features. Mountains frame their eastern and western edges, cradling a central region of vast plains.

When people first arrived on these plains, they found an immense sea—not of water, but of grass. Beneath the gently rolling landscape lay dark, fertile soil. In time, the grasslands were transformed into some of the world's most productive farmland.

To the east of the plains stand the ancient, rounded Appalachian Mountains. To the west are the much younger Rocky Mountains, a majestic ribbon of jagged, snowcapped peaks. Still farther west are the Pacific Ranges, which run along the Pacific coast.

Almost every imaginable type of climate— from tundra to desert to tropical savanna—can be found within the borders of these two diverse countries.

1 **Six-foot-tall sunflowers** thrive on this farm in North Dakota, in the heart of the Great Plains. North Dakota leads the United States in the production of sunflowers. The protein-rich seeds are turned into margarine and cooking oil.

BACKGROUND INFORMATION

The Yukon The Yukon Territory, located north of British Columbia and east of Alaska, is a region of high mountains and plateaus. People settled on a large central plateau encircled by some of the highest and most spectacular peaks in North America. There, Mount Logan rises 19,524 feet (5,951 m). In 1896 the discovery of gold on the Klondike River led to a gold rush that lasted only a few years. The territory still has great mineral wealth, but its remote location and arctic climate have been a barrier to development. Today, the Yukon is one of the few mostly unspoiled and sparsely populated wilderness regions in North America. 🌐 **EE2 Places and Regions: Standard 4**

② TEACH

L2 Location

Have students describe the climate and location where they live. Have them name some geographical features that distinguish their region, such as rivers and other bodies of water, mountains, plains, and deserts. **Ask:** If you were writing a brochure for your local Chamber of Commerce, what aspects of climate and physical features would you emphasize? Why do you think other people might choose your region as a place to live? Have students share their observations with the class.

☐ NATIONAL GEOGRAPHIC **GEOFACT**

▶ **Mammoth Cave in Kentucky is the most extensive cave system in the world.**

GLENCOE
TECHNOLOGY

☐ **NATIONAL GEOGRAPHIC**
WORLD REGIONS
VIDEO PROGRAM

Unit 2, The United States and Canada
The following segments enhance the study of this unit:
• **Preserving Wilderness**
• **Land of Immigrants**
• **Brass Bands**

2 Boats line the harbor of a fishing village in Nova Scotia, along Canada's Atlantic coast. Both Canadians and Americans harvest fish and other types of seafood from the Atlantic's bountiful waters.

3 Snow-dusted peaks surround a climber in the Canadian Rockies. The backbone of North America, the Rockies extend from the farthest reaches of Alaska and the Yukon Territory down into the southwestern United States.

4 The only deserts in the region are found in the southwestern United States, in an area of low basins and high, windswept plateaus sandwiched between the Pacific Ranges and the Rocky Mountains. These rippled dunes lie in Utah.

Unit 2   103

A TRAVELER'S LOG

Henry Gannett People of all types—poets, adventurers, outlaws—have long been drawn to Alaska, first in search of fur, then gold, and most recently, oil. Booms have come and gone, each luring new seekers to this frontier. The population has grown by three and a half times the national rate—49 percent since 1980. Yet the U.S. Congress almost passed up the chance to purchase Alaska from Russia in 1867.

Federal geographer and founder of the National Geographic Society Henry Gannett visited Alaska in 1904. He described the allure of this far northern frontier: "Its grandeur is more valuable than the gold or the fish or the timber, for it will never be exhausted."

⊕ EE2 Places and Regions: Standard 4

L2 Making Generalizations

Ask students in what ways they think the United States and Canada have been strengthened by being a region predominantly made up of immigrants. If they have difficulty coming up with answers, prompt them to name the contributions of certain ethnic groups—different types of architecture, music, food, and religion.

☐ NATIONAL GEOGRAPHIC **GEOFACT**

▶ **St. John's, Newfoundland, is closer to Europe than any other city in Canada. The city has long had a connecting role between the two sides of the Atlantic. In 1901 North America's first radio transmission from Europe was received there. In 1919 the first successful nonstop flight across the Atlantic started from St. John's and landed in Ireland more than 16 hours later.**

FYI

Quebec Food connoisseurs consider Quebec cuisine, with its definite French flavor, to be one of North America's best. The most famous foods of Quebec are pea soup, French pastries and breads, and highly spiced meat pies.

Region of Immigrants

Even the ancestors of Native Americans came from a distant shore. These ancient people may have crossed from Asia to North America by way of a land bridge that spanned what is now the Bering Strait.

Immigrants began arriving from Europe in the 1500s. In the centuries that followed, others came from Africa, Asia, and Latin America. Many made this land their home by choice. Others were forced to come as exiles or slaves.

Today, most people in the United States and Canada live in urban areas. Major cities are ethnically diverse, reflecting an immigrant heritage. The economic strength of both countries was built on the bounty of agriculture. Manufacturing, technology, and service industries have joined agriculture as the region's primary economic activities.

1 **The white walls** of a Spanish mission, or religious settlement, stand out against a blue New Mexico sky. Hoping to convert the area's native inhabitants to Christianity, the Spanish built many missions in what is now the southwestern United States.

2 **Red lights and blues music** illuminate a musician's face. The blues, a distinctively American musical style, was developed by African Americans. It sprang from spiritual music and from the wails and calls used by Southern plantation workers.

BACKGROUND INFORMATION

Cultural Values Contrary to what many people perceive, Canadians are not a homogeneous people. Their population is a diverse collection of ethnic and cultural groups. About half of Canadians are descended from the British or French. Historically, even before Canada became a country, friction arose between Quebec's French-speaking people and the country's English-speakers. In Quebec, all signs are in French, and there are strict requirements to use French in all commercial endeavors. English phrases are only allowed when there is no French equivalent. The Parti Quebecois continues to work for sovereignty, but the national government and the provinces of Canada have not yet come to an agreement about the issue. 🌐 **EE4 Human Systems: Standard 10**

3 **Lights of Toronto,** Ontario, stretch toward the horizon, brightening the night sky. With 4.7 million inhabitants in its metropolitan area, Toronto is Canada's largest city. It is a thriving center for service industries such as finance and communications.

4 **Freshly caught fish** chill in a snow bank outside an Inuit village in Canada's Northwest Territories. The Inuit have lived in the northern parts of Canada and Alaska for about a thousand years. Many still pursue traditional activities such as fishing and hunting.

Unit 2 **105**

Culture NOTE

Americans Individualism is often cited as an American characteristic. Even when working as a team, many Americans think of distinct individuals blending their efforts rather than the group working as a unit.

3 ASSESS

Ask: How is your place of residence typical of the region of the United States and Canada? What makes it different from other places?

4 CLOSE

Have students create illustrated postcards that highlight the cultural and geographical patterns associated with different places in the United States and Canada. Tell students to write descriptions of their places on the opposite side of their cards. They might focus on how cultural and physical patterns in their places helped create and spread new ideas and products.

UNIT PROJECT

Calendar Before students begin the study of this unit, tell them that they will be responsible for creating a calendar of the United States and Canada. They should begin collecting or drawing pictures of 12 landscapes that represent major regions of these two countries. Suggest that they choose an appropriate landscape for each month. Each picture should be accompanied by a caption that identifies its location and describes the climate during that month in the location they have chosen.
🌐 **EE2 Places and Regions: Standard 4**

These features and activities may be used as an introduction to the unit or as teaching tools throughout the course of the unit.

L1 Comparing

Direct students' attention to the physical map on this page. Ask them to compare the main landforms in the western, middle, and eastern United States with those of Canada. *(The two countries have similar physical features: the Rocky Mountains in the west, plains and lowlands in the middle, and low-lying mountains and highlands in the east.)*

INTERDISCIPLINARY
connection

ECONOMICS Some of the world's largest deposits of silver and zinc lie in the Canadian Shield. Intense mining and smelting in the area resulted in such a bleak terrain that U.S. astronauts once trained there before the landscape was restored.

Elevation Profile

In order to show a variety of physical features, this cross section begins at Vancouver Island and proceeds east near the U.S./Canada border until it reaches Lake Superior. From Lake Superior, it crosses the Canadian Shield to the southeast, and goes through Mt. Washington in the Appalachian Mountains in New Hampshire, before ending in the Atlantic Ocean.

The United States and Canada

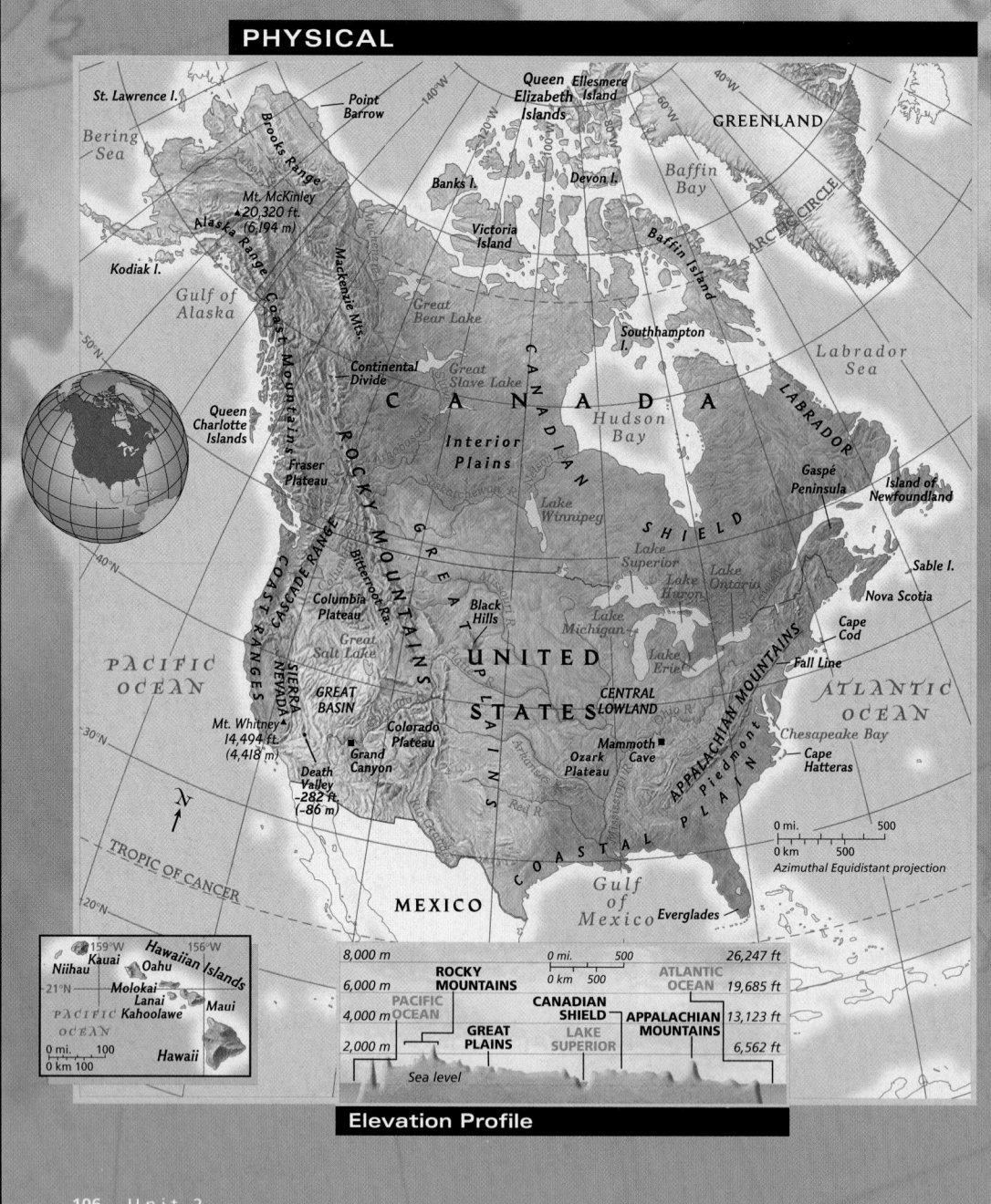

PHYSICAL

Elevation Profile

106 Unit 2

REGIONAL ATLAS ACTIVITY

Class Challenge Pair up students to write at least six questions about the physical geography of the United States and Canada with which to challenge another pair. Tell students to include direction, key, scale, or physical map questions such as: **In what direction would you travel from the Great Plains to Florida?** *(southeast)* **In the elevation profile, how do the Appalachian Mountains compare to the Rocky Mountains?** *(The Rocky Mountains have a higher elevation.)* **About how many miles would you have to travel between the Hawaiian Islands of Kauai and Maui?** *(about 200 miles)*
🌐 **EE1 The World in Spatial Terms: Standard 1**

POLITICAL

RUSSIA
180°

ARCTIC OCEAN

Greenland Sea

ARCTIC CIRCLE

20°W

40°W

60°W

Chukchi Sea

Bering Sea

Ellesmere Island

GREENLAND (KALAALLIT NUNAAT) Den.

ALASKA
•Anchorage

Beaufort Sea

Banks Island

Baffin Bay

Gulf of Alaska

YUKON TERRITORY

Victoria Island

NUNAVUT

Baffin Island

Davis Strait

Labrador Sea

NORTHWEST TERRITORIES

Southampton Island

Hudson Strait

Mackenzie R.

BRITISH COLUMBIA

C A N A D A

159°W   156°W

HAWAII

Honolulu•

21°N

PACIFIC OCEAN

0 mi.   100
0 km 100

ALBERTA

SASK.

Nelson R.

Saskatchewan R.

Hudson Bay

NEWFOUNDLAND AND LABRADOR

Edmonton•

QUEBEC

Vancouver •Calgary

Seattle•
WASH.

MANITOBA

Winnipeg•

ONTARIO

P.E.I.

N.B.   NOVA SCOTIA

Montreal•
Ottawa®   ME.

40°N

Missouri R.

OREGON

MONT.   N. DAK.

MINN.

MICHIGAN

Toronto•   VT. N.H.

IDAHO

S. DAK.

WIS.

N.Y.   MASS.
R.I. CONN.

PACIFIC OCEAN

WYO.

IOWA

Chicago•

OHIO

PA.

New York City
Philadelphia•

San Francisco•

NEVADA   UTAH

NEBR.

ILL. IND.

Ohio R.   W.   DEL.
VA.   MD.
Washington, D.C.

30°N

Los Angeles•

California R.

COLO.   KANSAS

St. Louis•
MO.   KY.   VA.

U N I T E D   S T A T E S

Arkansas R.

ARIZ.
Phoenix•

OKLA.

ARK.

TENN.

N.C.

ATLANTIC OCEAN

NEW MEXICO

Red R.

MISS. ALA.

S.C.

Atlanta•
GA.

TEXAS

Mississippi R.

LA.

● National capital
• Major city

MEXICO

Rio Grande

Houston•

FLORIDA

0 mi.   500
0 km   500

Miami•

Azimuthal Equidistant projection

Gulf of Mexico

TROPIC OF CANCER

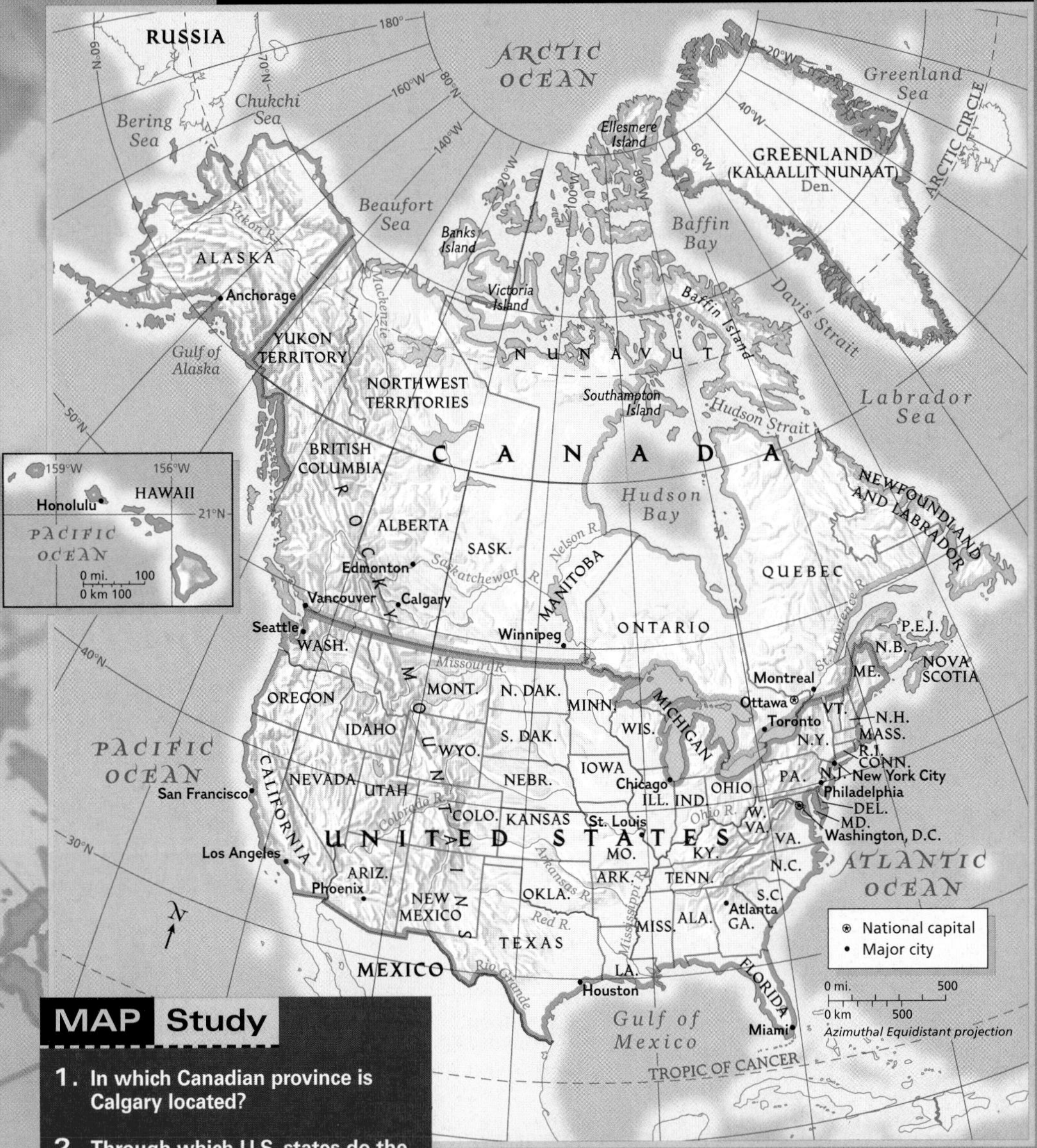

MAP Study

1. In which Canadian province is Calgary located?

2. Through which U.S. states do the Coast Ranges run?

L2 Location

Have students identify the main bodies of water that surround the United States and Canada and the principal waterways that are found within these countries. *(Surrounding bodies of water include the Pacific Ocean, Arctic Ocean, Atlantic Ocean, and Gulf of Mexico. Some of the principal waterways include Hudson Bay, St. Lawrence River and the Great Lakes, and the Mississippi and Missouri Rivers.)*

Native Languages More than 300 native languages once existed in the United States and Canada. Although two-thirds of these languages still survive, there are few speakers left. Native languages have left their imprint, though, on place names such as Chicago and Massachusetts.

MAP Study

Answers:

1. *Alberta*

2. *Washington, Oregon, and California*

Map Skills Practice
Location What Canadian territory borders the northwest part of Hudson Bay? *(Nunavut)*

REGIONAL ATLAS ACTIVITY

Studying Cultures Assign small groups of students to research the cultural contributions of one of the ethnic or indigenous groups that live in the United States or Canada. For students who need extra help, suggest one of the following ethnic groups: Ukrainians, Cajuns, Acadians, Cubans, Puerto Ricans, Filipinos, or Koreans. For indigenous groups, suggest the Inuit, Aleut, Iroquois, Sioux, or Cheyenne. Tell students to identify contributions—such as cuisine, architecture, music, clothing, government, or religion—and note their significance within the cultural group as well as the mainstream culture. Have students share their findings with the class. ▣ **EE4 Human Systems: Standard 10**

L1 Comparing

Have students look at the Population Density map on this page. Ask them to locate the most densely populated areas in the United States and compare them to densely populated areas in Canada. **Ask:** What geographical features appear most often in densely populated areas? *(Students should note that the most densely populated areas in both countries are in the east near water.)*

L2 Location

Refer students to the Natural Resources map on page 109. Tell them they are planning to invest in the Canadian forestry industry. **Ask:** What factors would you consider when deciding in which Canadian province to do business? *(Students should note that Canadian forests stretch from coast to coast. They should consider the location of population centers and waterways or railroads.)*

Megalopolis This word, coined in 1961, describes the densely populated 500-mile (805-km) long string of cities along the eastern seaboard stretching from Boston to Washington, D.C. The area continues to sprawl. New Jersey has more people per square mile— 1,042—than does crowded Japan with 871 people per square mile.

UNIT 2 REGIONAL ATLAS

The United States and Canada

POPULATION DENSITY

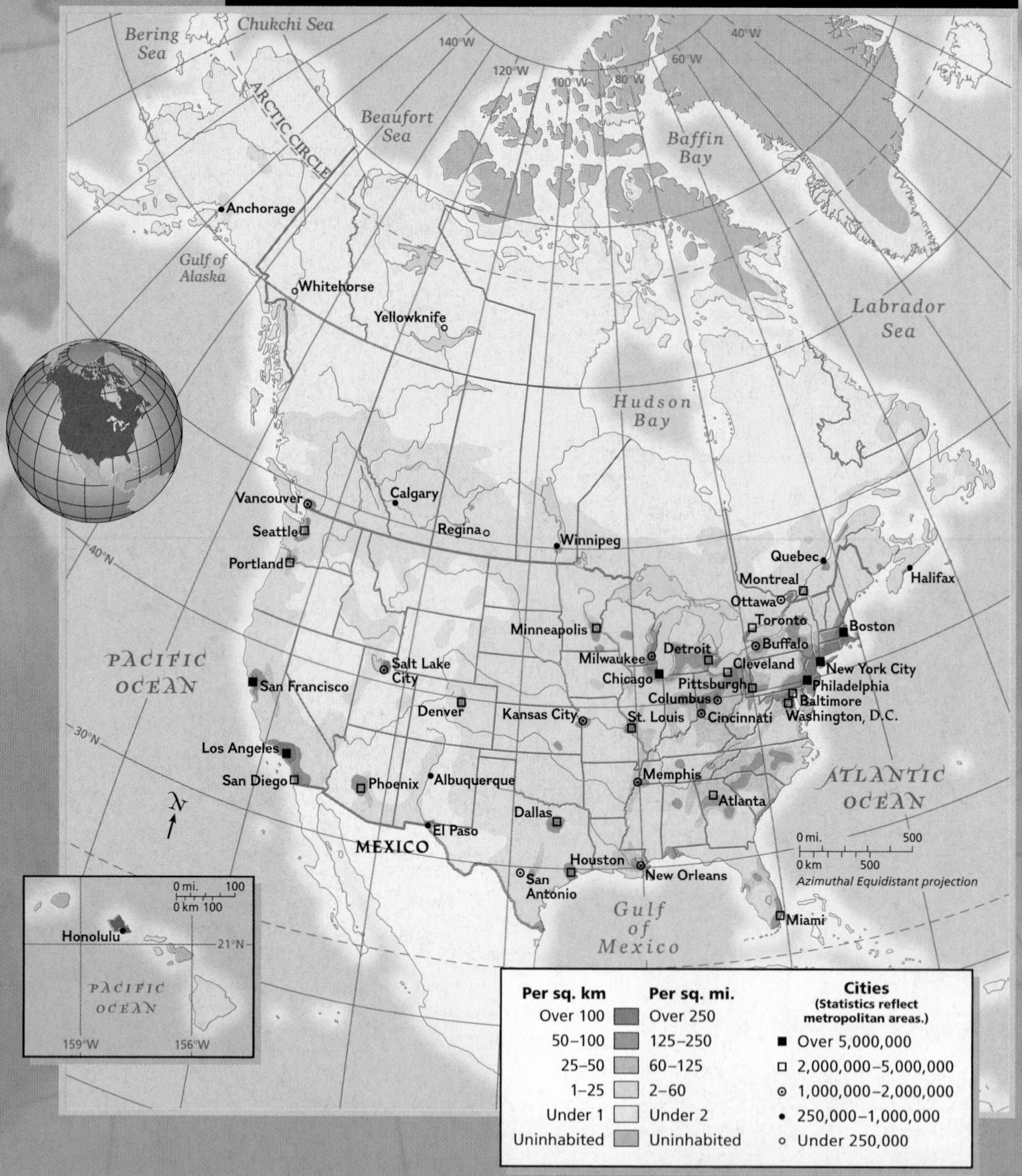

Per sq. km	Per sq. mi.	Cities (Statistics reflect metropolitan areas.)
Over 100	Over 250	■ Over 5,000,000
50–100	125–250	▫ 2,000,000–5,000,000
25–50	60–125	◉ 1,000,000–2,000,000
1–25	2–60	• 250,000–1,000,000
Under 1	Under 2	○ Under 250,000
Uninhabited	Uninhabited	

Azimuthal Equidistant projection

REGIONAL ATLAS ACTIVITY

Region Have students study the population density map on this page. Then give students a specified amount of time to write six geographic questions whose answers can be determined from the map. Model a population density question: **Which three northern states bordering Canada have the lowest population densities?** *(Idaho, Montana, North Dakota)* Be sure students know that Canada's political units are called provinces instead of states, so that they use the correct term in their questions. Organize the class into teams and have a competition similar to a spelling bee, using the questions.
🌐 **EE2 Places and Regions: Standard 4**

ECONOMIC ACTIVITY

GREENLAND

Beaufort Sea

Baffin Bay

Anchorage

Gulf of Alaska

ARCTIC CIRCLE

Davis Strait

Labrador Sea

Hudson Strait

C A N A D A

Hudson Bay

0 mi. 500
0 km 500
Azimuthal Equidistant projection

Vancouver

Calgary

Wheat

Seattle

Winnipeg

Portland

Wheat

Ottawa

Montreal

Potatoes

Minneapolis

Green Bay

Toronto

Boston

Sheep

Milwaukee

Detroit

Buffalo

Cattle

PACIFIC OCEAN

U N I T E D   S T A T E S

New York City

San Francisco

Salt Lake City

Des Moines

Corn

Chicago

Columbus

Pittsburgh

Philadelphia

Fruit

Denver

Kansas City

Corn

Indianapolis

Baltimore

Washington, D.C.

Wheat

St. Louis

Tobacco

Norfolk

Los Angeles

Cotton

Nashville

Raleigh

Phoenix

Memphis

Columbia

ATLANTIC OCEAN

Dallas

Birmingham

Atlanta

MEXICO

Cotton

Pecans

Cattle

Houston

New Orleans

Gulf of Mexico

Miami

Fruit

TROPIC OF CANCER

0 mi. 100
0 km 100

Sugarcane

Honolulu

HAWAII

PACIFIC OCEAN

Fruit

159°W   156°W

Resources

⚒	Iron ore	◆	Copper
⚑	Petroleum	⊡	Zinc
◊	Natural gas	▱	Gold
⬛	Coal	▱	Silver

Land Use

- ☐ Commercial farming
- ☐ Subsistence farming
- ☐ Livestock raising
- ☐ Nomadic herding
- ☐ Hunting and gathering
- ☐ Forests
- ☐ Manufacturing and trade
- ☐ Commercial fishing
- ☐ Little or no activity

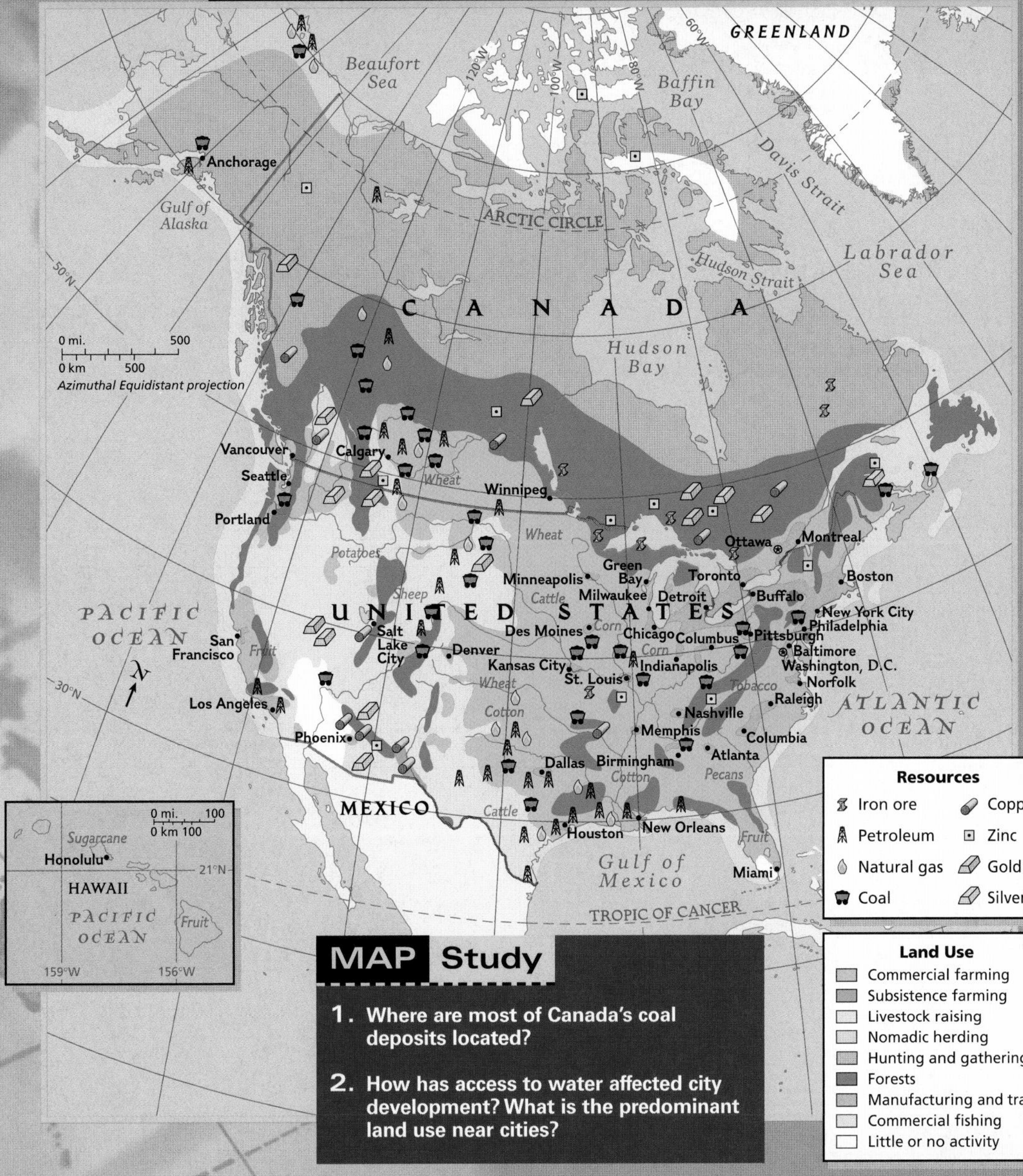

MAP Study

1. Where are most of Canada's coal deposits located?

2. How has access to water affected city development? What is the predominant land use near cities?

L2 Movement

Have students suppose they are planning an automobile tour of part of the United States or Canada. Tell them to plan their tour based on one of the following criteria: avoiding densely populated areas, visiting an area that is heavily forested, seeing a variety of land-forms in an area where there is also commercial farming, or visiting places on or near great waterways. Give students blank maps so they can plot their driving tours. Have students share their itineraries with the rest of the class.

global issues

Polar Bears In Manitoba's Wapusk National Park, polar bears are protected from humans by park boundaries and restricted hunting, yet they face other serious challenges. Chemicals pollute their food chain, and mining and offshore drilling could further encroach upon their habitat. Global warming may be causing accelerated melting of ice packs, cutting short the bears' seal hunting season.

MAP Study

Answers
1. *the Rocky Mountains*
2. *It has accelerated and promoted development; manufacturing and trade.*

REGIONAL ATLAS ACTIVITY

Place Allow students several minutes to look at the maps on pages 108–109. Have them generalize about how geographical characteristics determine population density and economic activity. Have students form the same groups as they did for the population density activity on the preceding page. Tell them to take their 10 best questions and revise them to include economic activities and natural resources. Give students this example as a model and ask them to identify the place: **Ask: Which state, located in the northwestern United States, is sparsely populated except for one area on the water and has economic activities that include coal mining and fishing?** *(Washington)* Repeat the game from the previous page using the new questions. 🎲 🖥 **EE4 Human Systems: Standard 12**

These features and activities may be used as an introduction to the unit or as teaching tools throughout the course of the unit.

L1 Identify

Direct students to the information on state and province names on pages 110–111. Say the name of a capital and have students identify the state or province. Continue until all of them have been called out. Next, read a "Meaning and Origin" fact and have students identify the state or province.

L2 Categorizing

Have students scan pages 110–111 to review how states and provinces received their names. Students should then put the name origins in categories, such as Native American or Indigenous, Spanish, French, and British. Students should note that about half the states have names of Native American origin.

Anglo Americans The United States and Canada are often called *Anglo America*, because many of their settlers came from England, and the main language of both countries is English.

UNIT 2 REGIONAL ATLAS

The United States and Canada

COUNTRY PROFILES

COUNTRY * AND CAPITAL	FLAG AND LANGUAGE	POPULATION** AND DENSITY	LANDMASS	MAJOR EXPORT	MAJOR IMPORT	CURRENCY	GOVERNMENT
UNITED STATES Washington, D.C.	English	291,500,000 78 per sq. mi. 30 per sq. km	3,717,796 sq. mi. 9,629,091 sq. km	Machinery	Crude Oil	U.S. Dollar	Federal Republic
CANADA Ottawa	English, French	31,600,000 8 per sq. mi. 3 per sq. km	3,849,670 sq. mi. 9,970,645 sq. km	Newsprint	Crude Oil	Canadian Dollar	Parliamentary Democracy

FOR AN ONLINE UPDATE OF THIS INFORMATION, VISIT GEOGRAPHY.GLENCOE.COM AND CLICK ON "TEXTBOOK UPDATES."

U.S. State Names: Meaning and Origin

ALABAMA — Montgomery
"thicket clearers" (Choctaw)

ALASKA — Juneau
"the great land" (Aleut)

ARIZONA — Phoenix
"little spring" (Papago), or "dry land" (Spanish)

ARKANSAS — Little Rock
"downstream people" (Quapaw)

CALIFORNIA — Sacramento
unknown meaning (Spanish)

COLORADO — Denver
"red" (Spanish)

CONNECTICUT — Hartford
"beside the long tidal river" (Native American)

DELAWARE — Dover
named for Virginia's colonial governor, Baron De La Warr

FLORIDA — Tallahassee
"feast of flowers" (Spanish)

GEORGIA — Atlanta
named for England's King George II

HAWAII — Honolulu
unknown meaning (Native Hawaiian)

IDAHO — Boise
unknown meaning (Native American)

ILLINOIS — Springfield
"tribe of superior men" (Native American)

INDIANA — Indianapolis
"land of Indians" (European American)

IOWA — Des Moines
unknown meaning (Native American)

KANSAS — Topeka
"people of the south wind" (Sioux)

KENTUCKY — Frankfort
"land of tomorrow" (Iroquoian)

LOUISIANA — Baton Rouge
named for France's King Louis XIV

MAINE — Augusta
named for an ancient French province

MARYLAND — Annapolis
named in honor of the wife of England's King Charles I

MASSACHUSETTS — Boston
"great mountain place" (Native American)

MICHIGAN — Lansing
"great lake" (Ojibway)

MINNESOTA — Saint Paul
"sky-tinted water" (Sioux)

MISSISSIPPI — Jackson
"father of the waters" (Native American)

* COUNTRIES, FLAGS, STATES, AND PROVINCES NOT DRAWN TO SCALE
** POPULATIONS ARE ROUNDED, *SOURCE: 2003 WORLD POPULATION DATA SHEET*

COUNTRY PROFILE ACTIVITY

Places Assign each student two states and one province. Have students draw or trace their states and province on three large note cards. Students should outline the shapes in red for states and blue for provinces but not label them. On the reverse side of the card, students should write a description of the physical shape of their state or province. Give students the following example to help them get started: *Oklahoma is shaped like a pan with its handle pointing west.* The cards should also list the capital and the meaning and origin of the state's or province's name. When they finish, have students read one of their descriptions to see if others can identify the state or province it describes.

🌐 EE2 Places and Regions: Standard 6

MISSOURI
Jefferson City
"town of the large canoes"
(Native American)

MONTANA
Helena
"mountainous" (Spanish)

NEBRASKA
Lincoln
"flat water"
(Native American)

NEVADA
Carson City
"snowcapped"
(Spanish)

NEW HAMPSHIRE
Concord
named for Hampshire,
a county in England

NEW JERSEY
Trenton
named for Isle of Jersey,
a British territory

NEW MEXICO
Santa Fe
named for the state's former
colonial ruler, Mexico

NEW YORK
Albany
named in honor of the
English Duke of York

NORTH CAROLINA
Raleigh
named in honor of
England's King Charles I

NORTH DAKOTA
Bismarck
named for the Dakota,
a Native American group

OHIO
Columbus
"great river"
(Native American)

OKLAHOMA
Oklahoma City
"red people" (Choctaw)

OREGON
Salem
unknown meaning
and origin

PENNSYLVANIA
Harrisburg
"Penn's woodland," named for
the father of Pennsylvania's
founder, William Penn

RHODE ISLAND
Providence
unknown meaning
and origin

SOUTH CAROLINA
Columbia
named for England's
King Charles I

SOUTH DAKOTA
Pierre
named for the Dakota,
a Native American group

TENNESSEE
Nashville
named for Tanasi,
"Cherokee villages"
(Cherokee)

TEXAS
Austin
"friends" (Tejas)

UTAH
Salt Lake City
"people of the
mountains" (Ute)

VERMONT
Montpelier
"green mountain"
(French)

VIRGINIA
Richmond
named for the unmarried
Queen Elizabeth I of England,
known as "the Virgin Queen"

WASHINGTON
Olympia
named in honor of
George Washington

WEST VIRGINIA
Charleston
began as the western
part of Virginia before
becoming a state in 1863

WISCONSIN
Madison
"grassy place"
(Chippewa)

WYOMING
Cheyenne
"upon the great plain"
(Delaware)

Canadian Province and Territory Names: Meaning and Origin

ALBERTA
Edmonton
named for the
daughter of England's
Queen Victoria

BRITISH COLUMBIA
Victoria
named for Christopher
Columbus and the
province's British
heritage

MANITOBA
Winnipeg
"strait of the great spirit"
(Algonquian)

NEW BRUNSWICK
Fredericton
named for English royal
family of Brunswick-Luneburg

NEWFOUNDLAND AND LABRADOR
St. John's
"new found land,"
named by explorer John
Cabot in 1497; lavrador,
"laborer" (Portuguese)

NORTHWEST TERRITORIES
Yellowknife
named for lands
north and west
of Lake Superior

NOVA SCOTIA
Halifax
Latin term for "New Scotland,"
based on province's
Scottish heritage

NUNAVUT
Iqaluit
"our land"
(Inuktitut)

ONTARIO
Toronto
meaning unknown
(Iroquoian)

PRINCE EDWARD ISLAND
Charlottetown
named for the son of
England's King George III

QUEBEC
Quebec
"place where the
river narrows"
(Algonquian)

SASKATCHEWAN
Regina
"fast flowing river"
(Cree)

YUKON TERRITORY
Whitehorse
"great river"
(Native American)

L3 Mapping
Help students understand the variety of political units in the region by having them fill in outline maps or prepare sketch maps showing their community with its various subdivisions, their state showing counties, and the United States and Canada showing states and provinces. Have students consult atlases or road maps for their research.

Caverns and Desert One-third of New Mexico is covered by federal land. Carlsbad Caverns is one of the world's deepest caverns. White Sands National Monument has the world's largest field of gypsum dunes. Other places of interest include Aztec Ruins, Bandelier, and Gila Cliff Dwellings.

NATIONAL GEOGRAPHIC GEOFACT
Alaska is so large that if you were to place it inside the lower 48 states, the lower parts of Alaska, including the Aleutian Islands, would stretch 2,260 miles (3,635 km) from northern Florida westward to California.

COUNTRY PROFILE ACTIVITY

Comparing Countries Although Canada and the United States are both democracies, significant differences exist between the two governments. Have students research such areas as the countries' leaders and methods of choosing them, political parties, elections, branches of the governments and their powers, and powers of the states and the provinces. Have students present their information during an informal discussion. Create a class comparison/contrast chart for the governments of the two countries.

EE4 Human Systems: Standard 13

① FOCUS

Have students recall ice hockey games they have seen or heard about. Allow a minute or two for students to volunteer adjectives and verbs that capture and explain the feelings they had during the game. Tell students to think about other outdoor activities that are popular during the winter. **Ask: How do outdoor winter activities in our region differ from those in Canada?**

② TEACH

L2 Explain

Ask students familiar with hockey to explain hockey terms and give a short description of how the game is played.

L2 Debate

Hockey critics have called the sport "legalized mayhem." Avid fans claim that hockey is "poetry on ice." Have students debate the issue, supporting their opinions with examples from games they have seen. At the end of the debate, have students compare hockey skills and violence to that in other sports—soccer, basketball, football, boxing, and so on.

GLOBAL ● CONNECTION
CANADA AND THE UNITED STATES

ICE HOCKEY !

Historians still debate the details, but everyone agrees that ice hockey was invented in Canada. The game seems to have originated in the early 1800s in Nova Scotia, one of Canada's easternmost provinces. Not content to spend long winters indoors, some of Nova Scotia's inhabitants began tinkering with an Irish game, similar to field hockey, that was played with sticks and a ball. The eager sportsmen realized that the slick surface of a frozen pond was a worthy alternative to a grassy playing field. They traded their shoes for skates, and ice hockey was born.

As the new game gained popularity, it spread west and north across Canada. By the turn of the century, ice hockey had become Canada's

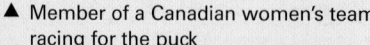

▲ Member of a Canadian women's team racing for the puck

▲ Pick-up game near Canada's Laurentian Mountains

BACKGROUND INFORMATION

Geography in History: Movement Hockey stars have attracted crowds throughout North America since the 1920s. Stars like Howie Morenz, dubbed "Lightning Legs" for his grace and speed, made hockey a major-league attraction on both sides of the border. Wayne Gretzky owned the ice in the 1980s. In 1989 he became the National Hockey League's all-time leading scorer with 1,851 points. Today, teams play in almost every U.S. state. The Kid Hockey system has divisions for boys and girls, men and women. At the boys' "Bantam" level (13–14 year olds), promising youngsters are scouted, and at the Junior level (17–19 year olds) talented U.S. players are prepared for the National Hockey League.

🌐 EE5 Environment and Society: Standard 15

▼ Getting a feel for skating on wheels

NATIONAL GEOGRAPHIC

national sport. And it was not just for men. The first all-female ice hockey game on record was played in Ontario in 1892.

Hockey fever spread southward, too, crossing the U.S.-Canadian border into northern states such as Minnesota, Michigan, Massachusetts, and New York. In 1924 the Boston Bruins became the first U.S. team to join Canada's National Hockey League. Other northern cities, including Chicago and Detroit, soon had teams on the League's roster as well.

At this point, geography checked ice hockey's southward spread. For nearly a quarter century, the game remained a northern pastime. It just didn't catch on in southern states where cold weather was rare and lakes never froze.

Eventually, however, indoor ice rinks, televised hockey games, and a steady influx of Canadian players into the United States overcame the geographic barriers, and the sport found a foothold in nearly every state. Hockey made headlines in 1980 when America's team beat the heavily favored Soviets in the Olympic Winter Games and then went on to win the gold medal. When Canadian superstar Wayne Gretzky came to play in the United States a few years later, hockey's popularity surged again.

Now in-line skates and roller hockey make it possible for would-be players to get a feel for the game no matter where they live or what the season. Many major U.S. cities have professional hockey teams, including Phoenix, Dallas, and Miami. In fact, America's Sun Belt alone is home to more hockey teams than there are in Canada! But ice hockey in the United States isn't just for professionals. It's played by kids—both boys and girls—and amateurs throughout the nation.

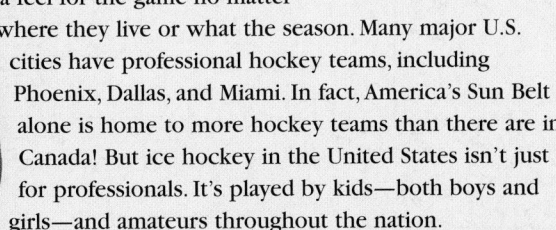
▲ Hockey legend Wayne Gretzky entering a rink

Unit 2   **113**

FYI

Hockey Pucks So powerful are the swings of hockey players that a puck, when struck, can travel across the ice at speeds faster than 100 miles (161 km) per hour.

③ ASSESS

Have students name as many ways as they can how sports such as ice hockey help define the United States and Canada as a region. List responses on the board.

④ CLOSE

Ask: How do enthusiastic sports fans help expand a sport? How did fans aid the spread of ice hockey?

🌐 Meeting National Standards

Geography for Life
The following standards are met in the Student Edition:

EE2 Places and Regions: Standard 6
EE4 Human Systems: Standards 10, 11
EE5 Environment and Society: Standards 15, 16
EE6 The Uses of Geography: Standard 18

CONNECTION ACTIVITY

Research Organize students into teams of five or six. Allow each team to choose a facet of hockey to research: history, equipment, teams, or heroes. Challenge teams to use books and magazine articles to "flesh out" the basic information they obtain from encyclopedias. Have students present their research in as graphic and interesting a way as possible: time lines, captioned photographs or drawings, equipment displays, a Hockey Heroes Hall of Fame, or a hockey trivia booklet. When students have completed their research, have them work together to create a hockey exhibit. Have them present information informally, as if they were museum guides. 🌐 **EE4 Human Systems: Standard 10**

PLANNING GUIDE

NOTE: The following materials may be used when teaching Chapter 5. Section-level support materials are shown at point-of-use in the margins of the Teacher Wraparound Edition.

TEACHING TRANSPARENCIES

Unit 2 Map Overlay Transparencies

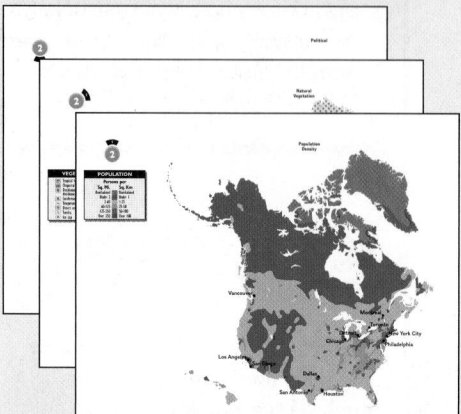

Political Map Transparency 2

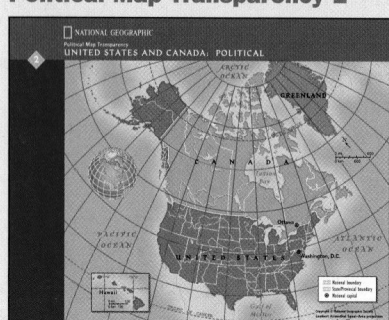

GEOGRAPHIC LITERACY

Focus on Geography Literacy

APPLICATION AND ENRICHMENT

L3 Enrichment Activity 5

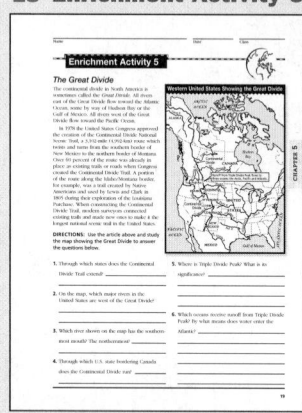

REVIEW AND REINFORCEMENT

L1 Vocabulary Activity 5   L1 Reinforcing   L1 Reteaching Activity 5
Skills Activity 5

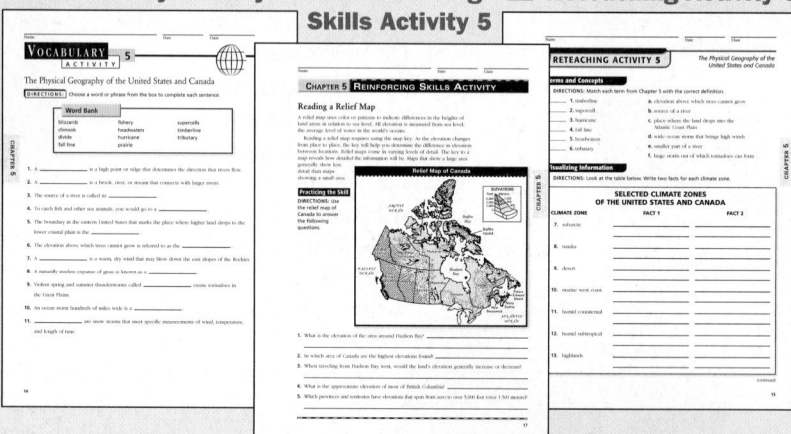

ASSESSMENT

L2 Chapter 5 Test Form A

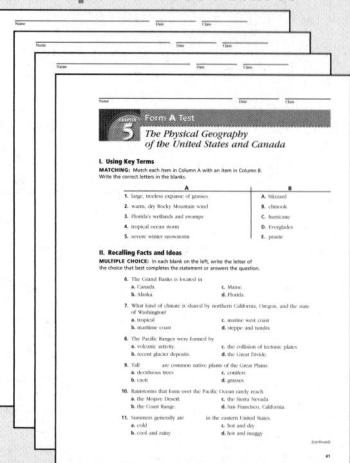

L2 Chapter 5 Test Form B

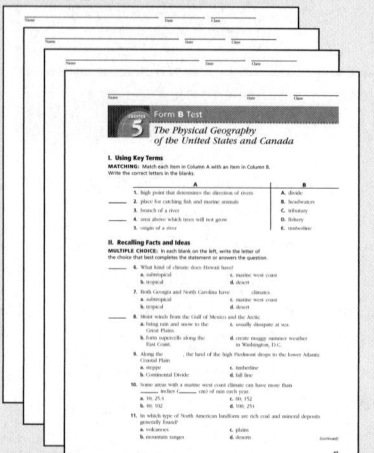

**L1/ELL Performance
Assessment Activity 5**

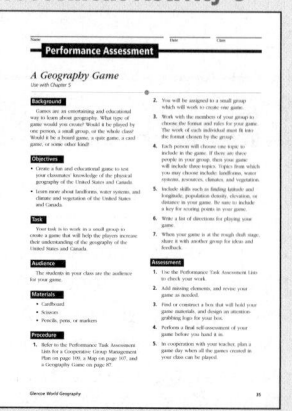

**ExamView® Pro
Testmaker**

SPANISH RESOURCES

The following Spanish language materials are available in the Spanish Resources binder:

- 📁 Spanish Vocabulary Activities
- 📁 Spanish Guided Reading Activities
- 📁 Spanish Reteaching Activities
- 📁 Spanish Summaries
- 📁 Spanish Quizzes and Tests
- 📁 Spanish Reading Essentials and Study Guide

MULTIMEDIA

- World Regions Video
- MindJogger Videoquiz
- Vocabulary PuzzleMaker CD-ROM
- Interactive Tutor Self-Assessment CD-ROM
- ExamView® Pro Testmaker CD-ROM
- Audio Program
- TeacherWorks CD-ROM
- Interactive Student Edition CD-ROM
- Glencoe Skillbuilder Interactive Workbook CD-ROM, Level 2
- Presentation Plus! CD-ROM

Timesaving Tools

TeacherWorks™ All-In-One Planner and Resource Center

- **Interactive Teacher Edition** Access your Teacher Wraparound Edition and your classroom resources with a few easy clicks.

- **Interactive Lesson Planner** Planning has never been easier! Organize your week, month, semester, or year with all the lesson helps you need to make teaching creative, timely, and relevant.

Use Glencoe's **Presentation Plus!** multimedia teacher tool to easily present dynamic lessons that visually excite your students. Using Microsoft PowerPoint® you can customize the presentations to create your own personalized lessons.

GEOGRAPHY Online

Use our Web site for additional resources. All essential content is covered in the Student Edition.

You and your students can visit geography.glencoe.com, the Web site companion to *Glencoe World Geography*. This innovative integration of electronic and print media offers your students a wealth of opportunities. The student text directs students to the Web site for the following options:

- Chapter Overviews
- Self-Check Quizzes
- Student Activities
- Textbook Updates

Answers are provided for you in the "Web Activity Lesson Plan." Additional Web resources and Interactive Tutor puzzles are also available.

Additional Glencoe Teacher Support

- Teaching Strategies for the Geography Classroom (including Block Scheduling Pacing Guides)

- Graphic Organizer Transparencies Strategies and Activities

- Outline Map Resource Book

- Reading in the Content Area

PLANNING GUIDE

SECTION RESOURCES

Daily Objectives	Reproducible Resources	Multimedia Resources

SECTION 1 The Land

1. Identify some key similarities and differences in the physical geography of the United States and Canada.
2. Explain why rivers have played such an important role in this region's development.
3. Examine geographic factors that have made the United States and Canada so rich in natural resources.

 Reproducible Lesson Plan 5-1
Daily Lecture Notes 5-1
Guided Reading Activity 5-1*
 Reading Essentials and Study Guide 5-1*
Section Quiz 5-1*

- Daily Focus Skills Transparency 5-1
- Political Map Transparency 2
- Unit 2 Map Overlay Transparencies
- Interactive Tutor Self-Assessment CD-ROM
- ExamView® Pro Testmaker CD-ROM*
- Presentation Plus! CD-ROM

SECTION 2 Climate and Vegetation

1. List the climate zones found in the United States and Canada.
2. Describe how winds, ocean currents, latitude, and landforms affect the region's climates.
3. Identify the kinds of weather hazards that affect the United States and Canada.
4. Discuss how human settlement has affected the natural vegetation of the United States and Canada.

 Reproducible Lesson Plan 5-2
Vocabulary Activity 5
Daily Lecture Notes 5-2
 Guided Reading Activity 5-2*
 Reading Essentials and Study Guide 5-2*
 Reteaching Activity 5*
Reinforcing Skills Activity 5
 Section Quiz 5-2*

- Daily Focus Skills Transparency 5-2
- Political Map Transparency 2
- Unit 2 Map Overlay Transparencies
- Vocabulary PuzzleMaker CD-ROM
- Interactive Tutor Self-Assessment CD-ROM
- ExamView® Pro Testmaker CD-ROM*
- Presentation Plus! CD-ROM

 Blackline Master

Transparency

Software

CD-ROM

Videocassette

DVD

Also available in Spanish

OUT OF TIME? 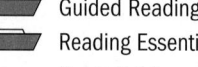 Assign the Chapter 5 **Reading Essentials and Study Guide.**

Block Schedule

Activities that are particularly suited to use within the block scheduling framework are identified throughout this chapter by the following designation:

KEY TO ABILITY LEVELS

Teaching strategies have been coded for various learning styles and abilities.

L1 **BASIC** activities for all students

L2 **AVERAGE** activities for average to above-average students

L3 **CHALLENGING** activities for above-average students

ELL **ENGLISH LANGUAGE LEARNER** activities

Teacher to Teacher

Kelly Park
Smethport Area
High School
Smethport, PA

Journeying Through North America

To combine a variety of disciplines into a project about the United States and Canada, have students write 15 journal entries that describe journeys to places in the region. The journal entries must contain geography facts, such as location and landforms. Entries should include visuals, such as maps, photographs, drawings or sketches, magazine or newspaper clippings, or CD-ROM or Internet images.

Students may select places they have firsthand knowledge of as well as places that require research. To help students begin, have them select a reason for their journey. For example, they might consider traveling with an athletic team, or a salesperson, or going on an archaeological search.

Remind students that their travel journals should include a specific route and that their entries might also include notes about their modes of transportation, the foods they sample along the way, and interesting events they might attend.

NATIONAL GEOGRAPHIC TEACHER'S CORNER

Index to National Geographic Magazine:

The following articles may be used for research relating to this chapter:

- "Living with Natural Hazards," by Michael Parfit, July 1998.
- "Prince Edward Island: A World Apart No More," by Ian Darragh, May 1998.

National Geographic Society Products:

To order the following products for use with this chapter, call National Geographic Society at 1-800-368-2728.

- *PictureShow: U.S. Regional Geography Library* (CD-ROM)
- *Physical Geography of North America Series* (Videos)
- *North America Political* (Map)
- *United States Political* (Map)
- *National Geographic Atlas of the World, Seventh Edition* (Book)

NGS ONLINE

Access National Geographic's Web site for current events, activities, links, interactive features, and archives.
www.nationalgeographic.com

Meeting National Standards

Geography For Life

The following standards are highlighted in Chapter 5:

Section 1	EE1 The World in Spatial Terms: Standard 1
	EE2 Places and Regions: Standard 4
	EE3 Physical Systems: Standards 7, 8
	EE5 Environment and Society: Standards 14, 15, 16
Section 2	EE2 Places and Regions: Standard 4
	EE3 Physical Systems: Standard 8
	EE4 Human Systems: Standard 11
	EE5 Environment and Society: Standard 15

Local Objectives

_____

_____

MEETING SPECIAL NEEDS

In addition to the Differentiated Instruction strategies found in each section, the following resources are also suitable for your special needs students:

- ***ExamView® Pro Testmaker CD-ROM*** allows teachers to tailor tests by reducing answer choices.
- The ***Audio Program*** includes the entire narrative of the student edition so that less-proficient readers can listen to the words as they read them.
- The ***Reading Essentials and Study Guide*** provides the same content as the student edition but is written two grade levels below the textbook.
- ***Guided Reading Activities*** give less-proficient readers point-by-point instructions to increase comprehension as they read each textbook section.
- ***Enrichment Activities*** include a stimulating collection of readings and activities for gifted and talented students.

Chapter Objectives

1. Describe the dominant land-forms and natural resources of the United States and Canada.

2. Discuss climate and vegetation in the United States and Canada.

GLENCOE TECHNOLOGY

Use *MindJogger Videoquiz* to preview the Chapter 5 content.

GeoJournal

For access to additional photos, maps, and information on the geographic features of the United States and Canada, go to www.nationalgeographic.com **(See Teacher pages in front for strategies for using journals in the geography classroom.)**

GEOGRAPHY Online

Introduce students to chapter content and key terms by having them access Chapter Overview 5 at geography.glencoe.com

FOLDABLES™
Study Organizer

Dinah Zike's Foldables are three-dimensional, interactive graphic organizers that help students practice basic writing skills, review key vocabulary terms, and identify main ideas. Have students complete the Foldable activity in the ***Dinah Zike's Reading and Study Skills Foldables*** booklet.

CHAPTER 5

The Physical Geography of the United States and Canada

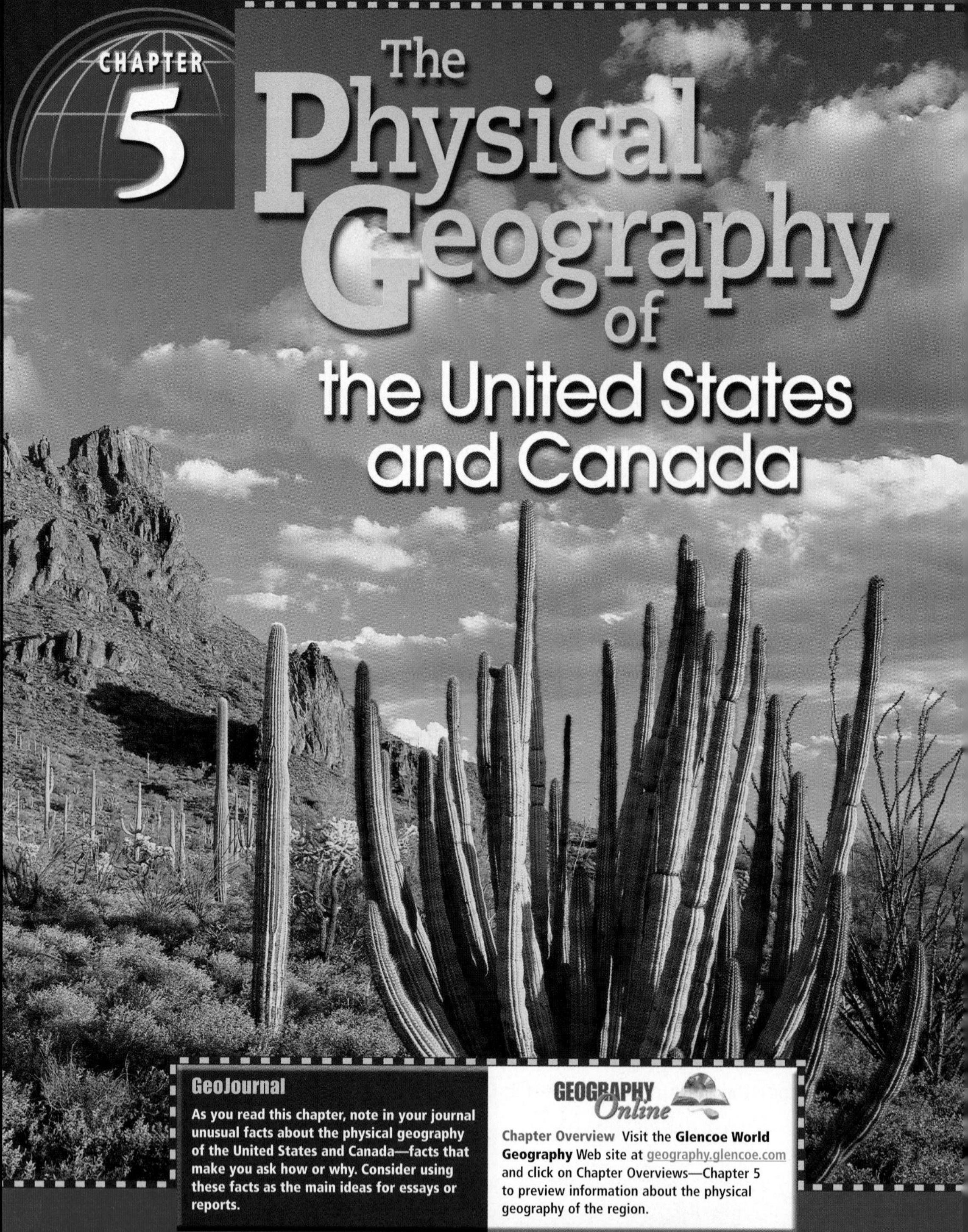

GeoJournal

As you read this chapter, note in your journal unusual facts about the physical geography of the United States and Canada—facts that make you ask how or why. Consider using these facts as the main ideas for essays or reports.

GEOGRAPHY Online

Chapter Overview Visit the **Glencoe World Geography** Web site at geography.glencoe.com and click on Chapter Overviews—Chapter 5 to preview information about the physical geography of the region.

ABOUT THE PHOTO

Visual Instruction Located near Ajo, Arizona, Organ Pipe Cactus National Monument spans 330,688 acres (133,929 ha) in the Sonoran Desert. The organ pipe cactus, pictured here, is seldom found in the United States. It is perfectly adapted to its environment, which includes extreme temperatures and very dry conditions. The plant's many stems store water for long periods of time in order to survive the desert's dry months. In spring the cactus varieties in the park bloom during the warm weather.

- EE2 Places and Regions: Standard 4
- EE3 Physical Systems: Standards 7, 8

Guide to Reading

Consider What You Know
The United States and Canada share the world's longest undefended border. What famous natural feature do both the United States and Canada claim as a tourist attraction?

Reading Strategy
Organizing Complete a web diagram similar to the one below by listing major minerals found in the United States and Canada.

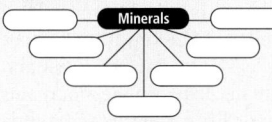

Read to Find Out
• What are some key similarities and differences in the physical geography of the United States and Canada?
• Why have rivers played such an important role in this region's development?
• What geographic factors have made the United States and Canada so rich in natural resources?

Terms to Know
• divide
• headwaters
• tributary
• fall line
• fishery

Places to Locate
• Mount McKinley
• Rocky Mountains
• Canadian Shield
• Appalachian Mountains
• Colorado River
• Rio Grande
• Mackenzie River
• Mississippi River
• St. Lawrence River
• Great Lakes

The Land

NATIONAL GEOGRAPHIC

A Geographic View

Carving Their Own Way

Grain fields spill their color across the badlands of the Missouri Breaks, a lonesome swatch of eastern Montana where the Great Plains roll to an abrupt and wild end. The Missouri River and its tributaries have cut deep paths through the underlying sandstone and shale, fracturing the open country. Rough and remote spaces rule the Breaks—perfect for folks who insist on carving their own way.

—John Barsness, "The Missouri Breaks," National Geographic, May 1999

Missouri Breaks, Montana

The rugged terrain of the Missouri Breaks bears witness to the geologic forces that have shaped the North American continent. The United States and Canada share the northern part of the continent. They form a geographic region of enormous physical variety and natural wealth. Together, Canada and the continental United States cover more than 7 million square miles (18 million sq. km), about 12 percent of Earth's land surface. In this section you will explore the physical geography of these two countries.

Landforms

Mountains rise at the eastern and western edges of both the United States and Canada. In the west young, sharp-edged mountain ranges tower above plateaus that descend to vast, rolling central plains. Mighty rivers and enormous lakes satisfy the thirst of cities, wildlife, and natural vegetation in the two countries' midsections. The fertile plains extend across the continent until they meet the lower, more eroded mountains in the east.

Organ Pipe Cactus National Monument, Arizona

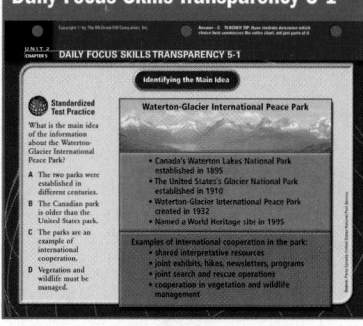

② TEACH

L1 Creating a Chart

Have students create a chart with the following headings: *Landforms, Water Systems,* and *Resources.* Under each heading, have students list features found in the United States and in Canada. Have them indicate with a star those features found in both countries.

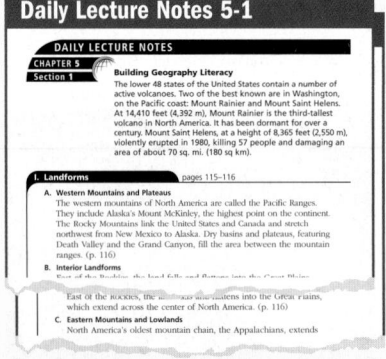

Daily Lecture Notes 5-1

DAILY LECTURE NOTES

CHAPTER 5
Section 1

Building Geography Literacy
The lower 48 states of the United States contain a number of active volcanoes. Two of the best known are in Washington, on the Pacific coast: Mount Rainier and Mount Saint Helens. At 14,410 feet (4,392 m), Mount Rainier is the third-tallest volcano in North America. It has been dormant for over a century. Mount Saint Helens, at a height of 8,365 feet (2,550 m), violently erupted in 1980, killing 57 people and damaging an area of about 70 sq. mi. (180 sq km).

I. **Landforms**   pages 115–116

A. **Western Mountains and Plateaus**
The western mountains of North America are called the Pacific Ranges. They include Alaska's Mount McKinley, the highest point on the continent. The Rocky Mountains link the United States and Canada and stretch northwest from New Mexico to Alaska. Dry basins and plateaus, featuring Death Valley and the Grand Canyon, fill the area between the mountain ranges. (p. 116)

B. **Interior Landforms**
East of the Rockies, the land falls and flattens into the Great Plains, which extend across the center of North America. (p. 116)

C. **Eastern Mountains and Lowlands**
North America's oldest mountain chain, the Appalachians, extends

□ NATIONAL GEOGRAPHIC **GEOFACT**

▶ The Appalachian Trail is a 2,000 mile (3,200 km) hiking path through some of the most beautiful scenery in the eastern United States. Earl V. Shaffer distinguished himself by being the first person to hike the entire trail alone in one trip in 1948; the first to hike it in both directions in 1965; and, in 1998, at the age of 79, the oldest person to complete the trek from Springer Mountain in Georgia to Mount Katahdin in Maine.

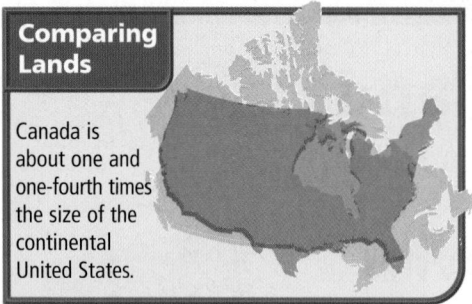

Comparing Lands

Canada is about one and one-fourth times the size of the continental United States.

Western Mountains and Plateaus

Collisions between the Pacific and the North American tectonic plates millions of years ago thrust up a series of impressive, sharp-peaked mountain ranges called the Pacific Ranges. Still young in geologic terms, the Pacific Ranges include the Sierra Nevada, the Cascade Range, the Coast Range, and the Alaska Range. The Alaska Range gives rise to the highest point on the continent, **Mount McKinley**, at 20,320 feet (6,194 m).

Like the Pacific Ranges, the **Rocky Mountains** grew as geologic forces heaved slabs of rock upward. The map on p. 117 shows that the snow-covered Rocky Mountains link the United States and Canada and stretch more than 3,000 miles (4,828 km) from New Mexico to Alaska. Some peaks of the Rockies soar to more than 14,000 feet (4,267 m).

Dry basins and plateaus fill the area between the Pacific Ranges and the Rockies. The Columbia Plateau in the north was formed by lava that seeped from cracks in the earth. The heavily eroded Colorado Plateau displays flat-topped mesas and the majestic Grand Canyon of the Colorado River. At its deepest the canyon's steep walls plunge 6,000 feet (1,829 m). The Great Basin cradles Death Valley, the hottest and lowest place in the United States. Canada's Nechako Plateau and Fraser Plateau are colder and narrower than the plateau areas in the United States.

Interior Landforms

East of the Rockies, the land falls and flattens into the Great Plains, which extend 300 to 700 miles (483 to 1,126 km) across the center of the region. The Great Plains are sometimes called the Interior Plains or the High Plains because of their location and elevation, which reaches up to 6,000 feet (1,829 m).

Although the Great Plains appear flat, the land slopes gradually downward at about 10 feet per mile (about 2 m per km) to the heart of the Central Lowlands along the Mississippi River.

Eastern Mountains and Lowlands

East of the Mississippi, the land rises slowly into the foothills of the Appalachian Mountains. At the edge of the Canadian plains, the **Canadian Shield**, a giant core of rock centered on the Hudson and James Bays, anchors the continent. The stony land of the Shield makes up the eastern half of Canada and the northeastern United States. In northern Quebec the Canadian Shield descends to the Hudson Bay.

The heavily eroded **Appalachian Mountains** are North America's oldest mountains and the continent's second-longest mountain range. They extend about 1,500 miles (2,414 km) from Quebec to central Alabama. Coastal lowlands lie east and south of the Appalachians. Between the mountains and the coastal lowlands lies a wide area of rolling hills. Many rivers cut through the Piedmont and flow across to the Atlantic Coastal Plain in the Carolinas. In the southeast the Gulf Coastal Plain extends westward to Texas.

Islands

Islands are important in the region. New York City's Manhattan Island, at the mouth of the Hudson River, is a major United States and world economic center. Volcanic mountaintops emerging from the Pacific Ocean formed Hawaii, creating 8 major and 124 smaller islands with a land area of 6,471 square miles (16,760 sq. km). Newfoundland, Prince Edward Island, and Cape Breton Island in the east and Vancouver Island in the west are Canada's most important islands. Near the coast of Canada's Ellesmere Island lies the world's largest island, Greenland. An overseas territory of Denmark, Greenland spans 840,325 square miles (2.2 million sq. km), an area about the size of Alaska and Texas combined.

A Fortune in Water

Freshwater lakes and rivers have helped make the United States and Canada wealthy. Abundant water satisfies the needs of cities and rural areas, provides power for homes and industries, and moves resources across the continent.

DIFFERENTIATED INSTRUCTION

Gifted and Talented Have students create a topographic model of the United States and Canada. First, students should work together to create an outline map on heavy poster board. Tell students to double check the accuracy of their outline maps before they go on to the next step. Next, have them use clay or other media to form mountain ranges. Students should paint the model, using a key to indicate elevation. They may also add details, such as bodies of water and deserts.

▦ EE1 The World in Spatial Terms: Standard 1
▦ EE3 Physical Systems: Standard 8
⬎ Refer to *Inclusion for the Social Studies Classroom Strategies and Activities.*

NATIONAL GEOGRAPHIC

MAP STUDY

The United States and Canada: Physical-Political

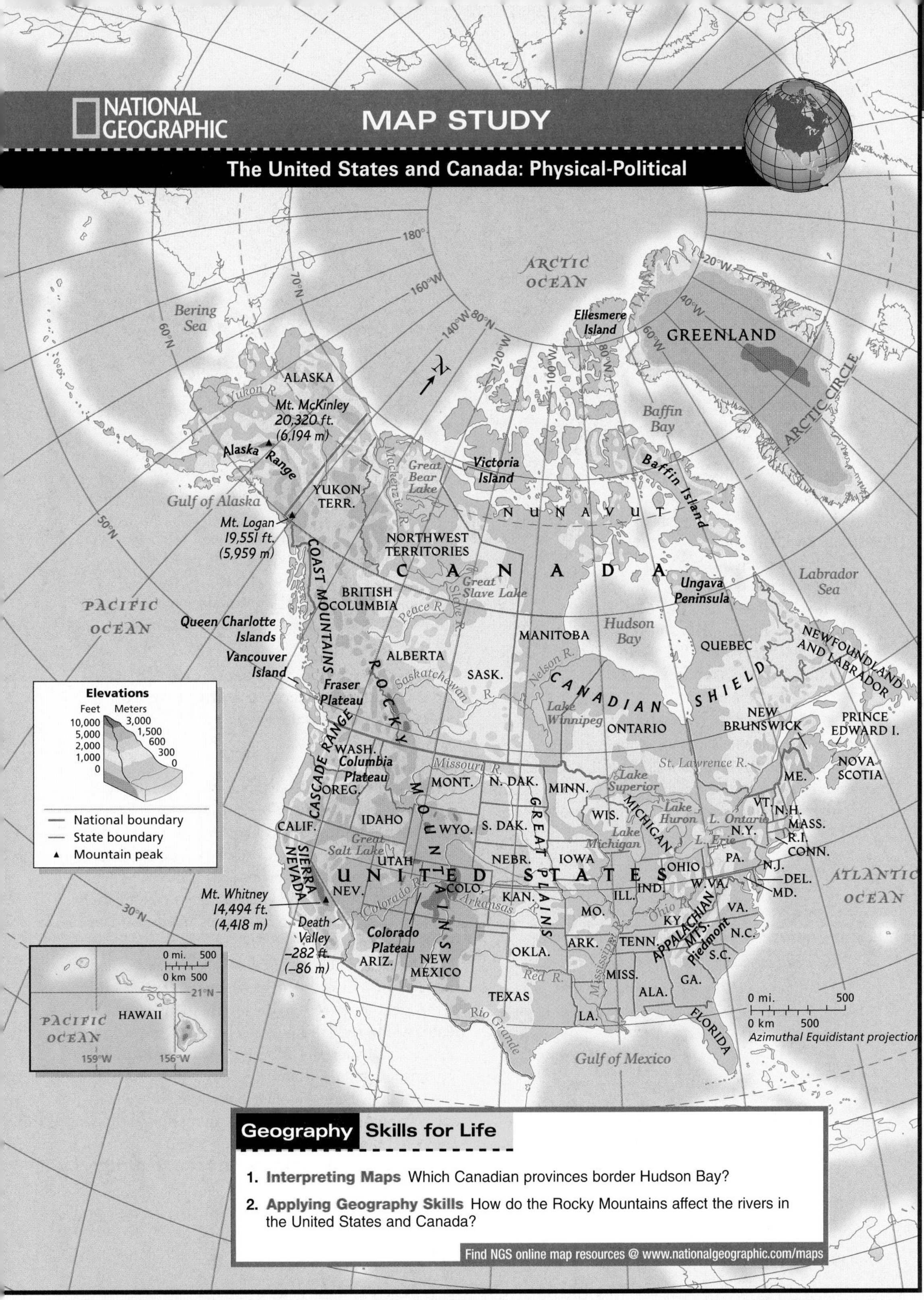

Elevations

Feet	Meters
10,000	3,000
5,000	1,500
2,000	600
1,000	300
0	0

— National boundary
— State boundary
▲ Mountain peak

Mt. McKinley 20,320 ft. (6,194 m)

Mt. Logan 19,551 ft. (5,959 m)

Mt. Whitney 14,494 ft. (4,418 m)

Death Valley –282 ft. (–86 m)

0 mi. 500
0 km 500

Azimuthal Equidistant projection

PACIFIC OCEAN
HAWAII
159°W   156°W   21°N

Geography | Skills for Life

1. **Interpreting Maps** Which Canadian provinces border Hudson Bay?

2. **Applying Geography Skills** How do the Rocky Mountains affect the rivers in the United States and Canada?

Find NGS online map resources @ www.nationalgeographic.com/maps

L2 Research

Tell students to study the physical map on page 117. Have students choose an interesting physical feature or location in the region that they would like to learn more about. Have them research their subject and write a brief report to share with the class.

L1/ELL

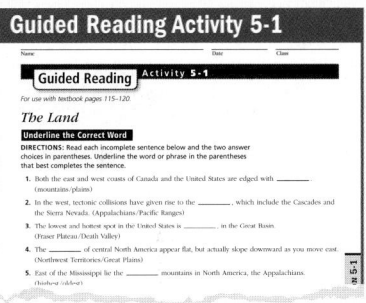

Guided Reading Activity 5-1

NATIONAL GEOGRAPHIC | MAP STUDY

Answers:

1. *Nunavut, Manitoba, Ontario, Quebec*

2. *They determine the directional flow of rivers.*

Map Skills Practice

Location Which three states are directly south of the Canadian province of Alberta? *(Washington, Idaho, Montana)*

COOPERATIVE LEARNING ACTIVITY

Mapping Have pairs of students draw an outline map of the United States and Canada. One student should map natural resources, including water systems, and the other should map population density. Each student should label or provide symbols for the map and provide a key. When they finish, have students exchange maps and agree to any needed changes. Then students should collaborate on a report, briefly describing and explaining the significance of each of their assigned parts. 📦 🌐 **EE2 Places and Regions: Standard 4**

World Explorer

Answer
Mackenzie, Missouri, Colorado, Rio Grande

More About the Photo More than 50 peaks in the southern Rocky Mountains rise higher than 14,000 feet (4,250 m).

L1/ELL

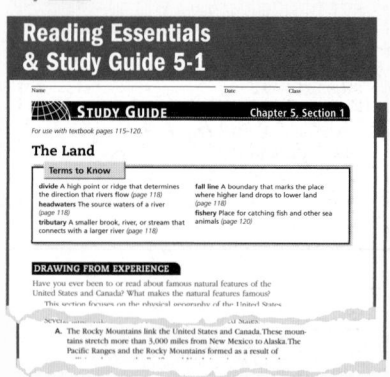

Reading Essentials & Study Guide 5-1

Rivers from the Rockies

In North America the high ridge of the Rockies is called the Continental Divide, or the Great Divide. A divide is a high point or ridge that determines the direction that rivers flow. East of the Continental Divide, waters flow toward the Arctic Ocean, Hudson Bay, the Atlantic Ocean, and the Mississippi River system into the Gulf of Mexico; to the west, waters flow into the Pacific Ocean. Rivers—such as the **Colorado** and the **Rio Grande**—have their headwaters, or source, in the Rockies, and many tributaries, or brooks, rivers, and streams, connect with one of these rivers. Northeast of the Rockies, the **Mackenzie River**—which flows from the Great Slave Lake to the Arctic Ocean—drains much of Canada's northern interior.

World Explorer

Geography **Skills for Life**

The Mighty Rockies Rising high into the sky, much of the Rocky Mountains are capped with snow year-round.

Place What major rivers have their headwaters in the Rockies?

The Mighty Mississippi

One of North America's longest rivers, the **Mississippi River**, flows 2,350 miles (3,782 km) from its source. It begins in Minnesota as a stream so narrow that a person can jump across it.

> 66 *When I was nine years old, I jumped across the Mississippi. . . . My parents let me know this modest stream I'd taken in stride was actually one of the Earth's great corridors, dominion of paddleboats and Huck Finn, prime mover of food, fertility, and commerce across our land.* 99
> Barbara Kingsolver, "San Pedro River: the Patience of a Saint," *National Geographic*, April 2000

The Mississippi, swelled to a width of a mile and a half (2.4 km), empties into the Gulf of Mexico. The Mississippi drains 1,200,000 square miles (3,108,000 sq. km) of land, including all or part of 31 U.S. states and 2 Canadian provinces. It is one of the world's busiest commercial waterways.

Eastern Rivers

The **St. Lawrence River**, one of Canada's most important rivers, flows for 750 miles (1,207 km) from Lake Ontario to the Gulf of St. Lawrence in the Atlantic, forming part of the border between Canada and the United States. The Canadian cities of Quebec, Montreal, and Ottawa grew up along the St. Lawrence River and its tributaries and depend on these waters as a transportation resource.

In the eastern United States, a boundary called the fall line marks the place where the higher land of the Piedmont drops to the lower Atlantic Coastal Plain. Along the fall line, eastern rivers break into rapids and waterfalls, blocking ships from traveling farther inland. Many key U.S. cities, such as Philadelphia, Pennsylvania; Baltimore, Maryland; and Washington, D.C., grew up along the fall line. They offer port facilities for oceangoing trading vessels. Smaller towns along the fall line, especially

INTERDISCIPLINARY
connection

GEOLOGY The Canadian Shield is a horseshoe-shaped expanse of rock that covers half of Canada. Some of the rock formations in the Canadian Shield are 2 billion to 4 billion years old, making them some of the oldest formations in the world.

CRITICAL THINKING ACTIVITY

Synthesizing Information Challenge students to synthesize information they have read about the physical geography of the United States and Canada. **Ask:** How has physical geography aided or hindered human settlement and economic development in the region? Have students analyze how the distribution and use of resources has affected the location and patterns of movement of products, capital, and people. (*Students should indicate the advantages or rich soil and water transport as well as the relationship of physical geography and population density. Encourage them to identify specific locations in the region to support their answers.*) 🌐 **EE5 Environment and Society: Standards 15, 16**

in New England and in the South, tap the water-power of the falls for textile mills and factories.

Niagara Falls is a popular tourist attraction on the Niagara River, which forms part of the border between Ontario, Canada, and New York State in the United States. Niagara Falls is also a major source of hydroelectric power for both countries. Two separate drops form the falls, the Horseshoe Falls adjoining the Canadian bank of the river, and the American Falls adjoining the U.S. bank.

From Glaciers to Lakes

In northern Canada glacial dams created Great Bear Lake and Great Slave Lake. Glaciers also gouged the Canadian Shield and tore at the central section of the continent, leaving glacial basins that became the **Great Lakes**. Lake Superior, Lake Huron, Lake Erie, Lake Ontario, and Lake Michigan

Geography Skills for Life

Copper Mining During the 1990s, this copper mine in Utah produced over 300,000 tons of copper annually.
Place What minerals are mined in the United States and Canada?

have had their current shapes for only about the last 14,000 years.

Providing a link between inland and coastal waterways has been crucial to the economic development of North America. The greatest of these connections is the Great Lakes–St. Lawrence Seaway, a series of canals, rivers, and other inland waterways linking the Great Lakes with the Atlantic Ocean. The seaway helped make cities along the Great Lakes, such as Chicago, powerful trade and industrial centers. Other important inland waterways include the Gulf Intracoastal Waterway, which connects cities from Florida to Texas with the Mississippi River, and the Atlantic Intracoastal Waterway, which provides sheltered inland channels for navigation between Norfolk, Virginia, and Key West, Florida.

Natural Resources

Ample freshwater is only one of the many natural resources of the United States and Canada. The same geologic processes that shaped the North American landscape left the region rich in a wide variety of resources. Access to this natural wealth has helped speed the industrialization of this region.

Fuels

The United States and Canada have important energy resources such as petroleum and natural gas. Texas and Alaska rank first and second in oil reserves in the United States. Texas also has the greatest reserves of natural gas. Most of Canada's oil and natural gas reserves lie in or near Alberta. Coal in the Appalachians, Wyoming, and British Columbia has been mined for more than 100 years.

Minerals

Mineral resources are also plentiful in the region. The Rocky Mountains yield gold, silver, and copper. Parts of the Canadian Shield are rich in iron and nickel. Deposits of low-grade iron ore exist in northern Minnesota and Michigan. Canada's minerals include 28 percent of the world's supply of potash (mineral salt used in fertilizers), 18 percent of its copper, 14 percent of its gold, and 12 percent of its silver.

Timber

Timber is vital for both countries. Forests and woodlands once covered much of the United

▶ **The National Geographic Society Tree, a coast redwood growing in California's Redwood National Park, is a leading contender for the world's tallest living tree. Measured in 1995 at 365.5 feet (111 m), the tree has branches that sweep in 50-foot (15-m) arcs.**

ASSESS

Assign Section 1 Assessment as homework or as an in-class activity.

🔘 Have students use **Interactive Tutor Self-Assessment CD-ROM.**

L2

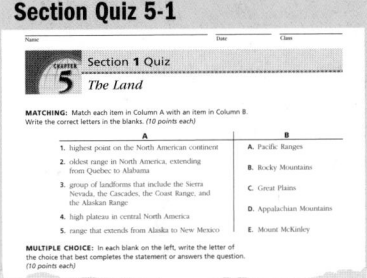

Section Quiz 5-1

Answer
gold, silver, copper, iron ore, nickel, potash

More About the Photo The Bingham Canyon copper mine is located near Salt Lake City, Utah. The mine is the world's largest human-made excavation.

TEAM-TEACHING ACTIVITY: SCIENCE

Building a Levee Tell students that levees, embankments built along waterways to prevent flooding, allow people to use the natural floodplain. When it rains, the level of the river contained by the levee rises, and the river flows faster. As the river's pressure increases, levees may break or overflow. Have students talk to a science teacher about what happens when a levee bursts. **Ask: Why is flood damage from a broken levee more severe than damage from a river overflowing its natural banks?** *(Levees enclose a river so that water is high above the surrounding land. A breached levee results in a wall of water rushing across the countryside.)* 🌐 **EE5 Environment and Society: Standard 14**

NATIONAL GEOGRAPHIC World Explorer

Answer
It is one of the world's richest fishing grounds.

More About the Photo The Great Lakes, which hold about 18 percent of the world's surface freshwater, face the continual challenge of contamination from many different sources.

Reteach

Have students work in pairs to make labels for major landforms, rivers, and lakes in the United States and Canada. Then have the partners take turns drawing a label from the pile and locating the feature on a map.

Enrich

Have students look through travel magazines for photos of a region of the United States or Canada. Have students identify the place and explain to the class why they think it is typical of the region.

 **CLOSE**

Have students reread "A Geographic View" on page 115 and then write a description about the photo they chose for the "Enrich" activity.

NATIONAL GEOGRAPHIC World Explorer

Geography Skills for Life

Catch of the Day This fisherman earns his livelihood fishing on Lake Michigan.
Place Why is the Grand Banks important to Canada?

States and Canada. Today, however, forests cover less than 50 percent of Canada and about one-third of the United States. Commercial lumbering operations face the challenge of harvesting the region's timber resources responsibly. Positive efforts to preserve the forests include planting new trees to replace those cut for lumber, cooperating to protect the 1,000 species of native animals in the forests, and preserving old-growth forests in areas set aside as national forests.

Economics
Fishing

The coastal waters of the Atlantic and Pacific Oceans and the Gulf of Mexico are important to the region's economy. Rich with fish and shellfish, these waters are important fisheries, or places for catching fish and other sea animals. The Grand Banks, once one of the world's richest fishing grounds, covers about 139,000 square miles (360,000 sq. km) off Canada's southeast coast. Fishers have harvested cod from the Grand Banks for at least 500 years. As these waters were overfished, however, stocks decreased, and the Canadian government banned cod fishing in 1992.

SECTION 1 ASSESSMENT

Checking for Understanding

1. **Define** divide, headwaters, tributary, fall line, fishery.
2. **Main Ideas** On a sheet of paper, fill in a chart like the one below. Then choose one example of landforms, water, of natural resources and describe its impact on the United States and Canada.

	Landforms	Water	Natural Resources
United States			
Canada			

Critical Thinking

3. **Drawing Conclusions** Why might fishing disputes arise in the region?
4. **Identifying Cause and Effect** How did the Great Lakes–St. Lawrence Seaway influence the development of cities in the region?
5. **Drawing Conclusions** In what ways did the actions of glaciers alter the physical geography of this region, and what effects did those alterations have on the region's development?

Analyzing Maps

6. **Location** Study the physical-political map on page 117. Describe the landscapes found in the following places: Montana, Texas, and Ontario.

Applying Geography

7. **Effects of Location** Write a paragraph describing the effects of a physical process, such as weather or gravity, on the flow of rivers in the United States and Canada.

SECTION 1 ASSESSMENT ANSWERS

1. All vocabulary terms are defined in the text.
2. Check charts and descriptions for accuracy and completeness.
3. Answers may include more intense competition for decreasing numbers of fish.
4. Early cities depended on the lakes and waterways for transportation.
5. Answers may include the observation that settlers could search for helpful geographic features, such as gaps or low-lying areas, through which they could pass.
6. Montana: plains, and mountains; Texas: plains, coastlines, hills, mountains; Ontario: lowlands lakes, plateau
7. **Applying Geography** Students might discuss topics such as the fall line, the Continental Divide, Mississippi River floods.

Guide to Reading

Consider What You Know

Think about the climate differences between the United States and Canada. Why do you think Canada is so much colder than the United States?

Reading Strategy

Organizing Complete a graphic organizer similar to the one below by listing the factors that contribute to the varying climate and vegetation found in the western climates of the United States and Canada.

Factors:

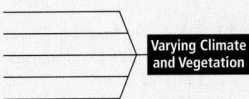

Varying Climate and Vegetation

Read to Find Out

- Which climate zones are found in the United States and Canada?
- In what ways do winds, ocean currents, latitude, and landforms affect the region's climates?
- What kinds of weather hazards affect the United States and Canada?
- How has human settlement affected the natural vegetation of the United States and Canada?

Terms to Know

- timberline
- chinook
- prairie
- supercell
- hurricane
- blizzard

Places to Locate

- Death Valley
- Great Plains
- Everglades
- Newfoundland
- Yukon Territory

Climate and Vegetation

NATIONAL GEOGRAPHIC

A Geographic View

Life Amid the Glaciers

The diversity of species on nunataks [mountains surrounded by glacial ice] takes patience to grasp. Only the showiest, such as moss campion and orange lichens, grab the eye. Wait and you might glimpse an alert wolf spider or resting butterfly. How did life reach these isolated peaks? Winds bore most pioneers over the glaciers. Plants were carried as seeds. Young spiders sailed in on strands of silk.

—Kevin Krajick, "Nunataks,"
National Geographic, *December 1998*

Moss campion, Yukon Territory, Canada

The ice fields of Canada's northwestern Yukon Territory seem at first to be Arctic wastelands. Studding the glaciers, though, are craggy summits encased in glacial ice. Although temperatures there can fall below zero, mini-climates shelter an amazing variety of life forms. Similar diversity characterizes the whole of Canada and the United States. In this section you will learn about the climate regions and natural vegetation of the United States and Canada.

A Varied Region

Much of the United States and Canada experiences exactly the types of climate one might expect from the countries' latitudes. Two thirds of Canada and the U.S. state of Alaska lie in higher latitudes and experience long, cold winters and brief, mild summers. Most of the continental United States and the southern one third of Canada lie within more temperate latitudes, where climate regions vary with elevation. Hawaii, the only non-continental U.S. state, has a tropical climate.

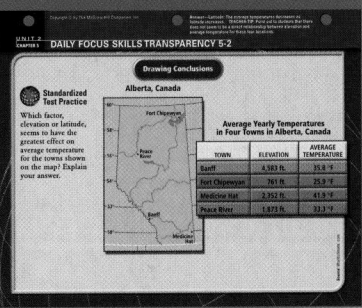

2 TEACH

L1 Identify

After students study the climate and vegetation maps on pages 122–123, give them a location, such as the region's west coast, and tell them to identify the climate and vegetation in that region. Invite a volunteer to name another area or location and continue the process until the entire region has been covered.

NATIONAL GEOGRAPHIC   MAP STUDY

Answers

1. *humid subtropical*

2. *Winds, ocean currents, and protective mountains along the Pacific coast help create a marine west coast climate.*

Map Skills Practice

Location Where can one find a tropical savanna region? *(southern tip of Florida)*

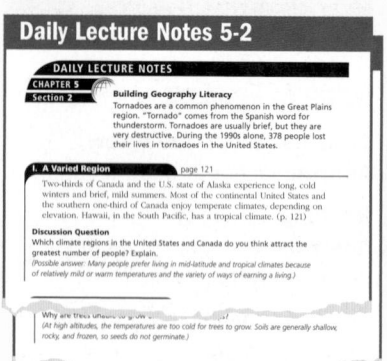

Daily Lecture Notes 5-2

DAILY LECTURE NOTES

CHAPTER 5
Section 2

Building Geography Literacy
Tornadoes are a common phenomenon in the Great Plains region. "Tornado" comes from the Spanish word for thunderstorm. Tornadoes are usually brief, but they are very destructive. During the 1990s alone, 378 people lost their lives in tornadoes in the United States.

I. A Varied Region   page 121

Two-thirds of Canada and the U.S. state of Alaska experience long, cold winters and brief, mild summers. Most of the continental United States and the southern one-third of Canada enjoy temperate climates, depending on elevation. Hawaii, in the South Pacific, has a tropical climate. (p. 121)

Discussion Question
Which climate regions in the United States and Canada do you think attract the greatest number of people? Explain.
(Possible answer: Many people prefer living in mid-latitude and tropical climates because of relatively mild or warm temperatures and the variety of ways of earning a living.)

Why are trees unable to grow _____?
(At high altitudes, the temperatures are too cold for trees to grow. Soils are generally shallow, rocky, and frozen, so seeds do not germinate.)

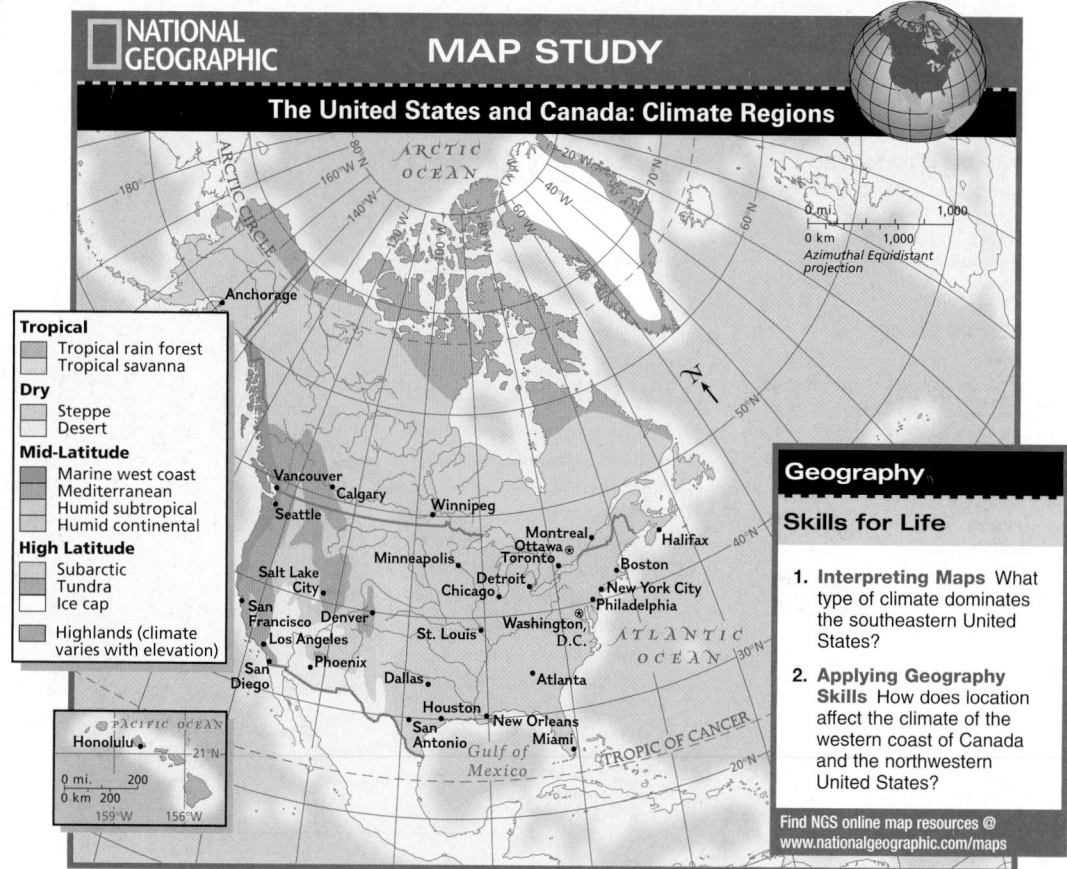

NATIONAL GEOGRAPHIC   MAP STUDY

The United States and Canada: Climate Regions

Tropical
- Tropical rain forest
- Tropical savanna

Dry
- Steppe
- Desert

Mid-Latitude
- Marine west coast
- Mediterranean
- Humid subtropical
- Humid continental

High Latitude
- Subarctic
- Tundra
- Ice cap

- Highlands (climate varies with elevation)

0 mi. 1,000
0 km 1,000
Azimuthal Equidistant projection

0 mi. 200
0 km 200

Geography

Skills for Life

1. **Interpreting Maps** What type of climate dominates the southeastern United States?

2. **Applying Geography Skills** How does location affect the climate of the western coast of Canada and the northwestern United States?

Find NGS online map resources @ www.nationalgeographic.com/maps

Northern Climates

Large parts of Canada and Alaska lie in a subarctic climate zone with very cold winters and extensive coniferous forests. Two-thirds of Canada has January temperatures that average below 0°F (–18°C). In winter, temperatures can fall to –70°F (–57°C) in some places. A persistently high atmospheric pressure area over the Canadian subarctic spawns the cold winds that chill much of the central United States during the winter.

Lands along the Arctic coastline fall into the tundra climate zone. Bitter winters and cool summers in this vast expanse of wilderness make it inhospitable for most plants, and few people live there. Greenland's tundra vegetation consists of sedge, cotton grass, and lichens. The island's small ice-free areas have few trees, but some dwarfed birch, willow, and alder scrubs do survive. As in other northern climate areas, few people inhabit Greenland because of its harsh climate conditions.

Western Climates

From the cool, wet coast of British Columbia to the hot, dry deserts of California and the snow-capped peaks of the Rocky Mountains, the climate and vegetation patterns in the western areas of the United States and Canada vary widely. This variation in climate and vegetation is the result of the combined effects of latitude, elevation, ocean currents, and rainfall.

DIFFERENTIATED INSTRUCTION

English Learners Help English language learners organize information by making a chart listing climate and vegetation regions of the U.S. and Canada. Tell students to copy the climates listed on the map on page 122 down the side of their chart. Next to each climate, have students list the type of vegetation characteristic of each climate region. Refer students to the vegetation map on page 123 and encourage them to look up unfamiliar terms. Pair an English language learner with a native speaker to evaluate the information under each heading and subheading. **ELL** ⊕ **EE3 Physical Systems: Standard 8**

⊳ Refer to *Inclusion for the Social Studies Classroom Strategies and Activities.*

NATIONAL GEOGRAPHIC — MAP STUDY

The United States and Canada: Natural Vegetation

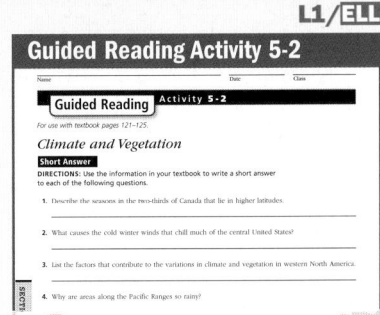

Legend:
- Tropical forest
- Chaparral
- Deciduous and mixed deciduous-coniferous forest
- Coniferous forest
- Temperate grassland
- Desert scrub and desert waste
- Tundra
- Ice cap

Geography

Skills for Life

1. **Interpreting Maps** What kind of vegetation can be found around the Great Lakes?

2. **Applying Geography Skills** In what climate region can most of Canada's forests be found?

Find NGS online map resources @ www.nationalgeographic.com/maps

---

Guided Reading Activity 5-2

L1/ELL

Guided Reading Activity 5-2

For use with textbook pages 121–125.

Climate and Vegetation

Short Answer

DIRECTIONS: Use the information in your textbook to write a short answer to each of the following questions.

1. Describe the seasons in the two-thirds of Canada that lie in higher latitudes.

2. What causes the cold winter winds that chill much of the central United States?

3. List the factors that contribute to the variations in climate and vegetation in western North America.

4. Why are areas along the Pacific Ranges so rainy?

NATIONAL GEOGRAPHIC — MAP STUDY

Answers

1. *temperate grassland and deciduous and mixed deciduous-coniferous forest*

2. *subarctic*

Map Skills Practice

Location What type of vegetation is found in Alaska? *(coniferous forest and tundra)*

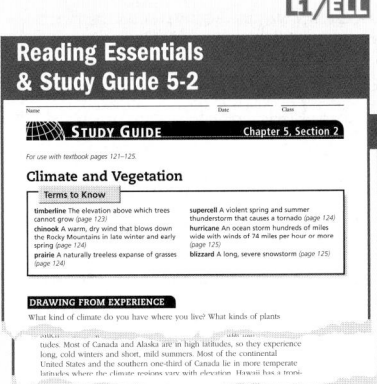

Culture NOTE

The Dust Bowl Writer John Steinbeck chronicled the plight of those who lost their farms in the Dust Bowl in his Pulitzer Prize-winning novel, *The Grapes of Wrath*, published in 1939.

L1/ELL

Reading Essentials & Study Guide 5-2

STUDY GUIDE Chapter 5, Section 2

For use with textbook pages 121–125.

Climate and Vegetation

Terms to Know

timberline The elevation above which trees cannot grow (page 123)
chinook A warm, dry wind that blows down the Rocky Mountains in late winter and early spring (page 124)
prairie A naturally treeless expanse of grasses (page 124)
supercell A violent spring and summer thunderstorm that causes a tornado (page 124)
hurricane An ocean storm hundreds of miles wide with winds of 74 miles per hour or more (page 125)
blizzard A long, severe snowstorm (page 125)

DRAWING FROM EXPERIENCE

What kind of climate do you have where you live? What kinds of plants

...tudes. Most of Canada and Alaska lie in high latitudes, so they experience long, cold winters and short, mild summers. Most of the continental United States and the southern one-third of Canada lie in more temperate latitudes where the climate regions vary with elevation. Hawaii has a tropic...

Marine West Coast

The interplay of ocean currents and winds with the Pacific Ranges gives the Pacific coast from California to southern Alaska a marine west coast climate. The mountains force the wet ocean air upward, where it cools and releases its moisture. As a result, more than 100 inches (254 cm) of rain soaks parts of this region each year. Coniferous forests, ferns, and mosses are common there. Southern California has a mild Mediterranean climate.

Plateaus, Basins, and Deserts

The rain shadow effect keeps the plateaus and basins between the Pacific Ranges and the Rocky Mountains hot and dry. This contributes to problems with water quality and quantity in states like New Mexico. Much of the area has a steppe or desert climate. U.S. desert lands in this area, including the Great Salt Lake Desert, Death Valley, the Mojave (moh•HAH•vee) Desert, and the Chihuahuan (chee•WAH•wahn) Desert, bake in the relentless sun. **Death Valley** had the highest temperature ever recorded in the United States, 134°F (57°C). The areas adjacent to these deserts usually experience a steppe climate with a mixture of desert scrub, grasslands, or coniferous forest, depending on latitude.

Elevation, not latitude, gives the higher reaches of the Rocky Mountains and Pacific Ranges their highlands climate. Coniferous forests cover the middle elevations of the western mountains, but

---

COOPERATIVE LEARNING ACTIVITY

Climate Organize students into groups and assign a major city in the region to each group. Make sure cities are scattered throughout different climate regions. Instruct members of each group to find information about the climate of their city, including average temperatures and precipitation. Have students identify physical geography features, position on the continent, latitude, elevation, ocean currents, and rainfall that influence the city's climate. Have each group write five questions and answers about the city and check them for accuracy. Groups should then create a chart to display their information, posting their questions somewhere on the chart. Have the class answer the questions.

🌐 **EE5 Environment and Society: Standard 15**

 **World Explorer**

Answer
Settlers plowed up the prairie to raise crops and left the topsoil exposed to wind.

More About the Photo The severe drought and ensuing dust storms in the 1930s resulted in the displacement of many farmers. Many became migrant workers in California.

③ ASSESS

Assign Section 2 Assessment as homework or as an in-class activity.

Have students use **Interactive Tutor Self-Assessment CD-ROM.**

L2

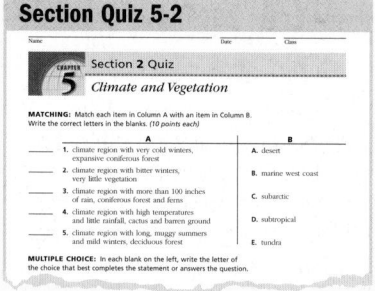

Section Quiz 5-2

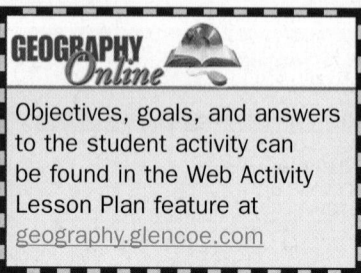

Objectives, goals, and answers to the student activity can be found in the Web Activity Lesson Plan feature at geography.glencoe.com

---

NATIONAL GEOGRAPHIC World Explorer

Geography Skills for Life

Dust Bowl to Recovery Farmland that turned to desert during the 1930s has been revived and today produces crops such as wheat and sorghum.
Human-Environment Interaction How did human activity bring about the Dust Bowl?

beyond the timberline, the elevation above which trees cannot grow, only lichens and mosses brave the ever-present cold. In late winter and early spring, a warm, dry wind called the chinook (shuh•NUK) may blow down the eastern slopes of the Rockies. Warming at a rate of about 1°F for every 180 feet (or about 1°C for every 99 meters) that it descends, the chinook rapidly melts and evaporates the snow at the base of the mountains.

Interior Climates

Far from large bodies of water that tend to moderate climate, the **Great Plains**, in the center of the continent, have a humid continental climate with bitterly cold winters and hot summers. Although western mountains do block moisture-bearing Pacific winds, the Great Plains benefit from moist winds that blow north along the Rockies from the Gulf of Mexico and south from the Arctic. The humid continental climate extends into southern Canada.

GEOGRAPHY Online

Student Web Activity Visit the **Glencoe World Geography** Web site at geography.glencoe.com and click on Student Web Activities— Chapter 5 for an activity about the physical features of North America.

Prairies

In the Great Plains of the United States and Canada, prairies, or naturally treeless expanses of grasses, spread across the continent's midsection. Each year, rainfall ranging from 10 to 30 inches (26 to 76 cm) waters tall prairie grasses, such as switchgrass and bluestem. Towering 6 to 12 feet (1.8 to 3.7 m) high, these grasses can grow as much as half an inch (1.3 cm) a day. In the Great Plains and the eastern United States, violent spring and summer thunderstorms called supercells spawn tornadoes, twisting funnels of air whose winds can reach 300 miles (483 km) per hour.

History
The Dust Bowl

The tangled roots of prairie grasses once formed dense, solidly packed layers of sod on the Great Plains. Then settlers broke up the sod to grow crops. When dry weather blanketed the plains in the 1930s, the wind eroded unprotected topsoil, reducing farmlands across several U.S. states to a barren wasteland called the Dust Bowl. The resulting economic hardships, made worse by the Great

---

CRITICAL THINKING ACTIVITY

Determining Cause and Effect Have students describe the Dust Bowl in terms of cause and effect. On the board, write *Causes* and *Effects* and ask students to give examples: Exposed topsoil, drought, and wind (causes) contributed to erosion (effect). Barren farmlands, no longer productive, (cause) forced families to move in search of work (effect).
Ask: How have physical features or environmental conditions influenced migration patterns in the past and shaped the distribution of culture groups today? *(Possible answers: changing climate as a factor in prehistoric migrations; many people today cluster in urban areas near waterways).* 🌐 EE4 Human Systems: Standard 11

Depression, caused mass migrations of people. Since the 1930s, improved farming and conservation methods have restored this region's soil.

Eastern Climates

The humid subtropical climate of the southeast has long, muggy summers and mild winters. Deciduous forests extend as far south as Louisiana, but land has been cleared for farming along the Mississippi River. Wetlands and swamps like Florida's **Everglades** shelter a great variety of vegetation and wildlife. In late summer and early autumn, hurricanes—ocean storms hundreds of miles wide with winds of 74 miles per hour (119 km per hour) or more—can pound the region's coastlines.

A humid continental climate extends from the northeastern United States into southeastern Canada. In Canada, a band of deciduous and mixed deciduous-coniferous forestland more than 1,375 miles (2,213 km) wide sweeps from **Newfoundland** into the subarctic **Yukon Territory**. In the United States, deciduous forests grow at lower elevations in the south. In winter, much of northern North America experiences blizzards with winds of more than 35 miles per hour (56 km per hour), heavy or blowing snow, and visibility of less than 1,320 feet (402 m) for three hours or more. On the East coast hazardous winter weather may disrupt travel.

Tropical Climates

Within the continental United States, only the extreme southern tip of Florida has a tropical savanna

NATIONAL GEOGRAPHIC World Explorer

Geography **Skills for Life**

New Hampshire Forest During autumn in the northeastern United States, deciduous forests show a dazzling display of colors.

Place Where are humid continental climate regions located in the United States and Canada?

climate. Hawaii, 2,400 miles (3,862 km) west of the mainland, and the Caribbean island of Puerto Rico have tropical rain forests. The wide variety of climates and vegetation in the United States and Canada has helped shape the region's history.

SECTION 2 ASSESSMENT

Checking for Understanding

1. **Define** timberline, chinook, prairie, supercell, hurricane, blizzard.

2. **Main Ideas** Use a Venn diagram to compare the climate and vegetation of the United States and Canada.

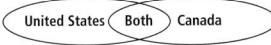

United States / Both / Canada

Critical Thinking

3. **Making Comparisons** How do the Pacific winds and the Arctic winds differ in their impact on climate?

4. **Problem Solving** How might the conditions that caused the 1930s Dust Bowl disaster have been avoided?

5. **Comparing and Contrasting** How do hurricanes and tornadoes differ?

Analyzing Maps

6. **Region** Study the map on page 122. Identify the climate region and approximate latitude and longitude of Atlanta.

Applying Geography

7. **Effects of Climate** Describe and explain the environmental factors that have affected human migration in the region.

NATIONAL GEOGRAPHIC World Explorer

Answer
east of the Rocky Mountains and in the northeastern United States and southeastern Canada

More About the Photo
Areas in Maine, Vermont, and New Hampshire attract thousands of tourists each autumn when deciduous forests display their foliage in a blaze of color before the leaves fall.

Reteach

Have students turn each heading in Section 2 into a complete sentence that summarizes the section.

Enrich

Read to students "The Cremation of Sam McGee," a humorous poem by Robert Service that is set during the Klondike gold rush.

4 CLOSE

Have students compare and contrast the environments of the U.S. and Canada.

SECTION 2 ASSESSMENT ANSWERS

1. All vocabulary terms are defined in the text.

2. Check for accuracy and completeness.

3. Pacific winds that warm the west coast of the region account for the mild winters there. Arctic winds chill the region's mid-section and east coast, bringing severe winter weather.

4. Conditions could have been avoided by using different farming and conservation methods.

5. Hurricanes are ocean storms hundreds of miles wide with winds of 74 mph (119 k/h) or more that occur in late summer and early autumn. Tornadoes—twisting funnels of air with winds of up to 300 mph (482 k/h)—result from violent spring and summer thunderstorms called supercells.

6. Atlanta is located in the mid-latitude, humid subtropical climate region at approximately 34°N, 84°W.

7. **Applying Geography** Students might discuss the role of harbors, waterways, climate and soil differences, and rugged, but passable, mountains.

Map & Graph SkillBuilder

Teaching the Skill

Tell students that a relief map provides a three-dimensional perspective of an area. Cartographers use aerial photographs to make topographic, or relief maps. Some maps show more detail than others, depending on their scale. Two common scales are 1:250,000 (also written 1/250,000) and 1:62,500. The first scale of 1:250,000 means one inch on the map equals 250,000 inches—almost 4 miles on the ground. The second scale of 1:62,500 means one inch on the map equals about one mile on the ground. **Ask: If you were planning a day hike, which scale would you prefer for your topographical map and why?**

Additional Practice
L1

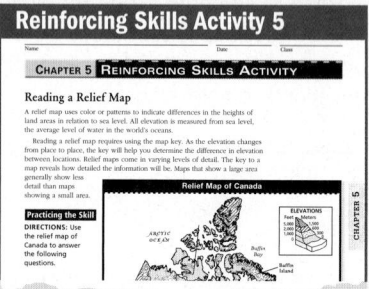

GLENCOE TECHNOLOGY

Glencoe Skillbuilder Interactive Workbook, Level 2

This interactive CD-ROM reinforces student mastery of essential social studies skills.

Reading a Relief Map

When you plan a walk, do you prefer an easy stroll along flat ground, or do you look for a challenging hike up and down steep hills? By using a relief map, you can determine the elevation of the terrain you are going to cover.

Learning the Skill

A **relief map** is a special purpose map that shows variation in height, or elevation, of land areas. All elevation is measured from sea level, the average level of water in the world's oceans. Mapmakers label this elevation level zero feet (0 m). The actual elevation of some places is shown as a negative number because they lie below sea level.

It is not possible for a relief map to show the elevation of every single inch of land. As a result, areas are grouped together. A map may show all areas with an elevation between sea level and 1,000 feet (305 m) colored green. Within that area no hill will be higher than 1,000 feet (305 m) and no valley lower than sea level.

Follow these steps to read a relief map:

• **Note the title of the map.**

• **Study the map key.** Relief maps generally use colors or shaded areas to identify elevation.

• **Compare the relief map with other maps.** Observe how elevation affects climate, population distribution, and economic activity in an area.

Practicing the Skill

Refer to the relief map shown here to answer these questions.

1. What is the color of the map's highest elevation?
2. What elevation range does the color green indicate in feet? In meters?
3. What color is the elevation range of 2,000 to 5,000 feet (600 m to 1,500 m)?
4. At what elevation is the state of Mississippi?
5. What are the elevation levels as you travel west from New Jersey to Ohio?

Appalachian Region: Physical–Political

Elevations

Feet	Meters
10,000	3,000
5,000	1,500
2,000	600
1,000	300
0	0

Applying the Skill

Compare the relief map of the United States and Canada on page 117 with the population density map on page 109. Then write a paragraph explaining how elevation affects population distribution.

Go To The Glencoe Skillbuilder Interactive Workbook, Level 2 provides instruction and practice in key social studies skills.

126 Unit 2

ANSWERS TO PRACTICING THE SKILL

1. brown
2. 0 to 1,000 feet; 0 to 300 meters
3. light orange
4. 0 to 1,000 feet
5. 0 to 5,000 feet

126

CHAPTER 5 SUMMARY & STUDY GUIDE

SECTION 2   The Land (pp. 115–120)

Terms to Know
- divide
- headwaters
- tributary
- fall line
- fishery

Key Points
- Canada and the continental United States have similar landforms, shaped by similar geologic processes. Both have high, sharp mountains and dry plateaus in the west; rolling, grassy plains in the center; and lower, older mountains and coastal lowlands in the east.
- The region's waterways, including rivers, lakes, coastal waters, and intracoastal channels, played a vital role in settling the land and continue to serve as commercial highways.
- The Continental Divide divides the region into two large drainage areas. To the east of the Divide, waters flow to the Arctic Ocean, to Hudson Bay, to the Atlantic Ocean, or to the Gulf of Mexico. To the west, they flow into the Pacific Ocean.
- Glacial movement shaped much of the North American landscape.
- The geologic factors that shaped the United States and Canada also provided the region with a wealth of natural resources.

Organizing Your Notes
Use a table like the one below to help you organize the notes you took as you read this section.

Physical Feature	Location
Cascade Range	
Great Plains	
Canadian Shield	
Appalachian Mountains	

SECTION 2   Climate and Vegetation (pp. 121–125)

Terms to Know
- timberline
- chinook
- prairie
- supercell
- hurricane
- blizzard

Key Points
- The region encompassing the United States and Canada experiences a great variety of climates.
- Some climate regions of the United States and Canada are influenced primarily by latitude.
- Wind, ocean currents, rainfall patterns, and elevation moderate the effects of latitude in other climate zones of the United States and Canada.
- Climatic factors cause hazardous seasonal weather patterns in the United States and Canada, including spring and summer tornadoes, and summer and fall hurricanes, and winter blizzards.
- The region's natural vegetation reflects its climatic variety, but human interaction with the environment has greatly altered natural vegetation.

Organizing Your Notes
Use diagrams like the one below to organize your notes under the following headings: Climate Regions, Seasonal Weather Patterns, and Vegetation.

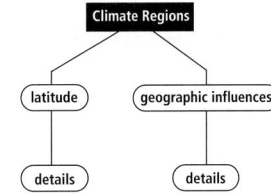

Climate Regions
- latitude
  - details
- geographic influences
  - details

Using the Chapter 5 Summary & Study Guide

Use the Chapter 5 Summary & Study Guide to preview, review, condense, or reteach the chapter.

Preview/Review

◉ **Vocabulary PuzzleMaker CD-ROM** reinforces "Terms to Know."

◉ **Interactive Tutor Self-Assessment CD-ROM** provides a review of Chapter 5 content.

Condense

Have students read the Chapter 5 Summary & Study Guide.

◉ Chapter 5 Audio Program

▱ Chapter 5 Guided Reading Activities

Reteach

▱ Chapter 5 Reteaching Activities (Spanish also available)

▱ Chapter 5 Reading Essentials and Study Guides

GLENCOE TECHNOLOGY

☐ NATIONAL GEOGRAPHIC
WORLD REGIONS VIDEO PROGRAM

Unit 2, The United States and Canada
The following segments enhance the study of this unit:
- **Preserving Wilderness**
- **Land of Immigrants**
- **Brass Bands**

CHAPTER CULMINATING ACTIVITY

Making Inferences Ask: How do the physical geography, climate, and vegetation of the United States and Canada help define the daily lives of the people who live there? Tell students their source material should come directly from this chapter. Have students answer the question in a travel article format that focuses on five different areas of the United States and Canada. Sketches, maps, or personal anecdotes can enrich the narrative. Remind students to review their notes, exercises, and activities as well as the text, maps, charts, and photographs from Chapter 5 to answer the question.

▦ EE2 Places and Regions: Standard 4

GEOGRAPHY
Online

Have students visit the Web site at geography.glencoe.com to review Chapter 5 and take the **Self-Check Quiz.**

GLENCOE TECHNOLOGY

Use *MindJogger Videoquiz* to review the Chapter 5 content.

Reviewing Key Terms

1. fisheries
2. chinook
3. timberline
4. supercell
5. prairies
6. headwaters, divide
7. fall line
8. tributary

Reviewing Facts

SECTION 1

1. by collisions between the Pacific and the North American tectonic plates millions of years ago
2. Waters west of the Continental Divide flow into the Pacific Ocean; waters east of the divide flow into the Mississippi River system and then into the Gulf of Mexico.

SECTION 2

3. climates typical of mid-latitudes that vary with elevation
4. mixed deciduous-coniferous forest and grasslands

Critical Thinking

1. collision of tectonic plates and the movement of glaciers
2. Possible answer: to prevent massive erosion and loss of topsoil such as that which occurred during the Dust Bowl era.
3. Check students' webs for accuracy.

Reviewing Key Terms

Write the key term that best completes each sentence. Refer to the Terms to Know in the Summary & Study Guide on page 127.

1. _____ supply great quantities of fish and other sea animals to North America.

2. The warm, dry wind, or _____, melts snow at the base of the Rockies.

3. Lichens and mosses grow above the _____.

4. Spring and summer tornadoes are spawned by a violent thunderstorm called a(n) _____.

5. Farmers on the wide grasslands, or _____, of the Great Plains broke up sod to grow crops.

6. Many North American rivers have their _____, or source, in the Rocky Mountains, where a(n) _____ determines the direction of the rivers' flow.

7. Important cities grew up along the _____, where the Piedmont drops to the Atlantic Coastal Plain.

8. A(n) _____ of the Mississippi River may be a stream or small river.

Reviewing Facts

SECTION 1

1. How were the Pacific Ranges formed?

2. What effect does the Continental Divide have on the direction rivers flow?

SECTION 2

3. What kind of climate is common in most of the United States and southern Canada?

4. Name two types of vegetation in this region.

Critical Thinking

1. **Analyzing Information** What geologic processes shaped much of this region?

2. **Drawing Conclusions** Why should the United States and Canada protect their natural vegetation?

3. **Classifying Information** On a web diagram, fill in information about the kinds of vegetation found in each of the region's climate zones.

Climate Zones and Vegetation

NATIONAL GEOGRAPHIC **Locating Places**

The United States and Canada: Physical Geography

Match the letters on the map with the physical features of the United States and Canada. Write your answers on a sheet of paper.

1. Rocky Mountains
2. Great Plains
3. Appalachian Mountains
4. Canadian Shield
5. Great Lakes
6. Mississippi River
7. Hudson Bay
8. Great Bear Lake
9. Pacific Ranges
10. Mackenzie River
11. Rio Grande
12. Great Slave Lake

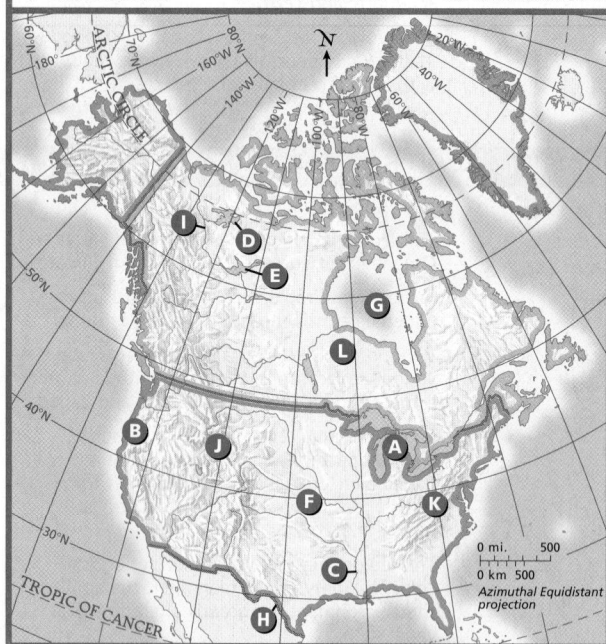

NATIONAL GEOGRAPHIC **Locating Places**

1. J	**3.** K	**5.** A	**7.** G	**9.** B	**11.** H
2. F	**4.** L	**6.** C	**8.** D	**10.** I	**12.** E

Using the Regional Atlas

1. Geologically, eastern regions have eroded mountains and western regions have young mountains; climates are warmer on the west coast.

2. Possible answers include timber, tobacco, and coal on the Ohio River; and timber, gold, coal, and agricultural and petroleum products on the Missouri River.

Using the Regional Atlas

Refer to the Regional Atlas on pages 106–109.

1. **Region** How are the eastern and western halves of the United States and Canada different?

2. **Location** On the physical map, locate rivers that flow into the Mississippi. Then use the economic activity map to make a list of products that might be shipped using these rivers.

Thinking Like a Geographer

The region of the United States and Canada possesses natural resources that people depend on for survival. Choose one section of the region, and write a paragraph explaining how people depend on a natural resource in that area.

Problem-Solving Activity

Group Research Project The flooding of the Mississippi River floodplain in 1993 caused billions of dollars worth of damage and raised questions about the wisdom of controlling the flow of major rivers with dams and levees. Should rivers be allowed to take their natural course? In your group, choose who will argue for controlling rivers and who will argue against it. Be sure to give a fair presentation of the data, including supportive evidence on the pros and cons.

GeoJournal

Expository Writing Using the information you logged in your GeoJournal as you read, write a paragraph explaining how one of the region's physical features affects its inhabitants. Use your textbook and Internet resources to make your explanation clear and accurate.

Technology Activity

Using the Internet for Research Think about the effects of physical processes, landforms, and climate. Then use reliable Internet resources to find out more about one way in which life in your area is shaped by physical geography. Write a report, and share it with the class.

Standardized Test Practice

Choose the best answer for the following multiple-choice question. If you have trouble answering the question, use the process of elimination to narrow your choices.

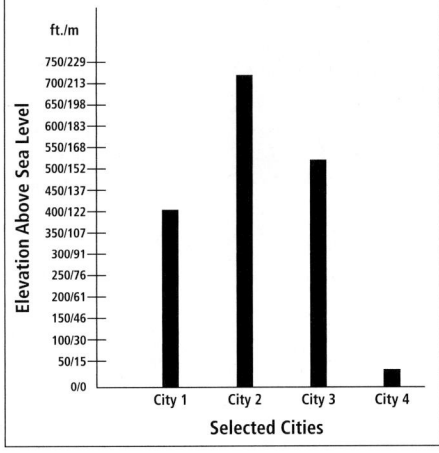

Elevations: Selected U.S. Cities

1. Given the information shown in the bar graph, which city is most likely located east of the fall line in the eastern United States?

   A City 1   C City 3
   B City 2   D City 4

Test-Taking Tip To determine which city is east of the fall line, remember that the fall line is where the higher land of the Piedmont drops to the lower Atlantic Coastal Plain to the east. Eliminate those choices that do not indicate a city on the coast, near sea level.

GeoJournal

Students' paragraphs should present accurate information in a logically organized and developed way.

Technology Activity

Students' reports should show evidence of reliable research and careful organization and development. Remind students to credit their sources.

Standardized Test Practice

1. D

Tested Objectives: making inferences analyzing information

Additional Practice and Test-Taking Tips

Standardized Test Practice Workbook

CHAPTER BONUS TEST QUESTION

Why is vegetation in the United States more varied than that in Canada? *(The United States has more climate zones, from subarctic to tropical. These zones help determine what types of vegetation will grow in a certain area.)*

Thinking Like a Geographer

Students' paragraphs should identify natural resources that characterize an area and explain how people depend on them. For example, Hawaii's natural resources include a tropical rain forest, which draws many visitors. The tourism industry provides a livelihood for many people.

Problem-Solving Activity

To gather material for the presentation of the pros and cons of using dams and levees to control flooding, suggest that students divide their research to cover basic information on dams and levees, historic efforts at flood control, and news stories about the 1993 Mississippi River flood.

1 FOCUS

Tell students that soil is an important natural resource and a basic part of our environment. Ask students to identify ways humans use soil. As students provide responses, note their suggestions on the board. *(Possible responses: soil is used to grow plants, which feed humans or animals; animals are, in turn, a part of our food supply. Soil is also used as a foundation upon which to build homes, public buildings, highways, and other structures. Humans drink water that has been filtered through soil or that runs off it.)*

Then ask students to consider how soil can affect a region's quality of life. *(Soil can affect stability of buildings put upon it; the quality of food grown on it, and the quality of the water which passes through it or over it.)*

2 TEACH

L1 Identify
Place different types of soil such as sand, clay, and potting soil in unmarked containers. Have students identify each soil type and note the differences among them. **Ask:** Which type of soil do you think holds moisture best? *(clay)* Which type do you think is least absorbent? *(sand)* What do you think would happen if coarse sand and clay were mixed? *(The clay soil would become more porous and the sandy soil less so.)*

Geography
Lab Activity

Comparing Soils

You may think that all soil is alike, but there are many different varieties. Several factors account for soil differences. The parent rock, or the type of rock from which soil is formed, is one factor. Weathering breaks down parent rock to produce different types of soil. For example, if limestone is the parent rock, it will produce a different soil than if sandstone were the parent rock. Climate, types of vegetation, and the slope of the land surface also affect soils.

The color of the soil indicates the presence of certain minerals or other substances. Sandy soil is usually light in color. Soil rich in humus is dark in color because of the presence of decaying plant and animal matter. Red soils are colored by large amounts of iron-bearing minerals. Different types of soil are found in the United States, including mountain soils, prairie soils, river soils, glacial soils, and desert soils.

▲ Students collect soil samples for experiments.

1 Materials

- Computers with Internet access
- Large map of your state, with counties outlined and identified
- Small plastic envelopes or bags for soil samples
- Labels for the plastic envelopes or bags
- Pushpin or thumbtacks

2 Procedures

In this activity, you will use the Internet and other resources to compare soils in your state and explain why differences exist among them.

1. Using the Internet, locate e-mail addresses for as many other schools throughout your state as you can. Save the e-mail addresses in your program's address book.

2. Collect the e-mail addresses and postal addresses of your friends and relatives throughout your state.

3. Coordinate all of the addresses to ensure that there is full coverage and that counties or regions are not duplicated.

4. Send e-mail messages or handwritten notes to all your partners, asking each to send you a small soil sample of his or her area. Ask partners to identify exactly where the soil came from (for example, "from my yard," or "from the hillside behind my house"). Explain that you are trying to identify why soil samples are different within an area. Ask that the soil samples be sent as soon as possible.

GEOGRAPHY IN THE REAL WORLD

Soil and Agriculture Taking care of the world's soil means finding new ways to use and preserve it as well as practicing time-honored agricultural methods. Rotating crops, such as corn and wheat, with nitrogen-fixing legumes—alfalfa and soybeans—reduces the need for chemical fertilizers. Crop rotation also helps control insects and plant diseases. Releasing beneficial insects or bacteria to control destructive pests is another method of natural pest control. Integrated pest management, or IPM, uses a combination of natural pest control with limited chemical pesticides. Soil scientists, called pedologists, are developing new ways to grow food with less fertilizer and pesticide use. 🌐 **EE5 Environment and Society: Standard 14**

5. Ask partners to sterilize the soil in a 350° oven for about 15 minutes before sealing the cooled soil sample in a small plastic bag.
6. As soil samples arrive, put each one in a separate plastic envelope or bag. Label each envelope or bag with the name and location of the person who sent it. Using the map below, try to identify the type of soil your partners sent.
7. Research to find the characteristics of that area's soils. Does the soil sample reflect information found in your research?
8. Using the pushpins, place each soil sample on the map in the area of its origin.
9. Describe how the location of where these soils were found affects how they are similar to or different from each other.

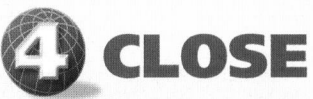

3 Lab Report

1. How many soil samples were collected?
2. What were some of the factors that accounted for the differences in the soils?
3. **Drawing Conclusions** Write a paragraph explaining how the differences in the soils collected do or do not reflect the economic activity of at least two areas of the state. Give reasons for your conclusions.

4 Find Out More

Identify a climate area in Canada or the United States, and research to find out, for example, how soils in that climate differ from each other. How has the climate affected the soil? The area's vegetation?

ARCTIC OCEAN
ARCTIC CIRCLE
GREENLAND
CANADA
PACIFIC OCEAN
UNITED STATES
HAWAII
PACIFIC OCEAN
0 mi. 200
0 km 200
159°W
156°W
21°N
MEXICO
TROPIC OF CANCER
0 mi. 500
0 km 500
Azimuthal Equidistant projection
Arctic
Desert
Glacial
Mountain
Prairie
River
Temperate
Tropical
Wetlands

◀ *Different types of soils are found in the United States.*

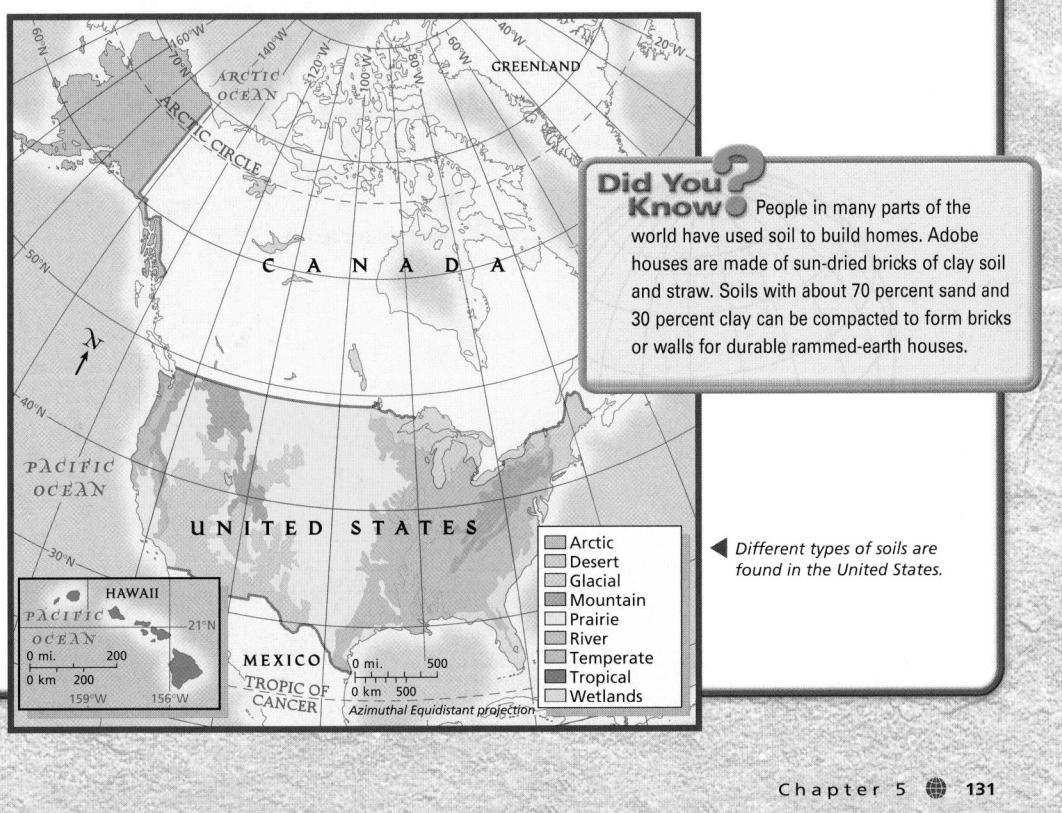

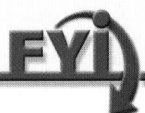

Did You Know? People in many parts of the world have used soil to build homes. Adobe houses are made of sun-dried bricks of clay soil and straw. Soils with about 70 percent sand and 30 percent clay can be compacted to form bricks or walls for durable rammed-earth houses.

ANSWERS TO LAB REPORT

1. Answers depend on the number of samples.
2. Students may mention color, mineral content, kinds of parent rock, and presence or absence of humus and clay, among many others.
3. Check to see that paragraphs have a topic sentence. Supporting details should illustrate how the soil types do or do not reflect the economic activity of at least two areas of the region. Possible activities include agricultural or industrial (cement making). If students state that soil types do not reflect the economic activity in that area, their reasons should reflect an understanding of the region's economic activities as well as physical geography.

3 ASSESS

Have students answer the **Lab Report** questions on this page.

4 CLOSE

Ask: How can assessing soil quality be helpful to urban and rural planners? *(It can help them determine if the soil needs amendment before engaging in certain activities such as construction or farming.)*

FYI

Soil Types North America's varied physical features and climate zones have contributed to the many different soil types in the United States and Canada. Together, the two countries represent all of the world's main soil groups.

Meeting National Standards

Geography for Life

The following standards are met in the Student Edition:

EE3 Physical Systems: Standards 7, 8

EE5 Environment and Society: Standards 14, 15, 16

PLANNING GUIDE

NOTE: The following materials may be used when teaching Chapter 6. Section-level support materials are shown at point-of-use in the margins of the Teacher Wraparound Edition.

TEACHING TRANSPARENCIES

L2 Unit 2 Map Overlay Transparencies

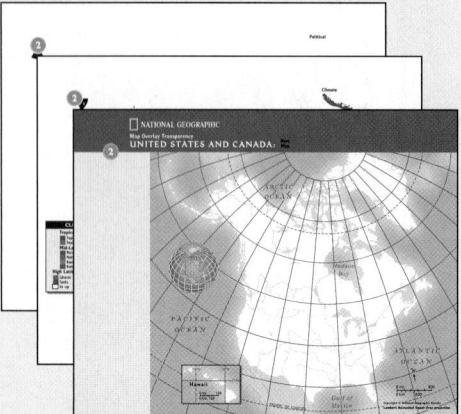

L2 Political Map Transparency 2

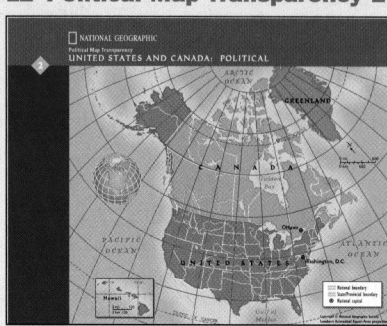

GEOGRAPHIC LITERACY

Focus on Geography Literacy

APPLICATION AND ENRICHMENT

L3 Enrichment Activity 6

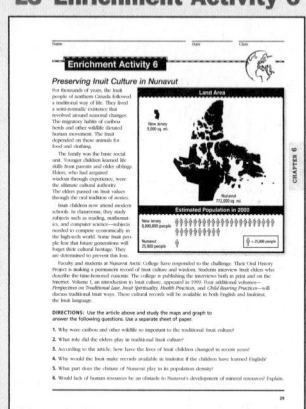

REVIEW AND REINFORCEMENT

L1 Vocabulary Activity 6   L1 Reinforcing Skills Activity 6   L1 Reteaching Activity 6

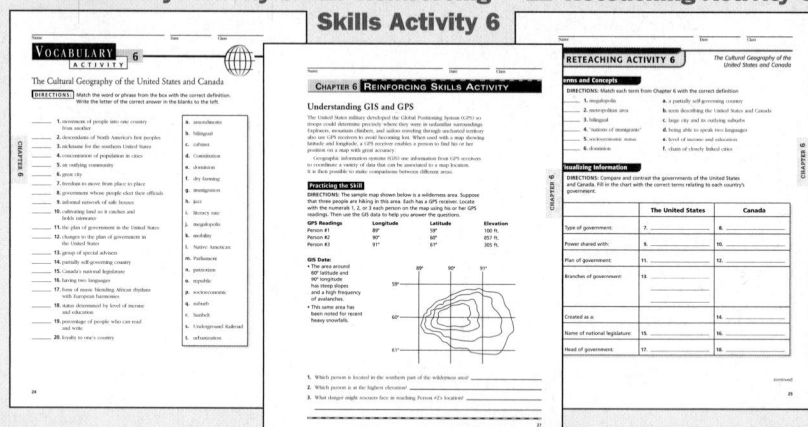

ASSESSMENT

L2 Chapter 6 Test Form A

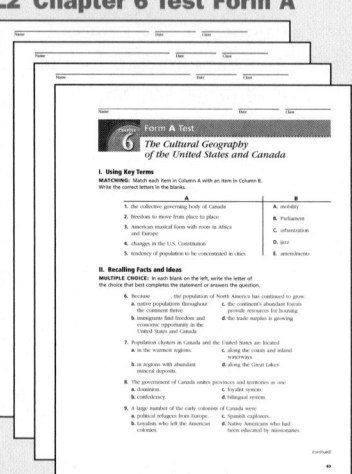

L2 Chapter 6 Test Form B

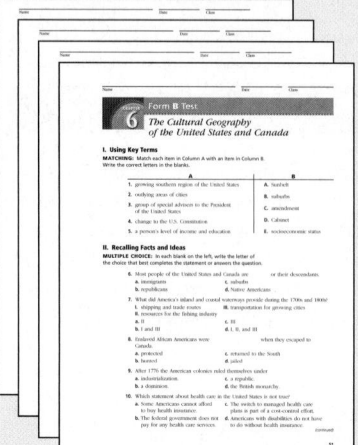

L1/ELL Performance Assessment Activity 6

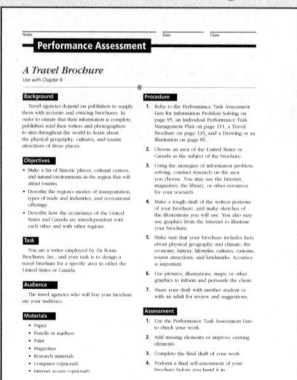

ExamView® Pro Testmaker

EXAMVIEW® PRO Testmaker CD-ROM

Glencoe

World Geography

WINDOWS/MACINTOSH

- QuickTest Wizard does all the work for you
- Choose ExamView tests or create your own
- Complete editing capability

SPANISH RESOURCES

The following Spanish language materials are available in the Spanish Resources binder:

- 📁 Spanish Vocabulary Activities
- 📁 Spanish Guided Reading Activities
- 📁 Spanish Reteaching Activities
- 📁 Spanish Summaries
- 📁 Spanish Quizzes and Tests
- 📁 Spanish Reading Essentials and Study Guide

MULTIMEDIA

- 📼 World Regions Video
- 📼 MindJogger Videoquiz
- 💿 Vocabulary PuzzleMaker CD-ROM
- 💿 Interactive Tutor Self-Assessment CD-ROM
- 💿 ExamView® Pro Testmaker CD-ROM
- 💿 Audio Program
- 💿 TeacherWorks CD-ROM
- 💿 Interactive Student Edition CD-ROM
- 💿 Glencoe Skillbuilder Interactive Workbook CD-ROM, Level 2
- 💿 Presentation Plus! CD-ROM

Timesaving Tools

TeacherWorks™ — All-In-One Planner and Resource Center

- **Interactive Teacher Edition** Access your Teacher Wraparound Edition and your classroom resources with a few easy clicks.
- **Interactive Lesson Planner** Planning has never been easier! Organize your week, month, semester, or year with all the lesson helps you need to make teaching creative, timely, and relevant.

Use Glencoe's **Presentation Plus!** multimedia teacher tool to easily present dynamic lessons that visually excite your students. Using Microsoft PowerPoint® you can customize the presentations to create your own personalized lessons.

PRESENTATION Plus!

GEOGRAPHY Online

Use our Web site for additional resources. All essential content is covered in the Student Edition.

You and your students can visit geography.glencoe.com, the Web site companion to *Glencoe World Geography*. This innovative integration of electronic and print media offers your students a wealth of opportunities. The student text directs students to the Web site for the following options:

- Chapter Overviews
- Student Activities
- Self-Check Quizzes
- Textbook Updates

Answers are provided for you in the "Web Activity Lesson Plan." Additional Web resources and Interactive Tutor puzzles are also available.

► Additional Glencoe Teacher Support

- **Teaching Strategies for the Geography Classroom** (including Block Scheduling Pacing Guides)
- **Graphic Organizer Transparencies Strategies and Activities**
- **Outline Map Resource Book**
- **Reading in the Content Area**

PLANNING GUIDE

SECTION RESOURCES

Daily Objectives	Reproducible Resources	Multimedia Resources

SECTION 1 Population Patterns

1. Identify the peoples of the United States and Canada.
2. Explain how population patterns in the United States and Canada are influenced by the region's physical geography.
3. Describe the geographic factors that encouraged the industrialization and urbanization of the United States and Canada.

Reproducible Lesson Plan 6-1
Daily Lecture Notes 6-1
Guided Reading Activity 6-1*
Reading Essentials and Study Guide 6-1*
Section Quiz 6-1*

Daily Focus Skills Transparency 6-1
Political Map Transparency 2
Unit 2 Map Overlay Transparencies
Interactive Tutor Self-Assessment CD-ROM
ExamView® Pro Testmaker CD-ROM*
Presentation Plus! CD-ROM

SECTION 2 History and Government

1. Describe what life was like for the earliest Americans and for European settlers.
2. Explain how industrialization and technology enabled westward expansion in North America.
3. Discuss how the governments of the United States and Canada differ.

Reproducible Lesson Plan 6-2
Daily Lecture Notes 6-2
Guided Reading Activity 6-2*
Reading Essentials and Study Guide 6-2*
Section Quiz 6-2*

Daily Focus Skills Transparency 6-2
Political Map Transparency 2
Unit 2 Map Overlay Transparencies
Interactive Tutor Self-Assessment CD-ROM
ExamView® Pro Testmaker CD-ROM*
Presentation Plus! CD-ROM

SECTION 3 Cultures and Lifestyles

1. Discuss how the religious practices and languages of the region reflect the immigrant history of the United States and Canada.
2. Describe how the arts of the United States and Canada reflect the region's colonial past.
3. Identify the kinds of educational and health care systems that serve the people of the region.

Reproducible Lesson Plan 6-3
Vocabulary Activity 6*
Daily Lecture Notes 6-3
Guided Reading Activity 6-3*
Reading Essentials and Study Guide 6-3*
Reteaching Activity 6*
Reinforcing Skills Activity 6
Section Quiz 6-3*

Daily Focus Skills Transparency 6-3
Unit 2 Map Overlay Transparencies
Vocabulary PuzzleMaker CD-ROM
World Music: A Cultural Legacy
World Art Prints
Interactive Tutor Self-Assessment CD-ROM
ExamView® Pro Testmaker CD-ROM*
Presentation Plus! CD-ROM

Blackline Master	Software	Videocassette	*Also available in Spanish
Transparency	CD-ROM	DVD	

OUT OF TIME? Assign the Chapter 6 Reading Essentials and Study Guide.

Block Schedule

Activities that are particularly suited to use within the block scheduling framework are identified throughout this chapter by the following designation:

KEY TO ABILITY LEVELS

Teaching strategies have been coded for various learning styles and abilities.

L1 **BASIC** activities for all students

L2 **AVERAGE** activities for average to above-average students

L3 **CHALLENGING** activities for above-average students

ELL **ENGLISH LANGUAGE LEARNER** activities

Teacher to Teacher

Anthony J. Williams
Baldwin
Middle/Senior School
Baldwin, FL

Highlighting Diversity

To help emphasize the presence and importance of ethnic groups within the United States and Canada, organize students into research groups of two or three. Have the groups choose an ethnic group represented in the region and use the Internet, e-mail, the library, and personal interviews to gather information about the group.

Remind the students that because many other regions of the world are also ethnically diverse, they should be specific when they choose an ethnic group from a particular region. For example, if students choose Latin America or Africa, they need to be aware that many cultures exist there. Suggest that students browse through other chapters in their textbook before choosing an ethnic group to research.

Direct the groups to prepare presentations for the class, encouraging them to dress in ethnic clothing, bring in food and music, and if practical, invite a speaker from that group to class. Encourage the class to ask questions about particular groups that focus on the contributions the group may have made to the culture of the United States and Canada.

NATIONAL GEOGRAPHIC TEACHER'S CORNER

Index to National Geographic Magazine:

The following articles may be used for research relating to this chapter:

- "The Way West," by John G. Mitchell, September 2000.
- "Rodeos—Behind the Chutes," by Michael Parfit, September 1999.
- "Tale of Three Cities," by Joel L. Swerdlow, August 1999.

National Geographic Society Products:

To order the following products for use with this chapter, call National Geographic Society at 1-800-368-2728.

- *PictureShow: U.S. Regional Geography Library* (CD-ROM)
- *GeoKit: American Revolution* (Kit)
- *Branches of Government Series* (Videos)
- *National Geographic Atlas of the World, Seventh Edition* (Book)

NGS ONLINE

Access National Geographic's Web site for current events, activities, links, interactive features, and archives.
www.nationalgeographic.com

Meeting National Standards

Geography For Life

The following standards are highlighted in Chapter 6:

Section 1 EE2 Places and Regions: Standard 4
EE4 Human Systems: Standard 10
EE5 Environment and Society:
Standards 14, 15, 16
EE6 The Uses of Geography: Standard 17

Section 2 EE4 Human Systems: Standards 10, 13
EE5 Environment and Society:
Standards 14, 15

Section 3 EE1 The World in Spatial Terms:
Standard 1
EE4 Human Systems: Standard 10

Local Objectives

_____

_____

MEETING SPECIAL NEEDS

In addition to the Differentiated Instruction strategies found in each section, the following resources are also suitable for your special needs students:

- *ExamView® Pro Testmaker CD-ROM* allows teachers to tailor tests by reducing answer choices.
- The *Audio Program* includes the entire narrative of the student edition so that less-proficient readers can listen to the words as they read them.
- The *Reading Essentials and Study Guide* provides the same content as the student edition but is written two grade levels below the textbook.
- *Guided Reading Activities* give less-proficient readers point-by-point instructions to increase comprehension as they read each textbook section.
- *Enrichment Activities* include a stimulating collection of readings and activities for gifted and talented students.

Chapter Objectives

1. Describe the peoples of the region, and explain how physical geography affected population and economic development patterns.

2. Identify factors that led to the rise and expansion of the region.

3. Explain how culture reflects the region's past, and discuss present-day educational and health care systems.

GLENCOE TECHNOLOGY

Use *MindJogger Videoquiz* to preview the Chapter 6 content.

GeoJournal

For access to additional photos, maps, and information on the cultural features of the United States and Canada, go to www.nationalgeographic.com (See Teacher pages in front for strategies for using journals in the geography classroom.)

GEOGRAPHY Online

Introduce students to chapter content and key terms by having them access **Chapter Overview 6** at geography.glencoe.com

FOLDABLES™
Study Organizer

Dinah Zike's Foldables are three-dimensional, interactive graphic organizers that help students practice basic writing skills, review key vocabulary terms, and identify main ideas. Have students complete the Foldable activity in the **Dinah Zike's Reading and Study Skills Foldables** booklet.

CHAPTER 6

The Cultural Geography of the United States and Canada

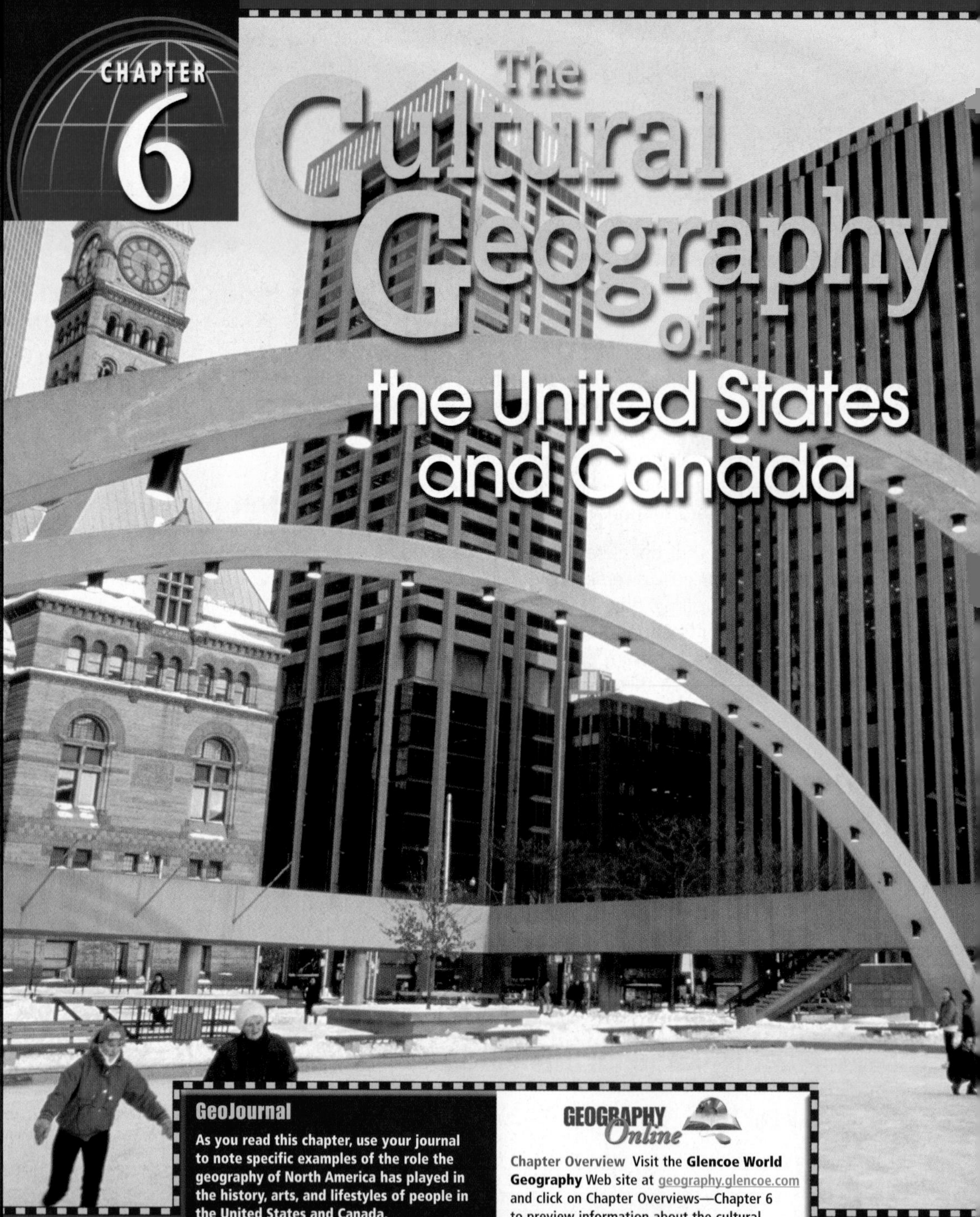

GeoJournal

As you read this chapter, use your journal to note specific examples of the role the geography of North America has played in the history, arts, and lifestyles of people in the United States and Canada.

GEOGRAPHY Online

Chapter Overview Visit the Glencoe World Geography Web site at geography.glencoe.com and click on Chapter Overviews—Chapter 6 to preview information about the cultural geography of the region.

ABOUT THE PHOTO

Visual Instruction Pictured above is an outdoor ice rink in Toronto, Ontario, Canada. Located in Nathan Phillips Square, this ice rink is used as a reflecting pool in the summer. People gather there for music and dance performances, outdoor art exhibits, and farmers' markets. Summer or winter, however, the square attracts those who enjoy outdoor activities and winter sports. **Ask: How does this scene reflect the cultural geography of people who live in North America?** (Students may answer that it depicts an outdoor physical activity in the midst of an urban area.) **EE2 Places and Regions: Standard 4**

Guide to Reading

Consider What You Know

Think about news reports, movies, and songs you know that feature large, densely populated cities as topics or settings. What factors make urban living appealing to people?

Reading Strategy

Organizing Complete a web diagram similar to the one below by listing the cities that comprise the megalopolis Boswash.

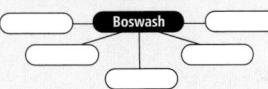

Read to Find Out

- Who are the peoples of the United States and Canada?
- How are population patterns in the United States and Canada influenced by the region's physical geography?
- What geographic factors encouraged the industrialization and urbanization of the United States and Canada?

Terms to Know

- immigration
- Native American
- Sunbelt
- urbanization
- metropolitan area
- suburb
- megalopolis
- mobility

Places to Locate

- Washington, D.C.
- Miami
- New Orleans
- Houston
- Los Angeles
- Vancouver
- Ottawa
- Detroit

◀ *The city skyline rises behind an outdoor ice rink in Toronto, Ontario, Canada.*

Population Patterns

A Geographic View

The Next Wave

For a century and a half this part of lower Manhattan has functioned as a catchment [holding place] for successive waves of poor immigrants, including Irish, Germans, Italians, and East European Jews. Each enclave [separate cultural community] dissolved as second and third generations seized the opportunities that education afforded them and then moved on to better neighborhoods, greener suburbs, or distant cities. But lower Manhattan, with its inexpensive housing, remained, ready to absorb the next wave.

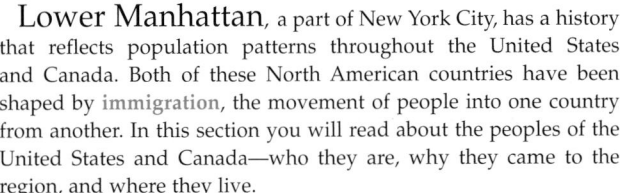
Chinatown, New York City

—Joel L. Swerdlow, "New York's Chinatown," National Geographic, *August 1998*

Lower Manhattan, a part of New York City, has a history that reflects population patterns throughout the United States and Canada. Both of these North American countries have been shaped by immigration, the movement of people into one country from another. In this section you will read about the peoples of the United States and Canada—who they are, why they came to the region, and where they live.

The People

About 5 percent of the world's population lives in the United States and Canada. The 291 million people of the United States and the 31.6 million people of Canada all are immigrants or descendants of immigrants. Some arrived only recently. Others belong to families whose ancestors came to North America centuries ago.

1 FOCUS

Section Overview

This section discusses the population of the United States and Canada and explains how geographic factors have influenced settlement patterns in the region.

BELLRINGER
Skillbuilder Activity

🎞 Project the transparency and have students answer questions.

📁 Available as blackline master.

Daily Focus Skills Transparency 6-1

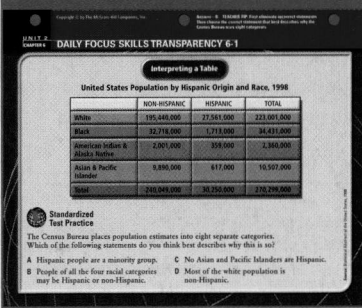

Guide to Reading

Consider What You Know
Answers *Answers may include cultural attractions and employment opportunities.*

Reading Strategy
Answers *Baltimore, Boston, New York City, Philadelphia, Washington, D.C.*

Preteaching Vocabulary
Discuss the following roots derived from Greek words: *polis* (city), *metro* (mother), and *mega* (great). Guide students to understand the meanings of *metropolitan* (major city) and *megalopolis* (great urban area).

RESOURCE MANAGER

📁 Reproducible Masters
- Reproducible Lesson Plan 6-1
- Daily Lecture Notes 6-1
- Guided Reading Activity 6-1
- Reading Essentials and Study Guide 6-1
- Section Quiz 6-1

🎞 Transparencies
- Daily Focus Skills Transparency 6-1
- Political Map Transparency 2
- Unit 2 Map Overlay Transparencies

Multimedia
- 💿 Interactive Tutor Self-Assessment CD-ROM
- 💿 ExamView® Pro Testmaker CD-ROM
- 💿 Presentation Plus! CD-ROM

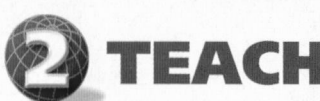

2 TEACH

L1 Locate

Project Unit Map Overlay Transparency 2-1, and have students locate the cities listed in the "Guide to Reading." Tell them the location of these cities reflects the region's population patterns.

NATIONAL GEOGRAPHIC World Explorer

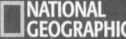

Answer
about 2.5 million; about 700,000

More About the Photo Fishing and logging are the Yurok's primary sources of income. Traditionally, the Yurok lived in permanent villages, were skilled woodworkers and basketweavers, and had a complex fishing technology.

Daily Lecture Notes 6-1

DAILY LECTURE NOTES
CHAPTER 6
Section 1

Building Geography Literacy
In 1998 about 661,000 immigrants were admitted for legal permanent residence in the United States. The country sending the largest number of immigrants—about 131,000—was Mexico. New York, Los Angeles, Miami, and Chicago were the top four destinations for immigrants in that year.

I. The People pages 133–134

North America's first immigrants may have come from Asia thousands of years ago. Because they were the first settlers, they are called Native Americans. In recent centuries, people have immigrated to North America from all parts of the world for various reasons—religious or political freedom and economic or educational opportunities. (p. 134)

Discussion Question
What would make you move permanently to a new country? What challenges do you think immigrants to the United States face?
(Students might move for some of the reasons listed above. Challenges include language and cultural barriers, economic hurdles, and prejudice from those already established here. Accept reasoned responses.)

inland cities, such as Dallas, Atlanta, Denver, and San Antonio in the United States and Regina and Calgary in Canada grew from agricultural or trading centers. (pp. 136–137)

GEOGRAPHY Online

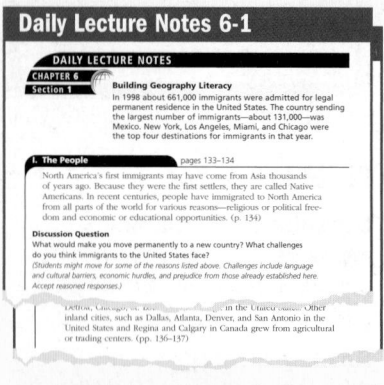

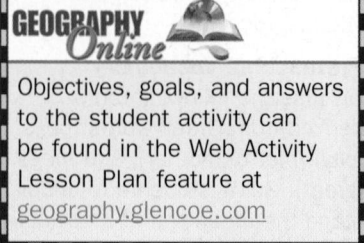

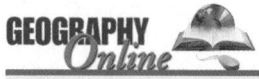

Objectives, goals, and answers to the student activity can be found in the Web Activity Lesson Plan feature at geography.glencoe.com

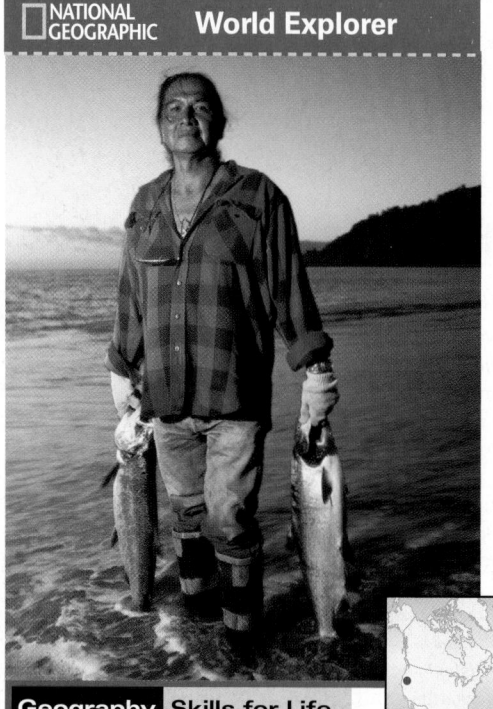

NATIONAL GEOGRAPHIC World Explorer

Geography Skills for Life

Northwest California The Yurok Native American group is only one of many groups that help define the populations of the United States and Canada.

Place About how many Native Americans are there in the United States? Canada?

History

Waves of Immigrants

North America's first immigrants probably moved into the region from Asia thousands of years ago. Today their descendants, known as **Native Americans**, number 2.5 million in the United States and 700,000 in Canada. Other peoples—Europeans, Asians, Africans, and Latin Americans—came later. As a result of these waves of immigrants, the populations of the United States and Canada are among the world's most diverse.

Some immigrants came to the United States and Canada to seek political and religious freedom and to find better economic opportunities. Others fled wars or natural disasters. For example, the Irish potato famine of the 1840s caused about 1.5 million Irish people to immigrate to the United States.

Rich natural resources and the region's rapid industrial and economic development made the United States and Canada attractive destinations. Popular songs among European immigrants in the 1800s referred to the United States as the land "where the streets are paved with gold." Chinese immigrants nicknamed it "Gold Mountain." The rumors of gold were exaggerated, but the opportunities were real. Some immigrants faced discrimination at first, but they offered hard work, talent, enthusiasm, and diverse cultural practices. Throughout their histories, the United States and Canada have benefited from the contributions of immigrants.

Population Density and Distribution

Although the United States and Canada are "nations of immigrants," their populations differ in terms of density and distribution. Slightly larger than the United States in land area, Canada has an average population density of only 8 people per square mile (3 people per sq. km). Much of Canada's vast territory is inhospitable to human settlement because of rugged terrain and a bitterly cold climate. About 90 percent of Canadians live in a narrow strip of land along Canada's border with the United States. The poor soil of the Canadian Shield steered settlement toward the fertile land and industrial resources of the Great Lakes–St. Lawrence lowlands. Other population centers include the farming and ranching areas along the southern sweep of the Prairie Provinces of Manitoba, Saskatchewan, and Alberta and the Pacific coast of British Columbia.

Compared with Canada, the United States, with an average population density of 78 people per

GEOGRAPHY Online

Student Web Activity Visit the **Glencoe World Geography** Web site at geography.glencoe.com and click on Student Web Activities—Chapter 6 for an activity about the history of immigration to the United States.

DIFFERENTIATED INSTRUCTION

Reading Support Before they read Section 1, have students who have trouble with identifying and organizing important concepts and information turn to page 137 and copy the graphic organizer from question 2 in the "Section Assessment" onto a sheet of paper. Tell students to look for information that is required as they read, so they can fill in the information needed in the graphic organizer. **EE4 Human Systems: Standard 10**

Refer to ***Inclusion for the Social Studies Classroom Strategies and Activities.***

square mile (30 people per sq. km), may seem relatively crowded. Outside large urban areas, however, the population is widely distributed. The Northeast and the Great Lakes regions are the most densely populated areas and the historic centers of American commerce and industry. Another population cluster lies on the Pacific coast, where pleasant climate, abundant natural resources, and economic opportunities attract residents.

Since the 1970s the American South and Southwest, including California, Arizona, and New Mexico, have become the country's fastest growing areas. Nicknamed the Sunbelt for its mild climate, the southern United States draws employees to its growing manufacturing, service, and tourism industries. Retirees choose the Sunbelt for its mild winters. The area's geographic closeness to Mexico and the Caribbean also draws immigrants from those two regions.

The least densely populated areas of the United States include the subarctic region of Alaska, the parched Great Basin, and parts of the arid or semi- arid Great Plains. These areas owe their sparse populations to difficult climate conditions.

The Cities

Although both the United States and Canada began as agricultural societies, they have experienced urbanization, the concentration of population in cities. Cities grew as the use of machines in agriculture gave rise to large commercial farms. As a result, fewer agricultural laborers were needed, sending people to urban areas to search for work. Jobs, education, health care, and cultural opportunities also have drawn people to large cities.

Today most people in the United States and Canada live in metropolitan areas. A metropolitan area includes a city with a population of at least 50,000 and outlying communities called suburbs. More than 80 percent of the population of the United States lives in the country's 276 metropolitan areas. Canada's 25 metropolitan areas are home to about 60 percent of the Canadian population.

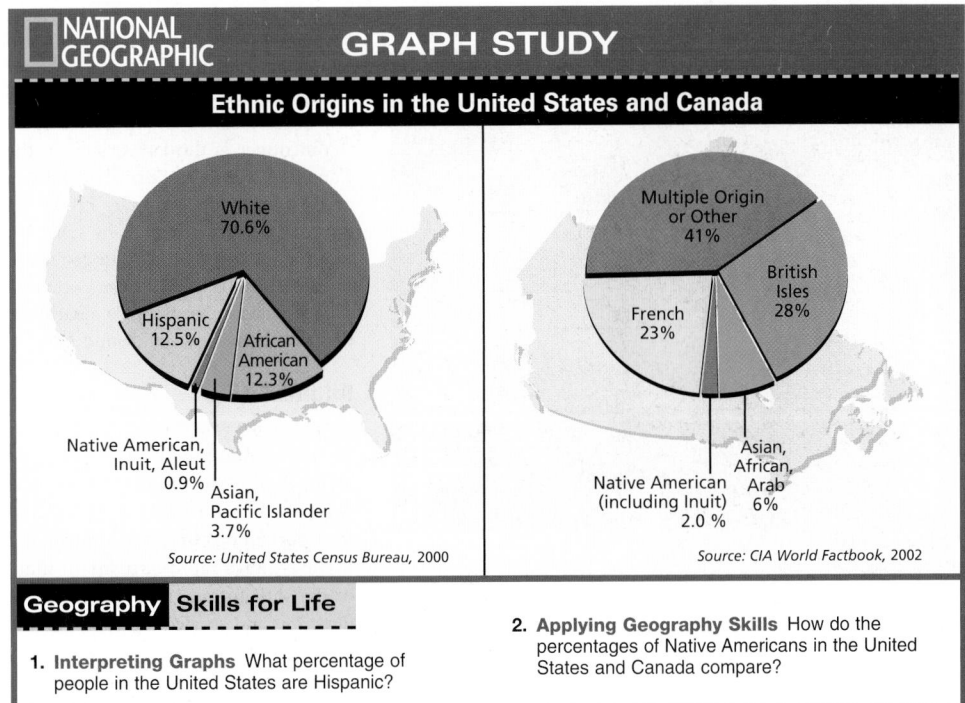

NATIONAL GEOGRAPHIC GRAPH STUDY

Ethnic Origins in the United States and Canada

White 70.6%
Hispanic 12.5%
African American 12.3%
Native American, Inuit, Aleut 0.9%
Asian, Pacific Islander 3.7%

Source: United States Census Bureau, 2000

Multiple Origin or Other 41%
British Isles 28%
French 23%
Native American (including Inuit) 2.0 %
Asian, African, Arab 6%

Source: CIA World Factbook, 2002

Geography Skills for Life

1. **Interpreting Graphs** What percentage of people in the United States are Hispanic?

2. **Applying Geography Skills** How do the percentages of Native Americans in the United States and Canada compare?

Guided Reading Activity 6-1

Name _____ Date _____ Class _____

Guided Reading   Activity 6-1

Population Patterns

Short Answer

DIRECTIONS: Use the information in your textbook to write a short answer to each of the following questions.

1. Approximately when did the first immigrants to North America begin to arrive, and from where did they come?

2. List the reasons people have immigrated to North America.

3. What made the United States and Canada attractive destinations to immigrants?

4. Where do most people in the United States and Canada live?

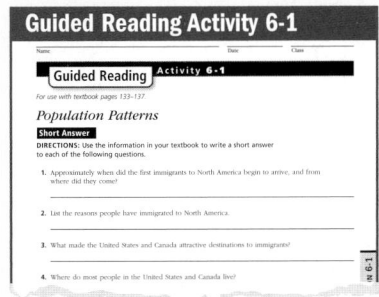
NATIONAL GEOGRAPHIC GRAPH STUDY

Answers:

1. *12.5 percent*

2. *The United States has a smaller percentage of Asians.*

Skills Practice

Place What percentage of Canadians trace their ancestry to the British Isles? *(28 percent)*

L1/ELL

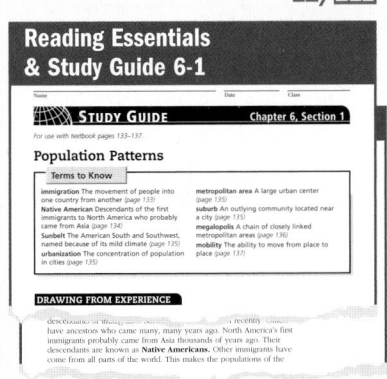
Reading Essentials & Study Guide 6-1

Name _____ Date _____ Class _____

STUDY GUIDE   Chapter 6, Section 1

For use with textbook pages 133-137.

Population Patterns

Terms to Know

immigration The movement of people into one country from another (page 133)
Native American Descendants of the first immigrants to North America who probably came from Asia (page 134)
Sunbelt The American South and Southwest, named because of its mild climate (page 135)
urbanization The concentration of population in cities (page 135)

metropolitan area A large urban center (page 135)
suburb An outlying community located near a city (page 135)
megalopolis A chain of closely linked metropolitan areas (page 136)
mobility The ability to move from place to place (page 137)

DRAWING FROM EXPERIENCE

COOPERATIVE LEARNING ACTIVITY

Tourism Organize students into groups of three. Assign, or allow each group to choose, one of the major cities in the United States or Canada. Instruct members of each group to prepare a one-minute commercial encouraging tourists to visit their city. Commercials should include interesting facts about the city's physical and human (political, economic, social, and cultural) characteristics. Provide time for each group to present its commercial to the class. Then, have the class analyze how each city's character is related to its physical and human characteristics.   **EE2 Places and Regions: Standard 4**

Assign Section 1 Assessment as homework or as an in-class activity.

🌐 Have students use **Interactive Tutor Self-Assessment CD-ROM** to review Section 1.

L2

Section Quiz 6-1

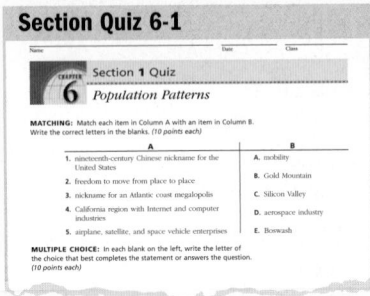

NATIONAL GEOGRAPHIC World Explorer

Answer
Cities are concentrated in parts of the eastern and western United States and Canada where there are more links to waterways.

More About the Photo
Satellite photos clearly reveal the outlines of coastal areas because of the lights. In the western mountains and plains, however, only a few major cities and roadways are illuminated. Can students guess which cities show up? *(Omaha and Denver, among others)*

Coastal Cities

Many population centers in the United States and Canada lie in coastal areas where healthy economies support large populations. Along the northern Atlantic coast of the United States, for example, a chain of closely linked metropolitan areas forms a megalopolis, or "great city." Home to about 42 million people, this megalopolis—nicknamed Boswash—includes the cities of Boston, New York, Philadelphia, Baltimore, and Washington, D.C. Four of the cities—Boston, New York, Philadelphia, and Baltimore—are important world trade centers because of their coastal or near coastal locations. The planned city of **Washington, D.C.**, established on the Potomac River near the Chesapeake Bay, is the country's capital. On the capital's 200th birthday, a native Washingtonian commended the city's chief designer:

❝ *Most American cities grew haphazardly . . . with little overall planning. . . . But our nation's capital became one of the most*

attractive low-rise cities . . . in the world . . . [because of] the vision of Pierre L'Enfant who conceived the plan for the capital. . . . ❞

Gilbert M. Grosvenor, "Washington, D.C., Reaches Its 200th Birthday," *National Geographic*, August 1991

Other important U.S. coastal cities include the busy ports of **Miami**, on the Atlantic coast, and **New Orleans** and **Houston**, on the Gulf of Mexico. Houston, connected to the Gulf of Mexico by the Houston Ship Channel, is the southern end of a developing megalopolis that stretches north to the Dallas/Fort Worth metropolitan area.

Pacific coast cities also provide important commercial links to the rest of the world, especially to the growing Asian economies of the Pacific Rim. A developing megalopolis stretches from San Francisco south through **Los Angeles** to San Diego. All three cities have major ports. Another western port city, Seattle, as well as San Francisco and the neighboring area nicknamed the Silicon Valley, features innovative computer and Internet industries. These latter two areas also have developed aerospace industries, enterprises that design and manufacture airplanes, satellites, and space vehicles.

Vancouver is the largest city in the Canadian province of British Columbia and an important shipping center for western Canada. Despite its northern location, Vancouver's harbor never freezes, so ships use the busy port year-round. Vancouver handles nearly all the trade between Canada and Asia.

Inland Cities

Rivers, lakes, and inland waterways promoted the growth of the region's inland cities. North America's waterways offered both natural resources and transportation routes that contributed to the region's rapid industrialization, or the shift from agriculture to manufacturing and service industries as the basis of an economy.

In Canada, ships reach the cities of Quebec, Montreal, Toronto, and **Ottawa**

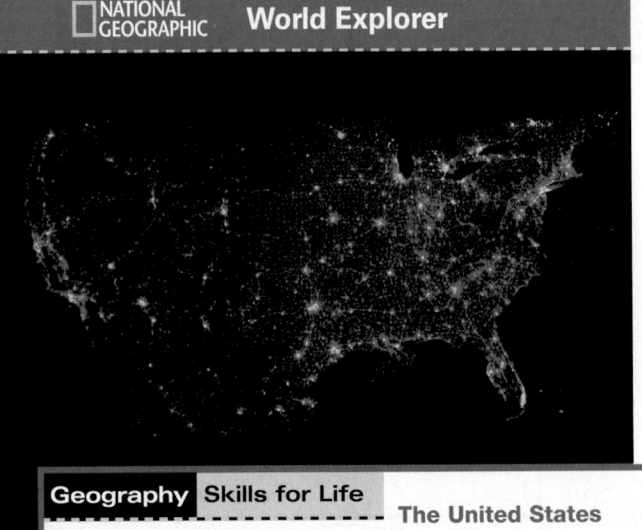

NATIONAL GEOGRAPHIC World Explorer

Geography **Skills for Life**
The United States at Night City lights as seen at night from space reveal dense population clusters in the east and on the west coast.
Region What pattern do you observe in the distribution of cities in the United States and Canada?

CRITICAL THINKING ACTIVITY

Evaluating Information Tell students that scientists continue to uncover evidence about America's first inhabitants. The theory generally accepted until the 1990s was that people crossed over to North America on a land bridge connecting Siberia to Alaska about 14,000 years ago, and then worked their way south to Middle and South America. New evidence suggests that humans may have arrived as many as 30,000 years ago. One theory argues that the first inhabitants may even have crossed the Pacific in boats. **Ask:** Is the following a valid statement? Archaeology is not a very reliable field of study if it is not an exact science. *(not valid; although archaeology is not exact, it has helped us understand our past)* 📋 **EE6 The Uses of Geography: Standard 17**

through the St. Lawrence River, the Ottawa River, and the Great Lakes. **Detroit**, the center of the United States automobile industry, uses the Great Lakes for shipping goods. A megalopolis links the U.S. Great Lakes cities of Chicago, Milwaukee, and Cleveland with Pittsburgh, a freshwater port on the Ohio River. Other U.S. river cities include Cincinnati, on the Ohio River, and Minneapolis and St. Louis, on the Mississippi River. Winnipeg, on the Red River, and Saskatoon and Edmonton, on the Saskatchewan River, are inland population centers in western Canada.

Other inland cities, such as Atlanta, Denver, Dallas, and San Antonio in the United States and Regina and Calgary in Canada, grew from agricultural and trading centers.

Future Trends

Like most developed countries, the United States and Canada have low birthrates, which increase the population by only 0.5 percent annually. Immigration accounts for most of the region's population growth. In 1998 more than 9 percent of the population of the United States was born in another country. Like earlier immigrants, however, the people of the United States and Canada cherish their mobility, the freedom to move from place to place. In a typical year, one in six U.S. residents of the United States relocates, often to cities. As immigration adds to population diversity, living with cultural differences and managing urban congestion are ongoing challenges.

Geography Skills for Life

The Grain Trade Workers load grain sacks for export from the port of Vancouver.
Movement How do port cities sustain an economy?

SECTION ❶ ASSESSMENT

Checking for Understanding

1. **Define** immigration, Native American, Sunbelt, urbanization, metropolitan area, suburb, megalopolis, mobility.

2. **Main Ideas** Create a word web like the one below, listing the various peoples of North America.

Peoples of North America

Critical Thinking

3. **Comparing and Contrasting** How are the population patterns of Canada and the United States similar? How do they differ?

4. **Making Inferences** What are some of the advantages and disadvantages of living in a megalopolis?

5. **Categorizing Information** Select three coastal and three inland cities and indicate the economic activities important to each city.

Analyzing Maps

6. **Human-Environment Interaction** Study the population density map on page 108. How many cities with populations over 1,000,000 lie along waterways? Explain.

Applying Geography

7. **Choosing a Destination** Imagine that you are an immigrant writing a letter to relatives about your new home in the United States. Explain your reasons for settling where you live.

NATIONAL GEOGRAPHIC **World Explorer**

Answer
Port cities are important transportation links for people and products.

More About the Photo
Historically, Canada's economic development was based on the export of raw materials and agricultural products, such as wheat. Today, about 75 percent of Canada's trade is with the U.S. and includes energy and manufactured goods.

Reteach
Have students make a list of similarities and differences between the populations of the United States and Canada.

Enrich
Have students use maps, LANDSAT maps, or other graphics of the United States and Canada to locate the region's largest metropolitan areas. Ask them to observe and point out patterns in the size and distribution of these urban areas.

❹ CLOSE

Have students list information they learned in this section and tell why they found it interesting or noteworthy.

SECTION ❶ ASSESSMENT ANSWERS

1. All vocabulary terms are defined in the text.

2. Check webs for accuracy and completeness. Answers should include Native Americans, Europeans, Africans, Asians, and Latin Americans.

3. They both have a low population density compared to other regions of the world. Most of Canada's population clusters near the U.S. border; the population of the United States is more widely distributed, with concentration along both coasts and near the Great Lakes.

4. advantages: jobs, education, health care, and cultural opportunities; disadvantages: pollution, traffic congestion, stress

5. Answers will depend on which cities are chosen.

6. A majority; waterways provide inexpensive transportation and water for drinking and irrigation.

7. **Applying Geography** Check letters for sufficient and accurate details. Make sure students use geographic terminology correctly.

GEOGRAPHY AND HISTORY

1 FOCUS

Have students look at the map on page 117. Tell them to compare the length of the border between the United States and Canada with the border between the United States and Mexico. *(Students should note that the border with Canada is about twice as long.)* Ask students what other factors besides length would make it difficult to defend our border with Canada if we were not on friendly terms. *(Students should note the varied geographical features that could make defending this border a challenge.)*

2 TEACH

L1 Math

As students look at the map on page 117, have them calculate the longitudinal span of the border between the United States and Canada, starting from Alaska and moving east. *(approximately 74°)*

L2 Identify

Refer students to the Regional Atlas maps on pages 106–109. Ask them to use information from the maps to identify possible economic purposes—tourism, sports, or trade—for border crossings in Alberta, Ontario, and Quebec. *(Students may note trade for Alberta and Ontario and tourism for Quebec.)*

GEOGRAPHY AND HISTORY

GIVE-AND-TAKE ACROSS THE BORDER

CANADA AND THE UNITED STATES share the longest undefended border in the world. The 3,987-mile (6,416-km) border runs through the middle of rivers and lakes, crosses fields and forests, and slices through towns and farms. Each year more than a hundred million tourists, truck drivers, sports fans, and other visitors pass through 96 official border crossings and thousands of unofficial ones. Even more impressive, though, is the value of goods and services that flow between the United States and Canada—a total that exceeds trade between any other two countries in the world.

A History of Trade

Trade has played an important role in the growth of both the United States and Canada. The fur trade in Canada began in the 1500s. Native Americans gave Europeans furs in exchange for such items as tools, weapons, and kettles. During the 1700s, colonists traded numerous raw materials—timber and furs—for Europe's manufactured goods. In the early 1800s, the quest for furs by American and Canadian companies pushed frontiers westward as trading posts sprang up in the wilderness.

Cars line up to enter Canada at Fort Erie, Ontario. ▶

BACKGROUND INFORMATION

Transportation, Communications, and Trade The vast size of the United States and Canada impelled both countries to develop their transportation and communications systems. These systems encouraged trade not only within each country but between them as well. The U.S. and Canada have similar levels of economic development and have much in common, geographically as well as culturally. Some regions of Canada have fewer geographical links with one another than with neighboring regions of the United States, which is why a large proportion of the industrial base of Canada attracted U.S. investments.
EE5 Environment and Society: Standards 14, 15, 16

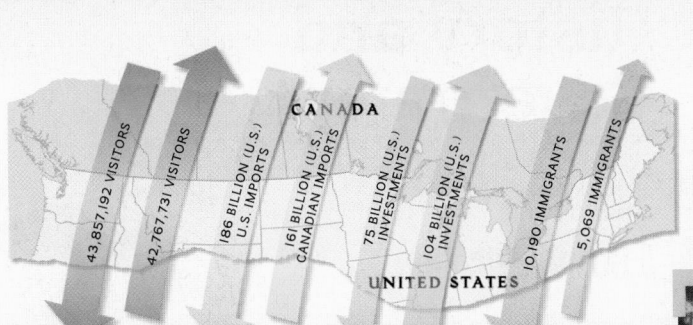

Each year, Canadians and Americans exchange products and people. Investors seek profits in real estate, mines, oil, and other ventures.

As the neighboring economies grew and prospered, so did cooperation. Since the late 1800s, trade has flourished between Canada and the United States. Most goods pass freely across the border, without tariffs of any kind. Two major agreements have sought to eliminate remaining tariffs and other trade barriers: the United States-Canada Free Trade Agreement (FTA) in 1989 and the North American Free Trade Agreement (NAFTA), which includes Mexico, in 1994.

Cooperation and Conflict

Today each country has a major stake in the other's economy. Canadian companies operate plants in the United States and vice versa. Joint business ventures proliferate. The open border and long history of cooperation between the United States and Canada have led to good relations and a friendly give-and-take between neighbors.

Trade disputes do occur, however. Many Canadians dislike the effect free trade with the United States has on their culture and way of life. Canadians struggle to maintain a separate identity while they're bombarded by American music and movies. Moreover, differences arise over shared resources, such as fishing grounds, and over solutions to joint problems, such as pollution.

Looking Ahead
Will the spirit of cooperation between the United States and Canada prevail in this century? Or will trade disputes, disagreements over cultural issues, and other problems lead to conflict?

1500s Fur trade starts between present-day Canada and Europe

1605 French explorers set up first trading post at Port Royal, Canada (photo above)

1608 French explorer Samuel de Champlain establishes settlement at Quebec

1700s American colonists trade raw materials for Europe's manufactured goods

1800s U.S.-Canada border (background photo) continues to be defined

1989 U.S.-Canada Free Trade Agreement takes effect

1994 North American Free Trade Agreement takes effect

INTERDISCIPLINARY
connection

ECONOMICS Canada encouraged its industries through protective tariffs on imports. To avoid the tariffs, many U.S. companies set up branch plants in Canada to supply the Canadian market.

3 ASSESS

Have students answer the **Looking Ahead** question on page 139.

4 CLOSE

Ask students to summarize the sources of conflict between the U.S. and Canada. *(trade and resource disputes, Canada's struggle to maintain a distinct culture)* **Ask:** How do you think differences between the United States and Canada compare in seriousness to those between other countries?

 Meeting National Standards

Geography for Life
The following standards are met in the Student Edition:

EE1 The World in Spatial Terms: Standards 1, 3
EE4 Human Systems: Standards 11, 13
EE5 Environment and Society: Standards 14, 15, 16

ANSWERS TO LOOKING AHEAD

Some students might say that the spirit of cooperation will continue to prevail in this century. They may cite historical ties of cooperation and the challenge of defending a 3,987-mile (6,416-km) border. Others may say that relations between the two countries will become more strained as trade, cultural, and other types of issues become more problematic. Environmental issues could become more important as population increases in both countries strain the two countries' shared natural resources.

SECTION 2

Section Overview

This section describes the life of early Native Americans and European settlers. It identifies factors that led to the rise and expansion of the United States and Canada and compares the governments of the two countries.

BELLRINGER
Skillbuilder Activity

Project the transparency and have students answer questions.

Available as blackline master.

Daily Focus Skills Transparency 6-2

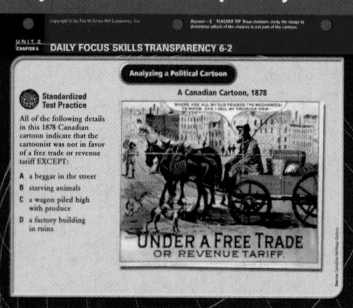

Guide to Reading

Consider What You Know
Answers *Answers may include that cities in the West are not as old as those in the East.*

Reading Strategy
Answers dry farming: *dry land is able to catch and hold rainwater;* steel plows: *stronger and better able to break hard prairie sod;* steam tractors: *possible to plant and harvest large areas of land faster and easier*

Preteaching Vocabulary
Explain that words often have multiple meanings. Have students use a dictionary to locate the various meanings of *constitution*. Have students predict which meaning applies to the "Terms to Know" listing.

Guide to Reading

Consider What You Know

The early history of Canada and the United States featured the movement of people from east to west. In what ways did that movement affect the place where you live?

Reading Strategy

Organizing Complete a graphic organizer similar to the one below by filling in the results of each innovation on farming the Great Plains.

Farming Innovations

| Dry Farming | Steel Plows | Steam Tractors |

Read to Find Out

- What was life like for the earliest Americans and for European settlers?
- How did industrialization and technology enable westward expansion in North America?
- How do the governments of the United States and Canada differ?

Terms to Know

- republic
- Underground Railroad
- dry farming
- Constitution
- amendment
- Bill of Rights
- cabinet
- dominion
- Parliament

Places to Locate

- Hudson Bay
- Quebec
- Ontario
- Nova Scotia
- New Brunswick
- Yukon Territory
- Northwest Territories
- Nunavut
- Texas
- Alaska
- Hawaii
- Pennsylvania
- Ohio

History and Government

NATIONAL GEOGRAPHIC

A Geographic View

Personality and History

History has bred the caricatures. The United States was born of rebellion and the cult of independence. It spread west two hops ahead of the law. Canada was formed by consensus among public servants. On its way west the law went first. Canadians never had a Wild West.

—Priit J. Vesilind, "Common Ground, Different Dreams: The U.S.–Canada Border," National Geographic, February 1990

Monument Valley, Arizona

The United States and Canada share much in terms of geography, but they have taken different historical and cultural paths. In this section you will learn how the vast northern part of North America, originally inhabited by Native Americans, then colonized by Europeans, eventually developed into these two independent countries. You also will discover the key role physical geography played in the emergence of the United States and Canada and their development as industrialized countries.

History

Archaeologists generally believe that nomads crossing a land bridge from Asia to Alaska first settled North America thousands of years ago. Recent evidence suggests, however, that nomads from Central and South America may have populated North America at the same time as—or even before—those from Asia. Whatever theory proves correct, we know that as of 10,000 years ago, people lived in almost every part of what is now the United States and Canada.

RESOURCE MANAGER

Reproducible Masters
- Reproducible Lesson Plan 6-2
- Daily Lecture Notes 6-2
- Guided Reading Activity 6-2
- Reading Essentials and Study Guide 6-2
- Section Quiz 6-2

Transparencies
- Daily Focus Skills Transparency 6-2
- Political Map Transparency 2
- Unit 2 Map Overlay Transparencies

Multimedia
- Interactive Tutor Self-Assessment CD-ROM
- ExamView® Pro Testmaker CD-ROM
- Presentation Plus! CD-ROM

Native Americans

Location and climate shaped the various cultures later known as Native American. For the peoples of the cold Arctic tundra, scarce resources and lack of farmland prompted them to hunt caribou and other animals for food and fur. By contrast, Pacific Coast peoples enjoyed a mild climate and abundant resources. They harvested salmon with fiber nets and used stone and copper tools to split cedar, fir, and redwood trees into planks for building houses and canoes.

In the high deserts of the Southwest, Native Americans used irrigation to farm the dry land. On the Great Plains, other groups hunted the buffalo, parts of which were used for food, clothing, shelter, and tools. Native Americans in the woodlands east of the Mississippi River built ceremonial mounds, hunted game, grew crops, and traded for shells and freshwater pearls. In the northeastern woodlands, Native American peoples hunted deer, turkeys, geese, and squirrels. These northeastern peoples lived in closely knit villages, developed systems of government, and traded throughout the region.

European Colonies

European migration had begun by the late 1500s. Europeans came to North America in search of land to farm, valuable minerals, and political and religious freedom. Most European migrants came from Spain, France, and England and settled in colonies.

The Spaniards controlled Florida and a large area west of the Mississippi River. Many Spanish settlements were founded as military posts or as missions—religious communities founded to convert Native Americans to Christianity. Spanish colonists also set up farms and huge cattle ranches.

The French came to North America primarily for the fur trade. French trappers canoed down rivers such as the St. Lawrence and the Mississippi. They set up trading posts, collecting beaver pelts and other furs from Native Americans to ship to Europe. Those who settled permanently lived along the St. Lawrence River and the Mississippi River near the Gulf of Mexico.

By the 1700s England had colonies or controlled land along much of the Atlantic coast and around **Hudson Bay**. The settlers in the northern English colonies found that the thin, rocky soil and short growing season made farming difficult. The area, however, had excellent harbors as well as good timber and fishing. Shipbuilding, trade, and fishing became important industries in this region. The middle English colonies had wide river valleys, level land, and fertile soil. They also had mild winters; long, warm summers; and an extended growing season. Many settlers there raised cash crops to be exported. The southern English colonies had mild climates, rich soils, and open land that encouraged plantation agriculture. Most

NATIONAL GEOGRAPHIC **World Explorer**

Geography Skills for Life

Fort Ticonderoga
French, British, and American forces fought over Fort Ticonderoga from 1758 through the American Revolution.
Human-Environment Interaction How did the physical geography of the United States influence settlement in the colonies?

Chapter 6 ● 141

② TEACH

L1 Locate
Display Unit Map Transparency 2. Have students mark areas of English, French, and Spanish settlement in North America. Discuss ways of describing the locations of these areas.

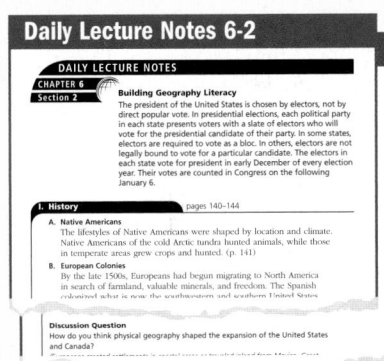

Daily Lecture Notes 6-2

DAILY LECTURE NOTES
CHAPTER 6
Section 2

Building Geography Literacy
The president of the United States is chosen by electors, not by direct popular vote. In presidential elections, each political party in each state presents voters with a slate of electors who will vote for the presidential candidate of their party. In some states, electors are required to vote as a bloc. In others, electors are not legally bound to vote for a particular candidate. The electors in each state vote for president in early December of every election year. Their votes are counted in Congress on the following January 6.

I. History   pages 140–144
A. Native Americans
The lifestyles of Native Americans were shaped by location and climate. Native Americans of the cold Arctic tundra hunted animals, while those in temperate areas grew crops and hunted. (p. 141)
B. European Colonies
By the late 1500s, Europeans had begun migrating to North America in search of farmland, valuable minerals, and freedom. The Spanish colonized what is now the southwestern and southern United States.

Discussion Question
How do you think physical geography shaped the expansion of the United States and Canada?

NATIONAL GEOGRAPHIC **World Explorer**

Answer
northern—rocky soil, good timber and harbors, fishing led to trade; middle—good agriculture for cash crops; southern—rich soil led to plantations

More About the Photo Fort Ticonderoga's name may come from an Iroquois term meaning "where waters meet." The fort's location on the LaChute River, a link between Lake George and Lake Champlain, gave it strategic importance for the French, British, and the young United States, all of whom controlled it at various times between 1755 and 1777.

DIFFERENTIATED INSTRUCTION

Gifted and Talented Invite students to speculate about what the region of the United States and Canada would have been like if political/territorial expansion had taken place from west to east instead of from east to west. **Ask: What would government/society have been like? Where would national capitals have been located? How would climate and physical geography have influenced expansion?** Invite students to write their revised versions of history and then share with the rest of the class.
🌐 **EE5 Environment and Society: Standards 14, 15**
📂 Refer to *Inclusion for the Social Studies Classroom Strategies and Activities.*

L2 Compare

After students read the "European Colonies" section on page 141, ask them to compare the English, French, and Spanish colonies in North America. Suggest that they consider the reasons each group had for coming and the kinds of settlements each group established. Have students make a chart to jot down their observations. **Ask: Which group was most successful in colonizing North America?** Be sure students support their answers with evidence from the text. Have students add to their charts as they continue to read the section.

L1/ELL

Guided Reading Activity 6-2

Name_____ Date_____ Class_____

Guided Reading Activity **6-2**

For use with textbook pages 140–145

History and Government

Fill in the Blanks

DIRECTIONS: Use the information in your textbook to fill in the blanks in the sentences below.

1. The cultures of various Native American groups were shaped primarily by location and _____

2. Spain controlled Florida and vast areas _____ of the Mississippi River.

3. By the 1700s the Atlantic coast and Hudson Bay were controlled by _____

4. Immigrants found that the Northeast had plentiful timber and fish and good _____

5. The war for independence from Great Britain began in _____

6. In the 1800s settlers in the United States and Canada expanded into the _____

7. Alaska was purchased from _____ in 1867.

Culture NOTE

Quebec The only walled city in North America north of Mexico, Quebec City is sometimes called the "Cradle of New France." It became the main base of early French explorers and missionaries on the continent.

---

plantation owners used enslaved Africans to provide the labor such large-scale farming required.

Two New Countries

In 1763 France was forced to give up much of its North American empire to Great Britain (formed by the union of England and Scotland in 1707). Conflicts soon arose between Native Americans and colonial settlers. Occupying the land, many settlers pushed out Native American communities and nearly destroyed their cultures.

During the 1760s the British government aroused the American colonists' anger by imposing new taxes and limiting their freedoms. Beginning in 1775, the thirteen British colonies, all of them along or near the Atlantic coast, fought a war for independence. The outcome was a new country—the United States of America. Rejecting monarchy, the Americans set up a republic, a government in which people elect their own officials, including their head of state. They elected George Washington as the first president of the United States.

Some American colonists, however, did not want to break ties with the British monarch. As many as 100,000 of these people, known as Loyalists, left the new country. Most settled in French-populated **Quebec,** which Great Britain controlled. During the early 1800s, English- and French-speaking communities in British North America constantly feuded about colonial government policies, but fears of a United States takeover forced them together. In 1867, under Prime Minister John A. Macdonald, four of the colonies—Quebec, **Ontario**, **Nova Scotia**, and **New Brunswick**—united as provinces of the Dominion of Canada, a new country within the British Empire. Neighboring areas—Manitoba, British Columbia, Alberta, and Saskatchewan in the west and Prince Edward Island and Newfoundland along the Atlantic coast—became provinces of Canada during the next 100 years. Today Canada encompasses these 10 provinces and 3 additional territories, the **Yukon Territory**, the **Northwest Territories**, and **Nunavut** (NOO•nuh•vut).

From Sea to Shining Sea

During the 1800s the United States and Canada expanded into western North America. In 1803, for example, the United States bought from France

---

nearly all the land between the Mississippi River and the Rocky Mountains. This agreement, known as the Louisiana Purchase, nearly doubled the size of the country and gave the United States control of the Mississippi River and access to the Far West.

The western lands were rich in natural resources. **Texas,** a former Mexican territory that became an independent republic in 1836 and joined the United States in 1845, was valued for cotton production and cattle ranching. In the late 1840s, as a result of a war with Mexico, the United States gained all of the present-day states of California, Utah, and Nevada and parts of Colorado, Wyoming, Arizona, and New Mexico. The discovery of gold and silver boosted settlement in the region. A traveler on the California Trail during the Gold Rush of 1849 captured the attraction of the West in his journal:

> *On, on, stay not for those who linger, on , on, look not for those behind. . . . America with one heave throws her life toward Sacramento!*
>
> C. B. Darwin, quoted in "The Way West," *National Geographic*, September 2000

By trade or treaty, the United States eventually gained control of land from the Atlantic to the Pacific coasts, and from the Canadian border in the north to the Rio Grande in the south. In 1867 the United States purchased its last great frontier, **Alaska,** from Russia. Later it acquired **Hawaii** and some other islands located in the Pacific and the Caribbean. During this period Canada also acquired western lands, spreading from the Atlantic to the Pacific Ocean and from the Arctic region in the north to the United States border to the south. For Native Americans, however, westward expansion by both countries signaled the steady loss of their lands and restrictions on their traditional ways of life.

Economics
Growth, Division, and Unity

In the 1800s industrialization transformed the United States and Canada. The first factories in North America arose in the northeastern United

---

COOPERATIVE LEARNING ACTIVITY

Native American Culture Regions Organize students into six groups, and assign one of the Native American culture regions to each group. Instruct each group to research the way of life for their particular culture region. They should create a diorama, poster, or some kind of visual aid that shows how North American ways of life related to the environment. Students also should prepare both written and oral analyses of topics, such as how Native American traditional economies operated. Each group member should contribute to the activity, either through research, creation of a visual aid, writing, or oral presentation.

EE4 Human Systems: Standard 10

States, which had many waterfalls that could be harnessed to produce power to run machines. Because waterpower was limited to a few places, people in industry later used steam as a source of power. Large supplies of coal in **Pennsylvania** and **Ohio**, which were used to power steam engines, made steam power cheap and manufacturing very profitable. The Midwestern United States and the Canadian provinces of Ontario and Quebec became leading centers of industry and business. The many rivers and lakes in these areas, improved by the building of canals, were used to transport goods from factories to port cities.

A growing demand for cotton by the textile industry in the northeastern United States made cotton production highly profitable. Cotton became the South's major cash crop. Swamps were drained and pine forests cleared for more cotton plantations. For plantation owners, the labor of enslaved Africans became more important than ever before.

Other people, however, worked to end slavery by enabling enslaved people to escape from bondage. The Underground Railroad, an informal network of safe houses, helped thousands of escaping enslaved people make their way north to freedom. Many escapees found shelter in Canada, which never practiced slavery and refused to honor U.S. laws that punished those who escaped.

Disputes over slavery, along with economic and political differences between Northern and Southern states, led to the American Civil War of 1861–1865. Under President Abraham Lincoln, the Northern states defeated the Southern states that had left the Union. After the war the United States abolished slavery and gave formerly enslaved African Americans citizenship, equal protection under the law, and the right to vote. Reunited, the United States set about rebuilding itself.

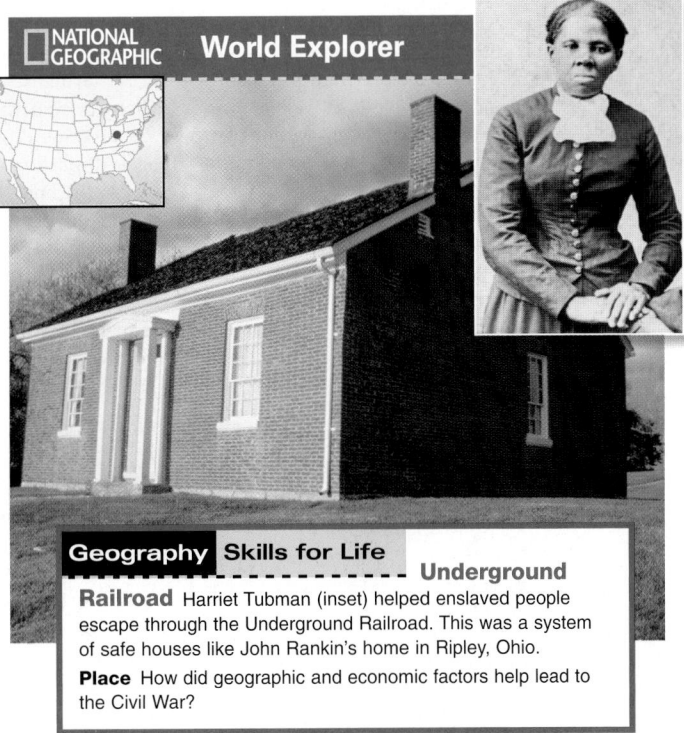

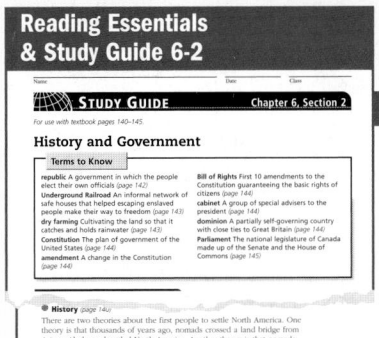

Geography **Skills for Life**

Underground Railroad Harriet Tubman (inset) helped enslaved people escape through the Underground Railroad. This was a system of safe houses like John Rankin's home in Ripley, Ohio.
Place How did geographic and economic factors help lead to the Civil War?

Technological and Social Change

During the late 1800s, the United States and Canada both encouraged settlement of the Great Plains. The United States and Canadian governments wanted to ease the crowding in eastern cities caused by immigration from Europe. They also wanted people to farm the region, thus providing more food for urban populations. Thousands of people from Atlantic coastal areas, as well as immigrants from eastern Europe and Scandinavia, started farms on the Great Plains.

Because of dry conditions, settlers on the Great Plains developed a special farming method, called dry farming, cultivating the land so that it caught and held rainwater. Strong steel plows, better able to break the hard prairie sod, soon replaced iron plows. Steam tractors made it possible to plant and harvest large areas of land faster and easier.

Chapter 6 🌐 143

CHAPTER 6
Section 2, pages 140–145

L1/ELL

Reading Essentials & Study Guide 6-2

STUDY GUIDE   Chapter 6, Section 2
For use with textbook pages 140–145

History and Government

Terms to Know

republic A government in which the people elect their own officials (page 142)
Underground Railroad An informal network of safe houses that helped escaping enslaved people make their way to freedom (page 143)
dry farming Cultivating the land so that it catches and holds rainwater (page 143)
Constitution The plan of government of the United States (page 144)
amendment A change in the Constitution (page 144)

Bill of Rights First 10 amendments to the Constitution guaranteeing the basic rights of citizens (page 144)
cabinet A group of special advisers to the president (page 144)
dominion A partially self-governing country with close ties to Great Britain (page 144)
Parliament The national legislature of Canada made up of the Senate and the House of Commons (page 145)

● History (page 140)
There are two theories about the first people to settle North America. One theory is that thousands of years ago, nomads crossed a land bridge from Asia to Alaska and settled North America. Another theory is that nomads...

NATIONAL GEOGRAPHIC **World Explorer**

Answer
The North's economy was based on industry, the South's on plantation agriculture. Disputes over slavery and economic differences caused conflict.

More About the Photo
The Underground Railroad dates from 1786 but was most active during the 1850s and 1860s. About 40,000 enslaved people used it to reach Canada. About half of those returned to the United States after the Civil War.

INTERDISCIPLINARY
connection

HISTORY After gold was discovered on Cherokee land in Georgia, federal soldiers rounded up Cherokee families in 1838 and relocated them to Oklahoma. During the forced march, called the Trail of Tears, thousands of Cherokee died.

CRITICAL THINKING ACTIVITY

Identifying Central Issues *Uncle Tom's Cabin*, a famous novel about the life of an enslaved person, was enormously popular when it appeared in the early 1850s. Written by Harriet Beecher Stowe, the novel was translated into more than 20 languages. Its dramatic adaptation played to large crowds. When Abraham Lincoln was introduced to Stowe, he is said to have commented, "So you are the little woman who wrote the book that started this great war!" **Ask: Why do you think Lincoln might have made this comment? How might a work of fiction be said to have helped start the Civil War?** *(Possible answers: It gave slavery a human face; it gave focus to the differences between the North and South.)*
🌐 **EE4 Human Systems: Standard 13**

ASSESS

Assign Section 2 Assessment as homework or as an in-class activity.

🌐 Have students use **Interactive Tutor Self-Assessment CD-ROM** to review Section 2.

L2

Section Quiz 6-2

Name	Date	Class

CHAPTER 6 Section **2** Quiz
History and Government

MATCHING: Match each item in Column A with an item in Column B. Write the correct letters in the blanks. *(10 points each)*

A	B
1. American colonists who protested the move toward independence from the British monarchy	A. Alaska
2. agreement that acquired territory between the Mississippi River and the Rocky Mountains for the United States	B. province
3. purchased from Russia in 1867	C. Louisiana Purchase
4. hiding places along the Underground Railroad	D. safe houses
5. political division within the Dominion of Canada	E. Loyalists

MULTIPLE CHOICE: In each blank on the left, write the letter of the choice that best completes the statement or answers the question.

NATIONAL GEOGRAPHIC **World Explorer**

Answer
Manufactured goods, food, and people traversed the country more efficiently, and immigrants were recruited to build railroads.

More About the Photo
Transcontinental railroad routes in Canada are located primarily in the south, although new routes have been constructed to serve timber and mining areas in the north. There is a major north-south line in British Columbia. Per capita, Canada has one of the highest railway mileages worldwide.

The late 1800s also saw the completion of transcontinental railroads in the United States and Canada. These made it possible to transport manufactured goods from east to west, as well as food products—especially beef cattle—from west to east. Immigrants from China, Ireland, Mexico, and other countries were recruited to help build the railroads.

During the early 1900s, the introduction of assembly lines for mass production cut the cost and the time needed to make many industrial products. Perhaps the most influential mass-produced item was the automobile. At this time people were becoming increasingly mobile, and more of them lived in urban areas than in rural areas.

Two world wars during the 1900s spurred economic growth in the United States and Canada. After 1940 both countries were linked in a close partnership that included increased trade between them. By the 1990s certain economic activities,

NATIONAL GEOGRAPHIC **World Explorer**

Geography Skills for Life

Growth of Railroads Thousands of Chinese workers, such as these on the Northern Pacific Railway, helped build the railroads across western North America in the late 1800s.

Movement How did the completion of transcontinental railroads affect the United States?

mining and steel production, for example, were less important than rising high-tech industries. Social changes also took place. Immigration increased from Latin America and Asia. Women, African Americans, Hispanics, and other groups began to participate in business and the political process. In both Canada and the United States, Native Americans have negotiated with governments over land claims, mineral rights, and other issues. In 1999 the Inuit, one of Canada's native peoples, won the right to their own territory, called Nunavut, carved from the eastern half of the Northwest Territories.

Government

The United States and Canada both are democracies with federal systems, in which the national government shares power with state or provincial governments. To create a strong national government while preserving the rights of individual states and citizens, United States leaders in 1787 drafted a plan of government called the Constitution. Over the years, changes in the Constitution, called amendments, have been made to meet the country's changing needs. The first 10 amendments, called the Bill of Rights, guarantee the basic rights of citizens, including the freedoms of speech, religion, and the press.

The national government of the United States has three branches: executive, legislative, and judicial. The executive branch includes the president, the vice president, and the executive departments that administer various divisions of the national government. The heads of these departments form the president's cabinet—a group of special advisers. Congress, consisting of elected state representatives to both the Senate and the House of Representatives, is the legislative branch. The Supreme Court and lower federal courts make up the judicial branch.

Canada was created as a dominion, a partially self-governing country with close ties to Great Britain. It gained full independence in 1931, but the British government kept the right to approve changes to Canada's constitution. In 1982 this legislative link to Great Britain finally ended. Canada at its founding had a strong central government with only minor powers given to the individual

---

TEAM-TEACHING ACTIVITY: WORLD HISTORY

Federal Systems of the United States and Canada Tell students that the governments of the United States and Canada include the same three branches of government: executive, legislative, and judicial. Their systems both also share power between the central government and the state or provincial governments. Students might request help from a history teacher in researching the answer to the following question: **In which country do the executive and legislative branches of government overlap?** *(Canada; the powers of the prime minister and the cabinet lie partly within the executive branch and partly within the legislative branch.)* Tell students to make a poster illustrating the three branches of government for each country. 📦 🖥 **EE4 Human Systems: Standard 13**

provinces. Over the years, the power of the provinces has increased.

Today the executive part of Canada's government includes the governor-general, the prime minister, and the cabinet. The British monarch still serves as the head of state, appointing a governor-general to act in his or her place. The national legislature, called Parliament, is made up of the Senate and the House of Commons. Canada's prime minister, who is leader of the majority political party in Parliament, is the actual head of government. Nine judges sit on the Supreme Court of Canada, the country's highest court.

In the next section, you will learn about the culture and lifestyles in the United States and Canada as they enter the new millennium.

NATIONAL GEOGRAPHIC World Explorer

Geography Skills for Life

House of Parliament
Ottawa's location on the border between Quebec and Ontario helped determine its role as Canada's capital city.
Place How does Canada's prime minister derive his or her position?

Reteach

Have students write a two-page section summary and then quiz each other on the material.

Enrich

Have students compare two similar political maps (U.S. presidential races or congressional apportionment). Ask students what geographic factors influenced the political changes shown on the maps.

4 CLOSE

Summarize the historical influences that shaped the United States and Canada.

NATIONAL GEOGRAPHIC World Explorer

Answer
by being the majority party's leader in Parliament

More About the Photo
The Canadian Senate has 104 members, appointed on a provincial basis. The House of Commons has 295 members elected for a maximum of five years.

SECTION 2 ASSESSMENT

Checking for Understanding

1. **Define** republic, Underground Railroad, dry farming, Constitution, amendment, Bill of Rights, cabinet, dominion, Parliament.

2. **Main Ideas** Create a time line like the one below, and label major events in the settlement and development of the United States and Canada.

Native Americans
settled in region

circa
8000 B.C.

Critical Thinking

3. **Identifying Cause and Effect** How did physical geography influence the cultures of the region's first settlers?

4. **Drawing Conclusions** Why is the influence of French culture more pronounced in Canada than in the United States?

5. **Making Generalizations** Trace the spread of railroads in the United States and Canada. Describe the effects of the railroad on cultural sharing and national unity in both the countries.

Analyzing Maps

6. **Region** Study the political map on page 107. Then, without looking at this map, label the U.S. states and Canadian provinces/territories on an outline map.

Applying Geography

7. **Effects of Technology** How did people meet the challenges of settling the West through innovation and change? Write a brief essay describing these changes and how they affected the region's physical and human geography.

SECTION 2 ASSESSMENT ANSWERS

1. All vocabulary terms are defined in the text.

2. Check time lines for accuracy and completeness.

3. tundra region: hunted animals such as caribou for food and fur; Pacific Coast: fished, used trees to build houses and canoes; Southwest deserts: irrigated crops; Great Plains: hunted buffalo for food, clothing, shelter, and tools; woodlands: built ceremonial mounds, hunted, farmed, and traded; northeastern woodlands: hunted, lived in close-knit villages, traded

4. The province of Quebec was populated largely by French settlers.

5. Railroads brought manufactured goods, foods, and people with the latest ideas, and unified the nations by making long-distance travel faster.

6. Students should label 50 U.S. states, 10 Canadian provinces, and 3 Canadian territories. Labels for smaller states and territories may be abbreviated.

7. **Applying Geography** Check paragraphs for topic sentence and accurate details.

FOCUS

Section Overview

This section discusses how religion, languages, and the arts reflect the cultural diversity of the United States and Canada.

BELLRINGER
Skillbuilder Activity

Project the transparency and have students answer questions.

Available as blackline master.

Daily Focus Skills Transparency 6-3

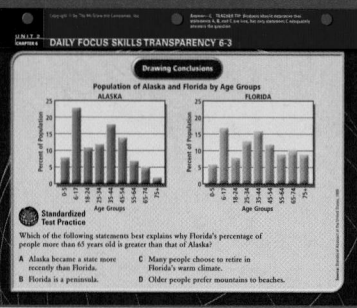

Guide to Reading

Consider What You Know
Answers *Answers may include modern popular music, fashions, music videos, and certain dances.*

Reading Strategy
Answers *Nathaniel Hawthorne, Edgar Allan Poe—Life in North America; Mark Twain—Life on the Mississippi River; Margaret Laurence—Prairies of central Canada; Willa Cather—Great Plains; Richard Wright, Toni Morrison—African American experience; Maxine Hong Kingston, Amy Tan—Asian immigrants' experiences; Isaac Bashevis Singer—Jewish Americans; Rudolfo Anaya, Sandra Cisneros—Hispanic Americans' lives and issues*

Preteaching Vocabulary
Use the **Vocabulary Puzzle-Maker CD-ROM** to create crossword and word-search puzzles.

Guide to Reading

Consider What You Know
The arts and popular entertainment of the United States and Canada influence other culture regions of the world. What cultural trends can you think of that began in this region and spread to other parts of the world?

Reading Strategy
Categorizing As you read about the literature of North America, complete a graphic organizer similar to the one below by listing authors and the topics they wrote about.

Author	Topic
James Fenimore Cooper	Life in North America

Read to Find Out
- How do the religious practices and languages of the region reflect the immigrant history of the United States and Canada?
- How do the arts of the United States and Canada reflect the region's colonial past?
- What kinds of educational and health care systems serve the people of the region?

Terms to Know
- bilingual
- jazz
- socioeconomic status
- literacy rate
- patriotism

Places to Locate
- New Mexico
- Hollywood

SECTION **3**

Cultures and Lifestyles

NATIONAL GEOGRAPHIC

A Geographic View

The Art of Everyday Life

Such attention to reality was at odds with artistic convention in [painter Winslow] Homer's time, as was his choice of subjects—barefoot boys, farm girls, working men, freed slaves, North Woods guides, ordinary soldiers, and women of leisure, all of whom represented everyday life in America. Early critics complained about it.... But like other American originals of his time—Walt Whitman and Mark Twain—Homer kept to his own path.

—Robert M. Poole, "Winslow Homer: American Original,"
National Geographic, *December 1998*

Fresh Eggs by Winslow Homer

Winslow Homer, known for his naturalistic style, was one of the greatest American painters of the 1800s. His paintings express the independent thinking and the enthusiasm for new frontiers that mark the cultures of the United States and Canada. The immigrant roots of these countries also gives them a respect for diversity. In this section you will read about the cultures and lifestyles of the United States and Canada.

Cultural Characteristics

The United States and Canada are countries of many cultures. Like the threads of a brightly colored blanket, the cultures of these countries blend into a new pattern without losing their individual qualities.

RESOURCE MANAGER

📂 Reproducible Masters
- Reproducible Lesson Plan 6-3
- Vocabulary Activity 6
- Daily Lecture Notes 6-3
- Guided Reading Activity 6-3
- Reading Essentials and Study Guide 6-3
- Reteaching Activity 6
- Reinforcing Skills Activity 6
- Section Quiz 6-3

🖳 Transparencies
- Daily Focus Skills Transparency 6-3
- Unit 2 Map Overlay Transparencies

Multimedia
- 💿 Vocabulary PuzzleMaker CD-ROM
- 💿 World Music: A Cultural Legacy
- 📕 World Art Prints
- 💿 Interactive Tutor Self-Assessment CD-ROM
- 💿 ExamView® Pro Testmaker CD-ROM

music of NORTH AMERICA

The music of North America stems from Native American, European, and African influences. Music from this region is extremely varied and has greatly influenced other types of music around the world.

Instrument Spotlight
The **Native American flute** originated among the peoples of the Great Plains, and it was often played by men to express their feelings of love to women. Each flute, made individually by hand, has its own unique look and sound. Traditional flutes are made from a piece of cedar, cut the same length as the distance between the armpit and the longest finger of the musician. In addition to five or six playing holes, four "direction" holes are added to send the sound in all directions.

 **World Music: A Cultural Legacy** Hear music of this region on Disc 1, Tracks 1–6.

History
Religious Freedom

Freedom of religion has always been valued in the United States and Canada. Many of the people who migrated to the region did so to worship freely. As early as 1774, the British Parliament passed a law recognizing the religious rights of Roman Catholic French Canadians. In 1791 the Bill of Rights, which became part of the United States Constitution, guaranteed Americans religious freedom in addition to a number of other rights.

Today most Americans and Canadians who are members of an organized religion are Christians. In the United States, the majority of Christians are Protestant, while in Canada most Christians are Roman Catholic. Judaism, Islam, and Buddhism are among other religions practiced in the United States and Canada.

Languages

English is the main language in the United States. In Canada, English and French are the official languages. Because of immigration from all over the world, however, people in the United States and Canada also speak or use various words and phrases of other languages. For example, street signs in ethnic neighborhoods of the region's port cities—New York, Los Angeles, San Francisco, and Vancouver—may be printed in Chinese, Korean, Russian, Arabic, or Hindi. A writer describes this mix of cultures and languages in New York:

> ❝ *Store owners [on Third Avenue] are often Asian. Corner groceries are run by families from the Dominican Republic. . . . Arabs operate the candy stores . . . Koreans run vegetable stands. . . . [Near 118th Street] Robert Kosches finished talking in Spanish to a young couple. . . . 'My grandfather, who came from Austria, started this [furniture] business,' he said, switching to English. . . .* ❞
>
> Jere Van Dyk, "Growing Up in East Harlem," *National Geographic*, May 1990

② TEACH

L1 Identify
Ask students to identify examples of cultural diversity that exist in their communities. Tell students to think about the different languages, religions, and ethnic foods they encounter as well as the various arts and leisure activities.

Music Notes
Although Plains Native Americans play the flageolet, or end-blown flute, their most common instrument is the large bass drum, played by all singers in a group. Rattles and bells made of natural materials like turtle shells and gourds are other Native American instruments.

🎵 **World Music: A Cultural Legacy**
Use the Teacher Guide for information about the music of this region.

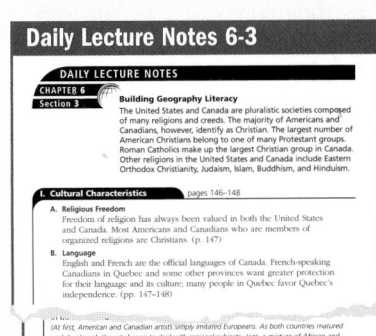

Daily Lecture Notes 6-3

DAILY LECTURE NOTES

CHAPTER 6
Section 3   **Building Geography Literacy**
The United States and Canada are pluralistic societies composed of many religions and creeds. The majority of Americans and Canadians, however, identify as Christian. The largest number of American Christians belong to one of many Protestant groups. Roman Catholics make up the largest Christian group in Canada. Other religions in the United States and Canada include Eastern Orthodox Christianity, Judaism, Islam, Buddhism, and Hinduism.

I. Cultural Characteristics   pages 146–148

A. **Religious Freedom**
Freedom of religion has always been valued in both the United States and Canada. Most Americans and Canadians who are members of organized religions are Christians. (p. 147)

B. **Language**
English and French are the official languages of Canada. French-speaking Canadians in Quebec and some other provinces want greater protection for their language and its culture; many people in Quebec favor Quebec's independence. (pp. 147–148)

(At first, American and Canadian artists simply imitated Europeans. As both countries matured and developed, the arts began to deal with regional subjects. Jazz, a mixture of African and European musical ideas, might not have developed without the blending of cultures reflected in the region's music and art.)

DIFFERENTIATED INSTRUCTION

English Learners Tell students that they can increase their comprehension of this section's content if they apply reading strategies before, during, and after reading. Before they begin, help students preview the text and make predictions about its content. Read each heading and subheading aloud and check for understanding. Be sure students understand the vocabulary and practice pronouncing terms. As they read, tell students to connect the text to their everyday knowledge. After they finish reading, confirm their understanding, and have them answer questions orally. **Ask:** Were your predictions correct? **ELL**

🌐 **EE4 Human Systems: Standard 10**
📁 Refer to *Inclusion for the Social Studies Classroom Strategies and Activities.*

World Explorer

Answer

to preserve their language and cultural identity

More About the Photo

Advocates of a separate Quebec sometimes point out that from 1791 to 1841 the province had, in a sense, a separate identity from the rest of Canada. Still, the majority of Canadians support a united Canada.

L1/ELL

Guided Reading Activity 6-3

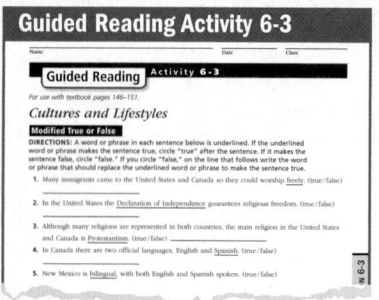

Quebec Fewer than one million people in Quebec speak English as their primary language. Most of the rest—6,400,000—speak French as their first language. Many Quebéçois are bilingual, and French and English are sometimes mixed in daily conversation—especially in urban areas.

NATIONAL GEOGRAPHIC World Explorer

Geography Skills for Life

Unity Rally

Supporters of Canadian unity rally in Hull, Quebec, prior to a 1995 referendum on Quebec independence.

Place Why do some Quebecois desire independence?

Immigrants from Great Britain brought the English language to the United States and much of Canada. In the Canadian province of Quebec, however, French is the official language because most of the province's population are descended from French settlers who arrived from the 1500s to the 1700s.

French-speaking Canadians in Quebec and some other provinces want greater protection for their language and culture. To achieve this goal, many Quebecois (kay•beh•KWAH) want Quebec's independence and support a movement for *separatism*—the breaking away of one part of a country to create a separate, independent country.

The Southwestern United States since colonial times has had a large Spanish-speaking population. In **New Mexico**, any communications with the state government or with local governments may be in Spanish or English. Thus, New Mexico is **bilingual**, meaning "having two languages." In California the presence of Asian communities is evident in the signs written in Chinese, Japanese, Korean, and other Asian languages.

The Arts

The arts of the United States and Canada go back to the first Americans, who interwove art and music into daily life. Native Americans made detailed carvings from shell and stone, used clay to produce pottery, and wove baskets, sandals, and mats from local plants. After European settlement the arts of the region were dominated by European traditions. By the mid-1800s, however, Americans and Canadians had begun to create art forms that reflected their own lives as North Americans.

Music

In their music Native Americans used drums, flutes, whistles, and vocal chanting. Europeans later brought European folk and religious music to the region. At the beginning of the 1900s, a distinctive form of music known as jazz developed in African American communities throughout the United States. Jazz blended African rhythms with

COOPERATIVE LEARNING ACTIVITY

Cultural Exchange Ask students to define "melting pot" and "mosaic." (*"Melting pot" implies that cultures blend together to form one; "mosaic" implies that each culture retains its identity within the whole.*) Organize the class into three groups to research British, French, and Spanish cultural influences. Each group should examine how its assigned culture shaped lifestyle and leisure activities in this region. Have the groups share what they have learned. Finally, ask the class to select and examine an aspect of American and Canadian cultures that has impacted other parts of the world—for example, English as a language of global communication. **EE4 Human Systems: Standard 10**

European harmonies. By the end of the century, country music and rock 'n' roll had become popular musical forms, not only in North America but around the world. In classical music, dancers and choreographers created a modern form of ballet.

The Visual Arts

Painting and sculpture in the United States and Canada moved away from their European roots and explored new themes. In the early 1900s, a group of American artists known as the Ashcan School painted the grim realities of urban life. A group of Canadian painters called the Group of Seven showed the rugged landscape of Canada's far north in bright, dynamic colors. American artist Georgia O'Keeffe gave the world new visions of the American West. In the mid-1900s many artists in the region adopted from Europe the abstract style, which expresses the artist's emotions and attitudes without depicting recognizable images.

Architects in the United States and Canada also developed innovations. The skyscraper, a tall building with many floors, first appeared in the United States. The architects Frank Lloyd Wright in the United States and Arthur Erickson in Canada were noted for designing buildings that harmonized with the region's natural environments.

Literature

Literature in the United States and Canada at first dealt mainly with European historical and religious themes. Later writers, such as James Fenimore Cooper, Nathaniel Hawthorne, and Edgar Allan Poe, wrote stories about life in North America. Since the late 1800s, many American and Canadian authors have written about different parts of the region. Mark Twain described life on the Mississippi River, Margaret Laurence focused on the prairies of central Canada, and Willa Cather described life on the Great Plains.

More recently, writers have concentrated on highlighting aspects of the region's cultures. For example, writers such as Richard Wright and Toni Morrison depict the African American experience, Maxine Hong Kingston and Amy Tan write about the experience of Asian immigrants, Isaac Bashevis Singer's stories reflect the world of Jewish Americans, and Rudolfo Anaya and Sandra Cisneros focus on Hispanic American lives and issues.

Popular Entertainment

The cultural influence of the United States and Canada on the rest of the world is strongest in the area of popular entertainment. During the 1900s the United States became the world's dominant source for entertainment and popular fashion, from jeans and T-shirts to rock stars, movies, and television programs. The motion picture industry began in New York City and later moved to southern California. Today the name of a Los Angeles district, **Hollywood**, has become synonymous with the movie business. Canada's film industry, supported by the government, is known for its innovative documentaries. In the performing arts, Canada is noted for its Shakespeare Festival, held annually in Stratford, Ontario. Broadway, a New York City street name, is internationally identified with popular theater. The musical, combining elements of

performing arts of THE UNITED STATES

Modern Dance Modern dance combines the techniques of social dance and ballet. One of modern dance's best known performers and choreographers, Twyla Tharp, uses movement to interpret everyday activities.

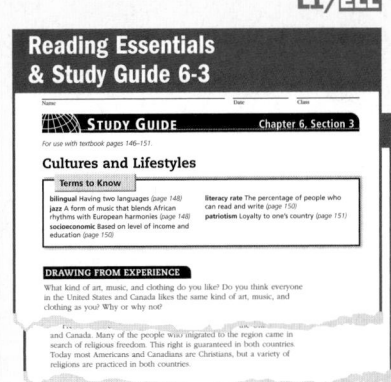

Reading Essentials & Study Guide 6-3

Name _____ Date _____ Class _____

STUDY GUIDE   Chapter 6, Section 3

For use with textbook pages 146–151.

Cultures and Lifestyles

Terms to Know

bilingual Having two languages *(page 148)*
jazz A form of music that blends African rhythms with European harmonies *(page 148)*
socioeconomic Based on level of income and education *(page 150)*
literacy rate The percentage of people who can read and write *(page 150)*
patriotism Loyalty to one's country *(page 151)*

DRAWING FROM EXPERIENCE

What kind of art, music, and clothing do you like? Do you think everyone in the United States and Canada likes the same kind of art, music, and clothing as you? Why or why not?

and Canada. Many of the people who migrated to the region came in search of religious freedom. This right is guaranteed in both countries. Today most Americans and Canadians are Christians, but a variety of religions are practiced in both countries.

Arts of the United States and Canada

Twyla Tharp's experimental work gained great popularity in the 1960s and 1970s. Her innovative choreography mixed athleticism with classical, modern, and popular genres.

 **World Art Prints**

Use these prints to introduce students to other arts of the region.

GEOGRAPHY AND THE HUMANITIES

 World Music: A Cultural Legacy

 World Art and Architecture Transparencies

 World Art Prints

CRITICAL THINKING ACTIVITY

Immigrants Have students write an essay discussing the effects of immigrants on cultures in the United States and Canada. Brainstorm the data students might need, and write contributions on the board. Model a graphic organizer, such as chart or web, to show students how to organize the data. Have students share their preliminary thesis sentences with the class to get feedback. Students can work with an English teacher during the writing process. Before students write their first drafts, check their thesis statements, supporting details, and organizational plans. Students may wish to add their work to the "Technology Activity" on page 155. 🌐 **EE4 Human Systems: Standard 10**

ASSESS

Assign Section 3 Assessment as homework or as an in-class activity.

Have students use **Interactive Tutor Self-Assessment CD-ROM** to review Section 3.

L2

Section Quiz 6-3

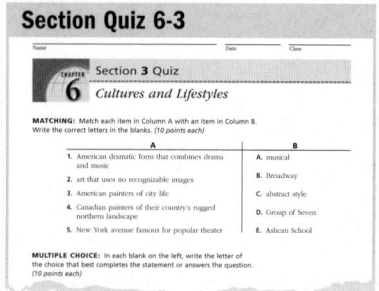

FYI

Baseball This most American of sports has become internationalized. During one recent spring training, rosters included 305 players from 17 countries and territories.

NATIONAL GEOGRAPHIC   **GRAPH STUDY**

Answers

1. *homes with electricity; own a TV*

2. *Both countries have highly developed economies.*

---

drama with music, became a popular form of theater in the United States.

Lifestyles

As citizens of two of the world's wealthiest countries, most people in the United States and Canada enjoy a high standard of living. Their socioeconomic status, or level of income and education, means having the advantage of many personal choices and opportunities. Because the region has an agricultural surplus, foods are relatively inexpensive. Housing varies to suit the needs of individuals and families, whether it be high-rise apartments, multifamily row houses, or suburban houses in a variety of styles.

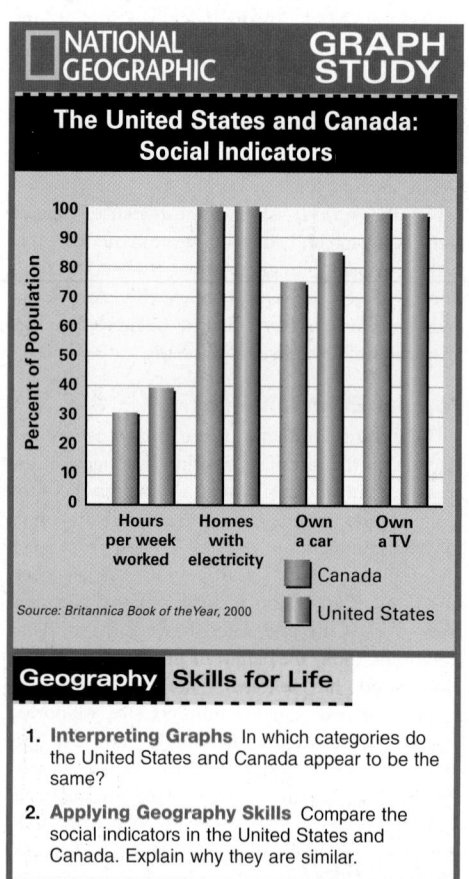

NATIONAL GEOGRAPHIC   **GRAPH STUDY**

The United States and Canada: Social Indicators

Source: Britannica Book of the Year, 2000

Canada
United States

Geography   **Skills for Life**

1. **Interpreting Graphs** In which categories do the United States and Canada appear to be the same?

2. **Applying Geography Skills** Compare the social indicators in the United States and Canada. Explain why they are similar.

Economics
Health Care

People in both the United States and Canada can expect to live longer, generally healthier lives than people in many other parts of the world. The region's high level of economic development enables governments to devote substantial resources to health care. Health care is administered differently in the two countries. In Canada, the government pays for health care. In the United States, most people are expected to pay for their own health care through health insurance provided by employers or other organizations. Federal and state governments, however, pay for some health insurance for people who are older, people with disabilities, or low-income families. Still, many people in the United States are unable to purchase insurance, and others cannot afford health care even with insurance. In the United States, the role of the government in providing health care for all citizens, regardless of their socioeconomic status, is currently under debate.

Education

The United States and Canada have similar educational systems, including networks of public and private schools. Both countries maintain compulsory education requirements. In the United States and most Canadian provinces, school systems have 12 grades. Colleges and universities exist in every state and province. In the United States, the literacy rate, the percentage of people who can read and write, is 97 percent; Canada's literacy rate is also 97 percent.

Sports and Recreation

Although a strong work ethic is woven into the culture of both the Americans and Canadians, they also enjoy plenty of leisure time. Some of the most popular activities involve watching and participating in sports. Most people associate baseball and football with the United States and ice hockey with Canada. Fans and players of these sports, however, come from both sides of the border. Basketball, soccer, golf, tennis, and competitive ice-skating also have their supporters in both countries.

Television transformed sports during the late 1900s. Many people in the United States and Canada share in exciting sports telecasts throughout the

---

CRITICAL THINKING ACTIVITY

Drawing Conclusions Have students analyze the graph "Social Indicators" on page 150. Then have students choose a diverse group of countries in other parts of the world and research the same kinds of data. Have students compare and contrast the social indicators of each of these countries with those of the United States and Canada. **Ask:** What does the data suggest about the relationship between the level of economic development and standard of living in any given country? What does the data particularly reveal about the level of economic development and the standard of living in both the United States and Canada?   **EE4 Human Systems: Standard 10**

year: baseball during the spring and summer and its World Series in the early fall; football during the fall, capped by the Super Bowl in January; and the National Basketball Association (NBA) championships in the spring. As a result, sports heroes, such as baseball's Derek Jeter, football's Brett Favre, and basketball's Michael Jordan, have become household names.

The vast North American landscape is ideal for camping, canoeing, and hiking. The first U.S. national park was created in 1872. Located in parts of Wyoming, Montana, and Idaho, Yellowstone National Park covers more than two million acres, and dazzles visitors from around the world with its spectacular physical features. Since then, the United States and Canada have set aside millions of acres as national parks for conservation and recreation.

Celebrations

Holiday celebrations in the United States and Canada are essentially similar. Both countries celebrate many of the same religious holidays, and many civic observances are similar although held on different dates. Celebrations such as American Independence Day (July 4) and Canada Day (July 1) are occasions for public displays of patriotism, or loyalty to one's country.

NATIONAL GEOGRAPHIC World Explorer

Geography Skills for Life

United States Patriotism A crowd enjoys a Fourth of July celebration in Baton Rouge, Louisiana. **Place** What Canadian holiday is associated with patriotism?

Reteach

Have students turn to the Guide to Reading on page 146 to answer the "Read to Find Out" questions, the "Terms to Know," and "Places to Locate."

Enrich

Have students find examples of music that have different regional or cultural styles, and have each student bring a musical sample to share with the class. You may wish to suggest styles such as jazz, blues, zydeco, bluegrass, and conjunto.

④ CLOSE

Have students describe how inventions and new technology have affected cultural changes in the United States and Canada since World War II.

NATIONAL GEOGRAPHIC World Explorer

Answer
Canada Day (July 1)

More About the Photo
As the capital of Louisiana, Baton Rouge is often the site of patriotic events, such as this Independence Day parade.

SECTION 3 ASSESSMENT

Checking for Understanding

1. **Define** bilingual, jazz, socioeconomic, literacy rate, patriotism.

2. **Main Ideas** Create a diagram like the one below, listing aspects of the cultures, arts, and lifestyles of the region.

Cultures and Lifestyles		
Cultural Characteristics	The Arts	Lifestyles
•	•	•
•	•	•
•	•	•

Critical Thinking

3. **Making Generalizations** What challenges are created for government, education, and business when a country has two official languages?

4. **Making Inferences** Why do you think immigrants to the United States and Canada did not develop new styles of art, music, and literature at first?

5. **Identifying Cause and Effect** How has the region's history of religious freedom contributed to the development of culturally diverse societies in the United States and Canada?

Analyzing Maps

6. **Place** Study the physical map in the Regional Atlas on page 106. Why does the physical geography of California make it ideal for both surfers and mountain climbers?

Applying Geography

7. **Sports as Culture** Think about the popularity of various sports in the region. Write a paragraph explaining how sports can increase cultural understanding among the peoples of Canada and the United States.

Chapter 6 🌐 151

SECTION 3 ASSESSMENT ANSWERS

1. All vocabulary terms are defined in the text.

2. Check charts for completeness and accuracy.

3. Possible answer: written materials, such as government forms, street signs, even menus, must be in both languages.

4. Possible answer: immigrants brought old art styles with them.

5. Religions have many cultural components, festivals, and celebrations that can be observed when immigrants are free to practice any religion they choose.

6. California has beaches and mountains.

7. **Applying Geography** Check paragraphs for topic sentences and adequate supporting details. Students may mention that sports bring diverse peoples together and promote understanding.

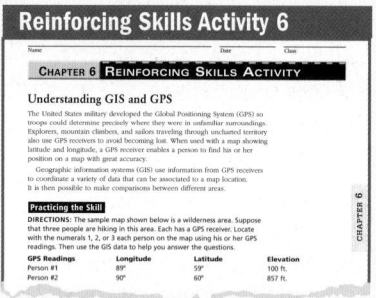

TECHNOLOGY
SkillBuilder

Understanding GIS and GPS

A Global Positioning System (GPS) can accurately determine a position on the earth to within .08 inches (2 mm). Geographic information systems (GIS) are computer tools for handling, processing, and analyzing geographic data. Both systems help us understand information about location.

Learning the Skill

GPS satellites in space continually broadcast signals to Earth. By tracking the signals from several satellites, a GPS receiver on the ground can determine its current latitude, longitude, and altitude. GPS measurements showed that Mt. Everest is actually 7 feet (2.1 m) higher than its official recorded height! The receiver can also report current time and the direction and speed of travel. The unit even has a feature that tells exact sunrise, sunset, and moon phase based on location and time.

Originally developed by the United States military, GPS is now available for many different uses:

- **Hikers** use GPS receivers with physical maps that show an area's surface features and elevations.

- **Drivers** use GPS receivers in cars to obtain digital street maps and plot travel routes.

- **Sailors** use GPS technology to plot a ship's course.

GPS receivers often feed data into geographic information systems (GIS). GIS are computer tools that gather, combine, and display information relevant to a specific geographic location. After information about an area is entered into the GIS database, the computer can create maps showing any combination of the data.

▲ *Soldier using GPS receiver*

Businesses use GIS to find prime locations to open franchises. Creating a database with information such as traffic patterns, competitors' locations, average income, and vacant lots for sale helps pinpoint the best location for a new store. Using data from various sources, GIS technology might display a map that shows the factories, air pollution count, and cancer rates in a particular neighborhood. GIS aid in information analysis by visually presenting the interaction among various factors in a given location.

GPS allows people to locate themselves inside the map, while GIS creates maps that highlight the elements affecting a location. GPS and GIS technology represents the state of the art in geography and mapmaking.

Practicing the Skill

Using the data you have read, answer the following questions.

1. What do GPS receivers use to plot exact locations?

2. Why was the military the original developer of GPS?

3. How does seeing various factors on a map help people make decisions?

4. How is GPS information used with a GIS database?

5. How could GPS and GIS improve traffic safety?

Applying the Skill

Your community is planning to build a recreation center. If you have access to a GIS program, use the program to help determine the best location. Use three types of data—such as roads, housing estates, and high school gyms—to create maps. Then analyze the maps and write your proposal.

ANSWERS TO PRACTICING THE SKILL

1. satellite signals
2. Answers may include the need for soldiers to track their location and the location of enemy weapons.
3. The more information available, the more accurate and profitable are the decisions that can be made.

4. GPS information is fed into a geographic information system (GIS), a computer tool that gathers, integrates, and displays relevant information in order to make maps showing any combination of the data.
5. Answers may include the ability to pinpoint areas of congestion and accidents.

SECTION 1 — Population Patterns (pp. 133–137)

Terms to Know
- immigration
- Native American
- Sunbelt
- urbanization
- metropolitan area
- suburb
- megalopolis
- mobility

Key Points
- Both Canada and the United States are home to various groups of native peoples and descendants of immigrants.
- Physical geography impacts the distribution and density of population in the U.S. and Canada.
- North America's settlements and its largest cities developed along waterways.
- Natural resources and waterways for transportation helped North America industrialize.

Organizing Your Notes
Use a table like the one below to help you organize your notes about the region's population patterns.

Peoples	Population Patterns

SECTION 2 — History and Government (pp. 140–145)

Terms to Know
- republic
- Underground Railroad
- dry farming
- Constitution
- amendment
- Bill of Rights
- cabinet
- dominion
- Parliament

Key Points
- Native Americans are North America's earliest people.
- Europeans set up colonies in North America for trading, conquest, and religious freedom.
- The thirteen British colonies won their independence from Britain in 1776 and formed their own republic, the United States of America.
- In 1867 the eastern provinces combined to form the Dominion of Canada. Canada today encompasses 10 provinces and 3 territories; it became an independent country in 1931.
- Industrialization and technology enabled westward expansion and spurred social change.

Organizing Your Notes
Create an outline using the format below to help you organize your notes for this section.

History and Government

I. History
  A. Native Americans
    1.
    2.
  B. European Colonies
    1.
    2.

SECTION 3 — Cultures and Lifestyles (pp. 146–151)

Terms to Know
- bilingual
- jazz
- socioeconomic status
- literacy rate
- patriotism

Key Points
- The immigrant roots of the United States and Canada make these two countries diverse.
- Both countries have a heritage of religious freedom.
- Musical and artistic expression began with immigrants and gradually became uniquely North American.
- Health care is supported by the governments of both countries but in different ways.
- Both countries in the region have high standards of living.

Organizing Your Notes
Use a cluster map like the one below to help you organize your notes for this section.

Region's Cultures

Using the Chapter 6 Summary & Study Guide

Use the Chapter 6 Summary & Study Guide to preview, review, condense, or reteach the chapter.

Preview/Review

Vocabulary PuzzleMaker CD-ROM reinforces "Terms to Know."

Interactive Tutor Self-Assessment CD-ROM provides a review of Chapter 6 content.

Condense

Have students read the Chapter 6 Summary & Study Guide.

Chapter 6 Audio Program

Chapter 6 Guided Reading Activities

Reteach

Chapter 6 Reteaching Activities (Spanish also available)

Chapter 6 Reading Essentials and Study Guides

GLENCOE TECHNOLOGY

NATIONAL GEOGRAPHIC
WORLD REGIONS
VIDEO PROGRAM

Unit 2, The United States and Canada
The following segments enhance the study of this unit:
- **Preserving Wilderness**
- **Land of Immigrants**
- **Brass Bands**

CHAPTER CULMINATING ACTIVITY

Identify and Locate Provide each student with a copy of the outline map of North America found on page 25 of the Outline Map Resource Book. Have students locate and label each of the places listed at the beginning of the sections in this chapter. Then have partners compare their completed maps, resolve any discrepancies, and revise as needed. Remind students to include a map key and compass rose on their maps. Display the completed maps on a classroom bulletin board. **EE1 The World in Spatial Terms: Standard 1**

GLENCOE TECHNOLOGY

Use *MindJogger Videoquiz* to review the Chapter 6 content.

Reviewing Key Terms

1. socioeconomic status
2. patriotism
3. literacy rate
4. immigration
5. metropolitan area
6. republic
7. megalopolis
8. dominion
9. bilingual
10. dry farming

Reviewing Facts

SECTION 1

1. Europe
2. near the United States border

SECTION 2

3. provided routes and safe houses
4. completion of transcontinental railroads, dry farming, and mass production, especially of the automobile

SECTION 3

5. Both countries are predominantly Christian. Canada mostly Roman Catholic; the United States, mostly Protestant
6. Writers began to focus on particular regions, such as Mark Twain describing the Mississippi River.

Reviewing Key Terms

On a sheet of paper, write the key term that matches the definition. Refer to the Terms to Know in the Summary & Study Guide on page 153.

1. level of income and education
2. loyalty to one's country
3. percentage of people who can read and write
4. the movement of people into one country from another
5. a central city and outlying communities
6. a government in which people elect their own officials
7. a chain of closely linked urban areas and suburbs
8. partially self-governing country with close British ties
9. ability to use two languages
10. cultivating land so that it catches and holds rainwater

Reviewing Facts

SECTION 1

1. Most settlers in the United States and Canada came from what region of the world?
2. Where is most of Canada's population concentrated?

SECTION 2

3. Explain how the Underground Railroad helped enslaved African Americans escape to freedom.
4. What three technological innovations led to the expansion and development of the United States?

SECTION 3

5. What is the most widely practiced religion in Canada? In the United States?
6. How did the literature of the United States begin to change in the late 1800s?

Critical Thinking

1. **Making Generalizations** How did physical features influence population patterns and urbanization in the United States and Canada?
2. **Drawing Conclusions** Explain how diverse ethnic groups influenced the development of the region's arts.
3. **Comparing and Contrasting** Use a Venn diagram to compare and contrast the governments of the United States and Canada.

Government

United States | Both | Canada

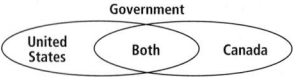

Locating Places
The United States and Canada: Physical-Political Geography

Match the letters on the map with the places and physical features of the United States and Canada. Write your answers on a sheet of paper.

1. Texas	5. Alberta	9. Detroit
2. Great Salt Lake	6. New Mexico	10. Nunavut
3. Nova Scotia	7. Miami	11. British Columbia
4. Quebec	8. Pennsylvania	12. Hudson Bay

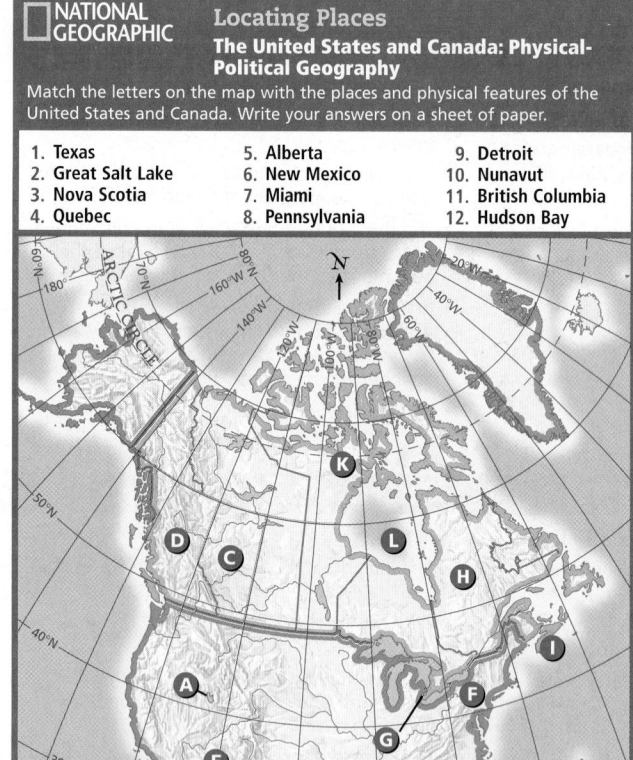

0 mi. 500
0 km 500
Azimuthal Equidistant projection

Critical Thinking

1. Some physical features, such as bodies of water, encouraged population growth, but others, such as deserts and mountains, inhibited population growth.
2. They helped create unique art forms, such as jazz, which blended African rhythms with European harmonies.
3. Diagrams should show that both countries have the same three branches of government, but there are differences in the executive branch.

Locating Places

1. B	**3.** I	**5.** C	**7.** J	**9.** G	**11.** D
2. A	**4.** H	**6.** E	**8.** F	**10.** K	**12.** L

Using the Regional Atlas

Refer to the Regional Atlas on pages 106–109.

1. **Human-Environment Interaction** Compare the political map to the economic activity map. What commercial crops are grown in the southern United States?

2. **Place** Compare the population density map to the political map. What states and provinces have the highest population density?

Thinking Like a Geographer

Describe the effects of cultural diffusion between the United States and Canada and other parts of the world in recent decades. Trace this process, using specific examples, such as films, music, foods, and American slang.

Problem-Solving Activity

Group Research Project Research U.S. voting patterns and the distribution of political power. Study a map showing the outcome of the latest congressional election, district by district. Then compare it to a map of a previous race. Write a report explaining the political changes from one election to the next as well as the factors shaping the formation of congressional voting districts.

GeoJournal

Expository Writing Using your GeoJournal data, write an essay analyzing the effects of processes, such as migration, on the territorial growth of the United States and Canada.

Technology Activity

Developing Multimedia Presentations Choose one Native American or immigrant group and describe its influences on the region's cultures and lifestyles. Include contributions such as religion, language, the arts, food, clothing, and celebrations. Create a multimedia presentation that displays examples of these contributions and explains their origins. To enhance your presentation, play music appropriate to the group you choose for the class.

Standardized Test Practice

Choose the best answer for each of the following multiple-choice questions. If you have trouble answering the questions, use the process of elimination to narrow your choices.

1. **Researchers using GIS and GPS technology to correlate water quality indexes, zoning maps, census figures, and maps of area rivers and aquifers are most likely trying to determine which of the following?**

   A The relationship between the location of industrial plants and water quality

   B The water pressure for new fire hydrants for a developing community

   C The location of scenic hiking trails

   D The lung disease rates for various areas in the region

Test-Taking Tip Several of the data elements correlated by the researchers relate to water. Eliminate those answers that do not relate to water.

2. **Ships at sea use GPS technology**

   F as a communication device.

   G as a navigational aid.

   H for inventory control.

   J to maintain personnel files.

Test-Taking Tip If you know that GPS technology deals with precise positioning data, you can eliminate choices H and J, and choose the best answer from the answer choices that remain.

GeoJournal

Students' essays should be organized and developed, using examples of migrations and their impact from their study of this chapter.

Technology Activity

Allow time for students to present their multimedia program to the class, answer questions, and receive feedback from their audience.

Standardized Test Practice

1. A
2. G

Tested Objectives:
analyzing information
recalling information

Additional Practice and Test-Taking Tips

 Standardized Test Practice Workbook

CHAPTER BONUS TEST QUESTION

What effect do you think physical geography has on the way of life of people in the United States and Canada?

(Answers should indicate that landscapes and climates influence housing, clothing, economic activities, and recreation. These factors may also influence human characteristics, such as etiquette or sociability.)

Using the Regional Atlas

1. cotton, tobacco, fruit, pecans
2. Massachusetts, Rhode Island, Connecticut, New York, New Jersey, Pennsylvania, Delaware, Maryland, California, Washington, Ontario, and British Columbia

Thinking Like a Geographer

Students should mention that today's global culture has been greatly shaped by the export of U.S. culture. The United States and Canada, however, have been transformed by other cultures.

Problem-Solving Activity

Be sure all students in each group have an assigned task. One or two students could research information for the more recent map. Other students might research data for the earlier map. After they gather information, each group could appoint one person to jot down brainstorming ideas, another to put together an outline or graphic organizer, one to write the rough draft, and another to make revisions and proofread the final draft.

PLANNING GUIDE

NOTE: The following materials may be used when teaching Chapter 7. Section-level support materials are shown at point-of-use in the margins of the Teacher Wraparound Edition.

TEACHING TRANSPARENCIES

L2 Unit 2 Map Overlay Transparencies

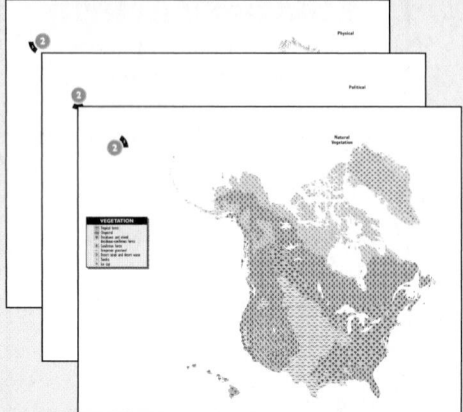

L2 Political Map Transparency 2

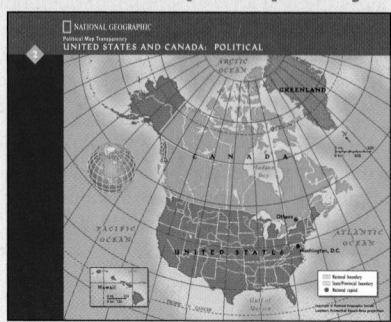

GEOGRAPHIC LITERACY

Focus on Geography Literacy

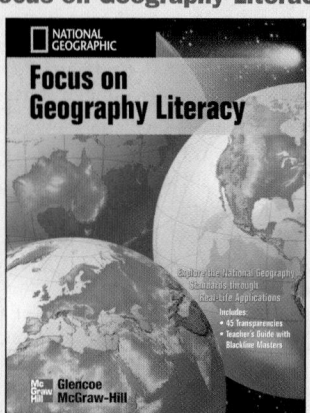

APPLICATION AND ENRICHMENT

L3 Enrichment Activity 7

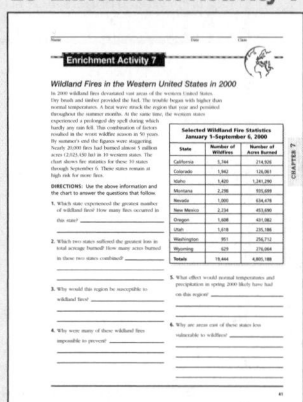

REVIEW AND REINFORCEMENT

L1 Vocabulary Activity 7   L1 Reinforcing Skills Activity 7   L1 Reteaching Activity 7

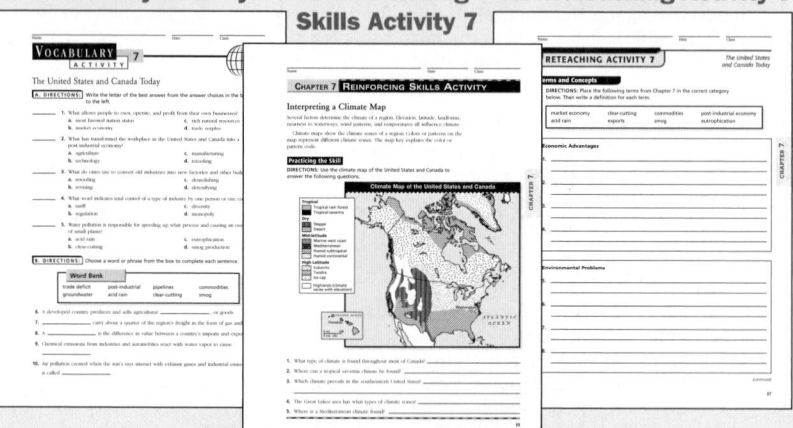

ASSESSMENT

L2 Chapter 7 Test Form A

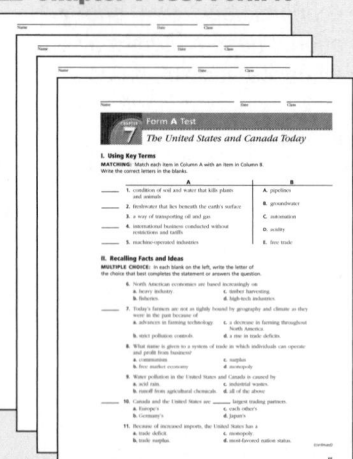

L2 Chapter 7 Test Form B

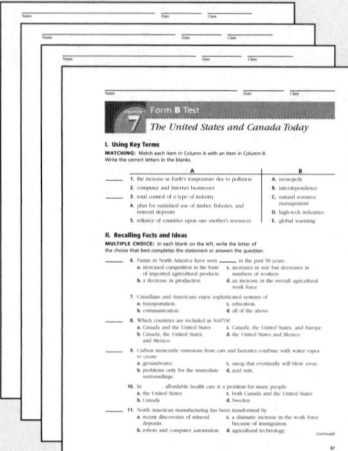

L1/ELL Performance Assessment Activity 7

ExamView® Pro Testmaker

SPANISH RESOURCES

The following Spanish language materials are available in the Spanish Resources binder:

- 📁 Spanish Vocabulary Activities
- 📁 Spanish Guided Reading Activities
- 📁 Spanish Reteaching Activities
- 📁 Spanish Summaries
- 📁 Spanish Quizzes and Tests
- 📁 Spanish Reading Essentials and Study Guide

MULTIMEDIA

- 📼 ⊙ World Regions Video
- 📼 MindJogger Videoquiz
- 💿 Vocabulary PuzzleMaker CD-ROM
- 💿 Interactive Tutor Self-Assessment CD-ROM
- 💿 ExamView® Pro Testmaker CD-ROM
- 💿 Audio Program
- 💿 TeacherWorks CD-ROM
- 💿 Interactive Student Edition CD-ROM
- 💿 Glencoe Skillbuilder Interactive Workbook CD-ROM, Level 2
- 💿 Presentation Plus! CD-ROM

Timesaving Tools

TeacherWorks™ All-In-One Planner and Resource Center

- **Interactive Teacher Edition** Access your Teacher Wraparound Edition and your classroom resources with a few easy clicks.

- **Interactive Lesson Planner** Planning has never been easier! Organize your week, month, semester, or year with all the lesson helps you need to make teaching creative, timely, and relevant.

Use Glencoe's **Presentation Plus!** multimedia teacher tool to easily present dynamic lessons that visually excite your students. Using Microsoft PowerPoint® you can customize the presentations to create your own personalized lessons.

GEOGRAPHY Online

Use our Web site for additional resources. All essential content is covered in the Student Edition.

You and your students can visit geography.glencoe.com, the Web site companion to *Glencoe World Geography*. This innovative integration of electronic and print media offers your students a wealth of opportunities. The student text directs students to the Web site for the following options:

- Chapter Overviews
- Self-Check Quizzes
- Student Activities
- Textbook Updates

Answers are provided for you in the "Web Activity Lesson Plan." Additional Web resources and Interactive Tutor puzzles are also available.

▶ Additional Glencoe Teacher Support

- Teaching Strategies for the Geography Classroom (including Block Scheduling Pacing Guides)
- Graphic Organizer Transparencies Strategies and Activities
- Outline Map Resource Book
- Reading in the Content Area

PLANNING GUIDE

SECTION RESOURCES

Daily Objectives	Reproducible Resources	Multimedia Resources

SECTION 1 Living in the United States and Canada

1. Explain the effects of physical geography on the region's agriculture.
2. Identify the kinds of transportation and communications systems in the region.
3. Describe how the economies of the United States and Canada are dependent on each other and interdependent with those in other parts of the world.

 Reproducible Lesson Plan 7-1
 Daily Lecture Notes 7-1
Guided Reading Activity 7-1*
Reading Essentials and Study Guide 7-1*
 Section Quiz 7-1*

- Daily Focus Skills Transparency 7-1
- Political Map Transparency 2
- Unit 2 Map Overlay Transparencies
- World Art and Architecture Transparencies
- Interactive Tutor Self-Assessment CD-ROM
- ExamView® Pro Testmaker CD-ROM*
- Presentation Plus! CD-ROM

SECTION 2 People and Their Environment

1. Explain how the United States and Canada are learning to manage their natural resources responsibly.
2. Identify causes and effects of pollution in the region, and discuss how it can be prevented.
3. Discuss the environmental challenges faced by the United States and Canada in the 2000s, both as individual countries and as a region.

 Reproducible Lesson Plan 7-2
Vocabulary Activity 7
 Daily Lecture Notes 7-2
 Guided Reading Activity 7-2*
 Reading Essentials and Study Guide 7-2*
 Reteaching Activity 7*
 Reinforcing Skills Activity 7
 Section Quiz 7-2*

- Daily Focus Skills Transparency 7-2
- Political Map Transparency 2
- Unit 2 Map Overlay Transparencies
- Vocabulary PuzzleMaker CD-ROM
- Interactive Tutor Self-Assessment CD-ROM
- ExamView® Pro Testmaker CD-ROM*
- Presentation Plus! CD-ROM

 Blackline Master   ■ Software   ▥ Videocassette   *Also available in Spanish*

 Transparency   ◉ CD-ROM   ◉ DVD

OUT OF TIME?  Assign the Chapter 7 **Reading Essentials and Study Guide.**

Block Schedule

Activities that are particularly suited to use within the block scheduling framework are identified throughout this chapter by the following designation: 🔲

KEY TO ABILITY LEVELS

Teaching strategies have been coded for various learning styles and abilities.

L1 BASIC activities for all students

L2 AVERAGE activities for average to above-average students

L3 CHALLENGING activities for above-average students

ELL ENGLISH LANGUAGE LEARNER activities

Teacher to Teacher

Jon Eno
Baldwin High School
Wailuku, HI

Comparison and Contrast Showdown

Gather students into cooperative learning groups of four. Further organize each group into two pairs. Ask one pair to come up with four similarities between the United States and Canada while the remaining pair lists four differences between the two countries.

After giving the class time to assemble their lists, have the pairs within the groups trade lists. Students who listed similarities should review the list of differences, for example, to see if differences trigger additional ideas for their list of similarities. Then the pairs should return the lists to the original authors for additions or changes.

When students have completed their lists, have them use the information to plan, organize, and develop an essay titled *Analyzing the Canadian Culture, Analyzing the United States Culture,* or *Comparing Cultures: the United States and Canada.* Encourage students to work with an English teacher if they need help in developing a thesis or organizing their materials.

TEACHER'S CORNER

Index to National Geographic Magazine:

The following articles may be used for research relating to this chapter:

- "Big Sur," by Pico Iyer, August 2000.
- "Playing the Slots," by Scott Thybony, July 2000.
- "Cape Hatteras Lighthouse," by Angus Phillips, May 2000.
- "San Pedro River," by Barbara Kingsolver, April 2000.

National Geographic Society Products:

To order the following products for use with this chapter, call National Geographic Society at 1-800-368-2728.

- *GeoKit: Pollution* (Kit)
- *Recycling: The Endless Circle* (Video)
- *Technology's Price* (Video)
- *An Ecosystem: A Struggle for Survival* (Video)
- *The Living Ocean* (Video)
- *Investigating Global Warming* (Video)

NGS ONLINE

Access National Geographic's Web site for current events, activities, links, interactive features, and archives.
www.nationalgeographic.com

Meeting National Standards

Geography For Life

The following standards are highlighted in Chapter 7:

Section 1   EE2 Places and Regions: Standard 6
EE4 Human Systems: Standards 9, 11
EE5 Environment and Society: Standard 14

Section 2   EE2 Places and Regions: Standard 4
EE3 Physical Systems: Standard 8
EE4 Human Systems: Standard 12
EE5 Environment and Society: Standards 14, 15

Local Objectives

_____

_____

MEETING SPECIAL NEEDS

In addition to the Differentiated Instruction strategies found in each section, the following resources are also suitable for your special needs students:

- **ExamView® Pro Testmaker CD-ROM** allows teachers to tailor tests by reducing answer choices.
- The **Audio Program** includes the entire narrative of the student edition so that less-proficient readers can listen to the words as they read them.
- The **Reading Essentials and Study Guide** provides the same content as the student edition but is written two grade levels below the textbook.
- **Guided Reading Activities** give less-proficient readers point-by-point instructions to increase comprehension as they read each textbook section.
- **Enrichment Activities** include a stimulating collection of readings and activities for gifted and talented students.

Chapter Objectives

1. Describe the economic activities of the United States and Canada, and identify the transportation and communications systems.

2. Discuss the challenges faced by the United States and Canada in managing their natural resources, preventing pollution, and facing environmental challenges.

GLENCOE TECHNOLOGY

Use *MindJogger Videoquiz* to preview the Chapter 7 content.

GeoJournal

For access to additional photos, maps, and information on the contemporary issues in the United States and Canada, go to www.nationalgeographic.com (See Teacher pages in front for strategies for using journals in the geography classroom.)

GEOGRAPHY Online

Introduce students to chapter content and key terms by having them access **Chapter Overview 7** at geography.glencoe.com

FOLDABLES™
Study Organizer

Dinah Zike's Foldables are three-dimensional, interactive graphic organizers that help students practice basic writing skills, review key vocabulary terms, and identify main ideas. Have students complete the Foldable activity in the **Dinah Zike's Reading and Study Skills Foldables** booklet.

CHAPTER

7

The United States and Canada Today

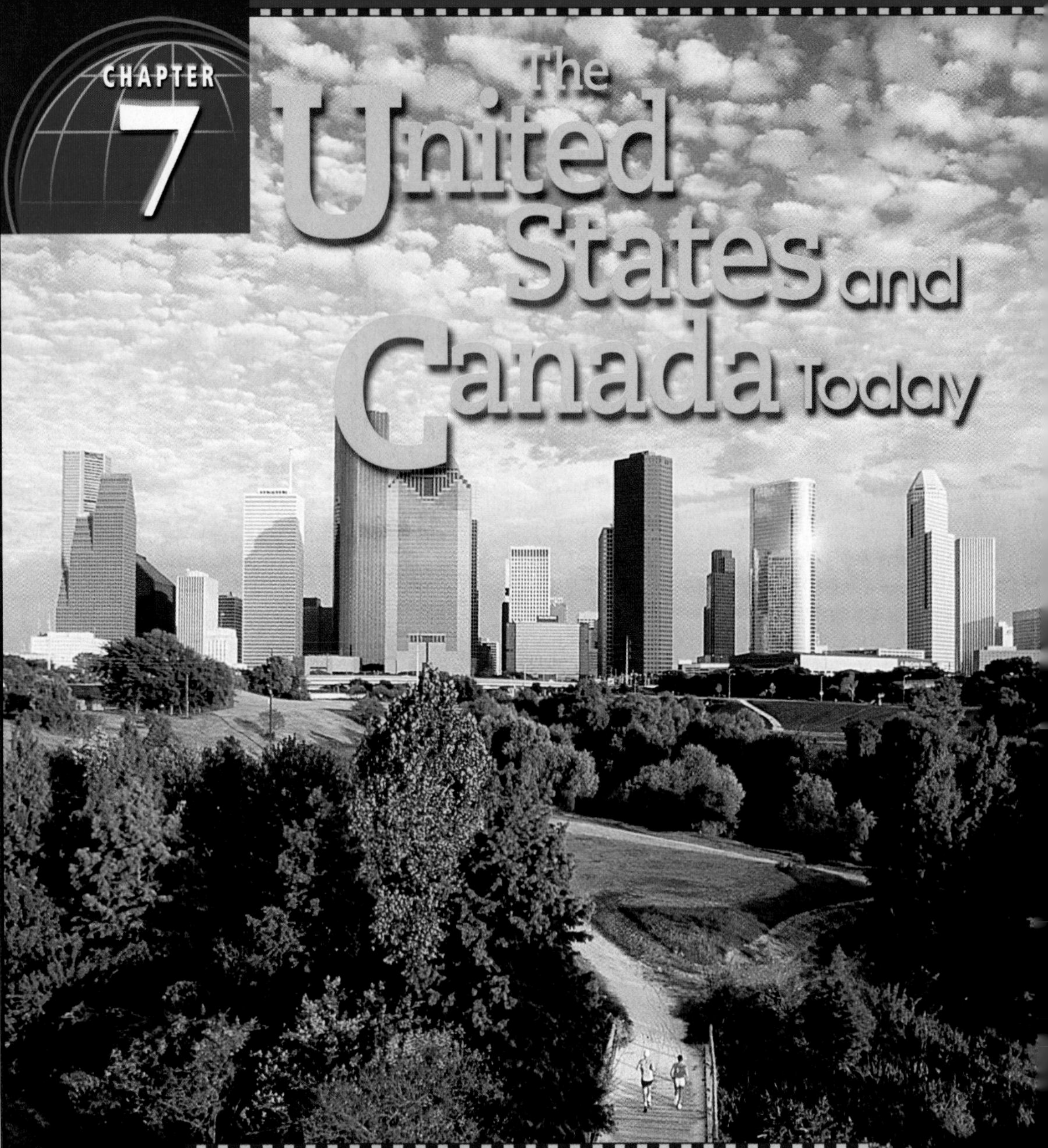

GeoJournal

As you read this chapter, take notes in your journal on the economic activities, transportation, communications, and environmental concerns of the United States and Canada.

GEOGRAPHY Online

Chapter Overview Visit the **Glencoe World Geography** Web site at geography.glencoe.com and click on Chapter Overviews—Chapter 7 to preview information about the region today.

ABOUT THE PHOTO

Visual Instruction Houston is the fourth largest city in the United States and one of the world's major seaports. An air-conditioned underground tunnel system, with its own stores and restaurants, connects many downtown buildings, enabling people to move about in comfort despite the hot, humid climate. In 1965 the world's first baseball and football stadium to be completely enclosed by a roof, the Astrodome, was built in Houston. Today, the Astrodome serves as an exhibition and conference hall and arena. **Ask**: Why do you suppose the Astrodome was completely enclosed when it was built? *(Fans could attend sporting events in air-conditioned comfort in Houston's hot, humid climate.)*

⊕ **EE4 Human Systems: Standard 11**

Guide to Reading

Consider What You Know

People in the United States and Canada depend heavily on the automobile for personal travel. How is travel by automobile different from travel by bus or train? How do you think dependence on automobiles has influenced the development of new neighborhoods?

Reading Strategy

Categorizing Complete a graphic organizer similar to the one below by identifying the location of the "belt" regions listed.

"Belt" Region	Location
Wheat Belt	
Corn Belt	
Rust Belt	
Sun Belt	

Read to Find Out

- What are the effects of physical geography on the region's agriculture?
- What kinds of transportation and communications systems does the region have?
- How are the economies of the United States and Canada interdependent with each other and those in other parts of the world?

Terms to Know

- market economy
- post-industrial
- commodity
- retooling
- pipeline
- monopoly
- trade deficit
- tariff
- trade surplus

Places to Locate

- Corn Belt
- New York State
- Minnesota
- Seattle
- Research Triangle
- Pittsburgh
- Trans-Canada Highway

◀ *The skyline of Houston, Texas*

Living in the United States and Canada

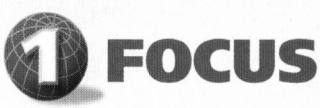

NATIONAL GEOGRAPHIC

A Geographic View

An Occasion to Celebrate

County fairs endure as an occasion to celebrate our agrarian traditions, to honor family, inventiveness, and hard work. More important, perhaps, they allow us, as communities, to come together and get to know one another. County fairs also give us a chance to glimpse the American past. Yet they have lasted not by being annual historical reenactments but by evolving as American society evolves and becomes more urban.

—*John McCarry, "County Fairs,"* National Geographic, *October 1997*

County fair, Vermont

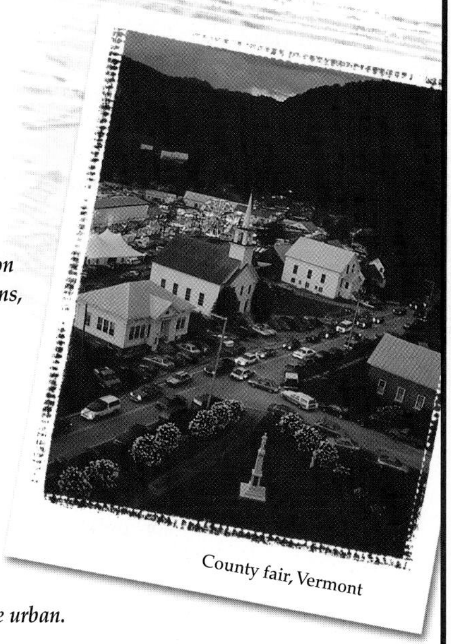

Urban lifestyles predominate in the United States and Canada, yet people in both countries continue to respect traditional rural values, such as inventiveness and hard work. Adhering to these values, Americans and Canadians have utilized their rich natural resources and technological skills, placing their countries among the world's top economic powers. In this section you will learn how people in the United States and Canada make their livings and how their economies are interrelated with each other and with the rest of the world.

Economic Activities

The United States and Canada both have free **market economies**, which allow people the freedom to own, operate, and profit from their own businesses. Businesses can hire employees and pay them for their work. Laws protect private property rights, employment

RESOURCE MANAGER

Reproducible Masters
- Reproducible Lesson Plan 7-1
- Daily Lecture Notes 7-1
- Guided Reading Activity 7-1
- Reading Essentials and Study Guide 7-1
- Section Quiz 7-1

Transparencies
- Daily Focus Skills Transparency 7-1
- Political Map Transparency 2
- Unit 2 Map Overlay Transparencies
- World Art and Architecture Transparencies

Multimedia
- Interactive Tutor Self-Assessment CD-ROM
- ExamView® Pro Testmaker CD-ROM
- Presentation Plus! CD-ROM

1 FOCUS

Section Overview

This section discusses the region's agriculture, transportation and communications networks, and the economies of the United States and Canada.

BELLRINGER
Skillbuilder Activity

Project the transparency and have students answer questions.

Available as blackline master.

Daily Focus Skills Transparency 7-1

Guide to Reading

Consider What You Know

Answers *Answers may include that the automobile is more convenient, but dependence on it has encouraged urban sprawl.*

Reading Strategy

Answers Wheat Belt: *Great Plains of United States and Prairie Provinces of Canada;* Corn Belt: *Ohio to Nebraska in United States and Quebec, Ontario, Manitoba in Canada;* Rust Belt: *Great Lakes cities, Buffalo, Cleveland, Detroit, Pittsburgh;* Sun Belt: *southern United States*

Preteaching Vocabulary

Have students identify the following word parts: *post (after), re (again), mono (one).* Tell them to find and explain three vocabulary words that contain these prefixes.

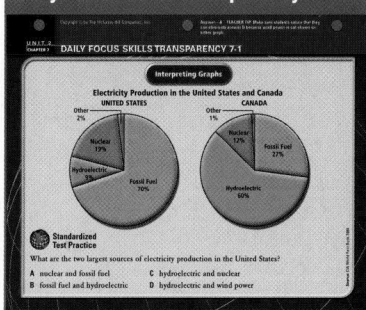

②TEACH

L1 Identify

Based on the map on page 109, have students identify the major economic activities of the state in which they live. Ask them to write one or more statements about their state's economy, using as many of the words in "Terms to Know" as possible.

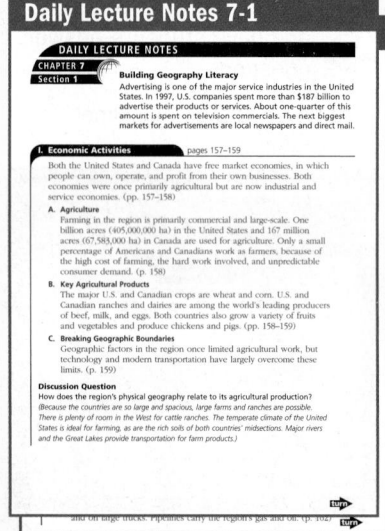

Daily Lecture Notes 7-1

NATIONAL GEOGRAPHIC World Explorer

Answer
in the Great Plains

More About the Photo
Today the Prairie Provinces of Alberta, Saskatchewan, and Manitoba produce most of Canada's wheat.

---

opportunities, and the health and safety of workers. Although their economies are similar, the United States and Canada take different approaches to the ownership of some corporations and the administration of some services. In Canada the government owns and administers many services, such as broadcasting and health care, that tend to be handled by private, nongovernmental corporations in the United States.

Like other developed countries, the United States and Canada have moved from primarily agricultural to primarily industrialized economies. As technology transforms the workplace, both countries are developing post-industrial economies, which place less emphasis on heavy industry and traditional manufacturing and more emphasis on service and high-tech businesses. Agriculture and manufacturing continue to play significant roles in the region's economic life, however.

Agriculture

As in most developed countries, farming in the United States and Canada is overwhelmingly commercial, with agricultural commodities, or goods, produced for sale. Large commercial corporations, however, account for only 5 percent of farm

NATIONAL GEOGRAPHIC World Explorer

Geography **Skills for Life**
------------------------------- **Wheat Harvest** The
Peace River area of British Columbia produces most of the grain harvested in the province.
Place Where is wheat grown in the United States?

ownership. Most farms in the United States and Canada, no matter what their size, are still owned by farming families, many of whom have formed cooperative operations.

The United States devotes about 1 billion acres (405,000,000 ha) of land to agriculture. A little less than half of that total is cropland—the largest cropland area of any country in the world—and the rest is used for the grazing of livestock. Canada, with much less arable land than the United States, still devotes 167 million acres (67,583,000 ha) to agriculture, evenly divided between crops and livestock.

Since the 1950s, although the average size of farms in the United States and Canada has risen, the number of people employed as farmers in the region has decreased. Today only 2 percent of Americans and 4 percent of Canadians work in agriculture. Among the factors contributing to this decline is the high cost of farming. Successful agriculture requires investing in expensive machinery, fertilizers, and chemical pesticides—all of which make farming easier but drive up costs and impact profits. Another factor is unpredictable consumer demand. If a farm product produced in large quantities—such as hogs or cranberries—does not sell well on the market, farmers have to lower their prices for the product and may lose money as a result. The risk of natural disasters and the time and hard work needed to run a farm also contribute to fewer farmers entering this segment of the economy.

Key Agricultural Products

The United States and Canada rank among the world's leading producers of beef, milk, and eggs, and of corn, wheat, and other grains. These agricultural products are shipped to markets across the country and around the world.

Cattle ranches operate mostly in the western, southern, and midwestern United States and in Canada's western Prairie Provinces. Other important livestock-producing areas include the north-central parts of the United States and the Canadian

---

DIFFERENTIATED INSTRUCTION

Verbal/Linguistic Bring to class a copy of *Blue Highways* by William Least Heat Moon. Explain that maps use different colors for different kinds of roads. The book title comes from the blue used for secondary road systems. Read two or three passages aloud to students and show them some of the author's photographs. Explain that the writer traveled blue highways, keeping a journal of his experiences. Have students think about journeys they have taken or would like to take and write a description of the trip. Encourage them to describe their emotional reactions to the people as well as to the locations. 📦

🌐 **EE2 Places and Regions: Standard 6**

📁 Refer to *Inclusion for the Social Studies Classroom Strategies and Activities.*

provinces of Quebec and Ontario. Hogs, chickens, and dairy products also lead the list of farm products from these areas.

Wheat is grown in the Prairie Provinces of Canada and on the Great Plains of the United States, a region often called the Wheat Belt. The type of wheat grown depends on the climate. Farmers in the northern plains, with their short growing season, concentrate on spring wheat, which is planted in the spring and harvested in the fall. Farther south, farmers plant winter wheat, which germinates before the ground freezes, grows with the spring rains, and is harvested in the early summer.

The **Corn Belt** of the United States consists of a band of farmland stretching from Ohio to Nebraska. Corn is also grown in the Canadian provinces of Quebec, Ontario, and Manitoba. About 50 percent of the corn crop is used to feed livestock; the rest is processed to make sweeteners and corn oil, used in industrial manufacturing, or used for food by people.

Fruits and vegetables are grown in many parts of the United States and Canada. Apples, peaches, and cherries flourish in the Great Lakes region and in the St. Lawrence River Valley. Potatoes are an important crop in the U.S. states of Maine, North Dakota, and Idaho as well as in the Canadian provinces of Prince Edward Island and New Brunswick. California ranks first among U.S. states in the production of tomatoes, lettuce, peas, asparagus, okra, avocados, grapes, and strawberries. Citrus fruits are grown in central and southern Florida, in the lower Rio Grande Valley of Texas, and in southern California. Sugarcane, pineapples, and bananas are grown in Hawaii.

Economics
Breaking Geographic Boundaries

Throughout much of the region's history, geographic factors often limited the type of agriculture that could be carried out in a particular area. Cattle ranching, for example, needed the wide open spaces and natural grasses of the western prairies and plains. Most American dairy farms were con-

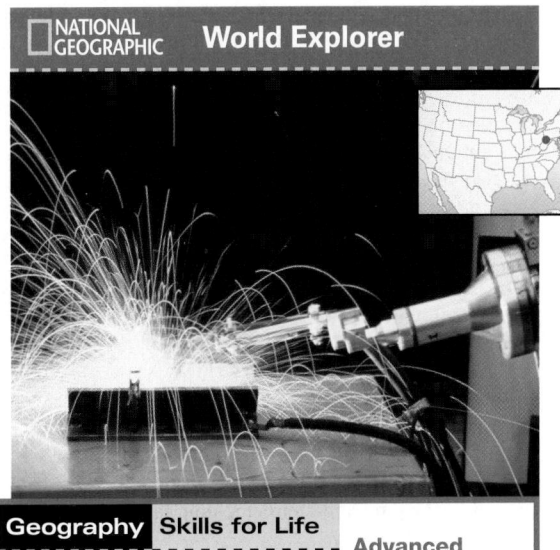

NATIONAL GEOGRAPHIC World Explorer

Geography | **Skills for Life**
Advanced
Technologies Automation and robotics have revolutionized heavy industry in the United States and Canada.
Place What kinds of industries might use robots for welding?

centrated in a belt of land stretching from upper **New York State** to **Minnesota**. This region, known as America's Dairyland, has cooler summers and native grasses ideal for dairy cattle.

Advances in agricultural technology have changed the traditional growing areas to include states like New Mexico. The development of breeds of cattle that need less room to roam has opened the southern United States to cattle ranching. Because of improved feed sources and automation, large productive dairy farms can now be found in every American state and many Canadian provinces.

Manufacturing and Service Industries

Manufacturing makes up about 20 percent of both the United States and Canadian economies and employs about 20 percent of the region's workforce. Advanced technologies, such as robotics and computerized automation, have transformed manufacturing in the region. As with farming, the region's factories produce greater quantities of goods with fewer workers than in the past.

Chapter 7 ⊕ 159

L3 Apply

Help students apply their understanding of the relationship between place characteristics and economic activity. **Ask: Why would people in Boston be less likely to buy Florida tomatoes in summer than in winter?** *(Local truck farms provide northeasterners with fresh vegetables in summer.)*

High-Tech Industry The strong U.S. economy of the 1990s made central Texas a leader in the high-tech industry. One of the world's largest direct-sale computer producers is headquartered in Austin, Texas, as are several computer chip manufacturing firms. Together, these companies employ tens of thousands of people. Their presence, in turn, has an impact on the state's shipping industry. Hundreds of trucks are dispatched daily with the finished products.

□ NATIONAL GEOGRAPHIC **GEOFACT**

▶ Route 66, the celebrated road from Chicago to southern California, lost much of its traffic and its allure after a number of more modern highways were built in the 1970s. The 2,448-mile (3,940-km) route is making a comeback, however. The U.S. Department of the Interior will spend $10 million by 2010 to preserve Route 66.

Transportation equipment and machinery are large export categories of both countries. In the United States, aircraft and aerospace equipment are produced in California and Washington, and factories in the Midwest produce most of the country's automobiles. United States auto manufacturers also operate plants in Quebec and Ontario. Food processing is another important economic activity in California and in the northeastern United States. Canada, especially Quebec, manufactures and exports a variety of wood-based products drawn from its timber resources.

Post-Industrial Economies

The largest area of economic growth in the United States and Canada is in service industries. About 75 percent of the region's workers are employed in service jobs, such as government, education, health care, tourism, entertainment, banking, and real estate.

The rising post-industrial economy is best reflected in the region's high-tech and biotechnology industries. Both countries produce high-tech equipment for use in computer sciences and telecommunications. California's Silicon Valley, for example, is home to around 20 of the world's 100 largest high-tech companies. Led by the development of high-tech industries in **Seattle**, the state of Washington has the sixth-highest concentration of high-tech businesses in the United States. Texas boasts more than 1,000 software companies in its capital city of Austin, and some of the fastest-growing high-tech companies are based in Dallas. Raleigh, Durham, and Chapel Hill, known as North Carolina's **Research Triangle**, have attracted prestigious biotechnology companies. Boston is a leading area in software, telecommunications, and media technology. In Canada, Ontario is home to many thriving telecommunications and Internet businesses.

Retooling the Rust Belt

During the last third of the 1900s, the switch from heavy industry and traditional manufacturing to service industries left cities in the east and near the Great Lakes, such as Buffalo, Pittsburgh, Cleveland, and Detroit, without their major economic bases. As corporations began to move

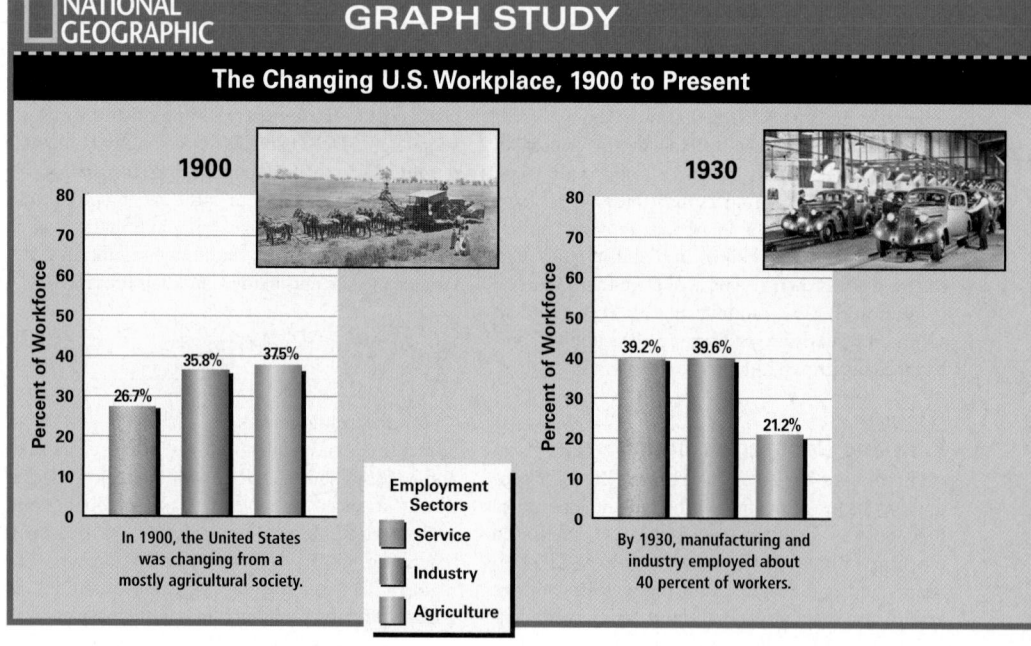

NATIONAL GEOGRAPHIC — **GRAPH STUDY**

The Changing U.S. Workplace, 1900 to Present

1900
Percent of Workforce: 26.7%, 35.8%, 37.5%
In 1900, the United States was changing from a mostly agricultural society.

1930
Percent of Workforce: 39.2%, 39.6%, 21.2%
By 1930, manufacturing and industry employed about 40 percent of workers.

Employment Sectors
Service
Industry
Agriculture

CRITICAL THINKING ACTIVITY

Analyzing Information Have students read the material under "Manufacturing and Service Industries" in this section and reflect on occupational trends that are discussed. Then ask them to identify three jobs that they think may have potential for growth in the 2000s. Students should support their choices with sound reasoning. In addition to the material in the book, students might consult a reference, such as the *Occupational Handbook*, for additional information and help in supporting their choices. Have students explain their choices in a class discussion. Write their choices on the board, and take a vote to determine the occupations students feel are most likely to have high rates of growth in the future. ▦ **EE4 Human Systems: Standard 11**

south to the Sunbelt, some older industrial areas were left with abandoned factories and rusting steel mills. Together they acquired the derogatory nickname "the Rust Belt." Today, however, many of these cities are converting old factories for use in new industries, a process called retooling, and transforming run-down areas into tourist attractions and public spaces. For cities such as Pittsburgh, this change has brought renewed energy:

❝ *shaken by the collapse of the steel industry, which had provided them with an unshakable sense of identity for more than a century, Pittsburghers hunkered down and built a new economy based on services, medicine, education, and technology. In the process, they transformed their community from one driven by quantity of production into one devoted to quality of life.* ❞

Peter Miller, "Pittsburgh: Stronger than Steel," *National Geographic*, December 1991

Transportation and Communications

Good transportation and reliable communications systems are the backbone of economic success in the United States and Canada. Both also contribute to the quality of life in the region today.

The Automobile

Since World War II, the most popular means of personal transportation in the United States and Canada has been the automobile. Extensive automobile use in the region has required heavy investment in the building and maintenance of highways, roads, and bridges. In the United States, more than 3,900,000 miles (6,276,442 km) of streets, roads, and highways carry about 208 million motor vehicles each year. Canada's smaller, more concentrated population relies on about 15 million motor vehicles and 550,000 miles (885,139 km) of roads. The **Trans-Canada Highway**, a well-maintained modern roadway, runs 4,860 miles (7,821 km) from Victoria, British Columbia, to St. John's, Newfoundland.

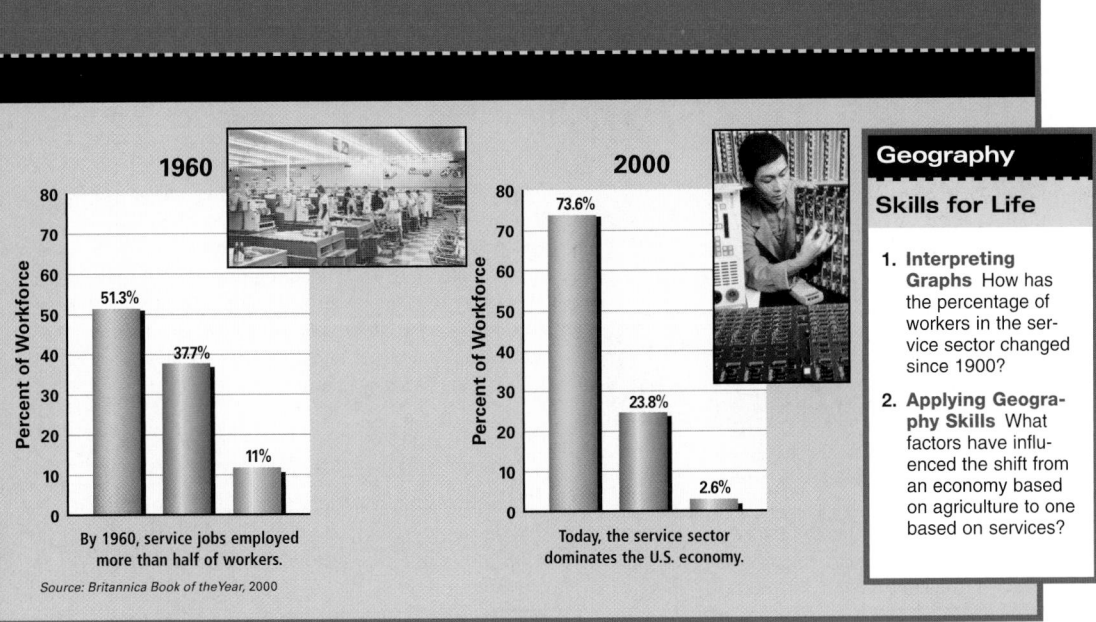

1960

Percent of Workforce

51.3%

37.7%

11%

By 1960, service jobs employed more than half of workers.

Source: Britannica Book of the Year, 2000

2000

Percent of Workforce

73.6%

23.8%

2.6%

Today, the service sector dominates the U.S. economy.

Geography

Skills for Life

1. **Interpreting Graphs** How has the percentage of workers in the service sector changed since 1900?

2. **Applying Geography Skills** What factors have influenced the shift from an economy based on agriculture to one based on services?

Chapter 7 ⊕ 161

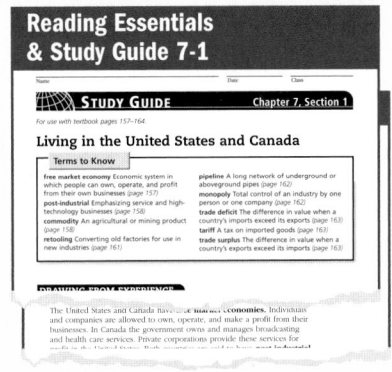

Reading Essentials & Study Guide 7-1

For use with textbook pages 157–164

STUDY GUIDE Chapter 7, Section 1

Living in the United States and Canada

Terms to Know

free market economy Economic system in which people can own, operate, and profit from their own businesses (page 157)
post-industrial Emphasizing service and high-technology industries (page 158)
commodity An agricultural or mining product (page 158)
retooling Converting old factories for use in new industries (page 161)

pipeline A long network of underground or aboveground pipes (page 162)
monopoly Total control of an industry by one person or one company (page 162)
trade deficit The difference in value when a country's imports exceed its exports (page 163)
tariff A tax on imported goods (page 163)
trade surplus The difference in value when a country's exports exceed its imports (page 163)

The United States and Canada have free market economies. Individuals and companies are allowed to own, operate, and make a profit from their businesses. In Canada the government owns and manages broadcasting and health care services. Private corporations provide these services for profit in the United States. Both economies are said to be post-industrial.

NATIONAL GEOGRAPHIC **GRAPH STUDY**

Answers

1. *It has gone from the lowest to the highest percentage.*

2. *Technological advances in agriculture and industry led to a decreased demand for workers, while advances in service industry led to increased demand for workers.*

Skills Practice

About how much larger was the service sector in 1998 than the industry and agriculture sectors combined? *(about 47 percent)*

Highway System The Federal Interstate Highway System was started in the 1950s during the Eisenhower administration. Under this system, even-numbered highways run east and west; odd-numbered highways run north and south.

TEAM-TEACHING ACTIVITY: JOURNALISM

Newspaper Writing Explain that many news stories begin with a "lead," an opening sentence that answers the following questions: *Who? What? When? Where? Why?* and *How?* Model a lead about the factors affecting closer U.S.-Canadian-Mexican trade links, based on in the text material on pages 163-164: The United States, Canada, and Mexico (*who*) moved to end trade barriers (*what*) in 1992 (*when*) by signing the North American Free Trade Agreement, or NAFTA (*how*). Tell students to use the topics in this section to write five sentences in the style of a newspaper lead. Encourage students to work with a journalism teacher to develop a lead into a news story.

🌐 **EE5 Environment and Society: Standard 14**

NATIONAL GEOGRAPHIC World Explorer

Answer
rail, water, air, pipelines

More About the Photo
About 80 percent of the truck traffic from Mexico enters the U.S. through Texas, a direct result of the 1994 trade agreement known as NAFTA (North American Free Trade Agreement). Interstate 35 carries much of this traffic through the country's heartland, starting at the U.S.-Mexico border in Laredo, Texas, and ending north of Duluth, Minnesota, near the Canadian border.

INTERDISCIPLINARY
connection

CLIMATOLOGY A computer model called the Integrated Biosphere Simulator analyzes interactions among humans, the earth's atmosphere, and the global ecosystem. Climatologists study land use to see how commercial agricultural practices, for example, can alter ecosystems, which in turn can alter the atmosphere. Replacing forests with pasture results in a drier climate because a pasture does not return as much water to the atmosphere as does a forest.

More than a simple means of getting from one place to another, the automobile has become a status symbol for many North Americans. Cars are marketed for the image they represent, and obtaining a driver's license has become an unofficial rite of passage for most teenagers in the United States and Canada. Reliance on the automobile, however, creates many challenges because automobile-related pollution affects most urban areas. Automakers and government agencies are working together to reduce the use of automobiles in certain urban districts and to find clean, efficient ways to use fuel.

Another challenge posed by automobile use is traffic congestion in the region's cities, where traffic jams can last for hours. Mass public transportation can help ease such congestion. Cities such as Montreal, New York, San Francisco, and Boston now have well-established subway systems. Los Angeles, which has some of the world's largest traffic jams, is completing a transport system that will combine subways with elevated trains, and Seattle and Dallas both use monorail systems. Urban areas also use buses and commuter trains to ease some of the congestion.

NATIONAL GEOGRAPHIC World Explorer

Geography Skills for Life

Transporting Goods Long-haul trucks are used heavily in the United States and Canada.
Region What other means of transporting goods are important to the region?

Other Means of Transportation

For long-distance travel, many people in the United States and Canada use the region's busy network of airports. In the United States, Atlanta's Hartsfield and Chicago's O'Hare International Airports vie for the title of the busiest airport in the country and in the world. Toronto's Pearson International Airport is Canada's busiest. Passenger railroads and long-distance buses account for only a small portion of the region's passenger travel.

The transport systems of the region move goods as well as people. Railroads move about 35 percent of the region's freight, and about 15 percent continues to be carried along inland waterways. More modern means of transport include long-haul trucks, which carry about 20 percent of the region's freight. Airplanes carry only a small portion of the region's heavy freight but do a growing amount of overnight delivery business. Finally, pipelines, long networks of underground or aboveground pipes, carry almost one-fourth of the region's freight in the form of gas and oil.

Communications

In the United States and Canada, telephone and mail services are the primary means of communication. While Canada's broadcasting and telephone services are publicly owned, private companies operate the same services in the United States. Federal government regulations, however, make sure that there is no monopoly, the total control of a type of industry by one person or one company.

Wireless microwave and satellite relays are increasingly used for long-distance contacts. Cellular and digital services have made telephone communication more mobile. Computer use is high, although efforts are underway to make this technology available to all people. In the midst of these advances, Americans and Canadians still rely on newspapers and magazines.

Trade and Interdependence

The United States and Canada are among the world's major trading countries. The United States is second only to the European Union in exports, providing more than 10 percent of all world exports. The U.S. economy supplies chemicals,

EXTENDING THE CONTENT

Bridges Twenty-nine percent of the 587,755 bridges in the United States fail to meet safety standards. In Massachusetts, Rhode Island, and Hawaii, the rate jumps to more than 50 percent. Increased volumes of traffic make existing problems worse. Bridges are structurally unsound, in need of repair, or obsolete. In Massachusetts, part of Lee's Bridge across the Sudbury River collapsed without warning in the late 1990s, and chunks of concrete the size of softballs regularly break off the Interstate 70 viaduct in Denver. In Texas more than 9,000 bridges are obsolete because they are too outdated or too narrow for the traffic they now serve. Congress has allocated billions of dollars for bridge repairs nationwide, but progress is slow. **EE4 Human Systems: Standard 11**

architecture of THE UNITED STATES

Empire State Building Completed in New York City in 1931, the Empire State Building was the tallest building in the world at 1,250 feet (381 m). It was created in the streamlined art deco style of geometric patterns that was popular in the 1920s and 1930s.

agricultural and manufactured goods, and raw materials, such as metals, iron ore, and cotton fiber. Canada exports many of the same goods, as well as large quantities of seafood and timber products. In 2000, the United States granted China—one of the world's largest potential markets—permanent normal trade relation status (PNTR, formerly called most-favored nation status), which gives China the same trading opportunities granted to other trading partners.

Exports and Imports

Despite its many resources, the United States spends more on imports than it earns from exports. The resulting trade deficit, or difference in value between a country's imports and its exports, is hundreds of billions of dollars. The U.S. trade deficit results from the country's large population and its growing industries that require costly energy purchases. Also, some countries charge high tariffs, or taxes, on imports, thus raising the price of U.S. products and reducing

their sales abroad. As a result, growth rates for U.S. exports are very slow.

Canada, by contrast, enjoys a trade surplus, earning more from exports than it spends for imports. Canada's smaller population makes its energy needs less costly. Although both countries are spending more on imports, Canada's export revenues have grown yearly at a higher rate than those of the United States.

NAFTA

The United States and Canada are each other's largest trade partners. In 1989, the two countries signed an agreement that removed trade restrictions between them. A 1994 pact—the North American Free Trade Agreement (NAFTA)—included these two countries and Mexico. Unlike the European Union, however, NAFTA prohibits the free flow of labor among member countries.

In recent years, businesses in the United States and other developed countries have sought lower production and labor costs by *outsourcing*, or setting up plants abroad to produce parts and products for domestic use or sale. Outsourcing provides cheaper goods for home markets, while offering jobs to foreign workers. Because of NAFTA, more American companies have set up assembly plants in Mexico, where labor costs are less expensive than in the United States.

United Against Terrorism

On September 11, 2001, terrorists hijacked four passenger planes, crashing two of them into New York City's World Trade Center and the third into the Pentagon, the defense department headquarters near Washington, D.C. A fourth plane plummeted into a Pennsylvania field. The devastation and loss of so many lives made the United States firmly resolved to rid the world of terrorism.

Student Web Activity Visit the **Glencoe World Geography** Web site at geography.glencoe.com and click on Student Web Activities—Chapter 7 for an activity on the economic interdependence of Canada and the United States.

Architecture of the United States The Empire State Building has riveted steel construction, a framework covered by limestone panels and an alloy of chrome, nickel, and steel.

World Art and Architecture

Use these transparencies to introduce students to other regional architecture.

③ ASSESS

Assign Section 1 Assessment as homework or as an in-class activity.

🅦 Have students use **Interactive Tutor Self-Assessment CD-ROM.**

L2

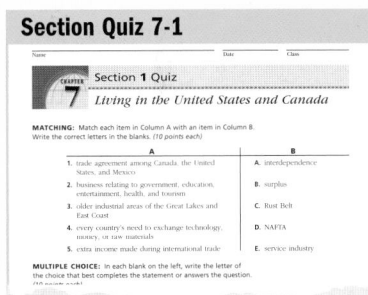

Section Quiz 7-1

Section 1 Quiz
Living in the United States and Canada

Objectives, goals, and answers to the student activity can be found in the Web Activity Lesson Plan feature at geography.glencoe.com

---

DIFFERENTIATED INSTRUCTION

Auditory/Musical Play the theme song to the television show *Route 66*. Explain that this highway is a symbol of the great love the people of the United States have for the open road and the freedom it represents. Tell students that travel and transportation are an important part of life in the United States and Canada. Work with students to brainstorm a list of songs that have as their theme a mode of transportation. **Ask: Is there a mode of transport that seems to capture the imagination more than others? Why do you think that is?** If time permits, have students bring songs to class.

🌐 **EE4 Human Systems: Standard 9**

Refer to *Inclusion for the Social Studies Classroom Strategies and Activities.*

NATIONAL GEOGRAPHIC World Explorer

Answer
U.S. forces readied for war; international support sought; investigative and security measures put in place

More About the Photo
Because of their valiant efforts, New York City's firefighters and police became heroes across the nation.

Reteach

Read a summary statement for each heading and subheading, and have students identify the one that is being summarized.

Enrich

Have students plan a cross-country trip on a highway system in Canada or in the United States. Provide road maps for students to consult as well as outline maps from the **Outline Map Resource Book**. Ask them to indicate the route they would take and write a travel itinerary listing the places they would visit and why.

4 CLOSE

Tell students to pair up and compose sentences that explain the significance of the "Places to Locate" words in terms of the economic activities that take place there. Call out a word and ask several volunteers to read the sentences they wrote.

NATIONAL GEOGRAPHIC World Explorer

Geography Skills for Life

American Heroes New York City firefighters raise the U.S. flag on the ruins of the World Trade Center.

Region What was the U.S. response to the terrorist attacks of September 11, 2001?

the country put up flags and held candlelight vigils and prayer services. The United States government also acted swiftly in dealing with the crisis. Military forces were put on high alert and security was increased at airports and other public places. President George W. Bush announced the creation of the Office of Homeland Security to organize efforts to protect Americans from further terrorist attacks. Congress later approved this office as a cabinet-level department.

The United States launched its first international effort against terrorism by attacking Afghanistan in October 2001. Afghanistan's rulers, known as the Taliban, had harbored Osama bin Laden and his terrorist network al-Qaeda, which had carried out the September 11th attacks. By December 2001, the Taliban had been forced from power, although many terrorists escaped.

The next target in the war on terrorism was Iraq, a country suspected of manufacturing weapons of mass destruction. In late 2002, the United Nations approved a resolution requiring Iraq to turn over all of its weapons of mass destruction or face serious consequences. The Iraqi government denied the existence of such weapons. After attempts to find a peaceful solution failed, war began in Iraq on March 20, 2003. By April 9, 2003, the regime had collapsed and United States forces occupied Baghdad. The long process of rebuilding Iraq's government began.

Although the attacks stunned Americans, they responded quickly to aid victims and rescue workers. To show their unity, Americans across

---

SECTION 1 ASSESSMENT

Checking for Understanding

1. **Define** market economy, post-industrial, commodity, retooling, pipeline, monopoly, trade deficit, tariff, trade surplus.

2. **Main Ideas** Use a table to organize details about agriculture, manufacturing, and trade in the United States and Canada.

Economic Activity	United States	Canada

Critical Thinking

3. **Analyzing Information** Describe how recent technological changes have affected the location and pattern of economic activities in the United States and Canada.

4. **Identifying Cause and Effect** What factors caused technological growth in the region? How did technology affect agriculture?

5. **Drawing Conclusions** Why do the United States and Canada have strong economies?

Analyzing Maps

6. **Region** Study the economic activity map on page 109. How are the locations of manufacturing centers related to the region's lakes and rivers?

Applying Geography

7. **Public Policies** Research an issue related to global trade and the United States and Canada. Identify different points of view in each country that affect public policy and decision making on the issue.

SECTION 1 ASSESSMENT ANSWERS

1. All vocabulary terms are defined in the text.
2. Check tables for completeness and accuracy.
3. The switch from heavy industry to high tech and service industries and the relocation of businesses to the Sunbelt have impacted economic activities.
4. Skilled workforce, an innovative culture, prosperous market economy. Machines applied to agriculture

raised production and lessened need for workers.
5. because of their rich natural resources and technological advances
6. Many of the manufacturing centers are located on or near waterways.
7. **Applying Geography** Students should choose an issue, such as NAFTA or the U.S.-China trade relationship, that has supporters and opponents.

People and Their Environment

Guide to Reading

Consider What You Know

Pollution of the air, water, and land in the United States and Canada is a well-known problem. Why does reducing pollution require regional cooperation?

Reading Strategy

Categorizing As you read about the types of pollution affecting the United States and Canada, complete a graphic organizer similar to the one below by listing the causes of pollution.

Causes of Pollution

Acid Rain	Smog	Water Pollution
•	•	•
•	•	•
•	•	•

Read to Find Out

• How are the United States and Canada learning to manage their natural resources more responsibly?

• What are the causes and effects of pollution in the region? How can pollution be prevented?

• What environmental challenges face the United States and Canada in the twenty-first century, both as individual countries and as a region?

Terms to Know

• clear-cutting
• acid rain
• smog
• groundwater
• eutrophication

Places to Locate

• Sudbury
• Banks Island

NATIONAL GEOGRAPHIC

A Geographic View

From Waste to Wetland

This is gold mining today, the ads proclaim—beautiful hills, waving fields of grass, prancing mule deer, a glimmering lake. . . . I saw waste rock piles shaped into eye-pleasing mounds, the milling operation that recycles and contains all processed water, and the huge [residue-collecting] pond that, over time, will become a 600-acre wetland. I saw the sophisticated monitoring system for the early detection of contamination in the groundwater. I even saw the gate placed over the mouth of a tunnel to protect the maternity roost for a local population of Townsend's big-eared bats.

—T. H. Watkins, "Hard Rock Legacy," National Geographic, *March 2000*

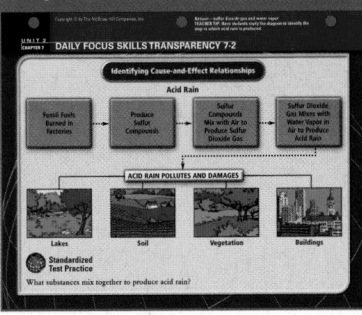

Gold mine in Nevada

◆

Strip mining made the American West rich, but it also left deep scars on the landscape. Today mining and other resource-based western industries are working to control ecological damage. In this section you will discover how people in the United States and Canada are managing scarce resources and seeking ways to overcome the effects of pollution.

Human Impact

The rich natural resources of the United States and Canada have not always been managed responsibly. The practice of clear-cutting, or taking out whole forests when harvesting timber, has destroyed

① FOCUS

Section Overview

This section describes how the United States and Canada are managing natural resources and facing environmental challenges.

BELLRINGER
Skillbuilder Activity

Project the transparency and have students answer questions.

Available as blackline master.

Daily Focus Skills Transparency 7-2

Guide to Reading

Consider What You Know
Answers *Answers may include that air pollution and water pollution often cross political boundaries.*

Reading Strategy
Answers acid rain: *chemical emissions react with water vapor in the air;* smog: *sun's rays interact with exhaust gases and industrial emissions;* water pollution: *water sources contaminated by sewage, industrial waste, and agricultural waste*

Preteaching Vocabulary
Use the **Vocabulary Puzzle-Maker CD-ROM** to create crossword and word-search puzzles.

RESOURCE MANAGER

Reproducible Masters
• Reproducible Lesson Plan 7-2
• Vocabulary Activity 7
• Daily Lecture Notes 7-2
• Guided Reading Activity 7-2
• Reading Essentials and Study Guide 7-2
• Reteaching Activity 7
• Reinforcing Skills Activity 7
• Section Quiz 7-2

Transparencies
• Daily Focus Skills Transparency 7-2
• Political Map Transparency 2
• Unit 2 Map Overlay Transparencies

Multimedia
 Vocabulary PuzzleMaker CD-ROM
Interactive Tutor Self-Assessment CD-ROM
ExamView® Pro Testmaker CD-ROM
Presentation Plus! CD-ROM

L2 Apply

Have students examine the causes of pollution discussed in this section. Then ask them to design a bumper sticker to promote public awareness of the issues. Display completed bumper stickers, and have students vote on the ones they think are the most effective.

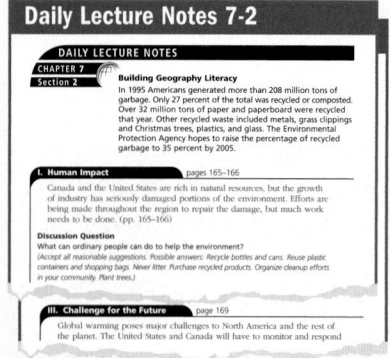

Daily Lecture Notes 7-2

NATIONAL GEOGRAPHIC — MAP STUDY

Answers

1. *major cities in southeastern Canada, cities on or near the Great Lakes and the St. Lawrence River, and many cities along the eastern seaboard of the United States*

2. *Florida; eastward winds from industrial areas do not reach Florida.*

Map Skills Practice

Which major city in the southwestern United States has high levels of acid rain concentration? *(Dallas)*

---

many of the region's old-growth forests, endangered wildlife, and left the land subject to erosion and flooding. Overfishing has depleted many of the region's freshwater and ocean fisheries. Although efforts to reverse the damage have begun, the region has a long way to go toward the sustainable use of its natural resources.

Natural resource management also includes evaluating the impact of human activity on the environment. In some cases, policies that appear to make good environmental sense must be rethought. For example, in the dry western regions of the United States and Canada, it used to be standard practice to extinguish wildfires as quickly as possible. The vegetation in these areas, however, needs periodic wildfires to clear overgrowth and to germinate seeds. Without burning, grasses and scrub grow thick and underbrush dries out. Too much burning, however, can be devastating. For example, when lightning from summer storms ignited brushfires in 2000, the result was explosive infernos that raged across several states, endangering human and animal life and destroying agricultural and grazing lands. One solution may be to follow the practice of the early Native American inhabitants of these dry areas, who set deliberate fires, known today as controlled burns, to clear dry brush before it became too dense.

Pollution

One of the unfortunate consequences of industrial development in the United States and Canada has been the increase in human-made pollution. Pollution, the introduction of harmful materials into the environment, damages the quality of water, air, and land. The kinds of pollution that trouble the United States and Canada are directly related to the region's physical geography and economic activities.

Acid Rain

Acid rain, precipitation that carries abnormally high amounts of acidic material, affects plants and fish in a large area of the eastern United States and Canada. Acid rain forms when chemical emissions from cars, power plants, factories, and refineries react with water vapor in the air. The reaction turns the chemicals, chiefly sulfur dioxide and nitrogen oxide, into their acidic forms. As the acid rain falls to

the ground, it corrodes stone and metal buildings, damages crops, and pollutes the soil. Acid rain is especially damaging to the region's waters, however. Plant life and fish cannot survive in highly acidic waters. Over time, lakes may become biologically dead, unable to support most organisms.

The winds that carry acid rain do not respect local or national boundaries. The source of the pollution may be quite distant from the place where acid rain falls. Carried by eastward winds, acid rain from the U.S. Midwest's coal-burning plants falls on the Adirondack Mountains, where it mixes with the runoff from melting acid snow. The result is that 26 percent of all lakes in the region are

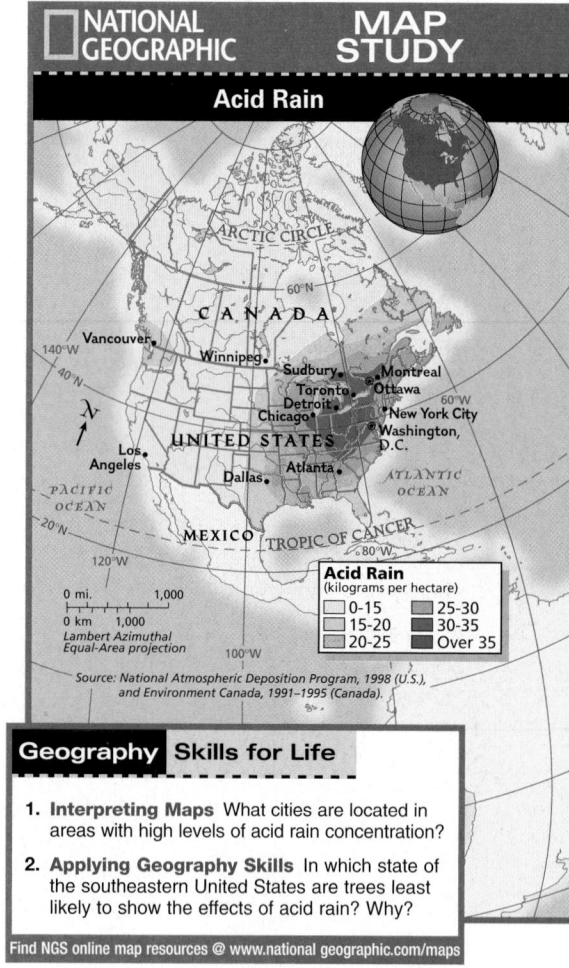

NATIONAL GEOGRAPHIC — MAP STUDY

Acid Rain

Acid Rain
(kilograms per hectare)
- 0-15
- 15-20
- 20-25
- 25-30
- 30-35
- Over 35

Source: National Atmospheric Deposition Program, 1998 (U.S.), and Environment Canada, 1991–1995 (Canada).

Geography Skills for Life

1. **Interpreting Maps** What cities are located in areas with high levels of acid rain concentration?

2. **Applying Geography Skills** In which state of the southeastern United States are trees least likely to show the effects of acid rain? Why?

Find NGS online map resources @ www.nationalgeographic.com/maps

---

DIFFERENTIATED INSTRUCTION

Reading Support Have students who have trouble organizing and remembering what they have read make a two-column chart titled *What I Know* and *What I Learned*. Then direct their attention to the title of Section 2, and have students tell you what they already know about the topic. Next, have them look at the major headings, tell you what they already know about these topics, and fill in the first column on their charts. Tell students to add what they learn as they read to their charts. Have students read silently, pausing at the end of each section to fill in the second column. **EE3 Physical Systems: Standard 8**
EE4 Human Systems: Standard 12
Refer to *Inclusion for the Social Studies Classroom Strategies and Activities.*

acidic, and hundreds are unsuitable for the survival of sensitive fish species. Emissions from the United States also result in acid rain in Canada, threatening important timber and water resources. Canada's eastern provinces—Ontario, Quebec, New Brunswick, and Nova Scotia—are the most vulnerable. Thousands of lakes throughout Canada, including 100 in Ontario alone, are so acidic that they are biologically dead.

About half of the acid rain in Canada comes from the United States. As a result, the two countries have begun cooperating to improve air quality. Improvement has already been noted. In Canada, 33 percent of the acidified lakes studied since the 1980s show reduced acid levels. In the **Sudbury** region of Ontario, for example, fish populations are rising, as are the number of fish-eating birds, such as loons.

Smog

The sulfur and nitrogen oxides that create acid rain also contribute to the type of air pollution known as smog. As the sun's rays interact with automobile exhaust gases and industrial emissions, a visible haze forms, damaging or killing plants and irritating people's eyes, throats, and lungs.

Health officials in many of the region's metropolitan areas now measure air quality on a daily basis. When emissions interact with climate conditions and create dangerous levels of smog, officials issue alerts, urging children, the elderly, and people with respiratory problems to stay indoors. Under these conditions authorities may prohibit nonessential driving and the use of lawnmowers, chainsaws, and other devices with gas-powered engines. Industrial activity may be restricted, and industries with excessive emissions may be fined. Some local and state governments in the United States require emissions testing as part of the automobile licensing process. In many parts of the United States and Canada, fuel pumps in service stations must have special nozzles that reduce the leakage of petroleum vapors into the air.

NATIONAL GEOGRAPHIC World Explorer

Geography | **Skills for Life**

Skyline of Smog Automobile and factory emissions combine with natural conditions to create smog in Los Angeles, California (shown), and other cities.
Human-Environment Interaction How has industrialization affected the environment?

Clean-air practices have substantially reduced air pollution in Los Angeles and other major cities, and still more is being done. Some car manufacturers are producing vehicles that run on electricity instead of fossil fuels. Engineers also continue to research air-, water-, and solar-powered cars. In the United States, proposed legislation would require the reduction of the sulfur content in diesel fuel by 97 percent. By 2007, officials hope to make all new diesel vehicles, such as trucks and buses, smoke free. Smog can also be reduced by encouraging the use of alternatives to automobiles, such as walking, bicycling, or using public transportation.

Water Pollution

Water systems in the United States and Canada become polluted not only by acid rain but also by the introduction of sewage and industrial and agricultural wastes into the water supplies. Industrial wastes, including toxic substances, may be illegally dumped into rivers and streams or may find their way through small, unnoticed leaks into the groundwater, freshwater that lies beneath the earth's surface. Industries also cause thermal pollution by releasing heated industrial waste water into cooler lakes and rivers. Runoff from agricultural

L3 Research
Give students the following list of books that depict the writer's passion for the environment: *Walden* by Henry David Thoreau, *A Sand County Almanac* by Aldo Leopold, and *Silent Spring* by Rachel Carson. Provide a copy or brief description of each book for students to scan. Tell students to research a synopsis of the book they chose and then state in their own words why the book is considered an environmental classic.

NATIONAL GEOGRAPHIC World Explorer

Answer
It has polluted the land, air, and water; killed sensitive plant and animal life; and affected people's health.

More About the Photo
Smog is related to human-environment interaction. The term *smog* was first used to describe the combination of smoke and fog over industrial cities. Today, smog also refers to a condition caused by the action of sunlight on exhaust gases from automobiles and factories.

L1/ELL

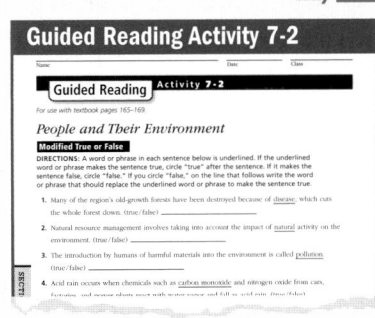

Guided Reading Activity 7-2

Guided Reading Activity 7-2

People and Their Environment

Modified True or False

DIRECTIONS: A word or phrase in each sentence below is underlined. If the underlined word or phrase makes the sentence true, circle "true" after the sentence. If it makes the sentence false, circle "false." If you circle "false," on the line that follows write the word or phrase that should replace the underlined word or phrase to make the sentence true.

1. Many of the region's old-growth forests have been destroyed because of disease, which cuts the whole forest down. (true/false)

2. Natural resource management involves taking into account the impact of natural activity on the environment. (true/false)

3. The introduction by humans of harmful materials into the environment is called pollution. (true/false)

4. Acid rain occurs when chemicals such as carbon monoxide and nitrogen oxide from cars, factories, and power plants react with water vapor and fall as acid rain. (true/false)

COOPERATIVE LEARNING ACTIVITY

Users Versus Conservers Assign each of four groups of students one of the following job titles: logger, forest conservationist, commercial fisher, and marine conservationist. Have each group share what they already know about their identity and determine what they need to find out. Assign tasks such as note taking and organizing research to each member. Then reorganize the class into groups that have at least one expert with each occupation. Students should share their areas of expertise with the group. Finally, have each new group summarize the environmental and economic issues that each occupation faces. 📦 🌐 **EE5 Environment and Society: Standard 14**

L1/ELL

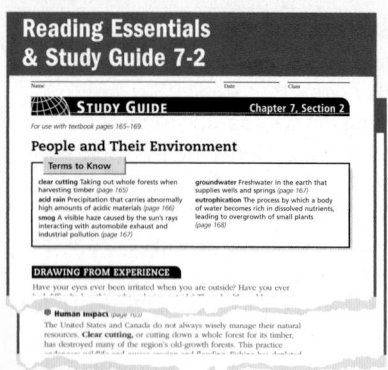

Reading Essentials
& Study Guide 7-2

□ NATIONAL GEOGRAPHIC **GEOFACT**

▶ The wildfires of 2000 scorched more than 6 million acres of land in the western United States, much of it in Montana and Idaho. Rehabilitating the burned land involves using bales of hay and coconut fiber mats to prevent soil erosion and reseeding with native prairie grasses to replace the nonnative cheatgrass, which dries out quickly and provides ample fuel for wildfires.

Yew Trees This valuable tree, which grows in the Pacific Northwest, was viewed as a trash tree until a cancer-battling chemical called *taxol* was discovered in the bark of the tree. Taxol may cause remission in some patients.

▲ The polluted Nashua River, Massachusetts, in the 1960s

▼ The present-day Nashua River, after cleanup

---

chemicals, such as fertilizers and pesticides, also pollutes the water resources of the region.

Water pollution has disastrous effects on marine life and on the birds and other animals that feed on fish or breed in wetlands. The toxic chemicals and wastes that pollute the water supply also endanger humans. In 2000 seven people in the Canadian farming town of Walkerton died and thousands became ill after being infected by *E. coli* bacteria in their drinking water. Groundwater contaminated with animal waste and other toxins had entered Walkerton's water supply through corroded pipes.

Water pollution also speeds eutrophication (yu•TROH•fuh•KAY•shuhn), the process by which a lake or other body of water becomes rich in dissolved nutrients, encouraging overgrowth of small plants, especially algae. In extreme cases the algae growth depletes the water's oxygen, leaving none for fish. Algae overgrowth can also turn a lake first into a swamp and later into dry land. Normally, eutrophication takes thousands of years, but pollution greatly speeds the process.

History
Back from the Brink

In the 1960s the region's waterways were under assault from pollution. The Cuyahoga River near Cleveland, Ohio, was so fouled by industrial chemicals that it burst into flames. Oil from a spill off the coast of Santa Barbara, California, coated beaches and wildlife. Eutrophication threatened Lake Erie. A biologist warned of serious consequences:

❝ *The most alarming of all man's assaults upon the environment is the contamination of air, earth, rivers, and sea with dangerous and even lethal materials.... The poisons ... kill vegetation, sicken cattle and ... travel from link to link of the food chain....* ❞

Rachel Carson, *Silent Spring*, 1962

In 1972 the United States and Canada signed the Great Lakes Water Quality Agreement to combat pollution in the lakes. The United States also passed

168 🌐 U n i t 2

CRITICAL THINKING ACTIVITY

Making Generalizations The forests of the Pacific Northwest in the United States hold some of the oldest plants on the continent. These old-growth forests have the following characteristics: the trees generally are older than 150 years, dead trees remain standing, and trees have never been harvested. **Ask:** How can a dead tree be vital to an ecosystem? *(When a tree dies, the trunk may remain standing, offering animals a place to live and a source of food. Insects help the wood decompose, which attracts more insects that are food for other animals. When the trunk falls to the ground, amphibians and fungi contribute to the rotting of the wood, which fertilizes the soil and enables young seedlings to grow.)*

🌐 **EE3 Physical Systems: Standard 8**

the Clean Water Act, mandating measures to restore the quality of the country's waters.

In New England, the Act forced an end to asbestos dumping in the Nashua River and spurred the construction of waste-water treatment plants. The facilities protected the river from paper pulp, chemical dyes, and other industrial wastes. Like many of the country's waterways, the Nashua slowly regained its health. Today it is once again safe for wildlife and people.

The passage of the North American Free Trade Agreement (NAFTA), however, has shifted some environmental concerns south to the U.S.–Mexico border. Along the Rio Grande, rapid industrial growth threatens the environment. The Commission for Environmental Cooperation, a nongovernmental agency with representation from Canada, the United States, and Mexico, is monitoring the environmental effects of NAFTA and suggesting ways to reduce pollution.

Challenge for the Future

Like people worldwide, those who live in the United States and Canada are concerned about the possible effects of global warming. The slight but steady rise in the earth's temperatures over the past century is not easily explained, nor are its consequences completely understood. Some effects of global warming, however, are easy to see, especially in the Arctic regions of Alaska and Canada. In these areas, the melting of polar ice is accelerating, a phenomenon with potentially disastrous consequences. In one Inuit community on the western tip of Canada's **Banks Island**, thinning sea ice has forced caribou, polar bears, and seals, on which the hunting lifestyle of the Inuit depends, to move farther north. More disturbing, the permafrost—the frozen soil of the tundra—is beginning to thaw, buckling the land and weakening the foundations of houses.

Global warming has a chain reaction of effects that threaten to alter life throughout the United States and Canada. When polar ice melts, ocean levels rise, increasing the danger of coastal flooding. For example, the city of New Orleans, much of which lies below sea level, is in danger of being completely submerged because of the combined effects of rising ocean waters and more frequent Mississippi River floods. Warmer, higher seas also alter climate patterns, leading to increased frequency and severity of weather events such as El Niño, which has been responsible for both flooding and drought. Monitoring and responding appropriately to the effects of global warming remains a critical challenge for the future of the region and for the world.

SECTION 2 ASSESSMENT

Checking for Understanding

1. **Define** clear-cutting, acid rain, smog, groundwater, eutrophication.

2. **Main Ideas** Copy the flowchart below on a sheet of paper. Complete the chart by listing causes, effects, and possible solutions for a regional environmental problem.

Problem → Causes → Effects → Solutions

Critical Thinking

3. **Analyzing Information** Why is it important for Canada and the United States to work together to reduce pollution?

4. **Drawing Conclusions** Why are more metropolitan areas of the United States and Canada beginning to experience smog?

5. **Identifying Cause and Effect** What are the short-term and long-term effects of water pollution on people and the environment?

Analyzing Maps

6. **Place** Study the map of acid rain on page 166. Which parts of the region have the greatest concentration of acid rain? Why?

Applying Geography

7. **Regional Cooperation** Think about the cooperation among the United States, Canada, and Mexico in NAFTA to promote free trade. Identify the human factors involved in the trade network created by this agreement.

SECTION 2 ASSESSMENT ANSWERS

1. All vocabulary terms are defined in the text.

2. Check flowcharts for completeness and accuracy.

3. Wind and water carry pollution across country borders.

4. Automobile exhaust gases and industrial emissions are increasing.

5. Short-term effects include poisoning the food chain from the smallest animals on up, including endangering the health of humans; long-term effects include eutrophication, which eventually can turn lakes into swamps and then into dry land.

6. Eastward winds carry the rain from the Midwest's coal-burning plants to the area around Lake Erie and to eastern Ohio and western Pennsylvania.

7. **Applying Geography** Students should consider the role and impact of governments, businesses, workers, and consumers in all three countries.

Assign Section 2 Assessment as homework or as an in-class activity.

Have students use **Interactive Tutor Self-Assessment CD-ROM.**

L2

Section Quiz 7-2

Reteach

Have students answer the questions on page 165 under "Read to Find Out."

Enrich

Have students prepare a calendar for the environment for each month of the year, designating at least one day each month as a "preserve the environment action day." The calendar should suggest an activity for the day, such as cleaning up school-yard litter.

④ CLOSE

Read aloud to students the quotation under "A Geographic View" on page 165. Ask them if they feel this optimism is unfounded or not, based on human problem-solving ability.

1 FOCUS

Direct students' attention to the heron on the facing page. Tell them that as communities grow, more demand is placed on developers to find land suitable for building. **Ask: What impact does development have on wetlands in the United States and Canada?** *(Increased development puts many wetlands in jeopardy.)*

2 TEACH

L1 Identify

After students read pages 170–171, have them list reasons why wetlands are important to the ecosystem. *(spawning grounds for fish and shellfish; feeding grounds; sanctuaries for endangered species; stabilize shorelines and riverbanks; serve as a filtering system; provide a buffer for storm tides and floodwaters.)*

L2 Ordering

Write the following uses of water on the board, and have students rate them in order of importance. Invite students to explain why they ranked them as they did.

- *recreation*
- *agriculture*
- *protected wetlands for wildlife*
- *domestic use (drinking water, bathing, watering lawns)*
- *hydroelectric power*

Viewpoint
CASE STUDY on the Environment

UNITED STATES

ALASKA

■ Wetlands

HAWAII

Source: USGS Water Supply Paper 2425

United States's Wetlands: Under Siege

Marsh. Bog. Swamp. Different words, but they all describe wetlands. A wetland is an area where water covers the soil, or lies just beneath its surface, for at least part of the year. For centuries, wetlands were regarded as smelly, insect-choked wastelands. They were places to eliminate. Across America, wetlands were filled in or drained. But in the 1970s, research confirmed what many had suspected—wetlands are valuable ecosystems that link water, life, and land. Laws were passed to protect wetlands. However, balancing wetlands preservation with development is controversial.

LOOKING TO THE FUTURE

Florida's Wetlands Everglades National Park is a watery sanctuary of saw grass prairie, hardwood hammock, and mangrove forest. Endangered species, such as the Florida panther and the manatee, have the Everglades as their habitat, as do more than 300 bird species, including the roseate spoonbill, a rare and colorful bird. More than 1,400 miles (2,253 m) of drainage canals and levees built in Florida to meet the demands of a growing population make the Everglades one of the most threatened of the U.S. national parks. There have been efforts to restore the natural flow of water through these wetlands, which will have a positive impact on other nearby wetlands.

▨ **EE3 Physical Systems: Standard 8**
▨ **EE5 Environment and Society: Standard 14**

A tricolored heron stands in the still, shallow water (left). It is early morning in Florida's Everglades National Park, one of the largest wetlands in the United States.

Wetlands teem with life. Spend a few hours in the Everglades and what might you see? Egrets, herons, and dozens of other birds. Scores of insects, fish, frogs, and snakes. Perhaps an alligator or two.

Wetlands rank among Earth's most productive ecosystems. They are nurseries, where fish and shellfish come to spawn. They are rich feeding grounds, where tiny plants and aquatic insects form the base of complex food webs. They are also sanctuaries, home to living things found nowhere else. About a third of all endangered or threatened species in the United States live in wetlands.

Wetlands are valuable in other ways, too. They slow erosion, thus stabilizing shorelines and riverbanks. They filter out pollutants that would other-

wise end up in lakes and rivers. Coastal wetlands buffer the impact of storm tides. Inland wetlands slow fast-moving floodwaters.

However, wetlands often occur where people want to grow crops. Before wetlands were recognized as valuable, the United States government encouraged farmers to drain these ecosystems to create cropland. In addition, wetlands frequently lie in the path of new housing developments, shopping malls, airports, roads, and reservoirs.

When Europeans arrived in North America, some 220 million acres (89 million ha) of wetlands existed in what are now the lower 48 states. Today slightly more than 100 million acres (40 million ha) remain. Wetlands are protected by law, but some wetlands development is allowed.

Supporters of wetlands development think the land where wetlands are found has more profitable uses. As cities and communities grow, people

need more housing, schools, businesses, and roads. Developers insist they often have no choice but to build in wetlands. In many instances, it is now legal for developers to destroy natural wetlands as long as they create "new" wetlands as replacements.

Opponents of wetlands development argue that wetlands are too valuable to lose. Without these unique habitats, some kinds of animals may become extinct. Opponents are concerned that human-made wetlands are not true replacements for existing ecosystems.

◀ In its wetland habitat, a bullfrog eyes the world.

> **What's Your Point of View?**
> Do you think it's acceptable to build on natural wetlands, as long as "new" wetlands are created? Or do you think wetlands should be completely protected?

A worker in an all-terrain tractor (below) digs ditches in wetlands in Florida. A waterfront housing development (right) abuts wetlands on Long Island in New York State.
▼

WHAT CAN YOU DO?

Become acquainted with public lands in your area, and let people know about the importance of preserving these lands.

- Volunteer your time or money. Many public lands do not have adequate funding for public education and upkeep of preserves.

- Model conservation practices. For example, don't waste water.
- Enjoy the beauty of the wetlands.

🌐 EE5 Environment and Society: Standard 14

Teaching the Skill

So that students can apply what they know about climate maps, be sure they understand that interpreting a climate map is a step-by-step process. Turn each bulleted item into a question, and have students answer orally. Explain that to get a complete picture of a place's climate, one must take into account all the factors listed in the opening paragraph: latitude, temperature, precipitation, altitude, wind patterns, and proximity to oceans. **Ask: How can the amount of precipitation affect climate?** *(Answers may include that large amounts of rain can contribute to a humid climate.)*

Additional Practice
L1

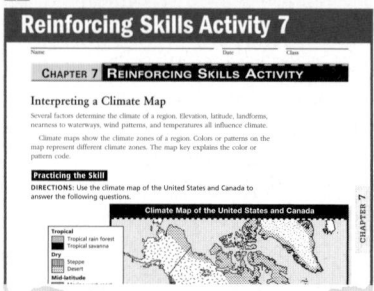

Reinforcing Skills Activity 7

GLENCOE
TECHNOLOGY

Glencoe Skillbuilder Interactive Workbook, Level 2

Interpreting a Climate Map

Climate helps determine how people live, work, dress, and play in a particular region. People on different continents may share similar climates. By reading a climate map, you can discover these similarities and differences among regions.

Learning the Skill

A climate map shows the climate zones of a region. Latitude, temperature, precipitation, altitude, wind patterns, and nearness to oceans help determine the climate of a region. Variation in precipitation also creates different types of climates, such as *rain forest* (very wet), *desert* (very dry), and *savanna* (wet and dry seasons).

On a climate map, colors represent different climate regions. The map key explains the color code. To interpret a climate map:

- Identify the area covered by the map.
- Study the key to identify the climate regions on the map.
- Locate the regions in each climate zone.
- Draw conclusions about the climate similarities and differences among regions.

Practicing the Skill

Study the climate map of eastern Canada. Use the information to answer the following questions.

1. What climate dominates the far northeast part of Canada?
2. Which area shown has a humid continental climate?
3. What climate does the coast of Newfoundland and Labrador have?

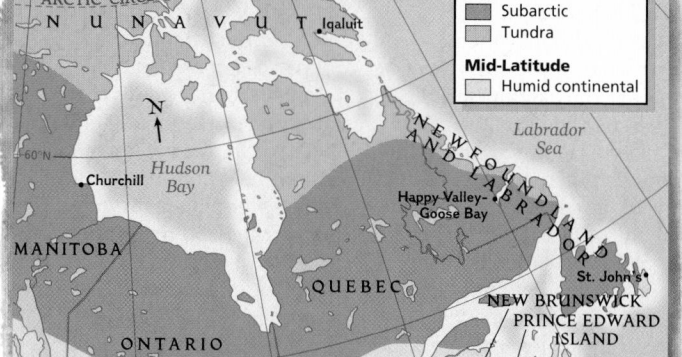

Eastern Canada: Climate Regions

High Latitude
- Subarctic
- Tundra

Mid-Latitude
- Humid continental

Azimuthal Equidistant projection

4. Why are so few major cities located in Nunavut and northern Quebec?
5. Why are there only three climate regions represented in eastern Canada? What factors of physical geography may account for this?
6. Compare the climate map on this page to the natural vegetation map on page 123. What is the relationship between climate patterns and vegetation patterns in eastern Canada?

Applying the Skill

Research to learn more about the climate of a place in the United States or Canada. Then write a paragraph describing how you think the location of the area affects its climate. Include examples of agricultural products or vegetation found in the area.

Go To The Glencoe Skillbuilder Interactive Workbook, Level 2 provides instruction and practice in key social studies skills.

ANSWERS TO PRACTICING THE SKILL

1. tundra
2. the area closest to the United States border
3. tundra
4. The tundra climate limits economic activities, discouraging the growth of large cities.
5. mainly because of its location in the high latitudes; the region does not receive warming westerly winds

6. Tundra has little vegetation; subarctic climates have coniferous forests; humid continental climates have mixed vegetation.

CHAPTER 7 SUMMARY & STUDY GUIDE

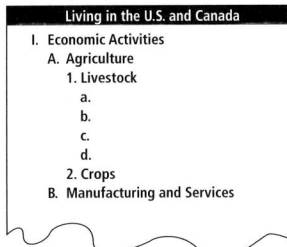

SECTION 1 — Living in the United States and Canada (pp. 157–164)

Terms to Know
- market economy
- post-industrial
- commodity
- retooling
- pipeline
- monopoly
- trade deficit
- tariff
- trade surplus

Key Points
- The region's economy has shifted from reliance on agriculture and traditional manufacturing to emphasis on service and high-tech industries.
- Agriculture is a key economic activity of the region, although it employs only a small percentage of the workforce.
- Technology and improved agricultural methods have helped farmers overcome the limitations of physical geography and climate.
- Dependable transportation and advanced communications systems help make the region an economic leader.
- The United States and Canada are among the world's leading exporters.
- The region's two countries are each other's largest trade partners. The region also trades with countries and trade blocs around the world.

Organizing Your Notes
Use an outline format similar to the one below to help you organize your notes for this section.

Living in the U.S. and Canada
I. Economic Activities
A. Agriculture
1. Livestock
a.
b.
c.
d.
2. Crops
B. Manufacturing and Services

SECTION 2 — People and Their Environment (pp. 165–169)

Terms to Know
- clear-cutting
- acid rain
- smog
- groundwater
- eutrophication

Key Points
- The United States and Canada are working to manage their rich natural resources responsibly.
- Acid rain, smog, and water pollution cause damage to the region's environment and affect human health.
- Cooperative efforts to address environmental concerns are making a difference in the region.

Organizing Your Notes
Use a web diagram like the one below to help you organize your notes for this section.

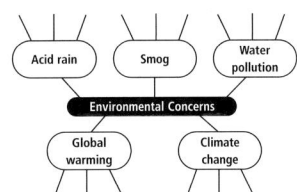

Acid rain — Smog — Water pollution — Environmental Concerns — Global warming — Climate change

◄ Workers guide a barge down the Erie Canal.

Chapter 7 🌐 173

Using the Chapter 7 Summary & Study Guide

Use the Chapter 7 Summary & Study Guide to preview, review, condense, or reteach the chapter.

Preview/Review

🔘 **Vocabulary PuzzleMaker CD-ROM** reinforces "Terms to Know."

🔘 **Interactive Tutor Self-Assessment CD-ROM** provides a review of Chapter 7 content.

Condense

Have students read the Chapter 7 Summary & Study Guide.

💿 Chapter 7 Audio Program

📁 Chapter 7 Guided Reading Activities

Reteach

📁 Chapter 7 Reteaching Activities (Spanish also available)

📁 Chapter 7 Reading Essentials and Study Guides

GLENCOE TECHNOLOGY

NATIONAL GEOGRAPHIC
WORLD REGIONS
VIDEO PROGRAM

Unit 2, The United States and Canada
The following segments enhance the study of this unit:
- **Preserving Wilderness**
- **Land of Immigrants**
- **Brass Bands**

CHAPTER CULMINATING ACTIVITY

Synthesizing Information To review what life is like in the United States and Canada today, have students create a poster or collage that illustrates the main ideas of the chapter. Students might start by reviewing the key points listed on this page and discussing how each one could be represented visually. Instruct students to include captions next to each drawing or picture to identify the point. 🌐 **EE2 Places and Regions: Standard 4**
🌐 **EE4 Human Systems: Standard 12**
🌐 **EE5 Environment and Society: Standards 14, 15**

GEOGRAPHY Online

Have students visit the Web site at geography.glencoe.com to review Chapter 1 and take the **Self-Check Quiz.**

GLENCOE TECHNOLOGY

Use *MindJogger Videoquiz* to review the Chapter 7 content.

Reviewing Key Terms

1. market economy
2. post-industrial
3. retooling
4. trade deficit
5. tariff
6. clear-cutting
7. acid rain
8. trade surplus

Reviewing Facts

SECTION 1

1. market economy
2. service industry

SECTION 2

3. emissions laws, production of cleaner automobiles, encouraging alternatives to automobile transportation
4. acid rain, auto and factory emissions, sewage, industrial and agricultural wastes
5. the area along the Rio Grande River

Critical Thinking

1. finding new job opportunities for those people who may not have a post-high school education; finding ways to renovate and reuse industrial property; filling high-tech positions
2. Increased transportation brings more pollution to an area because of emissions.

Reviewing Key Terms

Write the letter of the key term that best matches each definition below.

a. trade surplus   e. trade deficit
b. retooling   f. market economy
c. clear-cutting   g. post-industrial
d. acid rain   h. tariff

1. an economic system in which people can own and profit from their own businesses
2. reduced emphasis on heavy industry
3. converting old factories to new uses
4. loss of income through trade
5. a tax on imported trade goods
6. taking out whole forests when harvesting timber
7. precipitation that carries high amounts of acids
8. earning money through export sales

Reviewing Facts

SECTION 1

1. What type of economic system do the United States and Canada have?
2. What economic activity employs the most people in both the United States and Canada?

SECTION 2

3. What solutions have the United States and Canada implemented to deal with air pollution?
4. What factors contribute to water pollution in the region?
5. What part of the region is experiencing increased environmental problems as a result of NAFTA?

Critical Thinking

1. **Making Generalizations** What challenges will industrial cities face as the economy becomes more dependent on high-technology industries?

---

2. **Analyzing Information** Explain the connection between transportation patterns and air pollution.

3. **Identifying Cause and Effect** Use a chart like the one below to analyze the causes of acid rain and its effects on the environment.

Acid Precipitation	
Causes	Effects

NATIONAL GEOGRAPHIC Locating Places

The United States and Canada: Physical-Political Geography

Match the letters on the map with the places and physical features of the United States and Canada. Write your answers on a sheet of paper.

1. Midwest   5. Toronto   8. Alaska
2. Prairie Provinces   6. St. Lawrence River   9. Texas
3. California   7. Ohio River   10. Pacific Northwest
4. New York

---

3. Causes include human-made pollutants, such as fumes from industrial wastes and automobile exhaust; effects include increased stress upon vegetation and fish, corrosion of stone and metal buildings, crop damage, polluted soil and water, biologically dead lakes.

NATIONAL GEOGRAPHIC Locating Places

1. J	**3.** B	**5.** D	**7.** I	**9.** E
2. C	**4.** G	**6.** A	**8.** F	**10.** H

Using the Regional Atlas

Refer to the Regional Atlas on pages 106–109.

1. **Region** Describe the relationship between areas where livestock is raised and the population density in these areas.

2. **Human-Environment Interaction** What types of natural resources are clustered around large cities and manufacturing areas in the United States?

Thinking Like a Geographer

Study the economic activity map on page 109. Identify an activity that is represented in your area. Then, in geographic terms, explain why your area is suited to this activity and what other related activities might be developed there.

Problem-Solving Activity

Problem–Solution Proposal Identify a transportation problem in your community or state. Find examples of different points of view that affect decision making and the development of public policies on the problem. Then devise your own solution and present it to the class.

GeoJournal

Descriptive Writing Use your GeoJournal to write an essay describing how varying physical and cultural patterns in the region influenced the development and spread of new ideas and technologies. Use your textbook and the Internet as resources to make your essay accurate and interesting.

Technology Activity

Creating an Electronic Database Choose a region of the United States or Canada. Research that region and create an electronic database. Include types of industries, jobs, trading partners, major transportation routes, communications, land use, and environmental problems. Share your findings with the class, using charts, maps, and other graphics.

Standardized Test Practice

Study the bar graph below. Then choose the best answer for the following multiple-choice question. If you have trouble answering the question, use the process of elimination to narrow your choices.

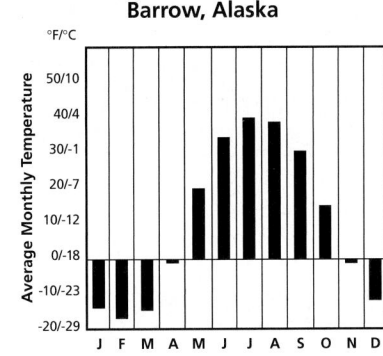

Barrow, Alaska

1. As a regional geographer for an oil company, you need to determine the best time for a survey team to work near Barrow, Alaska. Given the information on the bar graph, during which three-month period should the survey take place?

A January, February, March

B September, October, November

C March, April, May

D June, July, August

Test-Taking Tip Study the information shown on the bar graph for average monthly temperature. Look for three consecutive months in which temperatures would be the most favorable for people and equipment to function outside.

GeoJournal

Essays should contain a clear thesis statement and accurate details to support each of the listed topics.

Technology Activity

Check to see that databases support the graphic elements in students' presentations.

Standardized Test Practice

1. D

Tested Objectives: analyzing information synthesizing information

Additional Practice and Test-Taking Tips

 Standardized Test Practice Workbook

CHAPTER BONUS TEST QUESTION

Compare the economies of Canada and the United States. *(Both countries have highly developed market economies. In Canada, the government owns and administers broadcasting and health care services, whereas in the United States, private companies handle these services. Both countries are moving toward developing post-industrial economies with more emphasis on service and high-tech businesses. Agriculture and manufacturing also play important roles in the economies of both countries. Both countries export many of the same goods, and both are major importing countries.)*

Using the Regional Atlas

1. Generally, the population density is low in areas where livestock is raised.

2. water, fish, forests, coal, petroleum, copper

Thinking Like a Geographer

Students' answers will vary but should mention the area's particular geographic factors, such as location, climate, vegetation, and altitude, that influence the type of activity they identify.

Other related activities students mention should fit in with the physical geography of the area.

Problem-Solving Activity

Students might benefit from using a flowchart like the one on page 169 in the Section Assessment to help them organize their thoughts. Allow students to brainstorm issues and opinions, sharing any information they have about steps that have been taken to solve the problem. Check to see that students' solutions are reasonable.

PLANNING GUIDE

TEACHING TRANSPARENCIES

L2 Unit 3 Map Overlay Transparencies

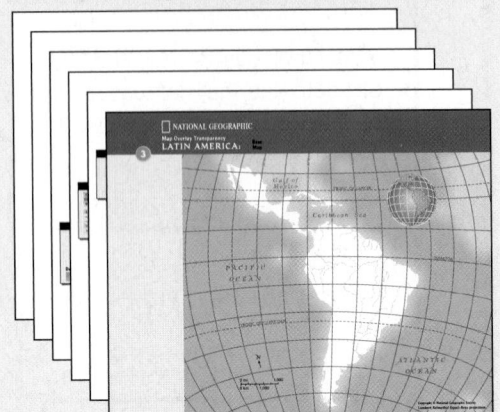

L2 Political Map Transparency 3

L2 World Cultures Transparencies 3, 4

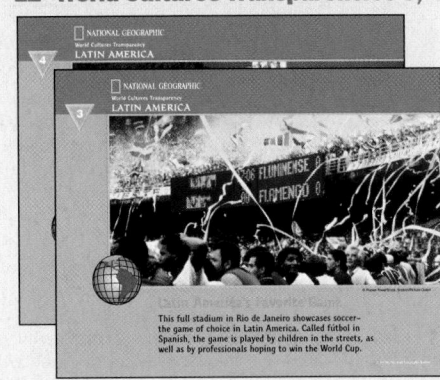

This full stadium in Rio de Janeiro showcases soccer—the game of choice in Latin America. Called fútbol in Spanish, the game is played by children in the streets, as well as by professionals hoping to win the World Cup.

APPLICATION AND ENRICHMENT

L2 Location Activity 3

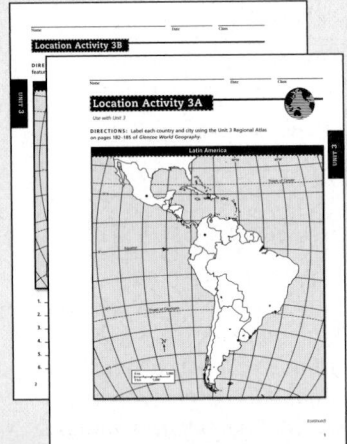

L2 Real-Life Applications and Problem-Solving Activity 3

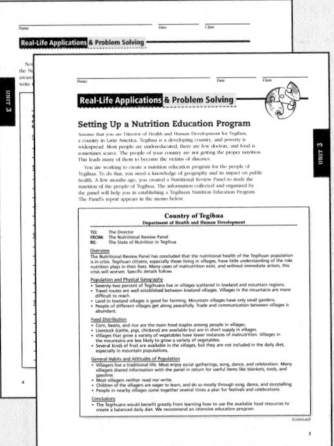

L2 GeoLab Activity 3

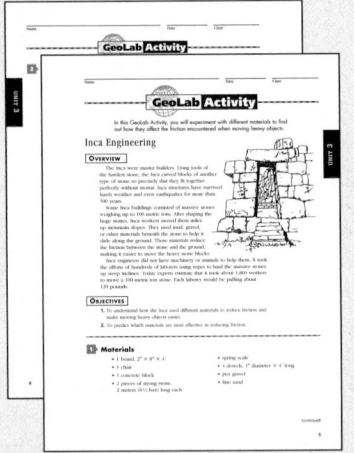

L2 Environmental Issues Case Study 3

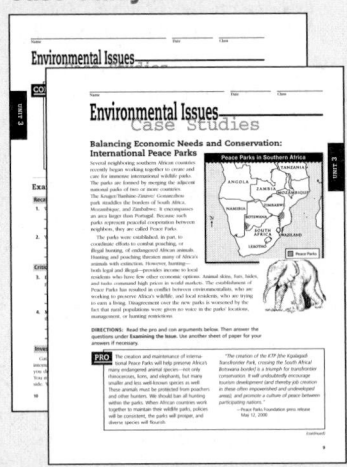

GEOGRAPHIC LITERACY

Focus on Geography Literacy

Building Geography Skills for Life

ASSESSMENT

Use the following to easily assess student learning in a variety of ways:

- Performance Assessment Activities and Rubrics
- Section Quizzes
- Chapter and Unit Tests
- Interactive Tutor Self-Assessment CD-ROM
- ExamView® Pro Testmaker
- MindJogger Videoquiz
- geography.glencoe.com
- Standardized Test Practice Workbook
- SAT I/II Test Practice

L2 Unit 3 Pretest and Tests

INTERDISCIPLINARY CONNECTIONS

L2 World Literature:
Contemporary Selection 3

Foods Around the World

Multimedia

- **World Art and Architecture Transparencies**
- **World Art Prints**
- **World Music: A Cultural Legacy**
- **World History Primary Source Document Library**

BIBLIOGRAPHY

Readings for the Student

A Brief History of the Caribbean: From the Arawak and the Carib to the Present, Facts on File, 1999.

Discovering the Inca Ice Maiden: My Adventures on Ampato. Washington, D.C.: National Geographic Society, 1998.

The Incas. New York, NY: Viking, 1996.

Readings for the Teacher

Exploring the Developing World: Life in Africa and Latin America. Denver, CO: Center for Teaching International Relations, 1994.

Latin American Popular Culture: An Introduction. Wilmington, DE: Scholarly Resources, 2000.

Progress, Poverty and Exclusion: An Economic History of Latin America in the Twentieth Century. Baltimore, MD: Johns Hopkins University Press, 1998.

Multimedia Resources

Amazon: Paradise Lost? Chicago, IL: Coronet/MTI, 1996. Videocassette, 25 minutes.

The Maya and the Inca. Time-Life Video, 1995. Videocassette, 60 minutes.

Secrets of the Aztecs and Maya. Alexandria, VA: Time-Life Video, 1994. Videocassette, 48 minutes.

READING SUPPORT FROM
JAMESTOWN EDUCATION

- *Timed Readings Plus in Social Studies* help students increase their reading rate and fluency while maintaining comprehension. The 400-word passages are similar to those found on state and national assessments.

- *Reading in the Content Area: Social Studies* concentrates on six essential reading skills that help students better comprehend what they read. The book includes 75 high-interest nonfiction passages written at increasing levels of difficulty.

- *Reading Fluency* helps students read smoothly, accurately, and expressively.

- *Jamestown's Reading Improvement,* by renowned reading expert Edward Fry, focuses on helping build your students' comprehension, vocabulary, and skimming and scanning skills.

- *Critical Reading Series* provides high-interest books, each written at three reading levels.

For more information about these products, see the Jamestown Education materials in the Classroom Solutions in the front of this Teacher Wraparound Edition.
To order these products, call Glencoe at 1-800-334-7344.

Background Information

CHAPTER 8 (pp. 192–207)

The Physical Geography of Latin America

At nearly 8 million square miles (21 million sq. km), Latin America is a region nearly equal to the size of North America. Made up of Mexico; Central America; the South American continent; and the island-countries in the Caribbean, Latin America encompasses a wide variety of landforms. Various landforms, a broad range of latitude, and extremes of elevation have resulted in unique climates and ecosystems and some of the world's most breathtaking and forbidding places. Ecotourists from around the world flock to many of these unique places, such as the Galápagos Islands, lush tropical rain forests of Costa Rica, Iguaçú Falls—a system of waterfalls that is arguably the most beautiful place on Earth—and some of the world's tallest mountains, the Andes.

Natural Resources

It is well known that Latin America supplies the world with an abundance of tropical produce—coffee, sugar, cocoa beans, and other commodities—that so many people enjoy on a daily basis. One of the world's greatest rivers, the Amazon River, courses through the rain forest that covers about one-third of the South American continent. How people manage this great resource has broad implications. The extremes and variety of its geography and its global importance help make Latin America a fascinating region to study.

CHAPTER 9 (pp. 210–235)

The Cultural Geography of Latin America

In 2000 archaeologists announced the stunning discovery of a Mayan city, a regional center for artistic creation and trade, that has been covered by dense vegetation for more than a millennium. The discovery has forced anthropologists to revise their theories of the Maya. The connection of North America to Latin America is rooted in history. As so-called "New World" archaeology—in contrast to the "Old World" archaeology of ancient Greece and Rome—attracts more scientific interest, Western people are beginning to shed a traditionally Eurocentric view of human history and to recognize Latin America's anthropological significance. In addition, nineteenth-century colonial rule, slavery, and subsequent independence movements in Latin America point to a shared experience with peoples of North America who fought to win their freedom. In Latin America the struggle for freedom is ongoing as countries work to establish strong democratic institutions and economic stability. Understanding Latin American cultures means examining their origins to see how Amerindian, Spanish, and African influences blend into unique forms. Latin America is fertile ground for new discoveries.

Population and Migration

Today more than 525 million people inhabit Latin America. By the year 2025, the number is expected to increase by 179 million, or 33 percent. Since the 1950s, many Latin Americans have migrated from rural areas to coastal cities. Recently, too, migration north has brought people in the United States in closer contact with Hispanic, or Latino, culture. In 1997 alone more than 340,000 people, representing all Latin American countries, had migrated to the United States. By examining the living conditions of Latin Americans today, we can begin to understand the phenomenon of northward migration, which impacts us intimately.

CHAPTER 10 (pp. 236–253)

Latin America Today

Historically, the economies of many Latin American countries have depended upon the exportation of one or two food crops, but this type of specialization is disadvantageous for several reasons. Economic suffering results when crops fail because of drought, disease, or other natural disasters. Insufficient farmland is set aside to grow the food needed to sustain the local population. A majority of farmers are poor, whether they work on *latifundia*, large estates owned by families or corporations, or *minifundia*, small farms that provide for a single family or for a local market.

Diversifying their economies so that they are less dependent on one or two exports challenges many Latin American countries. Mexico's oil reserves have helped the country become industrialized. Brazil, another industrial giant, produces tires, cement, and pharmaceuticals. Many of Brazil's prosperous industries, though, are controlled by multinational corporations, who take their profits out of the country. Industrialization, then, has not greatly alleviated Brazil's social and economic challenges.

GDP (gross domestic product) in Latin America falls below that in the United States and Europe—partly because Latin American countries must use their resources to repay foreign debts to the World Bank and other institutions. Although loans are necessary for a country's economic development, rising debts also hinder domestic spending and industrial investments.

The physical geography of the region also hampers the development of transportation and communications systems throughout Latin America. Outside of urban areas, high mountains and dense vegetation make construction difficult and expensive, but a few major roadways exist. The Pan American Highway runs the length of Mexico, Central America, and South America. The Trans-Amazon Highway in Brazil links the interior of the Amazon Basin with the rest of the country and with the surrounding countries of Colombia, Ecuador, Peru, and Bolivia. Ironically, the opening up of isolated regions of the Amazon rain forest has led to some of the region's and the world's most pressing challenges, including destruction of the rain forest and its biodiversity.

Regional and Global Challenges

Many of the challenges of industrialization—pollution, overcrowding, health care—are global in scope. The endangered Amazon rain forest, for example, has been recognized as one of the world's greatest conservation challenges.

Latin America's rapid population growth has implications beyond the region's borders. Overcrowding and low standards of living have encouraged large numbers of Latin Americans to migrate internally and to other countries, especially to the United States. At the same time, Latin American countries share the concern that sizable out-migration will drain talent essential to meeting the region's future challenges, especially in the development of strong economies.

The region's location along major fault lines makes it vulnerable to destructive earthquakes and volcanic eruptions. Hurricanes have recently devastated countries in Central America and South America. With international cooperation, however, Latin America's governments are working to meet these challenges.

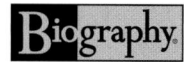

00:00 OUT OF TIME?

If time does not permit teaching each chapter in this unit, you may want to use the **Reading Essentials and Study Guide** summaries.

Unit Launch Activity

Ask: What Latin American influences do you see around you in daily life? What stories do you hear on TV or the radio or read about in the newspaper? Have the class brainstorm and write the responses on the board. Ask for one volunteer to copy the list and another to transfer it to a poster board. Display the poster board in class and encourage students to add to it throughout the course of the unit. At the end of the unit, revisit the expanded list and ask students to summarize why it is important to study Latin America.

GLENCOE TECHNOLOGY

◻ NATIONAL GEOGRAPHIC

WORLD REGIONS
VIDEO PROGRAM

Unit 3, Latin America
The following segments enhance the study of this unit:

- **Green Commerce**
- **The Inca**
- **Steel Drums**

 Available in DVD and VHS

Latin America

Maya ruins at Palenque, Mexico

176   Unit 3

 GETTING TO KNOW THE REGION

Map Activity Display Political Map Transparency 3 and **Ask: What continents form Latin America?** *(South America and part of North America)* **What part of North America is part of Latin America?** *(southwestern-most region)* **Why might this area also be called Middle or Central America?** *(geographically in the middle, or center, between North and South America)* **What other landforms are part of Latin America?** *(islands)* **In what part of Latin America are there groups of islands?** *(Caribbean)* **By what group names are these islands known?** *(West Indies, Caribbean Islands, Antilles)* **What body of water is west of the islands?** *(Gulf of Mexico)* **South?** *(Caribbean Sea)* **East?** *(Atlantic Ocean)*
🌐 **EE1 The World in Spatial Terms: Standard 1**

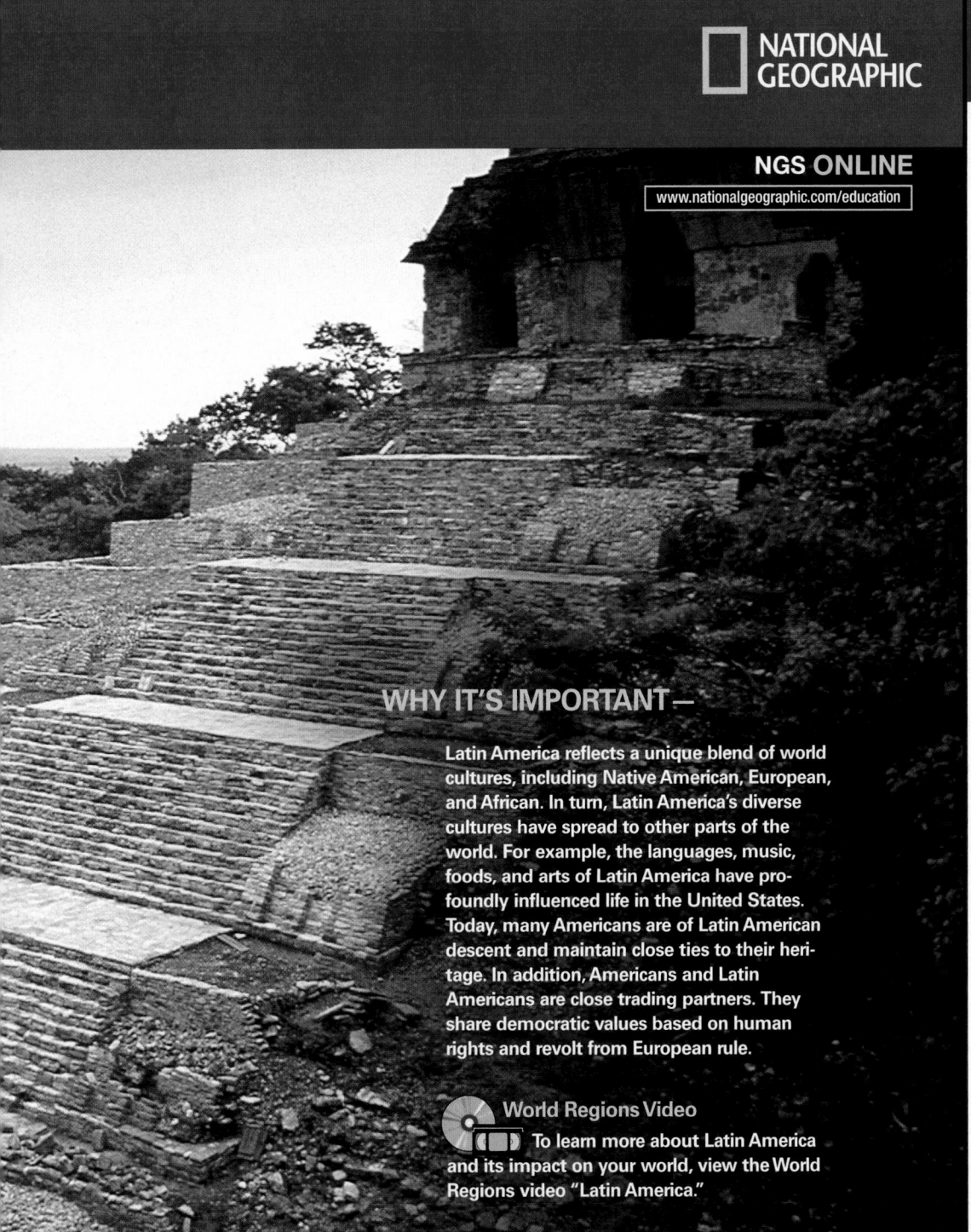

NGS ONLINE
www.nationalgeographic.com/education

WHY IT'S IMPORTANT—

Latin America reflects a unique blend of world cultures, including Native American, European, and African. In turn, Latin America's diverse cultures have spread to other parts of the world. For example, the languages, music, foods, and arts of Latin America have profoundly influenced life in the United States. Today, many Americans are of Latin American descent and maintain close ties to their heritage. In addition, Americans and Latin Americans are close trading partners. They share democratic values based on human rights and revolt from European rule.

World Regions Video
To learn more about Latin America and its impact on your world, view the World Regions video "Latin America."

NGS ONLINE
www.nationalgeographic.com/education

This online resource, brought to you by the National Geographic Society, provides lesson plans, atlas updates, cartographic activities with interactive maps, an online map store, and links to the boundless subjects of maps and geography.

Unit Overview

The three chapters that comprise this unit introduce students to the physical and cultural geography of Latin America as well as to the peoples and challenges of that region. Point out to students that although the countries of Latin America are diverse, most have the following features in common:

- a strong Spanish or Portuguese influence on language and culture
- a blend of Native American, African, and European heritages
- a mostly tropical or subtropical climate
- the world's largest zone of tropical rain forest

ABOUT THE PHOTO

Visual Instruction The Maya had one of the greatest civilizations of the Western Hemisphere. They built complex stone buildings and pyramid temples, practiced agriculture, worked in gold and copper, and developed hieroglyphic writing. One of the principal cities during the peak of Maya civilization (A.D. 250–A.D. 900) was Palenque, in what is today Mexico. Most surviving Maya structures, like those in the photo, were overlaid with limestone blocks and were decorated with reliefs and inscriptions. **Ask:** If you knew nothing about the Maya civilization, what might you conclude about it from looking at the ruins in the photo on this page? (the Maya were very skilled in math, engineering, and architecture)
🌐 EE2 Places and Regions: Standard 6

UNIT 3 REGIONAL ATLAS

① FOCUS

These features and activities may be used as an introduction to the unit or as teaching tools throughout the course of the unit.

L1 Using Flash Cards Activity

Before beginning the study of this unit, use the **Countries of the World Flash Cards** to preview students' knowledge of Latin America. Organize the students into two competing teams, and test their knowledge. At the end of the game, ask students to summarize any physical or cultural similarities they noticed among countries in the region.

L2 Photo Research Activity

Have students research to find out more information about the subjects of the photos on pages 178–181. You may assign this as an individual or group activity. Have students report findings.

INTERDISCIPLINARY
connection

GEOLOGY The west coasts of Mexico, Central America, and South America are part of a geologically active rim called the Ring of Fire. Great plates of the earth's crust move against each other along Latin America's western coasts, causing earthquakes and volcanic eruptions.

What Makes Latin America a Region?

Spanning more than 85 degrees of latitude, Latin America encompasses Mexico, Central America, the Caribbean Islands, and South America. It is a region of startling contrasts.

High mountains run from northern Mexico through the heart of Central America. The higher peaks of the Andes course down South America's western side.

Elsewhere, broad plateaus span huge areas. At still lower elevations, plains dominate the landscape. These great grasslands, such as the pampas in Argentina and the llanos in Venezuela and Colombia, are ideal for grazing cattle and sheep.

But when people think of Latin America, it's often rain forests that come to mind. Eternally wet, intensely green, and bursting with life, rain forests cover parts of many Caribbean islands and Central American countries. Yet none of these compare to the Amazon rain forest of Brazil. Drained by the Amazon River, this lowland forest covers one-third of South America and is home to nearly half of the world's plant and animal species.

1 Like a cartoon come to life, a brightly colored toucan calls out from a leafy perch in a Costa Rican rain forest. A toucan's enormous beak has serrated edges that help the bird get a good grip on slippery-skinned fruits.

178   Unit 3

BACKGROUND INFORMATION

Amazon River South America's mighty Amazon River begins high in the Andes, less than 100 miles (161 km) from the Pacific Ocean. The river flows nearly 4,000 miles (6,400 km) to empty into the Atlantic Ocean. Its length is about equal to the distance from New York City to Rome, Italy! This immense river carries a huge amount of water. Some scientists estimate that the Amazon River alone funnels about 20 percent of all the freshwater that flows over the earth.

The river was named by Spanish explorer Francisco de Orellana for the Amazons, a band of female warriors in Greek mythology. De Orellana supposedly chose the name after he was attacked by a group of female warriors.   🌐 **EE2 Places and Regions: Standard 4**

2 TEACH

L2 Location

Encourage students to discuss how geographic location affects their daily lives. **Ask:** Is your community near a body of water? How does this location affect what you eat or what leisure activities you enjoy? Is the climate moderate, hot, or cold? Mostly wet or mostly dry? How do these factors influence what clothes you wear or how much time you spend outdoors? Do you live in a city, a town, or in a more rural area? How does this location affect how you get to school or what you do after school? Have students make a list of the different ways that climate can affect people's lives. Have them refer to this list as they read about landforms and climate in Latin America.

GLENCOE TECHNOLOGY

NATIONAL GEOGRAPHIC

WORLD REGIONS VIDEO PROGRAM

Unit 3, Latin America
The following segments enhance the study of this unit:

- **Green Commerce**
- **The Inca**
- **Steel Drums**

 Available in DVD and VHS

2 **Rust-red terraces** curve around the Carajás iron mine, in Brazil. This mine boasts the world's largest deposit of high-quality iron ore. Tin, copper, silver, oil, and natural gas are among Latin America's other important natural resources.

3 **Like jagged teeth** in some enormous jaw, the snow-covered peaks of the Andes guard South America's western flank. The world's longest mountain chain, the Andes stretch the entire length of the continent.

4 **On the plains of Paraguay,** cowboys known as vaqueros round up cattle before driving them to fresh pastures. The western part of Paraguay, the Gran Chaco, is a grassland area where cattle roam on large ranches.

Unit 3 **179**

A TRAVELER'S LOG

Charles Darwin In 1831 Charles Darwin set off on a world voyage aboard the *HMS Beagle*. His research on the voyage formed the basis for his theory of evolution. In this passage from *The Voyage of the* Beagle (1845), Darwin describes his travels in the Galápagos Islands:

"As I was walking along I met two large tortoises, each of which must have weighed at least two hundred pounds: one was eating a piece of cactus, and as I approached, it stared at me and slowly walked away; the other gave a deep hiss, and drew in its head. These huge reptiles, surrounded by the black lava, the leafless shrubs, and large cacti, seemed to my fancy like some antediluvian animals. The few dull-coloured birds cared no more for me than they did for the great tortoises." **EE2 Places and Regions: Standards 4, 6**

L2 Making Predictions

Ask students in what ways they think Spanish and Portuguese cultures might have influenced the countries of Latin America. If they have difficulty coming up with answers, prompt them to name the influences they have read about in the text—language and religion—and seen in the photos —architecture.

FYI

Indigenous people have inhabited the Amazon region for 20,000 to 50,000 years. Anthropologists estimate that 200 groups of five million native inhabitants lived in the Amazon Basin. Although the Inca, Aztec, and Maya built great civilizations, the native peoples of the Amazon lived simply, moved frequently, and left few possessions. The few clues they left were quickly consumed by the rain forest. Today only about 200,000 of their descendants continue to follow a traditional lifestyle.

□ NATIONAL GEOGRAPHIC **GEOFACT**

▶ **The Amazon discharges so much freshwater at its mouth that it reduces the salt content of Atlantic Ocean water up to 100 miles (161 km) offshore!**

Mix of Old and New

Latin America is a region where cultures have collided and combined. Maya, Aztec, and Inca civilizations flourished here long ago. Then Europeans arrived in the late 1400s. For more than 300 years, Spain and Portugal controlled most of Latin America. They forced new laws, new languages, and a new religion onto the region's inhabitants. Yet native cultures survived by blending with those of the conquerors.

Today, the faces, costumes, and customs of many Latin Americans reveal their mixed heritage.

This is a region of developing nations—countries in the process of becoming industrialized. Latin America's urban population is increasing rapidly as people flock from the countryside to modern, bustling cities.

1 Music fills the air as a young Ecuadoran plays the panpipe, a traditional Andean instrument. Many of the people who live in the Andes are Native Americans—descendants of the Inca and other groups that flourished here before the arrival of Europeans.

BACKGROUND INFORMATION

Cultural Values One of the principal themes the Latin Americans inherited from their Iberian ancestors is *personalismo*, or personalism. They believe strongly that each individual is unique and has an inner dignity and personality. A strong sense of personal honor and sensitivity to praise, insult, and slight is just part of *personalismo*.

Personalismo is not concerned with outward signs of equality, such as equality before the law, but with a person's inner qualities. Social standing has no influence on *personalismo*. Every person has inner qualities that he or she can fulfill.

🌐 **EE4 Human Systems: Standard 10**

Culture NOTE

Brazil Soccer is Brazil's national sport. So passionate are Brazilians about it that they have closed businesses and schools during the Soccer World Cup or important national competitions.

FYI

Costa Ricans have no army because they despise militarism. In school, Costa Rican children learn that armies are created to oppress people. Military forces, however, may be organized for national defense if necessary.

③ ASSESS

Ask: How is the region where you live different from and similar to Latin America?

④ CLOSE

Have students create an illustrated travel brochure highlighting the cultural and geographic features of Latin America.

2 Villages and farms dot the highlands near Cuzco, Peru. The economies of many Latin American countries are still based largely on agriculture, though manufacturing and other industries play an increasingly important role.

3 Arms outstretched as if in blessing, a huge statue of Jesus keeps watch over the sprawling city of Rio de Janeiro, Brazil. Most Latin Americans are Catholic, a legacy from the days of Spanish and Portuguese rule.

4 A glass-covered bridge links a hotel to a convention center, part of a new business complex in Monterrey, Mexico. Among Latin American countries, Mexico has been one of the quickest to modernize and industrialize.

Unit 3 **181**

UNIT PROJECT

Festival Before students begin the study of this unit, tell them that they will be responsible for organizing a Latin American Festival at the conclusion of the unit. They will present the region of Latin America to their peers. Have students brainstorm and list on the board different features of the region they should highlight, such as physical geography, history, peoples, food, music, architecture, languages, and styles of clothing. Have students choose a category and collect information about it as they study the unit.

🌐 **EE4 Human Systems: Standard 10**

These features and activities may be used as an introduction to the unit or as teaching tools throughout the course of the unit.

L1 Comparing

Have students turn to the physical/political map of the world in the Reference Atlas at the front of the book. Ask them to compare the main landforms in western North America and South America. *(North America: wide bands of mountains in west with high plateaus between; South America: more narrow bands of mountains along the Pacific coast)*

L2 Location

Tell students that Latin America has the greatest latitudinal span of any world region; Mexico's northernmost part lies at about 33°N, and Tierra del Fuego at 56°S. Have them speculate on how this span from the Equator almost to the South Pole might affect the continent's geography, climate, and weather.

Elevation Profile

In order to show a variety of physical features, this cross section begins at the coast of Peru around 10°S latitude and moves east across the Andes, and through the Brazilian Selvas, northern Brazil, and the Mato Grosso Plateau and the Brazilian Highlands and ends at the coast of Brazil north of Salvador.

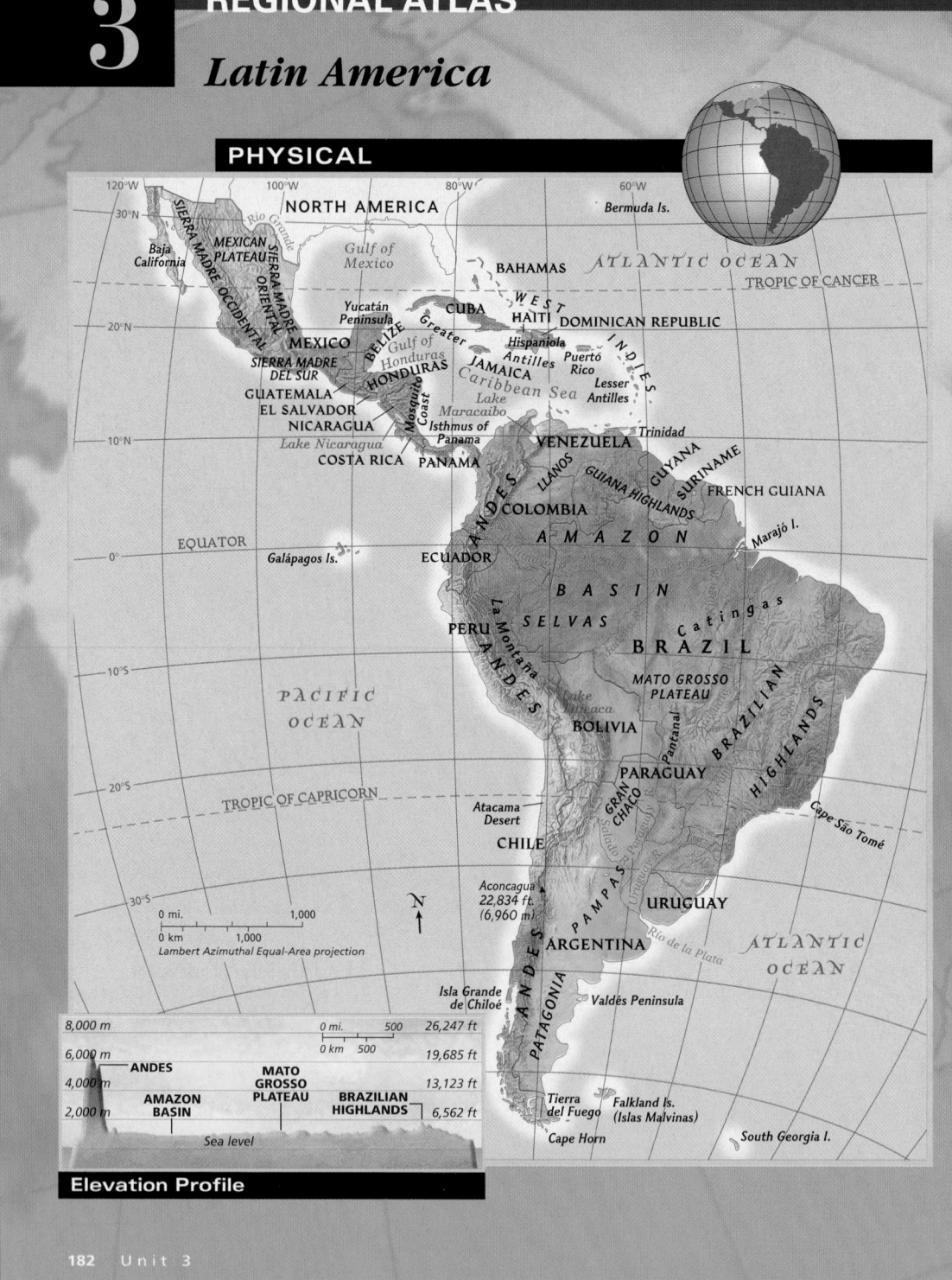

PHYSICAL

Elevation Profile

REGIONAL ATLAS ACTIVITY

Class Challenge Organize students into small groups to write at least five questions about the physical geography of Latin America with which to challenge another group. Tell students to include direction, key, scale, or physical map questions, such as the following: In what direction would you travel from the Yucatán Peninsula to Cuba? *(east)* In the elevation profile, how do the Brazilian Highlands compare in elevation to the Andes ranges? *(The Andes, at about 11,000 feet [3,353 m], are about five-and-one-half times higher than the Brazilian Highlands, at 2,000 feet [610 m].)* Allow time for groups to write questions and challenge one another. You may also want to repeat this activity at the end of the unit. **ELL**

🌐 **EE1 The World in Spatial Terms: Standard 1**

NATIONAL GEOGRAPHIC

POLITICAL

Map of Latin America showing countries and cities:

120°W · 100°W · 80°W · 60°W · 40°W

NORTH AMERICA

30°N

BERMUDA U.K.

Río Grande

Monterrey

MEXICO

Gulf of Mexico

ATLANTIC OCEAN

TROPIC OF CANCER

Guadalajara

Nassau

BAHAMAS

DOMINICAN REPUBLIC

Virgin Islands U.S. & U.K.

20°N

Mexico City

Havana

CUBA

HAITI

Santo Domingo

ANTIGUA AND BARBUDA

Cayman Is. U.K.

Port-au-Prince

Puerto Rico U.S.

Guadeloupe Fr.

DOMINICA

BELIZE JAMAICA

Kingston

Martinique Fr.

Belmopan

ST. KITTS AND NEVIS

ST. LUCIA

GUATEMALA HONDURAS

Caribbean Sea

ST. VINCENT AND THE GRENADINES

Guatemala City Tegucigalpa

BARBADOS

San Salvador

NICARAGUA

GRENADA

EL SALVADOR

Managua

Panama City

TRINIDAD AND TOBAGO

10°N

San José

Caracas

Port-of-Spain

COSTA RICA

PANAMA

VENEZUELA

Georgetown

Medellín

Bogotá

GUYANA

Paramaribo Cayenne

Cali

SURINAME

FRENCH GUIANA Fr.

COLOMBIA

EQUATOR

0°

Galápagos Islands Ecua.

Quito

ECUADOR

Negro R.

Amazon R.

PACIFIC OCEAN

AMAZON BASIN

Selvas

Recife

PERU

Madeira R.

10°S

Lima

ANDES

MATO GROSSO PLATEAU

BRAZIL

Salvador

Lake Titicaca

La Paz

BRAZILIAN HIGHLANDS

Brasília

BOLIVIA

Sucre

Belo Horizonte

PARAGUAY

20°S

TROPIC OF CAPRICORN

Paraná R.

Rio de Janeiro

Asunción

São Paulo

CHILE

Curitiba

Porto Alegre

⊛ National capital
⊙ Territorial capital
• Major city

ARGENTINA

Valparaíso Santiago

Rosario

URUGUAY

30°S

Buenos Aires

Montevideo

0 mi. 1,000

PAMPAS

Río de la Plata

ATLANTIC OCEAN

0 km 1,000

ANDES

PATAGONIA

Lambert Azimuthal Equal-Area projection

N

Falkland Islands (Islas Malvinas) U.K.

South Georgia Island U.K.

MAP Study

1. Through which country do most South American rivers flow?

2. What European and North American countries have territories in Latin America?

L2 Predicting Consequences

Remind students that Latin America has the greatest latitudinal span of any world region. Ask students to predict how the region's geographical location might affect settlement, clothing, housing, and leisure time activities. Students may wish to write predictions in their journals.

Culture NOTE

Argentina Most of Argentina's people are of Spanish or Italian ancestry. Native Americans—the original inhabitants—make up only a small part of the country's population.

MAP Study

Answers:

1. *Brazil*

2. *United States, United Kingdom, France*

Map Skills Practice
Location Locate and name the United Kingdom's southernmost territories in the region. *(Falkland Islands, South Georgia Island, both in the South Atlantic, east of Patagonia)*

REGIONAL ATLAS ACTIVITY

Travel Itinerary Have students form groups. Tell them to choose five Latin American countries to visit. Students will develop itineraries. They should plan in what order they will visit their chosen countries and explain why they chose that order. Students should also take into account the geography of the regions they will be touring and consider what travel methods they will use to get the most extensive and greatest viewing pleasure. For each country, students should list at least one reason for visiting that particular location. Students may wish to plot their itineraries on maps. Encourage students to share their plans orally with other class members. 🌐 **EE4 Human Systems: Standard 10**

L1 Comparing

Have students look at the population density map on this page. Ask them to compare the population of Brazil with that of Argentina. *(Students should note that, per square mile, Brazil has larger populated areas. In fact, about half of South America's population lives here.)*

L2 Location

Refer students to the economic activity map on page 185. Explain that students are investors, planning to invest in the zinc industry. Ask them to think about which countries to focus on in terms of supply as well as transportation costs to the United States. *(Students should note that zinc is plentiful in Mexico as well as Peru; it would be cheaper to transport from Mexico.)*

□ NATIONAL GEOGRAPHIC GEOFACT

▶ **Brazil is so huge that, although it faces the Atlantic Ocean along 4,600 miles (7,400 km) of coastline, it borders on every country of the South American continent except Chile and Ecuador.**

UNIT 3 REGIONAL ATLAS

Latin America

POPULATION DENSITY

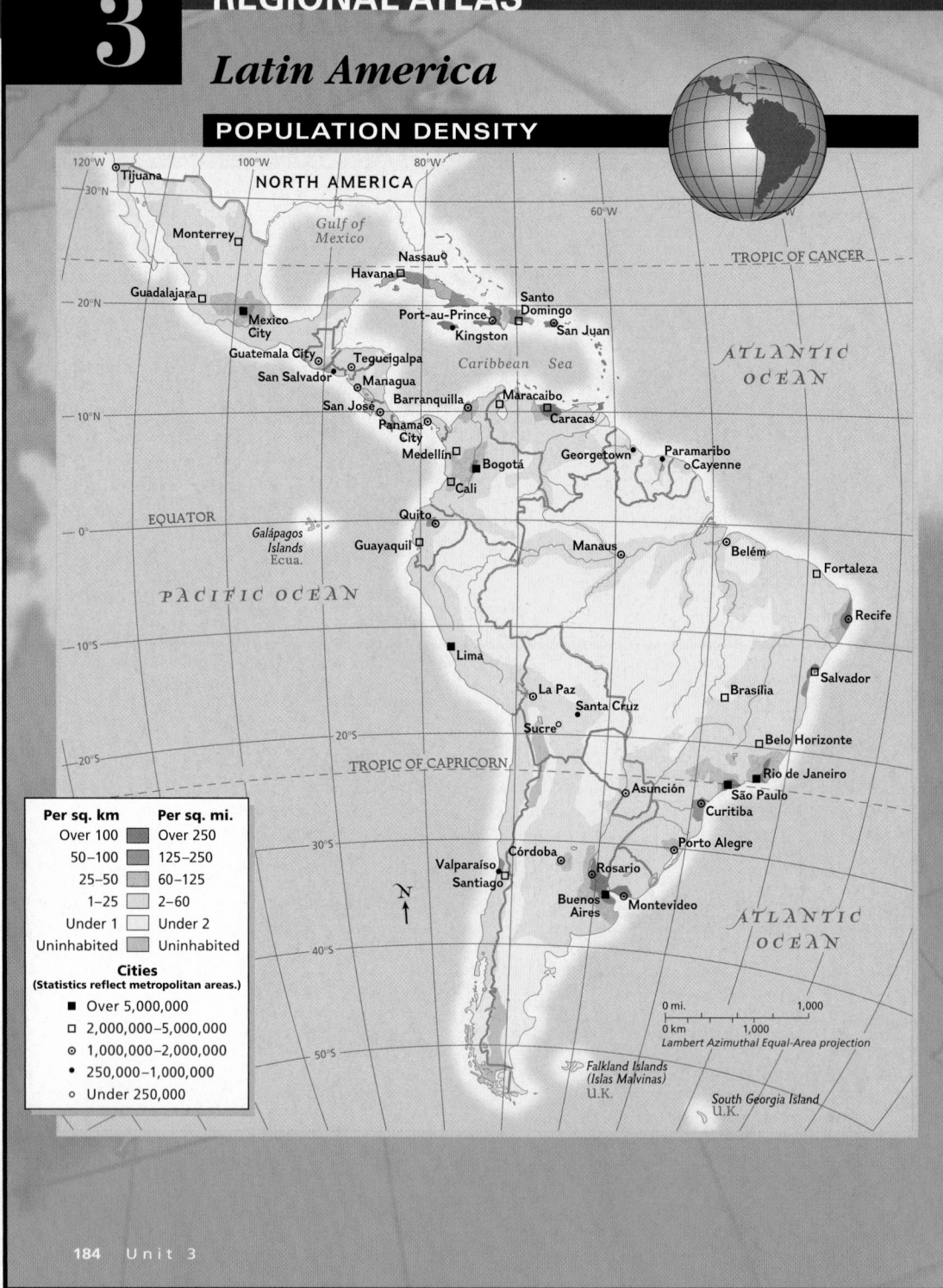

Per sq. km	Per sq. mi.
Over 100	Over 250
50–100	125–250
25–50	60–125
1–25	2–60
Under 1	Under 2
Uninhabited	Uninhabited

Cities
(Statistics reflect metropolitan areas.)

- ■ Over 5,000,000
- □ 2,000,000–5,000,000
- ◉ 1,000,000–2,000,000
- • 250,000–1,000,000
- ○ Under 250,000

Lambert Azimuthal Equal-Area projection

REGIONAL ATLAS ACTIVITY

Place Assign a country or island group to pairs of students. Have them research how the geographical characteristics of each country helped determine population density and the location of cities and towns. Students can note their findings on index cards and then use those notes to formulate clear, concise facts. Have students read their facts to other students, leaving out the name of the country. They can give other students a choice of three countries and ask them to decide which one it is.

◉ **EE4 Human Systems: Standard 9**
◉ **EE5 Environment and Society: Standard 15**

ECONOMIC ACTIVITY

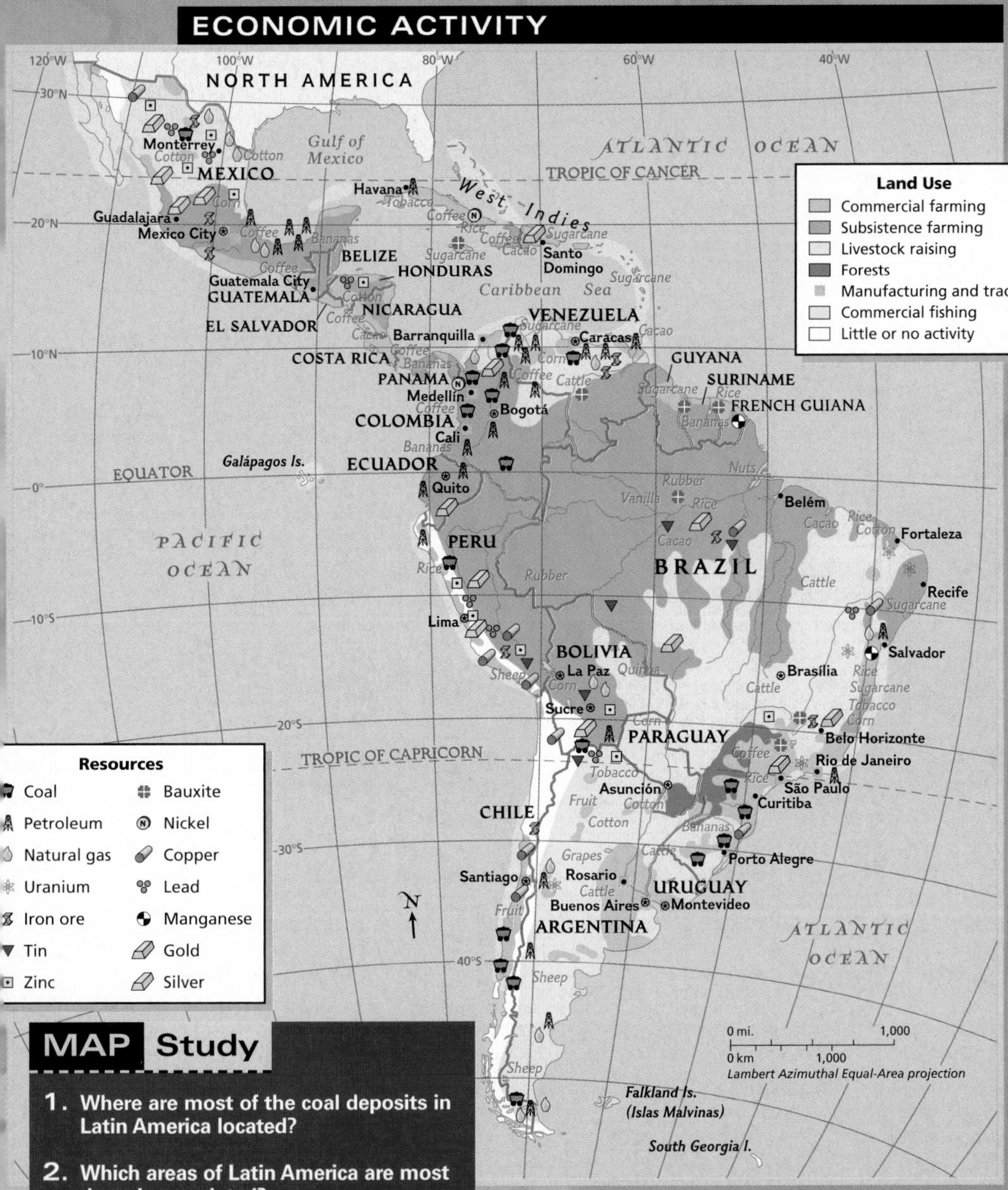

NORTH AMERICA

Monterrey
Cotton
MEXICO
Cotton

Guadalajara
Mexico City ®
Coffee
Bananas

Gulf of Mexico

Havana
Tobacco

ATLANTIC OCEAN

TROPIC OF CANCER

West Indies

Coffee

Santo Domingo

BELIZE
HONDURAS
Sugarcane
Guatemala City
GUATEMALA
Cotton
Coffee
EL SALVADOR
NICARAGUA
Coffee

Caribbean Sea

Sugarcane

VENEZUELA
Barranquilla
Cacao
Caracas
Sugarcane
COSTA RICA
Coffee
Bananas
PANAMA
Cattle
Medellín
Coffee
● Bogotá
COLOMBIA
Cali
Bananas
Corn

GUYANA
Sugarcane
SURINAME
Rice
FRENCH GUIANA
Bananas

EQUATOR
Galápagos Is.
ECUADOR
Quito
Rubber
Nuts
Vanilla
Rice

PACIFIC OCEAN

PERU
Rice
Rubber
Belém
Cacao
Rice
Cotton
Fortaleza

BRAZIL
Cacao
Cattle
Recife
Sugarcane

Lima

BOLIVIA
La Paz
Corn
Quinia
Brasília
Cattle
Salvador
Rice
Sugarcane
Tobacco
Corn

Sucre ®
Corn
Sheep

TROPIC OF CAPRICORN

PARAGUAY
Coffee
Rice
Belo Horizonte
Rio de Janeiro
São Paulo
Curitiba

CHILE
Asunción
Tobacco
Fruit
Cotton
Bananas
Cattle
Porto Alegre

Grapes
Santiago
Rosario
URUGUAY
Buenos Aires ®
● Montevideo
Fruit
Cattle
ARGENTINA

ATLANTIC OCEAN

N

Sheep

0 mi. 1,000
0 km 1,000
Lambert Azimuthal Equal-Area projection

Sheep
Falkland Is. (Islas Malvinas)

South Georgia I.

Land Use
- Commercial farming
- Subsistence farming
- Livestock raising
- Forests
- Manufacturing and trade
- Commercial fishing
- Little or no activity

Resources
- Coal
- Petroleum
- Natural gas
- Uranium
- Iron ore
- Tin
- Zinc
- Bauxite
- Nickel
- Copper
- Lead
- Manganese
- Gold
- Silver

MAP Study

1. Where are most of the coal deposits in Latin America located?

2. Which areas of Latin America are most densely populated?

L2 Movement
Ask students to consider how the geographic information they learn might affect them if they were touring Latin America.

☐ NATIONAL GEOGRAPHIC **GEOFACT**

▶ **Bananas and coffee, crops closely associated with Latin America, are not native to the Western Hemisphere. Bananas were brought from the Canary Islands (off the northwest coast of Africa) to the Americas shortly after Columbus sailed to the West Indies. Europeans brought coffee to Latin America from Africa in the 1700s.**

Latifundia Parts of Argentina and Brazil have farms known as *latifundia* that are larger than some countries.

MAP Study

Answers
1. *western South America*

2. *cities, especially those on the coast*

Map Skills Practice
Location Which country produces grapes? *(Argentina)*

REGIONAL ATLAS ACTIVITY

Place Organize students into small groups. Allow them a specified amount of time to write several geographic place questions whose answers can be determined from the map on this page. For example, "What country has petroleum near a densely populated capital city?" *(Cuba)* Encourage students to be creative in composing their questions. Allow time for groups to challenge each other with their material and then revise any questions that are confusing or unclear. ▦ **EE2 Places and Regions: Standard 4**

UNIT 3 REGIONAL ATLAS

Latin America

These features and activities may be used as an introduction to the unit or as teaching tools throughout the course of the unit.

L1 Identify

Direct students to the "Country and Capital" column on pages 186–187. Say the name of a country and have students identify its capital. Continue until all the countries have been called out. Then reverse the activity by calling out the capital and having students identify the country. Pair up students and have them repeat the activity together for pages 188–189.

☐ NATIONAL GEOGRAPHIC **GEOFACT**

▶ **In Quito, Ecuador, on October 5, 1999, a heavy shower of ash spewed from the 15,728-foot-tall (4,794-m-tall) volcano Guagua Pichincha for the first time since 1660. The cloud blocked out the sun and darkened the land. Two days later, without a tremor to alert residents, ash and steam rose from the peak, and the wind quickly swept the cloud away.**

Llamas The largest South American members of the camel family, llamas are useful pack animals because they can carry as much as 130 pounds (60 kg) and are sure-footed on mountain trails.

COUNTRY PROFILES

COUNTRY * AND CAPITAL	FLAG AND LANGUAGE	POPULATION ** AND DENSITY	LANDMASS	MAJOR EXPORT	MAJOR IMPORT	CURRENCY	GOVERNMENT
ANTIGUA AND BARBUDA — St. John's	English	100,000 436 per sq.mi. 168 per sq.km	170 sq.mi. 440 sq.km	Petroleum Products	Foods and Livestock	East Caribbean Dollar	Parliamentary Democracy
ARGENTINA — Buenos Aires	Spanish	36,900,000 34 per sq.mi. 13 per sq.km	1,073,514 sq.mi. 2,780,401 sq.km	Meat	Machinery	Peso	Republic
BAHAMAS — Nassau	English, Creole	301,000 58 per sq.mi. 22 per sq.km	5,359 sq.mi. 13,880 sq.km	Pharma-ceuticals	Foods	Bahamian Dollar	Parliamentary Democracy
BARBADOS — Bridgetown	English	300,000 1,524 per sq.mi. 588 per sq.km	166 sq.mi. 430 sq.km	Sugar	Manufactured Goods	Barbados Dollar	Parliamentary Democracy
BELIZE — Belmopan	English	300,000 31 per sq.mi. 12 per sq.km	8,865 sq.mi. 22,960 sq.km	Sugar	Machinery	Belize Dollar	Parliamentary Democracy
BOLIVIA — La Paz, Sucre	Spanish, Quechua, Aymara	8,600,000 20 per sq.mi. 8 per sq.km	424,162 sq.mi. 1,098,580 sq.km	Metals	Machinery	Boliviano	Republic
BRAZIL — Brasília	Portuguese	176,500,000 53 per sq.mi. 21 per sq.km	3,300,154 sq.mi. 8,547,399 sq.km	Iron Ore	Crude Oil	Real	Federal Republic
CHILE — Santiago	Spanish	15,800,000 54 per sq.mi. 21 per sq.km	292,135 sq.mi. 756,630 sq.km	Copper	Machinery	Peso	Republic
COLOMBIA — Bogotá	Spanish	44,200,000 100 per sq.mi. 39 per sq.km	439,734 sq.mi. 1,138,911 sq.km	Petroleum	Machinery	Peso	Republic

* COUNTRIES AND FLAGS NOT DRAWN TO SCALE   ** POPULATIONS ARE ROUNDED, *SOURCE: 2003 WORLD POPULATION DATA SHEET*

COUNTRY PROFILE ACTIVITY

Researching Economics Many countries in Latin America are considered to be developing countries that have yet to meet their full economic potential.

Assign a country to each student. Have them use world almanacs, encyclopedias, and atlases to compile an economic profile to put on charts titled "(Country): Economics at a Glance." The charts should include the gross domestic product (GDP), the economic activities of the country and corresponding percentages of the GDP, per capita income, areas of concern, and areas of strength. Have students present their findings to the class. Lead a discussion about the economic potential of these countries. Ask students to make economic generalizations or predictions.   📖 **EE4 Human Systems: Standard 11**

INTERDISCIPLINARY
connection

COUNTRY * AND CAPITAL	FLAG AND LANGUAGE	POPULATION ** AND DENSITY	LANDMASS	MAJOR EXPORT	MAJOR IMPORT	CURRENCY	GOVERNMENT
COSTA RICA San José	Spanish	4,200,000 211 per sq.mi. 81 per sq.km	19,730 sq.mi. 51,100 sq.km	Coffee	Raw Materials	Colón	Republic
CUBA Havana	Spanish	11,300,000 264 per sq.mi. 102 per sq.km	42,803 sq.mi. 110,860 sq.km	Sugar	Petroleum	Peso	Communist State
DOMINICA Roseau	English, French	100,000 242 per sq.mi. 93 per sq.km	290 sq.mi. 751 sq.km	Bananas	Manufactured Goods	East Caribbean Dollar	Republic
DOMINICAN REPUBLIC Santo Domingo	Spanish	8,700,000 463 per sq.mi. 179 per sq.km	18,815 sq.mi. 48,731 sq.km	Ferronickel	Foods	Peso	Republic
ECUADOR Quito	Spanish, Quechua	12,600,000 115 per sq.mi. 44 per sq.km	109,483 sq.mi. 283,561 sq.km	Petroleum	Transport Equipment	Sucre	Republic
EL SALVADOR San Salvador	Spanish	6,600,000 817 per sq.mi. 315 per sq.km	8,124 sq.mi. 21,041 sq.km	Coffee	Raw Materials	Colón	Republic
FRENCH GUIANA (FRANCE) Cayenne	French	200,000 5 per sq.mi. 2 per sq.km	34,749 sq.mi. 90,000 sq.km	Shrimp	Foods	French Franc	Overseas Department of France
GRENADA St. George's	English, French	100,000 800 per sq.mi. 309 per sq.km	131 sq.mi. 339 sq.km	Bananas	Foods	East Caribbean Dollar	Parliamentary Democracy
GUATEMALA Guatemala City	Spanish, Mayan Languages	12,400,000 294 per sq.mi. 114 per sq.km	42,042 sq.mi. 108,889 sq.km	Coffee	Petroleum	Quetzal	Republic

* COUNTRIES AND FLAGS NOT DRAWN TO SCALE   ** POPULATIONS ARE ROUNDED, *SOURCE: 2003 WORLD POPULATION DATA SHEET*

FOR AN ONLINE UPDATE OF THIS INFORMATION, VISIT GEOGRAPHY.GLENCOE.COM AND CLICK ON "TEXTBOOK UPDATES."

HISTORY The Inca of Peru were skillful builders. They constructed stone buildings that clung to steep mountain-sides. The stones for these buildings were cut so accurately that they fit together without using mortar.

Quinoa The Inca cultivated a grain high in the Andes called quinoa (pronounced *KEEN-wa*), which contains more protein than any other grain. It is a complete protein, similar to that found in milk. Today this supergrain is grown in Colorado.

Bolivia's Two Capitals Bolivia has two capitals, Sucre (founded in 1539) and La Paz. After attempts to move the capital from Sucre to La Paz in 1898, a civil war ensued. The factions settled their dispute by establishing two capitals. Sucre was kept as the seat of the supreme court, and La Paz became the center for the executive and legislative branches of the government.

COUNTRY PROFILE ACTIVITY

Places and Regions Latin America has some of the oldest Native American civilizations in the Western Hemisphere as well as many of the earliest European colonial sites.

Allow students to work in small groups to research an ancient Latin American civilization, such as the Aztec, Maya, or Inca. Have students share what they learned in an information-sharing session. Each group should take turns by first naming the civilization they researched and then stating one fact about it. Continue until all group members have had a chance to share a fact or give some additional information about a previously stated fact.
EE4 Human Systems: Standard 10

Culture NOTE

Peru Pre-Hispanic customs survive in the heart of the former Inca Empire in Peru. In remote villages many older people speak only Quechua, the language of their Inca ancestors. They also keep traditions in food, music, and religion that have all but died out in urban areas. Catholicism is part of daily life, but native beliefs and practices pervade its rituals.

UNIT 3 REGIONAL ATLAS

Latin America

COUNTRY PROFILES

COUNTRY * AND CAPITAL	FLAG AND LANGUAGE	POPULATION ** AND DENSITY	LANDMASS	MAJOR EXPORT	MAJOR IMPORT	CURRENCY	GOVERNMENT
GUYANA Georgetown	English	800,000 9 per sq.mi. 4 per sq.km	83,000 sq.mi. 214,970 sq.km	Sugar	Manufactured Goods	Guyana Dollar	Republic
HAITI Port-au-Prince	French, Creole	7,500,000 703 per sq.mi. 271 per sq.km	10,714 sq.mi. 27,750 sq.km	Manufactured Goods	Machinery	Gourde	Republic
HONDURAS Tegucigalpa	Spanish	6,900,000 159 per sq.mi. 61 per sq.km	43,278 sq.mi. 112,090 sq.km	Bananas	Machinery	Lempira	Republic
JAMAICA Kingston	English, Creole	2,600,000 624 per sq.mi. 241 per sq.km	4,243 sq.mi. 10,989 sq.km	Alumina	Machinery	Jamaican Dollar	Parliamentary Democracy
MEXICO Mexico City	Spanish, Native American Languages	104,900,000 139 per sq.mi. 54 per sq.km	756,062 sq.mi. 1,958,201 sq.km	Crude Oil	Machinery	Peso	Federal Republic
NICARAGUA Managua	Spanish	5,500,000 109 per sq.mi. 42 per sq.km	50,193 sq.mi. 130,000 sq.km	Coffee	Manufactured Goods	Cordoba	Republic
PANAMA Panama City	Spanish	3,000,000 102 per sq.mi. 32 per sq.km	29,158 sq.mi. 75,519 sq.km	Bananas	Machinery	Balboa	Republic
PARAGUAY Asunción	Spanish, Guaraní	6,200,000 39 per sq.mi. 15 per sq.km	157,046 sq.mi. 406,749 sq.km	Cotton	Machinery	Guaraní	Republic
PERU Lima	Spanish, Quechua, Aymara	27,100,000 55 per sq.mi. 21 per sq.km	496,224 sq.mi. 1,285,220 sq.km	Copper	Machinery	Nuevo Sol	Republic

* COUNTRIES AND FLAGS NOT DRAWN TO SCALE   ** POPULATIONS ARE ROUNDED, *SOURCE: 2003 WORLD POPULATION DATA SHEET*

COUNTRY PROFILE ACTIVITY

Researching Languages Have students work as a class to identify the official languages spoken in Latin America, along with the number of countries that speak each language. Have students construct a bar graph showing the results of their search. Have them use the completed graph to help them compose a paragraph concerning languages spoken in Latin America. To help students get started, tell them they can use the following sentence—or write one of their own—as their topic sentence: "A variety of languages are spoken in Latin America." (Students might prefer to assign a color to each language; then, on a map, shade each country the color that corresponds to the language that is spoken there.) 🖼 **EE4 Human Systems: Standard 10**

COUNTRY * AND CAPITAL	FLAG AND LANGUAGE	POPULATION ** AND DENSITY	LANDMASS	MAJOR EXPORT	MAJOR IMPORT	CURRENCY	GOVERNMENT
PUERTO RICO (U.S.) San Juan	Spanish, English	3,900,000 1,123 per sq.mi. 434 per sq.km	3,456 sq.mi. 8,951 sq.km	Pharma-ceuticals	Chemical Products	U.S. Dollar	U.S. Commonwealth
ST. KITTS AND NEVIS Basseterre	English	50,000 339 per sq.mi. 128 per sq.km	139 sq.mi. 360 sq.km	Machinery	Electronic Goods	East Caribbean Dollar	Parliamentary Democracy
ST. LUCIA Castries	English, French	200,000 667 per sq.mi. 261 per sq.km	239 sq.mi. 619 sq.km	Bananas	Foods	East Caribbean Dollar	Parliamentary Democracy
ST. VINCENT AND THE GRENADINES Kingstown	English, French	100,000 731 per sq.mi. 282 per sq.km	151 sq.mi. 391 sq.km	Bananas	Foods	East Caribbean Dollar	Parliamentary Democracy
SURINAME Paramaribo	Dutch	400,000 6 per sq.mi. 3 per sq.km	63,039 sq.mi. 163,271 sq.km	Bauxite	Machinery	Suriname Guilder	Republic
TRINIDAD AND TOBAGO Port-of-Spain	English	1,300,000 661 per sq.mi. 255 per sq.km	1,981 sq.mi. 5,131 sq.km	Petroleum	Machinery	Trinidad and Tobago Dollar	Republic
URUGUAY Montevideo	Spanish	3,400,000 49 per sq.mi. 19 per sq.km	68,498 sq.mi. 177,410 sq.km	Wool	Machinery	Peso	Republic
VENEZUELA Caracas	Spanish	25,700,000 73 per sq.mi. 28 per sq.km	352,143 sq.mi. 912,050 sq.km	Petroleum	Raw Materials	Bolivar	Federal Republic
VIRGIN ISLANDS (U.S.) Charlotte Amalie	English	123,498 922 per sq.mi. 356 per sq.km	134 sq.mi. 347 sq.km	Chemical Products	Crude Oil	U.S. Dollar	U.S. Territory

* COUNTRIES AND FLAGS NOT DRAWN TO SCALE   ** POPULATIONS ARE ROUNDED, *SOURCE: 2003 WORLD POPULATION DATA SHEET*

FOR AN ONLINE UPDATE OF THIS INFORMATION, VISIT GEOGRAPHY.GLENCOE.COM AND CLICK ON "TEXTBOOK UPDATES."

L2 Comparing

Have students choose one country from each region: Middle America, the Caribbean, and South America. Have them use a world almanac to compare the life expectancy of males and females in each country and share their findings with the class.

Bolivia Every community has its own traditions of dress—the shape of a hat or the design of a fabric indicates where each person comes from. Aymara women still dress like their ancestors, even when going to town. Men, who venture beyond their villages more often, are generally quicker to adopt modern ways.

☐ NATIONAL GEOGRAPHIC **GEOFACT**

▶ **The upper canopy of the Amazon rain forest is home to a whole world of plants that never root in soil. These *epiphytes*, or plants that live on the surfaces of other plants or objects, include ferns, mosses, and orchids. Strung like garlands on the highest tree branches, epiphytes get their nourishment solely from sunlight and moisture and nutrients in the air.**

COUNTRY PROFILE ACTIVITY

Comparing Statistics Organize students into pairs and have one student rank countries from greatest to least in population density. The other student will rank countries from greatest to least in terms of landmass. Have each pair compare their rankings to see what generalizations they can make about some countries based on these two factors. Ask students what correlation they see between population density and landmass in Barbados and Brazil. (*Barbados: small landmass, very densely populated; Brazil: the largest landmass in Latin America and a low population density*) Have students share observations with the class. ⊕ **EE4 Human Systems: Standard 9**

① FOCUS

Ask students if they have eaten any Latin American foods (fruits, vegetables, main dishes). **Ask: What were some of the ingredients of those foods? Are these same ingredients found in foods you often eat?**

② TEACH

Cultural Exchange Latin America was the original source of corn, potatoes, and cacao, which now grow and are food staples in many other parts of the world. Another staple of many countries, coffee, was originally brought to Latin America from Africa. Today coffee is the main export of several Latin American countries. Have students identify these countries by consulting the "Country Profiles" on pages 186–189. *(Costa Rica, El Salvador, Guatemala, Nicaragua)* Have students look at the physical map on page 182. **Ask: What characteristics of Central America's location and geography make it a good region for growing coffee?** *(abundant rainfall, high elevation)*

 Meeting National Standards

Geography for Life
The following standards are met in the Student Edition:

EE4 Human Systems:
 Standards 10, 11
EE5 Environment and Society:
 Standards 15, 16
EE6 The Uses of Geography:
 Standard 18

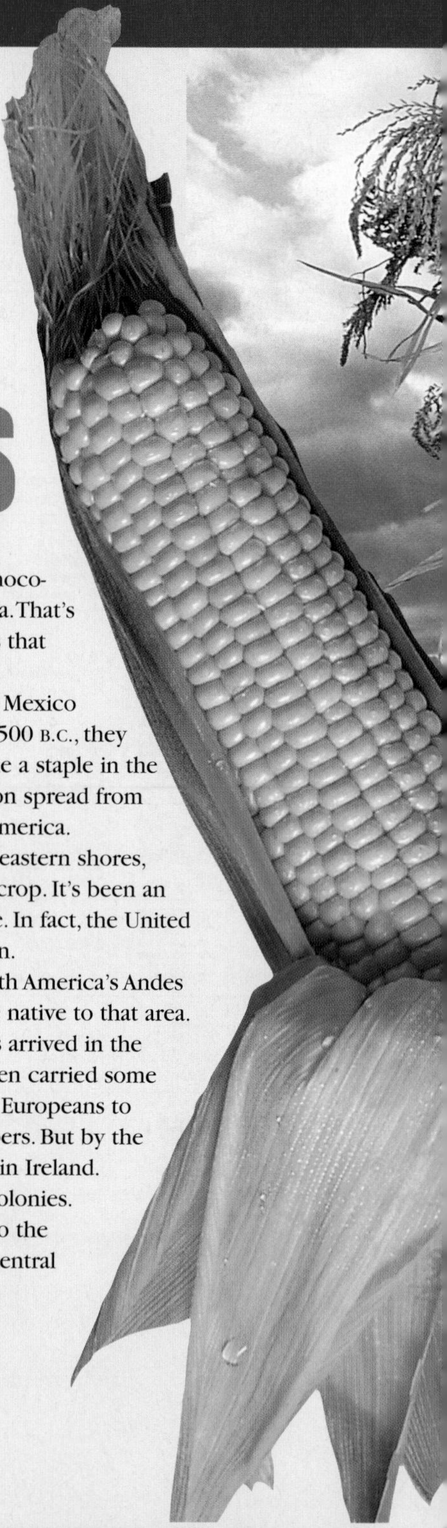

GLOBAL CONNECTION

LATIN AMERICA AND THE UNITED STATES

FOOD CROPS

 If you've had cornflakes, French fries, or a chocolate bar recently, you can thank Latin America. That's because these foods all are made from crops that originated there.

About 10,000 years ago, Native Americans in what is now Mexico gathered ears of wild corn for food. Between 5000 B.C. and 3500 B.C., they domesticated the plants and began raising them. Corn became a staple in the diets of the Maya and Aztec peoples. Gradually, corn cultivation spread from Mexico, eventually reaching the northeastern part of North America.

When European colonists arrived on America's eastern shores, Native Americans taught them how to grow this crop. It's been an important part of American agriculture ever since. In fact, the United States now leads the world in corn production.

Roughly 2,000 years ago, people in South America's Andes began cultivating potatoes, which are native to that area. When Spanish and English explorers arrived in the 1500s, they sampled potatoes and then carried some back to their homelands. It took a while for Europeans to develop a taste for these strange-looking tubers. But by the 1700s, potatoes were widely grown, especially in Ireland. Immigrants from Europe brought potatoes to the American colonies.

Chocolate is made from the seeds of cacao, a tree native to the Amazon River basin. How and when cacao seeds arrived in Central

190   Unit 3

BACKGROUND INFORMATION

Geography in History: Movement The potato, which originated in Latin America, had a profound effect on the history of Ireland and the United States. The potato became an important staple food in Ireland. When a fungus from North America was accidentally introduced into Ireland in 1845, and the country also had unusually cool, moist weather that year, the resulting blight nearly wiped out the potato crop. Between 1846 and 1849, repeated potato crop failures caused widespread famine, which caused many people to leave Ireland. As many as 1.5 million Irish people emigrated to Great Britain and to North America. Today people of Irish ancestry make up more than 15 percent of the United States population.
🌐 **EE5 Environment and Society: Standard 15**

NATIONAL GEOGRAPHIC

America remains a mystery, but we do know that cacao came to play a major role in Maya and Aztec cultures. The Aztec believed that cacao seeds were a gift from heaven. The seeds were ground up to make a rich beverage called *xocoatl* (shoh•KOH•ahtl). However, the drink wasn't sweet. It was rather bitter and spiced with chili peppers!

In 1519 the Spanish explorer Hernán Cortés was served a cup of *xocoatl* by an Aztec ruler. When Cortés returned home, he took cacao seeds with him and introduced the drink to Spain. The Spanish made a few alterations. Their "chocolate" was sweetened with sugar and flavored with cinnamon and vanilla. For about 80 years, the Spanish kept their new beverage a secret. Once word got out, though, a chocolate craze spread across Europe.

When chocolate first arrived in the American colonies, it was an expensive European delicacy that only the wealthy could afford. Then in 1765, cacao seeds began to be imported directly, and relatively cheaply, from the West Indies. Finally, the average American was able to afford what the Aztec believed was the "food of the gods."

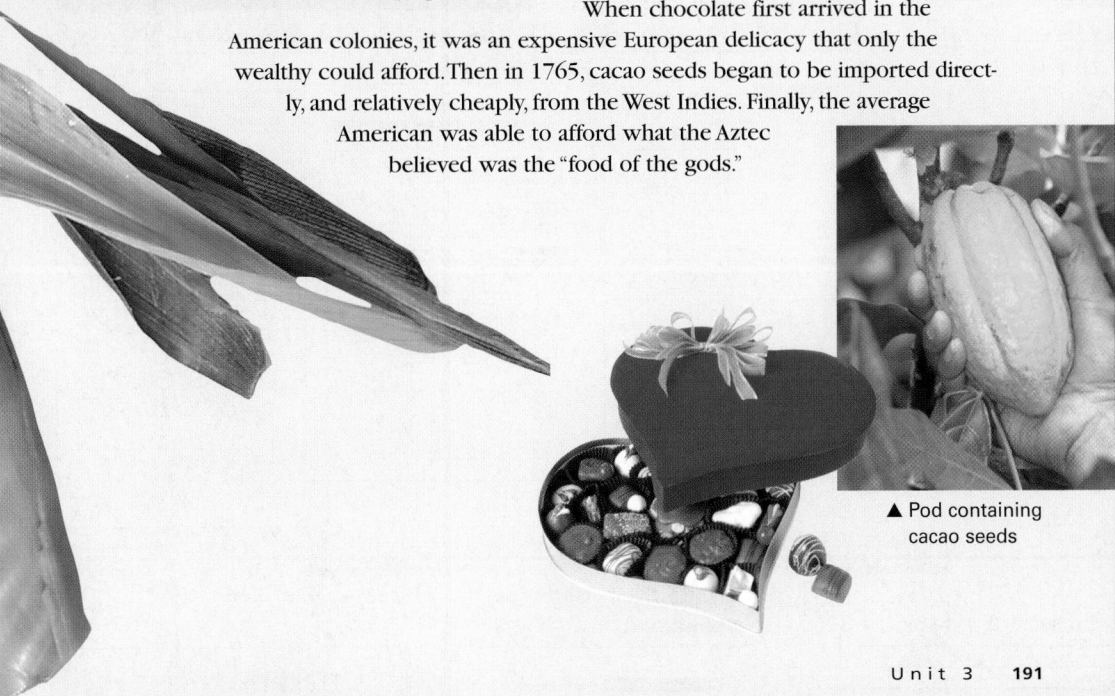

▲ Guatemalan farmer carrying cornstalks

▲ Pod containing cacao seeds

Unit 3 **191**

FYI

Potatoes Spanish explorers and conquistadors took the potato back to Europe. For almost 200 years, however, Europeans refused to grow or eat many potatoes. Some medical experts predicted that potatoes would cause leprosy or other diseases because they were so ugly and misshapen. Many religious leaders thought eating potatoes was sinful since they were not mentioned in the Bible. Some agriculturists believed that growing potatoes would destroy the soil.

❸ ASSESS

Have students brainstorm and write on the board a list of all the foods they eat that contain corn, potatoes, and chocolate or the variety of ways in which those items are prepared. *(corn—corn on the cob, cereal, tortilla chips; potatoes—french fries, potato salad; chocolate—candy, ice cream)* **Ask: Would your diet change drastically if these foods were no longer a part of it, or would there not be much difference? See if there is a consensus of opinion.**

❹ CLOSE

Have students evaluate the cultural effects that came with the global exchange of foods.

CONNECTION ACTIVITY

Foods Have students use resources from the media center, the Internet, or interviews with people from Latin America to assemble a Latin American cookbook. Each student should find a recipe for a typical dish in a Latin American country and then conduct research on at least one ingredient native to the country. Students should use the information they find about that ingredient as an introduction to their recipe. You may wish to have students sign up for their chosen country or dish to avoid duplication. Combine the recipes into a cookbook and encourage interested students to make some of these recipes.

🌐 **EE4 Human Systems: Standard 10**

PLANNING GUIDE

NOTE: The following materials may be used when teaching Chapter 8. Section-level support materials are shown at point-of-use in the margins of the Teacher Wraparound Edition.

TEACHING TRANSPARENCIES

L2 Unit 3 Map Overlay Transparencies

L2 Political Map Transparency 3

GEOGRAPHIC LITERACY

Focus on Geography Literacy

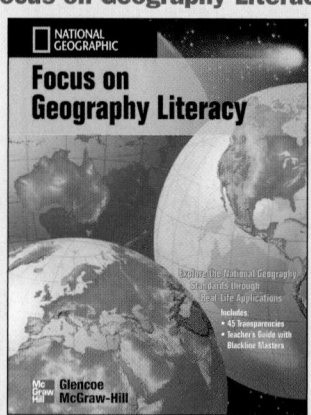

APPLICATION AND ENRICHMENT

L3 Enrichment Activity 8

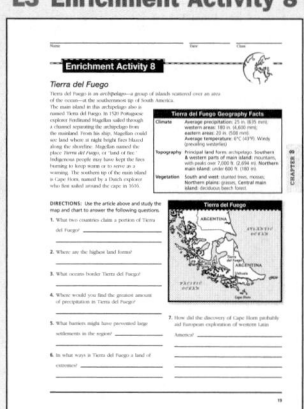

REVIEW AND REINFORCEMENT

L1 Vocabulary Activity 8   L1 Reinforcing Skills Activity 8   L1 Reteaching Activity 8

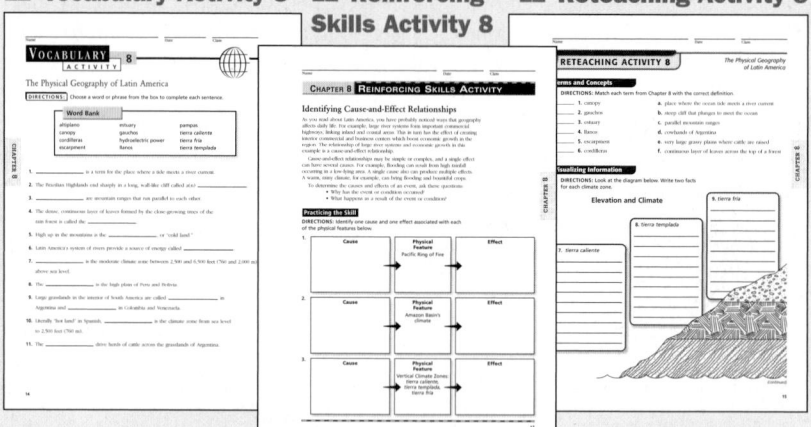

ASSESSMENT

L2 Chapter 8 Test Form A

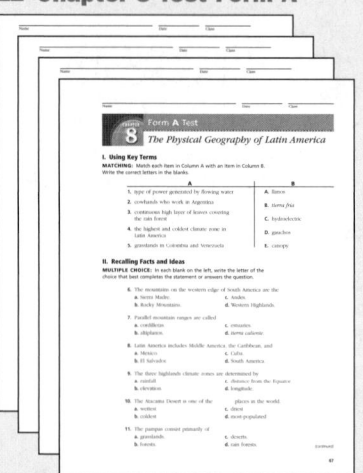

L2 Chapter 8 Test Form B

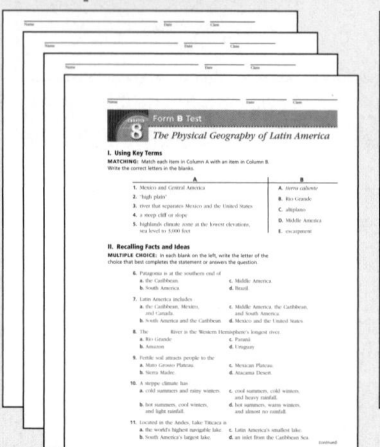

L1/ELL Performance Assessment Activity 8

ExamView® Pro Testmaker

The following Spanish language materials are available in the Spanish Resources binder:

- 📁 Spanish Vocabulary Activities
- 📁 Spanish Guided Reading Activities
- 📁 Spanish Reteaching Activities
- 📁 Spanish Summaries
- 📁 Spanish Quizzes and Tests
- 📁 Spanish Reading Essentials and Study Guide

- 📼 World Regions Video
- 📼 MindJogger Videoquiz
- 💿 Vocabulary PuzzleMaker CD-ROM
- 💿 Interactive Tutor Self-Assessment CD-ROM
- 💿 ExamView® Pro Testmaker CD-ROM
- 💿 Audio Program
- 💿 TeacherWorks CD-ROM
- 💿 Interactive Student Edition CD-ROM
- 💿 Glencoe Skillbuilder Interactive Workbook CD-ROM, Level 2
- 💿 Presentation Plus! CD-ROM

Timesaving Tools

TeacherWorks™
All-In-One Planner and Resource Center

- **Interactive Teacher Edition** Access your Teacher Wraparound Edition and your classroom resources with a few easy clicks.

- **Interactive Lesson Planner** Planning has never been easier! Organize your week, month, semester, or year with all the lesson helps you need to make teaching creative, timely, and relevant.

Use Glencoe's **Presentation Plus!** multimedia teacher tool to easily present dynamic lessons that visually excite your students. Using Microsoft PowerPoint® you can customize the presentations to create your own personalized lessons.

GEOGRAPHY Online

Use our Web site for additional resources. All essential content is covered in the Student Edition.

You and your students can visit geography.glencoe.com, the Web site companion to *Glencoe World Geography*. This innovative integration of electronic and print media offers your students a wealth of opportunities. The student text directs students to the Web site for the following options:

- • Chapter Overviews
- • Student Activities
- • Self-Check Quizzes
- • Textbook Updates

Answers are provided for you in the "Web Activity Lesson Plan." Additional Web resources and Interactive Tutor puzzles are also available.

▶ Additional Glencoe Teacher Support

- ■ Teaching Strategies for the Geography Classroom (including Block Scheduling Pacing Guides)
- ■ Graphic Organizer Transparencies Strategies and Activities
- ■ Outline Map Resource Book
- ■ Reading in the Content Area

PLANNING GUIDE

SECTION RESOURCES

Daily Objectives	Reproducible Resources	Multimedia Resources

SECTION 1   The Land

1. Explain how geographers divide the large region known as Latin America.
2. Identify the factors that have shaped the formation of Latin America's landforms.
3. Discuss how the Latin American landscape has influenced patterns of human settlement.
4. List the natural resources that make Latin America an economically important region.

 Reproducible Lesson Plan 8-1
Daily Lecture Notes 8-1
Guided Reading Activity 8-1*
Reading Essentials and Study Guide 8-1*
Section Quiz 8-1*

 Daily Focus Skills Transparency 8-1
Political Map Transparency 3
Unit 3 Map Overlay Transparencies
Interactive Tutor Self-Assessment CD-ROM
ExamView® Pro Testmaker CD-ROM*
Presentation Plus! CD-ROM

SECTION 2   Climate and Vegetation

1. List the climate regions that are represented in Latin America.
2. Describe how Latin America's location and landforms affect climates even within particular regions.
3. Discuss how the natural vegetation and agriculture of Latin America are influenced by climatic factors.

 Reproducible Lesson Plan 8-2
Vocabulary Activity 8*
Daily Lecture Notes 8-2
Guided Reading Activity 8-2*
Reading Essentials and Study Guide 8-2*
Reteaching Activity 8*
Reinforcing Skills Activity 8
Section Quiz 8–2*

 Daily Focus Skills Transparency 8-2
Political Map Transparency 3
Unit 3 Map Overlay Transparencies
Vocabulary PuzzleMaker CD-ROM
Interactive Tutor Self-Assessment CD-ROM
ExamView® Pro Testmaker CD-ROM*
Presentation Plus! CD-ROM

 Blackline Master   Software   Videocassette   *Also available in Spanish

 Transparency   CD-ROM   DVD

OUT OF TIME?  Assign the Chapter 8 **Reading Essentials and Study Guide.**

Block Schedule

Activities that are particularly suited to use within the block scheduling framework are identified throughout this chapter by the following designation: 📖

KEY TO ABILITY LEVELS

Teaching strategies have been coded for various learning styles and abilities.

L1   **BASIC** activities for all students

L2   **AVERAGE** activities for average to above-average students

L3   **CHALLENGING** activities for above-average students

ELL   **ENGLISH LANGUAGE LEARNER** activities

Teacher to Teacher

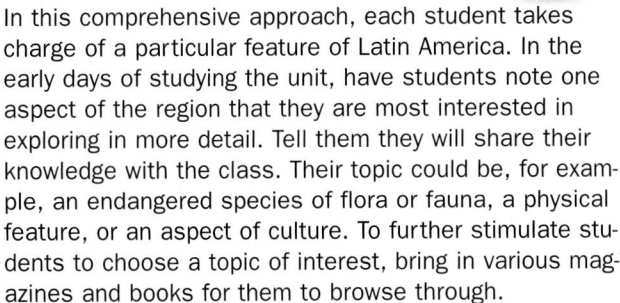

Walter Ryce
San Jose School District
San Jose, CA

Oral Reports

In this comprehensive approach, each student takes charge of a particular feature of Latin America. In the early days of studying the unit, have students note one aspect of the region that they are most interested in exploring in more detail. Tell them they will share their knowledge with the class. Their topic could be, for example, an endangered species of flora or fauna, a physical feature, or an aspect of culture. To further stimulate students to choose a topic of interest, bring in various magazines and books for them to browse through.

When students choose a topic of interest early in the course of study, it focuses their attention and helps them begin to take responsibility for their learning. During the semester, students conduct ongoing research on their topic and prepare to write a report. By the end of the semester, they are ready to do final research and writing on the topic that they have been thinking about for many weeks. Finally, each student gives an oral briefing of the report to the class, and takes questions from the audience.

NATIONAL GEOGRAPHIC   TEACHER'S CORNER

Index to National Geographic Magazine:

The following articles may be used for research relating to this chapter:

- "After the Deluge," by A. R. Williams, November 1999.
- "Uncovering Patagonia's Lost World," by James Shreeve, December 1997.
- "Amazon: South America's River Road," by Jere van Dyk, February 1995.

National Geographic Society Products:

To order the following products for use with this chapter, call National Geographic Society at 1-800-368-2728.

- *South America* (Video)
- *Central America* (Map)
- *South America Political* (Map)
- *National Geographic Desk Reference* (Book)
- *National Geographic Atlas of the World, Seventh Edition* (Book)

NGS ONLINE

Access National Geographic's Web site for current events, activities, links, interactive features, and archives.
www.nationalgeographic.com

Meeting National Standards

Geography For Life

The following standards are highlighted in Chapter 8:

Section 1   EE2 Places and Regions:
Standards 4, 6
EE5 Environment and Society:
Standard 14

Section 2   EE1 The World in Spatial Terms:
Standards 1, 3
EE2 Places and Regions: Standard 4
EE3 Physical Systems: Standard 8
EE5 Environment and Society: Standard 15
EE6 The Uses of Geography: Standard 17

Local Objectives

_____

_____

MEETING SPECIAL NEEDS

In addition to the Differentiated Instruction strategies found in each section, the following resources are also suitable for your special needs students:

- ***ExamView® Pro Testmaker CD-ROM*** allows teachers to tailor tests by reducing answer choices.
- The ***Audio Program*** includes the entire narrative of the student edition so that less-proficient readers can listen to the words as they read them.
- The ***Reading Essentials and Study Guide*** provides the same content as the student edition but is written two grade levels below the textbook.
- ***Guided Reading Activities*** give less-proficient readers point-by-point instructions to increase comprehension as they read each textbook section.
- ***Enrichment Activities*** include a stimulating collection of readings and activities for gifted and talented students.

CHAPTER OBJECTIVES

1. Describe the dominant landforms and natural resources of Latin America.
2. Discuss Latin America's climate and vegetation.

GLENCOE TECHNOLOGY

 Use *MindJogger Videoquiz* to preview the Chapter 8 content.

GeoJournal

For access to additional photos, maps, and information on the geographic features of Latin America, go to www.nationalgeographic.com (See Teacher pages in front for strategies for using journals in the geography classroom.)

GEOGRAPHY *Online*

Introduce students to chapter content and key terms by having them access **Chapter Overview 8** at geography.glencoe.com

FOLDABLES™
Study Organizer

Dinah Zike's Foldables are three-dimensional, interactive graphic organizers that help students practice basic writing skills, review key vocabulary terms, and identify main ideas. Have students complete the Foldable activity in the **Dinah Zike's Reading and Study Skills Foldables** booklet.

CHAPTER **8**

The Physical Geography of Latin America

GeoJournal

As you read this chapter, use your journal to describe the geographic features of Latin America. Choose strong, vivid terms to capture the beauty, grandeur, and economic importance of the physical features of the region.

GEOGRAPHY *Online*

Chapter Overview Visit the **Glencoe World Geography** Web site at geography.glencoe.com and click on Chapter Overviews—Chapter 8 to preview information about the physical geography of the region.

ABOUT THE PHOTO

Visual Instruction One of the world's great natural wonders, Iguaçu Falls is located on the Iguaçu River at the border of Argentina and Brazil. Water from the Iguaçu River plunges more than 269 feet (82 m) in 275 separate falls. The word *iguaçu* comes from the Guaraní word for "great water." At 1.7 miles (2.7 m) across, the horseshoe-shaped falls is almost three times wider than Niagara Falls, on the United States-Canada border. Both the Brazilian and Argentine governments have made Iguaçu Falls a national park, and UNESCO designated the falls a World Heritage site. **Ask: Why would Iguaçu Falls be made a national park and a World Heritage site?** *(to preserve an area of great beauty and to encourage tourism)*
🌐 **EE2 Places and Regions: Standard 6**

Guide to Reading

Consider What You Know
News accounts of natural disasters in Latin America describe the destruction caused by hurricanes, earthquakes, and volcanic eruptions. What geographic factors might make the region vulnerable to such natural disasters?

Reading Strategy
Organizing Complete a graphic organizer similar to the one below by listing the countries drained by the Amazon Basin.

Read to Find Out
- How do geographers divide the large region known as Latin America?
- What factors have shaped Latin America's landforms?
- How has the Latin American landscape influenced patterns of human settlement?
- What natural resources make Latin America an economically important region?

Terms to Know
- cordillera
- altiplano
- escarpment
- llano
- pampas
- gaucho
- hydroelectric power
- estuary

Places to Locate
- Amazon River
- Middle America
- Central America
- West Indies
- South America
- Sierra Madre
- Andes
- Mexican Plateau
- Patagonia
- Mato Grosso Plateau
- Rio Grande
- Río de la Plata

◀ *View from the top of the Iguaçu Falls, Brazil*

The Land

NATIONAL GEOGRAPHIC

A Geographic View

On the Amazon

I watched the river. Each boat carried a tiny cross-section of Amazon society. . . . Canoes drifted past. Small wooden passenger boats or traders mumbled their smoky way downstream. No matter how blue the sky, the river never caught the color in its reflection; it was loaded with sediment carved from the Andes. Logs and brush and whirlpools moved past in endless flow, and river dolphins rolled ahead of us.

—Jere van Dyk, "Amazon: South America's River Road," National Geographic, February 1995

Brazilian riverboat

From the headwaters of the Peruvian Andes to the Atlantic coast of Brazil, the **Amazon River** winds about 4,000 miles (6,400 km) through the heart of South America. This mighty river, the world's second longest, is only one prominent feature of Latin America's large and varied landscape. In this section you will explore the region's physical geography: mountains, islands, coastal lowlands, plains, and waterways.

A Vast Region

Located in the Western Hemisphere south of the United States, Latin America has a land area of about 8 million square miles (20,720,000 sq. km)—nearly 16 percent of Earth's land surface. The countries of the region share a heritage of settlement by Europeans, especially those from Spain and Portugal. Most of these settlers spoke Spanish or Portuguese—languages based on Latin, the language of the Roman Empire, which gives the region its name.

Chapter 8 🌐 **193**

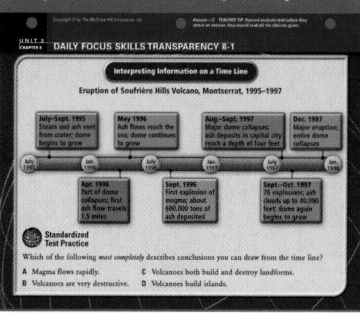

L1 Locate

Project Unit Map Overlay Transparency 3–5 and have students locate the following: the Andes, Sierra Madre Occidental, Sierra Madre Oriental, Guiana Highlands, Brazilian Highlands, Anáhuac, the altiplano, and Patagonia. **Ask:** How might these regions be classified? *(as highlands)*

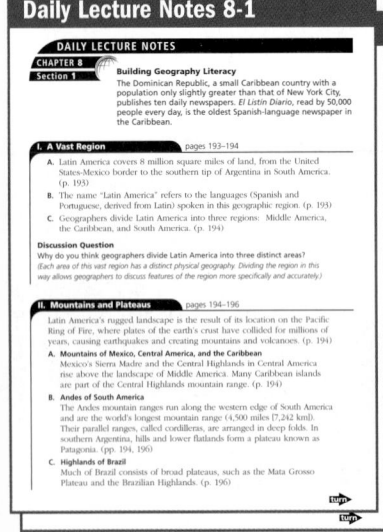

Daily Lecture Notes 8-1

☐ NATIONAL GEOGRAPHIC **GEOFACT**

▶ **Many nonvolcanic Caribbean islands are partially or completely composed of coral, the hard outer skeletons of tiny marine animals. The world's second-longest coral reef—a 180-mile (290-km) stretch popular with tourists and ecologists—lies off the coast of Belize in Central America.**

Geographers usually divide Latin America into three areas—Middle America, the Caribbean, and South America. **Middle America** consists of Mexico and the seven countries of **Central America**, the stretch of land that links the landmasses of North and South America. The Caribbean islands, also known as the **West Indies**, fall into three groups—the Bahamas, the Greater Antilles, and the Lesser Antilles. The continent of **South America** is by far the largest land area of Latin America. Among South America's 13 countries, Brazil is the largest in both land area and population.

Mountains and Plateaus

One of Latin America's most distinctive landforms is its towering mountains. Thrusting upward in countless folds and ridges, this mountainous profile begins in North America as the Rocky Mountains and extends all the way to South America's southern tip. The mountains' names change as you move south. In Mexico they are the **Sierra Madre**; in Central America, the Central Highlands; and in South America, the **Andes**.

Latin America has such a rugged landscape because much of the region sits along the Pacific Ring of Fire, where plates of the earth's crust have collided for billions of years. These collisions have formed mountains and volcanoes and have caused tremendous earthquakes. They continue to change the landscape today. In 1999, for example, a strong earthquake reduced to rubble many towns and villages in northwestern South America.

Despite obstacles, the mountains and plateaus of Latin America have been places of human settlement for thousands of years. People wanting to

Comparing Lands

Latin America is about three times the size of the continental United States.

escape the heat of the lowland areas have been drawn to cooler mountain climates. They also have been attracted by the mountains' rich natural resources—water, volcanic soil, timber, and minerals. Historically, Latin America's rugged terrain has tended to block movement and trade and to isolate regions and peoples. In recent decades radio, television, air transport, and the Internet have begun to break down old physical barriers.

Mountains of Mexico, Central America, and the Caribbean

Look at the physical-political map on page 195. Notice that Mexico's Sierra Madre consists of two mountain ranges—the Sierra Madre Oriental ("Eastern") and the Sierra Madre Occidental ("Western")—that meet near Mexico City to form the sharp-peaked Sierra Madre del Sur ("of the South"). These ranges surround the densely populated **Mexican Plateau**, which covers much of central Mexico. In the plateau's southern area, the mild climate, fertile volcanic soil, and adequate rainfall have attracted human settlement for thousands of years.

Farther south, the Central Highlands, a chain of volcanic mountains, rise like a backbone across Central America. Many Caribbean islands are also part of this mountain range, which extends across the bed of the Caribbean Sea. The islands are actually volcanic peaks that rise above sea level. Some of these volcanoes are still active, which can make living on these islands hazardous.

Andes of South America

None of Latin America's other mountains compare with the 4,500-mile (7,242-km) stretch of the Andes along the western edge of South America. Their extent makes the Andes the world's longest mountain range, as well as one of the highest, with some peaks rising to more than 20,000 feet (6,096 m) above sea level. The Andes consist of several ranges that run parallel to one another like deep folds in a carpet. Such parallel ranges are called cordilleras (KAWR•duhl•YEHR•uhs).

In Peru and Bolivia, the spectacular Andes peaks encircle a region called the altiplano, which means "high plain." In southern Argentina, hills and lower flatlands form the plateau of **Patagonia**.

DIFFERENTIATED INSTRUCTION

Reading Support For students who have problems with reading, direct them to the "Guide to Reading" at the beginning of the section on page 193. Remind them that this feature sums up the content of the section. Have students speculate on what the section will cover based on the information in "Guide to Reading." As they read the section, tell them to see if their predictions were correct. ▦ **EE2 Places and Regions: Standard 4**

 Refer to *Inclusion for the Social Studies Classroom Strategies and Activities.*

Latin America: Physical-Political Map

120°W · Río Grande · 100°W · 80°W · Bermuda Is. · 60°W · 40°W

30°N

Baja California · Mexican Plateau · Sierra Madre Oriental · Gulf of Mexico · ATLANTIC OCEAN · TROPIC OF CANCER

Sierra Madre Occidental · MEXICO · BAHAMAS · WEST INDIES

20°N · Yucatán Pen. · CUBA · DOMINICAN REPUBLIC · Virgin Is. · ANTIGUA AND BARBUDA

Sierra Madre del Sur · BELIZE · HAITI · JAMAICA · Greater Antilles · Puerto Rico · Lesser Antilles · Guadeloupe · DOMINICA · Martinique

HONDURAS · GUATEMALA · Caribbean · Sea · GRENADA · ST. LUCIA · ST. VINCENT AND THE GRENADINES · BARBADOS

EL SALVADOR · NICARAGUA · TRINIDAD AND TOBAGO

10°N · COSTA RICA · PANAMA · VENEZUELA · GUYANA · SURINAME

Isthmus of Panama · COLOMBIA · Orinoco R. · LLANOS · GUIANA HIGHLANDS · FRENCH GUIANA

EQUATOR · Galápagos Islands · ECUADOR · AMAZON · Amazon R.

0° · BASIN

BRAZIL

PERU · ANDES

10°S · PACIFIC OCEAN · Lake Titicaca · MATO GROSSO PLATEAU · São Francisco R. · BRAZILIAN HIGHLANDS

BOLIVIA · Paraguay R. · Paraná R.

GRAN CHACO · PARAGUAY · HIGHLANDS

20°S · TROPIC OF CAPRICORN · CHILE

ARGENTINA

Aconcagua 22,834 ft. ▲ (6,960 m) · URUGUAY · ATLANTIC OCEAN

Elevations

Feet	Meters
10,000	3,000
5,000	1,500
2,000	600
1,000	300
0	0

PAMPAS · Río de la Plata

— National boundary
▲ Mountain peak

PATAGONIA · ANDES

N

0 mi. 1,000
0 km 1,000
Lambert Azimuthal Equal-Area projection

Tierra del Fuego · Falkland Islands (Islas Malvinas) · South Georgia I.

Cape Horn

30°S
40°S
50°S

Geography Skills for Life

1. **Interpreting Maps** What physical features surround the Mexican Plateau?

2. **Applying Geography Skills** Which South American rivers flow through highlands areas? Lowlands areas?

Find NGS online map resources @ www.nationalgeographic.com/maps

L3 Math

Inform students that the distance from western Peru to eastern Brazil is about 47 degrees of longitude. Tell students that each degree of longitude corresponds to about 69 miles (111 km). Have students calculate the width of South America at this point. *(about 3,240 miles [47 × 69] or about 5,220 km [111 × 47])*

L1/ELL

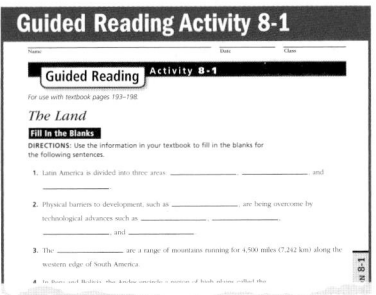

Guided Reading Activity 8-1

NATIONAL GEOGRAPHIC · **MAP STUDY**

Answers:

1. *Sierra Madre Occidental and Sierra Madre Oriental*

2. *Most begin in highlands areas but they mostly flow, except for the São Francisco River, through lowlands.*

Map Skills Practice

Movement What dominant physical feature that runs the length of western South America might make trade difficult? Why? *(Andes; they are high, rugged mountains, which make transportation difficult.)*

COOPERATIVE LEARNING ACTIVITY

Natural Resources Direct students' attention to the last subhead in the section, "Natural Resources," on page 198. Tell them to note that these resources include gold, copper, tin, silver, and bauxite. Have students list things that are made with these minerals on the board. Then organize the class into groups. Have each group copy the list from the board, and tell groups to "scavenge" for pictures in magazines of as many items on the list as they can. Have the groups return to the classroom and compare their collections. **Ask: Why do many cultures consider items made of precious metals such as gold and silver valuable?** *(Answers may include beauty and scarcity because these resources are nonrenewable.)* ◼ EE5 Environment and Society: Standard 16

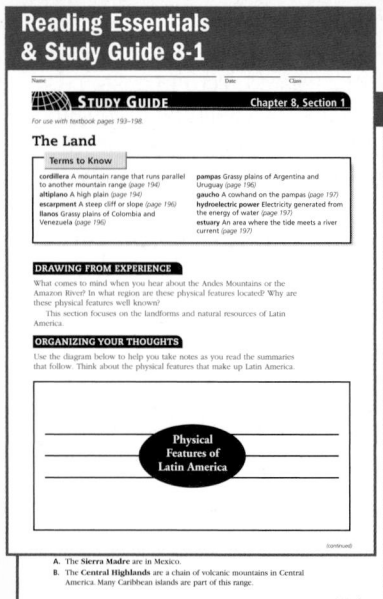
Wildlife expert William Franklin describes the
windswept Patagonia region at the southern end
of South America:

> 66 *The sky is full of mountains in this
> country. I often get a sore neck from
> admiring these Andean peaks as we
> trek on foot and horseback over the
> plains and hills. The wind is our con-
> stant companion; locals advise that if
> you want to see Patagonia, just stand
> still and it will all blow past you.* 99

William Franklin, "Patagonia Puma:
The Lord of Land's End," *National
Geographic*, January 1991

Highlands of Brazil

Eastern South America is marked by broad
plateaus and valleys. The **Mato Grosso Plateau**, a
sparsely populated plateau of forests and grasslands, spreads over much of Brazil and across the
west to Bolivia and Peru. East of the Mato Grosso
Plateau lie the Brazilian Highlands, a plateau so
vast that it spans several climate and vegetation
zones. On the eastern edge of the Brazilian
Highlands, the plateau plunges sharply to the
Atlantic Ocean, forming a steep cliff or slope called
an escarpment.

Lowlands and Plains

Narrow coastal lowlands wind their way along
the Gulf of Mexico and the Caribbean and also hem
the Atlantic and Pacific coasts of South America.
One of the longest strips of coastal plain in Latin
America lies along Brazil's Atlantic coast. In northeastern Brazil, this plain is about 40 miles (60 km)
wide but narrows considerably as it winds southward. Between Rio de Janeiro and the southeastern
seaport of Santos, the plain disappears entirely, only
to reappear and widen again near Brazil's borders
with Uruguay and Argentina. Hemmed in by highland escarpment, Brazil's coastal plain has been a
major area of settlement and economic activity
since the 1500s.

Inland areas of South America hold vast grasslands: the llanos (LAH•nohs) of Colombia and
Venezuela, and the pampas of Argentina and

NATIONAL GEOGRAPHIC World Explorer

Geography Skills for Life

The Coast of Brazil Ipanema Beach in
Rio de Janeiro is a popular tourist area.

Place Describe the physical environment in
which Rio de Janeiro is located.

CRITICAL THINKING ACTIVITY

Identifying Alternatives Direct students' attention to the political map on page 183,
and show them where Santiago, the capital of Chile, is located. Then list four other Latin
American capital cities—Mexico City, Bogotà, Quito, and Sucre—that are also at an elevation of 5,000 feet (1,500 m) and have students locate them on the map. **Ask:** What challenges might inhabitants of these cities face? How can they overcome the natural
limitations to economic development? *(isolation, which limits communication and transportation; these limitations may be minimized by using the Internet to improve communication and encouraging tourism.)* EE2 Places and Regions: Standard 4

NATIONAL GEOGRAPHIC **World Explorer**

Geography | **Skills for Life**

The Gaucho Argentine cowhands known as gauchos ride the pampas herding livestock, the major agricultural product of Argentina.
Human-Environment Interaction How does terrain in Argentina support cattle ranching?

Uruguay. Both plains areas provide wide grazing lands for beef cattle. Ranchers on large estates employ cowhands, called *llaneros* in the llanos and gauchos in the pampas, to drive great herds of cattle across the rolling terrain. Known for its fertile soil, the pampas region is one of the world's major "breadbaskets," producing an abundance of wheat and corn. Many people in the pampas region grow crops on small- and medium-sized farms.

Water Systems

Like a massive circulatory system, Latin America's many waterways serve as arteries that transport people and goods to different parts of the region and the world. Most of the region's major rivers are in South America. One important exception is the **Rio Grande**, or *Río Bravo del Norte* ("Wild River of the North"), which forms part of the long border between Mexico and the United States.

Economics
Rivers of South America

Middle America's rivers are generally small, but the rivers that cross South America are gigantic. The Amazon is the Western Hemisphere's longest river

and carries ten times the water volume of the Mississippi River. Hundreds of smaller rivers join the Amazon as it journeys from the Andes to the Atlantic Ocean. These rivers together form the Amazon Basin, which drains parts of Bolivia, Peru, Ecuador, Colombia, and Venezuela, as well as Brazil. Despite the tremendous force of water at its mouth, the Amazon is navigable. Oceangoing ships can travel upstream as far as 2,300 miles (3,701 km) from the Atlantic coast.

The Paraná, Paraguay, and Uruguay Rivers together form the second-largest river system in Latin America. This system drains the rainy eastern half of South America. Important commercial highways, these three rivers provide inland water routes and hydroelectric power—electricity generated from the energy of water—for Argentina, Bolivia, Brazil, Paraguay, and Uruguay. After coursing through inland areas, the three rivers flow into a broad estuary, an area where the tide meets a river

Student Web Activity Visit the **Glencoe World Geography** Web site at geography.glencoe.com and click on Student Web Activities—Chapter 8 for an activity about the physical geography of Costa Rica.

NATIONAL GEOGRAPHIC **World Explorer**

Answer
Extensive grasslands are ideal for grazing.

More About the Photo
Gauchos dominated the range from the middle 1700s until the late 1800s. Like the U.S. cowboy, they have their own mythology and heroes.

③ ASSESS

Assign Section 1 Assessment as homework or as an in-class activity.

✷ Have students use **Interactive Tutor Self-Assessment CD-ROM** to review Section 1.

L2

Section Quiz 8-1

CHAPTER 8	Section **1** Quiz
	The Land

MATCHING: Match each item in Column A with an item in Column B. Write the correct letters in the blanks. *(10 points each)*

A		B
1. the place where a tide meets a river current		A. Sierra Madre
2. mountain range in Mexico		B. altiplano
3. parallel mountain ranges		C. estuary
4. high plain		D. Andes
5. mountain range along the western edge of South America		E. cordilleras

MULTIPLE CHOICE: In each blank on the left, write the letter of the choice that best completes the statement or answers the question. *(10 points each)*

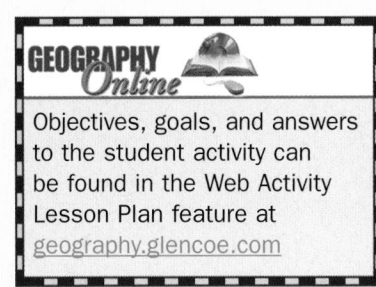

GEOGRAPHY *Online*

Objectives, goals, and answers to the student activity can be found in the Web Activity Lesson Plan feature at geography.glencoe.com

---

TEAM-TEACHING ACTIVITY: SCIENCE

Organizing Geographic Data Some scientists hypothesize that up to 20,000 species of plants and animals are becoming extinct around the world each year. A large percentage of these extinctions occur in tropical rain forests such as the Amazon River Basin. Loss of rain forest plants could have damaging effects on the entire planet, not just the local area. Rain forest plants provide atmospheric oxygen and remove carbon dioxide. The increased levels of carbon dioxide that result from deforestation could lead to global warming. Have students work with a science teacher to create a diagram of how the destruction of rain forests impacts the environment. **Ask:** How might this destruction affect your own lives? *(Destruction could change the local climate and increase severe weather.)*
🌐 **EE5 Environment and Society: Standard 14**

Reteach

Have students reread the section. Then tell them to include the following in a written summary of their reading: the answers to "Read to Find Out" questions, the "Terms to Know," and "Places to Locate."

Enrich

Read aloud the passage from Chapter 1 of Gabriel García Márquez's *One Hundred Years of Solitude* that begins, "Jose Arcadio Buendia was completely ignorant of the geography of a region." Identify García Márquez as a Colombian author who won the Nobel Prize for Literature in 1982. García Márquez served as a foreign correspondent in various regions of the world, including Mexico, Paris, and New York City. Have students locate Colombia on the map on page 195.

④ CLOSE

Have students reread "A Geographic View" on page 193 and write a similar descriptive paragraph about a landform or region of Latin America that interests them.

---

current. This estuary, the **Río de la Plata** ("River of Silver"), meets the Atlantic Ocean. Buenos Aires, the capital of Argentina, and Montevideo, the capital of Uruguay, lie along the Río de la Plata.

Lakes

Latin America has few large lakes. The region does include the world's highest navigable lake, Lake Titicaca (TEE•tee•KAH•kah), in the Andes of Bolivia and Peru. Lake Titicaca lies about 12,500 feet (3,810 km) above sea level. The area surrounding Lake Titicaca was one of the centers of early Native American civilization. It holds many architectural remains from the distant past. Lake Maracaibo (MAH•rah•KY• boh) in Venezuela is regarded as South America's largest lake, even though it is actually an inlet of the Caribbean Sea. Lake Maracaibo and the surrounding area contain the most important oil fields in Venezuela. The largest lake in Central America is Lake Nicaragua, which lies between Nicaragua and Costa Rica.

Natural Resources

Latin America has significant natural resources, including minerals, forests, farmland, and water. Major deposits of oil and natural gas lie in rock

Gold mask from Ecuador, about 500 B.C.–A.D. 500

beds located in mountain valleys and in offshore areas, especially along the Gulf of Mexico and in the southern Caribbean Sea. These deposits help make Mexico and Venezuela leading oil producers.

Latin America's mineral wealth was first mined by Native American peoples and later by European colonists. The foothills along Venezuela's Orinoco River contain large amounts of gold. Brazil also is rich in gold, while Peru and Mexico are known for silver. Mines in Colombia have been producing the world's finest emeralds—precious green stones composed of beryllium—for more than 1,000 years. Even Latin America's nonprecious minerals have great economic value. Chile is the world's largest exporter of copper, and Jamaica is a leading source of bauxite, the main ore of aluminum. Bolivia and Brazil have large reserves of tin.

Not all of Latin America's countries share equally in this bounty. Geographic inaccessibility, lack of capital for development, and deep social and political divisions keep many of the region's natural resources from being developed fully or distributed evenly. The challenge for Latin Americans in the future is how to overcome these obstacles and make the best use of the region's natural resources.

SECTION ❶ ASSESSMENT

Checking for Understanding

1. **Define** cordillera, altiplano, escarpment, llano, pampa, gaucho, hydroelectric power, estuary.

2. **Main Ideas** Use a table like the one below to describe Latin America's three main geographic areas. Then choose one area, and explain how it differs from the other two.

Geographic Area	Physical Features

Critical Thinking

3. **Identifying Cause and Effect** How do the physical features of Latin America affect everyday life? Give examples.

4. **Drawing Conclusions** Why does much of South America have the potential to produce hydroelectric power?

5. **Making Inferences** What factors make Latin America important to the global economy?

Analyzing Maps

6. **Region** Study the physical-political map on page 195. What part of South America is dominated by mountains?

Applying Geography

7. **Effects of Landforms** Think about the physical features of South America. Write a descriptive paragraph explaining how landforms affect the course of South America's water systems.

SECTION ❶ ASSESSMENT ANSWERS

1. All vocabulary terms are defined in the text.

2. Answers should include physical features for Middle America, the Caribbean, and South America.

3. Answers may include that mountains are rich in natural resources but also block movement/trade and isolate regions and people.

4. Mountainous terrain creates fast-moving rivers and streams that can be dammed for generating electricity.

5. Latin America has mineral wealth, such as gold, silver, emeralds, copper, aluminum, tin, and iron. It also has

forest products and good agricultural produce, oil, and natural gas. Swift rivers and geothermal regions have the potential to produce electricity.

6. The western part, especially near the coast, is dominated by the Andes.

7. **Applying Geography** Mountains and highlands at the sources of South America's rivers make them swift moving and channel their waters into tributaries that join to form larger rivers. For that reason, the rivers in South America tend to be large and swift.

Guide to Reading

Consider What You Know

Most of Latin America's people live in an area between the Tropic of Cancer and the Tropic of Capricorn, an area that includes the Equator. What types of climate and vegetation would you expect to find in this broad area?

Reading Strategy

Categorizing As you read about the climate of Latin America, complete a graphic organizer similar to the one below by filling in the characteristics of the three vertical climate zones.

Climate Zone	Characteristics
tierra caliente	

Read to Find Out

- Which climate regions are represented in Latin America?
- How do Latin America's location and landforms affect climates even within particular regions?
- How are the natural vegetation and agriculture of Latin America influenced by climatic factors?

Terms to Know

- canopy
- *tierra caliente*
- *tierra templada*
- *tierra fría*

Places to Locate

- Amazon Basin
- Colombia
- Venezuela
- Argentina
- Uruguay
- Atacama Desert

Climate and Vegetation

NATIONAL GEOGRAPHIC

A Geographic View

Exploring Chile's Mountains

Green was the color we least expected when we landed on [Chile's] Sarmiento [ranges].... Mosses and lichens carpeted the rocks above an iceberg-littered bay.... After several days of exploring, our progress thwarted by glacial canyons and snarly ice-falls, we discovered a route to the peaks.... To reach the ridge, we had to hack through rain forest, our skis catching on limbs, our boots slipping off logs.

Sarmiento peak and bay

—Jack Miller, "Chile's Uncharted Cordillera Sarmiento," National Geographic, April 1994

Diverse climates make Latin America a region of sharp contrasts. To reach the glacial peaks of Chile's Cordillera Sarmiento, for example, climbers must trek through thick, nearly impenetrable vegetation. Steamy rain forests, arid deserts, grassy plains, and sandy beaches are all part of the region. In this section you will learn about Latin America's various climate regions and how the region's climates and landforms together influence natural vegetation and the growing of crops.

Climate and Vegetation Regions

Much of Latin America lies between the Tropic of Cancer and the Tropic of Capricorn. As a result, vast areas of the region have some form of tropical climate with lush green vegetation. Yet, even within the Tropics, mountain ranges and wind patterns create a variety of climates and natural vegetation in Latin America. The

Section Overview

This section discusses the effect of location and landforms on climate regions in Latin America, as well as the influence of climatic factors on vegetation and agriculture.

BELLRINGER
Skillbuilder Activity

- Project transparency and have students answer questions.
- Available as blackline master.

Daily Focus Skills Transparency 8-2

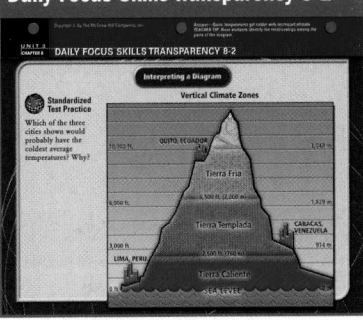

Guide to Reading

Consider What You Know

Answers Student answers will most likely list a tropical climate with rain forest vegetation. Other responses may include subtropical, desert, and steppe climate.

Reading Strategy

Answers tierra caliente: *hot land, sea level–2,500 ft., average temperature 68°–91°F;* tierra templada: *temperate land, 2,500–6,500 ft., 60°–72°F;* tierra fria: *cold land, 6,500–10,000 ft.*

Preteaching Vocabulary

Encourage a Spanish-speaking student to translate *tierra caliente, tierra templada,* and *tierra fría* for the rest of the class.

⊙ Use the **Vocabulary Puzzle-Maker CD-ROM.**

RESOURCE MANAGER

📂 Reproducible Masters

- Reproducible Lesson Plan 8-2
- Vocabulary Activity 8
- Daily Lecture Notes 8-2
- Guided Reading Activity 8-2
- Reading Essentials and Study Guide 8-2
- Reteaching Activity 8
- Reinforcing Skills Activity 8
- Section Quiz 8-2

🖳 Transparencies

- Daily Focus Skills Transparency 8-2
- Political Map Transparency 3
- Unit 3 Map Overlay Transparencies

Multimedia

- ⊙ Vocabulary Puzzlemaker CD-ROM
- ⊙ Interactive Tutor Self-Assessment CD–ROM
- ⊙ ExamView® Pro Testmaker CD–ROM
- ⊙ Presentation Plus! CD–ROM

TEACH

L1 Identify

After reading the section, give a clue to help a student identify a climate or vegetation region, such as "the Amazon River basin" for "tropical climate." If the student answers incorrectly, give a second clue to another student. Give three clues before revealing the answer.

NATIONAL GEOGRAPHIC **MAP STUDY**

Answers

1. *southeastern South America*
2. *tropical forest and tropical grasslands*

Map Skills Practice

Location What climate region in Chile has scrub vegetation? *(desert)*

Daily Lecture Notes 8-2

DAILY LECTURE NOTES

CHAPTER 8
Section 2

Building Geography Literacy
The rain forests of Latin America are the source of many medicines. For example, the poisonous bark of certain curare plants is used to treat such diseases as multiple sclerosis and other muscular disorders, and as a surgical anesthetic. Scientists use the chemical structures of rain forest plants as models from which they can synthesize drug compounds. Rain forest plants also aid in research. Some plant compounds show scientists how cancer cells grow, for example.

I. Climate and Vegetation Regions pages 199–202

Most of Latin America lies between the Tropic of Cancer and the Tropic of Capricorn; thus, much of its area has a tropical climate. However, there is a great variety of climates in the region. (pp. 199–200)

A. Tropical Regions
Mexico, eastern central America, some Caribbean islands, and such parts of South America as the Amazon Basin have a tropical rain forest climate and vegetation, with hot temperatures and abundant rainfall occurring year-round. (p. 200)

B. The Rain Forest
The Amazon Basin, with the earth's largest rain forest, covers one-third of South America, and has trees that form a dense canopy that soars as high as 130 feet (40 m) over the forest floor. (p. 200)

C. Tropical Savanna
In the tropical savanna climate typical of the coast of southwestern Mexico, most Caribbean islands, and north-central South America, the grasslands have hot temperatures, abundant rainfall, and a dry season lasting several months. (p. 201)

D. The Humid Subtropics
In the humid subtropical climate of southeastern South America, the winters are short and mild, and the summers are long, hot, and humid. (pp. 201–202)

E. Desert and Steppe Areas
Parts of northern Mexico and the southwestern climate of South America have desert climates and vegetation; in Chile the rain shadow effect of the Andes has produced the dry, arid Atacama Desert, whereas other areas have a steppe climate, with hot summers, cool winters, and light rainfall. (p. 202)

Discussion Question
What kinds of vegetation might be found in rain forest areas of Latin America?
(hardwood trees, palms, tree ferns, bamboo)

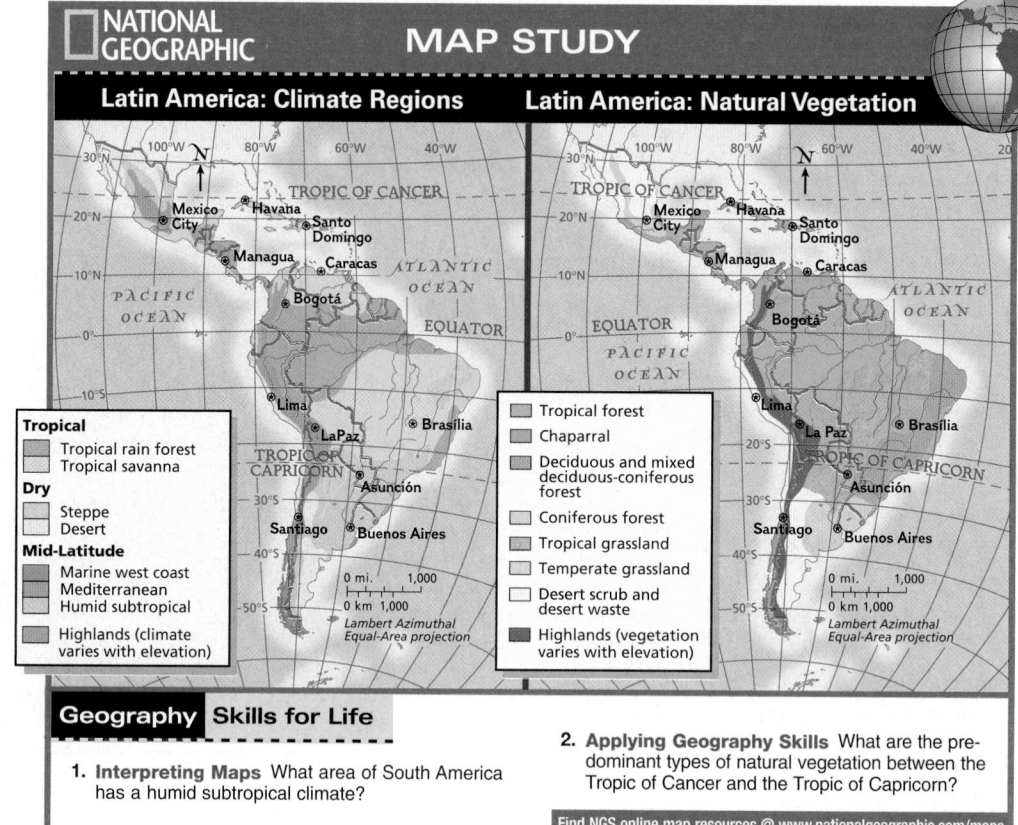

NATIONAL GEOGRAPHIC **MAP STUDY**

Latin America: Climate Regions   **Latin America: Natural Vegetation**

Tropical
Tropical rain forest
Tropical savanna

Dry
Steppe
Desert

Mid-Latitude
Marine west coast
Mediterranean
Humid subtropical

Highlands (climate varies with elevation)

Tropical forest
Chaparral
Deciduous and mixed deciduous-coniferous forest
Coniferous forest
Tropical grassland
Temperate grassland
Desert scrub and desert waste
Highlands (vegetation varies with elevation)

Lambert Azimuthal Equal-Area projection

Geography Skills for Life

1. **Interpreting Maps** What area of South America has a humid subtropical climate?

2. **Applying Geography Skills** What are the predominant types of natural vegetation between the Tropic of Cancer and the Tropic of Capricorn?

Find NGS online map resources @ www.nationalgeographic.com/maps

---

maps above show Latin America's climate regions and natural vegetation zones.

Tropical Regions

A tropical rain forest climate and vegetation dominate southern Mexico, eastern Central America, some Caribbean islands, and parts of South America. Hot temperatures and abundant rainfall occur year-round. In the **Amazon Basin**, this combination results from the area's location on the Equator and the patterns of the prevailing winds.

The Rain Forest

Wet tropical areas of Latin America have a dense cover of rain forest, or *selva* as it is called in Brazil. Latin American rain forests contain a variety of trees, including tropical hardwoods, palms,

tree ferns, and bamboos. In Latin America's tropical rain forest areas, broad-leafed and needle-leafed evergreen trees are so close together that their crowns form a dense canopy, or a continuous layer of leaves. The canopy may soar to 130 feet (40 m) and is so dense that sunlight seldom reaches the forest floor. Plants beneath the canopy must be shade tolerant.

The Amazon Basin, with Earth's largest rain forest, covers about one-third of South America. It is also the world's wettest tropical plain. Heavy rains drench much of the densely forested lowlands throughout the year, but especially between January and June. During the months of heavy rainfall, large areas crossed by the Amazon River are often severely flooded. In Brazil, the width of the river ranges between 1 and 6 miles (1.6 and

---

DIFFERENTIATED INSTRUCTION

Gifted and Talented Encourage students to recognize and organize patterns in the natural environment to help them classify information about Latin America. Have students refer to the climate and vegetation maps on this page. Point out that both maps organize information in different ways, and tell students they might wish to use a political map (see page 183) to help them identify the different climate and vegetation zones by country, or they might categorize the information according to latitude.

EE1 The World in Spatial Terms: Standard 3

Refer to *Inclusion for the Social Studies Classroom Strategies and Activities.*

10 km) but enlarges to 30 miles (48 km) or more during annual flooding.

The Amazon rain forest shelters more species of plants and animals per square mile than anywhere else on Earth. One journalist described a recent survey by scientists from the Smithsonian Institution in Washington, D.C.:

> ❝ Here at this one site on the Equator, in about 1,500 acres, scientists have counted 3,000 species of plants, 530 species of birds, nearly 80 species of bats, and 11 species of primates. There are jaguars and other wild cats, tapir, deer, otters, capybaras, and agoutis. . . . ❞
>
> Virginia Morell, "The Variety of Life," *National Geographic*, February 1999

The Amazon rain forest is also a habitat for many reptiles. The snakes there include boas and anacondas. Iguanas and crocodiles also are found in many rain forests. Rivers and streams teem with varied and abundant freshwater fish.

Tropical Savanna

A tropical savanna climate is typical of the coast of southwestern Mexico, most Caribbean islands, and north-central South America. These areas have hot temperatures and abundant rainfall but also experience an extended dry season. In many tropical savanna areas, vast grasslands flourish. Some of these grasslands, such as the llanos of **Colombia** and **Venezuela**, are covered with scattered trees and are considered transition zones between grasslands and forests.

History
The Humid Subtropics

A humid subtropical climate prevails over much of southeastern South America, from Rio de Janeiro, Brazil, to the pampas of **Argentina** and **Uruguay**. In this area, winters are short and mild, and summers are long, hot, and humid. Summers occasionally bring short dry periods.

The vast pampas today consist primarily of short grasses but once had scattered trees. Spanish settlers brought cattle and horses to the pampas and cut down trees to set up ranches. Overgrazing

L1/ELL

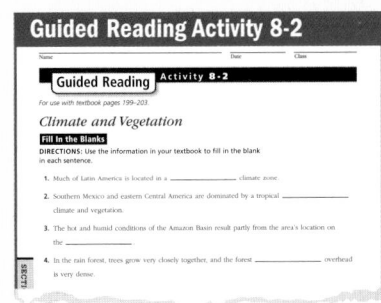

Guided Reading Activity 8-2

Name _____ Date _____ Class _____

Guided Reading Activity 8-2

For use with textbook pages 199–203.

Climate and Vegetation

Fill In the Blanks

DIRECTIONS: Use the information in your textbook to fill in the blank in each sentence.

1. Much of Latin America is located in a _____ climate zone.

2. Southern Mexico and eastern Central America are dominated by a tropical _____ climate and vegetation.

3. The hot and humid conditions of the Amazon basin result partly from the area's location on the _____.

4. In the rain forest, trees grow very closely together, and the forest _____ overhead is very dense.

NATIONAL GEOGRAPHIC **World Explorer**

Answer

They would be unpopulated or sparsely populated. In Dominica, the dense forest and the remote location make it difficult to acquire the necessities of life. The Atacama has little or no water and appears unfavorable for agriculture that would sustain human life.

More About the Photo
Although the Atacama Desert in the photo looks hot, it is relatively cool, with average summer temperatures of 66°F (19°C).

L1/ELL

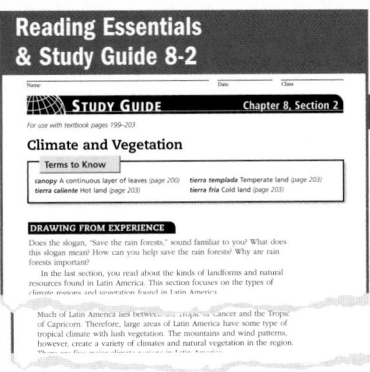

Reading Essentials & Study Guide 8-2

Name _____ Date _____ Class _____

STUDY GUIDE Chapter 8, Section 2

For use with textbook pages 199–203

Climate and Vegetation

Terms to Know

canopy A continuous layer of leaves (page 200) | tierra templada Temperate land (page 203)
tierra caliente Hot land (page 200) | tierra fria Cold land (page 203)

DRAWING FROM EXPERIENCE

Does the slogan, "Save the rain forests," sound familiar to you? What does this slogan mean? How can you help save the rain forests? Why are rain forests important?

In the last section, you read about the kinds of landforms and natural resources found in Latin America. This section focuses on the types of climate regions and vegetation found in Latin America.

Much of Latin America lies between the Tropic of Cancer and the Tropic of Capricorn. Therefore, large areas of Latin America have some type of tropical climate with lush vegetation. The mountains and wind patterns, however, create a variety of climates and natural vegetation in the region.

NATIONAL GEOGRAPHIC **World Explorer**

Geography Skills for Life

Diverse Vegetation Tropical forests (left) grow in the warm, rainy climate of Dominica in the Caribbean. In the arid Atacama Desert of Chile (right), low shrubs grow among steaming geysers.

Human-Environment Interaction Would you expect these places to be densely populated? Why or why not?

COOPERATIVE LEARNING ACTIVITY

Plant and Animal Life Assign small groups a climate region of Latin America, and have students research its animal and plant life. Tell students to draw or paste a picture of a plant or an animal onto an index card and label the region. Number each card on the blank side from 1–30. Pin the cards number side up on a bulletin board. Students take turns calling out the numbers of two cards. If the player chooses two cards from the same climate region, the cards are left picture side up. If the cards do not match, the cards are turned number side up and the team earns no points.

🌐 EE3 Physical Systems: Standard 8
🌐 EE5 Environment and Society: Standard 15

INTERDISCIPLINARY
connection

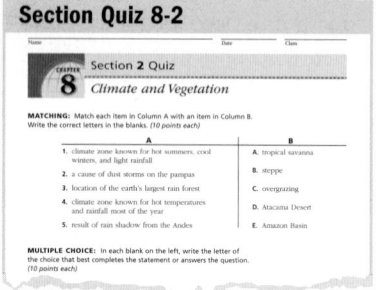

BIOLOGY There are many distinct varieties of ants in the Amazon rain forest. One variety, army ants, of which there are about 200 species, does not build permanent nests. Millions of them travel together in columns at speeds of up to 65 feet (20 m) per hour. A swarm can destroy crops as well as small animals.

L2

Section Quiz 8-2

③ ASSESS

Assign Section 2 Assessment as homework or as an in-class activity.

🌐 Have students use **Interactive Tutor Self-Assessment CD-ROM.**

NATIONAL GEOGRAPHIC — GRAPH STUDY

Answers

1. *52°F (11°C) in Buenos Aires and 80°F (27°C) in Dallas*

2. *supports cattle and grains*

---

eventually left only short clumps of grass to anchor the pampas soil, and dust storms periodically swept over the region. Argentine farmers now plant alfalfa, corn, and cotton to hold the topsoil in place.

Desert and Steppe Areas

Parts of northern Mexico, coastal Peru and Chile, and the southeastern coast of Argentina have desert climates and vegetation. In Chile the rain shadow effect of the Andes has produced the **Atacama Desert**, a region so arid that in some places no rainfall has ever been recorded. In the desert areas of Latin America, vegetation is sparse. Prickly cacti and drought-resistant shrubs, however, have adapted to the harsh environment.

Parts of Latin America—northern Mexico, northeastern Brazil, and south central South America—receive little rainfall but do not have desert climates and vegetation. Instead, they have steppe climates—hot summers, cool winters, and light rainfall—and grassy or lightly forested vegetation.

Elevation and Climate

Although Latin America lies in the Tropics, its varied climates are more affected by elevation than by distance from the Equator. Throughout the region, Spanish terms are used to describe three different vertical climate zones that occur as elevation increases. Each of these three zones has its own characteristic natural vegetation and crops.

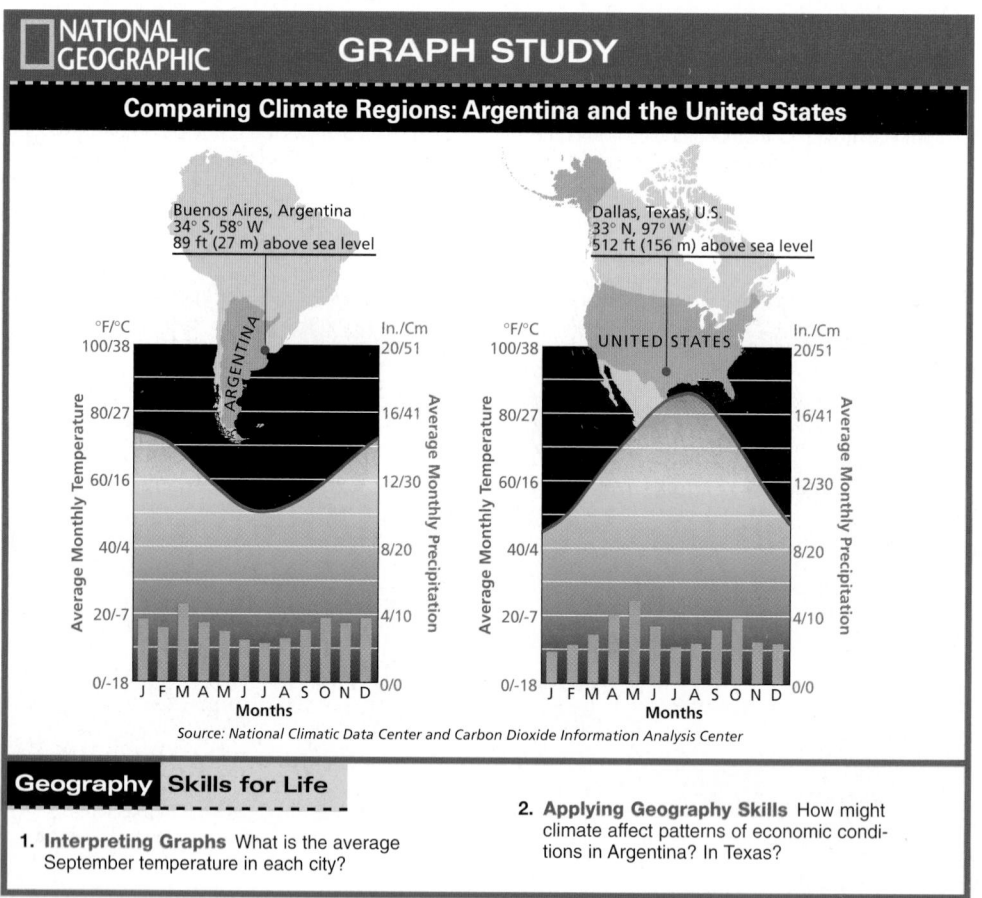

NATIONAL GEOGRAPHIC — GRAPH STUDY

Comparing Climate Regions: Argentina and the United States

Buenos Aires, Argentina
34° S, 58° W
89 ft (27 m) above sea level

Dallas, Texas, U.S.
33° N, 97° W
512 ft (156 m) above sea level

Source: National Climatic Data Center and Carbon Dioxide Information Analysis Center

Geography Skills for Life

1. Interpreting Graphs What is the average September temperature in each city?

2. Applying Geography Skills How might climate affect patterns of economic conditions in Argentina? In Texas?

CRITICAL THINKING ACTIVITY

Making Comparisons Refer students to the climate and vegetation maps on page 200. Tell students the capital cities of Mexico City, Mexico; Quito, Ecuador; and Sucre, Bolivia, are located in highlands climate zones and that altitude determines the kind of vegetation in this climate zone, including what crops can be grown. Have students find the approximate latitude for each of these cities. *(19°N, 0° latitude, and 19°S, respectively)* **Ask: How does the information about these three cities illustrate the effect of latitude and altitude on climate and vegetation?** *(Although all three cities are located in highlands, the climate zones at 19°N and 19°S do not have tropical climates and tropical vegetation or steppe as do areas of lower elevations on the same lattitude.)* 🌐 **EE1 The World in Spatial Terms: Standard 1**

NATIONAL GEOGRAPHIC — DIAGRAM STUDY

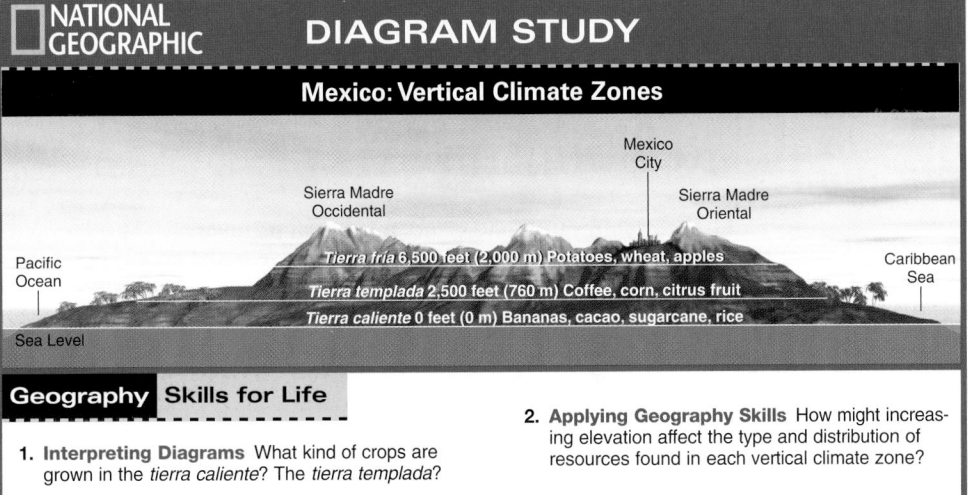

Mexico: Vertical Climate Zones

Mexico City

Sierra Madre Occidental

Sierra Madre Oriental

Pacific Ocean

Caribbean Sea

Tierra fría 6,500 feet (2,000 m) Potatoes, wheat, apples

Tierra templada 2,500 feet (760 m) Coffee, corn, citrus fruit

Tierra caliente 0 feet (0 m) Bananas, cacao, sugarcane, rice

Sea Level

Geography Skills for Life

1. **Interpreting Diagrams** What kind of crops are grown in the *tierra caliente*? The *tierra templada*?

2. **Applying Geography Skills** How might increasing elevation affect the type and distribution of resources found in each vertical climate zone?

The *tierra caliente*, or "hot land," lies at elevations between sea level and 2,500 feet (760 m). Average annual temperatures in these coastal areas and foothills range from 68° to 91°F (20° to 33°C). In the rain forests of the *tierra caliente*, the main crops include bananas, sugar, rice, and cacao.

The *tierra templada*, or "temperate land," lies between 2,500 and 6,500 feet (760 and 2,000 m). In this zone temperatures range between 60° and 72°F (16° and 22°C). Broad-leafed evergreen trees at lower levels give way to needle-leafed, cone-bearing evergreens at upper levels. In the *tierra templada*, the most densely populated of the vertical climate zones, coffee and corn are the main crops.

Land at 6,500 to 10,000 feet (2,000 to 3,048 m) is known as the *tierra fría*, or "cold land." At this elevation, frosts are common during winter months. However, crops such as potatoes and barley grow well here. Above the *tierra fría*, conditions are more difficult for agriculture or human habitation.

SECTION 2 ASSESSMENT

Checking for Understanding

1. **Define** canopy, *tierra caliente*, *tierra templada*, *tierra fría*.

2. **Main Ideas** Create a table to identify, locate, and describe Latin America's climate regions. Then write a sentence that describes each zone's features and vegetation.

Climate Region	Location	Characteristics
Humid Subtropical		

Critical Thinking

3. **Making Inferences** Why might some Latin Americans live in areas in which climate and agriculture are unfavorable?

4. **Determining Cause and Effect** How does elevation affect climate and vegetation in Latin America?

5. **Comparing and Contrasting** Compare the pampas to your region. How do climate and vegetation help define the economic activities in each place?

Analyzing Maps

6. **Place** Study the map on page 200. What is the approximate latitude and longitude of Bogotá?

Applying Geography

7. **Effects of Climate** Write a paragraph describing the effects of climate on economic activities in a particular Latin American country. Then map the locations of these activities.

SECTION 2 ASSESSMENT ANSWERS

1. All vocabulary terms are defined in the text.

2. Answers should include climate regions, locations, and characteristics for Middle America, the Caribbean, and South America.

3. possible answer: because of tradition and natural resources (for example, minerals, timber) that can support them economically

4. Possible answer: higher elevations have cooler temperatures and less varied vegetation.

5. Students should identify the climate and vegetation for the pampas as well as their region and connect them with the economic activity of each.

6. approximately 5°N, 74°W

7. **Applying Geography** Check to see that students correctly list sights and activities for the country they choose as well as appropriate clothing they would bring.

Teaching the Skill

Tell students that graphic organizers, such as the chart below illustrating the fossil fuels cause-and-effect chain, can help them more clearly sort through information and see the relationship among different things. Point out that the forest fire, which was the effect caused by hot weather and lack of rain, also caused loss of animal habitat. Show students the following graphic organizers, and ask them which one illustrates the forest fire begun because of a series of events. (#1)

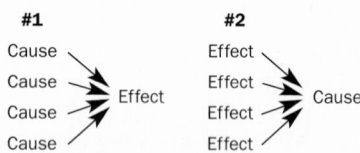

#1   #2

Cause   Effect
Cause   Effect
          Effect   Cause
Cause   Effect
Cause   Effect

Additional Practice
L1

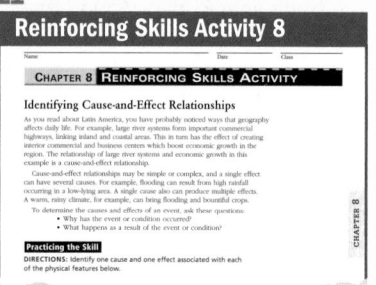

Reinforcing Skills Activity 8

Name   Date   Class

CHAPTER 8 REINFORCING SKILLS ACTIVITY

Identifying Cause-and-Effect Relationships

Practicing the Skill

DIRECTIONS: Identify one cause and one effect associated with each
of the physical features below.

Identifying Cause-and-Effect Relationships

Identifying cause-and-effect relationships involves considering how and why an event occurred. A *cause* is the action or situation that leads to the event. An *effect* is the result or consequence of an action or situation.

Learning the Skill

Cause-and-effect relationships may be simple or complex. Several causes can produce a single effect. For example, a forest fire may be caused by a series of events or conditions. Hot weather and lack of rain make grass and wood dry and flammable. The day the fire started might have been windy, and the wind might have blown sparks from a camper's fire to some dry grass.

Similarly, one event can produce several effects. A large forest fire can destroy animal habitats. It can also suddenly reduce plant cover, making the land more susceptible to erosion from wind and rain. A large fire can also be expensive to fight and damaging to homes and businesses, harming the economy of an entire region.

Sometimes one event causes several other events in a chain reaction. A traffic accident on a highway may cause another accident, which causes another accident, and so on. Strings of causal relationships are called *cause-and-effect chains.*

Follow these steps to identify cause-and-effect relationships:

- **Ask questions about why events occur.**

Causes →	Forest Fire →	Effects

- Hot weather and lack of rain make grass and wood dry and flammable.

- Natural factors such as lightning strikes or wind can ignite or fuel a fire.

- Careless campers and hikers may leave a fire unattended.

- Animal habitats destroyed.

- Soil erosion increases due to loss of plant cover.

- Expense of fighting the fire and the loss of homes and businesses harms the region's economy.

- **Identify the outcomes of events.**

- **Look for clues that indicate a cause-and-effect relationship.** Words and phrases such as *because, as a result of, brought about, as a consequence, therefore,* and *thus* can help you identify cause-and-effect relationships.

Practicing the Skill

Identify one cause and one effect associated with each of the events or conditions listed below.

1. The 1999 earthquake in Colombia

2. The formation of several Caribbean islands

3. Limited access to the rich mineral resources of the Amazon Basin

4. Cold temperatures in the *tierra fría*

Applying the Skill

Use the library or the Internet to research volcanic activity in Latin America. Then explain the causes and effects of a volcanic eruption by creating a graphic like the one above.

Go To The Glencoe Skillbuilder Interactive Workbook, Level 2 provides instruction and practice in key social studies skills.

ANSWERS TO PRACTICING THE SKILL

Possible answers appear below.
1. cause: location along the Ring of Fire makes region prone to earthquakes; effect: many people left homeless

2. cause: islands part of a chain of volcanic mountains; effect: some islands have active volcanoes that can harm inhabitants

3. cause: rain-drenched land is inaccessible for months each year; effect: slows economic development of the region

4. cause: high elevation; effect: frosts common during winter months

CHAPTER 8

SUMMARY & STUDY GUIDE

SECTION 1 — The Land (pp. 193–198)

Terms to Know
- cordillera
- altiplano
- escarpment
- llano
- pampas
- gaucho
- hydroelectric power
- estuary

Key Points
- Latin America includes Middle America, the Caribbean, and South America.
- Latin America's physical features include high mountain ranges, less rugged highlands, vast central plains, and volcanic islands.
- The water systems of Latin America, especially the mighty rivers of South America, are key to human activity in the region.
- Although the region is rich in natural resources, geographic, political, and economic obstacles have kept resources from being developed fully or shared equally.

Organizing Your Notes
Create a table like the one below to help you organize information about the physical features of Latin America.

Physical Feature	Location
Mexican Plateau	
Andes	
Rio Grande	
Amazon River	
Rio de la Plata	

SECTION 2 — Climate and Vegetation (pp. 199–203)

Terms to Know
- canopy
- *tierra caliente*
- *tierra templada*
- *tierra fría*

Key Points
- Much of Latin America lies in the Tropics; however, landforms and wind patterns give the region great climatic diversity.
- Tropical climates such as tropical forest and tropical savanna are the most common climates in Latin America.
- The natural vegetation of Latin America consists mainly of rain forests and grasslands.
- The tropical highlands in Latin America include three vertical climate zones that are based on latitude and elevation.

Organizing Your Notes
Create an outline using the format below to help you organize your notes for this section.

Climate and Vegetation
I. Climate and Vegetation Regions
   A. Tropical Regions
      1. The Rain Forest
II.

▶ Andean peaks in northern Chile

Using the Chapter 8 Summary & Study Guide

Use the Chapter 8 Summary & Study Guide to preview, review, condense, or reteach the chapter.

Preview/Review

🔵 **Vocabulary PuzzleMaker CD-ROM** reinforces "Terms to Know."

🔵 **Interactive Tutor Self-Assessment CD-ROM** provides a review of Chapter 8 content.

Condense

Have students read the Chapter 8 Summary & Study Guide.

🔵 Chapter 8 Audio Program

📁 Chapter 8 Guided Reading Activities

Reteach

📁 Chapter 8 Reteaching Activities (Spanish also available)
📁 Chapter 8 Reading Essentials and Study Guides

GLENCOE TECHNOLOGY

NATIONAL GEOGRAPHIC
WORLD REGIONS
VIDEO PROGRAM

Unit 3, Latin America
The following segments enhance the study of this unit:
- **Green Commerce**
- **The Inca**
- **Steel Drums**

CHAPTER CULMINATING ACTIVITY

Making Inferences Ask: How does the physical geography of Latin America shape the daily lives of the people who live there? Have students review their notes and the pages of Chapter 8 to answer the question. Students should answer the question by creating diary excerpts in the role of a person living in this region. Diary entries should include sketches, maps, and personal anecdotes to enrich the narrative. Have students review the chapter's photos and maps as well as the text and any exercises they have completed in their study of this chapter. 🌐 **EE2 Places and Regions: Standard 4**

NOTE: This activity may be completed separately, or you may wish students to incorporate it into their GeoJournals.

GEOGRAPHY Online

Have students visit the Web site at geography.glencoe.com to review Chapter 8 and take the **Self-Check Quiz.**

GLENCOE TECHNOLOGY

Use *MindJogger Videoquiz* to review the Chapter 8 content.

Reviewing Key Terms

1. cordilleras
2. altiplano
3. escarpment
4. llanos, pampas
5. estuary
6. *tierra caliente, tierra templada, tierra fría*

Reviewing Facts

SECTION 1

1. Middle America, the Caribbean, South America
2. the Bahamas, the Greater Antilles, the Lesser Antilles
3. Paraná, Paraguay, and Uruguay Rivers

SECTION 2

4. tropical rain forest, tropical savanna, steppe, desert, Mediterranean, humid subtropical, marine west coast, and highlands
5. elevation and latitude
6. Amazon Basin
7. llanos, pampas

Critical Thinking

1. The grasslands are ideal for grazing, and the rich prairie soil is ideal for agriculture.

Reviewing Key Terms

Write the key term that best completes each of the following sentences. Refer to the Terms to Know in the Summary & Study Guide on page 205.

1. The Andes consist of parallel mountain ranges, or _____.
2. The high plain encircled by the Andes of Bolivia and Peru is known as the _____.
3. The plateau of the Brazilian Highlands plunges sharply to the Atlantic Ocean, forming a steep cliff called an _____.
4. Cattle are raised on the broad grasslands called _____ in Colombia and Venezuela and _____ in Argentina and Uruguay.
5. The Río de la Plata is typical of an _____, an area where the tide meets a river current.
6. Highlands climates are divided into vertical zones, including the hot _____, the temperate _____, and the cold _____.

Reviewing Facts

SECTION 1

1. What are the three major geographic areas within Latin America?
2. What three island groups make up the West Indies?
3. Which three rivers flow into the Río de la Plata?

SECTION 2

4. What are the eight climate regions of Latin America?
5. What factors determine why Latin America's highlands climate is divided into three zones?
6. Where is the world's largest rain forest located?
7. What are South America's two main grassland areas called?

Critical Thinking

1. **Making Generalizations** Write a generalization that describes the kinds of economic activities you would expect to find in grasslands areas, using Latin America as an example.
2. **Analyzing Information** Identify and explain the factors affecting the location of different types of economic activities in Latin American countries.
3. **Comparing and Contrasting** Use a Venn diagram to compare the climate and vegetation found in Latin America's tropical areas.

Tropical Savanna (Both) Tropical Rain Forest

NATIONAL GEOGRAPHIC Locating Places

Latin America: Physical Geography

Match the letters on the map with the physical features of Latin America. Write your answers on a sheet of paper.

1. Amazon River
2. Lake Titicaca
3. Rio Grande
4. Hispaniola
5. Lake Maracaibo
6. Río de la Plata
7. Gulf of Mexico
8. Pampas
9. Caribbean Sea
10. Orinoco River
11. Mexican Plateau

2. Possible answer: Physical geography in some areas of the region often impedes economic development because geographic inaccessibility isolates people. Yet some areas, such as the pampas, are economically strong.
3. tropical savanna: hot, humid, a lot of rain, cool season, dry season, grasslands; tropical rain forest: dense forest with canopy, heavy rainfall, hot and humid most of the year, broad-leafed evergreen plants; both: high humidity, heavy rainfall, warm temperatures

NATIONAL GEOGRAPHIC Locating Places

1. D	**4.** E	**7.** G	**10.** A
2. I	**5.** H	**8.** F	**11.** B
3. C	**6.** K	**9.** J	

Using the Regional Atlas

Refer to the Regional Atlas on pages 182–185.

1. **Location** What river makes up a major part of the boundary between Mexico and the United States?

2. **Place** In terms of land use, why is there little to no activity along much of the Pacific coast of South America?

Thinking Like a Geographer

Review the economic activity map on page 187. Analyze the effects of physical and human geographic processes on the development of Latin America's resources. Make three practical suggestions for improving resource development in the region.

Problem-Solving Activity

Problem-Solution Proposal Working with a group, contact media services to find out more about a recent natural disaster in Latin America. Investigate accounts of the disaster to determine whether human activity made the disaster worse. In a report, describe the disaster's impact and propose ways to reduce the potential for damage in the future.

GeoJournal

Descriptive Writing Using the information you logged in your GeoJournal as you read, write a descriptive paragraph about one of the physical features of the region. Use your textbook and the Internet as resources to make your descriptions vivid, accurate, and interesting.

Technology Activity

Building an Electronic Database Collect facts about the countries of Latin America, such as natural resources, climate, average annual temperature, average annual rainfall, and natural vegetation. Create a database to organize and analyze the data. From the database, develop a table that presents your analysis.

Standardized Test Practice

Use the climograph below and your knowledge of geography to answer the question.

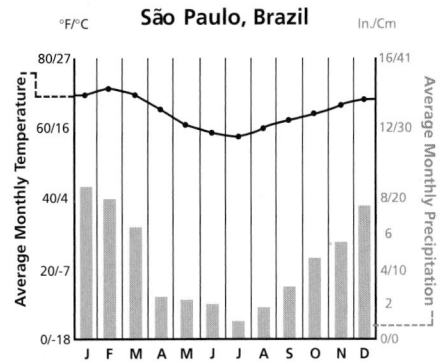

São Paulo, Brazil

1. Based on the information shown in the climograph, which statement about the months of April and November is accurate?

   A The average temperature and amount of rainfall are about the same.

   B It is hotter and drier in November.

   C The average temperature is about the same, but it is wetter in November.

   D The amount of rainfall is about the same, but it is hotter in November.

Test-Taking Tip Study the information shown on the climograph for average temperature and monthly precipitation. Then look carefully at the data for the months of April and November. Compare the amount of precipitation for the two months. As a result, you will be able to eliminate some of the statements.

Technology Activity

Students' databases and tables should reflect accurate information about the countries.

Standardized Test Practice

1. C

Tested Objectives:
making comparisons
analyzing information

Additional Practice and Test-Taking Tips

Standardized Test Practice Workbook

? CHAPTER BONUS TEST QUESTION

Which Latin American country supplies 25 percent of the world's coffee? *(Brazil)*

Using the Regional Atlas

1. Rio Grande (Río Bravo del Norte)
2. Much of the coast is desert.

Thinking Like a Geographer

Students' suggestions for development may vary; accept all reasonable answers, and use them as the basis for class discussion.

Problem Solving Activity

For students who need help in getting started, suggest they investigate Hurricane Mitch in 1998 or the severe flooding in Venezuela in 1999. Tell students to focus on cause and effect.

GeoJournal

Students' GeoJournal entries should contain descriptive language that appeals to all five senses.

① FOCUS

Ask students to consider what they would want to know about a site before building an amusement park with record-breaking roller coasters. As students provide responses, note their suggestions on the board. *(possible factors: soil conditions; wind conditions; rainfall amount; accessibility for thousands of tourist automobiles, charter buses, and trucks hauling supplies)*

Ask students to think about how they would find answers to their questions. Point out that GIS technology can provide geographic information about any location.

② TEACH

L1 Mapmaking

Without providing any type of measurements, ask students to draw the boundaries of their classroom. Have several students draw the desks in the classroom on their "map." Another group should include the room's shelves and windows. A third group should draw the overhead lighting on their map. Now put all three maps together for a complete picture of the classroom. Students should note that the three maps do not work together because they do not have the same boundary measurements.

Tell students that all the information in GIS must be input or scanned from existing maps. In order for map information to be properly compared and analyzed, GIS technology transforms all information to a common projection.

Geography Lab Activity

Simulating Geographic Information Systems

▲ *City planning is made easier with GIS technology.*

Geographic information systems (GIS) use computer software to create specialized maps that display a range of geographic information about an area. The user first creates a database with fields for images, such as digitized maps and satellite photos, and statistical information, such as census figures or property taxes. The GIS software can then generate maps to display the data, either separately or in combination.

GIS technology makes maps that can help people manage resources, select sites for buildings, and plan transportation routes. If Mexico City's government wants to add a new bus route, for example, an urban planner might input such data as population distribution, traffic patterns, congested areas, and existing bus routes. After examining these data, displayed in "layers" on a computerized map, the planner can analyze relationships and make an informed decision about the new bus route.

GIS technology allows layers of data drawn on a map to be turned on or off. ▶
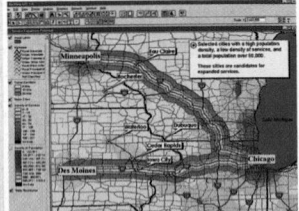

① Materials

- Overhead projector
- Transparency markers
- Seven blank 8½″ × 11″ transparencies
- Street map of your community
- Computer

② Procedures

In this activity, you will simulate a GIS map, using data about your community. As a class, you will analyze the data to determine the best emergency evacuation routes for your community.

1. Form three groups (A, B, and C). Each group will collect a different type of data.

2. Each group should copy a street map of the town or community onto a blank transparency. These will be the base maps. (Be sure that each group uses the same map.)

3. **Group A:** Determine the locations of major roads. Draw these roads on the blank overlay transparency placed on top of the base map. Color-code primary roads in black and secondary roads in purple. Be sure to note specific features such as bridges, railroads, and high-water crossings.

4. **Group B:** Gather information on the population distribution in the community. Locate residential areas, business districts, and shopping centers. Identify single-family homes and clusters of apartment buildings or college dormitories, and mark them on the overlay transparency. Color-code the areas or use symbols.

GEOGRAPHY IN THE REAL WORLD

Everyday Uses of GIS Global information systems enable businesses, governments, and individuals to incorporate the geographic perspective in making decisions. GIS affects the quality of daily life in ways we do not realize. For example, the electricity that runs the alarm clock that wakes you comes from your electric utility company, which uses GIS to plan and monitor its complex infrastructure and distribution lines. The juice you drank this morning was made from oranges watered by an irrigation system that uses GIS to maintain and operate hundreds of miles of waterways. Your local telephone company uses GIS to maximize coverage of mobile networks. The roads you use have become safer as the transportation infrastructure uses GIS for construction and special-event planning.

EE6 The Uses of Geography: Standard 17

List peak business hours and traffic rush hours, when roads may be crowded.

5. **Group C:** Gather information on the location of emergency shelters in the community. Use a symbol to indicate these shelters on the overlay transparency. Also, identify physical features of the town, such as rivers, creeks, or mountains.

6. As a class, layer the overlay transparencies of each group over one base map on the overhead projector. Analyze the map and the data to determine the best emergency evacuation routes. Using a blank transparency taped over the other layers, draw the suggested emergency evacuation route(s) in red.

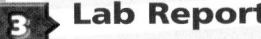

3 Lab Report

1. Which of the steps was the most time-consuming? Why?

2. Which of the overlays provided you with the most useful information? Explain.

3. What layers of information might you need to determine the best location for a new shopping center in your town?

4. **Drawing Conclusions** How do you think GIS technology might help scientists monitor earthquakes and perhaps prevent heavy earthquake damage in the future?

4 Find Out More

If you have access to an actual GIS program, use the program to determine the locations of new bridges, roads, or schools in your community. Is the information you gathered in questions 3 and 4 similar to or different from that of the actual GIS program?

Did You Know In Portland, Maine, researchers are working with the Federal Emergency Management Agency's Project Impact to help minimize flood damage. They are using GIS and handheld GPS (global positioning systems) to create a database of the city's drainage systems. The project is part of a nationwide effort to minimize damage from natural disasters.

◀ *Growing populations and limited roads may indicate a need for more emergency routes. City planners look at traffic patterns in the community and use GIS technology to help identify solutions.*

3 ASSESS

Have students answer the **Lab Report** questions on this page.

4 CLOSE

Encourage students to complete the **Find Out More** activity and summarize their findings. If you have access to a GIS Program, have students use the program to help plot a travel route from their community to another place. They may use data—such as roads, points of interest, and natural features—to create maps. Have students analyze the maps and then design and draw their own maps presenting their chosen route.

🌐 Meeting National Standards

Geography for Life
The following standards are met in the Student Edition:

EE1 The World in Spatial Terms: Standards 1, 2, 3
EE6 The Uses of Geography: Standards 17, 18

ANSWERS TO LAB REPORT

1. Students may say that preparing the transparencies was the most time consuming because they needed to gather data, develop appropriate symbols, and transfer information to the map.

2. Answers may vary depending on the size of the community and the degree to which evacuation might be necessary. Some students may say that the information about the roads and traffic were the most useful; others may say that the location of emergency shelters was most useful.

3. Answers may vary, but students should recognize that transportation routes and proximity to population centers are important considerations.

4. GIS technology may help scientists observe clusters of earthquake activity and define where faults are located. Then that information might be used to formulate building codes that could help prevent earthquake damage in those areas.

PLANNING GUIDE

NOTE: The following materials may be used when teaching Chapter 9. Section-level support materials are shown at point-of-use in the margins of the Teacher Wraparound Edition.

TEACHING TRANSPARENCIES

L2 Unit 3 Map Overlay Transparencies

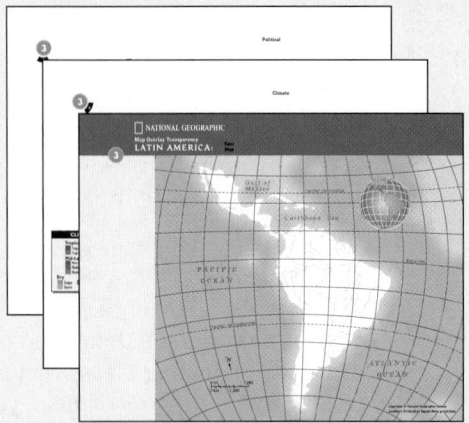

L2 Political Map Transparency 3

GEOGRAPHIC LITERACY

Focus on Geography Literacy

APPLICATION AND ENRICHMENT

L3 Enrichment Activity 9

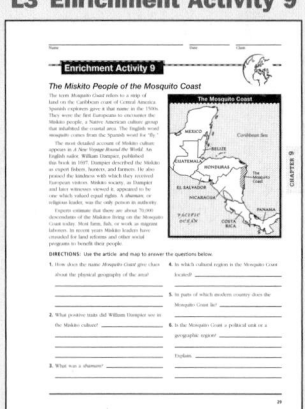

REVIEW AND REINFORCEMENT

L1 Vocabulary Activity 9   L1 Reinforcing Skills Activity 9   L1 Reteaching Activity 9

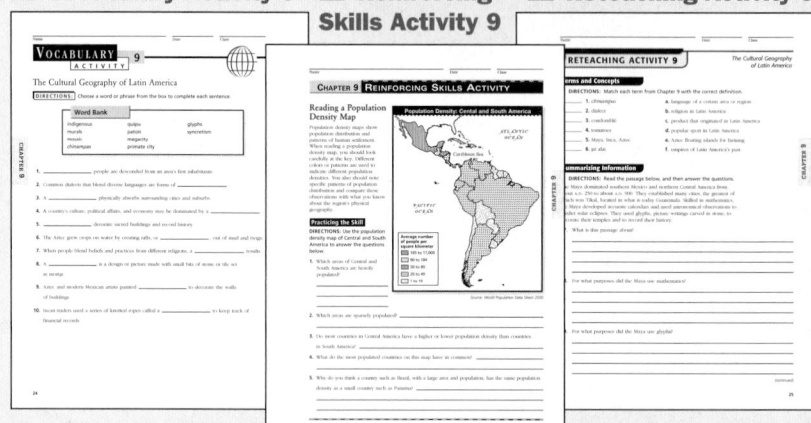

ASSESSMENT

L2 Chapter 9 Test Form A

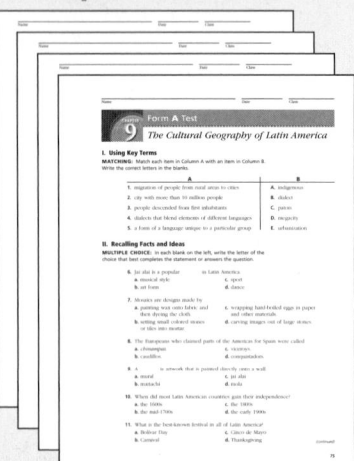

L2 Chapter 9 Test Form B

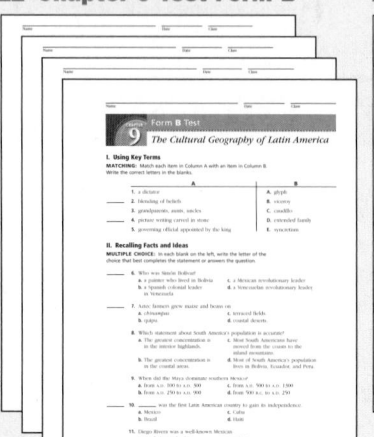

L1/ELL Performance Assessment Activity 9

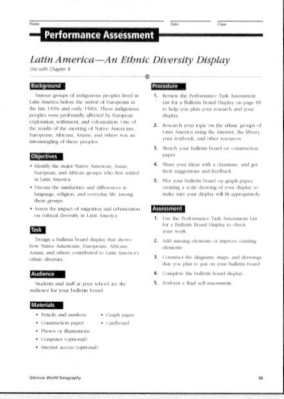

ExamView® Pro Testmaker

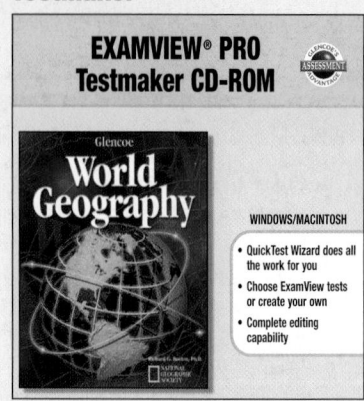

EXAMVIEW® PRO Testmaker CD-ROM

Glencoe World Geography

WINDOWS/MACINTOSH

- QuickTest Wizard does all the work for you
- Choose ExamView tests or create your own
- Complete editing capability

The following Spanish language materials are available in the Spanish Resources binder:

- 📂 Spanish Vocabulary Activities
- 📂 Spanish Guided Reading Activities
- 📂 Spanish Reteaching Activities
- 📂 Spanish Summaries
- 📂 Spanish Quizzes and Tests
- 📂 Spanish Reading Essentials and Study Guide

- 📼 World Regions Video
- 📼 MindJogger Videoquiz
- 💿 Vocabulary PuzzleMaker CD-ROM
- 💿 Interactive Tutor Self-Assessment CD-ROM
- 💿 ExamView® Pro Testmaker CD-ROM
- 💿 Audio Program
- 💿 TeacherWorks CD-ROM
- 💿 Interactive Student Edition CD-ROM
- 💿 Glencoe Skillbuilder Interactive Workbook CD-ROM, Level 2
- 💿 Presentation Plus! CD-ROM

Timesaving Tools

TeacherWorks™ — All-In-One Planner and Resource Center

- **Interactive Teacher Edition** Access your Teacher Wraparound Edition and your classroom resources with a few easy clicks.
- **Interactive Lesson Planner** Planning has never been easier! Organize your week, month, semester, or year with all the lesson helps you need to make teaching creative, timely, and relevant.

Use Glencoe's **Presentation Plus!** multimedia teacher tool to easily present dynamic lessons that visually excite your students. Using Microsoft PowerPoint® you can customize the presentations to create your own personalized lessons.

GEOGRAPHY Online

Use our Web site for additional resources. All essential content is covered in the Student Edition.

You and your students can visit geography.glencoe.com, the Web site companion to *Glencoe World Geography*. This innovative integration of electronic and print media offers your students a wealth of opportunities. The student text directs students to the Web site for the following options:

- Chapter Overviews
- Student Activities
- Self-Check Quizzes
- Textbook Updates

Answers are provided for you in the "Web Activity Lesson Plan." Additional Web resources and Interactive Tutor puzzles are also available.

▶ **Additional Glencoe Teacher Support**

- Teaching Strategies for the Geography Classroom (including Block Scheduling Pacing Guides)
- Graphic Organizer Transparencies Strategies and Activities
- Outline Map Resource Book
- Reading in the Content Area

PLANNING GUIDE

SECTION RESOURCES

Daily Objectives	Reproducible Resources	Multimedia Resources

SECTION 1 Population Patterns

1. Identify the ethnic groups that make up the population of Latin America.
2. Explain how geography and economics have influenced the distribution of Latin America's population.
3. Discuss the effects of migration on the Latin American culture region.
4. Describe the ways Latin America's cultural diversity presents both benefits and challenges for its people.

 Reproducible Lesson Plan 9-1
 Daily Lecture Notes 9-1
 Guided Reading Activity 9-1*
Reading Essentials and Study Guide 9-1*
 Section Quiz 9-1*

 Daily Focus Skills Transparency 9-1
Political Map Transparency 3
Unit 3 Map Overlay Transparencies
Interactive Tutor Self-Assessment CD-ROM
ExamView® Pro Testmaker CD-ROM*
Presentation Plus! CD-ROM

SECTION 2 History and Government

1. List the contributions Latin America's indigenous empires have made to the region's cultural development.
2. Explain how colonial rule influenced Latin America's political and social structures.
3. Discuss how most Latin American nations made the transition from colonialism to democracy.
4. Identify the political and social factors that continue to challenge the Latin American culture region.

 Reproducible Lesson Plan 9-2
 Daily Lecture Notes 9-2
 Guided Reading Activity 9-2*
 Reading Essentials and Study Guide 9-2*
Section Quiz 9-2*

 Daily Focus Skills Transparency 9-2
Unit 3 Map Overlay Transparencies
World Art and Architecture Transparencies
Interactive Tutor Self-Assessment CD-ROM
ExamView® Pro Testmaker CD-ROM*
Presentation Plus! CD-ROM

SECTION 3 Cultures and Lifestyles

1. Explain the role religion plays in Latin American culture.
2. Describe how Latin Americans have used the arts to express their history, their social struggles, and their cultural diversity.
3. Identify how Latin America's cultural diversity is reflected in family life, leisure activities, and public celebrations.

 Reproducible Lesson Plan 9-3
 Vocabulary Activity 9*
 Daily Lecture Notes 9-3
 Guided Reading Activity 9-3*
Reading Essentials and Study Guide 9-3*
 Reteaching Activity 9*
 Reinforcing Skills Activity 9
 Section Quiz 9-3*

 Daily Focus Skills Transparency 9-3
Unit 3 Map Overlay Transparencies
Vocabulary PuzzleMaker CD-ROM
World Music: A Cultural Legacy
Interactive Tutor Self-Assessment CD-ROM
ExamView® Pro Testmaker CD-ROM*
Presentation Plus! CD-ROM

 Blackline Master
 Transparency
Software
CD-ROM
Videocassette
DVD

Also available in Spanish

 **OUT OF TIME?** Assign the Chapter 9 Reading Essentials and Study Guide.

Block Schedule

Activities that are particularly suited to use within the block scheduling framework are identified throughout this chapter by the following designation:

KEY TO ABILITY LEVELS

Teaching strategies have been coded for various learning styles and abilities.

L1 **BASIC** activities for all students

L2 **AVERAGE** activities for average to above-average students

L3 **CHALLENGING** activities for above-average students

ELL **ENGLISH LANGUAGE LEARNER** activities

Teacher to Teacher

Renee West
Benjamin E. Mays
High School, Atlanta, GA

Latin American Festival

A good way to bring Latin American culture to life for students is to explore the community's resources. For example, students might visit several local Latin American sites, such as consulates, community centers, specialty food stores, and Latin American restaurants. They can sample the cuisine and explore the stimulating tastes characteristic of the region.

You may invite Latin American guests to the class to speak on some aspect of their culture, or Latin American musicians to give a demonstration of their regional music. After students learn about different Latin American countries, have them role play going into various Latin American countries to act out what is similar to our culture and what is different.

As a culminating activity, organize and host a whole-school geography fest, complete with traditional dress, foods, music, posters, and videos. Finally, create a Web page to showcase the experiences of students who have gone on trips to Latin American countries or students who are from Latin American countries. The Web page can include students' stories and photos of the places they have visited or lived. These activities add a dynamic dimension to the study of the vibrant Latin American culture.

Meeting National Standards

Geography For Life

The following standards are highlighted in Chapter 9:

Section 1   EE4 Human Systems:
Standards 9, 10, 11, 12
EE5 Environment and Society:
Standards 14, 15

Section 2   EE4 Human Systems:
Standards 10, 12, 13

Section 3   EE4 Human Systems:
Standard 10

Local Objectives

_____

_____

TEACHER'S CORNER

Index to National Geographic Magazine:

The following articles may be used for research relating to this chapter:

- "Lost Tombs of Peru," by Peter Lerche, September 2000.
- "Sierra Madre Pilgrimage," by Paul Salopek, June 2000.
- "Cuba," by John J. Putman, June 1999.

National Geographic Society Products:

To order the following products for use with this chapter, call National Geographic Society at 1-800-368-2728.

- *South America* (Video)
- *Mexico* (Video)
- *Lost City of the Maya* (Video)
- *South America Political* (Map)

NGS ONLINE

Access National Geographic's Web site for current events, activities, links, interactive features, and archives.
www.nationalgeographic.com

MEETING SPECIAL NEEDS

In addition to the Differentiated Instruction strategies found in each section, the following resources are also suitable for your special needs students:

- *ExamView® Pro Testmaker CD-ROM* allows teachers to tailor tests by reducing answer choices.
- The *Audio Program* includes the entire narrative of the student edition so that less-proficient readers can listen to the words as they read them.
- The *Reading Essentials and Study Guide* provides the same content as the student edition but is written two grade levels below the textbook.
- *Guided Reading Activities* give less-proficient readers point-by-point instructions to increase comprehension as they read each textbook section.
- *Enrichment Activities* include a stimulating collection of readings and activities for gifted and talented students.

Chapter Objectives

1. Explain how geography, economics, and cultural diversity affect the population of Latin America.

2. Discuss how Latin America's history continues to affect the region's politics today.

3. Describe how Latin American culture is affected by religion, the arts, and cultural diversity.

GLENCOE TECHNOLOGY

Use *MindJogger Videoquiz* to preview the Chapter 9 content.

GeoJournal

For access to additional photos, maps, and information on the cultural features of Latin America, go to www.nationalgeographic.com (See Teacher pages in front for strategies for using journals in the geography classroom.)

GEOGRAPHY Online

Introduce students to chapter content and key terms by having them access **Chapter Overview 9** at geography.glencoe.com

FOLDABLES
Study Organizer

Dinah Zike's Foldables are three-dimensional, interactive graphic organizers that help students practice basic writing skills, review key vocabulary terms, and identify main ideas. Have students complete the Foldable activity in the **Dinah Zike's Reading and Study Skills Foldables** booklet.

CHAPTER 9
The Cultural Geography of Latin America

GeoJournal

As you read this chapter, use your journal to list and describe the cultural influences that have shaped life in Latin America. Note how both native and imported cultures have formed a uniquely Latin American way of life.

GEOGRAPHY Online

Chapter Overview Visit the **Glencoe World Geography** Web site at geography.glencoe.com and click on Chapter Overviews—Chapter 9 to preview information about the cultural geography of the region.

ABOUT THE PHOTO

Visual Instruction The woman in the photograph wears a colorful hand-embroidered blouse typical of those produced by the indigenous people who live in the Guatemalan highlands. Notice the green birds. The quetzal, a native bird species, is the Guatemalan national bird, which also gives its name to Guatemala's currency. A large portion of Latin Americans earn their living through subsistence farming, while others work on large corporate-owned farms that produce cash crops. **Ask: Do the crops pictured appear to be for export or local consumption? How do you know?** (local consumption because it is a local market with small quantities for sale) 📖 EE4 Human Systems: Standard 10

Guide to Reading

Consider What You Know

Think about what you have read about the physical geography of Latin America. What geographic factors influence where people have settled in this region?

Reading Strategy

Categorizing Complete a graphic organizer similar to the one below by filling in the reasons Latin Americans migrate to the United States.

Reasons for Migrating North

Read to Find Out

- What ethnic groups make up the population of Latin America?
- How have geography and economics influenced the distribution of Latin America's population?
- How has migration affected the Latin American culture region?
- In what ways does Latin America's cultural diversity present both benefits and challenges for its people?

Terms to Know

- indigenous
- dialect
- patois
- urbanization
- megacity
- primate city

Places to Locate

- Ecuador
- Peru
- Bolivia
- Guyana
- Buenos Aires
- Caracas
- Santiago
- Patagonia
- Rio de Janeiro
- Barbados

◀ *Woman at a Guatemalan market*

Population Patterns

 NATIONAL GEOGRAPHIC

A Geographic View

A Flavorful Mix

More than any other Caribbean island, Trinidad is a multiethnic stew. Africans and East Indians, each with about 40 percent of the population, make up the base, while smaller groups add their own flavor. Spanish and French families trace their roots to the 18th century, when their ancestors came to clear the land for plantations or to trade. . . . Portuguese, Chinese, and Syrian immigrants became merchants and shopkeepers. Today Trinidadians compare the resulting mix to callaloo, a soup with many ingredients.

Trinidad's Laventille neighborhood

—A. R. Williams, "The Wild Mix of Trinidad and Tobago," National Geographic, March 1994

The island country of Trinidad and Tobago reflects in miniature Latin America's diverse population. In this section you will learn how Latin America's multiethnic population came about, how the land shaped patterns of human migration, and what benefits and challenges population growth and diversity bring to the region.

Human Characteristics

Latin America's 539 million people—about 9 percent of the world's population—live in 33 countries that span more than half of the Western Hemisphere. The region's population includes Native Americans, Europeans, Africans, Asians, and mixtures of these groups. The bar graph on page 212 shows you the ethnic diversity that characterizes Latin America today.

 FOCUS

Section Overview

This section discusses the population of Latin America, including its ethnic groups and languages, distribution of people, migration, and cultural diversity.

BELLRINGER
Skillbuilder Activity

📽 Project transparency and have students answer questions.

📁 Available as blackline master.

Daily Focus Skills Transparency 9-1

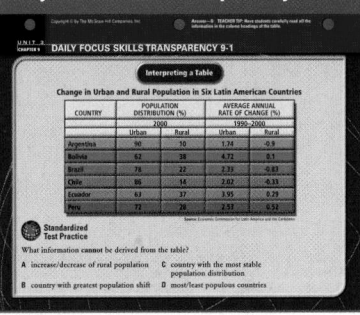

Guide to Reading

Consider What You Know

Answers *may include elevation, climate, and proximity to water.*

Reading Strategy

Answers *escape political unrest, improved living conditions, political freedom*

Preteaching Vocabulary

Direct students to page 212 to find the meaning of *indigenous*. Ask them to identify some indigenous groups of North America. *(Answers may include the Sioux, Apache, or other groups native to North America.)*

RESOURCE MANAGER

📁 **Reproducible Masters**
- Reproducible Lesson Plan 9-1
- Daily Lecture Notes 9-1
- Guided Reading Activity 9-1
- Reading Essentials and Study Guide 9-1
- Section Quiz 9-1

📽 **Transparencies**
- Daily Focus Skills Transparency 9-1
- Political Map Transparency 3
- Unit 3 Map Overlay Transparencies

Multimedia
- 💿 Interactive Tutor Self-Assessment CD-ROM
- 💿 ExamView® Pro Testmaker CD-ROM
- 💿 Presentation Plus! CD-ROM

2 TEACH

L1 Locate

Project Unit Map Overlay Transparency 3-4 and have students locate the following: Mexico City, the Yucatán Peninsula, Central America, Brazil, and Peru. Tell students that these are areas where Latin America's indigenous populations are or were located.

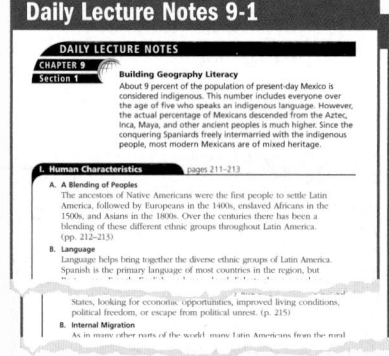

Daily Lecture Notes 9-1

DAILY LECTURE NOTES
CHAPTER 9
Section 1

Building Geography Literacy
About 9 percent of the population of present-day Mexico is considered indigenous. This number includes everyone over the age of five who speaks an indigenous language. However, the actual percentage of Mexicans descended from the Aztec, Inca, Maya, and other ancient peoples is much higher. Since the conquering Spaniards freely intermarried with the indigenous people, most modern Mexicans are of mixed heritage.

I. Human Characteristics pages 211–213

A. **A Blending of Peoples**
The ancestors of Native Americans were the first people to settle Latin America, followed by Europeans in the 1400s, enslaved Africans in the 1500s, and Asians in the 1800s. Over the centuries there has been a blending of these different ethnic groups throughout Latin America. (pp. 212–213)

B. **Language**
Language helps bring together the diverse ethnic groups of Latin America. Spanish is the primary language of most countries in the region, but

States, looking for economic opportunities, improved living conditions, political freedom, or escape from political unrest. (p. 215)

B. **Internal Migration**
As in many other parts of the world, many Latin Americans from the rural

NATIONAL GEOGRAPHIC **GRAPH STUDY**

Answers:

1. *Argentina*

2. *voluntary immigration and slavery*

Skills Practice

Place Which country has the second largest population of mixed ethnic groups?

(Venezuela)

History
A Blending of Peoples

The ancestors of Native Americans were the first people to settle Latin America. As a result, Native Americans today are known as an indigenous (ihn•DIH•juh•nuhs) group, people descended from an area's first inhabitants. Centuries ago three Native American groups—the Maya of the Yucatán Peninsula and parts of Central America, the Aztec of Mexico, and the Inca of Peru's highlands—developed great civilizations with important cities and ceremonial centers.

Today many Native American cultural features still remain in parts of Latin America. Most of Latin America's present-day Native Americans live in Mexico, Central America, and the Andes region of **Ecuador**, **Peru**, and **Bolivia**. In areas where they are a large part of the population, Native American peoples have worked to preserve their traditional cultures while adopting features of other cultures.

Europeans first arrived in what is now Latin America in the late 1400s. Since that time millions of European immigrants have come to the region. Most of these settlers were Spanish and Portuguese. Over the years other European groups—Italians, British, French, and Germans—came as well. In modern times so many Europeans settled in Argentina and Uruguay that these countries became known as *immigrant nations*. In Latin America today, descendants of European immigrants continue to follow many of the ways of life their ancestors brought with them.

Africans first came to Latin America in the 1500s. They arrived as enslaved people, brought forcibly by Europeans to work sugar and other cash crop plantations in Brazil and the Caribbean islands. The labor of enslaved Africans helped build Latin American economies. By the late 1800s, slavery had finally ended in the region. Many Africans whose families had been in Latin America for generations remained in parts of the region. They added their rich cultural

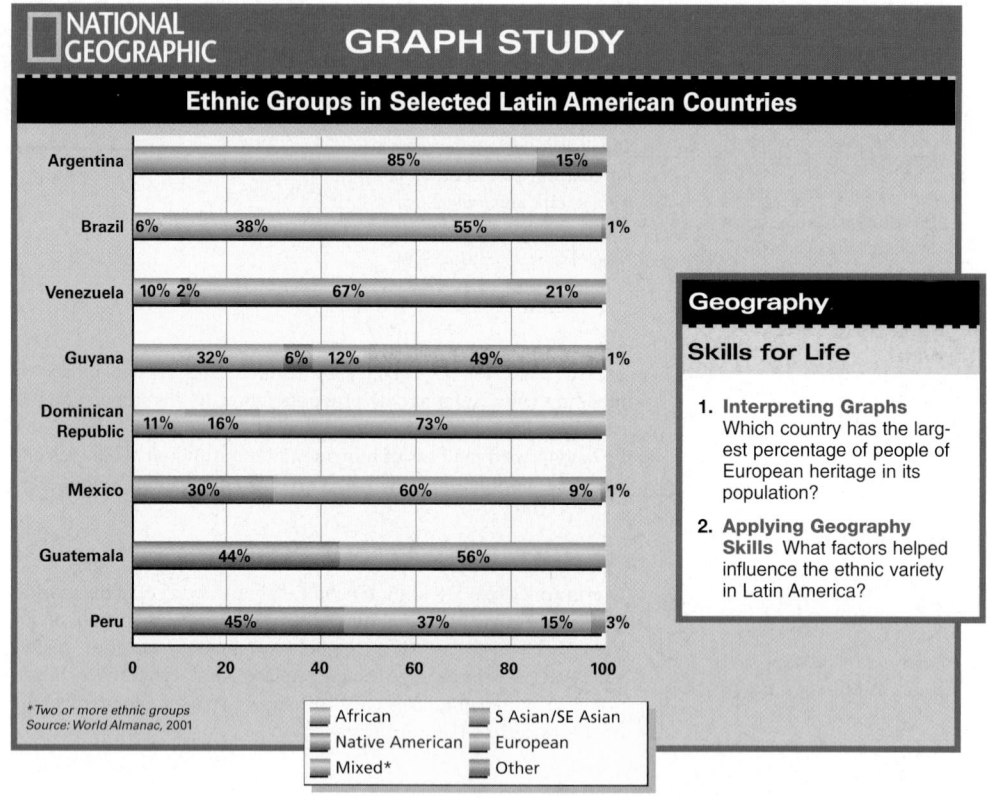

NATIONAL GEOGRAPHIC **GRAPH STUDY**

Ethnic Groups in Selected Latin American Countries

Argentina	85%	15%
Brazil	6% 38% 55%	1%
Venezuela	10% 2% 67%	21%
Guyana	32% 6% 12% 49%	1%
Dominican Republic	11% 16% 73%	
Mexico	30% 60% 9%	1%
Guatemala	44% 56%	
Peru	45% 37% 15%	3%

0   20   40   60   80   100

*Two or more ethnic groups
Source: World Almanac, 2001

☐ African
☐ Native American
☐ Mixed*
☐ S Asian/SE Asian
☐ European
☐ Other

Geography

Skills for Life

1. **Interpreting Graphs** Which country has the largest percentage of people of European heritage in its population?

2. **Applying Geography Skills** What factors helped influence the ethnic variety in Latin America?

DIFFERENTIATED INSTRUCTION

At-Risk Students For students who have trouble with reading comprehension, inform them that the information on ethnic groups and on languages in the first part of the section is summarized in the graph on page 212 and on the map on page 213. Before they read, have students study the graph and map and write two or three observations about each. As they read pages 211–213, have students check their observations.

🌐 **EE4 Human Systems: Standard 10**

📁 Refer to *Inclusion for the Social Studies Classroom Strategies and Activities.*

influences to the food, music, arts, and religions of Latin America.

Asians first settled in Latin America during the 1800s. They labored as temporary workers, and many remained to form ethnic communities. Today the Caribbean islands and some countries of South America have large Asian populations. In **Guyana** about one-half of the population is of South Asian or Southeast Asian descent. Many people of Chinese descent make their homes in Peru, Mexico, and Cuba, and many people of Japanese descent live in Brazil and Peru.

Over the centuries there has been a blending of these different ethnic groups throughout Latin America. For example, in countries such as Mexico, Honduras, and El Salvador, people of mixed Native American and European descent make up the largest part of the population. In other countries, such as Cuba and the Dominican Republic, people of mixed African and European descent form a large percentage of the population.

Language

Language is a major factor in bringing together the diverse ethnic groups of Latin America. Most people in the region have adopted the languages of the European countries that once colonized the region. Today Spanish is the primary language of most countries of Latin America. However, other languages also are spoken. For example, the official language of Brazil is Portuguese; of Haiti and Martinique, French; and of Jamaica, Belize, and Guyana, English.

Not all Latin Americans, however, speak these European languages the same way as, or even in a way similar to, the original European colonists. Each country has its own dialects, forms of a language unique to a particular place or group. Meanings of words and the words themselves often differ from one place to another.

In addition, millions of Latin Americans speak Native American languages. In Central America, Mayan dialects such as K'iche' (kee•CHAY) are common. Tupi-Guarani predominates in Paraguay and Brazil. Aymara is spoken in Bolivia, and Quechua (KEH•chuh•wuh) in Ecuador, Peru, and Bolivia.

Many Latin Americans are bilingual, speaking two languages—a European language and another language, either indigenous, African, or Asian. Other

Latin Americans speak one of many Latin American forms of **patois** (PA•TWAH), dialects that blend elements of indigenous, European, African, and Asian languages.

Where Latin Americans Live

In addition to having a diverse population, Latin America today has a high rate of population growth. By most estimates the region's population will soar to about 800 million by the year 2050—an increase of 55 percent. This high growth rate magnifies the challenges to human patterns of

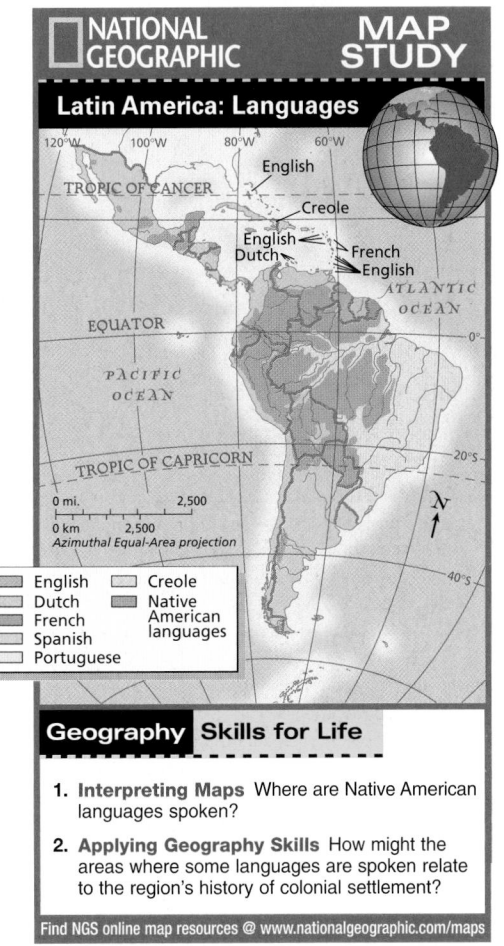

NATIONAL GEOGRAPHIC **MAP STUDY**

Latin America: Languages

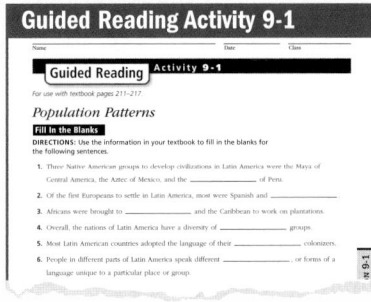

English
Creole
English
Dutch
French
English

- English
- Dutch
- French
- Spanish
- Portuguese
- Creole
- Native American languages

Geography Skills for Life

1. **Interpreting Maps** Where are Native American languages spoken?
2. **Applying Geography Skills** How might the areas where some languages are spoken relate to the region's history of colonial settlement?

Find NGS online map resources @ www.nationalgeographic.com/maps

L1/ELL

Guided Reading Activity 9-1

Name ___ Date ___ Class ___

Guided Reading Activity 9-1

For use with textbook pages 211–217.

Population Patterns

Fill in the Blanks

DIRECTIONS: Use the information in your textbook to fill in the blanks for the following sentences.

1. Three Native American groups to develop civilizations in Latin America were the Maya of Central America, the Aztec of Mexico, and the _____ of Peru.

2. Of the first Europeans to settle in Latin America, most were Spanish and _____.

3. Africans were brought to _____ and the Caribbean to work on plantations.

4. Overall, the nations of Latin America have a diversity of _____ groups.

5. Most Latin American countries adopted the language of their _____ colonizers.

6. People in different parts of Latin America speak different _____, or forms of a language unique to a particular place or group.

NATIONAL GEOGRAPHIC **MAP STUDY**

Answers

1. *parts of Middle America and much of central and western South America*

2. *The language of the dominant European colonizers is usually the language still spoken today.*

Map Skills Practice

Place What European country dominated Brazil during the colonial era? *(Portugal)*

Africans in Bolivia Spanish conquistadors forced enslaved Africans to work in the silver mines of Bolivia after thousands of Bolivians died from diseases brought from Spain. Many Africans, unable to adjust to the climate and high altitude, died more quickly than the indigenous Bolivians had. Surviving African descendants settled in the rain forests east of the Andes.

COOPERATIVE LEARNING ACTIVITY

Creating a Dictionary Have students work in small groups to compile a picture dictionary of Spanish words, starting with words from chapters in this unit, such as *tierra caliente, chicle, cordilleras, vaqueros,* and *jai alai.* Then add English words derived from Spanish to their list: *arroyo, bronco, corral, coyote, loco, palomino,* and *pronto.* Refer students to an English dictionary for the meanings of these words. If possible, have students interview community members or exchange students from Latin American countries to gather more words and phrases. Assign students to edit, type, and illustrate the pages, bind them into a dictionary, and donate their dictionary to the school library.

📖 **EE4 Human Systems: Standard 10**

L2 Locate

After the class reads "Where Latin Americans Live," project Unit Map Overlay Transparency 3-4. Ask volunteers to shade the populated areas where most South Americans live. Then add Unit Map Overlay Transparency 3-1 to check their accuracy.

NATIONAL GEOGRAPHIC World Explorer

Answer
to seek a better life

More About the Photo Brazil is a melting pot of different cultures and peoples.

L1/ELL

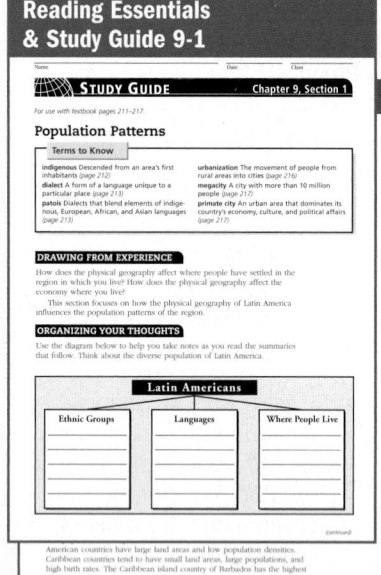

Reading Essentials & Study Guide 9-1

NATIONAL GEOGRAPHIC World Explorer

Geography | Skills for Life
Latin American Immigration These floral arrangers, in the state of São Paulo, Brazil, are part of a community of Japanese Brazilians.
Movement Why have Asian and European immigrants settled in Latin America?

settlement already presented by Latin America's physical geography.

Latin America's varied climates and landscapes have an impact on where Latin Americans live. Temperature extremes, dense rain forests, towering mountains, and arid deserts limit human habitation in many parts of Latin America. In fact, most of Latin America's population lives on only one-third of the region's land.

About 350 million people live in South America, generally along the coasts. Another 138 million people live in Central America and Mexico, either along Central America's Pacific coast or on the inland Mexican Plateau and Central Highlands. The Caribbean island countries are home to 37 million people.

South America's Populated Rim

Rain forests, deserts, and mountains dominate South America's interior. In these areas harsh living conditions and poor soil discourage human settlement. As a result, most South Americans live on the continent's edges, an area sometimes known as the "populated rim." The coastal regions provide favorable climates, fertile land, and easy access to transportation systems.

South America's eastern coast, from the mouth of the Amazon River in Brazil to the pampas around **Buenos Aires**, Argentina, is Latin America's largest populated area. A narrower strip of densely populated land stretches along the continent's northern and western coast from **Caracas**, Venezuela, to **Santiago**, Chile.

South America's populated rim does not encircle the entire continent, however. For example, the eastern coast between the Amazon's mouth and Caracas has a hot, rainy climate and is sparsely populated. Another area of low population density lies to the far south in the Andes and **Patagonia**, where the climate and land are harsh.

With the exception of Native Americans, few South Americans live in the continent's inland areas. To draw people away from the densely populated coast, the Brazilian government in 1960 moved the capital from coastal **Rio de Janeiro** to Brasília, a planned city built in the country's interior.

Population Density

As the population density map on page 184 shows, population density varies greatly throughout Latin America. One important factor in a country's population density is its area. South American countries, with their relatively large land areas, tend to have low population densities. In Ecuador, the most densely populated country in South America, an average of only 115 people share a square mile (44 people per sq. km). Brazil has a large population, but its enormous land area, over 3.3 million square miles (8.5 million sq. km), results in a population density averaging only 53 people per square mile (21 people per sq. km).

Caribbean countries, in contrast, combine small land areas with large populations that tend to grow at rapid rates. These factors make the Caribbean countries some of the most densely populated in Latin America. The tiny island nation of **Barbados** has the highest population density in

---

CRITICAL THINKING ACTIVITY

Predicting Consequences Read aloud the following passage from a news story: "In Petion-Ville, Port-au-Prince's hilltop suburb of contradiction, the elite live in luxury while the rest of the city starves. . . . 'Why do people think the rich are so bad? What did we do?' said a wealthy woman. . . . Others say the rich think only of themselves and need to start caring about the interests of others. They would like to see the rich pay taxes [and] . . . pay their maids and cooks, waiters and [domestic workers] more than subsistence wages."
Ask: What might happen if the conditions in Haiti do not change? *(Answers may include that the poor may suffer more, the economy will not improve, and people may rebel.)*
⊕ **EE4 Human Systems: Standard 11**

the Caribbean, with an average of 1,524 people per square mile (588 people per sq. km).

Population density also varies within countries. With 104.9 million people, Mexico is the world's most populous Spanish-speaking country, and it is the second most populous country in Latin America, after Brazil. Mexico's population and its land area of 756,062 square miles (1.9 million sq. km) give it a population density of 139 people per square mile (54 people per sq. km), making Mexico seem relatively uncrowded. This overall density rate is only an average, however. In metropolitan Mexico City, more than 18 million people live within an area of 597 square miles (1,547 sq. km). That makes the population density of Mexico City a staggering 30,150 people per square mile (11,641 people per sq. km)!

NATIONAL GEOGRAPHIC World Explorer

Geography Skills for Life

Street in La Paz A crowded street in La Paz, Bolivia, shows the effects of rapid urbanization. **Market**

Movement How does internal migration contribute to urbanization in the region?

Migration

Migration has been a major force shaping population patterns in Latin America. As a geography writer recently observed,

> " *Migration is . . . everyone's solution, everyone's conflict. . . . Unlike the flight of refugees, which is usually chaotic, economic movement is a chain that links the world. Migration . . . continues to push us toward change.* "
>
> Michael Parfit, "Human Migration," *National Geographic*, October 1998

In past centuries Europeans, Africans, and Asians migrated to Latin America in large numbers, either voluntarily or involuntarily. Today people from places such as Korea, Armenia, Lebanon, and Syria come to Latin America seeking economic and political opportunities.

Migrating North

In addition to receiving an inflow of migrants from foreign countries, Latin America also experiences an outflow of people to different parts of the world. For many Latin Americans, the desire for improved living conditions, political freedom, or an escape from political unrest leads them to move north to the United States. Latin Americans come to the United States primarily from Mexico, Central America, and the Caribbean islands. Immigrants from Latin America live in every state of the Union, with large numbers in California, Texas, New York, Illinois, and Florida. Many Latin American immigrants go through the process of legally entering the United States; others enter illegally. All of these immigrants bring elements of their culture with them. Most retain close ties with family and friends in their home countries, and many intend to return when economic conditions there improve.

Internal Migration

Internal migration, or movement within a region or country, also has shaped Latin America

Culture NOTE

Rio de Janeiro Many of the sidewalks of Rio are made of mosaic tiles with a distinctive swirling design. People often joke that the pattern of the walkways makes them late for appointments because the wavy pattern makes it difficult to walk in a straight line.

NATIONAL GEOGRAPHIC World Explorer

Answer
Migrating people flock to urban areas believing there is a chance for a better life in the city.

More About the Photo At an altitude of 12,000 feet (3,660 m), La Paz is the highest capital in the world. The city is nestled in a long, narrow valley cut by the La Paz River. Because of this physical location, La Paz could not be laid out in the traditional Spanish gridiron pattern. The city's main plaza, the Plaza Murillo, with the national palace, cathedral, and other buildings, is small. It includes only a few long, broad avenues, and the streets ascend steeply on either side of the plaza.

Chapter 9 🌐 215

TEAM-TEACHING ACTIVITY: LANGUAGE ARTS

Journal Tell students that they live in a Latin American country but plan to migrate to another part of the region. Have students record their experiences in a journal entry, using that point of view. They should describe their reasons for moving and discuss the ways the move will change their lives. After students write the first draft, have them provide feedback to each other by exchanging papers. Following revision and final rewrite, encourage students to share their journals with the class. Have them explain what factors (political, economic, social, and environmental) contribute to migration and how physical geography affects the routes, flows, and destinations of migrations. 📦 🌐 **EE4 Human Systems: Standards 9, 12**

NATIONAL GEOGRAPHIC — MAP STUDY

Answers

1. *United States, Brazil, Venezuela*

2. *Guatemala has the lowest level of urbanization, and Argentina has the highest.*

Map Skills Practice

Movement Which country had a 27 percent increase in urban growth between 1970 and 2001? *(Bolivia)*

③ ASSESS

Assign Section 1 Assessment as homework or as an in-class activity.

⊗ Have students use **Interactive Tutor Self-Assessment CD-ROM** to review Section 1.

L2

Section Quiz 9-1

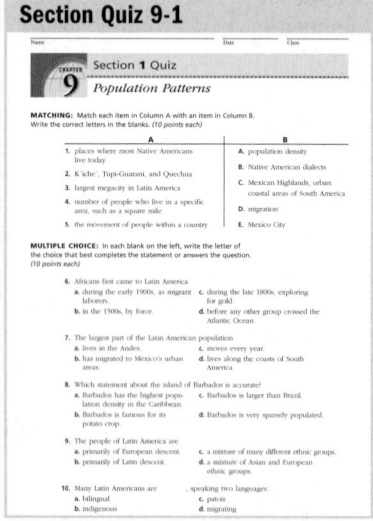

NATIONAL GEOGRAPHIC — MAP STUDY

Latin America: Migration and Urbanization

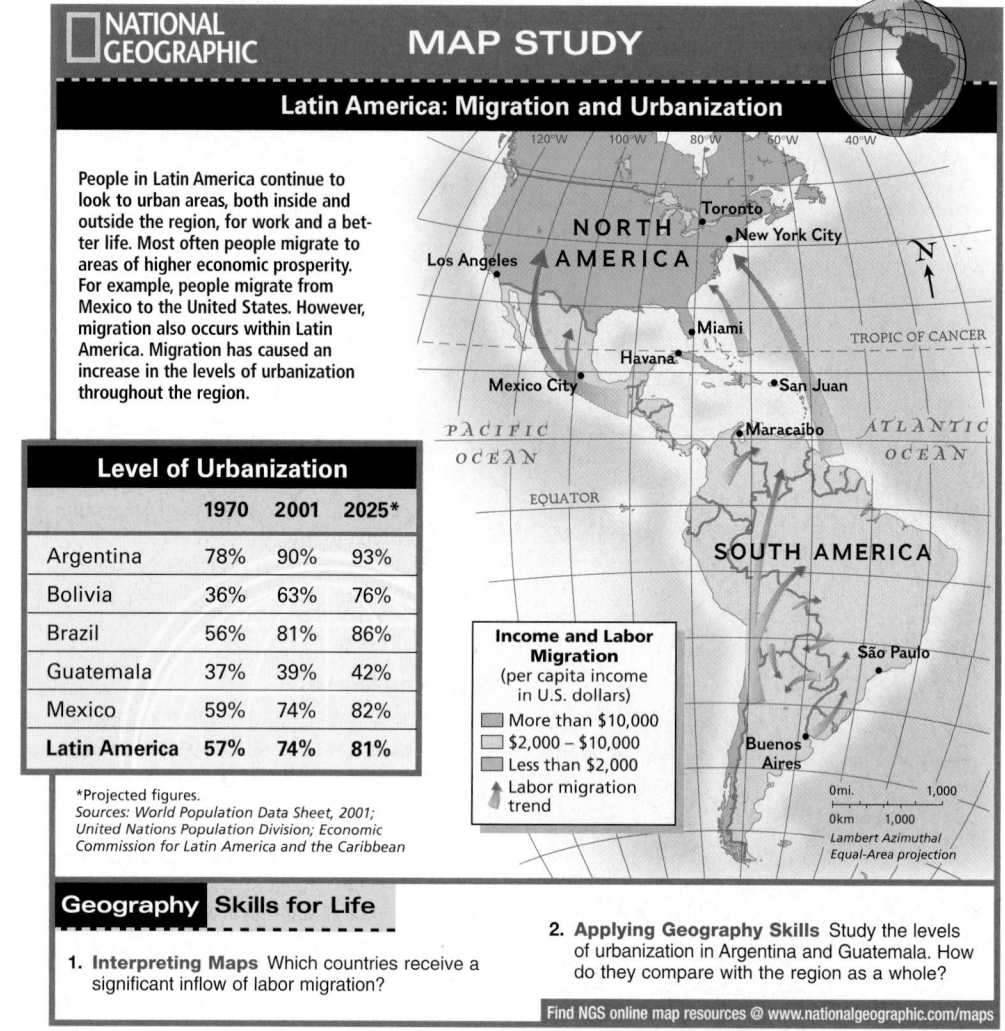

People in Latin America continue to look to urban areas, both inside and outside the region, for work and a better life. Most often people migrate to areas of higher economic prosperity. For example, people migrate from Mexico to the United States. However, migration also occurs within Latin America. Migration has caused an increase in the levels of urbanization throughout the region.

Level of Urbanization

	1970	2001	2025*
Argentina	78%	90%	93%
Bolivia	36%	63%	76%
Brazil	56%	81%	86%
Guatemala	37%	39%	42%
Mexico	59%	74%	82%
Latin America	**57%**	**74%**	**81%**

*Projected figures.
Sources: World Population Data Sheet, 2001; United Nations Population Division; Economic Commission for Latin America and the Caribbean

Income and Labor Migration
(per capita income in U.S. dollars)
■ More than $10,000
▫ $2,000 – $10,000
■ Less than $2,000
↟ Labor migration trend

0mi.   1,000
0km   1,000
Lambert Azimuthal Equal-Area projection

Geography Skills for Life

1. **Interpreting Maps** Which countries receive a significant inflow of labor migration?

2. **Applying Geography Skills** Study the levels of urbanization in Argentina and Guatemala. How do they compare with the region as a whole?

Find NGS online map resources @ www.nationalgeographic.com/maps

---

in recent decades. As in many parts of the world, migrants within Latin America usually move from rural to urban areas because of better job opportunities in the cities. This one-way migration also occurs because in many rural areas fertile land is in short supply or a small portion of the population controls access to the land. As the rural population rises, there is less fertile land to go around. Smaller farms can no longer support families. The result is continuing, rapid urbanization—

the migration of people from the countryside to cities as well as the change from a rural to an urban society that accompanies this movement.

Growth of Cities

In the past most Latin Americans lived in the countryside and worked the land. Today most live in urban areas. Four cities of Latin America—Mexico City, Mexico; São Paulo and Rio de Janeiro, Brazil;

EXTENDING THE CONTENT

Urban Poverty Natural disasters in the last quarter of the 1900s had a devastating effect on the population of Brazil. Frosts, droughts, and floods destroyed thousands of coffee trees and forced the migration of poor unskilled laborers to the cities. Because of economic problems in the 1980s, the government reduced public health spending. The poor were the hardest hit by this reduction. The bubonic plague appeared in several northern cities, and there was a dramatic increase in leprosy, yellow fever, and malaria. Severe flooding in 1986 and mudslides in 1988 left hundreds of thousands homeless.

⊞ **EE5 Environment and Society: Standard 15**

and Buenos Aires, Argentina—now rank among the world's 20 largest urban areas in population.

The Urban Setting

In some Latin American countries, as cities have grown they have absorbed surrounding cities and suburbs to create megacities, cities with more than 10 million people. The region's largest megacity is Mexico City, with a current population of more than 18 million. By 2015, the city is expected to have 19.2 million people. Mexico City's rapidly growing population already stresses the city's ability to provide safe drinking water, underground sewers, and utilities for new arrivals. Although the city has many areas with comfortable homes, its challenge for the future is to provide adequate housing for many who now live in cardboard shacks or makeshift houses made from sheets of metal.

Because of its size and influence, Mexico City is a primate city, an urban area that dominates its country's economy, culture, and political affairs. Other primate cities in Latin America include Caracas, Venezuela; Montevideo, Uruguay; Santiago, Chile; Buenos Aires, Argentina; and Havana, Cuba. Many primate cities began near waterways during the colonial era. Today these cities serve as central locations for gathering, collecting, and shipping resources overseas. They are especially powerful magnets for rural migrants seeking a higher standard of living.

Urban Challenges

Most rural Latin Americans migrate to cities to find a better life—higher incomes, more educational opportunities, better housing, and increased access to health care. In many cases people do not find what they seek. As a city's resources are strained by rapid population growth, jobs and housing become scarce. At the same time, many rural people lack the education and skills to obtain urban employment. Schools and health care centers are overwhelmed.

Despite disappointments, most rural migrants do not have the resources to return to their villages. They remain in the cities, forced by poverty to live in neighborhoods with substandard housing, poor sanitation, and little opportunity for improvement. Families sometimes split apart under the stress, leaving large numbers of homeless children to fend for themselves on the streets.

Many of Latin America's urban challenges arise from modern developments, such as the growth of cities. Others, however, stem from social and economic issues deeply rooted in the past. In the next section you will read about the historical factors that still shape current ways of life in Latin America.

SECTION 1 ASSESSMENT

Checking for Understanding

1. **Define** indigenous, dialect, patois, urbanization, megacity, primate city.

2. **Main Ideas** Create a web diagram like the one below, and fill in important information about Latin America's people.

- Who they are
- Latin America's People
- Where they live

Critical Thinking

3. **Analyzing Cause and Effect** What factors account for the differences in the way Spanish is spoken in various Latin American countries?

4. **Drawing Conclusions** Develop a hypothesis describing probable population patterns in Latin America in the year 2050. Defend your hypothesis, using present trends as evidence.

5. **Making Inferences** In what ways might physical geography influence the development of megacities in Latin America?

Analyzing Maps

6. **Region** Study the language map on page 213. What is the most widely spoken language in Central America?

Applying Geography

7. **Population Density** Consider the physical geography of Latin America. Write a paragraph suggesting suitable locations for constructing new cities to relieve population pressures in Latin America's existing cities. Consider the kinds of resources required to sustain large populations.

Reteach

Have students scan the section and turn each major heading into a question and then answer it. Model the first heading: **Ask: What are some characteristics of the Latin American population?** *(There is a blending of peoples and a variety of languages.)* Have students do this with the subheadings as well. Encourage students to share their questions and responses with each other.

Enrich

Have students consult reference sources to find examples of cultures in Latin America that maintain traditional ways. Ask them to write a paragraph that describes and analyzes their efforts to hold on to their traditions despite increasing modernization.

4 CLOSE

Have students include the terms in "Places to Locate" on page 211 as they write a sentence about the human characteristics, population and migration patterns, and urban growth for each of these places.

SECTION 1 ASSESSMENT ANSWERS

1. All vocabulary terms are defined in the text.

2. Refer students to the graph on page 212. Answers should include Native Americans, Europeans, Africans, Asians, and mixtures of these groups, and list some of the countries in which they live.

3. The blending of peoples and cultures throughout the region results in different Spanish dialects and forms of patois. The language spoken today also is greatly influenced by colonial settlers.

4. more densely urbanized with population distribution in roughly the same areas as today

5. Elevation and proximity to water could affect transportation and growth of industries.

6. Spanish

7. **Applying Geography** Suitable locations might include planned cities patterned after Brasília that are farther inland and linked by highways or rivers to existing coastal cities.

GEOGRAPHY AND HISTORY

① FOCUS

Have students locate the Isthmus of Panama on the map on page 182 or project Unit Map Overlay Transparency 3-5. Tell them to look at the approximate latitudes between which the country of Panama is located. *(between 5°N and 10°N latitude)* Based on that information, have them describe the climate of Panama. Ask students to identify any special problems that they think might occur if they were building a canal in that area. List student responses on the board. *(Students may mention dense vegetation, heavy rains, hot temperatures, and difficulty transporting materials.)*

② TEACH

Brainstorming Organize the class into two groups. Have one group brainstorm a list of the costs of building the Panama Canal. Remind the group that costs are not always monetary. *(The canal cost more than $300 million; thousands of workers died; it caused a revolution.)* Have the second group brainstorm a list of advantages that were gained from the building of the canal. *(improved trade; engineering skills advanced; dangerous trip around Cape Horn avoided; techniques for preventing several diseases developed)* Have students share and discuss their lists.

PASSAGE THROUGH PANAMA

THE PANAMA CANAL, a vital waterway connecting the Atlantic and Pacific Oceans, has been an important trade route since the day it opened. About 14,000 ships pass through the canal's system of locks and lakes each year. Using the canal, ships can avoid the treacherous waters around Cape Horn at the southern tip of South America and can shave 7,000 miles (11,265 km) off their trip. For most of the twentieth century, the United States controlled the canal. This changed on the last day of 1999, when control passed to the nation of Panama. Today the United States and other countries anxiously watch how Panama operates this international shortcut between the world's largest oceans.

Big Dreams and Political Shenanigans

Spanish explorer Vasco Núñez de Balboa was the first to grasp the unique geographic features of the land in Central America known today as Panama. In 1513, while exploring the isthmus, he climbed a peak and discovered a body of water as vast as the Atlantic, the ocean he had left behind. It wasn't long before thoughts turned to building a waterway to breach the slender neck of land that connects Central and South America. The limitations of manual labor, however, kept the idea in

A freighter winds its way through the Panama Canal. ▶

BACKGROUND INFORMATION

Diseases One reason for de Lesseps' failure to build the Canal was the French lack of medical knowledge to control the epidemics of tropical diseases that decimated the laborers. Beginning in 1904 Colonel William C. Gorgas, the United States physician who had wiped out yellow fever in Havana, Cuba, after the Spanish-American War, began an effort to eliminate malaria, yellow fever, and bubonic plague from the Isthmus of Panama. By destroying the mosquitoes that carry the first two diseases and the rats that carry the third, Gorgas dramatically lowered the death rate.
▨ **EE5 Environment and Society: Standards 14, 15**

◀ Canal enthusiast Theodore Roosevelt operates a steam shovel at a canal work site.

the realm of dreams for more than 300 years.

By the late 1800s, technology had caught up with the imagination. The first to try to build a waterway was Frenchman Ferdinand de Lesseps, who masterminded the Suez Canal. Cutting through the mountainous terrain proved extremely difficult, and de Lesseps failed. But one of his engineers, Philippe Jean Bunau-Varilla, refused to quit. In 1901 he pitched the idea to U.S. President Theodore Roosevelt, who was willing to pay the engineer's price if Colombia, of which Panama was a part, relinquished control of the proposed canal route. When Colombia refused, Bunau-Varilla supported Panamanian revolutionaries and persuaded the United States to intervene. The presence of American gunboats was enough to make Colombia give in. Panama became an independent country. Bunau-Varilla, Panama's new minister to the United States, negotiated a treaty giving the United States control of the land along the proposed route. In 1904 construction began.

Engineering Wonder of the World

Nearly 75,000 laborers from around the world built what is still regarded as one of the engineering wonders of the world. Instead of trying to make a cut through the rugged hills to carry ships across at sea level, the American solution was to build a system of locks to lift ships up to a newly created lake, and in the same way, lower them down the other side. The volcanic soil, heat and rain, dense vegetation, and disease-spreading insects conspired to make progress painfully slow. Thousands of workers lost their lives, and costs grew to more than $380 million. The canal was completed in 1914.

Looking Ahead

In acquiring the Panama Canal, the Panamanians gained a sizable investment. Do you think Panama will find the resources to maintain and operate the canal? How might the United States be affected by the change in command?

1500s First road built across isthmus

1855 American business interests build railroad across isthmus

1881 French company begins building a sea level canal; project abandoned in 1887

1903 Backed by U.S. President Theodore Roosevelt (cartoon above), Panama becomes independent country and signs treaty to create Panama Canal Zone

1904 Work begins on the Panama Canal (background photo)

1914 First ship passes through canal

1977 U.S. and Panama sign Panama Canal Treaty, gradually transferring ownership to Panama

1999 Canal ownership transfers to Panama

③ ASSESS

Have students answer the **Looking Ahead** questions on page 219.

④ CLOSE

Have students identify other endeavors where human knowledge has been advanced at great cost. What other advances in learning came with a "price tag"? *(the space program, medical advances such as organ transplantation, early air travel)* **Ask: Do you think advances in these areas have been worth the costs?**

🌐 Meeting National Standards

Geography for Life
The following standards are met in the Student Edition:

EE1 The World in Spatial Terms: Standard 3
EE4 Human Systems: Standard 13
EE5 Environment and Society: Standards 14, 15

ANSWERS TO LOOKING AHEAD

Some students may say that Latin American countries have a history of political instability, and it is risky to count on Panama's running the canal effectively. Others may say that the canal is on Panamanian territory, and that Panamanians have had ample opportunity to learn about the operation of the canal during the time the United States ran it. Possible ways the United States may be adversely affected include paying higher usage fees, loss of control, vulnerability to political instability within Panama, and vulnerability in the event of military conflicts. Positive effects might include improved relations with Panama, improved relations with Latin America in general, and less responsibility for upkeep on the canal.

① FOCUS

Section Overview

This section discusses the contributions of indigenous empires to the region's culture and the influences of colonial rule that still challenge this region.

BELLRINGER
Skillbuilder Activity

Project transparency and have students answer questions.

Available as blackline master.

Daily Focus Skills Transparency 9-2

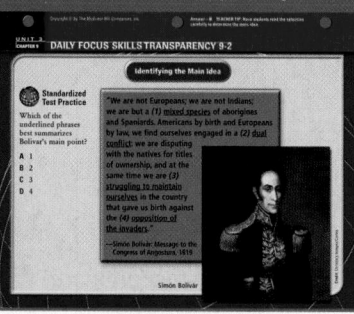

Guide to Reading

Consider What You Know
Answer *In general they are democracies. Cuba is a dictatorship.*

Reading Strategy
Answers Maya: *economy based on agriculture and trade, developed accurate calendars;* Aztec: *highly structured class system, grew crops on chinampas;* Inca: *constructed roads and irrigation systems*

Preteaching Vocabulary
Direct students to pages 221–222 to find the meanings of *glyph, chinampas,* and *quipu* and have them match the words with the indigenous group with which each word is associated. *(glyph—Maya, chinampas—Aztec, quipu—Inca)*

Guide to Reading

Consider What You Know
Latin American politics and social conflicts often make news in the United States. How are Latin American governments similar to or different from the United States government?

Reading Strategy
Organizing Complete a graphic organizer similar to the one below by filling in characteristics of the three Native American empires which existed in what is now Latin America.

Native American Empires
Maya
Aztec
Inca

Read to Find Out
- What contributions have Latin America's Native American empires made to the region's cultural development?
- How has colonial rule influenced Latin America's political and social structures?
- How did most Latin American countries make the transition from colonialism to democracy?
- What political and social factors continue to challenge the Latin American culture region?

Terms to Know
- glyph
- *chinampas*
- quipu
- conquistador
- viceroy
- caudillo

Places to Locate
- Mexico
- Tikal
- Tenochtitlán
- Cuzco
- Haiti
- Cuba

History and Government

NATIONAL GEOGRAPHIC

A Geographic View

Native Rights Protest

Drawn machetes slapped against trouser legs. Dark eyes stared in anger. About 40 Tojolabal Indian men and women surrounded two men. . . . They talked angrily, and the phrase that came through was, "This is our land." The sharp edges of the machetes gleamed. . . . These Indians might be Zapatistas, rebel Indian farmers named for Mexico's revolutionary war hero Emiliano Zapata. . . .

—Michael Parfit, "Chiapas: Rough Road to Reality," National Geographic, August 1996

Zapatista protesters, Chiapas, Mexico

In 1994 the Zapatistas attacked government troops and captured several towns in southern Mexico. One of their aims was to recover lands that Spanish conquerors had seized from their ancestors four centuries earlier. They finally succeeded in pressuring the Mexican government to introduce reforms giving Native Americans more power in Mexico's political system. Throughout Latin America today people struggle with unresolved issues rooted in the past. In this section you will learn about Latin America's long and often violent history, which includes ancient Native American civilizations, European colonial rule, and struggles for independence.

Native American Empires

Years before Christopher Columbus arrived in the Americas in 1492, three Native American empires—the Maya, the Aztec, and the Inca—flourished in the area that is present-day Latin America.

RESOURCE MANAGER

📂 Reproducible Masters
- Reproducible Lesson Plan 9-2
- Daily Lecture Notes 9-2
- Guided Reading Activity 9-2
- Reading Essentials and Study Guide 9-2
- Section Quiz 9-2

🖳 Transparencies
- Daily Focus Skills Transparency 9-2
- Unit 3 Map Overlay Transparencies
- World Art & Architecture Transparencies

Multimedia
- Interactive Tutor Self-Assessment CD-ROM
- ExamView® Pro Testmaker CD-ROM
- Presentation Plus! CD-ROM

The civilization of each empire left enduring marks on Latin American cultures.

The Maya

The Maya dominated southern **Mexico** and northern Central America from about A.D. 250 to 900. They established many cities, the greatest of which was **Tikal**, located in what is today Guatemala. Terraces, courts, and pyramid-shaped temples stood in these cities. Priests and nobles ruled the cities and surrounding areas. The Maya based their economy on agriculture and trade.

Skilled in mathematics, the Maya developed accurate calendars and used astronomical observations to predict solar eclipses. They used glyphs, picture writings carved in stone, on temples to honor their deities and record their history.

For reasons that are still a mystery, the Maya eventually abandoned their cities, which over time became lost beneath the vegetation of the rain forest. Archaeologists continue to search for more information about the ancient Maya. Researchers have uncovered the ruins of over 40 Mayan cities, but most of the glyphs remain untranslated. Today many temple ruins are popular tourist attractions. Descendants of the Maya still live in villages in southern Mexico and northern Central America, where they practice subsistence farming.

The Aztec

The Aztec civilization arose in central Mexico, in the A.D. 1300s. The Aztec founded their capital, **Tenochtitlán** (tay•NAWCH•teet•LAHN), today the site of Mexico City, on an island in a large lake. To feed the growing population, Aztec farmers grew beans and maize on *chinampas*—floating "islands" made from large rafts covered with mud from the lake bottom.

The Aztec developed a highly structured class system headed by an emperor and military officials. High-ranking priests performed rituals to win the deities' favor and to guarantee good harvests. At the bottom of Aztec society were the majority—farmers, laborers, and soldiers.

Culture
Gifts to the World's Tables

Several foods grown by the Aztec have become worldwide favorites. Corn, a staple food of Latin America, came from the maize cultivated by the Aztec. The tomato, later used in Mediterranean cuisine, was unknown in Europe until the European conquest of Latin America. From bitter cacao beans, the Aztec made a concoction called *xocoatl* (chocolate), or "food of the gods."

The Inca

During the time of the Aztec, the Inca established a civilization in the Andes mountain ranges of South America. At its height the Incan Empire stretched from what is today Ecuador to central

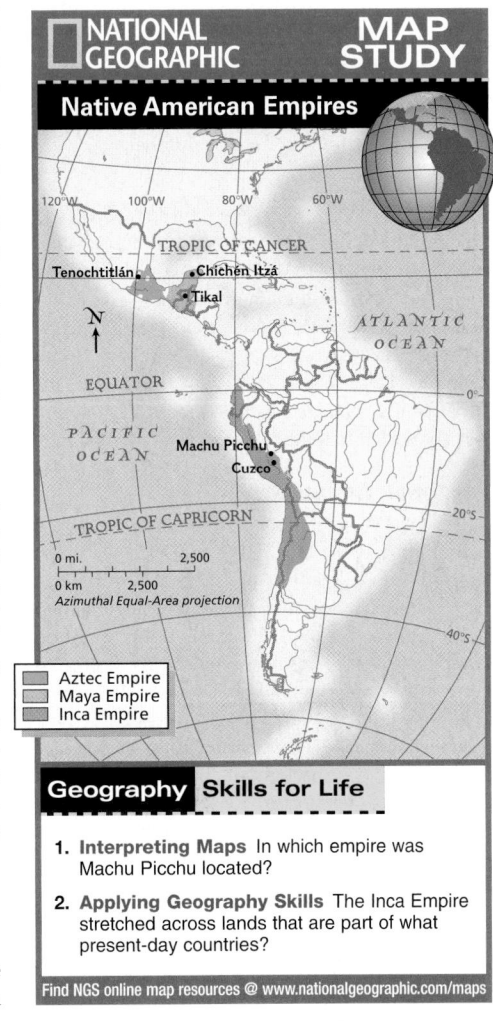

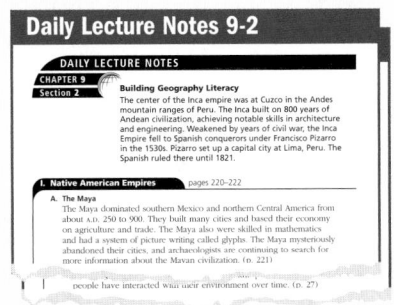

NATIONAL GEOGRAPHIC   **MAP STUDY**

Native American Empires

120°W   100°W   80°W   60°W

TROPIC OF CANCER

Tenochtitlán   •Chichén Itzá
    •Tikal

N

ATLANTIC OCEAN

EQUATOR   0°

PACIFIC OCEAN   Machu Picchu
    Cuzco•

TROPIC OF CAPRICORN   20°S

0 mi.   2,500
0 km   2,500
Azimuthal Equal-Area projection

40°S

☐ Aztec Empire
☐ Maya Empire
☐ Inca Empire

Geography   **Skills for Life**

1. **Interpreting Maps** In which empire was Machu Picchu located?

2. **Applying Geography Skills** The Inca Empire stretched across lands that are part of what present-day countries?

Find NGS online map resources @ www.nationalgeographic.com/maps

② TEACH

L1 Identify

After students read "Colonial Economies" on pages 222–223, ask them to list the colonists' economic activities in Latin America. Next to each activity, have them write *Spanish*, *Portuguese*, or *both* to identify which group engaged in that activity.

Daily Lecture Notes 9-2

DAILY LECTURE NOTES

CHAPTER 9
Section 2   **Building Geography Literacy**
The center of the Inca empire was at Cuzco in the Andes mountain ranges of Peru. The Inca built on 800 years of Andean civilization, achieving notable skills in architecture and engineering. Weakened by years of civil war, the Inca Empire fell to Spanish conquerors under Francisco Pizarro in the 1530s. Pizarro set up a capital city at Lima, Peru. The Spanish ruled there until 1821.

I. **Native American Empires**   pages 220–222

A. **The Maya**
The Maya dominated southern Mexico and northern Central America from about A.D. 250 to 900. They built many cities and based their economy on agriculture and trade. The Maya also were skilled in mathematics and had a system of picture writing called glyphs. The Maya mysteriously abandoned their cities, and archaeologists are continuing to search for more information about the Mayan civilization. (p. 221)

people have interacted with their environment over time. (p. 27)

NATIONAL GEOGRAPHIC   **MAP STUDY**

Answers
1. *Inca*
2. *Ecuador, Bolivia, Peru, Chile, Argentina*

Map Skills Practice
Location What modern-day countries were once occupied by the Inca? (*Argentina, Chile, Peru, and Ecuador*)

DIFFERENTIATED INSTRUCTION

Reading Support Before students read this section, help them understand the factors that contributed to the movement for Latin American independence. Have students read the opening paragraph on page 220. **Ask:** What unresolved past issue compelled the Zapatistas to attack troops and capture towns? (*desire to recover lands that Spanish conquerors seized from ancestors*) Have students think about how they would feel if someone took away their home. Tell students that the word *conquistador* reflects the theme of this section and encourage them to look for specific examples as they read.

🌐 **EE4 Human Systems: Standard 12**
  📁 Refer to *Inclusion for the Social Studies Classroom Strategies and Activities.*

L2 Essay

Have students use information from their textbook and the Internet to write an essay about the effects of European colonization on Latin America. For example, student might analyze the cultural changes that came to the region as a result of European rule.

L1/ELL

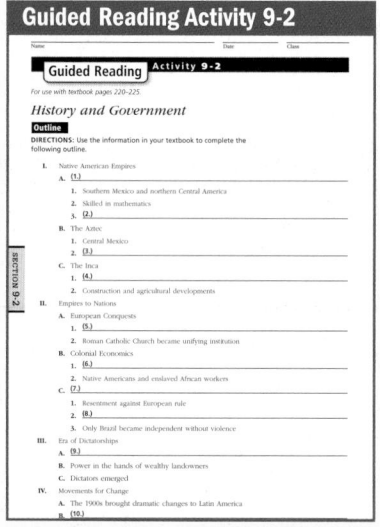

Guided Reading Activity 9-2

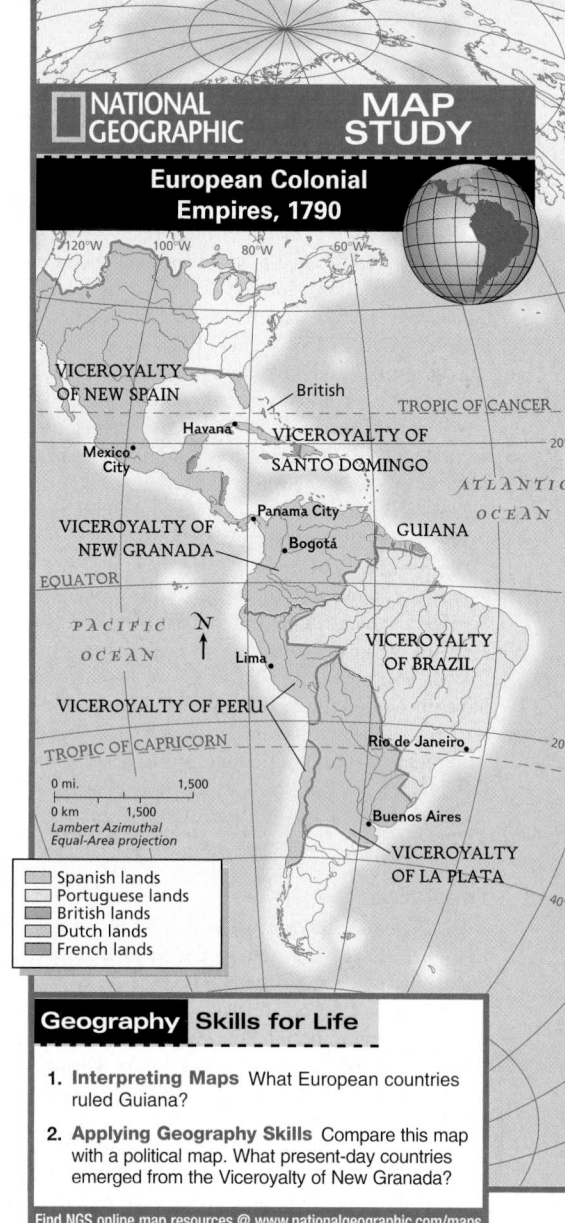

NATIONAL GEOGRAPHIC   MAP STUDY

European Colonial Empires, 1790

VICEROYALTY OF NEW SPAIN

British

TROPIC OF CANCER

Havana

Mexico City

VICEROYALTY OF SANTO DOMINGO

ATLANTIC OCEAN

Panama City

VICEROYALTY OF NEW GRANADA

Bogotá

GUIANA

EQUATOR

PACIFIC OCEAN

N

Lima

VICEROYALTY OF BRAZIL

VICEROYALTY OF PERU

TROPIC OF CAPRICORN

Rio de Janeiro

0 mi.   1,500
0 km   1,500
Lambert Azimuthal
Equal-Area projection

Buenos Aires

VICEROYALTY OF LA PLATA

Spanish lands
Portuguese lands
British lands
Dutch lands
French lands

Geography | Skills for Life

1. **Interpreting Maps** What European countries ruled Guiana?

2. **Applying Geography Skills** Compare this map with a political map. What present-day countries emerged from the Viceroyalty of New Granada?

Find NGS online map resources @ www.nationalgeographic.com/maps

---

NATIONAL GEOGRAPHIC   MAP STUDY

Answers

1. *the Netherlands, France*

2. *Panama, Venezuela, Colombia, Ecuador*

Map Skills Practice

Location In which part of Latin America was British rule and influence the greatest?

(the Caribbean)

Chile. The Inca built their capital, **Cuzco**, in what is now Peru and ruled their lands through a central government headed by an emperor.

Using precisely cut stones, Incan builders constructed massive temples and fortresses. They laid out a network of roads that crossed high mountain passes and penetrated dense forests. To keep soil from washing away, Incan farmers cut terraces into the steep slopes of the Andes and built irrigation systems to bring water to Pacific coast deserts. The Inca also domesticated the alpaca and the llama, which they used for wool. With no written language, the Inca used oral storytelling to pass on knowledge to each generation. To keep track of financial records, Incan traders used a quipu (KEE•poo), a series of knotted cords of various colors and lengths. Each knot represented a different item or number.

Empires to Nations

Beginning with Christopher Columbus's voyages from 1492 to 1504, Europeans explored and colonized vast areas of the Americas. The major European powers of Spain and Portugal ruled huge territories from Mexico to southern South America. Later Great Britain, France, and the Netherlands colonized in the Caribbean area and parts of northern South America.

European Conquests

From the West Indies, the Spaniards expanded into other parts of the Americas. Desiring riches, Spanish conquistador, or conqueror, Hernán Cortés in 1521 defeated the Aztec and claimed Mexico for Spain. In 1535 another conquistador, Francisco Pizarro, destroyed the Incan Empire in Peru and began Spain's South American empire. The Portuguese settled on the coast of Brazil.

As a result of these conquests, European colonies gradually arose throughout Latin America. In Spanish-ruled territories, for example, the conquerors set up highly structured political systems under royally appointed officials known as viceroys. The Roman Catholic Church became the major unifying institution in both Spanish and Portuguese colonies. Missionaries from Europe converted the Native Americans to Christianity and set up schools and hospitals.

Colonial Economies

The European colonies in the Americas became sources of wealth for the home countries. Some Spanish settlers prospered from the mining of gold and silver. The Portuguese discovered precious metals in Brazil and made use of brazilwood,

---

CRITICAL THINKING ACTIVITY

Making Reasoned Judgments Write these words by Simón Bolívar on the board: "Let us give our republic a fourth power . . . to watch over the education of the children, to supervise national education, to purify whatever may be corrupt in the republic, to denounce ingratitude, coldness in the country's service, egotism, sloth, idleness, and to pass judgment upon the first signs of corruption. . . ." Then have each student choose a phrase from the quote and frame a law that would enforce that ideal. For example, for "to denounce . . . sloth" a student might write, "All government workers loafing on the job will be fined." After volunteers write their laws on the board, have them explain whether the law violates people's rights. **EE4 Human Systems: Standard 10**

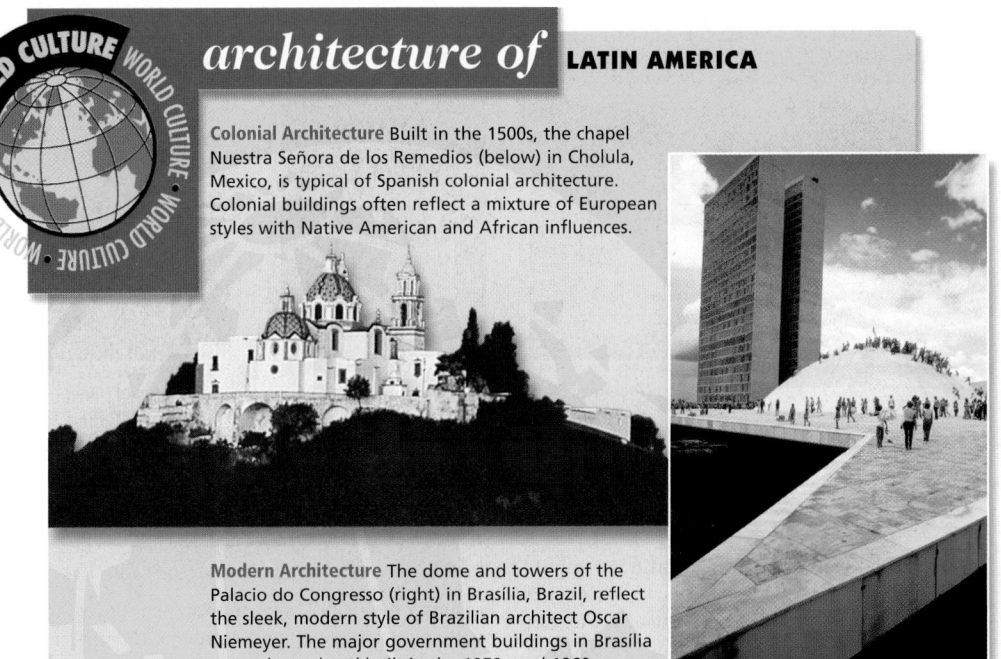

architecture of LATIN AMERICA

Colonial Architecture Built in the 1500s, the chapel Nuestra Señora de los Remedios (below) in Cholula, Mexico, is typical of Spanish colonial architecture. Colonial buildings often reflect a mixture of European styles with Native American and African influences.

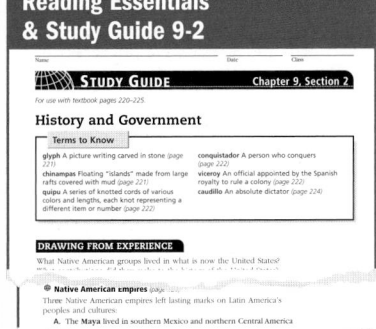

Modern Architecture The dome and towers of the Palacio do Congresso (right) in Brasília, Brazil, reflect the sleek, modern style of Brazilian architect Oscar Niemeyer. The major government buildings in Brasília were planned and built in the 1950s and 1960s.

a tree used to make red dye. Spanish and Portuguese colonists also built cities and towns that served as trade centers and seats of government. In the tropics their plantations grew coffee, bananas, and sugarcane for export to Europe. In cool highlands areas, they established farms and cattle ranches.

The Spaniards and Portuguese used Native Americans to work on the plantations and ranches. As epidemic diseases and hardships drastically reduced the numbers of Native Americans, the European colonists imported enslaved Africans to meet the labor shortage. Despite European dominance many aspects of the Native American and African ways of life survived, creating a blend of the cultures of three continents in Latin America.

Gaining Independence

In the late 1700s, resentment against European rule spread throughout Latin America. Wealthy colonists of European origin wanted self-rule. Those Europeans lower on the social scale demanded more rights. Native Americans and Africans simply yearned for freedom from servitude.

Encouraged by the revolutions in North America and France, many Latin Americans joined together to end European colonial rule.

The first Latin American country to gain its independence was **Haiti**, located on the Caribbean island of Hispaniola. In the 1790s François Toussaint-Louverture (frahn•SWAH TOO•SAN•LOO•vuhr•TYUR), a soldier born of enslaved parents, led a revolt by enslaved Africans. By 1804 Haiti had won its independence from France. The first Spanish-ruled country in Latin America to win independence was Mexico. The independence movement there began in 1810 and was led by a parish priest, Father Miguel Hidalgo. After a long struggle, Mexico became independent in 1821.

Other territories in Latin America also sought independence. By the mid-1800s most of them had achieved their goal under such leaders as Simón Bolívar of Venezuela and José de San Martín of Argentina. However, only one country—Brazil—became independent without a violent upheaval.

Except for Haiti, Caribbean island countries were the last territories in Latin America to achieve

---

L1/ELL

Reading Essentials & Study Guide 9-2

| STUDY GUIDE | Chapter 9, Section 2 |

For use with textbook pages 220–225

History and Government

Terms to Know

glyph A picture writing carved in stone (page 221)
chinampas Floating "islands" made from large rafts covered with mud (page 221)
quipu A series of knotted cords of various colors and lengths, each knot representing a different item or number (page 222)

conquistador A person who conquers (page 221)
viceroy An official appointed by the Spanish royalty to rule a colony (page 222)
caudillo An absolute dictator (page 224)

DRAWING FROM EXPERIENCE

What Native American groups lived in what is now the United States?

● **Native American empires** (page)
Three Native American empires left lasting marks on Latin America's peoples and cultures:
 A. The **Maya** lived in southern Mexico and northern Central America

Architecture of Latin America Colonial Latin American cities were built on a grid plan with a central rectangular plaza surrounded by houses.

✍ 📁 **World Art and Architecture**
Use these transparencies to show regional architecture.

INTERDISCIPLINARY
connection

HISTORY Bolivia's social revolution in 1952 brought some improvements in the lives of the *campesinos*. Some of their land, which had been confiscated by the Spaniards, was returned, and all adults were given the right to vote. Many of the reforms won in 1952 have since been taken away, and Bolivia's people continue their fight for reform.

CRITICAL THINKING ACTIVITY

Recognizing Ideologies Tell students that an ideology is a set of beliefs that guides a person or group of people. Being able to recognize an ideology helps us understand why people act the way they do. Ideologies become ingrained in a society over time and make it very difficult to change quickly or easily. Have students follow along silently as you read aloud the paragraphs under "Era of Dictatorships," on page 224. **Ask:** How did caudillos become so powerful in Latin America? *(Students should mention the rigid class structures that characterized Aztec and European traditions made it easy to ignore democratic principles.)* 🌐 **EE4 Human Systems: Standard 10**

③ ASSESS

Assign Section 2 Assessment as homework or as an in-class activity.

⊗ Have students use **Interactive Tutor Self-Assessment CD-ROM** to review Section 2.

L2

Section Quiz 9-2

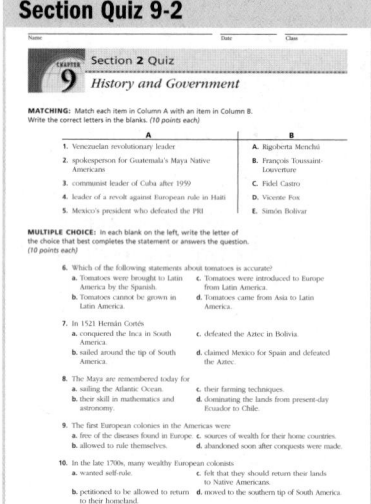

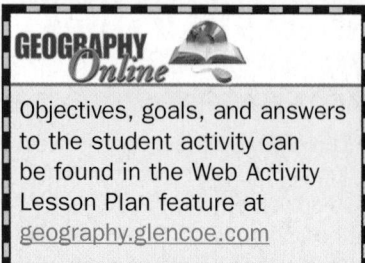

GEOGRAPHY *Online*

Objectives, goals, and answers to the student activity can be found in the Web Activity Lesson Plan feature at geography.glencoe.com

Latin America's Independence Leaders

François Toussaint-Louverture led enslaved Haitians in a violent revolt against French rule. He died in a French prison in 1803.

Called "the Liberator," Simón Bolívar of Venezuela won freedom for the present-day countries of Venezuela, Colombia, Ecuador, Peru, and Bolivia.

José de San Martín of Argentina led his Latin American forces across the Andes to win independence for Chile and Peru.

Father Miguel Hidalgo called on Mexicans to fight for "Independence and Liberty" from Spain. He was executed in 1811.

independence. **Cuba**, for example, did not win its freedom from Spain until 1898. British-ruled islands, such as Jamaica and Barbados, did not gain independence until well into the 1900s. Even today some islands remain under foreign control; for example, Martinique is a possession of France, the Cayman Islands of Great Britain, and Curaçao of the Netherlands. In addition, Puerto Rico and some of the Virgin Islands have political links to the United States.

Era of Dictatorships

Latin America's wars for independence ushered in a period of political and economic instability. During the 1800s some leaders in the region wanted to build democratic institutions and prosperous economies. However, they had to contend with the legacy of indigenous and European class structures, which stressed rank and privilege. As a result, political and economic power often remained in the hands of a small group of wealthy landowners, army officers, and clergy. Written constitutions were ignored, public dissatisfaction led to revolts, and governments relied on the military to keep order.

In this chaotic situation, a new kind of leader emerged—the **caudillo** (kow•DEE•yoh), or dictator. With the backing of military forces and wealthy landowners, caudillos became absolute rulers with sole authority to make decisions.

Movements for Change

During the 1900s Latin America experienced dramatic political, social, and economic changes. For example, after Panama became an independent country in 1903, the United States and Panama signed a treaty creating the Panama Canal Zone. The formation of industries, the building of railroads, and the expansion of trade all brought new wealth to the upper classes. However, for the vast majority of Latin Americans, especially rural dwellers, progress was limited.

As the gap between the rich and the poor widened, dissatisfaction with the peonage system spread. In 1915 a decree against peonage, the forced servitude of an individual because of debt, was issued in Mexico. However, the system continued in several countries until the 1930s. Conservative dictators and military governments resisted most demands for reform.

Reform did occur in Cuba, however, when a revolution in 1959 set up a communist state under Fidel Castro. During the 1990s communism remained entrenched in Cuba, but military dictatorships gave

GEOGRAPHY *Online*

Student Web Activity Visit the **Glencoe World Geography** Web site at geography.glencoe.com and click on Student Web Activities—Chapter 9 for an activity about the Panama Canal.

TEAM-TEACHING ACTIVITY: WORLD HISTORY

Indigenous People Have students choose a Native American empire—Maya, Aztec, or Inca—to explore more fully. A world history teacher can suggest two or more useful sources and narrowed topics. As they research their empire, students should keep their scope narrow. Possible topics may include daily life, technology, arts and crafts, architecture, the belief system, government, the conquistadors, writing, ceramics, and games. Tell students to write a brief report on their findings and provide at least one visual to accompany it. Have students sign up for a narrow topic so that a variety of areas in each empire are explored. Then have students share what they learned about the empire. 🎲

🌐 **EE4 Human Systems: Standard 13**

way to democratically elected governments in a number of countries. Today Latin American countries are struggling to end corrupt politics and bring economic benefits to all their citizens. In Mexico, for example, nearly 70 years of one-party rule ended in the year 2000 when the candidate of the ruling party PRI (*Partido Revolucionario Institucional*) lost the presidency to Vicente Fox of the opposition party PAN (*Partido Acción Nacional*).

As Latin America entered the 2000s, Native Americans, farmers, and workers demanded more political power and greater economic benefits. A spokeswoman for Guatemala's modern-day Maya people, Rigoberta Menchú, discusses the need for greater inclusion in political processes:

> *" National unity must be defined in the context of the right of the whole society to diversity, protected by and reflected in a democratic state. Eventually governments will have to tackle the issue of the self-determination of diverse peoples within national boundaries. . . .We must accept that humanity is a beautiful multicolored garden. "*
>
> Rigoberta Menchú (Ann Wright, trans.), *Crossing Borders*, 1998

NATIONAL GEOGRAPHIC World Explorer

Geography Skills for Life

New President In his campaign, Vicente Fox (shown here with Rigoberta Menchú) promised better public education and more attention to the poor.

Region What political issues are important in Latin America today?

CHAPTER 9
Section 2, pages 220–225

NATIONAL GEOGRAPHIC World Explorer

Answer
corruption, economic equality, and the rights of indigenous peoples

More About the Photo
Mexico's President Vicente Fox, who has reached out to all his country's people, here shakes hands with Rigoberta Menchú, the Nobel Prize winning spokesperson for Latin America's indigenous people.

Reteach
Have students reread the section. Ask them to list at least five cause-and-effect relationships from their reading.

Enrich
Have students assemble and display dioramas of Mayan cities Chichen Itzá and Tulum and include temples, plazas, and marketplaces.

 **CLOSE**

Tape a label of each "Terms to Know" from the section onto a different student's back so that only that student cannot read it. Have students ask questions about their key term such as "Am I a person?" or "Am I a place?" until they have enough facts to identify the term.

SECTION 2 ASSESSMENT

Checking for Understanding

1. **Define** glyph, *chinampas*, quipu, conquistador, viceroy, caudillo.

2. **Main Ideas** Create a web diagram like the one below for each Native American culture, and show its major achievements. Then choose one achievement and explain why it was important.

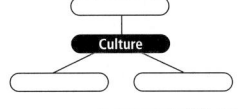

Culture

Critical Thinking

3. **Making Comparisons** How was the social structure of the Aztec Empire similar to the social structures of Latin America under European colonialism?

4. **Drawing Conclusions** Was the plantation system beneficial or harmful? Explain.

5. **Analyzing Information** According to Rigoberta Menchú, how can diversity bring unity? Do you agree or disagree with her assessment, and what steps would you take to bring about unity?

Analyzing Maps

6. **Region** Compare the maps of Latin America and the colonial empires on pages 195 and 222. Which Spanish viceroyalty was named for a geographic feature of Latin America?

Applying Geography

7. **Development and History** On a time line trace the development of indigenous and European empires in Latin America. Include at least one achievement that occurred during each empire.

Chapter 9 🌐 225

SECTION 2 ASSESSMENT ANSWERS

1. All vocabulary terms are defined in the text.

2. Students should list major achievements for the Maya, Aztec, and Inca, and explain why one of those achievements was important.

3. Both systems were highly structured with the majority of people at the bottom in each system. The Aztecs were ruled by an emperor and military officials. Under colonial rule, royally appointed viceroys ruled.

4. Europeans prospered; many Native Americans and Africans suffered and died.

5. Her definition of unity includes the rights of diverse peoples; accept reasonable responses.

6. Rio de la Plata

7. **Applying Geography** Time lines should include all indigenous and European empires with at least one change or achievement for each empire.

 **FOCUS**

Section Overview

This section discusses the roles religion and the arts play in Latin American culture, and how family life, leisure activities, and public celebrations reflect the region's cultural diversity.

BELLRINGER
Skillbuilder Activity

 Project transparency and have students answer questions.

 Available as blackline master.

Daily Focus Skills Transparency 9-3

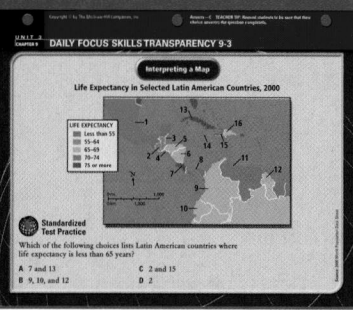

Guide to Reading

Consider What You Know
Answers *may include media and contact with Latin American immigrants and businesses.*

Reading Strategy
Answers Religion: *most people are Roman Catholic; many blend different religions into a single faith;* Arts: *art reflects ethnic heritage and focus has shifted to more traditional works;* Everday Life: *emphasis is placed on family and social events; many are passionate about fútbol*

Preteaching Vocabulary
Use the **Vocabulary Puzzle-Maker CD-ROM** to create crossword and word-search puzzles.

Guide to Reading

Consider What You Know
Latin American foods and music are popular in the United States and around the world. How do people today discover and learn about the cultural traditions of Latin America?

Reading Strategy
Categorizing Complete a graphic organizer similar to the one below by filling in a brief description of each aspect of Latin American culture.

Cultural Aspect	Description
Religion	
Arts	
Everyday Life	

Read to Find Out
- What role does religion play in Latin American culture?
- How have Latin Americans used the arts to express their history, their social struggles, and their cultural diversity?
- How is Latin America's cultural diversity reflected in family life, leisure activities, and public celebrations?

Terms to Know
- syncretism
- mural
- mosaic
- extended family
- malnutrition
- *fútbol*
- jai alai

Places to Locate
- West Indies
- Dominican Republic
- Guatemala
- Brasília
- Chile

Cultures and Lifestyles

NATIONAL GEOGRAPHIC

A Geographic View

Shadows of the Ancients

Doffing his mask, a member of Los Panchitos dance troupe takes a breather from the vigorous street dancing. . . . With its origins deep in the past, the dance pokes fun at figures of the present. . . . The finger of ridicule points to a landowner who abuses peasant workers, a judge who decides a case in favor of the rich. . . .

—Michael E. Long, "Enduring Echoes of Peru's Past," National Geographic, June 1990

Masked dancer at a Peruvian festival

The past and present intermingle in the lives of Latin Americans. Here, along Peru's northern coast, a masked dance blends Native American and European influences, music and visual arts, religion and social criticism. This interweaving of diverse elements is a hallmark of Latin American culture. In this section you will learn how Latin Americans express their culture through religion, the arts, and everyday life.

Religion

Religion has long played an important role in Latin American society. During the colonial era, most Latin Americans became Christians, and Christianity still has the most followers. In addition, other faiths are found in the region. For example, scores of traditional Native American and African religions thrive, often mixed with Christianity and other faiths. Islam, Hinduism, and Buddhism, brought by Asian immigrants, are practiced in the **West Indies** and coastal areas of South America. Judaism has followers in the largest Latin American cities.

RESOURCE MANAGER

Reproducible Masters
- Reproducible Lesson Plan 9-3
- Vocabulary Activity 9
- Daily Lecture Notes 9-3
- Guided Reading Activity 9-3
- Reading Essentials and Study Guide 9-3
- Reteaching Activity 9
- Reinforcing Skills Activity 9
- Section Quiz 9-3

Transparencies
- Daily Focus Skills Transparency 9-3
- Unit 3 Map Overlay Transparencies

Multimedia
- Vocabulary PuzzleMaker CD-ROM
- World Music: A Cultural Legacy
- Interactive Tutor Self-Assessment CD-ROM
- ExamView® Pro Testmaker CD-ROM
- Presentation Plus! CD-ROM

Roman Catholicism

Most Christians in Latin America are Roman Catholics, and Roman Catholic traditions influence daily life in the region. During colonial times Roman Catholicism was the official religion of the Spanish colonies and Brazil. Roman Catholic clergy had accompanied European conquerors and colonists to the Americas. They established Roman Catholicism throughout Latin America, converting many Native Americans to their faith. When European settlers arrived, the priests saw to their spiritual needs as well.

Before long, church leaders were playing an important role in political affairs in the region, and the Roman Catholic Church had become wealthy. When the fight for independence came, church officials backed the wealthy and powerful classes. During the late 1900s, however, Roman Catholics in Latin America began to support the concerns of the poor and the oppressed. In recent years many Roman Catholic clergy and laypeople have opposed dictatorships and worked to improve the lives of disadvantaged groups. For example, the Church has been active in movements for land reform and for improvements in education and health care.

Protestantism

Various forms of Protestant Christianity came to Latin America with British and Dutch settlers in the 1800s. In time American Protestant missionaries came and built hospitals, schools, and colleges. Protestants in the region were few in number until the late 1900s, when Protestantism grew rapidly. According to religious observers, many Latin Americans were drawn to Protestantism because it gave laypeople a major role in religious life and emphasized personal religious experience.

A Mixing of Religions

Throughout Latin America a mixing of religions has occurred since the colonial era. Many Latin

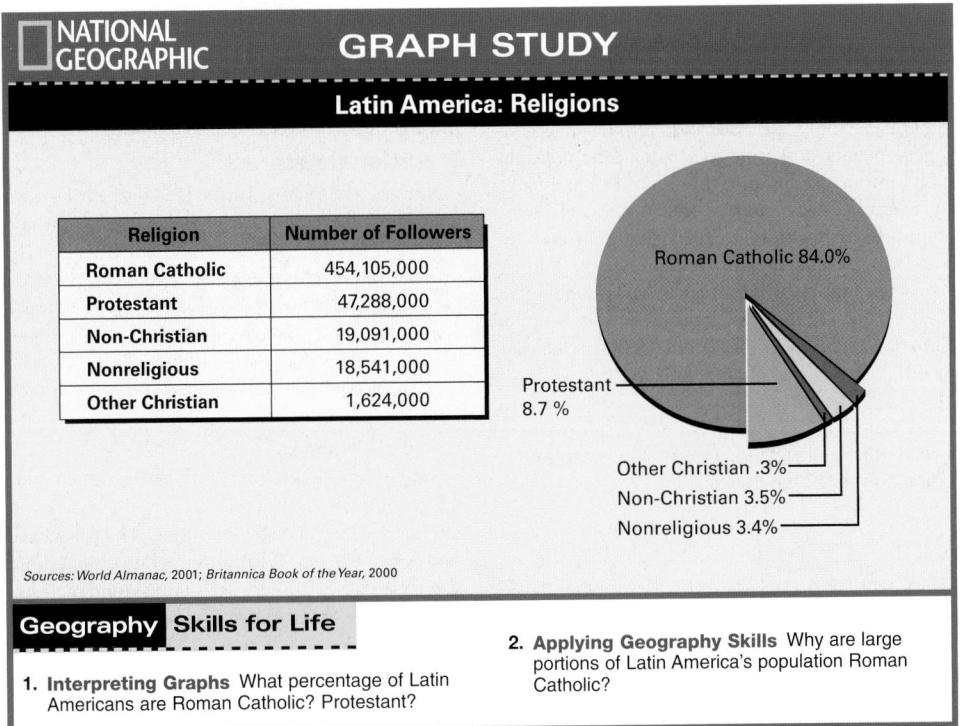

NATIONAL GEOGRAPHIC

GRAPH STUDY

Latin America: Religions

Religion	Number of Followers
Roman Catholic	454,105,000
Protestant	47,288,000
Non-Christian	19,091,000
Nonreligious	18,541,000
Other Christian	1,624,000

Roman Catholic 84.0%

Protestant 8.7 %

Other Christian .3%

Non-Christian 3.5%

Nonreligious 3.4%

Sources: World Almanac, 2001; Britannica Book of the Year, 2000

Geography Skills for Life

1. **Interpreting Graphs** What percentage of Latin Americans are Roman Catholic? Protestant?

2. **Applying Geography Skills** Why are large portions of Latin America's population Roman Catholic?

L1 Identify

Ask students to hypothesize about what language the word *fútbol* came from. *(Spanish)* Then have Spanish-speaking students share words with altered spellings or pronunciations in English. *(Answers may include tamale and rancho.)* **ELL**

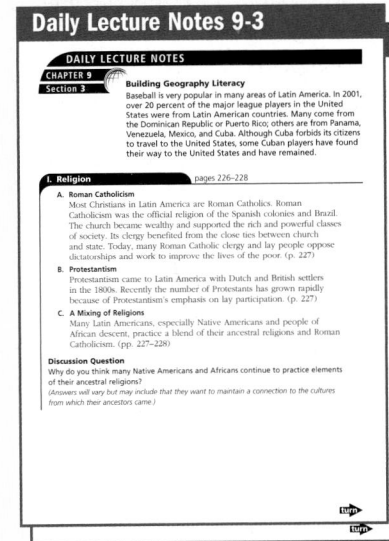

Daily Lecture Notes 9-3

DAILY LECTURE NOTES

CHAPTER 9
Section 3

Building Geography Literacy
Baseball is very popular in many areas of Latin America. In 2001, over 20 percent of the major league players in the United States were from Latin American countries. Many come from the Dominican Republic or Puerto Rico; others are from Panama, Venezuela, Mexico, and Cuba. Although Cuba forbids its citizens to travel to the United States, some Cuban players have found their way to the United States and have remained.

I. Religion pages 226–228

A. Roman Catholicism
Most Christians in Latin America are Roman Catholics. Roman Catholicism was the official religion of the Spanish colonies and Brazil. The church became wealthy and supported the rich and powerful classes of society. Its clergy benefited from the close ties between church and state. Today, many Roman Catholic clergy and lay people oppose dictatorships and work to improve the lives of the poor. (p. 227)

B. Protestantism
Protestantism came to Latin America with Dutch and British settlers in the 1800s. Recently the number of Protestants has grown rapidly because of Protestantism's emphasis on lay participation. (p. 227)

C. A Mixing of Religions
Many Latin Americans, especially Native Americans and people of African descent, practice a blend of their ancestral religions and Roman Catholicism. (pp. 227–228)

Discussion Question
Why do you think many Native Americans and Africans continue to practice elements of their ancestral religions?
(Answers will vary but may include that they want to maintain a connection to the cultures from which their ancestors came.)

NATIONAL GEOGRAPHIC

GRAPH STUDY

Answers

1. *82.3 percent, 8.6 percent*

2. *Spanish and Portuguese colonizers brought missionaries who spread Roman Catholicism.*

Skills Practice

Place What percentage of Latin Americans are nonreligious? *(2.9 percent)*

DIFFERENTIATED INSTRUCTION

Visual/Spatial Have students read the material under "Religion" before giving them a blank map to indicate religions practiced in Latin America. Have students create a list of the religions mentioned in the text. Next, have them create a color key for each of the religions practiced. Although most of Latin America is Roman Catholic, people practice syncretism in many places. From the paragraph titled "A Mixing of Religions," read aloud the following sentence: "*Some Latin Americans, for example, especially Native Americans, worship at Roman Catholic churches on Sunday but pray to nature deities during the week.*" **EE4 Human Systems: Standard 10**

➥ Refer to *Inclusion for the Social Studies Classroom Strategies and Activities.*

Take a Deep Breath Because the air is thin at high altitudes, the thoracic capacity of many Andean people may be up to 30 percent larger than those of lowland people. The added lung capacity helps them play the giant, mysterious-sounding panpipes.

🎵 **World Music: A Cultural Legacy** Use the accompanying Teacher Guide for background information, discussion questions, and worksheets about the music of this region.

L3 Comparison Essay

Have interested students research religion, the arts, or leisure activities for three Latin American countries and write a comparison-contrast essay about their findings.

L1/ELL

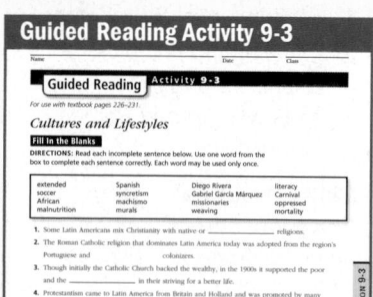

Guided Reading Activity 9-3

| Name | Date | Class |

Guided Reading Activity 9-3

For use with textbook pages 226-231.

Cultures and Lifestyles

Fill in the Blanks

DIRECTIONS: Read each incomplete sentence below. Use one word from the box to complete each sentence correctly. Each word may be used only once.

extended	Spanish	Diego Rivera	literacy
soccer	syncretism	Gabriel García Márquez	Carnival
African	machismo	missionaries	oppressed
malnutrition	murals	weaving	mortality

1. Some Latin Americans mix Christianity with native or _____ religions.
2. The Roman Catholic religion that dominates Latin America today was adopted from the region's Portuguese and _____ colonizers.
3. Though initially the Catholic Church backed the wealthy, in the 1900s it supported the poor and the _____ in their striving for a better life.
4. Protestantism came to Latin America from Britain and Holland and was promoted by many

---

music of LATIN AMERICA

A wide mix of music traditions in Latin America comes from the native inhabitants (wind and percussion instruments), the Europeans (strings, vocal harmonies), and the Africans (drums, varied rhythms).

Instrument Spotlight
Panpipes are one of the most common musical instruments from the Andean region of South America, dating from before the arrival of the Europeans. Often called *zampona* or *siku*, panpipes are made of bamboo in varying sizes and pitches. Individual bamboo stalks are cut precisely and lashed together in rows with strips of bamboo and string. The notes of a given scale often alternate from one set of pipes to another. For a complete melody to be played, the two rows of pipes are stacked one on top of the other.

Go To **World Music: A Cultural Legacy** Hear music of this region on Disc 1, Tracks 7–12.

Americans today practice syncretism—a blending of beliefs and practices from different religions into a single faith. Some Latin Americans, for example, especially Native Americans, worship at Roman Catholic churches on Sunday but pray to nature deities during the week. Among the descendants of enslaved Africans, belief in West African deities is combined with Roman Catholic devotion to the saints. Called *condomblé* in Brazil, Santería in Cuba, and voodoo in Haiti and the **Dominican Republic**, these African-based religions have thousands of followers in Latin America and among Latin American immigrants to the United States.

The Arts of Latin America

For centuries, the arts and literature of Latin America were shaped by European styles. Today's Latin American artists and writers have developed styles that often reflect their diverse ethnic heritages, blending European styles with those of Native American cultures.

History
Traditional Arts

Native Americans produced the earliest art forms in Latin America. They left a legacy of weaving, woodcarving, pottery, and metalwork. The intricate, colorful handwoven textiles produced in **Guatemala** and the Andes regions reflect Mayan symbols and Incan weaving. The work of contemporary goldsmiths, silversmiths, and jewelers is matched only by the sophisticated metalwork from the pre-Columbian era, the time before the arrival of Columbus.

Native Americans built temples decorated with colored murals, or wall paintings, and mosaics, pictures or designs made by setting small bits of colored stone, tile, or shell into mortar. Native Americans also created the region's earliest music and dance.

During colonial times the arts were largely inspired by European works. Most paintings had Christian themes. Murals, however, mixed the brightly colored abstract designs of the Native Americans with the more realistic European styles.

COOPERATIVE LEARNING ACTIVITY

Carnival Describe Carnival, the five-day festival Brazilians celebrate before Lent. Organize the class into groups and assign each group some aspect of Carnival. For example, have one group research the kinds of costumes worn during the festivities and have the members of the group create a display of photos and sketches, and make masks to distribute to other students. Have another group listen to *samba* music and learn to play some Latin American rhythms and research the *samba* step. One group might research and write a short report on the origins, function, and significance of Carnival float competitions. Designate a part of a class period for Carnival, and have the groups share what they have learned. 📦
🌐 **EE4 Human Systems: Standard 10**

Churches built in Spanish and Portuguese designs often were enlivened by the ethnic details added by Native American and African artists. Meanwhile, Africans brought to the region the rhythms, songs, and dances that evolved into today's Latin American musical styles and dances, such as calypso, reggae, and samba.

Modern Arts

During the 1900s Latin American artists mixed European, Native American, and African artistic traditions. Many of them also focused on social and political subjects. Diego Rivera, a well-known Mexican artist, created huge murals that illustrated key events in Mexico's history, especially the struggles of impoverished farmers to win social justice. Other noted Latin American painters included Mexico's Frida Kahlo, known for her self-portraits, and Colombia's Fernando Botero, who satirized the lifestyles of Latin America's upper classes.

Latin American music combines Native American, European, and African influences to create unique styles. These musical styles include Brazilian samba, Cuban salsa, and Mexican mariachi.

During the past 50 years, Latin American architects, dancers, and writers also have won international recognition. The Brazilian architect Oscar Niemeyer is known for the buildings he designed in the Brazilian capital of **Brasília**. Dance companies such as the Ballet Folklórico of Mexico fascinate audiences worldwide with their performances of traditional Native American and Spanish dances. Latin America also has produced outstanding novelists, such as Colombia's Gabriel García Márquez and Chile's Isabel Allende, who skillfully blend everyday reality with the mythical and fantastic in their writings. A continuing theme of Latin American literature is cultural identity. The Argentine poet Jorge Luis Borges wrote of this theme in his life:

> **“** From a lineage of Protestant ministers and South American soldiers who fought, with their incalculable dust, against the Spaniards and the desert lances, I am and am not . . . **”**
>
> "Yesterdays," *Jorge Luis Borges: Selected Poems,* Alexander Coleman, ed., Stephen Kessler, trans., 1999

Everyday Life

Latin Americans place great emphasis on social status and family life. They also cherish values such as personal honor and individual freedom.

Families

Most Latin Americans have a strong sense of loyalty to family. Each person is part of an extended family that includes grandparents, aunts, uncles, and cousins as well as parents and children. Latin American parents and children often share their home with grandparents and sometimes other members of the extended family. *Compadres*, or godparents, play an important role in family life. Godparents are people chosen by the mother and father to sponsor their new baby. Godparents are concerned with the child's religious and moral upbringing and help take care of the child if something happens to the parents.

Latin American society still displays traces of machismo, a Spanish and Portuguese tradition of male

▲ *Diego Rivera's mural* Teatro Insurgentes *depicts leaders of the Mexican Revolution.*

L1/ELL

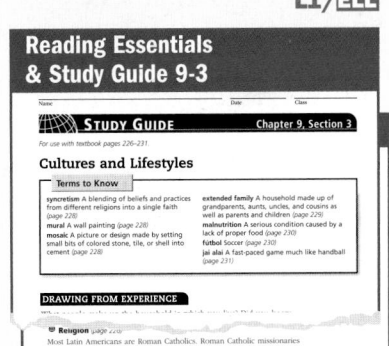

Reading Essentials & Study Guide 9-3

GEOGRAPHY AND THE HUMANITIES

 World Music: A Cultural Legacy

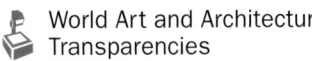 World Art and Architecture Transparencies

 World Art Prints

Ritual Dance A form of martial arts called *capoeira* was brought by enslaved peoples to Rio de Janeiro from Angola. It was disguised as a ritual dance, because enslaved peoples were not allowed to fight. Today the martial art-dance is performed for tourists and is characterized by thrusts, feints, and high kicks, which call for great flexibility and agility.

CRITICAL THINKING ACTIVITY

Making Generalizations Have students follow along silently as you read aloud the paragraph under "Protestantism" on page 227. Have students note the reason why Protestantism grew rapidly in the late 1900s. **Ask:** What changes will the Roman Catholic Church need to make to stem the growth of Protestantism in the early 2000s? *(The Church will need to give laypeople a bigger role in religious life and emphasize personal religious experience.)* ⬛ **EE4 Human Systems: Standard 10**

Answer

The family is central to Latin American life. Extended families are all responsible for the children's upbringing.

More About the Photo In addition to the important role of grandparents and godparents to children, godparents also have a customary relationship with each other. Called *compadres* in Spanish, godparents are obliged to offer support and money to each other in times of hardship.

③ ASSESS

Assign Section 3 Assessment as homework or as an in-class activity.

◉ Have students use **Interactive Tutor Self-Assessment CD-ROM** to review Section 3.
L2

Section Quiz 9-3

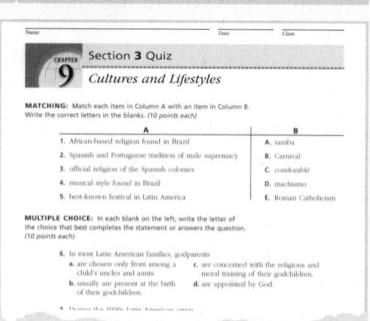

supremacy, although women have made rapid advances in public life in recent decades. Latin American women are in charge of home life, making important financial and family decisions. Each year more women attend universities and hold jobs in a variety of professions. Many have been elected as national legislators, as mayors of large cities, and as country leaders. For example, in 1999, Panama elected Mireya Elisa Moscoso as president.

Education and Health Care

The quality of education varies throughout Latin America. Children generally are required to complete elementary school, but they often do not because of long distances to school and lack of money for clothing and supplies. Also, many children drop out to help with family farming or to find jobs.

Despite such realities many Latin American countries have made gains in education. Adult literacy rates have risen steadily, governments now devote more funds to schools, and some countries have seen impressive gains in school attendance. University enrollment also is rising, as some public universities provide higher education at little or no cost to students. Although Latin America has lagged behind some other regions in computer literacy, Internet usage is beginning to transform education in countries such as **Chile** and Mexico.

In Latin America, as in other regions, health care is linked to standards of living. As people become employed and better educated, health concerns linked to poverty, lack of sanitation, and malnutrition, a serious condition caused by a lack of proper food, become much less severe. Today, despite a wide gap between the rich and the poor, Latin America overall is improving the health of its people. Infant mortality rates for

the region have fallen dramatically in recent years, and most people now have access to clean, treated water for drinking.

Still, health conditions vary from country to country. In lands with prosperous economies and high standards of living, such as Chile, people have access to better health care systems and are able to live healthier, longer lives. By contrast, countries with less developed economies, such as Haiti, have little money to spend on health care. Consequently, disease is more prevalent and life expectancy is low. In most Latin American countries, the quality of health care falls between these two extremes.

Sports and Leisure

Throughout Latin America fans are as passionate about *fútbol*, or soccer, as fans in the United States are about American football. In many Latin American countries it is the national sport. Thousands of dedicated spectators crowd into huge stadiums to watch their teams play. Baseball, basketball, and volleyball also have large followings, especially in the West Indies. Many Latin

NATIONAL GEOGRAPHIC World Explorer

Geography **Skills for Life**
Extended
Families Family celebrations such as birthdays and weddings are important traditions within extended families.
Region How do Latin Americans view families?

TEAM-TEACHING ACTIVITY: ART

Expressing Ethnic Heritage Show students several examples of traditional and modern Latin American art. Point out features that reflect the peoples and cultures of pre-Columbian times, such as designs of indigenous people or early history. Have students choose an artistic tradition—such as mural painting, sculpture, or mosaics—or a particular artist—such as Frida Kahlo, Diego Rivera, or Fernando Botero—to imitate in order to express their own ethnic heritage. Students whose ancestry includes several ethnic groups might portray that background in a mural where several elements can be depicted. Students can work with an art teacher in the initial stages designing and choosing an appropriate medium. 📦
🌐 **EE4 Human Systems: Standard 10**

American baseball stars, including home-run hitter Sammy Sosa from the Dominican Republic, have gone on to play in the North American major leagues. A favorite sport among many Mexicans and Cubans is *jai alai* (HY•LY), a fast-paced game much like handball, played with a ball and a long, curved basket strapped to each player's wrist.

Watching television, listening to the radio, and attending movies, concerts, and plays are leisure activities as popular in Latin America as they are around the world. The most popular Latin American leisure activity of all, however, may be celebrating. From impromptu gatherings of friends to special family dinners to religious feast days, and patriotic events, almost any social occasion is a party—a *fiesta*, or festival.

Perhaps the best-known festival is Carnival, celebrated in the week before the Roman Catholic observance of Lent, a 40-day period of fasting and prayer before Easter. In Rio de Janeiro, home of one of the largest Carnival celebrations, teams from different parts of the city compete to win the prize for the best hand-decorated float. People make their own brightly colored masks and elaborate costumes and then parade to samba music through the streets. Today Carnival draws people from around the world to Latin America.

NATIONAL GEOGRAPHIC World Explorer

Geography Skills for Life

Fútbol The Brazilian star Ronaldo breaks through the Italian defense during a tournament game.
Region What other sports have large followings in Latin America?

NATIONAL GEOGRAPHIC World Explorer

Answer
baseball, basketball, jai alai

More About the Photo
Soccer is considered the world's most popular sport. Brazil has one of the world's leading soccer teams and competes in the World Cup Championship, an international competition held every four years. There also is a women's World Cup; and soccer is included in the Olympic Games.

Reteach

Have students turn the section's subheads into questions, then answer each question.

Enrich

Play some calypso music for students and tell them that the oil industry on the Caribbean island of Trinidad provided calypso singers their instruments—the steel drums which characterize this type of music. Used oil drums were cut to different sizes which resulted in different tones.

 **CLOSE**

Challenge the class to write the name of a person, group, place, or sport from the section for each letter in the term *Latin America*.

SECTION 3 ASSESSMENT

Checking for Understanding

1. **Define** syncretism, mural, mosaic, extended family, malnutrition, *fútbol*, jai alai.

2. **Main Ideas** Create a chart like the one below, and fill in the influences that contributed to each aspect of Latin American culture.

Cultures and Lifestyles

Influences		Aspects of Culture
	→	
	→	
	→	

Critical Thinking

3. **Making Inferences** Why do you think Roman Catholicism has remained the predominant religion in Latin America?

4. **Drawing Conclusions** Why do you think Latin American arts imitated the arts of Europe?

5. **Making Generalizations** On an outline map, label the countries of South America. What factors do you think determine their political boundaries?

6. **Making Inferences** Why might parties—fiestas and festivals—be so popular in Latin America?

Analyzing Charts

7. **Place** Study the graph showing religions on page 227. Which religion in Latin America is second to Roman Catholicism in its number of followers?

Applying Geography

8. **Cultural Influences** Make a sketch map to show where the region's arts originated. Include representative examples of various art forms and examples from Africa, Europe, and Latin America. Provide notes about each example's ethnic origins.

SECTION 3 ASSESSMENT ANSWERS

1. All vocabulary terms are defined in the text.

2. Answers may include colonial influences on religion, indigenous influences on art, and European values on family life.

3. It was the traditional religion of Spanish and Portuguese colonies. Roman Catholic religious leaders became involved in politics. In the 1900s they began to support the concerns of the poor and oppressed and continue to work to improve the lives of the disadvantaged.

4. Colonials held European arts as models.

5. Students might point out physical features, such as rivers (Rio Grande) or mountains (Andes) that form parts of natural borders.

6. due to the importance of families and religion, as well as widespread poverty

7. Protestantism

8. **Applying Geography** Maps should include examples of each art form. Paragraphs should indicate each example's ethnic origin.

Teaching the Skill

Tell students that the first step in understanding a population density map is to look at map keys to understand what the colors and symbols represent. Have students answer the first two questions orally in "Practicing the Skill." Before students answer questions 3–5, have them read "Learning the Skill." Then ask them to write a concluding statement about population density patterns in both high and low population density areas. *(Student answers might include geographical features, such as proximity to water, as a predictor of dense population.)* Finally, tell students to think about what they already know about the region that will help them make generalizations about population density and answer the rest of the questions in "Practicing the Skill."

Additional Practice
L1

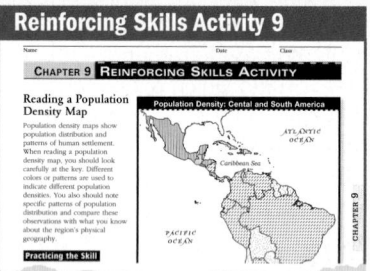

GLENCOE
TECHNOLOGY

**Glencoe Skillbuilder
Interactive Workbook,
Level 2**

Reading a Population Density Map

Population density measures how many people live within a certain unit area, such as a square mile or square kilometer. Population density may vary from place to place within a country or region. A population density map shows you these variations.

Learning the Skill

To determine a country's overall population density, divide the number of people within a country's boundaries by its land area in square miles or square kilometers. The map at right shows how population density differs within Brazil.

- **Study the map keys to determine what the colors and symbols represent.** Notice that the map uses colors to show population densities and symbols to show the populations of cities.

- **Look for patterns that might explain population density patterns.** Ask yourself what geographical features are shared by areas with high or low population densities.

- **Compare the map with other regional information,** such as natural resources and physical geography, to draw conclusions about the possible causes and effects of population density patterns.

Practicing the Skill

Use the population density map to answer the questions.

1. What does the dark orange color represent?

2. What symbol represents cities of more than 5,000,000 people?

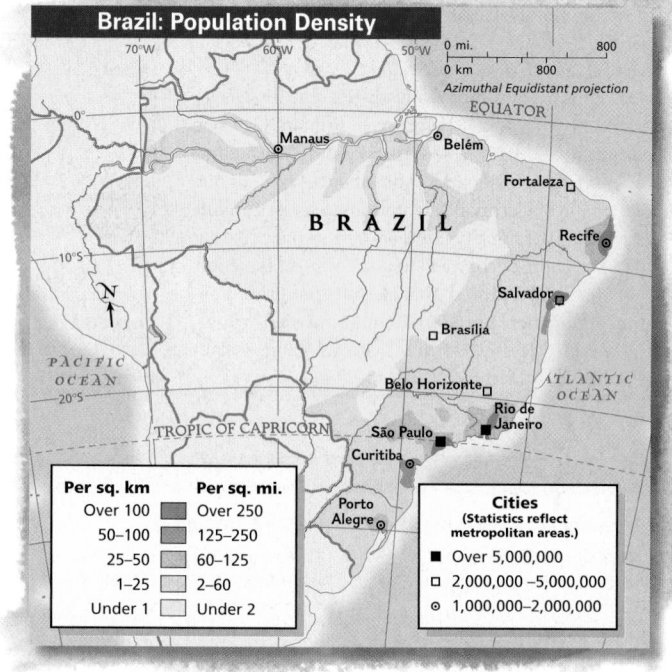

Brazil: Population Density

Per sq. km	Per sq. mi.
Over 100	Over 250
50–100	125–250
25–50	60–125
1–25	2–60
Under 1	Under 2

Cities
(Statistics reflect metropolitan areas.)
- ■ Over 5,000,000
- ▫ 2,000,000 –5,000,000
- ◉ 1,000,000–2,000,000

3. Which areas of Brazil have low population densities?

4. Which areas have the highest population densities?

5. Which two cities have the most people?

6. Which cities have fewer than 2 million people?

7. Why do you think the southern coast of Brazil is more densely populated?

Applying the Skill

Compare the physical map of Latin America with the population density map. Write a paragraph explaining how physical geography affects population density.

Go To The Glencoe Skillbuilder Interactive Workbook, Level 2 provides instruction and practice in key social studies skills.

ANSWERS TO PRACTICING THE SKILL

1. population of 125–250 people per square mile
2. colored square
3. inland areas
4. coastal areas

5. São Paulo and Rio de Janeiro
6. Manaus, Belém, Recífe, Porto Alegre, and Curitíba
7. The area has a milder climate than the interior, and ports make it more accessible.

SUMMARY & STUDY GUIDE

CHAPTER 9

SECTION 1 — Population Patterns (pp. 211–217)

Terms to Know
- indigenous
- dialect
- patois
- urbanization
- megacity
- primate city

Key Points
- Latin America's people descended from indigenous peoples, Europeans, Africans, and Asians.
- Latin Americans speak Spanish, Portuguese, other European languages, indigenous languages, and mixed dialects or patois.
- Latin America's population is mostly concentrated in coastal areas.
- Urbanization has created an imbalance in Latin America's population density.
- The region has some of the world's largest cities.

Organizing Your Notes
Use a graphic organizer like the one below to help you organize important details from this section.

Peoples	Population Patterns	Migration

SECTION 2 — History and Government (pp. 220–225)

Terms to Know
- glyph
- *chinampas*
- quipu
- conquistador
- viceroy
- caudillo

Key Points
- The Maya, the Aztec, and the Inca developed complex civilizations before Europeans arrived.
- Spanish and Portuguese colonization had lasting effects on Latin America's culture.
- Most Latin American countries achieved independence during the 1800s.
- Most Latin American countries developed democratic self-rule in the twentieth century.
- The political, economic, and cultural legacy of colonialism still challenges Latin America.

Organizing Your Notes
Use a time line like the one below to help you organize your notes on key historical events discussed in this section.

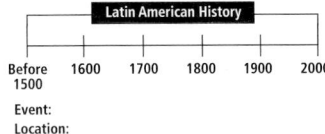

Latin American History

| Before 1500 | 1600 | 1700 | 1800 | 1900 | 2000 |

Event:
Location:

SECTION 3 — Cultures and Lifestyles (pp. 226–231)

Terms to Know
- syncretism
- mural
- mosaic
- extended family
- malnutrition
- *fútbol*
- jai alai

Key Points
- Religion plays an important role in Latin American life.
- Educational quality varies throughout the region.
- As each country improves its economy, nutrition, and sanitation, people's health improves.
- Latin American traditional arts, music, and literature reflect the region's cultural diversity.
- Deep divisions between economic and social classes still characterize Latin American life.
- Latin Americans value family activities, sports such as *fútbol* and jai alai, and holidays and festivals.

Organizing Your Notes
Create an outline using the format below to help you organize your notes for this section.

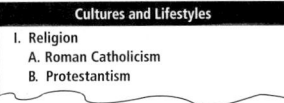

Cultures and Lifestyles
I. Religion
  A. Roman Catholicism
  B. Protestantism

Using the Chapter 9 Summary & Study Guide

Use the Chapter 9 Summary & Study Guide to preview, review, condense, or reteach the chapter.

Preview/Review

Vocabulary PuzzleMaker CD-ROM reinforces "Terms to Know."

Interactive Tutor Self-Assessment CD-ROM provides a review of Chapter 9 content.

Condense

Have students read the Chapter 9 Summary & Study Guide.

Chapter 9 Audio Program

Chapter 9 Guided Reading Activities

Reteach

Chapter 9 Reteaching Activities (Spanish also available)

Chapter 9 Reading Essentials and Study Guides

GLENCOE TECHNOLOGY

NATIONAL GEOGRAPHIC

WORLD REGIONS VIDEO PROGRAM

Unit 3, Latin America
The following segments enhance the study of this unit:
- **Green Commerce**
- **The Inca**
- **Steel Drums**

CHAPTER CULMINATING ACTIVITY

Synthesizing Information Have students use the pages of Chapter 9 in addition to outside sources, including the Internet, to help them design and create a poster about the culture of a Latin American country of their choice. The posters should include students' sketches or other artwork taken from magazines, as well as maps, and descriptions. The posters should reflect the country's cultural diversity, ethnic makeup, language, demographics, history, government, and other aspects studied in this chapter. Encourage students to review the chapter's photos and maps, as well as the text and any exercises they have completed in their study of this chapter to help them plan their poster and to synthesize what they have learned. **EE4 Human Systems: Standard 10**

GEOGRAPHY Online

Have students visit the Web site at geography.glencoe.com to review Chapter 9 and take the **Self-Check Quiz.**

GLENCOE TECHNOLOGY

Use *MindJogger Videoquiz* to preview the Chapter 9 content.

Reviewing Key Terms

1. indigenous
2. any two: baseball, basketball, volleyball, *fútbol,* jai alai
3. mosaic
4. extended family
5. dialect, patois
6. primate city
7. quipu
8. conquistadors
9. viceroys
10. megacity
11. syncretism
12. mural
13. glyphs
14. urbanization
15. malnutrition

Reviewing Facts

SECTION 1

1. mainly along the coasts
2. Temperature extremes, dense vegetation, deserts, and high mountains limit human habitation in the interior.

SECTION 2

3. Maya, Aztec, Inca
4. resentment against European rule, demand for more rights for lower classes, and examples of successful North American and French revolutions

SECTION 3

5. mural painting
6. *fútbol,* jai alai, baseball, basketball, and volleyball

Reviewing Key Terms

Write the key term that best matches each description. Refer to the Terms to Know in the Summary & Study Guide on page 233.

1. native; original inhabitant
2. two popular sports in Latin America
3. designs made by setting small pieces of colored stone, tile, or shell into mortar
4. grandparents, aunts, uncles, cousins
5. two language variations
6. a city that dominates its country's economy and government
7. knotted cords used for keeping accounts
8. Spanish or Portuguese conqueror
9. government officials appointed by European monarchs
10. a city with more than 10 million inhabitants
11. mixing of diverse religious traditions
12. wall painting
13. Mayan picture writing
14. migration from rural areas to cities
15. condition caused by lack of food

Reviewing Facts

SECTION 1

1. Where is most of South America's population located?
2. Why is the region's population density unbalanced?

SECTION 2

3. Name three indigenous Latin American empires.
4. What fueled the movement for Latin American independence?

SECTION 3

5. What ancient art form inspired the region's painters?
6. What sports are most popular in Latin America?

Critical Thinking

1. **Categorizing Information** Define the types of migration that occur in the region.
2. **Making Comparisons** Compare social and family life in Latin America and the United States.
3. **Identifying Cause and Effect** Use a diagram like the one below to fill in three lasting effects of colonialism.

Cultural Effects of Colonialism

NATIONAL GEOGRAPHIC **Locating Places**
Latin America: Political Geography

Match the letters on the map with the places of Latin America. Write your answers on a sheet of paper.

1. Caracas	5. Montevideo	9. Mexico City
2. Brasília	6. Bogotá	10. La Paz, Sucre
3. Port-au-Prince	7. Quito	11. Buenos Aires
4. Santiago	8. Havana	12. Lima

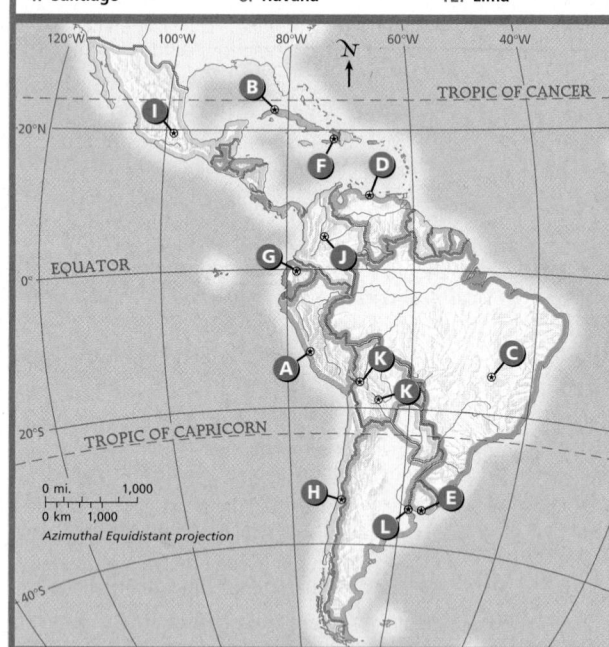

0 mi. 1,000
0 km 1,000
Azimuthal Equidistant projection

Critical Thinking

1. internal migration within a country or region, inflow of immigrants into the region, outflow of emigrants to other countries
2. The Latin American family is characterized by loyalty to an extended family; women's role is subordinate, while male dominance is the norm.
3. religion, arts, family values

NATIONAL GEOGRAPHIC **Locating Places**

1. D	**3.** F	**5.** E	**7.** G	**9.** I	**11.** L
2. C	**4.** H	**6.** J	**8.** B	**10.** K	**12.** A

Using the Regional Atlas

Refer to the Regional Atlas on pages 182–185.

1. **Place** What features draw a large population to the Buenos Aires area?
2. **Human-Environment Interaction** Study the physical and population density maps. Why are parts of Argentina and Bolivia uninhabited?

Thinking Like a Geographer

Trace the diffusion and exchange of foods between the Americas and other parts of the world. Describe the foods involved, their place of origin, and their effects on the places to which they spread.

Problem-Solving Activity

Contemporary Issues Case Study Using the Internet, research a democratic country in Latin America. Then write a report that discusses the spread and adaptation of democracy to that country. Also, explain how other countries in the region might learn from its experience. Use photos, charts, and other graphics in your report.

GeoJournal

Descriptive Writing Using the information you logged in your GeoJournal, write a paragraph describing European or African influences on the art or religion of a particular Latin American country. Use additional resources to make your descriptions as vivid and accurate as possible.

Technology Activity

Creating an Electronic Database Use reliable sources to gather population data for the past 10 years for three Latin American countries. Choose one category of information, such as literacy rates, population under age 18, or male/female ratio. Create an electronic computer database, and then use computer software to design and draw a graph or chart. Present your conclusions orally to the class, using the graph or chart to illustrate your findings.

Standardized Test Practice

Choose the best answer for each of the following multiple-choice questions. If you have trouble answering the questions, use the process of elimination to narrow your choices.

1. **Which of the following statements about languages in Latin America is true?**

   A Few Latin Americans speak Native American languages.

   B Portuguese is the official language of only one Latin American country.

   C French is the official language in most Latin American countries.

   D Few Latin Americans are bilingual.

Test-Taking Tip For multiple choice questions, remember to read each answer choice carefully. This question asks you to identify which statement is true. Eliminate the answer choices you know to be false in order to select the correct answer.

2. **Diego Rivera was a Mexican artist who was well known for his creation of**

   F folk dramas.

   G woven tapestry.

   H political and social satires in poetry.

   J large murals of historic events.

Test-Taking Tip This question is factual. Try to recall what you know about Rivera, considering that he was a popular modern artist and important political activist.

Technology Activity

Students' charts or graphs should accurately support the information on their databases. Oral presentations should be clear and accurate.

Standardized Test Practice

1. B
2. J

Tested Objectives:
making generalizations
identifying relevant
factual material

Additional Practice and Test-Taking Tips

 Standardized Test Practice Workbook

? CHAPTER BONUS TEST QUESTION

What measures would you suggest to improve health care in Latin America? *(Possible answers include improved sanitation, access to clean water, better environmental protection laws and their enforcement, better nutrition, immunization programs, better education. Students should elaborate on how they would accomplish these measures.)*

Using the Regional Atlas

1. Rio de la Plata's port advantages, fertile plains of the region to support commercial farming
2. The high peaks of the Andes and the desert in Patagonia are unfavorable to settlement.

Thinking Like a Geographer

Students' answers may include corn, potatoes, chocolate, and tomatoes (from the Americas); bananas, coffee, tea, sugarcane, and spices (from Asia and Africa). The exchange led to changes in diet in many places.

Problem-Solving Activity

For students who need help in getting started, consider assigning them a country and suggesting possible sources for their research. Accept all reasonable answers, and check to see that each group uses some type of graphic displays to show the class when they share the results of their research.

GeoJournal

Check students' paragraphs for accurate information and concrete details to support their descriptions.

PLANNING GUIDE

NOTE: The following materials may be used when teaching Chapter 10. Section-level support materials are shown at point-of-use in the margins of the Teacher Wraparound Edition.

TEACHING TRANSPARENCIES

L2 Unit 3 Map Overlay Transparencies

L2 Political Map Transparency 3

GEOGRAPHIC LITERACY

Focus on Geography Literacy

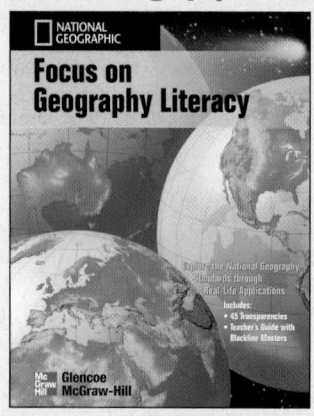

APPLICATION AND ENRICHMENT

L3 Enrichment Activity 10

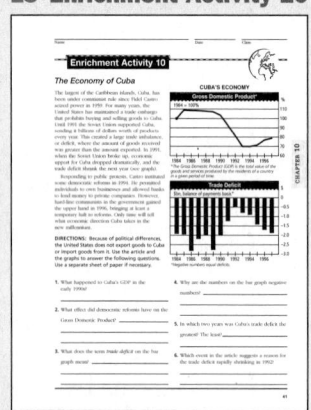

REVIEW AND REINFORCEMENT

L1 Vocabulary Activity 10   L1 Reinforcing

Skills Activity 10   **L1 Reteaching Activity 10**

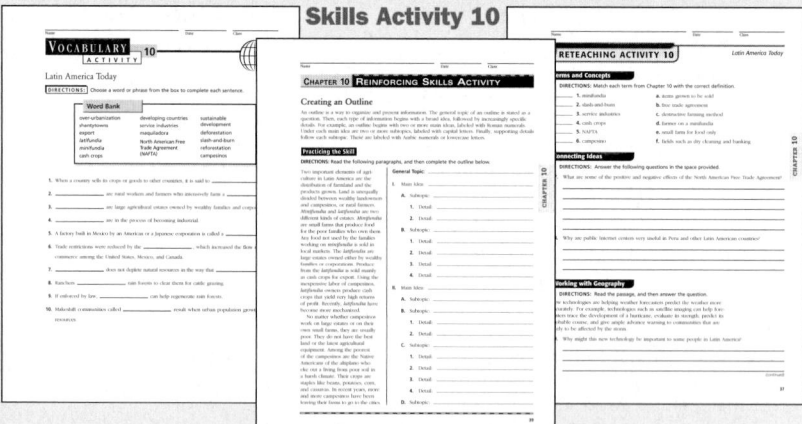

ASSESSMENT

L2 Chapter 10 Test Form A

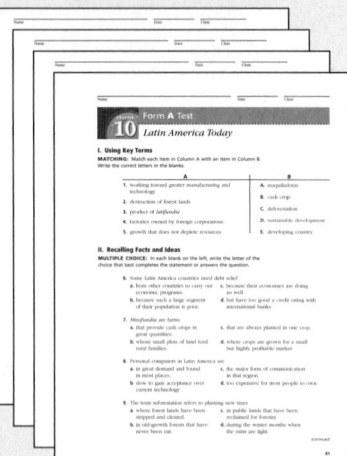

L2 Chapter 10 Test Form B

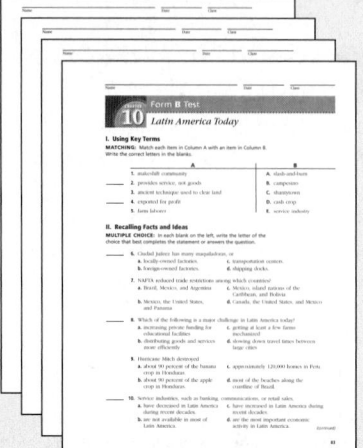

L1/ELL Performance Assessment Activity 10

ExamView® Pro Testmaker

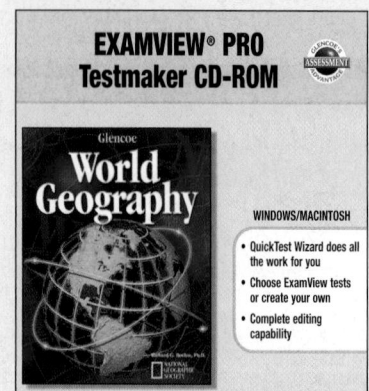

The following Spanish language materials are available in the Spanish Resources binder:

- 📁 Spanish Vocabulary Activities
- 📁 Spanish Guided Reading Activities
- 📁 Spanish Reteaching Activities
- 📁 Spanish Summaries
- 📁 Spanish Quizzes and Tests
- 📁 Spanish Reading Essentials and Study Guide

- 📼 World Regions Video
- 📼 MindJogger Videoquiz
- 💿 Vocabulary PuzzleMaker CD-ROM
- 💿 Interactive Tutor Self-Assessment CD-ROM
- 💿 ExamView® Pro Testmaker CD-ROM
- 💿 Audio Program
- 💿 TeacherWorks CD-ROM
- 💿 Interactive Student Edition CD-ROM
- 💿 Glencoe Skillbuilder Interactive Workbook CD-ROM, Level 2
- 💿 Presentation Plus! CD-ROM

Timesaving Tools

 **TeacherWorks™** All-In-One Planner and Resource Center

- **Interactive Teacher Edition** Access your Teacher Wraparound Edition and your classroom resources with a few easy clicks.
- **Interactive Lesson Planner** Planning has never been easier! Organize your week, month, semester, or year with all the lesson helps you need to make teaching creative, timely, and relevant.

Use Glencoe's **Presentation Plus!** multimedia teacher tool to easily present dynamic lessons that visually excite your students. Using Microsoft PowerPoint® you can customize the presentations to create your own personalized lessons.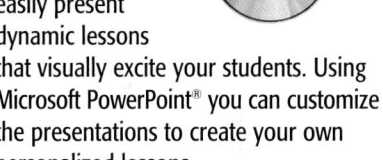

GEOGRAPHY Online

Use our Web site for additional resources. All essential content is covered in the Student Edition.

You and your students can visit geography.glencoe.com, the Web site companion to *Glencoe World Geography*. This innovative integration of electronic and print media offers your students a wealth of opportunities. The student text directs students to the Web site for the following options:

- Chapter Overviews
- Self-Check Quizzes
- Student Activities
- Textbook Updates

Answers are provided for you in the "Web Activity Lesson Plan." Additional Web resources and Interactive Tutor puzzles are also available.

▶ **Additional Glencoe Teacher Support**

- Teaching Strategies for the Geography Classroom (including Block Scheduling Pacing Guides)
- Graphic Organizer Transparencies Strategies and Activities
- Outline Map Resource Book
- Reading in the Content Area

PLANNING GUIDE

SECTION RESOURCES

Daily Objectives	Reproducible Resources	Multimedia Resources

SECTION 1   Living in Latin America

1. Identify the basis of the economy of many Latin American countries.
2. List the advantages and disadvantages for Mexico of the North American Free Trade Agreement (NAFTA).
3. Discuss the causes and consequences of Latin America's economically dependent status.
4. Explain how the region's physical geography has affected transportation and communications.

 Reproducible Lesson Plan 10-1
 Daily Lecture Notes 10-1
Guided Reading Activity 10-1*
Reading Essentials and Study Guide 10-1*
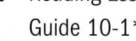 Section Quiz 10-1*

 Daily Focus Skills Transparency 10-1
Political Map Transparency 3
Unit 3 Map Overlay Transparencies
Interactive Tutor Self-Assessment CD-ROM
ExamView® Pro Testmaker CD-ROM*
Presentation Plus! CD-ROM

SECTION 2   People and Their Environment

1. Describe how development has affected Latin America's forest resources.
2. Explain how Latin American governments are working to balance forest conservation with human and economic development.
3. Discuss the challenges posed by the growth of Latin America's urban population.
4. Identify the regional and international issues that continue to pose challenges for Latin American countries.

 Reproducible Lesson Plan 10-2
Vocabulary Activity 10*
 Daily Lecture Notes 10-2
Guided Reading Activity 10-2*
 Reading Essentials and Study Guide 10-2*
Reteaching Activity 10*
 Reinforcing Skills Activity 10
 Section Quiz 10-2*

Daily Focus Skills Transparency 10-2
Political Map Transparency 3
Unit 3 Map Overlay Transparencies
Vocabulary PuzzleMaker CD-ROM
Interactive Tutor Self-Assessment CD-ROM
ExamView® Pro Testmaker CD-ROM*
Presentation Plus! CD-ROM

 Blackline Master
 Software
 Videocassette

Transparency
CD-ROM
DVD

Also available in Spanish

OUT OF TIME?  Assign the Chapter 10 **Reading Essentials and Study Guide.**

Block Schedule

Activities that are particularly suited to use within the block scheduling framework are identified throughout this chapter by the following designation:

KEY TO ABILITY LEVELS

Teaching strategies have been coded for various learning styles and abilities.

L1   **BASIC** activities for all students

L2   **AVERAGE** activities for average to above-average students

L3   **CHALLENGING** activities for above-average students

ELL **ENGLISH LANGUAGE LEARNER** activities

Teacher to Teacher

Lee Thomassen
Baltimore County
Public Schools
Baltimore, MD

Role-Playing

Role-playing can be a powerful tool to bring a new perspective to a complex situation such as the disappearing rain forests of Latin America.

After studying the rain forest issue, have students role-play different viewpoints regarding the fate of the Amazon rain forest. Present the situation of a world summit attended by mining and logging companies, world conservationist groups, bank officials, government leaders, scientists, and ranchers and farmers. Organize the class into groups representing each viewpoint to research the subject and present their arguments at a round-table discussion.

Tell students, for example, that the bankers might argue that they are supporting big hydroelectric projects and logging of exotic lumber, and that they deserve to make a profit. Encourage students to use visual aids in their discussions. In a second class session, reassign students to different groups. This time tell students to research and discuss viable solutions that will satisfy their new group and as many other viewpoints as possible. At a third session, have the whole class vote on the best solutions.

NATIONAL GEOGRAPHIC TEACHER'S CORNER

Index to National Geographic Magazine:

The following articles may be used for research relating to this chapter:

- "Madidi National Park," by Steve Kemper, March 2000.
- "Suriname," by John McCarry, June 2000.
- "Chiquibul Cave," by Thomas Miller, April 2000.

National Geographic Society Products:

To order the following products for use with this chapter, call National Geographic Society at 1-800-368-2728.

- *South America* (Video)
- *Mexico* (Video)
- *South America Political* (Map)
- *National Geographic Desk Reference* (Book)
- *National Geographic Atlas of the World, Seventh Edition* (Book)

NGS ONLINE

Access National Geographic's Web site for current events, activities, links, interactive features, and archives.
www.nationalgeographic.com

MEETING SPECIAL NEEDS

In addition to the Differentiated Instruction strategies found in each section, the following resources are also suitable for your special needs students:

- *ExamView® Pro Testmaker CD-ROM* allows teachers to tailor tests by reducing answer choices.
- The *Audio Program* includes the entire narrative of the student edition so that less-proficient readers can listen to the words as they read them.
- The *Reading Essentials and Study Guide* provides the same content as the student edition but is written two grade levels below the textbook.
- *Guided Reading Activities* give less-proficient readers point-by-point instructions to increase comprehension as they read each textbook section.
- *Enrichment Activities* include a stimulating collection of readings and activities for gifted and talented students.

Meeting National Standards

Geography For Life

The following standards are highlighted in Chapter 10:

Section 1   EE4 Human Systems: Standards 10, 11
EE5 Environment and Society: Standards 14, 15

Section 2   EE2 Places and Regions: Standard 4
EE3 Physical Systems: Standard 8
EE4 Human Systems: Standard 13
EE5 Environment and Society: Standard 14
EE6 The Uses of Geography: Standard 18

Local Objectives

_____

_____

Chapter Objectives

1. Discuss aspects of the Latin American economy and how geography affects transportation and communications.

2. Explain how Latin America's forest resources are affected by economic development and how the region's countries are working with other countries to solve economic and migration problems.

GLENCOE TECHNOLOGY

Use *MindJogger Videoquiz* to preview the Chapter 10 content.

GeoJournal

For access to additional photos, maps, and information on the contemporary issues of Latin America go to www.nationalgeographic.com (See Teacher pages in front for strategies for using journals in the geography classroom.)

GEOGRAPHY Online

Introduce students to chapter content and key terms by having them access **Chapter Overview 10** at geography.glencoe.com

FOLDABLES™
Study Organizer

Dinah Zike's Foldables are three-dimensional, interactive graphic organizers that help students practice basic writing skills, review key vocabulary terms, and identify main ideas. Have students complete the Foldable activity in the ***Dinah Zike's Reading and Study Skills Foldables*** booklet.

CHAPTER 10 Latin America Today

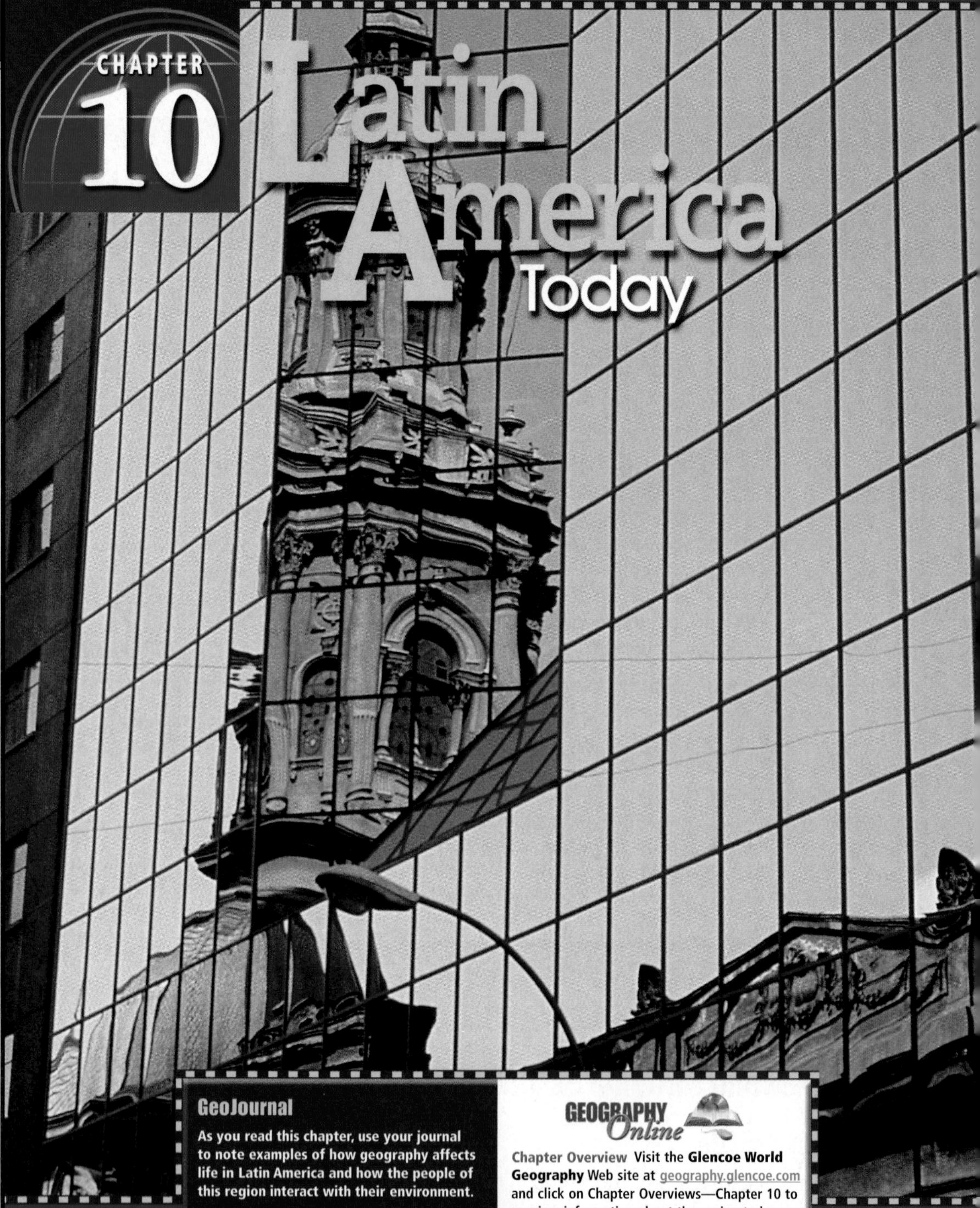

GeoJournal

As you read this chapter, use your journal to note examples of how geography affects life in Latin America and how the people of this region interact with their environment.

GEOGRAPHY Online

Chapter Overview Visit the **Glencoe World Geography** Web site at geography.glencoe.com and click on Chapter Overviews—Chapter 10 to preview information about the region today.

ABOUT THE PHOTO

Visual Instruction The reflective glass of this modern office building in Santiago, Chile's capital, mirrors an older, more ornate building with colonial-era architecture. Like most capital cities, Santiago is the center of government, business, and culture. **Ask: How does this photo symbolize an important aspect of Chile's culture?** (*Students may observe that the colonial-era building reflected in the glass of the modern building symbolizes the various influences, both historical and modern, that shape life in Chile and the rest of the region.*)
EE4 Human Systems: Standard 10

Guide to Reading

Consider What You Know

The North American Free Trade Agreement (NAFTA) has been the focus of economic and political news in recent years. What do you know about this agreement? How does NAFTA affect your community?

Reading Strategy

Organizing As you read about life in Latin America, complete a graphic organizer similar to the one below by listing factors that limit industrial growth.

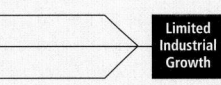

Read to Find Out

• What is the basis of the economies of many Latin American countries?

• What are the advantages and disadvantages of the North American Free Trade Agreement (NAFTA) for Mexico?

• What are the causes and consequences of Latin America's economically dependent status?

• How has the region's physical geography affected transportation and communications?

Terms to Know

• export
• campesino
• *latifundia*
• *minifundia*
• cash crop
• developing country
• service industry
• maquiladora
• North American Free Trade Agreement (NAFTA)

Places to Locate

• Honduras
• Tijuana

◀ *Modern Santiago, Chile, reflects the past.*

Living in Latin America

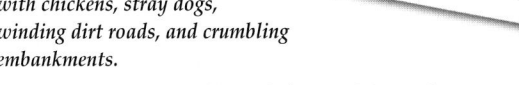

NATIONAL GEOGRAPHIC

A Geographic View

Unlikely Neighbors

Tijuana's character changes from street to street. In one colonia, or neighborhood, people wash laundry in tubs.... Up another road you pass dozens of modest homes built of concrete block and metal. Across town in wealthy Colonia Chapultepec, magnificent homes are built like fortresses right to the edge of the sidewalk.... Upper-middle-class sections abut neighborhoods of shacks with chickens, stray dogs, winding dirt roads, and crumbling embankments.

Tijuana, Mexico

—Michael Parfit, "Tijuana and the Border," National Geographic, August 1996

Like Mexico's Tijuana, many Latin American cities reveal the sharp divisions between the wealthy and the poor. These class differences stem from social, political, and economic factors, but they are also shaped by physical geography. In this section you will learn about the ways in which Latin America's physical environment relates to the region's economic development and quality of life.

Agriculture

Although about three-fourths of Latin America's people live in cities, most of the region's countries still depend on agriculture to supply a major portion of their incomes. Latin American countries export, or sell to other countries, much of what their farms produce, such as bananas, sugarcane, and coffee.

Chapter 10 **237**

 **FOCUS**

Section Overview

This section discusses both the economy of Latin America, including the role of trade and interdependence, and the region's developing transportation and communications networks.

BELLRINGER
Skillbuilder Activity

 Project transparency and have students answer questions.

 Available as blackline master.

Daily Focus Skills Transparency 10-1

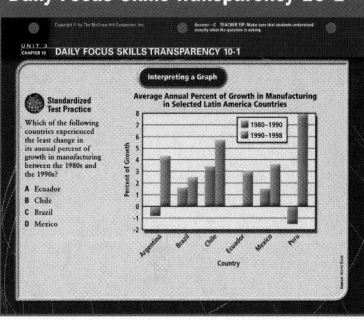

Guide to Reading

Consider What You Know
Answers *possible answers: removes tariffs, makes trade easier, could move jobs to Mexico; more goods we buy are assembled in Mexico*

Reading Strategy
Answer factors: *physical geography, ties to more developed regions, political instability*

Preteaching Vocabulary
Explain that *export* comes from a Latin word meaning "to carry out." Have students hypothesize about what kinds of goods exports are. *(those shipped out of the country)*

② TEACH

L1 Identify

After reading the section, review the words in "Terms to Know." Give students a definition and have them provide the vocabulary word. For further practice, give students a clue related to a word instead of the definition itself and have them provide the correct term. As a clue, you might say *coffee, bananas, sugarcane* to elicit the words *export* or *cash crop.*

Daily Lecture Notes 10-1

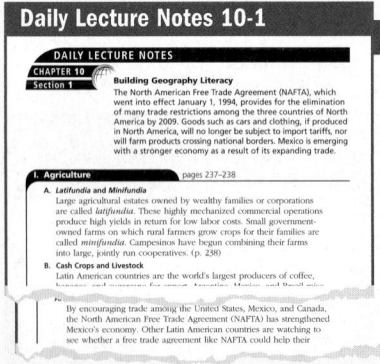

◼ NATIONAL GEOGRAPHIC World Explorer

Answer
Subsistence farming provides food for a family's needs; cash-crop farming produces crops to be sold for profit.

More About the Photo
Many of Mexico's food crops grown for export go to the United States. The majority of strawberries, oranges, melons, cucumbers, and tomatoes that the United States imports come from Mexico.

History
Latifundia and Minifundia

For centuries farmland in Latin America has been unevenly distributed between a small group of wealthy landowners and a much larger force of *campesinos* (KAM•puh•SEE•nohs), or rural farmers and workers. Large agricultural estates owned by wealthy families or corporations are called *latifundia*. Today's *latifundia* are highly mechanized commercial operations that yield high returns for low investment in labor. All other farms are called *minifundia*, small plots of land intensively farmed by campesinos to feed their families. Campesinos, though, rarely own these plots, which are held by either wealthy landowners or the government.

The centuries-old system of *latifundia* and *minifundia* is gradually breaking down, however. As *latifundia* become more mechanized, farmworkers are leaving the land for the cities. In addition,

◼ NATIONAL GEOGRAPHIC World Explorer

Geography Skills for Life

Mexican Countryside Farmers harvest limes on a *latifundium* near the Mexico-U.S. border.
Human-Environment Interaction What is the difference between subsistence farming and cash-crop farming?

---

reform-minded governments are passing laws to distribute farmland more fairly. Many campesinos have formed agricultural cooperatives, combining *minifundia* into large, jointly run farms. The legacy of economic inequality, however, is difficult to overcome completely, and Latin America's campesinos remain very poor.

Cash Crops and Livestock

Latin America's physical geography makes it a suitable region for growing cash crops, crops produced in large quantities to be sold or traded. Fertile highlands help make Brazil, Mexico, Guatemala, and Colombia among the world's leading coffee producers. Lush, tropical coastal areas enable Central America, as well as Jamaica, Honduras, Ecuador, and Brazil, to be major producers of bananas. Tropical climates and fertile soil also help make Brazil and Cuba the world's leading producers of sugarcane. These export crops, all grown most efficiently on *latifundia*, usually benefit large-scale commercial producers more than individual farmers. In addition to growing cash crops, some Latin American countries—Argentina, Mexico, and Brazil—raise cattle for export on large ranches located in grassland areas.

Countries run great risks, however, when they depend on just one or two export products. If droughts, floods, or volcanic eruptions destroy a country's cash crop, the damage to that country's economy causes great hardship. In 1998 Hurricane Mitch devastated parts of Central America and destroyed about 90 percent of the banana crop, the main export, in **Honduras.** Tragically, the storm hit Honduras just as it was beginning to make some economic progress.

Industry

Most of Latin America's countries are developing countries, or countries that are working toward greater manufacturing and technology use. Countries with skilled workforces, good energy supplies, efficient transportation networks, and many natural resources are industrializing more rapidly than countries without these advantages. In many Latin American countries, service industries, such as banking, which provide services rather than goods, have grown rapidly in recent decades.

DIFFERENTIATED INSTRUCTION

English Learners Help English language learners with unfamiliar vocabulary as they read Section 1. First, go over the pronunciation of "Terms to Know" and "Places to Locate" on page 237. Make sure students know that the words appear in blue type throughout the section. Then, have students look for boldface words in the section titled "Cash Crops and Livestock." **Ask:** Why do you suppose these words appear in this section? *(Students might answer that the countries listed are where cash crops, defined here, are grown and livestock is raised.)* ELL 🌐 EE5 Environment and Society: Standard 14

📂 Refer to *Inclusion for the Social Studies Classroom Strategies and Activities.*

Industrial Growth

Several factors have limited industrial growth in Latin America. Physical geography may present obstacles. The high Andes and the dense Amazon rain forest, for example, limit access to natural resources. Ties to more developed regions also have limited growth. Foreigners have brought new technology to the region, but many have drained local resources and profits. Finally, political instability in many Latin American countries has made investors wary of investing in Latin American enterprises.

Some Latin American countries, however, are overcoming these barriers. They combine the necessary human and natural resources with relatively stable governments and active business communities. Mexico, for example, is a major producer of motor vehicles, textiles, and processed foods. Brazil is a leading producer of iron and steel, cars, airplanes, textiles, and electrical goods. After weathering serious financial crises in the 1990s, both countries emerged with stronger economies because of their expanding global trade.

Other countries in the region also are developing industries. Argentina produces cars and processed meats. Venezuela refines oil, and Chile, Costa Rica, and Nicaragua all produce foods and textiles. Bolivia mines and refines tin, and Barbados, Cuba, and Saint Kitts and Nevis refine sugar.

Economics
Maquiladoras

During the past 50 years, American and Japanese firms have built manufacturing plants in Latin American countries. Most of these factories, known as maquiladoras (muh•KEE•luh•DOHR•uhs), lie along the Mexico–United States border—especially near the Mexican cities of Ciudad Juárez and **Tijuana**—where they employ many Mexicans. Maquiladoras benefit foreign corporations by allowing them to hire low-cost labor and to produce duty-free exports. They also offer the host country and its people employment opportunities and investment income. As one observer noted:

> 66 *. . . Tijuana lures foreign investors with cheap labor and proximity to U.S. markets, while beckoning workers from across Mexico with the chance for a new beginning. Here their dreams converge and sometimes collide, pulled hard by the magnet of the north.* 99
>
> Michael Parfit, "Tijuana and the Border," *National Geographic*, August 1996

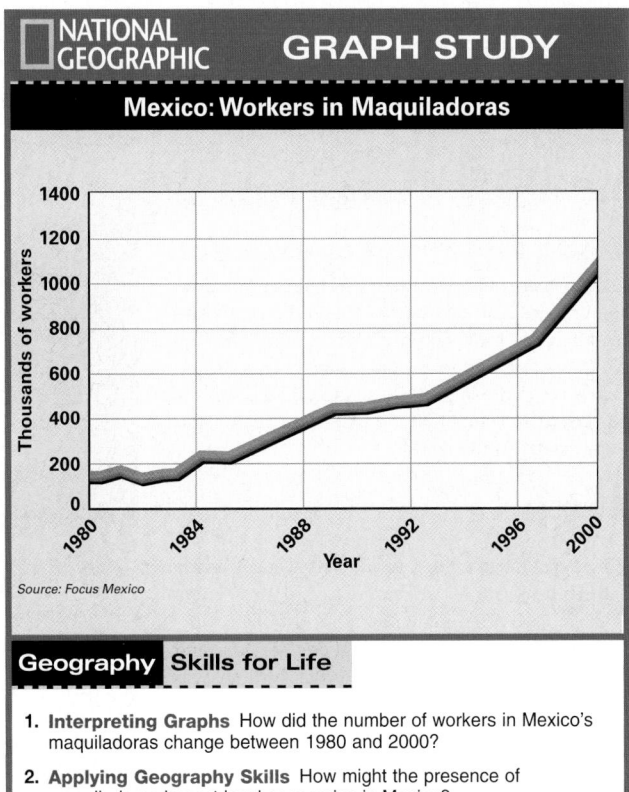

NATIONAL GEOGRAPHIC — GRAPH STUDY

Mexico: Workers in Maquiladoras

Source: Focus Mexico

Geography Skills for Life

1. **Interpreting Graphs** How did the number of workers in Mexico's maquiladoras change between 1980 and 2000?

2. **Applying Geography Skills** How might the presence of maquiladoras impact local economies in Mexico?

Chapter 10 🌐 **239**

L3 Problem Solving
After students have read the material under "Agriculture," have groups list the reasons that distributing farmland equitably and diversifying agricultural output is important. Tell students to look for cause-effect relationships.

L1/ELL

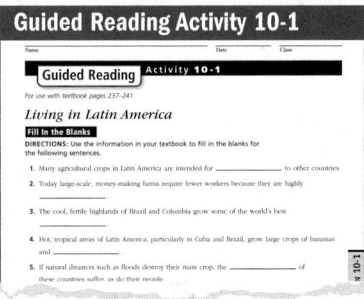

Guided Reading Activity 10-1

NATIONAL GEOGRAPHIC — GRAPH STUDY

Answers
1. *increased from about 200,000 in 1980 to more than one million in 1999*
2. *Maquiladoras provide jobs and income to the local economy. However, many argue that low-paying jobs are not worth the environmental damage some factories cause.*

L1/ELL

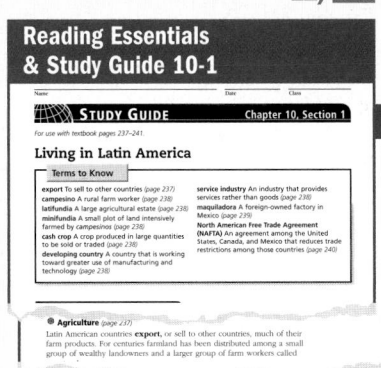

Reading Essentials & Study Guide 10-1

COOPERATIVE LEARNING ACTIVITY

Board Game Assign groups to create a board game about Latin American agriculture and industry. The players are international businesspeople, and the board represents the path to profits with windfalls and pitfalls along the way. Have each group create up to 10 items to be included on the game board squares. One item might read: *You buy copper in Peru for a song but lose time transporting it across unpaved roads. Miss a turn.* Another might read: *The North Dakota sugar beet crop fails, and the profits at your Caribbean sugar refinery go sky high. Collect $200.* Tell students to get their facts from Section 1 as well as other sources about Latin America. Have groups work together to choose the best 25 items for inclusion in the game. 📦 🖳 **EE5 Environment and Society: Standard 15**

□ NATIONAL GEOGRAPHIC **GEOFACT**

▶ **Environmentalists express concern over the possible effects of unregulated industrial growth brought about by NAFTA. The monarch butterfly, which migrates annually between Canada and Mexico, is serving as a monitor of environmental changes. Scientists keep track of the monarch butterfly to determine NAFTA's effects on the environment.**

③ ASSESS

Assign Section 1 Assessment as homework or as an in-class activity.

Have students use **Interactive Tutor Self-Assessment CD-ROM.**
L2

Section Quiz 10-1

Critics of maquiladoras charge that the system often ignores labor and environmental protection laws, damaging the environment and encouraging low-paying or dangerous jobs. As the world's economy becomes globalized, developing countries will weigh the benefits and drawbacks of their associations with industries of the developed world.

Trade and Interdependence

Like other countries of the world, Latin American countries depend on trade to obtain the goods and food that they cannot produce. Some Latin American countries, for example, import raw materials and expensive technology. In recent years Latin America has begun to promote trade within the region and with the rest of the world.

Economics
NAFTA

In 1992 Mexico, the United States, and Canada signed the North American Free Trade Agreement (NAFTA). NAFTA gradually reduced trade restrictions and increased the flow of goods, services, and people among these countries. After NAFTA was implemented, trade among the three countries grew by 10 to 15 percent annually.

NAFTA, however, has been controversial in the United States. American labor groups fear the loss of jobs to generally lower-paid Mexican workers. Still, U.S. companies have not yet relocated south of the border in large numbers because certain production costs, such as electricity, are higher in Mexico. From Mexico's viewpoint, NAFTA has helped boost exports and create thousands of new jobs. Other Latin American countries are watching Mexico's economy to see if an agreement like NAFTA could work for them.

Foreign Debts

Many Latin American countries borrow funds from foreign sources to finance industrial development. During the 1980s a worldwide economic slowdown caused a sharp decline in demand for Latin America's products. When their incomes fell, many Latin American governments threatened to default, or not pay back their loans on time. Lenders then rescheduled the loans, which lengthened the time allowed to repay them and decreased monthly

NATIONAL GEOGRAPHIC World Explorer

Geography | **Skills for Life**

Traditional Handicrafts Local potters in Peru produce clay jars and jugs to sell.
Region What other goods are produced in Latin America?

payments. However, this remedy also raised the total amount of interest on the debt. Repaying large foreign debts has halted needed domestic programs in some countries. Now international agencies are looking for other ways to offer debt relief.

Transportation

In Latin America building roads and railroads is difficult. Many governments cannot afford building projects that must cross rugged mountains, dense rain forests, and arid deserts. Even so, some Latin American countries do have good roads. The region's major road system, the Pan-American Highway, stretches from northern Mexico to southern

CRITICAL THINKING ACTIVITY

Making Comparisons On the board, copy the following profile of United States transportation and communications: 137,000 miles of railroads; 206 million motor vehicles; 834 airports with scheduled flights; one television per 1.18 persons; 2.1 radios per one person; 179,822 telephones; 215 newspapers per 1,000 people. Have volunteers read aloud similar statistics for Latin American countries from a world almanac and have students write these on the board. **Ask: How do the differences in transportation and communications reflect the economies of the United States and Latin America?** (Possible answer: The economy of the United States is stronger and that people can afford to buy more goods and services.) ▦ **EE4 Human Systems: Standard 11**

▲ *An Andean highway echoes the past when Inca roads crossed the area.*

Chile and links more than a dozen Latin American capitals. A trans-Andean highway runs through the Andes and links cities in Chile and Argentina. To develop the Amazon Basin's mineral resources, Brazil is building the Trans-Amazonian Highway.

Although physical barriers limit railroad use, Mexico, Panama, Argentina, and Brazil have well-developed rail systems. In some places, however, railways have fallen into disrepair. As a result, inland waterways such as the Amazon River, the Paraná-Paraguay Rivers, and the Panama Canal remain important. As air travel becomes more affordable it will help overcome geographic barriers. All Latin American capitals and most major cities receive domestic and international flights. Mexico City, Buenos Aires, Rio de Janeiro, and São Paulo have the region's busiest airports. Many private and military landing strips serve remote locations.

Communications

Latin America's developing communications networks include newspapers, radio, and television, but all may be censored by governments during political unrest. Millions of Latin Americans use telephones, but few have them in their homes. Some countries cannot afford the equipment needed to provide residential phone service. In larger cities though, many people, especially young people, use cellular phones.

Although computer technology is slowly changing communications in Latin America, most people cannot afford personal computers. In 1998, on average, only 34 of every 1,000 Latin Americans owned computers. Innovative ways to offer computer access, such as Peru's public Internet centers, are helping Latin Americans go online, however.

Reteach

Have students find each place name under "Places to Locate" on page 237, locate them on page RA12, and sum up why that place is significant.

Enrich

Display color photos in books about traditional arts from various Latin American countries. Encourage students to list characteristics and motifs they observe in the examples. Ask students to take a motif or design and create their own items or use the motif in a color drawing of their own. Students might discuss a project with an art teacher.

Have students reread the opening quotation and the first paragraph on page 237. Have students volunteer ways in which Latin America's physical environment relates to the region's economic development and quality of life.

Honduras Many Hondurans communicate by placing messages on the radio. They do so because only major cities in Honduras have telephones, while most towns have only one public telephone and a telegraph office.

SECTION **1** **ASSESSMENT**

Checking for Understanding

1. **Define** export, campesino, *latifundia*, *minifundia*, cash crop, developing country, service industry, maquiladora, North American Free Trade Agreement (NAFTA).

2. **Main Ideas** On a table, fill in examples of how five Latin American countries produce income.

Latin American Country	Chief Source of Income

Critical Thinking

3. **Drawing Conclusions** Why might political instability in a country discourage investors?

4. **Identifying Cause and Effect** What effects might defaulting on debt repayments have?

5. **Making Comparisons** How are *latifundia* and *minifundia* systems of farming alike? Different?

Analyzing Maps

6. **Place** Study the economic activity map on page 185. Which countries produce the most petroleum?

Applying Geography

7. **Industrialization** In a paragraph, discuss why industrialization requires good transportation and communications systems. Describe the impact of new technologies.

Chapter 10 ● **241**

SECTION 1 ASSESSMENT ANSWERS

1. All vocabulary terms are defined in the text.

2. Possible answers: Brazil: coffee, bananas, sugarcane, cattle, iron, steel, cars, airplanes, textiles, electrical goods; Bolivia: tin; Mexico: coffee, cattle, motor vehicles, textiles, processed foods; El Salvador: coffee; Colombia: coffee; Argentina: cattle, cars, processed meats; Honduras: bananas; Venezuela: oil; Chile, Costa Rica and Nicaragua: textiles, processed foods

3. A military government or dictator could decide to nationalize a foreign business.

4. discourages investors, hampers future borrowing ability

5. *latifundia*: large, mechanized commercial estates; *minifundia*: small subsistence farms; both owned by wealthy landowners

6. Venezuela, Colombia, Ecuador, and Mexico

7. **Applying Geography** Without good roads, trucks cannot transport raw materials and products; expanding telephone and Internet service could speed the flow of information.

SECTION 2

FOCUS

Section Overview

This section describes how human development of the Amazon River basin has impacted the rain forest. It also discusses major challenges presented by rapid urban growth in the region and discusses possible solutions.

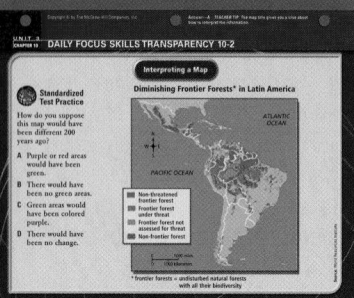
Guide to Reading

Consider What You Know
Answer *Rain forests benefit the entire planet. The local population however, must meet its needs.*

Reading Strategy
Answer Students should complete the outline by including all heads in the section.

Preteaching Vocabulary
Use the **Vocabulary Puzzle-Maker CD-ROM** to create crossword and word-search puzzles.

Guide to Reading

Consider What You Know

People around the world are concerned about the destruction of Latin America's rain forests. Why is the preservation of the rain forests important, and what makes this issue so complex?

Reading Strategy

Taking Notes As you read about concerns for the rain forest, use the major headings of the section to create an outline similar to the one below.

> I. Managing Rain Forests
>   A.
>   B.
> II. Urban Enviroments
>   A.
>   B.

Read to Find Out

- How has development affected Latin America's forest resources?
- How are Latin American governments working to balance forest conservation with human and economic development?
- What challenges are posed by the growth of Latin America's urban population?
- What regional and international issues continue to pose challenges for Latin American countries?

Terms to Know

- sustainable development
- deforestation
- slash-and-burn
- reforestation
- shantytown

Places to Locate

- São Paulo
- El Salvador

People and Their Environment

NATIONAL GEOGRAPHIC

A Geographic View

A Crucial Decision

Taking life slow, a three-toed sloth hangs out on an ambaibo tree along the Río Tuichi in Madidi National Park. A planned hydro-electric dam may permanently [flood] this area—claiming one of South America's most biologically diverse rain forests even before it has been fully explored.

—Steve Kemper, "Madidi,"
National Geographic, *March 2000*

Three-toed sloth

Bolivia and other Latin American countries face a difficult choice: whether to preserve large tracts of wilderness, such as Madidi National Park in northwestern Bolivia, or develop these areas for the purpose of raising peoples' standard of living. One way of resolving this dilemma is to work toward sustainable development—technological and economic growth that does not deplete the human and natural resources of a given area. In this section you will learn about the interrelationship of Latin Americans and their environment, and how the region is working to protect the environment while meeting human needs.

Managing Rain Forests

As you recall, extensive rain forests cover South America's Amazon River basin and the coastal areas of the Caribbean region. Like rain forests in other regions of the world, those in Latin America are disappearing as a result of deforestation, the clearing or destruction of forests. Although the threats to the world's rain forests are well known, the proposed strategies for preserving them are hotly debated.

RESOURCE MANAGER

Reproducible Masters
- Reproducible Lesson Plan 10-2
- Vocabulary Activity 10
- Daily Lecture Notes 10-2
- Guided Reading Activity 10-2
- Reading Essentials and Study Guide 10-2
- Reteaching Activity 10
- Reinforcing Skills Activity 10
- Section Quiz 10-2

Transparencies
- Daily Focus Skills Transparency 10-2
- Political Map Transparency 3
- Unit 3 Map Overlay Transparencies

Multimedia
- Vocabulary PuzzleMaker CD-ROM
- Interactive Tutor Self-Assessment CD-ROM
- ExamView® Pro Testmaker CD-ROM
- Presentation Plus! CD-ROM

Brazil's experience serves as an example of the complexity of the deforestation issue. During the past several decades, Brazil has worked to boost its economy by tapping the rain forest's vast mineral resources, such as petroleum, iron, copper, and tin. Roads have been carved out of the rain forest to open up Brazil's interior to settlement and development. For example, a 3,400-mile (5,472-km) east-west segment of the Trans-Amazonian Highway now crosses the region. This development of Brazil's interior, however, has proved disastrous for the Amazon rain forest and its indigenous human and animal inhabitants. The indigenous people of Brazil's interior have seen their homes and traditional ways of life disappear along with trees, other forms of vegetation, and animal life.

More than 13 percent of the Amazon rain forest has already been destroyed. (See the map below.) As the Amazon rain forest is depleted, the diversity of Earth's plant and animal species is threatened. Many of the world's key medicines are derived from rain forest plants and organisms, and deforestation risks the loss of compounds that have the potential to treat cancer and other illnesses. Because plants use carbon dioxide and produce oxygen, destroying rain forest plants could result in less carbon dioxide being used and more of it remaining in the atmosphere. Since carbon dioxide is a greenhouse gas that helps trap heat, catastrophic global warming, climate change, and rising ocean levels could result. Traditional wisdom has another way of expressing the value of rain forests, as one journalist notes:

> 'Who cuts the trees as he pleases cuts short his own life.' The Maya adage... is spoken in a language that uses the same word for both 'blood' and 'tree sap.'
>
> George E. Stuart, "Maya Heartland Under Siege," *National Geographic*, November 1992

Brazil and other rain forest countries are listening to the advice of scientists and environmentalists, but they still face pressing social and economic

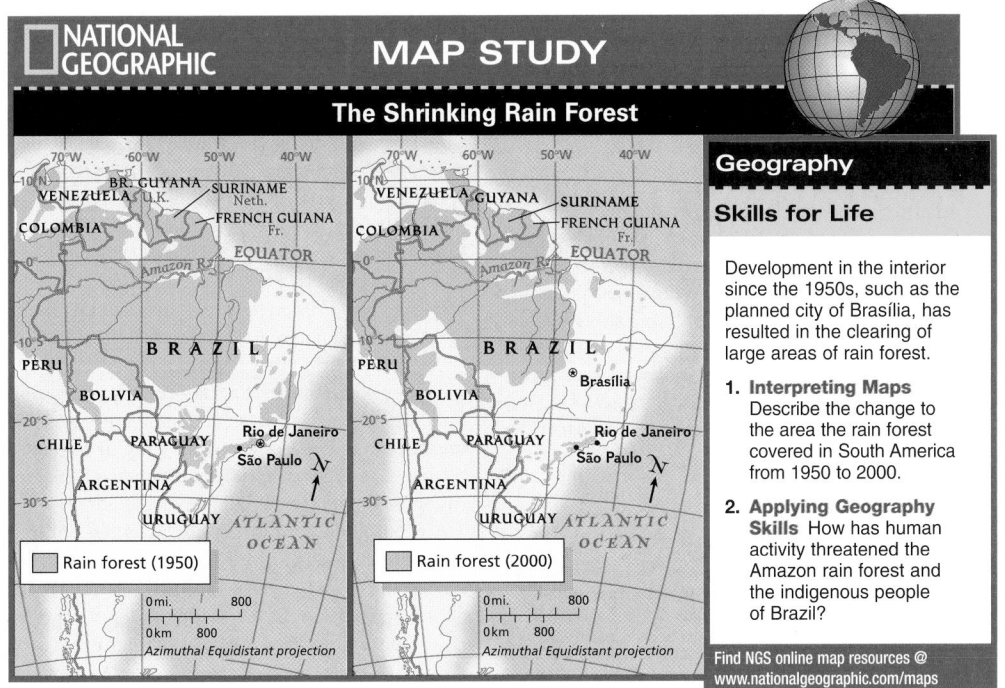

NATIONAL GEOGRAPHIC

MAP STUDY
The Shrinking Rain Forest

Rain forest (1950)
Rain forest (2000)

0 mi. 800
0 km 800
Azimuthal Equidistant projection

Geography
Skills for Life

Development in the interior since the 1950s, such as the planned city of Brasília, has resulted in the clearing of large areas of rain forest.

1. **Interpreting Maps** Describe the change to the area the rain forest covered in South America from 1950 to 2000.

2. **Applying Geography Skills** How has human activity threatened the Amazon rain forest and the indigenous people of Brazil?

Find NGS online map resources @ www.nationalgeographic.com/maps

Chapter 10   **243**

② TEACH

L2 Research
Have students research what individual Native American groups live in the Amazon rain forest. **Ask: How are these peoples reacting to development of the rain forest?** Hold a class discussion on findings.

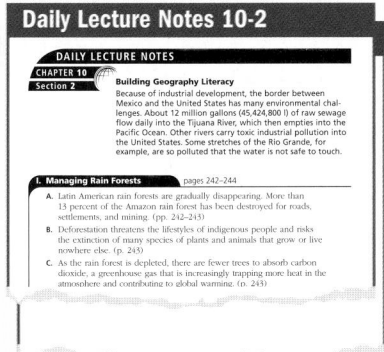

Daily Lecture Notes 10-2

DAILY LECTURE NOTES
CHAPTER 10
Section 2   **Building Geography Literacy**
Because of industrial development, the border between Mexico and the United States has many environmental challenges. About 12 million gallons (45,424,800 l) of raw sewage flow daily into the Tijuana River, which then empties into the Pacific Ocean. Other rivers carry toxic industrial pollution into the United States. Some stretches of the Rio Grande, for example, are so polluted that the water is not safe to touch.

I. **Managing Rain Forests**   pages 242–244
A. Latin American rain forests are gradually disappearing. More than 13 percent of the Amazon rain forest has been destroyed for roads, settlements, and mining. (pp. 242–243)
B. Deforestation threatens the lifestyles of indigenous people and risks the extinction of many species of plants and animals that grow or live nowhere else. (p. 243)
C. As the rain forest is depleted, there are fewer trees to absorb carbon dioxide, a greenhouse gas that is increasingly trapping more heat in the atmosphere and contributing to global warming. (p. 243)

NATIONAL GEOGRAPHIC   **MAP STUDY**

Answers
1. *receded significantly on all sides*
2. *Roads and development (ranching, farming, lumber, settlement) are reducing its size and displacing indigenous people.*

Map Skills Practice
Human-Environment Interaction What effect do you think Brasília will have on the rain forest? *(Population growth may increase pressure to develop the rain forest.)*

DIFFERENTIATED INSTRUCTION

Reading Support For students who have trouble locating answers to the section assessment questions, show them how they can profit from scanning, a form of rapid reading used to locate specific information quickly. To define the section's "Terms to Know," tell students to scan Section 2 to locate these words in blue type. Model the scanning procedure by sliding your finger rapidly down the middle of the column on page 242 and telling students that you see the first two vocabulary words on this page. Have students turn to page 244 and practice the procedure. 🌐 **EE5 Environment and Society: Standard 14**

📂 Refer to *Inclusion for the Social Studies Classroom Strategies and Activities.*

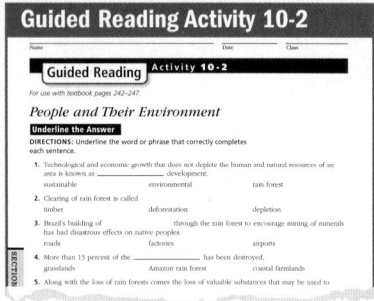

Guided Reading Activity 10-2

INTERDISCIPLINARY
connection

HEALTH The Brazil nut tree has the potential to treat or prevent health ailments. In the Amazon rain forest, indigenous people use the oil from this nut, which is rich in vitamin E and selenium, to treat skin conditions. Antioxidants may also help slow the progression of eye cataracts. Researchers are also studying the Brazil nut as possible treatments for Alzheimer's disease.

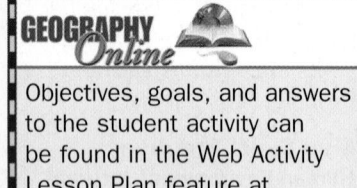

Objectives, goals, and answers to the student activity can be found in the Web Activity Lesson Plan feature at geography.glencoe.com

---

realities. If Brazil were to ban the use of rain forest lands, for example, how would it provide for all the people who would no longer have a way to support themselves? How would the country handle population growth in coastal areas if vast stretches of the interior were off-limits to its people?

Economics
Farms and Ranches Versus Forests

One of the most widespread activities in the Amazon Basin is the clearing of rain forest to provide more land for farming. To prepare the land, settlers use an ancient technique called **slash-and-burn** farming—but practiced on a larger scale. Farmers cut down all plants and strip any trees of bark. After the plants and trees have dried out, they are set on fire. The ash from the fire puts nutrients into the soil. Unfortunately, frequent rains leach away the benefits, and within one or two years, the soil loses its fertility or is washed away. Crop yields decline, and farmers move on to clear new parts of the forest.

Slash-and-burn methods are also used to carve huge cattle ranches out of the forest. Ranchers plant grasses in the charred ground for cattle grazing. After about four years, the grasses dry up and the ranchers, like the farmers, move on. The spent land supports little growth, and centuries-old rain forests have disappeared in just a few years.

Planting for the Future

Farming and ranching are not the only activities that contribute to deforestation in the Amazon area. Commercial logging operations harvest trees for timber and other products. Some estimates indicate that for every tree cut, two-thirds of the wood is wasted. Since colonial times, few attempts have been made to regulate the profitable logging industry. Today, however, the importance of conserving and restoring forest resources in Brazil and other Latin American

Student Web Activity Visit the **Glencoe World Geography** Web site at geography.glencoe.com and click on Student Web Activities—Chapter 10 for an activity about economic development in Brazil.

---

countries has become increasingly clear. Brazil has set aside about 10 percent of its Amazon rain forest for national forests or parks in which logging is banned. In Costa Rica concerned citizens are buying abandoned, burned-over tropical forests that were once home to old-growth mahogany and other trees. The citizens then donate the land to a conservation district for restoration.

Given time, rain forests will regenerate on their own but with a considerable loss of biodiversity. Laws requiring **reforestation**—the planting of young trees or the seeds of trees on the land that has been stripped—can help, especially if the laws are rigorously enforced. Developing new methods of farming, mining, and logging and combining conservation with responsible tourism can protect the forests while boosting local economies.

Urban Environments

Latin America also has environmental challenges in its urban areas. More of the region's people live in megacities or towns than in rural areas. In 2000 Mexico City and **São Paulo** (sown POW•loo) ranked as the world's second- and fourth-largest metropolitan areas.

Overcrowded Cities

As Latin America's rural workers migrate to cities, they often cannot find jobs or adequate housing. Some are forced to live in slums or **shantytowns**, makeshift communities on the edges of cities. Known in different cities by different names—the *favelas* of São Paulo, the *barriadas* of Bogotá, and the *villas miserias* of Buenos Aires—these shantytowns often rest on dangerous slopes and wetlands. Mudslides, floods, and other natural disasters can wipe out entire communities. Lacking running water and underground sewage systems, these areas are also unsanitary, so diseases can spread rapidly. Because people have little or no money to buy food, malnutrition is common, especially among children.

Air pollution affects people in cities without adequate clean air laws. Millions of vehicles clog city streets and release massive amounts of exhaust gases into the air. Added to that are pollutants from industrial smokestacks. In Mexico City, air pollution can become so severe that authorities

---

COOPERATIVE LEARNING ACTIVITY

Atlas of Latin America Have the class compile an atlas featuring special-purpose maps of places in Latin America. Assign each student a country and direct him or her to find land use, resource, and vegetation maps of that country as well as street maps of the country's major cities. Research resources include encyclopedias, back issues of *National Geographic* and other magazines, and travel books. Additional sources may include travel agencies and foreign embassies. Take apart a scrapbook and give pages to each student for attaching and labeling maps. After the students have finished, reassemble the scrapbook.

🧊 📱 **EE2 Places and Regions: Standard 4**

periodically order cars off the roads and children are not allowed to play outside.

Building a Better Life

Rapid urbanization creates environmental challenges for Latin American cities. Cities experience rapid urbanization when their rates of population growth far exceed the available resources for housing, sanitation, employment, education, and government services.

The trend toward urbanization is global and is not likely to be reversed. Governments and international agencies, however, are beginning to address the needs of Latin America's urban areas. For example, Mexico City's recent improvements include a new water supply system and expanded public transportation. The World Bank has targeted cities in Venezuela, Peru, Brazil, and Guatemala for intensive neighborhood improvements. Grassroots

efforts are even more promising. Groups of homeless people in cities such as Buenos Aires, Rio de Janeiro, and Santiago have successfully turned abandoned city buildings into affordable housing and commercial space.

Regional and International Issues

The quality of life in Latin America today continues to be shaped by geographic, economic, and historical realities that reach beyond national borders. Regional cooperation in addressing international issues will help move the region forward.

History
Disputed Borders

During the past 150 years, Latin America has faced a number of territorial conflicts. These

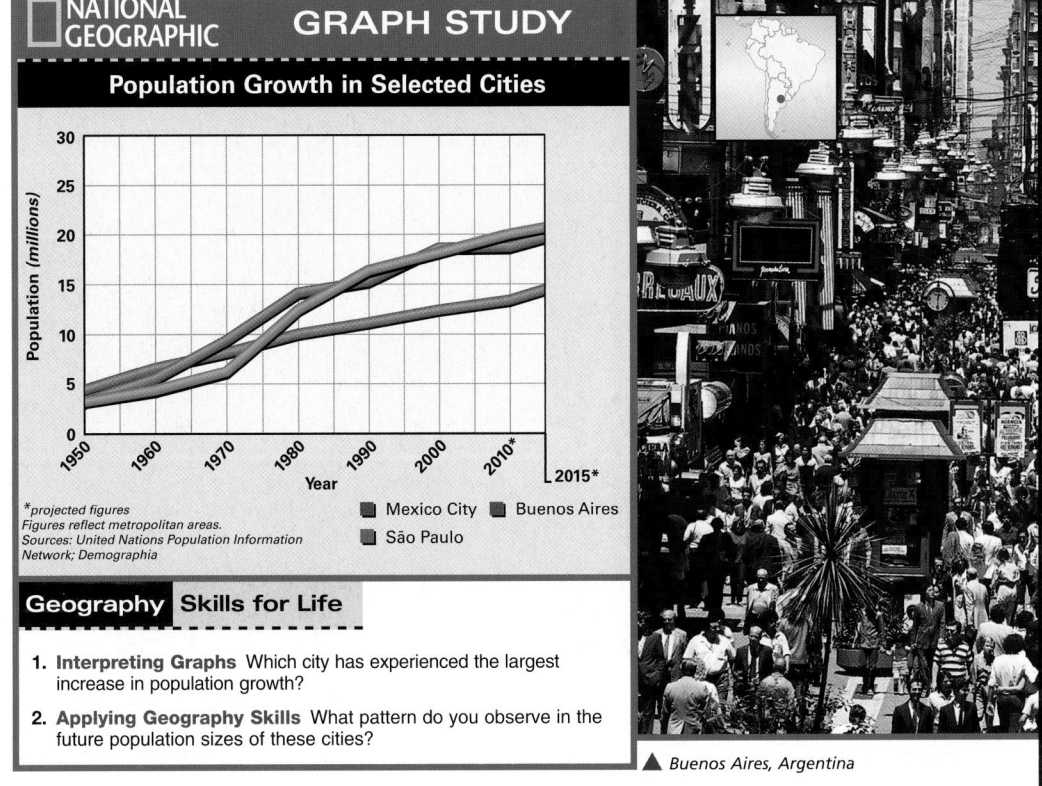

GRAPH STUDY

Population Growth in Selected Cities

*projected figures
Figures reflect metropolitan areas.
Sources: United Nations Population Information Network; Demographia

■ Mexico City ■ Buenos Aires
■ São Paulo

Geography Skills for Life

1. **Interpreting Graphs** Which city has experienced the largest increase in population growth?

2. **Applying Geography Skills** What pattern do you observe in the future population sizes of these cities?

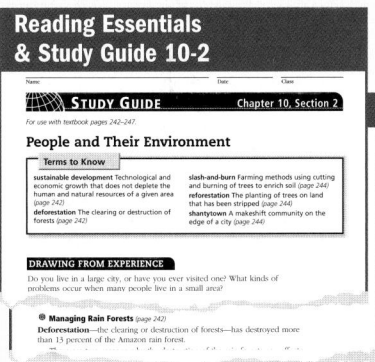

▲ *Buenos Aires, Argentina*

Chapter 10 🌐 245

L3 Finding Solutions
Have students form groups to analyze the problem of over-urbanization in Latin American cities. Tell students to list the causes and effects of this problem, and solutions that are already being implemented in several Latin American cities. Then have each group choose a different major Latin American city to gather and analyze information about its physical and human geography. Then, share with the class an overview of the city and a proposal to alleviate over-urbanization.

L1/ELL

Reading Essentials & Study Guide 10-2

NATIONAL GEOGRAPHIC **GRAPH STUDY**

Answers
1. *São Paulo*
2. *continued growth but not as much as in the 1970s*

Skills Practice
Which city might experience the fewest challenges in the future? Why? *(Buenos Aires; gradual growth rate allows services and infrastructure to keep pace with population.)*

CRITICAL THINKING ACTIVITY

Formulating Questions Formulating good questions can help students learn more about a problematic issue. Questions can lead to a greater understanding of a problem and point the way to a possible solution. After students have read pages 243–244, direct their attention to the two questions that appear just before the subhead "Farms and Ranches Versus Forests" on page 244. **Ask:** How can these questions direct people toward a possible solution to the problem of deforestation? *(These questions suggest issues in need of the most attention. By focusing attention on the challenges of overpopulation, perhaps people can find solutions.)* 🌐 **EE5 Environment and Society: Standard 14**

ASSESS

Assign Section 2 Assessment as homework or as an in-class activity.

🖥 Have students use **Interactive Tutor Self-Assessment CD-ROM** to review Section 2.

L2

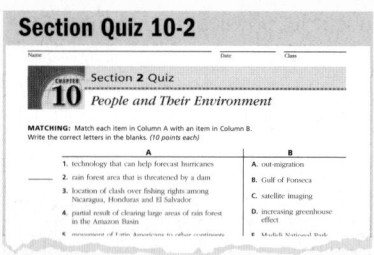

Section Quiz 10-2

NATIONAL GEOGRAPHIC **World Explorer**

Answer
Scientists are using satellite imaging and computer modeling to forecast the direction and severity of hurricanes. Early warnings may reduce the loss of human life.

More About the Photo
In 2000 Popocatépetl began spewing lava and ash over the countryside. About 40,000 people in villages within a 12-mile (20-km) radius of the volcano were forced to evacuate their homes. Most of them have returned. Although a major eruption did not occur, experts anticipate such an occurrence, but no one can say when that will happen.

---

conflicts occur over disputed regions involving strategic locations or rights to valuable natural resources. Nicaragua, Honduras, and **El Salvador**, for example, have quarreled over fishing rights in the Gulf of Fonseca. Venezuela and Guyana battle over petroleum holdings along their shared border. Border wars divert resources that might better be used for development, but economic incentives can encourage countries to resolve their differences. After going to war three times, Peru and Ecuador finally settled a 60-year-old border dispute in 1998. During the negotiations international investors offered more than $3 billion in aid to develop economies and human services on both sides of the border.

Population Growth and Migration

Through education and economic improvement, most Latin American countries have begun to lower the high birthrates that have led to overpopulation. In the 2000s Latin America's population challenges will likely involve balancing the distribution of goods and services. Migration within the region—for economic or political reasons, or to escape the devastation of natural disasters—will continue to strain the resources of overcrowded cities.

In addition, growing numbers of Latin Americans have migrated abroad, especially to the United States. Many of these migrants have come to the United States to find a better way of life, some entering without visas. Others are well-educated people or skilled workers who could make important contributions to their home countries. For example, if scientists or researchers leave Latin America, its countries may ultimately lack the human resources necessary to solve environmental problems. To stem this out-migration, Latin American leaders are seeking to create jobs for their people by attracting more foreign investment.

Latin American migrants, meanwhile, have brought many changes to the United States. Immigration from Latin America has made the United States the country with the fifth largest Spanish-

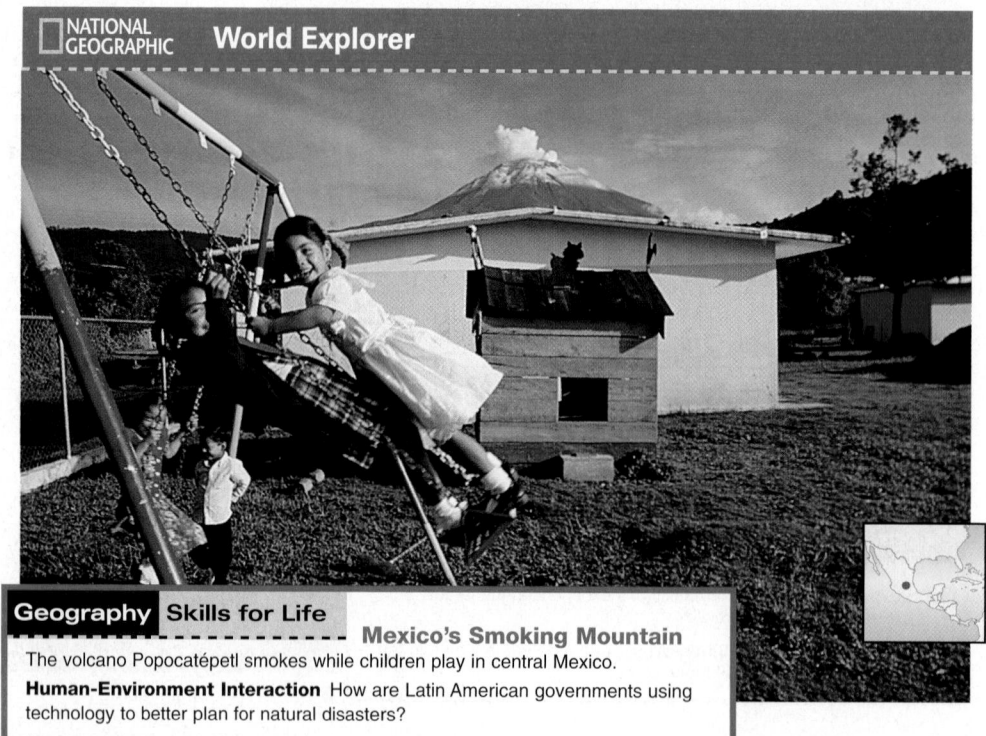

NATIONAL GEOGRAPHIC **World Explorer**

Geography **Skills for Life**
Mexico's Smoking Mountain
The volcano Popocatépetl smokes while children play in central Mexico.
Human-Environment Interaction How are Latin American governments using technology to better plan for natural disasters?

TEAM-TEACHING ACTIVITY: SCIENCE

Ethnobotany Tell students that ethnobotany is the study of how indigenous peoples use their local plants. Today ethnobotanists, schooled in the usage of plants as medicines, are racing to identify and learn the uses of the hundreds of thousands of plants throughout Latin America before they disappear. Tell students to imagine they are ecotourists who are attending a workshop in a Latin American rain forest to learn more about native uses for local plants. Have students identify a plant native to one of the region's rain forests that is known to have medicinal, culinary, or nutritional properties and describe its uses. A science teacher can suggest possible topics and direct students to helpful sources.
📖 **EE4 Human Systems: Standard 13**

speaking population in the world. Latin Americans have contributed much to the many communities in which they have settled—Mexicans in Texas, California, and Illinois; Cubans in Florida; and Puerto Ricans and Dominicans in New York.

Disaster Preparedness

Latin America's physical geography makes the region especially vulnerable to natural disasters, such as earthquakes, volcanic eruptions, and hurricanes, which take a huge toll in human life and economic resources. In order to increase the region's emergency preparedness, Latin American governments are cooperating in the use of sophisticated technology, such as satellite imaging and computer modeling, to forecast the direction and severity of hurricanes, for example. Such cooperative efforts can help Latin Americans anticipate emergencies rather than reacting after the fact. The savings in lives and economic resources are sure to be significant.

Industrial Pollution

Air and water pollution do not respect national boundaries. Multinational firms and free-trade agreements have increased industrial growth in some countries. Environmental laws, however, have not reduced the risks of increased pollution from new factories. Similarly, runoff from chemical fertilizers and pesticides used on commercial farms may cross borders to damage health or

endanger lives. Governments and international agencies are cooperating to help Latin America address these challenges.

NATIONAL GEOGRAPHIC World Explorer

Geography Skills for Life

Water Pollution Bauxite mining runoff covers a cove in Jamaica.
Human-Environment Interaction How can Latin America overcome the challenges of industrial pollution?

SECTION 2 ASSESSMENT

Checking for Understanding

1. **Define** sustainable development, deforestation, slash-and-burn, reforestation, shantytown.

2. **Main Ideas** Use a diagram similar to the one below to identify activities that have contributed to deforestation in Latin America.

Deforestation

Critical Thinking

3. **Predicting Consequences** How might the destruction of the Amazon rain forest affect your life?

4. **Making Comparisons** Compare the ways urban populations in Latin America and those in your state have modified their physical environments.

5. **Drawing Conclusions** What circumstances might make environmental protection a low priority for some Latin American governments?

Analyzing Maps

6. **Human-Environment Interaction** Study the maps of the Amazon rain forest on page 243. What kinds of activities are responsible for these changes?

Applying Geography

7. **Mental Mapping** Without consulting a map, identify the Latin American countries most at risk from hurricanes. Write a description of ways that a hurricane is a threat to these countries.

NATIONAL GEOGRAPHIC World Explorer

Answer
new laws and stricter enforcement of existing laws

More About the Photo
Although Jamaica is located in a favorable climate and has numerous natural harbors, its tourism industry has declined in recent years, and industrial waste has increasingly impacted the environment. Bauxite is mined within a 1,000-square-mile (2,590-sq-km) area in the central part of the island.

Reteach

Have pairs of students use the words in "Terms to Know" and "Places to Locate" in a paragraph titled "Latin American People and Their Environment." Encourage students to share their paragraphs with the rest of the class.

Enrich

Have students leaf through the pages of this section and choose a photo that they feel is a good representation of one aspect of Latin American environment. Then have students identify the photo and explain why they chose it.

4 CLOSE

Challenge students to create a crossword puzzle using one clue and word from each subhead in this section.

SECTION 2 ASSESSMENT ANSWERS

1. All vocabulary terms are defined in the text.
2. Activities may include road building to promote settlement, slash-and-burn agriculture, cattle ranching, and logging.
3. Answers may include urban expansion into rural areas; more transportation networks
4. Overcrowding and unaffordable housing are issues in both regions.

5. Leaders might see industrial and economic development as an immediate priority.
6. logging, slash-and-burn agriculture, mining, cattle ranching, resettlement
7. **Applying Geography** Paragraphs should list countries in the Caribbean and on the Atlantic and Gulf coasts and include specific details, such as destruction of housing and farmland.

1 FOCUS

Put the following headings on the board and have students brainstorm to list items for each category.

- *foods from the rain forest*
- *non-food rain forest products*
- *medicines from the rain forest*
- *animals of the rain forest*
- *people of the rain forest*
- *effects on global environment*

2 TEACH

Tell students that rain forest preservationists tend to view the fate of rain forests as an international issue, since people worldwide benefit from the products of rain forests and the stabilizing impact that rain forests have on the environment in which we all live. Some proponents of rain forest development are mostly concerned with profit. Those who live in the area are more concerned with the day-to-day need of families to work on rain forest land in order to feed their families.

L2 Debate

Have students identify as many pros and cons as they can to support the arguments of those who believe the issue should be resolved by Brazil and those who favor international involvement.

Viewpoint
CASE STUDY on the Environment

BRAZIL
Amazon R.
Tapajós R.
Tocantins R.
⊛ Brasília
Paraná R.

■ Rain forest

Brazil's Rain Forests: Biodiversity at Risk

Nowhere is "biodiversity"—the term biologists coined to describe our planet's bountiful variety of living things—more apparent than in a tropical rain forest. Rain forests harbor at least half of all species on Earth. However, deforestation severely threatens these biologically rich ecosystems. Worldwide, roughly 150 acres (61 ha) of rain forest are destroyed every minute. As the forests disappear, habitats are lost and Earth's biodiversity dwindles. The world's largest remaining expanses of tropical rain forest are in Brazil. But the fate of these forests, and their astounding array of plants and animals, is uncertain.

LOOKING TO THE FUTURE

The World's Medicine Chest Experts estimate that at least 328 new plant-based drugs are yet to be developed from rain forest plants. These new medicines will join the 121 pharmaceutical drugs already in use that were developed from such plants.

Almost three-fourths of these drugs are based on plants that native peoples have used for centuries to treat illnesses. As rain forests disappear, however, native shamans who may hold the key to the world's medicine chest are also disappearing. Today bioprospectors from more than 100 pharmaceutical companies are working with tribal shamans and herbal healers to compile records of their knowledge.
▨ **EE3 Physical Systems: Standard 8**

S mall enough to fit in the palm of your hand, a golden lion tamarin (left) is a blaze of orange against vivid rain-forest green. A tiny primate, the golden lion is one of four tamarin species that live in Brazil's Amazon and less-well-known Atlantic rain forests. All tamarins are endangered, but a successful captive-breeding program recently brought the golden lion tamarin back from the brink of extinction. The future of thousands of other plant and animal species also is in jeopardy as pressures on Brazil's rain forests intensify.

These forests boast the richest variety of plant life on the planet. A few acres might contain 450 different species of trees. Thousands of other types of plants—orchids, bromeliads, ferns, and vines—grow on, among, or beneath the trees.

Brazil's rain forests reverberate with the hum of countless insect species. A single tree might harbor 650 kinds of beetles. Sharing the forest with

Brazilian farmers (below) clear a field in the Amazon rain forest. Fire (right) destroys large areas of forest. ▼

these insect multitudes are snakes, such as anacondas and jararacas, and other animals, such as poison dart frogs, fruit bats, jaguars, and spider monkeys. But this biodiversity is rapidly disappearing.

Large areas of Brazil's rain forests are burned or cut down by farmers and ranchers to make way for cropland and cattle pastures. Loggers cut the fine hardwoods and export them for a profit. Growing cities, new roads, and industries encroach on the forests. Each year hundreds, perhaps thousands, of species are lost as their habitats are destroyed.

Rain forest preservationists want future generations to enjoy Earth's biodiversity. They point out that rain forest plants provide us with many things: foods, such as bananas and Brazil nuts; medicines, such as quinine and muscle relaxants; and substances, such as dyes and waxes. Scientists have identified only a fraction of rain forest species. Could a cure for cancer or AIDS lurk in a plant that has not yet been studied?

◀ The flowering four-o'clock contains substances used to treat rheumatism.

Rain forest developers argue that people living in or near Brazil's rain forests need to feed their families. For many, farming or raising cattle in clear-cut areas is the only way they can survive. Harvesting rain forest timber allows workers to lift their standard of living above the poverty line. With a growing population of more than 160 million, Brazil needs room for urban growth and industrial development. Some argue that Brazil's rain forests belong to Brazilians. Shouldn't they manage their forests as they see fit?

What's Your Point of View?
Only about 8 percent of Brazil's Atlantic rain forest remains. Do you think this remnant is worth saving? Why or why not?

③ **ASSESS**

Have students answer the **What's Your Point of View?** questions on this page.

④ **CLOSE**

Problem-Solving Have students work with a partner to create a plan that balances the need to preserve the biodiversity of the Amazon rain forest with Brazil's need to support its people.

global issues

Deforestation One rain forest plant, the Madagascar periwinkle, is now extinct in the wild because of deforestation in Madagascar, an island south of Africa in the Indian Ocean. Two drugs derived from that plant have helped increase the survival rate for children with leukemia from 20 percent to 80 percent.

🌐 **Meeting National Standards**

Geography for Life
The following standards are met in the Student Edition:

EE3 Physical Systems: Standard 8
EE4 Human Systems: Standards 10, 11, 12, 13

WHAT CAN YOU DO?

Plan and carry out a public awareness campaign about the destruction of the rain forests.

- Help groups who are trying to protect the rain forests by raising money.
- Plant a tree.
- Find out what natural lands might be threatened in your community.
- Use recycled paper and wood, and encourage others to do so.

- Make information posters about deforestation and its causes, and then place the posters in public places.
- Write a series of informational TV and radio announcements. Announce them on the school PA system.

 EE5 Environment and Society: Standard 14

Teaching the Skill

To model each of the bulleted outlining steps, have students help you set up part of a formal outline for Section 1 of this chapter. Tell students that the title of Section 1 gives the general topic of the section. Have students turn the title into a question. Write the question on the board. Tell students to identify the four main ideas by looking at the headings. *(Agriculture, Industry, Trade and Interdependence, Transportation)* Label them with Roman numerals. Next, ask students to identify two subtopics under the first main idea, Agriculture. *(Latifundia and Minifundia, Cash Crops and Livestock)* Label them with the capital letters A and B. Ask students to find at least two supporting details for subtopic A.

Additional Practice
L1

Reinforcing Skills Activity 10

CHAPTER 10 REINFORCING SKILLS ACTIVITY	

Creating an Outline

An outline is a way to organize and present information. The general topic of an outline is stated as a question. Then, each type of information begins with a broad idea, followed by increasingly specific details. For example, an outline begins with two or more main ideas, labeled with Roman numerals. Under each main idea are two or more subtopics, labeled with capital letters. Finally, supporting details follow each subtopic. These are labeled with Arabic numerals or lowercase letters.

Practicing the Skill

DIRECTIONS: Read the following paragraphs, and then complete the outline below.

GLENCOE
TECHNOLOGY

Glencoe Skillbuilder Interactive Workbook, Level 2

Creating an Outline

Outlining may be used as a starting point for a reader who wants to understand and organize information. The reader begins with the rough shape of the material and gradually fills in the details in a logical manner.

Learning the Skill

Outlining can be used as a method of note taking and organizing information. There are two types of outlines—informal and formal. An informal outline is similar to taking notes—you write words and phrases needed to remember main ideas. A formal outline has a standard format.

To make a formal outline, begin by thinking about big ideas and dividing them into units of information. Give each of these major ideas a *heading*—a word or phrase that will identify the concept. Each major idea will be followed by two or more *subtopics*, or parts of main ideas. Include *supporting details* within each subtopic.

To create a formal outline, follow these steps:

- **Identify the general topic of the outline, and write the topic as a question.** Refer to the topic question as you work to be sure you are recording the most important ideas.

- **Write the main ideas that answer this question.** Label these with Roman numerals.

- **Write subtopics under each main idea.** Label these with capital letters.

- **Write supporting details for each subtopic.** Label these

with Arabic numerals and lowercase letters.

Topic as a question:
_____?

I. Managing Rain Forests
  A. Rain Forests
    1. Location
    2. Brazil's experience
      a. Trans-Amazonian Highway
      b. Indigenous peoples
    3. World concerns
    4. Local challenges
  B. Farms and Ranches Versus Forests
    1. Slash-and-burn farming
    2. Future land value
  C. Planting for the Future
    1. _____
    2. _____
II. _____
  A. Overcrowded Cities
    1. Shantytowns
    2. _____

  B. Building a Better Life
    1. Rapid urbanization
III. Regional and International Issues
  A. _____
    1. _____
    2. _____
  B. Population Growth and Migration
    1. _____
    2. _____
  C. _____
    1. _____
    2. _____
  D. _____
    1. _____
    2. _____

Practicing the Skill

Study the incomplete outline of Chapter 10, Section 2, above. The main ideas generally correspond to the section headings in the chapter. Copy this outline on a sheet of paper, and fill in the missing information for Section 2 of Chapter 10.

When you have completed your outline, answer the following questions:

1. What are the most important topics in Chapter 10, Section 2?

2. What are the four main subtopics under the heading "Regional and International Issues"?

3. What are two situations in which an outline such as this might be useful?

4. In addition to being useful to readers, how would an outline help writers?

Applying the Skill

Create an outline for Chapter 10, Section 1. Use the section headings for your main ideas. Remember to include at least two subtopics for each main heading. When you have finished, use your outline to identify the main ideas of the section.

The Glencoe Skillbuilder Interactive Workbook, Level 2 provides instruction and practice in key social studies skills.

ANSWERS TO PRACTICING THE SKILL

1. Managing Rain Forests, Urban Environments, and Regional and International Issues
2. disputed borders, population growth and migration, disaster preparedness, and industrial pollution
3. Accept practical answers, such as giving a talk or taking notes.
4. It would help a writer stay organized.

CHAPTER **10**

SECTION 1 — Living in Latin America (pp. 237–241)

Terms to Know
- export
- campesino
- *latifundia*
- *minifundia*
- cash crop
- developing country
- service industry
- maquiladora
- North American Free Trade Agreement (NAFTA)

Key Points
- Latin America's economy is based on the export of agricultural products.
- A small group of wealthy families or businesses owns a large percentage of the agricultural land in Latin America.
- The economy of many Latin American countries is linked to one or two cash crops.
- The maquiladora system, trade agreements, and international borrowing are attempts to speed the industrialization of many Latin American countries.
- Geographic and economic realities have presented obstacles to developing transportation and communications in the region.

Organizing Your Notes
Use a graphic organizer like the one below to summarize your notes for this section.

Living in Latin America	
Agriculture	
Industry	
Trade and Interdependence	
Transportation and Communications	

SECTION 2 — People and Their Environment (pp. 242–247)

Terms to Know
- sustainable development
- deforestation
- slash-and-burn
- reforestation
- shantytown

Key Points
- A key challenge for the Latin American region is sustainable development.
- Damage to the Amazon rain forest has both local and global consequences.
- Slash-and-burn cultivation contributes to Latin America's environmental challenges.
- Latin America's urban environmental problems are a result of rapid urbanization.
- Solutions to the region's environmental concerns will come through cooperation among local, national, regional, and international governments and organizations.

Organizing Your Notes
Create graphic organizers like the one below for each of the following topics: deforestation, population growth, and international issues.

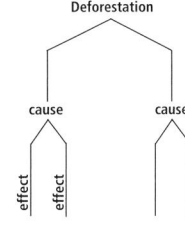

Deforestation

cause   cause

effect effect

◀ *Signing of NAFTA, 1992*

Using the Chapter 10 Summary & Study Guide

Use the Chapter 10 Summary & Study Guide to preview, review, condense, or reteach the chapter.

Preview/Review

🔘 **Vocabulary PuzzleMaker CD-ROM** reinforces "Terms to Know."

🔘 **Interactive Tutor Self-Assessment CD-ROM** provides a review of Chapter 10 content.

Condense

Have students read the Chapter 10 Summary & Study Guide.

💿 Chapter 10 Audio Program

📁 Chapter 10 Guided Reading Activities

Reteach

📁 Chapter 10 Reteaching Activities (Spanish also available)

📁 Chapter 10 Reading Essentials and Study Guides

GLENCOE TECHNOLOGY

NATIONAL GEOGRAPHIC
WORLD REGIONS
VIDEO PROGRAM

Unit 3, Latin America
The following segments enhance the study of this unit:
- **Green Commerce**
- **The Inca**
- **Steel Drums**

 Available in DVD and VHS

CHAPTER CULMINATING ACTIVITY

Determining Cause and Effect Have students review the chapter to find at least five causes and their effects that are examples of the challenges faced by this region today. If students have already outlined the chapter in the Skillbuilder Activity, tell them to review their outlines for information. Have students scan each main idea and subhead and list pertinent information. For example, for Section 1, in the subhead *Agriculture*, students might note that as the old agricultural system gradually changes *(cause)*, people leave rural areas in search of work *(effect)*. 🌐 **EE6 The Uses of Geography: Standard 18**

NOTE: This activity may be completed separately, or you may wish students to incorporate it into their GeoJournals.

CHAPTER
10
ASSESSMENT & ACTIVITIES

GLENCOE TECHNOLOGY

Use *MindJogger Videoquiz* to review the Chapter 10 content.

Reviewing Key Terms

Accept reasonable responses that explain relationships.

Reviewing Facts

SECTION 1

1. coffee, bananas, sugarcane
2. Natural disasters can wipe out an entire year's crops.
3. Investors are wary of doing business there.
4. lack of government funds and difficult geographical barriers

SECTION 2

5. deforestation, loss of the rain forest, leaching of soil nutrients by erosion
6. act as a filtering system for the atmosphere, produces oxygen, and decreases atmospheric carbon dioxide
7. building new water supply systems, expanding public transportation, using abandoned buildings to house the homeless
8. Disputes divert resources that could be better spent on human services and development.

Critical Thinking

1. positive: employing local people, offer investment incomes, making goods cheaper to buy; negative: damaging environment, ignoring labor laws, creating low-paying jobs

---

Reviewing Key Terms

Examine the sets of terms below. Then write a sentence explaining how each set is related.

a. export — cash crop
b. *latifundia — minifundia*
c. developing country — sustainable development
d. maquiladora — service industries — North American Free Trade Agreement (NAFTA)
e. deforestation — slash-and-burn — reforestation
f. shantytown — rapid urbanization

Reviewing Facts

SECTION 1

1. What three cash crops supply much of Latin America's income?
2. How can dependence on a single crop affect a country's economy?
3. How do unstable governments prevent industrial development?
4. What obstacles have slowed the development of Latin America's transportation and communications systems?

SECTION 2

5. What are the environmental effects of slash-and-burn cultivation?
6. Why do some people believe that preservation of the Amazon rain forest is a global concern?
7. How are Latin American countries addressing the problems resulting from rapid urbanization?
8. Why do border disputes slow the economic development of the Latin American region?

Critical Thinking

1. **Making Generalizations** Has the maquiladora system had a positive or a negative effect on Mexico's people? Explain.

---

2. **Predicting Consequences** How might the North American Free Trade Agreement (NAFTA) change migration patterns in Latin America? What are the implications?
3. **Identifying Cause and Effect** Complete a diagram by giving examples of how rapid urbanization in Latin America affects housing, employment, education, sanitation, and government services.

Rapid urbanization affects . . .

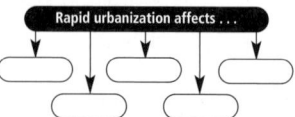

NATIONAL GEOGRAPHIC Locating Places

Latin America: Political Geography

Match the letters on the map with the places in Latin America. Write your answers on a sheet of paper.

1. Panama	5. Santiago	9. Mexico
2. Belém	6. Bogotá	10. Rio de Janeiro
3. Brazil	7. Costa Rica	11. Mexico City
4. São Paulo	8. Lima	

---

2. Answers might include slowing out-migration by creating jobs in local industries. Accept reasonable responses.
3. lack of affordable housing, not enough employment, overburdened education system, lack of sanitation in slums, not enough government services

NATIONAL GEOGRAPHIC Locating Places

1. D	**4.** G	**7.** J	**10.** K
2. E	**5.** I	**8.** A	**11.** C
3. B	**6.** F	**9.** H	

Using the Regional Atlas

1. All these areas are near water transportation and in coastal plains with good soil; population is concentrated in farming areas.
2. livestock raising, grapes

GEOGRAPHY
Online

Self-Check Quiz Visit the **Glencoe World Geography** Web site at <u>geography.glencoe.com</u> and click on Self-Check Quizzes—Chapter 10 to prepare for the Chapter Test.

Using the Regional Atlas

Refer to the Regional Atlas on pages 182–185.

1. **Region** What do the economic activity and population density maps suggest about where commercial farming occurs in Latin America?

2. **Location** Compare the economic activity and population density maps. What industry probably attracts settlers around Córdoba, Argentina?

Thinking Like a Geographer

Why do you think Latin American countries often depend on a single cash crop? As a geographer, what suggestions would you make to help governments make their agricultural output more varied?

GeoJournal

Descriptive Writing Review the data in your GeoJournal. Then write a paragraph comparing the ways Latin Americans in rural, urban, coastal, and highlands areas depend on or adapt to their environment. Focus on specific human activities.

Problem-Solving Activity

Problem-Solution Proposal In Latin America thousands of children spend most of their lives roaming the streets. Pick one Latin American city with street children, and learn more about them: how they survive, where they come from, how they spend their time, and where their families are. Then write a proposal in which you present your solution to the problem.

Technology Activity

Using the Internet for Research Search the Internet for photographs showing the destruction of a rain forest in Latin America. Narrow your search by using words such as *Amazon rain forest* or *Brazil*. Print the photographs, write captions to explain what is happening, and display your work on the classroom bulletin board. If possible, include charts, graphs, and maps.

Standardized Test Practice

Choose the best answer for the following multiple-choice question. If you have trouble answering the question, use the process of elimination to narrow your choices.

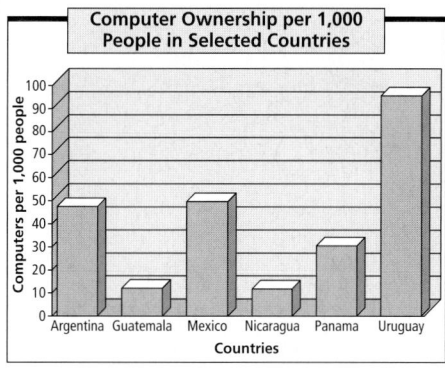

Computer Ownership per 1,000 People in Selected Countries

y-axis: Computers per 1,000 people (0, 10, 20, 30, 40, 50, 60, 70, 80, 90, 100)
x-axis: Countries — Argentina, Guatemala, Mexico, Nicaragua, Panama, Uruguay

1. **On average, 34 of every 1,000 Latin Americans owned computers in 1998. Which countries had higher rates of computer ownership than the regional average?**

   A Nicaragua and Panama

   B Argentina, Mexico, Panama, and Uruguay

   C Argentina, Mexico, and Uruguay

   D Guatemala, Nicaragua, and Panama

Test-Taking **Tip** Reread the title and x- and y-axis labels of the graph to determine the information the graph shows. Notice that Guatemala, Nicaragua, and Panama all fall short of the regional average. Tackle each answer choice one by one, eliminating those that contain even one country that has a lower rate than the regional average.

1. C

Tested Objectives: analyzing information using graphs

Additional Practice and Test-Taking Tips

 Standardized Test Practice Workbook

? CHAPTER BONUS TEST QUESTION

What would be the best way for the owner of a *latifundium* in Ecuador to ship a banana crop to the eastern United States?

(**1.** by truck on the Pan-American Highway

2. by freight car on a railway

3. on a barge through the Panama Canal

4. by boat on the Amazon River)

Thinking Like a Geographer

Students' answers may vary, but should mention that governments could encourage farmers to grow different crops by offering price supports or tax breaks.

GeoJournal

Paragraphs should demonstrate the relationships between physical and human geography and economic activities, using appropriate examples and illustrations.

Problem-Solving Activity

Check to see that students' proposals have sufficient background information about the street children for the city they picked. The proposals should also clearly state the issue before presenting a solution.

Technology Activity

Students' photo selections and captions should demonstrate careful research and insights into the causes and consequences of the destruction of the rain forest.

TEACHING TRANSPARENCIES

L2 Unit 4 Map Overlay Transparencies

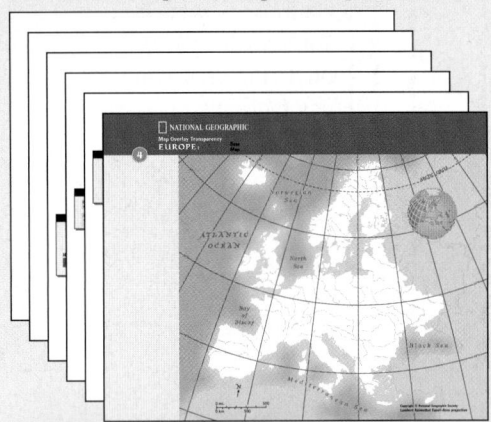

L2 Political Map Transparency 4

L2 World Cultures Transparencies 5, 6

French cuisine does not separate appearance from flavor. The entire culinary experience involves attention to the smallest detail, from the finest ingredients to exquisite presentation.

APPLICATION AND ENRICHMENT

L2 Location Activity 4

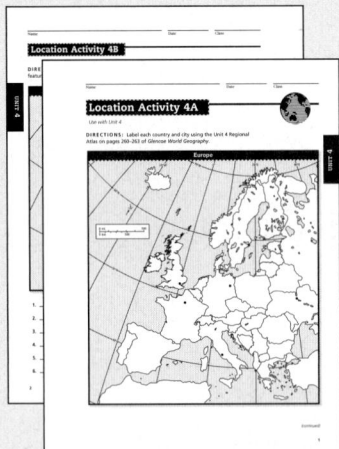

L2 Real-Life Applications and Problem-Solving Activity 4

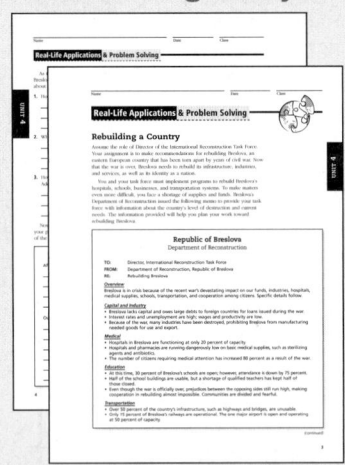

L2 GeoLab Activity 4

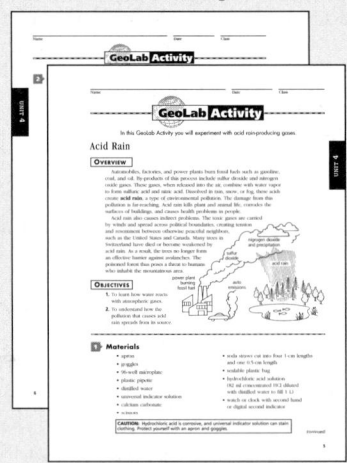

L2 Environmental Issues Case Study 4

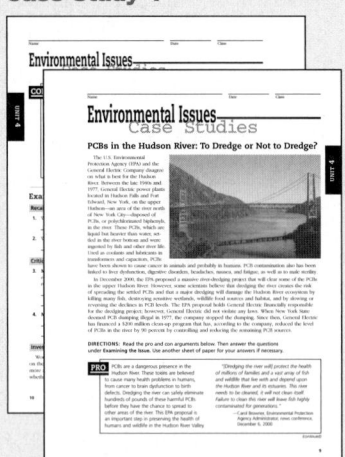

GEOGRAPHIC LITERACY

Focus on Geography Literacy

Building Geography Skills for Life

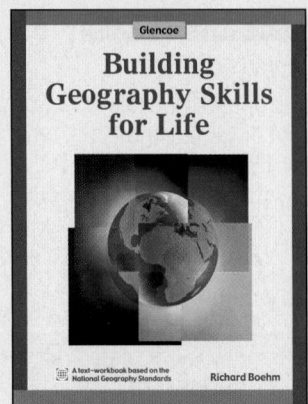

ASSESSMENT

Use the following to easily assess student learning in a variety of ways:

- Performance Assessment Activities and Rubrics
- Section Quizzes
- Chapter and Unit Tests
- Interactive Tutor Self-Assessment CD-ROM
- ExamView® Pro Testmaker
- MindJogger Videoquiz
- geography.glencoe.com
- Standardized Test Practice Workbook
- SAT I/II Test Practice

L2 Unit 4 Pretest and Tests

INTERDISCIPLINARY CONNECTIONS

L2 World Literature:
Contemporary Selection 4

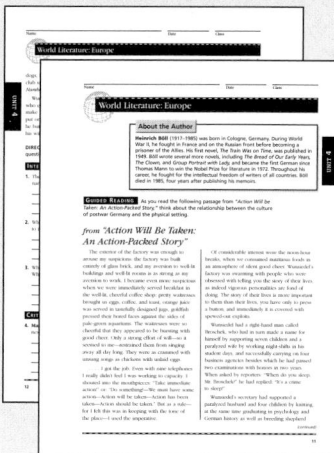

Foods Around the World

Glencoe
Foods Around the World

Multimedia

- **World Art and Architecture Transparencies**

- **World Art Prints**

- **World Music: A Cultural Legacy**

- **World History Primary Source Document Library**

BIBLIOGRAPHY

Readings for the Student

Longitude: The True Story of a Lone Genius Who Solved the Greatest Scientific Problem of His Time, by Dava Sobel. New York, NY: Viking Penguin, 1996.

The Pillars of Hercules: A Grand Tour of the Mediterranean, by Paul Theroux. New York, NY: Fawcett Books, 1996.

Readings for the Teacher

A Geography of the European Union, by John Cole and Francis Cole. London/New York, NY: Routledge, 1997.

The New Europe: Economy, Society and Environment, ed. David Pinder, New York, NY: John Wiley & Son, 1998.

A European Geography, by Tim Unwin. New York, NY: Addison-Wesley, 1998.

Multimedia Resources

Travel the World By Train: Europe Parts 1, 2, and 3. Long Beach, CA: Pioneer Entertainment. DVD, 60 minutes each. (Also available on videocassette)

Wild Europe—Tour the Natural Wonders of Wild Mountains. Boston, MA: WGBH, 1999. Videocassette, 60 minutes.

READING SUPPORT FROM
JAMESTOWN EDUCATION

- *Timed Readings Plus in Social Studies* help students increase their reading rate and fluency while maintaining comprehension. The 400-word passages are similar to those found on state and national assessments.

- *Reading in the Content Area: Social Studies* concentrates on six essential reading skills that help students better comprehend what they read. The book includes 75 high-interest nonfiction passages written at increasing levels of difficulty.

- *Reading Fluency* helps students read smoothly, accurately, and expressively.

- *Jamestown's Reading Improvement,* by renowned reading expert Edward Fry, focuses on helping build your students' comprehension, vocabulary, and skimming and scanning skills.

- *Critical Reading Series* provides high-interest books, each written at three reading levels.

For more information about these products, see the Jamestown Education materials in the Classroom Solutions in the front of this Teacher Wraparound Edition.
To order these products, call Glencoe at 1-800-334-7344.

Background Information

CHAPTER 11 (pp. 270–285)

The Physical Geography of Europe

With more than 40 countries, Europe comprises a diverse range of terrain, climate, history, and culture. The region's extensive coastlines, natural harbors, and overland trade routes encouraged Europeans of the past to explore and colonize other parts of the world. This expansion spread European ideas and ways abroad and also brought to Europe cultural influences from foreign lands.

Scenic beauty and a rich cultural and historical heritage have made Europe one of the world's popular travel destinations. Each year, millions of foreign visitors join Europeans in activities such as visiting art museums in Paris and Florence, snorkeling off Spain's Balearic Islands, and skiing in the Austrian Alps. Europeans host international athletic competitions, such as the annual Tour de France, a cycling race that covers over 2,250 miles (3,630 km) through the French countryside.

Natural Resources

Endowed with a temperate climate, navigable rivers, and an abundance of natural resources including fertile soil, forests, and mineral wealth, Europe is an international center of technology, industry, and commercial agriculture.

Europe's rivers are major historic, scenic, and commercial waterways. The Rhine River, for example, flows 820 miles (1,319 km) from Switzerland through Germany and the Netherlands before entering the North Sea near Rotterdam, one of the world's busiest ports. Large barges and ocean freighters can navigate the Rhine, and a network of canals links this major waterway to various other European rivers, such as the Danube and the Elbe.

CHAPTER 12 (pp. 286–311)

The Cultural Geography of Europe

Europe's cultural fabric is the result of influences spanning more than 2,000 years. The ancient Greeks and Romans developed cultural and political standards that still influence Europe today. Under the Roman Empire, Christianity spread across Europe. During the Middle Ages, Roman Catholicism and Eastern Orthodoxy shaped government, learning, and the arts. Contacts with Islamic Southwest Asia and North Africa also opened Europeans to new ideas in science, mathematics, philosophy, and the arts.

In the early modern period, the need for religious reform led to the rise of Protestantism and the renewal of Roman Catholicism. About the same time, the Renaissance gave birth to new cultural achievements and created a spirit of individualism and inquiry. From the 1400s to the 1800s, European explorations, scientific discoveries, artistic achievements, and political upheavals transformed Europe and much of the world.

During the late 1700s and 1800s, the Industrial Revolution made Europe the world's major economic center. Two world wars, however, devastated much of the region during the first half of the 1900s. The Cold War that followed divided Europe into two parts: communist eastern Europe, tied to the Soviet Union, and largely democratic western Europe, allied to the United States. While eastern Europe stagnated economically and politically, democratic western Europe rebuilt and prospered. Communism's fall in the 1990s unleashed nationalist hatreds that led to violence in the Balkan Peninsula of southeastern Europe. However, the eastern and western parts of Europe came closer together, and many European countries as a group worked toward economic and political unity within the European Union.

Population and Migration

Population shifts and migrations have been an important part of Europe's history for centuries. Waves of migrating peoples settled in Europe during the early Middle Ages, laying the foundations of the countries of modern Europe. The era of overseas exploration that began in the 1400s led to the emigration of many Europeans to the Americas, southern Africa, and the South Pacific region. The twentieth century's two world wars redrew national boundaries, displaced many people, and altered population patterns. Jews, Roma people (once called Gypsies), and others were systematically executed by the Nazis during World War II.

After communism's collapse in the 1990s, migration from eastern to western Europe increased as people sought jobs and a better standard of living. Meanwhile, western Europe's prosperity also drew migrants from Asia, Africa, and the Caribbean.

CHAPTER 13 (pp. 312–331)

Europe Today

Today, many European countries are putting aside centuries-old differences and working together to forge a united Europe. Still, nationalist loyalties remain, and in some cases, are powerful enough to create friction. This is especially the case in eastern Europe, where iron-fisted communist rule had once held down ethnic rivalries.

Regional Challenges

Since the collapse of communism, Europe has faced a number of political and economic challenges. While economic progress has been made, many eastern European countries have had difficulty in moving from government-controlled economies to free market economies, and their standards of living are lower than those of western Europe. Some

western Europeans are hesitant about admitting into the European Union countries whose economies are still shaky.

Another issue is how Europe in the future will relate to the United States and Russia. From the Marshall Plan in 1947, which helped rebuild post–World War II western Europe, to the latest military interventions in the Balkans, the United States has had major political, cultural, and economic ties to Europe. Some European countries, however, would like to develop their own international role while continuing this close relationship. In the case of Russia, eastern European countries are wary of traditional Russian expansionism, and some of them have joined NATO to increase their security.

Above all, Europe's countries are trying to reach agreement on the kind of union they want for their region. On the verge of admitting eastern European members, the European Union is also debating how to reform and strengthen its existing institutions. A major question is to what extent such changes will come at the expense of national sovereignty. While Germany would like to create an all-European government, some countries, such as the United Kingdom, are unwilling to yield too much of their independence to a supranational body. Whatever political path Europe chooses, its economic strength, trading ties, and cultural legacy will continue to make it one of the world's influential regions.

00:00 OUT OF TIME?

If time does not permit teaching each chapter in this unit, you may want to use the **Reading Essentials and Study Guide** summaries.

Unit Launch Activity

Ask: Which Europeans in the past 100 years have had the greatest effect on the world scientifically, politically, artistically, militarily, and athletically? *(Albert Einstein, Sigmund Freud, Adolf Hitler, Joseph Stalin, the Beatles, Martina Hingis, or Sir Winston Churchill, for example)* **What events originating in Europe have changed the world?** *(Russian Revolution, World Wars I and II, Chernobyl, the war in the Balkans, fall of the Berlin Wall, for example)* Display students' answers on a poster board. As the unit progresses, add names and events.

GLENCOE TECHNOLOGY

☐ NATIONAL GEOGRAPHIC
WORLD REGIONS VIDEO PROGRAM

Unit 4, Europe
The following segments enhance the study of this unit:

- **Mariners of the Mediterranean**
- **A Divided City**
- **City of Canals**

 Available in DVD and VHS

UNIT 4

Europe

WHY IT'S IMPORTANT—

In the 1990s, several nations of Europe formed the European Union, an alliance that works for the region's economic and political unity. Many European countries are replacing their national currencies with a common currency—the euro. As one of the world's leading economic powers, Europe has long had close political, cultural, and trading ties with the United States. Because of this important relationship, European ideas and practices have shaped your life and will continue to do so in the years ahead.

World Regions Video
To learn more about Europe and its impact on your world, view the World Regions video "Europe."

254 Unit 4

GETTING TO KNOW THE REGION

Map Activity Display Political Map Transparency 4, and have students also refer to the map on page 260 of their texts. **Ask: Which is the northernmost country in Europe?** *(Norway)* **Which countries in Europe could be called island countries?** *(United Kingdom, Ireland, Iceland, Malta, Cyprus)* **The boundary dividing Europe and Asia runs through which body of water?** *(Black Sea)* **Which four countries share the mountain range known as the Alps?** *(France, Italy, Austria, Switzerland)* **At which point is Europe closest to Africa?** *(Gibraltar)* **Which two countries are separated by the Pyrenees Mountains?** *(France and Spain)* **Which countries are bordered by the North Sea?** *(United Kingdom, France, Belgium, the Netherlands, Denmark, Norway)* **EE1 The World in Spatial Terms: Standard 1**

NATIONAL GEOGRAPHIC

Gondolier in Venice, Italy

This online resource, brought to you by the National Geographic Society, provides lesson plans, atlas updates, cartographic activities with interactive maps, an online map store, and links to the boundless subjects of maps and geography.

Unit Overview

The three chapters that comprise this unit introduce students to the physical and cultural geography of Europe as well as to the peoples of that region. Point out to students the following:

- the diverse range of languages and cultures as well as landforms and climates in Europe
- Europe as birthplace of science, industry, and democracy
- Europe's global role—past empires and present European Union

ABOUT THE PHOTO

Visual Instruction In the 1400s Venice was a powerful and wealthy seaport city-state that had established trade routes and colonies along the Mediterranean, Aegean, and Black Seas. Because Venice is built on a cluster of more than 100 islands, Venetians today still travel through the city by boat on a network of interconnected canals that serve as streets. Although gondolas are still used for tourists and special celebrations, today's boats are motorized rather than human powered. **Ask:** How has water transportation in Venice changed since the 1500s? *(Tourists still ride in gondolas, but the residents of Venice use motorized boats.)* ⊕ EE2 Places and Regions: Standard 6

1 FOCUS

These features and activities may be used as an introduction to the unit or as teaching tools throughout the course of the unit.

L1 Using Flash Cards Activity

Prior to beginning the study of this unit, use the **Countries of the World Flash Cards** to preview students' knowledge of Europe. Organize the class into groups. Have students share their knowledge about Europe with others in their group. Ask students to share their opinions of the characteristics that make Europe a distinct region.

L2 Photo Research Activity

Ask your students to study the photos and accompanying captions on pages 256–259. As a homework assignment, have them choose two of the photos to research and write one or two paragraphs about each. Ask students to share their research findings with the class.

FYI

Spain is a large country in land area, measuring more than 600 miles (965 km) from west to east—about the distance from London, England, to Prague in the Czech Republic. Spain is also diverse, with temperate wet mixed forests in the northwest and dry grasslands in the southeast.

What Makes Europe a Region?

E urope is a small continent with a long, jagged coastline. With watery fingers, the sea reaches deep into the land, embracing peninsulas and carving out bays, gulfs, and channels. Warm Atlantic winds and currents bathe European shores, helping to give this northerly landmass an unexpectedly mild climate. They also bring abundant rain that nurtures lush, green landscapes.

Fertile plains extend across much of northern Europe. Farther south, the plains become rugged hills, then mountains. The Alps are the continent's highest mountain range. They stretch across south-central Europe, forming a barrier that shelters the sunny Mediterranean area from moist northern winds.

Great rivers wind their way through Europe's landscapes, linking inland areas with the sea. The Danube flows through or along more countries than any other river in the world. The Rhine, with its source high in the Swiss Alps, is the continent's most important waterway.

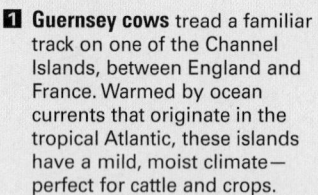

1 Guernsey cows tread a familiar track on one of the Channel Islands, between England and France. Warmed by ocean currents that originate in the tropical Atlantic, these islands have a mild, moist climate—perfect for cattle and crops.

256   Unit 4

BACKGROUND INFORMATION

Danube River This major European waterway rises from its source in Germany's Black Forest and runs for more than 1,700 miles (2,735 km) through or alongside Austria, the Slovak Republic, Hungary, Croatia, Serbia and Montenegro, Bulgaria, Moldova, Ukraine, and Romania, where it diffuses into a broad delta before spilling into the Black Sea. The Danube has about 300 tributaries and is one of Europe's major transport routes. The Danube can accommodate large ships and barges and is linked to other major rivers by a series of canals. In recent years pollution of the Danube has become a serious problem, adversely affecting fishing and making the river unsafe for drinking and irrigation.   **EE2 Places and Regions: Standard 4**

② TEACH

L2 Location

Have students discuss how geographic location has influenced their lives as well as those of others in their community. Encourage them to consider such things as climate, terrain, and proximity to a desert, prairie, plain, forest, body of water, or range of mountains. Ask students to make a list of how their specific geographic location has affected home design, clothing, typical foods, the models of cars or trucks, the holidays and festivities they celebrate, and even the kinds of music they favor. Throughout the study of this unit, have them refer to and add to their lists as they learn about Europe's geography.

GLENCOE TECHNOLOGY

NATIONAL GEOGRAPHIC

WORLD REGIONS
VIDEO PROGRAM

Unit 4, Europe
The following segments enhance the study of this unit:

- **Mariners of the Mediterranean**
- **A Divided City**
- **City of Canals**

 Available in DVD and VHS

2 Rows of bright umbrellas shelter beachgoers at Positano, Italy. Europe's unusually long coastline borders many seas. Countries along the Mediterranean Sea enjoy what is called a Mediterranean climate, with mild winters and hot, dry summers.

3 Ships and barges follow the snaking curves of the Rhine River in Germany. For centuries, the Rhine has provided an important transportation route through western Europe. Some of Germany's largest cities—and many medieval castles—lie along the Rhine and its tributaries.

4 Icy peaks in the Swiss Alps reflect the colors of the setting sun. The Alpine mountain system forms a broad arc that reaches from southern France to the Balkan Peninsula. The range's highest peak, Mont Blanc, lies in France, near the border with Switzerland and Italy.

Unit 4   257

A TRAVELER'S LOG

Paul Theroux, an American, wrote in his article, "A Circuit of Corsica" (*Atlantic Monthly*, November 1978): "Corsica is France, but it is not French. It is a mountain range moored like a great ship with a cargo of crags a hundred miles off the Riviera. In its three climates it combines the high Alps, the ruggedness of North Africa, and the choicest landscapes of Italy, but most dramatic are the peaks which are never out of view and show in the upheaval of rock a culture that is violent and heroic. . . . On the west are cliffs which drop straight and red into the sea; on the south there is a true fjord, on the east a long, flat, and formerly malarial coast with the island's only straight road, on the north a populous cape, and in the center the Gothic steeples of mountains, fringed by forests where wild boar are hunted."

🌐 EE2 Places and Regions: Standard 4

L2 Understanding Conflict

During the past century, Europe has been the site of some of the world's most brutal and destructive wars. Ask students to speculate on the geographic and cultural issues that may have contributed to these conflicts. If they have difficulty, you might prompt them with the possibilities such as: the distribution of natural resources or religious and ethnic differences. Also have students speculate on the impact of war on cultural and political changes (shifting boundaries, displaced populations, technological changes.)

FYI

The Euro On January 1, 1999, the euro became the currency for European Union countries. While the euro could be used for personal checks, traveler's checks, credit cards, and the trading of stocks and bonds, the actual release of euro notes and coins was January 1, 2002. During the three-year interim period, currencies such as the French franc and the German mark continued to be used along with the euro. The symbol for the euro resembles the letter "c" with two horizontal parallel lines across it.

Cultural Colossus

A mosaic of more than 40 countries, Europe enjoys a rich cultural heritage. Western traditions of art, architecture, science, and mathematics had their start in ancient Greece and Rome. In the centuries that followed, European culture spread far beyond the continent, aided by easy access to the sea. Modern European cities remain thriving centers for education and the arts.

Europe is home to people of many ethnic groups. Differences among those groups have led to frequent conflicts throughout European history. Toward the end of the twentieth century, political reforms greatly changed the face of Europe and brought new unity—as well as new challenges—to the region's inhabitants.

1 **Crates of cargo** stand on docks lining the harbor of Aberdeen, Scotland. The cargo awaits loading onto oceangoing ships. Europe's long coastline is dotted with busy ports. Access to the sea has helped spread European goods and culture worldwide.

258 Unit 4

BACKGROUND INFORMATION

Cultural Geography For centuries, European explorers—beginning more than 1,000 years ago with the Vikings—embarked on expeditions to the Americas, Asia, Africa, and the Pacific islands. That sense of adventure, which put Europeans in contact with cultures from around the world, persists today in Europe. Every year, thousands of European tourists travel to countries around the globe, from the rain forests of Panama to the mountains of Nepal to the Grand Canyon in the southwest United States. In shops and homes across Europe, batiks from Malaysia, jackets from Peru, masks from Korea, or tapestries from Pakistan are displayed. In cafes, restaurants, and coffee shops, music—often live performances—from musicians from Zimbabwe, Indonesia, and North Africa entertains customers.
EE4 Human Systems: Standard 10

NATIONAL GEOGRAPHIC

Culture NOTE

The Netherlands The Dutch export more than 60 percent of the world's cut flowers, primarily to other parts of western Europe. Dutch floral exports to the United States total $100 million annually.

③ ASSESS

Ask students to compare and contrast the physical and human geographic features of their state and a European country. Have them include the following in their considerations: landforms, cities, and other physical features as well as human cultural patterns. *(Texas and Spain, for example, both have semi-dry plains areas and ranching traditions.)*

④ CLOSE

Organize the class into small groups and assign each group a region or country of Europe. Ask each group to present a brief report on the region or country, focusing on terrain, culture, history, economy, and population.

2 **West Berliners batter** the wall that once separated the city into eastern and western sectors—and represented Europe's division into Communist and non-Communist camps. In 1989 several Communist governments were toppled, and the Berlin Wall began to come down.

3 **The extravagant Opéra Garnier,** one of the largest theaters in the world, stands near the center of Paris. Sometimes compared to a gilded wedding cake, this ornate structure was built in the mid-1800s. Originally an opera house, it now features mostly ballet.

4 **A young Basque boy** dons his father's cap and will carry on the elder's ethnic traditions. Three million Basques inhabit a wedge-shaped homeland that straddles the border between France and Spain. Basques speak an ancient tongue that is unrelated to any other known language.

Unit 4 259

UNIT PROJECT

Cultural Artifacts At the beginning of the unit, tell students to pick one country and research its distinctive cultural and physical characteristics. For example, the guitar evolved to its present form in Spain, and Spaniards have had a long affinity for flamenco music and dance. Throughout the country you will find Moorish influences in art and architecture. Ask students to enhance their research reports with illustrations or photos. Emphasize that although there are many common characteristics among European countries, there are also distinct differences. 📦 🌐 **EE4 Human Systems: Standard 10**

These features and activities may be used as an introduction to the unit or as teaching tools throughout the course of the unit.

L2 Region

Remind students that Europe's boundaries extend from the Arctic Circle to just north of Africa. Ask them to make geographic comparisons—including political, social, economic, and environmental changes—between the northern, central, and southern European countries.

The Roma, also known as Gypsies, are a traditionally nomadic people who have lived in Europe for about 500 years. Today, about 8 million Roma live in Europe, primarily in the Balkans, central Europe, and Russia. Over the centuries, the Roma have suffered relentless persecution. During World War II, about 500,000 Roma died in Nazi concentration camps.

Elevation Profile

In order to show a variety of physical features, this cross section begins at Lisbon and goes northeast through the Pyrenees to the Alps, crossing through Mont Blanc. From there, it continues northeast to the North European Plain, passing through Switzerland, southern Germany, the Czech Republic, and Poland, ending in Warsaw.

Europe

PHYSICAL

Lambert Azimuthal Equal-Area projection

Elevation Profile

8,000 m		26,247 ft
6,000 m	**NORTH EUROPEAN PLAIN**	19,685 ft
4,000 m **PYRENEES** **ALPS**		13,123 ft
2,000 m		6,562 ft
—Lisbon	Sea level Warsaw—	

260

REGIONAL ATLAS ACTIVITY

Student Challenge Arrange the class into small groups. Have each group write five or six questions about Europe's physical geography as challenges to the other students. Tell the groups to write questions that involve asking directions, measuring distances, and knowledge of other details about Europe's physical geography. An example might be: Using the elevation profile, compare the elevations of Lisbon, Portugal, to the Alps. *(The Alps, at over 15,000 feet [4,572 m] above sea level, are more than 30 times higher than Lisbon, at approximately 500 feet [152 m].)* Allow time for groups to write questions and challenge one another. ⬢ **EE1 The World in Spatial Terms: Standard 1**

POLITICAL

Jan Mayen
Nor.

North Cape

ARCTIC CIRCLE

Reykjavík
ICELAND

Faroe Islands
Den.

Shetland
Islands

Rockall
U.K.

Isle of Lewis

Orkney
Islands

Oslo

Stockholm

Helsinki

Tallinn
ESTONIA

ATLANTIC OCEAN

SCOTLAND

Edinburgh

N. IRE.

IRELAND
Dublin

Irish
Sea

UNITED

KINGDOM

WALES

Celtic
Sea

ENGLAND

Land's End

London

DENMARK
Copenhagen

North
Sea

Gotland

LATVIA
Rīga

LITHUANIA

RUSSIA

Vilnius

Minsk

RUSSIA

BELARUS

NETH.
Amsterdam

Hamburg

Berlin

POLAND
Warsaw

Kiev

Donetsk

Brussels

BELG.

GERMANY

UKRAINE

LUX.

Paris

Prague

CZECH REP.

Carpathian Mts.

FRANCE

Munich

LIECH.
Vienna

SLOVAKIA
Bratislava

MOLDOVA

AUSTRIA
Budapest

Chişinău

Odesa

Bern
SWITZ.

HUNGARY

Milan

SLOV.

ROMANIA

Sea of
Azov

Crimea

Bay of
Biscay

Ljubljana

Zagreb

CROATIA

BOSN. &
HERZG.

Belgrade

ROMANIA

Bucharest

Black Sea

Sarajevo

SERB.
&
MONT.

Danube

Balkan Mts.

Europe-Asia
boundary

MONACO

SAN
MARINO

ITALY

PORTUGAL

Lisbon

Madrid

ANDORRA

Corsica
Fr.

KOSOVO

BULGARIA

Sofia

Rome

VATICAN CITY
(Within Rome)

Tirana

Skopje

MACED.

TURKEY

Barcelona

SPAIN

Naples

ALBANIA

GREECE

Aegean
Sea

GIBRALTAR
U.K.

Balearic Is.
Sp.

Sardinia
It.

Tyrrhenian
Sea

Ionian
Sea

Athens

Sicily

Peloponnésus

Valletta
MALTA

Crete

Rhodes

Nicosia

CYPRUS

Mediterranean Sea

National capital
Major city

0 mi 500
0 km 500
Lambert Azimuthal Equal-Area projection

MAP Study

1. Which European countries border the Black Sea?

2. Which European countries are land-locked, or have no coastline?

L2 A Diverse Continent

Have your students plan an extended summer trip from Europe's Arctic region to the Mediterranean Sea. Ask them to speculate about the languages, climate, and terrain they would encounter on their travels. What kinds of attire and transportation might they find? What kinds of occupations and recreational activities would people be engaged in? What types of architecture would they see?

Hot dogs originated in Germany as frankfurters, or smoked sausages. The American name "hot dog" was adopted during World War I, when many Americans considered it unpatriotic to use German names.

MAP Study

Answers:

1. *Ukraine, Romania, Bulgaria*

2. *Andorra, Austria, Czech Republic, Hungary, Liechtenstein, Luxembourg, Macedonia, San Marino, Slovakia, Switzerland*

Map Skills Practice Location Which European countries border the Baltic Sea? *(Denmark, Germany, Poland, Lithuania, Latvia, Estonia, Finland, Sweden)*

REGIONAL ATLAS ACTIVITY

Influences of the Roman Empire At the height of its power in the A.D. 100s, the Roman Empire ruled over much of Europe and parts of North Africa and Southwest Asia. During this time, the empire's network of roads facilitated the spread of Roman ways and the new religion of Christianity to much of the Mediterranean world. Ask students to think of modern languages that were derived from Latin, the language of Rome (Romance languages such as Spanish, Italian, French, Romanian, and Portuguese), and where those languages are now spoken—in Europe and around the world. *(See "Country Profiles.")* **Ask:** What effects did Christianity have on Europe and the world? *(arts and learning; political, religious and social beliefs; societal unity and division)* 🌐 **EE4 Human Systems: Standard 10**

Europe

These features and activities may be used as an introduction to the unit or as teaching tools throughout the course of the unit.

L1 Population Density

Have students look at the population density map and its key. Ask students to identify which countries have cities of at least 2 million people. *(the United Kingdom, Spain, France, Italy, Greece, Germany, Poland, Austria, Hungary, Romania, and Ukraine)* Which countries have the greatest number of cities with more than 2 million people? *(Spain, Italy, Germany, Ukraine)* Which countries do not have any cities of at least 250,000 people? *(Iceland, Macedonia, Slovenia, Liechtenstein, Monaco, Andorra, Luxembourg, San Marino, Vatican City, Moldova)*

L2 Place

Remind students that Europe has a much greater population density than does the United States. Ask students to consider how population density might affect an individual's quality of life—environmentally, economically, and socially. Ask them to consider the benefits as well as the drawbacks of large concentrations of people.

Olives and olive oil are two of Italy's chief agricultural products. Italy's variety of climatic conditions allows for the cultivation of many different fruits, vegetables, and grains.

POPULATION DENSITY

Per sq. km	Per sq. mi.
Over 100	Over 250
50–100	125–250
25–50	60–125
1–25	2–60
Under 1	Under 2
Uninhabited	Uninhabited

Cities
(Statistics reflect metropolitan areas.)

■ Over 5,000,000
□ 2,000,000–5,000,000
◉ 1,000,000–2,000,000
● 250,000–1,000,000
○ Under 250,000

Reykjavík

ARCTIC CIRCLE

MERIDIAN OF GREENWICH (LONDON)

Norwegian Sea

Faroe Islands Den.

ATLANTIC OCEAN

Glasgow
Belfast
Dublin
Manchester
Birmingham
London

Celtic Sea

Oslo
Stockholm
Göteborg
Copenhagen
Amsterdam
Hamburg
Brussels
Cologne
Paris
Frankfurt

North Sea

Helsinki
Tallinn
Rīga
Vilnius
Minsk

Gulf of Bothnia

Baltic Sea

RUSSIA

Bay of Biscay

Munich
Zurich
Lyon
Turin
Milan
Genoa

Prague
Vienna
Bratislava
Budapest
Zagreb
Venice

Kraków
Lviv
Kiev
Kharkiv
Donetsk
Dnipropetrovsk
Odesa

Warsaw
Gdańsk
Berlin

Porto
Lisbon
Madrid
Valencia
Seville
Barcelona

Marseille
Nice
Corsica Fr.
Rome
Naples
Palermo

Belgrade
Sarajevo
Bucharest
Sofia
Tirana
Salonica
Athens

Black Sea

Strait of Gibraltar
Balearic Is. Sp.
Sardinia It.
Mediterranean Sea
Sicily
Ionian Sea
Crete
Rhodes
Nicosia
Cyprus

Adriatic Sea

AFRICA

0 mi. 500
0 km 500
Lambert Azimuthal Equal-Area projection

REGIONAL ATLAS ACTIVITY

People and Places Organize the class into small groups of three or four students each. Assign a European country to each group. Have the groups study physical, population density, and economic activity maps. Have each group create a two-column chart with the headers *Physical Features* and *Economic Activities.* The students should list possible reasons under these categories for their country's high or low population density. Ask students to explain why they think certain regions of a country are densely populated while others are sparsely inhabited. Students should consider such features as terrain, climate, and natural resources. ⊛ **EE4 Human Systems: Standard 12**

ECONOMIC ACTIVITY

Resources

- 🐖 Coal
- ⚡ Iron ore
- ⚗ Petroleum
- ✣ Bauxite
- ⬭ Copper
- ♉ Lead
- ⊡ Zinc
- ◰ Silver
- ✳ Uranium
- ⬘ Phosphate
- ◉ Nickel
- ◊ Natural gas
- ⟲ Manganese

Land Use

- Commercial farming
- Subsistence farming
- Nomadic herding
- Forests
- Manufacturing and trade
- Commercial fishing
- Little or no activity

MAP Study

1. Which European countries appear to have the highest population densities?

2. Describe the relationship between coal deposits and population density in Europe.

L3 Standards of Living

Northern European countries (such as Germany, Denmark, and the United Kingdom) generally have a higher standard of living (measured by gross domestic product, jobs, housing, education) than southern European countries (such as Greece, Portugal, Albania). Ask students to discuss how natural resources, climate, and geographic location may have contributed to this discrepancy between the north and the south.

MAP Study

Answers:

1. Belgium, Czech Republic, Germany, Italy, Liechtenstein, the Netherlands, Poland, San Marino, Switzerland, Ukraine, United Kingdom

2. Regions with significant coal resources, such as the United Kingdom, Czech Republic, Belgium, and Germany, offered a ready source of power for factories, businesses and homes. After the Industrial Revolution, when jobs in manufacturing increased dramatically in Europe, towns and cities in these areas grew in both size and population.

Map Skills Practice
Place In which European countries are olives grown? (Spain, France, Italy, Greece)

REGIONAL ATLAS ACTIVITY

Natural Resources and geographic location profoundly affect a country's economy—particularly its imports and exports. Organize the class into small groups and assign each group a country. Ask students to identify their country's resources and list the kinds of products that country would be most likely to export and import. For example, northern countries (Finland) and island countries (Iceland, the United Kingdom) need to import some food products. At the same time, Finland—with its vast forests—exports paper products, Iceland exports fish, and the United Kingdom—rich in coal and a leader in industry—exports manufactured goods. 🌐 **EE5 Environment and Society: Standard 16**

These features and activities may be used as an introduction to the unit or as teaching tools throughout the course of the unit.

INTERDISCIPLINARY
connection

HISTORY The Vikings, originally from the region now known as Scandinavia, were among Europe's earliest explorers. Adventurous and at times brutal, the Vikings sailed from their homelands from about A.D. 800 to 1100 in long, narrow galleys—single-masted boats propelled by sails and oarsmen—to raid or trade with European coastal villages and build settlements. The Danish Vikings went south toward Germany and Spain and into areas on the northwestern Mediterranean coast. Swedish Vikings went to eastern Europe, and Norwegian Vikings sailed to Greenland and North America.

Europe

COUNTRY PROFILES

COUNTRY * AND CAPITAL	FLAG AND LANGUAGE	POPULATION** AND DENSITY	LANDMASS	MAJOR EXPORT	MAJOR IMPORT	CURRENCY	GOVERNMENT
ALBANIA — Tirana	Albanian	3,100,000 282 per sq.mi. 109 per sq.km	11,100 sq.mi. 28,749 sq.km	Asphalt	Machinery	Lek	Republic
ANDORRA — Andorra la Vella	Catalan, French, Spanish	100,000 578 per sq.mi. 222 per sq.km	174 sq.mi. 451 sq.km	Electricity	Manufactured Goods	Euro	Parliamentary Democracy
AUSTRIA — Vienna	German	8,200,000 252 per sq.mi. 97 per sq.km	32,378 sq.mi. 83,859 sq.km	Machinery	Petroleum	Euro	Federal Republic
BELARUS — Minsk	Belarussian, Russian	9,900,000 123 per sq.mi. 47 per sq.km	80,154 sq.mi. 207,599 sq.km	Machinery	Fuels	Belarussian Ruble	Republic
BELGIUM — Brussels	Flemish, French	10,400,000 881 per sq.mi. 340 per sq.km	11,787 sq.mi. 30,528 sq.km	Iron and Steel	Fuels	Euro	Constitutional Monarchy
BOSNIA AND HERZEGOVINA — Sarajevo	Serbo-Croatian	3,900,000 197 per sq.mi. 76 per sq.km	19,741 sq.mi. 51,129 sq.km	N/A	N/A	Convertible Mark	Republic
BULGARIA — Sofia	Bulgarian	7,500,000 176 per sq.mi. 68 per sq.km	42,822 sq.mi. 110,909 sq.km	Machinery	Fuels	Lev	Republic
CROATIA — Zagreb	Serbo-Croatian	4,300,000 196 per sq.mi. 76 per sq.km	21,830 sq.mi. 56,540 sq.km	Transport Equipment	Machinery	Kuna	Republic
CYPRUS — Nicosia	Greek, Turkish	900,000 262 per sq.mi. 101 per sq.km	3,571 sq.mi. 9,249 sq.km	Citrus Fruits	Manufactured Goods	Cyprus Pound	Republic
CZECH REPUBLIC — Prague	Czech, Slovak	10,200,000 334 per sq.mi. 129 per sq.km	30,448 sq.mi. 78,860 sq.km	Machinery	Crude Oil	Koruna	Republic
DENMARK — Copenhagen	Danish	5,400,000 324 per sq.mi. 125 per sq.km	16,637 sq.mi. 43,090 sq.km	Machinery	Machinery	Krone	Constitutional Monarchy

*COUNTRIES AND FLAGS NOT DRAWN TO SCALE   **POPULATIONS ARE ROUNDED, SOURCE: 2003 WORLD POPULATION DATA SHEET

COUNTRY PROFILE ACTIVITY

National Economies The countries of Europe are prosperous compared to most other countries in the world. There are, however, some major economic differences among many of the European countries. Assign a country to each student in the class. Ask your students to do an economic assessment of their designated countries. Encourage students to consult encyclopedias, almanacs, atlases, magazines, and the Internet. Students should focus on gross domestic product, per capita income, industries, trade, arable land, transportation, communications, health and life expectancy, literacy rate, education, and natural resources. ⊕ **EE4 Human Systems: Standard 11**

COUNTRY * AND CAPITAL	FLAG AND LANGUAGE	POPULATION** AND DENSITY	LANDMASS	MAJOR EXPORT	MAJOR IMPORT	CURRENCY	GOVERNMENT
ESTONIA Tallinn	Estonian	1,400,000 78 per sq.mi. 30 per sq.km	17,413 sq.mi. 45,100 sq.km	Textiles	Machinery	Kroon	Republic
FINLAND Helsinki	Finnish, Swedish	5,200,000 40 per sq.mi. 15 per sq.km	130,560 sq.mi. 338,150 sq.km	Paper	Foods	Euro	Republic
FRANCE Paris	French	59,800,000 281 per sq.mi. 109 per sq.km	212,934 sq.mi. 551,499 sq.km	Machinery	Crude Oil	Euro	Republic
GERMANY Berlin	German	82,600,000 599 per sq.mi. 231 per sq.km	137,830 sq.mi. 356,980 sq.km	Machinery	Machinery	Euro	Federal Republic
GREECE Athens	Greek	11,000,000 216 per sq.mi. 83 per sq.km	50,950 sq.mi. 131,961 sq.km	Foods	Machinery	Euro	Republic
HUNGARY Budapest	Hungarian	10,000,000 282 per sq.mi. 109 per sq.km	35,919 sq.mi. 93,030 sq.km	Machinery	Crude Oil	Forint	Republic
ICELAND Reykjavík	Icelandic	300,000 7 per sq.mi. 3 per sq.km	39,768 sq.mi. 102,999 sq.km	Fish	Machinery	Icelandic Króna	Republic
IRELAND Dublin	English, Irish Gaelic	4,000,000 147 per sq.mi. 57 per sq.km	27,135 sq.mi. 70,280 sq.km	Chemicals	Foods	Euro	Republic
ITALY Rome	Italian	57,200,000 491 per sq.mi. 190 per sq.km	116,320 sq.mi. 301,269 sq.km	Metals	Machinery	Euro	Republic
LATVIA Riga	Latvian, Russian	2,300,000 93 per sq.mi. 36 per sq.km	24,942 sq.mi. 64,600 sq.km	Wood	Fuels	Lat	Republic
LIECHTENSTEIN Vaduz	German	40,000 567 per sq.mi. 219 per sq.km	62 sq.mi. 161 sq.km	Machinery	Machinery	Swiss Franc	Constitutional Monarchy

* COUNTRIES AND FLAGS NOT DRAWN TO SCALE **POPULATIONS ARE ROUNDED, *SOURCE: 2003 WORLD POPULATION DATA SHEET*

FOR AN ONLINE UPDATE OF THIS INFORMATION, VISIT GEOGRAPHY.GLENCOE.COM AND CLICK ON "TEXTBOOK UPDATES."

L2 Size and Population

Some European countries are similar in size but vastly different in population (for example, Poland and Norway). Others are similar in both size and population (for example, Austria and the Czech Republic). Have students find four countries that match the above criteria (similar in size, different in population; similar both ways), and then ask them to discuss what geographic factors may have contributed to those conditions.

□ NATIONAL GEOGRAPHIC **GEOFACT**

▶ **The Isles of Scilly [SIH•lee], part of the British Isles, are located 28 miles from the southwestern tip of England. Although the islands are situated at 50 degrees north latitude, about the same latitude as Newfoundland, they are warmed by the Gulf Stream. Flowers bloom in January, giving the islands a thriving winter flower industry.**

Culture NOTE

Finland is one of the world's cleanest countries. Helsinki, the capital, is called the White City of the North because of its cleanliness and its buildings of native white granite.

COUNTRY PROFILE ACTIVITY

Cultural Legacies Throughout Europe, a traveler will encounter hundreds of ruins—the remnants of once-great civilizations, kingdoms, and empires. There is ample evidence that many ancient cultures across Europe were inventive and technologically advanced. Ask students to choose the people of an ancient culture—the Moors, Celts, Vikings, Greeks, or Romans, for example—and report on a particular structure that is typical of that culture's technical and artistic expertise. Examples include the Alhambra in Granada, Spain, built by the Moors; the Viking ships, on display in Oslo, Norway; and the Colosseum in Rome, Italy. Students should use a variety of sources, including the Internet, and illustrate their presentation with drawings or photographs, if possible. 🖫 **EE4 Human Systems: Standard 10**

Europe

▶ More than half of the world's population speaks one of just ten major languages: Mandarin Chinese, Hindi, Spanish, English, Arabic, Bengali, Russian, Portuguese, Malay, or French. Twenty to 50 percent of the world's six thousand languages are in danger of being lost as the number of native speakers declines.

INTERDISCIPLINARY
connection

HISTORY In the A.D. 700s, the Moors—North African Islamic peoples of mixed ethnicity—conquered regions of Spain and Portugal. From their headquarters in Cordoba and Granada, Spain, they made advances in mathematics and architecture throughout the Iberian Peninsula. The Moors were driven from Spain in 1492, the same year Christopher Columbus completed his first explorations of the Bahamas and Cuba.

COUNTRY PROFILES

COUNTRY * AND CAPITAL	FLAG AND LANGUAGE	POPULATION** AND DENSITY	LANDMASS	MAJOR EXPORT	MAJOR IMPORT	CURRENCY	GOVERNMENT
LITHUANIA Vilnius	Lithuanian, Polish, Russian	3,500,000 137 per sq.mi. 53 per sq.km	25,174 sq.mi. 65,201 sq.km	Foods and Livestock	Minerals	Litas	Republic
LUXEMBOURG Luxembourg	Luxembourgian, German, French	500,000 452 per sq.mi. 175 per sq.km	999 sq.mi. 2,587 sq.km	Steel Products	Minerals	Euro	Constitutional Monarchy
MACEDONIA Skopje	Macedonian, Albanian	2,100,000 207 per sq.mi. 80 per sq.km	9,927 sq.mi. 25,711 sq.km	Manufactured Goods	Fuels	Denar	Republic
MALTA Valletta	Maltese, English	400,000 3,205 per sq.mi. 1,237 per sq.km	124 sq.mi. 321 sq.km	Machinery	Foods	Maltese Lira	Republic
MOLDOVA Chişinău	Moldovan, Russian	4,300,000 327 per sq.mi. 128 per sq.km	13,012 sq.mi. 33,701 sq.km	Foods	Petroleum	Moldovan Leu	Republic
MONACO Monaco	French	30,000 45,333 per sq.mi. 11,503 per sq.km	1 sq.mi. 2.6 sq.km	N/A	N/A	Euro	Constitutional Monarchy
NETHERLANDS Amsterdam	Dutch	16,200,000 1,030 per sq.mi. 398 per sq.km	15,768 sq.mi. 40,839 sq.km	Manufactured Goods	Raw Materials	Euro	Constitutional Monarchy
NORWAY Oslo	Norwegian	4,600,000 37 per sq.mi. 14 per sq.km	125,050 sq.mi. 323,880 sq.km	Petroleum	Machinery	Krone	Constitutional Monarchy
POLAND Warsaw	Polish	38,600,000 309 per sq.mi. 119 per sq.km	124,807 sq.mi. 323,250 sq.km	Manufactured Goods	Machinery	Zloty	Republic
PORTUGAL Lisbon	Portuguese	10,400,000 294 per sq.mi. 114 per sq.km	35,514 sq.mi. 91,981 sq.km	Clothing	Machinery	Euro	Republic

*COUNTRIES AND FLAGS NOT DRAWN TO SCALE   **POPULATIONS ARE ROUNDED, *SOURCE: 2003 WORLD POPULATION DATA SHEET*

COUNTRY PROFILE ACTIVITY

Musical Heritage Europe has a rich and diverse tradition of music. From the Scottish Highland bagpipers to the Italian opera to the Romany or gypsy fiddlers of Romania and the Balkans, European music has exerted a powerful influence on the world. Ask students to choose a country or region and research one of its distinctive kinds of music. Their reports should include the origins of the musical style and the kind(s) of instruments used in performances. Ask students to enhance their reports by bringing in a tape or CD of the music, or by playing a brief sample of a melody. *(See also* Glencoe's *World Music: A Cultural Legacy.)* 🌐 **EE4 Human Systems: Standard 10**

COUNTRY * AND CAPITAL	FLAG AND LANGUAGE	POPULATION** AND DENSITY	LANDMASS	MAJOR EXPORT	MAJOR IMPORT	CURRENCY	GOVERNMENT
ROMANIA Bucharest	Romanian, Hungarian	21,600,000 235 per sq.mi. 91 per sq.km	92,042 sq.mi. 238,389 sq.km	Textiles	Fuels	Leu	Republic
SAN MARINO San Marino	Italian	30,000 1,295 per sq.mi. 500 per sq.km	23 sq.mi. 60 sq.km	Building Stone	Manufactured Goods	Euro	Republic
SERBIA AND MONTENEGRO Belgrade	Serbo-Croatian, Albanian	10,700,000 271 per sq.mi. 105 per sq.km	39,448 sq.mi. 102,170 sq.km	Manufactured Goods	Machinery	Dinar, Euro	Republic
SLOVAKIA Bratislava	Slovak, Hungarian	5,400,000 283 per sq.mi. 110 per sq.km	18,923 sq.mi. 49,011 sq.km	Transport Equipment	Machinery	Koruna	Republic
SLOVENIA Ljubljana	Slovene, Serbo-Croatian	2,100,000 256 per sq.mi. 99 per sq.km	7,819 sq.mi. 20,251 sq.km	Transport Equipment	Machinery	Slovenian Tolar	Republic
SPAIN Madrid	Spanish, Catalan, Galician, Basque	41,300,000 212 per sq.mi. 82 per sq.km	195,363 sq.mi. 505,990 sq.km	Cars and Trucks	Machinery	Euro	Constitutional Monarchy
SWEDEN Stockholm	Swedish	9,000,000 52 per sq.mi. 20 per sq.km	173,730 sq.mi. 449,961 sq.km	Paper Products	Crude Oil	Krona	Constitutional Monarchy
SWITZERLAND Bern	German, French, Italian	7,300,000 460 per sq.mi. 178 per sq.km	15,942 sq.mi. 41,290 sq.km	Precision Instruments	Machinery	Swiss Franc	Federal Republic
UKRAINE Kiev	Ukrainian, Russian	47,810,000 205 per sq.mi. 79 per sq.km	233,089 sq.mi. 603,701 sq.km	Metals	Machinery	Hryvnya	Republic
UNITED KINGDOM London	English, Welsh, Scottish Gaelic	59,200,000 626 per sq.mi. 242 per sq.km	94,548 sq.mi. 244,879 sq.km	Manufactured Goods	Foods	Pound Sterling	Constitutional Monarchy
VATICAN CITY	Italian, Latin	1,000	0.2 sq.mi. 0.4 sq.km	N/A	N/A	Euro	Sovereign State Under the Pope

*COUNTRIES AND FLAGS NOT DRAWN TO SCALE   **POPULATIONS ARE ROUNDED, SOURCE: 2003 WORLD POPULATION DATA SHEET

FOR AN ONLINE UPDATE OF THIS INFORMATION, VISIT GEOGRAPHY.GLENCOE.COM AND CLICK ON "TEXTBOOK UPDATES."

L2 Comparing

Have students investigate and compare the various kinds of governments in Europe. Ask them to select European countries as examples of each of the following kinds of government: Republic, Federal Republic, and Constitutional Monarchy.

Monaco, an independent principality, is one of the most densely populated places in the world. The country is less than one square mile in area—smaller than New York City's Central Park—and has a population density of 30,000 people per square mile (11,539 people per sq. km).

Lapland This Arctic region encompasses about 150,000 square miles (388,500 sq. km) of Finland, Sweden, Norway, and Russia. The Sami people—also known as Lapps—rely on reindeer herding for much of their livelihood. In recent years their reindeer herds have become the prey of many protected species, such as the lynx, brown bear, and wolverine.

COUNTRY PROFILE ACTIVITY

Exotic Locales Although Europe is an industrialized and densely populated region, a journey across it will also reveal some of the world's most beautiful landscapes. From Portugal's Atlantic seacoast to Germany's Black Forest to Greece's sun-drenched islands, Europe offers hundreds of miles of intriguing landscapes for the adventurous traveler. Ask students to select a region of Europe and write a travelogue on a short excursion, such as an overland trek or a trip by bike, kayak, sailboat, or canoe, focusing on the route they take and the various environments they encounter on their excursion. Encourage students to consult magazines, books, and the Internet. 🎲   🌐 EE3 Physical Systems: Standard 8

1 FOCUS

Ask students if they have seen or visited any buildings or houses that have a distinctly European architectural style. **Ask: What details did you notice that indicated European designs and materials? What differed from what you might find in an American structure?**

2 TEACH

European Influences The ancient Greeks and Romans had profound influences on architecture in Europe. Other peoples also made contributions. For example, the Vikings built longhouses, and the Moors constructed palaces such as the Alhambra in Spain. Ask students to compare two types of European architecture: one classical style and the other reflecting another influence. Students need not compare entire structures—a roof, window, or other feature can be used as examples of the similarities and differences.

Meeting National Standards

Geography for Life

The following standards are met in the Student Edition:

EE2 Places and Regions:
    Standard 4
EE4 Human Systems:
    Standards 9, 10, 11, 12
EE6 The Uses of Geography:
    Standard 17

GLOBAL CONNECTION

EUROPE AND THE UNITED STATES

ARCHITECTURE

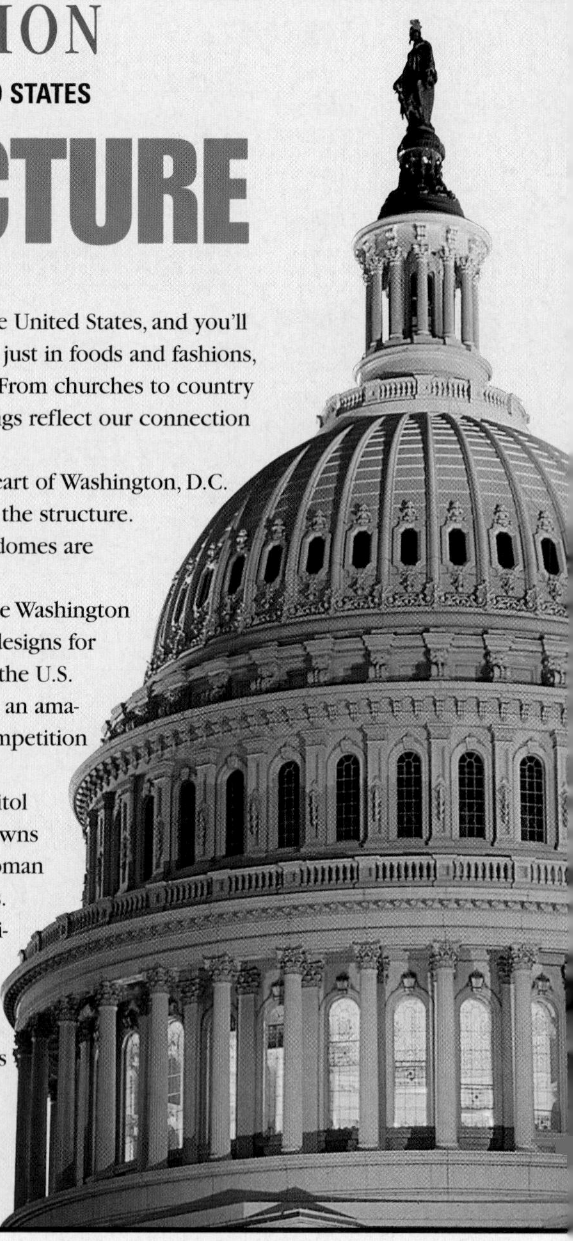

Wander through any city in the United States, and you'll see European influences—not just in foods and fashions, but in brick, wood, and stone. From churches to country homes, many American buildings reflect our connection to European cultures.

The Capitol is a national landmark in the heart of Washington, D.C. Its great dome, or large arched roof, dominates the structure. Roman architects favored arching shapes, and domes are their legacy.

In 1792 President George Washington asked architects to submit designs for a "federal Capitol" to house the U.S. Congress. William Thornton, an amateur draftsman, won the competition with a neo-Roman design. Thornton modeled the Capitol dome after the one that crowns the Pantheon, an ancient Roman temple built in the A.D. 100s.

The Gothic style of architecture originated in France in the 1100s and became the style of choice for cathedrals. Gothic cathedrals are huge and soaring, with

▲ Queen Anne house in Washington State

BACKGROUND INFORMATION

Classical Design: Architecture The ancient Greeks had an important influence on the development of one of the most crucial architectural components: the column. Columns were designed for ornamental or decorative purposes and to support roofs and enable the thickness of walls to be reduced. The Greeks developed three types of columns: the Doric, the Ionic, and the Corinthian. The simplest design was the Doric, which had a wide shaft, no base, and a simple top, called the capital. The Ionic column had a simple base, narrower shaft, and spiral-shaped capitals. The most complex and elaborate column—as seen in the picture above of the U.S. Capitol in Washington, D.C.—was the Corinthian, with its multileveled base and decorative capital.   ⬛ EE4 Human Systems: Standard 12

▲ Interior of Pantheon, in Rome

pointed arches, large stained glass windows, and towers and spires that seem to point toward heaven. Such cathedrals were built across western Europe during the Middle Ages.

Hundreds of years later, American architect James Renwick designed St. Patrick's Cathedral, which was built in New York City starting in 1858. It is considered one of the best examples of Gothic architecture in the United States. True to the Gothic style, the cathedral has pointed arches, stained glass windows, and a pair of enormous towers.

The Queen Anne style developed in England in the 1860s and 1870s. Queen Anne buildings tend to be asymmetrical and quirky, with prominent chimneys, steep roofs, dormer windows, and corner turrets jutting out. Ornamental details such as fancy brickwork and contrasting trim help give Queen Anne buildings their characteristic look.

Queen Anne houses became popular throughout the United States in the late 1800s. You probably wouldn't have to travel far to see a Queen Anne house. There might even be one in your neighborhood.

◄ Dome of U.S. Capitol

▲ St. Patrick's Cathedral

③ ASSESS

Have students brainstorm and list any notable building styles in the United States that have their origins in Europe, such as Classical, Gothic, and Queen Anne. Encourage students to consider subtle features—windows, doors, and arches—when they think about these structures. Remind them to consider different parts of the United States. **Ask: Why do you think different architectural styles developed in various regions of the world?**

④ CLOSE

Ask each student to choose a European style of architecture and discuss the geographic factors—for example, climate, terrain, or available natural resources—that may have influenced its design.

CONNECTION ACTIVITY

Functional Architecture While European architectural influences are evident in American cathedrals, museums, and government buildings, European design has also influenced the way homes, barns, and other outbuildings have been constructed. Throughout the United States, you can see A-framed chalets, log cabins, cottages, adobe bungalows, and Amish barns—all of which have a historic architectural link to Europe. Ask each of your students to research a building based on European design that interests them. Have students write a two-page report about the structure's origin, the type of resources needed to produce it, the building's uses, and any other interesting facts, including how the design has evolved over the centuries. ▩ **EE4 Human Systems: Standards 10, 12**

PLANNING GUIDE

NOTE: The following materials may be used when teaching Chapter 11. Section-level support materials are shown at point-of-use in the margins of the Teacher Wraparound Edition.

TEACHING TRANSPARENCIES

L2 Unit 4 Map Overlay Transparencies

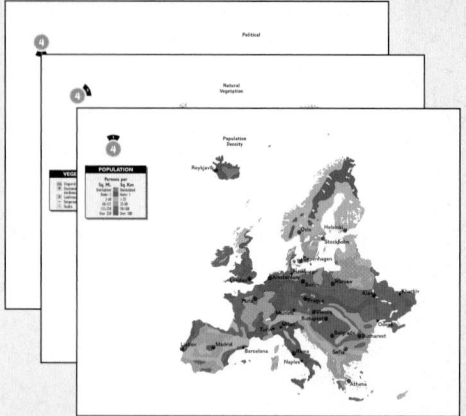

L2 Political Map Transparency 4

GEOGRAPHIC LITERACY

Focus on Geography Literacy

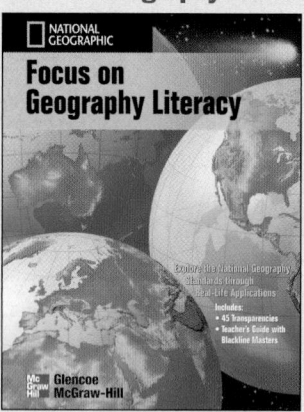

APPLICATION AND ENRICHMENT

L3 Enrichment Activity 11

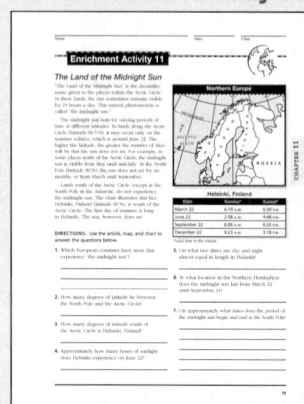

REVIEW AND REINFORCEMENT

L1 Vocabulary Activity 11 L1 Reinforcing L1 Reteaching Activity 11
Skills Activity 11

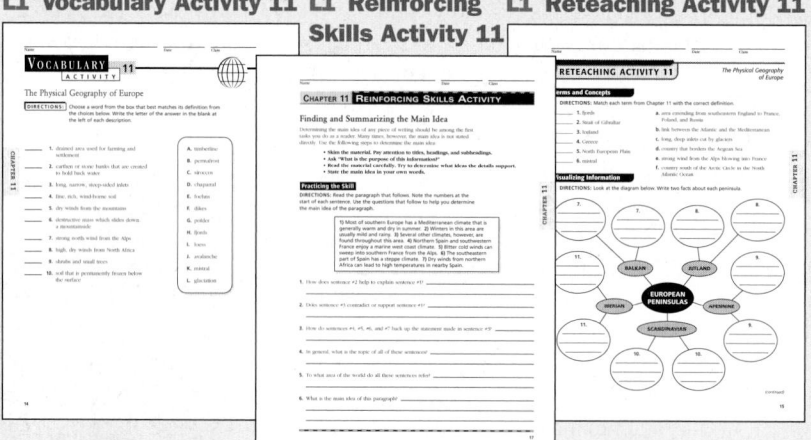

ASSESSMENT

L2 Chapter 11 Test Form A

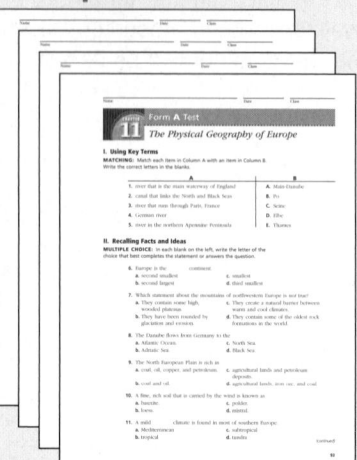

L2 Chapter 11 Test Form B

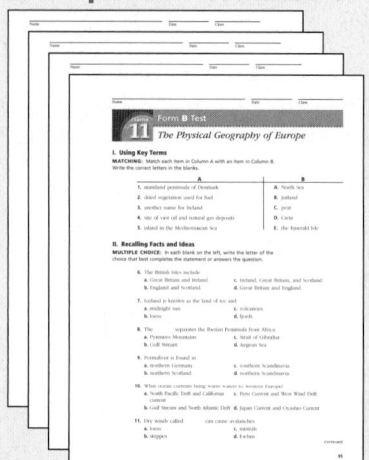

L1/ELL Performance Assessment Activity 11

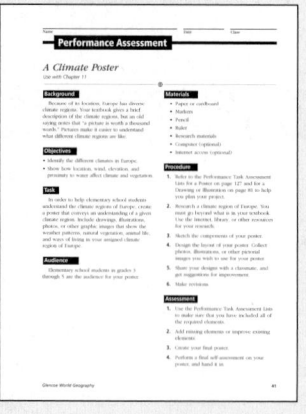

ExamView® Pro Testmaker

SPANISH RESOURCES

The following Spanish language materials are available in the Spanish Resources binder:

- 📁 Spanish Vocabulary Activities
- 📁 Spanish Guided Reading Activities
- 📁 Spanish Reteaching Activities
- 📁 Spanish Summaries
- 📁 Spanish Quizzes and Tests
- 📁 Spanish Reading Essentials and Study Guide

MULTIMEDIA

- 📽 World Regions Video
- 📽 MindJogger Videoquiz
- 💿 Vocabulary PuzzleMaker CD-ROM
- 💿 Interactive Tutor Self-Assessment CD-ROM
- 💿 ExamView® Pro Testmaker CD-ROM
- 💿 Audio Program
- 💿 TeacherWorks CD-ROM
- 💿 Interactive Student Edition CD-ROM
- 💿 Glencoe Skillbuilder Interactive Workbook CD-ROM, Level 2
- 💿 Presentation Plus! CD-ROM

Timesaving Tools

TeacherWorks™ — All-In-One Planner and Resource Center

- **Interactive Teacher Edition** Access your Teacher Wraparound Edition and your classroom resources with a few easy clicks.

- **Interactive Lesson Planner** Planning has never been easier! Organize your week, month, semester, or year with all the lesson helps you need to make teaching creative, timely, and relevant.

Use Glencoe's **Presentation Plus!** multimedia teacher tool to easily present dynamic lessons that visually excite your students. Using Microsoft PowerPoint® you can customize the presentations to create your own personalized lessons.

GEOGRAPHY Online

Use our Web site for additional resources. All essential content is covered in the Student Edition.

You and your students can visit geography.glencoe.com, the Web site companion to *Glencoe World Geography*. This innovative integration of electronic and print media offers your students a wealth of opportunities. The student text directs students to the Web site for the following options:

- Chapter Overviews
- Student Activities
- Self-Check Quizzes
- Textbook Updates

Answers are provided for you in the "Web Activity Lesson Plan." Additional Web resources and Interactive Tutor puzzles are also available.

▶ Additional Glencoe Teacher Support

- Teaching Strategies for the Geography Classroom (including Block Scheduling Pacing Guides)

- Graphic Organizer Transparencies Strategies and Activities

- Outline Map Resource Book

- Reading in the Content Area

CHAPTER 11 PLANNING GUIDE

SECTION RESOURCES

Daily Objectives	Reproducible Resources	Multimedia Resources

SECTION 1 The Land

1. Explain why Europe is sometimes called a "peninsula of peninsulas."
2. Identify some of the numerous islands surrounding the continent of Europe.
3. Reinforce the importance of rivers to Europe's economy.
4. Discuss some of Europe's most important natural resources.

Reproducible Resources:
- Reproducible Lesson Plan 11-1
- Daily Lecture Notes 11-1
- Guided Reading Activity 11-1*
- Reading Essentials and Study Guide 11-1*
- Section Quiz 11-1*

Multimedia Resources:
- Daily Focus Skills Transparency 11-1
- Political Map Transparency 4
- Unit 4 Map Overlay Transparencies
- Interactive Tutor Self-Assessment CD-ROM
- ExamView® Pro Testmaker CD-ROM*
- Presentation Plus! CD-ROM

SECTION 2 Climate and Vegetation

1. Discuss the climate regions in Europe.
2. Describe the physical features that influence Europe's climate.
3. Explain why most of Europe's original forests are gone.

Reproducible Resources:
- Reproducible Lesson Plan 11-2
- Vocabulary Activity 11*
- Daily Lecture Notes 11-2
- Guided Reading Activity 11-2*
- Reading Essentials and Study Guide 11-2*
- Reteaching Activity 11*
- Reinforcing Skills Activity 11
- Section Quiz 11-2*

Multimedia Resources:
- Daily Focus Skills Transparency 11-2
- Political Map Transparency 4
- Unit 4 Map Overlay Transparencies
- Vocabulary PuzzleMaker CD-ROM
- Interactive Tutor Self-Assessment CD-ROM
- ExamView® Pro Testmaker CD-ROM*
- Presentation Plus! CD-ROM

 Blackline Master   Software   Videocassette

Transparency   CD–ROM   DVD

Also available in Spanish

00:00 OUT OF TIME? Assign the Chapter 11 **Reading Essentials and Study Guide.**

Block Schedule

Activities that are particularly suited to use within the block scheduling framework are identified throughout this chapter by the following designation:

KEY TO ABILITY LEVELS

Teaching strategies have been coded for various learning styles and abilities.

L1   **BASIC** activities for all students

L2   **AVERAGE** activities for average to above-average students

L3   **CHALLENGING** activities for above-average students

ELL   **ENGLISH LANGUAGE LEARNER** activities

Teacher to Teacher

Susan Dennis
Anacostia Senior
High School
Washington, D.C.

How Climate Affects Europe

Have your students work with the maps in this unit to determine the various climates in Europe. Students can interpret the various colors on the map by studying the map key. Once students establish the region's climate, have them look at a world map to see where else similar climate regions are located. Then lead a class discussion on how climate affects the region. Discuss how climate is related to economic conditions, leisure-time activities, people's clothes, jobs, vegetation, or products that come from this region.

Remind students that precipitation has an important effect on vegetation. Have students graph Europe's precipitation over a year's time and identify seasonal patterns of precipitation to better understand how precipitation as an aspect of climate may affect European ways of life.

NATIONAL GEOGRAPHIC   TEACHER'S CORNER

Index to National Geographic Magazine:

The following article may be used for research relating to this chapter:

- "A History Forged by Disaster," by Rick Gore, July 2000.
- "Earthquake in Turkey," by Rick Gore, July 2000.

National Geographic Society Products:

To order the following products for use with this chapter, call National Geographic Society at 1-800-368-2728.

- *Europe* (Video)
- *Weather: Come Rain, Come Shine* (Video)
- *Europe Political* (Map)
- *National Geographic Desk Reference* (Book)
- *National Geographic Atlas of the World, Seventh Edition* (Book)

NGS ONLINE

Access National Geographic's Web site for current events, activities, links, interactive features, and archives.
www.nationalgeographic.com

Meeting National Standards

Geography For Life

The following standards are highlighted in Chapter 11:

Section 1   EE1 The World in Spatial Terms: Standard 1
EE2 Places and Regions: Standards 4, 5
EE3 Physical Systems: Standard 7
EE4 Human Systems: Standard 9
EE5 Environment and Society: Standard 15

Section 2   EE2 Places and Regions: Standard 5
EE5 Environment and Society: Standard 15

Local Objectives

_____

_____

MEETING SPECIAL NEEDS

In addition to the Differentiated Instruction strategies found in each section, the following resources are also suitable for your special needs students:

- *ExamView® Pro Testmaker CD-ROM* allows teachers to tailor tests by reducing answer choices.
- The *Audio Program* includes the entire narrative of the student edition so that less-proficient readers can listen to the words as they read them.
- The *Reading Essentials and Study Guide* provides the same content as the student edition but is written two grade levels below the textbook.
- *Guided Reading Activities* give less-proficient readers point-by-point instructions to increase comprehension as they read each textbook section.
- *Enrichment Activities* include a stimulating collection of readings and activities for gifted and talented students.

Chapter Objectives

1. Describe the dominant land-forms and natural resources of Europe.

2. Discuss the differences in climate and vegetation throughout Europe.

GLENCOE
TECHNOLOGY

 Use *MindJogger Videoquiz* to preview the Chapter 11 content.

GeoJournal

For access to additional photos, maps, and information on the geographic features of Europe, go to www.nationalgeographic.com (See page Teacher pages in front for strategies for using journals in the geography classroom.)

GEOGRAPHY Online

Introduce students to chapter content and key terms by having them access **Chapter Overview 11** at geography.glencoe.com

FOLDABLES
Study Organizer

Dinah Zike's Foldables are three-dimensional, interactive graphic organizers that help students practice basic writing skills, review key vocabulary terms, and identify main ideas. Have students complete the Foldable activity in the *Dinah Zike's Reading and Study Skills Foldables* booklet.

CHAPTER 11
The Physical Geography of Europe

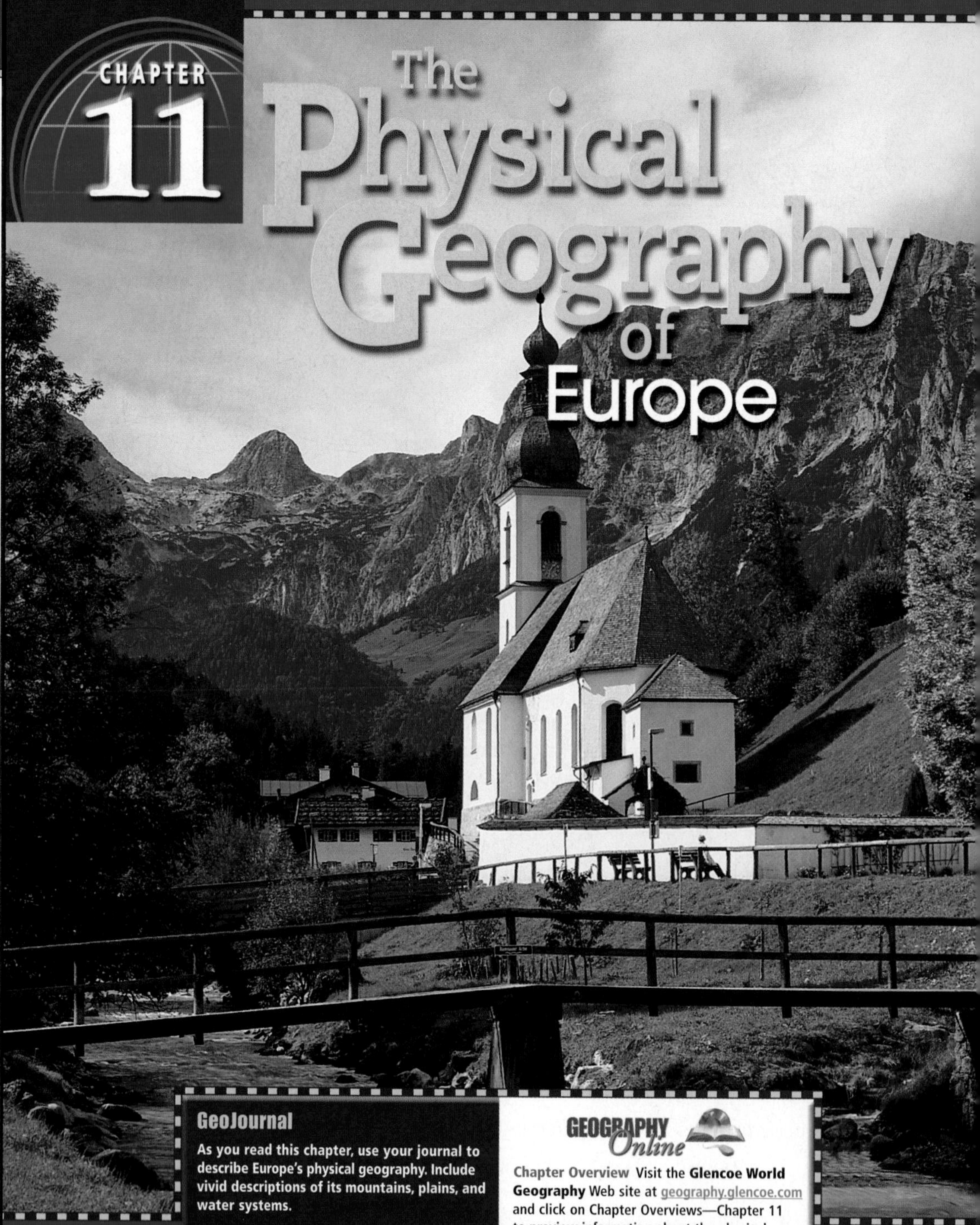

GeoJournal

As you read this chapter, use your journal to describe Europe's physical geography. Include vivid descriptions of its mountains, plains, and water systems.

GEOGRAPHY Online

Chapter Overview Visit the **Glencoe World Geography** Web site at geography.glencoe.com and click on Chapter Overviews—Chapter 11 to preview information about the physical geography of the region.

ABOUT THE PHOTO

Bavarian Alps This baroque church, with its onion tower and ornate interior, is nestled in the Bavarian Alps. Straddling the German-Austrian border, the Bavarian Alps extend east-northeast for 70 miles (110 km). The Bavarian Alps take their name from Bavaria, a large state in southeast Germany. The range's steep wall overlooks the Inn River valley to the south; its north slope, however, is gentler and allows for cattle grazing. Winter sports and tourism are the region's main activities, with a large national park that preserves the area's original Alpine landscape, vegetation, and animal life. Many older residents of the state still consider themselves Bavarians as well as Germans because Bavaria was once an independent kingdom. 🖵 **EE2 Places and Regions: Standard 4**

Guide to Reading

Consider What You Know

References to Europe are often in the news. What physical features come to mind when you think of Europe? What do you know about them?

Reading Strategy

Organizing Complete a web diagram similar to the one below by filling in the natural resources found in Europe.

Natural Resources

Read to Find Out

• Why is Europe sometimes called a "peninsula of peninsulas"?

• What are some of the numerous islands surrounding the continent of Europe?

• Why are rivers vital to Europe's economy?

• What are some of Europe's most important natural resources?

Terms to Know

• dike
• polder
• glaciation
• fjord
• loess

Places to Locate

• North Sea
• Iberian Peninsula
• Balkan Peninsula
• Alps
• Rhine River
• Po River
• North European Plain (Great European Plain)

◀ *Church in the Alps, Bavaria, Germany*

The Land

NATIONAL GEOGRAPHIC

A Geographic View

Fire in Iceland

. . . [O]ne of the largest volcanic eruptions to hit Iceland this century rumbled to life beneath the country's biggest ice cap. For two weeks ash and steam billowed skyward as elemental forces clashed in thermal battle. . . . [A]sh-laden runoff rushed from the eruption site, carving an ice canyon 500 feet deep and more than two miles long.

—Glenn Oeland, "Iceland's Trial by Fire," National Geographic, *May 1997*

Ice canyon, Iceland

Though few natural occurrences are as dramatic as Iceland's volcanic eruptions, physical forces continue to shape the landscape of Europe. In this section you will learn about the variety of Europe's landforms, water systems, and natural resources.

Seas, Peninsulas, and Islands

Unlike the world's other continents, Europe and Asia share a common landmass called Eurasia. Yet Europe, the second smallest of the continents after Australia, is a distinct region. Jutting westward from Asia, Europe has an unusually long, irregular coastline that touches a number of bodies of water, including the Atlantic Ocean and the Baltic, North, Mediterranean, and Black Seas.

History
Struggle With the Sea

Most of Europe lies within 300 miles (483 km) of a seacoast. This closeness to the sea has shaped the lifestyles of its peoples. In the

Chapter 11 🌐 271

Section Overview

This section discusses Europe's important land formations, including its rivers, mountains, plains, islands, and distinctive peninsular features. The section also summarizes some of the continent's important natural resources.

BELLRINGER
Skillbuilder Activity

🖅 Project transparency and have students answer questions.

🗀 Available as blackline master.

Daily Focus Skills Transparency 11-1

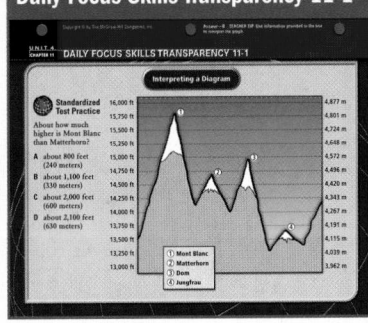

Guide to Reading

Consider What You Know
Answers *Responses may include the Alps or the Danube River, among many others. Associations will vary.*

Reading Strategy
Answers *bauxite, coal, gas, hydroelectric power, iron ore, manganese, oil, zinc*

Preteaching Vocabulary
Ask students to find the meanings of the following words: *fjord, dike, polder,* (page 272); and *loess,* (page 275).

RESOURCE MANAGER

🗀 **Reproducible Masters**
• Reproducible Lesson Plan 11-1
• Daily Lecture Notes 11-1
• Guided Reading Activity 11-1
• Reading Essentials and Study Guide 11-1
• Section Quiz 11-1

🖅 **Transparencies**
• Daily Focus Skills Transparency 11-1
• Political Map Transparency 4
• Unit 4 Map Overlay Transparencies

Multimedia
💿 Interactive Tutor Self-Assessment CD-ROM
💿 ExamView® Pro Testmaker CD-ROM
💿 Presentation Plus! CD-ROM

② TEACH

L1 Identify
Read a brief description of a part of Europe from a guidebook, magazine, newspaper, or novel that conveys a vivid sense of an area the students will study. Ask students to identify the area from the description.

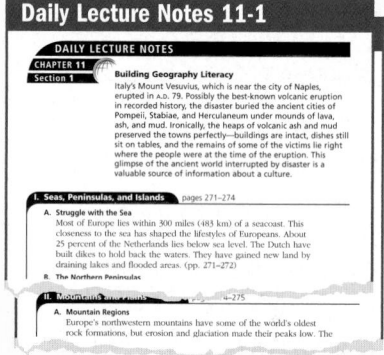

Daily Lecture Notes 11-1

NATIONAL GEOGRAPHIC World Explorer

Answer
Possible answer: Windpower is less dependable than other power sources.

More About the Photo
Although other power sources now pump water from lowlands, windmills have become a world-famous symbol of the Netherlands.

Netherlands, water can be friend or foe. About 25 percent of the Netherlands lies below sea level. Coastal dunes have not always been helpful in keeping out North Sea waters, so the Dutch since the Middle Ages have built dikes, large banks of earth and stone, to hold back water. With the dikes for protection, they have reclaimed new land from the sea. These reclaimed lands, called polders, once were drained and kept dry by the use of windmills. Today, other power sources run pumps to remove seawater. Polders provide hundreds of thousands of acres for farming and settlement. Still, from time to time, stormy seas breach the dikes, creating devastating floods.

The Northern Peninsulas
Europe is a large peninsula made up of smaller peninsulas. In the far north of Europe lies the scenic Scandinavian Peninsula. During the last Ice Age, in a process known as glaciation, glaciers formed and spread over the peninsula. They carved out long, narrow, steep-sided inlets called fjords

NATIONAL GEOGRAPHIC World Explorer

Geography Skills for Life

Dutch Windmills By the 1800s the Dutch had built about 9,000 windmills to pump seawater from low-lying areas.
Place Why do you think the Dutch shifted to other power sources to drain flooded areas?

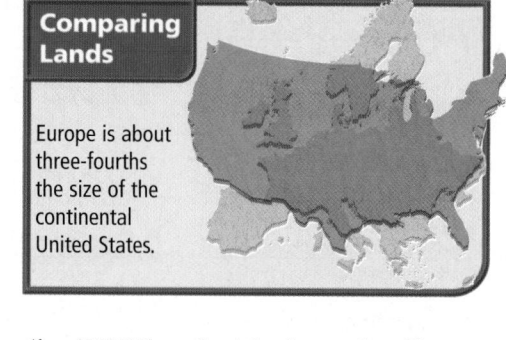

Comparing Lands
Europe is about three-fourths the size of the continental United States.

(fee•AWRDZ) on the Atlantic coastline. The map on page 273 shows Norway's jagged coastal strip, where many fjords provide fine harbors.

Much of Norway and northern Sweden is mountainous, but in southern Sweden, lowlands slope gently to the Baltic Sea. In both countries, and in Finland, Ice Age glaciers left behind thousands of sparkling lakes.

The peninsula of Jutland forms the mainland part of Denmark and extends into the **North Sea** toward Norway and Sweden. Glaciers deposited sand and gravel on Jutland's flat western side and carved fjords into the slightly higher coastline on the east. Flat plains or low hills make up most of Jutland's interior.

The Southern Peninsulas
The **Iberian Peninsula** extends off the southwestern edge of Europe. Home to Spain and Portugal, the peninsula separates the Atlantic Ocean from the Mediterranean Sea. Only 20 miles (32 km) of water at the Strait of Gibraltar, however, separates the peninsula's southern tip from Africa.

Most of the Iberian Peninsula is a semiarid plateau, rising above slender coastal plains. To the north, the Pyrenees (PIHR•uh•NEEZ) Mountains cut off the peninsula from the rest of Europe. Because of this rugged barrier, the people of the Iberian Peninsula until modern times were relatively isolated from the rest of Europe and were oriented toward the sea.

The Apennine (A•puh•NYN) Peninsula, where Italy is located, extends like a giant boot into the Mediterranean Sea. Its long coastline varies from high, rocky cliffs to long, sandy beaches. Forming the peninsula's spine are the Apennines, a geologically young mountain chain that includes an active

---

DIFFERENTIATED INSTRUCTION

Visual/Spatial To highlight some of the distinctive and varied physical features of Europe, bring to class some posters, photographs, or videos that illustrate the continent's valleys, mountains, rivers, coastlines, and forests. Excellent sources are listed in the "Teacher's Corner" on page 270D. Ask students to compare and contrast the physical geography of Europe with that of the United States.
- ⊕ EE1 The World in Spatial Terms: Standard 1
- ⊕ EE2 Places and Regions: Standard 4
- ⊕ EE3 Physical Systems: Standard 7
  - 🗁 Refer to *Inclusion for the Social Studies Classroom Strategies and Activities.*

MAP STUDY

NATIONAL GEOGRAPHIC

Europe: Physical-Political

Elevations

Feet	Meters
10,000	3,000
5,000	1,500
2,000	600
1,000	300
0	0

— National boundary
▲ Mountain peak

20°W

20°E

70°N

ARCTIC CIRCLE

60°N

ICELAND

Faroe Is.

Lapland

Shetland Is.

Orkney Is.

Ben Nevis
4,406 ft.
(1,343 m)

NORWAY

SCANDINAVIA

FINLAND

SWEDEN

Norwegian Sea

ATLANTIC OCEAN

North Sea

DENMARK
Jutland

ESTONIA

LATVIA

LITHUANIA

Baltic Sea

50°N

IRELAND

UNITED KINGDOM

Great Britain

Thames R.

NETH.

BELGIUM

GERMANY

NORTH EUROPEAN PLAIN

POLAND

BELARUS

Elbe R.

Loire R.

Seine R.

LUX.

CZECH REP.

SLOVAKIA

Carpathian Mountains

UKRAINE

Dnieper R.

Vistula R.

Dniester R.

MOLDOVA

Bay of Biscay

FRANCE

L. Geneva

SWITZ.

LIECH.

A L P S

AUSTRIA

HUNGARY

Great Hungarian Plain

ROMANIA

Black Sea

Massif Central

Mt. Blanc
15,771 ft.
(4,807 m)

Po R.

SLOV.

CROATIA

SAN MARINO

BOSN. & HERZG.

SERB. &
MONT.

Danube R.

PORTUGAL

Pyrenees

Ebro R.

MONACO

Corsica

ITALY

Apennines

Adriatic Sea

Balkan Mts.

Balkan Peninsula

BULGARIA

Bosporus

IBERIAN PENINSULA

ANDORRA

Meseta

SPAIN

Sardinia

MACED.

TURKEY

40°N

GIBRALTAR

Balearic Islands

Strait of Gibraltar

Vesuvius
4,190 ft.
(1,277 m)

Sicily

ALBANIA

GREECE

Aegean Sea

Dardanelles

M e d i t e r r a n e a n   S e a

Ionian Sea

Crete

Rhodes

CYPRUS

MALTA

MERIDIAN OF GREENWICH (LONDON)

N

0 mi. 500
0 km 500

Lambert Azimuthal Equal-Area projection

Geography Skills for Life

1. **Interpreting Maps** What body of water separates the United Kingdom from Denmark?

2. **Applying Geography Skills** Which country has areas of land below sea level? How might people live in these areas?

Find NGS online map resources @ www.nationalgeographic.com/maps

COOPERATIVE LEARNING ACTIVITY

Regional Identity Many of Europe's countries, peninsulas, and islands have geographic features, such as mountains, valleys, rivers, coasts, climate, resources, and location, that define them as regions. Organize the class into groups of four or five students and assign each group a region of Europe. Ask each group to identify the geographic features that distinguish that part of Europe and to find photos or illustrations of those features to share with the other groups. **Ask: How might these physical features influence the cultural, economic, and political development of the region?**

🌐 EE2 Places and Regions: Standard 5

L2 Comparing

Ask students to draw comparisons between two European cities: Lisbon, Portugal, and Reykjavík, Iceland, for example. Encourage students to use the Internet, the library, or other resources for their research and to consider each country's climate and physical features.

L1/ELL

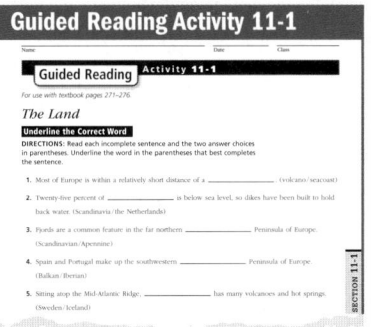

NATIONAL GEOGRAPHIC   **MAP STUDY**

Answers
1. *the North Sea*
2. *the Netherlands; dikes hold back waters from the sea, and polders were created from land once under water*

Map Skills Practice
Place Which islands and island countries are comprised of predominantly lowland terrain? *(the Balearic Islands, parts of the United Kingdom and Ireland)* Which islands and island countries are characterized by predominantly high elevations? *(Iceland, Corsica, Sardinia, Sicily, and Crete)*

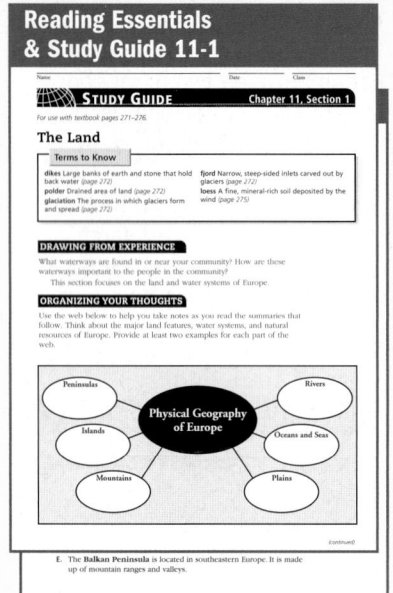

Reading Essentials & Study Guide 11-1

☐ NATIONAL GEOGRAPHIC GEOFACT

▶ The people of Sweden, who endure long, cold winters with few daylight hours, are united in their respect for their country's land. The Arctic blasts of winter are made bearable by the promise of summers in the country in the family's *stuga*, or cottage. Between June and August, many Swedes forsake the cities and, for five weeks, vacation in small farming towns.

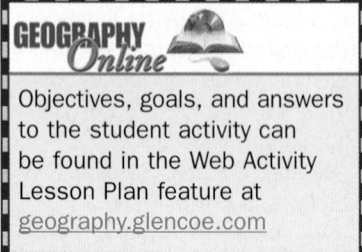

Objectives, goals, and answers to the student activity can be found in the Web Activity Lesson Plan feature at geography.glencoe.com

---

volcano—Mount Vesuvius, near the city of Naples. Plains cover only about one-third of the Apennine Peninsula, the largest being the fertile plain of Lombardy along the Po River in the north.

In southeastern Europe lies the **Balkan Peninsula**. Bounded by the Adriatic and Ionian Seas on the west and the Aegean and Black Seas on the east, the Balkan Peninsula holds a tangle of mountain ranges and valleys that stretch southward from the Danube River. Because of the region's craggy landscape, overland travel is difficult. Historically people moved along rivers and seas in this mountainous region.

Europe's Islands

In addition to peninsulas, Europe includes many islands. Iceland is located south of the Arctic Circle in the North Atlantic Ocean. Lying astride the Mid-Atlantic Ridge, Iceland has volcanoes, hot springs, and geysers. Because of Iceland's far northern location, glaciers are found next to the volcanoes and hot springs. Most of the homes and industries in the area of the capital, Reykjavík (RAY•kyah•VEEK), pipe in water from hot springs for heat. Grassy lowlands stretch along Iceland's coast, but the land rises sharply to form a large inland plateau.

The British Isles lie northwest of the European mainland. They consist of two large islands, Great Britain and Ireland, and thousands of smaller islands. Mountain ranges, plateaus, and deep valleys make up most of northern and western Great Britain, and low hills and gently rolling plains dominate in the south. Ireland, often called the Emerald Isle, is a lush green land of cool temperatures and abundant rainfall. In many places the rugged coastline of the British Isles features rocky cliffs that drop to deep bays. One visitor to the British coast writes:

> ❝ We hiked past . . . plenty of farms, and mile after mile of rocky cliffs, their long faces carved raw and craggy by the ocean's dull knife. All day we stayed close to Cornwall's serrated edge, weaving in and out like a conga line. ❞
> —Alan Mairson, "Saving Britain's Shore," *National Geographic*, October 1995

Islands also lie south of the European mainland, in the Mediterranean Sea. Rugged mountains form the larger islands of Sicily, Sardinia, Corsica, Crete, and Cyprus. Volcanic and earthquake activity are characteristic of the region. Mount Etna, Europe's highest active volcano, rises over Sicily. Smaller island groups in the Mediterranean area are Spain's Balearic Islands, Malta's 5 islands, and Greece's nearly 2,000 islands in the Aegean Sea. The scenic, rugged landscape and the sunny climate of Europe's Mediterranean islands draw tourists from around the world.

Mountains and Plains

Europe's mainland, in essence, consists of plains interrupted by mountains running through its interior and along its northern and southern edges. The map on page 273 shows the names and locations of some of these landforms.

Mountain Regions

Europe's northwestern mountains have some of the earth's most ancient rock formations. Rounded by eons of erosion and glaciation, these ranges feature relatively low peaks, such as Ben Nevis, the highest mountain in the British Isles at 4,406 feet (1,343 m). Extending from the Iberian Peninsula to eastern Europe, the central uplands consist of low, rounded mountains and high plateaus with scattered forests. This region includes the Meseta, Spain's central plateau, and the Massif Central, France's central highlands.

By contrast, southern Europe's geologically younger mountains are high and jagged. As the earth's crust lifted and folded, the Pyrenees Mountains were thrust upward to more than 11,000 feet (3,354 m). Created by glaciation and folding, the mountain system known as the **Alps** forms a crescent from southern France to the Balkan Peninsula. The highest peak in the Alps, Mont Blanc, stands at

Student Web Activity Visit the **Glencoe World Geography** Web site at geography.glencoe.com and click on Student Web Activities— Chapter 11 for an activity about the physical geography of the Netherlands.

CRITICAL THINKING ACTIVITY

Physical Processes Water is the essence of life. Since ancient times, human settlement has gravitated toward areas where freshwater is abundant. Europe contains many major river systems, from the Thames in England to the Po River in Italy. **Ask: What physical features make the Rhine and Danube Rivers the most important river systems for the people of western and eastern Europe?** (*Possible answers: Each river is long and runs through Europe, linking major cities; each river is deep and wide enough to accommodate ships and barges.*) 🌐 **EE3 Physical Systems: Standard 7**
🌐 **EE5 Environment and Society: Standard 15**

NATIONAL GEOGRAPHIC **World Explorer**

Answer

Short rivers, such as those in Scandinavia, are not easily navigable; long, navigable rivers, such as the Rhine and the Danube, link many industrial cities.

More About the Photo

Paths were built along both sides of the 106-mile (171-km) Main-Danube Canal to give access for repairs and emergencies and to open new scenic routes for cyclists and hikers.

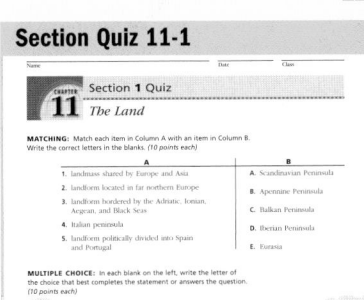 **ASSESS**

Assign Section 1 Assessment as homework or as an in-class activity.

Have students use **Interactive Tutor Self-Assessment CD-ROM** to review Section 1.

L2

Section Quiz 11-1

| | Name | Date | Class |

11 Section **1** Quiz
The Land

MATCHING: Match each item in Column A with an item in Column B. Write the correct letters in the blanks. *(10 points each)*

A	B
1. landmass shared by Europe and Asia	A. Scandinavian Peninsula
2. landform located in far northern Europe	B. Apennine Peninsula
3. landform bordered by the Adriatic, Ionian, Aegean, and Black Seas	C. Balkan Peninsula
4. Italian peninsula	D. Iberian Peninsula
5. landform politically divided into Spain and Portugal	E. Eurasia

MULTIPLE CHOICE: In each blank on the left, write the letter of the choice that best completes the statement or answers the question. *(10 points each)*

NATIONAL GEOGRAPHIC **World Explorer**

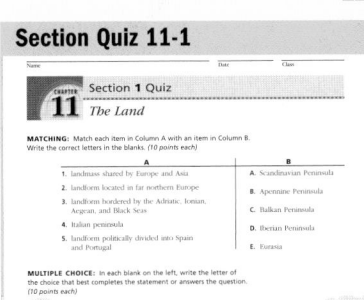

Geography Skills for Life

Main-Danube Canal

Rolling through rural Bavaria, the Main-Danube Canal offers a large lake for swimming and artificial ponds for wildlife along landscaped banks.

Region Describe the two different types of rivers that flow in Europe.

15,771 feet (4,807 m) on the border of France and Italy. Some of Europe's major rivers, such as the **Rhine** and the **Po**, originate in the Alps. The Alps also form a barrier that separates the warm, dry climate of the Mediterranean region from the cooler climates of the north. Another towering mountain chain, the Carpathians, runs through eastern Europe from Slovakia to Romania.

Plains Regions

Europe's broad plains curve around the highlands. Scoured by Ice Age glaciers, the **North European Plain**, or **Great European Plain**, stretches from southeastern England and western France eastward to Poland, Ukraine, and Russia. The plain's fertile soil and wealth of rivers originally drew farmers to the area. The southern edge is especially fertile because deposits of loess, a fine, rich, wind-borne soil, cover it.

Deposits of coal, iron ore, and other minerals found on the North European Plain led to western Europe's industrial development during the 1800s. Today many of Europe's largest cities, such as Paris and Berlin, are located on the plain.

Another fertile plains area, the Great Hungarian Plain, extends from Hungary to Croatia, Serbia,

and Romania. Farmers cultivate grains, fruit, and vegetables and raise livestock in the lowlands along the Danube River.

Water Systems

Many of Europe's water systems flow from inland mountain and highlands areas to the coasts. By connecting navigable rivers with canals, Europeans have greatly enhanced their natural waterways as transportation links. Europe's rivers and canals also provide water to irrigate farmland and to produce electricity.

Europe's rivers have differing characteristics. The rivers in Scandinavia are short and do not provide easy connections between cities. In the Iberian Peninsula, main rivers generally are too narrow and shallow for large ships. England's Thames (TEHMZ) River, on the other hand, allows ocean-going ships to reach the port of London.

In the heartland of Europe, however, relatively long rivers provide links between inland areas as well as to the sea. The Rhine is the most important river in western Europe. It flows from the Swiss

Chapter 11 **275**

TEAM-TEACHING ACTIVITY: WORLD HISTORY

Migration One of the more culturally diverse regions in Europe is the Balkan Peninsula. Over the past 2,000 years, a number of important civilizations have flourished in the region, including the Greek city-states and the Roman, Byzantine, and Ottoman Empires. Because of its proximity to Mediterranean sea routes and Asian land routes, this mountainous region has been overrun by many conquering peoples. Have students work with a history teacher to create a cause-and-effect chart illustrating how migration has influenced the cultural, religious, and political composition of the Balkans—influences that have caused much of the conflict in the region. **EE4 Human Systems: Standard 9**

Reteach

Have students identify the different areas of Europe and the countries within these areas. Ask them to identify Europe's important physical features—mountains, plains, rivers, peninsulas.

Enrich

Ask students to find out how three important bodies of water—the North Sea, the Black Sea, and the Mediterranean Sea—have historically affected Europe. Encourage students to consider trade routes, climate, and proximity to other regions of the world.

 **CLOSE**

Ask students to write a short essay on a part of Europe they would like to visit. Ask them to mention what physical features of the country, island, province, or region help make that place interesting to them.

Alps through France and Germany and into the Netherlands, connecting many industrial cities to the busy port of Rotterdam on the North Sea.

The Danube, which flows from Germany's Black Forest to the Black Sea, is eastern Europe's major waterway. Each year ships and barges carry millions of tons of cargo on the Danube. In 1992 the Main (MYN) River, a tributary of the Rhine, became connected to the Danube when the Main-Danube Canal was completed, thereby linking the North Sea with the Black Sea.

Other major European rivers include the Seine, Rhône, and Loire in France; the Elbe and Weser in Germany; the Vistula in Poland; the Po in Italy; and the Dnieper in Ukraine.

Natural Resources

Europe has a long history of utilizing its natural resources, including energy sources, agricultural areas, water, and especially minerals. Europe's abundant supply of coal and iron ore fueled the development of modern industry.

Major reserves of coal lie in the United Kingdom, Germany, Ukraine, and Poland as well as other European countries. Although coal is still an important fuel source, many coalfields in western Europe are depleted or are too expensive to mine. Large deposits of iron ore lie in northern Sweden,

▲ An Irish farmer digging peat

northeastern France, and southeastern Ukraine. Europe's other mineral resources include bauxite, zinc, and manganese.

In places where other fuels are scarce, Europeans burn peat, a kind of vegetable matter found in swamps and usually composed of mosses. Peat is dug up, chopped into blocks, and dried so it can be burned. Europeans, however, largely rely on coal, oil, gas, and nuclear and hydroelectric power. Vast oil and natural gas deposits under the North Sea contribute greatly to Europe's energy needs. France, which lacks large oil or gas reserves, has invested heavily in nuclear power.

SECTION 1 ASSESSMENT

Checking for Understanding

1. **Define** dike, polder, glaciation, fjord, loess.
2. **Main Ideas** Re-create the table below on a sheet of paper, and fill in examples of the physical features and natural resources of Germany, Norway, Ukraine, Italy, and France.

Country	Physical Features	Natural Resources

Critical Thinking

3. **Comparing and Contrasting** How does the landscape of the Jutland peninsula differ from that of the Balkan Peninsula?
4. **Making Generalizations** Europe's Mediterranean islands are popular vacation destinations. What physical features make these islands attractive to tourists?
5. **Drawing Conclusions** How does Europe's network of rivers and canals contribute to industrial development in the region?

Analyzing Maps

6. **Location** Study the physical-political map of Europe on page 273. What part of Europe has the lowest elevation? The highest?

Applying Geography

7. **Conflict Over Resources** Use the economic activity map on page 263 to identify three areas in which natural resources cross international boundaries. Describe the areas in which conflict could arise because of the management of these resources.

SECTION 1 ASSESSMENT ANSWERS

1. All vocabulary terms are defined in the text.
2. Answers should include at least two physical features and two natural resources of each country.
3. The Jutland Peninsula has lowlands in the west and fjords on its slightly elevated eastern coast. The Balkan Peninsula is more rugged, with mountain ranges and valleys.
4. A warm climate, beautiful coastlines, and ocean sports like snorkeling, water skiing, parasailing, and fishing draw tourists from around the world.
5. The Rhine and the Danube can accommodate large ships and barges. Because of their links to the North and Black Seas, Europe's rivers provide important trade outlets for the continent's cities and industries.
6. lowest is in the Netherlands; highest are the Pyrenees and the Alps
7. **Applying Geography** the North Sea; the borders of Germany, Belgium, and the Netherlands; Bulgaria and Romania. Conflict over resources would be less likely among European Union members.

Guide to Reading

Consider What You Know

Much of Europe borders oceans and seas. What kinds of climates would you expect in Europe?

Reading Strategy

Categorizing As you read about the climates of Europe, complete a graphic organizer similar to the one below by listing the types of climate regions found in the mid-latitudes.

Mid-Latitudes	

Read to Find Out

- What are the climate regions in Europe?
- What physical features influence Europe's climates?
- Why are most of Europe's original forests gone?

Terms to Know

- timberline
- foehn
- avalanche
- mistral
- sirocco
- chaparral
- permafrost

Places to Locate

- Gulf Stream
- North Atlantic Drift

Climate and Vegetation

A Geographic View

Power of the Wind

I stood on the shore of Als Sund, a saltwater sound . . . with [Flemming] Rieck, a maritime archaeologist at the National Museum of Denmark. . . . After a week of rain the spring sun radiated intense light but little heat. Chins tucked in our windbreakers, Rieck and I stared at sailboats bobbing on the whitecaps.

"At some point . . . ," he said, "Scandinavians began using sails." He spread his arms into the stiff breeze. "No one can say why it took so long for them to use the power of all this wind."

Sailboats on Als Sund

—Michael Klesius, "Mystery Ships From a Danish Bog," *National Geographic*, May 2000

Wind is only one of the factors affecting Europe's climates. Latitude, mountain barriers, ocean currents, and the distance from large bodies of water all help determine Europe's varied climates. In this section you will read about Europe's climate regions—from the sunny, dry Mediterranean climate to the frozen subarctic zone. You will also study the patterns of vegetation growth found in each region of Europe.

Water and Land

The climates and vegetation of Europe vary from the cold, barren tundra and subarctic stretches of Iceland, Norway, Sweden, and Finland to the warm, shrub-covered Mediterranean coasts of Italy, Spain, and Greece. What factors account for such variety in a relatively small area?

Guide to Reading

① FOCUS

Section Overview

This section discusses Europe's climate and vegetation regions.

BELLRINGER
Skillbuilder Activity

Project transparency and have students answer questions.

Available as blackline master.

Daily Focus Skills Transparency 11-2

Guide to Reading

Consider What You Know

Answers *Warm maritime winds of the Atlantic Ocean would probably make Europe's coastal climates more moderate.*

Reading Strategy

Answers *marine west coast, mediterranean, humid subtropical, humid continental*

Preteaching Vocabulary

Use the **Vocabulary Puzzle-Maker CD-ROM** to create crossword and word-search puzzles.

RESOURCE MANAGER

Reproducible Masters

- Reproducible Lesson Plan 11-2
- Vocabulary Activity 11
- Daily Lecture Notes 11-2
- Guided Reading Activity 11-2
- Reading Essentials and Study Guide 11-2
- Reteaching Activity 11
- Reinforcing Skills Activity 11
- Section Quiz 11-2

Transparencies

- Daily Focus Skills Transparency 11-2
- Political Map Transparency 4
- Unit 4 Map Overlay Transparencies

Multimedia

- Vocabulary PuzzleMaker CD-ROM
- Interactive Tutor Self-Assessment CD-ROM
- ExamView® Pro Testmaker CD-ROM
- Presentation Plus! CD-ROM

TEACH

NATIONAL GEOGRAPHIC   MAP STUDY

Answers

1. *marine west coast, humid continental, subarctic, tundra*

2. *Eastern Europe is not warmed by the maritime winds from the Atlantic.*

Map Skills Practice

Region What climate region includes eastern Switzerland and western Austria? *(highlands)*

L1 Comparing Vegetation

Have students select one Scandinavian country and compare the kinds of trees and other vegetation found in that region of Europe with vegetation near where they live. **Ask:** Which kinds are the same? Which kinds are different?

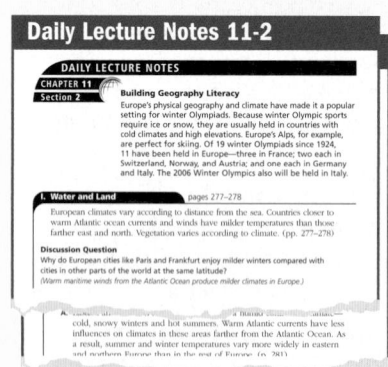

Daily Lecture Notes 11-2

DAILY LECTURE NOTES

CHAPTER 11
Section 2

Building Geography Literacy
Europe's physical geography and climate have made it a popular setting for winter Olympiads. Because winter Olympic sports require ice or snow, they are usually held in countries with cold climates and high elevations. Europe's Alps, for example, are perfect for skiing. Of 19 winter Olympiads since 1924, 11 have been held in France; two each in Switzerland, Norway, and Austria; and one each in Germany and Italy. The 2006 Winter Olympics also will be held in Italy.

I. Water and Land   pages 277–278
European climates vary according to distance from the sea. Countries closer to warm Atlantic ocean currents and winds have milder temperatures than those farther east and north. Vegetation varies according to climate. (pp. 277–278)

Discussion Question
Why do European cities like Paris and Frankfurt enjoy milder winters compared with cities in other parts of the world at the same latitude?
(Warm maritime winds from the Atlantic Ocean produce milder climates in Europe.)

a milder Atlantic cold, snowy winters and hot summers. Warm Atlantic currents have less influences on climates in these areas farther from the Atlantic Ocean. As a result, summer and winter temperatures vary more widely in eastern and northern Europe than in the rest of Europe. (p. 281)

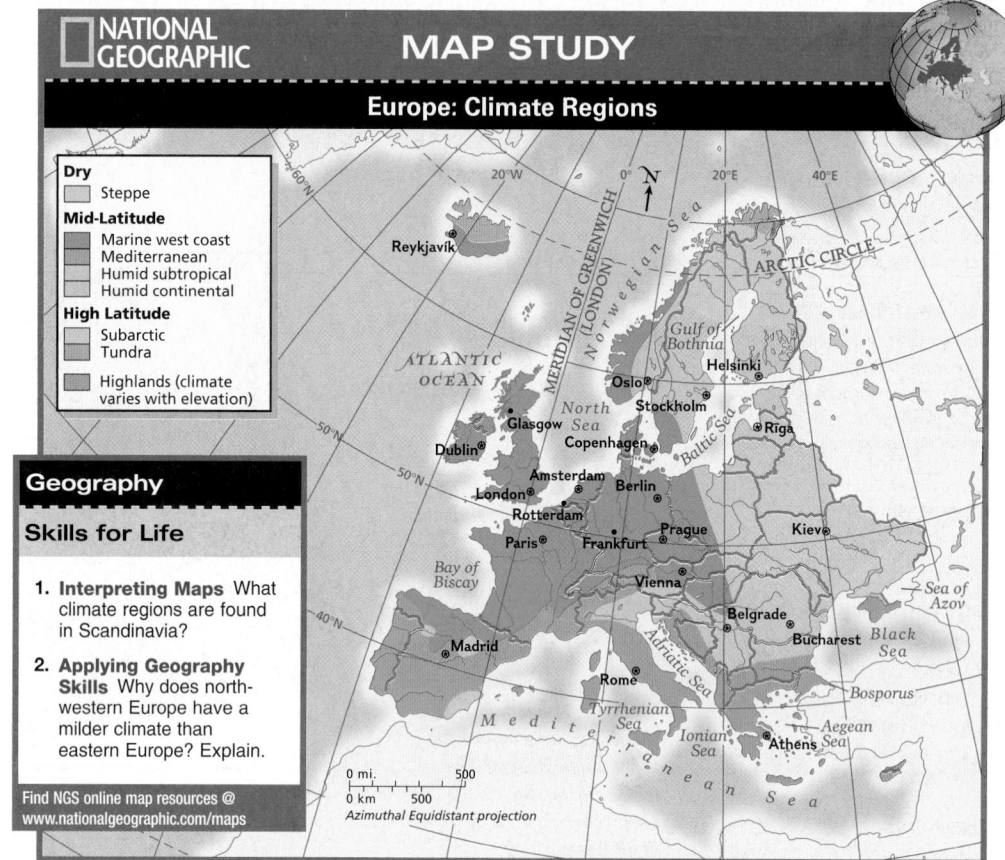

NATIONAL GEOGRAPHIC   MAP STUDY

Europe: Climate Regions

Dry
- Steppe

Mid-Latitude
- Marine west coast
- Mediterranean
- Humid subtropical
- Humid continental

High Latitude
- Subarctic
- Tundra

- Highlands (climate varies with elevation)

Geography

Skills for Life

1. **Interpreting Maps** What climate regions are found in Scandinavia?

2. **Applying Geography Skills** Why does northwestern Europe have a milder climate than eastern Europe? Explain.

Find NGS online map resources @ www.nationalgeographic.com/maps

0 mi. 500
0 km 500
Azimuthal Equidistant projection

Europe's northern latitude and its relationship to the sea influence its climates and vegetation. Western and southern parts of Europe, which lie near or along large bodies of water, benefit from warm maritime winds. These areas have a generally mild climate compared with other places in the world at the same latitude. Frankfurt, Germany, as well as Paris, France, and Boston, Massachusetts, are about the same distance from the Arctic Circle, yet January temperatures in Paris are milder than those in Boston. By contrast, parts of eastern and northern Europe have a colder climate than most of western and southern Europe because of their distance from the warming effects of the Atlantic Ocean.

As in other areas of the world, location influences vegetation patterns in Europe. Natural vegetation in the region varies from forests and grasslands to tundra plants and small shrubs. Compare the natural vegetation map on page 279 with the climate map above. Notice that the types of vegetation found in Europe are closely linked to the climate regions.

Western Europe

As the climate map on this page shows, much of western Europe has a marine west coast climate—mild winters, cool summers, and abundant rainfall. The Atlantic Ocean's **Gulf Stream** and its northern extension, the **North Atlantic Drift**, bring warm waters to this part of Europe from the Gulf of Mexico and regions near the Equator (see map on page 61). Prevailing westerly winds blowing over these currents carry warm, moist air across the surface of the European landmass.

DIFFERENTIATED INSTRUCTION

Reading Support For students who have trouble with reading comprehension, ask them to slowly read the first two sentences of each subsection in Section 2. Have them repeat the exercise. When they have read the selections twice, ask them to summarize the main idea of each subsection.

 Refer to *Inclusion for the Social Studies Classroom Strategies and Activities.*

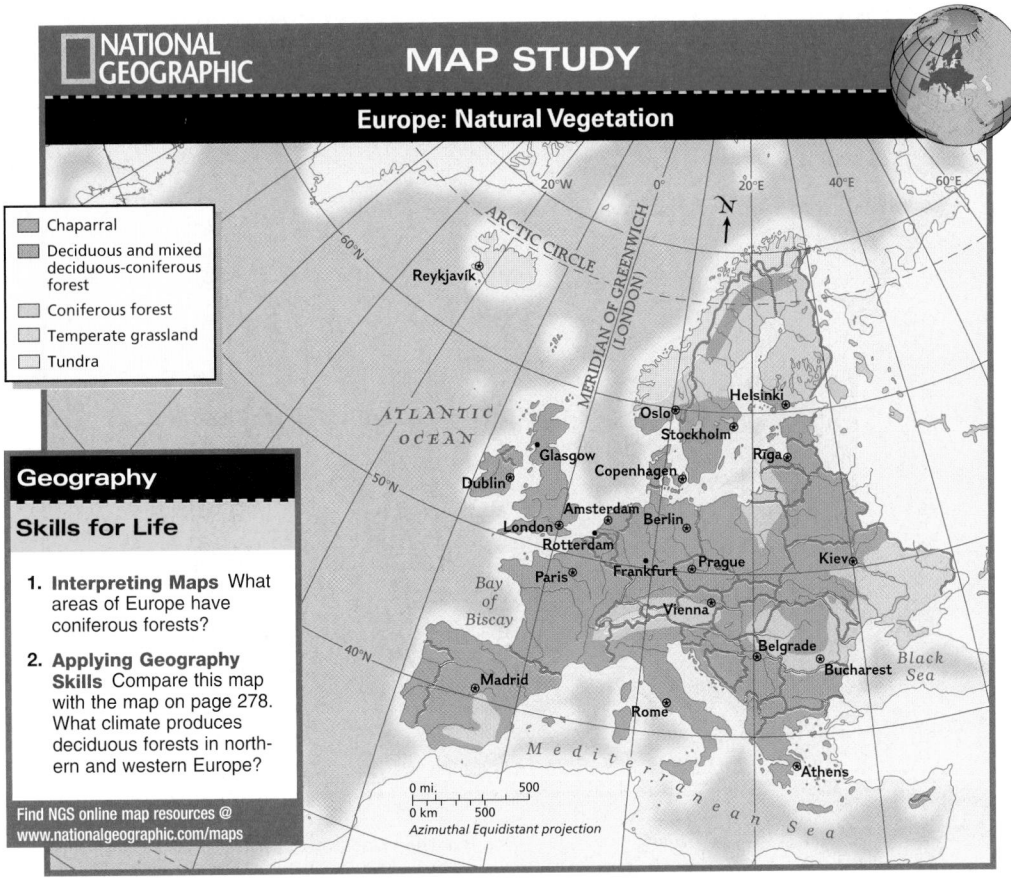

NATIONAL GEOGRAPHIC — MAP STUDY

Europe: Natural Vegetation

Legend:
- Chaparral
- Deciduous and mixed deciduous-coniferous forest
- Coniferous forest
- Temperate grassland
- Tundra

Geography

Skills for Life

1. **Interpreting Maps** What areas of Europe have coniferous forests?

2. **Applying Geography Skills** Compare this map with the map on page 278. What climate produces deciduous forests in northern and western Europe?

Find NGS online map resources @ www.nationalgeographic.com/maps

0 mi. 500
0 km 500
Azimuthal Equidistant projection

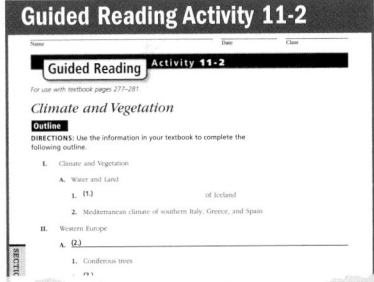

NATIONAL GEOGRAPHIC — MAP STUDY

Answers

1. *Norway, the Alps region, and parts of Poland, Lithuania, and Latvia*

2. *marine west coast*

Map Skills Practice

Location Which parts of Europe have large areas of grassland? *(the Iberian Peninsula [southeast Spain] and Eastern Europe [Hungary, Romania, and Bulgaria])*

L1/ELL

Guided Reading Activity 11-2

Guided Reading Activity **11-2**

For use with textbook pages 277–281

Climate and Vegetation

Outline

DIRECTIONS: Use the information in your textbook to complete the following outline.

I. Climate and Vegetation
   A. Water and Land
      1. (1.) _____ of Iceland
      2. Mediterranean climate of southern Italy, Greece, and Spain
II. Western Europe
   A. (2.) _____
      1. Coniferous trees
      (3.) _____

INTERDISCIPLINARY
connection

ECONOMICS Finland's economy was once based on lumber, Finland's major natural resource. The Finnish economy is now highly industrialized, with exports making up a quarter of the country's gross domestic product. The United States is one of Finland's main export markets.

Trees and Highlands

Western Europe's natural vegetation includes varieties of deciduous (dih•SIH•juh•wuhs) and coniferous (koh•NIH•fuh•ruhs) trees. Deciduous trees, those that lose their leaves, such as ash, maple, and oak, thrive in the area's marine west coast climate. Coniferous trees, cone-bearing fir, pine, and spruce, are found in cooler Alpine mountain areas up to the timberline, the elevation above which trees cannot grow.

The Alps have a highlands climate with generally colder temperatures and more precipitation than nearby lowland areas. Sudden changes can occur, however, when dry winds called foehns (FUHNZ) blow down from the mountains into valleys and plains. Foehns can trigger avalanches, destructive masses of ice, snow, and rock sliding down mountainsides. Avalanches threaten skiers and hikers, and often carry away everything in their paths. They represent a serious natural hazard in the Alps.

History
Ireland's Forests

Much of Europe was orginally covered by forest, but over the centuries human settlement and clearing of the land have transformed the vegetation. For example, prior to the 1600s, much of the midlands region of Ireland was covered with forests of broad-leaved trees. However, pressure from agriculture and the large-scale harvest of native lumber for firewood depleted the country's forests. By 1922, when Ireland gained independence, only 1 percent of the

Chapter 11 🌐 **279**

COOPERATIVE LEARNING ACTIVITY

Regional Identity Organize students into six groups. Assign one of the following locations and seasons to each group: Ireland—summer; Hungary—winter; Italy—summer; Finland—winter; Spain—summer; Greece—winter. Instruct each group to plan a vacation to its assigned location during the season specified. Have groups be sure to list the kinds of clothing they would take with them, based on the seasonal climate. Have each group share its vacation plan with other groups. Combine all vacation plans into a "travel brochure" and distribute it to the class. 🌐 **EE2 Places and Regions: Standard 5**

L1/ELL

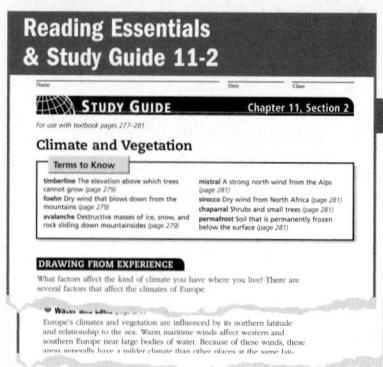

Reading Essentials & Study Guide 11-2

NATIONAL GEOGRAPHIC — GRAPH STUDY

Answers

1. *Paris: about 45°F, almost 2 inches of precipitation; Boston: about 40°F, 4 inches of precipitation*

2. *Paris has a marine west coast climate with mild winters and cool summers. Boston has a humid continental climate with cold winters and hot summers.*

Skills Practice
Location What is the absolute location of each city? *(Paris: 49°N, 2°E; Boston 42°N, 71°W)*

③ ASSESS

Assign Section 2 Assessment as homework or as an in-class activity.

⊙ Have students use **Interactive Tutor Self-Assessment CD-ROM** to review Section 2.

NATIONAL GEOGRAPHIC — GRAPH STUDY

Comparing Climate Regions: France and the United States

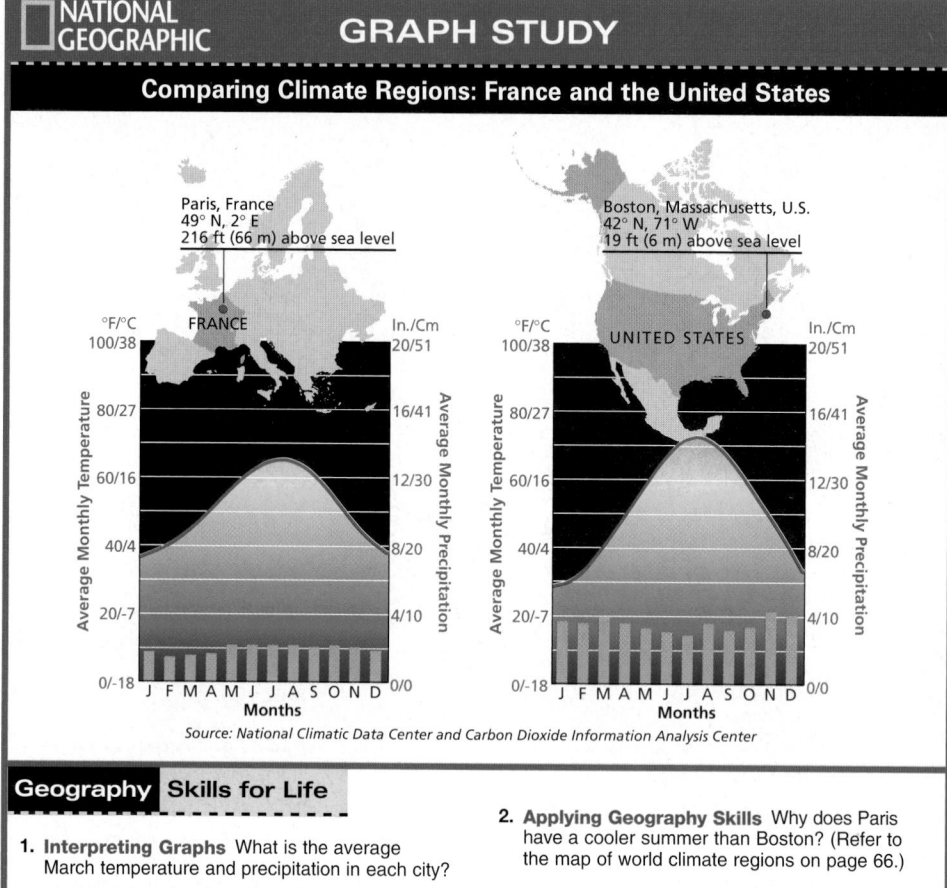

Paris, France
49° N, 2° E
216 ft (66 m) above sea level

Boston, Massachusetts, U.S.
42° N, 71° W
19 ft (6 m) above sea level

Source: National Climatic Data Center and Carbon Dioxide Information Analysis Center

Geography Skills for Life

1. **Interpreting Graphs** What is the average March temperature and precipitation in each city?

2. **Applying Geography Skills** Why does Paris have a cooler summer than Boston? (Refer to the map of world climate regions on page 66.)

---

country was woodland. Searching for old-growth forests can be challenging, as one traveler notes:

> *'Of course Tomies Wood is all second growth'.... The real thing, Padraig told me, was far more remote, far from the trails, in the heights of MacGillycuddy's Reeks, where even now few people ventured.*
>
> Rebecca Solnit, "The Lost Woods of Killarney," *Sierra*, March/April 1997

State-sponsored reforestation efforts since World War II have increased Ireland's woodland areas.

Southern Europe

Most of southern Europe has a Mediterranean climate—warm, dry summers and mild, rainy winters. Several other climates, however, are found in small areas of the region. For example, a humid subtropical climate stretches from northern Italy to the central part of the Balkan Peninsula. In addition, parts of Spain's Meseta have a drier steppe climate.

The Alps block moist Atlantic winds, so less precipitation falls in southern Europe than in northwestern Europe. Local winds in the region sometimes cause changes in the normal weather pattern. The **mistral**, a strong north wind from the Alps, sometimes sends gusts of bitterly cold air into southern France. By contrast, **siroccos** (suh•RAH•kohs),

---

CRITICAL THINKING ACTIVITY

Making Inferences Have students study the climate data about Paris in the climograph above as well as other geographic data about the French capital presented in the four maps on pages 260–263 of the Regional Atlas. **Ask:** What generalization can you make about Paris's climate? *(Paris has a marine west coast climate of mild winters and cool summers.)* How might a climate like that of Paris affect patterns of settlement, population and resource distribution, and political and economic conditions in a given area?
🌐 **EE5 Environment and Society: Standard 15**

high, dry winds from North Africa, may bring high temperatures to the region. The hot, dry summers in much of southern Europe support the growth of chaparral, or shrubs and small trees, such as the cork oak tree and the olive tree.

Eastern and Northern Europe

Eastern and certain northern areas of Europe have a generally humid continental climate—cold, snowy winters and hot summers. Warm Atlantic currents have less influence on climate in these areas farther from the Atlantic Ocean. As a result, summer and winter temperatures vary more widely in eastern and northern Europe than in the rest of Europe.

In eastern Europe the vegetation is generally a mix of deciduous and coniferous forests. Coniferous trees, which are able to survive long, cold winters, are found in parts of Scandinavia and the region around the Baltic Sea. Grasslands cover parts of eastern Europe, especially in Hungary, Serbia and Montenegro, and Romania.

Europe's far north—for example, Iceland, northern Scandinavia, and Finland—has subarctic and tundra climates of bitterly cold winters and short, cool summers. Tundra and subarctic regions have permafrost, soil that is permanently frozen below the surface.

NATIONAL GEOGRAPHIC **World Explorer**

Geography   Skills for Life

Land of Lakes Inari, in the far north of Finland, is one of some 60,000 lakes that dot the Finnish countryside.
Region What climates dominate Europe's far north?

Tundra areas support little vegetation, with the exception of mosses, small shrubs, and wildflowers that bloom during the brief summer. The subarctic supports a vast coniferous forest that broadens in the eastern part where Europe and Russia share a border.

SECTION 2 ASSESSMENT

Checking for Understanding

1. **Define** timberline, foehn, avalanche, mistral, sirocco, chaparral, permafrost.

2. **Main Ideas** Create an outline like the one below, showing the climates and vegetation found in three European countries.

Climate and Vegetation
I. Iceland
A. Climates: subarctic, tundra, and permafrost
B. Vegetation: conifers, lichens, moss

Critical Thinking

3. **Predicting Consequences** Prevailing westerly winds bring warm air from the North Atlantic Drift to the European continent. What do you think happens when the winds temporarily change course?

4. **Analyzing Information** What geographic factors contribute to vegetation differences between highlands and tundra climate regions?

5. **Identifying Cause and Effect** How has human interaction with the environment caused changes in Europe's vegetation patterns?

Analyzing Maps

6. **Location** Study the map of Europe's climate regions on page 278. Where are highlands climate regions found? What are their physical features?

Applying Geography

7. **Physical Processes** Describe the physical processes that affect Europe's climate and vegetation. Provide specific examples related to the variety of climates and vegetation found in the region.

Chapter 11   281

SECTION 2 ASSESSMENT ANSWERS

1. All vocabulary terms are defined in the text.
2. The outline should include at least three types of climate and vegetation.
3. A shift could bring cold, dry air and lower temperatures to the region.
4. Highland climate: high elevation, chaparral and coniferous vegetation; tundra climate: high latitude, little vegetation except for mosses, small shrubs, and wildflowers.

5. Large percentages of European forests have been lost to agriculture and urban development.
6. the Alps region; high elevations and mountain ranges
7. **Applying Geography** Western: Gulf Stream; moderate temperatures, deciduous/coniferous; Southern: drier climate, mistral, siroccos, chaparral; Northern/Eastern: far from moderating ocean effects; continental, subarctic, or tundra; deciduous/coniferous mix

L2

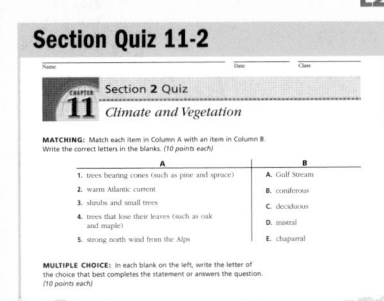

Section Quiz 11-2

Section 2 Quiz
11   *Climate and Vegetation*

MATCHING: Match each item in Column A with an item in Column B. Write the correct letters in the blanks. *(10 points each)*

	A		B
1.	trees bearing cones (such as pine and spruce)	A.	Gulf Stream
2.	warm Atlantic current	B.	coniferous
3.	shrubs and small trees	C.	deciduous
4.	trees that lose their leaves (such as oak and maple)	D.	mistral
5.	strong north wind from the Alps	E.	chaparral

MULTIPLE CHOICE: In each blank on the left, write the letter of the choice that best completes the statement or answers the question. *(10 points each)*

NATIONAL GEOGRAPHIC **World Explorer**

Answer
subarctic and tundra climates

More About the Photo
Today sailboating is a popular form of recreation on the Als Sund, located on the Jutland Peninsula of Denmark.

Reteach

Have a geography "spelldown" using review questions. Students remain standing until they miss an answer.

Enrich

Read aloud a passage from Paul Theroux's *The Pillars of Hercules: A Grand Tour of the Mediterranean.*

4 CLOSE

Ask: How might climate and vegetation affect the economy and culture in the different regions of Europe? *(Scandinavia: the timber industry; Switzerland: the ski industry; the Mediterranean area: the tourist industry)*

281

Teaching the Skill

On the board, copy the following outline. As you progress through this SkillBuilder, fill in the appropriate places on the outline, based on the passage and discussion with students.

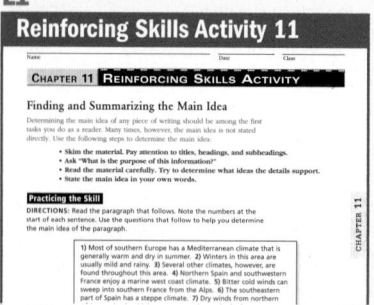

I. Main Idea

   A. Intended Audience

   B. Purpose of Passage

II. Supporting Details in First Paragraph

III. Supporting Details in Second Paragraph

Additional Practice
L1

Reinforcing Skills Activity 11

CHAPTER 11 REINFORCING SKILLS ACTIVITY

Finding and Summarizing the Main Idea

Determining the main idea of any piece of writing should be among the first tasks you do as a reader. Many times, however, the main idea is not stated directly. Use the following steps to determine the main idea.

- Skim the material. Pay attention to titles, headings, and subheadings.
- Ask "What is the purpose of this information?"
- Read the material carefully. Try to determine what ideas the details support.
- State the main idea in your own words.

Practicing the Skill

DIRECTIONS: Read the paragraph that follows. Note the numbers at the start of each sentence. Use the questions that follow to help you determine the main idea of the paragraph.

1) Most of southern Europe has a Mediterranean climate that is generally warm and dry in summer. 2) Winters in this area are usually mild and rainy. 3) Several other climates, however, are found throughout this area. 4) Northern Spain and southwestern France enjoy a marine west coast climate. 5) Bitter cold winds can sweep into southern France from the Alps. 6) The southeastern part of Spain has a steppe climate. 7) Dry winds from northern

GLENCOE
TECHNOLOGY

Glencoe Skillbuilder Interactive Workbook, Level 2

This interactive CD-ROM reinforces student mastery of essential social studies skills.

Finding and Summarizing the Main Idea

Finding and summarizing the main idea in an article or book will help you organize information. It will also help you identify the most important concepts to remember.

> … Patterdale lies within the 885 square miles of the Lake District National Park. …
> It is the largest of ten national parks in England and Wales (Scotland has none), but, as with the others, the designation is really a misnomer [incorrect name] since the land is neither owned by the nation nor is it in any conventional sense a park. It is, rather, a lived-in landscape, full of towns and farms, with a resident population of 40,000. All but a small fraction of the land is in private hands.
> Unlike U.S. national parks, which often aim to preserve wilderness, British parks inevitably include residents. These parks were created so there could be a way to exert some control over the speed and nature of change, not to prevent it altogether. Unfortunately, the various authorities have little power, relying primarily on persuasion to resolve myriad [numerous] demands.
>
> —Bill Bryson, "England's Lake District,"
> *National Geographic,* August 1994

Learning the Skill

To identify the main idea, you may need to "read between the lines" and interpret the facts and evidence that are presented. Review the important details, and decide which ones are central to the message. By looking closely at important details, you can infer an author's main meaning.

When looking for a main idea, follow these steps:

- **Skim the material to identify its general subject.** Look at any headings and subheadings.

- **Read the information to pinpoint the ideas that the details support.** Why is the author presenting these facts and this evidence?

- **Identify the main idea.** Ask yourself: How can I state the main idea in my own words?

Practicing the Skill

Read the passage above. Then answer the following questions.

1. What is the general subject of the passage?

2. What important facts and details does the passage include?

3. What is the main idea of the passage? State the main idea in your own words.

Applying the Skill

Bring to class a news article about an issue facing Europe. Summarize the main idea of the article, and explain why it is important.

The Glencoe Skillbuilder Interactive Workbook, Level 2 provides instruction and practice in key social studies skills.

ANSWERS TO PRACTICING THE SKILL

1. a description of a national park in England and how it differs from national parks in the United States

2. Patterdale is the largest national park in England and Wales; "national park" is a misnomer because it is neither nationally owned nor a park per se; rather, it is a lived-in landscape with a population of 40,000; British parks are intended to exert control over the speed and nature of change, not prevent it altogether; authorities really have little power over the parks.

3. The United Kingdom and the United States have different approaches to preserving wilderness.

CHAPTER 11

SECTION 1   The Land (pp. 271–276)

Terms to Know
- dike
- polder
- glaciation
- fjord
- loess

Key Points
- Europe is a huge peninsula extending westward from the Eurasian landmass.
- Europe has a long coastline with many peninsulas and islands.
- Europe has a large plains region in its northern areas; mountains are found along the continent's eastern and southern boundaries.
- Rivers provide important transportation in Europe, linking the interior of the continent with coastal ports.
- Europe has important deposits of minerals, oil, and natural gas.

Organizing Your Notes
Use a table like the one below to help you organize the notes you took as you read the chapter.

Country	Mountains	Rivers and Lakes	Other Features

SECTION 2   Climate and Vegetation (pp. 277–281)

Terms to Know
- timberline
- foehn
- avalanche
- mistral
- sirocco
- chaparral
- permafrost

Key Points
- Warm ocean currents give much of Europe a milder climate than other areas at similar latitudes.
- Areas of western Europe with a marine west coast climate have generally moderate temperatures.
- Much of southern Europe has a Mediterranean climate, with mild, rainy winters and warm, dry summers.
- Europe's interior has more extreme seasonal temperatures than do areas nearer the sea.
- Both climate and human activity affect the natural vegetation of Europe.

Organizing Your Notes
Create graphic organizers like the one below to help organize your notes about each of Europe's climate regions.

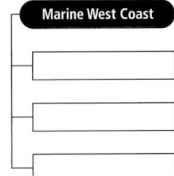

Marine West Coast

◀ *Reindeer herding, northern Sweden*

Chapter 11   🌐   **283**

Using the Chapter 11 Summary & Study Guide
Use the Chapter 11 Summary & Study Guide to preview, review, condense, or reteach the chapter.

Preview/Review
🔵 **Vocabulary PuzzleMaker CD-ROM** reinforces "Terms to Know."

🔵 **Interactive Tutor Self-Assessment CD-ROM** provides a review of Chapter 11 content.

Condense
Have students read the Chapter 11 Summary & Study Guide.

🔵 Chapter 11 Audio Program

🗂 Chapter 11 Guided Reading Activities

Reteach
🗂 Chapter 11 Reteaching Activities (Spanish also available)

🗂 Chapter 11 Reading Essentials and Study Guides

GLENCOE
TECHNOLOGY

🔲 **NATIONAL GEOGRAPHIC**

WORLD REGIONS
VIDEO PROGRAM

Unit 4, Europe
The following segments enhance the study of this unit:
- **Mariners of the Mediterranean**
- **A Divided City**
- **City of Canals**

CHAPTER CULMINATING ACTIVITY

Historical Implications Ask: How has physical geography affected the history of Europe? *(Over the centuries, climate and physical features have exerted influences on the growth of cities, trade, politics migrations, and wars in Europe. From the eruption of volcanoes in Italy to countless avalanches, droughts, and floods across Europe, many events in the region have been shaped by physical geography.)* Ask each student to write a brief report on an important European event that was significantly influenced by some aspect of the continent's physical geography. 🌐 **EE5 Environment and Society: Standard 15**

GEOGRAPHY Online

Have students visit the Web site at geography.glencoe.com to review Chapter 11 and take the **Self-Check Quiz.**

GLENCOE TECHNOLOGY

Use *MindJogger Videoquiz* to review the Chapter 11 content.

Reviewing Key Terms

1. e
2. c
3. a
4. d
5. b
6. f

Reviewing Facts

SECTION 1

1. Europe is a large peninsula made up of smaller peninsulas
2. North European Plain
3. They have built dams, introduced pollution, and completed canals that link rivers.

SECTION 2

4. Prevailing westerly winds blowing over the currents carry warm, moist air across the continent.
5. marine west coast, subarctic, tundra, and humid continental

Critical Thinking

1. Seacoasts and rivers facilitated trade and industrialization; mountain ranges created distinct regional and political boundaries; the Mediterranean Sea opened a link to African and Asian cultures; varying climates and vegetation allowed for distinct types of social, political, and economic developments.

Reviewing Key Terms

Write the letter of the key term that best matches each definition below.

a. sirocco   d. polder
b. fjord   e. timberline
c. foehn   f. mistral

1. elevation above which trees cannot grow
2. dry wind that blows in the Alps
3. hot wind that blows from North Africa to Europe's Mediterranean coast
4. drained area reclaimed from the sea
5. deep, water-filled valley carved by glaciers
6. strong north wind from the Alps that brings cold air to southern France

Reviewing Facts

SECTION 1

1. Why is Europe a "peninsula of peninsulas"?
2. What geographic area in Europe has rich, fertile farmland and is a center of industry?
3. How have human actions over the centuries changed Europe's waterways?

SECTION 2

4. How do the Gulf Stream and the North Atlantic Drift affect Europe's climate?
5. What kinds of climate regions are found in Iceland and the Scandinavian Peninsula?

Critical Thinking

1. Drawing Conclusions How did geographic features help shape European cultures? Provide examples to support your answers.

2. Identifying Cause and Effect Why did the North European Plain develop into a densely populated industrial center?

3. Drawing Conclusions Copy the diagram of European rivers, seas, and waterways below onto a sheet of paper. In each oval, write the name of a city that is located on or beside the body of water. Then draw lines to show how cities are linked by waterways.

North Sea –	Danube River –
Baltic Sea –	Thames River –
Rhine River –	Main-Danube Canal –

NATIONAL GEOGRAPHIC Locating Places
Europe: Physical Geography

Match the letters on the map with the physical features of Europe. Write your answers on a sheet of paper.

1. British Isles   5. Baltic Sea   8. Crete
2. Rhine River   6. Mediterranean Sea   9. Iberian Peninsula
3. Sicily   7. Scandinavia   10. Balkan Peninsula
4. Apennines

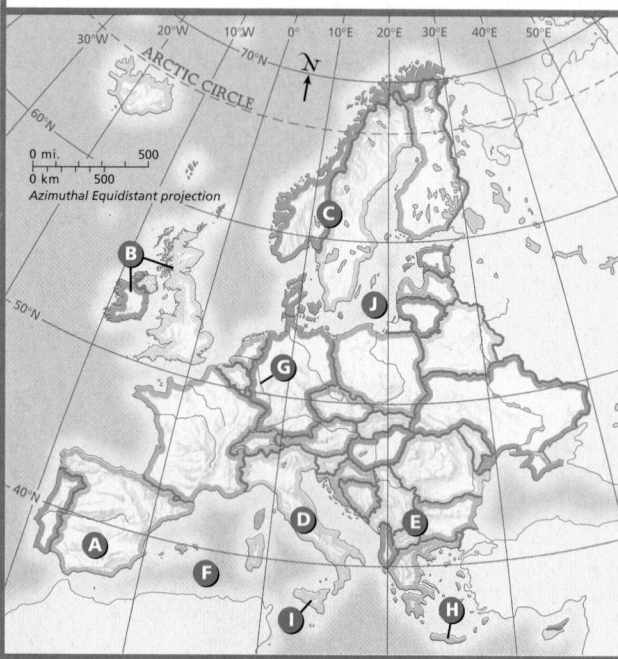

2. fertile soil, natural resources, and a major river linking that region to the North Sea
3. North Sea: Rotterdam, Netherlands; Baltic Sea: Gdańsk, Poland; Rhine River: Cologne, Germany; Danube River: Vienna, Austria; Thames River: London, England; Main-Danube Canal: Frankfurt, Germany. After locating key cities, students should show links by correct waterways.

NATIONAL GEOGRAPHIC Locating Places

| **1.** B | **3.** I | **5.** J | **7.** C | **9.** A |
| **2.** G | **4.** D | **6.** F | **8.** H | **10.** E |

Using the Regional Atlas

1. France
2. dairy, potatoes, grains

Using the Regional Atlas

Refer to the Regional Atlas on pages 260–263.

1. **Location** Through what country do the Seine, Loire, and Rhône Rivers flow?

2. **Place** What are three major agricultural products of the North European Plain?

Thinking Like a Geographer

Think about the physical geography of Europe. Identify Europe's energy resources, and where they are located. Which of these are nonrenewable resources? What future energy sources would you advise European countries to pursue?

Problem-Solving Activity

Group Research Activity People in Europe face many weather-related challenges, from avalanches in the mountains to flooding in the lowlands. Using the Internet and other resources, research an area in Europe that has successfully coped with weather-related events. Then report to the class on the solutions to these challenges. Include photos, charts, graphs, or any other visual elements to enhance your report.

GeoJournal

Creative Writing Using the information in your GeoJournal, describe an imaginary trip through a European country of your choice. Describe the country's physical features and the climate and natural vegetation you find. Use what you have learned in your reading to make your account detailed and colorful.

Technology Activity

Using an Electronic Spreadsheet Choose a city in each of Europe's climate regions, and find the average rainfall for each city. Use a spreadsheet program to organize your information, listing the cities in the first column and the rainfall amounts in the next column. Use the program's graphics feature to make a bar graph. Write a paragraph summarizing the variations in rainfall among the cities.

Standardized Test Practice

Choose the best answer for the following multiple-choice question. If you have trouble answering the question, use the process of elimination to narrow your choices.

> *"And so I have finally come to understand that while I am hopelessly American, accustomed to (and dependent on) the relentless pressures and fierce energies of the New World, . . . there are moments when I want to escape to a different place with a beauty and a beat of its own. And when that happens, when I want to disappear from who I am, and where I live, the place I think of is Paris."*
>
> —David Halberstam, "Paris," *National Geographic Traveler,* October 1999

1. **What kind of place does the author want to escape to sometimes?**

   A He wants a place where there is a lot of pressure and energy.

   B He wants a beautiful place halfway around the world.

   C He wants a unique, beautiful place that is different from where he lives.

   D He wants a place where he can disappear into the crowds.

 **Test-Taking Tip** When choosing an answer for a multiple-choice question, sometimes more than one option may seem correct. Read the question carefully, and then look in the reading for information about the kind of place. Compare each answer with that information.

GeoJournal

In this activity, students might imagine themselves traveling across a country by train, bicycle, motorcycle, or on foot. It might be helpful to tell them to consider a timeframe—a day hike, weekend bike trip, or cross-country ride on a train with several stops along the way.

Technology Activity

In the paragraph, students should consider a comparison and contrast approach. They could compare the seasonal rainfall changes in a cluster of cities in one region or compare different cities in different regions.

Standardized Test Practice

1. C

Tested Objectives:
analyzing information
process of elimination

Additional Practice and Test-Taking Tips

 Standardized Test Practice Workbook

❓ CHAPTER BONUS TEST QUESTION

In what country would you find Europe's highest and lowest points? *(European Russia; the highest is Mt. Elbrus at 18,510 ft. [5,642 m]; the lowest is at the Volga delta on the Caspian Sea at 92 ft. [28 m] below sea level.)*

Thinking Like a Geographer

Students should refer to the unit opener section and categorize Europe's natural resources. They should determine which regions have the highest concentrations of coal, iron ore, timber, petroleum, or other resources used for energy. Students should consider that some resources are renewable and others are not. They might also discuss the role that nuclear and solar energy will play in meeting Europe's future energy requirements.

Problem-Solving Activity

Students' reports should show knowledge of how to use the Internet for research, with accompanying visuals. Topics may include polders or land reclamation in the Netherlands or the building-up or reinforcement of Venice against sinking and flooding.

CHAPTER 12 PLANNING GUIDE

NOTE: The following materials may be used when teaching Chapter 12. Section-level support materials are shown at point-of-use in the margins of the Teacher Wraparound Edition.

TEACHING TRANSPARENCIES

L2 Unit 4 Map Overlay Transparencies

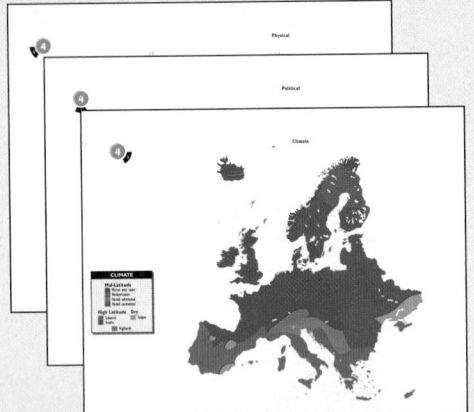

L2 Political Map Transparency 4

GEOGRAPHIC LITERACY

Focus on Geography Literacy

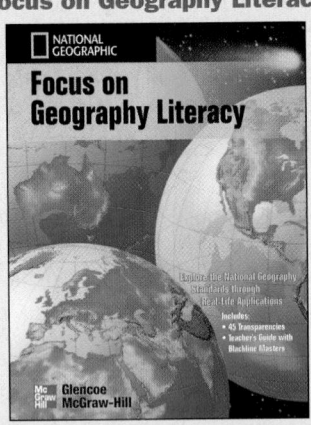

APPLICATION AND ENRICHMENT

L3 Enrichment Activity 12

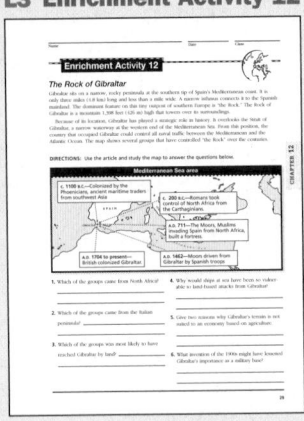

REVIEW AND REINFORCEMENT

L1 Vocabulary Activity 12 L1 Reinforcing Skills Activity 12 L1 Reteaching Activity 12

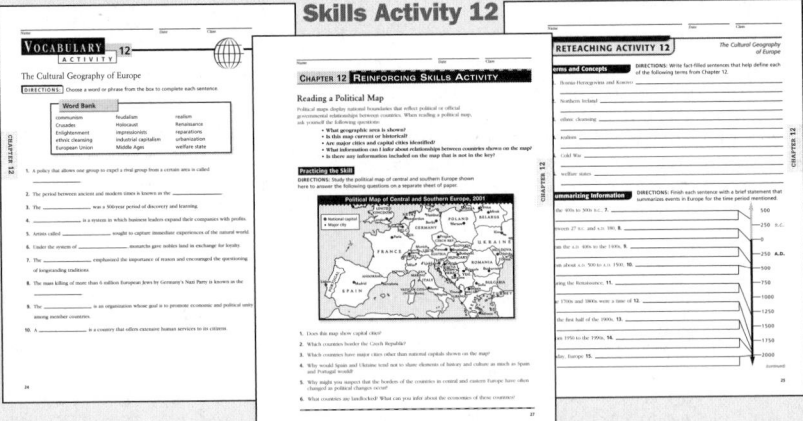

ASSESSMENT

L2 Chapter 12 Test Form A

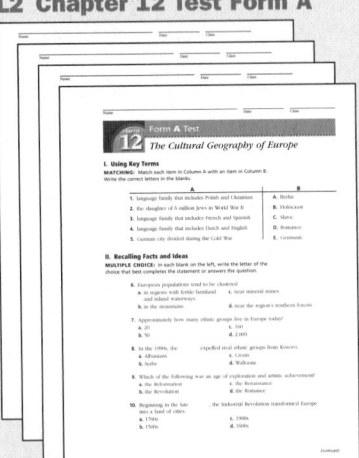

L2 Chapter 12 Test Form B

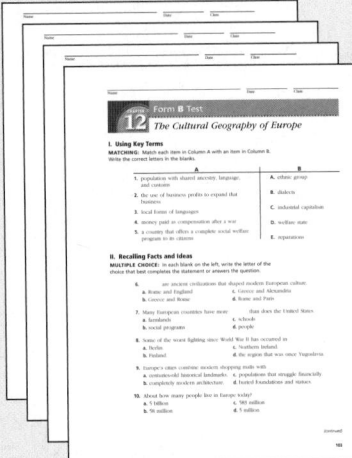

L1/ELL Performance Assessment Activity 12

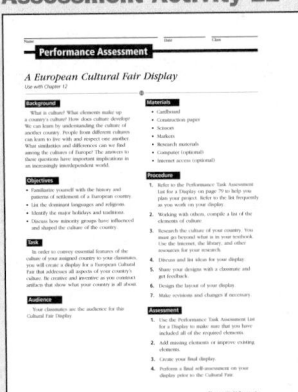

ExamView® Pro Testmaker

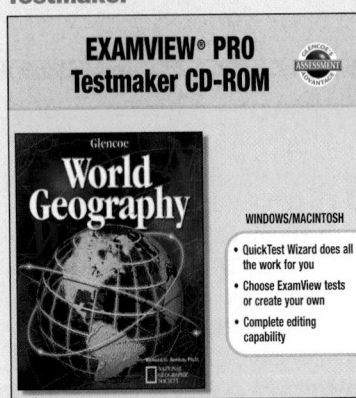

EXAMVIEW® PRO Testmaker CD-ROM

WINDOWS/MACINTOSH

- QuickTest Wizard does all the work for you
- Choose ExamView tests or create your own
- Complete editing capability

The following Spanish language materials are available in the Spanish Resources binder:

- 📁 Spanish Vocabulary Activities
- 📁 Spanish Guided Reading Activities
- 📁 Spanish Reteaching Activities
- 📁 Spanish Summaries
- 📁 Spanish Quizzes and Tests
- 📁 Spanish Reading Essentials and Study Guide

- 🎞 World Regions Video
- 🎞 MindJogger Videoquiz
- 💿 Vocabulary PuzzleMaker CD-ROM
- 💿 Interactive Tutor Self-Assessment CD-ROM
- 💿 ExamView® Pro Testmaker CD-ROM
- 💿 Audio Program
- 💿 TeacherWorks CD-ROM
- 💿 Interactive Student Edition CD-ROM
- 💿 Glencoe Skillbuilder Interactive Workbook CD-ROM, Level 2
- 💿 Presentation Plus! CD-ROM

Timesaving Tools

TeacherWorks™ All-In-One Planner and Resource Center

- **Interactive Teacher Edition** Access your Teacher Wraparound Edition and your classroom resources with a few easy clicks.
- **Interactive Lesson Planner** Planning has never been easier! Organize your week, month, semester, or year with all the lesson helps you need to make teaching creative, timely, and relevant.

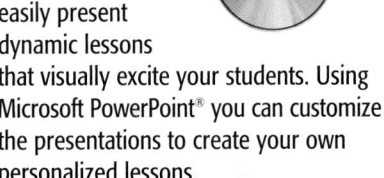

Use Glencoe's **Presentation Plus!** multimedia teacher tool to easily present dynamic lessons that visually excite your students. Using Microsoft PowerPoint® you can customize the presentations to create your own personalized lessons.

GEOGRAPHY Online

Use our Web site for additional resources. All essential content is covered in the Student Edition.

You and your students can visit geography.glencoe.com, the Web site companion to *Glencoe World Geography*. This innovative integration of electronic and print media offers your students a wealth of opportunities. The student text directs students to the Web site for the following options:

- Chapter Overviews
- Student Activities
- Self-Check Quizzes
- Textbook Updates

Answers are provided for you in the "Web Activity Lesson Plan." Additional Web resources and Interactive Tutor puzzles are also available.

▶ **Additional Glencoe Teacher Support**

- Teaching Strategies for the Geography Classroom (including Block Scheduling Pacing Guides)
- Graphic Organizer Transparencies Strategies and Activities
- Outline Map Resource Book
- Reading in the Content Area

SECTION RESOURCES

Daily Objectives	Reproducible Resources	Multimedia Resources

SECTION 1   Population Patterns

1. Explain how Europe's physical geography influences its population density and distribution.
2. Describe the effects of industrialization and urbanization on Europe's people.
3. Discuss how recent patterns of migration have influenced European culture.

- Reproducible Lesson Plan 12-1
- Daily Lecture Notes 12-1
- Guided Reading Activity 12-1*
- Reading Essentials and Study Guide 12-1*
- Section Quiz 12-1*

- Daily Focus Skills Transparency 12-1
- Political Map Transparency 4
- Unit 4 Map Overlay Transparencies
- Interactive Tutor Self-Assessment CD-ROM
- ExamView® Pro Testmaker CD-ROM*
- Presentation Plus! CD-ROM

SECTION 2   History and Government

1. Discuss the contributions early Europeans made to world culture.
2. Describe the ways Europe's geography has shaped its history.
3. Explain how world wars and economic and political revolutions affected Europe.

- Reproducible Lesson Plan 12-2
- Daily Lecture Notes 12-2
- Guided Reading Activity 12-2*
- Reading Essentials and Study Guide 12-2*
- Section Quiz 12-2*

- Daily Focus Skills Transparency 12-2
- Unit 4 Map Overlay Transparencies
- World Art and Architecture Transparencies
- Interactive Tutor Self-Assessment CD-ROM
- ExamView® Pro Testmaker CD-ROM*
- Presentation Plus! CD-ROM

SECTION 3   Cultures and Lifestyles

1. Explain how religion has influenced the cultural development of Europe.
2. Discuss the ways European art and culture have been influential throughout the world.
3. Describe how European governments meet the educational and healthcare needs of their peoples.

- Reproducible Lesson Plan 12-3
- Vocabulary Activity 12*
- Daily Lecture Notes 12-3
- Guided Reading Activity 12-3*
- Reading Essentials and Study Guide 12-3*
- Reteaching Activity 12*
- Reinforcing Skills Activity 12
- Section Quiz 12-3*

- Daily Focus Skills Transparency 12-3
- Unit 4 Map Overlay Transparencies
- Vocabulary PuzzleMaker CD-ROM
- World Music: A Cultural Legacy
- Interactive Tutor Self-Assessment CD-ROM
- ExamView® Pro Testmaker CD-ROM*
- Presentation Plus! CD-ROM

- Blackline Master
- Transparency
- Software
- CD-ROM
- Videocassette
- DVD

*Also available in Spanish

00:00 OUT OF TIME? Assign the Chapter 12 **Reading Essentials and Study Guide.**

Block Schedule

Activities that are particularly suited to use within the block scheduling framework are identified throughout this chapter by the following designation:

KEY TO ABILITY LEVELS

Teaching strategies have been coded for various learning styles and abilities.

L1   **BASIC** activities for all students

L2   **AVERAGE** activities for average to above-average students

L3   **CHALLENGING** activities for above-average students

ELL   **ENGLISH LANGUAGE LEARNER** activities

NATIONAL GEOGRAPHIC — TEACHER'S CORNER

Index to National Geographic Magazine:

The following articles may be used for research relating to this chapter:

- "Wrath of the Gods," by Rick Gore, July 2000.
- "Tale of Three Cities," by Joel L. Swerdlow, August 1999.
- "London," by Simon Worrall, June 2000.
- "Italy's Endangered Art," by Erla Zwingle, August 1999.

National Geographic Society Products:

To order the following products for use with this chapter, call National Geographic Society at 1-800-368-2728.

- *Europe* (Video)
- *Europe: The Road to Unity* (Video)
- *National Geographic Atlas of the World, Seventh Edition* (Book)

NGS ONLINE

Access National Geographic's Web site for current events, activities, links, interactive features, and archives.
www.nationalgeographic.com

Meeting National Standards

Geography For Life

The following standards are highlighted in Chapter 12:

Section 1 EE2 Places and Regions:
Standards 4, 6
EE4 Human Systems:
Standards 9, 10, 13

Section 2 EE4 Human Systems:
Standards 9, 10, 12, 13
EE5 Environment and Society:
Standards 14, 16

Section 3 EE2 Places and Regions: Standards 4, 6
EE4 Human Systems: Standards 9, 10, 13
EE5 Environment and Society: Standard 15

Local Objectives

_____

_____

MEETING SPECIAL NEEDS

In addition to the Differentiated Instruction strategies found in each section, the following resources are also suitable for your special needs students:

- *ExamView® Pro Testmaker CD-ROM* allows teachers to tailor tests by reducing answer choices.
- The *Audio Program* includes the entire narrative of the student edition so that less-proficient readers can listen to the words as they read them.
- The *Reading Essentials and Study Guide* provides the same content as the student edition but is written two grade levels below the textbook.
- *Guided Reading Activities* give less-proficient readers point-by-point instructions to increase comprehension as they read each textbook section.
- *Enrichment Activities* include a stimulating collection of readings and activities for gifted and talented students.

Chapter Objectives

1. Describe how physical geography and industrial growth have affected the distribution of Europe's population.

2. Explain how Europe's ethnic diversity has been both a cause of conflict and a source of unity.

3. Discuss the influence of European art and culture throughout the world.

GLENCOE TECHNOLOGY

Use *MindJogger Videoquiz* to preview the Chapter 12 content.

GeoJournal

For access to additional photos, maps, and information on the cultural features of Europe, go to www.nationalgeographic.com (See Teacher pages in front for strategies for using journals in the geography classroom.)

Introduce students to chapter content and key terms by having them access **Chapter Overview 12** at geography.glencoe.com

FOLDABLES™ Study Organizer

Dinah Zike's Foldables are three-dimensional, interactive graphic organizers that help students practice basic writing skills, review key vocabulary terms, and identify main ideas. Have students complete the Foldable activity in the **Dinah Zike's Reading and Study Skills Foldables** booklet.

CHAPTER 12

The Cultural Geography of Europe

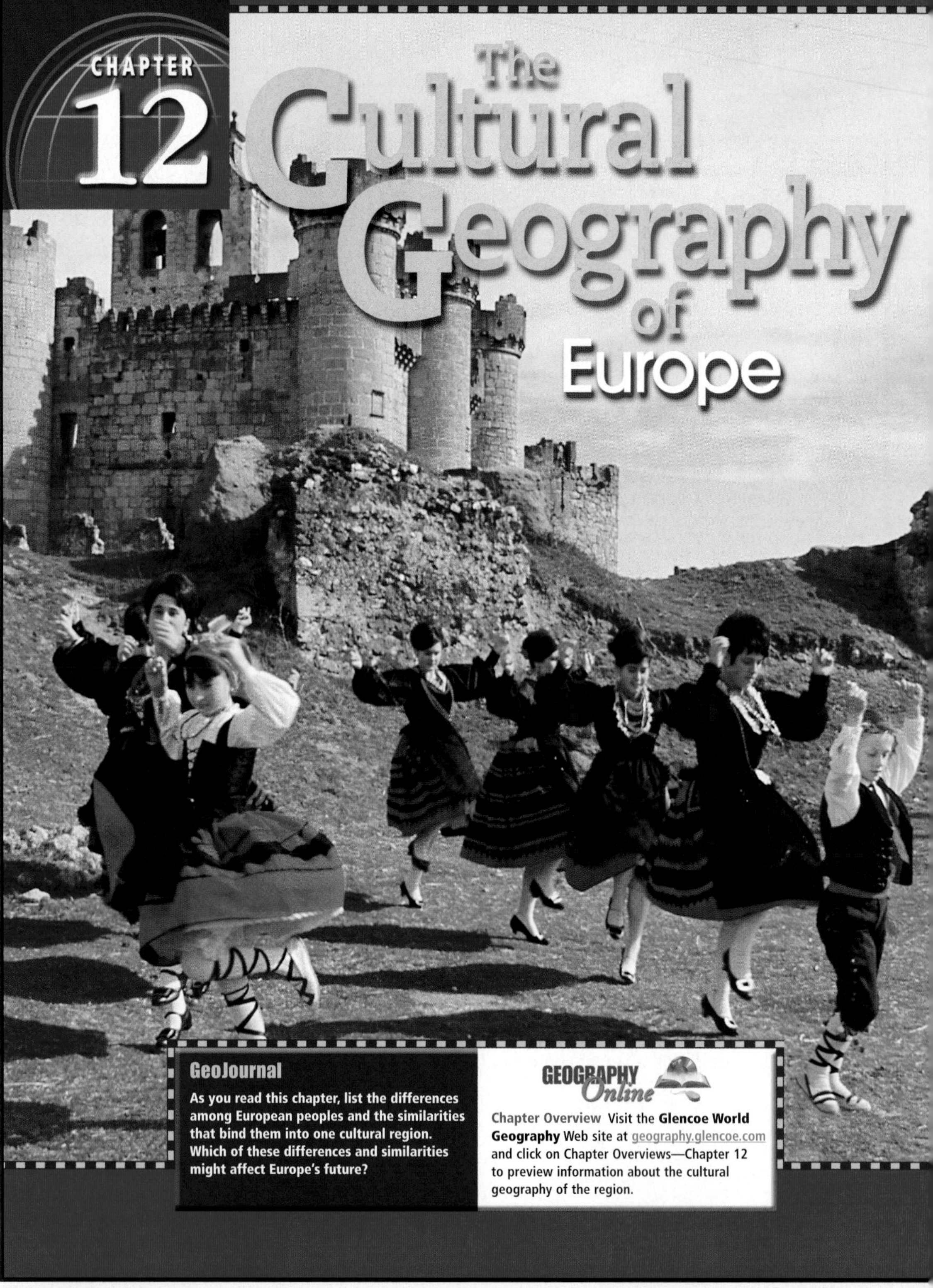

GeoJournal

As you read this chapter, list the differences among European peoples and the similarities that bind them into one cultural region. Which of these differences and similarities might affect Europe's future?

GEOGRAPHY Online

Chapter Overview Visit the **Glencoe World Geography** Web site at geography.glencoe.com and click on Chapter Overviews—Chapter 12 to preview information about the cultural geography of the region.

ABOUT THE PHOTO

Castilla Castilla-Leon is not only the largest region in Spain, it is also the largest region of the European Union. It is situated on elevated plains that are surrounded by mountain ranges to the east, south, and north, and the Duero River to the west, toward Portugal. The region's importance during Spanish medieval history is reflected by its many cathedrals, monasteries, castles, and fortified towns. **Ask: Do people in Spain generally dress like these dancers?** *(No)* **What groups in the United States might wear special kinds of clothing to perform folk dances?** *(possible answers: square dancers, Native American dancers)* **EE2 Places and Regions: Standards 4, 6**

Population Patterns

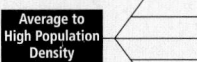
NATIONAL GEOGRAPHIC

A Geographic View

Search for a New Life

In a world of shifting demographics—where the poor, the dispossessed, and the war-ravaged are on the move—Western Europe has become the migrant's preferred destination.... There are nearly 20 million legal immigrants there—plus an estimated two million illegal aliens.... In 1992 more than 750,000 political asylum seekers crowded into Europe, more than half of them into Germany. Almost all become economic wards [dependents] of their adopted nations.

Immigrants shop at a London market.

—Peter Ross Range, "Europe Faces an Immigrant Tide,"
National Geographic, *May 1993*

Europe is home to more than 40 countries, whose peoples belong to many different cultural groups and speak a variety of languages. This diversity stems from centuries of migration, cultural diffusion, conflict, and changing borders. In this section you will learn about Europe's peoples, their ethnic characteristics, and where they live.

Ethnic Diversity

Europe's diverse population reflects a long history of migrations throughout the continent. Most Europeans are descended from various Indo-European and Mediterranean peoples who settled the continent centuries ago. Europe's population today also includes more recent immigrants from Asia, Africa, and the Caribbean area who arrived during the past 100 years. Many of these immigrants have come from areas of the world once ruled by European countries.

◀ *Turegano folk dancers, Spain*

Chapter 12 ● **287**

Guide to Reading

Consider What You Know

Recent conflicts in Europe's Balkan Peninsula frequently make newspaper headlines. How do these conflicts affect everyday life for people in the region today?

Reading Strategy

Categorizing Complete a graphic organizer similar to the one below by listing the features that contribute to an average to higher-than-average population density.

> Average to
> High Population
> Density

Read to Find Out

- How does the physical geography of Europe influence its population density and distribution?
- What effects have industrialization and urbanization had on Europe's people?
- How have recent patterns of migration influenced the region's cultures?

Terms to Know

- ethnic group
- refugee
- ethnic cleansing
- urbanization

Places to Locate

- Sweden
- United Kingdom
- Belgium
- France
- Bosnia-Herzegovina
- Czech Republic
- Poland
- Kosovo
- Paris
- Germany
- London
- Vatican City
- Naples

 **FOCUS**

Section Overview

This section discusses the effects of physical geography, industrialization, and recent patterns of migration in Europe.

BELLRINGER
Skillbuilder Activity

- Project transparency and have students answer questions.
- Available as blackline master.

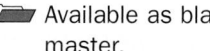
Daily Focus Skills Transparency 12-1

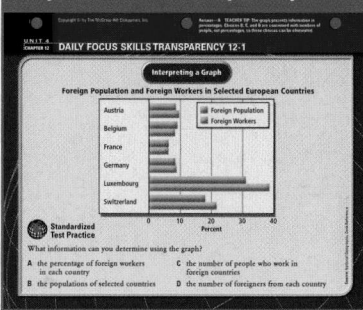

Guide to Reading

Consider What You Know

Answers *Responses may include loss of life and property; environmental damage; economic crises; shortages of food and medicine; and the threat of expanded hostilities.*

Reading Strategy

Answers *favorable climates, plains, fertile soil, mineral resources, inland waterways*

Preteaching Vocabulary

Ask students to find the meanings of the following terms: *ethnic cleansing* (page 288), *refugee* (page 288), and *urbanization* (page 290).

② TEACH

L2 Comparisons

Discuss some of the important social issues that have confronted the United States and Europe throughout their respective histories. Issues can be linked to ethnic conflicts, and religious and cultural differences. Ask students to compare how these issues were resolved, if at all, in Europe and the United States.

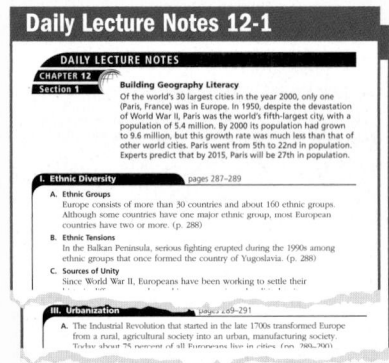

Daily Lecture Notes 12-1

DAILY LECTURE NOTES

CHAPTER 12
Section 1

Building Geography Literacy
Of the world's 30 largest cities in the year 2000, only one (Paris, France) was in Europe. In 1950, despite the devastation of World War II, Paris was the world's fifth-largest city, with a population of 5.4 million. By 2000 its population had grown to 9.6 million, but this growth rate was much less than that of other world cities. Paris went from 5th to 22nd in population. Experts predict that by 2015, Paris will be 27th in population.

I. Ethnic Diversity *pages 287–289*

A. **Ethnic Groups**
Europe consists of more than 30 countries and about 160 ethnic groups. Although some countries have one major ethnic group, most European countries have two or more. (p. 288)

B. **Ethnic Tensions**
In the Balkan Peninsula, serious fighting erupted during the 1990s among ethnic groups that once formed the country of Yugoslavia. (p. 288)

C. **Sources of Unity**
Since World War II, Europeans have been working to settle their

III. Urbanization *pages 289–291*

A. The Industrial Revolution that started in the late 1700s transformed Europe from a rural, agricultural society into an urban, manufacturing society. Today about 75 percent of all Europeans live in cities. (pp. 289–290)

📷 NATIONAL GEOGRAPHIC World Explorer

Answer

Unify: value of past; families; commitment to democracy; divide: ethnic differences

More About the Photo Les Galeries Lafayette is Paris's major department store. A center of luxury goods, Paris is known for high-fashion clothing, jewelry, and perfumes.

Ethnic Groups

Today Europe is home to more than 160 separate ethnic groups—groups of people with a shared ancestry, language, customs, and, often, religion. Some European countries have one major ethnic group. In **Sweden**, for example, 89 percent of the population are Swedes, descendants of Germanic and other groups that settled the peninsula of Scandinavia centuries ago. They share a common culture, the Swedish language, and a Lutheran religious heritage.

In other countries the population consists of two or more major ethnic groups. For example, **Belgium** has two leading ethnic groups—the Flemings and the Walloons. The Flemings make up about 56 percent of Belgium's population and the Walloons about 32 percent. The Flemings, closely related to the Dutch, are descended from Germanic groups who invaded the area of present-day Belgium during the A.D. 400s. The Walloons trace their ancestry to the Celts who lived in the area during the Germanic invasions. Flemings and Walloons are both Roman Catholic, but language differences have often led to bitter relations between them. Both groups, however, have been able to keep their disputes from endangering Belgium's national unity.

Ethnic Tensions

Tensions among some European ethnic groups have led to armed conflict. The Balkan Peninsula has long been a shatterbelt, a region caught between external and internal rivalries. In the 1990s, the Balkans was a battleground among Serbs, Croats, Bosnian Muslims, and Kosovar Albanians. Following World War II, these and other Balkan peoples had belonged to a communist-ruled land called Yugoslavia. For a time, hatreds were muted. But after the communist system's fall in the early 1990s, ethnic tensions erupted, resulting in Yugoslavia's breakup into separate independent republics.

Within some of the new republics, ethnic hatreds were serious enough to spark the worst fighting in Europe since World War II. The republic of **Bosnia-Herzegovina** (BAHZ•nee•uh HERT•seh•GAW•vee•nah) and the Serb-ruled territory of **Kosovo** (KAW•saw•VAW) were centers of the most brutal warfare. Following a policy called ethnic cleansing, Serb leaders expelled or killed rival ethnic groups in these areas. As a result, many people

became refugees—people who flee to a foreign country for safety. International peacemaking efforts, however, enabled many of these refugees to later return to their homes.

Sources of Unity

Although division and conflict have characterized much of Europe's history, Europeans in recent years have been working toward greater unity. Their efforts at cooperation rest on common attitudes and values. For example, most Europeans value the importance of the past and the cultural achievements of their ancestors. They also take pride in their families, which they place at the center of their social lives.

Despite having varying forms of government, the peoples of Europe generally share a commitment to

📷 NATIONAL GEOGRAPHIC World Explorer

Geography Skills for Life

Paris Shopping A world center of fashion, Paris, France, is known for its elegant shops and department stores.

Region What cultural factors unite Europeans? What cultural factors divide them?

DIFFERENTIATED INSTRUCTION

Reading Support Instruct students who may have reading difficulties to study the "Guide to Reading" at the beginning of the section on page 287. Tell them that this feature summarizes the content of Section 1. Have students speculate on what the section will cover based on the information in "Guide to Reading."

🌐 **EE4 Human Systems: Standard 13**

📁 Refer to *Inclusion for the Social Studies Classroom Strategies and Activities.*

democracy and free markets. Their sense of individualism, however, is combined with the belief that government should regulate economies and provide for social welfare. These similarities make it easier for residents to think of themselves as Europeans as well as members of ethnic or national groups.

Population Characteristics

Europe is smaller in land area than any other continent except Australia. Yet it is the third most populous continent, after Asia and Africa. In the year 2003, Europe's population (excluding Russia) was about 581.5 million. **Germany**, with 82.6 million people, is Europe's largest country in population, and **Vatican City** is the smallest, with only 1,000 people.

Population Density

Europe's large numbers of people are crowded into a relatively small space. In fact, Europe's population density is greater than that of any other continent except Asia. If Europe's population were distributed evenly throughout the continent, the average population density would be 255 people per square mile (98 people per sq. km). In Europe, however, as in other continents, the population is not distributed evenly. Most of Europe has far less than the average population density. The region's highly industrialized urban centers, however, are among the world's most densely populated areas.

Population Distribution

As in other parts of the world, Europe's population distribution is closely related to its physical geography. Compare the population density map on page 262 with the physical map on page 260. Notice that mountainous areas and cold northern areas in Europe are less populated than plains areas. In fact, the parts of Europe with average or higher than average population densities share one or more of the following features: favorable climates, plains, fertile soil, mineral resources, and inland waterways. One of the most densely populated parts of Europe extends from the **United Kingdom** into **France** and across the fertile North European Plain into the **Czech Republic** and **Poland**. Another densely

Geography Skills for Life

Vatican City This view of St. Peter's Square is from the top of St. Peter's Basilica, one of the world's largest Christian churches and a gathering place for many Roman Catholics.

Place What other European countries have small populations?

populated area extends from southeastern France into northern Italy. In addition to having rich farmland, these regions contain densely populated, industrial cities.

Urbanization

Beginning in the late 1700s, the Industrial Revolution transformed Europe from a rural, agricultural society to an urban, industrial society. Rural villagers moved in large numbers to urban areas

GEOGRAPHY Online

Student Web Activity Visit the **Glencoe World Geography** Web site at geography.glencoe.com and click on Student Web Activities—Chapter 12 for an activity on researching the cultural similarities and differences among Scandinavian countries.

NATIONAL GEOGRAPHIC **World Explorer**

Answer
Andorra, Liechtenstein, Monaco, and San Marino

More About the Photo Constructed from 1656 to 1667, St. Peter's Square (in reality, an oval) is encompassed by four rows of graceful Doric columns —284 altogether.

L1/ELL

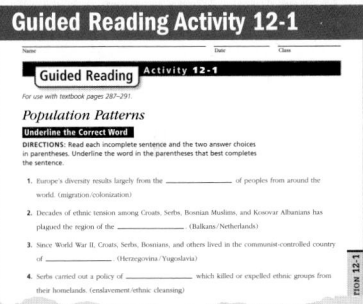

Guided Reading Activity 12-1

L1/ELL

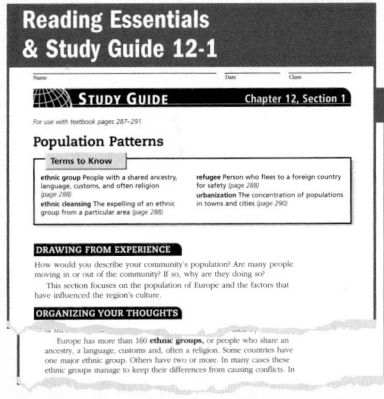

Reading Essentials & Study Guide 12-1

GEOGRAPHY Online

Objectives, goals, and answers to the student activity can be found in the Web Activity Lesson Plan feature at geography.glencoe.com

COOPERATIVE LEARNING ACTIVITY

Europe's Cities Organize students into six groups and assign one of the following European cities to each group: Paris, Amsterdam, Florence, Lisbon, Athens, or Prague. Members of each group should prepare an article for a book about some of Europe's cities. The article should include location, natural resources, economic activities, population, history, and landmarks. Organize the articles into a "book," and reproduce copies for students. Have students compare and contrast the information. Ask them to explain the processes that have caused these cities to grow over the centuries. *(Possible answers: location along transportation routes; availability of resources.)*
🌐 **EE4 Human Systems: Standard 9**

ASSESS

Assign Section 1 Assessment as homework or as an in-class activity.

Have students use **Interactive Tutor Self-Assessment CD-ROM** to review Section 1.

L2

Section Quiz 12-1

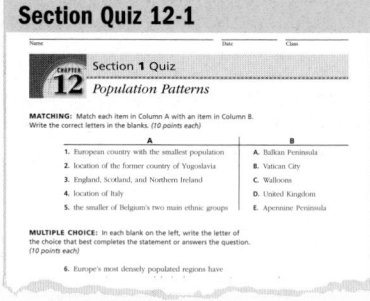

NATIONAL GEOGRAPHIC **World Explorer**

Answer
Answers should contain meaningful comparisons.

More About the Photo
Unlike much of Europe, Prague was spared serious damage in World War II. It remains one of Europe's most beautiful cities.

---

and became factory workers. This concentration of populations in towns and cities is known as **urbanization**. The growth of industries and cities began first in western Europe during the late 1700s. Later, after World War II, this process spread to eastern Europe.

Today about 75 percent of Europeans live in cities. **Paris** and **London** rank among the world's largest urban areas. Other European cities with large populations include Rome, Italy; Madrid, Spain; Berlin, Germany; Stockholm, Sweden; Budapest, Hungary; Athens, Greece; and Kiev, Ukraine.

Urban Features

Europe's largest cities, like cities everywhere, face the challenges of overcrowding and pollution. In spite of these problems, European cities

NATIONAL GEOGRAPHIC **World Explorer**

Geography Skills for Life

Historic Prague Prague, in the Czech Republic, is a city of churches and palaces.
Place How does Prague compare with major cities in your state?

provide a unique combination of old and new ways of life. Landmarks that date back hundreds of years stand near fast-food restaurants and shopping malls. **Naples**, Italy, is one city that reflects this coming together of past and present in modern Europe:

> One morning I went on a . . . walk through . . . the historic center of Naples. Here the grid plan remains from the original Greek settlement, with laundry-festooned streets barely the width of an average driveway. Lack of space has never presented any serious problem to the Neapolitan. . . . At any given moment there will be at least one car on the street, along with two motorbikes (coming from opposite directions), three girls walking arm in arm, and a family with a baby carriage, all of whom unaccountably manage to avoid collision. "
>
> Erla Zwingle, "Naples Unabashed," *National Geographic*, March 1998

Economics
Population Movements

Population movements have been a constant aspect of European life. During the 1800s and early 1900s, many Europeans migrated to the Americas and parts of Africa and the South Pacific region. Since the mid-1900s, far fewer Europeans have permanently left the region, but large numbers of foreigners have migrated to Europe.

When western Europe's economy boomed during the 1950s and 1960s, labor shortages developed. Many European countries invited guest workers from other countries to fill available jobs. Soon guest workers and immigrants began arriving, seeking the social and economic opportunities that western Europe had to offer. In France, for example, immigrants came from North African countries newly independent from France. In Germany guest workers from Turkey, Greece, and the Balkan countries of southeastern Europe filled industrial jobs. The United Kingdom also saw

---

CRITICAL THINKING ACTIVITY

Analyzing Information Since the end of World War II, Europe has seen a massive influx of immigrants from all over the world. Have students research the Internet and library resources for statistical data on immigration to the European Union. Have students design and draw a world map that uses arrows to show the inflow of migrants to the European Union from their places of origin. **Ask:** From where have migrants to the EU come? *(North Africa, the Balkans, the Caribbean, South Asia, Southwest Asia.)* Which EU countries have received the most immigrants? *(United Kingdom, France, Germany, Belgium)*
🌐 **EE4 Human Systems: Standard 13**

increased immigration from countries in South Asia and the Caribbean areas that had once been British but were now independent.

By the time Europe's economy had slowed in the 1970s, many guest workers had moved their families and established homes in host countries. Tensions rose as the immigrants and local residents competed for jobs, housing, and social services. As a result, many immigrants felt unwelcome in their new countries. Since the 1970s, European governments have tried to limit further immigration while protecting the rights of their immigrant communities.

Despite its growing immigrant populations and abundant resources, Europe's overall population is shrinking. Italy and Germany, for example, have the world's lowest birthrates. Experts predict that Italy's population will fall from 57.2 million today to about 52.3 million by 2050. In addition, older people are making up a larger percentage of Europe's population.

Europe's population continues to change even as it maintains and honors its historic traditions. In the next section you will learn how Europe's physical geography affected the settlement of its peoples and their cultural and economic development.

NATIONAL GEOGRAPHIC World Explorer

Geography Skills for Life

A Village in Ruins During the 1990s ethnic violence uprooted many people in the Balkan Peninsula.
Movement What major European country has hosted Balkan migrants since the 1950s?

SECTION  1 ASSESSMENT

Checking for Understanding

1. **Define** ethnic group, ethnic cleansing, refugee, urbanization.
2. **Main Ideas** On a sheet of paper, create a web diagram like the one below to show important details about Europe's population.

```
Population of Europe

Ethnic Diversity          Population Characteristics
•                         •
•                         •
•                         •
•                         •
```

Critical Thinking

3. **Making Generalizations** Why have people migrated to Europe from various parts of the world?
4. **Drawing Conclusions** What factors contribute to the patterns of population density and distribution in Europe?
5. **Identifying Cause and Effect** What effect has migration had on modern Europe?
6. **Predicting Consequences** What might be the consequences of falling birthrates in some European countries?

Analyzing Maps

7. **Region** Look at the population density map page 262. Find three regions in which population density varies within a country. Explain how climate and physical features contribute to these differences.

Applying Geography

8. **Geography and Population** Consider how physical geography has influenced population patterns in Europe. In an essay, describe one population group, and explain the impact of physical geography on the settlement of this group.

NATIONAL GEOGRAPHIC World Explorer

Answer
Germany

More About the Photo Some of the worst battles of Balkan ethnic conflicts were fought around Sarajevo—the city that hosted the Winter Olympic Games in 1984.

Reteach

Review the concepts of population density and distribution, so that students understand the reasons why for centuries people have been drawn to specific regions of Europe.

Enrich

Read a passage from a magazine or newspaper that recounts a refugee's experience during the 1990s war in Bosnia.

④ CLOSE

Ask students to write a short essay on how immigrants have influenced the cultures of the United States and Europe.

SECTION 1 ASSESSMENT ANSWERS

1. All vocabulary words are defined in the text.
2. Students' diagrams should reflect an understanding of ethnic diversity and population characteristics.
3. to find good jobs and a higher quality of life
4. Answers should focus on the effects of urbanization and the continent's physical features.
5. increased tension between immigrants and residents over jobs, housing, and social services
6. a high percentage of older people and a need to import "guest workers"
7. An example is in the Apennine Peninsula (Italy), where population density varies from more than 250 people per square mile (per 2.59 sq. km) to less than 50 people per square mile (per 2.59 sq. km). These variations in population density are the consequence of mountains, fertile soil, and urbanization.
8. **Applying Geography** Students should consider how mountain ranges, coastlines, rivers, altitude, and climate affected the historical and cultural development of the population group they select.

GEOGRAPHY AND HISTORY

① FOCUS

At different points during its past, the Balkan Peninsula has been subjected to rule by outsiders, from the Ottoman Turks in the 1300s to the German invaders in the 1900s. Have students refer to the map on page 261. Using the scale provided on the map, have students determine the proximity of Balkan cities such as Belgrade, Zagreb, and Sarajevo to Constantinople and Berlin. Have students consider what might have attracted the Turks and Germans to exert control over the Balkans.

② TEACH

Cultural Influences Ask students to discuss some of the causes of recent Balkan conflicts. In their discussions, students should consider the region's strategic location, cultural diversity, and years of foreign occupation. Point out to students that the term *balkanize*—to break up (as a unit) into smaller and often hostile units—is derived from the word Balkans, a region that has been steeped in conflict for centuries.

YUGOSLAVIA: THEN AND NOW

CAN YOU IMAGINE waking in the night to the sounds of soldiers and gunfire? Quickly you grab a few belongings and flee with your family from your home. This scenario may sound far-fetched, but if you lived on the Balkan Peninsula, it might be more believable. There, many people have been forced from their homes during the last decade. The peninsula has long been a region of instability and conflict. But since the beginning of the breakup of the former Yugoslavia in 1991–1992, long-held resentments among various ethnic groups have erupted into full-scale wars.

A New Nation Emerges

The Balkan Peninsula lies in southeast Europe, between the Black and Adriatic Seas. Towering mountain ranges—the Carpathian and Dinaric—dominate the area. Long ago, Slavic peoples moved south into the region from what are now southern Poland and Russia. Slavic groups established independent states—Croatia, founded by the Croats; Serbia, founded by the Serbs; and Slovenia, founded by the Slovenes. Foreign nations ruled these lands for centuries. The Ottomans, who were based in what is now

Families flee Rača, Yugoslavia, when fighting erupts in their village. Minority ethnic groups throughout the region have been forced to leave their homes. ▶

BACKGROUND INFORMATION

Serbia The 1389 defeat of the Serb army by the Ottoman Turks at the battle of Kosovo resulted in almost 500 years of Turkish dominance in the Balkan Peninsula, fueling Serb nationalism. Serbia gained independence in 1878 and later became the core of Yugoslavia, a new country formed after World War I. From 1944 until 1980, Josip Broz Tito's strong rule muted religious and ethnic tensions. In the 1990s, however, fighting broke out among the Serbs, Bosnians, and Croats as the former Federated Republic of Yugoslavia was dismantled. In 1999 Serbia's expulsion of ethnic Albanians from Kosovo triggered new hostilities on the Balkan Peninsula.
🌐 **EE4 Human Systems: Standard 10**

NATIONAL GEOGRAPHIC

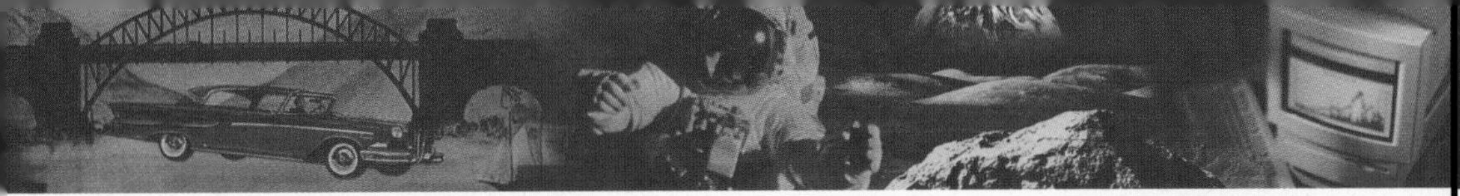

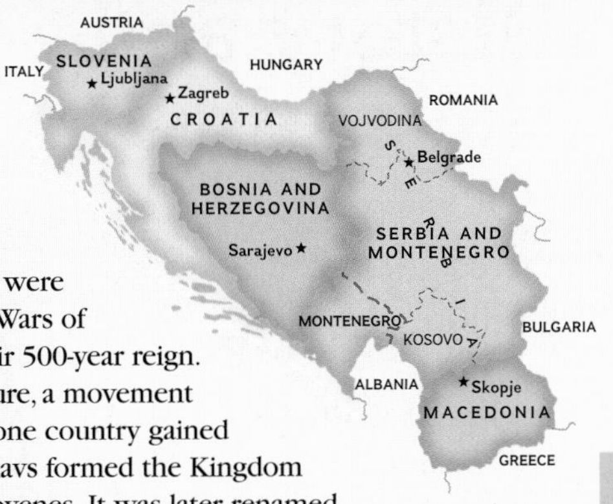

Turkey, controlled much of the region and gave the peninsula its name—*Balkan*, or "mountains."

The Ottoman Turks were defeated in the Balkan Wars of 1912–1913, ending their 500-year reign. Following their departure, a movement to unite the Slavs into one country gained strength. In 1918 the Slavs formed the Kingdom of Serbs, Croats, and Slovenes. It was later renamed Yugoslavia, "Land of the South Slavs."

During World War II, Nazi Germany's occupation of Yugoslavia divided the country. Throughout the war, an underground group headed by Croatian Josip Broz, who was code-named Tito, worked against Germany. At war's end, Yugoslavia emerged as a Communist country with Tito as its leader. It consisted of six republics—Croatia, Bosnia and Herzegovina, Slovenia, Montenegro, Serbia, and Macedonia.

The Nation Splinters

Tito ruled Yugoslavia with an iron hand and succeeded in holding the ethnically mixed republics together. One of his challenges was to prevent Serbia, the largest of the republics, from dominating the central government. To dilute Serb power, Tito gave greater autonomy to two provinces within Serbia—Kosovo and Vojvodina.

Yugoslavia's economy began to crumble in the 1970s. When Tito died in 1980, the country began to fracture along ethnic lines. In 1991 Serbia's president, Slobodan Milosevic, tried to assert Serb leadership over the republics. Slovenia, Macedonia, and Croatia declared independence. Fighting erupted in Croatia between Serbs and non-Serbs. When Bosnia and Herzegovina tried to secede, civil war broke out. In 2002, the remaining republics—Serbia and Montenegro—loosened ties, and Yugoslavia passed into history.

Looking Ahead
The hostilities are far from over. Minority ethnic groups throughout the region may be tomorrow's targets. How do the historic and geographic roots of the area shed light on the conflict?

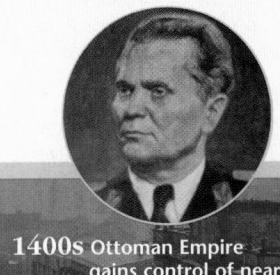

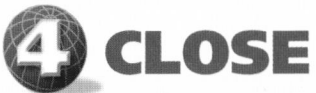

1400s Ottoman Empire gains control of nearly all lands in the Yugoslav region

1912–1913 Balkan Wars end Ottoman rule

1918 Slavs unite to form Kingdom of Serbs, Croats, and Slovenes

1929 Kingdom is renamed Yugoslavia

1945 World War II ends; Tito (photo above) and the Communists control Yugoslavia

1980 Tito dies

1991–1992 Several Yugoslav republics declare independence; civil wars ravage cities (background photo)

2002 Serbia and Montenegro loosen ties; Yugoslavia ends

3 ASSESS

Have students answer the **Looking Ahead** question on page 293. Ask them to speculate on possible solutions to the conflict in the region.

4 CLOSE

Have students research library resources, the Internet and media services for data about other places having cultural/religious conflicts, such as Northern Ireland and Cyprus. Have a student volunteer briefly describe one conflict, and then ask students to draw comparisons between it and the situation in the Balkans. **Ask: What are the similarities and differences between the two conflicts? Are these conflicts an unavoidable outcome of religious and cultural differences? Do any physical geographic factors, such as location or control of resources, contribute to the conflict?**

Meeting National Standards

Geography for Life
The following standards are met in the Student Edition feature:

EE2 Places and Regions: Standards 4, 6
EE4 Human Systems: Standard 13

ANSWERS TO LOOKING AHEAD

Historically, the Balkans have been a geographic bridge between Asia and Europe, and the region has been influenced by many migrants and cultures—Greek, Roman, Byzantine, Ottoman, and Slav. Located at the edge of Christian and Islamic worlds, the Balkans saw Roman Catholicism, Eastern Orthodoxy, and Islam take root. Therefore, over the centuries, brutal religious and cultural conflicts erupted in the Balkans. During World War II Germany and its allies (Hungary, Bulgaria, and Italy) occupied the Balkan Peninsula and reorganized Yugoslavia into puppet regimes. Serbs and Croats rekindled ethnic hostilities. The 35-year Cold War reign of Josip Broz Tito supressed these tensions, but they re-emerged in the 1990s and continued into the 2000s.

① FOCUS

Section Overview

This section provides an overview of Europe's history, from prehistory and the classical civilizations to the rise of the European Union.

BELLRINGER
Skillbuilder Activity

 Project transparency and have students answer questions.

 Available as blackline master.

Daily Focus Skills Transparency 12-2

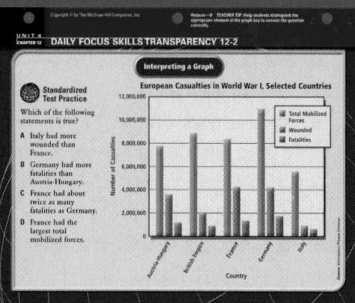

Guide to Reading

Consider What You Know
Answer *It has broadened their perspectives, enabling many Europeans to realize that despite differences, they share much in common.*

Reading Strategy
Answer *Students' time lines should include significant events.*

Preteaching Vocabulary
Direct students to learn the meanings of the following terms and to use each term in an original sentence: *city-state, feudalism, industrial capitalism, communism,* and *European Union.*

Guide to Reading

Consider What You Know
Europe, a relatively small continent, is home to a great variety of ethnic groups. How do you think being exposed to many different cultures has affected the way Europeans live?

Reading Strategy
Sequencing Complete a time line similar to the one below to record key events in Europe's history for each date.

Read to Find Out
- What contributions did early Europeans make to world culture?
- In what ways has Europe's geography shaped its history?
- What were the effects of world wars and economic and political revolutions in Europe?

Terms to Know
- city-state
- Middle Ages
- feudalism
- Crusades
- Renaissance
- Reformation
- Enlightenment
- industrial capitalism
- communism
- reparations
- Holocaust
- Cold War
- European Union

Places to Locate
- Greece
- Rome
- Athens
- Italy
- Constantinople
- Spain
- Portugal

History and Government

NATIONAL GEOGRAPHIC

A Geographic View

Layers of Culture

Bosnia and Herzegovina spreads across the gnarled reaches of the Dinaric Alps, a region possessed of enough bracing mountain beauty, enterprise, and gusto to have landed the 1984 Winter Olympics at its capital, Sarajevo. Even in this rugged corner of the Balkan Peninsula, the wash of empires—Roman, Byzantine, Ottoman, Austro-Hungarian— deposited layer upon layer of culture.

—Priit J. Vesilind, "In Focus: Bosnia," National Geographic, *June 1996*

Sarajevo, Bosnia and Herzegovina

The layering of cultures in the Balkans area is typical of Europe as a whole. Throughout the region, buildings, monuments, and local customs reflect the different periods of Europe's long history and the peoples that dominated its stage at these times. Through empire-building, immigration, and trade, Europe's cultures also have influenced other parts of the world. In this section you will learn about the contributions Europeans have made in learning, the arts, and technology.

The Rise of Europe

Physical geography in part has shaped Europe's history. The physical map on page 260 shows that several large bodies of water touch Europe. This closeness to the sea enabled Europeans to move beyond their own borders to other parts of the world. In addition, European mountain ranges contained passes and so did not severely

---

RESOURCE MANAGER

📁 Reproducible Masters
- Reproducible Lesson Plan 12-2
- Daily Lecture Notes 12-2
- Guided Reading Activity 12-2
- Reading Essentials and Study Guide 12-2
- Section Quiz 12-2

📊 Transparencies
- Daily Focus Skills Transparency 12-2
- Unit 4 Map Overlay Transparencies
- World Art and Architecture Transparencies

Multimedia
- 💿 Interactive Tutor Self-Assessment CD-ROM
- 💿 ExamView® Pro Testmaker CD-ROM
- 💿 Presentation Plus! CD-ROM

hinder contacts within the region as did mountain ranges in other parts of the world. Also, Europe's river-crossed fertile plains encouraged peaceful settlement as well as invasions and conflicts.

Early Peoples

Fossils found by archaeologists suggest that early humans lived in Europe more than a million years ago. Prehistoric Europeans moved from place to place in search of food. By about 6000 B.C., farming spread from Southwest Asia to southeastern Europe and then to all but the densely forested areas in the northern part of the continent. With the introduction of farming, early Europeans settled in agricultural villages, some of which later developed into Europe's first cities.

Ancient Greece and Rome

Two civilizations in the Mediterranean world laid the foundations of European—and Western—civilization. The first was ancient **Greece**, which reached its peak during the 400s and 300s B.C. The second civilization, whose capital was **Rome**, ruled a vast empire that reached its height of power between 27 B.C. and A.D. 180.

Greece's mountainous landscape and its closeness to the sea influenced the ancient Greeks to form separate communities called city-states. Each city-state was independent, but was linked to other city-states by Greek language and culture. Fleeing overpopulated areas and desiring new wealth, Greek merchants and sailors eventually colonized many parts of the Mediterranean coast.

The ancient Greeks laid the foundations of European government and culture. The city-state of **Athens** introduced the Western idea of democracy. Although women and enslaved persons could not vote, more people had a voice in Athens' government than in any earlier civilization. Greek art, literature, drama, and philosophy as well as mathematics and medicine also left a lasting impression on the Western world.

In **Italy** around 500 B.C., another Mediterranean people, the Romans, founded a republic. From the city of Rome, Roman armies went forth to conquer an empire that spanned much of Europe, some of Southwest Asia, and North Africa. The Romans imitated Greek art and literature, and borrowed from Greek science and architecture.

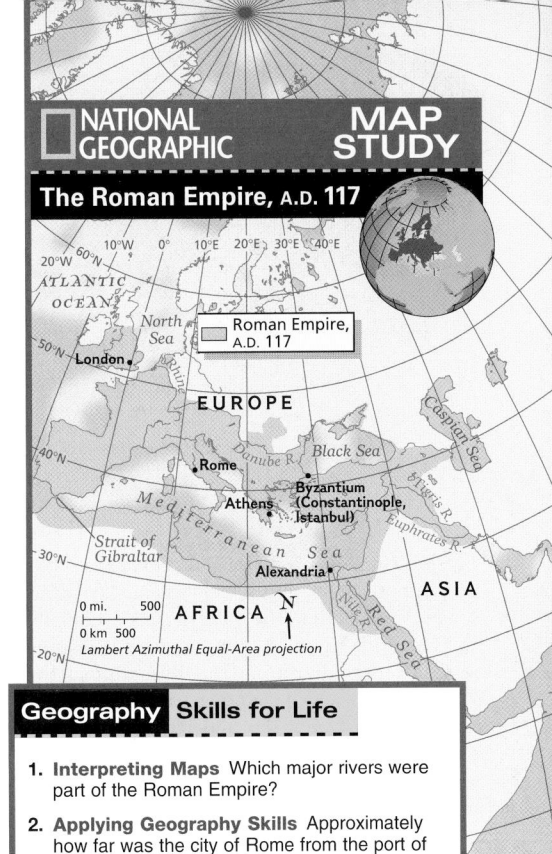

Geography Skills for Life

1. **Interpreting Maps** Which major rivers were part of the Roman Empire?

2. **Applying Geography Skills** Approximately how far was the city of Rome from the port of Byzantium?

Find NGS online map resources @ www.national geographic.com/maps

Roman developments in government, law, and engineering, however, influenced other cultures. Throughout the Roman Empire, for example, engineers built a vast network of roads, bridges, and aqueducts—artificial channels for carrying water.

A Christian Europe

In the late A.D. 300s, Christianity became the official religion of the Roman Empire and, later, one of the world's major religions. Although united in name, the empire came to be ruled by two emperors, one in the eastern half and the other in the western half. Eventually the two parts developed into eastern and western Europe, each with its own political, cultural, and religious traditions. During the 400s, Germanic groups from the north overthrew Roman rule in the western half and founded

Chapter 12 · **295**

2 TEACH

Answers
1. *the Rhine, Danube, Tigris, Euphrates, Nile*
2. *about 700 miles (1,126 km)*

Map Skills Practice
Location What climate regions did the Roman Empire encompass? What major bodies of water did the empire border? *(Mediterranean, humid continental, marine west coast, steppe, and highlands; Mediterranean, Black, Caspian, Red, and North Seas, Atlantic Ocean)*

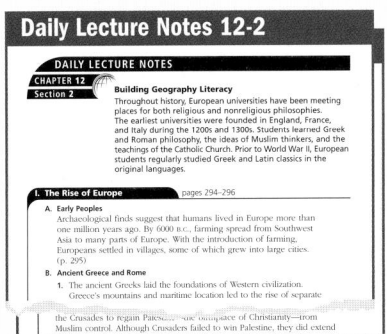

Daily Lecture Notes 12-2

DAILY LECTURE NOTES
CHAPTER 12 Section 2
Building Geography Literacy
Throughout history, European universities have been meeting places for both religious and nonreligious philosophies. The earliest universities were founded in England, France, and Italy during the 1200s and 1300s. Students learned Greek and Roman philosophy, the ideas of Muslim thinkers, and the teachings of the Catholic Church. Prior to World War II, European students regularly studied Greek and Latin classics in the original languages.

I. The Rise of Europe pages 294–296
A. Early Peoples
Archaeological finds suggest that humans lived in Europe more than one million years ago. By 6000 B.C., farming spread from Southwest Asia to many parts of Europe. With the introduction of farming, Europeans settled in villages, some of which grew into large cities. (p. 295)
B. Ancient Greece and Rome
1. The ancient Greeks laid the foundations of Western civilization. Greece's mountains and maritime location led to the rise of separate
the Crusades to regain Palestine—the birthplace of Christianity—from Muslim control. Although Crusaders failed to win Palestine, they did extend

L2 Cultural Exchange

Beginning in the A.D. 1400s, European explorers set out on expeditions to Africa, Asia, and the Americas. Ask students to list some of the ways European explorations influenced the world and how Europe was, in turn, affected by these voyages.

DIFFERENTIATED INSTRUCTION

Interpersonal Organize the class into small groups. Assign each student in the groups a specific subtopic of Section 2 (for example, Ancient Greece and Rome, the Middle Ages, European Explorations). Then ask each student to act as the authority on that subtopic and share his or her knowledge with the others in the group. Encourage the other students in the group to add their perspectives and ask questions.

EE4 Human Systems: Standards 10, 12
Refer to **Inclusion for the Social Studies Classroom Strategies and Activities.**

Architecture
Gothic architecture, popular throughout Europe between A.D. 1100 and 1300, is typified by the cathedral Notre Dame de Paris. Construction began in 1163, was performed in phases, and was not completed until 1345. Gothic architecture used heavy exterior decoration, flying buttresses, rib vaults, and stained glass.

World Art and Architecture

Use these transparencies to introduce students to other types of regional architecture.

L1/ELL

Guided Reading Activity 12-2

Guided Reading	Activity 12-2

For use with textbook pages 294–300

History and Government

Short Answer

DIRECTIONS: Use the information in your textbook to write a short answer to each of the following questions.

1. What physical features of Europe enabled its people to move easily beyond its borders to other parts of the world?

2. When did farming spread from Southwest Asia to southeastern Europe and then on to most of northern Europe?

3. What linked the independent city-states of ancient Greece together?

4. What territories were included in the Roman Empire?

Italy Italy's mountains divided it into regions, each with its own cultures and political structure. These regions often warred among themselves, and local ties became a strong force in Italy as a result.

architecture of EUROPE

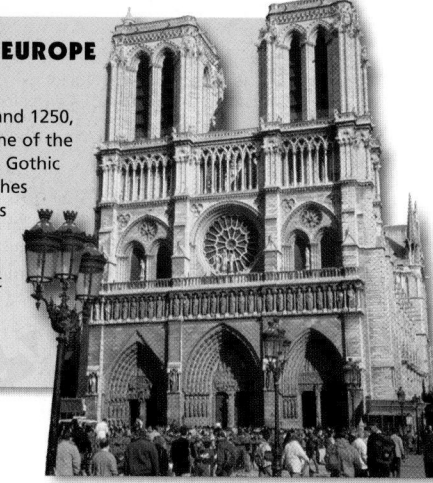

Notre Dame de Paris Built between 1163 and 1250, Notre Dame Cathedral in Paris, France, is one of the best known Gothic cathedrals in the world. Gothic architecture is characterized by pointed arches and flying buttresses—external stone beams that support the outer walls. High ceilings, beautiful stained glass windows, and open interiors are also typical elements of Gothic architecture. The western front of Notre Dame is adorned with fine carvings of biblical figures and events.

separate kingdoms. They also accepted the western form of Christianity, which became known as Roman Catholicism. The eastern half eventually was called the Byzantine Empire, with its capital at **Constantinople**, formerly Byzantium. The Byzantines developed their own Christian civilization that lasted until the mid-1400s. The eastern form of Christianity became known as Eastern Orthodoxy. During the 500s Slavic peoples migrated from Ukraine into eastern and central Europe. Some of them later accepted western European ways and Roman Catholicism, and others adopted Byzantine traditions and Eastern Orthodoxy.

The Middle Ages

After the fall of Rome, western Europe entered the Middle Ages, the period between ancient and modern times. During this era, from about A.D. 500 to 1500, feudalism—a system in which monarchs or lords gave land to nobles in return for pledges of loyalty—replaced centralized government. The Roman Catholic Church, western Europe's major religious body, brought Roman culture and principles of government and law to the region's Germanic peoples. During the Middle Ages, religious centers, such as cathedrals and monasteries, were major centers of learning. Meanwhile, in eastern Europe, the Byzantine Empire preserved ancient Greek and Roman cultures, and Byzantine missionaries spread Eastern Orthodoxy among many of the Slavic peoples.

Although generally Christian, Europe was influenced by other religious groups during the Middle Ages. Cities and towns in western Europe were home to Jewish communities that made contributions to European society. Many Christians, however, saw the Jews as outsiders and persecuted or discriminated against them. Expelled from much of western Europe, many Jews settled in eastern Europe, where they developed new communities based on their religious traditions.

Another influence on Christian Europe was Islam, a religion based on belief in one God and the preachings of Muhammad, a prophet who lived in Southwest Asia during the 600s. Within a century of Muhammad's death, Islam had spread from Southwest Asia through North Africa and into **Spain**. Muslims, the followers of Islam, developed a culture in Spain that passed on to Europeans many achievements in science, mathematics, and medicine.

Expansion of Europe

Beginning in the 1000s, western European armies fought the Crusades—a series of brutal religious wars—to win Palestine, the birthplace of Christianity, from Muslim rule. Europeans failed to win permanent control of the area but did extend trade routes to the eastern Mediterranean world. Spices and other products that came with increased trade sparked the interest of the small number of educated Europeans in other parts of the world. Beginning in the 1300s, the Renaissance (REH•nuh•SAHNTS)—a 300-year period of discovery and learning—brought about great advances in European civilization.

COOPERATIVE LEARNING ACTIVITY

Early Infrastructure By A.D. 200, Rome had constructed a network of durable roads that linked it to outlying areas like Britain and Spain. Another Roman achievement was the aqueduct. These large conduits channeled water from mountain sources to cities and towns miles away. Organize the class into small groups, and have each group assess how the two examples of Roman infrastructure listed below have affected patterns of migration and settlement: Watling Street, a Roman road in Great Britain, which runs from Dover to London and on to St. Albans; Calahorra, the site of a Roman aqueduct in northern Spain. Have each group offer a brief report of its findings.

 EE5 Environment and Society: Standard 14

The Renaissance

During the Renaissance, educated Europeans developed a new interest in the cultures of ancient Greece and Rome. They stressed the importance of people and their place in this world. Writers described human feelings, and artists created life-like paintings and sculptures. In addition to religious structures, architects designed buildings, such as palaces and villas, for private use. The Renaissance also led to scientific advances. For example, the invention of movable type in printing spread new ideas more quickly and easily.

The increased production of books and pamphlets aided a religious movement called the Reformation, which lessened the power of the Roman Catholic Church and led to the beginnings of Protestantism. By the mid-1500s, Protestant churches were dominant in northern Europe, but Roman Catholicism retained its hold on the southern, central, and northeastern parts of the region. Religious wars soon engulfed Europe, and European monarchs were able to strengthen their power over nobles and church leaders.

European Explorations

During the Middle Ages, Europe lagged behind the Chinese and Muslim empires in economic development. In the 1400s, however, western Europe began to emerge as a significant force in world affairs. At that time seafarers from **Portugal** developed new trade routes around Africa to Asia. Spanish rulers financed the Italian-born explorer Christopher Columbus, who reached the Americas in the late 1400s. England, France, and the Netherlands also sent out expeditions of explorers. These voyages resulted in conquests of foreign lands, often destroying the cultures already thriving there. Trade with colonies in the Americas, Asia, and Africa brought great wealth and power to western Europe.

A Changing Europe

During the late 1600s and early 1700s, many educated Europeans emphasized the importance of reason and began to question long-standing traditions and values. This movement, known as the Enlightenment, was followed by political and economic revolutions that swept the entire region.

Revolutions

At this time Europeans wanting a voice in government began political revolutions. In the late 1600s, the English Parliament, or lawmaking body, passed a Bill of Rights that limited the power of the monarch. The French Revolution in the late 1700s overthrew France's monarchy and spread the ideals of democracy. The 1800s saw many uprisings throughout the rest of Europe that challenged the power of monarchs and nobles. By 1900 most European countries had constitutions that limited rulers' powers and guaranteed at least some political rights to citizens.

During this time of political change, the Industrial Revolution began in England and rapidly spread to other countries. Power-driven machinery and new methods of production transformed life in Europe. Industrial cities and improved transportation and communication developed. These sweeping changes led to the rise of industrial capitalism, an economic system in which business leaders used profits to

NATIONAL GEOGRAPHIC World Explorer

Geography Skills for Life

Industrial Revolution Industrial cities, such as Mossley, England, developed as the Industrial Revolution spread across Europe.

Region How did the Industrial Revolution affect life in Europe?

L1/ELL

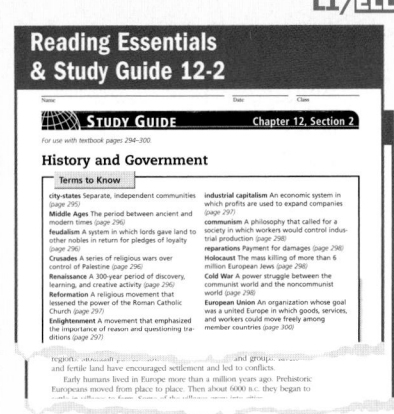

Reading Essentials & Study Guide 12-2

STUDY GUIDE Chapter 12, Section 2

For use with textbook pages 294–300

History and Government

Terms to Know

city-states Separate, independent communities (page 295)
Middle Ages The period between ancient and modern times (page 296)
feudalism A system in which lords gave land to other nobles in return for pledges of loyalty (page 296)
Crusades A series of religious wars over control of Palestine (page 296)
Renaissance A 300-year period of discovery, learning, and creative activity (page 297)
Reformation A religious movement that lessened the power of the Roman Catholic Church (page 297)
Enlightenment A movement that emphasized the importance of reason and questioning traditions (page 297)

industrial capitalism An economic system in which profits are used to expand companies (page 297)
communism A philosophy that called for a society in which workers would control industrial production (page 298)
reparations Payment for damages (page 298)
Holocaust The mass killing of more than 6 million European Jews (page 298)
Cold War A power struggle between the communist world and the noncommunist world (page 298)
European Union An organization whose goal is a united Europe in which goods, services, and workers could move freely among member countries (page 300)

region, structural population since and groups, and fertile land have encouraged settlement and led to conflicts.

Early humans lived in Europe more than a million years ago. Prehistoric Europeans moved from place to place. Then about 6000 b.c. they began to

NATIONAL GEOGRAPHIC World Explorer

Answer

It spawned new social groups, including middle-class factory owners and a working class of factory laborers.

More About the Photo

In England many factories were built during the Industrial Revolution. To find work, large numbers of people migrated from rural to urban areas. Social problems such as overcrowded living conditions, pollution, and crime increased.

INTERDISCIPLINARY
connection

HISTORY In 1900 Great Britain had the world's largest overseas empire. During the early 1930s, Canada, Australia, and New Zealand became fully independent. India and most other British-ruled areas were free by the end of the 1900s.

CRITICAL THINKING ACTIVITY

Identifying Causes Ask students to look at the photo on page 298. Reiterate how this picture illustrates the toll that World War II took on civilians as well as those in uniform. As a result of Hitler's policies in Nazi Germany, millions of Jews, Roma, political dissidents, and other people despised by the Nazis died during the Holocaust. Advise students that wars against civilians are not exclusive to Europe. Have students list some of the causes of wartime atrocities that occurred in Europe during World War II. Remind students that factors such as prejudice, economic and political instability, civil war, and revolution are often precursors to wars against civilians. Have students discuss their results.

🌐 **EE4 Human Systems: Standard 13**

NATIONAL GEOGRAPHIC World Explorer

Answer

Democratic systems of government developed or continued in most western European countries, and communist systems of government took hold in many eastern European countries.

More About the Photo

In 1993 the U.S. Holocaust Memorial Museum opened in Washington, D.C., as a permanent reminder of the atrocities of Nazi Germany and as a memorial to those who died there.

Culture NOTE

Hungary In Hungary the surname (last name) is listed before the given name (first name). The Hungarian musicians Franz Liszt and Béla Bartók are known in their homeland as Liszt Franz and Bartók Béla.

GEOGRAPHY AND THE HUMANITIES

 World Music:
A Cultural Legacy

 World Art and Architecture
Transparencies

 World Art Prints

NATIONAL GEOGRAPHIC World Explorer

Geography Skills for Life

Auschwitz Memorial In Auschwitz, Poland—site of infamous Nazi death camps—a Holocaust memorial exhibit shows piles of footwear worn by Jewish and other prisoners who lost their lives.

Region How did World War II impact the political landscape of Europe?

---

expand their companies. Under this system, new social groups emerged: a middle class of merchants and factory owners, and a working class of factory laborers. Although the middle class prospered, factory workers at first were poorly paid and lived in crowded, unhealthy conditions.

These social problems led in the mid-1800s to the birth of communism—a philosophy that called for a society based on economic equality in which the workers would control the factories and industrial production. By the end of the 1800s, various European governments began passing laws to improve conditions for workers in the workplace and to expand education, housing, and health care.

Conflict and Division

In the first half of the 1900s, two world wars resulted in major changes in Europe. Rivalries among European powers for colonies and economic power led to World War I, which lasted from 1914 to 1918. An American journalist,

---

Richard Harding Davis, described the German invasion of Belgium in these words:

> *... For three days and three nights the column of gray, with fifty thousand bayonets and fifty thousand lances, with gray transport wagons, gray ammunition carts, gray ambulances, gray cannons, like a river of steel cut Brussels in two.*
>
> quoted in John N. Chettle, "When War Called, Davis Answered," *Smithsonian*, April 2000

As a result of World War I, monarchies collapsed in Germany, Austria-Hungary, and Russia, and several central and eastern European countries won independence. The Versailles peace treaty in 1919 found Germany guilty of starting the war and demanded that Germany make reparations, or payment for damages.

The large number of unresolved political problems from World War I and a worldwide economic depression enabled dictators Benito Mussolini and Adolf Hitler to gain control of Italy and Germany, respectively. Following aggressive territorial expansion by these two countries, World War II broke out in 1939. By the time this conflict ended in 1945, most of Europe and much of the rest of the world were involved. A major horror of World War II in Europe was the Holocaust, the mass killing of more than 6 million European Jews and others by Germany's Nazi leaders.

World War II left Europe ruined and divided. Most of eastern Europe came under communist control of the Soviet Union, and most of western Europe backed democracy and received economic and military support from the United States. This division of Europe brought about the Cold War, a power struggle between the communist world, led by the Soviet Union, and the noncommunist world, led by the United States. A divided Germany—communist East Germany and democratic West Germany—became the "hot point" of the Cold War in Europe.

History
The Cold War in Europe

At the end of World War II, the victorious Allies, including the United States, the Soviet Union, the

---

TEAM-TEACHING ACTIVITY: WORLD HISTORY

History/Athletics The ancient Greeks created the Olympic Games, which included boxing, wrestling, distance running, discus throw, javelin throw, and chariot racing. Have students work with a history teacher or a coach to trace the evolution of the Olympic Games from ancient to modern times. **Ask:** How do the modern Olympics differ from the ancient ones? *(The modern games have more events; some ancient events are no longer observed.)* **Ask:** How has geography influenced the evolution of Olympic events? *(Beginning in 1924 winter events were added as more countries with cold-weather climates participated.)*
🌐 EE4 Human Systems: Standard 12; 🌐 EE5 Environment and Society: Standard 16

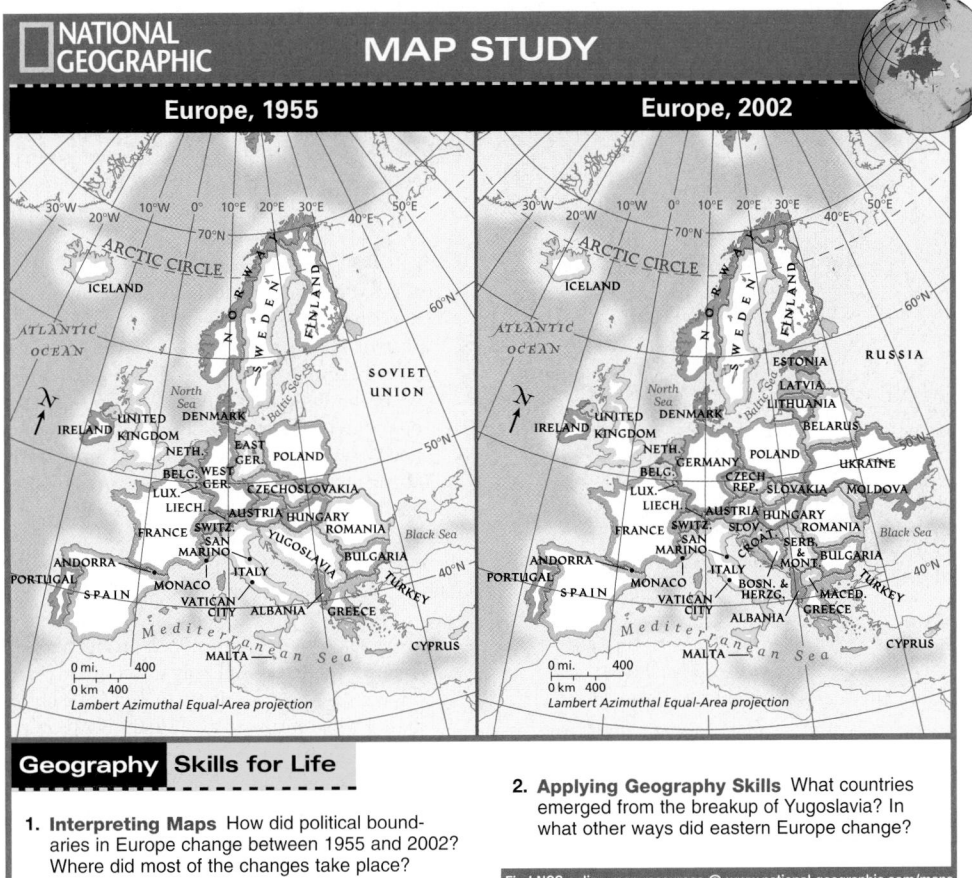

NATIONAL GEOGRAPHIC MAP STUDY

Europe, 1955 | Europe, 2002

Geography Skills for Life

1. **Interpreting Maps** How did political boundaries in Europe change between 1955 and 2002? Where did most of the changes take place?

2. **Applying Geography Skills** What countries emerged from the breakup of Yugoslavia? In what other ways did eastern Europe change?

Find NGS online map resources @ www.national geographic.com/maps

NATIONAL GEOGRAPHIC **MAP STUDY**

Answers

1. *New nations came from communism's fall; in central and eastern Europe*

2. *Slovenia, Croatia, Bosnia-Herzegovina, Macedonia, Serbia and Montenegro, Czechoslovakia split into the Czech Republic and Slovakia; Estonia, Latvia, Lithuania, Belarus, Ukraine, and Moldova emerged from the Soviet Union*

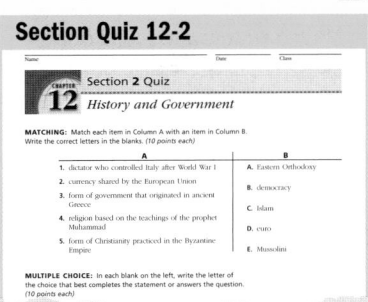

ASSESS

Assign Section 2 Assessment as homework or as an in-class activity.

Have students use **Interactive Tutor Self-Assessment CD-ROM**.

L2

Section Quiz 12-2

United Kingdom, and France, divided Germany into four zones. By 1949 the three western zones of Germany were combined into West Germany, with Bonn as its capital. The eastern zone, occupied by the Soviets, became East Germany with East Berlin as its capital. Throughout the decade following the division, many East Germans fled to the West to escape communism. In the 1960s, East Germany built the Berlin Wall and other barriers to stop this movement of people.

During the Cold War era, most western European democracies became more productive and economically secure than they had been before World War II. In contrast, communist governments in eastern Europe allowed people little voice in

government or the economy. Although eastern European communist countries pushed for industrial growth, their economies and standards of living lagged behind those of western Europe.

A New Era for Europe

From the 1950s to the 1980s, revolts against communist rule periodically swept eastern Europe. In Poland, Hungary, Czechoslovakia, East Germany, Romania, and Bulgaria, citizens demanded freedom and a better way of life. In the early 1980s, Polish workers founded Solidarity, the first free labor union in the communist world. In 1989, public demonstrations—and the refusal of reform-minded Soviet leaders to intervene—

Chapter 12 🌐 **299**

Reteach

Have students review the sections "Read to Find Out" and "Terms to Know." Encourage them to ask questions about any concept or event they do not understand.

EXTENDING THE CONTENT

Holocaust Poet Sonia Schreiber Weitz is a Holocaust survivor, educator, and poet. She suffered six years of her adolescence in five concentration camps in Poland, Germany, and Austria during World War II. For 50 years, Weitz has recounted her "six years of darkness" in interviews, articles, and public speakings. "The Holocaust was a crime without a language," Weitz said. "To try and describe it is almost impossible. I'm a poet, and it's easier to express what happened through poetry." 🌐 **EE4 Human Systems: Standard 9**

NATIONAL GEOGRAPHIC World Explorer

Answers
a united Europe in which goods, services, and workers can move freely among member countries

More About the Photo The Trabant automobile was manufactured in East Germany beginning in the 1950s. After Germany reunification in the 1990s, some Trabants were decorated with 15 stars, which represent the member countries of the European Union.

Enrich

Ask students to compare maps of Europe in 1900, 1940, 1955, and 2002. Have them explain how conflicts influenced political boundaries and the distribution of power.

 **CLOSE**

Have students explore one piece of European art that addresses a cultural or historical aspect of the region: the lyrics of a song, a poem, painting, photograph, or short story.

NATIONAL GEOGRAPHIC World Explorer

Geography Skills for Life

European Union A car in Germany is painted to display the logo of the European Union during a celebration of the new organization.
Region What is the goal of the European Union?

swiftly led to the fall of eastern Europe's communist governments. Dramatic changes followed. The infamous Berlin Wall came down, and in 1990, the two parts of Germany reunited. Three years later, Czechoslovakia split into two separate countries: the Czech Republic and Slovakia. Throughout much of eastern Europe during the 1990s, free elections installed democratic leaders, who encouraged the rise of market economies.

Changes also occurred in western Europe. During the 1950s, Belgium, France, Italy, Luxembourg, the Netherlands, and West Germany banded closer together economically and politically. By the 1990s this growing movement toward unity had led to the European Union (EU), an organization whose goal was a united Europe in which goods, services, and workers could move freely among member countries. The Maastricht Treaty, signed in 1992, set goals for a central bank and a common currency. Launched in 1999, that currency, the euro, replaced national currencies, such as the Italian lira and the German mark, in 2002. Currently comprising 25 member countries, the European Union had its biggest membership enlargement in 2004 when 10 countries officially joined. In the next section, you will learn about the variety of cultures and lifestyles that are found today in the new Europe.

SECTION 2 ASSESSMENT

Checking for Understanding

1. **Define** city-state, Middle Ages, feudalism, Crusades, Renaissance, Reformation, Enlightenment, industrial capitalism, communism, reparations, Holocaust, Cold War, European Union.

2. **Main Ideas** Create a section outline like the one below. Fill in headings from this section, and add supporting details.

European History and Government
I. The Rise of Europe
A. Early peoples
1. Prehistoric Europeans
2.
B. Ancient Greece and Rome

Critical Thinking

3. **Identifying Cause and Effect** How did the rise of communism and working-class movements affect the lives of workers in the 1800s?

4. **Drawing Conclusions** How were the countries of eastern Europe affected by World War I? By World War II?

5. **Predicting Consequences** How might an organization such as the European Union encourage unity among the various European countries? Provide examples to support your answer.

Analyzing Maps

6. **Region** Study the map of the Roman Empire on page 295. Compare it with the map of Europe 2002 on page 299. Which areas of Europe were not conquered by the Romans?

Applying Geography

7. **Causes of Political Change** Study the maps of Europe in 1955 and in 2002 on page 299. Choose one area whose boundaries changed between 1955 and 2002, and write a paragraph explaining the causes and effects of these changes.

SECTION 2 ASSESSMENT ANSWERS

1. All vocabulary terms are defined in the text.
2. Headings should follow a consistent pattern throughout the outline and match Section 2.
3. They set into motion laws that improved working conditions and expanded access to education, health care, and housing.
4. After World War I many of the old monarchies of eastern Europe collapsed and several countries won independence. After World War II

many eastern European countries succumbed to Soviet communist control.

5. by promoting a single currency, lowering trade barriers, and establishing common security and legal agreements; Students' examples should support their answers.

6. Scandinavia, the Baltic states, Iceland, Ireland, Scotland, Poland, and much of Germany and central Europe

7. **Applying Geography** Paragraphs may take into account the partition of Germany after World War II and the division of the continent between the Soviet Union and the Western powers (United States, Britain, France) following World War II. Students should also consider the collapse of the Soviet Union and the fall of communism that began in 1989.

Guide to Reading

Consider What You Know

The cultures of Europe have had a profound influence on the rest of the world. How many European artworks—paintings, sculptures, literary works, musical compositions, or works of architecture—can you list? Can you name the artist who created each work, and the country where the artist worked or lived?

Reading Strategy

Taking Notes As you read about the cultures of Europe, use the major headings of the section to create an outline similar to the one below.

```
I.  Expressions of Culture
    A.
    B.
    C.
II. Quality of Life
    A.
    B.
```

Read to Find Out

- How has religion influenced the cultural development of Europe?

- Why has European art and culture been so influential throughout the world?

- How do European governments meet the educational and health-care needs of their peoples?

Terms to Know

- dialect
- language family
- Good Friday Peace Agreement
- romanticism
- realism
- impressionist
- welfare state

Places to Locate

- Switzerland
- Northern Ireland
- the Netherlands
- Ukraine

Cultures and Lifestyles

NATIONAL GEOGRAPHIC

A Geographic View

Denmark's Two Seasons

Life in Denmark is divided into two parts, the Golden Summer and the Great Murk, which extends from late fall to mid-spring. The months of youth and beauty [are] when the sky is light until almost 11 p.m. and Danes take to the beaches, eat in their gardens, soak up the sun, feel sleek and smart. . . . [T]he other months [are] when they go to and from work in the dark and the rain and just try to keep putting one foot in front of the other and not get too glum.

Sidewalk café in Denmark

—Garrison Keillor, "Civilized Denmark," National Geographic, July 1998

In Denmark, as in other countries of Europe, people have developed distinct ways of life in response to their physical environment. At the same time that Europe becomes more united politically and economically, its peoples struggle to maintain their separate cultural identities. In this section you will learn about the cultural characteristics that both unite and divide Europeans as well as impact their everyday lives.

Expressions of Culture

Like people in other regions, Europeans express their values through language, religion, and the arts. A study of European languages, religions, and art forms reveals the rich diversity of culture in Europe today.

Section Overview

This section discusses cultures and ways of life of Europe, including language, art, religion, political and social systems, and recreational activities.

BELLRINGER
Skillbuilder Activity

Project transparency and have students answer questions.

Available as blackline master.

Daily Focus Skills Transparency 12-3

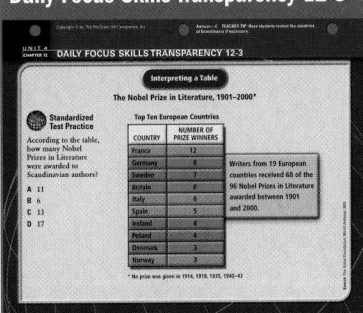

Guide to Reading

Consider What You Know
Answers *Responses may include: the Spanish painter Pablo Picasso, the Italian artist Leonardo da Vinci, the German composer Ludwig van Beethoven, the English playwright William Shakespeare, the Italian artist Michelangelo, the Dutch painter Rembrandt; examples of artists' works should be well known to most students.*

Reading Strategy
Answer Students should complete the outline by including all heads in the section.

Preteaching Vocabulary
Use the **Vocabulary Puzzle-Maker CD-ROM** to create crossword and word-search puzzles.

RESOURCE MANAGER

Reproducible Masters
- Reproducible Lesson Plan 12-3
- Vocabulary Activity 12
- Daily Lecture Notes 12-3
- Guided Reading Activity 12-3
- Reading Essentials and Study Guide 12-3
- Reteaching Activity 12
- Reinforcing Skills Activity 12
- Section Quiz 12-3

Transparencies
- Daily Focus Skills Transparency 12-3
- Unit 4 Map Overlay Transparencies

Multimedia
- Vocabulary PuzzleMaker CD-ROM
- World Music: A Cultural Legacy
- Interactive Tutor Self-Assessment CD-ROM
- ExamView® Pro Testmaker CD-ROM

TEACH

L1 Compare

Ask students to compare and contrast European soccer and American football, and consider why American football has not caught on in Europe, while soccer continues to grow in popularity across the United States.

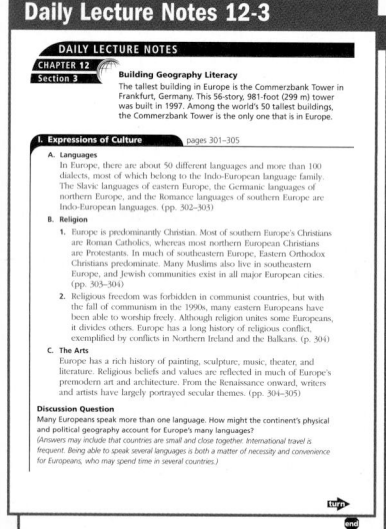

Daily Lecture Notes 12-3

NATIONAL GEOGRAPHIC MAP STUDY

Answers

1. *Scottish Gaelic, Welsh, Breton, Irish*

2. *Spain, Italy, Portugal, France, and Romania*

Map Skills Practice

Place Where is the Basque language spoken? *(Spain and France)*

Languages

In Europe there are about 50 different languages and more than 100 **dialects**, or local forms of languages. At times dialects are so different that even people speaking the same language have difficulty understanding one another. For example, a dialect of English called Orkney is spoken in the Orkney Islands off Scotland's northern coast:

> *[The Orkney dialect] combines Old Norse words with many unique or archaic English expressions in a way that leaves outsiders— known as 'eens fae aff,' literally 'ones from off'—hopelessly befuddled. [An Orkney resident observes:] "When someone says to you, 'We hid a quey caff yistreen' (We had a female calf last night), you know you are on the fringes of the English-speaking world."*
>
> Bill Bryson, "Orkney: Ancient North Sea Haven," *National Geographic*, June 1998

Almost all of Europe's languages and dialects, however, belong to the Indo-European language

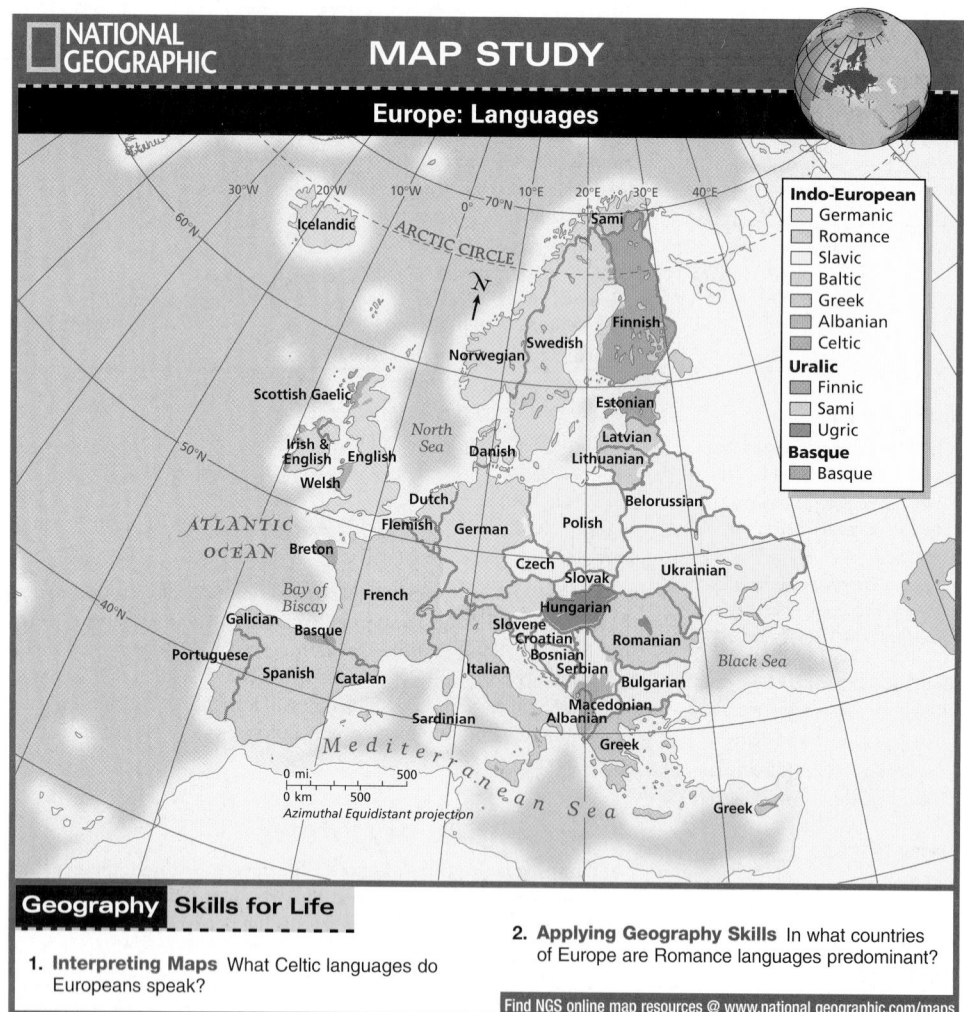

NATIONAL GEOGRAPHIC — MAP STUDY

Europe: Languages

Indo-European
- Germanic
- Romance
- Slavic
- Baltic
- Greek
- Albanian
- Celtic

Uralic
- Finnic
- Sami
- Ugric

Basque
- Basque

Geography Skills for Life

1. Interpreting Maps What Celtic languages do Europeans speak?

2. Applying Geography Skills In what countries of Europe are Romance languages predominant?

Find NGS online map resources @ www.national geographic.com/maps

---

DIFFERENTIATED INSTRUCTION

English Learners Students who have difficulty understanding unfamiliar words often skip over them. However, they often are successful in defining the words based on the context of the sentence. Ask students to scan Section 3 for words that are unfamiliar to them. Have them write the words in their notebooks and interpret the meanings from context.

ELL   **EE2 Places and Regions: Standard 4**

EE4 Human Systems: Standard 9

Refer to *Inclusion for the Social Studies Classroom Strategies and Activities.*

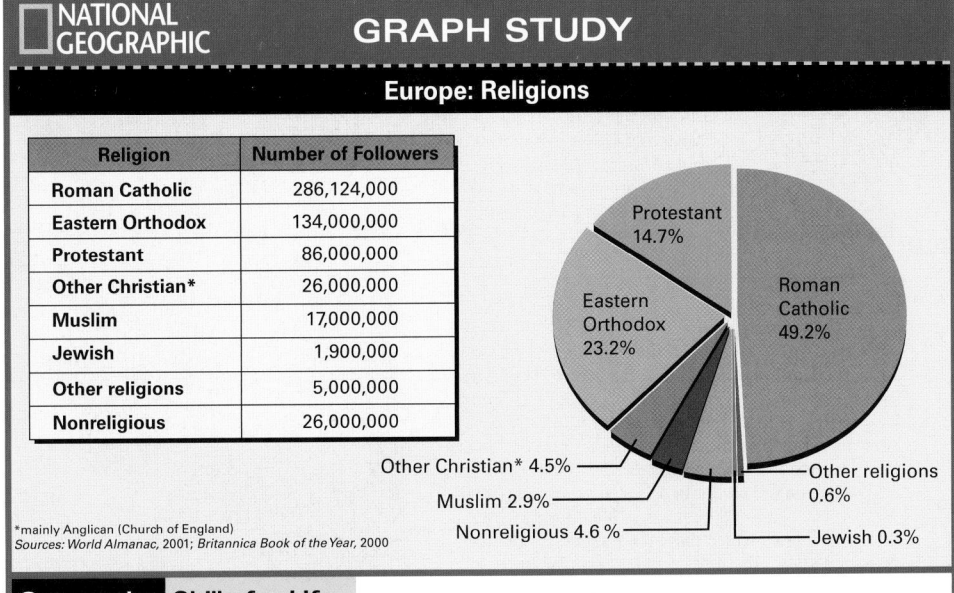

GRAPH STUDY

Europe: Religions

Religion	Number of Followers
Roman Catholic	286,124,000
Eastern Orthodox	134,000,000
Protestant	86,000,000
Other Christian*	26,000,000
Muslim	17,000,000
Jewish	1,900,000
Other religions	5,000,000
Nonreligious	26,000,000

Protestant 14.7%
Roman Catholic 49.2%
Eastern Orthodox 23.2%
Other Christian* 4.5%
Muslim 2.9%
Nonreligious 4.6 %
Other religions 0.6%
Jewish 0.3%

*mainly Anglican (Church of England)
Sources: World Almanac, 2001; Britannica Book of the Year, 2000

Geography Skills for Life

1. **Interpreting Graphs** How does the percentage of Europeans who are Roman Catholic compare with the percentage of those who are Protestant? Eastern Orthodox?

2. **Applying Geography Skills** Why do you think religion has both united and divided Europeans throughout their history? Provide examples to support your answer.

GRAPH STUDY

Answers

1. *There are about three times as many Roman Catholics as there are Protestants. There are about twice as many Roman Catholics as there are Eastern Orthodox.*

2. *Students' answers should indicate an understanding of the historical impact of religion on Europeans.*

Skills Practice

Region According to the graph, which two groups have the same number of people?
(Other Christian, Nonreligious)

L1/ELL

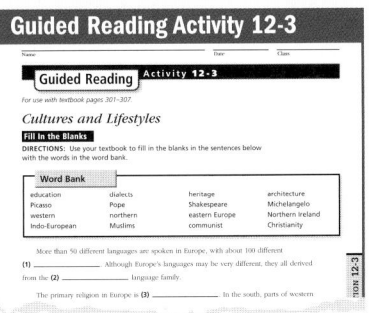

Guided Reading Activity 12-3

Guided Reading Activity 12-3

For use with textbook pages 301–307

Cultures and Lifestyles

Fill In the Blanks

DIRECTIONS: Use your textbook to fill in the blanks in the sentences below with the words in the word bank.

Word Bank

education	dialects	heritage	architecture
Picasso	Pope	Shakespeare	Michelangelo
western	northern	eastern Europe	Northern Ireland
Indo-European	Muslims	communist	Christianity

More than 50 different languages are spoken in Europe, with about 100 different
(1) _____. Although Europe's languages may be very different, they all derived from the (2) _____ language family.

The primary religion in Europe is (3) _____. In the south, parts of western

Beethoven The German composer Ludwig van Beethoven was completely deaf by the time he reached his late 40s. Nevertheless, he continued to compose symphonies—masterpieces that he was never able to hear performed.

---

family. A language family is a group of related languages that developed from an earlier language. The Indo-European family has several major branches in Europe. Most people in eastern Europe speak Slavic languages—including Bulgarian, Czech, Polish, Slovak, Ukrainian, Belorussian, and Serbo-Croatian—or Baltic languages, such as Latvian and Lithuanian. In northern Europe, most people speak Germanic languages—German, Dutch, English, Danish, Swedish, and Norwegian. The Romance languages, which come from Latin, the language of the Roman Empire, are widely spoken in southern Europe. They include Italian, Spanish, Portuguese, French, and Romanian. Other Indo-European branches are Greek, Albanian, and the Celtic languages. Two European language groups are not Indo-European—the Uralic languages (Finnish, Estonian, and Hungarian) and Basque, one of the world's few languages that is not related to any other.

Many European countries have one or more official languages, those that are recognized by the government, and a smaller number of the other languages. For example, Romanian is the official language of Romania, but Hungarian and German are also spoken there. **Switzerland** has three official languages—German, French, and Italian. A fourth language—Romansch, closely related to Latin—is spoken by a small number of Swiss.

Religion

Religion—primarily Christianity—has deeply shaped European values, societies, and cultures. Today many Europeans are not practicing members of a religious body, but they still maintain cultural links to the faiths of their ancestors, especially in celebrating religious holidays. Although many European countries have a largely Christian heritage, others are Muslim or have a diversity of faiths.

Chapter 12 **303**

COOPERATIVE LEARNING ACTIVITY

European Art Europe has produced some of the world's greatest art—including painting, music, sculpture, architecture, literature, film, theater, and dance. Organize the class into groups of three or four students each. Assign a category of art to each group, and have each group prepare a report on some of the important styles and artists within each category. Have each student within each group be responsible for a different example from that category. Ask the groups to illustrate their reports with posters, photographs, videocassettes, or audio recordings. Have the groups present their findings, with individual students within each group reporting on his or her style and artist.
EE4 Human Systems: Standard 10

Music Notes
Instruments such as the violin, cello, oboe, guitar, drums, and percussion—now considered part of the European classical tradition—were based on earlier instruments brought to the European continent by Turks and Arabs who invaded or influenced the Balkan, Iberian, and Apennine peninsulas. Before cultural contact with Southwest Asia, indigenous Europeans had limited knowledge of musical instruments and played almost exclusively on wind instruments such as bagpipes, horns, and flutes.

♫ **World Music:**
A Cultural Legacy
Use the accompanying Teacher Guide for information, and worksheets about the music of this region.

L1/ELL

Reading Essentials & Study Guide 12-3

music of EUROPE

European music has a history descending from the ancient Greeks through the Christian era and into Western classical music. Traditional music from Europe is based strongly on melody, with less emphasis on percussion and rhythm.

Instrument Spotlight
It is believed that **bagpipes** originated with early European shepherds. The bag traditionally is made from an animal's hide or stomach. Hollow sticks or bones are connected to it so the air can escape in a controlled way to produce different notes. With all bagpipes, sound is produced either by blowing air through an intake tube or by pumping with a bellows held under one arm. Most bagpipes create one or more steady drone notes, produced by pipes called "drones." The other pipe, which plays the melody, is called a "chanter." The most well-known types of bagpipes are from Scotland and Ireland.

 **Go To** World Music: A Cultural Legacy Hear music of this region on Disc 1, Tracks 13–19.

Most of Europe's Christians are Roman Catholics, who live in southern Europe, parts of western Europe, and the northern part of eastern Europe. Protestants, who generally belong to the Anglican, Lutheran, and Reformed churches, are dominant in northern and northwestern Europe. Eastern Orthodox churches are strongest in the southern part of eastern Europe. Many Muslims live in Albania, Bosnia-Herzegovina, and Bulgaria. Jewish communities are found in all major European cities.

Religious leaders, such as Pope John Paul II, head of the Roman Catholic Church, inspired religious believers in eastern Europe in the struggle against communist controls. With the fall of communism and its antireligious policies, religious freedom came to eastern Europeans during the 1990s.

Although religion unites some Europeans, it divides others. For years, hostility between Catholics and Protestants led to conflict in **Northern Ireland**, a part of the United Kingdom. Roman Catholics there wanted to become part of the largely Catholic Republic of Ireland, and Protestants favored keeping ties with the mostly Protestant United Kingdom. In 1998 the Good Friday Peace Agreement paved the way for Protestant and Roman Catholic communities to share political power. Though hopes for peace run high, the political situation in Northern Ireland remains unstable.

Religious and ethnic differences were at the heart of conflict in the Balkan Peninsula. During the early 1990s, Roman Catholic Croats, Eastern Orthodox Serbs, and Muslim Bosnians fought over land and political power in Bosnia-Herzegovina. Later in the decade, Eastern Orthodox Serbs fought the Albanian Muslim majority in the Serb province of Kosovo.

The Arts

As a result of Europe's global influence in the 1800s and 1900s, European art forms have spread around the world and influenced other cultures. The arts of Europe reflect its history as well as the ideas and values of its people.

Europe's temples and churches show the close relationship of religion and architecture. The

CRITICAL THINKING ACTIVITY

Comparing and Contrasting Since the end of the Cold War in the early 1990s, many European countries have eagerly embraced the idea of an integrated European Community. One important remaining obstacle to such unity is the disparity of education and health care levels. Compare and contrast literacy levels and levels of health care in Sweden and Croatia.
Ask: What factors help explain the disparity? *(Sweden has enjoyed more than two centuries of peace, so life expectancy and literacy rates are higher in Sweden. Because Croatia has fought its neighbors in the Balkans throughout the 1990s, it is still rebuilding its schools and health care services.)* 🌐 **EE4 Human Systems: Standard 13**

Parthenon in Athens and the Pantheon in Rome are examples of temples built by the ancient Greeks and Romans. The Roman Catholic cathedral in Córdoba, Spain, once was a mosque built by North African Muslims who brought Islam to Spain. The Church of the Holy Apostles in Salonica, Greece, is an example of Byzantine art that reflects Eastern Orthodox spirituality. Notre Dame Cathedral in Paris is an example of the Gothic architecture that flourished in Roman Catholic western Europe from the mid-1100s to the 1400s.

During the 1500s and 1600s, European artists and writers began to work with everyday subjects as well as religious themes. The paintings of Leonardo da Vinci and Michelangelo Buonarotti influenced generations of artists. England's William Shakespeare wrote numerous plays, and Spain's Miguel de Cervantes penned *Don Quixote*, a classic novel about a landowner who imagines himself a knight called to perform heroic deeds.

In the 1600s and 1700s, new music forms, such as opera and the symphony, emerged in Europe. In the 1800s artists such as French painter Eugène Delacroix, British writer Sir Walter Scott, and German composer Ludwig van Beethoven reflected the style of romanticism, which focused on the emotions, stirring historical events, and the exotic. During the mid-1800s, realism—an artistic style that focused on accurately depicting the details of everyday life—became prominent. Later in the century, a group of French painters called impressionists moved outdoors from their studios to capture immediate experiences, or "impressions," of the natural world.

During the 1900s, European artists and writers explored a variety of new forms and styles. Abstract painting and sculpture, which emphasized form and color over realistic content, became dominant. An important European artist who influenced modern art was the Spanish painter Pablo Picasso. In architecture, Germany's Bauhaus school of design emphasized clean geometric forms and the use of glass and concrete.

Quality of Life

Today western Europe, with its heritage of industrial and urban growth, generally enjoys a higher standard of living than southern and eastern Europe. Many eastern European countries especially struggle with problems inherited from the communist past or are rebuilding economies damaged by recent warfare or internal unrest. The

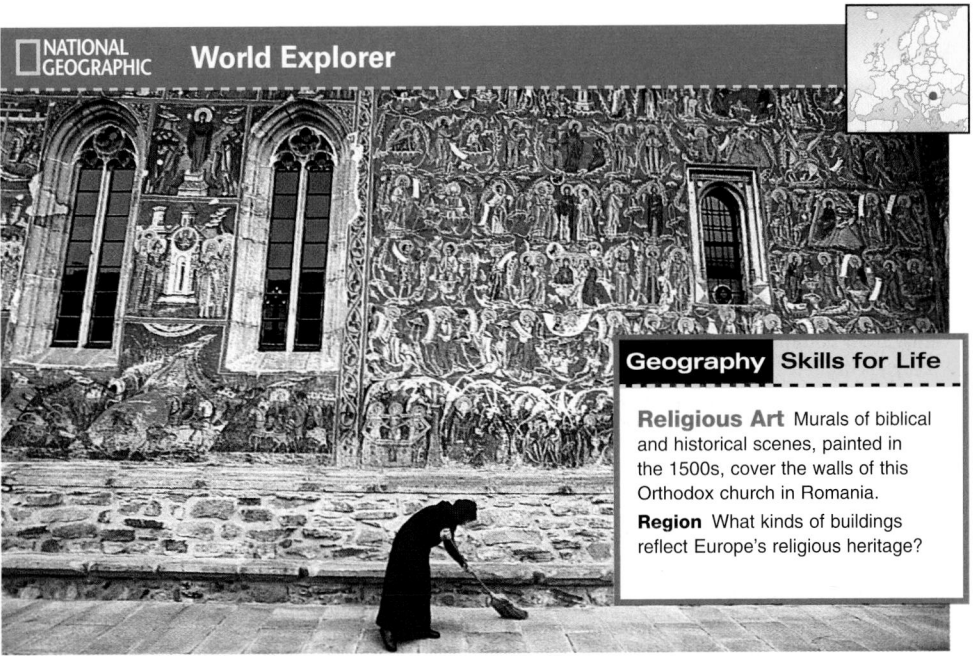

NATIONAL GEOGRAPHIC World Explorer

Geography Skills for Life

Religious Art Murals of biblical and historical scenes, painted in the 1500s, cover the walls of this Orthodox church in Romania.

Region What kinds of buildings reflect Europe's religious heritage?

Chapter 12 ● 305

L3 Literature

Have students read selections from *Don Quixote*, a Shakespearean play, the *Odyssey*, or *Canterbury Tales*. Ask students to share their selections with the class through dramatization, pantomime, illustrations, or other expressive form.

NATIONAL GEOGRAPHIC World Explorer

Answer
temples, such as the Parthenon; churches, such as Notre Dame; and mosques, such as the one in Córdoba, now a cathedral

More About the Photo
Today about 86 percent of Romanians belong to the Romanian Orthodox Church. A small number of Romanians, primarily in the area around Transylvania, are Roman Catholics.

NATIONAL GEOGRAPHIC **GEOFACT**

It is impossible to determine where the game of golf originated. In ancient Rome as well as in North American Native American societies, games played with sticks and balls were common. The first recorded reference to the sport occurred in 1457.

TEAM-TEACHING ACTIVITY: PHOTOGRAPHY

Influence of Photography The invention of photography in the early 1800s had a profound influence on the way Europeans were able to see events and people around the world. Prior to the invention of photography, people could have a visual understanding of the world only through frescoes, statues, and paintings. Have students work with an art or history teacher to write a report showing the relationship between photography and the artistic movement known as realism. **EE4 Human Systems: Standard 10**

NATIONAL
GEOGRAPHIC   **World Explorer**

Answer

families are more mobile; women have entered the work-force; government agencies now handle many social con-cerns once handled by families

More About the Photo A Greek Orthodox marriage cere-mony is also known as a ser-vice of the crowning. During the ceremony, the bride and groom exchange rings that symbolize the unbreakable bond of Christian marriage. Lighted candles symbolize the purity in their lives. A priest reads passages from the Bible. As hymns are chanted, the priest leads the bride and groom around a small table three times. The circular path symbolizes eternity.

ASSESS

Assign Section 3 Assessment as homework or as an in-class activity.

🌐 Have students use **Interactive Tutor Self-Assessment CD-ROM**.

L2

Section Quiz 12-3

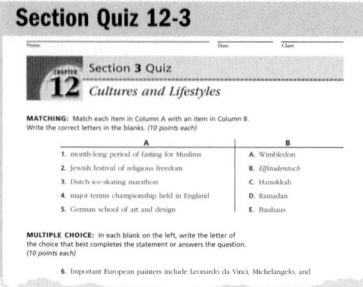

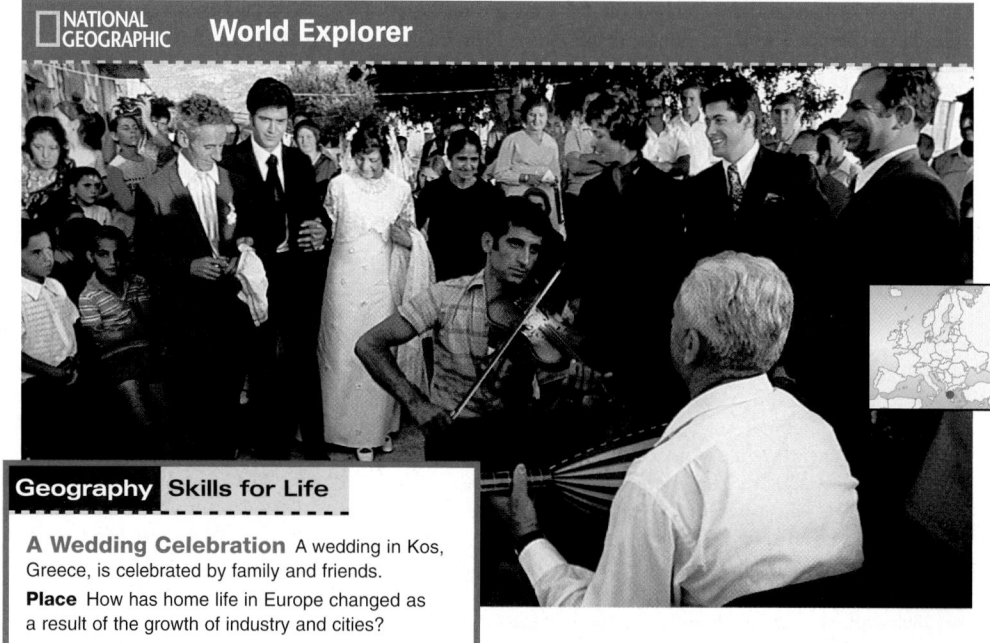

NATIONAL
GEOGRAPHIC   **World Explorer**

Geography | Skills for Life

A Wedding Celebration A wedding in Kos, Greece, is celebrated by family and friends.
Place How has home life in Europe changed as a result of the growth of industry and cities?

gap in the quality of life among various parts of Europe poses an obstacle to full European unity.

Education

Respect for education is a traditional European value. The quality of education in Europe, whose people are among the world's best educated, is linked to economic performance. Countries with a high standard of living can afford to improve schools and provide specialized training for students. With the exception of war-torn Balkan countries, European countries have literacy rates above 90 percent.

The number of years of required schooling varies from country to country. For example, in Portugal children must attend school for only 6 years, but the United Kingdom requires 12 years. Many European school systems provide prepara-tion for either college or vocational training.

Economics
State-Sponsored Human Services

Some European countries, such as Sweden and the United Kingdom, offer complete social welfare

programs to their citizens. These countries, known as **welfare states,** have tax-supported programs for higher education, health care, and social security. The government of Sweden is Europe's most wide-ranging provider of human services. For example, each Swedish family receives an allowance for every child under 16 years of age and for sec-ondary or university students. Also, single parents with low incomes can obtain allowances for family vacations.

Funding social programs is expensive for Euro-pean governments. Many countries, such as Swe-den and France, have spent large portions of their national budgets to provide social services. In recent years European governments have had to tighten their budgets and limit human services to citizens most in need. This cutback has met with opposition from trade unions and voters.

Lifestyles

Cultural and economic differences have produced a variety of lifestyles in Europe. These differences, however, have lessened as industrialization, urban-ization, and technological advances have brought a common culture to many places.

306   🌐   Unit 4

EXTENDING THE CONTENT

Economic Opportunities Have students use the Internet and other resources to research the role of women and various religious/ethnic groups in the European workforce today. Then ask them to select two other regions of the world and research the same infor-mation for women and various groups in these regions. Have students compare economic opportunities for women and religious/ethnic minorities among the three regions. They may present their information as a chart or in writing. 🌐 **EE4 Human Systems: Standard 10**

Home Life

Extended families often shared homes and economic resources in Europe before the Industrial Revolution. As the number of Europeans moving to the cities increased, this traditional pattern changed. Today women in most European countries have entered the workforce, families are more mobile, and government agencies tend to many social concerns once handled by families. Still, family life remains important in Europe. In many European cultures, life revolves around the extended family. Even when young people move away from home, they often maintain close family ties.

Sports and Recreation

Soccer is a major sport in Europe, and many countries have professional soccer teams. Rugby football is a popular team sport, especially in the United Kingdom, France, and Ireland. Many Europeans play tennis for recreation, and the British tennis tournament at Wimbledon is a major international championship.

Some European sports evolved in response to a country's climate, landscape, or culture. In Spain, soccer's popularity only recently surpassed that of bullfighting. In **the Netherlands**, the *Elfstedentocht*, or Eleven Cities Tour, is a Dutch ice-skating marathon along frozen rivers and canals. Winter sports, such as downhill skiing in the Alpine regions, cross-country skiing in Scandinavia, and

ice-skating in **Ukraine** (yoo•KRAYN), have made European athletes famous in the Winter Olympics.

Celebrations

Europeans celebrate many of the same religious holidays observed in other parts of the world, although their celebrations are marked by distinctive traditions. Greeks celebrate Easter with a feast of roast lamb, and Ukrainians share intricately decorated eggs called *pysanky*. European Jews make potato pancakes called latkes to eat during the eight-day festival of religious freedom known as Hanukkah. Muslim families gather for family feasting at the end of Ramadan, a month-long period of fasting during daylight hours.

European Roman Catholics celebrate local festivals in honor of patron saints. Many festivals blend Christian symbolism with customs that date back to pre-Christian times.

Other European holidays mark the change of seasons or patriotic events. In the British Isles, for example, Yule logs and mistletoe decorate homes at the winter solstice. On July 14 the French celebrate Bastille Day to commemorate the storming of the Bastille prison in 1789 and the start of the French Revolution. Countries such as Denmark and the Netherlands celebrate the birthdays of their reigning monarchs as national holidays. Celebrations help Europe's peoples maintain their cultural heritages even as they move toward greater unity.

SECTION 3 ASSESSMENT

Checking for Understanding

1. **Define** dialect, language family, Good Friday Peace Agreement, romanticism, realism, impressionist, welfare state.

2. **Main Ideas** Use a web to organize major cultural influences on the people of Europe.

Critical Thinking

3. **Making Generalizations** How has Europe influenced the arts of other cultures?

4. **Comparing and Contrasting** How do European welfare states differ from the social welfare systems in the United States?

5. **Predicting Consequences** How will recent political and economic developments in Europe produce greater similarities or differences in lifestyles and quality of life?

Analyzing Maps

6. **Region** Study the map of Europe's languages on page 302. Where are Germanic languages predominant?

Applying Geography

7. **Historical Geography** Research daily life in Rome today and as it was in ancient times. Describe the human characteristics of the city then and now. What are the similarities and the differences?

Reteach

Have students reread Section 3. Ask them to write down any topics, words, or locations that are confusing or unclear. Encourage students to ask questions.

Enrich

Share with the class an artistic piece that evokes an image of war, such as an excerpt from *War and Peace*, a copy of Picasso's *Guernica*, or the *1812 Overture*. Afterward, ask students to share their impressions of the piece.

Have students reread "Music of Europe" on page 304 and write a paragraph describing a European musical instrument they find interesting. They may want to use the library, the Internet, or other sources for their research.

SECTION 3 ASSESSMENT ANSWERS

1. All vocabulary terms are defined in the text.

2. Webs should link Language to language families such as Indo-European, Germanic, Slavic, and Romance; Religion to Orthodox, Roman Catholic, Jewish, and Islam; The Arts to architecture, sculpture, music, literature, and painting; and Lifestyles to families, sports, recreation, and festivities.

3. through cultural diversity, colonization, and immigration

4. European welfare states have tax-supported programs for such things as higher education, healthcare, and social security for all citizens. In contrast, social welfare systems in the United States are designed for citizens most in need.

5. The European Union will promote trade, increase cultural, scientific, and educational exchanges, help chart a common political course, and help deal with immigration, environmental challenges, and security.

6. Germany, Austria, Switzerland, the Netherlands, the United Kingdom, Denmark, Sweden, and Norway

7. **Applying Geography** Students might discuss Rome then and now in terms of the city's environment and buildings, living conditions, economic and social activities, means of transportation, and family life.

307

MAP & GRAPH
SkillBuilder

Reading a Political Map

Lines on a map that indicate counties, states, and countries are called political boundaries because they divide areas controlled by different governments. A political map illustrates these divisions.

Teaching the Skill

Ask: In what town or city do you live? Explain that a city, town, or township is the smallest political unit. **Ask: In what larger political units do you live?** Have students name their county, state, and country.

Have students read Learning the Skill on page 308. **Ask: What are the borders between countries called?** *(international boundaries)* **What causes political maps to change?** *(war, government changes)* **Would a political map of eastern Europe from 1985 be valid and useful today? Explain.** *(no; communism's fall brought sweeping changes)*

Additional Practice
L1

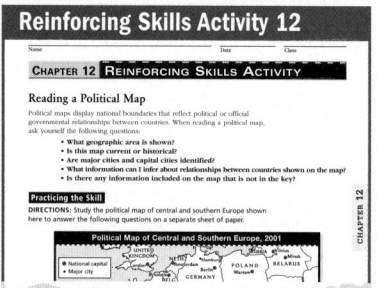

Reinforcing Skills Activity 12

GLENCOE
TECHNOLOGY

Glencoe Skillbuilder Interactive Workbook, Level 2

This interactive CD-ROM reinforces student mastery of essential social studies skills.

Learning the Skill

Unlike physical maps, which remain fairly constant over time, political maps change as political relationships shift. By comparing political maps from different historical periods, you can observe changes in political relationships over time.

On political maps of large areas, lines indicate boundaries between countries, or *national boundaries*. Political maps may also include cities, counties, or provinces. A map key can show the symbols for national boundaries, national capitals, and state or provincial capitals.

To interpret a political map:

• **Read the map's title to identify the geographic area.**

• **Note the time period the map reflects.**

• **Identify the countries or other political units named on the map.**

• **Use the information from the map to make generalizations about the history, government, and political geography of the region.**

Practicing the Skill

Use the political map of present-day Scandinavia to answer the following questions.

1. Which Scandinavian capital lies farthest south?

Scandinavia: Political

National boundary
National capital
Major city

Lambert Azimuthal Equal-Area projection

2. Which Scandinavian countries have port cities on the Baltic Sea?

3. Which Scandinavian country owns the Faroe Islands? Which country owns Jan Mayen Island?

4. Which Scandinavian country probably has the strongest historical and cultural ties to Germany? Explain your answer.

Applying
the Skill

Use an encyclopedia or the Internet to find a political map showing Scandinavia in the mid-1600s. Write a paragraph comparing this map to the present-day political map.

Go To The Glencoe Skillbuilder Interactive Workbook, Level 2 provides instruction and practice in key social studies skills.

ANSWERS TO PRACTICING THE SKILL

1. Copenhagen
2. Finland, Sweden, Denmark
3. Denmark; Norway
4. Denmark, since it borders northern Germany

CHAPTER 12

SUMMARY & STUDY GUIDE

SECTION 1 — Population Patterns (pp. 287–291)

Terms to Know
- ethnic group
- ethnic cleansing
- refugee
- urbanization

Key Points
- Europe's cultures and ethnic groups are diverse.
- Physical features, climate, and resources have affected the region's population density and distribution.
- Industrialization, urbanization, and patterns of migration have helped define Europe as a region.

Organizing Your Notes
Create a table like the one below. Fill in details about each aspect of Europe's population patterns.

Ethnic Diversity	Population Characteristics	Urbanization

SECTION 2 — History and Government (pp. 294–300)

Terms to Know
- city-state
- Middle Ages
- feudalism
- Crusades
- Renaissance
- Reformation
- Enlightenment
- industrial capitalism
- communism
- reparations
- Holocaust
- Cold War
- European Union

Key Points
- The contributions of Greek and Roman civilizations have influenced much of European history.
- During the Middle Ages, Christianity played a major role in shaping European societies.
- Trade, colonization, and immigration spread European cultures to other continents.
- After World War II, the Cold War divided communist-controlled eastern Europe from noncommunist western Europe.
- The European Union was formed to promote economic unity and stability among European countries.

Organizing Your Notes
Create a time line that shows key dates in European history. The time line below has been started for you.

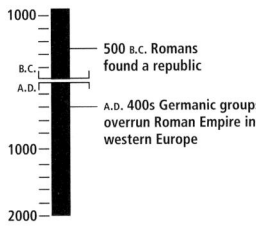

IMPORTANT DATES IN EUROPEAN HISTORY

1000 —
B.C. —   500 B.C. Romans found a republic
A.D. —
             A.D. 400s Germanic groups overrun Roman Empire in western Europe
1000 —
2000 —

SECTION 3 — Cultures and Lifestyles (pp. 301–307)

Terms to Know
- dialect
- language family
- Good Friday Peace Agreement
- romanticism
- realism
- impressionist
- welfare state

Key Points
- Most of Europe's various languages belong to one language family.
- Religion has influenced European values and has sometimes contributed to conflicts.
- Because of colonialism, European art and culture have profoundly influenced the Western world.
- Eastern and western European countries have differences in standards of living.
- Some European governments provide comprehensive social services to their citizens.

Organizing Your Notes
Create a table like the one below to help you organize your notes for this section. Give examples of each aspect of European culture.

European Culture	Examples
Language	
Religion	
The Arts	

Using the Chapter 12 Summary & Study Guide

Use the Chapter 12 Summary & Study Guide to preview, review, condense, or reteach the chapter.

Preview/Review

🔵 **Vocabulary PuzzleMaker CD-ROM** reinforces "Terms to Know."

🔵 **Interactive Tutor Self-Assessment CD-ROM** provides a review of Chapter 12 content.

Condense

Have students read the Chapter 12 Summary & Study Guide.

🔵 Chapter 12 Audio Program

📁 Chapter 12 Guided Reading Activities

Reteach

📁 Chapter 12 Reteaching Activities (Spanish also available)

📁 Chapter 12 Reading Essentials and Study Guides

GLENCOE TECHNOLOGY

▢ NATIONAL GEOGRAPHIC

WORLD REGIONS VIDEO PROGRAM

Unit 4, Europe
The following segments enhance the study of this unit:
- **Mariners of the Mediterranean**
- **A Divided City**
- **City of Canals**

CHAPTER CULMINATING ACTIVITY

Drawing Conclusions Ask: How has the geography, history, and cultural diversity of Europe affected the world in the 2000s? Have students review Chapter 12 and write a summary of their impressions about Europe's political, economic, military, and cultural influence around the globe. Students should consider the effects that colonization, democratic values, immigration, war, and the media had on the diffusion of technology, art, religion, and social systems that originated in Europe. 🔲 **EE2 Places and Regions: Standards 4, 6** 🔲 **EE4 Human Systems: Standard 10**

NOTE: This activity may be completed separately or you may wish students to incorporate it into their GeoJournals.

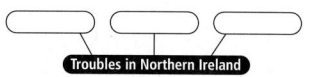

ASSESSMENT & ACTIVITIES

CHAPTER 12

Reviewing Key Terms

European Peoples: a, b, g, n
Historical Development: a, b, c, d, e, f, g, h, i, j, k, n
Art and Ways of Life: d, e, f, g, i, j, k, l, m, n

Reviewing Facts

SECTION 1

1. Asia, Africa, the Caribbean

2. regions of the United Kingdom, Germany, Holland, Belgium, Italy, France, Ireland, Spain, Portugal, Poland, and Hungary

3. The Industrial Revolution drew millions of people to cities in search of work.

SECTION 2

4. the Greeks and Romans

5. the French Revolution and Industrial Revolution

6. revolts against and the end of communist rule

SECTION 3

7. the Indo-European language family, including Germanic languages such as German and English; Romance languages such as French, Spanish, and many others

8. Christianity; Roman Catholic, Eastern Orthodox, and Protestant

Critical Thinking

1. In some communities, Jews made important contributions;

Reviewing Key Terms

On a sheet of paper, classify each of the lettered terms below into the following categories. (Some key terms may apply to more than one category.)

- **European Peoples**
- **Historical Development**
- **Art and Ways of Life**

a. romanticism
b. ethnic cleansing
c. city-states
d. Middle Ages
e. feudalism
f. Renaissance
g. urbanization
h. reparations
i. welfare state
j. European Union
k. Reformation
l. refugees
m. realism
n. Cold War

Reviewing Facts

SECTION 1

1. From which world regions have many of Europe's more recent immigrants arrived?

2. Which parts of Europe are the most densely populated?

3. What has contributed to the rapid rise of urbanization in Europe?

SECTION 2

4. What civilizations shaped early Europe?

5. What important revolutions changed Europe in the 1700s and 1800s?

SECTION 3

6. What political changes swept through Europe during the second half of the twentieth century?

7. What language family includes most of the European languages? Give examples.

8. Name the religion that most Europeans practice. What are its three major branches?

Critical Thinking

1. Drawing Conclusions How did Europe's Christians relate to Jews and Muslims during the Middle Ages?

2. Predicting Consequences How might the European Union affect the social services provided by European governments?

3. Identifying Cause and Effect Create a diagram that shows factors that led to conflicts in Northern Ireland. Then describe what has been done to resolve them.

◯ ◯ ◯

Troubles in Northern Ireland

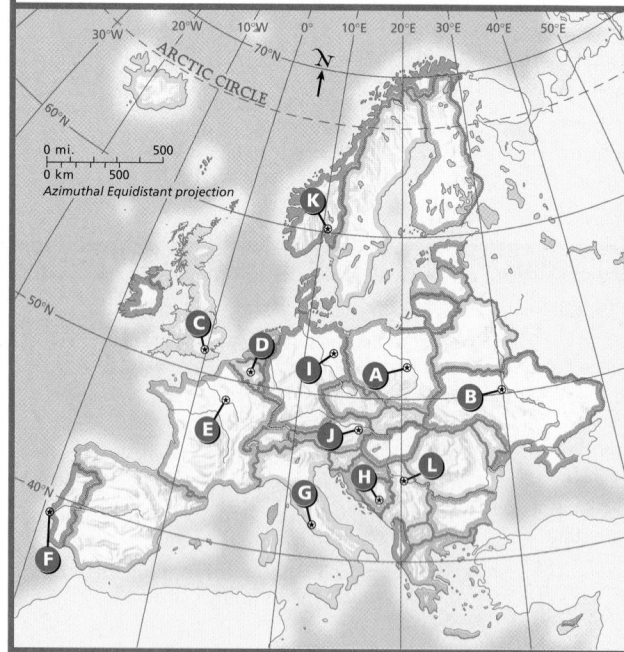

NATIONAL GEOGRAPHIC
Locating Places
Europe: Political Geography
Match the letters on the map with these capitals of European countries. Write your answers on a sheet of paper.

1. Berlin
2. Oslo
3. Brussels
4. Warsaw
5. Lisbon
6. Belgrade
7. Kiev
8. Sarajevo
9. London
10. Rome
11. Paris
12. Vienna

in others, they were persecuted and eventually expelled from much of western Europe. Although the Crusades were military campaigns intended to expel Muslims from Palestine, the Islamic religion and culture had strong influences in Europe, especially in Spain.

2. It may make some member countries lower debts, contribute funds to military expenditures, and introduce austerity measures. These changes might reduce the amount and types of social services that are currently provided by governments.

3. The three categories might include British Rule, Religious Differences (Catholics vs. Protestants), and Economic Disparity. Students may mention the Good Friday Agreement.

NATIONAL GEOGRAPHIC Locating Places					
1. I	**3.** D	**5.** F	**7.** B	**9.** C	**11.** E
2. K	**4.** A	**6.** L	**8.** H	**10.** G	**12.** J

Using the Regional Atlas

Refer to the Regional Atlas on pages 260–263.

1. **Human-Environment Interaction** Compare the population density map and the economic activity map. Describe the population patterns in manufacturing areas.

2. **Location** What capitals are located on the North European Plain? What are the advantages of this location?

Thinking Like a Geographer

Use your textbook, library sources, and the Internet to answer the following: How did Europe's culture spread overseas? How did physical geography affect Europe's expansion?

Problem-Solving Activity

Contemporary Issues Case Study Membership in the European Union offers many benefits but also many challenges. Choose one EU member country, and research the issues that were raised before it joined the EU. Then analyze the situation in the country today, highlighting the benefits and difficulties of EU membership. Present your findings as a case study.

GeoJournal

Expository Writing Using the information you logged in your GeoJournal, explain in a paragraph how two groups of Europeans are attempting to overcome the cultural differences that exist between them.

Technology Activity

Using the Internet for Research Search the Internet for the Web sites of European museums, such as the Louvre in Paris, France, and the Uffizi Gallery in Florence, Italy. Look for information about European architecture, sculpture, paintings, or historical artifacts. Choose one work that expresses the spirit of a particular European country or historical period, and explain your choice to the class. Provide photographs or illustrations of the work you chose.

Standardized Test Practice

Choose the best answer for the following multiple-choice question. If you have trouble answering the question, use the process of elimination to narrow your choices.

Selected Countries in Eastern Europe

1. Study the locations of the Czech Republic, Slovakia, and Hungary. How might the locations of these three countries affect their role in world trade?

   A They are smaller.
   B They are landlocked.
   C They are communist.
   D They have many resources.

 **Test-Taking Tip** Notice that the question asks you to base your answer on location. Three of the choices deal with resources, form of government, and size. Choice B, however, focuses on the countries' locations away from seas, which would influence their role in world trade.

GeoJournal

One way to promote cultural understanding would be to set up exchange visits—perhaps a work-study program—to gain firsthand insight into each country's way of life.

Technology Activity

Although museums such as the British Museum in London, the Louvre in Paris, and the Uffizi Gallery in Florence are rich sources of information, exploring smaller towns and villages might prove fruitful and lead to some interesting discoveries.

Standardized Test Practice

1. B

Tested Objectives: map skills

Additional Practice and Test-Taking Tips

 Standardized Test Practice Workbook

? CHAPTER BONUS TEST QUESTION

What European country has the lowest population density? *(Iceland)*

Using the Regional Atlas

1. There is a greater population density in manufacturing areas. Ask for examples.
2. Paris, Berlin, Warsaw, Amsterdam, Brussels, Prague, Budapest, Vilnius, Riga, and Tallinn; fertile soils and access to waterways

Thinking Like a Geographer

Key points in the essay should be exploration, colonization, trade, and war. The European continent has many navigable rivers, important mountain passes, proximity to Asia and Africa, and access to the Atlantic Ocean.

Problem-Solving Activity

Students' case studies should show a knowledge of the European Union and its member countries, as well as evidence of good research methods.

NOTE: The following materials may be used when teaching Chapter 13. Section-level support materials are shown at point-of-use in the margins of the Teacher Wraparound Edition.

TEACHING TRANSPARENCIES

L2 Unit 4 Map Overlay Transparencies

L2 Political Map Transparency 4

GEOGRAPHIC LITERACY

Focus on Geography Literacy

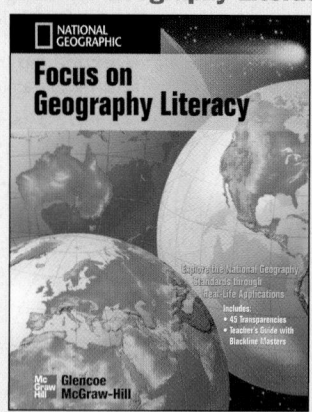

APPLICATION AND ENRICHMENT

L3 Enrichment Activity 13

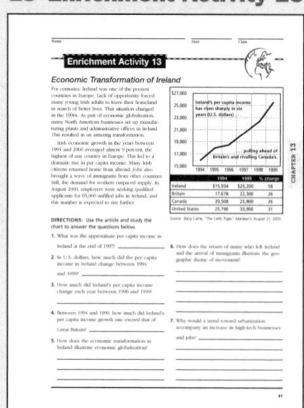

REVIEW AND REINFORCEMENT

L1 Vocabulary Activity 13 L1 Reinforcing Skills Activity 13   L1 Reteaching Activity 13

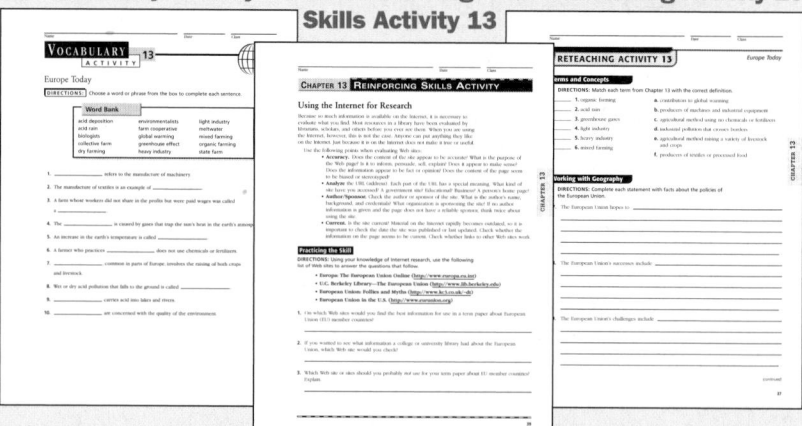

ASSESSMENT

L2 Chapter 13 Test Form A

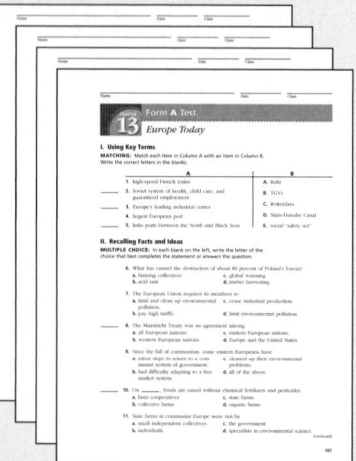

L2 Chapter 13 Test Form B

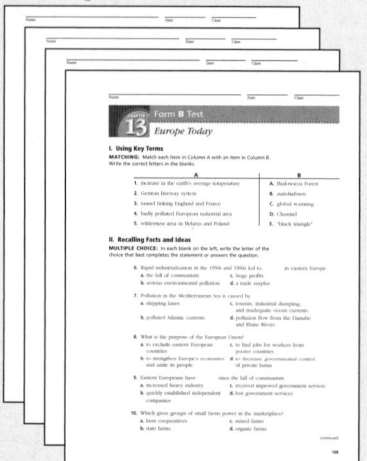

L1/ELL Performance Assessment Activity 13

ExamView® Pro Testmaker

The following Spanish language materials are available in the Spanish Resources binder:

- 📁 Spanish Vocabulary Activities
- 📁 Spanish Guided Reading Activities
- 📁 Spanish Reteaching Activities
- 📁 Spanish Summaries
- 📁 Spanish Quizzes and Tests
- 📁 Spanish Reading Essentials and Study Guide

- World Regions Video
- MindJogger Videoquiz
- Vocabulary PuzzleMaker CD-ROM
- Interactive Tutor Self-Assessment CD-ROM
- ExamView® Pro Testmaker CD-ROM
- Audio Program
- TeacherWorks CD-ROM
- Interactive Student Edition CD-ROM
- Glencoe Skillbuilder Interactive Workbook CD-ROM, Level 2
- Presentation Plus! CD-ROM

Timesaving Tools

TeacherWorks™ — All-In-One Planner and Resource Center

- **Interactive Teacher Edition** Access your Teacher Wraparound Edition and your classroom resources with a few easy clicks.
- **Interactive Lesson Planner** Planning has never been easier! Organize your week, month, semester, or year with all the lesson helps you need to make teaching creative, timely, and relevant.

Use Glencoe's **Presentation Plus!** multimedia teacher tool to easily present dynamic lessons that visually excite your students. Using Microsoft PowerPoint® you can customize the presentations to create your own personalized lessons.

GEOGRAPHY Online

Use our Web site for additional resources. All essential content is covered in the Student Edition.

You and your students can visit geography.glencoe.com, the Web site companion to *Glencoe World Geography*. This innovative integration of electronic and print media offers your students a wealth of opportunities. The student text directs students to the Web site for the following options:

- Chapter Overviews
- Self-Check Quizzes
- Student Activities
- Textbook Updates

Answers are provided for you in the "Web Activity Lesson Plan." Additional Web resources and Interactive Tutor puzzles are also available.

▶ Additional Glencoe Teacher Support

- Teaching Strategies for the Geography Classroom (including Block Scheduling Pacing Guides)
- Graphic Organizer Transparencies Strategies and Activities
- Outline Map Resource Book
- Reading in the Content Area

PLANNING GUIDE

SECTION RESOURCES

Daily Objectives	Reproducible Resources	Multimedia Resources

SECTION 1 Living in Europe

1. Discuss the types of economic systems found in Europe.
2. Explain why economic changes are taking place in Europe.
3. Describe how transportation and communications systems link European countries to one another and to the rest of the world.

Reproducible Resources:
 Reproducible Lesson Plan 13-1
 Daily Lecture Notes 13-1
Guided Reading Activity 13-1*
 Reading Essentials and Study Guide 13-1*
 Section Quiz 13-1*

Multimedia Resources:
- Daily Focus Skills Transparency 13-1
- Political Map Transparency 4
- Unit 4 Map Overlay Transparencies
- World Art and Architecture Transparencies
- Interactive Tutor Self-Assessment CD-ROM
- ExamView® Pro Testmaker CD-ROM*
- Presentation Plus! CD-ROM

SECTION 2 People and Their Environment

1. Explain how industry and farming practices have affected Europe's environment.
2. Identify the steps that are being taken to protect Europe's environment.
3. Discuss the successes Europeans have had in recent decades in reversing the effects of pollution.

Reproducible Resources:
 Reproducible Lesson Plan 13-2
 Vocabulary Activity 13*
 Daily Lecture Notes 13-2
Guided Reading Activity 13-2*
Reading Essentials and Study Guide 13-2*
 Reteaching Activity 13*
Reinforcing Skills Activity 13
 Section Quiz 13-2*
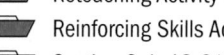

Multimedia Resources:
- Daily Focus Skills Transparency 13-2
- Unit 4 Map Overlay Transparencies
- Vocabulary PuzzleMaker CD-ROM
- Interactive Tutor Self-Assessment CD-ROM
- ExamView® Pro Testmaker CD-ROM*
- Presentation Plus! CD-ROM

 Blackline Master   Software   Videocassette

 Transparency   CD-ROM   DVD

Also available in Spanish

00:00 OUT OF TIME? Assign the Chapter 13 **Reading Essentials and Study Guide.**

Block Schedule

Activities that are particularly suited to use within the block scheduling framework are identified throughout this chapter by the following designation:

KEY TO ABILITY LEVELS

Teaching strategies have been coded for various learning styles and abilities.

L1 BASIC activities for all students

L2 AVERAGE activities for average to above-average students

L3 CHALLENGING activities for above-average students

ELL ENGLISH LANGUAGE LEARNER activities

Teacher to Teacher

Mike Walker
Moore County
High School
Lynchburg, TN

The Economies of Europe

To help students learn about European economies, have them work individually or with partners to gather research about a particular European country's major imports, exports, GDP, inflation rate, and other economic details. Students should use the Internet, encyclopedias, almanacs, magazines, or other library materials to obtain up-to-date information. After students gather their data, ask them to prepare a report about their assigned country's economic status. If possible, have students use illustrations, graphs, or other visuals to enhance their reports.

Once the economic information is collected, have students present their findings to the class. During the presentations, other students should be encouraged to ask questions to learn more about the particular country's economy. Collect the reports, and make them available throughout the course of studying this unit.

NATIONAL GEOGRAPHIC TEACHER'S CORNER

Index to National Geographic Magazine:

The following articles may be used for research relating to this chapter:

- "Wrath of the Gods," by Rick Gore, July 2000.
- *Biodiversity*, A National Geographic Special Edition, February 1999.
- "East Europe's Dark Dawn: The Iron Curtain Rises to Reveal a Land Tarnished by Pollution," by Jon Thompson, June 1991.

National Geographic Society Products:

To order the following products for use with this chapter, call National Geographic Society at 1-800-368-2728.

- *GeoKit: Pollution* (Kit)
- *Capitalism, Communism, Socialism Series* (Videos)
- *Recycling: The Endless Circle* (Video)
- *Pollution: World at Risk* (Video)
- *Technology's Price* (Video)
- *National Geographic Desk Reference* (Book)
- *National Geographic Atlas of the World, Seventh Edition* (Book)

NGS ONLINE

Access National Geographic's Web site for current events, activities, links, interactive features, and archives.
www.nationalgeographic.com

Meeting National Standards

Geography For Life

The following standards are highlighted in Chapter 13:

Section 1   EE4 Human Systems: Standards 10, 11
EE5 Environment and Society:
Standards 14, 16
EE6 The Uses of Geography:
Standard 18

Section 2   EE3 Physical Systems:
Standard 8
EE4 Human Systems:
Standards 12, 13
EE5 Environment and Society:
Standards 14, 15

Local Objectives

_____

_____

MEETING SPECIAL NEEDS

In addition to the Differentiated Instruction strategies found in each section, the following resources are also suitable for your special needs students:

- *ExamView® Pro Testmaker CD-ROM* allows teachers to tailor tests by reducing answer choices.
- The *Audio Program* includes the entire narrative of the student edition so that less-proficient readers can listen to the words as they read them.
- The *Reading Essentials and Study Guide* provides the same content as the student edition but is written two grade levels below the textbook.
- *Guided Reading Activities* give less-proficient readers point-by-point instructions to increase comprehension as they read each textbook section.
- *Enrichment Activities* include a stimulating collection of readings and activities for gifted and talented students.

Chapter Objectives

1. Examine recent economic changes in Europe as they relate to industry, agriculture, transportation, and communications.

2. Discuss the impact of industrialization and urban development on Europe's environment, focusing on the challenges of acid rain, global warming, and air and water pollution.

GLENCOE TECHNOLOGY

Use *MindJogger Videoquiz* to preview the Chapter 13 content.

GeoJournal

For access to additional photos, maps, and information on the contemporary issues of Europe, go to www.nationalgeographic.com (See Teacher pages in front for strategies for using journals in the geography classroom.)

GEOGRAPHY Online

Introduce students to chapter content and key terms by having them access **Chapter Overview 13** at geography.glencoe.com

FOLDABLES™ Study Organizer

Dinah Zike's Foldables are three-dimensional, interactive graphic organizers that help students practice basic writing skills, review key vocabulary terms, and identify main ideas. Have students complete the Foldable activity in the **Dinah Zike's Reading and Study Skills Foldables** booklet.

CHAPTER 13 Europe Today

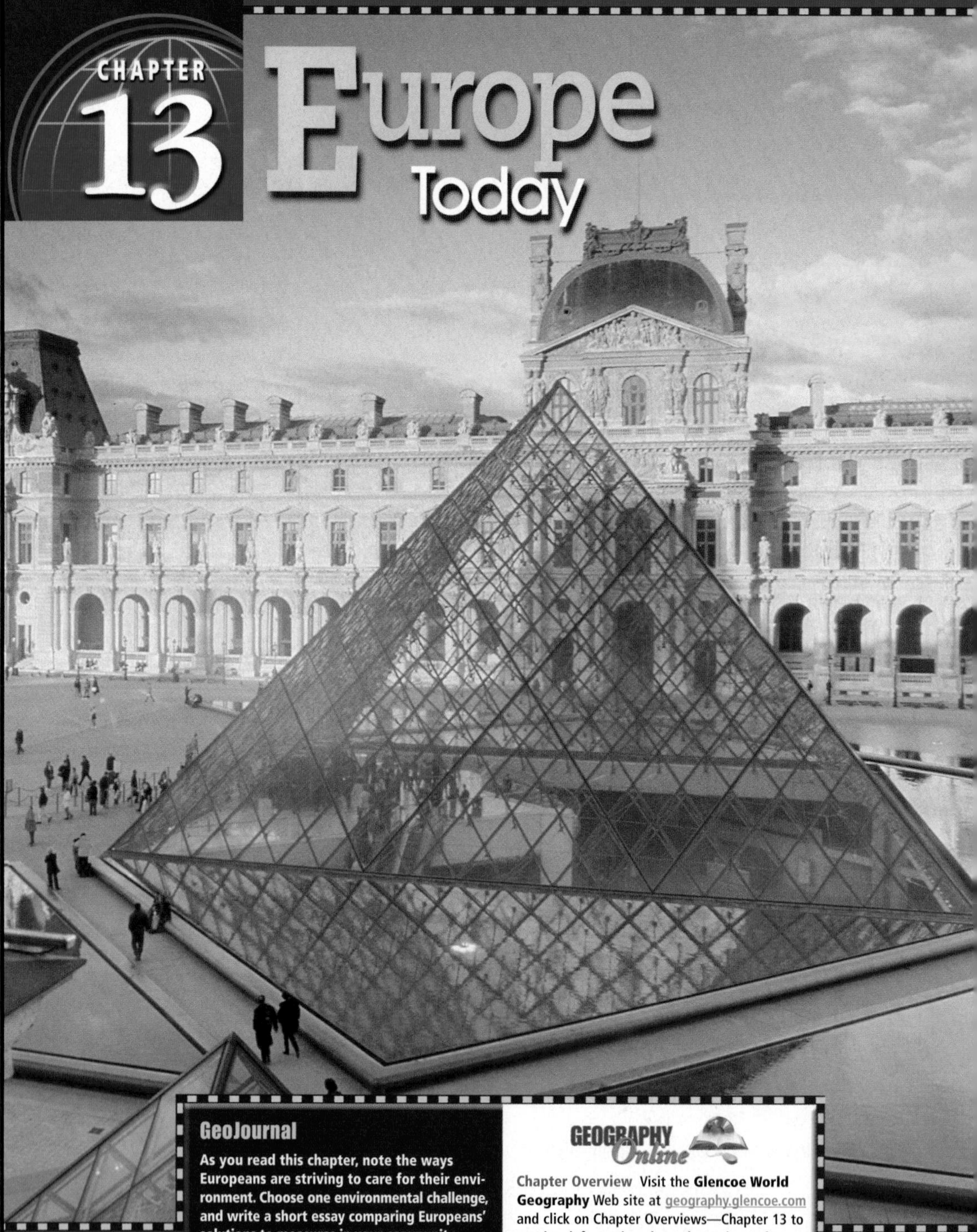

GeoJournal

As you read this chapter, note the ways Europeans are striving to care for their environment. Choose one environmental challenge, and write a short essay comparing Europeans' solutions to measures in your community.

GEOGRAPHY Online

Chapter Overview Visit the **Glencoe World Geography** Web site at geography.glencoe.com and click on Chapter Overviews—Chapter 13 to preview information about the region today.

ABOUT THE PHOTO

The Louvre Begun in 1546, the Louvre in Paris, France, was the palace of French monarchs until 1682, when King Louis XIV built the Palace of Versailles as his royal residence. In 1793 the Louvre was opened as a public museum. Undergoing several expansions through the years, the Louvre holds one of the world's finest art collections, including Leonardo da Vinci's *Mona Lisa*. Its modern glass pyramid entrance—designed by renowned American architect I. M. Pei—was added during renovations in the 1980s. Today the Louvre covers more than 98 acres (40 ha) in the center of Paris, with almost 650,000 square feet (60,000 sq. m) of exhibition rooms. ◆ EE4 Human Systems: Standard 10

Guide to Reading

Consider What You Know

Based on what you learned in Chapter 12, how do you think Europeans are adjusting to the changes caused by the fall of communism?

Reading Strategy

Organizing As you read about the European Union, complete a web diagram similar to the one below by filling in the goals of the European Union.

Goals of EU

Read to Find Out

• What economic systems are found in Europe?

• Why are economic changes taking place in Europe?

• How do transportation and communications systems link European countries to each other and to the rest of the world?

Terms to Know

• European Union (EU)
• Maastricht Treaty
• heavy industry
• light industry
• mixed farming
• farm cooperative
• collective farm
• state farm
• genetically modified food
• organic farming

Places to Locate

• Ruhr
• Denmark

◀ *Pyramid entrance of the Louvre Museum, Paris, France*

Living in Europe

NATIONAL GEOGRAPHIC

A Geographic View

A New Europe

By 5:30 A.M., 3,000 or 4,000 workers of the first shift are pouring through the gates of the iron and steel works on the Danube River island of Csepel. Expanded by ardent communists in the 1950s, it became Hungary's largest industrial site.... Today's worker wants to become part of the middle class, to own a car and a weekend cottage in the country. "That's what I want," says Gábor Szabó, a young welder, "to become a European."

Eastern European miners

—Tad Szulc, "Dispatches from Eastern Europe," National Geographic, March 1991

Like many eastern Europeans during the early 1990s, this factory worker in Hungary was eager to leave behind the dark legacy of communism and share in the prosperity that democratic western Europe enjoyed. Today, despite many difficulties, the countries of eastern Europe are building democracies and market economies. As standards of living rise, people in these countries also are developing closer ties to western Europe. Throughout Europe, people still remain proud of their individual national identities, but they are also beginning to identify with the region as a whole. In this section you will learn about Europe's social, political, and economic systems and the recent changes that are transforming them.

Changing Economies

Europe's economies, like its peoples, are diverse and changing. Today Europe is one of the world's major manufacturing and trading regions. The European Union (EU), which unites much of

Chapter 13 **313**

RESOURCE MANAGER

Reproducible Masters
• Reproducible Lesson Plan 13-1
• Daily Lecture Notes 13-1
• Guided Reading Activity 13-1
• Reading Essentials and Study Guide 13-1
• Section Quiz 13-1

Transparencies
• Daily Focus Skills Transparency 13-1

• Political Map Transparency 4
• Unit 4 Map Overlay Transparencies
• World Art and Architecture Transparencies

Multimedia
• Interactive Tutor Self-Assessment CD-ROM
• ExamView® Pro Testmaker CD-ROM
• Presentation Plus! CD-ROM

1 FOCUS

Section Overview

This section provides an economic overview of Europe, including the European Union, recent economic changes, and the features of Europe's key industries.

BELLRINGER
Skillbuilder Activity

 Project transparency and have students answer questions.

 Available as blackline master.

Daily Focus Skills Transparency 13-1

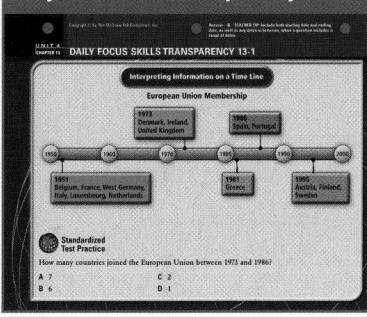

Guide to Reading

Consider What You Know
Answers *Students may say that initially economic, social, and political hardships were widespread in eastern Europe.*

Reading Strategy
Answers *a united Europe; make Europe's economies more efficient and productive; freer movement of goods, services, and people across borders; single European currency; a central bank; common foreign policy*

Preteaching Vocabulary
Direct students to pages 313–314 to learn about the term *European Union*; page 317 for *heavy* and *light industry*; and page 317 for *collective farm*, *state farm*, and *farm cooperative*.

2 TEACH

L2 Drawing Conclusions

Discuss with students the European Union's history, membership, and intended purpose. Ask students why the EU might be good for Europe and why it might not be. To offer a perspective, ask them to consider the consequences if the United States were 50 separate small countries instead of one large union.

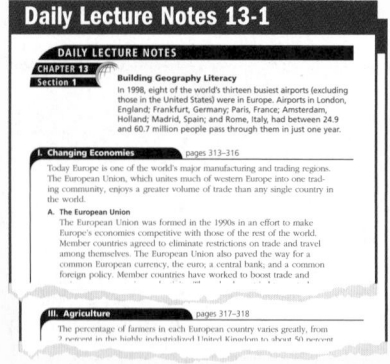

Daily Lecture Notes 13-1

DAILY LECTURE NOTES

CHAPTER 13
Section 1

Building Geography Literacy
In 1998, eight of the world's thirteen busiest airports (excluding those in the United States) were in Europe. Airports in London, England; Frankfurt, Germany; Paris, France; Amsterdam, Holland; Madrid, Spain; and Rome, Italy, had between 24.9 and 60.7 million people pass through them in just one year.

I. Changing Economies *pages 313–316*

Today Europe is one of the world's major manufacturing and trading regions. The European Union, which unites much of western Europe into one trading community, enjoys a greater volume of trade than any single country in the world.

A. The European Union
The European Union was formed in the 1990s in an effort to make Europe's economies competitive with those of the rest of the world. Member countries agreed to eliminate restrictions on trade and travel among themselves. The European Union also paved the way for a common European currency, the euro, a central bank, and a common foreign policy. Member countries have worked to boost trade and

III. Agriculture *pages 317–318*

The percentage of farmers in each European country varies greatly, from 2 percent in the highly industrialized United Kingdom to about 50 percent

Culture NOTE

Language Nearly 16 percent of European Union citizens are native English speakers. A survey of EU citizens taken in 2001 found that over half the survey respondents claimed to be able to converse in English.

---

western Europe into one trading community, enjoys a greater volume of trade than any single country in the world. Meanwhile, the former communist countries of eastern Europe are trying to build free market economies. Some also seek to eventually become part of the European Union.

Economics
The European Union

The movement for European unity arose from the ashes of World War II, as western European countries struggled to rebuild their ruined economies. In 1950 France proposed closer links among Europe's coal and steel industries, a move seen as the first step toward a united Europe.

Over the years more steps were taken toward that goal, but not until the 1990s did most Europeans agree that such a goal could ever be reached. In 1992 representatives from various European governments met in Maastricht, the Netherlands, and signed the **Maastricht Treaty**, which set up the European Union (EU). This new body aimed to make Europe's economies competitive with those of the rest of the world by getting rid of restrictions on the movement of goods, services, and people across its members' borders. It also paved the way for a single European currency, a central bank, and a common foreign policy.

Since the EU was formed, member countries have worked to boost trade and to make their economies more efficient and more productive. They have also tried to control government spending for many costly social welfare programs. Many Europeans, however, oppose scaling down the welfare state, believing that such a step would increase hardships on people during times of rising unemployment. The EU continues to work toward the goal of a stronger single economy in spite of the difficulties brought on by change. In the years ahead, the European Union plans to extend its membership to include a number of additional countries, mainly in eastern Europe.

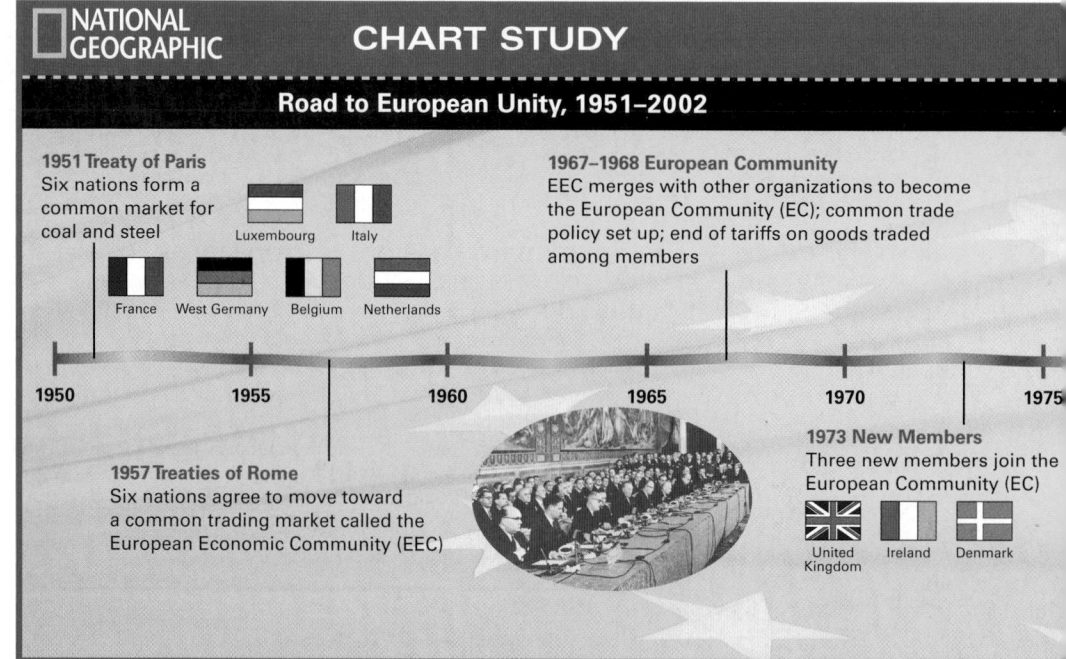

NATIONAL GEOGRAPHIC — **CHART STUDY**

Road to European Unity, 1951–2002

1951 Treaty of Paris
Six nations form a common market for coal and steel

Luxembourg   Italy
France   West Germany   Belgium   Netherlands

1967–1968 European Community
EEC merges with other organizations to become the European Community (EC); common trade policy set up; end of tariffs on goods traded among members

1950   1955   1960   1965   1970   1975

1957 Treaties of Rome
Six nations agree to move toward a common trading market called the European Economic Community (EEC)

1973 New Members
Three new members join the European Community (EC)

United Kingdom   Ireland   Denmark

DIFFERENTIATED INSTRUCTION

At-Risk Students Have students who may have trouble reasoning or organizing and interpreting information create a large chart with the following headings: *Heavy Industry, Light Industry, Agriculture, Services*. Have students reread the material from the text and list the facts they consider important under the appropriate headings. Then have each student choose one of the headings and write a paragraph using the facts listed on the chart.

EE5 Environment and Society: Standard 16

Refer to *Inclusion for the Social Studies Classroom Strategies and Activities.*

Eastern Europe

For more than 40 years after World War II, communist governments loyal to the Soviet Union ran eastern Europe's command economies. Under these systems, government planners made decisions about what goods to produce and how to produce them. Industries employed many more workers and managers than they needed, and many factories lacked modern technology.

Since the fall of communism in 1989, eastern European countries have been moving from command economies to market economies. To compete in global markets, eastern European industries are working to overcome the obstacles of outdated equipment and inefficient production methods. Many laid-off workers are being retrained, as industries try to acquire new technology and to adopt energy conservation measures to reduce pollution. Eastern European governments are seeking to attract investments and financial aid from western Europe and other parts of the world.

Eastern Europeans have realized, however, that change is often costly and difficult. Workers have lost part of their social "safety net"—the free health care, child care, lifetime jobs, and other social benefits—provided by the communist system. With reduced benefits, death rates among newborns have risen in some parts of eastern Europe, and life expectancy levels have declined. Despite these difficulties, however, people in eastern Europe are slowly adjusting to a new way of life. For example, Germany—reunited in 1990—has faced challenges in improving industrial and living conditions in its eastern part, once under

Student Web Activity Visit the **Glencoe World Geography** Web site at geography.glencoe.com and click on Student Web Activities— Chapter 13 for an activity about the European Union.

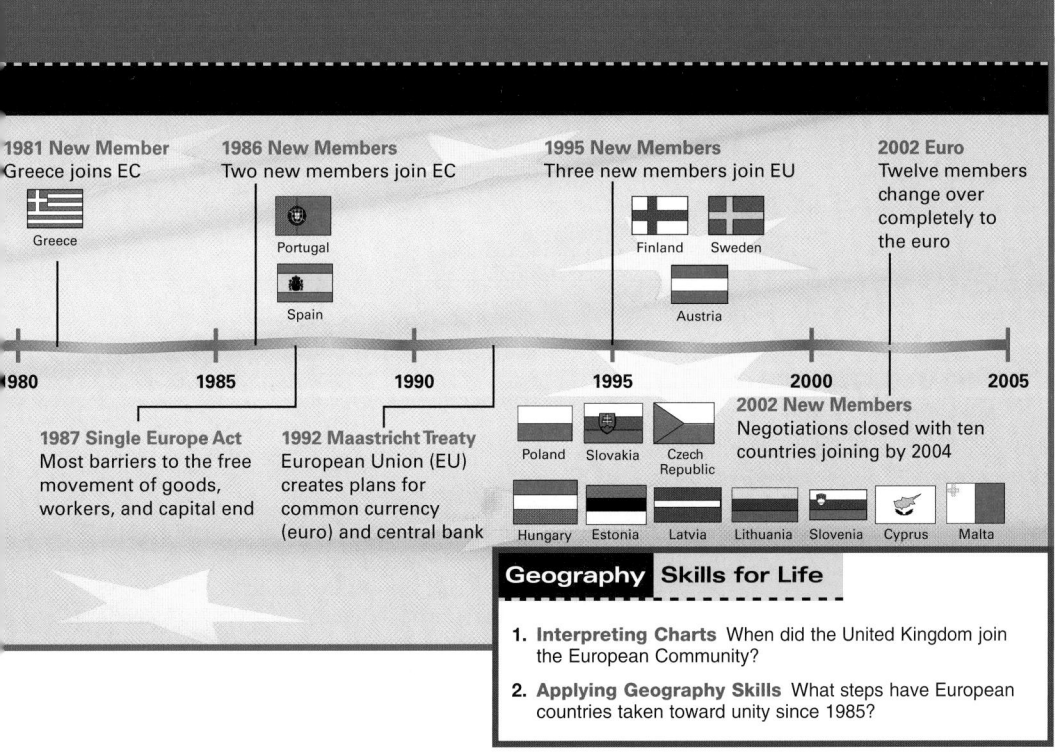

1981 New Member
Greece joins EC

Greece

1986 New Members
Two new members join EC

Portugal

Spain

1995 New Members
Three new members join EU

Finland   Sweden

Austria

2002 Euro
Twelve members change over completely to the euro

1980   1985   1990   1995   2000   2005

1987 Single Europe Act
Most barriers to the free movement of goods, workers, and capital end

1992 Maastricht Treaty
European Union (EU) creates plans for common currency (euro) and central bank

Poland   Slovakia   Czech Republic

2002 New Members
Negotiations closed with ten countries joining by 2004

Hungary   Estonia   Latvia   Lithuania   Slovenia   Cyprus   Malta

Geography Skills for Life

1. **Interpreting Charts** When did the United Kingdom join the European Community?
2. **Applying Geography Skills** What steps have European countries taken toward unity since 1985?

Chapter 13 ⊕ 315

CHAPTER 13
Section 1, pages 313–319

L1/ELL

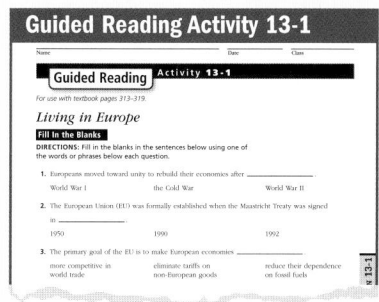

Guided Reading Activity 13-1

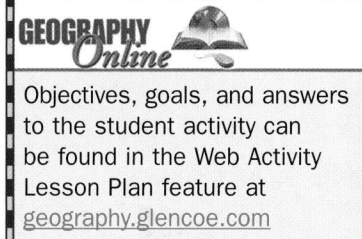

Objectives, goals, and answers to the student activity can be found in the Web Activity Lesson Plan feature at geography.glencoe.com

NATIONAL GEOGRAPHIC   **CHART STUDY**

Answers

1. *1973*

2. *eliminated most barriers to the movement of goods, workers, and services; made plans for a common currency and central bank*

Skills Practice

Location From what part of Europe are the majority EU member countries? *(western Europe)*

COOPERATIVE LEARNING ACTIVITY

European Products Organize students into six groups, and assign several European countries to each group. Using the Internet, encyclopedias, and other references, have students research the major products of their assigned countries. Provide each group with an outline map of Europe. Have students design symbols for the major products and place them in the appropriate places on their maps. Compare the completed maps, and ask students to draw conclusions about the relationship between geography and major products of European countries. ⊞ **EE5 Environment and Society: Standard 16**

NATIONAL GEOGRAPHIC MAP STUDY

Answers

1. *Austria, Belgium, Cyprus, Czech Republic, Denmark, Estonia, Finland, France, Germany, Greece, Hungary, Ireland, Italy, Latvia, Liechtenstein, Lithuania, Luxembourg, Malta, the Netherlands, Poland, Portugal, Slovakia, Slovenia, Spain, Sweden, and the United Kingdom*

2. *waterways: oceans, seas, and navigable rivers*

Map Skills Practice

Place Identify the landlocked European countries, and list the possible ways those countries would import and export products. *(Andorra, Austria, Czech Republic, Hungary, Liechtenstein, Luxembourg, Moldova, San Marino, Slovakia, Switzerland; They might use railroads, air, highways, rivers, and canals to move goods; treaties and trade agreements with neighboring countries.)*

L1/ELL

Reading Essentials & Study Guide 13-1

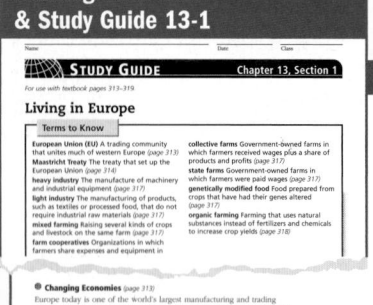

NATIONAL GEOGRAPHIC MAP STUDY

The European Union

Legend:
- ☐ European countries
- Members of the European Union, 2004
- Applicant countries, 2004

Geography

Skills for Life

1. **Interpreting Maps** What countries are members of the European Union?

2. **Applying Geography Skills** What physical features aid the movement of goods into and out of the European Union?

Find NGS online map resources @ www.nationalgeographic.com/maps

---

communist control. Yet for many people, life has improved:

 Despite the . . . joblessness in eastern Berlin, there are thousands of quiet success stories. . . . 'It was the fulfillment of a dream,' says Stefan Geissler, a 37-year-old former publishing clerk in the old East Berlin, who started the business with a partner, using their combined savings of $2,250. Despite a shaky beginning, Goethe & Co. is now making a small profit. 'Everybody I know is making it—somehow,' Geissler says with

conviction. 'People who say "Bring back the Wall" are talking nonsense. Most people are better off today.'
Peter Ross Range, "Reinventing Berlin," *National Geographic*, December 1996

Industry

The Industrial Revolution made Europe the birthplace of modern industry. Today large-scale manufacturing centers are found across Europe from the United Kingdom to Poland. In both heavy and light industries, Europe produces everything from computers and cellular phones to transportation equipment and packaged goods.

CRITICAL THINKING ACTIVITY

Problem Solving With the European Union promoting economic growth, energy shortages might arise for its member countries as more factories, businesses, cars, and homes compete for energy resources. Ask students to look at the Natural Resources map in the Unit Atlas on page 263 and list the kinds of energy resources found in Europe. **Ask:** Which areas have the kinds of resources that meet energy needs? *(For example, North Sea: petroleum; Spain and Sweden: uranium)* What alternative sources might the European Union promote to meet future energy demands and avoid energy problems? *(solar, wind, energy-efficient homes and businesses, additional railroad systems, and electric cars)*
🌐 EE6 The Uses of Geography: Standard 18

Manufacturing

The development of industry is often linked to the availability of raw materials. In the 1800s Europe's large deposits of coal and iron ore sparked the growth of heavy industry—the manufacture of machinery and industrial equipment. Today Europe's leading industrial centers include the **Ruhr** and the Middle Rhine districts in Germany, the Lorraine-Saar district in France, the Po basin in Italy, and the Upper Silesia-Moravia district in Poland and the Czech Republic. Vast mineral deposits help to make the United Kingdom, France, and Germany leaders in manufacturing. Countries lacking industrial raw materials, such as the Netherlands and Denmark, specialize in light industry, such as making textiles or processing food.

Service and Technology Industries

Service industries employ a large percentage of the workforce in most European countries—in fact, about 60 percent of workers in western Europe. International banking and insurance rank among Europe's top service industries. Switzerland and the United Kingdom are leaders in these fields. Belgium serves as the headquarters for hundreds of international companies. Tourism is another large service industry in Europe, especially in the United Kingdom, France, Germany, and Switzerland. As in the United States and Canada, high-technology industries are a growing sector of western Europe's economy. Ireland, for example, has become a leading manufacturer of computer products and software.

▲ *Harvesting wheat in Ukraine*

Agriculture

Although largely industrialized, Europe also has fertile farmland. More Europeans earn a living from farming than from any other single economic activity. Yet the percentage of farmers in each country varies widely. For example, about 50 percent of Albania's workers are farmers, but in the industrialized United Kingdom, fewer than 2 percent engage in agriculture.

Europe's crops vary from area to area. Olives, citrus fruits, dates, and grapes grow in warm Mediterranean areas. Farther north, in the cooler plains region, farmers raise wheat, rye, and other grains as well as livestock. Northern countries, such as Denmark and the Netherlands, are major producers of dairy products. The Scandinavian countries are among the world's leading suppliers of fish.

Farming Techniques

In western Europe, farmers use advanced technology to make the best use of limited agricultural space. Mixed farming—raising several kinds of crops and livestock on the same farm—is common. Most western European farmers own their own land, and the average farm covers about 30 acres (about 12 ha). In **Denmark** and some other countries, farm cooperatives, organizations in which farmers share in growing and selling products, reduce costs and increase profits.

In eastern Europe, the fall of communism has brought many changes to farming. Under communism, farmers worked either on government-owned collective farms, receiving wages plus a share of products and profits, or on state farms, not sharing in the profits but getting wages like factory workers. On both types of farms, outdated equipment and lack of incentive resulted in low crop yields. Since the shift to democracy, private ownership of land and food production has risen, and eastern European farmers are expected to increase yields and profits by using modern equipment and fertilizers.

Agricultural Issues

Throughout Europe, new farming methods have not escaped criticism. Many Europeans, for example, oppose genetically modified foods, foods with genes altered to make them grow bigger or faster or be more resistant to pests. Opponents claim that

L2 Tourism and Economics

Assign each student in the class one European country. Using the Internet and maps in this unit, have students create a travel brochure promoting their country. Have students consider the economic potential of tourism—a country's natural beauty is one way of attracting visitors and business investment.

Moldova Much of Moldova, formerly known as the Republic of Moldavia in the U.S.S.R., was created from captured Romanian lands. The Soviets forced the Moldavians to write their Romanian dialect in the Cyrillic alphabet instead of the Latin alphabet used in Romania.

GEOGRAPHY AND THE HUMANITIES

 World Music: A Cultural Legacy

 World Art and Architecture Transparencies

 World Art Prints

TEAM-TEACHING ACTIVITY: ECONOMICS

Common Currency In 2002 the euro became the legal tender for most members of the European Union, permanently replacing national currencies. For many Europeans this development is a major change after centuries of separate monetary systems defined by distinctive notes and coins. Have students work with a history, economics, or business teacher to learn more about how the euro works. Have students research the economic risks a common currency may entail as well as the probable benefits. Have students compare their findings with others in the class. **EE4 Human Systems: Standard 11**

Architecture of Europe Built in 1889 for the 100th anniversary of the French Revolution, the Eiffel Tower was, until 1930, the world's tallest building. There are 1,652 steps to the top.

World Art and Architecture Transparencies

Use these transparencies with accompanying strategies and activities to introduce students to other types of architecture of this region.

③ ASSESS

Assign Section 1 Assessment as homework or as an in-class activity.

⊕ Have students use **Interactive Tutor Self-Assessment CD-ROM**.

L2

Section Quiz 13-1

Reteach

Review with the class the major topics in Section 1, including Europe's changing economies and the significance of the European Union.

---

little is yet known about the safety of these foods. In addition, many consumers also avoid foods grown in fields treated with toxic chemicals to control insects or weeds. Because of the concern about chemical use, some farmers rely on organic farming, using natural substances instead of fertilizers and chemicals to increase crop yields.

Despite much agricultural success, western Europe today faces a livestock crisis. In 2001 an outbreak of foot-and-mouth disease in the United Kingdom required the killing of thousands of animals, severely crippling the country's livestock industry. The disease—highly contagious among animals but harmless to humans—then crossed to the European continent. As the disease threatened to spread across Europe, consumer panic led to plummeting beef sales. Fearing a global threat from the foot-and-mouth outbreak, the United States and other countries banned imports of animals, meat, and milk from Europe.

architecture of EUROPE

Eiffel Tower Built in Paris, France, the 984-foot (300-m) Eiffel Tower was an early example of modern architecture using wrought iron construction. French engineer Gustave Eiffel designed the tower for the Paris World's Fair in 1889. The lower section of the tower consists of four arched legs that curve inward until they rise together in a single tapered tower. Stairs and elevators allow people to visit the tower's three platform levels, each with an observation deck. Modern additions to the tower include a meteorological station and a radio station.

Transportation and Communications

Europe's network of highways, railroads, waterways, and airline routes is among the best in the world. Modern communications systems also link most parts of Europe to one another and to the rest of the world. Many of the continent's transportation and communications systems are government-owned, with standards and performance varying from one country to another. Eastern Europe, for example, is trying to improve its less advanced transportation and communications systems to match the quality of those in western Europe.

Railways and Highways

Throughout Europe, railroads move freight and passengers. Rail lines connect the region's major cities and airports as well as link natural resources to major industrial centers. Railroads provide easy access to downtown and suburban areas. Bridges and tunnels carry traffic over or through barriers posed by water, mountains, or valleys. For example, in 2000 Denmark and Sweden opened a rail and road bridge that links Sweden to western Europe for the first time since the last Ice Age.

France pioneered the use of high-speed trains with its introduction in 1981 of *trains à grand vitesse* (TGVs), which means "very fast trains." The fastest trains in the world, TGVs cause less damage to the environment than most other forms of transportation. High-speed rail lines, more economical than airline travel, now also operate in Germany, Italy, and Spain. A high-speed rail triangle links Paris, Brussels, and London, passing beneath the English Channel through the Chunnel, or Channel Tunnel.

A well-developed highway system also links Europe's major cities. Germany's four-lane superhighways, called *autobahnen*, are among Europe's best roads. Europe has the highest number of automobile owners in the world except for the United States. Bicycles and motorcycles also provide popular forms of transportation.

Seaports and Waterways

With its long coastline, Europe has a seafaring tradition. Europe handles more than half the world's international shipping at its bustling ports. Major ports include London, England; Antwerp, Belgium;

EXTENDING THE CONTENT

The Chunnel The Chunnel, the world's longest underwater tunnel system, connects France and England. Consisting of two train tunnels with a third smaller service tunnel in between, the Chunnel offers travelers the option of taking a regular passenger train or a train that carries vehicles. The last time that the British Isles were joined to mainland Europe was at the end of the last Ice Age, before water from melting glaciers covered the land bridge that linked them. ⊕ **EE5 Environment and Society: Standard 14**

Genoa, Italy; Le Havre and Marseille in France; Odesa, Ukraine; and Gdańsk, Poland. Rotterdam, the Netherlands, is the world's largest port in surface area, amount of freight handled, and numbers of ships that it can dock at one time.

Europe has many navigable rivers and human-built canals. The Rhine River and its tributaries carry more freight than any other river system in Europe, providing access to the North Sea for five European countries. The Kiel Canal cuts across southern Denmark and shortens the route between the North Sea and the Baltic Sea. The Main-Danube Canal in Germany links hundreds of inland ports between the North Sea and the Black Sea.

Communications Links

Communications systems bring information and programming to Europe. The International Tele-communications Satellite Organization uses a series of communications satellites (INTELSATs) to broadcast and receive television programs. The Eurovision network links most of western Europe, and the Intervision network operates in eastern Europe. The two networks sometimes exchange programming.

Telephone service and print media vary throughout Europe. High-quality telephone service is not as available in eastern Europe as it is in western Europe. Western European telephone systems include extensive cable and microwave radio relay, fiber optics, and satellite systems. A large percentage of western

NATIONAL GEOGRAPHIC **World Explorer**

Geography | Skills for Life

Rail Travel At London's Victoria Station, travelers wait to board a transcontinental train.
Movement Why do some Europeans use high-speed rail lines rather than airline travel?

Europeans use cellular phones, electronic mail, and the Internet. Books, magazines, and newspapers continue to shape public opinion in Europe. As democracy has grown in eastern Europe, government censorship of printed materials has ended. In the next section, you will read how people in Europe interact with the region's physical environment.

NATIONAL GEOGRAPHIC **World Explorer**

Answer
They provide easy access to cities and suburbs, are very fast, and are more economical.

More About the Photo
Victoria Station, built in 1859, is the busiest railway terminal in the United Kingdom. The station houses cafes and gift shops as well as facilities to exchange foreign currency.

Enrich

Ask students to name European products sold in the United States, such as food, cars, clothes, furniture, beverages, or music, and to identify the country of origin for each product.

 **CLOSE**

Ask students to reread "A Geographic View" on page 313. Ask students to write a paragraph explaining what Gábor Szabó meant by, "That's what I want . . . to become a European."

SECTION 1 ASSESSMENT

Checking for Understanding

1. **Define** European Union (EU), Maastricht Treaty, heavy industry, light industry, mixed farming, farm cooperative, collective farm, state farm, genetically modified food, organic farming.

2. **Main Ideas** Use a chart to organize data about factors affecting Europe's economy.

Economic Impact		
Industry	Agriculture	Transportation and Communications

Critical Thinking

3. **Making Comparisons** What different challenges do eastern and western Europeans face as they move toward a more unified Europe?

4. **Identifying Cause and Effect** Explain how physical geography influenced Europe's economic development.

5. **Drawing Conclusions** What are the advantages and disadvantages of Europe's communications systems?

Analyzing Maps

6. **Region** Study the map of the European Union on page 316. What common cultural and geographic features aided the formation of the EU?

Applying Geography

7. **Agriculture in Europe** Imagine that you are a farm-worker in eastern Europe. Write a description about how your work activities have changed since the fall of communism.

SECTION 1 ASSESSMENT ANSWERS

1. All vocabulary terms are defined in the text.
2. industry: technology, services, light and heavy products; agriculture: grains, fruits, vegetables, livestock, fishing; transportation and communications: railways, highways, airlines, waterways, telephone, TV, radio, Internet
3. western: reduce social welfare programs, promote a single currency, develop a common foreign policy; eastern: adjust to a market

economy and address serious environmental problems.
4. Answers should include the role of waterways, natural resources, and fertile lands.
5. Western Europe is linked by TV, radio, the Internet, and satellite services; those services are not as readily available in eastern Europe, which hinders economic growth.

6. cultural: language (Romance and Germanic), religion, history, education standards, democratic societies, market economies; geographical: an abundance of fertile land and natural resources and access to waterways
7. **Applying Geography** Descriptions may show the farmer thinking more like an entrepreneur and being concerned about competition and new developments in technology.

1 FOCUS

Section Overview

This section discusses the major environmental challenges in Europe today and some of the steps European countries are taking to address these issues.

BELLRINGER
Skillbuilder Activity

 Project transparency and have students answer questions.

Available as blackline master.

Daily Focus Skills Transparency 13-2

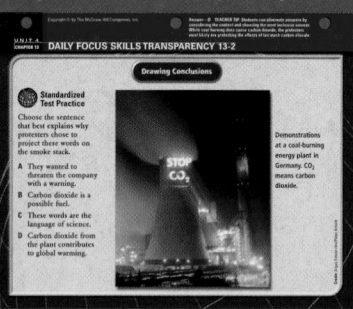

Guide to Reading

Consider What You Know

Answers *the Chernobyl nuclear power plant accident in Ukraine, pollution and oil spills in the Mediterranean and North Seas and the Danube River*

Reading Strategy

Answers *high concentration of industry and population; few laws to control pollution before 1989; communist emphasis on rapid industrial growth, not environmental safety*

Preteaching Vocabulary

Use the **Vocabulary Puzzle-Maker CD-ROM** to create crossword and word-search puzzles.

Guide to Reading

Consider What You Know

Environmental issues are frequently in the news in the United States. What threats to the environment in European countries have made headlines in U.S. newspapers?

Reading Strategy

Organizing Complete a graphic organizer similar to the one below by listing some of the reasons why Eastern Europe has pollution problems.

Pollution

Read to Find Out

- How have industry and farming practices affected Europe's environment?
- What steps are being taken to protect Europe's environment?
- What successes have Europeans had in recent decades in reversing the effects of pollution?

Terms to Know

- dry farming
- acid rain
- meltwater
- acid deposition
- environmentalist
- greenhouse effect
- global warming
- biologist

Places to Locate

- Romania
- Mediterranean Sea
- Strait of Gibraltar
- Carpathian Mountains

SECTION 2

People and Their Environment

NATIONAL GEOGRAPHIC

A Geographic View

A High Price

A Czechoslovak friend described what it was like in the 1950s. . . . "The bright future lay in industrializing as fast as possible. This way we would exploit all natural resources and gain mastery over nature. The technology was often out of date, but we were after short-term benefits—there was no thought of the future environmental consequences."

—Jon Thompson, "East Europe's Dark Dawn," National Geographic, June 1991

Factory worker in Czechoslovakia

When communism ended in eastern Europe, the results of nearly 40 years of rapid industrialization were shockingly clear: polluted air and rivers, acres of destroyed forests, and soot-covered, decaying buildings. In this section you will learn about the interaction of Europeans with their environment. You will also discover how Europeans are working together to reverse the effects of pollution, a problem that crosses national borders.

Humans and the Environment

As in other parts of the world, people in Europe face challenges posed by the physical environment. In southern Europe, about 40 million years ago, two tectonic plates collided, thrusting up great mountain ranges, including the Alps and the Apennines. The frequent occurrence of earthquakes in countries such as Italy, Greece, and Macedonia indicates that tectonic changes are still taking place today, and earthquakes may strike with devastating effects. Like peoples in other areas, Europeans affect and are affected by their environment.

RESOURCE MANAGER

Reproducible Masters
- Reproducible Lesson Plan 13-2
- Vocabulary Activity 13
- Daily Lecture Notes 13-2
- Guided Reading Activity 13-2
- Reading Essentials and Study Guide 13-2
- Reteaching Activity 13
- Reinforcing Skills Activity 13
- Section Quiz 13-2

Transparencies
- Daily Focus Skills Transparency 13-2
- Unit 4 Map Overlay Transparencies

Multimedia
- Vocabulary PuzzleMaker CD-ROM
- Interactive Tutor Self-Assessment CD-ROM
- ExamView® Pro Testmaker CD-ROM
- Presentation Plus! CD-ROM

People in parts of southern Europe also have to cope with low rainfall. For example, Spain's Meseta is so arid that streams dry up, the ground becomes scorched, and drought is common. The arid climate makes dry farming necessary in this area. Dry farming is a way of farming in dry areas that produces crops without any irrigation and relies on farming methods that conserve soil moisture.

The Delta Project

In northwestern Europe, violent Atlantic and North Sea storms strike countries that border the sea, such as the Netherlands and Denmark. During these storms, sea travel is often hazardous along these countries' coasts. In 1953 a severe Atlantic storm, combined with the North Sea's heavy spring tide, flooded the southwest corner of the Netherlands, killing about 1,800 people. For nearly the next 30 years, Dutch engineers carried out the Delta Plan, a project that aimed to prevent such severe flooding. Under the plan, a system of dams and dikes was built to seal off and protect the Netherlands' southwestern coast.

Floods

In recent years heavy rains have lashed much of Europe, causing widespread floods and mudslides. This extreme weather has led to loss of life, property damage, and disruption of transportation networks. Some scientists claim that the natural climate cycle accounts for the rains. Others believe that global warming is responsible.

Pollution

In some ways, Europeans have not dealt wisely with their environment. Over the years, Europe's high concentration of industry and population has had a devastating impact on the land, air, and water. For example, in central Europe's "black triangle," a heavily industrialized area in Poland, eastern Germany, and the Czech Republic, soot covers the ground, and the air bears the smell of sulfur from smokestacks.

Before 1989 eastern European countries had practically no laws to control pollution. With the communist emphasis on rapid industrial growth—not environmental safety—the pollution of the air, water, and soil increased until it affected public health. Although efforts are now under way to clean up the environment, the "black triangle" still bears the scars of poorly considered development from the communist era. Western European countries also have experienced serious environmental damage from the dumping of industrial wastes into the air and water. The European Union (EU) now requires environmental protection and cleanup from its members.

Acid Rain

In the 1960s industries in several European countries built high smokestacks to carry pollution away from industrial sites. This method worked locally, but the pollution directed away from the factories drifted across national borders. The pollution, containing acid-producing chemicals, combined with moisture in the air and fell as acid rain. Polluted clouds drifting from the industrial belt of Europe, for example, wither forests in other areas, and increase the trees' vulnerability to insects and disease.

The effects of acid rain are especially severe in eastern Europe, where lignite coal continues to serve as a main fuel source. Also called brown coal, lignite is found close to the earth's surface, making the cost of production low. Lignite, however, burns inefficiently and pollutes heavily. As a result, acid rain has ravaged 35 percent of Hungary's forests, 82 percent of Poland's, and 73 percent of the forests in the Czech Republic and Slovakia.

Acid rain damage is not limited to forests. Acid rain also falls on lakes and rivers. In winter, snow carries the industrial pollution to the ground. In spring, meltwater—the result of melting snow and ice—carries the acid into lakes and rivers. As acid concentrations build, fish and other aquatic life die. Nearly 20 percent of Sweden's lakes have no fish. A third of the rivers in the Czech Republic and half of those in Slovakia cannot support aquatic life.

Automobile exhaust also adds acid-forming compounds to the atmosphere. Acid deposition, wet or dry acid pollution that falls to the ground, harms not only Europe's natural environment but also its historic buildings. The Acropolis in Athens, the Tower of London, and Cologne Cathedral in Germany all show damage from acid deposition. Statues, bridges, and stained glass windows also show the harmful effects of this type of pollution.

② TEACH

L2 Environment

One reason the Mediterranean Sea is seriously polluted is that its only outlet to the Atlantic Ocean is through the narrow Strait of Gibraltar. Have students identify other European seas that may also be vulnerable to pollution and the possible sources of pollution in those seas. *(Black Sea: contamination flowing in from the Danube River; Baltic Sea: contamination from industrial wastes)*

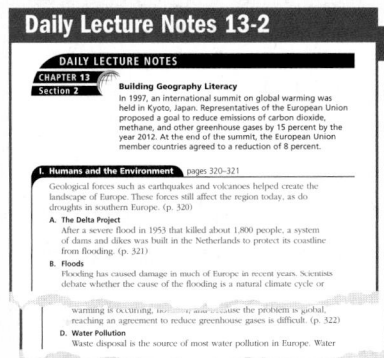

Daily Lecture Notes 13-2

DAILY LECTURE NOTES

CHAPTER 13
Section 2

Building Geography Literacy
In 1997, an international summit on global warming was held in Kyoto, Japan. Representatives of the European Union proposed a goal to reduce emissions of carbon dioxide, methane, and other greenhouse gases by 15 percent by the year 2012. At the end of the summit, the European Union member countries agreed to a reduction of 8 percent.

I. Humans and the Environment pages 320–321
Geological forces such as earthquakes and volcanoes helped create the landscape of Europe. These forces still affect the region today, as do droughts in southern Europe. (p. 320)

A. The Delta Project
After a severe flood in 1953 that killed about 1,800 people, a system of dams and dikes was built in the Netherlands to protect its coastline from flooding. (p. 321)

B. Floods
Flooding has caused damage in much of Europe in recent years. Scientists debate whether the cause of the flooding is a natural climate cycle or

warming is occurring, ... ause the problem is global, reaching an agreement to reduce greenhouse gases is difficult. (p. 322)

D. Water Pollution
Waste disposal is the source of most water pollution in Europe. Water

INTERDISCIPLINARY
connection

MEDICINE Lead poisoning poses a major medical problem in the coal mining and industrial regions of Europe. Health records indicate that babies born in these regions have twice the safe amount of lead in their bodies.

DIFFERENTIATED INSTRUCTION

English Learners Direct students to page 320, and ask them to review the sections "Terms to Know," "Places to Locate," "Read to Find Out," and "Consider What You Know." Have students learning English work together in small groups with a native English speaker. Encourage them to ask questions about the vocabulary terms and any other unfamiliar terms they encounter throughout this section. **ELL**

🌐 EE5 Environment and Society: Standards 14, 15

📂 Refer to *Inclusion for the Social Studies Classroom Strategies and Activities.*

L2 Health

Ask your class to think about what it would be like to live in a European city that has high levels of air and water pollution. Have them list the steps they might have to take in their day-to-day lives to protect their health.

L1/ELL

Guided Reading Activity 13-2

Name _____ Date _____ Class _____

Guided Reading Activity **13-2**

For use with textbook pages 320–325.

People and Their Environment

Short Answer

DIRECTIONS: Use the information in your textbook to write a short answer to each of the following questions.

1. How do people adapt their methods of agricultural production in arid areas like Spain's Meseta?

2. When about 1,800 people died in a flood in the Netherlands in 1953, how did the government respond to that natural disaster?

3. Why have the countries of eastern Europe had more severe problems with pollution than those of western Europe?

The **European Union** is developing laws to protect the environment against water and air pollution. The laws will control risks related to chemicals, biotechnology, and nuclear energy in member countries.

NATIONAL GEOGRAPHIC **World Explorer**

Geography **Skills for Life**
- - - - - - - - - - - - - - - - - - **Industrial**
Pollution Hearty agricultural fields surround a Polish factory whose smokestacks may carry pollution north into Scandinavia.
Human-Environment Interaction How does industrial pollution contribute to global warming?

Air Pollution

Air pollution is a problem throughout Europe. Traffic exhausts and industrial fumes cause eye irritations and asthma, and make respiratory infections worse in people who live in the industrial areas of western Europe. In the Netherlands—where people drive the greatest number of cars per square mile in Europe—high levels of air pollution also affect public health. In 2000 Swiss researchers estimated that pollution from automobiles and trucks was responsible for about 6 percent of all deaths across Austria, France, and Switzerland.

In eastern Europe, factories built in the communist era belch soot, sulfur, and carbon dioxide into the air by the hundreds of tons. As a result, Poland, **Romania**, and the Czech Republic are among the world's most polluted countries. Life expectancy is lower in eastern Europe than in environmentally cleaner regions, and cancer rates and birth defects are higher. Air pollution also has poisoned crops.

Although steps are being taken to reduce pollution, Europe still faces many challenges. For example, some former communist countries are closing polluting factories. Yet they are also putting more cars on the road, increasing air pollution from traffic.

Global Warming

The problems of air quality in Europe, like those in other industrialized regions, may have global consequences. Many **environmentalists**—people concerned with the quality of the environment—are studying the effects of increased carbon dioxide in the earth's atmosphere. Carbon dioxide and other gases trap the sun's heat near the earth's surface, creating the **greenhouse effect**. Without this greenhouse effect, the earth would be so cold that even the oceans would freeze. Plants would not grow, and life would not exist.

The burning of fossil fuels such as coal, oil, and gasoline, however, has significantly raised the amounts of carbon dioxide in the atmosphere, increasing the greenhouse effect. Some scientists estimate that the earth's average temperature may rise 2.5° to 10.4°F (1.4° to 5.8°C) by the year 2100, a trend called **global warming**. A warmer global climate, they claim, will melt polar ice caps and mountain glaciers and cause oceans to submerge coastal areas. Weather patterns might change, producing new extremes of rainfall and drought.

Although the potential destruction from global warming is more widespread than are other environmental issues, governments give it less attention than they do other environmental issues that are more regional or local. Facing the threat of global warming requires international cooperation. However, because not all scientists agree that global warming is occurring, the international community so far has done little to reduce its possible causes.

COOPERATIVE LEARNING ACTIVITY

Environmental Crisis On April 26, 1986, a fire at the Chernobyl nuclear reactor in Ukraine caused widespread environmental contamination. Organize the class into nine groups, and assign each group one of the following categories impacted by the Chernobyl disaster: residents, animals, vegetation, land, air, water, Europeans, government officials, and power company officials. Have each group prepare a report on the Chernobyl incident from their respective positions. After groups have prepared and presented their reports, combine all nine "chapters" into a booklet titled "Chernobyl's Aftereffects" and display it in the school library. 🌐 **EE5 Environment and Society: Standard 14**

Economics
Water Pollution

Water pollution is another issue facing Europe, particularly in the Mediterranean region. Countries bordering the **Mediterranean Sea** use the sea for transportation and recreation. They also use it for waste disposal, dumping sewage, garbage, and industrial waste there. In the past, bacteria in the Mediterranean Sea broke down most of the waste the sea received. In recent times, however, growing populations and tourism along the coast have increased the environmental problems of the Mediterranean. Small tides and weak currents tend to keep pollution where people discharge it. The Mediterranean Sea, open to the Atlantic only through the narrow **Strait of Gibraltar**, takes almost a century to renew itself completely.

Pollution contaminates marine and animal life and creates health hazards for people. The Mediterranean is overfished and cannot provide its former bounty. Only small schools of tuna enter from the Atlantic, and disease has claimed the last Mediterranean monk seals. Native species of seaweed and shellfish compete with foreign species carried into the Mediterranean by ships.

Water pollution affects Europe's rivers and lakes as well as its coastal waters. The Danube River, for example, is seriously affected by agricultural runoff. When fertilizers enter the river, they encourage algae growth. Algae, in turn, rob the river of so much oxygen that fish cannot survive. Another source of pollution is raw sewage, which is dumped into rivers in various places. In Warsaw, for example, only half of the sewage is treated. The other half is released untreated into the Vistula River. Industries in western Europe deposit wastes into the Meuse and Rhine Rivers; from there the pollutants flow into the North Sea. Consequently, pollution levels from the Netherlands to Denmark have doubled over the past few years.

Reducing Pollution

Europeans are working to solve environmental problems, such as pollution and waste disposal. They understand the economic impact of pollution, such as the loss of tourists and the high cost of cleanup. They also recognize the cultural effects, primarily the destruction of natural and historical sites.

Concern for the Environment

Today's Europeans feel responsible for protecting and preserving the environment and their national heritages for future generations. For example, many Europeans share a respect for nature. Those who live in densely populated areas value the opportunity to get away from urban areas and enjoy the natural landscape. Those who inhabit sparsely populated areas often depend on the natural environment to support their way of life.

The European concept of a natural environment is different from that in other parts of the world. Few

NATIONAL GEOGRAPHIC World Explorer

Geography Skills for Life

Water Pollution Children play in the Gulf of Gdańsk in Sopot, Poland. Nearby rivers dump agricultural and industrial waste into the gulf.

Human-Environment Interaction What happens when fertilizers enter lakes and rivers?

Chapter 13 323

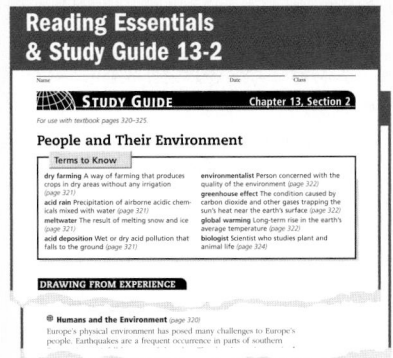

Reading Essentials & Study Guide 13-2

For use with textbook pages 320–325

STUDY GUIDE — Chapter 13, Section 2

People and Their Environment

Terms to Know

dry farming A way of farming that produces crops in dry areas without any irrigation (page 321)
acid rain Precipitation of airborne acidic chemicals mixed with water (page 321)
meltwater The result of melting snow and ice (page 321)
acid deposition Wet or dry acid pollution that falls to the ground (page 321)

environmentalist Person concerned with the quality of the environment (page 322)
greenhouse effect The condition caused by carbon dioxide and other gases trapping the sun's heat near the earth's surface (page 322)
global warming Long-term rise in the earth's average temperature (page 322)
biologist Scientist who studies plant and animal life (page 324)

DRAWING FROM EXPERIENCE

● Humans and the Environment (page 320)
Europe's physical environment has posed many challenges to Europe's people. Earthquakes are a frequent occurrence in parts of southern

Mythology In Roman mythology, Romulus was the founder and first king of Rome. According to legend, he and his twin brother, Remus, were abandoned by their father—Mars, the god of war—and then rescued and nursed by a female wolf.

NATIONAL GEOGRAPHIC World Explorer

Answer
They promote the growth of algae, which depletes these water systems of oxygen, endangering fish and other aquatic life.

More About the Photo For decades, this inlet of the Baltic Sea bordering Poland and a thin strip of Russia has been inundated with industrial and agricultural pollutants, the result of communist-era environmental neglect.

CRITICAL THINKING ACTIVITY

Problem Solving One of the countries being considered for membership in the European Union is Poland. In recent years the EU has established laws regulating air and water pollution, but for decades Poland has had a poor record of addressing its environmental issues. Ask students to use library and Internet resources to research this issue and then write an essay outlining the environmental issues Poland might first need to address before becoming a member of the EU. Essays should focus on the importance of protecting wildlife and waterways as well as the health of Polish citizens and other Europeans.

▦ EE3 Physical Systems: Standard 8

World Explorer

Answer
because of efforts to reintroduce the species

More About the Photo
Wolves inhabit forests and tundra. These pack hunters have specific territories, and each pack has a hierarchy with a top male and female.

③ ASSESS

Assign Section 2 Assessment as homework or as an in-class activity.

⊕ Have students use **Interactive Tutor Self-Assessment CD-ROM**.

L2

Section Quiz 13-2

[Section 2 Quiz reproduction: "Section 2 Quiz — People and Their Environment", with MATCHING and MULTIPLE CHOICE sections]

Reteach
Review key points of Section 2, emphasizing that environmental cleanup will be both costly and politically challenging.

Enrich
View one of the following National Geographic Society videos: *Pollution: The World at Risk; Recycling: The Endless Circle;* or *Technology's Price.*

---

areas in Europe remain unchanged by the clearing of forests, the drainage of seas, or the building of canals. Although much of Europe has been greatly altered by human activity, Europeans want to preserve what little wilderness area is left. One of the largest areas of Europe still in its natural state is the Bialowieza (bee•ahl•lah•WEH•zhah) Forest in Belarus and Poland. Today this area is home to animal species such as the wolf, lynx, and European bison, all of which are now rarely seen elsewhere in Europe.

An effort to reintroduce wolves—which help reduce large herds of musk oxen, elk, reindeer, and other deer—is under way in some parts of Europe. Spain recolonized the animals in the northwest areas of the country, and their number has tripled to more than 2,000. Wolves now live within 25 miles of Rome, where their reintroduction succeeded in part because Italian farmers are paid for livestock lost to wolves. Wolves also are thriving in Romania's **Carpathian Mountains**. About 2,500 wolves—weighing up to 150 pounds (68 kg) each—live in the heavily forested mountains, preying on chamois, roe deer, and red deer.

Cleanup Efforts
In recent decades Europeans have made more concerted efforts to clean up the environment. Member countries of the EU can face legal action if they do not respect environmental protection laws. For example, France was cited for violating the European Union's guidelines on nitrate pollution, and Greece is being taken to court for failing to protect a rare Mediterranean sea turtle. European countries are also addressing the consequences of pollution. Cities in western Europe now protect buildings and statues with acid-resistant coatings. Lime added to lakes in Scandinavia reduces acid levels. Biologists— scientists who study plant and animal life—are researching the effects of acid levels on fish.

England's Thames River cleanup is a notable success story. Until the 1960s, the river was lifeless, its fish destroyed by sewage and industrial pollution.

Factory closings and strict environmental controls have allowed the return of many fish and birds. After having disappeared for 150 years, even the giant conger eel, a traditional delicacy, returned in large numbers to the Thames.

Pollution that crosses national borders, however, presents a more complicated situation. For example, pollution in the Danube River, flowing through central and eastern Europe, threatens wildlife in its outlet—the Black Sea:

> ❝ *In the past 50 years the number of dolphins in the Black Sea has declined from an estimated million to about 200,000. We must improve the water quality, but how will it be possible financially and administratively when the Danube flows through eight countries, and 70 million people live within its drainage area?* ❞
>
> Jon Thompson, "East Europe's Dark Dawn," *National Geographic,* June 1991

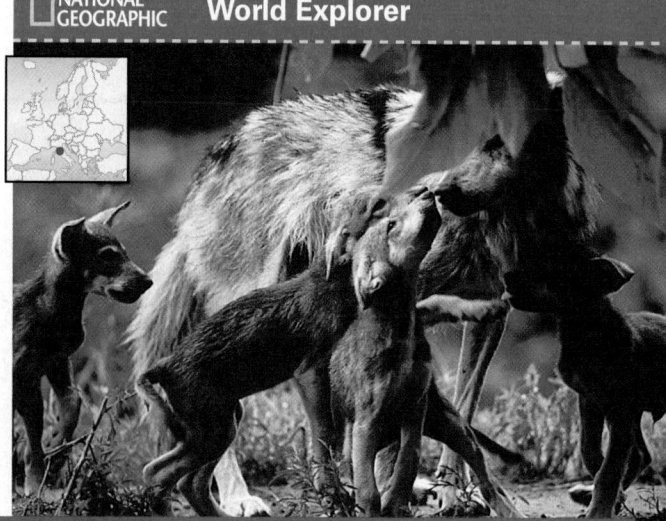

World Explorer

Geography | **Skills for Life** | **Preserving Wildlife**

A litter of wolves boosts hopes that fears of extinction are over as European countries seek to increase wolf populations.

Human-Environment Interaction Why have the wolf populations in Spain and Italy increased?

TEAM-TEACHING ACTIVITY: SCIENCE

Mapping Along with air, water, and noise pollution, Europeans confront naturally occurring environmental disasters. In northwestern Europe, storms and floods strike the low-lying regions of the Netherlands and Denmark. In southern Europe—in particular, Macedonia, Greece, and Italy—earthquakes are an ever-present threat. Have students work with a science teacher to create a map indicating areas of Europe most vulnerable to naturally occurring environmental disasters. Have students detail the consequences of an earthquake, flood, or volcanic eruption. ⊕ **EE5 Environment and Society: Standard 15**

Solving wide-ranging pollution problems requires international cooperation. The United Nations' Mediterranean Action Plan, which involves 20 countries and the European Union, is a model of international joint effort. In 1999 the EU approved guidelines to protect endangered species, increase protection from industrial waste, and prevent the dumping of pollutants by ships and aircraft into the Mediterranean. The EU also required large companies to recycle a portion of their packaging waste. As a result, over 9 billion pounds (over 4 billion kg) of waste plastics were recycled in 1998.

Plans for the Future

The EU and European governments continue to develop ways to protect the environment. Many power plants now burn clean natural gas instead of lignite coal. By 2010 the EU wants all member countries to lower emissions to 15 percent below 1990 levels to reduce greenhouse gases.

In order to be admitted to the EU, countries in eastern Europe are expected to meet EU environmental standards. Because they will need to spend about $120 billion on cleanup, eastern Europeans are now seeking financial aid from EU countries in western Europe. Pollution from eastern Europe also threatens western Europeans, so they and U.S. companies are also providing technology, expertise, and

investment to help modernize eastern Europe's industries. Such efforts highlight the global range of Europe's environmental concerns.

NATIONAL GEOGRAPHIC World Explorer

Geography | **Skills for Life**

Inspecting the Baltic Divers in the Baltic Sea off Finland inspect the water quality and measure pollution from nearby factories.

Human-Environment Interaction How have European countries improved the conditions of their physical environments?

NATIONAL GEOGRAPHIC World Explorer

Answer
implemented recycling programs, established rules regulating water pollution, and sewage runoff into waterways, modernized industries and upgraded technologies

More About the Photo
Agricultural runoff, auto emissions, and waste materials from industries such as chemical wood-processing and fish farming, have all polluted the Gulf of Finland.

④ CLOSE

Ask students to write a short essay on the consequences of forest destruction. Remind students that forests are home to thousands of species of animals, insects, and vegetation, and of the role that trees play in curtailing erosion.

SECTION ② ASSESSMENT

Checking for Understanding

1. **Define** dry farming, acid rain, meltwater, acid deposition, environmentalist, greenhouse effect, global warming, biologist.

2. **Main Ideas** On a table, list physical and human-made features affected by pollution. Then describe steps to counteract pollution's effects.

People and Their Environment		
Pollution Concern	Feature Affected	Steps Taken

Critical Thinking

3. **Identifying Cause and Effect** Why does eastern Europe have higher levels of industrial pollution than western Europe?

4. **Finding and Summarizing the Main Idea** Why do cleanup and preservation of the environment require cooperation in Europe?

5. **Making Generalizations** What are some of Europe's major challenges as its countries work to improve the environment?

Analyzing Maps

6. **Human-Environment Interaction** Refer to the population density map on page 262 and the map of Germany on page 326. In what ways are areas of dense population and areas affected by acid rain related?

Applying Geography

7. **Environmental Protection** Imagine that you live in a polluted area of Europe. Write a letter to the editor of a newspaper there, suggesting steps to halt environmental damage.

SECTION ② ASSESSMENT ANSWERS

1. All vocabulary terms are defined in the text.

2. pollution: air (acid rain and smog) and water (sewage, industrial and agricultural contaminants); features affected: soil, air, forests, waterways, historical sites; steps taken: recycling, improved sewage treatment, reduction of industrial and automobile emissions

3. a legacy of more than 50 years of environmental neglect by communist leaders

4. because pollution crosses political borders

5. upgrade factories responsible for water and air pollution; set standards in order to comply with EU laws; protect the Mediterranean Sea, which is vulnerable to pollution from tourism, industry, and agriculture; reduce automobile emissions

6. Densely populated areas are also the most industrialized. Forests in Scandinavia, Poland, Hungary, Slovakia, and the Czech Republic

have been seriously damaged from acid rain from pollutants that have drifted north and east.

7. **Applying Geography** Encourage students to balance economic realities and scientific fact about the risks to the continent's ecosystems and the preservation of Europe's natural habitats, historic sites, and pristine areas.

 **FOCUS**

Write the following terms on the board, and lead the class in a discussion about their implications:

- *Acid Rain Risk* (ask students to draw conclusions based on Europe's population densities, economic activity, and climatic features)
- *Fossil Fuels*
- *Emissions Regulations*
- *Alternative Energy* (discuss technological advances in automotive and factory designs that reduce air pollution)
- *European Union* (discuss its role in reducing air and water pollution in member countries)

 **TEACH**

Acid rain is a source of contention between countries that produce the contamination and those whose forests and waterways are harmed by it. In recent years there has been some agreement on the need to develop alternative energy sources that would be less polluting and more efficient. Some of these sources include wind, solar, geothermal, and fuel cell energy. Outline how some of these alternative energy sources work, discussing the pros and cons of each one.

L2 Cause and Effect
Have students compose a cause-and-effect outline to explain the acid rain situation in Europe.

Acid Rain Risk
- High risk
- Medium risk
- Low risk
- Little to no risk

Source: UNEP GRID-Arendal, Ed. Hatier, Paris, 1993.

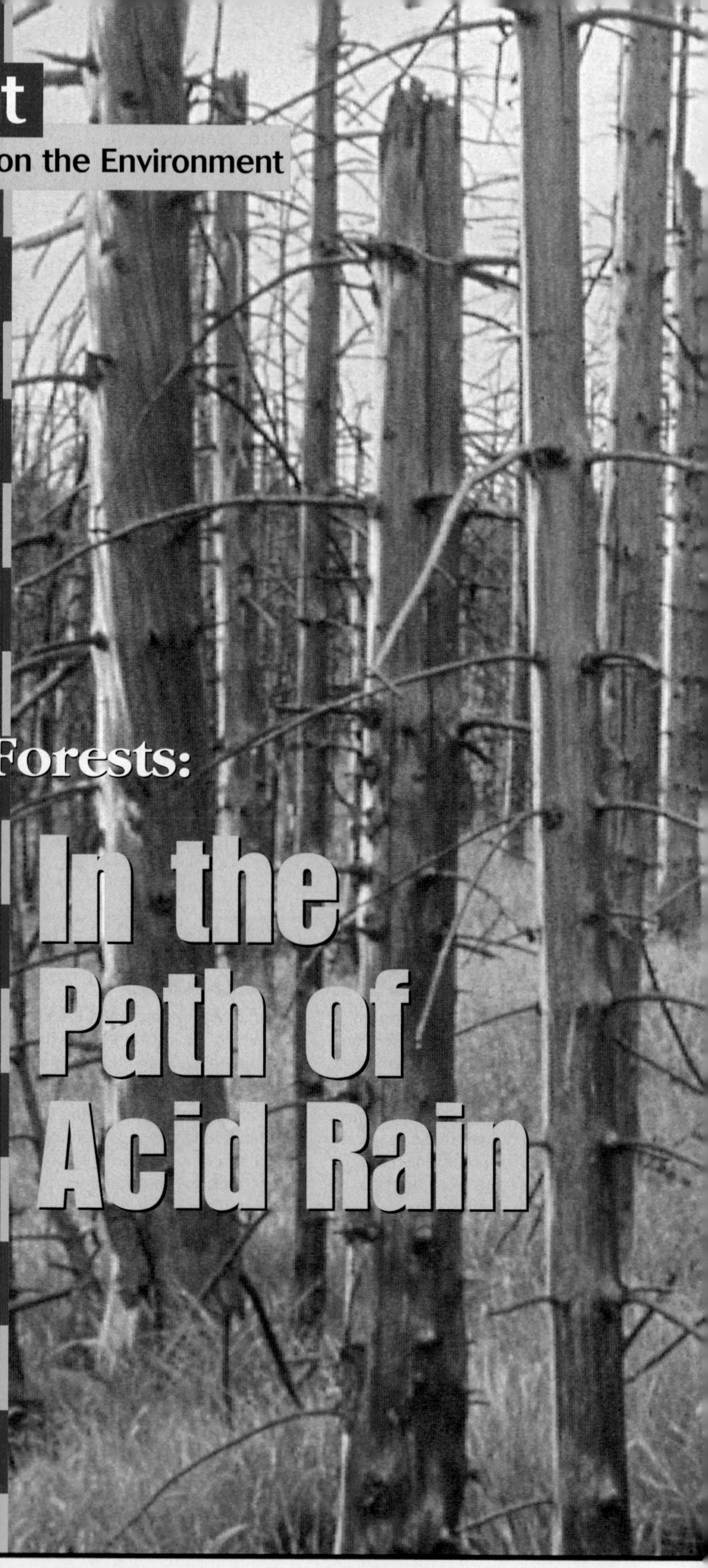

Germany's Forests:

It looks harmless as it falls, pattering softly on the ground. Yet acid rain is a quiet killer. It can turn a forest into a patch of leafless trunks and a pond into a lifeless pool. Human activities are to blame for most acid rain. Chemical gases emitted from power plants, factories, and cars are the chief causes. Acid rain has damaged many European forests and lakes. Germany's once-picturesque forests have been especially hard hit. Acid rain can be reduced. But to do so requires balancing environmental protection with the needs of modern industrialized societies.

In the Path of Acid Rain

LOOKING TO THE FUTURE

Encouraging Results While acid rain continues to be a problem, recent environmental laws seem to have reduced sulfur dioxide emissions in both Europe and the United States. In 1999 the U.S. Environmental Protection Agency released the results of a study that examined acidity in 205 lakes and streams in five regions in North America and in three regions in Europe between 1980 and 1995. The report concluded that the amount of acidic sulfates entering streams and lakes has declined in both the United States and Europe. However, the lakes and streams that were damaged by acid rain have not yet recovered.

🌐 **EE5 Environment and Society: Standard 14**

ike pale skeletons, dead evergreen trees (left) haunt the Ore Mountains near the border between rmany and the Czech public. What caused this struction? Acid rain.

When fossil fuels, such as al and gasoline, are burned, fur and nitrogen compounds e produced. Sulfur dioxide irls from the smokestacks coal-burning power plants. trogen oxides escape in the haust of gasoline-powered rs and trucks.

Wind carries these com- unds high into the sky. As the ses travel through air, they mbine with moisture to form lfuric acid and nitric acid. ese acids make rainwater uch more acidic than normal. e result is "acid rain"—a term plied to rain, snow, fog, or any rm of precipitation that con- ns abnormal amounts of acid. is precipitation can be as idic as battery acid!

Acid rain damages trees, pecially evergreens. High vels of acidity in streams and

German power plant (below) nits chemicals that cause acid n. But industries such as car mpanies (right) that use elec- city make essential products. ▼

lakes harm aquatic life, killing fish and plants. Acid rain also eats away at stone monuments and buildings.

Power plants, steel mills, and factories are found in or near most large European cities. Millions of cars and trucks travel European highways. The emissions from these industries and vehicles cause acid rain, which often falls hundreds of miles from its source. More than 25 percent of Germany's forests have been damaged by acid rain. Forests in Poland, the Czech Republic, Sweden, and Norway are also dying. Solutions to the problem do exist, but they often conflict with the needs of people.

Environmentalists want stricter emissions regulations for indus- tries and vehicles. This often involves equipping smoke- stacks and vehicle exhaust sys- tems with devices that remove sulfur and nitrogen com- pounds. Many people believe we should replace fossil fuels with alternative energy sources, such as solar and wind power.

◄ Industrial emissions contribute to acid rain.

Industrialists point out that modern societies cannot func- tion without the electricity and material goods produced by power plants and factories. People need vehicles to get from place to place. Devices that reduce acid-causing emis- sions are expensive. Further- more, solar power and other alternative energy sources are not yet realistic replacements for fossil fuels.

Despite these challenges, Germany is developing new technologies that will help reduce acid rain. German com- panies manufacture some of the world's most efficient gas turbines. Germans also built the first steel mill that does not burn coal to make steel.

What's Your Point of View?
Acid rain falling in Germany can be caused by another country's power plants. How does this complicate finding solutions to the acid rain problem?

③ ASSESS

Have students answer the **What's Your Point of View?** question on page 327.

④ CLOSE

Have students share personal opinions about the causes, effects, and possible solutions related to acid rain.

global issues

Wind Energy Non-polluting wind turbines are used in Germany and Denmark as well as in more than 20 U.S. states. Much more techno- logically advanced than the familiar Dutch windmills, wind turbines are taller, more effi- cient, and have slower-turning blades, allowing for fewer and more widely spaced wind machines.

⊕ Meeting National Standards

Geography for Life
The following standards are met in the Student Edition feature:

EE2 Places and Regions: Standard 4
EE4 Human Systems: Standards 11, 12, 13
EE5 Environment and Society: Standards 14, 15

WHAT CAN YOU DO?

Ask students to develop an environmental awareness plan that addresses the issue of acid rain. Have groups of students create posters that illustrate acid rain's causes (sources such as factory smoke and auto emissions) and its effects on forests, water- ways, and animal life in the United States and Europe. Illustrations may depict how pol- lution travels over hundreds of miles. Have other groups create posters and illustrations that compare alternative energy sources with fossil fuel sources, including the costs, effi- ciency, maintenance, and each system's basic components.
🌐 **EE5 Environment and Society: Standard 14**

Teaching the Skill

Working with students in small groups, help them become familiar with at least two Internet search engines, such as Google.com or Yahoo.com, and two Internet reference centers, such as the Encyclopedia Britannica online or the Internet Public Library.

Have students use the search engines and reference centers to perform simple searches using the key terms "acid rain" or "environmental pollution" and see the number of "hits" each search returns.

Additional Practice
L1

Reinforcing Skills Activity 13

Name_____ Date_____ Class_____

CHAPTER 13 REINFORCING SKILLS ACTIVITY

Using the Internet for Research

Because so much information is available on the Internet, it is necessary to evaluate what you find. Most resources in a library have been evaluated by librarians, scholars, and others before you ever see them. When you are using the Internet, however, this is not the case. Anyone can put anything they like on the Internet. Just because it is on the Internet does not make it true or useful.

Use the following points when evaluating Web sites:
- **Accuracy.** Does the content of the site appear to be accurate? What is the purpose of the Web page? Is it to inform, persuade, sell, explain? Does it appear to make sense? Does the information appear to be fact or opinion? Does the content of the page seem to be biased or stereotyped?
- **Analyze** the URL (address). Each part of the URL has a special meaning. What kind of site have you accessed? A government site? Educational? Business? A person's home page?
- **Author/Sponsor.** Check the author or sponsor of the site. What is the author's name, background, and credentials? What organization is sponsoring the site? If no author information is given and the page does not have a reliable sponsor, think twice about using the site.
- **Current.** Is the site current? Material on the Internet rapidly becomes outdated, so it is important to check the date the site was published or last updated. Check whether the information on the page seems to be current. Check whether links to other Web sites work.

CHAPTER 13

GLENCOE
TECHNOLOGY

Glencoe Skillbuilder Interactive Workbook, Level 2

This interactive CD-ROM reinforces student mastery of essential social studies skills.

Using the Internet for Research

Using the Internet for research is both easier and harder than using the library. It is easier because you can look through many different sources at one time. Internet research can sometimes be difficult because of the large amounts of information and the lack of organization to it.

Learning the Skill

Fortunately, you can search for information on the Internet in several ways. You can start your search with a search engine, such as www.yahoo.com or a reference center, such as Internet Public Library, at www.ipl.org.

Once you find information, however, you need to consider its reliability.

- **Evaluate the source of the information.** Avoid sources that do not provide facts or that are heavily slanted toward a particular view.

- **Keep records.** Always record the Web site title and address, the date you viewed the Web site, and the author's name (if available) so you can cite it.

The top level domain (TLD) at the end of a Web site address tells you what kind of site you have accessed. These are the most common TLDs:

1. **.gov**—government agencies, such as the Library of Congress or the U.S. State Department
2. **.edu**—educational sites, such as universities or the Smithsonian Institution
3. **.org**—nonprofit organizations, such as the United Nations and the World Wildlife Fund
4. **.com**—business sites, such as the National Geographic

▲ *Information and photographs about European wildlife, such as these Alpine ibexes, can be found on the Internet.*

Society or the Discovery Channel; search engines, such as Yahoo, are often .com sites

In 2000, seven new TLDs were introduced, including ".mus" for museums and ".biz", an additional TLD for businesses.

Practicing the Skill

Use an Internet search engine to search for information about the environmental policies of the European Union. Analyze the Web sites you find. Then choose three sites, and record the reference information about each site.

Applying the Skill

Search the Internet to find three sites that provide data and statistics on Europe's wildlife. Write a report analyzing and evaluating the sites' validity and usefulness. Then use reliable site data to answer the following questions: What kinds of wildlife does Europe have? How is wildlife being protected? What countries are the most committed to wildlife protection?

ANSWERS TO PRACTICING THE SKILL

Students' Web site information should show meaningful data about the European Union's environmental policies. Assess the Web sites to see if their TDLs are .gov, .org, .edu, or .com, and help students understand that .gov is a government-sponsored site, such as that of the census bureau. Sites ending in .org are sponsored by organizations, such as the National Red Cross. Sites with .edu often are sponsored by colleges and universities. Sites sponsored by businesses or other commercial operations have a .com ending.

SUMMARY & STUDY GUIDE

CHAPTER 13

SECTION 1 — Living in Europe (pp. 313–319)

Terms to Know

- European Union (EU)
- Maastricht Treaty
- heavy industry
- light industry
- mixed farming
- farm cooperative
- collective farm
- state farm
- genetically modified food
- organic farming

Key Points

- The countries of the European Union work toward bringing the continent economic and political unity.
- After years of communist rule, countries in eastern Europe face a difficult transition to market economies.
- Europe's economic activities include manufacturing, service and technology industries, and agriculture.
- Much of Europe has well-developed communications and transportation systems.

Organizing Your Notes

Create an outline using the format below to help you organize your notes for this section.

Living in Europe

I. Changing Economies
  A. The European Union
  B. Eastern Europe
II. Industry
  A.
  B.
  C.
III. Agriculture
IV.

SECTION 2 — People and Their Environment (pp. 320–325)

Terms to Know

- dry farming
- acid rain
- meltwater
- acid deposition
- environmentalist
- greenhouse effect
- global warming
- biologist

Key Points

- Acid rain is damaging Europe's forests, waterways, wildlife, and buildings.
- Air pollution from Europe's factories endangers public health and the environment.
- Greenhouse gases contribute to global warming.
- Pollution threatens the water quality and wildlife in the Mediterranean Sea and eastern Europe.
- European countries are taking steps to reduce pollution and clean up the environment.

Organizing Your Notes

Use charts like the one below to help you organize the notes you took as you read this section.

Polluted Countries or Areas
↓
Types of Pollution
↓
Sources of Pollution
↓
Cleanup Efforts
↓
Results

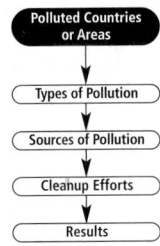

▲ *Bird rescued from oil-covered beach, Wales*

Using the Chapter 13 Summary & Study Guide

Use the Chapter 13 Summary & Study Guide to preview, review, condense, or reteach the chapter.

Preview/Review

🅥 **Vocabulary PuzzleMaker CD-ROM** reinforces "Terms to Know."

🅧 **Interactive Tutor Self-Assessment CD-ROM** provides a review of Chapter 13 content.

Condense

Have students read the Chapter 13 Summary & Study Guide.

🅐 Chapter 13 Audio Program

🗂 Chapter 13 Guided Reading Activities

Reteach

🗂 Chapter 13 Reteaching Activities (Spanish also available)

🗂 Chapter 13 Reading Essentials and Study Guides

GLENCOE TECHNOLOGY

▊ NATIONAL GEOGRAPHIC

WORLD REGIONS
VIDEO PROGRAM

Unit 4, Europe
The following segments enhance the study of this unit:

- **Mariners of the Mediterranean**
- **A Divided City**
- **City of Canals**

CHAPTER CULMINATING ACTIVITY

Problem Solvers Some of the most influential people in history were Europeans: William Shakespeare, Isaac Newton, Charles Darwin, Galileo Galilei, Christopher Columbus, and Albert Einstein. All were, in one way or another, problem solvers. Today, Europe is beset with changing economies and serious environmental challenges. **Ask:** What kind of person would it take to guide Europe through the 2000s: a scientist, economist, politician, or some combination of those and more? How would such a person address the challenges of air and water pollution, upgrading industries, and expanding the European Union?

🌐 **EE4 Human Systems: Standards 12, 13**
🌐 **EE5 Environment and Society: Standard 14**

CHAPTER
13
ASSESSMENT & ACTIVITIES

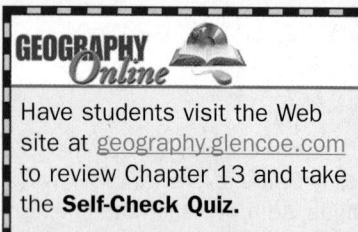
GLENCOE TECHNOLOGY

Use *MindJogger Videoquiz* to review the Chapter 13 content.

Reviewing Key Terms

1. acid deposition
2. acid rain
3. mixed farming
4. global warming
5. heavy industry
6. state farm
7. meltwater
8. Maastricht Treaty
9. greenhouse effect
10. light industry
11. organic farming

Reviewing Facts
SECTION 1

1. by eliminating the restrictions on the movement of goods, services, and people across its members' borders, and promoting a single currency, a central bank, and a common foreign policy
2. more privately owned farms and farms smaller than the former state-run farms

SECTION 2

3. the combination of traffic exhaust and industrial fumes, especially in formerly communist-controlled countries that had no environmental controls
4. by setting environmental standards for agriculture and industry for member countries and requiring that such standards be met as a condition for membership

Reviewing Key Terms

On a sheet of paper, write the key term that best completes each sentence. Refer to the Terms to Know in the Summary & Study Guide on page 329.

1. Wet or dry pollution that falls directly to the ground is also known as _____.
2. _____ is damaging Europe's forests.
3. Raising several types of crops and livestock is called _____.
4. _____ may cause the ice caps to melt.
5. _____ produces machinery.
6. Soviet officials managed a(n) _____, but did not share profits with the farmers.
7. _____ carries the acid precipitation into rivers and lakes in the spring.
8. The _____ set up the European Union (EU).
9. The _____ causes the sun's heat to be trapped near the earth's surface.
10. _____ is the production of textiles or processed food.
11. _____ uses natural substances to increase crop yield.

Reviewing Facts
SECTION 1

1. How is the European Union working toward economic and political unity for its members?
2. How has eastern European agriculture changed since the communist era ended?

SECTION 2

3. Why is air pollution in Europe so widespread?
4. How has the EU encouraged environmental protection and cleanup?

Critical Thinking

1. **Drawing Conclusions** Why are pollution problems most severe in eastern Europe?
2. **Making Predictions** How might global warming affect Europe? How do you think the countries of Europe will address the issue of global warming in the future?
3. **Comparing and Contrasting** On a Venn diagram, compare and contrast pollution in western and eastern Europe. Explain the interrelationships among physical and human processes regarding environmental change.

Western Europe — Both — Eastern Europe

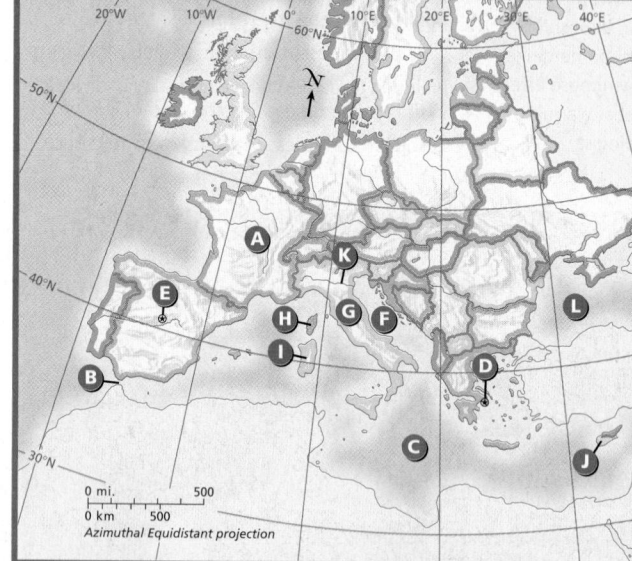

NATIONAL GEOGRAPHIC Locating Places
Europe: Physical-Political Geography
Match the letters on the map with the places and physical features of Europe. Write your answers on a sheet of paper.

1. Mediterranean Sea
2. Po River
3. Italy
4. Athens
5. Madrid
6. Corsica
7. France
8. Adriatic Sea
9. Cyprus
10. Sardinia
11. Black Sea
12. Strait of Gibraltar

Critical Thinking

1. because of rapid industrialization and a lax attitude toward environmental issues during the communist era
2. Global warming might cause rising sea levels and severe drought. Students should consider current European environmental policies when discussing future actions.
3. eastern Europe: cleanup of polluted land and water, refurbishing of old industries, compliance with environmental policies set by the European Union; western Europe: lowering industrial and automobile emissions, strict guidelines for agricultural and waste-water runoff, especially in the Mediterranean Sea; both: lowering industrial emissions

NATIONAL GEOGRAPHIC Locating Places

1. C	**3.** G	**5.** E	**7.** A	**9.** J	**11.** L
2. K	**4.** D	**6.** H	**8.** F	**10.** I	**12.** B

Using the Regional Atlas

Refer to the Regional Atlas on pages 260–263.

1. **Location** In what area of Europe is subsistence farming predominant?

2. **Place** Name three European capitals that have populations greater than 5,000,000.

Thinking Like a Geographer

Think about the physical and human geography of Europe. What factors helped establish the European Union? Research and identify different points of view that will shape the future structure and role of the European Union.

Problem-Solving Activity

Problem-Solution Proposal Choose a city located on the Mediterranean Sea. Imagine that you head a planning committee that wants to encourage tourism but also wants to reduce the pollution in the local bay. Research the industrial and tourism activities of the city, and then write a proposal suggesting ways to develop tourism while reducing pollution. Address the proposal to the city's industrial leaders, hotel managers, tourism directors, and water quality experts.

GeoJournal

Creative Writing Use the information in your GeoJournal to create an outline and storyboard for a television special on preserving the environment in Europe.

Technology Activity

Creating an Electronic Database Choose five countries from western Europe and five countries from eastern Europe. Using the Internet and other references, research the per capita income, or the average individual earnings in a year, for each country. Also find the percentage of the workforce involved in agriculture, manufacturing, and service industries for each country. Then use the information to create an electronic database. Write an essay explaining how these economic factors affect the standard of living in western and eastern Europe.

Standardized Test Practice

Choose the best answer for each of the following multiple-choice questions. If you have trouble answering the questions, use the process of elimination to narrow your choices.

1. **Lignite, or brown coal, is easily and inexpensively mined. Why should European cities be discouraged from using lignite as a main fuel source?**

   A Mining of lignite creates unsightly open pits that are dangerous to children.

   B Acid rain in European cities would be reduced by burning lignite.

   C European cities, especially in the east, use natural gas more than lignite.

   D Sulfur dioxide emissions from lignite cause high levels of air pollution.

2. **How do prevailing winds affect the acid rain that falls in Europe?**

   F Prevailing winds disperse acid rain across national borders.

   G Prevailing winds help clear away the acid rain, which results in less pollution.

   H Acid rain is heavier than air, so prevailing winds do not affect acid rain at all.

   J Europe's industrial belt lies in an area with no prevailing winds.

Test-Taking Tip For multiple-choice questions, remember to read each answer choice carefully. Some answer choices may not answer what the question asks. Sometimes, more than one answer may seem correct. Therefore, closely study the question so that you are sure of what it is asking, and then choose the answer choice that best answers the question.

Problem-Solving Activity

Proposals should show student understanding of the conflict between industries, economic development, tourism, and pollution.

Technology Activity

Check students' spreadsheets for accuracy and to make sure they understand how to use a spreadsheet.

Standardized Test Practice

1. D
2. F

Tested Objectives: analyzing information synthesizing information

Additional Practice and Test-Taking Tips

Standardized Test Practice Workbook

? CHAPTER BONUS TEST QUESTION

In the 1950s, what six European countries took the first step toward a united Europe? *(France, Germany, Italy, the Netherlands, Belgium, and Luxembourg)*

Using the Regional Atlas

1. the Balkans, Bulgaria, and Romania
2. London, Paris, Kiev

Thinking Like a Geographer

Democratic, free market societies, closeness to water, need for unity on global issues. Students should discuss whether power should remain with individual countries or be placed in an all-European government.

GeoJournal

Students may describe Europe's ecosystem prior to the Industrial Revolution. In the next section, they should explain, with examples, how the combination of industrialization, urban development, war, and decades of environmental neglect in the East have caused serious environmental and health problems across the continent. In the final section, students should offer solutions to some of Europe's most pressing environmental concerns.

TEACHING TRANSPARENCIES

L2 Unit 5 Map Overlay Transparencies

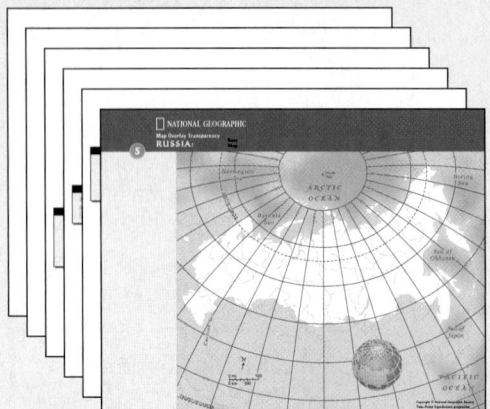

L2 Political Map Transparency 5

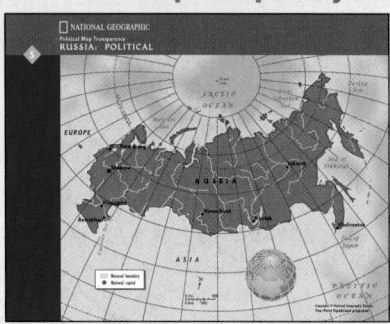

L2 World Cultures Transparencies 7, 8

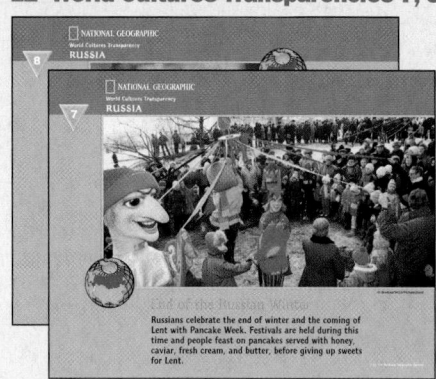

APPLICATION AND ENRICHMENT

L2 Location Activity 5

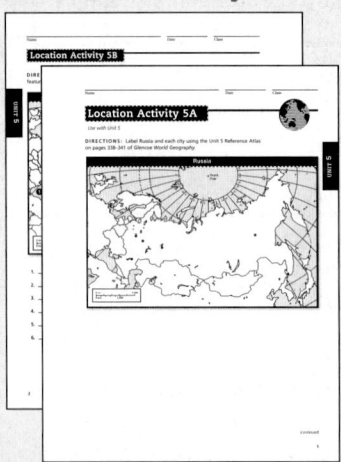

L2 Real-Life Applications and Problem-Solving Activity 5

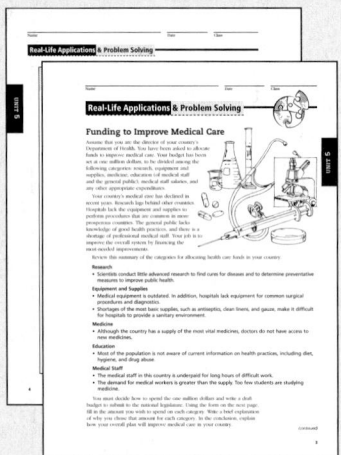

L2 GeoLab Activity 5

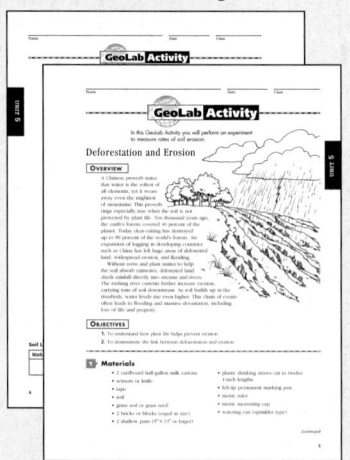

L2 Environmental Issues Case Study 5

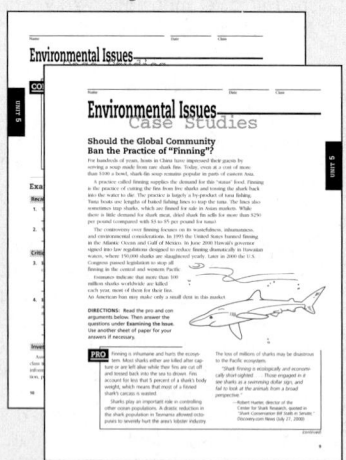

GEOGRAPHIC LITERACY

Focus on Geography Literacy

Building Geography Skills for Life

ASSESSMENT

Use the following to easily assess student learning in a variety of ways:
- Performance Assessment Activities and Rubrics
- Section Quizzes
- Chapter and Unit Tests
- Interactive Tutor Self-Assessment CD–ROM
- ExamView® Pro Testmaker
- MindJogger Videoquiz
- geography.glencoe.com
- Standardized Test Practice Workbook
- SAT I/II Test Practice

L2 Unit 5 Pretest and Tests

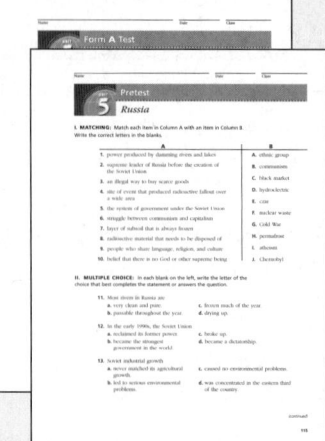

INTERDISCIPLINARY CONNECTIONS

L2 World Literature:
Contemporary Selection 5

Foods Around the World

Multimedia

- **World Art and Architecture Transparencies**
- **World Art Prints**
- **World Music: A Cultural Legacy**
- **World History Primary Source Document Library**

BIBLIOGRAPHY

Readings for the Student

Eyewitness Russia, by Kathleen Burton Murrell. New York, NY: DK Publishing, 2000.

Modern Nations of the World: Russia, by Kim Brown Fader. San Diego, CA: Lucent Books, 1998.

Readings for the Teacher

Cultural Atlas of Russia and the Former Soviet Union, by R. R. Milner-Gulland and Nikolai Dejevsky. New York, NY: Checkmark Books, 1998.

A History of Russia, by Nicholas Valentine Riasanovsky. New York, NY: Oxford University Press, 1999.

Multimedia Resources

Discovering Russia. San Ramon, CA: International Video Network, 1995. Videocassette, 60 minutes.

Great Railway Journeys: St. Petersburg to Tashkent with Natalia Makarova. Bethesda, MD: Atlas Video, 1994. Videocassette, 57 minutes.

READING SUPPORT FROM
JAMESTOWN EDUCATION

- *Timed Readings Plus in Social Studies* help students increase their reading rate and fluency while maintaining comprehension. The 400-word passages are similar to those found on state and national assessments.

- *Reading in the Content Area: Social Studies* concentrates on six essential reading skills that help students better comprehend what they read. The book includes 75 high-interest nonfiction passages written at increasing levels of difficulty.

- *Reading Fluency* helps students read smoothly, accurately, and expressively.

- *Jamestown's Reading Improvement,* by renowned reading expert Edward Fry, focuses on helping build your students' comprehension, vocabulary, and skimming and scanning skills.

- *Critical Reading Series* provides high-interest books, each written at three reading levels.

For more information about these products, see the Jamestown Education materials in the Classroom Solutions in the front of this Teacher Wraparound Edition.
To order these products, call Glencoe at 1-800-334-7344.

Background Information

The Physical Geography of Russia

Russia, the world's largest country, has qualities more commonly associated with a continent. Travelers crossing Russia from Vladivostok to St. Petersburg reset their watches ten times as they cross time zones.

Russia contains a variety of climates. In most of northern and western Russia, spring and autumn are short transitions between hot summers and frigid winters. Temperatures near Verkhoyansk, in the Siberian tundra, are colder than any other location outside of Antarctica.

The Ural Mountains, an aging mountain chain, extend some 1,500 miles (2,400 km) from the Arctic tundra to the Caspian Sea. They mark the traditional boundary between the North European Plain and the Siberian Plains. In the 1100s, a thriving fur trade first attracted settlers to this region.

Natural Resources

By the 1600s the Russians had established their first ironworks. Czar Peter I (the Great) encouraged the development of metallurgy. Iron is still mined in Russia today along with gold, silver, bauxite, lead, copper, nickel, and uranium. Russia is a leading producer of coal, oil, and natural gas. The country also has rich deposits of precious gems, such as diamonds, emeralds, topaz, and amethyst.

The Siberian taiga, a densely-wooded belt that covers nearly 40 percent of European Russia and portions of Siberia, is home to the world's largest coniferous forest. Only 8 percent of Russia's land is arable, yet the fertile area along the country's western border and tapering into Southwest Siberia yields wheat, barley, oats, rye, potatoes, and sugar beets.

The Cultural Geography of Russia

With its diverse population, Russia is a product of European and Asian cultures. From the A.D. 800s to the late 1300s, Slavic states under Scandinavian, and later, Mongol, influences developed in the western part of the region. Through conquest, the strongest state—Muscovy—laid the foundation of the empire of Russia. Because of its vast size and security concerns, Russia historically has been ruled by powerful leaders.

A Turbulent Past

During the 1400s and 1500s, Russian rulers increased their power with the support of the Russian Orthodox Church. In Moscow Czar Ivan III (the Great) had Italian architects and Russian workers build the Kremlin, a massive fortress with many churches and palaces. In the late 1500s, Czar Ivan IV (the Terrible, or the Awesome) became the first crowned czar and crushed opposition to his rule within the country. During the next 200 years, czars such as Peter I (the Great) and Catherine II (the Great) expanded Russia's territory and turned to western Europe for models in science, technology, and culture. While the nobles served the czars and accepted European ways, the peasant majority held to tradition and became bound as serfs to the nobles' land.

Mounting injustices fueled discontent among all groups in Russian society. In the 1800s czars made some reforms, such as freeing the serfs, but refused to yield any of their powers. In 1917 tensions exploded in a violent revolution that ended czarist rule, briefly installed a democracy, and brought to power a communist government. Under Lenin, and later, Stalin, Russia was transformed into a new empire—the Soviet Union.

The Soviet Union's communist rulers brought nearly all aspects of Soviet life under their control. Education expanded, and the country rapidly industrialized; however, millions of people labeled as enemies of the state were either killed or sent to prison labor camps. After a brutal but victorious struggle against the Nazis in World War II, the Soviet Union expanded into eastern Europe, where it set up communist governments. A cold war followed, in which the Soviet

Union rivaled the United States for global influence. During this time, Soviet officials spent heavily on defense, scientific research, space exploration, and heavy industry at the expense of Soviet consumers and the environment.

By the 1980s inflexible controls and the stifling of workers' initiative had crippled the Soviet economy. A reform-minded leader, Mikhail Gorbachev, tried in vain to halt Soviet decline. After the Soviet collapse in 1991, Russia under Boris Yeltsin emerged as an independent nation intent on fostering democracy and free enterprise. After 70 years of communism, however, Russia found it hard to shed old ways. With social disorder, crime, economic uncertainty, and secessionist challenges, Yeltsin's successor, Vladimir Putin, in 2001 seemed to centralize more power in his hands. His actions raised concerns about the fate of Russia's fragile democracy.

CHAPTER 16 (pp. 386–403)

Russia Today

Russia has the potential to tap its vast natural resources, including oil and natural gas, for economic development. Yet certain factors have made the transition from communism to a market economy difficult. For example, Russian companies must reinvest more than 50 percent of their profits to replace worn-out machinery inherited from the Soviet era. Another challenge is transporting people and goods in a country where frigid winters damage roads and rail lines. A shortage of funds has limited regular repairs or improvements to the country's infrastructure. Another major concern is widespread environmental damage caused by Soviet-era industrialization and military policies. For example, scientists estimate that the Soviet navy dumped large amounts of nuclear waste into the Barents Sea. Additionally, industrial and auto emissions are still largely unregulated in Russia. Only about 15 percent of Russians breathe unpolluted air.

Despite economic uncertainties, Russians today enjoy greater liberties than they did under communism. After years of communist censorship, many Russians show a renewed interest in religion and in the czarist past. As Russia struggles to become more globally involved, individual Russians are finding information increasingly available. Although Russians have always routinely read newspapers, news sources and opinions were limited. The fall of communism has allowed for more diverse views to be expressed, not only in print, but also on TV and in film. Despite recent media restrictions by the Putin government, the increased integration of global communications via the Internet precludes any complete return to the conditions of censorship that existed under communism.

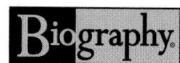

00:00 OUT OF TIME?

If time does not permit teaching each chapter in this unit, you may want to use the **Reading Essentials and Study Guide** summaries.

Unit Launch Activity

Tell students that they are going to initiate e-mail correspondence with students in Russia. Have small groups generate lists of questions they would ask their Russian peers. You may wish to assign each group a category of questions, such as physical geography, language and culture, history, government, economics, and contemporary challenges. Each group should list its questions on poster board so the questions are on display throughout the study of this unit. Cross off the questions as they are answered. Assign any remaining questions as extra-credit research.

GLENCOE TECHNOLOGY

NATIONAL GEOGRAPHIC
WORLD REGIONS
VIDEO PROGRAM

Unit 5, Russia
The following segments enhance the study of this unit:

- **Siberian Tigers**
- **The Tire Factory**
- **Bolshoi Ballet**

Available in DVD and VHS

UNIT 5

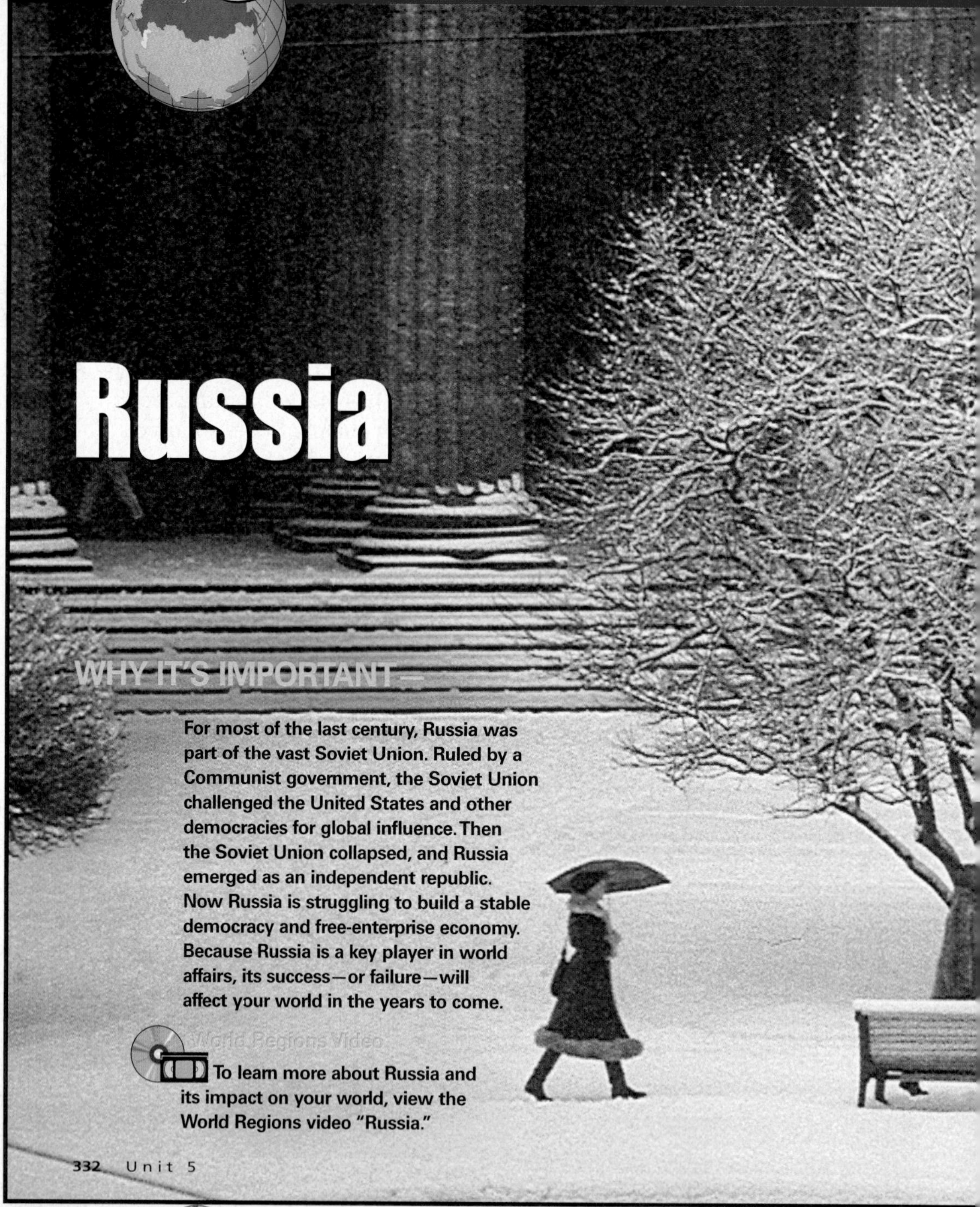

Russia

WHY IT'S IMPORTANT

For most of the last century, Russia was part of the vast Soviet Union. Ruled by a Communist government, the Soviet Union challenged the United States and other democracies for global influence. Then the Soviet Union collapsed, and Russia emerged as an independent republic. Now Russia is struggling to build a stable democracy and free-enterprise economy. Because Russia is a key player in world affairs, its success—or failure—will affect your world in the years to come.

World Regions Video

To learn more about Russia and its impact on your world, view the World Regions video "Russia."

GETTING TO KNOW THE REGION

Map Activity Display Political Map Transparency 5 and have students turn to the map on page RA24. **Ask:** **Across which two continents does Russia extend?** *(Europe, Asia)* **Between which lines of longitude does Russia extend?** *(from about 20°E to about 170°W)* **Which is the southernmost Russian city shown on the map?** *(Vladivostok)* **What is Russia's capital?** *(Moscow)* **Which body of water separates Russia from Alaska?** *(the Bering Strait, which connects the Bering Sea and the Chukchi Sea, a part of the Arctic Ocean)* **Which Russian city shown on the map is located on Lake Baikal?** *(Irkutsk)* **Which body of water gives Russian shipping access to the Mediterranean?** *(the Black Sea, through the Bosporus Strait, the Sea of Marmara, and the Dardanelles)* **EE1 The World in Spatial Terms: Standard 1**

Snow-covered trees in St. Petersburg

NGS ONLINE
www.nationalgeographic.com/education

This online resource, brought to you by the National Geographic Society, provides lesson plans, atlas updates, cartographic activities with interactive maps, an online map store, and links to the boundless subjects of maps and geography.

Unit Overview

The three chapters that make up this unit introduce students to the physical and cultural geography of Russia and its diverse peoples. Point out to students that although Russia is one country, several factors justify its being classified as a region of its own:

- Russia's huge size, an area of more than 6.5 million square miles (17 million sq. km), spans two continents.
- Russia's diverse population encompasses more than 100 ethnic groups in more than 80 autonomous republics, regions, and territories.
- Russia is important in world history and economics, and significant in global affairs.

ABOUT THE PHOTO

Visual Instruction Czar Peter the Great founded St. Petersburg, Russia's second largest city, in 1703. Located on the Gulf of Finland in northwestern Russia, the seaport is Russia's "window to the West," a link to Europe's culture and economy. Located at about 60°N latitude, St. Petersburg's seasonal extremes include the brief, frigid daylight hours of its long winter—shown in this photograph—and the "white nights" of perpetually bright skies in July. The former Winter Palace of the czars is now St. Petersburg's Hermitage museum. **Ask:** Why did St. Petersburg grow in importance despite its extreme climate? *(proximity to Europe, importance as a western seaport, role as a center of arts and culture)*
🌐 EE4 Human Systems: Standard 12

① FOCUS

These features and activities may be used as an introduction to the unit or as teaching tools throughout the course of the unit.

L1 Using Flash Cards Activity

Before beginning the study of this unit, use the **Countries of the World Flash Cards** to preview students' knowledge of Russia.

L2 Photo Research Activity

Ask each student to choose one of the photos from pages 334–337 and imagine that it is the photo on a postcard he or she is sending home from a visit to Russia. Have students research to find additional information about their chosen photos. Then have them incorporate what they have learned into written postcard messages. Display finished work.

☐ NATIONAL GEOGRAPHIC **GEOFACT**

▶ **Lake Baikal is famous as one of the world's most impressive natural wonders—and rightfully so. Lake Baikal is so large that, if it were emptied, all Earth's rivers combined would take an entire year to fill it back up.**

What Makes Russia a Region?

The world's largest country, Russia stretches almost halfway around the northern part of the globe, covering nearly half of two continents. It is a land of vast distances, bitter winters, and remote frontiers.

The ancient Ural Mountains separate European Russia in the west from Asian Russia, or Siberia, in the east. Most Russians live in the west, where several rivers course through rolling plains. East of the Urals, Siberia begins as a vast plain. It rises gradually to an immense plateau, then reaches higher still to rugged mountain ranges that border Russia's eastern shores. Siberia has abundant natural resources but few inhabitants.

North of the Arctic Circle, the land is treeless tundra where most of the ground is permanently frozen and winters are some of the coldest on Earth. South of the tundra lies the taiga, an enormous belt of dense coniferous forest. South of the trees is the Russian steppe, a rolling grassland with rich soil and a more hospitable climate.

1 Sparks flare against a dark January sky as lengths of pipe are welded in western Siberia. The pipeline will carry natural gas. Siberia is rich in natural resources, but its rugged terrain, harsh climate, and isolation make extracting and transporting those resources a tremendous challenge.

BACKGROUND INFORMATION

Ural Mountains Russia's oldest mountain chain has traditionally been considered one of the boundaries between the continents of Europe and Asia. The Urals have been an important source of Russia's mineral resources, from the gems that decorated the czars' imperial crowns to the iron used to make Soviet tanks in World War II. Salt has been mined from underground caves in the Urals since the 1500s, often by forced labor. The low, rounded Ural Mountains are in the latter stages of their second life span. The mountains were first formed about 300 million years ago, and were worn down almost to a plain over time. The present ranges are the remnants of a new chain that was formed about 200 million years ago.

🌐 **EE3 Physical Systems: Standard 7**

NATIONAL GEOGRAPHIC

② TEACH

L2 Human-Environment Interaction

Ask: What is the most significant fact about Russia's climate? *(It is extreme—for the most part, extremely cold.)* Encourage students to discuss how climate affects human activity. **Ask: How would your life be different if you lived in a climate like Russia's? What changes would you have to make in your lifestyle—what you wear, how you travel to school, what outdoor activities you enjoy? How would your home be different?** Ask students to keep this discussion in mind as they learn more about how Russians have adapted to their environment.

GLENCOE TECHNOLOGY

☐ NATIONAL GEOGRAPHIC
WORLD REGIONS
VIDEO PROGRAM

Unit 5, Russia
The following segments enhance the study of this unit:

- **Siberian Tigers**
- **The Tire Factory**
- **Bolshoi Ballet**

 Available in DVD and VHS

2 **The splendid skyline** of St. Petersburg, Russia's second largest city, forms a glowing backdrop for the Neva River. The Neva flows into the Gulf of Finland, an extension of the Baltic Sea. Like many of Russia's rivers, the Neva freezes over during the country's harsh winters.

3 **Worn down over time,** the rounded peaks of the Ural Mountains shelter a Russian village. The Urals extend 1,500 miles (2,400 km) from the Arctic Ocean south to Kazakhstan. They have long been a rich source of minerals, including gemstones such as emeralds, amethyst, and topaz.

4 **At home in the snow,** a trio of Siberian tigers roams through the frigid forests of eastern Siberia. Long, thick fur protects these big cats from the cold—but not from poaching and habitat loss, which have left Siberian tigers extremely endangered. Fewer than 500 survive in the wild.

Unit 5   335

A TRAVELER'S LOG

Jeffrey Tayler American National Public Radio correspondent Jeffrey Tayler lives in Moscow. In 1993 he traveled alone from Siberia to the Russian-Polish border. In his 1999 book, *Siberian Dawn: A Journey Across the New Russia,* Tayler wrote about crossing the Volga River.
   "An intoxicating warmth spread over me as I wandered around Ulyanovsk on my first day. . . . In some visceral way, I suddenly realized how European Russians are; I came to see the West *(western Russia)* as Russians did: it was civilization, it was home, it was where flowers scented warm breezes with nectars, and where nightingales trilled from the crests of drooping acacias. Russians belonged west of the Volga; the eastern territories . . . remained places of exile. . . ."
🌐 **EE2 Places and Regions: Standard 6**

L3 Economy

Invite one or more volunteers to use the Internet and recent financial publications to find current articles and information on the Russian economy. Have the volunteers summarize their findings for the class in an oral report or a visual presentation. Students should highlight information on how Russia's economy interacts with the rest of the world.

Czar The title *czar* (also spelled *tsar* or *tzar*) assumed by the Russian monarchs was a form of *Caesar*, the family name of Julius Caesar by which Roman emperors after Augustus were known. Between 1871 and 1918, the rulers of Germany bore a title with similar roots—*kaiser*. Ivan IV ("Ivan the Terrible") was the first Russian ruler to formally carry the title of czar. Today a person wielding great power or authority in a given field (such as banking, energy, or drug enforcement) also may be known as a czar.

From Empire to Free Enterprise

Most Russians are descended from Slavs, ancient European peoples who settled in western Russia. The settlements they established were eventually united under the rule of Ivan the Great, who ruled in the 1400s.

For centuries, autocratic czars governed what became a vast Russian empire. Revolution ended the czars' rule in 1917. Communism took its place, and Russia, along with neighboring republics, became part of the Soviet Union. Communist authorities controlled the Soviet economy. Everything from farms to steel mills was owned and operated by the government.

Since the Soviet Union disintegrated in 1991, Russians have struggled to establish a free-enterprise economy in their now independent nation.

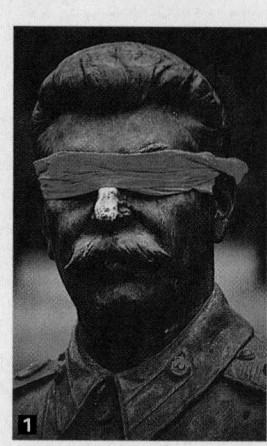

1 A blindfolded statue of Stalin symbolizes the end of Communist rule in Russia. Stalin was a brutal dictator who ruled the Soviet Union for some 30 years. Millions of Russians starved or were put to death under his totalitarian regime. Stalin died in 1953; the Communist system would last almost four decades more.

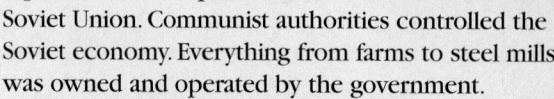

BACKGROUND INFORMATION

Russian Orthodoxy Much of Russia's art, architecture, music, and literature has been influenced by Eastern Orthodox Christianity, which developed its own unique expression in Russia. The Cyrillic alphabet used to write the Russian language was developed by Greek missionaries who brought Christianity to the Slavs of eastern Europe in the 800s. Russian Orthodox liturgical texts, which use an early form of Slavic language called Old Church Slavonic, have inspired internationally famous musical settings by Tchaikovsky, Rimsky-Korsakov, and Stravinsky. 🌐 **EE4 Human Systems: Standard 10**

NATIONAL GEOGRAPHIC

Culture NOTE

Russian California Russian fur traders left their cultural mark on the U.S. state of California, where onion-domed churches are still visible in towns along northern California's Russian River. Fort Ross, on the Pacific Coast north of San Francisco, was a Russian colony from 1812 until the early 1840s.

3 ASSESS

Ask: In what way is Russia different from other regions you have studied? Similar? *(different: region includes only one country; similar: has unique physical geography and culture)*

4 CLOSE

Organize the class into three groups: physical geography, cultural geography, and Russia today. Ask each group member to state an opinion about Russia appropriate to the group's title. Write the opinions on blank overhead transparencies. At the end of the Russia unit, use the transparencies to play a truth-or-misconception game with the class.

2 Snow-dusted sculptures inspire an artist in Peter the Great's Summer Garden, in St. Petersburg. Czar Peter the Great founded St. Petersburg in 1703. His goal: to create a Russian capital that rivaled Western cities such as London and Amsterdam.

3 Onion-shaped domes cap Russian Orthodox churches beside a lake in northwestern Russia. The Russian Orthodox faith has its roots in the ancient Byzantine Empire, which was centered in what is now Turkey. The domes are characteristic of Byzantine architecture.

4 Eager for customers, vendors on a Moscow street wait anxiously by their produce. After the disintegration of the Soviet Union, the Russian economy entered a period of great instability. Wages fell, while prices for food and other necessities soared.

Unit 5   337

UNIT PROJECT

Virtual Travel Before students begin the study of this unit, tell them they will be responsible at the conclusion of the unit for conducting a virtual tour of Russia. Have students form two groups. Have one group brainstorm and list features of the region—physical features and cultural expressions and landmarks—they would like to highlight. Have the other group brainstorm the logistics of the presentation, such as the use of Web pages, multimedia presentations, and posters or other graphic representations. Throughout the study of the unit, members of the first group should be responsible for researching and communicating information to the second group, who will incorporate it into the presentation.
EE2 Places and Regions: Standard 4

L1 Identifying Physical Features

Have students use their fingers to trace on the physical map the course of the following rivers and identify the bodies of water into which they empty: Volga *(Caspian Sea)*, Ob *(Kara Sea)*, N. Dvina *(Berents Sea)*, Don *(Black Sea)*, Lena *(Laptev Sea)*.

L2 Drawing Conclusions

Have students refer to the elevation profile of Russia on this page. Ask students to recall their knowledge of geologic forces. **Ask: Which mountains are higher, the Ural or the Sayan?** *(Sayan)* **What might account for the difference in elevation?** *(The Ural Mountains are older and have been worn away; the Sayan Mountains are younger, with higher peaks.)* **How do the shapes of the peaks in these two ranges support those conclusions?** *(Ural peaks are low and rounded, typical of older mountains; Sayan peaks are high and sharp, typical of newer mountains.)*

Elevation Profile

This cross section begins at the Belarus-Russia border around 55°N latitude. It crosses east through the Ural Mountains and the West Siberian Plain, continuing through the Sayan Mountains, Lake Baikal, and the Stanovoy Range at the coast of the Sea of Okhotsk, before ending on the Kamchatka Peninsula.

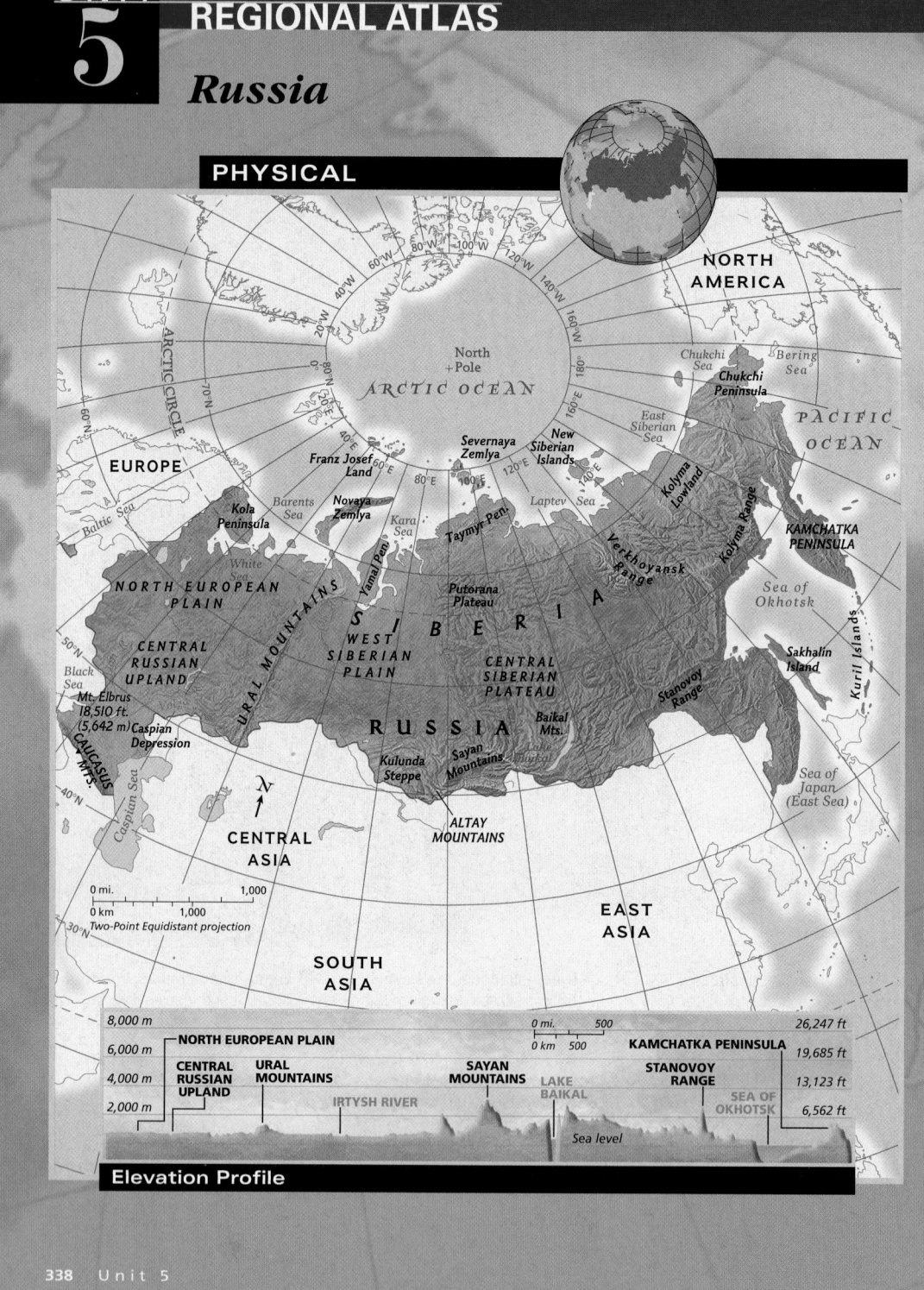

PHYSICAL

Elevation Profile

REGIONAL ATLAS ACTIVITY

Relative and Absolute Location Have a student draw a large unlabeled map of Russia and its surroundings. On separate slips of paper, put the names of all physical and political features identified on the two text maps (pages 338–339). Display the map and distribute the strips of paper to students. Give students a chance to study the text maps. Then ask students to attach their slips of paper to the appropriate places on the unlabeled map, working together and using relative location. When all items have been placed, have students evaluate the accuracy of the map they produced. Finally, have students make any needed adjustments to reflect absolute locations, using the text maps as a reference.
🌐 **EE1 The World in Spatial Terms: Standard 3**

NATIONAL GEOGRAPHIC

POLITICAL

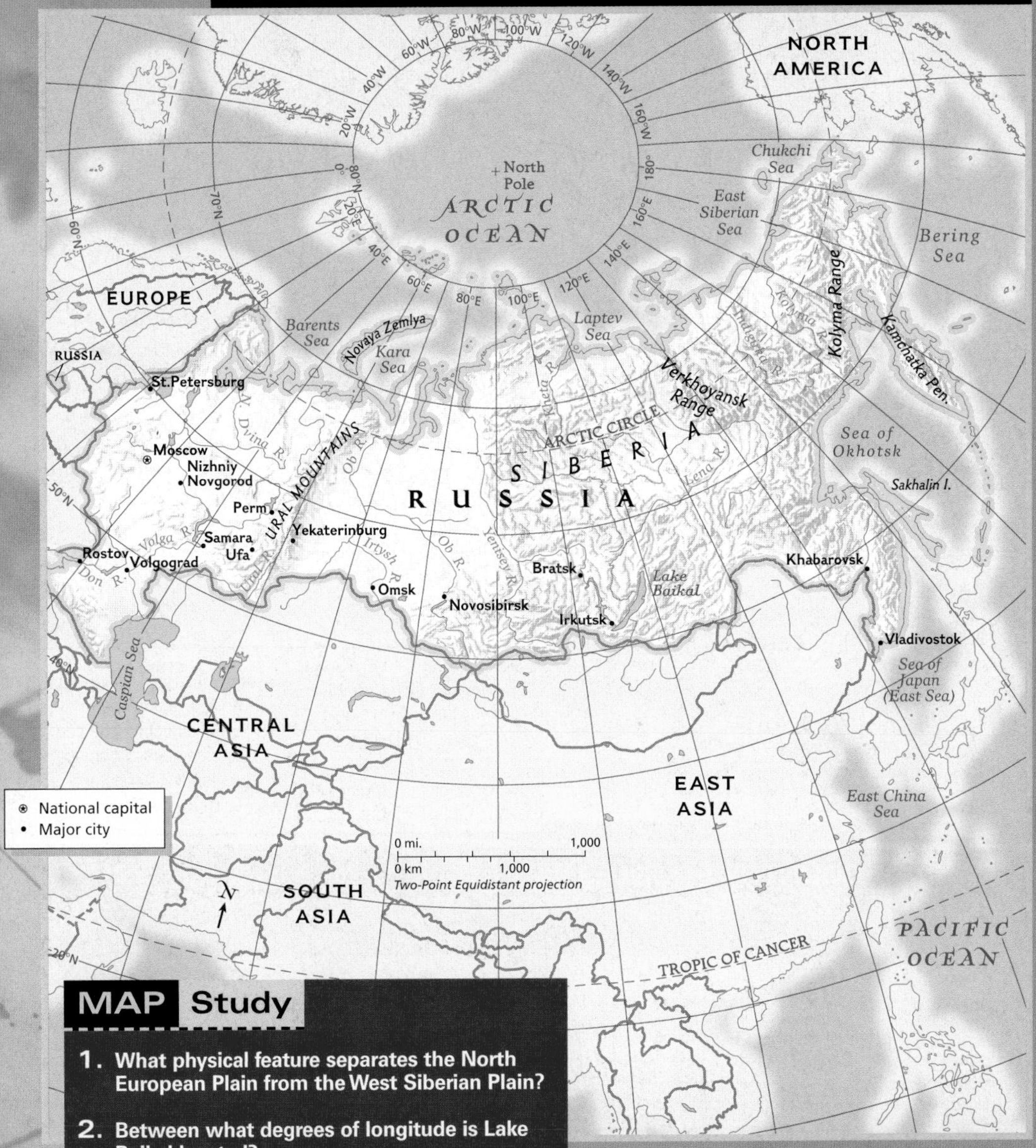

(Map of Russia and surrounding regions, showing:)

NORTH AMERICA

North Pole
ARCTIC OCEAN

Chukchi Sea
East Siberian Sea
Bering Sea

EUROPE
RUSSIA
St. Petersburg
Barents Sea
Novaya Zemlya
Kara Sea
Laptev Sea
ARCTIC CIRCLE
SIBERIA
Verkhoyansk Range
Kolyma Range
Kamchatka Pen.
Sea of Okhotsk
Sakhalin I.

Moscow
Nizhniy Novgorod
URAL MOUNTAINS
Dvina R.
Perm
Yekaterinburg
Ob R.
Yenisey R.
Lena R.
Khabarovsk
RUSSIA

Volga R.
Samara
Ufa
Rostov
Volgograd
Don R.
Omsk
Bratsk
Lake Baikal
Irkutsk
Novosibirsk
Vladivostok
Sea of Japan (East Sea)

Caspian Sea

CENTRAL ASIA

EAST ASIA
East China Sea

⊛ National capital
• Major city

0 mi. 1,000
0 km 1,000
Two-Point Equidistant projection

SOUTH ASIA

PACIFIC OCEAN
TROPIC OF CANCER

N

MAP Study

1. **What physical feature separates the North European Plain from the West Siberian Plain?**

2. **Between what degrees of longitude is Lake Baikal located?**

Unit 5 339

L2 Comparing

Have students turn to the World Political Map on pages RA4–RA5. Point out the countries that once formed the Soviet Union: Russia, Armenia, Azerbaijan, Belarus, Estonia, Georgia, Kazakhstan, Kyrgyzstan, Latvia, Lithuania, Moldova, Tajikistan, Turkmenistan, Ukraine, and Uzbekistan. Ask students to compare the area of the former Soviet Union with that of Russia today.

Culture NOTE

Beluga Caviar The white sturgeon, a fish found in the Caspian Sea, has traditionally been one of Russia's most prized luxury exports. The eggs, or roe, of the sturgeon, preserved in salt, make a delicacy known as beluga caviar. Overfishing and damming of the rivers that are sturgeon spawning grounds have made caviar rarer and more costly. In 2001 an ounce of high-grade beluga caviar cost $53.

MAP Study

Answers
1. *Ural Mountains*

2. *Between 100°E and 110°E longitude.*

Map Skills Practice
Location On which river is the city of Novosibirsk located? *(Ob River)*

REGIONAL ATLAS ACTIVITY

Map Puzzles Have students work in small groups to create puzzles based on the physical and political maps of Russia. Each group will develop a puzzle for members of another group to solve. Tell groups to be creative about the form of their puzzles. Possibilities include cutting a map into pieces (possibly squares of the latitude/longitude grid) and challenging students to put the pieces together accurately, or providing students with a list of Russian cities and asking them to put the cities in geographical order from west to east. Allow time for each group to attempt each puzzle.

🌐 **EE1 The World in Spatial Terms: Standard 1**

These features and activities may be used as an introduction to the unit or as teaching tools throughout the course of the unit.

L2 Determining Cause and Effect

Have students compare the population density map on this page with the physical map on page 338. **Ask:** Which part of Russia is most densely populated? *(western Russia)* What factors might account for this concentration of population? *(location on North European Plain, with the most temperate climate and agricultural land; closeness to other European countries for trade; presence of rivers with access to Mediterranean; abundant natural resources for industry)*

INTERDISCIPLINARY

connection

TECHNOLOGY In 1999 only one out of every 15 Russians owned a telephone. (You might have students use this formula and the population statistics in the country profile to approximate the number of privately owned phones in the country.) Although public telephones are widely available for long distance calls, economic and technological obstacles limit the number of traditional phone lines available for private homes. Cellular phones are growing in popularity as an alternative.

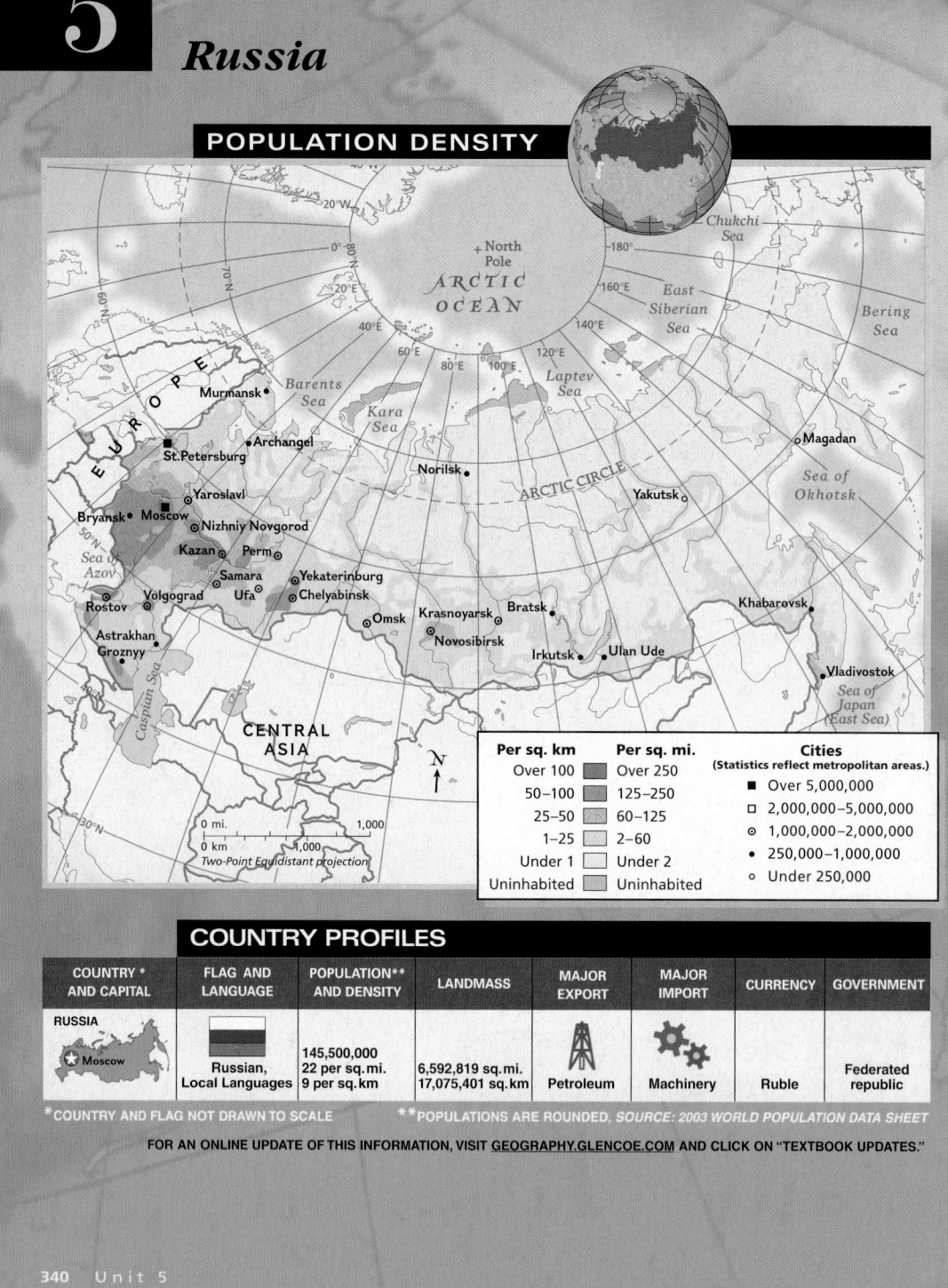

POPULATION DENSITY

Per sq. km	Per sq. mi.
Over 100	Over 250
50–100	125–250
25–50	60–125
1–25	2–60
Under 1	Under 2
Uninhabited	Uninhabited

Cities (Statistics reflect metropolitan areas.)
- ■ Over 5,000,000
- ◻ 2,000,000–5,000,000
- ◉ 1,000,000–2,000,000
- • 250,000–1,000,000
- ○ Under 250,000

0 mi. 1,000
0 km 1,000
Two-Point Equidistant projection

COUNTRY PROFILES

COUNTRY * AND CAPITAL	FLAG AND LANGUAGE	POPULATION** AND DENSITY	LANDMASS	MAJOR EXPORT	MAJOR IMPORT	CURRENCY	GOVERNMENT
RUSSIA Moscow	Russian, Local Languages	145,500,000 22 per sq.mi. 9 per sq.km	6,592,819 sq.mi. 17,075,401 sq.km	Petroleum	Machinery	Ruble	Federated republic

*COUNTRY AND FLAG NOT DRAWN TO SCALE   **POPULATIONS ARE ROUNDED, *SOURCE: 2003 WORLD POPULATION DATA SHEET*

FOR AN ONLINE UPDATE OF THIS INFORMATION, VISIT GEOGRAPHY.GLENCOE.COM AND CLICK ON "TEXTBOOK UPDATES."

COUNTRY PROFILE ACTIVITY

Cultural Regions Have students work in pairs to research Russia's many autonomous republics, regions, and territories. Each pair should use Internet resources and other reference materials to develop a profile of one cultural region, and include the following information: name and location of the region, principal ethnic or cultural group, language(s), religion(s), key cities, and principal land uses. Have the pairs present their information to the class using verbal and graphic forms. ▣ EE4 Human Systems: Standard 10

ECONOMIC ACTIVITY

NORTH AMERICA

ARCTIC OCEAN

North Pole

EUROPE

Barents Sea

Reindeer

Kara Sea

Laptev Sea

Reindeer

Chukchi Sea

East Siberian Sea

Bering Sea

RUSSIA

Baltic Sea

St. Petersburg

Moscow

Nizhniy Novgorod

Kazan

Perm

Corn

Oats

Barley

Rostov

Samara

Wheat

Chelyabinsk

Tyumen

ARCTIC CIRCLE

Sea of Okhotsk

RUSSIA

Wheat

Novosibirsk

Irkutsk

Lake Baikal

Sheep

Sea of Japan (East Sea)

Vladivostok

Caspian Sea

CENTRAL ASIA

East China Sea

EAST ASIA

PACIFIC OCEAN

Land Use
- Commercial farming
- Subsistence farming
- Livestock raising
- Nomadic herding
- Hunting and gathering
- Forests
- Manufacturing and trade
- Commercial fishing
- Little or no activity

Resources
- 🛒 Coal
- ⚡ Petroleum
- 💧 Natural gas
- ⚙ Iron ore
- Ⓝ Nickel
- ✚ Bauxite
- ◑ Manganese
- ◩ Tungsten
- ◆ Platinum
- Gold
- Copper
- Lead
- ⊡ Zinc
- ▼ Tin

0 mi. 1,000
0 km 1,000
Two-Point Equidistant projection

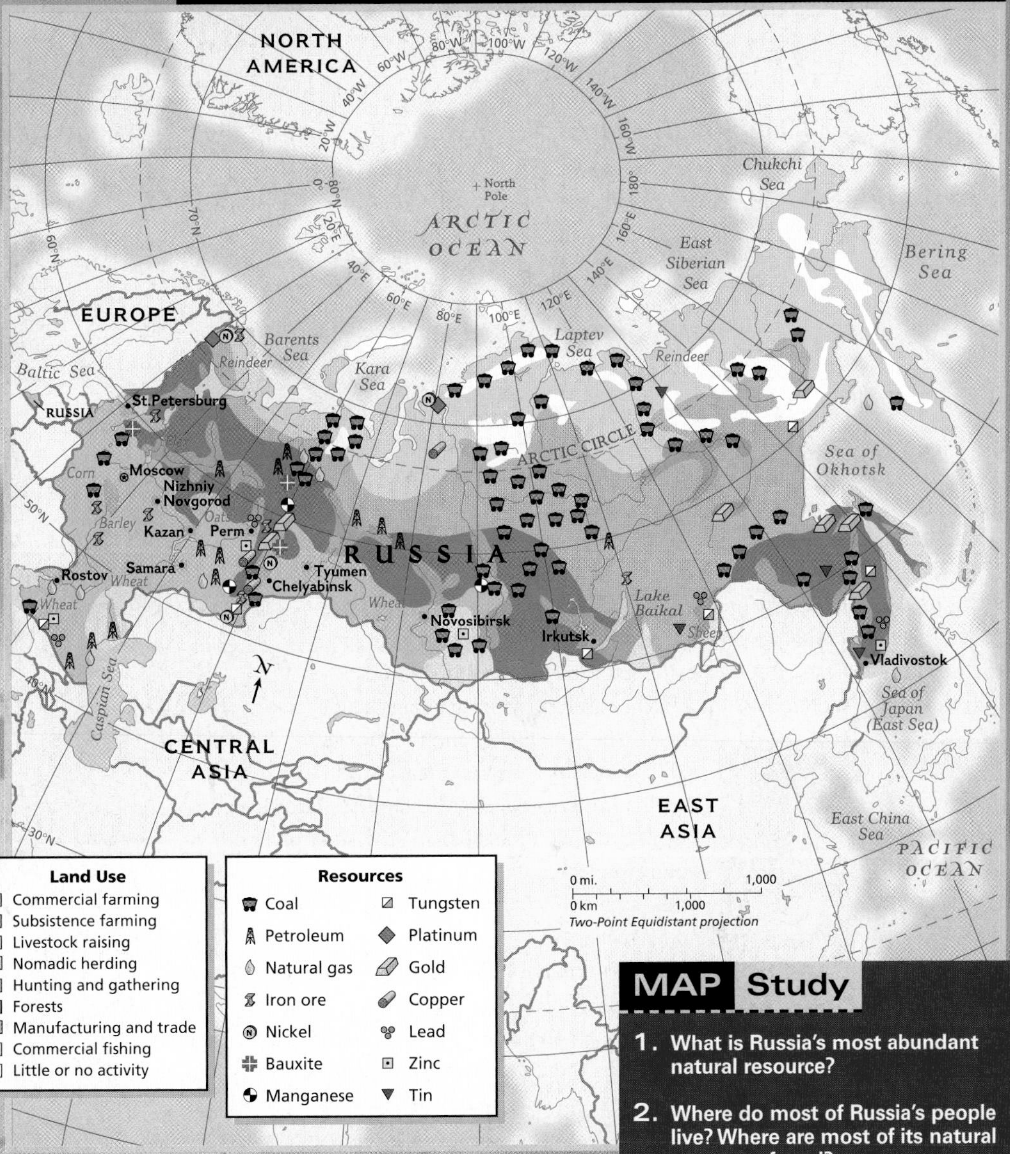

MAP Study

1. What is Russia's most abundant natural resource?

2. Where do most of Russia's people live? Where are most of its natural resources found?

 **Culture NOTE**

Borscht Russians and other eastern Europeans enjoy *borscht*, a soup made from beets and onions. Regional variations may incorporate potatoes, cabbage, or carrots. These vegetables grow well in Russia's soil, and—along with bread—play a key role in the diet of the Russian people.

FYI

Sculpture The world's tallest statue towers over Volgograd, Russia. Entitled "Motherland," the 270-foot (82-m) statue depicts a classically dressed female figure holding a sword aloft in her right hand while she beckons with her out-stretched left arm to an unseen army behind her.

MAP Study

Answers
1. *coal*
2. *the North European Plain and central Russian uplands; along mountains and rivers*

Map Skills Practice
Movement In which parts of Russia is nomadic herding a key land use? *(north and east)*

COUNTRY PROFILE ACTIVITY

Natural Resources Challenge Organize students into four groups, and assign each group three or four of Russia's natural resources. Have the groups use the maps on pages 338–341 to determine all the geographic locations for each of their assigned resources. Direct the groups to frame the information as written clues describing the location but not naming the resource. Students should make their descriptions as clear and accurate as possible. *(Example: This resource can be found on the northwestern shore of the Caspian Sea.)* Have groups take turns reading their clues aloud while other groups try to guess the resource. 📦 🌐 **EE1 The World in Spatial Terms: Standard 3**

① FOCUS

Ask students if they have ever seen a live or televised performance of *The Nutcracker*. Invite volunteers to share their impressions. Play selections for the class.

② TEACH

Cultural Exchange Explain that for many years, while the Soviet Union and the United States were engaged in the Cold War, visits from Russian ballet companies were one of the very few permitted cultural exchanges. Performances of *The Nutcracker* and other Russian ballets served as a bridge of understanding between the two countries. **Ask: Where do you get your ideas about the cultures and lifestyles of other regions of the world?** *(movies, television, and music)* **Ask: Based on what you know of American popular culture, what impressions about Americans might people in other countries form?**

Meeting National Standards

Geography for Life
The following standards are met in the Student Edition:

EE2 Places and Regions:
    Standard 6

EE4 Human Systems:
    Standard 10

EE6 The Uses of Geography:
    Standard 17

GLOBAL • CONNECTION

RUSSIA AND THE UNITED STATES

NUTCRACKER

Clara. The Mouse King. The Sugarplum Fairy. Do these names sound familiar? All across America, children and adults alike would instantly recognize them as the names of characters from *The Nutcracker* ballet. Although *The Nutcracker* originated in Russia more than a century ago, it has become a beloved holiday tradition in the United States.

In the late 1800s, elegant St. Petersburg was the world center for ballet. Peter Ilich Tchaikovsky, the famous Russian composer, was at the height of his career. A theater director in St. Petersburg asked Tchaikovsky to write music for a ballet based on a German fairy tale

called "The Nutcracker and the Mouse King." Tchaikovsky agreed, and in 1892 the Russian Imperial Ballet gave the first performance of this unconventional ballet—the story of a young girl's dream of Christmas presents that come to life in a magical kingdom of snowflakes and sweets.

The premiere of *The Nutcracker*, however, was far from a success. Critics sneered and audiences were unimpressed. The ballet wasn't seen outside Russia until 1934. Even then, it was only modestly popular.

◀ Peter Ilich Tchaikovsky

BACKGROUND INFORMATION

A World of Music and Dance Tchaikovsky's music for *The Nutcracker* reflects Russia's outward-looking perspective at the end of the 1800s. St. Petersburg was a cosmopolitan city, and Tchaikovsky's music gives a hint of the Russian elite's intense curiosity about all things exotic and foreign. The second act of the ballet, during which Clara is entertained at the court of the Sugarplum Fairy, features dances based on music from, or inspired by, Spain, China, Arabia, Italy, and England—as well as the Russian military dancers, with their memorable crouches, kicks, and leaps. These latter dancers provided many generations of Americans with their sole image of Russian culture.

🌐 **EE3 Places and Regions: Standard 6**

▲ Dancers performing *The Nutcracker* in Austin, Texas

In 1940, musical excerpts from *The Nutcracker* were included in the score of Walt Disney's animated film *Fantasia*. The movie was a hit, and as a result, Tchaikovsky's *Nutcracker* melodies were suddenly all the rage in the United States. The stage was set, so to speak, for a successful American production of the ballet.

It was George Balanchine, a Russian choreographer, who brought *The Nutcracker* to life for American audiences. Balanchine, whose given name was Georgi Melitonovitch Balanchivadze, was born in St. Petersburg and studied ballet there. As a boy, he danced the roles of the Mouse King and the Nutcracker Prince. In 1933 Balanchine came to the United States, where he helped found a ballet company that would become the famous New York City Ballet. In 1954 Balanchine directed the New York City Ballet in a lush and imaginative production of *The Nutcracker*. It was an immediate—and enormous—success.

In the years that followed, *The Nutcracker* became, and still remains, one of the most widely produced and widely attended ballets in American history—as much a part of December holiday celebrations as colored lights, carols, and presents under the tree.

Culture NOTE

1812 Tchaikovsky's popular *1812 Overture* commemorates the Russian triumph over Napoleon's besieging armies in that year. The work incorporates excerpts from the Russian and French national anthems and Russian hymns, as well as church bells and cannons.

③ ASSESS

Ask: How did George Balanchine help bridge the gap between Russia and the United States? *(He used ballet skills acquired in Russia to create new performances for his New York City Ballet company. As a result of Balanchine's efforts, the ballet became popular for the first time in the United States.)*

④ CLOSE

Have students watch a video of *The Nutcracker* and write a review.

343

CONNECTION ACTIVITY

Tchaikovsky Have students work in small groups to research and report on other examples of Tchaikovsky's music and ballets that have become popular in the U.S. Ballets include *The Sleeping Beauty* and *Swan Lake*. Musical compositions include the *1812 Overture,* the *Fantasy Overture for Romeo and Juliet,* the *Marche Slav,* and the *Symphony No. 6 in B minor (Pathetique).* Groups should obtain and listen to recordings of their chosen works, do research to determine information, such as the sources of inspiration and performance history, and prepare a class presentation. After the presentations, have students vote on the selection they most enjoyed. 📦 🌐 **EE4 Human Systems: Standard 10**

PLANNING GUIDE

NOTE: The following materials may be used when teaching Chapter 14. Section-level support materials are shown at point-of-use in the margins of the Teacher Wraparound Edition.

TEACHING TRANSPARENCIES

L2 Unit 5 Map Overlay Transparencies

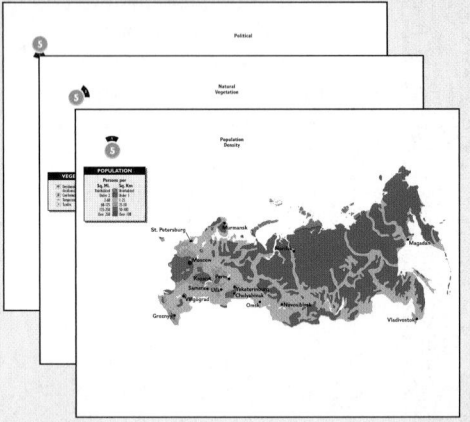

L2 Political Map Transparency 5

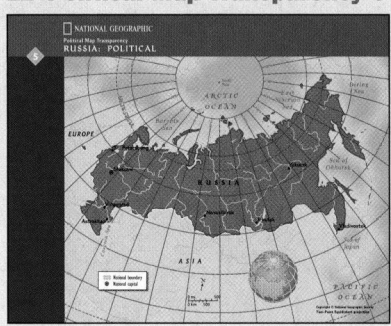

GEOGRAPHIC LITERACY

Focus on Geography Literacy

APPLICATION AND ENRICHMENT

L3 Enrichment Activity 14

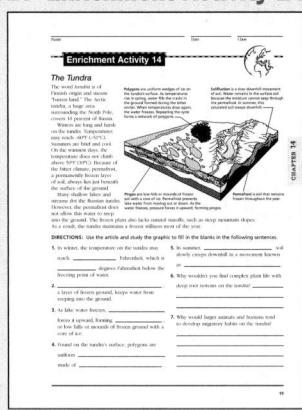

REVIEW AND REINFORCEMENT

L1 Vocabulary Activity 14 L1 Reinforcing   L1 Reteaching Activity 14
Skills Activity 14

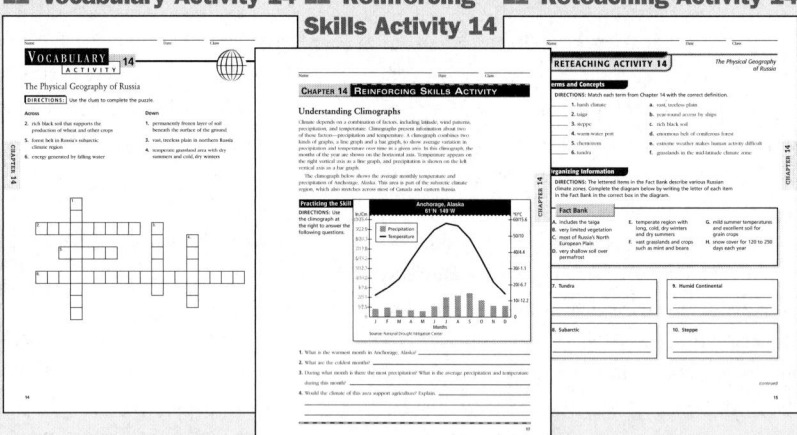

ASSESSMENT

L2 Chapter 14 Test Form A

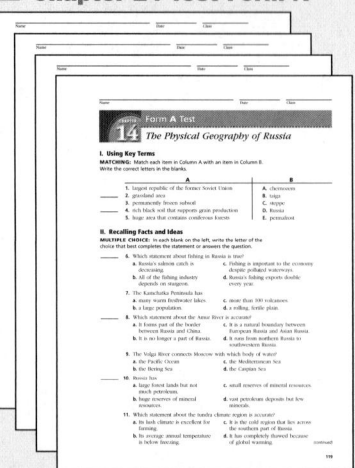

L2 Chapter 14 Test Form B

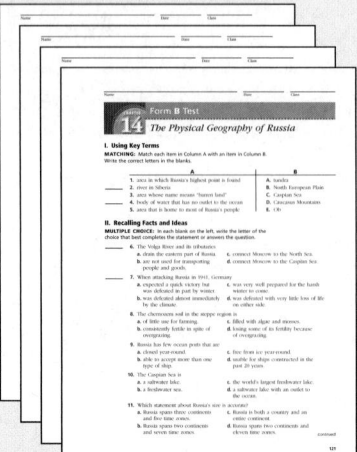

L1/ELL Performance Assessment Activity 14

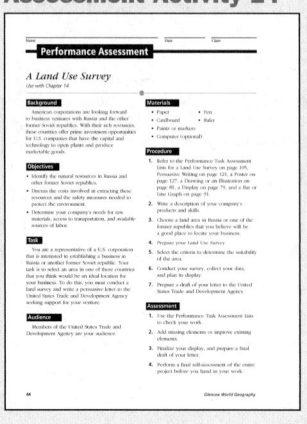

ExamView® Pro Testmaker

The following Spanish language materials are available in the Spanish Resources binder:

- 📁 Spanish Vocabulary Activities
- 📁 Spanish Guided Reading Activities
- 📁 Spanish Reteaching Activities
- 📁 Spanish Summaries
- 📁 Spanish Quizzes and Tests
- 📁 Spanish Reading Essentials and Study Guide

- 📼 World Regions Video
- 📼 MindJogger Videoquiz
- 💿 Vocabulary PuzzleMaker CD-ROM
- 💿 Interactive Tutor Self-Assessment CD-ROM
- 💿 ExamView® Pro Testmaker CD-ROM
- 💿 Audio Program
- 💿 TeacherWorks CD-ROM
- 💿 Interactive Student Edition CD-ROM
- 💿 Glencoe Skillbuilder Interactive Workbook CD-ROM, Level 2
- 💿 Presentation Plus! CD-ROM

Timesaving Tools

TeacherWorks™ All-In-One Planner and Resource Center

- **Interactive Teacher Edition** Access your Teacher Wraparound Edition and your classroom resources with a few easy clicks.
- **Interactive Lesson Planner** Planning has never been easier! Organize your week, month, semester, or year with all the lesson helps you need to make teaching creative, timely, and relevant.

Use Glencoe's **Presentation Plus!** multimedia teacher tool to easily present dynamic lessons that visually excite your students. Using Microsoft PowerPoint® you can customize the presentations to create your own personalized lessons.

GEOGRAPHY Online

Use our Web site for additional resources. All essential content is covered in the Student Edition.

You and your students can visit geography.glencoe.com, the Web site companion to *Glencoe World Geography.* This innovative integration of electronic and print media offers your students a wealth of opportunities. The student text directs students to the Web site for the following options:

- Chapter Overviews
- Student Activities
- Self-Check Quizzes
- Textbook Updates

Answers are provided for you in the "Web Activity Lesson Plan." Additional Web resources and Interactive Tutor puzzles are also available.

▶ Additional Glencoe Teacher Support

- Teaching Strategies for the Geography Classroom (including Block Scheduling Pacing Guides)
- Graphic Organizer Transparencies Strategies and Activities
- Outline Map Resource Book
- Reading in the Content Area

PLANNING GUIDE

SECTION RESOURCES

Daily Objectives	Reproducible Resources	Multimedia Resources

SECTION 1 The Land

1. Describe the size of Russia's land area.
2. Discuss how Russia's interconnected plains and mountain ranges shape settlement in the country.
3. Identify Russia's natural resources.

 Reproducible Lesson Plan 14-1
 Daily Lecture Notes 14-1
Guided Reading Activity 14-1*
Reading Essentials and Study Guide 14-1*
 Section Quiz 14-1*

- Daily Focus Skills Transparency 14-1
- Political Map Transparency 5
- Unit 5 Map Overlay Transparencies
- Interactive Tutor Self-Assessment CD-ROM
- ExamView® Pro Testmaker CD-ROM*
- Presentation Plus! CD-ROM

SECTION 2 Climate and Vegetation

1. List Russia's major climates.
2. State what seasons are like in Russia.
3. Explain how climate affects the way Russians live.
4. Classify the types of natural vegetation found in each of Russia's climate regions.

 Reproducible Lesson Plan 14-2
 Vocabulary Activity 14*
Daily Lecture Notes 14-2
 Guided Reading Activity 14-2*
Reading Essentials and Study Guide 14-2*
 Reteaching Activity 14*
Reinforcing Skills Activity 14
 Section Quiz 14-2*

- Daily Focus Skills Transparency 14-2
- Political Map Transparency 5
- Unit 5 Map Overlay Transparencies
- Vocabulary PuzzleMaker CD-ROM
- Interactive Tutor Self-Assessment CD-ROM
- ExamView® Pro Testmaker CD-ROM*
- Presentation Plus! CD-ROM

 Blackline Master   Software   Videocassette   *Also available in Spanish

Transparency   CD-ROM   DVD

OUT OF TIME?  Assign the Chapter 14 **Reading Essentials and Study Guide.**

`00:00`

Block Schedule

Activities that are particularly suited to use within the block scheduling framework are identified throughout this chapter by the following designation: 📖

KEY TO ABILITY LEVELS

Teaching strategies have been coded for various learning styles and abilities.

L1 **BASIC** activities for all students

L2 **AVERAGE** activities for average to above-average students

L3 **CHALLENGING** activities for above-average students

ELL **ENGLISH LANGUAGE LEARNER** activities

Teacher to Teacher

John Crawford
Lake Shore
Central Schools
Angola, NY

The Shrinking Sea

The object of this activity is to help students see how humans have helped change the planet. Direct students to create a report about the shrinking of the Aral Sea. In the report students should demonstrate an understanding of why the Aral Sea has shrunk, what the consequences of the shrinking sea have been for the people who live in the region, and what needs to be done in reaction to the shrinking of the sea—should it be left to die, should it be revived, or is there another mode of action that can be taken.

The report should also address the possible consequences of the action students suggest in regard to the shrinking of the sea. Students should focus on health, environmental, and economic consequences of the actions they suggest.

Direct students to use the Internet for their research, encouraging them to seek out unusual references such as satellite photos. Allow time for students to share their findings and ideas in a roundtable forum.

NATIONAL GEOGRAPHIC — TEACHER'S CORNER

Index to National Geographic Magazine:

The following articles may be used for research relating to this chapter:

- "Russia's Iron Road," by Fen Montaigne, June 1998.
- "An Arctic Breakthrough," by Don Belt, February 1997.
- "Siberian Tigers," by Maurice Hornocker, February 1997.

National Geographic Society Products:

To order the following products for use with this chapter, call National Geographic Society at 1-800-368-2728.

- *GeoKit: Weather* (Kit)
- *Asia* (Video)
- *Europe* (Video)
- *Asia Political* (Map)
- *Europe Political* (Map)
- *National Geographic Desk Reference* (Book)
- *National Geographic Atlas of the World, Seventh Edition* (Book)

NGS ONLINE

Access National Geographic's Web site for current events, activities, links, interactive features, and archives.
www.nationalgeographic.com

Meeting National Standards

Geography For Life

The following standards are highlighted in Chapter 14:

Section 1   EE2 Places and Regions: Standards 4, 6
EE3 Physical Systems: Standard 8
EE4 Human Systems: Standards 9, 10, 11
EE5 Environment and Society: Standards 15, 16

Section 2   EE2 Places and Regions: Standard 4
EE3 Physical Systems: Standard 8
EE6 The Uses of Geography: Standard 18

Local Objectives

_____

_____

MEETING SPECIAL NEEDS

In addition to the Differentiated Instruction strategies found in each section, the following resources are also suitable for your special needs students:

- *ExamView® Pro Testmaker CD-ROM* allows teachers to tailor tests by reducing answer choices.
- The *Audio Program* includes the entire narrative of the student edition so that less-proficient readers can listen to the words as they read them.
- The *Reading Essentials and Study Guide* provides the same content as the student edition but is written two grade levels below the textbook.
- *Guided Reading Activities* give less-proficient readers point-by-point instructions to increase comprehension as they read each textbook section.
- *Enrichment Activities* include a stimulating collection of readings and activities for gifted and talented students.

Chapter Objectives

1. Identify the physical features and natural resources of Russia.

2. Discuss the effects of Russia's climate and vegetation on life in the region.

GLENCOE TECHNOLOGY

Use *MindJogger Videoquiz* to preview the Chapter 14 content.

GeoJournal

For access to additional photos, maps, and information on the geographic features of Russia go to www.nationalgeographic.com (See Teacher pages in front for strategies for using journals in the geography classroom.)

GEOGRAPHY Online

Introduce students to chapter content and key terms by having them access **Chapter Overview 14** at geography.glencoe.com

FOLDABLES
Study Organizer

Dinah Zike's Foldables are three-dimensional, interactive graphic organizers that help students practice basic writing skills, review key vocabulary terms, and identify main ideas. Have students complete the Foldable activity in the **Dinah Zike's Reading and Study Skills Foldables** booklet.

CHAPTER

14 The Physical Geography of Russia

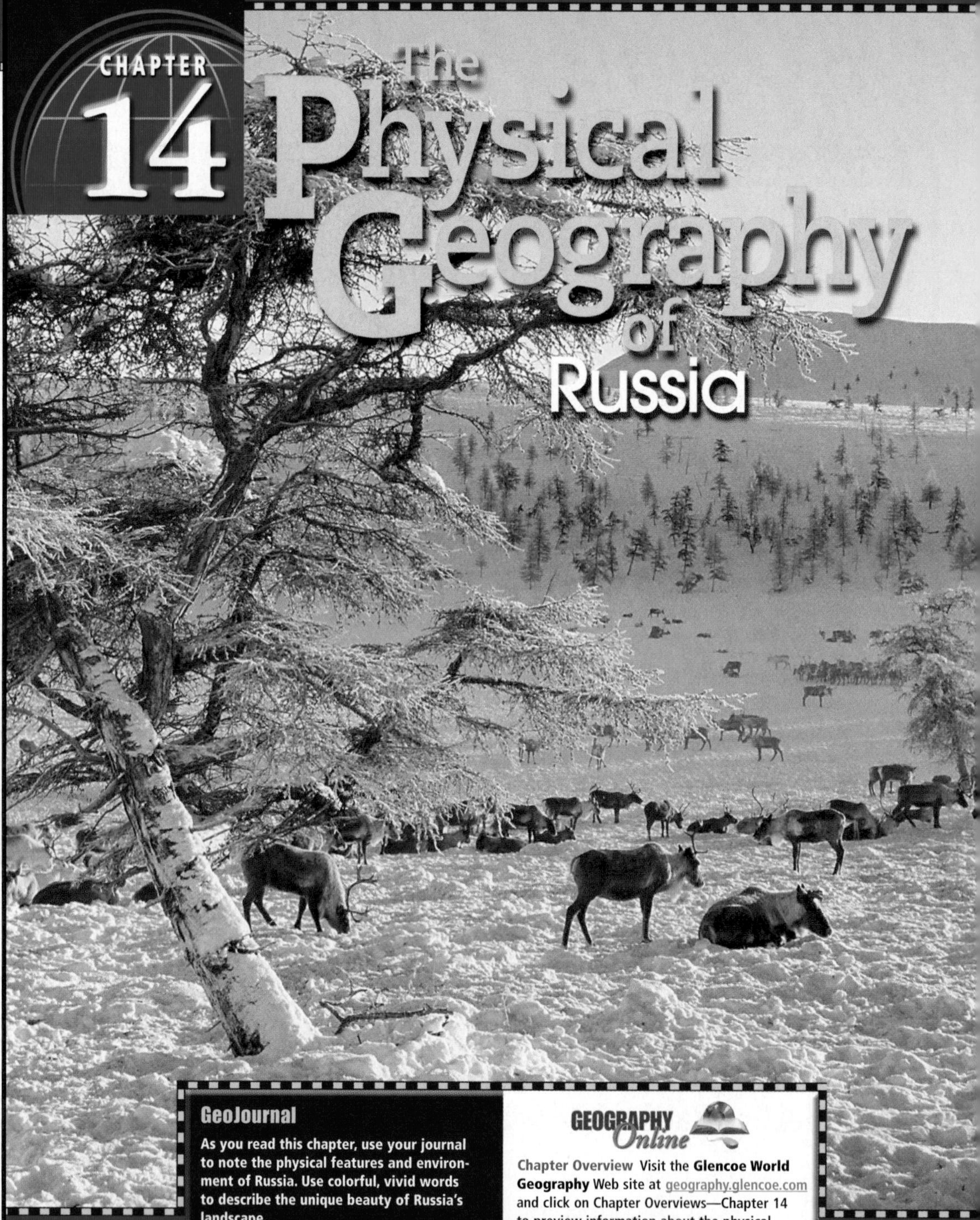

GeoJournal

As you read this chapter, use your journal to note the physical features and environment of Russia. Use colorful, vivid words to describe the unique beauty of Russia's landscape.

GEOGRAPHY Online

Chapter Overview Visit the **Glencoe World Geography** Web site at geography.glencoe.com and click on Chapter Overviews—Chapter 14 to preview information about the physical geography of the region.

ABOUT THE PHOTO

Visual Instruction The vast northern stretches of Russia are rich in animal life, including foxes, otters, wolves, hare, bears, elk, and reindeer. Native Siberian people in northern Russia still earn their living from herding reindeer, but traditional herding methods have changed since the 1950s. Today herders work in shifts, and the herders move the reindeer along planned routes. The herders communicate with one another using radios. Reindeer are herded for their milk, flesh, and hides. **EE2 Places and Regions: Standards 4, 6 EE4 Human Systems: Standards 9, 11**

Guide to Reading

Consider What You Know

Like Canada, Russia is a far northern country. How might Russia's location affect its connections to other parts of the world?

Reading Strategy

Taking Notes As you read about Russia's physical landscape, use the major headings of the section to create an outline similar to the one below.

```
I.  A Vast and Varied Land
    A.
    B.
    C.
II. Rivers
    A.
    B.
```

Read to Find Out

- How large is the land area of Russia?

- How do Russia's interconnected plains and mountain ranges shape settlement in the country?

- What are Russia's natural resources?

Terms to Know

- chernozem
- hydroelectric power
- permafrost

Places to Locate

- Caucasus Mountains
- Central Siberian Plateau
- North European Plain
- West Siberian Plain
- Volga River

◄ *Reindeer in winter pastures, Siberia, Russia*

The Land

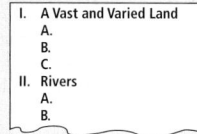
NATIONAL GEOGRAPHIC

A Geographic View

Swimming in the Volga

Crossing the Volga on a summer day, the ferry **Moskva-44** *took pale passengers to a sandy beach and brought away bathers red as lobsters. Upon this island Sahara were . . . boom boxes, sand castles, paper hats. . . . Yes, people still swim in the Volga, and I did, too. . . . You just forget about heavy metals and the 24 smokestacks vying on the horizon with the awesome Stalingrad memorial. The love of Mother Volga is real and has priority.*

—Mike Edwards, "Mother Russia on a New Course," National Geographic, February 1991

Sunbathers, Volga River

In 1991 the powerful Soviet Union broke up into 15 independent republics. Of these, Russia is by far the largest. In this section you will explore Russia, a gigantic and varied land of grassy and swampy plains divided and bordered by mountain ranges; tundra; subarctic forests; and wide, often frozen rivers and seas.

A Vast and Varied Land

In both total land area and geographic extent, Russia is the world's largest country. Covering about 6.6 million square miles (17.1 million sq. km), Russia stretches across parts of two continents—Europe and Asia. The country's greatest east-west extent is about 6,200 miles (about 9,980 km). This vast distance spans 11 time zones, contains 9 mountain ranges, and borders 13 seas, 2 oceans, and 14 other countries. The Russian landscape consists of an interrupted belt of rugged mountains and plateaus in the south and east and vast plains in the north and west.

Chapter 14 ● **345**

Section Overview

This section discusses the physical features and natural resources of Russia, the only world region that comprises just one country.

BELLRINGER
Skillbuilder Activity

Project transparency and have students answer questions.

Available as blackline master.

Daily Focus Skills Transparency 14-1

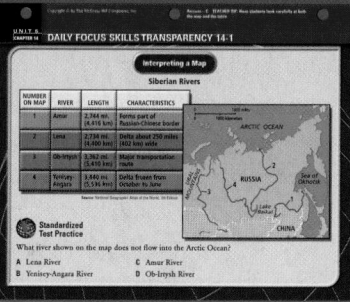

Guide to Reading

Consider What You Know
Answers *Ports might be inaccessible in winter; heavy snows might hamper overland travel.*

Reading Strategy
Answer Students should complete the outline by including all heads in the section.

Preteaching Vocabulary
Ask students to identify the word in "Terms to Know" that comes from the Russian language. *(chernozem)* Have them skim the section to locate this term and its definition, and practice pronouncing it aloud.

RESOURCE MANAGER

Reproducible Masters
- Reproducible Lesson Plan 14-1
- Daily Lecture Notes 14-1
- Guided Reading Activity 14-1
- Reading Essentials and Study Guide 14-1
- Section Quiz 14-1

Transparencies
- Daily Focus Skills Transparency 14-1
- Political Map Transparency 5
- Unit 5 Map Overlay Transparencies

Multimedia
- Interactive Tutor Self-Assessment CD-ROM
- ExamView® Pro Testmaker CD-ROM
- Presentation Plus! CD-ROM

② TEACH

L2 Place

Refer students to the "Comparing Lands" feature on this page.

Ask: If Alaska and Hawaii were included in the U.S. land area, how would the sizes of Russia and the United States compare? *(Russia would be a little less than twice the size of the United States; Alaska, the largest U.S. state, adds about 570,000 square miles (1,477,000 sq. km), and Hawaii's land area is about 6,400 square miles (16,576 sq. km)*

 **World Explorer**

Answer

Urals: create boundary between European and Asian Russia; Caucasus: lie between Black and Caspian Seas; mountains define border with China

More About the Photo

Although the Caucasus Mountains are Russia's southernmost landform, their towering peaks—many over 10,000 feet (3,000 m)—are covered with glaciers year-round.

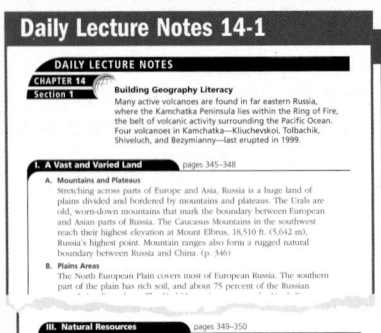

Daily Lecture Notes 14-1

DAILY LECTURE NOTES

CHAPTER 14
Section 1

Building Geography Literacy
Many active volcanoes are found in far eastern Russia, where the Kamchatka Peninsula lies within the Ring of Fire, the belt of volcanic activity surrounding the Pacific Ocean. Four volcanoes in Kamchatka—Kliuchevskoi, Tolbachik, Shiveluch, and Bezymianny—last erupted in 1999.

I. A Vast and Varied Land pages 345–348

A. Mountains and Plateaus
Stretching across parts of Europe and Asia, Russia is a huge land of plains divided and bordered by mountains and plateaus. The Urals are old, worn-down mountains that mark the boundary between European and Asian parts of Russia. The Caucasus Mountains in the southwest reach their highest elevation at Mount Elbrus, 18,510 ft. (5,642 m), Russia's highest point. Mountain ranges also form a rugged natural boundary between Russia and China. (p. 346)

B. Plains Areas
The North European Plain covers most of European Russia. The southern part of the plain has rich soil, and about 75 percent of the Russian

III. Natural Resources pages 349–350

A. Minerals and Energy

NATIONAL GEOGRAPHIC World Explorer

Geography Skills for Life

Treacherous Climb Hikers brave rugged terrain and glacial temperatures in the Caucasus Mountains of southern Russia.

Place How do mountain ranges help define Russia's territory?

Mountains and Plateaus

Mountains and plateaus punctuate the generally flat landscape of Russia. The Ural Mountains mark the traditional boundary between European Russia and Asian Russia. The Urals are an old, worn-down series of mountain ranges with an average height of about 2,000 feet (about 610 m). Though modest in height, the Urals are rich in iron ore and mineral fuels, such as oil and natural gas.

In southwestern Russia the rugged **Caucasus** (KAW•kuh•suhs) **Mountains** lie between the Black and Caspian Seas. The Caucasus reach their highest elevation at Mount Elbrus, an extinct volcano that reaches 18,510 feet (5,642 m), Russia's highest point.

Mountain ranges also form a rugged natural boundary between Russia and China. These mountains mark the southeastern edge of the **Central Siberian Plateau**. This rolling plateau has elevations ranging from 1,600 to 2,300 feet (480 to 700 m). Throughout the plateau's expanse, swiftly flowing rivers have carved out canyons.

Still farther east, mountains and basins extend to the Pacific Ocean. Temperatures in this remote area have plunged to a record –90°F (–68°C). In the easternmost part of Russia, on the Kamchatka Peninsula, there are more than 100 volcanoes, including 23 that are active.

Plains Areas

Vast plains span nearly half of Russia. Most of European Russia is part of the rolling **North European Plain** that sweeps across western and central Europe into Russia. In Russia, the northern part of this plain is very flat and poorly drained, resulting in many swamps and lakes. By contrast, the southern part has navigable waterways and a rich black soil, known as **chernozem** (cher•nuh•ZYAWM), that supports the production of wheat, barley, rye, oats, and other crops. About 75 percent of the Russian population lives on the North European Plain. This region holds Russia's most populous cities, including Moscow, the capital, and the port city of St. Petersburg.

Farther to the east, the Ural Mountains divide the North European Plain from another vast plains area—the **West Siberian Plain**. With almost 1 million square miles (2.6 million sq. km), the West Siberian Plain is one of the world's largest areas of flatland. At its widest this plain stretches from the Arctic Ocean in the north to the grasslands of central Asia in the south. Its lowland areas are poorly drained, with many swamps and marshes.

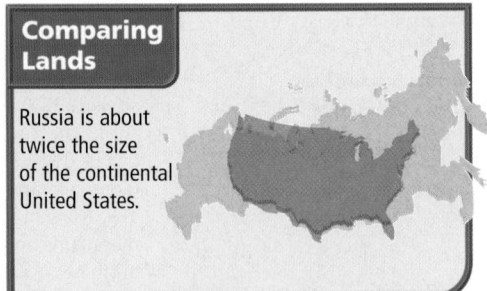

Comparing Lands

Russia is about twice the size of the continental United States.

DIFFERENTIATED INSTRUCTION

Auditory/Musical Have students research Russian folk songs that have become popular in English, such as "The Song of the Volga Boatmen." Ask students to play examples of these songs, or read their lyrics aloud, for the class. Discuss the references to Russia's landforms and resources found in the folk songs.

📖 **EE4 Human Systems: Standard 10**

🎵 For more examples of Russian folk songs, refer to Glencoe's *World Music: A Cultural Legacy* program.

📁 Refer to *Inclusion for the Social Studies Classroom Strategies and Activities.*

Coasts, Seas, and Lakes

Russia has the longest continuous coastline of any country in the world. Stretching 23,400 miles (37,650 km), Russia's coastline touches both the Arctic and Pacific Oceans. Other coasts lie along an arm of the Baltic Sea in the northwest and along the Black and Caspian Seas in the south. Because of Russia's far northern location, most of its coast lies along waters that are frozen for many months of the year. As a result, Russia has few ocean ports that are free of ice year-round.

In Russia's southwest corner, the Black Sea provides Russia with a warm-water outlet to the Aegean and Mediterranean Seas through three Turkish-controlled waterways—the Bosporus strait, the Sea of Marmara, and the Dardanelles (DAHRD•uhn•EHLZ). Despite sudden storms that sometimes strike the Black Sea, Russia's fishing industry has thrived in its waters.

The Caspian Sea, on Russia's southwestern border, is the largest inland body of water in the world. Although called a sea, it is actually a saltwater lake that occupies a deep depression. Rivers flow into the Caspian, but there is no outlet to the ocean. Water in the Caspian Sea evaporates over time, slowly shrinking the sea and leaving behind salts that accumulate and make the water saltier.

Another large body of water, Lake Baikal (by•KAHL), lies in southern Siberia. At nearly 400 miles (644 km) long, 40 miles (64 km) wide, and

NATIONAL GEOGRAPHIC
MAP STUDY
Russia: Physical-Political
North Pole
ARCTIC OCEAN
ARCTIC CIRCLE
60°N
70°N
80°N
0°
20°E
40°E
60°E
80°E
100°E
120°E
140°E
160°E
180°
N
Chukchi Peninsula
Bering Sea
East Siberian Sea
PACIFIC OCEAN
Kolyma Range
Laptev Sea
Barents Sea
Novaya Zemlya
Kara Sea
Kola Peninsula
Baltic Sea
Klyuchevskaya Sopka 15,584 ft. (4,750m)
KAMCHATKA PENINSULA
Sea of Okhotsk
Verkhoyansk Range
Lena R.
SIBERIA
NORTH EUROPEAN PLAIN
URAL MOUNTAINS
Ob R.
RUSSIA
CENTRAL SIBERIAN PLATEAU
WEST SIBERIAN PLAIN
Yenisey R.
Irtysh R.
Kuril Islands
Sakhalin Island
Amur R.
Yablonovyy Range
Don R.
Volga R.
Ural R.
50°N
Mt. Elbrus 18,510 ft. (5,642m)
Caspian Depression
Caspian Sea
Caucasus Mts.
40°N
0 mi. 1,000
0 km 1,000
Two-Point Equidistant projection
Lake Baikal
Sayan Mts.
Sea of Japan (East Sea)
Elevations
Feet Meters
10,000 3,000
5,000 1,500
2,000 600
1,000 300
0 0
National boundary
Mountain peak

Geography Skills for Life

1. **Interpreting Maps** Which area has the highest elevation, the West Siberian Plain or the Central Siberian Plateau?
2. **Applying Geography Skills** Which Russian peninsulas extend north of the Arctic Circle?

Find NGS online map resources @ www.nationalgeographic.com/maps

COOPERATIVE LEARNING ACTIVITY

Chart Soil Types Have small groups of students work together to develop a report on soil types found in Russia. Students should use encyclopedias or Internet resources to research chernozem, permafrost, and other soil types, and prepare a chart that notes principal locations and compares soil characteristics such as color, texture, and suitability for agriculture. Students should then prepare a map showing where different soil types are located in Russia. Group members should each complete different tasks that include researching soil types, preparing the chart, preparing the map, and compiling a report about soils in Russia.

EE3 Physical Systems: Standard 8

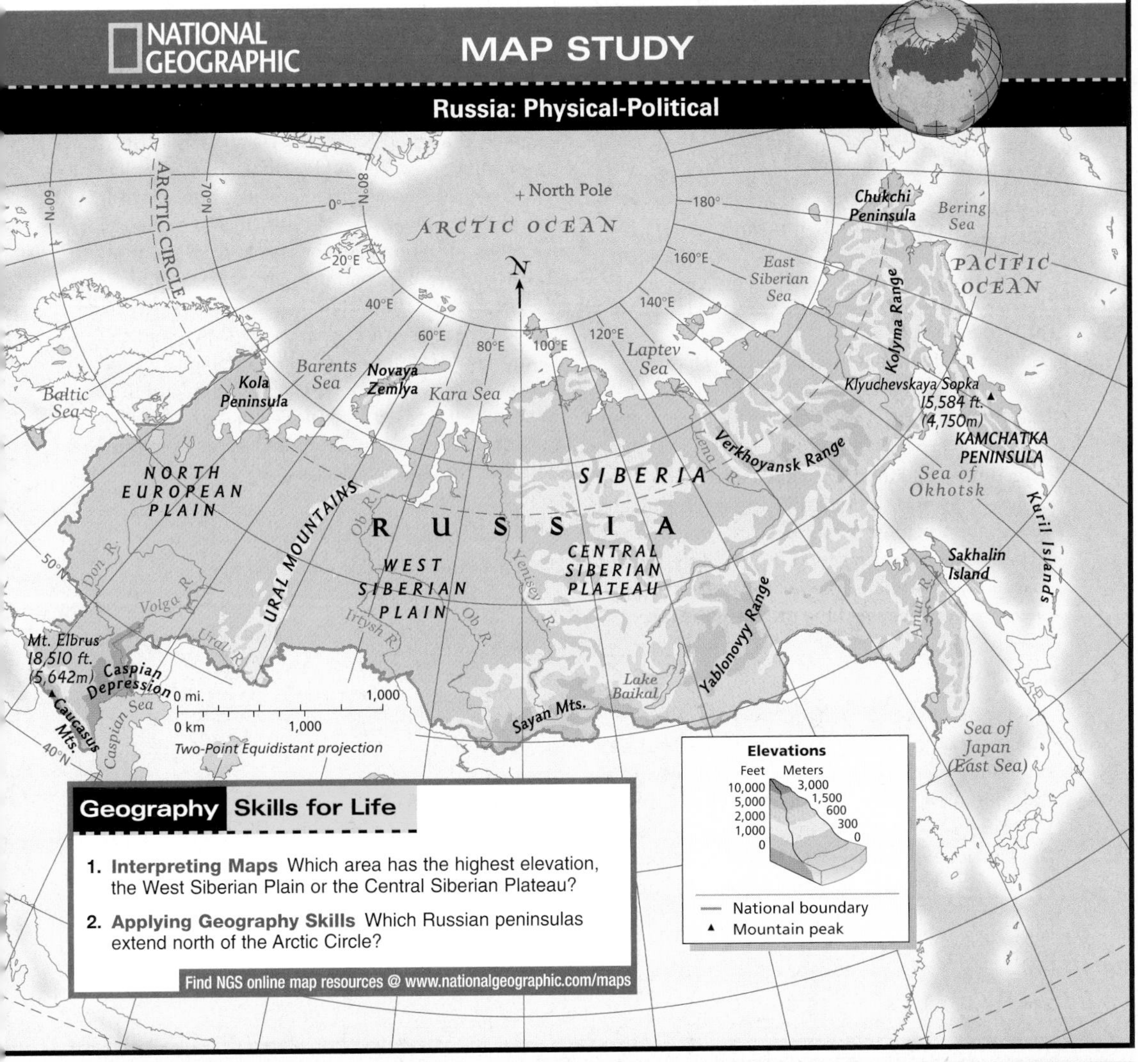

L3 Making Comparisons

Ask students to prepare a chart contrasting Russia's largest rivers with other major world rivers. Have them use almanacs or Internet resources to compare such characteristics as length and drainage area.

L1/ELL

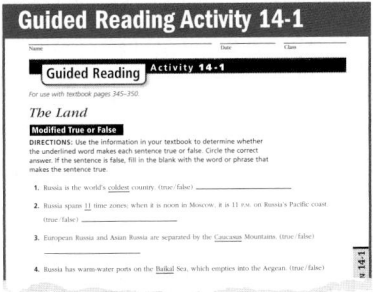

Guided Reading Activity 14-1

Guided Reading Activity 14-1

For use with textbook pages 345–350.

The Land

Modified True or False

DIRECTIONS: Use the information in your textbook to determine whether the underlined word makes each sentence true or false. Circle the correct answer. If the sentence is false, fill in the blank with the word or phrase that makes the sentence true.

1. Russia is the world's coldest country. (true/false)
2. Russia spans 11 time zones; when it is noon in Moscow, it is 11 P.M. on Russia's Pacific coast (true/false)
3. European Russia and Asian Russia are separated by the Caucasus Mountains. (true/false)
4. Russia has warm-water ports on the Baikal Sea, which empties into the Aegean. (true/false)

NATIONAL GEOGRAPHIC MAP STUDY

Answers

1. *Central Siberian Plateau*
2. *Kola, Chukchi*

Map Skills Practice

Location Which Russian city lies farthest west? *(Kaliningrad, between Poland and Lithuania on the Baltic coast)*

NATIONAL GEOGRAPHIC GEOFACT

About 500 Siberian tigers, most of the world's wild population of the animal, live in the forested mountains north of Vladivostok. Because poachers hunt the tigers and loggers destroy the tigers' habitat, the species has become endangered.

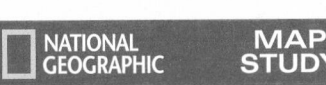

Lake Baikal has a unique ecosystem that is home to 1,500 types of animals and plants found nowhere else in the world.

Geography | **Skills for Life**

Lake Baikal At an estimated 20 to 25 million years old, Russia's Lake Baikal is the world's oldest existing freshwater lake.

Human-Environment Interaction How has industrial development affected Lake Baikal?

over 1 mile (1.6 km) deep, Lake Baikal is the third largest lake in Asia and the deepest freshwater lake in the world. It is estimated to contain about 20 percent of the earth's total supply of freshwater. In recent years runoff from nearby pulp and paper factories has threatened the purity of the lake.

Rivers

Some of the world's longest rivers flow through Russia, draining a large portion of the land and providing water for irrigation. They also serve as transportation routes or sources of electric power for densely populated urban areas. Most of Russia's longest rivers—which supply 84 percent of the country's water—are located in Siberia,

where only 25 percent of the population lives. Thus, people in Siberia enjoy a surplus of freshwater, but European Russians often face water shortages or problems with water quality.

The Volga River

The **Volga River** in European Russia is the fourth-longest river in Russia. Affectionately called *Matushka Volga*, or "Mother Volga," the river is vital to Russia. The Volga and its tributaries drain much of the eastern part of Russia's North European Plain. They connect Moscow to the Caspian Sea and, by way of the Volga-Don Canal, to the Sea of Azov and the Black Sea. Canals link the Volga to the Baltic Sea in the north, giving Russia a water route to northern Europe. Although frozen almost half of each year, the river provides hydroelectric power, or power generated by falling water, and water for drinking and irrigation.

Two-thirds of Russia's water traffic travels along the Volga. Heavy use of the river, however, has created challenges for Russia's people. Fed by melting snow, the wide, swift Volga supplies 33 percent of Russia's usable water, but half of it returns to the river carrying human and industrial waste. In addition, dams interrupt the river's flow, threatening wildlife and drinking water supplies.

Other rivers important to European Russia include the Western Dvina, the Dnieper, and the Don. Many fishing villages line the banks of the Don as it flows through rich farmland toward Rostov, where it empties into the Sea of Azov. A visitor to Veshenskaya, several hundred miles upstream, describes the river's peaceful flow:

> ❝ *It is indeed a quiet Don there, flowing dreamily at sunup under a diaphanous mist. Rowboats move upon the surface like water spiders, as geese waddle down to the edge, honking joyously.* ❞
>
> Mike Edwards, "A Comeback for the Cossacks," *National Geographic*, November 1998

Siberian Rivers

In Siberia, rivers such as the Ob, the Irtysh, the Yenisey, and the Lena rank among the world's largest river systems. They flow north through

---

CRITICAL THINKING ACTIVITY

Drawing Conclusions Have students work independently or in pairs to choose one of the following mineral resources found in Russia: coal, iron ore, nickel, bauxite, manganese, tungsten, platinum, gold, copper, lead, zinc, or tin. Have students research the uses for their assigned resources and report their findings to the class. Then have the class predict what kinds of industries Russia has based on these resources. Use almanacs, encyclopedias, and Internet resources to check the accuracy of the predictions.
🌐 **EE5 Environment and Society: Standard 16**

Siberia to the Arctic Ocean. Temperatures are warmer at the rivers' sources in the south than at their mouths in the north. Frozen rivers melt and land along the rivers thaws earlier in the south than in the north. Blocked by ice as they head northward, the meltwaters often flood the land, creating vast inland swamps and marshes.

The Amur River, which drains eastward, forms the border between Russia and China for about 1,000 miles (1,610 km). Influenced by summer monsoon winds from the southeast, the Amur River valley is warmer than the rest of Siberia and is Siberia's main food-producing area.

Natural Resources

Russia's physical geography is both a blessing and a challenge. The country holds an abundance of natural resources. Much of this wealth, however, lies in remote and climatically unfavorable areas and is difficult to tap or utilize.

Minerals and Energy

Russia has huge reserves of mineral resources. It is especially rich in mineral fuels. The country holds large petroleum deposits and 16 percent of the world's coal reserves. Russia produces more dry natural gas than any other country in the world. It also leads the world in nickel production and ranks among the top three producers of aluminum, gemstones, platinum group metals, sulfur, and tungsten. Russia's rivers make it a leading producer of hydroelectric power.

Soil and Forest Land

Because of Russia's generally cold climate, only about 10 percent of Russia's land can support agriculture. In the far north there is very little farming because of permafrost, a permanently frozen layer of soil beneath the surface of the ground, which underlies much of Russia. However, a wide, fertile band called the Black Earth Belt covers about 250 million acres (100 million ha) and stretches from Ukraine to southwestern Siberia. The chernozem soils of this farmland produce crops such as wheat, rye, oats, barley, and sugar beets that feed much of Russia.

About one-fifth of the world's remaining forest lands lie in Russia—75 percent of them in eastern Siberia. Second only to the Amazon rain forest in terms of the amount of oxygen returned to the

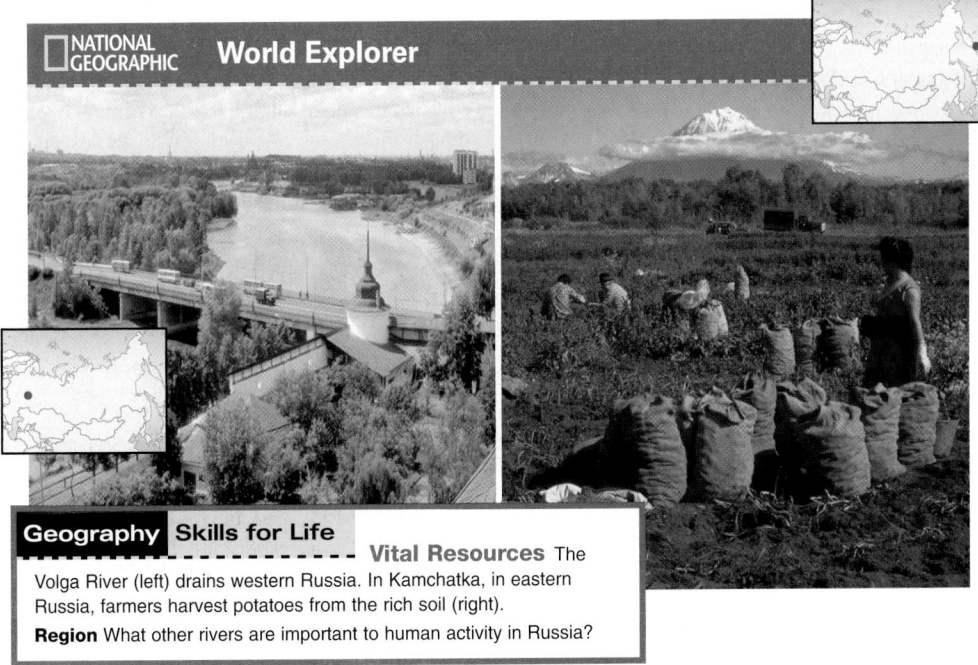

NATIONAL GEOGRAPHIC World Explorer

Geography Skills for Life
Vital Resources The Volga River (left) drains western Russia. In Kamchatka, in eastern Russia, farmers harvest potatoes from the rich soil (right).
Region What other rivers are important to human activity in Russia?

☐ NATIONAL GEOGRAPHIC **GEOFACT**

▶ In Siberia, buildings rest on pilings 6 to 8 feet (1.8–2.4 m) off the ground so that heat from within does not melt the permafrost. Melting permafrost can cause building foundations to shift and crack.

❸ ASSESS

Assign Section 1 Assessment as homework or as an in-class activity.

◑ Have students use **Interactive Tutor Self-Assessment CD-ROM**.

L2

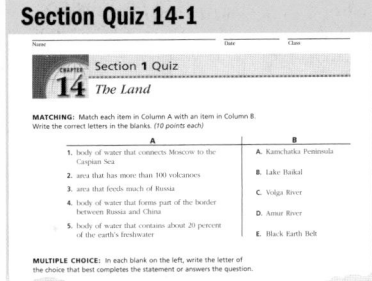

Section Quiz 14-1

NATIONAL GEOGRAPHIC World Explorer

Answer
the western Dvina, the Dnieper, the Don, the Ob, the Irtysh, the Yenisey, the Amur, and the Lena

More About the Photo The photos contrast the urbanized areas along the Volga River with rural areas in eastern Russia.

TEAM-TEACHING ACTIVITY: LANGUAGE ARTS

Russian Folktales Have students work with a language arts teacher to research, read, and discuss Russian folktales. Invite students to pay special attention to the setting of the stories. **Ask:** How has Russia's physical geography and climate influenced the region's storytellers? If time allows, have small groups of students choose folktales to present to the class in the form of short dramatizations, puppet shows, or theater presentations. 🗐
🌐 **EE5 Environment and Society: Standard 15**

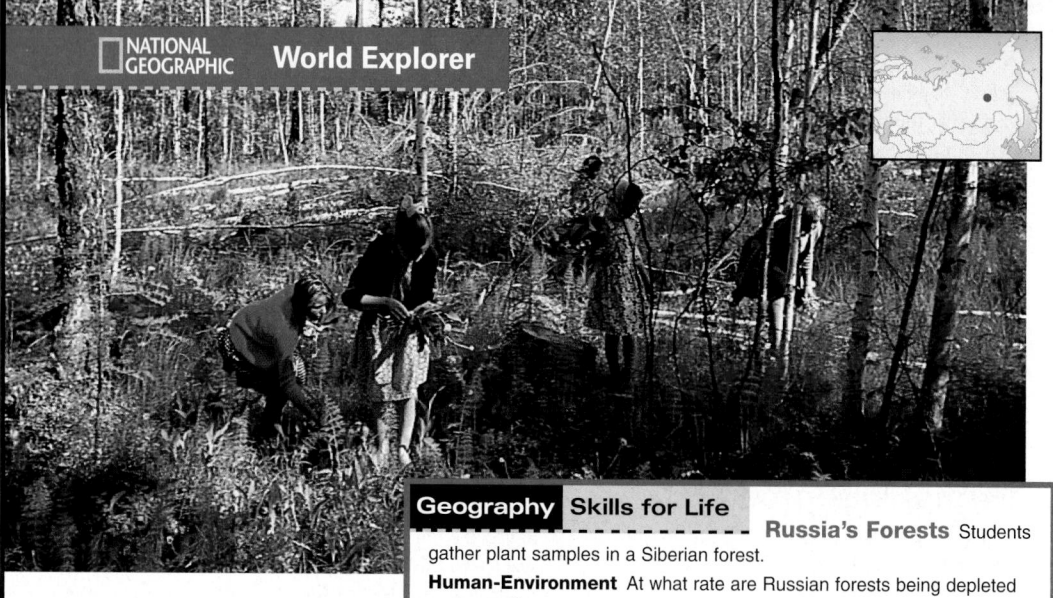

NATIONAL GEOGRAPHIC **World Explorer**

NATIONAL GEOGRAPHIC **World Explorer**

Answer
about 40 million acres (16 million ha) per year

More About the Photo
Russia's forests cover nearly 40 percent of the country. The forested areas consist of two kinds: a large, mainly coniferous forest in the north and a smaller area of mixed forest that lies in the south.

Reteach

Have students review the physical-political map of Russia on page 347 and then quiz one another on the location of Russia's key landforms and cities.

Enrich

Refer students to portions of Mark Twain's 1869 book *Innocents Abroad* that describes Russia from the point of view of an American tourist in the 1800s.

4 CLOSE

Have students work together to plan the itinerary for a 10-day class tour of Russia. Ask students to give reasons for their chosen destinations.

Geography | **Skills for Life**

Russia's Forests Students gather plant samples in a Siberian forest.
Human-Environment At what rate are Russian forests being depleted each year?

atmosphere, Russian forests also supply much of the world's timber, mainly pine, fir, spruce, cedar, and larch. As a result of commercial logging, however, Russian forests shrink by almost 40 million acres (16 million ha) each year—a rate of loss higher than that of the Amazon Basin.

Economics
Russia's Fishing Industry

Fish remain important to the Russian diet and economy, even though many of Russia's rivers and seas are overfished or polluted. Salmon from the Pacific Ocean and herring, cod, and halibut from the

Arctic Ocean support a flourishing fishing industry. However, the supply of world-famous Russian caviar, or salted fish eggs, has declined. Dams built on the Volga River have interrupted the migration of sturgeon, the fish that provide the eggs for caviar. Sturgeon is now being fished illegally to meet the global demand for this delicacy.

As you have learned, Russia's vast and varied land of plains, mountains, and great frozen tundra has both advantages and disadvantages. In the next section, you will learn in more detail how climate restricts access to the country's natural resources.

SECTION 1 ASSESSMENT

Checking for Understanding

1. **Define** chernozem, hydroelectric power, permafrost.

2. **Main Ideas** Use a Venn diagram like the one below to show how European Russia and Asian Russia are alike and different.

European Russia — Both — Asian Russia

Critical Thinking

3. **Drawing Conclusions** Why do 75 percent of Russians live west of the Ural Mountains?

4. **Identifying Cause and Effect** What problems arise as a result of the large number of Russians living on the North European Plain?

5. **Making Generalizations** Explain how Russia's geography affects access to natural resources.

Analyzing Maps

6. **Region** Study the map on page 347. What types of physical features form Russia's boundaries?

Applying Geography

7. **Effect of Location** Think about the locations of Russia's seas. Then write a descriptive paragraph explaining how the locations of these seas affect Russia's economy.

SECTION 1 ASSESSMENT ANSWERS

1. All vocabulary terms are defined in the text.

2. European Russia: densely populated, major cities, agricultural land, inland seas, limited freshwater supply; Asian Russia: sparsely populated, few cities, soil not fertile, many rivers, volcanoes; both: coniferous forests, cold, rich in natural resources

3. because of the milder climate and presence of fertile soil and navigable rivers, which led to the development of large cities

4. water shortages, pollution

5. Russia is rich in natural resources, but geographic and climatic obstacles make resources inaccessible or costly to develop.

6. seas, mountains, rivers

7. **Applying Geography** Most of Russia's seas are in the far north where ports are often icebound. The Black Sea provides Russia with warm-water ports for year-round shipping.

Climate and Vegetation

Guide to Reading

Consider What You Know

You can see on a map that Russia's vast landmass lies in the far northern latitudes. What effect do you think this location has on Russia's climate?

Reading Strategy

Categorizing As you read about Russia's physical geography, complete a graphic organizer similar to the one below by describing the climates and vegetation of Russia.

Region	Description
Tundra	
Taiga	
Steppe	

Read to Find Out

- What are Russia's major climates?
- What are the seasons like in Russia?
- How does climate affect the way Russians live?
- What types of natural vegetation are found in each of Russia's climate regions?

Terms to Know

- tundra
- taiga
- steppe

Places to Locate

- Siberia
- Arctic Circle

NATIONAL GEOGRAPHIC

A Geographic View

Ice or Mud

We had started on a fine summer day, but as we approached the coast, blue skies gave way to a bitter wind and soul-drenching fog. When Yuri stopped at a small outpost called Nizhne Kamchatsk . . . I was ready to accept his friend's offer of hot tea made from tree fungus ("Good for the kidneys!") and an all-purpose forecast: "Fickle, the weather," he growled. "In Kamchatka the earth is a piece of ice or a piece of mud."

—*Bryan Hodgson, "Kamchatka: Russia's Land of Fire and Ice,"* National Geographic, *April 1994*

Mountain range, Kamchatka Peninsula

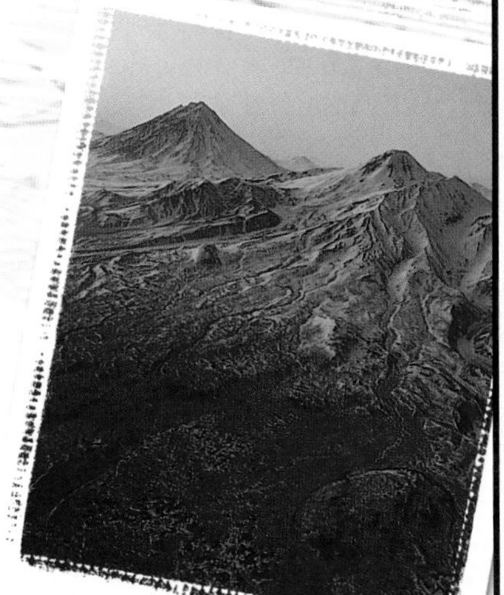

Shifting extremes of weather in the Kamchatka Peninsula challenge the people who live there. Much of Russia experiences extreme cold and long winters. In a land where it is frigid and dark for long periods of time and where the rivers do not move for months, people learn patience.

Russia's Climates and Vegetation

Most of Russia has a harsh climate with long, cold winters and short, relatively cool summers. The country's climate is characterized by temperature extremes. The coldest winter temperatures occur in eastern **Siberia**. Warmer air from the Atlantic Ocean moderates temperature to some extent in certain areas of European Russia. Most of the country, however, lies well within the Eurasian landmass, far

1 FOCUS

Section Overview

This section discusses Russia's climate regions and the vegetation found in each of them.

BELLRINGER
Skillbuilder Activity

Project transparency and have students answer questions.

Available as blackline master.

Daily Focus Skills Transparency 14-2

Guide to Reading

Consider What You Know

Answer *High latitudes make Russia's climate generally cold and often snowy.*

Reading Strategy

Answers Tundra: *vast, treeless plain that dominates Russia;* Taiga: *world's largest coniferous forest, covers two-fifths of European Russia, contains half of the world's soft timber;* Steppe: *temperate grassland, dry summers; long, cold dry winters; rich soil*

Preteaching Vocabulary

Use the **Vocabulary Puzzle-Maker CD-ROM** to create crossword and word-search puzzles.

RESOURCE MANAGER

Reproducible Masters

- Reproducible Lesson Plan 14-2
- Vocabulary Activity 14
- Daily Lecture Notes 14-2
- Guided Reading Activity 14-2
- Reading Essentials and Study Guide 14-2
- Reteaching Activity 14
- Reinforcing Skills Activity 14
- Section Quiz 14-2

Transparencies

- Daily Focus Skills Transparency 14-2
- Political Map Transparency 5
- Unit 5 Map Overlay Transparencies

Multimedia

- Vocabulary PuzzleMaker CD-ROM
- Interactive Tutor Self-Assessment CD-ROM
- ExamView® Pro Testmaker CD-ROM
- Presentation Plus! CD-ROM

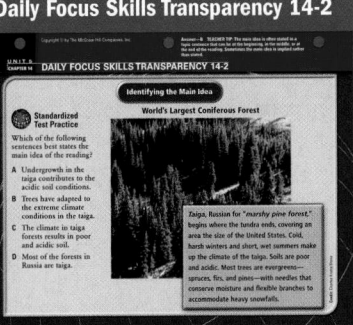

L2 Location

Ask: What is the relationship between latitude and Russia's climate regions? *(Warmer climates occur farther south, while most of Russia lies in cold, high latitudes, including the polar region.)* What factors moderate Russia's harsh climates? *(oceans, large bodies of water in coastal areas of European and far eastern Russia)*

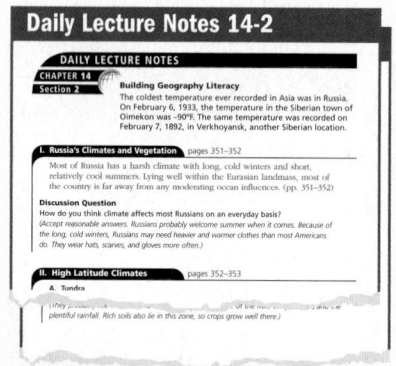

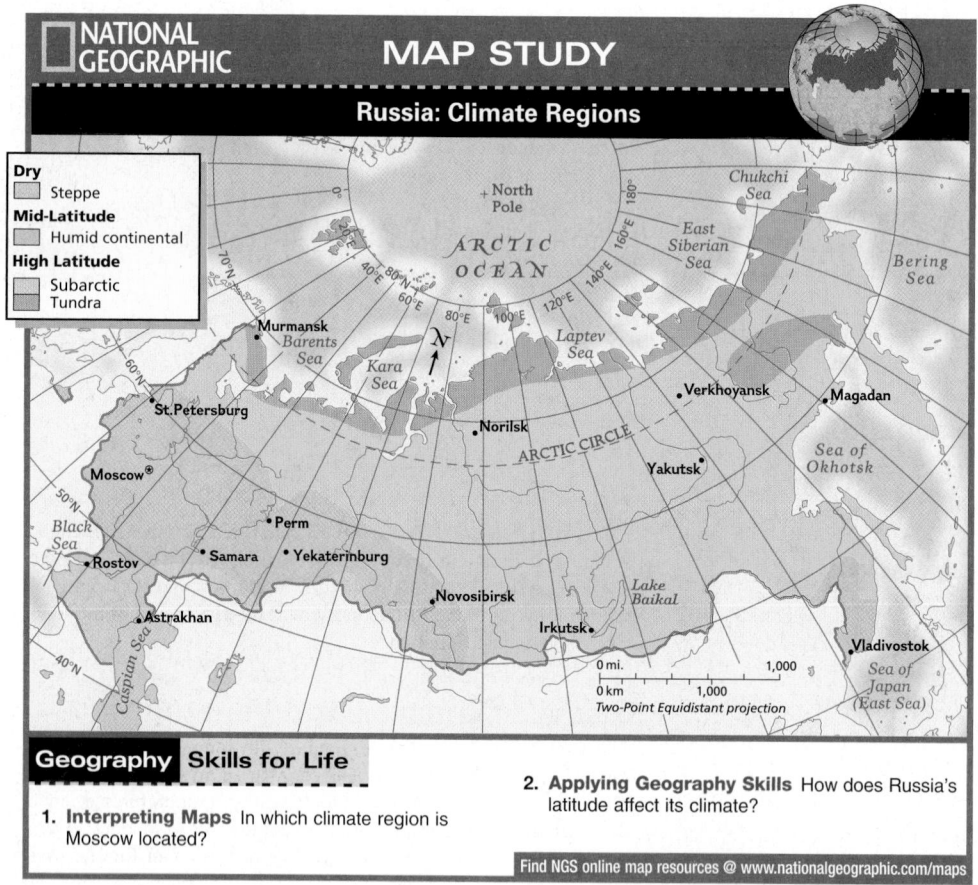

NATIONAL GEOGRAPHIC — MAP STUDY

Answers

1. *humid continental*

2. *Russia's high latitude results in cold winters and short summers.*

Map Study Skills

Location Why is Vladivostok's seaport ice-free nine months of the year? *(Vladivostok is located in a humid continental region on the Sea of Japan.)*

---

away from any moderating ocean influences. The Siberian city of Verkhoyansk, located at about 68°N latitude, has been called the "cold pole of the world" because of its bitter winters. January temperatures there have fallen to a low of –90°F (–68°C).

High Latitude Climates

Russia's high-latitude climates feature extremely cold winters and short summers. Seasonal temperatures across this broad landmass can vary greatly. In Yakutsk, in eastern Russia, for example, January temperatures often fall below –33°F (–36°C), and July temperatures average 64°F (18°C). Isolated from oceans and moisture-bearing air masses, Siberia's interior has very little precipitation.

Tundra

Far to the north, the tundra, a vast, treeless plain, dominates the Russian landscape. Hugging the edges of the Arctic seas, almost all of the tundra climate region lies north of the **Arctic Circle** (66½°N). An isolated patch of tundra in northeastern Siberia lies near the Sea of Okhotsk. *Tundra* in Finnish means "barren land," an apt term for a place where the average annual temperature is below freezing. In this region the sky stays dark for many weeks before and after December 22. Then, for several weeks during summer, there is continuous sunlight.

The tundra covers about 10 percent of Russia. Its short growing season and the thin, acidic soil lying just above the permafrost limit the kinds of plants

Geography | Skills for Life

1. **Interpreting Maps** In which climate region is Moscow located?

2. **Applying Geography Skills** How does Russia's latitude affect its climate?

Find NGS online map resources @ www.nationalgeographic.com/maps

---

DIFFERENTIATED INSTRUCTION

Reading Support For students who have trouble with reading comprehension and for English language learners, provide strategies for identifying new words in context. Students with reading comprehension difficulties often skip over words they cannot immediately identify. Encourage them to scan the section for these words, list them, search for context clues, and predict definitions. Examples of challenging words in this section may include: *frigid, moderates/moderating, coniferous, barren, dominant, interspersed,* and *assert.* **ELL**

📁 Refer to *Inclusion for the Social Studies Classroom Strategies and Activities.*

that can grow there. Only mosses, lichen, algae, and dwarf shrubs thrive in the tundra.

Subarctic

Russia's dominant climate region is the subarctic. Although the subarctic lies south of the tundra, some of the world's coldest temperatures occur there. For 120 to 250 days each year, snow covers the ground. The subarctic climate supports the taiga (TY•guh), a forest belt that covers two-fifths of European Russia and extends into much of Siberia. Roughly the size of the United States, the Russian taiga is the world's largest coniferous forest, containing about one-half of the world's softwood timber.

Culture
Living in a Cold Climate

Living in an extremely cold climate challenges Russians' creativity. Russians must make adjustments to the climate in all aspects of their lives—jobs, transportation, food and water supplies, heating, clothing, and plumbing. Keeping warm requires a great deal of energy from oil, gas, wood, or coal. Layers of clothing made of wool or fur protect those who brave the frigid outdoor temperatures.

Businesses and industries also must make adjustments to the extreme cold. Builders plan for the cold when they construct buildings. To make machinery and cars, manufacturers must use a special type of steel that will not crack in the cold.

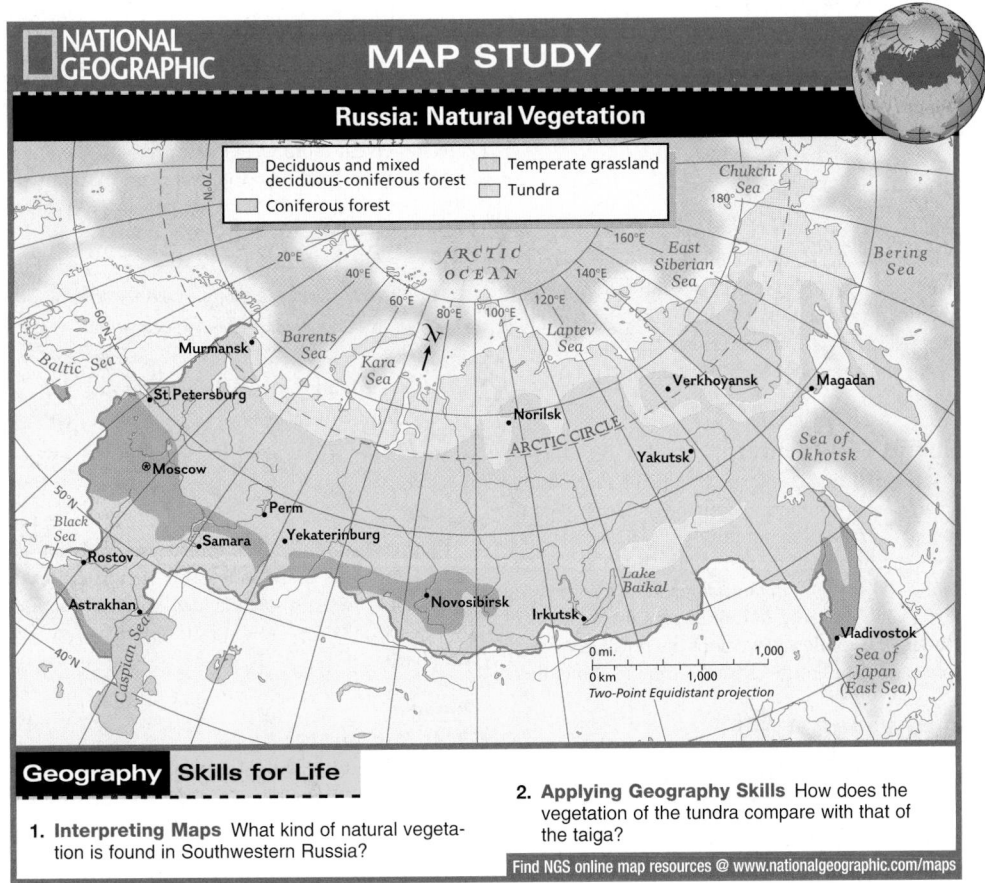

NATIONAL GEOGRAPHIC MAP STUDY

Russia: Natural Vegetation

- Deciduous and mixed deciduous-coniferous forest
- Coniferous forest
- Temperate grassland
- Tundra

Geography Skills for Life

1. **Interpreting Maps** What kind of natural vegetation is found in Southwestern Russia?

2. **Applying Geography Skills** How does the vegetation of the tundra compare with that of the taiga?

Find NGS online map resources @ www.nationalgeographic.com/maps

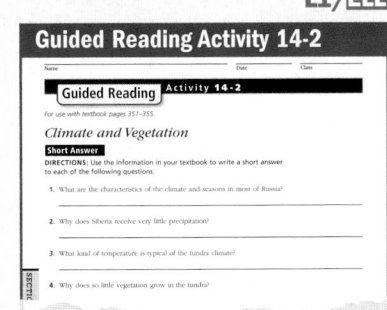

L1/ELL

Guided Reading Activity 14-2

Name ___ Date ___ Class ___

Guided Reading Activity 14-2

For use with textbook pages 351–355.

Climate and Vegetation

Short Answer

DIRECTIONS: Use the information in your textbook to write a short answer to each of the following questions.

1. What are the characteristics of the climate and seasons in most of Russia?

2. Why does Siberia receive very little precipitation?

3. What kind of temperature is typical of the tundra climate?

4. Why do so little vegetation grow in the tundra?

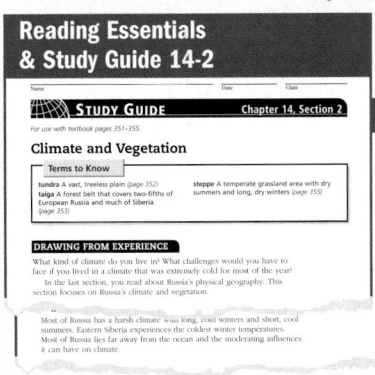

NATIONAL GEOGRAPHIC MAP STUDY

Answers

1. *deciduous and mixed deciduous-coniferous forest and temperate grasslands*

2. *tundra—mosses, lichens, algae, dwarf shrubs; taiga— coniferous forests*

Map Study Skills

Region What kind of soil would you expect to find along the shores of the Laptev Sea? *(thin, acidic soil over permafrost)*

L1/ELL

Reading Essentials & Study Guide 14-2

Name ___ Date ___ Class ___

🌐 **STUDY GUIDE** Chapter 14, Section 2

For use with textbook pages 351–355.

Climate and Vegetation

Terms to Know

tundra A vast, treeless plain *(page 352)*
taiga A forest belt that covers two-fifths of European Russia and much of Siberia *(page 353)*

steppe A temperate grassland area with dry summers and long, dry winters *(page 355)*

DRAWING FROM EXPERIENCE

What kind of climate do you live in? What challenges would you have to face if you lived in a climate that was extremely cold for most of the year?
In the last section, you read about Russia's physical geography. This section focuses on Russia's climate and vegetation.

Most of Russia has a harsh climate with long, cold winters and short, cool summers. Eastern Siberia experiences the coldest winter temperatures. Most of Russia lies far away from the ocean and the moderating influences it can have on climate.

COOPERATIVE LEARNING ACTIVITY

A Russian Botanical Garden Have students work in small groups to make a virtual Russian botanical garden in the classroom. Assign one climate region to each group, and ask group members to research the variety of vegetation found in their region of Russia. Groups should work together to determine how they will illustrate their virtual garden. Possibilities include drawing pictures, using photographs from old magazines, creating three-dimensional models from papier-mâché or clay, or developing a multimedia computer presentation. Remind students to label their displays with detailed descriptions. 📦

🗺️ **EE3 Physical Systems: Standard 8**

World Explorer

Answer
Siberia lies in high altitudes, unmoderated by the effects of oceans.

More About the Photos
Siberia, once considered one of the most remote areas on Earth, has urban areas, industry, and a growing economy. Residents still endure one of the harshest climates on the planet, however.

Objectives, goals, and answers to the student activity can be found in the Web Activity Lesson Plan feature at geography.glencoe.com

❸ ASSESS

Assign Section 2 Assessment as homework or as an in-class activity.

🌐 Have students use **Interactive Tutor Self-Assessment CD-ROM.**

L2

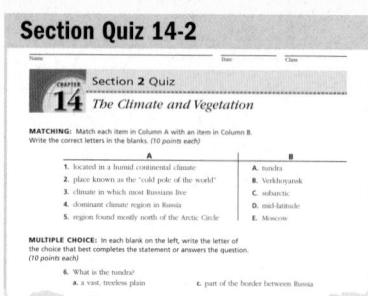

Section Quiz 14-2

World Explorer

Geography Skills for Life
Temperatures Arctic conditions are part of daily life in Siberia. The woman shown at right is carrying blocks of frozen milk to her home.
Place Why is the climate so cold in Siberia?

Mid-Latitude Climates

Russia's mid-latitude climates are much milder than the high-latitude climates, with milder winters and warmer summers. Although still relatively cold, these climates are where most Russians live and where much of Russia's agricultural production takes place.

Humid Continental

Most of Russia's North European Plain and a small part of southern Siberia have a humid continental climate. Temperatures in Moscow, which lies in a humid continental region, range from 9° to 21°F (–13° to –6°C) in January and from 56° to 75°F (13° to 24°C) in July. In humid continental areas of Russia, the coniferous taiga of the north gives way to mixed coniferous-deciduous forests. Soils there

Student Web Activity Visit the **Glencoe World Geography** Web site at geography.glencoe.com and click on Student Web Activities— Chapter 14 for an activity about Siberia.

---

are somewhat more fertile than those of the taiga, and farming methods and fertilizers have made them very productive. Here, one traveler takes note of the crops he sees in the region:

❝ *The train bored through a corridor of birch and pine interspersed every 15 minutes with a village. Each of these openings revealed, in the evening light, patches of cabbages, beets, onions, and tomatoes. . . .* ❞
Mike Edwards, "Playing by New Rules," *National Geographic*, March 1993

Farther south the mixed forests gradually merge into temperate grasslands. The rich chernozem soil makes these grasslands ideal for crop production, especially for growing grains such as wheat and barley.

History
War and Winter

Russia's cold climate played an important role in the defeat of Napoleon in 1812 and of German forces during World War II. In June 1812, a Grand Army of over 600,000 men entered Russia. The Russian forces retreated for hundreds of miles,

---

CRITICAL THINKING ACTIVITY

Identifying Alternatives Have students research the factors that are contributing to the deforestation of the Russian taiga. List these factors on the board. Then have students work in small groups to brainstorm practical alternatives to damaging practices and suggestions for limiting environmental damage to Russia's forests. Remind students to keep Russia's economic and climatic challenges in mind as they develop proposed solutions. 📦
🌐 **EE6 The Uses of Geography: Standard 18**

burning their own villages and countryside to keep Napoleon's army from finding food.

Lacking food and supplies, Napoleon began to retreat in terrible winter conditions. Less than 40,000 out of the original army managed to arrive back in Poland.

During World War II, Germans advanced into Moscow in December 1941. They unexpectedly encountered Russia's most effective weapon, its brutal cold. Winter arrived early, blanketing the front lines with temperatures as low as −40°F (−40°C). The frigid cold paralyzed the German tanks, mechanized vehicles, artillery, and aircraft. A combination of Russia's harsh winter and its military forces forced the Germans to retreat.

Steppe

A small area between the Black and Caspian Seas and a thin band along Russia's border with Kazakhstan make up Russia's steppe climate region. This temperate grassland area has dry summers and long, cold, dry winters with swirling, sparse snow. The steppe's chernozem soil is rich in organic matter that enables many plants to flourish. Rippling in the winds, seas of grass stretch to the horizon in every direction. Sunflowers, mint, and beans also flourish in the steppe region. In recent years, however, the introduction of foreign plants and overgrazing by animals have damaged the steppe ecosystem. As the

newly introduced plant species crowd out native grasses, soil fertility declines.

As you have learned, frigid climates dominate large areas of Russia. Nonetheless, in the pockets of more moderate climates, vegetation and human life coexist quite comfortably.

Geography Skills for Life

Russian Steppe Over the centuries, many nomadic invaders, including Attila the Hun, have crossed over Russia's steppe to invade territories to the west.
Region What allows plants to flourish in Russia's steppe region?

NATIONAL GEOGRAPHIC **World Explorer**

Answer
rich chernozem soil with abundant organic matter

More About the Photo
Russia's steppe consists of a mixture of grasses with a scattering of trees. Much of this region is now under cultivation.

Reteach
Project Map Overlay Transparencies 5-2 and 5-3. Ask students to identify Russia's major climate regions and vegetation types.

Enrich
Invite a zoologist from a local zoo, museum, or university to present information on the wildlife of Russia, including Siberian tigers, jerboas, Caspian sturgeon, reindeer, and sables.

④ CLOSE

Have students reread "A Geographic View" on page 351. Point out the colorful description of Kamchatka's climate in the last sentence, and challenge students to come up with similarly colorful one-sentence descriptions of the climate or vegetation in other parts of Russia.

SECTION ② ASSESSMENT

Checking for Understanding

1. Define tundra, taiga, steppe.

2. Main Ideas On a sheet of paper, create a table like the one below. Complete the table by filling in information on the climate regions and vegetation of Russia.

Climate Region	Description	Vegetation

Critical Thinking

3. Making Generalizations What generalization can you make about Russia's climate regions?

4. Making Inferences How does Russia's climates and short growing season affect food production?

5. Comparing and Contrasting What are the differences between the tundra and subarctic climate regions? Between the humid continental and steppe climate regions?

Analyzing Maps

6. Region Study the maps on pages 347 and 352. Which type of climate characterizes the North European Plain?

Applying Geography

7. Impact of Climate Write a paragraph describing physical processes, such as freezing and thawing, and the effect they have on the land and the people of Siberia and other northern parts of Russia.

SECTION ② ASSESSMENT ANSWERS

1. All vocabulary terms are defined in the text.

2. Table entries should reflect text information.

3. With some exceptions, Russia's climates and vegetation are typical of high latitudes—extremely cold temperatures, tundra and taiga vegetation.

4. Possible answer: limited agricultural land must be farmed intensely, fresh foods must be preserved, and some produce must be imported.

5. tundra: year-round cold temperatures, treeless, barren; subarctic: taiga vegetation (coniferous forests); humid continental: mixed forests, fertile soil, more moderate seasonal temperatures; steppe: short summer season, fertile soil, grasslands

6. humid continental, subarctic

7. Applying Geography Paragraphs should focus on the adjustments that individuals and businesses must make to conditions in Russia's cold climate areas.

MAP & GRAPH SkillBuilder

Teaching the Skill

Review with students examples of bar graphs and line graphs. **Ask:** If you were going to combine the information in a line graph and the information in a bar graph into one graph, what might it look like? Have volunteers sketch their ideas on the board. Then **Ask:** What are some circumstances that might call for such a combined graph? Lead students to see that studying information drawn from complex factors, such as climate, is best done using complex graphs.

Additional Practice
L1

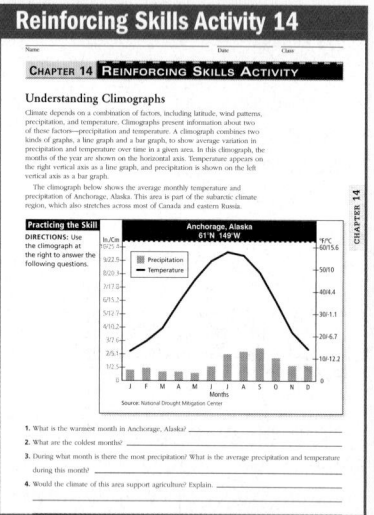

Reinforcing Skills Activity 14

GLENCOE TECHNOLOGY

Glencoe Skillbuilder Interactive Workbook, Level 2

MAP & GRAPH SkillBuilder

Understanding Climographs

Climate is the result of the complex interaction of latitude, wind patterns, temperature, and precipitation. Climographs allow us to compare and contrast different climates in different regions based on temperature and precipitation.

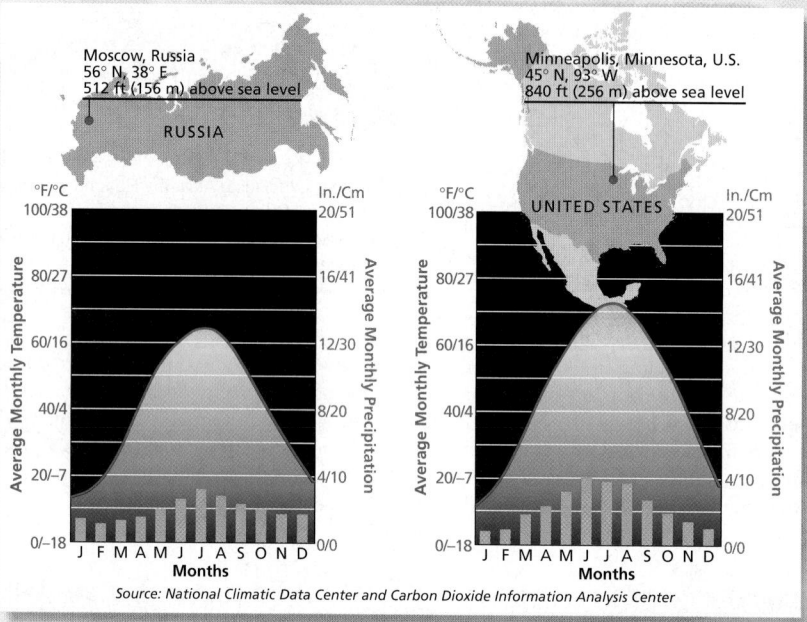

Source: National Climatic Data Center and Carbon Dioxide Information Analysis Center

Learning the Skill

A climograph combines a line graph and bar graph to show average variation in temperature and precipitation. In the graphs above, the months of the year are shown on the horizontal axis. Temperature appears on the left vertical axis as a line graph; precipitation appears on the right vertical axis as a bar graph.

To analyze the information in a climograph:

- **Identify highest and lowest temperatures.**
- **Determine the variation in annual precipitation.**
- **Use this information to describe and compare the two climates.**

Practicing the Skill

Answer the questions using the climographs above.

1. Which city is warmer year-round? Wetter?
2. Which city has the greater annual variation in temperature?
3. What kind of climate does Moscow have? Minneapolis?

Applying the Skill

Research the average monthly precipitation and temperature in your area using the library, a local newspaper, or the Internet. Use the data to make a climograph. How are the climates of your area and Moscow similar? Different?

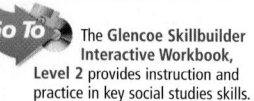

Go To The Glencoe Skillbuilder Interactive Workbook, Level 2 provides instruction and practice in key social studies skills.

ANSWERS TO PRACTICING THE SKILL

1. Minneapolis; Minneapolis
2. Minneapolis
3. Both cities have a humid continental climate.

SUMMARY & STUDY GUIDE

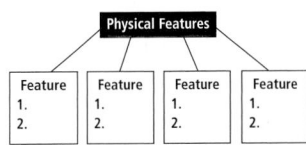

SECTION 1 — The Land (pp. 345–350)

Terms to Know
- chernozem
- hydroelectric power
- permafrost

Key Points
- Russia is the largest country in the world, spanning Europe and Asia.
- Russia's land consists of interconnected plains and plateaus and is bordered on the south and east by mountain ranges.
- Most rivers in Russia flow northward and are frozen for much of the year.
- Russia is rich in resources, such as petroleum, coal, minerals and gems, and timber.

Organizing Your Notes
Use a diagram like the one below to help you organize important details about Russia's physical features.

Physical Features

| Feature 1. 2. | Feature 1. 2. | Feature 1. 2. | Feature 1. 2. |

SECTION 2 — Climate and Vegetation (pp. 351–355)

Terms to Know
- tundra
- taiga
- steppe

Key Points
- Most of Russia has a harsh climate with wide extremes of temperatures, which creates challenges in all aspects of Russian life.
- Russian winters are long and cold, and its summers are short and relatively cool.
- Permanently frozen subsoil, or permafrost, lies beneath much of Siberia.
- The vegetation in Russia is varied, with treeless tundra in the far north, densely wooded taiga in the north and central areas, and temperate steppe grasslands in the southwest.

Organizing Your Notes
Create an outline using the format below to help you organize your notes for this section.

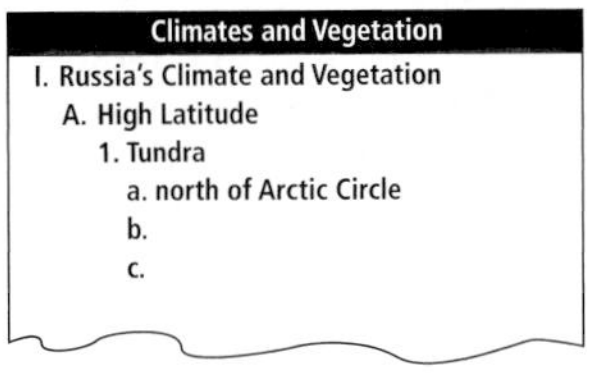

Climates and Vegetation
I. Russia's Climate and Vegetation
  A. High Latitude
    1. Tundra
      a. north of Arctic Circle
      b.
      c.

Birch tree forest in Siberia.

Chapter 14   357

Using the Chapter 14 Summary & Study Guide

Use the Chapter 14 Summary & Study Guide to preview, review, condense, or reteach the chapter.

Preview/Review

Vocabulary PuzzleMaker CD-ROM reinforces "Terms to Know."

Interactive Tutor Self-Assessment CD-ROM provides a review of Chapter 14 content.

Condense

Have students read the Chapter 14 Summary & Study Guide.

Chapter 14 Audio Program

Chapter 14 Guided Reading Activities

Reteach

Chapter 14 Reteaching Activities (Spanish also available)

Chapter 14 Reading Essentials and Study Guides

GLENCOE TECHNOLOGY

NATIONAL GEOGRAPHIC
WORLD REGIONS VIDEO PROGRAM

Unit 5, Russia
The following segments enhance the study of this unit:

- **Siberian Tigers**
- **The Tire Factory**
- **Bolshoi Ballet**

 Available in DVD and VHS

CHAPTER CULMINATING ACTIVITY

Russian ABCs Challenge students to write a children's book about Russia, with one place, landform, climate type, form of vegetation, or example of regional wildlife for each letter of the alphabet. Students may refer to their texts and do additional research with encyclopedias or Internet resources. **EE2 Places and Regions: Standard 4**

ASSESSMENT & ACTIVITIES

Reviewing Key Terms

1. permafrost
2. tundra
3. steppe
4. chernozem
5. taiga
6. hydroelectric power

Reviewing Facts

SECTION 1

1. Urals
2. North European, West Siberian
3. It provides hydroelectric power, transportation, and links for trade and agriculture.
4. oil, natural gas, and coal, as well as other minerals, forests, and fish

SECTION 2

5. long, cold winters and short, cool summers
6. tundra, subarctic, humid continental, steppe
7. subarctic
8. tundra: lichens, mosses, algae, dwarf shrubs; subarctic: taiga (coniferous forests); humid continental: deciduous and mixed deciduous-coniferous forests; steppe: grasslands

Reviewing Key Terms

Write the key term that best completes each of the following sentences. Refer to the Terms to Know in the Summary & Study Guide on page 357.

1. The permanently frozen _____ lies beneath much of northern Russia.
2. The frigid _____ stretches along Russia's northern boundary.
3. Many varieties of grasses grow in the _____ climate region.
4. The rich _____ soil of the North European Plain supports the production of grains.
5. Coniferous trees grow in the _____, a forest belt that covers most of Russia.
6. The Volga River provides western Russia with _____.

Reviewing Facts

SECTION 1

1. Which mountains form a natural dividing line between European Russia and Asian Russia?
2. What are Russia's two main plains?
3. Explain why the Volga River is so important to the people of Russia.
4. What are Russia's major natural resources?

SECTION 2

5. What are the main characteristics of Russian seasons?
6. What are the four climate regions in Russia?
7. Which climate region dominates Russia?
8. What kinds of vegetation are found in each of Russia's climate regions?

Critical Thinking

1. **Drawing Conclusions** Why do most Russians live on the North European Plain?
2. **Analyzing Information** Why is Russia's Volga River often called "Mother Volga"?
3. **Identifying Cause and Effect** Create a web diagram like the one below, and fill in effects of the cold climate on Russian life. Then write a paragraph describing one effect in detail.

effect | effect
Cold Russian Climate
effect | effect

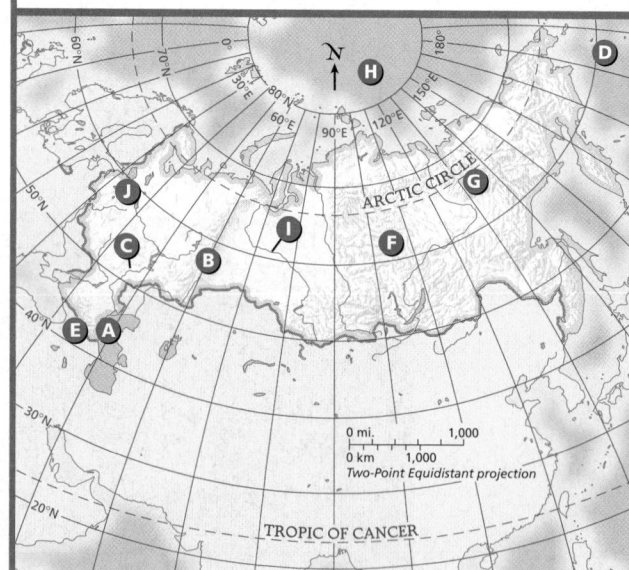

NATIONAL GEOGRAPHIC
Locating Places
Russia: Physical Geography

Match the letters on the map with the places and physical features of Russia. Write your answers on a sheet of paper.

1. Ural Mountains
2. Caucasus Mountains
3. Verkhoyansk Range
4. Central Siberian Plateau
5. Arctic Ocean
6. Bering Sea
7. Caspian Sea
8. Volga River
9. Ob River
10. North European Plain

Critical Thinking

1. navigable rivers, fertile soil, less harsh climate
2. The river is vital to Russia; it drains much of the eastern North European Plain and connects Moscow to northern Europe.
3. Webs should reflect text information.

NATIONAL GEOGRAPHIC **Locating Places**

| 1. B | 3. G | 5. H | 7. A | 9. I |
| 2. E | 4. F | 6. D | 8. C | 10. J |

GEOGRAPHY Online
Self-Check Quiz Visit the **Glencoe World Geography** Web site at geography.glencoe.com and click on Self-Check Quizzes—Chapter 14 to prepare for the Chapter Test.

Using the Regional Atlas

Refer to the Regional Atlas on pages 338–341.

1. **Location** What challenges do Russia's physical features create for mining and transporting coal?
2. **Region** What is the major natural resource found on the Central Siberian Plateau?

Thinking Like a Geographer

Think about the physical geography of Russia. What factors prevent Russia from being a major shipping country with many ports? As a geographer, which form of transportation within Russia do you think would be the best choice for further development?

Problem-Solving Activity

Decision Making Imagine you are a Russian engineer. A foreign automobile manufacturing company has asked you to recommend a location within Russia to build a new plant. List the resources and services needed for the factory. Then use your text, the Internet, or other sources to select one or two ideal areas for the plant. Write your recommendations in a letter to the president of the company.

GeoJournal

Descriptive Writing Using the information you logged in your GeoJournal as you read this chapter, write a descriptive paragraph about one of Russia's unique or beautiful physical features. Describe the feature in detail, using your textbook and the Internet as resources to make your descriptions as specific and vivid as possible.

Technology Activity

Using E-mail Locate an e-mail address for a youth organization in Russia. Write a letter requesting information about the land and climate in the youths' area and the effects on their lifestyle. Share the response you receive with your class.

Standardized Test Practice

Using the table below and your knowledge of geography, choose the best answer for the following multiple-choice question. If you have trouble answering the question, use the process of elimination to narrow your choices.

Arable Land in Selected Countries				
	Russia	Canada	United States	France
arable land	8%	5%	19%	33%
permanent crops	0%	0%	0%	2%
permanent pastures	4%	3%	25%	20%
forests and woodland	46%	54%	30%	27%
other	42%	38%	26%	18%

Source: CIA World Factbook 2000

1. What factor may help explain why Russia and Canada have a lower percentage of arable land than do the United States and France?

A Russia and Canada have been settled longer.

B Russia and Canada extend farther into cold northern regions.

C Russia and Canada have larger land masses.

D Russia and Canada are less industrialized.

 **Test-Taking Tip** Study the information shown in the table about land use. Then think about climate regions in the selected countries. Notice similarities or differences between figures for the four countries. Choice C is not relevant, so it can be eliminated.

Problem-Solving Activity

Student groups should consider the factory's shipping and supply needs and check maps to locate ports and rail lines which are open year-round. Check students' letters for standard grammar, spelling, sentence structure, punctuation, and accurate information.

GeoJournal

Students should explain why they chose to write about their location and describe its important features. Check paragraphs for clear topic sentences and good descriptive details.

Technology Activity

Students' letters should explain the purpose of their inquiries and offer information about their own location.

Standardized Test Practice
1. B

Tested Objectives: analyzing information

Additional Practice and Test-Taking Tips
Standardized Test Practice Workbook

CHAPTER BONUS TEST QUESTION

Due to the large amount of coal deposits, what precious gem is also a natural resource of Russia? *(diamond)*

Using the Regional Atlas

1. Mountains, frigid temperatures, and distance from navigable rivers or seaports create transportation challenges.
2. coal

Thinking Like a Geographer

Because of the country's high latitude location, most of Russia's coastal ports are frozen for much of the year. Air transportation might provide the best potential for development, because it is not limited by surface features.

359

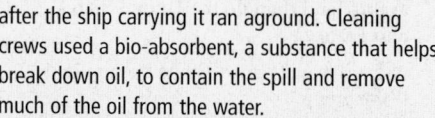
Geography Lab Activity

① FOCUS

Invite students to share their recollections of news reports about major oil spills. **Ask: Why do oil spills make news?** *(They can cause environmental damage and are difficult and costly to clean up.)* Invite students to speculate on whether the incidence of oil spills will increase or decrease in the future.

② TEACH

L2 Science Connections

Ask students to apply what they know about physical science (the properties of oil and water) and biology (the effects of oil on natural environments and wildlife) to a discussion of the challenges caused by oil spills. If possible, have students review relevant portions of their science texts.

③ ASSESS

Have students answer the **Lab Report** questions on page 361.

Cleaning Up Oil Spills

▲ *Approximately 30 tons (27,216 kg) of oil spilled into the Neva River in October 1999.*

Petroleum and water are both natural resources. However, when they mix, they pose a grave danger to the environment. In 1999 a massive oil spill on the Neva River in northwest Russia threatened to poison the water supply of St. Petersburg and damage the Gulf of Finland downstream. Russian officials immediately dispatched vessels equipped with floating barriers to contain the oil after the ship carrying it ran aground. Cleaning crews used a bio-absorbent, a substance that helps break down oil, to contain the spill and remove much of the oil from the water.

When oil mixes with water, a number of chemical changes may take place. Depending on the movement and temperature of the water and the presence of wind and sunlight, the oil may change its shape, density, and chemical composition. Cleanup crews have a limited number of tools to use against an oil spill. Pumps and sponges may suck up oil if it is not too heavy after mixing with water. Skimmers that look like conveyor belts draw oil off the water's surface. Oil-eating microbes and strong detergents are also used to dissolve oil.

① ▶ Materials

- Large, shallow, rectangular pan about 11 inches (28 cm) long
- Water
- 1 tablespoon vegetable or cooking oil
- String or dental floss, at least 36 inches (91 cm) long
- Ruler
- Timer
- Drinking straw
- 2 paper towels or several cotton balls
- 1 or 2 drops of dishwashing detergent
- Measuring cup
- Writing materials

② ▶ Procedures

In this activity, you will simulate an oil spill in order to observe how oil reacts in water. You also will experiment with two cleanup strategies.

1. Fill the pan about halfway with water, and set the pan on a level surface.

2. Gently pour the vegetable oil into the center of the water.

3. Use the string or dental floss to measure the size (the circumference) of the "oil slick." Record your measurement.

4. Wait 2 to $2\frac{1}{2}$ minutes, and then measure the oil spill again. Record your measurements.

5. Repeat step 4 three more times, until you have five measurements.

GEOGRAPHY IN THE REAL WORLD

Monitoring Oil Spills Observers from the United Nations and from environmental organizations use satellite imaging and GIS to monitor and track the cleanup of oil spills. While ocean spills from tankers are often dramatic, inland spills from pipelines can be even more difficult to control. A 1994 break in a Russian pipeline near Usink, in the Arctic, for example, released 25 million gallons—more than twice the amount of the 1989 *Exxon Valdez* spill. Because the frigid temperatures (−40°F) made traditional cleanup equipment unusable, workers burned the oil, releasing harmful gases into the atmosphere. Alerted to the spill by monitors, professional cleanup firms offered their services to the Russian government.

🌐 **EE6 The Uses of Geography: Standard 18**

6. Use the straw to blow gently across the surface of the water. Blow steadily for about 20 to 30 seconds. Record your observations.

7. Gently shake or vibrate the pan to create a wavelike motion. Do this for about 30 seconds to 1 minute. Record your observations.

8. Set a paper towel or cotton ball on the surface of the water in the pan until it is completely soaked, but do not let it sink.

9. Remove the paper towel or cotton ball, and repeat this step with a fresh paper towel or cotton ball. Record your observations.

10. Now mix the drops of dishwashing detergent into 4 ounces of water. Pour the mixture gently into the middle of the pan. Record your observations.

 **Lab Report**

1. Which of the steps was most time-consuming? Why?

2. What did measuring the oil slick demonstrate about the way oil behaves in water?

3. What did blowing on and shaking the water demonstrate about the way oil behaves in rivers, lakes, and oceans?

4. **Drawing Conclusions** Based on your observations, what oil cleanup strategy would you recommend for future oil spills? Why?

 **Find Out More**

Look in reference books or check Internet sources for more information about strategies for cleaning up oil spills. Take notes on the different strategies, including the way they work and how successful they are. Make a poster or multimedia presentation of the different strategies and their success rates, and then share your findings with the class.

Did You Know? Magnets may prove to be an effective tool against the effect of oil spills on wild birds. When oil coats birds' feathers, the birds lose their natural protection against the elements, and they cannot fly. Scientists have discovered that coating bird feathers with an iron powder and then applying magnets removed nearly all the oil in test cases.

 Water movement and air flow can affect the shape and density of an oil spill.

 **CLOSE**

Have students complete the **Find Out More** activity and summarize their findings.

FYI

Healthier Alternatives The amount of oil that tankers spill into the ocean each year is about 2.5 billion pounds (1.1 billion kg). Normal ship operations can be as damaging as accidental spills. For example, scientists are working to find alternatives to the regular discharge of oily seawater that ships carry in their holds for stabilization.

Meeting National Standards

Geography for Life
The following standards are met in the Student Edition:

EE6 The Uses of Geography: Standard 18

ANSWERS TO LAB REPORT

1. Possible answer: steps 3–5, measuring the oil spill, will be most time-consuming.

2. The oil spreads on the surface of the water.

3. Oil molecules are dispersed on the surface by wind and water motion, but not dissolved.

4. Students should be able to provide reasons to support their choices.

PLANNING GUIDE

NOTE: The following materials may be used when teaching Chapter 15. Section-level support materials are shown at point-of-use in the margins of the Teacher Wraparound Edition.

TEACHING TRANSPARENCIES

L2 Unit 5 Map Overlay Transparencies

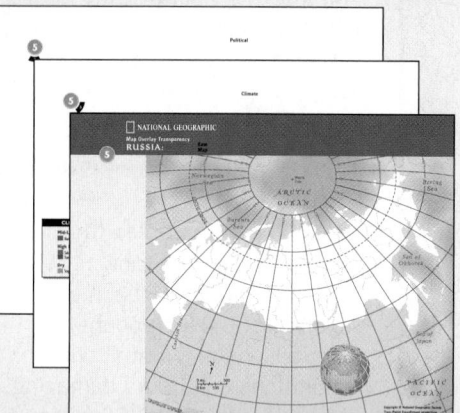

L2 Political Map Transparency 5

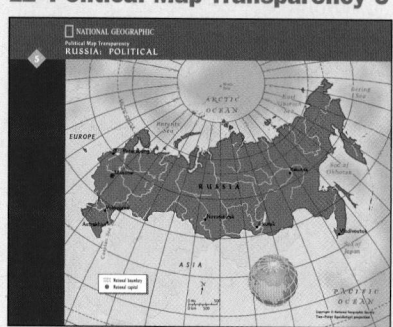

GEOGRAPHIC LITERACY

Focus on Geography Literacy

APPLICATION AND ENRICHMENT

L3 Enrichment Activity 15

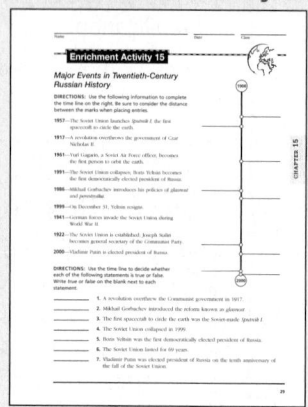

REVIEW AND REINFORCEMENT

L1 Vocabulary Activity 15 L1 Reinforcing L1 Reteaching Activity 15
Skills Activity 15

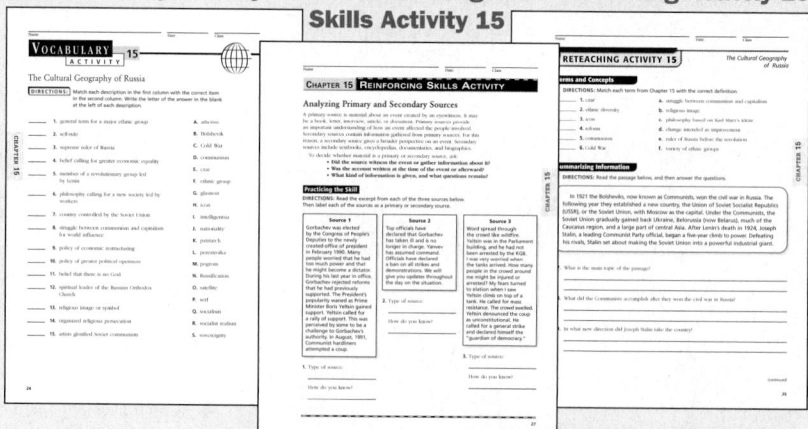

ASSESSMENT

L2 Chapter 15 Test Form A

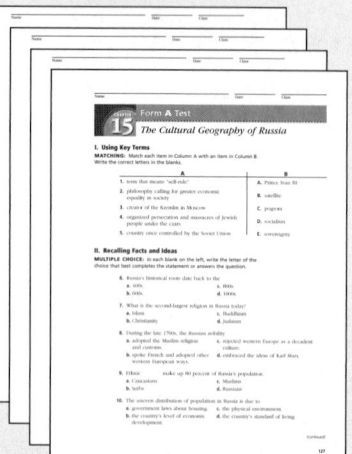

L2 Chapter 15 Test Form B

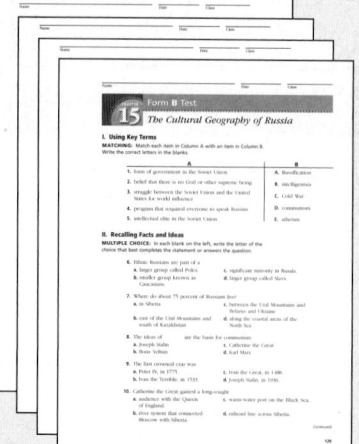

L1/ELL Performance Assessment Activity 15

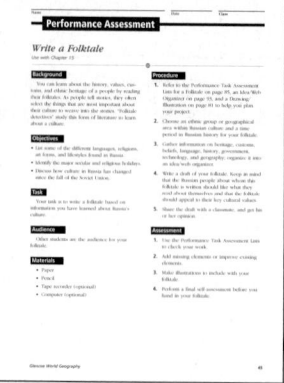

ExamView® Pro Testmaker

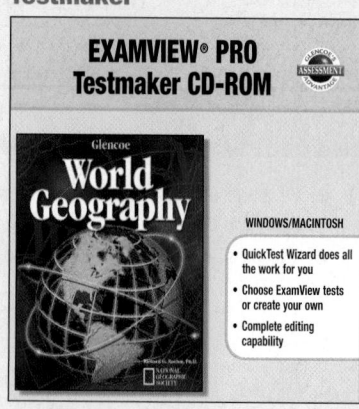

The following Spanish language materials are available in the Spanish Resources binder:

- 📁 Spanish Vocabulary Activities
- 📁 Spanish Guided Reading Activities
- 📁 Spanish Reteaching Activities
- 📁 Spanish Summaries
- 📁 Spanish Quizzes and Tests
- 📁 Spanish Reading Essentials and Study Guide

- 📼 World Regions Video
- 📼 MindJogger Videoquiz
- 💿 Vocabulary PuzzleMaker CD-ROM
- 💿 Interactive Tutor Self-Assessment CD-ROM
- 💿 ExamView® Pro Testmaker CD-ROM
- 💿 Audio Program
- 💿 TeacherWorks CD-ROM
- 💿 Interactive Student Edition CD-ROM
- 💿 Glencoe Skillbuilder Interactive Workbook CD-ROM, Level 2
- 💿 Presentation Plus! CD-ROM

Timesaving Tools

TeacherWorks™ **All-In-One Planner and Resource Center**

- **Interactive Teacher Edition** Access your Teacher Wraparound Edition and your classroom resources with a few easy clicks.

- **Interactive Lesson Planner** Planning has never been easier! Organize your week, month, semester, or year with all the lesson helps you need to make teaching creative, timely, and relevant.

Use Glencoe's **Presentation Plus!** multimedia teacher tool to easily present dynamic lessons that visually excite your students. Using Microsoft PowerPoint® you can customize the presentations to create your own personalized lessons.

GEOGRAPHY Online

Use our Web site for additional resources. All essential content is covered in the Student Edition.

You and your students can visit geography.glencoe.com, the Web site companion to *Glencoe World Geography*. This innovative integration of electronic and print media offers your students a wealth of opportunities. The student text directs students to the Web site for the following options:

- Chapter Overviews
- Self-Check Quizzes
- Student Activities
- Textbook Updates

Answers are provided for you in the "Web Activity Lesson Plan." Additional Web resources and Interactive Tutor puzzles are also available.

▶ **Additional Glencoe Teacher Support**

- Teaching Strategies for the Geography Classroom (including Block Scheduling Pacing Guides)

- Graphic Organizer Transparencies Strategies and Activities

- Outline Map Resource Book

- Reading in the Content Area

PLANNING GUIDE

SECTION RESOURCES

Daily Objectives	Reproducible Resources	Multimedia Resources

SECTION 1   Population Patterns

1. Identify the ethnic groups that make up Russia.
2. Explain the distribution of population in this country.
3. Describe the effect of climate on the culture and lifestyle of Russians.

 Reproducible Lesson Plan 15-1
 Daily Lecture Notes 15-1
 Guided Reading Activity 15-1*
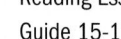 Reading Essentials and Study Guide 15-1*
Section Quiz 15-1*

Daily Focus Skills Transparency 15-1
Political Map Transparency 5
Unit 5 Map Overlay Transparencies
Interactive Tutor Self-Assessment CD-ROM
ExamView® Pro Testmaker CD-ROM*
Presentation Plus! CD-ROM

SECTION 2   History and Government

1. Describe the ancestry of the Russian people.
2. Explain the government rule of the czars and its effect on Russian society.
3. Identify the causes of the breakup of the Soviet Union.
4. List present and future challenges that Russia faces.

 Reproducible Lesson Plan 15-2
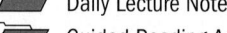 Daily Lecture Notes 15-2
 Guided Reading Activity 15-2*
Reading Essentials and Study Guide 15-2*
 Section Quiz 15-2*

Daily Focus Skills Transparency 15-2
Political Map Transparency 5
Unit 5 Map Overlay Transparencies
World Art Prints
Interactive Tutor Self-Assessment CD-ROM
ExamView® Pro Testmaker CD-ROM*
Presentation Plus! CD-ROM

SECTION 3   Cultures and Lifestyles

1. Describe the role of religion in Russian society.
2. Identify contemporary challenges for education and health care in Russia.
3. Describe the cultural heritage found in Russia's art, literature, and music.

 Reproducible Lesson Plan 15-3
 Vocabulary Activity 15*
 Daily Lecture Notes 15-3
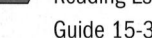 Guided Reading Activity 15-3*
Reading Essentials and Study Guide 15-3*
 Reteaching Activity 15*
 Reinforcing Skills Activity 15
 Section Quiz 15-3*

Daily Focus Skills Transparency 15-3
Unit 5 Map Overlay Transparencies
World Music: A Cultural Legacy
Vocabulary PuzzleMaker CD-ROM
Interactive Tutor Self-Assessment CD-ROM
ExamView® Pro Testmaker CD-ROM*
Presentation Plus! CD-ROM

 Blackline Master
 Transparency

Software
 CD-ROM

Videocassette
DVD

Also available in Spanish

 **OUT OF TIME?** Assign the Chapter 15 **Reading Essentials and Study Guide.**

 **Block Schedule**

Activities that are particularly suited to use within the block scheduling framework are identified throughout this chapter by the following designation:

KEY TO ABILITY LEVELS

Teaching strategies have been coded for various learning styles and abilities.

L1   **BASIC** activities for all students

L2   **AVERAGE** activities for average to above-average students

L3   **CHALLENGING** activities for above-average students

ELL   **ENGLISH LANGUAGE LEARNER** activities

Chapter Objectives

1. Describe Russia's population, including its makeup, density, and distribution.

2. Identify key developments in the history and government of Russia.

3. Discuss the role of religion, education, health care, and the arts in the cultural life of the region.

GLENCOE TECHNOLOGY

Use *MindJogger Videoquiz* to preview the Chapter 15 content.

GeoJournal

For access to additional photos, maps, and information on the cultural features of Russia go to www.nationalgeographic.com (See Teacher pages in front for strategies for using journals in the geography classroom.)

GEOGRAPHY Online

Introduce students to chapter content and key terms by having them access **Chapter Overview 15** at geography.glencoe.com

FOLDABLES™
Study Organizer

Dinah Zike's Foldables are three-dimensional, interactive graphic organizers that help students practice basic writing skills, review key vocabulary terms, and identify main ideas. Have students complete the Foldable activity in the *Dinah Zike's Reading and Study Skills Foldables* booklet.

CHAPTER 15

The Cultural Geography of Russia

GeoJournal

Create two columns in your journal. Label the first column "Questions" and the second "New Knowledge." First, list questions you have about Russian history and culture. Then, as you read this chapter, record the answers.

GEOGRAPHY Online

Chapter Overview Visit the **Glencoe World Geography** Web site at geography.glencoe.com and click on Chapter Overviews—Chapter 15 to preview information about the cultural geography of the region.

ABOUT THE PHOTO

Visual Instruction Lake Baikal's waters are cold, even in summer, but the lake begins to freeze in its shallow bays in late October. By midwinter a layer of ice about 3 to 4 feet (about 1 m) thick covers the entire lake. In summer the Lake Baikal area beckons other outdoor enthusiasts who hike along its shores, engage in whitewater sports, climb nearby mountains, and photograph the area's abundant wildlife, including the world's only freshwater seals. **Ask:** What winter sports might people enjoy on Lake Baikal? *(ice-skating, ice fishing)* 🌐 **EE2 Places and Regions: Standard 4;** 🌐 **EE3 Physical Systems: Standard 7**

Population Patterns

Guide to Reading

Consider What You Know
Throughout much of its history, Russia has been a land of many different peoples. The United States also has a diverse population. What do you think are the benefits and challenges of living in a country that has people of many different backgrounds?

Reading Strategy
Organizing Complete a web diagram similar to the one below by filling in the major ethnic groups in Russia.

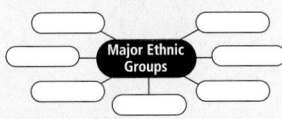

Read to Find Out
• What ethnic groups make up Russia's population?

• Why is Russia's population unevenly distributed?

• How does the climate east of the Ural Mountains affect the population distribution in this region?

Terms to Know
• ethnic group
• nationality
• sovereignty

Places to Locate
• Ural Mountains
• Moscow

 NATIONAL GEOGRAPHIC

A Geographic View

Russian Heartland

I have come back to Mother Russia, the old heartland from which had sprung the Russian Empire and its successor, the Union of Soviet Socialist Republics. . . . A modern land in many ways, yet profoundly tied to the past. . . . There is [today] a new quest for the much trampled Russian culture, for the "soul" that writers lauded for its breadth and warmth. The old love of the gentle landscape that 'spreads out evenly across half the world,' as [the writer] Nikolay Gogol saw it in [his novel] **Dead Souls,** *blooms anew—in the form of anger over polluted rivers and smoky vistas.*

Historic church in Moscow

—Mike Edwards, "Mother Russia on a New Course," National Geographic, February 1991

Over the centuries Russia's borders moved beyond Moscow to include vast territories inhabited by people of different ethnic backgrounds. Today, the citizens of Russia are not one people, but many. Each of the diverse groups within the country has its own cultural traditions, history, and language. In this section you will learn about the various culture groups of Russia—from the Arctic peoples in the north to the peoples of the Caucasus region in the south.

Russia's Ethnic Diversity

Russia has one of the widest varieties of ethnic groups in the world—in fact, more than a hundred! An ethnic group shares a common ancestry, language, religion, or set of customs, or a combination of these things. Despite Russia's ethnic diversity, more than 80 percent of the population are ethnic Russians, people who follow Russian customs and speak Russian as their first language. The percentage of

Children playing on ice, Lake Baikal

Chapter 15 🌐 363

FOCUS

Section Overview
This section discusses the ethnic diversity of Russia and the connection between physical geography and population distribution.

BELLRINGER
Skillbuilder Activity

Project transparency and have students answer questions.

Available as blackline master.

Daily Focus Skills Transparency 15-1

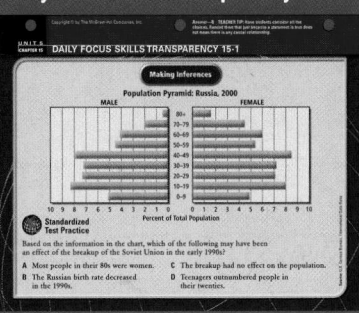

Guide to Reading

Consider What You Know
Answer *Benefits include richness of culture—foods, festivals, and so on. Challenges include helping people feel a sense of national unity, overcoming conflicts.*

Reading Strategy
Answers *Caucasian, Finnic, Mongolian, Ossetian, Russian, Turkic, Ukrainian*

Preteaching Vocabulary
Have students identify the root words *nation* and *sovereign* in the terms *nationality* and *sovereignty*. Ask students to define these roots and then predict the meaning of the terms based on their roots.

RESOURCE MANAGER

Reproducible Masters
• Reproducible Lesson Plan 15-1
• Daily Lecture Notes 15-1
• Guided Reading Activity 15-1
• Reading Essentials and Study Guide 15-1
• Section Quiz 15-1

Transparencies
• Daily Focus Skills Transparency 15-1
• Political Map Transparency 5
• Unit 5 Map Overlay Transparencies

Multimedia
• Interactive Tutor Self-Assessment CD-ROM
• ExamView® Pro Testmaker CD-ROM
• Presentation Plus! CD-ROM

② TEACH

L2 Region

Tell students that Russia is divided into many administrative units. Have students do research to identify those units and the factors involved in forming them.

NATIONAL GEOGRAPHIC — MAP STUDY

Answers

1. *near Urals and Barents Sea; near Lake Baikal*

2. *Regional boundaries often reflected the locations of ethnic groups.*

Map Skills Practice

Place Which ethnic group predominates in European Russia? *(Russian)*

Daily Lecture Notes 15-1

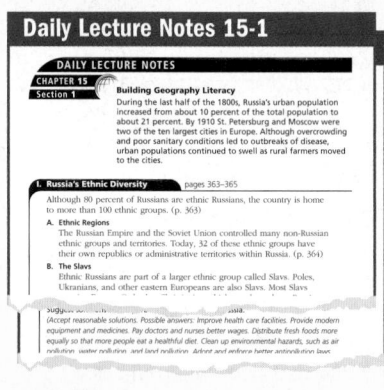

L1/ELL

Guided Reading Activity 15-1

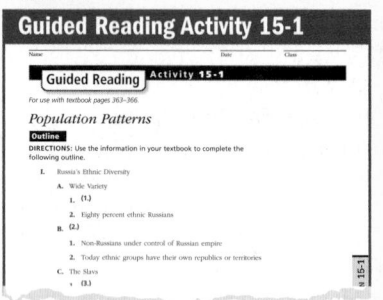

NATIONAL GEOGRAPHIC — MAP STUDY

Major Ethnic Groups of Russia

Major Ethnic Groups of Russia
- Russian
- Turkic
- Ukrainian
- Finnic
- Caucasian
- Ossetian
- Mongolian
- Uninhabited or sparsely populated

Geography Skills for Life

1. **Interpreting Maps** Where in Russia do most Finnic peoples live? Mongolians?

2. **Applying Geography Skills** How have the settlement patterns of ethnic groups affected regional boundaries in Russia?

Find NGS online map resources @ www.nationalgeographic.com/maps

---

the population that is not ethnic Russian usually became part of Russia's population as a result of conquest. This fact has made it difficult for some groups to consider themselves truly Russian.

Culture
Ethnic Regions

Over the centuries Russia grew from a small territory to a gigantic empire that stretched from the plains of Europe to the waters of the Pacific Ocean. In the process, many non-Russian ethnic groups came under its control. In some cases ethnic groups were concentrated in a single area. During the Soviet era, regional political boundaries often reflected the locations of major ethnic groups, or **nationalities**. In

1991, after the Soviet breakup, several of these larger republics, including Russia, became independent countries. Today 32 ethnic groups have their own republics or administrative territories within Russia.

The Slavs

Ethnic Russians are a part of a larger ethnic group known as Slavs, a family that also includes Poles, Serbs, Ukrainians, and other eastern Europeans.

Throughout Russia's history the Russian Slavs have dominated the country's politics and culture. Most Slavs practice Eastern Orthodoxy, a form of Christianity brought to Russia from the eastern Mediterranean area. Russian national identity has long been tied to the Slav, or ethnic Russian, culture.

364 ✦ Unit 5

DIFFERENTIATED INSTRUCTION

Reading Support For students who have trouble with reasoning, point out the logical structure of subsections within the text. Remind students that they can use visual cues such as the size and color of headlines to determine whether they are reading a main section or a subsection. Have students locate the topic sentences of each new paragraph in the section and restate them in their own words. Remind students that these topic sentences are like arrows directing readers to the most important information in a paragraph.

☞ Refer to *Inclusion for the Social Studies Classroom Strategies and Activities.*

Although more than 100 languages are spoken in Russia today, Russian is the country's official language. Ethnic Russians generally speak only this language, while people belonging to other ethnic groups speak both their own languages and Russian.

Turkic Peoples

Russia's second-largest family of ethnic groups, the Turkic peoples, live in the Caucasus area, in Siberia, and in the middle Volga area. Although Turkic peoples are mainly Muslims, their ethnicity is based primarily on language.

The Turkic peoples of Russia include the Tatars, Chuvash, Bashkirs, and Sakha. The most numerous of these groups are the Tatars, about one-third of whom live in Tatarstan (TA•tuhr•STAN) in east-central Russia. The Tatar population there, however, is growing rapidly, as this observer reveals:

> " *Tatars make up 48 percent of Tatarstan's 3.7 million population. Russians are 43 percent. The ratio is close, but the Russians are worried.... [T]he Tatar birthrate is 40 percent higher than the Russian, and efforts to revive Tatar ways ... will surely erode Russian influence.* "
>
> Mike Edwards, "Russia: Playing by New Rules," *National Geographic*, March 1993

Russia has ruled Tatarstan since the mid-1500s. In 1994, however, the Russian government granted Tatarstan a limited amount of sovereignty (SAH•vuh•ruhn•tee), or self-rule. The government hopes that this arrangement will dampen any desire the people of Tatarstan may have to separate from Russia.

Caucasian Peoples

Another large group of diverse peoples is classified as Caucasian (kaw•KAY•zhuhn) because they live in the Caucasus region of southeastern Russia. Mainly Muslims, the Caucasian peoples have similar languages and cultures, but local dialects often make communication among them difficult. Caucasian groups such as the Chechens, Dagestanis, and Ingushetians today are demanding independence or at least local self-rule.

Population Density and Distribution

Russia is the sixth most populous country in the world, after China, India, the United States, Indonesia, and Brazil. Russia does not, however, have a large population relative to its land area.

Population and the Environment

With a population of about 145.5 million people and an area of about 6.6 million square miles (about 17.1 million sq. km), Russia's average population density is about 22 people per square mile (9 per sq. km). Compare this figure with that of the United States, where an average of 78 people live within a square mile (30 per sq. km), and you can begin to appreciate how sparsely populated parts of Russia are.

Averages alone, however, can be misleading. About 75 percent of all Russians live in the area between the Belarus and Ukraine borders and the **Ural Mountains**, making the population density of European Russia about 120 people per square mile (46 per sq. km). Meanwhile, Russia's largest eastern republic, Sakha, averages less than 1 person per square mile.

NATIONAL GEOGRAPHIC World Explorer

Geography | Skills for Life

Kazan Marketplace Consumers shop at the poultry counter in the marketplace of Kazan, the major economic center of Tatarstan.

Place What is Tatarstan's political relationship with Russia?

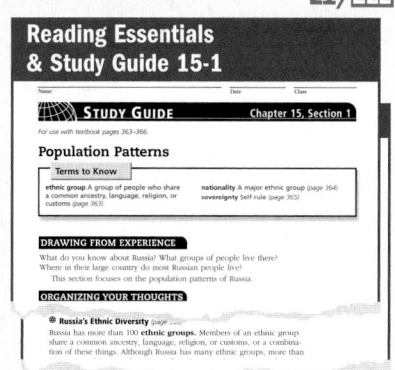

Reading Essentials & Study Guide 15-1

③ ASSESS

Assign Section 1 Assessment as homework or as an in-class activity.

🅘 Have students use **Interactive Tutor Self-Assessment CD-ROM**.

L2

Section Quiz 15-1

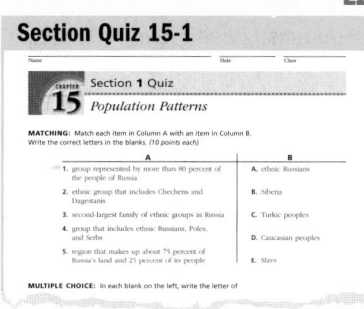

NATIONAL GEOGRAPHIC World Explorer

Answer
Tatarstan has limited self-rule.

More About the Photo The Tatars are descendants of Muslim Turkic peoples.

COOPERATIVE LEARNING ACTIVITY

Population Puzzle Project Political Map Transparency 5 onto a large poster board, and have students refer to the map on page 364 to sketch in the areas covered by each major ethnic group. Cut out the map, and then cut it into puzzle pieces along ethnic boundaries. Have students form seven groups, and give each group a puzzle piece representing an ethnic group. Groups should use encyclopedias and Internet resources to find out about their assigned ethnic population's language, typical dress, foods, and holidays. Have each group decorate its puzzle piece with words and drawings that reflect its ethnic culture. Then have students work together to reassemble and display their enhanced map of Russia. 🗐

🌐 **EE4 Human Systems: Standard 10**

NATIONAL GEOGRAPHIC **World Explorer**

Answer
Russian language, Eastern Orthodox Christianity

More About the Photo The posters and the newspaper the woman is reading are printed in Cyrillic letters, the alphabet used for writing Russian.

Reteach

Ask students to develop one question from each subsection with which to quiz one another.

Enrich

Show students a chart of the Cyrillic alphabet with each letter's Western equivalent, and have them practice writing their names phonetically using Cyrillic letters.

4 CLOSE

Have students reread "A Geographic View" on page 363 and identify the various ethnic and cultural influences mentioned in the passage.

NATIONAL GEOGRAPHIC **World Explorer**

Geography **Skills for Life**

Russian Language A poster in St. Petersburg announces the opening of an opera.

Region What two cultural characteristics give ethnic Russians a sense of identity?

The uneven distribution of Russia's population relates to its physical environment. East of the Ural Mountains, the Siberian climate is harsh. Mountains, frozen tundra, and forests there are unsuitable for farming. Although Siberia makes up about 75 percent of Russia's land area, only 25 percent of Russia's people live there.

By contrast, the more densely settled European Russia includes the region's industrialized cities, many of which are connected by waterways. The major industrial city is **Moscow**, Russia's capital. Other industrial centers include St. Petersburg, Nizhniy Novgorod, Kazan, Perm, Volgograd, and Yekaterinburg. Since 1990, urban population growth in most industrialized centers has leveled off or decreased, particularly in cities with more than 500,000 inhabitants.

Population Trends

During the Soviet era, many ethnic Russians migrated to non-Russian republics of the Soviet Union. In the 1970s this trend began to reverse. Since the breakup of the Soviet Union in 1991, more ethnic Russians have returned to their homeland. Most have settled in Moscow, St. Petersburg, and southwestern Russia. Because of this trend, the number of immigrants to Russia has been greater than the number of Russians leaving the country.

Still, Russia is currently experiencing a population crisis because of a rise in illnesses as the quality and availability of health care have declined. Infant mortality during the early 1990s rose from 17.4 deaths per 1,000 births to 19 per 1,000 births. Since 1992 the number of deaths has exceeded the number of births. In the 1990s, female life expectancy decreased from 74 years to 72 years. Male life expectancy also dropped, from 64 years to 59 years, but it is expected to rise slowly in the 2000s. One of the tasks facing Russia in the years ahead is to improve health care.

SECTION 1 ASSESSMENT

Checking for Understanding

1. **Define** ethnic group, nationality, sovereignty.

2. **Main Ideas** Copy the web below, and use it to fill in current information about Russia's population.

Population Patterns

Ethnic Diversity — Density and Distribution

Critical Thinking

3. **Categorizing Information** What would be the advantages and disadvantages of an ethnic group forming an independent country?

4. **Making Generalizations** How might improved health care help solve Russia's current population crisis?

5. **Predicting Consequences** What are some likely effects of changes in Russia's population in the future?

Analyzing Maps

6. **Human-Environment Interaction** Study the map of Russia's ethnic groups on page 364. Explain the pattern of settlement east of the Ural Mountains.

Applying Geography

7. **Migration** Consider past population trends in Russia. What might have drawn immigrants to settle in an area like Moscow?

SECTION 1 ASSESSMENT ANSWERS

1. All vocabulary terms are defined in the text.

2. Web details should reflect text information.

3. Advantages may include self-rule, sense of national identity, ethnic pride; disadvantages may include lack of the social services provided by a large central government, limited access to natural resources and economic activities.

4. Improved health care will improve life expectancy, decrease infant mortality, and help increase the population.

5. increased crowding, pollution, and strained resources in urban areas; decreasing quality of life, health care, life expectancy

6. Population is widespread, sparse, ethnically isolated, and limited to areas (mainly lands conquered by Russia) where climate and physical geography are favorable or where natural resources are located.

7. **Applying Geography** Moscow's favorable location on waterways and between forests and plains; its role as the traditional center of Russian political and religious life

Guide to Reading

Consider What You Know

Events in Russia are often in the news. What recent news events have helped you understand more about Russia's government and its challenges?

Reading Strategy

Sequencing As you read about Russia's history, complete a time line similar to the one below by recording major events in Russia's history.

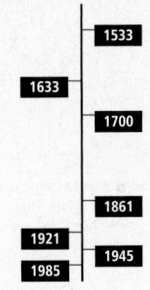

1533
1633
1700
1861
1921
1945
1985

Read to Find Out

- Who were the ancestors of the ethnic Russians?
- Why did the rule of the czars end in revolution?
- What were the causes of the Soviet Union's collapse?
- Why does Russia face an uncertain future?

Terms to Know

- czar
- serf
- Russification
- socialism
- Bolshevik
- communism
- satellite
- Cold War
- perestroika
- glasnost

Places to Locate

- Baltic Sea
- Black Sea
- St. Petersburg

History and Government

NATIONAL GEOGRAPHIC

A Geographic View

End of an Era

The Bolshevik dream finally ended with Mikhail Gorbachev's program of glasnost, or openness, which allowed citizens to speak freely for the first time in decades. All the carefully constructed "truths" began to unravel, and there was no turning back. Gorbachev's era passed. Russia's President, Boris Yeltsin, outlawed the Communist Party by signing a few pieces of paper. The Bolsheviks surrendered without a shot.

—Dusko Doder, "The Bolshevik Revolution," National Geographic, October 1992

Mikhail Gorbachev

Mikhail Gorbachev saw firsthand both the costs and benefits of political change, even changes that come with democratic reforms. As the last Soviet leader, Gorbachev tried to reform the Soviet system, but his efforts failed to prevent its collapse. The history of Russia, once the dominant republic of the Soviet Union, is a story of the rise and fall of great empires. Monarchs, Communist Party officials, and democratic politicians—as well as foreign invaders—have all shaped Russia's national character.

Early Peoples and States

Russia's historical roots go back to the A.D. 600s, when Slav farmers, hunters, and fishers settled near the waterways of the North European Plain. Over time, the Slavs separated into distinct cultural groups. The West Slavs eventually became the Poles, Czechs,

---

FOCUS

Section Overview

This section discusses the major turning points in Russia's tumultuous history and outlines Russia's changes in government over the centuries.

BELLRINGER
Skillbuilder Activity

- Project transparency and have students answer questions.
- Available as blackline master.

Daily Focus Skills Transparency 15-2

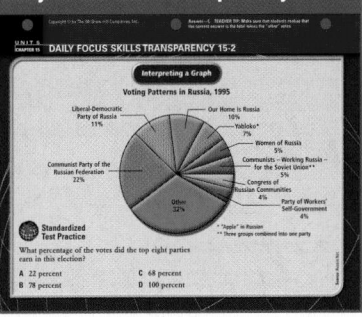

Guide to Reading

Consider What You Know
Answer *Possible events include elections, international diplomacy, pollution, war or internal strife, economic developments.*

Reading Strategy
Answer Students' time lines should include significant events from each year.

Preteaching Vocabulary
Share with students the meanings of the following Russian terms:
- *czar*—Caesar
- *Bolshevik*—greater party
- *perestroika*—restructuring
- *glasnost*—public voice

RESOURCE MANAGER

📁 Reproducible Masters
- Reproducible Lesson Plan 15-2
- Daily Lecture Notes 15-2
- Guided Reading Activity 15-2
- Reading Essentials and Study Guide 15-2
- Section Quiz 15-2

🖨 Transparencies
- Daily Focus Skills Transparency 15-2
- Political Map Transparency 5
- Unit 5 Map Overlay Transparencies

Multimedia
- 📖 World Art Prints
- 💿 Interactive Tutor Self-Assessment CD-ROM
- 💿 ExamView® Pro Testmaker CD-ROM
- 💿 Presentation Plus! CD-ROM

2 TEACH

NATIONAL GEOGRAPHIC — MAP STUDY

Answers

1. *1689–1917; 1689–1917*

2. *to consolidate power in the region, gain resources, provide defensive buffers against other powers*

L1 Sequence

Have a few students list on the board historical events from this section in random order. Ask the class to number the items in the order in which they happened.

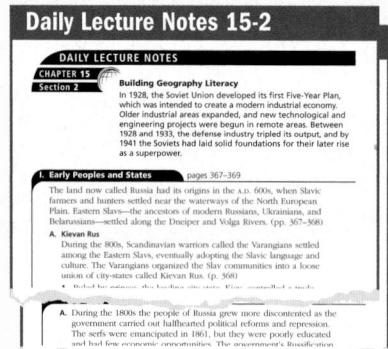

Daily Lecture Notes 15-2

Guided Reading Activity 15-2

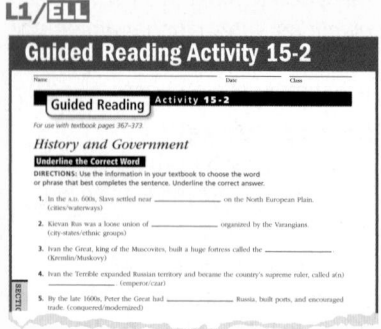

NATIONAL GEOGRAPHIC — MAP STUDY

Russia's Changing Borders, 1462–Present

Russian and Soviet Expansion
- 1462–1505 — Kievan Rus
- 1505–1689 — Muscovy of Ivan III, 1462
- 1689–1917 — Boundary of Soviet Union in 1945
- 1917–1945 — Present boundaries

Two-Point Equidistant projection

Geography Skills for Life

1. **Interpreting Maps** In what time period did Russia gain control of St. Petersburg? Omsk?

2. **Applying Geography Skills** What geographical factors influenced Russian leaders to expand their empire's boundaries?

Find NGS online map resources @ www.nationalgeographic.com/maps

---

and Slovaks. The South Slavs became the Bulgarians, Croats, Serbs, and Slovenes. The East Slavs became the Russians, Ukrainians, and Belarusians. These East Slav peoples remained settled along the Dnieper (NEE•puhr) River in the west and the Volga River in the east.

Kievan Rus

During the 800s Scandinavian warriors called the Varangians settled among the Slavs living near the Dnieper and Volga Rivers. Within a century the Varangians had adopted the Slav language and many Slav customs and had organized the Slav communities into a loose union of city-states known as Kievan Rus. Ruled by princes, the leading city-state, Kiev, controlled a prosperous trading route, using Russia's western rivers as a link between the **Baltic Sea** and the **Black Sea**.

Eventually, fighting among the city-states weakened Kievan Rus. Then, in the early 1200s, Mongol invaders from Central Asia conquered Kiev and many of the Slav territories. Although the Mongols allowed the Slavs self-rule, they continued to control the area for more than 200 years. During this period the Slav territories still remained in contact with western and central Europe. However, they

---

DIFFERENTIATED INSTRUCTION

English Learners Help English language learners distinguish among similar terms with different meanings, such as *capital* (the governmental center of a country) and *capitalist* (a market economic system), as well as the difference between *territory* as land and *territory* as an official administrative region. Conversely, have students watch for groups of synonyms—different words with the same meaning—such as *reign* and *rule*. Finally, ask students to use context clues to discern shades of difference among similar concepts such as *reform*, *revolution*, and *overthrow*. **ELL**

📁 Refer to *Inclusion for the Social Studies Classroom Strategies and Activities.*

followed their own distinctive cultural path based on the traditions of Eastern Orthodoxy.

The Rise of Russia

When the Mongols first overran Kiev, many Slavs fled into nearby forests, and some of them later settled along the Moskva River to the northeast. In time one of their settlements grew into the city of Moscow, which became the center of a territory called Muscovy (muh•SKOH•vee). Muscovy was linked by rivers to major trade routes and surrounded by lands good for farming and trapping fur-bearing animals.

For about two centuries, Muscovy's princes kept peace with the Mongols. Their territory grew in power as the princes helped the Mongols collect taxes from other Slav territories. By the late 1400s, however, the Muscovites became strong enough to refuse payments to the Mongols and to drive them out. Following this triumph, Muscovy's Prince Ivan III brought many Slav territories under his control, thus earning the title "the Great." Ivan's expanded realm eventually became known as Russia. In the heart of Moscow, Ivan built a huge fortress, called the Kremlin, and filled it with churches and palaces.

In 1533 Ivan the Great's grandson, Ivan IV, became Russia's first crowned czar (ZAHR), or supreme ruler. Called Ivan the Terrible, Ivan IV crushed all opposition to his power and expanded his realm's borders.

After Ivan's reign, however, the country faced foreign invasion, economic decline, and social upheaval. When the Romanov dynasty came to power in 1613, the government gradually tightened its grip on the people. By 1650 many peasants had become serfs, a virtually enslaved workforce bound to the land and under the control of nobility.

Romanov Czars

While Russia struggled through chaos and harsh rule, western Europe moved forward and left Russia behind, especially in the areas of science and technology. Then in the late 1600s, Czar Peter I—known as Peter the Great—came to power determined to modernize Russia. Under him, Russia enlarged its territory, built a strong military, and developed trade with Europe. To acquire seaports, Peter gained land along the Baltic Sea from Sweden. He also strengthened Russia's control of Siberia.

A new capital—**St. Petersburg**—was carved out of the wilderness. Built along the Gulf of Finland, St. Petersburg provided access to the Baltic Sea and gave Russia a "window to the West." Since most of Russia's other ports were icebound for almost half the year, St. Petersburg became a major port.

During the late 1700s, Empress Catherine the Great continued to expand Russia's empire and gained a long-sought-after warm-water port on the Black Sea. By that time the Russian nobility had adopted western European ways—for example, using French instead of Russian as their primary language. As a result, a cultural gap developed between the nobility and Russia's serfs, who followed traditional Russian ways. Meanwhile, poverty and heavy work fell even more harshly on the serfs. Russia's great expansion also brought

NATIONAL GEOGRAPHIC World Explorer

Geography **Skills for Life**

The Catherine Palace Along with other palaces, the summer residence of Catherine the Great is located outside of St. Petersburg.
Region How did Catherine the Great expand Russia's empire?

Slavs were often captured and forced into labor by other central European groups. The name for this practice—*slavery*—came from the name of this ethnic group, used by speakers of Middle English, Medieval Latin, and Late Greek.

L1/ELL

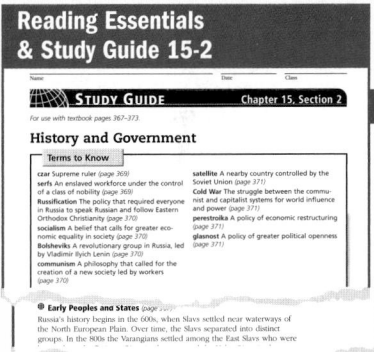

Reading Essentials & Study Guide 15-2

NATIONAL GEOGRAPHIC World Explorer

Answer
She gained a warm-water port on the Black Sea.

More About the Photo
Onion domes have a special advantage in the Russian climate; they do not allow snow to build up on roofs.

COOPERATIVE LEARNING ACTIVITY

Make a Time Line Have students work together to make an illustrated time line of the history of communism in Russia. Students may work in pairs or in small groups to complete the following tasks: (1) Use the textbook and other references to research the Russian communist period and identify about 20 of the most significant events. (2) Plot the key events on a large time line, illustrated with drawings or copies of old magazine photos. (3) Locate the key geographic focus of each event on a large map of Russia, identifying each location with a numbered sticker. 🧊 ⬛ **EE4 Human Systems: Standard 13**
⬛ **EE6 The Uses of Geography: Standard 17**

Arts of Russia

One of Fabergé's most remarkable works was a tiny gold model of a Trans-Siberian Express train that operated by clockwork. The passenger cars had crystal windows, and the engineer's lamp was a ruby. The entire train was enclosed in a gold egg engraved with a map of the railroad, the world's longest.

World Art Prints

Use these prints with accompanying strategies and activities to introduce students to other arts of the region.

Easter Eggs Fabergé's practice of hiding surprises inside his jeweled eggs gave a name to hidden graphics or bonus applications built into software by computer programmers. These surprises are known as *Easter eggs*.

the arts of RUSSIA

Fabergé Eggs Russian goldsmith and jeweler Peter Carl Fabergé created imaginative jeweled and enameled Easter eggs for the czars of Russia and other royalty in Europe and Asia. The eggs were often created to mark important events, such as coronations and marriages. Each egg was unique and contained a tiny surprise inside.

under its rule many non-Russians, including Poles, Ukrainians, Estonians, Baltic Germans, Jews, and Tatars in Crimea near the Black Sea.

The Russian Revolution

The 1800s saw a long cycle of popular discontent, half-hearted political reforms, and governmental repression. Inspired by the American and French Revolutions, educated Russians wanted to make Russian society more open. The government, however, held on tightly to power, and reforms were limited. Czar Alexander II freed the serfs in 1861, but they had no education and few ways to earn a living. Industrialization drew some peasants from the country to the cities, where they worked long hours in poor conditions for meager wages.

At the same time, non-Russian peoples were facing prejudice and hostility. Spurred by increasing nationalism, the government introduced the policy of Russification, which required everyone to speak Russian and follow Eastern Orthodox Christianity. People who refused were often persecuted. Harsh treatment was directed especially toward Jews, who were often blamed for Russia's problems.

Frustrated and discontented, many Russian thinkers and workers were attracted to socialism, a belief that calls for greater economic equality in society. Some Russians especially liked the socialist ideas of German philosopher Karl Marx. Marx advocated public ownership of all land and a classless society with an equal sharing of wealth. He claimed that continual struggle between the wealthy and working classes would lead to a worldwide revolution. This revolution, he thought, would be led by workers and end the power of the wealthy.

In the early 1900s, discontent with the iron rule of the czars spilled into the streets. Strikes and demonstrations in 1905 nearly ended the reign of Czar Nicholas II. One event, called Bloody Sunday, began with a peaceful crowd of workers desiring better working conditions and personal freedoms marching toward the czar's palace in St. Petersburg. The march ended abruptly when soldiers fired into the marchers, killing nearly 1,000 people.

Twelve years later, in 1917, the hardships of World War I brought even larger numbers of workers into the streets of the capital. With soldiers joining them, the workers demanded "bread and freedom." Finally, Nicholas II was forced to give up his throne, ending the rule of the czars in Russia.

The Soviet Era

The Russian Revolution of March 1917 established a representative government, but it was too weak to control the passion for change that had swept Russia. In November of that year, the Bolsheviks, a revolutionary group led by Vladimir Ilyich Lenin, seized control. The victorious Bolsheviks believed in communism, a philosophy based on Karl Marx's ideas that called for the violent overthrow of government and the creation of a new society led by workers.

Promising the Russian people "Peace, Land, and Bread!" the Bolsheviks withdrew Russia from World War I, surrendering much territory to Germany. They used their complete hold on political power to take over industry, direct food distribution, establish an eight-hour workday, and reform the army.

Not all Russians supported the Bolsheviks. To maintain power, the Bolsheviks dealt harshly with their opponents. A civil war soon divided the country, pitting the Bolshevik Red Army against the anti-Bolshevik White Army.

CRITICAL THINKING ACTIVITY

Drawing Conclusions In the late 1850s, 1,000 noble families owned about 175,000,000 acres (70,000,000 ha) of Russia's land. Serfs labored on that land and shared their crops with feudal lords. Unrest smoldered. In 1861 Czar Alexander II freed the serfs in order to forestall a peasant revolt. However, serfs only gained title to their homesteads; fields became the property of villages. Most serfs could not afford to "redeem" the land from the villages. After a revolt in 1905, the government tried to implement private ownership, but the action was "too little, too late." **Ask:** How might land ownership issues in Russia have set the stage for the overthrow of the czars? *(The majority of the people were desperate and had little to lose.)* ▦ EE2 Places and Regions: Standard 4; ▦ EE4 Human Systems: Standard 13

History

The Soviet Union

In 1921 the Bolsheviks, now known as Communists, won the civil war. The following year they established a new country, the Union of Soviet Socialist Republics (USSR), or the Soviet Union, with Moscow as the capital. Under the Communists the Soviet Union gradually gained back Ukraine, Belorussia (now Belarus), much of the Caucasus region, and a large part of Central Asia.

After Lenin's death in 1924, Joseph Stalin, a leading Communist Party official, began a five-year climb to power. Defeating his rivals, Stalin set about making the Soviet Union into a powerful industrial giant by ruthlessly taking control of farms and factories. Millions either were killed or died as a result of hunger, physical hardships, or the brutal conditions in labor camps. Stalin also eliminated from the party and the military those people who might threaten his power.

A Superpower

During World War II, the growth of industry—and the fierce Russian winter—helped the Russians push out the invading Germans, but at great cost. More than 27 million Russian soldiers and civilians died as a result of the war. At the war's end in 1945, the Soviet Union controlled much of eastern Europe. By 1949 most of the countries in the region had become Soviet satellites, countries controlled by the Soviet Union. These satellite states, notably East Germany, Hungary, Poland, and Czechoslovakia, strengthened the Soviet Union's military and supplied critically needed raw materials, such as coal and iron ore, as well as manufactured goods.

For the next four decades, the Soviet Union and the United States were engaged in the Cold War, the struggle between the two competing systems—communist and capitalist—for world influence and power. Since each country

had destructive nuclear weapons, outright conflict was avoided. Instead, the two countries used as "weapons" propaganda, the threat of force, and economic aid to developing countries.

The Soviet Breakup

During the Cold War, the Soviet economy weakened while many other economies grew. Soviet workers struggled with economic hardships, yet their leaders enjoyed great privileges. By the 1980s it was clear that communism was failing.

In 1985 Mikhail Gorbachev, a reform-minded official, assumed power in the Soviet Union. Gorbachev was keenly aware of the abuses of the past—Joseph Stalin had imprisoned both his grandfathers. Although Gorbachev remained a dedicated communist, he began a policy of economic restructuring called perestroika (PEHR•uh•STROY•kuh) and a policy of greater political openness called glasnost (GLAZ•nohst). Gorbachev's reforms, however, failed to save the Soviet Union.

Poland, Hungary, Czechoslovakia, and other communist countries overthrew their communist rulers in 1989. Meanwhile, nationalist fervor was rising in

NATIONAL GEOGRAPHIC **World Explorer**

Geography **Skills for Life**

Lenin's Plan Lenin and the Bolsheviks promised to build an economy in which each citizen shared equally in the wealth.

Place What conditions led many people to identify with the promises of Lenin?

INTERDISCIPLINARY
connection

SCIENCE Under Nikita Khrushchev, Soviet leader from 1958 to 1964, the Soviet Union invested heavily in space exploration. The first spacecraft to orbit the earth was the Soviet satellite Sputnik-1, launched in 1957. Soviet Air Force Colonel Yuri Gagarin became the first human to orbit the earth in 1961. These advances spurred competition from the United States and kicked off the so-called space race. Today U.S. and Russian teams work together on the International Space Station.

NATIONAL GEOGRAPHIC **World Explorer**

Answer
poverty, hunger, labor disputes, class differences, effects of World War I

More About the Photo After Lenin died in 1924, his body was preserved and put on display in a special tomb in Moscow's Red Square. With the end of communism in Russia, visitor attendance at Lenin's tomb has sharply declined, and the tomb's special honor guard has been removed. Plans to close the monument and bury Lenin's body in his family's plot in St. Petersburg have been proposed.

TEAM-TEACHING ACTIVITY: HISTORY & GOVERNMENT

The Cold War Have small groups of students work with an American history teacher to prepare simulated U.S. news broadcasts from the Cold War era. Student groups should research and include information on different United States–Russia interactions such as the arms race, the space race, and the Cuban missile crisis. Students might use a newscast formula or role-play interviews with noted Cold War figures from both countries.
🌐 EE6 The Uses of Geography: Standard 17

NATIONAL GEOGRAPHIC World Explorer

Answer
He called for economic restructuring (perestroika) and greater political openness (glasnost).

More About the Photo
It became known as Red Square in 1650, from the Russian word *Krasnaya*, meaning both "beautiful" and "red."

L2 Debate
Invite volunteers to come up with arguments that Catherine the Great, Joseph Stalin, and Mikhail Gorbachev might present to defend their forms of government. Have the volunteers present their arguments in the form of a debate. In conclusion, have the class consider how these arguments compare or contrast with those used to support a democratic system.

③ ASSESS

Assign Section 2 Assessment as homework or as an in-class activity.

⊙ Have students use **Interactive Tutor Self-Assessment CD-ROM**.

L2

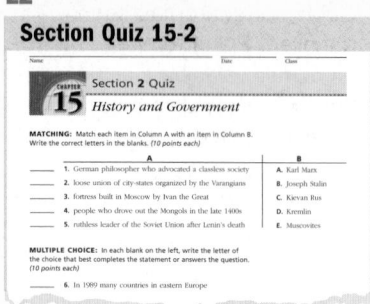

Section Quiz 15-2

NATIONAL GEOGRAPHIC World Explorer

Geography | **Skills for Life**

Red Square, Moscow A retired Russian colonel confronts an anti-communist demonstrator in the early 1990s.
Place How did Gorbachev seek to reform the Soviet system?

the non-Russian Soviet republics. The Baltic states of Latvia, Lithuania, and Estonia were the first Soviet republics to declare independence.

Then in 1991 loyal Communists tried to overthrow Gorbachev and preserve the Soviet Union. Boris Yeltsin, who had recently become the first democratically elected president of the Russian republic, rallied the people of Moscow to defy the plotters. A reporter described how Yeltsin's cause was helped by financier Konstantin Borovoy:

> ❝*On the first day..., few Russians knew that Yeltsin was resisting.... [Yeltsin] sent faxes to Borovoy's office.... Brokers copied them and spread leaflets.... Citizens...threw up barricades as tanks took positions.... 'The [secret police] came to arrest the Xerox machines,' Borovoy said, 'but we had already taken them to a safer place.'...*❞
> Mike Edwards, "Russia: Playing by New Rules," *National Geographic*, March 1993

The coup collapsed, and Gorbachev remained the leader of the Soviet Union. By year's end, however, all the remaining Soviet republics had declared independence. Boris Yeltsin remained president of Russia, the largest of the former Soviet republics. Russia, Belarus, and Ukraine formed the Commonwealth of Independent States (CIS) in 1991, and they eventually were joined by other former republics. On December 25, 1991, Gorbachev's presidency ended, and the Soviet Union ceased to exist.

A New Russia
Boris Yeltsin assumed the leadership of a devastated Russia. The economy was in shambles, and ethnic conflicts threatened the Caucasus region.

EXTENDING THE CONTENT

Chechnya The terrain of the Russian republic of Chechnya is ideally suited to guerrilla warfare. Located in the northern Caucasus, Chechnya is a rugged land of steep cliffs and gorges. Fighting is most intense during the spring and summer months, when the thickly wooded hillsides offer cover. Even Chechnya's urban areas have become dangerous wastelands after years of bombing. In Grozny, the republic's capital, few buildings are undamaged, and many abandoned ruins shelter rebel bands at night. Russian forces, unused to the rough terrain, are vulnerable to the guerrilla attacks. Since the renewal of fighting in 1999, about 10–30 Russians a week have been killed. 🌐 **EE4 Human Systems: Standard 13**

A Market Economy

On the economic front, Russia began moving from a command economy to a market economy. This transition caused massive unemployment as outdated and inefficient factories were closed and agriculture was restructured. By 2000, however, the Russian economy began to improve. The rate of inflation, at an unbelievable high of 1,500 percent in 1992, fell below 20 percent by 1997. In addition, Russia's currency, the ruble, which had been sharply losing value on international markets, began to stabilize.

Separatist Movements

After the fall of the Soviet Union, separatist movements and ethnic conflict threatened Russia's stability. Beginning in the 1990s, Tatarstan, Dagestan, Chechnya, and other Russian ethnic territories demanded greater self-rule or sought a complete break from Moscow. Although some conflicts have been settled by compromise, often violence or full-scale war has erupted. The bloody war between the Russian government and separatist forces in Chechnya is a tragic example. In 1991 the Chechens declared their independence. Fearing Russia's breakup if other groups did the same, Boris Yeltsin sent Russian troops into Chechnya in 1994. Under Yeltsin's successor, Vladimir Putin, Russia claimed to control much of the territory. Chechen resistance,

▲ Apartment building damaged during the Chechen conflict

however, continued in rural areas. By 2001 about 335,000 people had been displaced by the conflict, and Chechens faced severe food shortages.

The years of warfare have ravaged Chechnya's civilian population and the area's oil-based economy. The conflict has also drained economic-development funds from the rest of Russia.

SECTION ② ASSESSMENT

Checking for Understanding

1. Define czar, serf, Russification, socialism, Bolshevik, communism, satellite, Cold War, perestroika, glasnost.

2. Main Ideas List the key events in Russia or in the Soviet Union during each of the following time periods: Kievan Rus, Russian Empire, Soviet Union, and Russia.

Era	Dates and Key Events
Kievan Rus	

Critical Thinking

3. Making Inferences Why do you think Russians have almost always had a centralized government? What problems do you think the government had as Russia grew?

4. Comparing and Contrasting How was the government during czarist rule and the Soviet era similar? Different?

5. Predicting Consequences How might Russia be affected if separatist groups gain independence?

Analyzing Maps

6. Human-Environment Interaction Look at the map of Russia's changing borders on page 368. What geographic factors encouraged Russian expansion?

Applying Geography

7. Geography and History Think about ways that physical geography influenced the Russian people's history and culture. Write an essay explaining the impact of geography on one of Russia's ethnic groups.

1. All vocabulary terms are defined in the text.

2. Tables should reflect text information.

3. A centralized government can unite diverse ethnic groups over a wide area. As Russia grew, the government faced the problem of meeting diverse needs, distributing resources fairly, and maintaining the loyalty of ethnic groups and conquered peoples.

4. similarities: centralized, sometimes totalitarian, expansionist; differences: rule by monarchy/aristocracy (czarist) versus rule by party (Soviet), rigid class

distinctions (czarist) versus no class distinctions (Soviet), state religion (czarist) versus no religion (Soviet)

5. Russia would lose access to natural resources, territory, and prestige, and would be a less diverse society.

6. few physical obstacles (Urals are low, do not provide defense or obstacle to expansion), low population density in eastern regions

7. Applying Geography Essays should reflect text information.

① FOCUS

Have students look at the political map of Russia on page 339 of the Regional Atlas. Tell them that they are to plan a rail route that connects Moscow in the west with Vladivostok in the east. Have them trace potential routes on the map with their fingers. **Ask: What physical obstacles would you encounter?** *(mountains, rivers, Lake Baikal)* **What climatic obstacles would you expect to face in building the railroad?** *(severely cold temperatures, wind, permafrost or swampy ground in Siberia)* Tell students to keep their speculations in mind as they read this feature.

② TEACH

Writing Tell students that they are journalists working at the time the Trans-Siberian Railroad project was initiated. Organize the class into small groups. Have half the groups work on writing newspaper editorials in favor of the project, listing its advantages for the country. Have the other half of the groups work on writing editorials opposed to the project, citing anticipated costs or proposing alternate means of connecting the east and west. Allow time for groups to post their editorials or read them aloud.

GEOGRAPHY AND HISTORY

RUSSIA'S IRON ROAD

EASTWARD HO? Opening the Russian frontier meant traveling east—far east. But Conestoga wagons could not have crossed the frozen lands of Siberia. Encompassing more than half of Russia's total area, Siberia dwarfs the American West and ranks as one of Earth's coldest climates. Only the Trans-Siberian Railroad could accomplish Russia's eastward expansion.

Czar Alexander III approved plans for the railroad that would link the European and Asian parts of the Russian Empire and bring eastern lands under Russia's control. Construction of the world's longest railroad began in 1891. The builders hoped to connect Moscow to the port city of Vladivostok, on the Sea of Japan, by 1900. The distance between the cities is nearly 6,000 miles (9,650 km).

Get Me to Vladivostok on Time

Huge construction problems loomed from the start. Siberia's severe climate and rugged topography slowed progress. By the expected end date of 1900, two unfinished segments remained. The first was the section around Lake Baikal, the world's deepest freshwater lake. To lay track around the lake's southern tip, bridges spanning hundreds of gorges and 33 tunnels through

A train bound for Vladivostok rumbles over Trans-Siberian tracks. More passengers and freight move by train than by any other form of transportation in Russia. ▶

BACKGROUND INFORMATION

A New Role for the Iron Road Just as the future of the Trans-Siberian Railroad seems jeopardized by Russia's internal economic and political challenges, a new lease on life may come from outside Russia. Both South Korea and Japan have indicated strong interest in linking rail lines with the Trans-Siberian Railroad, which would result in a new trade connection between the Far East and Europe. One Korean official called this new link the Iron Silk Road, referring to the medieval caravan route between Asia and Europe. Japan's rail link would require the construction of the world's longest undersea tunnel, connecting the Japanese island of Kyushu with the Korean peninsula. Such a tunnel would cost approximately $77 billion. 🌐 **EE4 Human Systems: Standard 11**

◄ Workers built more than 200 bridges to span rivers and gorges along the railway's route.

rock would have to be built. Farther east, the Shilka and Amur Rivers presented similar challenges.

As a temporary solution, an icebreaking steam ferry about the size of a football field carried rail cars and up to 800 passengers at a time across Lake Baikal. Farther down the line, passengers and freight were loaded onto riverboats—ice sledges in winter—for the 1,400-mile (2,250-km) trip along the rivers whose banks had yet to be conquered by rail.

Eager to complete an east-west railway, Russia negotiated an alternate route through Chinese-controlled Manchuria that bypassed the Shilka and Amur Rivers. Completion of this shortcut, along with the Lake Baikal segment in 1904, made travel by rail between Moscow and Vladivostok possible for the first time. Twelve years later, the original route within Russia was completed.

A Driving Force

The railroad opened Russia's interior to homesteaders and developers who exploited Siberia's vast store of raw materials—including coal, timber, and gold. During World War II, rail cars carried supplies to the front and moved hundreds of factories from western sites in the Soviet Union to safer sites east of the Ural Mountains.

Since the 1950s much of the line has been electrified. From start to finish, passengers can make the trip in slightly less than a week across seven time zones.

Looking Ahead

Today the Trans-Siberian Railroad shows signs of wear. With Russia's political turmoil and shaky economy, passenger and freight traffic have steadily declined. Worker morale is low. Will the railroad withstand Russia's upheavals? If the railroad falls apart, how might that affect Russia's future?

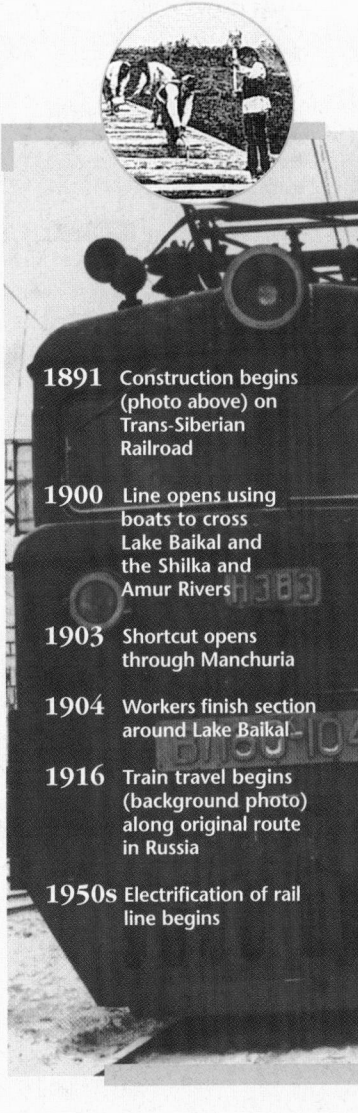

1891 Construction begins (photo above) on Trans-Siberian Railroad

1900 Line opens using boats to cross Lake Baikal and the Shilka and Amur Rivers

1903 Shortcut opens through Manchuria

1904 Workers finish section around Lake Baikal

1916 Train travel begins (background photo) along original route in Russia

1950s Electrification of rail line begins

FYI

Vulnerability In January 2001 citizens in the Siberian town of Razdolnoye attempted to halt rail traffic on the Trans-Siberian Railroad to protest government cuts in heating and electricity during one of the region's coldest winters, when temperatures reached –122°F (–50°C).

---

③ ASSESS

Have students answer the **Looking Ahead** questions on page 375.

④ CLOSE

Share with students parts of Paul Theroux's book *The Great Railway Bazaar: By Rail Across Asia* (Penguin, 1995) that deal with the writer's travels on the Trans-Siberian Railroad. **Ask: Would you like to take this same journey? Why?**

🌐 Meeting National Standards

Geography for Life
The following standards are met in the Student Edition:

EE5 Environment and Society: Standard 14

EE6 The Uses of Geography: Standard 18

ANSWERS TO LOOKING AHEAD

Some students may argue that the Trans-Siberian Railroad plays such a significant role in Russia's economic life that the government must take steps to assure its survival. Others may be more pessimistic, noting the enormous costs of maintaining the rail structure across so many miles and in such difficult climates, the low worker morale, and the railroad's vulnerability to attack by separatists. If the railroad does not survive, the consequences for Russia may include severe difficulties in transporting resources (with equally serious economic consequences) and loss of a main unifying force across the country's huge territory. One positive consequence of the railroad's demise might be efforts to upgrade Russia's internal air transport capabilities, although heavy cargoes will still require ground travel of some kind.

FOCUS

Section Overview

This section discusses how religion, education, health care, and the arts influence the lives of Russia's peoples.

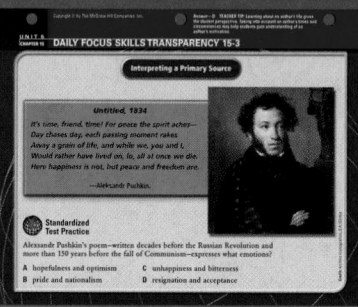
Guide to Reading

Consider What You Know

Answers *Have students brainstorm a list of impressions. Popular book/film choices may include Dr. Zhivago, Anna Karenina, Reds, and Anastasia.*

Reading Strategy

Answers *Christianity: recent resurgence of Russian Orthodox Church, reemergence of Roman Catholics and Protestants in the 1980s; Islam: second largest religion in Russia, highly concentrated in southern Russia and Caucasus region; Judaism: after years of persecution, religious practices and schools are slowly being restored; Buddhism: nearly half a million people, concentrated in two ethnic republics, are Buddhists*

Preteaching Vocabulary

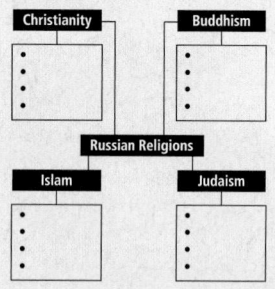 Use the **Vocabulary Puzzle-Maker CD-ROM** to create cross-word and word-search puzzles.

Guide to Reading

Consider What You Know

Think of books or movies about Russia that you may have read or seen. What images of life in Russia stand out in your mind?

Reading Strategy

Categorizing As you read about the cultures of Russia, complete a graphic organizer similar to the one below by filling in information about religions in Russia.

```
Christianity          Buddhism
  •                     •
  •                     •
  •                     •

      Russian Religions

Islam                 Judaism
  •                     •
  •                     •
  •                     •
```

Read to Find Out

• How has the role of religion changed in post-Soviet Russia?

• How are education and health care in Russia adjusting to the fall of communism?

• What role do art, music, and literature have in Russia's cultural heritage?

Terms to Know

• atheism
• patriarch
• icon
• pogrom
• intelligentsia
• socialist realism

Places to Locate

• Caspian Sea
• Lake Baikal

Cultures and Lifestyles

NATIONAL GEOGRAPHIC

A Geographic View

A Cultural Center

. . . [T]oday's Russian aristocracy of entrepreneurs and artists . . . [feel] nostalgia for a Russia long gone—an age of glittering accomplishment when St. Petersburg reigned as a world center of music, ballet, and literature. . . . Reflecting that legacy, the city counts some 30 theaters devoted to the performing arts. . . . Under communist rule, the arts . . . were lavishly subsidized. The Bolsheviks may have made Moscow the political capital of the Soviet Union, but St. Petersburg remained its cultural rival—a position Petersburgers are resolved to maintain.

—Steve Raymer, "St. Petersburg: Capital of the Tsars," National Geographic, *December 1993*

A Russian family reciting poems

Russia's adjustment to a new government and economic system has had a profound effect on all Russians. As they move into a new era, Russia's people are also looking for a cultural renewal. Now that the Soviet state no longer dictates their personal lives, millions of Russians are rediscovering their faiths and traditions, reeducating themselves, and expressing themselves creatively.

Religion in Russia

The Eastern Orthodox Church had been central to Russian culture for a thousand years before the communist revolution in 1917. After acquiring power, the Soviet government strictly discouraged religious practices. It actively promoted atheism (AY•thee•IH•zuhm), or the belief that there is no God or other supreme being, in schools and other public institutions. In the late 1980s, however, the government began to relax its restrictions on religion.

GRAPH STUDY

Russia: Religions

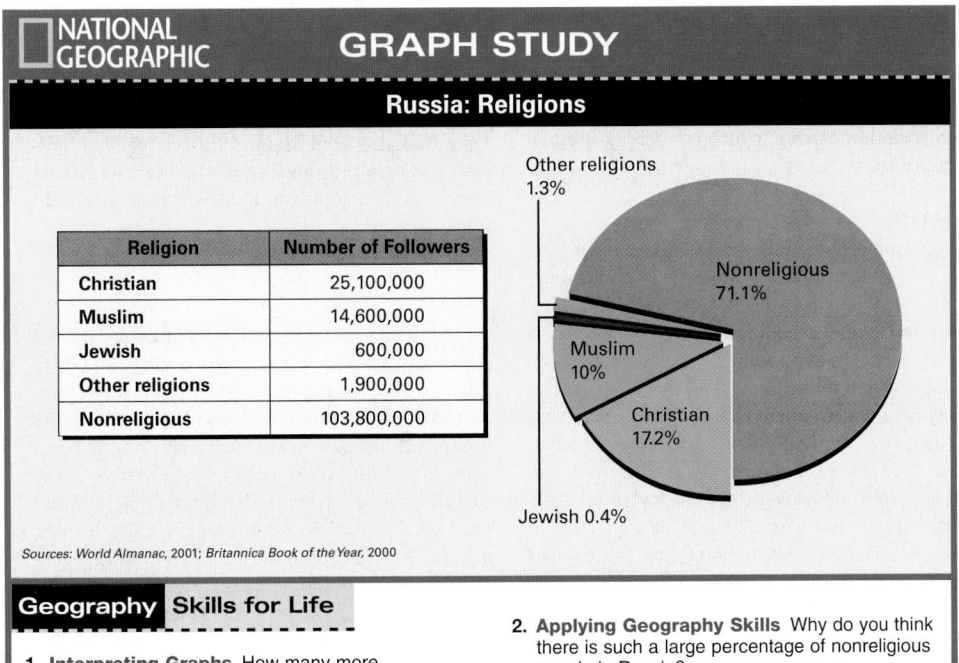

Religion	Number of Followers
Christian	25,100,000
Muslim	14,600,000
Jewish	600,000
Other religions	1,900,000
Nonreligious	103,800,000

Other religions 1.3%
Nonreligious 71.1%
Muslim 10%
Christian 17.2%
Jewish 0.4%

Sources: World Almanac, 2001; Britannica Book of the Year, 2000

Geography Skills for Life

1. **Interpreting Graphs** How many more Christians than Muslims live in Russia?

2. **Applying Geography Skills** Why do you think there is such a large percentage of nonreligious people in Russia?

L1 Charting Information

Have the class develop a chart displaying the following information on Russia's four officially recognized religions: *percentage of population represented, how the religion came to Russia, key points of the religion's history in Russia,* and *contributions of the religion to Russian culture.* Direct students to their textbooks and other reference works for information.

NATIONAL GEOGRAPHIC GRAPH STUDY

Answers

1. *10,500,000*

2. *Religion was discouraged under the Soviets.*

Skills Practice

Region What religions are considered as Russia's traditional faiths? *(Christianity, Islam, Judaism, and Buddhism)*

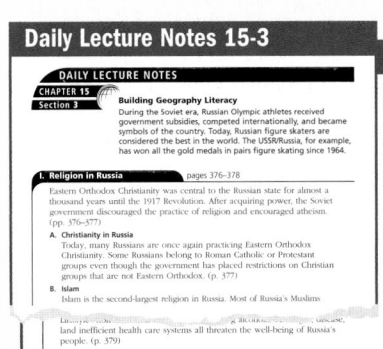

Daily Lecture Notes 15-3

DAILY LECTURE NOTES
CHAPTER 15
Section 3
Building Geography Literacy
During the Soviet era, Russian Olympic athletes received government subsidies, competed internationally, and became symbols of the country. Today, Russian figure skaters are considered the best in the world. The USSR/Russia, for example, has won all the gold medals in pairs figure skating since 1964.

I. Religion in Russia pages 376–378
Eastern Orthodox Christianity was central to the Russian state for almost a thousand years until the 1917 Revolution. After acquiring power, the Soviet government discouraged the practice of religion and encouraged atheism. (pp. 376–377)

A. **Christianity in Russia**
Today, many Russians are once again practicing Eastern Orthodox Christianity. Some Russians belong to Roman Catholic or Protestant groups even though the government has placed restrictions on Christian groups that are not Eastern Orthodox. (p. 377)

B. **Islam**
Islam is the second-largest religion in Russia. Most of Russia's Muslims

land inefficient health care systems all threaten the well-being of Russia's people. (p. 379)

Discussion Question

After the Soviet breakup, many Russians returned to religious practices. However, the influx of many foreign missionaries from Western Christian denominations prompted lawmakers in 1997 to place restrictions on the activities of newly established religious groups. Only Christianity, Islam, Judaism, and Buddhism were allowed full liberty as traditional religions of Russia.

History

Christianity in Russia

In 988 Prince Vladimir, leader of Kievan Rus, adopted Eastern Orthodox Christianity as Russia's official religion. By 1453 the Byzantine Empire, the center of the Eastern Orthodox Church, had fallen, and Russia asserted its claim as leader of the Orthodox Christian world.

During the 1900s the Soviet government weakened Orthodoxy's influence, but today the Russian Orthodox Church is enjoying a resurgence. Most Russians who claim a religious affiliation belong to the Russian branch of the Orthodox Church. The faithful have repaired or rebuilt many of the churches that were looted or destroyed during Soviet times. Like some other Eastern Orthodox churches, the Russian Church has a spiritual leader called a patriarch (PAY•tree•AHRK) and uses icons, or religious images or symbols, in its religious practices.

Despite recent government efforts to restore the dominant position of Eastern Orthodoxy and restrict other denominations, Russia is also home to many other Christian groups, including Roman Catholics and Protestants. Persecuted during the Soviet era along with members of all other religions, these groups have reemerged since the 1980s.

Islam

Islam, the second-largest religion in Russia, is also enjoying a rebirth. Islam is practiced mostly by people living in the southern regions of Russia, particularly in the Caucasus region and in areas north of Kazakhstan. Most Russian Muslims belong

Chapter 15 **377**

DIFFERENTIATED INSTRUCTION

Auditory/Musical Have students find and listen to recordings of the musical chants used in Russia's four official traditional religions: Eastern Orthodox Christianity, Islam, Judaism, and Buddhism. Ask students to listen for similarities and differences among these four kinds of religious music. Point out that all four musical styles developed from non-Western musical roots, and thus contain harmonies and rhythms unfamiliar to European and American listeners. For more information on this topic and specific music selections, consult Glencoe's *World Music: A Cultural Legacy.*

EE4 Human Systems: Standard 10

Refer to *Inclusion for the Social Studies Classroom Strategies and Activities.*

L1/ELL

FYI

English Most Russians under the age of 40 speak some English. Russian schools begin teaching English at the third-grade level. There are more teachers of English in Russia than speakers of Russian in the United States.

NATIONAL GEOGRAPHIC World Explorer

Answer
Soviet emphasis on free, mandatory education

More About the Photo
Although Russia once led the Western world in scientific and technological education, today few Russian schools can afford sophisticated computer equipment.

---

to the Sunni branch of Islam. Sunni Islam is also practiced by people in most Arab countries of Southwest Asia as well as Turkey and Afghanistan. Some citizens of Russia also practice other forms of Islam, including Sufism, which is a deeply spiritual branch of Islam.

Judaism

People practicing Judaism in Russia have long been persecuted. In czarist times Jews could settle only in certain areas and could not own land. They were often the targets of organized persecution and massacres known as **pogroms**. Yet Jewish communities managed to thrive in many of Russia's cities.

Events in the twentieth century took a tragic toll on Russia's Jews. During most of the communist era, Jews experienced discrimination and were discouraged from practicing their religion or celebrating their culture. As a result, many Jews migrated to Israel or the United States, though the process was difficult in some cases. By 1995, however, 700,000 Jews still lived in Russia. Despite lingering prejudice, Jewish communities in Russia are restoring their religious practices and organizing schools.

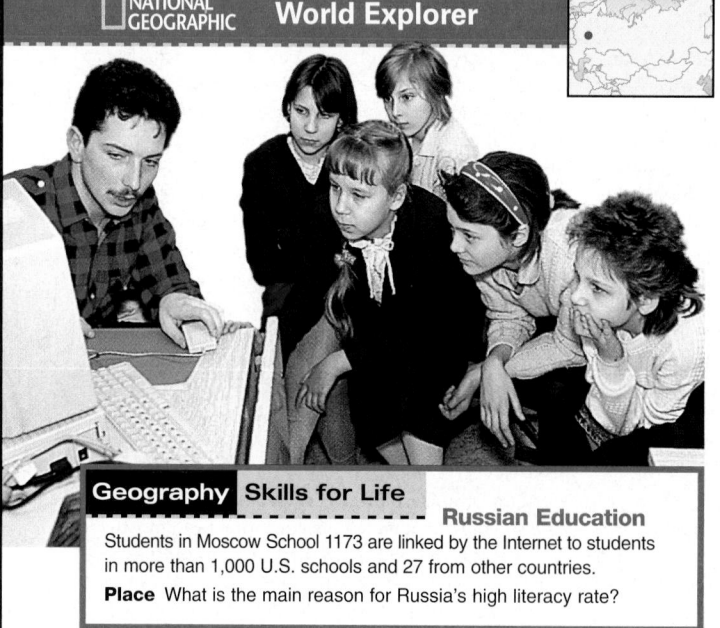

NATIONAL GEOGRAPHIC World Explorer

Geography | **Skills for Life**

Russian Education

Students in Moscow School 1173 are linked by the Internet to students in more than 1,000 U.S. schools and 27 from other countries.

Place What is the main reason for Russia's high literacy rate?

Buddhism

Russia has two ethnic republics that are mainly Buddhist. Kalmykia (kal•MIH•kee•uh), near the **Caspian Sea** in the southwest, and Buryatia, near **Lake Baikal** in south-central Russia, together have nearly half a million Buddhists. For this reason Buddhism is accepted in today's Russia as a traditional religion.

Education

During the 1900s education in Russia showed significant advances. Today the country's literacy rate is nearly 100 percent in most urban areas populated by ethnic Russians. This high rate is largely the result of the Soviet emphasis on free but mandatory education. During the Soviet era, the education system favored military, science, and engineering studies rather than language, history, and literature. This educational focus produced generations of technology-focused government officials. They, along with prominent educators, writers, and artists, made up the Soviet **intelligentsia** (in•TEH• luh•JEHN•see•uh), or intellectual elite.

In contrast, doctors and teachers were among the lowest-paid professionals in Soviet society.

When the Soviet Union collapsed, the curriculum in Russia's schools changed dramatically. Communist teachings disappeared, and schools emphasized a more objective and less authoritarian approach to learning. Today students in Russia have a choice of several different kinds of high schools, including traditional schools, schools specializing in elective studies such as languages, university preparatory schools, and alternative schools with experimental programs.

Unfortunately, Russia's unstable economy has severely limited budgets for schools. Many schools are overcrowded and in disrepair. Frustrated teachers

COOPERATIVE LEARNING ACTIVITY

The Economics of Education Organize students into two groups. One group should research the literacy rate and the amount of federal funding for education in the United States. The other group should research the same information for Russia. Students should use the library, newspapers, and the Internet as sources. Groups should draw conclusions based on the relationships between funding and literacy rates. Each group should create a multimedia presentation to share their research and conclusions with the rest of the class. Each member of the group should be responsible for one part of the presentation—organizing information or creating graphs, for example. **EE2 Places and Regions: Standard 4**

often abandon teaching because of low pay, lack of respect, and low morale. In an unstable economy, many young people focus on earning money rather than getting an education. Still, Russian students and teachers are reexamining Russia's traditions in education and the arts.

Health Care

Disease, lifestyle choices such as smoking tobacco and drinking alcoholic beverages, and inefficient health care systems all threaten the well-being of Russia's people. Russian birthrates fell after World War II because of the massive loss of life in the war. This drop, coupled with an aging population in the 1990s, is shrinking Russia's population, but the trend may be slowing. Male life expectancy in Russia is expected to rise slowly in the 2000s, moving from a low of 59 years in the late 1990s, compared with 74 years in the United States during the same period. However, infertility in Russia is increasing by more than 3 percent a year, and 75 percent of all pregnant women develop serious health problems. Concern about increasing rates of infectious disease, such as tuberculosis, typhoid, and diphtheria, has led some countries to carefully screen Russian immigrants.

Today the Russian health care system is struggling to meet people's needs. Privatization has helped, but the government still owns and manages many clinics and hospitals, and these are often inefficient. Doctors and nurses are giving up their professions because they can earn more money as cab drivers or store clerks. Better insurance funding and wiser health care management are among the many reforms needed to improve health care in Russia.

The Arts

Russians revere their artists, musicians, and writers not only for their creativity but also for their courage in expressing themselves in the face of censorship. Modern Russians are still devoted to their long and rich cultural heritage.

Russia's Artistic Golden Age

Before the late 1600s, Russian architects and artists often found inspiration in religion. They built beautiful churches, crowned with onion-shaped domes and filled with icons of Jesus, Mary, and the saints as well as wall paintings of biblical stories. When Peter the Great introduced western European culture to Russia in the early 1700s, Russian arts began to focus on nonreligious themes. By the early 1800s, Russia had entered an artistic golden age that lasted into the 1900s.

NATIONAL GEOGRAPHIC — CHART STUDY

State of Health

Country	Infant Mortality Rate (per 1000)	Life Expectancy Male	Life Expectancy Female	Rate of Natural Increase
Russia	16.0	59	72	–0.7
Poland	9.2	68	77	0.0
Czech Republic	4.1	71	78	–0.2
Albania	12.0	69	75	1.2
Ukraine	15.0	63	74	–0.7

Source: 2001 World Population Data Sheet

Geography | Skills for Life

1. **Interpreting Charts** Which country has the highest infant mortality rate?
2. **Applying Geography Skills** How are infant mortality rates and life expectancy related to the general state of health in a country?

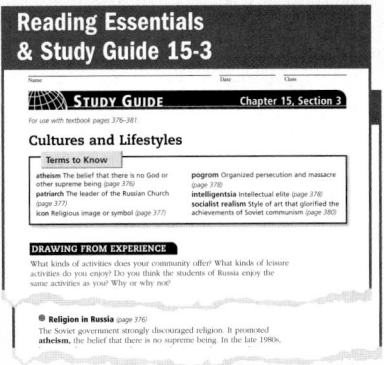

Reading Essentials & Study Guide 15-3

STUDY GUIDE — Chapter 15, Section 3

Cultures and Lifestyles

Terms to Know

atheism The belief that there is no God or other supreme being (page 376)
patriarch The leader of the Russian Church (page 377)
icon Religious image or symbol (page 377)

pogrom Organized persecution and massacre (page 378)
intelligentsia Intellectual elite (page 378)
socialist realism Style of art that glorified the achievements of Soviet communism (page 380)

DRAWING FROM EXPERIENCE
What kinds of activities does your community offer? What kinds of leisure activities do you enjoy? Do you think the students of Russia enjoy the same activities as you? Why or why not?

● **Religion in Russia** (page 376)
The Soviet government strongly discouraged religion. It promoted **atheism**, the belief that there is no supreme being. In the late 1980s,

Greetings When Russians ask *Kak dela?* ("How are you?"), it is not just a formality. Russians expect a detailed reply, and it is considered rude to ask unless you are ready to listen.

NATIONAL GEOGRAPHIC — CHART STUDY

Answers
1. *Russia*
2. *Where access to health care is limited and general health is poor, infant mortality rates go up and life expectancies go down.*

Skills Practice
Region What kind of population growth rate does Russia have? *(negative)* Why? *(Poor health care and rising rates of infertility mean death rates exceed birthrates.)*

CRITICAL THINKING ACTIVITY

Cultural Convergence Have students form groups, each researching an aspect of Russian daily life that has been influenced by American culture, such as fashion, fast-food restaurants, music and film, and sports activities. Have a volunteer from each group present its findings to the class. Have students evaluate in what ways Russian and American cultures have come together, and in what ways they remain different.

🌐 **EE4 Human Systems: Standard 10**

Music Notes
Although the balalaika is traditionally Russian, international groups encourage and support the use of these folk instruments. One group, The Balalaika and Dorma Association of America, has members from the United States and Canada, Europe, Russia, Ukraine, Belarus, Japan, and Australia.

World Music: A Cultural Legacy
Use the accompanying Teacher Guide for background information, discussion questions, and worksheets about the music of this region.

Objectives, goals, and answers to the student activity can be found in the Web Activity Lesson Plan feature at geography.glencoe.com

③ ASSESS

Assign Section 3 Assessment as homework or as an in-class activity.

⊙ Have students use **Interactive Tutor Self-Assessment CD-ROM** to review Section 3.

music of RUSSIA

Traditional Russian music includes many styles, from the rich folk traditions of the steppes to religious choral music performed in richly decorated urban churches. In the former Soviet Union, music and art were government-controlled, but individual artistic expression is very much alive today.

Instrument Spotlight
The **balalaika** appeared in Russia during the 1600s and was based on a two-string Tatar instrument from the 1200s. The instrument is crafted of pine in a rounded or triangular shape, and it has three strings, which are strummed or plucked. Balalaikas are often played in folk groups along with accordions, guitars, zithers, and percussion instruments. Today there is a wide range of balalaikas in different sizes, ranging from soprano to bass.

Go To World Music: A Cultural Legacy Hear music of this region on Disc 1, Tracks 20–23.

Russian painters such as Ilya Repin, Wassily Kandinksy, and Marc Chagall contributed to the wealth of Russian art. Composers Pyotr (Peter) Tchaikovsky, Nikolay Rimsky-Korsakov, and Modest Mussorgsky revolutionized Russian classical music and created memorable ballets. Many of their compositions used themes from Russian folk music. Today the Bolshoi and Kirov ballet companies are world famous for their stunning performances of traditional Russian ballet.

Russian literature owes a great debt to poets such as Alexander Pushkin, Boris Pasternak, and Anna Akhmatova, who wrote eloquently about their private lives and about historical events.

Student Web Activity Visit the **Glencoe World Geography** Web site at geography.glencoe.com and click on Student Web Activities—Chapter 15 for an activity on nineteenth-century Russian painters.

Novelists of the 1800s, such as Leo Tolstoy and Fyodor Dostoyevsky, became known for epic works filled with vivid characters caught up in the struggle between good and evil or between love and hate. These two literary giants also focused on social and political injustices of life under the czars. Tolstoy's *War and Peace* and Dostoyevsky's *Crime and Punishment* still captivate readers today.

Government
Culture and the Soviets

After 1917 the Soviet government severely limited individual artistic expression. It believed that all artists had the duty to glorify the achievements of Soviet communism in their works. This approach to art was called socialist realism. Writers, painters, and other artists who did not follow government guidelines were severely punished. The writer Alexander Solzhenitsyn, for example, was banished to a succession of labor camps and finally expelled from the country. He described the horrors of the labor camps in his famous work, *The Gulag Archipelago*.

TEAM-TEACHING ACTIVITY: ART

Russian Art Have students work with an art teacher to research examples of the work of Russia's painters, sculptors, architects, and craftspersons. Ask students to look for connections between Russian artworks and the region's physical geography, history, religion, and ethnic diversity. **Ask:** What do these artworks tell you about how the artists experienced the region? What insights about Russia can you gain from looking at Russian art?
⊕ EE2 Places and Regions: Standard 6

Post-Soviet Arts

Beginning in the mid-1980s, activity in the arts renewed, as loosening government controls allowed the printing of previously unpublished works and new materials. During the height of Soviet repression, some of these works had been smuggled from Russia and printed in other countries. In 1989, a journalist from the United States noted the frenzy of cultural activity that came with the dawn of freedom:

> ❝ On [Moscow's] Arbat pedestrian mall, would-be Pushkins and Pasternaks peddle their autographed poetry for a ruble or more a page. . . . More than 200 experimental studio theaters have sprouted in Moscow alone. The cultural explosion has been felt as far away as the Pacific port of Nakhodka, where local artists set up a puppet theater workshop, and in Yaroslavl in the Soviet heartland, scene of a rollicking street festival celebrating the arts. ❞
>
> John Kohan, "Freedom Waiting for Vision," *Time,* April 10, 1989

Life and Leisure

Daily life has always been difficult for ordinary people in Russia. During Soviet times apartment dwellers often found residential buildings crowded. Because of shortages of consumer goods, people spent many hours trying to purchase daily staples. Today, although some Russians are prospering and are building new homes in suburbs, others still live in crowded apartments and find it hard to pay the high prices charged for certain goods. Despite the frustrations, urban life offers many opportunities for people to enjoy the arts and culture. Reading, playing chess, and attending concerts, the ballet, and the theater all provide popular entertainment.

Both in cities and rural areas, Russians enjoy relaxing at mealtime with family and close friends. Sports, both amateur and professional, are quite popular with all age groups. Russia's tennis, track and field, and ice hockey athletes have had remarkable success in international events, as have figure skaters and gymnasts.

In the Soviet era, holidays were celebrated to honor Soviet workers or Soviet history. On May 1, the traditional workers' holiday known as May Day, great parades passed through Red Square, a large open area next to the Kremlin.

Today Russians observe May Day more as a spring festival than as a workers' holiday. Traditional religious holidays also have reemerged. In 1991, Christmas, celebrated by Eastern Orthodox Christians, became an official holiday in Russia for the first time since 1918.

SECTION 3 ASSESSMENT

Checking for Understanding

1. Define atheism, patriarch, icon, pogrom, intelligentsia, socialist realism.

2. Main Ideas Create a graphic organizer like the one below, and use it to fill in the key details for each aspect of Russian culture today.

Aspects of Russian Culture
- Religion
- Education
- Health Care
- The Arts

Critical Thinking

3. Making Inferences Why do you think Russian lawmakers have restricted activity by religious groups other than Russia's four traditional religions?

4. Comparing and Contrasting What was the education system like during the Soviet era, and what is it like today?

5. Making Generalizations How have Russian artists, musicians, and writers inspired the Russian people during difficult times?

Analyzing Graphs

6. Region Study the graph of religions in Russia on page 377. What percentage of people living in Russia today is Muslim? What percentage is nonreligious?

Applying Geography

7. Influence of Location In which part of Russia do most Russian followers of Islam live? Why do you think this is so? Write a paragraph to explain your reasoning.

Section Quiz 15-3

Name _____ Date _____ Class _____

CHAPTER 15 Section 3 Quiz
Cultures and Lifestyles

MATCHING: Match each item in Column A with an item in Column B. Write the correct letters in the blanks. *(10 points each)*

A	B
___ 1. Russian painter	A. Prince Vladimir
___ 2. second-largest religion in Russia	B. Leo Tolstoy
___ 3. leader who adopted Eastern Orthodox Christianity as Russia's official religion	C. Islam
___ 4. main religion of two republics: Kalmykia and Buryatia	D. Buddhism
___ 5. novelist known for his epic novels about Russian life	E. Wassily Kandinsky

MULTIPLE CHOICE: In each blank on the left, write the letter of the choice that best completes the statement or answers the question. *(10 points each)*

___ 6. During the 1900s the Soviet government

Reteach

List the following headings on the board: *Religion, Education, Health Care, The Arts, Life and Leisure.* Have students list as many facts as possible pertaining to Russia under each heading.

Enrich

Play a recording of *Peter and the Wolf,* written by Russian composer Sergei Prokofiev. Combining narration and orchestration, Prokofiev's composition uses a Russian folktale to teach children how to identify musical instruments by their sounds.

④ CLOSE

Ask each student to choose a popular Russian pastime or leisure activity, and write a GeoJournal entry about why he or she might enjoy participating in that activity.

SECTION 3 ASSESSMENT ANSWERS

1. All vocabulary terms are defined in the text.

2. Key details should reflect text information.

3. possible answers: traditional resistance to religion under Soviet system, fear of influence of Western missionaries, need to use religion to unite diverse peoples

4. Under the Soviet system, education was free, mandatory, and focused on science and technology. Today there is more variety in courses of study, but education is underfunded and teachers are poorly paid.

5. Russian artists have inspired patriotism, provided cultural and religious identity, offered hope in difficult times, and defended truth against efforts of government censors.

6. 10 percent; 71.1 percent

7. Applying Geography Most Islamic Russians live in southern Russia, in areas populated by Turkic peoples. The Turks brought Islam to the lands they conquered and populated.

Teaching the Skill

Ask two volunteers—one who participated in the event, and one who only heard or read about it in the school newspaper—to describe a school event such as a team competition, a concert, or a play. Tell the volunteers not to identify their levels of participation in the event. After the accounts have been presented, ask students to identify which was a first-person account and which was a second-hand description. **Ask: What key differences helped you decide?** *(vividness of detail, personal connection in first-person account, more general statements in second-hand account)* Explain that these same details can help distinguish between primary and secondary research sources.

Additional Practice
L1

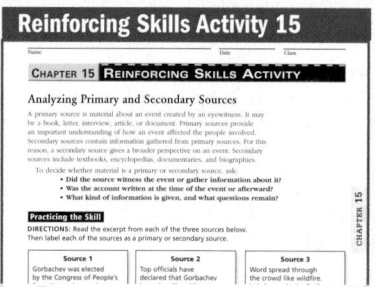

Reinforcing Skills Activity 15

CHAPTER 15 **REINFORCING SKILLS ACTIVITY**

Analyzing Primary and Secondary Sources

A primary source is material about an event created by an eyewitness. It may be a book, letter, interview, article, or document. Primary sources provide an important understanding of how an event affected the people involved. Secondary sources contain information gathered from primary sources. For this reason, a secondary source gives a broader perspective on an event. Secondary sources include textbooks, encyclopedias, documentaries, and biographies.

To decide whether material is a primary or secondary source, ask:
• Did the source witness the event or gather information about it?
• Was the account written at the time of the event or afterward?
• What kind of information is given, and what questions remain?

Practicing the Skill

DIRECTIONS: Read the excerpt from each of the three sources below. Then label each of the sources as a primary or secondary source.

Source 1	Source 2	Source 3
Gorbachev was elected by the Congress of People's	Top officials have declared that Gorbachev	Word spread through the crowd like wildfire.

GLENCOE
TECHNOLOGY

Glencoe Skillbuilder Interactive Workbook, Level 2

Analyzing Primary and Secondary Sources

When you read an account written by someone who witnessed an event, you are reading a primary source. If you read about the event based on a historian's research, you are reading a secondary source.

Learning the Skill

Knowing whether you are reading a primary or secondary source is important for evaluating the information. A primary source has the advantage of firsthand knowledge of an event. A secondary source often benefits from a broader perspective on the event.

Primary sources may include letters, interviews with eyewitnesses, photographs, and historical documents. Secondary sources rely on primary sources to create a broader picture. History books, encyclopedias, and documentary films are examples of secondary sources.

To analyze primary and secondary sources, ask yourself the following questions:

• **Did the source witness the event, or just gather information about it?**

• **When was the account written? At the time of, or after the event?**

• **Is the account valid? Do emotions, opinions, and biases influence the account?**

• **How useful is the source? What kind of information does the source provide, and what questions are left unanswered?**

▲ *This military hero who played a role in the 1917 Russian Revolution can be a primary source for historical research.*

Practicing the Skill

Read the following excerpt about the Bolshevik seizure of power in 1917, and then answer the questions.

"A tall iron gate surrounded the palace. One of the gates had not been locked. We saw this and opened the gate wide.... Like a wave of black lava, we moved into the palace, followed by workers and soldiers. There was no resistance, none at all. They surrendered their weapons. We arrested the members of the ... government."

—Karl G. Rianni, colleague of Lenin, quoted by Dusko Doder, "The Bolshevik Revolution," *National Geographic*, October 1992

1. What information does the source provide?

2. What is the writer's relationship to the information?

3. Is the source a primary or secondary source? How do you know?

Applying the Skill

Research a topic about Russia. Analyze your sources, and evaluate their validity and usefulness as primary or secondary sources.

The Glencoe Skillbuilder Interactive Workbook, Level 2 provides instruction and practice in key social studies skills.

ANSWERS TO PRACTICING THE SKILL

1. The source describes the effects of shelling on the city of Stalingrad during a World War II battle.

2. The writer of the book from which the source comes, Alexander Werth, presumably has no relationship to the information other than as a gatherer of facts, although we can presume that the person quoted within the source, a Russian military officer, was present to view the damages he describes.

3. It appears to be a primary source because the man quoted implies that he was present to see the damage by using terms like "here" and "now." This quote is included in a secondary source entitled *The Year of Stalingrad*.

CHAPTER 15

SUMMARY & STUDY GUIDE

SECTION 1 — Population Patterns (pp. 363–366)

Terms to Know
- ethnic group
- nationality
- sovereignty

Key Points
- More than 80 percent of Russia's population is ethnic Russian, and the remainder comprises about 100 different ethnic groups.
- Although more than 100 different languages are spoken in Russia, Russian is the official language.
- Russia is experiencing a population crisis, largely the result of health care problems.
- Russia's population is unevenly distributed, with 75 percent of Russians living west of the Urals.

Organizing Your Notes
Create an outline similar to the one started below to help you organize important details from this section.

Population Patterns
I. Russia's Ethnic Diversity
   A. Ethnic Regions
   B. Slavs
   C.

SECTION 2 — History and Government (pp. 367–373)

Terms to Know
- czar
- serf
- Russification
- socialism
- Bolshevik
- communism
- satellite
- Cold War
- perestroika
- glasnost

Key Points
- Kievan Rus, an early Slavic state, grew out of settlements of Slavs and Varangians.
- Under the czars Russia expanded its territory and became an enormous empire.
- In 1917 a revolution overthrew Czar Nicholas II. Later that year, the Bolsheviks, under Lenin, seized power.
- In 1922 the Communists formed the Union of Soviet Socialist Republics, or Soviet Union.
- In December 1991 the Soviet Union collapsed and was replaced by Russia and other independent republics.

Organizing Your Notes
Organize your notes for this section by listing the important events under each century of Russian history.

Russian History

Before 1600	1601–1700	1701–1800	1801–1900	1901–Present

SECTION 3 — Cultures and Lifestyles (pp. 376–381)

Terms to Know
- atheism
- patriarch
- icon
- pogrom
- intelligentsia
- socialist realism

Key Points
- Since the Soviet Union's collapse, many Russians have resumed their religious practices.
- Post-Soviet Russian schools are more open to new ideas and methods, but they face low budgets, overcrowding, and disrepair.
- Russia's artistic golden age began in the 1800s. After 1917 the Soviet government severely restricted certain kinds of artistic expression.
- Today Russians' respect for culture, traditions, and the arts has increased as a result of the new freedoms.

Organizing Your Notes
Create web diagrams like the one below to help you organize your notes for this section. Make separate diagrams for Religion, Education, Health Care, and the Arts.

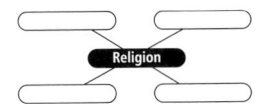
Religion

Using the Chapter 15 Summary & Study Guide

Use the Chapter 15 Summary & Study Guide to preview, review, condense, or reteach the chapter.

Preview/Review

🖳 **Vocabulary PuzzleMaker CD-ROM** reinforces "Terms to Know."

🖳 **Interactive Tutor Self-Assessment CD-ROM** provides a review of Chapter 15 content.

Condense

Have students read the Chapter 15 Summary & Study Guide.

💿 Chapter 15 Audio Program

📁 Chapter 15 Guided Reading Activities

Reteach

📁 Chapter 15 Reteaching Activities (Spanish also available)

📁 Chapter 15 Reading Essentials and Study Guides

GLENCOE TECHNOLOGY

NATIONAL GEOGRAPHIC
WORLD REGIONS VIDEO PROGRAM

Unit 5, Russia
The following segments enhance the study of this unit:
- **Siberian Tigers**
- **The Tire Factory**
- **Bolshoi Ballet**

CHAPTER CULMINATING ACTIVITY

Making Inferences Have students choose a key moment in Russian history. **Ask:** If things had gone differently at this particular moment, how might Russia be different today? Have students write stories in which they rewrite key moments in Russia's history, showing how the region's future might have been affected. If students need prompting, **Ask:** What if the Mongols had never invaded Kievan Rus? What if Russia had followed Western Christianity instead of Eastern Orthodoxy? What if the White Army had defeated the Bolsheviks? Encourage students to be creative in their choice of moments, but to depict the changes in history accurately.

🌐 **EE6 The Uses of Geography: Standards 17, 18**

NOTE: This activity may be completed separately or you may wish students to incorporate it in their GeoJournals.

Have students visit the Web site at geography.glencoe.com to review Chapter 15 and take the **Self-Check Quiz.**

GLENCOE TECHNOLOGY

Use *MindJogger Videoquiz* to review the Chapter 15 content.

Reviewing Key Terms

1. Bolshevik
2. czar
3. patriarch
4. intelligentsia
5. icon
6. perestroika
7. glasnost
8. serf
9. atheism

Reviewing Facts
SECTION 1

1. Russians
2. European Russia

SECTION 2

3. They expanded it to include many diverse populations.
4. goals: world influence and power, expansionism; events: World War II, Cold War, arms race, space race

SECTION 3

5. Eastern Orthodox Christianity, Islam, Judaism, Buddhism
6. loss of quality, low pay for teachers and doctors, outdated equipment

384

Reviewing Key Terms

Write the key term that best completes each of the following sentences. Refer to the Terms to Know in the Summary & Study Guide on page 383.

1. A person who was part of the revolutionary group led by Lenin was called a(n) _____.
2. A(n) _____ ruled Russia at the time of the Russian Revolution.
3. The _____ is the head of the Russian Orthodox Church.
4. The Soviet Union's intellectual elite was called the _____.
5. A religious symbol is called a(n) _____.
6. The Russian term for restructuring is _____.
7. The Russian term for political openness is _____.
8. A peasant worker who farmed a plot of land that was owned by someone else was called a(n) _____.
9. _____ is the belief that there is no God or supreme being.

Reviewing Facts
SECTION 1

1. Which ethnic group forms the majority in Russia?
2. Where do most of Russia's people live?

SECTION 2

3. How did princes and czars change Russia's territory?
4. What were the major goals and events of the Soviet era?

SECTION 3

5. What major religions are found in Russia?
6. How have education and health care changed since the Soviet breakup?

Critical Thinking

1. **Drawing Conclusions** Explain why you agree or disagree with the following statement: "The Soviet Union was a 74-year-long experiment that failed."
2. **Making Inferences** Why do you think many people in Russia have returned to earlier traditions?
3. **Finding and Summarizing the Main Idea** Fill in four key events in Russian history in the order they occurred, on a flowchart. Then explain why each event was a turning point in Russia's history.

Key Events

□ → □ → □ → □

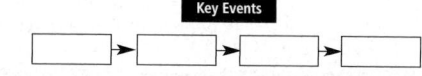

NATIONAL GEOGRAPHIC   Locating Places
Russia: Physical-Political Geography

Match the letters on the map with the places and physical features of Russia. Write your answers on a sheet of paper.

1. St. Petersburg
2. Baltic Sea
3. Barents Sea
4. Volga River
5. Moscow
6. Yenisey River
7. Yekaterinburg
8. Black Sea
9. Lake Baikal

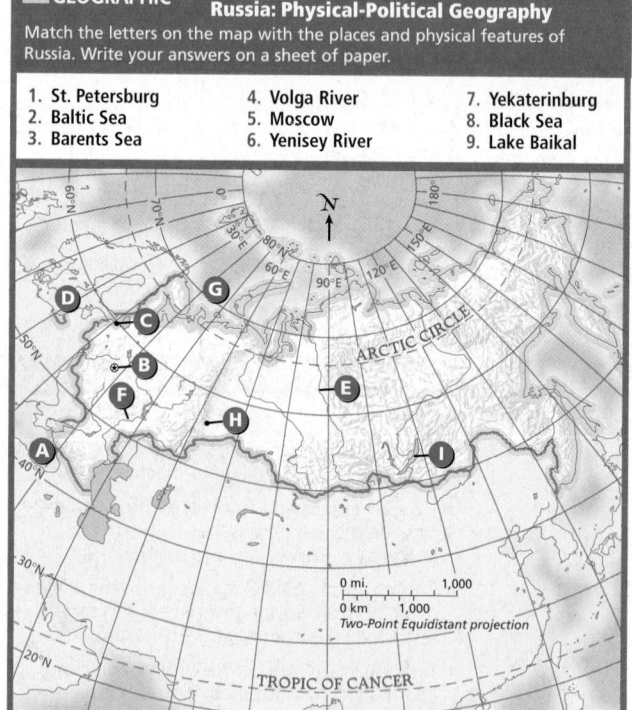

Critical Thinking

1. Students should offer logical supporting arguments.
2. nostalgia for pre-Soviet days, rise of ethnic identity and nationalism, freedom of religious expression
3. Flowcharts should reflect text information.

NATIONAL GEOGRAPHIC   Locating Places

1. C	**3.** G	**5.** B	**7.** H	**9.** I
2. D	**4.** F	**6.** E	**8.** A	

Using the Regional Atlas

1. Dnieper, Volga, Moskva
2. More Russians live west of the Urals, which has navigable waterways and plains. Few people live in eastern Russia, which has a harsher environment.

Using the Regional Atlas

Refer to the Regional Atlas on pages 338–341.

1. **Human-Environment Interaction** Which important rivers have helped in Russia's development?

2. **Place** What physical processes have affected migration and patterns of settlement in Russia?

Thinking Like a Geographer

Russia's population is spread unevenly across an enormous country. What physical features influence population density? How might human action affect population density? Design and draw a chart of elements that encourage population and those that discourage it.

Problem-Solving Activity

Contemporary Issues Case Study Choose one aspect of Russian culture today in which Russian and foreign cultural traits have converged, or come together. Research your topic in news magazines and newspapers or on the Internet to find a specific example, such as growth of U.S.-based fast-food restaurants or the spread of Western religions. Then write a one-page essay describing your example.

GeoJournal

Summarizing Return to the chart you made in your GeoJournal before you started reading this chapter. Write a brief summary of what you learned about Russia from reading the textbook. Use your chart, the textbook, and the Internet to prepare your summary.

Technology Activity

Using the Internet for Research The Soviet government required all artists to portray communism in a positive way. Use the Internet to locate examples of socialist realism in Russian art. Develop a brochure to educate people about this style of art. Download examples, and use them as illustrations in your brochure.

Standardized Test Practice

Read the quote by Zina Popova below, and then choose the best answer for each of the following multiple-choice questions. If you have trouble answering the questions, use the process of elimination to narrow your choices.

> *"That hero stuff was a millstone around [my mother's] neck. Mama told me she knew nothing about Lenin and Marxism when she joined the revolutionaries. They were spurred by hunger. My mother believed in the myth of the October Revolution but only for a few years. Then there was no exit. She put in her time, like most of the others."*
>
> —Zina Popova, in "The Bolshevik Revolution," *National Geographic*, October 1992

1. The quote above could be used by a geographer to learn more about a country's

   A cultural geography.
   B foreign policy.
   C ethnic minorities.
   D physical geography.

2. Zina Popova's perspective on the Bolshevik Revolution comes from

   F the Communist Party.
   G her own experience.
   H her mother.
   J a reference book.

Test-Taking **Tip** In answering questions about quotations, make sure that you have a clear understanding of the quote. Also make sure that you understand the perspective of the person being quoted. Often, as in this case, you can find this information after the person's name.

❓ CHAPTER BONUS TEST QUESTION

One of Russia's most important and well-known cities has had many names throughout history. What is the name of this city today, and by what names has it been known in the past? *(Originally called St. Petersburg, the city has also been known as Petrograd, Leningrad, Stalingrad, and once again, St. Petersburg.)*

Thinking Like a Geographer

Charts should reflect the relationship between Russia's population densities and its physical features and climate, as well as the influence of human activity such as historic conquests and urbanization on population patterns.

Problem-Solving Activity

Students may carry out their research individually, in pairs, or in small groups. Allow time for reports to be shared with the class.

GeoJournal

Invite students to illustrate their written summaries or to prepare their charts in a form that can be displayed for the class. Check for use of standard grammar, spelling, sentence structure, and punctuation.

Technology Activity

Guide students to Internet art resources such as museum Web sites.

PLANNING GUIDE

NOTE: The following materials may be used when teaching Chapter 16. Section-level support materials are shown at point-of-use in the margins of the Teacher Wraparound Edition.

TEACHING TRANSPARENCIES

L2 Unit 5 Map Overlay Transparencies

L2 Political Map Transparency 5

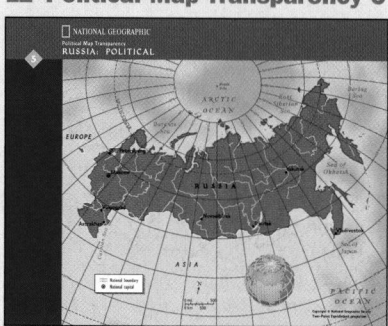

GEOGRAPHIC LITERACY

Focus on Geography Literacy

APPLICATION AND ENRICHMENT

L3 Enrichment Activity 16

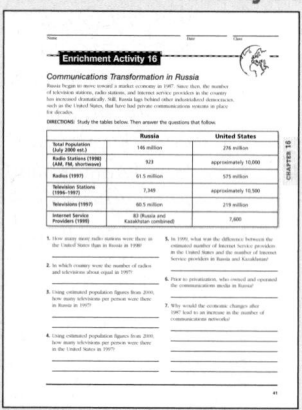

REVIEW AND REINFORCEMENT

L1 Vocabulary Activity 16 L1 Reinforcing Skills Activity 16 L1 Reteaching Activity 16

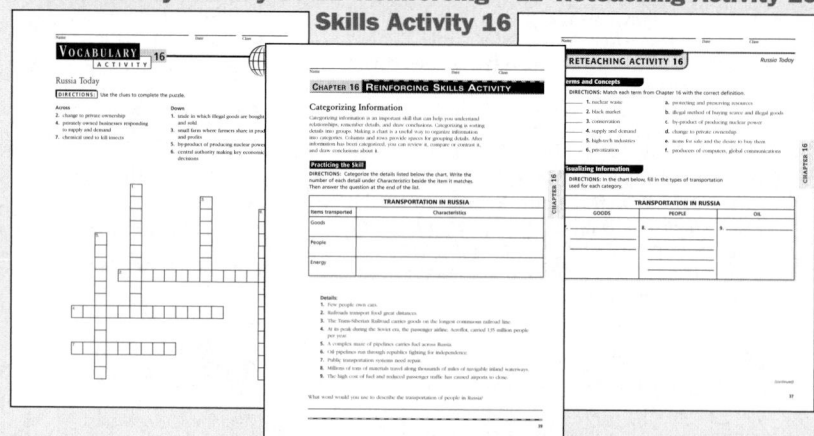

ASSESSMENT

L2 Chapter 16 Test Form A

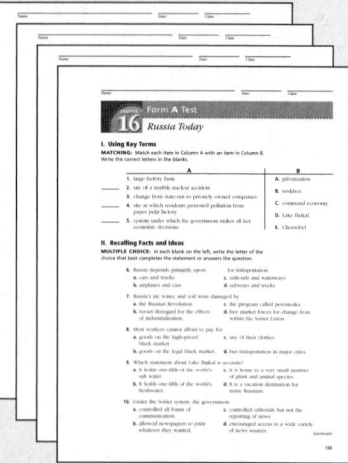

L2 Chapter 16 Test Form B

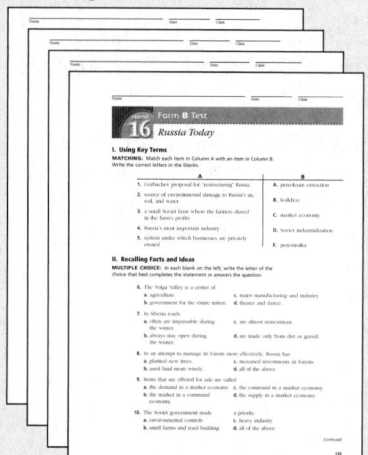

L1/ELL Performance Assessment Activity 16

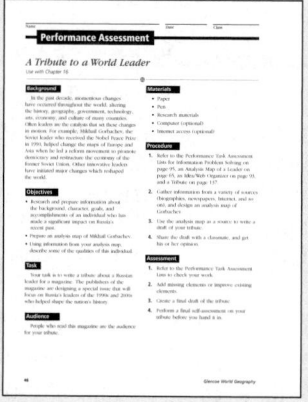

ExamView® Pro Testmaker

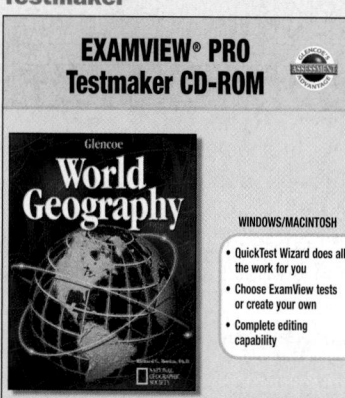

The following Spanish language materials are available in the Spanish Resources binder:

- 📁 Spanish Vocabulary Activities
- 📁 Spanish Guided Reading Activities
- 📁 Spanish Reteaching Activities
- 📁 Spanish Summaries
- 📁 Spanish Quizzes and Tests
- 📁 Spanish Reading Essentials and Study Guide

- World Regions Video
- MindJogger Videoquiz
- Vocabulary PuzzleMaker CD-ROM
- Interactive Tutor Self-Assessment CD-ROM
- ExamView® Pro Testmaker CD-ROM
- Audio Program
- TeacherWorks CD-ROM
- Interactive Student Edition CD-ROM
- Glencoe Skillbuilder Interactive Workbook CD-ROM, Level 2
- Presentation Plus! CD-ROM

Timesaving Tools

TeacherWorks™ All-In-One Planner and Resource Center

- **Interactive Teacher Edition** Access your Teacher Wraparound Edition and your classroom resources with a few easy clicks.
- **Interactive Lesson Planner** Planning has never been easier! Organize your week, month, semester, or year with all the lesson helps you need to make teaching creative, timely, and relevant.

Use Glencoe's **Presentation Plus!** multimedia teacher tool to easily present dynamic lessons that visually excite your students. Using Microsoft PowerPoint® you can customize the presentations to create your own personalized lessons.

GEOGRAPHY Online

Use our Web site for additional resources. All essential content is covered in the Student Edition.

You and your students can visit geography.glencoe.com, the Web site companion to *Glencoe World Geography*. This innovative integration of electronic and print media offers your students a wealth of opportunities. The student text directs students to the Web site for the following options:

- Chapter Overviews
- Self-Check Quizzes
- Student Activities
- Textbook Updates

Answers are provided for you in the "Web Activity Lesson Plan." Additional Web resources and Interactive Tutor puzzles are also available.

▶ **Additional Glencoe Teacher Support**

- Teaching Strategies for the Geography Classroom (including Block Scheduling Pacing Guides)
- Graphic Organizer Transparencies Strategies and Activities
- Outline Map Resource Book
- Reading in the Content Area

PLANNING GUIDE

SECTION RESOURCES

Daily Objectives	Reproducible Resources	Multimedia Resources

SECTION 1 Living in Russia

1. Explain how Russia has moved toward a market economy.
2. List changes in agriculture, industry, transportation, and communications since the breakup of the Soviet Union.
3. Describe Russia's role in the global community.

Reproducible Resources:
- Reproducible Lesson Plan 16-1
- Daily Lecture Notes 16-1
- Guided Reading Activity 16-1*
- Reading Essentials and Study Guide 16-1*
- Section Quiz 16-1*

Multimedia Resources:
- Daily Focus Skills Transparency 16-1
- Political Map Transparency 5
- Unit 5 Map Overlay Transparencies
- Interactive Tutor Self-Assessment CD-ROM
- ExamView® Pro Testmaker CD-ROM*
- Presentation Plus! CD-ROM

SECTION 2 People and Their Environment

1. Discuss how Russia manages its natural resources.
2. Describe some of the effects of pollution on the people of Russia.
3. Identify some of the environmental challenges Russia faces.

Reproducible Resources:
- Reproducible Lesson Plan 16-2
- Vocabulary Activity 16*
- Daily Lecture Notes 16-2
- Guided Reading Activity 16-2*
- Reading Essentials and Study Guide 16-2*
- Reteaching Activity 16*
- Reinforcing Skills Activity 16
- Section Quiz 16-2*

Multimedia Resources:
- Daily Focus Skills Transparency 16-2
- Political Map Transparency 5
- Unit 5 Map Overlay Transparencies
- Vocabulary PuzzleMaker CD-ROM
- Interactive Tutor Self-Assessment CD-ROM
- ExamView® Pro Testmaker CD-ROM*
- Presentation Plus! CD-ROM

	Blackline Master		Software		Videocassette	*Also available in Spanish
	Transparency		CD-ROM		DVD	

OUT OF TIME? Assign the Chapter 16 **Reading Essentials and Study Guide.**

Block Schedule

Activities that are particularly suited to use within the block scheduling framework are identified throughout this chapter by the following designation:

KEY TO ABILITY LEVELS

Teaching strategies have been coded for various learning styles and abilities.

L1   **BASIC** activities for all students

L2   **AVERAGE** activities for average to above-average students

L3   **CHALLENGING** activities for above-average students

ELL   **ENGLISH LANGUAGE LEARNER** activities

Teacher to Teacher

Grant Lane
Ellinwood High School
Ellinwood, KS

Comparing Governments

Organize students into three groups, assigning each group one form of government—communism, socialism, or democracy. Direct the groups to research their forms of government and take notes on how different kinds of governments meet their people's needs.

Suggest several issues that students might address, such as property ownership, health care, education, social welfare, environmental protection laws, and foreign affairs. Groups should assign specific issues to individual members and then share what they discovered.

Then ask a volunteer from each group to state how their form of government addresses each issue. After covering all relevant issues, have the class discuss the strengths and weaknesses of each form of government. Finally, ask students to write individual essays in which they design an ideal government system for Russia, drawing on what they have learned about government systems and Russian physical and human geography.

Meeting National Standards

Geography For Life

The following standards are highlighted in Chapter 16:

Section 1   EE2 Places and Regions:
Standards 4, 6
EE4 Human Systems:
Standards 11, 13
EE5 Environment and Society:
Standard 16
EE6 The Uses of Geography:
Standard 18

Section 2   EE4 Human Systems:
Standard 11
EE5 Environment and Society:
Standards 14, 16

Local Objectives

_____

_____

NATIONAL GEOGRAPHIC   TEACHER'S CORNER

Index to National Geographic Magazine:
The following articles may be used for research relating to this chapter:

- "The Caspian Sea," by Robert Cullen, May 1999.
- "Stellar's Sea-Eagles," by Klaus Nigge, March 1999.
- *Biodiversity*, a National Geographic Special Edition, February 1999.

National Geographic Society Products:
To order the following products for use with this chapter, call National Geographic Society at 1-800-368-2728.

- *GeoKit: Pollution* (Kit)
- *Asia* (Video)
- *Europe* (Video)
- *Russia: Then and Now Series* (Videos)
- *Europe: The Road to Unity* (Video)
- *Capitalism, Communism, Socialism Series* (Videos)
- *Pollution: World at Risk* (Video)
- *Healing the Earth* (Video)
- *National Geographic Desk Reference* (Book)
- *National Geographic Atlas of the World, Seventh Edition* (Book)

NGS ONLINE

Access National Geographic's Web site for current events, activities, links, interactive features, and archives.
www.nationalgeographic.com

MEETING SPECIAL NEEDS

In addition to the Differentiated Instruction strategies found in each section, the following resources are also suitable for your special needs students:

- *ExamView® Pro Testmaker CD-ROM* allows teachers to tailor tests by reducing answer choices.
- The *Audio Program* includes the entire narrative of the student edition so that less-proficient readers can listen to the words as they read them.
- The *Reading Essentials and Study Guide* provides the same content as the student edition but is written two grade levels below the textbook.
- *Guided Reading Activities* give less-proficient readers point-by-point instructions to increase comprehension as they read each textbook section.
- *Enrichment Activities* include a stimulating collection of readings and activities for gifted and talented students.

Chapter Objectives

1. Describe the economic changes Russia has experienced in its move from a command economy to a market economy, and the effects of those changes on agriculture, transportation, and communications.

2. Identify the challenges Russia faces as the region struggles to manage its resources and control environmental damage.

GLENCOE TECHNOLOGY

Use *MindJogger Videoquiz* to preview the Chapter 16 content.

GeoJournal

For access to additional photos, maps, and information on the contemporary issues of Russia, go to www.nationalgeographic.com (See Teacher pages in front for strategies for using journals in the geography classroom.)

GEOGRAPHY Online

Introduce students to chapter content and key terms by having them access **Chapter Overview 16** at geography.glencoe.com

FOLDABLES
Study Organizer

Dinah Zike's Foldables are three-dimensional, interactive graphic organizers that help students practice basic writing skills, review key vocabulary terms, and identify main ideas. Have students complete the Foldable activity in the **Dinah Zike's Reading and Study Skills Foldables** booklet.

CHAPTER 16 Russia Today

GeoJournal

As you read this chapter, make notes in your journal about life in Russia today. Use clear, specific language to explain how recent economic and political changes have affected the people of Russia.

GEOGRAPHY Online

Chapter Overview Visit the **Glencoe World Geography** Web site at geography.glencoe.com and click on Chapter Overviews—Chapter 16 to preview information about the region today.

ABOUT THE PHOTO

Visual Instruction In Russia, Red Square is called *Krasnaya Ploschad*. The word *krasnaya* means both "red" and "beautiful." Although the teenagers in the photo might blend into many large cities around the world, the beautiful onion domes in the photo's background are distinctly Russian. Today Red Square is lined with blue spruces along the Kremlin wall, its granite paving stones are blue-gray, and the colorful Cathedral of St. Basil displays all the colors of the rainbow. Red Square is certainly both colorful and beautiful.

Ask: What other visual clues tell you this photo is of a location in Russia? (*Students may mention the writing on the shopping bag. They should note that the teenagers themselves could be in any large city.*) ▣ EE2 Places and Regions: Standards 4, 6

Guide to Reading

Consider What You Know

Russia continues to adjust to dramatic and sometimes difficult political and economic changes. How do you think these changes probably affect Russians' attitudes toward the old Soviet government?

Reading Strategy

Organizing Complete a graphic organizer similar to the one below by listing changes in Russia's economic system and the effect of each.

Economic System	Effect
Command Economy	
Market Economy	

Read to Find Out

- How has Russia made the transition to a market economy?
- How have agriculture, industry, transportation, and communications in Russia changed since the breakup of the Soviet Union?
- What is Russia's relationship to the global community?

Terms to Know

- command economy
- consumer goods
- black market
- market economy
- privatization
- kolkhoz
- sovkhoz

Places to Locate

- Siberia
- Vladivostok

◀ *Teens walking through Red Square, Moscow*

Living in Russia

A Geographic View

The Price of Freedom

Not long ago . . . I met a woman named Larissa Pavlova. She was a teacher who now sold old clothes evenings and weekends to supplement her family's income. Countless thousands of Muscovites work second and third jobs to get by. . . . "Moscow is filled with what our good Comrade Lenin called contradictions," she said. "The rich get richer and the rest of us tread water or drown. I work much harder than I did in the old days, and sometimes that makes it hard to remember what we've gained. Freedom is sweet, but it's also a heavy, heavy load."

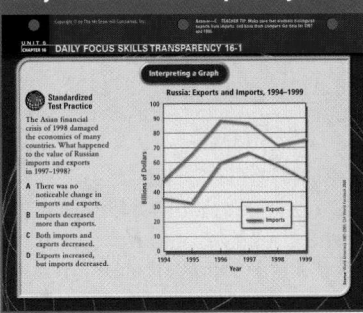
Muscovites selling food on the street

—*David Remnick, "Moscow: The New Revolution,"* National Geographic, *April 1997*

Russians hoped that the end of the Soviet-controlled economy and the birth of Russian independence would bring quick and painless economic change. As the teacher from Moscow discovered, however, shifting toward a freer economy could also bring hard times. Russia continues its efforts to create a working economy that will provide for its people and maintain its place in the global marketplace.

Changing Economies

Since the fall of communism, Russia has faced many economic challenges, such as providing more jobs for its citizens, increasing food production at home, and expanding trade internationally. As Russia works to strengthen its economy, its citizens also face ethnic unrest, rising crime, and declining health and social services.

Chapter 16 🌐 387

1 FOCUS

Section Overview

This section discusses Russia's changing economy and the effects of those changes on everyday life in the region.

BELLRINGER
Skillbuilder Activity

🖳 Project transparency and have students answer questions.

🗁 Available as blackline master.

Daily Focus Skills Transparency 16-1

Guide to Reading

Consider What You Know
Answer *Some people may be nostalgic for the old system's centralized control. Others may blame the old system for the region's continued challenges.*

Reading Strategy
Answers Command: *central authority makes decisions, emphasis on heavy industry, low unemployment but low wages;* Market: *businesses privately owned, production and prices based on supply and demand, more consumer goods available, increase in government corruption and organized crime*

Preteaching Vocabulary
Direct students to an economics text or dictionary to find the meaning of the first five terms. Ask students to predict the significance these terms will have in their study of life in Russia today.

RESOURCE MANAGER

🗁 Reproducible Masters
- Reproducible Lesson Plan 16-1
- Daily Lecture Notes 16-1
- Guided Reading Activity 16-1
- Reading Essentials and Study Guide 16-1
- Section Quiz 16-1

🖳 Transparencies
- Daily Focus Skills Transparency 16-1
- Political Map Transparency 5
- Unit 5 Map Overlay Transparencies

Multimedia
- 💿 Interactive Tutor Self-Assessment CD-ROM
- 💿 ExamView® Pro Testmaker CD-ROM
- 💿 Presentation Plus! CD-ROM

TEACH

L1 Vocabulary

Have students locate the terms *kolkhoz* and *sovkhoz* on page 390. Write the terms on the board, and have students list distinguishing characteristics of each kind of farm ownership under the relevant term. **Ask:** What part of the word *sovkhoz* might help you understand that it means a large, centrally run system? *(the prefix* sov, *which also appears in* Soviet*)* What part of the word *kolkhoz* might help you remember that it is a collective form of ownership? *(the prefix* kol, *which sounds like, and means, "collective")*

L2 Making Comparisons

Have each student make a list of the consumer goods he or she used so far today. Brainstorm categories, such as personal grooming items, medicines, food, and school supplies. **Ask:** Which of these consumer goods would you be able to do without in a time of economic shortages? For which consumer goods would you be willing to stand in long lines or pay high prices?

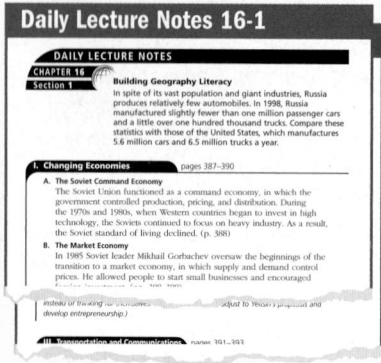

Daily Lecture Notes 16-1

The Soviet Command Economy

Under Communist leaders, the Soviet Union operated as a command economy. In a command economy, a central authority makes key economic decisions. The government owned banks, factories, farms, mines, and transportation systems. Members of the State Planning Committee, known as *Gosplan*, decided what and how much to produce, how to produce it, and who would benefit from the profits. *Gosplan* also controlled the pricing of most goods and decided where they would be sold.

The Soviet government emphasized heavy industry—the manufacture of goods such as tanks and other military hardware, machinery, and electric generators. As a result, the Soviet Union became an industrial giant and a world power, but its people could not buy many consumer goods, or goods needed for everyday life.

Unemployment in the Soviet Union was low, but so were wages, because most men and women worked at state-run factories and farms. People often could not afford the few consumer goods that factories produced. Even when people had enough money, such goods were hard to find. Some items could be bought on the black market, an illegal trade in which scarce or illegal goods are sold at prices even higher than those set by the government. Most workers, however, could not afford to pay such high prices with their limited incomes.

By the 1970s and 1980s, Western countries and some Asian countries had turned away from heavy industry to focus on computer technology and global communications. The Soviet system during this time, however, focused on increased industrial production and did not invest in developing new high-technology industries. As a result, the Soviet Union's economy stagnated, and its standard of living declined while the global economy entered a dynamic new era of change.

The Market Economy

When Mikhail Gorbachev came to power in 1985, the Soviet Union's economy was in serious trouble. To remedy the crisis, Gorbachev began to move away from a command economy toward a market economy, in which businesses are privately owned. Production and prices in a market economy depend on supply and demand. Things offered for sale are *supply*; people's desire to buy those things is *demand*. As part of his program of

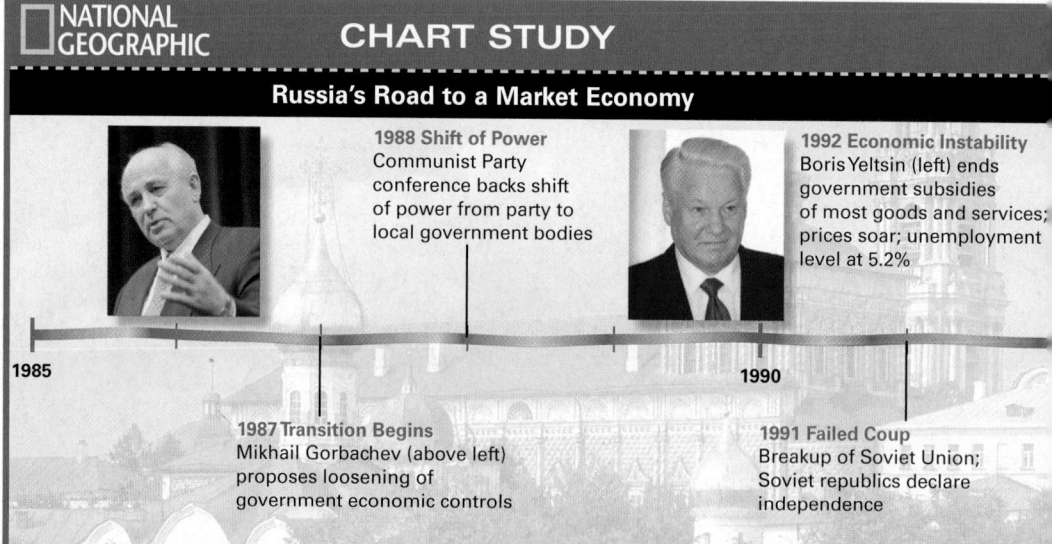

NATIONAL GEOGRAPHIC CHART STUDY

Russia's Road to a Market Economy

1988 Shift of Power Communist Party conference backs shift of power from party to local government bodies

1992 Economic Instability Boris Yeltsin (left) ends government subsidies of most goods and services; prices soar; unemployment level at 5.2%

1985

1990

1987 Transition Begins Mikhail Gorbachev (above left) proposes loosening of government economic controls

1991 Failed Coup Breakup of Soviet Union; Soviet republics declare independence

388 🌐 Unit 5

DIFFERENTIATED INSTRUCTION

English Learners This section contains several examples of idiomatic speech which may be confusing to English language learners. List the following examples on the board: *to get by, to tread water, black market, privatization, political insiders, shortfalls, organized crime, fast-food chain, high-tech, skyrocketing.* Ask students to work with fluent English speakers or use dictionaries to ascertain the literal meaning of these idiomatic terms and phrases and make predictions about their contextual meanings. **ELL**

📁 Refer to *Inclusion for the Social Studies Classroom Strategies and Activities.*

perestroika, or restructuring, Gorbachev reduced some government controls, allowed people to start small businesses, and encouraged foreign investment. Boris Yeltsin, Gorbachev's successor, expanded this process.

Economics
Privatization

Russia's economy continued to change after the Soviet Union officially ceased to exist in 1991. When Russia and the other Soviet republics became independent, they eliminated most remaining economic controls. Russian President Boris Yeltsin removed 90 percent of price controls and encouraged the mass privatization—a change to private ownership—of state-owned companies and industries, such as mining and oil extraction and processing. This process of privatization favored important businesspeople, political insiders, and foreign investors, all of whom could afford to purchase large companies. Rather than reinvest in Russia and its economy, many of these people invested their profits outside the country. Most average Russian workers did not benefit from this changing economic system: they neither earned nor were spending the new wealth.

> ❝ By 1995 privatization had gained a negative reputation with ordinary Russians, who coined a slang word prikhvatizatsiya, a combination of the Russian word for 'grab' and the Russianized English word 'privatize,' producing the equivalent of 'grabification.' ❞
>
> Glenn E. Curtis (ed.), *Russia: A Country Study*, 1996

Widespread corruption complicated the privatization process in the new Russia. Organized crime groups and corrupt public officials operated throughout the country, especially in Moscow. Some people grew rich through special government favors that allowed them to buy property at far below its true value. This illegal behavior damaged the economy and absorbed investment funds that could have been used to rebuild the country.

The Transition Continues

The Russian economy experienced ups and downs throughout the 1990s. Russians could find

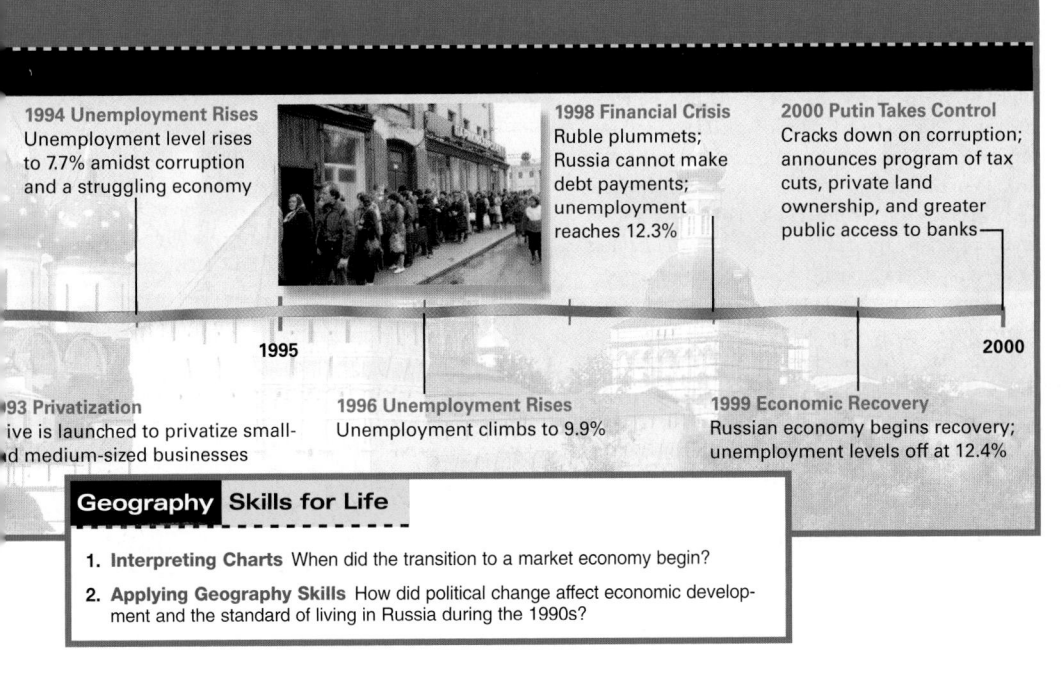

1994 Unemployment Rises Unemployment level rises to 7.7% amidst corruption and a struggling economy

1998 Financial Crisis Ruble plummets; Russia cannot make debt payments; unemployment reaches 12.3%

2000 Putin Takes Control Cracks down on corruption; announces program of tax cuts, private land ownership, and greater public access to banks

1995

2000

93 Privatization ive is launched to privatize small- d medium-sized businesses

1996 Unemployment Rises Unemployment climbs to 9.9%

1999 Economic Recovery Russian economy begins recovery; unemployment levels off at 12.4%

Geography Skills for Life

1. **Interpreting Charts** When did the transition to a market economy begin?
2. **Applying Geography Skills** How did political change affect economic development and the standard of living in Russia during the 1990s?

Chapter 16 🌐 389

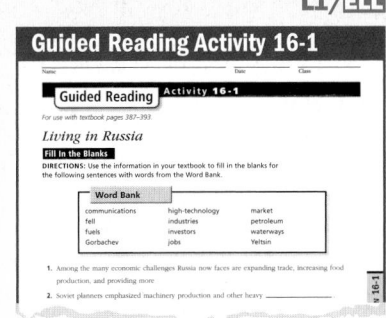

Guided Reading Activity 16-1

Guided Reading Activity 16-1
For use with textbook pages 387-393

Living in Russia

Fill in the Blanks
DIRECTIONS: Use the information in your textbook to fill in the blanks for the following sentences with words from the Word Bank.

Word Bank

communications	high-technology	market
fell	industries	petroleum
fuels	investors	waterways
Gorbachev	jobs	Yeltsin

1. Among the many economic challenges Russia now faces are expanding trade, increasing food production, and providing more _____.

2. Soviet planners emphasized machinery production and other heavy _____.

L3 Recognizing Bias

Ask interested students to analyze recent news articles to determine Russia's current level of economic development and standard of living and its future prospects. Have them write simulated "quotes" representing a range of opinions, such as those of officials, wealthy businesspeople, workers, and foreign investors.

NATIONAL GEOGRAPHIC | **CHART STUDY**

Answers
1. *1987*
2. *Privatization allowed for private ownership of farms and property, although very few could afford the cost.*

Skills Practice
Region What trend can you identify in unemployment rates for the years shown in the chart? (*Unemployment rates rose steadily from 5.2 percent in 1992 to 12.4 percent in 1999, when they leveled off.*)

COOPERATIVE LEARNING ACTIVITY

Research News Stories Have students work in small groups to research news stories about changes in the Soviet/Russian economy from each of the years annotated on the time line on pages 388–389. Direct students to Internet sources or the *Readers' Guide to Periodical Literature*. Ask students to find at least one nationally published news story and one internationally published news story for each year. Have students recreate the time line on the board or poster board and attach printouts of their news stories at the appropriate points. Compare internal and external news accounts. Ask students to trace the change in tone of internal stories as freedom of the press widened in Russia.

📖 **EE4 Human Systems: Standard 11**

NATIONAL GEOGRAPHIC World Explorer

Answer
Russia has moved toward a market economy with greater opportunities for private enterprise but also higher inflation and unemployment rates.

More About the Photo
The open-air market, similar to farmer's markets in the United States, is an economic feature of many developed and developing countries. The small scale and low overhead allow individuals and families to maximize profits.

INTERDISCIPLINARY
connection

MATHEMATICS Have students use Internet resources to research the following: the price, in rubles, of a new Russian-made car; the current value, in American dollars, of the Russian ruble; the present rate of inflation in Russia. Have students calculate how much the car costs in American dollars today and how much the same car would sell for in a year if the rate of inflation remained the same.

GEOGRAPHY *Online*

Objectives, goals, and answers to the student activity can be found in the Web Activity Lesson Plan feature at geography.glencoe.com

NATIONAL GEOGRAPHIC World Explorer

Geography Skills for Life

Kaliningrad, Russia To supplement their income, many Russians sell hard-to-find goods, such as car parts, in open-air markets.
Place Describe the characteristics of Russia's economy in 1991 and today.

more consumer goods in shops. However, without controls, prices soared, and many people could not afford to buy the goods that were available. Between 1990 and 1995, the total value of goods and services produced in Russia fell by 50 percent, a far greater drop than the United States experienced during the Great Depression of the 1930s. Following a 1998 financial crisis, the ruble, Russia's currency, lost 71 percent of its value. Prices, which had dropped, rose once again. The international community made large loans to aid the Russian economy.

Yeltsin resigned as president of Russia in 1999. His successor, Vladimir Putin, inherited an unstable economy. Russia's economy needed money and a stronger banking system, which would help keep more Russian money at home. Putin also needed to improve the Russian military. However, he needed to do so without overspending on the armed forces at the expense of overall economic growth, a problem experienced previously by Soviet leaders.

An inefficiently managed government, budget shortfalls, unclear property rights, an unstable currency, corruption, and organized crime all threaten Russia's economic stability. However, there is also potential for success. Russia can rebuild its economy by relying on its vast natural resources, developed industries, and well-educated citizens.

Agriculture and Industry

Under the Soviet system, farms were organized into state-controlled kolkhozes (kahl•KAW•zehz) and sovkhozes (sahf•KAW•zehz). The **kolkhozes** were small farms worked by farmers who shared, to a degree, in the farm's production and profits. **Sovkhozes** were large farms run more like factories, with the farm workers receiving wages. However, prices and production in both the agricultural and industrial sectors were controlled by the government. Both the agricultural and industrial sectors suffered because the system did not motivate workers. As a result, long before the 1980s Soviet agriculture did not produce enough food to feed its people, and the government had to import additional grain and other foods.

In 1991 President Yeltsin started to restructure state-run farms so they could function better in a market economy. However, Russian farmers—accustomed to the stability of Soviet controls—continued to operate many of Russia's farms as kolkhozes or sovkhozes. Most farmers could not afford to buy land, and they worried that wealthy Russians or foreign investors might use the land for nonagricultural development. Because of these concerns, progress toward a market economy for agriculture has been slow, and crop and livestock production has fallen. Recently, however, gains in farm productivity have helped reduce the need for agricultural imports.

Like agriculture, Russian industry has also been transformed since the early 1990s. For many years

GEOGRAPHY *Online*

Student Web Activity Visit the **Glencoe World Geography** Web site at geography.glencoe.com and click on Student Web Activities—Chapter 16 for an activity about living in Russia today.

CRITICAL THINKING ACTIVITY

Formulating Questions Tell students that they are part of a student delegation being sent to Russia to learn about life in the region. Direct students to work in small groups to generate lists of questions they would ask the Russian people they encounter about each of the following areas: the state of Russia's economy, education in Russia, Russia and the high-tech revolution, and feelings about life after the breakup of the Soviet Union. Have students rely on the information in their texts to help shape the direction of their questions. Allow time for all groups to share their lists. ⊕ **EE2 Places and Regions: Standard 6**

Russia's state-owned aerospace industry and its military-industrial system were its economic and technical focus. Many of these components have become privately owned and provide export income. Russia has also encouraged foreign investment by selling shares of ownership in some Russian companies and by opening Russia's markets to Western companies. A popular American fast-food chain, for example, now has 52 restaurants in 17 Russian cities.

Russia's most important industry is petroleum extraction and processing, and the country is one of the world's largest producers of crude oil. Russia's domestic oil provides its other industries with vital energy at a reasonable cost. The country is also a major producer of iron ore, manganese, and nickel. Huge forests in Russia produce one-fifth of the world's softwood, and Russian fish-factory ships process catches from both the Atlantic and Pacific Oceans. Other major manufacturing industries include steel milling; auto and truck production; aircraft construction; and the manufacturing of chemicals, heavy machinery, and agricultural equipment. Most of these industries are in the Volga Valley, near Moscow and St. Petersburg, and in the Ural Mountains. Although Russia's industries still face difficulties, industrial production is now rising.

Transportation and Communications

Russian transportation and communications systems lag behind those of most of the world's developed countries. In an age of speedy transportation, the Internet, and a global economy, Russia struggles to find funds for new highways and high-tech communications.

Transporting Goods

Russia's transportation systems must move food and other resources great distances to reach consumers. A major highway system links Moscow with other major Russian cities, but many roads are in poor repair. Harsh winters in places like **Siberia** often make roads impassable.

Because of its great size and climate extremes, Russia depends on railroads and waterways for most of its transportation needs. Not surprisingly, Russia boasts the world's longest continuous railroad line. The Trans-Siberian Railroad is the greater part of the rail route from Moscow through the Siberian steppes to the Pacific port city of **Vladivostok**. Major cities are found where the Trans-Siberian Railroad crosses large rivers, such as the Ural, Irtysh, Ob, and Yenisey. Millions of tons of materials travel along thousands of miles of navigable inland waterways, which connect seaports and inland cities.

Transporting People

Most Russians live in cities and many do not own cars, so public transportation, such as trains, buses, and, in several large cities, subways, is common. Private car ownership doubled in the 1990s, but public transportation remains a practical option for Russians, in part because the government helps pay for it. The systems and equipment, however, need repair and improvements.

The Soviet Union used jet airplanes for passenger traffic, and the government

NATIONAL GEOGRAPHIC World Explorer

Geography Skills for Life

Russian Agriculture Outdated farm equipment makes farming labor-intensive for humans and animals.
Place Why have farmers in Russia been reluctant to accept a market economy system?

L1/ELL

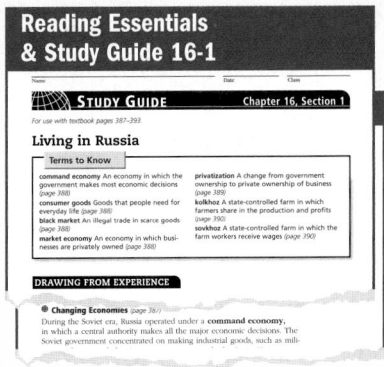

Reading Essentials & Study Guide 16-1

STUDY GUIDE — Chapter 16, Section 1
For use with textbook pages 387–393

Living in Russia

Terms to Know

command economy An economy in which the government makes most economic decisions (page 388)
consumer goods Goods that people need for everyday life (page 388)
black market An illegal trade in scarce goods (page 388)
market economy An economy in which businesses are privately owned (page 388)

privatization A change from government ownership to private ownership of business (page 389)
kolkhoz A state-controlled farm in which farmers share in the production and profits (page 390)
sovkhoz A state-controlled farm in which farm workers receive wages (page 390)

DRAWING FROM EXPERIENCE

● **Changing Economies** (page 387)
During the Soviet era, Russia operated under a **command economy**, in which a central authority makes all the major economic decisions. The Soviet government concentrated on making industrial goods, such as mili-

Military Music The Red Army Chorus—allowed the rare freedom of international travel during the Cold War—continues to sell CDs and perform around the world.

NATIONAL GEOGRAPHIC World Explorer

Answer
Farmers who could not afford to buy land feared that wealthy Russians and foreign businesses would buy the land for nonagricultural purposes, so they kept the old system of collective land ownership.

More About the Photo
Increasing the productivity of Russia's farms would require large investments in gasoline-powered equipment and agricultural chemicals, both of which have environmental drawbacks.

TEAM-TEACHING ACTIVITY: ECONOMICS

Role-play Have students work with an economics teacher to carry out a simulation of the two kinds of economies experienced by Russia in the last century. Organize the class into two groups. Have one group role-play everyday transactions to explain how the Soviet command economy operated. Have the other group role-play the same transactions under a newly developing market economy, such as that of Russia. Have the two groups compare and contrast their experiences. 🌐 **EE4 Human Systems: Standard 11**

NATIONAL GEOGRAPHIC World Explorer

Answer
energy fuels, lumber, metals, and chemicals

More About the Photo
The Baltic port of Kaliningrad is located between Poland and Lithuania and is separated from the rest of Russia. Kaliningrad was founded in 1255 by German knights, and was originally known as Konigsberg.

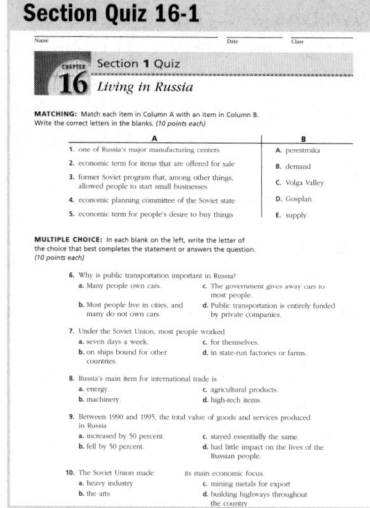
3 ASSESS

Assign Section 1 Assessment as homework or as an in-class activity.

Have students use **Interactive Tutor Self-Assessment CD-ROM** to review Section 1.

L2

Section Quiz 16-1

NATIONAL GEOGRAPHIC World Explorer

Geography Skills for Life

Russian Waterways Cargo cranes along the Pregolya River in Kaliningrad assist in shipping goods for export.
Place What goods does Russia export?

financially supported air travel for many years. The passenger airline Aeroflot was once the only one in the Soviet Union and at its peak carried 135 million people a year. After the fall of the Soviet Union, Aeroflot split into numerous smaller airlines. The high cost of fuel and reduced passenger traffic because of skyrocketing ticket prices have forced about 60 percent of Russia's airports to close.

Transporting Energy

Russia's large size also affects how it transports natural gas, crude oil, and other petroleum products. Pipelines are effective, although constructing and maintaining them can be difficult in areas of harsh climate. A complex maze of pipelines crisscrosses Russia, providing major Russian cities and parts of western Europe with fuel.

The oil pipelines run through Chechnya and Dagestan (DAH•guh•STAHN), ethnic republics in southwestern Russia. Because people in these republics are fighting for their independence from Russia, control of the area's oil reserves and working pipelines is a major concern.

History
Mass Communications

Under the Soviet Union, the state owned and controlled all the mass communications systems, including newspapers, magazines, television, the postal service, and the telegraph and telephone systems. State agencies reviewed all print and broadcast materials to make sure that they contained no criticism of the government. Since the breakup of the Soviet Union, Russians have heard and read new voices and fresh views. Most families own radios and television sets, and by 1995 Russians could choose from among 10,000 newspapers and journals.

Telephone service in Russia has also grown. As a result of Russia's vast size, only 22 percent of rural households have telephones, compared with 56 percent of urban households. However, communications companies are increasingly offering services such as the Internet, e-mail, and cellular phones. These advances in communications systems will make

---

EXTENDING THE CONTENT

Russia and the World Since the breakup of the Soviet Union, Russia has attempted to strengthen its economic and political ties with other parts of the world. Russia is a member of Asia-Pacific Economic Cooperation (APEC), a consortium of countries located on the Pacific Rim. Russia maintains diplomatic ties with, and receives aid from, the European Union (EU). Some propose that Russia be invited to join the EU—contingent on Russia's improving its economy and ending the strife in Chechnya. Russia continues to hope for admission to the World Trade Organization (WTO), but one large obstacle to Russia's joining the WTO is its failure to successfully privatize agriculture. 🌐 **EE4 Human Systems: Standard 13**

vital contributions to the successful transition to a market economy.

Global Interdependence

After independence Russia and the other former Soviet republics began to increase their interdependence with other countries. By expanding international trade and building political and financial relations, Russia has increasingly focused on becoming a full partner in the global community.

Trade

Russia has already established trade relations in world markets and is a major source of energy and fuels, which make up 48 percent of its exports. Lumber, metals, and chemicals are also important Russian exports. The United States, the European Union, the other former Soviet republics, China, and Japan are among Russia's major trading partners. These countries provide Russia with the consumer goods, medicines, meat, and sugar it needs.

Energy is expected to remain Russia's main item of international trade until its manufactured goods, such as machinery and light industrial products, improve in quality and become more competitively priced. Working to strengthen its industries, Russia became a member of the Asia-Pacific Economic Cooperation (APEC) forum in 1998. Negotiations

are continuing for Russia's membership in the World Trade Organization (WTO). As Russian manufacturing makes further gains, these trading networks will become even more important for the Russian economy.

International Relations

Despite its political and economic challenges at home, Russia maintains its important role in world affairs. Russia benefits from occupying the former Soviet Union's seat in the United Nations Security Council. The country has also joined European organizations that support security and cooperation. Russia has helped settle conflicts and has supported peace efforts in several countries, especially in former Soviet republics. Even as Russia asserts itself internationally, however, economic problems have drained money from its military. As a result, military forces have old equipment, and soldiers' morale is low.

Adequate financial resources are vitally important to Russia's stability and progress in the global community. Other countries and world organizations have provided loans, and foreign investors have made funds available to Russian industry. With foreign help, Russia is trying to create secure and workable systems for banking, farming, manufacturing, transportation, and communications. Although Russia has a long way to go, the economic gains made in recent years are positive signs.

SECTION 1 ASSESSMENT

Checking for Understanding

1. **Define** command economy, consumer goods, black market, market economy, privatization, kolkhoz, sovkhoz.

2. **Main Ideas** On a chart like the one below, fill in details about agriculture, industry, transportation, and communications in the Soviet command economy and the Russian market economy.

	Soviet Command Economy	Russian Market Economy
Agriculture		

Critical Thinking

3. **Predicting Consequences** How might Russia's agricultural and industrial sectors be affected by Russia's growing global interdependence?

4. **Comparing and Contrasting** How did the Soviet command economy and the Russian market economy affect the Russian people?

5. **Making Inferences** What can you infer about Russia's goals, based on changes in Russia's trade and international relations since the Soviet breakup?

Analyzing Maps

6. **Human-Environment Interaction** Study the economic activity map on page 341. In what area is the raising of livestock concentrated? How is this related to the physical geography of the region?

Applying Geography

7. **Effects of Size and Distance** Think about the physical geography of Russia. Write a paragraph analyzing how Russia's vast size affects the availability of natural resources and the country's ability to develop them.

Reteach

Have students choose partners and challenge one another by taking turns describing characteristics of Russian agriculture, transportation, and communications. Each student should ask his or her partner whether each characteristic describes life under communism or life after 1991.

Enrich

Have students research the Internet and other sources to compare and contrast Soviet and Russian systems of education with those found in the United States, Europe, East Asia, or other regions of the world.

4 CLOSE

Have students attempt to establish an e-mail link with a Russian school to exchange information about everyday life with students there.

SECTION 1 ASSESSMENT ANSWERS

1. All vocabulary terms are defined in the text.
2. Chart entries should reflect text information.
3. Both sectors may become more productive with free trade and foreign aid.
4. Command economy: unemployment was low but so were wages; consumer goods were scarce; some sectors were undeveloped. Market economy: private economic opportunities and the supply of some goods increased, but

so did unemployment; profits were invested outside the country; crime and corruption increased.

5. Russia is hoping to become part of Western economic and trade groups in order to secure further investments. Russia inherited the Soviet Union's seat on the United Nations's Security Council. It hopes to play a leading role in settling conflicts.

6. Most livestock grazes in southern Russia, on the grasslands of the steppe.

7. **Applying Geography** Paragraphs should reflect an understanding of the obstacles to resource development: distance, terrain, climate, and inadequate transportation.

1 FOCUS

Ask students to identify the kinds of fish they have eaten recently. Explain that the most widely consumed meals containing fish in the United States include fish sticks and other processed, battered fish pieces (normally made from pollack and cod), fast-food fish sandwiches, canned tuna, and imitation crab and lobster (also made from pollack). Tell students that these kinds of fish are among those most likely to be commercially caught by large fishing fleets.

2 TEACH

Tell students that between 1970 and 1990, the number of the world's fishing fleets increased at twice the rate of increase of the world's fishing catch. **Ask: What might be some of the consequences of this situation?** *(increased economic competition, overfishing, increased government regulation, reduced income for fishers)*

3 ASSESS

Have students answer the **What's Your Point of View?** questions on this page.

Viewpoint
CASE STUDY on the Environment

Russia's Supertrawlers: Factories at Sea

More than a million fishing vessels scour the oceans for fish. As a result, fish populations are shrinking worldwide. Enormous ships called supertrawlers are largely to blame. Towing huge trawl nets—some large enough to scoop up a whale—supertrawlers are floating fish factories. These ships can catch and process more than 400 tons (360 t) of fish a day. No one knows how many fish swim the oceans. However, if too many are caught, some species may not recover. Is sustainable fishing possible with supertrawlers harvesting the seas?

394 Unit 5

LOOKING TO THE FUTURE

Alternatives to Trawling In response to shrinking fish resources, many countries have tightened restrictions on fishing in their coastal waters. Today, however, more than 90 percent of the world's commercial fishing is carried out by six "distant-waters" countries—Russia, Japan, Spain, Poland, South Korea, and Taiwan—that send their fleets of supertrawlers around the world. Fishing provides large portions of these countries' income. Proposed alternatives to trawling include replacing high-seas fishing with aquaculture—"farming" fish under controlled conditions.
▣ **EE5 Environment and Society: Standard 16**

State-of-the-art electronic gear allows super-trawlers to track schools of fish with pinpoint accuracy. Trawl nets may stretch half a mile behind the ships, engulfing everything in their paths.

The first factory trawler was built in Scotland in 1954. By 1970 the Soviet Union had 400 trawlers, the world's largest fleet at that time. Other countries, including the United States, China, and Japan, soon launched their own trawler fleets. Marine harvests soared as these enormous vessels went to work in the world's richest fishing grounds. But after a few years of bounty, there were signs of trouble at sea.

In the western Bering Sea, for example, Soviet (later Russian) supertrawlers initially harvested large numbers of sole, perch, herring, and especially pollock—the fish used in frozen fish sticks and fast-food fish sandwiches. As catches started to outpace reproduction rates, fish populations plummeted. Data gathered by Russian marine biologists show

A Russian supertrawler (below) searches for fish in the Sea of Okhotsk. Aboard these vessels, workers (right) prepare fish for a global market. ▼

that pollock catches are declining by 10 percent every year. American scientists raise similar concerns about the impact of American supertrawlers working the eastern Bering Sea.

Supertrawlers are usually after certain kinds of fish. Everything else hauled up in the nets gets discarded. Millions of fish and other marine animals die unnecessarily every year. Many trawlers also drag nets along the seafloor, destroying countless organisms and their habitats. Animals higher on the food chain are affected, too. Seals, sea lions, and kittiwakes can starve if there are fewer fish to eat. Since the 1970s these mammal and bird populations in the Bering Sea have declined.

Opponents of supertrawlers argue that the ships are doing irreparable damage to fish stocks and marine habitats. Opponents feel the unnecessary slaughter of healthy marine organisms is wasteful. Even though there are some restrictions on supertrawlers, opponents maintain that the

◄ Using a huge net, a Russian fisherman empties a load of fish into his boat.

laws are hard to enforce. Furthermore, since smaller boats can't compete with supertrawlers, the big ships threaten traditional fishing cultures on every continent.

Supporters of supertrawlers cite the growing global demand for fish and fish products. They point out that their catches supply high-protein food to millions of people. Some trawler operators dispute data that show a decline in fish populations. Others say that if trawlers reduce their catches, other ships will simply harvest what's left behind. Russian officials must balance the risk of destroying fish stocks with Russia's need for a profitable fishing industry.

What's Your Point of View? Should further restrictions be placed on supertrawlers? Should they be banned worldwide?

4 CLOSE

Problem Solving Challenge small groups of students to create an international plan for protecting fish populations and preventing economic hardship to fishers.

global issues

Oceans and Fishing Approximately 7 million people—mostly Asians—rely on fish to supply at least a third of their animal protein. At least 200 million people worldwide depend on fishing for their income. Marine goods and services contribute $21 trillion annually to the world's income. Overfishing, pollution, and climate changes threaten these important resources.

Meeting National Standards

Geography for Life
The following standards are met in this feature:

EE3 Physical Systems:
   Standard 8
EE4 Human Systems:
   Standards 11, 13
EE5 Environment and Society:
   Standards 14, 16
EE6 The Uses of Geography:
   Standard 18

WHAT CAN YOU DO?

Share these strategies for promoting effective management of ocean resources:

- Learn more about the issue. Contact the National Oceanic and Atmospheric Administration (NOAA) and other Internet resources for information.
- Support efforts toward environmentally responsible fishing. Choose fish products with labels indicating compliance with

environmental standards and practices.
- Control pollution and waste that may eventually reach the oceans.
- Share your concerns in letters to the editors of popular magazines and in messages to the directors of corporations that profit from ocean fishing.

🌐 **EE6 The Uses of Geography: Standard 18**

FOCUS

Section Overview

This section discusses Russia's environmental and economic challenges as the region struggles to manage its resources.

BELLRINGER
Skillbuilder Activity

 Project transparency and have students answer questions.

 Available as blackline master.

Daily Focus Skills Transparency 16-2

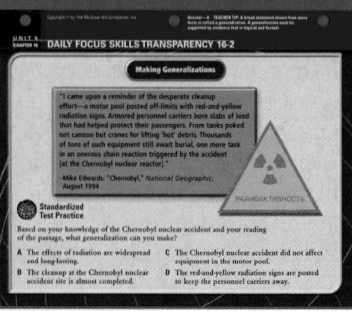

Guide to Reading

Consider What You Know
Answer *Soviet-era industrialization led to pollution; the economic chaos following the switch to a market economy has not allowed Russia to invest in environmental repair and conservation.*

Reading Strategy
Answers Kamchatka: *mining operation in region is a possible threat to salmon spawning grounds;* Lake Baikal: *factories dump waste into lake, endangering 1,500 native species of plants and animals;* Chernobyl: *site of 1986 nuclear reactor fire, tons of radioactive particles released into atmosphere*

Preteaching Vocabulary
Use the **Vocabulary Puzzle-Maker CD-ROM** to create crossword and word-search puzzles.

Guide to Reading

Consider What You Know
You have read about the Soviet government's development of heavy industry and about Russia's development of a market economy after the breakup of the Soviet Union. How do you think these activities have affected the quality of Russia's environment?

Reading Strategy
Organizing As you read about Russia's environment, complete a graphic organizer similar to the one below by describing the environmental issues and concerns for each location.

Location	Description
Kamchatka	
Lake Baikal	
Chernobyl	

Read to Find Out
- How does Russia manage its natural resources?
- How has pollution affected the lives of Russia's people?
- What are the environmental challenges in Russia's future?

Terms to Know
- radioactive material
- pesticide
- nuclear waste

Places to Locate
- Kamchatka
- Lake Baikal

People and Their Environment

NATIONAL GEOGRAPHIC

A Geographic View

The Aftermath

I found little likelihood that things [would] improve soon; the economies of Russia and most of the other . . . former Soviet republics are in shambles. "They used to show us films of the corrupted West with its polluted waters, like your Great Lakes," a Siberian environmental worker said. "Now the situation you had in the 1960s is here. But if the chaos continues, we will need two or three times as many years as you needed just to decide it's necessary to clean up."

—Mike Edwards, "Lethal Legacy,"
National Geographic, *August 1994*

Steel plant in Siberia

The world's expanding industries and rapidly growing population often strain the natural environment. Careless management of natural resources for short-term gain destroys economic opportunities for future generations, damages the environment, threatens people's health, and jeopardizes people's quality of life. In this section you will learn how Russia is managing its resources and balancing economic growth with environmental conservation.

Managing Resources

Russia is trying to make the best use of its vast and abundant natural resources in order to strengthen its economy and improve its standard of living. Unfortunately, the country has inherited a legacy of environmental damage. Russia's main challenge is to manage its resources without repeating its past disregard for the environment.

RESOURCE MANAGER

📁 Reproducible Masters
- Reproducible Lesson Plan 16-2
- Vocabulary Activity 16
- Daily Lecture Notes 16-2
- Guided Reading Activity 16-2
- Reading Essentials and Study Guide 16-2
- Reteaching Activity 16
- Reinforcing Skills Activity 16
- Section Quiz 16-2

📠 Transparencies
- Daily Focus Skills Transparency 16-2
- Political Map Transparency 5
- Unit 5 Map Overlay Transparencies

Multimedia
- Vocabulary PuzzleMaker CD-ROM
- Interactive Tutor Self-Assessment CD-ROM
- ExamView® Pro Testmaker CD-ROM
- Presentation Plus! CD-ROM

A second challenge is to improve the environment and repair damage that has already been done. One target for improvement is the timber industry. Russia contains the world's largest forest reserve, and the World Bank's Sustainable Forestry Pilot Project is helping Russia manage its forests more effectively. Using land more wisely, protecting forests, planting new trees, and increasing private forestry investment all help Russia's environment and economy. Higher taxes paid by Russian citizens provide income for the government to help protect the environment. Increased employment opportunities in the forest industry and more stable local economies will be possible only if steps to conserve the forest are taken. It is in the best interest of the people to protect the forests because the timber industry provides jobs and economic resources for communities.

Individual Russians are becoming more aware of the value of good environmental management. People have banded together to oppose a mining operation located in remote **Kamchatka** (kuhm•CHAWT•kuh), a region of Siberia in eastern Russia. The Kamchatka Committee for the Protection of the Environment and Natural Resources has demanded that the mining company meet strict environmental standards. The possible threat to the area's salmon spawning grounds prompted the local fishing industry to support the effort. The mine also caused concern among local residents and environmentalists because it was close to a nature park that was recently named a United Nations World Heritage site.

Pollution

The Soviets' disregard for the environmental effects of industrialization damaged Russia's water, air, and soil. By the 1990s, 40 percent of Russia's vast territory was under "ecological stress," with the health of millions of Russians affected by unchecked pollution and radiation.

Water Quality

Although Russia has one of the world's largest supplies of freshwater, industrialization has polluted most of its lakes and rivers. Fertilizer runoff, sewage, metals such as aluminum, and radioactive material—material contaminated by residue from the generation of nuclear energy—all contribute to poor water quality. The waters of the Moskva and Volga Rivers, for instance, pose severe health risks. The many dams along the Volga have trapped contaminated water. Moscow has also reported cholera-causing bacteria in its water. Pollution even threatens the Caspian Sea.

Lying on the southeastern edge of the Central Siberian Plateau, **Lake Baikal** (by•KAWL) is the world's oldest and deepest lake. It contains one-fifth of the world's freshwater, and 1,500 native species of aquatic plants and animals make their home there. Calling it "the Pearl of Siberia," Russians consider the lake a natural wonder. A recent traveler learned from a local resident what Baikal means to Russians:

> ❝ Lake Baikal is a symbol, Sasha told me once, of all the things that give Siberian life its distinct sweetness—the natural beauty, the purity of open air, the hardy generosity of people and the poetry in their collective soul. 'This is what Russians mean when they talk about the Motherland,' he said. 'And nothing, nothing is more precious to us than that'. ❞
>
> Don Belt, "Russia's Lake Baikal: The World's Great Lake," *National Geographic*, June 1992

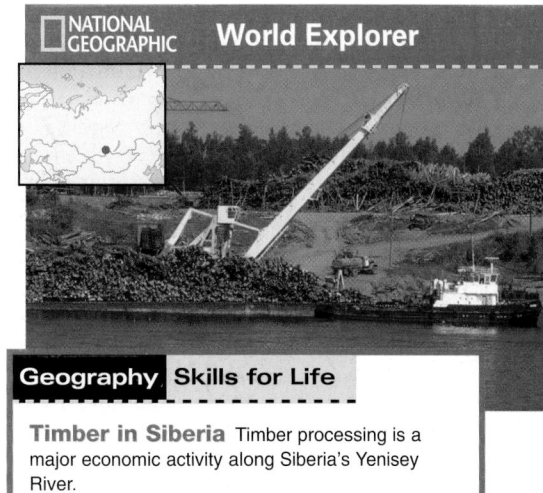

NATIONAL GEOGRAPHIC **World Explorer**

Geography Skills for Life

Timber in Siberia Timber processing is a major economic activity along Siberia's Yenisey River.

Human-Environment Interaction How does the proper management of forests affect a country?

② TEACH

L1 Determining Cause and Effect

Invite students to discuss the causes and effects of the Chernobyl accident.

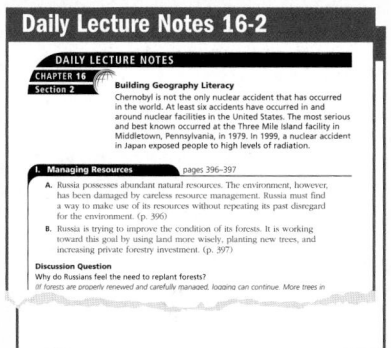

Daily Lecture Notes 16-2

DAILY LECTURE NOTES

CHAPTER 16
Section 2

Building Geography Literacy
Chernobyl is not the only nuclear accident that has occurred in the world. At least six accidents have occurred in and around nuclear facilities in the United States. The most serious and best known occurred at the Three Mile Island facility in Middletown, Pennsylvania, in 1979. In 1999, a nuclear accident in Japan exposed people to high levels of radiation.

I. Managing Resources pages 396–397

A. Russia possesses abundant natural resources. The environment, however, has been damaged by careless resource management. Russia must find a way to make use of its resources without repeating its past disregard for the environment. (p. 396)

B. Russia is trying to improve the condition of its forests. It is working toward this goal by using land more wisely, planting new trees, and increasing private forestry investment. (p. 397)

Discussion Question
Why do Russians feel the need to replant forests?
If forests are properly renewed and carefully managed, logging can continue. More trees in

L1/ELL

Guided Reading Activity 16-2

Guided Reading Activity 16-2

For use with textbook pages 396–399

People and Their Environment
Short Answer
DIRECTIONS: Use the information in your textbook to write a short answer to each of the following questions.

1. What is the main challenge for Russia and its abundant natural resources?

2. What is one example of Russia's second challenge—to repair environmental damage?

3. What were the concerns of Russians who opposed the Kamchatka mining operation?

4. How has the Soviets' disregard for the environmental effects of industrialization affected Russia's

NATIONAL GEOGRAPHIC **World Explorer**

Answer
It contributes to economic growth and environmental quality.

More About the Photo To be certified as environmentally sustainable, timber producers must replace timber reserves at the same or greater rates as they are harvesting them.

DIFFERENTIATED INSTRUCTION

Visual/Spatial Have students work together to create a visual model of the effects of pollution and overlogging on the Russian taiga. Direct students to use their textbooks as well as printed and Internet references to obtain information about the taiga, its significance to the global environment and to Russia's economy, and the effects of acid rain and poor timber management. Students may use any form of graphic display, such as three-dimensional models, posters, or multimedia presentations. 🌐 **EE5 Environment and Society: Standards 14, 16**

📁 Refer to *Inclusion for the Social Studies Classroom Strategies and Activities.*

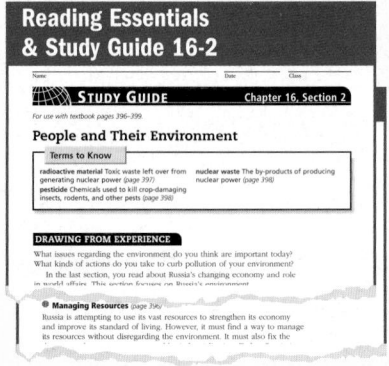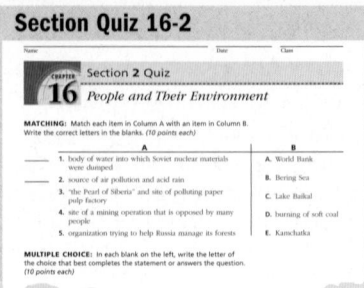

NATIONAL GEOGRAPHIC **World Explorer**

Geography Skills for Life

Lake Baikal Efforts to protect Lake Baikal include closing paper mills and installing waste-water treatment plants.
Human-Environment Interaction How has industrial development affected Lake Baikal?

In 1957 the Soviet Union announced a plan to build a paper pulp factory in Baikalsk along Lake Baikal's southwestern shores. Although this plan was opposed by citizens in the area, their protests were ignored and the factory was built. This factory and others that followed continue to dump industrial waste into the lake. However, in response to the ongoing protests of local residents, the most serious polluters either have been closed or are in the process of reducing pollution. Pollution levels in the lake are now relatively low compared with many lakes in Europe and the United States.

Soil and Air Quality

For decades toxic waste dumps and airborne pollution poisoned Russia's soil. Aging storage containers cracked and leaked toxic wastes into the soil. Petroleum pipelines also often broke and tainted the land. Overuse of fertilizers and pesticides—chemicals used to kill crop-damaging insects, rodents, and other pests—has damaged farmland.

Russian experts believe that during the 1990s only 15 percent of Russia's urban population lived

with acceptable air quality. Industries, emissions from vehicles, and the soft coal burned for fuel are all sources of air pollution. In addition to releasing soot, sulfur, and carbon dioxide into the air, burning coal leads to another harmful agent—acid rain. Experts estimate that the combination of acid rain and chemical pollution has reduced Russian forests by about 1.5 million acres (607,500 ha) since the early 1970s.

Nuclear Wastes

Between 1949 and 1987, the Soviet Union set off more than 600 nuclear explosions. Soviets developed and then stockpiled nuclear weapons throughout the Cold War. Today, the condition and fate of those weapons concern Russia and the rest of the world.

Nuclear wastes are the by-products of producing nuclear power. Some of these wastes can remain radioactive for thousands of years, posing great dangers to people and the environment. The Soviets placed most nuclear wastes in storage facilities, but they also dumped some radioactive nuclear materials directly into Russia's northern waters, such as the Baltic and Bering Seas.

History
Chernobyl

During the Cold War, nuclear power generated much-needed electricity in the Soviet Union. It also provided power for building military weapons and vehicles. The urgency of keeping pace with the West during the Cold War often resulted in substandard nuclear plants and reactors that employed poorly trained workers who ignored proper safeguards. In 1986 a fire in a nuclear reactor in the town of Chernobyl (chuhr•NOH•buhl), 60 miles (97 km) north of Kiev, Ukraine, released tons of radioactive particles into the local environment. This radiation was then carried great distances by the wind, and contaminated other countries.

Thousands of people were exposed to deadly levels of radiation because Soviet officials were slow to alert the public to the crisis and did not evacuate people soon enough. By the mid-1990s

---

COOPERATIVE LEARNING ACTIVITY

Problem Solving Have students work in groups to research Russia's energy resources—both for internal use and for export income. Then, direct the groups to develop plans that show how Russia's energy needs might be met without relying on outmoded nuclear facilities or other environmentally dangerous means. Remind students to consider what they know about Russia's economy and physical geography when proposing solutions. Have each group prepare a poster advertising its proposed solutions.
🌐 **EE5 Environment and Society: Standard 16**

over 8,000 people had died as a direct result of radiation poisoning. Millions more continue to suffer from cancer, stomach diseases, and immune system disorders. Radiation covered thousands of acres of farmland and forests in Belarus, Ukraine, and Russia. In Russia alone, radiation covered over 19,300 square miles (50,000 sq. km), where more than 30 million people lived. Because of prevailing winds, other countries suffered as well, most notably Finland, Sweden, Poland, and the former Czechoslovakia.

After the Chernobyl accident, international pressure prompted Soviet leaders to improve nuclear safety standards and to shut down dangerous plants. In response to these demands, Soviet officials never opened some newly built reactors and abandoned plans for building others. Despite concerns from other countries, 28 nuclear reactors continue to operate at nine sites throughout Russia. Much of Russia's electricity continues to come from these plants. In late 2000, however, the remaining reactor at Chernobyl was shut down. Experts in Western countries as well as in Russia and Ukraine think that many remaining Soviet-era reactors are poorly designed, unsafe, and should be made secure.

NATIONAL GEOGRAPHIC World Explorer

Geography Skills for Life

The Chernobyl Reactor The explosion at Chernobyl resulted in a total meltdown of the core.
Human-Environment Interaction How did the Soviet government improve nuclear safety standards after the Chernobyl accident?

SECTION 2 ASSESSMENT

Checking for Understanding

1. **Define** radioactive material, pesticide, nuclear waste.

2. **Main Ideas** Create a graphic organizer like the one below, and fill in information about each of the topics. Then choose one of the topics, and summarize efforts currently under way in Russia to address the situation.

```
                Pollution
   ┌───────────────┼────────────────┐
 Water       Soil & Air      Nuclear Waste
  •               •                •
  •               •                •
  •               •                •
```

Critical Thinking

3. **Making Generalizations** What generalizations can you make about the relationship between economic development and the environment in Russia?

4. **Problem Solving** Assume the role of the Russian president, and identify an environmental problem in your country. What steps would you take to solve this problem?

5. **Predicting Consequences** Think about what you know about the Russian economy. What is the likelihood of a dramatic improvement in Russia's environmental problems in the near future?

Analyzing Maps

6. **Human-Environment Interaction** Study the economic activity map on page 341. Think about the regions of Russia in which pollution is a problem. Describe the relationship between the location of manufacturing centers and pollution.

Applying Geography

7. **Influence of Location** Think about the challenges Russia faces concerning water quality. Write a paragraph explaining why Russians do not use more water from Lake Baikal to supply their freshwater needs.

Chapter 16 🌐 399

NATIONAL GEOGRAPHIC World Explorer

Answer
shut down dangerous plants; never opened some completed plants; dropped plans for building some new plants

More About the Photo
Measurements indicate that Chernobyl radiation far exceeds that released by the atomic bombs dropped on Hiroshima and Nagasaki.

Reteach

Have students list Russia's environmental challenges and then propose possible solutions for each challenge.

Enrich

Share with students poems of Pushkin, Akhmatova, Pasternak, and Yevtushenko that describe Russia's environment.

4 CLOSE

Have students write poems or paint pictures celebrating the future restoration of one facet of the Russian environment.

SECTION 2 ASSESSMENT ANSWERS

1. All vocabulary terms are defined in the text.

2. Graphic organizers and summaries should reflect text information.

3. Generally, Russian economic development has harmed the environment. Recent attempts to improve the economy without harming the environment have been challenging.

4. Students' responses should reflect an understanding of the environmental challenges facing Russia, and should apply logical remedies.

5. No dramatic improvement is likely, though some improvement will occur.

6. Pollution is often concentrated in mining and manufacturing areas and in cities, although agricultural runoff also causes water pollution.

7. **Applying Geography** Paragraphs should indicate an understanding of the impracticality of transporting freshwater from Lake Baikal over great distances to the west, where water supplies are limited. Other reasons include the fact that only one river flows out of Lake Baikal, and the desire of Russia's people to preserve the lake's unique ecosystems.

Teaching the Skill

Line up a number of unrelated objects on a desk or table. Ask students to study the objects and attempt to group them into logical categories. Invite volunteers to share their categories and explain the basis on which they made their choices. Allow time for the class to evaluate each attempt at categorization. **Ask: Which categorization did you find most effective? Does the effectiveness of the categorizing depend on the purpose for which you will be using the categories?** Have students suggest ways they can use the categories they developed. *(to compare and contrast objects, to organize information)*

Additional Practice
L1

Reinforcing Skills Activity 16

Name _____ Date _____ Class _____

CHAPTER 16 REINFORCING SKILLS ACTIVITY

Categorizing Information

Categorizing information is an important skill that can help you understand relationships, remember details, and draw conclusions. Categorizing is sorting details into groups. Making a chart is a useful way to organize information into categories. Columns and rows provide spaces for grouping details. After information has been categorized, you can review it, compare or contrast it, and draw conclusions about it.

Practicing the Skill

DIRECTIONS: Categorize the details listed below the chart. Write the number of each detail under *Characteristics* beside the item it matches. Then answer the question at the end of the list.

TRANSPORTATION IN RUSSIA	
Items transported	Characteristics
Goods	

GLENCOE
TECHNOLOGY

Glencoe Skillbuilder Interactive Workbook, Level 2

This interactive CD-ROM reinforces student mastery of essential social studies skills.

CRITICAL THINKING
SkillBuilder

Categorizing Information

When you read a map, you make sense of the data you see—the symbols, words, and different-colored lines and shapes—by categorizing the information. Categorizing means grouping information and details together in a way that helps you understand and compare two or more ideas or concepts.

Learning the Skill

Categorizing information helps you make connections and retain information. This skill helps you answer questions such as *What is it? What parts does it have?* and *How is this like or unlike something else?*

When you categorize, you sort details into groups. You may be looking at a map, reading an informative article, or watching a basketball game. Once you understand how the details are grouped, you can make comparisons and draw conclusions. One way to keep track of the different details is to create a chart.

Follow these steps to categorize written information, using a chart.

- **As you read a section of a chapter, identify its main categories.** Make a two-column chart with one row for titles and one row for each category.
- **Spend a few minutes reading the section.** Record the title for each category in the first column of the chart. Then note some details and characteristics that you found for each category. List these in the second column of the chart.
- **Review the details in the second column of the chart.** Use them to write a summary statement about each category and to compare the categories with each other.

The Changing Economy of Russia

Type of Economy	Characteristics
Command (Soviet)	• Central authority owns banks, factories, farms, mines, and transportation systems. • Production and prices depend on decisions of the central authority. • Meets the basic needs of consumers but not designed to meet their wants.
Market	• Businesses are privately owned. • Production and prices depend on supply and demand. • A high degree of individual freedom allows producers to make whatever they think they will sell.

Practicing the Skill

Use the information about Russia on pages 388–390 and the chart on this page to answer the questions below.

1. What are the main categories of information on pages 388–390?

2. What are two other characteristics you could list in the chart?

3. How are these systems alike? How are they different?

4. What are two ways that a chart similar to the one above could help you?

Applying the Skill

Use library or Internet research and the information in Chapters 7 and 16 to categorize information about pollution in Russia, the United States, and Canada. Use a chart like the one on this page to list details about the sources of air, water, and soil pollution and proposed solutions for these challenges.

 The Glencoe Skillbuilder Interactive Workbook, Level 2 provides instruction and practice in key social studies skills.

ANSWERS TO PRACTICING THE SKILL

1. the soviet command economy, the market economy

2. command economy: emphasized heavy industry; market economy: many government controls eliminated

3. Alike: both systems supply jobs; both create products. Different: command systems have ownership of production facilities by a central authority, which also sets priorities and pricing; market systems have private ownership of production facilities, which set prices based on supply and demand and make products to satisfy consumers' wants as well as their needs.

4. Possible answers include making comparisons for research or reports, studying for tests, or organizing notes.

CHAPTER 16 | SUMMARY & STUDY GUIDE

SECTION 1 — Living in Russia (pp. 387–393)

Terms to Know
- command economy
- consumer goods
- black market
- market economy
- privatization
- kolkhoz
- sovkhoz

Key Points
- The Soviet economy was a command economy controlled by government agencies.
- Since the 1980s the Russians have been making the difficult transition from the Soviet command economy to a market economy.
- After the breakup of the Soviet Union, Boris Yeltsin encouraged privatization of state-owned farms and businesses.
- Transportation and communications systems must improve in order to support a strong market economy.
- To take its place as a full partner in the global community, Russia needs good international trade and strong political and economic relations.

Organizing Your Notes
Create an outline like the one below, using the section headings to help you organize your notes for this section.

Living in Russia
I. Changing Economies
A. The Soviet Command Economy
1.
2.

SECTION 2 — People and Their Environment (pp. 396–399)

Terms to Know
- radioactive material
- pesticide
- nuclear waste

Key Points
- Soviet leaders' drive for an industrial-based economy caused major and lasting damage to Russia's water, soil, and air.
- Russia needs to manage its use of natural resources properly in order to avoid more environmental damage.
- Radioactivity from nuclear waste, nuclear accidents, and aging nuclear weapons poses a grave danger to Russia's environment and its people's health.

Organizing Your Notes
Use a graphic organizer like the one below to help you organize information about the challenges facing Russia today.

Environmental Challenges		
Water	Soil and Air	Nuclear Waste

Russian passengers wait to board a train.

Chapter 16 🌐 **401**

Using the Chapter 16 Summary & Study Guide

Use the Chapter 16 Summary & Study Guide to preview, review, condense, or reteach the chapter.

Preview/Review

🔘 **Vocabulary PuzzleMaker CD-ROM** reinforces "Terms to Know."

🔘 **Interactive Tutor Self-Assessment CD-ROM** provides a review of Chapter 16 content.

Condense

Have students read the Chapter 16 Summary & Study Guide.

🔘 Chapter 16 Audio Program

📁 Chapter 16 Guided Reading Activities

Reteach

📁 Chapter 16 Reteaching Activities (Spanish also available)

📁 Chapter 16 Reading Essentials and Study Guides

GLENCOE TECHNOLOGY

📷 NATIONAL GEOGRAPHIC
WORLD REGIONS
VIDEO PROGRAM

Unit 5, Russia
The following segments enhance the study of this unit:
- **Siberian Tigers**
- **The Tire Factory**
- **Bolshoi Ballet**

CHAPTER CULMINATING ACTIVITY

Letter to the Editor Tell students that the year is 1991. Ask them to put themselves in the position of a Russian leader, telling the Russian people what might be expected from the change to a market economy. Have students include information about the challenges Russia will face, but also provide encouragement and make suggestions for addressing the challenges that will arise. 🌐 **EE4 Human Systems: Standard 11**

NOTE: This activity may be completed separately or you may wish students to incorporate it in their GeoJournals.

GLENCOE TECHNOLOGY

Use *MindJogger Videoquiz* to review the Chapter 16 content.

Reviewing Key Terms

Soviet Era: command economy; After Independence: market economy, privatization; Both: consumer goods, black market, kolkhoz, sovkhoz, radioactive material, pesticide, nuclear waste

Reviewing Facts
SECTION 1

1. The central government controlled all prices and wages, and businesses and industries were run by the state.

2. economic and political instability, rising unemployment and inflation, corruption, crime, loss of foreign investment income, environmental damage

3. Privatization has not benefited the average Russian. Private ownership of agriculture has been particularly slow. Only the wealthy have been able to invest in factories and business opportunities.

4. They have widened trade relationships with other countries and attempted to join international organizations.

SECTION 2

5. serious health challenges and environmental damage

6. cleaning up contaminated air, water, soil; providing clean water and electrical power; aging equipment; harsh climate; separatist

Reviewing Key Terms

On a sheet of paper, classify each of the lettered terms below into the following categories. (Some terms may apply to both categories.)

• Soviet Era   • After Independence

a. command economy   f. kolkhoz
b. consumer goods   g. sovkhoz
c. black market   h. radioactive material
d. market economy   i. pesticide
e. privatization   j. nuclear waste

Reviewing Facts
SECTION 1

1. What was the role of the government in the Soviet command economy?

2. How has the transition to a market economy challenged Russian society?

3. How did privatization impact daily life in Russia?

4. What steps has Russia taken to become part of the global community?

SECTION 2

5. What problems have been created by pollution in Russia?

6. What challenges with the environment and natural resources does Russia face today?

7. How did the Cold War contribute to Russia's environmental problems?

Critical Thinking

1. Making Inferences Study the chart on pages 388–389. How might political and economic reforms in Russia eventually affect the distribution of the country's resources?

2. Problem Solving Identify one kind of pollution affecting Russia. Describe the cause or origin of the pollution. What steps do you think would be necessary to reduce its effects? Explain the reasons for your answer.

3. Categorizing Information Complete a diagram like the one below to show the changes in Russian life after independence. Then write a paragraph explaining the change you think had the greatest impact on Russian life.

Changes After Russian Independence

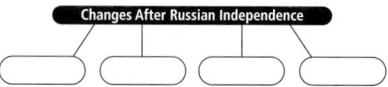

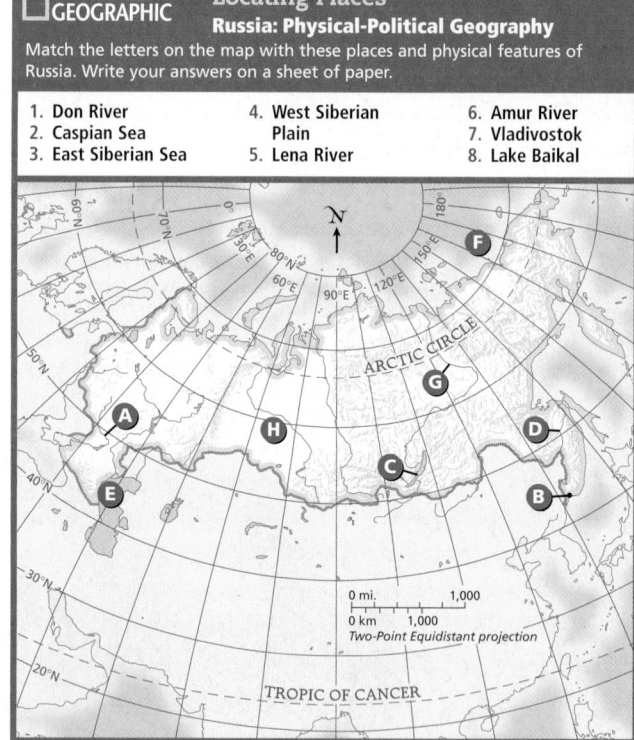

NATIONAL GEOGRAPHIC **Locating Places**
Russia: Physical-Political Geography

Match the letters on the map with these places and physical features of Russia. Write your answers on a sheet of paper.

1. Don River
2. Caspian Sea
3. East Siberian Sea
4. West Siberian Plain
5. Lena River
6. Amur River
7. Vladivostok
8. Lake Baikal

activities; sustainable forest management

7. During the Cold War, the Soviet government concentrated on industrial buildup and military spending at the expense of the environment. Radioactive waste has contaminated Russia's water and soil.

Critical Thinking

1. Economic decision-making becomes more decentralized; supply and demand determines distribution of resources.

2. Responses should reflect an understanding of the roots of the problem and suggest practical solutions.

3. Graphic organizers should reflect information in the text.

NATIONAL GEOGRAPHIC **Locating Places**

1. A	**3.** F	**5.** G	**7.** B
2. E	**4.** H	**6.** D	**8.** C

Using the Regional Atlas

Refer to the Regional Atlas on pages 338–341.

1. **Location** Which manufacturing areas are located along the Volga River? Along the Ob and Irtysh Rivers?

2. **Human-Environment Interaction** Compare the population density map and the economic activity map. Describe the correlation between commercial farmland and population density.

Thinking Like a Geographer

Think about the population distribution in Russia. How do you think the shift from a command economy to a market economy might affect migration patterns and population density? Write a paragraph about the most significant effect.

Problem-Solving Activity

Contemporary Issues Case Study Russia remains an influential international power despite its recent political and economic changes. Learn more about Russia's policies toward the expansion of the European Union. Then focus on ways Russian and European interests are similar and different. In an essay, present your conclusions about the future of Russian-European relations.

GeoJournal

Expository Writing Use your GeoJournal, your textbook, and the Internet to research and write an essay that analyzes how Moscow's character as a city is related to its political, social, economic, and cultural features.

 ## Technology Activity

Developing Multimedia Presentations Compile information about people's work, school, community, home life, and leisure activities in Russia. Use various media to introduce Russian life to other students or people in your community. For example, you might play recordings of popular Russian music or show a film that presents an aspect of Russian culture, in addition to your oral report.

Standardized Test Practice

Use your knowledge of Russia to choose the best answer for each of the following multiple-choice questions. If you have trouble answering the questions, use the process of elimination to narrow your choices.

1. **In Russia which of these challenges affects the transportation of both petroleum products and other goods?**

   A Poorly repaired roads
   B Harsh weather and vast distances
   C Frozen waterways
   D Separatist movements

 **Test-Taking Tip** First determine what choices you can eliminate. Since petroleum products are transported through pipelines, choices A and C do not apply and can be eliminated. Choose the best answer from the remaining options.

2. **In Russia, nuclear power plants built during the Soviet era**

   F have been shut down.
   G provide much of Russia's electricity.
   H are now safer than ever before.
   J have been replaced by coal-fired generators.

 **Test-Taking Tip** Only one answer is completely true. Some reactors have been shut down, and some safety standards were improved. Choose the answer that is completely true.

GeoJournal

Invite interested students to share their work.

Technology Activity

Have students work on this activity in five small groups, one for each aspect of Russian life being researched.

Standardized Test Practice

1. B
2. G

Tested Objectives:
analyzing information
synthesizing information

Additional Practice and Test-Taking Tips

 Standardized Test Practice Workbook

? CHAPTER BONUS TEST QUESTION

How do you think growing Russian nationalism will affect international relations in the future? *(Russia may feel it deserves a larger role on the world scene, it may resist separatist movements and suppress diversity, and it may increase military spending.)*

Using the Regional Atlas

1. Kazan, Samara; Tyumen, Novosibirsk
2. Commercial farming takes place in the most densely populated areas of Russia, on the North European Plain. This area has a mild climate and fertile soil.

Thinking Like a Geographer

Paragraphs might consider urban/rural differences and migration of ethnic Russians to Russia from former Soviet republics. Check for use of standard grammar, spelling, sentence structure, and punctuation.

Problem-Solving Activity

Student groups might consider the pros and cons of Russian membership in the EU, debate this issue, and then vote on Russia's future ties with Europe.

TEACHING TRANSPARENCIES

L2 Unit 6 Map Overlay Transparencies

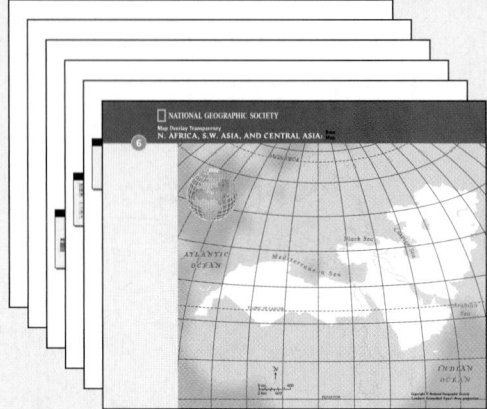

L2 Political Map Transparency 6

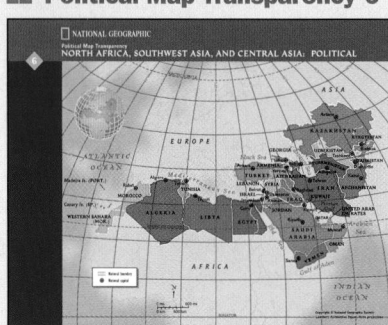

L2 World Cultures Transparencies 9, 10

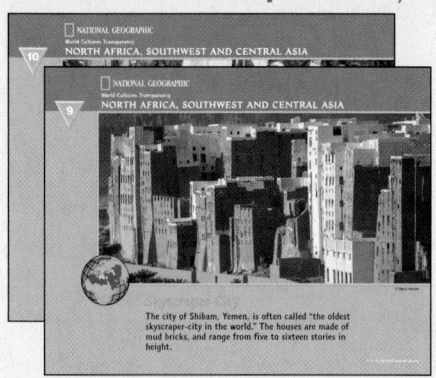

The city of Shibam, Yemen, is often called "the oldest skyscraper-city in the world." The houses are made of mud bricks, and range from five to sixteen stories in height.

APPLICATION AND ENRICHMENT

L2 Location Activity 6

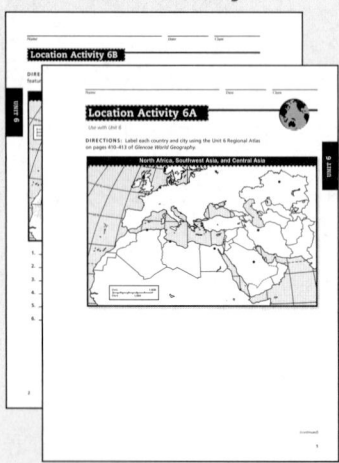

L2 Real-Life Applications and Problem-Solving Activity 6

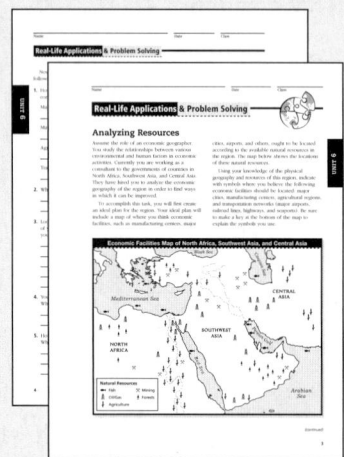

L2 GeoLab Activity 6

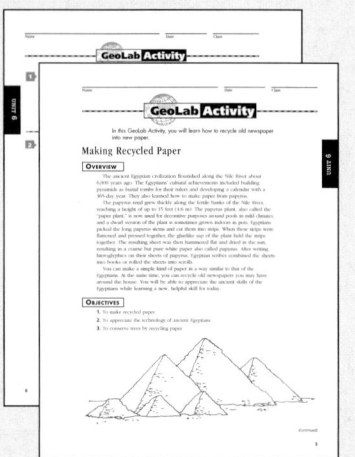

L2 Environmental Issues Case Study 6

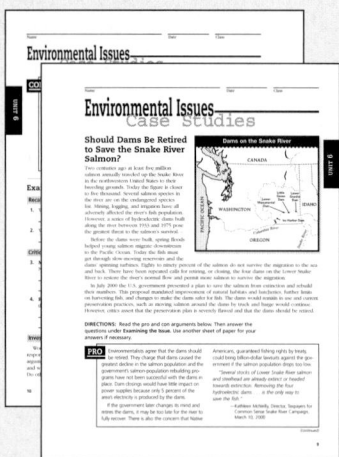

GEOGRAPHIC LITERACY

Focus on Geography Literacy

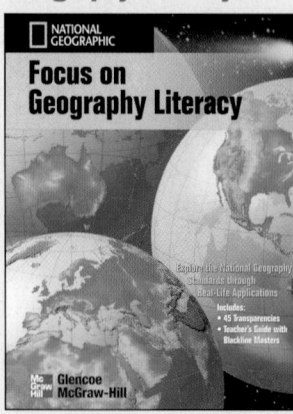

Building Geography Skills for Life

ASSESSMENT

Use the following to easily assess student learning in a variety of ways:
- Performance Assessment Activities and Rubrics
- Section Quizzes
- Chapter and Unit Tests
- Interactive Tutor Self-Assessment CD–ROM
- ExamView® Pro Testmaker
- MindJogger Videoquiz
- geography.glencoe.com
- Standardized Test Practice Workbook
- SAT I/II Test Practice

L2 Unit 6 Pretest and Tests

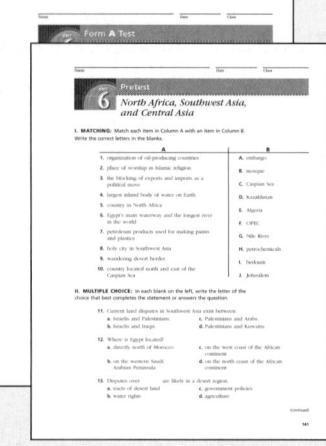

INTERDISCIPLINARY CONNECTIONS

L2 World Literature:
Contemporary Selection 6

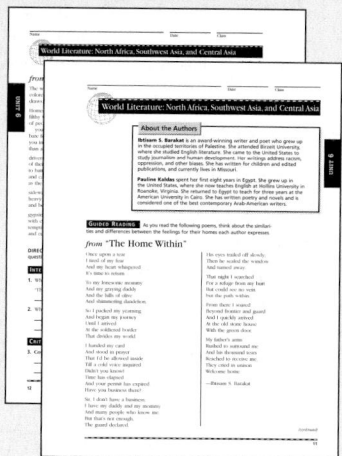

Foods Around the World

Multimedia

🖼 **World Art and Architecture Transparencies**

📕 **World Art Prints**

🎵 **World Music: A Cultural Legacy**

💿 **World History Primary Source Document Library**

BIBLIOGRAPHY

Readings for the Student

Cyprus: Divided Island, by Tom Streissguth. Mahwah, NJ: World Almanac Books, 1998.

Kurdistan: Region Under Siege, by Kari Bodnarchuk. Mahwah, NJ: World Almanac Books, 2000.

The Middle East, by Mary E. Williams. San Diego, CA: Greenhaven Press, 2000.

Readings for the Teacher

A History of the Middle East, by Peter Mansfield. New York, NY: Penguin USA, 1996.

Understanding the Contemporary Middle East, by Deborah J. Gerner, ed. London, UK: Lynne Rienner, 2000.

Multimedia Resources

Egypt: Valley of the Nile. Mahwah, NJ: World Almanac Education, 1999. Videocassette, 30 minutes.

The Search for Peace in the Middle East: 20th Century With Mike Wallace. Culver City, CA: Social Studies School Service, 1998. Videocassette, 50 minutes.

READING SUPPORT FROM JAMESTOWN EDUCATION

- *Timed Readings Plus in Social Studies* help students increase their reading rate and fluency while maintaining comprehension. The 400-word passages are similar to those found on state and national assessments.

- *Reading in the Content Area: Social Studies* concentrates on six essential reading skills that help students better comprehend what they read. The book includes 75 high-interest nonfiction passages written at increasing levels of difficulty.

- *Reading Fluency* helps students read smoothly, accurately, and expressively.

- *Jamestown's Reading Improvement,* by renowned reading expert Edward Fry, focuses on helping build your students' comprehension, vocabulary, and skimming and scanning skills.

- *Critical Reading Series* provides high-interest books, each written at three reading levels.

For more information about these products, see the Jamestown Education materials in the Classroom Solutions in the front of this Teacher Wraparound Edition.
To order these products, call Glencoe at 1-800-334-7344.

Background Information

The Physical Geography of North Africa, Southwest Asia, and Central Asia

The continents of Africa, Europe, and Asia meet in the dry, sprawling region of North Africa, Southwest Asia, and Central Asia. Reaching as far west as Morocco's Atlantic coast and as far east as the steppes of Kazakhstan, the region is a patchwork of grassy plains, highlands, and deserts. Included in this region is the world's largest hot desert, the Sahara, where the highest temperature on Earth was recorded—136°F (58°C).

Symbolically and literally this region is defined by water and oil. Although the region has several seas, including the saltiest body of water on Earth, the Dead Sea, it is the region's scarce freshwater rivers that help sustain the region's people. The Tigris, the Euphrates, and the Nile—the world's longest river—provide freshwater for drinking and irrigation along the fertile strips of arable land that line their banks.

Other fertile areas are the coastal plains along the Mediterranean and Caspian Seas, and along the Persian Gulf. Because the plains can be farmed, they are home to most of the region's people. A crown of mountains rings much of the coastal plains.

Severe earthquakes often shake the region's mountains, including the Atlas Mountains, Africa's longest range. Strong earthquakes also rip through Turkey and Iran, whose mountain ranges were born when the African and Arabian tectonic plates collided with the giant Eurasian plate.

Natural Resources

The region's petroleum and natural gas reserves are a source of wealth and global power for many of the countries located here. An unknown amount of oil awaits exploration under the waters of the Caspian Sea.

Minerals are another of the region's resources. Turkmenistan has the world's largest deposits of sulfur, and Morocco is the second biggest producer of phosphate, which is used in fertilizers.

The Cultural Geography of North Africa, Southwest Asia, and Central Asia

The region of North Africa, Southwest Asia, and Central Asia is a kaleidoscope of ethnic diversity that includes Arabs, Jews, Turks and other Turkic peoples, Greeks, Iranians, Afghanis, Caucasian peoples, and Kurds.

Most of the people of the region live near water. For example, most Egyptians live along the Nile River or near the Suez Canal. The least densely populated areas include countries with little arable lands, such as Saudi Arabia, Turkmenistan, and the most sparsely populated of all, Kazakhstan.

Cities such as Bukhara, Uzbekistan; Istanbul, Turkey; and Cairo, Egypt have existed for centuries. Yet the population of North Africa, Southwest Asia, and Central Asia has always been mostly rural.

History

The region has seen the rise of some of the world's greatest civilizations—the Egyptians, Sumerians, Persians, and Phoenicians—as well as the birth of three of the world's major religions—Judaism, Christianity, and Islam. Farmers of the region were the first to raise many of the grains, vegetables, and animals that are still used as staple foods in much of the world. Unfortunately, the region also has a long history of intense conflicts over land and resources, and such conflicts continue today among the region's countries.

Cultures and Lifestyles

Arabic—the language of the Muslim faith's sacred text, the Quran—is the main language in the region. Other languages include Hebrew, Berber, Pushtu, Kurdish, Farsi, Greek, and Turkic languages.

The region's arts reflect the influences of Judaism, Christianity, and Islam. Although early civilizations produced fine metal craftswork and sculptures, they are best known for their architecture. The monumental pyramids in Egypt are just one example of the region's ancient building skills.

Beginning in the 1900s, the ways of life of the peoples of North Africa, Southwest Asia, and Central Asia changed dramatically. Population in the region has grown, and there have been many lifestyle changes as more people have moved from rural to urban areas.

Population growth in countries such as Iran, Afghanistan, and Egypt has surpassed economic growth. As a result, governments often cannot meet people's basic needs.

CHAPTER 19 (pp. 462–479)

North Africa, Southwest Asia, and Central Asia Today

The economies within this region vary from some of the world's richest countries to some of its poorest. Although the wealthier countries use revenues from oil and other resources to buy food from other countries, for others in this mostly arid region, producing enough food and access to freshwater for their rapidly growing populations is a major concern.

Cereal crops, citrus fruits, grapes, and dates are major products in countries with a Mediterranean climate. Kazakhstan is an important grain-producing area.

The fishing industry is another source of food, with good harvests available in the Atlantic Ocean, the Mediterranean, Black, and Caspian Seas, and the Persian Gulf.

The most important natural resource in the region, however, is petroleum. Wealth from oil has brought industrial growth to parts of the region, but most oil-producing countries still export crude petroleum to be refined elsewhere. Eight countries in the region belong to the Organization of Petroleum Exporting Countries (OPEC), and have great control over the production and price of their oil.

Despite their wealth, however, physical geography limits communications and transportation in this region. Telephone communication is difficult over vast stretches of desert, but satellite technology and solar-powered radiophones are improving service. In 1998 the longest telecommunications highway in the world opened along the ancient Silk Road trade route that once connected Europe with Central Asia. This new road gives 20 countries cable access.

People and Their Environment

For thousands of years, rivers, oases, and wells that draw from aquifers have provided freshwater to these parched lands. As the region's population has grown, however, these sources are no longer enough. Some countries

Additional Resources

The following videotape programs are available from Glencoe:

- **Israel: Birth of a Nation** 0-7670-1107-4
- **Legends of the Arabian Nights** 0-7670-0232-6
- **Pyramids of Giza** 0-7670-0703-4
- **Cleopatra: Destiny's Queen** 1-56501-454-5
- **King Tut: The Face of Tutankhaman** 1-56501-159-7
- **Ramses the Great** 0-7670-0665-8

To order, call Glencoe at 1-800-334-7344. To find classroom resources to accompany many of these check:

A&E Television:
www.aetv.com

The History Channel:
www.historychannel.com

are using oil wealth to fund desalination facilities that turn seawater into precious freshwater.

Nuclear, chemical, and biological weapons testing conducted by the former Soviet Union has caused health problems in Central Asia. Sewage wastes, oil tanker accidents in the seas, and fertilizer runoff threaten the region's air, soil, and water. Some of the countries in North Africa, Southwest Asia, and Central Asia are taking steps to solve their environmental problems.

6

OF TIME?

...not permit teach-
...apter in this unit,
...ant to use the
Essentials and
Guide summaries.

Launch Activity
. What have you heard on
or the radio about places in
...orth Africa, Southwest Asia,
...and Central Asia? What have
you read about the region in
the newspaper? Have students
relate news stories of any countries in the region and then summarize their stories on index
cards. Use the cards as a springboard for discussion on why it
is important to study North Africa,
Southwest Asia, and Central Asia.
Tack the cards on a bulletin board.
Encourage students to add cards
to the display throughout the
course of the unit.

GLENCOE
TECHNOLOGY

□ NATIONAL GEOGRAPHIC
WORLD REGIONS
VIDEO PROGRAM

Unit 6, North Africa,
Southwest Asia, and
Central Asia
The following segments
enhance the study of this unit:

- **Heart of Egypt**
- **Three Religions**
- **Oil Boom**

Available in DVD and VHS

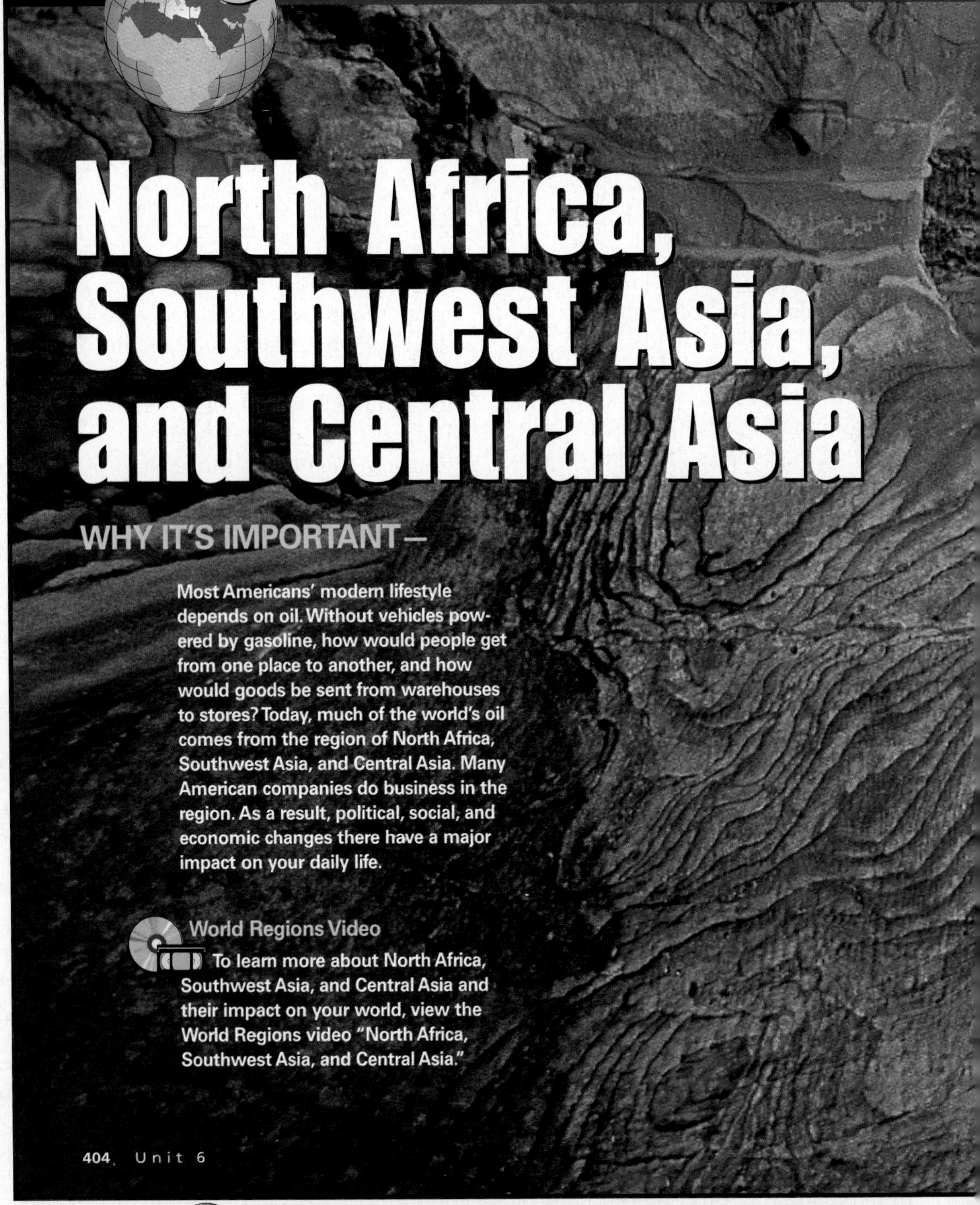

North Africa, Southwest Asia, and Central Asia

WHY IT'S IMPORTANT—

Most Americans' modern lifestyle
depends on oil. Without vehicles powered by gasoline, how would people get
from one place to another, and how
would goods be sent from warehouses
to stores? Today, much of the world's oil
comes from the region of North Africa,
Southwest Asia, and Central Asia. Many
American companies do business in the
region. As a result, political, social, and
economic changes there have a major
impact on your daily life.

World Regions Video

To learn more about North Africa,
Southwest Asia, and Central Asia and
their impact on your world, view the
World Regions video "North Africa,
Southwest Asia, and Central Asia."

404 Unit 6

GETTING TO KNOW THE REGION

Map Activity Display Political Map Transparency 6 and **Ask:** What three continents
meet in the region of North Africa, Southwest Asia, and Central Asia? *(Europe, Africa, and
Asia)* What country is partly in Europe, but mostly in Asia? *(Turkey)* What North African
country is closest to Europe? *(Morocco)* Which country lies farthest east in the region?
(Kazakhstan) Which country is farthest north? *(Kazakhstan)* Which countries border the
Caspian Sea? *(Turkmenistan, Azerbaijan, Iran, Russia, and Kazakhstan)*
⊕ EE1 The World in Spatial Terms: Standard 1

NGS ONLINE
www.nationalgeographic.com/education

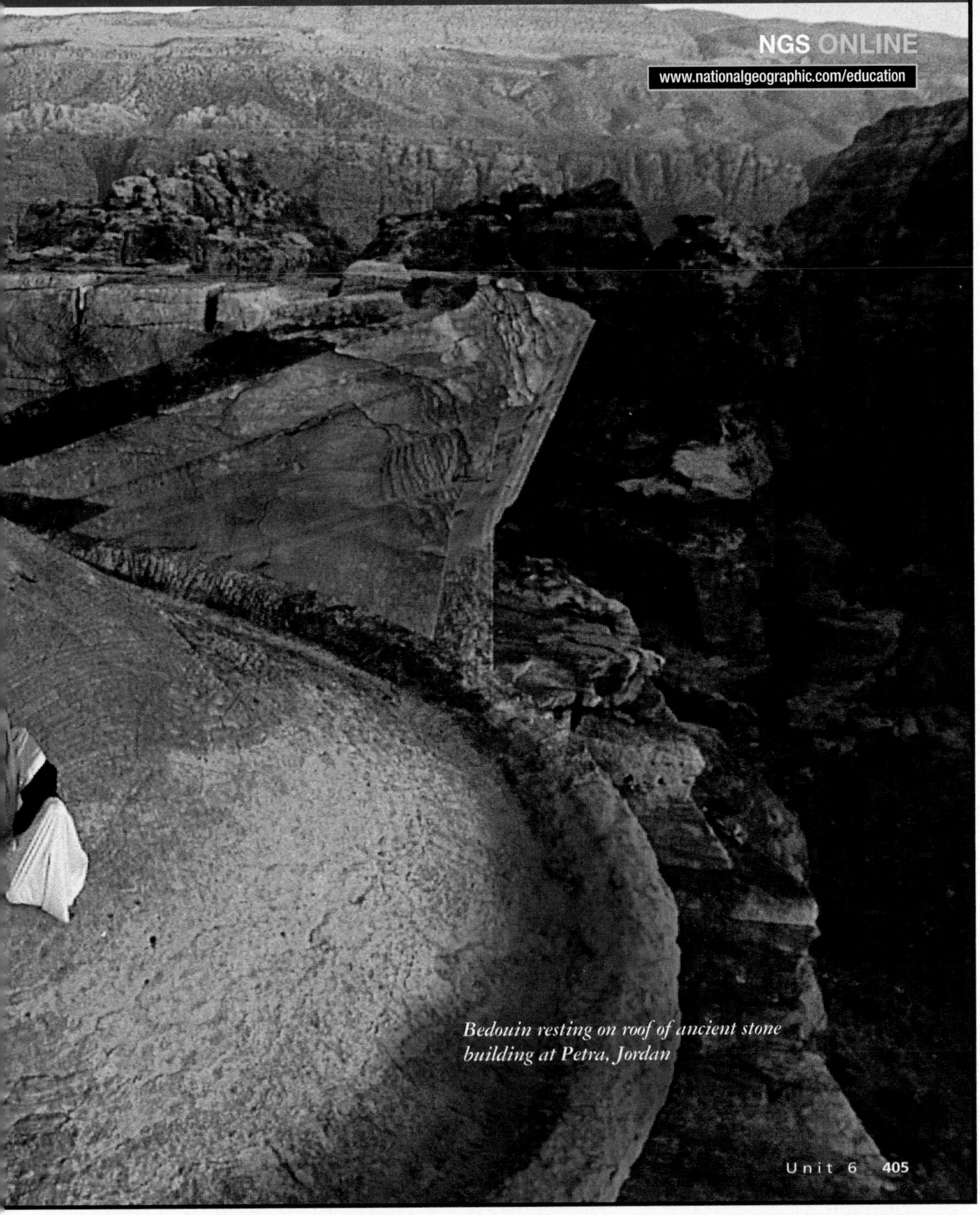

Bedouin resting on roof of ancient stone building at Petra, Jordan

NGS ONLINE
www.nationalgeographic.com/education

This online resource, brought to you by the National Geographic Society, provides lesson plans, atlas updates, cartographic activities with interactive maps, an online map store, and links to the boundless subjects of maps and geography.

Unit Overview

The three chapters that comprise this unit introduce students to the physical and cultural geography of North Africa, Southwest Asia, and Central Asia, as well as to the peoples of that region. Point out to students that although the countries of North Africa, Southwest Asia, and Central Asia are diverse, most have the following features in common:

- a mostly arid climate
- a lack of sufficient freshwater for drinking and irrigation
- strong religious influences, predominantly Islamic
- political unrest and conflicts

ABOUT THE PHOTO

Visual Instruction In ancient times, caravans from the regions around the Mediterranean and Red Seas and the Persian Gulf crisscrossed Jordan, often stopping at Petra, the name meaning "city of rock" in Greek. Petra's entrance, a narrow pass flanked by steep rock walls, protected the city from invasion, making it a stronghold for the treasures of ancient kingdoms. Today Petra is a popular stop for tourists—so popular, in fact, that Jordan is struggling to preserve the ancient site from crumbling beneath the feet of its thousands of visitors.
Ask: Why are tourist sites such as Petra especially important to countries like Jordan? *(Tourism helps the country's economy and increases global understanding of its history.)*
⊕ EE2 Places and Regions: Standard 6

UNIT 6 REGIONAL ATLAS

① FOCUS

These features and activities may be used as an introduction to the unit or as teaching tools throughout the course of the unit.

L1 Using Flash Cards Activity

Before beginning the study of this unit, use the **Countries of the World Flash Cards** to preview students' knowledge of North Africa, Southwest Asia, and Central Asia. Arrange students into teams of three or four to compete in a geography bee. Allow team members to talk over their answers before responding to clues. Used cards may be reshuffled into the deck, but clues may not be used twice.

L1 Location

Use the title question as a discussion opener. **Ask: What makes North Africa, Southwest Asia, and Central Asia a region?** Have students list the physical characteristics of the region, based on pages 406–407. Have students add to this list as they read Unit 6.

□ NATIONAL GEOGRAPHIC GEOFACT

▶ The Dead Sea differs from all other bodies of water in the world. It is the lowest place on Earth, at 1,312 feet (400 m) below sea level, and its water, the world's saltiest, holds nine times the salt of an ocean.

What Makes North Africa, Southwest Asia, and Central Asia a Region?

Arid and often forbidding, the region of North Africa, Southwest Asia, and Central Asia stretches from Morocco to Kazakhstan. Rugged mountain ranges surround vast, dry plateaus and some of Earth's greatest deserts. Through these parched landscapes flow a handful of life-sustaining rivers. The Nile, the world's longest river, slices northward through Egypt to the Mediterranean Sea. The Tigris and Euphrates flow southeast across Turkey, Syria, and Iraq. These two rivers cradle the "Fertile Crescent," an area of rich soil where some of the world's earliest agricultural societies took root.

Where slightly more rain falls, deserts give way to grass-covered steppes where nomadic herders roam with their flocks. Only coastal areas and highlands enjoy a moister, milder Mediterranean climate. On the whole, water, perhaps the most precious resource, is very scarce in this region. Oil, in contrast, is one of the region's most abundant resources.

1 A bedouin girl holds a baby goat on an arid plain in Jordan. Bedouins traditionally are nomadic herders of goats, sheep, and camels. Nomadic herding is common—and practical—in the vast parts of this region that are too dry for growing crops.

BACKGROUND INFORMATION

The Hindu Kush Even though its snowcapped peaks rise more than 20,000 feet (6,000 m), the forbidding Hindu Kush mountain range was once part of the main route between Europe and Asia. Conquerors from Alexander the Great to Tamerlane forced their armies across the steep passes of the Hindu Kush. For hundreds of years, caravans of merchants struggled across the mountains to bring goods and new ideas from east to west. The name Hindu Kush means "slayer of Hindus," so named, according to legend, because travelers from the east, many of whom were Hindu, often died in the mountains' snow and freezing temperatures. **⊕ EE2 Places and Regions: Standard 4**

② TEACH

L2 Photo Research Activity

Assign the photographs on pages 406–409 to individuals or groups of students. Have students gather enough information about their assigned photo to write two paragraphs about its subject. Have students share their paragraphs with the class.

FYI

Sahara winds do more than carve sand dunes. Without trees to break their path, windstorms race through the Sahara at incredible speeds. Clouds of dust from the Sahara have even been known to cross the Atlantic Ocean, bringing a golden glow to Florida's sunsets.

GLENCOE TECHNOLOGY

NATIONAL GEOGRAPHIC

WORLD REGIONS
VIDEO PROGRAM

Unit 6, North Africa, Southwest Asia, and Central Asia

The following segments enhance the study of this unit:

- **Heart of Egypt**
- **Three Religions**
- **Oil Boom**

4

2 Gleaming pipes surround an oil refinery in Kuwait. This tiny country and its neighbors on the Arabian Peninsula produce much of the world's oil. An elaborate system of pipelines transports the oil from refineries to seaports where huge oil tankers dock.

3 Wind-carved sand dunes surround a small oasis in the Algerian Sahara. The world's largest hot desert, the Sahara covers most of North Africa. Surprisingly, sand dunes are relatively rare in the Sahara. Far more common are windswept expanses of rock and gravel.

4 Muslims pause to pray high in the mountains of Afghanistan's Hindu Kush, one of the region's many mountain ranges. Other ranges include the Atlas Mountains, which span Morocco and Algeria, and the glacier-crowned Tian Shan of Kyrgyzstan.

Unit 6   407

A TRAVELER'S LOG

Marco Polo To Marco Polo, an adventurous European merchant of the 1200s, Southwest Asia and Central Asia meant the Silk Road that led him to the silks and spices of East Asia. Polo's tales of his travels gave many Europeans their first glimpse of lands east of the Mediterranean. Here is how he described part of Southwest Asia: "The merchants . . . are obliged to pass extensive deserts and tracts of sand, where no kind of herbage is to be met with, and where, on account of the distance between the wells or other watering places, it is necessary to make long journeys in the course of the day . . ."

EE2 Places and Regions: Standard 6

L2 Making Predictions

Ask students how they think the three world religions that began in the region may have influenced the countries in North Africa, Southwest Asia, and Central Asia. Refer students to the text on page 408 to find the names of the region's two Christian countries and its Jewish state. Ask students to predict the predominant religion in the other countries.

Ask: What do the photographs on pages 408–409 suggest about the influence of religion on dress, custom, and architecture?

Culture NOTE

Islamic Countries In many Islamic countries, businesses are closed on Fridays, Islam's holy day. Many businesses are closed on Thursdays, as well. The workweek begins again on Saturday and continues to Wednesday.

Cradle of Civilization

Along the banks of the Nile River, colossal stone statues are mute reminders of the ancient Egyptian civilization. Many other great civilizations, including those of the Sumerians, Persians, and Phoenicians, also arose in this region. So did three of the world's great religions—Judaism, Christianity, and Islam. Today, Islam claims the greatest number of followers here. Yet Georgia and Armenia remain Christian strongholds, and Israel is the Jewish state.

Ethnic diversity is a hallmark of this region, which has long been a cultural crossroads linking Europe, Africa, and Asia. Just as cultures mix in this part of the world, so tradition intermingles with the newest technology. Ancient customs persist even in the most modern cities.

1 A man wearing a traditional headdress chats on a cellular phone in the Israeli desert. Scenes like this one are most common in countries with oil- or industry-based economies that support high standards of living.

BACKGROUND INFORMATION

Arabic Names Have you ever noticed a *bin* in the middle of an Arab person's name? Perhaps you thought it was "Ben" used as a middle name. Actually, it is a preposition. In Arabic the words *al* and *bin* mean "from." Some Arabs use these terms between their first name and last name, meaning "son of," and the female preposition *bint* means "daughter of." *Al* or *bin* can also mean "from the town of" or "from the family of." For example, King Fahd bin Abdul-Aziz al-Saud of Saudi Arabia is Fahd, son of Abdul-Aziz, from the family of Saud.
🌐 **EE4 Human Systems: Standard 10**

L1 Human-Environment Interaction

Explain to students that the great civilization of the ancient Egyptians never would have existed if it had not been for the Nile River. The river and its floodplain enabled Egypt's farmers to grow the food that allowed their civilization to develop. **Ask: How else do you think the Nile could have contributed to the development of the Egyptian civilization?** *(Answers may include the importance of the river as a source of transportation and trade.)*

 **ASSESS**

Ask: **How is the region of North Africa, Southwest Asia, and Central Asia different from the region where we live?** *(Accept reasonable answers that are appropriate to your location.)*

4 CLOSE

Ask students to speculate on the kinds of problems facing North Africa, Southwest Asia, and Central Asia, based on what they have learned so far.

2 Draped in flowing *chadris,* or body veils, women shop for shoes in a market in Kabul, Afghanistan. The women practice a conservative form of Islam, which encourages women to conceal their bodies under these traditional full-length garments.

3 Straddling the Bosporus Strait, Istanbul, Turkey, is the only major city to stand on two continents—Asia and Europe. The magnificent, domed Hagia Sophia was initially built as a Christian cathedral. Nearly a thousand years later, it was converted into a mosque. It now serves as a museum.

4 Standing guard for centuries, giant stone figures flank the entrance to an ancient temple in Egypt. Pharaoh Ramses II built this and a neighboring temple beside the Nile River during the 1200s B.C. When the Aswan High Dam was built in the 1960s, the temples were moved to higher ground.

Unit 6 **409**

UNIT PROJECT

A Regional Library Explain to students that they will be creating a library of information about North Africa, Southwest Asia, and Central Asia as they study the unit. Help students list categories to cover in their library, such as ethnic groups, history, physical geography, architecture and arts, governments, religion, food, languages, clothing, and customs. Supply folders for each of the categories and have students collect information for the library as they study the unit. Explain that the library is available for them to use while doing reports or projects during the study of this unit.

EE2 Places and Regions: Standard 4

These features and activities may be used as an introduction to the unit or as teaching tools throughout the course of the unit.

L1 Comparing

Have students study the physical and political maps of North Africa, Southwest Asia, and Central Asia on pages 410–411. **Ask: How does the overall size of the region compare with that of Europe?** *(It is twice the size.)* **How do most of the countries of North Africa, Southwest Asia, and Central Asia compare in size with the countries of Europe?** *(Most European countries are smaller.)*

□ NATIONAL GEOGRAPHIC **GEOFACT**

▶ **Twenty-eight percent of the Nile's waters come from the White Nile, starting at Uganda's Lake Victoria. Fifty-eight percent of the Nile's waters come from the Blue Nile, which begins at Ethiopia's Lake Tana. The rest is from the Atbarah River, also out of Ethiopia.**

Elevation Profile

This cross section begins in western Africa around 30 degrees north latitude, crossing the Atlas Mountains in Morocco, the Great Western Erg, and the Great Eastern Erg of Algeria. It continues east through Libya and Egypt, crossing the Nile River and Cairo, through the Suez Canal and the Sinai Peninsula. It continues east through the Arabian Peninsula and the Euphrates River near Kuwait. It then crosses the Zagros Mountains in Iran before ending at the Afghanistan/Pakistan border.

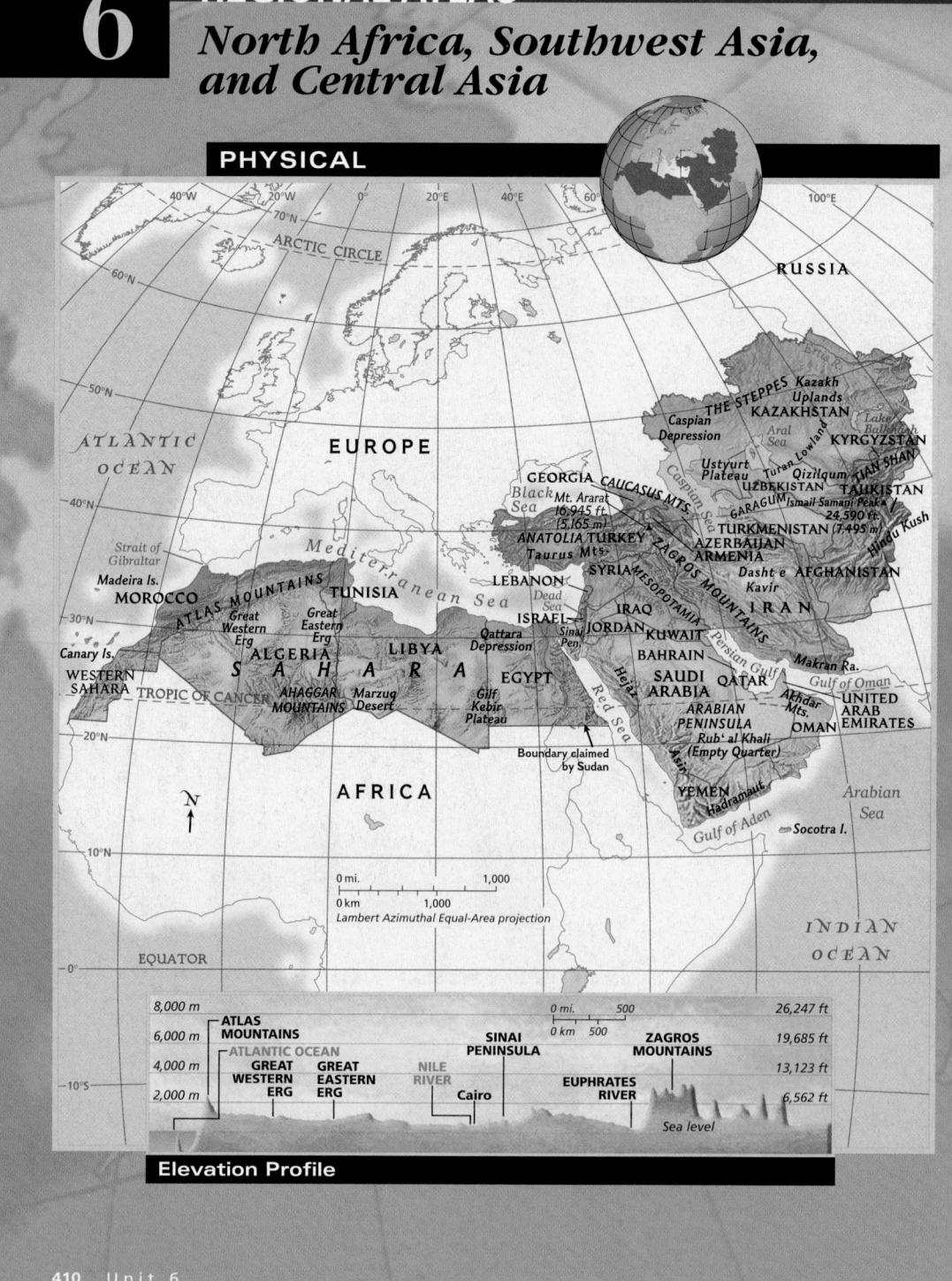

UNIT
6 REGIONAL ATLAS
North Africa, Southwest Asia, and Central Asia

PHYSICAL

Elevation Profile

410   Unit 6

REGIONAL ATLAS ACTIVITY

Predicting the Weather Have students study the maps on pages 410–411. Ask each student to choose three capital cities from the region and speculate on today's weather in the cities they chose. Suggest that they consider which capitals might be closest to the Equator, which might get the most precipitation, and whether the precipitation might include snow. Remind them to take into account the season, extreme elevations, and proximity to large bodies of water while forming their predictions. Then have students check their predictions with weather reports on the Internet, in newspapers, or on television. Have students who made the most accurate predictions tell the class what map clues they used.
🌐 **EE3 Physical Systems: Standard 7**

POLITICAL

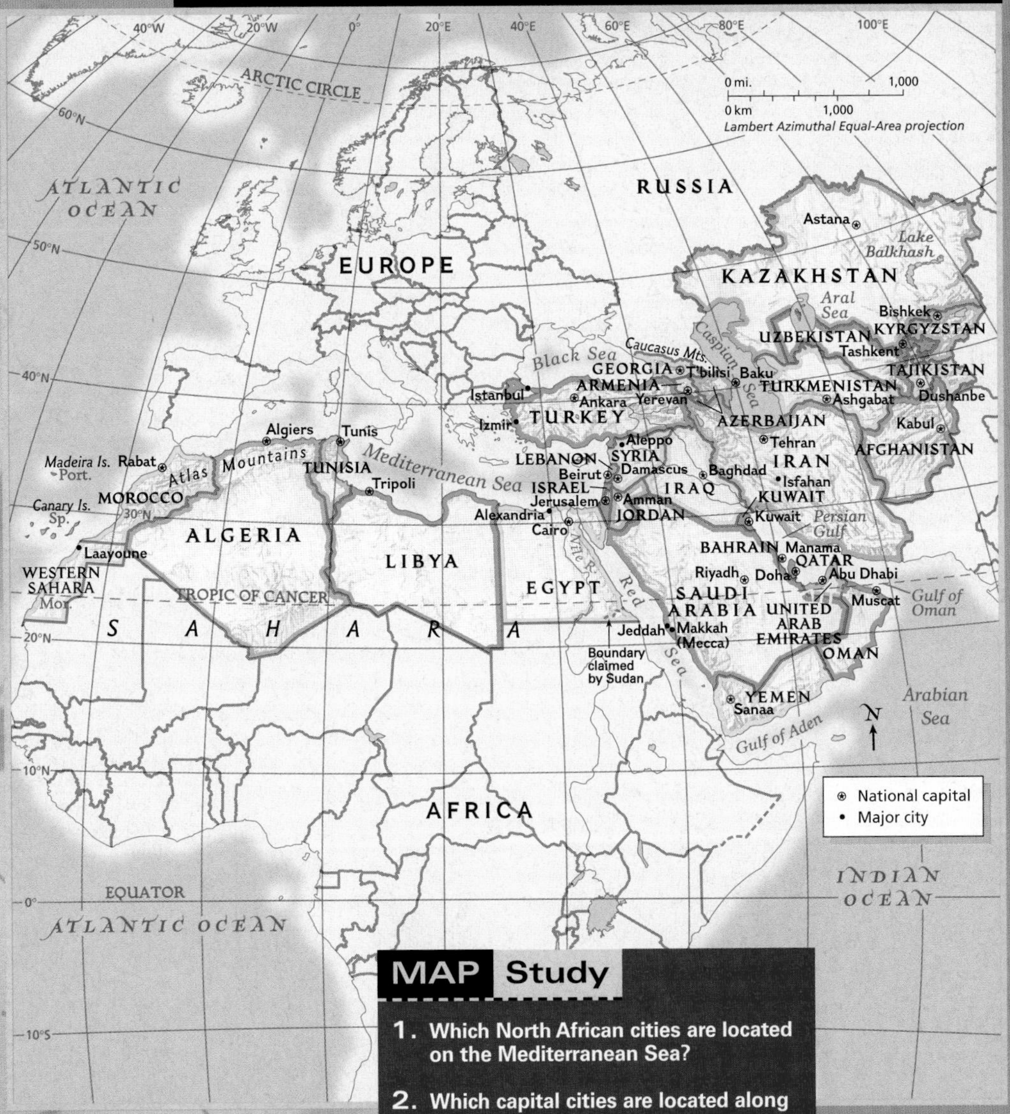

(Map of Europe, Africa, and the Middle East / Central Asia region showing national capitals and major cities)

0 mi. 1,000
0 km 1,000
Lambert Azimuthal Equal-Area projection

ARCTIC CIRCLE

ATLANTIC OCEAN

EUROPE

RUSSIA

Astana ⊛ — Lake Balkhash

KAZAKHSTAN

Aral Sea

Black Sea — Caspian Sea

Caucasus Mts.

UZBEKISTAN — Bishkek ⊛ KYRGYZSTAN

GEORGIA ⊛ T'bilisi Baku ⊛ Tashkent ⊛ TAJIKISTAN

ARMENIA Ankara ⊛ Yerevan ⊛ TURKMENISTAN Ashgabat ⊛ Dushanbe ⊛

Istanbul ● Aleppo ● AZERBAIJAN Kabul ⊛ AFGHANISTAN

Izmir ● TURKEY Kandahar

Algiers ⊛ Tunis ⊛

Madeira Is. Rabat ⊛ Atlas Mountains TUNISIA LEBANON SYRIA Tehran ⊛ IRAN

Port. Mediterranean Sea Tripoli ● Beirut ● Damascus ⊛ Baghdad ⊛ Isfahan ●

Canary Is. MOROCCO ISRAEL IRAQ KUWAIT

Sp. Jerusalem ⊛ Amman ⊛ JORDAN Kuwait ⊛ Persian Gulf

ALGERIA Alexandria ● Cairo ⊛

WESTERN SAHARA LIBYA BAHRAIN Manama ⊛ QATAR

Laayoune ● Mor. EGYPT Riyadh ⊛ Doha ⊛ Abu Dhabi ⊛ Gulf of Oman

TROPIC OF CANCER SAUDI UNITED Muscat ⊛

S A H A R A ARABIA ARAB OMAN

Jeddah ● Makkah ● EMIRATES

Boundary claimed by Sudan (Mecca) Red Sea

YEMEN Arabian Sea

Sanaa ⊛ N

Gulf of Aden ↑

AFRICA

INDIAN OCEAN

EQUATOR

ATLANTIC OCEAN

⊛ National capital
● Major city

MAP Study

1. Which North African cities are located on the Mediterranean Sea?

2. Which capital cities are located along the Persian Gulf?

L1 Coordinating Maps

Have students use the political map on this page together with the population density map on page 412 to answer the following questions. **Ask:** *What cities have over 5 million people? (Istanbul, Cairo, and Tehran) Which of those three cities is not its country's capital? (Istanbul)*

MAP Study

Answers:

1. *Algiers, Tunis, Tripoli, Alexandria*

2. *Abu Dhabi, Manama, Kuwait, Doha*

Map Skills Practice
Location What countries in the region border Russia? *(Georgia, Azerbaijan, and Kazakhstan)*

Ancient Map One of the oldest maps in the world is a small clay tablet that was found in Iraq. It is thought to be about 4,000 years old. Shown on the tablet are hills and a river in Mesopotamia.

REGIONAL ATLAS ACTIVITY

Flora and Fauna Assign each student a country from the region. Have students use the Internet, the library, encyclopedias, almanacs, or other resources to make maps that show the native plant and animal life of their countries. Students should tell whether any species are endangered and, if so, why. Have students present their findings to the class. For those plants and animals that are found in more than one part of the region, have students compare how well the species are faring in the different countries. Maps and information sheets may be included in the class's regional library.

🌐 **EE3 Physical Systems: Standard 8**

L2 Location

Write the names of countries in the region on slips of paper. Place the names in a box and have each student choose a country. Then have students use the map on this page and the Gazetteer at the back of the book to write detailed descriptions of their country's location. Group the class into teams and have students take turns reading their descriptions aloud. Award a point to the team that identifies a country first.

INTERDISCIPLINARY
connection

HISTORY The great capitals of the ancient world had small populations by today's standards. Around 1850 B.C., the grand city of Babylon had about 30,000 people. A rival city of the time, Ashkelon, in what is now Israel, had about 15,000 inhabitants. Estimates place world population at only about 150 million people in 1000 B.C., with very little change for the next 2,500 years.

Culture NOTE

Language Cultural interactions among Southwest Asians and Europeans resulted in Arabic and Persian words becoming part of the English language. Examples of these words are *algebra, bazaar, coffee, cotton, guitar, lemon, lute, sofa, taffeta,* and *tambourine.*

POPULATION DENSITY

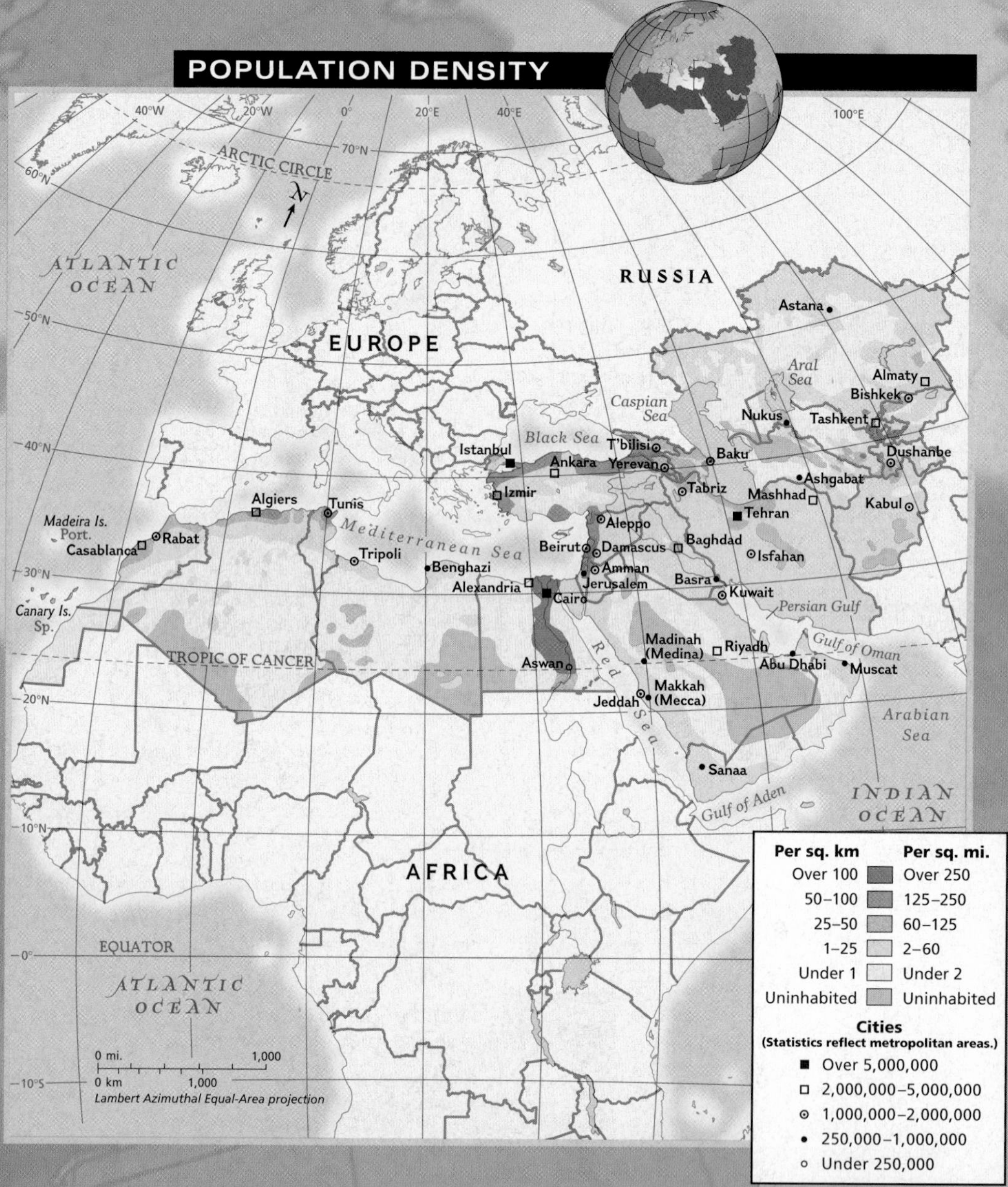

ARCTIC CIRCLE

ATLANTIC OCEAN

EUROPE

RUSSIA

Astana

Aral Sea

Almaty

Bishkek

Caspian Sea

Nukus

Tashkent

Black Sea

Istanbul

Ankara

T'bilisi

Yerevan

Baku

Dushanbe

Izmir

Tabriz

Mashhad

Ashgabat

Kabul

Algiers

Tunis

Aleppo

Tehran

Madeira Is. Port.

Casablanca

Rabat

Mediterranean Sea

Beirut

Damascus

Baghdad

Isfahan

Tripoli

Benghazi

Amman

Jerusalem

Basra

Canary Is. Sp.

Alexandria

Cairo

Kuwait

Persian Gulf

TROPIC OF CANCER

Madinah (Medina)

Riyadh

Gulf of Oman

Abu Dhabi

Muscat

Aswan

Makkah (Mecca)

Jeddah

Red Sea

Arabian Sea

Sanaa

INDIAN OCEAN

Gulf of Aden

AFRICA

EQUATOR

ATLANTIC OCEAN

0 mi. 1,000

0 km 1,000

Lambert Azimuthal Equal-Area projection

Per sq. km	Per sq. mi.
Over 100	Over 250
50–100	125–250
25–50	60–125
1–25	2–60
Under 1	Under 2
Uninhabited	Uninhabited

Cities
(Statistics reflect metropolitan areas.)
- ■ Over 5,000,000
- □ 2,000,000–5,000,000
- ◉ 1,000,000–2,000,000
- • 250,000–1,000,000
- ○ Under 250,000

REGIONAL ATLAS ACTIVITY

Puzzle Maps Have groups of students make jigsaw puzzles of the region. First have each group take a turn projecting Unit Map Overlay Transparency 6 on a half sheet of poster board and outline the borders of the countries. Assign the groups one of the maps in the Unit 6 Regional Atlas to use as a guide for labeling, drawing, and coloring details. Students will be designing and drawing a physical map, a population density map, a political map, or an economic activity map. Have students cut the poster board apart jigsaw-fashion. Have groups exchange puzzles and challenge each other to reassemble the puzzles.
🌐 EE1 The World in Spatial Terms: Standard 1

ECONOMIC ACTIVITY

[Map of North Africa, Southwest Asia, and Central Asia showing economic activity with labeled countries, seas, and resource/land use symbols]

Land Use
- Commercial farming
- Subsistence farming
- Livestock raising
- Nomadic herding
- Hunting and gathering
- Manufacturing and trade
- Commercial fishing
- Little or no activity

Resources
- Coal
- Petroleum
- Natural gas
- Iron ore
- Copper
- Lead
- Zinc
- Bauxite
- Manganese
- Phosphate
- Tungsten
- Gold
- Silver
- Chromite

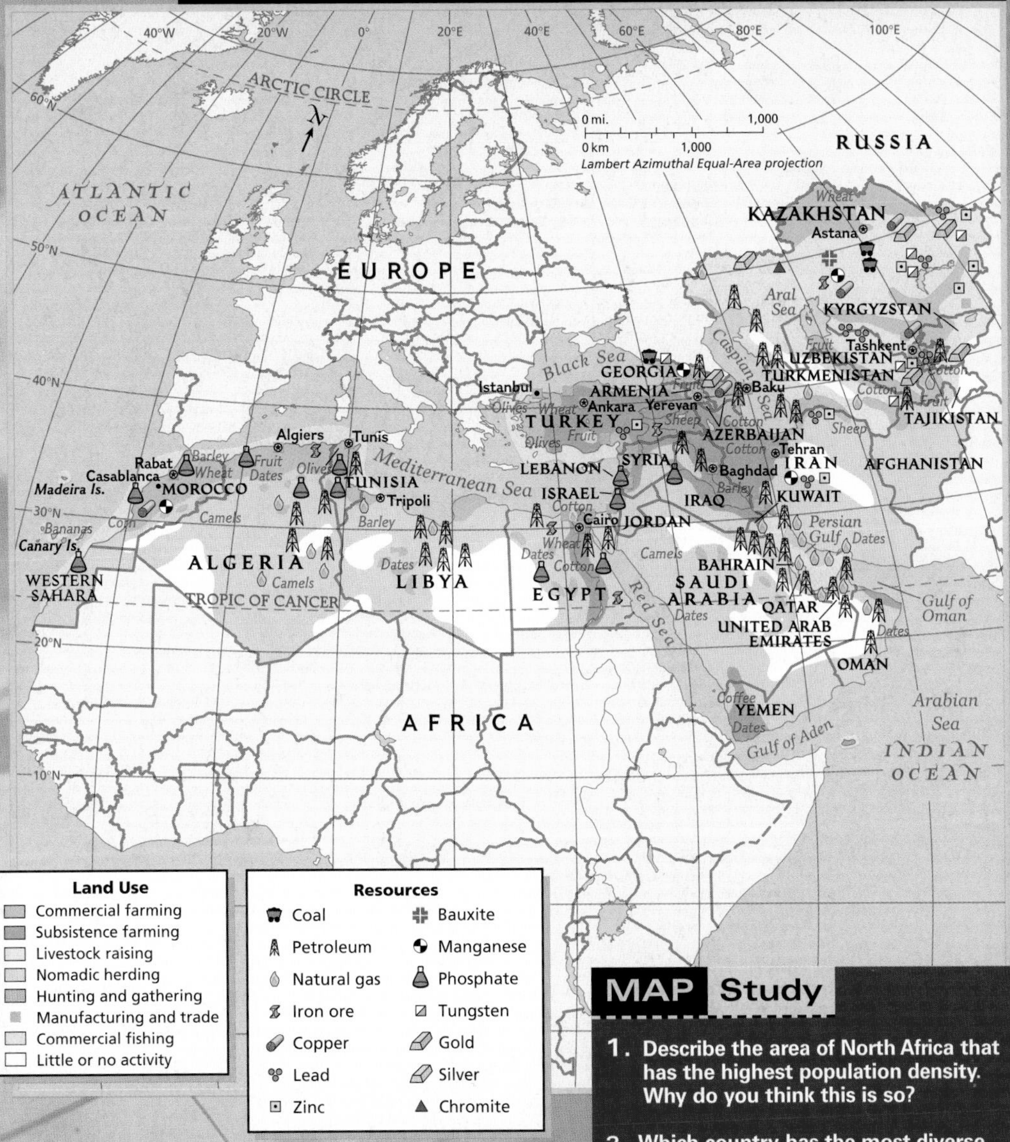

MAP Study

1. Describe the area of North Africa that has the highest population density. Why do you think this is so?

2. Which country has the most diverse natural resources?

Unit 6 **413**

L2 Comparing

On the board make a Venn diagram to compare the natural resources of two of the region's countries. Draw two intersecting circles and list resources from one of the countries in the left circle, and resources from the other in the right circle. Resources that the countries have in common can be listed in the overlapping section. Discuss the diagram and then have students make similar diagrams comparing other countries in the region.

L2 Interdependence

Have students find examples of products from North Africa, Southwest Asia, and Central Asia in their homes, local stores, newspaper advertisements, or on the Internet. The products may be grown or manufactured in the region. Have students label, group, and display their findings on posters.

MAP Study

Answers:
1. *the Nile River valley because it has the most arable land*
2. *Kazakhstan*

Map Skills Practice
Location Manganese is a natural resource of which countries in the region? *(Morocco, Georgia, Iran, Kazakhstan)*

REGIONAL ATLAS ACTIVITY

Geography Contest Have each student write a question about the geography of North Africa, Southwest Asia, and Central Asia to use in a class geography game. Tell students that they may write questions about landforms, location, population, natural resources, capitals, borders, or any combination of these. Give students the following models: What country has its capital on the Caspian Sea? *(Azerbaijan)* In what direction would you travel from the Arabian Peninsula to the Caucasus Mountains? *(north)* Organize the class into two teams and have each team challenge the other with questions. **ELL**

🌐 **EE1 The World in Spatial Terms: Standard 1**

North Africa, Southwest Asia, and Central Asia

These features and activities may be used as an introduction to the unit or as teaching tools throughout the course of the unit.

L2 Flags and Symbols

On the board draw a crescent and star and explain that it is the symbol of Islam. **Ask: Which of the region's flags contain some variation of the crescent and star?** *(Algeria, Azerbaijan, Tunisia, Turkey, Turkmenistan, and Uzbekistan)* **What do you think the symbol in these flags implies?** *(These countries have large Muslim populations.)* **What country includes the symbol of Judaism on its flag?** *(Israel)* **Judging by the flags shown, what country do you think is known for its cedar trees?** *(Lebanon)*

INTERDISCIPLINARY connection

HEALTH As the Aral Sea dried up, winds blew the salts and other dried chemical residue from the sea bed across the landscape. Drinking water in the area now contains four times the amount of salt recommended by the World Health Organization, resulting in increases in kidney diseases, diarrhea, and other health problems.

COUNTRY PROFILES

COUNTRY * AND CAPITAL	FLAG AND LANGUAGE	POPULATION** AND DENSITY	LANDMASS	MAJOR EXPORT	MAJOR IMPORT	CURRENCY	GOVERNMENT
AFGHANISTAN Kabul	Pashto, Dari	28,700,000 114 per sq.mi. 44 per sq.km	251,772 sq.mi. 652,090 sq.km	Fruits and Nuts	Foods	Afghani	Islamic Republic
ALGERIA Algiers	Arabic, French, Berber	31,700,000 35 per sq.mi. 14 per sq.km	919,591 sq.mi. 2,381,741 sq.km	Petroleum	Machinery	Algerian Dinar	Republic
ARMENIA Yerevan	Armenian, Russian	3,200,000 280 per sq.mi. 108 per sq.km	11,506 sq.mi. 29,801 sq.km	Gold	Grain	Dram	Republic
AZERBAIJAN Baku	Azeri, Russian, Armenian	8,200,000 246 per sq.mi. 95 per sq.km	33,436 sq.mi. 86,599 sq.km	Petroleum	Machinery	Manat	Republic
BAHRAIN Manama	Arabic	700,000 2,545 per sq.mi. 983 per sq.km	266 sq.mi. 689 sq.km	Petroleum	Machinery	Bahrain Dinar	Traditional Monarchy
EGYPT Cairo	Arabic	72,100,000 186 per sq.mi. 72 per sq.km	386,660 sq.mi. 1,001,449 sq.km	Crude Oil	Machinery	Egyptian Pound	Republic
GEORGIA T'bilisi	Georgian, Russian	4,700,000 173 per sq.mi. 67 per sq.km	26,911 sq.mi. 69,699 sq.km	Citrus Fruits	Fuels	Lari	Republic
IRAN Tehran	Persian, Kurdish	66,600,000 106 per sq.mi. 41 per sq.km	630,575 sq.mi. 1,633,189 sq.km	Petroleum	Machinery	Rial	Islamic Republic
IRAQ Baghdad	Arabic, Kurdish	24,200,000 143 per sq.mi. 55 per sq.km	169,236 sq.mi. 438,321 sq.km	Crude Oil	Machinery	Iraqi Dinar	Republic
ISRAEL Jerusalem***	Hebrew, Arabic	6,700,000 825 per sq.mi. 319 per sq.km	8,131 sq.mi. 21,059 sq.km	Polished Diamonds	Chemicals	Shekel	Republic

*COUNTRIES AND FLAGS NOT DRAWN TO SCALE
**POPULATIONS ARE ROUNDED.
SOURCE: 2003 WORLD POPULATION DATA SHEET

***Israel has proclaimed Jerusalem as its capital, but many countries' embassies are located in Tel Aviv. The Palestinian Authority has assumed all governmental duties in non-Israeli-occupied areas of the West Bank and Gaza Strip.

COUNTRY PROFILE ACTIVITY

Political Systems Assign each student or pair of students a country. Using the Internet, library, and other resources, have students find the country's official name, title and name of the country's leader, the leader's powers, the country's present form of government, and when this government came into being. Have students list this information in columns on the board. When every country has been accounted for, have students survey the information and generalize on the role that religion has in that country, the power of the leader, as well as the role of women in the country.
EE4 Human Systems: Standard 9

COUNTRY * AND CAPITAL	FLAG AND LANGUAGE	POPULATION** AND DENSITY	LANDMASS	MAJOR EXPORT	MAJOR IMPORT	CURRENCY	GOVERNMENT
JORDAN Amman	Arabic	5,500,000 155 per sq.mi. 61 per sq.km	34,444 sq.mi. 89,210 sq.km	Phosphates	Crude Oil	Jordanian Dinar	Constitutional Monarchy
KAZAKHSTAN Astana	Kazakh, Russian	14,800,000 14 per sq.mi. 5 per sq.km	1,049,151 sq.mi. 2,717,301 sq.km	Petroleum	Machinery	Tenge	Republic
KUWAIT Kuwait	Arabic	2,400,000 346 per sq.mi. 134 per sq.km	6,880 sq.mi. 17,819 sq.km	Petroleum	Foods	Kuwaiti Dinar	Constitutional Monarchy
KYRGYZSTAN Bishkek	Kirghiz, Russian	5,000,000 66 per sq.mi. 25 per sq.km	76,641 sq.mi. 198,500 sq.km	Cotton	Grain	Som	Republic
LEBANON Beirut	Arabic, French	4,200,000 1,045 per sq.mi. 403 per sq.km	4,015 sq.mi. 10,399 sq.km	Paper	Machinery	Lebanese Pound	Republic
LIBYA Tripoli	Arabic	5,500,000 8 per sq.mi. 3 per sq.km	679,359 sq.mi. 1,759,540 sq.km	Crude Oil	Machinery	Libyan Dinar	Military Dictatorship
MOROCCO*** Rabat	Arabic, French, Berber	30,700,000 178 per sq.mi. 69 per sq.km	269,757 sq.mi. 698,671 sq.km	Foods	Manufactured Goods	Dirham	Constitutional Monarchy
OMAN Muscat	Arabic	2,600,000 32 per sq.mi. 12 per sq.km	82,031 sq.mi. 212,460 sq.km	Petroleum	Machinery	Omani Rial	Traditional Monarchy
QATAR Doha	Arabic	600,000 148 per sq.mi. 57 per sq.km	4,247 sq.mi. 11,000 sq.km	Petroleum	Machinery	Qatari Riyal	Traditional Monarchy

*COUNTRIES AND FLAGS NOT DRAWN TO SCALE
**POPULATIONS ARE ROUNDED.
SOURCE: 2003 WORLD POPULATION DATA SHEET

***Morocco claims the Western Sahara area, but other countries do not accept this claim.

FOR AN ONLINE UPDATE OF THIS INFORMATION, VISIT GEOGRAPHY.GLENCOE.COM AND CLICK ON "TEXTBOOK UPDATES."

Unit 6 **415**

L2 Size and Population

Have students use the "Country Profiles" to answer the following questions. **Ask: Which is the largest country in the region?** (*Kazakhstan*) **Which is the smallest?** (*Bahrain*) **Which country is most similar in landmass to Lebanon?** (*Qatar*) **List in order the three countries that have the largest populations.** (*Egypt, Iran, Turkey*) **Which country in the region is most densely populated?** (*Bahrain*) **Which is the least densely populated?** (*Libya*) **Look back at the physical map of the region. Why do you think Libya is so lightly populated?** (*It is mostly desert.*)

Egyptians Egyptians are generally comfortable with less personal space than people in the United States are used to, and they will stand quite close to a listener when speaking. Egyptians also generally prefer being close to others in public places. If you were the only person in a theater or bus, an Egyptian would probably come and sit next to you rather than sit alone.

COUNTRY PROFILE ACTIVITY

Making a Time Line Assign each student a country of the region. Have them use encyclopedias, the Internet, and history books to research the history of their assigned countries. Have students write short reports that include the approximate dates of the country's settlement, major historical events, and milestones in its culture or civilizations. Have all students combine their research to create a time line that illustrates the important dates for each country, from the rise of the first civilizations in the region to the present day. During a class-wide report, individual students can point out to the class their country's milestones on the time line. **EE4 Human Systems: Standard 12**

L2 Location

Have students find out which countries in the region have the longest coastlines. *(Turkey, Libya, Morocco and Western Sahara, Saudi Arabia, and Algeria)* Then have students investigate which economic activities of these countries are linked to their coastlines. *(fishing, trade, tourism)*

Oil In the early 1900s, half the oil used in the world came from Azerbaijan. The country's oil potential was developed by Robert and Ludwig Nobel of Sweden, along with their other brother, Alfred, who was the founder of the Nobel Prizes.

INTERDISCIPLINARY
connection

HISTORY The first coins were made around 600 B.C. by the ancient Lydians in the country now known as Turkey. Each coin, a mixture of gold and silver, was stamped with a picture that told its worth.

UNIT 6 REGIONAL ATLAS
North Africa, Southwest Asia, and Central Asia

COUNTRY PROFILES

COUNTRY * AND CAPITAL	FLAG AND LANGUAGE	POPULATION** AND DENSITY	LANDMASS	MAJOR EXPORT	MAJOR IMPORT	CURRENCY	GOVERNMENT
SAUDI ARABIA ★Riyadh	Arabic	24,100,000 29 per sq. mi. 11 per sq. km	829,996 sq. mi. 2,149,690 sq. km	Petroleum	Machinery	Riyal	Traditional Monarchy
SYRIA ★Damascus	Arabic, Kurdish, Armenian	17,500,000 245 per sq. mi. 95 per sq. km	71,498 sq. mi. 185,180 sq. km	Petroleum	Machinery	Syrian Pound	Republic
TAJIKISTAN ★Dushanbe	Tajik, Russian	6,600,000 119 per sq. mi. 46 per sq. km	55,251 sq. mi. 143,100 sq. km	Aluminum	Fuels	Tajik Ruble	Republic
TUNISIA ★Tunis	Arabic, French	9,900,000 158 per sq. mi. 61 per sq. km	63,170 sq. mi. 163,610 sq. km	Petroleum Products	Machinery	Tunisian Dinar	Republic
TURKEY ★Ankara	Turkish, Kurdish	71,200,000 238 per sq. mi. 92 per sq. km	299,158 sq. mi. 774,819 sq. km	Foods and Livestock	Machinery	Turkish Lira	Republic
TURKMENISTAN ★Ashgabat	Turkmen, Russian, Uzbek	5,700,000 30 per sq. mi. 12 per sq. km	188,456 sq. mi. 488,101 sq. km	Natural Gas	Machinery	Manat	Republic
UNITED ARAB EMIRATES Abu Dhabi	Arabic, Persian	3,900,000 120 per sq. mi. 46 per sq. km	32,278 sq. mi. 83,600 sq. km	Petroleum	Manufactured Goods	Emirian Dirham	Federal Monarchy
UZBEKISTAN ★Tashkent	Uzbek, Russian, Tajik	25,700,000 149 per sq. mi. 58 per sq. km	172,741 sq. mi. 447,399 sq. km	Cotton	Machinery	Som	Republic
YEMEN ★Sanaa	Arabic	19,400,000 95 per sq. mi. 37 per sq. km	203,849 sq. mi. 527,969 sq. km	Cotton	Textiles	Rial	Republic

* COUNTRIES AND FLAGS NOT DRAWN TO SCALE   **POPULATIONS ARE ROUNDED, *SOURCE: 2003 WORLD POPULATION DATA SHEET*

FOR AN ONLINE UPDATE OF THIS INFORMATION, VISIT GEOGRAPHY.GLENCOE.COM AND CLICK ON "TEXTBOOK UPDATES."

▶ Traffic speeds by eastern harbor, Alexandria, Egypt

COUNTRY PROFILE ACTIVITY

Researching Industries The economies of many of the region's countries are dependent on their exports. Have each student research and report on a country and its major export product. Reports should cover the history of the industry in that country, the state of the export at present, as well as the country's plans for the future. Students should evaluate the global economic impact of the country's policies relating to the production and use of its resources and to the development of scarce natural resources. Students should gain information from Internet and library resources to design and draw graphs that can be used in an oral presentation to the class.

▦ **EE4 Human Systems: Standard 11**

L3 Population Density

Ask students to compose cause-and-effect statements about the physical geography of the region to explain its uneven population distribution. Then have students choose one of the region's countries and write a paragraph in which they apply the cause-and-effect statements to the country and use details to support the statements.

☐ NATIONAL GEOGRAPHIC **GEOFACT**

▶ **Along with the development of irrigation, the introduction of better varieties of grain in the region greatly increased agricultural production, which in turn led to the rise of cities. Around 5500 B.C. in Egypt and Southwest Asia, a new robust variety of wheat was introduced. Because its hulls came off easily, this new wheat processed easily into flour.**

Literacy Although a recent education campaign has raised the literacy rate in Saudi Arabia to over 50 percent, many older Saudis, especially those in rural areas, remain illiterate. Outside Saudi post offices one can still find scribes busily writing letters for those who cannot read or write.

ABOUT THE PHOTO

Alexandria Built in 332 B.C. by Alexander the Great, Alexandria soon became an important city. Capital of Egypt in the days of Queen Cleopatra (69–30 B.C.), ancient Alexandria was also the site of the largest library in the world at that time, housing nearly 500,000 books. Ancient Alexandria is also remembered for its lighthouse—built around 280 B.C.—which was one of the seven wonders of the ancient world. The lighthouse's beacon, a fire that was made brighter by mirrors, could be seen 35 miles (56 km) away.

Pictured above is modern Alexandria, Egypt's second largest city and main port. Over 80 percent of Egypt's imports and exports pass through Alexandria.

🌐 **EE2 Places and Regions: Standard 4**

1 FOCUS

Have volunteers who are familiar with a religious object or place in the photographs on pages 418–419 explain its significance to the class. *(Shown is a rosary, a string of beads used by Roman Catholics to count prayers. The Western Wall, also called the "Wailing Wall," is all that remains of a Jewish temple destroyed in A.D. 70. Jews gather there and pray and hold religious ceremonies. The Muslim women are near the Dome of the Rock, an important Muslim shrine in Jerusalem.)*

Culture NOTE

Rosaries Americans generally associate rosaries with Roman Catholic practice. Yet strings of beads used to count prayers are also used by Muslims and Eastern Orthodox Christians.

 Meeting National Standards

Geography for Life
The following standards are met in the Student Edition:

EE4 Human Systems:
   Standards 9, 10, 13
EE6 The Uses of Geography:
   Standards 17, 18

GLOBAL ● CONNECTION

SOUTHWEST ASIA AND THE UNITED STATES

RELIGIONS

 Chances are there's a church, a synagogue, or a mosque in your community. These places of worship represent three of the most widespread religions in the United States: Christianity, Judaism, and Islam. All three have their roots in Southwest Asia and profess belief in one God.

Jews trace their ancestry to a herder named Abraham, who lived at least 3,500 years ago in what is now Iraq. According to Jewish scripture, God instructed Abraham to settle in the area that became known as Israel and promised to bless Abraham's descendants if they worshiped one God.

Around 1000 B.C., Israel was united under a powerful king, David, who made Jerusalem his capital. Political strife later divided Israel into two parts, Israel and Judah, which were conquered by other nations. Many of the people of Judah—the Jews—left their homeland, and their descendants scattered around the world. The first Jews in North America arrived in the American colonies in the 1650s. Today, the United States is home to the world's largest Jewish population.

The Jews believed that God would send a Messiah to unite and lead them. Jesus was a Jew who was born in Judah when it was under Roman rule. Jesus interpreted Jewish teachings in a new way. His message made him unpopular with the authorities, and the Romans executed him around A.D. 30.

▲ Christmas celebration in Bethlehem, birthplace of Jesus

BACKGROUND INFORMATION

Geography in History: Place The Old City in Jerusalem contains holy sites for Jews, Muslims, and Christians. Near what is known as the Temple Mount, a magnificent Jewish temple was built during the first century B.C. Jews from around the world pray before the temple's remaining Western Wall, the holiest site of Judaism. For Muslims, the Temple Mount is holy because it is said to be the place from where the Prophet Muhammad made a night journey to heaven and back again. Muslim pilgrims pray there at the Dome of the Rock, a shrine that was built on the site. Also within the Old City is the Church of the Holy Sepulchre, which was built on what is said to be the tomb of Jesus Christ. Many Christian pilgrims visit the site each year. 🌐 **EE2 Places and Regions: Standard 6**

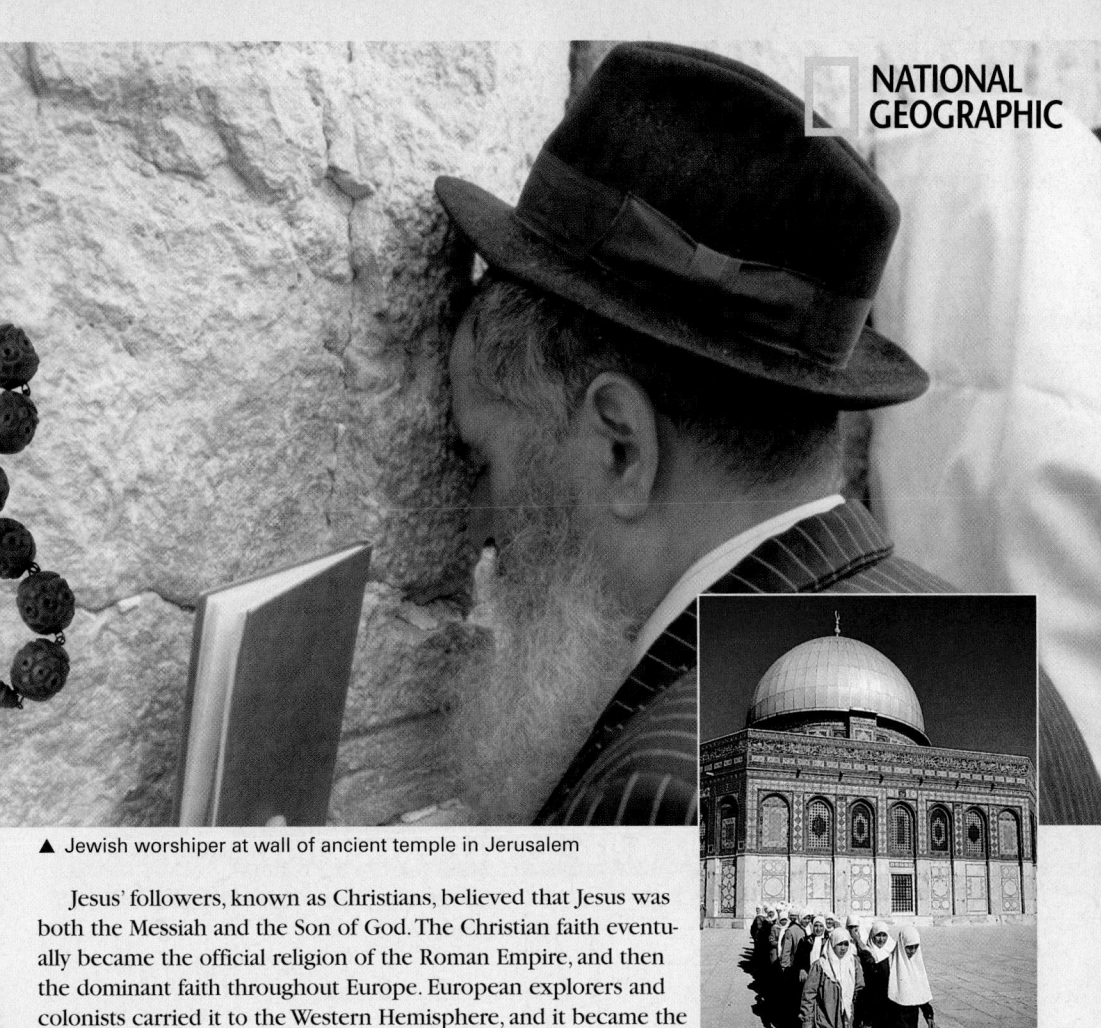

NATIONAL GEOGRAPHIC

▲ Jewish worshiper at wall of ancient temple in Jerusalem

Jesus' followers, known as Christians, believed that Jesus was both the Messiah and the Son of God. The Christian faith eventually became the official religion of the Roman Empire, and then the dominant faith throughout Europe. European explorers and colonists carried it to the Western Hemisphere, and it became the most widely practiced religion in the United States.

More than 500 years after Jesus died, the prophet Muhammad was born on the Arabian Peninsula. According to Muslim tradition, Muhammad received revelations from God and began to teach lessons to his followers. The heart of his teachings form the basis of Islam, which revolves around belief in a single God who periodically communicates through prophets. For believers of Islam, Muhammad was the last in a series of prophets that included Abraham and Jesus.

After Muhammad's death in A.D. 632, Islam spread quickly. Unlike Judaism and Christianity, however, Islam remained the dominant faith in the region where it originated. Islam has more than a billion followers worldwide, and its numbers are growing in the United States.

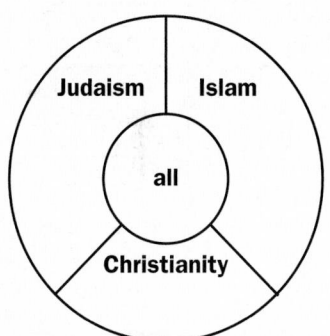

▲ Muslim women leaving shrine in Jerusalem

Unit 6 **419**

2 TEACH

Religious Influences Discuss with students the many ways in which Christianity, Judaism, and Islam affect the lives of Americans. Include in the discussion the areas of the world to which the religions later spread from Southwest Asia, and the means by which they spread beyond their place of origin.

3 ASSESS

Draw a large diagram on the board like the one below and have students suggest ways that Judaism, Christianity, and Islam are alike and ways that they are different to fill in the diagram.

Judaism | Islam

all

Christianity

4 CLOSE

Encourage students to find out more about Christianity, Islam, and Judaism. Suggest that they browse through the Bible or the Quran, or visit a church, mosque, or synagogue.

CONNECTION ACTIVITY

Holidays Organize the class into three groups. Assign each group to one of the following holidays—Christian: Christmas (Dec. 25)/birth of Jesus; Jewish: Hanukkah/Judah Maccabee; or Muslim: Id al-Adha (Feast of the Sacrifice)/Abraham. Have groups use resources from the library, the Internet, or interviews with practicing Christians, Jews, or Muslims to research the holiday and its connection to the person named. Then have students give presentations that tell the history and religious significance of the holiday and explain how it is celebrated. Presentations may include foods, illustrations, games, or music. 📦

🌐 **EE4 Human Systems: Standard 10**

CHAPTER 17 PLANNING GUIDE

NOTE: The following materials may be used when teaching Chapter 17. Section-level support materials are shown at point-of-use in the margins of the Teacher Wraparound Edition.

TEACHING TRANSPARENCIES

L2 Unit 6 Map Overlay Transparencies

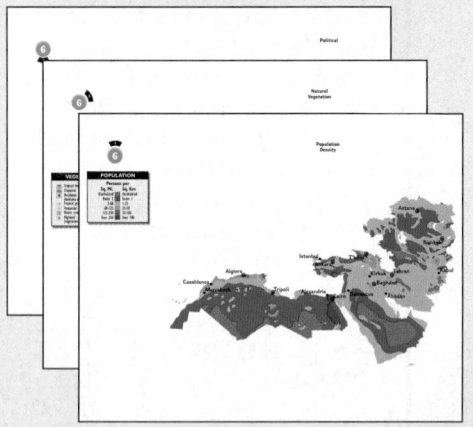

L2 Political Map Transparency 6

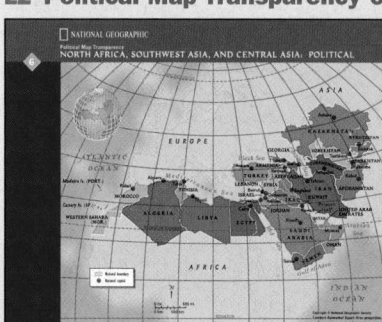

GEOGRAPHIC LITERACY

Focus on Geography Literacy

APPLICATION AND ENRICHMENT

L3 Enrichment Activity 17

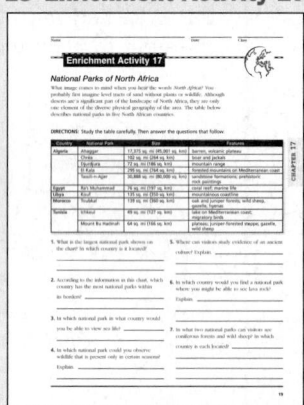

REVIEW AND REINFORCEMENT

L1 Vocabulary Activity 17 L1 Reinforcing Skills Activity 17 L1 Reteaching Activity 17

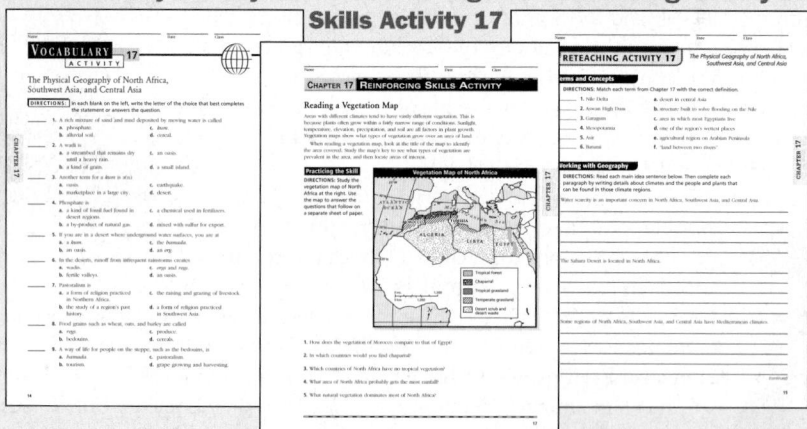

ASSESSMENT

L2 Chapter 17 Test Form A

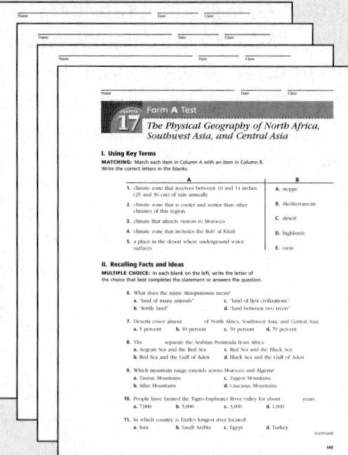

L2 Chapter 17 Test Form B

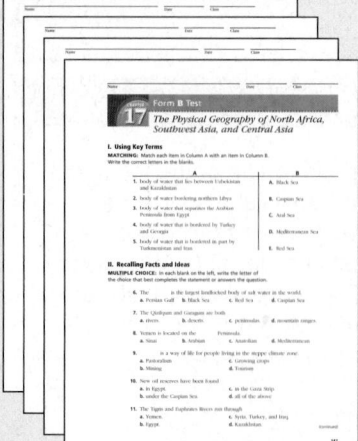

L1/ELL Performance Assessment Activity 17

ExamView® Pro Testmaker

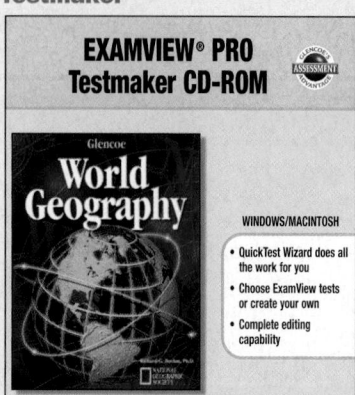

The following Spanish language materials are available in the Spanish Resources binder:

- 📁 Spanish Vocabulary Activities
- 📁 Spanish Guided Reading Activities
- 📁 Spanish Reteaching Activities
- 📁 Spanish Summaries
- 📁 Spanish Quizzes and Tests
- 📁 Spanish Reading Essentials and Study Guide

- World Regions Video
- MindJogger Videoquiz
- Vocabulary PuzzleMaker CD-ROM
- Interactive Tutor Self-Assessment CD-ROM
- ExamView® Pro Testmaker CD-ROM
- Audio Program
- TeacherWorks CD-ROM
- Interactive Student Edition CD-ROM
- Glencoe Skillbuilder Interactive Workbook CD-ROM, Level 2
- Presentation Plus! CD-ROM

Timesaving Tools

TeacherWorks™ All-In-One Planner and Resource Center

- **Interactive Teacher Edition** Access your Teacher Wraparound Edition and your classroom resources with a few easy clicks.

- **Interactive Lesson Planner** Planning has never been easier! Organize your week, month, semester, or year with all the lesson helps you need to make teaching creative, timely, and relevant.

Use Glencoe's **Presentation Plus!** multimedia teacher tool to easily present dynamic lessons that visually excite your students. Using Microsoft PowerPoint® you can customize the presentations to create your own personalized lessons.

GEOGRAPHY Online

Use our Web site for additional resources. All essential content is covered in the Student Edition.

You and your students can visit geography.glencoe.com, the Web site companion to *Glencoe World Geography*. This innovative integration of electronic and print media offers your students a wealth of opportunities. The student text directs students to the Web site for the following options:

- Chapter Overviews
- Self-Check Quizzes
- Student Activities
- Textbook Updates

Answers are provided for you in the "Web Activity Lesson Plan." Additional Web resources and Interactive Tutor puzzles are also available.

▶ **Additional Glencoe Teacher Support**

- Teaching Strategies for the Geography Classroom (including Block Scheduling Pacing Guides)

- Graphic Organizer Transparencies Strategies and Activities

- Outline Map Resource Book

- Reading in the Content Area

CHAPTER 17 PLANNING GUIDE

SECTION RESOURCES

Daily Objectives	Reproducible Resources	Multimedia Resources

SECTION 1   The Land

1. Identify which land and water features dominate the region.
2. Discuss how the region's major rivers are important to its people.
3. Explain why much of the world is economically dependent on the region.

 Reproducible Lesson Plan 17-1
 Daily Lecture Notes 17-1
Guided Reading Activity 17-1*
Reading Essentials and Study Guide 17-1*
 Section Quiz 17-1*

- Daily Focus Skills Transparency 17-1
- Political Map Transparency 6
- Unit 6 Map Overlay Transparencies
- Interactive Tutor Self-Assessment CD-ROM
- ExamView® Pro Testmaker CD-ROM*
- Presentation Plus! CD-ROM

SECTION 2   Climate and Vegetation

1. Explain how the climates of the region differ.
2. Describe how the needs of a growing population have affected the natural vegetation of the region.

 Reproducible Lesson Plan 17-2
Vocabulary Activity 17*
 Daily Lecture Notes 17-2
 Guided Reading Activity 17-2*
 Reading Essentials and Study Guide 17-2*
 Reteaching Activity 17*
Reinforcing Skills Activity 17
 Section Quiz 17-2*

- Daily Focus Skills Transparency 17-2
- Political Map Transparency 6
- Unit 6 Map Overlay Transparencies
- Vocabulary PuzzleMaker CD-ROM
- Interactive Tutor Self-Assessment CD-ROM
- ExamView® Pro Testmaker CD-ROM*
- Presentation Plus! CD-ROM

Blackline Master   Software   Videocassette

Transparency   CD-ROM   DVD

*Also available in Spanish

 OUT OF TIME? Assign the Chapter 17 **Reading Essentials and Study Guide.**

Block Schedule

Activities that are particularly suited to use within the block scheduling framework are identified throughout this chapter by the following designation:

KEY TO ABILITY LEVELS

Teaching strategies have been coded for various learning styles and abilities.

L1   **BASIC** activities for all students

L2   **AVERAGE** activities for average to above-average students

L3   **CHALLENGING** activities for above-average students

ELL   **ENGLISH LANGUAGE LEARNER** activities

Teacher to Teacher

Gabe Estrada
Onate High School
Las Cruces, NM

What Do You Know?

A good introductory exercise to learn what students already know about the region—and one that is fun for students—is to ask them a series of questions concerning the region's physical geography, climate, and vegetation. A familiar feature and one that provides a good starting point is the Sahara. Ask if students know in which countries the Sahara is located, what kinds of vegetation might be found there, and if the Sahara is completely made up of sand. Students may remember seeing movies or reading books in which the Sahara is featured.

After students reveal what they think they already know about the region, locate passages in the chapter and have students read aloud the facts presented on the pages. Students may be surprised to learn that, for instance, sand covers less than 10 percent of the Sahara.

Have students then work in groups of four to research the physical geography, climate, and vegetation of one of the countries in the region. Have groups present oral reports to the class. Ask students to include in their reports interesting or little-known features about the country.

TEACHER'S CORNER

Index to National Geographic Magazine:
The following articles may be used for research relating to this chapter:

- *Biodiversity*, A National Geographic Special Edition, February 1999.
- "The Imperiled Nile Delta," by Peter Theroux, January 1997.
- "The Desert Sea," by David Doubilet, November 1993.

National Geographic Society Products:
To order the following products for use with this chapter, call National Geographic Society at 1-800-368-2728.

- *Africa* (Video)
- *Asia* (Video)
- *Pollution: World at Risk* (Video)
- *Healing the Earth* (Video)
- *Physical Earth* (Map)
- *National Geographic Desk Reference* (Book)
- *National Geographic Atlas of the World, Seventh Edition* (Book)

NGS ONLINE

Access National Geographic's Web site for current events, activities, links, interactive features, and archives.
www.nationalgeographic.com

Meeting National Standards

Geography For Life

The following standards are highlighted in Chapter 17:

Section 1 EE2 Places and Regions:
Standards 4, 5
EE3 Physical Systems:
Standard 7

Section 2 EE2 Places and Regions:
Standard 4
EE3 Physical Systems:
Standard 8
EE5 Environment and Society:
Standards 14, 15

Local Objectives

_____

_____

MEETING SPECIAL NEEDS

In addition to the Differentiated Instruction strategies found in each section, the following resources are also suitable for your special needs students:

- *ExamView® Pro Testmaker CD-ROM* allows teachers to tailor tests by reducing answer choices.
- The *Audio Program* includes the entire narrative of the student edition so that less-proficient readers can listen to the words as they read them.
- The *Reading Essentials and Study Guide* provides the same content as the student edition but is written two grade levels below the textbook.
- *Guided Reading Activities* give less-proficient readers point-by-point instructions to increase comprehension as they read each textbook section.
- *Enrichment Activities* include a stimulating collection of readings and activities for gifted and talented students.

Chapter Objectives

1. Describe the major landforms and natural resources of North Africa, Southwest Asia, and Central Asia.

2. Discuss the climate and vegetation of North Africa, Southwest Asia, and Central Asia.

GLENCOE
TECHNOLOGY

Use *MindJogger Videoquiz* to preview the Chapter 17 content.

GeoJournal

For access to additional photos, maps, and information on the geographic features of North Africa, Southwest Asia, and Central Asia, go to www.nationalgeographic.com **(See Teacher pages in front for strategies for using journals in the geography classroom.)**

GEOGRAPHY *Online*

Introduce students to chapter content and key terms by having them access **Chapter Overview 17** at geography.glencoe.com

FOLDABLES
Study Organizer

Dinah Zike's Foldables are three-dimensional, interactive graphic organizers that help students practice basic writing skills, review key vocabulary terms, and identify main ideas. Have students complete the Foldable activity in the **Dinah Zike's Reading and Study Skills Foldables** booklet.

CHAPTER 17

The Physical Geography of North Africa, Southwest Asia, and Central Asia

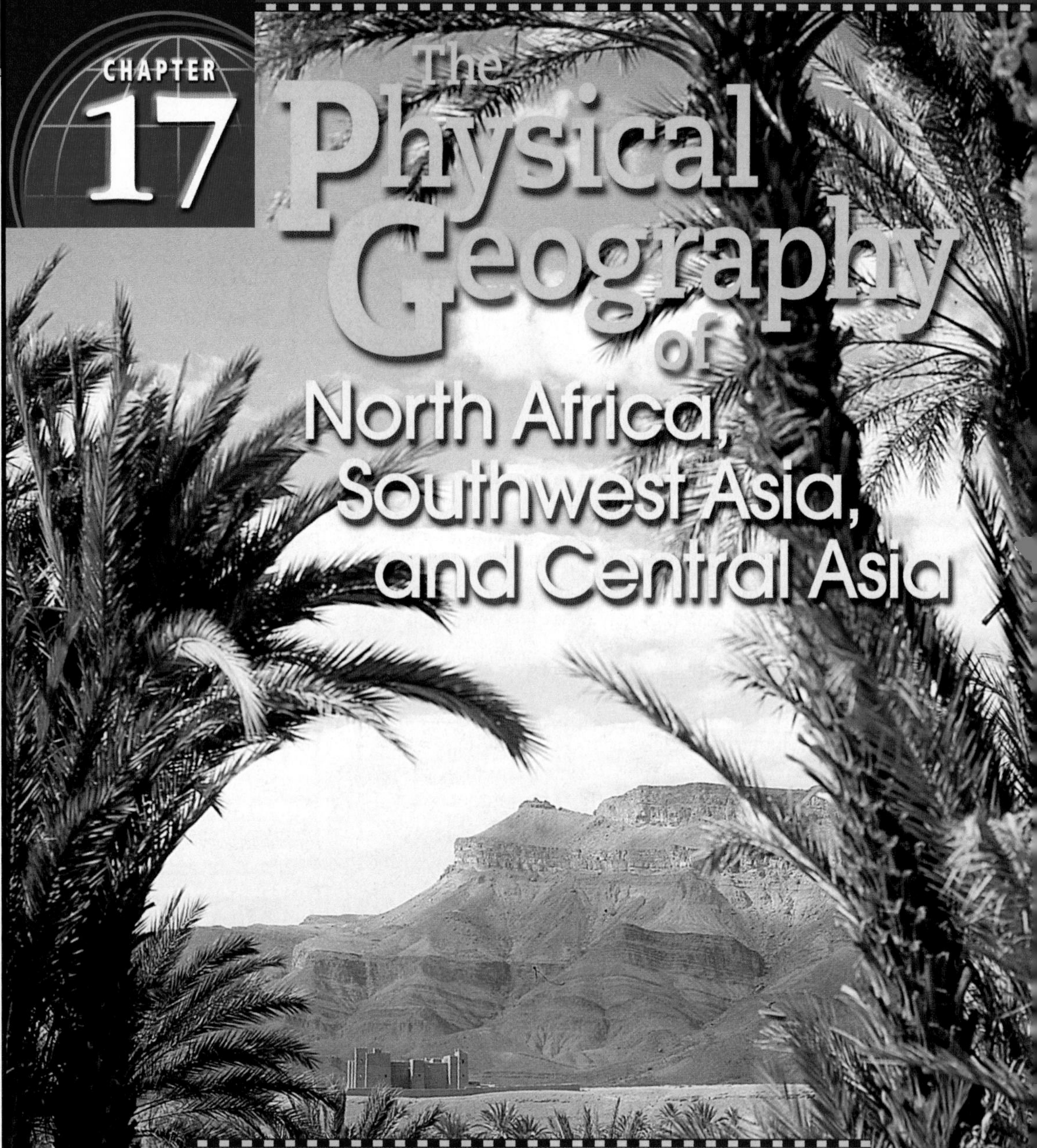

GeoJournal

As you read this chapter, list ways the physical geography of North Africa, Southwest Asia, and Central Asia shapes the lives of people in the region. Include examples you discover in media sources.

GEOGRAPHY *Online*

Chapter Overview Visit the **Glencoe World Geography** Web site at geography.glencoe.com and click on Chapter Overviews—Chapter 17 to preview information about the physical geography of the region.

ABOUT THE PHOTO

Morocco A Muslim country at the northwest corner of Africa, Morocco is remarkably diverse in its geography and climates. The Sahara extends along the far south of the country. Morocco is bordered on its north and west by the Mediterranean Sea and the Atlantic Ocean, and encompasses sand, snow, mountains, plains, and plateaus along with dozens of fertile oases. Temperatures in the mountains are frigid, while Morocco's interior and coastal regions can be very hot. Crops—mainly dates, olives, lemons, oranges, and almonds, as well as grains such as barley, wheat, alfalfa, and maize—are plentiful around the oases that dot the Moroccan landscape. **EE2 Places and Regions: Standard 4**

The Land

NATIONAL GEOGRAPHIC

A Geographic View

Timeless Travel

Men and boys of the caravan form a ragged rank, facing distant Mecca.... In unison the caravanners kneel, then bow, pressing their foreheads into the sand. In the cool shadows of morning they rejoin the line of beasts tethered head to tail and wait for a signal.... The **madougou,** *or caravan boss, raises his staff, jerks the rope halter on his lead camel, and, to shouts and the clanging of pans and bowls, the half-mile-long train grudgingly lurches forward.*

—*Thomas J. Abercrombie, "Ibn Battuta, Prince of Travelers,"* National Geographic, *December 1991*

Camel caravan, Sahara

Joining a camel caravan in the Sahara, writer Thomas J. Abercrombie followed in the footsteps of the Muslim traveler Ibn Battuta, who crisscrossed the lands of North Africa, Southwest Asia, and Central Asia more than five centuries ago.

People, goods, and ideas have come together in this part of the world for thousands of years because of its location on or near the Mediterranean Sea. This section examines the varied landscape and the wealth of natural resources of the region where the continents of Europe, Africa, and Asia meet.

Seas and Peninsulas

North Africa, Southwest Asia, and Central Asia form an intricate jigsaw puzzle of seas and peninsulas. Edging the coast of North Africa as far as the Strait of Gibraltar, the Mediterranean Sea separates Africa and Europe.

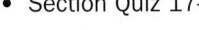

Desert fort and oasis, Morocco

Chapter 17 **421**

Guide to Reading

Consider What You Know

The vast region of North Africa, Southwest Asia, and Central Asia spans portions of Africa and Asia. Considering this great expanse, what landforms would you expect to discover in the region?

Reading Strategy

Organizing Complete a graphic organizer similar to the one below by filling in a description of each body of water listed.

Body of Water	Description
Dead Sea	
Caspian Sea	
Aral Sea	

Read to Find Out

- What land and water features dominate the region?
- Why are the region's major rivers important to its people?
- Why is much of the world economically dependent on the region?

Terms to Know

- alluvial soil
- *kum*
- wadi
- phosphate

Places to Locate

- Red Sea
- Arabian Peninsula
- Persian Gulf
- Sinai Peninsula
- Anatolia
- Dead Sea
- Caspian Sea
- Aral Sea
- Nile River
- Tigris River
- Euphrates River
- Atlas Mountains
- Caucasus Mountains

FOCUS

Section Overview

This section discusses the major land and water features of North Africa, Southwest Asia, and Central Asia, as well as the region's natural resources.

BELLRINGER
Skillbuilder Activity

- Project transparency and have students answer questions.

- Available as blackline master.

Daily Focus Skills Transparency 17-1

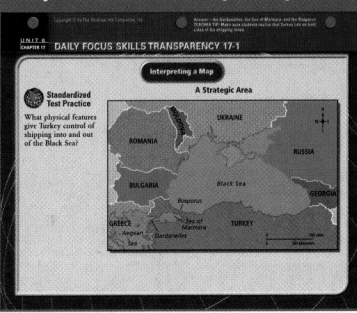

Guide to Reading

Consider What You Know
Answers *Answers may include coastal regions, vast plains, plateaus, deserts, and mountains.*

Reading Strategy
Answers Dead Sea: *located at mouth of Jordan River, part of Israeli-Jordanian border, source of chemical products such as potash;* Caspian Sea: *largest inland body of water on Earth, reaches both Asia and Europe;* Aral Sea: *began shrinking in the 1960s, only a fraction of its original size due to diversion of tributaries*

Preteaching Vocabulary
Direct students to page 424 for the meaning of *wadi* and explain that similar geographic features are found in many regions of the world.

RESOURCE MANAGER

Reproducible Masters
- Reproducible Lesson Plan 17-1
- Daily Lecture Notes 17-1
- Guided Reading Activity 17-1
- Reading Essentials and Study Guide 17-1
- Section Quiz 17-1

Transparencies
- Daily Focus Skills Transparency 17-1
- Political Map Transparency 6
- Unit 6 Map Overlay Transparencies

Multimedia
- Interactive Tutor Self-Assessment CD-ROM
- ExamView® Pro Testmaker CD-ROM
- Presentation Plus! CD-ROM

② TEACH

L1 Identify

Write the following geographic features on the board: *sea, peninsula, plateau, mountain, river, desert*. Ask students to describe each term and give examples from the region.

Daily Lecture Notes 17-1

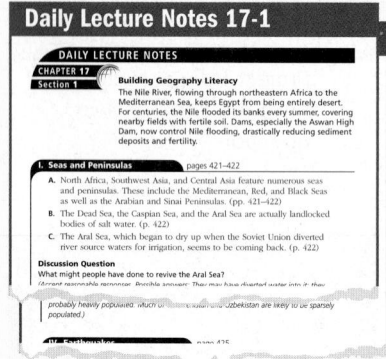

DAILY LECTURE NOTES

CHAPTER 17
Section 1

Building Geography Literacy
The Nile River, flowing through northeastern Africa to the Mediterranean Sea, keeps Egypt from being entirely desert. For centuries, the Nile flooded its banks every summer, covering nearby fields with fertile soil. Dams, especially the Aswan High Dam, now control Nile flooding, drastically reducing sediment deposits and fertility.

I. Seas and Peninsulas   pages 421–422

A. North Africa, Southwest Asia, and Central Asia feature numerous seas and peninsulas. These include the Mediterranean, Red, and Black Seas as well as the Arabian and Sinai Peninsulas. (pp. 421–422)

B. The Dead Sea, the Caspian Sea, and the Aral Sea are actually landlocked bodies of salt water. (p. 422)

C. The Aral Sea, which began to dry up when the Soviet Union diverted river source waters for irrigation, seems to be coming back. (p. 422)

Discussion Question
What might people have done to revive the Aral Sea?
(Accept reasonable answers. Possible answers: They may have diverted water into it; they probably heavily populated. Much of ... ... Uzbekistan are likely to be sparsely populated.)

NATIONAL GEOGRAPHIC World Explorer

Answer
The Aswan High Dam and other dams control the river's water, reducing flooding and deposits of alluvial soil.

More About the Photo
Around 4000 B.C., a simple irrigation system in which Nile floods were dammed in shallow pools allowed Egyptians to grow wheat and barley in the soaked fields. In the 1800s continuous irrigation enabled Egyptians to expand their farming to include crops of cotton, sugarcane, and peanuts.

Comparing Lands

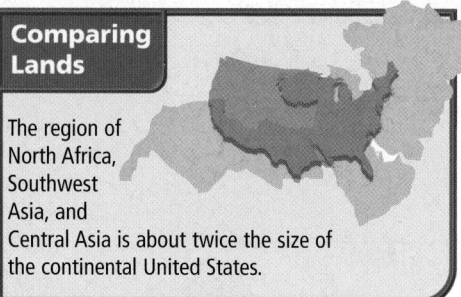

The region of North Africa, Southwest Asia, and Central Asia is about twice the size of the continental United States.

To the east, the **Red Sea** and the Gulf of Aden separate Southwest Asia's **Arabian Peninsula** from Africa. The **Persian Gulf** frames this peninsula on the east, and the Arabian Sea borders it on the south. Northwest of the Arabian Peninsula, the Gulf of Suez and the Gulf of Aqaba flank the smallest piece in the puzzle, the **Sinai Peninsula**.

To the north the peninsula of **Anatolia** points west to the Aegean Sea. Two more seas—the Black Sea and the Mediterranean Sea—lie at the peninsula's north and south. The Dardanelles, the Sea of Marmara, and the Bosporus strait, which together separate Europe and Asia, connect the Aegean and Black Seas.

Three landlocked bodies of salt water lie east of the Mediterranean Sea. The smallest of these, the **Dead Sea**, sits at the mouth of the Jordan River,

forming part of the Israeli-Jordanian border. It is a source of chemical products such as potash. In Central Asia, the **Caspian Sea** is the largest inland body of water on Earth. Stretching for almost 750 miles (1,207 km), this landlocked sea laps the shores of both Asia and Europe. As you read in Unit 4, evaporation and decreased flow from feeder rivers have resulted in the Caspian Sea's lower water levels. Irrigation and industry also cut the flow of other rivers flowing into the Caspian Sea, further reducing water levels.

East of the Caspian Sea, in the heart of Central Asia, is the **Aral Sea**. Until the 1960s the Aral Sea was the world's fourth-largest inland sea, and it supported a healthy fishing community. Now it is just a fraction of its former size and looks more like a desert than a sea. The Aral Sea began to dry up when the Soviet Union diverted huge amounts of water for irrigation from the major rivers flowing into the sea. Today the Aral Sea seems to be coming back. By building small dams in parts of the former sea, local people plan to create smaller freshwater basins with water from the rivers.

Rivers

Rivers are the lifeblood of North Africa, Southwest Asia, and Central Asia. Their lush and productive valleys have always welcomed travelers

---

NATIONAL GEOGRAPHIC World Explorer

Geography Skills for Life

Gift of the Nile The fertile flood plain of the Nile has sustained Egyptian life for thousands of years. The ancient drawing (inset) depicts the wheat harvest. In the photograph (left), an Egyptian harvests sugarcane.
Place How are the Nile's waters controlled today?

DIFFERENTIATED INSTRUCTION

Reading Support For students who have problems with reading, point out the "Guide to Reading" at the beginning of the section on page 421. Remind students that this feature sums up the content of the section. Call students' attention to each heading in this feature, and have them speculate on what the section will cover. Remind them to watch for the "Terms to Know" as they read, and suggest that they write definitions for any unfamiliar terms.

Refer to *Inclusion for the Social Studies Classroom Strategies and Activities.*

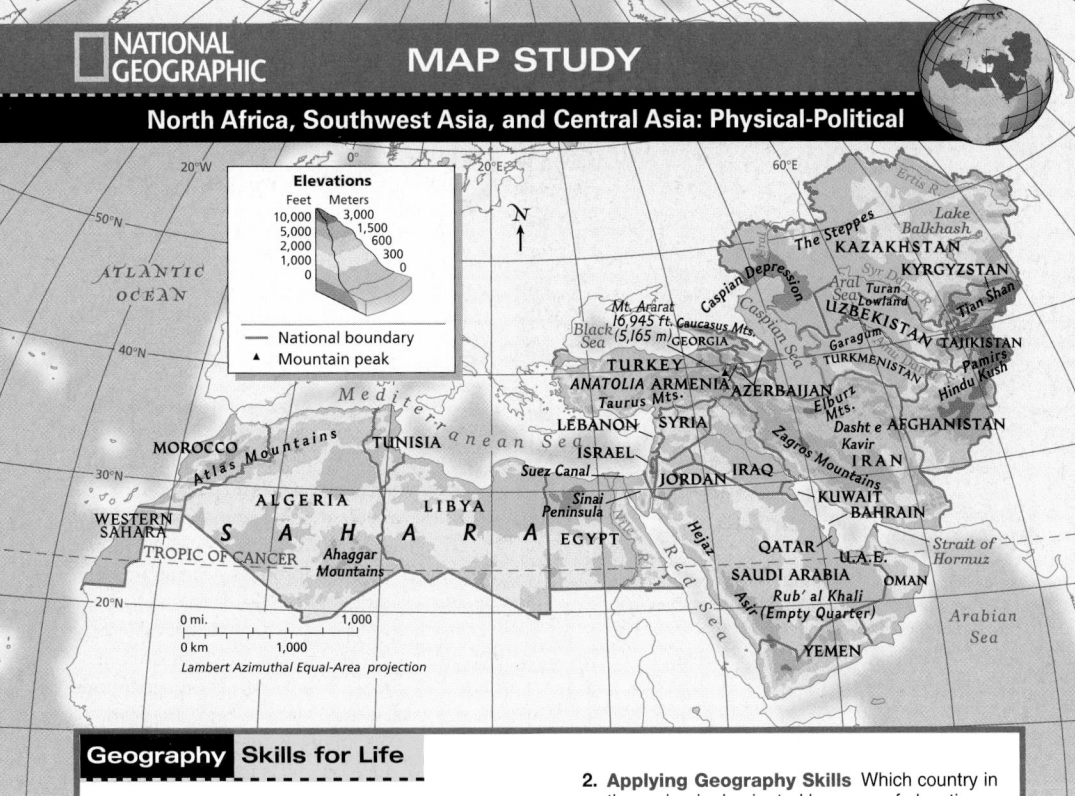

NATIONAL GEOGRAPHIC — MAP STUDY

North Africa, Southwest Asia, and Central Asia: Physical-Political

Elevations

Feet	Meters
10,000	3,000
5,000	1,500
2,000	600
1,000	300
0	0

— National boundary
▲ Mountain peak

Lambert Azimuthal Equal-Area projection

Geography Skills for Life

1. **Interpreting Maps** Where are the Zagros Mountains located? The Atlas Mountains?

2. **Applying Geography Skills** Which country in the region is dominated by areas of elevations of more than 5,000 feet (1,500 meters)?

Find NGS online map resources @ www.nationalgeographic.com/maps

---

and provided food for local peoples. Egypt's **Nile River** is the world's longest river at 4,160 miles (6,695 km). The Tigris (TY•gruhs) and Euphrates (yu•FRAY•teez) Rivers, which flow mainly through Iraq, are also important to the region.

Culture
Major Rivers: Cradles of Civilization

The Nile Delta and the fertile land along the river's banks gave birth to one of the world's earliest civilizations. Today more than 90 percent of Egypt's people live in the Nile Delta or along the course of the river on only 3 percent of Egypt's land. The Aswan High Dam and other modern dams farther up the Nile now control the river's flow, reducing both flooding and deposits of

alluvial soil, rich soil made up of sand and mud deposited by moving water.

Early civilizations also thrived in the Tigris-Euphrates river valley, a fertile farming valley in Central Asia. Known by ancients as Mesopotamia, which is Greek for "land between two rivers," this valley owes its fertile character to the **Tigris** and **Euphrates Rivers**. A complex irrigation network has watered the valley and supported farming there for 7,000 years. Today the Tigris and Euphrates help irrigate farms throughout Syria, Turkey, and Iraq.

Originating only 50 miles (80 km) from each other in eastern Turkey, the Tigris and Euphrates Rivers join in Iraq to form the Shatt al Arab, which empties into the Persian Gulf. The Euphrates is the longer river, flowing 1,700 miles (2,736 km) toward the sea.

Chapter 17 🌐 **423**

NATIONAL GEOGRAPHIC — MAP STUDY

Answers

1. *Iran; Morocco, Algeria, small part of Tunisia*

2. *Kyrgyzstan*

Map Skills Practice

Place Which countries have mountains of 10,000 feet (3,000 m) or more? *(Georgia, Iran, Kyrgyzstan, Tajikistan, Yemen, Afghanistan, Saudi Arabia, Morocco, Turkey, Armenia, Israel)*

L2 Latitude and Longitude

Have students identify the countries on the map on this page through which the 30°E longitude line runs. *(Turkey and Egypt)* Then have students identify the countries through which the 30°N latitude line runs. *(Morocco, Algeria, Libya, Egypt, Jordan, Saudi Arabia, Iraq, Iran, Afghanistan)*

L1/ELL

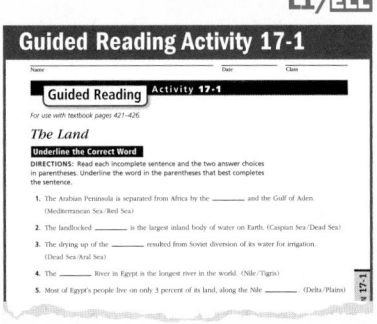

Guided Reading Activity 17-1

Guided Reading Activity 17-1

For use with textbook pages 421–426

The Land

Underline the Correct Word

DIRECTIONS: Read each incomplete sentence and the two answer choices in parentheses. Underline the word in the parentheses that best completes the sentence.

1. The Arabian Peninsula is separated from Africa by the _____ and the Gulf of Aden. (Mediterranean Sea/Red Sea)

2. The landlocked _____ is the largest inland body of water on Earth. (Caspian Sea/Dead Sea)

3. The drying up of the _____ resulted from Soviet diversion of its water for irrigation. (Dead Sea/Aral Sea)

4. The _____ River in Egypt is the longest river in the world. (Nile/Tigris)

5. Most of Egypt's people live on only 3 percent of its land, along the Nile _____. (Delta/Plains)

COOPERATIVE LEARNING ACTIVITY

Physical Processes List on the board and have volunteers briefly describe the physical processes that occur in arid environments: salt accumulation, soil erosion, sand movement, dust storms, flash floods, and desertification. Organize the class into six groups and assign each group a process from the list. Have groups research to find out which areas of the region are particularly prone to the processes. Finally, have groups list their findings on the board so that the class may see which areas experience more than one of those processes. Allow time for a class discussion of their findings. Offer extra credit to students who choose to research what an area is doing to protect itself from the effects of those processes. 📦

🌐 **EE3 Physical Systems: Standard 7**

World Explorer

Answer
farming, fishing, raising livestock

More About the Photo The Atlas Mountains stretch about 1,500 miles (2,410 km) and are most rugged and highest in Morocco, where Jebel Toubkal, the highest peak, reaches 13,671 feet (4,167 m).

L1/ELL

Reading Essentials & Study Guide 17-1

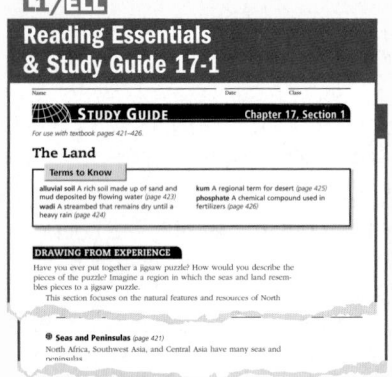

Comparing Deltas The Aswan High Dam and other dams in Egypt now reduce alluvial soil deposits from the Nile, but the free-flowing Mississippi River in the United States still carries more than 170 million tons of sediment annually to an ever-growing delta.

Objectives, goals, and answers to the student activity can be found in the Web Activity Lesson Plan feature at geography.glencoe.com

---

World Explorer

Geography Skills for Life

Snowy Desert Morocco's Atlas Mountains lie near the Sahara, but mountain travelers must be prepared for cold, snowy weather.
Place What are Morocco's most important economic activities?

The Tigris extends about 1,180 miles (1,899 km). Dams control the flow of both rivers.

Streambeds

Many streams in arid North Africa and Southwest Asia flow only intermittently, appearing suddenly and disappearing just as quickly. In the region's deserts, runoff from infrequent rainstorms creates wadis (WAH•dees)—streambeds that remain dry until a heavy rain. Irregular rainstorms often produce flash flooding. During a flash flood, wadis fill with so much sediment that they can rapidly become mud flows, or moving masses of wet soil, which are a danger to humans and animals.

Plains, Plateaus, and Mountains

A traveler in North Africa, Southwest Asia, and Central Asia could expect to see varied and dramatic landforms. Low plains extend to the horizon and sometimes rise to a plateau or mountains.

Study the map on page 423 to see elevation patterns within the region.

Coastal Plains

In a region dominated by deserts and mountains, lush coastal plains stand out. The region's agricultural base is rooted in fertile plains along the Mediterranean Sea, such as those stretching east to west along the Moroccan and Algerian coasts and those along the Caspian Sea and Persian Gulf.

Highlands

Africa's longest mountain range, the **Atlas Mountains**, reaches across Morocco and Algeria, in the westernmost part of the region. Enough precipitation falls on the northern side of these mountains to water the coastal regions and make them hospitable to settlement and farming. Despite Morocco's generally rugged terrain, for example, the fertile farmlands of the Atlas's northern slopes produce an abundance of crops typical of the Mediterranean climate. About 50 percent of Morocco's people engage in agriculture, producing barley, oats, and wheat. In years of drought, as in 1999, the economy suffers. With more rain predicted, the economy is expected to grow by about 6 percent per year. Fishing and raising livestock also play a large role in Morocco's economy.

In Southwest Asia, two mountain ranges, the Hejaz and the Asir, stretch along the western coast of the Arabian Peninsula. The taller Asir Mountains receive more rainfall than the Hejaz, accumulating up to 19 inches (48 cm) annually. This precipitation makes the Asir region the most agriculturally productive on the Arabian Peninsula. In contrast, the Central Plateau to the east of the Asir Mountains averages between 0 and 4 inches (0 and 10 cm) of rain per year, mainly because of the rain shadow effect.

Student Web Activity Visit the Glencoe World Geography Web site at geography.glencoe.com and click on Student Web Activities—Chapter 17 for an activity about physical processes in North Africa, Southwest Asia, and Central Asia.

CRITICAL THINKING ACTIVITY

Drawing Conclusions Have students suggest characteristics or features that define regions. Write their ideas on the board. *(list should include physical features, climate, economic activities, and culture)* **Ask:** What conclusions can you draw about why North Africa, Southwest Asia, and Central Asia are considered a region? *(Answers should include similar landforms, location, climate, resources, economic activity, history, and culture.)* Ask students to provide examples of characteristics or features that are shared by two or more countries in the region. **Ask:** Why is this region called a "crossroads"? *(It joins Europe, Asia, and Africa.)* 🌐 EE2 Places and Regions: Standard 5

The Pontic Mountains and the Taurus Mountains rise from the Turkish landscape. Between these ranges, the Anatolian Plateau stands 2,000 to 5,000 feet (610 to 1,524 m) above sea level. East of the Pontic range, camel-backed Mount Ararat, at almost 17,000 feet (5,182 m), overlooks the Turkish-Iranian border.

As the map on page 423 shows, the **Caucasus Mountains** rise north of Mount Ararat between the Black Sea and Caspian Sea. The grandeur and beauty of this mountain range and surrounding country are captured in a journalist's words:

> 66 *To glimpse the landscape of the . . . Caucasus . . . is to imagine Eden. Beneath the icy summits of its mountain range, grapevines and pomegranate trees hang [heavy] with fruit.* 99
>
> Mike Edwards, "The Fractured Caucasus," *National Geographic*, February 1996

West of the Tian Shan range, the Turan Lowland provides some irrigated farmland. To the south, dune-covered *kums* (KOOMZ), or deserts, offer a stark contrast to the cultivated fields of the lowland. The Garagum (Kara Kum), or black sand desert, covers most of Turkmenistan. The Qizilqum (Kyzyl Kum), or red sand desert, blankets half of Uzbekistan. Farther west, the Ustyurt Plateau has salt marshes, sinkholes, and caverns.

Earthquakes

The African, Arabian, and Eurasian plates come together in the lands of North Africa, Southwest Asia, and Central Asia. As the plates move, they build mountains, shift landmasses, and cause earthquakes. Tectonic movement built the Zagros Mountains of southern Iran and the Taurus Mountains of Turkey. The movement continues to shape the region. For example, the shifting of the African and Arabian plates causes the widening of the Red Sea.

Earthquakes rumble throughout the region regularly. Turkey, lying at the boundary of the Arabian and Eurasian plates, experienced a 1999 earthquake measuring 7.4 on the Richter scale. It toppled more than 76,000 buildings and killed nearly 20,000 people.

NATIONAL GEOGRAPHIC · World Explorer

Geography Skills for Life
Nature's Wrath Survivors survey the destruction caused by an earthquake in Turkey.
Human-Environment Interaction What factor accounts for frequent earthquakes in this region?

Chapter 17 ⊕ **425**

L1 Locating Features
Have pairs of students list major land and water features mentioned in this section. Then have them locate each feature on a map of the region and give its absolute location. **ELL**

③ ASSESS

Assign Section 1 Assessment as homework or as an in-class activity.

● Have students use **Interactive Tutor Self-Assessment CD-ROM** to review Section 1.

L2

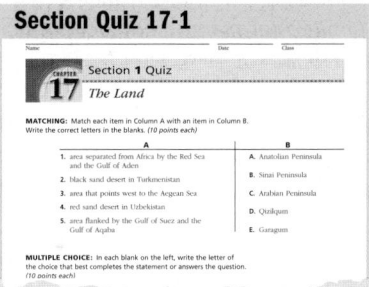

Section Quiz 17-1

NATIONAL GEOGRAPHIC World Explorer

Answer
The movements of three tectonic plates—the African, Arabian, and Eurasian—come together in this region.

More About the Photo The North Anatolian Fault, which runs through western Turkey, caused 13 major earthquakes between 1939 and 1999.

TEAM-TEACHING ACTIVITY: SCIENCE

Desert-causing Conditions Rain shadows are one of the causes of deserts. As moist air approaches mountain ranges, it rises over the peaks. As it rises, it cools and loses its ability to retain moisture so rain falls on the upwind side of a mountain. The downward side, however, often stays dry because the moisture has already fallen on the mountain's upwind side. The dry, downwind side of the mountain is said to lie in the rain shadow. Other deserts exist because ocean winds lose their moisture as they travel great distances. Have students work with a science teacher to make illustrations or models that show how the deserts of North Africa, Southwest Asia, and Central Asia were formed.

⊕ **EE3 Physical Systems: Standard 7**

Reteach

Have students write a review question for each section heading. Then have partners exchange papers and answer the questions.

Enrich

Challenge students to find out why the region is so rich in fossil fuels. Suggest that students research what the region was like millions of years ago.

4 CLOSE

Ask students to speculate on the kinds of challenges that the region of North Africa, Southwest Asia, and Central Asia faces. *(limited farmland; shrinking seas; earthquakes and flash floods)*

▲ *Working in the oil fields of Azerbaijan*

Natural Resources

The lands of North Africa, Southwest Asia, and Central Asia contain many natural resources. Petroleum and natural gas, the region's most abundant resources, are important to the economies of countries around the world.

Economics
Oil and Natural Gas

Seventy percent of the world's known oil reserves and 33 percent of the world's known natural gas reserves lie beneath the region. Unmeasured reserves include newly discovered gas fields in the Gaza Strip and Egypt and under the Caspian Sea.

Although North Africa, Southwest Asia, and Central Asia produced little oil before World War II, production increased dramatically after 1945. Petroleum exports have enriched the region, but heavy reliance on petroleum exports is risky. When oil prices fluctuate on world markets, as they did between 1997 and 1999, the region's economies suffer. By the time oil prices rose from a low of $7 per barrel to about $30 per barrel in early 2000, oil-exporting countries' economies had been damaged.

Minerals

Minerals also provide revenue for the region. Turkmenistan has the world's largest deposits of sulfate used in paperboard, glass, and detergents, and the largest deposits of sulfur. Morocco ranks third in the production of phosphate—a chemical used in fertilizers. Deposits of chromium, gold, lead, manganese, and zinc are sprinkled across the region. Discoveries of iron ore and copper deposits indicate that the region may contain up to 10 percent of the world's iron ore reserves.

Building Diverse Economies

Some countries in the region are diversifying their economies to decrease their reliance on oil and minerals exports. The United Arab Emirates, for example, is investing oil earnings in banking, information technology, and tourism. Libya, which relies on oil for 98 percent of its export income, is investing in infrastructure, agriculture, and fisheries.

SECTION 1 ASSESSMENT

Checking for Understanding

1. **Define** alluvial soil, wadi, *kum*, phosphate.

2. **Main Ideas** Complete the table by listing physical features found in this region. Then describe how the physical features of one part of the region influence people's lives.

Region	Physical Features
North Africa	

Critical Thinking

3. **Comparing and Contrasting** How are the Caspian Sea and the Aral Sea alike? How are they different?

4. **Predicting Consequences** How might development of oil fields in the Caspian Sea affect the region of North Africa, Southwest Asia, and Central Asia?

5. **Analyzing Information** How has diversification affected the economies of countries in the region?

Analyzing Maps

6. **Place** Study the physical-political map on page 423. What physical feature dominates western Iran?

Applying Geography

7. **Benefits of Rivers** Write a descriptive paragraph explaining how the major rivers of North Africa, Southwest Asia, and Central Asia benefit people in the region.

SECTION 1 ASSESSMENT ANSWERS

1. All vocabulary terms are defined in the text.

2. Physical features: waterways, peninsulas, deserts, some arable land, plains, mountains, plateaus; an example of a feature affecting people's lives is the Nile River which makes its banks fertile for farming.

3. Alike: landlocked bodies of saltwater that have suffered from a decrease in the flows of feeder rivers; different: the Aral is smaller and has shrunk a great deal more than the Caspian Sea.

4. It may improve the economies of countries that share the Caspian, but it may also increase pollution in the area.

5. Oil-producing countries, such as Libya and the UAE, are shifting to banking, tourism, and other areas to support their economies when the oil runs out.

6. the Zagros Mountains

7. **Applying Geography** Paragraphs should mention that the rivers of the region supply freshwater for drinking and irrigation and create fertile farmland along their banks and through their valleys.

Guide to Reading

Consider What You Know

In much of North Africa, Southwest Asia, and Central Asia, rainfall averages 10 inches (25 cm) or less annually. How does lack of precipitation affect the growth of vegetation in this region?

Reading Strategy

Categorizing Complete a web diagram similar to the one below by filling in the three mid-latitude climate regions of North Africa, Southwest Asia, and Central Asia.

Read to Find Out

- How do the climates of North Africa, Southwest Asia, and Central Asia differ?
- How have the needs of a growing population affected the natural vegetation of the region?

Terms to Know

- oasis
- pastoralism
- cereal

Places to Locate

- Sahara
- Rub' al Khali
- Garagum (Kara Kum)

Climate and Vegetation

A Geographic View

Algeria's Desert Art

From the mouth of this cave Algeria stretches dry and desolate before me, but the paintings inside . . . tell of a time, perhaps 7,000 years ago, when this land was wet and green enough to support cattle and a community of herders. Today our only evidence of this rich life is an ancient artist's rendering of it. . . . Amazingly, even after thousands of years the colors are still vibrant.

—David Coulson, "Ancient Art of the Sahara," National Geographic, *June 1999*

Desert scene, Algeria

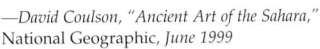

The North African landscape is commonly associated with images of vast stretches of sand, huge dunes, and the occasional watering hole. However, as David Coulson suggests, ancient cave paintings tell us that this part of the African continent was once wet and green. This section explores how differences and changes in climate across the region affect vegetation and human activities in North Africa, Southwest Asia, and Central Asia today.

Water: A Precious Resource

Water scarcity defines the region's climates. Rainfall in some areas is plentiful. The southern edge of the Caspian Sea receives more than 78 inches (198 cm) of rainfall per year. Elsewhere, however, water evaporation rates far exceed rainfall, making water very precious. Desert predominates, although steppe, Mediterranean, and highlands climates are also present in North Africa, Southwest Asia, and Central Asia.

Chapter 17 427

① FOCUS

Section Overview

This section discusses the various climates of North Africa, Southwest Asia, and Central Asia and looks at how the needs of the region's growing populations have affected its natural vegetation.

BELLRINGER
Skillbuilder Activity

 Project transparency and have students answer questions.

 Available as blackline master.

Daily Focus Skills Transparency 17-2

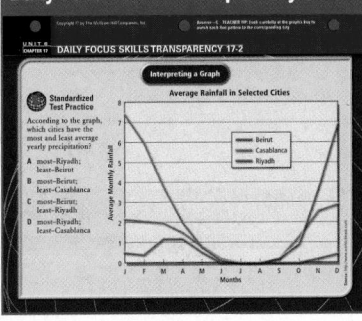

Guide to Reading

Consider What You Know
Answers *Varieties of natural vegetation would be limited, and farming would be difficult without irrigation.*

Reading Strategy
Answers Mediterranean, humid subtropical, highlands

Preteaching Vocabulary
① Use the **Vocabulary Puzzle-Maker CD-ROM** to create crossword and word-search puzzles.

RESOURCE MANAGER

📁 Reproducible Masters
- Reproducible Lesson Plan 17-2
- Vocabulary Activity 17
- Daily Lecture Notes 17-2
- Guided Reading Activity 17-2
- Reading Essentials and Study Guide 17-2
- Reteaching Activity 17
- Reinforcing Skills Activity 17
- Section Quiz 17-2

🎞 Transparencies
- Daily Focus Skills Transparency 17-2
- Political Map Transparency 6
- Unit 6 Map Overlay Transparencies

Multimedia
- Vocabulary PuzzleMaker CD-ROM
- Interactive Tutor Self-Assessment CD-ROM
- ExamView® Pro Testmaker CD-ROM
- Presentation Plus! CD-ROM

② TEACH

Answers

1. *Tigris-Euphrates valley, uplands areas, and the coastal plains of the Mediterranean, Black, and Caspian Seas*

2. *By blocking rainfall, they create Mediterranean climates along the coast and steppe or desert climates inland.*

Map Skills Practice

Human-Environment Interaction Compare the map on this page with the population density map on page 412. What effect does climate have on the patterns of human settlement? *(Desert areas are sparsely populated.)*

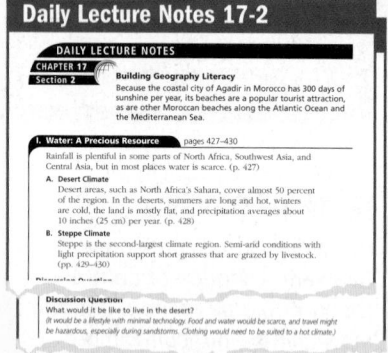

Daily Lecture Notes 17-2

DAILY LECTURE NOTES

CHAPTER 17
Section 2

Building Geography Literacy
Because the coastal city of Agadir in Morocco has 300 days of sunshine per year, its beaches are a popular tourist attraction, as are other Moroccan beaches along the Atlantic Ocean and the Mediterranean Sea.

I. Water: A Precious Resource pages 427–430

Rainfall is plentiful in some parts of North Africa, Southwest Asia, and Central Asia, but in most places water is scarce. (p. 427)

A. **Desert Climate**
Desert areas, such as North Africa's Sahara, cover almost 50 percent of the region. In the deserts, summers are long and hot, winters are cold, the land is mostly flat, and precipitation averages about 10 inches (25 cm) per year. (p. 428)

B. **Steppe Climate**
Steppe is the second-largest climate region. Semi-arid conditions with light precipitation support short grasses that are grazed by livestock. (pp. 429–430)

Discussion Question
What would it be like to live in the desert? Food and water would be scarce, and travel might be hazardous, especially during sandstorms. Clothing would need to be suited to a hot climate.

☐ NATIONAL GEOGRAPHIC **GEOFACT**

► The highest temperature recorded on Earth occurred in the Sahara at Al-Aziziah, Libya, on September 13, 1922. It was 136°F (58°C)!

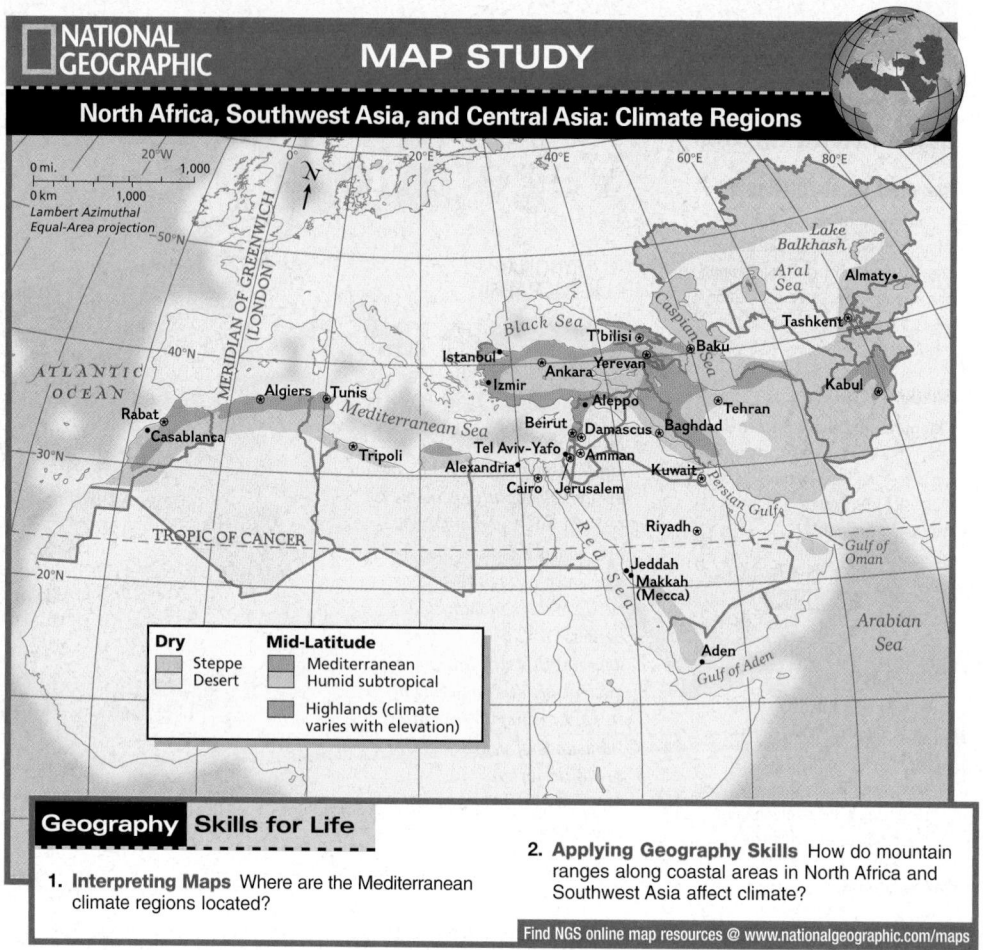

NATIONAL GEOGRAPHIC | **MAP STUDY**

North Africa, Southwest Asia, and Central Asia: Climate Regions

Dry
Steppe
Desert

Mid-Latitude
Mediterranean
Humid subtropical
Highlands (climate varies with elevation)

Geography | **Skills for Life**

1. **Interpreting Maps** Where are the Mediterranean climate regions located?

2. **Applying Geography Skills** How do mountain ranges along coastal areas in North Africa and Southwest Asia affect climate?

Find NGS online map resources @ www.nationalgeographic.com/maps

Desert Climate

In prehistoric times a grassy plain extended across North Africa, and the climate was moderate. Today the climate in the area is hot and dry. The **Sahara**, the largest desert in the world at about 3.5 million square miles (about 9.1 million sq. km), covers most of North Africa. How much of the entire region is desert? Scientists define a desert climate as one in which precipitation averages 10 inches (25 cm) or less per year. By that definition deserts encompass almost 50 percent of the lands in North Africa, Southwest Asia, and Central Asia. In recent decades, droughts have expanded the Sahara.

Weather patterns in the desert tend to be extreme. The deserts of Central Asia and northern parts of the Sahara and the Arabian Desert have relatively cold winters with freezing temperatures. Winters in the southern Sahara and the Arabian Desert are generally milder. Summers in all these desert regions are long and hot. In July, daytime temperatures in the Central Asian deserts sometimes exceed 120°F (49°C) in the shade. At night, however, temperatures drop significantly because of the air's lack of moisture.

A traveler crossing any of the region's deserts would probably see only a few *ergs*, or sandy, dune-covered areas. *Regs*, stony plains covered with

---

DIFFERENTIATED INSTRUCTION

Gifted and Talented Group students into one of the following climate exploration groups: Mediterranean, humid subtropical, desert, highlands, or steppe. Explain that each group will choose and explore a major city in North Africa, Southwest Asia, or Central Asia that is in their assigned climate region. Have students search for Web sites or individuals from their cities and send e-mails asking about climate and weather. Alternatively, have students interview community members who have lived in or traveled to the region. Then have students present their findings to the class. Suggest that they include visuals in their presentations.

⊕ **EE2 Places and Regions: Standard 4**

🗁 Refer to *Inclusion for the Social Studies Classroom Strategies and Activities.*

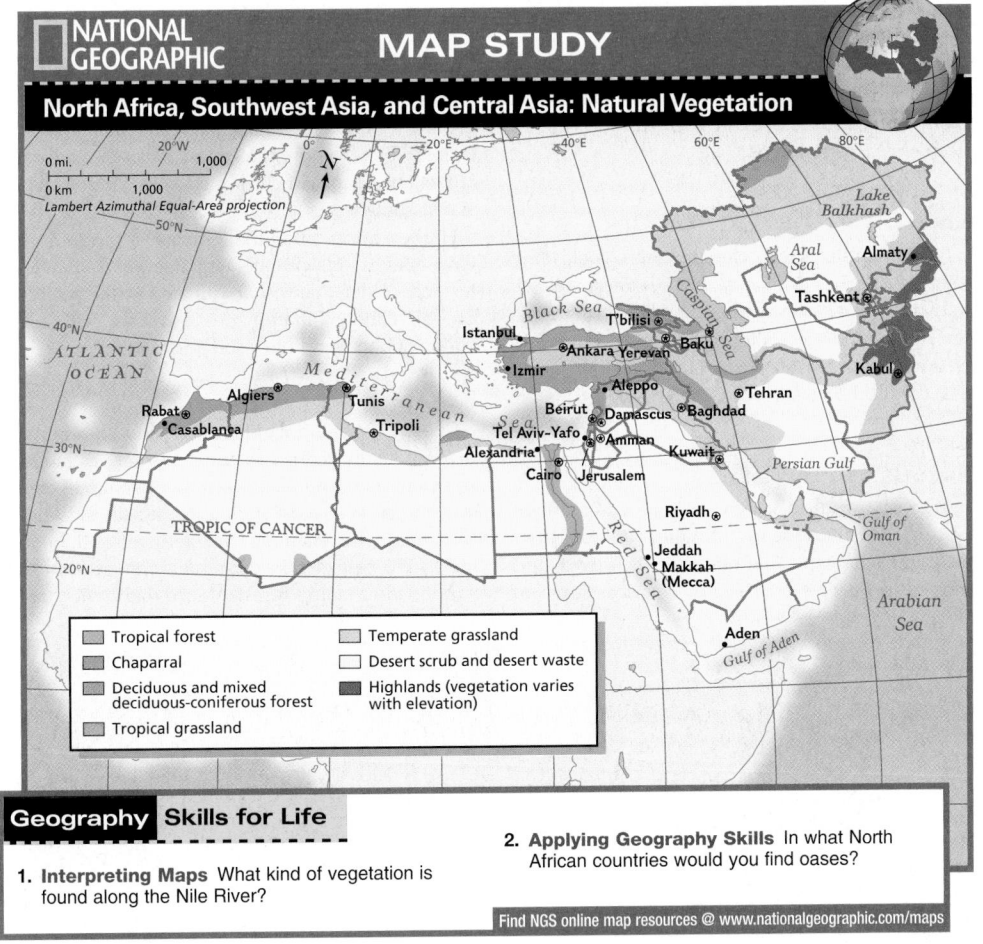

NATIONAL GEOGRAPHIC   **MAP STUDY**

North Africa, Southwest Asia, and Central Asia: Natural Vegetation

0 mi. [scale] 1,000
0 km [scale] 1,000
Lambert Azimuthal Equal-Area projection

Legend:
- Tropical forest
- Chaparral
- Deciduous and mixed deciduous-coniferous forest
- Tropical grassland
- Temperate grassland
- Desert scrub and desert waste
- Highlands (vegetation varies with elevation)

Geography **Skills for Life**

1. **Interpreting Maps** What kind of vegetation is found along the Nile River?

2. **Applying Geography Skills** In what North African countries would you find oases?

Find NGS online map resources @ www.nationalgeographic.com/maps

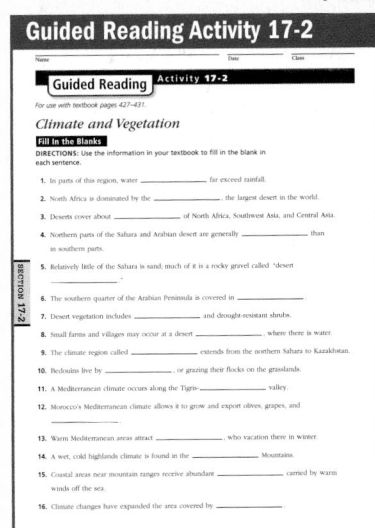

NATIONAL GEOGRAPHIC   **MAP STUDY**

Answers
1. *plants typical of a tropical forest*
2. *Algeria, Libya, Egypt*

Map Skills Practice
Region What climate regions support forests?
(Mediterranean, some steppe)

L2 Natural Vegetation

Have students collect illustrations, photos, descriptions, or actual samples of natural vegetation found in the region. Display student findings and allow students time to look over the collection. Then lead a discussion comparing the kinds of vegetation, their uses, and the climate regions in which they are found.

L1/ELL

Guided Reading Activity 17-2

rocky gravel called "desert pavement," and an occasional *hamada*, or flat, sandstone plateau, would be more common. Sand covers less than 10 percent of the Sahara; desert pavement, mountains, and barren rock cover the rest.

The 250,000-square-mile (647,500-sq.-km) **Rub' al Khali**, or Empty Quarter, has the largest area of sand in the region. One of several deserts on the Arabian Peninsula, the Rub' al Khali covers almost the entire southern quarter of the peninsula.

Despite their arid conditions, the Sahara and other deserts in the region support vegetation such as cacti and drought-resistant shrubs. Nomadic herds of

sheep, goats, and camels graze on brush in Central Asia's **Garagum (Kara Kum)**. Small-scale farming is possible in an oasis, a place in the desert where underground water surfaces. Villages, towns, and cities have risen around many Saharan oases.

Steppe Climate

Steppe is the second-largest climate region in the lands of North Africa, Southwest Asia, and Central Asia. The steppe borders the Sahara to the north and snakes between other climate regions from Turkey to eastern Kazakhstan. Precipitation in this semi-arid climate region usually averages less than 14

COOPERATIVE LEARNING ACTIVITY

Climate and Agricultural Areas Organize the class into groups of four students each. Assign each group an agricultural area in North Africa, Southwest Asia, or Central Asia—a pastoral steppe area in Central Asia, a fruit-producing area in Southwest Asia, or an area of North Africa where cereal grains are major crops, for example. Have students in each group choose from the following topics on which to report: geographic features that influence the climate, average temperature and precipitation, natural vegetation, kinds of agriculture, and whether irrigation is needed. Instruct groups to compile the information they gather into a booklet about the area. Circulate finished booklets. 📔
🌐 **EE3 Physical Systems: Standard 8;** 🌐 **EE5 Environment and Society: Standard 15**

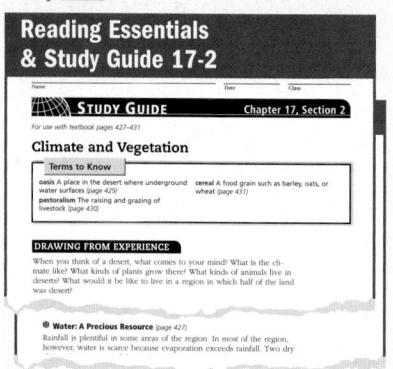

Reading Essentials & Study Guide 17-2

NATIONAL GEOGRAPHIC | **World Explorer**

Answer
chaparral, deciduous and mixed deciduous-coniferous forest

More About the Photo
Farmers raise sheep, goats, cattle, camels, and chickens and grow such crops as alfalfa on fertile hills or in valleys.

③ ASSESS

Assign Section 2 Assessment as homework or as an in-class activity.

◉ Have students use **Interactive Tutor Self-Assessment CD-ROM**.

L2

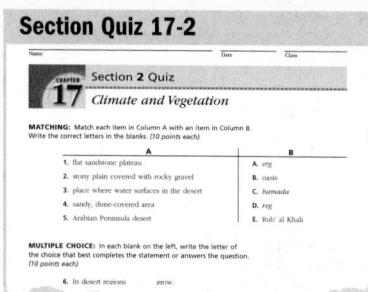

Section Quiz 17-2

---

inches (36 cm) annually. This amount is enough to support short grasses in the steppe climate, providing pasture for sheep, goats, and camels, as well as shrubs and some trees. Pastoralism, the raising and grazing of livestock, is a way of life for the steppe's people, such as bedouins.

Climatic Variations

In the Mediterranean climate zones, cool, rainy winters alternate with hot, dry summers. As the map on page 428 shows, this climate is common in the Tigris-Euphrates valley and in uplands areas as well as on the coastal plains of the Mediterranean Sea, the Black Sea, and the Caspian Sea.

Culture
Exports and Tourists

Morocco, Tunisia, Syria, and other countries having Mediterranean climates boost their economies by exporting citrus fruits, olives, and grapes to Europe and North America. Some of these Mediterranean countries also benefit from tourism, as people from colder climates seek the sun and warmth. Morocco's city of Agadir, with 360 days of sunshine per year, attracts many of the country's 2 million tourists, who come mainly from Europe. Travelers in Morocco also visit the cultural attractions of ancient cities such as Fès, Marrakech, and Casablanca.

Higher areas, like the Caucasus Mountains, have a highlands climate, which is generally wetter and colder than other climates in the region. The highlands climate varies, however, with elevation and exposure to wind and sun.

Rainfall

Coastal and highlands areas near mountain ranges usually receive the most rainfall, as moist, warm air is driven off the sea by prevailing westerly winds. The North African coast near the Atlas Mountains, for example, averages more than 30 inches (76 cm) of rain each year, enough rain to support flourishing forests. More than twice that

NATIONAL GEOGRAPHIC | **World Explorer**

Geography | **Skills for Life**

Mediterranean Climate The bushes and short trees of the landscape around this Moroccan village typify the Mediterranean climate region.

Region What type of natural vegetation is found in Mediterranean climate regions?

CRITICAL THINKING ACTIVITY

Finding and Summarizing the Main Idea Have students write a question based on the text using each of the five subheads in Section 2. Have students also write one question for each of the two maps and three photographs in the section. Organize students into two teams and have students use their questions in a game-show type contest. Explain that one contestant from each team will be asked a question by the other team. The student answering may request help from teammates, but will lose half a point for doing so. Questions that are too similar to those already asked should be skipped. 🔲
🌐 **EE3 Physical Systems: Standard 8**

amount falls each year at the foot of the Elburz Mountains. Batumi, in the Republic of Georgia, one of the region's wettest places, receives more than 100 inches (254 cm) of rain a year. In areas where more than 14 inches (36 cm) of rain falls yearly, farmers can raise cereals—food grains such as barley, oats, and wheat—without irrigation.

A Sign of Things to Come?

Landscapes can change with variations in climate and with people's activities. Under the pressure of climate changes, grassy plains in the region turned into desert, as explorer Thor Heyerdahl observed:

> ❝ The desert, encroaching upon the spring-green marshes from all sides, has swallowed up the former Sumerian homeland [in Mesopotamia] and all that it contained. . . . The landscape which once throbbed with life is today as silent and lifeless as the North Pole. ❞
>
> Thor Heyerdahl, *The Tigris Expedition,* 1981

Will other fertile lands give way to the desert as the grasslands of North Africa and Mesopotamia did? Will pollution threaten other bodies of water as it has the Aral and Caspian Seas? The answers depend on future world climate changes and the interactions of people with their environments.

NATIONAL GEOGRAPHIC **World Explorer**

Geography **Skills for Life**

Grape Harvest Grape vineyards, such as this one in Georgia, have been cultivated for food and wine for 8,000 years.

Human-Environment Interaction In what areas can farmers raise cereals without irrigation?

NATIONAL GEOGRAPHIC **World Explorer**

Answer
areas of more than 14 inches of yearly rainfall

More About the Photo
Wine grapes are Georgia's second most important crop after cereals. Other major products include tea and citrus fruit.

Reteach

Have students work with a partner to make an outline of the climates in the region, including temperatures, precipitation, agricultural activities, and natural vegetation for each climate.

Enrich

Have students reread "A Geographic View" on page 427. Then challenge students to research the Sahara's history, including its formation and expansion. Have students report their findings to the class.

④ CLOSE

Ask a volunteer to name a country in the region and have the class identify its climate region(s) and typical vegetation. Continue with other students naming countries until each country has been reviewed.

SECTION ② ASSESSMENT

Checking for Understanding

1. **Define** oasis, pastoralism, cereal.

2. **Main Ideas** On a web diagram, fill in the climate regions found in North Africa, Southwest Asia, and Central Asia. Then describe the characteristics of one region.

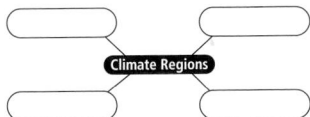

Critical Thinking

3. **Comparing and Contrasting** Compare and contrast agriculture in steppe climate regions with that of Mediterranean climate regions.

4. **Analyzing Cause and Effect** Why has natural vegetation declined in areas of North Africa, Southwest Asia, and Central Asia?

5. **Drawing Conclusions** How did climate changes in the Sahara centuries ago affect its people?

Analyzing Maps

6. **Region** Study the map of climate regions on page 429. What city is located at approximately 10°E, 37°N?

Applying Geography

7. **Climate and Population** Write a paragraph explaining the possible effects of climate on settlement patterns in North Africa, Southwest Asia, and Central Asia.

Chapter 17 🌐 **431**

SECTION ② ASSESSMENT ANSWERS

1. All vocabulary terms are defined in the text.

2. regions: desert, steppe, Mediterranean, and highlands; characteristics should be in chosen climate region

3. steppe: short grasses as pasture for livestock; Mediterranean: cereals and food grains, fruits, olives, and grapes

4. Climatic changes and human activity have turned grassy plains into desert.

5. Climate change led to raising of brush-grazing sheep, goats, and camels instead of grass-hungry cattle; relocation toward the coast, rivers, and oases

6. Tunis

7. **Applying Geography** While oil has increased desert settlement, desert areas are still sparsely settled. Most people live where food, water, and fertile land are available, such as in Mediterranean climate areas.

Teaching the Skill

Ask students to turn to the vegetation map on page 429. Have them compare the key for that map with the one on page 432.
Ask: What types of vegetation are found in parts of the region other than Central Asia? *(tropical forest, chaparral, tropical grassland)* Based on what you know about the climate in which chaparral and tropical vegetation grow, what can you conclude about the climate in the lands shown on page 432? *(It is much colder.)*

Additional Practice
L1

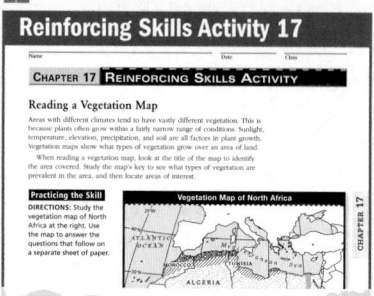

Reinforcing Skills Activity 17

GLENCOE
TECHNOLOGY

Glencoe Skillbuilder Interactive Workbook, Level 2

This interactive CD-ROM reinforces student mastery of essential social studies skills.

Reading a Vegetation Map

Geographers call the plant life that grows naturally in an area **natural vegetation. Variations in vegetation can make areas of the same country look very different.**

Learning the Skill

Climate greatly affects natural vegetation. For example, thick layers of plants that make up tropical forest vegetation grow only in tropical rain forest climates. Likewise, areas with less than 10 inches (25 cm) of rain support only desert scrub vegetation.

Elevation also affects vegetation. Forests grow at the bases of mountains. At higher elevations, grasses, small trees, and shrubs grow. Where elevation makes it too cold for trees and shrubs, only mosses thrive.

On a vegetation map, colors indicate different vegetation types. The map key explains the color code. To read a vegetation map:

- **Identify the area covered on the map.**
- **Study the key to identify the vegetation types that the map depicts.**
- **Locate the regions covered by each vegetation type.**
- **Draw conclusions about the similarities and differences between the types of vegetation found in different areas of the map.**

Practicing the Skill

Use the map showing the vegetation of Central Asia to answer the following questions.

1. What geographic area does this map show?

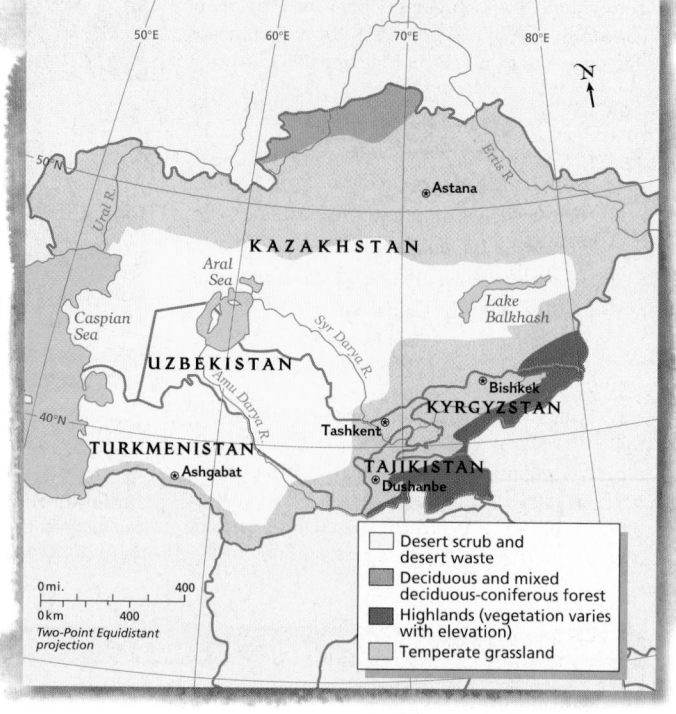

Desert scrub and desert waste
Deciduous and mixed deciduous-coniferous forest
Highlands (vegetation varies with elevation)
Temperate grassland

0 mi. 400
0 km 400
Two-Point Equidistant projection

2. In which vegetation region is the capital of Kyrgyzstan located?

3. What kinds of vegetation are found along the coast of the Caspian Sea?

4. What factors would explain the distribution of vegetation throughout the region?

5. Of the areas shown on the vegetation map, where do you think irrigation is used for cultivating crops?

Applying the Skill

Look at the vegetation map on page 429. Compare the vegetation types of North Africa, Southwest Asia, and Central Asia with those of the United States and Canada, found on page 123. How are they similar? Different?

Go To The Glencoe Skillbuilder Interactive Workbook, **Level 2** provides instruction and practice in key social studies skills.

ANSWERS TO PRACTICING THE SKILL

1. Central Asia
2. temperate grassland
3. desert scrub and desert waste, and temperate grassland
4. A variety of climates—steppe, desert, and highlands—contribute to the variation in vegetation.
5. Answers should relate to the dryness of climate and the availability of water resources.

Answers to Applying the Skill: Similar: Both regions have desert scrub and desert waste, deciduous and mixed deciduous-coniferous forest, highlands vegetation types, and temperate grassland. Different: The United States (including Hawaii) and Canada also have all the remaining vegetation types.

CHAPTER 17
SUMMARY & STUDY GUIDE

SECTION 1 — **The Land** (pp. 421–426)

Terms to Know
- alluvial soil
- wadi
- *kum*
- phosphate

Key Points
- North Africa, Southwest Asia, and Central Asia are located at the crossroads of Asia, Africa, and Europe.
- The region is a jigsaw puzzle of peninsulas and seas.
- Rivers feed the inland seas and supply irrigation to parched lands. Their alluvial soil deposits enrich the land, especially in the Nile River Valley and delta.
- The movement of tectonic plates forms mountains, moves landforms, and causes earthquakes in the region.
- The region contains much of the world's oil and natural gas reserves.

Organizing Your Notes
Use a table like the one below to help you organize the notes for this section. Complete the table by listing and describing the location of the region's important physical features.

Feature	Location
Sahara	
Atlas Mountains	
Nile River	

SECTION 2 — **Climate and Vegetation** (pp. 427–431)

Terms to Know
- oasis
- pastoralism
- cereal

Key Points
- Rainfall in North Africa, Southwest Asia, and Central Asia varies widely. Most of the region contains arid areas.
- The four climate regions in North Africa, Southwest Asia, and Central Asia are desert, steppe, Mediterranean, and highlands.
- Natural vegetation in the region varies widely and is closely related to rainfall and irrigation patterns.

Organizing Your Notes
Create an outline using the format below to help you organize your notes for this section.

Climate and Vegetation
I. Water: A Precious Resource
  A. Desert Climate
    1. Sahara
    2.
  B. Steppe Climate

► *Mosque in Afghanistan*

CHAPTER CULMINATING ACTIVITY

Physical Profiles Have students use the information from this chapter, along with their research notes from projects in the chapter, to create one-page physical profiles of the countries of North Africa, Southwest Asia, and Central Asia. Have students work in groups of four or five to identify and list the data they want to include in their profiles. Then have each student within the groups choose a country, and produce a profile. Have the small groups present each of their profiles to the rest of the class, and encourage all students to participate in the presentations. ▣ **EE2 Places and Regions: Standard 4**

Using the Chapter 17 Summary & Study Guide

Use the Chapter 17 Summary & Study Guide to preview, review, condense, or reteach the chapter.

Preview/Review

🔘 **Vocabulary PuzzleMaker CD-ROM** reinforces "Terms to Know."

🔘 **Interactive Tutor Self-Assessment CD-ROM** provides a review of Chapter 17 content.

Condense

Have students read the Chapter 17 Summary & Study Guide.

🔘 Chapter 17 Audio Program

🗂 Chapter 17 Guided Reading Activities

Reteach

🗂 Chapter 17 Reteaching Activities (Spanish also available)

🗂 Chapter 17 Reading Essentials and Study Guides

GLENCOE TECHNOLOGY

▯ NATIONAL GEOGRAPHIC
WORLD REGIONS
VIDEO PROGRAM

Unit 6, North Africa, Southwest Asia, and Central Asia
The following segments enhance the study of this unit:

- **Heart of Egypt**
- **Three Religions**
- **Oil Boom**

CHAPTER **17** ASSESSMENT & ACTIVITIES

GLENCOE TECHNOLOGY

Use *MindJogger Videoquiz* to review the Chapter 17 content.

Reviewing Key Terms

1. oasis
2. wadi
3. pastoralism
4. phosphate
5. *kum*
6. cereal
7. alluvial soil

Reviewing Facts

SECTION 1

1. the Red Sea and the Gulf of Aden
2. the Dardanelles, the Sea of Marmara, the Bosporus
3. the Garagum; the Qizilqum

SECTION 2

4. almost 50 percent
5. short grasses, shrubs, and some trees
6. Along the Nile River; it is in the desert climate area, but the river gives enough water for farming and diverse vegetation.

Critical Thinking

1. Countries producing petroleum and natural gas greatly influence the economies of countries around the world by controlling the supply and prices of these exports.
2. People live where food and water are available and where there is a chance for livelihood, such as the arable lands in the Mediterranean climate region.
3. Increased irrigation diverts water from rivers that feed inland seas, which in turn causes those seas to shrink or even dry up.

Reviewing Key Terms

Write the key term that best completes each of the following sentences. Refer to the Terms to Know in the Summary & Study Guide on page 433.

1. In the Sahara, a place where underground water surfaces is a(n) _____.
2. Runoff from infrequent rainstorms creates _____, or dry streambeds.
3. _____, or the raising and grazing of livestock, is a way of life on the steppe.
4. Morocco produces _____, which is used in fertilizers.
5. Much of the region is covered by sandy deserts, or _____.
6. Barley is an example of a _____ grain.
7. _____ is rich soil deposited by running water.

Reviewing Facts

SECTION 1

1. What physical features separate the Arabian Peninsula from the African continent?
2. What physical features separate Europe and Asia and connect the Aegean and Black Seas?
3. What desert covers most of Turkmenistan? What desert covers about half of Uzbekistan?

SECTION 2

4. About how much of North Africa, Southwest Asia, and Central Asia experience desert climate?
5. Describe the natural vegetation of steppe areas.
6. In what part of the region does tropical vegetation flourish? What climate factors allow this kind of vegetation to grow in that area?

Critical Thinking

1. **Drawing Conclusions** How do you think the region's resources affect the global economy?
2. **Analyzing Information** Compare the climate map on page 428 with the population density map on page 412. How does climate influence where people live in the region?
3. **Identifying Cause and Effect** On a sheet of paper, complete a chart like the one below to show how increased irrigation affected the region's inland seas.

Locating Places
North Africa, Southwest Asia, and Central Asia: Physical Geography

Match the letters on the map with the physical features of North Africa, Southwest Asia, and Central Asia. Write your answers on a sheet of paper.

1. Arabian Peninsula	5. Aral Sea	9. Caspian Sea
2. Sahara	6. Red Sea	10. Black Sea
3. Atlas Mountains	7. Persian Gulf	11. Gulf of Aden
4. Nile River	8. Mediterranean Sea	12. Tian Shan

TROPIC OF CANCER

EQUATOR

0 mi. 1,000
0 km 1,000
Lambert Azimuthal Equal-Area projection

Locating Places

| 1. A | 3. E | 5. K | 7. F | 9. G | 11. B |
| 2. I | 4. C | 6. D | 8. J | 10. H | 12. L |

Using the Regional Atlas

Refer to the Regional Atlas on pages 410–413.

1. **Region** In which area of the region is livestock raising practiced? Subsistence farming?

2. **Place** Compare the physical map on page 410 with the population density map on page 412. What do the gray areas on the population map represent? How does the physical map help explain the distribution of the population in these areas?

Thinking Like a Geographer

Think about the areas in North Africa, Southwest Asia, and Central Asia that do not have enough freshwater. As a geographer, where would you recommend desalination plants to be built? Consider population centers, energy needs, and water sources.

Problem-Solving Activity

Group Research Project As a group, choose an oil-producing country from this region and investigate possible ways the country could diversify its economy. Present your research in a written report that gives reasons for your recommendations. Be sure to include photos, maps, charts, or graphs to help illustrate your findings.

GeoJournal

Descriptive Writing Select three physical features in North Africa, Southwest Asia, or Central Asia. Then, using your GeoJournal data, describe and analyze in writing how these physical features shape the distribution of culture groups in the region.

 Technology Activity

Using the Internet for Research
Use the Internet to research the natural resources of one of the countries in this region. Identify factors affecting the location of the economic activities there. Create a bulletin board display about the country, including a list of its primary imports and exports.

Standardized Test Practice

Choose the best answer for the following multiple-choice questions. If you have trouble answering the questions, use the process of elimination to narrow your choices.

1. **Part of Uzbekistan has a desert climate. What kind of vegetation can grow in a desert climate?**

   A No vegetation at all

   B Drought-resistant shrubs and cacti

   C Drought-resistant shrubs, cacti, and occasional small-scale farm crops in areas with underground water

   D Short grasses for grazing

 *Test-Taking* **Tip** Note that the directions ask you to choose the best answer to the question. The best answer will contain the most precise information for answering the question.

2. **In part of the region of North Africa, Southwest Asia, and Central Asia, people earn their living by growing citrus fruits, olives, and grapes, as well as from the tourist trade. This region probably has a**

   F highlands climate.

   G steppe climate.

   H Mediterranean climate.

   J desert climate.

 *Test-Taking* **Tip** Think about the conditions needed to grow the specific crops. Desert climates are too dry, as are steppe climates. Highlands climates are wet but may be too cold. Eliminating wrong choices helps you choose the correct answer.

GeoJournal

Check students' answers for their understanding of the physical features in the region.

Technology Activity

Check students' display to see if their reports are accurate, and if they are comfortable using the Internet for research.

Standardized Test Practice

1. C
2. H

Tested Objectives:
analyzing information
synthesizing information

Additional Practice and Test-Taking Tips

 Standardized Test Practice Workbook

? CHAPTER BONUS TEST QUESTION

Why do the farming techniques in some of the region's coastal areas differ from those practiced in the Nile River valley? *(Precipitation in coastal areas is adequate for farming. Irrigation is usually required along the Nile.)*

Using the Regional Atlas

1. Livestock is raised in Kazakhstan, Kyrgyzstan, Uzbekistan, and Turkmenistan; subsistence farming is found along the Nile River, other parts of Egypt, in Turkey, Iraq, Yemen, Iran, and Azerbaijan.

2. The gray areas, which are uninhabited, are mostly in deserts.

Thinking Like a Geographer

Students' suggestions for placement of desalination plants should be logical (that is, plants need to be near saltwater, for example); accept all reasonable answers and use them as the basis for class discussion.

Problem-Solving Activity

Reports should include well-researched facts that support students' recommendations.

435

① FOCUS

Discuss with students some everyday activities that require freshwater. (*drinking; washing clothes, dishes, cars, floors, and streets; bathing and personal hygiene; cooking; watering lawns and plants; fire fighting*) Explain that industry and agriculture also use great quantities of water. For example, it can take 62,600 gallons of water to produce a ton of steel, and 115 gallons to grow the wheat needed to bake just one loaf of bread! Yet only 3 percent of the world's water is fresh. Ninety-seven percent is too salty for drinking, farming, or industry.

② TEACH

L2 Alternatives

Explain that freezing saltwater is another method of desalination. Have students fill a cup with saltwater and set it in the freezer. When half the water is frozen, remove the container, wipe off the ice with a paper towel, and place the ice in a second cup. Allow the ice to melt, and put this water into another cup to freeze. Repeat these steps several times. **Ask: What happened to the salt during each freezing?** (*The salt remained in the unfrozen water, not in the ice. As each solution was refrozen, the concentration of salt in the ice decreased.*) Discuss with students whether it would be worth attempting to tow icebergs to the region and thaw them out for water. Point out that icebergs would need to be small enough to fit through the Strait of Gibraltar.

Geography Lab Activity

Desalination

▲ *Students distill salt water.*

In spite of the location of large river systems in North Africa, Southwest Asia, and Central Asia, most of the usable water comes from regional river basins such as the Jordan and the Nile and from aquifers. Aquifers are underground layers of porous rock, gravel, or sand that contain water. Although abundant, seawater is not usable because of its salt content. Countries in the region are searching for new sources of water as well as increasing their use of desalination—the removal of salt from seawater. These countries produce about 75 percent of the world's desalinated water. Worldwide, more than 2 billion gallons (7.5 billion liters) of freshwater were produced daily at desalination plants at the end of the twentieth century.

Distillation is the most widely used desalination method. The process of distillation purifies water by imitating the way ocean water evaporates into clouds, condenses, and falls back to Earth as precipitation. The distillation process varies little whether producing one cup or millions of gallons of freshwater. Salt water is heated until the water evaporates. The vapor condenses into freshwater in a second container, while the salt remains in the first container.

① Materials

- Table salt
- Water
- 1 flask
- Rubber stopper
- Plastic tubing
- Rubber tubing
- Scissors
- Cardboard
- Metal washers (for weight)
- Beaker
- Ice
- Shallow pan
- Hot plate
- Measuring cup
- Thermal mitt

CAUTION: Be careful when using the hot plate. It should be cool before the flask is moved.

② Procedures

In this activity, you will distill salt water to make drinking water.

1. In the flask, dissolve 2 teaspoons (10 ml) of salt in 1 cup (237 ml) of water. Swish the salt and water mixture around until no salt crystals remain.

2. Insert the plastic tubing into the rubber stopper, and then insert the stopper into the flask. Be sure the plastic tubing is above the surface of the saltwater solution.

GEOGRAPHY IN THE REAL WORLD

Emergency Water For years, lifeboats have been installed on all large ships. Yet thousands of people die of thirst in the lifeboats. To aid shipwreck victims, small desalination devices are being developed for use in lifeboats and in other emergency situations. How can seawater be heated in a lifeboat? Some emergency systems are using solar power or other fuels to distill the saltwater. One belt-like invention even uses the survivor's own body heat. A completely different kind of device is a hollow globe that can be lowered into the seawater. Made from a special material, the globe actually strains the salt out of the seawater seeping into it and becomes a vessel full of fresh, drinkable, life-saving water.

🌐 **EE5 Environment and Society: Standard 14**

3. Attach one end of the rubber tubing to the plastic tubing. Insert the other end of the rubber tubing through a small hole cut in the cardboard. The hole in the cardboard should be small enough that the tubing fits snugly.

4. Place the cardboard over the beaker. Add several washers to the cardboard to hold it in place.

5. Place the beaker in the shallow pan filled with ice water to speed up the condensation process.

6. Set the flask on the hot plate. Bring the saltwater solution to a boil, and continue boiling until the solution is almost boiled away. You will notice a salt residue forming as the boiling water evaporates.

7. Turn off the hot plate. After letting it cool, remove the flask.

8. Pour the water you collected in the beaker into a measuring cup.

9. Taste the water in the measuring cup. Does the water still taste salty?

3 Lab Report

1. What happened to the water in the flask as you boiled the solution?
2. What happened inside the beaker?
3. Why did the water, and not the salt, move from the flask to the beaker?
4. **Drawing Conclusions** How could this process be used to extract minerals from seawater?
5. **Predicting Consequences** Based on your observations, what do you think might be the biggest drawback to using this process?

4 Find Out More

Research where desalination is used in the United States. What other places in the country would benefit from desalination plants? Create a map showing existing plants and areas where you would propose building new plants.

 Did You Know? Today's desalination plants produce 15 times as much freshwater as they did 20 years ago. Saudi Arabia, a world leader in desalination projects, relies on about 30 desalination plants to change seawater to freshwater. One plant turns out 250 million gallons (950 million liters) of freshwater daily for human use!

◀ As stagnant water evaporated, it left behind a crust of salt in this field in southern Iraq.

3 ASSESS

Have students answer the **Lab Report** questions on page 437.

4 CLOSE

Have students complete the **Find Out More** activity. Ask them to find out where, besides Saudi Arabia, desalination is used in North Africa, Southwest Asia, and Central Asia. Have students mark the desalination plants on a map of the region. Then have students compare the number and production of desalination plants in the region with those in the United States.

⊕ Meeting National Standards

Geography for Life
The following standards are met in the Student Edition feature:

EE5 Environment and Society: Standards 14, 15
EE6 The Uses of Geography: Standard 18

ANSWERS TO LAB REPORT

1. The volume of water decreased, and it became much more salty.
2. Water began to collect in the beaker as the water vapor condensed.
3. The salt cannot evaporate.
4. Evaporation and condensation can remove freshwater from seawater, leaving the minerals behind and making freshwater available for drinking.
5. It is time consuming, and the amount of water and salt obtained is rather minimal.

CHAPTER 18 PLANNING GUIDE

NOTE: The following materials may be used when teaching Chapter 18. Section-level support materials are shown at point-of-use in the margins of the Teacher Wraparound Edition.

TEACHING TRANSPARENCIES

L2 Unit 6 Map Overlay Transparencies

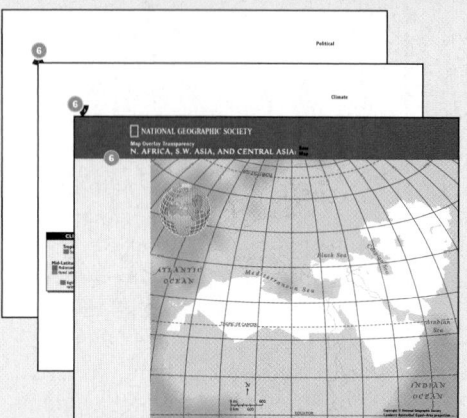

L2 Political Map Transparency 6

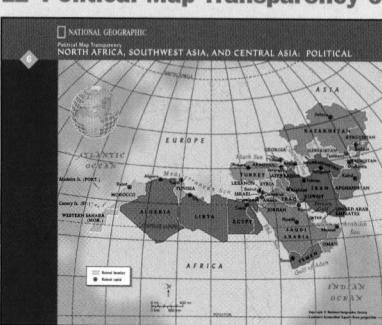

GEOGRAPHIC LITERACY

Focus on Geography Literacy

APPLICATION AND ENRICHMENT

L3 Enrichment Activity 18

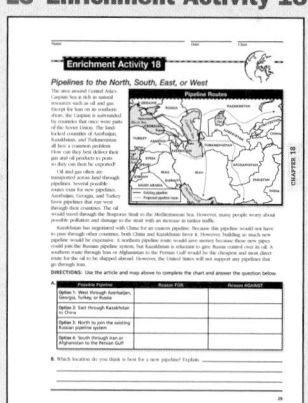

REVIEW AND REINFORCEMENT

L1 Vocabulary Activity 18 L1 Reinforcing L1 Reteaching Activity 18

Skills Activity 18

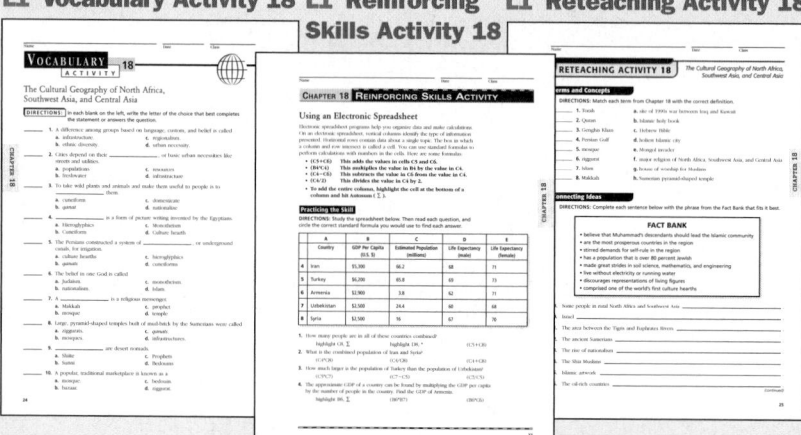

ASSESSMENT

L2 Chapter 18 Test Form A

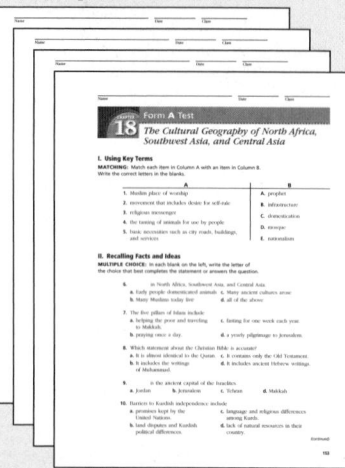

L2 Chapter 18 Test Form B

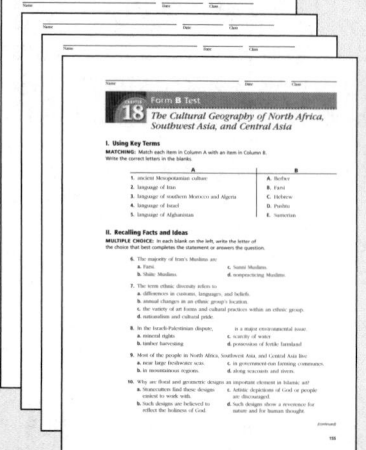

L1/ELL Performance Assessment Activity 18

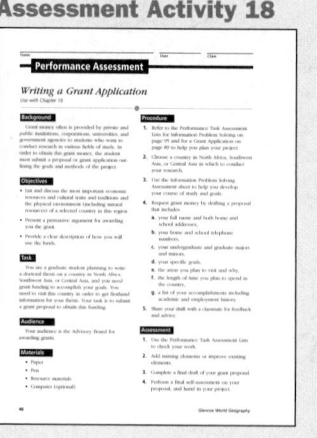

ExamView® Pro Testmaker

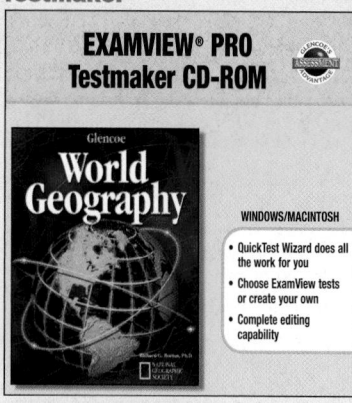

The following Spanish language materials are available in the Spanish Resources binder:

- 📁 Spanish Vocabulary Activities
- 📁 Spanish Guided Reading Activities
- 📁 Spanish Reteaching Activities
- 📁 Spanish Summaries
- 📁 Spanish Quizzes and Tests
- 📁 Spanish Reading Essentials and Study Guide

- 🎞️ World Regions Video
- 🎞️ MindJogger Videoquiz
- 💿 Vocabulary PuzzleMaker CD-ROM
- 💿 Interactive Tutor Self-Assessment CD-ROM
- 💿 ExamView® Pro Testmaker CD-ROM
- 💿 Audio Program
- 💿 TeacherWorks CD-ROM
- 💿 Interactive Student Edition CD-ROM
- 💿 Glencoe Skillbuilder Interactive Workbook CD-ROM, Level 2
- 💿 Presentation Plus! CD-ROM

Timesaving Tools

TeacherWorks™ All-In-One Planner and Resource Center

- **Interactive Teacher Edition** Access your Teacher Wraparound Edition and your classroom resources with a few easy clicks.
- **Interactive Lesson Planner** Planning has never been easier! Organize your week, month, semester, or year with all the lesson helps you need to make teaching creative, timely, and relevant.

Use Glencoe's **Presentation Plus!** multimedia teacher tool to easily present dynamic lessons that visually excite your students. Using Microsoft PowerPoint® you can customize the presentations to create your own personalized lessons.

GEOGRAPHY Online

Use our Web site for additional resources. All essential content is covered in the Student Edition.

You and your students can visit geography.glencoe.com, the Web site companion to *Glencoe World Geography*. This innovative integration of electronic and print media offers your students a wealth of opportunities. The student text directs students to the Web site for the following options:

- Chapter Overviews
- Student Activities
- Self-Check Quizzes
- Textbook Updates

Answers are provided for you in the "Web Activity Lesson Plan." Additional Web resources and Interactive Tutor puzzles are also available.

► Additional Glencoe Teacher Support

- **Teaching Strategies for the Geography Classroom** (including Block Scheduling Pacing Guides)
- **Graphic Organizer Transparencies Strategies and Activities**
- **Outline Map Resource Book**
- **Reading in the Content Area**

SECTION RESOURCES

Daily Objectives	Reproducible Resources	Multimedia Resources

SECTION 1   Population Patterns

1. Examine how movement and interaction in North Africa, Southwest Asia, and Central Asia led to ethnic diversity.
2. Explain how the region's seas, rivers, and oases influence where people live.
3. Discuss how growing migration into cities has affected the region.

- Reproducible Lesson Plan 18-1
- Daily Lecture Notes 18-1
- Guided Reading Activity 18-1*
- Reading Essentials and Study Guide 18-1*
- Section Quiz 18-1*

- Daily Focus Skills Transparency 18-1
- Political Map Transparency 6
- Unit 6 Map Overlay Transparencies
- Interactive Tutor Self-Assessment CD-ROM
- ExamView® Pro Testmaker CD-ROM*
- Presentation Plus! CD-ROM

SECTION 2   History and Government

1. Name the great civilizations that arose in North Africa, Southwest Asia, and Central Asia.
2. Discuss the three major world religions that originated in the region.
3. Explain how countries of the region gained independence in modern times.

- Reproducible Lesson Plan 18-2
- Daily Lecture Notes 18-2
- Guided Reading Activity 18-2*
- Reading Essentials and Study Guide 18-2*
- Section Quiz 18-2*

- Daily Focus Skills Transparency 18-2
- Political Map Transparency 6
- Unit 6 Map Overlay Transparencies
- Interactive Tutor Self-Assessment CD-ROM
- ExamView® Pro Testmaker CD-ROM*
- Presentation Plus! CD-ROM

SECTION 3   Cultures and Lifestyles

1. Explain how religion and language have both unified and divided the peoples of North Africa, Southwest Asia, and Central Asia.
2. Describe arts that are popular in the region.
3. Discuss the characteristics of everyday life in the region.

- Reproducible Lesson Plan 18-3
- Vocabulary Activity 18*
- Daily Lecture Notes 18-3
- Guided Reading Activity 18-3*
- Reading Essentials and Study Guide 18-3*
- Reteaching Activity 18*
- Reinforcing Skills Activity 18
- Section Quiz 18-3*

- Daily Focus Skills Transparency 18-3
- Unit 6 Map Overlay Transparencies
- World Art and Architecture Transparencies
- Vocabulary PuzzleMaker CD-ROM
- Interactive Tutor Self-Assessment CD-ROM
- ExamView® Pro Testmaker CD-ROM*
- Presentation Plus! CD-ROM

Blackline Master	Software	Videocassette
Transparency	CD-ROM	DVD

Also available in Spanish

OUT OF TIME? Assign the Chapter 18 **Reading Essentials and Study Guide.**

Block Schedule

Activities that are particularly suited to use within the block scheduling framework are identified throughout this chapter by the following designation:

KEY TO ABILITY LEVELS

Teaching strategies have been coded for various learning styles and abilities.

L1   **BASIC** activities for all students

L2   **AVERAGE** activities for average to above-average students

L3   **CHALLENGING** activities for above-average students

ELL   **ENGLISH LANGUAGE LEARNER** activities

Teacher to Teacher

Linda Archer
Ouachita High School
Donaldson, AR

Food and Dress in North Africa, Southwest Asia, and Central Asia

Have students work together in groups of four or five to research countries in North Africa, Southwest Asia, or Central Asia. The student groups will make food or bring in recipes from countries in the region. They will also create traditional dress of the country or design a "paper doll" and dress it in traditional cultural attire.

Students should use the Internet, the library, and other resources—especially people they may know from countries in the region—to find recipes of foods they can make and to learn about traditional dress of their assigned country. Students' research should be focused on the physical environment, family life, religion, population, economy, and other aspects that make up cultural geography.

Students then give a presentation—complete with food—on their assigned country. Encourage students to give presentations in a variety of ways so that students of all learning abilities may understand.

TEACHER'S CORNER

Index to National Geographic Magazine:

The following articles may be used for research relating to this chapter:

- "Ancient Greece III," by Caroline Alexander, March 2000.
- "Valley of the Mummies," by Donovan Webster, October 1999.
- "Tale of Three Cities," by Joel L. Swerdlow, August 1999.

National Geographic Society Products:

To order the following products for use with this chapter, call National Geographic Society at 1-800-368-2728.

- *Africa* (Video)
- *Asia* (Video)
- *Who Built the Pyramids?* (Video)
- *National Geographic Desk Reference* (Book)
- *National Geographic Atlas of the World, Seventh Edition* (Book)

NGS ONLINE

Access National Geographic's Web site for current events, activities, links, interactive features, and archives.
www.nationalgeographic.com

Meeting National Standards

Geography For Life

The following standards are highlighted in Chapter 18:

Section 1   EE2 Places and Regions:
Standards 4, 5
EE4 Human Systems:
Standards 9, 10, 12
EE5 Environment and Society:
Standard 16

Section 2   EE4 Human Systems:
Standards 9, 10, 12, 13
EE6 The Uses of Geography:
Standard 17

Section 3   EE3 Physical Systems: Standard 8
EE4 Human Systems:
Standards 10, 12

Local Objectives

_____

_____

MEETING SPECIAL NEEDS

In addition to the Differentiated Instruction strategies found in each section, the following resources are also suitable for your special needs students:

- *ExamView® Pro Testmaker CD-ROM* allows teachers to tailor tests by reducing answer choices.
- The *Audio Program* includes the entire narrative of the student edition so that less-proficient readers can listen to the words as they read them.
- The *Reading Essentials and Study Guide* provides the same content as the student edition but is written two grade levels below the textbook.
- *Guided Reading Activities* give less-proficient readers point-by-point instructions to increase comprehension as they read each textbook section.
- *Enrichment Activities* include a stimulating collection of readings and activities for gifted and talented students.

Chapter Objectives

1. Explain population patterns found in North Africa, Southwest Asia, and Central Asia.

2. Discuss the history and governments of North Africa, Southwest Asia, and Central Asia.

3. Describe the cultures and lifestyles of the people in the region.

GLENCOE TECHNOLOGY

Use *MindJogger Videoquiz* to preview the Chapter 18 content.

GeoJournal

For access to additional photos, maps, and information on the cultural features of North Africa, Southwest Asia, and Central Asia, go to www.nationalgeographic.com (See Teacher pages in front for strategies for using journals in the geography classroom.)

GEOGRAPHY Online

Introduce students to chapter content and key terms by having them access **Chapter Overview 18** at geography.glencoe.com

FOLDABLES™
Study Organizer

Dinah Zike's Foldables are three-dimensional, interactive graphic organizers that help students practice basic writing skills, review key vocabulary terms, and identify main ideas. Have students complete the Foldable activity in the **Dinah Zike's Reading and Study Skills Foldables** booklet.

CHAPTER 18

The Cultural Geography of North Africa, Southwest Asia, and Central Asia

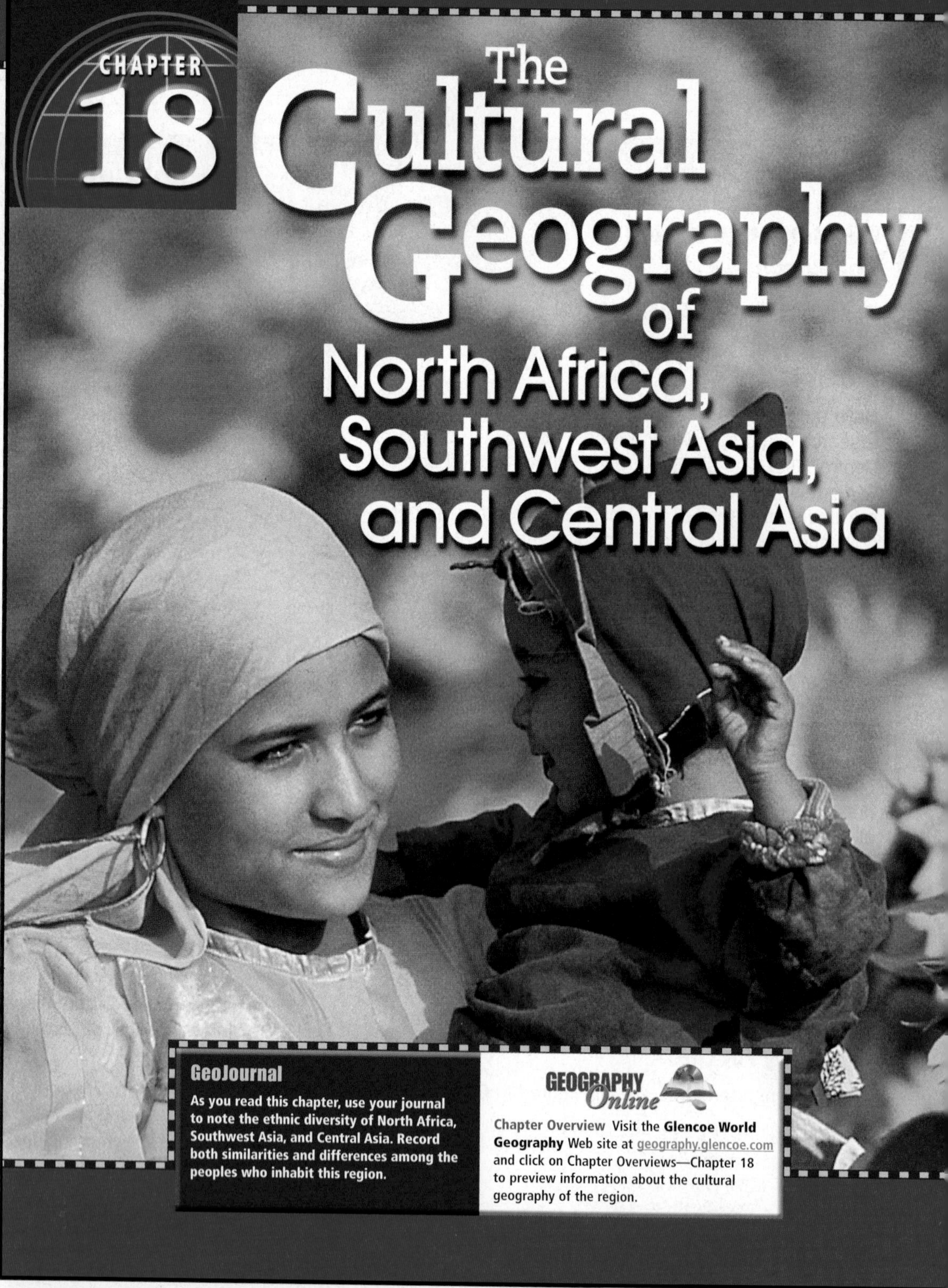

GeoJournal

As you read this chapter, use your journal to note the ethnic diversity of North Africa, Southwest Asia, and Central Asia. Record both similarities and differences among the peoples who inhabit this region.

GEOGRAPHY Online

Chapter Overview Visit the **Glencoe World Geography** Web site at geography.glencoe.com and click on Chapter Overviews—Chapter 18 to preview information about the cultural geography of the region.

ABOUT THE PHOTO

El Faiyum lies west of the Nile River in an area completely below sea level. The oasis is an irrigated, richly fertile agricultural area that utilizes canals originally constructed around 1800 B.C., as well as 200 huge, wooden waterwheels to distribute the water throughout the oasis. Cereal grains, fruit, and cotton grow in the oasis. In ancient times El Faiyum was named "Crocodilopolis," since it was the location where people worshipped the crocodile god, Sobek. **Ask: What conditions might make it practical to use wooden waterwheels for distributing water throughout the oasis?** *(Students may suggest its elevation, the kind of energy that is available, the size of the community.)*
🌐 **EE2 Places and Regions: Standard 4**

Guide to Reading

Consider What You Know

As you know, the region of North Africa, Southwest Asia, and Central Asia is made up of a variety of physical features and climates. Many different peoples live in the region. How does the diversity of ethnic groups affect life in North Africa, Southwest Asia, and Central Asia?

Reading Strategy

Categorizing Complete a web diagram similar to the one below by naming the major ethnic groups of North Africa, Southwest Asia, and Central Asia.

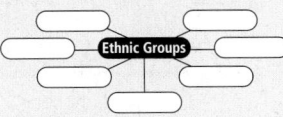
Ethnic Groups

Read to Find Out

• How have movement and interaction of people in the region led to ethnic diversity?

• How do the region's seas, rivers, and oases influence where people live?

• What effect does the growing migration into the cities have on the region?

Terms to Know

• ethnic diversity
• infrastructure

Places to Locate

• Turkey
• Afghanistan
• Armenia
• Georgia
• Kazakhstan
• Tajikistan
• Uzbekistan
• Tehran

◀ *El Faiyum oasis, Egypt*

Population Patterns

NATIONAL GEOGRAPHIC

A Geographic View

Refuge of Peoples

A refuge since the last period of Eurasian glaciation, the Caucasus region has been a gateway for travel, trade, and conquest. [Despite the numerous power struggles] the Caucasus has remained a [stronghold] of peoples whose identities are tied to the 50-some languages they speak.... The persistence of the enduring identities of ethnic groups has been aided by the rugged terrain and by societies whose loyalties are to clan and family as much as to nation or region.

—Mike Edwards, "The Fractured Caucasus," National Geographic, *February 1996*

Family in the Caucasus

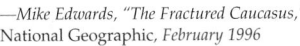

Like North Africa, Southwest Asia, and Central Asia as a whole, the Caucasus area has long been home to many peoples. Some of these peoples vanished long ago—defeated in wars, wiped out by famines, or absorbed by more powerful groups. Others have survived for hundreds of years and flourish today because of contact with travelers, merchants, and conquerors from distant places. The result is a tapestry as rich and varied as the region's much-sought-after carpets.

Many Peoples

The region of North Africa, Southwest Asia, and Central Asia has served as the crossroads for Asia, Africa, and Europe. As a result, the region has remarkable **ethnic diversity**, or differences among groups based on their languages, customs, and beliefs.

① FOCUS

Section Overview

This section discusses how movement and interaction of people in North Africa, Southwest Asia, and Central Asia have led to ethnic diversity, how the region's water resources influence where people live, and the consequences of urbanization.

BELLRINGER
Skillbuilder Activity

 Project transparency and have students answer questions.

 Available as blackline master.

Daily Focus Skills Transparency 18-1

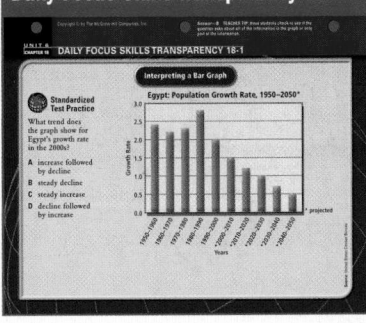

Guide to Reading

Consider What You Know
Answer *The different ethnic groups bring a variety of religions, languages, customs, and loyalties and conflict to the region.*

Reading Strategy
Answers Arabs, Israelis, Iranians, Afghans, Caucasian peoples, Turkic peoples, Kurds

Preteaching Vocabulary
On the board write the term *ethnic diversity*. Then have a volunteer read the paragraph under "Many Peoples" on page 439. Discuss ethnic diversity.

RESOURCE MANAGER

📁 Reproducible Masters
• Reproducible Lesson Plan 18-1
• Daily Lecture Notes 18-1
• Guided Reading Activity 18-1
• Reading Essentials and Study Guide 18-1
• Section Quiz 18-1

📠 Transparencies
• Daily Focus Skills Transparency 18-1
• Political Map Transparency 6
• Unit 6 Map Overlay Transparencies

Multimedia
• Interactive Tutor Self-Assessment CD-ROM
• ExamView® Pro Testmaker CD-ROM
• Presentation Plus! CD-ROM

② TEACH

Answer
Libya, Tunisia, Algeria, Morocco

More About the Photo
During the A.D. 1000s bedouins from Southwest Asia invaded North Africa. Bedouin herds devoured the green pastures that Berbers there had maintained, turning grasslands into semidesert wastelands. Today, fewer than 10 percent of bedouins engage in a fully nomadic lifestyle; some travel seasonally.

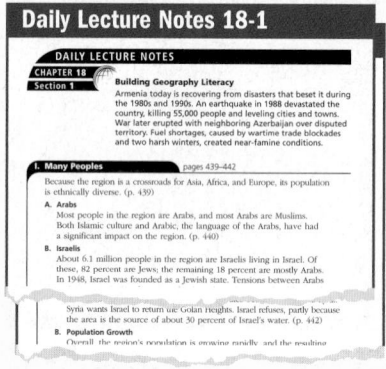

Daily Lecture Notes 18-1

L1 Location

Have students reread "A Geographic View" on page 439. Instruct students to locate the Caucasus region on the maps in the Regional Atlas on pages 410–411. **Ask:** What countries are in the Caucasus region? *(Georgia, Azerbaijan, Armenia)* What bodies of water is the region near? *(Black and Caspian Seas)*

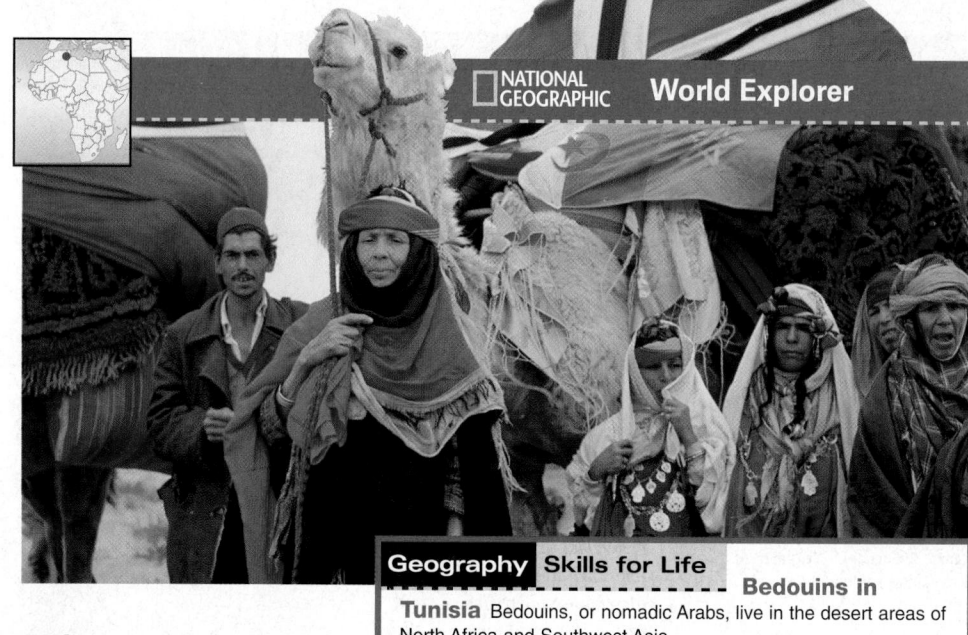

NATIONAL GEOGRAPHIC World Explorer

Geography **Skills for Life**

Bedouins in Tunisia Bedouins, or nomadic Arabs, live in the desert areas of North Africa and Southwest Asia.
Place Which countries are part of the Maghreb?

Arabs

Most people of the region—about 275 million—are Arabs. Most Arabs are Muslims, followers of the religion of Islam, but a small percentage follow Christianity or other religions. Both Islamic culture and Arabic, the language of the Arabs, have had a significant impact in this region.

Before the spread of Islam in the A.D. 600s, Arabic-speaking peoples inhabited the Arabian Peninsula and a few areas to its north. Many Arabic-speaking people today, however, descend from ancient groups such as the Egyptians, Phoenicians, Saharan Berbers, and peoples speaking Semitic languages. Currently, Arabs live in 16 countries, including Libya, Tunisia, Algeria, and Morocco—the countries known as the Maghreb—"the West" in Arabic.

Israelis

About 6.4 million people of the region are Israelis living in Israel. Of these, 82 percent are Jewish. The remaining 18 percent are mostly Arabs who are Muslim or Christian.

Jews living in Israel and elsewhere trace their religious heritage to the Israelites, who in ancient times settled Canaan, the land shared today by Israel and Lebanon. The Israelites believed that God had given them this area as a permanent homeland. Over the centuries, wars, persecution, and trade led many Jews—as the descendants of the Israelites are called—to settle in other countries. Their religious identity, however, kept alive their link to the ancestral homeland. Finally, in 1948, Israel was founded as a Jewish state. Today half of Israel's Jews were born in Israel, and half have emigrated from elsewhere.

The Arabs of the region, however, did not want a Jewish state in territory that had been their homeland for centuries. Tensions between Arabs and Jews resulted in four wars that brought severe hardship to all the people of the area, including the Palestinians—Arabs living in the territory in which Israel was established. During this period of conflict, many Palestinians were displaced from their homes and lived in refugee settlements in neighboring Arab countries.

Today agreements between Israeli and Palestinian leaders have led to greater Palestinian self-rule. Nevertheless, peace is still elusive. Issues such as the ownership of the Old City of Jerusalem, the return of Palestinian refugees, and ownership of water and other natural resources remain unresolved.

DIFFERENTIATED INSTRUCTION

English Learners Explain that in English certain words and phrases signal time changes, sequences, and other relationships among ideas or events. On the board write the following: *of these, in ancient times, today, over the centuries, however, finally, during this period, nevertheless.* Then read aloud the material under "Israelis." Stop after each paragraph to ask if there were words or phrases from the list on the board. **Ask:** What relationships among events or ideas do the words point out? **ELL**

🗂 Refer to *Inclusion for the Social Studies Classroom Strategies and Activities.*

Turks

Over the past 8,000 years, many peoples have occupied Anatolia, the Asian part of what is today the country of **Turkey**. Each group added its own customs and beliefs to the cultural blend. Turkic peoples migrated to the peninsula in the A.D. 1000s from Central Asia. One Turkic group, known as the Ottoman Turks, later built the Ottoman Empire, which ruled much of the eastern Mediterranean world for more than 600 years. When a group of Turkish citizens was asked to define who a Turk is today, one of them responded this way:

> ❝ *'I don't believe anybody is Turkish, whatever that means,' he said. Then, swinging his arms to take in the lunch crowd, he exclaimed, 'Look at us! A mix of Turks, Arabs, Jews, Greeks, Iranians, Armenians, Kurds.'* ❞
>
> Thomas B. Allen, "Turkey Struggles for Balance," *National Geographic*, May 1994

Most Turks practice Islam and speak the Turkish language. They have a culture that blends Turkish, Islamic, and Western elements.

Iranians and Afghans

About 66.6 million people live in Iran, once called Persia. The word *Iran* means "land of the Aryans." Many Iranians believe they are descendants of the Aryans (AR•ee•uhnz), Indo-Europeans who migrated into the region from southern Russia about 1000 B.C. Iranians speak Farsi, and almost 90 percent of them are Shiite (SHEE•EYET) Muslims.

On the eastern border of Iran is **Afghanistan**. This mountainous country is home to many ethnic groups that reflect centuries of migrations and invasions by different peoples. People in Afghanistan speak many languages, and most practice Islam.

Caucasian Peoples

More than 50 ethnic groups and nationalities live in the Caucasus area. Armenians and Georgians are among the largest ethnic groups.

Armenians make up more than 90 percent of the population of the republic of **Armenia**, which became independent after the Soviet

Union dissolved in 1991. The Armenians have had their own language and literature for more than 15 centuries, and in the A.D. 300s most accepted Christianity.

In ancient times the Armenians ruled a large, powerful kingdom. For much of their later history, however, the Armenians were ruled by others—Arabs, Persians, Turks, and Russians. In 1915 about 1 million Armenians in Turkey were massacred, were deported, or died of illness at the hands of the Ottoman Turks. Many survivors fled to Southwest Asia, Europe, and the United States.

The republic of **Georgia** also became independent after the fall of the Soviet Union in 1991. Like the Armenians, most Georgians became Christian in the A.D. 300s. Today they have their own Orthodox Christian Church. The Georgian language, with its unique alphabet, is related to other Caucasian languages, which suggests that the Georgians probably originated in the Caucasus region.

Turkic Peoples

Most Turkic peoples outside of Turkey, including Uzbeks and Kazakhs, live in the republics of Central Asia. All of these peoples speak Turkic languages, and almost all are Muslims.

The Uzbeks form the largest Turkic group in the Central Asian republics. Of the Central Asian Turkic peoples, only the Kazakhs are a minority in their own country, **Kazakhstan**. Under Russian and, later, Soviet rule, Kazakhstan was settled by large numbers of Russians, Ukrainians, and Germans. Since the end of the Soviet era, the proportion of Kazakhs has increased for two reasons: a high birthrate and the movement of many non-Kazakhs out of Kazakhstan.

The Tajiks (tah•JIHKS), a predominantly Muslim non-Turkic group in the Central Asian republics, make up most of the population of **Tajikistan**. Tajiks also live in **Uzbekistan** and Afghanistan and speak a language similar to Farsi.

Student Web Activity Visit the **Glencoe World Geography** Web site at geography.glencoe.com and click on Student Web Activities—Chapter 18 for an activity about visiting Egypt's cultural and historic sites.

Refugees Afghanis make up the world's largest single refugee population, with about 3 to 4 million people living mainly in Pakistan and Iran.

L1/ELL

Israel Israel's immigrant Jews come from many places around the world—especially Russia, Yemen, North Africa, North America, and Europe. They bring to Israel a wide mix of cultural traditions.

Objectives, goals, and answers to the student activity can be found in the Web Activity Lesson Plan feature at geography.glencoe.com

COOPERATIVE LEARNING ACTIVITY

Cultural Exchange Organize students into nine groups. Assign each group one of the following peoples: Arabs, Israeli Jews, Turks, Iranians, Afghanis, Armenians, Georgians, Turkic peoples of Central Asia, or Kurds. Have each group investigate the cultures of their assigned peoples, including customs related to family life, eating, greetings, visiting, dating, and business. Have them also explore their peoples' ancestral roots to discover the effects of various migrations on the ethnic groups. Then provide time for a "cultural exchange" during which students can share information about the peoples of North Africa, Southwest Asia, and Central Asia. 🌐 **EE4 Human Systems: Standards 9, 10, 12**

L1/ELL

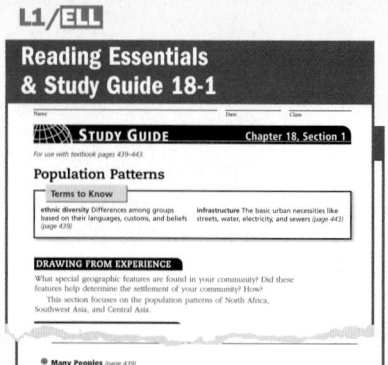

③ ASSESS

Assign Section 1 Assessment as homework or as an in-class activity.

🖱 Have students use **Interactive Tutor Self-Assessment CD-ROM**.

L2

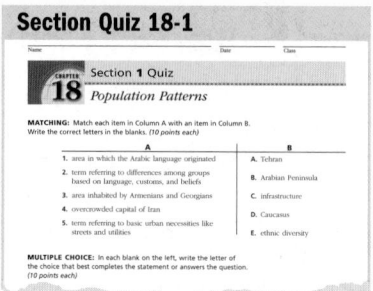

NATIONAL GEOGRAPHIC **World Explorer**

Answer
Most Egyptians live along the Nile and irrigated areas nearby. Areas lacking water have few people.

More About the Photo
Trenches bring water from the canal to crops.

Kurds

The Kurds also speak a language related to Farsi, and most Kurds are Muslims. They live in the border areas of Turkey, Iraq, Iran, Syria, and the Caucasian republics, in an area that is sometimes called Kurdistan. However, the Kurds have no country of their own. Their efforts to win self-rule have been repeatedly crushed by their Turkish and Arab rulers.

NATIONAL GEOGRAPHIC **World Explorer**

Geography Skills for Life

Water and Population A canal supplies water to farms near Luxor, Egypt.
Place How does the availability of water affect human settlement in Egypt?

Population and Resources

Geographic factors, especially the availability of water, help determine where the region's people have settled. Because water is scarce, people have for centuries settled along seacoasts and rivers, near oases, or in rain-fed highlands where drinking water is readily available. For example, many people live along the Nile River in Egypt or in the Tigris-Euphrates Valley in Iraq. Desert areas remain largely unpopulated except where oil is abundant. Nomadic herders live in or near the desert oases or where there is enough vegetation to support their herds.

Government
Control of a Vital Resource

Water has been a major issue in border disputes between Israel and Syria. As much as 30 percent of Israel's water comes from the Sea of Galilee, which is partly fed by streams beginning in the Golan Heights, a Syrian area that Israel conquered in the 1967 Arab-Israeli War. The Jordan River carries the water south, where Israeli farmers use it to irrigate their crops. Some 15,000 Israelis live in the Golan Heights. The area also has about 17,000 Arabs. Syria wants Israel to return the Golan Heights, but Israel is reluctant to give up needed water resources.

Population Growth

The region's most populous countries are Turkey, Egypt, and Iran, each with more than 66 million people. Morocco, Uzbekistan, Algeria, Iraq, Saudi Arabia, and Afghanistan each have between 24 million and 31.7 million people. Other countries each have about 19.5 million or fewer people.

Overall, the region's population is growing rapidly. The result is that many citizens in some countries, especially those in North Africa, are unemployed and must migrate to other countries to find work. This migration serves as a safety valve for some countries, helping to diffuse political discontent.

Urbanization

Large urban areas, such as Istanbul, Turkey; Cairo, Egypt; Tehran, Iran; and Baghdad, Iraq, dominate social and cultural life in their respective countries. Cities like these have been growing rapidly as villagers move there in search of a better life. Problems

---

CRITICAL THINKING ACTIVITY

Analyzing Information Have students use the maps on pages 410–411 along with data on current events to answer the following questions. **Ask:** In what areas have physical features historically kept ethnic groups apart? How might physical features or processes influence the formation of political boundaries today? *(Answers: Students should understand how features, such as Iran's Zagros Mountains, have historically isolated peoples, with the exception of armies and merchant caravans. Oil and water resources shape the formation of boundaries or have been the cause of boundary disputes, such as that between Iraq and Kuwait.)* 🌐 **EE2 Places and Regions: Standard 5**
🌐 **EE4 Human Systems: Standards 9, 10, 12**

have arisen, however, because cities have grown too fast to supply enough jobs and housing or improve the infrastructure—basic urban necessities like streets and utilities. Poverty, snarled traffic, and pollution have resulted. Families moving to a city sometimes crowd into single rooms or live in makeshift shelters far from the city's center, and they overload public resources. For example, illegal developments without water or waste services have cropped up on the outskirts of Cairo, adding to the city's sanitation problems.

Some cities have tried to cope by installing traffic control systems and improving public transportation. Iran has tried another solution—decentralizing its government. It has set up many government offices in various towns and villages away from the capital, **Tehran**. By doing so, Iran hopes to improve services in outlying areas and slow Tehran's rapid growth.

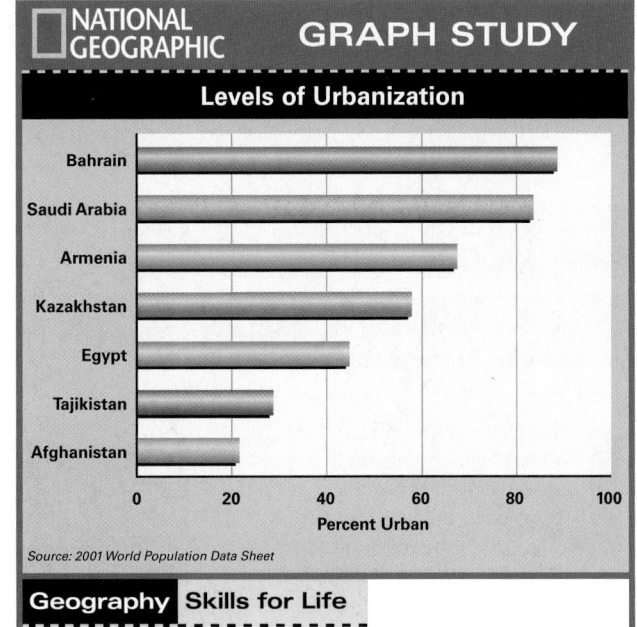

NATIONAL GEOGRAPHIC **GRAPH STUDY**

Levels of Urbanization

Bahrain, Saudi Arabia, Armenia, Kazakhstan, Egypt, Tajikistan, Afghanistan

Percent Urban — 0, 20, 40, 60, 80, 100

Source: 2001 World Population Data Sheet

Geography Skills for Life

1. **Interpreting Graphs** Which countries are less than 60 percent urban? More than 60 percent?

2. **Applying Geography Skills** Why do you think some countries are more urbanized than others?

NATIONAL GEOGRAPHIC **GRAPH STUDY**

Answers
1. *Kazakhstan, Egypt, Tajikistan, Afghanistan; Bahrain, Saudi Arabia, Armenia*

2. *less arable land; locations may encourage settlement; natural resources may provide jobs*

Skills Practice
Place Compare the graphic data with the country profiles on pages 414–416. How does Bahrain's level of urbanization compare with its size and population? *(Highly urbanized Bahrain has a small population and landmass.)*

Reteach
Display Political Map Transparency 6. Have students identify the region's most populated areas and summarize information about the ethnic groups who live there.

Enrich
Assign each student a major city in the region. Have them write the name of the city and describe its location on one side of a card and a list of important facts about the city on the other. Have students use their cards to quiz one another.

4 CLOSE

Have groups of students make travel brochures about a major city in the region.

SECTION 1 ASSESSMENT

Checking for Understanding
1. **Define** ethnic diversity, infrastructure.

2. **Main Ideas** Create a table like the one below, and fill it in to show information about the diverse peoples, religions, and languages of this region.

	North Africa	Southwest Asia	Central Asia
Peoples			
Religions			
Languages			

Critical Thinking
3. **Comparing and Contrasting** In what ways is the population of Turkey similar to and different from the population of Iran? What may account for these differences and similarities?

4. **Identifying Cause and Effect** What historical event accounts for the large number of Armenians living outside their homeland?

5. **Predicting Consequences** What might happen if Israel returns the Golan Heights to Syria? How would this affect life in Israel? In Syria?

Analyzing Maps
6. **Location** Study the population density map on page 412. Where are the largest concentrations of people in the region? Why are they concentrated there?

Applying Geography
7. **Ethnic Diversity** Think about the diverse groups of people you have read about. Write a paragraph describing positive aspects of ethnic diversity in the region. Also mention any drawbacks to ethnic diversity.

SECTION 1 ASSESSMENT ANSWERS

1. All vocabulary terms are defined in the text.

2. Answers should include the peoples, religions, and languages mentioned in this section.

3. Both are mostly Muslim, but they speak different languages and have different cultures. Most Turks descend from Turkic peoples from Central Asia. Iranians descend from the Aryans of southern Russia.

4. In 1915 the Turks killed or deported about 1 million Armenians in Turkey. Many survivors fled the country.

5. Syria would control Israel's access to freshwater from the Golan Heights. Israel could suffer a water shortage, while Syria could gain water resources.

6. Most people live near seacoasts, rivers, or the highlands where drinking water is available.

7. **Applying Geography** Paragraphs should mention that ethnic diversity gives people of the region an opportunity for a wide exchange of ideas and customs. Unfortunately, it often creates conflict among groups.

GEOGRAPHY
AND HISTORY

① FOCUS

Ask students to name some things that use petroleum. *(heating systems, hot water heaters, automobiles, trucks, factories, lawnmowers)* Mention that petroleum is also used to produce CDs and other everyday products. Discuss how modern life would be changed if oil supplies were limited. Include in the discussion the necessity of reducing traveling due to oil shortages.

② TEACH

L2 Comparing and Contrasting

Organize students into seven groups and assign one of the following areas to each group: Central Asia; North America; Latin America; Europe; Africa; Russia; or Australia, Oceania, and Antarctica. Have groups use the Internet, almanacs, newspapers, magazines, the library, and other resources to research oil production in their assigned areas. Ask groups to compose a comparison/contrast outline about oil production in the countries of the Persian Gulf region and their assigned areas. Have groups post their outlines on the bulletin board and allow time for all groups to read one another's outlines.

BLACK GOLD IN THE PERSIAN GULF

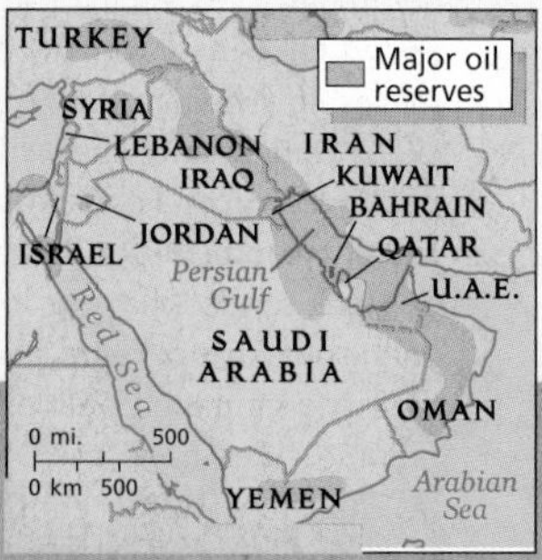

LIKE THE GENIE IN ALADDIN'S LAMP, oil has brought unimagined riches to the nations of the Persian Gulf. Trapped in pockets beneath the region's sandy soils are two-thirds of the world's known petroleum reserves. This "black gold" provides the raw material for everyday products such as compact discs, crayons, and house paint. In addition, oil supplies more than half of the energy used worldwide. Almost overnight, oil profits transformed villages in Saudi Arabia, Kuwait, Bahrain, and other Gulf countries from watering holes for camel caravans into gleaming, modern cities.

The discovery of oil in the early 1900s, however, did not immediately bring riches to the region. Nor did drilling wells to extract oil from the ground. The American and European companies who owned the wells paid host countries only about 20 cents a barrel, and the quantity of oil tapped was small.

Boom Times
Low oil prices in the late 1950s caused Western companies to cut payments to the oil-producing countries. In 1960 Venezuela joined with four Gulf states—Iran, Iraq, Kuwait, and Saudi Arabia—to form the

▶ Massive pipelines carry tons of crude oil from wells in Saudi Arabia.

444 Unit 6

BACKGROUND INFORMATION

Saudi Oil The 1930s were the turning point for the land now known as Saudi Arabia. In 1932, after thirty years of conflicts, Abd al-Aziz of the powerful family of Saud completed his conquest of most of the Arabian Peninsula and declared himself absolute monarch. He named his kingdom Saudi Arabia. Just four years later, when American oil companies discovered oil on his land, King Ibn Saud sold the rights to his country's oil fields for a mere $50,000! It was not until 1974, after Saudi Arabia had taken a strong stance against the United States during the 1973 Arab oil embargo, that the Saudis regained a 60 percent controlling ownership of Saudi Arabia's oil.
🌐 **EE5 Environment and Society: Standard 16**

◀ **Money from oil profits builds new schools for children in the Persian Gulf region.**

NATIONAL GEOGRAPHIC

Organization of Petroleum Exporting Countries (OPEC). The OPEC nations agreed to reduce oil production in an effort to cut supplies and increase prices. As demand grew, the group gradually assumed more power. They set their own prices for oil and mandated production quotas for each country. In 1973 the Arab oil embargo, sparked by the Arab-Israeli War, reduced supplies and further boosted prices. In less than a year, prices increased fourfold.

With money pouring in, Gulf countries took over ownership of their oil operations. Big budgets meant big spending. Billions were used to build highways, airports, and telecommunications systems. Hospitals and schools sprang up, and governments showered their citizens with free medical care, low-cost housing, and lifetime jobs.

Planning for Post-Oil Days

Beginning in the early 1980s, however, oil prices started to decline. Why? Reduced consumption and increased oil production outside the Middle East led to a surplus of oil. As oil profits shrank, collaboration among OPEC members began to break down. Quota disputes and other disagreements led Iraq to invade Kuwait in 1990, igniting the Persian Gulf War. Many Gulf countries have cut spending—an unpopular move among citizens accustomed to subsidies.

While OPEC members manipulate current oil prices, they also know they must prepare for the day their oil reserves will run out. Today Gulf countries are investing in foreign real estate and creating new businesses at home, from cement factories to theme parks.

Looking Ahead

Persian Gulf leaders expect their oil to run out within this century. Many are reconsidering their dependence on oil. Will oil prove to be a genie of good or bad fortune? What will be oil's legacy in the Persian Gulf?

GAS SHORTAGE! Sales Limited to 10 GALS. OF GAS. PER CUSTOMER

1908	Workers discover oil in Persia (Iran)
1960	Four Gulf countries and Venezuela form OPEC
1960s	OPEC members press for oil price increases
1970s	Gulf countries acquire their oil production facilities (background photo)
1973	Arab oil embargo leads to gas rationing in United States (photo above)
1991	Persian Gulf War; Embargo on Iraqi oil limits exports
2003	Embargo lifted following war in Iraq
2090s	Experts predict Persian Gulf oil supplies will be depleted

Unit 6   **445**

ASSESS

Have students write essays expressing their opinions to the **Looking Ahead** questions on page 445.

CLOSE

Ask students to consider how the world will meet its energy needs after the oil reserves in the Persian Gulf area are depleted. *(reserves from other areas and alternate energy sources)* Have students speculate on how new technology may help the world find needed energy. *(new ways of locating and retrieving oil, more energy-efficient automobiles and furnaces, new energy sources, and improvements on sources such as solar and nuclear power)*

Meeting National Standards

Geography for Life
The following standards are met in the Student Edition feature:

EE5 Environment and Society: Standards 14, 15, 16

EE6 The Uses of Geography: Standards 17, 18

ANSWERS TO LOOKING AHEAD

Some students may say that when the Persian Gulf area's oil supplies become depleted the area will enter a phase of economic depression, joblessness, famine, and even war. They may say that although some oil-rich families are investing their profits now for future generations, the average citizen does not have such long-term investments. Others may say that the Persian Gulf countries will have developed plenty of other profit-making businesses by then to keep their economies healthy.

1 FOCUS

Section Overview

This section discusses the early civilizations of North Africa, Southwest Asia, and Central Asia; the three world religions that developed there; and how countries of the region gained their independence in the modern era.

BELLRINGER
Skillbuilder Activity

 Project transparency and have students answer questions.

 Available as blackline master.

Daily Focus Skills Transparency 18-2

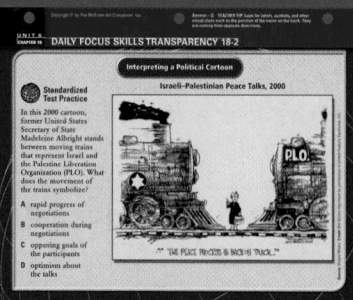

Guide to Reading

Consider What You Know
Answer *Answers may include the pharaohs, the pyramids, and well-known figures such as Tutankhamen and Cleopatra.*

Reading Strategy
Answer Sumerian: *irrigation canals, established cities and code of law, writing system;* Egyptian: *irrigation systems, 365-day calendar, hieroglyphics, impressive pyramids and tombs;* Phoenician: *alphabet of letters representing sounds, underground canals*

Preteaching Vocabulary
Have students find the definitions for the "Terms to Know" in the text. Point out that the word *qanat* is spelled without the *u* that usually follows a *q* in English words.

Guide to Reading

Consider What You Know
The Egyptian civilization was one of several civilizations that arose in this region. Ancient Egypt is a popular subject in films and books. What can you recall about its history and government?

Reading Strategy
Organizing Complete a graphic organizer similar to the one below by listing the achievements of each ancient civilization listed.

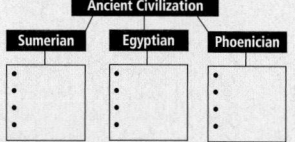

Read to Find Out
- What great civilizations arose in North Africa, Southwest Asia, and Central Asia?
- What three major world religions originated in the region?
- How did countries of the region gain independence in the modern era?

Terms to Know
- domesticate
- culture hearth
- cuneiform
- hieroglyphics
- *qanat*
- monotheism
- prophet
- mosque
- nationalism
- nationalize
- embargo

Places to Locate
- Mesopotamia
- Fertile Crescent
- Persian Empire
- Silk Road
- Samarqand
- Jerusalem
- Makkah (Mecca)
- Iraq
- Iran

History and Government

NATIONAL GEOGRAPHIC

A Geographic View

A Long History

Tucked away at the bottom of the Arabian Peninsula, . . . Yemen [is] . . . [d]ivided by nature into three distinct geographical regions—coastal plains, highlands, and desert. . . . Yemen has for much of its long history been no less divided politically by the shifting fortunes of its fiercely independent inhabitants. Kingdoms and empires have risen and fallen here for more than 3,000 years.

—Andrew Cockburn, "Yemen United," National Geographic, *April 2000*

Yemeni woman in traditional clothing

Yemen is only one of many young countries with a long history in the region of North Africa, Southwest Asia, and Central Asia. This region saw the rise of some of the world's greatest civilizations and the birth of three of the world's major religions. Sadly, the region also has a long history of intense conflicts.

Prehistoric Peoples

Hunters and gatherers settled throughout North Africa, Southwest Asia, and Central Asia by the end of the last Ice Age, about 10,000 years ago. By 6000 B.C. farming communities had arisen in areas along the Nile River, the Mediterranean Sea, and the Taurus and Zagros Mountains.

The region's farmers were among the first in the world to domesticate plants and animals, or take them from the wild and make them useful to people. These farmers captured and herded cattle, sheep, goats, pigs, and camels. Some of the animals were used for food. Farmers used the hides to make clothes and shelters.

RESOURCE MANAGER

📁 Reproducible Masters
- Reproducible Lesson Plan 18-2
- Daily Lecture Notes 18-2
- Guided Reading Activity 18-2
- Reading Essentials and Study Guide 18-2
- Section Quiz 18-2

🎬 Transparencies
- Daily Focus Skills Transparency 18-2
- Political Map Transparency 6
- Unit 6 Map Overlay Transparencies

Multimedia
- Interactive Tutor Self-Assessment CD-ROM
- ExamView® Pro Testmaker CD-ROM
- Presentation Plus! CD-ROM

Early Civilizations

Although much of North Africa, Southwest Asia, and Central Asia has dry land, important civilizations developed there. These civilizations began to grow in the region's most fertile areas about 6,000 years ago.

The civilizations that arose in **Mesopotamia**, the area between the Tigris and Euphrates Rivers, comprised one of the world's first culture hearths, or centers where cultures developed and from which ideas and traditions spread outward. Part of a larger, rich agricultural region known as the **Fertile Crescent**, the area was home to the Sumerian civilization. The Sumerians mastered farming by growing crops year-round and using canals to irrigate them. The Sumerians made great strides in soil science, mathematics, and engineering. They also established at least 12 cities and created a code of law to keep order. They kept records by using a writing system called cuneiform (kyu•NEE•uh•FAWRM), wedge-shaped symbols written on wet clay tablets that were then baked to harden them.

Egyptian civilization flourished along the Nile River. Annual floods from the Nile deposited rich soils on the flood plain. During dry seasons Egyptians used sophisticated irrigation systems to water crops, enabling farmers to grow two crops each year. The Egyptians also developed a calendar with a 365-day year, built impressive pyramids as tombs for their rulers, and invented a form of picture writing called hieroglyphics (HY•ruh•GLIH•fihks).

Empires and Trade

The Phoenician civilization, which arose along the eastern Mediterranean coast, developed an alphabet in which letters stood for sounds. It formed the basis for many alphabets used in much of the Western world today.

During the 500s B.C., the **Persian Empire** extended from the Nile River and the Aegean Sea in the west to Central Asia's Amu Darya in the east. Realizing that irrigation water would evaporate in surface canals, the Persians constructed a system of qanats, or underground canals, to carry water from the mountains across the desert to farmlands.

Beginning about 100 B.C., parts of Central Asia and Southwest Asia prospered from the **Silk Road**, a trade route connecting China with the Mediterranean Sea. Many cities in the region, such as **Samarqand** in present-day Uzbekistan, thrived as trading stations along the Silk Road. At these stations travelers and merchants traded Chinese silks and Indian cotton as well as ideas and inventions. Because of the Silk Road, with its cultural and commercial exchange, the region became known as the "crossroads of civilization."

Today, as they did hundreds of years ago, nomads travel across the steppes of Central Asia seeking grasslands for their herds. Sometimes nomadic peoples, including the Mongols, invaded these lands. During the late 1100s, a leader known as Genghis Khan united the nomadic Mongol tribes living north of China. In the 1200s they invaded Central Asia, establishing a vast empire. The Mongols killed tens of thousands of people to gain control, but later they brought many improvements to the region, such as paper money and safer trade routes.

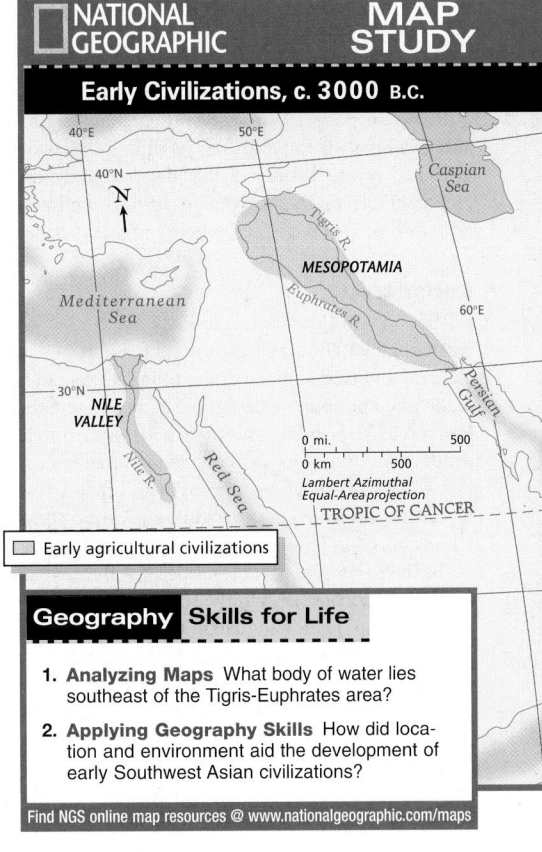

NATIONAL GEOGRAPHIC **MAP STUDY**

Early Civilizations, c. 3000 B.C.

Early agricultural civilizations

Geography Skills for Life

1. **Analyzing Maps** What body of water lies southeast of the Tigris-Euphrates area?

2. **Applying Geography Skills** How did location and environment aid the development of early Southwest Asian civilizations?

Find NGS online map resources @ www.nationalgeographic.com/maps

② TEACH

L1 Identify

Display Unit Map Overlay Transparencies 6-4 and 6-5. Have students identify the areas where the following civilizations began: Sumerian *(Mesopotamia)*, Egyptian *(along the Nile)*, Phoenician *(Mediterranean coast of present-day Israel and Lebanon)*, and Persian *(present-day Iran [Persia]).*

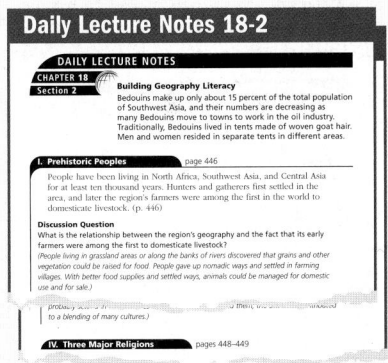

Daily Lecture Notes 18-2

DAILY LECTURE NOTES

CHAPTER 18
Section 2

Building Geography Literacy
Bedouins make up only about 15 percent of the total population of Southwest Asia, and their numbers are decreasing as many Bedouins move to towns to work in the oil industry. Traditionally, Bedouins lived in tents made of woven goat hair. Men and women resided in separate tents in different areas.

I. Prehistoric Peoples page 446

People have been living in North Africa, Southwest Asia, and Central Asia for at least ten thousand years. Hunters and gatherers first settled in the area, and later the region's farmers were among the first in the world to domesticate livestock. (p. 446)

Discussion Question
What is the relationship between the region's geography and the fact that its early farmers were among the first to domesticate livestock?
(People living in grassland areas or along the banks of rivers discovered that grains and other vegetation could be raised for food. People gave up nomadic ways and settled in farming villages. With better food supplies and settled ways, animals could be managed for domestic use and for sale.)

... to a blending of many cultures.)

IV. Three Major Religions pages 448–449

NATIONAL GEOGRAPHIC **MAP STUDY**

Answers
1. *Persian Gulf*
2. *Warm climate, proximity to rivers, and fertile soils provided a reliable food supply.*

Map Skills Practice
Region How were the early civilizations geographically similar? *(They developed in river valleys with access to seas.)*

DIFFERENTIATED INSTRUCTION

Visual/Spatial For students who tend to perceive information through images and are able to process graphic information easily, a web diagram is an especially useful note-taking tool. To help students remember relationships among civilizations, have them create five web diagrams: one each for the Sumerians, Egyptians, Phoenicians, Persians, and Mongols. Ask students to fill in facts about the civilization in the center of each diagram. Then have them compare webs and draw lines connecting similarities, such as locations of settlements, or other features. 🌐 **EE4 Human Systems: Standard 9**

📁 Refer to *Inclusion for the Social Studies Classroom Strategies and Activities.*

L2 Making Comparisons

Have students choose one of the following topics to write about in a paragraph comparing these three religions. Suggest that they use information from other resources as well as from the text.

- Houses of worship: synagogue, church, mosque
- Major figures: Abraham, Jesus, Muhammad
- Holy books: Bible, Quran

L1/ELL

Guided Reading Activity 18-2

Name _____ Date _____ Class _____

Guided Reading Activity **18-2**

For use with textbook pages 446–452.

History and Government

Fill in the Blanks

DIRECTIONS: Use the information in your textbook to fill in the blank in each sentence.

1. Farmers in this region were among the first to _____ plants and animals.
2. One of the oldest civilizations developed in Mesopotamia, in the rich agricultural region known as the _____.
3. The _____ civilization flourished along the Nile River.
4. The alphabet we use today is based on the one conceived by the ancient _____ of the eastern Mediterranean.
5. The ancient trade route connecting China with the Mediterranean is called the _____.
6. As in ancient times, _____ lead their herds across the steppes of Central Asia.
7. Genghis Khan was a _____ leader who invaded many lands in Central Asia in the late 1100s.
8. Ancient Jews set up their capital at _____, which was also a religious center.
9. Christianity, based on the teachings of Jesus, uses as its scriptures the Hebrew Bible and the _____.
10. Islam is a monotheistic religion based on the teachings of _____.
11. Islam spread widely, and today about _____ of the world's people are Islamic.
12. Over the centuries, many _____ empires rose and fell in this region.
13. _____ is the belief in the right of an ethnic group to have its own independent country.
14. Israel is a _____ state in the midst of predominantly Muslim countries.
15. Four major wars have been fought between Israel and its _____ neighbors.
16. Today, many _____ want an independent state of their own in the West Bank and Gaza Strip areas.
17. After World War I the Allies failed to keep their promise to provide the _____ with a country of their own.
18. For several years Iran and _____ were at war over national boundaries.
19. Eight countries in this region are ruled by _____.

SECTION 18-2

□ NATIONAL GEOGRAPHIC **GEOFACT**

▶ Proximity to water is especially important in the region because 16 of its 29 countries contain less than 10 percent arable land.

Three Major Religions

Three major religions began in the region: Judaism, Christianity, and Islam. All three share many beliefs, especially monotheism, or belief in one God.

Judaism

Judaism is the oldest of the monotheistic faiths. Followers of Judaism, known as Jews, trace their origin to the ancient Israelites, who set up the kingdom of Israel along the eastern Mediterranean coast. There they made **Jerusalem** their capital and religious center.

Despite political division, conquest, and exile to Mesopotamia, Jews and Judaism continued to survive and flourish. Many Jews eventually left Mesopotamia and returned to their homeland, now known as Judah. Others settled elsewhere in the Mediterranean. As they scattered, the Jews took their beliefs with them.

Judaism teaches obedience to God's laws and the creation of a just society. Believing that events have a divine purpose, the Jews recorded their history and examined it for meaning. Writings based on laws and on the history of the Jews make up the Hebrew Bible, or Torah. Worship services are traditionally held in synagogues, where a rabbi officiates.

Christianity

About A.D. 30, in the territory of Judah, a Jewish teacher named Jesus began preaching a message of renewal and God's mercy. Some of Jesus' teachings made him unpopular with people in power, and the Roman officials ruling the area had Jesus put to death. Jesus' followers soon proclaimed that he was the world's savior, alive in heaven, and that a new life in the world to come would be given to those who believed in Jesus and followed his teachings.

The life and teachings of Jesus became the basis of a new religion—Christianity. The Christian scriptures came to include the Hebrew Bible as the Old Testament, and writings on the life and teachings of Jesus as well as on the experiences of the earliest Christian communities as the New Testament. As the centuries passed, Christians spread the message of Jesus throughout the Mediterranean world and into Asia, Africa, and Europe, and eventually to the Americas.

Islam

Islam today is the major religion of Southwest Asia, North Africa, and Central Asia. Islamic tradition states that in A.D. 610, revelations from God came to Muhammad, a merchant in the city of **Makkah (Mecca)** in the Arabian Peninsula. Muhammad began preaching that people should turn away from sin and worship the one true God. Various groups in the peninsula accepted Muhammad's message, acknowledging him as the last in a line of prophets, or messengers, that included Abraham and Jesus.

By the 800s, Islam had spread to North Africa, Central Asia, South Asia, Southwest Asia, and parts of Europe. Islam had profound religious, political, and cultural influences in these areas. One of the new features seen in the region's cities was the mosque, a house of worship where Muslims pray. Muslim scholars also made important contributions:

> 66 *During Europe's [Middle Ages], the light of Islam shone, unifying, stimulating the cultures of many lands with the currents of trade and the bond of a common language, Arabic. Ibn Sina of Bukhara, known to the West as Avicenna, wrote his Canon, which remained Europe's medical textbook for more than 500 years. Mathematician al-Khwarizmi of Baghdad introduced 'Arabic' numerals and the decimal system from India and wrote the standard treatise on al-jabr—algebra.* 99
>
> Thomas J. Abercrombie, *Great Religions of the World*, 1971

The geographer Ibn Battuta traveled extensively throughout the Muslim world in the 1300s. He described the peoples and places of the region in his famous book, the *Rihlah*. Other Muslim scholars wrote about Islamic achievements and translated Greek writings into Arabic, works that later added to European knowledge about the ancient world.

Today around one-fifth of the world's population follows Islam and is called Muslim, a term meaning "those who submit to God's will." Muslims follow their faith's principles set down in the Quran, Islam's holy book. They also fulfill five duties known as the Five Pillars of Islam: professing faith in

COOPERATIVE LEARNING ACTIVITY

Early Peoples Organize students into five groups and assign one of the following peoples to each group: Sumerians, Egyptians, Phoenicians, Persians, or Mongols. Have group members investigate the ways of life of each civilization or empire, concentrating on how the people adapted to the environment of the region. Provide time for sharing insights. Lead a discussion on how these civilizations helped make North Africa, Southwest Asia, and Central Asia a crossroads of culture. 📦

🌐 **EE4 Human Systems: Standards 9, 10, 12**
🌐 **EE6 The Uses of Geography: Standard 17**

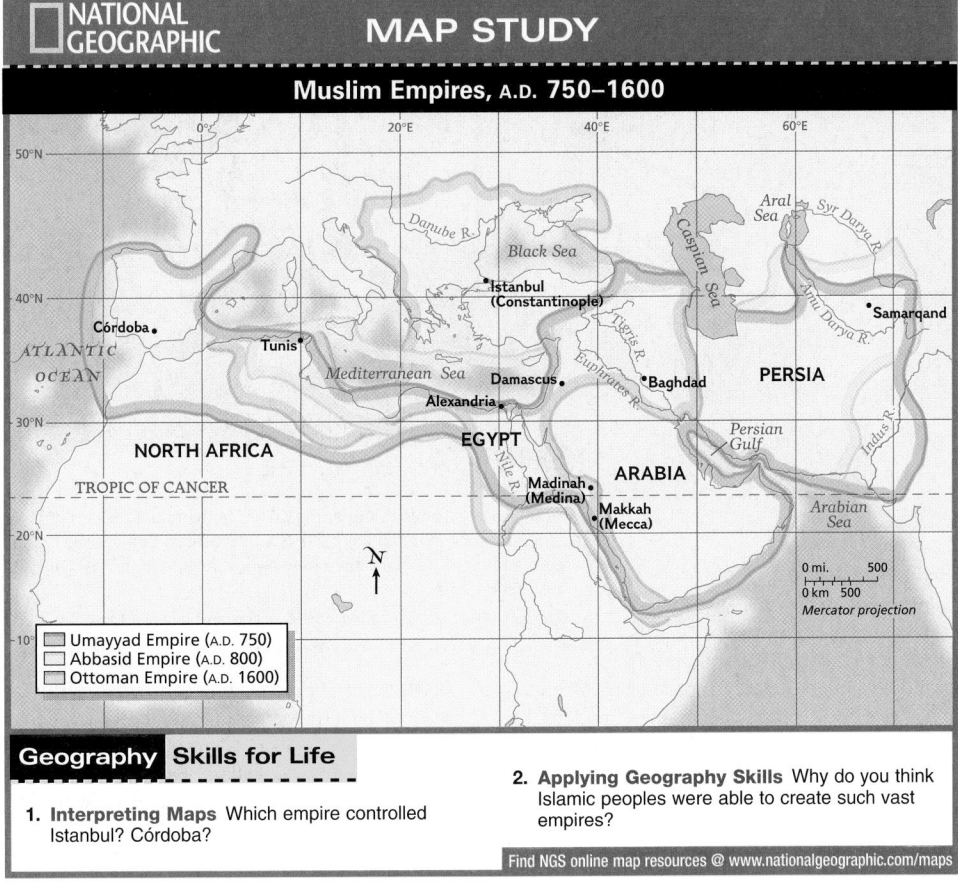

NATIONAL GEOGRAPHIC — MAP STUDY

Muslim Empires, A.D. 750–1600

☐ Umayyad Empire (A.D. 750)
☐ Abbasid Empire (A.D. 800)
☐ Ottoman Empire (A.D. 1600)

Geography Skills for Life

1. **Interpreting Maps** Which empire controlled Istanbul? Córdoba?

2. **Applying Geography Skills** Why do you think Islamic peoples were able to create such vast empires?

Find NGS online map resources @ www.nationalgeographic.com/maps

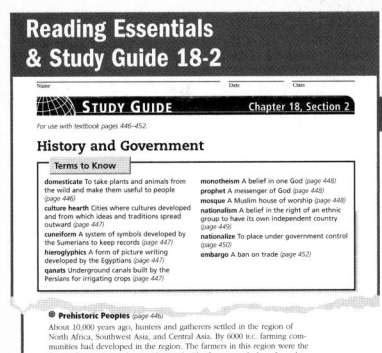

NATIONAL GEOGRAPHIC — MAP STUDY

Answers

1. *Ottoman; Umayyad Empire*

2. *By spreading Islam, Muslims were able to unify people politically.*

Map Skills Practice

Location Which empire reached farthest north into Europe? *(Ottoman)* What body of water is Makkah near? *(Red Sea)*

L1/ELL

Reading Essentials & Study Guide 18-2

Decline of the Sumerians
Around 2100 B.C., after centuries of irrigation, salts began to soak down to root level and destroy crops in southern Mesopotamia. Within 400 years, the lower Tigris-Euphrates Valley was producing only one-fourth of its previous harvests. Without enough food, Sumerian cities declined.

God and the prophet Muhammad, praying five times a day, helping the poor and needy, fasting during the ninth month of the Islamic calendar, and making a pilgrimage to Makkah, Islam's holiest city.

The Modern Era

As the centuries passed, Muslim empires in North Africa, Southwest Asia, and Central Asia rose and fell. Major conflicts, including the Crusades and the Mongol invasions, brought challenges to the region. Physical geography sometimes placed limits on economic development. For example, empires in North Africa and Southwest Asia lacked resources such as minerals, wood, and coal to fuel an industrial revolution like that of western Europe. By the late 1800s, western European powers controlled large areas of North Africa and Southwest Asia, and the Russian Empire took much of Central Asia.

Although the Caucasus area prospered under the Russians, peoples in other parts of the region were discontented under foreign control. During the 1800s a well-educated urban middle class developed in North Africa and Southwest Asia. Trained in European ways, this new middle class adopted European ideas about nationalism, or a belief in the right of an ethnic group to have its own independent country. This development stirred demands for self-rule that provided the basis for the modern countries that have emerged in the region.

Chapter 18 ⊕ **449**

CRITICAL THINKING ACTIVITY

Drawing Conclusions Ask: In what ways has religion influenced government, public policies, and citizenship in the region? *(Answers might include: political parties based on religion; Israel as a Jewish state; Iran as an Islamic republic)*; Has religion been a unifying or dividing force in the region? Ask students to provide entries for each category, and then present specific examples. Have students use the data to form an opinion and write a paragraph supporting their opinion with facts from references. Provide time for class discussion of differing viewpoints. 📺 **EE4 Human Systems: Standards 9, 13**

NATIONAL GEOGRAPHIC World Explorer

Geography Skills for Life

War and Peace

From the late 1940s to the early 1970s, Arabs and Israelis fought a series of wars, such as the 1967 Six-Day conflict (left). Since then, Arab and Israeli leaders have held peace talks to try to resolve their differences.

Region What major issues divide Arabs and Israelis today?

NATIONAL GEOGRAPHIC World Explorer

Answer

the status of Palestinian refugees; Palestinian statehood; the status of Jerusalem

More About the Photo

Israeli Foreign Minister Shimon Peres (left) met Palestinian leader Yasir Arafat (right) in June 2001. No progress was made in the talks, as conflict between Israeli forces and Palestinians spread through the West Bank and Gaza Strip.

L2 Governments

Have students turn to the regional atlas on pages 414–416. Ask them to classify the countries of the region according to their political systems. **Ask: In what area of the region are most of the monarchies?** *(the Arabian Peninsula)* **Which kind of government do most countries in North Africa, Southwest Asia, and Central Asia have?** *(republics)* **Why is Libya an exception?** *(It has a military dictatorship.)*

Independence

In North Africa and Southwest Asia, the continuing rise of nationalism after World Wars I and II gradually ended direct European colonial rule. By the 1960s most territories in these regions had achieved political freedom. Independence has been a more recent development in Muslim Central Asia, where countries did not win their freedom until the breakup of the Soviet Union in 1991. Even after gaining independence, the regional economies of countries often remained under European control. Regional governments sometimes retaliated by seizing European property. Leaders in Iran, Iraq, and Libya nationalized, or placed under government control, the foreign-owned oil companies within their borders.

Arab-Israeli Conflict

Not all the independent countries in the region are Arab or Muslim. An exception is Israel, founded in 1948 as a Jewish state. About 1,900 years earlier, the Romans had expelled most Jews from their ancestral homeland, known as Palestine. These Jewish migrants eventually settled in communities scattered around the world. In their adopted countries, the Jews often faced persecution by the majority population around them. In the late 1800s, a fierce wave of persecution drove many European Jews to call for the return of the Jews to Palestine and for the creation of a Jewish homeland there. Many of these Jews, known as Zionists, began to settle in Palestine, which was then largely Arab and under Ottoman Turkish rule.

After World War I, the British gained control of Palestine. They supported a Jewish homeland there while claiming to give equal attention to the interests of the majority Arab population. These conflicting goals, as well as increasing Jewish immigration into Palestine, sparked conflict between Palestine's Arab and Jewish communities. Later, the murder of 6 million European Jews by the Nazis in the Holocaust increased Western sympathy for the Zionist cause.

After World War II, hostilities broke out in Palestine among Jews, Arabs, and British forces. Finally, the United Nations decided in 1947 to divide Palestine into separate Jewish and Arab states. When the British withdrew from Palestine, the Jews proclaimed the independent state of Israel in 1948. During the next 25 years, Arab opposition to Israel and Israel's concern for its security led to four major wars in the region. In the 1948 and 1967 Arab-Israeli

TEAM-TEACHING ACTIVITY: WORLD HISTORY

Ancient Cultures Along with the Sumerians, Egyptians, Phoenicians, Persians, and Mongols, there were many other ancient peoples that left their mark on the region, including the Hittites, Assyrians, Babylonians, Greeks, and Romans. Have students ask a history teacher for help in researching the ways ancient civilizations changed the region. Allow pairs of students to research the civilization that interests them most and report their findings to the class. ⊛ **EE4 Human Systems: Standards 9, 10, 12, 13**

conflicts, victorious Israeli forces took over Arab lands that had been part of Palestine. Since its formation, Israel has drawn many Jewish immigrants from around the world.

Israelis and Palestinians

The wars that followed the birth of Israel forced many Palestinian Arabs from their homes to live as refugees or settlers in other lands. The status of the Palestinian refugees is an ongoing issue in the Arab-Israeli dispute. In addition, the Palestinians—both refugees and those living in Israeli-occupied areas—want an independent state of their own in the West Bank and Gaza Strip areas. The West Bank lies west of the Jordan River, between Israel and Jordan. The Gaza Strip is a territory bordered on the south by Egypt, on the west by the Mediterranean Sea, and on the north and east by Israel.

The goal of Palestinian independence is complicated by the many Jewish settlements that have been built on the West Bank since the 1967 war. The challenge, says one West Bank resident, is straightforward: "Israelis and Palestinians claim the right of return to the same land."

Israel and the Palestinians finally agreed to the first stages of a peace settlement in 1993. Under its terms the Palestinians would gain limited self-rule in return for Arab recognition of Israel's right to exist as a nation. Another stage began with the Wye River Agreement, signed in 1998. It called for Israeli troop withdrawals from Israeli-held areas in the West Bank and Gaza Strip in order to increase Palestinian self-rule.

By 2002, disagreements had halted this peace process. Palestinian militants then staged suicide bombings in Israel. In response, Israeli forces reoccupied West Bank towns.

War in Afghanistan

In past centuries, Hindu Kush mountain passes brought waves of invaders and traders to Afghanistan. Having an ethnically diverse population, Afghanistan in recent years has seen conflict involving foreign forces and rival Afghan groups. In the 1990s, radical Muslims known as the Taliban won control of most of the country. Taliban leaders were criticized internationally for human rights abuses, especially in limiting education and jobs for women, and for sheltering terrorists, such as wealthy Saudi exile Osama bin Laden.

In October 2001, American and British warplanes began bombing Afghan targets in the first military

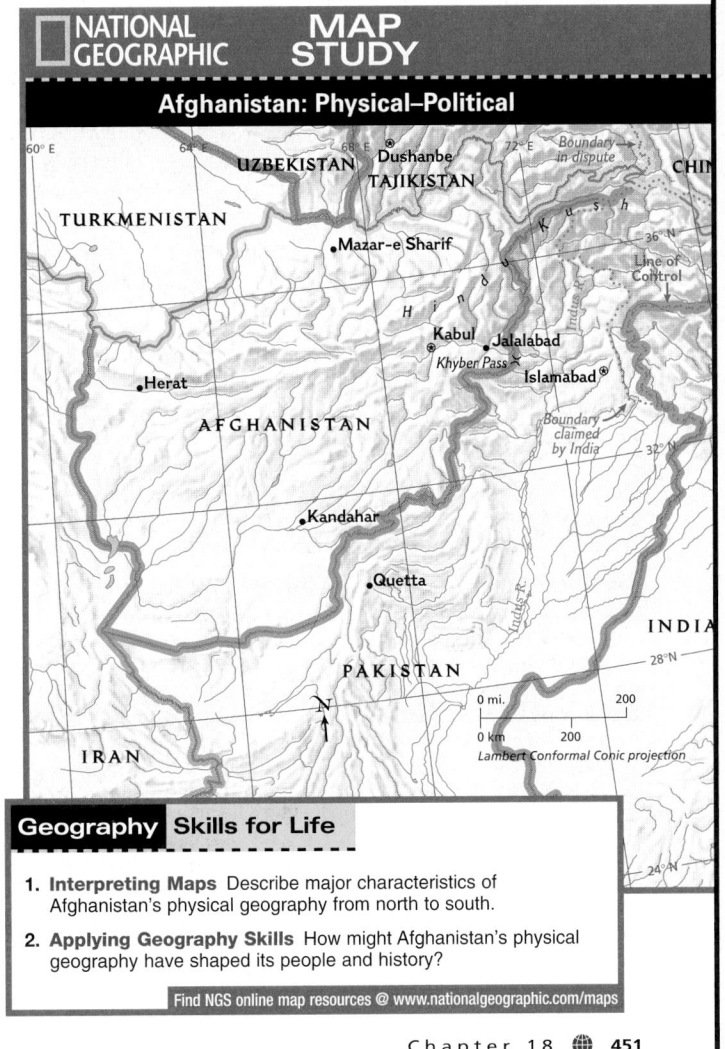

NATIONAL GEOGRAPHIC   MAP STUDY

Afghanistan: Physical–Political

Geography Skills for Life

1. **Interpreting Maps** Describe major characteristics of Afghanistan's physical geography from north to south.

2. **Applying Geography Skills** How might Afghanistan's physical geography have shaped its people and history?

Find NGS online map resources @ www.nationalgeographic.com/maps

Chapter 18 ⊕ 451

L3 Place

Ask students to research why Jerusalem has been the center of continuing conflict between Palestinian Arabs and Israeli Jews. Ask students to suggest solutions, supporting their ideas with facts.

③ ASSESS

Assign Section 2 Assessment as homework or as an in-class activity.

🔘 Have students use **Interactive Tutor Self-Assessment CD-ROM.**

L2

Section Quiz 18-2

8 Section 2 Quiz
Climate and Vegetation

MATCHING: Match each item in Column A with an item in Column B. Write the correct letters in the blanks. (10 points each)

A	B
1. climate zone known for hot summers, cool winters, and light rainfall	A. tropical savanna
2. a cause of dust storms on the pampas	B. steppe
3. location of the earth's largest rain forest	C. overgrazing
4. climate zone known for hot temperatures and rainfall most of the year	D. Atacama Desert
5. result of rain shadow from the Andes	E. Amazon Basin

MULTIPLE CHOICE: In each blank on the left, write the letter of the choice that best completes the statement or answers the question. (10 points each)

NATIONAL GEOGRAPHIC   MAP STUDY

Answers

1. *Rugged mountains in the north; plains in the south*

2. *Mountain passes, trade routes encouraged migration and ethnic diversity.*

Map Skills Practice
Location How might Afghanistan's landscape affect warfare there? *(Rugged and remote terrain, especially mountain caves, provide shelters for warriors.)*

EXTENDING THE CONTENT

Religions at the Crossroads Although most Afghanis have been Muslims since the 700s, two gigantic Buddhist statues have stood as silent reminders of Afghanistan's historical place as a crossroads of cultures. In 2001, however, Afghanistan's Muslim ruling group, the Taliban, decided to destroy the statues, claiming they were an affront to Islam's prohibition against the making of images. Targeted in the demolition was the world's tallest statue in which the Buddha is depicted standing—a 175-foot (53-m) high work of art from about the A.D. 400s. The statue was made during the time of the Silk Road, when Afghanistan was a crossroads of trade between China and India.
🌐 **EE4 Human Systems: Standards 9, 10, 13**

Reteach

List the five major headings from this section on the board. Under each heading, call on students to write the "Terms to Know" that apply to that part of the text. Then have students use the terms to review the main ideas of each subsection.

Enrich

Challenge students to find out how the Rosetta stone provided a key to understanding the language of ancient Egypt.

Ask students if they think North Africa, Southwest Asia, and Central Asia is still a crossroads of civilization. *(Answers should reflect an understanding of the region today.)*

operation of the war on terrorism. The United States also gave ground and air support to the Northern Alliance, a group of Afghan rebels fighting the Taliban. With this help, the Northern Alliance in November captured major Afghan cities and routed most Taliban forces. Talks then began to form a new Afghan government. Meanwhile, bin Laden and some of his followers remained at large. Reports suggested that they had taken refuge in the region's mountain caves. The United States and other nations expressed resolve to defeat them and bring them to justice.

Border Conflicts

Since World War II, various nations in Southwest Asia, North Africa, and Central Asia have fought each other over land and water resources. In 1980 a border dispute led to years of war between **Iraq** and **Iran**. Ten years later, Iraq's invasion of its oil-rich neighbor Kuwait forced the world community to impose an embargo, or a ban on trade, against Iraq. During the Persian Gulf War in early 1991, the United States and other countries forced Saddam Hussein, then Iraq's leader, to withdraw his army from Kuwait. For years, the region's 20 million Kurds, most of whom live in border areas of Armenia, Iraq, Iran, Syria, and Turkey, have sought a country of their own. Political differences among the Kurds themselves and opposition by the governments ruling them have kept the Kurds from realizing this goal.

Government
Today's Governments

The countries of North Africa, Southwest Asia, and Central Asia have various forms of government. Traditionally the region was under the rule of dynasties. Today monarchs with varying degrees of power still rule in eight countries, including Bahrain, Oman, Qatar, and Saudi Arabia.

The rest of the region's countries call themselves republics, although their republican governments differ greatly. Israel is a parliamentary democracy with a president as head of state and a prime minister as head of government. In the West Bank and Gaza Strip, a body known as the Palestinian National Authority is laying the foundation of statehood for Arab Palestinians.

Elsewhere, powerful presidents rule in Egypt, Syria, Kazakhstan, Turkmenistan, Uzbekistan, and Georgia. A military-based dictator governs Libya. United States–led forces removed Iraq's military-based dictator, Saddam Hussein, from power in 2003. The process of rebuilding Iraq's government began soon thereafter.

In some countries, such as Algeria and Egypt, Islamist, or politically Islamic, groups have opposed secular, or non-religious, governments. Some of these movements have been successful. Under Shiite Muslim religious leaders, Iran's Islamic government was set up in 1979 after a revolution toppled the country's shah, or monarch.

SECTION 2 ASSESSMENT

Checking for Understanding

1. **Define** domesticate, culture hearth, cuneiform, hieroglyphics, *qanat*, monotheism, prophet, mosque, nationalism, nationalize, embargo.

2. **Main Ideas** Re-create a web diagram like the one below, and write in the features of one of the major religions that began in Southwest Asia.

[ ]
[ ]—(Major Religion)—[ ]
[ ]

Critical Thinking

3. **Drawing Conclusions** Why was the domestication of plants and animals so important for the early peoples in the region?

4. **Comparing and Contrasting** How are Judaism, Christianity, and Islam alike, and how do they differ? Describe the similarities and differences.

5. **Identifying Cause and Effect** What are the main causes of conflict in the region today?

Analyzing Maps

6. **Place** Study the map of Afghanistan on page 451. What challenges might military forces face in fighting a war there?

Applying Geography

7. **Expansion and Geography** Look at the map of Muslim empires on page 449. Consider the physical geography of the region. Then write a paragraph explaining why the locations of the three empires are similar.

SECTION 2 ASSESSMENT ANSWERS

1. All vocabulary terms are defined in the text.

2. Answers should include monotheism, the religion's founder and holy book, the major teaching or belief, and the place of worship.

3. It enabled people to settle in one area and led to the growth of cities and civilizations.

4. Answers might include that they all are monotheistic, have designated places of worship, books of scriptures, and similar origins. Differences

might include that they revere different religious leaders, practice different rituals, and have different standards of behavior.

5. religious differences, border conflicts, and competition for homelands and resources

6. Rugged terrain hinders combat, but provides hideouts for military groups.

7. **Applying Geography** The three empires controlled the Tigris and Euphrates, the Nile, and the Persian Gulf, as well as the important cities of Baghdad, Makkah, Madinah, Alexandria, and Damascus.

Guide to Reading

Consider What You Know

As you have learned, North Africa, Southwest Asia, and Central Asia have diverse geographic features, climate zones, and ethnic groups. How might these aspects of the region affect its culture?

Reading Strategy

Organizing As you read about the region's culture, create a web diagram similar to the one below by listing some of the region's famous literary works.

Read to Find Out

- How have religion and language both unified and divided the peoples of North Africa, Southwest Asia, and Central Asia?
- What arts are popular in the region?
- What are some characteristics of everyday life in the region?

Terms to Know

- ziggurat
- bedouin
- bazaar

Places to Locate

- Qatar
- United Arab Emirates

Cultures and Lifestyles

A Geographic View

City of Tradition Meets the Modern World

Smoke and the fragrance of roasting quail float up from long charcoal grills lining the perimeter of Suq el-Attarine, the Market of Scents in Alexandria, Egypt. . . . Along sidewalks men sit on benches. . . . Some play dominoes. Above us hang the purple flowers of jacaranda trees.

The tranquil scene recalls earlier times in the city that Alexander the Great founded more than 2,300 years ago. But as I stroll from the marketplace toward the harbor, I am clearly in a modern city. Apartment buildings . . . surround me. Traffic jams the streets. Supermarkets, cell phones, motorcycles, and teenagers in baseball caps are everywhere.

Alexandria, Egypt

—Joel L. Swerdlow, "Tale of Three Cities," National Geographic, *August 1999*

Everyday scenes in Alexandria, Egypt, and elsewhere in the region reflect both tradition and change. In this section you will look at aspects of culture that have long shaped the lives and experiences of peoples in the region. You will also consider how the peoples of the region balance tradition and change in their daily lives.

Religion

Religion both unifies and divides the peoples of the region. The great majority of the people are Muslims. Most belong to the Sunni branch of Islam, which believes that leadership should be in the hands of the

Section Overview

This section discusses how religion and language have shaped cultural life in North Africa, Southwest Asia, and Central Asia.

BELLRINGER
Skillbuilder Activity

- Project transparency and have students answer questions.

- Available as blackline master.

Daily Focus Skills Transparency 18-3

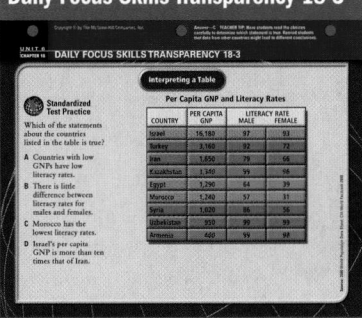

Guide to Reading

Consider What You Know
Answers *The diversity allows for variation in agriculture, resources, and settlements, creating a cultural mosaic.*

Reading Strategy
Answers *Shahnameh (King of Kings), Rubaîyat, The Knight in the Panther's Skin, The Thousand and One Nights*

Preteaching Vocabulary
Use the **Vocabulary Puzzle-Maker CD-ROM** to create crossword and word-search puzzles.

RESOURCE MANAGER

📁 Reproducible Masters
- Reproducible Lesson Plan 18-3
- Vocabulary Activity 18
- Daily Lecture Notes 18-3
- Guided Reading Activity 18-3
- Reading Essentials and Study Guide 18-3
- Reteaching Activity 18
- Reinforcing Skills Activity 18
- Section Quiz 18-3

Transparencies
- Daily Focus Skills Transparency 18-3
- Unit 6 Map Overlay Transparencies
- World Art and Architecture Transparencies

Multimedia
- Vocabulary PuzzleMaker CD-ROM
- Interactive Tutor Self-Assessment CD-ROM
- ExamView® Pro Testmaker CD-ROM

TEACH

Answers

1. *91 percent are Muslims.*

2. *Both follow the teachings of the Quran; Sunnis believe that leadership should be held by the community; Shiites believe only Muhammad's descendants should lead.*

Skills Practice

Location What do you think is included in the 4 percent "other religions" group? *(smaller religions and non-religious people)*

L2 Languages

Have students use the information in the Country Profiles on pages 414–416, as well as the Internet and other resources to create a circle graph for a given country, showing the percentages of people by language.

Daily Lecture Notes 18-3

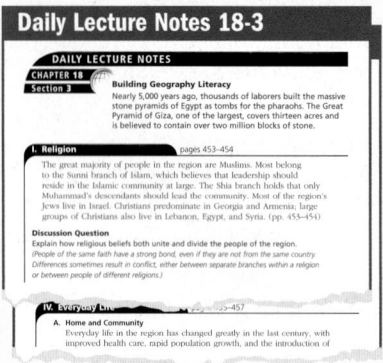

NATIONAL GEOGRAPHIC — **GRAPH STUDY**

North Africa, Southwest Asia, and Central Asia: Religions

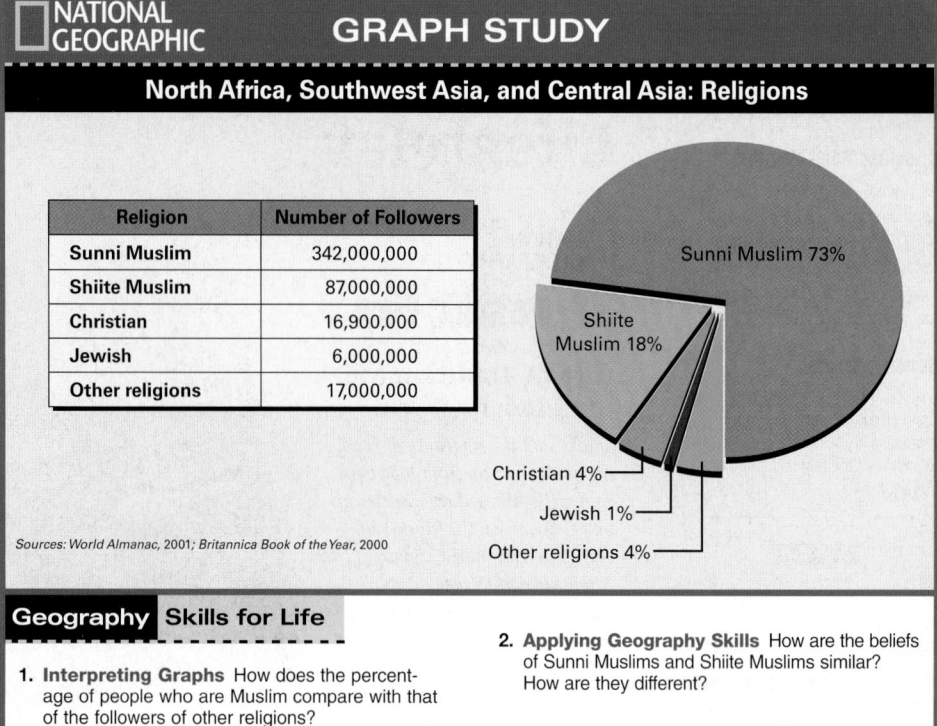

Religion	Number of Followers
Sunni Muslim	342,000,000
Shiite Muslim	87,000,000
Christian	16,900,000
Jewish	6,000,000
Other religions	17,000,000

Sources: World Almanac, 2001; Britannica Book of the Year, 2000

Sunni Muslim 73%
Shiite Muslim 18%
Christian 4%
Jewish 1%
Other religions 4%

Geography | Skills for Life

1. **Interpreting Graphs** How does the percentage of people who are Muslim compare with that of the followers of other religions?

2. **Applying Geography Skills** How are the beliefs of Sunni Muslims and Shiite Muslims similar? How are they different?

Islamic community at large. In Iran, Azerbaijan, Iraq, and parts of Syria and Lebanon, however, most Muslims follow the Shia branch of Islam. The Shia, or Shiites, believe that only Muhammad's descendants should lead the Islamic community.

Although Judaism and Christianity originated in the region, their followers make up only a small percentage of the population. Most Jews in the area live in Israel. Christians predominate in Armenia and Georgia, and large groups of Christians also live in Lebanon, Egypt, and Syria.

Languages

As Islam spread across the region, so did the Arabic language. Non-Arab Muslims learned Arabic in order to read Islam's holy book, the Quran. As more people became Muslims, Arabic became the region's main language. Other major languages in the region include Hebrew in Israel, Berber in south-

ern Morocco and Algeria, and Turkish in Turkey. The languages of the Iranians, the Afghanis, and the Kurds include Farsi, Pashto, and Kurdish, respectively. Turkic languages are spoken in most of Central Asia.

The Arts

From earliest times, the peoples of the region have expressed themselves through the arts and architecture. Architects, artists, and writers later found inspiration in Judaism, Christianity, and Islam. Today the region's cultural expressions reflect the influence of both East and West.

Art and Architecture

The region's early civilizations created sculptures, fine metalwork, and buildings. In Mesopotamia the Sumerians built large, mud-brick temples called **ziggurats**, which were shaped like pyramids and

---

DIFFERENTIATED INSTRUCTION

Logical/Mathematical Ask students to analyze the information provided in the graph on page 454. Then have them look at the paragraph under the subheading, "Education and Health Care" on page 456. Instruct students to show the information in that paragraph in graph form. **EE4 Human Systems: Standard 12**

Refer to *Inclusion for the Social Studies Classroom Strategies and Activities.*

rose above the flat landscape. The Egyptians built towering pyramids from massive stone blocks to serve as royal tombs. The Persians erected great stone palaces decorated with beautiful textiles.

Mosques and palaces are the best-known examples of Islamic architecture. Because Islam discourages depicting living figures in religious art, Muslim artists work in geometric patterns and floral designs. They also use calligraphy, or elaborate writing, for decoration. Passages from the Quran adorn the walls of many mosques.

Literature

Based on a strong oral tradition, epics and poetry are the region's dominant literary forms. The epic *Shahnameh (King of Kings)* describes heroic events in early Persian history. The *Rubaiyat* by the Persian poet Omar Khayyam is one of the few world masterpieces that has been translated into most languages. *The Knight in the Panther's Skin*, a Georgian epic by the writer Shota Rustaveli, paints a picture of brave warriors and their battles during the reign of Georgia's Queen Tamara. *The Thousand and One Nights*, a well-known collection of Arab, Indian, and Persian stories, reflects life in the early period of the Muslim empires.

Today rhythmic patterns in the region's poetry show an increased Western influence. Much modern literature has nationalistic themes. Many writers also focus on the challenges of change in traditional society. Kyrgyz writer Chingiz Aitmatov, for example, defends his homeland's traditional values against modernization. The Egyptian writer Naguib Mahfouz's novels about Cairo's recent past portray the conflicts between traditional village life and the new urban environment. In 1988 Mahfouz became the first winner of the Nobel Prize in literature whose native language is Arabic.

Everyday Life

The lives of people in Southwest Asia, North Africa, and Central Asia have changed dramatically in the last century. The population has grown rapidly with improved health care and a high birthrate. In most countries more than one-third of the population is under 15 years of age. Many people also have moved to urban areas. For example, less than 50 percent of North Africans and Southwest Asians still cultivate the land, and only a small percentage are bedouins (BEH•duh•wuhnz), or desert nomads. Contact with other regions of the world through travel, trade, and the Internet is also changing lifestyles. Even so, cherished customs and traditions survive. Daily life still revolves around family, home, education, religion, and recreation.

Home and Community

In the region's largest cities, many people live in high-rise apartments. In the older parts of cities, however, people may live in stone or mud-brick buildings hundreds of years old. Similarly, many rural people in North Africa and Southwest Asia reside in stone or wooden structures. Some of these dwellings still lack running water or electricity.

Many families are very close-knit, often gathering at midday for their main meal. The menu might feature grains such as wheat and barley as well as

architecture of SOUTHWEST ASIA

Ishtar Gate Built about 575 B.C., the Ishtar Gate was built over the main entrance to the ancient city of Babylon (now in Iraq). Thirty-eight feet (12 m) in height, the gate is covered in colored, glazed bricks adorned with reliefs, or raised sculptures, of animals. Rows of bulls and dragons seem to parade around and through the gate. Each of the bricks forming the figures had to be cast separately.

L2 The Arts

Have students share photographs of works of art from the region. Instruct them to include brief descriptions about each piece of art. Then lead a discussion comparing the kinds of art, their creators and time period, and the regions in which they were made.

L1/ELL

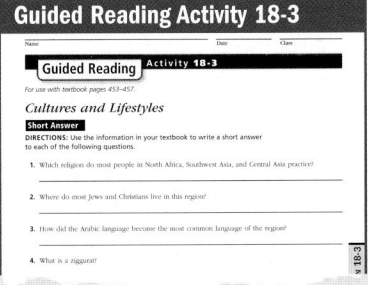

Guided Reading Activity 18-3

Name _____ Date _____ Class _____

Guided Reading Activity 18-3

For use with textbook pages 453–457.

Cultures and Lifestyles

Short Answer

DIRECTIONS: Use the information in your textbook to write a short answer to each of the following questions.

1. Which religion do most people in North Africa, Southwest Asia, and Central Asia practice?

2. Where do most Jews and Christians live in this region?

3. How did the Arabic language become the most common language of the region?

4. What is a ziggurat?

Architecture of North Africa, Southwest Asia, and Central Asia The first structure a visitor to ancient Babylon would see was Etemenanki, a seven-story ziggurat overlooking the city. To the north was the giant Ishtar Gate, its glazed brick tiles glistening under the sun. The gate and walkways were excavated for a German museum.

World Art and Architecture

Use these transparencies and activities to introduce students to other types of architecture of this region.

COOPERATIVE LEARNING ACTIVITY

Religious Art Organize students into four groups and assign each group one of these topics: religions of early civilizations, Judaism, Christianity, or Islam. Instruct members of each group to investigate ways in which the arts of North Africa, Southwest Asia, and Central Asia have been influenced by their assigned religion. Students may present an in-depth study of one example, or they may find several different examples. Students may create models, drawings, or obtain illustrations to go with their reports. Provide time for groups to share their work. 🔲 🌐 **EE4 Human Systems: Standard 10**

L1/ELL

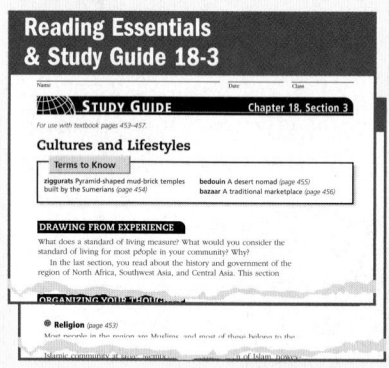

Reading Essentials & Study Guide 18-3

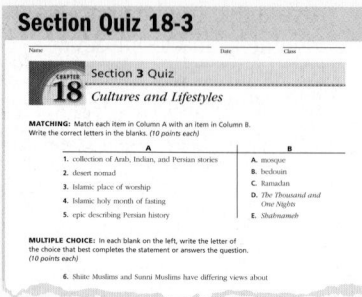

③ ASSESS

Assign Section 3 Assessment as homework or as an in-class activity.

⊗ Have students use **Interactive Tutor Self-Assessment CD-ROM.**

L2

Section Quiz 18-3

NATIONAL GEOGRAPHIC World Explorer

their shops. Lights make the glass, beads, and brass trays sparkle. The dimly lit twisting streets and alleys that curve off into the unknown add a . . . sense of adventure. **99**

Stewart G. McHenry, "Markets, Bazaars, and Suqs," *Focus*, Summer 1993

Geography Skills for Life

Pilgrims in Makkah This Asian couple eating a meal in front of the holy al-Haram Mosque is among the two million pilgrims that visit the city of Makkah each year.
Location Why is the direction they face when praying important to Muslims?

---

fruits, vegetables, and dairy products. Meat, especially lamb or mutton, is also a part of the diet of most of the region's peoples.

Rural dwellers often depend on their own farms or the village market for food. City dwellers can shop at supermarkets, but the bazaar is still popular. This traditional marketplace is a bustling area ranging from a single street of stalls to an entire district in a large city. The bazaar of Istanbul, for example, extends along miles of passageways:

> **66** *Sizzling hot kebabs give off an aroma. . . . The pounding of the hammers on copper pots assails our ears. . . . Merchants . . . wave and call out hoping to lure us into*

Economics
Standards of Living

Standards of living vary widely across the region and even within countries. Urbanized countries with economies based on oil production or manufacturing and trade have relatively high standards of living. In Israel and **Qatar**, for example, the majority of people have access to the material goods they need. They can also afford additional goods that they want. Some oil-rich countries, such as the **United Arab Emirates**, are so prosperous that they have labor shortages and depend on foreign workers from India, Sri Lanka, the Philippines, and other countries.

In developing countries, however, much of the population does not share in the benefits of the available natural resources. Population growth in countries such as Egypt and Afghanistan has surpassed the ability of their economies to meet citizens' needs. Prosperity and poverty often exist alongside each other. For example, cellular phones and foreign cars may be a common sight in Azerbaijan's capital of Baku, but many other Azeris live in poverty.

Education and Health Care

Most young people in the region attend school. Primary education is free, and enrollment is increasing. Many students now complete both primary and secondary school, and a small percentage attend university. Eighteen of the region's 28 countries have literacy rates above 75 percent; in 10 countries, more than 90 percent of the people can read and write. Before 1979, when revolution in Iran established an Islamic government, less than 50 percent of Iranians could read or write; today, 79 percent can. Women have advanced especially in education, now making up fully half of new university admissions.

CRITICAL THINKING ACTIVITY

Predicting Consequences Ask: What might have been the future of the countries in North Africa, Southwest Asia, and Central Asia if oil had not been discovered there? Have students develop a hypothesis to answer this question, using facts about countries in the region that do not have oil supplies, and historical data about life in regional OPEC countries before the discovery of oil. Provide time for students with differing views to discuss their ideas. *(Answers may include that people in the various countries in the region might have had a much slower pace of development.)*
🌐 **EE3 Physical Systems: Standard 8**

In recent decades health care also has improved and expanded in the region. People needing medical treatment usually go to government-owned hospitals. In wealthier countries, the hospital stay is often free, but doctor shortages in the rural areas of many countries mean that treatment is available mainly in large towns and cities. So despite improvements, average life expectancies have remained low in much of the region.

Celebrations and Leisure Time

Calls to worship occur five times each day in countries with large Muslim populations. A muezzin, or crier, calls the faithful to prayer from the minaret, or tower, of each local mosque. Men gather in rows on the mosque's mats or carpets after leaving their shoes at the entrance. Following the movements of the imam, or prayer leader, they bow and kneel, touching their foreheads to the ground in the direction of the holy city of Makkah in Saudi Arabia.

Religious holidays and observances often bring family and community together. Many Muslims mark Id al Adha, the Feast of Sacrifice, by making a pilgrimage to Makkah. They also observe Ramadan, a holy month of fasting from dawn to dusk ordained by the Quran. Yom Kippur, the Jews' most solemn holy day, is also a time of fasting and prayer. Passover and Hanukkah are other important holy days for Jews. Christians observe the holy days of Christmas and Easter, with special services at the places associated with Jesus' life.

People also visit with family members during their leisure time, often daily. Simple activities such as watching television or going to the movies bring young and old together. Soccer matches draw many spectators, and hunting and fishing are also popular. Board games such as backgammon and chess amount to unofficial national pastimes in countries like Armenia.

Interpretations of Islamic law have prevented Muslim women in some countries from fully participating in certain public activities such as sports. Some Muslim women, however, have begun to protest these restrictions. For example, women gather daily in Tehran's Mellat Park for a morning aerobic session, but in public places they must cover themselves completely. In sports where such dress is not practical, women perform in separate areas where the only spectators are female. Today Iranian women are active in many sports, including skiing, bodybuilding, shooting, and soccer. Their enthusiasm helped launch the first Islamic Women's Games in Tehran in 1993. Women competing in the games represented many predominantly Muslim countries, including Afghanistan, Azerbaijan, Kazakhstan, Kyrgyzstan, Oman, Syria, Turkmenistan, and Yemen.

Reteach

Have students make an outline of important section topics including religion, language, art, and everyday life in North Africa, Southwest Asia, and Central Asia.

Enrich

Challenge students to research the Seven Wonders of the Ancient World, including the Lighthouse of Alexandria and the Hanging Gardens of Babylon. Have them report their findings to the class.

 **CLOSE**

Have students identify changes in the ways of life of people in the region since 1900. Ask students to classify each change as generally positive or negative. Discuss differences of opinion.

SECTION 3 ASSESSMENT

Checking for Understanding

1. **Define** ziggurat, bedouin, bazaar.
2. **Main Ideas** Use a diagram like the one below to organize information about religion, language, the arts, and everyday life in the region.

| Cultures and Lifestyles |

Critical Thinking

3. **Making Generalizations** How has religion been expressed in the arts from earliest times in North Africa, Southwest Asia, and Central Asia?
4. **Predicting Consequences** What are two possible effects of recent increases in literacy in Iran?
5. **Identifying Cause and Effect** Why does a large segment of the region's population live in poverty, even in oil-rich countries?

Analyzing Graphs

6. **Region** Study the graph of religions on page 454. How does the percentage of Sunni Muslims compare to the percentage of Shiite Muslims in the region?

Applying Geography

7. **Ways of Life** Think about the language, religion, systems of education, and customs in this region. Then write a paragraph comparing the ways of life there with your own.

SECTION 3 ASSESSMENT ANSWERS

1. All vocabulary terms are defined in the text.
2. Answers should include the three main religions of the region along with the major languages, arts, and aspects of modern life.
3. through religious sculpture and architecture, including temples, ziggurats, churches, and mosques; also in art and literature
4. possible answers: more exposure to non-Islamic ideas and a new interest in the West;

more study of the Quran and a tightening of religious fundamentalism; a change in the status of some groups, such as women

5. Much of the population does not share in the benefits of the available natural resources, and population growth has surpassed the ability of some economies to meet citizens' needs.

6. There are about four times as many Sunni Muslims as there are Shiite Muslims.

7. **Applying Geography** Answers should include discussions of dominant languages and religions. Most countries in the region have a literacy rate of at least 75 percent. Close-knit families use meals and religious holidays to spend time together. Students should contrast these areas with their own cultures.

TECHNOLOGY SkillBuilder

Teaching the Skill

Ask students to turn to the circle graph of religions in North Africa, Southwest Asia, and Central Asia on page 454. Have them compare the figures in that graph with the one showing religions in Europe on page 303. **Ask:** How can you set up the information from these graphs to develop a spreadsheet comparing religions in the two regions? *(Religions could be listed in column A, and the other columns could list the numbers for each region.)* How would figures about religions in another region be added to the graph? *(Another column would be added.)*

Additional Practice
L1

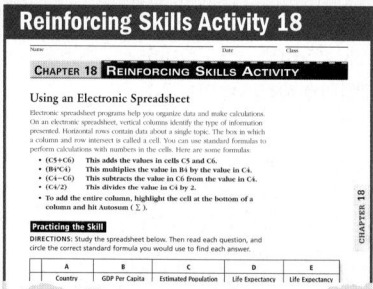

GLENCOE
TECHNOLOGY

Glencoe Skillbuilder Interactive Workbook, Level 2

This interactive CD-ROM reinforces student mastery of essential social studies skills.

Using an Electronic Spreadsheet

Electronic spreadsheets are used to manage numbers quickly and easily. Formulas may be used to add, subtract, multiply, and divide the numbers in the spreadsheet. If you make a change to one number, the totals are recalculated automatically.

Learning the Skill

An electronic spreadsheet is a worksheet for numerical information. All spreadsheet programs follow the same basic design of rows and columns. Columns, arranged vertically, are assigned letters. Rows, arranged horizontally, are assigned numbers. The point where a column and a row intersect is called a *cell*. The cell's position on the spreadsheet is labeled according to its column and row. For example, the cell at the intersection of Column A and Row 1 is labeled A1.

Spreadsheets use *standard formulas* to perform calculations using numbers in the cells. To create an equation using the standard formulas, you should first select the cell in which you want to display the results of your calculation. Here are some examples of equations you can build:

- **The equation = B4 + B5 applies a standard formula to add the values in cells B4 and B5.**
- **The equation = B5/B6 divides the value in cell B5 by the value in cell B6.**
- **An asterisk (*) signifies multiplication. The equation = (B7 * C4) + D4 means you want to multiply the value in cell B7 by the value in cell**

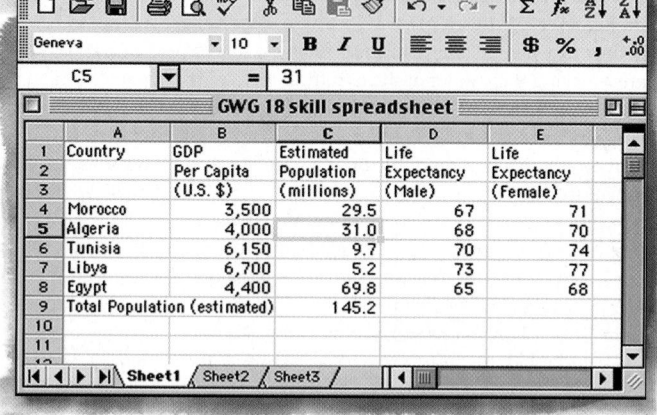

C4, and then add the value in cell *D4* to the total.

Because adding is the most common function of spreadsheets, most spreadsheet programs have an *AutoSum* key (Σ) that you can click on to place a sum in a highlighted cell.

Practicing the Skill

To practice using an electronic spreadsheet, follow these steps.

1. Open a new spreadsheet file.
2. Enter the information in Columns A through E as shown above.
3. In cell *C9*, use the *AutoSum* function (Σ) to calculate total population in millions for North Africa.

4. Print your results and share them with the class.

Applying the Skill

Use the information on pages 414–416 to develop a spreadsheet on the land area and population for all countries in the region. Use the *AutoSum* function to create calculations showing the total land area and the total number of people in the region. Then create an equation to calculate the population density of the entire region.

ANSWERS TO PRACTICING THE SKILL

Answer 145.2

Applying the Skill Check students' spreadsheets to make sure they include information on landmass and population for all countries in the region, and that they have used the formulas correctly.

CHAPTER 18

SUMMARY & STUDY GUIDE

Using the Chapter 18 Summary & Study Guide

Use the Chapter 18 Summary & Study Guide to preview, review, condense, or reteach the chapter.

Preview/Review

🔘 **Vocabulary PuzzleMaker CD-ROM** reinforces "Terms to Know."

🔘 **Interactive Tutor Self-Assessment CD-ROM** provides a review of Chapter 18 content.

Condense

Have students read the Chapter 18 Summary & Study Guide.

💿 Chapter 18 Audio Program

📁 Chapter 18 Guided Reading Activities

Reteach

📁 Chapter 18 Reteaching Activities (Spanish also available)

📁 Chapter 18 Reading Essentials and Study Guides

SECTION 1 — Population Patterns (pp. 439–443)

Terms to Know
- ethnic diversity
- infrastructure

Key Points
- Movement and interaction of people have created the region's ethnic diversity.
- The largest concentrations of population are in coastal and river valley areas where water is readily available.
- Urbanization has caused increased pollution and overcrowding, challenges that cities and regional governments are addressing in many ways.

Organizing Your Notes

Use a cause-and-effect chart like the one below to help reinforce your understanding of how change affects population patterns in the region.

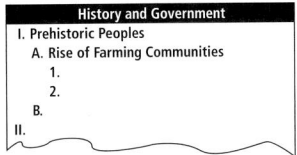

Cause	Effect
Movement of people	→
	→
	→

SECTION 2 — History and Government (pp. 446–452)

Terms to Know
- domesticate
- culture hearth
- cuneiform
- hieroglyphics
- qanat
- monotheism
- prophet
- mosque
- nationalism
- nationalize
- embargo

Key Points
- Early peoples in the region were among the first to domesticate plants and animals.
- Two of the world's earliest civilizations arose in Mesopotamia and the Nile River valley.
- Three of the world's major religions—Judaism, Christianity, and Islam—trace their origins to Southwest Asia.
- After centuries of foreign rule, independent states arose in North Africa, Southwest Asia, and Central Asia during the 1900s.

Organizing Your Notes

Create an outline using the format below to help you organize important details from this section.

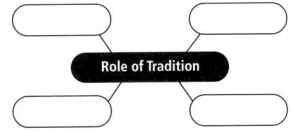

History and Government

I. Prehistoric Peoples
   A. Rise of Farming Communities
       1.
       2.
   B.
II.

SECTION 3 — Cultures and Lifestyles (pp. 453–457)

Terms to Know
- ziggurat
- bedouin
- bazaar

Key Points
- Islam and the Arabic language have been unifying forces in much of North Africa, Southwest Asia, and Central Asia.
- Many people in the region speak Arabic. Other major languages in the region include Hebrew, Berber, Greek, Farsi, Pushtu, Kurdish, and various Turkic languages.
- The peoples of North Africa, Southwest Asia, and Central Asia have expressed themselves from the earliest times through the arts and architecture.
- Tradition, especially religious observance, plays an important role in everyday life in the region.

Organizing Your Notes

Use a graphic organizer like the one below to fill in examples of the role tradition plays in different aspects of everyday life in the region.

Role of Tradition

GLENCOE TECHNOLOGY

🟦 NATIONAL GEOGRAPHIC

WORLD REGIONS VIDEO PROGRAM

Unit 6, North Africa, Southwest Asia, and Central Asia

The following segments enhance the study of this unit:

- **Heart of Egypt**
- **Three Religions**
- **Oil Boom**

CHAPTER CULMINATING ACTIVITY

Class Challenge Organize students into small groups. Have each group develop at least five questions about the cultural geography of North Africa, Southwest Asia, and Central Asia with which to challenge the other groups. Tell students to include questions about religion, art, economics, history, government, and population patterns. Allow time for groups to write questions and challenge one another.

🌐 **EE4 Human Systems: Standard 10**

CHAPTER **18**

ASSESSMENT & ACTIVITIES

ASSESSMENT & ACTIVITIES

GEOGRAPHY Online

Have students visit the Web site at geography.glencoe.com to review Chapter 18 and take the **Self-Check Quiz.**

GLENCOE TECHNOLOGY

Use *MindJogger Videoquiz* to review the Chapter 18 content.

Reviewing Key Terms

1. b
2. c
3. a
4. e
5. f
6. h
7. g
8. d

Reviewing Facts

SECTION 1
1. Arabs, Israelis, Turks, Iranians, Afghanis, Caucasian peoples, Turkic peoples, Kurds
2. Cities have been growing rapidly as rural residents move there in search of a better life. Cities have grown too fast to supply enough jobs and housing or improve the infrastructure. Poverty, snarled traffic, and pollution have resulted.

SECTION 2
3. rivers, rich fertile soil, and proximity to other waterways
4. monotheism
5. the West Bank and Gaza Strip areas

SECTION 3
6. Religion and language both unify and divide the peoples of the region.
7. Customs and traditions still survive despite contact with others through travel, trade, and the Internet.

460

Reviewing Key Terms

Match the following terms with their definitions.

a. cuneiform　　e. monotheism
b. culture hearth　f. ziggurat
c. hieroglyphics　g. bedouin
d. *qanat*　　　　h. bazaar

1. center where cultures developed and from which ideas and traditions spread outward
2. form of picture writing
3. writing system developed by the Sumerians
4. belief in one God
5. large, mud-brick temple shaped like a pyramid
6. traditional public marketplace
7. desert nomad
8. underground canal

Reviewing Facts

SECTION 1
1. What groups of people live in the region?
2. How has urbanization affected cities in North Africa, Southwest Asia, and Central Asia?

SECTION 2
3. What physical features allowed areas in Mesopotamia and the Nile Valley to become culture hearths?
4. What basic idea is shared by Judaism, Christianity, and Islam?
5. In which areas of Israel do the Palestinians want an independent state of their own?

SECTION 3
6. How do religion and language influence the region's cultures?
7. How does tradition blend with modern ways in everyday life?

Critical Thinking

1. Comparing and Contrasting How are Armenians and Georgians similar? Different?
2. Predicting Consequences How might the impact of new technologies affect the region's ways of life?
3. Categorizing Information Create a web diagram like the one below to explain reasons for varying standards of living in the region.

Standards of Living

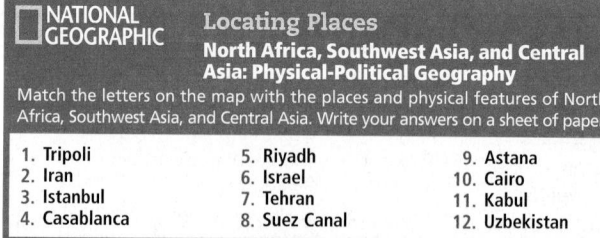

NATIONAL GEOGRAPHIC Locating Places

North Africa, Southwest Asia, and Central Asia: Physical-Political Geography

Match the letters on the map with the places and physical features of North Africa, Southwest Asia, and Central Asia. Write your answers on a sheet of paper.

1. Tripoli	5. Riyadh	9. Astana
2. Iran	6. Israel	10. Cairo
3. Istanbul	7. Tehran	11. Kabul
4. Casablanca	8. Suez Canal	12. Uzbekistan

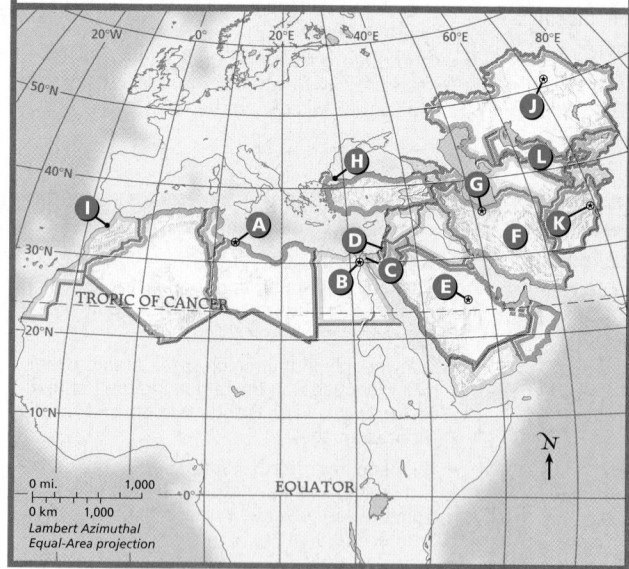

Critical Thinking

1. They are both in the Caucasus and were both part of the Soviet Union, but they have different religions, languages, and customs.
2. Technology will increase contact with other peoples throughout the world and will change lifestyles. It may also improve the standard of living.
3. Webs should include population growth, natural resources, education, health care, and manufacturing and trade.

NATIONAL GEOGRAPHIC Locating Places

1. A	**3.** H	**5.** E	**7.** G	**9.** J	**11.** K
2. F	**4.** I	**6.** D	**8.** C	**10.** B	**12.** L

Using the Regional Atlas

1. Turkish coasts, especially north and northeast; rugged terrain inland; more possibilities for irrigation near coasts
2. Turkey, Egypt, Iran

Using the Regional Atlas

Refer to the Regional Atlas on pages 410–413.

1. **Location** Where do most people in Turkey live? What accounts for this pattern?

2. **Place** Which countries' capitals have populations of more than 5 million?

Thinking Like a Geographer

Think about how language both unites and divides the region's peoples. Prepare a map of North Africa, Southwest Asia, and Central Asia, using different colors to show specific language areas. Use one color for areas where Arabic is the main language, another for Turkish and Turkic languages, and a third color for Farsi-related languages. As a geographer, what might you suggest to improve communication within the region?

Problem-Solving Activity

Group Research Project Working in a small group, simulate a meeting of delegates from four or five oil-producing countries. Each group member should research and report to the group on his or her country's oil production, oil revenues, and ways the revenues should be spent. Group members should then work together to create a chart or a graph to present the information to the class.

GeoJournal

Descriptive Writing Use details from your journal to write a descriptive paragraph about one of the culture groups of North Africa, Southwest Asia, or Central Asia. Share your paragraph with the class.

Technology Activity

Using E-Mail Search the Internet for the e-mail address of a museum or university in one of the region's countries. Compose and send an e-mail message requesting information about some aspect of the country's culture, such as architecture, religion, art, or language. Write a short report from the response you receive.

Standardized Test Practice

The following question refers to the accompanying quotation. Read the quotation carefully and then answer the question.

"Censorship in Saudi Arabia is even more overt. Under a system that took two years to develop, all Internet connections in the country have been routed through a hub outside Riyadh, where high-speed government computers block access to thousands of sites catalogued on a rapidly expanding blacklist."

—Douglas Jehl, "The Internet's 'Open Sesame' Is Answered Warily," *New York Times on the Web* (online), March 18, 1999

1. **Which of the following statements can be inferred about Saudi Arabia from the excerpt above?**

   F Only Saudi men have access to technology.

   G There is a great amount of censorship in Saudi Arabia.

   H The Saudi Arabian government provides scholarships to poor students who want to study abroad.

   J Only Internet sites related to Islam are allowed in Saudi Arabia.

Test-Taking Tip Many questions ask you to identify information that can be inferred from a passage. Eliminating answers that are not directly referred to in the passage helps narrow the possible choices. Ask yourself: Which of the statements are true about the passage, and which of the statements are false? Eliminate statements that you are certain cannot refer directly to the passage above.

Standardized Test Practice

1. G

Tested Objectives:
making inferences
analyzing information
synthesizing information

Additional Practice and Test-Taking Tips

Standardized Test Practice Workbook

CHAPTER BONUS TEST QUESTION

In the 1980s King Fahd of this country adapted the title Guardian of the Two Holy Shrines. Which country does King Fahd rule, and why is this title appropriate? *(Saudi Arabia; both of Islam's holiest cities, Madinah and Makkah, are located in Saudi Arabia.)*

Thinking Like a Geographer

Check students' maps for accuracy; possible answer—encourage people to learn others' languages.

Problem-Solving Activity

Check students' charts to assess their understanding of who the oil-producing countries are and the accuracy or logic of their recommendations.

GeoJournal

Check students' paragraphs for main ideas and accurate supporting details.

Technology Activity

Check students' work for their knowledge of how to use e-mail and their success in finding an address in the region.

PLANNING GUIDE

NOTE: The following materials may be used when teaching Chapter 19. Section-level support materials are shown at point-of-use in the margins of the Teacher Wraparound Edition.

TEACHING TRANSPARENCIES

L2 Unit 6 Map Overlay Transparencies

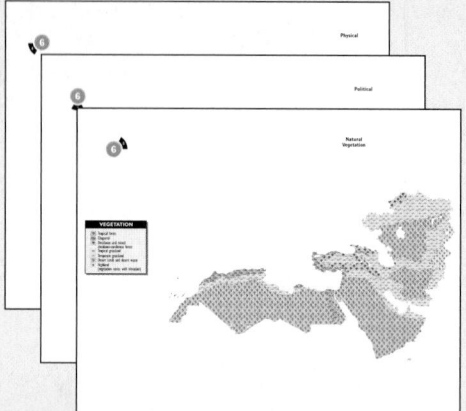

L2 Political Map Transparency 6

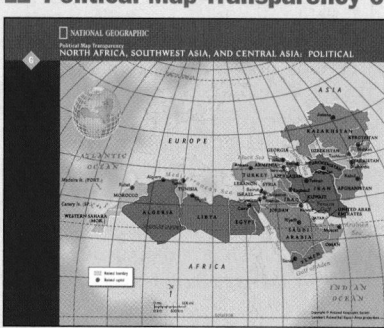

GEOGRAPHIC LITERACY

Focus on Geography Literacy

APPLICATION AND ENRICHMENT

L3 Enrichment Activity 19

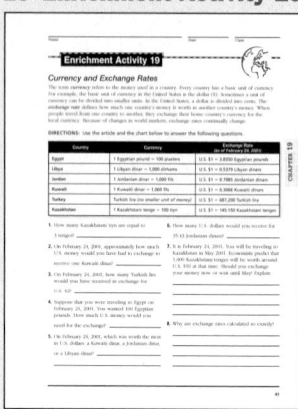

REVIEW AND REINFORCEMENT

L1 Vocabulary Activity 19 L1 Reinforcing   L1 Reteaching Activity 19
Skills Activity 19

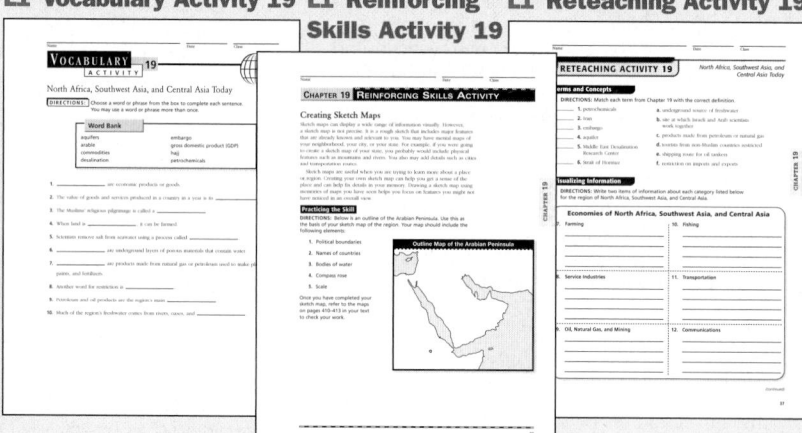

ASSESSMENT

L2 Chapter 19 Test Form A

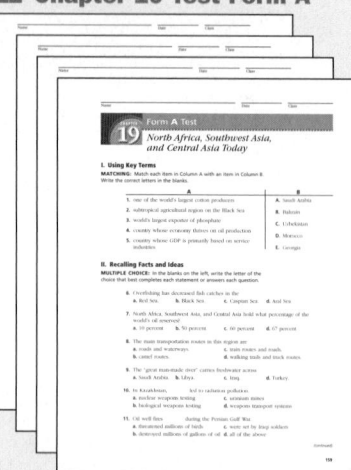

L2 Chapter 19 Test Form B

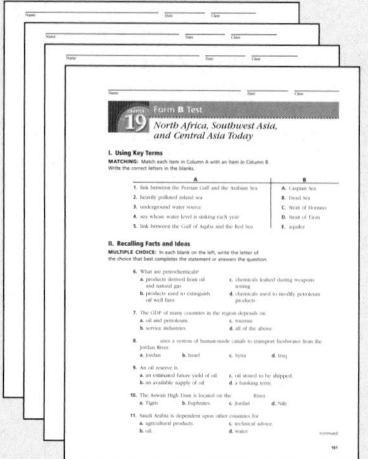

L1/ELL Performance Assessment Activity 19

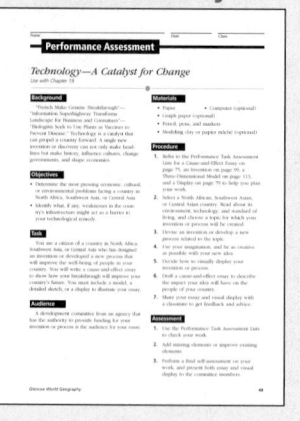

ExamView® Pro Testmaker

The following Spanish language materials are available in the Spanish Resources binder:

- 📁 Spanish Vocabulary Activities
- 📁 Spanish Guided Reading Activities
- 📁 Spanish Reteaching Activities
- 📁 Spanish Summaries
- 📁 Spanish Quizzes and Tests
- 📁 Spanish Reading Essentials and Study Guide

- World Regions Video
- MindJogger Videoquiz
- Vocabulary PuzzleMaker CD-ROM
- Interactive Tutor Self-Assessment CD-ROM
- ExamView® Pro Testmaker CD-ROM
- Audio Program
- TeacherWorks CD-ROM
- Interactive Student Edition CD-ROM
- Glencoe Skillbuilder Interactive Workbook CD-ROM, Level 2
- Presentation Plus! CD-ROM

Timesaving Tools

TeacherWorks™ — All-In-One Planner and Resource Center

- **Interactive Teacher Edition** Access your Teacher Wraparound Edition and your classroom resources with a few easy clicks.
- **Interactive Lesson Planner** Planning has never been easier! Organize your week, month, semester, or year with all the lesson helps you need to make teaching creative, timely, and relevant.

Use Glencoe's **Presentation Plus!** multimedia teacher tool to easily present dynamic lessons that visually excite your students. Using Microsoft PowerPoint® you can customize the presentations to create your own personalized lessons.

GEOGRAPHY Online

Use our Web site for additional resources. All essential content is covered in the Student Edition.

You and your students can visit geography.glencoe.com, the Web site companion to *Glencoe World Geography*. This innovative integration of electronic and print media offers your students a wealth of opportunities. The student text directs students to the Web site for the following options:

- Chapter Overviews
- Self-Check Quizzes
- Student Activities
- Textbook Updates

Answers are provided for you in the "Web Activity Lesson Plan." Additional Web resources and Interactive Tutor puzzles are also available.

Additional Glencoe Teacher Support

- Teaching Strategies for the Geography Classroom (including Block Scheduling Pacing Guides)
- Graphic Organizer Transparencies Strategies and Activities
- Outline Map Resource Book
- Reading in the Content Area

SECTION RESOURCES

Daily Objectives	Reproducible Resources	Multimedia Resources

SECTION 1 Living in North Africa, Southwest Asia, and Central Asia
 	
 1. Discuss how physical geography affects farming and fishing in North Africa, Southwest Asia, and Central Asia.
 2. List the region's important industries.
 3. Explain how improvements in transportation and communications are changing life in the region.
	Reproducible Lesson Plan 19-1
	  Daily Lecture Notes 19-1
	 Guided Reading Activity 19-1*
	 Reading Essentials and Study Guide 19-1*
	  Section Quiz 19-1*
		Daily Focus Skills Transparency 19-1
		 Political Map Transparency 6
		 Unit 6 Map Overlay Transparencies
		 Interactive Tutor Self-Assessment CD-ROM
		 ExamView® Pro Testmaker CD-ROM*
		 Presentation Plus! CD-ROM

SECTION 2 People and Their Environment
 	
 1. Describe how the peoples in North Africa, Southwest Asia, and Central Asia have dealt with scarce water resources.
 2. Discuss the causes and effects of environmental problems in the region.
	Reproducible Lesson Plan 19-2
	  Vocabulary Activity 19*
	 Daily Lecture Notes 19-2
	  Guided Reading Activity 19-2*
	 Reading Essentials and Study Guide 19-2*
	 Reteaching Activity 19*
	 Reinforcing Skills Activity 19
	  Section Quiz 19-2*
		Daily Focus Skills Transparency 19-2
		 Unit 6 Map Overlay Transparencies
		 Vocabulary PuzzleMaker CD-ROM
		 Interactive Tutor Self-Assessment CD-ROM
		 ExamView® Pro Testmaker CD-ROM*
		 Presentation Plus! CD-ROM

Blackline Master	💾 Software	📼 Videocassette
Transparency	💿 CD-ROM	⊙ DVD

Also available in Spanish

OUT OF TIME? Assign the Chapter 19 **Reading Essentials and Study Guide.**

Block Schedule

Activities that are particularly suited to use within the block scheduling framework are identified throughout this chapter by the following designation:

KEY TO ABILITY LEVELS

Teaching strategies have been coded for various learning styles and abilities.

L1 BASIC activities for all students

L2 AVERAGE activities for average to above-average students

L3 CHALLENGING activities for above-average students

ELL ENGLISH LANGUAGE LEARNER activities

TEACHER'S CORNER

Index to National Geographic Magazine:

The following articles may be used for research relating to this chapter:

- "Iran: Testing the Waters of Reform," by Fen Montaigne, July 1999.

National Geographic Society Products:

To order the following products for use with this chapter, call National Geographic Society at 1-800-368-2728.

- *Africa* (Video)
- *Asia* (Video)
- *National Geographic Desk Reference* (Book)
- *National Geographic Atlas of the World, Seventh Edition* (Book)

NGS ONLINE

Access National Geographic's Web site for current events, activities, links, interactive features, and archives.
www.nationalgeographic.com

 Meeting National Standards

Geography For Life

The following standards are highlighted in Chapter 19:

Section 1 EE2 Places and Regions:
Standard 6
EE4 Human Systems:
Standards 11, 13
EE5 Environment and Society:
Standards 5, 15, 16

Section 2 EE2 Places and Regions:
Standard 4
EE4 Human Systems: Standard 11
EE5 Environment and Society:
Standards 14, 15, 16
EE6 The Uses of Geography:
Standard 18

Local Objectives

_____

_____

_____

Chapter Objectives

1. Describe ways of life in North Africa, Southwest Asia, and Central Asia.

2. Discuss efforts to improve the region's supply of freshwater and to meet environmental challenges.

GLENCOE TECHNOLOGY

Use *MindJogger Videoquiz* to preview the Chapter 19 content.

GeoJournal

For access to additional photos, maps, and information on the contemporary issues of North Africa, Southwest Asia, and Central Asia, go to www.nationalgeographic.com (See Teacher pages in front for strategies for using journals in the geography classroom.)

GEOGRAPHY Online

Introduce students to chapter content and key terms by having them access **Chapter Overview 19** at geography.glencoe.com

FOLDABLES™
Study Organizer

Dinah Zike's Foldables are three-dimensional, interactive graphic organizers that help students practice basic writing skills, review key vocabulary terms, and identify main ideas. Have students complete the Foldable activity in the **Dinah Zike's Reading and Study Skills Foldables** booklet.

CHAPTER 19 North Africa, Southwest Asia, and Central Asia Today

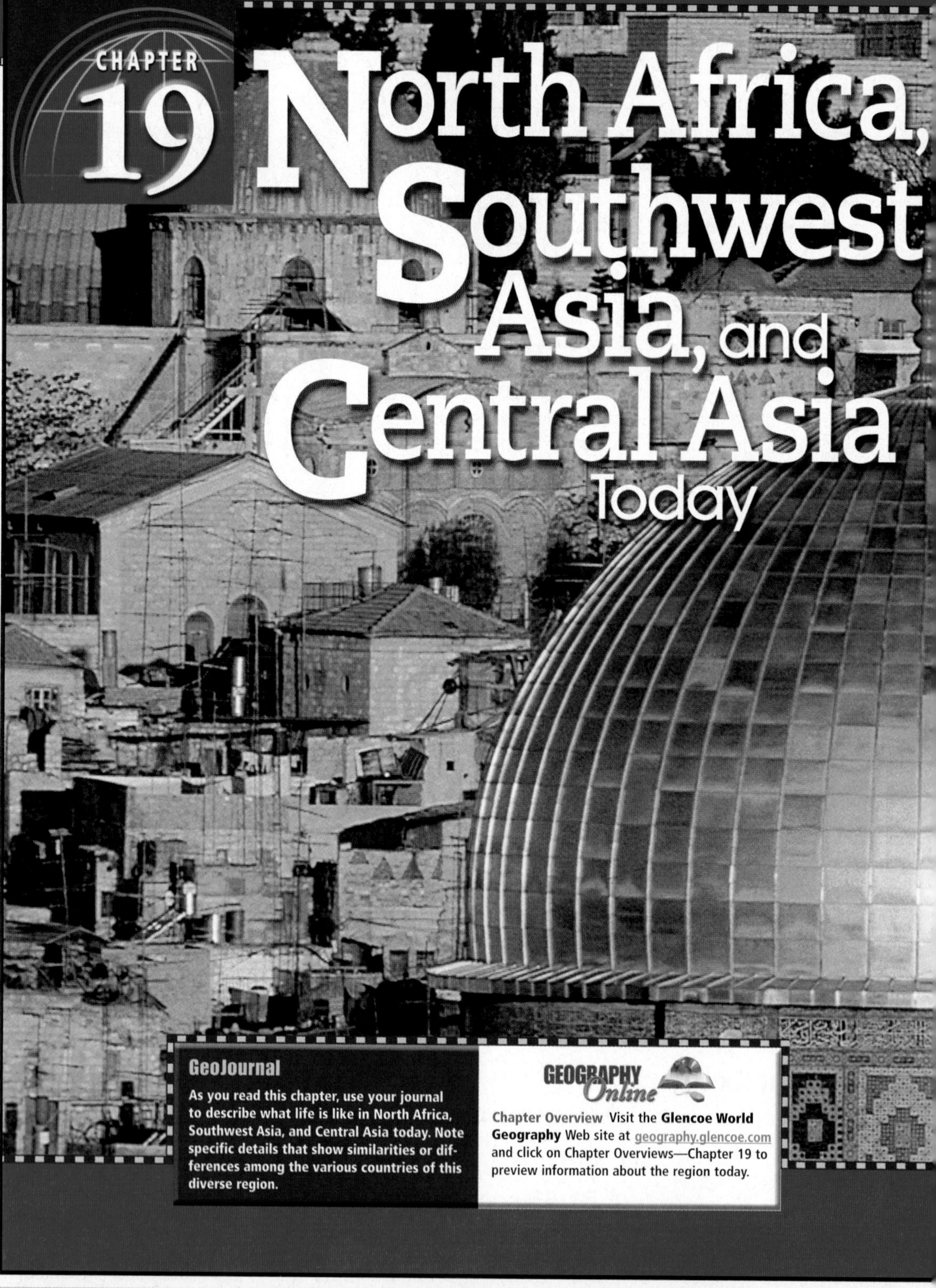

GeoJournal

As you read this chapter, use your journal to describe what life is like in North Africa, Southwest Asia, and Central Asia today. Note specific details that show similarities or differences among the various countries of this diverse region.

GEOGRAPHY Online

Chapter Overview Visit the **Glencoe World Geography** Web site at geography.glencoe.com and click on Chapter Overviews—Chapter 19 to preview information about the region today.

ABOUT THE PHOTO

Jerusalem *Jerusalem* comes from two Hebrew words, *ir* meaning "city" and *shalom* meaning "peace." Arab Muslims and Christians call Jerusalem *Al Quds*, "the Holy City." A section of Jerusalem, known as the Old City, holds many religious sites sacred to Jews, Christians, and Muslims. The Temple Mount—once site of the First and Second Temples of Israel—includes the Western Wall, where Jews come to offer prayers. Muslims honor the Temple Mount as the place from which Muhammad made a night journey to heaven. Today, the Dome of the Rock and the Al Aqsa Mosque stand on this site. Also in the Old City is the Church of the Holy Sepulchre, located where many Christians believe Jesus was crucified, buried, and resurrected. 🌐 **EE2 Places and Regions: Standard 6**

Guide to Reading

Consider What You Know

Reflect on what you have learned about the physical geography of North Africa, Southwest Asia, and Central Asia. Which countries in the region do you think have experienced the greatest economic development? Why?

Reading Strategy

Taking Notes Create an outline similar to the one below by using the major headings of the section.

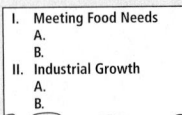

I. Meeting Food Needs
   A.
   B.
II. Industrial Growth
   A.
   B.

Read to Find Out

• How does physical geography affect farming and fishing in North Africa, Southwest Asia, and Central Asia?

• What kinds of industries are important in the region?

• How are improvements in transportation and communications changing life in the region?

Terms to Know

• arable
• commodity
• petrochemical
• gross domestic product (GDP)
• hajj
• embargo

Places to Locate

• Saudi Arabia
• Israel
• Kuwait
• Morocco
• Istanbul
• Gulf of Aqaba
• Strait of Hormuz
• Baku

◀ *The Old City of Jerusalem*

Living in North Africa, Southwest Asia, and Central Asia

NATIONAL GEOGRAPHIC

A Geographic View

Oil Boom

On a clear, warm Sunday . . . Jamshid Khalilov, a 22-year-old student at the Azerbaijan State Oil Academy, rose early to study. Jamshid lives on the third floor of a dormitory a mile from the Caspian Sea in the Azerbaijani capital of Baku. In Baku Bay oil derricks spike the horizon like dead trees, and water seems to carry a gray, viscous film. . . . "As a boy I wanted to be a doctor," he said. "But then I decided there were better opportunities in oil."

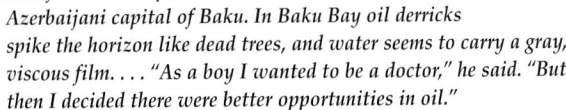

Baku oil derricks, Azerbaijan

—Robert Cullen, "The Rise and Fall of the Caspian Sea," National Geographic, May 1999

────────◆────────

Jamshid wants a job in the oil industry. His future, however, depends on the Caspian Sea's oil potential. Like other areas in North Africa, Southwest Asia, and Central Asia, the Caspian Sea has great oil reserves that encourage economic activities such as oil production. Improved transportation and communications also link the region and its global neighbors.

Meeting Food Needs

Producing food for a rapidly growing population is a challenge in many parts of the region. More developed countries, such as

---

 FOCUS

Section Overview

This section discusses agriculture, fishing, and various industries in North Africa, Southwest Asia, and Central Asia, and the impact of transportation and communications on the region.

BELLRINGER
Skillbuilder Activity

 Project transparency and have students answer questions.

Available as blackline master.

Daily Focus Skills Transparency 19-1

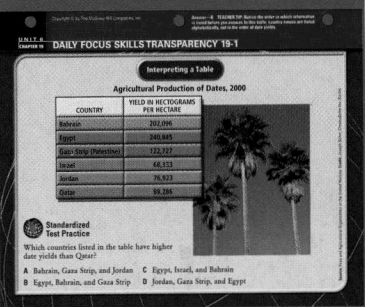

Guide to Reading

Consider What You Know
Answers *Answers may include countries producing petroleum and natural gas.*

Reading Strategy
Answer Students should complete the outline by including all heads in the section.

Preteaching Vocabulary
Have students find the meanings of the "Terms to Know" in the text. Then ask them to list petroleum-based industries. Help them understand how such industries relate to a country's gross domestic product.

RESOURCE MANAGER

📂 Reproducible Masters
• Reproducible Lesson Plan 19-1
• Daily Lecture Notes 19-1
• Guided Reading Activity 19-1
• Reading Essentials and Study Guide 19-1
• Section Quiz 19-1

🖥 Transparencies
• Daily Focus Skills Transparency 19-1
• Political Map Transparency 6
• Unit 6 Map Overlay Transparencies

Multimedia
🎵 World Music: A Cultural Legacy
💿 Interactive Tutor Self-Assessment CD-ROM
💿 ExamView® Pro Testmaker CD-ROM
💿 Presentation Plus! CD-ROM

TEACH

L1 Agricultural Products

Assign each student a country from the region. Have students make charts or pictographs illustrating what products their assigned country produces—both for export and domestic use.

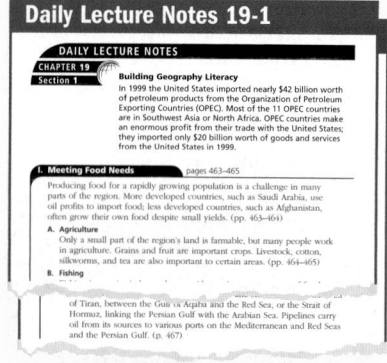

Daily Lecture Notes 19-1

NATIONAL GEOGRAPHIC **CHART STUDY**

Answers

1. *1 percent; 2 percent*

2. *Answers may include irrigation, mining, and development of other industries.*

Skills Practice

Place Which country on the chart has the smallest total land area? *(Lebanon)* Which three countries have the greatest percentage of land used for herding? *(Saudi Arabia, Morocco, Afghanistan)*

Saudi Arabia, buy food with oil profits. Less developed countries, such as Afghanistan, often grow their own food, but yields are usually small because of unreliable rainfall or poor soil. Farmers in some countries, such as **Israel**, however, take advantage of better climate and soils or use effective irrigation to grow food for export.

Agriculture

Only a small part of the region's land is **arable**, or suitable for farming, yet a large percentage of the population works in agriculture. In Afghanistan, for example, where only 12 percent of the land is arable, 67 percent of the people farm for a living. Agriculture plays a smaller role in many countries, such as **Kuwait**, that have economies based on oil.

Areas of North Africa and Southwest Asia that have a Mediterranean climate are best suited for cereal crops, citrus fruits, grapes, olives, and dates. When rainfall is below normal, however, harvests of major crops such as wheat, barley, and corn seldom meet people's needs. Countries such as Tunisia, Morocco, and Egypt that grow these crops often import grains to feed their people. Other crops of North Africa and Southwest Asia, like citrus fruits, are important exports. For example, Georgia, located at the eastern end of the Black Sea, has a subtropical climate that is good for producing citrus fruits, grapes, tobacco, and cotton.

Farmers in Central Asia raise both crops and livestock. Uzbekistan is one of the world's largest cotton producers. Both Uzbekistan and Turkmenistan are

---

NATIONAL GEOGRAPHIC **CHART STUDY**

Land Use in Selected Countries

Country	Total Land Area sq. mi.	(sq. km)	Arable Land†	Forests and† Woodlands	Herding†
Afghanistan	251,772	(652,090)	12	3	46
Algeria	919,591	(2,381,741)	3	2	13
Egypt	386,660	(1,001,450)	2	*	*
Iran	630,575	(1,633,190)	10	7	27
Israel	8,131	(21,060)	17	6	7
Jordan	34,444	(89,210)	4	1	9
Lebanon	4,015	(10,399)	18	8	1
Morocco	279,757	(724,571)	21	20	47
Saudi Arabia	829,996	(2,149,690)	2	1	56
Tunisia	63,170	(163,610)	19	4	20
Turkey	299,158	(774,820)	32	26	16

* Less than 1 percent
† Data represent a percentage of the total land area of each country. Columns will not total 100 percent, as some land uses are omitted.
Sources: 2001 World Population Data Sheet; CIA World Fact Book, 2000

Geography Skills for Life

1. Interpreting Charts What percentage of Saudi Arabia's land is forested? What percentage of Egypt's land is suitable for farming?

2. Applying Geography Skills How might a country with relatively little arable land, forests and woodlands, or grasslands for herding make up for these deficiencies?

DIFFERENTIATED INSTRUCTION

At-Risk Students For students who have trouble with reasoning, illustrate the use of headings and subheadings as a means of understanding the main ideas of a section. For example, read aloud the first heading in the section. **Ask:** How do people in North Africa, Southwest Asia, and Central Asia meet food needs? Students should use subheads to answer: "Agriculture" and "Fishing." Have students ask and answer similar questions based on the remaining headings and subheadings in Section 1.

Refer to *Inclusion for the Social Studies Classroom Strategies and Activities.*

important centers for raising silk-worms. Wheat, cotton, potatoes, and tea earn Azerbaijan substantial export income, even though less than one-eighth of its land is cultivated. Kazakhstan, which has fertile soil, is a major grain producer.

Fishing

Fish serve as an important food source in the region. Fishing boats ply the region's waters. Moroccan fishing boats bring in sardines and mackerel from the Atlantic Ocean. The majority of Israel's annual fish catch consists of freshwater fish raised in human-made ponds. Fishers from other countries harvest fish from the Persian Gulf, which is home to about 150 edible species. The size of fish catches has declined in the Caspian Sea because of overfishing and pollution. Still, Iran and several other countries have flourishing fishing industries.

Industrial Growth

Petroleum and oil products are the main export commodities, or economic goods, of North Africa, Southwest Asia, and Central Asia. The region holds about 70 percent of the world's oil and is likely to continue to supply much of the world's fossil fuels. In addition to significant oil reserves (the amount that can be recovered for use), the region also holds about 33 percent of the world's natural gas reserves.

Oil, Natural Gas, and Mining

Wealth from oil has helped build industry in the region. **Iran** and Saudi Arabia operate large oil-refining and oil-shipping facilities, and most other oil-producing countries export crude oil to industrialized countries. Natural gas has also advanced the region, powering steel, textile, and electricity production in various countries. Some countries have developed industries using petrochemicals—products derived from petroleum or natural gas—to make fertilizers, medi-

cines, plastics, and paints. The economic growth brought by industries provides thousands of jobs and helps improve the region's standard of living.

Mining also contributes to the region's economic growth. Coal and copper mining and cement production are important in both Southwest Asia and Central Asia. In North Africa, Morocco is the world's largest exporter of phosphate, an essential ingredient in agricultural fertilizers.

Service Industries

Service industries—banking, real estate, insurance, financial services, and tourism—play significant roles in the region's economies. For example, the banking, real estate, and insurance industries amount to more than 60 percent of Bahrain's gross domestic product (GDP). GDP is the value of goods and services produced in a country in a year.

NATIONAL GEOGRAPHIC **GRAPH STUDY**

World Oil Reserves (Billions of Barrels)

Source: World Almanac, 2001

NORTH AFRICA, SOUTHWEST ASIA, CENTRAL ASIA
677.9

NORTH AMERICA **26.6**

EUROPE **25.7**

RUSSIA **55.1**

SOUTH ASIA **3.2**

EAST ASIA **33.5**

LATIN AMERICA **91.8**

AFRICA, SOUTH OF THE SAHARA **33.3**

SOUTHEAST ASIA **17.9**

AUSTRALIA, OCEANIA, ANTARCTICA **2.5**

Numbers represent oil reserves in billions of barrels

Geography Skills for Life

1. **Interpreting Graphs** About how much greater are oil reserves in North Africa, Southwest Asia, and Central Asia than those in the rest of the world?

2. **Applying Geography Skills** How might having large oil reserves affect a region's relations with other world regions?

Chapter 19 🌐 **465**

NATIONAL GEOGRAPHIC **GRAPH STUDY**

Answers

1. *more than twice as much oil as the rest of the world combined*

2. *High oil reserves can give a country great influence in the global market.*

Skills Practice
Region Which regions have less oil reserves than North America? *(Europe, South Asia, Southeast Asia, and Australia, Oceania, Antarctica)*

Caspian Sea In the early 1980s, when the Soviet Union controlled fishing in the Caspian Sea, sturgeon catches averaged 20,000 to 26,000 tons per year. Today, because of overfishing, the official catch for all Caspian Sea countries totals only about 3,000 tons.

L1/ELL

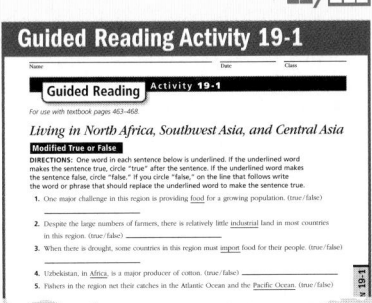

Guided Reading Activity 19-1

Guided Reading Activity **19-1**

For use with textbook pages 463-468

Living in North Africa, Southwest Asia, and Central Asia

Modified True or False

DIRECTIONS: One word in each sentence below is underlined. If the underlined word makes the sentence true, circle "true" after the sentence. If the underlined word makes the sentence false, circle "false." If you circle "false," on the line that follows write the word or phrase that should replace the underlined word to make the sentence true.

1. One major challenge in this region is providing food for a growing population. (true/false)

2. Despite the large numbers of farmers, there is relatively little industrial land in most countries in this region. (true/false)

3. When there is drought, some countries in this region must import food for their people. (true/false)

4. Uzbekistan, in Africa, is a major producer of cotton. (true/false)

5. Fishers in the region net their catches in the Atlantic Ocean and the Pacific Ocean. (true/false)

COOPERATIVE LEARNING ACTIVITY

Industry-Related Jobs Assign a country in North Africa, Southwest Asia, or Central Asia to each student. Have students form groups of four or five students each. Tell each student to write a "want ad" for a job opening in their assigned country—for example, a farmer in Kazakhstan, a worker in an oil field in Saudi Arabia, a miner in Morocco, or a fisher in Iran. Groups should combine their ads onto a poster to represent a "page" from a newspaper. Have groups compare their ads. Lead a discussion about economic activities in the region.

🌐 **EE5 Environment and Society: Standards 15, 16**

What You See Is Not What You Get
In the West virtually all melodies are composed of twelve tones. In Southwest Asian music, semi-tones, or notes that lie between the black and white keys of a piano are common. Instruments are designed to play these notes, and singers are trained to hit them perfectly. A violinist in this region may convey moods to music that a European violinist might not know how to play.

♫ **World Music: A Cultural Legacy**
Use the accompanying Teacher Guide for information about the music of this region.

L1/ELL

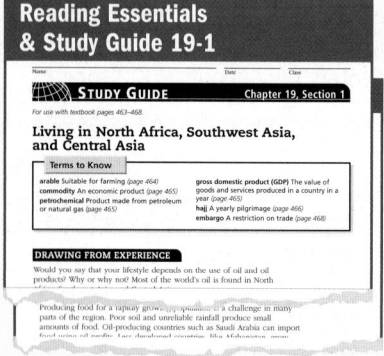

Reading Essentials & Study Guide 19-1

GEOGRAPHY AND THE HUMANITIES

♫ World Music: A Cultural Legacy

World Art and Architecture Transparencies

World Art Prints

music of NORTH AFRICA, SOUTHWEST ASIA, AND CENTRAL ASIA

The region of North Africa, Southwest Asia, and Central Asia is home to a wide variety of music that is divided into three general cultural categories: Arabic, Turkish, and Persian. Islam is an important unifying influence of the music of this region.

Instrument Spotlight
The **oud** is the most popular stringed instrument of North Africa, Southwest Asia, and Central Asia. The body of the oud is pear-shaped, with a thin neck that bends sharply backward toward the player. The oud is made of various kinds of wood and is usually decorated with ebony, ivory, and other materials. Often used in solos, the oud is also an important ensemble instrument and is used to accompany classical pieces. It is said that the instrument owes its special tone to the birdsongs absorbed by the wood from which the oud is crafted.

Go To **World Music: A Cultural Legacy** Hear music of this region on Disc 1, Tracks 24–29.

Tourism also benefits some of the region's economies. North Africa and Southwest Asia are popular travel destinations because of their historical importance. Ancient monuments and religious sites have attracted millions of visitors, especially followers of the three major religions that began in the region. Christians and Jews tour Israel, Jordan, and other countries with deep roots in the heritage of the Bible. Muslims make a hajj, or pilgrimage, to Makkah in Saudi Arabia. Other visitors come to enjoy sunny Mediterranean beaches or the vibrant music and other cultural traditions of the region. Tourism is especially vital to **Morocco**:

❝ *Tourism is Morocco's third largest industry. . . . Europeans come for hiking and skiing in the Atlas Mountains, or to the beaches around Agadir. . . . Americans come for the culture, . . . the medieval medina [quarter] of Fez, where they comb the market. . . .* ❞
Erla Zwingle, "Morocco," *National Geographic*, October 1996

Some countries, however, discourage visitors in order to limit unwanted foreign influences. After the Islamic revolution in 1979, the Iranian government placed restrictions on tourists from non-Muslim countries. Regional conflicts and political instability in places such as Algeria, Syria, and Lebanon have also affected tourism.

Transportation and Communications

Advances in transportation and communications systems in the region are bringing the peoples closer together. Countries in the eastern Mediterranean area have experienced the region's greatest expansion in transportation and communications.

Roads, Railroads, and Airlines

Extensive road systems cross Iran, Turkey, and Egypt, connecting their major cities with oil fields and seaports. More than 200,000 miles (321,869 km) of roads span Turkey alone. In some countries of the region, mountains and deserts

---

CRITICAL THINKING ACTIVITY

Identifying Cause and Effect Have students list the physical factors that affect economies in North Africa, Southwest Asia, and Central Asia. (*climate, soil, landforms, water resources, petroleum and other mineral resources*) Have them also list the cultural factors that affect the economies. (*war, political unrest, fast-growing populations, an influx of refugees*) Then have students explain in a short essay how these factors have helped cause the great differences in wealth and standards of living among countries in the region.
⊕ **EE4 Human Systems: Standards 11, 13**
⊕ **EE5 Environment and Society: Standards 15, 16**

make road building difficult and costly. However, the growing number of vehicles and the need to link cities fosters highway development. In parts of the Caucasus area, roads provide the only access to the outside world. To ease traffic congestion in crowded urban areas and to improve urban-rural connections, some governments have built rapid transit systems and railroads. A new subway in **Istanbul**, Turkey, a city of some 9.5 million people, carries commuters to and from the city's center. National rail lines also connect urban areas and seaports. In 1998 Tajikistan unveiled part of a major railway system, which is designed to make trade and travel easier throughout Central Asia.

Since World War II, the growth in the air travel industry has benefited North Africa and Southwest Asia. In recent years Central Asia also has benefited from increased air traffic. Before the breakup of the Soviet Union, Central Asian countries relied on the Soviet airline Aeroflot, but now some Central Asian countries have their own airlines.

Waterways and Pipelines

Water transportation is vital to the region. Ships load and unload cargo at ports on the Mediterranean and Black Seas. The Strait of Tiran—between the **Gulf of Aqaba** and the Red Sea—and the **Strait of Hormuz**—linking the Persian Gulf with the Arabian Sea—are of strategic and economic importance. Oil tankers entering and leaving the Persian Gulf must pass through the Strait of Hormuz. The **Suez Canal**, a major human-made waterway lying between the Sinai Peninsula and the rest of Egypt, enables ships to pass from the Mediterranean Sea to the Red Sea.

An elaborate system of pipelines transports oil overland to ports on the Mediterranean and Red Seas and the Persian Gulf. In Central Asia, pipelines carry oil from **Baku**, Azerbaijan's capital, to Batumi, Georgia, on the Black Sea coast. The recent discovery of large oil and natural gas reserves in the Caspian Sea has prompted governments to plan for the building of more pipelines.

Communications

Throughout the region, television and radio broadcasting is expanding, although government control of the media in many places limits programming.

Communication is difficult in some areas because of vast stretches of desert. Satellite technology, however, is helping countries improve communications services. Technologies such as wireless service and solar-powered radiophones are bringing telephone service to more people. Cellular phones are a common sight on the streets of major cities. Although service is limited, more and more people in the region have computer and Internet access. In Dubai, a territory of the United Arab Emirates, plans are in place to build a computer-based "cybercity" that will include a free trade zone, a research center, a science and technology park, and a university.

Economics
Two New Silk Roads

The year 1998 marked the opening of the world's longest telecommunications highway. The "highway" is actually a 16,767-mile (26,984-km) cable

NATIONAL GEOGRAPHIC World Explorer

Geography Skills for Life

Road Construction Workers build a bridge across a riverbed in Tajikistan.

Human-Environment Interaction What new development in Central Asia has made trade and travel easier in the area?

L2 Transportation

Have students state the advantages and disadvantages of using different modes of transportation for the region's products. Suggest that they look back at the Country Profiles on pages 414–416 for major exports and imports. *(barges and trains for nonperishable items; airplanes for perishable foods; pipelines for oil and natural gas)*

③ ASSESS

Assign Section 1 Assessment as homework or as an in-class activity.

◉ Have students use **Interactive Tutor Self-Assessment CD-ROM.**

L2

Section Quiz 19-1

19 Section **1** Quiz
Living in North Africa, Southwest Asia, and Central Asia

MATCHING: Match each item in Column A with an item in Column B. Write the correct letters in the blanks. (10 points each)

A	B
1. overland carrier of oil	A. Kuwait
2. group of oil-producing countries	B. Dubai
3. country with petroleum-based economy	C. pipeline
4. network of road, rail, and air transportation systems	D. TRACECA
5. location where a "cybercity" is planned	E. OPEC

MULTIPLE CHOICE: In each blank on the left, write the letter of the choice that best completes the statement or answers the question. (10 points each)

NATIONAL GEOGRAPHIC World Explorer

Answer
a major railway system in Tajikistan

More About the Photo
Tajikistan's mountains make it difficult to reach the east or north by road during the winter without taking a detour through Uzbekistan and Kyrgyzstan.

TEAM-TEACHING ACTIVITY: SCIENCE

Environmental Dangers from Oil Spills Through the 19-mile (31-km) Bosporus Strait—a narrow, busy waterway connecting the Black Sea and the Sea of Marmara—cruise giant oceangoing tankers filled with oil from Central Asia. Because of swift currents, the Bosporus, which separates the European and Asian parts of Istanbul, Turkey, is regarded as a very difficult strait to navigate and environmentalists worry about the potential for an oil spill disaster. Have students work with a science teacher to find out how a spill would affect the area's people and environment, and what measures are being taken to safeguard against spills. ▣ **EE5 Environment and Society: Standard 5**

INTERDISCIPLINARY
connection

ECONOMICS OPEC showed its economic might when it raised the price of oil from $2 per barrel in 1973 to almost 20 times that by 1981. To buy oil, the poorer countries of the world had to borrow great sums at high interest rates.

Reteach

Have students write one paragraph about each chart, graph, and photograph in this section to review the main ideas.

Enrich

Have students find out how the Israelis have cultivated the Negev Desert. Provide time for them to share their findings.

4 CLOSE

Have each student complete the following statement: The most significant influence on the economies of North Africa, Southwest Asia, and Central Asia is ____.

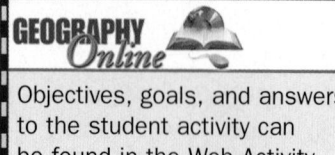

Objectives, goals, and answers to the student activity can be found in the Web Activity Lesson Plan feature at geography.glencoe.com

---

that follows the route of the Silk Road, the ancient trade route that linked Europe, Central Asia, and China. The cable provides the 20 countries along its path with digital circuits for voice, data, fax, and video transmissions.

Plans are also under way to build a network of road, rail, and air transportation systems tracing the Silk Road's path. The Transport Corridor Europe-Caucasus-Asia (TRACECA) will extend from Moldova in Europe eastward to Mongolia in East Asia. The more than 30 countries involved hope the project will promote peace in this vast area and provide access to newly discovered oil and gas deposits in the Caspian region.

Interdependence

Good transportation and communications networks go a long way toward increasing interaction between North Africa, Southwest Asia, and Central Asia and the rest of the world. Interdependence is also growing within the region, as developed countries provide foreign aid, trade deals, and development loans to less developed countries. Following the breakup of the Soviet Union, for example, Turkey, Iran, and Saudi Arabia helped smooth the new Central Asian republics' transition to independence.

Eight of the region's oil-producing countries—Algeria, Libya, Iran, Iraq, Kuwait, Qatar, Saudi Arabia, and United Arab Emirates—have become a majority in the 11-member Organization of Petroleum Exporting Countries (OPEC). Founded in 1960, OPEC has given member countries more control over oil production and prices. Because other countries depend heavily on the region's oil, OPEC has considerable influence in global affairs. It exercised political muscle by restricting oil shipments to the United States because of its aid to Israel during the 1973 Arab-Israeli war. OPEC raised oil prices during the 1970s. It also placed and later canceled an embargo, or restriction, on oil shipments to the United States and other industrialized countries. In 1999 and again in 2000, OPEC cut back oil production, forcing up oil prices around the world.

The countries of North Africa, Southwest Asia, and Central Asia and the rest of the world depend on one another. Industrialized countries, such as the United States, need oil from the region, and the region needs industrial products for its markets. For these reasons, both sides recognize that, despite political and economic disagreements, they must work together to ensure the well-being of all.

Student Web Activity Visit the **Glencoe World Geography** Web site at geography.glencoe.com and click on Student Web Activities—Chapter 19 for an activity about OPEC.

SECTION 1 ASSESSMENT

Checking for Understanding

1. **Define** arable, commodity, petrochemical, gross domestic product (GDP), hajj, embargo.

2. **Main Ideas** Use a graphic organizer like the one below to list ways that the activities listed help meet food needs in the region.

```
     Meeting Food Needs
       /           \
  Agriculture    Fishing
```

Critical Thinking

3. **Drawing Conclusions** Why does this region refine only a small amount of the oil it produces?

4. **Predicting Consequences** How might recent advances in communications technology help unify the region and change its cultures?

5. **Identifying Cause and Effect** Why do oil prices rise and fall? How do these changes affect global consumers?

Analyzing Maps

6. **Region** Study the economic activity map on page 413 of the Regional Atlas. In what areas of the region are oil deposits most abundant?

Applying Geography

7. **Effects of Transportation** List recent changes in global transportation and communications. Then create a graphic organizer showing how these changes have affected everyday life in the region.

SECTION 1 ASSESSMENT ANSWERS

1. All vocabulary terms are defined in the text.

2. Answers should show the relationship between the activities and food production.

3. It is easier and cheaper for other countries to simply import crude oil.

4. Answers may include that greater trade and an exchange of ideas may modernize lifestyles.

5. OPEC controls the prices and sometimes raises them for political reasons. High prices can cripple the economic development of countries and make them dependent on the oil-producing countries.

6. the Persian Gulf and Caspian Sea areas, Algeria, Libya, Egypt

7. **Applying Geography** Students should include changes listed in the text. Graphic organizers should show cause-and-effect relationships and students' understanding of how these changes affect life in the region.

Guide to Reading

Consider What You Know

North Africa, Southwest Asia, and Central Asia produce much of the world's oil. Because of this commodity, what particular environmental problems do you think people in this region face?

Reading Strategy

Organizing As you read about the environmental concerns of the region, complete a graphic organizer similar to the one below by describing the environmental challenges of the Caspian Sea, Dead Sea, and Aral Sea.

Body of Water	Challenges
Caspian Sea	
Dead Sea	
Aral Sea	

Read to Find Out

- How have peoples in the region dealt with scarce water resources?
- What are the causes and effects of environmental problems in the region?

Terms to Know

- aquifer
- desalination

Places to Locate

- Tripoli
- Aswan High Dam
- Elburz Mountains
- Dead Sea
- Aral Sea

People and Their Environment

NATIONAL GEOGRAPHIC

A Geographic View

Resources in Danger

An ocean of yellow sand covers Egypt, divided by the dark green vein of the Nile River. The river injects life into the bright green fan at its mouth, while the gray, man-made mass of Cairo eats away at the fan's delicate stem. . . . Cairo's commercial and residential sprawl has locked priceless soil beneath miles of concrete; the discharge of chemicals into delta lakes threatens the fishing industry and the supply of clean drinking water.

Satellite view of the Nile Delta

—Peter Theroux, "The Imperiled Nile Delta," National Geographic, *January 1997*

Human actions in North Africa, Southwest Asia, and Central Asia, like human actions in many places, often threaten the environment. These actions take many forms—oil spills, urban sprawl, and overuse of water supplies. The dilemma faced by people in the region is how to meet human needs while protecting the environment.

The Need for Water

Because more than 70 percent of the earth is covered by water, we often think of it as an abundant natural resource. However, about 2 percent of the earth's water is frozen, and 97 percent is salt water. According to the United Nations, about 1.2 billion people worldwide cannot obtain clean drinking water. About two-thirds of the world's households do not have a nearby source of freshwater. Some experts predict that by the year 2050 about 10 billion people will be living on the earth, producing an even greater strain on water resources.

Chapter 19 🌐 **469**

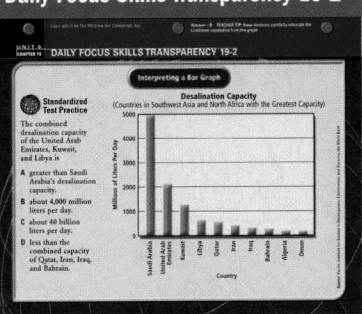

NATIONAL GEOGRAPHIC — MAP STUDY

Answers

1. *Algeria, Turkey, Georgia*

2. *Agriculture would be limited; resources—which could be used for other economic or domestic programs—would have to be spent on obtaining water from elsewhere.*

Map Skills Practice

Human-Environment Interaction Compare the map on this page with the population density map on page 412. What effect does precipitation generally have on patterns of human settlement in the region? *(Areas with greater precipitation are more densely populated.)*

② TEACH

L1 Compare

Have students use almanacs or the Internet to find out the average annual precipitation in the area where they live or in the nearest city. Then have them compare that figure with the annual precipitation for various areas shown on the map on page 470.

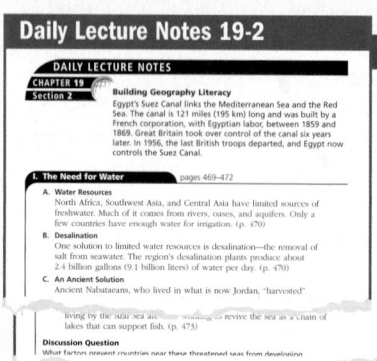

Daily Lecture Notes 19-2

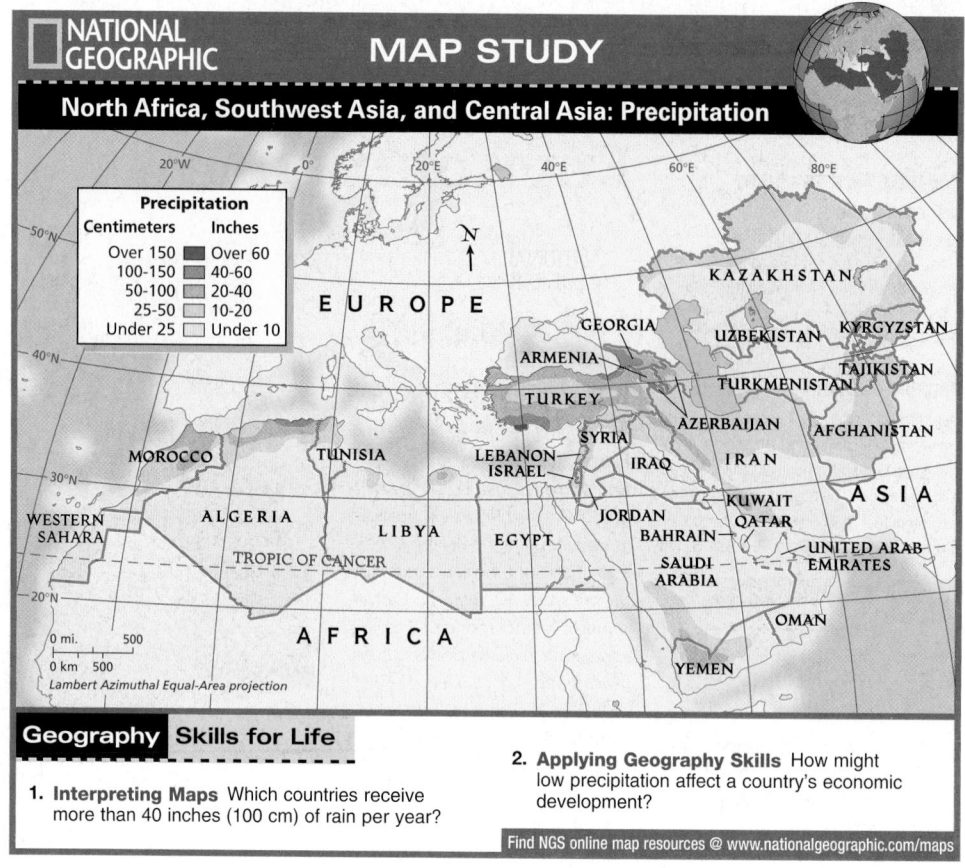

NATIONAL GEOGRAPHIC — MAP STUDY

North Africa, Southwest Asia, and Central Asia: Precipitation

Precipitation

Centimeters	Inches
Over 150	Over 60
100-150	40-60
50-100	20-40
25-50	10-20
Under 25	Under 10

Lambert Azimuthal Equal-Area projection

0 mi. 500
0 km 500

Geography Skills for Life

1. **Interpreting Maps** Which countries receive more than 40 inches (100 cm) of rain per year?

2. **Applying Geography Skills** How might low precipitation affect a country's economic development?

Find NGS online map resources @ www.nationalgeographic.com/maps

---

Water Resources

Much of the freshwater in North Africa, Southwest Asia, and Central Asia comes from rivers, oases, and aquifers—underground layers of porous rock, gravel, or sand that contain water. As the population grows, demand for water taxes these aquifers and other water resources.

The Nile, Tigris, Euphrates, Jordan, Amu Darya, and Syr Darya are the area's only major rivers, so only a few of the region's countries have enough freshwater for irrigation. Israel, for instance, uses an elaborate system of human-made canals to funnel the freshwater of the Jordan River from north to south. In the rest of the region, people turn to smaller rivers and other sources for water.

Desalination

Limited water resources have prompted scientists to develop ways to remove salt from seawater, a process called desalination. As the world's population increases and becomes more highly concentrated in urban areas, desalination helps meet the need for more freshwater. Within the region, Israel was the first country to attempt desalination. Other countries soon followed. The region now has about 60 percent of the world's freshwater-producing capacity, producing more than 2.4 billion gallons (9.1 billion l) a day. Many countries, particularly those near the Persian Gulf, depend on desalination plants. At the new Middle East Desalination Research Center, freshwater needs have brought Israeli and Arab scientists together.

DIFFERENTIATED INSTRUCTION

English Learners Have students create diagrams or graphs that show amounts of annual precipitation in assigned countries from the region. Have students label the diagrams and charts using words that explain the numbers and illustrations, such as "very dry," or "not as dry." Invite volunteers to share their work with the class. Suggest that they first write out what they want to say and have an English proficient student review the presentation before it is given to the class. **ELL** 🌐 **EE2 Places and Regions: Standard 4** 🌐 **EE6 The Uses of Geography: Standard 18**

🗂 Refer to *Inclusion for the Social Studies Classroom Strategies and Activities.*

History
An Ancient Solution

Creative solutions to the scarce water supply in North Africa, Southwest Asia, and Central Asia are an ongoing need. Scientists are now looking to the region's past for insights into possible solutions for the future. The ancient Nabataeans built the city of Petra, located in present-day Jordan, in a desert canyon that receives only about six inches of rain each year. To supply the 30,000 residents of Petra with the water they needed, the Nabataeans harvested rainwater, collecting and storing it in an amazingly intricate system of pipes, dams, terraces, and cisterns, or other artificial reservoirs.

> *Hundreds of cisterns kept Petra from dying of thirst in times of drought, while masonry dams in the surrounding hills protected the city from flash floods after bursts of rain. . . . That kind of planning is called for again today.*
>
> Don Belt, "Petra: Ancient City of Stone," *National Geographic*, December 1998

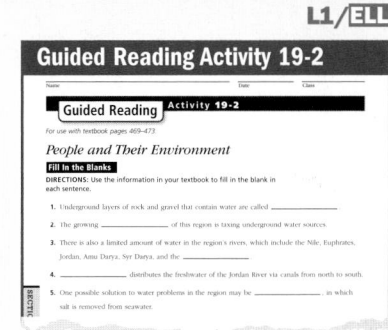

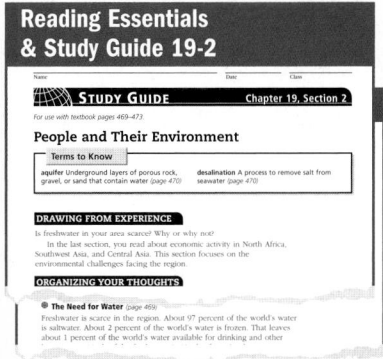

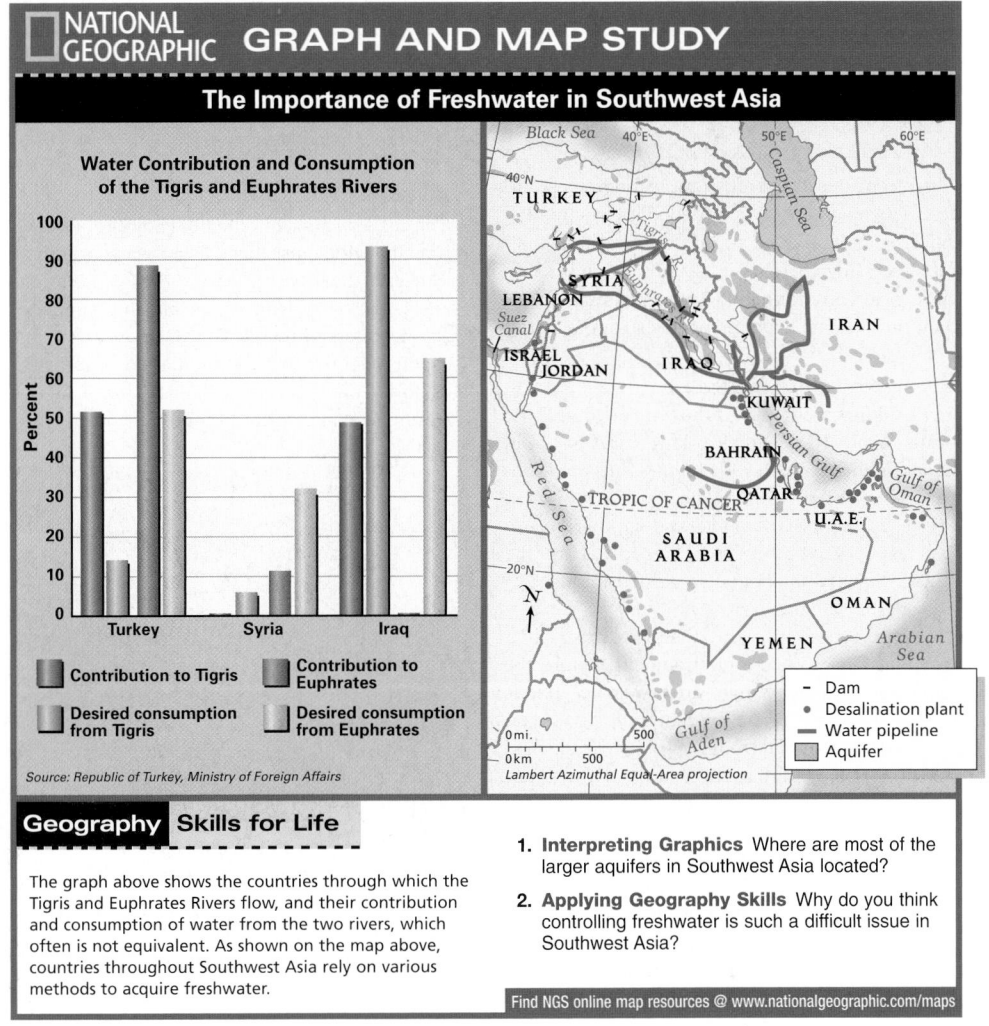

NATIONAL GEOGRAPHIC GRAPH AND MAP STUDY

The Importance of Freshwater in Southwest Asia

Water Contribution and Consumption of the Tigris and Euphrates Rivers

Legend:
- Contribution to Tigris
- Contribution to Euphrates
- Desired consumption from Tigris
- Desired consumption from Euphrates

Source: Republic of Turkey, Ministry of Foreign Affairs

Map legend:
- Dam
- Desalination plant
- Water pipeline
- Aquifer

Lambert Azimuthal Equal-Area projection

Geography Skills for Life

The graph above shows the countries through which the Tigris and Euphrates Rivers flow, and their contribution and consumption of water from the two rivers, which often is not equivalent. As shown on the map above, countries throughout Southwest Asia rely on various methods to acquire freshwater.

1. **Interpreting Graphics** Where are most of the larger aquifers in Southwest Asia located?

2. **Applying Geography Skills** Why do you think controlling freshwater is such a difficult issue in Southwest Asia?

Find NGS online map resources @ www.nationalgeographic.com/maps

NATIONAL GEOGRAPHIC   MAP STUDY

Answers

1. *Iraq, northwest Iran, Yemen*

2. *Water is precious in the region; disputes arise because rivers travel through several countries and cross borders.*

Map Skills Practice

Location Where does Saudi Arabia have most of its desalination plants? *(along its coast of the Red Sea)*

Chapter 19 471

COOPERATIVE LEARNING ACTIVITY

Water Resources Organize the class into three groups and assign one of the following water resources to each group: rivers, aquifers, or desalinated seawater. Have students research the region's water sources within their group's topic—that is, specific rivers, aquifers, or desalination plants. Have groups discuss among themselves how each source contributes water for the peoples of the region. Have each group present its findings to the class, using maps, diagrams, or other graphic aids.
EE5 Environment and Society: Standards 14, 15, 16

ASSESS

Assign Section 3 Assessment as homework or as an activity.

Have students use **Interactive Tutor Self-Assessment CD-ROM**.

L2

Section Quiz 19-2

[Section 2 Quiz — Chapter 19 — People and Their Environment — MATCHING: Match each item in Column A with an item in Column B. Write the correct letters in the blanks. (10 points each) Column A: 1. Libyan freshwater pipeline 2. ancient desert city that harvested rainwater 3. Egypt's main waterway 4. polluted region at the southern end of the Caspian Sea 5. site for control of flood and irrigation waters in Egypt Column B: A. Petra B. Aswan High Dam C. Elburz Mountains D. Nile River E. "great man-made river" MULTIPLE CHOICE: In each blank on the left, write the letter of the choice that best completes the statement or answers the question. (10 points each)]

NATIONAL GEOGRAPHIC World Explorer

Answer
controls the Nile's floods; irrigates about 3 million acres (1.2 million ha)

More About the Photo
The Aswan High Dam took ten years and over $1 billion to construct. It sits about 4 miles (6 km) upstream from the original Aswan Dam, built in 1902.

Reteach

With student input, make an outline of the region's water problems and possible solutions.

Enrich

Invite someone who served in the Persian Gulf War to share his or her views of the environmental damage caused by the conflict.

The "Great Man-Made River"

Libya's "great man-made river" is an ambitious effort to supply freshwater. This multibillion-dollar project uses two pipelines to carry water from large aquifers beneath the Sahara to farms near the Mediterranean. The first pipeline, completed in 1991, brings freshwater across eastern Libya to the coast, and plans are under way to extend the pipeline to other areas. A second pipeline, completed in 1996, carries water to areas near **Tripoli** (TRIH•puh•lee), the country's capital, from an aquifer in the west. Yet pipelines may create environmental challenges. Scientists fear that the pipelines could drain aquifers in Libya and neighboring countries and that pumping aquifers near the Mediterranean could draw in salt water from the sea, contaminating the freshwater.

Environmental Concerns

In recent decades both new technologies and destructive wars have heightened environmental concerns in the region. Today countries must balance accessing their natural resources with preserving the environment. Egypt's **Aswan High Dam** provides an example of this struggle.

The Aswan High Dam

In 1970 Egypt completed the Aswan High Dam, located about 600 miles (966 km) south of Cairo. Started in the 1950s, the 364-foot (111-m) dam controls the Nile's floods, irrigates around 3 million acres (1.2 million ha) of land, and supplies nearly 50 percent of Egypt's electrical power. To boost the fishing industry, the dam also created the world's largest artificial lake.

In spite of these successes, the project also had a negative impact on the environment. Before the dam's construction, the annual Nile floods deposited fertile alluvial soil along the floodplain and washed away salt from the soil. Now the dam traps the soil, and Egyptian farmers must use expensive fertilizers. The land also retains salt because floodwaters no longer cleanse the soil.

The health of people and their livestock also suffers. After the dam was completed, parasite-related diseases and deaths around the dam and downriver increased. With aid from other countries and international organizations, however,

Egypt is overcoming many of the difficulties created by the dam.

History
The Persian Gulf War

War in the region has also had a negative effect on the environment. During the Persian Gulf War, Iraqi troops retreating from Kuwait set fire to more than 700 oil wells. Huge black clouds of smoke polluted the area. Iraqi troops also dumped about 250 million gallons (947 million l) of oil into the Persian Gulf.

Scientists do not yet know what long-term effects these events will have. Thousands of fish and other marine life died when the oil spill spread 350 miles (563 km) along the Persian Gulf coastline. Smoke from oil-well fires threatened millions of birds. Oil pollution from routine shipping also adversely affects the Persian Gulf environment.

Nuclear and Chemical Dangers

Central Asia also inherited the Soviet era's environmental problems. Kazakhstan was once home to Soviet nuclear bases. During the Cold War, the Soviets tested nuclear, chemical, and biological weapons there. In 1989 it was found that this weapons testing had caused radiation leaks. Scientists think many years will pass before all the resulting contamination disappears.

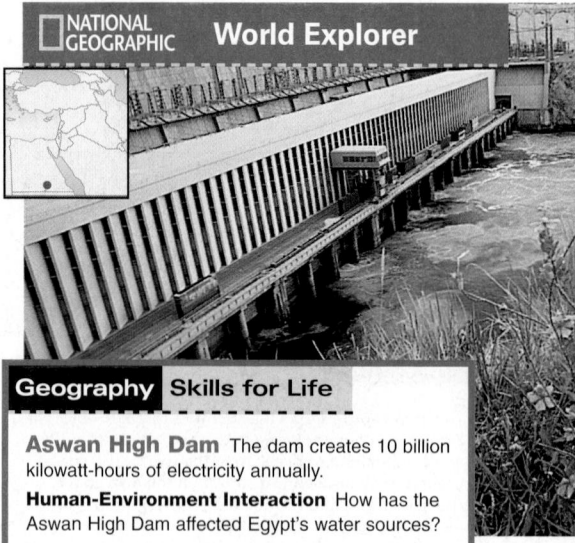

NATIONAL GEOGRAPHIC World Explorer

Geography Skills for Life

Aswan High Dam The dam creates 10 billion kilowatt-hours of electricity annually.

Human-Environment Interaction How has the Aswan High Dam affected Egypt's water sources?

CRITICAL THINKING ACTIVITY

Problem Solving Experts claim that water scarcity may someday lead to armed conflicts in various parts of the world. One factor contributing to the water crisis is rapid population growth and the increasing demand it places on available water supplies. Adding to population pressure is the continuing increase in water pollution. **Ask: What alternatives to conflict might countries take in dealing with their water problems? How might international groups help defuse disputes over water sources?** *(Answers may include negotiations and agreements toward sharing water resources, international monitoring of water agreements, and global efforts for desalination.)*
EE5 Environment and Society: Standards 15, 16

Soviet planners also chose Kazakhstan as a site for heavy industry, which polluted the air with toxic chemicals. Scientists have linked increased infant mortality in Kazakhstan directly to industrial pollution. The people of Kyrgyzstan, another site of Soviet heavy industry, have suffered similar effects.

Three Troubled Seas

The Caspian Sea, the Dead Sea, and the Aral Sea also face severe environmental challenges. Pollution at the Caspian Sea's southern end, near the **Elburz Mountains** of Iran, is especially severe. Pollution and overfishing threaten fish, like sturgeon, whose products are important exports.

The water level of the **Dead Sea** has dropped more than 262 feet (80 m) over the past 40 years. Ninety percent of the water from the sea's feeder rivers is diverted for irrigation and to hydroelectric plants. Scientists have suggested pumping water into the Dead Sea from the Gulf of Aqaba, but the $5 billion price is too high. To reduce the amount of water diverted from the Dead Sea, planners recommend building a desalination plant on Israel's Mediterranean coast.

Like the Dead Sea, the **Aral Sea** has had water diverted from feeder rivers to irrigate cropland. Once the world's fourth-largest body of inland water, by the year 2000 it had become separate, smaller lakes. These changes destroyed the sea's fishing industries, and dust storms have spread disease. People living by the Aral Sea are now working to revive their sea as a chain of lakes that can support fish.

NATIONAL GEOGRAPHIC   MAP STUDY

The Shrinking Aral Sea

0 mi. 150
0 km 150
Albers Conic Equal-Area projection

N

KAZAKHSTAN

— Shoreline in 1999
-- Shoreline in 1960
▓ Desert

Syr Darya

45°N

Aral Sea

Amu Darya

UZBEKISTAN

60°E

Geography Skills for Life

1. **Interpreting Maps** How has the Aral Sea changed since 1960?
2. **Applying Geography Skills** What factors have affected the size of the Aral Sea?

Find NGS online map resources @ www.nationalgeographic.com/maps

NATIONAL GEOGRAPHIC   MAP STUDY

Answers

1. *It has shrunk into separate, smaller lakes.*
2. *Water was diverted from feeder rivers to irrigate cropland.*

Map Skills Practice

Location What two countries are most affected by the Aral Sea disaster? *(Kazakhstan and Uzbekistan)*

④ CLOSE

Have students write brief cause-and-effect reports on various environmental concerns in North Africa, Southwest Asia, and Central Asia. Allow time for volunteers to share their reports with the class.

SECTION ② ASSESSMENT

Checking for Understanding

1. **Define** aquifer, desalination.
2. **Main Ideas** Re-create the web diagram below on a sheet of paper, and fill in ways the region meets its freshwater needs.

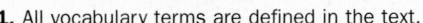

Meeting Freshwater Needs

Critical Thinking

3. **Drawing Conclusions** Have the effects of the Aswan High Dam been mostly positive or mostly negative? Explain.
4. **Predicting Outcomes** What problems might occur if new sources of water are not found for the region?
5. **Comparing and Contrasting** How are the problems facing this region's seas similar? Different?

Analyzing Maps

6. **Region** Study the precipitation map on page 470. What kind of vegetation would you expect to find in most of Kazakhstan? Why?

Applying Geography

7. **Planning for the Future** Think about the needs of this region. Write a plan to address its water needs in the future.

SECTION ② ASSESSMENT ANSWERS

1. All vocabulary terms are defined in the text.
2. Answers should include rivers, aquifers, pipelines, and desalination projects.
3. The negative effects are generally outweighed by the positive effects of flood control; continual irrigation which allows for a year-round growing season, and the generation of electricity.
4. Answers may include an increase in disease and famine, or even war.
5. All three seas have had water from their feeder rivers diverted for irrigation. The Caspian's main problem, however, is pollution. The Dead Sea and Aral Sea suffer most from shrinkage.
6. Short grasses, brush, and some trees as found in steppe climates; most of the area receives less than 20 inches of precipitation a year.
7. **Applying Geography** Answers may include plans for desalination plants and water pipelines.

Viewpoint
CASE STUDY on the Environment

1 FOCUS

Ask students to read page 474 and describe some uses of water. Have them hypothesize about the effects of widespread water loss to an area. List their speculations on the board.

2 TEACH

L2 Consider Both Sides

In this case study, have students identify and discuss both sides of the Euphrates water dispute. Ask them to explore both Turkey's needs and the concerns of Syria and Iraq, and encourage further research.

global issues

Shared Waters The Euphrates is just one river that has caused controversy between Southwest Asian countries. Syria, Jordan, and Israel, for example, have long-standing disputes over sharing waters of the Yarmuk River, which is a boundary between Syria and Jordan, and the Jordan River, which runs between Israel and Jordan. Damming, diverting, or draining the rivers concern more than just those countries that border the rivers. Countries downstream are often those most affected.

TURKEY *Atatürk Dam*
SYRIA
IRAQ
Tigris R.
Euphrates R.

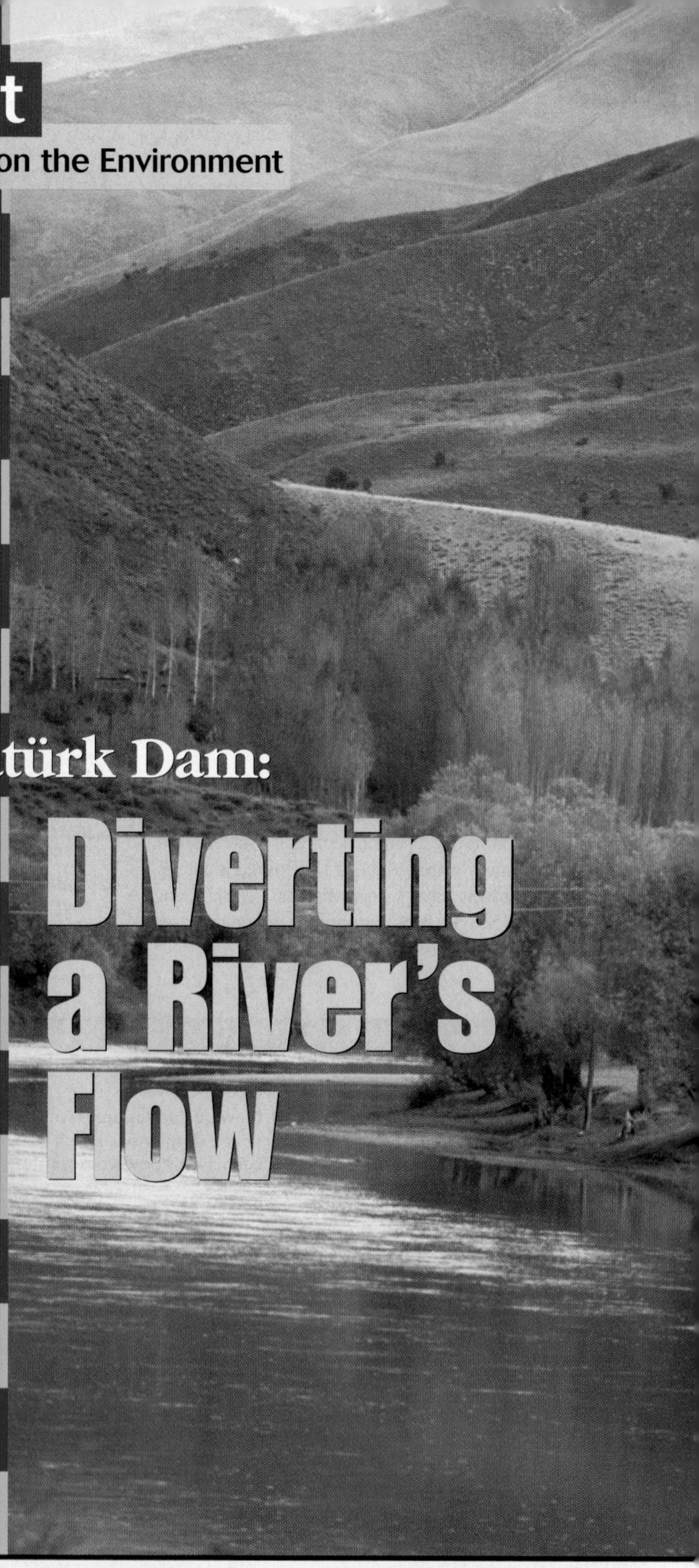

Turkey's Atatürk Dam:

Diverting a River's Flow

Rivers are the lifeblood of arid regions. As rivers wind through parched landscapes, they supply precious water to millions of people. Anything that disrupts a river's flow can be a threat to life itself. So it is with Turkey's Atatürk Dam on the Euphrates River. The Atatürk restrains the Euphrates and diverts some of its water for irrigation. For the Turks, the dam is turning barren plains into lush croplands. Downstream, however, Syria and Iraq worry that the Atatürk project will rob their countries of a vital lifeline.

474   Unit 6

LOOKING TO THE FUTURE

Needed Safeguards Along with irrigation problems and the reduction of water to Syria and Iraq, the Atatürk Dam poses potential disaster in the event of an earthquake. Turkey, which lies in an area of high seismic activity, claims that the dam has been built to withstand quakes measuring 8 on the Richter scale. But if the dam should ever break, the resulting flooding could be catastrophic. How can countries be protected from such dangers? Money is not always the answer. The World Bank refused to fund the building of the Atatürk Dam, but Turkey went ahead with the project anyway. Invite students to share their ideas and suggestions for dealing with the problem.
▦ **EE6 The Uses of Geography: Standard 18**

Like a silver ribbon, the Euphrates River (left) winds down through Turkey's Anti-Taurus Mountains. It skirts the western edge of the Harran Plain, then crosses the border into Syria. From Syria, the Euphrates flows into Iraq, where it eventually joins the Tigris River and empties into the Persian Gulf.

In the early 1980s, Turkey embarked on the Southeastern Anatolia Project, a plan to bring water from both the Euphrates and Tigris Rivers to Turkey's arid southeast region. The Atatürk Dam is the centerpiece of this massive irrigation project. Completed in 1990, the Atatürk is one of the world's largest dams. Water held in the dam's reservoir is channeled into two huge irrigation tunnels that lead to the Harran Plain 40 miles (64 km) away.

Eventually 21 other dams will be constructed along the Euphrates and Tigris Rivers. Nineteen hydroelectric power plants associated with the dams will generate about 27 billion kilowatt-hours of electricity

A Syrian farmer (below) relies on river water to grow crops. Turkey's Atatürk Dam (right) may reduce his share of irrigation waters. ▼

each year—about twice Turkey's current output.

Yet the project is creating tension downstream. People in Syria and Iraq worry that Turkey's dams will reduce the precious flow of water through their lands. They were outraged when Turkey stopped the flow of the Euphrates for a month in 1990 while filling the Atatürk reservoir. Despite Turkey's assurances that its southern neighbors will receive a fair share of river water, Syria and Iraq remain unconvinced.

Supporters of the Atatürk Dam claim that the Southeastern Anatolia Project will help Turkey expand its agricultural base and raise its standard of living. They note that every country has the right to control river water within its borders. Before the dam's reservoir was filled, Turkey increased water flow from the Euphrates for two months to prevent adverse effects to Syria and Iraq. Supporters say that while Syria and Iraq rely on petroleum deposits for energy, oil-poor Turkey needs hydroelectric power.

◄ Woman in Turkey hauls water to her family.

Opponents of the dam claim that once the Anatolia Project is complete, Syria's share of Euphrates waters could be reduced by 40 percent and Iraq's by 60 percent. Reduced flow will make it harder for Syria's hydroelectric plants to maintain current levels of production. Irrigation-based agriculture in both Syria and Iraq could also be jeopardized. Opponents believe that because the Turks stopped the flow of the Euphrates once, they may do it again—whenever it suits their needs. Archaeologists in the region also oppose the project because the dams are destroying unexplored ancient cities.

What's Your Point of View?
Does Turkey have the right to restrict the flow of river water to its downstream neighbors?

3 ASSESS

Have students answer the **What's Your Point of View?** question on this page.

4 CLOSE

Problem Solving Have students work in pairs to find out how the United States and Mexico have handled water issues related to the Rio Grande.

 NATIONAL GEOGRAPHIC **GEOFACT**

▶ There is about 30 times more groundwater in the earth than all the water in the world's lakes and streams combined.

Meeting National Standards

Geography for Life
The following standards are met in the Student Edition feature:

EE4 Human Systems: Standard 13
EE5 Environment and Society: Standards 14, 15
EE6 The Uses of Geography: Standard 18

WHAT CAN YOU DO?

Have students find out about the health of rivers that affect their state or community. If the rivers are polluted, have students explore the sources of pollution and find out what measures, if any, are being taken to clean the rivers. **Ask:** Are the waters being dammed or diverted? What other communities or states are affected by human alterations to the natural flow of the rivers? Have students write a letter to the editor of the local newspaper with suggestions for cleanup or correction of problems. ⦿ EE5 Environment and Society: Standard 14

Teaching the Skill

Have students read the lesson on page 476. **Ask: What is the purpose of a sketch map?** (It helps with organization and can display a wide range of useful information at a glance.) **Why might people's perceptions differ?** (People view places differently and would therefore place varying degrees of emphasis on different locations.) **What effects could this have?** (Sketch maps may have different focal points or show different streets or features more prominently and not proportionately.) Using an overhead projector, draw a sketch map—with input from students—of a familiar place in the community. Have students name and suggest placement of well-known sites. Make adjustments as needed.

Additional Practice
L1

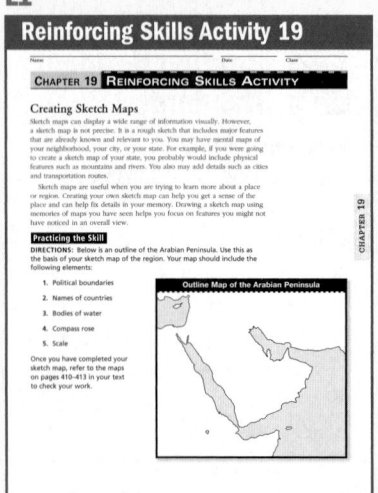

GLENCOE
TECHNOLOGY

 Glencoe Skillbuilder Interactive Workbook, Level 2

This interactive CD-ROM reinforces student mastery of essential social studies skills.

Creating Sketch Maps

While traveling, it is often much easier to follow visual images on a map than directions given in words. A simple sketch map can display a wide range of useful information.

Learning the Skill

Think about how you get from place to place each day. In your mind you have mentally mapped your route. You could probably draw sketch maps of many familiar places. Making mental maps and sketching them are also useful skills in the study of geography. They can help you remember and organize information about the regions you study.

To create a sketch map, follow these steps:

- **When a country or city name is mentioned, find it on a map to get an idea of where it is and what it is near.** Look for important features, such as highways, mountains, buildings, or bodies of water.

- **Draw a sketch map of the area.** Include a compass rose to show direction. Include these important features and political boundaries on your map.

- **As you read or hear information about the place, picture where on your sketch map you would fill in this information.** Add the information to your sketch map. Use colors and symbols to show different kinds of information, and add a legend, or key.

- **Compare your sketch to an actual map of the place.** Change your sketch if you need to by adjusting the locations of places or including additional information.

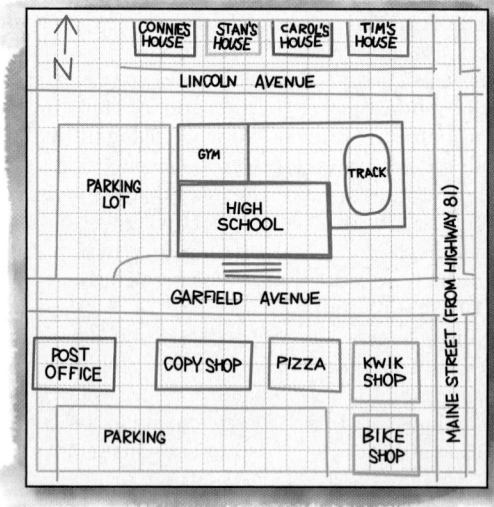

Practicing the Skill

Study the map above. Use it to answer the following questions.

1. If you are at the post office, what is the quickest route to Tim's house?

2. How many blocks apart are the bike shop and Carol's house?

3. Suppose your classroom is in the southeast corner of this high school. Could you have a view of the school's parking lot from the classroom?

4. Suppose you deliver pizzas for the pizza shop on Garfield Avenue. You have deliveries to the post office, Connie's house, the high school gym, and the bike shop. What is the best route?

Applying the Skill

Without looking back at this chapter, draw a sketch map that shows the locations of important physical features of the region. Compare your sketch map with other students' maps. How do your perceptions of the region differ? Compare your sketch map with an actual map of the region. Revise your sketch if needed. Then create three questions based on your sketch map, and have another student use your map to answer them.

 The Glencoe Skillbuilder Interactive Workbook, Level 2 provides instruction and practice in key social studies skills.

ANSWERS TO PRACTICING THE SKILL

1. Garfield Avenue to Maine Street to Lincoln Avenue
2. two
3. No.
4. Accept reasonable answers.

Applying the Skill Sketch maps should include a compass rose, important features, and political boundaries. Students should recognize differences between their maps.

CHAPTER 19 SUMMARY & STUDY GUIDE

SECTION 1 — Living in North Africa, Southwest Asia, and Central Asia (pp. 463–468)

Terms to Know
- arable
- commodity
- petrochemical
- gross domestic product (GDP)
- hajj
- embargo

Key Points
- Although North Africa, Southwest Asia, and Central Asia have limited arable land, a relatively large percentage of the region's people work in agriculture.
- The oil-producing countries in North Africa, Southwest Asia, and Central Asia have experienced greater economic growth than other countries in the region.
- Expanded and more advanced transportation and communications systems are helping connect the region's urban and economic centers with one another and with the world.
- Interdependence is increasing among the countries of the region, especially in controlling oil production and prices.

Organizing Your Notes
Use a chart like the one below to help you organize the notes you took as you read this section. Under each head, fill in the important supporting details.

Food Production	Industrial Growth	Transportation and Communications	Inter-dependence

SECTION 2 — People and Their Environment (pp. 469–473)

Terms to Know
- aquifer
- desalination

Key Points
- Countries in the region have modified their environments to meet people's needs for water for drinking and irrigation.
- New technologies and destructive wars have subjected the region's environment to stress.
- People are working to revive areas damaged by past events.

Organizing Your Notes
Create an outline using the format below to list ways in which the people of North Africa, Southwest Asia, and Central Asia use their environment.

People and Their Environment
I. Need for Water
  A. Water Resources
    1. Population

▶ Business district, Ankara, Turkey

Using the Chapter 19 Summary & Study Guide

Use the Chapter 19 Summary & Study Guide to preview, review, condense, or reteach the chapter.

Preview/Review

◉ **Vocabulary PuzzleMaker CD-ROM** reinforces "Terms to Know."

◉ **Interactive Tutor Self-Assessment CD-ROM** provides a review of Chapter 19 content.

Condense

Have students read the Chapter 19 Summary & Study Guide.

◉ Chapter 19 Audio Program

🗀 Chapter 19 Guided Reading Activities

Reteach

🗀 Chapter 19 Reteaching Activities (Spanish also available)

🗀 Chapter 19 Reading Essentials and Study Guides

GLENCOE TECHNOLOGY

▢ NATIONAL GEOGRAPHIC
WORLD REGIONS VIDEO PROGRAM

Unit 6, North Africa, Southwest Asia, and Central Asia
The following segments enhance the study of this unit:
- **Heart of Egypt**
- **Three Religions**
- **Oil Boom**

CHAPTER CULMINATING ACTIVITY

Write to Describe Have each student choose a country in North Africa, Southwest Asia, or Central Asia and write two paragraphs describing its economy or environment. Encourage students to use the Internet, current magazines and newspapers, and other resources for their research. Invite volunteers to share their paragraphs with the class.

🌐 EE2 Places and Regions: Standard 4
🌐 EE4 Human Systems: Standard 11

NOTE: This activity may be completed separately or you may wish students to incorporate it into their GeoJournals.

GEOGRAPHY *Online*

Have students visit the Web site at geography.glencoe.com to review Chapter 19 and take the **Self-Check Quiz.**

GLENCOE TECHNOLOGY

Use *MindJogger Videoquiz* to review the Chapter 19 content.

Reviewing Key Terms

1. aquifers
2. gross domestic product
3. desalination
4. embargoes
5. petrochemical
6. hajj
7. arable
8. commodities

Reviewing Facts
SECTION 1

1. by powering steel, textile, and electricity production in various countries
2. to limit unwanted foreign influences
3. Roads are the only access to the outside world.

SECTION 2

4. Libya's multibillion-dollar freshwater pipeline
5. Smoke polluted the area and oil polluted the water of the Persian Gulf; thousands of fish and other marine life died, as did birds.
6. diversion of feeder rivers

Critical Thinking

1. Countries without wealth from oil or other major exports cannot afford the materials and fuel needed for industrialization.
2. Opportunities range from favor-

Reviewing Key Terms

Write the key term that best completes each of the following sentences. Refer to the Terms to Know in the Summary & Study Guide on page 477.

1. Underground layers of porous rock, gravel, or sand that contain water are called _____.
2. _____ is the value of goods and services produced in a country in a year.
3. _____ is the process that removes salt from seawater.
4. Government restrictions on buying or selling certain goods are called _____.
5. _____ are products derived from petroleum or natural gas.
6. The _____ is the pilgrimage to Makkah made by many Muslims.
7. Land that is suitable for farming is _____.
8. Petroleum is one of the main economic goods, or _____, exported by the region.

Reviewing Facts

SECTION 1

1. How has natural gas helped advance the region's industrial growth?
2. Why do some countries in North Africa, Southwest Asia, and Central Asia discourage tourism?
3. Why is most freight carried by road in Armenia?

SECTION 2

4. What, and where, is the "great man-made river" project?
5. How did the Persian Gulf War affect the environment of the region?
6. What has caused the water levels of the Dead and Aral Seas to drop?

Critical Thinking

1. **Making Inferences** Why is industrial growth limited in some parts of the region?
2. **Analyzing Information** How does the region of North Africa, Southwest Asia, and Central Asia compare with other world regions in terms of economic opportunities for women?
3. **Identifying Cause and Effect** List examples of economic growth in the region and the effects of each on the environment. Then write a paragraph that explains the impact of one of them.

Examples	Effects on Environment

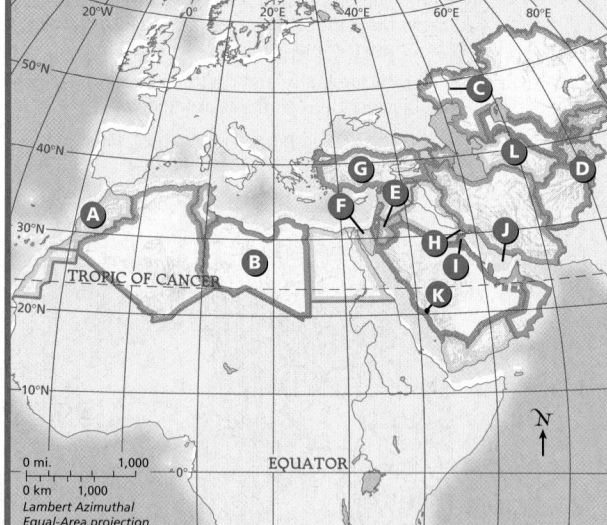

NATIONAL GEOGRAPHIC **Locating Places**

North Africa, Southwest Asia, and Central Asia: Physical-Political Geography

Match the letters on the map with the places and physical features of North Africa, Southwest Asia, and Central Asia. Write your answers on a sheet of paper.

1. Libya
2. Turkey
3. Kuwait
4. Shatt al Arab
5. Jordan
6. Morocco
7. Persian Gulf
8. Ural River
9. Hindu Kush
10. Sinai Peninsula
11. Turkmenistan
12. Makkah

able in Israel and Turkey to poor in Afghanistan. The less developed the economy, the less opportunities.

3. Answers may include that economic growth has provided money for desalination plants and has led further development of natural resources, which has sometimes polluted the environment.

NATIONAL GEOGRAPHIC **Locating Places**

1. B	**3.** I	**5.** E	**7.** J	**9.** D	**11.** L
2. G	**4.** H	**6.** A	**8.** C	**10.** F	**12.** K

Using the Regional Atlas

1. areas near the Mediterranean, the Red Sea, and the Persian Gulf

Using the Regional Atlas

Refer to the Regional Atlas on pages 410–413.

1. **Location** For which densely populated areas in North Africa, Southwest Asia, and Central Asia are desalination plants practical?

2. **Human-Environment Interaction** What is the relationship between the locations of commercial farms and water resources in North Africa and Southwest Asia?

Thinking Like a Geographer

Consider human-environment interaction in the region. How have people's views about the environment there changed since ancient times? How have these changing viewpoints led to changes in lifestyles? Give examples.

Problem-Solving Activity

Contemporary Issues Case Study Research an OPEC member country. Find statistics that illustrate how important petroleum and natural gas are to the country's economy. Share a written summary of your findings with the class.

GeoJournal

Cause and Effect Using your GeoJournal data and other resources, write an essay that compares an environmental trouble spot in North Africa, Southwest Asia, and Central Asia with that in another region. Focus on the relationship between technology and environmental change.

 ## Technology Activity

Using the Internet for Research On the Internet, search for an online news source with articles about North Africa, Southwest Asia, and Central Asia. Find a recent article about an environmental issue, and summarize the article. Be sure to cite source information on which the summary is based. Identify any biases, if present, in the article, and make sure the source is reliable. Then evaluate the impact of the issue on the region.

Standardized Test Practice

Choose the best answer for each of the following multiple-choice questions. If you have trouble answering the questions, use the process of elimination to narrow your choices.

1. **Imagine that you are hired to create a sketch map of Egypt to show the importance of the Nile River to Egypt's people. What combination of information would be the most useful to show?**

   A Coastal areas, mountains, and oil and phosphate resources

   B Population density, commercial farming, and deserts

   C Population density, subsistence farming, and city locations

   D Deserts, plateaus, and mountains

Test-Taking Tip Use the Process of Elimination (POE) to answer this question. First, consider the physical features, land use, resources, and population patterns near the Nile River. Then, eliminate answer choices that contain even one feature or resource that is not likely to be found along the river. Choose your answer from those that remain.

2. **What set of latitude lines would be best to use on your sketch map of Egypt and the Nile River?**

   F 40°N, 50°N, 60°N   H 30°S, 0°N, 30°N

   G 20°S, 25°S, 30°S   J 20°N, 35°N, 70°N

Test-Taking Tip Use POE to answer this question. First, visualize where Egypt lies in relation to the Equator on a map. Then, eliminate coordinates that are likely to be too far from Egypt.

Technology Activity

Check students' work to see that they use the Internet properly and can identify biases and reliability of the source.

Standardized Test Practice

1. C

2. H

Tested Objectives: process of elimination analyzing information synthesizing information

Additional Practice and Test-Taking Tips

 Standardized Test Practice Workbook

? CHAPTER BONUS TEST QUESTION

How have changes in transportation and communication affected the pattern of economic activities in the region? *(Improvements have overcome barriers imposed by deserts and mountains.)*

---

2. Commercial farms are typically located near rivers, aquifers, or major desalination projects.

Thinking Like a Geographer

Students' answers will vary but should include environmental challenges and the use of technology to meet them. Examples might include irrigation projects and the oil industry.

Problem-Solving Activity

Students' reports should include well-researched facts that support students' findings.

GeoJournal

Essays should show that students understand the environmental problems of the regions.

TEACHING TRANSPARENCIES

L2 Unit 7 Map Overlay Transparencies

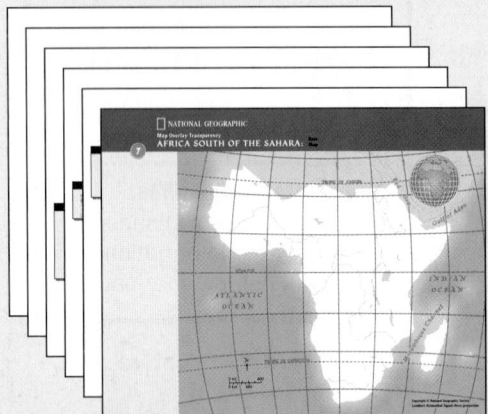

L2 Political Map Transparency 7

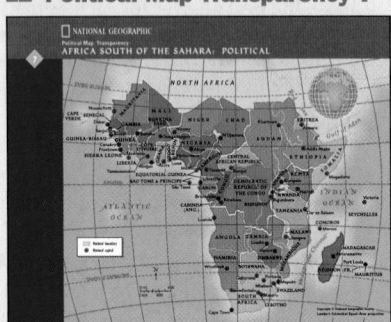

L2 World Cultures Transparencies 11, 12

APPLICATION AND ENRICHMENT

L2 Location Activity 7

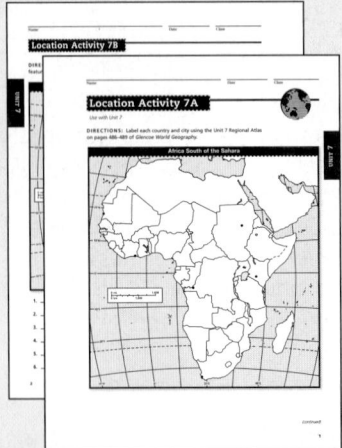

L2 Real-Life Applications and Problem-Solving Activity 7

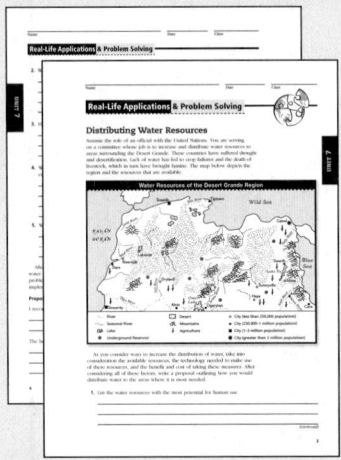

L2 GeoLab Activity 7

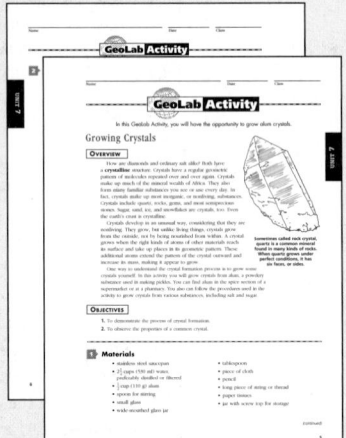

L2 Environmental Issues Case Study 7

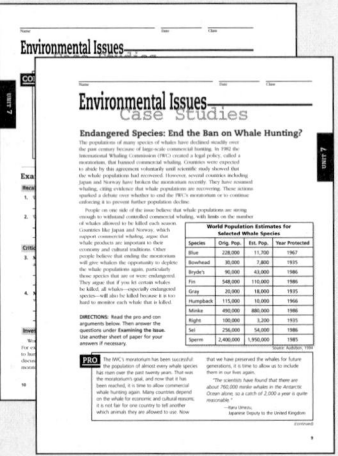

GEOGRAPHIC LITERACY

Focus on Geography Literacy

Building Geography Skills for Life

ASSESSMENT

Use the following to easily assess student learning in a variety of ways:

- Performance Assessment Activities and Rubrics
- Section Quizzes
- Chapter and Unit Tests
- Interactive Tutor Self-Assessment CD-ROM
- ExamView® Pro Testmaker
- MindJogger Videoquiz
- geography.glencoe.com
- Standardized Test Practice Workbook
- SAT I/II Test Practice

L2 Unit 7 Pretest and Tests

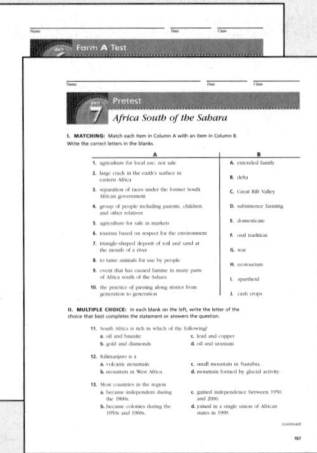

INTERDISCIPLINARY CONNECTIONS

L2 World Literature:
Contemporary Selection 7

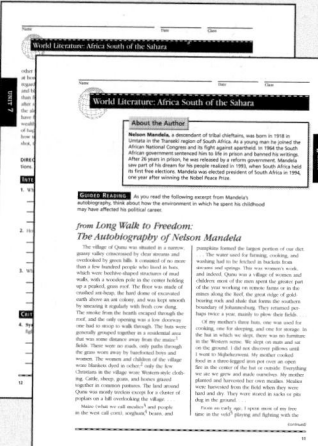

Foods Around the World

Multimedia

🖌 **World Art and Architecture Transparencies**

📖 **World Art Prints**

🎵 **World Music: A Cultural Legacy**

🌐 **World History Primary Source Document Library**

BIBLIOGRAPHY

Readings for the Student

Africa: A Biography of the Continent, by John Reader. New York, NY: Vintage Books, 1999.

Peoples of Africa. The Diagram Group. New York, NY: Facts on File, 1997.

Readings for the Teacher

Africa 2000, by Charles H. Cutter. The World Today Series. Harper's Ferry, WV: Stryker-Post, 2000.

Into the House of the Ancestors: Inside the New Africa, by Karl Maier. New York, NY: John Wiley & Sons, 1999.

Multimedia Resources

Okavango: Africa's Wild Oasis. Questar, Inc., 1996. Videocassette, 57 minutes.

East Africa, Tanzania and Zanzibar. Lonely Planet, 1997. Videocassette, 47 minutes.

READING SUPPORT FROM JAMESTOWN EDUCATION

- *Timed Readings Plus in Social Studies* help students increase their reading rate and fluency while maintaining comprehension. The 400-word passages are similar to those found on state and national assessments.

- *Reading in the Content Area: Social Studies* concentrates on six essential reading skills that help students better comprehend what they read. The book includes 75 high-interest nonfiction passages written at increasing levels of difficulty.

- *Reading Fluency* helps students read smoothly, accurately, and expressively.

- *Jamestown's Reading Improvement,* by renowned reading expert Edward Fry, focuses on helping build your students' comprehension, vocabulary, and skimming and scanning skills.

- *Critical Reading Series* provides high-interest books, each written at three reading levels.

For more information about these products, see the Jamestown Education materials in the Classroom Solutions in the front of this Teacher Wraparound Edition. To order these products, call Glencoe at 1-800-334-7344.

Background Information

The Physical Geography of Africa South of the Sahara

Africa south of the Sahara is dominated by a large inland plateau. In many parts of the region, this high, flat land falls in dramatic cliffs to narrow, unbroken coastlines having few inlets, large bays, gulfs, or natural harbors. In eastern Africa's interior, the plateau descends to the Great Rift Valley, a long, narrow break in the earth's surface that stretches through the region from the Red Sea to southern Africa. Formed by the folding and fracturing of Earth's crust over the last 60 million years, the valley area holds chains of sparkling lakes, such as Lake Victoria, Africa's largest lake. The valley's rich volcanic soil creates some of Africa's best farmland. East of the valley, rising above plateau areas, are lofty, snowcapped mountains. One of the most impressive of these is Kilimanjaro—Africa's tallest mountain, with a height of 19,340 feet (5,895 m).

Extensive river systems such as the Congo, the Niger, and the Zambezi—wind through Africa south of the Sahara. The Congo, Africa's second-longest river, and its tributaries traverse the vast rain forests of the Congo Basin, eventually draining into the South Atlantic Ocean. Awesome rapids and waterfalls on some rivers have posed obstacles to travel over the centuries. Limited river travel and few natural harbors isolated early African civilizations and made foreign invasions difficult in some areas. Rivers, however, have long been an important means of local transportation for people in the region, especially in areas where dense rain forest prevails.

Climate and Resources

Africa's major climate and vegetation areas can be roughly identified by the amount of rainfall each area receives. Early civilizations developed where rainfall was plentiful, or near lakes or along rivers. Warm, humid rain forests—so thick that sunlight cannot reach the forest floor—stretch across central Africa near the Equator from the Atlantic to the Great Rift Valley. To the north and south of the rain forests lie the drier savanna grasslands. Farther north and south of the savannas are semiarid lands and desert. In southern Africa deserts give way to a cool fertile highland rimmed by coastal plains having a Mediterranean-type climate.

Africa south of the Sahara is rich in mineral resources—fossil fuels, ores, and gems. The region also has an abundance of plant and animal species. The preservation of these diverse biological resources has become a global concern. Countries in the region, meanwhile, are working hard to achieve a balance between conserving habitats and meeting economic needs.

The Cultural Geography of Africa South of the Sahara

Fossil remains and stone tools found in sites in eastern Africa point to Africa south of the Sahara as the home of humankind's earliest known ancestors. Later, the development of agriculture and trade led to the rise of African city-states, kingdoms, and empires. These African civilizations left few written records of their achievements. Through oral traditions, legends, and history, early African peoples passed down knowledge about their cultures. Thus, archaeologists and historians have had to rely on these traditions and artifacts to learn about early African civilizations. African cultures developed technologies, such as iron making, and trade based on regional natural resources, such as gold. Civilizations rose and declined, and were influenced by the movement of peoples and by the way in which natural resources were developed.

Today, nearly 673 million people live in Africa south of the Sahara. Africans belong to many different ethnic groups, most of which are indigenous to the region. Language, religion, and ways of life unite members of each group and define ethnic homelands that cross the boundaries of the countries of Africa today. With more than 1,000 languages, communication among ethnic groups can be a challenge.

Millions of people in the region speak more than one language, however, and Arabic, Hausa, Swahili, and various European languages are used widely.

Movement and Change

From the A.D. 1500s to the 1800s, Europeans explored the African continent, enslaved many Africans, and sent them across the Atlantic Ocean to Brazil, the Caribbean islands, and the southern part of the present-day United States. By 1914 Europeans had divided nearly all of Africa among themselves. They often established colonial borders without regard to the different ethnic groups living in the area.

In many parts of Africa, however, Africans resisted European rule. By the late 1960s, most of Africa south of the Sahara was made up of independent nations. Descendants of European settlers, however, continued to rule the country of South Africa, carrying out the policy of apartheid that withheld many rights from black Africans and other non-Europeans. In the early 1990s, South Africa became a genuine democracy, extending civil rights and the right to vote to all of its citizens.

Since independence, African countries have struggled to forge national identities and to diversify and develop their economies. Saddled with colonial-era boundaries, many nations have diverse populations, often bitterly divided by their ethnic differences. In many countries, loyalty to an ethnic group is more important than loyalty to a national government. Ethnic

tensions have engulfed countries such as Nigeria, Liberia, Sudan, Rwanda, and Burundi in devastating civil wars. Meanwhile, economic hardships and the desire for a better life have drawn rural people to Africa's cities, now the world's fastest-growing urban areas.

CHAPTER 22 (pp. 536–553)

Africa South of the Sahara Today

Africans south of the Sahara today are the first to acknowledge the huge challenges their region faces. Improving standards of living, fighting diseases such as AIDS, raising literacy rates, and settling regional conflicts are among these challenges.

Over the last 30 years, African leaders have tried to promote industrialization while pushing the export of cash crops and raw materials. A lack of capital, skilled workers, and transportation systems, however, have stood in the way of industrial growth. Seeking to overcome these obstacles, African countries have turned to foreign governments and banks for loans to build factories, airports, harbors, and roads. With economies geared for export, many African countries have not produced enough food for domestic needs. As a result, their governments also have borrowed from foreign sources to buy food. Other causes of food shortages in Africa are drought, civil war, or misuse of agricultural and

grazing land. Population pressures have also taken their toll on food resources, although population increases are now being offset by the loss of life due to AIDS.

Regional Cooperation

Some African countries are joining together to deal with the issues that affect the region as a whole. One of the foremost cooperative institutions is the Organization of African Unity (OAU), founded in 1963. It promotes economic cooperation among members and tries to settle regional disputes and conflicts. Another African organization is the West African Economic Community, which supports joint economic ventures among members. These and other signs of international and regional cooperation have helped bolster Africans' hopes for the future.

Introducing Unit 7

00:00 Out of Time?

If time does not permit teaching each chapter in this unit, you may want to use the **Reading Essentials and Study Guide** summaries.

Unit Launch Activity

Prompt students to name countries in Africa south of the Sahara. **Ask:** **What do you know about life in these or other places in the region?** Have students share what they have learned about the region from news reports and other media sources. As they share their ideas, draw a K-W-L chart on the board and record what students *know* in the chart's first column. Have them copy the chart and list what they *want to know* about life in the region in the second column. When they have finished the unit, students may record what they *learned* about the region in the third column.

GLENCOE TECHNOLOGY

NATIONAL GEOGRAPHIC
WORLD REGIONS
VIDEO PROGRAM

Unit 7, Africa South of the Sahara
The following segments enhance the study of this unit:

- **Namib Desert**
- **Living With Elephants**
- **Baaba Maal: Musician of the World**

Available in DVD and VHS

UNIT 7

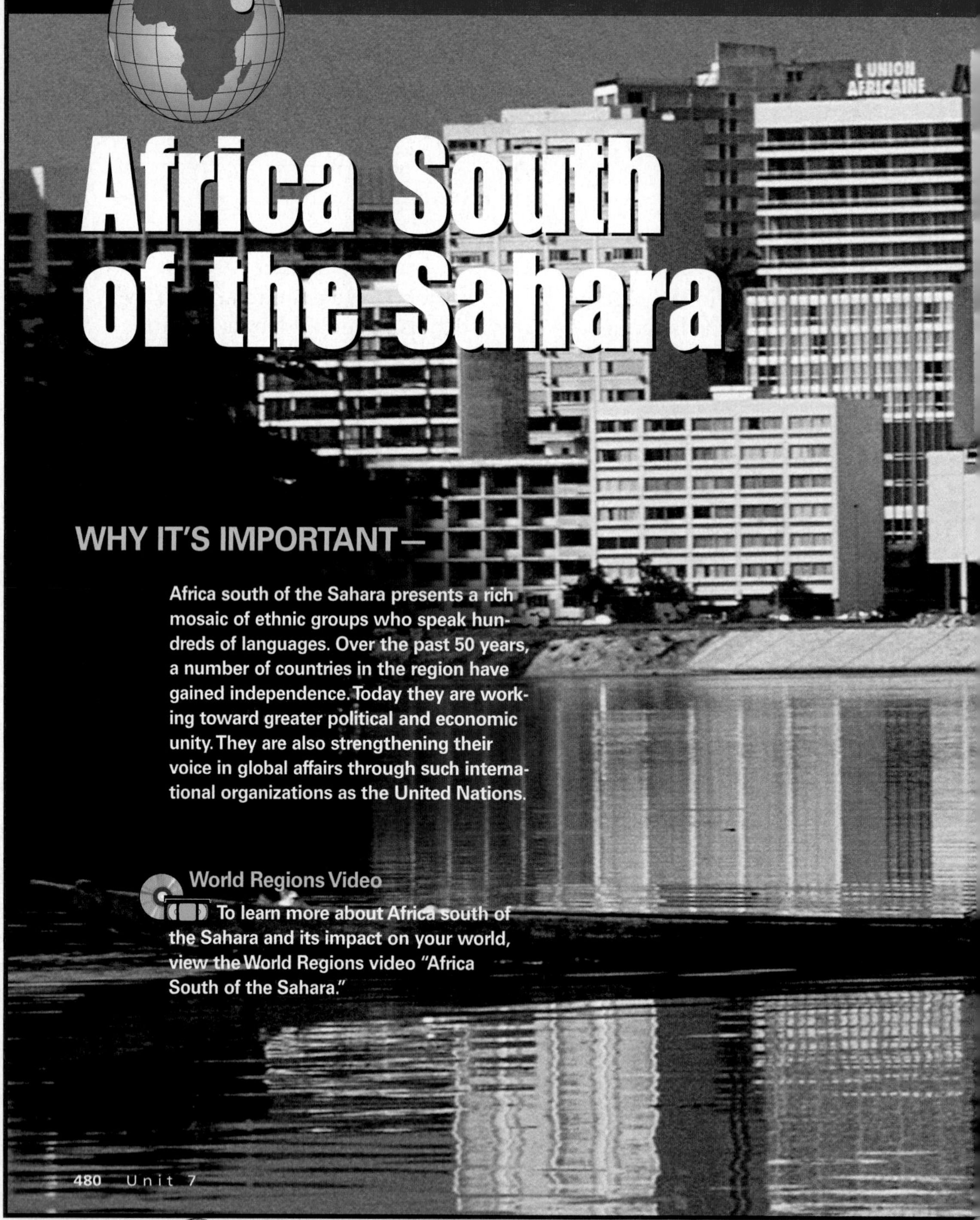

Africa South of the Sahara

WHY IT'S IMPORTANT—

Africa south of the Sahara presents a rich mosaic of ethnic groups who speak hundreds of languages. Over the past 50 years, a number of countries in the region have gained independence. Today they are working toward greater political and economic unity. They are also strengthening their voice in global affairs through such international organizations as the United Nations.

World Regions Video
To learn more about Africa south of the Sahara and its impact on your world, view the World Regions video "Africa South of the Sahara."

480 Unit 7

GETTING TO KNOW THE REGION

Map Activity Have students look at the maps of physical features and political boundaries of Africa south of the Sahara on pages 486 and 487. Display Map Overlay Transparency 7-5 and **ask:** **What major rivers are found in Africa south of the Sahara?** *(Nile, Congo, Niger)* **Where is Victoria Falls?** *(on the Zambezi River on the border of Zambia and Zimbabwe)* **What countries in the region are affected by the Sahara?** *(Mauritania, Mali, Niger, Chad, Sudan, Eritrea)* **What other deserts are found in the region?** *(Namib and Kalahari Deserts)* **What large island is part of Africa south of the Sahara?** *(Madagascar)*
EE1 The World in Spatial Terms: Standard 1; EE2 Places and Regions: Standard 4

Port city of Abidjan, Côte d'Ivoire

Unit 7   481

This online resource, brought to you by the National Geographic Society, provides lesson plans, atlas updates, cartographic activities with interactive maps, an online map store, and links to the boundless subjects of maps and geography.

Unit Overview

The first two chapters of the unit survey the physical and cultural geography of Africa south of the Sahara, and the third chapter provides insights about life in the region today. Emphasize to students that although many countries comprise Africa south of the Sahara, most share the following features:

- a tropical location and climate
- plentiful natural resources, including minerals and wildlife
- many ethnic groups with their own languages, religions, and ways of life
- a colonial history in the 1800s and 1900s

ABOUT THE PHOTO

Visual Instruction From small beginnings as a fishing village on the Atlantic coast of West Africa, Abidjan in Côte d'Ivoire has become a busy commercial and cultural center. In less than 100 years, Abidjan's population has grown to over 2.8 million. The city boasts many broad, tree-shaded avenues and public squares accented with gardens. Abidjan has a museum of traditional African art and is home to various research institutes. Coffee, cocoa, timber, manganese, and fruit are exported from Abidjan's deepwater port. **Ask: What does this photo suggest about life in Abidjan?** *(Possible answer: traditional ways of life continue to be practiced even in the modern cities.)* 🌐 **EE2 Places and Regions: Standard 4**
🌐 **EE4 Human Systems: Standard 12**

UNIT 7 REGIONAL ATLAS

① FOCUS

These features and activities may be used as an introduction to the unit or as teaching tools throughout the course of the unit.

L1 Using Flash Cards Activity

Before starting the unit, use the **Countries of the World Flash Cards** to preview students' knowledge of Africa south of the Sahara. Organize students into several teams and test their knowledge. At the end of the game, have students locate countries in the region on a map and provide a fact about each.

L2 Photo Research Activity

Direct students to gather additional information about the people, places, and activities shown in the photos on pages 482–485. Have students pursue their research independently or in small groups. Allow time for individual students to share their findings with the rest of the class.

What Makes Africa South of the Sahara a Region?

Straddling the Equator, Africa south of the Sahara encompasses about 9.5 million square miles (24.6 million sq. km) and nearly 50 countries. It is a region of immense plateaus that rise, like steps, from west to east across the continent. Several great rivers flow across this landscape. As the rivers journey to the sea, they cascade from one plateau to the next, creating spectacular waterfalls.

The Great Rift Valley, formed by the movement of the Earth's crust, slices through the plateaus of eastern Africa. Along the valley's rim stand some of the region's isolated mountain peaks, including the highest: snowcapped Kilimanjaro.

Most of this region lies within the Tropics. Closest to the Equator are steamy rain forests, second in size only to those of the Amazon River basin. At higher latitudes lie grasslands, home to many of Africa's famous wild animals. Beyond the grasslands, deserts stretch out under the fierce African sun.

1 **Sculpted sand dunes** rise in the Namib, one of Africa's deserts. The Namib lies in western Namibia, bordering the Atlantic Ocean. Eastern Namibia is home to another desert, the Kalahari, which stretches far into neighboring Botswana.

482 Unit 7

BACKGROUND INFORMATION

Kilimanjaro Three inactive volcanoes form Kilimanjaro. Kibo, the highest and central cone, rises to a height of 19,340 feet (5,895 m). Thousands of climbers each year try to scale Kibo, and many succeed, as no special mountain-climbing equipment is needed. Kibo alone has a permanent ice cap, but all three cones are blanketed with snow in season. German missionaries to Africa in 1848 at first were not believed when they reported sighting these snow-capped peaks near the Equator. Mount Kilimanjaro National Park, which includes the surrounding forests, teems with wildlife. The Chaga, Pare, Kahe, and Mbugu peoples live in the region surrounding Kilimanjaro, and grow crops such as coffee, barley, wheat, sugar, and sisal.
🌐 **EE2 Places and Regions: Standard 4**

② TEACH

L2 Physical and Human Characteristics

Help students distinguish between physical and human characteristics of a place. Then have them analyze how physical and human (political, economic, social, and cultural) characteristics define the place where they live. Finally, have students analyze how physical and human patterns and processes have changed these characteristics over time. Ask students to compare and contrast the causes and effects of changes in their community with those in Africa south of the Sahara.

GLENCOE TECHNOLOGY

▢ NATIONAL GEOGRAPHIC

WORLD REGIONS
VIDEO PROGRAM

Unit 7, Africa South of the Sahara

The following segments enhance the study of this unit:

- **Namib Desert**
- **Living With Elephants**
- **Baaba Maal: Musician of the World**

 Available in DVD and VHS

---

2 **Covered in mineral-rich mud,** a South African miner drills for gold. In the late 1800s, huge deposits of gold and diamonds were discovered in South Africa. Mining has made this country the wealthiest and most developed in the region.

3 **A rainbow dances** in the spray of Victoria Falls, on the Zambezi River. The river plummets 355 feet (108 m) as it spills over the edge of a steep cliff. The spray and the roar prompted local people to call the falls *Mosi oa Tunya*—"smoke that thunders."

4 **Like regal lords,** two male lions stride across an African savanna, or tropical grassland. Some savannas support huge herds of antelope, buffalo, wildebeests, and zebras, which are hunted by lions, cheetahs, and other predators.

Unit 7 **483**

A TRAVELER'S LOG

Mary Kingsley Journeying alone to West Africa in 1893, British explorer Mary Kingsley marveled at the biodiversity of the region. In her book *Travels in West Africa*, Kingsley writes: "Sometimes for hours we passed among thousands upon thousands of gray-white columns of uniform height (about 100–150 feet); at the top of these the boughs branched out and interlaced among each other, forming a canopy or ceiling, which dimmed the light even of the equatorial sun to such an extent that no undergrowth could thrive in the gloom. . . . From their far-away summits hung great bush-ropes . . . coiled round, and intertwined among each other, until one could fancy one was looking on some mighty battle between armies of gigantic serpents." ▤ **EE3 Physical Systems: Standard 8**

UNIT 7 REGIONAL ATLAS

L1 Ordering Events

Have students make a simple time line showing the major regional developments mentioned on this page. Then encourage students to discuss the chronology of these events. **Ask:** What was the first significant event in the cultural geography of Africa? *(the beginning of the human race)* When did it occur? *(millions of years ago)* When did empires first develop in Africa south of the Sahara? *(before the arrival of Europeans)* How long were Europeans active in the region? *(about 500 years)* When did the European colonial powers leave? *(in the 1900s)*

FYI

Incomes vary widely across Africa south of the Sahara. Gabon, one of the richest countries in the region, boasts an annual per capita income of about $6,500. Gabon's wealth comes from its oil and mineral deposits. By contrast, in Malawi, a poor country almost entirely dependent on agriculture, annual per capita income is less than $1,000.

Rich in Resources and Challenges

Many scientists believe that the human race originated in Africa millions of years ago. Ever since, the lands south of the Sahara have been home to diverse peoples, cultures, and empires. Europeans arrived in the 1400s and quickly began to exploit the region's abundant natural resources. By the 1800s, Africa was a patchwork of European colonies. Colonial rule ended in the twentieth century, leaving independent, but struggling, nations in its wake.

In Africa south of the Sahara, most of the people depend on small-scale agriculture or herding for their livelihood. Drought, disease, illiteracy, political instability, and poor transportation systems make economic development difficult in this region—the poorest of all world regions.

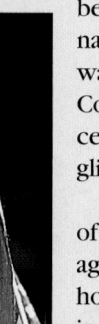

1 **A proud heritage** is reflected in the face of a young Afar woman. The Afar inhabit northeastern Ethiopia, an ethnically complex country in which about 70 different languages and 200 dialects are spoken. The nomadic Afar make their living by herding livestock.

484 Unit 7

BACKGROUND INFORMATION

Traditional Activities Ethnic groups in Africa south of the Sahara cherish special traditions. Among certain groups of the Nuba, who live in the remote and rugged hills of Sudan, ceremonial wrestling is a time-honored sport, going back generations. Teenage boys train as wrestlers away from their families and villages in special all-male camps. A boy's passage through the ranks of wrestling skill is marked by various rituals. When a young man reaches the highest rank, he may compete in tournaments with the best wrestlers from neighboring villages. ● **EE4 Human Systems: Standard 10**

L2 Cause and Effect

Prompt students to identify or hypothesize about the causes and effects of historical developments described on page 484. List their ideas in a cause-and-effect chart on the board.

Madagascar Most people on the island of Madagascar are of Indonesian origin. Their ancestors migrated across the Indian Ocean to Madagascar more than 1,000 years ago.

❸ ASSESS

Have students use what they have learned to write a paragraph about what makes Africa south of the Sahara a region. Tell students to name both physical and cultural characteristics that define the region.

❹ CLOSE

Have student pairs locate and read a news article about people, places, or developments in Africa south of the Sahara on the Internet or in a newspaper or magazine. Then ask students to summarize the main ideas in the article orally for their classmates.

❷ Mud-brick walls of an old mosque rise behind a busy market in Djenné, Mali. Five centuries ago, Djenné was a center of commerce and Muslim scholarship in the Songhai Empire, a wealthy and powerful trading kingdom.

❸ Table Mountain rises steeply behind Cape Town, in South Africa. The city was established in 1652 as a port of call for Dutch ships sailing from Europe to India. Today, Cape Town is an important shipping center as well as the legislative capital of South Africa.

❹ Waist-deep in tea plants, a Kenyan man picks leaves that will go into making one of the world's most popular drinks. Most farms in Africa are small, but Kenya has several large plantations that grow cash crops of tea and coffee for export.

Unit 7   **485**

UNIT PROJECT

Regional Conference Tell students that at the end of the unit they will participate in a mock regional conference of countries in Africa south of the Sahara. Have each student choose a country in the region to represent at the conference. Direct students to gather information about the physical features, ethnic groups, history, and government of their countries over the course of the unit. Explain that students will use the information they collect to make a brief presentation about their country at the conference. Then they will use what they have learned about their countries and the region as a whole to take part in a discussion of the challenges facing the region today and possible solutions.
🌐 **EE2 Places and Regions: Standard 4**

These features and activities may be used as an introduction to the unit or as teaching tools throughout the course of the unit.

L1 Comparing

Have students identify and locate the major physical features of Africa south of the Sahara. Then have them compare the physical map of the region with the population density map on page 488. Ask students to name the physical features that correspond to areas of low population density.

☐ NATIONAL GEOGRAPHIC **GEOFACT**

▶ **The dense reeds of Botswana's Okavango Delta harbor the tsetse fly. This deadly insect, which carries a parasite that causes sleeping sickness in humans and a disease called nagana in domestic animals, has kept large numbers of people from settling in the Okavango Delta.**

Elevation Profile

In order to show a variety of physical features, this cross section follows the Equator east from Gabon on the west coast of Africa, crossing the Congo River and the Congo Basin. It continues east to the Mitumba Mountains, through Lake Victoria, the Great Rift Valley, and Mt. Kenya, before ending in Somalia at the coast of the Indian Ocean.

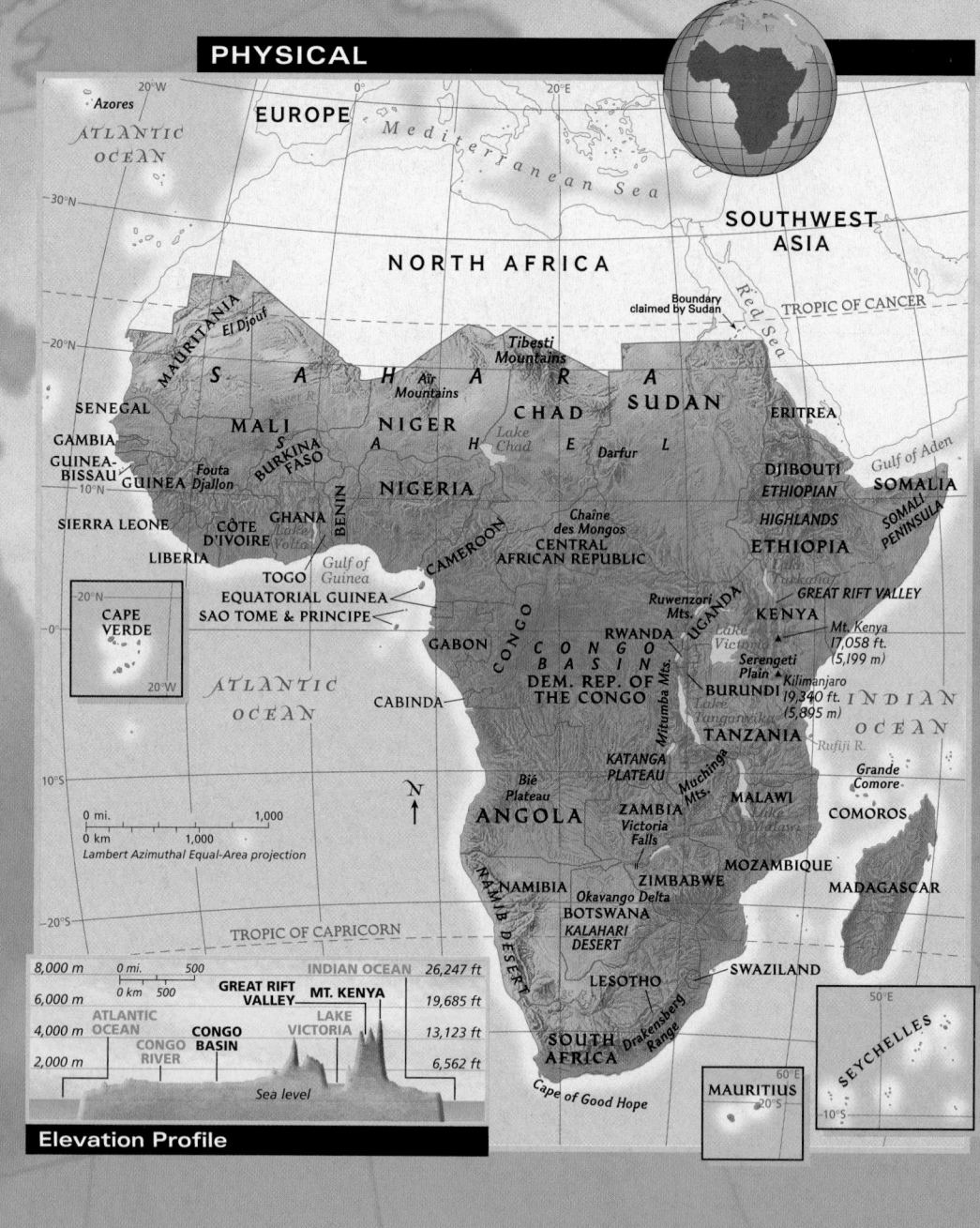

PHYSICAL

Elevation Profile

486   Unit 7

REGIONAL ATLAS ACTIVITY

Physical Fact Swap Allow two class periods or one block for groups of students to gather facts about the various physical features of Africa south of the Sahara shown on the map. They may use encyclopedias, almanacs, atlases, and other resources. Students should create a fact sheet for each feature as they find them. Then set aside one class period or block for a fact swap. As you name a physical feature or point to it on a wall map, call on each group to volunteer a fact. If another group has listed the same fact, ask members of that group to raise their hands. Continue to call on groups until they have exhausted their facts about a particular feature. Repeat for other features.

🌐 **EE2 Places and Regions: Standard 4**

POLITICAL

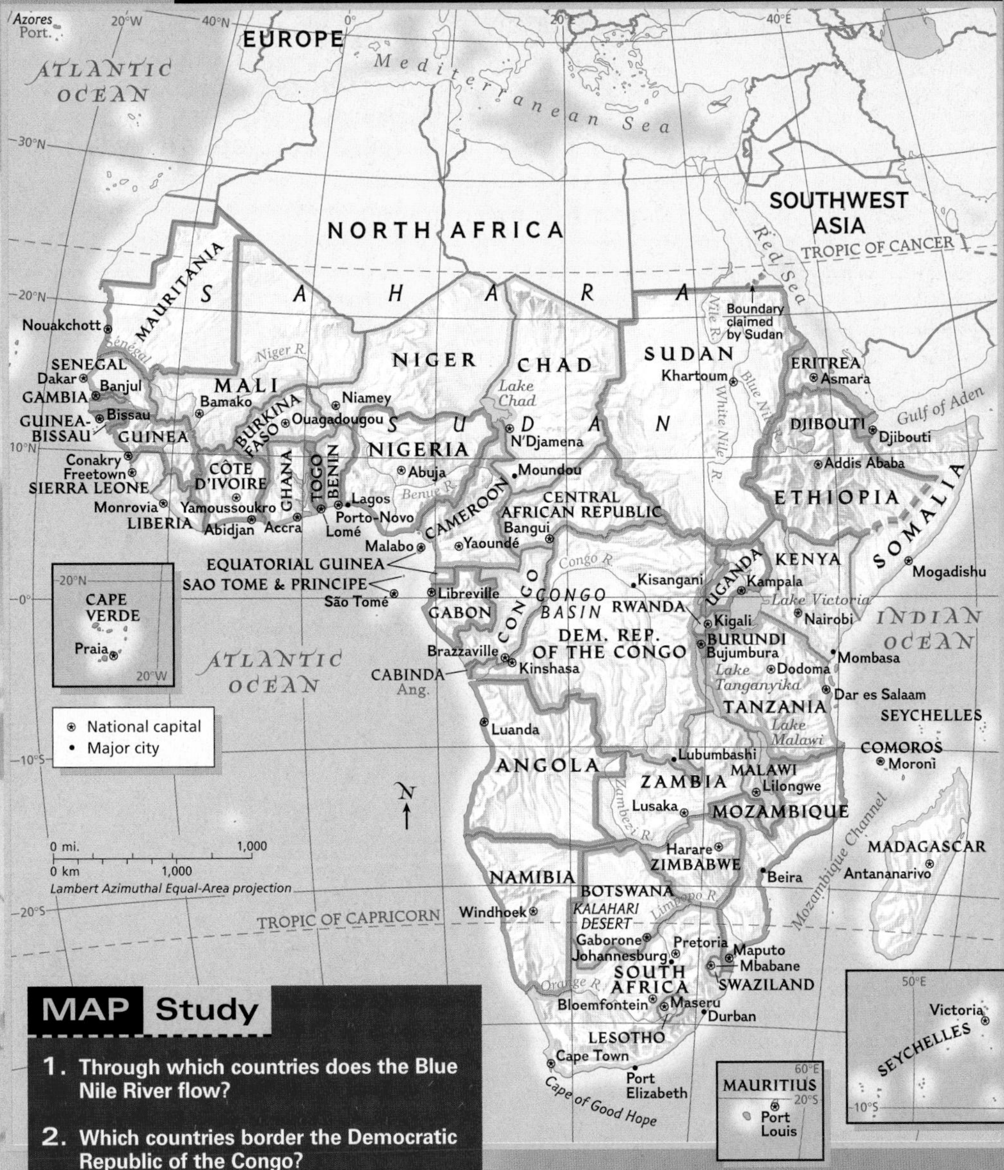

Azores
Port.
20°W   40°N   EUROPE   40°E   ATLANTIC OCEAN
Mediterranean Sea
30°N
20°N
NORTH AFRICA
SOUTHWEST ASIA
TROPIC OF CANCER
Nouakchott
MAURITANIA   S   A   H   A   R   A
Red Sea
SENEGAL   Niger R.   NIGER   CHAD   SUDAN   ERITREA   Asmara
Dakar   MALI   Bamako   Niamey   Lake Chad   Khartoum   DJIBOUTI   Gulf of Aden   Djibouti
GAMBIA   Banjul   BURKINA FASO   Ouagadougou   N'Djamena   Blue Nile
Bissau   GUINEA   NIGERIA   Abuja   Moundou   Addis Ababa   White Nile   ETHIOPIA
GUINEA-BISSAU   10°N
Conakry   CÔTE   GHANA   TOGO   BENIN   Lagos   CAMEROON   CENTRAL AFRICAN REPUBLIC   Bangui   SOMALIA   Mogadishu
Freetown   D'IVOIRE   Porto-Novo   Yaoundé   UGANDA   KENYA
SIERRA LEONE   Monrovia   Yamoussoukro   Accra   Lomé   Malabo   Congo R.   Kisangani   Kampala   Nairobi   INDIAN OCEAN
LIBERIA   Abidjan   EQUATORIAL GUINEA   Libreville   CONGO BASIN   RWANDA   Lake Victoria
0°   SAO TOME & PRINCIPE   São Tomé   GABON   DEM. REP. OF THE CONGO   Kigali   BURUNDI   Bujumbura   Dodoma   Mombasa
20°N   CAPE VERDE   Brazzaville   Kinshasa   Lake Tanganyika   Dar es Salaam   SEYCHELLES
Praia   20°W   CABINDA Ang.   TANZANIA   Lake Malawi
ATLANTIC OCEAN   Luanda   COMOROS   Moroni
● National capital   Lubumbashi   MALAWI
• Major city   ANGOLA   ZAMBIA   Lilongwe
10°S   Lusaka   MOZAMBIQUE
N   MADAGASCAR
0 mi.   1,000   Harare   ZIMBABWE   Beira   Antananarivo
0 km   1,000   NAMIBIA   BOTSWANA   Limpopo R.
Lambert Azimuthal Equal-Area projection   KALAHARI DESERT   50°E
TROPIC OF CAPRICORN   Windhoek   Gaborone   Pretoria   Maputo   Victoria   SEYCHELLES
20°S   Johannesburg   Mbabane   SWAZILAND   10°S
SOUTH AFRICA   Maseru
Bloemfontein   Durban   60°E
LESOTHO   MAURITIUS   20°S
Cape Town   Port Elizabeth   Port Louis
Cape of Good Hope

Unit 7   487

L1 Location

Have students use latitude and longitude to describe the location of cities or countries in the region. Students should estimate latitude and longitude where necessary. Students may also locate places by indicating what parallels and meridians cross or bisect them.

L2 Calculating Distance

Challenge students to use the map scale to calculate the distance of various places from the Equator and the Tropics of Cancer and Capricorn. Then prompt them to make inferences about the climate and vegetation of places based on their calculations.

MAP Study

Answers:
1. Sudan, Ethiopia

2. Congo, Central African Republic, Sudan, Uganda, Rwanda, Zambia, Angola

Map Skills Practice
Location Which countries are located on the Equator? (Gabon, Congo, Democratic Republic of the Congo, Uganda, Kenya, Somalia)

REGIONAL ATLAS ACTIVITY

Cultural Diversity Assign one or two countries to each student. Direct students to use various references to identify ethnic groups in these countries. Have students write the name of each group on a slip of paper. Provide a large wall map of Africa south of the Sahara. Have students read the name of each group and attach it to the appropriate country. As students make their contributions, have students keep a running tally of the number of different groups. After students have located all the groups on the map, make a final tally of ethnic groups that live in the region. Use the final total to stimulate discussion about what effects the large number of ethnic groups could have on the region.
🌐 **EE4 Human Systems: Standard 10**

L1 Making Generalizations

Have students examine the map of population density in Africa south of the Sahara and make generalizations about population patterns in the region. Remind students that to make generalizations they should combine information provided in the map with what they know from their own experience.

L2 Place

Ask: Why do so many people live in cities in Africa south of the Sahara? *(They want the services and opportunities available in cities.)* Then prompt students to use what they know about the physical features of the region and physical geography in general to explain why the following are so densely populated: the area north of Khartoum and areas along the eastern and southern coasts of Africa.

INTERDISCIPLINARY
connection

HISTORY Some place names in Africa south of the Sahara originated during the region's colonial period. Windhoek and Johannesburg (Afrikaans, primarily Dutch), Durban, Cape Town and Freetown (British) are a few examples of cities named by Europeans. Monrovia, the capital of independent Liberia, was named for U.S. President James Monroe, during whose administration it was founded.

Africa South of the Sahara

POPULATION DENSITY

Per sq. km / **Per sq. mi.**
- Over 100 / Over 250
- 50–100 / 125–250
- 25–50 / 60–125
- 1–25 / 2–60
- Under 1 / Under 2
- Uninhabited / Uninhabited

Cities
(Statistics reflect metropolitan areas.)
- ■ Over 5,000,000
- ▢ 2,000,000–5,000,000
- ◉ 1,000,000–2,000,000
- • 250,000–1,000,000
- ○ Under 250,000

Lambert Azimuthal Equal-Area projection

COUNTRY PROFILE ACTIVITY

Graphing Population Growth Have student pairs select two or three cities shown on the map on this page. Direct students to consult an almanac or other up-to-date resource to find population figures for different years for each city. Then have students design and draw bar graphs showing their results. Have students use the bar graphs in a discussion of urban population growth in the region. To engage students in the discussion, **Ask: By how much have city populations increased? Why do you think these populations are growing? How will countries' rural-urban population distribution be affected? What factors might slow—or advance—future population growth?**

⊞ **EE4 Human Systems: Standard 9**

NATIONAL GEOGRAPHIC

ECONOMIC ACTIVITY

Resources
- ◈ Diamonds
- ◢ Gold
- ◖ Copper
- ✳ Uranium
- ◆ Manganese
- ▲ Cobalt
- ⊡ Zinc
- ⚲ Petroleum
- ◢ Silver

Land Use
- Commercial farming
- Subsistence farming
- Livestock raising
- Nomadic herding
- Manufacturing and trade
- Commercial fishing
- Little or no activity

EUROPE

Mediterranean Sea

SOUTHWEST ASIA

NORTH AFRICA

Boundary claimed by Sudan

TROPIC OF CANCER

MAURITANIA

Camels

Camels

Camels

Pearls

Dates

SENEGAL
Dakar
GAMBIA
GUINEA-BISSAU
GUINEA
SIERRA LEONE
LIBERIA

Rice

Rice

MALI

Sheep

Goats

Cattle

NIGER

CHAD

SUDAN

Khartoum

ERITREA

DJIBOUTI

Gulf of Aden

BURKINA FASO

Peanuts

Cattle

Cotton

NIGERIA

Kano

Sorghum

Millet

Wheat

Goats

Fruit
Rubber
Coffee
Cacao
CÔTE
D'IVOIRE
Cacao
GHANA
TOGO
BENIN

Ibadan

Lagos

Cotton

Cacao

CAMEROON

CENTRAL AFRICAN REPUBLIC

Cotton

Addis Ababa
Corn
Coffee

ETHIOPIA

Sheep
Goats

SOMALIA

Abidjan
Accra

Douala

Cacao

EQUATORIAL GUINEA
SAO TOME & PRINCIPE

GABON

CONGO

Corn
Cotton
Rubber

Coffee

Kisangani

RWANDA

UGANDA

Tea
Coffee

KENYA

Kisumu
Nairobi

Tea
Coffee

Sugarcane
Bananas
Fruits

CAPE VERDE

CABINDA

Kinshasa

DEM. REP. OF THE CONGO

Cotton

Cotton
Coffee

BURUNDI

Cattle Cloves

Dar es Salaam

SEYCHELLES

Coffee
Cotton
Palm oil

Luanda

Sugarcane

TANZANIA

Tea Tobacco

Pearls

COMOROS
& Vanilla

ANGOLA

Corn

MALAWI

Cashews
Tea

Rice

MERIDIAN OF GREENWICH (LONDON)

ZAMBIA

MOZAMBIQUE

Coconuts

Vanilla

MADAGASCAR

Antananarivo

Cloves
Cattle
Rice

0 mi. 1,000
0 km 1,000
Lambert Azimuthal Equal-Area projection

N

Harare
ZIMBABWE

Coffee

NAMIBIA

Cattle

BOTSWANA

Bananas

Corn

Mozambique Channel

Coffee

Goats

TROPIC OF CAPRICORN

Sheep

Maputo
SWAZILAND

Johannesburg
Corn
Sugarcane
LESOTHO
Durban
Cotton
Sheep

SOUTH AFRICA

Cape Town
Port Elizabeth

MAURITIUS
Sugarcane

SEYCHELLES
Coconuts

MAP Study

1. What natural resources are located in South Africa?

2. What are the centers of manufacturing and trade in Africa south of the Sahara?

Unit 7 **489**

L2 Making Predictions

Before students look at the map of economic activity on this page, prompt them to recall the kinds of areas where mineral resources and resources needed for agriculture are usually found. Ask students to point to such places on the map on page 486.

MAP Study

Answers:

1. diamonds, gold, copper, uranium, manganese, zinc

2. Dakar, Abidjan, Lagos, Kano, Douala, Kinshasa, Kisangani, Cape Town, Port Elizabeth, Durban, Johannesburg, Maputo, Harare, Nairobi, Antananarivo, Kisumu, Khartoum

Map Skills Practice
Place How can you explain the lack of agriculture in parts of the countries bordering North Africa? (*The Sahara extends into these areas, and the dry conditions there do not support agriculture.*)

FYI

Camels are a source of milk, meat, and hides for nomadic herders and their families. An essential mode of transportation in drier parts of the region, camels are also used to cultivate land and pump water.

REGIONAL ATLAS ACTIVITY

Exploring Interdependence Have students use the map above to identify resources and agricultural products that the countries of Africa south of the Sahara might supply to the rest of the world. Then ask students to describe the transportation networks that might be used to export these items. Students should be specific, naming bodies of water, ports, and so on that might form part of such networks. Have students form small groups to investigate the worldwide demand for and supply of an African resource or product. Students should use both Internet and print resources to gather information and should display their findings on a poster, illustrating the resource or product, its uses, and countries importing it.
🌐 **EE4 Human Systems: Standard 11**

Africa South of the Sahara

These features and activities may be used as an introduction to the unit or as teaching tools throughout the course of the unit.

L1 Formulating Questions

Have students examine the "Country Profiles" on pages 490–495 and list any questions they have about the information provided. On the board compile a master list of questions, with each student contributing one question. Use the questions as a basis for the "Country Profile Activity" below.

The coast of Africa appears extensive, but at 18,950 miles (30,497 km) in length, it is actually shorter than the coast of Europe. Few inlets, bays, or gulfs cut into the African continent.

COUNTRY PROFILES

COUNTRY * AND CAPITAL	FLAG AND LANGUAGE	POPULATION** AND DENSITY	LANDMASS	MAJOR EXPORT	MAJOR IMPORT	CURRENCY	GOVERNMENT
ANGOLA Luanda	Portuguese, Local Languages	13,100,000 27 per sq.mi. 10 per sq. km	481,351 sq. mi. 1,246,699 sq. km	Crude Oil	Machinery	Kwanza	Republic
BENIN Porto-Novo	French, Fon, Yoruba	7,000,000 162 per sq. mi. 63 per sq. km	43,483 sq. mi. 112,621 sq. km	Cotton	Foods	CFA Franc	Republic
BOTSWANA Gaborone	English, Setswana	1,600,000 7 per sq. mi. 3 per sq. km	224,606 sq. mi. 581,730 sq. km	Diamonds	Foods	Pula	Republic
BURKINA FASO Ouagadougou	French, Local Languages	13,200,000 125 per sq. mi. 48 per sq. km	105,792 sq. mi. 274,001 sq. km	Cotton	Machinery	CFA Franc	Republic
BURUNDI Bujumbura	Kirundi, French	6,100,000 567 per sq. mi. 219 per sq. km	10,745 sq. mi. 27,830 sq. km	Coffee	Machinery	Burundi Franc	Republic
CAMEROON Yaoundé	French, English, Local Languages	15,700,000 86 per sq. mi. 33 per sq. km	183,568 sq. mi. 475,441 sq. km	Crude Oil	Machinery	CFA Franc	Republic
CAPE VERDE Praia	Portuguese, Crioulo	500,000 305 per sq. mi. 118 per sq. km	1,556 sq. mi. 4,030 sq. km	Shoes	Foods	Cape Verdean Escudo	Republic
CENTRAL AFRICAN REPUBLIC Bangui	French, Sango, Arabic, Hunsa	3,700,000 15 per sq. mi. 6 per sq. km	240,533 sq. mi. 622,981 sq. km	Diamonds	Foods	CFA Franc	Republic
CHAD N'Djamena	French, Arabic, Sara, Sango	9,300,000 19 per sq. mi. 7 per sq. km	495,753 sq. mi. 1,284,000 sq. km	Cotton	Machinery	CFA Franc	Republic
COMOROS Moroni	Arabic, French, Comoran	600,000 735 per sq. mi. 284 per sq. km	861 sq. mi. 2,230 sq. km	Vanilla	Rice	CFA Franc	Republic

*COUNTRIES AND FLAGS NOT DRAWN TO SCALE   **POPULATIONS ARE ROUNDED, *SOURCE: 2003 WORLD POPULATION DATA SHEET*

COUNTRY PROFILE ACTIVITY

Locating Information Have each student research to find an answer to the question he or she contributed to the master list of questions about data in the country profiles. Direct students to appropriate references: encyclopedias, world almanacs, atlases, and reliable online news and information sources. Instruct students to write their questions and the answers or relevant information they have located and the sources of the information on index cards. Students may share their findings in a bulletin board display titled *Africa South of the Sahara: Q & A.* Have students post their cards around a map of Africa and use yarn or string as leaders to connect their cards to countries on the map.
🌐 **EE2 Places and Regions: Standard 4**

COUNTRY * AND CAPITAL	FLAG AND LANGUAGE	POPULATION** AND DENSITY	LANDMASS	MAJOR EXPORT	MAJOR IMPORT	CURRENCY	GOVERNMENT
CONGO Brazzaville	French, Lingala, Monokutuba	3,700,000 28 per sq. mi. 11 per sq. km	132,046 sq. mi. 341,999 sq. km	Crude Oil	Machinery	CFA Franc	Republic
CONGO, DEMOCRATIC REPUBLIC OF THE Kinshasa	French, Lingala, Kingwana	56,600,000 63 per sq. mi. 24 per sq. km	905,351 sq. mi. 2,344,859 sq. km	Diamonds	Manufactured Goods	Congolese Franc	Republic
CÔTE D'IVOIRE Yamoussoukro Abidjan	French, Dioula	17,000,000 136 per sq. mi. 53 per sq. km	124,502 sq. mi. 322,460 sq. km	Cocoa	Foods	CFA Franc	Republic
DJIBOUTI Djibouti	French, Arabic	700,000 73 per sq. mi. 28 per sq. km	8,958 sq. mi. 23,201 sq. km	Hides and Skins	Foods	Djibouti Franc	Republic
EQUATORIAL GUINEA Malabo	Spanish, French, Fang, Bubi, Ibo	500,000 47 per sq. mi. 18 per sq. km	10,830 sq. mi. 28,050 sq. km	Petroleum	Machinery	CFA Franc	Republic
ERITREA Asmara	Afar, Amharic, Arabic, Tigre	4,400,000 96 per sq. mi. 37 per sq. km	45,405 sq. mi. 117,599 sq. km	Livestock	Processed Foods	Nakfa	Republic
ETHIOPIA Addis Ababa	Amharic, Tigrinya, Orominga	70,700,000 166 per sq. mi. 64 per sq. km	426,371 sq. mi. 1,104,301 sq. km	Coffee	Foods and Livestock	Birr	Federal Republic
GABON Libreville	French, Local Languages	1,300,000 13 per sq. mi. 5 per sq. km	103,347 sq. mi. 267,669 sq. km	Crude Oil	Machinery	CFA Franc	Republic
GAMBIA Banjul	English, Mandinka, Fula	1,500,000 344 per sq. mi. 133 per sq. km	4,363 sq. mi. 11,300 sq. km	Peanuts	Foods	Dalasi	Republic
GHANA Accra	English, Local Languages	20,500,000 222 per sq. mi. 86 per sq. km	92,100 sq. mi. 238,539 sq. km	Gold	Machinery	Cedi	Republic

*COUNTRIES AND FLAGS NOT DRAWN TO SCALE   **POPULATIONS ARE ROUNDED, *SOURCE: 2003 WORLD POPULATION DATA SHEET*

FOR AN ONLINE UPDATE OF THIS INFORMATION, VISIT GEOGRAPHY.GLENCOE.COM AND CLICK ON "TEXTBOOK UPDATES."

L1 Location

To help orient students, ask volunteers to locate the island countries of the region on a world map or globe. Have students tell the absolute location (latitude and longitude) of each country and describe its location in relation to the continent of Africa using cardinal or intermediate directions.

NATIONAL GEOGRAPHIC GEOFACT

The highest and lowest points in the region are located in East Africa. Kilimanjaro soars 19,340 feet (5,895 m) above the rest of the landscape in Tanzania. Lake Assal dips 515 feet (157 m) below sea level in Djibouti.

Culture NOTE

Cape Verde Islands Singing is a favorite part of social gatherings and celebrations in the Cape Verde Islands, where Portuguese customs and African traditions have blended to form a unique culture. The *morna*, a song form that captures the sorrows of love and leaving home, is heard only on these islands.

COUNTRY PROFILE ACTIVITY

Analyzing Economic Indicators Assign a country or two to each student. In two class periods, have students research a variety of other sources to obtain statistical data for each country, such as GDP, GDP per capita, sectors of the economy, and percentages of workers employed in each sector. Students may record this data on index cards. Then, in the next period or block, have students compare and contrast their findings, ranking their countries from most to least prosperous. Post index for the different countries in that order on a classroom wall. Follow up by asking students to compare the prosperity of Africa south of the Sahara with that of other world regions. ⊕ **EE4 Human Systems: Standard 11**

L2 Types of Government

Probe students' understanding of the different types of government found in countries in Africa south of the Sahara. **Ask: What is a republic?** *(a government in which representatives elected by voters govern)* Point out that in a federal republic the powers of government are shared between representatives elected to serve on the national level and representatives elected to serve on a state or provincial level. Ask students to name a country outside of Africa that is a federal republic. *(United States)*

INTERDISCIPLINARY
connection

GOVERNMENT Mauritania is an Islamic republic. Since 1980 magistrates and qadis (Islamic judges) have administered and enforced the principles of Shari'ah, or Islamic law, through the courts of Mauritania.

Dinosaur bones some 230 million years old have been found on the island of Madagascar. These gigantic animals roamed the island at a time when it was still joined with the continent of Africa in a huge landmass.

Africa South of the Sahara

COUNTRY PROFILES

COUNTRY * AND CAPITAL	FLAG AND LANGUAGE	POPULATION** AND DENSITY	LANDMASS	MAJOR EXPORT	MAJOR IMPORT	CURRENCY	GOVERNMENT
GUINEA — Conakry	French, Local Languages	9,000,000 — 95 per sq.mi. — 37 per sq.km	94,927 sq.mi. — 245,861 sq.km	Bauxite	Petroleum Products	Guinean Franc	Republic
GUINEA-BISSAU — Bissau	Portuguese, Crioulo, Fula	1,300,000 — 92 per sq.mi. — 36 per sq.km	13,946 sq.mi. — 36,120 sq.km	Cashews	Foods	CFA Franc	Republic
KENYA — Nairobi	English, Swahili	31,600,000 — 141 per sq.mi. — 54 per sq.km	224,081 sq.mi. — 580,370 sq.km	Tea	Machinery	Kenyan Shilling	Republic
LESOTHO — Maseru	English, Sesotho, Zulu, Xhosa	1,800,000 — 153 per sq.mi. — 59 per sq.km	11,718 sq.mi. — 30,350 sq.km	Clothing	Corn	Loti	Constitutional Monarchy
LIBERIA — Monrovia	English, Local Languages	3,300,000 — 77 per sq.mi. — 20 per sq.km	43,000 sq.mi. — 111,370 sq.km	Diamonds	Natural Gas	Liberian Dollar	Republic
MADAGASCAR — Antananarivo	French, Malagasy	17,000,000 — 75 per sq.mi. — 29 per sq.km	226,656 sq.mi. — 587,039 sq.km	Coffee	Machinery	Malagasy Franc	Republic
MALAWI — Lilongwe	Chewa, English	11,700,000 — 255 per sq.mi. — 98 per sq.km	45,745 sq.mi. — 118,480 sq.km	Tobacco	Foods	Kwacha	Republic
MALI — Bamako	French, Bambara	11,600,000 — 24 per sq.mi. — 9 per sq.km	478,838 sq.mi. — 1,240,190 sq.km	Cotton	Machinery	CFA Franc	Republic
MAURITANIA — Nouakchott	Hasaniya Arabic, Wolof	2,900,000 — 7 per sq.mi. — 3 per sq.km	395,954 sq.mi. — 1,025,521 sq.km	Fish	Foods	Ouguiya	Islamic Republic
MAURITIUS — Port Louis	English, Creole, Bhojpuri, French	1,200,000 — 1,550 per sq.mi. — 598 per sq.km	788 sq.mi. — 2,041 sq.km	Sugar	Foods	Mauritian Rupee	Republic

*COUNTRIES AND FLAGS NOT DRAWN TO SCALE   **POPULATIONS ARE ROUNDED, *SOURCE: 2003 WORLD POPULATION DATA SHEET*

COUNTRY PROFILE ACTIVITY

Gauging Health Have students research health statistics for one or two countries in the region (perhaps the same countries they investigated in the activity on page 491). Instruct students to record each country's birthrate, infant mortality rate, life expectancy, and any other health characteristics of the population on a sheet of paper with the head *[Country Name]: Bill of Health.* Then moderate a health forum in which students compare and contrast the data they have gathered and decide on criteria for ranking the countries. Conclude the forum with a discussion of the possible connections between each country's economic profile and the health of its population.   ■ **EE2 Places and Regions: Standard 4**

COUNTRY * AND CAPITAL	FLAG AND LANGUAGE	POPULATION** AND DENSITY	LANDMASS	MAJOR EXPORT	MAJOR IMPORT	CURRENCY	GOVERNMENT
MOZAMBIQUE Maputo	Portuguese, Local Languages	17,500,000 56 per sq.mi. 22 per sq.km	309,494 sq.mi. 801,590 sq.km	Cashews	Foods	Metical	Republic
NAMIBIA Windhoek	English, Afrikaans, Local Languages	1,900,000 6 per sq.mi. 2 per sq.km	318,259 sq.mi. 824,291 sq.km	Diamonds	Construction Materials	Namibian Dollar	Republic
NIGER Niamey	French, Hausa, Djerma	12,100,000 25 per sq.mi. 10 per sq.km	489,189 sq.mi. 1,267,000 sq.km	Uranium	Manufactured Goods	CFA Franc	Republic
NIGERIA Abuja	English, Hausa, Yoruba, Igbo	133,900,000 375 per sq.mi. 145 per sq.km	356,668 sq.mi. 923,770 sq.km	Petroleum	Machinery	Naira	Federal Republic
RWANDA Kigali	Kinyarwanda, French, English	8,300,000 817 per sq.mi. 315 per sq.km	10,170 sq.mi. 26,340 sq.km	Coffee	Foods	Rwanda Franc	Republic
SAO TOME AND PRINCIPE São Tomé	Portuguese, Crioulo	200,000 475 per sq.mi. 183 per sq.km	371 sq.mi. 961 sq.km	Cocoa	Textiles	Dobra	Republic
SENEGAL Dakar	French, Wolof, Pulaar, Diola	10,600,000 139 per sq.mi. 54 per sq.km	75,954 sq.mi. 196,721 sq.km	Fish	Foods	CFA Franc	Republic
SEYCHELLES Victoria	English, French, Creole	100,000 501 per sq.mi. 193 per sq.km	174 sq.mi. 451 sq.km	Fish	Foods	Seychelles Rupee	Republic
SIERRA LEONE Freetown	English, Mende, Temne, Krio	5,700,000 207 per sq.mi. 80 per sq.km	27,699 sq.mi. 71,740 sq.km	Diamonds	Foods	Leone	Republic
SOMALIA Mogadishu	Somali, Arabic	8,000,000 33 per sq.mi. 13 per sq.km	246,201 sq.mi. 637,661 sq.km	Livestock	Textiles	Somali Shilling	Republic

*COUNTRIES AND FLAGS NOT DRAWN TO SCALE   **POPULATIONS ARE ROUNDED, SOURCE: 2003 WORLD POPULATION DATA SHEET

FOR AN ONLINE UPDATE OF THIS INFORMATION, VISIT GEOGRAPHY.GLENCOE.COM AND CLICK ON "TEXTBOOK UPDATES."

L2 Drawing Conclusions

Have students draw conclusions about the status of different countries in the region during the colonial period based on the language information provided in the country profiles. Call on students at random to identify the European power that claimed a particular African country as a colony.

Nigeria City living has always been popular in what is now Nigeria. People crowded the urban centers of Kano, Katsina, and Zaria as early as the eleventh century. Benin City was a booming metropolitan area in the late 1500s.

□ NATIONAL GEOGRAPHIC **GEOFACT**

▶ The city and valley of Great Zimbabwe may have supported a population of 20,000 people between A.D. 1100 and 1500. The Shona trading empire's economy relied on cattle, crop farming, and gold trading on Africa's east coast. The word *zimbabwe* means "stone houses."

COUNTRY PROFILE ACTIVITY

Rating Education Have students find out the literacy rate, education levels and opportunities in one or two countries in the region. (Students may continue to research the same countries assigned previously, adding new information to the data they have already gathered.) Direct students to use the information they find to make a report card for each country. After students have presented their report cards to the rest of the class, ask them to speculate on the relationship between economic and health conditions in each country and its educational profile. Encourage students to predict how higher literacy rates and increased educational opportunities might affect the countries' economies and the health of their populations. 🔳 🌐 **EE2 Places and Regions: Standard 4**

L2 Population Density

Ask: Which is the most densely populated country in the region? *(Mauritius)* The least densely populated country? *(Namibia)* Prompt students to suggest reasons for the high and low population densities of these countries.

Culture NOTE

Sudan Many West Africans of Fulani, Hausa, and Borno background have relocated to Sudan to work on cotton farms. These West African immigrants, known as the Fellata in Sudan, form a large minority group.

Triangular trade is the term for the trade network that linked enslaved Africans, plantations in the Americas, and European manufacturing. The triangular trade benefited the British, French, and Dutch economies from the late 1600s through the 1700s, when it reached its peak.

UNIT 7 REGIONAL ATLAS

Africa South of the Sahara

COUNTRY PROFILES

COUNTRY * AND CAPITAL	FLAG AND LANGUAGE	POPULATION** AND DENSITY	LANDMASS	MAJOR EXPORT	MAJOR IMPORT	CURRENCY	GOVERNMENT
SOUTH AFRICA Pretoria Bloemfontein Cape Town	Afrikaans, English, Zulu	44,000,000 93 per sq.mi. 36 per sq.km	471,444 sq.mi. 1,221,038 sq.km	Gold	Transport Equipment	Rand	Republic
SUDAN Khartoum	Arabic, Nubian, Ta Bedawie	38,100,000 39 per sq.mi. 15 per sq.km	967,494 sq.mi. 2,505,809 sq.km	Cotton	Petroleum Products	Sudanese Pound	Republic
SWAZILAND Mbabane	English, Swazi	1,200,000 173 per sq.mi. 67 per sq.km	6,703 sq.mi. 17,361 sq.km	Soft Drink Concentrates	Machinery	Lilangeni	Monarchy
TANZANIA Dodoma Dar es Salaam	Swahili, English	35,400,000 97 per sq.mi. 38 per sq.km	364,900 sq.mi. 945,087 sq.km	Coffee	Machinery	Tanzanian Shilling	Republic
TOGO Lomé	French, Ewe, Mina, Kabye	5,400,000 248 per sq.mi. 96 per sq.km	21,927 sq.mi. 56,791 sq.km	Phosphates	Manufactured Goods	CFA Franc	Republic
UGANDA Kampala	English, Ganda	25,300,000 271 per sq.mi. 105 per sq.km	93,066 sq.mi. 241,041 sq.km	Coffee	Machinery	Ugandan Shilling	Republic
ZAMBIA Lusaka	English, Local Languages	10,400,000 37 per sq.mi. 14 per sq.km	290,583 sq.mi. 752,610 sq.km	Copper	Manufactured Goods	Kwacha	Republic
ZIMBABWE Harare	English, Shona, Sindebele	12,600,000 83 per sq.mi. 32 per sq.km	150,873 sq.mi. 390,761 sq.km	Gold	Machinery	Zimbabwean Dollar	Republic

*COUNTRIES AND FLAGS NOT DRAWN TO SCALE   **POPULATIONS ARE ROUNDED, *SOURCE: 2003 WORLD POPULATION DATA SHEET*

FOR AN ONLINE UPDATE OF THIS INFORMATION, VISIT GEOGRAPHY.GLENCOE.COM AND CLICK ON "TEXTBOOK UPDATES."

▶ Crowd in Burundi market wearing colorful traditional clothing

COUNTRY PROFILE ACTIVITY

Identifying Issues Ask students to review the statistics they have collected in the previous activities. Then challenge them to identify problems or issues they think all or most countries in Africa south of the Sahara face. List the problems or issues on the board as students suggest them. Have students make a two-column chart on a sheet of paper, copying the list of issues in the first column. As they proceed through the unit, have students make notes in the second column when they discover through their reading and study that the issues identified in the first column match issues the region's leaders and people are actually encountering and dealing with. ▦ **EE6 The Uses of Geography: Standard 18**

L3 Making Inferences

Challenge students to make observations about economic development in the countries listed. Students should use the information supplied about exports and imports and their own knowledge to make inferences about economic conditions in selected countries. Discuss factors that may affect the economies of these countries.

FYI

Togo has a very young population. Almost half the population is less than 15 years old.

INTERDISCIPLINARY connection

THE ARTS Storytelling is a popular art form in Africa south of the Sahara. Storytellers use pitch, pacing, and a variety of sound effects to entertain their audience. Those listening often respond with comments and their own sound effects and sing the songs that accompany many stories. Tales about animal-tricksters, such as Anansi the spider, and myths explaining natural phenomena have been popular for generations.

Unit 7 495

COUNTRY PROFILE ACTIVITY

Interpreting Symbols Direct students to appropriate resources to research the flags of countries in the region. (Students may investigate a flag that interests them, the flag of the country they will represent in the regional conference for the Unit Project, or the flags of the countries assigned in previous country profile activities.) Students should find out when the flag was adopted and the meaning of the symbols and colors used on it. Have students make a replica of the flag on poster board with markers, paint, or construction paper. Tell students to record the name of the country, the date of the flag's adoption, and an interpretation of the flag on the reverse of the flag. Display the flags so that students can learn about each one. ⊕ EE4 Human Systems: Standard 10

① FOCUS

Write the word *jazz* on the board. **Ask:** What does this word mean to you? Organize students' ideas in a concept map around the word *jazz.*

② TEACH

Active Listening Play selections from various recordings of jazz for students. Works by Louis Armstrong, Duke Ellington, Ella Fitzgerald, and John Coltrane are good introductions to jazz music. **Ask:** How would you describe *jazz music?* Discuss the sounds of jazz and the subjects of jazz lyrics. Help students identify African elements in the music: strong rhythms, different beats on top of each other, call-and-response patterns, sliding-pitch tones, and improvisation. **Ask:** What kinds of music today do you think compare to jazz? *(rap, hip-hop)*

Meeting National Standards

Geography for Life
The following standards are met in the Student Edition:

EE4 Human Systems:
    Standards 9, 10, 12
EE6 The Uses of Geography:
    Standard 17

GLOBAL CONNECTION

AFRICA SOUTH OF THE SAHARA AND THE UNITED STATES

ROOTS OF JAZZ

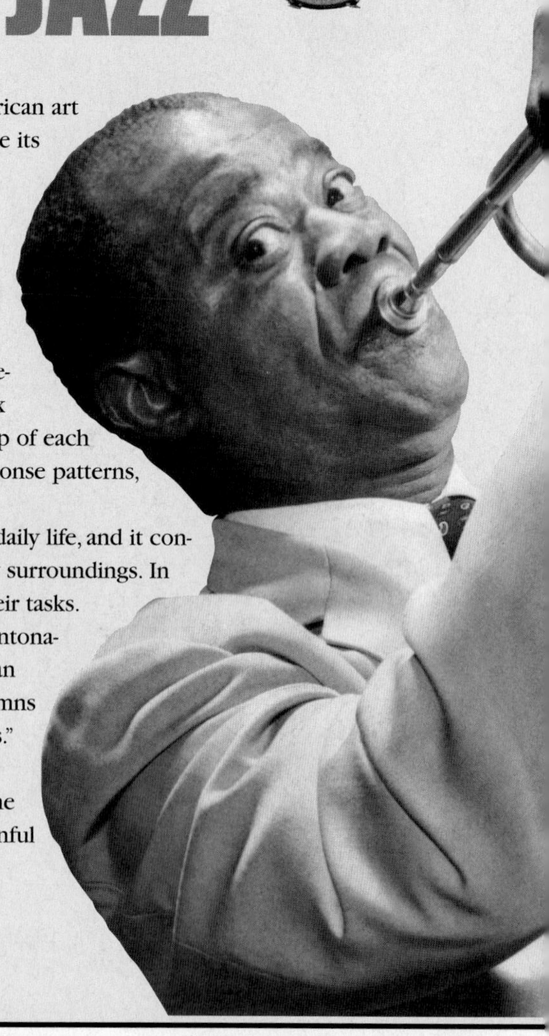

It's been called the only truly American art form. However, jazz music can trace its roots straight back to Africa.

Beginning in the 1600s, thousands of black Africans, mostly from West Africa, were forcibly brought to the American colonies as slaves. Torn from their homelands, these enslaved Africans held tightly to the only possessions they retained—their cultural traditions, especially their music. That music had strong, complex rhythms, with layers of different beats built on top of each other. Other characteristics included call-and-response patterns, sliding-pitch tones, and improvisation.

In Africa, music had been an essential part of daily life, and it continued to be for the enslaved people in their new surroundings. In the fields, they sang to relieve the drudgery of their tasks. Their work songs echoed with the rhythms and intonations of their homelands. Forced to adopt Christian beliefs, the enslaved people altered traditional hymns to suit their own tastes, creating soulful "spirituals."

After the Civil War, work songs, spirituals, and other influences came together to give birth to the blues—simple, repeated harmonies set to a mournful

496   Unit 7

BACKGROUND INFORMATION

Geography in History: Movement During World War I many African Americans migrated from the South to northern cities. Northern factories needed workers because the war had slowed the flow of European immigrants, who had provided much of industry's cheap labor. Between 1.5 million and 2 million African Americans moved north in the period from 1914 to 1930. They were fleeing failing cotton crops, which had been their main income source, and seeking higher wages. Jazz spread from New Orleans and other parts of the South to northern cities with the movement of African Americans. In New York City, jazz became an integral part of the Harlem Renaissance, an important cultural movement.
🌐 EE4 Human Systems: Standard 9

scale. Close on the heels of the blues came ragtime—a jaunty style of piano music with a distinctly African rhythmic undertone.

It was in New Orleans that blues and ragtime blended with Creole, European, and other influences to become jazz. By 1917, the new music echoed throughout New Orleans.

In the 1920s, the center of jazz began shifting northward, first to Chicago and then to New York. In the decades that followed, jazz underwent many changes. New forms of jazz emerged, such as big band swing, bebop, and cool jazz. Jazz continues to develop today. No matter what variations appear, however, the roots of jazz remain firmly planted in Africa.

◀ American jazz innovator Louis Armstrong

▲ West African musicians

Unit 7 **497**

Louis Armstrong helped support his family as a young man by working at odd jobs all over New Orleans. He sang on street corners and came into contact with all kinds of music and musicians. Soon he was performing with bands at clubs and playing in parades and funerals. As a boy, Armstrong learned to play the cornet, and later he became a well-known trumpet player. He played jazz on the Mississippi riverboats with some of the greatest musicians in the genre. In 1922 Armstrong joined Joe Oliver's Creole Jazz Band in Chicago and began a lifetime of touring. Louis Armstrong is celebrated as the greatest of jazz innovators.

❸ ASSESS

Ask: What is the most interesting thing you have learned about jazz? Encourage all students to contribute ideas in a class discussion. Ask students to write a brief paragraph about what they like or dislike about jazz.

❹ CLOSE

Have students share their presentations of music influencing or influenced by jazz with other students in a school assembly.

CONNECTION ACTIVITY

Tracing Music Roots Organize the class into small groups and have each group research a type or style of music that was incorporated into or was influenced by jazz: traditional African music, spiritual, blues, ragtime, rap, hip-hop. Students should consult various resources for information, including the Internet. Ask students to prepare an oral presentation on the type of music they have chosen or been assigned. In addition to reporting on the type of music, students should play selections for their classmates if appropriate. For their presentations, encourage students to use props that are appropriate to the music they have researched. 🌐 **EE4 Human Systems: Standard 10**

CHAPTER 20 PLANNING GUIDE

NOTE: The following materials may be used when teaching Chapter 20. Section-level support materials are shown at point-of-use in the margins of the Teacher Wraparound Edition.

TEACHING TRANSPARENCIES

L2 Unit 7 Map Overlay Transparencies

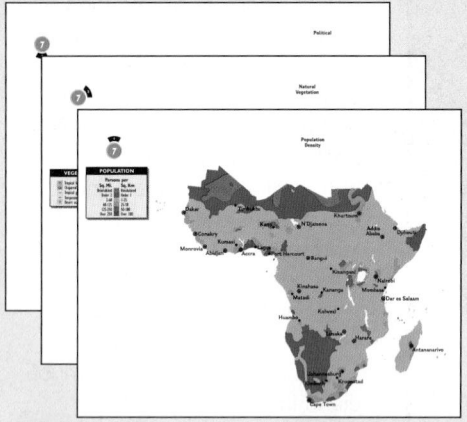

L2 Political Map Transparency 7

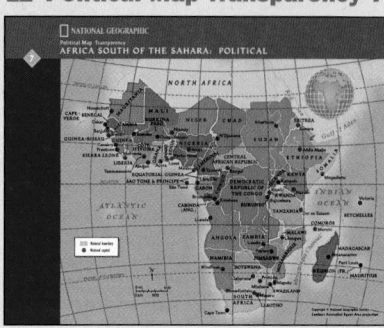

GEOGRAPHIC LITERACY

Focus on Geography Literacy

APPLICATION AND ENRICHMENT

L3 Enrichment Activity 20

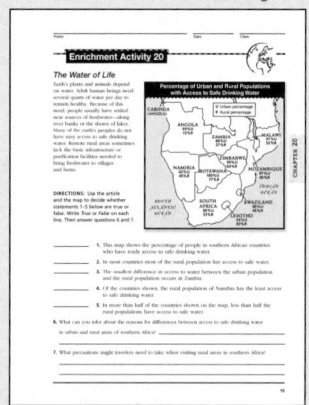

REVIEW AND REINFORCEMENT

L1 Vocabulary Activity 20 L1 Reinforcing L1 Reteaching Activity 20
Skills Activity 20

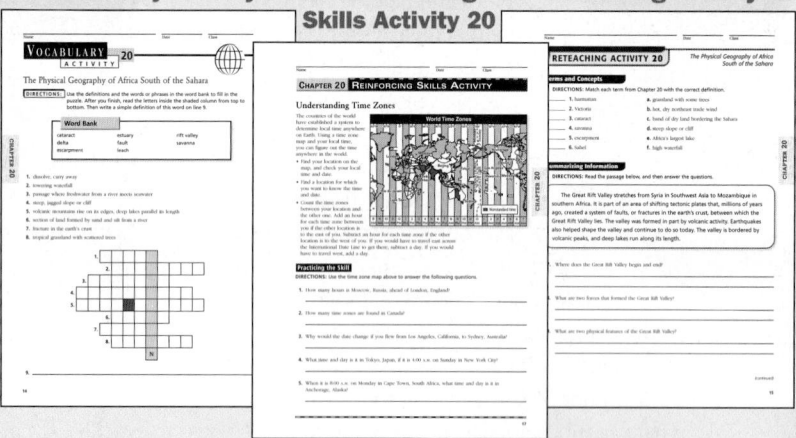

ASSESSMENT

L2 Chapter 20 Test Form A

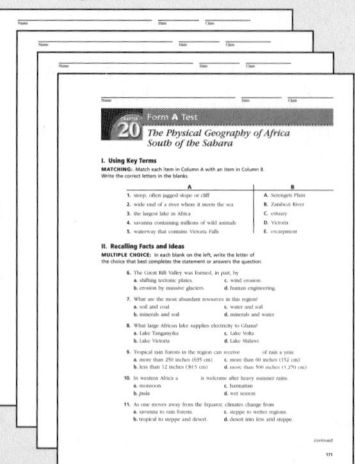

L2 Chapter 20 Test Form B

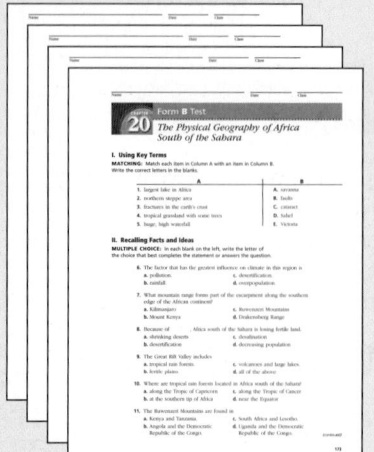

L1/ELL Performance Assessment Activity 20

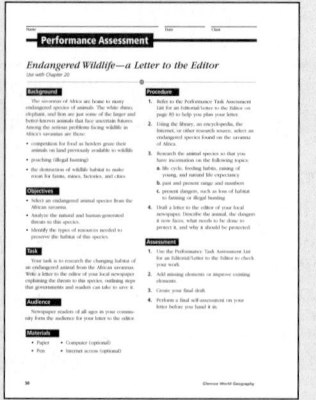

ExamView® Pro Testmaker

The following Spanish language materials are available in the Spanish Resources binder:

- 📁 Spanish Vocabulary Activities
- 📁 Spanish Guided Reading Activities
- 📁 Spanish Reteaching Activities
- 📁 Spanish Summaries
- 📁 Spanish Quizzes and Tests
- 📁 Spanish Reading Essentials and Study Guide

- World Regions Video
- MindJogger Videoquiz
- Vocabulary PuzzleMaker CD-ROM
- Interactive Tutor Self-Assessment CD-ROM
- ExamView® Pro Testmaker CD-ROM
- Audio Program
- TeacherWorks CD-ROM
- Interactive Student Edition CD-ROM
- Glencoe Skillbuilder Interactive Workbook CD-ROM, Level 2
- Presentation Plus! CD-ROM

Timesaving Tools

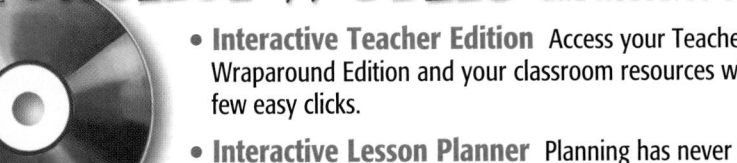 **TeacherWorks™** All-In-One Planner and Resource Center

- **Interactive Teacher Edition** Access your Teacher Wraparound Edition and your classroom resources with a few easy clicks.

- **Interactive Lesson Planner** Planning has never been easier! Organize your week, month, semester, or year with all the lesson helps you need to make teaching creative, timely, and relevant.

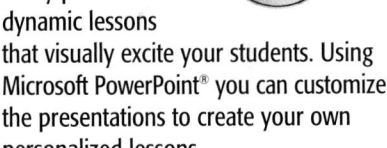 Use Glencoe's **Presentation Plus!** multimedia teacher tool to easily present dynamic lessons that visually excite your students. Using Microsoft PowerPoint® you can customize the presentations to create your own personalized lessons.

 **GEOGRAPHY** *Online*

Use our Web site for additional resources. All essential content is covered in the Student Edition.

You and your students can visit geography.glencoe.com, the Web site companion to *Glencoe World Geography*. This innovative integration of electronic and print media offers your students a wealth of opportunities. The student text directs students to the Web site for the following options:

- Chapter Overviews
- Student Activities
- Self-Check Quizzes
- Textbook Updates

Answers are provided for you in the "Web Activity Lesson Plan." Additional Web resources and Interactive Tutor puzzles are also available.

▶ **Additional Glencoe Teacher Support**

- Teaching Strategies for the Geography Classroom (including Block Scheduling Pacing Guides)
- Graphic Organizer Transparencies Strategies and Activities
- Outline Map Resource Book
- Reading in the Content Area

CHAPTER 20 PLANNING GUIDE

SECTION RESOURCES

Daily Objectives	Reproducible Resources	Multimedia Resources

SECTION 1   The Land

1. Describe the major landforms in Africa south of the Sahara.
2. Explain how the land affects the water systems of Africa south of the Sahara.
3. List the most important natural resources of Africa south of the Sahara.

Reproducible Resources
- Reproducible Lesson Plan 20-1
- Daily Lecture Notes 20-1
- Guided Reading Activity 20-1*
- Reading Essentials and Study Guide 20-1*
- Section Quiz 20-1*

Multimedia Resources
- Daily Focus Skills Transparency 20-1
- Political Map Transparency 7
- Unit 7 Map Overlay Transparencies
- Interactive Tutor Self-Assessment CD-ROM
- ExamView® Pro Testmaker CD-ROM*
- Presentation Plus! CD-ROM

SECTION 2   Climate and Vegetation

1. Relate the geographic factors that affect climate in Africa.
2. Identify the kinds of climate and vegetation that are found in Africa south of the Sahara.

Reproducible Resources
- Reproducible Lesson Plan 20-2
- Vocabulary Activity 20*
- Daily Lecture Notes 20-2
- Guided Reading Activity 20-2*
- Reading Essentials and Study Guide 20-2*
- Reteaching Activity 20*
- Reinforcing Skills Activity 20
- Section Quiz 20-2*

Multimedia Resources
- Daily Focus Skills Transparency 20-2
- Political Map Transparency 7
- Unit 7 Map Overlay Transparencies
- Vocabulary PuzzleMaker CD-ROM
- Interactive Tutor Self-Assessment CD-ROM
- ExamView® Pro Testmaker CD-ROM*
- Presentation Plus! CD-ROM

Blackline Master	Software	Videocassette	*Also available in Spanish
Transparency	CD-ROM	DVD	

OUT OF TIME? Assign the Chapter 20 **Reading Essentials and Study Guide.**

Block Schedule

Activities that are particularly suited to use within the block scheduling framework are identified throughout this chapter by the following designation:

KEY TO ABILITY LEVELS

Teaching strategies have been coded for various learning styles and abilities.

L1   **BASIC** activities for all students

L2   **AVERAGE** activities for average to above-average students

L3   **CHALLENGING** activities for above-average students

ELL   **ENGLISH LANGUAGE LEARNER** activities

Teacher to Teacher

Eva M. Doyle
Campus West
Buffalo, NY

Map Projections

Because it is impossible to accurately depict the spherical earth on a flat map, all flat maps will have distortions of distance, shape, area, or direction. Geographers use different map projections for different purposes.

Display a selection of world maps that use different map projections. Show students a map that uses the Peters projection. Point out that the Peters map accurately represents the sizes of the continents, although it distorts the shapes. Students can easily see that Africa is the second largest continent. Have students use the Peters map to list the continents in order of size.

The old Mercator projection was created to show accurate distances for navigation. It is now rarely used as a world map because its size distortions become very large away from the Equator. The National Geographic Society began using the Winkel Tripel map projection in 1998. Have students locate maps that use the Winkel Tripel and other projections. Tell them to look at Africa on all the maps and compare the shape of the continent on each with a globe.

Meeting National Standards

Geography For Life

The following standards are highlighted in Chapter 20:

Section 1 EE2 Places and Regions:
Standard 4
EE3 Physical Systems:
Standard 7
EE5 Environment and Society:
Standards 14, 16

Section 2 EE2 Places and Regions:
Standard 4
EE3 Physical Systems:
Standard 7
EE5 Environment and Society:
Standards 14 and 15

Local Objectives

_____

_____

NATIONAL GEOGRAPHIC

TEACHER'S CORNER

Index to National Geographic Magazine:

The following articles may be used for research relating to this chapter:

- "Photographing the Sahara from Aloft," by George Steinmetz, March 1999.

National Geographic Society Products:

To order the following products for use with this chapter, call National Geographic Society at 1-800-368-2728.

- *Africa* (Video)
- *Physical Earth* (Map)
- *National Geographic Desk Reference* (Book)
- *National Geographic Atlas of the World, Seventh Edition* (Book

NGS ONLINE

Access National Geographic's Web site for current events, activities, links, interactive features, and archives.
www.nationalgeographic.com

MEETING SPECIAL NEEDS

In addition to the Differentiated Instruction strategies found in each section, the following resources are also suitable for your special needs students:

- *ExamView® Pro Testmaker CD-ROM* allows teachers to tailor tests by reducing answer choices.
- The *Audio Program* includes the entire narrative of the student edition so that less-proficient readers can listen to the words as they read them.
- The *Reading Essentials and Study Guide* provides the same content as the student edition but is written two grade levels below the textbook.
- *Guided Reading Activities* give less-proficient readers point-by-point instructions to increase comprehension as they read each textbook section.
- *Enrichment Activities* include a stimulating collection of readings and activities for gifted and talented students.

Chapter Objectives

1. Identify the major landforms, water systems, and natural resources of Africa south of the Sahara.

2. Describe the relationship between climate and vegetation in the region.

GLENCOE
TECHNOLOGY

Use *MindJogger Videoquiz* to preview the Chapter 20 content.

GeoJournal

For access to additional photos, maps, and information on the geographic features of Africa south of the Sahara, go to www.nationalgeographic.com **(See Teacher pages in front for strategies for using journals in the geography classroom.)**

GEOGRAPHY
Online

Introduce students to chapter content and key terms by having them access Chapter Overview 20 at geography.glencoe.com

FOLDABLES™
Study Organizer

Dinah Zike's Foldables are three-dimensional, interactive graphic organizers that help students practice basic writing skills, review key vocabulary terms, and identify main ideas. Have students complete the Foldable activity in the **Dinah Zike's Reading and Study Skills Foldables** booklet.

CHAPTER 20

The Physical Geography of Africa South of the Sahara

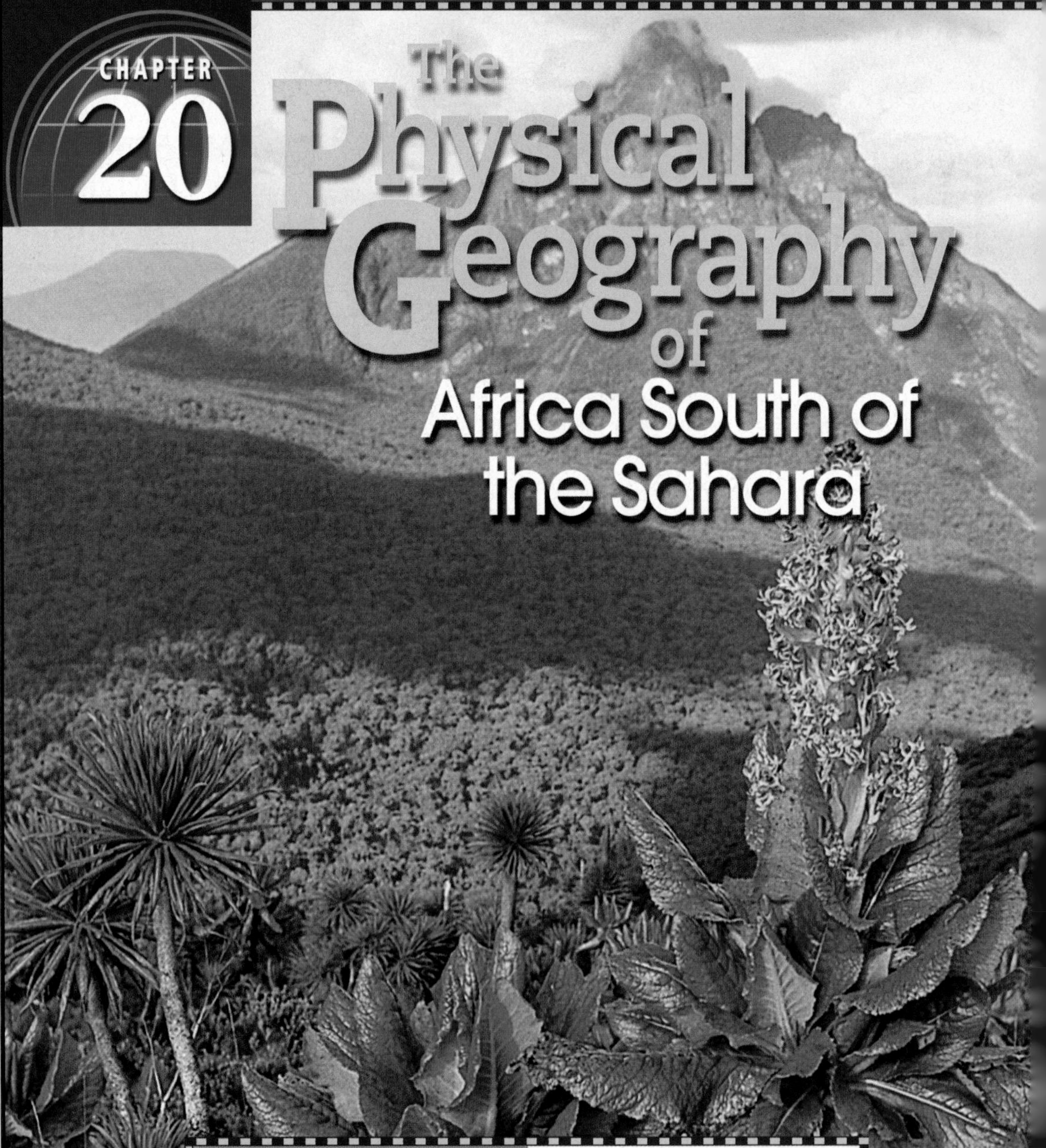

GeoJournal

As you read this chapter, use your journal to compare and contrast the physical geography of Africa south of the Sahara with that of Latin America. List similarities and differences in your journal.

GEOGRAPHY
Online

Chapter Overview Visit the **Glencoe World Geography** Web site at geography.glencoe.com and click on Chapter Overviews—Chapter 20 to preview information about the physical geography of the region.

ABOUT THE PHOTO

Visual Instruction Located near the borders of the Democratic Republic of the Congo, Rwanda, and Uganda, 14,370-foot (4,380-meter) Mt. Mikeno is one of the southernmost volcanoes of the Virunga Mountains. The area is home to groups of mountain gorillas that people worldwide have been working to protect.

Hundreds of thousands of refugees fleeing the civil wars in Rwanda and the Democratic Republic of the Congo came to the area in the 1990s. These refugees have cut down forests for wood and killed thousands of animals for food. The future of the mountain gorilla population remains uncertain. 🌐 **EE2 Places and Regions: Standard 4**

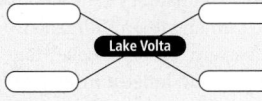
The Land

Guide to Reading

Consider What You Know

Africa south of the Sahara is known throughout the world for its extraordinary physical geography as well as its wildlife. What animals do you associate with the region? What landforms do you think are present in the places where those animals live?

Reading Strategy

Organizing Complete a web diagram similar to the one below by filling in the many uses of Lake Volta.

Lake Volta

Read to Find Out

- What are the major landforms in Africa south of the Sahara?
- How does the land affect the water systems of Africa south of the Sahara?
- What are the region's most important natural resources?

Terms to Know

- escarpment
- cataract
- rift valley
- fault
- delta
- estuary

Places to Locate

- Ruwenzori Mountains
- Drakensberg Range
- Great Rift Valley
- Lake Victoria
- Niger River
- Zambezi River
- Congo River

◀ *Mt. Mikeno, Democratic Republic of the Congo*

NATIONAL GEOGRAPHIC

A Geographic View

Across the Great Rift

The road has risen swiftly as we leave Nakuru, a town that sits just south of the Equator in Kenya. . . . We drive beneath cool gray rain clouds. . . . Abruptly the clouds break, and before our windshield the red earth drops away. A gash 700 meters (2,300 feet) deep and 16 kilometers (ten miles) across— an offshoot of Africa's Great Rift—lies before us. Far to the left, stretching beyond the horizon, I see a glimmering expanse of water—Lake Victoria.

—Curt Stager, "Africa's Great Rift," National Geographic, May 1990

Lake Victoria, East Africa

Nothing in his research prepared biologist Curt Stager for the breathtaking views on the road out of Nakuru, Kenya, in East Africa. Along the Great Rift, long troughs and deep lakes slash the land in the shadow of majestic volcanic mountains. In this section you will read about the dramatic physical features and the rich natural resources of Africa south of Sahara.

Landforms

Africa south of the Sahara is an immense region covering about 9.5 million square miles (24.6 million sq. km). Bounded on the north by the Sahara, the region extends to the sea in all other directions. To its northeast is the Red Sea, to its west the Atlantic Ocean, and to its east the Indian Ocean. On the southern edge of Africa south of the Sahara, the waters of the Atlantic and Indian Oceans meet at the Cape of Good Hope. This vast region embraces a broad variety of physical features.

1 FOCUS

Section Overview

This section surveys the landforms, water systems, and most important natural resources of Africa south of the Sahara.

BELLRINGER
Skillbuilder Activity

- Project transparency and have students answer questions.

- Available as blackline master.

Daily Focus Skills Transparency 20-1

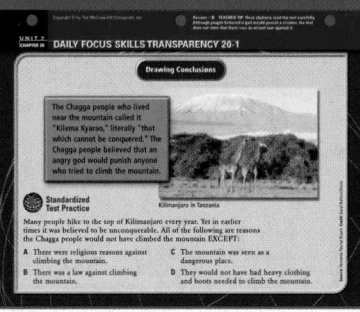

Guide to Reading

Consider What You Know

Answers *may include lions, rhinoceroses, and giraffes on plains or plateaus; hippopotamuses and crocodiles near rivers; and gorillas in the mountains.*

Reading Strategy

Answers *stores 124 million acre-feet of water; irrigation; fishing; hydroelectric power*

Preteaching Vocabulary

Read aloud several dictionary definitions for *fault*. Then ask the class to predict which meaning defines the word as it is used in the section.

RESOURCE MANAGER

📂 Reproducible Masters

- Reproducible Lesson Plan 20-1
- Daily Lecture Notes 20-1
- Guided Reading Activity 20-1
- Reading Essentials and Study Guide 20-1
- Section Quiz 20-1

🖥 Transparencies

- Daily Focus Skills Transparency 20-1
- Political Map Transparency 7
- Unit 7 Map Overlay Transparencies

Multimedia

- 💿 Interactive Tutor Self-Assessment CD-ROM
- 💿 ExamView® Pro Testmaker CD-ROM
- 💿 Presentation Plus! CD-ROM

L1 Interpret a Map

Assign each student a country in Africa south of the Sahara. Then have students take turns making statements about the physical geography of their countries based on the information in the map.

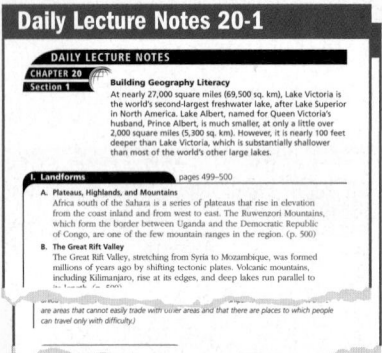

Daily Lecture Notes 20-1

DAILY LECTURE NOTES

CHAPTER 20
Section 1

Building Geography Literacy
At nearly 27,000 square miles (69,500 sq. km), Lake Victoria is the world's second-largest freshwater lake, after Lake Superior in North America. Lake Albert, named for Queen Victoria's husband, Prince Albert, is much smaller, at only a little over 2,000 square miles (5,300 sq. km). However, it is nearly 100 feet deeper than Lake Victoria, which is substantially shallower than most of the world's other large lakes.

I. Landforms   pages 499–500

A. Plateaus, Highlands, and Mountains
Africa south of the Sahara is a series of plateaus that rise in elevation from the coast inland and from west to east. The Ruwenzori Mountains, which form the border between Uganda and the Democratic Republic of Congo, are one of the few mountain ranges in the region. (p. 500)

B. The Great Rift Valley
The Great Rift Valley, stretching from Syria to Mozambique, was formed millions of years ago by shifting tectonic plates. Volcanic mountains, including Kilimanjaro, rise at its edges, and deep lakes run parallel to its length. (p. 500)

are areas that cannot easily trade with other areas and that there are places to which people can travel only with difficulty.)

□ NATIONAL GEOGRAPHIC **GEOFACT**

▶ **Ngorongoro Crater formed when an ancient volcano to the west of Kilimanjaro exploded and collapsed on itself, leaving a hollow measuring 10–12 miles (16–19 km) across and 2,000 feet (610 m) deep. The crater has been a popular tourist destination for more than half a century. Elephants, rhinoceroses, leopards, zebras, and other wildlife range across its open grasslands.**

Plateaus, Highlands, and Mountains

Seen from space, Africa south of the Sahara might be described as a series of steps. These steps are actually plateaus that rise in elevation from the coast inland and from west to east. Ranging in elevation from 500 feet (152 m) in the west to 8,000 feet (2,438 m) or more in the east, the plateaus are outcroppings of the solid rock that makes up most of Africa.

The edges of the continent's plateaus are marked by escarpments—steep, often jagged slopes or cliffs. Most of the escarpments are located less than 20 miles (32 km) from the coast. Rivers crossing the plateaus plunge suddenly down the sides of the escarpments in cataracts, or towering waterfalls.

Although Africa's overall surface is higher in average elevation than that of every other continent, it has relatively few mountains. Most African mountains dot the Eastern Highlands, an area that stretches from Ethiopia almost to the Cape of Good Hope. These highland areas include the Ethiopian Highlands as well as volcanic summits, such as Kilimanjaro and Mount Kenya.

West of the Eastern Highlands, the **Ruwenzori (ROO•wuhn•ZOHR•ee) Mountains** divide Uganda and the Democratic Republic of the Congo. Covered with snow and cloaked in clouds, these mountains, also called the "Mountains of the Moon," have fascinated observers since ancient times. The writer Christopher Ondaatje, who traveled to East Africa in the 1990s, recorded these impressions of the legendary range:

❝ *One can feel the water in the air. It is damp, dank, grey, and cold.... [T]he clouds seldom clear so the upper slopes remain veiled. Still, we were constantly aware of them, a powerful presence brooding over the surrounding countryside.* ❞
— Christopher Ondaatje,
Journey to the Source of the Nile, 1999

Moist air from the Indian Ocean creates the clouds that wrap around the Ruwenzoris and give these mountains their wondrous appearance.

Farther south are the Cape Mountains, which include the **Drakensberg Range** in South Africa

---

and Lesotho. These mountains rise to more than 11,000 feet (3,353 m) and form part of the sharp escarpment along the southern edge of the continent.

The Great Rift Valley

An amazing natural wonder known as the **Great Rift Valley** stretches from Syria in Southwest Asia to Mozambique (MOH•zahm•BEEK) in the southeastern part of Africa. A rift valley is a large crack in the earth's surface formed by shifting tectonic plates. Millions of years ago, plate movements created the system of faults or fractures in the earth's crust within which the Great Rift Valley lies. Volcanic eruptions as well as earthquakes helped create the valley's striking landscape, and they continue to shape it today.

In East Africa, the Great Rift Valley forms two branches, with volcanic mountains rising at its edges and deep lakes that run parallel to its length. The main volcanic cones, among them Kilimanjaro, are found along the eastern branch. Lake Tanganyika, one of the deepest and longest freshwater lakes in the world, lies on the western branch. To the south is Lake Malawi, a mountain-rimmed lake that looks much like a fjord. Like the glacier-cut valleys of seawater in northern Europe, Lake Malawi lies well below the land surrounding it. It is also very deep, its floor dropping to more than 2,300 feet (700 m) at its deepest point.

Water Systems

The land has influenced the water systems of Africa south of the Sahara in important ways. The lakes and rivers that drain the region are located in huge basins formed millions of years ago by the uplifting of the land. The great rivers of Africa

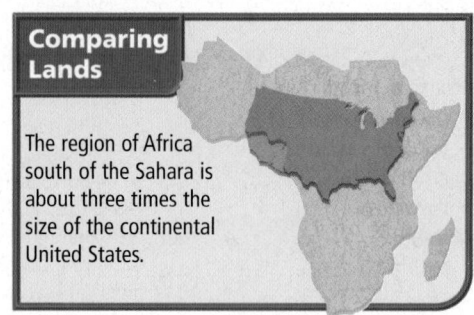

Comparing Lands

The region of Africa south of the Sahara is about three times the size of the continental United States.

DIFFERENTIATED INSTRUCTION

English Learners Students may demonstrate their grasp of the section vocabulary terms and other words in the section related to the physical geography of Africa south of the Sahara by creating a visual glossary. Direct students to draw a picture illustrating each word. **ELL** 🌐 **EE2 Places and Regions: Standard 4**
📁 Refer to *Inclusion for the Social Studies Classroom Strategies and Activities.*

NATIONAL GEOGRAPHIC — MAP STUDY

Africa South of the Sahara: Physical/Political

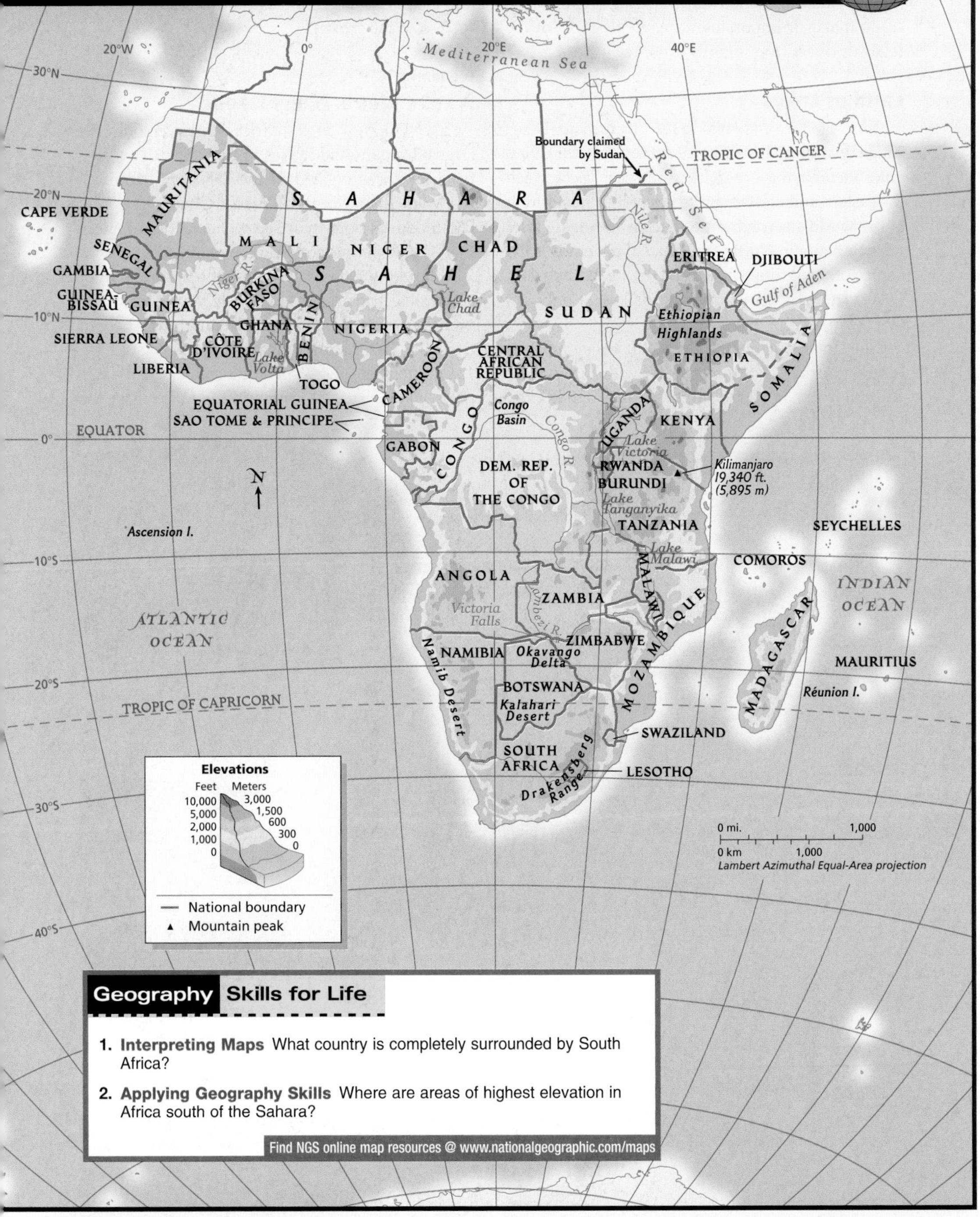

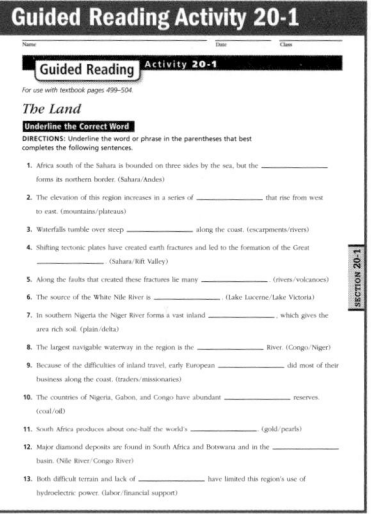

Boundary claimed by Sudan

TROPIC OF CANCER

Elevations

Feet	Meters
10,000	3,000
5,000	1,500
2,000	600
1,000	300
0	0

— National boundary
▲ Mountain peak

0 mi.   1,000
0 km   1,000
Lambert Azimuthal Equal-Area projection

Geography Skills for Life

1. **Interpreting Maps** What country is completely surrounded by South Africa?

2. **Applying Geography Skills** Where are areas of highest elevation in Africa south of the Sahara?

Find NGS online map resources @ www.nationalgeographic.com/maps

L1 Making Comparisons

Name pairs of lakes or rivers described in the section. Have students compare and contrast the pairs of lakes or rivers based on facts in the text.

L1/ELL

Guided Reading Activity 20-1

Guided Reading Activity 20-1

For use with textbook pages 499–504

The Land

Underline the Correct Word

DIRECTIONS: Underline the word or phrase in the parentheses that best completes the following sentences.

1. Africa south of the Sahara is bounded on three sides by the sea, but the _____ forms its northern border. (Sahara/Andes)

2. The elevation of this region increases in a series of _____ that rise from west to east. (mountains/plateaus)

3. Waterfalls tumble over steep _____ along the coast. (escarpments/rivers)

4. Shifting tectonic plates have created earth fractures and led to the formation of the Great _____. (Sahara/Rift Valley)

5. Along the faults that created these fractures lie many _____. (rivers/volcanoes)

6. The source of the White Nile River is _____. (Lake Lucerne/Lake Victoria)

7. In southern Nigeria the Niger River forms a vast inland _____ which gives the area rich soil. (plain/delta)

8. The largest navigable waterway in the region is the _____ River. (Congo/Niger)

9. Because of the difficulties of inland travel, early European _____ did most of their business along the coast. (traders/missionaries)

10. The countries of Nigeria, Gabon, and Congo have abundant _____ reserves. (coal/oil)

11. South Africa produces about one-half the world's _____. (gold/pearls)

12. Major diamond deposits are found in South Africa and Botswana and in the _____ basin. (Nile River/Congo River)

13. Both difficult terrain and lack of _____ have limited this region's use of hydroelectric power. (labor/financial support)

NATIONAL GEOGRAPHIC — MAP STUDY

Answers

1. *Lesotho*

2. *in northern Chad, in the east from Ethiopia to Tanzania, and in the south in South Africa, Lesotho, Angola, Namibia, and Madagascar*

Map Skills Practice

Location What is the elevation of Lake Chad? (*less than 1,000 feet [305 m]*)

COOPERATIVE LEARNING ACTIVITY

Forces Shaping the Earth Have small groups further investigate how landforms in and around the Great Rift Valley were formed. Separate groups should research volcanoes, earthquakes, or glaciers and their effect on this part of the region. Direct groups to use library and reliable Internet resources to gather information. When they have completed their research, groups should pool their findings to create a bulletin board display about the forces that have shaped the landforms in East Africa. Encourage students to include illustrative visuals (diagrams, pictures, and so on) in the display.

EE3 Physical Systems: Standard 7

L1/ELL

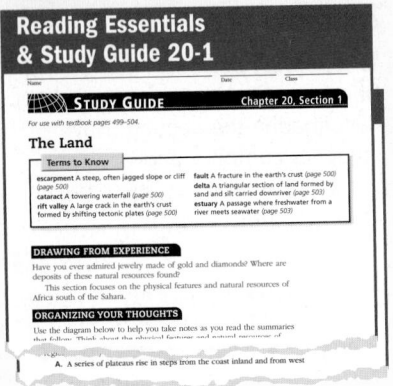
L2 Make a Graph

Have students make bar graphs to compare these elevations in Africa south of the Sahara:

Kilimanjaro	19,340 feet (5,895 m)
Mount Kenya	17,058 feet (5,199 m)
Ruwenzori Mountains	16,795 feet (5,119 m)
Drakensberg Range	11,358 feet (3,462 m)

NATIONAL GEOGRAPHIC World Explorer

Answer
the Niger, Zambezi, and Congo Rivers

More About the Photo The Niger Delta is one of the world's largest wetlands. People continue to protest against pollution caused by local oil and natural gas industries.

---

originate high in the plateaus and eventually make their way to the sea. Escarpments and ridges, also created long ago by movements of the earth's crust, frequently break the rivers' paths to the ocean with rapids, waterfalls, and cataracts. This broken landscape makes it impossible to navigate most of the region's rivers from mouth to source.

Land of Lakes

Most of the region's lakes, including Lakes Tanganyika and Malawi, are near the Great Rift Valley. **Lake Victoria**, the largest lake in Africa, lies between the eastern and western branches of the Great Rift. It is the world's second largest freshwater lake, after Lake Superior in North America. Lake Victoria is the source of the White Nile River. Despite its large size, Lake Victoria is comparatively shallow at only 270 feet (82 m) deep.

Lake Chad, outside the Great Rift Valley in west-central Africa, is threatened with extinction. Although fed by three large streams, landlocked Lake Chad is shrinking. Droughts in the 1970s completely dried up the northern portion of the lake, and the water level continues to be shallow even during years when rainfall is normal. Because of the arid climate, much of the lake's water evaporates or seeps into the ground.

Economics
A Lake Meets Many Needs

Lake Volta in West Africa ranks among the largest human-made lakes in the world. This artificial lake was created in the 1960s by damming the Volta River south of Ajena, Ghana. The new lake flooded more than 700 villages, forcing more than 70,000 people to find new places to live.

Although the dam was originally built as part of a hydroelectric project to provide power to an aluminum plant, the people of Ghana today benefit from the lake in many ways. Capable of storing 124 million acre-feet (153 billion cubic m) of water, Lake Volta supplies irrigation for farming in the

NATIONAL GEOGRAPHIC **World Explorer**

Geography Skills for Life

Niger River The Niger River spreads into a vast inland delta. The river is important for farming, travel, trade, and fishing (inset).

Place What are the longest rivers in Africa south of the Sahara?

CRITICAL THINKING ACTIVITY

Determining Cause and Effect Prompt students to identify causes and effects of the construction of Lake Volta. **Ask: Why was Lake Volta created?** *(Hydroelectric power was needed for an aluminum plant.)* **How did people benefit from the construction of the lake?** *(The lake supplies water for irrigation and a fishing industry; the hydroelectric plant also supplies electricity to people throughout Ghana.)* **What happened as a result of the damming of the Volta River?** *(Villages were flooded, and many people had to find new places to live.)* Have students organize the information in a cause-and-effect diagram.
🌐 **EE5 Environment and Society: Standard 14**

plains below the dam and is well stocked with fish. In addition to supplying power to the aluminum industry in the port of Tema, the hydroelectric plant now generates electricity used throughout Ghana.

River Basins

The **Niger** (NY•juhr) **River** is known by many names along its course, but all its names have roughly the same meaning—"great river." The Niger is the main artery in western Africa, extending about 2,600 miles (4,184 km) in length. Originating in the highlands of Guinea only 150 miles (241 km) inland from the Atlantic Ocean, the river forms a great arc. It flows northeast and then curves southeast to meet the Atlantic Ocean at the coast of Nigeria. In addition to being vitally important to agriculture, the Niger River is a major means of transportation for people in the region. It also provides a leisurely means of travel for tourists.

This great river does not flow as one well-defined stream into the sea. At Aboh in southern Nigeria, the Niger splits into a vast inland delta, a triangular section of land formed by sand and silt carried downriver. The Niger Delta stretches 150 miles (241 km) north to south and extends to a width of about 200 miles (322 km) along the shore of the Gulf of Guinea.

The **Zambezi River** of south-central Africa also meets the ocean in a delta. The Zambezi flows 2,200 miles (3,540 km) from its source near the Zambia-Angola border in the west to the Indian Ocean in the east, where it fans out in a delta that is 37 miles (60 km) wide. The Zambezi's course to the sea is interrupted in many places by waterfalls. At Victoria Falls, on the border of Zambia and Zimbabwe, the Zambezi plummets a sheer 355 feet (108 m), about twice the drop of Horseshoe Falls on the Niagara River between Canada and the United States. The water at Victoria Falls flows at 35,400 cubic feet (1,002 cubic m) per second.

Unlike the Niger, the Zambezi, and most other African rivers, the Congo River reaches the sea through a deep estuary (EHS•chuh•WEHR•ee), or passage where freshwater from a river meets

seawater. The Congo's estuary is 6 miles (10 km) wide and is easily navigated by ocean vessels, making it an important waterway. The 2,900 miles (4,667 km) of the Congo form the largest network of navigable waterways on the continent. Some parts of the river, however, such as rapids and waterfalls, present serious obstacles to traffic. The river plunges almost 900 feet (274 m) in numerous cataracts not far from where it meets the Atlantic Ocean. The cataracts are a major barrier to travel from the estuary upriver.

History

Daunting Physical Barriers

Although North Africans enjoyed relatively easy access to Europe and Southwest Asia across the Mediterranean and Arabian Seas, the Sahara prevented most land travel to and from central and southern Africa. The daunting physical geography

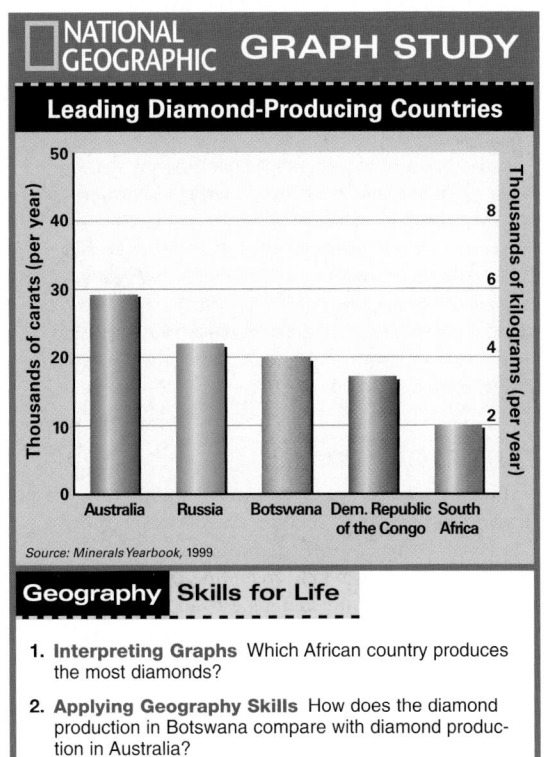

NATIONAL GEOGRAPHIC GRAPH STUDY

Leading Diamond-Producing Countries

Source: Minerals Yearbook, 1999

Geography Skills for Life

1. **Interpreting Graphs** Which African country produces the most diamonds?

2. **Applying Geography Skills** How does the diamond production in Botswana compare with diamond production in Australia?

Chapter 20 ● 503

Answers

1. *Botswana*

2. *Production in Australia is one third more than that of Botswana*

Skills Practice

What is the total annual diamond production of the African countries shown on the graph? *(about 48 thousand carats or 9.6 thousand kilograms)*

ASSESS

Assign Section 1 Assessment as homework or as an in-class activity.

⊗ Have students use **Interactive Tutor Self-Assessment CD-ROM** to review Section 1.

L2

Section Quiz 20-1

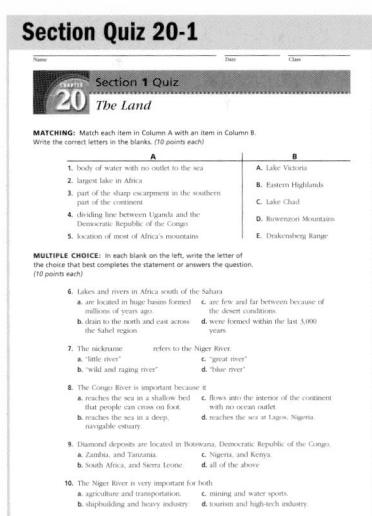

TEAM-TEACHING ACTIVITY: SCIENCE

Elements, Compounds, and Mixtures Display a periodic table of the elements and have students circle gold, copper, uranium, manganese, cobalt, chromium, and zinc—the elements that are resources in Africa south of the Sahara. Explain that elements are substances that cannot be broken down further into simpler substances by ordinary physical or chemical means. To extend understanding, ask a science teacher to design an experiment in which students can identify characteristics of elements, compounds, and mixtures and use the characteristics to classify selected objects.

⊕ **EE5 Environment and Society: Standard 16**

Reteach

With students, make an outline of the section using the section heads for Roman numeral divisions (*I, II, III*) and the section subheads for lettered divisions (*A, B, C*). Help students identify the main ideas under each subhead, and include them in the outline as numbered facts (*1, 2, 3,* and so on).

Enrich

Have students design a postage stamp for one of the countries of Africa south of the Sahara. Students' stamps should show a physical feature of the country they have chosen. To draw the feature, students may work from a photo or other illustration or from their own ideas about what the physical feature looks like.

 **CLOSE**

Tell students that they are traveling to Africa south of the Sahara for the first time. **Ask: What physical feature do you most want to see?** Have students write a letter to a friend or family member explaining why they want to see their chosen feature.

along the West African coast made travel inland by river very difficult for European traders, who began arriving in the late 1400s. Sand and silt deposits made navigation through the deltas treacherous. At certain times of the year, those who tried to sail inland often encountered shallows, sandbars, and even dry riverbeds. Farther upstream, rapids and waterfalls made travel upriver almost impossible. As a result, between the late 1400s and the late 1700s, most Europeans conducted trade with Africans from offshore islands or coastal forts, and regional African leaders maintained control of goods and trade routes in the interior of the continent.

Natural Resources

Mineral resources are abundant throughout Africa south of the Sahara. Angola, Nigeria, Gabon, and Congo have plentiful oil reserves. Deposits of various metals, including chromium, cobalt, copper, iron ore, manganese, and zinc, are scattered across the region. South Africa has about half the world's gold. Zimbabwe, the Democratic Republic of the Congo, Tanzania, and Ghana are additional sources of this precious metal. Uranium, usually found with gold, is abundant in South Africa as well as in Niger, Gabon, the Democratic Republic of the Congo, and Namibia. South Africa, Botswana, and the Congo River basin hold major diamond deposits. Diamonds also are mined in Angola, the Democratic Republic of the Congo, and Sierra Leone.

Water is an abundant resource in parts of Africa south of the Sahara, and it has tremendous potential for agricultural and industrial uses. Areas in the west of the region and near the Equator receive abundant rainfall. Controlling water for practical uses, such as irrigation and hydroelectric power, is difficult because rainfall often is irregular and unpredictable. Because of these physical challenges, combined with a lack of financial support, Africa has a great deal of unused hydroelectric power potential. The Congo River, for instance, has more potential hydroelectric power than all the lakes and rivers in the United States combined, but this resource has remained underdeveloped. Despite these challenges, some development has occurred, however. For example, most of the electricity generated in Kenya, Tanzania, Zambia, Ghana, and many other countries comes from hydroelectric power.

Solar power is another renewable energy source that has been harnessed in the region. In Kenya, rural electrification programs resulted in the installation of more than 20,000 small-scale solar power systems from 1986 to 1996. In the next section, you will read about the climate and vegetation of this vast region and their role in the development of Africa south of the Sahara.

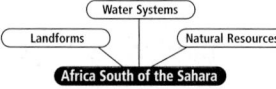 **SECTION 1 ASSESSMENT**

Checking for Understanding

1. **Define** escarpment, cataract, rift valley, fault, delta, estuary.
2. **Main Ideas** Create a web like the one below to record and organize information about the region's physical geography.

> Water Systems
> Landforms
> Natural Resources
> **Africa South of the Sahara**

Critical Thinking

3. **Identifying Cause and Effect** Physical features such as the Sahara to the north and oceans to the east and west isolated Africa south of the Sahara from other regions. What effects did this isolation have?
4. **Making Inferences** Considering the region's physical geography, what advancement in transportation do you think has contributed the most to improved travel in Africa?

Analyzing Maps

5. **Place** Study the map on page 501. What do most of the countries with elevations of less than 1,000 feet (300 m) have in common?

Applying Geography

6. **Identifying Cause and Effect** As a geographer from Kenya, write a paper on the geological process that caused the formation of the Great Rift Valley to deliver to the National Council for Geographic Education.

SECTION 1 ASSESSMENT ANSWERS

1. All vocabulary terms are defined in the text.
2. Students' webs should incorporate information about the landforms, water systems, and natural resources of the region.
3. For some time, goods, ideas, people, and conflicts from other regions did not easily spread to Africa south of the Sahara.
4. Air travel has greatly improved travel in the region. Travelers can cross areas where roads and rivers are not navigable.
5. They are located along the coast.
6. **Applying Geography** The Great Rift Valley was formed millions of years ago by a shift in tectonic plates, which created a system of faults in the earth's crust. Volcanic eruptions and earthquakes also contributed to the unique landscape of the valley and continue to shape it today.

Guide to Reading

Consider What You Know

The continent of Africa straddles the Equator. How do you think this location affects climate and vegetation in Africa south of the Sahara?

Reading Strategy

Organizing As you read about the landscape of Africa south of the Sahara, complete a graphic organizer similar to the one below by describing each geographical area.

Area	Description
Serengeti Plain	
Sahel	
Namib Desert	
Kalahari Desert	

Read to Find Out

- What geographic factors affect climate in Africa?
- What kinds of climate and vegetation are found in Africa south of the Sahara?

Terms to Know

- leach
- harmattan
- savanna

Places to Locate

- Serengeti Plain
- Sahel
- Namib Desert
- Kalahari Desert

Climate and Vegetation

NATIONAL GEOGRAPHIC

A Geographic View

Desert Delta

The Kalahari spread out below us. . . . Thunderheads spread cobras' hoods on the horizon, and the air was heavy with the musk of rain-wet earth somewhere up the breeze. There would be lightning that night, flashing on the burnished hills, then wind and finally, perhaps, the water that the whole land craved like a kind of forgiveness, like a blessing long withheld.

Kalahari sand dune, South Africa

—Douglas B. Lee, "Okavango Delta: Old Africa's Last Refuge," *National Geographic,* December 1990

"Pula"—in Botswana's Okavango Delta, this word, meaning "rain," is also used as a greeting. Rain is so important to the area, in fact, that *pula* is also the word for the country's currency and the word for blood, or life. In many places in Africa south of the Sahara, water is such a precious resource that rain and life are considered one and the same. In this section you will discover how rain helps determine climate, and thus vegetation, in every part of the region—its deserts, steppes, savannas, and tropical forests.

Tropical Climate

In addition to rainfall, other factors—ocean currents, prevailing wind patterns, elevation, and latitude—cause great variations in climate and vegetation throughout Africa south of the Sahara. However, as the map on page 506 shows, much of the region lies in the Tropics and has tropical climate and vegetation areas.

Chapter 20 🌐 505

① FOCUS

Section Overview

This section describes the kinds of climate and vegetation found in Africa south of the Sahara.

BELLRINGER
Skillbuilder Activity

Project transparency and have students answer questions.

Available as blackline master.

Daily Focus Skills Transparency 20-2

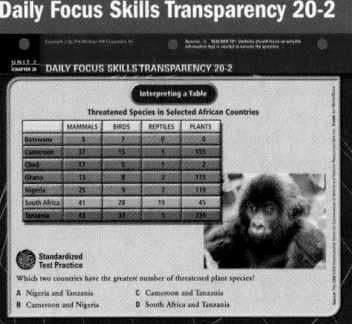

Guide to Reading

Consider What You Know

Answer *The climate of Africa south of the Sahara is generally warm to hot near the Equator with plenty of rain and vegetation that thrives in such conditions.*

Reading Strategy

Answer Serengeti: *savanna plain consisting of trees and tall grasses, abundance of animals;* Sahel: *4–8 inches of annual rainfall concentrated in June, July, August; low-growing grasses and shrubs;* Namib: *Atlantic coast of Namibia; rocks, dunes, scattered desert plants;* Kalahari: *mostly sand, little rain, extremely high daytime temperatures*

Preteaching Vocabulary

Use the **Vocabulary Puzzle-Maker CD-ROM** to create crossword and word-search puzzles.

RESOURCE MANAGER

📂 **Reproducible Masters**
- Reproducible Lesson Plan 20-2
- Vocabulary Activity 20
- Daily Lecture Notes 20-2
- Guided Reading Activity 20-2
- Reading Essentials and Study Guide 20-2
- Reteaching Activity 20
- Reinforcing Skills Activity 20
- Section Quiz 20-2

🖨 **Transparencies**
- Daily Focus Skills Transparency 20-2
- Political Map Transparency 7
- Unit 7 Map Overlay Transparencies

Multimedia
- 💿 Vocabulary PuzzleMaker CD-ROM
- 💿 Interactive Tutor Self-Assessment CD-ROM
- 💿 ExamView® Pro Testmaker CD-ROM
- 💿 Presentation Plus! CD-ROM

TEACH

L1 Visualizing

Have students draw or paint a picture of a tropical rain forest. As they create their illustrations, students should refer to the information in the text about the levels of vegetation in the rain forest.

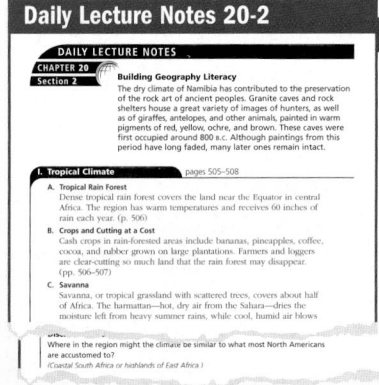

Daily Lecture Notes 20-2

DAILY LECTURE NOTES

CHAPTER 20
Section 2

Building Geography Literacy
The dry climate of Namibia has contributed to the preservation of the rock art of ancient peoples. Granite caves and rock shelters house a great variety of images of hunters, as well as of giraffes, antelopes, and other animals, painted in warm pigments of red, yellow, ochre, and brown. These caves were first occupied around 800 B.C. Although paintings from this period have long faded, many later ones remain intact.

I. Tropical Climate pages 505–508

A. **Tropical Rain Forest**
Dense tropical rain forest covers the land near the Equator in central Africa. The region has warm temperatures and receives 60 inches of rain each year. (p. 506)

B. **Crops and Cutting at a Cost**
Cash crops in rain-forested areas include bananas, pineapples, coffee, cocoa, and rubber grown on large plantations. Farmers and loggers are clear-cutting so much land that the rain forest may disappear. (pp. 506–507)

C. **Savanna**
Savanna, or tropical grassland with scattered trees, covers about half of Africa. The harmattan—hot, dry air from the Sahara—dries the moisture left from heavy summer rains, while cool, humid air blows

Where in the region might the climate be similar to what most North Americans are accustomed to?
(Coastal South Africa or highlands of East Africa.)

NATIONAL GEOGRAPHIC   **MAP STUDY**

Answers

1. *highlands of East Africa and the mid-latitude climates in southern Africa*

2. *The sequence is the same both north and south of the Equator: tropical rain forest, tropical savanna, steppe, desert.*

Map Skills Practice

Region What climate region extends across much of central Africa? *(tropical rain forest)*

Tropical Rain Forest

Tropical rain forest climate, located near the Equator, is the wettest climate region in Africa. Warm temperatures prevail in this zone. More than 60 inches (150 cm) of rainfall per year soak the dense forests. Rainfall amounts vary seasonally, but the tropical rain forests do not experience a truly dry season. Daily, rain falls on an amazing number and variety of life forms.

Shrubs, ferns, and mosses grow together at the lowest level of the rain forest, which rises 6 to 10 feet (2 to 3 m). A layer of trees and palms reaching as high as 60 feet (18 m) tops this undergrowth.

Arching over all is a canopy of leafy trees with a maximum height of 150 feet (46 m). Orchids, ferns, and mosses grow among the branches of the canopy, and woody vines link the trees in a tangle.

Economics
Crops and Cutting at a Cost

Although heavy rains in the tropical rain forest leach, or dissolve and carry away, nutrients from the soil, various crops are still grown in this zone. Bananas, pineapples, cocoa, tea, coffee, palms for oil, rubber, and cotton are grown as cash crops on large plantations. As farmers clear more land,

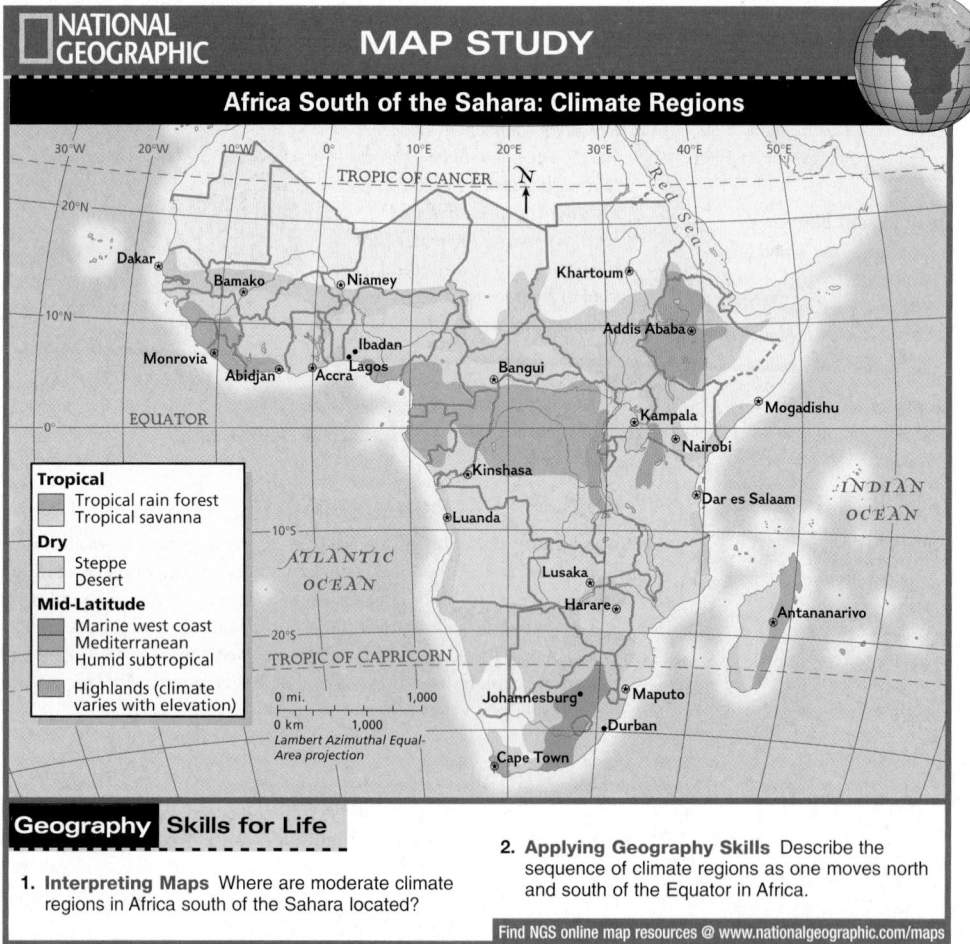

NATIONAL GEOGRAPHIC   **MAP STUDY**

Africa South of the Sahara: Climate Regions

Tropical
- Tropical rain forest
- Tropical savanna

Dry
- Steppe
- Desert

Mid-Latitude
- Marine west coast
- Mediterranean
- Humid subtropical

- Highlands (climate varies with elevation)

0 mi.   1,000
0 km   1,000
Lambert Azimuthal Equal-Area projection

Geography Skills for Life

1. **Interpreting Maps** Where are moderate climate regions in Africa south of the Sahara located?

2. **Applying Geography Skills** Describe the sequence of climate regions as one moves north and south of the Equator in Africa.

Find NGS online map resources @ www.nationalgeographic.com/maps

---

DIFFERENTIATED INSTRUCTION

At-Risk Students Students who have trouble with reading may find it helpful to approach the section in smaller portions and to set a purpose for reading each subsection. Before students begin reading, help them recast the heads and subheads in the section as questions. Then have students read each subsection to find an answer to each question. As students read, have them take notes related to each question. Then ask students to use their notes to write an answer to the question.

Refer to *Inclusion for the Social Studies Classroom Strategies and Activities.*

agriculture seriously threatens the rain forests. In addition, commercial loggers diminish the rain forest by clear-cutting tropical timber. The deforestation of Africa's tropical rain forests concerns people worldwide, who fear that if the clear-cutting continues the rain forests may disappear. In Chapter 22 you will read about steps that governments, groups, and individuals are taking to protect Africa's rain forest environments.

Savanna

Tropical grassland with scattered trees—known as savanna—covers almost half of the continent of Africa. Rainfall is seasonal in this climate zone, with alternating wet and dry seasons. In the wettest areas, which are closest to the Equator, six months of almost daily rain is followed by a six-month dry season. Average annual rainfall in the savanna is about 35 to 45 inches (90 to 115 cm).

Dueling winds affect the savanna climate of western Africa. Hot, dry air streams in from the Sahara on a northeast trade wind known as a harmattan. Although dusty, a harmattan is welcome in the summer because it dries up moisture left by heavy summer rains. Around the same time of year, cool, humid air blows in from the southwest.

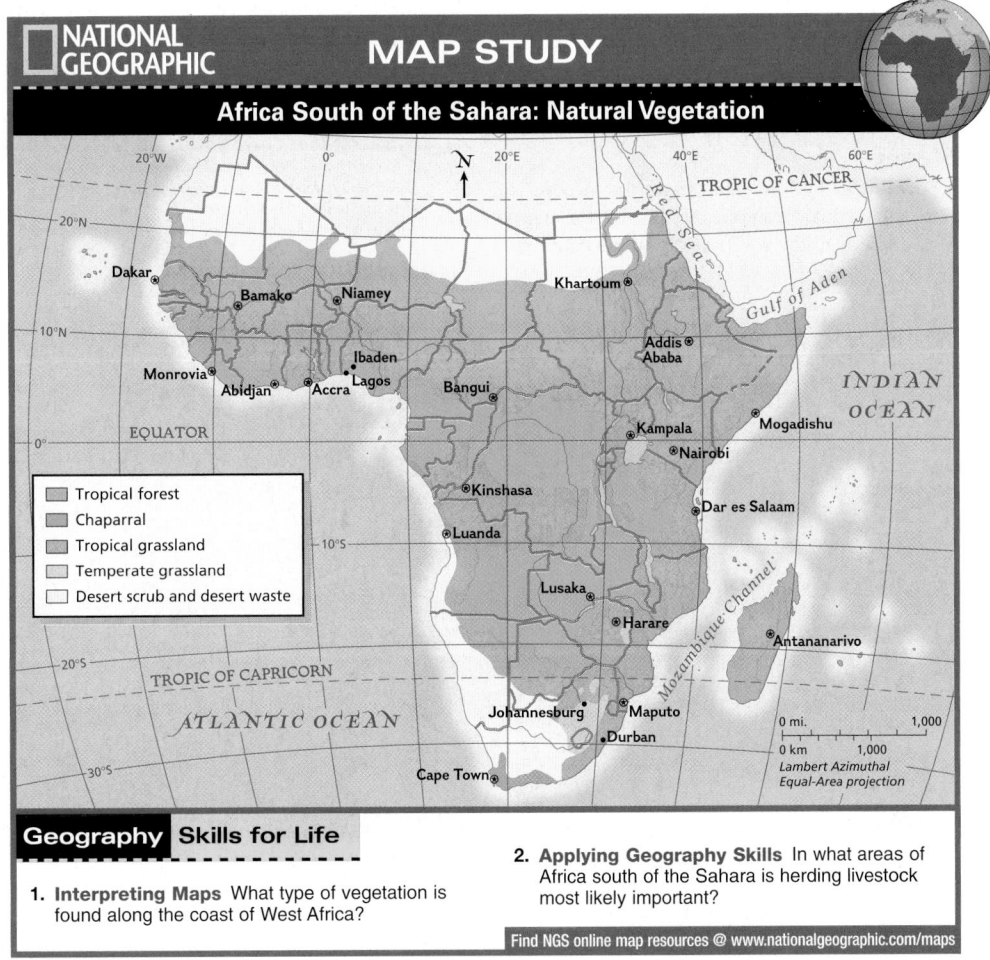

NATIONAL GEOGRAPHIC **MAP STUDY**

Africa South of the Sahara: Natural Vegetation

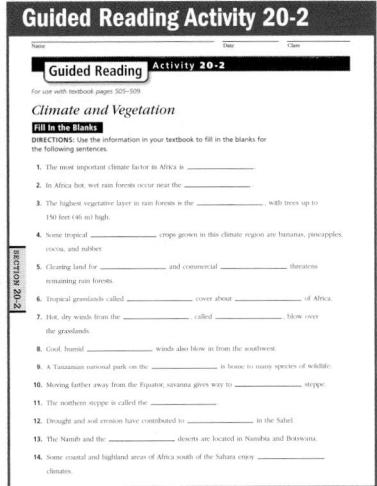

TROPIC OF CANCER

Red Sea

Gulf of Aden

Dakar
Bamako · Niamey · Khartoum
Monrovia · Abidjan · Accra · Ibaden · Lagos · Bangui
Addis Ababa
INDIAN OCEAN
EQUATOR
Kampala · Mogadishu
Nairobi
Kinshasa
Luanda
Lusaka
Harare
Antananarivo
TROPIC OF CAPRICORN
ATLANTIC OCEAN
Johannesburg · Maputo
Durban
Cape Town

Tropical forest
Chaparral
Tropical grassland
Temperate grassland
Desert scrub and desert waste

0 mi. 1,000
0 km 1,000
Lambert Azimuthal Equal-Area projection

Geography Skills for Life

1. **Interpreting Maps** What type of vegetation is found along the coast of West Africa?

2. **Applying Geography Skills** In what areas of Africa south of the Sahara is herding livestock most likely important?

Find NGS online map resources @ www.nationalgeographic.com/maps

L3 Expressing a Viewpoint

Prompt students to express a viewpoint about clear-cutting in the rain forest. **Ask:** Do you share other people's concern about the deforestation of the rain forest? Why or why not? Students may research to support their position.

L1/ELL

Guided Reading Activity 20-2

Name _____ Date _____ Class _____

Guided Reading Activity **20-2**

For use with textbook pages 505–509

Climate and Vegetation

Fill in the Blanks

DIRECTIONS: Use the information in your textbook to fill in the blanks for the following sentences.

1. The most important climate factor in Africa is _____.
2. In Africa hot, wet rain forests occur near the _____.
3. The highest vegetative layer in rain forests is the _____ with trees up to 150 feet (46 m) high.
4. Some tropical _____ crops grown in this climate region are bananas, pineapples, cocoa, and rubber.
5. Clearing land for _____ and commercial _____ threatens remaining rain forests.
6. Tropical grasslands called _____ cover about _____ of Africa.
7. Hot, dry winds from the _____ called _____ blow over the grasslands.
8. Cool, humid _____ winds also blow in from the southwest.
9. A Tanzanian national park on the _____ is home to many species of wildlife.
10. Moving farther away from the Equator, savanna gives way to _____ steppe.
11. The northern steppe is called the _____.
12. Drought and soil erosion have contributed to _____ in the Sahel.
13. The Namib and the _____ deserts are located in Namibia and Botswana.
14. Some coastal and highland areas of Africa south of the Sahara enjoy _____ climates.

NATIONAL GEOGRAPHIC **MAP STUDY**

Answers

1. *tropical forest and tropical grassland*
2. *in regions of tropical grassland where they overlap with steppe climate—near desert*

Map Skills Practice

Place What conclusion can you draw from the map key about vegetation along the southwestern coast? *(There is little or no vegetation in this area.)*

COOPERATIVE LEARNING ACTIVITY

Matching Climate and Vegetation Have groups of students make a puzzle map that shows climate and vegetation in layers. Pass out outline maps of Africa south of the Sahara that show country borders. Have one group create a colored replica of the climate map on page 506. Have another group make a colored replica of the vegetation map on page 507 and then cut their map into smaller pieces of large countries and groups of smaller countries. Have another group assemble the vegetation map pieces on top of the climate zone map. Students should pick a kind of vegetation and predict the climate where it grows. Then have them remove the country pieces to check their predictions.

EE3 Physical Systems: Standard 7

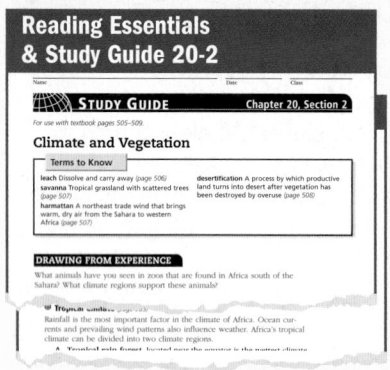

Reading Essentials
& Study Guide 20-2

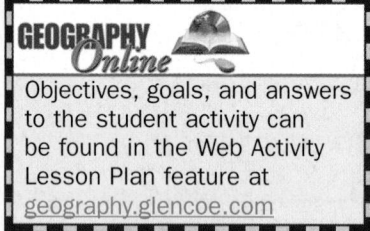

GEOGRAPHY
Online

Objectives, goals, and answers
to the student activity can
be found in the Web Activity
Lesson Plan feature at
geography.glencoe.com

NATIONAL GEOGRAPHIC **World Explorer**

Answer
*gnu, zebras, gazelles, hyenas,
lions, giraffes, and cheetahs*

More About the Photo The
plants and animals of both of
these regions are threatened
by growing human populations.

ASSESS

Assign Section 2 Assessment as
homework or as an in-class activity.

Have students use **Interactive
Tutor Self-Assessment CD-ROM.**

Tornadoes sometimes form when a harmattan and the southwest winds collide.

Trees are the main feature of the landscape in some parts of the savanna, while tall grasses cover other areas. Animals of many species graze in this zone. On the **Serengeti Plain**, one of the world's largest savanna plains, more than 1 million gnu, 60,000 zebras, and 150,000 gazelles roam, as well as hyenas, lions, giraffes, cheetahs, and other animals. Many of these animals live in the protected Serengeti National Park in Tanzania.

Dry Climates

Away from the Equator, tropical climates fade into semiarid steppe areas, which finally give way to the driest climate region of all—desert. Declining rainfall and growing populations have contributed to the expansion of the region's deserts.

Steppe

Separating the savanna from the deserts of Africa is semiarid steppe. In the south, steppe land extends to the southern tip of the continent.

The northern steppe is called the **Sahel**—literally "shore" or "edge" in Arabic. This band of dry land, which extends from Senegal to Sudan, represents the southern "coast" of the Sahara. The Sahel has natural pastures of low-growing grasses, shrubs, and acacia trees. On average, 4 to 8 inches (10 to 20 cm) of rain falls annually, but this rainfall is concentrated in June, July, and August. The remaining months are generally very dry.

Economics
Desertification

Over the past 50 years, the Sahel has undergone much desertification—a process by which productive land turns into desert following the destruction

GEOGRAPHY
Online

Student Web Activity Visit the **Glencoe World Geography** Web site at geography.glencoe.com and click on Student Web Activities—Chapter 20 for an activity on touring the physical features in Tanzania.

NATIONAL GEOGRAPHIC **World Explorer**

Geography **Skills for Life**
Tropical Climates
Eastern Africa includes both tropical savanna (left) and tropical rain forest (right) climates.
Place What animals live on the Serengeti Plain?

CRITICAL THINKING ACTIVITY

Expressing Problems Clearly After students have read pages 508–509, discuss the problem of desertification in the Sahel. Use these key questions to frame the discussion: **What is the problem? Where is the problem? What is causing the problem? What are the effects of the problem?** Then draw a problem-solution chart on the board and lead students to summarize the problem in one sentence. Write the sentence in the problem portion of the chart. Then prompt students to think about solutions to the problem with these questions: **Who might be trying to solve the problem? What are possible solutions? What might be the results of these solutions?** Write students' ideas in the solution portion of the chart.

EE5 Environment and Society: Standards 14 and 15

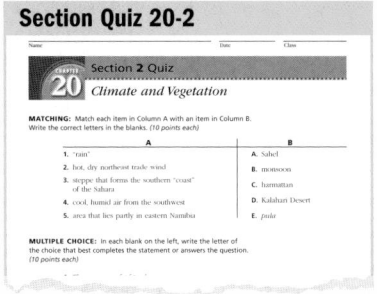

of vegetation. Some scientists claim that the Sahel's desertification is caused mainly by climate change that brings long periods of extreme dryness and water shortages. Lands managed well during drought periods can usually recover once rains return. Other scientists, however, believe that human and animal activities also contribute to desertification. People strip trees for firewood and clear too much land for farming, while livestock overgraze the short grasses. As a result, the land is depleted and topsoil is further eroded, reducing both the land's productivity and its ability to recover from drought.

▲ Desertification in the Sahel of West Africa

Desert

Isolated parts of southern Africa swelter in a desert climate. In the east, hot, dry weather prevails in much of Kenya and Somalia. Along the Atlantic coast of Namibia, rocks, dunes, and scattered desert plants cover the **Namib Desert**. Joining the Namib, the **Kalahari Desert** occupies eastern Namibia, most of Botswana, and part of South Africa. A sand-swept expanse with few other features, most of the Kalahari

is true desert, but parts of it do support some animals and a variety of plants, including grass and trees. In general, little rain falls in the desert, and average monthly temperatures are extremely high. Daily temperatures in the Kalahari vary greatly, however, ranging from 120°F (49°C) during the day to 50°F (10°C) at night.

Moderate Climates

Although less extensive than the main climate zones, moderate climate zones also exist in Africa south of the Sahara. As the map on page 506 shows, coastal areas of South Africa and highlands regions in East Africa enjoy moderate climates with comfortable temperatures and enough rainfall for farming. In the highlands, temperatures are somewhat lower, snow is not uncommon at high elevations, and vegetation abounds. The highlands areas can seem almost lush, as Curt Stager observed on his journey through East Africa:

> ❝ *The Ethiopian Highlands are far cooler and [more moist] than the surrounding lowlands. Although plagued in recent years by drought, this area is, in normal times, an agricultural island in a desert sea.* ❞
>
> Curt Stager, "Africa's Great Rift," *National Geographic*, May 1990

Reteach

Give each student a blank outline map of the region. Project Unit Map Overlay Transparency 7-3 and have students draw bands on their maps showing the arrangement of climate regions on either side of the Equator. Have students label each band and within it write statements about the climate and vegetation there.

Enrich

The name "Africa" comes from the ancient Romans. The Latin word *aprica* means "sunny" and the Greek word *aphrike* means "without cold." Ask students what parts of Africa south of the Sahara fit such descriptions.

④ CLOSE

Have students summarize orally what they have learned about climate and vegetation in Africa south of the Sahara. **Ask:** What questions do you still have about the region's climate and vegetation? Encourage students to look for answers in various resources.

SECTION ② ASSESSMENT

Checking for Understanding

1. **Define** leach, savanna, harmattan.

2. **Main Ideas** Use a table like the one below to fill in characteristics of Africa south of the Sahara. Then write a short description of one of the region's climate zones.

Climate Zone	Climate	Vegetation

Critical Thinking

3. **Making Predictions** Do you think desertification will continue in Africa south of the Sahara? Explain your answer.

4. **Identifying Cause and Effect** In what ways are people affecting Africa's tropical rain forests?

5. **Making Generalizations** How does physical geography affect the climate and vegetation in this region?

Analyzing Maps

6. **Region** Study the maps on pages 506 and 507. Which climate regions lie on the Equator? What kind of vegetation thrives there?

Applying Geography

7. **Rainfall's Impact** As a geographer studying rainfall in Africa south of the Sahara, write a report explaining how precipitation defines climate and vegetation there.

SECTION ② ASSESSMENT ANSWERS

1. All vocabulary terms are defined in the text.

2. Tables should contain details about the climate and vegetation of each climate zone, and descriptions should incorporate information from the table.

3. Possible answer: Desertification will continue—vegetation has been destroyed by people, their animals, and the climate, and without rain it is unlikely that new vegetation will grow.

4. People are using more land for farming, and commercial loggers are clear-cutting tropical timber.

5. Areas at higher elevations have cooler temperatures and receive plentiful precipitation, which results in lush vegetation.

6. tropical rain forest, tropical savanna, steppe, highlands, and desert; tropical forest and tropical grassland

7. **Applying Geography** Papers should reflect information about the amount of precipitation in the different climate zones and the resulting vegetation.

Teaching the Skill

As students look carefully at the time zone map, draw their attention to places where time zones accommodate political borders or geographic features. Remind students to match the color of each time zone band with the location, since time zones do not always follow straight lines. Then, in addition to questions like those in "Practicing the Skill," have students solve time zone problems, such as the following: "If you take a six-hour flight from London to New York City, leaving London at 10:00 A.M., what time will it be in New York City when you arrive?" *(11 A.M.)* Why? *(As you fly west, you cross five time zones, and the time is five hours earlier.)* Challenge students to test each other with similar time zone problems.

Additional Practice
L1

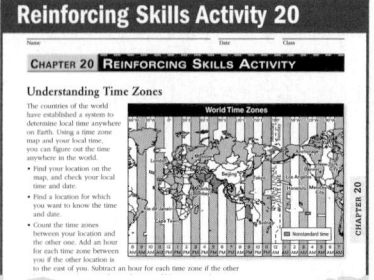

Reinforcing Skills Activity 20

GLENCOE
TECHNOLOGY

Glencoe Skillbuilder Interactive Workbook, Level 2

MAP & GRAPH
SkillBuilder

Understanding Time Zones

As the earth rotates on its axis, half of the planet experiences day and the other half experiences night. By international agreement there are 24 time zones around the world.

Learning the Skill

Each of the 24 time zones represents 15° longitude, or the distance that the earth rotates in one hour. The base time zone, called Greenwich Mean Time (GMT) or Universal Time, is set at the Prime Meridian (0°). As one travels west from Greenwich, the time becomes earlier; as one travels east, the time becomes later. The international date line generally follows the 180° meridian. Traveling west across this imaginary line, you add a day. Traveling east, you subtract a day.

The imaginary lines that divide time zones sometimes curve or form angles. The lines are drawn to allow for geographic or political needs. For example, certain lines curve around Pacific island groups so that island countries that cover relatively small areas will not have multiple time zones.

To determine the time and day of the week in different time zones, follow these steps:

- **Locate on the map a place for which you already know the time and day of the week.**
- **Locate the place for which you wish to know the time and day of the week.**
- **Count the time zones between the two places.**
- **Calculate the time by either adding or subtracting an hour for each time zone, depending on whether you are moving east or west.**

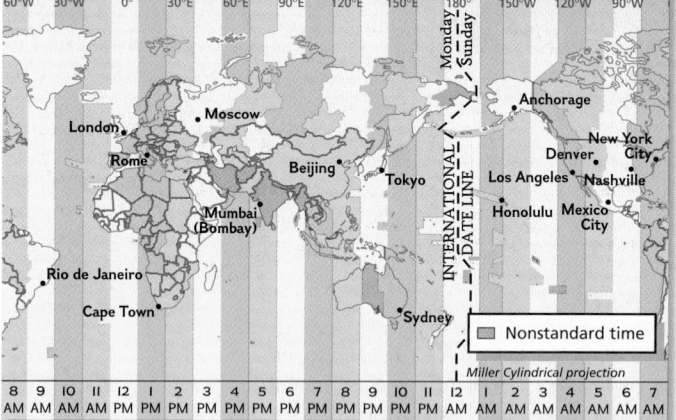

World Time Zones

Nonstandard time

Miller Cylindrical projection

- **If you have crossed the International Date Line, identify the day.**

Practicing the Skill

Study the map and answer the questions.

1. How many time zones does continental Africa have?
2. Does Africa have more, fewer, or the same number of time zones as the United States?
3. If it is 4:00 P.M. Saturday in Cape Town, South Africa, what time and what day is it in Rio de Janeiro, Brazil?
4. If it is 10:00 A.M. Tuesday in Sydney, Australia, what time and what day is it in Honolulu, Hawaii?

5. Notice that some time zones have crooked boundaries. Why do you think that is?

Applying the Skill

Use a reference book or Internet sources to find a more detailed map of Africa's time zones. Notice how the lines are drawn in relation to cities, political divisions, or physical features. Then make a list of locations where adjusted lines occur. Write the reasons you think the adjustments were made.

Go To The Glencoe Skillbuilder Interactive Workbook, Level 2 provides instruction and practice in key social studies skills.

ANSWERS TO PRACTICING THE SKILL

1. five
2. Fewer; the United States has six zones.
3. 11:00 A.M. Saturday
4. 2:00 P.M. Monday
5. They follow political boundaries so people in a common political unit will be in the same time zone.

SUMMARY & STUDY GUIDE

SECTION 1   The Land (pp. 499–504)

Terms to Know
- escarpment
- cataract
- rift valley
- fault
- delta
- estuary

Key Points
- Africa south of the Sahara is a series of step-like plateaus, rising in a few places to mountains and slashed in the east by a rift valley.
- High elevations and narrow coastal plains characterized by escarpments have made traveling to Africa's interior very difficult.
- The region's water systems include numerous long, large, or deep lakes; spectacular waterfalls; and great rivers that drain expansive basins.
- Minerals and water are the region's most abundant natural resources.

Organizing Your Notes
Use a table like the one below to help you organize important details about the physical features of Africa south of the Sahara.

Physical Feature	Location

SECTION 2   Climate and Vegetation (pp. 505–509)

Terms to Know
- leach
- savanna
- harmattan

Key Points
- Rainfall, tropical latitudes, nearness to the Equator, ocean air masses, and elevation are the main factors influencing climate variations in Africa south of the Sahara.
- The region can be divided into four main climate zones: tropical rain forest, savanna, steppe, and desert.
- Moderate climates such as humid subtropical and marine west coast are also found in Africa south of the Sahara.

Organizing Your Notes
Use a graphic organizer like the one below to organize your notes about each of the climate zones described in this section.

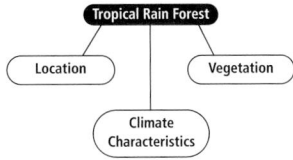

Tropical Rain Forest — Location — Vegetation — Climate Characteristics

◀ African wild dogs hunt in the Okavango Delta, Botswana

Using the Chapter 20 Summary & Study Guide

Use the Chapter 20 Summary & Study Guide to preview, review, condense, or reteach the chapter.

Preview/Review

🔘 **Vocabulary PuzzleMaker CD-ROM** reinforces "Terms to Know."

🔘 **Interactive Tutor Self-Assessment CD-ROM** provides a review of Chapter 20 content.

Condense

Have students read the Chapter 20 Summary & Study Guide.

🔘 Chapter 20 Audio Program

📂 Chapter 20 Guided Reading Activities

Reteach

📂 Chapter 20 Reteaching Activities (Spanish also available)

📂 Chapter 20 Reading Essentials and Study Guides

GLENCOE TECHNOLOGY

🔲 NATIONAL GEOGRAPHIC

WORLD REGIONS
VIDEO PROGRAM

Unit 7, Africa South of the Sahara
The following segments enhance the study of this unit:

- **Namib Desert**
- **Living With Elephants**
- **Baaba Maal: Musician of the World**

CHAPTER CULMINATING ACTIVITY

Synthesizing Information Direct students to use what they have learned in this chapter to write brief descriptions about the physical geography of Africa south of the Sahara. Write the following cue words and phrases on the board: *landforms, water systems, natural resources, tropical climate, dry climates.* For each cue have students write a one-paragraph summary of what they have learned about the topic as it relates to Africa south of the Sahara. When students have completed the assignment, you may wish to have them read aloud their descriptions when you call out the cues. 🔲 **EE2 Places and Regions: Standard 4**

NOTE: This activity may be completed separately or you may wish students to incorporate it into their GeoJournals.

CHAPTER
20

ASSESSMENT & ACTIVITIES

Reviewing Key Terms

1. fault
2. savanna
3. cataract
4. delta
5. escarpment
6. harmattan
7. leach
8. estuary
9. rift valley

Reviewing Facts
SECTION 1

1. in the eastern highlands from Ethiopia almost to the Cape of Good Hope
2. Niger, Zambezi, Congo
3. water, oil, gold, uranium, and diamonds; along the western coast and in southern Africa

SECTION 2

4. The Sahel has lost much of its vegetation. People have stripped the trees for firewood and cleared land for farming, and livestock have eaten the short grasses of the Sahel.
5. scattered trees and tall grasses
6. tropical rain forest, tropical forest

Critical Thinking

1. Minerals; the region's minerals are in demand because supplies of many of them are limited elsewhere in the world.

Reviewing Key Terms

On a sheet of paper, write the term that matches each definition. Refer to the Terms to Know in the Summary & Study Guide on page 511.

1. a crack in the earth's surface created by shifting of the earth's tectonic plates
2. tropical grassland with scattered trees
3. a towering waterfall
4. a triangular section of land formed by sand and silt carried downriver to a river's mouth
5. a steep, often jagged slope or cliff
6. a northeast trade wind crossing the Sahara
7. to dissolve and carry away
8. a passage where freshwater meets seawater
9. a long valley between faults in the earth, with volcanic mountains and deep lakes

Reviewing Facts

SECTION 1

1. Where are the main highlands areas and mountains in Africa south of the Sahara?
2. What three great river basins are located in Africa south of the Sahara?
3. What natural resources are especially plentiful in Africa south of the Sahara? Describe the locations of these resources.

SECTION 2

4. Describe vegetation changes in the Sahel and the causes that contribute to these changes.
5. What kind of vegetation grows in the savannas of this region?
6. What is the wettest climate zone in Africa south of the Sahara, and what types of vegetation grow there?

Critical Thinking

1. **Drawing Conclusions** What resources make Africa important to the world economy? Why?
2. **Making Generalizations** What general observations can you make about the areas of the region that have moderate climates?
3. **Drawing Conclusions** Create a Venn diagram to compare causes of rain forest deforestation and of desertification in the Sahel. Then propose steps to solve the problem.

Deforestation ── Both ── Desertification

NATIONAL GEOGRAPHIC **Locating Places**
Africa South of the Sahara: Physical Geography

Match the letters on the map with the physical features of Africa south of the Sahara. Write your answers on a sheet of paper.

1. Lake Chad
2. Kilimanjaro
3. Kalahari Desert
4. Lake Malawi
5. Great Rift Valley
6. Okavango Delta
7. Lake Victoria
8. Zambezi River
9. Lake Tanganyika
10. Congo River
11. Niger River
12. Namib Desert

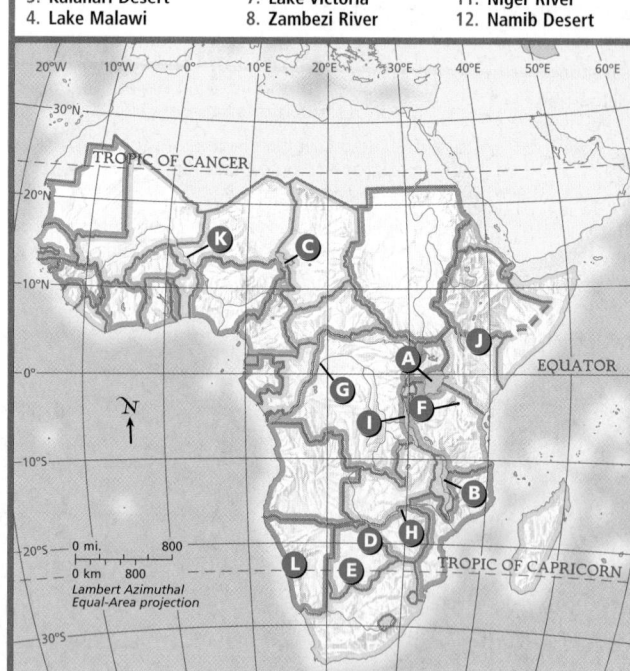

2. Areas in the region with moderate climates are usually close to the coast or at higher elevations.
3. Venn diagram: cause of deforestation alone—trees clear-cut by commercial loggers; causes of both—land cleared for farming, trees used for firewood; cause of desertification alone—grasses eaten by livestock. Students should hypothesize about steps being taken to slow or halt these processes.

NATIONAL GEOGRAPHIC **Locating Places**

1. C	**4.** B	**7.** A	**10.** G
2. F	**5.** J	**8.** H	**11.** K
3. E	**6.** D	**9.** I	**12.** L

Using the Regional Atlas

1. Zambezi, Okavango, Limpopo, Orange
2. uranium; diamonds, cobalt, copper, zinc, uranium, gold

Using the Regional Atlas

Refer to the Regional Atlas on pages 486–489.

1. **Region** What rivers drain much of southern Africa?
2. **Location** What natural resources are found in the Ethiopian Highlands? The Katanga Plateau?

Thinking Like a Geographer

What challenges does the physical geography of Africa south of the Sahara pose to the development and distribution of the area's natural resources?

Problem-Solving Activity

Group Research Project Africa south of the Sahara has enormous potential for producing hydroelectric power. Work with a group to learn more about hydroelectricity in the region. Find out where water power has already been harnessed, and identify other sites that might be good for hydroelectric power plants. What problems might the physical geography pose to generating and distributing hydroelectricity? Suggest solutions to one or more problems, and share your findings with the class.

GeoJournal

Comparison-Contrast Essay Using the information you logged in your GeoJournal, write a descriptive paragraph about one of the significant physical features of Africa south of the Sahara. Then write a second paragraph comparing this feature with a similar physical feature of Latin America.

Technology Activity

Developing Multimedia Presentations Select a land or water feature of Africa south of the Sahara, and develop a multimedia presentation about it. Use Internet and library resources to gather information. Then design and draw maps and other visual aids to illustrate your work, and make your presentation to the class.

Standardized Test Practice

Study the time zone map below. Then choose the best answer for the following multiple-choice questions. If you have trouble answering the questions, use the process of elimination to narrow your choices.

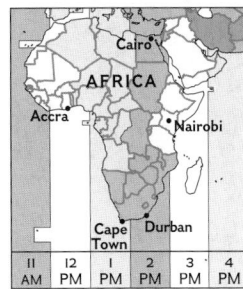

1. **If it is noon in Accra, Ghana, what time is it in Cape Town, South Africa?**

   A 2 P.M.   C 10 P.M.

   B 2 A.M.   D 11 P.M.

2. **If you were standing in Nairobi, Kenya, at 2:00 in the afternoon, what time would it be in Durban, South Africa?**

   F 2 P.M.   H 1 P.M.

   G 11 A.M.   J 4 P.M.

Test-Taking Tip Be sure to pay close attention to the locations mentioned in the question. By studying the map, you can see that the time zone in which Nairobi lies is located next to the time zone in which Durban is located. Therefore, the difference between the times should be one hour. Notice that the sample times shown on the map are different from those in the question, however, so you will need to subtract to find the correct answer.

GeoJournal

Students' descriptions should be vivid and accurate and their comparisons well chosen and well developed.

Technology Activity

Presentations and visuals should be engaging and appropriate to the land or water features chosen.

Standardized Test Practice

1. A
2. H

Tested Objectives:
analyzing information interpreting a diagram

Additional Practice and Test-Taking Tips

 Standardized Test Practice Workbook

? CHAPTER BONUS TEST QUESTION

Many of the plant and animal species on Madagascar are found nowhere else in Africa south of the Sahara. How would you explain this? *(Madagascar is an island; vegetation and animal species there developed separately from those on the continent of Africa; and those that developed on the island were never carried to the mainland.)*

Thinking Like a Geographer

Accept all reasonable answers, and prompt students to support their answers in class discussion. However, students may observe that sudden rises in land, waterfalls and rapids, and thick vegetation in the tropical rain forest prevent easy access to and transportation of the area's natural resources.

Problem-Solving Activity

Students' research and solutions should reflect an understanding of the requirements for generating power from hydroelectric plants and the barriers to their construction in Africa south of the Sahara.

CHAPTER 21 PLANNING GUIDE

NOTE: The following materials may be used when teaching Chapter 21. Section-level support materials are shown at point-of-use in the margins of the Teacher Wraparound Edition.

TEACHING TRANSPARENCIES

L2 Unit 7 Map Overlay Transparencies

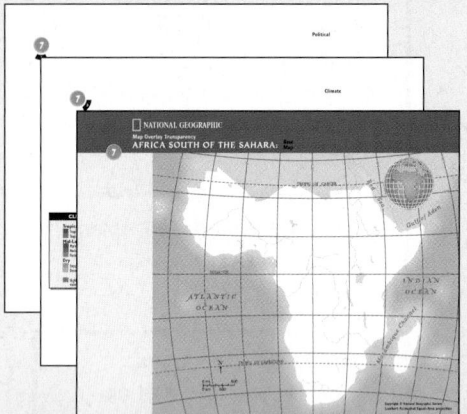

L2 Political Map Transparency 7

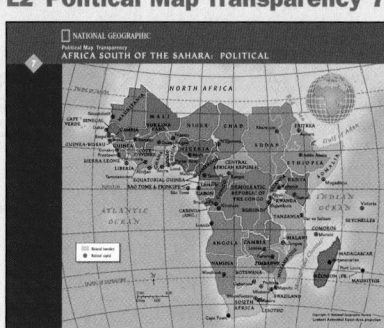

GEOGRAPHIC LITERACY

Focus on Geography Literacy

APPLICATION AND ENRICHMENT

L3 Enrichment Activity 21

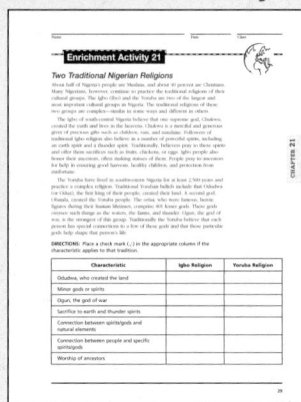

REVIEW AND REINFORCEMENT

L1 Vocabulary Activity 21 L1 Reinforcing Skills Activity 21 L1 Reteaching Activity 21

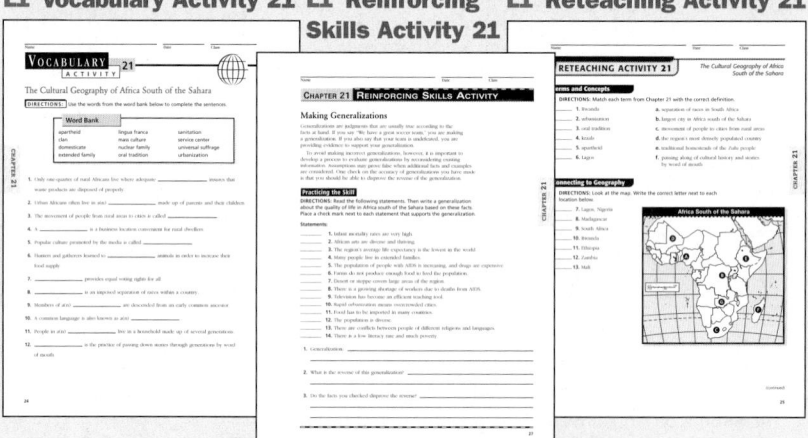

ASSESSMENT

L2 Chapter 21 Test Form A

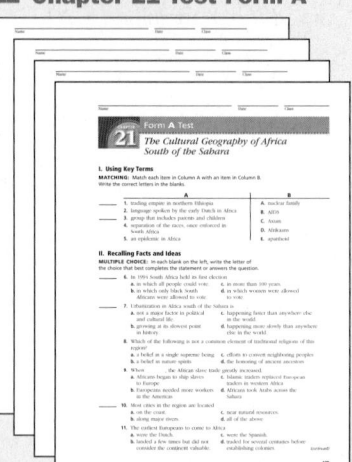

L2 Chapter 21 Test Form B

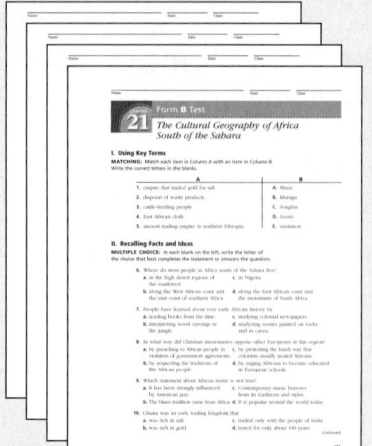

L1/ELL Performance Assessment Activity 21

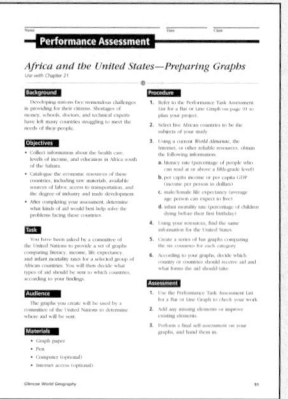

ExamView® Pro Testmaker

514A

SPANISH RESOURCES

The following Spanish language materials are available in the Spanish Resources binder:

- Spanish Vocabulary Activities
- Spanish Guided Reading Activities
- Spanish Reteaching Activities
- Spanish Summaries
- Spanish Quizzes and Tests
- Spanish Reading Essentials and Study Guide

MULTIMEDIA

- World Regions Video
- MindJogger Videoquiz
- Vocabulary PuzzleMaker CD-ROM
- Interactive Tutor Self-Assessment CD-ROM
- ExamView® Pro Testmaker CD-ROM
- Audio Program
- TeacherWorks CD-ROM
- Interactive Student Edition CD-ROM
- Glencoe Skillbuilder Interactive Workbook CD-ROM, Level 2
- Presentation Plus! CD-ROM

Timesaving Tools

TeacherWorks™ **All-In-One Planner and Resource Center**

- **Interactive Teacher Edition** Access your Teacher Wraparound Edition and your classroom resources with a few easy clicks.
- **Interactive Lesson Planner** Planning has never been easier! Organize your week, month, semester, or year with all the lesson helps you need to make teaching creative, timely, and relevant.

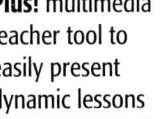

Use Glencoe's **Presentation Plus!** multimedia teacher tool to easily present dynamic lessons that visually excite your students. Using Microsoft PowerPoint® you can customize the presentations to create your own personalized lessons.

GEOGRAPHY Online

Use our Web site for additional resources. All essential content is covered in the Student Edition.

You and your students can visit geography.glencoe.com, the Web site companion to *Glencoe World Geography.* This innovative integration of electronic and print media offers your students a wealth of opportunities. The student text directs students to the Web site for the following options:

- **Chapter Overviews**
- **Student Activities**
- **Self-Check Quizzes**
- **Textbook Updates**

Answers are provided for you in the "Web Activity Lesson Plan." Additional Web resources and Interactive Tutor puzzles are also available.

▶ **Additional Glencoe Teacher Support**

- **Teaching Strategies for the Geography Classroom (including Block Scheduling Pacing Guides)**
- **Graphic Organizer Transparencies Strategies and Activities**
- **Outline Map Resource Book**
- **Reading in the Content Area**

CHAPTER 21 PLANNING GUIDE

SECTION RESOURCES

Daily Objectives	Reproducible Resources	Multimedia Resources
SECTION 1 Population Patterns 1. Explain why parts of Africa south of the Sahara are densely populated. 2. Name obstacles to economic growth in the region. 3. Identify the diverse peoples of Africa south of the Sahara. 4. Explain why the region's cities are growing so rapidly.	Reproducible Lesson Plan 21-1 Daily Lecture Notes 21-1 Guided Reading Activity 21-1* Reading Essentials and Study Guide 21-1* Section Quiz 21-1*	Daily Focus Skills Transparency 21-1 Political Map Transparency 7 Unit 7 Map Overlay Transparencies Interactive Tutor Self-Assessment CD-ROM ExamView® Pro Testmaker CD-ROM* Presentation Plus! CD-ROM
SECTION 2 History and Government 1. Describe the main achievements of the ancient civilizations of Africa south of the Sahara. 2. Explain how European colonization disrupted African patterns of life. 3. Discuss challenges countries of the region faced after independence.	Reproducible Lesson Plan 21-2 Daily Lecture Notes 21-2 Guided Reading Activity 21-2* Reading Essentials and Study Guide 21-2* Section Quiz 21-2*	Daily Focus Skills Transparency 21-2 Political Map Transparency 7 Unit 7 Map Overlay Transparencies Interactive Tutor Self-Assessment CD-ROM ExamView® Pro Testmaker CD-ROM* Presentation Plus! CD-ROM
SECTION 3 Cultures and Lifestyles 1. List languages spoken by people in Africa south of the Sahara. 2. Identify the major religions in Africa south of the Sahara. 3. Describe art forms developed by peoples of the region. 4. Examine similarities and differences in the lifestyles of people in the region.	Reproducible Lesson Plan 21-3 Vocabulary Activity 21* Daily Lecture Notes 21-3 Guided Reading Activity 21-3* Reading Essentials and Study Guide 21-3* Reteaching Activity 21* Reinforcing Skills Activity 21 Section Quiz 21-3*	Daily Focus Skills Transparency 21-3 Unit 7 Map Overlay Transparencies Vocabulary PuzzleMaker CD-ROM World Music: A Cultural Legacy Interactive Tutor Self-Assessment CD-ROM ExamView® Pro Testmaker CD-ROM* Presentation Plus! CD-ROM

Blackline Master	▣ Software	� Videocassette	*Also available in Spanish
Transparency	◉ CD-ROM	◉ DVD	

OUT OF TIME? Assign the Chapter 21 **Reading Essentials and Study Guide.**

Block Schedule

Activities that are particularly suited to use within the block scheduling framework are identified throughout this chapter by the following designation:

KEY TO ABILITY LEVELS

Teaching strategies have been coded for various learning styles and abilities.

L1   BASIC activities for all students

L2   AVERAGE activities for average to above-average students

L3   CHALLENGING activities for above-average students

ELL   ENGLISH LANGUAGE LEARNER activities

Teacher to Teacher

Sharon Goins
Colonel White School
of the Arts
Dayton, OH

Presenting Africa
South of the Sahara

Organize students into groups. Have each group choose an area of pre-colonial Africa south of the Sahara to research in the library or on the Internet. Research should include commerce, religion, government, landforms, and other cultural, geographic, and political features of their area. Each group should then conduct similar research about the same area in contemporary Africa.

Once the research is complete, have each group put together a presentation. These presentations must include a visual, such as a poster or a simulation of a village, and a written brief to hand out to the rest of the class. The presentations should also include maps students have made of their area. When they make their presentations, students may choose to dress in elements of traditional clothing, and bring in samples of foods, symbols, and artifacts of pre-colonial Africa.

NATIONAL GEOGRAPHIC TEACHER'S CORNER

Index to National Geographic Magazine:

The following articles may be used for research relating to this chapter:

- "People of Heaven," by Peter Godwin, August 2000.
- "African Marriage Rituals," by Carol Beckwith and Angela Fisher, November 1999.
- "Preserving the Sahara's Art," by David Coulson, September 1999.

National Geographic Society Products:

To order the following products for use with this chapter, call National Geographic Society at 1-800-368-2728.

- *South Africa: After Apartheid* (Video)
- *Africa* (Video)
- *National Geographic Desk Reference* (Book)

NGS ONLINE

Access National Geographic's Web site for current events, activities, links, interactive features, and archives.
www.nationalgeographic.com

Meeting National Standards

Geography For Life

The following standards are highlighted in Chapter 21:

Section 1	**EE1 The World in Spatial Terms:** Standard 1 **EE2 Places and Regions:** Standard 4 **EE4 Human Systems:** Standard 9
Section 2	**EE4 Human Systems:** Standards 11, 13
Section 3	**EE4 Human Systems:** Standards 10, 13

Local Objectives

_____

_____

MEETING SPECIAL NEEDS

In addition to the Differentiated Instruction strategies found in each section, the following resources are also suitable for your special needs students:

- *ExamView® Pro Testmaker CD-ROM* allows teachers to tailor tests by reducing answer choices.
- The *Audio Program* includes the entire narrative of the student edition so that less-proficient readers can listen to the words as they read them.
- The *Reading Essentials and Study Guide* provides the same content as the student edition but is written two grade levels below the textbook.
- *Guided Reading Activities* give less-proficient readers point-by-point instructions to increase comprehension as they read each textbook section.
- *Enrichment Activities* include a stimulating collection of readings and activities for gifted and talented students.

Chapter Objectives

1. Examine population patterns in Africa south of the Sahara.

2. Explain the effect of the movement of people on the region past and present.

3. Describe aspects of African culture.

GLENCOE TECHNOLOGY

Use *MindJogger Videoquiz* to preview the Chapter 21 content.

GeoJournal

For access to additional photos, maps, and information on the cultural features of Africa south of the Sahara go to www.nationalgeographic.com (See Teacher pages in front for strategies for using journals in the geography classroom.)

GEOGRAPHY Online

Introduce students to chapter content and key terms by having them access **Chapter Overview 21** at geography.glencoe.com

FOLDABLES™ Study Organizer

Dinah Zike's Foldables are three-dimensional, interactive graphic organizers that help students practice basic writing skills, review key vocabulary terms, and identify main ideas. Have students complete the Foldable activity in the **Dinah Zike's Reading and Study Skills Foldables** booklet.

CHAPTER **21**

The Cultural Geography of Africa South of the Sahara

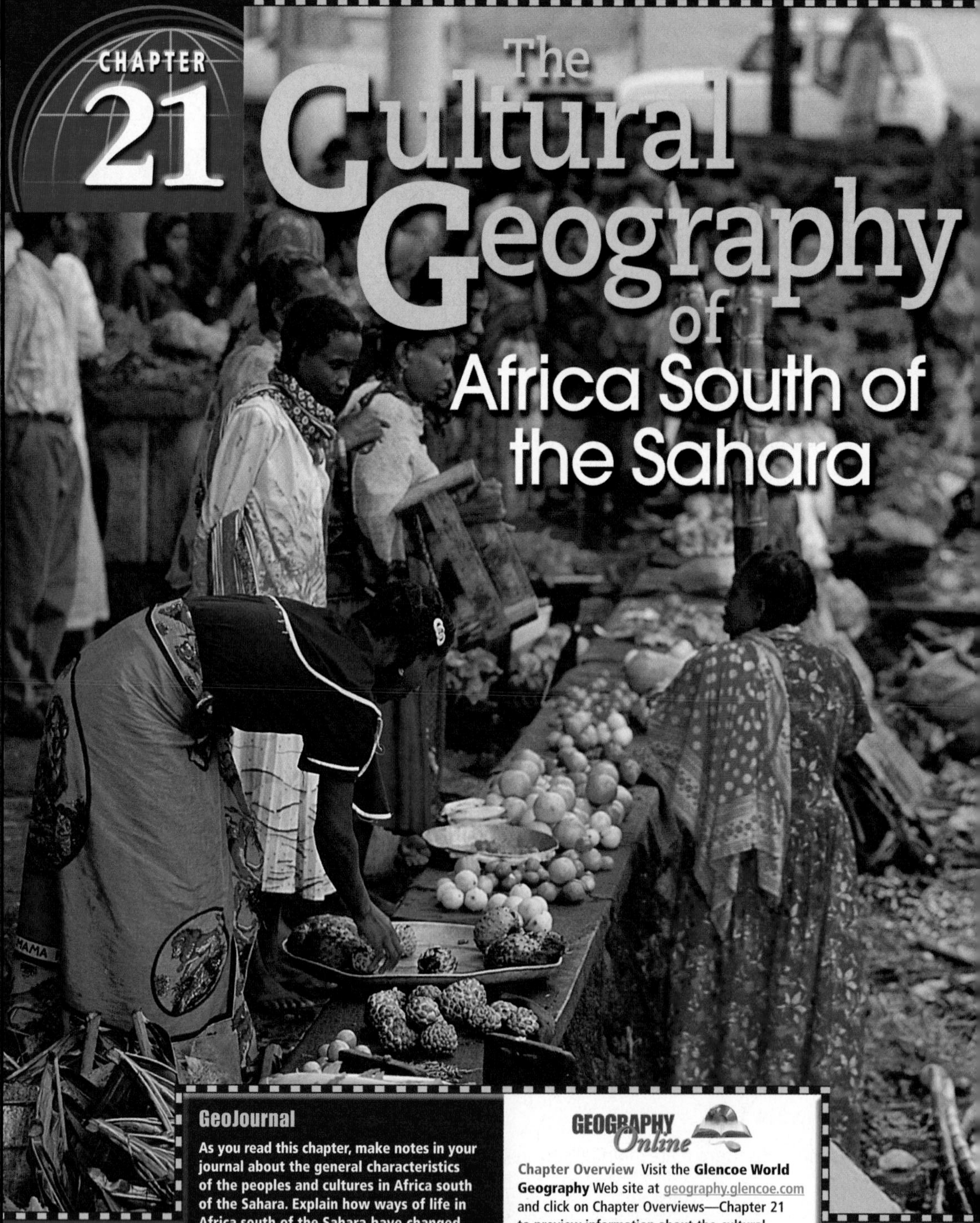

GeoJournal

As you read this chapter, make notes in your journal about the general characteristics of the peoples and cultures in Africa south of the Sahara. Explain how ways of life in Africa south of the Sahara have changed in recent years.

GEOGRAPHY Online

Chapter Overview Visit the **Glencoe World Geography** Web site at geography.glencoe.com and click on Chapter Overviews—Chapter 21 to preview information about the cultural geography of the region.

ABOUT THE PHOTO

Visual Instruction In markets such as this one in the islands of Comoros, shoppers might find vanilla beans, coconuts, coffee, cloves, and cacao as well as cassava, sweet potatoes, bananas, and rice. Traditional arts, including basketry, wood carving, and elaborately embroidered clothing are also common in Comoros. **Ask: What foods do you think people from these islands off the coast of Africa near Madagascar might prepare?** *(Comorian people eat root-based stews common in East Africa and rice-based curries common in South Asia.)* 🌐 **EE2 Places and Regions: Standard 4**

Guide to Reading

Consider What You Know

As in other world regions you have studied, people in Africa south of the Sahara are moving from rural areas to cities. What changes might a new city resident face?

Reading Strategy

Organizing Complete a web diagram similar to the one below by filling in reasons for food production problems in Africa south of the Sahara.

Food Production Problems

Read to Find Out

• Why are parts of Africa south of the Sahara densely populated?

• What are the obstacles to economic growth in the region?

• Who are the diverse peoples of Africa south of the Sahara?

• Why are the region's cities growing so rapidly?

Terms to Know

• sanitation
• urbanization
• service center

Places to Locate

• Nigeria
• Rwanda
• Namibia
• Zimbabwe
• Lagos
• Accra
• Kinshasa
• Nairobi
• Johannesburg

◀ *A market in the Comoros Islands*

Population Patterns

NATIONAL GEOGRAPHIC

A Geographic View

To Market

The [riverside market] in Lukulu [Zambia] bustled with swarms of people picking through baskets of fish and used clothes lying in enormous piles or draped on racks or else flapping like pennants on long lines.

Julius Nkwita was selling small piles of dried fish, about 60 cents for a handful. But sometimes he swapped his fish for cups of flour or an item of clothing.... His wife and four of his children were in his home village, ... while he stayed in his seasonal fishing camp—just a reed hut—with his son, fishing intensively.

Seasonal fishing camp, central Africa

—Paul Theroux, "Down the Zambezi," National Geographic, October 1997

A small market town, a village, a temporary fishing camp—this is Julius Nkwita's world. On a trip through central Africa on the Zambezi River, writer Paul Theroux met Julius Nkwita and many others whose lives revolve around a small community. Like these people of the Zambezi River basin, the majority of Africans south of the Sahara live in rural areas. In this section you will trace population patterns in Africa south of the Sahara—the fastest-growing and third most populous region in the world.

Rapid Population Growth

Home to more than 711 million people, Africa south of the Sahara has about 11 percent of the world's population. It has both the highest birthrate and the highest death rate in the world. It also has the world's highest infant mortality rate and shortest life expectancy.

Section Overview

This section explains population patterns in Africa south of the Sahara and their effect on life in the region.

BELLRINGER
Skillbuilder Activity

Project transparency and have students answer questions.

Available as blackline master.

Daily Focus Skills Transparency 21-1

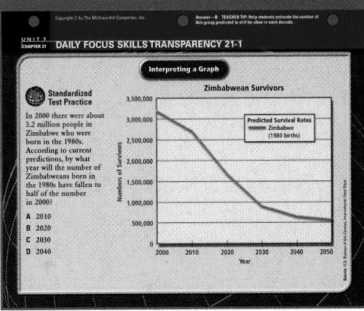

Guide to Reading

Consider What You Know
Answers *better job opportunities, overcrowding, and inadequate public services*

Reading Strategy
Answers *government geared economy towards importing too much of food suply, intensive cultivation has resulted in loss of soil fertility, drought*

Preteaching Vocabulary
Have selected students write their own definitions for the section vocabulary terms. Read aloud both the proposed and dictionary definitions, and have students vote for those they think are correct. Students earn a point for each correct choice.

RESOURCE MANAGER

Reproducible Masters
• Reproducible Lesson Plan 21-1
• Daily Lecture Notes 21-1
• Guided Reading Activity 21-1
• Reading Essentials and Study Guide 21-1
• Section Quiz 21-1

Transparencies
• Daily Focus Skills Transparency 21-1
• Political Map Transparency 7
• Unit 7 Map Overlay Transparencies

Multimedia
• Interactive Tutor Self-Assessment CD-ROM
• ExamView® Pro Testmaker CD-ROM
• Presentation Plus! CD-ROM

❷ TEACH

L3 Predicting Population

Challenge students to provide probable population figures for Africa south of the Sahara in 2010, 2020, and 2030. Direct students to use the population figure for 2000 (629 million) and an average rate of growth of 2 percent a year to predict the region's population for these intervals.

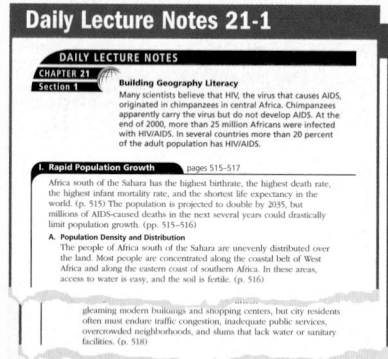

Daily Lecture Notes 21-1

L1/ELL

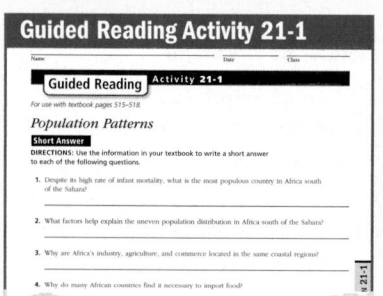

Guided Reading Activity 21-1

Despite a high death rate, births outnumber deaths in this region. In fact, population growth in Africa south of the Sahara surpasses that of every other region in the world, increasing at an average rate of 2.5 percent a year. At this rate, the total population of Africa south of the Sahara will more than double in just 35 years.

Nigeria, the most populous African country south of the Sahara, is one example of the region's rapid population growth. In 2003 about 133.9 million people lived in Nigeria. With an expected growth rate of 2.8 percent a year, it is likely that in 50 years Nigeria's population will reach more than 300 million.

One factor, however, may drastically limit population growth in the region over the next 10 years. The disease AIDS (acquired immunodeficiency syndrome) has spread rapidly. About 70 percent of the estimated 36 million people in the world currently carrying HIV, the virus that causes AIDS, live in Africa south of the Sahara. At the end of 2000, about 17 million Africans had already died of AIDS-related diseases.

Population Density and Distribution

Despite rapid population growth, Africa south of the Sahara has few people in relation to its vast land area. If the population were evenly spread across the region, there would be about 76 people per square mile (47 people per sq. km). However, the population of the region is not evenly distributed. **Rwanda**, one of the region's most densely populated countries, has 817 people per square mile (315 people per sq. km), whereas **Namibia** has only 6 people per square mile (2 people per sq. km).

Land and climate help explain this uneven distribution of people. Desert or steppe covers large areas of Africa south of the Sahara. Because living conditions there are difficult, few, if any, people live there. The land is generally too dry to support agriculture or the raising of livestock. As the map on page 488 shows, most of the region's people are crowded in the coastal belt of West Africa along the Gulf of Guinea and along the eastern coast of southern Africa. They are drawn to these areas because of easy access to water, fertile soil, and mild climates. As a result, agriculture, industry, and commerce are concentrated in these areas.

Population and Food Production

Soaring population growth combined with economic challenges have made it difficult for Africa south of the Sahara to feed its people. Agriculture—both subsistence and cash-crop farming—ranks as the region's main economic activity. About 70 percent of people in the region work as farmers. Yet they are producing less and eating less, while the population has almost tripled.

Factors such as the actions of governments and some farmers and the effects of climate have contributed to this critical situation. In recent years governments have geared their economies for exporting in order to boost national incomes. However, not enough food has been produced for domestic needs, making it necessary to import food. In addition, huge expanses of farmland in the region have been exhausted through intensive cultivation, loss of soil fertility, and devastating droughts.

Population and Health Care

In recent years, Africa south of the Sahara has made many advances in health care. However, famine and poor nutrition claim many lives, especially among infants and young children. Impure water is another cause of death. Only a third of rural Africans have clean water to drink, and only a fourth live where there is adequate sanitation, or disposal of waste products. Diseases such as malaria are widespread. Insects such as the mosquito and tsetse (SEHT•see) fly transmit viruses to people and animals.

AIDS, a worldwide disease caused by a virus that is spread from person to person, has reached epidemic proportions in the region. A child born in **Zimbabwe**, for instance, is more likely to die of AIDS than of any other cause. Treatments with drugs that help control the disease are available to patients in developed countries, but these treatments cost too much for most Africans or their governments to purchase. As a result of the lack of treatment, this deadly disease has drastically cut the average life expectancy throughout Africa south of the Sahara. In Zimbabwe, average life expectancy has fallen from 65 years to 41 years because of AIDS.

The disease is expected to reduce the populations of many of the region's countries significantly, with disastrous consequences. Workers

---

DIFFERENTIATED INSTRUCTION

Visual/Spatial Have students compare the populations of Nigeria, Rwanda, Namibia, and Zimbabwe by creating a pictograph on the board. Tell students to make different-colored stick figures to represent different numbers of people, such as a red figure for 1 million people and a blue figure for 100,000 people. Supply students with colored chalk and the following data: Nigeria (pop. 133,900,000); Rwanda (pop. 8,300,000); Namibia (pop. 1,900,000); Zimbabwe (pop. 12,600,000).

🖼 **EE1 The World in Spatial Terms: Standard 1**

🖼 **EE4 Human Systems: Standard 9**

📂 Refer to *Inclusion for the Social Studies Classroom Strategies and Activities*.

will be in short supply, and industries may be forced to close. Families and communities will suffer as adults in the prime of life are lost to the disease. Children will lack caregivers. The United Nations estimates that by the year 2010, 10.7 million children in Africa under the age of 15 will have lost at least one parent to AIDS.

A Diverse Population

In both urban and rural areas, Africa south of the Sahara has a very diverse population. In fact, Africa is home to more ethnic groups than any other continent. Some 3,000 African ethnic groups make up the population. Other groups living in Africa include Europeans, South Asians, Arabs, and people of mixed backgrounds.

Culture
People Without Borders

A people known as the Sena live in a wide area in the marshes near the Zambezi River, which divides Zambia and Zimbabwe. The Sena often travel up the Zambezi in dugout canoes to sell fish and to buy

needed items, such as nets, at markets in Malawi. They float downriver to Mozambique to trade fish for sugar. Writing about the Sena, noted travel author Paul Theroux observes:

> ❝ They come and go, from country to country, without passports—without even saying where they are going. ❞
>
> Paul Theroux, "Down the Zambezi," National Geographic, October 1997

As in other parts of Africa, country borders separate people politically, but they do not usually disturb daily patterns of life. Throughout Africa south of the Sahara, members of individual ethnic groups speak the same language and share other cultural features, such as religion. They also have common ways of organizing community and family activities.

Growing Cities

Africa south of the Sahara is one of the least urbanized regions in the world, with only 30 percent of the population living in cities. The region's urban areas, however, are growing so rapidly that Africa has the world's fastest rate of urbanization, or movement of people from rural areas to cities. In 1950 only about 35 million Africans lived in cities. Today it is estimated that about 270 million Africans are urban dwellers.

Africans leave their rural villages for urban areas in order to find better job opportunities, health care, and public services. At the same time, population growth has caused cities to spread out into the countryside. Areas once made up of villages and towns

NATIONAL GEOGRAPHIC World Explorer

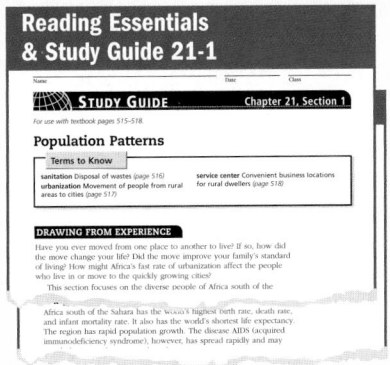

Geography | Skills for Life

Medical Services In Botswana, one of the wealthiest countries in the region, government funds help support a growing health-care system.

Region How does Botswana's health-care system compare with other health-care systems in this region?

Reading Essentials & Study Guide 21-1

🌐 STUDY GUIDE   Chapter 21, Section 1

For use with textbook pages 515–518

Population Patterns

Terms to Know

sanitation Disposal of wastes (page 516)   service center Convenient business locations
urbanization Movement of people from rural   for rural dwellers (page 518)
areas to cities (page 517)

DRAWING FROM EXPERIENCE

Have you ever moved from one place to another to live? If so, how did the move change your life? Did the move improve your family's standard of living? How might Africa's fast rate of urbanization affect the people who live in or move to the quickly growing cities?

This section focuses on the diverse people of Africa south of the

Africa south of the Sahara has the world's highest birth rate, death rate, and infant mortality rate. It also has the world's shortest life expectancy. The region has rapid population growth. The disease AIDS (acquired immunodeficiency syndrome), however, has spread rapidly and may

---

NATIONAL GEOGRAPHIC World Explorer

Answer
Students should infer that Botswana's health-care system is among the best in the region.

More About the Photo
Botswana gains much revenue from diamonds. Some diamond companies pay for drugs for employees with HIV/AIDS.

❸ASSESS

Assign Section 1 Assessment as homework or as an in-class activity.

Ⓐ Have students use **Interactive Tutor Self-Assessment CD-ROM.**

Reteach

Have students reread the section one subsection at a time. After each subsection, have students close their books, list the most important points, and then return to the text to correct their lists as needed. Students should use their lists to write a summary.

COOPERATIVE LEARNING ACTIVITY

Making a Bar Graph Explain that the movement of people from rural areas to cities has created large metropolitan areas in various countries of Africa south of the Sahara. Discuss the concept of a metropolitan area. Then have small groups research the populations of the 10 most-populated cities in the region in an almanac or other reliable source. When students have collected this data, have the groups work together to make a bar graph of the cities' populations. When it is complete, have students use the graph to compare and contrast the populations of cities in the region. 📦
🌐 **EE4 Human Systems: Standard 9**

L2

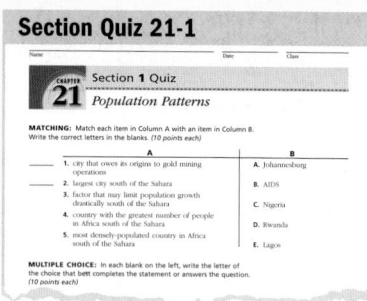

NATIONAL GEOGRAPHIC **World Explorer**

Answer

better job opportunities, health care, and public services in the cities

More About the Photo Once a village of the Tigre people, Asmara today is a manufacturing center, a transportation hub, a bustling marketplace for area farmers, and the location of Asmara University.

Enrich

To give students insight into the mixed emotions a move to the city can evoke, read excerpts from *Weep Not, Child* by Kenyan novelist Ngugi wa Thiong'o.

4 CLOSE

Challenge students to ask each other questions about population patterns in Africa south of the Sahara. When a student supplies a correct or reasonable answer to a question, he or she may ask a question of another student.

NATIONAL GEOGRAPHIC **World Explorer**

Geography **Skills for Life**
Asmara, Eritrea
Like other African cities, Asmara—Eritrea's capital—is rapidly urbanizing. It has a population of about 500,000.
Region What drives rapid urbanization in Africa south of the Sahara?

have mushroomed into service centers, convenient business locations for rural dwellers, who travel there by foot, bus, or boat.

Most cities in the region lie on the coast, along major rivers, or near areas rich in valuable resources. They developed largely as trading centers. The largest city in the region is the bustling seaport of **Lagos** (LAY•GAHS) in Nigeria, which has a population of more than 10 million. Other important cities include Cape Town, South Africa; Abidjan, Côte d'Ivoire; **Accra**, Ghana; and Dar es Salaam, Tanzania. **Kinshasa**, on the southern bank of the Congo River, is the political, cultural, and economic hub of the Democratic Republic of the Congo. In East Africa, inland cities—such as **Nairobi**, Kenya, and Addis Ababa, Ethiopia—have prospered from trade. **Johannesburg**, South Africa, also an inland city, owes its origins and growth to the mining of gold.

As in other regions of the world, Africa south of the Sahara faces many challenges because of rapid urbanization. Many African cities have towering skyscrapers and trendy shopping areas, but city residents often must endure traffic congestion, inadequate public services, overcrowded neighborhoods, and slums that lack water or sanitary facilities. In Chapter 22 you will learn how Africans south of the Sahara are meeting the challenges of their surroundings.

SECTION 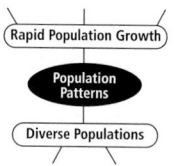 **1** **ASSESSMENT**

Checking for Understanding

1. **Define** sanitation, urbanization, service center.

2. **Main Ideas** In a diagram like the one below, make notes about population patterns in Africa south of the Sahara. Then write a brief paragraph about the region's population.

Rapid Population Growth
Population Patterns
Diverse Populations

Critical Thinking

3. **Drawing Conclusions** How can Africa south of the Sahara have rapid population growth and yet have relatively few people?

4. **Identifying Cause and Effect** How do you think declining agricultural production in Africa south of the Sahara contributes to urbanization? Explain your answer.

5. **Predicting Consequences** How will inadequate health care ultimately affect economies in this region? What steps would you recommend to help solve this problem?

Analyzing Maps

6. **Region** Study the population density map on page 488. Which countries have low population densities? What physical features account for this fact? Might these countries' population patterns change in the future? Explain.

Applying Geography

7. **Uneven Population Density** Think about the population patterns in Africa south of the Sahara. Brainstorm the reasons most people in the region settle in coastal areas. Then write a paragraph that explains this pattern.

518 Unit 7

SECTION **1** **ASSESSMENT ANSWERS**

1. All vocabulary terms are defined in the text.
2. Students' diagrams should incorporate information from the text.
3. While many areas, such as cities, have growing populations, large areas of the region are only sparsely populated because their terrain and climate are inhospitable to settlement.
4. Most people in rural areas are farmers; as agricultural production declines, people move to the city

to find new job opportunities.
5. Poor health care leads to a sick and slow-growing workforce, which hinders economic growth.
6. Mauritania, Mali, Niger, Chad, Sudan, Angola, Namibia, Botswana; desert
7. **Applying Geography** Coastal areas tend to have fertile soil, mild climates, and easy access to water. Agriculture, industry, and commerce are concentrated in coastal areas.

Guide to Reading

Consider What You Know

Global regions influence one another through trade, migration, and the exchange of ideas. What effect do you think new contacts, products, and ideas have on cultural traditions in each region?

Reading Strategy

Categorizing As you read about the history of Africa south of the Sahara, complete a graphic organizer similar to the one below by describing the ancient trading empires.

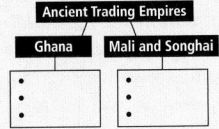

Read to Find Out

• What were the main achievements of the ancient civilizations of Africa south of the Sahara?

• How did European colonization disrupt African patterns of life?

• What challenges did countries of the region face after independence?

Terms to Know

• domesticate
• apartheid
• universal suffrage

Places to Locate

• Kush
• Axum
• Ghana
• Kumbi
• Mali
• Songhai
• Timbuktu
• Ethiopia
• Liberia

History and Government

NATIONAL GEOGRAPHIC

A Geographic View

Home of the Zulu

The [South African] district of Msinga, . . . as deep into deep Zululand as you can go, is the strongest bastion [place of survival] of inherited Zulu culture. . . . As you drive from Greytown . . . through the Mpanza Valley, . . . the avocado, pecan, and macadamia plantations give way to aloes and thorn trees. You wind down the escarpment, and there below is a sweeping view over the green folds and steep valleys of Zululand, dotted with thatch huts and small patches of corn.

Rural community, South Africa

—Peter Godwin, "Zulu: People of Heaven, Heirs to Violence," National Geographic, *August 2000*

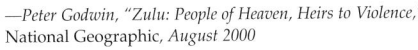

Kraals—the traditional homesteads of the Zulu people—have long been a familiar sight in what is now South Africa. Like many other ethnic groups in Africa south of the Sahara, the Zulu are descendants of the Bantu peoples. Massive Bantu migrations and movements of other peoples shaped the region's early history and are still influential today.

African Roots

Tens of thousands of years ago, people were already moving from place to place across Africa to hunt and gather food. No written records exist of these people, but early paintings in places as widespread as Niger in the north and Namibia in the south offer clues to their ways of life. Scenes painted in caves and on rocks are filled with

① FOCUS

Section Overview

This section surveys the history of the region and identifies the challenges countries faced after independence.

BELLRINGER
Skillbuilder Activity

▣ Project transparency and have students answer questions.

▭ Available as blackline master.

Daily Focus Skills Transparency 21-2

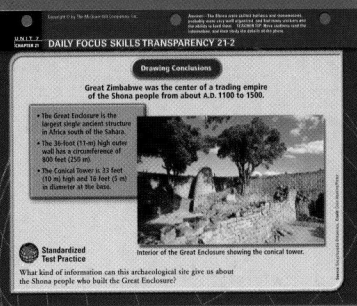

Guide to Reading

Consider What You Know

Answer *New contacts, products, and ideas may change or replace cultural traditions.*

Reading Strategy

Answers Ghana: *traded gold for salt, capital city Kumbi, developed tax collection system and charged tariffs on imports;* Mali/Songhai: *Mali was larger than Egypt, Timbuktu was wealthy center, also benefited from salt-gold trade, replaced by Songhai*

Preteaching Vocabulary

Write the vocabulary terms on the board and ask students what they know about each. Help students decode the terms by looking at their parts, such as *domestic* in *domesticate*. Have students use a dictionary to check and correct their definitions.

RESOURCE MANAGER

▭ Reproducible Masters

• Reproducible Lesson Plan 21-2
• Daily Lecture Notes 21-2
• Guided Reading Activity 21-2
• Reading Essentials and Study Guide 21-2
• Section Quiz 21-2

▣ Transparencies

• Daily Focus Skills Transparency 21-2
• Political Map Transparency 7
• Unit 7 Map Overlay Transparencies

Multimedia

ⓝ Interactive Tutor Self-Assessment CD-ROM
ⓝ ExamView® Pro Testmaker CD-ROM
ⓝ Presentation Plus! CD-ROM

2 TEACH

L1 Cause and Effect

Have students explain *why* people migrated to Africa south of the Sahara around 2000 B.C. Then ask them to explain *what* happened as a result of this migration. Organize the information in a cause-and-effect chain. *(cause: climate became hotter and drier; effect/ cause: people moved south to survive; effect: knowledge of agriculture spread south of the Sahara)*

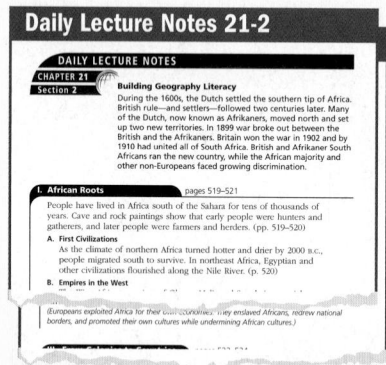

Daily Lecture Notes 21-2

DAILY LECTURE NOTES

CHAPTER 21
Section 2

Building Geography Literacy
During the 1600s, the Dutch settled the southern tip of Africa. British rule—and settlers—followed two centuries later. Many of the Dutch, now known as Afrikaners, pushed north and set up two new territories. In 1899 war broke out between the British and the Afrikaners. Britain won the war in 1902 and by 1910 had united all of South Africa. British and Afrikaner South Africans ran the new country, while the African majority and other non-Europeans faced growing discrimination.

I. African Roots pages 519–521

People have lived in Africa south of the Sahara for tens of thousands of years. Cave and rock paintings show that early people were hunters and gatherers, and later people were farmers and herders.

A. First Civilizations
As the climate of northern Africa turned hotter and drier by 2000 B.C., people migrated south to survive. In northeast Africa, Egyptian and other civilizations flourished along the Nile River. (p. 520)

B. Empires in the West

(Europeans exploited Africa for their own economies, they enslaved Africans, redrew national borders, and promoted their own cultures while undermining African cultures.)

NATIONAL GEOGRAPHIC   MAP STUDY

Answers

1. *on the Mediterranean coast*

2. *The kingdoms developed near gold-rich areas. Plentiful gold allowed them to buy goods and create strong kingdoms.*

Map Skills Practice

Location Which kingdoms were not in a location to profit from the gold-for-salt trade? *(Axum and Kush)*

---

people hunting, fishing, and celebrating. Later paintings show new peoples involved in new activities—farming and herding.

First Civilizations

Around 2000 B.C. migrants fleeing a dramatic shift in climate joined other settlers in Africa south of the Sahara. For thousands of years, the climate to the north had been mild and wet. People who once hunted and scavenged for food learned to plant seeds and domesticate, or tame, animals. They developed agriculture in the Sahara area. Around 3000 to 2500 B.C., however, the climate became hotter and drier. Plants shriveled, forests perished, and rivers evaporated. Forced to move in order to survive, many people migrated south. They took with them their knowledge of raising crops and animals.

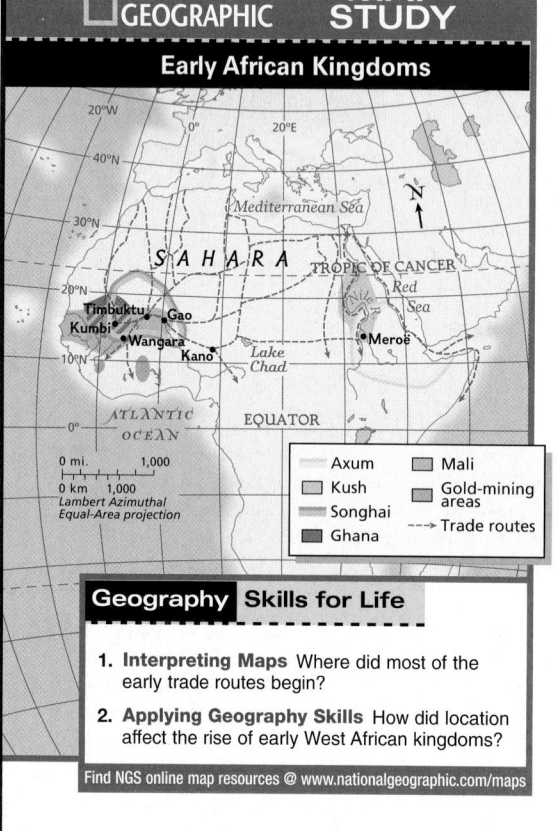

NATIONAL GEOGRAPHIC   MAP STUDY

Early African Kingdoms

Axum
Kush
Songhai
Ghana
Mali
Gold-mining areas
- - -> Trade routes

Geography Skills for Life

1. **Interpreting Maps** Where did most of the early trade routes begin?

2. **Applying Geography Skills** How did location affect the rise of early West African kingdoms?

Find NGS online map resources @ www.nationalgeographic.com/maps

---

In northeast Africa, the Nile Valley remained fertile and gave life to the great Egyptian civilization. Between 2000 and 1000 B.C., the Egyptians pressed south, bringing various cultures along the Nile under their control. When Egyptian civilization began to fade, the cultures under its sway rose to power. The kingdom of **Kush**, in what is now Sudan, extended its rule north into Egyptian territory. The Kushites then pushed south along the Nile, building a civilization around a new capital called Meroë (MEHR•oh•WEE). Kush flourished until the A.D. 300s, when its trade routes were attacked by **Axum**, a powerful trading empire in northern Ethiopia.

Empires in the West

Several centuries later, trading empires began to gain strength in West Africa. Today the West African countries of Ghana and Mali are named after two of these ancient empires. **Ghana**, one of the earliest of these trading kingdoms, emerged around A.D. 700. Its empire grew rich by trading gold for salt brought by camel caravans across the Sahara. Peoples south of the Sahara highly valued salt for use as a food preservative.

Gold was plentiful in Ghana. The Spanish-Arab geographer al-Bakri, who traveled to West Africa in the 1000s, reported, for example, that even the king's dogs wore collars of gold and silver. Ghana's wealth was reflected in its large capital, **Kumbi**. This prosperous empire, which created a tax collection system and charged tariffs on imports, flourished for almost 500 years.

The trading empires of **Mali** and **Songhai** (SAWNG•HY) succeeded Ghana and also grew rich from the gold-for-salt trade. Mali, which extended west to the Atlantic and was larger than Egypt, had as its center the wealthy city of **Timbuktu**. Songhai eventually took over Mali and then stretched east, prospering until about 1600, when it was overrun by Moroccans, a people from the north.

Bantu Migrations

In central and southern Africa, Bantu-speaking peoples had established settlements by A.D. 800. Although the origins of the Bantu and their routes of migration are debated, many historians believe that they spread across one-third of the continent. In addition to founding the central African kingdoms

---

DIFFERENTIATED INSTRUCTION

At-Risk Students Create a tasks checklist to help students who are easily distracted organize their time and approach to the material in this section. Closely monitor students' work on the various tasks on the checklist. Tasks may include rereading the text under each subhead, taking notes on the main ideas, writing a brief summary of each subsection based on the notes, and locating places mentioned on maps. To help students further organize information in the section, you may wish to distribute graphic organizers such as cause-and-effect and sequence diagrams for students to complete.

Refer to *Inclusion for the Social Studies Classroom Strategies and Activities.*

of Kongo (Congo), Luba, and Luanda, the Bantu established states to the southeast in what are today Tanzania, Malawi, Zambia, and Zimbabwe. The influence of the Bantu migration continues, with about 150 million Bantu speakers living in Africa today.

European Colonization

Slowly, word of the wealth of Africa's kingdoms reached Europe. Europeans began trading with Africans as early as the 1200s, bringing gold and other African goods to Europe. By the time Columbus set sail, Portuguese explorers were sailing along the African coast. They set up trading posts and way stations along coastal areas, where enslaved Africans were held for transport. Foreign travelers who reached the trading centers of Timbuktu, Kano, Gao, and Wangara in the west and Kilwa, Mombasa, and Sofala in the east were impressed with the bustling, abundant markets and cultural life.

The Slave Trade in Africa

By the 1600s and 1700s, Europeans were trading extensively with Africans. They sought African gold, ivory, textiles, and enslaved workers. African chiefs and kings had enslaved and traded prisoners of war for centuries. Arab traders had brought enslaved Africans to the Islamic world since the A.D. 800s. The slave trade greatly increased when Europeans began shipping Africans to the Americas to work on large plantations where sugar, tobacco, rice, and cotton were cultivated.

Huge numbers of people from the African interior were sold into slavery. As early as 1526, Nzinga

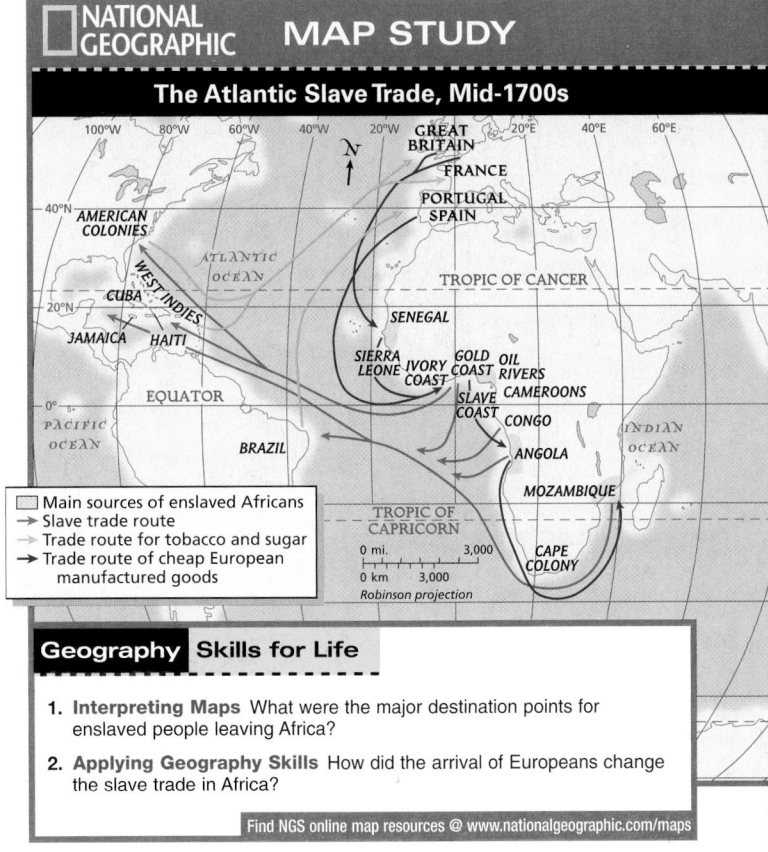

NATIONAL GEOGRAPHIC — MAP STUDY

The Atlantic Slave Trade, Mid-1700s

- ☐ Main sources of enslaved Africans
- → Slave trade route
- → Trade route for tobacco and sugar
- → Trade route of cheap European manufactured goods

0 mi. 3,000
0 km 3,000
Robinson projection

Geography Skills for Life

1. **Interpreting Maps** What were the major destination points for enslaved people leaving Africa?

2. **Applying Geography Skills** How did the arrival of Europeans change the slave trade in Africa?

Find NGS online map resources @ www.nationalgeographic.com/maps

Mbemba, the king of Kongo, deplored the actions of some African rulers. He also complained to the king of Portugal about Portuguese slave merchants:

> ❝ [They] seize upon our subjects . . . and cause them to be sold; and so great, Sir, is their corruption . . . that our country is being utterly depopulated. ❞
>
> Nzinga Mbemba, quoted by Basil Davidson, in *African Kingdoms*, 1966

Once captured and sold, enslaved Africans faced a terrible trip across the Atlantic Ocean as human cargo in a ship's hold. This passage from Africa claimed millions of African lives. The loss of so

Chapter 21 🌐 521

L2 Primary Sources

Check comprehension of the quotation on this page. **Ask:** Who is speaking? Who are "they"? What is the speaker complaining about? To whom is he complaining? Have volunteers paraphrase the quotation. Then have students speculate about what the king of Kongo wanted the king of Portugal to do.

NATIONAL GEOGRAPHIC — MAP STUDY

Answers

1. *the American colonies, the West Indies, and Brazil*

2. *The slave trade was greatly increased.*

Map Skills Practice

Movement Why did traders carry European manufactured goods to Africa? *(to trade for enslaved persons)*

L1/ELL

Guided Reading Activity 21-2

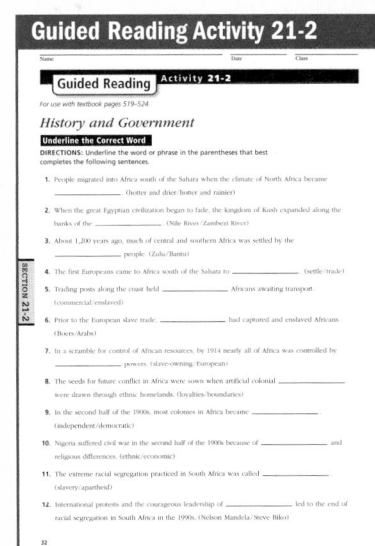

COOPERATIVE LEARNING ACTIVITY

The Slave Trade Point out that different parties were involved in the Atlantic slave trade: African rulers, enslaved Africans, European traders, and plantation owners in the Americas. Organize the class into four groups and have the different groups pose as a different party to the slave trade. Have students use library and Internet resources to gather information about their assigned party's participation in the slave trade. Tell the groups to use the information they find to create a script for a simulated television interview in which a modern news magazine host challenges a spokesperson from each group to defend their actions or, in the case of enslaved persons, to explain the pain of enslavement.

🌐 **EE4 Human Systems: Standard 11**

NATIONAL GEOGRAPHIC — MAP STUDY

Answers

1. *French and British*
2. *Local economies met European needs, and boundaries did not recognize ethnic groups.*

Map Skills Practice

Region Which country became independent most recently? *(Eritrea)*

L1/ELL

Reading Essentials & Study Guide 21-2

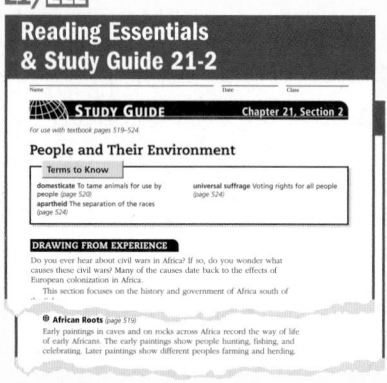

L2 Making Inferences

Have students research the African role in World War II. **Ask: How might African participation in this war have aided freedom movements?** *(Wars fought for democracy boosted African demands for freedom for themselves.)*

Liberia was founded as a colony for freed slaves under the direction of the American Colonization Society. The country declared its independence in 1847.

NATIONAL GEOGRAPHIC — MAP STUDY

African Independence

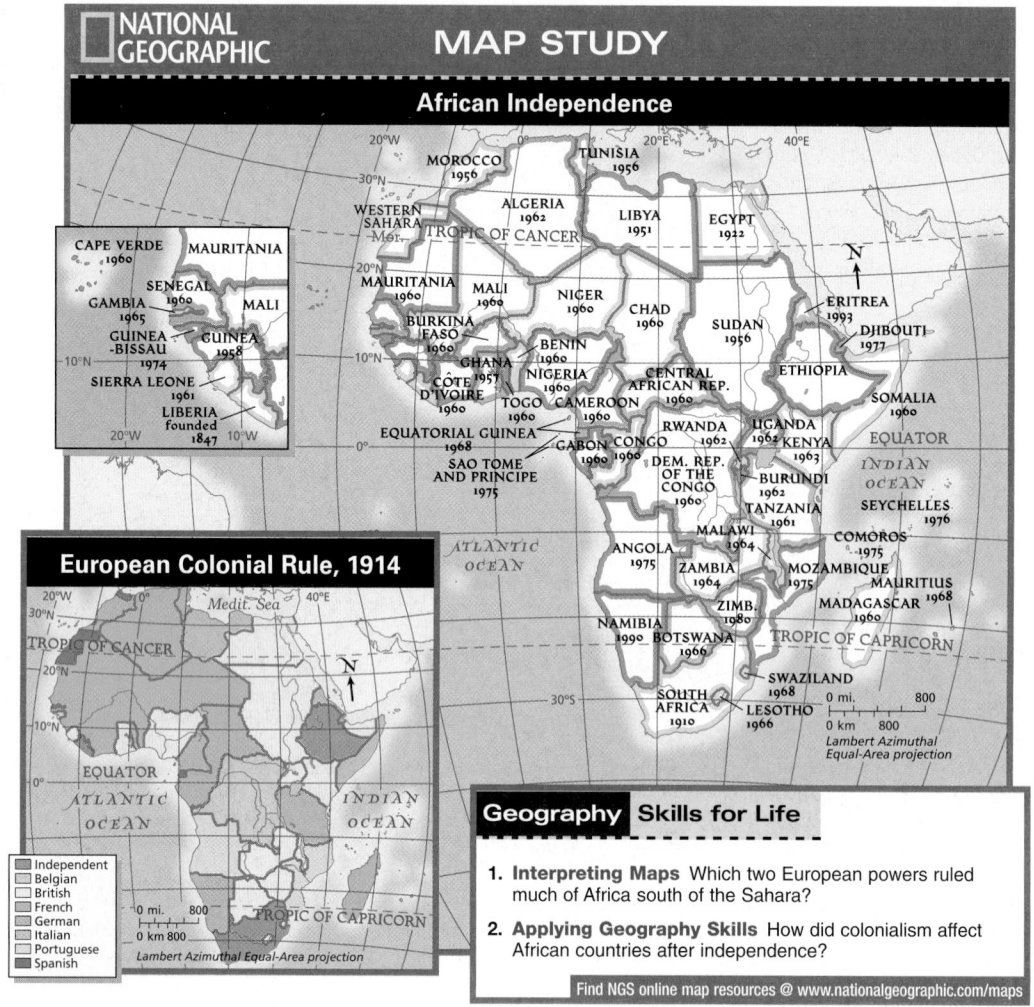

European Colonial Rule, 1914

Independent
Belgian
British
French
German
Italian
Portuguese
Spanish

Lambert Azimuthal Equal-Area projection

Geography Skills for Life

1. **Interpreting Maps** Which two European powers ruled much of Africa south of the Sahara?

2. **Applying Geography Skills** How did colonialism affect African countries after independence?

Find NGS online map resources @ www.nationalgeographic.com/maps

---

many young people to the slave trade was a major setback to the societies they left behind.

Government

Europe Divides and Rules

In the 1800s European powers regarded the region as a source of raw materials for their growing industries and a potential market for European goods. European countries laid claim to African territory, and by 1914, all of Africa except **Ethiopia, Liberia,** and **South Africa** was under European control.

In setting up their colonies, Europeans ignored African objections and created boundaries that often cut across ethnic homelands. By doing so they set African groups against one another and strengthened European rule in the region.

Among the earliest foreigners to explore Africa's interior, European missionaries often opposed the harsh treatment of Africans by the colonial traders and officials. Yet they, too, promoted European culture and weakened traditional African ways. European businessmen also disrupted African village

---

CRITICAL THINKING ACTIVITY

Predicting Consequences Tell students that in 1652 the Dutch East India Company built a supply base at the Cape of Good Hope in what is now South Africa and that, soon after, European settlers arrived. Read aloud this excerpt from a Dutch diary: "[The Khoikhoi, an African people] strongly insisted that we had been appropriating more and more of their land. . . . They asked if they would be allowed to do such a thing supposing they went to Holland." Then say: In 1652 the Khoikhoi set up a supply base in Amsterdam. **Ask: What happened next?** Continue the story by having each student add a sentence or two. Have a student volunteer record the story of what might have happened if Africans had settled in Europe.
EE4 Human Systems: Standard 13

NATIONAL GEOGRAPHIC — MAP STUDY

Ethnic Groups, Colonial Rule, and Conflict

Case Study: Conflict in Nigeria

1960	Nigeria becomes independent; ethnic tensions divide the country.
1966	Military officials take control of Nigeria's government.
1967	The Eastern Region secedes from Nigeria; its largely Ibo population sets up the Republic of Biafra.
1967–1970	A civil war between Nigerian government forces and Biafran rebels results in Biafra's defeat; war casualties number about 1 million.
1970s	Military officials rule harshly; corruption and mismanagement squander Nigeria's oil wealth.
1980s	Brief period of civilian rule is followed by a return to military dictatorship.
1993	Military allows free elections but annuls vote; riots sweep Nigeria.
1998–1999	Nigeria returns to civilian rule; free elections are held.
2000	Tensions increase between Nigeria's Muslim and Christian communities.

Language/Ethnic Groups
- Congo-Kordofanian
- Nilo-Saharan
- Afro-Asiatic
- Khoisan
- Afrikaans
- Malayo-Polynesian

Ibo Ethnic groups

0 mi. 1,000
0 km 1,000
Lambert Azimuthal Equal-Area projection

Geography Skills for Life

1. **Interpreting Maps** List three examples in which political boundaries divide an ethnic group.

2. **Applying Geography Skills** What problems might result from the political divisions created by colonial powers?

Find NGS online map resources @ www.nationalgeographic.com/maps

NATIONAL GEOGRAPHIC — MAP STUDY

Answers

1. *the Dogon, Ashanti, and the Masai*

2. *language difficulties, conflicts between ethnic groups in one country, problems governing people of diverse cultures*

Map Skills Practice

Place Where are Malayo-Polynesian languages spoken? *(Madagascar)*

③ ASSESS

Assign Section 2 Assessment as homework or as an in-class activity.

🖥 Have students use **Interactive Tutor Self-Assessment CD-ROM.**

L2

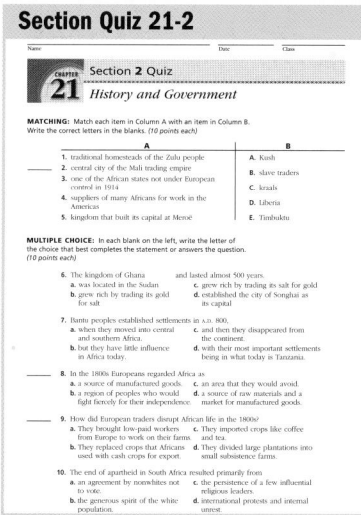

Section Quiz 21-2

---

life by replacing locally centered agriculture with huge plantation economies. These economies focused on the production of cash crops like coffee and tea for world markets.

From Colonies to Countries

Although European rule dealt serious blows to African life, many Africans benefited from new educational opportunities and city development. Soon some Africans demanded a share in government. By the mid-1900s, educated Africans had launched independence movements, and in the second half of the century, the colonies became independent. (See map on page 522.) These new countries faced difficult challenges, often the result of their colonial legacy. European powers, for example, had used African colonies as a source of raw materials for their industries. They also set up colonial economies that met European, rather than African, needs. Colonial governments did not involve Africans much in government, nor did they give Africans models for democracy. At independence, many of the new African countries adopted the political boundaries set earlier by the colonial powers. As the map above shows, these boundaries divided people of similar

Chapter 21 🌐 **523**

TEAM-TEACHING ACTIVITY: GOVERNMENT

African Governments Have students work individually, with partners, or in small groups to find out more about current governments in Africa south of the Sahara and the issues they are facing. Assign students one or more countries and have them use encyclopedias and recent newspaper and magazine articles to learn about the government(s) of their countries. Students should gather such information as types of government, government leaders, and political parties and at least one issue facing the current government. Students may present their findings orally in an "Africa South of the Sahara" assembly. Have students use graphics as part of their presentation. 📦 🌐 **EE4: Human Systems: Standard 13**

Reteach

As a class, create a sequence chain that shows events in the history of Africa south of the Sahara. Have students skim the text to identify significant events. Use the completed chain as a springboard to discussion.

Enrich

Show scenes from the movie *Cry Freedom* or read selected passages from Nelson Mandela's autobiography *Long Walk to Freedom* to give students a view of South Africa under apartheid.

4 CLOSE

To provide context for the events described in this section, discuss events in other world regions that occurred around the same time. For example, in the 1600s wealthy Dutch merchants formed the Dutch East India Company and ultimately used military force to further their goals for trade in Southeast Asia. In Europe competition for empires resulted in wars. The English civil war began in 1642.

language and ethnic background. Within the new countries, rival ethnic groups struggled for power, and civil wars erupted.

Nigeria: A Colonial Legacy

An example of ethnic conflict in the region is Nigeria. The time line next to the map on page 523 shows key events in Nigeria's ongoing ethnic struggles since independence. Nigeria's problems stem from its colonial past.

In 1914 the British had formed the colony of Nigeria from several smaller ethnic territories. As a result, many different ethnic and religious groups lived within Nigeria's boundaries. In the north, various peoples had developed cultures based on centuries-old Islamic influences from North Africa. Those in the south had created ways of life based on traditional African religions or on Christianity. Despite these differences, Nigerians united to resist British rule. In 1960 the colony of Nigeria finally became an independent country. The ethnic and religious differences inherited from the past soon erupted in civil war, however. Although the civil war eventually ended, ethnic and religious divisions continue to plague Nigeria today as it moves from harsh military rule to democracy.

Nelson Mandela

South Africa: Road to Freedom

During the early 1900s, South Africa became independent of British rule. For most of the century, however, the country's white minority population ran the government. It imposed a policy known as **apartheid** (uh•PAHR•tayt), or separation of the races, on South Africa's black majority and racially mixed peoples. Under apartheid, nonwhite South Africans were denied political rights and equality with whites in education, jobs, and housing. They were segregated into communities with substandard housing and few government services.

Internal unrest and international pressures finally forced South Africa to end apartheid in the early 1990s. Nelson Mandela, the country's most popular anti-apartheid leader, was released after 27 years in prison. In 1994 South Africa held its first election based on **universal suffrage**, or voting rights for all adult citizens. Nelson Mandela became South Africa's first black president. Within a short time, South Africa moved from a repressive society to one committed to democracy. Today, South Africa faces the challenge of ensuring a better quality of life for many nonwhite South Africans.

SECTION 2 ASSESSMENT

Checking for Understanding

1. **Define** domesticate, apartheid, universal suffrage.

2. **Main Ideas** Complete a time line of Africa's history based on the model below. Then use your time line to write a summary of the region's achievements and experiences of the past and present.

Important Dates in Africa South of the Sahara

2000 B.C.   A.D. 2000

Critical Thinking

3. **Making Generalizations** How did contact with other empires influence the West African empires?

4. **Drawing Conclusions** Why do you think the West African trading kingdoms were willing to trade gold for salt?

5. **Identifying Cause and Effect** In what ways did colonialism affect the region's development and set the stage for current conflicts in Africa south of the Sahara?

Analyzing Maps

6. **Movement** Study the map of early African kingdoms on page 520. To what seas and oceans did the early trade routes lead? What river was a major trade route?

Applying Geography

7. **Movement of People** List some of the major human migrations in Africa south of the Sahara. Then choose one migration, and write a paragraph about the motivation for and the effects of the migration.

SECTION 2 ASSESSMENT ANSWERS

1. All vocabulary terms are defined in the text.
2. Students should plot significant events in the history of the region on their time lines.
3. Initially, they grew rich through trade. Then the slave trade grew, and empires were taken over by Europeans.
4. West African kingdoms needed salt because, unlike gold, which was abundant in the region, salt, used to preserve food, was in short supply.

5. The European colonial powers set up economies in the region that met their needs instead of the needs of Africans, they created political boundaries that divided ethnic groups, and they did not provide models of democratic government.
6. Atlantic Ocean, Mediterranean Sea, Red Sea, Indian Ocean; the Nile River

7. **Applying Geography** Major migrations include farmers migrating into the region from the Sahara around 2000 B.C. (motivation: climate change; effect: spread of agriculture) and the Bantu migrations to central and southern Africa prior to A.D. 800 (possible motivation: food and land needed for a growing population; effect: spread of Bantu culture).

Guide to Reading

Consider What You Know

Think about ways in which Africans influence global culture. How do you think aspects of African culture have spread to other parts of the world?

Reading Strategy

Categorizing As you read about the religions of Africa south of the Sahara, complete a graphic organizer similar to the one below by filling in the common elements of traditional religions in the region.

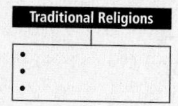

Traditional Religions

Read to Find Out

- What languages do people in Africa south of the Sahara speak?
- What are the major religions in Africa south of the Sahara?
- What art forms have peoples of the region developed?
- How do lifestyles among peoples of the region differ? How are they similar?

Terms to Know

- mass culture
- lingua franca
- oral tradition
- extended family
- clan
- nuclear family

Places to Locate

- Eritrea
- Madagascar
- Tanzania
- Dar es Salaam

Cultures and Lifestyles

A Geographic View

Wedding Traditions

Guests begin to arrive . . . [for] a wedding week of camel racing, dancing, and feasting on goat meat, wheat porridge, and sweet tea.

Bekitta, the bride, stays in seclusion, veiled behind an elaborate mask called a burqa, which she has painstakingly decorated. . . .

When the day cools at sunset, a woman breaks into a dance. Clapping out the rhythm, the men sing: "The sun is setting, so we sing before the dark!" As she swirls in perfumed skirts, they punctuate their song with shouts of tribal pride: "Rashaida! Rashaida!"

Rashaida woman of Eritrea

—*Carol Beckwith and Angela Fisher, "African Marriage Rituals,"* National Geographic, *November 1999*

Ethnic groups such as the Rashaida of **Eritrea** find their identity in such traditions as wedding customs. People in Africa south of the Sahara share a history of colonial rule and struggle for independence. A further bond is mass culture, or popular culture promoted by the media. Despite general similarities, however, the region's ethnic groups are as diverse as they are numerous. In this section you will learn about the languages, religions, arts, and lifestyles of Africa south of the Sahara.

Languages

More than 800 different languages are spoken in Africa today. As the map on page 523 shows, language experts put the many ethnic groups and languages of Africa south of the Sahara into six major

---

1 FOCUS

Section Overview

This section describes various aspects of cultures and lifestyles in Africa south of the Sahara.

BELLRINGER
Skillbuilder Activity

 Project transparency and have students answer questions.

 Available as blackline master.

Daily Focus Skills Transparency 21-3

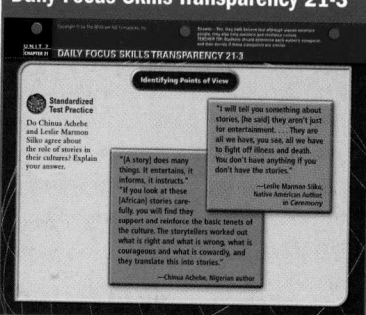

Guide to Reading

Consider What You Know
Answers *Enslaved Africans brought aspects of their culture to the Americas. Other Africans and foreigners who spent time in Africa have also spread African culture worldwide.*

Reading Strategy
Answers *belief in Supreme Being with a ranked order of lesser deities, belief in existence of nature spirits, honor distant ancestors and deceased family members*

Preteaching Vocabulary
Use the **Vocabulary Puzzle-Maker CD-ROM** to create crossword and word-search puzzles.

RESOURCE MANAGER

Reproducible Masters
- Reproducible Lesson Plan 21-3
- Vocabulary Activity 21
- Daily Lecture Notes 21-3
- Guided Reading Activity 21-3
- Reading Essentials and Study Guide 21-3
- Reteaching Activity 21
- Reinforcing Skills Activity 21
- Section Quiz 21-3

Transparencies
- Daily Focus Skills Transparency 21-3
- Unit 7 Map Overlay Transparencies

Multimedia
- Vocabulary PuzzleMaker CD-ROM
- World Music: A Cultural Legacy
- Interactive Tutor Self-Assessment CD-ROM
- ExamView® Pro Testmaker CD-ROM
- Presentation Plus! CD-ROM

TEACH

L2 Hypothesizing

Discuss the concept of a *lingua franca*, or universal language. Point out that English and French are commonly spoken in many other parts of the world today, as they are in Africa. Ask students to hypothesize about why Africans would need a *lingua franca*.

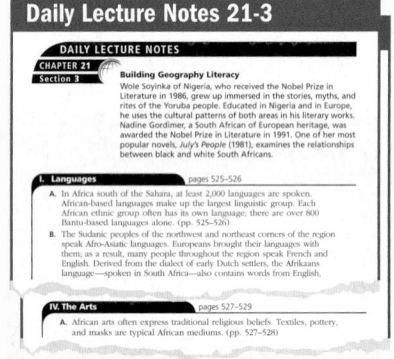

Daily Lecture Notes 21-3

DAILY LECTURE NOTES

CHAPTER 21
Section 3

Building Geography Literacy

Wole Soyinka of Nigeria, who received the Nobel Prize in Literature in 1986, grew up immersed in the stories, myths, and rites of the Yoruba people. Educated in Nigeria and in Europe, he uses the cultural patterns of both areas in his literary works. Nadine Gordimer, a South African of European heritage, was awarded the Nobel Prize in Literature in 1991. One of her most popular novels, *July's People* (1981), examines the relationships between black and white South Africans.

I. Languages pages 525–526

A. In Africa south of the Sahara, at least 2,000 languages are spoken. African-based languages make up the largest linguistic group. Each African ethnic group often has its own language; there are over 800 Bantu-based languages alone. (pp. 525–526)

B. The Sudanic peoples of the northwest and northeast corners of the region speak Afro-Asiatic languages. Europeans brought their languages with them; as a result, many people throughout the region speak French and English. Derived from the dialect of early Dutch settlers, the Afrikaans language—spoken in South Africa—also contains words from English,

IV. The Arts pages 527–529

A. African arts often express traditional religious beliefs. Textiles, pottery, and masks are typical African mediums. (pp. 527–528)

NATIONAL GEOGRAPHIC **GRAPH STUDY**

Answers

1. *Christianity*

2. *the many ethnic groups, European colonization, and the large Muslim population of the neighboring area of North Africa*

Skills Practice

How does the number of Muslims in the region compare to the number of people practicing traditional religions? *(There are almost twice as many Muslims as there are followers of traditional religions.)*

---

categories: Congo-Kordofanian, Nilo-Saharan, Afro-Asiatic, Khoisan, Malayo-Polynesian, and Afrikaans, an Indo-European language.

Languages in the African groups—Congo-Kordofanian, Nilo-Saharan, Afro-Asiatic, and Khoisan—are the most widely spoken and the most diverse. Originating on the African continent, these languages include hundreds of Bantu-based Congo-Kordofanian languages spoken by peoples in central, eastern, and southern Africa. Among these are Swahili, Zulu, and Kongo. The Bantu-related languages of Guinea coast peoples also belong to the Congo-Kordofanian group.

The Sudanic peoples of the northwest and northeast corners of the region speak Afro-Asiatic languages. The Afro-Asiatic group includes African languages, such as Hausa and Fulani, as well as languages of North Africa and Southwest Asia, such as Berber and Arabic.

Some languages spoken in the region are non-African. People on the island of **Madagascar** speak the Malagasy language in the Malayo-Polynesian language group. Indo-European languages spoken in Africa include English, French, and Afrikaans. Derived from the dialect of early Dutch settlers in South Africa, Afrikaans also contains words adapted from English, French, German, and African languages. Africa's Indo-European languages were introduced by European traders, administrators, and missionaries. Some have become the official languages of today's African countries. French or English often serves as a lingua franca, or common language, throughout the region.

Religions

A variety of religions claim followers in Africa south of the Sahara. Most people are Christian or Muslim. Christians make up the largest religious group. Missionaries and traders from Egypt and the Mediterranean area introduced Christianity to Ethiopia in the A.D. 300s. The Ethiopian Coptic

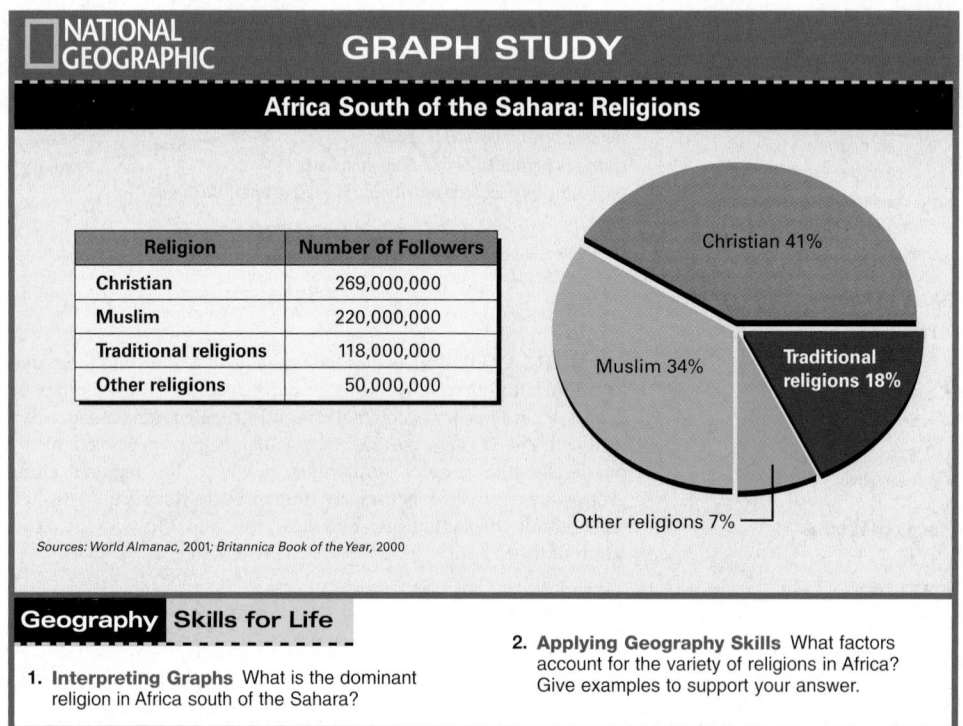

NATIONAL GEOGRAPHIC **GRAPH STUDY**

Africa South of the Sahara: Religions

Religion	Number of Followers
Christian	269,000,000
Muslim	220,000,000
Traditional religions	118,000,000
Other religions	50,000,000

Christian 41%

Muslim 34%

Traditional religions 18%

Other religions 7%

Sources: World Almanac, 2001; Britannica Book of the Year, 2000

Geography **Skills for Life**

1. Interpreting Graphs What is the dominant religion in Africa south of the Sahara?

2. Applying Geography Skills What factors account for the variety of religions in Africa? Give examples to support your answer.

DIFFERENTIATED INSTRUCTION

At-Risk Students One of the most common problems of students with language difficulties is an inability to ask questions of their teachers. Have students who have trouble formulating questions form small groups. Direct students to read a subsection of the text and work together to develop questions about it. Encourage groups to produce a variety of questions. Have each group share its list of questions, and make a master list of the questions on the board.

Refer to *Inclusion for the Social Studies Classroom Strategies and Activities.*

Church has played an important role in Ethiopian life ever since. Christian beliefs did not spread among other African peoples until the colonial period, however. Since then, many Africans have adopted Christianity, especially along the coasts, where Africans had greater contact with foreigners. Most Muslims in the region live in West Africa, where Muslims ruled the kingdoms of Mali and Songhai along the Niger River during the 1400s and 1500s. Today Nigeria has the largest Islamic population of any African country south of the Sahara.

Traditional religions in Africa south of the Sahara are numerous and diverse, but they have many common elements. For example, most traditional religions profess a belief in the existence of a supreme being and a ranked order of lesser deities. In the late 1700s, Olaudah Equiano, an African known for his vivid account of slavery, stated that the supreme god of his people, the Igbo, was "one Creator of all things, and he lives in the sun, . . . and governs all events, especially . . . deaths." These same characteristics describe the supreme beings of other African groups. Most followers of traditional African religions also believe in the existence of nature spirits and honor distant ancestors and family members who have recently died.

Religion plays an integral role in everyday life in Africa. Although many followers of different religions live together peacefully, conflict sometimes occurs between competing religious groups. In recent years Nigeria and Sudan have been scenes of conflict among Christians, Muslims, and followers of traditional African religions.

Education

Africans have always valued education, but it has taken many different forms. In the past, African children did not attend school but apprenticed to trades such as wood carving and metalworking. Large-scale, formal schooling became widespread in the early 1900s, as European powers sought to fill civil service and industrial jobs with African workers.

Educational Advances

Since independence, higher education has expanded. In 1960 only 120,000 students in the region enrolled in universities, but by the late 1990s more than 2 million had. Public school attendance and literacy have also increased, but only about 60 percent of people aged 15 and older can read and write. Rural areas, which often are short of schools, materials, and qualified teachers, generally have lower literacy rates than do urban areas. In some places few children receive even an elementary education; parents there are too poor to send their children to school.

Culture
New Ways of Learning

Television has become an efficient teaching tool, but exposure to newer technology is limited. Fewer than 10 personal computers per 1,000 people exist in the region, and Internet service is not yet widely available. In some countries, such as South Africa and Zambia, however, use of the Internet is becoming more widespread.

The Arts

African art, often expressing traditional religious beliefs, comes in many forms, from ritual masks to

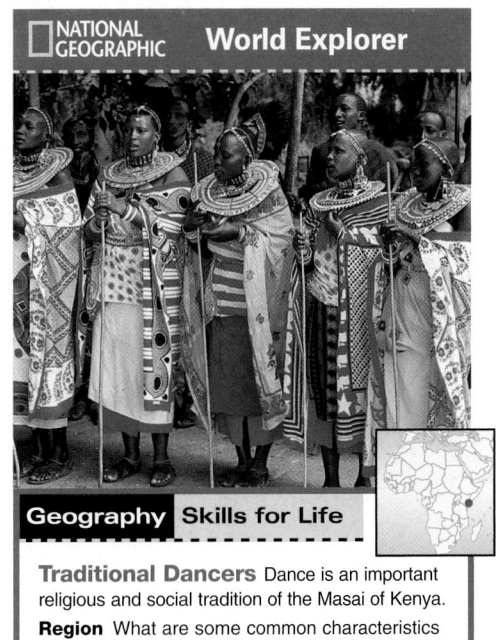

NATIONAL GEOGRAPHIC **World Explorer**

Geography **Skills for Life**

Traditional Dancers Dance is an important religious and social tradition of the Masai of Kenya.
Region What are some common characteristics of traditional African religions?

L1/ELL

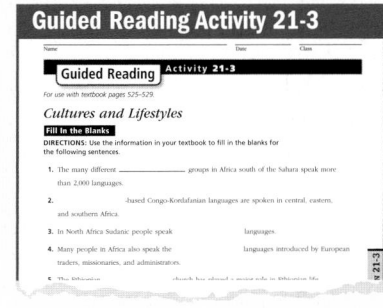

Guided Reading Activity 21-3

Name_____ Date_____ Class_____

Guided Reading **Activity 21-3**

For use with textbook pages 525–529.

Cultures and Lifestyles

Fill in the Blanks
DIRECTIONS: Use the information in your textbook to fill in the blanks for the following sentences.

1. The many different _____ groups in Africa south of the Sahara speak more than 2,000 languages.
2. _____-based Congo-Kordofanian languages are spoken in central, eastern, and southern Africa.
3. In North Africa Sudanic people speak _____ languages.
4. Many people in Africa also speak the _____ languages introduced by European traders, missionaries, and administrators.
5. The Ethiopian _____ church has played a great role in Ethiopian life.

NATIONAL GEOGRAPHIC **World Explorer**

Answer
belief in the existence of a supreme being, lesser deities, and nature spirits; and honoring ancestors

More About the Photo
In many African cultures, a dancer is judged by his or her ability to follow the rhythms of percussion instruments such as drums.

L1/ELL

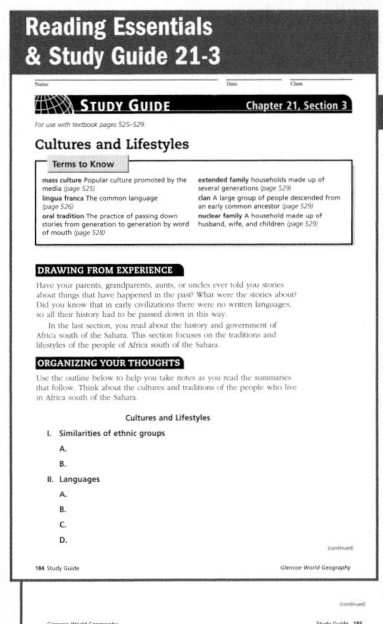

Reading Essentials & Study Guide 21-3

Name_____ Date_____ Class_____

🌐 **STUDY GUIDE** Chapter 21, Section 3

For use with textbook pages 525–529.

Cultures and Lifestyles

Terms to Know

mass culture Popular culture promoted by the media (page 525)	**extended family** households made up of several generations (page 529)
lingua franca The common language (page 526)	**clan** A large group of people descended from an early common ancestor (page 529)
oral tradition The practice of passing down stories from generation to generation by word of mouth (page 528)	**nuclear family** A household made up of husband, wife, and children (page 529)

DRAWING FROM EXPERIENCE
Have your parents, grandparents, aunts, or uncles ever told you stories about things that have happened in the past? What were the stories about? Did you know that in early civilizations there were no written languages, so all their history had to be passed down in this way.
In the last section, you read about the history and government of Africa south of the Sahara. This section focuses on the traditions and lifestyles of the people of Africa south of the Sahara.

ORGANIZING YOUR THOUGHTS
Use the outline below to help you take notes as you read the summaries that follow. Think about the cultures and traditions of the people who live in Africa south of the Sahara.

Cultures and Lifestyles
I. Similarities of ethnic groups
  A.
  B.
II. Languages
  A.
  B.
  C.
  D.
(continued)

184 Study Guide   Glencoe World Geography

(continued)
Glencoe World Geography   Study Guide 185

COOPERATIVE LEARNING ACTIVITY

Participating in a Multimedia Event Direct students' attention to the subsection titled "The Arts." On the board list the different art forms mentioned in the text: *visual arts, music, dance,* and *literature.* Organize the class into four groups. Have each group explore one of the four art forms and decide on a way to share the art form with the entire class. One group might make a ritual mask or draw the traditional patterns of a textile such as *kente* cloth. Other groups might play a recording of African drum music, demonstrate a form of African dance, or retell a folktale. Allow time for a question-and-answer session at the end of each presentation. 📦 🌐 **EE4 Human Systems: Standard 10**

The Earliest Telegraph

Africans traditionally communicated over long distances using a series of hollowed giant logs known as slit drums. Situated in just the right acoustic locations, these drums worked very much like a telegraph system. Even now, a master drummer using a talking drum can carry on a regular conversation with his or her listeners.

World Music: A Cultural Legacy

Use the accompanying Teacher Guide for background information and worksheets about the music of this region.

Objectives, goals, and answers to the student activity can be found in the Web Activity Lesson Plan feature at geography.glencoe.com

**ASSESS**

Assign Section 3 Assessment as homework or as an in-class activity.

Have students use **Interactive Tutor Self-Assessment CD-ROM.**

music of **AFRICA SOUTH OF THE SAHARA**

Important elements in African music are complex rhythms, improvisation, call-and-response singing, and the major role of dance.

Instrument Spotlight

The **talking drum** has an hourglass shape and a body carved from wood. On the open ends of the body, skins are held together by leather thongs or strings that stretch from one rim to the other. The drum is held under the arm and against the upper torso, and the drum head is struck with a curved wooden mallet. As the strings are squeezed down with the arm, the heads are stretched tighter and the pitch of the drum becomes higher. Many different pitches can be achieved by loosening and tightening the strings, and this gives the drum its characteristic "talking" sound.

Go To **World Music: A Cultural Legacy** Hear music of this region on Disc 2, Tracks 1–6.

rhythmic drum music to folktales. Strong examples of African visual arts include 2000-year-old terracotta heads produced by the Nok culture and bronze plaques that appeared in the palace courtyard of the Benin kingdom. Another art medium flourishing today is textiles, with patterns reflecting distinct ethnic groups—Ghana's *kente* cloth or East Africa's *khanga* cloth, for example.

Music and dance are art forms that are part of everyday African life. Entire communities participate, while dancers wearing masks honor specific deities, spirits of their ancestors, or a special occasion, such as a birth. Today African music is popular around the world and has influenced contemporary music. Paul Simon, Sting, and Peter Gabriel are only a few of the popular Western musicians who have borrowed from African music. In fact, the entire blues and jazz tradition of North America has its roots in the music enslaved Africans brought with them.

Oral literature, which is chanted, sung, or recited, has a strong tradition in Africa south of the Sahara. Oral tradition, the practice of passing down stories from generation to generation by word of mouth, is evident in folktales, myths, and proverbs and has helped preserve African history. Storytellers command great respect with tales of how the world began. In Mali, the Fulani people have this version:

Student Web Activity Visit the **Glencoe World Geography** Web site at geography.glencoe.com and click on Student Web Activities—Chapter 21 for an activity about West African textiles.

> At the beginning there was a huge
>   drop of milk.
> Then Doondari came and created the stone.
> Then the stone created iron;
> And iron created fire;
> And fire created water;
> And water created air.
>
> Ulli Beier, trans. in *The Origins of Life and Death*, 1966

528 🌐 Unit 7

CRITICAL THINKING ACTIVITY

Making Comparisons Have students compare and contrast the Fulani creation myth with similar stories around the world. If students are familiar with other creation stories, invite them to share these with the rest of the class. You may also collect versions of a variety of creation stories from other cultures to share with students. After reading them aloud, prompt students to identify their similarities and differences. Point out that in African stories about the origins of the world, the earth already existed. According to some creation stories in Asia and North America, water is the source of the earth and of life. In others, life begins with the sky and the earth acting as the world's parents or even with an egg.

EE4 Human Systems: Standard 10

Written literature developed mainly in northeast Africa, where societies came in contact with early Mediterranean systems of writing. In recent times written literature has become prominent in Africa south of the Sahara as well. Three Africans from the region have won the Nobel Prize in literature—Wole Soyinka of Nigeria in 1986 and Nadine Gordimer in 1991 and J.M. Coetzee in 2003, both of South Africa.

Varied Lifestyles

Lifestyles in the region are as varied as the ethnic groups who live there. **Tanzania**, with some 120 ethnic groups, is a perfect example. The Sukuma farm the land south of Lake Victoria, and the Chaggas grow coffee in the plains around Kilimanjaro. In the north live the nomadic cattleherders, the Masai, and in major cities, such as **Dar es Salaam**, Western urban lifestyles and dress prevail.

No matter how different their lifestyles, most Africans value strong family ties. In rural areas, most people still live in extended families, or households made up of several generations. Families also are organized into clans, large groups of people descended from an early common ancestor. Individuals often marry within their clan. In the cities, however, the nuclear family—made up of husband, wife, and children—is rapidly replacing the extended family.

NATIONAL GEOGRAPHIC World Explorer

Geography Skills for Life

Urban Shopping A supermarket in Gaborone, Botswana, provides shoppers with a variety of food products.

Place In which areas of Africa south of the Sahara do Western lifestyles prevail?

SECTION 3 ASSESSMENT

Checking for Understanding

1. **Define** mass culture, lingua franca, oral tradition, extended family, clan, nuclear family.

2. **Main Ideas** On a web diagram like the one below, fill in information about the cultural features of this region. Then write a paragraph describing one cultural feature.

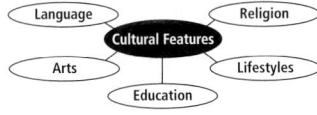

Language
Religion
Cultural Features
Arts
Lifestyles
Education

Critical Thinking

3. **Comparing and Contrasting** How are urban families in the region different from rural families? How are they similar?

4. **Making Inferences** Why do you think storytellers are respected figures in African communities?

5. **Making Generalizations** Write three general statements to summarize religion in Africa south of the Sahara. Support your generalizations with specific examples from your reading.

Analyzing Maps

6. **Place** Study the map on page 523. What language/ethnic groups are common in countries bordering the Sahara?

Applying Geography

7. **Lifestyles** Think about the varied lifestyles in Africa south of the Sahara, and study the population density map on page 488. Would people living in extended families be more common in Namibia or South Africa? Explain.

SECTION 3 ASSESSMENT ANSWERS

1. All vocabulary terms are defined in the text.
2. Webs should incorporate main ideas about the languages, religions, arts, lifestyles, and education of people in the region.
3. In the cities, nuclear families—husband, wife, children—are beginning to replace extended families, which are still more common in rural areas.
4. They help preserve the community's traditions by passing on the people's history and literature in the traditional way.
5. Students should support their generalizations with specific details from the text.
6. Afro-Asiatic and Nilo-Saharan
7. **Applying Geography** Namibia; Namibia is more rural than South Africa.

L2

Section Quiz 21-3

[Section 3 Quiz reproduction]

21 Section 3 Quiz
Cultures and Lifestyles

MATCHING: Match each item in Column A with an item in Column B. Write the correct letters in the blanks. *(10 points each)*

A	B
1. textile with distinct patterns found in Ghana	A. Masai people
2. Nobel prize-winning author	B. Wole Soyinka
3. producers of 2,000-year-old terra cotta sculpted heads	C. apprenticeship
4. traditional African way of education	D. Nok culture
5. nomadic cattle herders of Tanzania	E. kente cloth

MULTIPLE CHOICE: In each blank on the left, write the letter of the choice that best completes the statement or answers the question. *(10 points each)*

6. In Africa south of the Sahara, storytellers

Reteach

Have students work in pairs. Tell each student to prepare questions about the section content for his or her partner. Students should answer each other's questions orally or in writing.

Enrich

Have students read excerpts from Nobel Prize winner Wole Soyinka's book of memoirs, *Ake: The Years of Childhood*. Discuss details shared about African culture.

NATIONAL GEOGRAPHIC World Explorer

Answer
in big cities

More About the Photo
Gaborone has no real central business district, so people shop in suburban malls.

4 CLOSE

Ask students to name features that define African culture. Organize their ideas in a cluster on the board. Have students create a cluster of features they think defines their own culture.

① FOCUS

Direct students' attention to the map showing African ethnic groups on page 523. Have them identify the ethnic groups in Rwanda and Burundi. *(Hutu and Tutsi)* Remind students that the political boundaries set up by European colonial powers in Africa south of the Sahara rarely coincided with the homelands of Africa's ethnic groups. Have students evaluate the problems that colonial policies and influences have created for the peoples of Africa. *(Colonial boundaries divided ethnic groups; in some African countries today, rival ethnic groups struggle for political control.)*

② TEACH

L3 Panel Discussion

Organize the class into three groups representing the following parties: Hutu, Tutsi, and Europeans. Allow students time to gather further information about their group's involvement in or contribution to the current conflict in central Africa. Have the groups participate in a panel discussion and respond to questions such as the following: **Why were you able to live peacefully with the other group for centuries? How did you think you would benefit from favoring one group over the other? What is your goal in the current conflict? Why are you unwilling to compromise?**

CONFLICT IN CENTRAL AFRICA: HUTU VERSUS TUTSI

THE STORY OF AFRICA in the last two centuries includes the tale of European conquest and its aftermath. Beginning in the late 1800s, European nations set up colonies in most of Africa. Although African nations have since gained independence, the lingering effects of European rule have caused instability and conflict in many regions.

Central Africa, home to the peoples of Rwanda and Burundi, is one of Africa's most unstable regions. Hutu and Tutsi peoples lived there peacefully for centuries. Since the late 1950s, however, the two groups have been at war. Their conflict has its roots in a tortured history in which Europe played a key role.

Exploration and Colonization

In the early 1800s, Africa was a mystery to Europeans. Few who ventured into Africa's interior came out alive. But with improved steam-powered transportation and new medicines to treat disease, mid-century explorers successfully made their way inland. One of the first explorers was British doctor and missionary David Livingstone. Besides finding unspoiled beauty and rich

Soldiers patrol in the Democratic ▶ Republic of the Congo, where Rwandans have come seeking refuge.

BACKGROUND INFORMATION

Hutu and Tutsi The largest ethnic group in Rwanda and Burundi, the Hutu are farmers by tradition. The Tutsi, by contrast, are warriors and cattle owners. For centuries, both groups coexisted relatively peacefully in a feudal relationship in which the Tutsi were dominant. Under European colonial rule, the Tutsi were favored over the Hutu.

In 1960 the Hutu in Rwanda overthrew the Tutsi king, sending 200,000 Tutsi into exile.

After independence, Rwanda was controlled by the Hutu, while Burundi remained under Tutsi control. In 1994 Tutsi forces gained power in Rwanda; two years later, civil war erupted in Burundi between Tutsi and Hutu forces.

🌐 **EE4 Human Systems: Standards 10, 13**

◀ Foreign ministers of 14 European nations decide the future of Africa at the Berlin Conference in 1884.

ethnic cultures, he discovered a flourishing slave trade. Livingstone called for Europeans to spread commerce, Christianity, and their civilization throughout Africa to stop the evil trade.

The European powers—mainly Britain, France, Portugal, and Germany—were competing to expand their empires and to protect trade routes. With the outcry against slavery, Europeans moved swiftly into Africa. In less than 40 years, they carved the continent into more than 40 colonies.

Europe's Legacy

The Europeans introduced new crops, legal systems, basic schooling, roads, and medicine—all of which brought benefits to Africans. For many Africans, however, especially those in Central Africa, European commercial and labor practices caused hardships and great loss of life.

At the Berlin Conference of 1884–1885, where European powers divided Africa, Rwanda and Burundi were given to Germany. In 1919 the lands were awarded to Belgium. Both the Germans and Belgians viewed the Tutsi as a superior people. Hence the Tutsi were favored and were promoted in society. Most Hutu were exploited farmers. They were denied positions of authority. The stage was set for conflict.

The killing began in 1959 with a Hutu uprising in Rwanda. When Burundi and Rwanda achieved independence in 1962, Hutu and Tutsi political groups began a struggle for control of the two countries. Violence led to more violence, spilling into the neighboring countries of Tanzania, Uganda, and the Democratic Republic of the Congo. Since the 1960s, more than a million Hutu and Tutsi men, women, and children have lost their lives. Millions more have been driven from their homes in a cycle of violence that seems to have no end.

1850s Dr. Livingstone (photo above) explores Africa

1884–1885 Berlin Conference gives Rwanda and Burundi to Germany

1881–1912 Europe occupies Africa

1919 Belgium controls Rwanda and Burundi

1959 Hutu rebel in Rwanda

1962 Rwanda and Burundi gain independence

1970s–1980s Violence escalates; refugees (background photo) flee to neighboring countries

1990s Rwandan and Burundian governments work toward democracy; fighting continues

1997 War crimes trials begin

2002 Violence in Burundi continues; Rwandan government signs new peace agreement

> **Looking Ahead**
> Much of Africa today bears the scars of colonial rule. Why are peace and prosperity in Central Africa difficult to achieve?

Have students answer the **Looking Ahead** question on page 531.

Have students gather current articles about conflict in Africa south of the Sahara from newspapers and Internet news sources. Set aside time for students to share their articles and discuss causes and effects of current developments in the region.

🌐 Meeting National Standards

Geography for Life
The following standards are met in the Student Edition feature:

EE1 The World in Spatial Terms: Standard 3

EE4 Human Systems: Standards 10 and 13

ANSWER TO LOOKING AHEAD

Students may observe that ethnic rivalries have a long history in central Africa and that conflict creates long-term instability, disrupting daily activities and thus damaging the economy.

531

Teaching the Skill

Emphasize that one or two facts or examples are not enough support for a generalization. Many supporting details are needed. Help students distinguish between valid generalizations and overgeneralizations. Point out that limiting words such as *usually, often, most,* and *many* signal valid generalizations, while words with a broader reference, such as *all, always,* and *never,* are usually signs of overgeneralizations. Provide examples of generalizations from newspaper and magazine articles and advertisements, and have students identify them as valid generalizations or overgeneralizations. Students should explain their reasoning.

Additional Practice
L1

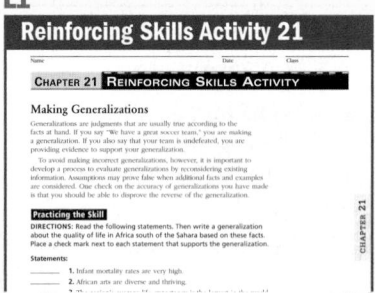

Reinforcing Skills Activity 21

GLENCOE
TECHNOLOGY

Glencoe Skillbuilder Interactive Workbook, Level 2

This interactive CD-ROM reinforces student mastery of essential social studies skills.

Making Generalizations

Suppose a friend says, "Both times I've been to Philadelphia, I heard someone on the street speaking Spanish. Philadelphia must have had a recent wave of immigrants from Spain." Your friend formed a generalization about Philadelphia. Whether the generalization is valid, or true, depends largely on the supporting details.

Learning the Skill

Generalizations are conclusions or judgments that people form based on the facts at hand. Using knowledge and experience, people make generalizations to help understand and explain the world. Geographers, like scientists, develop generalizations based on observation. Then they test these theories against further evidence they collect. This process is key to the scientific method.

Generalizations help us understand the world, but they can sometimes be misleading. For example, the generalization about Philadelphia was based on only two visits. But what are the real reasons the friend heard people speaking Spanish while visiting that city? Were the speakers long-time citizens who grew up speaking Spanish in a traditionally Hispanic neighborhood? To say that Philadelphia has had a recent wave of immigrants from Spain may be an *overgeneralization*, or a statement that is too broad.

Use the following steps to make useful generalizations:

• **Gather facts, examples, or statements related to the topic.**

• **Identify similarities or patterns among these facts.**

• **Use these similarities or patterns to form generalizations about the topic.**

▲ *South Africans line up to vote in the country's historic election of 1994.*

• **Test your generalizations against other facts and examples.**

Practicing the Skill

Complete the following activities about making generalizations.

1. Identify a generalization you have recently heard.

2. Describe ways you can avoid making an overgeneralization.

3. Write a generalization based on the following statements:

In 1994 Nelson Mandela succeeded F.W. de Klerk as president of South Africa. Mandela's party, the African National Congress, received 63 percent of the vote; de Klerk's party, the National Party, received only 20 percent.

Applying
the Skill

Read an article about Africa south of the Sahara in a newspaper or on an Internet news site. Write a generalization based on what you read. Provide details from the article to support your generalization.

Go To The Glencoe Skillbuilder Interactive Workbook, Level 2 provides instruction and practice in key social studies skills.

ANSWERS TO PRACTICING THE SKILL

1. Accept reasonable responses.
2. Gather enough facts or examples to support generalizations, and check that evidence is accurate.
3. Most South African voters wanted a change in leadership in 1994.

CHAPTER 21

SUMMARY & STUDY GUIDE

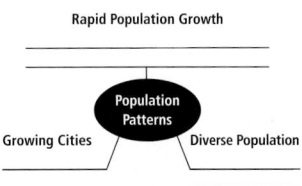

Using the Chapter 21 Summary & Study Guide

Use the Chapter 21 Summary & Study Guide to preview, review, condense, or reteach the chapter.

SECTION 1   Population Patterns (pp. 515–518)

Terms to Know
- sanitation
- urbanization
- service center

Key Points
- The uneven distribution of the 711 million people in Africa south of the Sahara is linked to the region's physical geography.
- The spread of AIDS has significantly impacted health and economic development in the region.
- Africa south of the Sahara is urbanizing faster than any other region in the world.
- Thousands of ethnic groups make up the population of Africa south of the Sahara.

Organizing Your Notes
Use a diagram like the one below to help you organize your notes for this section.

Rapid Population Growth

Population Patterns

Growing Cities   Diverse Population

SECTION 2   History and Government (pp. 519–524)

Terms to Know
- domesticate
- apartheid
- universal suffrage

Key Points
- The movement of different groups, including the migrations of Bantu peoples, helped shape the history of Africa south of the Sahara.
- From the A.D. 700s to the 1600s, powerful trading empires arose and prospered in West Africa.
- European colonization cut across traditional ethnic territories.
- Most of the countries in Africa south of the Sahara won independence in the second half of the 1900s.

Organizing Your Notes
Use a table like the one below to organize your notes about each major stage in the history of Africa south of the Sahara.

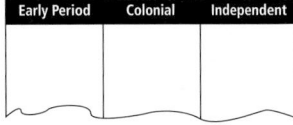

Early Period	Colonial	Independent

SECTION 3   Cultures and Lifestyles (pp. 525–529)

Terms to Know
- mass culture
- lingua franca
- oral tradition
- extended family
- clan
- nuclear family

Key Points
- The many languages of Africans south of the Sahara contribute to the diversity of the region.
- The peoples of the region are followers of Christianity, Islam, or traditional African religions.
- The various art forms created by Africans south of the Sahara have influenced cultures around the world.
- Although they have diverse lifestyles, most peoples in the region value family ties, and many live in extended families.

Organizing Your Notes
Create an outline using the format below to help you organize your notes for this section.

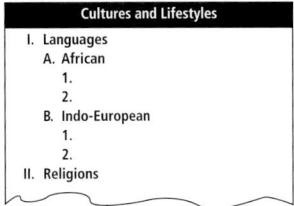

Cultures and Lifestyles
I. Languages
  A. African
    1.
    2.
  B. Indo-European
    1.
    2.
II. Religions

Chapter 21   533

Preview/Review

🔘 **Vocabulary PuzzleMaker CD-ROM** reinforces "Terms to Know."

🔘 **Interactive Tutor Self-Assessment CD-ROM** provides a review of Chapter 21 content.

Condense

Have students read the Chapter 21 Summary & Study Guide.

🔘 Chapter 21 Audio Program

📁 Chapter 21 Guided Reading Activities

Reteach

📁 Chapter 21 Reteaching Activities (Spanish also available)

📁 Chapter 21 Reading Essentials and Study Guides

GLENCOE TECHNOLOGY

◻ NATIONAL GEOGRAPHIC
WORLD REGIONS
VIDEO PROGRAM

Unit 7, Africa South of the Sahara
The following segments enhance the study of this unit:
- **Namib Desert**
- **Living With Elephants**
- **Baaba Maal: Musician of the World**

CHAPTER CULMINATING ACTIVITY

Writing an Essay Discuss with students the definition of "mosaic." *(an intricate design or picture made from different-colored pieces of glass, stone, or tile)* Then write the following on the board: *Africa South of the Sahara: A Vibrant Cultural Mosaic.* Direct students to use what they have learned about the cultural geography of the region to write a brief essay with the title you have written on the board. 🌐 **EE4 Human Systems: Standard 10**

NOTE: This activity may be completed separately or you may wish students to incorporate it into their GeoJournals.

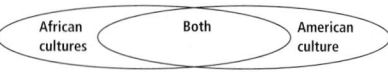

Have students visit the Web site at geography.glencoe.com to review Chapter 21 and take the **Self-Check Quiz.**

GLENCOE
TECHNOLOGY

Use *MindJogger Videoquiz* to review the Chapter 21 content.

Reviewing Key Terms

1. oral tradition
2. extended family
3. apartheid
4. universal suffrage
5. mass culture
6. urbanization
7. nuclear family
8. sanitation
9. domesticate

Reviewing Facts
SECTION 1

1. Large areas of the region are covered by desert and steppe, where living conditions are difficult; in other areas the land is fertile, there is access to water, and climates are generally moderate and support farming.
2. Much farmland has been exhausted through intensive cultivation, loss of fertile soils, and droughts.

SECTION 2

3. East Africa: Axum, Kush; West Africa: Ghana, Mali, Songhai
4. Africans won their independence from European colonial powers.

SECTION 3

5. Christianity, Islam, and traditional African religions
6. traditional religious beliefs

Reviewing Key Terms

Write the key term that best completes each of the following sentences. Refer to the Terms to Know in the Summary & Study Guide on page 533.

1. A strong _____ has helped preserve many literary forms in Africa south of the Sahara.
2. A(n) _____ includes several generations.
3. The strict separation of races in South Africa was called _____.
4. Under _____, or equal voting rights, all adults of voting age may cast a vote.
5. _____ unites African people of different ethnic backgrounds.
6. Rapid _____ has caused problems in the region's cities.
7. A(n) _____ includes a husband and wife and their children.
8. _____ and disease are important health issues in Africa south of the Sahara.
9. People began to _____ animals many years ago.

Reviewing Facts
SECTION 1

1. What physical features influence population density in Africa south of the Sahara?
2. Why is food production in the region inadequate?

SECTION 2

3. What ancient kingdoms and empires developed in East Africa? In West Africa?
4. What was the major development in Africa after World War II?

SECTION 3

5. What religions are practiced in Africa south of the Sahara?
6. What is the origin of many of the art forms of Africa south of the Sahara?

Critical Thinking

1. Predicting Consequences In what ways has urbanization affected traditional ways of life in Africa south of the Sahara? Explain.
2. Drawing Conclusions How did trade play a major role in early African societies?
3. Comparing and Contrasting Use a Venn diagram like the one below to compare and contrast the role of music in African cultures and in American culture. Then write a paragraph summarizing your conclusions.

African cultures — Both — American culture

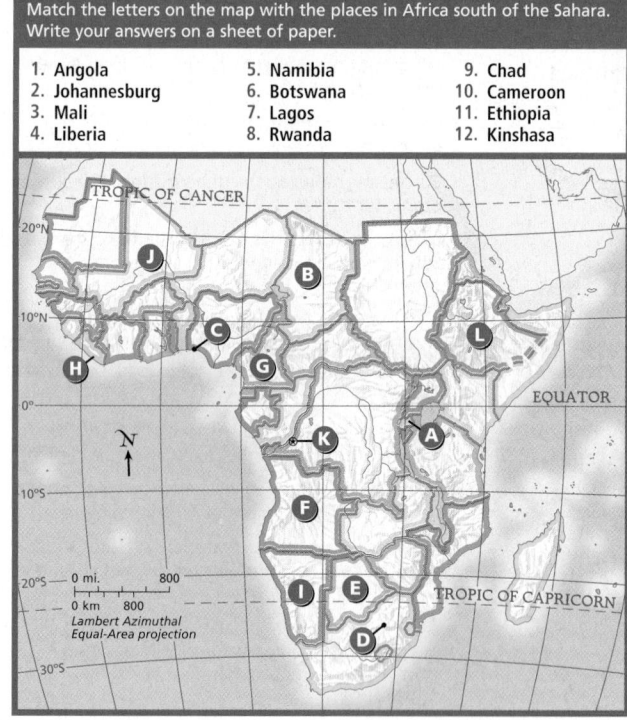

NATIONAL GEOGRAPHIC **Locating Places**
Africa South of the Sahara: Political Geography

Match the letters on the map with the places in Africa south of the Sahara. Write your answers on a sheet of paper.

1. Angola
2. Johannesburg
3. Mali
4. Liberia
5. Namibia
6. Botswana
7. Lagos
8. Rwanda
9. Chad
10. Cameroon
11. Ethiopia
12. Kinshasa

Critical Thinking

1. Traditional ways of life have been lost; movement to the cities breaks up the clan and extended family, both of which protect traditions; families formed in the city tend to be nuclear families, which may have no memory or experience of traditional ways of life and thus will not practice them or pass them on to the next generation.
2. Trade provided the peoples of early societies with needed goods and built up their economies through the export of plentiful local goods to places where they were in demand.
3. Students should compare and contrast the role of music in African and American culture and record their ideas in a Venn diagram.

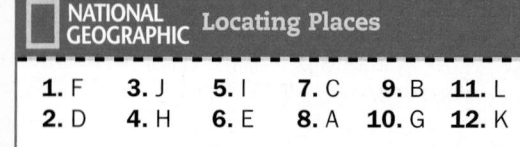

NATIONAL GEOGRAPHIC **Locating Places**

1. F	**3.** J	**5.** I	**7.** C	**9.** B	**11.** L
2. D	**4.** H	**6.** E	**8.** A	**10.** G	**12.** K

Using the Regional Atlas

Refer to the Regional Atlas on pages 486–489.

1. **Human-Environment Interaction** What is the relationship between areas of high population density and bodies of water?

2. **Location** Where are many of the capitals of West African countries located? Why do you think this pattern emerged?

Thinking Like a Geographer

How did past climate changes in the Sahara affect population patterns? What predictions can you make about future climate changes in the region?

Problem-Solving Activity

Contemporary Issues Case Study Many cities in Africa south of the Sahara have rapidly growing populations. Research and write a case study about an African city. Identify the processes causing the city's growth, such as location, resources, and transportation. Then describe the challenges the city faces and outline solutions. Design and draw maps and graphics for presentation.

GeoJournal

Newspaper Article Use your GeoJournal to write a newspaper article about an aspect of the cultural geography of Africa south of the Sahara. Remember to answer the 5-W questions (Who? What? Where? When? Why?). Your article should be impartial and factual, but be sure to include details that will hold your readers' interest.

Technology Activity

Using an Electronic Spreadsheet Using a world almanac, select 10 countries in Africa south of the Sahara, and find information about their birthrates, death rates, life expectancies, and rates of population change. Create a spreadsheet to compare and contrast these figures. If possible, also create graphs to illustrate your findings. Then write a summary of your analysis and possible explanations for your statistical findings.

Standardized Test Practice

Choose the best answer for the following multiple-choice question. If you have trouble answering the question, use the process of elimination to narrow your choices.

Facts About Tanzania

	1996	2003
Population	29,058,470	35,400,000
Percent urban	21	22
Percent rural	79	78
Population density of entire country	80 per sq. mi. (31 per sq. km)	97 per sq. mi. (38 per sq. km)
Population of current capital, Dar es Salaam	1,400,000	2,347,000

Sources: World Almanac, 1997, 2001; 2003 World Population Data Sheet

1. **Which of the following statements regarding Tanzania's population is implied by the chart?**

   A Dar es Salaam's population increased by about 100,000 people.

   B Tanzania's population density was lower in 1996 than it was in 2003.

   C The percentage of Tanzanians living in urban areas increased from 21 percent to 40 percent.

   D Between 1996 and 2003, many of Tanzania's residents moved from cities to rural areas.

 **Test-Taking Tip** Some standardized test questions ask you to answer a question using a chart. Do not try to answer these types of questions from memory. First, read the question. Then skim the chart. Next, read each answer choice, deciding whether it is correct or incorrect by referring to the chart. Finally, choose the answer choice that is correct according to the chart.

Technology Activity

Check students' spreadsheets, graphs, and analyses for accuracy.

Standardized Test Practice

1. B

Tested Objectives: analyzing information

Additional Practice and Test-Taking Tips

 Standardized Test Practice Workbook

CHAPTER BONUS TEST QUESTION

How did European colonial rule prevent African countries south of the Sahara from developing industry? *(Colonial powers used African raw materials for European industries and made Africans dependent on manufactured goods from Europe.)*

Using the Regional Atlas

1. Most areas of high population density are near water sources that are needed for drinking, agriculture, and transportation.
2. on the coast; they began as ports

Thinking Like a Geographer

Students may predict that people will move south and into urban areas because of climate changes in the Sahel today.

Problem-Solving Activity

Students' case studies should reflect accurate information about the cities they chose and be accompanied by reasoned suggestions to meet population challenges, and appropriate graphic elements.

GeoJournal

Check students' news stories for accuracy and impartiality as well as attention to the who, what, where, when, why, and how questions.

CHAPTER 22 PLANNING GUIDE

NOTE: The following materials may be used when teaching Chapter 22. Section-level support materials are shown at point-of-use in the margins of the Teacher Wraparound Edition.

TEACHING TRANSPARENCIES

L2 Unit 7 Map Overlay Transparencies

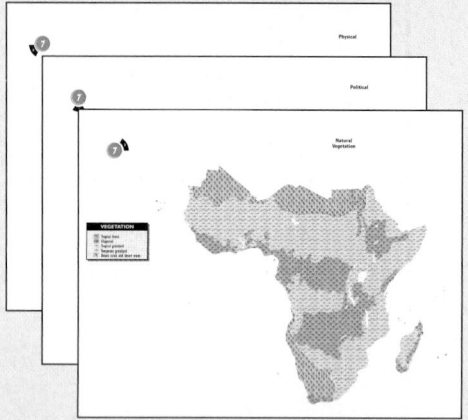

L2 Political Map Transparency 7

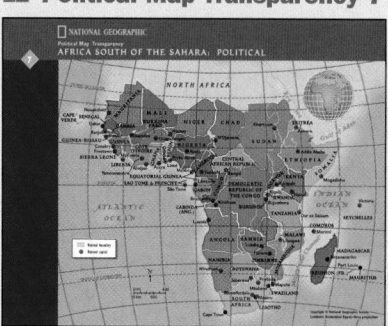

GEOGRAPHIC LITERACY

Focus on Geography Literacy

APPLICATION AND ENRICHMENT

L3 Enrichment Activity 22

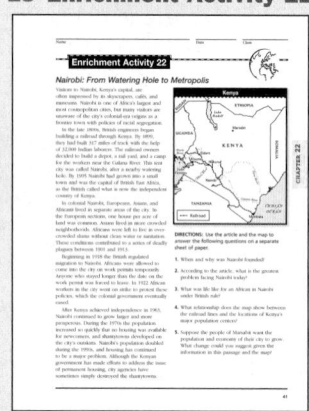

REVIEW AND REINFORCEMENT

L1 Vocabulary Activity 22 L1 Reinforcing Skills Activity 22 L1 Reteaching Activity 22

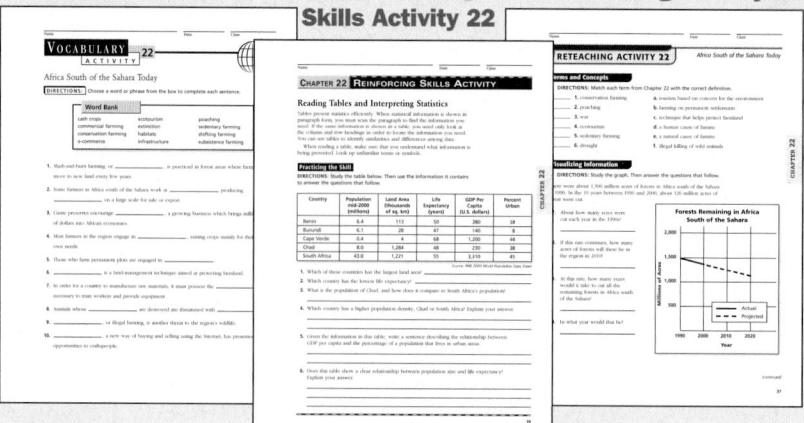

ASSESSMENT

L2 Chapter 22 Test Form A

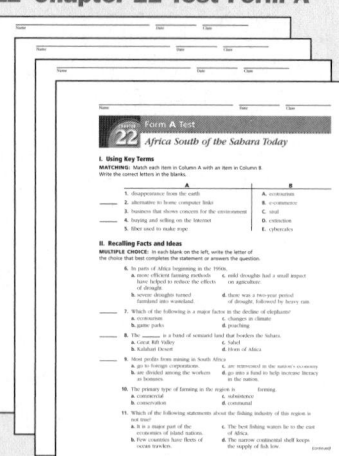

L2 Chapter 22 Test Form B

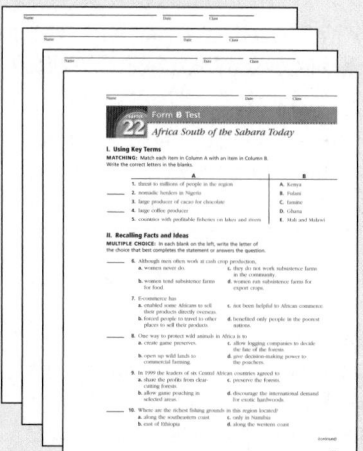

L1/ELL Performance Assessment Activity 22

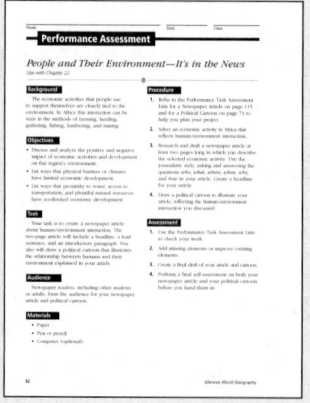

ExamView® Pro Testmaker

WINDOWS/MACINTOSH

- QuickTest Wizard does all the work for you
- Choose ExamView tests or create your own
- Complete editing capability

The following Spanish language materials are available in the Spanish Resources binder:

- 📁 Spanish Vocabulary Activities
- 📁 Spanish Guided Reading Activities
- 📁 Spanish Reteaching Activities
- 📁 Spanish Summaries
- 📁 Spanish Quizzes and Tests
- 📁 Spanish Reading Essentials and Study Guide

- World Regions Video
- MindJogger Videoquiz
- Vocabulary PuzzleMaker CD-ROM
- Interactive Tutor Self-Assessment CD-ROM
- ExamView® Pro Testmaker CD-ROM
- Audio Program
- TeacherWorks CD-ROM
- Interactive Student Edition CD-ROM
- Glencoe Skillbuilder Interactive Workbook CD-ROM, Level 2
- Presentation Plus! CD-ROM

Timesaving Tools

TeacherWorks™ All-In-One Planner and Resource Center

- **Interactive Teacher Edition** Access your Teacher Wraparound Edition and your classroom resources with a few easy clicks.

- **Interactive Lesson Planner** Planning has never been easier! Organize your week, month, semester, or year with all the lesson helps you need to make teaching creative, timely, and relevant.

Use Glencoe's **Presentation Plus!** multimedia teacher tool to easily present dynamic lessons that visually excite your students. Using Microsoft PowerPoint® you can customize the presentations to create your own personalized lessons.

GEOGRAPHY Online

Use our Web site for additional resources. All essential content is covered in the Student Edition.

You and your students can visit geography.glencoe.com, the Web site companion to *Glencoe World Geography*. This innovative integration of electronic and print media offers your students a wealth of opportunities. The student text directs students to the Web site for the following options:

- Chapter Overviews
- Self-Check Quizzes
- Student Activities
- Textbook Updates

Answers are provided for you in the "Web Activity Lesson Plan." Additional Web resources and Interactive Tutor puzzles are also available.

Additional Glencoe Teacher Support

- Teaching Strategies for the Geography Classroom (including Block Scheduling Pacing Guides)

- Graphic Organizer Transparencies Strategies and Activities

- Outline Map Resource Book

- Reading in the Content Area

PLANNING GUIDE

SECTION RESOURCES

Daily Objectives	Reproducible Resources	Multimedia Resources

SECTION 1 Living in Africa South of the Sahara

1. Describe the most common farming methods in Africa south of the Sahara.
2. Explain how mineral resources benefit the peoples of the region.
3. Identify the reasons industrial development has been slow in Africa south of the Sahara.
4. Describe how transportation and communications are changing in the region.

 Reproducible Lesson Plan 22-1
 Daily Lecture Notes 22-1
 Guided Reading Activity 22-1*
Reading Essentials and Study Guide 22-1*
Section Quiz 22-1*

Daily Focus Skills Transparency 22-1
Political Map Transparency 7
Unit 7 Map Overlay Transparencies
Interactive Tutor Self-Assessment CD-ROM
ExamView® Pro Testmaker CD-ROM*
Presentation Plus! CD-ROM

SECTION 2 People and Their Environment

1. Examine why food shortages have occurred in parts of Africa south of the Sahara.
2. List steps the African countries south of the Sahara are taking to protect their environment.
3. Discuss the outlook for the region's future development.

 Reproducible Lesson Plan 22-2
 Vocabulary Activity 22*
 Daily Lecture Notes 22-2
 Guided Reading Activity 22-2*
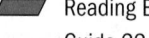 Reading Essentials and Study Guide 22-2*
 Reteaching Activity 22*
 Reinforcing Skills Activity 22
 Section Quiz 22-2*

Daily Focus Skills Transparency 22-2
Unit 7 Map Overlay Transparencies
Vocabulary PuzzleMaker CD-ROM
World Art Prints
Interactive Tutor Self-Assessment CD-ROM
ExamView® Pro Testmaker CD-ROM*
Presentation Plus! CD-ROM

 Blackline Master   Software   Videocassette   *Also available in Spanish

Transparency   CD-ROM   DVD

OUT OF TIME? Assign the Chapter 22 **Reading Essentials and Study Guide.**

Block Schedule

Activities that are particularly suited to use within the block scheduling framework are identified throughout this chapter by the following designation:

KEY TO ABILITY LEVELS

Teaching strategies have been coded for various learning styles and abilities.

L1 **BASIC** activities for all students

L2 **AVERAGE** activities for average to above-average students

L3 **CHALLENGING** activities for above-average students

ELL **ENGLISH LANGUAGE LEARNER** activities

Teacher to Teacher

Lynda Abner
Lee County High School
Beattyville, KY

Development and Culture

As students begin to learn more about the ways people in Africa south of the Sahara make a living, have students bring to class news clippings or articles about the cultures of the region. Some students may wish to do further research on the Internet or in the library.

Use the information students have collected to find examples of how economic changes have affected the lives of people in the region. Give students time to come up with their own ideas. Then have them get together to compare and contrast their findings. Discuss the effect growing industries can have on the environment, the economic opportunities available to women, or child labor issues, for example.

Students may mention that some developing countries have poor school systems, no labor laws to protect working children, and no agencies to regulate environmental protection. Students may also want to discuss why people from developing countries accept jobs with poor pay and unsafe working conditions. **Ask:** What changes in the economies of Africa will take place in the future? (Use students' answers as a basis for class discussion.)

NATIONAL GEOGRAPHIC
TEACHER'S CORNER

Index to National Geographic Magazine:

The following articles may be used for research relating to this chapter:

- "Monsters of Madagascar," by John Flynn and David Krause, August 2000.
- "Masai Passage to Manhood," by Carol Beckwith and Angela Fisher, September 1999.
- "Journey to the Heart of the Sahara," by Donovan Webster, March 1999.

National Geographic Society Products:

To order the following products for use with this chapter, call National Geographic Society at 1-800-368-2728.

- *Africa* (Video)
- *South Africa: After Apartheid* (Video)
- *Endangered Animals: Survivors on the Brink* (Video)
- *Healing the Earth* (Video)
- *National Geographic Atlas of the World, Seventh Edition* (Book)

NGS ONLINE

Access National Geographic's Web site for current events, activities, links, interactive features, and archives.
www.nationalgeographic.com

Meeting National Standards

Geography For Life

The following standards are highlighted in Chapter 22:

Section 1   EE2 Places and Regions: Standard 4
EE3 Physical Systems: Standard 8
EE4 Human Systems: Standard 11
EE5 Environment and Society: Standard 14
EE6 The Uses of Geography: Standard 18

Section 2   EE3 Physical Systems: Standard 8
EE5 Environment and Society: Standards 14, 15
EE6: The Uses of Geography: Standard 18

Local Objectives

_____

_____

MEETING SPECIAL NEEDS

In addition to the Differentiated Instruction strategies found in each section, the following resources are also suitable for your special needs students:

- *ExamView® Pro Testmaker CD-ROM* allows teachers to tailor tests by reducing answer choices.
- The *Audio Program* includes the entire narrative of the student edition so that less-proficient readers can listen to the words as they read them.
- The *Reading Essentials and Study Guide* provides the same content as the student edition but is written two grade levels below the textbook.
- *Guided Reading Activities* give less-proficient readers point-by-point instructions to increase comprehension as they read each textbook section.
- *Enrichment Activities* include a stimulating collection of readings and activities for gifted and talented students.

Chapter Objectives

1. Describe how people make a living in Africa south of the Sahara.
2. Examine environmental challenges and their effect on life in the region.

GLENCOE TECHNOLOGY

Use *MindJogger Videoquiz* to preview the Chapter 22 content.

GeoJournal

For access to additional photos, maps, and information on life today in Africa south of the Sahara go to www.nationalgeographic.com (See Teacher pages in front for strategies for using journals in the geography classroom.)

GEOGRAPHY Online

Introduce students to chapter content and key terms by having them access **Chapter Overview 22** at geography.glencoe.com

CHAPTER 22 Africa South of the Sahara Today

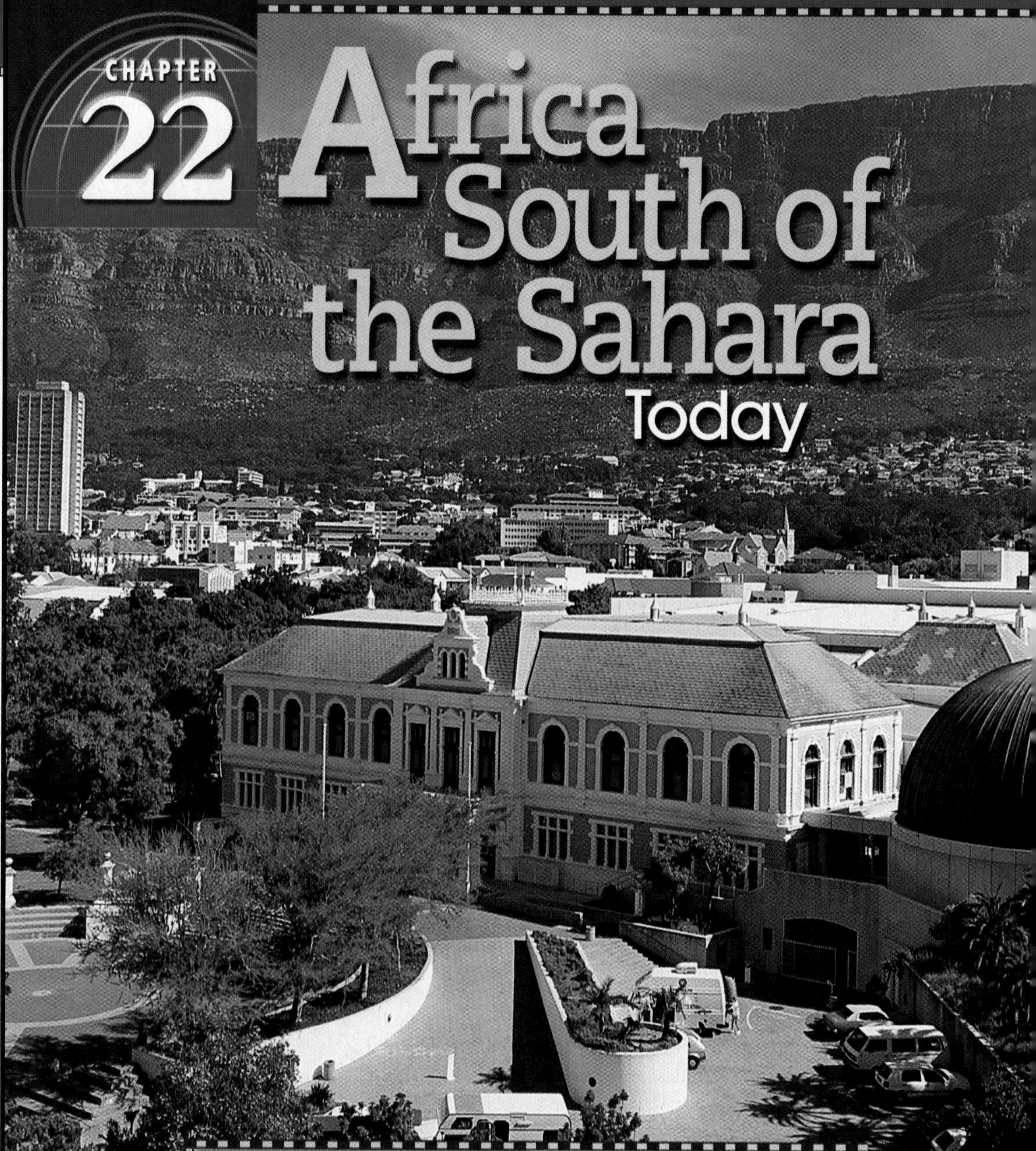

GeoJournal

As you read this chapter, use your journal to log information about life in Africa south of the Sahara today. Include interesting and descriptive details that reflect the region's unique characteristics.

GEOGRAPHY Online

Chapter Overview Visit the **Glencoe World Geography** Web site at geography.glencoe.com and click on Chapter Overviews—Chapter 22 to preview information about the region today.

ABOUT THE PHOTO

Visual Instruction The South African Museum in Cape Town, pictured above, has a long tradition of collecting and exhibiting specimens of South Africa's natural history. Established in 1825, the museum has attracted millions of visitors to its exhibits that feature the earth's biodiversity. In the background another popular tourist attraction, Table Mountain, rises 3,563 feet (1,086 m) above sea level. The massive sandstone feature is home to 1,470 species of plants. **Ask: How might South Africa benefit from people's interest in natural history?** *(It could use people's interest to educate them about the value of biodiversity and to encourage conservation.)* 🌐 **EE3 Physical Systems: Standard 8**

Guide to Reading

Consider What You Know

Think about the resources and products that come from Africa south of the Sahara and how people make their livings from them. If you wanted to create a mural showing what life in the region is like today, what images would you include?

Reading Strategy

Organizing Complete a web diagram similar to the one below by filling in the obstacles farmers face in Africa south of the Sahara.

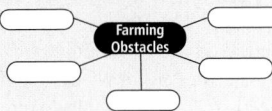

Farming Obstacles

Read to Find Out

- What are the most common farming methods in Africa south of the Sahara?
- How do mineral resources benefit the peoples of the region?
- Why has industrial development been slow in Africa south of the Sahara?
- How are transportation and communications in the region changing?

Terms to Know

- subsistence farming
- shifting farming
- sedentary farming
- commercial farming
- cash crop
- conservation farming
- infrastructure
- e-commerce

Places to Locate

- Zimbabwe
- Zambia
- South Africa
- Guinea
- Nigeria
- Kampala

◀ *View of South African Museum, Cape Town, South Africa*

Living in Africa South of the Sahara

A Geographic View

Leap into the Future

With seven children, [Kawab Bulyar Lago] sold his animals and saddled himself with debt to send his son Paul to. . . school outside Marsabit [Kenya]. Now awaiting the results of the national exams that will determine his fate, Paul hopes to attend university and become either a doctor, a civil engineer, a teacher, or even a tour guide. "I'd prefer to be a doctor," he tells me one morning, "but anything would be all right.". . .

Ariaal people, Kenya

In the old days [Paul] would have inherited his father's herd. Today he inherits his hopes and dreams.

—Wade Davis, "Vanishing Cultures," National Geographic, *August 1999*

Whichever career he pursues, Paul Lago's life will be different from his father's life. Like many other rural Africans, Paul's father herded camels and goats for a living. Today the lives of people throughout Africa south of the Sahara are changing as the region becomes more closely involved in the global economy. In this section you will learn about the region's changing economic activities— changes that offer new opportunities and challenges for the region's people.

Agriculture

Farming is the main economic activity in Africa south of the Sahara. More than two-thirds of the working population is involved in some form of agriculture. Some countries in the region still depend

Chapter 22 🌐 537

① FOCUS

Section Overview

This section examines economic activity and growth in Africa south of the Sahara.

BELLRINGER
Skillbuilder Activity

- Project transparency and have students answer questions.
- Available as blackline master.

Daily Focus Skills Transparency 22-1

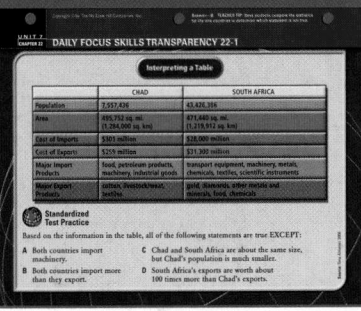

Guide to Reading

Consider What You Know
Answers *farming, herding, and mining; people working in service and industry in cities*

Reading Strategy
Answers *over-grazing, over-worked soil, lack of farming technology, soil erosion, desertification*

Preteaching Vocabulary
Challenge students to define the words *subsistence, shifting, sedentary,* and *conservation.* Use a dictionary to check and revise if necessary. Then ask students to explain the different kinds of farming based on these descriptive words.

RESOURCE MANAGER

📁 Reproducible Masters
- Reproducible Lesson Plan 22-1
- Daily Lecture Notes 22-1
- Guided Reading Activity 22-1
- Reading Essentials and Study Guide 22-1
- Section Quiz 22-1

🎞 Transparencies
- Daily Focus Skills Transparency 22-1
- Political Map Transparency 7
- Unit 7 Map Overlay Transparencies

Multimedia
- 💿 Interactive Tutor Self-Assessment CD-ROM
- 💿 ExamView® Pro Testmaker CD-ROM
- 💿 Presentation Plus! CD-ROM

TEACH

L1 Identify Products

Have students turn to the "Country Profiles" on pages 490–495 in the Unit Regional Atlas. As you name agricultural products of the region, have students identify countries that export them.

NATIONAL GEOGRAPHIC   GRAPH STUDY

Answers

1. *Ethiopia*

2. *subsistence farming*

Skills Practice

In which countries do agricultural workers make up more than half the population?
(Ethiopia, Mozambique, Central African Republic, Angola, Gabon, Sierra Leone)

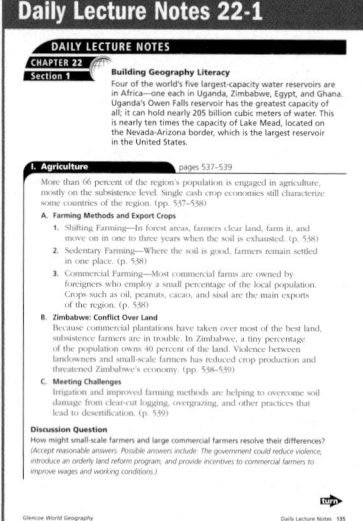

Daily Lecture Notes 22-1

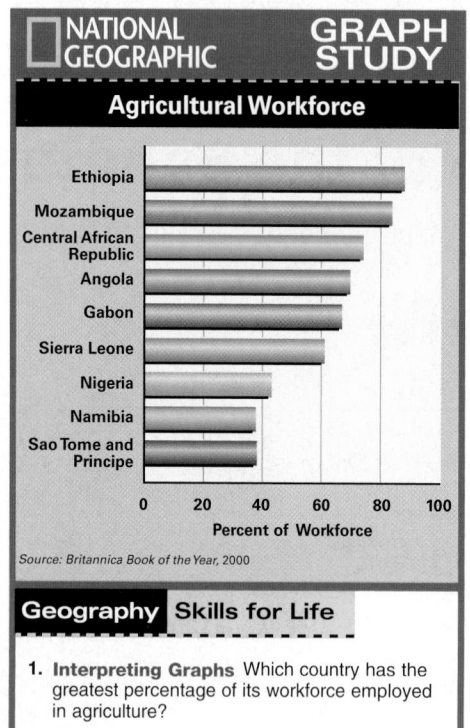

NATIONAL GEOGRAPHIC   GRAPH STUDY

Agricultural Workforce

Ethiopia
Mozambique
Central African Republic
Angola
Gabon
Sierra Leone
Nigeria
Namibia
Sao Tome and Principe

0   20   40   60   80   100
Percent of Workforce

Source: Britannica Book of the Year, 2000

Geography   Skills for Life

1. **Interpreting Graphs** Which country has the greatest percentage of its workforce employed in agriculture?

2. **Applying Geography Skills** Which farming method employs the largest number of workers in Africa?

---

on single-crop economies created during the colonial era. Others, however, produce a variety of agricultural goods.

Farming Methods and Export Crops

Most Africans south of the Sahara engage in subsistence farming, or small-scale agriculture that provides primarily for the needs of just a family or village. After they have met their own needs, farmers often sell any extra harvest or animals at a local market for cash or trade for other items they need or want.

African farmers use various methods to work the land. The Masai in Kenya and Tanzania and the Fulani in Nigeria and other parts of West Africa are nomadic herders. In the forest areas, farmers support themselves by shifting farming, a method in which farmers move every one to three

years to find better soil. People practicing this method—also known as slash-and-burn farming—use basic tools, often just an ax and a hoe, to clear and cultivate land. They burn the trees and brush they have cut and then plant seeds in the ash-enriched soil. When the soil is no longer fertile, they move on, sometimes returning to a location after the soil has had time to renew itself. This method has been used to clear land for a variety of plantation crops, such as rubber in Liberia, cacao in Ghana, and coffee in Burundi.

Other farmers depend on sedentary farming, or agriculture conducted at permanent settlements. Sedentary farming is most common in areas with good soil. The Kikuyu in Kenya and the Hausa in Nigeria, for instance, farm permanent plots. Many people of European descent who have made their homes in South Africa, Kenya, and Zimbabwe also practice sedentary farming.

A small percentage of the population works at commercial farming, in which farms produce crops on a large scale. These cash crops are grown to be sold for profit instead of used by the farmer. Most commercial farms, such as those in Zimbabwe and South Africa, are large, foreign-owned plantations. They supply much of the world's palm oil, peanuts, cacao, and sisal, a vegetable fiber used for making rope.

The colonial economic systems played an important role in the growth of commercial farms in the region. Today the same commercial crops are the region's main agricultural exports. Côte d'Ivoire (KOHT dee•VWAHR), Nigeria, Ghana, and Cameroon, for instance, depend heavily on the sale of cacao, which is used to make cocoa and chocolate. Kenya, Tanzania, and Madagascar are large producers of coffee. Most of today's cash crops leave Africa to be processed elsewhere, just as they did during the colonial period.

The continued practice of cash-crop production has created problems for African economies. Reliance on one or two export crops is extremely risky. An unfavorable growing season or a drop in prices on the world market can have a disastrous effect on a country's entire economy.

Zimbabwe: Conflict Over Land

Cash-crop production also creates problems for farmers trying to meet their own food needs, because plantations and other large-scale farms take

---

DIFFERENTIATED INSTRUCTION

English Learners Pair English language learners with students fluent in English and have students use the SQ3R (survey, question, read, recite, review) strategy together to approach and study material in this section. Direct partners to read the section independently and collaborate for the recite step, with English language learners orally sharing with fluent speakers answers they found to the questions raised before reading. For review, partners should return to the text and work together to refine or expand on answers to questions.

ELL 🌐 **EE4 Human Systems: Standard 11**

Refer to *Inclusion for the Social Studies Classroom Strategies and Activities.*

all the best land. For example, in **Zimbabwe**, a country with more than 11 million people, 40 percent of the farmland is controlled by only 4,000 commercial farmers and ranchers, descendants of Europeans who controlled the land in colonial times. Although the government has proposed land reform to distribute land more evenly, violence has broken out as small-scale farmers have tried to take over large-scale farms. The resulting conflict has slowed or completely halted production on commercial farms. These developments threaten Zimbabwe's economy, which currently depends heavily on commercial agriculture.

Meeting Challenges

Whether involved in large-scale or small-scale agriculture, farmers in the region face many challenges. Overgrazing, overworked soils, and a lack of technology have made farming difficult in many places. The use of heavy farm machinery, frequent tilling, and the clearing of forests for timber have caused soil erosion and desertification. Most subsistence farming in the region depends largely on human labor alone. Although men work primarily in cash-crop production, women often work at traditional subsistence farming, using basic tools and techniques. Food production has fallen far short of the needs of the region's booming population.

Gradually, however, farmers are beginning to employ new methods and tools. Farmers in **Zambia** have started to practice conservation farming, a land-management technique that helps protect farmland. By planting different crops where they will grow best, Zambian farmers actually conserve, or save, land for farming. In addition, better fertilizers and seeds have increased yields of maize and other crops. In Nigeria and other countries, farmers who depended solely on rain to water their fields now use irrigation to increase production.

Logging and Fishing

Although forests cover almost 25 percent of Africa south of the Sahara, human activities are destroying the region's forests at an alarming rate, upsetting unique ecosystems. The demand for farmland has led agricultural settlements to open up some of this land, using the slash-and-burn method of shifting farming. People in the region also cut wood from the rain forest and savanna woodlands to use as fuel. Logging companies also harvest and export valuable hardwoods, such as Rhodesian teak, ebony, African walnut, and rosewood.

Although logging creates serious consequences for Africa's forests, the lumber industry has a relatively small output. Logging in the region accounts for less than 10 percent of the world's lumber supply. Coastal countries with rain forests, such as Gabon and Equatorial Guinea, do export significant amounts of lumber and pulp.

Commercial fishing also represents only a small portion of the region's economic activity. Few countries build and support fleets of commercial fishing vessels. Africa also has a very narrow continental shelf, the shallow ocean area near a

NATIONAL GEOGRAPHIC **World Explorer**

Geography | **Skills for Life**

Fresh Sardines Fishing is a major activity along Zimbabwe's Lake Kariba, one of the world's largest human-made lakes.

Human-Environment Interaction What inland countries in Africa south of the Sahara profit from fisheries on lakes and rivers?

Chapter 22 ● 539

L2 Freewriting

Ask: Why haven't the people of Africa south of the Sahara really benefited from their mineral resources? Have students freewrite for three minutes in response to the question. Encourage students to write everything they know that is relevant to the question.

L1/ELL

Guided Reading Activity 22-1

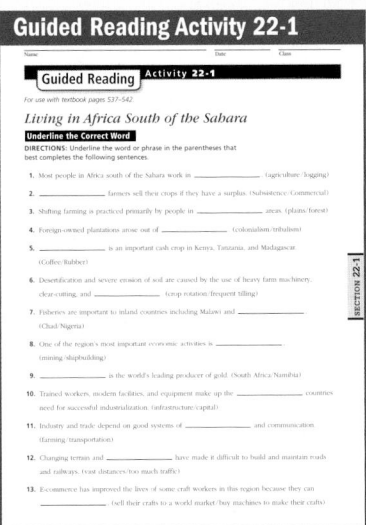

NATIONAL GEOGRAPHIC **World Explorer**

Answer
Malawi, Uganda, Chad, Mali

More About the Photo Lake Kariba covers approximately 2,000 square miles (5,200 sq. km). When built, the lake was heavily stocked with tilapia, a fast-growing freshwater fish raised in Africa for food since the time of the ancient Egyptians.

COOPERATIVE LEARNING ACTIVITY

Agricultural Solutions Remind students that chemical fertilizers are polluting agents. Then have students form small groups to research less harmful and expensive alternatives for enriching exhausted soil. Assign one of the following topics related to the problem or the solution to each group: monoculture, salination, sustainable agriculture, organic farming, crop rotation, strip farming, integrated pest management. Have groups report their findings at a simulated environmental conference titled "Agriculture in Africa South of the Sahara: Problems and Solutions." ● **EE5 Environment and Society: Standard 14**

□ NATIONAL GEOGRAPHIC **GEOFACT**

▶ As a result of increasing worldwide demand for organic produce, companies in the United States and the United Kingdom have approached Ghana about growing cacao using organic methods.

L3 Making a Flowchart

Have students research slash-and-burn farming and create a flowchart explaining the method step by step.

L1/ELL

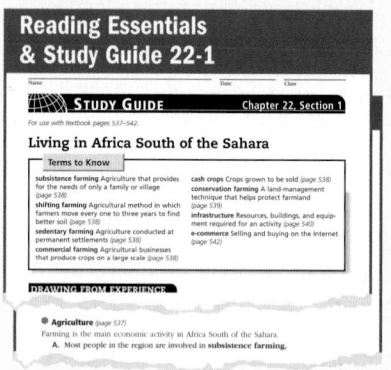

Reading Essentials & Study Guide 22-1

STUDY GUIDE
Chapter 22, Section 1

For use with textbook pages 537–542.

Living in Africa South of the Sahara

Terms to Know

subsistence farming Agriculture that provides for the needs of only a family or village (page 538)

shifting farming Agricultural method in which farmers move every one to three years to find better soil (page 538)

sedentary farming Agriculture conducted at permanent settlements (page 538)

commercial farming Agricultural businesses that produce crops on a large scale (page 538)

cash crops Crops grown to be sold (page 538)

conservation farming A land-management technique that helps protect farmland (page 539)

infrastructure Resources, buildings, and equipment required for an activity (page 540)

e-commerce Selling and buying on the Internet (page 542)

DRAWING FROM EXPERIENCE

● **Agriculture** (page 537)
Farming is the main economic activity in Africa South of the Sahara.
   A. Most people in the region are involved in **subsistence farming**.

Diamonds are extremely hard. In industry they are used for cutting rock, glass, and other hard materials and for polishing and grinding. Their brilliance makes them a highly prized gemstone.

---

continent's coast that usually contains abundant fish. Along the southwestern coast, commercial fishing vessels do catch large quantities of herring, sardines, and tuna for export. The richest fishing grounds in the region lie off the region's west coast. Countries bordering oceans—South Africa, Namibia, Angola, Nigeria, Ghana, and Senegal—haul in the largest catches. The economies of island countries in the region depend on the export of fish and fish products. In addition, the inland countries of Malawi, Uganda, Chad, and Mali profit from fisheries on lakes and rivers.

Mining Resources

Difficult and risky, mining is an important economic activity in the region. Gold mining is particularly dangerous. The extremely narrow seams of the valuable mineral are located deep in the earth. Such depths greatly increase the risk of rock bursts, or breaks in the earth's crust, under the stress of explosives and power tools, but mine workers need the wages to help support their families.

Mineral Wealth

The Witwatersrand, a gold deposit 300 miles (483 km) long, makes **South Africa** the world's largest producer of gold. The country also is a world leader in the production of gems and industrial diamonds mined from beneath the grassy plateau of Gauteng Province. South African miners also extract large quantities of coal, platinum, chromium, vanadium, and manganese for export.

Although South Africa's mineral wealth makes it one of the region's richest countries, foreign investors or companies owned by white South Africans reap the most benefits. Little money reaches black South African mine workers. Since the steady decline in gold prices that began in the 1980s, however, gold has also contributed less to South Africa's economy.

An Imbalance of Riches

The uneven distribution of mineral resources causes economic imbalances in Africa south of the Sahara. Most known mineral deposits lie along the Atlantic coast and south of the Equator. For example, **Guinea** (GIH•nee) has about one-third of the world's known reserves of bauxite, the main ore

used in making aluminum. Immense oil reserves make **Nigeria** the region's only member of the Organization of Petroleum Exporting Countries (OPEC). In spite of rich mineral resources, many people in these two countries do not benefit directly from local resources, and they remain poor. Governments have badly managed the income from mineral wealth, and foreign mine owners often send their profits abroad.

Industrialization

Despite its large reserves of bauxite, Guinea cannot manufacture aluminum because it lacks the cheap energy, capital, and infrastructure—resources such as trained workers, facilities, and equipment—to build a refinery. Guinea is not unique. Most of the region's countries never developed manufacturing industries to process their natural resources. Today many countries in Africa south of the Sahara receive foreign loans to industrialize, but progress has been slow. Few countries have industrial centers for processing raw materials. As a result, most countries in the region continue to act as suppliers of raw materials for the industrialized countries of the world.

Development of Manufacturing

Since the 1960s the governments of newly independent African countries have encouraged industrial expansion. Demand for manufactured goods has increased, and locally produced goods have replaced some imported items. Today the region's industrial workers process food or produce textiles, paper goods, leather products, and cement. Some assemble electric motors, tractors, airplanes, and automobiles. Yet compared to manufacturing in other developing areas, such as Latin America, the economic role of manufacturing is small. By the late 1990s, only 15 percent of the region's GDP came from manufacturing.

Overcoming Obstacles

Africa south of the Sahara faces many obstacles to industrialization, including the lack of skilled workers. Educational systems are relatively new, and training programs are limited. Hydroelectric resources are plentiful but untapped, and power shortages often occur. Political conflicts interrupt economic planning and divert resources from

---

CRITICAL THINKING ACTIVITY

Identifying Central Issues Ask students to draw an editorial cartoon that focuses on one of the main economic issues in Africa south of the Sahara today. Students may focus on an issue discussed in the text or an issue they read about in a newspaper or a magazine. Remind students that an editorial cartoon expresses a viewpoint about an issue. Before students design their cartoons, you may wish to share a sampling of editorial cartoons with them, pointing out the elements of such illustrations (symbolism, caricature, dialogue balloons, labels, and so on). Post students' cartoons for the whole class to interpret and enjoy. ⊞ **EE6 The Uses of Geography: Standard 18**

development projects. In addition, countries must import food to feed their growing populations.

Although African products still do not reach many parts of the world, exports have been growing since World War II. Some countries in the region trade with Japan and the United States, but most rely on trading ties established with Western European countries before independence. Some countries are breaking old trading patterns to trade within the region. Various countries, for example, have formed regional trading associations, such as the Economic Community of West African States (ECOWAS), to exchange ideas and to protect their interests.

Transportation and Communications

Good transportation and communications systems are essential to industry and trade as well as to everyday life in the region. New transportation networks and technology are beginning to change lifestyles, but much remains to be done.

Creating and maintaining transportation systems in the region is difficult. Roads and railways must cross vast distances and changing terrain. Water transportation is limited because most rivers cannot be navigated from source to mouth, and the region has few natural harbors. In addition, there are few experts and skilled managers to plan and supervise transportation systems. In recent years wars and lack of money have kept many roads and rail lines from being repaired.

Roads and Railroads

Several countries, however, consider roads and railroads a top priority. Nigeria plans to link all parts of its railroad system, and Uganda is scheduling repairs on the heavily traveled Trans-African Highway, which runs from Mombasa, Kenya, to Lagos, Nigeria. Mauritania, Senegal, and the North African country of Morocco are discussing plans for a highway between Tangiers in Morocco

World Explorer

Geography Skills for Life

Early Morning Travelers A 400-mile-long (644-km-long) railway links eastern Botswana to Zimbabwe and South Africa.

Region What factors challenge the development of transportation in the region?

and Dakar in Senegal that would eventually reach Lagos. This important project would link people and ideas in different parts of Africa.

Communications

In the area of communications, the region has long relied on radio, with state-run stations providing global programming. Television reaches fewer people because the land-relay systems for transmitting TV signals become very costly outside urban areas. Satellite technology should improve television's reach, however. Low literacy rates limit traditional media like newspapers and magazines, and in many countries, governments restrict the number of issues that can be published.

Telephone service is also limited, especially in rural areas. Across the region, only 14 main telephone lines serve each 1,000 people. However, satellite and wireless technology is expected to improve access to phone service and the Internet in Africa south of the Sahara.

Chapter 22 **541**

World Explorer

Answer
vast distances, difficult terrain, lack of skilled people to plan and supervise transportation systems, lack of funds

More About the Photo
Although completed in 1897, the railway did not serve many people in what is now Botswana until the 1970s, when rails were run out to mining areas.

③ ASSESS

Assign Section 1 Assessment as homework or as an in-class activity.

Have students use **Interactive Tutor Self-Assessment CD-ROM.**

L2

Section Quiz 22-1

Section 1 Quiz
22 *Living in Africa South of the Sahara*

MATCHING: Match each item in Column A with an item in Column B. Write the correct letters in the blanks. (10 points each)

A	B
1. city at one end of the Trans-African Highway	A. Nigeria
2. 300-mile-long gold deposit in South Africa	B. Guinea
3. regional trading association in Africa south of the Sahara	C. ECOWAS
4. country that has about one-third of the world's reserves of bauxite	D. Witwatersrand
5. country that has large oil deposits and is a member of OPEC	E. Mombasa

MULTIPLE CHOICE: In each blank on the left, write the letter of the choice that best completes the statement or answers the question. (10 points each)

_____ 6. Most of the profits from mining minerals in many African countries south of the

Reteach

Have students scan the text to locate facts about Africa today that surprised them. Call on students to share their facts with the class, and continue until everyone has contributed at least once.

TEAM-TEACHING ACTIVITY: LANGUAGE ARTS

Analyzing Advantages and Disadvantages Have students visualize a situation in which most people in their community do not have telephones or televisions, few if any have computers, and radio is the main form of communication—as is a common occurrence in Africa south of the Sahara. **Ask:** How would your life be different? Then have students write essays analyzing the advantages and disadvantages of limited communications. Tell students to use the block method to organize and present their ideas, focusing on advantages in one paragraph, and disadvantages in another. Students' essays should also include an engaging introductory sentence stating the main idea and a conclusion restating it.

🌐 **EE2 Places and Regions: Standard 4**

NATIONAL GEOGRAPHIC World Explorer

Answer

It allows customers from around the world to shop for and buy unique products.

More About the Photo

African baskets command higher prices on the international markets, where they are regarded as works of art.

Enrich

Have small groups gather samples of textile designs typical of the region to share with the class. Students should conduct research to present additional information on African textiles.

4 CLOSE

Name an economic activity in the region, and call on students at random to state one fact about it. Continue to call on students until they can no longer supply facts. Then name another activity and proceed in the same way.

Economics

Internet Commerce

Helen Mutono runs a small business selling baskets made by Ugandan women. Using **e-commerce**, or selling and buying on the Internet, Helen Mutono set up a Web site at a cybercafe in the Ugandan capital, **Kampala**, to sell baskets to customers around the world. Cybercafes provide Internet access for people who lack their own computers. For a fee, cybercafes allow customers to use Internet technology. The Internet broadens the market for locally made products, allowing customers from around the world to purchase unique products. As Helen Mutono notes:

❝ *You can imagine trying to sell a basket that everybody can make locally. [The weavers] probably wouldn't be able to sell very many baskets, but to be able to market [the baskets] worldwide is . . . the greatest thing that could have happened for them.* ❞

quoted in "E-commerce: Uganda's Entrepreneurs Go Global," *BBC World Service* (online)

NATIONAL GEOGRAPHIC World Explorer

Geography Skills for Life

E-Commerce By selling baskets worldwide via the Internet, Helen Mutono and others have been able to buy needed clothes and send their children to school.

Region How does the Internet broaden the market for locally made products?

SECTION 1 ASSESSMENT

Checking for Understanding

1. **Define** subsistence farming, shifting farming, sedentary farming, commercial farming, cash crop, conservation farming, infrastructure, e-commerce.

2. **Main Ideas** Copy the web diagram below. List details about each of the five major economic activities in the region. Then choose one type, and write a paragraph about it.

Logging and Fishing

Transportation and Communications

Africa South of the Sahara

Agriculture   Mining   Industry

Critical Thinking

3. **Making Generalizations** What economic features do many countries in Africa south of the Sahara share? How have these shared features affected their economies?

4. **Making Predictions** What role might the Internet play in the region's economic development? Explain.

5. **Comparing and Contrasting** Compare and contrast the roles agriculture and industry each play in the region. Consider changes in the region's economies before and after independence as part of your analysis.

Analyzing Graphs

6. **Human-Environment Interaction** Study the graph on page 538. What can you conclude about the importance of agriculture in the economies of the countries represented in the graph?

Applying Geography

7. **Obstacles to Development** Think about the challenges to economic development in Africa south of the Sahara. Write a speech in which you define one of the most critical challenges, propose a way to overcome it, and explain why your proposal is a good idea.

SECTION 1 ASSESSMENT ANSWERS

1. All vocabulary terms are defined in the text.

2. Students should list details from the text for each activity and use the details they have listed to write about an activity of their choice.

3. Subsistence farming, reliance on crops or resources developed during the colonial period, trading patterns; many countries have not yet experienced much economic growth.

4. open new markets for products from the region and be a source of ideas and information to help Africans develop their economies

5. Agriculture has played a greater role in the region, although industrial expansion has been encouraged since independence.

6. Agriculture is less important to the economies of Nigeria, Namibia, and Sao Tome and Principe than in those of the rest of the countries shown.

7. **Applying Geography** Accept reasonable responses backed by evidence from the text, including reliance on crops and resources developed during the colonial period, lack of technology, lack of capital, lack of infrastructure, government mismanagement, and conflict.

Guide to Reading

Consider What You Know

Imagine that you are going to create a series of TV specials about Africa south of the Sahara. What issues would you include in the segment about the environment?

Reading Strategy

Categorizing Complete a graphic organizer similar to the one below by describing the farming methods used in the region.

Farming Methods	Description
Subsistence	
Shifting	
Sedentary	
Commercial	
Conservation	

Read to Find Out

- Why have food shortages occurred in parts of Africa south of the Sahara?
- What steps are the African countries south of the Sahara taking to protect their environment?
- What is the outlook for the region's future development?

Terms to Know

- habitat
- extinction
- poaching
- ecotourism

Places to Locate

- Somalia
- Ethiopia
- Djibouti
- Sahel
- Sudan
- Eritrea
- Côte d'Ivoire
- Madagascar

People and Their Environment

NATIONAL GEOGRAPHIC

A Geographic View

Saving Forestlands

Traditional farmers use[d] slash-and-burn methods [in Madagascar], and a growing population . . . led to the clearing of more land. In the worst cases nearly a hundred tons of topsoil an acre were being lost each year. And while that flow has yet to be fully [stopped,] some progress has been made. Still, . . . unless these farming methods change, virtually all the island's forests will be gone within 25 years.

Village meeting in Madagascar

—Virginia Morell, "Restoring Madagascar," National Geographic, *February 1999*

Africans south of the Sahara, like their neighbors around the globe, look to the future with hope. Yet the people in this region face tremendous difficulties in achieving a better life. Many environmental challenges threaten the region's supply of food, its health care, and its plant and animal life. In this section you will learn about these problems and the solutions proposed to deal with them.

Shadow of Hunger

Today millions of people in the region must focus on survival. Hunger is one of their bitterest enemies. In the 1990s, for example, many thousands of people died of starvation in the Horn of Africa—the bulge of land that juts into the Indian Ocean and includes the countries of **Somalia, Ethiopia,** and **Djibouti** (jih•BOO•tee). Drought and human activities, such as wars, contributed to the famine, or extreme

1 FOCUS

Section Overview

This section discusses the interaction between the people of Africa south of the Sahara and their environment.

BELLRINGER
Skillbuilder Activity

 Project transparency and have students answer questions.

 Available as blackline master.

Daily Focus Skills Transparency 22-2

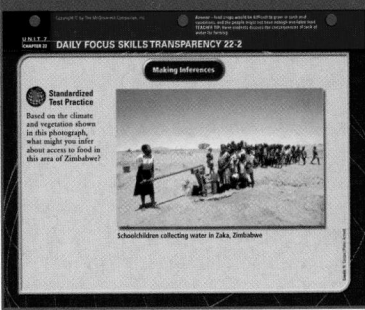

Guide to Reading

Consider What You Know
Answers *famine, rain forest destruction, endangered animals*

Reading Strategy
Answers subsistence: *small-scale agriculture to feed a family or village, only surplus is sold or traded;* shifting: *use basic tools, move every 1–3 years, slash-and-burn, ash temporarily enriches soil;* sedentary: *permanent plots, soil must be fertile;* commercial: *crops produced for sale, usually large plantations;* conservation: *land management farming used to help protect and conserve land*

Preteaching Vocabulary
🟡 Use the **Vocabulary Puzzle-Maker CD-ROM** to create cross-word and word-search puzzles.

RESOURCE MANAGER

📁 Reproducible Masters
- Reproducible Lesson Plan 22-2
- Vocabulary Activity 22
- Daily Lecture Notes 22-2
- Guided Reading Activity 22-2
- Reading Essentials and Study Guide 22-2
- Reteaching Activity 22
- Reinforcing Skills Activity 22
- Section Quiz 22-2

📠 Transparencies
- Daily Focus Skills Transparency 22-2
- Unit 7 Map Overlay Transparencies

Multimedia
- 🟡 Vocabulary PuzzleMaker CD-ROM
- 🖥 World Art Prints
- 🟡 Interactive Tutor Self-Assessment CD-ROM
- 🟡 ExamView® Pro Testmaker CD-ROM
- 🟡 Presentation Plus! CD-ROM

TEACH

L2 Current Events
Have students use newspapers and the Internet to track and report on conflict in Africa south of the Sahara. Set aside some time weekly for updates.

NATIONAL GEOGRAPHIC   **MAP STUDY**

Answers
1. *Sierra Leone, Liberia, Chad, Central African Republic, Eritrea, Ethiopia, Djibouti, Somalia, Kenya, Uganda, Rwanda, Burundi, Angola, Zambia, Zimbabwe, Mozambique*

2. *slows or halts economic growth; hampers food distribution*

Map Skills Practice
Region What countries in the region have more than 3,000 calories available per person per day? *(none)*

Daily Lecture Notes 22-2

DAILY LECTURE NOTES
CHAPTER 22
Section 2

Building Geography Literacy
During the late 1970s and 1980s, Ethiopia suffered from a series of droughts that steadily lowered food production. As the droughts became prolonged, the country faced widespread famine. A brutal civil war and obstacles imposed by the government hindered global efforts to provide food and medical aid to Ethiopia. During the 1980s, about 1 million Ethiopians died from starvation and disease.

I. Shadow of Hunger pages 543–545

Hunger is one of the leading concerns of people living in Africa south of the Sahara. Drought and wars have contributed to famine in many parts of the region. (pp. 543–544)

A. Desertification
The Sahel, a semiarid region of land in West Africa, once supported nomadic herding and farming. Today a wide area of the Sahel has become desert. Among the primary causes of this change are a drier climate and the stripping of the Sahel's vegetation by people and animals. Severe droughts in other parts of Africa have helped turn farmland into

2. European hunters reduced the animal population during the colonial period. Today poaching continues to threaten the region's wildlife. (p. 546)

C. Conservation and Tourism

---

scarcity of food. Today famine threatens many parts of Africa, which must look to the international community for food. Food donations often can help relieve famine if there are no barriers to distribution. However, they cannot end hunger caused by years of conflicts and natural disasters.

Desertification

Although never as fertile as land to the south and east, the **Sahel** region of West Africa once supported life. The Sahel is a band of semiarid land extending across the northern part of the region and bordering the Sahara. Not so long ago, nomadic peoples grazed livestock in the Sahel. Their animals helped fertilize the soil, and farming was possible. Today, however, a wide area of the Sahel has become desert. As the climate has become drier and as people and animals have stripped the Sahel of its vegetation, the desert has crept farther south, spreading in the countries of Mauritania, Mali, Niger, Chad, and Sudan.

Droughts, which have always occurred in the semiarid Sahel, have recently become severe there and in other parts of Africa south of the Sahara. Beginning in the 1960s, severe droughts in these areas helped turn farmland into wasteland. For example, in the early 1990s, drought in the Horn of Africa caused widespread famine. Since 1998 drought has killed crops and livestock across East Africa, threatening the lives of hundreds of thousands of people.

In 2000 the United Nations Food and Agriculture Organization (FAO) warned that famine could become a problem in central Africa because of unpredictable weather patterns and large numbers of refugees. In West Africa good harvests have boosted food supplies in most countries. Civil war, however, threatens to disrupt the distribution of food in Sierra Leone, Liberia, and Guinea.

Conflict and Hunger

War continues to be a major cause of hunger and malnutrition in Africa south of the Sahara. Since 1990, conflicts in countries such as Liberia, Sudan, Somalia, and Rwanda have halted economic growth, caused widespread starvation, and cost the lives of countless Africans. Huge refugee populations fleeing war-torn areas have strained already meager food resources. Today civil conflict in

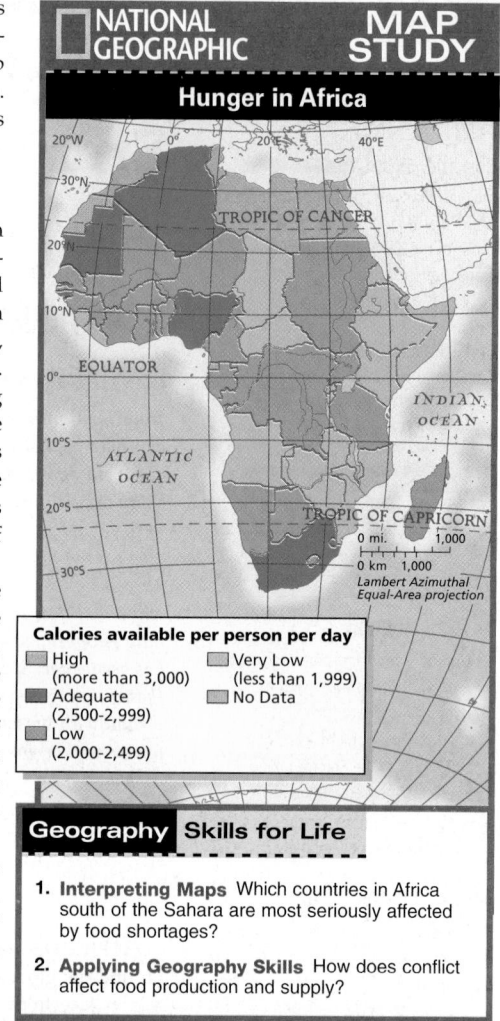

NATIONAL GEOGRAPHIC   **MAP STUDY**

Hunger in Africa

Calories available per person per day
- High (more than 3,000)
- Adequate (2,500–2,999)
- Low (2,000–2,499)
- Very Low (less than 1,999)
- No Data

Geography Skills for Life

1. **Interpreting Maps** Which countries in Africa south of the Sahara are most seriously affected by food shortages?

2. **Applying Geography Skills** How does conflict affect food production and supply?

Find NGS online map resources @ www.nationalgeographic.com/maps

Somalia endangers more than one million people, including relief workers. Looting and fighting severely hamper food distribution.

In **Sudan** about 2 million people are on the verge of starvation, according to UN estimates. Most of Sudan's people depend on subsistence farming, making them vulnerable to the country's periodic droughts. In addition, more than a decade of civil war between the Muslim Arab government and non-Muslim rebels in the south has torn Sudan

---

DIFFERENTIATED INSTRUCTION

Logical/Mathematical Point out that loss of vegetation in the Sahel has caused massive soil erosion, which has made farming nearly impossible. Explain that plants stop desertification not only by holding soil in place but also by releasing moisture into the air. Tell students that a houseplant, for example, releases up to $1\frac{1}{2}$ pints of water into the air every 24 hours. Explore this idea with the following experiment and record observations: (1) Set a houseplant in a clear plastic bag large enough not to crush the plant, and tie the bag shut. (2) After 24 hours, check the bag and record what you observe.

🔲 **EE3 Physical Systems: Standard 8**

📁 Refer to ***Inclusion for the Social Studies Classroom Strategies and Activities.***

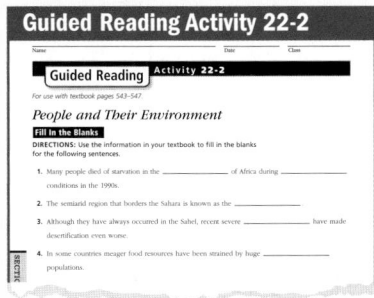

L1/ELL

Guided Reading Activity 22-2

Name _____ Date _____ Class _____

Guided Reading   Activity 22-2

For use with textbook pages 543-547.

People and Their Environment

Fill in the Blanks
DIRECTIONS: Use the information in your textbook to fill in the blanks for the following sentences.

1. Many people died of starvation in the _____ of Africa during conditions in the 1990s.

2. The semiarid region that borders the Sahara is known as the _____

3. Although they have always occurred in the Sahel, severe _____ have made desertification even worse.

4. In some countries meager food resources have been strained by huge _____ populations.

NATIONAL GEOGRAPHIC World Explorer

Geography Skills for Life

International Aid A Red Cross worker helps a Hutu mother in Rwanda find her lost children.
Region What factors lead to food shortages in Africa south of the Sahara?

earthen dams to store precious rainwater. Grain crops thrived in their fields. In Eritrea, crops were so abundant that the government was able to reduce its request for relief from other countries by 50 percent.

When Ethiopia and Eritrea went to war over their shared border, however, many people lost their homes or lives. Then one of the worst droughts in years struck the region. Although drought continues, a shaky peace is allowing farmers to restore the land, bringing hope to the area's people.

Medical teams and relief workers with humanitarian organizations like Doctors Without Borders (Médecins Sans Frontières) and the International Red Cross have helped. Feeding centers, for example, have nursed many malnourished children and adults back to health in war-torn countries.

Land Use

People in the region are also struggling with problems of land use. At the start of the 2000s, tropical rain forests in the region were disappearing at a rate of more than 12 million acres (4.8 million ha) per year. The environmental impact of hunting and tourism has also raised difficult questions about the region's land use.

Destruction of the Rain Forest

In 1990 rain forests covered almost 1.5 billion acres (607 million ha) in this region. By 2000 126 million acres (51 million ha) of that forest had disappeared. **Côte d'Ivoire** has lost more than

NATIONAL GEOGRAPHIC World Explorer

Answer
war, drought, desertification

More About the Photo
Ethnic fighting in east central Africa has led to massive migrations and loss of life for hundreds of thousands of people.

apart and created the world's largest refugee population. International aid workers have tried to meet the enormous food needs of the refugees, but warring factions continue to raise obstacles. In 2000, for example, rebel groups began to tax relief work, forcing many aid agencies to leave the country.

If the problem of hunger is to be solved, peace within the region is critical. Some countries and groups are moving toward peace. In 2002 peace talks were held between warring factions in Sudan. Ethiopia and **Eritrea** signed a peace agreement in 2000 after two years of conflict. Tensions remain high, and maintaining peace will be a great challenge in both cases. However, the Eritreans and Ethiopians have been working to undo the damage caused by drought and civil war.

History
Farming in Peace

After Eritrea gained its independence from Ethiopia in 1993, farmers in both countries worked to improve the land. Farmers in the northern Ethiopian province of Tigray terraced more than 250,000 acres (about 101,172 ha) of land and planted 42 million young trees to hold soil in place. They also built

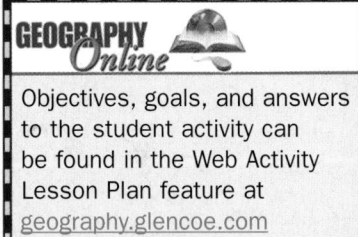

GEOGRAPHY *Online*

Objectives, goals, and answers to the student activity can be found in the Web Activity Lesson Plan feature at geography.glencoe.com

GEOGRAPHY *Online*

Student Web Activity Visit the **Glencoe World Geography** Web site at geography.glencoe.com and click on Student Web Activities—Chapter 22 for an activity about life today in Africa south of the Sahara.

L1/ELL

Reading Essentials & Study Guide 22-2

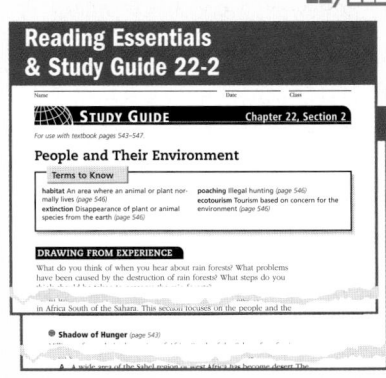

Name _____ Date _____ Class _____

STUDY GUIDE   Chapter 22, Section 2

For use with textbook pages 543-547.

People and Their Environment

Terms to Know

habitat An area where an animal or plant normally lives (page 546)
extinction Disappearance of plant or animal species from the earth (page 546)
poaching Illegal hunting (page 546)
ecotourism Tourism based on concern for the environment (page 546)

DRAWING FROM EXPERIENCE

What do you think of when you hear about rain forests? What problems have been caused by the destruction of rain forests? What steps do you _____ in Africa South of the Sahara. This section focuses on the people and the _____

● **Shadow of Hunger** (page 543)

COOPERATIVE LEARNING ACTIVITY

People Helping People Invite a Red Cross representative to tell the class about the agency's relief work around the world, including in Africa south of the Sahara. Identify other organizations that are active in the region, such as Doctors Without Borders and UNICEF. Then organize the class into groups and have each group find out more about one organization's work in the region. Have students present their findings in the form of an interview with a relief worker. The group should write a script for the interview and choose two members of the group to perform the interview for the rest of the class.
🌐 **EE5 Environment and Society: Standard 15**

❸ ASSESS

Assign Section 2 Assessment as homework or as an in-class activity.

🖥 Have students use **Interactive Tutor Self-Assessment CD-ROM.**

L2

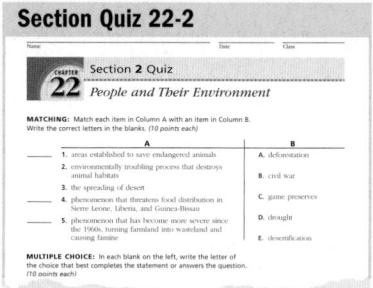

Section Quiz 22-2

Arts of Africa South of the Sahara Much of the stone—serpentine, steatite, and others—used in Shona sculpture is mined in the mountainous regions of Zimbabwe. After sculpting the figure with chisels, the sculptor uses sand and beeswax to polish the stone and then heats it with fire to bring out the stone's color. Many artists in Zimbabwe make a living through sales of their works in foreign galleries.

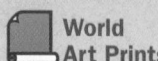
World Art Prints
Use these prints to introduce students to other regional arts.

90 percent of its rain forest, and **Madagascar**, at one time a heavily wooded island, has also seen more than 90 percent of its rain forest disappear. On the continent as a whole, about half of the original rain forests are gone. Nearly 15,000 square miles (38,850 sq. km), an area almost the size of Switzerland, is being cleared every year.

Such statistics have alerted people in the region to the severity of the problem. Today various countries have created forest preserves to help save the rain forests. Many logging companies are also getting involved, using scientific tree farming and replanting projects to protect and renew forests.

Endangered Animals

As the rain forests disappear, many plant and animal species are put at risk. Deforestation destroys animal habitats, or living areas. Today hundreds of animal species in Madagascar that exist nowhere else are in danger of extinction, or disappearance from the earth.

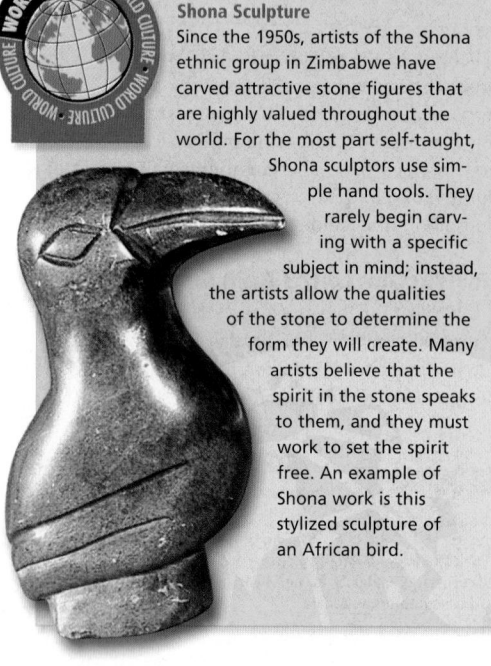

the arts of **AFRICA SOUTH OF THE SAHARA**

Shona Sculpture
Since the 1950s, artists of the Shona ethnic group in Zimbabwe have carved attractive stone figures that are highly valued throughout the world. For the most part self-taught, Shona sculptors use simple hand tools. They rarely begin carving with a specific subject in mind; instead, the artists allow the qualities of the stone to determine the form they will create. Many artists believe that the spirit in the stone speaks to them, and they must work to set the spirit free. An example of Shona work is this stylized sculpture of an African bird.

The threat to wildlife exists elsewhere too. As the region's population grows, farmers have moved into some forested areas to find land for planting and grazing. Some grassy savannas, home to huge herds of animals such as elephants, giraffes, antelopes, and lions, are being plowed for farming. As a result, many species have greatly decreased in number.

Hunting also threatens the region's wildlife. During the colonial period, European hunters reduced animal populations significantly. For instance, during the 1900s the numbers of Zambian black lechwe, a kind of antelope, dwindled from 1 million to fewer than 8,000. In recent years hunters have continued to pursue African game for sport and profit. Two million elephants roamed the region in the early 1970s. Today fewer than 600,000 remain, largely because of poaching, or illegal hunting. Ivory from elephant tusks brings high prices despite international bans on its trade. Other animals at risk include the Cape Mountain zebra and the mountain gorilla.

Economics
Conservation and Tourism

To save endangered species, some countries have created huge game preserves. These preserves—which include Tanzania's Serengeti National Park, Kenya's Masai Mara, and Rwanda's Parc National des Volcans—have helped some animals make a comeback. The parks also attract millions of tourists each year. Ecotourism, or tourism based on concern for the environment, has become a big business in parts of the region, bringing millions of dollars into African economies. Despite the profits earned from such preserves, many people in the region, like V.N. Mthembu, object to them:

❝ *My family lived in Ndumu [Game Reserve] until around 1960. They were moved outside when the park brought in rhinos. There is not enough land for everyone outside now and not enough water, especially in droughts. But the park has plenty of water and game. Why can't we come back inside to build homes and live?* ❞
quoted by Douglas H. Chadwick, "A Place for Parks in the New South Africa," *National Geographic,* July 1996

CRITICAL THINKING ACTIVITY

Predicting Consequences Have students identify a challenge in Africa south of the Sahara that requires a decision, such as protecting animal and plant habitats. Ask students to research and gather information on the issue. Then have students form groups to identify options in making a decision to solve the problem and to predict the consequences related to each option. Moderate a panel discussion in which group representatives present their conclusions to the class. Have the class brainstorm the actions to be taken to implement the decision. 🌐 **EE5 Environment and Society: Standard 14**
🌐 **EE6 The Uses of Geography: Standard 18**

Governments have tried to respond to such concerns by giving rural peoples an economic stake in the preserves. Some train to work in the preserves as trail guides or become involved in development planning.

Toward the Future

In Africa south of the Sahara, people are working to overcome some of the region's serious challenges, many of them inherited from the colonial period. The region has already taken important steps, however, toward preserving the environment and its precious natural resources. Efforts to encourage private enterprise have also had positive results. New ranching laws, for example, have allowed people to engage in crocodile farming, a highly profitable business that has also brought this species back from near extinction. Rhinoceroses and elephants are also beginning to thrive again as their habitats are protected and poaching is discouraged by stricter laws.

Increasingly, the protection of rain forests is a priority in the region. In 1999 leaders from six central African countries signed an agreement to preserve the forests. The effects of this and similar efforts have yet to be seen, but they are a strong signal that Africans today are moving toward a more positive future.

NATIONAL GEOGRAPHIC **World Explorer**

Geography | Skills for Life

Protecting Wildlife A conservationist measures the growth of a young cheetah in Namibia.
Human-Environment Interaction How have African countries addressed the problem of endangered species?

SECTION 2 ASSESSMENT

Checking for Understanding

1. **Define** habitat, extinction, poaching, ecotourism.

2. **Main Ideas** Use a diagram like the one below for each challenge facing the people of Africa south of the Sahara. Then write a paragraph about one of the challenges, and write a proposal for meeting the challenge.

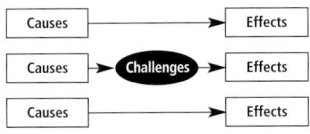

Critical Thinking

3. **Decision Making** List actions that governments in Africa south of the Sahara take to help eliminate hunger. Then arrange the items by order of importance and explain your reasoning.

4. **Finding and Summarizing the Main Idea** What is the central issue in the debate over the creation of game preserves?

5. **Problem Solving** How would you encourage logging companies and governments to help prevent deforestation? Consider the advantages and disadvantages.

Analyzing Maps

6. **Region** Study the map of hunger in Africa on page 544. What countries in Africa south of the Sahara generally have the least problem with hunger?

Applying Geography

7. **Global Issues** Think about the challenges Africa south of the Sahara faces today. Choose one problem in the region that might have an impact on the rest of the world. Make a chart or diagram that explains why the problem is a global issue.

Answer
They have established game preserves and created laws to protect them.

More About the Photo The African cheetah, now considered endangered, is a long-legged cat renowned for its speed. It has been clocked at 60 miles (100 km) per hour.

Reteach

Have a student describe the impact of an environmental hazard, such as a drought, and analyze its effects on the physical and human characteristics of the region.

Enrich

Have students create bumper stickers drawing attention to specific endangered species in the region.

 **CLOSE**

Ask: What are some positive developments in Africa south of the Sahara today? Have students write a paragraph in response.

SECTION 2 ASSESSMENT ANSWERS

1. All vocabulary terms are defined in the text.
2. Students should identify causes and effects mentioned in the text and make inferences about others. Students may use the information in one of their diagrams to write their paragraphs.
3. Ending conflict, restoring farmland, setting up feeding centers; students should support their ranking.
4. People disagree about whether scarce land should be set aside to protect endangered animals or to provide living and farming area for the region's booming population.
5. by explaining the economic consequences of deforestation
6. Nigeria, South Africa, and Mauritania
7. **Applying Geography** Students' charts or diagrams should focus on the broader, global impact of famine, deforestation, or extinction of plant and animal species.

1 FOCUS

Have students read the title of the feature and examine the photograph. Explain that a dilemma is a problem that involves a difficult choice. Have students use the title and photograph to predict the choice that the countries of southern Africa face.

2 TEACH

L1 Location
Direct students' attention to the map on page 548. Then, have them turn to the map of Africa on page 487 in the Unit Regional Atlas, and locate the part of the region shown on page 548. Ask students to identify and locate the countries affected by the ivory trade.

L2 Cause and Effect
After students have read the text on page 549, create a cause-and-effect diagram on the board showing causes and effects of the ivory trade in Africa. Remind students that some developments have more than one cause or effect and that effects can be causes of other developments.

3 ASSESS

Have students answer the **What's Your Point of View?** question on page 549.

Viewpoint
CASE STUDY on the Environment

Okavango Delta
NAMIBIA
ZIMBABWE
MOZAMBIQUE
BOTSWANA
SWAZILAND
LESOTHO
SOUTH AFRICA

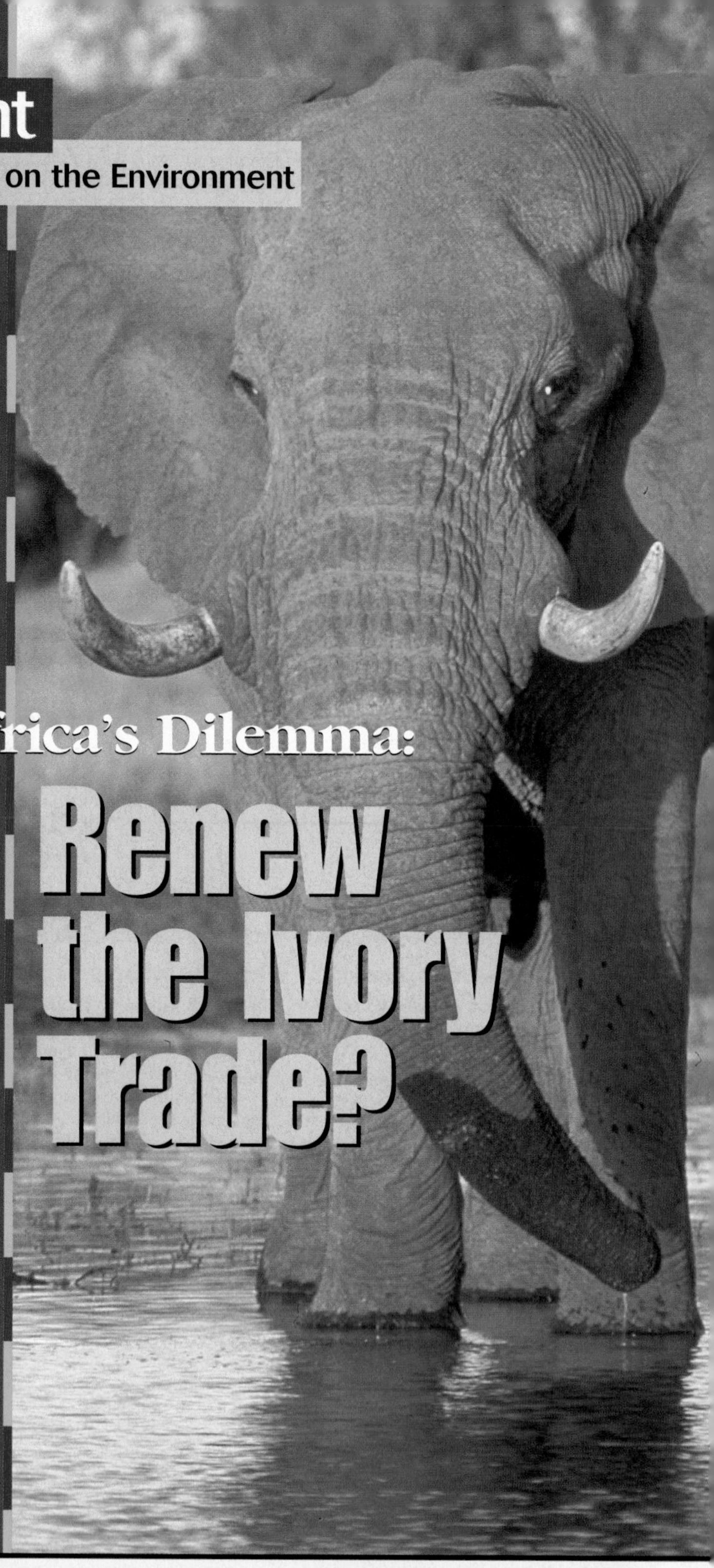

Southern Africa's Dilemma:
Renew the Ivory Trade?

African elephants—the biggest and strongest of all living land animals—once roamed in great numbers across the continent. During the last century, however, elephants were slaughtered by the tens of thousands for meat, for sport, and especially for their ivory tusks. In 1989 African elephants were placed on the endangered species list. Trade in elephant ivory was banned worldwide. Recently, however, three southern African nations were given approval to sell their stockpiles of ivory. Critics worry that these legalized sales will renew the demand for ivory and increase the killing of elephants for their tusks.

548   Unit 7

LOOKING TO THE FUTURE

Lives in Sync Instead of Conflict
Conservationists believe that the survival of the African elephant and that of other endangered animal species around the world will depend in large part on whether people and animals can live together in a way that benefits them both. Today people and elephants in southern Africa come into conflict in many ways. They compete for food, water, and land. Elephants destroy crops, and people destroy elephant habitats. Conservationists suggest a variety of changes, including substituting ecotourism for logging and farming in areas inhabited by elephants.

EE5 Environment and Society: Standard 15

Standing more than 10 feet (3 m) tall and weighing nearly 10,000 pounds (4,500 kg), an African elephant (left) wades into the waters of the Okavango Delta in Botswana. Both male and female African elephants grow tusks—the world's main source of ivory. A lustrous, creamy-white material, ivory was once carved into everything from figurines and jewelry to billiard balls and piano keys.

Biologists estimate that in 1930, Africa was home to 5 to 10 million elephants. When the price of ivory soared in the 1970s, elephants became very valuable. Gun-carrying ivory poachers began illegally killing elephants for their tusks. By 1979 the elephant population had dropped to 1.3 million. As many as 80,000 elephants a year were shot for their ivory. By the late 1980s, only about 600,000 elephants were left in Africa.

In 1989 the nations that make up CITES—the Convention on International Trade in Endangered Species—placed

Tons of tusks (below) are being sold to Japan. Will their sale lead carvers (right) and collectors to renew their interest in ivory? ▼

the African elephant on the endangered species list. The sale of ivory was banned worldwide. During the 1990s, the ban was successful in protecting elephants. Demand for ivory dwindled, prices fell, and poaching declined. Many elephant populations began to increase, particularly in southern Africa.

In fact, elephants grew so plentiful in Botswana, Namibia, and Zimbabwe that in 1997, CITES changed the elephant's status in these countries from endangered to threatened. This change allowed the three nations to sell government stockpiles of ivory to Japan, as long as each country adopted strict anti-poaching measures. The sales went forward in 1999, but not without controversy.

Supporters of the sale of ivory stress that only government stockpiles are being sold and that no elephants will be killed for ivory. Supporters argue that money from the sales can be spent on elephant conservation

◄ Watch out for elephants! Officials in southern Africa want to use money from ivory sales to protect elephants.

and on national parks. Further, a strict monitoring program will track poaching. If poaching increases, ivory sales will end.

Opponents of the ivory sales fear that even a partial lifting of the ban will lead to more poaching of elephants. Opponents argue that there are better ways to raise money, such as increasing park entrance fees. Moreover, opponents claim that programs to monitor and to report increased poaching of elephant populations could take years—too long to save the elephants.

What's Your Point of View? Do you agree with the decision to allow limited ivory trade in southern Africa? Will resumption of trade give the green light to poachers?

WHAT CAN YOU DO?

MAP & GRAPH SkillBuilder

Teaching the Skill

To check comprehension, ask students these questions about statistics shown in the table: **How is population density calculated?** *(by dividing the total population of a place by the place's total area)* **What does the annual growth rate show?** *(the percentage of increase in population each year)* **What does "percent urban" refer to?** *(the percentage of the population living in cities)*

Remind students that GDP refers to Gross Domestic Product—the total value of goods and services produced within a country. GDP per capita is the total value of goods and services produced per individual in that country. Point out that life expectancy and the categories listed under it reflect a country's standard of living.

Additional Practice
L1

Reinforcing Skills Activity 22

GLENCOE TECHNOLOGY

Glencoe Skillbuilder Interactive Workbook, Level 2

This interactive CD-ROM reinforces student mastery of essential social studies skills.

MAP & GRAPH SkillBuilder

Reading Tables and Interpreting Statistics

Reading lists of facts and figures can be confusing. For this reason, statistics are often organized in tables, which display numerical information in rows and columns.

Learning the Skill

In a table, similar kinds of information are organized into columns and rows. Labels across the top and left-hand side give information about the figures in the table. Identifying patterns and relationships among the figures can reveal a great deal about a topic. In this table, several kinds of statistical data for different countries are compared. The left row of labels shows what specific information is included in the comparison, such as population density or infant mortality rate. The top row identifies the countries being compared.

To read tables and interpret statistics, follow these steps:

- **Read headings and labels to determine the kinds of information included in the table.**
- **Look up any unfamiliar terms in the table.**
- **Identify similarities, differences, and other relationships among the data.**
- **Use the data to draw conclusions.**

Practicing the Skill

Study the table, and answer the following questions.

1. What countries are being compared in the table?
2. How do the countries rank according to total population? According to population density?
3. Which country has the highest GDP per capita?
4. Which country has the lowest annual population growth?
5. What is the relationship between infant mortality rate and life expectancy? Explain.
6. What is the relationship between infant mortality rate and GDP per capita? Explain.
7. What is the relationship between urbanization and the number of automobiles?

Population Information for Selected African Countries

	South Africa	Chad	Senegal
Total population	44,000,000	9,300,000	10,600,000
Population density	93/sq. mi.	19/sq. mi.	139/sq. mi.
Annual population growth	0.9%	3.2%	2.7%
Percent urban	53%	21%	43%
GDP (US dollars)	$290.6 billion	$7.5 billion	$15.6 billion
GDP per capita	$6,800	$1,000	$1,600
Life expectancy	53 years	49 years	53 years
Infant mortality rate (per 1,000 births)	57	103	68
Population per physician	1,529	27,765	14,825
Literacy rate	82%	48%	33%
Number of automobiles	4,350,000	9,630	110,000

Sources: 2003 World Population Data Sheet; World Almanac, 2001

Applying the Skill

Choose three countries in Africa south of the Sahara. Using an almanac, identify three statistics about the countries. Then use these statistics to make a table that allows you to compare and contrast the countries. Discuss with a partner the relationships among data that your table reveals.

 The Glencoe Skillbuilder Interactive Workbook, Level 2 provides instruction and practice in key social studies skills.

ANSWERS TO PRACTICING THE SKILL

1. South Africa, Chad, Senegal
2. total population, from largest to smallest: South Africa, Senegal, Chad; population density, from most to least densely populated: Senegal, South Africa, Chad
3. South Africa
4. South Africa
5. Countries with higher infant mortality rates have lower life expectancies. These countries may lack good health care and have a low standard of living.
6. Countries with higher per capita GDP have lower infant mortality rates. These countries are wealthier and may have better health care systems.
7. Countries with more people living in cities have more automobiles.

SUMMARY & STUDY GUIDE

Using the Chapter 22 Summary & Study Guide

Use the Chapter 22 Summary & Study Guide to preview, review, condense, or reteach the chapter.

Preview/Review

🅐 **Vocabulary PuzzleMaker CD-ROM** reinforces "Terms to Know."

🅐 **Interactive Tutor Self-Assessment CD-ROM** provides a review of Chapter 22 content.

Condense

Have students read the Chapter 22 Summary & Study Guide.

🅐 Chapter 22 Audio Program

📁 Chapter 22 Guided Reading Activities

Reteach

📁 Chapter 22 Reteaching Activities (Spanish also available)

📁 Chapter 22 Reading Essentials and Study Guides

SECTION 1 — Living in Africa South of the Sahara (pp. 537–542)

Terms to Know
- subsistence farming
- shifting farming
- sedentary farming
- commercial farming
- cash crop
- conservation farming
- infrastructure
- e-commerce

Key Points
- Most people in Africa south of the Sahara engage in subsistence farming, and most countries in the region depend on the export of one or two cash crops.
- Mineral resources are not evenly distributed across Africa south of the Sahara, causing economic imbalances among the region's countries.
- Africa south of the Sahara has taken actions to break its dependence on old trading patterns, and manufacturing is gaining strength in the economies of some countries in the region.
- New transportation networks and new forms of communication are changing the lives of Africans south of the Sahara.

Organizing Your Notes
Use an outline like the one below to organize the notes you took as you read about living in Africa south of the Sahara.

Living in Africa South of the Sahara

I. Agriculture
  A. Farming Methods and Export Crops
    1.
    2.

SECTION 2 — People and Their Environment (pp. 543–547)

Terms to Know
- habitat
- extinction
- poaching
- ecotourism

Key Points
- Desertification, drought, and conflict have contributed to hunger in Africa south of the Sahara.
- Deforestation, hunting, tourism, and meeting the basic needs of people are all issues in the debate over land use in the region.
- Africans south of the Sahara are working toward political stability and economic independence in the twenty-first century.

Organizing Your Notes
Use a diagram like the one below to organize your notes about each of the issues described in this section.

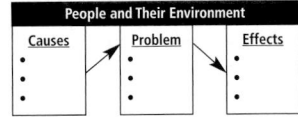

People and Their Environment

Causes	Problem	Effects
•	•	•
•	•	•
•	•	•

◀ Children in a refugee camp, Democratic Republic of the Congo

GLENCOE
TECHNOLOGY

🔲 NATIONAL GEOGRAPHIC
WORLD REGIONS
VIDEO PROGRAM

Unit 7, Africa South of the Sahara
The following segments enhance the study of this unit:
- **Namib Desert**
- **Living With Elephants**
- **Baaba Maal: Musician of the World**

Chapter 22 🌐 551

CHAPTER CULMINATING ACTIVITY

Evaluating the Present, Looking Toward the Future Tell students to write a brief description of life in Africa south of the Sahara today to be included in a time capsule. In addition to describing how people make a living in the region today and the challenges the region faces, students should comment on what they imagine are the hopes of Africans for the future. Before writing, have students review the chapter and take notes on relevant material. 🔲 **EE6 The Uses of Geography: Standard 18**

NOTE: This activity may be completed separately or you may wish students to incorporate it into their GeoJournals.

ASSESSMENT & ACTIVITIES

Have students visit the Web site at geography.glencoe.com to review Chapter 22 and take the **Self-Check Quiz.**

GLENCOE TECHNOLOGY

Use *MindJogger Videoquiz* to review the Chapter 22 content.

Reviewing Key Terms

1. subsistence farming
2. ecotourism
3. shifting farming
4. cash crops
5. infrastructure
6. poaching
7. habitats
8. sedentary farming
9. extinction
10. e-commerce
11. conservation farming

Reviewing Facts

SECTION 1

1. uneven distribution, government mismanagement, foreign ownership
2. reliance on colonial economic models and trading partners, lack of capital, few skilled workers
3. low literacy rates and limited access to other media

SECTION 2

4. drier climates, farming, livestock grazing
5. Forests, an animal habitat, are being destroyed.
6. It encourages countries to protect animals in game preserves.

Reviewing Key Terms

Write the key term that best matches each description. Refer to the Terms to Know in the Summary & Study Guide on page 551.

1. agriculture that provides for the needs of only a family or village
2. tourism based on concern for the environment
3. a method in which farmers move every one to three years to find better soil
4. crops grown for sale, not for use by the farmer
5. resources such as facilities and equipment
6. illegal hunting of animals
7. areas with conditions suitable for certain animals or plants
8. agriculture conducted at permanent settlements
9. the disappearance of a species from the earth
10. doing business on the Internet
11. a land-management technique that helps protect farmland

Reviewing Facts

SECTION 1

1. Why do Africans south of the Sahara share unequally in mineral wealth?
2. Why has Africa south of the Sahara been slow to industrialize?
3. Why have many people in the region relied primarily on radio for news and information?

SECTION 2

4. What factors have contributed to desertification in the Sahel?
5. What is the relationship between deforestation and endangered animals?
6. How does ecotourism affect the region's wildlife?

Critical Thinking

1. **Categorizing Information** What are the key elements shared by the region's economies? How important is each one?
2. **Making Inferences** How does conflict affect the region's overall quality of life?
3. **Predicting Consequences** Create a web diagram that lists the region's main challenges. Then list consequences for each one if no action is taken.

Regional Challenges

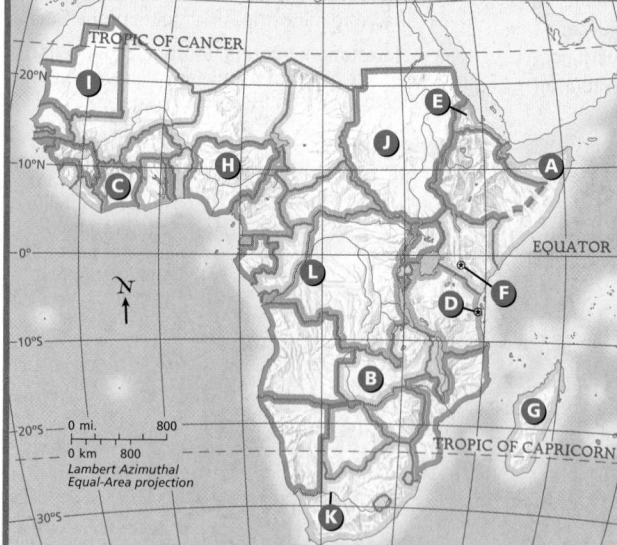

NATIONAL GEOGRAPHIC

Locating Places

Africa South of the Sahara: Physical-Political Geography

Match the letters on the map with the places and physical features of Africa south of the Sahara. Write your answers on a sheet of paper.

1. Mauritania	5. Côte d'Ivoire	9. Dar es Salaam
2. Nigeria	6. Sudan	10. Somalia
3. Madagascar	7. Zambia	11. Congo Basin
4. Eritrea	8. Nairobi	12. Orange River

Critical Thinking

1. agriculture, most important; mining, important; industry, least important
2. Conflict upsets everyday activities and has a negative effect on quality of life in the region, especially by contributing to hunger.
3. Students should list the main challenges and the probable outcomes resulting from not addressing these issues.

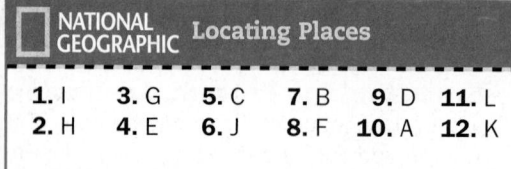

NATIONAL GEOGRAPHIC Locating Places

1. I	**3.** G	**5.** C	**7.** B	**9.** D	**11.** L
2. H	**4.** E	**6.** J	**8.** F	**10.** A	**12.** K

Using the Regional Atlas

1. Nomadic herding often takes place near desert areas; overgrazing causes desertification.
2. diamonds and gold

Using the Regional Atlas

Refer to the Regional Atlas on pages 486–489.

1. **Human-Environment Interaction** Describe the relationship between nomadic herding and the location of deserts.

2. **Region** Which two resources are concentrated in western and southern Africa?

Thinking Like a Geographer

As a geographer, would you favor setting aside more or less land for game preserves in Africa? Consider both the human and environmental concerns associated with the game preserves. What arguments would you present in support of your position?

Problem-Solving Activity

Problem-Solution Proposal The coastal zones of Africa south of the Sahara have great potential as sources of food, energy, and minerals. However, rapid, uncontrolled development of resources has led to environmental damage. Research to find out the specific causes of this damage and the ways in which it threatens the future of the region's ocean resources. Then write a proposal suggesting possible steps to prevent future harm to this environment.

GeoJournal

Public Service Announcement Use the information you logged in your GeoJournal to write a public service announcement explaining one of the efforts to address an environmental challenge in Africa south of the Sahara.

Technology Activity

Developing Multimedia Presentations Identify and research an endangered African animal. Collect information about the animal's habitat. Use mapping software, photographs, and other visual aids you download from Web sites to create a multimedia presentation. Show how the animal's location and habitat have been influenced by humans.

Standardized Test Practice

Use the table below to choose the best answer for the following multiple-choice question. If you have trouble answering the question, use the process of elimination to narrow your choices.

Population Change in Selected African Countries				
	Deaths per 1,000 people		Life Expectancy	
	1996	2000	1996	2000
Botswana	17	22	46	40
Namibia	8	19	65	41
South Africa	10	15	60	54
Uganda	21	18	41	44
Zimbabwe	18	22	42	39

Sources: World Almanac, 1997; World Almanac, 2001

1. What is the relationship between the change in the death rate (number of deaths per 1,000 people) and the change in life expectancy in the countries listed in the table?

A An increase in the death rate causes an increase in life expectancy.

B There is not a consistent relationship between changes in the death rate and changes in life expectancy.

C In countries where the life expectancy decreased, the death rate increased.

D Both the death rate and life expectancy are decreasing in these countries.

 **Test-Taking Tip** Before you read the answer choices, study the relationship between the death rate and the life expectancy of the African countries. Once you have drawn a conclusion about the relationship, read through the answer choices. Choose the one that most accurately supports the data in the chart.

? CHAPTER BONUS TEST QUESTION

How might developing hydroelectric energy in Africa south of the Sahara help slow deforestation? *(Hydroelectricity could replace wood for fuel, and fewer trees would be cut.)*

Thinking Like a Geographer

More land: need to protect endangered animals and to promote ecotourism for economic growth; less land: people living in the region need to use the land to support themselves.

Problem-Solving Activity

Accept reasonable responses based on research. Students' proposals should present strong arguments in support of their ideas.

GeoJournal

Students' public service announcements should be accurate and compelling.

Technology Activity

You may want to direct students' choices to avoid duplications. Presentations should reflect careful research and make good use of appropriate visuals.

TEACHING TRANSPARENCIES

L2 Unit 8 Map Overlay Transparencies

L2 Political Map Transparency 8

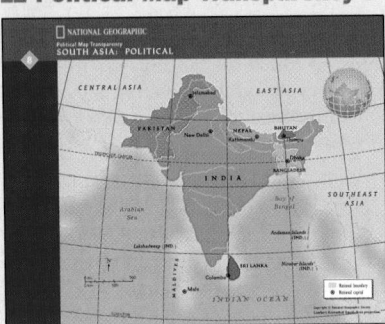

L2 World Cultures Transparencies 13, 14

APPLICATION AND ENRICHMENT

L2 Location Activity 8

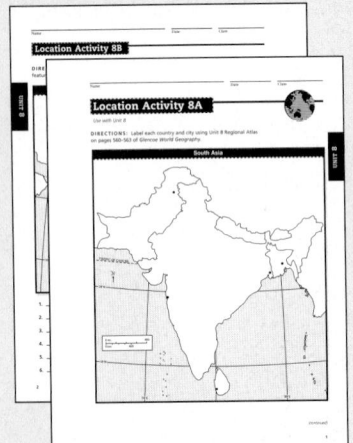

L2 Real-Life Applications and Problem-Solving Activity 8

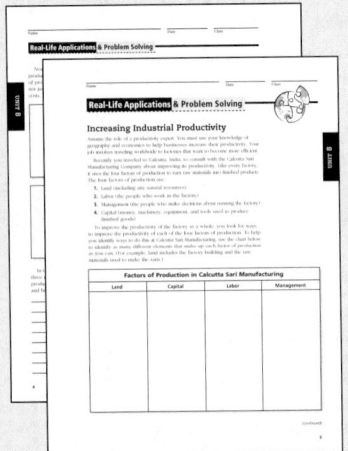

L2 GeoLab Activity 8

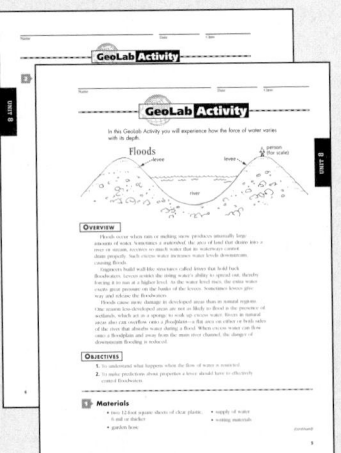

L2 Environmental Issues Case Study 8

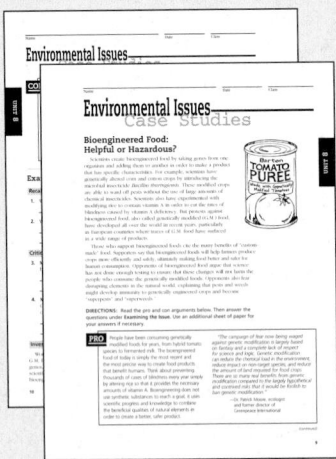

GEOGRAPHIC LITERACY

Focus on Geography Literacy

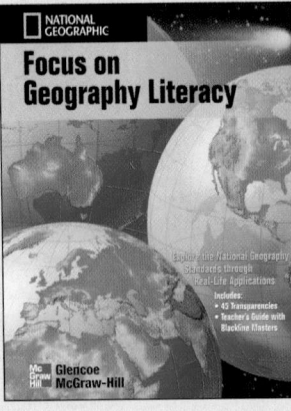

Building Geography Skills for Life

ASSESSMENT

Use the following to easily assess student learning in a variety of ways:

- Performance Assessment Activities and Rubrics
- Section Quizzes
- Chapter and Unit Tests
- Interactive Tutor Self-Assessment CD–ROM
- ExamView® Pro Testmaker
- MindJogger Videoquiz
- geography.glencoe.com
- Standardized Test Practice Workbook
- SAT I/II Test Practice

L2 Unit 8 Pretest and Tests

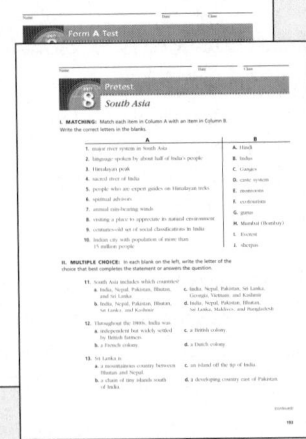

INTERDISCIPLINARY CONNECTIONS

L2 World Literature:
Contemporary Selection 8

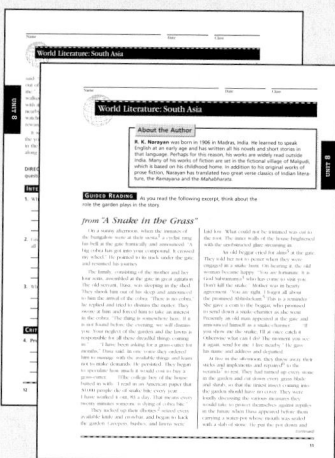

Foods Around the World

Glencoe

Foods Around the World

Multimedia

- World Art and Architecture Transparencies
- World Art Prints
- World Music: A Cultural Legacy
- World History Primary Source Document Library

BIBLIOGRAPHY

Readings for the Student

Celebrate! in South Asia, by Joseph F. Viesti. New York, NY: Lothrop Lee & Shepard, 1996.

India: The Land, by Bobbie Kalman. New York, NY: Crabtree Publishing, 2000.

Readings for the Teacher

India: A History, by John Keay. New York, NY: Atlantic Monthly Press, 2000.

New Cambridge History of India, Vol. IV: An Agrarian History of South Asia, by David Ludden. Columbia, MO: South Asia Books, 1999.

Multimedia Resources

A Migrant's Heart. S. Burlington, VT: Annenberg/CPB Collection, 1996. Videocassette, 27 minutes.

North India: Varanasi to the Himalayas. London: International Video Network, 1995. Videocassette, 47 minutes.

READING SUPPORT FROM
JAMESTOWN ⚓ EDUCATION

- *Timed Readings Plus in Social Studies* help students increase their reading rate and fluency while maintaining comprehension. The 400-word passages are similar to those found on state and national assessments.

- *Reading in the Content Area: Social Studies* concentrates on six essential reading skills that help students better comprehend what they read. The book includes 75 high-interest nonfiction passages written at increasing levels of difficulty.

- *Reading Fluency* helps students read smoothly, accurately, and expressively.

- *Jamestown's Reading Improvement,* by renowned reading expert Edward Fry, focuses on helping build your students' comprehension, vocabulary, and skimming and scanning skills.

- *Critical Reading Series* provides high-interest books, each written at three reading levels.

For more information about these products, see the Jamestown Education materials in the Classroom Solutions in the front of this Teacher Wraparound Edition.
To order these products, call Glencoe at 1-800-334-7344.

Background Information

CHAPTER 23 (pp. 568–583)

The Physical Geography of South Asia

South Asia contains some of the most varied landforms on Earth. In the north, the lofty Himalaya, Karakoram, and Hindu Kush ranges dominate the landscape. These mountain chains together create a formidable barrier between the region and the rest of Asia. In the past, invaders from the north could enter South Asia through only a few narrow passes. The mountain kingdoms of Nepal and Bhutan managed to remain isolated from the outside world well into the 1900s.

From the "abode of snows," as the Himalaya are called in Nepal, South Asia's landmass spreads southward in the form of a subcontinent. Within this upside-down triangular area are plains watered by three great river systems— the Indus, the Ganges, and the Brahmaputra. There are also arid deserts, vast plateaus, rugged hills, and eroded mountains. In addition, South Asia includes islands, such as Sri Lanka and the Maldives, in the Indian Ocean.

In the northern part of the subcontinent, the fertile soil of the Ganges River supports some of the planet's most densely populated areas. Farther south, the relatively arid Deccan Plateau holds fewer people, but well-watered coastal areas of southern India are densely populated.

Waiting for the Rains

Water—in the form of seas, rivers, and seasonal rains—is the key to life in South Asia. The region's largely tropical location makes it dependent on the monsoons. These seasonal wind patterns bring drenching rains that relieve the intense heat and nourish crops. South Asia is vulnerable, however, to weather-related disasters, such as drought, flooding, and typhoons.

South Asia's rich natural resources—iron ore, gemstones, and industrial minerals—for centuries have attracted outside conquerors, traders, and colonizers. Today, the region's seven countries are working to balance environmental preservation with economic development.

CHAPTER 24 (pp. 586–609)

The Cultural Geography of South Asia

With a population of more than 1.3 billion, South Asia is home to more than one-fifth of the world's people. The region's population is as diverse as its land, evidenced in the range of languages, religions, and ethnic groups. Several religious traditions—Hinduism, Buddhism, Jainism, and Sikhism—have their origins in the region. Other religions, such as Islam and Christianity, were brought to South Asia by migrants, conquerors, and colonizers. In India, where the ancient Hindu "caste" system still influences daily life, people commonly identify themselves by *jati*, or occupational groups, each with its own rules and customs.

South Asia's Long Past

South Asia was home to one of the world's earliest culture hearths— the Indus River valley civilization in what is now Pakistan. During the centuries after Aryan invaders entered the subcontinent, a succession of Hindu and Buddhist kingdoms and empires developed in the region. Greek, Central Asian, and Islamic groups added to the cultural mix. From the 1700s to the early 1900s, the British ruled or controlled most of South Asia. Independence came to the region's peoples after World War II. Religious and cultural differences led to the creation of two, and eventually three, countries—India, Pakistan, and Bangladesh—from the area that was once British India. Control of Kashmir, a largely Muslim region in the subcontinent's northwest, has been disputed between India and Pakistan since the late 1940s.

The literature, art, music, dance, and architecture of South Asia reflect the region's cultural diversity, and a variety of regional foods and other products have become known internationally. Tea, curries, spices, the practice of yoga, and textiles and patterns such as cashmere, calico, and paisley are just a few of South Asia's contributions to the world.

CHAPTER 25 (pp. 610–629)

South Asia Today

The geography and history of South Asia contribute greatly to the challenges the region faces today. How will a densely populated region, in which most people practice subsistence farming, move into an increasingly technological age? The stresses that large populations place on the environment are compounded in South Asia by the region's ethnic, religious, and political divisions and the wide gap between rich and poor.

The challenge of feeding the region's enormous population has begun to be met through scientific breakthroughs such as the green revolution, which has raised food production and improved people's diets. Concerns remain, however, about pesticide runoff, genetically modified seeds, and the increased energy use demanded by advanced technology. Cash crops such as tea still take up a disproportionate share of the region's agricultural land.

Changing global weather patterns bring special challenges to South Asia, where delayed or torrential monsoon rains can cost hundreds of thousands of lives and cause widespread devastation. Rising ocean levels, possibly from global warming, threaten island countries such as the Maldives and low-lying countries such as Bangladesh.

Further Challenges

Other challenges to South Asia come from growing urbanization, the environmental effects of deforestation and pollution, and the threat of a confrontation between India and Pakistan over Kashmir as well as other differences.

By 2000 both India and Pakistan had acquired nuclear weapons capability, a situation that poses dangers not only for the region but for the world. The escalation of a nuclear arms race in South Asia has diverted funds from social and economic development projects. As a source of raw materials, a destination for ecotourists, and a producer of high-technology products, South Asia will be an important player in the global economy of the twenty-first century.

00:00 OUT OF TIME?

If time does not permit teaching each chapter in this unit, you may want to use the **Reading Essentials and Study Guide** summaries.

Unit Launch Activity

Ask: What South Asian influences are part of your everyday life? *(foods such as tea and spices, textiles such as cashmere, practices such as yoga or meditation)* What kinds of news stories about South Asia have you seen or read? *(coverage of weather-related disasters, conflict between India and Pakistan, stories about the Himalaya or Everest climbs)* If students have difficulty identifying influences or news stories, ask them to pay special attention to these areas during the study of this unit.

GLENCOE TECHNOLOGY

☐ NATIONAL GEOGRAPHIC
WORLD REGIONS
VIDEO PROGRAM

Unit 8, South Asia
The following segments enhance the study of this unit:

• **Monsoon**
• **Sherpas of Nepal**
• **Bollywood**

[▭▭] Available in DVD and VHS

South Asia

554   Unit 8

GETTING TO KNOW THE REGION

Map Activity Have students refer to pages RA24–RA27 in the front of their texts. **Ask:** Which two South Asian countries are located in the Himalaya? *(Nepal, Bhutan)* Which South Asian countries are not located on the Indian subcontinent? *(Sri Lanka, Maldives, part of eastern India)* Which South Asian capital is farthest north? *(Islamabad)* Which country is located on the delta of the Ganges and Brahmaputra Rivers? *(Bangladesh)* What physical feature forms much of the boundary between India and Pakistan? *(Great Indian Desert)* Which bodies of water surround the Indian subcontinent? *(Arabian Sea, Indian Ocean, Bay of Bengal)*   ▣ EE1 The World in Spatial Terms: Standard 1

WHY IT'S IMPORTANT—

Many of the countries of South Asia have earned their independence relatively recently, but they have their roots in very ancient civilizations. The rich culture, minerals, and spices of the area have attracted foreign invaders for hundreds of years. Since the subcontinent shook off the cloak of British colonial rule in the 20th century, political and religious rivalries within the region have threatened its peace and stability. The governments of South Asia are struggling to overcome their differences and increase the region's role in trade and technological development.

World Regions Video
To learn more about South Asia and its impact on your world, view the World Regions video "South Asia."

Monk in front of dome of
Buddhist shrine, Nepal

This online resource, brought to you by the National Geographic Society, provides lesson plans, atlas updates, cartographic activities with interactive maps, an online map store, and links to the boundless subjects of maps and geography.

Unit Overview

This unit introduces students to the physical and cultural geography of South Asia. Point out the factors that make South Asia a significant region:

- one of the largest and most diverse populations on Earth
- a landscape having the world's highest mountain ranges and some of the world's great river systems
- the birthplace of two major world religions, Hinduism and Buddhism
- regional challenges that include a large population, limited and environmentally threatened resources, and national and ethnic tensions

ABOUT THE PHOTO

Visual Instruction The boy is clothed in the robes of a Buddhist monk. Most boys in Nepal spend time in Buddhist monasteries for religious training. The *stupa,* or domed shrine topped with a stepped tower, reflects elements of South Asian religious architecture. The eyes depicted on all sides of the shrine symbolize the presence of the Buddha, or Enlightened One, who watches over pilgrims as they circle the shrine in prayer and meditation. The flags flying from the shrine carry inscriptions of sacred texts called *sutras.*
Ask: What impressions does this photo give you of Buddhism? Of the role that religion plays in South Asian life? EE4 Human Systems: Standard 10

① FOCUS

These features and activities may be used as an introduction to the unit or as teaching tools throughout the course of the unit.

L1 Using Flash Cards Activity

Before beginning the study of this unit, use the **Countries of the World Flash Cards** to preview students' knowledge of South Asia. Organize the students into two teams, and test their knowledge. At the end of the game, ask students to summarize physical and cultural similarities and differences among the countries of the region.

L2 Photo Research Activity

Have students do research to find out more about the subjects of the photos on pages 556–559. Assign one photo per student or per small group, and challenge the student or group to discover three facts about the photo's subject not covered in the caption. Share information.

INTERDISCIPLINARY
connection

> **LANGUAGE ARTS** Ask interested students to read and report on personal accounts of climbing Mount Everest, such as *Into Thin Air*, by Jon Krakauer or *Within Reach: My Everest Story*, by Mark Phetzer.

What Makes South Asia a Region?

Like a giant pointed tooth, South Asia juts out of the Asian continent and into the salty waters of the Arabian Sea, the Indian Ocean, and the Bay of Bengal. Towering mountains separate this region from the rest of Asia. The greatest of these are the mountains of the Himalaya, which include Mount Everest—the tallest peak on Earth.

South of the Himalaya, the land descends to fertile lowlands that are watered by the Indus, Brahmaputra, and Ganges River systems. South Asia's southern tip is outlined by the Eastern and Western Ghats, ranges of low mountains that frame an arid tableland called the Deccan Plateau.

From snowy highlands to sun-scorched deserts, South Asia has a variety of climate zones. The climate is greatly affected by monsoons—seasonal winds that bring cycles of wet and dry weather to the region.

① Bright bridles and nose rings adorn a camel in the Thar, or Great Indian, Desert. Straddling northwestern India and eastern Pakistan, the desert lies beyond the reach of heavy monsoon rains. Camels are a traditional means of transportation in this arid part of South Asia.

556   Unit 8

BACKGROUND INFORMATION

Ganges River One of the world's most geographically and culturally important rivers, the Ganges flows some 1,560 miles (2,510 km) from its source in a Himalayan ice cave to its mouth in the Bay of Bengal. The Hindus of India consider the Ganges sacred; its waters, like a great mother, nourish the life of the land. People seeking physical or spiritual healing travel to holy cities such as Varanasi (Benares) to bathe in the river's waters. People with terminal illnesses often arrange to die in the Ganges or on its banks. Hindu funerals include cremation, and the ashes are scattered on the Ganges—a sign of the Hindu belief in the cycle of death and rebirth. 🌐 **EE5 Environment and Society: Standard 15**

NATIONAL GEOGRAPHIC

② TEACH

L2 Human-Environment Interaction

Ask: What would your life be like if it rained 60 days in a row every summer—and very little for the rest of the year? Have students brainstorm a list of ways their lives would be different if they lived in a monsoon climate.

Tenzing Norgay was a Nepalese Sherpa who aided a 1953 British Commonwealth effort to climb Mount Everest. On May 29, 1953, Norgay and Edmund Hillary, a New Zealand climber later knighted by Queen Elizabeth II, became the first people known to reach the 29,035-foot (8,850-m) peak and return successfully.

② Water swirls down a street in Delhi during India's wet monsoon season. Each year as summer approaches, wind patterns shift and moist air from the Indian Ocean sweeps over the subcontinent. Once the rains begin, they may continue for 60 days or more.

③ Whitewashed walls echo the brilliance of snow-covered peaks in Namche Bazaar, a Sherpa village in Nepal. Sherpas are a people who live mainly among the mountains of the Himalaya, where they have won fame as guides on climbing expeditions.

④ Up to their knees in green shoots, a farmer and his cow pause in a paddy in Bangladesh. The rich soil of the Ganges River delta spreads across much of Bangladesh, helping to make this tiny country one of the world's leading producers of rice.

Unit 8 **557**

GLENCOE TECHNOLOGY

NATIONAL GEOGRAPHIC
WORLD REGIONS
VIDEO PROGRAM

Unit 8, South Asia
The following segments enhance the study of this unit:
- **Monsoon**
- **Sherpas of Nepal**
- **Bollywood**

A TRAVELER'S LOG

Hugues de Montalembert, a French writer, painter, and filmmaker, lost his sight, but blindness did not prevent him from using his other senses. In a 1991 magazine article entitled "Missing Nothing," de Montalembert wrote about a houseboat journey through Kashmir.

"The mountains on the north horizon, the lake, all are still. Only the birds move over the evening waters. The boatman's hook hits the hull at regular intervals with a thud. Without seeing, I perceive all this beauty—the mountains, the lake, the floating islands, the sunset blurring softly. The houseboat is built entirely of sandalwood and smells like a pencil sharpener. All around, the creaking of floorboards. . . . A breeze coming down from the glaciers makes the lake shiver." 🌐 **EE2 Places and Regions: Standard 6**

557

L2 Making Predictions

Ask students to speculate on aspects of South Asian life that may have been influenced by conquerors and colonizers from other parts of the world. Have students note evidence in the photos and captions—such as Islamic influence on architecture and British cultivation of tea as a cash crop—and make predictions based on other information they may have about the region.

Culture NOTE

Sri Lanka In Sri Lanka, the traditional gestures for yes and no are reversed from their Western counterparts. A nod means no, and shaking the head from side to side means yes.

□ NATIONAL GEOGRAPHIC **GEOFACT**

▶ The Hindi term *ghat* means "step." India's Eastern and Western Ghats are old mountain ranges named for their stair-step profiles.

Population Giant

Over the centuries, the fertile floodplains of the Indus and Ganges Rivers have attracted many immigrants and invaders to South Asia, giving the region great diversity in peoples, languages, customs, and religious beliefs.

Hinduism and Buddhism both originated in South Asia, whereas Islam arrived from the west. The British brought colonial rule, which lasted for nearly two centuries. The region won its independence in the mid-1900s, but not without political, religious, and economic upheaval.

South Asia remains culturally rich, but its burgeoning population—over one billion in India alone—struggles with a low standard of living. Subsistence farming and labor-intensive traditional industries form the basis of the region's economy.

1 **Red powder** coats the face of an Indian boy during the festival of Ganesh Chaturthi. The festival celebrates the birth of Ganesh, an elephant-headed Hindu god. Hinduism is the most widespread religion in South Asia today.

BACKGROUND INFORMATION

Cultural Values Indigenous religions of South Asia, such as Hinduism, Buddhism, and Jainism, share a profound respect for all forms of life. Most Hindus, Buddhists, and Jains follow a vegetarian diet. Almost all Hindus regard cows as sacred; throughout India, cows wander freely through crowded city streets. Shoes, belts, purses, and clothing made of leather are not permitted within temple areas. Jains practice *ahimsa*, the belief that all violence must be renounced to avoid harming life. As a result, Jains refrain from stepping on ants and other insects; Jain monks carry peacock feathers to gently sweep insects from their path.   ⊕ **EE4 Human Systems: Standard 10**

L2 Movement

Have volunteers research on the Internet to find out how much of the world's tea product is grown in South Asia and which South Asian countries export tea.

Greeting In India and Sri Lanka, the handshake is often replaced by the traditional Hindu greeting, the *namaste* (NAH•mahs•TAY). The palms of the hands are placed together (as in prayer) under the chin, and the head is nodded or bowed slightly.

❸ ASSESS

Ask: What aspects of physical geography shape life in South Asia? *(elevation, seasonal monsoons, mighty rivers)* What major cultural characteristics define South Asia? *(high population, religious diversity, conquest and colonization)*

❹ CLOSE

Have students write GeoJournal entries about a part of South Asia they would most like to visit.

2 Filled to overflowing, a gaily painted city bus takes on passengers in a crowded street in Dhaka, the capital of Bangladesh. With a population of about 134 million, Bangladesh is one of the most densely populated countries in the world—and also one of the poorest and least developed.

3 Mirrored in still water, the Taj Mahal stands serenely outside the city of Agra, in northern India. The Taj Mahal was built in the 1600s by a Muslim ruler as a tomb for his favorite wife. Constructed of white marble, the building is decorated with verses from the Quran, the holy book of Islam.

4 Tender tea leaves are plucked by hand on a plantation in Sri Lanka, formerly called Ceylon. A legacy of British colonial rule, plantations produce much of the famous Ceylon tea that is a major product of this island nation. Sri Lanka gained its independence from Britain in 1948.

Unit 8 **559**

UNIT PROJECT

South Asian Cookbook Before students begin the study of this unit, tell them that they will be responsible for developing a South Asian cookbook. Assign students to or invite them to volunteer for a group representing each South Asian country. (You may wish to assign India to more than one group, subdividing the country by region or religious tradition.) Ask each group to research recipes reflecting the cuisine of its assigned country. Groups should also research the foods that are common ingredients as well as the country's etiquette and customs related to meals. Each group should print and illustrate its recipes for inclusion in a class cookbook. You may wish to conclude the unit study by preparing and sampling recipes.

 🌐 **EE4 Human Systems: Standard 10**

UNIT 8 REGIONAL ATLAS

South Asia

These features and activities may be used as an introduction to the unit or as teaching tools throughout the course of the unit.

L2 Making Comparisons

Have students compare the elevation profile of South Asia with that of the United States and Canada, shown on page 106. Ask students to speculate about what geologic factors might be responsible for the differences in elevation profiles between the two regions. *(age of mountains; varying means of erosion, such as glacial activity and wind patterns)*

☐ NATIONAL GEOGRAPHIC **GEOFACT**

▶ **The Himalaya are young mountains, and they are still growing—rising in geologic thrust at a rate of 0.5 centimeters per year. Earth tremors associated with this thrust action contribute to landslides and, indirectly, to the deforestation of the Himalayan slopes.**

Elevation Profile

In order to show a variety of physical features, this cross section starts just west of the Indus River at around 28°N and heads east across the Indus River, the Great Indian Desert, and the Ganges Plain. It crosses the Himalaya and Mt. Everest and continues east through the Brahmaputra River, stopping at the border of India and Myanmar.

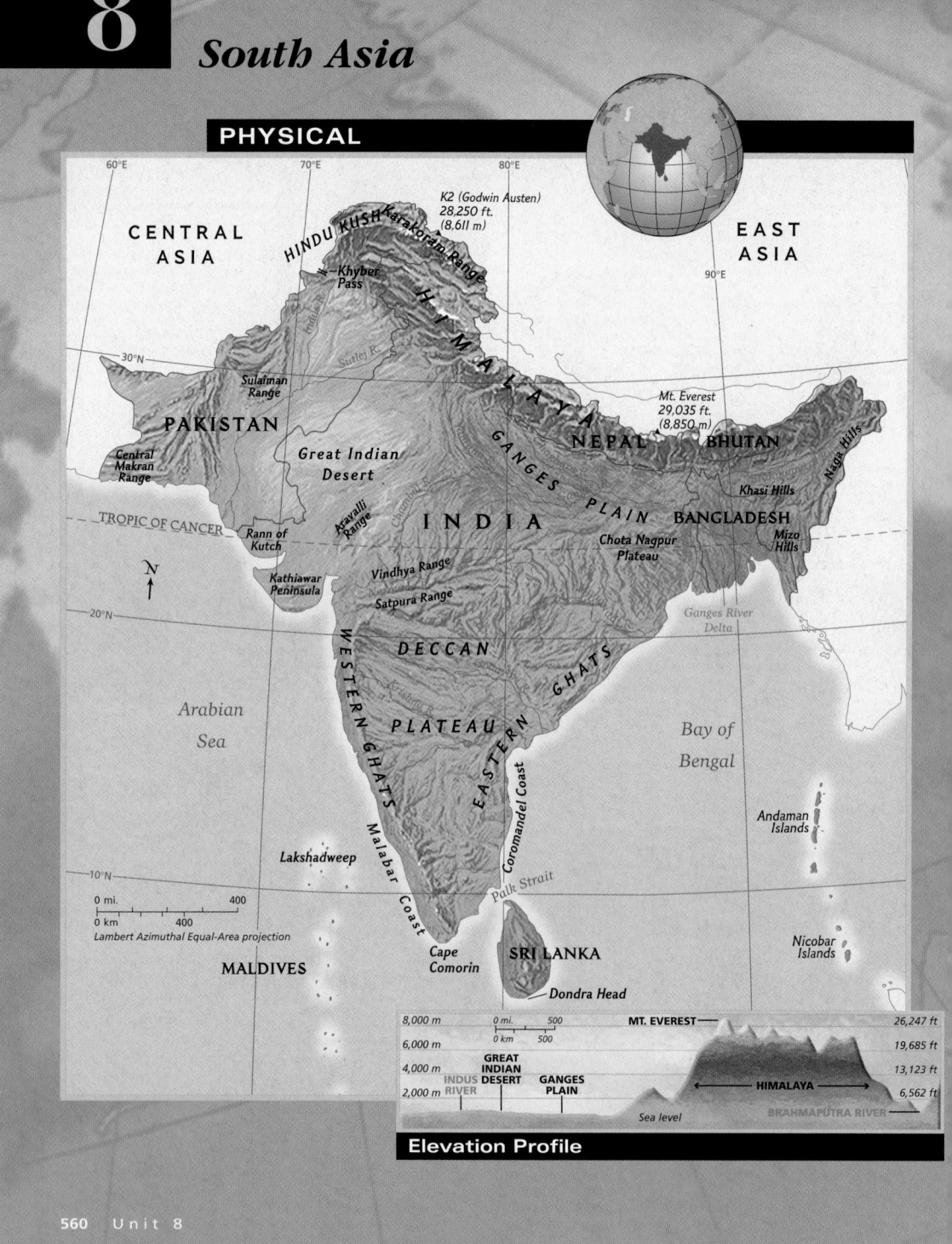

PHYSICAL

K2 (Godwin Austen) 28,250 ft. (8,611 m)

Mt. Everest 29,035 ft. (8,850 m)

CENTRAL ASIA

EAST ASIA

HINDU KUSH · Karakoram Range · HIMALAYA

Khyber Pass

PAKISTAN

Sulaiman Range

Central Makran Range

Great Indian Desert

GANGES PLAIN

NEPAL · BHUTAN

Naga Hills

Khasi Hills

BANGLADESH

Mizo Hills

TROPIC OF CANCER

Rann of Kutch

Aravalli Range

INDIA

Chota Nagpur Plateau

Kathiawar Peninsula

Vindhya Range

Satpura Range

Ganges River Delta

DECCAN PLATEAU

WESTERN GHATS

EASTERN GHATS

Bay of Bengal

Arabian Sea

Coromandel Coast

Andaman Islands

Lakshadweep

Malabar Coast

Palk Strait

Nicobar Islands

0 mi. 400
0 km 400
Lambert Azimuthal Equal-Area projection

Cape Comorin

SRI LANKA

MALDIVES

Dondra Head

Elevation Profile

8,000 m · 6,000 m · 4,000 m · 2,000 m

0 mi. 500 · 0 km 500

MT. EVEREST — 26,247 ft · 19,685 ft · 13,123 ft · 6,562 ft

INDUS RIVER · GREAT INDIAN DESERT · GANGES PLAIN · HIMALAYA · BRAHMAPUTRA RIVER · Sea level

---

REGIONAL ATLAS ACTIVITY

Physical Features Challenge Organize the class into two teams, one for South Asia above the Tropic of Cancer and one for South Asia below the Tropic of Cancer. For its assigned area, each team should list the physical features named on the map on this page. Have the teams research and write detailed descriptions of each of their listed features. Allow both teams to study the map for a specified time. Then have the teams take turns reading aloud their written descriptions as clues for the other team to guess the appropriate features. 📦 🌐 **EE1 The World in Spatial Terms: Standard 1**

POLITICAL

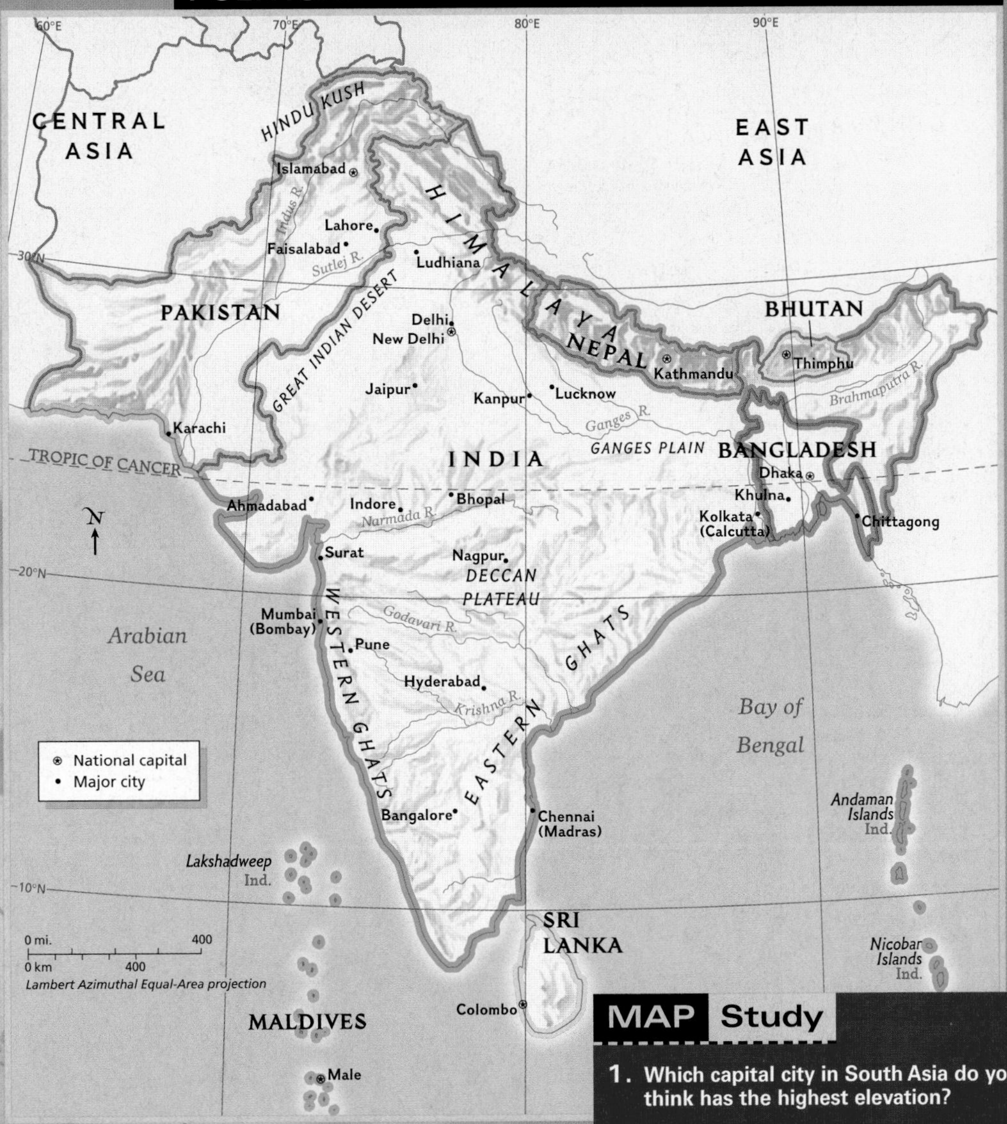

60°E 70°E 80°E 90°E

CENTRAL ASIA

EAST ASIA

HINDU KUSH

Islamabad ⊛

HIMALAYA

30°N

Lahore •
Faisalabad •

Sutlej R.

Ludhiana •

PAKISTAN

GREAT INDIAN DESERT

Delhi •
New Delhi ⊛

NEPAL

BHUTAN

Kathmandu ⊛

Thimphu ⊛

Jaipur •

Kanpur •
Lucknow •

Ganges R.

Brahmaputra R.

• Karachi

GANGES PLAIN

BANGLADESH

TROPIC OF CANCER

INDIA

Dhaka ⊛

N
↑

Ahmadabad •

Indore •
Narmada R.

Bhopal

Khulna •

Kolkata
(Calcutta)

• Chittagong

20°N

• Surat

Nagpur •

DECCAN
PLATEAU

Mumbai
(Bombay)

Godavari R.

WESTERN GHATS

• Pune

Hyderabad •

Krishna R.

EASTERN GHATS

Bay of
Bengal

Arabian
Sea

Andaman
Islands
Ind.

⊛ National capital
• Major city

Bangalore •

• Chennai
(Madras)

Lakshadweep
Ind.

10°N

0 mi.   400
0 km   400
Lambert Azimuthal Equal-Area projection

SRI
LANKA

Nicobar
Islands
Ind.

MALDIVES

Colombo ⊛

• Male

MAP Study

1. Which capital city in South Asia do you think has the highest elevation?

2. What rivers join to form the Ganges River delta?

L2 Location

Refer students to the political map of South Asia on this page. Remind them that national capitals and other major cities often are located on or near water because this facilitates trade and transportation. **Ask: Which South Asian capitals are located on or near water?** (*Dhaka, New Delhi, Colombo, Male*) Then have students compare the political map with the physical map on page 560. **Ask: What might explain the location of those South Asian capitals not found near major bodies of water?** (*Kathmandu and Thimphu are both located in sheltered valleys of the mountainous Himalayan region; Islamabad, which was built as a planned government city in the twentieth century, is also located in a mountain valley. Islamabad replaced Karachi, a crowded seaport city, as Pakistan's capital.*)

MAP Study

Answers

1. *Thimphu, Bhutan (7,708 feet/2,350 m); students may also suggest Kathmandu, Nepal, at 4,344 feet (1,325 m) because it is also located in the Himalaya.*

2. *Ganges, Brahmaputra*

Map Skills Practice
Region Which countries of South Asia are landlocked? (*Nepal, Bhutan*)

REGIONAL ATLAS ACTIVITY

Locating South Asian Cities On slips of paper, write the names of all cities listed on the political map of South Asia. (Do not include country information.) Display a large physical map of South Asia (with no cities identified), or sketch the region on the board. Invite students to study the political map on this page for a designated time. Then have students close their books. Have students take turns choosing a slip of paper with a city name and attaching it to the map or board in the appropriate location. If a student has difficulty, the class can give hints such as "warmer" or "colder."

🌐 **EE1 The World in Spatial Terms: Standard 2**

L2 Interpreting Map Legends

Review with students the legend for the population density map on this page. **Ask:** What color is used to indicate areas with a population density of 60–125 per square mile? *(orange)* Which South Asian capitals have populations of one million or fewer? *(Thimphu, Kathmandu, Islamabad)*

L2 Region

Ask volunteers to review the population density map of South Asia. Then have them mark out a space approximating South Asia on a classroom or gym floor or on the school grounds and form clusters of students to simulate South Asian population density patterns. **Ask:** Which areas are least densely populated? *(Himalayan highlands, Great Indian Desert)*

Sikhs As part of their tradition, India's Sikhs adopt religious last names. Men add the name *Singh* ("Lion") to their birth name. Women add the name *Kaur* ("Prince" or "Princess"). These names express the Sikhs' devotion to their faith.

UNIT 8 REGIONAL ATLAS

South Asia

POPULATION DENSITY

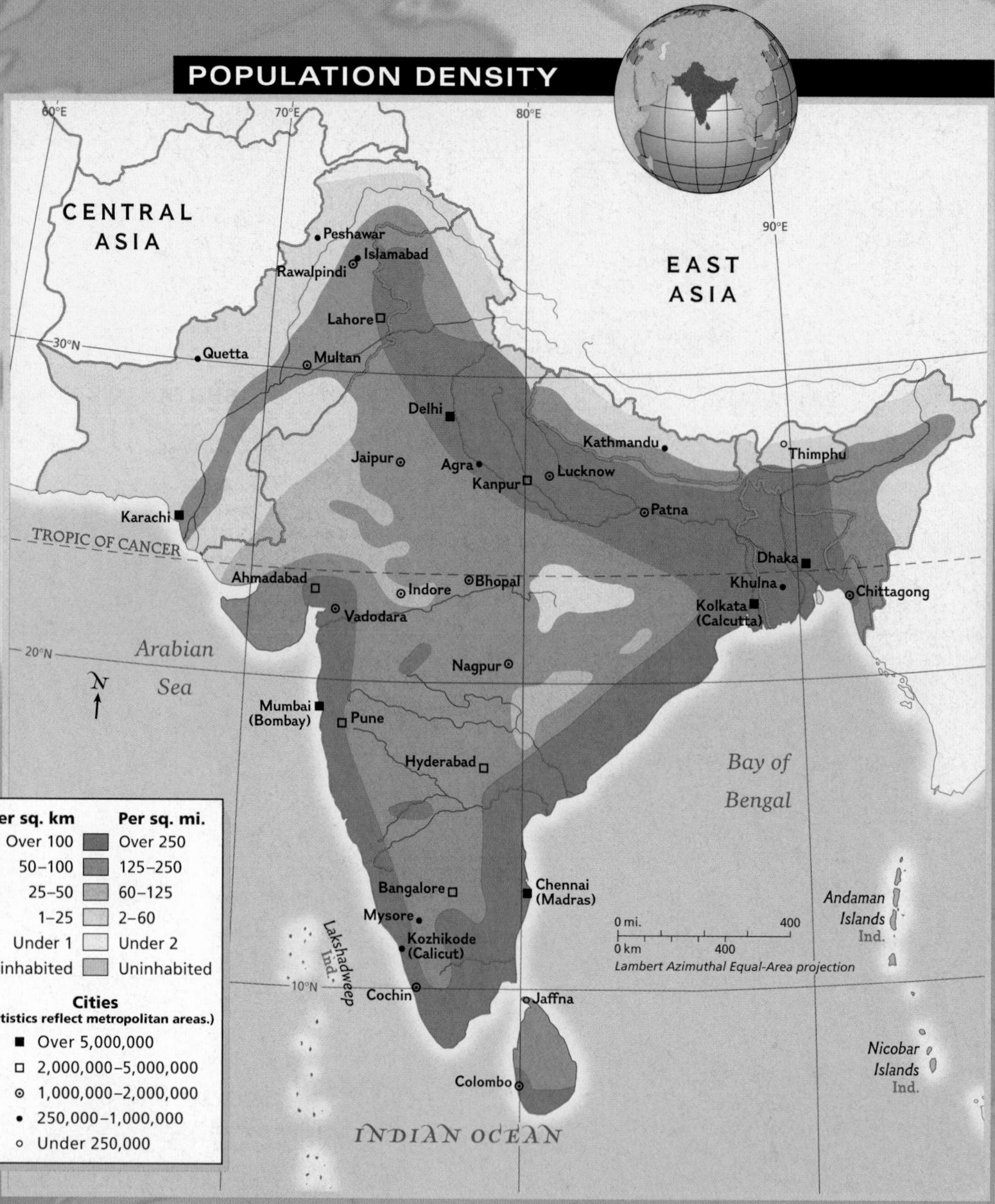

CENTRAL ASIA

EAST ASIA

Peshawar
Rawalpindi • Islamabad
Lahore □
Quetta • Multan
Delhi ■
Jaipur ⊙ Kathmandu
Agra • Thimphu
Kanpur ⊙ Lucknow
Karachi ■ Patna
TROPIC OF CANCER
Dhaka ■
Ahmadabad □ Khulna ■
Indore ⊙ Bhopal ⊙ Kolkata (Calcutta) ■ Chittagong
Vadodara ⊙
Nagpur ⊙
Arabian Sea
Mumbai (Bombay) ■ Pune •
Hyderabad □
Bay of Bengal
Bangalore □ Chennai (Madras) ■
Mysore • Andaman Islands Ind.
Kozhikode (Calicut) •
Lakshadweep Ind.
Cochin •
Jaffna •
Nicobar Islands Ind.
Colombo •
INDIAN OCEAN

Per sq. km / **Per sq. mi.**

Per sq. km	Per sq. mi.
Over 100	Over 250
50–100	125–250
25–50	60–125
1–25	2–60
Under 1	Under 2
Uninhabited	Uninhabited

Cities
(Statistics reflect metropolitan areas.)

■ Over 5,000,000
□ 2,000,000–5,000,000
⊙ 1,000,000–2,000,000
• 250,000–1,000,000
○ Under 250,000

0 mi. 400
0 km 400
Lambert Azimuthal Equal-Area projection

REGIONAL ATLAS ACTIVITY

Analyzing Population Patterns Organize the class into five groups. Assign each group one of the population density levels indicated on the map on this page. (Omit uninhabited areas.) Have each group research to determine the physical, climatic, or political factors responsible for the population density pattern. Remind students that population density areas cross national borders, and factors may differ in different countries. Allow time for groups to present the results of their research to the class.
🌐 **EE4 Human Systems: Standard 9**

ECONOMIC ACTIVITY

Map of South Asia showing economic activity.

Labels on map: CENTRAL ASIA, EAST ASIA, PAKISTAN, Rawalpindi, Corn, Lahore, Cotton, Wheat, Sheep, Delhi, NEPAL, BHUTAN, Cattle, Lucknow, Sheep, Goats, Rice, Cattle, Jute, Kanpur, Patna, Cattle, Karachi, Cotton, INDIA, Barley, BANGLADESH, Dhaka, Jute, TROPIC OF CANCER, Kolkata (Calcutta), Rice, Chittagong, Cotton, Rice, Arabian Sea, Mumbai (Bombay), Pune, Sheep, Wheat, Hyderabad, Bay of Bengal, Rice, Andaman Islands, Cotton, Bangalore, Chennai (Madras), Tea, Lakshadweep, Coconuts, Pearls, Nicobar Is., Rubber, MALDIVES, Colombo, SRI LANKA, Tea, Coconuts

60°E, 70°E, 80°E, 90°E, 30°N, 20°N, 10°N

Resources
- Ⱥ Petroleum
- ◊ Natural gas
- ▬ Coal
- ✳ Uranium
- ⚡ Iron ore
- ▲ Chromite
- ⬡ Gemstones
- ⬭ Copper

Land Use
- Commercial farming
- Subsistence farming
- Nomadic herding
- Hunting and gathering
- Forests
- Manufacturing and trade
- Commercial fishing
- Little or no activity

0 mi. 400
0 km 400
Lambert Azimuthal Equal-Area projection

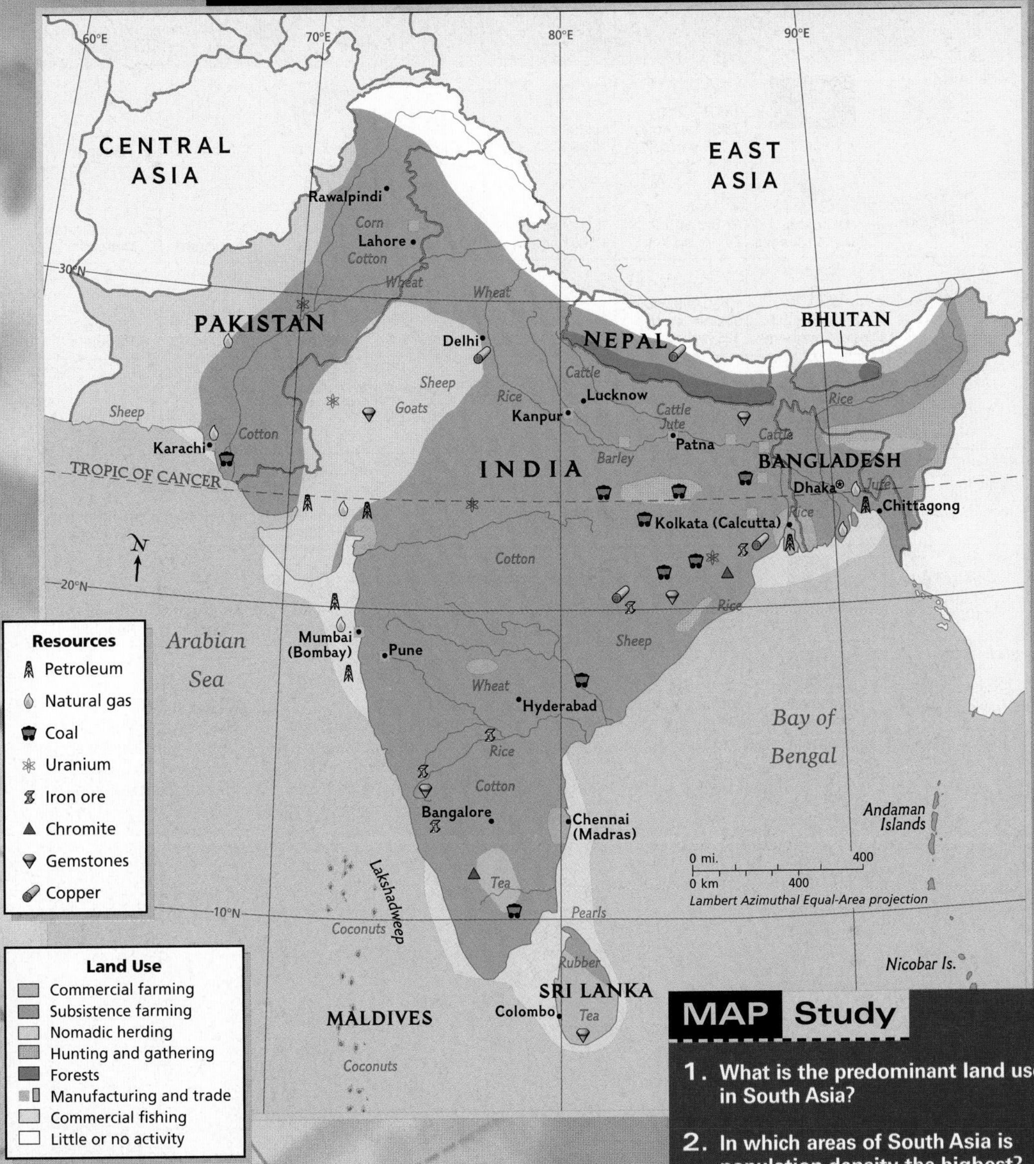

MAP Study

1. What is the predominant land use in South Asia?

2. In which areas of South Asia is population density the highest?

Unit 8 **563**

□ NATIONAL GEOGRAPHIC **GEOFACT**

▶ The terrace farming of rice is a practice that is thousands of years old. Terrace farming requires intensive labor, which is a relatively inexpensive commodity, and produces high yields. Today, nearly two billion people worldwide are fed by terrace farming.

Jute, one of the key natural resources of Bangladesh, is used to make burlap bags, or *gunny* sacks. The word *gunny* comes from the Punjabi word *guni*, meaning "sack." Jute fabrics are also used for upholstery lining and carpet backing.

MAP Study

Answers

1. *subsistence farming*

2. *along the Ganges River, most of India's coast, northwest India, southern Sri Lanka*

Map Skills Practice
Movement What physical factor might make South Asia's uranium resources difficult to develop? *(location in relatively inaccessible desert and interior areas)*

REGIONAL ATLAS ACTIVITY

Natural Resources Organize the class into two teams. Assign one team South Asia's mineral resources and the other South Asia's agricultural products (including animals). Have each group prepare a chart listing each resource or product and supplying the following information: where it is found or grown (list all applicable South Asian areas), how much of the region's export income is derived from the resource or product, and at least one example of how the resource or product is used. Students should use their textbooks, almanacs, encyclopedias, and Internet resources for reference. Display the completed charts. 📦 🖥 **EE5 Environment and Society: Standard 16**

South Asia

These features and activities may be used as an introduction to the unit or as teaching tools throughout the course of the unit.

L3 Language Roots

Explain to students that the Indo-European language family to which most South Asian languages belong also includes many European languages, such as English. Ask interested students to use an etymological dictionary or Internet reference to find examples of common English words that have Indo-European roots and similar-sounding equivalents in other European languages. (An example is the word *father*.)

Urdu, an official language of Pakistan, is a blend of Hindi with Persian, the language of the Islamic Mogul Empire that once ruled South Asia.

COUNTRY PROFILES

COUNTRY * AND CAPITAL	FLAG AND LANGUAGE	POPULATION** AND DENSITY	LANDMASS	MAJOR EXPORT	MAJOR IMPORT	CURRENCY	GOVERNMENT
BANGLADESH — Dhaka	Bengali	146,700,000 2,639 per sq.mi. 1,019 per sq.km	55,598 sq.mi. 143,999 sq.km	Clothing	Machinery	Taka	Republic
BHUTAN — Thimphu	Dzonkha, Local Languages	900,000 52 per sq.mi. 20 per sq.km	18,147 sq.mi. 47,001 sq.km	Cardamom	Fuels	Ngultrum	Constitutional Monarchy
INDIA — New Delhi	Hindi, English, Local Languages	1,069,000,000 842 per sq.mi. 325 per sq.km	1,269,340 sq.mi. 3,287,591 sq.km	Gems & Jewelry	Crude Oil	Rupee	Federal Republic
MALDIVES — Male	Maldivian Divehi, English	300,000 2,461 per sq.mi. 950 per sq.km	116 sq.mi. 300 sq.km	Fish	Machinery	Maldivian Rufiyaa	Republic
NEPAL — Kathmandu	Nepali	25,200,000 443 per sq.mi. 171 per sq.km	56,826 sq.mi. 147,179 sq.km	Clothing	Petroleum Products	Nepalese Rupee	Constitutional Monarchy
PAKISTAN — Islamabad	Urdu, English, Punjabi, Sindhi	149,100,000 485 per sq.mi. 187 per sq.km	307,375 sq.mi. 796,101 sq.km	Cotton	Petroleum	Pakistan Rupee	Federal Republic
SRI LANKA — Colombo	Sinhalese, Tamil, English	19,300,000 761 per sq.mi. 294 per sq.km	25,332 sq.mi. 65,610 sq.km	Textiles	Machinery	Sri Lanka Rupee	Republic

*COUNTRIES AND FLAGS NOT DRAWN TO SCALE   **POPULATIONS ARE ROUNDED, *SOURCE: 2003 WORLD POPULATION DATA SHEET*

FOR AN ONLINE UPDATE OF THIS INFORMATION, VISIT <u>GEOGRAPHY.GLENCOE.COM</u> AND CLICK ON "TEXTBOOK UPDATES."

▶ Boarding school students in Nepalganj, Nepal, study a computer.

COUNTRY PROFILE ACTIVITY

South Asian Governments Have students form three groups, one for each form of government found in South Asia—parliamentary republic, military government, and constitutional monarchy. Have each group use published and Internet references to research the way its assigned form of government functions in the South Asian countries to which it applies. Groups should find out the name of the current head of state or head of government in each relevant country and summarize any challenges to the system of government a South Asian country is facing. Allow time for groups to share their findings.

🌐 **EE6 The Uses of Geography: Standard 18**

FYI

High-tech India is the second leading exporter of computer software in the world. Many major U.S. high-tech firms have offices in India or have made investments in Indian companies.

Culture NOTE

India Boarding schools, such as the one attended by students shown in the photo on this page, are a legacy of India's British past. In India, as in England, the British public school system—in reality a network of private boarding schools—served to educate the children of the upper classes and to develop civil servants, scientists, teachers, and politicians. Although efforts to broaden access to education have increased since India's independence, literacy rates and school enrollments remain low among rural populations and the urban poor.

NATIONAL GEOGRAPHIC

Unit 8   565

COUNTRY PROFILE ACTIVITY

South Asian Flags Have students form seven small groups, and assign a South Asian country to each group. Ask each group to do research on the national flag of its assigned country. Groups should try to answer the following questions: When was the flag adopted? What significance do its colors and symbols have? What aspects of the country's physical or cultural geography are reflected in its flag's design? Have each group prepare a poster displaying the information, and allow time for groups to share their findings.
EE2 Places and Regions: Standard 6

① FOCUS

Ask students to estimate how much of their personal wardrobe is made up of cotton or cotton-blend fabrics. If students need help, remind them that two wardrobe staples—denim jeans and T-shirts—are usually made from cotton or cotton blends.

② TEACH

Cultural Exchange Explain to students that South Asia's textile industries have been supplying fabric, clothing, and rugs to the rest of the world for centuries. Have students refer to the country profiles on page 564. **Ask:** **Which South Asian countries today have raw cotton, textiles, or clothing as their primary export item?** *(Bangladesh, Nepal, Pakistan, Sri Lanka)*

Meeting National Standards

Geography for Life
The following standards are met in the Student Edition:

EE4 Human Systems:
    Standards 10, 11
EE5 Environment and Society:
    Standard 16
EE6 The Uses of Geography:
    Standards 17, 18

UNIT 8 REGIONAL ATLAS

GLOBAL CONNECTION

SOUTH ASIA AND THE UNITED STATES

TEXTILES

▲ Freshly printed fabric drying in Jodhpur, India

There are few things more comfortable than a pair of well-worn blue jeans. Denim—that soft, strong cotton fabric with the rich blue color—has become an integral part of modern life. But "indigo-dyed" textiles are nothing new—they were being produced in India many centuries ago. In fact, the word *indigo* comes from the name "India"!

South Asia has been a world center of textile production for thousands of years. As long ago as 2700 B.C., people in the Indus River valley were cultivating cotton plants and weaving cotton fibers into cloth. Ancient Indian artisans elevated spinning and weaving to art forms. They were among the first in the world to master techniques for dyeing cotton and other types of fabric. Using extracts from more than 300 different native plants, along with other natural substances, the artisans created beautiful, brilliant fabric dyes. The dark blue dye known as indigo, for example, came from the indigo plant.

Indian textile makers pioneered another important technique—making dyes

BACKGROUND INFORMATION

Oriental Rugs Another important South Asian textile industry and export is the so-called oriental rug. Using designs and techniques developed in Persia and brought to India by Mogul conquerors, Indian rugmakers create intricate, richly colored creations replicating flowery gardens and scroll-like architectural decorations. The best oriental rugs are made by hand knotting pile fibers through a woven background. An oriental carpet may contain from 50 to 500 knots per square inch (8–78 knots per sq. cm).
🌐 **EE4 Human Systems: Standard 10**

ART Archaeologists have found remains of 5,000-year-old printed cotton fabrics in the Indus River Valley. The patterns were made by block printing—carving or building up a design on a wooden block, inking the surface, and stamping it onto the fabric. Block printing was the basis for all later mechanical printing, whether in fine arts, textiles, or publishing. Some Indian fabrics are still block printed by hand today.

▲ Colorful dyes for sale on a street stand in Bangalore, India

permanent, or "colorfast," so they would not wash out. The colorfastness of Indian fabrics, combined with their vivid colors and intricate woven and printed patterns, made these fabrics highly prized in Europe, Asia, and other regions. By the 1700s, India was the greatest exporter of textiles the world had ever known.

In England, printed Indian fabrics known as calico and chintz became wildly popular for both fashions and furnishings. Eventually, such fabrics made their way to the American colonies. So precious were these imported textiles that scraps of calico and chintz were saved and made into patchwork quilts—a thrifty gesture that would eventually become an American craft tradition.

Fabrics and patterns that originated in South Asia are now made in other places. However, India is still one of the world's leading producers of cotton, and the textile industry remains India's most important industry. India's eastern neighbor, Bangladesh, also has a thriving garment industry. Check the labels in your cotton clothes—chances are some were made in South Asian countries.

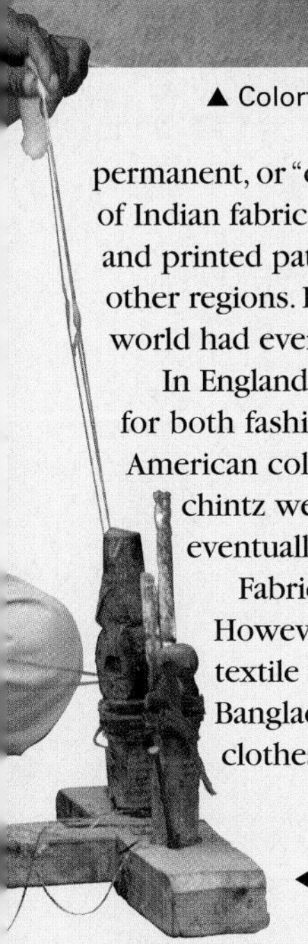

◀ Indian woman spinning cotton thread

③ ASSESS

Have students work together to identify and chart on the board the various colors and patterns of the clothing they are wearing. (If students wear school uniforms, ask them to list the colors and patterns of their favorite clothing.) **Ask: How would life be different without fabric dyes and patterns? Would your ability to express your personal tastes be limited? What factors influence your choice of clothing color and pattern?**

④ CLOSE

Have students check their clothing labels at home and tally the number of items made or assembled in South Asian countries.

CONNECTION ACTIVITY

South Asian Textiles Have students form small groups to research the South Asian origins of the following textiles or styles of clothing: calico cotton, madras plaids, cashmere, paisley and pashmina shawls, Indian rugs, pajamas, and jodhpurs (trousers worn for horseback riding). Have each group present its findings to the class using a combination of oral report and graphic display of information.
🌐 EE4 Human Systems: Standard 10

NOTE: The following materials may be used when teaching Chapter 23. Section-level support materials are shown at point-of-use in the margins of the Teacher Wraparound Edition.

TEACHING TRANSPARENCIES

L2 Unit 8 Map Overlay Transparencies

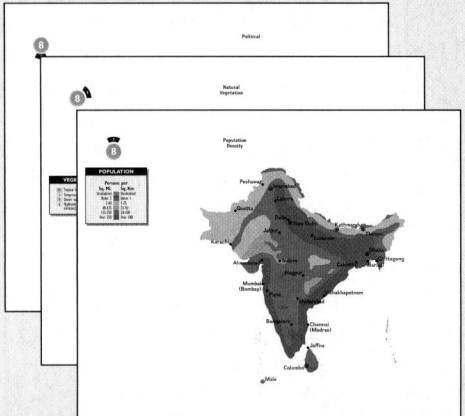

L2 Political Map Transparency 8

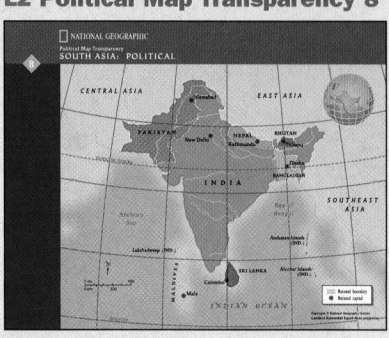

GEOGRAPHIC LITERACY

Focus on Geography Literacy

APPLICATION AND ENRICHMENT

L3 Enrichment Activity 23

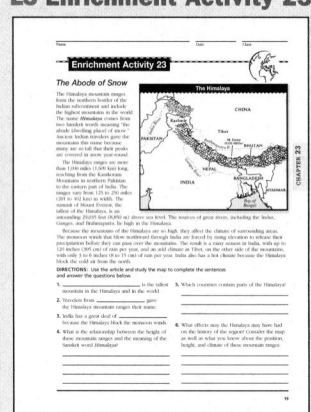

REVIEW AND REINFORCEMENT

L1 Vocabulary Activity 23   L1 Reinforcing   L1 Reteaching Activity 23
Skills Activity 23

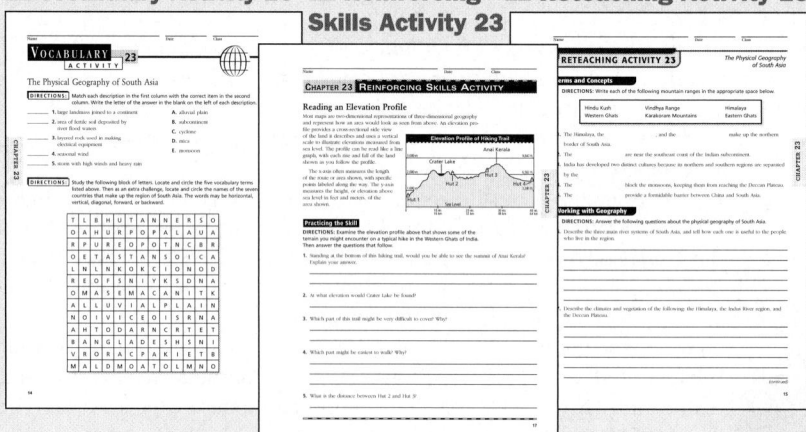

ASSESSMENT

L2 Chapter 23 Test Form A

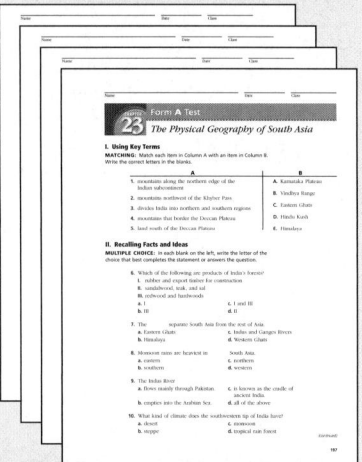

L2 Chapter 23 Test Form B

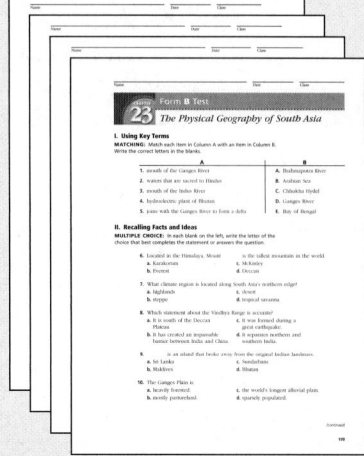

L1/ELL Performance Assessment Activity 23

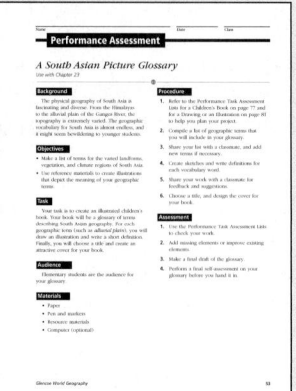

ExamView® Pro Testmaker

The following Spanish language materials are available in the Spanish Resources binder:

- 📁 Spanish Vocabulary Activities
- 📁 Spanish Guided Reading Activities
- 📁 Spanish Reteaching Activities
- 📁 Spanish Summaries
- 📁 Spanish Quizzes and Tests
- 📁 Spanish Reading Essentials and Study Guide

- 📼 ⊙ World Regions Video
- 📼 MindJogger Videoquiz
- 💿 Vocabulary PuzzleMaker CD-ROM
- 💿 Interactive Tutor Self-Assessment CD-ROM
- 💿 ExamView® Pro Testmaker CD-ROM
- 💿 Audio Program
- 💿 TeacherWorks CD-ROM
- 💿 Interactive Student Edition CD-ROM
- 💿 Glencoe Skillbuilder Interactive Workbook CD-ROM, Level 2
- 💿 Presentation Plus! CD-ROM

Timesaving Tools

TeacherWorks™ All-In-One Planner and Resource Center

- **Interactive Teacher Edition** Access your Teacher Wraparound Edition and your classroom resources with a few easy clicks.
- **Interactive Lesson Planner** Planning has never been easier! Organize your week, month, semester, or year with all the lesson helps you need to make teaching creative, timely, and relevant.

Use Glencoe's **Presentation Plus!** multimedia teacher tool to easily present dynamic lessons that visually excite your students. Using Microsoft PowerPoint® you can customize the presentations to create your own personalized lessons.

GEOGRAPHY Online

Use our Web site for additional resources. All essential content is covered in the Student Edition.

You and your students can visit geography.glencoe.com, the Web site companion to *Glencoe World Geography*. This innovative integration of electronic and print media offers your students a wealth of opportunities. The student text directs students to the Web site for the following options:

- **Chapter Overviews**
- **Self-Check Quizzes**
- **Student Activities**
- **Textbook Updates**

Answers are provided for you in the "Web Activity Lesson Plan." Additional Web resources and Interactive Tutor puzzles are also available.

Additional Glencoe Teacher Support

- Teaching Strategies for the Geography Classroom (including Block Scheduling Pacing Guides)
- Graphic Organizer Transparencies Strategies and Activities
- Outline Map Resource Book
- Reading in the Content Area

PLANNING GUIDE

SECTION RESOURCES

Daily Objectives	Reproducible Resources	Multimedia Resources

SECTION 1   The Land

1. Identify the major landforms in South Asia.
2. Describe the three great river systems of South Asia.
3. Explain how the peoples of South Asia use the region's natural resources.

Reproducible Lesson Plan 23-1
Daily Lecture Notes 23-1
Guided Reading Activity 23-1*
Reading Essentials and Study Guide 23-1*
Section Quiz 23-1*

Daily Focus Skills Transparency 23-1
Political Map Transparency 8
Unit 8 Map Overlay Transparencies
Interactive Tutor Self-Assessment CD-ROM
ExamView® Pro Testmaker CD-ROM*
Presentation Plus! CD-ROM

SECTION 2   Climate and Vegetation

1. List the five major climate regions of South Asia.
2. Discuss how seasonal weather patterns present challenges to the region's economy.
3. Explain how altitude and rainfall affect South Asia's vegetation.

Reproducible Lesson Plan 23-2
Vocabulary Activity 23*
Daily Lecture Notes 23-2
Guided Reading Activity 23-2*
Reading Essentials and Study Guide 23-2*
Reteaching Activity 23*
Reinforcing Skills Activity 23
Section Quiz 23-2*

Daily Focus Skills Transparency 23-2
Political Map Transparency 8
Unit 8 Map Overlay Transparencies
Vocabulary PuzzleMaker CD-ROM
Interactive Tutor Self-Assessment CD-ROM
ExamView® Pro Testmaker CD-ROM*
Presentation Plus! CD-ROM

Blackline Master	Software	Videocassette	*Also available in Spanish
Transparency	CD-ROM	DVD	

OUT OF TIME? Assign the Chapter 23 **Reading Essentials and Study Guide.**

Block Schedule

Activities that are particularly suited to use within the block scheduling framework are identified throughout this chapter by the following designation:

KEY TO ABILITY LEVELS

Teaching strategies have been coded for various learning styles and abilities.

L1   **BASIC** activities for all students

L2   **AVERAGE** activities for average to above-average students

L3   **CHALLENGING** activities for above-average students

ELL   **ENGLISH LANGUAGE LEARNER** activities

Teacher to Teacher

Patricia Diaz
Lopez High School
Brownsville, TX

Land, Water, and Population

Give each student a blank outline map of India and have students identify India's physical features on their maps. They should use information from the maps in the Regional Atlas on pages 560–563 and shade in areas of desert, the Ganges Plain, and the Deccan Plateau. Students should label the major rivers and indicate the direction in which they flow. Then have students use the population density map on page 562 to add major cities with populations greater than one million people.

Lead a class discussion about how physical features and climate patterns in India affect the way people live. Discuss how a physical feature such as a river can be sacred for the people as well as a necessity for life.

Have students work in pairs to role-play challenges people face in India today. Two students might be Indian farmers, for example. The pair will have a discussion in front of the class about the monsoon season. For example, they may discuss when to plant in order for crops to have time to grow before the coming of the monsoon rains.

Meeting National Standards

Geography For Life

The following standards are highlighted in Chapter 23:

Section 1 EE1 The World in Spatial Terms:
Standard 1
EE2 Places and Regions:
Standard 4
EE3 Physical Systems: Standard 7
EE5 Environment and Society:
Standard 14

Section 2 EE2 Places and Regions:
Standards 4, 5
EE3 Physical Systems:
Standards 7, 8
EE6 The Uses of Geography:
Standard 18

Local Objectives

_____

_____

NATIONAL GEOGRAPHIC — TEACHER'S CORNER

Index to National Geographic Magazine:

The following articles may be used for research relating to this chapter:
- "Rana Tharu Women," by Debra Kellner, September 2000.
- "Golden Harvest of the Raj," by Eric Valli, June 1998.

National Geographic Society Products:

To order the following products for use with this chapter, call National Geographic Society at 1-800-368-2728.

- *Asia* (Video)
- *Asia Political* (Map)
- *National Geographic Desk Reference* (Book)
- *National Geographic Atlas of the World, Seventh Edition* (Book)

NGS ONLINE

Access National Geographic's Web site for current events, activities, links, interactive features, and archives.
www.nationalgeographic.com

MEETING SPECIAL NEEDS

In addition to the Differentiated Instruction strategies found in each section, the following resources are also suitable for your special needs students:

- *ExamView® Pro Testmaker CD-ROM* allows teachers to tailor tests by reducing answer choices.
- The *Audio Program* includes the entire narrative of the student edition so that less-proficient readers can listen to the words as they read them.
- The *Reading Essentials and Study Guide* provides the same content as the student edition but is written two grade levels below the textbook.
- *Guided Reading Activities* give less-proficient readers point-by-point instructions to increase comprehension as they read each textbook section.
- *Enrichment Activities* include a stimulating collection of readings and activities for gifted and talented students.

Chapter Objectives

1. Identify the physical features and natural resources of South Asia.

2. Discuss the effects of South Asia's climates on life in the region.

GLENCOE
TECHNOLOGY

Use *MindJogger Videoquiz* to preview the Chapter 23 content.

GeoJournal

For access to additional information on the physical geography of South Asia go to www.nationalgeographic.com **(See Teacher pages in front for strategies for using journals in the geography classroom.)**

GEOGRAPHY *Online*

Introduce students to chapter content and key terms by having them access Chapter Overview 23 at geography.glencoe.com

FOLDABLES™
Study Organizer

Dinah Zike's Foldables are three-dimensional, interactive graphic organizers that help students practice basic writing skills, review key vocabulary terms, and identify main ideas. Have students complete the Foldable activity in the ***Dinah Zike's Reading and Study Skills Foldables*** booklet.

CHAPTER 23
The Physical Geography of South Asia

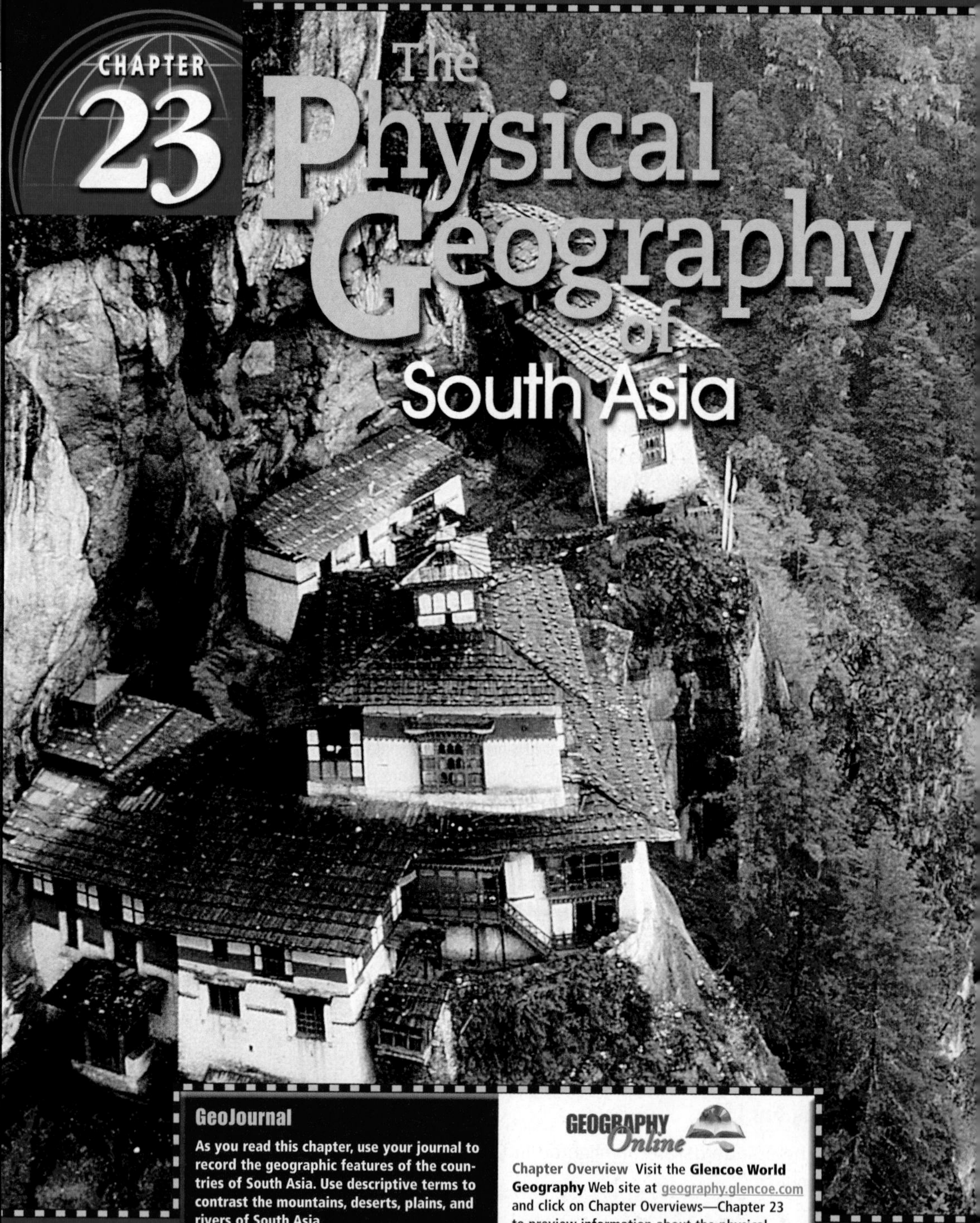

GeoJournal

As you read this chapter, use your journal to record the geographic features of the countries of South Asia. Use descriptive terms to contrast the mountains, deserts, plains, and rivers of South Asia.

GEOGRAPHY *Online*

Chapter Overview Visit the **Glencoe World Geography** Web site at geography.glencoe.com and click on Chapter Overviews—Chapter 23 to preview information about the physical geography of the region.

ABOUT THE PHOTO

Visual Instruction In mountainous Bhutan, ancient fortified monasteries called *dzong* are spiritual sanctuaries for Buddhist monks, but they are also centers of Buddhist learning and arts. The doors and pillars of temples in these castle-like structures often exhibit fine metalwork in bronze, silver, and other metals. Every temple has painted or gilded statues of the Buddha, and the low chants of Buddhist monks echo across Himalayan valleys. In Bhutan, religious festivals include dances accompanied by the music of drums, cymbals, and long horns. ⊕ **EE2 Places and Regions: Standard 4**

The Land

◀ *Buddhist monastery in Bhutan*

NATIONAL GEOGRAPHIC

A Geographic View

India by Train

The valleys and these hillsides [in the north of India] are open to the distant plains, and so the traveler on the toy train has a view that seems almost unnatural, it is so dramatic. At Sonada it is like standing at the heights of a gigantic outdoor amphitheater and looking down and seeing the plains and the rivers, roads and crops printed upon it and flattened by the yellow heat.

Train passing through Himalayan foothills

—Paul Theroux, "By Rail Across the Indian Subcontinent," National Geographic, June 1984

Novelist Paul Theroux described the varied and dramatic landscapes he saw while traveling South Asia by train. In this section you will explore the physical geography of South Asia—its majestic mountains, mighty rivers, and fertile plains.

A Separate Land

The seven countries that make up South Asia are separated from the rest of Asia by mountains. As a result, South Asia is called a subcontinent, a large, distinct landmass that is joined to a continent. In geologic terms South Asia contains some of the oldest and some of the youngest landforms on Earth.

Most of South Asia forms a peninsula of about 1.7 million square miles (4.4 million sq. km) touched by three bodies of water—the Arabian Sea to the west, the Indian Ocean to the south, and the Bay of Bengal to the east. The region also includes many small islands and the large island country of Sri Lanka, which lies off India's southern tip.

Chapter 23 ⊕ 569

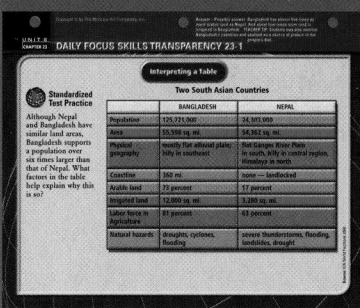

L1 Location

Project Map Overlay Transparencies 8-4 and 8-5. Have students take turns describing a physical feature of South Asia by using relative location and challenging the class to identify the feature.

Mount Everest was named for a man who may have never seen it. British scientist George Everest headed the Great Trigonometrical Survey that measured the Indian subcontinent in the 1800s. Mistakenly thinking the peak had no local name, British mapmakers assigned Everest's name to it.

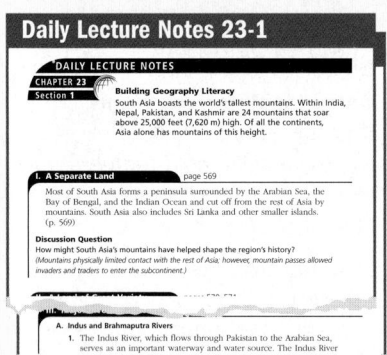

Daily Lecture Notes 23-1

DAILY LECTURE NOTES
CHAPTER 23
Section 1

Building Geography Literacy
South Asia boasts the world's tallest mountains. Within India, Nepal, Pakistan, and Kashmir are 24 mountains that soar above 25,000 feet (7,620 m) high. Of all the continents, Asia alone has mountains of this height.

I. A Separate Land   page 569

Most of South Asia forms a peninsula surrounded by the Arabian Sea, the Bay of Bengal, and the Indian Ocean and cut off from the rest of Asia by mountains. South Asia also includes Sri Lanka and other smaller islands. (p. 569)

Discussion Question
How might South Asia's mountains have helped shape the region's history?
(Mountains physically limited contact with the rest of Asia; however, mountain passes allowed invaders and traders to enter the subcontinent.)

A. Indus and Brahmaputra Rivers
1. The Indus River, which flows through Pakistan to the Arabian Sea, serves as an important waterway and water source. The Indus River

A Land of Great Variety

South Asia reveals a varied landscape. In the far north, some of the world's highest mountain ranges raise sharp, icy peaks above terraced foothills, high desert plateaus, and rich valleys. The older southern lands include eroded mountains and flat plateaus.

The Himalaya

According to the theory of continental drift, about 60 million years ago the Indian subcontinent was part of the same large landmass as Africa. After the subcontinent broke away, it collided with the southern edge of Asia. The force of this collision thrust up new mountain ranges, the **Himalaya**. These ranges spread more than 1,000 miles (1,609 km) across the northern edge of the peninsula and are hundreds of miles wide. Mount Everest, the world's highest peak, rises to 29,035 feet (8,850 m) above sea level in the Himalaya. A teenager describes climbing in the Himalaya:

> ❝ . . . I'm standing alone on a portion of the summit. . . . On very clear days like this, some from Everest have claimed to see the curvature of the earth; others say they can see the Indian Ocean, hundreds of miles away. . . . [I]t makes me feel very small. . . . ❞
>
> Mark Phetzer, *Within Reach: My Everest Story*, 1998

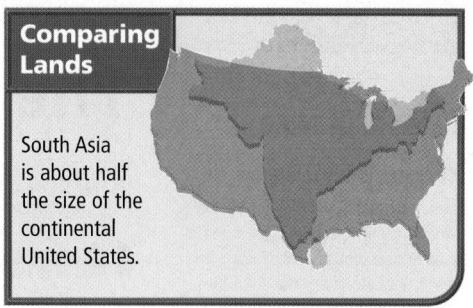

Comparing Lands

South Asia is about half the size of the continental United States.

Other Northern Landforms

The Himalaya meet the Karakoram Mountains in the northernmost part of South Asia. Farther west, the Hindu Kush range completes the chain. Together, they create a high wall of mountains between the subcontinent and the rest of Asia. In the past, invaders from the north could only enter the region through a few narrow crossing places, such as the famous **Khyber Pass** between Pakistan and Afghanistan. The Himalaya also protected Nepal and Bhutan from outside influence until the 1900s.

At the foot of the Himalaya ranges, wide fertile plains are watered by the region's great rivers—the Indus, the Ganges (GAN•JEEZ), and the Brahmaputra. One-tenth of the world's people live in this crowded northern area referred to as the **Ganges Plain** (or Indo-Gangetic Plain). In the northeast of India lies the Chota Nogpur Plateau, a high tableland of forests.

Culture
Central Landforms

The collision between the Indian subcontinent and Asia also pushed up a mountain range in central India. Not as tall as the Himalaya, the **Vindhya Range** divides India into northern and southern regions. This physical division separates the two distinct cultures that have developed in India. The cuisine, architecture, and religious practices of the peoples of northern and southern India differ markedly, as you will read in the next chapter.

Southern Landforms

The southern regions of South Asia contrast with those of the north. At the base of the subcontinent, two chains of eroded mountains—the Eastern

◀ *Fierce winds blow Buddhist prayer flags in Nepal.*

DIFFERENTIATED INSTRUCTION

Verbal/Linguistic Have students assume the role of writers for travel magazines or outdoor sports journals. Invite them to compose first-person accounts of one of the following South Asian journeys: trekking (hiking at levels where supplementary oxygen is not required) in the Himalaya, sailing and diving in the Maldives, collecting botanical specimens in the Sri Lankan rain forest, visiting archaeological digs in the Indus Valley. Have students do research for their writing. Ask them to use vivid language and to incorporate appropriate vocabulary terms from this unit in their presentations.
🌐 **EE2 Places and Regions: Standard 4**

📂 Refer to *Inclusion for the Social Studies Classroom Strategies and Activities.*

NATIONAL GEOGRAPHIC MAP STUDY

South Asia: Physical-Political

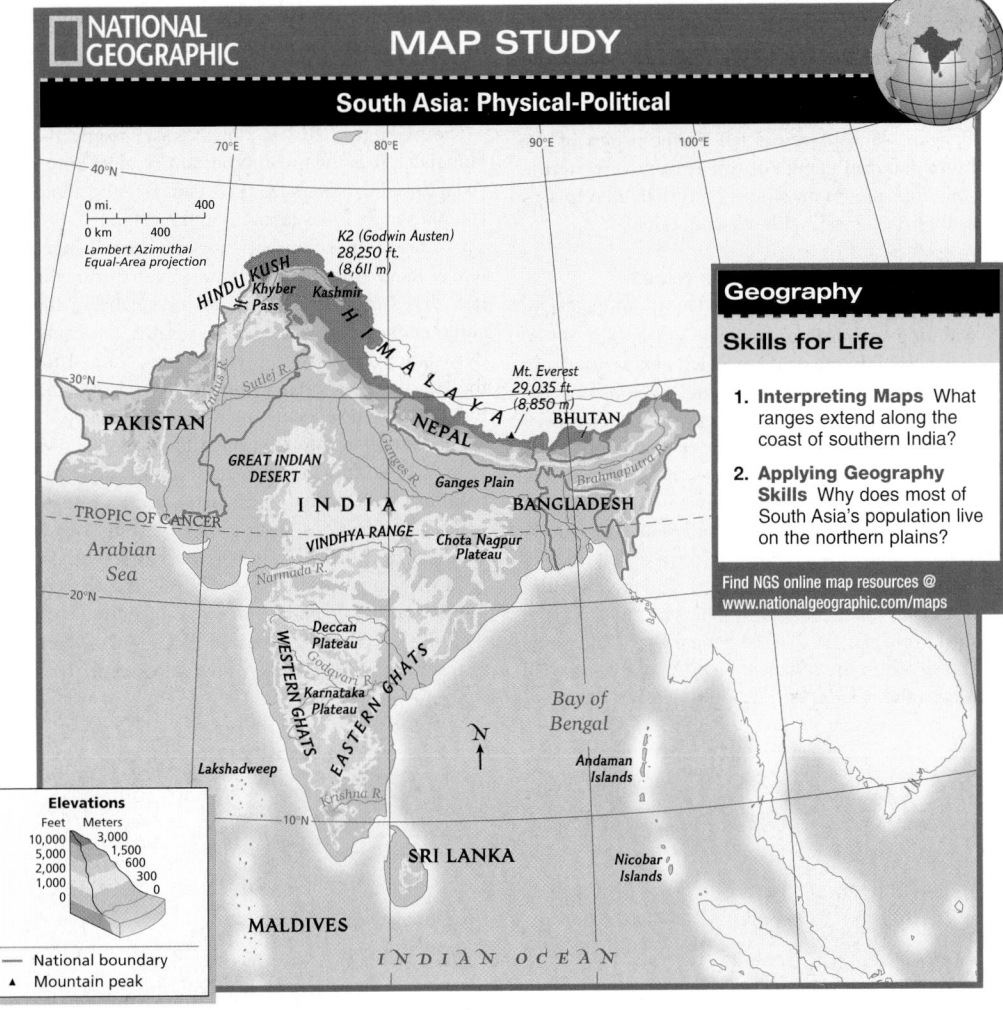

Geography

Skills for Life

1. **Interpreting Maps** What ranges extend along the coast of southern India?

2. **Applying Geography Skills** Why does most of South Asia's population live on the northern plains?

Find NGS online map resources @ www.nationalgeographic.com/maps

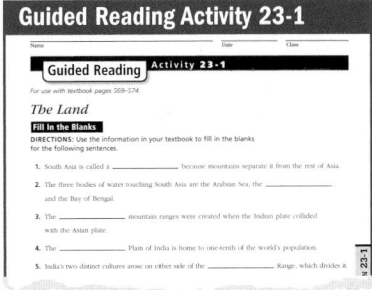

NATIONAL GEOGRAPHIC MAP STUDY

Answers

1. *Eastern Ghats, Western Ghats*

2. *The alluvial soil of the Ganges Plain supports agriculture.*

Map Skills Practice

Place What landform divides the Deccan Plateau from northern India? *(Vindhya Range)*

L1/ELL

Guided Reading Activity 23-1

L1 Description

Have students note and list the adjective-noun combinations used in one or more subsections to provide physical descriptions of South Asia's features. (examples: icy peaks, fertile plains, eroded mountains, teardrop-shaped island, snowcapped peaks, mountainous Nepal, layered rock) Have students look up the meanings of the adjectives in order to increase their comprehension of the phrases. **ELL**

Ghats and Western Ghats—form a triangle of rugged hills. Between them lies the **Deccan Plateau**. This plateau was part of the landmass from which the subcontinent broke away and is hundreds of millions of years old. Once covered with lava, the Deccan Plateau today has rich, black soil. The Western Ghats, however, prevent yearly rainy winds from reaching the plateau, leaving it arid, or extremely dry. The Karnataka Plateau south of the Deccan Plateau receives these rains instead, so hills there are lush and green. Spices

growing on plantations in this area scent the air, and wild elephants move through the foliage of the plateau's dense rain forests.

Sri Lanka (SREE LAHN•kuh) is a teardrop-shaped island that broke away from the original Indian landmass. Maldives (MAWL•DEEVZ), the southernmost country in South Asia, is a chain of tiny coral atolls and volcanic outcroppings. Although Maldives covers 35,200 square miles (90,000 sq. km) of ocean, its land area totals only 116 square miles (300 sq. km).

Chapter 23 🌐 **571**

COOPERATIVE LEARNING ACTIVITY

Make a Relief Map Have groups of students work together to prepare relief maps of South Asia. Students may use air-dried modeling clay, papier-mâché, plaster, or another medium of their choice. The maps should show major landforms and bodies of water to a relative scale. Have students paint the maps, label major physical features, and create keys to indicate elevation. Individual students should be responsible for each of these roles. Retain the maps as a classroom display. Then, as students continue to study South Asia, have them add different information to each map—vegetation types, economic activities, mineral resources, or population information are a few possibilities.

🌐 **EE1 The World in Spatial Terms: Standard 1**

L2 Natural Resources

Have students work in small groups to develop posters advertising products made from South Asian natural resources. *(examples: diamond, sapphire, or ruby jewelry; pencils; wrought iron fencing; teak furniture)*

L1/ELL

Reading Essentials & Study Guide 23-1

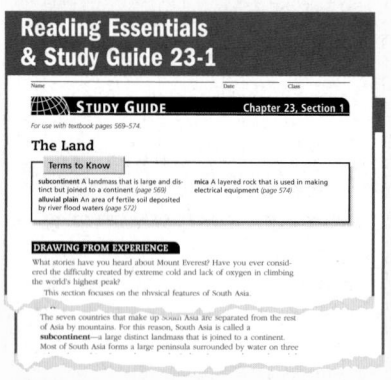

NATIONAL GEOGRAPHIC World Explorer

Answer

rice, sesame, sugarcane, jute, beans

More About the Photo The Hindu holy city of Varanasi, on the banks of the Ganges, draws people with illnesses who come to bathe in the river waters. Pilgrims, both healthy and ill, crowd the steps, called *ghats*, that lead into the river.

Major River Systems

Rivers are the key to life in South Asia. From sources high in the Himalaya, three major river systems—the Indus, the Brahmaputra, and the Ganges—fan out across the northern part of the Indian subcontinent. All three rivers carry fertile soil from mountain slopes onto their floodplains as the rivers swell with seasonal rains.

Indus and Brahmaputra Rivers

The **Indus River** flows mainly through Pakistan, watering orchards of peaches and apples before emptying into the Arabian Sea. It also serves as an important transportation route. Historically, the Indus River valley is known as the cradle of ancient India, which, with Mesopotamia and Egypt, was one of the world's earliest civilizations.

The **Brahmaputra River** flows east through the Himalaya and then west into India and Bangladesh. There it joins the Ganges—to form a delta before emptying into the Bay of Bengal. The Brahmaputra is a major inland waterway. Ships can navigate the river from the the Bay of Bengal as far inland as Dibrugarh in the Indian state of Assam, about 800 miles (about 1,290 km) from the sea. The Brahmaputra also provides Bangladesh with 50 percent of its power through hydroelectricity.

Ganges River

The **Ganges River** flows east from the Himalaya. It is the most important river of South Asia, drawing waters from a basin covering about 400,000 square miles (about 1 million sq. km). Fed by water from snowcapped peaks, the Ganges retains its size throughout the year, even during the hot, dry season from April to June. During the summer monsoon period, heavy rains can cause devastating floods along the Ganges. Named for the Hindu goddess Ganga, the Ganges is revered by Hindus, who consider its waters to be sacred.

The land area through which the Ganges flows is known as the Ganges Plain. Almost all of the plain has been cleared of grasslands and forests to make way for crops, such as rice, sesame, sugarcane, jute, and beans. As India's most agriculturally productive area, the Ganges Plain is the world's longest **alluvial plain**, an area of fertile soil deposited by river flood waters. The Ganges Plain also is India's most densely populated area.

NATIONAL GEOGRAPHIC World Explorer

Geography Skills for Life **The Holy River** The Ganges River is important to fishing, commerce, and agriculture. Millions of Hindus visit the river for ritual bathing (inset).

Human-Environment Interaction What crops are grown on the Ganges Plain?

CRITICAL THINKING ACTIVITY

Demonstrating Reasoned Judgment Have students work together to research the construction and operation of dams as well as the effects damming has on the environment. Then have the class gather information on a dam project in South Asia currently being debated. Choose two teams, and have them debate the question of whether the dam should be constructed. Invite students to determine the most convincing argument, based on the information they have gathered. 🔲 **EE5 Environment and Society: Standard 14**

NATIONAL GEOGRAPHIC **World Explorer**

Geography Skills for Life

Waterfalls in Nepal Twin waterfalls in the Annapurna region of Nepal cut through the sheer rock face of a Himalayan peak.

Human-Environment Interaction How might waterfalls benefit Nepal's economy?

Natural Resources

South Asia has a variety of natural resources. Dependent on these resources for their livelihood, South Asia's large populations and the fragile nature of some of their environments are ongoing challenges.

Water

The rivers of South Asia provide alluvial soil, drinking water, transportation, and hydroelectric power to the region's large, growing population. They also provide fish for local use and export.

Water resource management challenges South Asia because rivers cross national boundaries. Still, countries in the region sometimes work together on various projects. For example, India funded the Chhukha Hydel hydroelectric project in Bhutan. In return, India receives some of the energy generated there. Countries in the region also build dams to provide hydroelectric power and to open up

new farmlands by ensuring consistent levels of water for irrigation. Mountainous Nepal, with its many waterfalls, has the potential for creating large amounts of hydroelectricity.

Such massive projects, however, often have drawbacks as well as benefits. Dam projects in India meet with resistance when they threaten to flood existing settlements. In Pakistan one of the largest dams in the world, the Tarbela Dam, will soon be unusable, choked with built-up silt from the Indus River.

Energy Resources

Petroleum reserves are known to lie along India's northwest coast, near the Ganges Delta, and in northern Pakistan. Offshore exploration in the Arabian Sea may eventually yield oil. Overall, though, South Asia depends on imported oil.

Student Web Activity Visit the **Glencoe World Geography** Web site at geography.glencoe.com and click on Student Web Activities—Chapter 23 for an activity on the formation of the Himalaya and attempts to reach the summit of Mount Everest.

Chapter 23 🌐 573

NATIONAL GEOGRAPHIC **World Explorer**

Answer
Nepal could build hydroelectric power plants and sell to other countries.

More About the Photo
The Annapurna region is named for one of the world's highest peaks. Nepalese farmers call the 26,504-foot (8,078-m) Annapurna "the goddess of harvests." Streams from Annapurna provide water to farms in the foothills below.

L2

Section Quiz 23-1

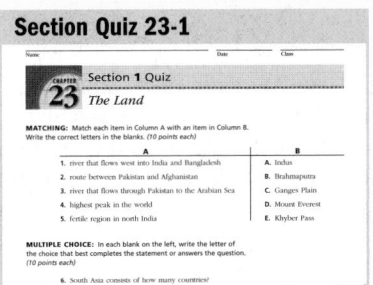

 **ASSESS**

Assign Section 1 Assessment as homework or as an in-class activity.

🖱 Have students use **Interactive Tutor Self-Assessment CD-ROM.**

Objectives, goals, and answers to the student activity can be found in the Web Activity Lesson Plan feature at geography.glencoe.com

TEAM-TEACHING ACTIVITY: SCIENCE

Geologic Processes Have students work with an earth science teacher to review the geologic forces and processes that have shaped South Asia's landscape. Name the following South Asian features, and have teams take turns identifying the force or process that shaped them: Himalaya *(continental drift, plate tectonics, subduction)*, Ganges Delta *(river erosion and deposit of silt)*, Ganges Plain *(alluvial deposit)*, Maldives Islands *(undersea volcanic activity)*, Sri Lanka island *(continental drift)*, Great Indian Desert *(rain shadow)*, Eastern and Western Ghats *(folding, wind and water erosion)*, Siachen Glacier *(glaciation)*, Vindhya Range *(plate tectonics)*, Deccan Plateau *(volcanic activity, erosion)*. The team with the most correct answers wins. 🌐 **EE3 Physical Systems: Standard 7**

NATIONAL GEOGRAPHIC World Explorer

Answer
Overcutting can result in massive erosion.

More About the Photo
Bhutan's forests grow in zones corresponding to elevation, from the pine and oak of the lower slopes, through the economically significant cypress, fir, spruce, and juniper in the mid-ranges, up to the stands of birch that grow as high as the timberline at 14,000 feet (4,270 m).

Reteach
Have students take turns naming South Asia's natural resources or physical features and challenging other students to identify their locations.

Enrich
Show students portions of a video or DVD such as *IMAX: The Greatest Places* (Image Entertainment, 1999) that explores the breathtaking landscape of the Himalaya.

CLOSE
Have students choose a photograph from this chapter (not limited to this section) and assume the role of visitors there. Have them write letters to friends describing their chosen sites.

Natural gas fields are found in southern Pakistan, in India's Ganges Delta, and in Bangladesh. India has a major uranium deposit north of the Eastern Ghats. Most South Asians, however, rely on energy from hydroelectricity, fuel wood, and coal.

Minerals
South Asia's mineral resources are rich, diverse, and widespread. India is a leading exporter of iron ore, and supplies 90 percent of the world's mica, a layered rock used in making electrical equipment. Deposits of manganese, chromite, and gypsum still await development. Nepal produces mica and small amounts of copper. Sri Lanka is one of the world's largest producers of graphite, the material used for the "lead" in pencils. Sri Lanka's other major mineral resources include sapphires, rubies, and about 40 other varieties of precious and semiprecious stones.

Timber
Timber is important to South Asia. The forests of Nepal and Bhutan contain conifers, including silver fir, and hardwoods such as oak, magnolia, beech, and birch. Severe overcutting threatens Nepal's timber, however, and could result in massive soil erosion. To preserve the fragile Himalayan environment, the government of Nepal is implementing conservation plans.

Timber resources also include India's prized sandalwood. Rain forests in southwest India yield sal and teak woods for export. To protect its rain forests, Sri Lanka since 1977 has banned timber exports.

NATIONAL GEOGRAPHIC World Explorer

Geography **Skills for Life**
Timber
Plantation In Bhutan, 90 percent of the workforce makes its living in agriculture and forestry.
Human-Environment Interaction How does overcutting impact the environment?

SECTION 1 ASSESSMENT

Checking for Understanding
1. **Define** subcontinent, alluvial plain, mica.
2. **Main Ideas** On a table like the one below show examples of the physical features and natural resources of South Asia.

Country	Physical Features	Natural Resources

Critical Thinking
3. **Making Comparisons** How does the landscape of the Himalaya differ from that of the Deccan Plateau? How do these differences affect people's lives?
4. **Identifying Cause and Effect** Why are population densities so high on the Ganges Plain?
5. **Problem Solving** How would you address the problem of overcutting trees in Nepal? How does your solution affect the timber industry?

Analyzing Maps
6. **Region** Study the physical-political map on page 571. What areas of South Asia would you expect to be most agriculturally productive? Why?

Applying Geography
7. **Managing Resources** Think about the physical geography of South Asia. Create a sketch map highlighting potential sites of conflict over water management among the countries of South Asia.

SECTION 1 ASSESSMENT ANSWERS

1. All vocabulary terms are defined in the text.
2. Table entries should reflect text information.
3. Himalaya: mountainous, steep, high altitudes, cold, forested; Deccan Plateau: dry, hot, flat; landscape and climate would influence clothing, housing, and agriculture, among other aspects of everyday life.
4. The alluvial soil of the Ganges Plain supports agriculture.
5. Responses should indicate an understanding of the effects of overcutting and suggest practical solutions that can address environmental and economic concerns.
6. Ganges Plain, Bangladesh, area between rivers in northern Pakistan, Sri Lanka; presence of rivers, alluvial soil, climate favorable to agriculture, absence of landforms that block rain
7. **Applying Geography** Sketch maps should show areas likely to experience droughts, or areas of joint-river ownership.

Guide to Reading

Consider What You Know

The countries of South Asia often are affected by natural disasters of some kind. For example, in 1998 Bangladesh suffered the effects of a terrible flood. What problems can flooding cause?

Reading Strategy

Categorizing As you read about the climate of South Asia, complete a web diagram similar to the one below by identifying the three seasons that occur in the region.

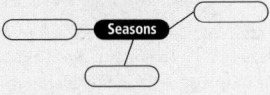

Read to Find Out

- What are the five major climate regions of South Asia?
- How do seasonal weather patterns present challenges to the region's economy?
- How do elevation and rainfall affect South Asia's vegetation?

Terms to Know

- monsoon
- cyclone

Places to Locate

- Bay of Bengal
- Great Indian Desert (Thar Desert)

Climate and Vegetation

NATIONAL
GEOGRAPHIC

A Geographic View

The Breath of Life

The eagle soared even higher in the updraft as I picked my way along the dark rocks beside the Arabian Sea. The winds shifted with promise, deepening the resonance of the surf, muffling even the crows that cackled and lurched along the seawalls. The water grew choppy, and the black thorns of fishermen's sails scratched the horizon. Surely the time [of the monsoon] was at hand.

Rain-swollen Mahandi River, India

—Priit J. Vesilind, "Monsoons: Life Breath of Half the World," National Geographic, *December 1984*

Journalist Priit Vesilind captures in words the tension of waiting for South Asia's seasonal rains. The region, with its hot climates, comes alive when the rain-bearing winds sweep in.

South Asia's Climates

South Asia's climate and vegetation regions are a study in contrasts. Much of the subcontinent lies south of the Tropic of Cancer and has tropical climates with diverse vegetation. In the north and the west, however, the climate varies widely, from the highlands of the Himalaya to the deserts around the Indus River, where little vegetation grows.

Tropical and Subtropical Climates

Tropical rain forest climates, with a variety of vegetation, are located along the western coast of India, near the Ganges Delta in Bangladesh,

Chapter 23 🌐 575

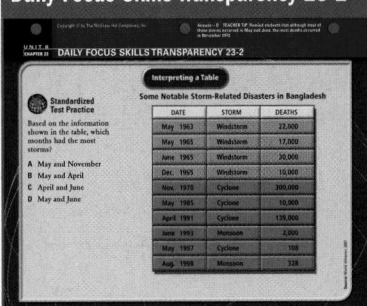

② TEACH

L2 Making Comparisons

Ask: Which climate zone of South Asia most closely resembles the climate zone you live in? What similarities and differences in vegetation are there?

Answers

1. *western Sri Lanka, southwest India, north of the Bay of Bengal*

2. *It has a highlands climate and vegetation.*

Map Skills Practice
Region Where are South Asia's driest climates found? *(western India, eastern and extreme western Pakistan)*

L3 Region

Have interested students develop a design for a South Asian botanical garden. Students should map the areas of the garden and list appropriate types of vegetation.

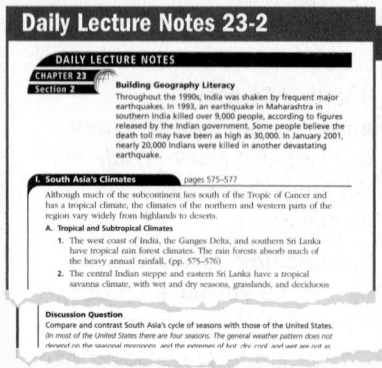

Daily Lecture Notes 23-2

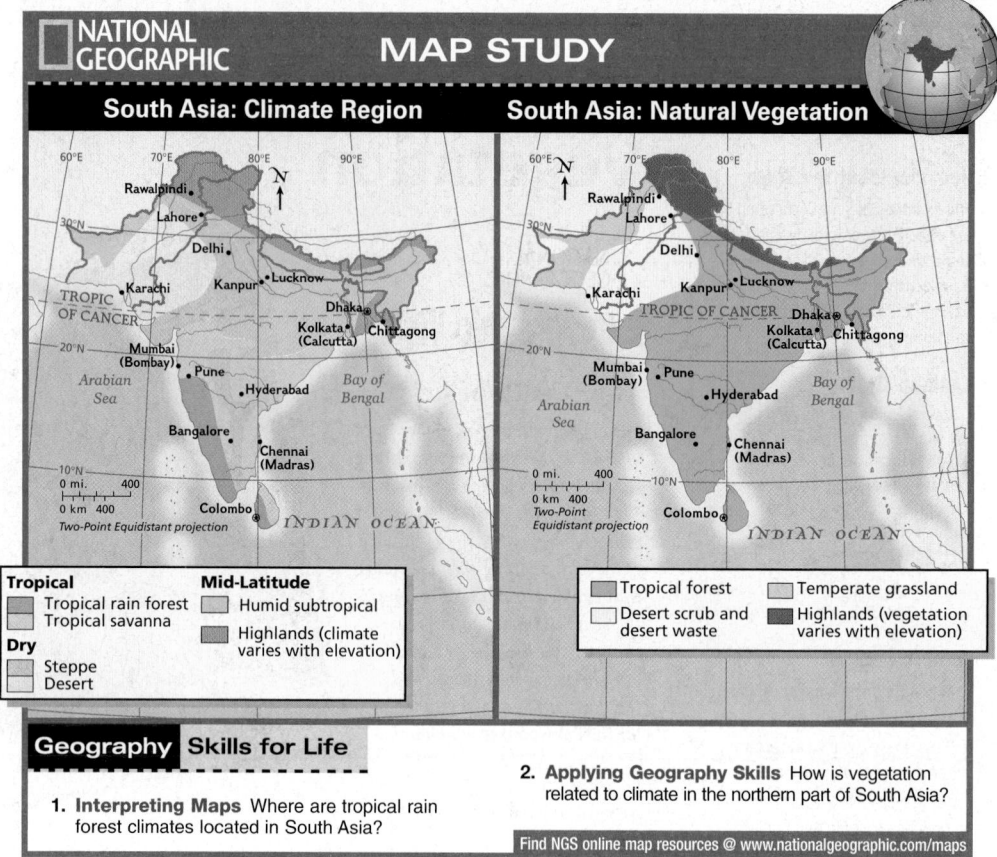

NATIONAL GEOGRAPHIC — MAP STUDY

South Asia: Climate Region

South Asia: Natural Vegetation

Tropical
- Tropical rain forest
- Tropical savanna

Dry
- Steppe
- Desert

Mid-Latitude
- Humid subtropical
- Highlands (climate varies with elevation)

- Tropical forest
- Desert scrub and desert waste
- Temperate grassland
- Highlands (vegetation varies with elevation)

Geography — Skills for Life

1. **Interpreting Maps** Where are tropical rain forest climates located in South Asia?

2. **Applying Geography Skills** How is vegetation related to climate in the northern part of South Asia?

Find NGS online map resources @ www.nationalgeographic.com/maps

---

and in southern Sri Lanka. In the path of seasonal rains from the southwest, South Asia's rain forests absorb great quantities of moisture. The rain forests in western Sri Lanka, in southwest India, and in areas north of the **Bay of Bengal** have ebony trees, lush vines, and orchids. Tropical coniferous and deciduous trees surround the rain forests near the Western Ghats. In hot, damp Bangladesh, tropical forests of bamboo, mango, and palm trees thrive. The Sundarbans, a swampy area in southwestern Bangladesh, has the world's largest protected mangrove forest.

A tropical savanna climate surrounds the central Indian steppe and also is found in eastern Sri Lanka. The grasslands and tropical-moist deciduous forests of the savanna experience wet and dry seasons. In Sri Lanka dry evergreen forests and moist

deciduous forests give way to drier grasslands at higher elevations.

A band of humid subtropical climate extends across Nepal, Bhutan, Bangladesh, and the northeastern part of India. Temperate mixed forests stretch across the borders of these countries in this area.

Highlands Climates

The coldest climate region of South Asia lies along its northern edge. In the Himalayan highlands and Karakoram peaks, snow never disappears. At the highest elevations, little vegetation can survive. Farther down these slopes, however, the climate turns milder and more temperate. In the upper area of this more temperate zone, coniferous and hardwood trees flourish. Grasslands and stands of bamboo cover the lower Himalayan foothills.

DIFFERENTIATED INSTRUCTION

At-Risk Students For students with attention deficit disorder (ADD), provide interventions to help them stay on task. Have students divide a sheet of paper into two columns labeled *On-task* and *Off-task*. During silent reading of this section, call out "Check" at intervals, and have students put a check in the appropriate column to indicate whether they were paying attention or their attention was wandering. Review the exercise with students to help them evaluate their attention levels and identify possible sources of distraction.
🌐 **EE2 Places and Regions: Standards 4, 5**
🗂 Refer to *Inclusion for the Social Studies Classroom Strategies and Activities.*

Dry Climates

Along the lower Indus River, a desert climate keeps the land arid and windswept. The **Great Indian Desert** (Thar Desert) lies to the east of the Indus. The vegetation here is desert scrub, low, thorny trees, and grasses. Livestock graze in some areas, and irrigation makes it possible to grow wheat near the Indus River. Much of this area, however, remains wasteland.

Surrounding this desert, except on the coast, is a steppe. Few trees grow in this semiarid grassland.

In northwestern India annual rainfall averages less than 20 inches (51 cm). Another steppe area runs through the center of the Deccan Plateau between the Eastern and Western Ghats. The Ghats block rainfall here, making the area relatively arid. Dry, deciduous forests cover vast stretches of India's interior.

Monsoons

Much of South Asia experiences three distinct seasons—hot (from late February to June), wet (from June or July until September), and cool (from

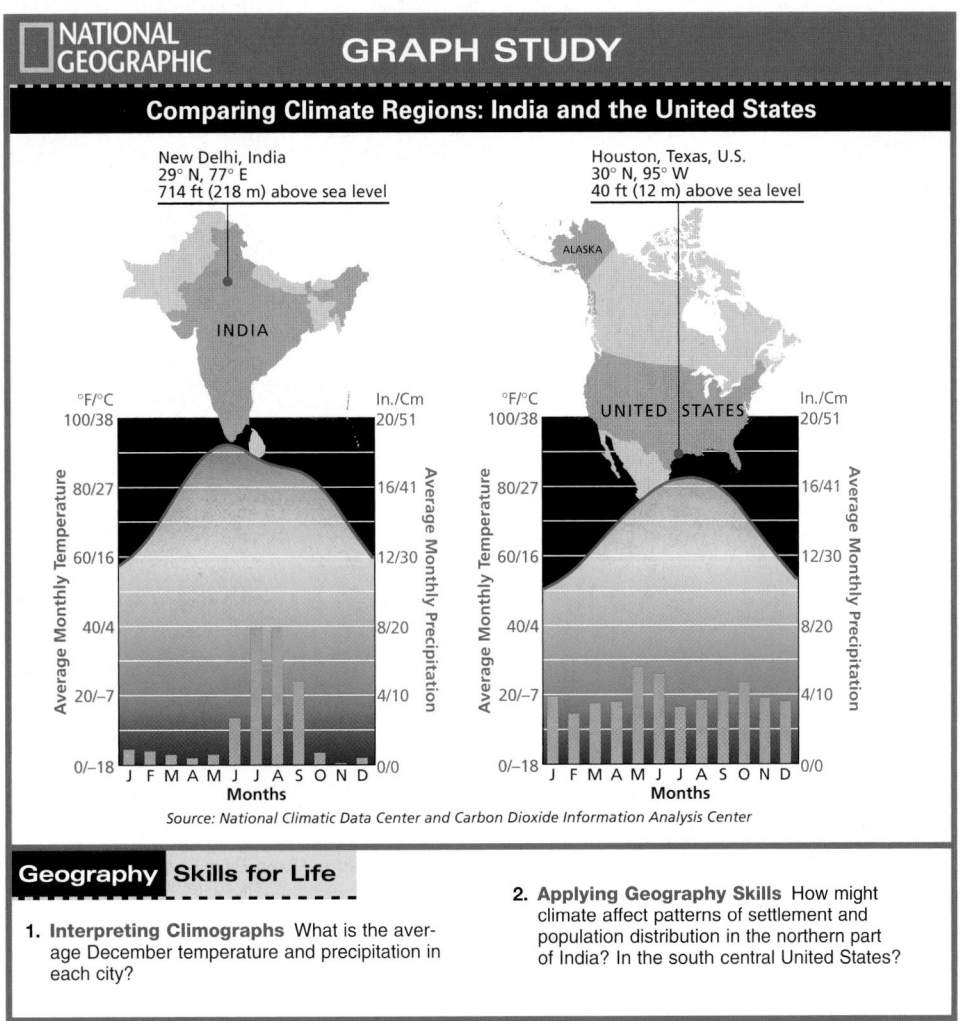

NATIONAL GEOGRAPHIC   GRAPH STUDY

Comparing Climate Regions: India and the United States

New Delhi, India
29° N, 77° E
714 ft (218 m) above sea level

Houston, Texas, U.S.
30° N, 95° W
40 ft (12 m) above sea level

Source: National Climatic Data Center and Carbon Dioxide Information Analysis Center

Geography Skills for Life

1. **Interpreting Climographs** What is the average December temperature and precipitation in each city?

2. **Applying Geography Skills** How might climate affect patterns of settlement and population distribution in the northern part of India? In the south central United States?

L1/ELL

Guided Reading Activity 23-2

Guided Reading Activity 23-2

Climate and Vegetation

Outline

DIRECTIONS: Use the information in your textbook to complete the following outline.

I. Climates of South Asia
  A. **(1)** _____
    1. Tropical rain forest climate
    2. **(2)** _____
    3. Humid subtropical climate
  B. **(3)** _____
    Little vegetation at highest elevations

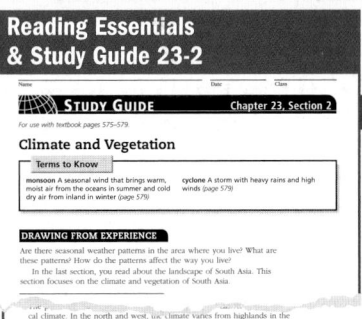

NATIONAL GEOGRAPHIC   GRAPH STUDY

Answers

1. *New Delhi: 60°F (16°C), about 0.5 inches (1.3 cm); Houston: 55°F (13°C), about 3.5 inches (8.9 cm)*

2. *Students should consider the relationship of rainfall and temperatures on settlement. They might note that temperatures are higher overall and that rainfall averages are more extreme in New Delhi than in Houston.*

L1/ELL

Reading Essentials & Study Guide 23-2

STUDY GUIDE   Chapter 23, Section 2

For use with textbook pages 575–579

Climate and Vegetation

Terms to Know

monsoon A seasonal wind that brings warm, moist air from the oceans in summer and cold dry air from inland in winter (page 579) **cyclone** A storm with heavy rains and high winds (page 579)

DRAWING FROM EXPERIENCE

Are there seasonal weather patterns in the area where you live? What are these patterns? How do the patterns affect the way you live?

In the last section, you read about the landscape of South Asia. This section focuses on the climate and vegetation of South Asia.

...cal climate: In the north and west, the climate varies from highlands in the Himalaya to deserts around the Indus River.

  A. A tropical rain forest climate with diverse vegetation covers the western coast of India, the Ganges Delta in Bangladesh, and southern Sri

COOPERATIVE LEARNING ACTIVITY

Prepare Climographs Organize students into groups of three or four. Assign each group, or have each group choose, a major city in South Asia. Have group members work together to research average monthly temperatures and precipitation levels for their cities. Each group should prepare a climograph displaying its findings. Remind groups to label their climographs with the name of the city, its location, and its elevation, and to cite the reference sources they used. Display the completed climographs, and invite students to make generalizations about South Asian climates based on the graphs. 📦

🌐 **EE2 Places and Regions: Standard 4**

NATIONAL GEOGRAPHIC **MAP STUDY**

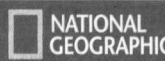

Answers

1. *northeast; dry*
2. *They bring moist ocean air from the southwest, which triggers rainfall that supports agriculture.*

Map Skills Practice

Human-Environment Interaction What are the benefits of monsoon rains for the people of Bangladesh? What are the drawbacks? *(they water the rice crop; may cause disastrous flooding)*

Culture NOTE

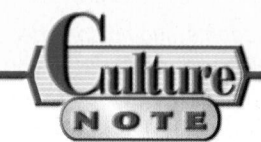

India Rice is so important to South Asian culture that the Hindi phrase for "Have you eaten?" translates literally as "Have you taken rice?"

3 ASSESS

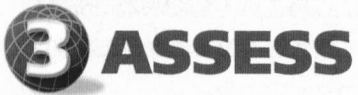

Assign Section 2 Assessment as homework or as an in-class activity.

Have students use **Interactive Tutor Self-Assessment CD-ROM.**

NATIONAL GEOGRAPHIC

MAP STUDY

South Asia: Monsoons

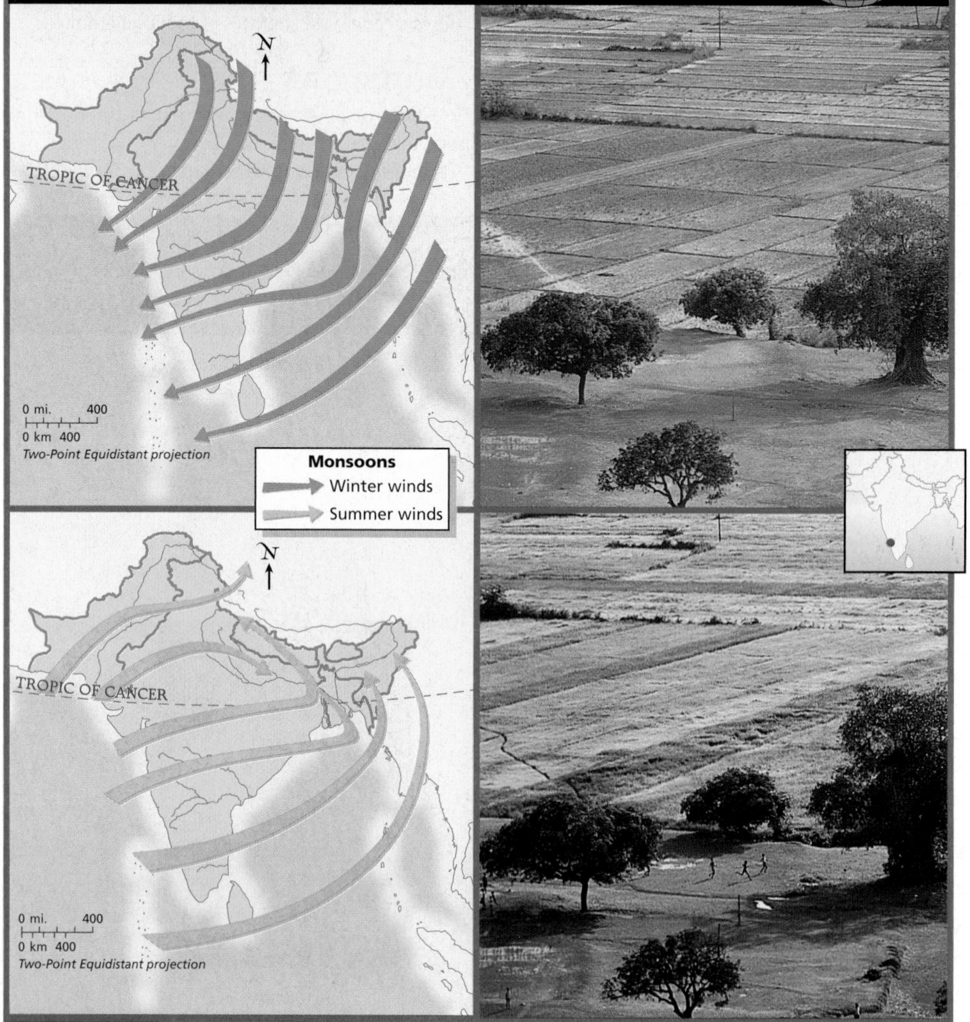
N
TROPIC OF CANCER
0 mi. 400
0 km 400
Two-Point Equidistant projection
Monsoons
Winter winds
Summer winds
N
TROPIC OF CANCER
0 mi. 400
0 km 400
Two-Point Equidistant projection

Geography Skills for Life

The same fields in west central India before (top right) and after (bottom right) the arrival of the monsoon rains reveal a stunning contrast between the dry and wet seasons.

1. **Interpreting Maps** From what direction do the winter monsoon winds come? What kind of weather do they bring?
2. **Applying Geography Skills** Describe the impact of the summer monsoon winds on South Asia.

Find NGS online map resources @ www.nationalgeographic.com/maps

CRITICAL THINKING ACTIVITY

Predicting Consequences Have students work in small groups to research recent monsoon patterns in South Asia. Ask students to identify any notable variations in the patterns (such as delays in the arrival of summer rainfall) and to list reasons suggested (such as changes in global climate patterns caused by global warming). Have groups share their findings. As a class, make a list of the possible consequences to South Asia's peoples of these changing monsoon patterns. **EE6 The Uses of Geography: Standard 18**

October to late February). These periods depend on seasonal winds called monsoons. During the cool season, dry monsoon winds blow from the north and northeast. In the hot season, warm temperatures heat the air, which rises and triggers a change in wind direction. Moist ocean air then moves in from the south and southwest, bringing monsoon rains.

Monsoon Rains

The monsoon rains are heaviest in eastern South Asia. When the rains sweep over the Ganges-Brahmaputra delta, the Himalaya block them from moving north. As a result, the rains move west to the Ganges Plain, bringing rainfall needed for crops. It is no wonder, then, that people celebrate the monsoon rains, as an Indian writer describes:

> ❝ Kulfi [a woman shopping] watched with unbelieving elation as the approaching smell of rain spiked the air like a flower, as the clouds shifted in from the east. . . . Outside, she could hear the sound of cheering from the bazaar. 'Rain, rain, rain, rain.' And in the streets, she watched the children leap like frogs, unable to keep still in their excitement. ❞
>
> Kiran Desai, *Hullabaloo in the Guava Orchard*, 1997

Economics
Natural Disasters

Both the high temperatures of the hot season and the heavy rains of the wet season are mixed blessings in South Asia. High temperatures allow farmers to produce crops, including the rice that many in Bangladesh and India depend on, year-round as long as water supplies are good. The extreme heat can result in evaporation and dried-out, nutrient-poor soils, however.

The monsoon winds also have benefits and drawbacks. Rainfall waters crops, but areas outside the path of the monsoon, such as the Deccan Plateau and western Pakistan, may receive little or no rainfall during the year. When the people of Bangladesh are planting rice, and those on the Ganges Plain are planting their winter crops, other areas are scorched by drought.

Too much rain also can be a problem. In the low-lying delta country of Bangladesh, monsoons may cause flooding that kills people and livestock, leaves thousands homeless, and ruins crops.

Another kind of weather catastrophe sometimes strikes South Asia. A cyclone is a storm with high winds and heavy rains. A 1999 cyclone struck Orissa, India, with winds of more than 160 miles per hour (257 km per hour) and waves over 20 feet (6 m) high. The storm killed nearly 10,000 people and caused more than $20 million in damages.

SECTION 2 ASSESSMENT

Checking for Understanding

1. **Define** monsoon, cyclone.

2. **Main Ideas** On a chart like the one below, fill in the names of different areas of South Asia, and then write in the type of climate and vegetation found in each area.

Location	Climate	Vegetation

Critical Thinking

3. **Analyzing Information** Analyze the reaction of South Asia's environment to the monsoons.

4. **Decision Making** Suppose that you wanted to establish a lumber business in South Asia. Where would you locate it? Why?

5. **Comparing and Contrasting** Are the effects of the very hot temperatures in much of South Asia more positive or more negative? Explain.

Analyzing Maps

6. **Region** Compare the maps of South Asia's climate and vegetation on page 576. Explain how climate and vegetation are related in the region.

Applying Geography

7. **Visiting Sri Lanka** Think about the attractions of Sri Lanka's climate and vegetation. Write a descriptive paragraph urging people to visit and enjoy Sri Lanka's natural features.

Section Quiz 23-2

Name _____ Date _____ Class _____

23 Section 2 Quiz
Climate and Vegetation

MATCHING: Match each item in Column A with an item in Column B. Write the correct letters in the blanks. (10 points each)

A	B
1. climate zone marked by grasslands and deciduous forests	A. the Sundarbans
2. swampy area in southwest Bangladesh	B. Great Indian Desert
3. climate zone marked by lush, dense vegetation	C. Deccan Plateau
4. area that lies to the east of the Indus River	D. tropical savanna
5. arid area between the Eastern and Western Ghats	E. tropical rain forest

MULTIPLE CHOICE: In each blank on the left, write the letter of the choice that best completes the statement or answers the question. (10 points each)

Reteach
Ask students to generate a topical outline of this section, using the text heads and subheads as divisions of the outline and supplying at least two details under each heading or subheading.

Enrich
Ask students to find and share examples of South Asian poetry that describes the region's climate or vegetation.

④ CLOSE

Tell students they live in a part of South Asia dependent upon monsoon rainfalls. Have them work together to create a festival celebrating the coming of the rains.

SECTION 2 ASSESSMENT ANSWERS

1. All vocabulary terms are defined in the text.

2. Chart entries should reflect text information.

3. The summer monsoon winds bring moist ocean air from the southwest, which triggers rainfall that supports agriculture in a region without much other annual precipitation. These winds can also trigger flooding. Winter monsoons bring dry air that may cause droughts.

4. Accept reasonable answers.

5. probably more negative, because of the effects on the soil (drying it out, removing nutrients) and the possibility of drought in a region with limited fresh-water access

6. Each climate has vegetation typical of its area. Highlands climate vegetation varies with elevation.

7. **Applying Geography** Paragraphs should reflect text information about Sri Lanka.

Teaching the Skill

If students made relief maps of South Asia for the Cooperative Learning Activity on page 571, have them use the maps to make a rough approximation of an elevation profile. Ask students to hold the model horizontally, level with the board and use a strong flashlight or projector lamp to cast a silhouette on the board. Have a student trace this silhouette on the board. Compare the silhouette with an elevation profile of South Asia from an atlas.

If students did not make maps, have them demonstrate the principle of elevation profiles by carefully cutting into a prepared, prebaked pizza crust or other irregularly surfaced substance to make a cross section, and then tracing the profile on paper.

Additional Practice
L1

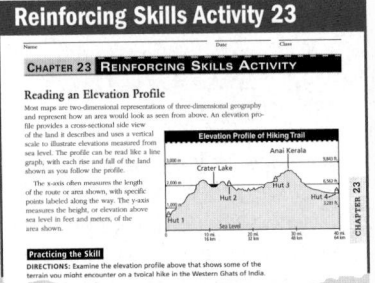

Reinforcing Skills Activity 23

GLENCOE
TECHNOLOGY

Glencoe Skillbuilder Interactive Workbook, Level 2

This interactive CD-ROM reinforces student mastery of essential social studies skills.

Reading an Elevation Profile

If you were planning a long-distance cycling expedition, you might want to check elevations of places along your route. Elevation, the vertical distance above sea level of a place or landform, can be shown in a number of ways. An elevation profile gives you elevation information in a visual form.

Learning the Skill

An elevation profile presents visual information about the elevation of a particular area, route, or landform in a two-dimensional way. The base of an elevation profile is sea level, the point from which land elevation is measured. A vertical scale measures elevation above sea level.

Reading an elevation profile is similar to reading a line graph. The vertical scale corresponds to the y-axis. In some elevation profiles, a horizontal scale, corresponding to the x-axis, measures the length of the route, area, or landform in miles or kilometers. The profile, or top edge of the landscape shown, corresponds to the line in a line graph. This line shows elevation at specific points. Some elevation profiles provide information on more than one route, area, or landform, using different colors or patterns to distinguish each profile.

Follow these steps to read an elevation profile:

- **Look at the landscape profile as a whole.** This will give you a general sense of the variations in elevation shown.

- **Find the highest and lowest points.** Use the vertical scale to find their elevations. Calculate the approximate difference in elevation between the highest and lowest points.

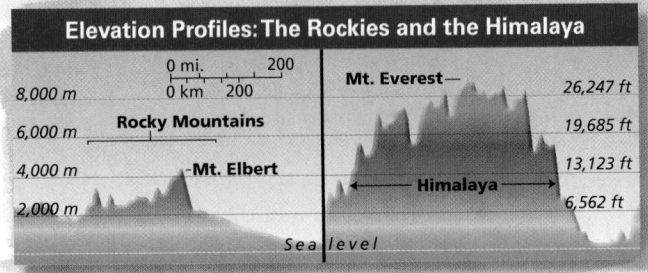

Elevation Profiles: The Rockies and the Himalaya

0 mi. — 200
0 km — 200

8,000 m
6,000 m — Rocky Mountains
4,000 m — Mt. Elbert
2,000 m

Mt. Everest — 26,247 ft
19,685 ft
Himalaya — 13,123 ft
6,562 ft

Sea level

- **Use your finger to trace the profile.** If your finger must jump up and down to follow the profile, the area has dramatic differences in elevation.

- **If more than one area or landform is profiled, follow the procedure for each profile.** Then use the information to compare the profiled areas.

Practicing the Skill

Study the elevation profile contrasting the Rocky Mountains with the Himalaya. Then answer these questions.

1. What is the highest peak in the Rocky Mountains? About how many feet above sea level does it rise?

2. What is the approximate elevation of the highest peak in the Himalaya?

3. What is the approximate difference in elevation between the highest point in the Rocky Mountains and

the highest point in the Himalaya?

4. Which range contains the greater variation in elevation?

5. Which range stretches over a greater distance?

6. What does the elevation profile reveal about the relative elevations of these mountain ranges?

Applying the Skill

Use a map to choose a bicycle route across your state. Identify several key points along your route, and check the elevations for each one. Then create an elevation profile of your route. Note the highest and lowest points on your profile. Where would your bike ride be easiest? Most difficult?

Go To The Glencoe Skillbuilder Interactive Workbook, Level 2 provides instruction and practice in key social studies skills.

ANSWERS TO PRACTICING THE SKILL

1. Mount Elbert; 14,433 feet
2. 29,035 feet (8,850 m)
3. 14,595 feet
4. Himalaya
5. Rockies

6. While the variations between the high and low points of the Himalaya are greater than those of the Rockies, overall, the peaks of the Himalaya are closer to the same height.

CHAPTER 23 SUMMARY & STUDY GUIDE

SECTION 1 — The Land (pp. 569–574)

Terms to Know
- subcontinent
- alluvial plain
- mica

Key Points
- The landforms of South Asia include mountains, plateaus, plains, and islands.
- South Asia has three great river systems—the Indus, Brahmaputra, and Ganges—and the world's longest alluvial plain.
- South Asia has few significant oil reserves, but has substantial mineral deposits, including iron ore and mica.

Organizing Your Notes
Create an outline using the format below to help you organize your notes for this section.

South Asia's Land
I. A Separate Land
II. A Land of Great Variety
A. The Himalaya
B. Other Northern Landforms

SECTION 2 — Climate and Vegetation (pp. 575–579)

Terms to Know
- monsoon
- cyclone

Key Points
- South Asia has highlands, tropical, and desert climates.
- The monsoon is a seasonal change in wind direction that brings heavy rainfall to much of South Asia from June to September.
- South Asia's vegetation is affected by elevation, rainfall, and human activity.

Organizing Your Notes
Use a table like the one below to help you organize the notes you took as you read this section.

Climate Region	Vegetation	Country or Area
tropical rain forest	ebony trees, lush vines, orchids	

▶ Along the Ganges, Varanasi, India

Chapter 23 🌐 581

Using the Chapter 23 Summary & Study Guide

Use the Chapter 23 Summary & Study Guide to preview, review, condense, or reteach the chapter.

Preview/Review

🔊 **Vocabulary PuzzleMaker CD-ROM** reinforces "Terms to Know."

💿 **Interactive Tutor Self-Assessment CD-ROM** provides a review of Chapter 23 content.

Condense

Have students read the Chapter 23 Summary & Study Guide.

🔊 Chapter 23 Audio Program

📁 Chapter 23 Guided Reading Activities

Reteach

📁 Chapter 23 Reteaching Activities (Spanish also available)

📁 Chapter 23 Reading Essentials and Study Guides

GLENCOE TECHNOLOGY

NATIONAL GEOGRAPHIC
WORLD REGIONS VIDEO PROGRAM

Unit 8, South Asia
The following segments enhance the study of this unit:
- **Monsoon**
- **Sherpas of Nepal**
- **Bollywood**

CHAPTER CULMINATING ACTIVITY

Drawing Conclusions Ask students to predict what would have happened if the collision of the South Asian landmass with the continent of Asia had never occurred. In an essay have students explain how South Asia's physical geography would be different, and how those differences would affect the region. (*Possible conclusions: Himalaya would not have formed, great rivers would have no source, rains would not be diverted to Ganges Plain, all of South Asia would resemble today's Deccan Plateau, population might be greatly reduced, some of the area might become largely desert.*) 🌐 **EE3 Physical Systems: Standards 7, 8**

NOTE: This activity may be completed separately or you may wish students to incorporate it in their GeoJournals.

ASSESSMENT & ACTIVITIES

CHAPTER 23

GLENCOE TECHNOLOGY

Use *MindJogger Videoquiz* to review the Chapter 23 content.

Reviewing Key Terms

1. d
2. e
3. c
4. a
5. b

Reviewing Facts

SECTION 1

1. many different landforms, climates, and types of vegetation

2. By separating India into distinct northern and southern parts, the Vindhya Range has given rise to two different Indian cultures.

3. The major rivers cross international boundaries. Access to freshwater is limited in much of the region, and most rainfall is limited to seasonal monsoons.

SECTION 2

4. on the Deccan Plateau, and surrounding the Great Indian Desert except on the coast

5. late February to June (hot), June or July until September (wet), October to late February (cool)

6. being directly in the path of the monsoon rains, with no mountains to block them

Reviewing Key Terms

Write the letter of the key term that best matches each definition below.

a. subcontinent   d. monsoons
b. alluvial plain   e. cyclone
c. mica

1. seasonal winds

2. a storm with high winds and heavy rains

3. a layered mineral used to make electrical components

4. a very large, distinct landmass that is part of a continent

5. an area of rich, fertile soil found along a river

Reviewing Facts

SECTION 1

1. Why might the region of South Asia be referred to as "a land of great variety"?

2. How have the mountains of the Vindhya Range affected the people of India?

3. Why is the management of water resources important in South Asia?

SECTION 2

4. Where can you find a steppe climate region in South Asia?

5. When do the three seasons found in much of South Asia occur, and how would you describe each?

6. What factors enable South Asia's rain forests to thrive?

Critical Thinking

1. Identifying Cause and Effect In what way are the Himalaya responsible for the richness of the soil in the northern plains of the Indian subcontinent?

2. Comparing and Contrasting What are the advantages and disadvantages of the monsoons to South Asia?

3. Predicting Consequences Using a web diagram like the one below, show the consequences to the people of South Asia of possible weather conditions. Then choose one consequence and describe it in detail.

South Asia's Weather

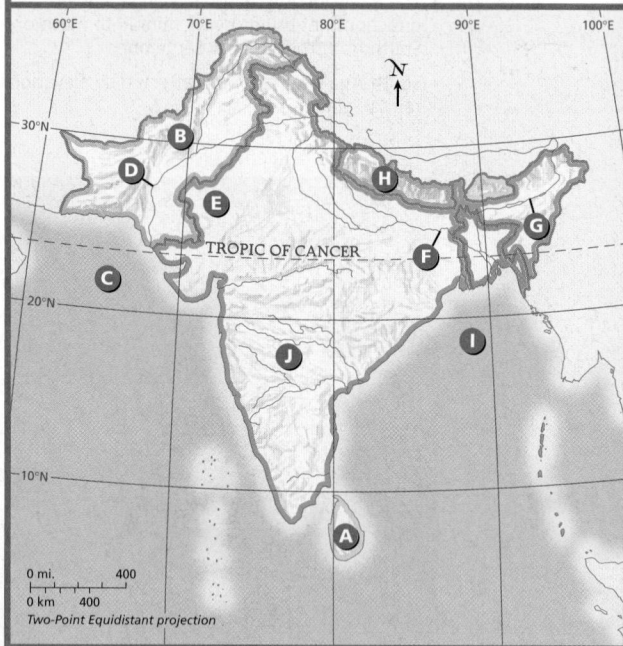

Locating Places
South Asia: Physical-Political Geography

Match the letters on the map with the places and physical features of South Asia. Write your answers on a sheet of paper.

1. Arabian Sea   5. Sri Lanka   8. Great Indian
2. Bay of Bengal   6. Himalaya   Desert
3. Ganges River   7. Brahmaputra   9. Pakistan
4. Deccan Plateau   River   10. Indus River

Critical Thinking

1. The Himalaya block the summer monsoon winds and redirect the rainfall to the plains.

2. The summer monsoon winds bring moist ocean air from the southwest, which triggers rainfall that supports agriculture. These winds can also trigger flooding. Winter monsoons bring dry air that may cause droughts.

3. Webs should factor in different climates, including varying amounts of rainfall.

Locating Places

1. C	**3.** F	**5.** A	**7.** G	**9.** B
2. I	**4.** J	**6.** H	**8.** E	**10.** D

Using the Regional Atlas

1. the Himalaya
2. at the northernmost point along the border, in the Hindu Kush

Using the Regional Atlas

Refer to the Regional Atlas on pages 560–563.

1. **Location** What mountains form the border between East Asia and South Asia?

2. **Place** Compare the political map with the population density map. Where is the area of lowest average population density along the India-Pakistan border?

Thinking Like a Geographer

Analyze the effects of physical geographic patterns on population in South Asia. What patterns favor high population density? Low population density?

Problem-Solving Activity

Contemporary Issues Case Study When natural disasters strike populated areas, their impact is worse in areas of high population density. In a group, research a recent natural disaster in South Asia, such as the 1999 cyclone in Orissa or the 1998 flood in Bangladesh. Find out the causes of the disaster and how it affected the area's population and natural resources. What efforts were taken following the disaster? Then, focusing on one of these efforts, present your group's findings to the class.

GeoJournal

Descriptive Writing Using your GeoJournal, write a description about the ways South Asians have adapted to or modified their environment. Then compare human-environment interaction in South Asia with that in your state and local community.

Technology Activity

Using an Electronic Spreadsheet
Use a spreadsheet program to organize information about elevations in South Asia. List at least six South Asian countries in the left column of a spreadsheet. Use a world atlas to find the highest point in each country. Then list the heights in the second column of the spreadsheet. Use the graphics feature of the program to make a bar graph to compare heights.

Standardized Test Practice

Study the elevation profile. Then choose the best answer for the following multiple-choice questions. If you have trouble answering the questions, use the process of elimination to narrow your choices.

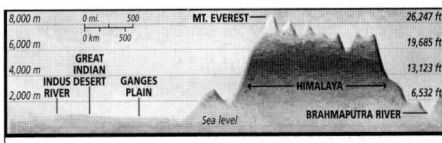

1. About how much higher is Mt. Everest than the Indus River?

   A 2,500 feet   C 25,000 feet
   B 19,000 feet   D 1,900 feet

Test-Taking Tip Note that the question asks for the difference in height between the two locations. You can arrive at the answer by subtracting.

2. Based on elevation, which locations on the profile would be unsuited for farming?

   F Ganges Plain
   G Great Indian Desert
   H Mt. Everest and the Great Indian Desert
   J Mt. Everest

Test-Taking Tip Read the question carefully. The phrase *based on elevation* is important. The Great Indian Desert is unsuited to farming, but not because of its elevation. Once you apply the standard asked for in the question, it is easy to eliminate wrong answers.

? CHAPTER BONUS TEST QUESTION

Which of South Asia's natural resources hold the most potential for further economic development? *(hydroelectric power, offshore petroleum deposits, natural gas, uranium)*

Thinking Like a Geographer

high population density: rivers, alluvial plains, coasts, islands; low population density: high mountains, desert, dense rain forests

Problem-Solving Activity

After groups have made their presentations, have students work together as a class to evaluate the success of the countries' post-disaster efforts.

GeoJournal

Students should describe human activities related to land/resource use and the building of dams, roads, and human settlements.

Technology Activity

Check students' spreadsheets and bar graphs for accuracy.

1 FOCUS

Ask students to recall what they know about the river cycle. **Ask: What factors influence the volume and flow speed of a river?** *(age of the river, distance from the source or mouth, width of the stream, differences in elevation along the course, amount of rainfall in the area, quantity of suspended material carried in the water)* **Why might people need to be able to calculate the volume and flow speed of a river or stream?** *(agriculture, flood planning, monitoring municipal water supplies, planning for public works programs, determining whether the stream is navigable)*

2 TEACH

L1 Human-Environment Interaction

Explain to students that scientists have developed sophisticated means of measuring the velocity and volume of rivers and streams, but that simple, low-tech methods have been used by farmers, sailors, and surveyors for centuries. **Ask: Why might it be important to know how to measure these factors without the use of sophisticated technology?** *(Understanding the principles involved helps people better interpret the data received from technology. In emergency situations, such as imminent danger from flooding, or in field situations in developing countries or remote areas, technology may be unavailable.)*

Geography
Lab Activity

River and Stream Speed

▲ *Flow calculations help people make effective use of river systems.*

Measuring the speed of a river or stream is the first step in determining the river's flow—the volume of water discharged over a period of time. Flow is calculated by multiplying the velocity, or speed, of a river (measured in feet or meters per second) by the area of the cross section of the river (a cutting made across, measured in square feet or square meters). Further calculations will yield the average flow in cubic feet per second or in gallons per day.

Why measure the flow of a river or stream? This information can help water management engineers plan for emergencies such as drought or flooding.

Natural flow varies throughout the year, especially in South Asia, where seasonal weather patterns and human interaction with the environment affect the great river systems.

1 Materials

- Tape measure
- Ball of string or twine
- 4 wooden dowels or sticks
- Several medium-sized oranges or large craft sticks painted in bright colors
- Stopwatch
- Writing materials

2 Procedures

In this activity, you will use a simple method to measure the approximate speed (velocity) at which water moves in a stream.

1. Take all materials to a local stream that is no more than a few yards wide and is relatively free from vegetation and rocks.

2. Set up the measuring marks. Fix a dowel or stick in the ground, and tie one end of the string to it. Then toss the ball of string to a student on the opposite bank of the stream. Have the second student pull the string taut, tie it to another dowel fixed in the ground, and cut the end of the string. This will be Mark 1.

3. Use the tape measure to determine a point 10 feet (3 m) downstream from Mark 1. Insert another dowel at this point, and repeat the process of stringing a line across the stream, parallel to Mark 1. This will be Mark 2. If the stream you are measuring is very shallow or slow-moving, set the two lines only 5 (1.5 m) feet apart. If the stream is very fast, set the two lines 15 (4.6 m) feet apart.

GEOGRAPHY IN THE REAL WORLD

Calculating Instream Flow Because flow rates and volumes are so important to river science, ecology, and economy—from recreation to habitat protection to hydroelectric power to the resolution of local and international conflicts—there have been continued efforts to improve measurement technology. Before the advent of the Acoustic Doppler Current Profiler (ADCP), scientists used a Venturi flume, named for the inventor Giovanni Battista Venturi. A Venturi flume is a short tube with a constricted interior. When water enters the tube, its flow is constricted. By measuring the resulting drop in pressure and increase in velocity, scientists can use formulas to calculate the stream's velocity.

🌐 **EE6 The Uses of Geography: Standard 18**

4. Position an observer at Mark 1. Position another observer with the stopwatch at Mark 2. Have a third student go to a point several feet upstream and toss an orange or a painted craft stick into the water.

5. When the object crosses under the string at Mark 1, the first observer stationed there yells "Go!" and the second observer starts the stopwatch. When the object crosses under the string at Mark 2, the second observer stops the stopwatch.

6. Record the time, in seconds, that it took the object to pass from Mark 1 to Mark 2.

7. Repeat the process several times, recording the elapsed seconds. Calculate the average elapsed time in seconds. Then divide the distance in feet or meters between Mark 1 and Mark 2 by the average elapsed time. The result is the average stream speed, measured in feet or meters per second.

8. Note the weather for the days preceding your measurements. Did it rain, or were the days sunny? Why might this information be important?

3 ▸ Lab Report

1. Did you expect to find a faster or slower average stream speed, or were your findings consistent with what you expected?

2. How much variation in elapsed time did you observe when taking repeated measurements at the same site?

3. If you were asked to measure the speed of a river 100 yards (91 m) wide, how would you adapt this activity?

4. **Predicting Consequences** How might your measurement change if you dammed off the right half of the stream in the 10-foot (3-m) span you measured?

4 ▸ Find Out More

Contact a public works department for information on how flow calculations are used in your area (possibilities include environmental management, flood control, recreational use, agricultural irrigation, and urban water resource management). Choose one of these uses to research. Share your findings with the class.

Did You Know? Scientists have used the Acoustic Doppler Current Profiler (ADCP) to measure the flow of the Brahmaputra River in Bangladesh. The Brahmaputra often has severe floods. The ADCP allows scientists to measure river flow safely and accurately during flood conditions. The ADCP attaches to a boat and is connected to a computer that computes the river's flow, using data about depth, current, and direction.

◂ *Flow calculations are used to help design the irrigation systems that make South Asian desert lands able to be farmed.*

 **ASSESS**

Have students answer the **Lab Report** questions on page 585.

 CLOSE

Have students complete the **Find Out More** activity and summarize their findings.

🌐 Meeting National Standards

Geography for Life
The following standards are met in the Student Edition feature:

EE1 The World in Spatial Terms:
   Standard 1
EE3 Physical Systems:
   Standard 3
EE5 Environment and Society:
   Standards 14, 15
EE6 The Uses of Geography:
   Standard 18

ANSWERS TO LAB REPORT

1. Answers depend on student expectations.

2. Answers depend on the volume of the stream, force of the current, and other factors.

3. One possible method is to use observers stationed at various points instead of string markers and to toss a larger, more visible object (such as a brightly colored beach ball or pool float) from a bridge into the river upstream from the first observer.

4. Narrowing a stream generally increases the rate of flow. If the point you are observing is near the mouth of the stream, however, large quantities of suspended material may actually slow the rate of flow.

CHAPTER 24

PLANNING GUIDE

NOTE: The following materials may be used when teaching Chapter 24. Section-level support materials are shown at point-of-use in the margins of the Teacher Wraparound Edition.

TEACHING TRANSPARENCIES

L2 Unit 8 Map Overlay Transparencies

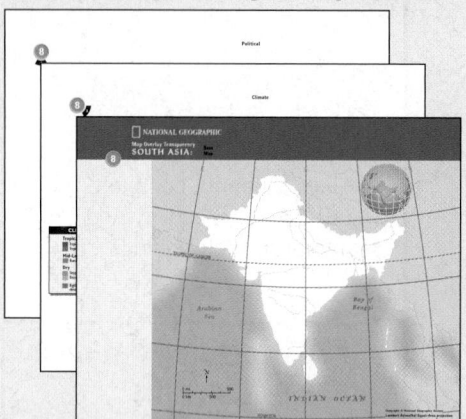

L2 Political Map Transparency 8

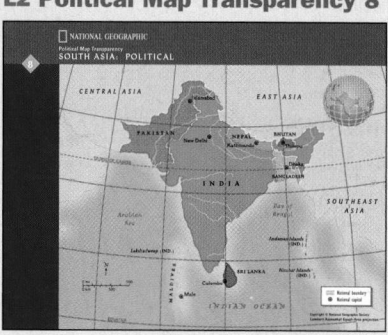

GEOGRAPHIC LITERACY

Focus on Geography Literacy

APPLICATION AND ENRICHMENT

L3 Enrichment Activity 24

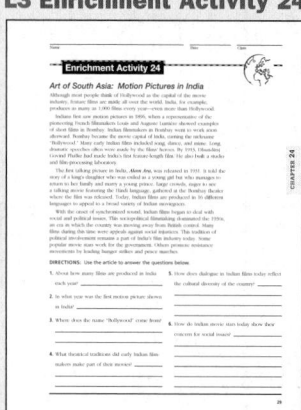

REVIEW AND REINFORCEMENT

L1 Vocabulary Activity 24 L1 Reinforcing L1 Reteaching Activity 24
Skills Activity 24

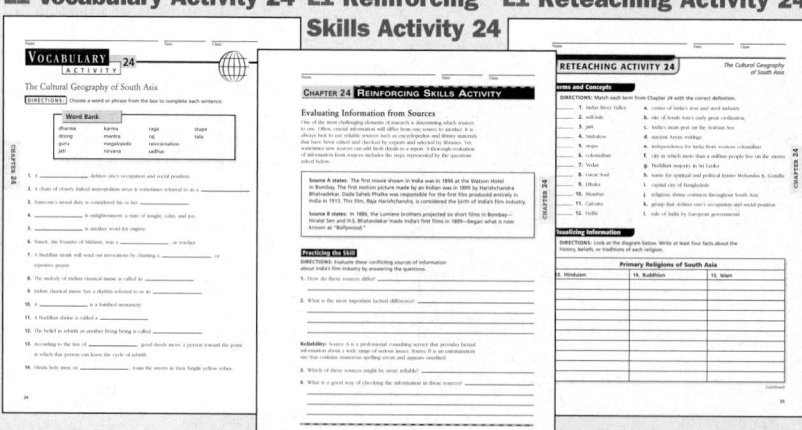

ASSESSMENT

L2 Chapter 24 Test Form A

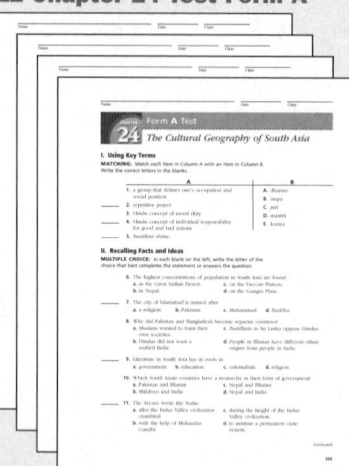

L2 Chapter 24 Test Form B

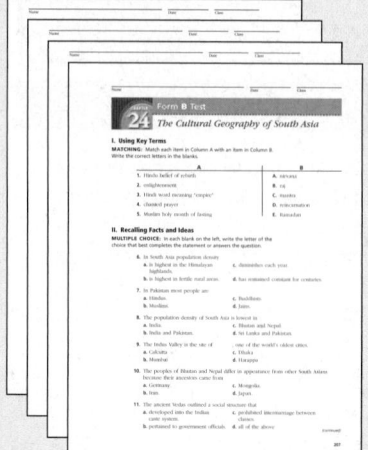

L1/ELL Performance Assessment Activity 24

ExamView® Pro Testmaker

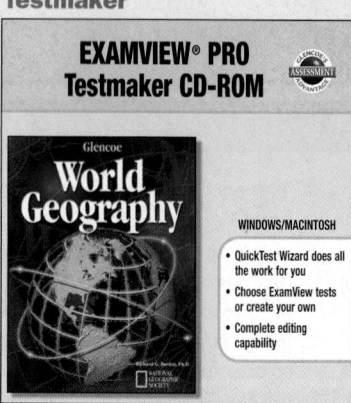

586A

SPANISH RESOURCES

The following Spanish language materials are available in the Spanish Resources binder:

- 📁 Spanish Vocabulary Activities
- 📁 Spanish Guided Reading Activities
- 📁 Spanish Reteaching Activities
- 📁 Spanish Summaries
- 📁 Spanish Quizzes and Tests
- 📁 Spanish Reading Essentials and Study Guide

MULTIMEDIA

- 📼 World Regions Video
- 📼 MindJogger Videoquiz
- 💿 Vocabulary PuzzleMaker CD-ROM
- 💿 Interactive Tutor Self-Assessment CD-ROM
- 💿 ExamView® Pro Testmaker CD-ROM
- 💿 Audio Program
- 💿 TeacherWorks CD-ROM
- 💿 Interactive Student Edition CD-ROM
- 💿 Glencoe Skillbuilder Interactive Workbook CD-ROM, Level 2
- 💿 Presentation Plus! CD-ROM

Timesaving Tools

TeacherWorks™ — All-In-One Planner and Resource Center

- **Interactive Teacher Edition** Access your Teacher Wraparound Edition and your classroom resources with a few easy clicks.
- **Interactive Lesson Planner** Planning has never been easier! Organize your week, month, semester, or year with all the lesson helps you need to make teaching creative, timely, and relevant.

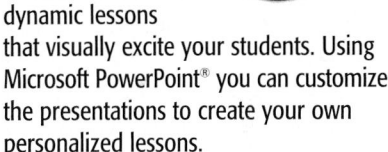

Use Glencoe's **Presentation Plus!** multimedia teacher tool to easily present dynamic lessons that visually excite your students. Using Microsoft PowerPoint® you can customize the presentations to create your own personalized lessons.

GEOGRAPHY Online

Use our Web site for additional resources. All essential content is covered in the Student Edition.

You and your students can visit geography.glencoe.com, the Web site companion to *Glencoe World Geography*. This innovative integration of electronic and print media offers your students a wealth of opportunities. The student text directs students to the Web site for the following options:

- Chapter Overviews
- Student Activities
- Self-Check Quizzes
- Textbook Updates

Answers are provided for you in the "Web Activity Lesson Plan." Additional Web resources and Interactive Tutor puzzles are also available.

▶ Additional Glencoe Teacher Support

- Teaching Strategies for the Geography Classroom (including Block Scheduling Pacing Guides)
- Graphic Organizer Transparencies Strategies and Activities
- Outline Map Resource Book
- Reading in the Content Area

PLANNING GUIDE

SECTION RESOURCES

Daily Objectives	Reproducible Resources	Multimedia Resources

SECTION 1 Population Patterns

1. Explain how the peoples of South Asia reflect diversity.
2. Describe how South Asia's large population is distributed.
3. Discuss how life in the region's cities compares with life in traditional rural villages.

Reproducible Lesson Plan 24-1
Daily Lecture Notes 24-1
Guided Reading Activity 24-1*
Reading Essentials and Study Guide 24-1*
Section Quiz 24-1*

Daily Focus Skills Transparency 24-1
Political Map Transparency 8
Unit 8 Map Overlay Transparencies
Interactive Tutor Self-Assessment CD-ROM
ExamView® Pro Testmaker CD-ROM*
Presentation Plus! CD-ROM

SECTION 2 History and Government

1. Explain where South Asia's first civilization developed.
2. Name the two major world religions that originated in South Asia.
3. Examine how invasions and conquests shaped South Asia.
4. Discuss what types of challenges South Asian countries face today.

Reproducible Lesson Plan 24-2
Daily Lecture Notes 24-2
Guided Reading Activity 24-2*
Reading Essentials and Study Guide 24-2*
Section Quiz 24-2*

Daily Focus Skills Transparency 24-2
Political Map Transparency 8
Unit 8 Map Overlay Transparencies
Interactive Tutor Self-Assessment CD-ROM
ExamView® Pro Testmaker CD-ROM*
Presentation Plus! CD-ROM

SECTION 3 Cultures and Lifestyles

1. Identify ways the region's linguistic and religious diversity is reflected in the lives of South Asia's peoples.
2. Describe South Asia's contributions to the arts.
3. List ways South Asian countries are meeting challenges to improve the quality of life of the region's people.
4. Point out how distinctive celebrations reflect the rich cultural diversity of South Asia.

Reproducible Lesson Plan 24-3
Vocabulary Activity 24*
Daily Lecture Notes 24-3
Guided Reading Activity 24-3*
Reading Essentials and Study Guide 24-3*
Reteaching Activity 24*
Reinforcing Skills Activity 24
Section Quiz 24-3*

Daily Focus Skills Transparency 24-3
Unit 8 Map Overlay Transparencies
Vocabulary PuzzleMaker CD-ROM
Interactive Tutor Self-Assessment CD-ROM
ExamView® Pro Testmaker CD-ROM*
Presentation Plus! CD-ROM

Blackline Master   Software   Videocassette   *Also available in Spanish
Transparency   CD-ROM   DVD

OUT OF TIME? Assign the Chapter 24 **Reading Essentials and Study Guide.**

Block Schedule

Activities that are particularly suited to use within the block scheduling framework are identified throughout this chapter by the following designation:

KEY TO ABILITY LEVELS

Teaching strategies have been coded for various learning styles and abilities.

L1 **BASIC** activities for all students
L2 **AVERAGE** activities for average to above-average students
L3 **CHALLENGING** activities for above-average students
ELL **ENGLISH LANGUAGE LEARNER** activities

Teacher to Teacher

Michael Crull
Jay School Corporation
Dunkirk, IN

An International Trade Fair

Have students simulate an international trade fair. The school band and choir can perform, and parents, community leaders, and school board members can be invited to attend the trade fair.

Organize students into groups, with one group for each of the seven South Asian countries. If there are more than seven groups, the extra groups may focus on other topics such as an ethnic conflict or an environmental issue. Each group will make a country display using graphs, charts, and pictures. Each group also should make an artifact or a food that represents their country and prepare a presentation that tells about the language, government, social groups, religion, economic aspects, food, and other information. They should also report about the trade relationship between their country and the United States.

Make passport booklets for students with pages for each country. The pages should have room for the students to answer questions about each country. Enlist student input to select the questions. Students will find answers as they visit each country's display.

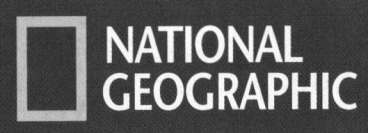

TEACHER'S CORNER

Index to National Geographic Magazine:

The following articles may be used for research relating to this chapter:

- "Rana Tharu Women," by Debra Kellner, September 2000.
- "Indus Civilization," by Mike Edwards, June 2000.

National Geographic Society Products:

To order the following products for use with this chapter, call National Geographic Society at 1-800-368-2728.

- *Asia* (Video)
- *National Geographic Desk Reference* (Book)
- *National Geographic Atlas of the World, Seventh Edition* (Book)

NGS ONLINE

Access National Geographic's Web site for current events, activities, links, interactive features, and archives.
www.nationalgeographic.com

MEETING SPECIAL NEEDS

In addition to the Differentiated Instruction strategies found in each section, the following resources are also suitable for your special needs students:

- *ExamView® Pro Testmaker CD-ROM* allows teachers to tailor tests by reducing answer choices.
- The *Audio Program* includes the entire narrative of the student edition so that less-proficient readers can listen to the words as they read them.
- The *Reading Essentials and Study Guide* provides the same content as the student edition but is written two grade levels below the textbook.
- *Guided Reading Activities* give less-proficient readers point-by-point instructions to increase comprehension as they read each textbook section.
- *Enrichment Activities* include a stimulating collection of readings and activities for gifted and talented students.

Meeting National Standards

Geography For Life

The following standards are highlighted in Chapter 24:

Section 1 EE2 Places and Regions: Standard 4
EE4 Human Systems:
Standards 9, 10, 11, 13

Section 2 EE2 Places and Regions: Standard 4
EE4 Human Systems:
Standards 10, 13
EE6 The Uses of Geography:
Standard 17

Section 3 EE4 Human Systems: Standard 10
EE6 The Uses of Geography:
Standard 18

Local Objectives

_____

_____

Chapter Objectives

1. Describe South Asia's population profile, density, and distribution.

2. Identify key developments in the history of the region and its countries' governments.

3. Discuss the role of religion, education, health care, and the arts in South Asia.

GLENCOE TECHNOLOGY

Use *MindJogger Videoquiz* to preview the Chapter 24 content.

GeoJournal

For access to additional information on the cultural geography of South Asia go to www.nationalgeographic.com (See Teacher pages in front for strategies for using journals in the geography classroom.)

GEOGRAPHY Online

Introduce students to chapter content and key terms by having them access **Chapter Overview 24** at geography.glencoe.com

FOLDABLES™
Study Organizer

Dinah Zike's Foldables are three-dimensional, interactive graphic organizers that help students practice basic writing skills, review key vocabulary terms, and identify main ideas. Have students complete the Foldable activity in the *Dinah Zike's Reading and Study Skills Foldables* booklet.

CHAPTER 24

The Cultural Geography of South Asia

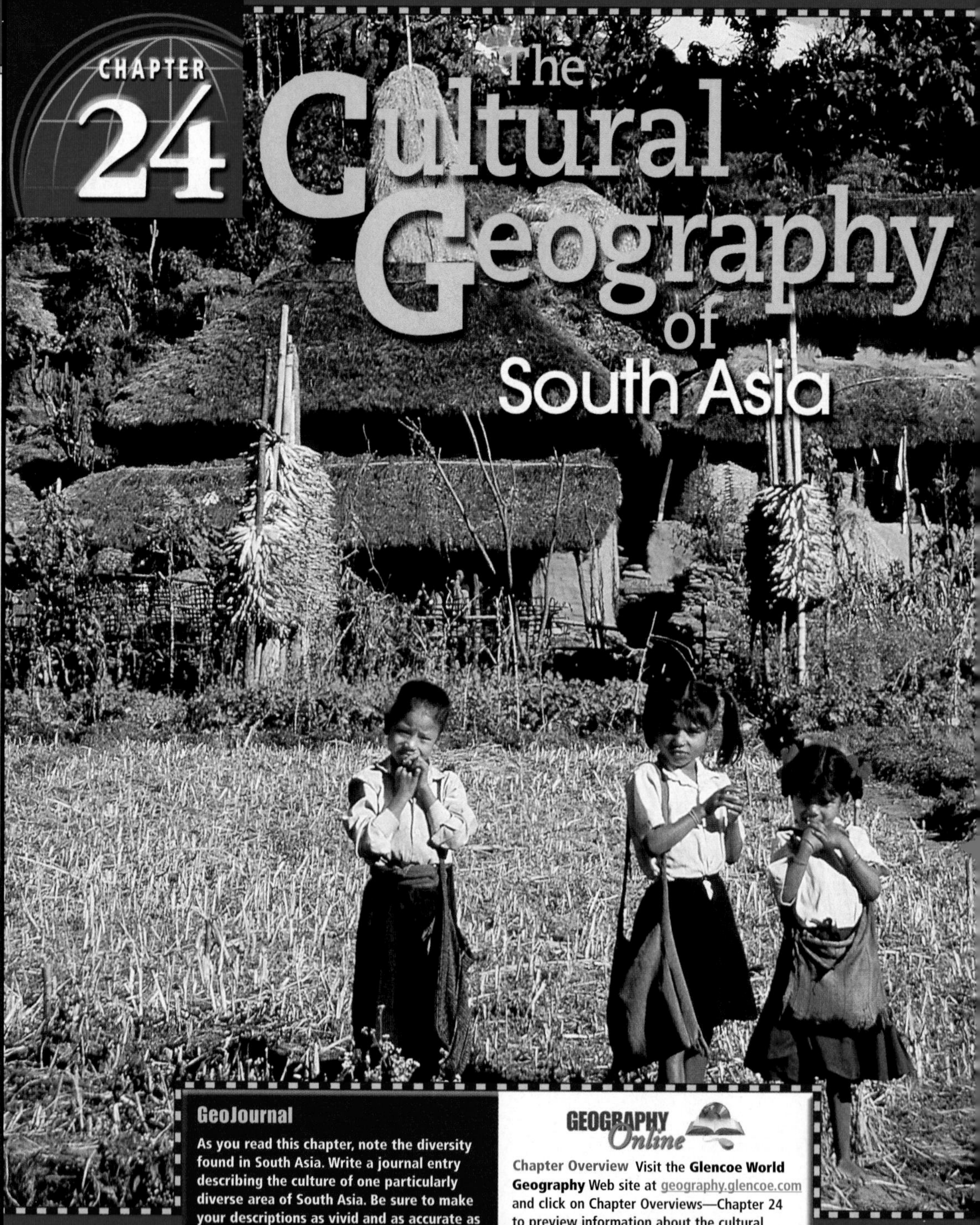

GeoJournal

As you read this chapter, note the diversity found in South Asia. Write a journal entry describing the culture of one particularly diverse area of South Asia. Be sure to make your descriptions as vivid and as accurate as possible.

GEOGRAPHY Online

Chapter Overview Visit the **Glencoe World Geography** Web site at geography.glencoe.com and click on Chapter Overviews—Chapter 24 to preview information about the cultural geography of the region.

ABOUT THE PHOTO

Visual Instruction The Pokhara Valley in Nepal lies near the Annapurna mountain range. At one time the city of Pokhara was an important stop on the trade route between Tibet and central Nepal. Because Pokhara is located at 2,950 feet (900 m) above sea level, it has a relatively mild climate—comfortable in winter, cooled by mountain breezes in the summer, although it is still hot. **Ask: What kinds of activities do you think these children might enjoy?** (Accept students' suggestions. Then explain that Pokhara is near several lakes, a waterfall, an impressive limestone cave, and of course, the Himalaya. The city of about 100,000 people also has a historic bazaar area, impressive Hindu and Buddhist temples, and a museum.) ⬤ **EE2 Places and Regions: Standard 4**

Guide to Reading

Consider What You Know

India is South Asia's most populous country—with more than one billion people—and the second most populous country in the world. Do you know which country has more people than India?

Reading Strategy

Categorizing Complete a graphic organizer similar to the one below by describing India's main cities.

City	Description
Mumbai (Bombay)	
Kolkata (Calcutta)	
Delhi	

Read to Find Out

- How do the peoples of South Asia reflect diversity?
- How is South Asia's large population distributed?
- How does life in the region's cities compare with life in traditional rural villages?

Terms to Know

- *jati*
- *megalopolis*

Places to Locate

- Islamabad
- Mumbai (Bombay)
- Kolkata (Calcutta)
- Delhi
- Dhaka
- Karachi

Schoolchildren in Pokhara, Nepal

Population Patterns

NATIONAL GEOGRAPHIC

A Geographic View

Scenes Along the Brahmaputra

[On a side stream of the Brahmaputra] there were men in long skirts, the descendants of ancient Aryans and Arab, Turkish, and Burmese traders.... Nearby, children bathed, men walked down planks with wicker baskets of coconuts, melons, and squash.... Three women fixed dinner in metal pots over a fire. The smell of mango, diesel fumes, and spices filled the air.

Hindu temple near the Brahmaputra, India

—Jere Van Dyk, "Long Journey of the Brahmaputra," National Geographic, November 1988

Imagine taking a boat down the Brahmaputra River. You see great cities and small villages. You meet travelers on steep mountains and talk with families tending green rice fields. Life along the Brahmaputra reflects the color and diversity of all South Asia. In this section you will get a sense of that color and diversity as you learn about the peoples of this region.

Human Characteristics

One of the most significant characteristics of South Asia's population is its size. Over 1.4 billion people—more than one-fifth of the world's population—live in the region. Size is not the only distinguishing factor of South Asia's population, however. Diversity—the complex mix of religious, social, and cultural influences—is reflected in this region as in almost no other area on Earth. The peoples of the region speak hundreds of languages and practice several major religions. The region's diversity has fostered both tolerance and conflict.

Chapter 24 ⬤ 587

① FOCUS

Section Overview

This section discusses the composition, density, and distribution of South Asia's diverse population.

BELLRINGER
Skillbuilder Activity

- Project transparency and have students answer questions.
- Available as blackline master.

Daily Focus Skills Transparency 24-1

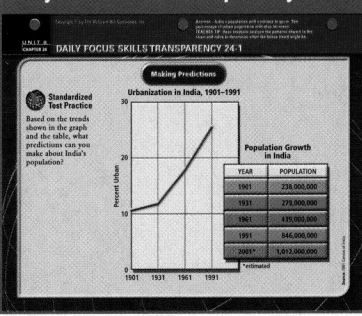

Guide to Reading

Consider What You Know
Answer *China*

Reading Strategy
Answers Mumbai: *largest city in India and main port, population over 18.1 million, leading industrial, financial, and filmmaking center;* Kolkata: *port city, center of India's iron and steel industries;* Delhi: *India's third largest city, part of megalopolis, part old city and part new*

Preteaching Vocabulary
Write the word *megalopolis* on the board. Underline *megalo*, and explain that it is a Greek prefix meaning "very large or gigantic." Tell students the Greek word *polis* means "city." Ask volunteers to name U.S. cities that include this word in their name. *(Indianapolis, Minneapolis, Annapolis)*

L1 Chart

Have students work together to chart on the board the ethnic diversity of South Asia. Have students list two identifying characteristics of each ethnic group and state where each ethnic group is located.

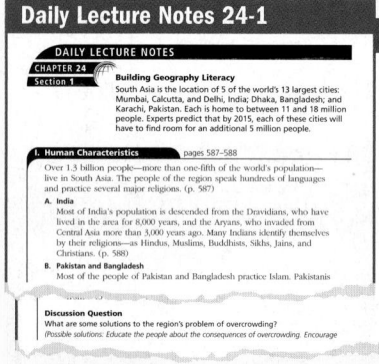

Daily Lecture Notes 24-1

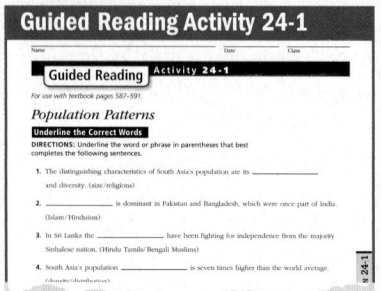

NATIONAL GEOGRAPHIC World Explorer

Answer
Tenzing Norgay

More About the Photo
"Sherpa" is the Westernized version of the word *Shar-wa*, one of the 18 clan names of the Sherpa people.

L1/ELL

Guided Reading Activity 24-1

India

India's population includes people from diverse groups. The largest number of Indians are descended from the Dravidians, who have lived in the south of India for 8,000 years, and the Aryans, who invaded from Central Asia more than 3,000 years ago. Also contributing to India's population mix are the descendants of British and Portuguese colonists as well as recent refugees from Tibet and Sri Lanka. Many Indians traditionally identify themselves by their religion—as Hindus, Muslims, Buddhists, Sikhs, Jains, or Christians. Hindus also identify themselves by a *jati*, a group that defines one's occupation and social position.

Pakistan and Bangladesh

Two South Asian countries—Pakistan and Bangladesh—were once part of British India. Pakistan and, later, Bangladesh became separate countries because of their distinct Muslim and ethnic heritages. More than 90 percent of the people of Pakistan and Bangladesh practice Islam. **Islamabad**, Pakistan's capital, is even named for the faith. This religious uniformity overshadows other cultural differences in Pakistan, which has at least five main ethnic groups. In Bangladesh most people are Bengali, an ethnic background they share with some of their Hindu neighbors in the Indian state of Bengal.

History
Sri Lanka's Sinhalese and Tamils

Sri Lanka has two main groups, which are fiercely divided along ethnic and religious lines. They speak different languages and live in different parts of the island country. The Buddhist Sinhalese are the majority and control the government. The other group—Hindu Tamils—have been fighting for an independent Tamil state in northern Sri Lanka since the early 1980s. Clashes between government forces and violent separatist groups like the Tamil Tigers have made this once peaceful, green island a war zone. Since 1984, more than 100,000 Sri Lankans have been killed or have disappeared. Almost a million people have been driven from their homes by ethnic violence—one of the largest such numbers ever recorded. The violence has disrupted the area's economy and demoralized its people.

Bhutan and Nepal

The peoples of Bhutan and Nepal differ in appearance from other South Asians, because their ancestors came from Mongolia. Bhutan's population is fairly evenly divided between the Bhote (BO•tay) people and those of Tibetan ancestry. Nepal, once a federation of tiny kingdoms, is home to a complex mix of ethnic groups. The group most familiar to people outside Nepal are the Sherpas, who are known for their mountaineering skills. One Sherpa, Tenzing Norgay, made the first successful ascent of Mount Everest with Sir Edmund Hillary in 1953.

Population Density and Distribution

With 814 people per square mile (314 people per sq. km), South Asia's population density is almost seven times the world average. Population growth rates in South Asia have traditionally been high, although educational and economic assistance efforts have slowed population growth

NATIONAL GEOGRAPHIC World Explorer

Geography | Skills for Life

Himalayan Trekkers The mountain-dwelling Sherpas, such as the woman at right, are famed as guides to foreign expeditions in the Himalaya.

Human-Environment Interaction Which Sherpa made the first successful ascent of Mount Everest?

DIFFERENTIATED INSTRUCTION

Interpersonal Ask interested students to research conflicts between South Asian ethnic/religious groups such as the Tamils and Sinhalese in Sri Lanka or the Sikhs and Hindus in northwestern India. Have students choose partners and role-play encounters between representatives of the two conflicting groups, with a third student acting as a mediator. **Ask:** What happens when large-scale conflicts are viewed as interpersonal conflicts? ⊞ EE4 Human Systems: Standards 10, 13

⊏ Refer to *Inclusion for the Social Studies Classroom Strategies and Activities.*

NATIONAL GEOGRAPHIC — GRAPH STUDY

Population of Pakistan by Age and Gender

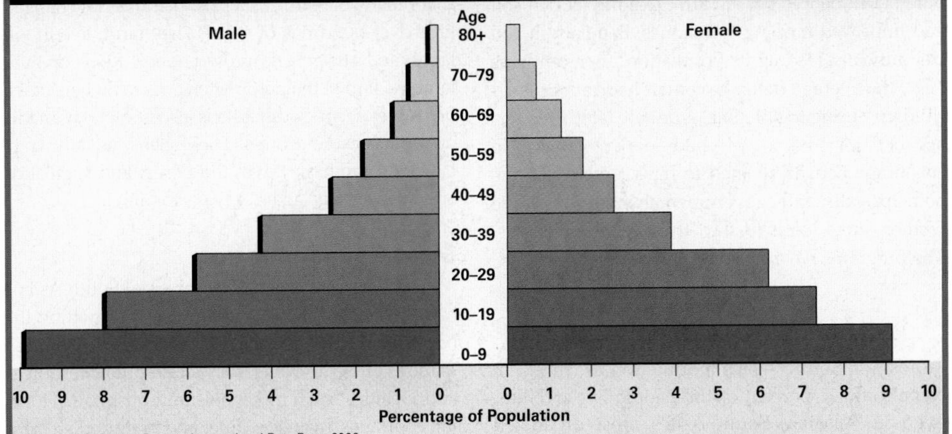

Male	Age	Female
	80+	
	70–79	
	60–69	
	50–59	
	40–49	
	30–39	
	20–29	
	10–19	
	0–9	

10 9 8 7 6 5 4 3 2 1 0   0 1 2 3 4 5 6 7 8 9 10

Percentage of Population

Source: U.S. Census Bureau, International Data Base, 2000

Geography | Skills for Life

1. **Interpreting Graphs** Population pyramids show the age and gender characteristics of a country's population. Describe the age distribution of Pakistan's population. Is the majority of the population young or old?

2. **Applying Geography Skills** What challenges might this age distribution present for Pakistan's future?

3. **Applying Geography Skills** Research age and gender data for another country on the Internet. Construct a population pyramid for that country.

---

in some countries. Still, at present rates, South Asia will nearly double its current population by the year 2050.

Regional Variation

Although population densities are generally high throughout South Asia, the distribution of population varies from region to region. Factors such as climate, vegetation, and physical features have an impact on the number of people the land can support. The Great Indian Desert (Thar Desert) is sparsely populated, as are the mountainous highlands of western Pakistan. In southern Bhutan and Nepal, average population densities vary between 44 and 447 people per square mile (17 and 173 people per sq. km). To the north, however, population decreases as the elevation increases. An average of only 25 people per square mile (10 people per sq. km) make their homes in

the Himalayan highlands because of unfavorable living conditions there.

The highest concentrations of population in South Asia are found on the fertile Ganges Plain (Indo-Gangetic Plain) and along the monsoon-watered coasts of the Indian peninsula. Because rice is an abundant and important food source, it is only natural that most South Asians live where rice is grown. Within parts of these agriculturally productive areas, densities exceed more than 2,000 people per square mile (772 people per sq. km). India's Deccan Plateau—not as populous as the Ganges Plain—supports up to 250 people per square mile (97 people per sq. km).

The large tea and rubber plantations of Sri Lanka require numerous workers. They come from the many villages that cluster around the plantations. The tiny coral islands of the Maldives are packed with 2,461 people per square mile (950 people per sq. km)!

Chapter 24   589

L2 Making Comparisons

Have students research population growth rates over the last 10 years for Karachi, Mumbai, Calcutta, Dhaka, and Kathmandu, and list their findings in a table on the board. Have students suggest reasons for these growth rates and explain how the role and function of cities change with size.

NATIONAL GEOGRAPHIC — GRAPH STUDY

Answers

1. *each older age group is smaller than the preceding younger group; young*

2. *stress on resources, especially in education, jobs, and health care*

3. *Research based on Internet and library resources.*

L1/ELL

Reading Essentials & Study Guide 24-1

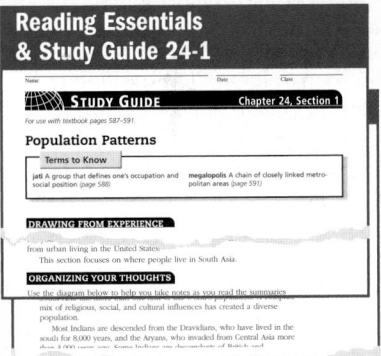

STUDY GUIDE   Chapter 24, Section 1

For use with textbook pages 587–591.

Population Patterns

Terms to Know

jati A group that defines one's occupation and social position (page 588)   **megalopolis** A chain of closely linked metropolitan areas (page 591)

DRAWING FROM EXPERIENCE

from urban living in the United States

This section focuses on where people live in South Asia.

ORGANIZING YOUR THOUGHTS

Use the diagram below to help you take notes as you read the summaries.

mix of religious, social, and cultural influences has created a diverse population.

Most Indians are descended from the Dravidians, who have lived in the souls for 8,000 years, and the Aryans, who invaded from Central Asia more than 4,000 years ago. Some Indians are descendants of British and

INTERDISCIPLINARY connection

ECONOMICS The Grameen Bank (village bank) system makes very small loans to poor people, mostly women, so they can start small businesses.

COOPERATIVE LEARNING ACTIVITY

Visualizing Population Statistics Organize students into seven groups. Assign one South Asian country to each group. Have each group develop a map, chart, or other graphic representation of the following population characteristics of its assigned country: size of population, population density, geographic distribution, and ethnic composition. Students may use encyclopedias, almanacs, atlases, and Internet references to obtain information, and groups should label their graphics with the sources used. Each student should have an assigned area of responsibility. Display the finished work on a bulletin board.

EE4 Human Systems: Standard 9

ASSESS

Assign Section 1 Assessment as homework or as an in-class activity.

Have students use **Interactive Tutor Self-Assessment CD-ROM.**

L2

Section Quiz 24-1

[Section 1 Quiz worksheet image showing:]
CHAPTER 24 Section 1 Quiz
Population Patterns

MATCHING: Match each item in Column A with an item in Column B. Write the correct letters in the blanks. *(10 points each)*

A	B
1. capital of Bangladesh	A. Islamabad
2. sprawling megalopolis containing the Old City and New Delhi	B. Mumbai (Bombay)
3. thriving port city on the Ganges River	C. Calcutta
4. capital of Pakistan	D. Delhi
5. India's main port on the Arabian Sea	E. Dhaka

MULTIPLE CHOICE: In each blank on the left, write the letter of the choice that best completes the statement or answers the question. *(10 points each)*

NATIONAL GEOGRAPHIC **World Explorer**

Answer
climate, vegetation, terrain, employment opportunities

More About the Photo
Although located in the flood-prone Ganges-Brahmaputra delta, Dhaka is a major manufacturing center of South Asia.

Reteach
Organize the class into four groups, assigning each group a topic related to South Asia's population patterns. Have each group use the textbook to write questions to quiz the other groups.

Economics
Bangladesh Slows Its Growth

Bangladesh is the second most densely populated country in South Asia, with 2,639 people per square mile (1,019 people per sq. km). Despite its rich soil and improved farming techniques, Bangladesh still has difficulty feeding its population. As recently as 1991, the average Bengali woman had more than 4 children during her lifetime. A decade later, the average had lowered to 2.8 children per woman. To encourage Bengali women to have fewer children, both private and governmental programs give women small loans to start their own businesses. The programs have achieved some success.

Urban and Rural Life

Most of South Asia's population is rural. In Nepal only 11 percent of the people live in cities. Even in Pakistan, South Asia's most urbanized country, nearly two-thirds of the population lives in

NATIONAL GEOGRAPHIC **World Explorer**

Geography **Skills for Life**
Dhaka, Bangladesh
Although Bangladesh is one of the least urbanized countries in the region, its capital of Dhaka has a high population density.
Human-Environment Interaction What factors influence population density?

rural areas. The sharp differences between urban and rural life add to the region's many contrasts.

Rural Life

For many of South Asia's peoples, life has changed little over hundreds of years. They farm, live in villages, and struggle to grow enough food for their families. Part of their crop often goes to owners of the fields they farm. South Asia is also home to nomadic or seminomadic groups. These clans, usually large extended families, travel the desert and highlands and herd camels, goats, or yaks for a living.

Growing Urbanization

In recent years growing numbers of South Asians have been migrating to urban areas, drawn by the hope of better jobs and higher wages. As urban populations grow, however, they strain public resources and facilities, such as schools and hospitals. Housing shortages, overcrowding, and pollution are serious problems resulting from rapid urbanization.

South Asia's Cities

South Asian cities are among the world's most densely populated urban areas. **Mumbai (Bombay)** is India's main port on the Arabian Sea as well as its largest city, with a population of more than 18.1 million. The city is also a leading industrial, financial, and filmmaking center. During the day, millions more people from outlying areas enter Mumbai to work. An American visiting Mumbai noted:

❝ . . . [M]ost of [Mumbai's] newest citizens are from rural villages. Many of them are refugees from natural disasters such as floods and droughts. Others are refugees from the exacting demands of their own local societies. ❞
John McCarry, "Bombay," *National Geographic,* March 1995

CRITICAL THINKING ACTIVITY

Drawing Conclusions The Grameen Bank system of Bangladesh has loaned billions of dollars to millions of poor Bangladeshis. Most loans are very small, averaging $160, and more than 95 percent are repaid. In 1999 Muhammad Yunus, founder of the bank, said "Banking has been built on the principle that the more you have, the more you get. Well, we have reversed that process and decided that the less you have, the more you get." The system has spread to other developing countries, and has even been adapted for the United States. **Ask:** Do you think the Grameen Bank system can succeed in the United States? Have students discuss their conclusions with the class.
🌐 **EE4 Human Systems: Standard 11**

Kolkata (Calcutta), a thriving port city on a branch of the Ganges River, is the center of India's iron and steel industries. Here crumbling public buildings and high-rise slums contrast sharply with modern office towers and a modern subway system. Millions of people use the subway to travel to jobs in the city.

Delhi (DEH•lee), India's third largest city, is part of a **megalopolis**, or chain of closely linked metropolitan areas. Its sprawling land area encompasses the Old City, dating from the mid-1600s, and New Delhi, the modern capital built by British colonial rulers in the early 1900s. More than a million Delhi newcomers from rural areas have become "pavement dwellers"—people living on the streets in temporary settlements called *jhuggi bastis*.

The cities of Bangladesh and Pakistan are also crowded. **Dhaka**, the capital of Bangladesh, is the world's second most densely populated urban area after Lagos, Nigeria. Rural Pakistanis are drawn to the modern capital, Islamabad, where new housing projects struggle to keep up with a growing population, and to the booming port city of **Karachi**.

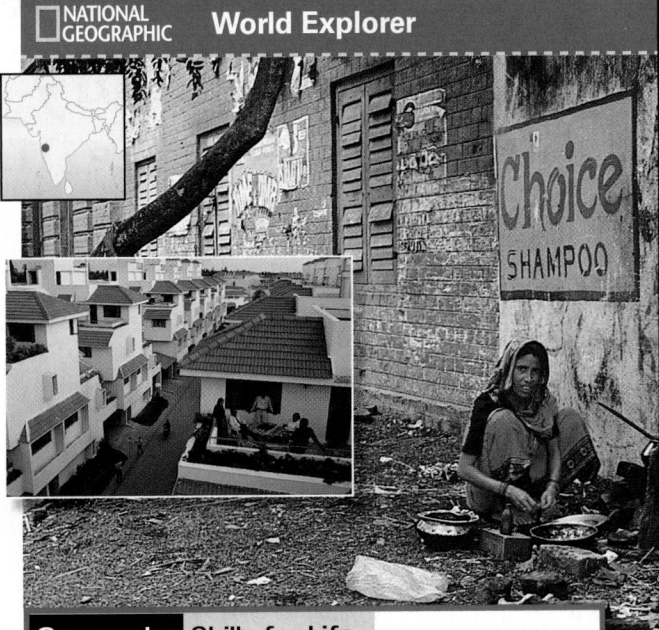

NATIONAL GEOGRAPHIC World Explorer

Geography | **Skills for Life**

Urban Contrasts

A growing middle class lives comfortably in India's suburbs (inset), but the poor in India's cities must struggle to survive.

Movement Why do people in South Asia leave their families and rural villages to move to urban areas?

NATIONAL GEOGRAPHIC World Explorer

Answer
to look for better jobs and higher wages, better public services

More About the Photo
India's urban population increased by more than 60 million people in the 1990s.

Enrich

Show students a portion of the video *A Migrant's Heart* (Annenberg/CPB Collection, 1996), which documents the return to South Asia of an Indian who emigrated to the United States.

④ CLOSE

Ask students to name the South Asian city they would most enjoy visiting, and to share the reasons for their choices.

SECTION ① ASSESSMENT

Checking for Understanding

1. **Define** *jati*, megalopolis.
2. **Main Ideas** Re-create the table below on a sheet of paper, and fill in the characteristics of the population in each South Asian country.

South Asian Countries	Population Characteristics

Critical Thinking

3. **Making Generalizations** Would you say that diversity has been more of a problem or a benefit for countries in South Asia? Why?
4. **Predicting Consequences** How might life in South Asia be affected in the next 50 years if present population growth rates and urbanization trends continue?
5. **Identifying Cause and Effect** What factors have contributed to the growth of South Asia's cities?

Analyzing Graphs

6. **Place** Study the graph on page 589. What percentage of people in Pakistan age 9 or under are female?

Applying Geography

7. **Effects of Geography** Study the population density map on page 562. Write a paragraph explaining how climate, physical features, and resources contribute to differences in population density.

Chapter 24 🌐 591

SECTION ① ASSESSMENT ANSWERS

1. All vocabulary terms are defined in the text.
2. Table entries should reflect text information.
3. a problem: including clashes over social roles, religious differences, and national boundaries; a benefit: including the richness of the region's cultures and the relative tolerance of diversity
4. Already limited resources will be strained beyond the region's ability to cope with issues of health care,

housing, education, and employment. The environment will also suffer.

5. immigration to cities by rural South Asians looking for better jobs and higher wages; high birthrates
6. about 9.2 percent
7. **Applying Geography** Paragraphs should demonstrate an understanding of how geographic features affect population density.

SECTION **2**

FOCUS

Section Overview

This section discusses the history of South Asia, from the Indus River valley civilization to the formation of today's South Asian governments.

BELLRINGER
Skillbuilder Activity

 Project transparency and have students answer questions.

Available as blackline master.

Daily Focus Skills Transparency 24-2

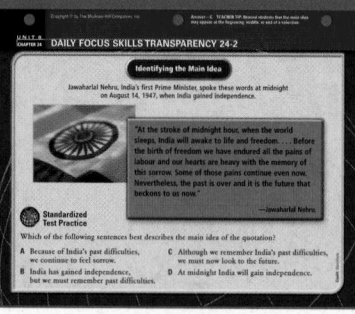

Guide to Reading

Consider What You Know
Answer *Most students will be familiar with images of the Buddha seated in the cross-legged lotus position.*

Reading Strategy
Answer Students should complete the outline by including all heads in the section.

Preteaching Vocabulary
Ask students to predict the meaning of *dharma, karma,* and *nirvana.* These words have very different meanings in American popular culture than they do in South Asia. Have students check the definitions in the text.

Guide to Reading

Consider What You Know

Many people who are not familiar with the Buddhist religion are nonetheless able to recognize the image of the Buddha. How have you seen the Buddha pictured?

Reading Strategy

Taking Notes As you read about the history of South Asia, use the major headings of the section to create an outline similar to the one below.

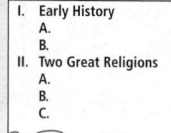

I. Early History
    A.
    B.
II. Two Great Religions
    A.
    B.
    C.

Read to Find Out

- Where did South Asia's first civilization develop?
- What two major world religions originated in South Asia?
- How did invasions and conquests shape South Asia?
- What types of challenges are South Asian countries facing today?

Terms to Know

- dharma
- reincarnation
- karma
- nirvana
- raj

Places to Locate

- Indus River valley
- Mohenjo Daro
- Harappa
- Khyber Pass
- Mauryan Empire
- Gupta Empire

History and Government

NATIONAL GEOGRAPHIC

A Geographic View

History as Architecture

Lahore [in Pakistan] . . . is an architectural accumulation of all of those who have conquered it. Mogul mosques stand next to Sikh temples, which stand next to British administration buildings. . . . Sitting near the Alamgiri Gate, a once private entrance to the royal quarters built by the emperor Aurangzeb in 1674 that is big enough for elephants to pass through, I fell into conversation with three college students. . . . Despite all the history around them . . . the young men were more interested in discussing the future than the past.

—John McCarry, "The Promise of Pakistan," National Geographic, October 1997

Badshahi Mosque, Lahore

Modern life in Lahore unfolds amidst the architectural reminders of the city's fabled past. In fact, throughout all of South Asia, the past and present meet in many different and surprising ways. In this section you will explore South Asia's fascinating history—the story of a series of groups drawn to the region by its wealth of natural resources. Each successive group left its own permanent mark, making South Asia a region of great political and cultural diversity.

Early History

The earliest South Asians left few written records, but evidence of their great achievements in building and trade has been discovered in modern times. As the centuries passed, invaders from the northwest succeeded these early peoples. The influence of all these groups is still felt in South Asia today.

RESOURCE MANAGER

Reproducible Masters
- Reproducible Lesson Plan 24-2
- Daily Lecture Notes 24-2
- Guided Reading Activity 24-2
- Reading Essentials and Study Guide 24-2
- Section Quiz 24-2

Transparencies
- Daily Focus Skills Transparency 24-2
- Political Map Transparency 8
- Unit 8 Map Overlay Transparencies

Multimedia
- Interactive Tutor Self-Assessment CD-ROM
- ExamView® Pro Testmaker CD-ROM
- Presentation Plus! CD-ROM

The Indus Valley Civilization

Around 2500 B.C. one of the world's great civilizations arose in the **Indus River valley**. This culture developed a writing system, a strong central government, and a thriving overseas trade. People built what may have been the world's first cities, **Mohenjo Daro** and **Harappa**. Made of bricks hardened by fire in kilns, these cities boasted sophisticated plumbing, sanitation systems, and other technology that would not be matched again for centuries.

Environmental changes may have led to the decline of this civilization between 1700 and 1500 B.C. The cities were most likely lost to flooding or drought as the Indus River changed its course.

The Aryans

As the Indus Valley civilization crumbled, a group of hunters and herders entered the region from the northwest. These people, the Aryans, settled down and began to farm. They left behind sacred writings called the Vedas.

The Vedas reveal Aryan ideas about religion and social structure. Society was organized into four groups—priests, warriors (or nobles), artisans and farmers, and enslaved people. At first the boundaries between groups were somewhat flexible; people of different classes could intermarry and change professions. Gradually, the social structure developed into a complex system of ranks that dictated from birth one's social status. This "caste" system prevailed in India for centuries and only now is gradually weakening.

Two Great Religions

Understanding the basic beliefs of Hinduism and Buddhism is a key to understanding South Asia's history and culture. These two religions, as well as other faiths, have had profound influence in the region.

Hinduism

Growing out of Aryan culture and religion, Hinduism is both a religion and a way of life. Hindu belief requires every person to carry out his or her dharma (DUHR•muh), or moral duty. Hindus also believe that after death people undergo reincarnation, or rebirth as another living being. This process occurs repeatedly until the individual overcomes personal weaknesses and earthly desires. At that point, a person leaves the cycle of rebirth and becomes reunited with the eternal being. In the law of karma, good deeds—actions in accord with one's dharma—move one toward this point, while bad deeds chain a person to the cycle of rebirth.

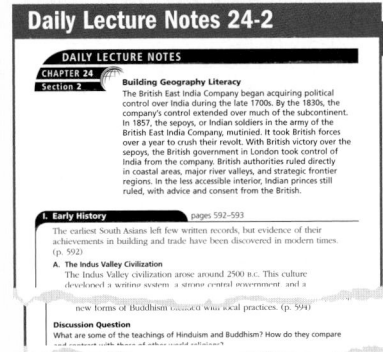

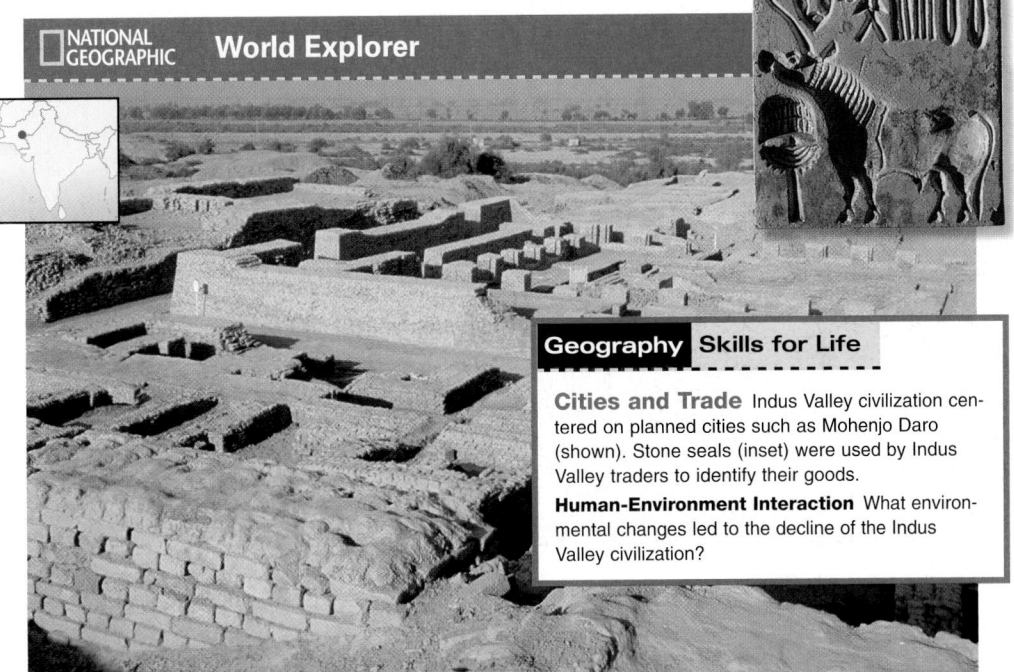

NATIONAL GEOGRAPHIC World Explorer

Geography | Skills for Life

Cities and Trade Indus Valley civilization centered on planned cities such as Mohenjo Daro (shown). Stone seals (inset) were used by Indus Valley traders to identify their goods.

Human-Environment Interaction What environmental changes led to the decline of the Indus Valley civilization?

② TEACH

L2 Making Comparisons

Have students compare what they know about the world's other great culture hearths with what they learn about the Indus River valley civilization. **Ask:** What physical features do culture hearths have in common? *(rivers, temperate climates)*

Daily Lecture Notes 24-2

DAILY LECTURE NOTES

CHAPTER 24
Section 2

Building Geography Literacy
The British East India Company began acquiring political control over India during the late 1700s. By the 1830s, the company's control extended over much of the subcontinent. In 1857, the sepoys, or Indian soldiers in the army of the British East India Company, mutinied. It took British forces over a year to crush their revolt. With British victory over the sepoys, the British government in London took control of India from the company. British authorities ruled directly in coastal areas, major river valleys, and strategic frontier regions. In the less accessible interior, Indian princes still ruled, with advice and consent from the British.

I. Early History pages 592–593
The earliest South Asians left few written records, but evidence of their achievements in building and trade have been discovered in modern times. (p. 592)

A. The Indus Valley Civilization
The Indus Valley civilization arose around 2500 B.C. This culture developed a writing system, a strong central government, and a ... new forms of Buddhism mixed with local practices. (p. 594)

Discussion Question
What are some of the teachings of Hinduism and Buddhism? How do they compare ...

NATIONAL GEOGRAPHIC World Explorer

Answer
possibly flooding or drought

More About the Photo
The Indus River valley civilization had a written language and systems for counting, weighing, and measuring.

DIFFERENTIATED INSTRUCTION

Kinesthetic Both Hinduism and Buddhism have contributed to the world systems of physical training that began as forms of spiritual discipline. Have interested students research some of the simpler postures of Hindu yoga or Buddhist circumambulation (walking meditatively in a circle) and teach these to the class.

🌐 **EE4 Human Systems: Standard 10**

📂 Refer to *Inclusion for the Social Studies Classroom Strategies and Activities.*

L1/ELL

Guided Reading Activity 24-2

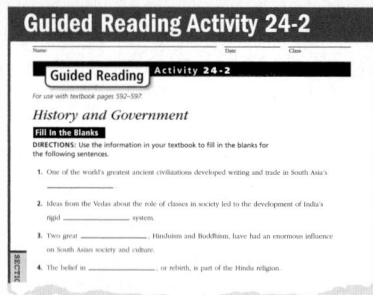

Guided Reading Activity 24-2

For use with textbook pages 592–597

History and Government

Fill In the Blanks

DIRECTIONS: Use the information in your textbook to fill in the blanks for the following sentences.

1. One of the world's greatest ancient civilizations developed writing and trade in South Asia's _____

2. Ideas from the Vedas about the role of classes in society led to the development of India's rigid _____ system.

3. Two great _____, Hinduism and Buddhism, have had an enormous influence on South Asian society and culture.

4. The belief in _____, or rebirth, is part of the Hindu religion.

The Raji, a semi-nomadic tribe in Nepal, make their living as "honey hunters." Wrapped in layers of protective cloth, Raji men, women, and children climb trees up to 150 feet (45.7 m) high to raid bees' nests for the sweetener.

NATIONAL GEOGRAPHIC World Explorer

Answer
Hindus generally exercise tolerance and respect toward other religions as different paths to the same goal.

More About the Photo
Buddhist stupas often entertain sacred relics related to the Buddha. This large ornately decorated stupa at Sanchi, India, was built between 200 B.C. and A.D. 100.

Hindus honor many gods and goddesses, which are often seen as different forms of the one eternal being. Many Hindus are tolerant of other religions, viewing them as different paths to the same goal.

Buddhism

Siddhartha Gautama (sih•DAHR•tuh GOW•tuh•muh) was born around 563 B.C. in what is today Nepal. Belonging to a noble Hindu family, Siddhartha lived a life of luxury. As he grew to manhood, however, he became aware of human suffering. Leaving his wealth and power behind, he went on a pilgrimage. Years of meditation and spiritual seeking led to the moment when Siddhartha perceived what he understood to be the true nature of human existence. He then became known as the Buddha, or the Awakened One.

The Buddha spent the rest of his life sharing his insights with others. He taught that people suffer because they are too attached to material things, which are temporary. The Buddha also taught people to think clearly, work diligently, and show compassion for all living things in order to escape desire and suffering and to be liberated from endless rebirth.

Like Hinduism, Buddhism developed a system of religious rituals, but it was primarily a practical way to achieve human happiness. By following Buddhist teachings, people could become enlightened, entering a state of insight, calm, and joy called nirvana (nir•VAHN•uh).

Culture
A Marriage of Influences

Because the Buddha rejected the rigid social system of his day, women and people of lower social classes embraced his teachings. Eventually, Buddhism spread from India to other countries. Sri Lanka became a Buddhist kingdom. In Nepal and Bhutan, new forms of Buddhism emerged that blended Hindu rituals with local practices. In India, Hinduism absorbed Buddhism but retained a tradition of honoring the Buddha.

Invasions and Empires

After the Aryans, other groups with new cultures invaded South Asia through the **Khyber Pass** in the northwestern Hindu Kush mountains. The **Mauryan Empire**, established by the first of these

NATIONAL GEOGRAPHIC World Explorer

Geography Skills for Life

Religions Hindu temples show Ganesh (inset), the god of good fortune, and other deities. A stupa, or domed shrine, honors the site where the Buddha first preached.
Place How does Hinduism regard other religions?

COOPERATIVE LEARNING ACTIVITY

Reporting Current Events Have students form small groups, and assign each group a South Asian country. Tell students to assume the role of television news teams sent to cover the most recent elections or changes in government. After the groups have gathered information using the Internet, ask each group to develop a script for its news broadcast, complete with graphics. Scripts should answer the following questions: (1) What change occurred in the country's government? (2) What are the implications of this change within and outside of the country? Allow time for the groups to present their broadcasts.
EE2 Places and Regions: Standard 4

groups, maintained control from about 320 to 180 B.C. and ruled all but the southernmost parts of the Indian peninsula. Asoka, the last and greatest Mauryan emperor, promoted Buddhism and nonviolence.

About 500 years later, the **Gupta Empire** came into power. From about A.D. 320 to 550, this Hindu civilization was one of the most advanced in the world. Science, technology, and the arts flourished. The numerals we call Arabic today were most likely developed in India during the Gupta period and introduced to Europe by Arab traders.

Muslim missionaries and traders first entered India in the 700s. By the 1100s Muslim armies from Mongolia, Turkey, and Persia had conquered northern India. The Muslim-led Mogul Empire dominated the Indian subcontinent for several centuries. During this era, many South Asians converted to Islam.

The final invaders, Europeans, came by sea. Portuguese traders arrived first in about 1500. They were followed by the French and the British. In the late 1700s, the British expelled the French. Though Portuguese strongholds remained, the British were the major European power in South Asia at this time. The British called their Indian empire the British raj, the Hindi word for empire. The British introduced the English language to South Asia, restructured the educational system, built railroads, and developed a civil service. British influence is still seen in some elements of Indian culture.

Modern South Asia

Today South Asia is free of European control. Independence did not come easily, however, and these growing countries still struggle with the aftereffects of colonialism.

Independence

In the early and mid-1900s, India's fight for independence was led by Mohandas K. Gandhi. Using nonviolent methods, such as boycotting British products and staging peaceful demonstrations,

Gandhi inspired the peoples of India to seek self-rule. A Hindu, Gandhi worked to end the rigid social system and promote local industry, such as spinning and weaving. Enduring prison and hunger strikes in the struggle for independence, Gandhi earned the name Mahatma, or "Great Soul." According to Gandhi,

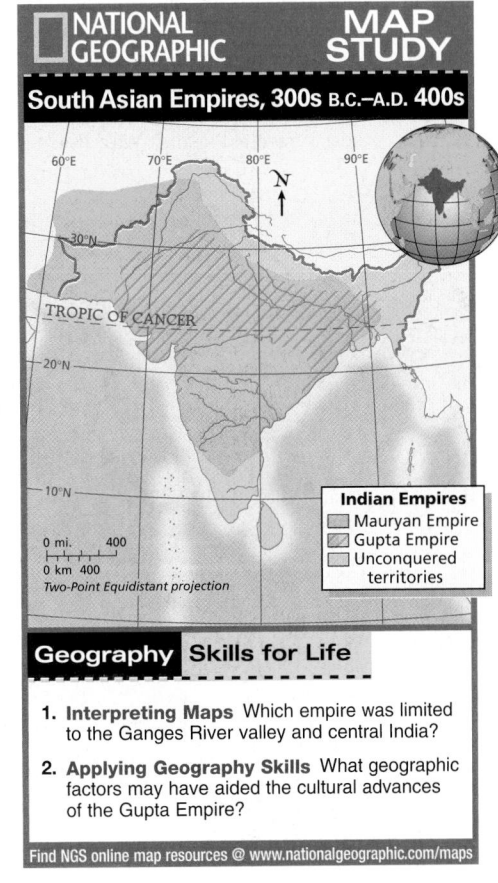

> **❝** *Nonviolence and truth* (Satya) *are inseparable and presuppose one another. There is no god higher than truth.* **❞**
>
> S. Hobhouse, ed., *True Patriotism: Some Sayings of Mahatma Gandhi*, 1939

Lion sculpture from the palace of Asoka

NATIONAL GEOGRAPHIC MAP STUDY

South Asian Empires, 300s B.C.–A.D. 400s

TROPIC OF CANCER

Indian Empires
- Mauryan Empire
- Gupta Empire
- Unconquered territories

0 mi. 400
0 km 400
Two-Point Equidistant projection

Geography Skills for Life

1. **Interpreting Maps** Which empire was limited to the Ganges River valley and central India?

2. **Applying Geography Skills** What geographic factors may have aided the cultural advances of the Gupta Empire?

Find NGS online map resources @ www.nationalgeographic.com/maps

Chapter 24 🌐 595

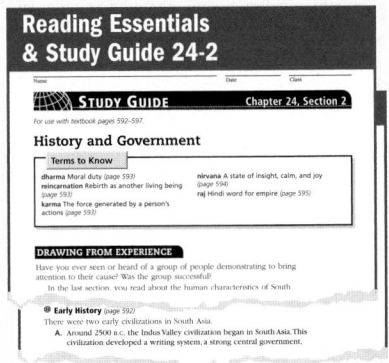

CRITICAL THINKING ACTIVITY

Making Inferences Tell students that India today is a democratic republic that includes features of the political systems of the United Kingdom and the United States. Like the United States, India has a federal system of government. The country is divided into 28 states and 7 territories. Most of India's states have large populations that share a common language and culture. **Ask:** What can you infer from this information about the primary political loyalty of many Indians? (*Many Indians feel a greater sense of attachment to their particular state with its common language and culture than to the country as a whole, which comprises a great diversity of language and cultural groups.*)

🌐 **EE4 Human Systems: Standards 10, 13**

Objectives, goals, and answers to the student activity can be found in the Web Activity Lesson Plan feature at geography.glencoe.com

③ ASSESS

Assign Section 2 Assessment as homework or as an in-class activity.

Ⓧ Have students use **Interactive Tutor Self-Assessment CD-ROM.**

L2

Section Quiz 24-2

[Section 2 Quiz worksheet image]

Name ___ Date ___ Class ___

24 Section 2 Quiz
History and Government

MATCHING: Match each item in Column A with an item in Column B. Write the correct letters in the blanks. *(10 points each)*

A	B
1. disputed territory between Pakistan and India	A. Harappa
2. name of Sri Lanka before 1972	B. Mogul Empire
3. advanced Hindu civilization, A.D. 320–550	C. Gupta Empire
4. empire that converted Asians to Islam	D. Kashmir
5. possibly one of the world's first cities	E. Ceylon

MULTIPLE CHOICE: In each blank on the left, write the letter of the choice that best completes the statement or answers the question. *(10 points each)*

6. South Asia's earliest civilizations arose in

NATIONAL GEOGRAPHIC **World Explorer**

Answer
ethnic and religious differences, border disputes

More About the Photo
The division of British India into largely Hindu India and Muslim Pakistan, resulted in the displacement of 10 million people. About 500,000 people were killed in rioting that accompanied the separation.

In 1947 Britain finally granted independence to British India, and the land became two new countries. Areas with a Hindu majority became India, and those with a Muslim majority became Pakistan. Pakistan actually consisted of two isolated sections—East Pakistan and West Pakistan—separated by about 1,000 miles (1,609 km) of land belonging to India.

Dividing British India split many families. Hundreds of thousands of Hindus in Pakistan moved to India, and a similar number of Muslims in India moved to East or West Pakistan. Violence often marked the movements. Religious violence also claimed the life of Gandhi, who was assassinated in 1948 by a Hindu nationalist opposed to the division of India.

One year after granting India self-rule, Britain gave independence to Ceylon. In 1972 the island took back its ancient name, Sri Lanka. Nepal and Bhutan had always been independent of European rule. The Maldives, a group of islands in the Indian Ocean, won independence from Britain in 1965. In 1971 East Pakistan revolted against West Pakistan and became the new country of Bangladesh. The western part retained the name Pakistan.

Regional Conflicts

Tensions between India and Pakistan continued after independence. Some border areas, especially the former Indian provinces of Jammu and Kashmir, are still hotly disputed. Today both India and Pakistan have nuclear weapons, adding to the complexity of the conflict. Ethnic and religious tensions also trouble other parts of South Asia. Hindu and Muslim groups within India have clashed. Since the 1980s the Sri Lankan government has been troubled by ethnic Tamil rebel groups seeking a separate Tamil state.

Student Web Activity Visit the **Glencoe World Geography** Web site at geography.glencoe.com and click on Student Web Activities—Chapter 24 for an activity on Kashmir.

NATIONAL GEOGRAPHIC **World Explorer**

Geography Skills for Life

Migrations, 1947 Mohandas Gandhi (inset) mourned the violence between Hindus and Muslims that came with British India's division and the mass migration of people.
Place What are the causes of conflict in South Asia today?

TEAM-TEACHING ACTIVITY: HISTORY

Civil Disobedience Have students work with teachers of American history and world history to research and compare two incidents of civil disobedience that strengthened independence movements against British rule: the American colonists' 1773 Boston Tea Party and Gandhi's 1930 Salt March. Have students prepare a chart listing similarities and differences between the two actions. It might be pointed out that the Boston Tea Party was sparked by a British decision to allow the East India Company operating in India to sell its tea cheaply and directly to the American colonies, an action that undercut American colonial traders and merchants. ▦ **EE6 The Uses of Geography: Standard 17**

Today's Governments

Today's South Asian governments are diverse. India, often called the world's largest democracy, is a federal parliamentary republic. For 40 years following India's independence, members of the Nehru (NAY•roo) family headed India's government. Jawaharlal (jah•wah•HAR•lahl) Nehru was India's prime minister from 1947 until his death in 1964. His daughter, Indira Gandhi, and later his grandson, Rajiv Gandhi, also led the country, but growing ethnic and religious conflict led to assassinations of Indira in 1984 and Rajiv in 1991. Since then, India's prime ministers have had less influence than the Nehru "dynasty." Workable parliamentary institutions have made India's democracy more secure.

Like India, Pakistan is a parliamentary republic, but instability and military rule have prevailed since 1971. A more stable democracy seemed likely in the 1990s under Benazir Ali Bhutto, the country's first female prime minister, and later under her successor, Nawaz Sharif. In 1999, however, charges of official corruption led to a military coup. Pakistan's new leader, General Pervez Musharraf, pledged to have a more democratic government.

Sri Lanka and Bangladesh also are parliamentary republics. Intense political or ethnic rivalries, however, have made stable political rule difficult. After independence, political assassinations or military takeovers marked both countries. In recent years

▲ Sheikh Hasina Wazid (right), prime minister of Bangladesh, shown here with Megawati Sukarnoputri, president of Indonesia

democratic rule has been strengthened. In 1994 Chandrika Bandaranaike Kumartungah (chahn•DREE•kah BAHN•dah•rahn•EYE•keh KOO•mahr•TOON•gah) was elected Sri Lanka's first female president. Two years later, Sheikh Hasina Wazid was elected as Prime Minister in Bangladesh.

A few countries in the region today have traditional forms of government. For example, Bhutan and Nepal have monarchies that are trying to modernize and still keep some power. Once ruled by a sultan, the Maldives became a republic in 1968.

SECTION 2 ASSESSMENT

Checking for Understanding

1. **Define** dharma, reincarnation, karma, nirvana, raj.

2. **Main Ideas** Re-create the graphic organizer below on a sheet of paper, and complete it by filling in information about the successive groups that influenced South Asia.

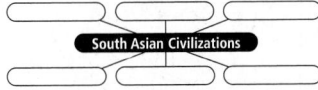

South Asian Civilizations

Critical Thinking

3. **Making Inferences** Describe characteristics of South Asia during ancient, colonial, and modern eras.

4. **Comparing and Contrasting** In what ways are Hinduism and Buddhism similar? Different?

5. **Identifying Cause and Effect** How do present-day political borders in South Asia reflect ethnic and religious conflicts?

Analyzing Maps

6. **Location** Study the map of South Asian empires on page 595. Which empire extended beyond the borders of present-day Pakistan?

Applying Geography

7. **Geography and Religion** Think about the influences of religion on the history and culture of South Asia. How has the geography of the region impacted South Asia's religions?

Chapter 24 🌐 597

L2 Government

Have students form small groups. **Ask:** Why do you think many South Asian countries have elected women heads of state? Why has the United States never elected a woman head of state? Have groups discuss these questions and share their opinions with the class.

Reteach

Have students work together on a time line of South Asian historical events. Students might use the board or large poster boards.

Enrich

Have students look through cookbooks and the Internet for South Asian recipes. Ask students to identify the cultural origins of their chosen recipes.

4 CLOSE

Ask students to write brief essays answering these questions: Which aspect of the region's past do you think South Asians most need to remember as they move toward the future? Why?

SECTION 2 ASSESSMENT ANSWERS

1. All vocabulary terms are defined in the text.

2. Groups should include Indus River valley, Aryans, Maurya, Gupta, Moguls, Europeans.

3. Ancient: series of Hindu, Buddhist, and Muslim empires; colonial: European rule of subcontinent; modern: independent countries

4. Both arose out of Indian culture, developed religious rituals, and see human life as a cycle of reincarnation or rebirth until enlightenment is reached. Buddhism, however, was primarily a practical way to achieve human happiness or enlightenment.

5. Hindu-Muslim differences led to British India's partition into Muslim Pakistan and largely Hindu India. Kashmir is still disputed between India and Pakistan. Ethnic divisions between eastern and western parts of Pakistan led to the independence of East Pakistan as Bangladesh in 1971.

6. Mauryan

7. **Applying Geography** Possible answer: Hinduism in southern India was protected from Muslim invaders by the Vindhya Range.

1 FOCUS

Bring to class or invite students to bring examples of cashmere clothing and fabrics. Remind students that cashmere is woven from the hair of rare mountain goats that are raised in the South Asian territory of Kashmir. **Ask: In what other context might you hear Kashmir mentioned in the news?** *(as the site of conflict between Pakistan and India)*

2 TEACH

L1 Location

Have students locate Kashmir and the Line of Control on the map on page 598. Ask them to research the Internet and other resources for geographical and historical information about Kashmir. **Ask: Why might Kashmir's location make it a source of conflict?** (India: a buffer against China; Pakistan: a source of water) **What are the historic/ cultural sources of conflict?** (Hindu-Muslim tensions; nationalism; colonial legacy)

□ NATIONAL GEOGRAPHIC GEOFACT

▶ **History's highest battleground is part of contested Kashmir. Soldiers from both India and Pakistan have been stationed and sometimes have clashed on the ice fields at altitudes greater than 20,000 feet (6,096 m).**

GEOGRAPHY
AND HISTORY

MOUNTAIN MADNESS: STRUGGLE FOR KASHMIR

A CASHMERE SWEATER, made of soft wool from the undercoat of the Kashmir goat, is a prized possession. So, too, is the Kashmir region, where the goat got its name. The problem: two countries claim Kashmir. No wonder, for Kashmir, situated high in the Himalaya on the northern tips of India and Pakistan, is renowned for its beauty and climate. Ancient mountain villages are reflected in the waters of its crystalline lakes. Fields of crocuses are harvested for the world's most expensive spice—saffron. However, decades of fighting have shattered this idyllic realm.

Tale of Two Religions

For centuries, Kashmir was part of the Indian kingdoms, ruled by maharajas, or princes. In 1846 Kashmir became the British Indian state of Jammu and Kashmir. When predominantly Hindu India won independence in 1947, Britain partitioned the western part of India to create Pakistan as a homeland for South Asia's Muslims. As the leaders of the existing Indian states decided which country to join, widespread rioting broke out between

Kashmiri Muslims struggle violently against Hindu India's rule. ▶

BACKGROUND INFORMATION

Kashmir's Young People The despair caused by the region's continuing tensions is felt most strongly by Kashmir's younger generation. Children growing up in disputed Kashmir have never known peace. The conflict has left an estimated 100,000 Kashmiri children without families. With few social services available, many orphaned children are on their own and work as child laborers in the region's textile industries. Teens and young adults also suffer because they are unable to assume lives that are appropriate to people of their ages.
🌐 **EE4 Human Systems: Standard 13**

◀ A flower merchant rows down a river in Kashmir, where years of warfare have shattered the calm.

Hindus and Muslims.

In the face of the chaos, the prince of Jammu and Kashmir sought to remain autonomous. As a Hindu, his loyalties were with India, but the majority of the population was Muslim. A Muslim uprising, perhaps supported by Pakistan, sent the prince fleeing to Delhi, where he signed his state over to India. India then sent troops to put down the uprising. The Pakistani army responded, and the first India-Pakistan war began.

India claimed a legal and historical right to Kashmir, but Pakistan insisted it would be a better homeland for the Muslim enclave. Each side also has strategic needs: India wants Kashmir as a buffer between itself and China, while Pakistan relies on river waters flowing from Kashmir for irrigation and electricity.

Demand for Independence

In 1949 the United Nations arranged a truce, which established a cease-fire line that split Kashmir unequally between India and Pakistan. But peace did not last. War broke out again in 1965. In 1972 an accord reaffirmed the original cease-fire line, now called the line of control. Yet troops on both sides regularly fire across it, killing civilians and wrecking villages.

In the late 1980s, a new crisis engulfed Kashmir. Muslim groups within Kashmir, demanding independence, began killing Indian soldiers and Kashmiri Hindus. India responded with force. Then the stakes were raised. In 1998, first India, then Pakistan confirmed the world's worst fears by conducting underground nuclear weapons tests. Today tensions continue between India and Pakistan, the world's newest nuclear powers, as they vie for Kashmir.

Looking Ahead

With nuclear weapons in the mix, other nations must pay attention. Why is this dispute so difficult for India and Pakistan to resolve? Why is it important to the world that they resolve it?

1947 Britain partitions India to create Pakistan; war erupts over Kashmir

1949 UN establishes cease-fire line, dividing Kashmir between India and Pakistan

1965 Second India-Pakistan war

1972 Agreement restores line of control

1980s Kashmiri Muslims (background photo) press for Kashmir's union with Pakistan

1988 Kashmiri Muslims seek independence; scores of refugees (photo above) crowd camps

1998 India and Pakistan conduct nuclear tests

2002 Kashmiri militant attacks raise fears of war between India and Pakistan

FYI

Kashmiri Separatists Tensions in Kashmir are further heightened by the presence of some 125,000 militants representing neither Pakistan nor India. These insurgent groups include Kashmiris fighting for an independent state as well as representatives of international Islamic movements.

3 ASSESS

Have students answer the **Looking Ahead** questions on page 599.

4 CLOSE

Problem Solving Challenge students to work with a partner to create a plan for easing tensions in Kashmir.

Meeting National Standards

Geography for Life
The following standards are met in the Student Edition:

EE2 Places and Regions:
  Standard 6

EE4 Human Systems:
  Standards 9, 12, 13

EE6 The Uses of Geography:
  Standards 17, 18

ANSWERS TO LOOKING AHEAD

India and Pakistan find it difficult to resolve the dispute over Kashmir because it has its roots in ancient religious and cultural differences and was fueled by British colonialism and partition. Resolution of the conflict is critically important to the region because of the continuing loss of life and diversion of key resources to warfare, and to the world because disputes between nuclear powers always have the potential to threaten international security, human health, and the environment.

SECTION 3

1 FOCUS

Section Overview

This section discusses the importance of language, religion, and the arts in the daily life of South Asia.

BELLRINGER
Skillbuilder Activity

Project transparency and have students answer questions.

Available as blackline master.

Daily Focus Skills Transparency 24-3

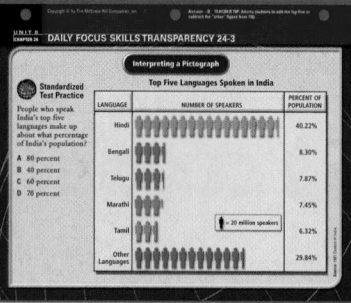

Guide to Reading

Consider What You Know
Answer *dialects*

Reading Strategy
Answer *Urdu, Hindi, Bengali*

Preteaching Vocabulary
Use the **Vocabulary Puzzle-Maker CD-ROM** to create crossword and word-search puzzles.

Guide to Reading

Consider What You Know

Indians speak many variations of the same basic language. What are such language variations called?

Reading Strategy

Categorizing As you read about the languages of South Asia, complete a web diagram similar to the one below by filling in the three Indo-European languages.

Read to Find Out

- How do the lives of South Asia's peoples reflect the region's linguistic and religious diversity?
- What contributions to the arts has the region made?
- How are South Asian countries meeting challenges to improve the quality of life in the region?
- How is the rich cultural diversity of South Asia reflected in distinctive celebrations?

Terms to Know

- guru
- mantra
- sadhu
- stupa
- *dzong*

Places to Locate

- Taj Mahal
- New Delhi

Cultures and Lifestyles

NATIONAL GEOGRAPHIC

A Geographic View

A South Asian Celebration

Diwali, the five-day Festival of Lights, was my family's favorite among all the religious observances that crowd the Indian calendar. . . . It commemorates to the Hindus of the north the return to India of Lord Ram and his wife, Sita, after their victory over the . . . king of Sri Lanka. Tiny earthen oil lamps are lit to outline every house and hut to guide them on the journey home. Sikhs also celebrate on this night of Diwali. Even Muslim families sometimes join in.

—*Jeffrey C. Ward, "India: Fifty Years of Independence,"* National Geographic, *May 1997*

Diwali celebration

South Asia's ethnic diversity has produced a rich cultural blend, a mix of contrasting elements much like the spicy Indian stew ingredient called *masala* or the mixture of pungent spices that make up curry. As you read this section, note the gifts of art, music, architecture, and dance that South Asia shares with the world.

Languages

The peoples of South Asia speak 19 major languages and hundreds of local dialects. In India alone the government officially recognizes 14 languages, although Hindi is chief among them. English, the common language of international business and tourism, is also widely spoken in the parts of South Asia that were once under British rule.

RESOURCE MANAGER

Reproducible Masters

- Reproducible Lesson Plan 24-3
- Vocabulary Activity 24
- Daily Lecture Notes 24-3
- Guided Reading Activity 24-3
- Reading Essentials and Study Guide 24-3
- Reteaching Activity 24
- Reinforcing Skills Activity 24
- Section Quiz 24-3

Transparencies

- Daily Focus Skills Transparency 24-3
- Unit 8 Map Overlay Transparencies

Multimedia

- Vocabulary PuzzleMaker CD-ROM
- Interactive Tutor Self-Assessment CD-ROM
- ExamView® Pro Testmaker CD-ROM
- Presentation Plus! CD-ROM

Indo-European Languages

Most languages spoken in Pakistan, Bangladesh, and northern India fall into the Indo-European family of languages. These languages—Hindi, Urdu, and Bengali—trace their roots to the Aryan invaders of 3,000 years ago and are related to most of the major languages of Europe.

About half of India's people, especially those in the northern and central states, speak Hindi as their primary language. Urdu is Pakistan's official language, and Bengali is the official language of Bangladesh. In many northern areas, Indians speak Hindustani, a mixture of Hindi and Urdu. Nepali, Sinhalese, and Divehi, the official languages of Nepal, Sri Lanka, and the Maldives, respectively, also have Indo-European roots. Sanskrit, the classical Aryan language of the Vedas, is still used for religious, literary, and musical purposes.

Other Languages

Most of the population in southern India and Sri Lanka speak languages of the Dravidian family, whose roots go back to the earliest inhabitants of southern South Asia. Dravidian languages include Tamil, Telugu, Kannada, and Malayalam. In the north the languages of Bhutan and parts of Nepal reflect these countries' close ethnic and historical ties to East Asia.

Religions

Hinduism, Islam, and Buddhism are the major religions of South Asia. Most people in India and Nepal are Hindus. Hinduism is also practiced, to a lesser extent, in Bhutan, Sri Lanka, Pakistan, and Bangladesh. Pakistan, Bangladesh, and the Maldives were all founded as Islamic states, and the majority of the people in these countries are Muslims. India's 120 million Muslims form the country's second-largest religious group. Buddhism, although no longer a significant religion in India, remains strong in Sri Lanka, Bhutan, and Nepal.

Other religions practiced in South Asia include Jainism, Sikhism, Christianity, and Zoroastrianism. Jainism was founded in the 500s B.C. by Mahariva, a Hindu teacher. India's more than 3 million Jains practice strict nonviolence, believing that every living thing has a soul. Sikhism, founded in the early A.D. 1500s by a guru, or teacher, named Nanak, teaches that there is one God and that

good deeds and meditation bring release from the cycle of reincarnation. Most of South Asia's 20 million Sikhs live in northwestern India, and many want an independent Sikh state there.

About 17 million Christians also live in South Asia, concentrated in urban areas in southern and northeastern India. The Indian city of Mumbai is home to some of the last living Zoroastrian followers, known as the Parsis, whose religious and cultural heritage comes from ancient Persia.

Culture
Religion and Daily Life

The influence of religion is ever present in South Asia. In Bhutan and Nepal, for example, colorful prayer flags wave in the wind, and prayer wheels twirl on many corners, sending out invocations. Monks chant mantras, or repetitive prayers. In India, Hindu holy men called

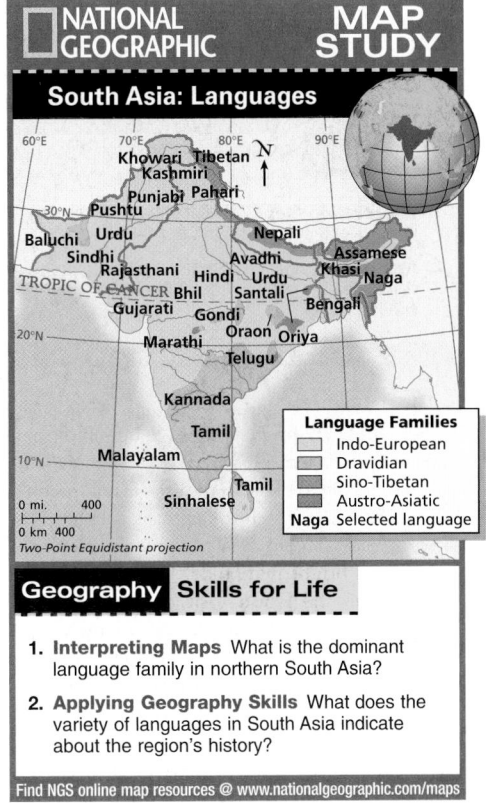

NATIONAL GEOGRAPHIC   MAP STUDY

South Asia: Languages

Language Families
- Indo-European
- Dravidian
- Sino-Tibetan
- Austro-Asiatic
- **Naga** Selected language

Two-Point Equidistant projection

Geography Skills for Life

1. **Interpreting Maps** What is the dominant language family in northern South Asia?

2. **Applying Geography Skills** What does the variety of languages in South Asia indicate about the region's history?

Find NGS online map resources @ www.nationalgeographic.com/maps

L2 Language Arts
Have students research the meanings of the following English words that have roots in South Asian languages: *curry, jungle, khaki, orange, mulligatawny, pajamas, Parcheesi, polo, pundit.* After identifying the original language of each word, have students locate on a map the areas where that language is spoken.

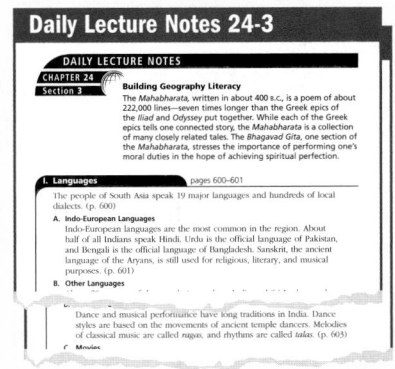

Daily Lecture Notes 24-3

DAILY LECTURE NOTES

CHAPTER 24
Section 3

Building Geography Literacy
The *Mahabharata*, written in about 400 B.C., is a poem of about 222,000 lines—seven times longer than the Greek epics of the *Iliad* and *Odyssey* put together. While each of the Greek epics tells one connected story, the *Mahabharata* is a collection of many closely related tales. The *Bhagavad Gita*, one section of the *Mahabharata*, stresses the importance of performing one's moral duties in the hope of achieving spiritual perfection.

I. Languages   pages 600–601

The people of South Asia speak 19 major languages and hundreds of local dialects. (p. 600)

A. Indo-European Languages
Indo-European languages are the most common in the region. About half of all Indians speak Hindi. Urdu is the official language of Pakistan, and Bengali is the official language of Bangladesh. Sanskrit, the ancient language of the Aryans, is still used for religious, literary, and musical purposes. (p. 601)

B. Other Languages

Dance and musical performance have long traditions in India. Dance styles are based on the movements of ancient temple dancers. Melodies of classical music are called *ragas*, and rhythms are called *talas*. (p. 603)

C. Movies

NATIONAL GEOGRAPHIC   MAP STUDY

Answers

1. *Indo-European*

2. *It experienced many waves of immigrants and invaders.*

Map Skills Practice

Place Which two languages are spoken in Sri Lanka?
(Tamil and Sinhalese)

DIFFERENTIATED INSTRUCTION

At-Risk Students For students who have problems with mathematics, supply hints for interpreting the Map Study and the Graph Study on pages 602–603. Have students notice that all three parts of the studies—the map, the table, and the circle graph—show the same information. Advise them to look for general information first and have them determine which religions are most widely practiced in South Asia. Refer students to the map key to see which colors cover the most territory. On the table, have them begin at the top, pointing out that the religions are listed in order from the greatest number to the least. On the circle graph, ask students to look for the largest section. 🔲 **EE4 Human Systems: Standard 10**

📂 Refer to *Inclusion for the Social Studies Classroom Strategies and Activities.*

NATIONAL GEOGRAPHIC — MAP STUDY

Answers

1. *Buddhism*

2. *Hinduism*

Map Skills Practice

Place In which parts of South Asia are local religions commonly practiced? *(in eastern Bangladesh and in the northeastern part of India)*

L1/ELL

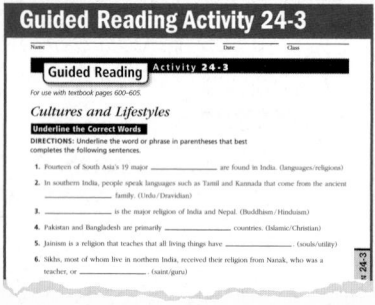

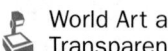

GEOGRAPHY AND THE HUMANITIES

🎵 World Music: A Cultural Legacy

🖼 World Art and Architecture Transparencies

📖 World Art Prints

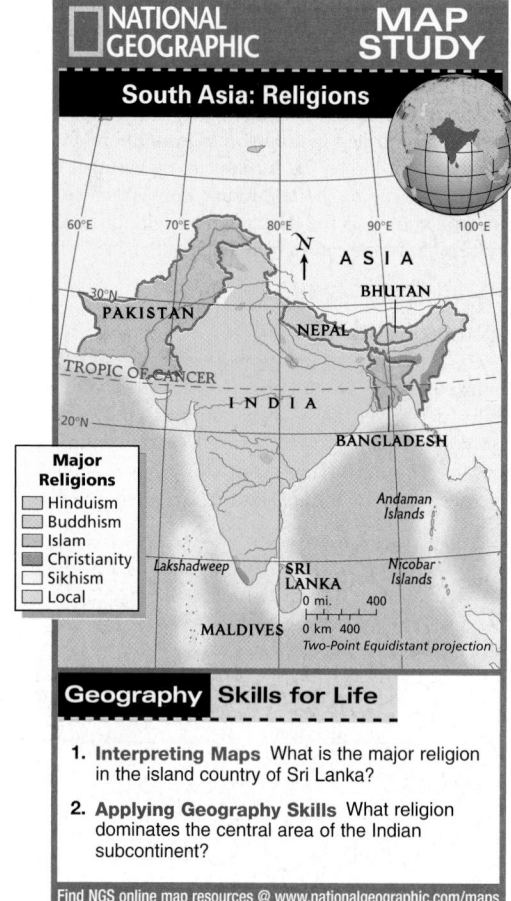

NATIONAL GEOGRAPHIC — MAP STUDY

South Asia: Religions

Major Religions
- Hinduism
- Buddhism
- Islam
- Christianity
- Sikhism
- Local

Geography Skills for Life

1. **Interpreting Maps** What is the major religion in the island country of Sri Lanka?

2. **Applying Geography Skills** What religion dominates the central area of the Indian subcontinent?

Find NGS online map resources @ www.nationalgeographic.com/maps

sadhus dress in bright yellow robes and roam from temple to temple, carrying only their blankets and begging bowls. In the streets and roads of India, where Hindus consider cattle sacred, thousands of cows roam freely, sometimes wearing garlands of bright marigolds. Buddhist pilgrims from around the world visit the shrines of Sri Lanka. In Pakistan and Bangladesh, many Muslim women wear the *chador*, the enveloping robe and veil that Islamic tradition requires for modesty.

Local communities of all these religions maintain places of worship, schools, clubs, and charitable foundations. Many religious groups, such as Hindus, have formed their own political parties.

Through such organizations they try to influence the government to pass laws that deal with religious or social issues.

The Arts

Artistic expression is as much a part of South Asian life as religious practice. The South Asian environment, with its rich appeal to all the senses, nurtures a variety of distinctive, artistic expressions.

Literature

The South Asian literary tradition has its roots in religion. India's two great epic poems, the *Mahabharata* (muh•hah•BAH•ruh•tuh) and the *Ramayana* (rah•MAH•yah•nuh), combine Hindu social and religious beliefs with intricate plots and richly detailed characters. These two works, composed between 1500 and 500 B.C., endure today in public readings, mask and puppet theater, and even television series. An especially treasured portion of the *Mahabharata* is the *Bhagavad Gita* (BAH•guh•vahd GEE•tuh), or "song of the lord." In this dialogue between a warrior and his chariot driver, the Indian god-hero Krishna, the reader finds a message of devotion to duty and courage in the face of death.

Among writers in the 1900s, South Asia boasts the Muslim poet and philosopher Muhammad Iqbal, who wrote in the early part of the century. He was the first to propose the idea of an Islamic state in South Asia. The 1913 Nobel laureate Rabindranath Tagore was an Indian who wrote poetry, fiction, and drama in both English and Bengali. Tagore wrote India's national anthem, whose third verse proclaims:

> *Eternal charioteer, thou drivest man's history along the road rugged with rises and falls of Nations. Amidst all tribulations and terror thy trumpet sounds to hearten those that despair and droop, and guide all people in their paths of peril and pilgrimage. Thou dispenser of India's destiny, victory, victory, victory to thee.*
>
> Rabindranath Tagore,
> "Jana Gana Mana," 1911

COOPERATIVE LEARNING ACTIVITY

South Asian Religions Have the class form three groups, and assign each group one of South Asia's important religious traditions: Hinduism, Buddhism, and Islam. Tell the groups that they are South Asian representatives of these religions and have been invited to give presentations to U.S. high schools. Assign tasks and have group members work together to research and answer the following questions: (1) When and where did your religious tradition start? (2) Who began it? (3) What are your major beliefs and rituals? (4) Where in South Asia is your religious tradition practiced today? Have each group present its report while the other students serve as the audience, asking questions to clarify as needed.

🌐 **EE4 Human Systems: Standard 10**

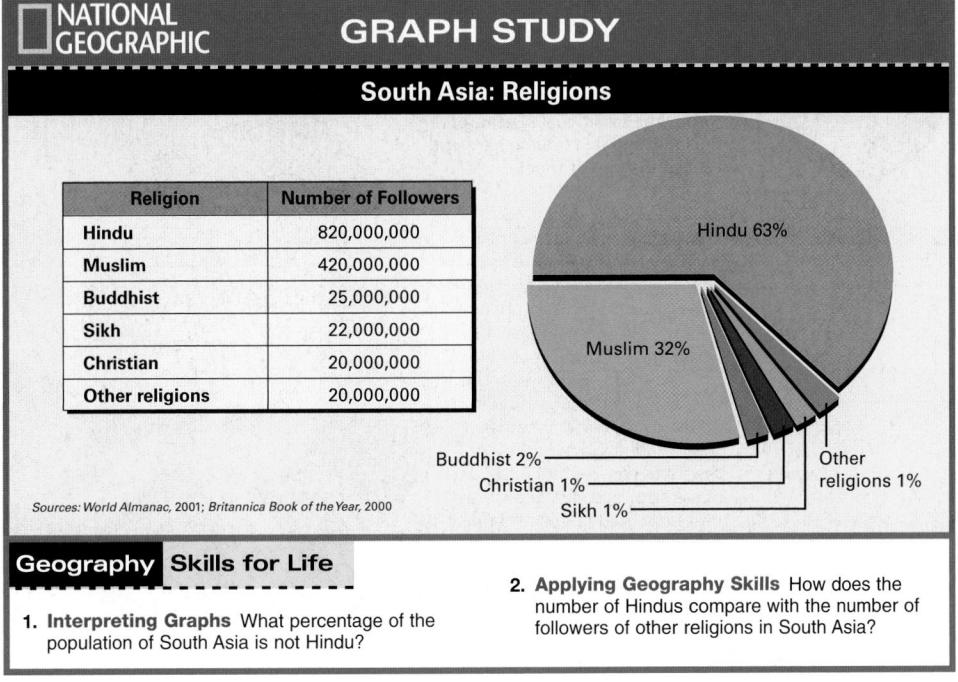

NATIONAL GEOGRAPHIC — GRAPH STUDY

South Asia: Religions

Religion	Number of Followers
Hindu	820,000,000
Muslim	420,000,000
Buddhist	25,000,000
Sikh	22,000,000
Christian	20,000,000
Other religions	20,000,000

Hindu 63%
Muslim 32%
Buddhist 2%
Christian 1%
Sikh 1%
Other religions 1%

Sources: World Almanac, 2001; Britannica Book of the Year, 2000

Geography Skills for Life

1. **Interpreting Graphs** What percentage of the population of South Asia is not Hindu?

2. **Applying Geography Skills** How does the number of Hindus compare with the number of followers of other religions in South Asia?

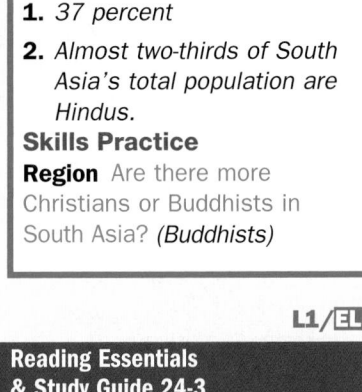

NATIONAL GEOGRAPHIC — GRAPH STUDY

Answers
1. *37 percent*
2. *Almost two-thirds of South Asia's total population are Hindus.*

Skills Practice
Region Are there more Christians or Buddhists in South Asia? *(Buddhists)*

L1/ELL

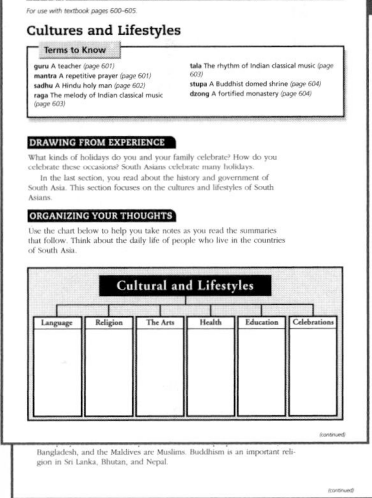

Reading Essentials & Study Guide 24-3

Some contemporary South Asian novelists live in other countries but continue to write from a uniquely South Asian perspective. Salman Rushdie, born in Mumbai, has written controversial novels on Indian history and Islamic politics. Michael Ondaatje, born in Sri Lanka but now living in Canada, won England's prestigious Booker Prize for his novel *The English Patient*, which became an Academy Award-winning film.

Dance and Music

India has numerous classical dance styles, most of which are based on themes from Hindu mythology. The style known as *Bharata Natyam* (bah•RAH•tah NAHT•yam) is practiced mainly in the south. Based on the devotional postures of sacred temple dancers, these dances involve rapid whirling, stamping feet, and an elaborate language of hand gestures called mudras. The dancers, usually women, wear bright silk saris and jingling gold jewelry.

On India's west coast, an ancient style of dance called *Kathakali* (kah•tha•KAHL•lee) is now being revived. The male dancers wear huge, colorful masks, and their violent movements are rooted in martial arts postures.

Indian classical music is divided into two basic types: Hindustani, in the north, and Karnatic, in the south. The melody of each is called the raga, and the rhythm is called the tala.

Movies

Since 1896 when motion pictures first arrived in India, movies have been a popular form of entertainment in India and Bangladesh. India's film industry, centered in Mumbai (nicknamed "Bollywood," a combination of Bombay and Hollywood), is the world's largest, producing more than 800 full-length feature films a year. When Satyajit Ray, India's most renowned director, died in 1992, more than half a million people joined his funeral procession.

Visual Arts and Architecture

Traditionally South Asians have used the visual arts to express religious beliefs and to document daily life. Stone carving and sculpture exist from as far back as the Indus Valley civilization, and some

L3 Literature

Students may wish to read Michael Ondaatje's novel, *Anil's Ghost*, which is set in the author's native Sri Lanka during the present Tamil-Sinhalese conflict.

Chapter 24 • 603

CRITICAL THINKING ACTIVITY

Analyzing Information Have students work in small groups to research the lives of the following figures associated with South Asia: Mother Teresa of Calcutta (Roman Catholic nun and Nobel Prize winner honored for her work with India's poor and dying), Bhimrao Ramji Ambedkar (member of an "untouchable" family who played a key role in writing India's constitution), Professor Muhammad Yunus (founder of Bangladesh's Grameen Bank system), Rabindranath Tagore (Indian poet and Nobel Prize winner), and Muhammad Iqbal (Islamic writer who proposed the founding of Pakistan). After groups have reported on their findings, have students vote on which figure they believe contributed most to life in the region.

EE6 The Uses of Geography: Standard 18

The Language of Rhythm To play drums in India, you must learn how to "speak the sounds" of the drum. Depending on hand position, number of fingers used, and the part of the drum that is struck, a great variety of sounds are attainable. Each of these "hits" has a name. Examples of this "language of rhythm" are featured on tracks 8 and 13 of Disc II in Glencoe's World Music program.

🎵 **World Music: A Cultural Legacy** Use the accompanying Teacher Guide for background information, discussion questions, and worksheets about the music of this region.

3 ASSESS

Assign Section 3 Assessment as homework or as an in-class activity.

🌐 Have students use **Interactive Tutor Self-Assessment CD-ROM.**

L2

Section Quiz 24-3

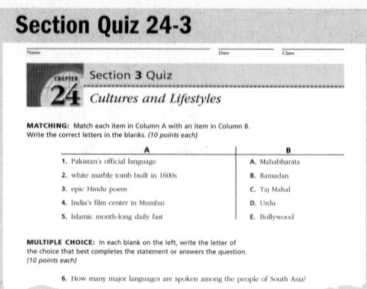

---

music of SOUTH ASIA

The Indian subcontinent is the birthplace of some of the world's oldest and most complex musical forms. The traditional systems of raga (melody) and tala (rhythm) are at the root of the music of India.

Instrument Spotlight: The **tabla** is the most popular percussion instrument of India. The cylindrical right-hand drum is carved of wood and is tuned by hammering wooden pegs underneath leather straps that hold the skin to the drum's top. The left-hand drum has a wider skin surface attached to a kettle-shaped metal bowl. Although the tabla first evolved in India about 500 years ago and is traditionally used in Indian classical music, these drums are now used in modern pop, jazz, and fusion music all over the world.

Go To **World Music: A Cultural Legacy** Hear music of this region on Disc 2, Tracks 7–13.

Mauryan Empire techniques for polishing marble have never been duplicated. Under Mogul emperors, traditional Muslim restrictions against depicting the human form loosened, and portraits and decorative miniature paintings flourished.

The elaborate Hindu temples of India, the Buddhist stupas, or domed shrines, of Nepal and Sri Lanka, and the fortified monasteries, or *dzong*, of Bhutan illustrate South Asia's artistic spirit. The **Taj Mahal** in Agra, India, and the Golden Temple of the Sikhs in Amritsar (UHM•RIHT•suhr), India, are world famous. A Muslim emperor built the Taj Mahal (shown on page 559) in the 1600s as a tomb for his beloved wife. Made of white marble, with towers and domes in the Islamic style, the structure has delicate screens, carved in the Hindu style.

Modern South Asian arts and architecture blend traditional and Western styles. By the mid-1900s South Asian painting and sculpture had an international flavor, and South Asian artists worked in a variety of different media. The mixture of traditional and modern forms is especially apparent in architecture. For example, the modern city of **New Delhi**, with its well-laid-out streets and Western-style government buildings, sits next to the historic city of Delhi, known for its mosques, ancient forts, and busy bazaars.

Quality of Life

The governments and economies of South Asia are still developing. Lifestyles there are a complicated mixture of the traditional and the modern, challenging South Asia's quality of life.

Health

Life expectancies in South Asia are generally lower than those in industrialized countries. Only Sri Lanka's life expectancy of 72 years comes close to that of the United States. Nepal's life expectancy, about 57 years, is the region's lowest, and in India, life expectancy is only about 61 years. In most countries in the region, figures for males and females are fairly close.

TEAM-TEACHING ACTIVITY: ART

South Asian Arts Have students work with an art teacher to research examples of South Asian arts and crafts, such as textile design, Islamic or Sanskrit calligraphy, miniature painting, maskmaking, and sculpture. After students have studied examples, have them work individually or in pairs to create original artworks in a South Asian style. Display students' works in a showcase, in the media center, or in the classroom for others to enjoy. Include a "museum card" explaining the style and origin of the piece. 📦
🌐 **EE4 Human Systems: Standard 10**

Tropical diseases, such as malaria, were once widespread but have been brought under control in much of South Asia. Other health problems continue, however. For example, South Asia and Southeast Asia together have the second-highest rate of HIV infection and AIDS in the world.

The scarcity of clean water in South Asia makes waterborne diseases such as cholera and dysentery common. About one-third of Nepal's infants die from dysentery before their first birthdays. Infant mortality rates are also high in Pakistan.

Food

Although improved farming techniques and government policies now make it theoretically possible for most of South Asia to feed its people, poor nutrition is still a problem. Almost one-third of South Asia's people are too poor to buy high-quality protein foods. To obtain needed protein, some South Asians eat soy-based tofu or beans.

Religious dietary restrictions prohibit Muslims from eating pork. Hindus cannot eat beef, and Jains and many Buddhists are vegetarian. Nevertheless, many South Asians enjoy cuisines of great variety.

Education

South Asia's standard of living is likely to rise with improved education. The region's governments are committed to raising literacy rates and extending educational opportunities to women and members of lower social classes.

▲ A middle school in Hyderabad, Pakistan

Celebrations

South Asia's cultural mix is underscored by its many celebrations. Muslims mark the end of the month-long daily Ramadan fast with feasting and family visits. Buddhists celebrate the birthday of Siddhartha. Hindus, Christians, Jains, and Sikhs all celebrate their traditional holidays. South Asians commemorate national holidays as well. For example, Indians mark the anniversary of the adoption of their constitution on January 26, known as Republic Day.

L2 Holidays

Have students research South Asian holidays such as the Hindu festival Diwali, the celebration of the Buddha's birth, or the Islamic festival that ends Ramadan, the Islamic holy month of fasting. **Ask:** Why are so many South Asian holidays rooted in religious traditions? *(Religion is an important part of everyday life in South Asia, where Hinduism and Buddhism began.)*

Reteach

Write the headings *Language, Religion, Art, Education,* and *Health* on the board. Invite students to list as many details as they can under each heading.

Enrich

Show portions of director Peter Brooks' version of the *Mahabharata* (BBC Video, 1989). Explain that this ancient story cycle has been performed in almost every art form—dance, song, drama, puppetry, film, and television—and continues to enthrall Indian audiences of all ages today.

④ CLOSE

Have students write and share poems or song lyrics about an aspect of South Asian cultural geography.

SECTION 3 ASSESSMENT

Checking for Understanding

1. **Define** guru, mantra, sadhu, stupa, *dzong.*

2. **Main Ideas** Create a graphic organizer like the one below, and fill in information about South Asian arts.

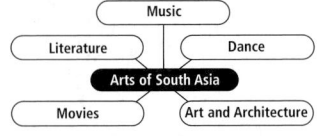

Music
Literature
Dance
Arts of South Asia
Movies
Art and Architecture

Critical Thinking

3. **Making Generalizations** What are the major languages of South Asia, and what do they have in common?

4. **Comparing and Contrasting** How might job opportunities for religious minorities in South Asia compare with those for religious minorities in other parts of the world?

5. **Problem Solving** What improvements in health and education might enrich the quality of life in South Asia?

Analyzing Maps

6. **Place** Look at the map of South Asian languages on page 601. What is the dominant language family in Pakistan? In Bhutan?

Applying Geography

7. **Identifying Relationships** Write a short essay describing the relationship among language families, religious groups, and national identities in South Asia.

SECTION 3 ASSESSMENT ANSWERS

1. All vocabulary terms are defined in the text.
2. Graphic organizers should reflect text information.
3. Hindi, Urdu, Bengali; all are Indo-European languages.
4. Student answers should focus on the extent to which religious tolerance is upheld in law and carried out in practice. As in many other regions, religious minorities in South Asia often play major roles in business, trade, and the military.

5. efforts to control the spread of HIV/AIDS, greater access to clean water, better nutrition, wider access to education and literacy programs
6. Indo-European; Sino-Tibetan
7. **Applying Geography** Essays should reflect text information, and use correct grammar and punctuation.

Teaching the Skill

Write the following topic on the board: *Health Care in South Asia.* Give students time to search their textbooks, published reference works, and Internet resources for data on this topic. Have students share their results. Then ask the class to evaluate the validity and utility of the information: **Ask: How reliable and useful is this information? How trustworthy are the sources? Can you tell whether what you found was fact or opinion? Why are these questions important?** *(because the quality of research and reports hinges on the quality and reliability of information)*

Additional Practice
L1

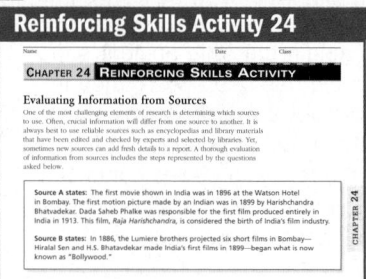

Reinforcing Skills Activity 24

Name _____ Date _____ Class _____

CHAPTER 24 REINFORCING SKILLS ACTIVITY

Evaluating Information from Sources

One of the most challenging elements of research is determining which sources to use. Often, crucial information will differ from one source to another. It is always best to use reliable sources such as encyclopedias and library materials that have been edited and checked by reports and selected by libraries. Yet, sometimes new sources can add fresh details to a report. A thorough evaluation of information from sources includes the steps represented by the questions asked below.

Source A states: The first movie shown in India was in 1896 at the Watson Hotel in Bombay. The first motion picture made by an Indian was in 1899 by Harishchandra Bhatvadekar. Dada Saheb Phalke was responsible for the first film produced entirely in India in 1913. This film, Raja Harishchandra, is considered the birth of India's film industry.

Source B states: In 1886, the Lumiere brothers projected six short films in Bombay— Hiralal Sen and H.S. Bhatavdekar made India's first films in 1899—began what is now known as "Bollywood."

GLENCOE
TECHNOLOGY

Glencoe Skillbuilder Interactive Workbook, Level 2

Evaluating Information and Sources

You live in a world saturated with information and opinions. Finding information on any topic is not a problem. But how can you decide which information is useful and accurate?

Learning the Skill

Information that you find while researching can come from a variety of sources. However, not all of the information that you find may be useful or even accurate. It is important to evaluate the information you find in order to determine whether it is valid information. To evaluate information and sources:

- **Identify the reliability of the source.** Consider whether the source may be biased. For example, a statement published by an environmental group and one published by a large energy company may have different biases.

- **Summarize the key points of the information in a few sentences.**

- **Distinguish fact from opinion.** Look for ways that facts are chosen or left out to support the stated opinions.

- **Verify facts by cross-checking them in other sources.** Check encyclopedias, almanacs, and other references to be sure the information is accurate. Make sure you are getting complete information from your sources.

- **Follow up with additional research.** Look for additional information about your source and about the issue.

> "British rule in India was not malign [or] needlessly cruel. . . . [T]he purpose of British rule was to educate Indians to be able to rule themselves and for the British to retire. . . . When freedom came, the British left us valuable legacies, which have come in very useful to us in ruling ourselves to some purpose."
>
> —M.R. Masani, former opposition leader of the Indian Parliament

> "[The British] tried to educate a certain middle class and allowed it all the facilities; but the basic reforms they did not carry out. Our literacy rates were so poor, and our technology has taken years to catch up with modern developments. . . . They needn't have left us to chaos, as they did, and divided our country. That was the worst—the partition of India. That was criminal: all the poisonous weeds have grown on that. . . ."
>
> —Aruna Asaf Ali, Indian nationalist leader

Practicing the Skill

Read the passages about the effect of British rule in India. Then answer the questions.

1. How reliable are the speakers as sources of information?

2. Summarize each speaker's position.

3. Is the information in this source primarily fact or opinion? Explain.

4. What evidence does each speaker present?

5. What other information might you need to gain a deeper understanding of the topic?

Applying the Skill

Research a current South Asian issue in multiple sources—magazines, newspapers, or Internet sites. Analyze the usefulness of the articles as sources of information. Determine whether the articles present primarily facts or opinions. Also, evaluate the articles' validity, and identify any biases.

Go To The Glencoe Skillbuilder Interactive Workbook, Level 2 provides instruction and practice in key social studies skills.

ANSWERS TO PRACTICING THE SKILL

1. Both speakers are writing from experience, but each has a personal bias that affects his opinion.

2. M. R. Masani: British rule was not intentionally harmful and left India with important gifts; Aruna Asaf Ali: British rule did more harm than good, especially in the legacy of partition.

3. The information is primarily opinion—both cases are writers' views of the same facts.

4. Masani: India was able to use British legacies to rule well when independence came; Araf Ali: evidence of educational and technological fallout from colonialism and the partition of the country.

5. factual accounts of conditions in British-controlled South Asia before and after independence (encyclopedia and almanac resources, for example)

CHAPTER 24 — SUMMARY & STUDY GUIDE

SECTION 1 — Population Patterns (pp. 587–591)

Terms to Know
- *jati*
- megalopolis

Key Points
- The population of South Asia reflects a rich and complex mix of religions, languages, and social groupings.
- South Asia has a high overall population density, but population distribution varies from region to region according to climate and terrain.
- There is a sharp contrast between urban and rural life in South Asia.

Organizing Your Notes
Create an outline using the format below to help you organize your notes for this section.

Population Patterns
I. Human characteristics
A. India
1. Descended from diverse groups
2.
3.
B. Pakistan

SECTION 2 — History and Government (pp. 592–597)

Terms to Know
- dharma
- reincarnation
- karma
- nirvana
- raj

Key Points
- One of the world's first civilizations developed in the Indus River valley.
- South Asia gave birth to two of the world's major religions, Hinduism and Buddhism.
- South Asia was shaped by a series of invasions and conquests, including the expansion of the British Empire into the region.
- South Asian countries today face the challenges of independence and establishing new governments.
- Several South Asian countries have had female leaders after becoming independent.

Organizing Your Notes
Use a table like the one below to help you organize important details from this section.

Country or Area	Early History	Government	Religions

SECTION 3 — Cultures and Lifestyles (pp. 600–605)

Terms to Know
- guru
- mantra
- sadhu
- stupa
- *dzong*

Key Points
- South Asia is a land of many languages and religions.
- The diverse cultures of South Asia have made rich contributions to the arts.
- South Asia faces the challenge of improving the quality of life for much of its population.
- Even with the challenges it faces, South Asia benefits from its cultural diversity.

Organizing Your Notes
Use a web diagram like the one below to help you organize your notes for this section.

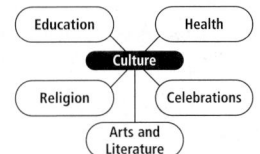

Education — Health — Culture — Religion — Celebrations — Arts and Literature

Chapter 24 🌐 607

Using the Chapter 24 Summary & Study Guide

Use the Chapter 24 Summary & Study Guide to preview, review, condense, or reteach the chapter.

Preview/Review

🖿 **Vocabulary PuzzleMaker CD-ROM** reinforces "Terms to Know."

🖿 **Interactive Tutor Self-Assessment CD-ROM** provides a review of Chapter 24 content.

Condense

Have students read the Chapter 24 Summary & Study Guide.

🖿 Chapter 24 Audio Program

📁 Chapter 24 Guided Reading Activities

Reteach

📁 Chapter 24 Reteaching Activities (Spanish also available)

📁 Chapter 24 Reading Essentials and Study Guides

GLENCOE TECHNOLOGY

📺 NATIONAL GEOGRAPHIC

WORLD REGIONS
VIDEO PROGRAM

Unit 8, South Asia
The following segments enhance the study of this unit:
- **Monsoon**
- **Sherpas of Nepal**
- **Bollywood**

CHAPTER CULMINATING ACTIVITY

Creative Writing Ask students to assume the identity of an individual from South Asian history. (They may choose famous or known individuals, or unnamed people from particular times and places.) Have them write journal entries describing an important day in their lives. Encourage students to use descriptive language to capture a sense of their character's time, culture, and physical setting. Invite volunteers to share their work.

🌐 **EE4 Human Systems: Standard 10**

NOTE: This activity may be completed separately or you may wish students to incorporate it in their GeoJournals.

Have students visit the Web site at geography.glencoe.com to review Chapter 24 and take the **Self-Check Quiz.**

GLENCOE TECHNOLOGY

Use *MindJogger Videoquiz* to review the Chapter 24 content.

Reviewing Key Terms

1. a   4. f
2. e   5. b
3. d   6. c

Reviewing Facts

SECTION 1

1. by religion or *jati* (occupational or social group)
2. on the Ganges Plain, the Ganges Delta, coastal cities of India, and Maldives islands
3. industry, finance, filmmaking; iron and steel industries

SECTION 2

4. Indus River valley
5. the Gupta Empire
6. the British

SECTION 3

7. Hindi, Urdu, Bengali
8. Jainism
9. moviemaking

Critical Thinking

1. It allowed intermixing of successive waves of immigrants and conquerors on the Ganges Plain, and preserved other unique cultures in the isolation of the Himalaya.
2. Religion influences clothing people wear; architectural styles; the treatment of livestock, such

Reviewing Key Terms

Write the letter of the key term that best matches each definition below.

a. *jati*   d. reincarnation
b. megalopolis   e. guru
c. karma   f. *dzong*

1. a social group that defines a person's occupation and standing in the community
2. a teacher
3. rebirth
4. fortified monasteries
5. a large metropolitan area
6. good or bad deeds and their effects

Reviewing Facts

SECTION 1

1. How do many Indians traditionally identify themselves?
2. Where are the highest population densities in South Asia found?
3. What economic activities are important to Mumbai? What economic activities are important to Kolkata?

SECTION 2

4. Where did the first South Asian civilization develop?
5. Which ancient South Asian empire was one of the most advanced civilizations in the world?
6. Which European power ruled much of South Asia until the mid-1900s?

SECTION 3

7. Name the primary languages of Pakistan, Bangladesh, and northern India.
8. What religion teaches nonviolence and holds that every living being has a soul?
9. What art form is a major industry in India?

Critical Thinking

1. **Making Generalizations** How has the physical geography of South Asia contributed to the development of diverse cultures?
2. **Drawing Conclusions** What are some religious influences on South Asia's peoples?
3. **Categorizing Information** Create a time line showing important dates and events in South Asian history.

Important Dates in South Asia's History

2500 B.C.	2000 B.C.	1500 B.C.	1000 B.C.
Indus Valley civilization flourishes		1700 B.C. Indus Valley civilization declines	

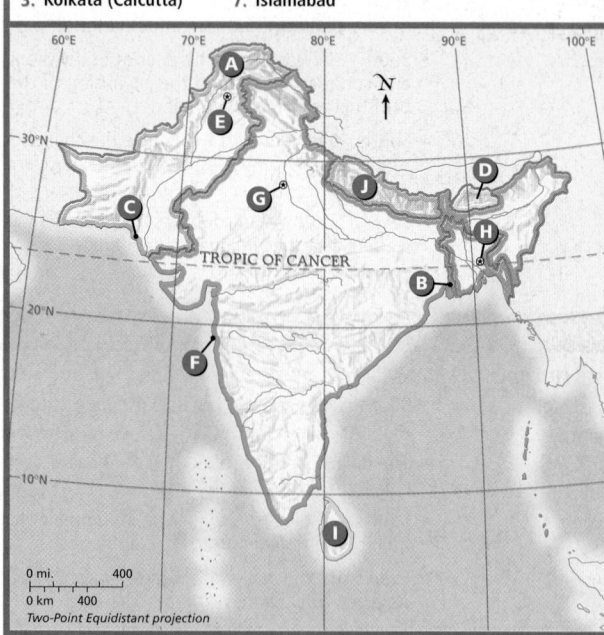

NATIONAL GEOGRAPHIC
Locating Places
South Asia: Physical-Political Geography

Match the letters on the map with the places and physical features of South Asia. Write your answers on a sheet of paper.

1. Sri Lanka   4. New Delhi   8. Karachi
2. Mumbai (Bombay)   5. Nepal   9. Bhutan
3. Kolkata (Calcutta) 6. Hindu Kush   10. Dhaka
                      7. Islamabad

as cows; education and political parties; as well as diet.
3. Time lines should reflect text information.

NATIONAL GEOGRAPHIC **Locating Places**

1. I	3. B	5. J	7. E	9. D
2. F	4. G	6. A	8. C	10. H

Using the Regional Atlas

1. on the Ganges Plain, the Ganges Delta, and the seacoasts
2. the high elevation, steep terrain, and very cold climates of the Himalaya and other northern ranges

Using the Regional Atlas

Refer to the Regional Atlas on pp. 560–563.

1. **Location** Where are most of South Asia's largest cities located?

2. **Human-Environment Interaction** What physical features might account for the areas of low population density in the northern part of the region?

Thinking Like a Geographer

What factors, including physical geography, helped the process of diffusion of South Asian cultural influences to other parts of the world?

Problem-Solving Activity

Problem-Solution Proposal Using information from your text, the school library, or the Internet, write a report that proposes a solution to one of the following problems of South Asia: urban population density, conflicts in Sri Lanka or the Kashmir region, or nutrition and health. Your report should include an outline of the problem, recommendations for a solution to the problem, and a course of action. Design and draw graphic elements, such as charts, as needed.

GeoJournal

Persuasive Writing Using your GeoJournal data, write a short speech urging American high school students to become familiar with South Asian history and culture. Use descriptive language, appropriate vocabulary terms, and powerful verbs to convince your audience of the value of learning about South Asia.

Technology Activity

Developing Multimedia Presentations Work with a team to develop a multimedia presentation on one aspect of South Asia's history or culture. (Examples include the Gupta Empire, Indian dance, or Buddhism in Bhutan.) Use reference works and the Internet to develop your presentation. Present your work to the class.

Standardized Test Practice

Read the passage and choose the best answer for the following multiple-choice question. If you have trouble answering the question, use the process of elimination to narrow your choices.

———— ■ ————

"Raindrops keep falling on the head of anyone who takes a summer trip to Mawsynram, a hill town in northeast India. And falling. And falling. Two Indian meteorologists claim, and many U.S. specialists agree, that Mawsynram has ousted Hawaii's Waialeale as [the] earth's wettest spot, measured by average annual rainfall. Mawsynram gets an average 467.44 inches of rain a year, compared with 459.99 for Waialeale."

"Geographica," National Geographic, May 1993

1. **According to the reading, which of the following statements is a fact?**

   A All Indian and U.S. meteorologists agree that the average annual rainfall in Mawsynram, India, is greater than that in Waialeale, Hawaii.

   B Mawsynram and Waialeale have always been wetter than other places on Earth.

   C The average annual rainfall in Waialeale, Hawaii, is less than that of Mawsynram, India.

   D In the view of many Indians, the town of Mawsynram is Earth's wettest spot.

 **Test-Taking Tip** Learn to distinguish facts from nonfacts. Sometimes nonfacts contain phrases such as *I believe* or *in my view* or broad generalizations such as *every, all,* or *never.*

Technology Activity

Students' presentations should be engaging, well-researched, and varied.

Standardized Test Practice

1. C

Tested Objectives: analyzing information synthesizing information

Additional Practice and Test-Taking Tips

Standardized Test Practice Workbook

? CHAPTER BONUS TEST QUESTION

During the monsoon, two-thirds of this low-lying country may be under floodwaters. At that time, floodwaters may rise to 20 feet above sea level. Flooding is even worse when the Ganges, Jamuna, and Meghna Rivers are swollen by heavy rain and melting snow in the Himalaya.

What country is being described in this passage, and under these conditions, what would you expect to be the country's major economic activity? *(Bangladesh; agriculture because regular floods enrich the soil for farming, but would destroy factories and manufacturing equipment.)*

Thinking Like a Geographer

Successive waves of immigrants and conquerors brought their own cultural influences to South Asia and carried South Asian influences elsewhere. The region's location on the major land and sea trade routes linking Europe, Asia, and North Africa helped spread South Asian influences, especially Buddhism, and opened South Asia to Islamic influence.

Problem-Solving Activity

Have students work in pairs or small groups to prepare their reports. Allow time for reports to be shared. Invite students to evaluate the potential success of one another's proposals.

GeoJournal

Students' speeches should be factually accurate and persuasive.

PLANNING GUIDE

NOTE: The following materials may be used when teaching Chapter 25. Section-level support materials are shown at point-of-use in the margins of the Teacher Wraparound Edition.

TEACHING TRANSPARENCIES

L2 Unit 8 Map Overlay Transparencies

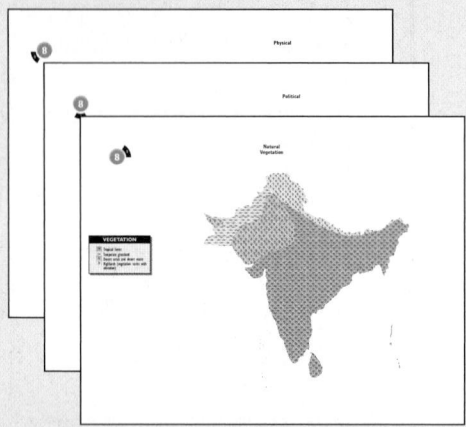

L2 Political Map Transparency 8

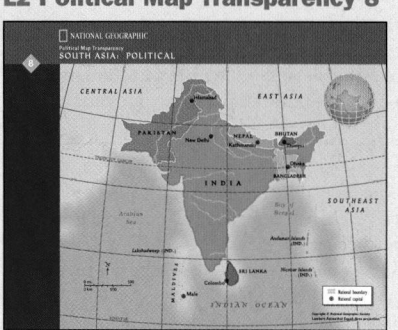

GEOGRAPHIC LITERACY

Focus on Geography Literacy

APPLICATION AND ENRICHMENT

L3 Enrichment Activity 25

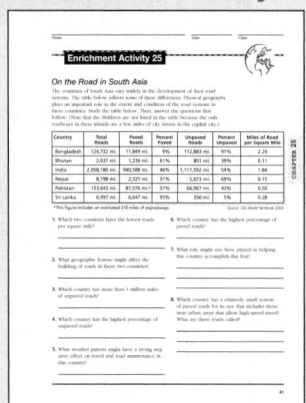

REVIEW AND REINFORCEMENT

L1 Vocabulary Activity 25 **L1 Reinforcing** **L1 Reteaching Activity 25**
Skills Activity 25

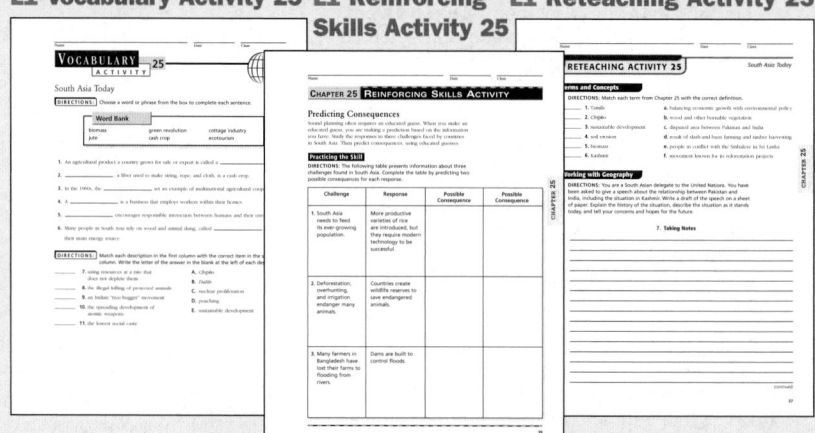

ASSESSMENT

L2 Chapter 25 Test Form A

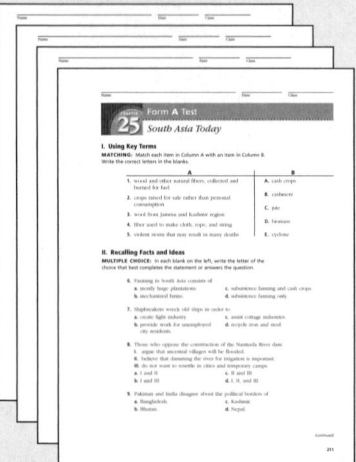

L2 Chapter 25 Test Form B

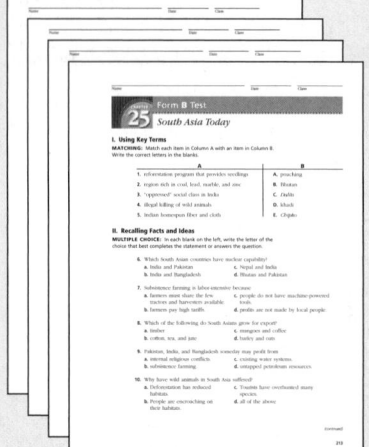

L1/ELL Performance Assessment Activity 25

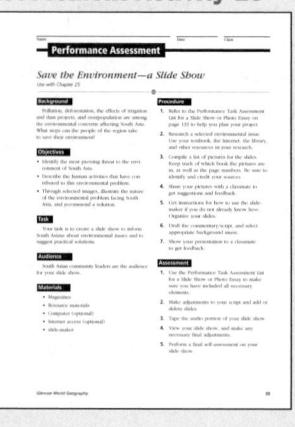

ExamView® Pro Testmaker

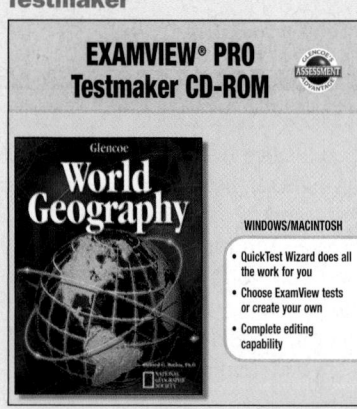

The following Spanish language materials are available in the Spanish Resources binder:

- 📁 **Spanish Vocabulary Activities**
- 📁 **Spanish Guided Reading Activities**
- 📁 **Spanish Reteaching Activities**
- 📁 **Spanish Summaries**
- 📁 **Spanish Quizzes and Tests**
- 📁 **Spanish Reading Essentials and Study Guide**

- 📼 ◉ **World Regions Video**
- 📼 **MindJogger Videoquiz**
- 💿 **Vocabulary PuzzleMaker CD-ROM**
- 💿 **Interactive Tutor Self-Assessment CD-ROM**
- 💿 **ExamView® Pro Testmaker CD-ROM**
- 💿 **Audio Program**
- 💿 **TeacherWorks CD-ROM**
- 💿 **Interactive Student Edition CD-ROM**
- 💿 **Glencoe Skillbuilder Interactive Workbook CD-ROM, Level 2**
- 💿 **Presentation Plus! CD-ROM**

Timesaving Tools

TeacherWorks™ All-In-One Planner and Resource Center

- **Interactive Teacher Edition** Access your Teacher Wraparound Edition and your classroom resources with a few easy clicks.

- **Interactive Lesson Planner** Planning has never been easier! Organize your week, month, semester, or year with all the lesson helps you need to make teaching creative, timely, and relevant.

Use Glencoe's **Presentation Plus!** multimedia teacher tool to easily present dynamic lessons that visually excite your students. Using Microsoft PowerPoint® you can customize the presentations to create your own personalized lessons.

GEOGRAPHY Online

Use our Web site for additional resources. All essential content is covered in the Student Edition.

You and your students can visit geography.glencoe.com, the Web site companion to *Glencoe World Geography*. This innovative integration of electronic and print media offers your students a wealth of opportunities. The student text directs students to the Web site for the following options:

- **Chapter Overviews**
- **Self-Check Quizzes**
- **Student Activities**
- **Textbook Updates**

Answers are provided for you in the "Web Activity Lesson Plan." Additional Web resources and Interactive Tutor puzzles are also available.

▶ **Additional Glencoe Teacher Support**

- **Teaching Strategies for the Geography Classroom** (including Block Scheduling Pacing Guides)
- **Graphic Organizer Transparencies Strategies and Activities**
- **Outline Map Resource Book**
- **Reading in the Content Area**

PLANNING GUIDE

CHAPTER 25

SECTION RESOURCES

Daily Objectives	Reproducible Resources	Multimedia Resources

SECTION 1   Living in South Asia

1. Explain how agriculture provides a living for most of South Asia's people.
2. Describe the role of fisheries and mines in South Asian economies.
3. Identify where rapid industrial development is taking place in South Asia.
4. List issues raised by tourism in South Asia.

Reproducible Resources:
- Reproducible Lesson Plan 25-1
- Daily Lecture Notes 25-1
- Guided Reading Activity 25-1*
- Reading Essentials and Study Guide 25-1*
- Section Quiz 25-1*

Multimedia Resources:
- Daily Focus Skills Transparency 25-1
- Political Map Transparency 8
- Unit 8 Map Overlay Transparencies
- Interactive Tutor Self-Assessment CD-ROM
- ExamView® Pro Testmaker CD-ROM*
- Presentation Plus! CD-ROM

SECTION 2   People and Their Environment

1. Examine how South Asia is handling the complex task of managing its rich natural resources.
2. Describe how seasonal weather patterns present challenges to the region's economy.
3. Explain how geographic factors impact the political and economic challenges of South Asia's future.

Reproducible Resources:
- Reproducible Lesson Plan 25-2
- Vocabulary Activity 25*
- Daily Lecture Notes 25-2
- Guided Reading Activity 25-2*
- Reading Essentials and Study Guide 25-2*
- Reteaching Activity 25*
- Reinforcing Skills Activity 25
- Section Quiz 25-2*

Multimedia Resources:
- Daily Focus Skills Transparency 25-2
- Political Map Transparency 8
- Unit 8 Map Overlay Transparencies
- Vocabulary PuzzleMaker CD-ROM
- Interactive Tutor Self-Assessment CD-ROM
- ExamView® Pro Testmaker CD-ROM*
- Presentation Plus! CD-ROM

 Blackline Master   💾 Software   📼 Videocassette   *Also available in Spanish

🖼 Transparency   💿 CD-ROM   💿 DVD

⏱ OUT OF TIME? 🗂 Assign the Chapter 25 **Reading Essentials and Study Guide.**

Block Schedule

Activities that are particularly suited to use within the block scheduling framework are identified throughout this chapter by the following designation: 🗂

KEY TO ABILITY LEVELS

Teaching strategies have been coded for various learning styles and abilities.

L1   BASIC activities for all students

L2   AVERAGE activities for average to above-average students

L3   CHALLENGING activities for above-average students

ELL   ENGLISH LANGUAGE LEARNER activities

Teacher to Teacher

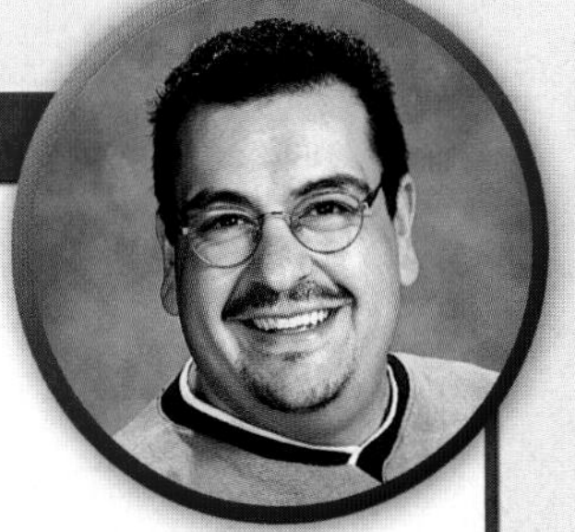

Keith Lucero
Denver East High School
Denver, CO

Briefing the President

Have each student select a country in South Asia. Tell them that they are to act as geography advisors to the president of the United States. Each student will write a presidential briefing book and a short presidential speech on an issue facing their selected country. Students must collect information about their selected country: its physical geography, its political and cultural environment, and most important, any issues, conflicts, or particular challenges faced by the country. Students may choose to do further research on one of the many issues described in the textbook, such as the Kashmir conflict or environmental concerns.

The briefing book each student assembles will contain background information and summaries for the president and offer suggestions as to what the president should do about one of the challenges the South Asian country faces. The briefing book should also include a three- to five-minute speech the president can give on the chosen issue.

Have several student volunteers give their speeches to the class.

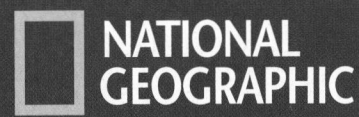

Meeting National Standards

Geography For Life

The following standards are highlighted in Chapter 25:

Section 1
- EE2 Places and Regions: Standard 4
- EE4 Human Systems: Standards 10, 11
- EE5 Environment and Society: Standards 14, 16

Section 2
- EE2 Places and Regions: Standards 4, 6
- EE3 Physical Systems: Standard 8
- EE4 Human Systems: Standards 10, 13
- EE5 Environment and Society: Standard 14, 16
- EE6 The Uses of Geography: Standard 18

Local Objectives

____

____

NATIONAL GEOGRAPHIC TEACHER'S CORNER

Index to National Geographic Magazine:

The following articles may be used for research relating to this chapter:

- "Nepal: Changed For Good, For Bad, Forever," by T. D. Allman, November 2000.
- "In Search of the Clouded Leopard," by Jesse Oak Taylor-Ide, September 2000.
- "Kashmir: Trapped in Conflict," by Lewis M. Simons, September 1999.
- *Biodiversity,* a National Geographic Special Edition, February 1999.

National Geographic Society Products:

To order the following products for use with this chapter, call National Geographic Society at 1-800-368-2728.

- *Asia* (Video)
- *Healing the Earth* (Video)
- *Endangered Animals: Survivors on the Brink* (Video)
- *National Geographic Desk Reference* (Book)
- *National Geographic Atlas of the World, Seventh Edition* (Book)

NGS ONLINE

Access National Geographic's Web site for current events, activities, links, interactive features, and archives.
www.nationalgeographic.com

MEETING SPECIAL NEEDS

In addition to the Differentiated Instruction strategies found in each section, the following resources are also suitable for your special needs students:

- ***ExamView® Pro Testmaker CD-ROM*** allows teachers to tailor tests by reducing answer choices.
- The ***Audio Program*** includes the entire narrative of the student edition so that less-proficient readers can listen to the words as they read them.
- The ***Reading Essentials and Study Guide*** provides the same content as the student edition but is written two grade levels below the textbook.
- ***Guided Reading Activities*** give less-proficient readers point-by-point instructions to increase comprehension as they read each textbook section.
- ***Enrichment Activities*** include a stimulating collection of readings and activities for gifted and talented students.

Chapter Objectives

1. Identify the key economic activities of South Asia.
2. Discuss the major environmental and social challenges the region faces.

GeoJournal

For access to additional photos, maps, and information on the contemporary issues of South Asia, go to www.nationalgeographic.com (See Teacher pages in front for strategies for using journals in the geography classroom.)

GEOGRAPHY Online

Introduce students to chapter content and key terms by having them access **Chapter Overview 25** at geography.glencoe.com

FOLDABLES™
Study Organizer

Dinah Zike's Foldables are three-dimensional, interactive graphic organizers that help students practice basic writing skills, review key vocabulary terms, and identify main ideas. Have students complete the Foldable activity in the *Dinah Zike's Reading and Study Skills Foldables* booklet.

CHAPTER 25 South Asia Today

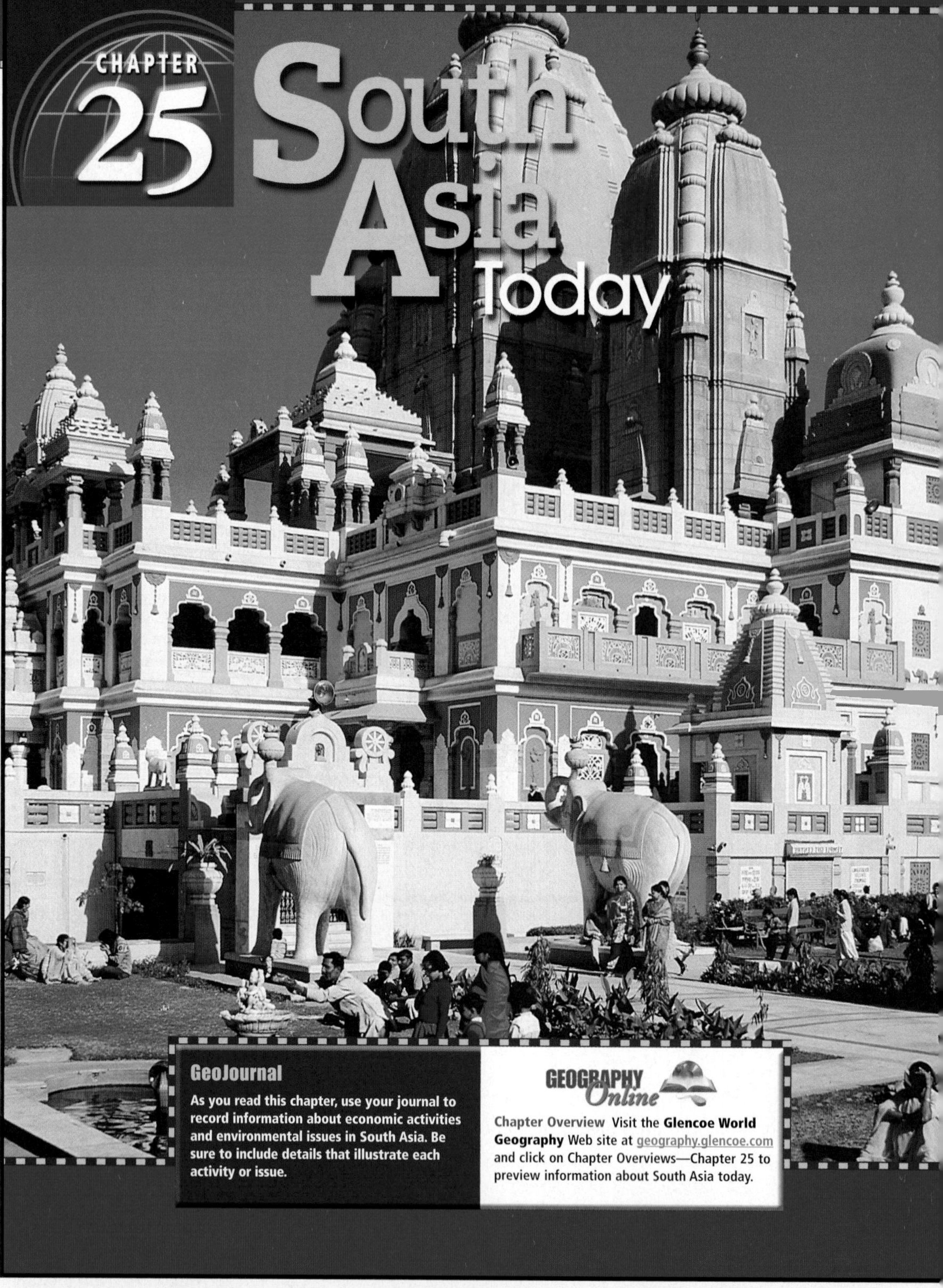

GeoJournal

As you read this chapter, use your journal to record information about economic activities and environmental issues in South Asia. Be sure to include details that illustrate each activity or issue.

GEOGRAPHY Online

Chapter Overview Visit the **Glencoe World Geography** Web site at geography.glencoe.com and click on Chapter Overviews—Chapter 25 to preview information about South Asia today.

ABOUT THE PHOTO

Visual Instruction The Laxmi Narayan Temple in Delhi, India, is an example of modern Indian architecture using traditional elements. The temple is built in Orissan style, which comes from the state of Orissa in east central India. This style is known for its horizontal patterns and beehive-shaped towers crowned with flat or round tops. The earliest temples in the Orissan style date back to the A.D. 700s. ⬛ EE2 Places and Regions: Standard 4 ⬛ EE4 Human Systems: Standard 10

Guide to Reading

Consider What You Know

South Asia is world-renowned for its many fine fabrics—soft pashminas and cashmeres, bright cottons, and finely spun silks. What other items from South Asia might you find in stores in your community?

Reading Strategy

Categorizing Complete a web diagram similar to the one below by filling in obstacles new farming methods create for the people of South Asia.

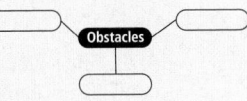

Read to Find Out

- How does agriculture provide a living for most of South Asia's people?
- What role do fisheries and mines have in South Asian economies?
- Where in South Asia is rapid industrial development taking place?
- What issues are raised by tourism in South Asia?

Terms to Know

- cash crop
- jute
- green revolution
- biomass
- cottage industry
- ecotourism

Places to Locate

- Bangalore
- Chittagong
- Hyderabad

◀ *Hindu temple, Delhi, India*

Living in South Asia

NATIONAL GEOGRAPHIC

A Geographic View

Ancient Rhythms

Despite . . . signs of change, much of Bhutan remains as it has always been, an unspoiled land of farmers and herders of yaks and cattle. Some 90 percent of Bhutanese live . . . as their [ancestors] did, following livestock through the high summer meadows, planting plots of rice and chiles in the valleys. People like . . . a woman I met in the northern village of Soe . . . still follow the ancient rhythms. . . . Together we watched pine smoke curl from her kitchen fire, sipped warm bowls of yak-butter tea, and talked about the sorts of things that concern farmers everywhere— the price of meat, the cost of clothing, [and] the health of the herd.

Bhutanese farmer drying chiles

—Bruce W. Bunting, "Bhutan: Kingdom in the Clouds,"
National Geographic, *May 1991*

———————◆———————

Throughout South Asia, agriculture is the most common occupation. More than 60 percent of the labor force in India and Bangladesh are employed in agriculture. In this section you will learn how South Asians today are using new agricultural methods to increase food production. You will also learn about other ways in which the peoples of South Asia earn a living.

Living From the Land

Most people in South Asia practice subsistence farming. Subsistence farmers often rely on labor-intensive farming methods. They may use digging sticks or hand plows to break up the soil, and they often sow

Chapter 25 ⊕ 611

FOCUS

Section Overview

This section discusses the key economic activities of the South Asian region.

BELLRINGER
Skillbuilder Activity

Project transparency and have students answer questions.

Available as blackline master.

Daily Focus Skills Transparency 25-1

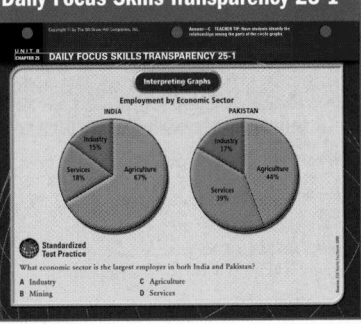

Guide to Reading

Consider What You Know
Answer *tea, clothing and shoes, spices, software*

Reading Strategy
Answer *monsoon rains only allow for one planting cycle per year; modernization is expensive; fuel is expensive and not enough is available*

Preteaching Vocabulary
Have students create pictogram clues for each of the "Terms to Know" in this section. Have students choose partners and guess one another's clues.

RESOURCE MANAGER

Reproducible Masters
- Reproducible Lesson Plan 25-1
- Daily Lecture Notes 25-1
- Guided Reading Activity 25-1
- Reading Essentials and Study Guide 25-1
- Section Quiz 25-1

Transparencies
- Daily Focus Skills Transparency 25-1
- Political Map Transparency 8
- Unit 8 Map Overlay Transparencies

Multimedia
- 💿 Interactive Tutor Self-Assessment CD-ROM
- 💿 ExamView® Pro Testmaker CD-ROM
- 💿 Presentation Plus! CD-ROM

2 TEACH

L1 Economy

Have students scan this section for examples of ways South Asians have been working in recent years to improve the region's economy. *(improving agriculture and commercial fishing; ship breaking; developing untapped resources; producing computer software and hardware)* After students have finished reading the section, **Ask: In what ways is South Asia's economy receiving help from outside the region?** *(outside investment, international loans, foreign aid, scientific and technical advice)*

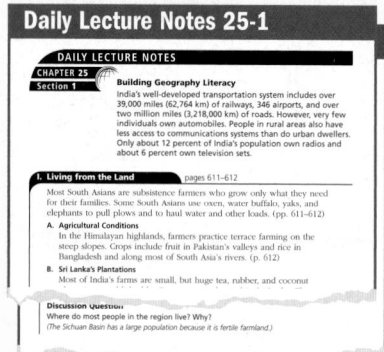

Daily Lecture Notes 25-1

NATIONAL GEOGRAPHIC World Explorer

Answer
to meet food needs of their own population, to avoid dependence on only a few crops

More About the Photo
Agriculture, which makes up 25 percent of India's GDP, remains an important sector of the economy.

---

seed by hand. To water their crops, farmers may hand-carry water for miles from a well or river, although some areas have irrigation systems.

Subsistence farmers also use animal power. Oxen and water buffalo pull wooden plows, carry heavy loads, and turn simple waterwheels for irrigation and mills for grinding grain. South Asians also use yaks, the long-haired cattle that flourish at high elevations; camels in desert areas; and elephants, which can do the heavy work of a tractor.

Farming depends on many changeable factors, such as rainfall, that are beyond the farmers' control. A family can lose its entire food supply in one season of drought, or crops might be eaten by wild animals. Even with the risks, however, subsistence farming allows many South Asians to be economically independent.

Agricultural Conditions

Farms in South Asia vary widely in size and appearance, based on geographic, historic, and cultural factors. In the Himalayan highlands of Nepal and Bhutan, farmers practice terracing, making use of every available inch of arable land on the steep slopes. Fruit orchards line the fertile highland valleys of Pakistan. In most of Bangladesh's delta region and along many of South Asia's great rivers, farmers work in water above their knees to grow rice. Farms in India are generally very small, with over one-third of them covering less than an acre.

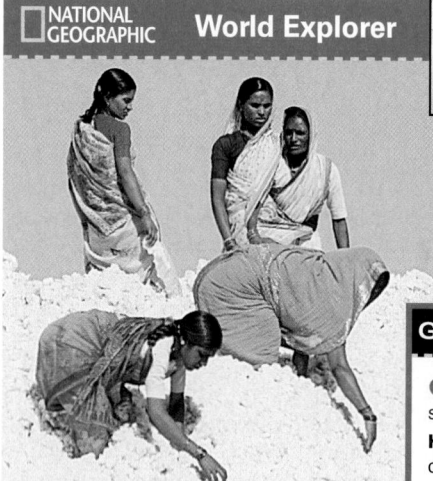

NATIONAL GEOGRAPHIC World Explorer

History
Sri Lanka's Plantations

India's tiny farm plots stand in sharp contrast to the huge tea, rubber, and coconut plantations where many Sri Lankans work. British and Dutch colonizers established these large, technically sophisticated agricultural operations. The British moved their tea plantations from India to Sri Lanka (then called Ceylon) when Indian workers demanded better working conditions.

Although the European planters left Sri Lanka when the country gained its independence from the United Kingdom in 1948, plantations continue to employ about three-fourths of Sri Lanka's workers. The profitable plantations leave little land for growing crops to feed the country's own people, however, so Sri Lanka must import large quantities of basic foods, such as rice.

South Asian Crops

Cash crops bring much-needed income to South Asia. The tea, rubber, and coconuts of Sri Lanka are cash crops, farm products grown for sale or export. India also grows large quantities of cashews, coffee, and tea for export. Tea plants grow well in northeastern India's temperate highlands. However, balancing the physical needs of hungry people with the economic needs of growing countries is a challenge to the region.

Cotton is a key cash crop in South Asia. India and Pakistan are among the world leaders in cotton production. Jute, a fiber used to make string, rope, and cloth, is the major cash crop of Bangladesh and is grown mainly in the western lowlands bordering India. Sales of this fiber, called the "golden crop" for its color and value, account for a large part of Bangladesh's export income, although demand for jute is decreasing.

Geography **Skills for Life**

Cotton Production Workers pile cotton by hand to be stored in outdoor warehouses in India.
Human-Environment Interaction Why is it important for countries to raise other crops in addition to cash crops?

DIFFERENTIATED INSTRUCTION

English Learners As students read this section, have them list nouns that name agricultural or manufacturing products of South Asia. Alert students to watch for context clues such as forms of the verbs *export*, *manufacture*, and *produce*. Ask students to place a check mark next to the nouns with which they are already familiar. **ELL**

🌐 **EE4 Human Systems: Standard 11**

📁 Refer to *Inclusion for the Social Studies Classroom Strategies and Activities.*

India is one of the world's largest producers of bananas. Citrus fruits, chiles, and spices are grown for export in the steppe areas of India, Pakistan, and Bangladesh.

Grains provide South Asia with important food sources as well as profitable exports. Rice, the major food crop of South Asia, grows in the tropical rain forest climate of the Ganges Delta and along the peninsula's western Malabar Coast. India is second only to China in rice production, and Bangladesh ranks fourth in the world. Wheat is the main crop in the western Ganges Plain (Indo-Gangetic Plain) and in Pakistan's Indus River valley, but millet, corn, and sorghum also grow there. Peanuts grow along the Malabar Coast and the southern Deccan Plateau, and farmers grow sugarcane in most of India's lowlands.

Agricultural Improvements

Even with some success in slowing the population growth, feeding South Asia's people is an enormous challenge. Farmers are being trained to use modern technology and methods for irrigation, pest control, and fertilization to increase productivity. More planting cycles, for example, have been successful in Bangladesh, where farmers usually can harvest three rice crops per year. In Nepal's Kathmandu Valley, farmers are planting and harvesting winter wheat following the rice harvest.

Educational and governmental efforts have increased agricultural productivity. Research stations in Bhutan, for example, have helped farmers establish fruit orchards, and government-funded irrigation systems and higher rice prices encourage Sri Lankan farmers to grow more food crops.

The Green Revolution

Since the 1960s, an effort known as the green revolution has sought to increase and diversify crop yields in the world's developing countries. In India, as elsewhere, the green revolution has involved using carefully managed irrigation, fertilizers, and high-yielding varieties of crops. As a result, India's wheat and rice production has greatly increased. India is now able to store—and even export—grain. Not all the new methods work everywhere in South Asia, however. In parts of the region, monsoon rains allow only one planting cycle per year. Modernization also has costs.

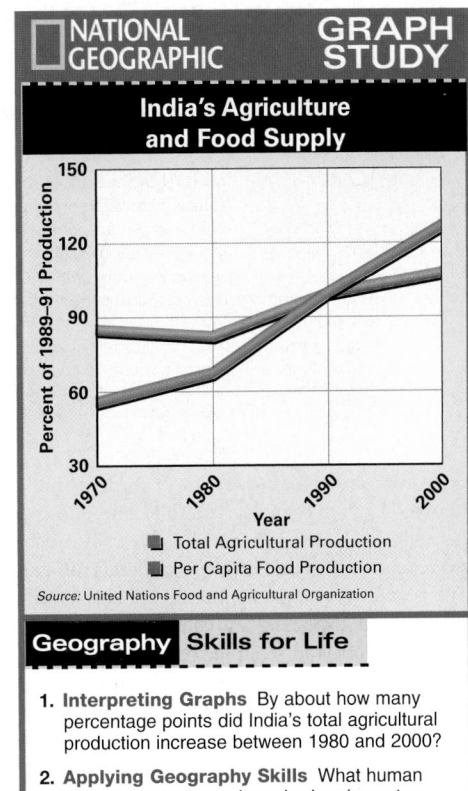

NATIONAL GEOGRAPHIC — **GRAPH STUDY**

India's Agriculture and Food Supply

Percent of 1989–91 Production (y-axis: 30, 60, 90, 120, 150)

Year (x-axis: 1970, 1980, 1990, 2000)

- ■ Total Agricultural Production
- ■ Per Capita Food Production

Source: United Nations Food and Agricultural Organization

Geography **Skills for Life**

1. **Interpreting Graphs** By about how many percentage points did India's total agricultural production increase between 1980 and 2000?
2. **Applying Geography Skills** What human factors or processes have had an impact on India's agriculture and food supply?

Irrigation and mechanization require expensive fuel, and in a region where not enough petroleum is available and many people burn biomass—plant materials and animal dung—as their only energy source, the costs are often too high.

Mining and Fishing

In addition to farming the soil, South Asians reap benefits from other natural resources in the region. Mining and fishing are profitable industries with the potential for growth in years to come.

Mineral Wealth

The Ganges Plain and parts of eastern India yield some of South Asia's richest mineral deposits. Iron ore, low-grade coal, bauxite, and copper are all

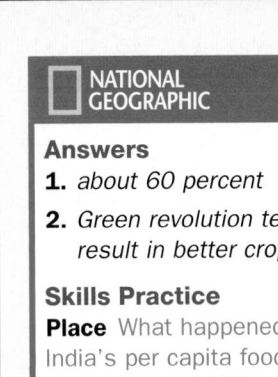

NATIONAL GEOGRAPHIC — **GRAPH STUDY**

Answers
1. *about 60 percent*
2. *Green revolution techniques result in better crop yields.*

Skills Practice
Place What happened to India's per capita food production between 1970 and 1980? *(It decreased.)*

L1/ELL

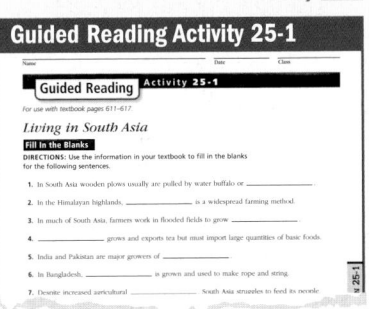

Guided Reading Activity 25-1

Guided Reading Activity 25-1

For use with textbook pages 611–617

Living in South Asia

Fill in the Blanks

DIRECTIONS: Use the information in your textbook to fill in the blanks for the following sentences.

1. In South Asia wooden plows usually are pulled by water buffalo or _____.
2. In the Himalayan highlands, _____ is a widespread farming method.
3. In much of South Asia, farmers work in flooded fields to grow _____.
4. _____ grows and exports tea but must import large quantities of basic foods.
5. India and Pakistan are major growers of _____.
6. In Bangladesh, _____ is grown and used to make rope and string.
7. Despite increased agricultural _____, South Asia struggles to feed its people.

Farm Size In India families divide their land equally among their sons. As generations pass, the inherited farms become smaller and more widely scattered. Some Indian states now set minimum sizes for farms.

COOPERATIVE LEARNING ACTIVITY

Research Agriculture Organize students into six groups, and assign each group one of the following important South Asian export crops: rice, tea, peanuts, jute, rubber, cotton. Have each group research climate, soil type, length of growing season, and planting, cultivation, and harvest methods for its assigned crop. Each group should create an illustrated display of its information. 🌐 **EE5 Environment and Society: Standard 16**

Food
Curry, the smoky-sweet seasoning of India, has spread to other parts of the world. Curry—from the Tamil *kari*—is a blend of dried chilies and spices that usually includes cumin, coriander, fenugreek, and turmeric.

📁 **Foods Around the World**
Use this booklet for more information about the foods of South Asia.

L1/ELL

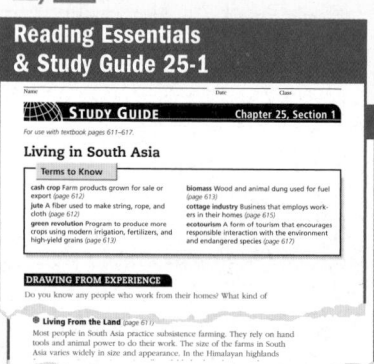

Reading Essentials & Study Guide 25-1

Child labor is common in many South Asian industries, especially textiles and clothing assembly. International trade regulations and the pressure of public opinion have begun to cause changes, but many South Asian families depend for their survival on the wages their children earn.

foods of SOUTH ASIA

Foods in South Asia usually consist of a staple grain: rice in the south and east, wheat in the north and west. Seasonal vegetables are often part of meals throughout the region, while fruits are considered a dessert. Meat and fish are common but not usually eaten daily.

One of the most important ingredients in South Asian cooking is curry, a blend of spices added to fish, meat, vegetables, and grain dishes. Curry is made by mixing from 2 to 20 different spices, and can be sweet and mild or hot and tangy.

mined in mountainous areas of eastern India. Bhutan is rich in coal, lead, marble, zinc, and copper, although its mountainous terrain makes extracting and processing these minerals difficult. The island of Sri Lanka supports a large graphite mining and exporting industry. Sri Lanka also mines precious and semiprecious stones.

Petroleum and natural gas reserves are found in several South Asian countries. India's oil fields are concentrated in the northeastern and northwestern areas of the country. Oil fields located in northeastern and southern Pakistan supply much of the country's energy needs. Pakistan also has significant natural gas reserves, especially in the western state of Baluchistan. Bangladesh, too, is rich in natural gas, a resource that offers an as-yet-untapped potential for export income to supplement the declining market for jute.

Fishing

Bordered partly by oceans and watered by great rivers, South Asia has rich fishing resources that provide needed income. Pakistan and Sri Lanka export shrimp, lobsters, and fresh and dried fish. Many people in India and Bangladesh fish for food. Bangladesh also has growing commercial fisheries, producing shrimp and frogs' legs for export.

In recent years the Indian government has encouraged deep-sea fishing by building processing plants and giving aid to oceangoing ships and fleets. More traditional local fishers see these developments as a threat to their livelihood.

South Asian Industries

Industrialization has proceeded along very different time lines in various South Asian countries. In India, industrialization began under British rule and was funded by European companies. In contrast, Bhutan, closed off from the outside world until 1975, still remains relatively isolated. Bhutan's government is moving ahead with industrial development slowly in order to preserve the country's natural and cultural resources.

Economics
India's Evolving Economy

After gaining independence in 1947, India introduced socialism, an economic policy that emphasized central planning. The government set goals for and closely regulated private industry. Many large industries were placed under direct government control, while others were partnerships between private owners and the government.

Wary of outside influences, India turned its back on foreign investment. It expanded home industries and reduced dependence on foreign trade to promote self-sufficiency. At first growth was steady, but by the 1960s the economy slowed, and India began to see the limitations of its policies in an increasingly global economy. Still, change came slowly. In the late 1980s, India's government still regulated or operated mining, banking and insurance, transportation, manufacturing, and construction industries. Then, in 1991, a financial crisis

CRITICAL THINKING ACTIVITY

Determining Cause and Effect Ask students to brainstorm a list of the effects of history and culture on agriculture in South Asia. *(Examples: British and Dutch colonial governments set up a plantation structure in Sri Lanka; traditional Indian inheritance practices result in small, widely scattered family farms.)* Have students work together to chart cause-and-effect relationships on the board. 🌐 **EE5 Environment and Society: Standard 14**

pushed India toward major economic reforms. It began moving toward a market economy.

> ❝ In 1991 India began opening its economy to wider trade, and the United States quickly became its primary trading and investment partner.... Foreign companies were thrilled by sheer numbers—an estimated 150 million potential middle-income consumers.... [F]oreign companies have also brought better job opportunities.... ❞
>
> Erla Zwingle, "A World Together," *National Geographic*, August 1999

The government also deregulated many industries and turned over government-run companies to private ownership. These changes sparked economic growth that helped expand the middle class, which was believed to make up 20 to 25 percent of India's population by the late 1990s. As a result, the demand for consumer goods from shoes to luxury cars has expanded rapidly. Today India, along with the rest of South Asia, struggles to balance national interest and global interdependence.

Light Industry

Many South Asians work in light industry, producing consumer goods. Textiles are a major part of South Asia's manufacturing base, as they have been in India for hundreds of years. India's 38 million textile workers manufacture cotton, silk, and wool fabrics in a dazzling variety of patterns, colors, and styles. India's textile industry, centered in Mumbai, Nagpur, and Sholapur, also produces garments for export. Bangladesh entered the textile industry in 1979, and sales of finished garments provide the country with export income.

Some of the world's most prized wools—cashmere and pashmina—come from a rare breed of goat found only in the Jammu and Kashmir region. Used in high-quality, high-fashion garments, these wools are in great demand.

Other light industries throughout South Asia manufacture shoes, carpets, bicycles, and bicycle parts. These small industries are generally housed in factories employing fewer than 100 people, and they use traditional production techniques.

South Asia's broad involvement in light industry grows out of its history of cottage industries, businesses that employ workers in their homes. Indian villagers weave textiles and make shoes, jewelry, woodcarvings, furniture, and bowls. Cottage industries in India, Nepal, and Bhutan provide jobs, encourage traditional crafts, and supply needed export income.

Mohandas Gandhi, the leader of India's independence movement, chose the spinning wheel as a symbol of the strength India could draw from its cottage industries. In his later years, Gandhi dressed only in simple robes of *khadi* (KAW•dee), traditional homespun cotton fabric,

NATIONAL GEOGRAPHIC World Explorer

Geography Skills for Life

Selling Shawls These women selling shawls in Bangladesh are a few of the millions of textile workers and merchants in South Asia.

Place How do cottage industries contribute to the export income of countries in the region?

L2 Interdependence

Challenge students to look in their homes or local stores for products that were grown, manufactured, or assembled in South Asia. Have students list the items they find on sticky notes and attach the notes to the appropriate countries on a wall map of South Asia.

 GEOGRAPHY AND THE HUMANITIES

 World Music: A Cultural Legacy

 World Art and Architecture Transparencies

 World Art Prints

NATIONAL GEOGRAPHIC World Explorer

Answer
Cottage industries provide export income through the sale of home manufactured crafts, clothing, and other goods.

More About the Photo True pashmina shawls are made from the thick, soft hair that Kashmir goats grow in the winter. Because the goat hairs are only 12–14 microns thick (one-sixth the thickness of human hair), pashminas have silk fibers woven in for added strength.

TEAM-TEACHING ACTIVITY: ART

South Asian Textile Art Have students work with an art teacher to research some of the typical patterns and printing methods used in the manufacture of South Asian textiles. Invite students to create their own patterned textiles based on South Asian designs and using one of the following techniques: block printing, batik, silk painting, embroidery, or weaving. Display students' work in showcases or around the classroom.
🌐 **EE4 Human Systems: Standard 10**

ASSESS

Assign Section 1 Assessment as homework or as an in-class activity.

🖥 Have students use **Interactive Tutor Self-Assessment CD-ROM.**

L2

Section Quiz 25-1

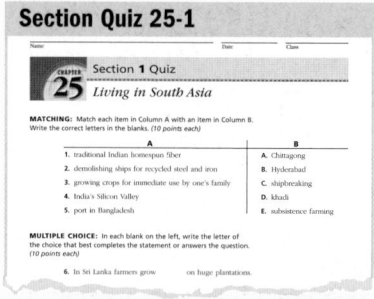

World Explorer

Answer
about 60 percent per year

More About the Photo In addition to computer hardware and software, plants in India assemble televisions, radios, and other electronic equipment for sale around the world.

Reteach

Have students write a paragraph comparing and contrasting cottage industries and commercial industries.

Enrich

Have students choose South Asian recipes from **Foods Around the World** to prepare and share.

---

and was often pictured sitting at the spinning wheel where he spun *khadi* thread. Gandhi urged the Indian people to maintain their traditional, family-centered industries even as the country developed.

Heavy Industry

South Asia's industrial base includes heavy industries geared toward mass production. India manufactures iron, steel, cement, and heavy machinery in Bhadravati and **Bangalore**. Bangladesh also produces iron, steel, and cement.

India, Pakistan, and Bangladesh also recycle iron and steel in a unique industry called "ship breaking." In Bangladesh's port of **Chittagong**, thousands of workers use sledgehammers and blowtorches to dismantle aging or damaged ships from around the world. Melted-down parts are

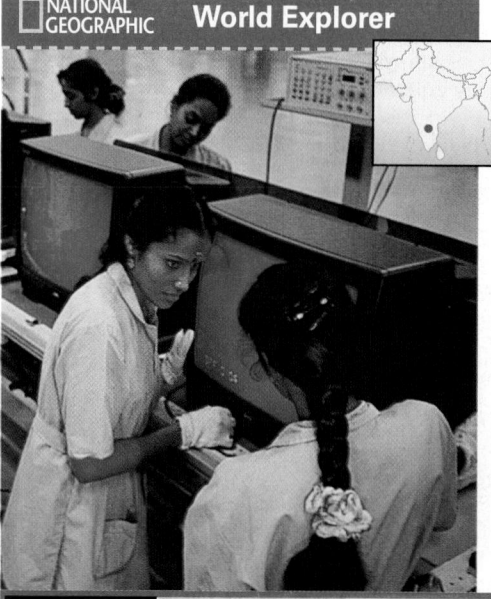
NATIONAL GEOGRAPHIC **World Explorer**

Geography **Skills for Life**

Technology Factories in India today produce a variety of electronic products such as televisions.
Place By how much is India's software trade with the United States expected to grow each year?

reforged into new iron and steel. In Bangladesh alone, ship breaking and related industries employ more than 1.3 million people.

Service Industries

Since the late 1990s, service industries—transport, real estate, banking and insurance, and public administration—have become increasingly important in South Asia. India and, to a lesser extent, Pakistan have benefited the most. In India wholesale and retail trade and government services rank as the leading contributors to the country's service economy. The Indian government provides a variety of social services to its people, especially in health, education, and public administration.

The High-Technology Sector

High technology—including the manufacture of equipment for the computer, communications, and aerospace industries and the creation of computer software—is a growing industry in South Asia. Millions of Indians use the Internet, and Indian computer professionals are in high demand around the world. The southern Indian cities of Bangalore and **Hyderabad** (HY•duh•ruh•BAD) are called "India's Silicon Valley," a reference to the part of California where many computer industries flourish. Software manufacturing in these cities has helped make India the world's second-largest exporter of software. In 2000 the software trade between India and the United States alone yielded $5 billion in income for India, with a projected growth rate of about 60 percent per year.

India also has strong potential to be a developer of computer hardware. The increasing use of copper rather than aluminum in microchip manufacturing benefits India because of its abundant copper deposits. India already has a strong and growing industry in the manufacture of televisions and other communications equipment.

Tourism

Tourism income is important in several South Asian countries. Nepal draws tourists to hike and climb the Himalayan slopes and to hunt or photograph wild animals. India's temples and festivals attract more than 2 million visitors each year.

EXTENDING THE CONTENT

Ship Breaking Bangladesh's port city of Chittagong is known as a "ship graveyard." By 2005 more than 1,400 vessels a year will have been taken out of service and broken down for parts. While the ship breaking business yields high profits for the country and helps ship owners recycle their fleets, workers are exposed to toxic materials and industrial accidents, and the chemical residue of ship breaking pollutes coastal areas. These challenges must be addressed by the governments involved as the industry continues to grow.
🌐 **EE4 Human Systems: Standard 11**

Continuing conflicts may discourage tourists, however. Sri Lanka's lush rain forests and tropical beaches once drew many tourists, but since the 1980s, violence between Hindu Tamils and Buddhist Sinhalese has emptied luxury hotels. Ongoing border disputes between India and Pakistan have all but eliminated tourism in Kashmir. Sporadic violence among religious groups in India also has discouraged foreign visitors.

In some South Asian countries, governments regulate tourism to protect threatened natural and cultural resources. For example, to preserve the Himalayan environment and its traditional culture, Bhutan issues fewer than 5,000 tourist visas each year. The Maldives restricts tourists to certain islands so that tourists do not interact with Maldivians who follow strict Islamic customs. Ecotourism, a form of tourism that encourages responsible interaction with the environment and endangered species, can support preservation efforts while contributing to South Asian economies.

GEOGRAPHY *Online*

Student Web Activity Visit the **Glencoe World Geography** Web site at geography.glencoe.com and click on Student Web Activities— Chapter 25 for an activity about business and tourism in India.

NATIONAL GEOGRAPHIC World Explorer

Geography Skills for Life

Beachside Paradise Among the most beautiful islands in the world, the Maldives also supports a diverse marine life.

Place Why does the Maldives restrict tourist access to some islands?

SECTION 1 ASSESSMENT

Checking for Understanding

1. Define cash crop, jute, green revolution, biomass, cottage industry, ecotourism.

2. Main Ideas Create a table like the one below, and fill in economic activities in South Asia and the challenges each represents.

South Asian Economic Activity	
Activity	Challenges

Critical Thinking

3. Comparing and Contrasting Compare and contrast cottage industries and commercial industries in the ways of operation, especially in regard to India's economy.

4. Categorizing Information Which of the region's industries focus on domestic needs, and which focus on exporting?

5. Predicting Consequences How might increased tourism affect life in the region?

Analyzing Maps

6. Movement Using the economic activity map on page 563, identify areas where nomadic herding is common. Explain why herding is the dominant economic activity in each of these areas.

Applying Geography

7. Effects of Physical Geography Think about farming methods in South Asia. Explain how farming methods are influenced by the region's physical geography.

NATIONAL GEOGRAPHIC World Explorer

Answer
To protect Maldivians who follow Islamic customs.

More About the Photo
Only about 200 of the Maldives' 1,190 islands are inhabited. More than 80 islands are tourist resorts.

GEOGRAPHY *Online*

Objectives, goals, and answers to the student activity can be found in the Web Activity Lesson Plan feature at geography.glencoe.com

④ CLOSE

Have students work in pairs to design pages for a catalog of South Asian exports. Display the completed pages.

SECTION 1 ASSESSMENT ANSWERS

1. All vocabulary terms are defined in the text.

2. Table entries should reflect text information.

3. Both cottage and commercial industries produce consumer goods for export, especially textiles. Cottage industries are small-scale, employing workers in their homes. Commercial industries are large in scale and operate in factories.

4. domestic needs: subsistence farming, fishing, some manufacturing; export: commercial agriculture (cash crops), mining, textiles, high-tech manufacturing

5. Increased tourism could bring more income, but may also damage the South Asian environment.

6. steppes in western Pakistan and in Pakistan and India near the Great Indian Desert; steppe climates provide grasses for herds but lack the climate and fertile soil for farming

7. **Applying Geography** South Asian farming methods are suited to physical geography: terracing in mountains and highlands, traditional or mechanized farming on plains and plantations, and wet farming (rice paddies) in the Ganges Delta and Bangladesh.

①FOCUS

Section Overview

This section discusses the environmental and social challenges South Asia faces as the region moves into the future.

BELLRINGER
Skillbuilder Activity

 Project transparency and have students answer questions.

 Available as blackline master.

Daily Focus Skills Transparency 25-2

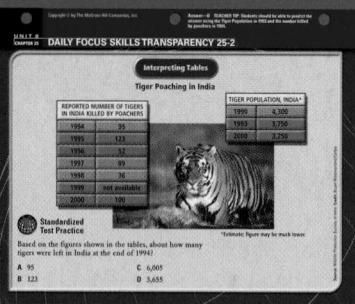

Guide to Reading

Consider What You Know
Answer *Increased tourism could damage the South Asian environment.*

Reading Strategy
Answers Pros: *stabilize course of river, reroute water for irrigation, control flooding;* Cons: *trap silt that would enrich soil downstream, can trap bacteria and disease, floods surrounding area, destroying homes and animal habitats*

Preteaching Vocabulary
🖭 Use the **Vocabulary Puzzle-Maker CD-ROM** to create crossword and word-search puzzles.

Guide to Reading

Consider What You Know
Tourism's growth rate in India is higher than the world average, and the Indian government considers tourism a high-priority industry. What effects do you think increased tourism might have on India's environment?

Reading Strategy
Categorizing Complete a web diagram similar to the one below by listing the pros and cons of building a dam.

Building a Dam	
Pros	**Cons**
•	•
•	•
•	•

Read to Find Out
• How is South Asia handling the complex task of managing its rich natural resources?

• What environmental challenges does South Asia face in the years ahead?

• How do geographic factors impact the political and economic challenges of South Asia's future?

Terms to Know
• sustainable development
• poaching
• *Chipko*
• nuclear proliferation
• *Dalits*

Places to Locate
• Narmada River
• Bay of Bengal

People and Their Environment

NATIONAL GEOGRAPHIC

A Geographic View

A Threatened Treasure

I have been climbing since well before dawn, and now I am alone at 17,000 feet. . . . Around me in a vast arc stand the snowy crests of the majestic Annapurna Range. The day is cloudless, not a breath of wind. The solitary splendor is dazzling—until I glance down at my feet. There, frozen into the ice cap of Tharpu Chuli, lies a miniature garbage dump: discarded candy wrappers, film cartons, plastic bags, wads of tissue, and half-empty food cans, all of it left by foreign climbing groups. It is a familiar and sickening sight to old Himalaya hands— the growing pollution of a priceless heritage.

—*Galen Rowell, "Annapurna: Sanctuary for the Himalayas,"* National Geographic, *September 1989*

Annapurna Range, Nepal

The tourism generated by trekking the Himalayan trails brings needed income to the kingdom of Nepal, but it also endangers the Himalayan ecosystem on which the entire Indian subcontinent depends. In this section you will learn about environmental and other challenges faced today by the countries of South Asia.

Managing Natural Resources

As you have learned, people and the environment interact and affect each other throughout the world. This interaction is especially significant in South Asia, where high population densities meet fragile ecosystems. As a result, South Asian countries seek to manage their resources wisely rather than just using them. A key to successful

---

RESOURCE MANAGER

📁 Reproducible Masters
• Reproducible Lesson Plan 25-2
• Daily Lecture Notes 25-2
• Guided Reading Activity 25-2
• Reading Essentials and Study Guide 25-2
• Reteaching Activity 25
• Reinforcing Skills Activity 25
• Section Quiz 25-2

🖭 Transparencies
• Daily Focus Skills Transparency 25-2
• Political Map Transparency 8
• Unit 8 Map Overlay Transparencies

Multimedia
🖭 Vocabulary PuzzleMaker CD-ROM
🖭 Interactive Tutor Self-Assessment CD-ROM
🖭 ExamView® Pro Testmaker CD-ROM
🖭 Presentation Plus! CD-ROM

resource management is sustainable development, or using resources at a rate that does not deplete them for future generations.

Wildlife

South Asia is home to an astonishing variety of wildlife. Elephants, water buffalo, and monkeys flourish in the rain forests of India and Sri Lanka. Crocodiles and Bengal tigers roam in Bangladesh. In the high mountain passes of the Himalaya, the elusive snow leopard hunts alone above fields crowded with blue sheep, exotic birds, and rare butterflies.

The Hindu, Buddhist, and Jain traditions of South Asia promote respect for all living things. However, many of South Asia's animals have become endangered through contact with the region's growing human population. Deforestation and irrigation have reduced animals' natural habitats, driving them into areas where people live. Some animals have been overhunted by tourists or by farmers and herders seeking to protect their crops and flocks.

Governments in the region, assisted by international conservation organizations, are working to reverse some of South Asia's wildlife losses. The creation of wildlife reserves—protected habitats—and the passage of laws controlling hunting and logging have begun to make a difference. Providing South Asians with economic incentives to cooperate in conservation efforts may also be effective. However, challenges still remain. Farmers' crops often are threatened by foraging elephants, and poachers can realize huge profits by selling the hides of Bengal tigers. To eliminate poaching, or the illegal killing of protected animals, governments in the region need to find ways to encourage people to respect wildlife.

Water

Water is one of the most precious resources on the planet. Lack of access to clean water is a persistent problem in South Asia. Even in

India, the most developed country in the region, 80 percent of the population has no access to sanitation facilities and must rely on water that is polluted by human waste and chemical runoff. The situation is worse in parts of Pakistan and in Bangladesh.

Because South Asia's climate varies greatly, the villagers of Rajasthan in northwestern India may be watching their crops and livestock perish from drought at the same time that farmers in Bangladesh are losing their homes to flooding. Building dams is one way to balance these extremes. Dams can change the course of rivers, reroute water for irrigation, and control flooding by holding water in reserve for times of drought.

Like many uses of technology, however, the building of dams has drawbacks as well as benefits. Dams trap silt that would otherwise flow downriver to enrich the soil. Reservoirs can trap bacteria, too, and become a source of disease. Also, building a dam usually results in the flooding of surrounding areas, displacing whole villages and disturbing the balance of wildlife and vegetation.

NATIONAL GEOGRAPHIC **World Explorer**

Geography **Skills for Life**

Bengal Tiger Some South Asian animals, such as this Bengal tiger, face extinction because of human activities such as poaching and clearing forests.

Human-Environment Interaction What steps are being taken to protect South Asia's wildlife?

---

2 TEACH

L2 Determining Cause and Effect

Have students work together to create a flowchart on the board illustrating the causes and effects of deforestation in South Asia. Have students note the effects of deforestation on the region's people, wildlife, and land.

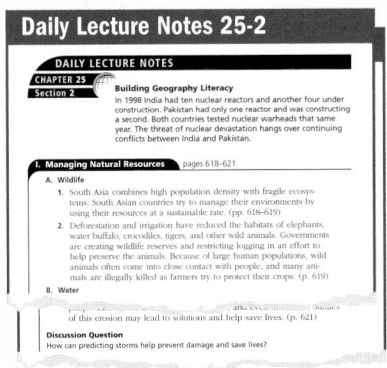

Daily Lecture Notes 25-2

DAILY LECTURE NOTES

CHAPTER 25
Section 2

Building Geography Literacy
In 1998 India had ten nuclear reactors and another four under construction. Pakistan had only one reactor and was constructing a second. Both countries tested nuclear warheads that same year. The threat of nuclear devastation hangs over continuing conflicts between India and Pakistan.

I. Managing Natural Resources pages 618–621

A. Wildlife
1. South Asia combines high population density with fragile ecosystems. South Asian countries try to manage their environments by using their resources at a sustainable rate. (pp. 618–619)
2. Deforestation and irrigation have reduced the habitats of elephants, water buffalo, crocodiles, tigers, and other wild animals. Governments are creating wildlife reserves and restricting logging in an effort to help preserve the animals. Because of large human populations, wild animals often come into close contact with people, and many animals are illegally killed as farmers try to protect their crops. (p. 619)

B. Water

of this erosion may lead to solutions and help save lives. (p. 621)

Discussion Question
How can predicting storms help prevent damage and save lives?

NATIONAL GEOGRAPHIC **World Explorer**

Answer
Governments are setting aside protected habitats and instituting antipoaching laws.

More About the Photo The tiger's stripes provide protective coloration in the grasslands. Though tigers can survive in almost any climate, they are found in the wild only in Asia.

DIFFERENTIATED INSTRUCTION

Visual Have students visit a local zoo or use Internet resources to develop an illustrated report on South Asian wildlife. The report should highlight several species, including some that are endangered, and should provide the following information about each: where the animal is found, typical habitat, food sources, threats to survival. Allow time for students to present their reports to the class.

🌐 **EE2 Places and Regions: Standard 4;** 🌐 **EE3 Physical Systems: Standard 8**
📂 Refer to *Inclusion for the Social Studies Classroom Strategies and Activities.*

NATIONAL GEOGRAPHIC World Explorer

Geography **Skills for Life**

Protesting the Dam
Activists concerned about environmental problems protest the building of a dam near Bhopal, India.
Human-Environment Interaction What are advantages and disadvantages of building dams?

NATIONAL GEOGRAPHIC World Explorer

Answer
Dams control flooding, collect water for irrigation, and sustain people during droughts, but they also displace homes and prevent silt from enriching the soil.

More About the Photo
In 2000 India's Supreme Court ruled that construction of this dam on the Narmada River could begin again after a five-year halt. Many protesters believe that displaced people will not receive fair compensation.

L1/ELL

Guided Reading Activity 25-2

Name_____ Date_____ Class_____

Guided Reading Activity **25-2**

For use with textbook pages 618–623.

People and Their Environment

Underline the Correct Words
DIRECTIONS: Underline the word or phrase in parentheses that best completes the following sentences.

1. In South Asia, a key to successful resource management is _____ development. (sustainable/limited)

2. The habitats of South Asia's wildlife have been reduced because of _____ and irrigation. (industrialization/deforestation)

3. Dams can reroute water for irrigation and _____ by holding water in reserve for times of drought. (change river courses/control flooding)

4. Dam building deprives downstream areas of _____ that nourishes the soil. (silt/wildlife)

Government
The Narmada River Dilemma

The 25-year effort to build a dam in India's **Narmada River** basin is a good example of the challenges of water management. Supporters of the project point out the benefits, including the irrigation of millions of acres of land currently subject to severe drought and the creation of hydroelectric power.

At the heart of the opposition to the project are environmentalists and the thousands of local peoples whose ancestral villages will be flooded as a result of the project. They point to other such projects in which farmers were uprooted and forced to resettle in cities or temporary camps. As work continues on the project, people on both sides of the controversy have begun talks to resolve their differences.

Forests

Centuries ago, much of South Asia was covered with forests. Today the region is in a state of environmental crisis because of deforestation. The problem has accelerated in recent years, driven by South Asia's growing population and the increasing interaction of humans with their environment. Commercial timber operations, an industry that began under British rule, have destroyed many of South Asia's old-growth forests. Other forest areas have been cleared to make way for human settlements.

Some deforestation is a result of traditional practices in South Asia. Slash-and-burn agriculture, no longer permitted in many places, is an ancient technique used by many hill peoples. In drought-stricken regions, villagers allow livestock to feed on leaves, slowly killing the trees. Most damaging of all is the widespread reliance on burning biomass, including the wood from trees, for fuel.

The effects of deforestation are devastating. The mangrove forests of Bangladesh's Sundarbans region, the area of swamp land near the Ganges River Delta, have over the years provided a barrier against erosion caused by cyclones. As the mangrove trees are cut, however, much of this protection against storms vanishes. Losing tropical rain forests also has other damaging effects. Rain forests usually grow in poor soil, where the trees' complex root systems efficiently absorb available nutrients and hold the topsoil in place. As rainfall filters slowly through layers of leafy branches, the surrounding air is cooled. When rain forests disappear, soil erodes, rains produce floods, and temperatures rise.

COOPERATIVE LEARNING ACTIVITY

Resource Management Organize students into three groups, and assign each group one of the following South Asian resources: forests, water, wildlife. Have each group research opposing South Asian viewpoints about appropriate management of its assigned resource. Each student should have specific responsibilities for different aspects of the research. Once groups have completed their research, ask group members to determine the best way to safeguard resources while allowing necessary economic development in the region. Allow time for groups to report their conclusions.

🌐 **EE5 Environment and Society: Standard 16**

Culture
Protecting the Forests

Reforestation efforts, under way throughout South Asia, build on the region's traditional respect for trees. India's *Chipko,* or "tree-hugger," movement was founded by Sunderlal Bahaguna, a follower of Gandhi. Bahaguna has succeeded by reminding villagers of the importance of trees. *Chipko* nurseries provide seedlings for reforestation. The government ban on timber production in the Himalayan forests of Uttar Pradesh, advocated by Bahaguna, was the first of many such government efforts in the region.

Protecting forests is at the heart of the region's culture. As the poet Rabindranath Tagore wrote,

> " *India's civilization has been distinctive in locating its source of regeneration, material and intellectual, in the forest, not the city. India's best ideas have come when man is in communion with trees.* "
>
> Rabindranath Tagore, quoted by Gita Mehta, *Snakes and Ladders: Glimpses of Modern India,* 1998

Seeking Solutions

As industrialization increases in South Asia, so does air pollution. Delhi, India, is now the world's fourth most polluted city. Scientists are studying the region to try to solve this and other problems.

Meteorologists are studying monsoon patterns in the **Bay of Bengal** in the hopes of reducing the devastation caused by these storms. The ability to predict with some accuracy the coming of the monsoon rains and their intensity could make enormous differences to South Asia's people.

Geographers are using satellite imaging to study the erosion in coastal deltas in Bangladesh. Millions of Bengali people live on thin, crusted islands formed from silt, which float on the surface of coastal waters. When the rains come, the rivers move silt—2 billion tons (1.8 billion metric tons) a year—into the Bay of Bengal. As a result, the average Bengali is displaced from his or her home seven times in a lifetime. If studies of silt erosion can identify solutions, scientists will be improving people's lives.

Finally, South Asia has the potential to help study global environmental issues. For example, an experimental station in the Maldives is measuring the possible effects of global warming on ocean levels.

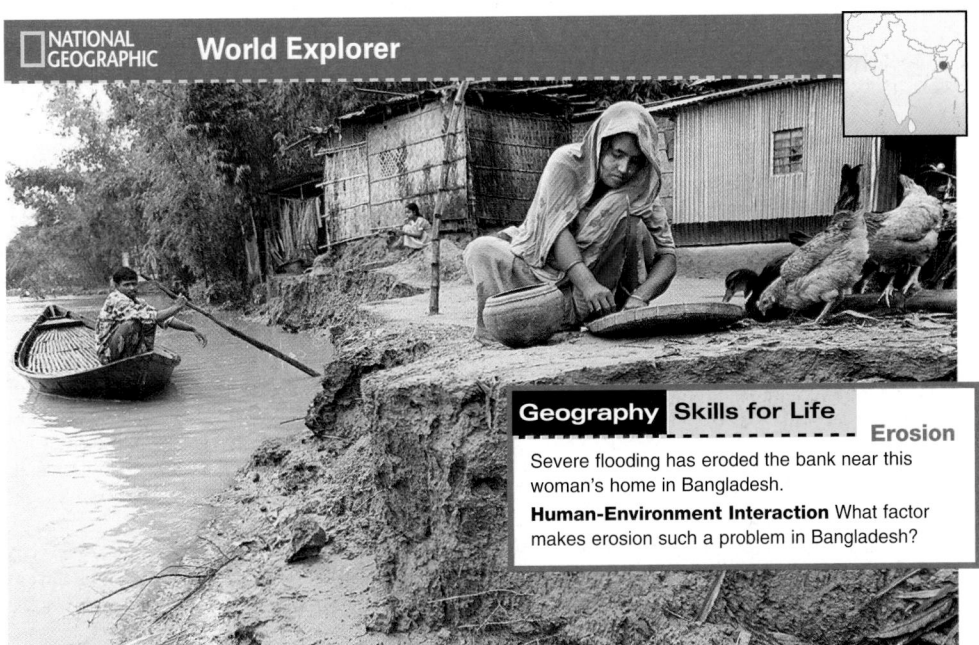

NATIONAL GEOGRAPHIC World Explorer

Geography | Skills for Life

Erosion

Severe flooding has eroded the bank near this woman's home in Bangladesh.

Human-Environment Interaction What factor makes erosion such a problem in Bangladesh?

L2 Art

Have students work in pairs to design posters promoting one of the following South Asian environmental efforts: the Chipko movement, wildlife conservation, river cleanups, or ecotourism. Display the completed posters.

L1/ELL

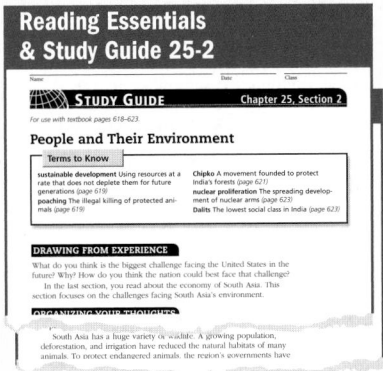

Reading Essentials & Study Guide 25-2

NATIONAL GEOGRAPHIC World Explorer

Answer
Many people live on islands made of silt, which is easily eroded during floods.

More About the Photo The government of Bangladesh's rural uplift infrastructure program in 2001 began a project to construct roads and embankments in the area near this woman's home in Manikganj.

CRITICAL THINKING ACTIVITY

Recognizing Bias Have students collect news articles and Internet resources on several South Asian environmental challenges. Be sure students note the source of each article or resource. Then have students work in teams to read and evaluate the information. Have students identify articles, resources, or statements that indicate bias, and discuss what bias is being shown in each. Remind students to watch for particular agendas and interests. ▣ **EE5 Environment and Society: Standard 14**

Answer

1. *Iran*

2. *Nuclear proliferation would probably increase tensions between India and Pakistan as well as among other countries, and would shift even more spending from social to military programs.*

Map Skills Practice

Region Which country bordering South Asia has acknowledged nuclear capacity? *(China)*

Assign Section 2 Assessment as homework or as an in-class activity.

🌐 Have students use **Interactive Tutor Self-Assessment CD-ROM** to review Section 2.

L2

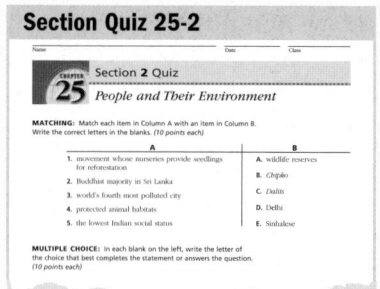

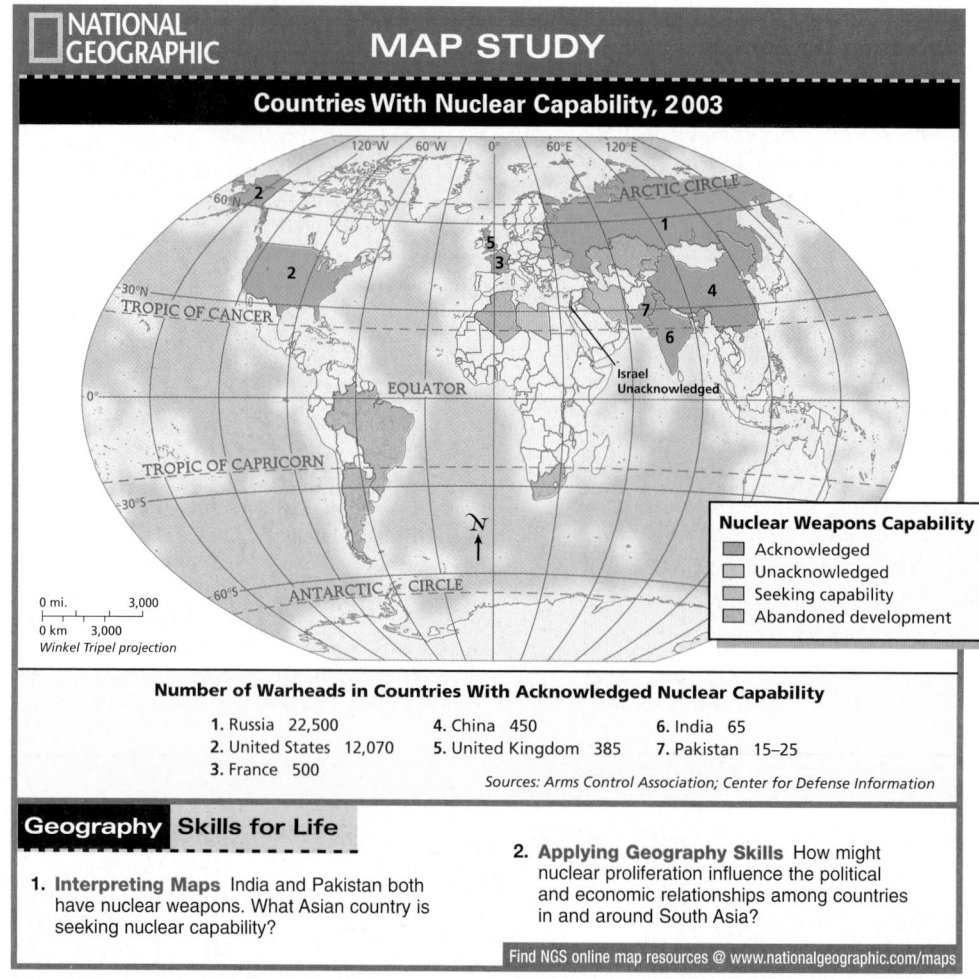

NATIONAL GEOGRAPHIC — **MAP STUDY**

Countries With Nuclear Capability, 2003

ARCTIC CIRCLE
TROPIC OF CANCER
EQUATOR
Israel Unacknowledged
TROPIC OF CAPRICORN
ANTARCTIC CIRCLE

0 mi. 3,000
0 km 3,000
Winkel Tripel projection

Nuclear Weapons Capability
- Acknowledged
- Unacknowledged
- Seeking capability
- Abandoned development

Number of Warheads in Countries With Acknowledged Nuclear Capability

1. Russia 22,500
2. United States 12,070
3. France 500
4. China 450
5. United Kingdom 385
6. India 65
7. Pakistan 15–25

Sources: Arms Control Association; Center for Defense Information

Geography **Skills for Life**

1. Interpreting Maps India and Pakistan both have nuclear weapons. What Asian country is seeking nuclear capability?

2. Applying Geography Skills How might nuclear proliferation influence the political and economic relationships among countries in and around South Asia?

Find NGS online map resources @ www.nationalgeographic.com/maps

---

South Asia's Challenges

Geography holds a key to other challenges now facing South Asia. Conflict in the region has deep roots in issues of national autonomy and religious and ethnic concerns.

Conflict in Kashmir

Since 1947, India and Pakistan have disputed ownership of the largely Muslim territory of Kashmir. During the past 50 years, two of the three wars fought between India and Pakistan have focused on this territory. Today, Pakistan controls one-third of Kashmir; the remainder is held by India.

Indian and Pakistani troops patrol the Line of Control, the border between the two parts of Kashmir. Despite occasional peace talks, India and Pakistan accuse each other of violating this border. In 2002 armed attacks by Kashmiri militants in India and Indian-ruled Kashmir brought India and Pakistan to the brink of war.

The potential danger from this enduring conflict has escalated since 1998, when both India and Pakistan tested nuclear warheads. The map above shows the

---

TEAM-TEACHING ACTIVITY: GOVERNMENT

International Community Have students work with a government teacher to research the response of the international community to nuclear proliferation in South Asia. Students should work in small groups to research and discuss the following questions: (1) What was the response by foreign countries to nuclear proliferation in India and Pakistan? (2) To which international alliances do India and Pakistan belong? (3) What is the policy of these organizations toward nuclear proliferation? (4) Where did India and Pakistan receive the most support for their nuclear policies? Where did they encounter the most criticism?

🌐 **EE4 Human Systems: Standard 13**

world's countries that have nuclear capability, including India and Pakistan. Both countries have spent huge sums to develop nuclear missiles. This new example of nuclear proliferation—the spreading development of nuclear arms—aroused international alarm. The costs of these nuclear programs hurt the people of both countries through the loss of much-needed funding for food and other human needs. In addition, economic sanctions leveled by the world's economic powers against India and Pakistan intensified the hardships of South Asia's people.

Internal Conflicts

Some South Asian conflicts occur within countries. The majority of people in Sri Lanka are Buddhist Sinhalese, who control the government. Tamils, who are Hindu, represent only about 20 percent of the population. Tamils accuse the government of discrimination, and some have taken up arms to create a separate Tamil state. In India differences between Hindu, Muslim, and Sikh militants often erupt into violence.

India also suffers from the legacy of its ancient system of social classes. Those traditionally assigned to the lowest social status—called the *Dalits*, or "oppressed"—continue to experience discrimination and even, in some areas, violent assault. *Dalits* are denied housing, educational opportunities, and jobs, even though India's constitution outlaws such discrimination.

Promise and Possibility

South Asia's history of conflict rests side-by-side with its long tradition of tolerance for diversity. On the fiftieth anniversary of his country's independence, one Indian writer posed this challenge for the future. His comments could also apply to the rest of South Asia:

> *In a country as diverse as India, the interests of various groups of Indians will tend to diverge, and political contention is inevitable. The major challenge for Indian democracy is therefore to absorb and resolve the clashes that may arise from contending interests, while ensuring the freedom, safety, and prosperity of all Indians.*
>
> Shashi Tharoor, *India: From Midnight to the Millennium*, 1997

CHAPTER 25
Section 2, pages 618–623

Reteach

Have students work in groups to develop crossword puzzles with which to quiz one another on section content.

Enrich

Have students research environmental changes in a South Asian city, an African city, and an American city. Ask students to compare and evaluate the cities in terms of the impact of these changes.

4 CLOSE

Invite students to write descriptions or draw pictures of one South Asian natural area as it would appear when all environmental threats are removed.

SECTION 2 ASSESSMENT

Checking for Understanding

1. **Define** sustainable development, poaching, *Chipko*, nuclear proliferation, *Dalits*.

2. **Main Ideas** Create a web like the one below on a sheet of paper. Use it to fill in the information about how natural resources and conflicts present challenges in South Asia.

South Asia's Challenges → Resources, Conflicts

Critical Thinking

3. **Making Decisions** Which of the region's resource issues do you think should receive the most funding and attention? Explain your choice.

4. **Comparing and Contrasting** List examples from your reading to contrast the region's tolerance for diversity with its ongoing religious and ethnic conflicts.

5. **Making Inferences** In what ways does nuclear proliferation further complicate the already intense conflicts in South Asia? Give examples to support your answer.

Analyzing Maps

6. **Location** Study the map of countries with nuclear capability on page 622. On which continent are the most nuclear warheads located? The most countries with nuclear capability?

Applying Geography

7. **Writing a Letter** Imagine you are a local official writing to a South Asian government about a village hard hit by floods or drought. Analyze the environmental impact and suggest ways to resolve the problem.

SECTION 2 ASSESSMENT ANSWERS

1. All vocabulary terms are defined in the text.
2. Graphic organizers should reflect text information.
3. Answers should reflect text information and make reasonable arguments.
4. tolerance: Hinduism's overall attitude toward other religions, South Asia's diverse cultural mix (such as the many cultures celebrating Diwali); conflict: Kashmir, Sri Lanka, social class discrimination, Indian strife between Hindus, Muslims, and Sikhs
5. Nuclear proliferation brings added strains to economic development and regional conflicts, as well as increasing the potential for human and environmental catastrophe.
6. Asia or Europe, depending on the location of Russia's warheads; Asia
7. **Applying Geography** Students' letters should reflect reasonable steps toward a solution based on text information.

1 FOCUS

Have students brainstorm a list of the effects of widespread malnutrition on a country's population and economy. *(poor general health, high infant mortality rates, reduced ability to learn affecting education, weakened labor force, high demand for social welfare)*

2 TEACH

L1 Making Comparisons

Make two columns on the board labeled *Traditional Agriculture* and *Green Revolution*. Ask volunteers to list under each heading the equipment and resources it requires. Then have students speculate about the positive and negative aspects for South Asia of each form of agriculture.

global issues

GM Seeds The controversy over the use of genetically modified (GM) seeds continues worldwide. In the United States in 2000, genetically modified corn approved only for animal feed accidentally cross-pollinated nearby cornfields that grew corn for human consumption. This accident resulted in huge economic losses for farmers and seed developers.

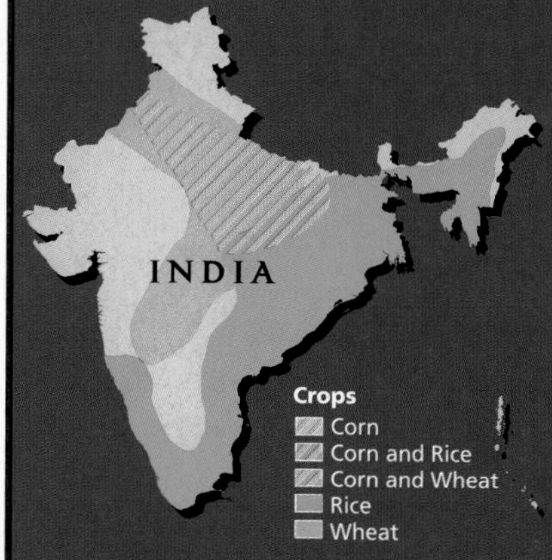

INDIA

Crops
- Corn
- Corn and Rice
- Corn and Wheat
- Rice
- Wheat

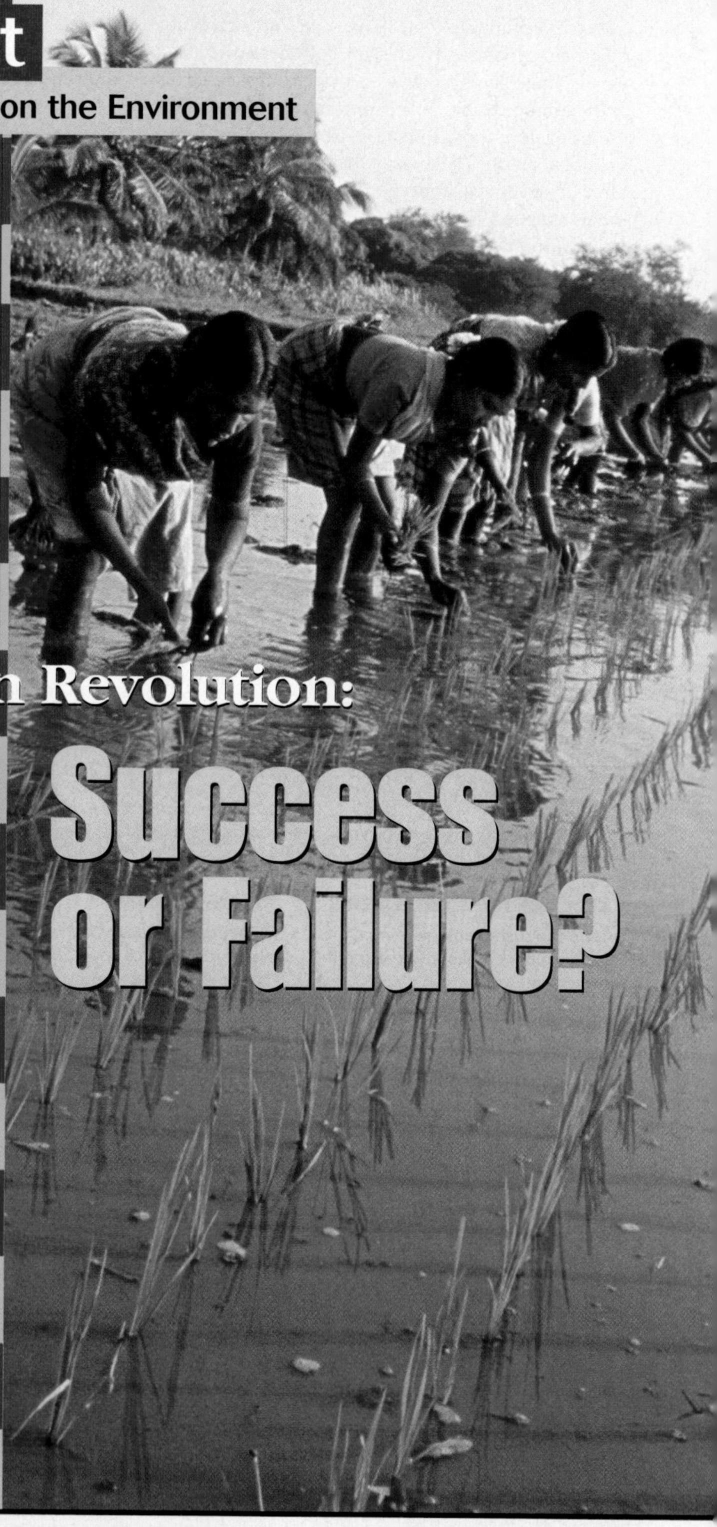

India's Green Revolution: Success or Failure?

Several decades ago, India's people were dying of starvation. Then came the green revolution. Hailed as the solution to India's chronic food shortages, the green revolution was an international effort to increase food production in less-developed countries. Starting in the 1960s, Indian farmers planted high-yield varieties of crops and used large amounts of fertilizers and pesticides to help the plants grow. By the 1970s, India was producing record harvests. Yet India's green revolution also has caused environmental damage and dependence on costly chemicals. Is India's green revolution a success or a failure?

LOOKING TO THE FUTURE

Weighing Tough Choices Even with the new techniques instituted by the Green Revolution, India still faces a nutritional crisis. In 1999 the World Health Organization estimated that half of all Indian children under 4 years old were malnourished and 60 percent of India's women showed signs of anemia. Science may hold some answers, such as the development of a strain of bioengineered rice that contains genetic proteins from corn and increases yields by 35 percent. But technology also has drawbacks. The high-yield seeds of the Green Revolution have all but driven out the crops Indians traditionally relied upon for protein—lentils, peas, and beans.

EE5 Environment and Society: Standard 16

At India's Rice Research Institute, scientists experiment with various methods of growing rice. The Institute's research aids Indian farmers (left) by introducing them to green revolution agricultural techniques.

The green revolution was designed to increase agricultural production and end hunger. In India, green revolution techniques encouraged farmers to turn more fields into cropland, raise more than one crop per year, and plant new high-yield variety (HYV) seeds—mainly wheat and rice.

India's green revolution has worked as people hoped it would. Grain harvests have soared, and India no longer imports grain. Yet there are problems. Compared with older strains of wheat and rice, new high-yield varieties need far more water, fertilizer, and pesticides to flourish. Huge irrigation projects deliver water to thirsty HYV plants. In some places, this has led to a buildup of

Indian farmers (below) harvest an abundant crop of rice. But abundance comes with a price—reliance on spraying crops with costly pesticides (right). ▼

salt in the soil, damaging once-fertile fields. Poor Indian farmers often go into debt to pay for expensive chemicals. Overuse of pesticides has gradually poisoned the soil and water in some areas. The chemicals also have led to pesticide-resistant crop pests.

India's growing population of one billion is the second-largest in the world. The country faces a critical decision: Should it continue to rely on green revolution technology?

Supporters of the green revolution point out that its techniques dramatically increased food production and alleviated hunger in India. They claim that new genetically engineered seeds will produce even higher yields. These new varieties will be resistant to pests, reducing the need for pesticides. Supporters also say that despite some exceptions, the green revolution has helped most farmers earn more money and raise their standards of living.

◄ Thanks to the green revolution, fewer children in India starve today.

Opponents of the green revolution argue that the new methods caused much environmental damage and widened the gap between rich and poor. Excessive use of chemicals pollutes water, poses health hazards, and leads to pest resistance. Opponents point out that farmers get caught in a cycle of using more and more chemicals to achieve healthy crops. Furthermore, some scientists warn that genetically modified seeds carry unknown risks and may create new environmental problems.

What's Your Point of View? Should India continue to practice and improve upon green revolution techniques? Or should the country seek a new approach?

③ ASSESS

Have students answer the **What's Your Point of View?** questions on page 625.

④ CLOSE

Writing Have students prepare a position paper on genetically modified foods.

Meeting National Standards

Geography for Life
The following standards are met in the Student Edition feature:

EE3 Physical Systems: Standard 8

EE4 Human Systems: Standard 11

EE5 Environment and Society: Standards 14, 16

EE6 The Uses of Geography: Standard 18

WHAT CAN YOU DO?

Share with students the following strategies for learning more about issues of nutrition, the Green Revolution, and genetically modified foods:

- Visit a farm or farmers' market to find out more about where the foods you eat come from. Check ingredients lists on prepared food packages.

- Use the Internet to find out more about India's Green Revolution and the controversy over genetically modified foods.
- Research and support organizations that work to end world hunger.
- Write letters to government leaders to express your opinion on these issues.

🌐 **EE6 The Uses of Geography: Standard 18**

Teaching the Skill

Have volunteers set up a row of dominoes or similar tiles in a straight line. Ask students to study the pattern and predict how many dominoes will fall when the first domino is knocked over. Then repeat the exercise, this time setting up the dominoes in a more complex pattern, including several turns. **Ask: Which pattern was easier to predict?** (*Most students will choose the straight-line pattern.*)

Tell students that this exercise models predicting consequences, but remind them that predicting the consequences of human events and activities can be much more difficult than predicting the fall of dominoes, then **Ask: Why?** (*because human events and activities are far more complicated and may be connected in many more ways than patterns of dominoes, which follow the laws of physical science*)

Additional Practice
L1

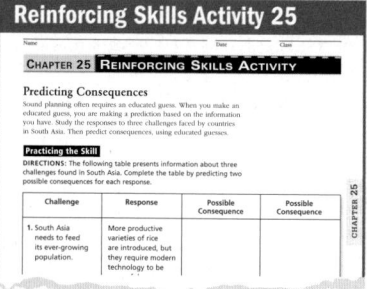

GLENCOE
TECHNOLOGY

**Glencoe Skillbuilder
Interactive Workbook,
Level 2**

Predicting Consequences

Making educated guesses about the outcome or consequences of an event or situation is useful in almost every area of life. Making good educated guesses is essential for successful decision making, problem solving, and planning.

Learning the Skill

Consequences are the results of actions or choices we make. For example, scoring high on an exam is one likely consequence of studying the night before. Often, predicting consequences is not so straightforward. An action or decision can have far-reaching or unintended consequences. One country's decision to provide aid to farmers, for instance, could lower the price of produce across an entire region. This would make it more difficult for farmers in other regions to compete.

Follow these steps to help you analyze information in order to predict consequences:

- **Gather information about the decision or action.**

- **Use your knowledge of history and human behavior to identify what consequences could result.**

- **Analyze each of the consequences by asking: How likely is it that this will occur?**

- **Determine whether this consequence will have other important consequences.**

- **Make a prediction using the information you have gathered.**

Practicing the Skill

Read and study the passage, and then answer the questions that follow.

"India is counting on information technology to create millions of new jobs and add billions of dollars to export earnings in the coming years. Yet it appears that unless more training and investment in education is made available, there may not be enough skilled workers to meet these ambitious goals. . . .

Most of the top schools producing computer and software workers send their graduates abroad to the United States and Europe, where Indian high technology professionals are in high demand. . . . Indian companies say they cannot compete with their counterparts abroad in salaries or benefits. . . . This is all happening while India's unemployment rate among unskilled workers is soaring. Economists say the only answer is a massive investment in primary and secondary education. But, with the Indian budget deep in deficit for years to come, it is hard to see where the money is going to come from."

— *Daniel Lak, "India at Risk of Tech Worker Shortage,"*
BBC News (online), April 15, 2000

1. What trend does the passage describe?

2. Do you think the trend the writer describes is likely to continue?

3. On what do you base this prediction?

4. What occurrences might have an effect on changing the trend?

5. What are three possible consequences or outcomes of this trend?

6. What are the possible benefits and drawbacks of the solution proposed by economists who study the issue?

Applying
the Skill

Find a newspaper or news magazine article that describes a political, economic, or social problem in South Asia. Analyze the article, and describe how the people of South Asia are trying to solve the problem. Predict three consequences of the actions described. On what do you base your prediction?

 The Glencoe Skillbuilder Interactive Workbook, Level 2 provides instruction and practice in key social studies skills.

ANSWERS TO PRACTICING THE SKILL

1. India's high-tech worker shortage
2. The trend will most likely continue.
3. India lacks resources to keep skilled workers or to train new ones.
4. increased funding for education, investment in keeping skilled workers from emigrating, a slowdown in the high-tech industry
5. India will have too few highly skilled workers to profit from growth in high-tech industries; skilled Indians will continue to find jobs in other countries; the economy will lose income from high-tech industries and bear the social costs of unemployment.
6. benefits: skilled workers do not emigrate; more skilled workers through education, more jobs for unemployed unskilled workers who receive training; drawbacks: money diverted from other needs such as social welfare and international debt repayment

SUMMARY & STUDY GUIDE

SECTION 1 — Living in South Asia (pp. 611–617)

Terms to Know
- cash crop
- jute
- green revolution
- biomass
- cottage industry
- ecotourism

Reviewing Key Points
- Agriculture provides a living for most of South Asia's people, and it also provides cash crops for export.
- South Asia's mines and fisheries contribute to its exports.
- South Asia is experiencing rapid growth in the high-tech sector and continues to develop light and heavy industries.
- Tourism offers both benefits and challenges to the South Asian economy.

Organizing Your Notes
Create an outline, using the format below, to help you organize your notes for this section.

Living in South Asia
I. Living From the Land
A. Agricultural Conditions
1.
2.
B.
1.
2.
II. South Asian Crops

SECTION 2 — People and Their Environment (pp. 618–623)

Terms to Know
- sustainable development
- poaching
- *Chipko*
- nuclear proliferation
- *Dalits*

Reviewing Key Points
- South Asia faces the complex task of managing its rich and varied natural resources.
- South Asia is seeking scientific solutions to its environmental challenges.
- Conflict in South Asia stems from issues of nationalism, religion, and ethnicity.

Organizing Your Notes
Use a table like the one below to help you organize important details from this section.

Natural Resources	Solutions	Conflicts

◀ Shopping district, New Delhi, India

Using the Chapter 25 Summary & Study Guide

Use the Chapter 25 Summary & Study Guide to preview, review, condense, or reteach the chapter.

Preview/Review

🕮 **Vocabulary PuzzleMaker CD-ROM** reinforces "Terms to Know."

🕮 **Interactive Tutor Self-Assessment CD-ROM** provides a review of Chapter 25 content.

Condense

Have students read the Chapter 25 Summary & Study Guide.

🕮 Chapter 25 Audio Program

📁 Chapter 25 Guided Reading Activities

Reteach

📁 Chapter 25 Reteaching Activities (Spanish also available)

📁 Chapter 25 Reading Essentials and Study Guides

GLENCOE TECHNOLOGY

📺 NATIONAL GEOGRAPHIC

WORLD REGIONS VIDEO PROGRAM

Unit 8, South Asia
The following segments enhance the study of this unit:

- **Monsoon**
- **Sherpas of Nepal**
- **Bollywood**

CHAPTER CULMINATING ACTIVITY

Creative Writing Have students imagine that they live in one of South Asia's seven countries. Have them write autobiographical profiles that answer the following questions: Where do you live? What does the landscape around your home look like? How does your family make a living? What are your greatest concerns about your country's future? What positive contribution do you think your country can bring to the world?

🌐 **EE2 Places and Regions: Standards 4, 6;** 🌐 **EE4 Human Systems: Standard 10**

NOTE: This activity may be completed separately or you may wish students to incorporate it in their GeoJournals.

GEOGRAPHY *Online*

Have students visit the Web site at geography.glencoe.com to review Chapter 25 and take the **Self-Check Quiz.**

GLENCOE TECHNOLOGY

Use *MindJogger Videoquiz* to review the Chapter 25 content.

Reviewing Key Terms

1. nuclear proliferation
2. ecotourism
3. sustainable development
4. Dalits
5. cottage industry
6. Green Revolution

Reviewing Facts

SECTION 1

1. terracing in the mountains and highlands, traditional or mechanized on plains and plantations, wet farming (paddies) in delta regions
2. Both mining and fishing are sources of export revenue for South Asia.
3. increased income, but also potential environmental damage

SECTION 2

4. forests in Himalayan highlands and Sri Lanka, wildlife throughout the region, water (mainly in rivers with sources in the Himalaya)
5. for the dam: increased irrigation possibilities, increased access to freshwater; against the dam: destruction of traditional villages and damage to the ecosystem
6. causes: religious tensions, ethnic strife, nationalism, class discrimination; effects: loss of life, high defense spending,

Reviewing Key Terms

Write the key term that best completes each of the following sentences. Refer to the Terms to Know in the Summary & Study Guide on page 627.

1. The spread of nuclear weapons is called _____.
2. _____ is a type of tourism that encourages responsible interaction with the environment.
3. Using resources at a rate that does not deplete them is called _____.
4. _____ are India's lowest social class.
5. People making products such as jewelry or textiles at home are working in a(n) _____.
6. The movement to increase food productivity through the use of experimental high-yield crops is called the _____.

Reviewing Facts

SECTION 1

1. What kinds of agricultural methods are used in South Asia?
2. How do mining and fishing contribute to the region's economy?
3. What are the benefits and challenges of tourism to the region today?

SECTION 2

4. What are South Asia's key natural resources, and where are they located?
5. What are the conflicting issues over India's Narmada River dam?
6. What are the causes and effects of the Kashmir conflict?

Critical Thinking

1. **Making Generalizations** What would you say is the greatest challenge facing South Asia today?

2. **Predicting Consequences** What might be the results of ongoing nuclear proliferation in South Asia?
3. **Identifying Cause and Effect** Create a cause-and-effect diagram like the one below for each of South Asia's current environmental challenges. Then fill in the details about the causes and effects of each.

Causes → Environmental Challenge → Effects

Causes → Environmental Challenge → Effects

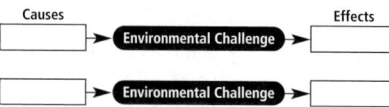

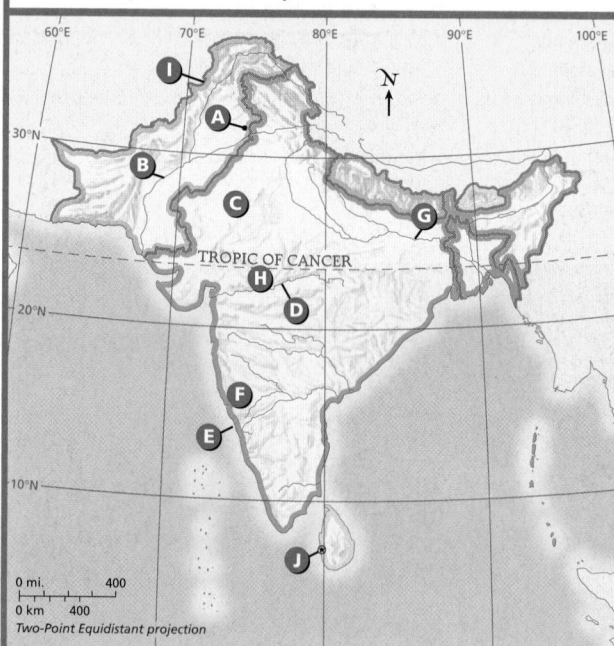

NATIONAL GEOGRAPHIC Locating Places

South Asia: Physical-Political Geography

Match the letters on the map with the places and physical features of South Asia. Write your answers on a sheet of paper.

1. Colombo
2. Lahore
3. Narmada River
4. Indus Valley
5. Western Ghats
6. Malabar Coast
7. Vindhya Range
8. Khyber Pass
9. Ganges Plain
10. Great Indian Desert

displacement of refugees, diversion of needed social resources

Critical Thinking

1. Possible answers include lack of access to freshwater, nuclear proliferation, poor education and health care, environmental destruction, or internal and external conflicts.
2. added strains on economic development and regional conflicts, increasing potential for human and environmental catastrophe

3. Diagrams should reflect accurate cause-and-effect relationships based on text information.

NATIONAL GEOGRAPHIC Locating Places

1. J	**3.** D	**5.** F	**7.** H	**9.** G
2. A	**4.** B	**6.** E	**8.** I	**10.** C

Using the Regional Atlas

Refer to the Regional Atlas on pages 560–563.

1. **Place** Which major physical feature allows subsistence farming west of the Great Indian Desert?

2. **Human-Environment Interaction** What natural resource do Pakistan and Bangladesh have in common?

Thinking Like a Geographer

Think about the diverse cultures and physical geography of South Asia. What do you think contributes to some of the problems or conflicts in South Asia today? Based on your understanding of this region's physical and human geography, what solutions might you propose?

Problem-Solving Activity

Contemporary Issues Case Study Prepare a case study on the use of the English language in South Asia. Gather data from print and electronic resources, and summarize the history and current status of English in the region. Also, consider why English today serves as a major international medium of communication.

GeoJournal

Creative Writing Referring to the notes you made in your journal, choose one economic activity. Imagine that you are employed in this activity, and write a description of a typical work day. If necessary, conduct additional research to add details to your account. Make your description as detailed as possible to capture the sense of what your job is like.

Technology Activity

Using E-Mail Choose an environmental issue in South Asia that you have read about in your text or in other news sources. List the important points about the issue, and then compose an e-mail letter to the editor of your local newspaper to bring the issue to the attention of others.

Standardized Test Practice

Read the passage and answer the question that follows. If you have trouble answering the question, use the process of elimination to narrow your choices.

South Asia is taking several steps to increase food production in the region's agricultural areas. Steps include increased planting cycles in Bangladesh and the use of technology such as modern irrigation techniques, pest control, soil fertilization, and new varieties of grain that increase crop yields. Farmers in Nepal now plant winter wheat in fields that used to lie fallow after the rice harvest. Research stations in Bhutan have helped farmers establish fruit orchards, and government-funded programs in Sri Lanka have encouraged farmers to grow more food crops.

1. Which of the following reasons explains why South Asian countries are changing agricultural methods and using modern technology?

   F South Asia is taking steps to increase manufacturing production.

   G Countries want to raise more food for their people.

   H Nepal does allow its agricultural fields to lie fallow.

   J Modern irrigation techniques will eliminate the threat of floods.

 **Test-Taking Tip** Never rely on your memory to answer questions derived from a passage. If you refer to the passage before you choose the correct answer, you will be less likely to make careless errors.

Technology Activity

Students' letters should reflect accurate information, presented in a persuasive way.

Standardized Test Practice

1. G

Tested Objectives:
analyzing cause and effect

Additional Practice and Test-Taking Tips

Standardized Test Practice Workbook

CHAPTER BONUS TEST QUESTION

If South Asia has so many rivers, why is access to freshwater so limited? *(Many people live in areas far from rivers; in some monsoon areas, underground springs are only replenished by rains once a year; water is diverted from human use to commercial irrigation; sanitation facilities are limited, so rivers and wells are polluted by human waste; rivers and wells are polluted by industrial waste and runoff from agricultural chemicals.)*

Using the Regional Atlas

1. the Indus River
2. natural gas

Thinking Like a Geographer

Have students work in groups to complete this exercise, citing arguments from their textbooks.

Problem-Solving Activity

Have students research Internet and library resources to find out about the role of English in today's world, especially in South Asia. Then have students brainstorm why English is a major language of international communication.

TEACHING TRANSPARENCIES

L2 Unit 9 Map Overlay Transparencies

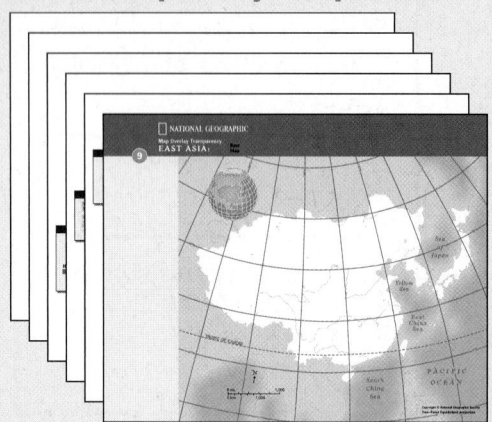

L2 Political Map Transparency 9

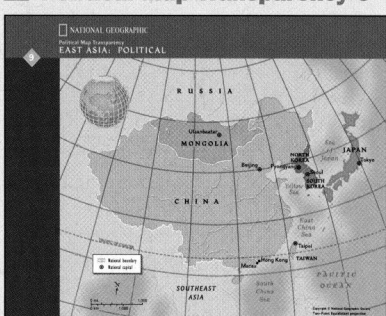

L2 World Cultures Transparencies 15, 16

APPLICATION AND ENRICHMENT

L2 Location Activity 9

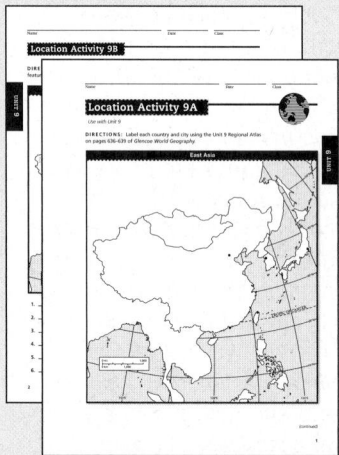

L2 Real-Life Applications and Problem-Solving Activity 9

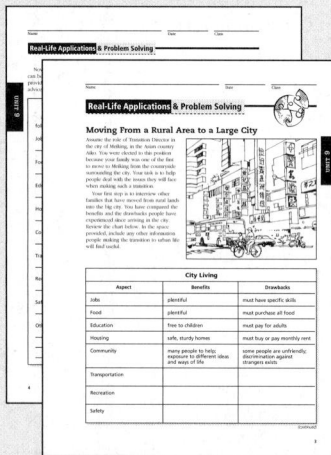

L2 GeoLab Activity 9

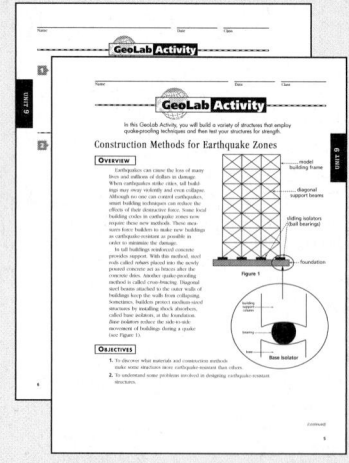

L2 Environmental Issues Case Study 9

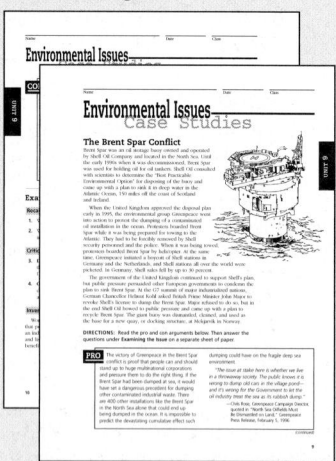

GEOGRAPHIC LITERACY

Focus on Geography Literacy

Building Geography Skills for Life

ASSESSMENT

Use the following to easily assess student learning in a variety of ways:

- Performance Assessment Activities and Rubrics
- Section Quizzes
- Chapter and Unit Tests
- Interactive Tutor Self-Assessment CD-ROM
- ExamView® Pro Testmaker
- MindJogger Videoquiz
- geography.glencoe.com
- Standardized Test Practice Workbook
- SAT I/II Test Practice

L2 Unit 9 Pretest and Tests

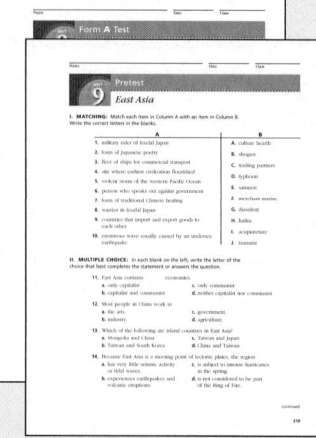

INTERDISCIPLINARY CONNECTIONS

L2 World Literature:
Contemporary Selection 9

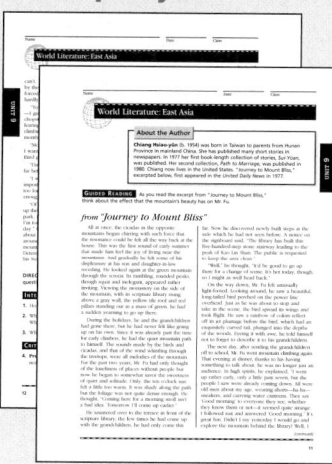

Foods Around the World

Multimedia

- **World Art and Architecture Transparencies**

- **World Art Prints**

- **World Music: A Cultural Legacy**

- **World History Primary Source Document Library**

BIBLIOGRAPHY

Readings for the Student

Ancient China, by Arthur Cotterell. New York, NY: Alfred A. Knopf, 1994.

The Boy and the Samurai, by Erik C. Haugaard. Boston, MA: Houghton Mifflin, 1991.

Japan: A Modern Land with Ancient Roots, by Irene Flum Galvin. Tarrytown, NY: Marshall Cavendish, 1996.

Readings for the Teacher

East Asia at the Center: Four Thousand Years of Engagement with the World, by Warren I. Cohen. New York, NY: Columbia University Press, 2001.

A History of Japan: From Stone Age to Superpower, by Kenneth G. Henshall. New York, NY: Palgrave, 1999.

Multimedia Resources

China: A Century of Revolution, New York, NY: Fox Lorber; 1997. Videocassette (3), 6 hours. (ASIN: 1572521902)

Tug of War: The Story of Taiwan, Boston, MA: WGBH, 1998. Videocassette. (ASIN: 6305374775)

READING SUPPORT FROM
JAMESTOWN EDUCATION

- *Timed Readings Plus in Social Studies* help students increase their reading rate and fluency while maintaining comprehension. The 400-word passages are similar to those found on state and national assessments.

- *Reading in the Content Area: Social Studies* concentrates on six essential reading skills that help students better comprehend what they read. The book includes 75 high-interest nonfiction passages written at increasing levels of difficulty.

- *Reading Fluency* helps students read smoothly, accurately, and expressively.

- *Jamestown's Reading Improvement,* by renowned reading expert Edward Fry, focuses on helping build your students' comprehension, vocabulary, and skimming and scanning skills.

- *Critical Reading Series* provides high-interest books, each written at three reading levels.

For more information about these products, see the Jamestown Education materials in the Classroom Solutions in the front of this Teacher Wraparound Edition.
To order these products, call Glencoe at 1-800-334-7344.

Background Information

The Physical Geography of East Asia

East Asia spreads across more than 4.5 million square miles (11.7 million sq. km) of territory. Of the region's six countries, China is the largest—with a land area slightly larger than that of the United States. China, however, has more than four times as many people.

In eastern China, lowlands and coastal areas are heavily populated and cultivated. Highlands in the west have rugged mountains, scattered human settlements, and extreme climates. This western region also includes Asia's largest desert, the Gobi, and the world's highest mountain, Mount Everest, located on the China-Nepal border. Across northern China stretches the country's most notable landmark and national symbol, the Great Wall, named in 1987 as one of UNESCO's World Heritage sites.

Volcanic activity and earthquakes along part of the Pacific Ocean's Ring of Fire helped form Taiwan and the Japanese islands. Natural forces continue to affect East Asia. A wide range in latitude from southern China and Taiwan in the Tropics to Siberia in the north gives the region a great variety of climates and vegetation.

Natural Resources

For centuries East Asia has been a source of tea, rice, bamboo, ginseng, ginkgo trees, and silk. Freshwater and ocean resources are so important to the livelihoods of people in coastal areas that water and fish are East Asia's traditional symbols of prosperity. South Korea, Taiwan, and Japan have few mineral resources, and Japan especially relies heavily on imports of coal and oil. By contrast China has rich deposits of minerals widely distributed throughout the country.

The Cultural Geography of East Asia

East Asia's earliest civilization developed in China thousands of years ago. Other civilizations later arose in Korea and Japan. For centuries nearly impassable mountains, vast deserts, and expanses of ocean often isolated East Asia from the rest of the world. Isolation and other factors led to the development of relatively homogeneous and highly refined cultures in the region.

China greatly influenced the cultures of Korea and Japan, which went on to develop their own styles in such art forms as ceramics, painting, and calligraphy. For thousands of years, caravans journeyed on the Silk Road, an extensive network of trading routes that linked China, central parts of Asia, and Southwest Asia. Traders carried with them not only goods but also ideas and religions, especially Buddhism, Islam, and Christianity. By way of the Silk Road, Chinese inventions, such as paper, printing, and fireworks, as well as food products—rice, tea, soybeans, and noodles—eventually reached the West.

Modernization

From the 1500s to the 1800s, East Asia's civilizations were challenged by the global expansion of Western nations. After a long period of political isolation, China and Japan both were forced to open their borders to Western trade and influences. Unlike China, which suffered military defeats and some loss of sovereignty, Japan faced the Western challenge by modernizing many of its institutions and building industries. Although Japan's military expansion later brought about its defeat in World War II, Japan quickly rebounded economically under its postwar democratic government. A period of Cold War tensions followed the rise of communism in China and the division of Korea into communist and non-communist states. However, during the late 1900s, East Asia as a whole emerged as a major world economic force. Even the region's communist countries wanted a share in new opportunities for global trade.

Society and Art

Most of East Asia's people today live in bustling, crowded, urban settings. Their traditional values and arts, however, stress the serenity and simplicity often associated with rural living. Traditional art forms include Chinese tai chi and qigong exercises, the Japanese tea ceremony, calligraphy, and landscape painting. Many of these practices derive from East Asia's major religions—Confucianism, Daoism, Buddhism, and Shintoism.

CHAPTER 28 (pp. 684–703)

East Asia Today

During the past century, migration and trade have facilitated an exchange of ideas and practices between East Asia and other parts of the world. Japan, Taiwan, and South Korea have become modern industrial nations, with a major stake in the global economy. China pursues economic modernization, although its communist government's harsh treatment of dissidents has been criticized by democratic countries, including the United States. In 2000, however, the United States granted full trading rights to China.

Some East Asian cities, especially in China, have grown tremendously in population as a result of migration from rural areas. A major factor in this population shift is the availability of jobs in new and growing industries. Industrial progress, however, has taken its toll on the environment, mirroring similar worldwide problems—pollution, acid rain, deforestation, and depletion of ocean and land resources. East Asian countries recently have become more active in addressing environmental issues.

World Trade

Despite great economic advances, East Asian countries faced a major financial crisis in the late 1990s that sapped their economic growth. The economies of two "Asian Tigers," Taiwan and South Korea, have improved faster than the economy of Japan, which has yet to implement reforms.

The financial crisis has had less of an impact on China, which has a developing economy promoted by nearly two decades of pro-market economic reforms. China now represents one of the world's largest emerging markets for consumer goods. The country's prosperity, however, is confined to coastal cities and market economic zones. In China's countryside, where 64 percent of the population lives, farmers have less opportunity to share in the material rewards of prosperity. China's unregulated industrial expansion—with widespread use of coal—has contributed to environmental damage. As a result of industrial and urban growth, many areas of East Asia suffer from air, water, and soil pollution.

Severe traffic congestion is a major problem in large urban centers, such as Tokyo, Taipei, and Shanghai. Clear-cutting of forests and careless practices in farming and mining have caused soil erosion, deforestation, and flooding. Added to these environmental issues is the threat of violent natural forces, such as earthquakes, tsunamis, and typhoons, that cause extensive loss of life and damage to property.

00:00 OUT OF TIME?

If time does not permit teaching each chapter in this unit, you may want to use the **Reading Essentials and Study Guide** summaries.

Unit Launch Activity

Ask: **What countries do you think make up East Asia?** *(China, Japan, Mongolia, North Korea, South Korea, Taiwan)* Have students locate these countries on a world map or globe. List each country's name as a column heading on the board. **Ask:** **What traditions, products, or ideas come to mind when you think of East Asian countries? What news stories have you heard about each one?** Have students brainstorm responses, and list them on the board. Have volunteers use the lists to create a bulletin board on East Asia that can be added to throughout the study of Unit 9. Encourage students to bring in news articles about East Asia to post on the bulletin board.

GLENCOE
TECHNOLOGY

☐ NATIONAL GEOGRAPHIC
WORLD REGIONS
VIDEO PROGRAM

Unit 9, East Asia
The following segments enhance the study of this unit:

- **Treasures of the Gobi**
- **Haenyo of Cheju**
- **A-Mei: Princess of Pop**

 Available in DVD and VHS

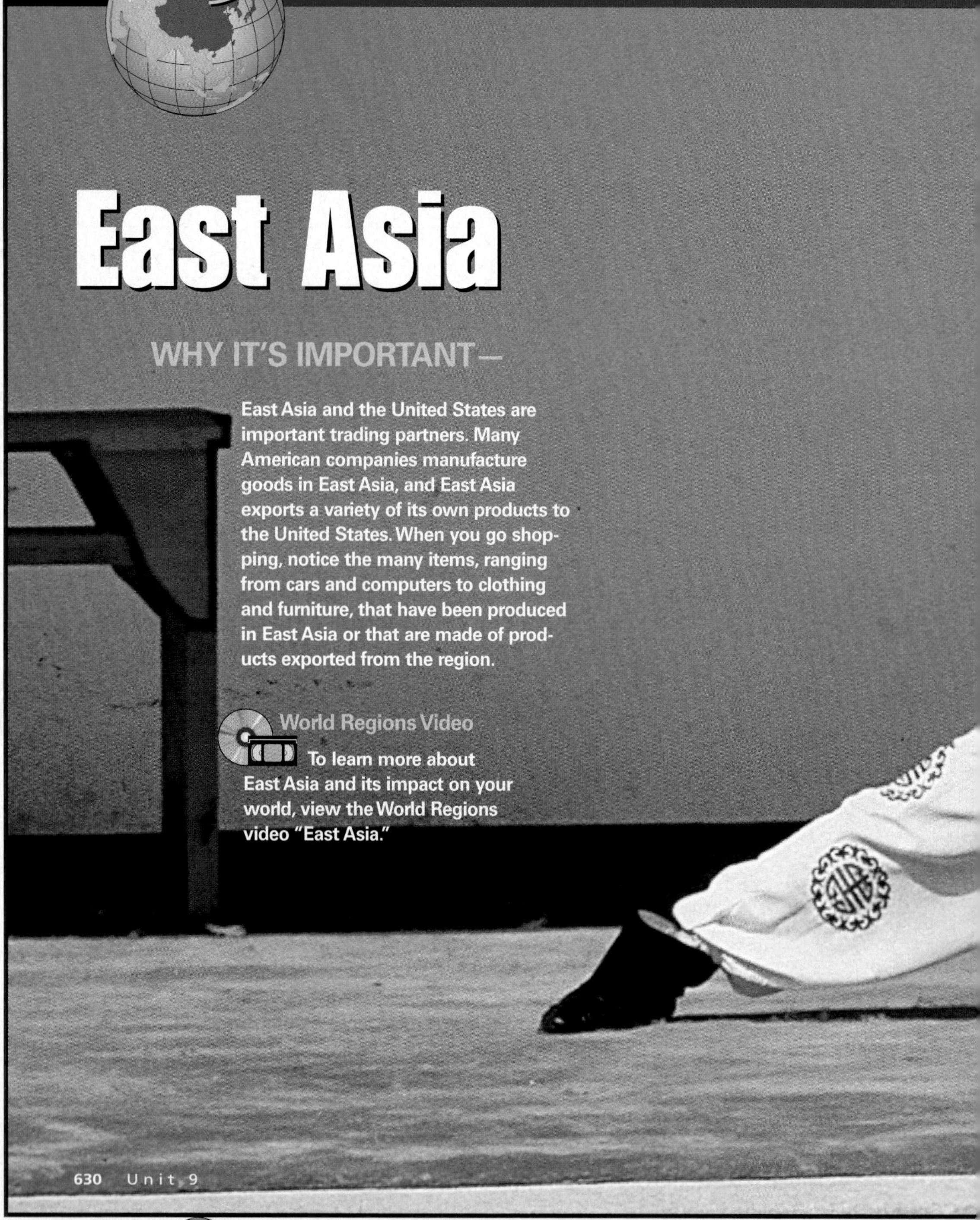

East Asia

WHY IT'S IMPORTANT—

East Asia and the United States are important trading partners. Many American companies manufacture goods in East Asia, and East Asia exports a variety of its own products to the United States. When you go shopping, notice the many items, ranging from cars and computers to clothing and furniture, that have been produced in East Asia or that are made of products exported from the region.

World Regions Video
To learn more about East Asia and its impact on your world, view the World Regions video "East Asia."

 GETTING TO KNOW THE REGION

Map Activity Display Political Map Transparency 9 and have students locate places in East Asia. **Ask:** **On what continent, and in which part of that continent, is East Asia located?** *(the eastern part of Asia)* **Which country occupies most of East Asia?** *(China)* **Which country is landlocked?** *(Mongolia)* **What rivers provide water for inland areas of China?** *(Yangtze River, Yellow River, Xi River)* **What landforms are to the east of the mainland?** *(islands and peninsulas)* **By what country names are the island countries known?** *(Taiwan, Japan)*
▦ **EE1 The World in Spatial Terms: Standard 1;** ▦ **EE2 Places and Regions: Standard 5**

NATIONAL GEOGRAPHIC

Dancer in Hong Kong

This online resource, brought to you by the National Geographic Society, provides lesson plans, atlas updates, cartographic activities with interactive maps, an online map store, and links to the boundless subjects of maps and geography.

Unit Overview

The three chapters that comprise this unit introduce students to the physical and cultural geography of East Asia. Point out that although East Asian countries and peoples are extremely diverse in many ways, they have the following features in common:

- Their populations are relatively homogeneous.
- Chinese heritage has profoundly influenced the language, religion, and arts of the region.
- The region's highly refined cultural development was generally isolated from Western cultures until the 1800s.

ABOUT THE PHOTO

Visual Instruction East Asia's traditional theater and dance are elaborate and stylized. East Asian dancers keep their feet firmly on the floor and often move in slow, highly geometric patterns with many arm and hand movements. Since the 1700s military plays and dueling have been popular subjects for Chinese opera, which often features acrobatic or pantomimed fighting. Actors typically specialize in a single role type, such as a *ching* (painted-face warrior), a *tan* (female), or a *ch'uo* (clown). Each character type is identified by costumes, headgear, makeup, and a few standarized props such as a sword for the warrior.
🌐 **EE2 Places and Regions: Standard 4;** 🌐 **EE4 Human Systems: Standard 10**

REGIONAL ATLAS

① FOCUS

These features and activities may be used as an introduction to the unit or as teaching tools throughout the course of the unit.

L1 Using Flash Cards Activity

Prior to studying this unit, preview students' knowledge of East Asia using the **Countries of the World Flash Cards.** Organize students into teams, and quiz them using the cards for the East Asian countries. After students study pages 632–635, have each team discuss the answers and make up additional flash card questions for each country. Then play the game again, incorporating each team's new questions into the game. ELL

L2 Photo Research Activity

Have students, individually or in groups, conduct research to find out more about the subjects of the photos on pages 632–635. Have students study the details of the photographs and read the captions to make a list of topics to research.

FYI

China Flood control and irrigation are extremely important in China. China is believed to have more than 80,000 dams. More than 22,000 of these dams are higher than four stories—the most of any country in the world.

What Makes East Asia a Region?

East Asia occupies much of the Asian mainland south of Russia. China takes up four-fifths of this region. With the exception of Mongolia, the other East Asian countries—Japan, North Korea, South Korea, and Taiwan—all lie on peninsulas and islands.

Towering mountains, such as the Himalaya and the Kunlun Shan, dominate the region's western landscape. Between these two ranges lies the Plateau of Xizang, the world's highest plateau. Two major rivers—the Yellow and the Yangtze—begin on the plateau and flow down onto fertile plains in eastern China.

Vast East Asia encompasses great variety in climate and vegetation, from the subarctic forests of northern Mongolia to the tropical rain forests on China's southernmost tip. Monsoons bring rain to coastal areas each summer, but the moist winds rarely reach the region's deep interior. In this arid heartland lie the parched and windswept Gobi and Taklimakan deserts.

1 **A snug coat warms a boy** in the chill, high-elevation air of Tibet, an area in southwestern China. Often called the "roof of the world," Tibet is perched on the lofty Plateau of Xizang, also known as the Plateau of Tibet. Valleys in Tibet are higher than the mountains of most countries.

632 Unit 9

BACKGROUND INFORMATION

Yangtze River China's Yangtze River is Asia's longest river and the third longest river in the world, after the Nile and the Amazon. It begins high in the Tibetan Plateau and descends more than 17,000 feet (5,182 m) over a total course of 3,915 miles (6,300 km). Along its middle section are deep, scenic gorges. Nearer the river's mouth are its basins and lowlands. The river empties into the East China Sea at Shanghai, China's most populous city. Millions of Chinese live along the Yangtze. Its basins and lowlands provide more than half of China's crops. The river also supports a huge fishing industry.

🌐 **EE2 Places and Regions: Standard 4;** 🌐 **EE3 Physical Systems: Standard 7**

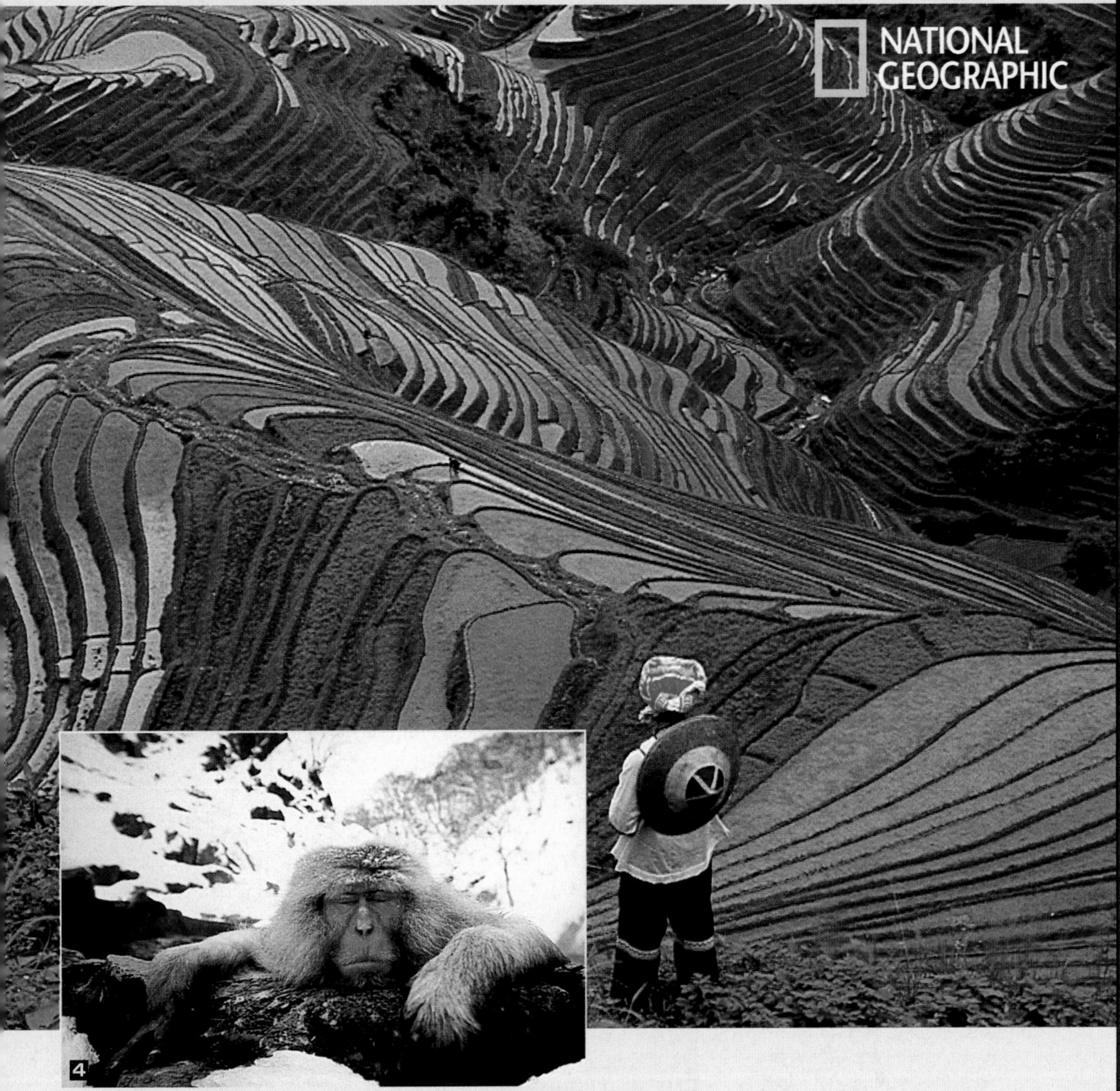

② TEACH

L2 Making Inferences

Have students study the photos and their captions on pages 632–633. Direct them to look for clues about the effects of physical environment on East Asians and ways that East Asians have affected their physical environment. **Ask: What can you infer from these pictures about the ways that humans interact with the physical environment in East Asia? What can you infer about the climate of the areas shown?** Ask students to explain the reasons for their inferences. *(Possible answers: The climate of Tibet is very cold, as shown by the boy's warm clothing. The terraces show human effort to increase limited croplands. Northern Japan has a cold climate, as shown by the frost on the macaque's fur. Fishing is an important human use of lakes in China; some East Asians depend on lakes as a food source.)*

2 **Ancient limestone hills** rise behind a rafter on the Li River, in southeastern China. On the raft are two large birds called cormorants, which are trained to dive for fish. Rivers and seas are important sources of food throughout East Asia.

3 **Neatly terraced paddies** follow the contours of steep hillsides in China. China is a huge country, but only about 10 percent of its land can be used for growing crops. Terraces allow farmers to grow rice in places that are fertile but sloping.

4 **With frost on its fur,** a Japanese macaque snoozes in a hot spring. Also called snow monkeys, Japanese macaques are adapted to the chilly climate of northern Japan, where cold winds scoop up moisture from the Sea of Japan (East Sea) and fling it back to Earth as snow.

Unit 9 **633**

GLENCOE TECHNOLOGY

NATIONAL GEOGRAPHIC

WORLD REGIONS
VIDEO PROGRAM

Unit 9, East Asia
The following segments enhance the study of this unit:

• **Treasures of the Gobi**
• **Haenyo of Cheju**
• **A-Mei: Princess of Pop**

A TRAVELER'S LOG

Elisabeth B. Booz In 1979 Elisabeth B. Booz traveled from the United States to Kunming, China, to teach at Yunnan University, which had been closed during Mao Zedong's "Cultural Revolution" of the 1960s. Ms. Booz describes her experience:

"Yunnan, which means 'south of the clouds,' is a border province surrounded on the south and west by Vietnam, Laos, and Burma. It has 23 different national minorities, with distinctive costumes, cultures, and languages. . . . We had not been in Kunming long before a joke was making the rounds: "Now we have a twenty-fourth national minority—the Americans!"

🌐 **EE2 Places and Regions: Standard 4;** 🌐 **EE4 Human Systems: Standards 9, 10**

L2 Research

Organize students into six groups, representing each East Asian country. Have individual students or pairs within each group research one of the following categories: literature and drama, arts and crafts, weapons, transportation, architecture, and agriculture. Research should focus on the country's achievements in each area, as well as outside influences, such as that of China or the West. Have each group report the results of their research to the class. English-language learners may be paired with students proficient in English. **ELL**

The Japanese enjoy a mixture of Eastern and Western cultures. Their favorite spectator sports, for example, are baseball and sumo wrestling.

China's arts and technology, for many centuries before contact with the West, spread to and were adapted by most of its neighbors. They benefited from China's advanced knowledge in metalworking, pottery, weapons, transportation, architecture, and agriculture.

Descended from Dynasties

East Asia can trace many of its cultural features to an ancient civilization that arose in China around 2000 B.C. In the centuries that followed, powerful dynasties ruled China, creating an enormous empire that influenced the cultural development of the entire region.

Today, East Asia is home to about one-fourth of the world's people. Most live crowded together in the region's fertile river valleys and coastal plains. Within each country, people tend to be ethnically similar.

During the twentieth century, the political and economic paths of East Asian countries diverged. China and North Korea adopted communist forms of government, while Japan, South Korea, and Taiwan developed capitalist, free-market economies.

1 A huge portrait of Communist leader Mao Zedong hangs above the Gate of Heavenly Peace, overlooking Tiananmen Square, in Beijing, China. In 1949 Mao stood at this site and established the People's Republic of China under Communist rule.

634   Unit 9

BACKGROUND INFORMATION

Cultural Values Confucianism, the ethical and moral system based on the teachings of the Chinese scholar and statesman Confucius (Konfuzi) over 2,000 years ago, still greatly influences East Asians. The Confucian system stresses virtuous conduct and rules of responsibility. Key among the virtues are kindness, propriety, intelligence, and faithfulness. Confucianism emphasizes the duties between children and parents, elder siblings and younger siblings, husband and wife, friends, rulers and subjects, and stresses the importance of avoiding shame or embarrassment to another or to one's family or self. As a result, respect for age, rank, and family continue to be important aspects of East Asian cultures.   **EE4 Human Systems: Standards 9 and 10**

INTERDISCIPLINARY
connection

GOVERNMENT In Japan the local divisions of the country that can be compared to states in the United States are called prefectures. China and the Koreas, on the other hand, are divided into provinces. The island of Taiwan is divided into counties.

3 ASSESS

Have students identify physical factors, such as climate, vegetation, river systems, and other trade networks, that define East Asia as a region. Ask them to describe the ways East Asia's culture is different and unique from those of other regions of the world.

4 CLOSE

Have students work in groups to create sets of postcards that describe key physical and cultural features of East Asia. Students should illustrate one side of each postcard and write a description on the other side.

2 Built as a barrier to stop invaders from the north, China's Great Wall was started around 221 B.C., during the Qin dynasty. The wall winds for thousands of miles over plains and mountains and along desert borders. Erected entirely by hand, it is the longest structure ever built.

3 Neon lights glow as the sun sets over Tokyo, the capital of Japan. One of the largest, busiest, and most crowded cities in the world, Tokyo is Japan's center of commerce and culture. About one-fourth of Japan's population lives in the Tokyo area.

4 Standing serenely, an offshore torii, or gate, marks the entrance to one of Japan's most famous Shinto shrines. Shinto is an ancient religion that originated in Japan. Its followers worship *kami*—deities found in rivers, rocks, trees, and other elements of nature.

Unit 9   635

UNIT PROJECT

Knowledge Bowl Have students study the photographs and captions on pages 632–635, and then compose three or more questions about each photo, writing each set of questions on a separate sheet of paper. For example, their page about the photo of the Great Wall might read: *China's Great Wall: Where exactly is the Great Wall? When was it completed? Was it successful in stopping invaders?* Have students brainstorm possible sources for finding the answers. Remind students on occasion to review the questions and write down answers as they read the unit. At the end of the unit, use students' questions to hold a Knowledge Bowl on East Asia. ▓ **EE2 Places and Regions: Standard 4**

These features and activities may be used as an introduction to the unit or as teaching tools throughout the course of the unit.

L1 Calculating Distance

Share with students the information from the GeoFact below. Have students turn to the maps in the Regional Atlas. Ask them to calculate the approximate length of the world's longest overland telecommunications cable. Inform students that they may need to combine information from more than one map to estimate the distance from Shanghai to Frankfurt. **Ask:** Which maps will you need to consult in order to complete your calculation? *(Answers may include World Physical/Political, East Asia, Russia, and/or Europe maps.)*

□ NATIONAL GEOGRAPHIC **GEOFACT**

▶ The world's longest overland telecommunications cable, linking 20 countries from Shanghai, China, to Frankfurt, Germany, follows the ancient Silk Road trading route. The fiber-optic super-link was opened in late 1998 and transmits digital voice, video, fax, and data communications.

Elevation Profile

In order to show a variety of physical features, this cross section starts at just east of K2 and crosses the Plateau of Tibet to the east. At the eastern edge of the plateau, it turns northeast to Beijing, crosses the Yellow Sea to Seoul, and then crosses the Sea of Japan to Mount Fuji.

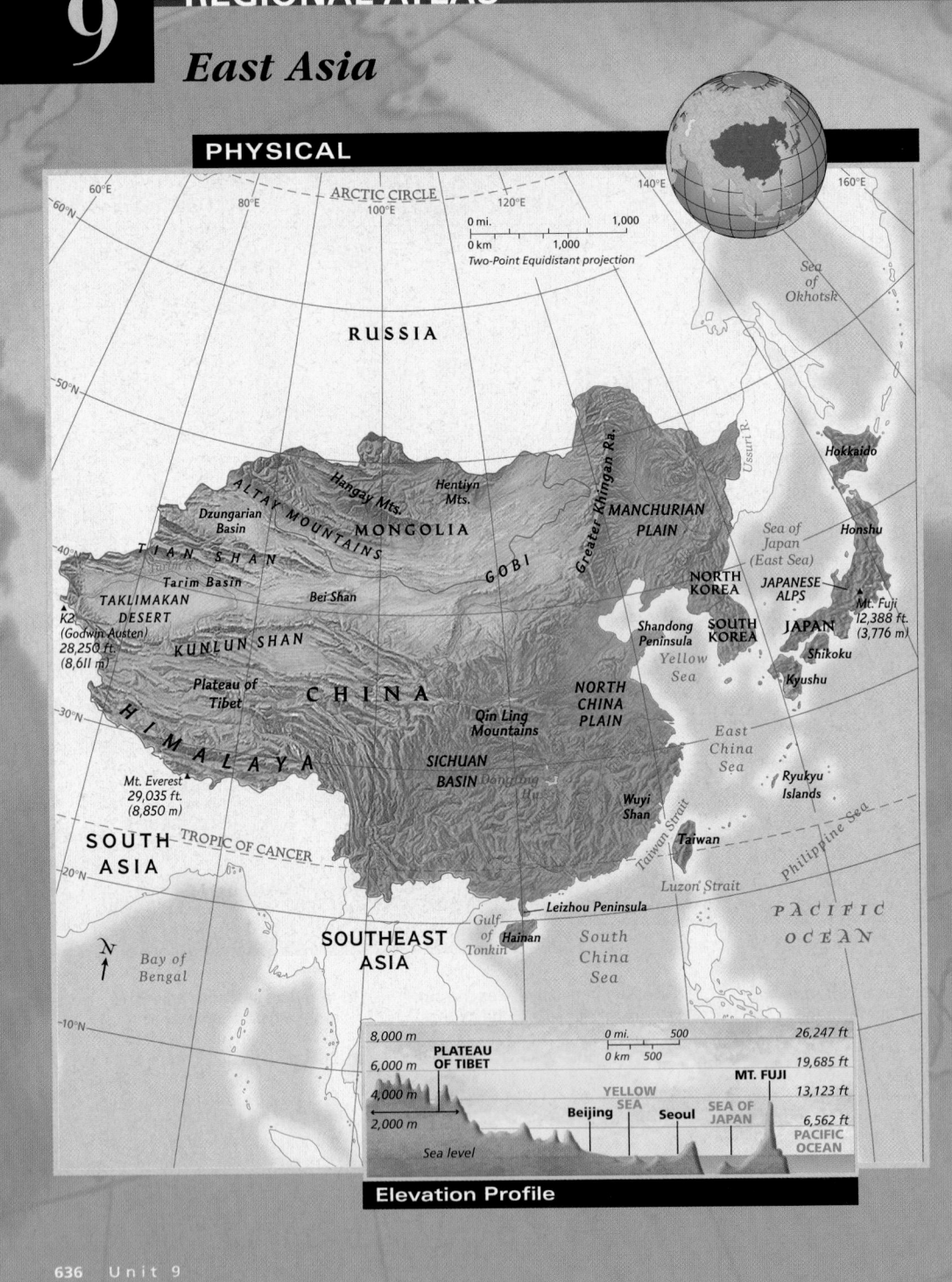

PHYSICAL

Elevation Profile

636 Unit 9

REGIONAL ATLAS ACTIVITY

Question Exchange Have students write questions based on the physical and political maps of East Asia. Model the questions. **Ask: In the elevation profile, what is the highest point in eastern East Asia?** *(Mount Fuji)* **How does it compare to the highest point in western East Asia?** *(The highest western peaks are nearly 6,500 feet [2,000 m] higher.)* **In which direction, and what distance, must one travel to reach Harbin from Chongqing?** *(northeast, about 2,200 miles or 3,541 km)* Encourage students to use information from all parts of the map to create questions. Then have pairs of students quiz each other. **ELL**

🌐 **EE1 The World in Spatial Terms: Standards 1, 3**
🌐 **EE2 Places and Regions: Standards 4, 5**

UNIT 9 REGIONAL ATLAS

POLITICAL

60°E 80°E ARCTIC CIRCLE 120°E 140°E 160°E
100°E

60°N

0 mi.   1,000
0 km   1,000
Two-Point Equidistant projection

⊛ National capital
• Major city

RUSSIA

CENTRAL ASIA

50°N

Sea of Okhotsk

ALTAY MOUNTAINS

Amur R.

Ulaanbaatar

MONGOLIA

Songhua R.

Hokkaido

Sapporo•

40°N TIAN SHAN

Tarim R.

G O B I

Liao

Harbin

Shenyang•

Honshu

Sea of Japan (East Sea)

JAPAN

TAKLIMAKAN DESERT

KUNLUN SHAN

Beijing⊛

•Tianjin

NORTH KOREA

Pyongyang

⊛Seoul

SOUTH KOREA

Taegu

Pusan

Tokyo•
Yokohama•

Kyoto•
Kobe•
Osaka•

Shikoku

30°N

HIMALAYA

Taiyuan•

Zibo•

North China Plain

Zhengzhou•

C H I N A

Yellow R.

Yellow Sea

Fukuoka•

Kyushu

Nanjing•

Shanghai•

Salween R.

•Chengdu

Wuhan•

Hangzhou•

East China Sea

Ryukyu Is.

Chongqing•

Yangtze R.

Okinawa

SOUTH ASIA

TROPIC OF CANCER

Red R.

Taipei•

TAIWAN

The People's Republic of China claims Taiwan as its 23rd province.

Philippine Sea

20°N

N

Bay of Bengal

SOUTHEAST ASIA

•Guangzhou

Macau• •Hong Kong

Hainan

South China Sea

PACIFIC OCEAN

10°N

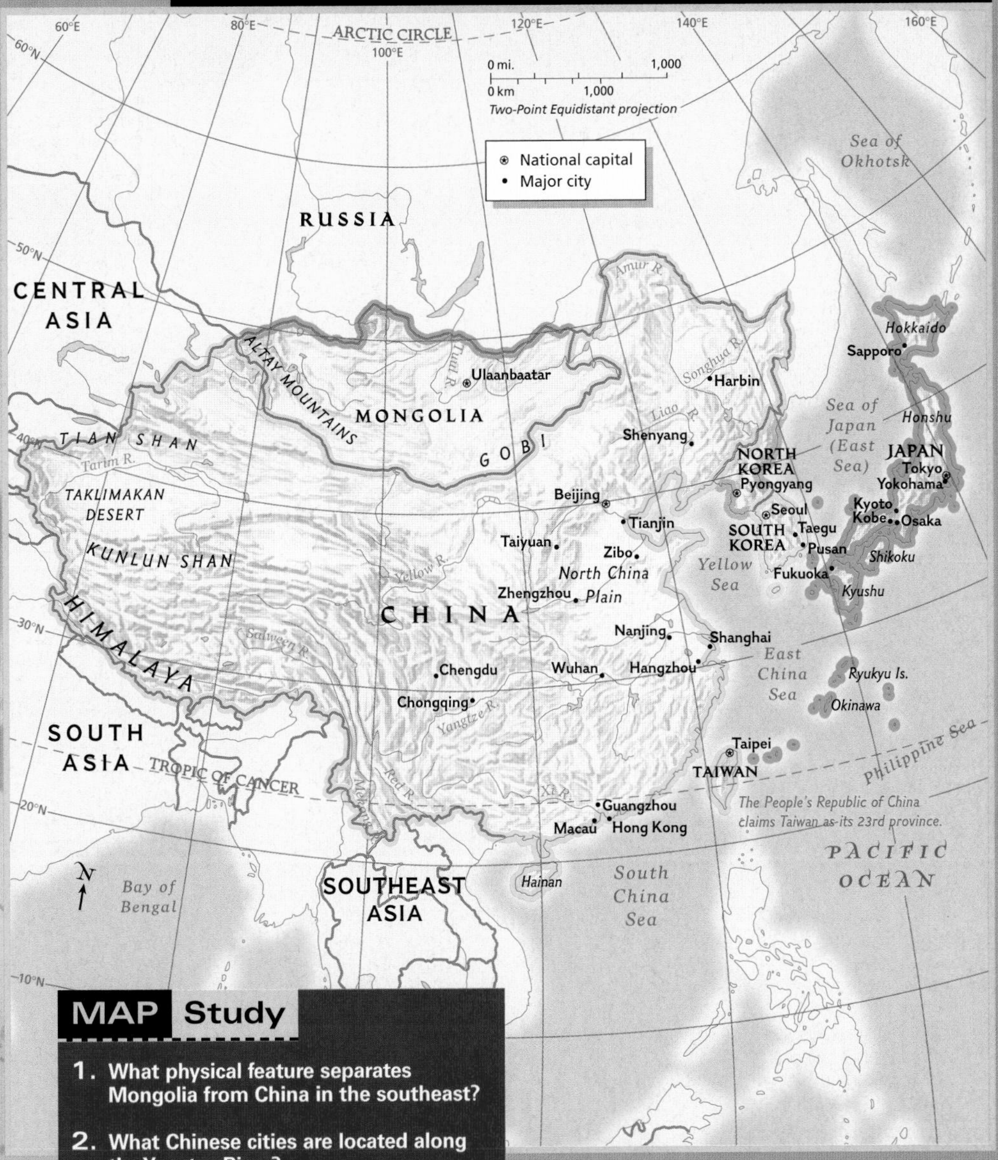

MAP Study

1. What physical feature separates Mongolia from China in the southeast?

2. What Chinese cities are located along the Yangtze River?

Unit 9 637

L2 Predicting Consequences

Ask: Which East Asian countries have coastlines? *(China, South Korea, Japan, Taiwan, North Korea)* Ask students to predict the effects of having coastlines on each country's natural resources, climate, and trade with other countries. Note students' responses on the board, and have students write their predictions in their notebooks. Later in Unit 9, have students review and refine their predictions.

Livestock Like the United States, China has a "wild west"—western lands that are drier and more sparsely settled than its eastern lands. The western mountains and deserts are home to ethnic groups such as the Tibetans and Mongols, who herd livestock.

MAP Study

Answers:

1. *the Gobi*

2. *Chongqing, Wuhan, Nanjing, and Shanghai*

Map Skills Practice Mental Mapping Have students sketch and label from memory a rough map of the East Asian countries.

REGIONAL ATLAS ACTIVITY

Ethnic Groups Explain that although the vast majority of people in East Asia are Han Chinese, the region's population includes well over 50 other ethnic groups, including Mongol, Uygur, Tibetan, Buyi, Tai, Miao, Hui, Yi, and Manchu peoples. Have students work as a class to research the names, locations, and population sizes of at least the above-listed ethnic groups. Have students create a circle graph to compare the population sizes of China's ethnic groups. 🌐 **EE1 The World in Spatial Terms: Standards 1, 3**
🌐 **EE4 Human Systems: Standards 9, 10**

637

L1 Identifying

Have students use the population density map to: **(1)** Name the cities with populations of over 2 million. *(Students' responses should show they understand the map key.)* **(2)** Describe the locations of areas that have the lowest population per square mile. *(Mongolia; China's northern and western regions; northern Japan; eastern Taiwan; eastern Korea)* **(3)** Describe the physical features of areas that have the highest population per square mile. *(coastal areas and river basins)* ELL

L1 Making Comparisons

Have students compare the population density and the economic activity maps on pages 638–639. Discuss the ways that land use and population density are related.

global issues

Population and Environment
More than 50 percent of China's population does not have access to clean water and consumes water dangerously contaminated by human and animal wastes. Air pollution in some Chinese cities is 10 times greater than safe levels.

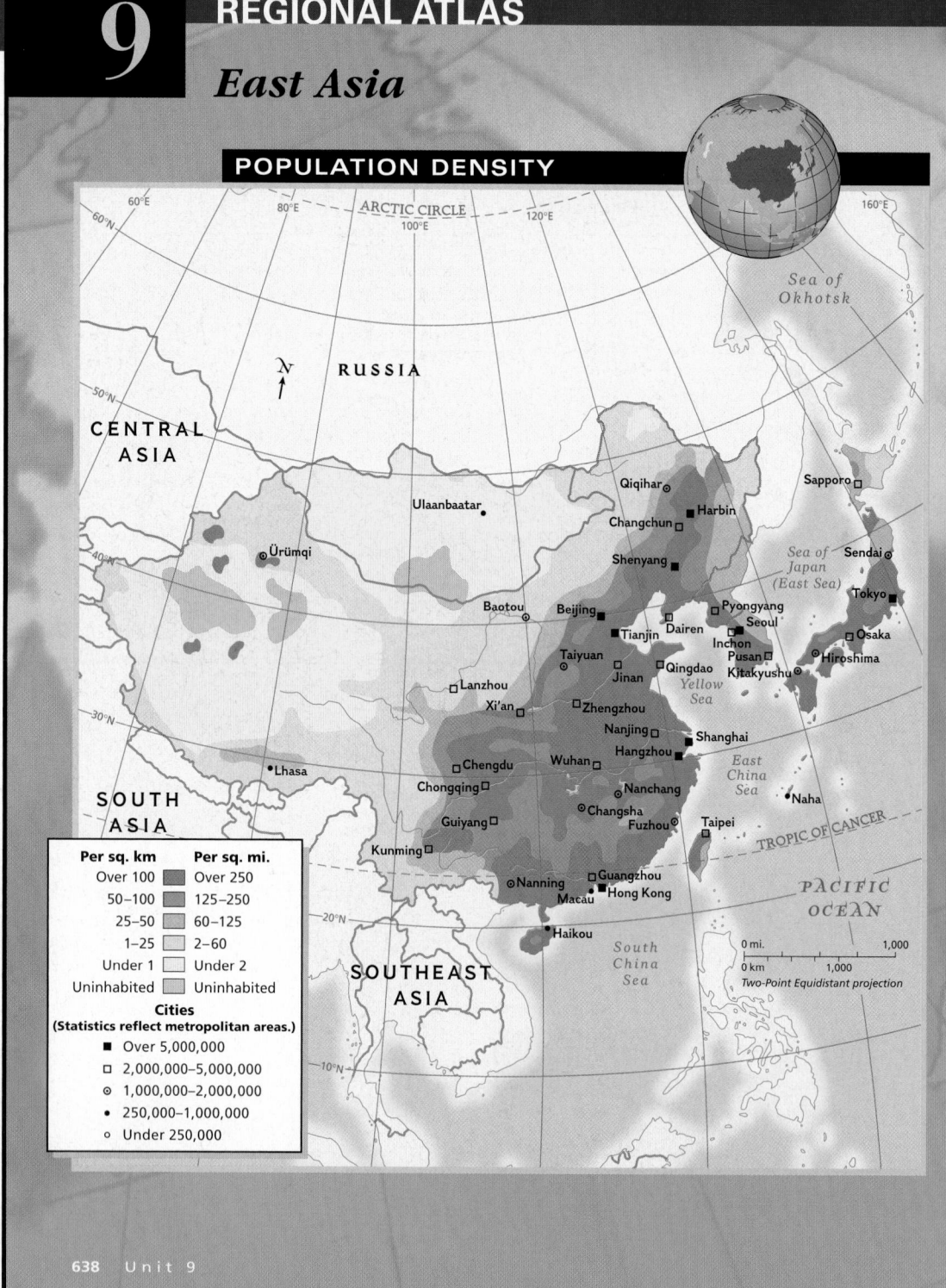

POPULATION DENSITY

Per sq. km	Per sq. mi.
Over 100	Over 250
50–100	125–250
25–50	60–125
1–25	2–60
Under 1	Under 2
Uninhabited	Uninhabited

Cities
(Statistics reflect metropolitan areas.)
- ■ Over 5,000,000
- ▫ 2,000,000–5,000,000
- ◉ 1,000,000–2,000,000
- • 250,000–1,000,000
- ◦ Under 250,000

REGIONAL ATLAS ACTIVITY

Analyzing Land Uses and Resources Organize students into seven groups, one each for Japan, western China, eastern China, Mongolia, Tibet, North Korea, and South Korea. Have each group identify and discuss land uses and natural resources shown on the map. Have speakers from each group describe to the class the land uses and resource reserves for their country or region. In conclusion, the class should analyze how the distribution and use of resources affect the location and patterns of movement of products, capital, and people in each area. ELL

⊕ **EE1 The World in Spatial Terms: Standards 1, 3**
⊕ **EE2 Places and Regions: Standard 4**

ECONOMIC ACTIVITY

ARCTIC CIRCLE

Sea of Okhotsk

RUSSIA

CENTRAL ASIA

Ulaanbaatar

MONGOLIA

Qiqihar

Changchun · Harbin

Camels

Soybeans

Shenyang

Wheat Corn

Sea of Japan (East Sea)

Ürümqi

Camels

NORTH KOREA

Pyongyang

Tokyo

Yokohama

Corn

Wheat

Sheep

Beijing · Tianjin

Seoul

SOUTH KOREA Pusan

Kyoto Kobe JAPAN

Osaka

Hiroshima

Goats

Lanzhou

CHINA

Taiyuan

Qingdao

Kitakyushu

Yellow Sea

Oats

Wheat

Barley

Nanjing

Yaks

Rice

Wuhan · Shanghai

East China Sea

Ryukyu Is.

Lhasa

Chongqing

Rice

Tea

Sugarcane

Hogs

Rice

Taipei

TROPIC OF CANCER

Rice

TAIWAN

Guangzhou

Rice

Hong Kong

SOUTH ASIA

South China Sea

SOUTHEAST ASIA

0 mi. 1,000
0 km 1,000
Two-Point Equidistant projection

Resources

- ⚒ Petroleum
- ⛏ Coal
- 🏭 Iron ore
- ▼ Tin
- ☑ Tungsten
- ✚ Bauxite
- Copper

Land Use

- Commercial farming
- Subsistence farming
- Nomadic herding
- Hunting and gathering
- Manufacturing and trade
- Commercial fishing
- Little or no activity

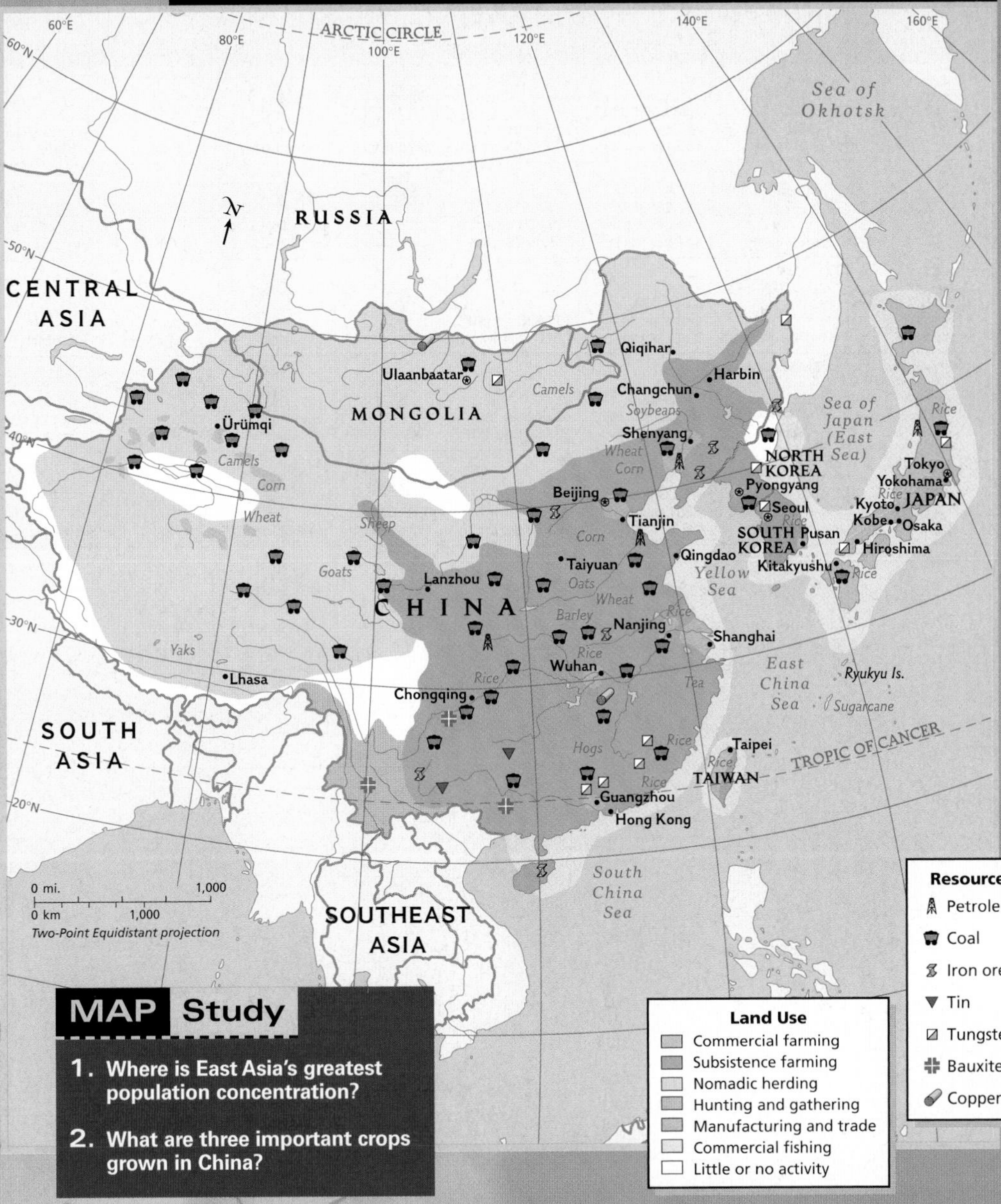

MAP Study

1. Where is East Asia's greatest population concentration?

2. What are three important crops grown in China?

L2 Drawing Conclusions

Have students study the physical map on page 636 and the population density map on page 638 to draw conclusions about what geographic features might account for the uneven population density in East Asia.

L3 Synthesizing Information

Have students combine information and facts from the four maps on pages 636–639 into descriptive sentences about various East Asian countries. Encourage students to write compound/complex sentences, and to include as many facts as possible in their sentences. Direct students to use standard grammar, spelling, sentence structure, and punctuation.

MAP Study

Answers:

1. *eastern China, southern Japan, western Korea, western Taiwan*

2. *rice, wheat, corn, soybeans, barley, oats, sugarcane*

Map Skills Practice Making Comparisons Have students determine the chief differences in land use between Japan and the other populous sections of the continent. *(Answers may include continent: large areas of subsistence farming; Japan's land: manufacturing, trade, and commercial farming.)*

REGIONAL ATLAS ACTIVITY

Economic Profiles Organize students into six groups and assign an East Asian country to each group. Have groups use available reference resources to find out each country's leading economic sectors, exports and imports, and trading partners. Have each group create charts that show the relationships between physical geography features and the country's economic activities, and then present the information to the class.

🌐 **EE4 Human Systems: Standard 11**

🌐 **EE5 Environment and Society: Standards 15, 16**

These features and activities may be used as an introduction to the unit or as teaching tools throughout the course of the unit.

Culture NOTE

China When eating out in China, tipping is not necessary. In fact, a tip is considered an insult; it implies that the giver feels superior to the person receiving the tip.

Bicycles in China are more common than cars because they are affordable, convenient, easily repaired, and take up relatively little space. Roads in China often are crowded with throngs of bicycle riders. Motor scooters also are popular.

□ NATIONAL GEOGRAPHIC **GEOFACT**

▶ **Japan's territory includes four principal islands and more than 3,000 smaller islands. The Kuriles Islands in the north are disputed territory between Russia and Japan.**

UNIT 9 REGIONAL ATLAS

East Asia

COUNTRY PROFILES

COUNTRY * AND CAPITAL	FLAG AND LANGUAGE	POPULATION** AND DENSITY	LANDMASS	MAJOR EXPORT	MAJOR IMPORT	CURRENCY	GOVERNMENT
CHINA — Beijing	Mandarin Chinese	1,289,000,000 349 per sq.mi. 135 per sq. km	3,696,100 sq.mi. 9,572,899 sq. km	Machinery	Machinery	Yuan	Communist State
JAPAN — Tokyo	Japanese	127,500,000 874 per sq.mi. 337 per sq. km	145,869 sq.mi. 377,801 sq. km	Machinery	Manufactured Goods	Yen	Constitutional Monarchy
MONGOLIA — Ulaanbaatar	Khalkha Mongol	2,500,000 4 per sq.mi. 2 per sq. km	604,826 sq.mi. 1,566,499 sq. km	Copper	Fuels	Tugrik	Republic
NORTH KOREA — Pyongyang	Korean	22,700,000 487 per sq.mi. 188 per sq. km	46,541 sq.mi. 120,541 sq. km	Minerals	Petroleum	Won	Communist State
SOUTH KOREA — Seoul	Korean	47,900,000 1,251 per sq.mi. 483 per sq. km	38,324 sq.mi. 99,259 sq. km	Electronic Equipment	Machinery	Won	Republic
TAIWAN*** — Taipei	Mandarin Chinese	22,600,000 1,616 per sq.mi. 624 per sq. km	13,969 sq.mi. 36,180 sq. km	Textiles	Machinery	New Taiwan Dollar	Republic

*COUNTRIES AND FLAGS NOT DRAWN TO SCALE
***The People's Republic of China claims Taiwan as its 23rd province.

**POPULATIONS ARE ROUNDED, *SOURCE: 2003 WORLD POPULATION DATA SHEET*

FOR AN ONLINE UPDATE OF THIS INFORMATION, VISIT GEOGRAPHY.GLENCOE.COM AND CLICK ON "TEXTBOOK UPDATES."

▶ Women inspecting cloth in textile mill, Kyoto, Japan

COUNTRY PROFILE ACTIVITY

Cultural Tour East Asia has a rich history and many cultural traditions reaching back thousands of years. Have students plan a hypothetical two-week tour of an East Asian country of their choice. Encourage students to gather information from many sources before setting their itinerary. Students may use tour guides, photographic reference books, travel magazines, videos, or interviews with travelers to that area. Have students create a colorful brochure and descriptive itinerary for their tour. Students should emphasize cultural or historic events or sites. Display the brochures on the classroom bulletin board.
🌐 **EE2 Places and Regions: Standard 4;** 🌐 **EE4 Human Systems: Standard 10**

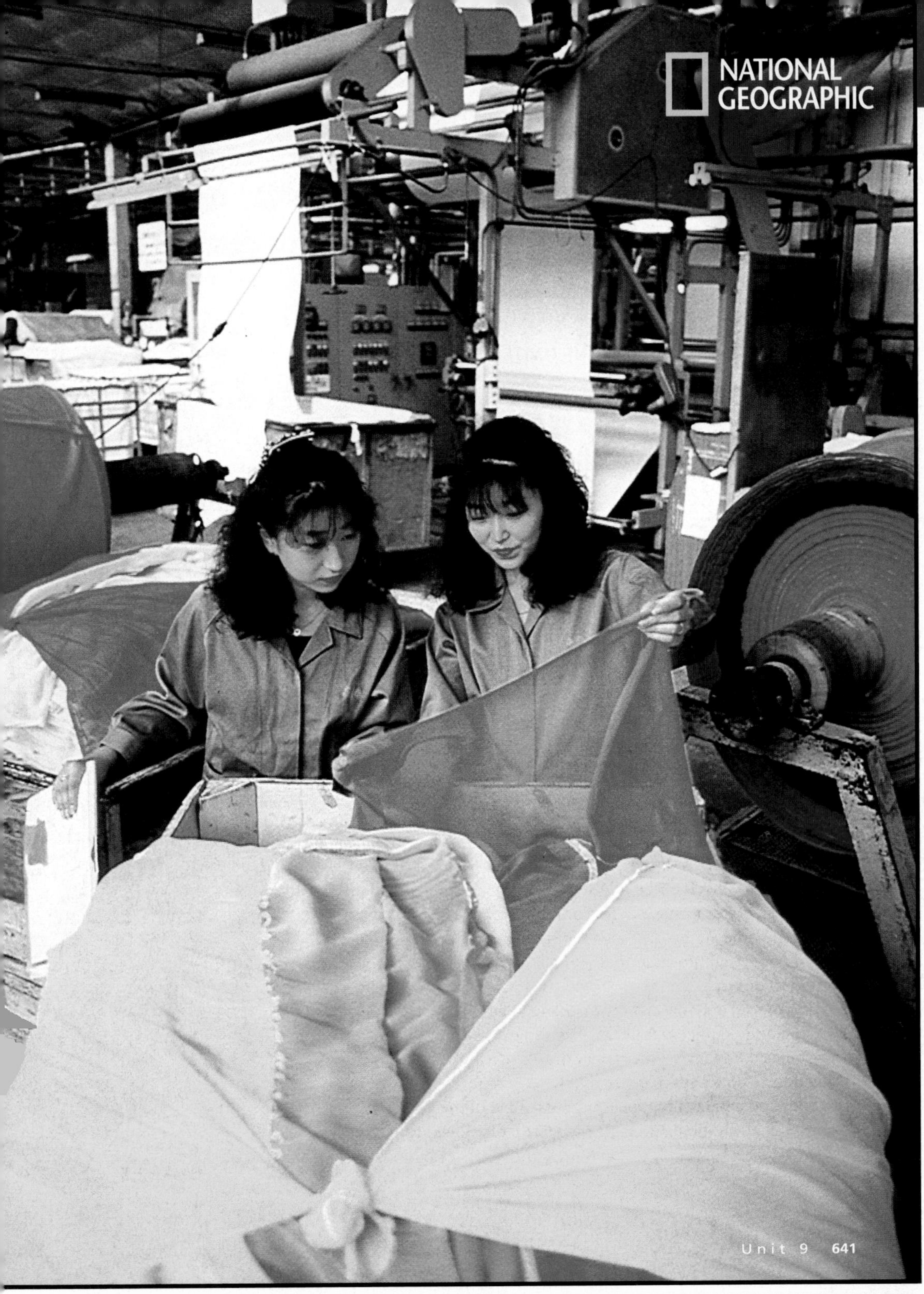

The Chinese language is tonal. Each word can have five to seven meanings, depending on the tone used when speaking the word. *Ma*, for example, can mean "horse," "mother," or function as a question mark, depending on the tone of voice in which it is uttered.

INTERDISCIPLINARY
connection

HEALTH The diet of most Mongolians consists of fatty meats and dairy products from camels, cattle, goats, and sheep. Many Mongolians relish animal fat—the more fat, the better, in most meals. Despite this fact, Mongolians generally do not have excessively high levels of blood cholesterol, which in the West is considered to be a major cause of heart disease. According to dietician B. Baljmaa, Mongolians are thought to have a genetic compatibility for this food.

Unit 9 **641**

COUNTRY PROFILE ACTIVITY

Effects of Culture and Experience on Perception War and military occupation have often embittered relations between different peoples in East Asia. For example, the occupation of Korea by Japan in the 1900s has caused mistrust and resentment in many Koreans toward the Japanese. Have students locate and share news articles that illustrate tensions among East Asian countries and efforts to overcome these differences. Hold a roundtable discussion regarding the ways that a society's culture and experience can influence the development or success of economic activities such as tourism, business, and trade. **EE2 Places and Regions: Standard 6**

1 FOCUS

Have students brainstorm a list of electronic devices that are popular in the United States. If possible, have students identify some of the countries where the items are made.

2 TEACH

Raw Materials Display personal electronic items. Locate an old or broken electronic item that can be taken apart and the components viewed. Have students analyze the components and speculate what raw materials went into the making of each component. List students' ideas on the board. **Ask: Where did the raw materials for the parts come from?** Have groups of students create maps and written explanations of their findings.

Meeting National Standards

Geography for Life
The following standards are met in the Student Edition:

EE4 Human Systems:
    Standard 11
EE5 Environment and Society:
    Standard 16
EE6 The Uses of Geography:
    Standard 17

GLOBAL CONNECTION

EAST ASIA AND THE UNITED STATES

ELECTRONICS

Turn on your TV, pop a tape into your VCR, play a CD on your stereo—chances are you're using a product that was made in Japan. Japan is one of the world's leading manufacturers of electronic goods.

Not only are many of our electronic gadgets made in Japan—quite a few were also invented there. That's the case with the portable personal stereo, the small tape or CD player with the lightweight headphones that people wear just about everywhere.

It's hard to imagine that a little over 20 years ago, personal stereos didn't exist. If you wanted to listen to music, your options were limited to home stereos, bulky boom boxes, or car audio systems. And, of course, all those around you had to listen, too, whether they wanted to or not.

Akio Morita and Masaru Ibuka changed all that. These two Japanese engineers founded one of Japan's largest electronics companies. One day in the 1970s, Ibuka walked into Morita's office lugging a heavy tape recorder and a pair of big headphones—state-of-the-art equipment at the time. Ibuka explained that he loved to

---

BACKGROUND INFORMATION

Economic Interdependence Sony, founded by Akio Morita and Masaru Ibuka, developed the first transistor radio in 1955 using a United States-developed technology, the transistor. It was the first radio small enough to fit in a pocket. In the 1960s and 1970s, the same company pioneered VCRs, high-resolution color TVs, and video camcorders, leading the way for other Japanese companies to develop consumer electronics for global export. Video games and playing systems have become a huge success for Japanese companies. Akio Morita's company worked in partnership with a European company, Philips, to bring out the first CDs in Japan in 1982. In 1996 the same partnership launched DVDs.
🌐 **EE4 Human Systems: Standard 11**

▲ Personal stereos for sale in a kiosk in Japan

listen to music, but he didn't want to disturb other people. It was the clunky tape recorder and earmuff headphones, or nothing at all.

Ibuka's dilemma made Morita think more seriously about an idea he'd been considering. Why not create a small, lightweight tape player with tiny headphones, so that people could conveniently take their music everywhere without bothering others? Morita instructed his engineers to remove the recording unit and speaker from a small cassette tape player, replace them with a tiny stereo amplifier, and then develop a very compact set of headphones to go with the device.

Others at the company shook their heads, doubting that anyone would buy a tape machine that couldn't record. Still, in 1979, the first portable personal stereo hit the market. Within months, it was a runaway success. Morita's company could hardly keep pace with the demand.

Now many companies make personal stereos, which are among the most popular electronic devices in the world. This Japanese invention has changed the way people everywhere listen to music.

California surfers listening to personal stereos ▶

FYI

Digital Technology Since 1975 consumer electronic products have become increasingly based on digital technology, which uses numbers to represent objects or concepts in communications devices and computers. East Asian, especially Japanese, digital products include musical instruments with built-in teaching systems, music-playing cameras, and MP3 (digital music files downloaded from the Internet) players.

③ ASSESS

Ask students to use their knowledge of history and of current trends in electronics to make predictions about future developments. Have students explain their predictions.

④ CLOSE

Have students brainstorm a list of electronic and non-electronic items that come from Japan and are used daily in the United States. *(automobiles, motorcycles, bicycles, cameras, animated television programs, video games, karaoke machines, toys, and so on)*

CONNECTION ACTIVITY

Electronics Fair Allow students to set up an electronics fair. Have them bring in and demonstrate the use of various types of personal electronic equipment, including personal stereos, pagers, cellular phones, walkie-talkies, video games, VCRs, video cameras, digital cameras, notebook or palmtop computers, and electronic dictionaries, calculators, or address books. Students can set up stations in the classroom for demonstrations of various types of equipment. Encourage students to create informational displays, including brochures, magazine articles, or other printed information about the items being demonstrated. Ask students to identify the country where each item was manufactured.

🌐 EE4 Human Systems: Standard 11

PLANNING GUIDE

NOTE: The following materials may be used when teaching Chapter 26. Section-level support materials are shown at point-of-use in the margins of the Teacher's Wraparound Edition.

TEACHING TRANSPARENCIES

L2 Unit 9 Map Overlay Transparencies

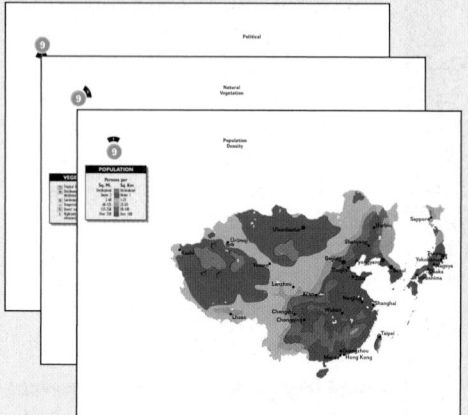

L2 Political Map Transparency 9

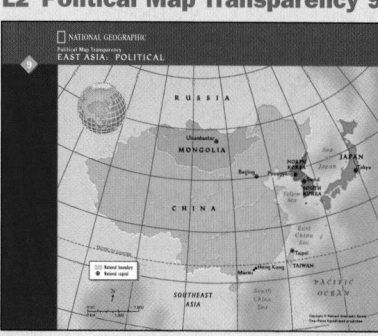

GEOGRAPHIC LITERACY

Focus on Geography Literacy

APPLICATION AND ENRICHMENT

L3 Enrichment Activity 26

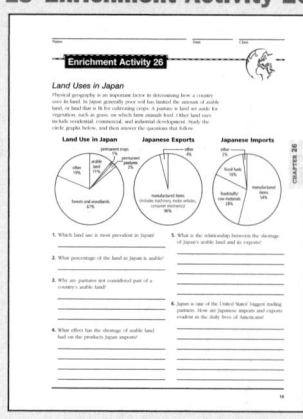

REVIEW AND REINFORCEMENT

L1 Vocabulary Activity 26 L1 Reinforcing L1 Reteaching Activity 26
Skills Activity 26

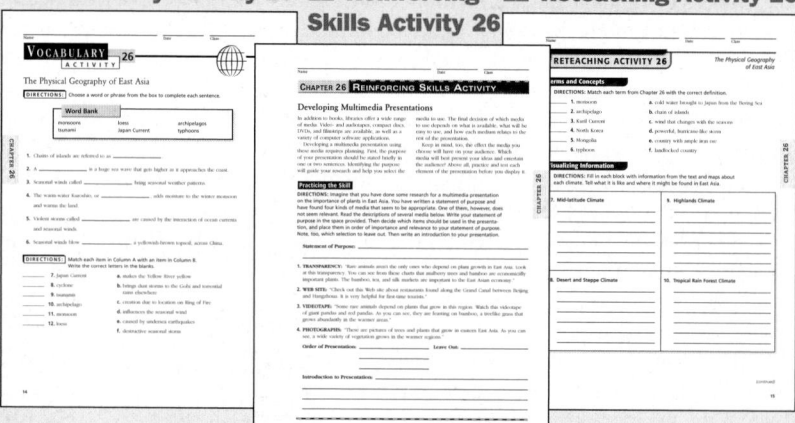

ASSESSMENT

L2 Chapter 26 Test Form A

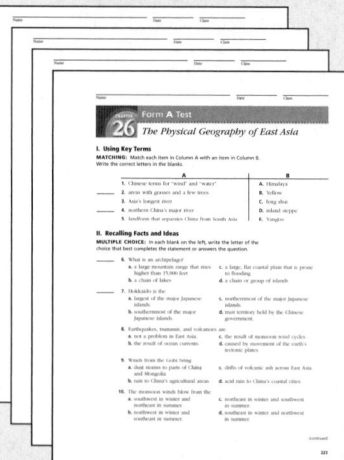

L2 Chapter 26 Test Form B

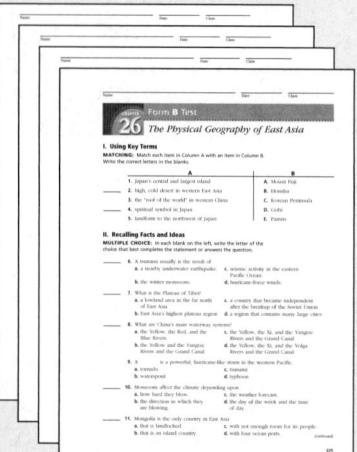

L1/ELL Performance Assessment Activity 26

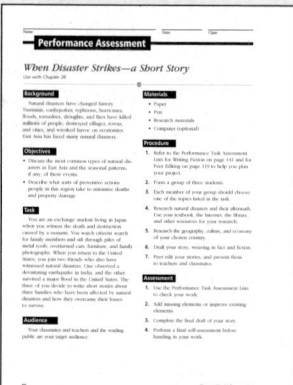

ExamView® Pro Testmaker

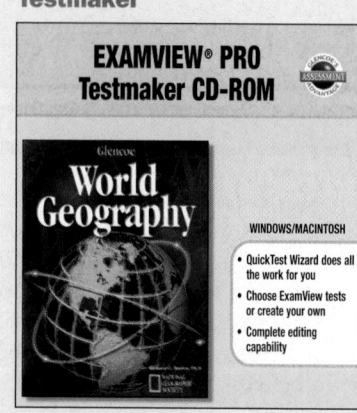

The following Spanish language materials are available in the Spanish Resources binder:

- Spanish Vocabulary Activities
- Spanish Guided Reading Activities
- Spanish Reteaching Activities
- Spanish Summaries
- Spanish Quizzes and Tests
- Spanish Reading Essentials and Study Guide

- World Regions Video
- MindJogger Videoquiz
- Vocabulary PuzzleMaker CD-ROM
- Interactive Tutor Self-Assessment CD-ROM
- ExamView® Pro Testmaker CD-ROM
- Audio Program
- TeacherWorks CD-ROM
- Interactive Student Edition CD-ROM
- Glencoe Skillbuilder Interactive Workbook CD-ROM, Level 2
- Presentation Plus! CD-ROM

Timesaving Tools

TeacherWorks™ — All-In-One Planner and Resource Center

- **Interactive Teacher Edition** Access your Teacher Wraparound Edition and your classroom resources with a few easy clicks.
- **Interactive Lesson Planner** Planning has never been easier! Organize your week, month, semester, or year with all the lesson helps you need to make teaching creative, timely, and relevant.

Use Glencoe's **Presentation Plus!** multimedia teacher tool to easily present dynamic lessons that visually excite your students. Using Microsoft PowerPoint® you can customize the presentations to create your own personalized lessons.

GEOGRAPHY Online

Use our Web site for additional resources. All essential content is covered in the Student Edition.

You and your students can visit geography.glencoe.com, the Web site companion to *Glencoe World Geography.* This innovative integration of electronic and print media offers your students a wealth of opportunities. The student text directs students to the Web site for the following options:

- **Chapter Overviews**
- **Self-Check Quizzes**
- **Student Activities**
- **Textbook Updates**

Answers are provided for you in the "Web Activity Lesson Plan." Additional Web resources and Interactive Tutor puzzles are also available.

▶ Additional Glencoe Teacher Support

- Teaching Strategies for the Geography Classroom (including Block Scheduling Pacing Guides)
- Graphic Organizer Transparencies Strategies and Activities
- Outline Map Resource Book
- Reading in the Content Area

SECTION RESOURCES

Daily Objectives	Reproducible Resources	Multimedia Resources

SECTION 1 The Land

1. Describe how East Asia's landforms are affected by the region's location on the Ring of Fire.
2. Compare the landforms of China with those in the rest of East Asia.
3. List the important natural resources that are present in East Asia.

Reproducible Lesson Plan 26-1
Daily Lecture Notes 26-1
Guided Reading Activity 26-1*
Reading Essentials and Study Guide 26-1*
Section Quiz 26-1*

Daily Focus Skills Transparency 26-1
Political Map Transparency 9
Unit 9 Map Overlay Transparencies
Interactive Tutor Self-Assessment CD-ROM
ExamView® Pro Testmaker CD-ROM*
Presentation Plus! CD-ROM

SECTION 2 Climate and Vegetation

1. State the reasons for East Asia's wide variety of climates.
2. Explain how winds, ocean currents, and mountains influence the climates of East Asia.
3. Identify the conditions that cause the extreme climates in much of China.
4. List the kinds of natural vegetation that are found in East Asia's varied climate regions.

Reproducible Lesson Plan 26-2
Vocabulary Activity 26*
Daily Lecture Notes 26-2
Guided Reading Activity 26-2*
Reading Essentials and Study Guide 26-2*
Reteaching Activity 26*
Reinforcing Skills Activity 26
Section Quiz 26-2*

Daily Focus Skills Transparency 26-2
Political Map Transparency 9
Unit 9 Map Overlay Transparencies
Vocabulary PuzzleMaker CD-ROM
Interactive Tutor Self-Assessment CD-ROM
ExamView® Pro Testmaker CD-ROM*
Presentation Plus! CD-ROM

Blackline Master	Software	Videocassette	*Also available in Spanish
Transparency	CD-ROM	DVD	

OUT OF TIME? Assign the Chapter 26 **Reading Essentials and Study Guide.**

Block Schedule

Activities that are particularly suited to use within the block scheduling framework are identified throughout this chapter by the following designation:

KEY TO ABILITY LEVELS

Teaching strategies have been coded for various learning styles and abilities.

L1 **BASIC** activities for all students

L2 **AVERAGE** activities for average to above-average students

L3 **CHALLENGING** activities for above-average students

ELL **ENGLISH LANGUAGE LEARNER** activities

Teacher to Teacher

Anne L. Crotty
Independence High School
Charlotte, NC

Comparing for Context: Using What Students Already Know

Use tools readily available to help give students a quick idea of cultural differences and similarities among countries.

For example, use the photos in the book to create a list of 10 or 12 questions. Have students take a quick trip through East Asia. **Ask:** What does a photo of a pagoda next to a high-rise tell us about this country? *(We see how a modern country with advanced engineering and architecture can also be steeped in tradition.)*

This technique also works well with map-reading skills. Open class every day with a map comparison activity. For example, when we compare a climate map of East Asia and one of North America, students readily see the similarities and differences more sharply. Parts of southeastern China and the southeastern United States are subtropical. Many students have experienced or are familiar with southern Florida and may be better able to imagine what Taiwan's climate is like.

 **NATIONAL GEOGRAPHIC**   **TEACHER'S CORNER**

Index to National Geographic Magazine:

The following articles may be used for research relating to this chapter:

- "Black Dragon River," by Simon Winchester, February 2000.
- "China's Three Gorges," by Arthur Zich, September 1997.
- "The Mekong: A Haunted River's Season of Peace," by Thomas O'Neill, February 1993.

National Geographic Society Products:

To order the following products for use with this chapter, call National Geographic Society at 1-800-368-2728.

- *Asia* (Video)
- *The Living Ocean* (Video)
- *Asia Political* (Map)
- *National Geographic Desk Reference* (Book)
- *National Geographic Atlas of the World, Seventh Edition* (Book)

NGS ONLINE

Access National Geographic's Web site for current events, activities, links, interactive features, and archives.
www.nationalgeographic.com

Meeting National Standards

Geography For Life

The following standards are highlighted in Chapter 26:

Section 1   EE1 The World in Spatial Terms: Standard 1
EE2 Places and Regions: Standards 4, 6
EE3 Physical Systems: Standards 7, 8
EE4 Human Systems: Standard 11
EE5 Environment and Society: Standard 16

Section 2   EE2 Places and Regions: Standards 4, 6
EE3 Physical Systems: Standard 7
EE4 Human Systems: Standards 10, 12
EE5 Environment and Society: Standard 15

Local Objectives

_____

_____

MEETING SPECIAL NEEDS

In addition to the Differentiated Instruction strategies found in each section, the following resources are also suitable for your special needs students:

- *ExamView® Pro Testmaker CD-ROM* allows teachers to tailor tests by reducing answer choices.
- The *Audio Program* includes the entire narrative of the student edition so that less-proficient readers can listen to the words as they read them.
- The *Reading Essentials and Study Guide* provides the same content as the student edition but is written two grade levels below the textbook.
- *Guided Reading Activities* give less-proficient readers point-by-point instructions to increase comprehension as they read each textbook section.
- *Enrichment Activities* include a stimulating collection of readings and activities for gifted and talented students.

Chapter Objectives

1. Identify East Asia's varied landforms, water systems, and natural resources.

2. Explain the factors that influence East Asia's diverse climates and vegetation.

GLENCOE TECHNOLOGY

 Use *MindJogger Videoquiz* to preview the Chapter 26 content.

GeoJournal

For access to additional photos, maps, and information on East Asia's geographic features go to www.nationalgeographic.com (See Teacher pages in front for strategies for using journals in the geography classroom.)

GEOGRAPHY Online

Introduce students to chapter content and key terms by having them access **Chapter Overview 26** at geography.glencoe.com

FOLDABLES
Study Organizer

Dinah Zike's Foldables are three-dimensional, interactive graphic organizers that help students practice basic writing skills, review key vocabulary terms, and identify main ideas. Have students complete the Foldable activity in the **Dinah Zike's Reading and Study Skills Foldables** booklet.

CHAPTER

26
The Physical Geography of East Asia

GeoJournal

As you read this chapter, use your journal to note the landforms and climate regions of East Asia. Write a series of descriptive paragraphs about these geographic features. Be sure to create a vivid, detailed description of each feature.

GEOGRAPHY Online

Chapter Overview Visit the **Glencoe World Geography** Web site at geography.glencoe.com and click on Chapter Overviews—Chapter 26 to preview information about the physical geography of the region.

ABOUT THE PHOTO

Visual Instruction People in Japan often refer to Mount Fuji as *Fuji-san*, a term of respect for the dormant volcano whose perfect cone has become an important spiritual symbol to many Japanese. Although legends say that Mount Fuji rose from the plain in 286 B.C., the volcano is actually much older. Mount Fuji has not erupted for almost 300 years, and its slopes contain numerous shrines and temples. ▦ **EE2 Places and Regions: Standard 6**
▦ **EE3 Physical Systems: Standard 7**

Guide to Reading

Consider What You Know

Earthquakes, volcanic eruptions, and ocean flooding occur frequently in East Asia. What geographic factors are the most likely causes of these natural hazards?

Reading Strategy

Organizing Complete a web diagram similar to the one below by identifying the three tectonic plates that form the Ring of Fire.

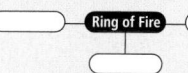

Read to Find Out

- How are East Asia's landforms affected by the region's location on the Ring of Fire?
- How do the landforms of China differ from the rest of East Asia?
- What important natural resources are present in the region?

Terms to Know

- archipelago
- tsunami
- loess

Places to Locate

- Mongolia
- Hong Kong
- Macau
- South China Sea
- Korean Peninsula
- Japan
- Pamirs
- Himalaya
- Plateau of Tibet (Plateau of Xizang)
- Tarim Basin
- Taklimakan Desert
- Gobi
- Yellow River (Huang He)
- Yangtze River (Chang Jiang)
- Xi (West) River

◀ *Mt. Fuji, Japan*

The Land

NATIONAL GEOGRAPHIC

A Geographic View

China's Wild West

The curving road went on for another two miles across barren, rocky ground and ended at a meadow dotted with grazing yaks. We had entered a vast valley edged by a massive mountain, more shoulder than peak, its flank half-buried in sand. The meadow had been touched by spring, and at that seam of whitish sand and faint new green was a village. The low houses, strung along the base of the mountain, looked as if they had been there since the beginning of time.

—Thomas B. Allen, "Xinjiang," National Geographic, March 1996

Outdoor classroom in Xinjiang, China

The wild and varied landscape of the western Chinese province of Xinjiang (SHIHN•JYAHNG) reflects the many contrasts and paradoxes of East Asia's physical geography. East Asia encompasses high mountains, rugged highlands, long and mighty rivers, barren deserts, fertile deltas and floodplains, miles of coastline, and countless islands dotting many seas. In this section you will read about East Asia's landforms and rich natural resources.

Land and Sea

The People's Republic of China makes up about 80 percent of the land area of East Asia and has the world's largest population—about 1.3 billion people. Of the world's countries, only Russia and Canada cover more land area than China. **Mongolia**, China's northern neighbor, occupies about 13 percent of East Asia's land. Mongolia's

Chapter 26 **645**

Section Overview

This section examines the region of East Asia and its landforms, water systems, and natural resources.

BELLRINGER
Skillbuilder Activity

- Project transparency and have students answer questions.

- Available as blackline master.

Daily Focus Skills Transparency 26-1

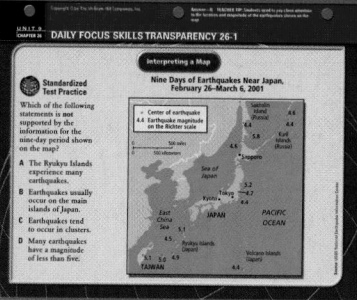

Guide to Reading

Consider What You Know
Answers *may include movements of the earth's tectonic plates or the region's location on the Ring of Fire.*

Reading Strategy
Answers *Pacific Plate, Eurasian Plate, Philippine Plate*

Preteaching Vocabulary
Write the "Terms to Know" and their pronunciations on the board. Direct students to these pages to find their meanings: archipelago, page 646; tsunami, page 646; loess, page 648.

RESOURCE MANAGER

Reproducible Masters
- Reproducible Lesson Plan 26-1
- Daily Lecture Notes 26-1
- Guided Reading Activity 26-1
- Reading Essentials and Study Guide 26-1
- Section Quiz 26-1

Transparencies
- Daily Focus Skills Transparency 26-1
- Political Map Transparency 9
- Unit 9 Map Overlay Transparencies

Multimedia
- Interactive Tutor Self-Assessment CD-ROM
- ExamView® Pro Testmaker CD-ROM
- Presentation Plus! CD-ROM

② TEACH

L1 Identify the Main Ideas

On the board, write the following as main headings for an outline: *Mountain Ranges, Plains, Plateaus, Basins, Deserts, Peninsulas, Islands, Rivers, Seas.* Have students add the names of several examples of each physical feature and include details. **ELL**

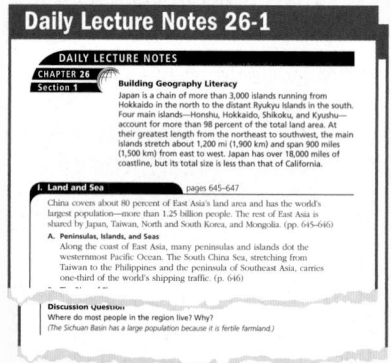

Daily Lecture Notes 26-1

DAILY LECTURE NOTES

CHAPTER 26
Section 1

Building Geography Literacy
Japan is a chain of more than 3,000 islands running from Hokkaido in the north to the distant Ryukyu Islands in the south. Four main islands—Honshu, Hokkaido, Shikoku, and Kyushu—account for more than 98 percent of the total land area. At their greatest length from northeast to southwest, the main islands stretch about 1,200 mi (1,900 km) and span 900 miles (1,500 km) from east to west. Japan has over 18,000 miles of coastline, but its total size is less than that of California.

I. Land and Sea   pages 645–647

China covers about 80 percent of East Asia's land area and has the world's largest population—more than 1.25 billion people. The rest of East Asia is shared by Japan, Taiwan, North and South Korea, and Mongolia. (pp. 645–646)

A. Peninsulas, Islands, and Seas
Along the coast of East Asia, many peninsulas and islands dot the westernmost Pacific Ocean. The South China Sea, stretching from Taiwan to the Philippines and the peninsula of Southeast Asia, carries one-third of the world's shipping traffic. (p. 646)

Discussion Question
Where do most people in the region live? Why?
(The Sichuan Basin has a large population because it is fertile farmland.)

NATIONAL GEOGRAPHIC   World Explorer

Answer
Tectonic plates meet in this region, creating conditions that favor the formation of volcanoes and cause earthquakes.

More About the Photo
Tsunamis may form when undersea earthquakes send fast-moving waves through the water. In open seas, tsunamis may be only slightly larger than ordinary waves, but when they reach the shallow waters along coastlines, tsunamis rise to great heights and wash over coastal communities.

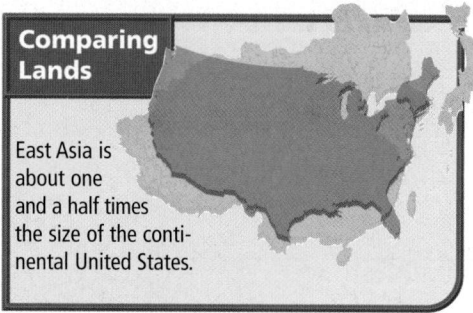

Comparing Lands

East Asia is about one and a half times the size of the continental United States.

---

population is less than 1 percent of China's, making the country one of the world's most sparsely populated. The rest of East Asia is shared by the countries of Japan, Taiwan, North Korea, and South Korea. **Hong Kong** and **Macau**, two bustling ports on China's southern coast, were once European colonies and are now part of China.

Peninsulas, Islands, and Seas

Along the coast of East Asia, many peninsulas and islands dot the westernmost Pacific Ocean. These landforms divide the ocean into smaller bodies of water, including the Yellow Sea, the Sea of Japan (East Sea), and the East China Sea. The **South China Sea**, stretching south from the island of Taiwan to the Philippines and the peninsula of Southeast Asia, carries one-third of the world's shipping traffic.

The **Korean Peninsula** juts southeast from China's Manchurian Plain, separating the Sea of Japan (East Sea) from the Yellow Sea. The peninsula, home to North Korea and South Korea, consists mainly of mountains surrounded by coastal plains.

Four large, mountainous islands and thousands of smaller ones form the **archipelago** (AHR•kuh•PEH•luh•GO), or island chain, of **Japan**. Honshu is the central and largest island, with Hokkaido to the north and Kyushu and Shikoku to the south. Most of Japan's major cities are on Honshu. Surrounding Japan are the Sea of Okhotsk on the north, the Sea of Japan (East Sea) and the East China Sea on the west, and the Philippine Sea on the south. On the east and southeast is the Pacific Ocean.

The Ring of Fire

An arc of islands east of China marks where the Pacific, Philippine, and Eurasian tectonic plates

---

meet. These islands are part of the Ring of Fire, a circle of volcanoes bordering the Pacific Ocean. Most of these mountainous islands, including Japan and Taiwan, were formed by volcanic activity. Plate movements there cause frequent and often violent earthquakes and volcanic eruptions. Japan has about 50 active volcanoes and numerous hot springs formed through volcanic activity.

More than 1,000 small earthquakes shake Japan every year. Major quakes occur less often, but they may cause disastrous damage and loss of life in Japan's crowded cities. When an undersea earthquake generates a **tsunami** (soo•NAH•mee)—a huge tidal wave that gets higher and higher as it

NATIONAL GEOGRAPHIC   World Explorer

Geography   Skills for Life

Tsunami Damage Waves as high as an eight-story building caused devastation to Okushiri, Japan, in 1993.

Region What factors make the Ring of Fire susceptible to earthquakes and volcanic eruptions?

DIFFERENTIATED INSTRUCTION

English Learners Pair English language learners with English-proficient students, and have the pairs create flash cards of the physical features of East Asia. On one side of the card have students write a question that names an East Asian feature. *(Example: What is the Gobi?)* On the other side, have students write clues describing the feature and its location. *(Example: a dry, cold, high, inland desert; frequent dust storms; located in eastern Mongolia and northeastern China.)* Then have paired students identify the question using the clues. **ELL**   🌐 **EE2 Places and Regions: Standard 4**
🌐 **EE3 Physical Systems: Standard 8**
📂 Refer to *Inclusion for the Social Studies Classroom Strategies and Activities.*

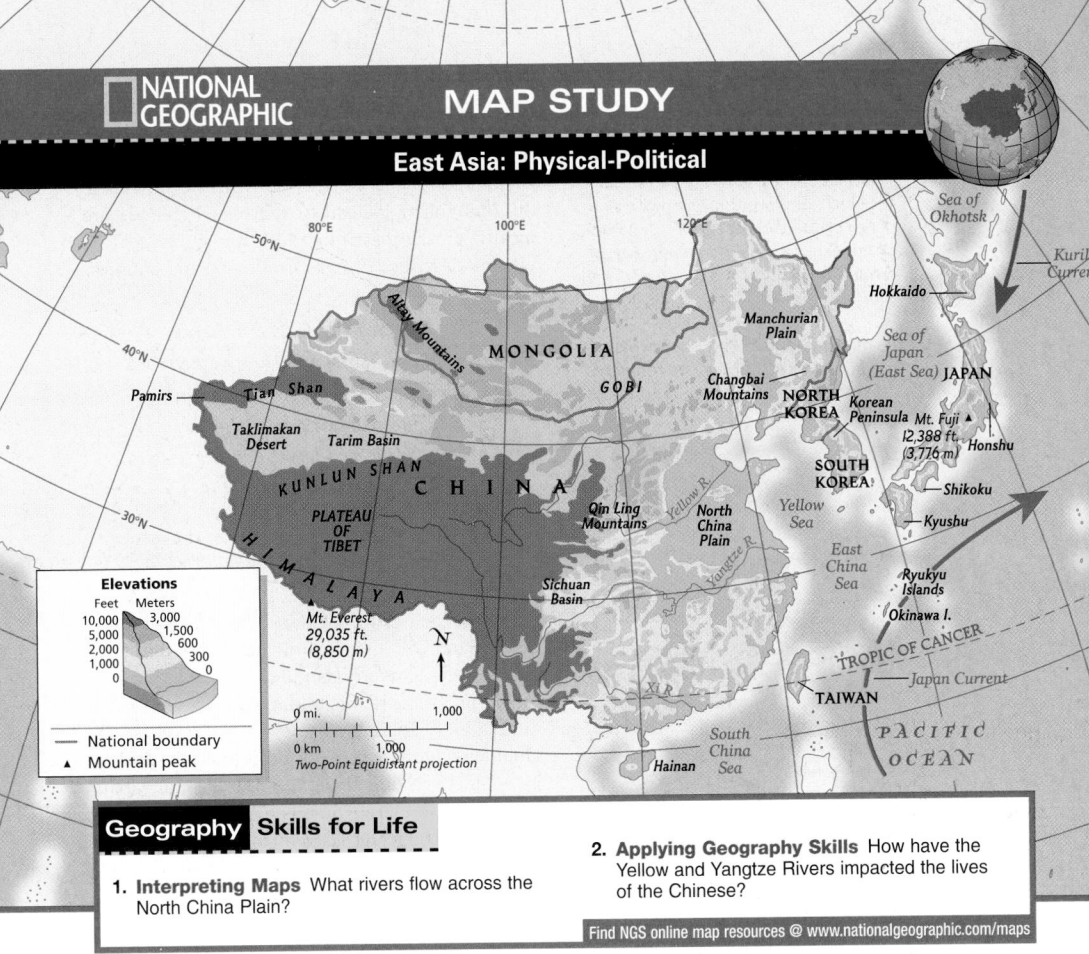

NATIONAL GEOGRAPHIC — MAP STUDY

East Asia: Physical-Political

Elevations

Feet	Meters
10,000	3,000
5,000	1,500
2,000	600
1,000	300
0	0

— National boundary
▲ Mountain peak

0 mi. 1,000
0 km 1,000
Two-Point Equidistant projection

Geography Skills for Life

1. **Interpreting Maps** What rivers flow across the North China Plain?

2. **Applying Geography Skills** How have the Yellow and Yangtze Rivers impacted the lives of the Chinese?

Find NGS online map resources @ www.nationalgeographic.com/maps

NATIONAL GEOGRAPHIC — MAP STUDY

Answers

1. Yangtze River, Yellow River

2. *The Yellow River has deposited fertile soil, but flooding has often destroyed villages. The Yangtze River irrigates cropland and provides a transport route.*

Map Skills Practice

How do rivers change the land over time? *(They create features such as gorges, deltas, and waterfalls, and they flood the land, depositing silt. They wash away soil during floods.)*

L1/ELL

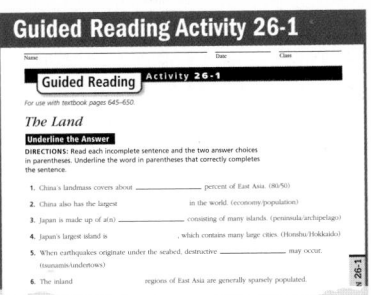

Guided Reading Activity 26-1

---

approaches the coast—many lives may be lost. A tsunami that struck the Japanese island of Hokkaido in 1993 took 200 lives. Because earthquakes and tsunamis are difficult to predict, people along the Ring of Fire rely on special building methods and emergency preparedness to help reduce casualties.

Mountains, Highlands, and Lowlands

Mountain ranges and highlands mark the inland regions of East Asia. Most extremely rugged highlands areas are sparsely populated and have formed barriers to the movement of people and ideas. The region's only extensive lowland areas are China's Manchurian Plain and North China Plain. Narrow lowland plains also line many coastal areas.

East Asian Mountains

Numerous mountain ranges fan out from an area of high peaks and deep valleys called the **Pamirs** in western China. The ranges that begin in this remote interior region include the Kunlun Shan and Tian Shan. (*Shan* is Chinese for "mountains.") Farther north, the Altay Mountains form a natural barrier between Mongolia and China. To the south and west, the world's highest mountains, the **Himalaya**, separate China from South Asia. They include many peaks higher than 25,000 feet

Mountains cover one-third of China. Only 14 mountain peaks in the world are higher than 26,400 feet (8,000 m). Of these, 9 are in China or along its southeastern border.

Chapter 26 **647**

COOPERATIVE LEARNING ACTIVITY

Compare and Contrast Organize students into eight groups. Assign each group a 10° longitudinal section of the region (70°E–80°E through 140°E–150°E). Have each group start at the northern end of their section (50°N or higher) and discuss how the physical geography changes as one travels south. Have students from each group take turns explaining the contrasts in physical geography to the class, using display maps as visual aids if available. Repeat the exercise, until all groups have had a turn.

🌐 **EE1 The World in Spatial Terms: Standard 1;** 🌐 **EE2 Places and Regions: Standard 4**

The Arts of East Asia

Artist Utagawa Toyokuni (1769–1825) was a master printmaker of the *ukiyo-e* school or "pictures of the floating world" movement in Japan. He first popularized the woodblock printmaking technique, producing art for mass consumption.

World Art Prints

Use these prints with accompanying strategies and activities to introduce students to other arts of the region.

L1/ELL

Reading Essentials & Study Guide 26-1

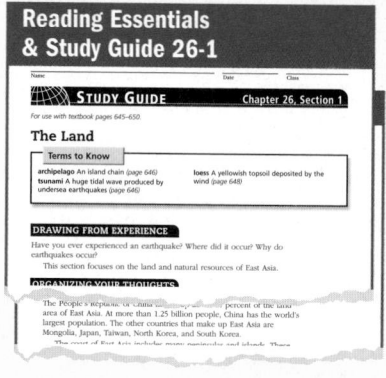

Name _____ Date _____ Class _____

STUDY GUIDE Chapter 26, Section 1

For use with textbook pages 645–650.

The Land

Terms to Know

archipelago An island chain (page 646)   **loess** A yellowish topsoil deposited by the
tsunami A huge tidal wave produced by   wind (page 649)
undersea earthquakes (page 646)

DRAWING FROM EXPERIENCE

Have you ever experienced an earthquake? Where did it occur? Why do
earthquakes occur?
This section focuses on the land and natural resources of East Asia.

ORGANIZING YOUR THOUGHTS

The People's Republic of China is _____ percent of the land
area of East Asia. At more than 1.25 billion people, China has the world's
largest population. The other countries that make up East Asia are
Mongolia, Japan, Taiwan, North Korea, and South Korea.
The coast of East Asia includes many peninsulas and islands. There

GEOGRAPHY AND THE HUMANITIES

 World Music:
A Cultural Legacy

 World Art and Architecture
Transparencies

World Art Prints

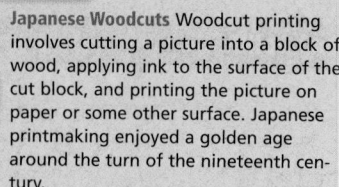

the arts of EAST ASIA

Japanese Woodcuts Woodcut printing involves cutting a picture into a block of wood, applying ink to the surface of the cut block, and printing the picture on paper or some other surface. Japanese printmaking enjoyed a golden age around the turn of the nineteenth century.

Evening Snow, Mt. Fuji (about 1830) by Toyokuni II depicts a natural harmony within the environment that is typical of Japanese art. Compare this view with the photograph on page 644.

(7,620 m) above sea level. Mount Everest, the world's tallest peak at 29,035 feet (8,850 m), spans the border between China and Nepal.

The Kunlun Shan bends to become the Qin (CHIHN) Ling Mountains, crossing central China from west to east. To the east, the lower Changbai Mountains of Manchuria extend into the Korean Peninsula, where they are called the Northern Mountains. Coastal plains surround the high mountain interiors of Japan and Taiwan. Mount Fuji, at 12,388 feet (3,776 m), is a dramatic, cone-shaped, dormant volcano rising above the central plains of Japan's Honshu Island. Also called Fujiyama, Mount Fuji is an important spiritual symbol to Japan's people.

China's Plateaus, Basins, and Deserts

China contains the region's most diverse landforms. The **Plateau of Tibet**, in China's southwest quarter, is East Asia's highest plateau region. Because the Chinese name for Tibet is Xizang

---

(SHEE•ZAHNG), the plateau is also known as the Plateau of Xizang. Its average elevation is about 15,000 feet (4,600 m). Other rugged highlands stretch north and eastward at lower elevations, averaging 4,900 feet (1,494 m). In the far north, the Mongolian Plateau's extensive highlands are mostly grassy pasture, ideal for grazing. Two visitors described the vast landscape and animals:

❝ *They appeared suddenly from a ravine, two nomad horsemen driving a herd of sheep across the path of our truck. On and on the animals came, a sea of brown, black, and white against the golden grasses of the broad plain.* ❞
Cynthia Beall and Melvyn Goldstein, "Past Becomes Future for Mongolian Nomads," *National Geographic*, May 1993

Broad expanses of flat wastelands, including the deserts and salt marshes of the **Tarim Basin**, lie between the Kunlun Shan and Tian Shan. West of the Tarim Basin is the **Taklimakan Desert**, a dry, sandy desert. To the northeast is another desert, the **Gobi**, whose frequent dust storms make life difficult in southern Mongolia and north central China. China's high, interior deserts are dry and cold. By contrast, the huge, fertile Sichuan Basin between the Plateau of Tibet and the North China Plain has a mild climate and long growing season, making it an important agricultural area.

River Systems

East Asia's rivers serve densely populated urban centers as transport routes. They provide hydroelectric power for energy, and the fertile soil in their basins is used for farming.

China's Rivers

China's major rivers begin in the Plateau of Tibet and flow eastward to the Pacific Ocean. The **Yellow River**, known in Chinese as Huang He (HWAHNG HUH), is northern China's major river system. This river is called "yellow" because it carries tons of fine, yellowish-brown topsoil called loess (LEHS), blown by winds from the western deserts into the air and water. When deposited, the rich soil—along with water from the river—makes the

---

CRITICAL THINKING ACTIVITY

Making Generalizations Have students reread "The Ring of Fire" on pages 646–647. Point out the generalization in the first paragraph: "Plate movements there cause frequent and often violent earthquakes and volcanic eruptions." **Ask:** Which facts and details in the text support the generalization? *(islands were formed by volcanic activity; hot springs and 50 active volcanoes in the area; frequent earthquakes; undersea earthquakes causing tsunamis)* Have students research the history of earthquakes, volcanic eruptions, and tsunamis in the region, and have them create graphs or time lines from their research results. Then have students write additional generalizations about the frequency, strength, or impact of the events. **EE2 Places and Regions: Standard 4**

North China Plain a major wheat-farming area. Also called "China's sorrow," the Yellow River often floods its basin. Throughout history, it has flooded large areas, killing hundreds of thousands of people.

Central China's **Yangtze** (YANG•SEE) **River**, known in Chinese as the Chang Jiang, is Asia's longest river at 3,965 miles (6,380 km). It flows through spectacular gorges and broad plains and empties into the ocean at Shanghai. The Yangtze, a major transport route, provides water for a large agricultural area where more than half of China's rice and other grains grow. When completed in 2009, the river's Three Gorges Dam will be the world's largest dam (see the feature on pages 698–699).

The **Xi** (SHEE), or West, **River** is southern China's most important river system. Near the ports of Guangzhou and Macau, the soil deposits of the Xi form a huge, fertile delta, one of China's fast-developing areas.

The world's longest artificial waterway, China's Grand Canal, was begun in the 400s B.C. Over the centuries, the canal has been expanded and rebuilt. Today, the Grand Canal moves people and goods along a 1,085-mile (1,746-km) course from Beijing in the north to Hangzhou in the south.

Rivers in Japan and Korea

In contrast to China's long rivers, the rivers of Japan and Korea are short and swift. They flow through mountainous terrain, often forming spectacular waterfalls. During the wet season, they provide hydroelectric power. South Korea's chief rivers flow from inland mountains westward toward the Yellow Sea. The Han River flows through South Korea's capital, Seoul. In North Korea the Amnok (or Yalu) River flows west, forming the border with China.

Culture
The Power of Wind and Water

For centuries East Asians have chosen building sites and designed homes using feng shui (FUHNG

Student Web Activity Visit the **Glencoe World Geography** Web site at geography.glencoe.com and click on Student Web Activities—Chapter 26 for an activity about the physical geography of East Asia.

SHWAY), from the Chinese words for "wind" and "water." By combining observations of the natural landscape with traditional spiritual teachings, the Chinese harmonize their buildings with the surrounding landforms, especially mountains and rivers. First used to locate favorable gravesites, feng shui is now used by architects, real estate agents, building contractors, and interior decorators worldwide.

Natural Resources

East Asia's rich mineral resources are unevenly distributed. China's huge land area contains the greatest share and widest range of minerals, including sizable reserves of iron ore, tin, tungsten, and

Geography | **Skills for Life**

Yellow River Tributary A tributary of the Yellow River winds through central China, carrying the sediment that gives the Yellow River its name.

Place How do China's rivers compare with those in Japan and Korea?

NATIONAL GEOGRAPHIC **World Explorer**

Answer
China's rivers are long; Japan's and Korea's are short and swift.

More About the Photo
The Yellow River is sometimes referred to as the cradle of civilization in China because the earliest Chinese settlements originated there more than 4,000 years ago.

③ ASSESS

Assign Section 1 Assessment as homework or as an in-class activity.

ⓘ Have students use **Interactive Tutor Self-Assessment CD-ROM** to review Section 1.

L2

Section Quiz 26-1

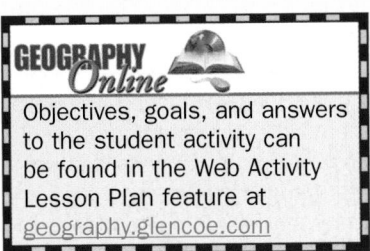

GEOGRAPHY *Online*

Objectives, goals, and answers to the student activity can be found in the Web Activity Lesson Plan feature at geography.glencoe.com

---

TEAM-TEACHING ACTIVITY: ECONOMICS

Predicting Consequences After reading the section on natural resources, have students create a country-by-country chart of resources that are abundant or scarce. China may be broken into regions. Based on their charts, have students predict what resources the country or area may need to import, and what resources they may be able to export. Have students work with an economics teacher to research additional facts about each country's resources, imports, and exports. Then ask students to add these facts to the data in their charts, and refine their predictions based on their research. 📦

📖 **EE4 Human Systems: Standard 11;** 📖 **EE5 Environment and Society: Standard 16**

NATIONAL GEOGRAPHIC World Explorer

Answer

Japan, South Korea, Taiwan, China

More About the Photo The Japanese eat one-sixth of the world's seafood catch—so much that Japan's coastal waters are overfished. The catch in the photo may have come from the mid-zone of the Sea of Japan, a prime squid-fishing area.

Reteach

Have students list the countries of East Asia and identify major mountains, highlands, lowlands, river systems, and natural resources for each one.

Enrich

Order take-out East Asian food or bring in rice, bamboo shoots, chopsticks, and so on, and have students practice using chopsticks. Display Japanese specialty foods such as *sushi* and *sashimi* and have the class examine them.

4 CLOSE

Have students reread "A Geographic View" on page 645. Have them write a description of an East Asian land or water feature that intrigues them, as if they were seeing it in person for the first time.

gold. Large oil deposits lie in the South China Sea and in the Takli-makan Desert in the west. Abundant coal deposits also lie in northeastern China. Coal is mined in the Korean Peninsula and Mongolia. North Korea's rich deposits of economically useful minerals include iron ore and tungsten. South Korea has relatively few mineral reserves, though large deposits of graphite are found there. Taiwan's mineral reserves are small, and its coal reserves are almost exhausted.

Productive farmlands and forests are unevenly distributed in East Asia. For example, only 10 percent of China's land is suitable for agriculture. The southern "rice bowl" yields two harvests per year, making China the world's leading producer of rice. With nearly 25 percent of its land suitable for farming, South Korea produces two crops per year, one of rice and one of barley, in the prime farmland of the coastal south. By contrast, Mongolia can use less than 1 percent of its land for crops. Japan also has very limited farmland and poor soil. Only one-fourth of Taiwan's land is suitable for farming, but every available space is planted, chiefly with rice. Taiwan has valuable forests of cedar, hemlock, and oak.

NATIONAL GEOGRAPHIC World Explorer

Geography Skills for Life

Squid Harvest Coastal fishers in Japan dry their squid catch in the sun.

Region Which countries have the biggest deep-sea fishing industries?

East Asia's island countries and coastal areas depend on the sea for food. Japan, South Korea, Taiwan, and China have the world's biggest deep-sea fishing industries. China alone harvests about 18 million tons (16.3 million metric tons) of fish each year. Seafood farming has become a major industry in East Asia.

SECTION 1 ASSESSMENT

Checking for Understanding

1. **Define** archipelago, tsunami, loess.

2. **Main Ideas** On a table, fill in details about major features of the physical geography for each country in East Asia.

Area	Physical Geography

Critical Thinking

3. **Comparing and Contrasting** How are East Asia's coastal, island, and peninsula areas similar? How do they differ from inland areas?

4. **Drawing Conclusions** How does the technique of feng shui reflect East Asian beliefs about humans and their environment?

5. **Predicting Consequences** What consequences do you think will result from East Asia's use of its ocean resources?

Analyzing Maps

6. **Place** Study the physical-political map on page 647. How does the elevation of the North China Plain compare with that of the Plateau of Tibet?

Applying Geography

7. **Soil Building** Describe the soil-building process that takes place in northern China's Yellow River basin. How does this process influence the natural environment, the people, and economy of the area?

SECTION 1 ASSESSMENT ANSWERS

1. All vocabulary terms are defined in the text.

2. Tables should include major physical features named or described in the text or maps.

3. similar: close to the sea; different: no long rivers and less farmland on islands

4. Humans are part of their environment and should be in harmony with it.

5. Students may predict that current practices will result in overfishing or depletion of ocean resources.

6. The North China Plain, at 0 to 1,000 feet (0–300 m) above sea level, is at a much lower elevation than the Plateau of Tibet, located at 10,000 feet (3,000 m) above sea level.

7. **Applying Geography** Students should focus on the loess carried by wind and the Yellow River, the depositing of the fertile soil that makes the North China Plain a major wheat-farming area, and the effects of the river's floods.

Climate and Vegetation

Guide to Reading

Consider What You Know

As you read in the last section, large areas of East Asia border the sea. How do you think climate and vegetation in coastal areas differ from those in inland areas?

Reading Strategy

Taking Notes As you read about the climate and vegetation of East Asia, use the major headings of the section to create an outline similar to the one below.

I. Climate Regions
A.
B.
C.

Read to Find Out

- What accounts for East Asia's wide variety of climates?
- How do winds, ocean currents, and mountains influence the climates of East Asia?
- What conditions cause the extreme climates in much of China?
- What kinds of natural vegetation are found in East Asia's varied climate regions?

Terms to Know

- monsoon
- Japan Current
- typhoon

Places to Locate

- Taiwan
- Hainan
- Qin Ling Mountains

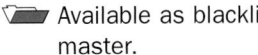

NATIONAL GEOGRAPHIC

A Geographic View

Weathering Uncertainty

Of course, living with uncertain circumstances is nothing new for Mongolia's nomads. For centuries they have weathered one of the earth's harshest and least predictable environments. Winter winds at camps high in mountain valleys can howl at minus 20°F to minus 50°F, and sudden blizzards can bury pastures and starve herds.

—*Cynthia Beall and Melvyn Goldstein, "Past Becomes Future for Mongolian Nomads,"* National Geographic, *May 1993*

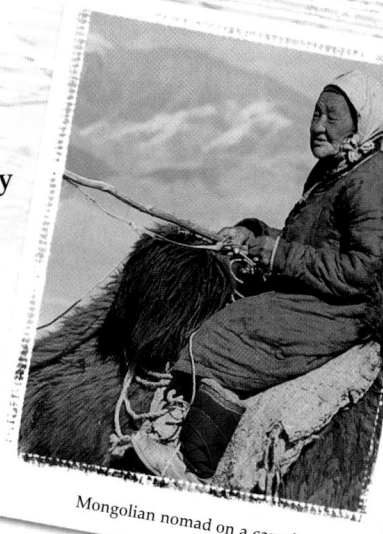

Mongolian nomad on a camel

The nomads of Mongolia are among the few peoples who have adapted to living in East Asia's harshest climate regions. Following their herds across the high grasslands, these nomadic peoples take shelter in tentlike structures called yurts, built to be portable yet withstand the howling winter winds. Wind is a powerful force throughout East Asia, a region that depends on seasonal wind patterns for life-giving rains. In this section you will learn how physical features shape the climate and vegetation of this vast region.

Climate Regions

Latitude and physical features—such as mountain barriers, highlands, and coastal regions—shape East Asia's climates. Each climate region has distinct characteristics and unique vegetation. Dry highlands and grasslands dominate the north and west, with humid and temperate forests to the south and east.

1 FOCUS

Section Overview

This section discusses the climate and vegetation of East Asia, and how these factors affect the people of the region.

BELLRINGER
Skillbuilder Activity

Project transparency and have students answer questions.

Available as blackline master.

Daily Focus Skills Transparency 26-2

Guide to Reading

Consider What You Know

Answer *Climate near the ocean may be warmer and more moist. Vegetation would be more lush.*

Reading Strategy

Answer Students should complete the outline by including all heads in the section.

Preteaching Vocabulary

Explain that the English word *typhoon* (page 655) comes from the Chinese term *tai-fung*, meaning "great wind," and that *monsoon* (page 654) is derived from the Arabic *mausim*, meaning "season."

Use the **Vocabulary PuzzleMaker CD-ROM**.

RESOURCE MANAGER

Reproducible Masters

- Reproducible Lesson Plan 26-2
- Vocabulary Activity 26
- Daily Lecture Notes 26-2
- Guided Reading Activity 26-2
- Reading Essentials and Study Guide 26-2
- Reteaching Activity 26
- Reinforcing Skills Activity 26
- Section Quiz 26-2

Transparencies

- Daily Focus Skills Transparency 26-2
- Political Map Transparency 9
- Unit 9 Map Overlay Transparencies

Multimedia

- Vocabulary PuzzleMaker CD-ROM
- Interactive Tutor Self-Assessment CD-ROM
- ExamView® Pro Testmaker CD-ROM
- Presentation Plus! CD-ROM

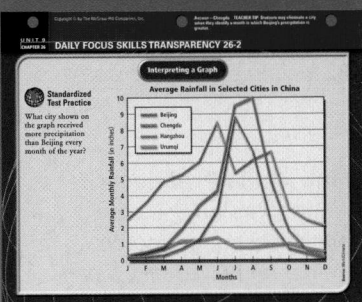

TEACH

L1 Identify

Direct students to the maps on pages 652–653. Name a city labeled on the maps, and call on students to describe the climate and vegetation for that locale. Give extra points to students who can name the country and describe the major land and water features at that location.

NATIONAL GEOGRAPHIC **MAP STUDY**

Answers

1. Northern Japan, northeastern China, North Korea, northern South Korea

2. Moisture from the coast is blocked by the rain shadow effect.

Map Skills Practice

What areas have a humid subtropical climate? *(southwestern China, southwestern Japan, southern South Korea)*

Daily Lecture Notes 26-2

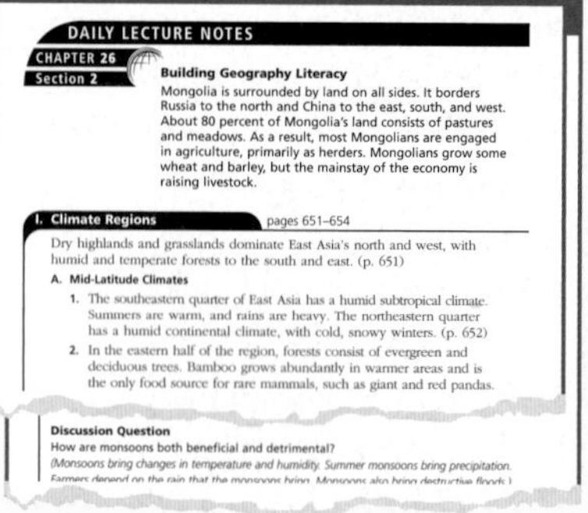

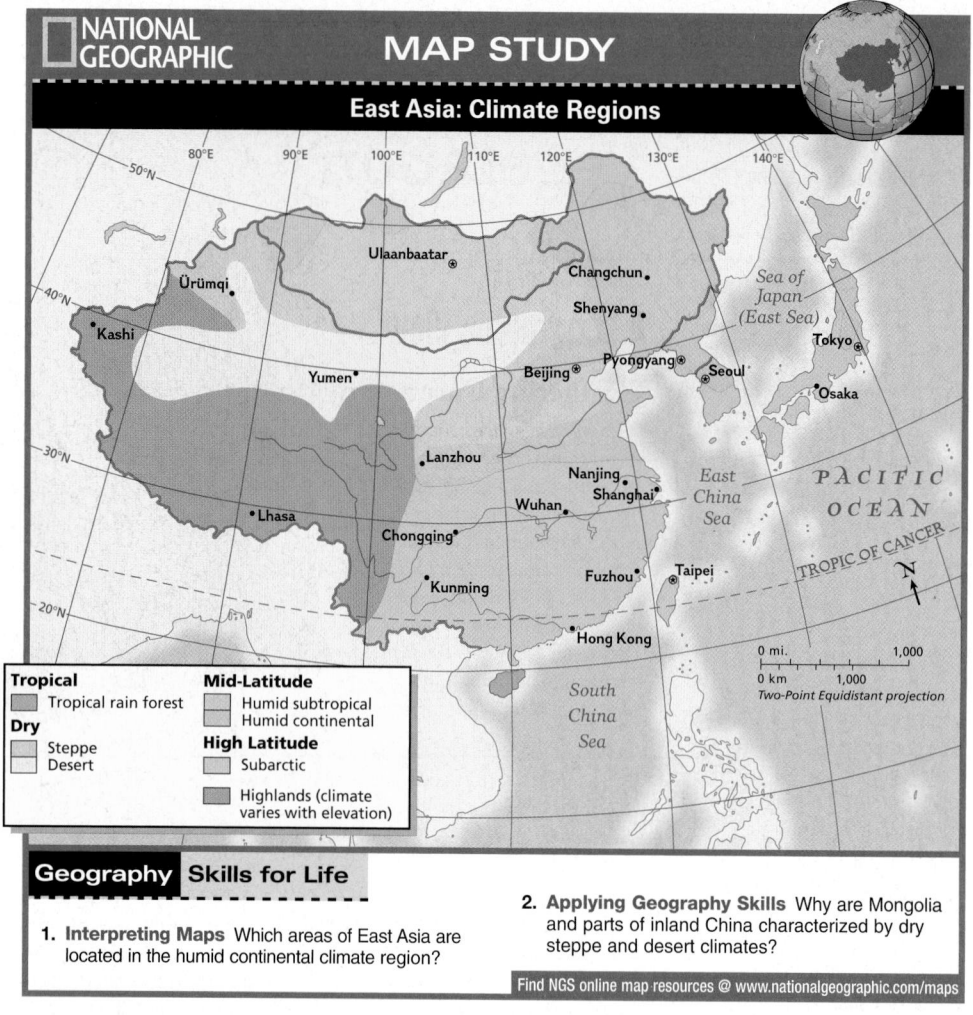

NATIONAL GEOGRAPHIC **MAP STUDY**

East Asia: Climate Regions

Tropical
- Tropical rain forest

Dry
- Steppe
- Desert

Mid-Latitude
- Humid subtropical
- Humid continental

High Latitude
- Subarctic
- Highlands (climate varies with elevation)

0 mi. 1,000
0 km 1,000
Two-Point Equidistant projection

Geography **Skills for Life**

1. **Interpreting Maps** Which areas of East Asia are located in the humid continental climate region?

2. **Applying Geography Skills** Why are Mongolia and parts of inland China characterized by dry steppe and desert climates?

Find NGS online map resources @ www.nationalgeographic.com/maps

Mid-Latitude Climates

The southeastern quarter of East Asia, including **Taiwan** and parts of China, the Koreas, and Japan, has a humid subtropical climate, with warm or hot summers and heavy rains from the Pacific monsoon. In contrast, the northeastern quarter, including the northern parts of the Koreas and Japan, has a cooler, humid continental climate. Summers may be warm, but winters are cold and snowy.

Natural forests in mid-latitude climates consist of needle-leaved and broad-leaved evergreens and broad-leaved deciduous trees. Deciduous trees and broad-leaved evergreens also flourish in the humid subtropical regions. Bamboo, a treelike grass, grows abundantly in many of the warmer areas. This tough, versatile plant has more than a thousand uses, from herbal medicine, food, and decoration to construction of homes, skyscrapers, and bridges. Bamboo also provides the only food source for two of East Asia's rare mammals, the giant panda and the smaller, raccoon-like red panda. Other economically important native plants are the

---

DIFFERENTIATED INSTRUCTION

At-Risk Students For students who have trouble categorizing information, or students who have trouble relating information from more than one source, help students create a chart with category headings such as *summer precipitation, winter precipitation, summer temperatures, winter temperatures, elevation,* and *vegetation.* Guide students as needed in searching for information to put under these categories, using the chapter's maps, text, and Unit Atlas, as well as additional reference resources.

EE3 Physical Systems: Standard 7

Refer to *Inclusion for the Social Studies Classroom Strategies and Activities.*

MAP STUDY

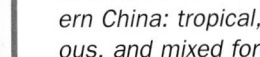

NATIONAL GEOGRAPHIC

East Asia: Natural Vegetation

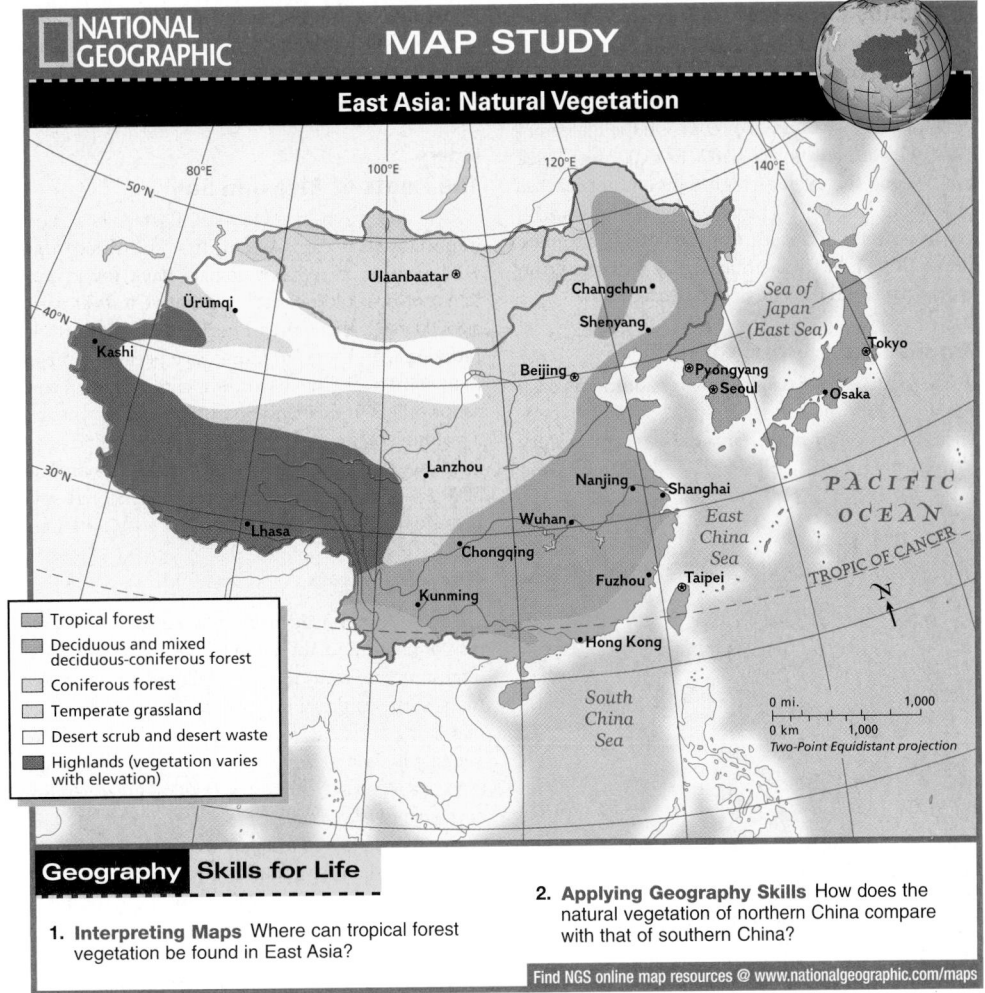

Tropical forest

Deciduous and mixed deciduous-coniferous forest

Coniferous forest

Temperate grassland

Desert scrub and desert waste

Highlands (vegetation varies with elevation)

Geography Skills for Life

1. **Interpreting Maps** Where can tropical forest vegetation be found in East Asia?

2. **Applying Geography Skills** How does the natural vegetation of northern China compare with that of southern China?

Find NGS online map resources @ www.nationalgeographic.com/maps

NATIONAL GEOGRAPHIC — MAP STUDY

Answers

1. *southern coast of China, Taiwan, Hainan*

2. *northern China: grasses, desert, some forest; southern China: tropical, deciduous, and mixed forest*

Map Skills Practice

At what longitude does elevation begin to affect vegetation in central China? *(100°N)*

Mongolia With an average of over 257 cloudless days per year, Mongolia is known as the "Land of Blue Sky." Winters are bitter cold, but with air so dry that very little snow falls.

L1/ELL

Guided Reading Activity 26-2

Guided Reading Activity 26-2

For use with textbook pages 651-655

Climate and Vegetation

Short Answer

DIRECTIONS: Use the information in your textbook to write a short answer to each of the following questions.

1. Which factors shape East Asia's climates?

2. In which climate region do people experience the Pacific monsoon?

3. What types of vegetation can be found in the forests of the mid-latitude climates?

4. How is the Gobi Desert an example of the rain shadow effect?

☐ NATIONAL GEOGRAPHIC **GEOFACT**

▶ **Bamboo grows more rapidly than any other living thing. Near Kyoto, Japan, scientists measured one bamboo culm, or stem, that grew almost 4 feet (1.2 m) in 24 hours.**

---

mulberry tree, whose leaves provide food for silkworms, and the tea bush. Bamboo, tea, and silk are significant to East Asia's culture and economy and have become identified worldwide with the region.

Desert and Steppe Climates

Far away from the moist winds of the coast, deserts spread across Mongolia and inland northern China. Moisture that might reach these areas is blocked by the rain shadow effect caused by the surrounding mountains. Deserts are not always hot—the Gobi and Taklimakan are often cold and windy. In the northern and northwestern desert and steppe climates, temperature variation can be extreme, falling as much as 55°F (31°C) from daytime to nighttime. In the Gobi, temperatures average 73°F (23°C) in summer and 0°F (−18°C) in winter, but they may range from 100°F to −30°F (38°C to −34°C). Grasses and sparse trees are the natural vegetation of the large steppe climate east of the deserts and in most of Mongolia.

Chapter 26 ● 653

COOPERATIVE LEARNING ACTIVITY

Poetry Explain that *haiku* is a non-rhyming form of Japanese poetry. Traditional haiku has three lines of five, seven, and five syllables, respectively, and often has nature as a subject. Write the following haiku on the board and read it to students: *Slender, silver grove,/ Bamboo, filtering sunlight,/Whispers ancient myths.*

Have students work in groups to locate photographs of East Asian scenery, and then write haiku about the photographs, focusing on the climate or vegetation depicted. Have groups create booklets of their haiku and read them or distribute the booklets to the class.
🔲 EE2 Places and Regions: Standard 6; 🔲 EE4 Human Systems: Standard 10

Reading Essentials & Study Guide 26-2

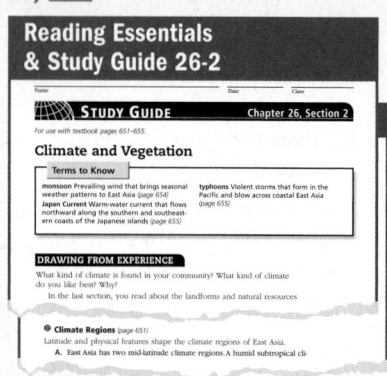

Answer

Rice is a staple of the diet of most of the population.

More About the Photo

A good rice harvest can mean the difference between prosperity and hardship.

③ ASSESS

Assign Section 2 Assessment as homework or as an in-class activity.

⚫ Have students use **Interactive Tutor Self-Assessment CD-ROM.**

L2

Section Quiz 26-2

Highlands Climates

The climate in mountainous areas changes with elevation. Generally, the higher the elevation of an area, the cooler it is. East Asia's highlands climates, therefore, are usually cool or cold. On the Plateau of Tibet, with an elevation of 13,000 to 15,000 feet (3,962 to 4,572 m), the average high temperature reaches only about 58°F (14°C). Small alpine meadows with grass, flowers, and trees dot the lower mountain slopes. Above the timberline, where no trees grow, only mosses and colorful lichens thrive.

Tropical Rain Forest Climate

The island of **Hainan**, off China's southern coast, has a tropical rain forest climate. This area experiences year-round high temperatures and a very rainy summer monsoon. In tropical areas palms and tropical hardwoods thrive alongside broad-leaved evergreens and tropical fruit trees. Lush rain forest covers much of Hainan.

History
The Roots of Rice and Soy

Rice and soybeans—two of East Asia's most important food crops—were first cultivated from wild vegetation. Archaeologists have found evidence of rice cultivation in southern China as early as 5000 B.C. It then spread north to Japan, south to Indonesia, and west to India. Rice became a major food source for China's ancient civilization as well as for others in East and Southeast Asia. Soybeans, a valuable source of protein for people and livestock, were also first cultivated in East Asia around 5000 B.C. China's ancient peoples considered soybeans one of the five foods necessary for long life.

Monsoons

In East Asia the air mass above the world's largest continent and the air mass above the world's largest ocean meet. The movement of these air masses causes prevailing winds, called monsoons, that bring seasonal weather patterns to East Asia. Along with inland highlands, mountains, and ocean currents in coastal areas, monsoons greatly influence East Asia's climate.

Monsoons blow in a steady direction for approximately half the year and then switch directions. The summer monsoon in East Asia blows from southeast to northwest, bearing heat and humidity from the Pacific Ocean. From April through October, especially near the coast and occasionally as far northwest as Mongolia, the winds cause intense downpours that provide more than 80 percent of the region's annual rainfall. From November to March, the winter monsoon brings cold, arctic air that usually blows from northwest to southeast. Inland, the winds tend to be dry, carrying clouds of dust from the Gobi. Along the coast, these winds pick up moisture in the Sea of Japan (East Sea) and bring heavy snow to Japan and the Korean Peninsula, especially in the north.

The East Asian economy depends on summer monsoons to bring the rains for crops. If the summer monsoons are late or do not bring enough rain,

Geography Skills for Life

Rice Seedlings A farmer tends to rice plants in a flooded paddy.

Region How is rice important to East Asian culture?

CRITICAL THINKING ACTIVITY

Determining Cause and Effect Organize the class into seven groups. Assign one of the following places or countries to each group: China's eastern highlands, Mongolia, China's Sichuan Basin, North China Plain, South Korea, Japan, and Taiwan. Ask each group to research the diet of the people in their assigned area, focusing on locally grown foods rather than imported foods. Have each group create a presentation explaining how climate, physical geography, and other natural factors affect what the people of the area eat.
🌐 **EE5 Environment and Society: Standard 15**

serious crop failures may occur. Too much rain brings disastrous flooding, as occurred in 1998 in the Chinese city of Harbin:

> *In north east China, Harbin . . . faced another [overflow] as the third flood crest in recent weeks swept down the Songhua River.*
>
> "China Floods 'Worst Ever'," *BBC News*, August 22, 1998

▲ *The Gobi*

In some parts of East Asia, mountains weaken the effects of the monsoons. The **Qin Ling Mountains** of central China, for example, act as a clear dividing line. South of the Qin Ling, the climate is warm and humid, and rice is the chief crop. To the north the mountains block the summer monsoons, so the climate north of the Qin Ling is cooler and drier, and wheat is the chief crop. The high mountains of the eastern Korean Peninsula act as a similar barrier against the winter monsoons, giving Korea's east coast warmer winters and lighter snowfalls.

Ocean Currents

Ocean currents, too, influence climate. Two such currents shape Japan's climate. The warm-water Japan Current, or Kuroshio, flows northward along the southern and southeastern coasts of the Japanese islands and adds moisture to the winter monsoon as it warms the land. The cold Kuril Current, or Oyashio, flows southwest from the Bering Sea along the Pacific coasts of Japan's northernmost islands. It brings harsh, cold winters to Hokkaido's east coast. In summer, when the cold ocean current meets the warm one near Hokkaido, a dense sea fog develops.

The interaction of ocean currents and winds frequently gives rise to violent storms called typhoons, which form in the Pacific and blow across coastal East Asia. Like hurricanes in the western Atlantic and Caribbean, typhoons tend to be most severe between late August and October. High winds, storm surges, and torrential rains during typhoons may cause heavy damage. Occasionally, though, a winter typhoon brings welcome rains during the normally dry part of the year.

SECTION 2 ASSESSMENT

Checking for Understanding

1. **Define** monsoon, Japan Current, typhoon.

2. **Main Ideas** Draw a Venn diagram like the one shown below. Use it to describe the similarities and differences in climate for western and eastern parts of East Asia.

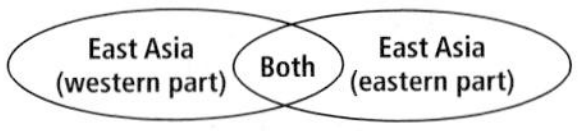

East Asia (western part) — Both — East Asia (eastern part)

Critical Thinking

3. **Analyzing Information** Why is Mongolia more suitable for herding than for farming?

4. **Predicting Consequences** What economic effects would occur if the summer monsoon arrived months late in China?

5. **Identifying Cause and Effect** How do ocean currents affect East Asia's climate?

Analyzing Maps

6. **Region** Compare the maps on pages 652 and 653. What kinds of vegetation characterize high latitude climates?

Applying Geography

7. **Effects of Elevation** Write a paragraph analyzing how mountains, plateaus, and lowlands affect East Asia's climate and vegetation.

Chapter 26 🌐 655

TECHNOLOGY SkillBuilder

Teaching the Skill

Explain that creating multimedia presentations is a skill that can be helpful not only in school but also in the workplace. Using a variety of media helps convey information in a way that engages the attention and interest of an audience.

Be prepared to demonstrate any available media tools, such as slide or overhead projectors, CD or cassette players, videos, as well as handouts, maps, graphs or charts mounted on display boards, or computer presentation software.

After students read the page, have them list some unique qualities of various media, such as those listed above. Discuss with students each of the points under "Practicing the Skill."

Additional Practice
L1

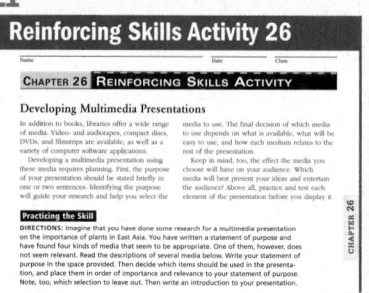

Reinforcing Skills Activity 26

Name ___ Date ___ Class ___

CHAPTER 26 REINFORCING SKILLS ACTIVITY

Developing Multimedia Presentations

In addition to books, libraries offer a wide range of media. Video- and audiotapes, compact discs, DVDs, and filmstrips are available, as well as a variety of computer software applications.

Developing a multimedia presentation using these media requires planning. First, the purpose of your presentation should be stated briefly in one or two sentences. Identifying the purpose will guide your research and help you select the

media to use. The final decision of which media to use depends on what is available, what will be easy to use, and how each medium relates to the rest of the presentation.

Keep in mind, too, the effect the media you choose will have on your audience. Which media will best present your ideas and entertain the audience? Above all, practice and test each element of the presentation before you display it.

Practicing the Skill

DIRECTIONS: Imagine that you have done some research for a multimedia presentation on the importance of plants in East Asia. You have written a statement of purpose and have found four kinds of media that seem to be appropriate. One of them, however, does not seem relevant. Read the descriptions of several media below. Write your statement of purpose in the space provided. Then decide which items should be used in the presentation, and place them in order of importance and relevance to your statement of purpose. Note, too, which selection to leave out. Then write an introduction to your presentation.

CHAPTER 26

GLENCOE TECHNOLOGY

Glencoe Skillbuilder Interactive Workbook, Level 2

This interactive CD–ROM reinforces student mastery of essential social studies skills.

Developing Multimedia Presentations

You can take advantage of all available technologies and media forms to create classroom presentations. A multimedia presentation can engage the senses and capture the attention of your audience.

Learning the Skill

A multimedia presentation uses several types of media to present information. These media may include audio, text, and graphics, such as slides, transparencies, animation, or videos.

Any multimedia presentation should have a definite purpose. Before you begin to develop a presentation, state the purpose briefly in one or two sentences. Identifying the purpose will guide your research and help you select the media to use.

Choosing the appropriate media from those available will help you communicate information most effectively. Showing a videotape of a graph during a presentation will probably not capture your audience's attention. An overhead transparency might be a better tool for displaying a graph. To prepare a presentation on the recent migration patterns of East Asians, for example, you might display a combination of maps and photos showing past and present migrations.

Use these questions to develop multimedia presentations:

• **What is my purpose?**
• **Which forms of media will best show the kind of information I want to present?**

• **Which media are available?**
• **What computer software programs do I need, if any?**
• **Does my computer support these software programs?**

3. What are some possible advantages and disadvantages of showing a Web site during a multimedia presentation?

Practicing the Skill

Answer the following questions about developing multimedia presentations.

1. What media tools would be most effective for a presentation about an important leader in East Asia?

2. What media tools would be most effective for explaining population changes in East Asia?

Applying the Skill

Work with a group to plan and produce a multimedia presentation on a political, economic, or social issue in an East Asian country. Use the information in this chapter, and research print and Web sources to prepare your presentation. Share each presentation with the class.

ANSWERS TO PRACTICING THE SKILL

1. graphics, such as slides or video
2. transparencies, including graphs, tables, or maps
3. advantages: colorful, dynamic, engaging; disadvantages: may contain unwanted messages, hard to see if screen is small, technical difficulties

SUMMARY & STUDY GUIDE

Use the Chapter 26 Summary & Study Guide to preview, review, condense, or reteach the chapter.

Preview/Review

🌐 **Vocabulary PuzzleMaker CD-ROM** reinforces "Terms to Know."

🌐 **Interactive Tutor Self-Assessment CD-ROM** provides a review of Chapter 26 content.

Condense

Have students read the Chapter 26 Summary & Study Guide.

🌐 Chapter 26 Audio Program

📁 Chapter 26 Guided Reading Activities

Reteach

📁 Chapter 26 Reteaching Activities (Spanish also available)
📁 Chapter 26 Reading Essentials and Study Guides

SECTION 1 — ## The Land (pp. 645–650)

Terms to Know
- archipelago
- tsunami
- loess

Key Points
- East Asia's location at the meeting point of tectonic plates leaves the region vulnerable to earthquakes, volcanic eruptions, and tsunamis.
- The region of East Asia consists of China, Mongolia, and North and South Korea on the Asian continent, plus the island countries of Japan and Taiwan.
- East Asia's rivers provide important transportation systems and support fertile farmlands.
- East Asia is rich in minerals, but they are unevenly distributed.
- Limited farmlands, long coastlines, and large populations have made the region dependent on the sea for food.

Organizing Your Notes
Create an outline using the format below to help you organize your notes for this section.

The Land
I. Land and Sea
A. Peninsulas, Islands, and Seas
B.
II. Mountains, Highlands, and Lowlands
A.
B.
III. River Systems
A.
B.
C.
IV. Natural Resources

SECTION 2 — ## Climate and Vegetation (pp. 651–655)

Terms to Know
- monsoon
- Japan Current
- typhoon

Key Points
- East Asia's natural vegetation tends to parallel the region's climate zones.
- East Asian countries rely on seasonal winds known as monsoons. The summer monsoons bring more than 80 percent of the region's rainfall.
- Ocean currents affect the climates of coastal and island regions. Powerful typhoons form in the Pacific and blow across coastal East Asia in later summer and early fall.
- East Asia's varied vegetation includes needle-leaved and broad-leaved evergreen trees, tropical plants, bamboo, tea, mulberry trees, and grasses as well as tropical rain forest vegetation.

Organizing Your Notes
Use a table like the one below to help you organize important details from this section.

Climate Zone	Location	Type of Vegetation
Humid Subtropical		
Humid Continental		
Desert		
Steppe		
Highlands		
Tropical Rain Forest		

◀ Li River, China

GLENCOE TECHNOLOGY

▢ NATIONAL GEOGRAPHIC
WORLD REGIONS
VIDEO PROGRAM

Unit 9, East Asia
The following segments enhance the study of this unit:
- **Treasures of the Gobi**
- **Haenyo of Cheju**
- **A-Mei: Princess of Pop**

CHAPTER CULMINATING ACTIVITY

Determining Cause and Effect Have students review their notes and the pages of Chapter 26 to answer the following question. **Ask: How do East Asia's prominent mountain ranges shape climates, human settlement patterns, and economic activities?** Before students answer, suggest that they respond as if they were a reporter traveling in the region. Have students write their answers as an article or program to educate people about East Asia's physical characteristics. Encourage students to do additional research and to include sketches, maps, and anecdotes from their imagined travels as a reporter.
▣ EE2 Places and Regions: Standard 4; ▣ EE4 Human Systems: Standard 12

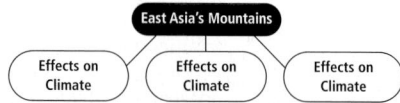

ASSESSMENT & ACTIVITIES
CHAPTER 26

GLENCOE TECHNOLOGY

Use *MindJogger Videoquiz* to review the Chapter 26 content.

Reviewing Key Terms

1. b
2. a
3. d
4. f
5. e
6. c

Reviewing Facts

SECTION 1

1. Korean Peninsula
2. Honshu
3. volcanoes, earthquakes, tsunamis
4. from the Pamirs area in western China
5. Yellow River, Yangtze River, Xi River, and the Grand Canal

SECTION 2

6. bamboo, tea bush, the mulberry tree (Students may also mention deciduous and evergreen trees.)
7. summer and winter monsoons
8. The economy depends on monsoons to bring rains for the crops. Crops may fail if there is too much or too little rain.
9. Kuril (Oyashio) Current

Critical Thinking

1. Answers may include: smaller countries, such as Japan, Taiwan, and Korea, import and conserve limited resources,

---

Reviewing Key Terms

Write the letter of the key term that best matches each description.

a. archipelago   **d.** monsoon
b. tsunami   **e.** Japan Current
c. loess   **f.** typhoon

1. large, fast-moving wave caused by an undersea earthquake
2. chain or group of islands
3. seasonal wind
4. powerful, hurricane-like storm generated in the western Pacific
5. warm-water stream that affects the climate in Japan
6. fine, windblown topsoil

Reviewing Facts

SECTION 1

1. On what landform are North and South Korea located?
2. What is the largest and most densely populated of the Japanese islands?
3. Describe the natural hazards that result from East Asia's location at the meeting point of three tectonic plates?
4. From which part of China do most of the region's great mountain ranges extend?
5. What are China's four major river or waterway systems?

SECTION 2

6. Which economically important plants thrive in East Asia's midlatitudes?
7. What climate factor influences East Asia in seasonal cycles?
8. How are economic activities affected by climate in East Asia?
9. Which ocean current brings cold winters to Hokkaido?

Critical Thinking

1. Making Generalizations How has the uneven distribution of natural resources most likely affected the economies of countries in the region?
2. Analyzing Information Why might the countries surrounding the South China Sea compete for control of its waters?
3. Identifying Cause and Effect Use a graphic organizer like the one below to fill in the effects that mountains have on the climate of East Asia.

East Asia's Mountains
Effects on Climate   Effects on Climate   Effects on Climate

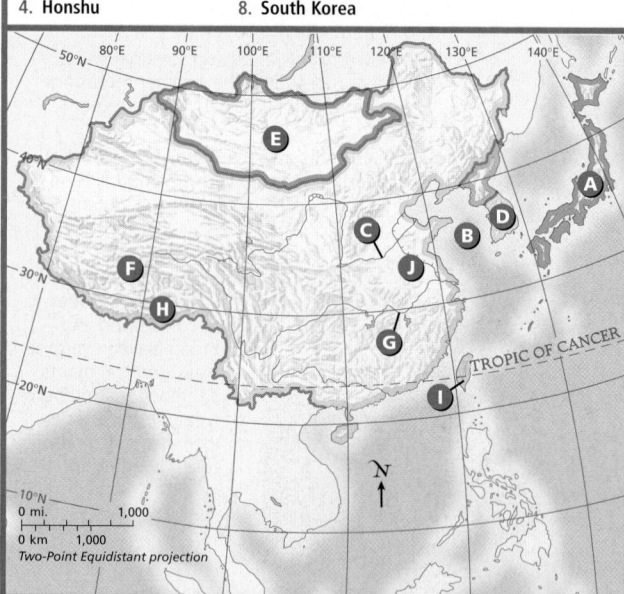

NATIONAL GEOGRAPHIC **Locating Places**
East Asia: Physical-Political Geography

Match the letters on the map with the places and physical features of East Asia. Write your answers on a sheet of paper.

1. Yellow River	5. Yellow Sea	9. Taiwan
2. Yangtze River	6. Plateau of Tibet	10. North China Plain
3. Mongolia	7. Himalaya	
4. Honshu	8. South Korea	

---

thus relying on trade; abundant resources may enable China to be independent or to profit from exporting natural resources.
2. It is an important shipping area.
3. Mountains block the humid summer monsoon, causing a cooler, drier climate north of the Qin Ling range; rain shadow causes desert conditions in Mongolia and inland northern China; cool or cold in highlands, depending on elevation.

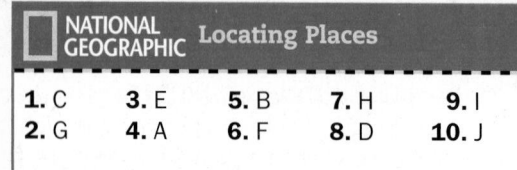

NATIONAL GEOGRAPHIC Locating Places

1. C	**3.** E	**5.** B	**7.** H	**9.** I
2. G	**4.** A	**6.** F	**8.** D	**10.** J

Using the Regional Atlas

1. coal, petroleum
2. Songhua, Liao, and Yalu Rivers

Using the Regional Atlas

Refer to the Regional Atlas on pages 636–639.

1. **Region** What rivers drain the Manchurian Plain?

2. **Location** Compare the physical and economic activity maps. What fossil fuels are found on the North China Plain?

Thinking Like a Geographer

Flooding on China's Yellow River periodically causes damage and loss of life. Use what you know about the physical geography of the region to write a paragraph explaining the causes of the flooding and suggesting possible solutions.

Problem-Solving Activity

Problem-Solution Proposal Conduct research on the growth of urbanization and manufacturing in East Asia. Analyze the effects of these processes on the climate of the region. Determine to what extent climate changes in East Asia can be related to global warming. Then prepare a proposal that suggests ways to avoid or reverse the causes or harmful consequences of climatic changes.

GeoJournal

Comparison-Contrast Essay Use GeoJournal data from this and previous units to write a descriptive essay that compares and contrasts cultural patterns of East Asia to those of two other global regions you have already studied.

Technology Activity

Creating an Electronic Database Use Internet and library resources to research recent significant earthquakes, tsunamis, volcanic eruptions, and typhoons in East Asia. Use a database program to organize your data into a table with headings for location, type, and severity of each event. Then write a paragraph describing the effects of physical processes, such as the wave action of tsunamis, on the specific locations.

Standardized Test Practice

Choose the best answer for the following multiple-choice question. If you have trouble answering the question, use the process of elimination to narrow your choices.

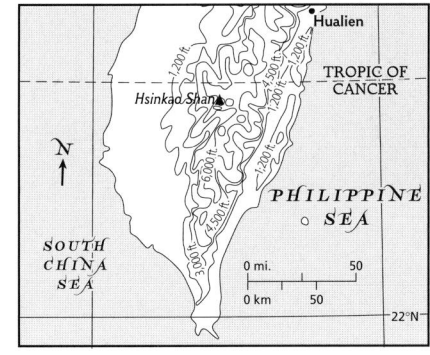

1. **If you were to hike straight up Hsinkao Shan, what would be the most gradual route to take?**

   A From the west
   B From the south
   C From the north
   D From the east

Test-Taking TiP On a contour map, the closer the lines that show elevation (isolines), the faster the terrain rises and the steeper the topography. Where lines are far apart, the change in elevation is more gradual. To answer the question correctly, first find Hsinkao Shan on the map. Determine the side of the mountain where the lines seem farthest apart. Then choose the answer that best describes your observation. It also may be helpful to notice where the map lines are closest. You can then eliminate these choices from the answers.

Thinking Like a Geographer

Students' answers might include deforestation or heavy monsoon rains as causes of flooding and reforestation or building dams and levees as possible solutions.

Problem-Solving Activity

Students' answers should be supported by information from research sources; solutions should be practical and focused on the problem's sources, both local and global.

GeoJournal

Students' answers should show insight into specific characteristics of East Asia's cultures and those of two other regions.

Technology Activity

Databases should be organized to clearly show relationships and comparisons of events. Paragraphs should demonstrate the student's ability to interpret data.

PLANNING GUIDE

NOTE: The following materials may be used when teaching Chapter 27. Section-level support materials are shown at point-of-use in the margins of the Teacher Wraparound Edition.

TEACHING TRANSPARENCIES

L2 Unit 9 Map Overlay Transparencies

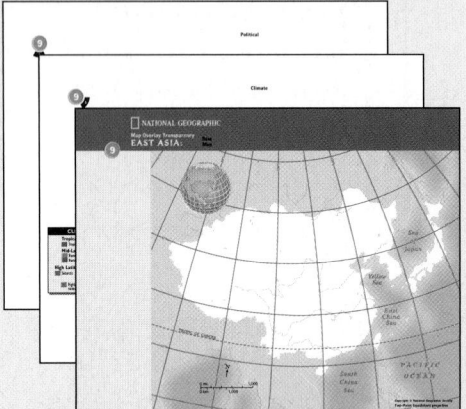

L2 Political Map Transparency 9

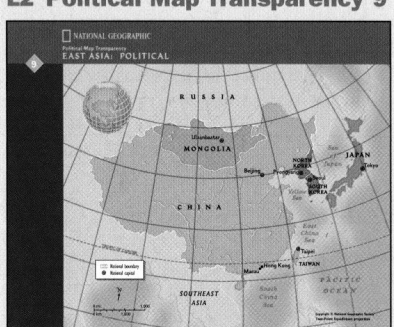

GEOGRAPHIC LITERACY

Focus on Geography Literacy

APPLICATION AND ENRICHMENT

L3 Enrichment Activity 27

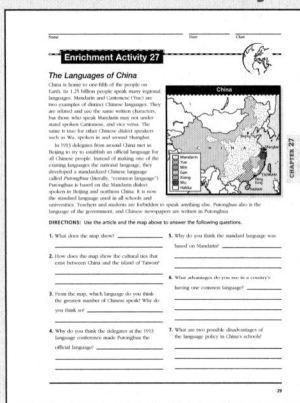

REVIEW AND REINFORCEMENT

L1 Vocabulary Activity 27 L1 Reinforcing L1 Reteaching Activity 27
Skills Activity 27

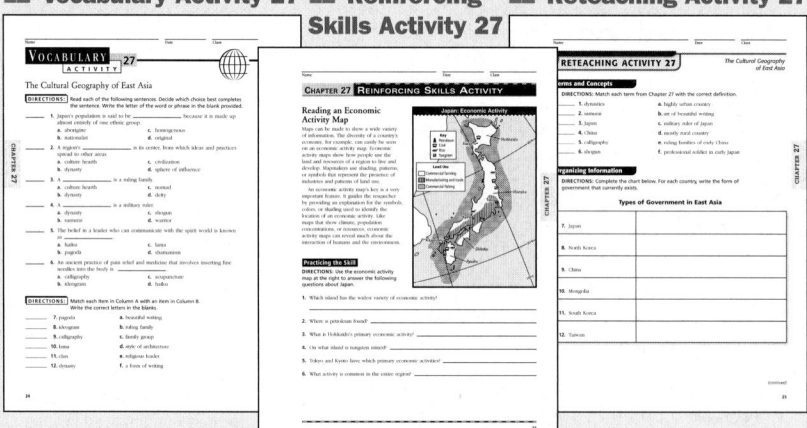

ASSESSMENT

L2 Chapter 27 Test Form A

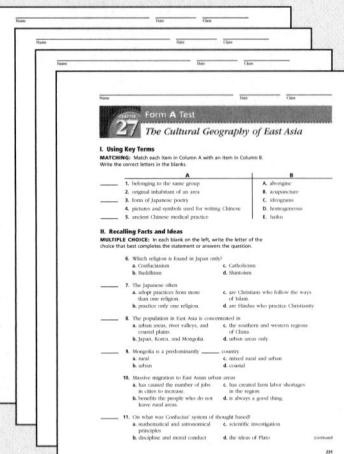

L2 Chapter 27 Test Form B

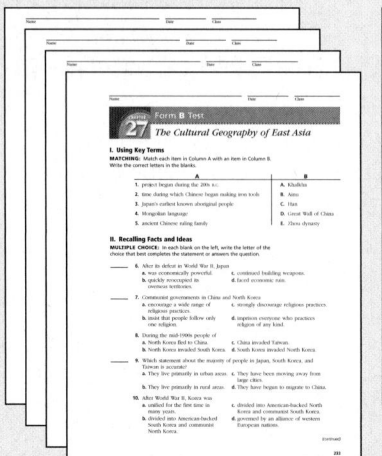

L1/ELL Performance
Assessment Activity 27

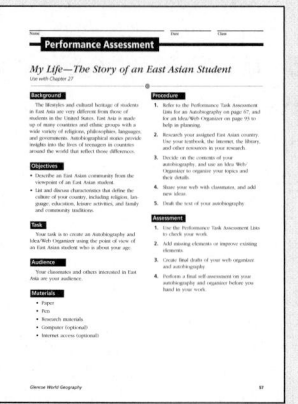

ExamView® Pro
Testmaker

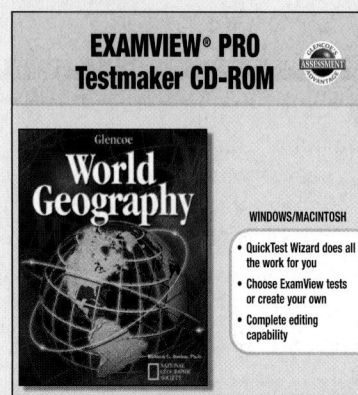

SPANISH RESOURCES

The following Spanish language materials are available in the Spanish Resources binder:

- 📁 Spanish Vocabulary Activities
- 📁 Spanish Guided Reading Activities
- 📁 Spanish Reteaching Activities
- 📁 Spanish Summaries
- 📁 Spanish Quizzes and Tests
- 📁 Spanish Reading Essentials and Study Guide

MULTIMEDIA

- 📼 World Regions Video
- 📼 MindJogger Videoquiz
- 💿 Vocabulary PuzzleMaker CD-ROM
- 💿 Interactive Tutor Self-Assessment CD-ROM
- 💿 ExamView® Pro Testmaker CD-ROM
- 💿 Audio Program
- 💿 TeacherWorks CD-ROM
- 💿 Interactive Student Edition CD-ROM
- 💿 Glencoe Skillbuilder Interactive Workbook CD-ROM, Level 2
- 💿 Presentation Plus! CD-ROM

Timesaving Tools

TeacherWorks™ All-In-One Planner and Resource Center

- **Interactive Teacher Edition** Access your Teacher Wraparound Edition and your classroom resources with a few easy clicks.

- **Interactive Lesson Planner** Planning has never been easier! Organize your week, month, semester, or year with all the lesson helps you need to make teaching creative, timely, and relevant.

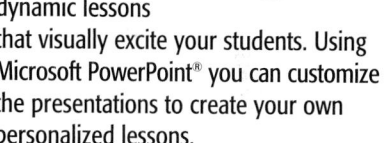

Use Glencoe's **Presentation Plus!** multimedia teacher tool to easily present dynamic lessons that visually excite your students. Using Microsoft PowerPoint® you can customize the presentations to create your own personalized lessons.

GEOGRAPHY Online

Use our Web site for additional resources. All essential content is covered in the Student Edition.

You and your students can visit geography.glencoe.com, the Web site companion to *Glencoe World Geography*. This innovative integration of electronic and print media offers your students a wealth of opportunities. The student text directs students to the Web site for the following options:

- **Chapter Overviews**
- **Student Activities**
- **Self-Check Quizzes**
- **Textbook Updates**

Answers are provided for you in the "Web Activity Lesson Plan." Additional Web resources and Interactive Tutor puzzles are also available.

▶ **Additional Glencoe Teacher Support**

- Teaching Strategies for the Geography Classroom (including Block Scheduling Pacing Guides)
- Graphic Organizer Transparencies Strategies and Activities
- Outline Map Resource Book
- Reading in the Content Area

PLANNING GUIDE

SECTION RESOURCES

Daily Objectives	Reproducible Resources	Multimedia Resources

SECTION 1   Population Patterns

1. Name the ethnic groups that make up East Asia's population.
2. Identify the country in which the majority of East Asians live.
3. Describe how the population in East Asia is distributed.

- Reproducible Lesson Plan 27-1
- Daily Lecture Notes 27-1
- Guided Reading Activity 27-1*
- Reading Essentials and Study Guide 27-1*
- Section Quiz 27-1*

- Daily Focus Skills Transparency 27-1
- Political Map Transparency 9
- Unit 9 Map Overlay Transparencies
- Interactive Tutor Self-Assessment CD-ROM
- ExamView® Pro Testmaker CD-ROM*
- Presentation Plus! CD-ROM

SECTION 2   History and Government

1. Explain where East Asia's ideas and traditions originated.
2. Discuss East Asia's first reaction to contact with the West.
3. Cite the major wars and revolutions that have occurred in East Asia.

- Reproducible Lesson Plan 27-2
- Daily Lecture Notes 27-2
- Guided Reading Activity 27-2*
- Reading Essentials and Study Guide 27-2*
- Section Quiz 27-2*

- Daily Focus Skills Transparency 27-2
- Political Map Transparency 9
- Unit 9 Map Overlay Transparencies
- Interactive Tutor Self-Assessment CD-ROM
- ExamView® Pro Testmaker CD-ROM*
- Presentation Plus! CD-ROM

SECTION 3   Cultures and Lifestyles

1. List the languages that the people of East Asia speak.
2. Describe the religions and philosophies that many people of East Asia follow.
3. Discuss how the living standards of East Asians compare with one another.
4. Compare education in East Asia with education in North America.
5. Identify the traditional arts that make East Asia unique.

- Reproducible Lesson Plan 27-3
- Vocabulary Activity 27*
- Daily Lecture Notes 27-3
- Guided Reading Activity 27-3*
- Reading Essentials and Study Guide 27-3*
- Reteaching Activity 27*
- Reinforcing Skills Activity 27
- Section Quiz 27-3*

- Daily Focus Skills Transparency 27-3
- Unit 9 Map Overlay Transparencies
- Vocabulary PuzzleMaker CD-ROM
- World Music: A Cultural Legacy
- Interactive Tutor Self-Assessment CD-ROM
- ExamView® Pro Testmaker CD-ROM*
- Presentation Plus! CD-ROM

Blackline Master	Software	Videocassette	*Also available in Spanish*	
Transparency	CD-ROM	DVD		

OUT OF TIME? Assign the Chapter 27 **Reading Essentials and Study Guide.**

Block Schedule

Activities that are particularly suited to use within the block scheduling framework are identified throughout this chapter by the following designation:

KEY TO ABILITY LEVELS

Teaching strategies have been coded for various learning styles and abilities.

L1   **BASIC** activities for all students

L2   **AVERAGE** activities for average to above-average students

L3   **CHALLENGING** activities for above-average students

ELL   **ENGLISH LANGUAGE LEARNER** activities

Teacher to Teacher

Jake McNally
Deering High School
Portland, ME

Ancient Beliefs, Modern Challenges

After introducing the ancient belief systems of China—Taoism, Confucianism, and Legalism—have students work in groups of three to apply each teaching to a set of real-life challenges faced by China today.

Give each group a list of three or four questions about modern-day China, such as: Why do you approve or disapprove of the one-child policy? How should we as a society deal with criminals? Would you build the Three Gorges Dam? How would you raise your children in this philosophy? Students should first research the facts of each issue and the teachings of each belief system. Student groups then work out the solutions based on the different belief systems and make class presentations. Each member of the group answers the questions from the point of view of one of the ancient philosophies.

By applying each belief system to a life situation, the activity brings into striking relief the implications of each system and gives students a richer understanding of them.

NATIONAL GEOGRAPHIC   TEACHER'S CORNER

Index to National Geographic Magazine:

The following articles may be used for research relating to this chapter:

- "Beijing," by Todd Carrell, March 2000.
- "Tibet Embraces the New Year," by Ian Baker, January 2000.
- "Hunting with Eagles," by Candice S. Millard, September 1999.

National Geographic Society Products:

To order the following products for use with this chapter, call National Geographic Society at 1-800-368-2728.

- *Asia* (Video)
- *The Living Ocean* (Video)
- *National Geographic Desk Reference* (Book)
- *National Geographic Atlas of the World, Seventh Edition* (Book)

NGS ONLINE

Access National Geographic's Web site for current events, activities, links, interactive features, and archives.
www.nationalgeographic.com

Meeting National Standards

Geography For Life

The following standards are highlighted in Chapter 27:

Section 1 EE1 The World in Spatial Terms:
Standards 1, 3
EE4 Human Systems:
Standards 9, 10, 11, 12, 13

Section 2 EE4 Human Systems:
Standards 10, 11, 13

Section 3 EE2 Places and Regions:
Standard 4
EE4 Human Systems:
Standards 9, 10, 11, 13

Local Objectives

_____

_____

MEETING SPECIAL NEEDS

In addition to the Differentiated Instruction strategies found in each section, the following resources are also suitable for your special needs students:

- *ExamView® Pro Testmaker CD-ROM* allows teachers to tailor tests by reducing answer choices.
- The *Audio Program* includes the entire narrative of the student edition so that less-proficient readers can listen to the words as they read them.
- The *Reading Essentials and Study Guide* provides the same content as the student edition but is written two grade levels below the textbook.
- *Guided Reading Activities* give less-proficient readers point-by-point instructions to increase comprehension as they read each textbook section.
- *Enrichment Activities* include a stimulating collection of readings and activities for gifted and talented students.

Chapter Objectives

1. Discuss the ethnic groups that comprise East Asia's peoples and the population distribution of the region.

2. Explain how East Asians have been influenced by China since ancient times and, in more recent times, by contact with the West.

3. Describe how, despite Chinese influences, each country in East Asia has its own unique cultural traditions.

GLENCOE TECHNOLOGY

Use *MindJogger Videoquiz* to preview the Chapter 27 content.

GeoJournal

For access to additional photos, maps, and information on East Asia's cultural features go to www.nationalgeographic.com (See Teacher pages in front for strategies for using journals in the geography classroom.)

GEOGRAPHY Online

Introduce students to chapter content and key terms by having them access **Chapter Overview 27** at geography.glencoe.com

FOLDABLES™
Study Organizer

Dinah Zike's Foldables are three-dimensional, interactive graphic organizers that help students practice basic writing skills, review key vocabulary terms, and identify main ideas. Have students complete the Foldable activity in the **Dinah Zike's Reading and Study Skills Foldables** booklet.

CHAPTER 27

The Cultural Geography of East Asia

GeoJournal

As you read this chapter, record details in your journal that will allow you to compare and contrast the various countries of East Asia. Organize details under the following heads: population patterns, history and government, and cultures and lifestyles.

GEOGRAPHY Online

Chapter Overview Visit the **Glencoe World Geography** Web site at geography.glencoe.com and click on Chapter Overviews—Chapter 27 to preview information about the cultural geography of the region.

ABOUT THE PHOTO

Visual Instruction Dance plays an important role in the daily lives of Tibetans. Some dances have religious significance, expressing Tibetan Buddhism, while others are secular and are performed at public celebrations and festivals, as in the picture. One of Tibet's most famous dances features the Tibetan Buddhist goddess Tara, whose qualities include the ability to protect and heal, great beauty, and wisdom. In the Tara dance, various female dancers portray the goddess's different aspects. **Ask: Why might people perform their traditional dances in public?** (to share their beliefs and practices with others; to express pride in their traditional culture) 🌐 **EE4 Human Systems: Standard 10**

Guide to Reading

Consider What You Know

In many parts of the world, people are migrating from rural areas to cities. What advantages and disadvantages do you think this trend brings?

Reading Strategy

Organizing Complete a graphic organizer similar to the one below by describing China's "one-child" policy.

China's "One-Child" Policy
•
•
•

Read to Find Out

• What ethnic groups make up East Asia's population?

• In what country do the majority of East Asians live?

• How is population in East Asia distributed?

Terms to Know

• aborigine

• homogeneous

Places to Locate

• Taipei

• Seoul

• Pyongyang

• Tokaido corridor

• Tokyo

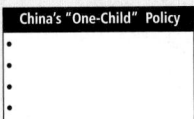
◀ Tibetan dancers, Beijing, China

SECTION 1

Population Patterns

NATIONAL GEOGRAPHIC

A Geographic View

Torrent of Commuters

There seems to be no end to Tokyo's congestion, no time of day when the city slackens pace to catch its breath. By 8 a.m., three million commuters are coursing through train and subway stations, joining 12 million residents of Tokyo proper on their purposeful way to work. . . . One rush hour morning . . . I got swept away in a pedestrian torrent . . . flowing in the opposite direction, and I was carried the distance of a city block. . . .

—Arthur Zich, "Japan's Sun Rises Over the Pacific," National Geographic, *November 1991*

Tokyo street at night

In Japan, as in other parts of East Asia, people are crowded onto relatively small lowland areas along rivers or on seacoasts. There, the largest cities are located. In this section you will learn what peoples make up East Asia's population, where East Asians live, and why many of them are migrating from rural areas to cities.

Human Characteristics

East Asia has more than 1.5 billion people—about 25 percent of the world's population. East Asians form many different ethnic groups, each with its own language and cultural traditions. Among the region's major ethnic groups are the Chinese, Tibetan, Japanese, Korean, and Mongolian.

China

When people in China say someone is Chinese, they use the Chinese word that means "a person of the Middle Kingdom." About 92 percent

Chapter 27 🌐 **661**

① FOCUS

Section Overview

This section examines present-day population patterns of East Asia, including ethnicity, population distribution, and migration.

BELLRINGER
Skillbuilder Activity

Project transparency and have students answer questions.

Available as blackline master.

Daily Focus Skills Transparency 27-1

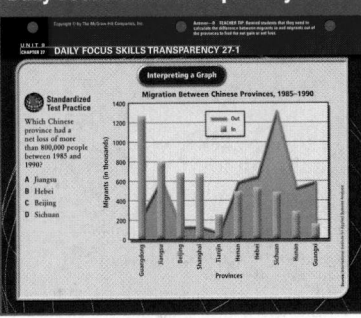

Guide to Reading

Consider What You Know
Answer *advantages: economic opportunity, better access to health care and education; disadvantages: farm labor shortages, urban overcrowding, and pollution*

Reading Strategy
Answer *program began in 1979; each family allowed only one child; factor in slowing China's population growth rate; no longer strictly enforced; population growth rate increasing again*

Preteaching Vocabulary
Have students look up the meaning of *aborigine* (page 662). Point out that the word aborigine contains the root *origin*, referring to a place's original inhabitants.

RESOURCE MANAGER

Reproducible Masters
• Reproducible Lesson Plan 27-1
• Daily Lecture Notes 27-1
• Guided Reading Activity 27-1
• Reading Essentials and Study Guide 27-1
• Section Quiz 27-1

Transparencies
• Daily Focus Skills Transparency 27-1
• Political Map Transparency 9
• Unit 9 Map Overlay Transparencies

Multimedia
🔘 Interactive Tutor Self-Assessment CD-ROM
🔘 ExamView® Pro Testmaker CD-ROM
🔘 Presentation Plus! CD-ROM

② TEACH

L1 Identify

Draw a two-column table on the board. Label the columns *Country* and *Ethnic Groups.* Call on students to name the various ethnic groups in each East Asian country and list them in the table. Have students name and highlight each country's major ethnic group. **ELL**

GRAPH STUDY

Answers
1. *China*

2. *China: a younger population and higher birthrate; Japan: higher life expectancy and aging workforce*

Skills Practice
Predicting In 20 years, which age groups in China and Japan will be the largest? *(China: males and females ages 40–49; Japan: males and females ages 40–49.)*

Daily Lecture Notes 27-1

DAILY LECTURE NOTES

CHAPTER 27
Section 1

Building Geography Literacy
Tokyo, Japan; Beijing, China; Shanghai, China; and Seoul, South Korea are four of the largest cities in the world. The United Nations projects that Tokyo will have a population of nearly 29 million in 2015. The four cities combined then will be home to about 76 million people.

I. Human Characteristics *pages 661–663*

East Asia has about 1.5 billion people—about 25 percent of the world's population. Among the region's major ethnic groups are the Han Chinese, Tibetan, Japanese, Korean, and Mongolian. (p. 661)

A. China
About 92 percent of China's population belong to the Han ethnic group. The remaining 8 percent belongs to about 55 different ethnic groups. (pp. 661–663)

B. Japan, Korea, and Mongolia
1. About 99 percent of Japan's population is ethnic Japanese, descendants of Asian migrants who crossed the Korean peninsula to Japan centuries ago. (p. 663)

on vacations. The Japanese also have developed a system of etiquette to reduce tensions in social relationships.)

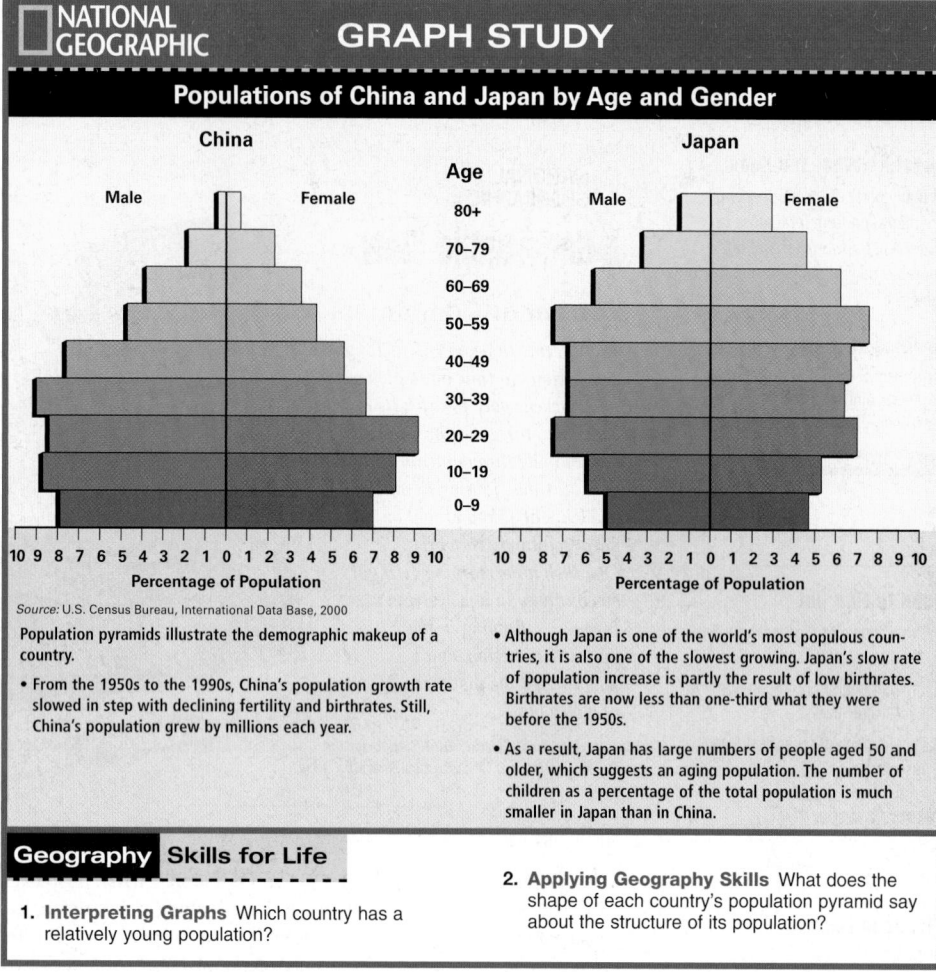

NATIONAL GEOGRAPHIC   **GRAPH STUDY**

Populations of China and Japan by Age and Gender

China   **Age**   **Japan**

Male   Female

| 80+ |
| 70–79 |
| 60–69 |
| 50–59 |
| 40–49 |
| 30–39 |
| 20–29 |
| 10–19 |
| 0–9 |

10 9 8 7 6 5 4 3 2 1 0 1 2 3 4 5 6 7 8 9 10   10 9 8 7 6 5 4 3 2 1 0 1 2 3 4 5 6 7 8 9 10

Percentage of Population   **Percentage of Population**

Source: U.S. Census Bureau, International Data Base, 2000

Population pyramids illustrate the demographic makeup of a country.

• From the 1950s to the 1990s, China's population growth rate slowed in step with declining fertility and birthrates. Still, China's population grew by millions each year.

• Although Japan is one of the world's most populous countries, it is also one of the slowest growing. Japan's slow rate of population increase is partly the result of low birthrates. Birthrates are now less than one-third what they were before the 1950s.

• As a result, Japan has large numbers of people aged 50 and older, which suggests an aging population. The number of children as a percentage of the total population is much smaller in Japan than in China.

Geography Skills for Life

1. **Interpreting Graphs** Which country has a relatively young population?

2. **Applying Geography Skills** What does the shape of each country's population pyramid say about the structure of its population?

---

of China's 1.3 billion people belong to the Han, an ethnic group named for a powerful ancient Chinese ruling family. From 206 B.C. to A.D. 220, Han rulers developed a culture whose influence has lasted to the present.

The remaining 8 percent of China's population belong to about 55 different ethnic groups, most of whom live mainly in western and northern China. Although ruled by China, non-Chinese peoples such as the Tibetans have their own separate histories and cultures. For example, the Tibetan homeland of Tibet, located on a high Himalayan plateau, was once a Buddhist kingdom. Since China's takeover of Tibet in 1950, the Tibetans have resisted Chinese efforts to destroy their culture.

Off China's southeastern coast lies the island of Taiwan. Taiwan and China share a long history. Most of Taiwan's people are descended from Chinese who migrated to the island several hundred years ago. Another 15 percent of the Taiwanese population descend from Chinese who fled from China to Taiwan in 1949, after the Communists in China defeated the Nationalist government in a civil war. Taiwan's original inhabitants, or aborigines,

---

DIFFERENTIATED INSTRUCTION

Auditory/Musical For students whose learning style reflects a sensitivity to pitch, melody, rhythm, and tone, help them locate recorded examples of East Asian ethnic music. Have students listen to the various examples, identifying how they are similar or different in terms of instruments, rhythms, tone, and so on. Allow students to prepare a presentation that summarizes facts about East Asian music. They may discuss different styles, instruments, or performers that are found in each country of the region.

🌐 **EE4 Human Systems: Standard 10**

Refer to *Inclusion for the Social Studies Classroom Strategies and Activities.*

are related to peoples in Southeast Asia and the Pacific area. They make up only about 2 percent of Taiwan's population.

Japan, Korea, and Mongolia

The populations of other East Asian countries have distinct ethnic groups. Japan is ethnically **homogeneous** (HOH•muh•JEE•nee•uhs)—having a population belonging to the same ethnic group. About 99 percent of Japan's population is ethnic Japanese, descendants of Asian migrants who crossed the Korean Peninsula to reach Japan centuries ago. The migrants forced Japan's earliest-known aboriginal people, the Ainu (EYE•noo), to move gradually north. Small numbers of Ainu still live on the island of Hokkaido (hoh•KY•doh).

Like Japan, Korea has long been ethnically homogeneous. Koreans trace their origins to early peoples from northern China and Central Asia. They have maintained their common identity despite long periods of foreign rule and today's division of the Korean Peninsula into communist North Korea and democratic South Korea.

The people of Mongolia are mostly ethnic Mongolians. Centuries ago their Mongol ancestors ruled the world's largest land empire, which stretched from China to eastern Europe. Today the Mongolians are divided into separate linguistic groups, but about 90 percent of them speak the Khalkha Mongolian language.

Where East Asians Live

Physical geography influences where East Asians live. Because much of East Asia is barren and mountainous, the region's population is distributed unevenly. Most East Asians settle in coastal areas or in fertile areas along rivers. In these places, among the most densely populated on Earth, the land and climate are favorable for agriculture, industry, and urban growth.

Population Distribution and Density

Despite China's large land area, more than 90 percent of Chinese live on only one-sixth of the land. Most inhabit the fertile valleys and plains of China's three great rivers: the Yellow (Huang He), Yangtze (Chang Jiang), and Xi. Large urban centers, such as Shanghai, Beijing, Tianjin, and Guangzhou, lie in river valleys or coastal plains.

They have populations ranging from 6 million to more than 13.5 million. By contrast, the rugged western province of Xinjiang has a sparse population of farmers and herders living on scattered oases. About 2.5 million people live in Mongolia's vast interior steppes, a population density of only 4 people per square mile (2 people per sq. km).

Space is limited on Taiwan, where most of the island's 22.6 million people live in cities such as **Taipei** (TY•PAY) that lie on or close to the coast. In North and South Korea, most people inhabit coastal plains that wrap around the Korean Peninsula's mountainous interior. About two-thirds of the Korean population lives in rapidly growing cities, such as **Seoul** (SOHL) and **Pyongyang**.

Japan has limited land area for its large population. Forested mountains cover the central part of the country, leaving only valleys and coastal plains for settlement. About 78 percent of Japan's 127.5 million people live in coastal urban areas, such as the **Tokaido corridor**—a series of cities crowded together on the main island of Honshu. One of these cities, **Tokyo**, is the world's most populous urban area, with more than 26 million people. By contrast, Japan's northernmost large island, Hokkaido, remains rural with few people.

Culture
Japan's Urban Lifestyle

Urbanization shapes the physical surroundings and lifestyles of the Japanese people. Hundreds of skyscrapers tower over the busy streets of Japan's modern cities. Glaring neon signs advertise cars, electronics, and watches. As in most of East Asia's crowded cities, a childless couple might live in a tiny one- or two-bedroom apartment. Because of Japan's high population density and costly land, suburban homes are small compared to those in other developed countries.

The Japanese have adapted to their crowded conditions with an efficient transportation system. Commuters board the Shinkansen express, or bullet train, to get to their destinations. As the electric train pulls out of the station, its movement gently presses passengers back into their seats. In a few moments, the train reaches speeds of over 160 miles per hour (257 km per hour) along the Tokaido corridor. The westbound train cruises from Tokyo through the urban,

Chapter 27 🌐 663

East Asian Greetings Bowing is a common means of respectful greeting in East Asia, yet there are differences between countries. The Japanese bow and lower the eyes—bowing to a depth that reflects the relationship between the two people. The Chinese nod or bow slightly—or more deeply to superiors; Koreans bow slightly to everyone, and Korean men may shake hands without breaking eye contact. Taiwanese bow slightly or nod the head upon being introduced. Mongolians shake hands.

L1/ELL

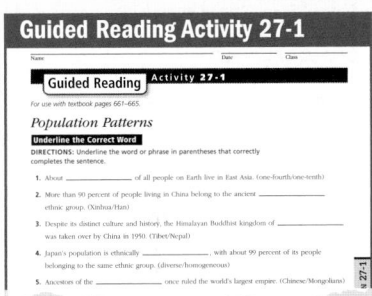

Guided Reading Activity 27-1

Name _____ Date _____ Class _____

Guided Reading Activity **27-1**

For use with textbook pages 661–665.

Population Patterns

Underline the Correct Word

DIRECTIONS: Underline the word or phrase in parentheses that correctly completes the sentence.

1. About _____ of all people on Earth live in East Asia. (one-fourth/one-tenth)

2. More than 90 percent of people living in China belong to the ancient _____ ethnic group. (Xinhua/Han)

3. Despite its distinct culture and history, the Himalayan Buddhist kingdom of _____ was taken over by China in 1950. (Tibet/Nepal)

4. Japan's population is ethnically _____, with about 90 percent of its people belonging to the same ethnic group. (diverse/homogeneous)

5. Ancestors of the _____ once ruled the world's largest empire. (Chinese/Mongolian)

☐ NATIONAL GEOGRAPHIC **GEOFACT**

▶ **The world's longest escalator system runs one-half mile (800 m) between downtown Hong Kong and the neighborhoods of Victoria Peak, a nearby mountain. Built to ease rush-hour traffic congestion, the covered, outdoor network carries 34,000 people daily.**

COOPERATIVE LEARNING ACTIVITY

Where Do They Live? Have students work in four groups, and assign each group one of the following countries or regions: China, Japan, Taiwan, and North and South Korea. Then using the population density map on page 638, the text, and reference resources, have them research where each country's population density is highest and why. Have each group create a poster-sized population density map and write one or more generalizations about the population distribution in their assigned country. Each group should write a list of reasons for the current population distribution. 📦

🌐 **EE1 The World in Spatial Terms: Standards 1, 3**
🌐 **EE4 Human Systems: Standards 9, 10, 12**

World Explorer

Answer
train

More About the Photo
Many Japanese institutions promote recreation at national vacation villages. However, the cost of these vacations is high, and the Japanese are increasingly turning to Europe and America for their vacations.

L1/ELL

Reading Essentials & Study Guide 27-1

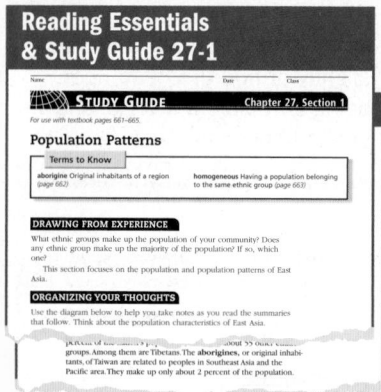

World Explorer

Geography Skills for Life
Traveling in Japan Japan's high standard of living enables vacationers to go abroad or to seaside and mountain resorts.
Place What form of public transportation is popular in Japan today?

ASSESS

Assign Section 1 Assessment as homework or as an in-class activity.

Have students use **Interactive Tutor Self-Assessment CD-ROM** to review Section 1.

industrial areas of Nagoya, Osaka, and Kobe, to Fukuoka on the island of Kyushu, 664 miles (1,069 km) away. A trip that takes more than 11 hours of hectic driving and delays by car takes only about 5 hours by high-speed train.

Migration

In recent decades many people in China and South Korea have moved from rural, desert, or mountainous areas to cities. Although most Chinese still live and work on farms, millions of people continue to migrate to high-growth urban areas. Many are especially drawn to southeastern China, where China's communist government allows privately owned businesses in Hong Kong and in special economic zones. For factories in these special zones, the arrival of migrants means plenty of available labor, as one observer notes:

> *These* wailai gongren—*literally, external coming workers—outnumber the Dongguan population, with more arriving all the time. 'When I need workers,' a sweater factory manager said, 'I just put a sign outside the gate.'*
>
> Mike Edwards, "Boom Times on the Gold Coast of China," *National Geographic*, March 1997

In South Korea many people also have moved from rural areas, seeking industrial jobs in coastal cities. Politics, however, has affected migration on the Korean Peninsula. To escape communism, many people in the mid-1900s fled from North Korea to South Korea or to other countries, especially the United States and Canada, seeking political and economic freedom. Today South Korea has 48.8 million people, more than twice as many as North Korea, where the standard of living is much lower.

CRITICAL THINKING ACTIVITY

Problem Solving Have students review the text about the following population issues in East Asia: population growth rate, migration, and urbanization. Remind students that solutions begin with a clear expression of a concern and may include causes and effects. Organize the class into groups, and have each group analyze one of the issues listed above.
Ask: What is the history of the issue? Why is it a concern now? What are its apparent causes and effects? What is expected to happen in the future? What are East Asians doing about the issue? What else could be done? Have each group write a composition that clearly outlines the challenge, and share what they wrote with the class.
⊕ **EE4 Human Systems: Standard 9**

Challenges of Growth

Population changes and increasing urbanization have brought challenges to East Asia. In China and South Korea, for example, the steady migration from rural villages to cities has led to urban overcrowding. This population shift has contributed to farm labor shortages in the countryside. To stem migration from rural areas to already overcrowded urban areas, China, for example, has built dozens of new agricultural towns in remote areas. These towns are designed to provide more social services and a better quality of life for rural people. The Chinese government hopes that the benefits of the new towns will encourage people to stay on their farms.

▲ A family in Xi'an, China

Ever-growing populations in East Asia have put a strain on limited resources and services. Some of East Asia's governments see population control as another way to meet the challenges of population growth. In 1979 China began a policy that allowed each family to have no more than one child. Although not followed by all Chinese, the "one-child" policy until recently had been a factor in slowing China's population growth rate. Now that the policy is no longer strictly enforced,

China's population growth rate is increasing once again. Statistics presented in the population pyramid of China on page 662 suggest that a higher birthrate is largely responsible for the increased population growth rate.

Population changes will continue to play an important part in East Asia's future. In the next section, you will learn about the values and traditions that sustain East Asians as they face the many challenges of the future.

SECTION 1 ASSESSMENT

Checking for Understanding

1. **Define** aborigine, homogeneous.

2. **Main Ideas** Create a graphic organizer like the one below, and fill in key points about population distribution and density, ethnic groups, and migration. Summarize one of the three topics in terms of population patterns in East Asia.

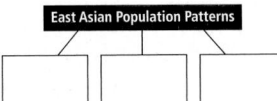
East Asian Population Patterns

Critical Thinking

3. **Drawing Conclusions** How does high-speed transportation in Japan affect daily life and the economy?

4. **Identifying Cause and Effect** Why has migration to urban areas increased in East Asia in recent years?

5. **Making Inferences** How might population growth and the continued migration of people from rural to urban areas affect East Asia's agricultural future?

Analyzing Graphs

6. **Place** Study the graph on page 662. How might China's demographic makeup affect the rural/urban distribution of its population?

Applying Geography

7. **Geography and Cities** Study the physical and political maps on pages 636–637. Describe the type of physical feature East Asia's major cities have in common.

Chapter 27 🌐 665

Section Quiz 27-1

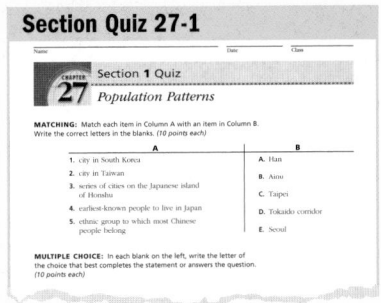

Reteach

Have students create a map of East Asia, adding icons, symbols, or shading to represent the percentages of ethnic groups in each country. Ask students to identify which countries are mostly homogeneous.

Enrich

Help students appreciate the cramped living conditions in Japan. Distribute floor plan grids of a three-room house. Have students arrange pictures of the furniture and appliances necessary to accommodate a family of four.

 **CLOSE**

Have pairs of students role-play a conversation between a travel agent and a person who wants to travel to East Asia. Each pair should ask and answer questions about one country in East Asia.

SECTION 1 ASSESSMENT ANSWERS

1. All vocabulary terms are defined in the text.

2. Diagrams should include key details about migration, population density, and ethnic variety in East Asia. Summaries should reflect the rural-to-urban migration trend; densely populated cities, coastal and river valley areas, and sparsely populated western areas; or the variety of ethnic groups in the region, despite relative homogeneity within each country.

3. enables commuters to travel great distances to work easily; increases the number of people working;

commute times may be long; personal or family time may be sacrificed

4. to find employment and a higher standard of living

5. It might result in farm labor and crop shortages.

6. China, with a relatively young population would have increased migration from rural to urban areas.

7. **Applying Geography** Most are located on lowlands, on coastlines or waterways.

GEOGRAPHY AND HISTORY

Have students locate the island of Taiwan on the inset map and on the Regional Atlas map on page 637. Have students use visuals and data from the "Country Profiles" on page 640 to compare and contrast basic facts about China and Taiwan. *(For example, China is 267 times larger than Taiwan in landmass and 57 times larger in population; China is a communist state, while Taiwan has a democratic form of government.)*

② TEACH

Inform students that in 2001 Taiwan dropped its ban on trade links with China. However, China still sees Taiwan as a renegade province. **Ask: What effects do you think Taiwan's action will have on China's attitude? Will it bring China and Taiwan closer or tend to divide them further?** *(Possible responses: Economic interdependence could bring one of the world's most valuable and active trading relationships; it will force both countries to have more direct trade, investment, political, and communication links; eventually, China might not declare war if it would jeopardize its trade relationship with other countries.)*

A TALE OF TWO CHINAS

WOULD YOU VOTE FOR A PRESI-DENTIAL CANDIDATE who occasionally donned a Superman costume? The citizens of Taiwan did when they elected Chen Shui-bian as their president. Neighboring China was infuriated, though not just because of the costume.

An Island Republic of China

Taiwan is a mountainous island located 90 miles (145 km) off China's coast. For most of its history, Taiwan has belonged to China. In 1949 the Chinese Nationalist Party, led by Chiang Kai-shek, lost its civil war against Mao Zedong's Communists. The battered Nationalist army fled to Taiwan with two million refugees. From Taipei, its capital-in-exile, the Nationalist regime maintained that it was the legitimate government of one China and vowed to recover control of the mainland. Taiwan called itself the Republic of China, while the Communist mainland took the name of the People's Republic of China.

United States intervention in the 1950s kept the more powerful Communists from conquering Taiwan. In step with the mainland, Taiwan pursued a goal of "one China"—two parts of one nation moving toward reunification. Taiwan wanted China's Communist government to change and to negotiate with Taiwan as an equal. Communist leaders, however, said no.

PEOPLE'S REPUBLIC OF CHINA

Taipei ⊛

Taiwan Strait

TAIWAN

N ↑

0 mi. 200
0 km 200

Taiwan's capital of Taipei bustles with economic activity. ▶

BACKGROUND INFORMATION

Economic Ties For decades Taiwan resisted the opening of direct trade, transportation, and communication with China, fearing that increasingly it would lead to Chinese domination. China favored direct trade with Taiwan, as a step toward reunification. In 1987 Taiwan began allowing people to conduct business with and visit family members in China. However, China continues to threaten to declare war with Taiwan unless Taiwan begins discussing the possibility of reunification. Nonetheless, economic ties between Taiwan and China continue to increase rapidly. In 2000 alone, trade between Taiwan and China increased by more than 22 percent, amounting to over $29 billion.

🌐 **EE4 Human Systems: Standards 11, 13**

◀ President Chen Shui-bian and Taiwan's first female vice president, Annette Lu, celebrate their win.

NATIONAL GEOGRAPHIC

From Rice Fields to Computer Chips

As the two sides haggled, many nations shifted their allegiance from Taiwan to China. The United States improved its relations with China in the 1970s and ended diplomatic relations with Taiwan. Meanwhile, life on the island was changing as dramatically as its alliances.

When the Nationalists first arrived in Taiwan, they found farmers cultivating rice fields in fertile valleys and a small population of native people living in the mountains. Taipei was an overgrown shantytown. The Nationalists quickly and brutally seized power. They allowed no local representation, and freedoms were limited.

In 1975 President Chiang Kai-shek died. When his son Chiang Ching-kuo was elected president in 1978, he began to institute democratic reforms. He ended martial law and legalized opposition political parties. By the 1990s Taiwan was a shining example of democracy in Asia. Prosperity transformed the island into an economic powerhouse. By comparison, China's communist economy was stagnant.

In 2000 Chen Shui-bian of the Democratic Progressive Party became the first ethnic Taiwanese and the first non-Nationalist to be elected president. Chen supports Taiwanese independence from the mainland—a stance that evokes angry reactions and military threats from China. Ever mindful of China's threats of war, Chen is working to improve ties with the mainland.

Today the economies of China and Taiwan are intertwined. Taiwan has invested billions of dollars in factories on the mainland. China, and the rest of the world, relies on Taiwan for key computer parts. With its strategic location and hardworking population, Taiwan is an important player in the global economy.

Looking Ahead

China advocates a "one country, two systems" approach to reunification with Taiwan. Most Taiwanese, however, would prefer to remain separate from China. How might China and Taiwan reconcile their differences for a better future for both countries?

1949 Chinese Nationalists, defeated by Chinese Communists, flee to Taiwan and establish government

1975 Nationalist leader Chiang Kai-shek (photo above) dies

1978 Chiang Ching-kuo elected president of Taiwan

1980s Taiwan institutes democratic reforms

1990s Taiwanese demonstrators (background photo) call for independence from China

1996 Taiwan holds first presidential elections; tensions with China escalate

2000 Chen Shui-bian wins presidential election; China threatens war unless Taiwan resumes reunification talks

FYI

Jobs As of 2001 over 30,000 factories owned or invested in by Taiwanese in China have provided a total of 3 million or more jobs for mainland Chinese.

❸ ASSESS

Have students answer the **Looking Ahead** question on page 667.

❹ CLOSE

Some observers believe the United States maintains somewhat contradictory policies regarding the two Chinas. On one hand, it cut off official diplomatic relations with Taiwan in 1979; on the other, Congress has passed laws to provide military support to Taiwan, a move that angers China. Have students debate the issue of United States military support of Taiwan.

🌐 Meeting National Standards

Geography for Life
The following standards are met in the Student Edition:

EE2 Places and Regions: Standard 4

EE4 Human Systems: Standards 9, 10, 11, 12, 13

EE6 The Uses of Geography: Standards 17, 18

ANSWERS TO LOOKING AHEAD

Some students may say that Taiwan should give up its claims of independence and accept being governed by China, because the Taiwanese are, in many ways, Chinese. Other students may say that Taiwan has become very different from communist China in the last 50 years, increasingly prosperous and democratic, and that the Taiwanese should be allowed to govern themselves. Some students may suggest that both China and Taiwan continue working together in business and trade and seek to avoid confrontation because they are mutually dependent. Students may argue that it is in China's best interest not to invade Taiwan, because a free Taiwan represents more future economic opportunities for China than a Taiwan whose economy is in shambles as a result of military takeover and a resentful population.

FOCUS

Section Overview

This section presents an overview of the history and governments of East Asia from ancient times to the present.

BELLRINGER
Skillbuilder Activity

Project transparency and have students answer questions.

Available as blackline master.

Daily Focus Skills Transparency 27-2

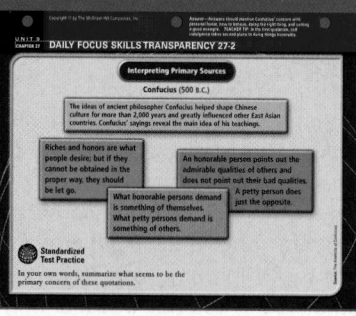

Guide to Reading

Consider What You Know
Answer *may include lack of contact due to great distances and natural barriers.*

Reading Strategy
Answers *ruled for 900 years; culture spread, trade grew, iron tools made; time of Confucius—system of thought based on discipline and moral conduct; time of Laozi—living in simplicity and harmony with nature*

Preteaching Vocabulary
Have students look up the definitions of *culture hearth* (page 668); *dynasty* (page 669); and *clans, shogun,* and *samurai* (page 670). Call on students to read aloud the sentences containing the definitions. Have other students use each term in a new sentence.

Guide to Reading

Consider What You Know
Many of the inventions we take for granted, such as printing, gunpowder, paper money, the compass, and the wheelbarrow, originated in ancient East Asia. Why do you think these ideas did not spread to the West until many centuries later?

Reading Strategy
Organizing Complete a graphic organizer similar to the one below by filling in details about the Zhou Dynasty.

The Zhou Dynasty
•
•
•

Read to Find Out
• Where did East Asia's ideas and traditions originate?

• How did East Asia first react to contact with the West?

• What major wars and revolutions occurred in East Asia?

Terms to Know
• culture hearth
• dynasty
• clan
• shogun
• samurai

Places to Locate
• Great Wall of China
• Guangzhou

History and Government

NATIONAL GEOGRAPHIC

A Geographic View

China's Buried Army

"A creation of awesome scale and accomplishment—an unforgettable symbol of the power of China's first emperor . . . Qin Shi Huang [Di] wanted an army with him after he died," says museum director Yuan. "His underground empire was a miniature of his real one." More than 700,000 laborers toiled 36 years building his monument.

—*O. Louis Mazzatenta, "China's Warriors Rise From the Earth,"* National Geographic, *October 1996*

Army of clay soldiers, China

In the Chinese city of Xi'an, archaeologists have unearthed thousands of life-size clay statues of soldiers and horses positioned as an army ready for battle. These burial statues were to protect the ancient Chinese ruler Qin Shi Huang Di (CHIHN SHIHR HWAHNG DEE) from threats in the afterlife. During the 200s B.C., Qin Huang Di ordered the building of the **Great Wall of China** to protect his empire. Archaeological finds, such as that of Qin Huang Di's tomb, reveal much about East Asia's long history and political heritage.

Ancient East Asia

East Asia is home to some of the world's oldest continuous civilizations. China, where the earliest East Asian civilization emerged, became the region's culture hearth, or a center from which ideas and practices spread to surrounding areas. Throughout history, China's influence helped shape East Asia's cultures. The Koreans and the Japanese, for example, blended Chinese ways with their own to form distinct cultural traditions.

RESOURCE MANAGER

Reproducible Masters
• Reproducible Lesson Plan 27-2
• Daily Lecture Notes 27-2
• Guided Reading Activity 27-2
• Reading Essentials and Study Guide 27-2
• Section Quiz 27-2

Transparencies
• Daily Focus Skills Transparency 27-2
• Political Map Transparency 9
• Unit 9 Map Overlay Transparencies

Multimedia
Interactive Tutor Self-Assessment CD-ROM
ExamView® Pro Testmaker CD-ROM
Presentation Plus! CD-ROM

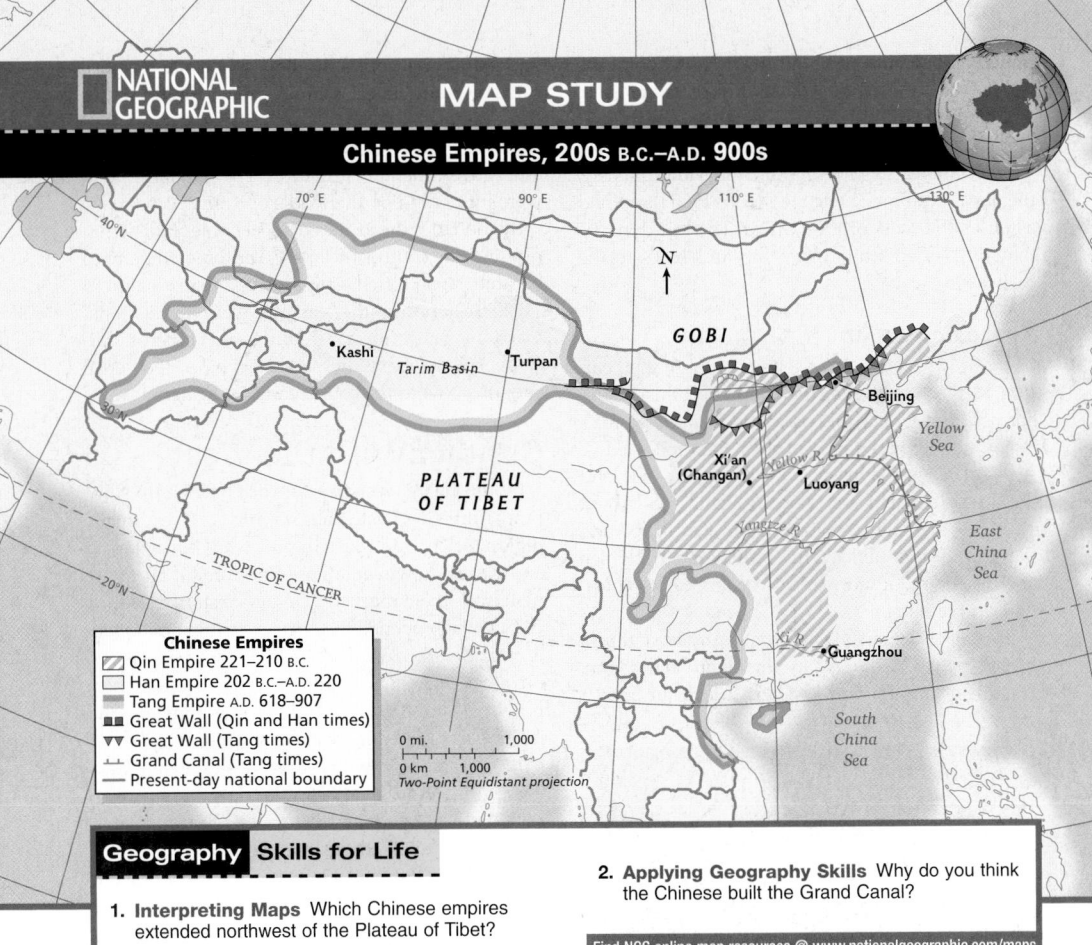

NATIONAL GEOGRAPHIC — MAP STUDY

Chinese Empires, 200s B.C.–A.D. 900s

Chinese Empires
- Qin Empire 221–210 B.C.
- Han Empire 202 B.C.–A.D. 220
- Tang Empire A.D. 618–907
- Great Wall (Qin and Han times)
- Great Wall (Tang times)
- Grand Canal (Tang times)
- Present-day national boundary

0 mi. 1,000
0 km 1,000
Two-Point Equidistant projection

Geography Skills for Life

1. **Interpreting Maps** Which Chinese empires extended northwest of the Plateau of Tibet?

2. **Applying Geography Skills** Why do you think the Chinese built the Grand Canal?

Find NGS online map resources @ www.nationalgeographic.com/maps

---

Government

China's Dynasties

Although China's culture began more than 5,000 years ago in the valley of the Wei River, a tributary of the Yellow River, historical records were first kept under the Shang **dynasty**. The dynasty, or ruling family, took power about 1600 B.C. in the North China Plain. Like all succeeding dynasties, the Shang faced rebellions by local lords, attacks by Central Asian nomads, and natural disasters such as floods. When the government was stable, it could defend its people against some of these problems. Eventually, however, the dynasty weakened and fell. According to the Chinese, a fallen

dynasty had lost "the mandate of heaven," the approval of the gods and goddesses.

After the Shang, the Zhou (JOH) dynasty ruled for 900 years, beginning about 1122 B.C. During the era of the Zhou dynasty, Chinese culture spread, trade grew, and the Chinese began making iron tools. China's best-known philosopher, Confucius (or Kongfuzi), lived during this time. He founded a system of thought based on discipline and moral conduct that for centuries influenced East Asian life. Another thinker, Laozi (or Lao-tzu), helped found Daoism, a philosophy of living in simplicity and harmony with nature.

After the Zhou, powerful dynasties expanded China's territory. In the 200s B.C., Qin Shi Huang Di

Chapter 27 🌐 **669**

TEACH

L1 Extending Content

Have students read the following: *The relationship between superiors and inferiors is like that between the wind and the grass. The grass must bend when the wind blows across it.* Invite students to discuss what the saying means, stating their personal interpretations, and whether they agree or disagree.

NATIONAL GEOGRAPHIC — MAP STUDY

Answers

1. *the Han and the Tang empires*

2. *to link the northern inland with seaports and the south; to link a north-south water route to east-west flowing rivers*

Map Skills Practice

Using the map scale, about how long was the Great Wall in Tang times? *(Answers will vary, accept 1,500–2,000 miles [2,414–3,219 km].)*

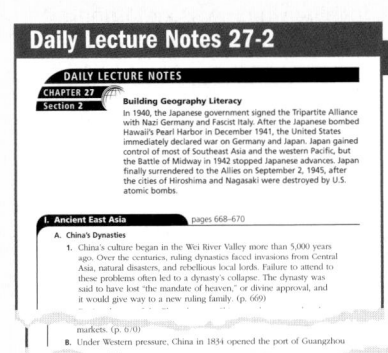

Daily Lecture Notes 27-2

DAILY LECTURE NOTES

CHAPTER 27
Section 2

Building Geography Literacy
In 1940, the Japanese government signed the Tripartite Alliance with Nazi Germany and Fascist Italy. After the Japanese bombed Hawaii's Pearl Harbor in December 1941, the United States immediately declared war on Germany and Japan. Japan gained control of most of Southeast Asia and the western Pacific, but the Battle of Midway in 1942 stopped Japanese advances. Japan finally surrendered to the Allies on September 2, 1945, after the cities of Hiroshima and Nagasaki were destroyed by U.S. atomic bombs.

I. Ancient East Asia pages 668–670

A. China's Dynasties

1. China's culture began in the Wei River Valley more than 5,000 years ago. Over the centuries, ruling dynasties faced invasions from Central Asia, natural disasters, and rebellious local lords. Failure to attend to these problems often led to a dynasty's collapse. The dynasty was said to have lost "the mandate of heaven," or divine approval, and it would give way to a new ruling family. (p. 669)

markets. (p. 670)

B. Under Western pressure, China in 1854 opened the port of Guangzhou

---

DIFFERENTIATED INSTRUCTION

At-Risk Students For students who have difficulty distinguishing the differences between similar words, this activity will help students provide better written responses to questions. Help students understand the differences between each direction word by providing the following hints. Students may wish to write each hint on a cue card.

Identify: name or describe. **Explain:** give reasons, tell how something works.
Describe: give qualities or characteristics. **List:** write examples. **Discuss:** includes all the above, plus personal opinions.

📁 Refer to *Inclusion for the Social Studies Classroom Strategies and Activities.*

L2 Time Line

Draw a long line across the board and write a date along the line for every 200-year period between 2000 B.C. and A.D. 2000. As students read the section, have volunteers mark and label each event named in the text in sequence along the line. Students may use this master time line to create individual time lines in their notebooks or journals for each East Asian country.

L1/ELL

Guided Reading Activity 27-2

Name _____ Date _____ Class _____

Guided Reading Activity 27-2

for use with textbook pages 668-672.

History and Government

Outline

DIRECTIONS: Use the information in your textbook to complete the following outline.

I. Ancient East Asia
   A. (1)
      1. Shang dynasty
      2. (2)
      3. Han dynasty
      4. Tang dynasty
      5. (3)
   B. Korea and Japan
      1. Chinese influences
      2. Korean Peninsula a cultural bridge

NATIONAL GEOGRAPHIC World Explorer

Answer
They helped shoguns govern the country.

More About the Photo
Samurai followed a strict code of conduct, including stoicism, bravery, honor, and personal loyalty, which was held dearer than life itself.

---

united all of China and built the first section of the Great Wall to ward off attacks from Central Asia. Under the Han and Tang dynasties, traders and missionaries took Chinese culture to all of East Asia. In the early 1400s, under the Ming dynasty, the naval explorer Zheng He (JUNG HUH) reached as far as the coast of East Africa. The last dynasty, the Qing, ruled China from the mid-1600s to the early 1900s.

Korea and Japan

About 1200 B.C. Chinese settlers brought their culture to the neighboring Koreans. Buddhism later spread from China to Korea and became Korea's major religion. In the centuries that followed, a series of Korean dynasties, including the Silla and the Koryo, united the Korean Peninsula. About A.D. 1300 the Chinese seized control of Korea and introduced the philosophy of Confucius, which became the model for Korea's government, education, and family life.

The Korean Peninsula was for centuries a cultural bridge between the Asian mainland and Japan. As a result, China and Korea had a major impact

NATIONAL GEOGRAPHIC World Explorer

Geography Skills for Life

Japanese History A Japanese man performs as a samurai in a historical reenactment.
Region Why were samurai important to Japanese history?

---

on Japan's civilization. In the A.D. 400s Japan, once ruled by many **clans**, or family groups, united under the Yamato dynasty. Yamato rulers adopted China's philosophy, writing system, art, sciences, and governmental structure. The Japanese also were influenced by the works of Korean scholars.

By the 1100s the armies of local nobles had begun fighting for control of Japan. Yoritomo Minamoto became Japan's first **shogun**, or military ruler, in 1192. Supporting the shogun were professional warriors, or **samurai**. Although an emperor officially ruled Japan, the samurai helped powerful shoguns govern the country until the late 1800s.

Contact With the West

By the 1600s Western countries had set up shipping routes to East Asia, hoping to share in the region's rich trade in silk and tea. China, Japan, and Korea, however, all rejected foreign efforts to penetrate their markets. Under Western pressure, China finally opened the port of **Guangzhou** to limited trade in 1834. Dissatisfied, Europeans used powerful warships to force China to open more ports. By the 1890s, European governments and Japan had claimed large areas of China as *spheres of influence*—areas in which they had exclusive trading rights. Deadlocked by rivalries, these powers reluctantly agreed in 1899 to a U.S. proposal to open China to all countries for trade.

During the 1800s the United States also worked to open Japan for trade. In 1854 U.S. naval officer Matthew C. Perry pressured the Japanese to change their policy. He and Japanese officials negotiated a treaty that ended centuries of Japanese isolation and opened Japan to trade with the United States. Not long afterward, rebel samurai forced shoguns to return full authority to the emperor. Japan's new government rapidly modernized the country's economy, government, and military forces.

Modern East Asia

During the 1900s East Asia as a whole was involved in two world wars. Meanwhile, each East Asian country faced its own internal upheavals.

Revolutionary China

In 1911 a revolution led by Sun Yat-sen ended the rule of emperors in China. By 1927 a military

---

COOPERATIVE LEARNING ACTIVITY

Regional Summit Organize students into six groups, one each for China, Taiwan, Japan, Mongolia, North Korea, and South Korea. Based on information in this section and available references, groups should prepare a mock regional summit to discuss their type of government and clarify their relationships with each other. Allow time for groups to research current foreign policy issues and prepare speeches or presentations. Have representatives meet to compose an agenda and order of speakers. Then hold the mock regional summit conference. Each speaker should begin by describing the country's type of government and explaining its current foreign policy. Students can work toward treaties that solve disagreements. **EE4 Human Systems: Standards 11, 13**

NATIONAL GEOGRAPHIC — MAP STUDY

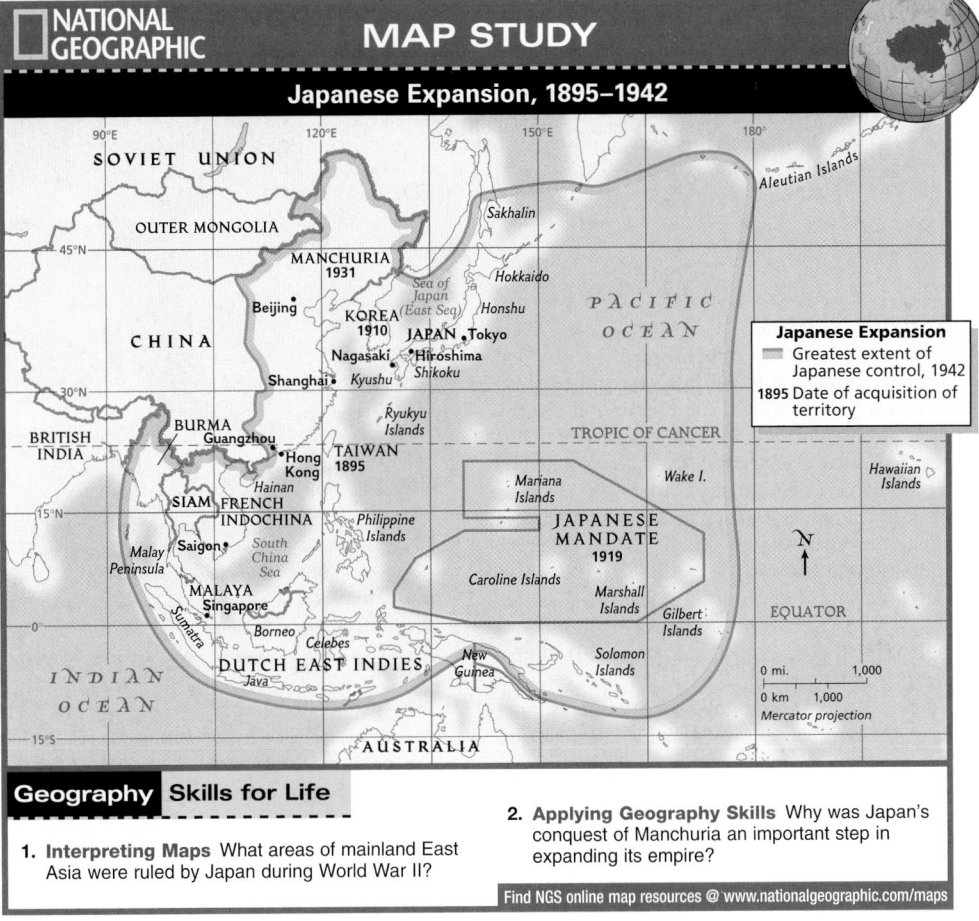

Japanese Expansion, 1895–1942

Japanese Expansion
- Greatest extent of Japanese control, 1942
- **1895** Date of acquisition of territory

Mercator projection

Geography — Skills for Life

1. **Interpreting Maps** What areas of mainland East Asia were ruled by Japan during World War II?

2. **Applying Geography Skills** Why was Japan's conquest of Manchuria an important step in expanding its empire?

Find NGS online map resources @ www.nationalgeographic.com/maps

---

leader, Chiang Kai-shek, had formed the Nationalist government. Meanwhile, Chiang's communist rival, Mao Zedong, gained support from China's farmers. After years of civil war, the Communists won power in 1949 and set up the People's Republic of China on the Chinese mainland. The Nationalists fled to Taiwan and set up a government called the Republic of China.

In the late 1900s, the People's Republic of China maintained strict communist political rule. However, pressures to modernize gradually opened China's economy to free-market influences. Meanwhile, Taiwan built a powerful, export-based economy and carried out democratic reforms.

Japan's Transformation

From the 1890s to the 1940s, Japan used diplomacy and military force to build an empire that included Taiwan (then called Formosa), Korea, other parts of mainland Asia, and numerous Pacific islands. This expansion was one factor that led Japan to fight the United States and other Allied countries in World War II. After its defeat in 1945, Japan became a democracy. Stripped of its overseas territories and military might, Japan rebuilt its shattered economy and society. By the late 1900s, it had emerged as a global economic power with worldwide trading and business links. One retired official described the change this way:

NATIONAL GEOGRAPHIC — MAP STUDY

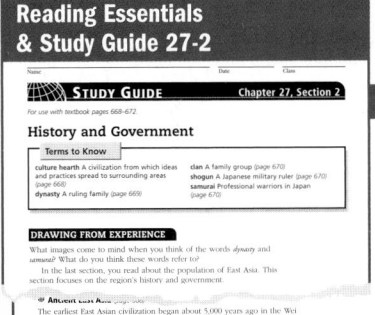

Answers

1. *Manchuria and coastal China, Korea, parts of Southeast Asia and Pacific area*

2. *It led to Japan's expansion into China.*

Map Skills Practice

Location What is the approximate longitude and latitude of Shanghai? *(about 122° east longitude, 32° north latitude)*

L1/ELL

Reading Essentials & Study Guide 27-2

STUDY GUIDE — Chapter 27, Section 2

For use with textbook pages 668–672

History and Government

Terms to Know

culture hearth A civilization from which ideas and practices spread to surrounding areas (page 668)
dynasty A ruling family (page 669)
clan A family group (page 670)
shogun A Japanese military ruler (page 670)
samurai Professional warriors in Japan (page 670)

DRAWING FROM EXPERIENCE

What images come to mind when you think of the words *dynasty* and *samurai*? What do you think these words refer to?

In the last section, you read about the population of East Asia. This section focuses on the region's history and government.

Ancient East Asia (page 668)

The earliest East Asian civilization began about 5,000 years ago in the Wei River valley of China. It became the region's **culture hearth**, or a center from which ideas and practices spread to surrounding areas. Historical records were first kept under the Shang **dynasty**, or ruling family. This

---

□ **NATIONAL GEOGRAPHIC** **GEOFACT**

▶ The Demilitarized Zone that separates North and South Korea has become an unofficial nature preserve. Untouched by humans for nearly 50 years, the region is home to some rare and endangered species.

ASSESS

Assign Section 2 Assessment as homework or as an in-class activity.

🌐 Have students use **Interactive Tutor Self-Assessment CD-ROM**.

CRITICAL THINKING ACTIVITY

Making Inferences Remind students that reading a textbook often requires the reader to infer the meanings of terms used. Have students reread the paragraph that begins at the end of page 670. Ask students to infer and explain the meaning of "cultural bridge" from information in the paragraph. *(Cultural ideas in philosophy, sciences, technology, arts, writing, and government spread from China through Korea to Japan.)* Repeat the process for the following phrases: "the mandate of heaven" on page 669, "spheres of influence" on page 670; "market economy" and "democratic constitution" on page 672.

🌐 **EE4 Human Systems: Standards 10, 13**

 **NATIONAL GEOGRAPHIC** **World Explorer**

Answer
The two countries have been enemies for more than 50 years, and negotiations may improve relations.

More About the Photo Religious practices in North Korea are nearly non-existent. In South Korea, 47 percent of the people practice Buddhism.

L2

Section Quiz 27-2

Reteach

Have students copy the questions provided in "Read to Find Out" (page 668) on a blank sheet of paper. Have them reread pages 668–672 and note details that answer the questions.

Enrich

Show scenes from the films *The Last Emperor* (1987) and *The Seven Samurai* (1954) to provide glimpses into East Asia's history.

4 CLOSE

Have teams write questions on one side of an index card and the answers on the other side. Have teams quiz each other.

> *After the war, Japan was in chaos. There was regret, suffering. There were no rich then, only poor. We pulled together, worked hard, geared our economy for export. . . . Now we're prosperous, and we're bringing that prosperity to others.* "
>
> Arthur Zich, "Japan's Sun Rises Over the Pacific," *National Geographic*, November 1991

A Divided Korea

After World War II ended, Korea was divided into American-backed South Korea and communist-ruled North Korea. Wanting to unite Korea, North Korea invaded South Korea in 1950. During the Korean War, United Nations forces, led by the United States, rushed to South Korea's defense. By June 1951, each army had dug in along the thirty-eighth parallel. The stalemate ended with a truce in 1953. Millions of Koreans had died and both countries were devastated. Today, North Korea and South Korea are still separated by the cease-fire line along the thirty-eighth parallel.

North Korea's communist society often cannot meet the basic needs of its people. South Korea has become a democracy with a prosperous market economy. In 2000, talks between North Korea and South Korea helped to improve their relations. This progress ended, however, when North Korea reactivated its nuclear reactor in 2002.

NATIONAL GEOGRAPHIC **World Explorer**

Geography | **Skills for Life**

A Historic Meeting A monk reads about the historic meeting of North Korea's Kim Jong Il and South Korea's Kim Dae Jung in June 2000.
Place Why was the meeting between the two leaders considered historic?

A Free Mongolia

Under the Soviet Union's influence, Mongolia was a communist state from 1924 to 1991. After the collapse of Soviet communism, the Mongolians adopted a democratic constitution that opened the way for free elections and a market economy, reflecting a growing openness to new ideas in East Asia.

SECTION 2 ASSESSMENT

Checking for Understanding

1. **Define** culture hearth, dynasty, clan, shogun, samurai.
2. **Main Ideas** On tables like the one below, summarize each East Asian country's history and government during each time period.

Country: _____

Ancient Times (3000 B.C. to A.D. 1600)	
Contact With the West (1600s–1900s)	
Modern Times (1900s to present)	

Critical Thinking

3. **Drawing Conclusions** Why were European powers dissatisfied with China's opening of the port of Guangzhou?
4. **Comparing and Contrasting** How were economic developments in Taiwan and South Korea during the 1900s similar and different?
5. **Making Inferences** Why do you think the Chinese Nationalists who fled to Taiwan called their government the Republic of China?

Analyzing Maps

6. **Human-Environment Interaction** Study the map of Chinese empires on page 669. Which rivers are linked by the Grand Canal?

Applying Geography

7. **Spread of Culture** Draw a map of East Asia to show the spread of Chinese culture in the region. Use arrows to show key movements. Then write an explanation of your map.

SECTION 2 ASSESSMENT ANSWERS

1. All vocabulary terms are defined in the text.
2. Tables should contain details for each time period.
3. They wanted other ports to open.
4. Possible answers: similar—both experienced effects of communist uprisings, both countries prospered under a market economy; different—China and Taiwan developed informal economic ties, North and South Korea did not.
5. They wished to be identified as the freely elected government of the Chinese people.
6. the Yellow River and the Yangtze River
7. **Applying Geography** Students' maps and paragraphs should include facts on the movement of Chinese culture through Korea to Japan.

Cultures and Lifestyles

NATIONAL GEOGRAPHIC

A Geographic View

A Spiritual Journey

As early as the [A.D. 400s], caves were carved into the sandstone cliffs of the Tian Shan range as shrines and places of worship for [Buddhists]. . . . Worshipers built these shrines in hopes of . . . personal well-being, a safe and prosperous journey, advancement in the next life, or perhaps the birth of many healthy sons. . . .

—Reza, "Pilgrimage to China's Buddhist Caves," National Geographic, April 1996

Worshipers at Buddhist shrine, China

The peoples of East Asia have a long and rich cultural heritage. Since ancient times the ideas and practices of three religious traditions—Confucianism, Buddhism, and Shintoism—have profoundly influenced the region. In the modern era, communism also has had a major impact on the peoples and cultures of China, North Korea, and Mongolia. East Asians also have adopted many aspects of Western culture. In this section you will learn about the variety of cultures and lifestyles found in East Asia today.

East Asia's Languages

Because of their diverse backgrounds, people in East Asia speak languages from several different language families. The largest, Sino-Tibetan, which includes Chinese and Tibetan, comprises languages spoken by more than 1.2 billion people. Other principal languages of East Asia include Japanese, Korean, Khalkha Mongolian, and Uygur—spoken in western China.

Chapter 27 🌐 **673**

Guide to Reading

Consider What You Know

East Asian food, art, pottery, and sports have become popular around the world. What foods and other products from East Asia are found in your community?

Reading Strategy

Taking Notes Use the major headings of the section to create an outline similar to the one below.

> I. East Asia's Languages
>   A.
>   B.
> II. Religion and Philosophy

Read to Find Out

- What languages do the peoples of East Asia speak?
- What religions and philosophies do many people of East Asia follow?
- How do the standards of living of East Asians compare with one another?
- How does education in East Asia compare with education in North America?
- What traditional arts make East Asia unique?

Terms to Know

- ideogram
- shamanism
- lama
- acupuncture
- haiku
- calligraphy
- pagoda

Places to Locate

- Mongolia
- Tibet

FOCUS

Section Overview

This section discusses the beliefs, lifestyles, and traditional arts of East Asia.

BELLRINGER
Skillbuilder Activity

📽 Project transparency and have students answer questions.

🗀 Available as blackline master.

Daily Focus Skills Transparency 27-3

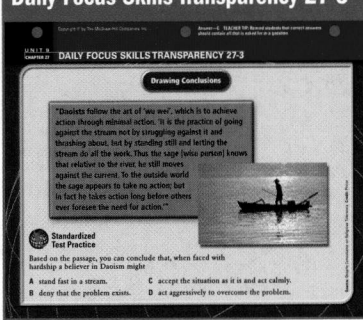

Guide to Reading

Consider What You Know
Answer *foods such as stir-fry vegetables and egg rolls, electronic equipment, cars, household appliances, acrobatics, karate, taiji (tai chi), and sumo wrestling*

Reading Strategy
Answer Students should complete the outline by including all heads in the section.

Preteaching Vocabulary
🔵 Use the **Vocabulary Puzzle-Maker CD-ROM** to create crossword and word-search puzzles.

RESOURCE MANAGER

🗀 **Reproducible Masters**
- Reproducible Lesson Plan 27-3
- Vocabulary Activity 27
- Daily Lecture Notes 27-3
- Guided Reading Activity 27-3
- Reading Essentials and Study Guide 27-3
- Reteaching Activity 27
- Reinforcing Skills Activity 27
- Section Quiz 27-3

📽 **Transparencies**
- Daily Focus Skills Transparency 27-3
- Unit 9 Map Overlay Transparencies

Multimedia
- 💿 Vocabulary PuzzleMaker CD-ROM
- 🎵 World Music: A Cultural Legacy
- 💿 Interactive Tutor Self-Assessment CD-ROM
- 💿 ExamView® Pro Testmaker CD-ROM
- 💿 Presentation Plus! CD-ROM

2 TEACH

L1 Identify

After students read pages 673–674, have them make a list of the principal East Asian languages named in the text. Using an outline map of East Asia, ask students to create a regional map and map key showing the locations where each language is most common.

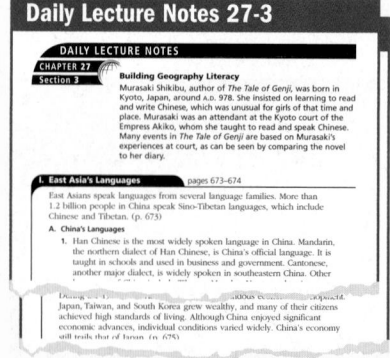

Daily Lecture Notes 27-3

DAILY LECTURE NOTES

CHAPTER 27
Section 3

Building Geography Literacy
Murasaki Shikibu, author of *The Tale of Genji*, was born in Kyoto, Japan, around A.D. 978. She insisted on learning to read and write Chinese, which was unusual for girls of that time and place. Murasaki was an attendant at the Kyoto court of the Empress Akiko, whom she taught to read and speak Chinese. Many events in *The Tale of Genji* are based on Murasaki's experiences at court, as can be seen by comparing the novel to her diary.

I. East Asia's Languages pages 673–674

East Asians speak languages from several language families. More than 1.2 billion people in China speak Sino-Tibetan languages, which include Chinese and Tibetan. (p. 673)

A. China's Languages

1. Han Chinese is the most widely spoken language in China. Mandarin, the northern dialect of Han Chinese, is China's official language. It is taught in schools and used in business and government. Cantonese, another major dialect, is widely spoken in southeastern China. Other...

...Japan, Taiwan, and South Korea grew wealthy, and many of their citizens achieved high standards of living. Although China enjoyed significant economic advances, individual conditions varied widely. China's economy still trails that of Japan. (p. 675)

NATIONAL GEOGRAPHIC — GRAPH STUDY

Answers

1. *Chinese religion (Confucianism/Daoism) and Buddhism*

2. *They have suppressed religious practice.*

Skills Practice

Why is there such a large "nonreligious" sector? *Communist governments in China and North Korea discourage religion, and most people in these countries do not openly profess a faith.*

China's Languages

Han Chinese, the most widely spoken language of China, has many dialects. Mandarin, the northern dialect, has become China's official language. It is taught in schools and used in business and government. Cantonese, another major dialect, is widely spoken in southeastern China. Other languages of China include Tibetan, Manchu, Uygur, and Mongolian dialects.

Unlike Western languages that use letters to stand for sounds in spoken language, Chinese languages use **ideograms**, pictures or symbols that stand for ideas. Chinese has thousands of ideograms. Each ideogram has one meaning, but combining it with other ideograms gives it a new meaning. For example, the ideogram for "man" next to the ideogram for "word" means standing by one's word, or "sincerity." Spoken Chinese languages also depend on tone, or pitch. Similar syllables, pronounced with different tones or inflections, take on different meanings.

Japanese and Korean Languages

Although the Japanese language developed in isolation, experts believe it may be distantly related to Korean and Mongolian. Over centuries, both Japanese and Korean languages borrowed words from Chinese. Japanese had no written form until the A.D. 400s, when Chinese writing and literature were introduced into Japan. Japan's first writing system was based on Chinese characters. Western languages, especially English, have also influenced Japanese and Korean languages.

Religion and Philosophy

East Asians hold a variety of philosophical and religious beliefs, including Confucianism, Buddhism, and Daoism. They also may follow more than one religion. Many Japanese, for example, practice both Buddhism and Shintoism, an ancient Japanese religion that stresses reverence for nature. Other religions of East Asia include Christianity,

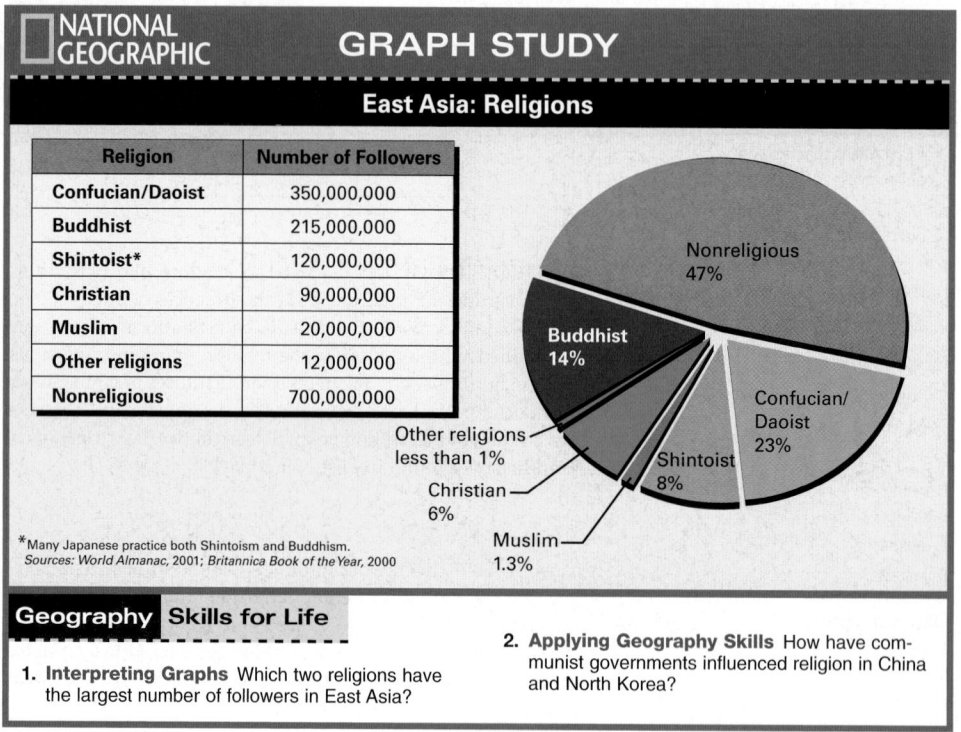

NATIONAL GEOGRAPHIC — **GRAPH STUDY**

East Asia: Religions

Religion	Number of Followers
Confucian/Daoist	350,000,000
Buddhist	215,000,000
Shintoist*	120,000,000
Christian	90,000,000
Muslim	20,000,000
Other religions	12,000,000
Nonreligious	700,000,000

Nonreligious 47%
Buddhist 14%
Confucian/Daoist 23%
Shintoist 8%
Muslim 1.3%
Christian 6%
Other religions less than 1%

*Many Japanese practice both Shintoism and Buddhism.
Sources: World Almanac, 2001; Britannica Book of the Year, 2000

Geography Skills for Life

1. **Interpreting Graphs** Which two religions have the largest number of followers in East Asia?

2. **Applying Geography Skills** How have communist governments influenced religion in China and North Korea?

DIFFERENTIATED INSTRUCTION

English Learners Pair English language learners with English-proficient students. Have students take turns reading paragraphs aloud to each other while the other follows along in the text. When students finish a section, have them practice summarizing the main points of the section aloud in their own words. Suggest that one student explain the main idea(s), followed by the other student describing at least three details that support each main idea. Remind students that main ideas are often stated in one or two sentences at or near the beginning of a paragraph, usually followed by examples or details. **ELL**

Refer to **Inclusion for the Social Studies Classroom Strategies and Activities.**

widely practiced in Korea, and Islam, which has many followers among the Uygur people of western China. Some East Asians also practice shamanism, faith in leaders believed to have powers to heal the sick and to communicate with spirits.

Communist governments in China and North Korea strongly discourage all religious practices, but many people still hold to their traditional faiths. Before communism, Buddhist religious leaders called lamas ruled in Mongolia and Tibet. When communist governments came to power, they began to persecute Buddhists. Mongolia is now a democracy, and Mongolian citizens are again free to engage in religious practices.

In Tibet, however, the Chinese government continues to place harsh restrictions on the Buddhist population. For example, Tibetans risk arrest just for owning photographs of the Dalai Lama, Tibet's exiled spiritual leader. The Dalai Lama currently leads a worldwide movement in support of Tibetan rights from his place of exile in neighboring India.

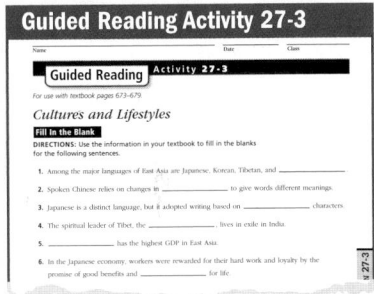

The Dalai Lama

Standard of Living

During the late 1900s, booming economies in East Asia improved standards of living for many of the region's peoples. In wealthy countries, such as Japan, Taiwan, and South Korea, lifestyles have improved dramatically in the last few decades. Yet large gaps remain between the rich and the poor. In economically developing countries, such as China, glittering steel-and-glass skyscrapers in the cities stand in sharp contrast to the mud houses in the surrounding rural areas.

One indicator of a country's standard of living is gross domestic product (GDP) per capita, or the value of goods and services each person produces. By 2000, for example, Japan's GDP per capita was $32,350, the highest in the region. By comparison, China's GDP, at $750 per capita, was one of the lowest.

Economy
Japan's Downturn and Recovery

The Japanese traditionally have valued individual loyalty to society in return for society's protection and support. Japanese businesses often ran on the principles of teamwork and cooperation. White-collar workers had secure lifetime jobs with benefits, such as insurance programs, leave-of-absence policies, and opportunities to buy company stock.

In 1997 many of these traditions were pushed aside when Japan, along with other Asian countries, suffered a severe economic downturn. Thousands of companies went bankrupt, and financial pressures forced the companies that survived to operate more efficiently. For the first time, companies had to lay off large numbers of workers.

Since 2000, Japan's economy has still been faltering. Declining sales continue to force companies to lay off workers, and huge debts threaten to cripple the banking industry. Hesitant to spend, many Japanese consumers face housing shortages because of higher costs and lack of confidence in the economy. Meanwhile, Japan's business practices have changed. As companies focus more on profits and less on workers' job security, workers, in turn, have less loyalty to their companies.

China's New Direction

During the 1970s a new communist leadership came to power in China after the death of Mao Zedong. The most prominent leader, Deng Xiaoping (DUHNG SHOW•PIHNG), took China in a new economic direction, summed up in his phrase, "To get rich is glorious." After years of strict control

 GEOGRAPHY *Online*

Student Web Activity Visit the **Glencoe World Geography** Web site at geography.glencoe.com and click on Student Web Activities—Chapter 27 for an activity about cultures and traditions of China, Japan, and the Koreas.

Chapter 27 ⊕ **675**

L2 Math
Have students create a circle graph to compare the standards of living in East Asian countries, using the per capita GDP figures on page 675 and additional figures from a world almanac. Students can compare a country's total GDP, which represents 100 percent, calculate the percentage of the total that each of the GDPs represents, and portray and label each percentage in the circle.

L1/ELL

Guided Reading Activity 27-3

Name	Date	Class

Guided Reading Activity 27-3

For use with textbook pages 673–679

Cultures and Lifestyles

Fill in the Blank

DIRECTIONS: Use the information in your textbook to fill in the blanks for the following sentences.

1. Among the major languages of East Asia are Japanese, Korean, Tibetan, and _____.
2. Spoken Chinese relies on changes in _____ to give words different meanings.
3. Japanese is a distinct language, but it adopted writing based on _____ characters.
4. The spiritual leader of Tibet, the _____, lives in exile in India.
5. _____ has the highest GDP in East Asia.
6. In the Japanese economy, workers were rewarded for their hard work and loyalty by the promise of good benefits and _____ for a time.

Japan Keeping alive the traditional arts is so important that the government recognizes some individual artists, performers, or artisans with the title of "living national treasure." These distinguished artists receive financial support to practice and teach their arts.

GEOGRAPHY *Online*

Objectives, goals, and answers to the student activity can be found in the Web Activity Lesson Plan feature at geography.glencoe.com

---

COOPERATIVE LEARNING ACTIVITY

Cultural Fair Assign small groups of students a topic based on the subheadings found on pages 677–679. Have students work together to present an East Asian cultural fair. Allow time for students to further research each topic, and to prepare a creative presentation or display. Students may gather photographs of East Asian life today, read excerpts of traditional literature and drama, play and comment on a recording of East Asian music, or prepare traditional East Asian foods to share with the class.

⊕ **EE2 Places and Regions: Standard 4**
⊕ **EE4 Human Systems: Standard 10**

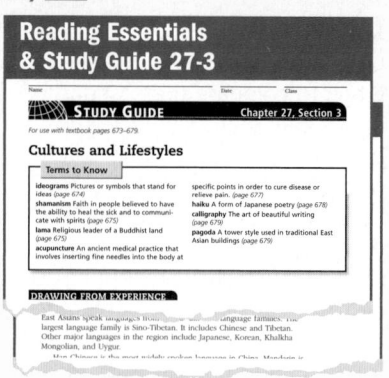

L1/ELL

Reading Essentials & Study Guide 27-3

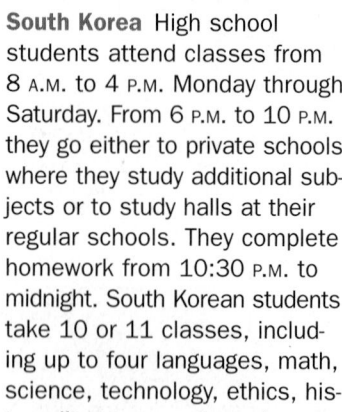

Culture NOTE

South Korea High school students attend classes from 8 A.M. to 4 P.M. Monday through Saturday. From 6 P.M. to 10 P.M. they go either to private schools where they study additional subjects or to study halls at their regular schools. They complete homework from 10:30 P.M. to midnight. South Korean students take 10 or 11 classes, including up to four languages, math, science, technology, ethics, history, literature, and music.

NATIONAL GEOGRAPHIC World Explorer

Answer
The country has an agricultural economy, and past government control of businesses and farms failed to improve the economy.

More About the Photo Once the capital of the Shu dynasty (A.D. 221), Chengdu today remains a major cultural center, with several universities and colleges and a thriving electronics industry.

over China's economy, China's communist leaders began allowing some free enterprise as a result of economic and political setbacks during the 1950s and 1960s.

During the "Great Leap Forward" campaign of the 1950s, large government-owned farms had replaced the small-scale farm cooperatives. The new farms, however, failed to produce enough food for the country. About 20 million Chinese died of starvation, and the economy crumbled.

To move China forward, Deng Xiaoping allowed private ownership of businesses and farms. Chinese officials welcomed foreign businesses and technology to China. Foreign investment flowed into special economic zones where foreigners could own and operate businesses with little government interference. The resulting economic growth raised the standards of living of some Chinese. Despite progress, China's economy is still agricultural, and the majority of Chinese have a lower standard of living than do other East Asians.

Education and Health

Most East Asians highly value learning. Today elementary education is free throughout the region, and opportunities for higher education have expanded greatly. Better education and higher standards of living have also improved the region's health care.

Literacy and Learning

In the several East Asian countries that spend the most money for education, the literacy rate is high. Nearly all Japanese can read and write, and South Korea has a literacy rate of 98 percent. The literacy rate for Taiwanese and North Koreans is 95 percent. China and Mongolia, however, have a lower literacy rate of about 82 percent.

In the past only the wealthiest Chinese learned to read and write, but China's communist government has pushed to increase literacy. During the Cultural Revolution, a period of upheaval in the late 1960s,

NATIONAL GEOGRAPHIC World Explorer

Geography Skills for Life
Chinese Life The sharp contrasts of Chinese life can be seen in the bustling city of Chengdu in Sichuan Province and in the quiet rural landscape that surrounds the city.
Place Why do the majority of Chinese have a lower standard of living than do other East Asians?

CRITICAL THINKING ACTIVITY

Making Comparisons Have students create a bar graph or pictograph that compares the literacy rates in East Asian countries. Students may write generalizations about East Asian countries, based on the graph. (*Example: Japan and South Korea have the highest literacy rates in East Asia, while Mongolia and China have the lowest.*) Next, have students add a bar to the graph for the United States literacy rate. Have students write a generalization comparing the United States literacy rate to those in East Asia. **Ask:** What factors might account for the differences between the United States and Asian countries? (*Accept reasonable responses.*) **EE4 Human Systems: Standard 10**

the growth of literacy, however, suffered a brief setback. During this time, schools and factories closed and people believed to be enemies of Mao Zedong's form of communism were persecuted. After Mao's death the Chinese government again emphasized education, and literacy has steadily risen.

Young South Koreans spend an average of 14 years in school and are among East Asia's best-educated students. South Korea and Taiwan believe that educational excellence supports the high performance of their economies.

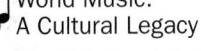
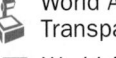

▲ *Chinese New Year celebrations (above) and Japanese professional baseball (right)*

Health Care

Better health care has raised life expectancies, and infant mortality has declined in East Asia. The average life expectancy is about 74 years for women and 70 years for men. Communist governments generally pay for medical treatment. As China moves toward a market economy, however, its government no longer guarantees equal access to health care. As a result, the gap in the quality of health care between urban areas and rural areas is widening.

Many East Asians rely on both Western and traditional medical care, including herbal medicines. Acupuncture, an ancient practice that involves inserting fine needles into the body at specific points in order to cure disease or relieve pain, is popular in China. Both herbal medicine and acupuncture are widely accepted around the world.

Leisure Activities

East Asians engage in a variety of leisure activities, ranging from music to sports. Recreation frequently involves family activities. Because of small living quarters in many urban areas, people often socialize in public parks and restaurants.

Food

Although cooking styles vary throughout the region, East Asians prefer staple foods, such as rice, wheat, and millet. Many East Asians maintain vegetarian diets or get protein from fish. Western foods, such as beef, chicken, and dairy products, recently have become popular. As a result, more East Asians now have health problems associated with a Western diet.

Sports and Festivals

East Asians of all ages practice traditional exercises and martial arts, such as tai chi, tae kwon do, *gongfu* (kung fu), or karate. Japan's ancient sport of sumo wrestling draws thousands of fans to several tournaments each year. East Asians also enjoy many Western sports, such as baseball, soccer, and volleyball. Olympic champions in skiing, swimming, gymnastics, table tennis, and other sports have come from East Asia.

Colorful celebrations mark the seasons of the year, national holidays, and religious ideas or events in East Asia. Many people participate in parades and ceremonies related to the Confucian, Daoist, Buddhist, and Shintoist religions. People in East Asia also commemorate the Lunar New Year, which begins in late January or early February. The Lunar New Year reflects the lunar calendar, which is based on the phases of the moon instead of Earth's movements around the sun.

INTERDISCIPLINARY
connection

MATH As early as the 1500s B.C., the Chinese inscribed numerals on bones and tortoise shells, with specific characters representing units for tens, hundreds, thousands, and ten thousands. The *suan pan*, a Chinese abacus or calculating device, is a forerunner of modern calculators and computers. It has been in use since about A.D. 1200. The Japanese abacus, or *soroban*, developed from the Chinese abacus in the A.D. 1600s. Expert users of these devices can perform calculations more rapidly than some mechanical calculating machines.

GEOGRAPHY AND THE HUMANITIES

♫ World Music: A Cultural Legacy

World Art and Architecture Transparencies

World Art Prints

TEAM-TEACHING ACTIVITY: LANGUAGE ARTS

Writing a Biographical Sketch Have students scan through Section 3 (pages 673–679) to locate the names of religious leaders, writers, and artists. List the names on the board as students find them. Have each student research one of these or other people who have made significant cultural contributions to East Asia. After students have done their research, have them work with an English teacher to write a biographical sketch of their person, highlighting key events and contributions.
▦ **EE4 Human Systems: Standard 10**

Music Notes
Traditional East Asian music is linear, having melody, but no harmony. It often seeks to create the maximum effect from few sources (a solo instrument, a small ensemble). Objectives are quite different than in the West, and like East Asian ink drawings and poetry, plenty of space is left in order to bring out the simplicity and beauty of each component.

World Music: A Cultural Legacy
Use the accompanying Teacher Guide for information and worksheets about the music of this region.

③ ASSESS

Assign Section 3 Assessment as homework or as an in-class activity.

🌐 Have students use **Interactive Tutor Self-Assessment CD-ROM** to review Section 3.

L2

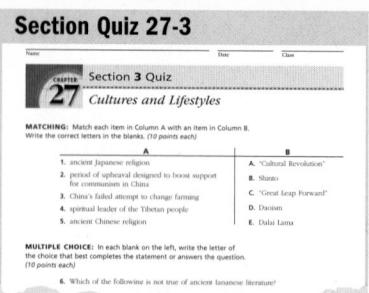

Section Quiz 27-3

music of EAST ASIA

Under Chinese influence, music in East Asia has evolved over thousands of years. Used for both spiritual and entertainment purposes, music of the region is characterized by the use of strings, wind instruments, and percussion.

Instrument Spotlight
The **shakuhachi** is a bamboo flute from Japan with five finger holes. This unique wind instrument arrived in Japan through China during the A.D. 600s and 700s. Unlike other instruments, the shakuhachi developed a strong collection of solo pieces and was used by Zen Buddhist monks as a form of spiritual practice and for meditation. This music usually has a peaceful effect on both the player and the listener.

Go To **World Music: A Cultural Legacy** Hear music of this region on Disc 2, Tracks 14–18.

The Arts

Over the centuries East Asians have excelled in the arts. Their artistic and literary achievements are deeply rooted in the long history of the region. During ancient times Chinese styles in art and architecture influenced all of East Asia. Religions such as Confucianism, Daoism, Buddhism, and Shintoism also have inspired great art in the region. In modern times Mao Zedong's Cultural Revolution tried to wipe out the traditional arts of China in favor of communist-inspired art forms. After Mao's death, however, Chinese artists returned to their traditions.

Literature

In ancient China and Japan, poetry flourished among the educated members of society. Li Bo and Du Fu, for example, created some of China's best poetry. In their works these poets described human relationships and the beauty of nature. In A.D. 1010 a Japanese noblewoman, Lady Murasaki Shikibu, wrote one of the world's first novels, *The Tale of Genji,* about the life and loves of a prince at the emperor's court. The Japanese also developed a form of poetry called **haiku** that originally had

only 3 lines and 17 syllables but now is written in many line and syllable combinations. A major theme is the fragile beauty of nature, as this example of haiku from the 1600s reveals:

> 66 *The red maple leaves shine so bright*
> *The wings of flying birds are scorched.* 99
> "In a Japanese Garden," *National Geographic,* November 1989

East Asia still produces notable writers. In 1994 Japanese writer Kenzaburo Oe won the Nobel Prize in literature for his works that connect the myths of traditional Japanese village life with life in the modern era. Exiled Chinese writer Gao Xingjian also won the Nobel Prize in literature in 2000.

Music and Theater

East Asian music is based on a five-tone scale with a melody line but no harmony. Over the centuries, instruments such as flutes, drums, and gongs accompanied dancers in temple rituals. Stringed instruments included the lute, the guitar, and the koto, a type of zither.

EXTENDING THE CONTENT

Taiji (Tai Chi) Originally a Daoist martial art, taiji is also widely practiced as a healthy discipline. Traditional taiji forms involve up to 108 connected movements, usually performed at a slow, even pace, somewhat like a slow-motion dance. The purpose of taiji is to combine exercise with relaxation. Throughout China, early in the morning hundreds of thousands of people can be seen gathered in parks and plazas, practicing the movements silently and simultaneously. Taiji exercises have their roots in Daoist principles of peacefully adapting to the cycles of nature and bringing *yin* and *yang,* the opposing forces, into harmony. The movements are said to stimulate the life force, called *chi,* and benefit circulation, balance, and stamina. 📖 **EE4 Human Systems: Standard 10**

East Asians have many forms of drama. Chinese traditional opera uses elaborate costumes, music, and acrobatics or martial arts displays. Japan's lively Kabuki theater uses costumes, song, and dance. By contrast, the Japanese Noh drama has actors who tell stories only through precise movements. Traditional art in Korea may involve group folk dances. Most East Asian countries produce movies.

▲ *The ancient art of making porcelain is still practiced in China today.*

Visual Arts

Throughout history, East Asians have developed their own unique art forms. In China, Korea, and Japan, artists have painted the rugged landscapes of their countries. These paintings often include a verse made in elegant brush-stroke calligraphy, the art of beautiful writing. The Japanese also created vivid prints using carved wood blocks. Influential print artists include Hiroshige and Hokusai. Other Japanese art forms include origami, in which paper is folded into the shapes of animals and birds; the tea ceremony; formal landscaping; and ikebana, or flower arranging. In East Asia elegant Chinese pottery developed into a fine art over thousands of years. During the Tang dynasty, Chinese potters created the fine, thin porcelain known today as china. In Korea, during the Koryo dynasty, artists made graceful vases with a pale green glaze called celadon still highly valued all over the world. Buddhist temples in China, Korea, and Japan contain many statues and sculptures in stone, bronze, or jade.

Architecture

Except for skyscrapers, most East Asian architecture uses wood, brick, and stone. Bamboo is important in the architecture of Japan and southern China. Traditional East Asian buildings often have gracefully curved tile roofs in the pagoda, or tower, style.

Despite the changes and pressures brought by modernization, East Asians have kept alive their ancient art forms. These traditions help unite East Asia's diverse peoples into a cultural region.

SECTION 3 ASSESSMENT

Checking for Understanding

1. **Define** ideogram, shamanism, lama, acupuncture, haiku, calligraphy, pagoda.

2. **Main Ideas** On a table like the one below, fill in details about each country's languages, religions, education, health, standard of living, leisure, and arts.

China	Japan	N. Korea	S. Korea

Critical Thinking

3. **Comparing and Contrasting** Describe health care in East Asia. How is it different from health care in the United States?

4. **Making Generalizations** How have rising standards of living changed the lives of people in East Asia?

5. **Drawing Conclusions** How do East Asia's religions influence its art forms?

Analyzing Graphs

6. **Region** Study the graph on East Asia's religions on page 674. Christianity accounts for about what percentage of religious followers in East Asia?

Applying Geography

7. **Chinese Culture** Write a paragraph explaining the impact of the "Great Leap Forward" and the Cultural Revolution on Chinese culture.

Reteach

List the headings from this section on the board and have students identify three facts from the text for each heading. Have students copy the list of headings and facts in their notebooks, then write a sentence summarizing the information or main points under each heading.

Enrich

Take students to an art gallery or museum exhibit featuring East Asian art, or suggest that they visit one on their own. As an alternative, students may be able to locate a "virtual tour" of East Asian art by visiting museum Web sites on the Internet.

4 CLOSE

Write *EAST ASIA* vertically on the board and challenge students to copy a term related to East Asian cultural traditions or lifestyles from Section 3 that begins with each letter. For example, students might choose *acuncture* next to an "A" in *ASIA*.

Chapter 27 🌐 **679**

SECTION 3 ASSESSMENT ANSWERS

1. All vocabulary terms are defined in the text.

2. Tables should include details about each cultural topic for each country.

3. Many East Asians rely on herbal cures as well as Western-style medical doctors. Communist governments pay for most medical care. The U.S. government does not pay for most people's medical care, and most people rely primarily on medical doctors for treatment.

4. Many people have more money but the gap between rich and poor has grown; in Japan, traditions of loyalty and job security have been weakened and many suffer during an economic downturn; in China, some people have a better standard of living but in general are behind the rest of East Asia.

5. Since many of the religions stress simplicity, beauty, and reverence for nature, many of the art forms include renderings of nature.

6. 6 percent

7. **Applying Geography** Industrialization has created overcrowding, growth of cities, migration from farmlands and countryside, and serious pollution, sanitation, and traffic problems, along with economic prosperity and the development of global trading ties.

MAP & GRAPH SkillBuilder

Teaching the Skill

Ask: What region is shown on this map? *(the Korean Peninsula; North Korea and South Korea)*

- Ask students what two types of economic activities are shown on this map. *(Land Use and Resources)* Have students name each symbol listed in the two boxes or map keys.
- Ask students to describe the economic value of each land use or resource in the list and how they are useful.
- Have students scan the map for examples of each symbol and describe their locations.
- Have students compare places that are relatively rich or poor in resources and the range of land uses on the map.

Additional Practice
L1

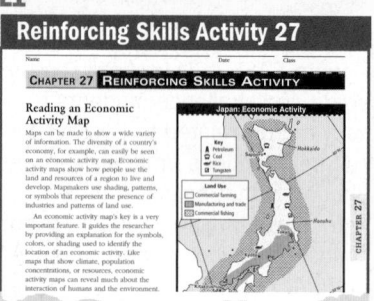

Reinforcing Skills Activity 27

GLENCOE
TECHNOLOGY

Glencoe Skillbuilder Interactive Workbook, Level 2

This interactive CD-ROM reinforces student mastery of essential social studies skills.

Reading an Economic Activity Map

Geographers and researchers use economic activity maps as well as other specialized maps to help them understand a region. An economic activity map gives a quick overview of economic resources and activities.

Learning the Skill

By comparing activities on an economic activity map with information on other types of maps, such as political, climate, or population density maps, geographers can quickly see the distribution of economic resources. Geographers can also get an idea about a country's economic potential and the people's standard of living.

Economic activity maps use colors to represent dominant economic activities. Other maps may use patterns or symbols instead of colors. In all economic activity maps, the key or legend defines the colors and symbols.

To read an economic activity map, follow these steps:

- **Identify the geographic region shown on the map.**
- **Study the map key to understand all colors, symbols, and patterns used on the map.**
- **Study the map to determine what resources and economic activities are predominant in each area.**
- **Compare the map with other maps showing landforms, climate, and natural vegetation of the region.** Draw conclusions about the interaction of humans with the environment.

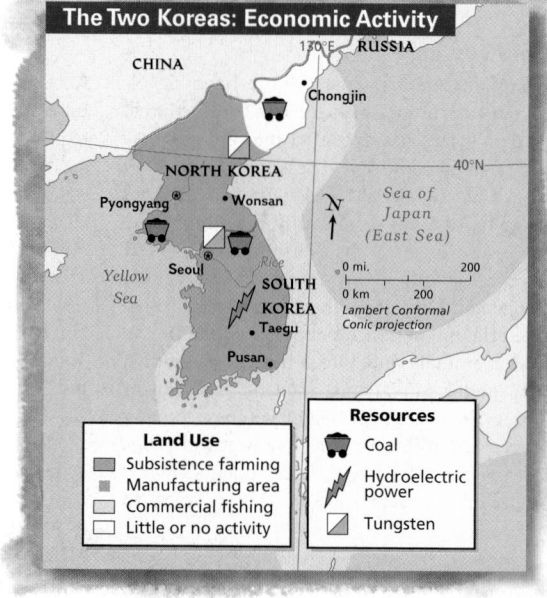

The Two Koreas: Economic Activity

Practicing the Skill

Use the economic activity map above to answer the following questions.

1. Which color on the map represents subsistence farming?

2. Which country has more coal deposits?

3. Which area has little or no economic activity?

4. Which part of the region probably has the lowest standard of living? The highest? Explain your answer.

Applying the Skill

Use a reference book or Internet sources to create an economic activity map for your city or county. Draw an outline map of your region, and create symbols and colors to represent economic activities in your area. Be sure to include a map key.

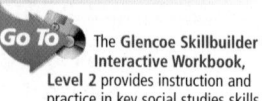

The Glencoe Skillbuilder Interactive Workbook, Level 2 provides instruction and practice in key social studies skills.

ANSWERS TO PRACTICING THE SKILL

1. green
2. North Korea
3. northeast North Korea
4. lowest standard of living: area of little or no economic activity and areas of subsistence farming; highest standard of living: the cities because they are manufacturing centers and have higher populations and resources

CHAPTER 27

SUMMARY & STUDY GUIDE

SECTION 1 — Population Patterns (pp. 661–665)

Terms to Know
- aborigine
- homogeneous

Key Points
- East Asia's 1.5 billion people are made up of many different ethnic groups with a variety of religions, languages, and cultures.
- Population in East Asia is unevenly distributed. It is concentrated in urban areas, in river valleys, and on coastal plains.
- Japan, Taiwan, and South Korea are highly urbanized countries. Mongolia is predominantly rural. In China most people live in rural areas.
- Massive migration from rural to urban areas has caused farm labor shortages in parts of East Asia.

Organizing Your Notes
Create a chart like the one below to help you organize your notes for this section. Fill in details for ethnic groups found in each country.

Ethnic Group	Chief Population Distribution	Largest Area of Concentration
China		

SECTION 2 — History and Government (pp. 668–672)

Terms to Know
- culture hearth
- dynasty
- clan
- shogun
- samurai

Key Points
- Confucianism and Daoism developed in China about 500 B.C. Buddhism spread from India throughout East Asia.
- China was ruled by a succession of dynasties until the early 1900s.
- Contact with the West forced East Asians to modernize.
- Revolutions and wars transformed East Asia in the 1900s.
- By the end of the 1900s, East Asian countries had important roles in the global economy.

Organizing Your Notes
On a web diagram like the one below, fill in important events in East Asia's history, including its various forms of government systems.

East Asia's History and Government
- Ancient East Asia
- Contact With West
- Modern East Asia

SECTION 3 — Cultures and Lifestyles (pp. 673–679)

Terms to Know
- ideogram
- shamanism
- lama
- acupuncture
- haiku
- calligraphy
- pagoda

Key Points
- Sino-Tibetan languages and Korean and Japanese are the region's main languages.
- East Asians often adopt practices from more than one religious tradition.
- Rising standards of living since 1945 have brought dramatic improvements in education and health care for some countries.
- East Asians have a long history of traditional arts and activities.

Organizing Your Notes
Create an outline using the format below to help you organize your notes for this section.

East Asia's Languages and Religions
I. Languages
  A. China
    1. Mandarin
    2. Cantonese

Chapter 27   681

Using the Chapter 27 Summary & Study Guide

Use the Chapter 27 Summary & Study Guide to preview, review, condense, or reteach the chapter.

Preview/Review

Vocabulary PuzzleMaker CD-ROM reinforces "Terms to Know."

Interactive Tutor Self-Assessment CD-ROM provides a review of Chapter 27 content.

Condense

Have students read the Chapter 27 Summary & Study Guide.

Chapter 27 Audio Program

Chapter 27 Guided Reading Activities

Reteach

Chapter 27 Reteaching Activities (Spanish also available)

Chapter 27 Reading Essentials and Study Guides

GLENCOE TECHNOLOGY

NATIONAL GEOGRAPHIC

WORLD REGIONS VIDEO PROGRAM

Unit 9, East Asia
The following segments enhance the study of this unit:
- **Treasures of the Gobi**
- **Haenyo of Cheju**
- **A-Mei: Princess of Pop**

CHAPTER CULMINATING ACTIVITY

Making Predictions Have students work in pairs or groups to brainstorm and predict what East Asia will be like in 50 years. Have them use the entire chapter as a basis for the predictions. Suggest to students that they examine issues such as population growth, migration, political changes, the impact of world trade and new markets, and technological change. Tell them to give reasons for their predictions. Have students share their predictions in class.

◾ **EE2 Places and Regions: Standard 4**
◾ **EE4 Human Systems: Standards 9, 10, 11, 13**

NOTE: This activity may be completed separately or you may wish students to incorporate it into their GeoJournals.

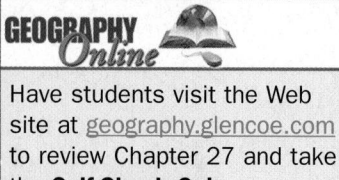

GLENCOE TECHNOLOGY

Use *MindJogger Videoquiz* to review the Chapter 27 content.

Reviewing Key Terms

1. samurai
2. shogun
3. calligraphy
4. culture hearth
5. dynasty
6. clans

Reviewing Facts
SECTION 1

1. Japan, Korea, and Mongolia
2. the western part of China and Mongolia; rugged mountains, deserts hinder settlement
3. the "Tokaido Corridor," a string of cities on the island of Honshu; most of Japan is mountainous, except for narrow coastal plains

SECTION 2

4. the Zhou dynasty
5. Japan used diplomacy and military force to build its empire, which came to an end after World War II.
6. Communists overthrew the nationalists.

SECTION 3

7. Confucianism, Buddhism, Daoism, and Shintoism
8. because of the belief that it leads to economic success
9. haiku, calligraphy, formal landscaping, origami, and ikebana

---

CHAPTER 27 ASSESSMENT & ACTIVITIES

Reviewing Key Terms

Write the key term that best completes each of the following sentences. Refer to the Terms to Know in the Summary & Study Guide on page 681.

1. A _____ was a professional soldier in early Japan.
2. Soldiers of ancient Japan were loyal to a military ruler known as a(n) _____.
3. _____ is the art of beautiful writing.
4. China was East Asia's _____, the center from which ideas spread.
5. A ruling family known as a(n) _____ formed China's early government.
6. Before ruling families, tribal groups, or _____, ruled in China.

Reviewing Facts

SECTION 1

1. Which countries in the region of East Asia are the most ethnically homogeneous?
2. What portions of East Asia are relatively unpopulated? Why?
3. What is Japan's most populous region? Why?

SECTION 2

4. During which dynasty did the philosophies of Confucius and Laozi emerge?
5. How did Japan build an empire in the early 1900s, and how did the empire come to an end?
6. How did the Communists in China come to power?

SECTION 3

7. Name four religious or philosophical traditions of East Asia.
8. Why is education a high priority in Taiwan and South Korea?
9. Name five art forms important in East Asia.

Critical Thinking

1. **Comparing and Contrasting** How do the standards of living vary among East Asian countries and between rural and urban areas?
2. **Making Inferences** Why are farmlands and the food supply of critical importance to China?
3. **Analyzing Consequences** Create a web diagram like the one below to show the effects of migration to urban areas in East Asian countries. Then write a paragraph explaining those effects.

Effects of Urbanization

NATIONAL GEOGRAPHIC **Locating Places**
East Asia: Physical-Political Geography

Match the letters on the map with the places and physical features of East Asia. Write your answers on a sheet of paper.

1. Wuhan
2. Shanghai
3. Taipei
4. Yangtze
5. Tokyo
6. Beijing
7. Guangzhou
8. Ulaanbaatar
9. Seoul
10. Kyoto

Critical Thinking

1. communist countries: low standard; free market: high standard; urban: higher; rural: lower
2. to help feed its large and growing population
3. Webs should demonstrate an understanding of urbanization.

NATIONAL GEOGRAPHIC **Locating Places**

1. C	**3.** E	**5.** H	**7.** G	**9.** B
2. F	**4.** A	**6.** J	**8.** I	**10.** D

Using the Regional Atlas

1. Harbin, Shen Yang, Beijing, Tianjin, Shanghai, Hangzhou, Hong Kong, Tokyo, Seoul
2. coal deposits

Using the Regional Atlas

Refer to the Regional Atlas on pages 636–639.

1. **Place** Which East Asian cities have populations over 5,000,000?

2. **Human-Environment Interaction** What natural resource may account for the areas of high population density in western China?

Thinking Like a Geographer

Think about the thousands of migrant workers settling in China's special economic zones. What are some of the problems created by this influx of people? As a geographer, what strategies would you suggest to help solve these problems? Explain your answer.

Problem-Solving Activity

Group Research Project Work with a group to research and evaluate the Chinese government's international reputation on human rights. Issues include the treatment of religious dissidents, political prisoners, ethnic Tibetans and exiled leaders, and students during the 1989 pro-democracy demonstrations at Tiananmen Square. Consider the following: What is China's current status on human rights? How will the Internet and communications technology affect this issue? Prepare a report stating your opinions and predicting future developments.

GeoJournal

Compare and Contrast Use the information you noted in your GeoJournal to write an essay comparing cultural aspects of two East Asian countries. Include specific examples.

Technology Activity

Creating an Electronic Database Create a database of the population densities of several East Asian countries, regions, or cities. Then use the database to help you draw an outline map to show population distribution using color codes, and include a map key.

Standardized Test Practice

Study the table. Then choose the best answer for the following multiple-choice question. If you have trouble answering the question, use the process of elimination to narrow your choices.

Economic Activities in East Asia

Economic Activity	Taiwan %	China %	Japan %	South Korea %
Agriculture	2.9	18.4	1.7	4.9
Industry	34.0	48.7	36.0	43.5
Services	63.1	32.9	62.3	51.6
Labor Force				
Agriculture	8.0	50.0	5.0	12.0
Mining & Manufacturing	37.0	23.0	32.0	27.0
Services & Other	55.0	27.0	63.0	61.0

Source: The Economist Pocket World in Figures, 2001

1. Based on the chart, which two countries have economic activities that are the most similar in all areas?

A South Korea and Taiwan
B Taiwan and Japan
C Taiwan and China
D China and Japan

Test-Taking Tip Charts and tables may reveal patterns or trends. Look for similarities in groups of numbers before you draw conclusions. In addition, numbers need not be exactly alike in a question such as this one. For example, although both China and South Korea have the same percentage for Services under Economic Activity, the other figures vary widely.

CHAPTER BONUS TEST QUESTION

Which country has a Communist government, a mostly rural population, traditional herbal medicine and acupuncture, and a literacy rate of 82 percent? *(China)*

Thinking Like a Geographer

Overcrowding causes a strain on services and resources. Accept reasonable solutions.

Problem-Solving Activity

Students' responses should be backed by evidence drawn from their research.

GeoJournal

Essays should focus on the population patterns, history and government, and culture and lifestyles of the students' chosen countries.

Technology Activity

Students' maps should accurately reflect the database figures.

PLANNING GUIDE

NOTE: The following materials may be used when teaching Chapter 28. Section-level support materials are shown at point-of-use in the margins of the Teacher Wraparound Edition.

TEACHING TRANSPARENCIES

L2 Unit 9 Map Overlay Transparencies

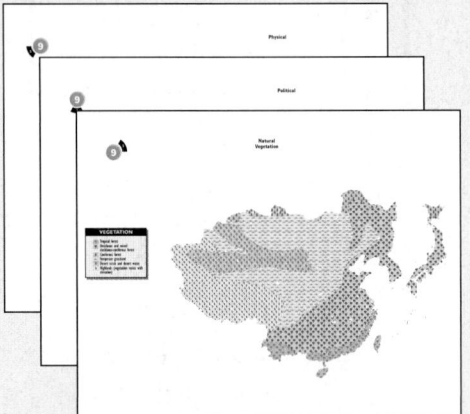

L2 Political Map Transparency 9

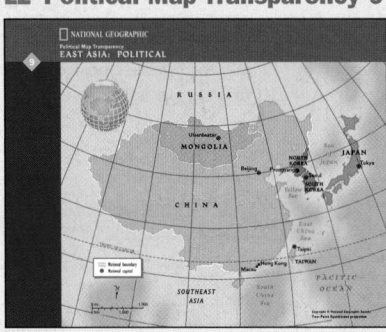

GEOGRAPHIC LITERACY

Focus on Geography Literacy

APPLICATION AND ENRICHMENT

L3 Enrichment Activity 28

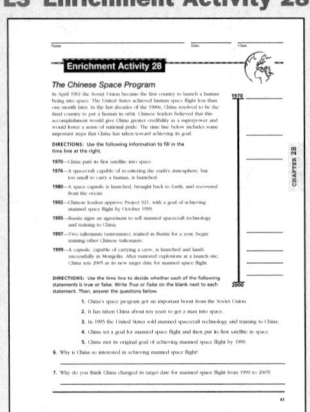

REVIEW AND REINFORCEMENT

L1 Vocabulary Activity 28 L1 Reinforcing L1 Reteaching Activity 28
Skills Activity 28

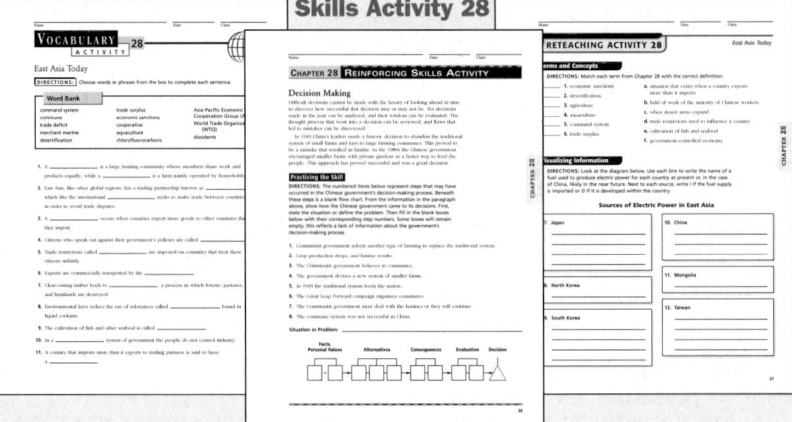

ASSESSMENT

L2 Chapter 28 Test Form A

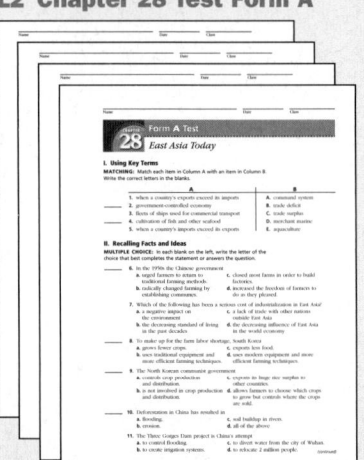

L2 Chapter 28 Test Form B

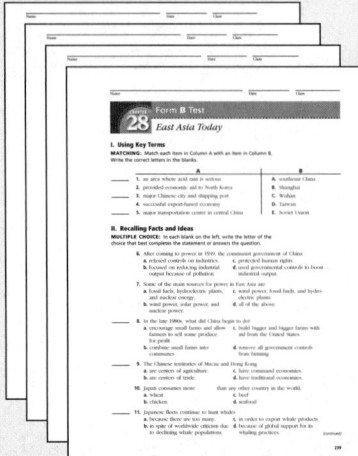

L1/ELL Performance Assessment Activity 28

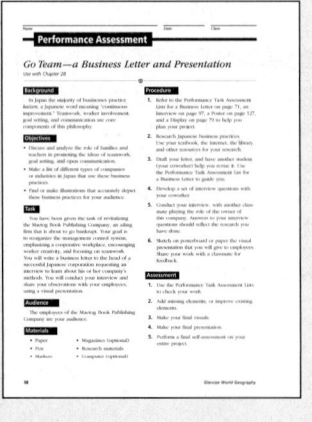

ExamView® Pro Testmaker

SPANISH RESOURCES

The following Spanish language materials are available in the Spanish Resources binder:

- 📁 Spanish Vocabulary Activities
- 📁 Spanish Guided Reading Activities
- 📁 Spanish Reteaching Activities
- 📁 Spanish Summaries
- 📁 Spanish Quizzes and Tests
- 📁 Spanish Reading Essentials and Study Guide

MULTIMEDIA

- 📼 World Regions Video
- 📼 MindJogger Videoquiz
- 💿 Vocabulary PuzzleMaker CD-ROM
- 💿 Interactive Tutor Self-Assessment CD-ROM
- 💿 ExamView® Pro Testmaker CD-ROM
- 💿 Audio Program
- 💿 TeacherWorks CD-ROM
- 💿 Interactive Student Edition CD-ROM
- 💿 Glencoe Skillbuilder Interactive Workbook CD-ROM, Level 2
- 💿 Presentation Plus! CD-ROM

Timesaving Tools

TeacherWorks™ All-In-One Planner and Resource Center

- **Interactive Teacher Edition** Access your Teacher Wraparound Edition and your classroom resources with a few easy clicks.
- **Interactive Lesson Planner** Planning has never been easier! Organize your week, month, semester, or year with all the lesson helps you need to make teaching creative, timely, and relevant.

Use Glencoe's **Presentation Plus!** multimedia teacher tool to easily present dynamic lessons that visually excite your students. Using Microsoft PowerPoint® you can customize the presentations to create your own personalized lessons.

GEOGRAPHY Online

Use our Web site for additional resources. All essential content is covered in the Student Edition.

You and your students can visit geography.glencoe.com, the Web site companion to *Glencoe World Geography*. This innovative integration of electronic and print media offers your students a wealth of opportunities. The student text directs students to the Web site for the following options:

- Chapter Overviews
- Student Activities
- Self-Check Quizzes
- Textbook Updates

Answers are provided for you in the "Web Activity Lesson Plan." Additional Web resources and Interactive Tutor puzzles are also available.

▶ Additional Glencoe Teacher Support

- **Teaching Strategies for the Geography Classroom** (including Block Scheduling Pacing Guides)
- **Graphic Organizer Transparencies Strategies and Activities**
- **Outline Map Resource Book**
- **Reading in the Content Area**

PLANNING GUIDE

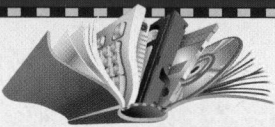

SECTION RESOURCES

Daily Objectives	Reproducible Resources	Multimedia Resources

SECTION 1 Living in East Asia

1. Discuss the types of governments and economies that East Asian countries have.
2. Identify the economic activities that play an important role in East Asia.
3. Describe how other countries in the region are challenging Japan's economic dominance.
4. Explain how the countries of East Asia are economically interdependent.

 Reproducible Lesson Plan 28-1
 Daily Lecture Notes 28-1
Guided Reading Activity 28-1*
Reading Essentials and Study Guide 28-1*
 Section Quiz 28-1*

Daily Focus Skills Transparency 28-1
Political Map Transparency 9
Unit 9 Map Overlay Transparencies
Interactive Tutor Self-Assessment CD-ROM
ExamView® Pro Testmaker CD-ROM*
Presentation Plus! CD-ROM

SECTION 2 People and Their Environment

1. Explain how East Asia's industrialization and urbanization have affected the environment.
2. Identify the steps that East Asians are taking to solve environmental problems.
3. Examine the naturally occurring destructive forces that East Asia regularly faces.

 Reproducible Lesson Plan 28-2
 Vocabulary Activity 28*
 Daily Lecture Notes 28-2
 Guided Reading Activity 28-2*
Reading Essentials and Study Guide 28-2*
 Reteaching Activity 28*
 Reinforcing Skills Activity 28
 Section Quiz 28-2*

 Daily Focus Skills Transparency 28-2
Political Map Transparency 9
Unit 9 Map Overlay Transparencies
Vocabulary PuzzleMaker CD-ROM
Interactive Tutor Self-Assessment CD-ROM
ExamView® Pro Testmaker CD-ROM*
Presentation Plus! CD-ROM

Blackline Master   Software   Videocassette   *Also available in Spanish*

Transparency   CD-ROM   DVD

OUT OF TIME? Assign the Chapter 28 **Reading Essentials and Study Guide.**

Block Schedule

Activities that are particularly suited to use within the block scheduling framework are identified throughout this chapter by the following designation:

KEY TO ABILITY LEVELS

Teaching strategies have been coded for varying learning styles and abilities.

L1   **BASIC** activities for all students

L2   **AVERAGE** activities for average to above-average students

L3   **CHALLENGING** activities for above-average students

ELL   **ENGLISH LANGUAGE LEARNER** activities

Teacher to Teacher

Tim Jacobson
Nikolaevsk School
Nikolaevsk, AK

Learn with Mnemonics

Students can use mnemonics to learn and retain factual material that may be difficult or unfamiliar. Ask volunteers to share examples of mnemonics they have used in their studies. Explain to students that they can create mnemonics by using letters, words, images, or rhymes. Emphasize that the most effective mnemonics are humorous, exaggerated, or colorful.

Write the following mnemonic on the board as an example for remembering the economic systems of countries in East Asia:

Ned's **K**itchen has a **commanding** view, where
Jane **S**hould **K**eep **T**omatoes from the **market.**
Charlie and **M**oe use them to **mix** a salad.

Guide students in looking at the initial letters and key words to recognize that North Korea has a command economy; Japan, South Korea, and Taiwan have market economies; and China and Mongolia have mixed economies. Students can picture the mnemonic or say it to themselves, depending on individual learning styles. Have students choose material from the chapter or unit and create and share individual mnemonics.

NATIONAL GEOGRAPHIC TEACHER'S CORNER

Index to National Geographic Magazine:

The following articles may be used for research relating to this chapter:

- "Beijing," by Todd Carrell, March 2000.
- "Tibet Embraces the New Year," by Ian Baker, January 2000.
- "Hunting with Eagles," by Candice S. Millard, September 1999.
- *Biodiversity*, a National Geographic Special Edition, February 1999.

National Geographic Society Products:

To order the following products for use with this chapter, call National Geographic Society at 1-800-368-2728.

- *GeoKit: Pollution* (Kit)
- *Natural Disasters* (Video)
- *Pollution: World at Risk* (Video)
- *Technology's Price* (Video)
- *National Geographic Desk Reference* (Book)
- *National Geographic Atlas of the World, Seventh Edition* (Book)

NGS ONLINE

Access National Geographic's Web site for current events, activities, links, interactive features, and archives.
www.nationalgeographic.com

Meeting National Standards

Geography For Life

The following standards are highlighted in Chapter 28:

Section 1 EE1 The World in Spatial Terms:
Standard 1
EE2 Places and Regions:
Standard 4
EE4 Human Systems:
Standards 10, 11, 13

Section 2 EE3 Physical Systems:
Standard 7
EE5 Environment and Society:
Standards 14, 15
EE6 The Uses of Geography:
Standard 18

Local Objectives

_____

_____

MEETING SPECIAL NEEDS

In addition to the Differentiated Instruction strategies found in each section, the following resources are also suitable for your special needs students:

- *ExamView® Pro Testmaker CD-ROM* allows teachers to tailor tests by reducing answer choices.
- The *Audio Program* includes the entire narrative of the student edition so that less-proficient readers can listen to the words as they read them.
- The *Reading Essentials and Study Guide* provides the same content as the student edition but is written two grade levels below the textbook.
- *Guided Reading Activities* give less-proficient readers point-by-point instructions to increase comprehension as they read each textbook section.
- *Enrichment Activities* include a stimulating collection of readings and activities for gifted and talented students.

Chapter Objectives

1. Describe the governments and economies of the East Asian countries.

2. Explain the environmental challenges and recurring natural disasters East Asians face and the steps they are taking to meet those challenges.

GLENCOE TECHNOLOGY

Use *MindJogger Videoquiz* to preview the Chapter 28 content.

GeoJournal

For access to additional photos, maps, and information on life today in East Asia go to www.nationalgeographic.com (See Teacher pages in front for strategies for using journals in the geography classroom.)

GEOGRAPHY *Online*

Introduce students to chapter content and key terms by having them access **Chapter Overview 28** at geography.glencoe.com

FOLDABLES™ Study Organizer

Dinah Zike's Foldables are three-dimensional, interactive graphic organizers that help students practice basic writing skills, review key vocabulary terms, and identify main ideas. Have students complete the Foldable activity in the *Dinah Zike's Reading and Study Skills Foldables* booklet.

CHAPTER 28

East Asia Today

GeoJournal

As you read this chapter, use your journal to summarize and reflect on the ways East Asians are working to meet economic and environmental challenges in the region today. Be sure to note specific examples.

GEOGRAPHY *Online*

Chapter Overview Visit the Glencoe World **Geography** Web site at geography.glencoe.com and click on Chapter Overviews—Chapter 28 to preview information about East Asia today.

ABOUT THE PHOTO

Visual Instruction The glitter of bright lights and glass in downtown Hong Kong reflect the city's image as one of the world's most prosperous financial and manufacturing centers. Hong Kong entered a new era in 1999 when 156 years of British rule ended and the city officially reverted to Chinese sovereignty. Hong Kong has retained its market economy under China's "one country, two systems" policy. **Ask:** What fears might the people of Hong Kong have felt when China took over the city? (*concern that China would impose harsh restrictions, and that Hong Kong would lose control of its economy*)
🌐 **EE4 Human Systems: Standard 13**

Guide to Reading

Consider What You Know

People in East Asia, like those in other world regions, are experiencing rapid economic changes. What impact do you think rapid economic change has on the lives of people today?

Reading Strategy

Organizing Complete a web diagram similar to the one below by filling in the East Asian members of the Asia-Pacific Economic Cooperation Group (APEC).

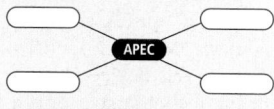

Read to Find Out

- What types of governments and economies do East Asian countries have?
- What economic activities play an important role in East Asia?
- How are other countries in the region challenging Japan's economic dominance?
- How are the countries of East Asia economically interdependent?

Terms to Know

- command system
- commune
- cooperative
- Asia-Pacific Economic Cooperation Group (APEC)
- trade surplus
- trade deficit
- dissident
- economic sanctions
- World Trade Organization (WTO)
- merchant marine

Places to Locate

- Wuhan
- Tianjin
- Guangzhou

◀ *Hong Kong at night*

Living in East Asia

A Geographic View

Japan's Economic Boom

. . . Out of the ashes [of Hiroshima's atomic bombing in 1945] has arisen a fully modern city. . . . The new Hiroshima is a self-proclaimed City of Peace, with a towering skyline, cosmopolitan shopping arcades, and more than 700 manicured parks. Its port sends out to New York, Shanghai, and London . . . the latest in consumer and industrial products.

—Ted Gup, "Up From Ground Zero: Hiroshima," National Geographic, *August 1995*

Bullet train in Hiroshima, Japan

Beginning in the 1960s, East Asian countries such as Japan, South Korea, and Taiwan experienced tremendous economic growth. Then, in the 1990s, a severe economic downturn jolted much of East Asia, shaking public confidence and causing widespread hardships. By 2001 financial aid from Western countries and economic reforms at home had brought a slow recovery to the region. In this section you will learn how East Asians are adjusting to the challenges of living and working in the global economy.

Political and Economic Systems

As in other world regions, governments and economies are closely related in East Asia. East Asian economies include market systems based on private ownership; command systems, which are controlled by governments; and a mix of both systems. During the mid- to late 1900s, Japan, South Korea, and Taiwan developed democratic governments, prospered under market systems, and became global economic powers. Meanwhile, communist-ruled China and democratic Mongolia shifted from strict command systems to mixed economies with both command

FOCUS

Section Overview

This section examines East Asian economies, their role in world markets, and the transportation and communications networks that support them.

BELLRINGER
Skillbuilder Activity

Project transparency and have students answer questions.

Available as blackline master.

Daily Focus Skills Transparency 28-1

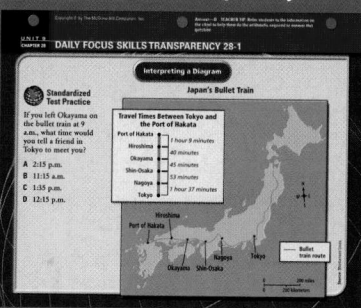

Guide to Reading

Consider What You Know
Answer *increased income, new technologies, more jobs, greater variety of products, access to global information through media, job losses, decay of valued traditions, increased stress*

Reading Strategy
Answers *China, Japan, South Korea, Taiwan*

Preteaching Vocabulary
Write the headings *Economic* and *Political* on the board. Ask students to study "Terms to Know" and group the terms under these two categories.

RESOURCE MANAGER

Reproducible Masters
- Reproducible Lesson Plan 28-1
- Daily Lecture Notes 28-1
- Guided Reading Activity 28-1
- Reading Essentials and Study Guide 28-1
- Section Quiz 28-1

Transparencies
- Daily Focus Skills Transparency 28-1
- Political Map Transparency 9
- Unit 9 Map Overlay Transparencies

Multimedia
- Interactive Tutor Self-Assessment CD-ROM
- ExamView® Pro Testmaker CD-ROM
- Presentation Plus! CD-ROM

②TEACH

L1 Identify

After students read this section, list on the board the countries of the region as column headings for a table. Have students call out whether each country uses a traditional, command, market, or mixed economic system, as well as the type of government and type of agriculture in each country. List the responses.

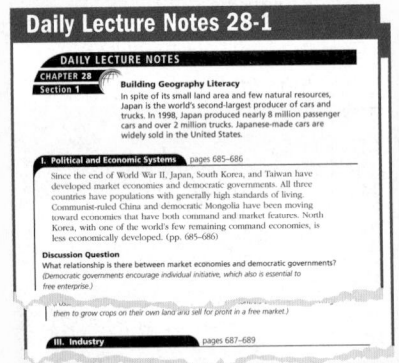

Daily Lecture Notes 28-1

DAILY LECTURE NOTES

CHAPTER 28
Section 1

Building Geography Literacy
In spite of its small land area and few natural resources, Japan is the world's second-largest producer of cars and trucks. In 1998, Japan produced nearly 8 million passenger cars and over 2 million trucks. Japanese-made cars are widely sold in the United States.

I. Political and Economic Systems   pages 685–686

Since the end of World War II, Japan, South Korea, and Taiwan have developed market economies and democratic governments. All three countries have populations with generally high standards of living. Communist-ruled China and democratic Mongolia have been moving toward economies that have both command and market features. North Korea, with one of the world's few remaining command economies, is less economically developed. (pp. 685–686)

Discussion Question
What relationship is there between market economies and democratic governments? (Democratic governments encourage individual initiative, which also is essential to free enterprise.)

them to grow crops on their own land and sell for profit in a free market.)

III. Industry   pages 687–689

GEOGRAPHY Online

Objectives, goals, and answers to the student activity can be found in the Web Activity Lesson Plan feature at geography.glencoe.com

▲ *Women making terraces to grow rice, China*

and market features. By 2001 North Korea had one of the world's few remaining command economies. Less economically developed than South Korea, North Korea is slowly reentering the global markets.

Agriculture

Since the mid-1900s most East Asian countries have shifted dramatically from rural-based agricultural economies to urban-based industrial ones. Agriculture, however, is still important in the region.

China

China has East Asia's most rural economy. About 50 percent of China's workers are farmers. Large numbers of people are needed to work the land because many farmers still use traditional tools. Still, China is a leading producer of rice, wheat, and tea. Chinese farmers also produce soybeans, cotton, jute, and silk and raise livestock.

Since 1949 China's communist government has made many changes to the country's agriculture. The Great Leap Forward campaign of the 1950s organized farmers into huge communes, large farming communities whose members shared work and products equally, but the government decided which farming methods to use. The results were disastrous. When crop production dropped, famines swept the country.

Then in the 1980s, Chinese leaders reversed their agricultural policies. They encouraged smaller farms,

jointly run by households but with private garden plots. Farmers could sell and profit from any extra crops or animals. Chinese farmers now can grow enough food to feed the country.

Despite these agricultural reforms, large numbers of rural workers have begun moving to cities such as Shanghai, Hong Kong, and Beijing to take jobs in industry and commerce, where earnings are better.

Mongolia

Most of Mongolia is used for grazing herds of sheep, goats, camels, and cattle. Until the early 1990s, Mongolia modeled its command economy on the Soviet Union's. Large goverment-owned farms set targets for producing milk and wool, and grew food for people and fodder for animals. Although Mongolia's government still owns much of the country's limited farmland, Mongolian farmers and herders are slowly adapting to a market economy.

South and North Korea

Largely urbanized, with many industries, South Korea's agricultural workforce makes up only 12 percent of its population. Most South Korean farmers work on small family farms, but a farm labor shortage has developed as people continue to move to urban areas. To make up for this loss, South Korean agriculture increasingly uses modern machinery and more efficient farming practices.

In North Korea agriculture makes up 25 percent of the economy and employs about 40 percent of all workers. Farms in North Korea are organized into cooperatives, farms jointly operated by households. The communist government, however, controls crop

GEOGRAPHY Online

Student Web Activity Visit the **Glencoe World Geography** Web site at geography.glencoe.com and click on Student Web Activities—Chapter 28 for an activity about China's modern history.

DIFFERENTIATED INSTRUCTION

Visual/Spatial Have students create a map of East Asia, using color-coding to show which countries have a command system, market system, or a mixed economic system. Have students add symbols to the map to represent the type of government that rules in each East Asian country. Make sure students include a map key. **ELL**

⊕ **EE1 The World in Spatial Terms: Standard 1**
⊕ **EE4 Human Systems: Standard 11**
  📁 Refer to *Inclusion for the Social Studies Classroom Strategies and Activities.*

production and distribution and rations agricultural products. Corn, wheat, and milk are in short supply, and North Korea cannot fully meet its own demand for rice, the country's major crop.

In the 1990s severe flooding destroyed North Korea's rice crop, causing food shortages. This disaster was heightened by government mismanagement of the economy and resulted in widespread famine. For the first time, North Korea accepted food aid from countries with market economies, such as the United States, Japan, and South Korea.

Japan and Taiwan

Japan and Taiwan are largely industrialized, but agriculture does play a role in their economies. Physical geography challenges farmers in both countries. Four-fifths of Japan is mountainous, so farmers have used terracing, modern machinery, fertilizers, and irrigation to dramatically raise Japan's crop yields since World War II. Japan's government also provides farmers with financial support to equalize rural and urban incomes. Despite such improvements, Japan still must import about 35 percent of its food.

Like Japan, Taiwan is mountainous. Rice, sugarcane, tea, bananas, and pineapples grow on limited, often terraced, farmland. Once an exporter of these crops, Taiwan now focuses on industrial exports and imports some food products.

Industry

Since the 1960s, East Asian countries such as Japan, South Korea, and Taiwan have become important industrial and trading countries. Although rich in minerals, North Korea lags far behind these three countries in industrial development. China is primarily agricultural but has a rapidly developing industrial economy. Mongolia also is building its industries, but its factories mostly process livestock and farm products.

Japan

With the aid of the United States, Japan's economy recovered quickly after World War II. A highly skilled workforce and the latest technology helped Japan dramatically develop its industries. Within a few decades, the Japanese were leading producers of ships, cars, cameras, computers, telecommunications products, and consumer goods. By the 1990s world demand for Japan's high-quality goods had made it a global economic power.

Japan, like other countries, faces challenges from the fast-paced, constantly changing global economy. Despite its overall success record, Japan and other parts of Asia suffered from a global economic slump in the 1990s. Japanese banks had invested in risky businesses. When they could not collect on their loans, they failed. Meanwhile, industrial production at home dropped, and unemployment soared. By 2001, Japan was considering banking and other economic reforms to get its sluggish economy moving again.

South and North Korea

After the Korean War, South Korea rapidly moved from an agricultural to an industrial economy. By the 1980s South Korean industries had begun exporting

NATIONAL GEOGRAPHIC **World Explorer**

Geography Skills for Life
Old and New

The economic boom in Taiwan has brought many changes, including the modern farm equipment now used on traditional farms.
Place What trend characterizes Taiwan's agriculture?

L2 Compare and Contrast

After students read pages 686–688, have them review the text and note details about the economic activities in each country. Ask students to create a table, chart, or map that lists or illustrates each country's economic activities, including the types of agriculture, and the products manufactured in each country.

L1/ELL

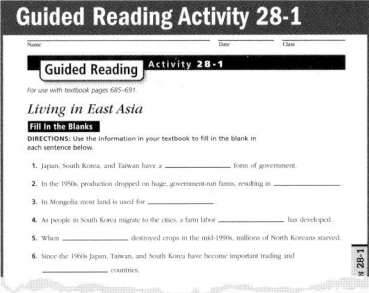

Guided Reading Activity 28-1

Name _____ Date _____ Class _____

Guided Reading Activity 28-1

Living in East Asia

Fill in the Blanks

DIRECTIONS: Use the information in your textbook to fill in the blank in each sentence below.

1. Japan, South Korea, and Taiwan have a _____ form of government.

2. In the 1990s, production dropped on huge, government-run farms, resulting in _____.

3. In Mongolia most land is used for _____.

4. As people in South Korea migrate to the cities, a farm labor _____ has developed.

5. When _____ destroyed crops in the mid-1990s, millions of North Koreans starved.

6. Since the 1960s Japan, Taiwan, and South Korea have become important trading _____ countries.

NATIONAL GEOGRAPHIC **World Explorer**

Answer

shifting from an exporter to an importer of food products

More About the Photo Since the 1960s Taiwan's farm labor force has dwindled as farmers have taken jobs in the growing industrial sector. With a shortage of laborers, farmers have depended more on technology to operate.

COOPERATIVE LEARNING ACTIVITY

Analyzing Trends Have students read Section 1 (pages 685–691). **Ask:** Which countries are challenging Japan's economic dominance of East Asia? (*South Korea, Taiwan, China*) Explain. Have students work in small groups to review the text for information to answer this question. Ask them to create a country-by-country chart in which to note details. Have students add to their charts by researching recent news articles on East Asian economic developments and forecasts for the region. Remind students to note the sources of all the facts they cite in their charts. Then have each group write or present a forecast of the comparative economic positions of each country in five years, including facts and reasons to support their predictions. 📖 **EE4 Human Systems: Standard 11**

L1/ELL

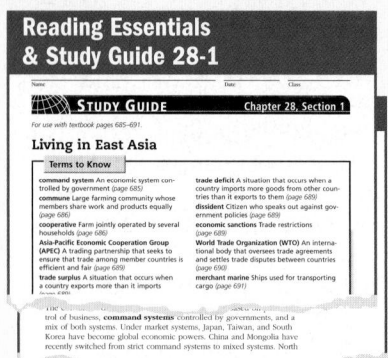

Reading Essentials
& Study Guide 28-1

For use with textbook pages 685-691.

Name_____ Date_____ Class_____

STUDY GUIDE   Chapter 28, Section 1

Living in East Asia

Terms to Know

command system An economic system controlled by government *(page 685)*
commune Large farming community whose members share work and products equally *(page 686)*
cooperative Farm jointly operated by several households *(page 686)*
Asia-Pacific Economic Cooperation Group (APEC) A trading partnership that seeks to ensure that trade among member countries is efficient and fair *(page 689)*
trade surplus A situation that occurs when a country exports more than it imports *(page 689)*

trade deficit A situation that occurs when a country imports more goods from other countries than it exports to them *(page 689)*
dissident Citizen who speaks out against government policies *(page 689)*
economic sanctions Trade restrictions *(page 689)*
World Trade Organization (WTO) An international body that oversees trade agreements and settles trade disputes between countries *(page 690)*
merchant marine Ships used for transporting cargo *(page 691)*

...the ...trol of business, **command systems** controlled by governments, and a mix of both systems. Under market systems, Japan, Taiwan, and South Korea have become global economic powers. China and Mongolia have recently switched from strict command systems to mixed systems. North

L2 Predicting

Have a volunteer read aloud the last paragraph under the heading "China" on page 688. Ask students to predict some possible consequences of the widening economic gap in terms of daily life. *(rural unemployment, tensions, and unrest; some government services, like health care and education, favor urban areas; urban pollution and health problems)*

NATIONAL GEOGRAPHIC   **GRAPH STUDY**

Answers

1. *It gradually increased from zero to about $48 billion.*

2. *It imported more goods than it exported (trade deficit) until 1996, when it began to export more than it imported (trade surplus).*

Skills Practice

How does the United States's trade balance compare to that of Japan and China during this period? *(The United States suffered a significant and increasing trade deficit, while Japan and China had increasing trade surpluses.)*

---

ships, steel, electronic equipment, and motor vehicles. Like other Asian countries, South Korea suffered an economic downturn in the 1990s. With international financial aid, however, South Korea soon began rebuilding its economy.

In North Korea, government-owned heavy industries produce machinery, chemicals, and military equipment. Because so many resources go to North Korea's military forces, production of consumer goods suffers. Before the early 1990s, North Korea had depended on the Soviet Union for economic aid. When the Soviet Union broke up, North Korea's

industrial output fell by half, forcing its communist leaders to trade with countries such as Japan and South Korea.

In 2000, relations improved between North Korea and South Korea. The leaders of the two countries agreed to trade with each other, and South Korea pledged economic aid to North Korea. Their governments also allowed a limited number of family visits across the border for the first time since the Korean War.

Taiwan

Taiwan has one of the world's most successful export-based economies. Until the 1960s, the island had exported a surplus of agricultural products, and invested the profits, as well as American and Japanese financial aid, in manufacturing. Taiwan's new industries specialized in textiles, plastics, and electronic goods for export. Their economic boom transformed Taiwan into a major trading country. Today about 60 percent of Taiwan's people work in service industries, such as finance and communications. Technology-based products, such as computers and precision instruments, are replacing traditional manufactured goods as Taiwan's major source of income.

China

When Chinese communist leaders came to power in 1949, they used government controls to boost industrial output. Today the Chinese government still controls major industries, such as textiles, clothing, footwear, toys, and plastics manufacturing. Many state-run factories, however, lack updated technology and incentives for improved performance.

To stimulate the economy, Chinese leaders since the 1970s have adopted some features of a market economy. For example, small, privately owned businesses are permitted to operate, and foreign companies and investments are welcomed. Many of China's most prosperous industries now lie in special economic zones along the southeastern coast, where they can operate without government controls on prices, production, or distribution.

With market reforms, China's economy is growing at a remarkably high annual rate of 8 percent. Standards of living have risen, especially in urban areas, but the country still faces economic challenges.

NATIONAL GEOGRAPHIC   **GRAPH STUDY**

Selected Countries: Balance of Trade

Billions of U.S. Dollars (y-axis: 150, 100, 50, 0, -50, -100, -150, -200, -250)

Year (x-axis: 1994, 1995, 1996, 1997, 1998)

■ Japan   ■ China   ■ USA

Sources: The World Almanac, 1995–2001

Geography   **Skills for Life**

1. **Interpreting Graphs** How did China's balance of trade change between 1994 and 1998?

2. **Applying Geography Skills** Why do you think the Japanese balance of trade decreased and then increased between 1994 and 1998?

CRITICAL THINKING ACTIVITY

Making Comparisons Remind students that marked differences exist in the availability and development of various means of land transportation throughout the region. Have them use the Internet and print resources to research types of existing land transportation as well as transportation projects underway in each of the region's countries. Tell students to create a chart to compare and contrast the information they find. Charts should include three columns, one for each type of transportation, a second listing the geographic features affecting each country's land transportation, and a third column detailing the impact of land transportation on economic activities.

🌐 **EE2 Places and Regions: Standard 4**

A large gap separates wealthier industrial areas on the coast from poorer agricultural regions in the interior. As unprofitable state-run industries close, unemployment increases. Industrial growth and few environmental safeguards have contributed to rising pollution.

Government

Hong Kong and Macau

The Chinese territories of Hong Kong and Macau are major industrial and trading centers. After more than 150 years of British rule,

▲ A student protester faces down tanks in Beijing's Tiananmen Square.

control of Hong Kong returned to China in 1997. Despite restricted political freedoms, Hong Kong is maintaining a market economy. Hong Kong's economic success provides great wealth to China. In 1999 Macau became part of China after centuries of Portuguese rule. Like Hong Kong, Macau's prosperous market economy benefits China.

Trade

In recent decades East Asian countries have become more interdependent with one another and the rest of the world. As in other world regions, East Asia has formed trading partnerships. For example, China, Japan, South Korea, and Taiwan are members of the Asia-Pacific Economic Cooperation Group (APEC), which ensures that trade among member countries is efficient and fair. Still, trade disputes and deeply rooted political differences continue to affect the region's international relations.

Japan: Trade Surpluses

With few mineral resources, Japan depends on international trade for its economic well-being. To produce its vast range of products for foreign buyers, Japanese industries import raw materials such as iron ore and fuels. The Japanese government, however, places high taxes on many imported finished goods. These taxes protect many Japanese industries from foreign competition, but they restrict what other countries can sell to Japan.

The term *balance of trade* refers to the difference in value over time between a country's imports and exports. High import taxes, along with the high global demand for Japanese goods, cause Japan to have trade surpluses with other countries. A trade surplus occurs when exports exceed imports.

Trade surpluses bring increased wealth to Japan, but the resulting trade imbalances mean lower profits for Japan's trading partners. A trade deficit occurs when a country imports more goods from other countries than it exports to them. In recent years the United States and other countries have tried to persuade Japan to open its market. Results are mixed. Trade policy, therefore, continues to complicate Japan's relations with other countries.

China: Trade and Human Rights

In an effort to modernize its economy, China has sought increased trade with the United States and other countries with market economies. The United States also favors increased trade because of China's growing economy and more than a billion potential customers. A major stumbling block, however, is China's harsh treatment of dissidents, or citizens who speak out against government policies. For example, in 1989, Chinese students wanting democratic reform held a massive demonstration in Beijing's Tiananmen Square. The government sent in troops to brutally end the protest. This action brought China severe criticism.

The United States, Japan, and other important trading countries have tried to influence China to respect human rights. In response to the Tiananmen crackdown, these countries placed economic sanctions, or trade restrictions, on China. In response to economic losses, China released several dissidents from prison, and the United States lifted sanctions.

L2 Cause and Effect

Ask volunteers to provide the meanings of these terms: *trading partners, trade surplus, trade imbalance* (page 689). **Ask:** What factors have caused Japan's trade imbalance with other countries? (*high import taxes that restrict what other countries can sell to Japan, high global demand for Japan's products*)

global
issues

Human Rights The U.S. Department of State noted that China's human rights record worsened in 2000. Serious abuses continue to occur through crackdowns on religion and political dissent, increased imprisonment in labor camps and psychiatric hospitals, and torture and beatings in custody. The Chinese government cites improvements in employment, social security, and education to counter international human rights pressure and to emphasize its view that civil rights are secondary to economic, social, and cultural rights.

▢ NATIONAL GEOGRAPHIC **GEOFACT**

▶ Japan's 34-mile-long (55 km) Seikan railway tunnel, completed in 1988, connects the islands of Honshu and Hokkaido. All four of Japan's major islands are now connected to each other, either by railway tunnel, road tunnel, suspension bridge, or combination railway-road bridge.

TEAM-TEACHING ACTIVITY: TECHNOLOGY

Internet Use in East Asia Have students work with a science teacher or computer instructor to research the Internet's impact on communications, culture, and politics in East Asia. Encourage students to use all available media services and the Internet itself for research. Have students create a multimedia presentation based on their findings. Suggested topics include: impact of the Internet in spreading political information and influencing public opinion; impact on global information exchange; or a description of how Internet and other electronic technology has affected the location and patterns of economic activities in the region.

🌐 EE2 Places and Regions: Standard 4; 🌐 EE4 Human Systems: Standard 10

NATIONAL GEOGRAPHIC MAP STUDY

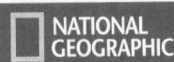

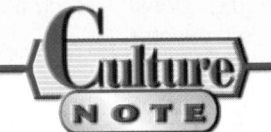

Answers

1. *bullet train*
2. *moving raw materials and goods quickly and efficiently to seaports for export*

Culture NOTE

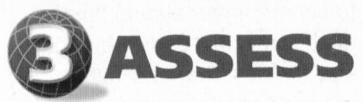

Japan The most common rice produced and consumed in Asia is long-grain rice, which has grains that remain separate after cooking. The Japanese, however, prefer short-grain "sticky rice," or cooked rice mixed with a blend of rice vinegar, sugar, and salt. The coated grains of rice stick together and are easier to pick up with chopsticks and to form into rolls wrapped with seaweed, as in *sushi*.

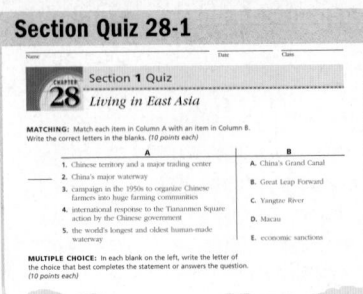

3 ASSESS

Assign Section 1 Assessment as homework or as an in-class activity.

Have students use **Interactive Tutor Self-Assessment CD-ROM.**

L2

Section Quiz 28-1

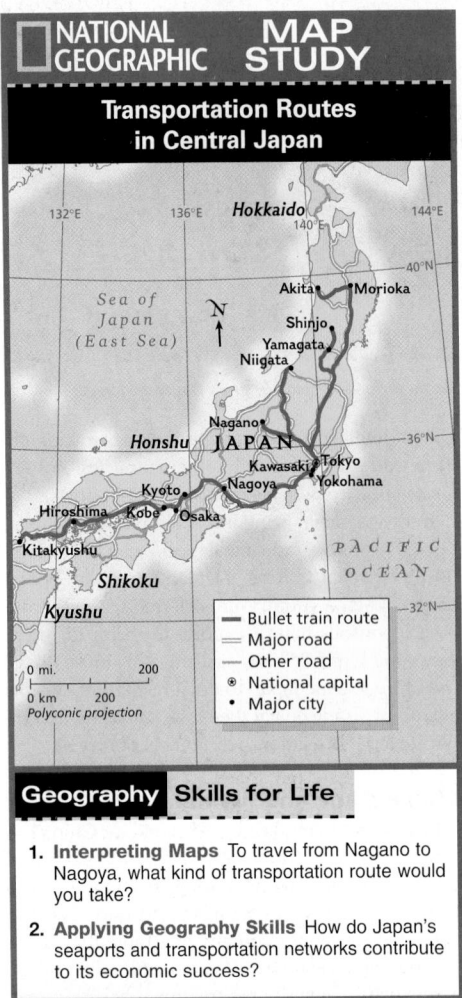

Name Date Class

CHAPTER 28 Section 1 Quiz
Living in East Asia

MATCHING: Match each item in Column A with an item in Column B. Write the correct letters in the blanks. *(10 points each)*

A	B
1. Chinese territory and a major trading center	A. China's Grand Canal
2. China's major waterway	B. Great Leap Forward
3. campaign in the 1950s to organize Chinese farmers into huge farming communities	C. Yangtze River
4. international response to the Tiananmen Square action by the Chinese government	D. Macau
5. the world's longest and oldest human-made waterway	E. economic sanctions

MULTIPLE CHOICE: In each blank on the left, write the letter of the choice that best completes the statement or answers the question. *(10 points each)*

NATIONAL GEOGRAPHIC MAP STUDY

Transportation Routes in Central Japan

Geography Skills for Life

1. **Interpreting Maps** To travel from Nagano to Nagoya, what kind of transportation route would you take?
2. **Applying Geography Skills** How do Japan's seaports and transportation networks contribute to its economic success?

Find NGS online map resources @ www.nationalgeographic.com/maps

Many, however, remain dissatisfied with China's human rights record. The United States government hopes that trade might open China to democratic change. In 2000 the United States Congress granted full trading privileges to China. In the near future, China expects to be admitted to the **World Trade Organization (WTO)**, an international body that oversees trade agreements and settles trade disputes among countries. Western countries believe that China's human rights record will improve as it has more frequent contact with other countries.

Transportation and Communications

Before air travel became common, rugged mountains isolated most of East Asia. Today every country in the region has modern air services. Overland travel in mainland East Asia, however, involves long journeys by railroad or highway. Transportation and communications networks are concentrated in heavily populated areas, and rural areas often have little access to communications networks.

Land Travel

Land transportation varies throughout East Asia. Japan, South Korea, and Taiwan have nationwide highway and railroad networks. Japan's rail system includes high-speed trains, commuter trains, and subways. Elsewhere in the region, transportation links, especially highways, are not as developed. For example, Mongolia's roads are mostly unpaved, and people rely on the Trans-Mongolian Railway. Lack of inland transport has slowed the development of western China, which remains poor despite large oil and coal deposits.

The Chinese, however, have made progress in building roads and rail lines. In 2001, work began on what is hailed as the world's highest railway, linking Tibet to China's national rail system. The Chinese claim the railway will lessen Tibet's isolation and boost its economy. The railway's critics, however, say that it will draw more Chinese to Tibet, further diluting Tibet's culture.

Water Travel

China's rivers provide important routes from inland areas to seaports. The Yangtze River is China's most important waterway. The major port of Shanghai lies at its mouth:

> *"Today the port [of Shanghai] handles more than 160 million tons of cargo a year through loadings and unloadings along the 40 miles of wharves on the [Yangtze River]. . . ."*
>
> William Ellis, "Shanghai," *National Geographic*, March 1994

EXTENDING THE CONTENT

Riding the Bullet Train In 1964 the high-speed shinkansen, or bullet train, began service between Tokyo and Shin-Osaka, a distance of 309 miles (515 km), traveling at speeds up to 131 mph (210 km/hr). The current bullet train's speed record is 277 mph (443 km/hr), with top commercial speeds of 186 mph (300 km/hr). Looking out the window, passengers riding from Tokyo to Nagoya see what seems like a vast city, with rice paddies and fields sandwiched between sprawling areas of housing and factories. Watching the view may not be possible for long, though, as the great speed can cause motion sickness.

EE2 Places and Regions: Standard 4

Large oceangoing ships travel 680 miles (1,094 km) inland on the Yangtze to the transportation center of **Wuhan** in central China. Other major ports are at the mouths of rivers—**Tianjin** (TYEHN•JIHN) on a tributary of the Yellow River and **Guangzhou** (GWAHNG•JOH) on the Xi River. The Grand Canal, the world's longest and oldest human-made waterway, runs from north to south, linking the Yangtze and Yellow Rivers.

Major seaports and merchant marine fleets used for commercial transport are vital to East Asia's export trade. Japan has more than 7,000 merchant vessels, and China's merchant marine fleet numbers about 2,400.

Communications

In North Korea and China, communist governments control communications, the news media, and citizens' access to the Internet. By contrast, people in democratic Japan, South Korea, and Taiwan enjoy a free press, and most own radios, televisions, and telephones (including pagers and cellular phones). In these countries, a wide variety of books, magazines, and newspapers is available, as is access to the Internet.

East Asian countries have overcome many obstacles in order to develop their economies. In the next section, you will learn of the environmental challenges that economic growth has brought to East Asia.

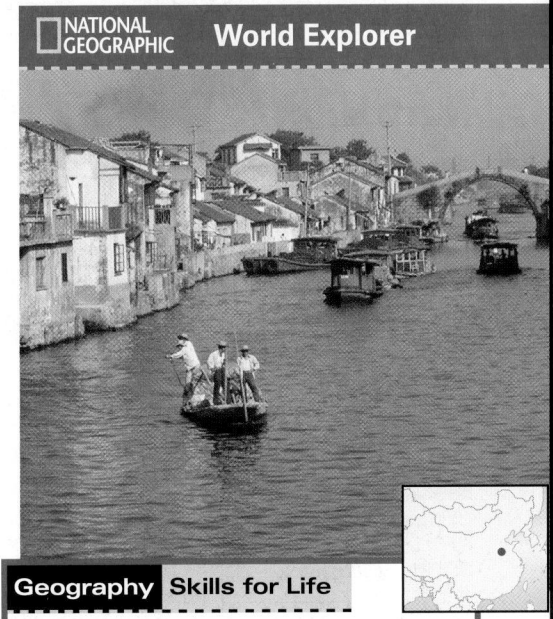

NATIONAL GEOGRAPHIC World Explorer

Geography Skills for Life

The Grand Canal The oldest part of the Grand Canal was built in the 400s B.C. Between 1958 and 1964, the Chinese government rebuilt or repaired vast stretches of the canal.
Movement How far inland can oceangoing ships travel on the Yangtze River?

NATIONAL GEOGRAPHIC World Explorer

Answer
680 miles (1,094 km)

More About the Photo The Grand Canal really is a series of waterways extending 1,085 miles (1,746 km) and linking Hangzhou and Beijing. The world's longest human-made waterway, the canal links several natural waterways; actually only parts of it are human-made.

Reteach

Have students work in pairs to find main ideas and details. Taking a paragraph at a time, have one student rewrite the first sentence of the paragraph as a question. Have the other student find information in the paragraph to write an answer to the question.

Enrich

Bring in and allow students to examine a copy of a Japanese, Chinese, or Korean book, magazine, or newspaper.

4 CLOSE

Bring to class some examples of products made in East Asia, such as electronic goods, decorative chopsticks, or art, ceramics, or porcelain china. Display these items, and invite students to share their impressions.

SECTION 1 ASSESSMENT

Checking for Understanding

1. **Define** command system, commune, cooperative, Asia-Pacific Economic Cooperation Group (APEC), trade surplus, trade deficit, dissident, economic sanctions, World Trade Organization (WTO), merchant marine.

2. **Main Ideas** On a chart like the one below, describe the economy of each East Asian country.

Country	Type of Economy

Critical Thinking

3. **Identifying Cause and Effect** How did the Asian financial crisis of the 1990s affect the economies of China, Japan, and South Korea?

4. **Problem Solving** How might various East Asian countries provide food for their populations, despite their limited farmlands?

5. **Drawing Conclusions** What conclusions can you draw about the economic differences between North and South Korea? Explain your answer.

Analyzing Graphs

6. **Place** Study the graph on page 688. How does the U.S. balance of trade compare to that of Japan? China?

Applying Geography

7. **Economic Reform** Write a paragraph that compares China's economy before and after the economic reforms of the 1980s. Explain how the reforms have affected the lives of China's people.

SECTION 1 ASSESSMENT ANSWERS

1. All vocabulary terms are defined in the text.

2. Students' charts should include details about the economy of all six East Asian countries.

3. Countries were affected differently depending on their level of economic development; Japan and South Korea suffered more severely than China.

4. possible responses: increase sea farming, increase use of high-tech machinery and efficient farming methods, adopt Japanese farming methods; pay farmers to produce crops rather than move to cities

5. possible response: Communist isolation (North Korea) causes depressed economies, and free enterprise (South Korea) results in more prosperity.

6. China and Japan: positive trade balance; the U.S.: increasingly negative trade balance

7. **Applying Geography** Under communism, farms failed to produce; under market conditions, China's economy is growing.

FOCUS

Section Overview

This section focuses on the effects of industrial and urban growth on East Asia's environment.

BELLRINGER
Skillbuilder Activity

 Project transparency and have students answer questions.

Available as blackline master.

Daily Focus Skills Transparency 28-2

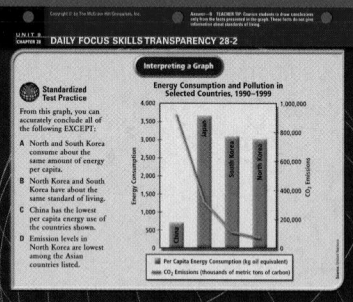

Guide to Reading

Consider What You Know
Answer *pollution, overuse of resources, desertification*

Reading Strategy
Answers China: *mostly coal, only about 1% nuclear power;* Japan: *30–40% generated by 750 nuclear power generators, about 65% from burning mostly imported coal;* Mongolia: *mostly coal;* North Korea: *mostly coal;* South Korea: *30–40% generated by 16 nuclear power generators, about 60% from mostly imported coal;* Taiwan: *primary source is imported petroleum, about 30–40% is generated by 8 nuclear power generators*

Preteaching Vocabulary
Use the **Vocabulary Puzzle-Maker CD-ROM** to create cross-word and word-search puzzles.

Guide to Reading

Consider What You Know
Given East Asia's crowded cities and rapid industrial growth, what environmental challenges do you think the region might face?

Reading Strategy
Organizing As you read about sources of electric power in East Asia, complete a graphic organizer similar to the one below by describing the power sources of each country.

Country	Power Sources
China	
Japan	
Mongolia	
North Korea	
South Korea	
Taiwan	

Read to Find Out
• How have industrialization and urbanization in East Asia affected the environment?

• What steps are East Asians taking to solve environmental problems?

• What naturally occurring destructive forces does East Asia regularly face?

Terms to Know
• desertification
• chlorofluorocarbons
• aquaculture

Places to Locate
• Three Gorges Dam
• Inland Sea
• Kobe

SECTION **2**

People and Their Environment

NATIONAL GEOGRAPHIC

A Geographic View

The Price of Modernization

The most tangible cost of modernization is environmental. . . . Today greater Taipei's population has swollen to almost six million—nearly 30 percent of the island's total. . . . The city chokes on the fumes of 460,000 cars, 7,300 buses, 38,000 taxis, and 869,000 motorcycles, whose drivers park all over the sidewalks and often drive down them too.

— *Arthur Zich, "Taiwan: The Other China Changes Course,"* National Geographic, November 1993

Family on motor scooter, Taiwan

Modernization has brought higher standards of living and increasing global influence to the peoples of East Asia. Yet the benefits have come with serious costs, especially to the region's environment. For example, industrial expansion and urban development have heightened pollution of the air, land, and water throughout the region. In addition to environmental hazards, East Asians also regularly face both the dangers and the challenges of devastating natural disasters, such as floods, earthquakes, and typhoons.

The Power Dilemma

Throughout East Asia, economic growth has increased the demand for electric power to operate businesses and industries. In addition, rising standards of living mean that people tend to buy and use more appliances and electronic devices. Thus, finding adequate sources of electric power has become a vital issue for the countries of the region.

RESOURCE MANAGER

Reproducible Masters
• Reproducible Lesson Plan 28-2
• Vocabulary Activity 28
• Daily Lecture Notes 28-2
• Guided Reading Activity 28-2
• Reading Essentials and Study Guide 28-2
• Reteaching Activity 28
• Reinforcing Skills Activity 28
• Section Quiz 28-2

Transparencies
• Daily Focus Skills Transparency 28-2
• Political Map Transparency 9
• Unit 9 Map Overlay Transparencies

Multimedia
• Vocabulary PuzzleMaker CD-ROM
• Interactive Tutor Self-Assessment CD-ROM
• ExamView® Pro Testmaker CD-ROM
• Presentation Plus! CD-ROM

Fossil Fuels

Some of East Asia's power comes from hydroelectric plants, but most is produced from the burning of fossil fuels such as coal, oil, or natural gas. China, North Korea, and Mongolia produce most of their power using coal from large reserves. Japan, South Korea, and Taiwan, however, have few coal, natural gas, or oil deposits, so they must import these resources to produce energy. About 65 percent of Japan's electricity comes from plants burning coal, natural gas, or petroleum, as does roughly 60 percent of South Korea's power. Coal reserves have dwindled in Taiwan, so the country relies on imported petroleum as its primary source of energy.

Burning fossil fuels, however, leads to acid rain, air pollution, and possibly global warming. East Asian governments have begun to search for cleaner power sources. China's massive **Three Gorges Dam** project on the Yangtze River, for example, aims to supply a huge amount of hydroelectric power to China's interior regions. The project should be completed by 2009.

Nuclear Energy

Japan, South Korea, and Taiwan rely on nuclear energy for 30 to 40 percent of their electrical power. Japan has more than 50 nuclear power generators, South Korea has 16, and Taiwan has 8. North Korea is not known to have any nuclear power facilities. China's few reactors currently produce just 1 percent of the country's electricity, but China's plans for the future include 100 more nuclear plants.

During the late 1990s, a series of accidents in Japan and South Korea exposed hundreds of people to radiation and raised public fears about the safety of nuclear power. People also worried that the earthquakes and volcanic activity common in the region could cause reactors to crack and release radiation.

After a 1999 nuclear accident, Japan began searching for alternatives to both nuclear and hydroelectric power. Since then, Japan has opened several plants that generate electricity from wind and solar energy.

Environmental Concerns

In many parts of East Asia, industrial and economic growth have been given more consideration than other issues. The effects of this growth on the region's environment have been largely ignored. Environmental challenges range from air pollution to the depletion of natural resources. East Asians are just beginning to take seriously issues dealing with health, environment, and quality of life.

China

In China's urban areas, the use of outdated technology in transportation and industry has caused major air pollution. In fact, 9 of the 10 cities worldwide with the worst air pollution are located in China. One major cause is China's heavy reliance on its huge reserves of relatively inexpensive coal. In northern industrial areas, windblown dust adds to the air pollution. As a result, large numbers of people living in the area suffer from lung disease.

Geography | **Skills for Life**

Nuclear Energy

A cargo ship delivers plutonium, a radioactive element used to produce nuclear power, to a nuclear power plant in central Japan. **Human-Environment Interaction** What are the positive and negative consequences of using nuclear power?

Chapter 28 **693**

---

② TEACH

L1 Math
Have students use facts from the text on page 693 to create a bar graph or pictograph of the number of nuclear power generators in each East Asian country. **ELL**

NATIONAL GEOGRAPHIC World Explorer

Answer
Positive: cheap, clean energy source; negative: danger of nuclear accidents, radioactive leakage, waste disposal

More About the Photo
Currently Japan is building two new nuclear plants, and the government plans to build 20 more by 2010. However, citizens groups are acting to stop their construction. Some Japanese cities have passed referenda that prohibit new reactors.

Daily Lecture Notes 28-2

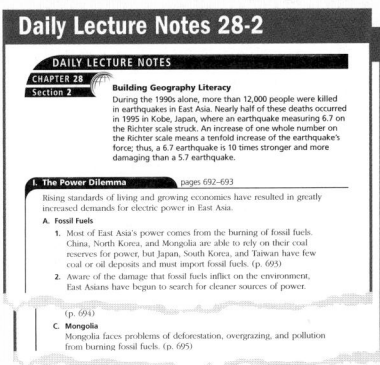

DIFFERENTIATED INSTRUCTION

At-Risk Students For students who have trouble staying on task or completing work, create a routine with structured tasks and time limits for studying. For example, create a guide page consisting of a checklist of the section headings, feature activities, and assessments in Section 2. Assign a certain number of check marks to complete within each study session, limiting the study session to a set period of time. Also, set a time limit—for example, 6 minutes—to complete the reading of two to four paragraphs of text under any given heading.

Refer to *Inclusion for the Social Studies Classroom Strategies and Activities.*

L2 Compare

After students have read Section 2, have them compare the environmental challenges and concerns in East Asia with those in the United States. Ask them to examine the causes of these challenges in each region and whether the causes are alike or different.

L1/ELL

Guided Reading Activity 28-2

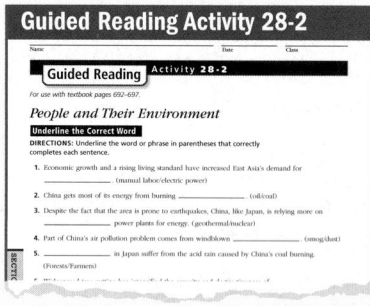

NATIONAL GEOGRAPHIC World Explorer

Answer

Japanese automakers have introduced a hybrid car engine; the government has issued very strict air pollution control laws and has urged factories to reduce emissions of chlorofluorocarbons. Other countries are just beginning to respond to the challenge.

More About the Photo

Bamboo planted in groves along roadsides in Hunan Province provide craftspeople with necessary supplies for their crafts.

Acid rain from burning coal also is a serious problem in the industrial region of southeast China.

Neighboring countries are affected by China's acid rain as well. Forests in Japan, for example, suffer not only from Japan's own coal-burning power plants but also from China's coal-generated pollution.

China and other rapidly urbanizing countries like Taiwan and South Korea also have trouble disposing of waste products. For example, 80 percent of the cities in China have no sewage treatment facilities.

Industrial waste from factories poses health risks to urban populations in parts of China. For many years an important metal company in the Chinese city of Shenyang spewed huge amounts of sulfur dioxide and other harmful chemicals into the atmosphere. In 2000 China responded to pleas from city residents who had long complained of health problems caused by the plant's toxic emissions. For the first time, China closed down a state-run factory for environmental reasons.

China has begun responding to other serious environmental issues, including deforestation. Each year China clears thousands of acres of forests and vegetation to meet the country's high demand for lumber. Deforestation caused by clear-cutting timber leads to soil erosion.

Without trees to slow runoff from rain, large-scale soil erosion and flooding occur. As heavy rains wash away large amounts of unprotected soil in deforested areas, soil deposits build up in rivers. The buildup causes waters to rise even higher than they otherwise might have, and flooding becomes more severe. In the late 1990s, a series of unusually heavy rains caused the Yangtze and Yellow Rivers to flood. Floodwaters destroyed property, altered the landscape of vast areas, and killed thousands of people.

In response to these disasters, China has begun planting trees on millions of acres along the deforested riverbanks. To help control flooding, the government ordered a major dam construction project along the Yellow River. Other steps in China's conservation and restoration plan include the creation of nature and wetland reserves and wildlife protection zones.

A related concern is **desertification**, the process in which grasslands became drier and desert areas expand. Along China's western borders with Mongolia, grasslands and desert meet. The grasses there are drought-resistant, but overgrazing and soil erosion have depleted much of the vegetation. The resulting desertification has contributed to dust and sand storms in northern and western areas of China.

North Korea, South Korea, and Taiwan

Urban areas of North Korea, South Korea, and Taiwan are plagued with air and water pollution due to lax industrial controls. Untreated sewage contaminates water supplies and threatens the health of humans and wildlife. For example, North Korea's safe drinking water supplies are inadequate.

Although nuclear energy provides inexpensive power for South Korea, the waste from such plants remains radioactive for tens of thousands of years and is difficult to dispose of safely. Nonetheless, South Korea continues to build nuclear power plants to meet its energy needs. Because North Korea has no nuclear power facilities, it is spared the task of managing nuclear waste, but the country still must confront the hazardous effects of using fossil fuels.

NATIONAL GEOGRAPHIC **World Explorer**

Geography **Skills for Life**
- - - - - - - - - **Endangered**

Forests Bamboo forests such as this one in southern China are threatened by air pollution.

Human-Environment Interaction How have East Asian countries tried to control air pollution?

COOPERATIVE LEARNING ACTIVITY

Pro and Con Organize the class into two teams to debate the issue of economic development versus environmental protection. Have one team support the need to promote economic growth and new technology, and the other team back the necessity of environmental protection. Remind each side to emphasize as many persuasive points as possible, defending each point with facts, examples, and reasons. Review the rules of debate with the entire class, and allow teams time for brainstorming, research, and practice with debate procedures before staging the debates. Have students vote on the most persuasive presentations.

EE5 Environment and Society: Standard 14

Mongolia

Environmental challenges in Mongolia resemble those of western China. Deforestation caused by logging and desertification caused by overgrazing have contributed to soil erosion. Burning coal pollutes the air, and safe drinking water supplies are limited.

Government
Japan Leads the Cleanup

Japan's highly industrialized, crowded society was criticized for years for ignoring the environmental problems created by rapid technological growth. Since the 1970s, however, the Japanese government has encouraged industries to curb pollution. Japan today has emerged as a world leader in addressing environmental issues. By 2000 two Japanese automakers had introduced a hybrid car powered by a battery and a supplemental gasoline engine. The car uses less fuel, so it emits fewer pollutants. It may be years, however, before use of this new technology becomes widespread.

Pollution control has taken on a national urgency in Japan, where environmental laws are among the world's strictest. The government has urged other countries to reduce emissions of carbon dioxide and chlorofluorocarbons (CFCs), gaseous substances found in liquid coolants. Once CFCs enter the atmosphere, they significantly contribute to the destruction of the earth's protective ozone layer.

Japan also offered "clean" technology and financial help for environmental projects to neighboring East Asian countries and other developing countries. Japan's 1990 Action Program to Arrest Global Warming required that 10 percent of its country's cars be replaced with less-polluting vehicles and that overall waste be reduced by 25 percent by the year 2000. Despite this resolve, Japan's total carbon dioxide emissions had increased in 1994 by more than 7 percent from 1990 levels.

Managing Ocean Resources

Another environmental issue in East Asia is the management of ocean resources. In most East Asian countries, oceans and seas provide an important source of food for local consumption and for export. Commercial fishing is a major industry in China,

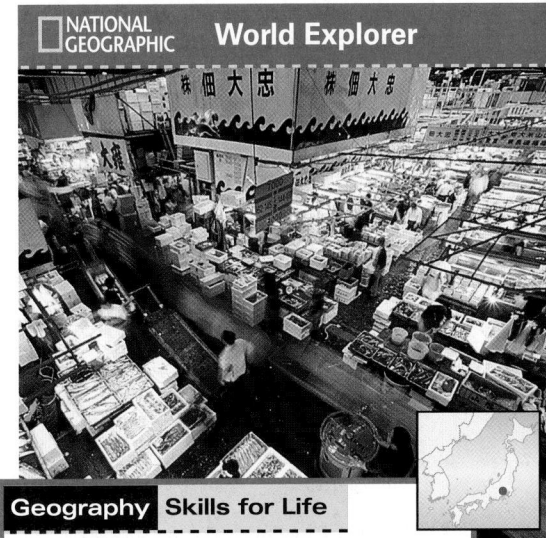

NATIONAL GEOGRAPHIC World Explorer

Geography Skills for Life

Fish Market Shoppers can find herring, salmon, trout, squid, and other seafoods at this Tokyo market.
Human-Environment Interaction How can countries in overfished sea areas obtain seafood?

Japan, and South Korea. Fleets from these countries catch tons of snapper, tuna, squid, shrimp, and other seafood. Now, however, Japan imports large quantities of seafood because of decreasing quantities of fish in the region. The Japanese must find other ways to obtain seafood because they consume more seafood than any other people in the world.

In recent years East Asia's coastal waters, such as Japan's **Inland Sea**, have become overfished or polluted. As a result, commercial fishing companies from several countries have begun fishing farther from shore, in international waters. Many of these companies have giant factory ships that follow fishing fleets to quickly clean and freeze large catches of fish. The use of factory ships is discouraged internationally because the practice allows fishing fleets to harvest huge catches, leading to overfishing. One solution to overfishing is aquaculture, or the cultivation of fish and other seafood. Several countries in the region raise seafood, such as prawns, in ponds for export.

Japan, East Asia's largest consumer of whale meat, remains the target of global criticism for its

L3 Research a Documentary
Have students research current events related to East Asia's environment (including natural disasters), and then prepare a TV or radio news feature.

NATIONAL GEOGRAPHIC World Explorer

Answer
develop aquaculture; restrict commercial fishing until supplies are replenished

More About the Photo
Every day, more than 400 types of seafood weighing 5 million pounds are auctioned at Tokyo's Central Wholesale Market, totaling $28 million per day.

L1/ELL

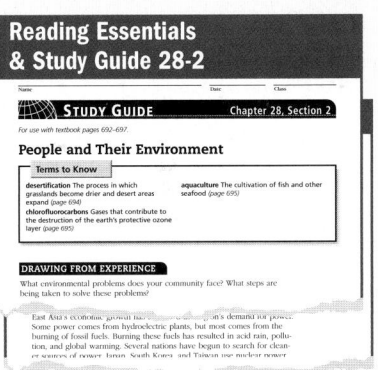

Reading Essentials & Study Guide 28-2

STUDY GUIDE   Chapter 28, Section 2

People and Their Environment

Terms to Know

desertification The process in which grasslands become drier and desert areas expand *(page 694)*
chlorofluorocarbons Gases that contribute to the destruction of the earth's protective ozone layer *(page 695)*
aquaculture The cultivation of fish and other seafood *(page 695)*

DRAWING FROM EXPERIENCE
What environmental problems does your community face? What steps are being taken to solve these problems?

CRITICAL THINKING ACTIVITY

Identifying Alternatives Challenge students to suggest energy alternatives to existing environmentally-troublesome technologies, such as nuclear, coal, or fossil fuel power generators. Have students brainstorm a list of alternatives, encouraging them to be creative in suggesting a wide range of ideas. Alternatives could include, but not be limited to, hydroelectric, solar, geothermal, or wind power; conservation practices and technologies; and the return to simpler ways of life. Have some students work with partners to research existing alternative technologies, or to present their creative ideas to the class, preparing graphics, posters, or media advertisements to promote or explain their ideas. 📦

🌐 EE5 Environment and Society: Standard 14

INTERDISCIPLINARY
c o n n e c t i o n

TECHNOLOGY In early 2000 China and Japan jointly initiated a high-tech flood- and environmental-monitoring system. The computerized remote-sensing system is designed to help predict natural disasters and provide environmental information.

 **ASSESS**

Assign Section 2 Assessment as homework or as an in-class activity.

⊙ Have students use **Interactive Tutor Self-Assessment CD-ROM.**

L2

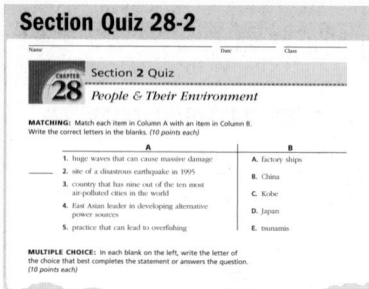

Section Quiz 28-2

NATIONAL GEOGRAPHIC   **MAP STUDY**

Answers

1. *five*

2. *It lies next to a plate boundary of the Ring of Fire.*

Map Skills Practice

Where did most of China's major earthquakes occur in the 1900s? *(central region)*

---

whaling practices. According to international conservation groups, overhunting has caused a serious decline in the whale population. Despite a 1986 international treaty limiting whaling, Japanese fleets continue to hunt whales, including endangered species, in large numbers to satisfy the high demand for the expensive delicacy.

Natural Disasters

Because of its location and physical geography, East Asia has faced catastrophic natural disasters. China's Yellow and Yangtze Rivers can produce disastrous flooding. Attempts to control flooding have included building networks of drainage channels and irrigation canals to transport or redirect water quickly. Dams, dikes, and levees also have been built. Despite these measures, severe floods continue. More than 30,000 of China's dams, hastily built during the 1950s and 1960s, are now defective and at risk of failing.

To address these problems, China is dredging rivers and creating more flood-control projects. The world's largest public works project, and one of the most controversial, is the Three Gorges Dam, under construction upriver from Wuhan on the Yangtze River in central China. When finished, it will create a huge reservoir nearly 400 miles (644 km) long. The dam's critics argue that the project will force the relocation of almost 2 million people, put countless farms, villages, scenic canyons, and ancient temples underwater, and destroy the natural habitats for Siberian cranes and snub-nosed dolphins.

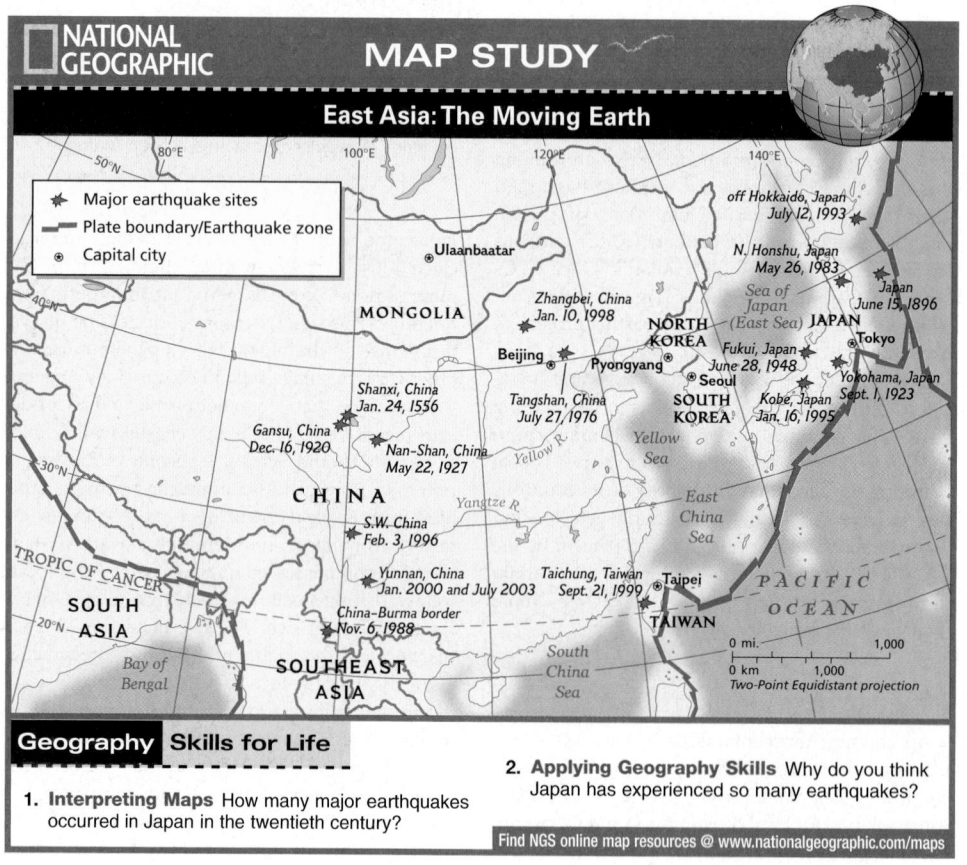

NATIONAL GEOGRAPHIC   **MAP STUDY**

East Asia: The Moving Earth

Geography Skills for Life

1. Interpreting Maps How many major earthquakes occurred in Japan in the twentieth century?

2. Applying Geography Skills Why do you think Japan has experienced so many earthquakes?

Find NGS online map resources @ www.nationalgeographic.com/maps

---

TEAM-TEACHING ACTIVITY: SCIENCE

Earthquakes, Tsunamis, and Volcanic Eruptions Have students work with a science teacher to deepen their understanding of how earthquakes, volcanoes, and tsunamis occur; investigating the various types of wave motion caused by different types of earthquakes; and the differing ways that volcanoes erupt. Have students create diagrams with captions that explain the dynamics of the earth's crust or the sequence of events during earthquakes, tsunamis, and volcanic eruptions. Some students may enjoy researching the construction technology of so-called earthquake-proof buildings, such as those built atop giant ball-bearings. ⊞ ⊕ **EE3 Physical Systems: Standard 7**

Most East Asian countries experience destructive earthquakes. A series of major earthquakes struck Taiwan in late 1999 and China's Yunnan Province in early 2000 and mid-2003. Each year, about 1,500 small earthquakes shake Japan, which is located at plate boundaries and is part of the Pacific Ocean's Ring of Fire. In 1995 a severe earthquake caused widespread damage around **Kobe** (koh•bay), a major Japanese port:

> ❝ *In the aftermath of Kobe, the government has tried to improve prediction of quakes, but scientists still cannot provide crucial details of imminent jolts, such as when and where [they] will occur.* ❞
>
> "Japan Recalls Quake Disaster," *BBC News* (online), January 17, 2000

Japan also has more than 80 active volcanoes. Undersea volcanoes or earthquakes can trigger huge tsunamis—waves that grow larger as they approach land and often cause massive destruction and loss of life when they hit land. Typhoons, violent tropical storms with circular winds of at least 74 miles per hour (119 km per hour), cause periodic devastation from high winds and flooding along East Asia's coasts.

NATIONAL GEOGRAPHIC **World Explorer**

Geography Skills for Life

Earthquake in Kobe The Kobe earthquake of 1995 destroyed about 100,000 buildings in the metropolitan area.
Human-Environment Interaction How many earthquakes shake Japan each year?

East Asia has begun to address environmental issues. However, other challenges, such as flooding, erosion, desertification, and famine, continue to loom on East Asia's horizon.

SECTION 2 ASSESSMENT

Checking for Understanding

1. **Define** desertification, chlorofluorocarbons, aquaculture.

2. **Main Ideas** Use a graphic organizer like the one below to fill in examples of environmental concerns and natural disasters common in East Asia.

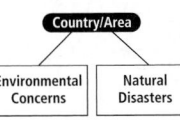

Country/Area

Environmental Concerns — Natural Disasters

Critical Thinking

3. **Identifying Cause and Effect** What are some possible positive and negative aspects of using nuclear power in East Asia?

4. **Classifying Information** What are the leading sources of power in each East Asian country? Which of the countries use nuclear power?

5. **Drawing Conclusions** How are environmental challenges in other developing countries similar to those in East Asia?

Analyzing Maps

6. **Location** Study the map on page 696. When did the most recent earthquake in China occur? Where did it occur?

Applying Geography

7. **Environmental Solutions** Choose one of East Asia's environmental challenges, such as pollution, deforestation, or desertification. Write a paragraph outlining possible solutions.

Chapter 28 ⊕ 697

SECTION 2 ASSESSMENT ANSWERS

1. All vocabulary items are defined in the text.

2. Students' charts should list examples of environmental concerns and natural disasters.

3. positive: abundant power; negative: hazardous nuclear waste, disposal problems, possibility of radioactive leaks in areas prone to earthquakes

4. coal: China, North Korea, Mongolia; imported fossil fuels (coal, natural gas, petroleum): Japan, South Korea, Taiwan; nuclear power: Japan, South Korea, Taiwan

5. Answers may include the need for power and that industrialization results in overlooking the harm some forms of cheap power can cause.

6. Sept. 21, 1999, in Taichung, Taiwan

7. **Applying Geography** Best paragraphs will clearly state the environmental concerns, identify their causes, effects, and the regions they impact within East Asia. It will suggest multiple solutions.

1 FOCUS

Point out that people living in the Three Gorges region may have different responses to the building of the dam.

- A couple who must move their family are probably concerned about their new home and how they will make a living.
- A tradesperson or fisher who depends on the Yangtze for a livelihood could face problems finding work.
- An entrepreneur may see opportunities when the dam makes it possible for tourists to travel farther north.

Ask students for additional ideas or viewpoints.

2 TEACH

Explain the opposing viewpoints regarding the Three Gorges project:

- China's government claims that the dam will prevent flood disasters, while environmentalists claim that a series of smaller dams would provide the same benefit with less environmental impact.
- Officials claim the dam will cause minimal environmental damage, while critics predict that pollution levels will double when the Yangtze no longer carries wastes from factories and cities out to sea.

L2 Identify Central Issues

Have students make a two-column chart listing advantages and disadvantages of the Three Gorges project.

698

Viewpoint
CASE STUDY on the Environment

CHINA

Beijing ★

Fengdu ● Three Gorges Dam ● Shanghai

Yangtze River

China's Three Gorges:

Before the Flood

The Chinese call it Chang Jiang—"Long River." Elsewhere, most people know it as the Yangtze River. Nearly 4,000 miles (6,400 km) long, the Yangtze is the longest river in China. For thousands of years, the Yangtze has been both a positive and a negative force in the lives of many Chinese. The river provides water for 380 million people, and half of China's food is grown along its banks. Yet when the Yangtze overflows, its floodwaters can kill thousands of people and leave millions homeless. Now the Chinese government is trying to tame the Yangtze with a huge—and hugely controversial—dam.

698   Unit 9

LOOKING TO THE FUTURE

Relocation Problems The challenges involved in relocating nearly two million people appear to be increasing. In 2000 nearly 100 Chinese officials were convicted of having stolen millions of dollars earmarked for helping people relocate their homes, towns, and businesses. Many people have been forced to go into debt in order to move. Farmers, promised good land, have been moved to rocky, steep areas practically impossible to farm. Some critics say a series of smaller dams could have provided the needed electricity without relocating millions of people and destroying countless historic sites. They warn that the dire problems people are facing may result in great social instability in the region.

🌐 **EE5 Environment and Society: Standards 14, 15**

Boatman Ma Linyou (left) deftly steers his wooden craft along the Yangtze, as it winds among the limestone cliffs of the scenic Three Gorges region. In less than a decade, these canyons will vanish forever under a huge volume of water when the Three Gorges Dam blocks the Yangtze's vigorous flow. The dam will create a deep reservoir nearly 400 miles (640 km) long.

Construction of the Three Gorges Dam began in 1994. Scheduled for completion in 2009, it will be the largest dam in the world. The dam is China's most ambitious construction project since building the Great Wall. The Chinese government claims that the dam's positive impact on the region will justify its staggering $25 billion price tag. The Three Gorges Dam could put an end to the devastating floods along the lower portions of the river. For centuries the floods have claimed lives, destroyed settlements, and damaged agricultural lands.

The dam will also be the world's largest hydroelectric plant, designed to generate more than 18 million kilowatts of electricity—an output equal to 18 nuclear power plants. China needs clean, renewable energy to replace the enormous amounts of coal the country burns, a practice that has led to severe air pollution and acid rain.

Supporters of the Three Gorges Dam emphasize its energy and commercial benefits. As China moves toward the future, it faces crippling power shortages. The dam will help solve the problem, generating 20 percent of China's electrical power. In addition, say supporters, the reservoir behind the dam will make more water available for irrigation. The reservoir also will allow large ships and tourist vessels to reach cities far upstream, thus sparking economic growth.

Opponents of the Three Gorges Dam object to its huge environmental and human costs. Environmentalists fear that as

A displaced villager lugs his belongings downriver to a new home.

the water rises, pollutants in soil and chemicals in abandoned factories will leach into the river, threatening aquatic life and drinking water. Critics point out that the reservoir will submerge hundreds of farms, villages, and some 13 major cities. Nearly two million people will have to abandon their homes. In addition, archaeologists estimate that 8,000 unexcavated sites will be lost forever in a tomb of water.

Despite the opposition, China's government seems determined to finish the Three Gorges Dam. As the controversy rages, work continues on the great concrete barrier that will tame the Yangtze's flow.

> **What's Your Point of View?**
> Do you think the Three Gorges Dam is a good idea? Why or why not?

The city of Fengdu today (below, left) and as it will look when the dam is complete (below, right). ▼

Before

After

WHAT CAN YOU DO?

Educate yourself in depth about the Three Gorges project, and keep aware of its progress in the coming years. Research news, media articles, and television programs that already exist about the project, and continue to update your knowledge.

Investigate the opposing claims of those who criticize or defend different aspects of the project, keeping in mind the authors' biases as you evaluate their claims.
🌐 **EE5 Environment and Society: Standard 14**
🌐 **EE6 The Uses of Geography: Standard 18**

③ ASSESS

Have students answer the **What's Your Point of View?** question on page 699.

④ CLOSE

Remind students that a major cause of flooding is the silting of riverbeds, and that silt is expected to build up over time in the reservoir behind the dam. **Ask:** What long-range effects could silting of the Three Gorges reservoir cause? (*Towns located along the shore of the reservoir could flood; water levels could eventually rise above the level of the dam, causing a disaster.*)

global
issues

Endangered Species The Yangtze River system is home to at least two threatened species, the rare snub-nosed dolphin and the Siberian crane.

🌐 Meeting National Standards

Geography for Life
The following standards are met in the Student Edition:

EE3 Physical Systems: Standard 7
EE4 Environment and Society: Standards 14, 15
EE6 The Uses of Geography: Standards 17, 18

Teaching the Skill

Ask a volunteer to identify a decision he or she has made recently, or pose the following situation:
Ask: Suppose your parents are not home when your friend calls to ask for a ride to work. Should you use your parents' car to help your friend?

Lead students through the bulleted steps on page 700, using a web diagram to lay out the options:

- Write the question on the board as the center of a web. Students can brainstorm a list of factors that influence the decision; list these under the question.
- Have students brainstorm options; add these as branches of the web. For each option, have students list consequences. Discuss and note the influence of personal values.
- Have students vote on the options to reach a decision.

Additional Practice
L1

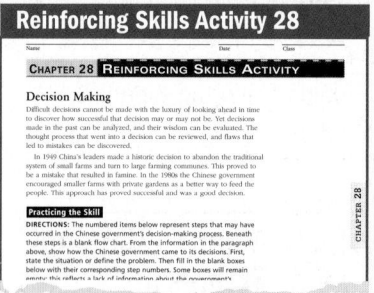

Reinforcing Skills Activity 28

Name ___ Date ___ Class ___

CHAPTER 28 REINFORCING SKILLS ACTIVITY

Decision Making

Difficult decisions cannot be made with the luxury of looking ahead in time to discover how successful that decision may or may not be. Yet decisions made in the past can be analyzed, and their wisdom can be evaluated. The thought process that went into a decision can be reviewed, and flaws that led to mistakes can be discovered.

In 1949 China's leaders made a historic decision to abandon the traditional system of small farms and turn to large farming communes. This proved to be a mistake that resulted in famine. In the 1980s the Chinese government encouraged smaller farms with private gardens as a better way to feed the people. This approach has proved successful and was a good decision.

Practicing the Skill

DIRECTIONS: The numbered items below represent steps that may have occurred in the Chinese government's decision-making process. Beneath these steps is a blank flow chart. From the information in the paragraph above, show how the Chinese government came to its decisions. First, state the situation or define the problem. Then fill in the blank boxes below with their corresponding step numbers. Some boxes will remain empty. This reflects a lack of information about the government's...

CHAPTER 28

GLENCOE
TECHNOLOGY

Glencoe Skillbuilder Interactive Workbook, Level 2

CRITICAL THINKING
SkillBuilder

Decision Making

From deciding what to eat for lunch to choosing a career goal, young people must make decisions every day. Some decisions are easier to make than others because they are less complex and have minor consequences. Thinking logically and carefully about more important decisions will help you choose wisely.

Learning the Skill

Decisions involve making a choice between alternatives. Each alternative has a likely consequence, or result. To make good decisions, consider as many of the likely consequences as possible before you take action. You can learn to improve your decision-making skills by following these basic steps:

- **State the situation or define the problem.** Ask: Why do I have to make a decision in this matter?
- **Gather all of the facts.** Ask: What information should influence my decision?
- **Identify and evaluate alternatives.** Ask: What are all of my options?
- **Predict future consequences.** Weigh the likely outcomes of each alternative.
- **Consider your personal values.** Use your values as guidelines for making the right decision.
- **Make your decision and act on it.** You should now feel confident that you have thought about the issue carefully.
- **Evaluate your decision.** Analyze whether you made the right choice. Ask: Would I make the same decision again?

▲ Chinese president Jiang Zemin (left) confers with Premier Li Peng.

Practicing the Skill

Answer the following questions about decision making.

1. Why is it important to consider more than one alternative when making a decision?

2. What are two reasons for predicting the possible consequences of each alternative you consider?

3. What might be the result of making a decision that conflicts with your values?

4. What can you learn from evaluating a decision you have made?

Applying the Skill

Identify a problem or issue in an East Asian country that requires a decision, and gather information about it. Write down the options available to the country, and assess the consequences of each option. Then write a paragraph explaining how you think the country should decide on the problem or issue.

Go To The Glencoe Skillbuilder Interactive Workbook, Level 2 provides instruction and practice in key social studies skills.

ANSWERS TO PRACTICING THE SKILL

Accept reasonable and thoughtful responses.

1. There may be more than one good option available; some options are more suitable than others; you might not think of the best options first.

2. Looking ahead can help you see if the result may cause any problems; doing so may help spark additional options; it can help you plan the steps to take once you make a decision.

3. If a decision conflicts with your values, you might not be comfortable with your decision after you take action; it could affect you for a long time.

4. Evaluating can help you improve your decision making and your choices in the future. As with other things, you get better with practice.

CHAPTER 28

SUMMARY & STUDY GUIDE

SECTION 1 — Living in East Asia (pp. 685–691)

Terms to Know

- command system
- commune
- cooperative
- Asia-Pacific Economic Cooperation Group (APEC)
- trade surplus
- trade deficit
- dissident
- economic sanctions
- World Trade Organization (WTO)
- merchant marine

Key Points

- East Asian economies include market and command systems, as well as a mix of both.
- East Asia was once mainly agricultural, but trade and industry have brought prosperity and economic growth to most of its countries.
- Most Chinese work in agriculture, although industry and commerce are thriving in certain areas as a result of government-sponsored economic reforms.
- Japan is East Asia's leading industrial country, followed by Taiwan and South Korea.
- Trade and business investments bring together capitalist and communist countries in East Asia.

Organizing Your Notes

Create an outline using the format below to help you organize your notes for this section.

Governments and Economies
I. Political and Economic Systems
A.
B.
C.
II. Agriculture
A. China
B.
C.

SECTION 2 — People and Their Environment (pp. 692–697)

Terms to Know

- desertification
- chlorofluoro-carbons
- aquaculture

Key Points

- Rapid industrial growth in East Asia has caused environmental challenges that were ignored for decades.
- Japan, with its strict anti-pollution laws, has become a leader in protecting and cleaning up the environment.
- China's economic development and the needs of its large population have a decisive impact on the environment.
- East Asia is subject to natural disasters such as flooding, earthquakes, tsunamis, and typhoons.
- Human activities in East Asia—such as clear-cutting forests, farming, and mining—have caused environmental disasters such as erosion, desertification, and flooding.

Organizing Your Notes

Create a chart like the one below to help you organize important details from this section.

Locations	Problems/Causes	Effects/Solutions
	air pollution	
	deforestation	
	desertification	
	nuclear hazards	
	earthquakes	
	floods	

Using the Chapter 28 Summary & Study Guide

Use the Chapter 28 Summary & Study Guide to preview, review, condense, or reteach the chapter.

Preview/Review

- **Vocabulary PuzzleMaker CD-ROM** reinforces "Terms to Know."

- **Interactive Tutor Self-Assessment CD-ROM** provides a review of Chapter 28 content.

Condense

Have students read the Chapter 28 Summary & Study Guide.

- Chapter 28 Audio Program

- Chapter 28 Guided Reading Activities

Reteach

- Chapter 28 Reteaching Activities (Spanish also available)

- Chapter 28 Reading Essentials and Study Guides

GLENCOE TECHNOLOGY

NATIONAL GEOGRAPHIC

WORLD REGIONS VIDEO PROGRAM

Unit 9, East Asia
The following segments enhance the study of this unit:

- **Treasures of the Gobi**
- **Haenyo of Cheju**
- **A-Mei: Princess of Pop**

CHAPTER CULMINATING ACTIVITY

Making Comparisons Remind students of their earlier discussion that compared East Asia's environmental challenges with those of the United States. Organize the class into two groups. Have one group review their notes and Chapter 28 to identify environmental issues in East Asia and the other group review their notes and pages 165–171 for environmental issues in the United States. Have groups prepare and present summaries to the class. **Ask: Which region do you think has greater environmental concerns? Why?** Have students write an essay in which they explain and defend a position on the issue.
EE5 Environment and Society: Standard 14

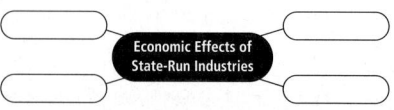

ASSESSMENT & ACTIVITIES

CHAPTER 28

Reviewing Key Terms

1. Both refer to farms under communist systems.
2. Both refer to trade imbalance.
3. Economic sanctions may result from the treatment of dissidents, as with U.S. sanctions against China.
4. Both are related to environmental concerns.
5. Both are international associations to encourage and regulate trade.

Reviewing Facts

SECTION 1

1. market: Taiwan, South Korea, Japan; command: North Korea; mixed: China, Mongolia
2. They allow some private businesses and foreign businesses; investments are encouraged, and government-free economic zones have been created.
3. high import taxes on finished goods, high global demand for Japanese goods
4. China, Japan, South Korea, Taiwan
5. economic sanctions, increased trade relationships

SECTION 2

6. deforestation, acid rain, air pollution, sewage treatment, flooding, desertification
7. a nuclear power accident in 1999 that caused a significant radiation leak

---

Reviewing Key Terms

Examine the pairs of words below. Then explain what each of the pairs has in common.

1. commune/cooperative
2. trade surplus/trade deficit
3. dissident/economic sanctions
4. desertification/chlorofluorocarbons
5. APEC/WTO

Reviewing Facts

SECTION 1

1. Explain how economies operate in each of the following East Asian countries: Japan, China, Taiwan, and North Korea.
2. What economic reforms have Chinese leaders introduced?
3. What contributes to Japan's trade surplus with other countries?
4. Which East Asian countries are members of APEC?
5. How have the United States and other countries tried to influence China's stance on human rights?

SECTION 2

6. Describe six serious environmental challenges facing East Asia.
7. Japan is looking for alternative electric power sources. What event helped cause Japanese interest in these alternatives?
8. Which three East Asian countries rely on nuclear power to meet at least 30 percent of their electricity needs?
9. How does China's heavy reliance on coal contribute to air pollution in the region?
10. How have commercial fishing companies and factory ships intensified overfishing in the region?

Critical Thinking

1. **Predicting Consequences** Study the map on page 639. What impact might a railroad between Tibet and the rest of China have on Tibet's economy?
2. **Comparing and Contrasting** Examine Japan's environmental record since 1990. In what ways has this record improved? What areas still need improvement?
3. **Identifying Cause and Effect** Complete the diagram below to show how China's state-run industries affect economic growth. Which effect do you think is most important?

Economic Effects of State-Run Industries

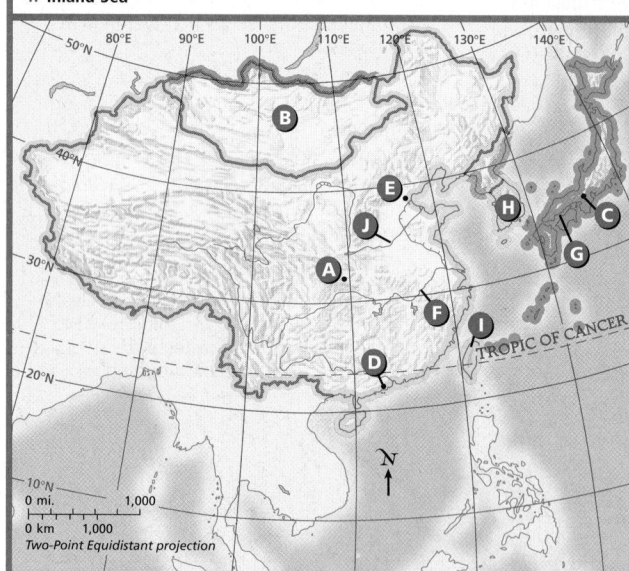

NATIONAL GEOGRAPHIC
Locating Places
East Asia: Physical-Political Geography

Match the letters on the map with the places and physical features of East Asia listed below. Write your answers on a sheet of paper.

1. Mongolia
2. Yangtze River
3. Macau
4. Inland Sea
5. Kobe
6. Wuhan
7. Tianjin
8. Taiwan
9. South Korea
10. Yellow River

---

8. Japan, South Korea, Taiwan
9. It is a major source of acid rain.
10. Their huge catches deplete fish resources.

Critical Thinking

1. Answers should focus on what economic changes will take place in Tibet in the short and long run, and why.
2. Students may mention improvements such as laws, clean technologies, and assistance to other countries. Areas needing improvement may include whaling, overfishing, and increased carbon dioxide emissions.
3. Answers may include drops in crop production, inefficient production, outdated technology, and little incentive to produce.

NATIONAL GEOGRAPHIC Locating Places

1. B	3. D	5. C	7. E	9. H
2. F	4. G	6. A	8. I	10. J

Using the Regional Atlas

Refer to the Regional Atlas on pages 636–639.

1. **Place** By giving the names of areas or countries, identify where each of the following natural resources in East Asia is found: tungsten, iron ore, copper, petroleum, tin, bauxite.

2. **Location** List the capitals of the East Asian countries and their absolute locations.

Thinking Like a Geographer

How might more and improved roads and railroads affect patterns of settlement, population distribution, and resource use in China's interior areas?

Problem-Solving Activity

Group Research Project In June 2000, North and South Korea entered into peaceful negotiations for the first time in 50 years. Work with a group to research the agreement the two countries reached. Evaluate whether unifying Korea is a realistic prospect for the future. Then write an editorial explaining your position.

GeoJournal

Evaluating Information Review the information you logged in your GeoJournal as you read this chapter. Choose one of the economic or environmental challenges. Then write an essay evaluating East Asia's success in using technology to meet and solve the challenge.

Technology Activity

Creating a Web Site Collect information, graphics, and photos for each country in East Asia, including examples of modern and traditional architecture, art, flags, clothing, and scenes from both rural and urban areas. Compose a fact sheet about each country that includes statistics on population, major cities, economic GNP or GDP, literacy rate, and other interesting information. Place your images and facts on your own Web site. Be sure to cite all your sources.

Standardized Test Practice

Read the excerpt below about Chinese writer Gao Xingjian, who won the Nobel Prize for literature in 2000. Then choose the best answer for the following multiple-choice question. If you have trouble answering the question, use the process of elimination to narrow your choices.

"Born in 1940 in Jiangxi province in eastern China, Mr. Gao earned a degree in French in Beijing and embarked on a life of letters [writing literature]. During the Cultural Revolution [1966-1976], he was sent to a re-education camp, where he spent six years at hard labor in the fields. He also burned a suitcase full of his early manuscripts. . . . [In] 1979 . . . he was first able to publish his work and to travel abroad. . . ."

—New York Times On the Web (online), October 12, 2000

1. Xingjian's relationship with the Chinese government can best be described as

A subservient.
B manipulative.
C passive.
D turbulent.

 **Test-Taking Tip** Return to the passage, and underline the parts that represent decisions Xingjian had to make or actions Xingjian had to take. Based on what you underline, try to summarize the government's role in Xingjian's life. Then read the answer choices, eliminating those that you know are incorrect. Last, determine an answer from the answer choices that remain.

GeoJournal

Solutions should be clearly stated and supported by persuasive reasoning.

Technology Activity

You may wish to organize country assignments to avoid duplication. Web sites should show accurate and representative information in both written and visual form.

Standardized Test Practice
1. D

Tested Objectives:
analyzing information
making inferences
determining relevance
making comparisions

Additional Practice and Test-Taking Tips
 Standardized Test Practice Workbook

CHAPTER BONUS TEST QUESTION

Fast-paced, well-informed, and *environmental leadership* are terms associated with the Japanese lifestyle. Give at least one example of each characteristic. *(fast-paced: bullet trains, subways, traffic congestion; well-informed: large print industry of books, magazines, and newspapers; environmental leadership: pollution control laws, developing alternative energy sources.)*

Using the Regional Atlas

1. tungsten: Japan, southeast China, North Korea, South Korea; iron ore: China; copper: Mongolia, China; petroleum: eastern China, Japan; tin: southern China; bauxite: southern China
2. Pyongyang: about 126°E, 39°N; Seoul: about 127°E, 37°N; Tokyo: about 140°E, 36°N; Ulaanbaatar: about 107°E, 47°N; Taipei: about 122°E, 25°N; Beijing: about 116°E, 40°N

Thinking Like a Geographer

Answers should demonstrate an awareness of the limitations presented by physical barriers.

Problem-Solving Activity

Accept reasonable answers based on supporting evidence.

TEACHING TRANSPARENCIES

L2 Unit 10 Map Overlay Transparencies

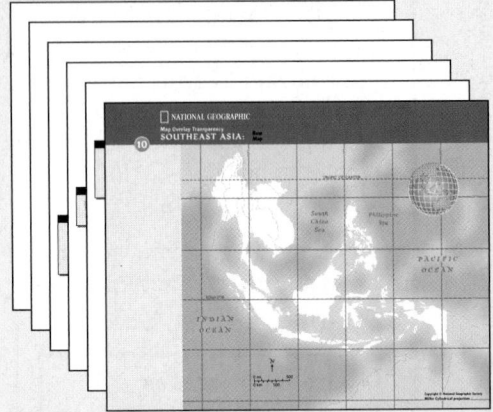

L2 Political Map Transparency 10

L2 World Cultures Transparencies 17, 18

APPLICATION AND ENRICHMENT

L2 Location Activity 10

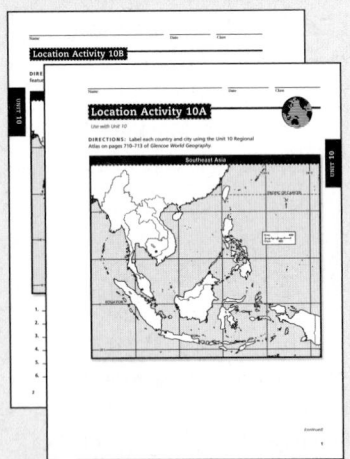

L2 Real-Life Applications and Problem-Solving Activity 10

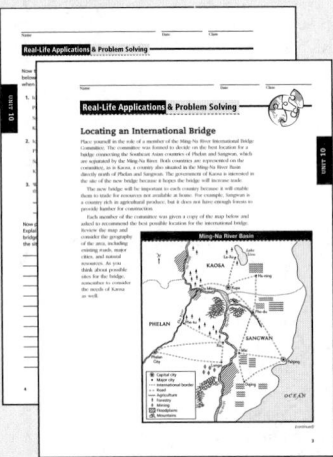

L2 GeoLab Activity 10

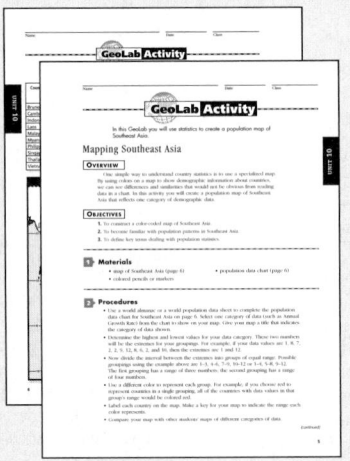

L2 Environmental Issues Case Study 10

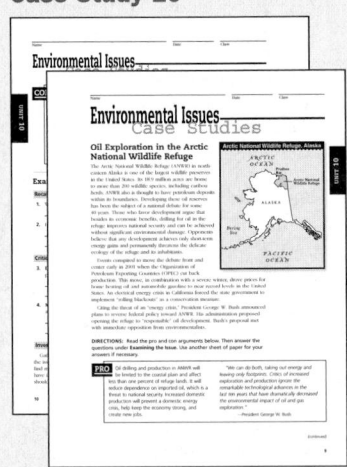

GEOGRAPHIC LITERACY

Focus on Geography Literacy

Building Geography Skills for Life

GLENCOE'S ASSESSMENT ADVANTAGE ASSESSMENT

Use the following to easily assess student learning in a variety of ways:
- Performance Assessment Activities and Rubrics
- Section Quizzes
- Chapter and Unit Tests
- Interactive Tutor Self-Assessment CD–ROM
- ExamView® Pro Testmaker
- MindJogger Videoquiz
- geography.glencoe.com
- Standardized Test Practice Workbook
- SAT I/II Test Practice

L2 Unit 10 Pretest and Tests

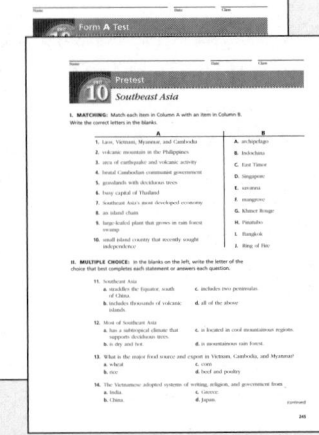

INTERDISCIPLINARY CONNECTIONS

L2 World Literature:
Contemporary Selection 10

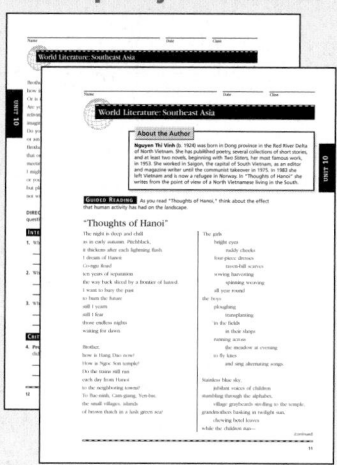

Foods Around the World

Multimedia

- World Art and Architecture Transparencies

- World Art Prints

- World Music: A Cultural Legacy

- World History Primary Source Document Library

BIBLIOGRAPHY

Readings for the Student

Southeast Asia by Anthony Mason. New York, NY: Steck-Vaughn, World in View Series, 1992.

Southeast Asia: A Concise History by Mary Somers Heidhues. London: Thames & Hudson, 2000.

Readings for the Teacher

South-East Asia: A Modern History by Nicholas Tarling. London: Oxford University Press, 2001.

Democratization in Southeast and East Asia, Anek Laothamatas (ed.). Bangkok: Institute of Southeast Asian Studies, Singapore, and Silkworm Books, 1997.

Multimedia Resources

Indochina: The Heart of Southeast Asia. Educational Video Network, 2000. VHS, 25 minutes (with teacher's guide online)

Vietnam: A Case Study for Critical Thinking. Both Sides of the Vietnam War. VHS, 52 minutes.

READING SUPPORT FROM JAMESTOWN EDUCATION

- *Timed Readings Plus in Social Studies* help students increase their reading rate and fluency while maintaining comprehension. The 400-word passages are similar to those found on state and national assessments.

- *Reading in the Content Area: Social Studies* concentrates on six essential reading skills that help students better comprehend what they read. The book includes 75 high-interest nonfiction passages written at increasing levels of difficulty.

- *Reading Fluency* helps students read smoothly, accurately, and expressively.

- *Jamestown's Reading Improvement,* by renowned reading expert Edward Fry, focuses on helping build your students' comprehension, vocabulary, and skimming and scanning skills.

- *Critical Reading Series* provides high-interest books, each written at three reading levels.

For more information about these products, see the Jamestown Education materials in the Classroom Solutions in the front of this Teacher Wraparound Edition.
To order these products, call Glencoe at 1-800-334-7344.

Background Information

The Physical Geography of Southeast Asia

Southeast Asia's islands and peninsulas cover an area of about 1,750,000 square miles (4,536,000 sq. km). Including its seas, Southeast Asia spreads over an area of about 5 million square miles (13 million sq. km).

The region's mainland mountains form a natural barrier between peninsular countries, such as Vietnam and Myanmar, and their larger neighbors, China and India.

In highlands areas below these mountain ranges rise three great rivers: the Mekong, the Irrawaddy, and the Chao Phraya. Southeast Asia's rivers have influenced human settlement and economic activities. Flowing southward through heavily forested areas, the rivers form the principal means of transportation. Their wet, fertile floodplains support the growing of rice, Southeast Asia's staple crop.

Rain forests cover many Southeast Asian islands. These lush habitats are home to thousands of species of rare plants and animals, among them the orangutan and the Komodo dragon, the world's largest lizard.

Natural Resources

Southeast Asia is rich in natural resources. The region's fertile soil yields rubber, rice, tea, and spices; its forests provide valuable woods, such as teak; and coastal waters have large quantities of fish.

Parts of Southeast Asia also have rich petroleum deposits and tin and gem mines. For example, Indonesia and Brunei are leading exporters of oil and natural gas.

The Cultural Geography of Southeast Asia

About 520 million people inhabit Southeast Asia today. Most Southeast Asians have Malay or Chinese ancestry, and about 65 percent of them live in rural areas.

In recent years a growing number of rural residents have moved to urban areas, seeking better economic opportunities. The largest cities in Southeast Asia are Jakarta, Indonesia; Bangkok, Thailand; Ho Chi Minh City, Vietnam; and the city-state of Singapore.

Southeast Asia as a whole has a high population growth rate, and some countries have carried out programs to slow population growth or to move people away from heavily populated areas. In some places, however, emigration and a declining birthrate may make it difficult to find enough skilled workers to meet future needs.

Islam and Buddhism are Southeast Asia's major faiths. Islam is the largest religion in Malaysia and Indonesia, while Buddhism predominates in Myanmar, Thailand, and Vietnam. Most people in the Philippines are Christians, primarily Roman Catholics.

Past and Present

Before the A.D. 1500s, powerful seafaring empires emerged in Southeast Asia under the influence of Hindu, and later, Arab Muslim traders. Europeans, attracted by such spices as pepper and cloves, occupied much of Southeast Asia in the early modern period. By the late 1800s, all of the region, except Siam (later Thailand), was under European rule.

During World War II, Japan, eager for tin and rubber, took over much of Southeast Asia. After Japan's defeat, the Philippines and major British colonies gained their freedom under relatively peaceful circumstances.

Elsewhere in Southeast Asia, nationalist and communist groups fought for independence. In 1975 after the long and bitter Vietnam War, all of Vietnam became communist. Beginning in the 1980s, the manufacture of export goods helped boost Southeast Asian economies.

Today, tradition and innovation coexist in Southeast Asia. Angkor Wat and the Petronas Twin Towers illustrate this meeting of past and present. In the forests of Cambodia lie the ruins of Angkor Wat, a magnificent temple complex built more than 800 years ago. Carved into its stone walls are detailed images that reveal the grandeur of the powerful Khmer Empire and its Hindu-Buddhist traditions.

In the Malay Peninsula to the south, a modern architectural wonder—the Petronas Twin Towers—rises 1,483 feet (452 m) above the streets of Kuala Lumpur, Malaysia's capital. These matching skyscrapers are among the tallest buildings in the world.

CHAPTER 31 (pp. 758–777)

Southeast Asia Today

Rice farming is the most important agricultural activity in Southeast Asia. For centuries farmers in the region followed traditional agricultural practices. In the 1960s Southeast Asian countries began to take part in what became known as the "green revolution," an undertaking to help farmers in developing countries increase production through technology and improved agricultural methods, including chemical fertilizers and pesticides. Rice production rose, which helped to feed the growing population.

In recent years Southeast Asian countries have tried to diversify their economies. Singapore, Thailand, and Malaysia took great strides toward industrialization. Malaysia, in fact, has become a leading manufacturer of microchips for the computer industry. Malaysia, Thailand, and Singapore now rank high among the world's newly industrialized countries, those with high economic growth and significant improvement in the standard of living.

Southeast Asian leaders realize that interdependence is a key as the region competes in the global economy. In 1967 the Association of Southeast Asian Nations (ASEAN) was formed to promote economic cooperation and development among countries of the Southeast Asian region. Before 2030 ASEAN hopes to share in the creation of a united Asian trading bloc to link the economies of Southeast Asia, China, Japan, and South Korea.

Regional and Global Challenges

Southeast Asia faces many of the same challenges that confront other regions. Globalization has brought a measure of prosperity. Fast-paced economic development, however, has taken a disastrous toll on plant and animal life.

Only 25 percent of Thailand's original forest cover remains. Of that, only about 17 percent is healthy. Careless fishing methods have destroyed vast areas of coral reef. These changes may have a negative impact on human health. Medical researchers believe that certain chemicals in coral and other sea life may have great potential for the treatment of cancer and other diseases.

Industrialization also has spawned the unregulated growth of urban areas with associated problems, such as air pollution and over-crowding. Expanding cities have encroached on rural areas, destroying farmland and rain forests. The movement of rural people to cities has placed a strain on groundwater supplies. Public awareness of environmental issues, however, has grown in recent years.

00:00 OUT OF TIME?

If time does not permit teaching each chapter in this unit, you may want to use the **Reading Essentials and Study Guide** summaries.

Unit Launch Activity

Ask: What do you know about Southeast Asia and its people? What have you learned about the region from TV, radio, newspapers, or movies? Have the class brainstorm and write the responses on the board. Ask for one volunteer to copy the list and another to transfer it to a poster board. Display the poster board in class and encourage students to add to it throughout the course of the unit. At the end of the unit, revisit the expanded list and ask students to summarize, in their own words, why it is important to study Southeast Asia.

GLENCOE
TECHNOLOGY

☐ NATIONAL GEOGRAPHIC

WORLD REGIONS
VIDEO PROGRAM

Unit 10, Southeast Asia
The following segments enhance the study of this unit:

- **Rice**
- **Tet in Hanoi**
- **Design for the Future**

 Available in DVD and VHS

Southeast Asia

704 Unit 10

 GETTING TO KNOW THE REGION

Map Activity Display Political Map Transparency 10. **Ask:** What landforms are part of Southeast Asia? *(a peninsula and islands)* How many countries in the region lie entirely on the Asian mainland? *(five)* How many countries occupy only island territory? *(five)* Which country has both mainland and island territory? *(Malaysia)* Which mainland country is landlocked? *(Laos)* What is the smallest country in the region? *(Singapore)* What imaginary line does the region straddle? *(the Equator)* What effect would proximity to this line have on the region's climate? *(The climate would be mostly tropical.)* Why might Europeans have called Southeast Asia's islands the "East Indies"? *(They are located east of India and the Indian Ocean.)* ▦ EE1 The World in Spatial Terms: Standard 1

NATIONAL GEOGRAPHIC

NGS ONLINE
www.nationalgeographic.com/education

WHY IT'S IMPORTANT—

Southeast Asia is a vital crossroads of trade and commerce. The region is rich in natural resources such as tin, petroleum, rubber, tea, spices, and valuable woods. In recent years, many Southeast Asians have migrated to the United States, bringing their own religions and cultures with them. You are probably familiar with the flavors of many Southeast Asian dishes, available now in restaurants in the United States.

World Regions Video
To learn more about Southeast Asia and its impact on your world, view the World Regions video "Southeast Asia."

Terraced rice fields on the island of Bali, Indonesia

NGS ONLINE
www.nationalgeographic.com/education

This online resource, brought to you by the National Geographic Society, provides lesson plans, atlas updates, cartographic activities with interactive maps, an online map store, and links to the boundless subjects of maps and geography.

Unit Overview

The three chapters that comprise this unit introduce students to the physical and cultural geography of Southeast Asia, as well as to the peoples of that region. Point out to students that although the countries of Southeast Asia are diverse, most have the following features in common:

- a strong Chinese and Indian cultural and religious influence
- European influences that carried over from a colonial period
- a mostly tropical climate and extensive rice fields
- rain forests and abundant natural resources

ABOUT THE PHOTO

Visual Instruction Although relatively small, Bali is one of Indonesia's most agriculturally profitable islands. Terraced gardens make it possible for farmers to irrigate land without the use of pumps or other complex machinery. Water stored above a terrace can be released into a sluice, or artificial channel fitted with a gate. The water flows through the sluice to the plants. By opening or closing the gate, the farmer can control the flow of water. **Ask:** What can you infer about the terrain of Bali from the use of terraced gardens? *(mountainous terrain or one with limited level ground)*

🌐 EE2 Places and Regions: Standard 6
🌐 EE6 The Uses of Geography: Standard 17

UNIT 10 REGIONAL ATLAS

① FOCUS

These features and activities may be used as an introduction to the unit or as teaching tools throughout the course of the unit.

L1 Using Flash Cards Activity

Before beginning the study of this unit, use the **Countries of the World Flash Cards** to preview students' knowledge of Southeast Asia. Organize the students into two teams and test their knowledge. At the end of the game, ask students to summarize any physical or cultural similarities they noticed among countries in the region.

L2 Photo Research Activity

Have students research the subjects of the photos on pages 706–709. Encourage them to find other photos with captions about life in Southeast Asia. Students should report their findings.

INTERDISCIPLINARY connection

GEOLOGY In his book, *Catastrophe*, historian David Keys describes a violent volcanic eruption in A.D. 535. It occurred in almost the same location as Krakatau. A contemporary Indonesian account reported that this blast split the original Java in two, creating Sumatra.

What Makes Southeast Asia a Region?

Lying east of India and south of China, Southeast Asia juts out from the rest of the Asian continent and then fragments into a jumble of islands that straddle the Equator. Two peninsulas form the mainland—the bulbous Indochina Peninsula and the narrow Malay Peninsula, which extends southward from the other like a long, gnarled finger. Millions of years ago, tectonic plates collided to form parallel mountain ranges that span the mainland from north to south. Great rivers, such as the Irrawaddy, Mekong, Chao Phraya, and Red, course through the valleys between these ranges and create fertile deltas where they meet the sea.

Most of the region's islands are mountainous, too, but their peaks were spawned by ancient volcanic eruptions. Active volcanoes remain a threat on these islands, which lie along the Pacific Ring of Fire.

Rain forests cover parts of Southeast Asia. Watered by monsoon rains, these forests—valued for their timber and wildlife—are decreasing because of extensive logging.

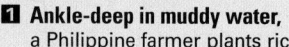

1 Ankle-deep in muddy water, a Philippine farmer plants rice seedlings in a flooded paddy. Southeast Asia's fertile soils and warm, wet climate are ideal for growing rice. Most farmers in Southeast Asia plant and harvest their crops by hand.

706 Unit 10

BACKGROUND INFORMATION

Vu Quang Nature Reserve Southeast Asia's rain forests are a source of wonder. Vu Quang, in northern Vietnam, is so remote and impenetrable that few humans venture there. In 1992 biologists found skulls of a previously unknown, long-horned mammal in the forest. The Vu Quang ox is a large mammal genus, a distant relative of sheep and cattle. A calf was later captured and taken to Hanoi for study. It was the first live specimen of the Vu Quang ox that scientists had seen. A second newly discovered species, the giant muntjac, was located at Vu Quang in 1993. A muntjac is a nocturnal deer with huge canine teeth. Smaller species of this "barking deer" are found in other parts of Southeast Asia, China, and India.
🌐 **EE2 Places and Regions: Standard 4**

② TEACH

L2 Human-Environment Interaction

Point out the importance of water in Southeast Asia and have students suggest the positive and negative ways that water affects the region. **Ask: What benefits might rivers, lakes, and seas bring to Southeast Asians?** *(water for transportation and for raising crops; fishing; the development of trade networks)* **What influence might water have on settlement patterns?** *(encourages settlement along the waterways and seacoasts, where transportation, trade, and fishing are available)* Tell students to make a list of the ways that the water might affect life in Southeast Asia. Have them refer to this list and confirm their predictions as they read about the region.

GLENCOE *TECHNOLOGY*

☐ NATIONAL GEOGRAPHIC

WORLD REGIONS
VIDEO PROGRAM

Unit 10, Southeast Asia
The following segments enhance the study of this unit:

* **Rice**
* **Tet in Hanoi**
* **Design for the Future**

 Available in DVD and VHS

2 **Using trunk and tusks,** an Asian elephant piles up teak logs along a river in Myanmar. The lush forests of this country supply more than three-fourths of the world's teak, a beautiful, durable wood often used for furniture. Some Southeast Asian loggers use tractors, but elephants are cheaper and don't require roads.

3 **Steering with slender paddles,** a Vietnamese woman guides her boat through a shallow waterway on the delta of the Mekong River. From its source in China, the Mekong flows 2,600 miles (4,180 km) to the South China Sea. Like rivers throughout this region, the Mekong is a vital transportation route for people and goods.

4 **Like a fountain of fire,** Krakatau hurls lava into the night sky. One of Indonesia's many active volcanoes, Krakatau lies between the islands of Sumatra and Java. In 1883, 36,000 people died when Krakatau erupted violently, generating huge tidal waves that swept over the nearby islands.

Unit 10 **707**

A TRAVELER'S LOG

Marco Polo Italian trader Marco Polo's account of his travels in the A.D. 1200s includes this description of the island of Java:
"This is the biggest island in the world, having a circumference of more than 3,000 miles [4,827 km]. . . . It is a very rich island, producing pepper, nutmegs, spikenard [plant used for making perfume], galingale [ginger-like root], cubebs [Java peppers], and cloves, and all the precious spices that can be found in the world. . . . The quantity of treasure in the island is beyond all computation. . . . [T]his is the source of most of the spice that comes into the world's markets." ⊕ EE2 Places and Regions: Standards 4, 6

UNIT 10 REGIONAL ATLAS

L3 Making Comparisons

Ask students to compare and contrast Southeast Asia and the United States. Have them refer to the text and use the following prompts: European colonization, ethnic diversity, forms of government, economic activities.

FYI

Southeast Asian Waterways One-third of all the world's goods transported by ship go through Southeast Asian waters. The busiest commercial waterways are the Malacca Straits (between the Malay Peninsula and Sumatra) and the South China Sea through which 600 vessels a day pass.

□ NATIONAL GEOGRAPHIC **GEOFACT**

Smoking volcanoes pepper the landscape of Sulawesi, one of Indonesia's larger islands. Coral reefs fringe the island's four long peninsulas.

Culture NOTE

Film Production The Philippines is one of the world's leading producers of films. Residents of this region spend much of their leisure time at the movies.

Ethnic Mosaic

Rugged mountains and rolling seas could not hold back the outsiders that have been drawn to Southeast Asia throughout its history. Some came to trade, some to settle, and others to forge empires. Beginning in the 1500s, Europeans laid claim to various parts of the region.

Eventually, every Southeast Asian country except Thailand was a European colony.

Colonial rule ended in the mid-1900s, but the region was left fragmented and in turmoil. Struggles among ethnic groups and between Communist and non-Communist powers claimed thousands of lives.

Today, more than 500 million people live in this culturally diverse region. They speak hundreds of languages and dialects and practice several major religions. Despite rapid urbanization and industrialization in some places, most Southeast Asians still make their living traditionally, as farmers.

1 **A white scarf** covers the head of a Muslim girl in Malaysia. Arab and Indian traders brought the faith of Islam to Southeast Asia in the 1300s and 1400s. Today, Islam is the dominant religion on the Malay Peninsula and in Indonesia. In fact, Indonesia has more Muslims than any other country in the world.

BACKGROUND INFORMATION

Cultural Values Buddhism has had a major impact on the cultural values of Southeast Asia. There are 300 Buddhist temples in the city of Bangkok alone. Buddhism is based on the teachings of Siddhartha Gautama, an ancient Indian teacher. According to legend, Gautama was a noble by birth. Moved by the suffering around him, he gave up a life of luxury to become a wandering monk. As Gautama's fame spread, he became known as the Buddha, which means "Enlightened One." Gautama taught that suffering was an inescapable part of life. People, however, could be freed from its pain. This liberation could be achieved by renouncing desires, practicing mental discipline, and striving for moral purification.
⬛ EE4 Human Systems: Standard 10

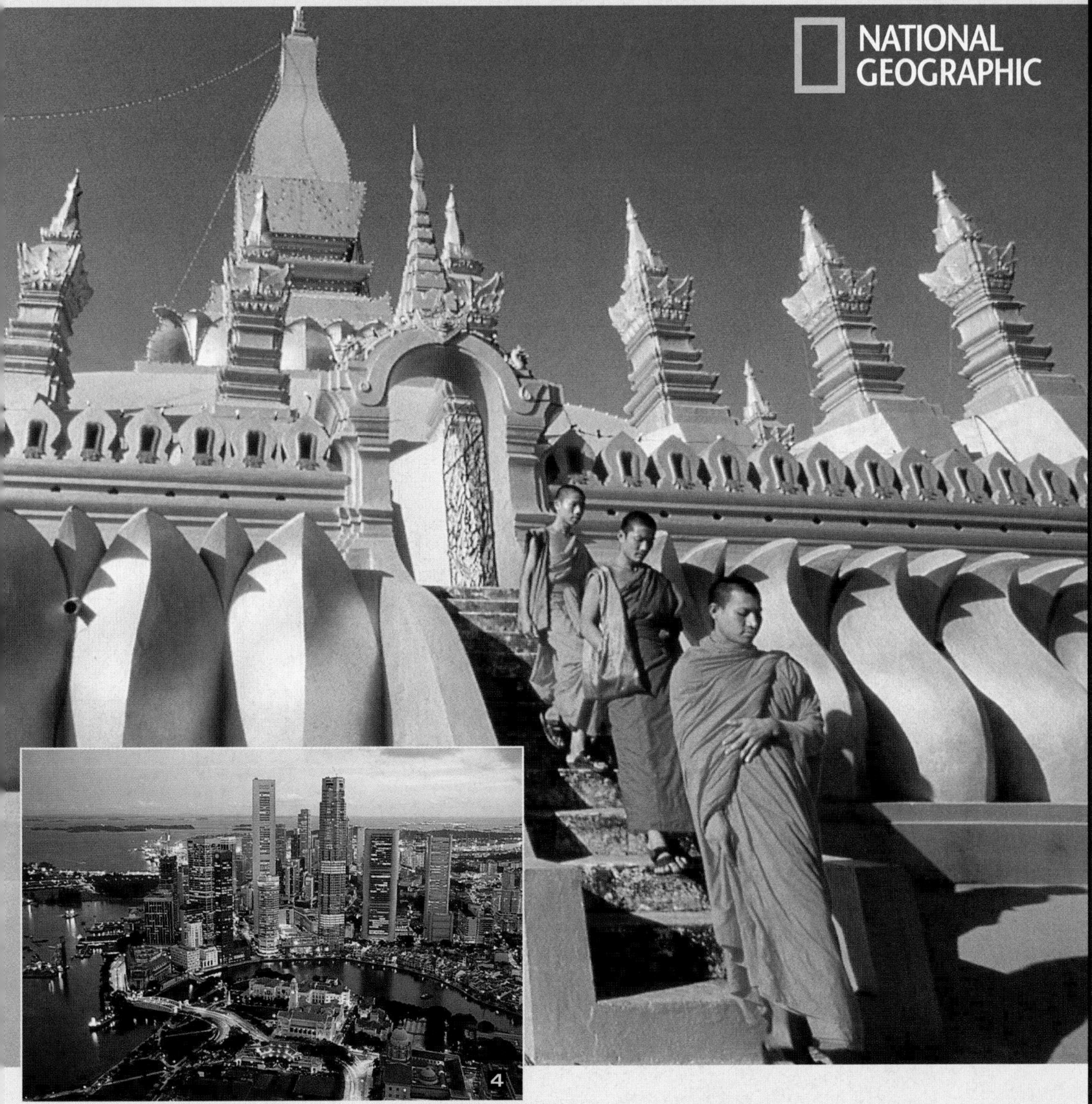

Culture
NOTE

Stupas are a chief characteristic of Buddhist temples. A stupa is a dome, or rounded tower, supported by a base. The interior of the stupa often contains holy relics.

③ ASSESS

Ask: How would your life be different if you lived in Southeast Asia? *(Encourage students to think of climate, travel, communications, social customs, and economic factors.)*

④ CLOSE

Have students discuss traditional and modern ways of earning a living in Southeast Asia. Tell them to support their ideas with evidence from the economic activity map on page 713.

2 Fruit vendors on bicycles offer bounty from the fields to buyers on the streets of Hanoi, Vietnam. Most Vietnamese, like other Southeast Asians, are farmers who raise rice, fruit, and other crops on small plots of land. Only a small percentage of Vietnamese people work in industry.

3 Beneath gilded towers, Buddhist monks descend the steps of a temple in Vientiane, the capital and largest city of Laos. After Islam, Buddhism is the second most widespread religion in Southeast Asia. It is the primary religion in Laos and on the rest of the Indochina Peninsula.

4 Southeast Asia's busiest port, Singapore lies at the tip of the Malay Peninsula, along the Strait of Malacca, the main shipping route between the Indian Ocean and the South China Sea. From this strategic location, the city handles much of the flow of goods into and out of Southeast Asia.

UNIT PROJECT

Southeast Asia Exposition Before students begin their study of Southeast Asia, tell them that they will be responsible for "hosting" a Southeast Asia Exposition at the conclusion of the unit. They will create exhibits to present key features of Southeast Asian countries. Have students brainstorm and list on the board different features about each country, such as physical geography, history, food, music, festivals, architecture, languages, and styles of clothing. Assign or have each student choose a country and collect information about it as they study the unit. Have students present findings in a multimedia show. 🎁

🌐 **EE4 Human Systems: Standard 10**

UNIT 10 REGIONAL ATLAS
Southeast Asia

These features and activities may be used as an introduction to the unit or as teaching tools throughout the course of the unit.

L1 Physical Geography

Have small groups study the maps on pages 710–713. Then have members take turns composing sentences that tell about the region. Each member should create at least one sentence based on each map. *(Answers may include: The Mekong River Delta is located in southern Vietnam; Petroleum is a natural resource of the region.)* Remind students to use standard grammar, sentence structure, and punctuation.

Mediterranean Comparison An outstanding quality of Southeast Asia's geography is its intermingling of land and water. The region is sometimes called the "Asian Mediterranean" because the region's peninsulas and islands are often compared to those in the Mediterranean.

Elevation Profile

In order to show a variety of physical features, this cross section starts at the mouth of the Irawaddy River in Myanmar and goes east through Yangon. There, it heads northeast through Thailand, crossing the Mekong River before heading over the Annam Cordillera. It ends at the mouth of the Red River south of Hanoi, where the river enters the Gulf of Tonkin.

PHYSICAL

EAST ASIA

MYANMAR
Shan Plateau
Naga Hills
Arakan Yoma
Tenen Ra.
Annam Cordillera
LAOS
Gulf of Tonkin
Bay of Bengal
THAILAND
KHORAT PLATEAU
Chao Phraya R.
Bilauktaung Range
Dangrek Ra.
Tonle Sap
VIETNAM
CAMBODIA
Andaman Sea
Isthmus of Kra
Gulf of Thailand
Mekong River Delta
Paracel Islands
Spratly Islands
South China Sea
Luzon Strait
Luzon
Mindoro
Palawan
PHILIPPINES
Samar
Leyte
Negros
Sulu Sea
Mindanao
Balabac Str.
Philippine Sea
PACIFIC OCEAN
TROPIC OF CANCER
Great Channel
Strait of Malacca
MALAYSIA
Malay Peninsula
Natuna Is.
BRUNEI
SINGAPORE
Karimana Str.
Borneo
Celebes Sea
Makassar Strait
Celebes (Sulawesi)
Molucca Sea
Moluccas
Ceram Sea
Ceram
New Guinea
Jaya Peak 16,500 ft. (5,029 m)
EQUATOR
Sumatra
Barisan Mts.
INDIAN OCEAN
GREATER SUNDA ISLANDS
Java Sea
INDONESIA
Java
Bali
Flores Sea
Banda Sea
Aru Is.
Savu Sea
EAST TIMOR
Arafura Sea
Lesser Sunda Islands
Timor Sea
AUSTRALIA

Elevation Profile

8,000 m	0 mi.	500	26,247 ft
6,000 m	0 km	500	19,685 ft
4,000 m			13,123 ft
2,000 m			6,562 ft

IRRAWADDY RIVER
MEKONG RIVER
ANNAM CORDILLERA
Yangon (Rangoon)
BAY OF BENGAL
Sea level
GULF OF TONKIN

0 mi. 400
0 km 400
Miller Cylindrical projection

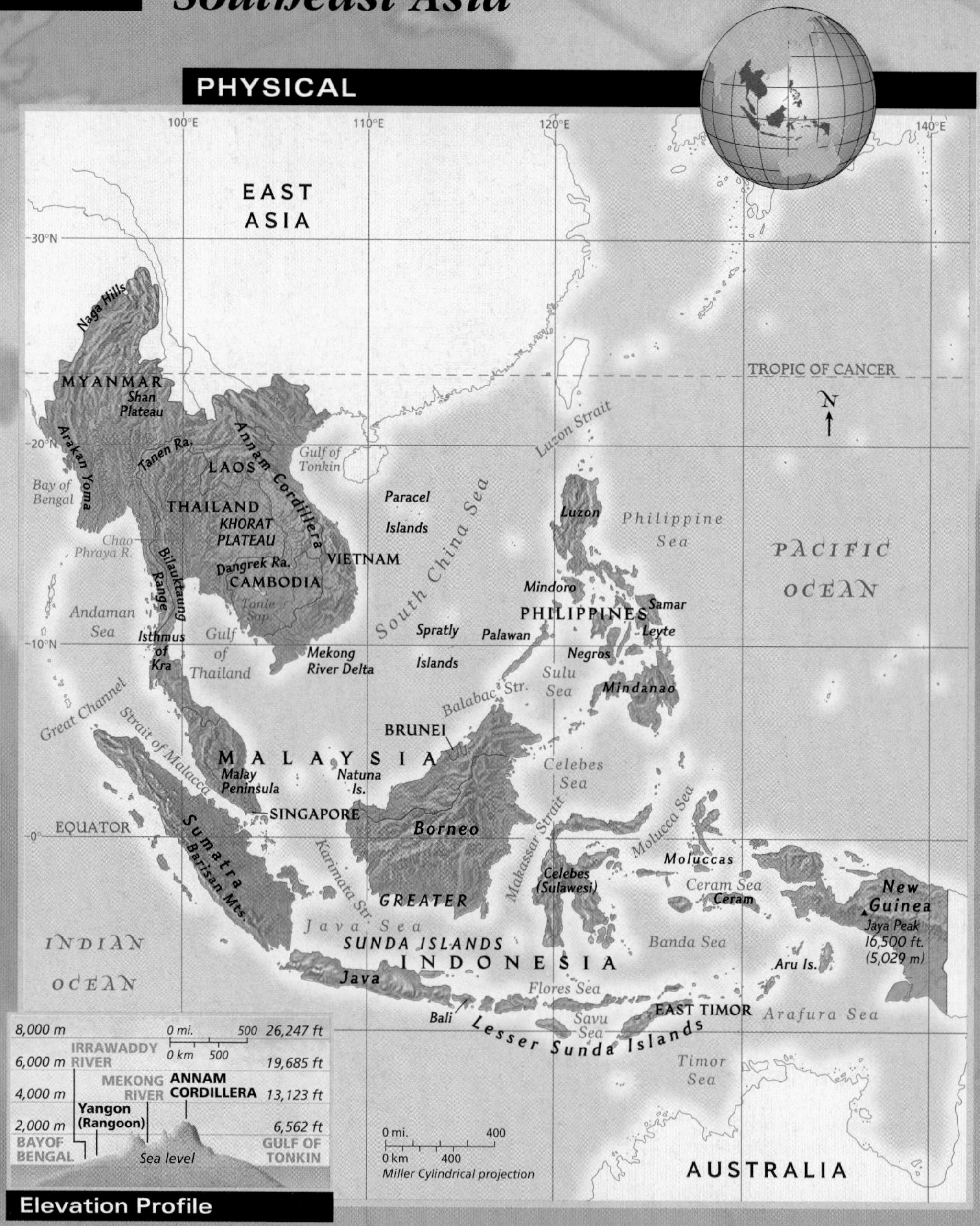

REGIONAL ATLAS ACTIVITY

Class Challenge Provide small groups of students copies of the political map on page 711. Have members paste the map to poster board. Next, they should cut the map into 16 squares using the latitude/longitude grid as a guide. Then, have them scramble the order and place the squares upside down on a table. Members can take turns picking a square and trying to place it in the correct position on a poster board outline of the grid. One point is awarded for placing a square in the correct position. An additional point may be awarded for stating one fact about the physical geography of the region. **ELL**

🌐 **EE1 The World in Spatial Terms: Standards 1, 3**

NATIONAL GEOGRAPHIC

POLITICAL

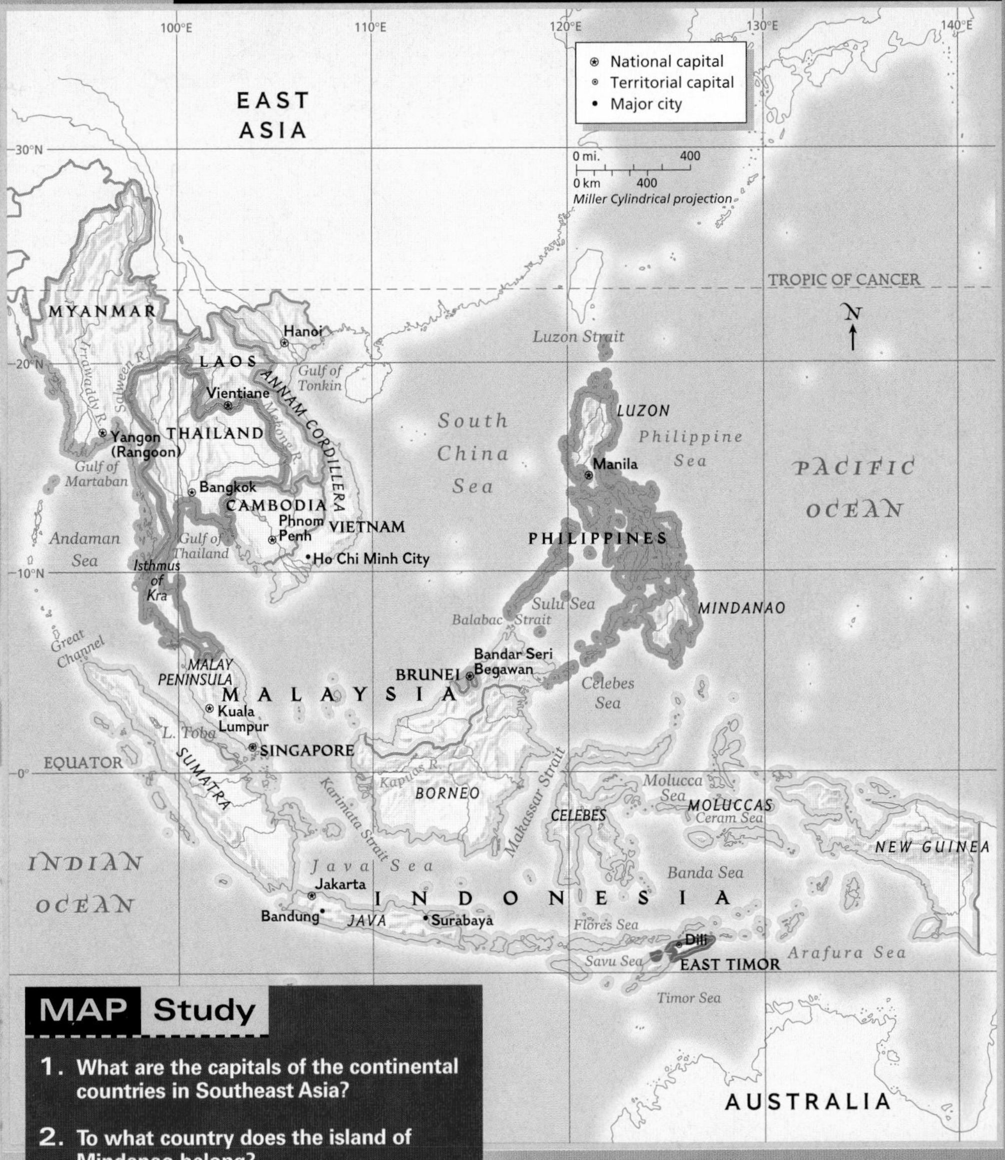

EAST ASIA

- ⊛ National capital
- ⊙ Territorial capital
- • Major city

0 mi.   400
0 km   400
Miller Cylindrical projection

TROPIC OF CANCER

N ↑

MYANMAR

Irrawaddy R.

Salween R.

Hanoi

LAOS

Gulf of Tonkin

Vientiane

ANNAM CORDILLERA

Luzon Strait

LUZON

Yangon (Rangoon)

THAILAND

South China Sea

Philippine Sea

PACIFIC OCEAN

Gulf of Martaban

Bangkok

CAMBODIA

Phnom Penh

VIETNAM

Manila

Andaman Sea

Gulf of Thailand

Ho Chi Minh City

PHILIPPINES

Isthmus of Kra

Sulu Sea

MINDANAO

Great Channel

Balabac Strait

MALAY PENINSULA

Bandar Seri Begawan

BRUNEI

Celebes Sea

MALAYSIA

Kuala Lumpur

L. Toba

SINGAPORE

SUMATRA

EQUATOR

Karimata Strait

Kapuas R.

BORNEO

Makassar Strait

CELEBES

Molucca Sea

MOLUCCAS

Ceram Sea

NEW GUINEA

INDIAN OCEAN

Java Sea

Banda Sea

Jakarta

INDONESIA

Bandung

JAVA

Surabaya

Flores Sea

Dili

EAST TIMOR

Savu Sea

Arafura Sea

Timor Sea

AUSTRALIA

MAP Study

1. What are the capitals of the continental countries in Southeast Asia?

2. To what country does the island of Mindanao belong?

L2 Comparing

Have students look at the political map on this page. Ask them to make statements contrasting two different places on the map. *(Answers may include: The Philippines is made up of several islands; Brunei is one part of one island; Hanoi is north of the Equator; Jakarta is south of the Equator.)*

MAP Study

Answers

1. *Phnom Penh (Cambodia); Vientiane (Laos); Yangon (Myanmar); Bangkok (Thailand); Hanoi (Vietnam)*

2. *The Philippines*

Map Skills Practice
Location In what direction would you travel going from Bangkok to Yangon? *(northwest)* from Yangon to Vientiane? *(northeast)* from Vientiane to Surabaya? *(southeast)*

Culture NOTE

Laos The phrase *Bo pen nyang,* "never mind," expresses Laotians' attitude toward life—it should be enjoyed at the moment; problems should not be allowed to hinder this enjoyment.

REGIONAL ATLAS ACTIVITY

Travel Itinerary Have students form small groups. Tell members to choose six Southeast Asian countries to visit, including a mix of mainland and island countries. Students will develop itineraries for each country. They should list physical features, cities, regions, and ancient and modern cultural sites they must see. Tell them to explain why they "can't miss" these stops along the way. They should also explain how they will get from place to place. Encourage them to use different means of transportation. Students may wish to plot their itineraries on maps. Allow time for students to share their plans orally.

🌐 **EE2 Places and Regions: Standard 4**
🌐 **EE4 Human Systems: Standard 10**

L2 Predicting Consequences

Note that overcrowding is a problem in many Southeast Asian cities. Have students predict what consequences overcrowding might have for residents of the region and what steps national governments might take to address these challenges. Students may wish to write predictions in their GeoJournals.

L2 Geographic Themes

Have students write three incorrect statements about Southeast Asian countries. Tell them to base each statement on one of the five geographic themes. Ask them to read their statements aloud. Challenge classmates to find the error in each statement and correct it. Those making corrections must support them with verified information.

☐ NATIONAL GEOGRAPHIC **GEOFACT**

▶ **The highest peak in the region is Indonesia's 16,024-foot (4,885-m) Puncak Jaya, located in the province of Irian Jaya.**

UNIT 10 REGIONAL ATLAS
Southeast Asia

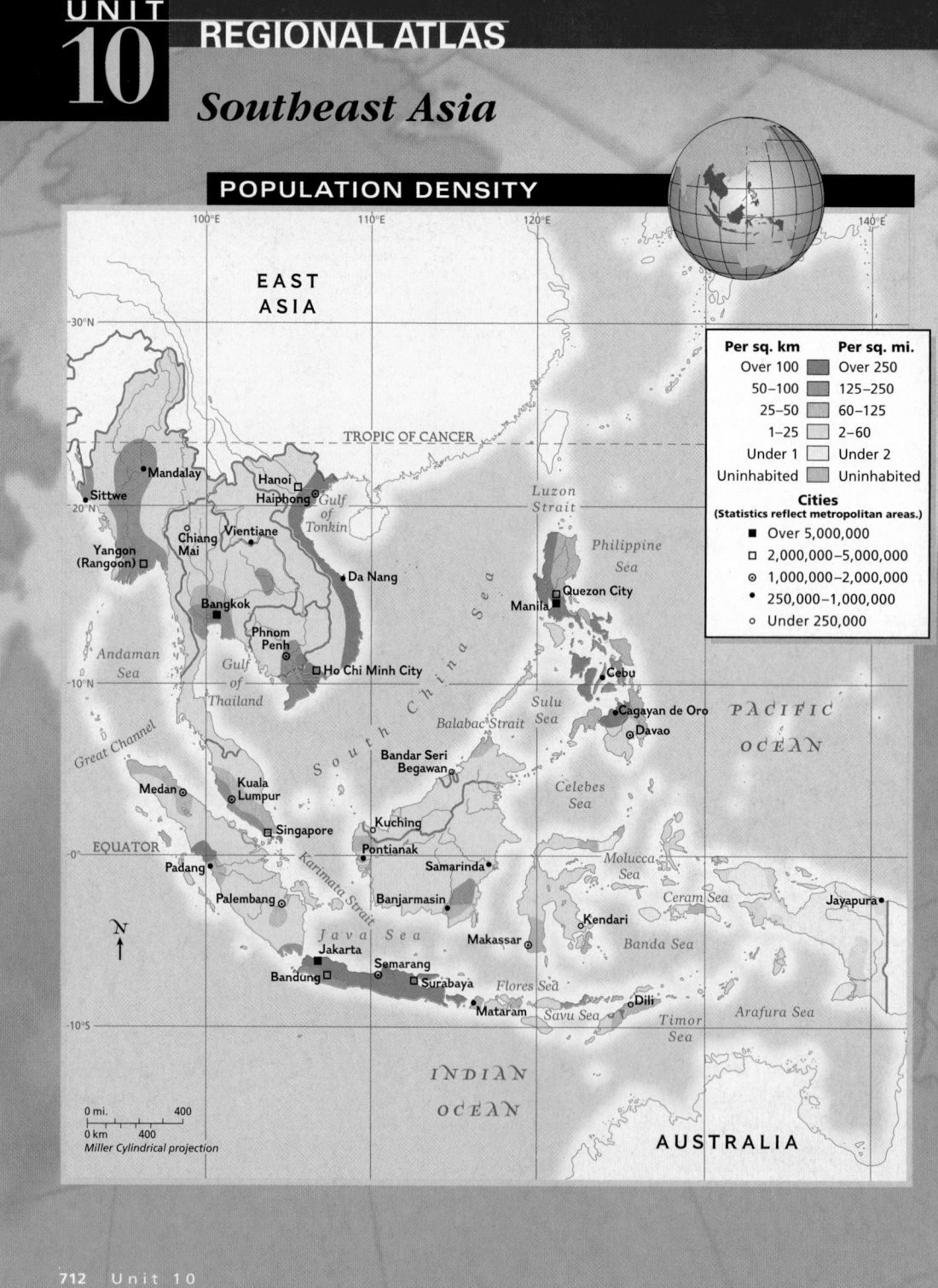

POPULATION DENSITY

Per sq. km	Per sq. mi.
Over 100	Over 250
50–100	125–250
25–50	60–125
1–25	2–60
Under 1	Under 2
Uninhabited	Uninhabited

Cities
(Statistics reflect metropolitan areas.)
- ■ Over 5,000,000
- ☐ 2,000,000–5,000,000
- ◉ 1,000,000–2,000,000
- • 250,000–1,000,000
- ○ Under 250,000

712 Unit 10

REGIONAL ATLAS ACTIVITY

Place Assign partners one country in the region. Have them plan, organize and complete a research project on how the geographical characteristics of each country influence population density—the location of urban and rural areas. Students can note their findings on index cards, and then use those notes to formulate clear, concise facts. Have students read their facts to another set of partners, leaving out the name of the country. They can give the other pair a choice of three countries and ask them to decide which one it is.

🌐 **EE4 Human Systems: Standard 9**
🌐 **EE5 Environment and Society: Standard 15**

L2 Movement

Tell students they are employers who are attempting to attract young emigrants back to the region. What geographic, economic, or cultural reasons would employers use to persuade young adults to return?

MAP Study

Answers
1. gold: Philippines, Malaysia; gemstones: Myanmar, Thailand, Cambodia, Vietnam
2. Indonesia, Philippines, Singapore

Map Skills Practice
Land Use To what use is the vast majority of land on peninsular Southeast Asia put? *(subsistence farming)*

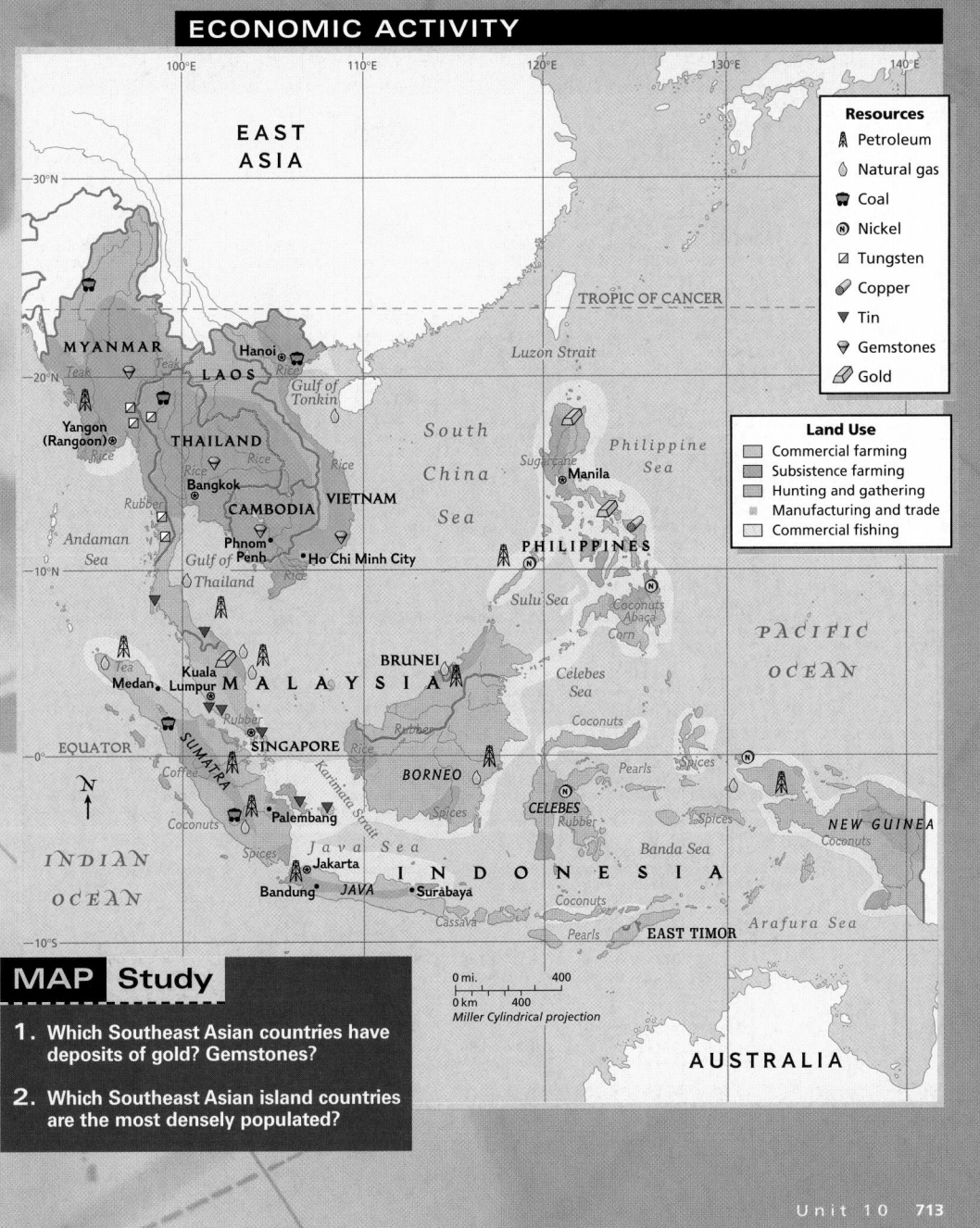

ECONOMIC ACTIVITY

Resources
- Petroleum
- Natural gas
- Coal
- Nickel
- Tungsten
- Copper
- Tin
- Gemstones
- Gold

Land Use
- Commercial farming
- Subsistence farming
- Hunting and gathering
- Manufacturing and trade
- Commercial fishing

0 mi. 400
0 km 400
Miller Cylindrical projection

MAP Study

1. Which Southeast Asian countries have deposits of gold? Gemstones?

2. Which Southeast Asian island countries are the most densely populated?

Unit 10 **713**

REGIONAL ATLAS ACTIVITY

Economics Have students study the map on this page and identify natural resources that are abundant in this region. List their responses on the board. Brainstorm with them the kinds of economic pursuits that would make effective use of these resources. Guide them to include farming, logging, fishing, and mining. Organize students into small groups and assign each group a country. Have each group research their country's principal economic activities and map the locations of these activities. Allow time for students to share their findings. Then, ask groups to contribute to a class chart showing the percentage of the population in each country that is engaged in each activity.

🌐 **EE5 Environment and Society: Standard 16**

UNIT 10 REGIONAL ATLAS

Southeast Asia

These features and activities may be used as an introduction to the unit or as teaching tools throughout the course of the unit.

L1 Identify

Group students in pairs, and have them refer to the chart on this page as they complete this activity. One partner should identify a category at the top of the chart and one fact from any row in the column below that category. *(Example: Currency—Kyat)* The other partner should use the chart to find the name of the country to which that fact applies. *(Example: Myanmar)* Partners then reverse roles and continue the process. Challenge them to include facts that apply to more than one country.

Languages of Myanmar More than two-thirds of Myanmar's people are ethnic Burman and speak Burmese, the country's official language. The rest of the population consists of a number of small ethnic groups that speak over 100 different languages.

COUNTRY PROFILES

COUNTRY * AND CAPITAL	FLAG AND LANGUAGE	POPULATION** AND DENSITY	LANDMASS	MAJOR EXPORT	MAJOR IMPORT	CURRENCY	GOVERNMENT
BRUNEI — Bandar Seri Begawan	Malay, English, Chinese	400,000 — 162 per sq.mi. — 63 per sq. km	2,228 sq.mi. — 5,771 sq. km	Crude Oil	Machinery	Brunei Dollar	Constitutional Monarchy
CAMBODIA — Phnom Penh	Khmer, French	12,600,000 — 180 per sq.mi. — 69 per sq. km	69,900 sq.mi. — 181,041 sq. km	Timber	Construction Materials	Riel	Constitutional Monarchy
EAST TIMOR — Dili	Tetun, Javanese, Portuguese	800,000 — 136 per sq.mi. — 53 per sq. km	5,741 sq.mi. — 14,869 sq. km	Coconut Products	Manufactured Goods	Indonesian Rupiah	Republic
INDONESIA — Jakarta	Bahasa Indonesia, Javanese	220,500,000 — 300 per sq.mi. — 116 per sq. km	735,355 sq.mi. — 1,904,569 sq. km	Crude Oil	Manufactured Goods	Rupiah	Republic
LAOS — Vientiane	Lao, French	5,600,000 — 61 per sq.mi. — 24 per sq. km	91,429 sq.mi. — 236,801 sq. km	Wood Products	Machinery	Kip	Communist State
MALAYSIA — Kuala Lumpur	Malay, English, Chinese	25,100,000 — 197 per sq.mi. — 76 per sq. km	127,317 sq.mi. — 329,751 sq. km	Electronic Equipment	Machinery	Ringgit	Constitutional Monarchy
MYANMAR — Yangon (Rangoon)	Burmese, Local Languages	49,500,000 — 189 per sq.mi. — 73 per sq. km	261,228 sq.mi. — 676,581 sq. km	Beans	Machinery	Kyat	Military Dictatorship
PHILIPPINES — Manila	Tagalog, English	81,600,000 — 704 per sq.mi. — 272 per sq. km	115,830 sq.mi. — 300,000 sq. km	Electronic Equipment	Raw Materials	Philippine Peso	Republic
SINGAPORE — Singapore	Chinese, Malay, Tamil, English	4,200,000 — 17,528 per sq.mi. — 6,624 per sq. km	239 sq.mi. — 619 sq. km	Computer Equipment	Aircraft	Singapore Dollar	Republic
THAILAND — Bangkok	Thai, Local Languages	63,100,000 — 318 per sq.mi. — 123 per sq. km	198,116 sq.mi. — 513,120 sq. km	Manufactured Goods	Machinery	Baht	Constitutional Monarchy
VIETNAM — Hanoi	Vietnamese, Local Languages	80,800,000 — 631 per sq.mi. — 244 per sq. km	128,066 sq.mi. — 331,691 sq. km	Crude Oil	Machinery	Dong	Communist State

*COUNTRIES AND FLAGS NOT DRAWN TO SCALE

**POPULATIONS ARE ROUNDED, *SOURCE: 2003 WORLD POPULATION DATA SHEET*

FOR AN ONLINE UPDATE OF THIS INFORMATION, VISIT GEOGRAPHY.GLENCOE.COM AND CLICK ON "TEXTBOOK UPDATES."

COUNTRY PROFILE ACTIVITY

Synthesizing Information Form small groups of three or four students. Assign each group a country. Have groups refer to pages 704–714 to find, organize, and synthesize information about their assigned countries. Remind them that interpretation of maps and graphs is an excellent way to supplement the written text. Ask the groups to compile their gathered data with thumbnail sketches of their countries. Then, have them examine their sketches and decide if they need to clarify any facts or conclusions. Encourage the groups to make additions and changes throughout the unit. ▣ **EE1 The World in Spatial Terms: Standard 3;** ▣ **EE2 Places and Regions: Standard 4;** ▣ **EE4 Human Systems: Standard 12**

◀ Ruins of Buddhist temple
c. A.D. 1000–1200,
Pagan, Myanmar

FYI

Influences Europeans once referred to the eastern mainland countries of Southeast Asia as *Indochina*. This name was derived from the subregion's location between India and China.

L2 Identify

Explain that Islam, Buddhism, Hinduism, and Christianity are the four great religious influences on Southeast Asian culture. Have students identify specific countries in this region and research to find the estimated numbers of people in that region who practice each of these religions.

INTERDISCIPLINARY
connection

HISTORY The town of Pagan (now Bagan) was a walled city located on the banks of the Irrawaddy River. It served as the capital of a mighty empire that ruled the land now known as Myanmar centuries ago. The Mongol armies of Kublai Khan captured Pagan in A.D. 1287. The capital and its fabled architecture eventually fell into ruin.

COUNTRY PROFILE ACTIVITY

Culture and History Structures that match Greek and Roman classical architecture in magnificence can be found in regions such as Southeast Asia. Allow students to work in small groups to research one of four architectural wonders found in this region: Angkor Wat, Cambodia; Ayutthaya, Thailand; Pagan, Myanmar; or Borobudur, Indonesia. Have students compile a booklet with background information and captioned illustrations. Ask a member of each group to present its findings to the class. Allow time for other students to ask questions and permit any member of the presentation group to respond.

🌐 **EE4 Human Systems: Standard 10**
🌐 **EE6 The Uses of Geography: Standard 17**

Ask students whether they have eaten any Southeast Asian foods (fruits, vegetables, main dishes). **Ask: What were some of the ingredients of those foods? Are similar ingredients found in foods you often eat?**

TEACH

Cultural Exchange Point out that Thailand and Vietnam are among the world's major rice producers. Many people believe that rice is a "near perfect" food because of its nutritional value. Have students research to identify the nutrients found in rice and their beneficial effects on the human body. They should then create a chart showing the nutritional value of rice. Tell students to think about what they have learned in this Unit Opener. **Ask: What characteristics of Southeast Asia's location and geography make it a good region for growing rice?** *(tropical or subtropical climate and abundant rainfall)*

 Meeting National Standards

Geography for Life
The following standards are met in the Student Edition:

EE2 Places and Regions:
    Standard 4
EE4 Human Systems:
    Standard 10

GLOBAL
CONNECTION

SOUTHEAST ASIA AND THE UNITED STATES

CUISINE

What's for dinner? Twenty or thirty years ago, the answer probably would have been "steak," "meatloaf," or "hamburgers." But now, you might hear "lemon grass chicken" or "laab moo"! Americans have developed a taste for foods from other lands. And the cuisines of two Southeast Asian countries—Thailand and Vietnam— have become especially popular in the United States.

Thai and Vietnamese cooks themselves have borrowed foods, flavors, and preparation methods from several of their neighbors, especially China and India. For example, many Thai and Vietnamese dishes are stir-fried, as is much Chinese food. Coconut milk is an ingredient picked up from India. Nevertheless, Thai and Vietnamese cuisines have their own distinctive flavors and characteristics.

Some of the common ingredients in Thai food are lemon grass, shrimp paste, Siamese ginger, and chilies—very hot chilies! These and other ingredients are combined to create complex and tantalizing tastes. Laab moo, for example, is a dish of minced pork seasoned with lemon juice, fish sauce, fresh mint, and green chilies. In a single forkful of a Thai dish, you might taste sweet, sour, salty, and hot flavors all at once.

Vietnamese food is often described as being similar to Thai food, but less intense,

▼ Enjoying a meal in Hanoi, Vietnam

716 Unit 10

BACKGROUND INFORMATION

Movement When people move to a new region, their way of life often absorbs different cultural elements from their new surroundings. They also retain important aspects of their original heritage. During Tet, the Vietnamese Lunar New Year celebration, Vietnamese in the United States celebrate much as the Vietnamese do in Southeast Asia. The holiday lasts from three to seven days. Women dress in red and yellow, the colors of the Vietnamese flag. Men wear black clothing. Special foods also are served. The Vietnamese believe that when a watermelon is cut open the redness of the fruit inside is directly related to good fortune in the coming year. ● **EE4 Human Systems: Standards 9, 10**

▲ Floating produce market in Thailand

with more subtle flavors. Some Vietnamese dishes might seem more like salads than main dishes to most Americans. Bits of cooked meat or fish are typically served with a platter of fresh lettuce, herbs, and vegetables. One ingredient found in almost all Vietnamese dishes is nuoc mam, a salty fish sauce. What salt is to American food and soy sauce is to Chinese dishes, nuoc mam is to Vietnamese cuisine.

How did Thai and Vietnamese foods get to the United States? In the 1970s, after the Vietnam War, Vietnamese refugees flocked to America. Many opened small restaurants. Thais had been coming to the United States as students since the 1960s. Many of the Thais settled in Los Angeles, where the climate may have reminded them of home. By 1990, there were more Thais living in greater Los Angeles than any other place outside Thailand—and the city had at least 200 Thai restaurants.

Now Thai and Vietnamese restaurants can be found in cities all across the United States. From the fiery flavors of Thailand to the more delicate tastes of Vietnam, Southeast Asian cuisines have found a home in America.

CONNECTION ACTIVITY

Foods Have students use library resources, the Internet, or interviews with people from Southeast Asia to compile a Southeast Asian cookbook. Each student should find a recipe for a typical food in a Southeast Asian country and then conduct research on at least one ingredient that is native to the country and one ingredient that was introduced through cultural exchange. Students should use the information they find about those ingredients as an introduction to their recipe. Combine the recipes into a cookbook and encourage students to try making some of these recipes.

🌐 **EE4 Human Systems: Standard 10**

Peppers The peppers that give so many Southeast Asian dishes their zesty flavor are an excellent example of cultural exchange. Peppers are native to Central and South America. They first found their way to Southeast Asia when European explorers brought products from the Americas. Today, Thailand is one of the world's leading producers of peppers.

3 ASSESS

Write the words *Thai* and *Vietnamese* on the board. Have students brainstorm and list ingredients that are typically found in dishes from each cuisine. *(Thai: lemongrass, shrimp paste, Siamese ginger, hot chilies, seasoned pork, lemon juice, fish sauce, mint; Vietnamese: meat, fish, lettuce, herbs, vegetables, nuoc mam [salty fish sauce])* After completing the list, **Ask: Which of these ingredients, if any, would you like to add to a favorite dish? Why?**

4 CLOSE

Have students find one Thai and one Vietnamese recipe. Have groups of four make a Venn diagram showing ingredients unique to each recipe and those found in both national cuisines.

PLANNING GUIDE

NOTE: The following materials may be used when teaching Chapter 29. Section-level support materials are shown at point-of-use in the margins of the Teacher Wraparound Edition.

TEACHING TRANSPARENCIES

L2 Unit 10 Map Overlay Transparencies

L2 Political Map Transparency 10

GEOGRAPHIC LITERACY

Focus on Geography Literacy

APPLICATION AND ENRICHMENT

L3 Enrichment Activity 29

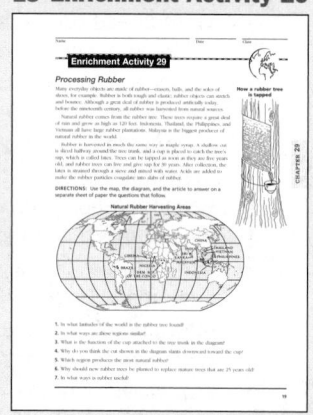

REVIEW AND REINFORCEMENT

L1 Vocabulary Activity 29   L1 Reinforcing   L1 Reteaching Activity 29
Skills Activity 29

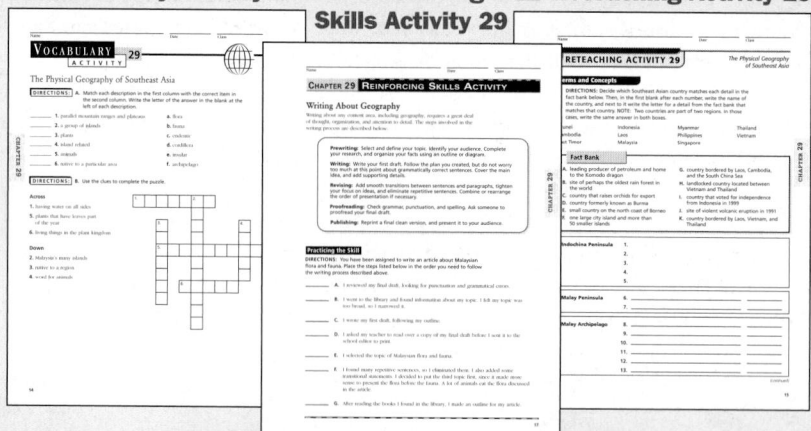

ASSESSMENT

L2 Chapter 29 Test Form A

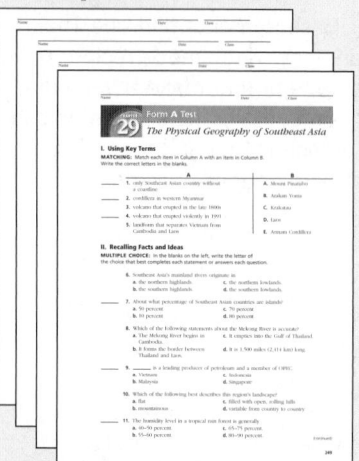

L2 Chapter 29 Test Form B

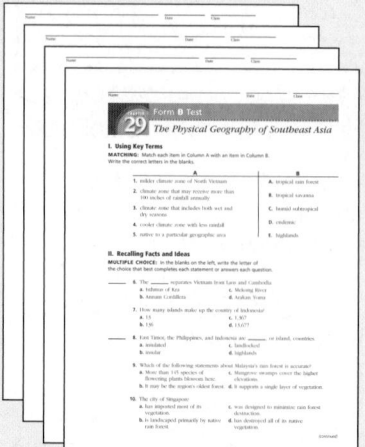

L1/ELL Performance
Assessment Activity 29

ExamView® Pro
Testmaker

EXAMVIEW® PRO
Testmaker CD-ROM

WINDOWS/MACINTOSH

- QuickTest Wizard does all the work for you
- Choose ExamView tests or create your own
- Complete editing capability

The following Spanish language materials are available in the Spanish Resources binder:

- 📁 Spanish Vocabulary Activities
- 📁 Spanish Guided Reading Activities
- 📁 Spanish Reteaching Activities
- 📁 Spanish Summaries
- 📁 Spanish Quizzes and Tests
- 📁 Spanish Reading Essentials and Study Guide

- World Regions Video
- MindJogger Videoquiz
- Vocabulary PuzzleMaker CD-ROM
- Interactive Tutor Self-Assessment CD-ROM
- ExamView® Pro Testmaker CD-ROM
- Audio Program
- TeacherWorks CD-ROM
- Interactive Student Edition CD-ROM
- Glencoe Skillbuilder Interactive Workbook CD-ROM, Level 2
- Presentation Plus! CD-ROM

Timesaving Tools

 **TeacherWorks™** All-In-One Planner and Resource Center

- **Interactive Teacher Edition** Access your Teacher Wraparound Edition and your classroom resources with a few easy clicks.
- **Interactive Lesson Planner** Planning has never been easier! Organize your week, month, semester, or year with all the lesson helps you need to make teaching creative, timely, and relevant.

 Use Glencoe's **Presentation Plus!** multimedia teacher tool to easily present dynamic lessons that visually excite your students. Using Microsoft PowerPoint® you can customize the presentations to create your own personalized lessons.

GEOGRAPHY Online

Use our Web site for additional resources. All essential content is covered in the Student Edition.

You and your students can visit geography.glencoe.com, the Web site companion to *Glencoe World Geography*. This innovative integration of electronic and print media offers your students a wealth of opportunities. The student text directs students to the Web site for the following options:

- Chapter Overviews
- Student Activities
- Self-Check Quizzes
- Textbook Updates

Answers are provided for you in the "Web Activity Lesson Plan." Additional Web resources and Interactive Tutor puzzles are also available.

▶ **Additional Glencoe Teacher Support**

- Teaching Strategies for the Geography Classroom (including Block Scheduling Pacing Guides)
- Graphic Organizer Transparencies Strategies and Activities
- Outline Map Resource Book
- Reading in the Content Area

PLANNING GUIDE

SECTION RESOURCES

Daily Objectives	Reproducible Resources	Multimedia Resources

SECTION 1   The Land

1. Describe how tectonic plates and activity from volcanoes and earthquakes formed Southeast Asia.
2. Explain why the region's waterways are important to its peoples.
3. Summarize how rich natural resources affect Southeast Asia's economy.

Reproducible Lesson Plan 29-1
Daily Lecture Notes 29-1
Guided Reading Activity 29-1*
Reading Essentials and Study Guide 29-1*
Section Quiz 29-1*

Daily Focus Skills Transparency 29-1
Political Map Transparency 10
Unit 10 Map Overlay Transparencies
Interactive Tutor Self-Assessment CD-ROM
ExamView® Pro Testmaker CD-ROM*
Presentation Plus! CD-ROM

SECTION 2   Climate and Vegetation

1. Identify the weather pattern that influences Southeast Asia's climate.
2. List the region's main climate types.
3. State the main type of natural vegetation found in Southeast Asia.

Reproducible Lesson Plan 29-2
Vocabulary Activity 29*
Daily Lecture Notes 29-2
Guided Reading Activity 29-2*
Reading Essentials and Study Guide 29-2*
Reteaching Activity 29*
Reinforcing Skills Activity 29
Section Quiz 29-2*

Daily Focus Skills Transparency 29-2
Political Map Transparency 10
Unit 10 Map Overlay Transparencies
Vocabulary PuzzleMaker CD-ROM
Interactive Tutor Self-Assessment CD-ROM
ExamView® Pro Testmaker CD-ROM*
Presentation Plus! CD-ROM

	Blackline Master		Software		Videocassette	*Also available in Spanish
	Transparency		CD-ROM		DVD	

OUT OF TIME?   Assign the Chapter 29 **Reading Essentials and Study Guide.**

Block Schedule

Activities that are particularly suited to use within the block scheduling framework are identified throughout this chapter by the following designation:

KEY TO ABILITY LEVELS

Teaching strategies have been coded for various learning styles and abilities.

L1   **BASIC** activities for all students

L2   **AVERAGE** activities for average to above-average students

L3   **CHALLENGING** activities for above-average students

ELL   **ENGLISH LANGUAGE LEARNER** activities

Teacher to Teacher

Eric Mitchell
Smithville High School
Smithville, MO

Geography Ads

Before beginning this unit, have students name as many countries in Southeast Asia as they can. Then give each student a blank map of the region and have him or her plot where he or she thinks these countries are located. When students are finished, have them use the maps in the text to correct their own maps. Then have each student choose one Southeast Asian country that especially interests him or her. While studying the chapter, ask students to keep notes about their countries, noting facts about physical and cultural geography, and listing any questions they might have for further exploration.

As a concluding activity have students write ads that describe the Southeast Asian countries they have chosen. Each ad should include geographical information about the chosen country such as rivers, mountain ranges, climate regions, and vegetation. Encourage students to add any information they have located from other sources. Country names do not go on the ads. Have students exchange ads, and based on the information given in each ad, guess what country they are reading about.

Meeting National Standards

Geography For Life

The following standards are highlighted in Chapter 29:

Section 1 EE1 The World in Spatial Terms:
Standards 1, 2
EE2 Places and Regions:
Standard 4
EE3 Physical Systems:
Standards 7, 8
EE5 Environment and Society:
Standard 14

Section 2 EE1 The World in Spatial Terms:
Standards 1, 2, 3
EE2 Places and Regions:
Standards 4, 6
EE3 Physical Systems:
Standards 7, 8

Local Objectives

_____

_____

MEETING SPECIAL NEEDS

In addition to the Differentiated Instruction strategies found in each section, the following resources are also suitable for your special needs students:

- ***ExamView® Pro Testmaker CD-ROM*** allows teachers to tailor tests by reducing answer choices.
- The ***Audio Program*** includes the entire narrative of the student edition so that less-proficient readers can listen to the words as they read them.
- The ***Reading Essentials and Study Guide*** provides the same content as the student edition but is written two grade levels below the textbook.
- ***Guided Reading Activities*** give less-proficient readers point-by-point instructions to increase comprehension as they read each textbook section.
- ***Enrichment Activities*** include a stimulating collection of readings and activities for gifted and talented students.

Chapter Objectives

1. Describe the dominant land-forms and natural resources of Southeast Asia.

2. Discuss Southeast Asia's climate and vegetation.

GLENCOE
TECHNOLOGY

Use *MindJogger Videoquiz* to preview the Chapter 29 content.

GeoJournal

For access to additional photos, maps, and information on Southeast Asia's geographic features go to www.nationalgeographic.com (See Teacher pages in front for strategies for using journals in the geography classroom.)

Introduce students to chapter content and key terms by having them access Chapter Overview 29 at geography.glencoe.com

FOLDABLES™
Study Organizer

Dinah Zike's Foldables are three-dimensional, interactive graphic organizers that help students practice basic writing skills, review key vocabulary terms, and identify main ideas. Have students complete the Foldable activity in the *Dinah Zike's Reading and Study Skills Foldables* booklet.

CHAPTER 29

The Physical Geography of Southeast Asia

GeoJournal

As you read the chapter, visualize places in Southeast Asia that are discussed in the chapter. Write entries in your journal that describe the region's prominent physical features. Use vivid images and details in your entries.

GEOGRAPHY
Online

Chapter Overview Visit the **Glencoe World Geography** Web site at geography.glencoe.com and click on Chapter Overviews—Chapter 29 to preview information about the physical geography of the region.

ABOUT THE PHOTO

Visual Instruction In the 1500s when Islam became the dominant religion in Java, many Hindus fled to Bali, a small island 1 mile (1.6 km) east of Java. Because of the influence of Hindu nobles, priests, and thinkers, Bali continues to center its religious life on Hinduism, the only Indonesian area to do so. The Saivite sect of Hinduism is particularly influential on Bali, and a firm belief in reincarnation is held by many of Bali's people. All Balinese villages have temples such as the one pictured here.
EE5 Environment and Society: Standard 14

Guide to Reading

Consider What You Know

You have learned how the physical geography of a region affects its economy. Southeast Asia is rich in tropical rain forests and water resources. What products do you know about that come from this region?

Reading Strategy

Taking Notes Use the major headings of the section to create an outline similar to the one below.

I. Peninsulas and Islands
   A.
   B.
II. Physical Features
   A.
   B.
   C.

Read to Find Out

- How did tectonic plate movement, volcanic activity, and earthquakes form Southeast Asia?
- Why are the region's waterways important to its peoples?
- How do rich natural resources affect Southeast Asia's economy?

Terms to Know

- cordillera
- archipelago
- insular
- flora
- fauna

Places to Locate

- Indochina Peninsula
- Malay Peninsula
- Annam Cordillera
- Irrawaddy River
- Chao Phraya River
- Red River
- Mekong River

◀ *Pura (temple) Ulun Danu, Bali, Indonesia*

The Land

NATIONAL GEOGRAPHIC

A Geographic View

Journey to the Interior

At dawn the next day I set off upriver in a hollowed-out tree trunk with my guide. . . . [He] poles the dugout through the tea-colored water while I watch birds—kingfishers darting from the riverbanks, flocks of hornbills skimming above the treetops, their wings sounding like runners panting for breath.

The banks sprout wild bread-fruits, bananas, and a host of palm trees, all tangled up with hanging vines. As the heat of the day intensifies, the river's green walls vibrate with the ringing of cicadas. Then the river grows shallower, forcing us to push the dugout over rocks. It is the dry season, something hard to fathom in a place drenched with more than 200 inches of rain a year.

—Thomas O'Neill, "Irian Jaya, Indonesia's Wild Side," National Geographic, *February 1996*

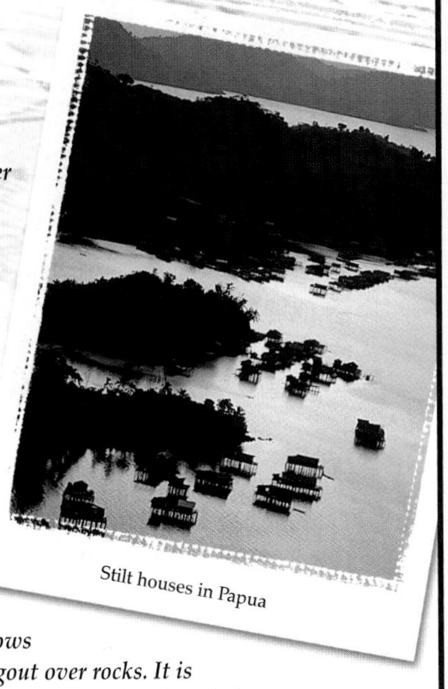

Stilt houses in Papua

Lush rain forests, tangled swamps, and rugged mountains characterize the province of Papua (formerly Irian Jaya) in the Southeast Asian country of Indonesia. In this section you will explore the physical geography of Southeast Asia: its beginnings, its natural barriers of mountains and water, its tempestuous volcanoes, and its abundant natural resources.

Peninsulas and Islands

When the Eurasian, Philippine, and Indo-Australian tectonic plates collided millions of years ago, they formed the landmasses that are known today as Southeast Asia. The upheaval formed cordilleras,

Chapter 29 ● **719**

② TEACH

L1 Locate

Have students identify where Southeast Asia is in relation to China and India. Ask students to infer how this region came to be called Southeast Asia. *(It is south of China and east of India.)*

NATIONAL GEOGRAPHIC World Explorer

Answer

Vietnam, Cambodia, Laos, Thailand, and Myanmar

More About the Photo

Hue was the royal capital of Vietnam from 1802 until 1945. The *Ngo Mon,* or Noon Gate, is the chief entrance to the Citadel. Inside the Citadel's ramparts was the Forbidden Purple City where the Vietnamese royal family lived.

Daily Lecture Notes 29-1

DAILY LECTURE NOTES

CHAPTER 29
Section 1

Building Geography Literacy
Although the Philippines includes over 7,000 islands, the archipelago's total area is only 115,831 square miles (300,001 sq. km), about the size of Arizona. The islands that make up the Philippines together have a coastline that measures 22,554 miles (36,289 km). The two large islands of Luzon and Mindanao account for about 66 percent of the country's land area.

I. Peninsulas and Islands pages 719–721

The collision of three tectonic plates millions of years ago produced the peninsulas and islands of Southeast Asia. Straddling the Equator, Southeast Asia has mountainous terrain with a predominately tropical climate.

A. Mainland Southeast Asia
About half of Southeast Asia's 14 countries are located on the mainland. Malaysia is both a mainland and an island country. Laos is the only landlocked country in the region. (p. 720)

B. Island Southeast Asia
Southeast Asia's island nations include Brunei, East Timor, Indonesia, Singapore, and the Philippines. Indonesia—the largest island country

Compare and contrast the physical features of these islands with those of other islands you have studied, such as Great Britain, various Mediterranean islands, or Hawaii. *(Accept reasonable answers. Possible answers: Great Britain is much cooler and has no volcanoes. It does have a network of rivers, like those on these islands. Hawaii is very much like the*

NATIONAL GEOGRAPHIC World Explorer

Geography Skills for Life

Hue, Vietnam Farmers tend their fields near Hue, a historic city in central Vietnam.
Place What countries lie on the Indochina Peninsula?

or parallel mountain ranges and plateaus, that extend into the Indochina Peninsula. Activity from related volcanoes and earthquakes created a series of archipelagos in the South Pacific. An **archipelago** is a group of islands.

Straddling the Equator, the peninsulas and islands of Southeast Asia combine mountainous terrain with a predominantly tropical climate. The region stretches from the Asian mainland almost to Australia and covers 1,735,448 square miles (4,512,165 sq. km). Two large land areas, the **Indochina Peninsula** and the **Malay Peninsula,** make up mainland Southeast Asia. South and east of this area lies the vast Malay Archipelago,

Comparing Lands

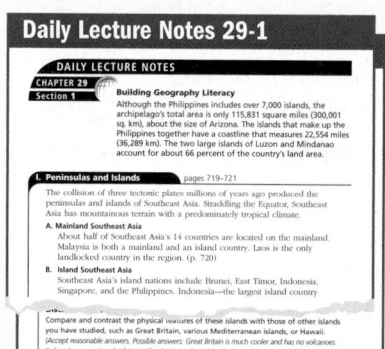

Southeast Asia is about half the size of the continental United States.

sometimes called the East Indies. The Malay Archipelago, containing 20,000 islands, stretches from the Indian Ocean to the Pacific Ocean.

Mainland Southeast Asia

About half of Southeast Asia's 11 countries are located on the mainland. The rest are island countries, except for Malaysia, which is both a mainland and an island country. Laos is the region's only country without a coastline. The four mainland countries of Vietnam, Laos, Cambodia, and Myanmar (formerly called Burma) lie entirely on the Indochina Peninsula. Most of Thailand also is located there, but part of that country trails southward to the Malay Peninsula. Malaysia shares the Malay Peninsula with Thailand, while the rest of Malaysia is located on Borneo, an island east of the Malay Peninsula.

Island Southeast Asia

The **insular,** or island, countries of Southeast Asia include Brunei, East Timor, Indonesia, Singapore, and the Philippines. Brunei, almost surrounded by Malaysia, is a small country on the northern coast of Borneo. Indonesia is the largest island country

---

DIFFERENTIATED INSTRUCTION

At-Risk Students Have students who have problems with reading, study the "Guide to Reading" at the beginning of the section on page 719. Remind students that this feature sums up the content of the section. Discuss terms, such as *tectonic plates*, that may need clarification. Have students predict answers to the questions in "Read to Find Out." As they read the section, tell them to see if their predictions were correct.

🌐 **EE2 Places and Regions: Standard 4**
🌐 **EE3 Physical Systems: Standards 7, 8**
🗀 Refer to *Inclusion for the Social Studies Classroom Strategies and Activities.*

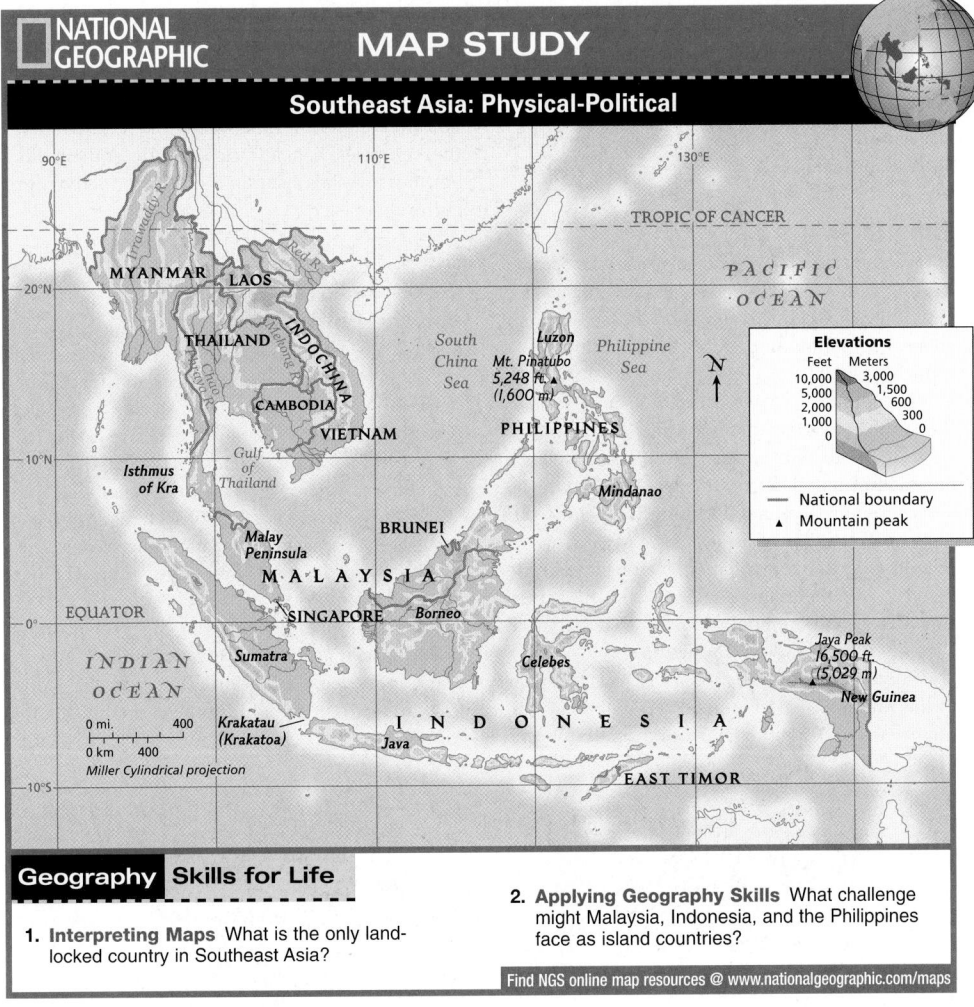

MAP STUDY

NATIONAL GEOGRAPHIC

Southeast Asia: Physical-Political

Geography Skills for Life

1. **Interpreting Maps** What is the only land-locked country in Southeast Asia?

2. **Applying Geography Skills** What challenge might Malaysia, Indonesia, and the Philippines face as island countries?

Find NGS online map resources @ www.nationalgeographic.com/maps

L2 Inference

Remind students that the region is made up of mainland countries and island countries. **Ask:** Why are the island countries considered part of Asia? *(Offshore islands are considered part of the continent to which they are closest.)*

NATIONAL GEOGRAPHIC **MAP STUDY**

Answers

1. *Laos*

2. *Answers may include that population centers could become overcrowded because of the lack of space for growth; limitation or transportation.*

Map Skills Practice

Place Which Southeast Asian countries are located on peninsulas? *(Indochina Peninsula: Vietnam, Laos, Cambodia, and Myanmar; Malay Peninsula: Malaysia and part of Thailand)*

L1/ELL

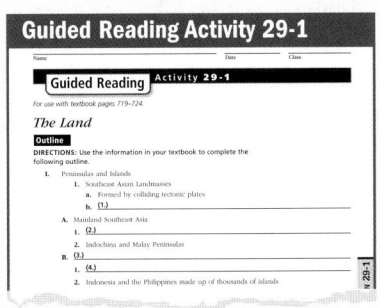

Guided Reading Activity 29-1

---

in the region. Its more than 13,500 islands span 3,000 miles (4,827 km) and two oceans, the Indian and the Pacific. Only about 6,000 islands are named, and fewer than 1,000 are permanently settled. East Timor, formerly a part of Indonesia, voted to become independent in 1999. Three years later, East Timor became a fully independent nation.

The country of Singapore, a collection of one large island and more than 50 smaller ones, sits just off the southern tip of the Malay Peninsula. The country's capital is on the large island, and both the

island and the capital city are called Singapore. The size of the islands varies greatly. The total area of the island of Singapore is 221 square miles (572 sq. km), and the total area of all the other islands is about 18 square miles (47 sq. km). Half of those islands are uninhabited.

Although more than 7,000 islands make up the Philippines, only around 900 are settled, and 11 islands account for over 95 percent of the country's area. As in Indonesia and Singapore, many of the Philippine islands have not been named.

Chapter 29   721

COOPERATIVE LEARNING ACTIVITY

Students Teaching Have students form small groups. Assign one or more Southeast Asian countries to each group. Tell students to study the location and physical features of their assigned countries and prepare a lesson plan to teach this information to the class. Suggest that students think of devices to help others remember the physical geography of this region. *(For example, some people think Thailand resembles the head and trunk of an elephant.)* Display Unit Map Overlay Transparency 29. Have members in each group take turns teaching specific sections of the lesson plan they have prepared.
EE1 The World in Spatial Terms: Standards 1, 2

L1/ELL

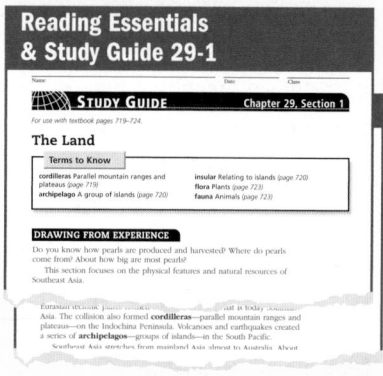

Reading Essentials & Study Guide 29-1

World Explorer

Answer

those in the Ring of Fire

More About the Photo

Ash spewing from Mt. Pinatubo, 50 miles (90 km) from Manila, Philippines, left 100,000 Filipinos homeless.

Cambodia During the rainy season, overflow from the Mekong River increases the depth of Cambodia's *Tonle Sap*, or Great Lake, from about 7 feet (2.2 m) to as much as 35 feet (11 m).

Physical Features

Cordilleras loom above fertile fields. Rivers create transportation routes through lush vegetation. Majestic volcanoes add to the scenery. These physical features create Southeast Asia's colorful and varied landscapes.

Mountains

Mountains dominate Southeast Asian landscapes, although most peaks crest below 10,000 feet (3,048 m). Throughout the region these mountains create geographic and political boundaries. The Indochina Peninsula's western and northern highlands separate the region from India and China. To the south and east, three cordilleras run mainly north to south, forming natural barriers between and within mainland Southeast Asian countries. These parallel mountain ranges include the Arakan Yoma Range in western Myanmar; the Bilauktaung Range, which runs along the border between Myanmar and Thailand; and the **Annam Cordillera**, the mountain range that separates Vietnam from Laos and Cambodia.

Mountains on Southeast Asia's islands form part of the Ring of Fire, an area of volcanic and earthquake activity roughly surrounding the Pacific Ocean. These mountains are actually volcanoes, many of which are still active. Some islands of Indonesia and the Philippines are marked with craters formed by these volcanoes. Mineral-rich volcanic material that has broken down over the centuries has left rich, fertile soil, making Southeast Asia's islands highly productive agricultural areas.

History
Volcanoes of Indonesia and the Philippines

Three hundred twenty-seven volcanoes stretch across Indonesia. Java, an Indonesian island, is one of the Ring of Fire's most active areas. This geologic hot spot is home to 17 of Indonesia's 100 active volcanoes. In 1883, the eruption of Krakatau (Krakatoa) in Indonesia caused massive destruction and great loss of life. To avoid a repeat of such disastrous consequences, observers in Java monitor volcanic activity, prepared to alert the population when an eruption threatens.

Some scientists believe that the 1991 eruption of Mount Pinatubo was the twentieth century's most powerful eruption. Located 55 miles (89 km) north of the Philippine capital of Manila, Mount Pinatubo churned out lava that severely

NATIONAL GEOGRAPHIC **World Explorer**

Geography Skills for Life

Pinatubo Eruption Heavy mudflows from the 1991 eruption of Mount Pinatubo forced thousands of people to evacuate the area (inset) and caused the deaths of more than 700 people.

Region What countries in Southeast Asia are likely to experience volcanic eruption?

CRITICAL THINKING ACTIVITY

Making Comparisons Ask students to consider the effects that physical processes—hurricanes, volcanic eruptions and earthquakes—have on Southeast Asia's environment and people. Have students supply entries under the categories *Positive Effects* and *Negative Effects* (*Positive effects: creating new land, lava becomes rich soil, scenic and scientific attraction; negative effects: loss of life and property; tsunamis created by quakes and eruptions*) Then ask students to compare the ways Southeast Asians depend on, adapt to, or modify their environment with those of people living in other volcanic and earthquake- or storm-prone regions. 📘 **EE2 Places and Regions: Standard 4**

damaged the town of Angeles. The volcano also blanketed the United States's Clark Air Force Base with volcanic ash nearly a foot deep.

Rivers

Southeast Asia's people rely on waterways for transportation, communication, and food. The rivers' silt and deposits of sediment also create fertile agricultural regions. Mainland rivers originate in the northern highlands of Southeast Asia and in southern China. Most of these rivers flow southward toward the Gulf of Thailand.

Major mainland rivers include the **Irrawaddy** in Myanmar, the **Chao Phraya** (chow PRY•uh) in Thailand, and the **Red (Hong)** in Vietnam. The **Mekong**, which begins its 2,600-mile (4,184-km) journey in China, forms the border between Thailand and Laos and then meanders through Cambodia and southern Vietnam before emptying into the South China Sea. Sediment deposited by the Mekong increases the shoreline around the delta by as much as 50 feet (15 m) per year.

Generally shorter than their mainland counterparts, rivers on Southeast Asia's islands flow in various directions. Most rivers in Indonesia run south to north, cutting vertically across the narrow islands. Borneo's rivers tend to start near the island's center, running outward toward the sea like spokes on a wheel. As one writer notes, traveling on Borneo's rivers reveals a dense, vibrant ecosystem:

> 66 *Poling our way along the inky green waterway, we glided upstream through quiet still-water bends in the river, where mats of fragrant white flowers had gathered, closing behind the stern of our 24-inch-wide dugout and concealing any sign of our passage.* 99
>
> Eric Hansen, *Stranger in the Forest: On Foot Across Borneo*, 1988

Natural Resources

In addition to the remarkable features found in the landscape, Southeast Asia also has rich natural resources. Fossil fuels, natural steam, minerals,

Geography Skills for Life

River Highway Two tugboats pull a chain of logs to a sawmill on the island of Borneo.
Place What are some important rivers in the region?

and gems can be found in the region. The flora and fauna, or plants and animals, of Southeast Asia are among the most diverse on the earth and also a valuable natural resource of the region.

Energy Sources

The region has a plentiful supply of fossil fuels—coal, oil, and natural gas. Malaysia's second major export is petroleum, and the country's production of oil and natural gas has increased since the 1970s. Indonesia, Vietnam, and the Philippines mine coal, and Vietnam also has rich oil reserves offshore. Oil and natural gas deposits off Borneo's northern coast have made the sultan, or ruler, of Brunei one of the world's richest people. Indonesia also has large petroleum reserves. The island of Sumatra supplies two-thirds of Indonesia's oil, and oil and gas are the country's main exports. One of the leading producers of oil in the Far East, Indonesia is a member of OPEC (Organization of Petroleum Exporting Countries).

Minerals and Gems

Southeast Asia has an abundance of minerals. Indonesia mines nickel and iron, and the

NATIONAL GEOGRAPHIC World Explorer

Answer
the Irrawaddy, the Chao Phraya, the Red, the Mekong

More About the Photo Rain forests cover most of Borneo. Some are so dense that their interior remains unexplored to this day. Because of the landscape, Borneo's rivers are the main means of transportation for people and goods.

③ ASSESS

Assign Section 1 Assessment as homework or as an in-class activity.
🖱 Have students use **Interactive Tutor Self-Assessment CD-ROM**.

L2

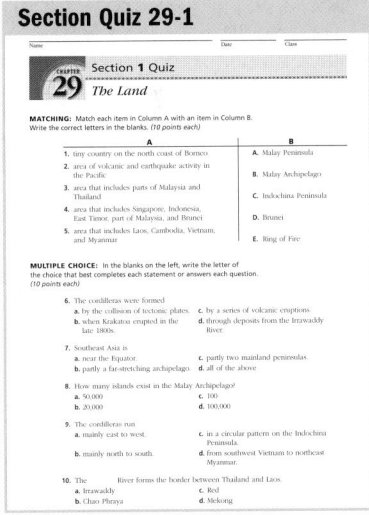

Section Quiz 29-1

TEAM-TEACHING ACTIVITY: SCIENCE

Creating a Volcano Model Remind students that parts of this region are located in the most active volcanic area on Earth. Organize students into small groups, and have each group make a portion of a two-part diorama. One model will be a cutaway of a volcano's interior before an explosion, including the magma chamber and the top or main vent. The second model will show the exterior and interior of the mountain during an eruption. Consult with a science teacher to create a flow chart of the eruption process, and display it. **Ask:** What short-term effect does an eruption have on mountain slopes? (*destroys vegetation*) What long-term effect does an eruption have on the surrounding area? (*makes the soil more fertile*) 📦 🖥 **EE5 Environment and Society: Standard 14**

Reteach

Have students answer the questions in "Read to Find Out" on page 719. Use their responses as a basis for discussion of points that seem to need reinforcement or clarification.

Enrich

Reread for students the passage from Marco Polo in "A Traveler's Log" on page 707. Tell them to assume the role of someone backpacking or traveling on a boat through Southeast Asia. They should select one physical feature of a Southeast Asian country and write a descriptive paragraph. Have them include an accurate description of its geographical characteristics and significance as well as their emotional reaction on seeing it for the first time.

4 CLOSE

Have students reread "A Geographic View" on page 719. Have students tell how they visualize the landforms, flora and fauna of Southeast Asia based on this written description.

Philippines mines copper. Thailand, Laos, Indonesia, and Malaysia mine tin. Indonesia and Malaysia are among the world's leading producers of tin.

Gems also are plentiful in the region. Sapphires and rubies can be found in Myanmar, Thailand, Cambodia, and Vietnam. In the Philippines pearls are harvested in the province of Sulu and on the island of Palawan. A giant pearl found off Palawan in 1934 weighed about 14 pounds (6.4 kg), making it the largest natural pearl ever harvested. Although most countries take advantage of the wealth provided by nature, some countries' resources remain underdeveloped. Myanmar, for example, has substantial deposits of tin, zinc, and other minerals, as well as jade, rubies, and sapphires, but mining employs less than 1 percent of Myanmar's workers.

Flora and Fauna

Southeast Asia's plant life is exotic and diverse. The region boasts the world's largest flower, the *Rafflesia arnoldii*, a spectacular plant with a blossom three feet wide. Southeast Asian flora, however, is more than just beautiful—it also contributes to the region's economy. For example, Thailand cultivates over 1,000 species of orchids, a valuable trade commodity. Workers tap rubber trees from Malaysia and process woods for export such as mahogany from the Philippines and teak from Myanmar. Indonesia is the world's largest supplier of plywood.

Like the region's flora, Southeast Asian fauna is varied and distinctive. Elephants, tigers, rhinoceroses, and orangutans roam the region's wildlife sanctuaries and national parks. Southeast Asia is home to animals found nowhere else in the world, including Borneo's bearded pig, the Malaysian lacewing butterfly, and the Komodo dragon, an Indonesian native and the world's largest lizard.

Economics
Fishing

More than 2,500 species of fish swim the tropical waters of Southeast Asia. Fish thrive in the mainland rivers and in seas near the Philippines, Indonesia, and Myanmar. Fish farming is an important part of the region's economy. Southeast Asians consume seafood at almost twice the world's average rate. The region's fishers, who have traditionally maintained small operations, now compete with large fleets of trawlers. This competition has produced an increased fish yield that helps meet demand, and so overfishing is a concern. Luckily, demand for exported seafood has started to level off, which may ease the pressure to fish excessively.

As in other parts of the world, Southeast Asia's diverse landforms shape the climate and vegetation of the region. The next section will examine these features—the lush tropical vegetation of the region's rain forest, the seasonal grasslands of its savannas, and its highlands.

SECTION 1 ASSESSMENT

Checking for Understanding

1. **Define** cordillera, archipelago, insular, flora, fauna.

2. **Main Ideas** Re-create the table below, and fill in five Southeast Asian countries and examples of their physical features and natural resources.

Country	Physical Features	Natural Resources
Malaysia		

Critical Thinking

3. **Identifying Cause and Effect** Rich soil makes Southeast Asia a productive agricultural region. What makes this soil so fertile?

4. **Drawing Conclusions** Southeast Asia has a diversity of peoples and cultures. How might physical geography have shaped this diversity?

5. **Making Generalizations** What special challenges does the location of Laos, the only country in the region without a coastline, present?

Analyzing Maps

6. **Location** Review the text and analyze the physical-political map on page 721. Note the geographic features found on Southeast Asia islands. What geographic features do the islands of Borneo, Celebes, and New Guinea share?

Applying Geography

7. **Effects of Water** Write a paragraph explaining why the abundance of water in Southeast Asia can be both an asset and a challenge for the region's population.

SECTION 1 ASSESSMENT ANSWERS

1. All vocabulary terms are defined in the text.

2. Answer should include physical features and natural resources of five Southeast Asian countries.

3. Answer may include fertile river plains and deltas and the effects of volcanic lava.

4. Answer should show understanding that physical diversity leads to different cultural adaptations and natural physical barriers create

isolation that fosters diverse customs. Ideas should be supported by specific examples.

5. Answer may include that mountains to the north are an obstacle, lack of a coastline limits trade and other interactions with island countries, and absence of river deltas means limited access to the delta's fertile soil.

6. They all are large islands with mountainous interiors.

7. **Applying Geography** Benefits may include that abundant water contributes to meeting basic human needs, fertile soil, and transportation through rugged terrain, and dense forests. Challenges include danger to people and destruction to property from flooding, as well as barriers to trade and communications.

Guide to Reading

Consider What You Know

You have learned that much of Southeast Asia lies near the Equator. Based on this knowledge, what types of climate and vegetation do you suppose dominate the region?

Reading Strategy

Categorizing As you read about the vegetation of Southeast Asia, complete a web diagram similar to the one below by filling in the three types of vegetation found in the region.

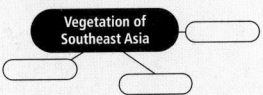

Read to Find Out

- What weather pattern influences the region's climate?
- What are the region's main climate types?
- What is the main type of natural vegetation found in the region?

Terms to Know

- endemic
- deciduous

Places to Locate

- Shan Plateau
- Myanmar
- New Guinea
- Borneo

Climate and Vegetation

NATIONAL GEOGRAPHIC

A Geographic View

World in Balance

This is the forest primeval. . . . The dappled splotches of sun and shade filtering through the leafy canopy 200 feet above wash over a rain forest that has been here since before humans appeared on earth. . . . It is a world in such careful balance that the mix of vegetation in these undisturbed jungle tracts has been essentially the same . . . for millions and millions of years.

—*T. R. Reid, "Malaysia: Rising Star," National Geographic, August 1997*

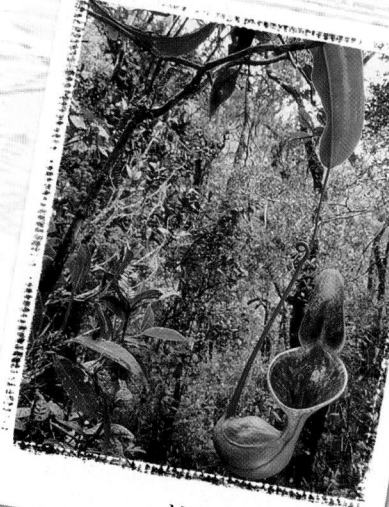

Malaysian rain forest

The rain forests of Southeast Asia owe much of their ancient beauty to an equally ancient climate pattern—monsoons, or seasonal winds that blow over the northern part of the Indian Ocean and the land nearby. In summer, moist monsoons blow in from the cooler sea in the south and west toward the warmer land and bring abundant rain, enough to support the region's tropical rain forests. The ample rain falls on lush tropical plants whose exotic flowers perfume the air. In winter, air over the land is cooler than that over the sea, so the wind blows out to sea from the northeast as a dry monsoon. The rain forests themselves are aptly named. They are generally wet all year long.

Tropical Climate Regions

Tropical rain forest climate dominates Southeast Asia. Parts of the mainland and some of the islands have a tropical savanna or humid subtropical climate. These climate regions are characterized by grasslands and tropical forests that support a diverse ecosystem.

1 FOCUS

Section Overview

This section discusses the effect of monsoons, location and landforms on climates and vegetation in Southeast Asia.

BELLRINGER
Skillbuilder Activity

Project transparency and have students answer questions.

Available as blackline master.

Daily Focus Skills Transparency 29-2

UNIT 10 CHAPTER 29 DAILY FOCUS SKILLS TRANSPARENCY 29-2

Interpreting a Table

Deforestation of Tropical Rain Forests

ECONOMIC ACTIVITY	FACTORS	TIME TO REGROW FOREST
Slash-and-Burn Agriculture	fields abandoned after brief use	less than 50 years
Shade Agriculture (e.g. coffee)	some trees left standing	about 20 years
Intensive Agriculture (plantation)	heavy pesticide use, alteration of water balance	more than 50 years
Cattle Grazing	soil degradation	more than 50 years
Selective Logging	few trees cut	less than 50 years
Clearcut Logging	no trees and few soil nutrients left	more than 50 years

Standardized Test Practice

Which economic activity is the least damaging to a rain forest?

A Intensive Agriculture
B Clearcut Logging
C Shade Agriculture
D Cattle Grazing

Guide to Reading

Consider What You Know

Answer *Students' answer may include tropical rain forest vegetation and broad leafed, evergreen vegetation of humid subtropical and tropical savanna climates.*

Reading Strategy

Answers *tropical forest, tropical grassland, deciduous and deciduous/coniferous forest*

Preteaching Vocabulary

Use the **Vocabulary Puzzle-Maker CD-ROM** to create crossword and word-search puzzles.

RESOURCE MANAGER

Reproducible Masters

- Reproducible Lesson Plan 29-2
- Vocabulary Activity 29
- Daily Lecture Notes 29-2
- Guided Reading Activity 29-2
- Reading Essentials and Study Guide 29-2
- Reteaching Activity 29
- Reinforcing Skills Activity 29
- Section Quiz 29-2

Transparencies

- Daily Focus Skills Transparency 29-2
- Political Map Transparency 10
- Unit 10 Map Overlay Transparencies

Multimedia

- Vocabulary PuzzleMaker CD-ROM
- Interactive Tutor Self-Assessment CD-ROM
- ExamView® Pro Testmaker CD-ROM
- Presentation Plus! CD-ROM

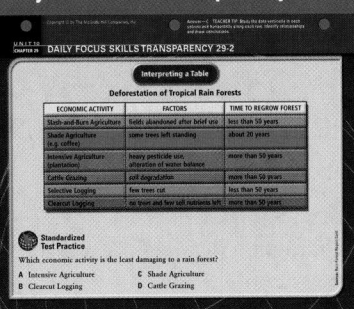

2 TEACH

L1 Language

Allow students whose native language is not English to work with an English language student who has shown mastery of geographic concepts. Have them develop a bilingual glossary that lists "Terms to Know," climate types, and vegetation categories in the primary language with English equivalents. **ELL**

NATIONAL GEOGRAPHIC MAP STUDY

Answers

1. *Myanmar, New Guinea, and on the island of Borneo*

2. *Mainland is mostly humid subtropical and tropical savanna; islands are mostly tropical rain forest.*

Map Skills Practice

Location Which country in the region has land that extends beyond the area of the tropics? (*Myanmar*)

Daily Lecture Notes 29-2

DAILY LECTURE NOTES

CHAPTER 29
Section 2

Building Geography Literacy
Malaysia includes mainland and island areas: West Malaysia, primarily on the southern part of the Malay Peninsula, and East Malaysia, on the northern part of the island of Borneo. Both areas, however, have similar natural features: coastal swamps or mangrove forests, lowland rain forests, and interior mountains.

I. Tropical Climate Regions   pages 725–729

Southeast Asia's rain forests depend on the moisture brought by the summer monsoons blowing in from the south and west.

A. Tropical Rain Forest Climate

   1. Most of Southeast Asia has a tropical rain forest climate. Temperatures are fairly constant, averaging 79°F (26°C). Humidity is always high, and annual rainfall is between 79 and 188 inches (201 and 478 cm). (p. 726)

   2. The rain forests feature more than 145,000 species of flowering plants. Other types of vegetation include peat swamp forests, mangrove swamp forests, and evergreen trees. (p. 727)

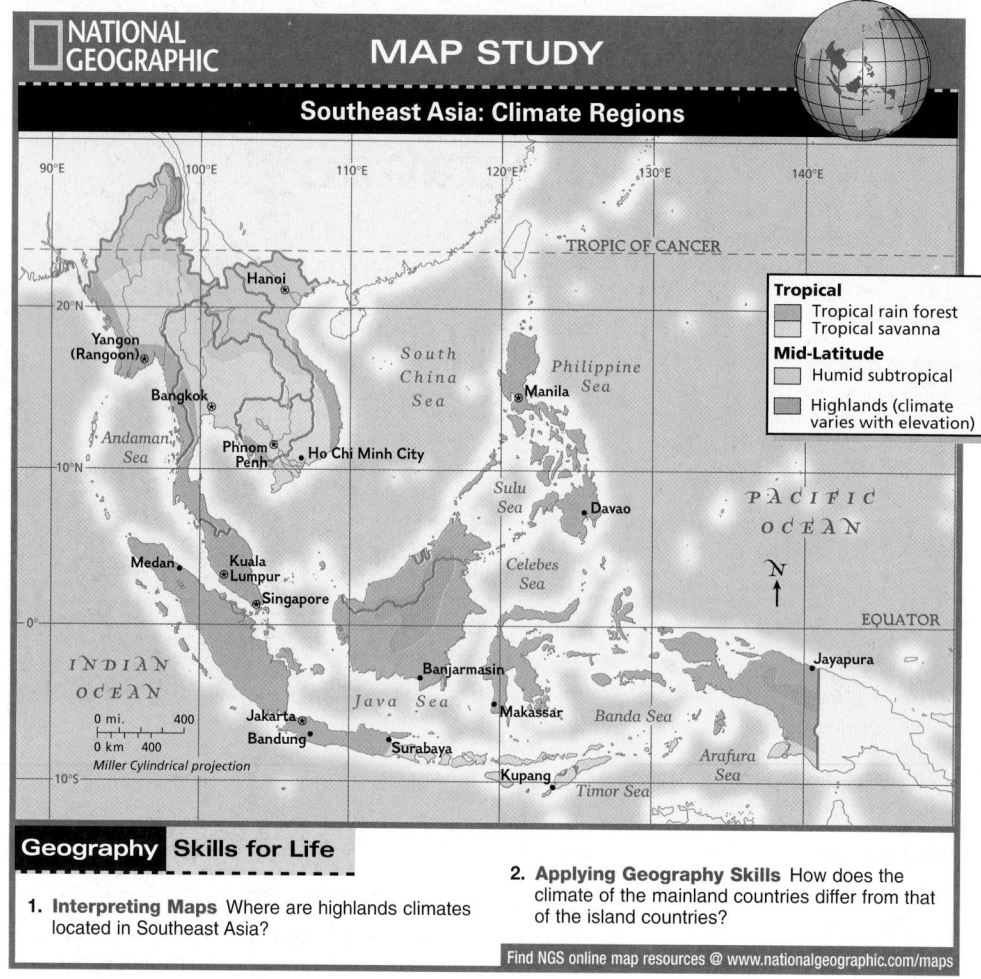

NATIONAL GEOGRAPHIC MAP STUDY

Southeast Asia: Climate Regions

Tropical
- Tropical rain forest
- Tropical savanna

Mid-Latitude
- Humid subtropical
- Highlands (climate varies with elevation)

Miller Cylindrical projection

Geography Skills for Life

1. **Interpreting Maps** Where are highlands climates located in Southeast Asia?

2. **Applying Geography Skills** How does the climate of the mainland countries differ from that of the island countries?

Find NGS online map resources @ www.nationalgeographic.com/maps

Tropical Rain Forest Climate

Most of the region, including the islands and coastal areas, has a tropical rain forest climate. This climate is characterized by little variation in temperature and mostly wet conditions almost year-round. The 79°F (26°C) average daily temperature creates hot, humid, and rainy conditions. Rainfall averages between 79 and 188 inches (201 and 478 cm) per year, and the humidity hovers between 80 and 90 percent. Even more rain falls near the summit of Mount Isarog in the Philippines, described here by journalist Virginia Morell:

 Thick mats of spongy mosses cover every rock, tree trunk, and branch, forming an emerald carpet for the orchids and ferns that drape the limbs overhead—a lush testament to the 35 feet [420 inches, or 1,067 cm] of rain that can annually drench this mountain's summit. 99

Virginia Morell, "In Search of Solutions," *National Geographic*, February 1999

DIFFERENTIATED INSTRUCTION

Visual/Spatial Encourage students to recognize patterns in the natural environment in Southeast Asia. Have students refer to the climate and vegetation maps on pages 726–727. Have interested students locate photos or make drawings of plants that are typical of each climate region shown on the map. Using the vegetation map as the central element, students should create a display on a bulletin board to illustrate the various kinds of vegetation. For example, students might tack one end of a piece of yarn to a vegetation type on the map and the other end to photos or drawings of its typical plants.

EE2 Places and Regions: Standard 6

Refer to *Inclusion for the Social Studies Classroom Strategies and Activities.*

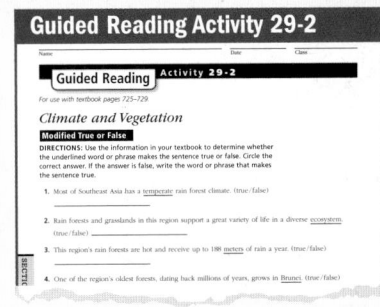

NATIONAL GEOGRAPHIC — MAP STUDY

Southeast Asia: Natural Vegetation

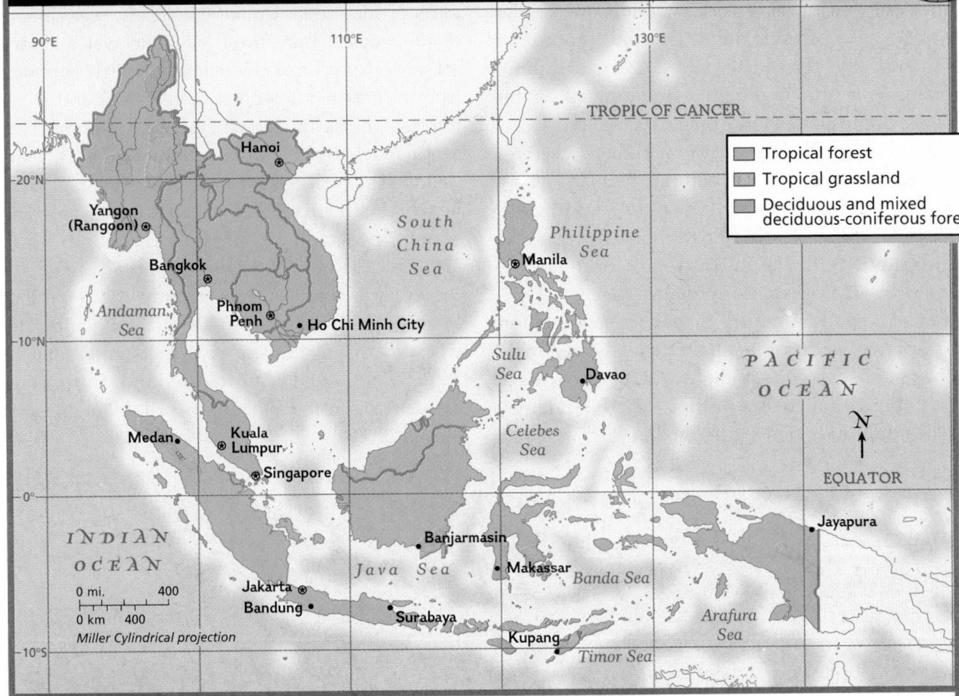

TROPIC OF CANCER

Hanoi

Yangon (Rangoon)

Bangkok

Phnom Penh

Ho Chi Minh City

South China Sea

Philippine Sea

Manila

Andaman Sea

Medan

Kuala Lumpur

Singapore

Sulu Sea

Davao

Celebes Sea

PACIFIC OCEAN

N

EQUATOR

Banjarmasin

Makassar

Jayapura

INDIAN OCEAN

0 mi. 400
0 km 400
Miller Cylindrical projection

Jakarta

Bandung

Surabaya

Java Sea

Banda Sea

Arafura Sea

Kupang

Timor Sea

Legend:
- Tropical forest
- Tropical grassland
- Deciduous and mixed deciduous-coniferous forest

Geography Skills for Life

1. **Interpreting Maps** What is the dominant natural vegetation in Southeast Asia?

2. **Applying Geography Skills** What type of climate produces tropical grasslands on Indonesia's eastern islands?

Find NGS online map resources @ www.nationalgeographic.com/maps

---

The tropical rain forest climate supports a diverse ecosystem. More than 14,500 species of flowering plants blossom in Malaysia alone. The Malaysian rain forest, where vegetation types mix, may be the region's oldest forest, dating back many millions of years. Here there are several layers of vegetation between river valleys and higher elevations. Peat swamp forests thrive in the river valleys. Sandy coastal soil supports various shrubs, and mangrove swamp forests cover the tidal mud flats. Lowland areas with poor or shallow soil support forests of tall trees with leathery, evergreen leaves. Some of these trees produce aromatic resins, or organic compounds. Such resins are used to make medicines and varnishes, or chemicals that protect wood from water damage.

GEOGRAPHY Online

Student Web Activity Visit the **Glencoe World Geography** Web site at geography.glencoe.com and click on Student Web Activities—Chapter 29 for an activity about writing a visitor's journal about the physical features of Southeast Asia.

Chapter 29 ⬤ 727

NATIONAL GEOGRAPHIC — MAP STUDY

Answers

1. *tropical forest*

2. *tropical savanna*

Map Skills Practice

Place What type of climate produces deciduous and mixed forests in northeastern Myanmar? *(humid subtropical)*

GEOGRAPHY Online

Objectives, goals, and answers to the student activity can be found in the Web Activity Lesson Plan feature at geography.glencoe.com

L1/ELL

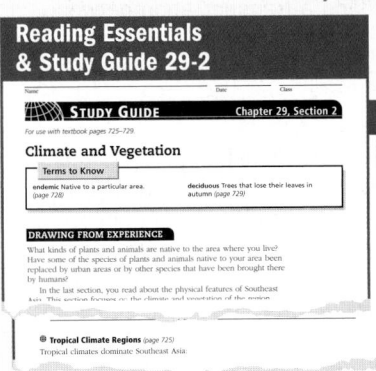

COOPERATIVE LEARNING ACTIVITY

Seasonal Weather Outlooks Organize the class into groups of three or four. Assign one of the following locations to each group: northern Laos, southern Thailand, Sumatra, or the Philippines. Instruct group members to prepare seasonal weather forecasts for their assigned location. Allow time for each group to research and present its forecast. Students might assume the roles of television weather forecasters and point out specifics on a wall map of this region.

▣ **EE1 The World in Spatial Terms: Standard 1**
▣ **EE2 Places and Regions: Standard 4**

3 ASSESS

Assign Section 2 Assessment as homework or as an in-class activity.

Have students use **Interactive Tutor Self-Assessment CD-ROM**.

L2

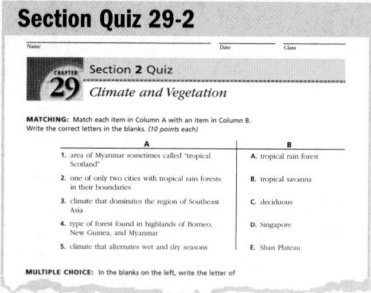

Section Quiz 29-2

Name	Date Class

CHAPTER 29 Section 2 Quiz
Climate and Vegetation

MATCHING: Match each item in Column A with an item in Column B. Write the correct letters in the blanks. *(10 points each)*

A	B
1. area of Myanmar sometimes called "tropical Scotland"	A. tropical rain forest
2. one of only two cities with tropical rain forests in their boundaries	B. tropical savanna
3. climate that dominates the region of Southeast Asia	C. deciduous
4. type of forest found in highlands of Borneo, New Guinea, and Myanmar	D. Singapore
5. climate that alternates wet and dry seasons	E. Shan Plateau

MULTIPLE CHOICE: In the blanks on the left, write the letter of

---

NATIONAL GEOGRAPHIC World Explorer

Answer
Summer monsoons bring warm, moist air; winter monsoons bring cold, dry air.

More About the Photo
Monsoons make it difficult for Thailand to develop a road system. The country's canals provide a transportation network.

Reteach

Assign small groups of students to scan each main heading in Section 2 to make a list of important terms and concepts. Then have the groups quiz one another by asking why the term is important in this region.

History
Singapore

Once an island covered by dense rain forest and surrounded by mangrove trees, **Singapore** developed into an urban area containing one of the world's highest population densities, more than 17,155 people per square mile (6,624 per sq. km). Towering apartment buildings now house Singapore's population of more than 4,000,000 people.

As Singapore grew, an urbanized setting replaced much of its natural habitat. Many *endemic* species—those native to a particular area—are gone. Nearly 80 percent of the trees and shrubs now growing in Singapore are imported, some originating from such distant places as Central and South America. Singapore's vegetation makes it exceptional in another way. Singapore is one of only two cities in the world that have areas of tropical rain forests within their boundaries. (The other is Rio de Janeiro, Brazil.)

Tropical Savanna Climate

The second most prominent climate zone, the tropical savanna, sweeps southeastward across the Indochina Peninsula and along the southeastern parts of Indonesia. Unlike the steady, wet climate of the tropical rain forest, alternate wet and dry seasons characterize this climate, which supports tropical grasslands with scattered trees and some forests. On the Indochina Peninsula, the dry season may last from four to eight months each year.

On the mainland from around May through September, summer monsoon winds bring rain. The winter dry season extends from October to April. The first few months of this period are generally cooler, but the last few months become hot. In southern Indonesia, south of the Equator, the wet and dry cycles are reversed. From May to September, South Pacific tradewinds bring the hot, dry season. From October to April, the monsoons bring rain.

NATIONAL GEOGRAPHIC World Explorer

Geography Skills for Life

Monsoon Rains Commuters in Thailand travel by boat, using a plastic sheet to protect themselves against the torrential rains of the summer monsoons.
Region How do the summer monsoons differ from winter monsoons?

CRITICAL THINKING ACTIVITY

Determining Cause and Effect Remind students that one cause might have several effects and each effect might cause still other effects. Strings of such cause-and-effect relationships are called cause-and-effect chains. Give students the following example: Deforestation (cause) allows rain to leach nutrients from the soil (effect). After several seasons, the soil becomes infertile (effect). Infertile soil (cause) forces farmers to find new lands for growing crops. They cut and burn forests for farm lands (effect). Meanwhile, the abandoned infertile areas erode (effect). Have students review the content of Section 2 to develop cause-and-effect chains related to monsoons, landforms, and locations in Southeast Asia.
EE1 The World in Spatial Terms: Standard 1

Humid Subtropical Climate

Parts of Southeast Asia's mainland, including most of Laos, a small part of Thailand, and northern Myanmar and Vietnam, have a humid subtropical climate. The northern reaches of Laos, Thailand, and Vietnam provide relief from the hot, humid temperatures. From November to April, the cool, dry temperatures there average around 61°F (16°C). In Myanmar the elevated **Shan Plateau** has lower temperatures than the rest of the country. The climate there resembles cooler climates elsewhere, and the plateau is sometimes called "tropical Scotland."

Highlands Climate

In mountainous areas of **Myanmar**, **New Guinea**, and **Borneo**, highlands climates predominate. The much cooler temperatures of these areas set them apart from surrounding climate regions. Deciduous forests with moss-covered tree trunks are found on lower slopes. **Deciduous** trees lose their leaves in autumn. Evergreen forests appear at higher elevations. In Myanmar's highlands climate, forests of rhododendrons grow.

Geography Skills for Life

Highlands Forest Tropical deciduous forests are found in some highlands areas of Borneo (shown), Myanmar, and New Guinea.
Place What other kind of vegetation is found in the highlands areas of Myanmar?

SECTION 2 ASSESSMENT

Checking for Understanding

1. **Define** endemic, deciduous.

2. **Main Ideas** Create a web like the one below. In the boxes, list each Southeast Asian climate region, its location, the kinds of vegetation found there and any identifying traits.

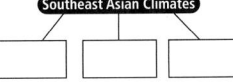

Southeast Asian Climates

Critical Thinking

3. **Analyzing Information** How do monsoon winds impact climates and seasonal changes in Southeast Asia?

4. **Identifying Cause and Effect** Why are wet and dry seasons in Southeast Asia reversed on different sides of the Equator?

5. **Analyzing Information** How does a humid subtropical climate differ from a tropical rain forest climate?

Analyzing Maps

6. **Climate Regions** Study the map of climate regions on page 726. Which of the countries in Southeast Asia has the most varied climate?

Applying Geography

7. **Climate and Vegetation** Review Southeast Asia's climate regions and natural vegetation. How might these features influence the region's economic activities?

SECTION 2 ASSESSMENT ANSWERS

1. All vocabulary terms are defined in the text.

2. Answer should include location of three Southeast Asian climates and traits of each.

3. North of the Equator, monsoons bring rain from May through October. The rains benefit agriculture, but can endanger lives and damage property.

4. Answer should reflect understanding that the time of the seasons is reversed in the Southern Hemisphere.

5. Tropical rain forest climate is hot and wet throughout the year; humid subtropical has hot, humid conditions for six months of the year.

6. Myanmar and Indonesia

7. **Applying Geography** Heavy rains limit transportation and industry, but are favorable to certain kinds of agriculture, such as rice farming.

Answer
rhododendrons; evergreen forests

More About the Photo
Southeast Asian forests contain more than 500 species of plants that yield aromatic oils and resins.

Enrich

Tell students that the Moluccas in this region once were known as the Spice Islands. Have interested students conduct research to find out what common spices come from the "spice islands," how they are used, and how the spice trade contributes to the islands' economy.

 **CLOSE**

Have volunteers predict what they will learn about the region in the rest of this unit, based on what they know about the region's physical geography. Record their predictions on a piece of poster board or overhead transparencies, and refer to them as students study the reminder of the unit.

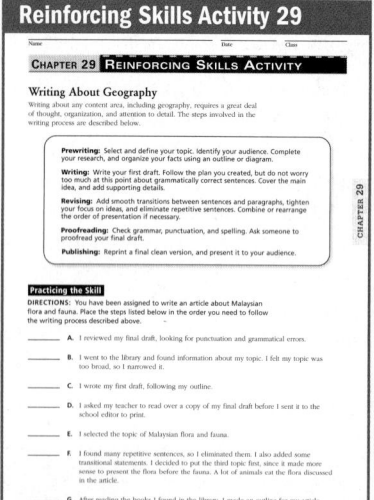

STUDY & WRITING SkillBuilder

Teaching the Skill

Tell students that using the writing process can help them plan and carry out their ideas in the most effective manner. Point out and discuss each step in that process. On the board, create a flowchart of the steps with students.

Additional Practice
L1

Reinforcing Skills Activity 29

Name _____ Date _____ Class _____

CHAPTER 29 REINFORCING SKILLS ACTIVITY

Writing About Geography

Writing about any content area, including geography, requires a great deal of thought, organization, and attention to detail. The steps involved in the writing process are described below.

Prewriting: Select and define your topic. Identify your audience. Complete your research, and organize your facts using an outline or diagram.

Writing: Write your first draft. Follow the plan you created, but do not worry too much at this point about grammatically correct sentences. Cover the main idea, and add supporting details.

Revising: Add smooth transitions between sentences and paragraphs, tighten your focus on ideas, and eliminate repetitive sentences. Combine or rearrange the order of presentation if necessary.

Proofreading: Check grammar, punctuation, and spelling. Ask someone to proofread your final draft.

Publishing: Reprint a final clean version, and present it to your audience.

Practicing the Skill

DIRECTIONS: You have been assigned to write an article about Malaysian flora and fauna. Place the steps listed below in the order you need to follow the writing process described above.

____ **A.** I reviewed my final draft, looking for punctuation and grammatical errors.

____ **B.** I went to the library and found information about my topic. I felt my topic was too broad, so I narrowed it.

____ **C.** I wrote my first draft, following my outline.

____ **D.** I asked my teacher to read over a copy of my final draft before I sent it to the school editor to print.

____ **E.** I selected the topic of Malaysian flora and fauna.

____ **F.** I found many repetitive sentences, so I eliminated them. I also added some transitional statements. I decided to put the third topic first, since it made more sense to present the flora before the fauna. A lot of animals eat the flora discussed in the article.

____ **G.** After reading the books I found in the library, I made an outline for my article.

CHAPTER 29

GLENCOE
TECHNOLOGY

Glencoe Skillbuilder Interactive Workbook, Level 2

This interactive CD-ROM reinforces student mastery of essential social studies skills.

Writing About Geography

Writing well is an essential skill. In school you write research papers and answers to essay questions. Beyond the classroom you may have to write business letters or reports. The writing process can help you put your thoughts on paper.

Learning the Skill

The writing process has several steps: prewriting, writing, revising, proofreading, and publishing. Following this process allows you to organize your ideas and complete the writing task in a logical manner. Use the following steps to help you write about geography:

▲ *The newsroom of the* Chicago Defender

- **Prewriting is the research, writing, and organization you do before you begin your essay or report.** Select a topic, and define your purpose for writing about it. Identify the audience who will read your final product. Then do research to gather information. Organize your ideas using a graphic organizer such as a chart, a web diagram, or an outline.

- **Write your first draft.** As you write, follow the plan you created during the prewriting step. Do not worry about grammatically correct sentences in this stage. Focus on getting your main ideas and supporting details down on paper.

- **Revise your draft.** Look for places where you can add transitions between ideas, combine or rearrange paragraphs or sentences, or cut repetitive or unnecessary sections.

- **Proofread your draft.** Check your draft for grammar, spelling, and punctuation errors.

- **Publish your draft.** Create a clean draft, and present it to your audience.

Practicing the Skill

You have been assigned to write a travel brochure for a Southeast Asian country for an advertising agency. Answer the following questions about the writing process.

1. What will you need to do before you begin writing the first draft of your brochure?

2. Why might it be a good idea to let a day pass between writing and revising your brochure?

3. What are two resources you might use while proofreading your brochure?

Applying the Skill

Prewrite and then create a draft of a brief guide for someone who has just moved to the United States from Southeast Asia. Include information about the geography and life in the United States. Read your first draft carefully, and mark places that need to be revised. After revising, proofread and publish your writing.

The Glencoe Skillbuilder Interactive Workbook, Level 2 provides instruction and practice in key social studies skills.

ANSWERS TO PRACTICING THE SKILL

Possible answers appear below.

1. Prewriting, including researching to gather information and organizing ideas using a graphic organizer.

2. Waiting a day allows the writer to step back and look at the draft with a fresh perspective. This may inspire new ideas and make it easier to see points that need clarification or additional information.

3. a dictionary, a thesaurus, or a grammar and composition handbook

SUMMARY & STUDY GUIDE

CHAPTER 29

SECTION 1 — The Land (pp. 719–724)

Terms To Know
- cordillera
- archipelago
- insular
- flora
- fauna

Key Points
- Southeast Asia's mountains were formed when the Indo-Australian, Philippine, and Eurasian tectonic plates collided.
- Straddling the Equator, Southeast Asia includes the Indochina and Malay Peninsulas as well as the 20,000 islands of the Malay Archipelago.
- About half of Southeast Asia's 11 countries are located on the mainland. The rest are island countries, except for Malaysia, which is both a mainland and an island country.
- Mountains and rivers dominate the region's landscape. The island mountains are part of the Pacific Ring of Fire.
- Rivers on the mainland of Southeast Asia are important for agriculture, communication, and transportation.
- Southeast Asia contains abundant natural resources, including fossil fuels, natural steam, minerals, and gems.

Organizing Your Notes
Use a web diagram like the one below to organize your notes about the islands and peninsulas, physical features, and natural resources of Southeast Asia.

> Physical Features of Southeast Asia

SECTION 2 — The Climate and Vegetation (pp. 725–729)

Terms To Know
- endemic
- deciduous

Key Points
- Monsoons cause two main seasons in Southeast Asia, one wet and one dry.
- Southeast Asia's major climate is tropical rain forest, although parts of the mainland and some of the islands have other types of climate.
- Humid subtropical climates predominate in Laos and in northern areas of Myanmar, Thailand, and Vietnam.
- Highlands climates are found in the mountains of Myanmar, Borneo, and New Guinea.
- Southeast Asia's lush vegetation is characteristic of tropical rain forest and tropical savanna climate regions.

Organizing Your Notes
Create an outline like the one below to help you organize your notes for this section. Copy the boldface headings and subheadings that appear in Section 2, and then list important points under each head.

> **Climate and Vegetation**
> I. Tropical Climate Regions
>   A. Tropical rain forest climate
>   1. steady rain and humidity
>   2. average daily temperature of 79°F (26°C)
>   B.

Chapter 29 731

Using the Chapter 29 Summary & Study Guide

Use the Chapter 29 Summary & Study Guide to preview, review, condense, or reteach the chapter.

Preview/Review

Vocabulary PuzzleMaker CD-ROM reinforces "Terms to Know."

Interactive Tutor Self-Assessment CD-ROM provides a review of Chapter 29 content.

Condense

Have students read the Chapter 29 Summary & Study Guide.

Chapter 29 Audio Program

Chapter 29 Guided Reading Activities

Reteach

Chapter 29 Reteaching Activities (Spanish also available)

Chapter 29 Reading Essentials and Study Guides

GLENCOE TECHNOLOGY

NATIONAL GEOGRAPHIC
WORLD REGIONS
VIDEO PROGRAM

Unit 10, Southeast Asia
The following segments enhance the study of this unit:

- **Rice**
- **Tet in Hanoi**
- **Design for the Future**

CHAPTER CULMINATING ACTIVITY

Making Inferences Ask: In what ways does the physical geography of Southeast Asia shape the daily lives of the people who live there? As a response, have students create brief feature or news articles. Ask them to assume the role of journalists traveling through this region. Students can arrange their articles to resemble a page from a newspaper. Articles should include sketches, maps, or charts and tables to enrich the narrative. Encourage students to review the chapter's photos and maps, as well as the text and any exercises they have completed in their study of this chapter. **EE1 The World in Spatial Terms: Standards 1, 2, 3**
EE2 Places and Regions: Standards 4, 6
EE3 Physical Systems: Standards 7, 8

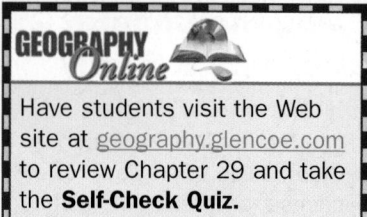

CHAPTER 29

ASSESSMENT & ACTIVITIES

GLENCOE TECHNOLOGY

Use *MindJogger Videoquiz* to review the Chapter 29 content.

Reviewing Key Terms

1. archipelago
2. cordillera
3. insular
4. endemic
5. deciduous
6. flora and fauna

Reviewing Facts
SECTION 1

1. Vietnam, Cambodia, Thailand, Laos, Myanmar
2. Brunei, East Timor, Indonesia, Singapore, and the Philippines
3. volcanoes and earthquakes
4. transportation, communications, and food
5. underground: minerals such as petroleum and gold; underwater: fish; tropical forest: wood, spices

SECTION 2

6. tropical rain forest, tropical savanna, humid subtropical, highlands
7. Malaysia
8. Myanmar, Borneo, New Guinea
9. The wet and dry cycles are reversed.
10. Nearly 80 percent is imported.

Reviewing Key Terms

Write the letter of the key term that best matches each definition below.

a. cordillera
b. archipelago
c. flora and fauna
d. insular
e. deciduous
f. endemic

1. group of islands
2. system of parallel mountain ranges
3. island
4. native to a particular area
5. trees that lose leaves in autumn
6. plants and animals

Reviewing Facts
SECTION 1

1. Which Southeast Asian countries lie partially or entirely on the Indochina Peninsula?
2. Name the five insular countries.
3. What geologic activities created Southeast Asia?
4. Explain why waterways are important to Southeast Asia's people.
5. Name a Southeast Asian resource found underground, another resource found underwater, and a third resource found in a tropical rain forest.

SECTION 2

6. What are the four main climate regions of Southeast Asia?
7. Where are the region's oldest forests found?
8. Where can highlands climates be found?
9. How is weather north of the Equator different from weather south of the Equator?
10. What is unusual about most of Singapore's vegetation?

Critical Thinking

1. **Drawing Conclusions** What geographic factors explain the large number of islands in Southeast Asia?
2. **Making Inferences** How might volcanoes affect the region's economy?
3. **Identifying Cause-and-Effect** Copy the web diagram below onto a sheet of paper. Complete the diagram to show how the tropical climate affects human activities in Southeast Asia. Then choose one effect, and write a paragraph explaining its impact on the people of Southeast Asia.

Tropical Climate

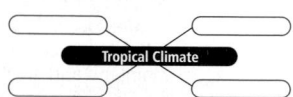

NATIONAL GEOGRAPHIC **Locating Places**
Southeast Asia: Physical-Political Geography

Match the letters on the map with the places and physical features of Southeast Asia. Write your answers on a sheet of paper.

1. Singapore
2. Irrawaddy River
3. Thailand
4. Malay Peninsula
5. Mekong River
6. Vietnam
7. Philippines
8. Java
9. Sumatra
10. Borneo

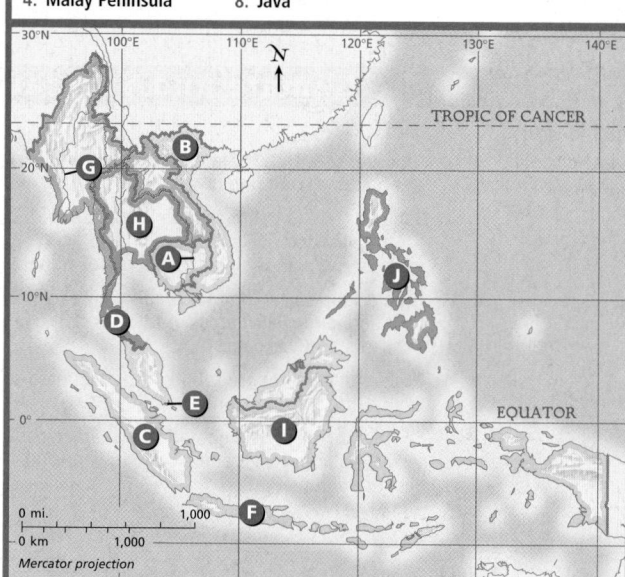

Critical Thinking

1. volcanoes and earthquakes
2. Volcanoes produce fertile soil and could be a source of geothermal energy.
3. Answers may include that abundant rain supports an agricultural economy; heat and humidity dictate hours of work; rain forests limit transportation; and rain forests impede trade and communications. Students' paragraphs should demonstrate understanding of causal relationships.

NATIONAL GEOGRAPHIC **Locating Places**

1. E	**3.** H	**5.** A	**7.** J	**9.** C
2. G	**4.** D	**6.** B	**8.** F	**10.** I

732

Using the Regional Atlas

Refer to the Regional Atlas on pages 710–713.

1. **Movement** What river provides Laos with its chief means of transportation?
2. **Place** Study the physical, economic activity, and population maps of the region. What three generalizations could you make about Borneo, given the information on these maps?

Thinking Like a Geographer

Think about the physical geography of Southeast Asia. Why do you suppose the capital cities of the region are located on or near water? As a geographer, would you encourage people to relocate to other areas in order to avoid overcrowding these cities? Explain.

Problem-Solving Activity

Group Research Project Working in a group of four, plan a trip through Southeast Asia. Decide what areas to visit, noting the kinds of landforms you would see in each place. Determine how to get from one place to another, and work together to create a map that shows your travel routes. Prepare a written itinerary, and present your travel plans to the class.

GeoJournal

Descriptive Writing Using the information you wrote in your GeoJournal as you read this chapter, write a newspaper story about the landscape of the region. You may wish to focus on a recent event, such as a volcanic eruption, flood, or other natural disaster.

Technology Activity

Using E-mail Use library or Internet resources to locate a postal or e-mail address for the United States Embassy in Manila, the Philippines. Compose and send a letter requesting information about the February 2000 eruption of the Mayon Volcano. Use the information you receive to create a bulletin board about the eruption.

Standardized Test Practice

Choose the best answer for the following multiple-choice question. If you have trouble answering the question, use the process of elimination to narrow your choices.

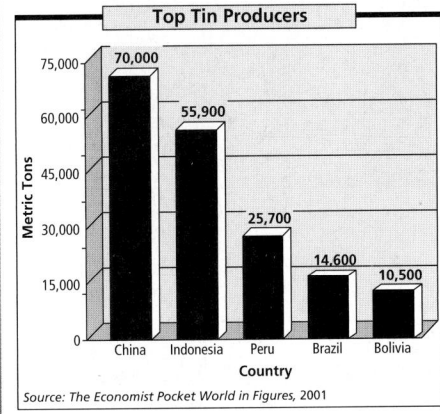

Top Tin Producers

Source: The Economist Pocket World in Figures, 2001

1. **About how much tin does Indonesia produce each year?**

   A 55,900 metric tons
   B 55,000,900 metric tons
   C 55.9 million metric tons
   D 55.9 billion metric tons

 Test-Taking Tip In order to understand any type of graph, look carefully around the graph for keys that show how it is organized. On this bar graph, the numbers along the left side represent the exact number shown. You do not have to multiply by millions or billions to find the number of metric tons.

Technology Activity

Remind students that their e-mails should be polite, appropriate to the person who receives it, and mechanically correct. You may want to assign small groups of students to do this activity cooperatively.

Standardized Test Practice
1. A

Tested Objectives:
reading graphs

Additional Practice and Test-Taking Tips

 Standardized Test Practice Workbook

CHAPTER BONUS TEST QUESTION

What do you think is a good reason for classifying the nations of Southeast Asia as a region? *(location, similar climate and vegetation, similar landforms)*

Using the Regional Atlas

1. Mekong
2. Responses should be based on evidence from the maps.

Thinking Like a Geographer

Students' suppositions may include that water provides a significant means of transportation and communications. Students' suggestions for relocation will vary; accept all reasonable answers.

Problem-Solving Activity

The itinerary should name specific places, identify landforms and means of transportation, and be accompanied by a map.

GeoJournal

Students' journal entries should be factually accurate and focus on the journalists' questions: *who, what, where, when, why,* and *how.* Check students' articles for standard grammar, spelling, sentence structure, and punctuation.

PLANNING GUIDE

NOTE: The following materials may be used when teaching Chapter 30. Section-level support materials are shown at point-of-use in the margins of the Teacher Wraparound Edition.

TEACHING TRANSPARENCIES

L2 Unit 10 Map Overlay Transparencies

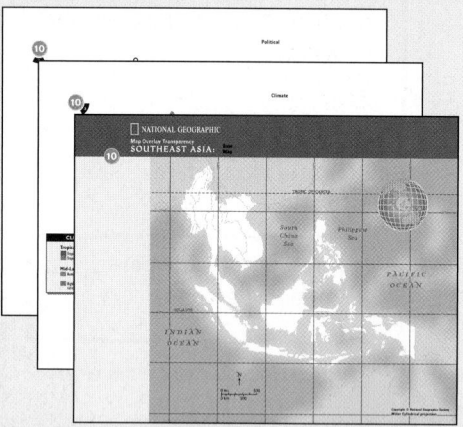

L2 Political Map Transparency 10

GEOGRAPHIC LITERACY

Focus on Geography Literacy

APPLICATION AND ENRICHMENT

L3 Enrichment Activity 30

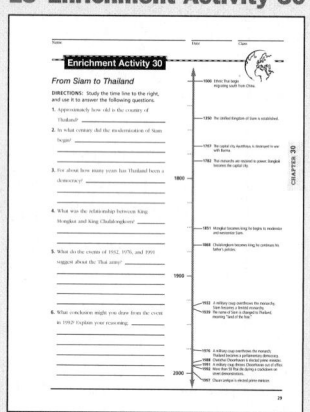

REVIEW AND REINFORCEMENT

L1 Vocabulary Activity 30 L1 Reinforcing Skills Activity 30 L1 Reteaching Activity 30

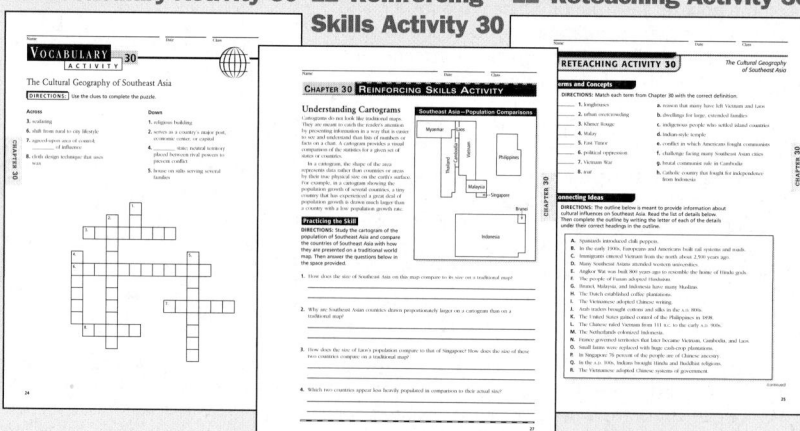

ASSESSMENT

L2 Chapter 30 Test Form A

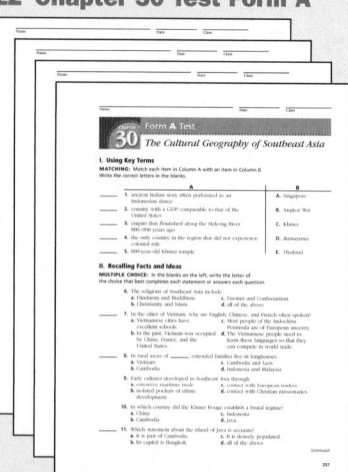

L2 Chapter 30 Test Form B

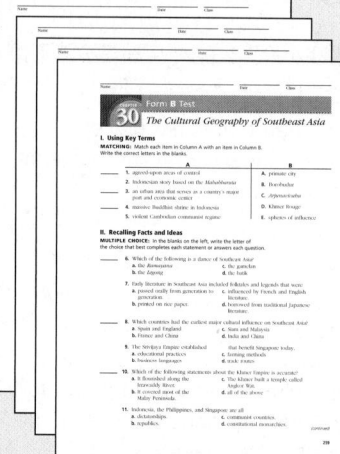

L1/ELL Performance Assessment Activity 30

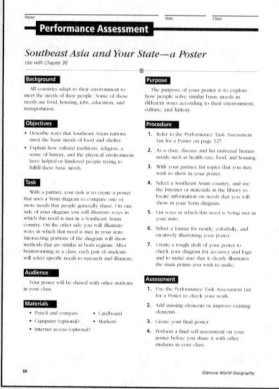

ExamView® Pro Testmaker

The following Spanish language materials are available in the Spanish Resources binder:

- 📁 Spanish Vocabulary Activities
- 📁 Spanish Guided Reading Activities
- 📁 Spanish Reteaching Activities
- 📁 Spanish Summaries
- 📁 Spanish Quizzes and Tests
- 📁 Spanish Reading Essentials and Study Guide

- World Regions Video
- MindJogger Videoquiz
- Vocabulary PuzzleMaker CD-ROM
- Interactive Tutor Self-Assessment CD-ROM
- ExamView® Pro Testmaker CD-ROM
- Audio Program
- TeacherWorks CD-ROM
- Interactive Student Edition CD-ROM
- Glencoe Skillbuilder Interactive Workbook CD-ROM, Level 2
- Presentation Plus! CD-ROM

Timesaving Tools

TeacherWorks™ All-In-One Planner and Resource Center

- **Interactive Teacher Edition** Access your Teacher Wraparound Edition and your classroom resources with a few easy clicks.

- **Interactive Lesson Planner** Planning has never been easier! Organize your week, month, semester, or year with all the lesson helps you need to make teaching creative, timely, and relevant.

Use Glencoe's **Presentation Plus!** multimedia teacher tool to easily present dynamic lessons that visually excite your students. Using Microsoft PowerPoint® you can customize the presentations to create your own personalized lessons.

GEOGRAPHY Online

Use our Web site for additional resources. All essential content is covered in the Student Edition.

You and your students can visit geography.glencoe.com, the Web site companion to *Glencoe World Geography*. This innovative integration of electronic and print media offers your students a wealth of opportunities. The student text directs students to the Web site for the following options:

- Chapter Overviews
- Self-Check Quizzes
- Student Activities
- Textbook Updates

Answers are provided for you in the "Web Activity Lesson Plan." Additional Web resources and Interactive Tutor puzzles are also available.

▶ Additional Glencoe Teacher Support

- **Teaching Strategies for the Geography Classroom** (including Block Scheduling Pacing Guides)
- **Graphic Organizer Transparencies Strategies and Activities**
- **Outline Map Resource Book**
- **Reading in the Content Area**

PLANNING GUIDE

SECTION RESOURCES

Daily Objectives	Reproducible Resources	Multimedia Resources

SECTION 1 Population Patterns

1. Identify the various ethnic roots of Southeast Asia's peoples.
2. Explain why the majority of Southeast Asians live in river valley lowlands or on coastal plains.
3. Specify how population movements and settlement patterns have affected the region.

 Reproducible Lesson Plan 30-1
 Daily Lecture Notes 30-1
 Guided Reading Activity 30-1*
Reading Essentials and Study Guide 30-1*
 Section Quiz 30-1*

 Daily Focus Skills Transparency 30-1
Political Map Transparency 10
Unit 10 Map Overlay Transparencies
Interactive Tutor Self-Assessment CD-ROM
ExamView® Pro Testmaker CD-ROM*
Presentation Plus! CD-ROM

SECTION 2 History and Government

1. Describe how location influenced the development of empires in Southeast Asia.
2. Name cultural influences that have affected the region's people.
3. Chart events that led to the independence of Southeast Asian countries.

 Reproducible Lesson Plan 30-2
 Daily Lecture Notes 30-2
Guided Reading Activity 30-2*
Reading Essentials and Study Guide 30-2*
Section Quiz 30-2*

Daily Focus Skills Transparency 30-2
Political Map Transparency 10
Unit 10 Map Overlay Transparencies
World Art and Architecture Transparencies
Interactive Tutor Self-Assessment CD-ROM
ExamView® Pro Testmaker CD-ROM*
Presentation Plus! CD-ROM

SECTION 3 Cultures and Lifestyles

1. Consider what makes Southeast Asia such an ethnically diverse region.
2. Describe how outside influences affected the region's arts.
3. Examine how people's lifestyles reflect the region's diversity.

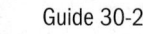 Reproducible Lesson Plan 30-3
Vocabulary Activity 30*
Daily Lecture Notes 30-3
Guided Reading Activity 30-3*
Reading Essentials and Study Guide 30-3*
 Reteaching Activity 30*
 Reinforcing Skills Activity 30
 Section Quiz 30-3*

 Daily Focus Skills Transparency 30-3
Political Map Transparency 10
Unit 10 Map Overlay Transparencies
Vocabulary PuzzleMaker CD-ROM
World Music: A Cultural Legacy
Interactive Tutor Self-Assessment CD-ROM
ExamView® Pro Testmaker CD-ROM*
Presentation Plus! CD-ROM

 Blackline Master   Software   Videocassette

 Transparency   CD-ROM   DVD

*Also available in Spanish

OUT OF TIME? Assign the Chapter 30 **Reading Essentials and Study Guide.**

 **Block Schedule**

Activities that are particularly suited to use within the block scheduling framework are identified throughout this chapter by the following designation:

KEY TO ABILITY LEVELS

Teaching strategies have been coded for various learning styles and abilities.

L1 **BASIC** activities for all students

L2 **AVERAGE** activities for average to above-average students

L3 **CHALLENGING** activities for above-average students

ELL **ENGLISH LANGUAGE LEARNER** activities

Teacher to Teacher

Julie Lindgren
Evergreen High School
Seattle, WA

Six Essential Elements

Have pairs of students choose a Southeast Asian country and create a poster to describe the country in geographic terms.

To describe Thailand, for example, students might show scenes typical of the place and region. They create a map to show location. For human-environment interaction, students might draw examples of farming or fishing. Photos or drawings of physical systems might include damage from volcanic activity, earthquakes, or typhoons. Illustrations of the country's transportation systems might show how people organize space and move about the country. Photos of logging operations or dams might show how people change the environment, and examples of housing or farming show how humans adapt to Thailand's physical systems. Finally, students include any examples they can find to show how Thailand's people might use geography. The resulting poster shows a geographic portrait of the country, and students have learned how to ask geographic questions; acquire, organize and analyze geographic information; and provide answers to geographic questions.

TEACHER'S CORNER

Index to National Geographic Magazine:

The following articles may be used for research relating to this chapter:

- "Wild Gliders of Borneo," by Tim Laman, October 2000.
- "Tam Dao—Vietnam's Sanctuary Under Siege," by Michael J. McRae, June 1999.
- "Irian Jaya: Indonesia's Wild Side," by Thomas O'Neill, February 1996.

National Geographic Society Products:

To order the following products for use with this chapter, call National Geographic Society at 1-800-368-2728.

- *Asia* (Video)
- *National Geographic Desk Reference* (Book)
- *National Geographic Atlas of the World, Seventh Edition* (Book)

NGS ONLINE

Access National Geographic's Web site for current events, activities, links, interactive features, and archives.
www.nationalgeographic.com

Meeting National Standards

Geography For Life

The following standards are highlighted in Chapter 30:

Section 1	EE4 Human Systems: Standards 9, 10, 12
	EE5 Environment and Society: Standard 16
	EE6 The Uses of Geography: Standards 17, 18
Section 2	EE2 Places and Regions: Standard 6
	EE3 Physical Systems: Standard 8
	EE4 Human Systems: Standards 9, 12, 13
	EE6 The Uses of Geography: Standard 17
Section 3	EE4 Human Systems: Standards 9, 10
	EE5 Environment and Society: Standard 14

Local Objectives

_____

_____

MEETING SPECIAL NEEDS

In addition to the Differentiated Instruction strategies found in each section, the following resources are also suitable for your special needs students:

- *ExamView® Pro Testmaker CD-ROM* allows teachers to tailor tests by reducing answer choices.
- The *Audio Program* includes the entire narrative of the student edition so that less-proficient readers can listen to the words as they read them.
- The *Reading Essentials and Study Guide* provides the same content as the student edition but is written two grade levels below the textbook.
- *Guided Reading Activities* give less-proficient readers point-by-point instructions to increase comprehension as they read each textbook section.
- *Enrichment Activities* include a stimulating collection of readings and activities for gifted and talented students.

Chapter Objectives

1. Recognize the various ethnic and religious influences on Southeast Asia's population and cultures.

2. Understand the historical development of Southeast Asia.

3. Describe the diverse languages, arts, and lifestyles of Southeast Asia.

GLENCOE
TECHNOLOGY

Use *MindJogger Videoquiz* to preview the Chapter 30 content.

GeoJournal

For access to additional photos, maps, and information on the cultural features of Southeast Asia, go to www.nationalgeographic.com (See Teacher pages in front for strategies for using journals in the geography classroom.)

GEOGRAPHY Online

Introduce students to chapter content and key terms by having them access **Chapter Overview 30** at geography.glencoe.com

FOLDABLES™
Study Organizer

Dinah Zike's Foldables are three-dimensional, interactive graphic organizers that help students practice basic writing skills, review key vocabulary terms, and identify main ideas. Have students complete the Foldable activity in the **Dinah Zike's Reading and Study Skills Foldables** booklet.

CHAPTER 30
The Cultural Geography of Southeast Asia

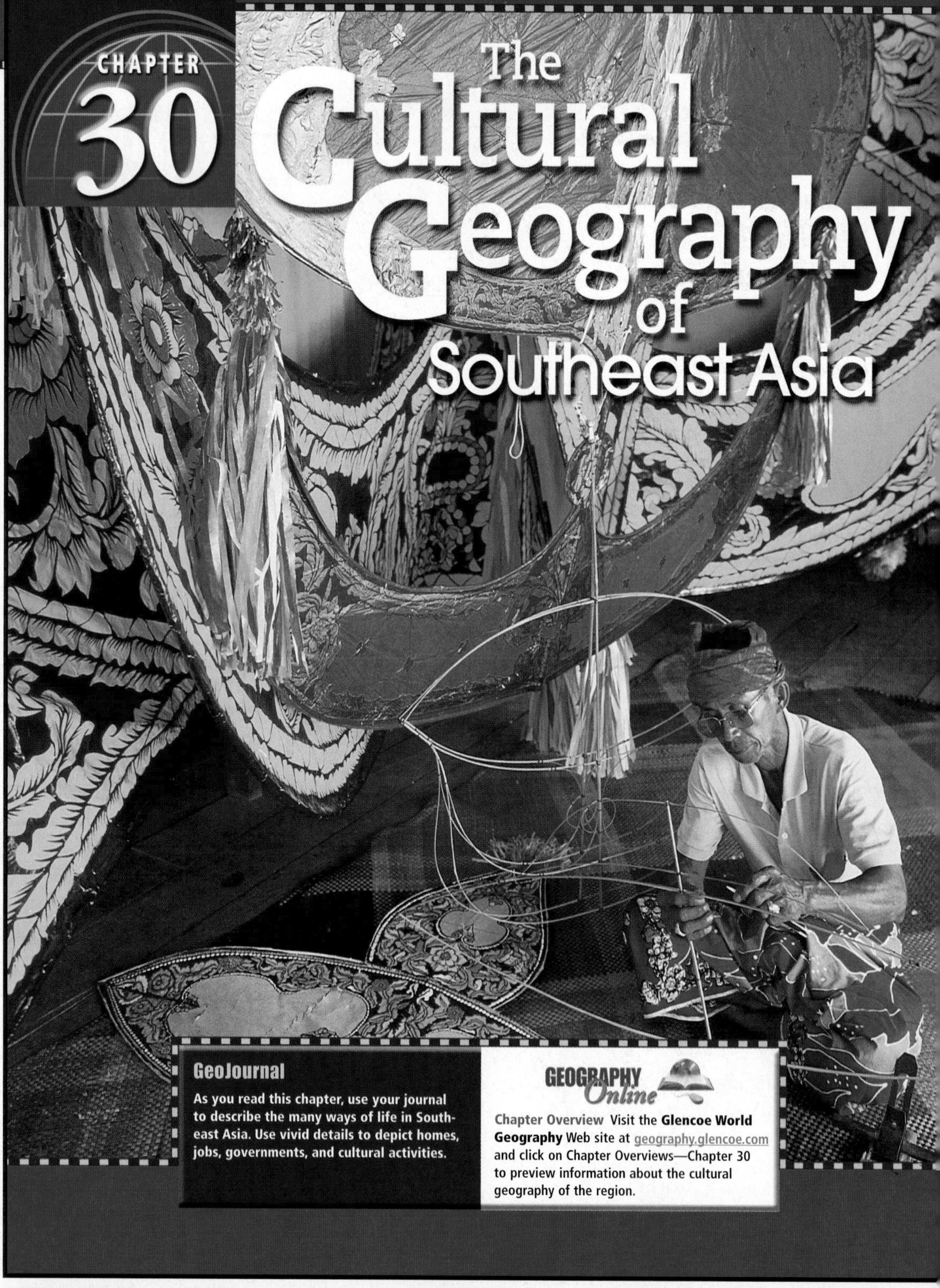

GeoJournal

As you read this chapter, use your journal to describe the many ways of life in Southeast Asia. Use vivid details to depict homes, jobs, governments, and cultural activities.

GEOGRAPHY Online

Chapter Overview Visit the **Glencoe World Geography** Web site at geography.glencoe.com and click on Chapter Overviews—Chapter 30 to preview information about the cultural geography of the region.

ABOUT THE PHOTO

Visual Instruction Kites come from an ancient tradition begun in China more than 3,000 years ago. From China, the art of making kites spread to other parts of Asia, and eventually to the rest of the world. Kites originally were made of silk stretched on a bamboo frame. Today they come in all kinds of designs and colors. They also vary from inexpensive children's toys made of light-weight wood and paper to elaborate creations like those shown in the photograph. Kite enthusiasts around the world participate in kite festivals to exhibit their custom-made kites. **Ask: Why do you think kites originally were made of silk and bamboo?** *(These light materials are ideal for flight.)* 	 EE4 Human Systems: Standard 10

Population Patterns

NATIONAL GEOGRAPHIC

A Geographic View

Traces of History

Home to nearly five million people, making it one of the world's most populated urban areas, Ho Chi Minh City [formerly Saigon, Vietnam] still bears traces of past foreign occupants. France, which made Saigon its first foothold in Indochina, left boulevards and a cathedral. The U.S., which based its military here during the Vietnam War, built an embassy complex and greatly expanded the airport. Now the Vietnamese take a turn, erecting hotels and factories.

Hotel in Ho Chi Minh City, Vietnam

—*Tracy Dahlby, "The New Saigon,"* National Geographic, *April 1995*

Vietnam's Western-style buildings are recent examples of a series of cultural influences—Chinese, Indian, Islamic, European, and American—that have shaped Southeast Asia over thousands of years. Each culture has added its own unique flavor to Southeast Asia's cultural mix. In this section you will learn about the diverse peoples of Southeast Asia, how physical geography affects where they live, and what challenges population changes are bringing to the region.

Human Characteristics

Southeast Asia's cultural geography is as varied as its physical geography. About 544 million people live on the many peninsulas and islands of Southeast Asia. Southeast Asia's population today includes descendants of indigenous peoples, Indians, Chinese, Arabs, and European colonists.

◀ *Master kite maker at work in Malaysia*

Guide to Reading

Consider What You Know
Many Southeast Asians have migrated to other countries, including the United States. What impact do you think migrants have on the cultures of their adopted countries?

Reading Strategy
Categorizing Complete a graphic organizer similar to the one below by filling in four examples of primate cities in Southeast Asia.

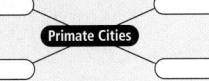
Primate Cities

Read to Find Out
- What are the various ethnic roots of Southeast Asia's peoples?
- Why do the majority of Southeast Asians live in river valley lowlands or on coastal plains?
- How have population movements and settlement patterns affected Southeast Asia?

Terms to Know
- urbanization
- primate city

Places to Locate
- Cambodia
- Vietnam
- Myanmar
- Indonesia
- Java
- Singapore
- Thailand
- Philippines
- Bangkok
- Jakarta

---

① FOCUS

Section Overview
This section discusses Southeast Asia's peoples—their human characteristics, the impact of outside influences on their cultures, and current population trends.

BELLRINGER
Skillbuilder Activity

- Project transparency and have students answer questions.
- Available as blackline master.

Daily Focus Skills Transparency 30-1

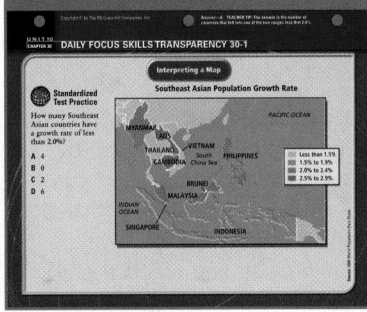

Guide to Reading

Consider What You Know
Answer *Students' answers may include influences on clothing styles, new foods, and holiday celebrations.*

Reading Strategy
Answers *Bangkok, Thailand; Jakarta, Indonesia; possible answers include Manila, Philippines; Yangon, Myanmar; Singapore*

Preteaching Vocabulary
Point out that *prime* (in *primate*) means "first in importance." **Ask: In what ways might a city be of prime importance to a country?** *(economic center, political capital, cultural center)*

RESOURCE MANAGER

📁 Reproducible Masters
- Reproducible Lesson Plan 30-1
- Daily Lecture Notes 30-1
- Guided Reading Activity 30-1
- Reading Essentials and Study Guide 30-1
- Section Quiz 30-1

🖥 Transparencies
- Daily Focus Skills Transparency 30-1
- Political Map Transparency 10
- Unit 10 Map Overlay Transparencies

Multimedia
- 💿 Interactive Tutor Self-Assessment CD-ROM
- 💿 ExamView® Pro Testmaker CD-ROM
- 💿 Presentation Plus! CD-ROM

② TEACH

L1 Locate

Project Political Map Transparency 10. Have students locate Manila, (Philippines), Jakarta (Indonesia), Bangkok (Thailand), Ho Chi Minh City (Vietnam), and Surabaya (Indonesia). Note they are among the world's largest cities. **Ask: Are the cities concentrated in one area? Explain.** *(No, two are on the mainland; three are on islands.)*

 **World Explorer**

Answer
western China and eastern Tibet

More About the Photo
The Iban people comprise the largest indigenous group in Sarawak, a state in northwestern Borneo. The Iban live in longhouses and practice shifting agriculture.

Daily Lecture Notes 30-1

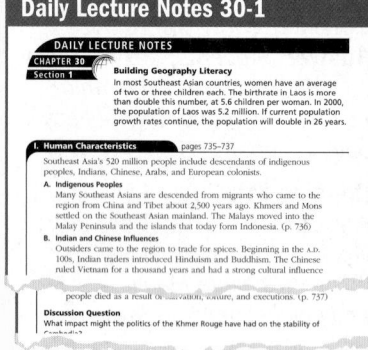

DAILY LECTURE NOTES

CHAPTER 30
Section 1

Building Geography Literacy
In most Southeast Asian countries, women have an average of two or three children each. The birthrate in Laos is more than double this number, at 5.6 children per woman. In 2000, the population of Laos was 5.2 million. If current population growth rates continue, the population will double in 26 years.

I. Human Characteristics pages 735–737

Southeast Asia's 520 million people include descendants of indigenous peoples, Indians, Chinese, Arabs, and European colonists.

A. Indigenous Peoples
Many Southeast Asians are descended from migrants who came to the region from China and Tibet about 2,500 years ago. Khmers and Mons settled on the Southeast Asian mainland. The Malays moved into the Malay Peninsula and the islands that today form Indonesia. (p. 736)

B. Indian and Chinese Influences
Outsiders came to the region to trade for spices. Beginning in the A.D. 100s, Indian traders introduced Hinduism and Buddhism. The Chinese ruled Vietnam for a thousand years and had a strong cultural influence

people died as a result of starvation, torture, and executions. (p. 737)

Discussion Question
What impact might the politics of the Khmer Rouge have had on the stability of Cambodia?

■ NATIONAL GEOGRAPHIC   **World Explorer**

Geography | Skills for Life
------------------------------- **Indigenous People**

The young woman wearing a headdress (left) and the elderly people (right) are Iban, an indigenous group in East Malaysia.
Movement From which areas did people migrate to Southeast Asia 2,500 years ago?

Indigenous Peoples

Humans have lived in Southeast Asia for tens of thousands of years. About 2,500 years ago, groups of migrants from western China and eastern Tibet arrived in the region. Many of today's Southeast Asians are descendants of these early peoples. On the Southeast Asian mainland, the Khmers settled **Cambodia** and **Vietnam**, the Mons moved into **Myanmar**, and the Malays settled the Malay Peninsula. Some Malay groups also undertook sea voyages, settling the many islands that today form **Indonesia**. These indigenous peoples developed agricultural civilizations and borrowed from other peoples without losing their own identities.

Indian and Chinese Influences

Valuable spices grown in Southeast Asia drew outside traders to the region. While exchanging goods with Southeast Asians, these foreigners passed on new ideas and practices that blended with Southeast Asian traditions. Beginning in the A.D. 100s, merchants from India introduced the Hindu and Buddhist religions, art forms inspired by these religions, and a concept of government that glorified kings as both political and spiritual leaders. Meanwhile, Chinese traders and soldiers brought Chinese cultural influences to the region through Vietnam. During a thousand years of Chinese rule, the Vietnamese adopted China's writing system, Confucian traditions, and system of government. Today Indian and Chinese ethnic communities are scattered throughout Southeast Asia, particularly in Brunei, Malaysia, Thailand, and Vietnam. In Singapore today, people of ethnic Chinese ancestry make up 76 percent of the country's total population.

Islamic Influence

In search of spices, Arab and Indian traders brought cottons and silks to Southeast Asia beginning in the A.D. 800s. They and locally based Malay traders set up trade routes that linked Southeast Asia with other parts of Asia. During the 1200s, Southeast Asians—especially those in port towns—began to convert to Islam, the religion of these traders. Over the centuries, Islam spread from coastal areas to interior areas of the Indonesian islands and the Malay Peninsula. Today Muslims form the majority of the population in Brunei, Malaysia, and Indonesia.

DIFFERENTIATED INSTRUCTION

English Learners Java, with an area of 48,000 square miles (124,320 sq. km), is slightly larger than Louisiana. Yet its population is larger than the combined populations of California, Texas, Pennsylvania, Illinois, Florida, and Ohio. To help English language learners understand population data and become familiar with individual U.S. states, pair English language learners with English proficient students. Have the pairs use an almanac or other sources to find and rank the land area and population of these states. Then have them calculate their combined populations. **ELL**

⊕ **EE4 Human Systems: Standards 9, 10**

📂 Refer to *Inclusion for the Social Studies Classroom Strategies and Activities.*

Western Colonization

During the 1400s and 1500s, European explorers, like others before them, sought new sea routes to acquire Southeast Asia's spices and other rich natural resources. Their voyages eventually brought nearly all of the region, with the exception of Thailand, under European control. While exporting nutmeg, cloves, and pearls to Europe, European traders brought new products to Southeast Asia. For example, from Latin America the Spaniards introduced various chili peppers that added new flavor to Southeast Asian cooking. When drinking coffee became popular in Europe during the 1600s, the Dutch began cultivating coffee trees—originally from the Arabian Peninsula—on various Southeast Asian islands.

Population Growth

Many of Southeast Asia's 544 million people live in fertile river valleys or on the coastal plains. A ready supply of water, fertile land, adequate transportation, and available jobs have all contributed to these concentrations of people. In general, highlands areas have fewer people than lowlands, and rural areas have fewer people than the cities.

Population Density

Population density varies widely throughout Southeast Asia. Indonesia, the world's fourth most populous country, has more than 220 million people living on more than 13,500 scattered islands. The Indonesian island of **Java** is one of the most densely populated islands in the world. The overall population density of Indonesia is 300 people per square mile (116 people per sq. km). **Singapore**, the region's smallest country in land area, has the greatest population density—17,528 people per square mile (6,624 people per sq. km).

Population Growth Rates

The population of Southeast Asia is growing at a rate of 1.6 percent per year compared with the 1.3 percent average growth rate for the world. Some estimates indicate that more than 790 million people will live in the region by 2050, representing about a 50 percent increase over the number of people living there today. Some countries, such as **Thailand,** Indonesia, and Singapore, are working to slow their population growth rates. Singapore, in fact, has succeeded so well in reducing its population growth rate that there is concern the country may not have enough young workers to replace and support its aging population. As a result, married couples are now encouraged to have more children.

History
Cambodia: Population Decline

Since the 1970s Cambodia's population growth rate has been below the region's average. Between 1975 and 1979, Cambodia lost 38 percent of its population as a result of harsh rule by the Khmer Rouge communist government. Many people died as a result of starvation, torture, and executions. People considered to be intellectuals were often the first targets of the violence as described below:

Even someone who as much [as] wore glasses was considered an intellect, [and] was killed. Thus began a vast extermination of all the wealthy and educated people in Cambodia. ... The Khmer Rouge watched over the people constantly, making sure everything they did was right, and if they showed any signs of an education, they would be first tortured to confess, and then executed.

Jerry Adler, "Pol Pot's Last Days," *Newsweek*, April 27, 1998

Movement to the Cities

For centuries, the majority of Southeast Asians lived in rural villages and farmed the land. Today increasing numbers of the region's people are moving from rural areas to urban centers. This population shift has resulted from political conflicts and government policies, but greater economic and educational opportunities available in cities have also been factors. The **Philippines**, for example, reflects this trend toward urbanization, or the shift from rural to urban lifestyles, in Southeast Asia. At the beginning of the 1900s, more than 80 percent of Filipinos lived in rural areas. Today about 53 percent of the Philippines' population lives in the countryside.

L3 Math
Remind students that the population of Southeast Asia today is about 544 million people. Have them calculate the region's population for the next two years at the current annual growth rate of 1.7 percent. *(year one: 544,000,000 + [.017 x 544,000,000] = 636,480,000; year two: 636,480,000 + [.017 x 636,480,000] = 744,681,600)*

L1/ELL

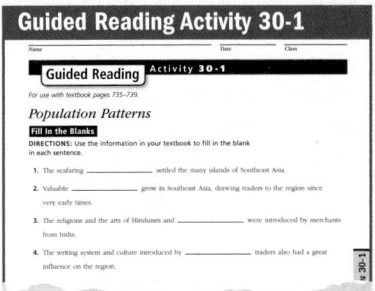

Guided Reading Activity 30-1

Guided Reading Activity 30-1

For use with textbook pages 735–739.

Population Patterns

Fill in the Blanks

DIRECTIONS: Use the information in your textbook to fill in the blank in each sentence.

1. The seafaring _____ settled the many islands of Southeast Asia.

2. Valuable _____ grow in Southeast Asia, drawing traders to the region since very early times.

3. The religions and the arts of Hinduism and _____ were introduced by merchants from India.

4. The writing system and culture introduced by _____ traders also had a great influence on the region.

☐ NATIONAL GEOGRAPHIC **GEOFACT**

▶ **The Sultan of Brunei, one of the world's wealthiest individuals, spent $450 million to build the world's largest palace at Bandar Seri Begawan, Brunei's capital. Oil and gas reserves account for the country's high standard of living.**

L1/ELL

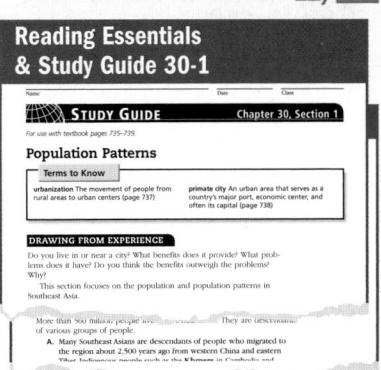

Reading Essentials & Study Guide 30-1

🌐 STUDY GUIDE — Chapter 30, Section 1

For use with textbook pages 735–739.

Population Patterns

Terms to Know

| urbanization The movement of people from rural areas to urban centers (page 737) | primate city An urban area that serves as a country's major port, economic center, and often its capital (page 738) |

DRAWING FROM EXPERIENCE

Do you live in or near a city? What benefits does it provide? What problems does it have? Do you think the benefits outweigh the problems? Why?

This section focuses on the population and population patterns in Southeast Asia.

More than 500 million people are _____. They are descendants of various groups of people.

A. Many Southeast Asians are descendants of people who migrated to the region about 2,500 years ago from western China and eastern Tibet. Indigenous people such as the Khmers in Cambodia and

---

COOPERATIVE LEARNING ACTIVITY

Ethnic Composition Organize the class into groups, and assign a Southeast Asian country to each group. Have students use the Internet and other resources to research ethnic groups of their assigned countries. Have students prepare a report to the class about the origins and present makeup of the country's ethnic groups, including data on their populations, future growth trends, and cultural traits. Reports should include pictures, charts, and graphs. You may combine this activity with the poster project suggested in the Teacher-to-Teacher activity on page 734D.

🌐 **EE5 Environment and Society: Standard 16**

NATIONAL GEOGRAPHIC | **CHART STUDY**

Answers

1. *Singapore; Cambodia*

2. *Laos is growing more than twice as fast as Thailand in urban population. Thailand's rural growth is .2 percent, compared with Laos's 2 percent rural growth rate.*

Skills Practice
Urban and Rural Growth

What countries have the fastest urban growth? *(Laos, Cambodia, Myanmar, and Indonesia)*
What effect does that growth have on cities? *(roads, housing, water and electric systems, and other public services are often not adequate for increased number of people)*

ASSESS

Assign Section 1 Assessment as homework or as an in-class activity.

⊕ Have students use **Interactive Tutor Self-Assessment CD-ROM.**

L2

Section Quiz 30-1

NATIONAL GEOGRAPHIC | **CHART STUDY**

Southeast Asia: Urban and Rural Growth (Selected Countries)

Country	Percent Urban	Percent Rural	Annual Urban Growth %	Annual Rural Growth %
Indonesia	40	60	3.4	0.3
Malaysia	57	43	2.9	0.1
Thailand	31	69	2.5	0.2
Vietnam	25	75	2.4	1.3
Philippines	47	53	3.1	0.1
Myanmar	27	73	3.4	0.9
Cambodia	16	84	4.4	1.0
Laos	17	83	5.2	2.0
Singapore	100	0	1.0	0.0

Sources: 2003 World Population Data Sheet; United Nations Population Division, 2000

Geography **Skills for Life**

1. **Interpreting Charts** Which country is the most urbanized? The least urbanized?

2. **Applying Geography Skills** How might migration and other human processes affect patterns of settlement in the region?

At least 11 Southeast Asian cities now have populations of more than 1 million. In some countries in the region, a single major city leads all other cities in attracting people, resources, and commerce. Such a magnet is called a **primate city**, an urban area that serves as a country's major port, economic center, and often its capital.

Bangkok, Thailand, and Jakarta, Indonesia, are examples of primate cities. Rapid growth in these and other urban areas has brought challenges as well as benefits. Thailand's capital, **Bangkok**, grew by 650 percent between 1950 and 1998, but the city's roads, housing, water and electric systems, and other public services could not adequately support all of the new migrants. About 1 million residents of Bangkok live in densely populated areas characterized by poor housing and poverty. Thailand is trying to solve these urban challenges by encouraging people to return to rural areas. The Thai government has offered incentives for industries to locate outside of cities. In spite of these efforts, however, the lure of urban jobs and lifestyles continues to drain small villages.

Indonesia also faces a movement of people from rural to urban areas. The major attraction for migrants in Indonesia is its capital, **Jakarta**, a city of more than 10 million on the densely populated island of Java. Some of these migrants are temporary residents seeking seasonal employment in the cities.

In an attempt to reduce urban overcrowding, Indonesia's government during the past 40 years has relocated 3 million people to the country's less densely populated outer islands. Although relocation has increased the rural population in some parts of Indonesia, it has done little to lessen overcrowding on Java. In addition, the mixing of peoples of different ethnic backgrounds has sparked conflict as groups compete for jobs, housing, and social services.

Outward Migrations

Since the 1970s, a number of Southeast Asians have left their homelands to settle in other parts of the world. Between 1975 and 1990, thousands of

---

CRITICAL THINKING ACTIVITY

Migration Tell students that they live in a Southeast Asian country and are considering migration either to another part of Southeast Asia or to another region. Have students work together to identify and explain the various push-pull factors related to migration. *(Examples: push factors—unemployment, ethnic discrimination, or political unrest; pull factors—better job opportunities, higher standard of living, freedom of religion).* Tell students to write a plan of action, explaining the challenges to be anticipated and the ways to meet these challenges. Have them share their ideas with the class.
📠 **EE4 Human Systems: Standards 9, 12**
📠 **EE6 The Uses of Geography: Standards 17, 18**

people left Vietnam to escape the widespread economic distress and political oppression that gripped the country. Since the mid-1970s, many people have left their homeland in Laos for similar reasons. Many of these Southeast Asian migrants came to settle in the United States. By 2000, for example, the United States population included 955,264 Vietnamese, 176,148 Cambodians, and 331,340 people of the Hmong and Lao ethnic groups. One effect of these outward migrations is that the countries of Southeast Asia lose skilled and educated workers who could contribute some of the valuable skills that their home countries

▲ Yawaraj Road, in the heart of Bangkok's busy Chinese district

need for sustained economic growth. Outward migration is only one factor that shapes the region's population patterns, however.

Southeast Asia's physical features—the many islands and peninsulas—as well as its growing cities have also shaped the region's population patterns. In the next section, you will learn how historical events, such as migration and colonization, and contemporary politics have left their marks on Southeast Asia.

SECTION 1 ASSESSMENT

Checking for Understanding
1. **Define** urbanization, primate city.
2. **Main Ideas** On a web like the one below, list the factors that have influenced rural and urban settlement patterns for each country in Southeast Asia.

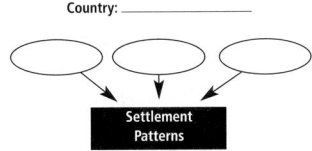

Critical Thinking
3. **Identifying Cause and Effect** Why have so many different peoples migrated to Southeast Asia over the centuries? How has this migration influenced the region's culture?
4. **Making Inferences** What do countries such as Indonesia hope to gain by slowing population growth?
5. **Comparing and Contrasting** How do migration patterns affect Indonesia's urban and rural populations?

Analyzing Maps
6. **Location** Study the political map on page 711 and the urban/rural growth chart on page 738. Are the countries with the lowest urban populations located on the mainland or on the islands?

Applying Geography
7. **Economic Effects** Think about population distribution in Southeast Asia. Write a paragraph explaining how environmental and economic factors have shaped settlement in the region.

Chapter 30 ● 739

SECTION 1 ASSESSMENT ANSWERS

1. All vocabulary terms are defined in the text.
2. Factors may include a ready water supply, fertile land, adequate transportation, and job availability.
3. relieve overcrowded cities, reduce unemployment, and increase living standards
4. Movement to cities causes urban centers to grow and become overcrowded; rural populations decrease.
5. The native spices and other rich natural resources of Southeast Asia have attracted traders and colonists.
6. mainland
7. **Applying Geography** Possible answer: Traditional occupations, such as farming and fishing, drew people to fertile river valleys and coastal plains. Industrialization is drawing people to the cities.

Section Overview

This section discusses the history of Southeast Asia from early seafaring civilizations to present-day forms of government.

BELLRINGER
Skillbuilder Activity

 Project transparency and have students answer questions.

 Available as blackline master.

Daily Focus Skills Transparency 30-2

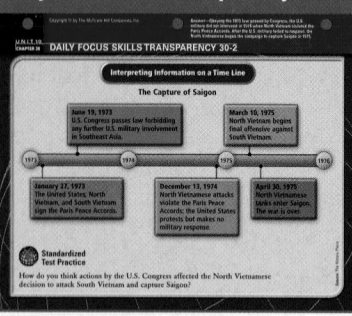

Guide to Reading

Consider What You Know
Answer *Students' answers may include: exposure to Western ways, conflict between traditions and new ideas; support for nationalist movements.*

Reading Strategy
Answers *built railroads, paved roads, and improved harbors; expanded tin mining and oil drilling; replaced small farms with large commercial plantations; increased military conflict as a result*

Preteaching Vocabulary
Use each of the "Terms to Know" in a sentence and have students infer the meaning from context.

Guide to Reading

Consider What You Know

Your history class may have taught you about the period of colonial rule that existed in Southeast Asia before the region's countries gained independence. What effects might foreign rule have on the people living in a colony?

Reading Strategy

Organizing Complete a graphic organizer similar to the one below by listing the effects of Western rule in Southeast Asia.

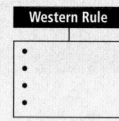

Western Rule
- •
- •
- •
- •

Read to Find Out

- How did location influence the development of empires in Southeast Asia?
- What cultural influences have affected the region's peoples?
- What events led to the independence of Southeast Asian countries?

Terms to Know

- maritime
- sphere of influence
- buffer state

Places to Locate

- Mekong River
- Gulf of Thailand
- Indochina Peninsula
- Malay Peninsula
- Angkor Wat
- Strait of Malacca
- Sunda Strait
- East Timor

History and Government

NATIONAL GEOGRAPHIC

A Geographic View

A Mighty Waterway

From its source, the Mekong [River] travels about half its length in China; then it borders or moves through Myanmar (formerly Burma), Laos, Thailand, Cambodia, and Vietnam. I would find it called by many names: River of Stone, Dragon Running River, Turbulent River, Mother River Khong, Big Water, the Nine Dragons. Along it empires, kingdoms, and colonial realms have risen and fallen. . . .

—*Thomas O'Neill, "The Mekong,"*
National Geographic, February 1993

Boat traffic, Mekong River, Vietnam

The many names given to the **Mekong River** serve as reminders of Southeast Asia's rich and colorful history. Over the centuries the Mekong River has been a major waterway for the different civilizations that have flourished along its banks. In this section you will learn about Southeast Asia's ancient kingdoms, its era of European colonial rule, and its struggles for independence and democracy. You will also learn about the regional conflicts that have taken place in Southeast Asia during the past 50 years.

Early Civilizations

Early peoples in Southeast Asia were highly skilled farmers. Rice was the staple grain of these agricultural societies, as it is in Southeast Asia today. During this early period, farmers in the region grew vegetables and domesticated cattle and pigs. Early Southeast Asians also were advanced metalworkers. Bronze was first cast in Thailand in 3000 B.C., nearly one thousand years before the Chinese developed the same skill.

RESOURCE MANAGER

Reproducible Masters
- Reproducible Lesson Plan 30-2
- Daily Lecture Notes 30-2
- Guided Reading Activity 30-2
- Reading Essentials and Study Guide 30-2
- Section Quiz 30-2

Transparencies
- Daily Focus Skills Transparency 30-2
- Political Map Transparency 10
- Unit 10 Map Overlay Transparencies
- World Art & Architecture Transparencies

Multimedia
- 💿 Interactive Tutor Self-Assessment CD-ROM
- 💿 ExamView® Pro Testmaker CD-ROM
- 💿 Presentation Plus! CD-ROM

architecture of SOUTHEAST ASIA

Angkor Wat The temple complex at Angkor Wat forms the largest single religious building in the world. The complex covers nearly one square mile (2.6 sq. km) and is surrounded by an extensive moat. To ensure order and harmony in the universe, carvings depicting the Hindu gods and the Buddha cover the walls. At the center of the complex, the sanctuary stands 130 feet (40 m) high. The distinct style of Khmer architecture shows in the roof towers. Each pyramid-shaped tower consists of a series of tiers stacked one on top of the other, each smaller than the one beneath.

TEACH

L1 Locate
Have students refer to the map on page 742. **Ask:** What bodies of water might Funan's ships have used to reach India? *(Gulf of Siam, Strait of Malacca, Bay of Bengal)*

Many Southeast Asian cultural traditions arose during this period. Early Southeast Asians worshiped their ancestors as well as animal and nature spirits. In society, power and wealth were passed down through the mother's family.

Kingdoms and Empires

Many civilizations in early Southeast Asia developed on waterways or around strategic ports. Maritime, or seafaring, empires gained power by controlling shipping and trade. Land-based empires gained wealth from crops grown in fertile soil.

Funan

During the A.D. 100s, traders from India set up trading posts along what is today the **Gulf of Thailand** (Siam). Southeast Asians living in the area blended Indian traditions with their own. By the A.D. 200s, they had established the kingdom of Funan. The people of Funan adopted Hinduism and the Indian model of a centralized government under one powerful ruler. They became skillful goldsmiths and jewelers and developed an impressive irrigation system. As a maritime power, Funan traded with regions as far away as India, China, and Persia.

Khmer

An abundance of crops grown in fertile river valleys and deltas brought wealth to mainland Southeast Asia. During the A.D. 1100s and 1200s, the Khmer Empire flourished along the Mekong River and covered most of the **Indochina Peninsula** and the northern part of the **Malay Peninsula**. Technologically advanced in irrigation and agriculture, the Khmer used a complex system of lakes, canals, and irrigation channels to grow three or four rice crops annually.

Although agriculturally advanced, the Khmer are best known for their magnificent architecture. Located in present-day Cambodia, **Angkor Wat**, a Khmer temple more than 800 years old, was designed to resemble the home of the Hindu gods and goddesses. A mixture of Indian and local styles, Angkor Wat is both a Hindu temple and a tomb for Suryavarman II—the Khmer ruler who built it.

Srivijaya Empire

Based on the island of Sumatra, the Srivijaya Empire controlled the seas bordering Southeast Asia from A.D. 600 to 1300. Ancient trade routes from Africa and Southwest Asia to East Asia went through the **Strait of Malacca** and the **Sunda Strait** and linked the Indian Ocean, the Java Sea, and the South China Sea. The Srivijaya Empire used its navy to control these straits. Once its power was established, the empire gained wealth by taxing traders whose ships passed through these waters.

By the 1300s, the Srivijaya Empire had declined, but its legacy shaped later maritime territories in Southeast Asia. Today Singapore owes its economic prosperity to these same trade routes.

Architecture of Southeast Asia
Angkor Wat, begun in the 1100s to honor the Hindu god Vishnu, later became the tomb of the Khmer ruler, Suyavarman II. When the Khmer were defeated by the Chams in the late 1100s, Angkor Wat became a Buddhist monastery.

World Art and Architecture Transparencies

Use these transparencies and activities to introduce students to more regional architecture.

Daily Lecture Notes 30-2

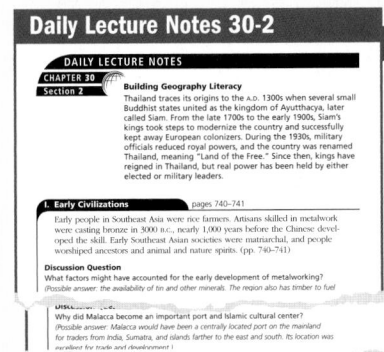

DIFFERENTIATED INSTRUCTION

Visual/Spatial Have students use the map on page 742 to create a table listing early empires and the names of modern Southeast Asian countries whose land lay entirely or partially within each empire. Have students label each column with the name of one of the empires, and list Southeast Asian countries beneath each heading. Have students also use the map on page 744 to create a similar table listing colonizing powers and colonies in Southeast Asia. ● **EE2 Places and Regions: Standard 6**
● **EE4 Human Systems: Standards 9, 12, 13**
🗁 Refer to *Inclusion for the Social Studies Classroom Strategies and Activities.*

MAP STUDY

Answers

1. East Asia, South Asia, Southwest Asia

2. They are port stops for trading vessels.

Map Skills Practice

Place Have students identify the early mainland empires (*Funan, Khmer*) and the empire that was based on an island but extended onto the mainland (*Srivijaya*).

L2 Interpretation

Ask: How did trade and the diffusion of ideas and motivations affect cultural change in Southeast Asia? (*Hindu, Buddhist, and Muslim influences came to Southeast Asia, affecting all areas of life*)

L1/ELL

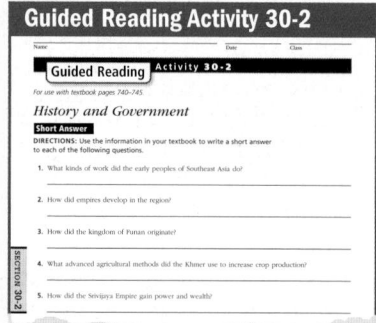

Guided Reading Activity 30-2

NATIONAL GEOGRAPHIC — MAP STUDY

Southeast Asia: Kingdoms and Trade Routes, A.D. 100s–1300s

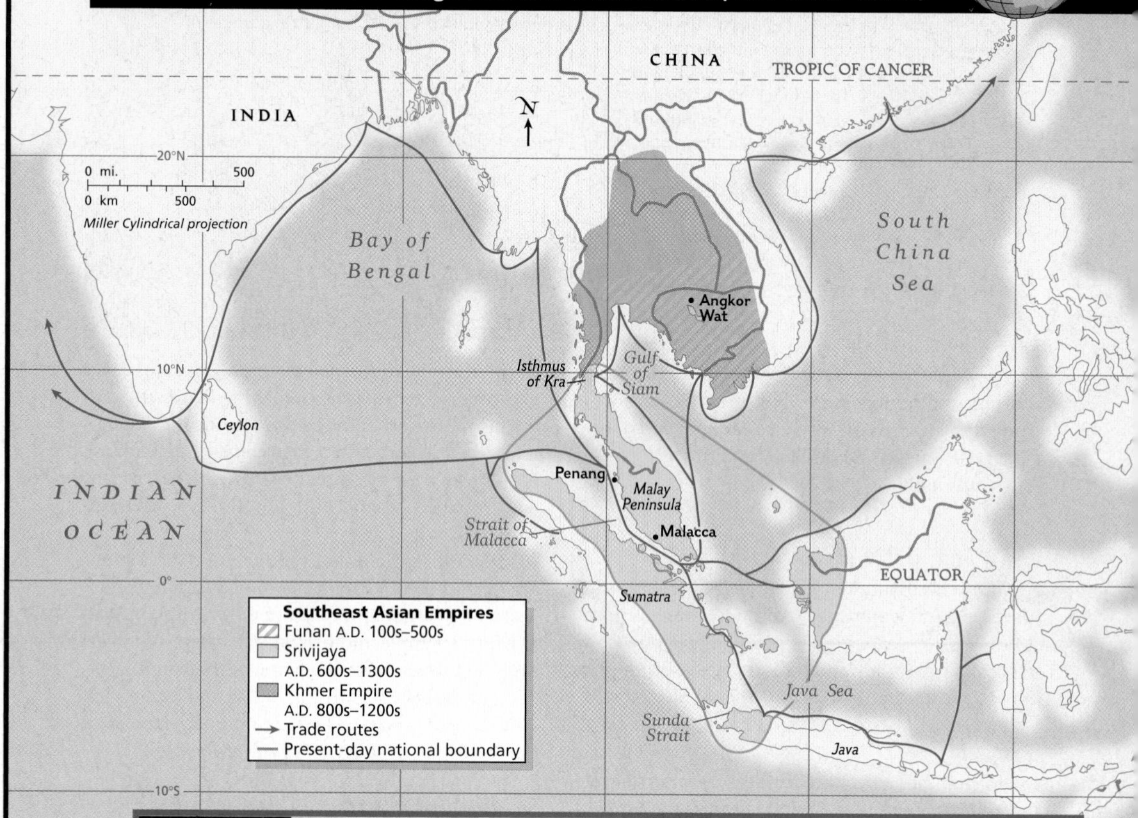

CHINA

TROPIC OF CANCER

INDIA

N

20°N

0 mi. 500
0 km 500

Miller Cylindrical projection

Bay of Bengal

South China Sea

• Angkor Wat

10°N

Isthmus of Kra

Gulf of Siam

Ceylon

INDIAN OCEAN

Penang

Malay Peninsula

Strait of Malacca

• Malacca

0°

Sumatra

EQUATOR

Java Sea

Sunda Strait

Java

10°S

Southeast Asian Empires
- ▨ Funan A.D. 100s–500s
- ▫ Srivijaya A.D. 600s–1300s
- ▪ Khmer Empire A.D. 800s–1200s
- → Trade routes
- — Present-day national boundary

Geography Skills for Life

1. **Analyzing Maps** What regions of the world traded with early Southeast Asian civilizations?

2. **Applying Geography Skills** Why do you think settlements such as Penang and Malacca prospered?

Find NGS online map resources @ www.nationalgeographic.com/maps

Vietnam

The Vietnamese people controlled the Indochina Peninsula from the Red (Hong) River delta in the north to coastal lands in the center. Throughout their history, the Vietnamese struggled against Chinese invaders. Finally, in 111 B.C. the Chinese emperor Wudi conquered the territory. The Chinese introduced their writing system and ideas about religion, philosophy, and government. Their control of the Vietnamese ended during the early A.D. 900s.

Islam

Muslim Arab merchants and missionaries from Southwest Asia traded and settled in Southeast Asian coastal areas during the A.D. 800s and 900s. Because of this influence, many coastal Southeast

---

COOPERATIVE LEARNING ACTIVITY

Evaluating Information Review with students the meaning and purpose of the concept of a *buffer state* (*a neutral territory lying between two potentially hostile or rival powers*). Then organize students into small groups. Tell groups to brainstorm and list reasons why the colonial powers might have wanted Siam (present-day Thailand) to serve as a buffer state in Southeast Asia. (*Answers may include the following: Colonial powers might not have wanted to devote their military forces to wars with other colonial powers when soldiers are needed to control indigenous groups. Wars, especially those fought at sea, disrupted trade.*)

🌐 **EE4 Human Systems: Standard 13**
🌐 **EE6 The Uses of Geography: Standard 17**

Asians adopted Islamic ways and converted to the religion of Islam. After 1400, Islam quickly spread from coastal to interior areas in the Malay Peninsula and neighboring islands. During the 1400s, Malacca, on the Malay Peninsula, was an important seaport and Islamic cultural center.

Western Colonization

By the 1500s Europeans had arrived in Southeast Asia to trade, spread Christianity, and claim territory. The European powers at first set up spheres of influence—agreed-upon areas of control. They later acquired Southeast Asian lands as colonies. Dividing British- from French-ruled territories, the kingdom of Siam (present-day Thailand) served as a buffer state, or neutral territory between rival powers. Because of its position, Siam was the only Southeast Asian territory that remained free of European rule.

Western Holdings

During the early 1900s, the Netherlands, the United Kingdom, France, and the United States dominated Southeast Asia. The Netherlands claimed most of the islands that today make up Indonesia. The United Kingdom controlled what is now Myanmar, Malaysia, Singapore, and Brunei. France governed territories in Indochina that later became Cambodia, Vietnam, and Laos. The United States gained control of the Philippines in a war with Spain in 1898.

Economics
Effects of Western Rule

Europeans and Americans brought widespread changes to Southeast Asia. They built railroads, paved roads, and improved harbors to speed the movement of people and goods throughout the region. Westerners expanded tin mining and oil drilling, and they replaced small farms with large commercial plantations. The production of rice, rubber, coffee, and other products soared, and Westerners received enormous profits.

NATIONAL GEOGRAPHIC World Explorer

Geography Skills for Life

Islamic Influences Over half of Malaysians practice Islam, including most ethnic Malays. **Movement** When did Islam spread to the Malay Peninsula?

Western rivalries for control of resources and territory, however, increased military conflict in Southeast Asia. Western influences also altered traditional lifestyles. Colonial landowners and trading companies forced Southeast Asians—who received low, if any, wages—to grow cash crops, work in the mines, and cut trees for timber.

Southeast Asian agricultural workers alone could not meet the growing Western demand for labor. Plantation owners imported machinery, but they also hired Indian and Chinese immigrants to work in the mines and fields. Many of the migrant laborers and their families settled permanently in Southeast Asia, contributing to the ethnic diversity of the region.

Struggle for Freedom

During World War II, Japan forced Western countries out of Southeast Asia. After Japan's defeat in 1945, the Western countries tried to regain control. They met opposition, however, from Southeast Asians determined to gain their freedom. By 1965,

NATIONAL GEOGRAPHIC World Explorer

Answer
after 1400

About the Photo Among Malaysia's Muslims, styles of dress, food preparation, and other social practices usually conform to Islamic law and traditions.

L1/ELL

Reading Essentials & Study Guide 30-2

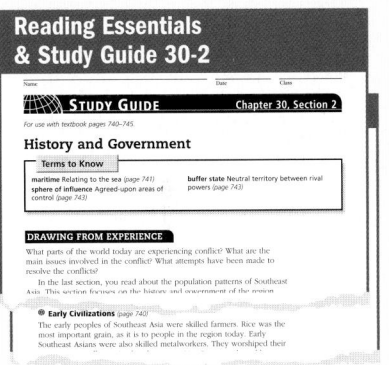

For use with textbook pages 740–745

History and Government

Terms to Know

| maritime Relating to the sea (page 741) | buffer state Neutral territory between rival powers (page 743) |
| sphere of influence Agreed-upon areas of control (page 743) | |

DRAWING FROM EXPERIENCE

What parts of the world today are experiencing conflict? What are the main issues involved in the conflict? What attempts have been made to resolve the conflict?

In the last section, you read about the population patterns of Southeast Asia. This section focuses on the history and government of the region.

⦿ **Early Civilizations** *(page 740)*
The early peoples of Southeast Asia were skilled farmers. Rice was the most important grain, as it is to people in the region today. Early Southeast Asians were also skilled metalworkers. They worshiped their

INTERDISCIPLINARY
connection

HISTORY Two reform-minded kings ruled Thailand (formerly known as Siam) between 1851 and 1910. Mongkut practiced religious tolerance and improved working conditions for his people. His son, Chulalongkorn, abolished slavery, instituted legal and financial reforms, built railroads, and created a modern postal service.

CRITICAL THINKING ACTIVITY

Recognizing Ideologies Explain that an ideology is a set of ideas or a way of thinking about human life or culture. An ideology usually is integrated into a sociopolitical program such as communism, Nazism, or democracy. Have students reread the section "Cambodia: Population Decline." **Ask: How would you describe the ideology and actions of the Khmer Rouge?** *(anti-intellectual, repressive, cruel)* **Why do you think the Khmer Rouge targeted educated and intellectual people?** *(Thinkers and educated people are harder to control.)* Have students define the principles of the following ideologies: communism *(government control of economy, rule by single political party)*; democracy *(free elections, human rights, private ownership of property)*. Use the answers as a basis for further discussion. 🌐 **EE4 Human Systems: Standard 13**

NATIONAL GEOGRAPHIC — MAP STUDY

Answers
1. *the Dutch*
2. *Laos, Cambodia, Vietnam*

Map Skills Practice
Location Ask: Which European country controlled the least amount of land in Southeast Asia? *(Portugal)*

③ ASSESS

Assign Section 2 Assessment as homework or as an activity.

◐ Have students use **Interactive Tutor Self-Assessment CD-ROM.**
L2

Section Quiz 30-2

Section 2 Quiz
30
History and Government

MATCHING: Match each item in Column A with an item in Column B. Write the correct letters in the blanks. *(10 points each)*

A	B
1. Southeast Asian country ruled by invading Chinese, 111 B.C. to A.D. 900	A. East Timor
2. Sumatran empire with naval strength, A.D. 600–1300	B. Srivijaya
3. Roman Catholic region that recently broke from Indonesia	C. Khmer
4. Mekong River empire with advanced architecture and agriculture, A.D. 1100s and A.D. 1200s	D. Vietnam
5. Hindu maritime power, A.D. 200	E. Funan

MULTIPLE CHOICE: In the blanks on the left, write the letter of the choice that best completes each statement or answers each question.

Reteach

Have students answer the questions in "Read to Find Out" on page 740.

---

after two decades of struggle, all of the countries of Southeast Asia had gained independence.

Culture
Regional Conflicts

After independence, political conflicts and wars raged throughout Southeast Asia. Local Communists fought other political groups in Indochina. In 1954 communist forces defeated the French in Vietnam, which was then divided into two independent parts: communist North Vietnam and non-communist South Vietnam. Vietnamese Communists used force to unite all of Vietnam under their rule by the mid-1970s. In Laos and Cambodia,

Communists also fought newly independent governments for control. During the 1960s and early 1970s, the United States intervened in these Southeast Asian conflicts to block the spread of communism. The feature on pages 746–747 describes the Vietnam War and the United States's involvement in Southeast Asia.

Other Southeast Asian countries have faced various kinds of conflicts. In Malaysia, ethnic Malays controlling the government have clashed with Chinese and Indian groups, who run the economy. Sometimes ethnic groups have waged struggles for independence. **East Timor**, a former Portuguese colony seized by Indonesia in 1975, is an

NATIONAL GEOGRAPHIC — MAP STUDY
Foreign Colonies in Southeast Asia, 1914

1914 Colonies: British, French, Dutch, U.S., Portuguese, Independent

Geography Skills for Life

1. **Analyzing Maps** Which European group controlled most of the island areas of Southeast Asia?
2. **Applying Geography Skills** What present-day countries were part of French Indochina?

Find NGS online map resources @ www.nationalgeographic.com/maps

---

TEAM-TEACHING ACTIVITY: SCIENCE

Studying the Orchid Point out that more than 1,000 different varieties of orchids grow in Thailand. Have partners research to discover more about Thailand's orchids. Consult a science teacher to find appropriate reference material on orchids, and have students research and write a report about special climate conditions and growing requirements for orchids to thrive. Ask students to focus on particular orchid varieties and, if possible, how they impact Thailand's economy. Students should include an illustration. Combine the projects to create a class booklet titled *Thailand: Land of Orchids.* Display the booklet in the classroom or school library. 📦 🌐 **EE3 Physical Systems: Standard 8**

example. Over 20 years, about 200,000 of the largely Roman Catholic East Timorese died in fierce combat against the largely Muslim Indonesians. A journalist visiting East Timor in the late 1980s described the fighting at that time:

> The consequences [of fighting] have been devastating. . . . 'Practically speaking,' [stated a local official], 'every family in East Timor has lost someone in this civil war.' 99
>
> Arthur Zich, "Indonesia: Two Worlds, Time Apart," *National Geographic,* January 1989

When Indonesia's dictatorship fell in 1999, East Timor broke away. The UN administered East Timor until the country became fully independent in 2002. Meanwhile terrorist groups based in Southeast Asia have carried out attacks against Westerners in the region. In the fall of 2002, terrorist bombings killed about 200 people—many of them foreign tourists—on the Indonesian island of Bali.

Forms of Government

Forms of government vary in Southeast Asia. Indonesia, the Philippines, and Singapore are democratic republics. In 1998 Indonesia moved toward democracy after years of dictatorship. Myanmar's military government has tried to crush the efforts of opposition leader Aung San Suu Kyi (AWNG SAHN SOO CHEE) to bring democracy peacefully to the country. Brunei, Cambodia, Malaysia, and Thailand are constitutional monarchies. Communist governments rule in Laos and Vietnam.

NATIONAL GEOGRAPHIC World Explorer

Geography **Skills for Life**

Voting for Freedom East Timorese greet a UN official sent to supervise a 1999 election in which East Timor's voters decided to separate their territory from Indonesia.

Place How did religion affect East Timor's relationship with Indonesia?

NATIONAL GEOGRAPHIC World Explorer

Answer
The largely Roman Catholic East Timorese resented being absorbed by largely Muslim Indonesia.

More About the Photo
After the vote for independence, pro-Jakarta militia massacred hundreds of East Timorese, destroyed entire towns, and forced more than 250,000 people to flee into West Timor.

Enrich

Point out that Aung San Suu Kyi is the daughter of General Aung San, the hero of the Burmese struggle to gain independence from Great Britain. **Ask:** What award did Aung win and why? *(1991 Nobel Peace Prize; called for peaceful democratic change)* Have students research to find the answer.

4 CLOSE

Have students explain how conflicts during the past 100 years have shaped governments and territorial boundaries in Southeast Asia.

SECTION 2 ASSESSMENT

Checking for Understanding

1. **Define** maritime, sphere of influence, buffer state.

2. **Main Ideas** On a table like the one below, fill in and describe influences of outside cultures on the development of Southeast Asia.

Culture	Influences on Southeast Asia

Critical Thinking

3. **Comparing and Contrasting** How were the region's three early empires alike? Different?

4. **Making Inferences** What physical and human factors have shaped Southeast Asia's current political borders?

5. **Predicting Consequences** How might East Timor's independence influence the region?

Analyzing Maps

6. **Region** Study the map on page 742. Why were the Strait of Malacca and the Sunda Strait vital to maritime development?

Applying Geography

7. **Interpreting Historical Maps** Write a paragraph explaining how the map of foreign colonies on page 744 helps us understand the region's cultural diversity.

Chapter 30 🌐 745

SECTION 2 ASSESSMENT ANSWERS

1. All vocabulary terms are defined in the text.

2. Answers may include Indian, Chinese, Muslim, and European influences.

3. alike: developed on waterways; became wealthy through advanced technologies or shipping and trading skills; influenced by different cultures and religions; different: some were primarily seafaring empires; some were primarily agricultural; practiced different religions

4. Island locations, mainland cordilleras, and rivers are physical factors. Political factors include ethnic and ideological conflicts as well as the colonial legacy.

5. Possible answer: other groups may try to gain independence.

6. These bodies of water lead to the Indian Ocean and trade/cultural exchange with other regions.

7. **Applying Geography** Answers should show an understanding of the influence of colonization on the cultural make-up of the region.

Ask students to write and pose questions to older family members about the Vietnam War. Have students tell what they have learned about the war from their questionnaires as well as from books, movies and television. *(Answers may include contrasting viewpoints on the war's merits; the reasons for the outcome; and the impact of antiwar protests.)* Have students discuss why the Vietnam War remains controversial.

L2 The Domino Theory

Bring a set of dominoes to class. Demonstrate how a row of dominoes, when lined up, will fall one after another if the first is toppled. Then, read the following quote from a 1954 speech by President Dwight D. Eisenhower: "You have a row of dominoes set up, and you knock over the first one, and what will happen to the last one is the certainty that it will go over very quickly." Tell students that the president was referring to Southeast Asia. Guide students to understand the belief that, if all of Vietnam fell to the communists, Cambodia, Laos, Thailand, and Burma would follow.

THE LONG WAR: AMERICA IN VIETNAM

WITHIN THE JUNGLES OF VIETNAM, slim shafts of light penetrate the dense vegetation. In the 1960s and 1970s, American soldiers fought a war in these jungles, while their nation's leaders struggled over how to end it.

The United States became concerned about Vietnam after World War II, when the Cold War split the world's nations into two groups—those favoring the democratic United States, and those aligned with the Soviet Union and communism. Each side feared the other's dominance, and U.S. President Truman vowed to help any country threatened by communism. This policy, expanded by Presidents Eisenhower, Kennedy, and Johnson, led America to war in Vietnam.

America Intervenes

France ruled Vietnam from the late 1800s to the early 1940s. Japan occupied Vietnam during most of World War II. After the war, the United States supported France as it tried to resume rule. But Ho Chi Minh, a Communist and a Soviet ally, organized a revolt in northern Vietnam. In 1954 the Vietnamese won control, ending French rule. All parties signed a peace agreement, and Vietnam was divided into Communist North Vietnam, led by Ho Chi Minh, and non-Communist South Vietnam, eventually led by Ngo Dinh Diem.

Soldiers in Vietnam battled harsh terrain, as well as the enemy. ▶

BACKGROUND INFORMATION

United States Involvement The United States at first sent only financial aid to the non-communist government of South Vietnam. Next, it sent small numbers of military advisers. The number of military advisers increased from 900 in 1960 to 11,000 by the end of 1962. In 1967, 389,000 American troops were in the country.

United States commitment reached its highest level by 1969 with more than 540,000 troops in Vietnam. Have partners research information and create a line graph of United States involvement in Vietnam from 1961 until 1973.

EE4 Human Systems: Standard 13

◄ A former soldier demonstrates a trapdoor in the network of tunnels near Saigon (now Ho Chi Minh City). Today the tunnels are a tourist attraction.

NATIONAL GEOGRAPHIC

Diem proved unpopular, and rebel groups formed. Having North Vietnam's support, the rebels were called Viet Cong, or "Vietnamese Communists." In 1963 a military coup overthrew Diem. After U.S. President Lyndon Johnson announced that North Vietnam had attacked American ships in the Gulf of Tonkin, the United States took action. Soon American planes were bombing North Vietnam. In 1965 the first American troops landed to support South Vietnam.

A Losing Battle

American pilots flew B-52 bombers in air strikes against North Vietnam. In the south, Americans used helicopters, tanks, and well-armed ground troops to seek out Viet Cong. Chemicals, such as Agent Orange, were sprayed to kill the thick jungle vegetation. Modern weaponry, however, did not deter the Communist forces. Viet Cong and North Vietnamese fighters relied on guerrilla tactics, on knowledge of the terrain, and on weapons from the Soviet Union and China. Viet Cong hid out and attacked from 200 miles (320 km) of underground tunnels. Many American soldiers lost their lives trying to infiltrate the jungles and tunnels of Vietnam.

As the war dragged on, antiwar protests erupted in the United States. Under pressure to end the war, U.S. President Nixon began withdrawing troops. The last American forces left Vietnam in 1973. By war's end in 1975, more than 50,000 Americans and as many as 2 million Vietnamese were dead. By 1976 Vietnam was reunited, and Hanoi imposed harsh reforms on Saigon, which was renamed Ho Chi Minh City. In the following decade, more than a million refugees fled Vietnam's shores by boat. Tragically, half of these "boat people" died.

Today Americans still study lessons of the war. In Vietnam, north and south remain vastly different, with little economic development in the north and foreign investment pouring into the south.

Looking Ahead
The United States established diplomatic ties with Vietnam in 1995. What role might the United States play in Vietnam's economic recovery?

1954 Ho Chi Minh (photo above) and Communist fighters defeat France

1964 Gulf of Tonkin incident; U.S. bombs North Vietnam

1965 U.S. sends ground forces to aid South Vietnam

1967–1972 War continues; Americans protest (background photo)

1973 Paris Accords establish cease-fire; U.S. troops withdraw

1975 North Vietnam conquers South Vietnam

1978–1980s Boat people flee

1995 U.S. normalizes relations with Vietnam

❸ ASSESS

Have students answer the **Looking Ahead** question.

❹ CLOSE

Tell students to reread the feature's last paragraph. Have them brainstorm "lessons" that they think the U.S. learned from the Vietnam War. (*Superior technology does not guarantee victory; people's resolve to fight despite the cost should not be underestimated.*)

🌐 Meeting National Standards

Geography for Life
The following standards are met in the Student Edition:

EE4 Human Systems: Standards 9, 13
EE5 Environment and Society: Standard 14

ANSWERS TO LOOKING AHEAD

Answers may include the following: The United States could help Vietnam develop its petroleum resources and buy oil from the country. It could provide loans or other forms of financial assistance. The government could encourage U.S. businesses to invest in Vietnam's economy, trade with Vietnamese companies, or locate Southeast Asian branch offices and plants in the country.

 **FOCUS**

Section Overview

This section discusses diversity in Southeast Asian arts, religion, and lifestyles.

BELLRINGER
Skillbuilder Activity

 Project transparency and have students answer questions.

Available as blackline master.

Daily Focus Skills Transparency 30-3

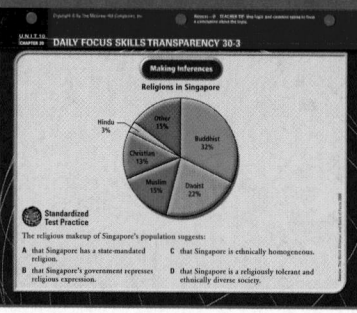

Guide to Reading

Consider What You Know
Answer *Students' answers may include food items and clothing styles. Religions should include Buddhism, Hinduism, and Islam.*

Reading Strategy
Answers *Myanmar, Thailand, Cambodia, Vietnam, Laos*

Preteaching Vocabulary
Use the **Vocabulary Puzzle-Maker CD-ROM** to create crossword and word-search puzzles.

Guide to Reading

Consider What You Know
Southeast Asia is a culturally diverse region. Increasingly, Southeast Asian cultural influences are present in the Western world. What foods, clothing, or religions do you know of that are from Southeast Asian cultures?

Reading Strategy
Categorizing As you read about the religions of Southeast Asia, complete a web diagram similar to the one below by filling in the countries where Buddhism is the major religion.

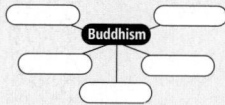

Read to Find Out
- What makes Southeast Asia such an ethnically diverse region?
- How have outside influences affected the arts in Southeast Asia?
- How do people's lifestyles reflect Southeast Asia's diversity?

Terms to Know
- *wat*
- *batik*
- *longhouse*

Places to Locate
- Irrawaddy River
- Kuala Lumpur

Cultures and Lifestyles

NATIONAL GEOGRAPHIC

A Geographic View

Rural Progress

Thailand's economic success is most obvious in the cities, but it filters into the countryside as well. Where families once tended small [rice] paddies just outside Bangkok, large tractors now groom sweeping fields of commercial farms.... On the quiet side roads where I once slowed for water buffalo, I now dodged motorcycles piloted by young Thai men in love with speed.

—Noel Grove, "The Many Faces of Thailand," National Geographic, *February 1996*

Shrimp farm outside Bangkok, Thailand

Throughout their history, Southeast Asians have successfully adapted new ideas and practices to indigenous cultural traditions. Today the peoples of Southeast Asia are learning to blend their cultural heritage with the fast-paced changes brought by the region's participation in a global economy. In this section you will learn about Southeast Asia's many cultures and lifestyles.

Cultural Diversity

Cultures in Southeast Asia reflect the region's ethnic diversity. In Vietnam, for example, a number of cultural traditions—Chinese, Hmong, Tai, Khmer, Man, and Cham—exist alongside the predominant Vietnamese culture. Indonesia has the region's largest number of ethnic and cultural groups. About 300 ethnic groups with more than 250 distinct languages live on Indonesia's many islands. Since independence, the Indonesian government has struggled to hold the country together. The collapse of its dictatorship

---

RESOURCE MANAGER

Reproducible Masters
- Reproducible Lesson Plan 30-3
- Vocabulary Activity 30
- Daily Lecture Notes 30-3
- Guided Reading Activity 30-3
- Reading Essentials and Study Guide 30-3
- Reteaching Activity 30
- Reinforcing Skills Activity 30
- Section Quiz 30-3

Transparencies
- Daily Focus Skills Transparency 30-3
- Political Map Transparency 10
- Unit 10 Map Overlay Transparencies

Multimedia
- Vocabulary PuzzleMaker CD-ROM
- World Music: A Cultural Legacy
- Interactive Tutor Self-Assessment CD-ROM
- ExamView® Pro Testmaker CD-ROM

and the breaking away of East Timor have encouraged independence movements in other parts of Indonesia to increase their demands.

History
Languages

Hundreds of languages and dialects are spoken in Southeast Asia. Most of the region's languages stem from three major language families—Malayo-Polynesian, Sino-Tibetan, and Mon-Khmer.

Many of the languages spoken in Southeast Asia are the result of migration or colonization. In the Philippines, for example, Pilipino, English, and Spanish are the major languages. Pilipino, an official language of the Philippines, belongs to the Malayo-Polynesian language family and evolved from the speech of early migrants. Spanish was brought to the Philippines during the years of rule by Spain. English, the second official language, came later with rule by the United States.

Chinese, Malay, Tamil, and English are the official languages of Singapore, reflecting the importance of global trade to this tiny island country. In Malaysia, where British influence was strong during the 1800s and early 1900s, English is the language most often used in business and daily life. Affirming the country's traditional culture, however, the Malaysian government has made Malay the country's official language, especially in schools and universities. In Vietnam urban residents speak Vietnamese, Chinese dialects, French, or English. The presence of the three non-Vietnamese languages is a daily reminder of the influence that China, France, and the United States have had on Vietnam's history and culture.

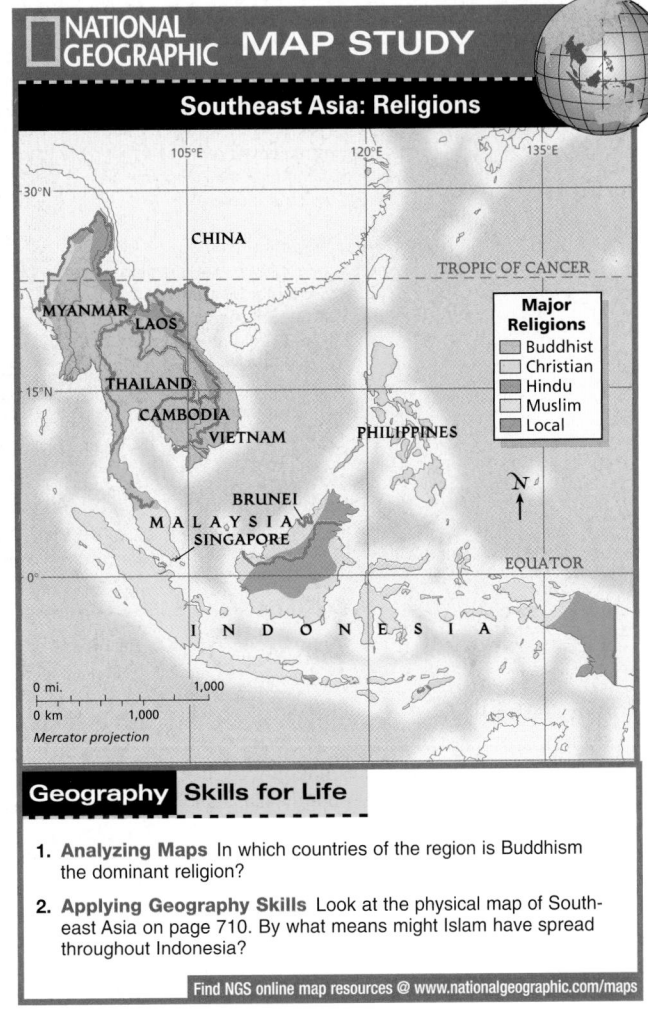

Southeast Asia: Religions

Major Religions
- Buddhist
- Christian
- Hindu
- Muslim
- Local

0 mi. 1,000
0 km 1,000
Mercator projection

Geography | Skills for Life

1. **Analyzing Maps** In which countries of the region is Buddhism the dominant religion?

2. **Applying Geography Skills** Look at the physical map of Southeast Asia on page 710. By what means might Islam have spread throughout Indonesia?

Find NGS online map resources @ www.nationalgeographic.com/maps

Religions

Because of the many cultures that exist in Southeast Asia, nearly all of the world's major religions are represented in the region. Buddhism is the major religion of Myanmar, Thailand, Cambodia, Laos, and Vietnam. Many people living in Malaysia and Indonesia practice Islam. The majority of people in the Philippines are Roman Catholic. This Christian influence began when the Philippines came under the control of Spain during the 1500s. A great number of Southeast

Chapter 30 ● 749

DIFFERENTIATED INSTRUCTION

At-Risk Students Students who are having difficulty grasping the main concepts of this section may wish to use an outline to organize the information. Outlining will enable students to organize information more clearly and precisely. Have students work with a partner who has demonstrated mastery of geographic concepts to develop the main heads under which details will be grouped.

📁 Refer to *Inclusion for the Social Studies Classroom Strategies and Activities.*

---

② TEACH

L1 Cultural Diversity
Write the words *cultural diversity* on the board. Have students use what they learned from the first two sections of this chapter to predict how that term might apply to Southeast Asia.

NATIONAL GEOGRAPHIC | **MAP STUDY**

Answers
1. *Thailand, Cambodia, Laos, Vietnam, Myanmar*
2. *traders arriving by sea*

Map Skills Practice
Place What major religions are practiced in Laos? *(Buddhism and local)* Which country has the greatest concentration of Hindus? *(Indonesia, on the island of Bali)*

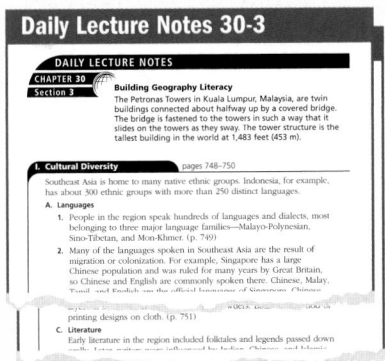

Daily Lecture Notes 30-3

DAILY LECTURE NOTES

CHAPTER 30
Section 3

Building Geography Literacy
The Petronas Towers in Kuala Lumpur, Malaysia, are twin buildings connected about halfway up by a covered bridge. The bridge is fastened to the towers in such a way that it slides on the towers as they sway. The tower structure is the tallest building in the world (1,483 feet (453 m).

I. Cultural Diversity pages 748–750

Southeast Asia is home to many native ethnic groups. Indonesia, for example, has about 300 ethnic groups with more than 250 distinct languages.

A. Languages
1. People in the region speak hundreds of languages and dialects, most belonging to three major language families—Malayo-Polynesian, Sino-Tibetan, and Mon-Khmer. (p. 749)
2. Many of the languages spoken in Southeast Asia are the result of migration or colonization. For example, Singapore has a large Chinese population and was ruled for many years by Great Britain, so Chinese and English are commonly spoken there. Chinese, Malay, Tamil, and English are the official languages of Singapore, Chinese...
...printing designs on cloth. (p. 751)

C. Literature
Early literature in the region included folktales and legends passed down orally. Later, writing was influenced by Indian, Chinese, and Islamic...

L2 Religion and Art
Remind students that religions from other regions influenced the art and architecture of Southeast Asia. **Ask:** What four religions do you think contributed to these influences? *(Hinduism, Buddhism, Islam, and Christianity)*

Music of Southeast Asia

The music, dance, and theater of Bali are linked for the most part to the Hindu religion. The Trance Dance, for example, is performed when a village suffers from an epidemic, a bad harvest, or some other natural misfortune. The aim of the dance is to win the favor of gods and goddesses for the village.

♪ World Music: A Cultural Legacy

Use the accompanying Teacher Guide for information and worksheets about the music of this region.

L1/ELL

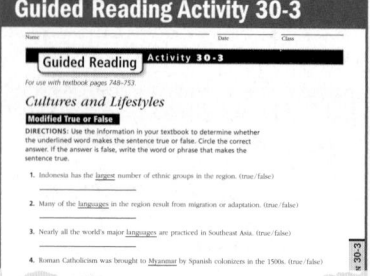

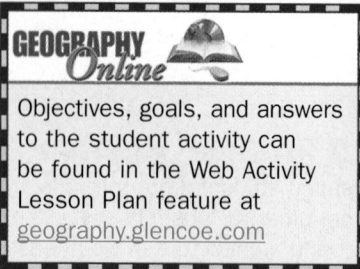

Objectives, goals, and answers to the student activity can be found in the Web Activity Lesson Plan feature at geography.glencoe.com

---

WORLD CULTURE

music of SOUTHEAST ASIA

A variety of instruments, chants, vocal styles, and dances are found throughout Southeast Asia. The use of bronze and bamboo instruments is common in Thailand, Cambodia, the Philippines, Malaysia, and Indonesia.

Instrument Spotlight

A metal gong known as a **gamelan** is the most popular instrument of Indonesia. These bronze gongs are made in many shapes and sizes and are usually featured in ensembles along with drums, percussion, flutes, singers, and dancers. Gamelans originated in Java prior to the 1400s, and by the 1700s they were an important part of the royal courts. From Java this music tradition spread to Bali and other neighboring islands.

Go To **World Music: A Cultural Legacy** Hear music of this region on Disc 2, Tracks 19–24.

Asians—mainly those of Chinese ancestry—follow Confucianism or Daoism.

These different religious beliefs not only coexist but also mingle throughout Southeast Asia. In Vietnam people blend Buddhism, Confucianism, and, in some cases, Catholicism. A housewarming ceremony in Thailand might include blessings by a Buddhist monk and a Hindu priest, followed by offerings to ancestors and nature spirits. Hinduism, influenced by Buddhism and indigenous religions, is the basis for elaborate ceremonies on the Indonesian island of Bali.

The Arts

The civilizations of early India and China significantly shaped Southeast Asia's cultural development. Over the centuries, local artists and writers creatively adapted Indian and Chinese styles to their own needs. Hinduism and Buddhism also inspired literature, art, and architecture in Southeast Asia. During the era of Western colonization, European artistic and literary styles began to influence Southeast Asian arts and literature.

Architecture

Many beautiful examples of religious architecture exist throughout Southeast Asia. Elaborate Chinese-style pagodas and Indian-style *wats*, or temples, dot the landscape. Thousands of these religious buildings are located on the Indochina Peninsula alone.

Borobudur, a Buddhist shrine in Indonesia, is a stunning example of Southeast Asian religious art and architecture. Built of gray volcanic stone around A.D. 800 on the island of Java, this temple is larger than Europe's great cathedrals. A large tower shaped like a bell tops the pyramid-shaped monument. The shrine's three levels, connected by stairs, represent the three stages of the Buddha's journey to enlightenment.

GEOGRAPHY Online

Student Web Activity Visit the **Glencoe World Geography** Web site at geography.glencoe.com and click on Student Web Activities—Chapter 30 for an activity about Malaysia.

COOPERATIVE LEARNING ACTIVITY

Creating and Dramatizing a Folktale Have students form small groups. Each group should research and report on, read aloud, or enact a folktale from Southeast Asia. Group members also could collaborate and write an original folktale based on themes and traditions found in the folklore of the region. Encourage group members to adapt their original work for a recitation or dramatic performance. One member could serve as narrator while others play the parts of characters. Allow time for a question-and-answer session in which the performers can clarify the relationship between their work and Southeast Asian culture.

📖 **EE4 Human Systems: Standard 10**

The royal city of Pagan (puh•GAHN) in Myanmar was the ancient capital of an early Burmese empire. From A.D. 1044 to about 1300, kings and commoners honored the Buddha by building more than 5,000 pagodas. More than 2,000 pagodas still stand along 8 miles (13 km) of the **Irrawaddy River.** Many of these ancient structures remain in excellent condition.

Christianity and Islam also have influenced Southeast Asian architecture. In the Philippines you can find Roman Catholic churches built in the Spanish colonial style. In Malaysia, Brunei, and Indonesia, where Islam is the major religion, the minarets of many beautiful mosques are prominent.

Modern architecture dominates the skyline of major Southeast Asian cities, such as Bangkok, Jakarta, Singapore, and Kuala Lumpur. **Kuala Lumpur,** Malaysia's capital, has an area called the Golden Triangle that includes luxury hotels, multi-storied office buildings, and a development project known as the Kuala Lumpur City Center (KLCC). The KLCC has one of the world's tallest office buildings, the Petronas Twin Towers.

Crafts

The rich cultures of Southeast Asia have produced many fine crafts. Artisans in Myanmar and Vietnam produce glossy lacquerware. Boxes, trays, dishes, and furniture are covered with many layers of resin from the Asian sumac tree. Colored powders are used to paint designs on the pieces.

Creating lacquerware is time-consuming. Several weeks must pass between applications of layers of lacquer, and a piece may take up to a year to complete. An observer explains the state of mind an artisan requires to create this traditional craft:

> ❝ Good lacquer requires a mood of timelessness that even the visitor senses. Workers' time clocks, if such existed, would be marked in months, not hours. ❞
>
> W. E. Garrett, "Pagan, on the Road to Mandalay," *National Geographic,* March 1971

Using a method known as batik (buh•TEEK), Indonesians and Malaysians produce beautiful designs and patterns on cloth. First, they use wax or rice paste to create designs on the cloth. Then, they dye the fabric. The dyes form a pattern, coloring only the untreated parts of the cloth. Finally, the cloth is boiled to remove the wax. A colorful pattern or picture remains.

Literature

Early literature in Southeast Asia consisted of folktales, legends, and love stories passed orally from generation to generation. Indian, Chinese, and Islamic literature later had a great influence on local writers, whose works still showed their own distinct character. For example, in *Arjunavivaha*, a story about the life of a king in Java, the court poet Mpu Kanwa modified the Indian epic *Mahabharata* to fit Southeast Asian circumstances.

In recent times Southeast Asian authors have used Western styles and themes in their works. Many

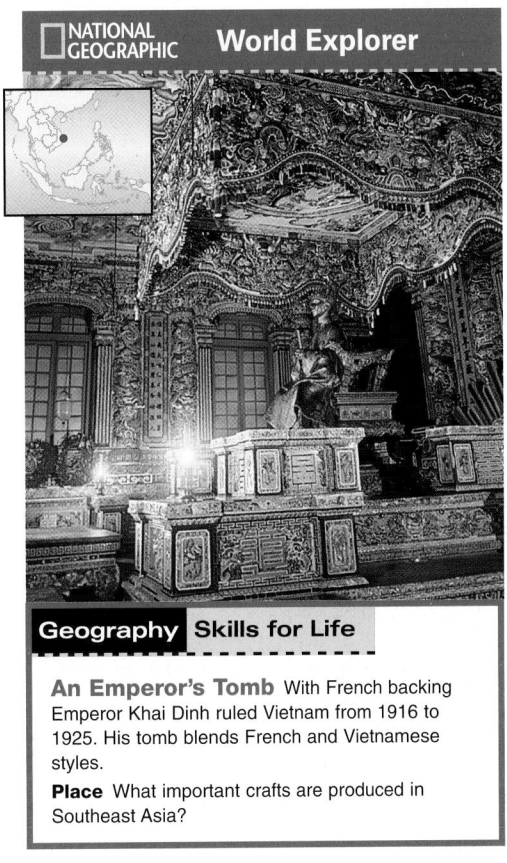

NATIONAL GEOGRAPHIC World Explorer

Geography Skills for Life

An Emperor's Tomb With French backing Emperor Khai Dinh ruled Vietnam from 1916 to 1925. His tomb blends French and Vietnamese styles.

Place What important crafts are produced in Southeast Asia?

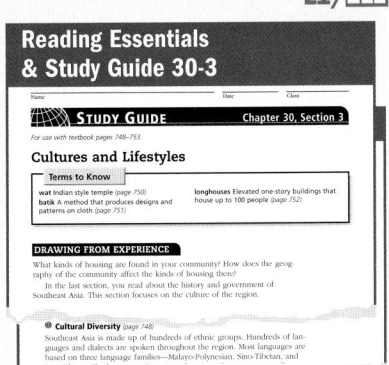

Reading Essentials & Study Guide 30-3

Name ___ Date ___ Class ___

🌐 **STUDY GUIDE** Chapter 30, Section 3

For use with textbook pages 748–753

Cultures and Lifestyles

Terms to Know

wat Indian style temple (page 750)
batik A method that produces designs and patterns on cloth (page 751)
longhouses Elevated one-story buildings that house up to 100 people (page 752)

DRAWING FROM EXPERIENCE

What kinds of housing are found in your community? How does the geography of the community affect the kinds of housing there?

In the last section, you read about the history and government of Southeast Asia. This section focuses on the culture of the region.

⊙ **Cultural Diversity** (page 748)
Southeast Asia is made up of hundreds of ethnic groups. Hundreds of languages and dialects are spoken throughout the region. Most languages are based on three language families—Malayo-Polynesian, Sino-Tibetan, and

Balinese drama is almost entirely dance, and there is no outward change of scene. The actors/dancers perform formal hand gestures to show scene changes, and facial gestures give the audience clues as to the location of the action.

NATIONAL GEOGRAPHIC World Explorer

Answer
lacquerware and batik

More About the Photo
Khai Dinh's tomb lies near Hue, Vietnam's old imperial capital. Inside Hue are historical buildings and other tombs associated with Vietnamese royalty.

CRITICAL THINKING ACTIVITY

Making Predictions Refer students to page 752 for information on housing in rural Malaysia. Have students form small groups and have group members predict how climate might have influenced traditional housing in other countries in Southeast Asia. Have students investigate different housing styles in Southeast Asia using media resources. Were students' predictions correct? Have students write a brief explanation of how architecture in different countries in the region reflects the location's climate.
🌐 **EE5 Environment and Society: Standard 14**

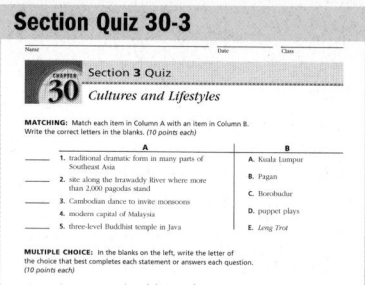

③ ASSESS

Assign Section 3 Assessment as homework or as an in-class activity.

🌐 Have students use **Interactive Tutor Self-Assessment CD-ROM**.

L2

Section Quiz 30-3

---

of the region's writers, however, have translated classic Southeast Asian literature into modern forms of language that can be read and understood by people today.

Culture
Dance and Drama

Performance arts remain immensely popular in Southeast Asia. Dance and drama are combined to retell legends or re-create historical events.

Traditional dances often make use of religious themes. On the island of Bali, in Indonesia, young women perform a dance called the *Legong*. Making graceful gestures, the dancers reenact episodes from the *Ramayana*, an ancient Indian story. Dances can also serve as reminders of the region's agricultural roots. In Cambodia, when the monsoon rains are late, dancers perform a type of rain dance called the *Leng Trot*.

Puppet plays are popular in many parts of Southeast Asia. These plays use historical and religious characters to perform tales. Sometimes a human dancer who imitates a puppet's movement performs the play.

Lifestyles

Southeast Asia's ethnic diversity leads to a wide variety of lifestyles in the region. Yet as global contacts have increased, similarities have also developed among the ways people in Southeast Asia live.

Health and Education

Since achieving independence, many Southeast Asian countries have enjoyed an improved quality of life. Industry has spread throughout the region, and per capita incomes have risen. Singapore's per capita gross domestic product (GDP) of $26,300 is comparable to that of the United States. The per capita GDPs of Laos, Cambodia, and Vietnam, however, are all lower than $2,000.

Life expectancy and infant mortality rates also have improved. The general levels of health in Southeast Asia still vary widely, with Singapore having the best overall health conditions. For example, average life expectancy is 78 years in Singapore, compared with only 52 years in Laos.

Since 1945, literacy has increased dramatically in the region, although educational opportunities are still limited in many areas. Governments continue efforts to make education available to everyone. Thailand has the highest literacy rate in the region (95 percent), and Laos has the lowest (57 percent).

Housing

Housing in Southeast Asia varies throughout the region, depending on physical geography. In cities, people often live in traditional brick or wooden houses. Some urban residents make their homes in high-rise apartments. Although many Southeast Asians still live in poor conditions, government-funded housing projects have improved the situations in some places.

Despite rapid urban growth, many Southeast Asians still live in small farming villages. A typical village consists of about 25 to 30 homes made of bamboo or wood. These houses are built to suit the environment. Most have roofs made of tiles, corrugated iron, or tin to keep out heavy rains. Most of these dwellings lack running water and electricity.

In some rural areas of Indonesia and Malaysia, people live in longhouses—elevated one-story buildings that house up to 100 people. Elevating the houses on poles helps ventilate and cool the structures and offers protection from insects, animals, and

NATIONAL GEOGRAPHIC World Explorer

Geography Skills for Life
— — — — — — — — — — — — — **Cramped**
Housing Thousands of people live aboard floating homes in Sabah, a region of Malaysia.
Region What are typical farming communities like in Southeast Asia?

TEAM-TEACHING ACTIVITY: HISTORY & GOVERNMENT

Comparing the Governments of Thailand and Brunei Note that both Brunei and Thailand have hereditary rulers. In Brunei, this ruler is a sultan; in Thailand, the leader is a king. Have students research to learn more about the governments of these two Southeast Asian countries and how forms of government affect cultures and lifestyles there. Students can use a Venn diagram to compare and contrast the two governments. They might include term of office, method of selection, extent of powers, and their effects on religions, lifestyles, and the arts. Consult with a history or government teacher on the project, and have students contrast these two systems with that of the United States in an essay.
🌐 **EE4 Human Systems: Standard 10**

flooding. The residents of longhouses are usually members of several extended or related families.

Food, Recreation, and Celebrations

Most rural Southeast Asians live on the food they raise themselves. Throughout the region rice is the staple food and is usually served with spicy fish, chicken, vegetables, and sauces. Various countries have their own specialties. Some use curry and other spices; some make use of coconut milk.

Southeast Asians enjoy a variety of leisure activities. In large cities, such as Bangkok, Jakarta, and Singapore, people visit museums, theaters, parks, restaurants, and nightclubs. In rural areas people enjoy visiting their neighbors and celebrating family occasions such as weddings and birthdays.

People throughout the region enjoy sports such as soccer, basketball, and badminton. Traditional sports and pastimes are also popular. In Myanmar, people play a game called *chinlon*, in which players form a circle and try to keep a rattan ball in the air without using their hands. Indonesians practice a combination of dancing and self-defense known as *silat*. Thais enjoy a form of "kick" boxing that uses the feet as well as the hands.

Many Southeast Asian holidays are tied to religious observances. For example, Thailand celebrates *Songkran*, or the Water Festival, during the Buddhist New Year. People bathe statues of the Buddha and bless one another with a sprinkling of water. In January or February, Vietnam celebrates its New Year, called Tet. The celebration begins at the start of the lunar year and lasts three days.

Geography Skills for Life

Thailand's Monkey Feast Thais regard monkeys as symbols of good fortune. At a yearly festival in their honor, monkeys are provided with an abundance of food.
Region What kinds of celebrations do Southeast Asians enjoy?

SECTION 3 ASSESSMENT

Checking for Understanding

1. **Define** *wat*, batik, longhouse.

2. **Main Ideas** In a graphic organizer like the one below, list cultural groups that migrated to the region in one column and their contributions in the other.

Cultural Group	Cultural Contribution

Critical Thinking

3. **Making Generalizations** What cultural features reflect Southeast Asia's ethnic diversity?

4. **Problem Solving** How might a new art museum ensure that it reflects Southeast Asia's culture?

5. **Comparing and Contrasting** How might standards of living differ between rural and urban Southeast Asia?

Analyzing Maps

6. **Location** Look at the map of Southeast Asia's religions on page 749. In which country is Christianity the predominant religion?

Applying Geography

7. **Diversity** Trace the spread of foreign influences in Southeast Asia. How have these influences shaped Southeast Asian life and culture?

Answer
those tied to religious observances

More About the Photo The monkeys live in the ruins of the Buddhist temple in the background. In 1989 a local hotelier began providing a yearly 10-course meal for the monkeys, who symbolize good fortune.

Reteach

Have students answer the questions in "Read to Find Out" on page 748. Use their responses as a basis for discussion of points that seem to need reinforcement or clarification.

Enrich

Tell students that flora and fauna of Malaysia are protected in the Kuala Selangor Nature Park. Have groups of students plan a nature park to protect their regional ecosystem.

4 CLOSE

Have students reread "A Geographic View" about Thailand on page 748. Tell them to select another Southeast Asian country and write a paragraph about the culture and lifestyles found there. Suggest that they use the feature on page 748 as a model.

SECTION 3 ASSESSMENT ANSWERS

1. All vocabulary terms are defined in the text.

2. Answers should include at least three groups and at least one contribution made by each.

3. diverse languages, multiple ethnic groups, several religions, and arts and celebrations

4. Possible answer: develop a list of the diverse groups that need to be represented; organize revolving exhibits to represent various groups.

5. Urban areas: tremendous population growth and economic change, variety of residential areas based on social/economic status, overcrowding; rural areas: maintain traditional ways; less use of running water or electricity.

6. the Philippines

7. **Applying Geography** Hindu and Muslim traders, Chinese contacts, and Western colonization brought diversity to Southeast Asia.

MAP & GRAPH SkillBuilder

Teaching the Skill

Have students compare the cartogram on this page with the political map on page 711 and note the differences. *(In the cartogram, countries appear as rectangular shapes and relative sizes of countries differ.)* Explain that in the cartogram on this page, country size is not based on land area. It represents some other value. Then, have students read the SkillBuilder and answer the questions in "Practicing the Skill." Use the answers as a basis for a class discussion of cartograms.

Additional Practice

L1

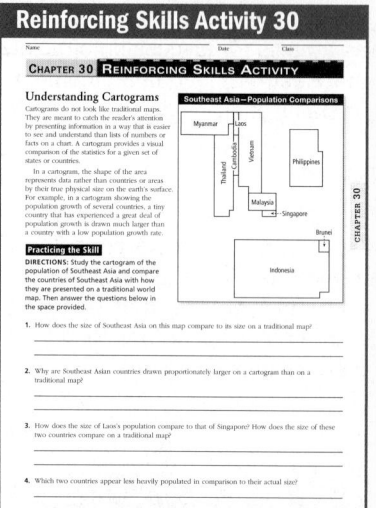

Reinforcing Skills Activity 30

Name Date Class

CHAPTER 30 REINFORCING SKILLS ACTIVITY

Understanding Cartograms

Cartograms do not look like traditional maps. They are meant to catch the reader's attention by presenting information in a way that is easier to see and understand than lists of numbers or facts on a chart. A cartogram provides a visual comparison of the statistics for a given set of states or countries.

In a cartogram, the shape of the area represents data rather than countries or areas by their true physical size on the earth's surface. For example, in a cartogram showing the population growth of several countries, a tiny country that has experienced a great deal of population growth is drawn much larger than a country with a low population growth rate.

Southeast Asia—Population Comparisons
Myanmar
Laos
Thailand
Cambodia
Vietnam
Philippines
Malaysia
Singapore
Brunei
Indonesia

CHAPTER 30

Practicing the Skill

DIRECTIONS: Study the cartogram of the population of Southeast Asia and compare the countries of Southeast Asia with how they are presented on a traditional world map. Then answer the questions below in the space provided.

1. How does the size of Southeast Asia on this map compare to its size on a traditional map?
2. Why are Southeast Asian countries drawn proportionately larger on a cartogram than on a traditional map?
3. How does the size of Laos's population compare to that of Singapore? How does the size of these two countries compare on a traditional map?
4. Which two countries appear less heavily populated in comparison to their actual size?

GLENCOE TECHNOLOGY

Glencoe Skillbuilder Interactive Workbook, Level 2

This interactive CD-ROM reinforces student mastery of essential social studies skills.

MAP & GRAPH SkillBuilder

Understanding Cartograms

On most maps, land areas are drawn in proportion to their actual surface areas on the earth. A cartogram is a map in which size is based on some characteristic other than land area, such as population or economic factors.

Learning the Skill

A cartogram provides clear visual comparisons of the characteristic it measures. To read a cartogram, apply the following steps:

- **Read the map title and key to identify the kind of information presented in the cartogram.**
- **Look for relationships among the countries.** Determine which countries are largest and smallest.
- **Compare the cartogram with a standard land-area map.** Determine the degree of distortion of particular countries.
- **Study these relationships and comparisons.** Identify the most important information presented in the cartogram.

Southeast Asia: Population Cartogram

VIETNAM
80,800,000
MYANMAR
49,500,000
LAOS
5,600,000
THAILAND
63,100,000
PHILIPPINES
81,600,000
CAMBODIA
12,600,000
SINGAPORE
4,200,000
BRUNEI
400,000
MALAYSIA
25,100,000
INDONESIA
220,500,000
EAST TIMOR
800,000
POPULATION GROWTH RATE
(excluding effects of migration)
2–2.9%
1–1.9%
Each square represents one million people.
2003 data

Practicing the Skill

Use the cartogram on this page to answer the following questions.

1. What data determine the relative sizes of countries on this cartogram?
2. What characteristics determine the color of the squares on this cartogram?
3. Compare the cartogram with the standard land-area map on page 721. How has the relative size of Singapore been changed on the cartogram? How would you explain this change?
4. From the information in this cartogram, would you expect Laos to have more squares than Vietnam in a cartogram based on 2010 data? Explain.
5. Suppose you want to compare the population densities of two countries in this region. Can this cartogram help you make this comparison? Explain.

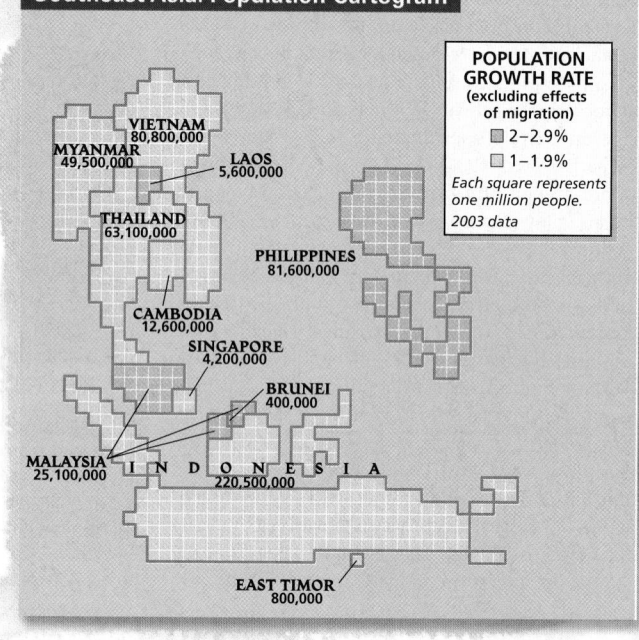

Applying the Skill

Research the gross domestic product (GDP) of each country in Southeast Asia. Then create a cartogram that compares the GDP of these countries. Include a key for the symbols you use.

Go To The **Glencoe Skillbuilder Interactive Workbook, Level 2** provides instruction and practice in key social studies skills.

ANSWERS TO PRACTICING THE SKILL

Possible answers appear below.

1. population
2. population growth rates
3. Singapore is larger on the cartogram because of its high population.
4. No; even with a higher growth rate, the population of Laos is so much smaller than that of Vietnam that the one percent difference in growth rate would not result in the population of Laos surpassing that of Vietnam over an 11-year period.
5. No; population density is related to the number of people in a known area, such as so many people per square mile (sq. km). The cartogram, alone, does not provide information on land area.

CHAPTER 30

SUMMARY & STUDY GUIDE

SECTION 1 — Population Patterns (pp. 735–739)

Terms to Know
- urbanization
- primate city

Key Points
- Southeast Asia has a diversity of ethnic and cultural groups.
- Most Southeast Asians live either in river valley lowlands or on coastal plains.
- Southeast Asian cities are growing rapidly as a result of migration from rural to urban areas.
- Since the 1970s, large numbers of Southeast Asians have migrated to escape political oppression and economic distress.

Organizing Your Notes
Use a web like the one below to help you organize the notes you took as you read this section. Fill in information about the population patterns of Southeast Asia.

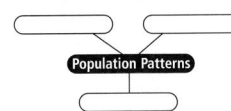

Population Patterns

SECTION 2 — History and Government (pp. 740–745)

Terms to Know
- maritime
- sphere of influence
- buffer state

Key Points
- Southeast Asia's early empires and kingdoms controlled shipping and trade that linked East Asia, South Asia, and Southwest Asia.
- European countries colonized all of Southeast Asia except Thailand (Siam). All of the region's countries are now independent.
- During the late 1900s, political conflict between communist and noncommunist forces divided much of Southeast Asia.

Organizing Your Notes
Use a cause-effect chart like the one below to help you organize the information you read in this section.

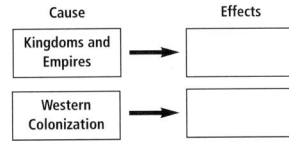

Cause → Effects

Kingdoms and Empires →

Western Colonization →

SECTION 3 — Cultures and Lifestyles (pp. 748–753)

Terms to Know
- *wat*
- batik
- longhouse

Key Points
- Southeast Asian culture reflects the ways of life of peoples who migrated from other regions as well as those of indigenous peoples.
- Buddhism, Hinduism, and Islam greatly influenced Southeast Asian art, architecture, drama, and celebrations.
- In spite of rapid population growth, Southeast Asia's economic development has led to many improvements in the region's quality of life.

Organizing Your Notes
Use an outline like the one below to help you organize information in this section about cultures and lifestyles.

I. Cultural Diversity
  A. Languages
    1. Hundreds of languages
    2.

Chapter 30 ⊕ 755

Using the Chapter 30 Summary & Study Guide

Use the Chapter 30 Summary & Study Guide to preview, review, condense, or reteach the chapter.

Preview/Review

🔘 **Vocabulary PuzzleMaker CD-ROM** reinforces "Terms to Know."

🔘 **Interactive Tutor Self-Assessment CD-ROM** provides a review of Chapter 30 content.

Condense

Have students read the Chapter 30 Summary & Study Guide.

🔘 Chapter 30 Audio Program

📁 Chapter 30 Guided Reading Activities

Reteach

📁 Chapter 30 Reteaching Activities (Spanish also available)

📁 Chapter 30 Reading Essentials and Study Guides

GLENCOE TECHNOLOGY

☐ NATIONAL GEOGRAPHIC

WORLD REGIONS VIDEO PROGRAM

Unit 10, Southeast Asia
The following segments enhance the study of this unit:
- **Rice**
- **Tet in Hanoi**
- **Design for the Future**

CHAPTER CULMINATING ACTIVITY

Future Flashback Diary **Ask: How have the demands of the modern world affected the cultural geography of Southeast Asia?** Have students review the text, photos, and maps in Chapter 30 to answer the question. Then, have students create diary excerpts in the role of a person who has returned to the region after living abroad for several years. Diary entries may include reminiscences about the past and predictions concerning lifestyle changes over the next 10 years. 🔲 **EE4 Human Systems: Standards 9, 10**

NOTE: This activity may be completed separately, or you may wish students to incorporate it into their GeoJournals.

GEOGRAPHY Online

Have students visit the Web site at geography.glencoe.com to review Chapter 30 and take the **Self-Check Quiz.**

GLENCOE TECHNOLOGY

Use *MindJogger Videoquiz* to review the Chapter 30 content.

Reviewing Key Terms

1. primate city
2. longhouse
3. spheres of influence
4. maritime
5. *wats*
6. buffer state

Reviewing Facts

SECTION 1

1. ready water supply, fertile land, adequate transportation, and job availability

2. rapid urbanization and increasing urban population with a decreasing rural population

SECTION 2

3. Maritime empires controlled shipping and trade on key waterways. Land-based empires acquired power and wealth from farming on fertile soil.

4. Colonization brought cultural diversity, modern transportation systems, improved harbors, expanded mining and oil drilling, development of large plantations, and migrant workers.

SECTION 3

5. Chinese, Indian, and European literature, art, and architecture; Indian epics; and western styles of life

6. Answers may include increased per capita income,

Reviewing Key Terms

Write the key term that best completes each of the following sentences. Refer to the Terms to Know in the Summary & Study Guide on page 755.

1. Kuala Lumpur is Malaysia's _____.

2. A(n) _____ often houses a large, extended family.

3. Western countries set up _____ in Southeast Asia.

4. Southeast Asian _____, or seafaring, empires controlled shipping and trade.

5. Southeast Asian architecture includes _____, or temples inspired by India.

6. A neutral territory called a(n) _____ can prevent conflict between rival powers.

Reviewing Facts

SECTION 1

1. What geographic factors influence where Southeast Asians live?

2. Describe the characteristics of the region's urban and rural populations.

SECTION 2

3. Why did the early Southeast Asian kingdoms prosper?

4. How did colonization by Western countries affect the region?

SECTION 3

5. What foreign influences can be seen in Southeast Asia's arts?

6. How has the quality of life in Southeast Asia improved?

Critical Thinking

1. Making Generalizations Why are small farms unable to compete with plantations?

---

2. Problem Solving Identify Southeast Asia's greatest challenge, and propose a solution.

3. Identifying Cause and Effect Complete a flowchart like the one below to show the history of Southeast Asia from colonization to independence.

| Europeans arrive | → | | → | |

Using the Regional Atlas

Refer to the Regional Atlas on pages 710–713.

1. Region What areas of Southeast Asia are the most densely populated?

2. Location What Southeast Asian cities have populations of more than 2 million? What geographic factors do most of these cities have in common?

NATIONAL GEOGRAPHIC Locating Places
Southeast Asia: Physical-Political Geography

Match the letters on the map with the places and physical features of Southeast Asia. Write your answers on a sheet of paper.

1. Cambodia	5. Gulf of Thailand	9. Indian Ocean
2. Bangkok	6. Manila	10. South China Sea
3. Hanoi	7. Sumatra	
4. Strait of Malacca	8. Kuala Lumpur	

---

life expectancy, infant survival rates, and higher literacy rates.

Critical Thinking

1. Small farms cannot grow large quantities for sale, and they lack the resources of plantations.

2. Students may say competing in a global economy, settling regional conflicts, or urbanization. Accept reasonable solutions.

3. Check flowcharts for accuracy.

NATIONAL GEOGRAPHIC Locating Places

1. F	**3.** I	**5.** G	**7.** J	**9.** E
2. C	**4.** B	**6.** H	**8.** D	**10.** A

Using the Regional Atlas

1. Yangon, Hanoi, Bangkok, Ho Chi Minh City, Singapore, Jakarta, Bandung, Surabaya, Manila, Quezon City

2. locations on major waterways or ports

Thinking Like a Geographer

Use your textbook, library sources, and the Internet to answer the following questions about Southeast Asia: What geographic factors might have drawn foreigners to the region? How might foreign influences have shaped forms of government in the region?

Problem-Solving Activity

Contemporary Issues Case Study *Push factors*, such as unemployment or famine, are the unsatisfactory features of a place that cause people to emigrate. *Pull factors*, such as fertile soil or better job opportunities, are a place's attractive features that draw migrants from other areas. Research Southeast Asia's national and international migration patterns, and write a report explaining how push, pull, or both push-and-pull factors shape Southeast Asian migration today.

GeoJournal

Descriptive Writing Using the details you logged in your GeoJournal as you read this chapter, write a letter to a friend or relative about one cultural element in the region. Imagine that you are visiting the region and you want your friend or relative to have a vivid picture of the places you describe. Include word pictures that appeal to as many of the five senses as possible. Explain how this cultural element differs from that found in different parts of the United States.

Technology Activity

Developing Multimedia Presentations Use the Internet or the library to conduct research about one typical example of Southeast Asian religious architecture. Create a multimedia presentation about your temple or *wat* that uses narration, music, and images. Be sure to cite all the sources that you used to prepare your presentation, including print and Internet sources for text and photographs.

Standardized Test Practice

Choose the best answer for each of the following multiple-choice questions. If you have trouble answering the questions, use the process of elimination to narrow your choices.

1. **Which countries' cultures most influenced Southeast Asia's religions?**

   A Japan and Korea

   B China and the United States

   C India and China

   D Arabia and India

Test-Taking Tip Think about what major religions are practiced in Southeast Asia. The answer that includes the cultures where those religions originated probably is the correct answer.

2. **Which of the following is a reason why Southeast Asia is a region of highly diverse cultures?**

   F High population density in many areas causes a variety of traditions.

   G Similar physical geography encouraged peoples to create their own traditions.

   H Trade and colonization from many regions spread new ideas.

   J Lack of contact with the outside world enabled many local cultures to develop.

Test-Taking Tip First determine what choices you can eliminate. Since Southeast Asia has a diverse physical geography and many outside contacts, choices G and J do not apply and can be eliminated. Choose the best answer from the remaining options.

GeoJournal

Students' descriptive words should appropriately reflect the culture and region of the chosen place.

Technology Activity

Students should select the appropriate media for an effective presentation of the topic.

Standardized Test Practice

1. C
2. H

Tested Objectives:
drawing conclusions
making inferences

Additional Practice and Test-Taking Tips

 Standardized Test Practice Workbook

❓ CHAPTER BONUS TEST QUESTION

What cultural impact did the different peoples migrating to or colonizing Southeast Asia have on the region? *(Southeast Asia has been greatly influenced by people from China, India, and the West. The Chinese brought much of their own culture including business skills and styles of dress. The Indians brought their culture and religion. Westerners brought culture, religion, and forms of education and government.)*

Thinking Like a Geographer

Students should focus on Southeast Asia's position as a crossroads of trade and its abundant natural resources. Students might look at concepts of Hindu-Buddhist kingship, Chinese political and social influences, Western concepts of democracy and republicanism, and Communist structures of government.

Problem-Solving Activity

Students should deal with both push and pull factors in either a regional or international setting. Students might focus on urban-rural differences and the impact of war and political upheavals. Check reports for standard grammar, spelling, sentence structure, and punctuation.

PLANNING GUIDE

NOTE: The following materials may be used when teaching Chapter 31. Section-level support materials are shown at point-of-use in the margins of the Teacher Wraparound Edition.

TEACHING TRANSPARENCIES

L2 Unit 10 Map Overlay Transparencies

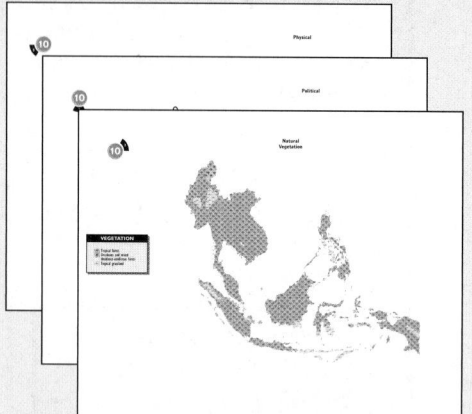

L2 Political Map Transparency 10

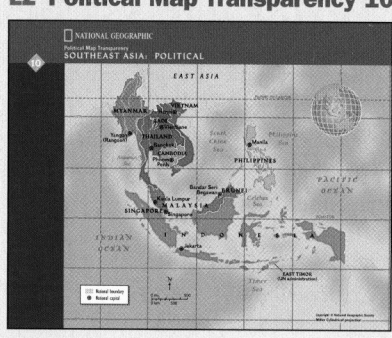

GEOGRAPHIC LITERACY

Focus on Geography Literacy

APPLICATION AND ENRICHMENT

L3 Enrichment Activity 31

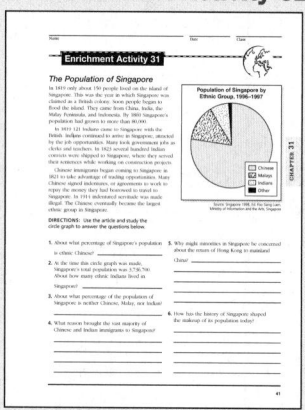

REVIEW AND REINFORCEMENT

L1 Vocabulary Activity 31 L1 Reinforcing Skills Activity 31 L1 Reteaching Activity 31

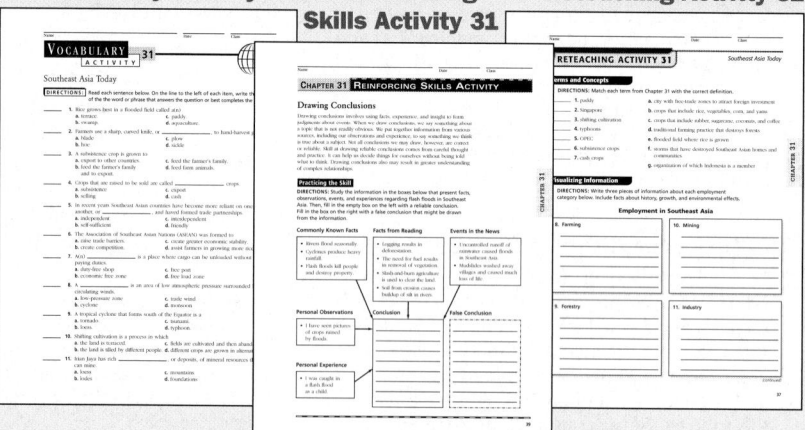

ASSESSMENT

L2 Chapter 31 Test Form A

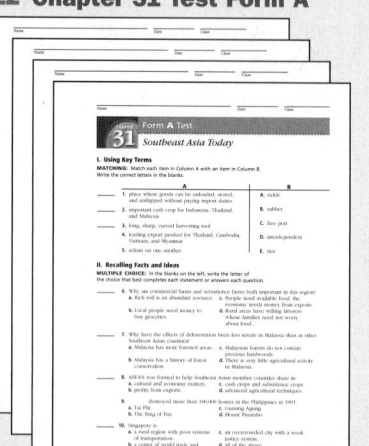

L2 Chapter 31 Test Form B

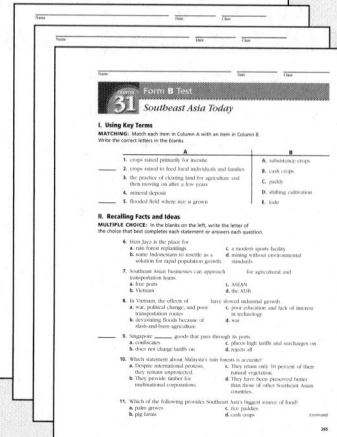

L1/ELL Performance Assessment Activity 31

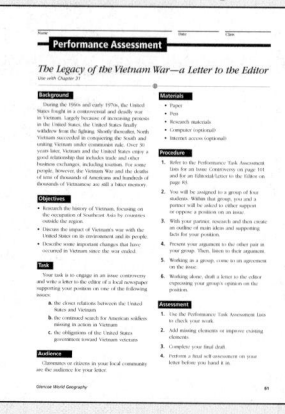

ExamView® Pro Testmaker

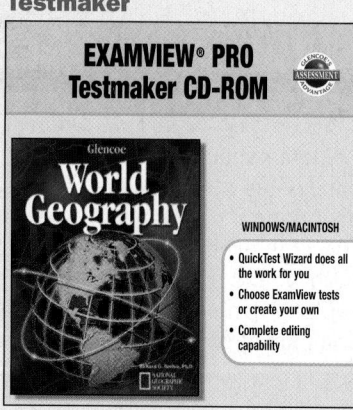

EXAMVIEW® PRO Testmaker CD-ROM

Glencoe
World Geography

WINDOWS/MACINTOSH

- QuickTest Wizard does all the work for you
- Choose ExamView tests or create your own
- Complete editing capability

SPANISH RESOURCES

The following Spanish language materials are available in the Spanish Resources binder:

- 📁 Spanish Vocabulary Activities
- 📁 Spanish Guided Reading Activities
- 📁 Spanish Reteaching Activities
- 📁 Spanish Summaries
- 📁 Spanish Quizzes and Tests
- 📁 Spanish Reading Essentials and Study Guide

MULTIMEDIA

- World Regions Video
- MindJogger Videoquiz
- Vocabulary PuzzleMaker CD-ROM
- Interactive Tutor Self-Assessment CD-ROM
- ExamView® Pro Testmaker CD-ROM
- Audio Program
- TeacherWorks CD-ROM
- Interactive Student Edition CD-ROM
- Glencoe Skillbuilder Interactive Workbook CD-ROM, Level 2
- Presentation Plus! CD-ROM

Timesaving Tools

TeacherWorks™ All-In-One Planner and Resource Center

- **Interactive Teacher Edition** Access your Teacher Wraparound Edition and your classroom resources with a few easy clicks.
- **Interactive Lesson Planner** Planning has never been easier! Organize your week, month, semester, or year with all the lesson helps you need to make teaching creative, timely, and relevant.

Use Glencoe's **Presentation Plus!** multimedia teacher tool to easily present dynamic lessons that visually excite your students. Using Microsoft PowerPoint® you can customize the presentations to create your own personalized lessons.

PRESENTATION Plus!

GEOGRAPHY Online

Use our Web site for additional resources. All essential content is covered in the Student Edition.

You and your students can visit geography.glencoe.com, the Web site companion to *Glencoe World Geography*. This innovative integration of electronic and print media offers your students a wealth of opportunities. The student text directs students to the Web site for the following options:

- **Chapter Overviews**
- **Student Activities**
- **Self-Check Quizzes**
- **Textbook Updates**

Answers are provided for you in the "Web Activity Lesson Plan." Additional Web resources and Interactive Tutor puzzles are also available.

▶ Additional Glencoe Teacher Support

- Teaching Strategies for the Geography Classroom (including Block Scheduling Pacing Guides)
- Graphic Organizer Transparencies Strategies and Activities
- Outline Map Resource Book
- Reading in the Content Area

SECTION RESOURCES

Daily Objectives	Reproducible Resources	Multimedia Resources

SECTION 1 Living in Southeast Asia

1. Explain why rice farming is the most important agricultural activity in Southeast Asia.
2. Examine why the countries of the region are industrializing at different rates.
3. Discuss how the economies of Southeast Asia are becoming more interdependent.

Reproducible Resources
- Reproducible Lesson Plan 31-1
- Daily Lecture Notes 31-1
- Guided Reading Activity 31-1*
- Reading Essentials and Study Guide 31-1*
- Section Quiz 31-1*

Multimedia Resources
- Daily Focus Skills Transparency 31-1
- Political Map Transparency 10
- Unit 10 Map Overlay Transparencies
- Interactive Tutor Self-Assessment CD-ROM
- ExamView® Pro Testmaker CD-ROM*
- Presentation Plus! CD-ROM

SECTION 2 People and Their Environment

1. Identify dangers posed by volcanoes, floods, and typhoons in Southeast Asia.
2. Describe how economic progress has increased environmental pollution in the region.
3. Discuss the efforts underway to protect the environment in Southeast Asia.

Reproducible Resources
- Reproducible Lesson Plan 31-2
- Vocabulary Activity 31*
- Daily Lecture Notes 31-2
- Guided Reading Activity 31-2*
- Reading Essentials and Study Guide 31-2*
- Reteaching Activity 31*
- Reinforcing Skills Activity 31
- Section Quiz 31-2*

Multimedia Resources
- Daily Focus Skills Transparency 31-2
- Political Map Transparency 10
- Unit 10 Map Overlay Transparencies
- Vocabulary PuzzleMaker CD-ROM
- Interactive Tutor Self-Assessment CD-ROM
- ExamView® Pro Testmaker CD-ROM*
- Presentation Plus! CD-ROM

| Blackline Master | Software | Videocassette | *Also available in Spanish |
| Transparency | CD-ROM | DVD | |

OUT OF TIME? 🗂 Assign the Chapter 31 **Reading Essentials and Study Guide.**

Block Schedule

Activities that are particularly suited to use within the block scheduling framework are identified throughout this chapter by the following designation: 🧊

KEY TO ABILITY LEVELS

Teaching strategies have been coded for various learning styles and abilities.

L1 **BASIC** activities for all students

L2 **AVERAGE** activities for average to above-average students

L3 **CHALLENGING** activities for above-average students

ELL **ENGLISH LANGUAGE LEARNER** activities

Teacher to Teacher

Dora Bradley
North Little Rock
School District
North Little Rock, AR

Population Pyramids

Creating and analyzing population pyramids is an effective way for students to analyze a country's demographics.

Students can build a population pyramid about Southeast Asia by using the data provided in the country profiles on pages 714–715.

Have students research the Internet for more detailed information, such as age groups and gender, to draw conclusions and make predictions. They might analyze the data to determine what challenges the countries in the region may face in the future. If, for example, a country has a large group of 1- to 15-year-olds, it can be inferred that the country needs to create more jobs, address food and housing issues, and prepare to educate proportionately more children. Population pyramids also can be used to correlate demographic changes to the country's history. For example, a decreasing number of males in the population might be explained by a recent devastating war.

NATIONAL GEOGRAPHIC   TEACHER'S CORNER

Index to National Geographic Magazine:

The following articles may be used for research relating to this chapter:

- "Wild Gliders: The Creatures of Borneo's Rain Forest Go Airborne," by Tim Laman, October 2000.
- "Tam Dao—Vietnam's Sanctuary Under Siege," by Michael J. McRae, June 1999.
- *Biodiversity*, a National Geographic Special Edition, February 1999.

National Geographic Society Products:

To order the following products for use with this chapter, call National Geographic Society at 1-800-368-2728.

- *GeoKit: Pollution* (Kit)
- *Asia* (Video)
- *Healing the Earth* (Video)
- *Natural Disasters* (Video)
- *National Geographic Atlas of the World, Seventh Edition* (Book)

NGS ONLINE

Access National Geographic's Web site for current events, activities, links, interactive features, and archives.
www.nationalgeographic.com

Meeting National Standards

Geography For Life

The following standards are highlighted in Chapter 31:

Section 1 EE1 The World in Spatial Terms: Standard 3
EE2 Places and Regions: Standard 4
EE3 Physical Systems: Standard 8
EE4 Human Systems: Standard 11

Section 2 EE3 Physical Systems: Standard 8
EE4 Human Systems: Standard 10, 11, 13
EE5 Environment and Society: Standards 14, 15
EE6 The Uses of Geography: Standard 18

Local Objectives

_____

_____

In addition to the Differentiated Instruction strategies found in each section, the following resources are also suitable for your special needs students:

- ***ExamView® Pro Testmaker CD-ROM*** allows teachers to tailor tests by reducing answer choices.
- The ***Audio Program*** includes the entire narrative of the student edition so that less-proficient readers can listen to the words as they read them.
- The ***Reading Essentials and Study Guide*** provides the same content as the student edition but is written two grade levels below the textbook.
- ***Guided Reading Activities*** give less-proficient readers point-by-point instructions to increase comprehension as they read each textbook section.
- ***Enrichment Activities*** include a stimulating collection of readings and activities for gifted and talented students.

Chapter Objectives

1. Describe traditional and modern economic activities in Southeast Asia.

2. Explain the kinds of human-environmental interactions that occur in Southeast Asia, and the challenges that the region faces.

GLENCOE TECHNOLOGY

Use *MindJogger Videoquiz* to preview the Chapter 31 content.

GeoJournal

For access to additional photos, maps, and information on the contemporary issues of Southeast Asia, go to www.nationalgeographic.com (See Teacher pages in front for strategies for using journals in the geography classroom.)

GEOGRAPHY Online

Introduce students to chapter content and key terms by having them access **Chapter Overview 31** at geography.glencoe.com

FOLDABLES™
Study Organizer

Dinah Zike's Foldables are three-dimensional, interactive graphic organizers that help students practice basic writing skills, review key vocabulary terms, and identify main ideas. Have students complete the Foldable activity in the **Dinah Zike's Reading and Study Skills Foldables** booklet.

CHAPTER 31 Southeast Asia Today

GeoJournal

As you read this chapter, use your journal to log information about the economies and the environmental challenges in Southeast Asia. Note interesting details that show similarities and differences among the region's countries.

GEOGRAPHY Online

Chapter Overview Visit the **Glencoe World Geography** Web site at geography.glencoe.com and click on Chapter Overviews—Chapter 31 to preview information about the region today.

ABOUT THE PHOTO

Visual Instruction In Kuala Lumpur, Malaysia, a gleaming new building towers over the domes and clock tower of the century-old Sultan Abdul Samad Building, once a center of British colonial rule and now a Malaysian government office. Founded as a small settlement by Chinese tin miners in 1857, Kuala Lumpur today is one of Southeast Asia's major manufacturing and commercial centers, with a population of more than one million. **Ask: What can you tell about the climate of Kuala Lumpur from the vegetation in this photo? About the architecture?** *(Palm trees suggest a tropical climate; onion-shaped domes, Islamic influence; clock tower, European influence.)* ◉ EE2 Places and Regions: Standard 4

Guide to Reading

Consider What You Know

Southeast Asia is a region of peninsulas and islands. How do you think people living in such areas earn their incomes?

Reading Strategy

Organizing Complete a graphic organizer similar to the one below by filling in the reasons why Singapore has Southeast Asia's most developed economy.

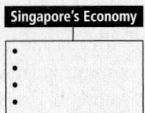

Singapore's Economy
- •
- •
- •
- •

Read to Find Out

- Why is rice farming the most important agricultural activity in Southeast Asia?
- Why are the countries in the region industrializing at different rates?
- How are the economies of Southeast Asia becoming more interdependent?

Terms to Know

- paddy
- sickle
- subsistence crop
- cash crop
- lode
- interdependent
- Association of Southeast Asian Nations (ASEAN)
- free port

Places to Locate

- Brunei
- Manila

◀ *Buildings at night in Kuala Lumpur, Malaysia*

Living in Southeast Asia

 NATIONAL GEOGRAPHIC

A Geographic View

Open-Air Market

. . . I visited the . . . colorful open-air market in Kota Baharu, way up north near [Malaysia's] border with Thailand. The merchants were nearly all women. Wearing full-length batik sarongs of bright red, orange, pink, and purple, with coordinated scarves of emerald green or royal blue around their heads, they sat beside huge piles of fruit and vegetables, truckloads of fish and chicken, mountains of rice, and tall wicker baskets filled with eggs—turtle eggs, stork eggs, even chicken eggs.

—T. R. Reid, "Malaysia: Rising Star," National Geographic, *August 1997*

Market in Malaysia

This market scene takes place in Malaysia, one of Southeast Asia's most rapidly developing countries. Like some other countries in the region, Malaysia is setting up new industries, yet it continues to rely on agriculture for its economic well-being. In this section you will learn about how people live and work in Southeast Asia today. You will also see how the region's countries face many of the same challenges and have come to depend on one another for increased economic growth.

Agriculture

Southeast Asia's fertile river valleys and plains are a major source of livelihood for its people. Southeast Asians depend on the rich variety of crops grown in these areas to supply their own food needs as well

Section Overview

This section discusses the agricultural and industrial aspects of Southeast Asian economies and the region's growing role in the global market.

BELLRINGER
Skillbuilder Activity

 Project transparency and have students answer questions.

▭ Available as blackline master.

Daily Focus Skills Transparency 31-1

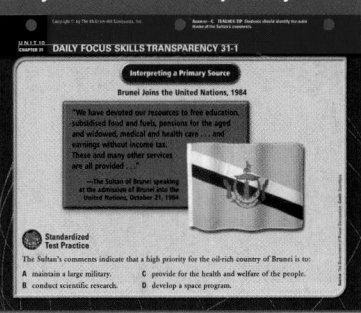

Guide to Reading

Consider What You Know
Answer *fishing, shipping, farming*

Reading Strategy
Answers *major port and manufacturing center due to location and harbors; free trade zones attracted foreign investment; focus on developing communications, information, and financial services; moved away from labor-intensive industries; government made strong commitment to education*

Preteaching Vocabulary
Direct students' attention to the definitions of *subsistence crop* and *cash crop* (page 760). Have them use the information to contrast lifestyles in the United States and Southeast Asia. (*Today little, if any, subsistence farming exists in the U.S.*)

RESOURCE MANAGER

▭ Reproducible Masters
- Reproducible Lesson Plan 31-1
- Daily Lecture Notes 31-1
- Guided Reading Activity 31-1
- Reading Essentials and Study Guide 31-1
- Section Quiz 31-1

Transparencies
- Daily Focus Skills Transparency 31-1
- Political Map Transparency 10
- Unit 10 Map Overlay Transparencies

Multimedia
- ◉ Interactive Tutor Self-Assessment CD-ROM
- ◉ ExamView® Pro Testmaker CD-ROM
- ◉ Presentation Plus! CD-ROM

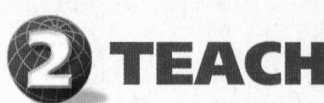

2 TEACH

L1 Supporting Details

Have students suggest reasons why rice is the most important agricultural product in Southeast Asia. Tell them to use their texts to find supporting details for their conclusions.

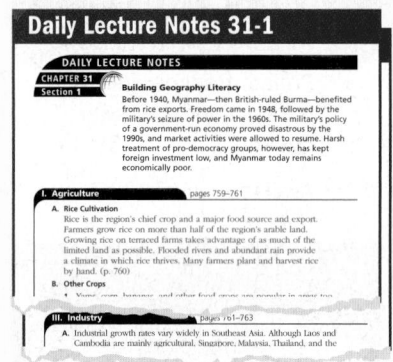

Daily Lecture Notes 31-1

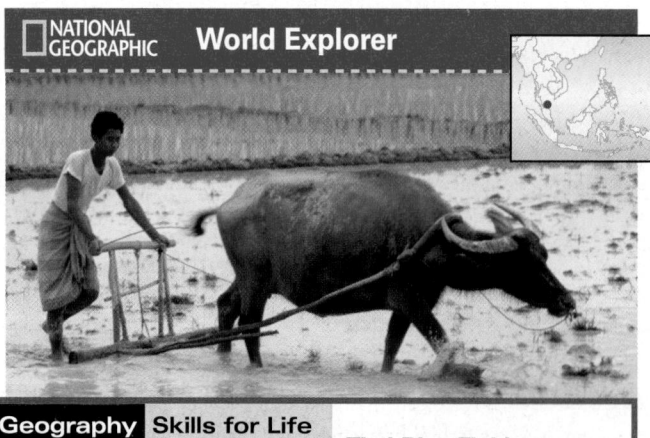

DAILY LECTURE NOTES
CHAPTER 31
Section 1

Building Geography Literacy
Before 1940, Myanmar—then British-ruled Burma—benefited from rice exports. Freedom came in 1948, followed by the military's seizure of power in the 1960s. The military's policy of a government-run economy proved disastrous by the 1990s, and market activities were allowed to resume. Harsh treatment of pro-democracy groups, however, has kept foreign investment low, and Myanmar today remains economically poor.

I. Agriculture pages 759–761

A. **Rice Cultivation**
Rice is the region's chief crop and a major food source and export. Farmers grow rice on more than half of the region's arable land. Growing rice on terraced farms takes advantage of as much of the limited land as possible. Flooded rivers and abundant rain provide a climate in which rice thrives. Many farmers plant and harvest rice by hand. (p. 760)

B. **Other Crops**

III. Industry pages 761–763

A. Industrial growth rates vary widely in Southeast Asia. Although Laos and Cambodia are mainly agricultural, Singapore, Malaysia, Thailand, and the

NATIONAL GEOGRAPHIC World Explorer

Answer
fertile soil; abundant water supply; warm, wet climate

More About the Photo In Southeast Asia rice production is accomplished by manual labor, which is plentiful. Oxen and water buffalo sometimes are used.

as to sell for income. Although Southeast Asia is industrializing rapidly, most of its workforce is still involved in agriculture. More than two-thirds of all workers in Cambodia and Laos are farmers.

Rice Cultivation

For 2,000 years, the Ifugao people of the Philippines have worked in terraced fields that follow the contours of the mountains. They plant their fields with rice, the most important crop in Southeast Asia. Southeast Asian farmers use more than half of the region's farmable land to grow this crop. A major food source for the region, rice is also a leading export product of Thailand, Cambodia, Vietnam, and Myanmar. A journalist traveling in Southeast Asia describes Thailand's rice trade:

> *"Since most rice is eaten in the countries where it's grown, the amount in world trade is small, only about 4 percent. The biggest exporter is Thailand, with 4.5 million tons a year. . . . [A]t Bangkok . . . [m]illed rice arrives by truck from the north—I see 100-kilo bags stacked 27 high—to be . . . packed for shipment to the Middle East, Europe, Africa."*
>
> Peter T. White, "Rice, the Essential Harvest," *National Geographic*, May 1994

NATIONAL GEOGRAPHIC World Explorer

Geography Skills for Life

Thai Rice Field A farmer uses the simple technology of a water buffalo and a wooden plow to prepare his field for planting.

Region Why does rice grow well in the region?

Rice grows well in Southeast Asia because most of the region has fertile soil, an abundant water supply, and a warm, wet climate. Some kinds of rice plants need a continuous supply of water from the time they are planted until just before harvest. Flooded rivers and abundant rainfall provide this water to Southeast Asia. In parts of Thailand, Cambodia, and Vietnam, seasonal flooding of the Chao Phraya and Mekong Rivers irrigates **paddies**, or flooded fields in which rice is grown. Rain also provides enough water to grow rice in the Irrawaddy River delta in Myanmar and in parts of the Philippines.

Farmers plant rice at the start of the rainy season, usually in May, and the crop is ready to harvest in October. They can then grow a second rice crop during the dry season by irrigating rice fields with water stored from rains and flooding rivers. Rice farming can be difficult work because many farmers do not use modern machinery. They plant and harvest their crops by hand, using simple tools such as **sickles**—long, sharp, curved knives. Water buffalo or oxen are often used to pull plows.

Other Crops

Southeast Asian farmers grow cassava, yams, corn, bananas, and other food crops in areas too dry for a second planting of rice. Some Indonesian farmers have begun to grow cassava, an edible root, as an alternative subsistence crop because it is easier to grow than rice. A **subsistence crop** is a crop grown mainly to feed the farmer's family. Many families in Southeast Asia have small subsistence garden plots that produce a variety of vegetables, and some people also raise pigs and poultry for food.

Plantations in Southeast Asia's coastal lowlands provide many of the region's **cash crops**—crops raised to be sold for profit. Rubber is an important cash crop, and Thailand, Indonesia, and Malaysia lead the world in natural rubber production. Sugarcane grows in the Philippines and on the Indonesian island of

DIFFERENTIATED INSTRUCTION

English Learners Pair English language learners with proficient English speakers prior to classroom activities. Partners can compare class notes and discuss vocabulary, syntax, or cultural concepts in the text that may challenge English language learners. For vocabulary and syntax challenges, suggest that English language learners create bilingual glossaries and paraphrased or translated passages that will help them review material or complete activities. ELL

Refer to ***Inclusion for the Social Studies Classroom Strategies and Activities.***

Java. The Philippines is also one of the largest producers and exporters of coconuts. Other regional exports include coffee, palm oil, and spices.

Forests and Mines

Forestry, which includes jobs in logging, transporting logs, and manufacturing finished goods, is important to many Southeast Asian countries. It is a major industry in Vietnam, where factories produce plywood and lumber, pulp and paper, and furniture products. Myanmar leads the world in teakwood exports. Teakwood, ebony, mahogany, and bamboo, in the form of lumber and finished products, are vital to the economies of Malaysia, the Philippines, Indonesia, and Thailand. Although excessive logging has contributed to deforestation in the region, several Southeast Asian countries are working to make their economic goals compatible with environmental goals.

NATIONAL GEOGRAPHIC World Explorer

Geography | **Skills for Life**

Timber in Malaysia

Logging is a major economic activity in East Malaysia.

Place Which economies are dependent on lumber and finished products?

Mineral Wealth

Rich mineral deposits lie within Southeast Asia's numerous mountains. Workers in several countries drill and blast their way to deposits of tin, iron ore, manganese, and tungsten. Malaysia, Thailand, and Indonesia are three of the world's leading producers of tin. Iron ore is excavated in Malaysia and the Philippines. Manganese, used to strengthen steel, is mined in the Philippines and Indonesia. Tungsten, used for electrical materials and in steel alloys, is found in Myanmar and Thailand.

The economies of Southeast Asia also benefit from oil extraction. Malaysia is rich in petroleum and natural gas reserves. Crude oil, natural gas, and petroleum products account for 95 percent of the export income of **Brunei** (bru•NY). This small country also has one of the world's largest natural gas plants. Indonesia, the largest producer of petroleum in the region, is one of the top ten producers in the Organization of Petroleum Exporting Countries (OPEC). Economic development in the Indonesian-owned western part of New Guinea and on the Indonesian islands of Sumatra, Java, and Borneo has been spurred by the building of pipelines. These pipelines carry oil from drilling sites to the coasts for shipping.

Economics
Papua's Resources

Indonesia's government has set aside large areas of Papua for resource development. Located on the western half of New Guinea, Papua has timber resources and rich lodes, or deposits of minerals. Many international companies are logging in mangrove swamps in Papua and surveying for gold, natural gas, oil, and uranium elsewhere.

Although Papua is rich in minerals, many of its people are poor. Groups favoring independence claim that the Indonesian government has allowed foreigners to extract resources but has invested little in improving health, education, and public services.

Industry

Industry is growing rapidly in Southeast Asia. In many places, workers are leaving farms to work

L2 Interpretation
Have students compare trade in ancient and modern Southeast Asia. Ask them to develop a hypothesis to explain any differences/similarities in the region's global trading position then and now. (*Students should focus on valuable natural resources and the region's crossroads location.*)

NATIONAL GEOGRAPHIC World Explorer

Answer
Myanmar

More About the Photo
Tropical hardwoods, such as mahogany and teak, are among Malaysia's most important natural resources. Malaysia is a leading exporter of this valuable timber used in building construction and furniture manufacturing.

L1/ELL

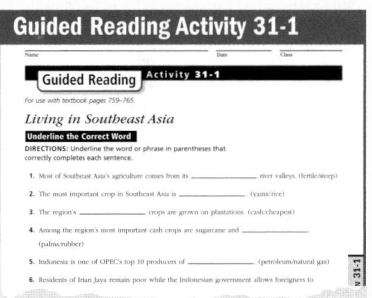

Guided Reading Activity 31-1

Guided Reading Activity 31-1

For use with textbook pages 759–765.

Living in Southeast Asia

Underline the Correct Word

DIRECTIONS: Underline the word or phrase in parentheses that correctly completes each sentence.

1. Most of Southeast Asia's agriculture comes from _____ river valleys. (fertile/steep)

2. The most important crop in Southeast Asia is _____. (yams/rice)

3. The region's _____ crops are grown on plantations. (cash/cheapest)

4. Among the region's most important cash crops are sugarcane and _____. (palms/rubber)

5. Indonesia is one of OPEC's top 10 producers of _____. (petroleum/natural gas)

6. Residents of Irian Jaya remain poor while the Indonesian government allows foreigners to

The Philippines exports chemicals, machinery, and petroleum to its main trading partners, the United States and Japan.

COOPERATIVE LEARNING ACTIVITY

Creating Posters Have students form small groups. Assign each group one of the following topics about Southeast Asia: *Forestry and Mining, Agriculture,* or *Transportation and Communications.* Members should work together to design and create a poster that shows important information about their topic. Tell them to include a title, photographs, drawings, and appropriate charts, maps, or graphs. Display finished posters and have the class discuss the interrelations between economic activities and transportation and communications.

🧊 📖 **EE2 Places and Regions: Standard 4;** 📖 **EE3 Physical Systems: Standard 8**

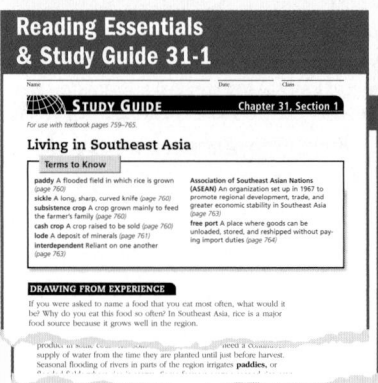

NATIONAL GEOGRAPHIC World Explorer

Answer
timber, rich lodes, potentially gold, oil, natural gas, and uranium

More About the Photo Most of the people of Papua are involved in farming. Chief products include cocoa, rice, and vegetables.

☐ **NATIONAL GEOGRAPHIC GEOFACT**

▶ **It is estimated that the Indonesian province of Papua has the largest single gold reserve in the world—an estimated 40 million ounces—and copper deposits of 28 billion pounds.**

L1/ELL

Reading Essentials & Study Guide 31-1

Name _____ Date _____ Class _____

🌐 **STUDY GUIDE**   Chapter 31, Section 1

For use with textbook pages 759–765.

Living in Southeast Asia

Terms to Know

paddy A flooded field in which rice is grown *(page 760)*
sickle A long, sharp, curved knife *(page 760)*
subsistence crop A crop grown mainly to feed the farmer's family *(page 760)*
cash crop A crop raised to be sold *(page 760)*
lode A deposit of minerals *(page 761)*
interdependent Reliant on one another *(page 763)*

Association of Southeast Asian Nations (ASEAN) An organization set up in 1967 to promote regional development, trade, and greater economic stability in Southeast Asia *(page 763)*

free port A place where goods can be unloaded, stored, and reshipped without paying import duties *(page 764)*

DRAWING FROM EXPERIENCE

If you were asked to name a food that you eat most often, what would it be? Why do you eat this food so often? In Southeast Asia, rice is a major food source because it grows well in the region.

produce in some countries. Farmers need a continuous supply of water from the time they are planted until just before harvest. Seasonal flooding of rivers in parts of the region irrigates **paddies**, or

NATIONAL GEOGRAPHIC World Explorer

Geography Skills for Life

Terraced Farming In hilly areas such as in Papua, terracing makes steep and rugged land suitable for agriculture.

Human-Environment Interaction In addition to farmland, what other resources are found in Papua?

in urban manufacturing and service industries. Still, the industrial growth rate varies widely throughout the region. While Laos and Cambodia are mainly agricultural, Singapore, Malaysia, Thailand, and the Philippines are Southeast Asia's major industrializing countries. A center of world trade, Singapore focuses on producing goods for export. Factories in Malaysia, the Philippines, Indonesia, and Thailand manufacture textiles, clothing, and automobiles.

During the 1980s and early 1990s, the industrializing countries of Southeast Asia enjoyed an economic boom. This prosperity was based on plentiful natural resources, an abundant supply of inexpensive labor, and increased foreign investment. Massive debts, political corruption, and financial mismanagement, however, led to an economic crisis in the region in late 1997. Economic reforms allowed Thailand to emerge fairly quickly from the crisis. Since the crisis, both Thailand and the Philippines have had to balance industrial growth with investment in traditional economic activities such as agriculture and fish farming.

Economics
Singapore and Malaysia

Singapore has Southeast Asia's most developed economy. Its location and harbors make it a major port and manufacturing center. In addition, Singapore's government and businesses have carried out several policies that have led to strong economic growth. After independence in 1965, Singapore set up free-trade zones that attracted foreign investment. More recently, businesses have focused on developing communications, information, and financial services—activities less dependent on foreign investment. Singapore's economy also has moved away from labor-intensive industries, such as textiles, into electronics and oil refining. To ensure a supply of skilled workers for these industries, the government has made a strong commitment to education.

Singapore's neighbor, Malaysia, also has diversified, or increased its economic activities. Although Malaysia remains a major producer of natural rubber and palm oil, it now also manufactures a variety of goods, such as electronic and electrical products, cement, chemicals, and processed foods. The country also has developed heavy industries, such as steelmaking and automobile assembly. These manufactured products—along with natural rubber and palm oil—account for most of Malaysia's export earnings. Malaysia is also the world's largest exporter of microchips, making it an important center for information technology.

Less Industrialized Countries

Since the late 1990s, political instability and a rapidly growing population have slowed economic growth in Indonesia. The country supplies raw materials for world markets and is a major exporter of textiles and garments. Its labor force, however, currently lacks the technical skills and knowledge required for industrialization. Therefore, Indonesia depends heavily on foreign aid and investment to develop its industries.

Industrialization in other Southeast Asian countries, such as Laos, Vietnam, Cambodia, and Myanmar, is developing even more slowly than in Indonesia. Wars and political changes slowed economic growth in Laos, Vietnam, and Cambodia for many years. Landlocked and without ocean harbors, Laos remains largely agricultural. However,

CRITICAL THINKING ACTIVITY

Demonstrating Reasoned Judgment Organize the class into two groups. Write on the board: *Will movement to a market economy in Vietnam weaken its communist political system?* Explain to students that this question will be the topic for a debate. Assign a *yes* response to one group and a *no* response to the other. Have each group research to find reasons supporting its position. Then, hold a class debate in which each side must defend its position. Allow ample time for responses to questions and rebuttals. 📦

🌐 **EE4 Human Systems: Standard 11**

the attempt by its communist leaders to collectivize farming reduced incentives for farmers to produce. The country is rich in mineral resources but lacks up-to-date mining technology. Laos's future economic growth may depend on its rivers, which could provide hydroelectric power for the region.

Rapid population growth and inadequate transportation have hurt Vietnam's economic development. The country, however, has a large potential workforce in its literate population. Another possible boost to Vietnam's economy is its beautiful coastline, which is well suited to the development of tourism. Cambodia's economy suffers from outdated factories and the lack of a trained, experienced workforce. Myanmar's self-imposed isolation from world markets has long slowed its economic growth. Myanmar's gross national product per person is one of the lowest in the world, and manufacturing accounts for just one-tenth of the country's gross domestic product.

Interdependence

In recent years Southeast Asian countries have become more interdependent, or reliant on one another. As they draw closer together, economic and political developments in one country can affect other countries in the region. Two organizations formed to promote regional development, trade, and greater economic stability reflect this increasing interdependence. They are the Asian Development Bank (ADB) and the Association of Southeast Asian Nations (ASEAN).

The ADB, based in the Philippines's capital of **Manila**, provides international loans to aid the economies of Asian member countries. In Southeast Asia these ADB loans support agricultural, transportation, and industrial development projects.

Indonesia, Malaysia, the Philippines, Singapore, and Thailand formed ASEAN in 1967 as an economic and political alliance. Brunei joined in 1984, and Vietnam, Cambodia, Laos, and Myanmar all became members by the late 1990s. ASEAN's main goals are to promote economic growth and to encourage cultural exchanges among member countries. ASEAN also provides an outlet for cooperation in a region that has long known economic and political conflict, although full political or economic unity is not its main focus.

ASEAN's founding members generally have had greater economic success than have other countries in Southeast Asia. Development has been slow or nonexistent in countries that joined ASEAN later and also in East Timor, which has not yet joined. ASEAN member countries try to balance diverse national goals while struggling

NATIONAL GEOGRAPHIC World Explorer

Geography Skills for Life

Making Silk A worker in Vietnam feeds mulberry leaves to silkworms. The fiber that silkworms produce is valuable in making finished silk (see inset above right).
Place What factors have hindered economic development in Vietnam?

NATIONAL GEOGRAPHIC World Explorer

Answer
rapid population growth and inadequate transportation

More About the Photo
Silk comes from the cocoon spun by a caterpillar known as a "silkworm," which feeds on the leaves of mulberry trees. Today silkworms are raised on farms. After hatching, large numbers of young silkworms are placed on a germ-free tray and fed mulberry leaves round the clock so that they will grow quickly and begin spinning silk cocoons.

TEAM-TEACHING ACTIVITY: SCIENCE

Hydroelectric Power and Laos Remind students that *hydroelectric power* is generated from falling water. Have small groups of students work with a science teacher to research and write a report about hydroelectric power, focusing on how it is produced and why it is environmentally superior to burning fossil fuels. *(It is renewable and, if used properly, does not cause pollution.)* Reports should also explain the relationship between elevation changes from north to south in Laos, the direction in which the Mekong River flows, and the potential for hydroelectric power. *(In Laos, the land elevation drops between the mountains in the north and a plateau area in the south. The Mekong River flows south.)*

🌐 **EE1 The World in Spatial Terms: Standard 3**

Assign Section 1 Assessment as homework or as an in-class activity.

Have students use **interactive Tutor Self-Assessment CD-ROM**.

L2

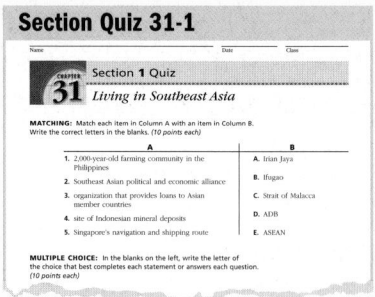

Objectives, goals, and answers to the student activity can be found in the Web Activity Lesson Plan feature at geography.glencoe.com

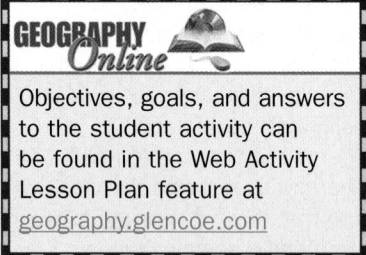

NATIONAL GEOGRAPHIC World Explorer

Answer
dense forests, rugged terrain, and seas that separate the region's coastline

More About the Photo
About 90 percent of the people of Myanmar are Buddhist.

---

for regional unity. In 1992 they agreed to establish a free-trade area and to reduce tariffs on nonagricultural products by 2008.

Transportation

Southeast Asia's peninsulas, islands, long coastlines, and many rivers make water transportation the most common way to move people and goods in the region. However, rain-swollen rivers in the tropical forests sometimes make travel slow and difficult. In some remote areas, such as Indonesia's territory of Papua, people receive supplies by air as well as by water.

Southeast Asia has long been the crossroads of major ocean trade routes. Today most shipping between Europe and East Asia passes through the Strait of Malacca, near Singapore. This transportation "choke point," or strategic location, enables Singapore to prosper as a **free port**, a place where goods can be unloaded, stored, and reshipped free of import duties. Other regional ports include the Indonesian cities of Palembang, on Sumatra, and the national capital, Jakarta, on Java. Manila, in the Philippines, is a major center for maritime trade in Asia. Vietnam's major international shipping port is Ho Chi Minh City.

Throughout Southeast Asia the quality of land transportation varies widely, partly because of differences in economic development. For example, Cambodia's original highway network was designed by French planners to link agricultural areas to the port of Saigon (now Ho Chi Minh City, Vietnam). Although the network no longer serves Cambodia's economic needs, the country lacks the resources to dramatically redesign the system. In contrast, the industrializing countries of Malaysia, Singapore, and Thailand, with their more successful economies, are able to fund improvements to roads.

Highways and railroads on Southeast Asia's peninsulas and larger islands generally link only major cities. Many people travel on bicycles, motor scooters, and oxcarts. In urban centers such as Jakarta, Indonesia, and Bangkok, Thailand, paved roads are also choked with trucks, automobiles, motorcycles, and buses.

Student Web Activity Visit the **Glencoe World Geography** Web site at geography.glencoe.com and click on Student Web Activities—Chapter 31 for an activity about life in Vietnam.

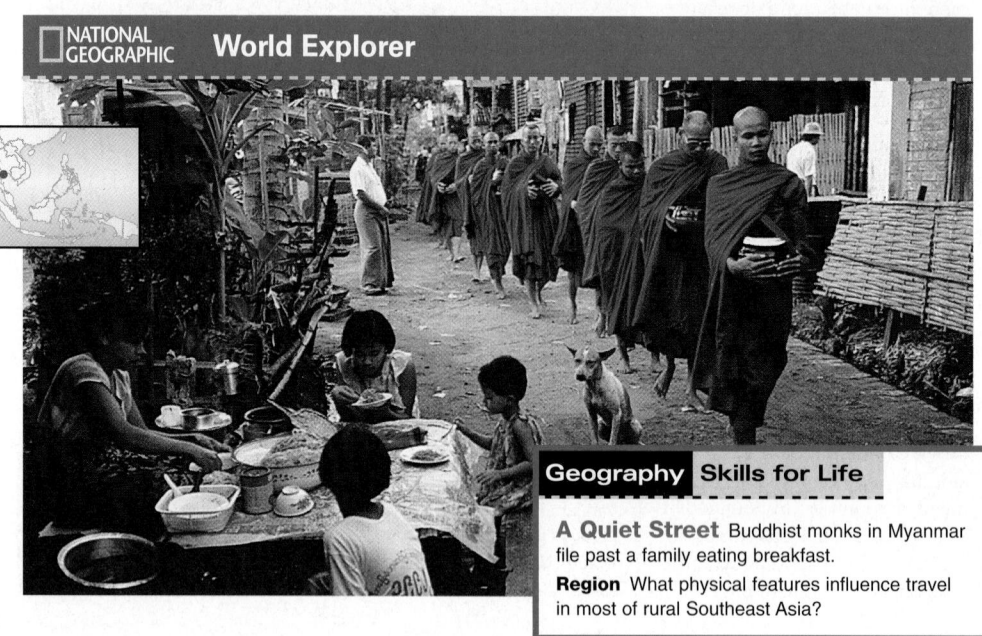

NATIONAL GEOGRAPHIC World Explorer

Geography Skills for Life

A Quiet Street Buddhist monks in Myanmar file past a family eating breakfast.
Region What physical features influence travel in most of rural Southeast Asia?

EXTENDING THE CONTENT

Animals and Habitats Southeast Asia is challenged by the need to balance improvements in people's quality of life with the preservation of animal habitats. Form small groups of students to research and identify at least three endangered species of animals found in Southeast Asia. Members should work together to write a report. Tell them to include areas of Southeast Asia where each species is found, estimates of how many once existed in the wild, how many remain, and efforts being made to ensure the animal's survival.
🌐 **EE2 Places and Regions: Standard 4;** 🌐 **EE3 Physical Systems: Standard 8**

In most parts of rural Southeast Asia, travel is difficult because of dense forests, rugged terrain, and the seas that separate the region's islands. Outside major urban areas, unpaved roads are often impassable during heavy rains.

Communications

As with transportation, communications in Southeast Asia depend on a country's level of industrialization. Singapore's largely prosperous and urbanized population has a well-developed communications system. Rural dwellers in parts of Cambodia and Laos, however, have little access to newspapers, television, or the Internet.

In Southeast Asia's cities, good communications services help advance economic growth. The Internet and wireless communication have also benefited Southeast Asian commerce. Partly because of the region's rugged terrain, telecommunications service remains poor in rural areas. Satellite communication, however, is improving television and telephone transmissions.

Post offices, newspapers, books, and magazines are located in major urban centers such as Bangkok, Jakarta, Kuala Lumpur, and Singapore. Governments typically own and control radio stations and television networks. Most people own or have access to a radio, but television sets are less common. Singapore, Brunei, and the Philippines have the greatest number of television sets per person.

NATIONAL GEOGRAPHIC World Explorer

Geography Skills for Life

Urban Transportation City streets in Jakarta, Indonesia, are crowded with automobiles, buses, and pedestrians.

Region How is the distribution of communications similar to that of transportation in the region?

Although most of Southeast Asia's countries are developing modern communications systems, it will take time for effective communications to reach every part of the region.

SECTION 1 ASSESSMENT

Checking for Understanding

1. **Define** paddy, sickle, subsistence crop, cash crop, lode, interdependent, Association of Southeast Asian Nations (ASEAN), free port.

2. **Main Ideas** On a table like the one below, list products and industries that support the economies of each of the region's countries.

Country	Products/Industries

Critical Thinking

3. **Making Comparisons** How is a country's workforce affected by growing cash crops? Subsistence crops?

4. **Making Generalizations** What might other Southeast Asian countries learn from Singapore's economic success?

5. **Predicting Consequences** How might rural ways of life change in Southeast Asia as communications services are developed? Provide examples to support your answer.

Analyzing Maps

6. **Place** Study the economic activity map on page 713. What geographic feature is common among most manufacturing and trade centers? Explain this relationship.

Applying Geography

7. **Water Transportation** Think about different kinds of transportation in Southeast Asia. Write a paragraph in which you discuss the day-to-day impacts of relying on water transportation.

SECTION 1 ASSESSMENT ANSWERS

1. All vocabulary terms are defined in the text.

2. Answers should list each country in the region and identify its most important products.

3. Cash crops provide money for national economic development; subsistence crops feed the country's farm families.

4. diversify the economy; establish free trade zones; improve communications; commit to education

5. Telephone, Internet, TV and newspaper access would increase. Economic growth would advance. Example: Singapore

6. They are on rivers or ocean ports and are ideal for transportation.

7. **Applying Geography** Possible answer: Water transportation is often slower and less dependable than land transportation. Storms, droughts, and other natural events or conditions affect it.

Reteach

Have students answer the questions in "Read to Find Out" on page 759. Use their responses as a basis for discussion of points that seem to need reinforcement or clarification.

NATIONAL GEOGRAPHIC World Explorer

Answer
strained resources, increased pollution, made cheap labor available

More About the Photo
Jakarta draws many people from the rest of Indonesia— an estimated 250 emigrants daily, most between the ages of 15 to 39.

Enrich

Have students find out more about communications in Southeast Asia. Tell students to use the Internet or other sources to discover the number of telephones, television sets, radios, and newspapers in Indonesia, Cambodia, and Vietnam. Suggest that students organize their information on a chart.

4 CLOSE

Call on volunteers to identify one country in Southeast Asia and share the most interesting fact that they learned about it.

① FOCUS

Section Overview

This section discusses various environmental challenges that Southeast Asia faces as well as the causes and effects.

BELLRINGER
Skillbuilder Activity

 Project transparency and have students answer questions.

📁 Available as blackline master.

Daily Focus Skills Transparency 31-2

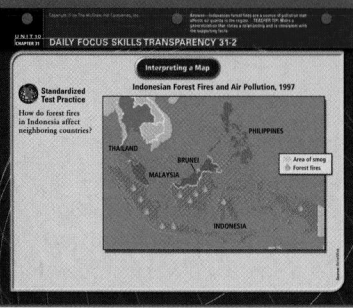

Guide to Reading

Consider What You Know
Answer *air pollution, overcrowded cities, and destruction of land and water resources*

Reading Strategy
Answer Students should complete the outline by including all heads in the section.

Preteaching Vocabulary
🕸 Use the **Vocabulary Puzzle-Maker CD-ROM** to create crossword and word-search puzzles.

Guide to Reading

Consider What You Know
Much of Southeast Asia has experienced rapid industrialization. What effect might industrial growth have on a region's natural surroundings?

Reading Strategy
Taking Notes Create an outline similar to the one below by using the major headings of the section.

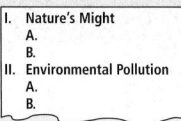

I. Nature's Might
 A.
 B.
II. Environmental Pollution
 A.
 B.

Read to Find Out
• What dangers are posed by volcanoes, floods, and typhoons in Southeast Asia?

• How has economic progress increased environmental pollution in the region?

• What efforts are under way to protect the environment in Southeast Asia?

Terms to Know
• cyclone
• typhoon
• shifting cultivation

Places to Locate
• Ring of Fire
• Bali

People and Their Environment

NATIONAL GEOGRAPHIC

A Geographic View

Traffic Ballet

Nikorn Phasuk, a Bangkok policeman who is also known as Plastic Man, steps onto a stage of asphalt under the glare of a blazing sun. He crouches, then retreats with mincing footwork as he coaxes vehicles toward him with fluid arm gestures, part of an artful ballet he uses to keep traffic rolling, no small feat in the city that may have the most congested streets in the world.

—Noel Grove, "The Many Faces of Thailand,"
National Geographic, *February 1996*

Rush hour in Bangkok, Thailand

In the heart of Bangkok, Thailand's capital, you can experience noisy, crowded, traffic-choked streets and intense heat rising from sunbaked pavement. Like other places in Southeast Asia, Bangkok faces a variety of environmental challenges. In this section you will learn about the natural and human factors that affect Southeast Asia's environment. You will also learn about the efforts of governments and citizens' groups to protect it.

Nature's Might

As you learned in Chapter 29, much of Southeast Asia is part of the **Ring of Fire**, the area of earthquake and volcanic activity that rims the Pacific Ocean. Residents of places along the Ring of Fire periodically face volcanic eruptions, flash floods, and typhoons. These natural disasters take their toll on human lives and on economic development. People's efforts to cope with the effects of disasters are part of everyday life in many parts of Southeast Asia.

RESOURCE MANAGER

📁 Reproducible Masters
• Reproducible Lesson Plan 31-2
• Vocabulary Activity 31
• Daily Lecture Notes 31-2
• Guided Reading Activity 31-2
• Reading Essentials and Study Guide 31-2
• Reteaching Activity 31
• Reinforcing Skills Activity 31
• Section Quiz 31-2

📠 Transparencies
• Daily Focus Skills Transparency 31-2
• Political Map Transparency 10
• Unit 10 Map Overlay Transparencies

Multimedia
🕸 Vocabulary PuzzleMaker CD-ROM
🕸 Interactive Tutor Self-Assessment CD-ROM
🕸 ExamView® Pro Testmaker CD-ROM
🕸 Presentation Plus! CD-ROM

Volcanoes

Volcanic mountains rise on most of the larger islands in the Philippines. Several of the volcanoes are active, and many Filipinos must cope with the constant threat of volcanic activity. In February 2000, thousands fled their homes as the Mayon Volcano, which had last erupted in 1993, spewed ash and lava over the landscape.

Another Philippine volcano, the 5,770-foot (1,759-m) Mount Pinatubo, erupted in June 1991. Scientists in the Philippines predicted the eruption, and government authorities ordered the evacuation of nearby towns. Still, the eruption killed about 800 people and destroyed about 100,000 homes. Clouds of ash and dust blown into the atmosphere affected weather patterns worldwide.

> *... Mount Pinatubo ... spewed 15 million tons of ash, rock, and sulfuric acid 22 miles into the stratosphere. Within three weeks, the debris had veiled the globe, reflecting sunlight back into space and chilling that year's winter by at least a full degree....*
>
> Jack McClintock, "Under the Volcano," *Discover*, November 1999

Volcanoes also figure prominently in the culture of some Southeast Asian countries. For example, the Indonesian island of **Bali** (BAH•lee) is famous for a volcano that reaches 10,308 feet (3,142 m) high—Gunung Agung. The Balinese people regard the volcano as the sacred centerpiece of their Hindu faith, and they leave offerings of food and flowers on the crater's rim. Despite a 1963 eruption that took more than 1,500 lives, many Balinese still live near Gunung Agung, risking their lives and property.

Geography | **Skills for Life**
- - - - - - - - - - - - - **Flooding**
Southeast Asians, such as these Buddhist monks in Cambodia, cope with flooded streets during the rainy season.
Human-Environment Interaction What human activity contributes to the problem of flooding?

Floods and Typhoons

Flash floods in Southeast Asia kill hundreds of people a year and ruin about 10 million acres (4 million ha) of crops. Human activity often magnifies the effects of these floods. In 1991 and 1995, for example, major storms struck the Philippines. Because so much land had been cleared of forest, the storms caused widespread runoff and mudslides.

The rivers of mainland Southeast Asia undergo seasonal flooding every year. Flooding poses a particular threat to Bangkok, which is built on unstable land. Some sections of the city sink as much as 25 inches (64 cm) each year. The city's most recent serious flooding occurred in 1983, when one-fourth of its area was under water.

Tropical storms also often strike various parts of Southeast Asia. A **cyclone** is an area of low

---

② TEACH

L1 Locate
Have students use the physical map on page 710 to locate the major rivers of Southeast Asia. Then, have them suggest areas that might be vulnerable to flooding and explain their reasoning.

NATIONAL GEOGRAPHIC **World Explorer**

Answer
deforestation

More About the Photo
Parts of Cambodia receive 200 inches (500 cm) of rain per year, and the central lowlands receive 55 inches (140 cm).

Daily Lecture Notes 31-2

> **DAILY LECTURE NOTES**
> **CHAPTER 31** **Building Geography Literacy**
> **Section 2**
> Along coastal regions of northern Java in Indonesia, villagers have created ponds of the salty tidal waters of mangrove forests. In recent years, these ponds—used for farming fish and prawns—have been expanded into nearby inland paddies. There mechanical pumps mix seawater and freshwater that help fish and prawns produce in abundance.
>
> **I. Nature's Might** pages 766–768
> Much of Southeast Asia is part of the Ring of Fire and is subject to earthquakes and volcanic activity. Flash floods and typhoons occur periodically. Natural disasters and their effects are part of everyday life in many parts of Southeast Asia.
> **A. Volcanoes**
> Volcanic eruptions are common throughout the region. The Mayon Volcano in the Philippines erupted in 1993 and again in 2000. Mount Pinatubo, also in the Philippines, erupted in 1991, killing more than 900 people. Gunung Agung, a towering volcano on the Indonesian island of Bali, last erupted in 1993, killing more than 1,500 people.
>
> What do you think are the positive and negative aspects of Singapore's environmental laws?
> *(Possible answers: Positive: Strict law enforcement helps reduce pollution; Negative: Singapore's laws reflect a government that overregulates citizens' lives.)*

L2 Interpretation
Note that the city of Bangkok was founded in the late 1700s. **Ask:** **What characteristics of a city built in the 1700s might add to traffic problems?** *(Streets often are narrow and unsuited to modern traffic.)*

DIFFERENTIATED INSTRUCTION

At-Risk Students Have students who have difficulty organizing information use the boldface subsection heads—*Volcanoes, Floods and Typhoons*, for example—to create an outline. As they read, have students copy each head onto a sheet of paper. When they have finished reading each paragraph following that head, they should complete the outline by writing the main idea or important details from that part of the text beneath the heading.
📁 Refer to *Inclusion for the Social Studies Classroom Strategies and Activities.*

Guided Reading Activity 31-2

Name _____ Date _____ Class _____

Guided Reading Activity **31-2**

For use with textbook pages 766–771.

People and Their Environment

Short Answer

DIRECTIONS: Use the information in your textbook to write a short answer to each of the following questions.

1. What kinds of natural disasters occur in Southeast Asia?

2. What are some effects of volcanic eruptions in the region?

3. What are the causes of flash floods?

4. Where do Southeast Asia's typhoons form, and where do they travel?

5. What benefits and challenges do increased manufacturing and greater wealth bring?

6. What are the sources of pollution in Southeast Asia's rural areas?

7. Why is deforestation a major concern throughout Southeast Asia?

8. How has mining contributed to environmental challenges?

9. What steps have some countries taken to protect and preserve their forests?

10. How are Southeast Asian governments dealing with the impact of urban growth on the environment?

INTERDISCIPLINARY
connection

SCIENCE Typhoons strike
the Philippines from June to
November. In 1991 Typhoon
Thelma caused flash floods
that killed about 3,000 people. Typhoon Angela struck
the Philippines in 1995 and
killed more than 700 people.

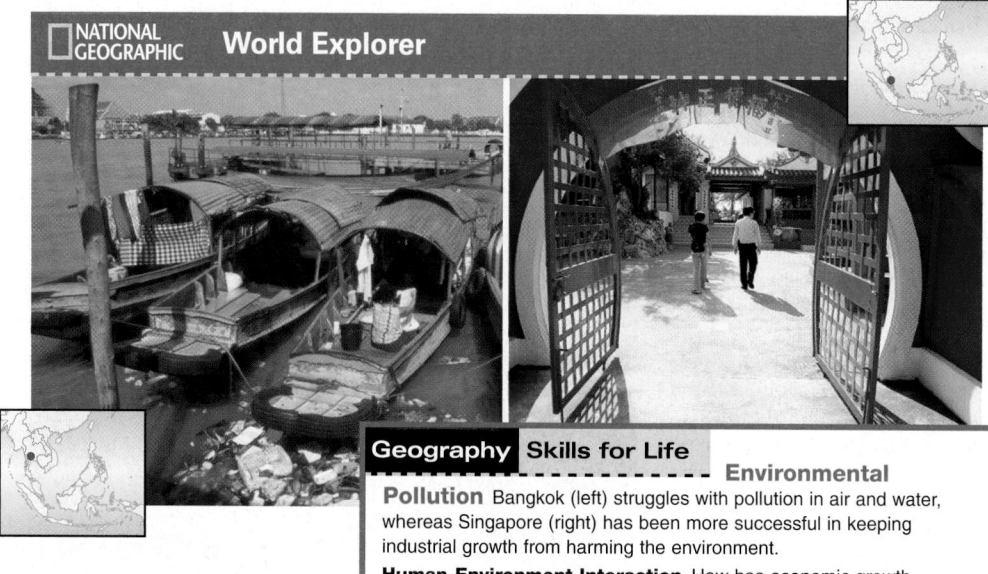

NATIONAL GEOGRAPHIC World Explorer

Geography Skills for Life

Environmental Pollution Bangkok (left) struggles with pollution in air and water, whereas Singapore (right) has been more successful in keeping industrial growth from harming the environment.

Human-Environment Interaction How has economic growth affected the environment and levels of pollution in Southeast Asia?

atmospheric pressure surrounded by circulating winds extending out from 100 to 1,000 miles (161 to 1,609 km). Tropical cyclones are particularly deadly storms. A typhoon is a tropical cyclone that forms in the Pacific Ocean 8° to 15° N of the Equator, often between July and November. Typhoon winds circulate in a counterclockwise direction.

Southeast Asia's typhoons form in the western Pacific Ocean, north of the island of New Guinea. Some travel north to Japan, while others move through the northern islands of the Philippines and then on to the Chinese mainland. Still others pass through the Philippines and reach Vietnam. Typhoons may have winds from 150 to 180 miles per hour (241 to 290 km per hour) and may be accompanied by rain, thunder, lightning, and high ocean waves that disrupt shipping.

Southeast Asians are taking steps to control the damage from typhoons. In Thailand, for example, planners in Bangkok are building dams to prevent typhoon-related flooding.

Environmental Pollution

Whether facing the commotion of a busy city, coaxing a modest crop from a small family plot, or taming a river's floodwaters to protect a cash crop, Southeast Asians, like people every-

where, affect their environments. In the face of technological advances and widespread air, water, and noise pollutants, Southeast Asia's people today try to balance environmental concerns with economic needs.

Cities

Increased prosperity in Southeast Asia has raised people's expectations about their quality of life. Economic growth, however, also depletes limited environmental resources. Increased manufacturing, for example, raises standards of living but also creates industrial waste. As societies become wealthier and more people buy automobiles, exhaust systems send toxic fumes into the air.

Growing populations and crowded conditions in cities such as Bangkok, Manila, and Jakarta raise concerns about adequate housing, water supplies, sanitation, and traffic control. Bangkok, for example, is a busy city of skyscrapers, factories, noisy expressways, and traffic jams. Dramatic population increases and industrialization even appear to be overheating Bangkok. In recent years, the city's heat, humidity, and pollution levels have increased at a rate higher than the global average. Higher

COOPERATIVE LEARNING ACTIVITY

Researching Natural Disasters Organize the class into groups to research one natural disaster, such as a hurricane, flood, or volcanic eruption, that has struck Southeast Asia in the last three years. Students should gather information such as the date(s) the disaster hit, where it caused the most damage, the death toll, the extent of property damage, and the rebuilding efforts. Have students analyze ways new technologies are helping people adapt to life in disaster-prone areas. Each group should prepare and present an oral report to the class, using graphic aids. 📦

🌐 **EE5 Environment and Society: Standard 15**

temperatures affect both humans and their environment, causing health problems and trapping pollutants in the air that contribute to acid rain.

Because of strict law enforcement, Singapore is an exception in a region of polluted cities. One observer describes Singapore as a "world of almost surrealistic cleanliness and good behavior, prompted on every public wall by slogans of a watchful state." In Singapore, littering the sidewalk can bring a $250 fine.

Rural Areas

In some parts of Southeast Asia, pollution extends into the countryside, including the region's national parks. In one of Thailand's national parks, for example, 80 percent of the fresh-water wells are contaminated as a result of poor waste disposal. The dumping of toxic wastes has created problems in other countries of Southeast Asia. In 1998, thousands of people in rural Cambodia fled their homes after finding out that tons of toxic materials, mislabeled as cement, had been dumped nearby. The waste, containing poisonous mercury, threatened their water supplies.

Volcanic eruptions and forest fires also pollute in rural areas, sometimes affecting cities as well. Forest fires on several islands of Indonesia in the 1990s, for example, created pollution and respiratory problems for people as far away as mainland Malaysia (see chart below). The smoke disrupted air traffic and shipping across the region.

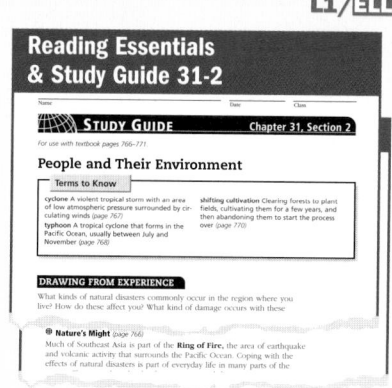

Reading Essentials & Study Guide 31-2

L3 Locate
Have students use the physical map on page 710 and text information on page 768 to track the two paths typhoons may follow from the ocean north of New Guinea to other parts of Southeast Asia.

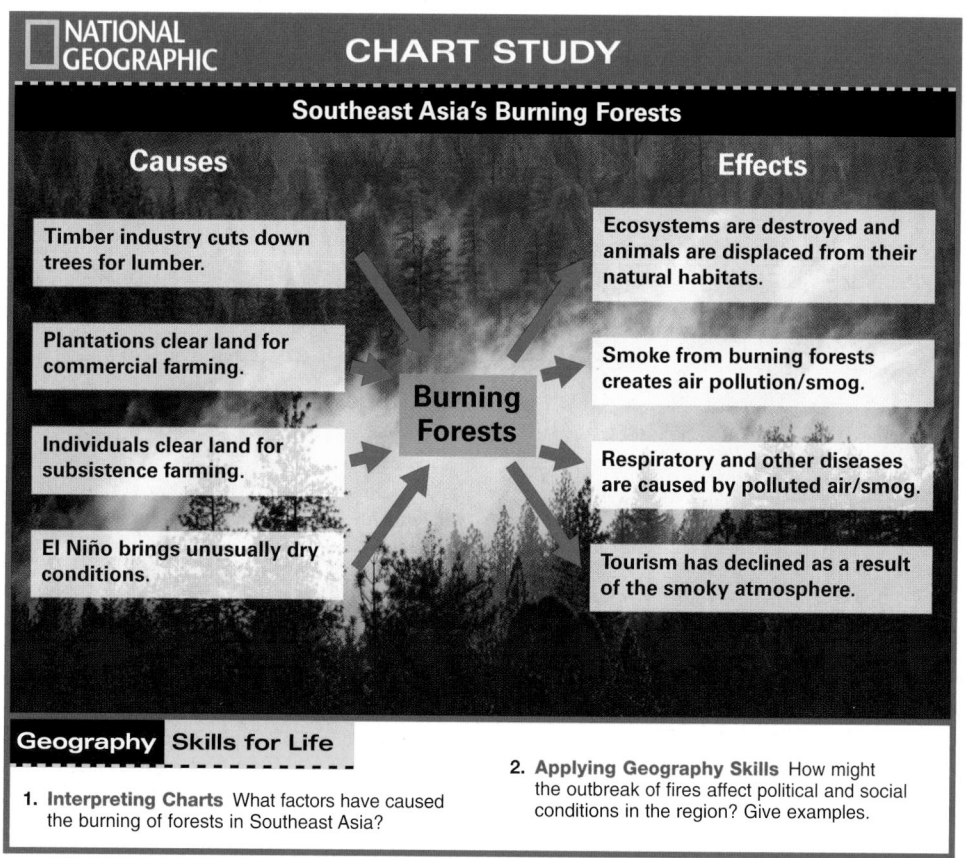

NATIONAL GEOGRAPHIC — **CHART STUDY**

Southeast Asia's Burning Forests

Causes

- Timber industry cuts down trees for lumber.
- Plantations clear land for commercial farming.
- Individuals clear land for subsistence farming.
- El Niño brings unusually dry conditions.

Burning Forests

Effects

- Ecosystems are destroyed and animals are displaced from their natural habitats.
- Smoke from burning forests creates air pollution/smog.
- Respiratory and other diseases are caused by polluted air/smog.
- Tourism has declined as a result of the smoky atmosphere.

Geography Skills for Life

1. **Interpreting Charts** What factors have caused the burning of forests in Southeast Asia?

2. **Applying Geography Skills** How might the outbreak of fires affect political and social conditions in the region? Give examples.

NATIONAL GEOGRAPHIC — **CHART STUDY**

Answers
1. *trees cut for lumber, land cleared for farming, El Niño brings dry conditions*

2. *Air pollution and smog cause respiratory problems; homes can be damaged and population displaced; economic uncertainty and political unrest*

Chapter 31 🌐 769

CRITICAL THINKING ACTIVITY

Demonstrating Reasoned Judgment Organize students into small groups. Review with them the information in the text concerning littering laws in Singapore. Tell each group to list advantages and disadvantages of having strict laws concerning matters such as litter. Then they should decide if the advantages outweigh the disadvantages or vice versa. Tell groups to be ready to defend their position. Have a member present his or her group's findings to the class. Allow time for a question and answer period during which findings can be challenged. 🔲 **EE4 Human Systems: Standards 10, 13**

Answer
erosion; clogged rivers; flooding; air pollution

More About the Photo A street vendor peddles cloth masks to pedestrians in the smoke-filled streets.

③ ASSESS

Assign Section 2 Assessment as homework or as an in-class activity.

⊗ Have students use **Interactive Tutor Self-Assessment CD-ROM** to review Section 2.

L2

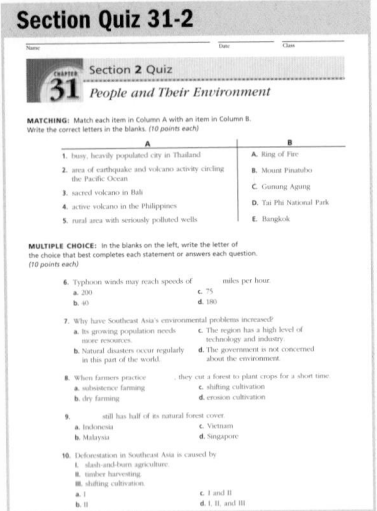

Logging, Farming, and Mining

In Southeast Asia, some logging, farming, and mining practices have harmed the environment. The destruction of habitats and the demand for certain food items also endanger the region's wildlife.

Economies
Deforestation

Deforestation is a major concern throughout Southeast Asia. In Laos, Thailand, and Myanmar, teak and other timber provides important sources of income. Since the 1960s, commercial logging companies have set up modern logging processes and provided training and jobs for many Southeast Asians. The region's economies have benefited, but the widespread cutting of trees has steadily diminished the region's forests. Until recently, companies made few efforts to replant as they harvested. Without the trees' root systems, topsoil is no longer held in place. Heavy tropical rains easily erode topsoil, washing it into streams that crisscross the region. The topsoil clogs rivers and reduces the amount of water available for irrigation.

Geography Skills for Life

Avoiding Pollution A vendor sells air masks to protect against air pollution in Indonesia.

Place What are some of the negative results of burning forests for agriculture?

Excessive logging also has caused major flooding. Without forests to absorb downpours, flash floods on bare, muddy slopes have swept into valleys, killing hundreds of people and leaving thousands more injured and homeless.

Some farming methods contribute to deforestation and soil erosion. Throughout Southeast Asia, farmers carry out slash-and-burn agriculture—cutting down vegetation, burning it, and using the ashes for fertilizer. In highlands areas, farmers grow food crops by a method known as shifting cultivation, clearing forests to plant fields, cultivating the land for a few years, and then abandoning it. They then repeat the process in a new area.

Fires also have destroyed forested areas. Plantation owners in Southeast Asia often burn large areas of land in order to plant profitable cash crops. These fires are becoming more frequent, and they often destroy large areas of forests when, during periods of drought, they blaze out of control.

Mining

The mining of valuable minerals and metals has also led to environmental abuses. At Indonesia's largest gold mine, workers dump large amounts of rock waste into the Ajkwa River in Papua. This dumping will eventually divert the river from its original course, flooding more than 50 square miles (130 sq. km) of forest and displacing many people. Pollution from the rock waste has already begun to kill vegetation in the surrounding rain forest.

Environmental Protection

In recent years, some Southeast Asian countries have taken steps to protect their environments. To prevent further loss of rain forests, Thailand, Indonesia, the Philippines, and Malaysia have limited certain timber exports and have introduced reforestation programs. Such efforts, however, have proved difficult to enforce or carry out, and illegal logging is still taking its toll on the region's forests. Scientists predict that many unique environments—with their variety of plant and animal species—will be lost within a few years.

In Indonesia, for example, the government in the early 1980s introduced a plan to set aside large parts of the country as conservation areas. In recent years, however, this plan has been largely

---

TEAM-TEACHING ACTIVITY: ART

Malaysian Kites Explain that making and flying kites has been popular in Malaysia for 600 years. Malaysian kites, like those in this country, come in different shapes and sizes. The colored figures on the kites, however, reflect local cultural symbols. Peacocks and the moon are among the favorite designs. Have students research these and other kite designs popular with Malaysians. Ask an art teacher to provide reference materials on kite-making and suggestions for art materials. Allow students to make kites using an original design based on what they have learned about Malaysian kites. Set aside a class period (on a windy day, if possible) for students to display their projects in flight. 🪁

🏛 **EE4 Human Systems: Standard 10**

abandoned because of the government's grant of logging rights to timber companies and the outbreak of political turmoil.

In addition, illegal logging operations on the Indonesian islands of Sumatra and Kalimantan have destroyed much of the forests bordering national parks. Scientists visiting these areas state that the Indonesian government must enforce its own environmental laws, and the army may have to be used to stop illegal logging.

In other Southeast Asian countries, planned migration or resettlement has balanced environmental protection and economic development. Laos, for example, has tried to limit shifting cultivation by resettling highlands peoples on more fertile and arable plains.

Southeast Asian governments also are starting to deal with the impact of urban growth on the environment. Bangkok, Thailand, for example, is a major example of urban warming, caused by industrialization, crowded living and working areas, and the increased use of automobiles and other vehicles. To handle this problem, scientists have proposed several solutions. One includes the creation of "green zones," or areas within a city that are granted special environmental protection. Another suggests banning the construction of tall

NATIONAL GEOGRAPHIC World Explorer

Geography Skills for Life

Farming Deforested Land Tropical forests continue to be cleared for settlement and agriculture, creating major ecological problems in Indonesia.
Human-Environment Interaction What steps have Southeast Asian countries taken to protect the forests?

buildings near the sea, allowing winds to blow farther into the city and provide more ventilation. Despite enormous challenges, these and other proposals are helping Southeast Asians realize that they must work hard to protect the environment while developing their economies.

SECTION 2 ASSESSMENT

Checking for Understanding

1. **Define** cyclone, typhoon, shifting cultivation.

2. **Main Ideas** On a cause-effect chart, fill in events, their causes, and their effects on Southeast Asia's environment.

Human Impact on the Environment		
Event	Cause	Effect

Critical Thinking

3. **Making Inferences** How do governments in Southeast Asia prepare for natural disasters?

4. **Predicting Consequences** What might be the consequences of clearing rain forests for housing in Indonesia?

5. **Drawing Conclusions** What might happen as Southeast Asia's less-industrialized countries develop manufacturing industries? Explain.

Analyzing Charts

6. **Human-Environment Interaction** Study the chart on page 769. What types of economic activities cause the burning of forests in Southeast Asia?

Applying Geography

7. **Using Resources** Evaluate the geographic impact of Southeast Asian government policies related to the use of resources.

NATIONAL GEOGRAPHIC World Explorer

Answer
limits on certain timber exports, reforestation programs, conservation areas

More About the Photo
Notice the haze along the horizon in this photo. In many areas such as this one, the odor of smoke hangs in the air for months during planting season.

Reteach

Read aloud each section subhead, and have students summarize the main idea in a sentence. Use their responses as a basis for reinforcement of the chapter content.

Enrich

Freshwater fish are an important food source for Indonesians. Favorites include tilapia. Because of its delicate flavor, tilapia has become popular in the United States in recent years and is now sold in supermarkets. Have students find an authentic Indonesian recipe for the preparation of tilapia.

4 CLOSE

Have students discuss whether environmental pollution or natural disasters are a greater threat to Southeast Asia. Tell them to support their opinions with facts.

SECTION 2 ASSESSMENT ANSWERS

1. All vocabulary terms are defined in the text.

2. one possible answer: deforestation caused by demand for agricultural land and lumber causes flooding—an effect

3. possible answers: tracking storms, providing safety information, setting up professional and volunteer emergency help units, and broadcasting information on radio and TV

4. increased soil erosion, flooding, threats to wildlife

5. Pollution and other threats to the region's ecosystem may increase; rapid urbanization

6. logging and agriculture

7. **Applying Geography** Industrial and urban growth have developed but also strained natural resources.

Viewpoint
CASE STUDY on the Environment

1 FOCUS

Ask: How do the ocean's living resources help meet people's needs and wants? Put the following headings on the board and have students brainstorm to list items for each category: *foods, medicines,* and *ecosystem.*

2 TEACH

Explain that scientists believe that methods of harvesting exotic fish along coral reefs may have grave global environmental implications. Scientists warn that these methods threaten the continued existence of the reefs, and loss of the reefs will disrupt the ocean's food chain. Many fishers argue that the economic opportunities outweigh any environmental consequences.

L2 Debate

Have students identify as many pros and cons as they can to support the arguments of those who believe that the fate of the coral reefs should be decided by the people of Southeast Asia and those who favor international involvement.

Viewpoint
CASE STUDY on the Environment

South China Sea
Philippine Sea

Risk Level of Reefs
- High
- Medium
- Low

Sources:
United Nations Environment Program,
World Conservation Monitoring Centre.

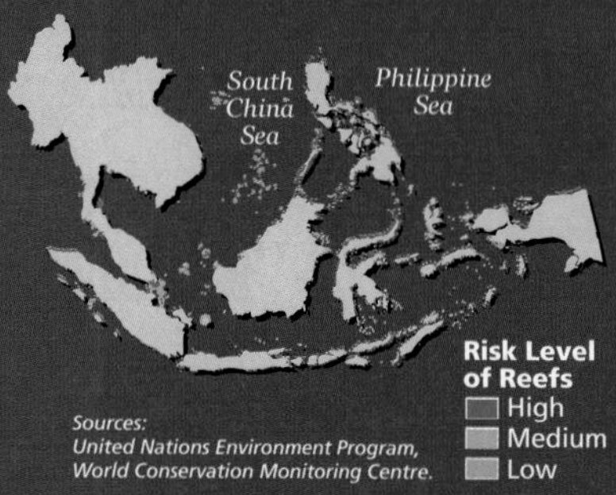

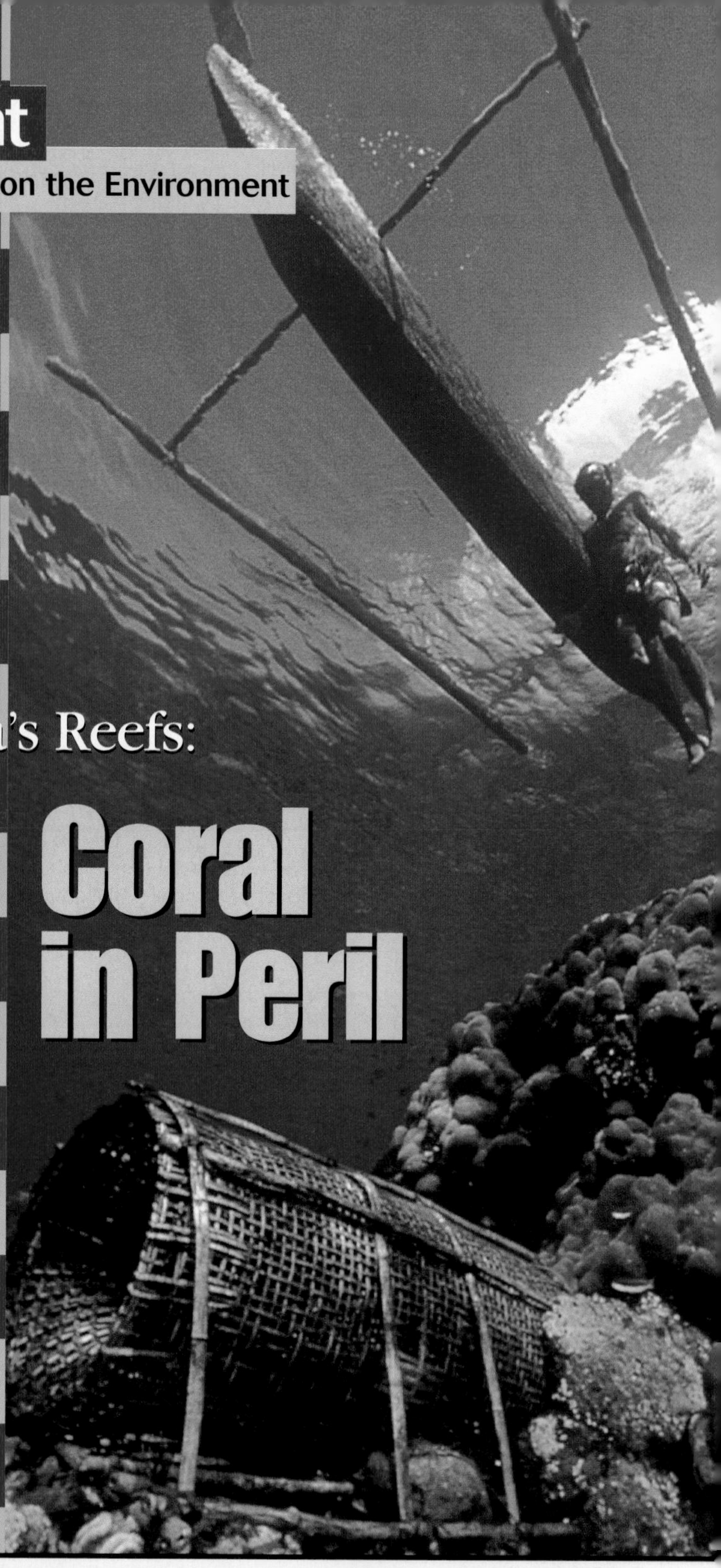

Southeast Asia's Reefs:

Coral in Peril

Like underwater cities, coral reefs swarm with life in the warm, shallow oceans banding the Equator. Home to a fourth of all known marine species, coral reefs rival tropical rain forests in biodiversity. Like rain forests, too, coral reefs are at risk worldwide. Nowhere are these fragile habitats in more danger than in Southeast Asia, where local people use poisons and explosives to capture certain kinds of fish. These fish supply Asian restaurants and a worldwide aquarium industry. The trade generates huge profits for many people in the region, but their fishing methods are destroying the reefs.

772 Unit 10

LOOKING TO THE FUTURE

The World's Survival Kit? Some scientists believe that the ocean may contain important keys to improving quality of life for future generations and even for the survival of the human race. Medical researchers have discovered that organisms found in the defense systems of coral, algae, and sponges also attack human cancer cells. They are excited about dramatic results that they have seen in early trial treatments. Other scientists believe that simple ocean life may help prevent future famines. These experts think that developing food for humans from these abundant sources may hold the key to meeting the nutritional demands of an ever-increasing world population.

📖 **EE3 Physical Systems: Standard 8**
📖 **EE6 The Uses of Geography: Standard 18**

Suspended in crystal clear waters, an Indonesian fisherman (left) drifts over a bamboo fish trap nestled among colorful corals. Corals look like rocks, but they are actually colonies of tiny animals called coral polyps. Each polyp secretes a limestone cup around itself, forming a limestone skeleton. The polyps attach to the skeletons of dead polyps, and the limestone formations—called coral reefs—grow larger and larger. Despite their rock-hard appearance, however, coral reefs are easily damaged. Worldwide, reefs are dying because of pollution, overfishing, coastal development, diseases, and rising ocean temperatures.

The reefs of Southeast Asia are among the world's richest—and some of the most endangered. The thriving trade in live reef fishes is largely to blame. Colorful tropical fish captured on coral reefs end up in collectors' aquariums. Fashionable restaurants in

A coral grouper (below) lives and feeds on coral reefs in the Philippines. Many such fish end up in skillets, as Asian diners (right) pay top dollar for live reef fish. ▼

Hong Kong, Taiwan, and China are also to blame. Diners there pay big money to select live reef fish from a tank, and then have them killed, cooked, and served on the spot.

To capture fish alive, many Southeast Asian fishers use dynamite to stun fish—a technique called blast fishing. In addition, fishers squirt fish with cyanide. The poison temporarily immobilizes a fish, making it easy to catch. Explosives and cyanide, however, kill countless other fish and ocean creatures, including corals. Scientists estimate that 50 percent of Indonesian reefs and 80 percent of Philippine reefs are turning into aquatic graveyards.

Environmentalists claim that the use of explosives and cyanide to capture live reef fish is destroying entire coral reef ecosystems. Scientists warn that the loss of coral reefs will harm other ocean food chains, which could affect oceans worldwide. Concerned officials point out that once the reefs are gone,

◀ Philippine divers squirt deadly cyanide to stun and net fish—a practice that also kills corals.

local communities will lose a primary source of food and a lucrative tourist industry.

Fishers working in the live reef-fish trade see it as an opportunity to raise their standard of living. Cyanide fishers often earn three times the salary of college-educated workers in the region. Some fishers claim that if they don't catch the reef fish now in demand, others will. Local people point out that Southeast Asia's coral reefs belong to Southeast Asian countries and that decisions about how to use their reef resources should be made by people living in the region.

> **What's Your Point of View?**
> Should people around the world be concerned about Southeast Asia's coral reefs? What might be done to restrict trade in live reef fish?

③ ASSESS

Have students answer the **What's Your Point of View?** questions on page 773.

④ CLOSE

Challenge partners to create a plan that balances the need to preserve coral reefs with the needs of Southeast Asian fishers.

global issues

A Review of Global Fisheries
The United Nations Food and Agriculture Organization has concluded that 15 to 18 percent of the world's fish populations are "overexploited." If overfishing of certain species does not end, future populations of these fish will be in jeopardy.

🌐 Meeting National Standards

Geography for Life
The following standards are met in the Student Edition:

EE3 Physical Systems: Standard 8
EE5 Environment and Society: Standard 14

WHAT CAN YOU DO?

Create a display that explains the importance of coral reefs and highlights the practices that threaten their survival. Mount the display in a central location at your school or in your community. Consider including a variety of items to make your display appealing and informative.

- color images of reefs and the species they support
- key information in question and answer format
- graphs of statistics on the biodiversity of reefs
- names of organizations working for the protection of coral reefs
- brochures or sample letters to the editor for viewers to pick up

Teaching the Skill

Have students draw conclusions by participating in the following game. Form small groups. Have members choose a location that they would like to "portray." Each group will give clues to the location without using words or sounds. To show a supermarket, for example, students might push carts, take items from shelves, and run a cash register. Have other students draw conclusions about each location being portrayed based on the clues. Then, ask them to identify clues that helped them identify the location.

Additional Practice
L1

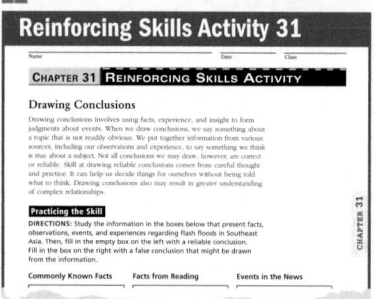

Reinforcing Skills Activity 31

CHAPTER 31 REINFORCING SKILLS ACTIVITY

Drawing Conclusions

Drawing conclusions involves using facts, experience, and insight to form judgments about events. When we draw conclusions, we say something about a topic that is not readily obvious. We put together information from various sources, including our observations and experience, to say something we think is true about a subject. Not all conclusions we may draw, however, are correct or reliable. Skill at drawing reliable conclusions comes from careful thought and practice. It can help us decide things for ourselves without being told what to think. Drawing conclusions also may result in greater understanding of complex relationships.

Practicing the Skill

DIRECTIONS: Study the information in the boxes below that present facts, observations, events, and experiences regarding flash floods in Southeast Asia. Then, fill in the empty box on the left with a reliable conclusion. Fill in the box on the right with a false conclusion that might be drawn from the information.

Commonly Known Facts | Facts from Reading | Events in the News

GLENCOE
TECHNOLOGY

Glencoe Skillbuilder Interactive Workbook, Level 2

This interactive CD-ROM reinforces student mastery of essential social studies skills.

Drawing Conclusions

Drawing conclusions involves studying facts and details to understand how they are related and what they mean. By putting this information together, you can better understand an action or event.

Learning the Skill

When you draw a conclusion, you use facts, observation, and experience to form a judgment about an event. Drawing conclusions allows you to understand indirectly stated ideas and events, so you can apply your knowledge to similar situations.

Sometimes, however, people draw incorrect conclusions based on the information they have. Often the facts and details of a situation could logically lead to more than one conclusion. For example, if you see someone sweating, you might conclude that the person has been exercising. You might also conclude that this person may be sick with a fever. To determine which conclusion is correct, you would need to obtain and evaluate further information. To determine the accuracy of any conclusion, it is important to gather information that will prove or disprove it.

Follow these steps when drawing conclusions:

- **Review the facts that are stated directly.**

- **Use your own knowledge, experience, and insight to form conclusions about the facts.**

- **Find information that would help prove or disprove your conclusions.**

Asked to form an expedition overnight, Tu'o is ready by dawn. With six young Penan as our companions and Tu'o as guide, we leave Long Iman [in Malaysia] traveling up the Tutok by longboat to reach a trail that climbs steeply through gingers and wild durian [fruit]. . . .

For two long days we walk farther into the forest, following a route that rises and falls with each successive ridge. Delighted to be away from the settlement, the Penan watch the forest for signs, hunting hornbills at dusk, tracking deer and sun bears, gathering ripe fruits of mango trees. On the third morning our party crests a steep hill; we have reached the nomads. It is just after dawn, and the sound of the gibbons howling runs across the canopy. Smoke from cooking fires mingles with the cool mist. A hunting party returns. Tu'o bows his head in morning prayer. "Thank you for the sun rising, for the trees and the forest of abundance, the trees that were not made by man, but by you."

—Wade Davis, "Vanishing Cultures,"
National Geographic, August 1999

Practicing the Skill

Read the excerpt above about traveling with the Penan people of Malaysia, and answer the following questions.

1. What important facts does the author include?
2. What information does Tu'o's morning prayer provide about his attitude toward the forest?
3. What conclusion can you draw about the Penan people based on this author's description?
4. What evidence do you have to support this conclusion?

Applying the Skill

Bring to class an article from a magazine, newspaper, or Internet source describing a current conflict in Southeast Asia. Using the steps on this page, draw conclusions about the causes of the conflict and its likely outcome. Summarize your conclusions in a paragraph.

Go To The Glencoe Skillbuilder Interactive Workbook, Level 2 provides instruction and practice in key social studies skills.

ANSWERS TO PRACTICING THE SKILL

1. Answers may include facts that relate to the location and nature of the trip, the activities and attitudes of the Penan people.
2. appreciation, reverence, humility, and belief in a supreme being
3. Answers may include that they live close to nature, have the skills to survive in the forest, are physically fit, and respect the resources found in the environment.
4. Answers should account for the things the Penan do to make their way successfully through the forest.

SUMMARY & STUDY GUIDE

SECTION 1 — Living in Southeast Asia (pp. 759–765)

Terms to Know
- paddy
- sickle
- subsistence crop
- cash crop
- lode
- interdependent
- Association of Southeast Asian Nations (ASEAN)
- free port

Key Points
- Agriculture is the leading economic activity in Southeast Asia.
- The countries of the region are industrializing at different rates, which causes great variation in economies, occupations, transportation, and communications.
- Through ASEAN and other organizations that were formed to promote regional development and trade, the countries of Southeast Asia are becoming more interdependent.

Organizing Your Notes
Create an outline using the format below to help you organize your notes for this section.

Living in Southeast Asia
I. Agriculture
A. Rice cultivation
1. Most important crop

SECTION 2 — People and Their Environment (pp. 766–771)

Terms to Know
- cyclone
- typhoon
- shifting cultivation

Key Points
- Volcanic eruptions, flash floods, and typhoons have serious effects on Southeast Asians' lives.
- Industrialization and economic development in Southeast Asia often result in the pollution of air, land, and water.
- The region's countries are taking steps to protect the environment.

Organizing Your Notes
Use a web diagram like the one below to help you organize important details from this section.

 Nature's Might Environmental Pollution Environmental Protection

◀ A Thai family stands by their house, built on a canal in Bangkok.

Using the Chapter 31 Summary & Study Guide
Use the Chapter 31 Summary & Study Guide to preview, review, condense, or reteach the chapter.

Preview/Review
🔘 **Vocabulary PuzzleMaker CD-ROM** reinforces "Terms to Know."

🔘 **Interactive Tutor Self-Assessment CD-ROM** provides a review of Chapter 31 content.

Condense
Have students read the Chapter 31 Summary & Study Guide.

🔘 Chapter 31 Audio Program

📁 Chapter 31 Guided Reading Activities

Reteach
📁 Chapter 31 Reteaching Activities (Spanish also available)

📁 Chapter 31 Reading Essentials and Study Guides

GLENCOE
TECHNOLOGY

■ NATIONAL GEOGRAPHIC
WORLD REGIONS
VIDEO PROGRAM

Unit 10, Southeast Asia
The following segments enhance the study of this unit:
- **Rice**
- **Tet in Hanoi**
- **Design for the Future**

CHAPTER CULMINATING ACTIVITY

Problem Solving Ask: What environmental problems must Southeast Asia solve to ensure that environmental protection goes hand-in-hand with economic development? To answer the question, students should review their notes and Chapter 31. Then have students assume the role of a United Nations observer who is traveling throughout the region. Students should write a report suggesting possible solutions to perceived problems and include appropriate supporting materials such as charts, graphs, maps, or photographs. ■ **EE4 Human Systems: Standard 11**
■ **EE5 Environment and Society: Standard 14**

CHAPTER
31
ASSESSMENT & ACTIVITIES

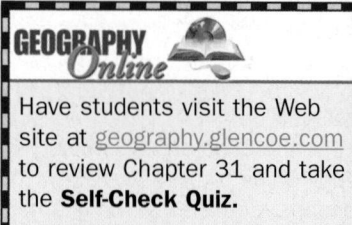

Reviewing Key Terms

1. lodes
2. Cash crops
3. paddy
4. free port
5. interdependent
6. Association of Southeast Asian Nations
7. cyclone
8. sickle
9. shifting cultivation

Reviewing Facts
SECTION 1

1. farming
2. textile and clothing manufacturing, automobile assembly, electronics, oil refining, cement, chemicals

SECTION 2

3. air pollution, overcrowding of cities, and dumping of toxic wastes
4. slash-and-burn agriculture and shifting cultivation

Critical Thinking

1. Logging and mining may continue to benefit foreign investors without improving the people's standard of living.
2. Answers may include that interdependence promotes economic stability and cultural exchange.

Reviewing Key Terms

Write the key term that best completes each of the following sentences. Refer to the Terms to Know in the Summary & Study Guide on page 775.

1. Papua has rich _____, or deposits of minerals.
2. _____ in the Philippines include coconuts and sugarcane.
3. A flooded field in which rice is grown is a _____.
4. Countries involved in oceangoing trade are attracted by a(n) _____ such as Singapore.
5. By becoming _____, the countries of Southeast Asia can build the region's economy.
6. Indonesia, Malaysia, the Philippines, Singapore, and Thailand were the first countries to join the _____.
7. Southeast Asia experiences a specific kind of _____ known as a typhoon.
8. A hand tool called a(n) _____ is still used to harvest crops.
9. In _____ farmers abandon their fields after a few years.

Reviewing Facts
SECTION 1

1. What is the occupation of most people in Southeast Asia?
2. What types of industries are the countries of Southeast Asia developing?

SECTION 2

3. List three negative impacts of industrialization in Southeast Asia. Give examples.
4. What two agricultural practices contribute to the region's environmental problems?

Critical Thinking

1. Identifying Cause and Effect What effects might continued mining and logging have on Papua's people?
2. Making Inferences How does interdependence help Southeast Asia's economic development and trade?
3. Comparing and Constrasting Using a Venn diagram like the one below, compare the environmental challenges that occur in Southeast Asian cities and rural areas.

Urban — Both — Rural

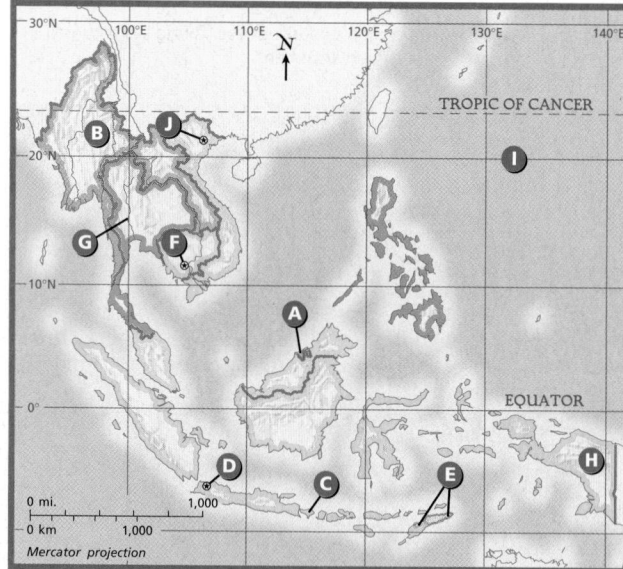
NATIONAL GEOGRAPHIC **Locating Places**
Southeast Asia: Physical-Political Geography
Match the letters on the map with the places and physical features of Southeast Asia. Write your answers on a sheet of paper.

1. Chao Phraya River   5. Bali   9. Jakarta
2. Brunei   6. East Timor   10. New Guinea
3. Myanmar   7. Hanoi
4. Phnom Penh   8. Pacific Ocean

3. possible answers: cities: overurbanization, air pollution, waste disposal; rural: deforestation; combined: air pollution from burning

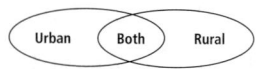
NATIONAL GEOGRAPHIC **Locating Places**

1. G	**3.** B	**5.** C	**7.** J	**9.** D
2. A	**4.** F	**6.** E	**8.** I	**10.** H

Using the Regional Atlas

1. Gulf of Tonkin
2. subsistence farming; hunting and gathering

Using the Regional Atlas

Refer to the Regional Atlas on pages 710–713.

1. **Location** What body of water separates northern Vietnam from the South China Sea?

2. **Human-Environment Interaction** What are the two main types of land use in mountainous areas in Southeast Asia?

Thinking Like a Geographer

Think about the physical geography of Southeast Asia. What is one of the region's important physical assets? As a geographer, how might you suggest that people utilize this asset to improve their lives?

Problem-Solving Activity

Group Research Project Work with a group to research how people in various world regions adapt to or modify their environment in order to control flooding. Compare methods of flood control in other regions with those used in Southeast Asia. Evaluate whether a method used in another region is workable in Southeast Asia.

GeoJournal

Expository Writing Using the information you logged in your GeoJournal as you read this chapter, choose one economic or environmental characteristic of Southeast Asia. Then write a short essay that compares and contrasts the characteristic among the region's countries. Use your textbook and the Internet as resources.

Technology Activity

Creating an Electronic Database Make a fact sheet for each Southeast Asian country. Include data about agriculture, industries, transportation, communications, and environmental challenges. Put this information into a database, and then write a paragraph comparing and contrasting two Southeast Asian countries. If possible, create graphic elements such as bar graphs or circle graphs to support your conclusions.

Standardized Test Practice

Study the bar graph below. Then choose the best answer for the multiple-choice question. If you have trouble answering the question, use the process of elimination to narrow your choices.

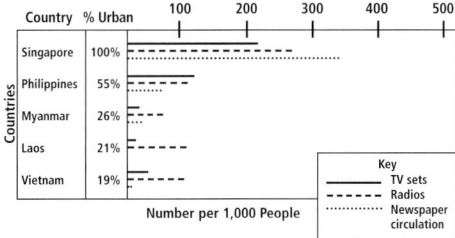

Media in Selected Southeast Asian Countries

Source: The World Almanac and Book of Facts, 2000

1. **What conclusions can you draw from the graph?**

   A Newspapers are censored in Laos.

   B People in rural areas have less access to literacy programs.

   C Urban populations have more access to news sources.

   D Televisions are less expensive in Singapore than in other countries in Southeast Asia.

 **Test-Taking Tip** Study the title and labels on the graph to see what information is being presented. Note the important facts, and look at the relationships among the countries. Remember, an answer choice that may be true cannot be the correct answer if there is no information to support it in the graph.

GeoJournal

Essays should be well organized, clearly written, and focused on one characteristic. Students should include accurate information for each country in the region.

Technology Activity

Students' fact sheets should include accurate, current data on each topic for each country in the region. Paragraphs should describe the similarities of and differences between two countries.

Standardized Test Practice
1. C

Tested Objectives:
reading a bar graph
synthesizing information

Additional Practice and Test-Taking Tips
Standardized Test Practice Workbook

? CHAPTER BONUS TEST QUESTION

What country was temporarily governed by the United Nations? *(East Timor)*

Thinking Like a Geographer

Major cities are or are near ocean ports. These locations can facilitate trade with other countries. Rivers are abundant and provide the best means of transportation between rural and urban areas; rivers have hydroelectric potential.

Problem-Solving Activity

Students should state the type of flood control method selected, how it works, and why it is or is not a viable solution for a country in Southeast Asia.

TEACHING TRANSPARENCIES

L2 Unit 11 Map Overlay Transparencies

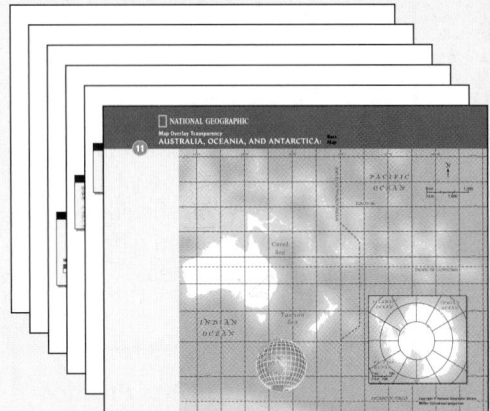

L2 Political Map Transparency 11

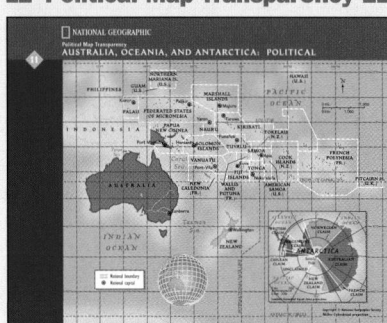

L2 World Cultures Transparencies 19, 20

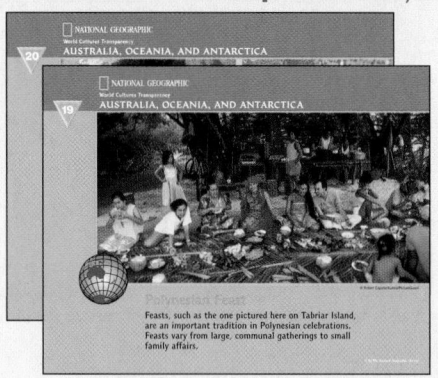

APPLICATION AND ENRICHMENT

L2 Location Activity 11

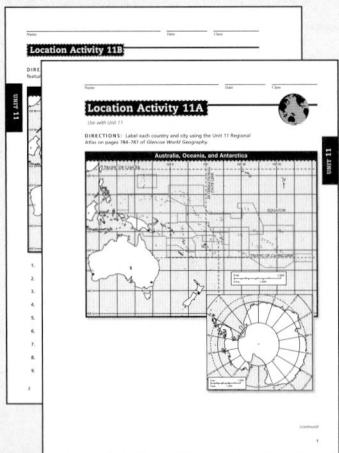

L2 Real-Life Applications and Problem-Solving Activity 11

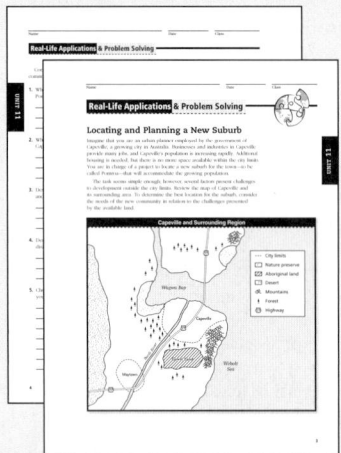

L2 GeoLab Activity 11

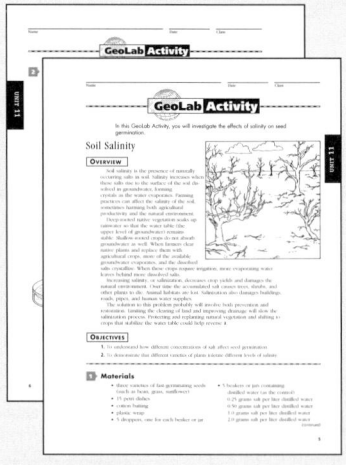

L2 Environmental Issues Case Study 11

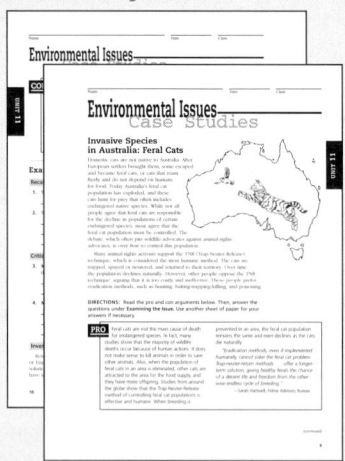

GEOGRAPHIC LITERACY

Focus on Geography Literacy

Building Geography Skills for Life

ASSESSMENT

Use the following to easily assess student learning in a variety of ways:
- Performance Assessment Activities and Rubrics
- Section Quizzes
- Chapter and Unit Tests
- Interactive Tutor Self-Assessment CD–ROM
- ExamView® Pro Testmaker
- MindJogger Videoquiz
- geography.glencoe.com
- Standardized Test Practice Workbook
- SAT I/II Test Practice

L2 Unit 11 Pretest and Tests

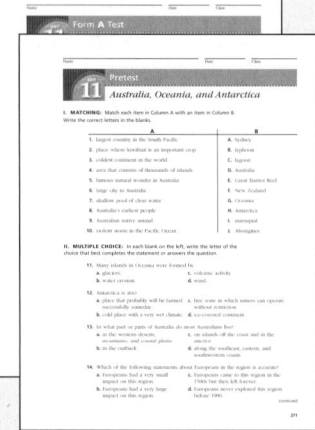

INTERDISCIPLINARY CONNECTIONS

L2 World Literature:
Contemporary Selection 11

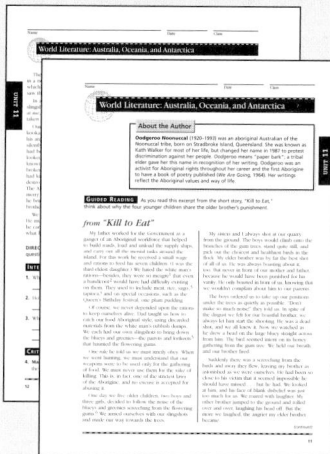

Foods Around the World

Multimedia

- **World Art and Architecture Transparencies**

- **World Art Prints**

- **World Music: A Cultural Legacy**

- **World History Primary Source Document Library**

BIBLIOGRAPHY

Readings for the Student

Cultures of the World: Australia by Vijeya & Sundran Rajendra. Tarrytown, NY: Benchmark Books, 1994.

Antarctica: The Last Continent, by Kim Heacox. Washington, D.C.: National Geographic Society, 1998.

Blue Horizons: Paradise Isles of the Pacific. Washington, D.C.: National Geographic Society, 1985.

Readings for the Teacher

The Fatal Shore by Robert Hughes. New York, NY: Alfred A. Knopf, 1994.

A Natural History of Australia, by Tim M. Berra. San Diego, CA: Academic Press, 1998.

A Natural History of the Antarctic by Alastair Fothergill. New York, NY: Sterling Publishing Company, 1995.

Multimedia Resources

History and Culture of Australia. Fairfield, CT: Queue, 1995. CD-ROM.

Australia's Great Barrier Reef. Washington, D.C.: National Geographic Society, 1993. Videocassette, 60 minutes.

Heart of Antarctica: 1998 Scientific Expedition. Venice, CA: TMW, 1998. Videocassette, 40 minutes.

READING SUPPORT FROM JAMESTOWN EDUCATION

- *Timed Readings Plus in Social Studies* help students increase their reading rate and fluency while maintaining comprehension. The 400-word passages are similar to those found on state and national assessments.

- *Reading in the Content Area: Social Studies* concentrates on six essential reading skills that help students better comprehend what they read. The book includes 75 high-interest nonfiction passages written at increasing levels of difficulty.

- *Reading Fluency* helps students read smoothly, accurately, and expressively.

- *Jamestown's Reading Improvement,* by renowned reading expert Edward Fry, focuses on helping build your students' comprehension, vocabulary, and skimming and scanning skills.

- *Critical Reading Series* provides high-interest books, each written at three reading levels.

For more information about these products, see the Jamestown Education materials in the Classroom Solutions in the front of this Teacher Wraparound Edition. To order these products, call Glencoe at 1-800-334-7344.

Background Information

CHAPTER 32 (pp. 792–807)

The Physical Geography of Australia, Oceania, and Antarctica

With a land area of 2,988,888 square miles, (7,741,220 sq. km) Australia is the earth's smallest continent, but its sixth largest country. Two of the Seven Natural Wonders of the World are located in Australia: the massive rock known as Uluru (Ayers Rock) and the Great Barrier Reef, the world's largest deposit of coral. The Great Barrier Reef, made up of billions of tiny organisms, is home to about 2,000 species of fish.

Although surrounded by water, Australia receives less precipitation than any continent except Antarctica. Deserts cover two-thirds of Australia's land, even though more than 100 inches (254 cm) of rain may fall each year on areas near the northeastern coast.

The continent of Antarctica, too, is unique. Its elevation is the highest of any continent. In places, the ice cap that covers Antarctica's surface is 14,000 feet (4,267 m) deep and 100,000 years old. Antarctica's elevation and location make it the coldest place on Earth. The world's lowest yearly air temperatures, averaging about -126°F (-88°C), are recorded in eastern Antarctica.

Natural Resources

Physical geography often makes developing natural resources difficult in the South Pacific region. For example, Papua New Guinea's rugged terrain makes building roads and railroads expensive. The lack of good transportation limits access to mining and makes transporting the country's rich copper and other mineral resources difficult. In addition, the 1997 *El Niño* caused droughts that damaged the country's coffee, cocoa, and coconut crops.

An international treaty bans exploitation of mineral resources on the frozen continent until 2041, but even then extraction in such a harsh environment may still be a challenge.

CHAPTER 33 (pp. 810–831)

The Cultural Geography of Australia, Oceania, and Antarctica

The 2000 Summer Olympic Games in Sydney, Australia, gave Australians an opportunity to display their cultural diversity. The opening ceremonies highlighted the contributions of Australia's indigenous and immigrant populations. Later, during the competition, Cathy Freeman, a running champion and one of the country's most admired athletes, became the first Aborigine to win an individual gold medal.

Throughout the South Pacific region, there is a diversity of peoples and languages. At one time, Australia's Aborigines may have spoken about 250 languages with as many as 700 dialects. Many of these languages have been lost because Aborigines did not have a written alphabet and because Aboriginal children began learning English in school. In 1970, however, the Australian government began providing bilingual education. Many different languages are spoken in Oceania. Some experts believe that roughly 40 percent of the 3,000 languages used worldwide are found in the Pacific islands.

Population and Migration

The movement of peoples has long been a part of the South Pacific's development. More than 90 percent of Australians have European ancestors, although in the last quarter of the 1900s, more than 125,000 Southeast Asians migrated to Australia. Many came to escape political turmoil in their homelands. At century's end, Australia's population was growing at a rate of about 1 percent per year. Even so, fewer people live in Australia than on any of the other inhabited continents. The vast majority of Australians live in cities near the coast.

As in Australia, New Zealand's population is growing at a rate of about 1 percent per year. Some of the larger Pacific islands, however, are growing much faster. Nauru's population has been increasing by

1.4 percent annually; Papua New Guinea's, by 2.3 percent. In the Solomon Islands the annual growth rate exceeds 3 percent.

CHAPTER 34 (pp. 832–847)

Australia, Oceania, and Antarctica Today

For decades Australia was associated with a "rough and ready" frontier or unusual native animals such as the kangaroo. Today, however, Australians are quick to point out that Nobel Prize–winning author Patrick White, the acclaimed opera singer Dame Joan Sutherland, and filmmaker Peter Weir are Australian. The Sydney Opera House, one of the architectural wonders of the modern world, contains state-of-the-art acoustics and an ultra-modern architectural form. Its design evokes the sailing ships that were an important part of Australia's past. Australians also like to boast that art museums on the island continent are even more popular with residents than is Australian football. Magnificent Aboriginal paintings and sculptures are among the most prized exhibits.

In New Zealand filmmakers Jane Campion and Lee Tamahori have fostered an appreciation of New Zealand's culture. Movies such as Campion's *The Piano* and Tamahori's *Once Were Warriors* (about the Maori) have won worldwide critical acclaim.

The island countries of Oceania are trying to develop their natural resources, improve living standards, and strengthen global ties. However, high costs of fuel imports, a limited range of agricultural exports, heavy dependence on food imports, and overreliance on foreign aid make island economies vulnerable to changes in the global marketplace. Coconut products form the principal export. Farming is based on family-owned agriculture and cash crop plantations. Larger island countries or territories—such as Fiji, Papua New Guinea, the Solomon Islands, and New Caledonia—benefit from the export of mineral deposits, such as gold, copper, and nickel. Since the 1970s, tourism has opened up new sources of revenue and opportunities for employment.

Regional and Global Challenges

Today the South Pacific region is seeking to overcome economic and environmental challenges. In recent decades, New Zealand's government has sought to decrease the country's dependence on agriculture and to develop industries, but South Pacific countries are also concerned about their environment.

During the Cold War, Western countries tested nuclear weapons in parts of Oceania. Environmental concerns and increased awareness of long-term effects of radiation brought international protests. The United States and Great Britain discontinued nuclear testing in this region in the 1960s. The United

States, in fact, paid millions of dollars to residents of Bikini Atoll in the Marshall Islands as compensation for damages done to their area and their people during nuclear testing. However, France continued nuclear testing in Oceania into the mid-1990s.

Since the 1980s, an increase in cases of cancer and stillbirths has alarmed Tahiti's people. To date, however, France has not conceded that there is any relationship between the rise in specific diseases and the nuclear tests.

Like the rest of the world, the countries of Australia and Oceania are looking for ways to reconcile the need for economic growth with concerns for the health and safety of their people and their environment.

00:00 OUT OF TIME?

If time does not permit teaching each chapter in this unit, you may want to use the **Reading Essentials and Study Guide** summaries.

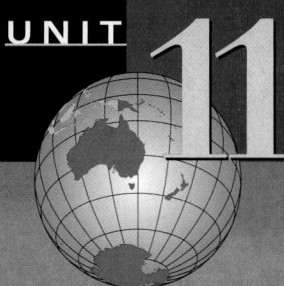

Unit Launch Activity

Ask: **What images come to mind when you think of Australia? The South Pacific islands? Antarctica? What do you know about these places from TV, radio, newspapers, or magazines?** Have the class brainstorm, and write responses on the board. Tell students to summarize their impressions in writing and to keep their papers. Encourage them to add information from the unit that reinforces their ideas or provides new insights. At the end of the unit, have students revisit their original summary and revise it based on what they have learned. Use the finished summaries as the basis for a class discussion of the region.

GLENCOE TECHNOLOGY

NATIONAL GEOGRAPHIC
WORLD REGIONS
VIDEO PROGRAM

Unit 11, Australia, Oceania, and Antarctica
The following segments enhance the study of this unit:

- **Dream of a Lifetime**
- **Australia's Pioneers**
- **Haka Tradition**

Available in DVD and VHS

UNIT 11

Australia, Oceania, and Antarctica

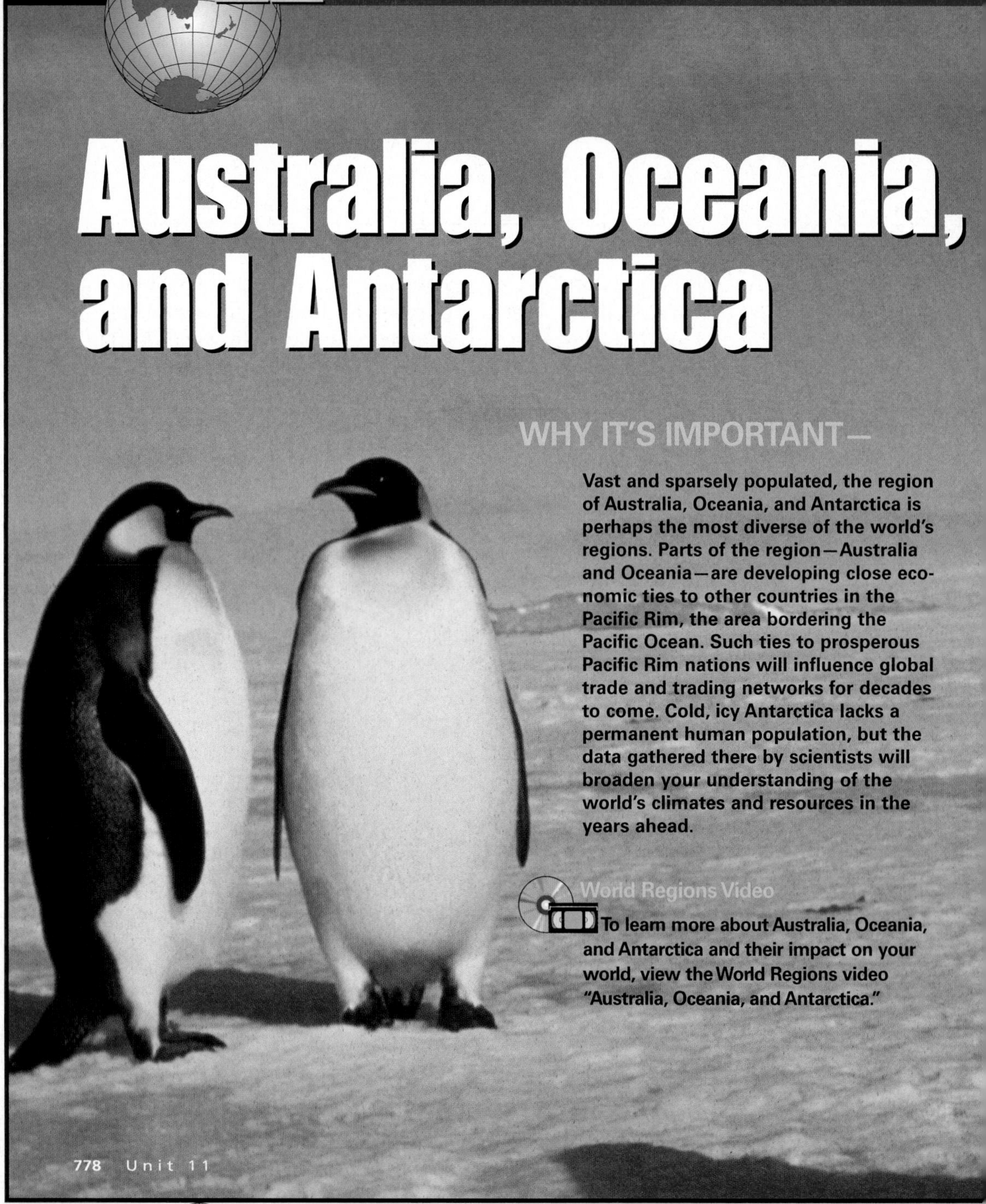

WHY IT'S IMPORTANT—

Vast and sparsely populated, the region of Australia, Oceania, and Antarctica is perhaps the most diverse of the world's regions. Parts of the region—Australia and Oceania—are developing close economic ties to other countries in the Pacific Rim, the area bordering the Pacific Ocean. Such ties to prosperous Pacific Rim nations will influence global trade and trading networks for decades to come. Cold, icy Antarctica lacks a permanent human population, but the data gathered there by scientists will broaden your understanding of the world's climates and resources in the years ahead.

World Regions Video

To learn more about Australia, Oceania, and Antarctica and their impact on your world, view the World Regions video "Australia, Oceania, and Antarctica."

GETTING TO KNOW THE REGION

Map Activity Refer students to the political map on page 785 of the Unit Atlas. **Ask:** **What is the largest landmass in the region?** *(Antarctica)* **What unifying characteristic do all the individual lands in this region share?** *(Each is surrounded by water.)* **If Australia is the "land down under," what is it below?** *(the Equator)* **What imaginary line runs from north to south through the region?** *(the International Date Line)* **How does longitude change when you cross this line traveling toward Asia?** *(Degrees of longitude change from west to east.)* **What two major landmasses are part of New Zealand?** *(North Island and South Island)* **What is the northernmost landmass in the region?** *(the Northern Mariana Islands)* **Easternmost?** *(Pitcairn Island)* **EE1 The World in Spatial Terms: Standard 1**

Penguins in Antarctica

This online resource, brought to you by the National Geographic Society, provides lesson plans, atlas updates, cartographic activities with interactive maps, an online map store, and links to the boundless subjects of maps and geography.

Unit Overview

This unit introduces students to the physical and cultural geography of Australia and Oceania as well as to the physical geography of Antarctica. Point out to students that although the countries of this region are diverse, most have the following features in common:

- a blend of indigenous and European influences on language and culture
- a location in the Southern Hemisphere that is remote from the industrialized regions of the world
- striking and unusual animal and plant species

ABOUT THE PHOTO

Visual Instruction Penguins are flightless birds that appear clumsy on land. They are superb swimmers, however, admirably adapted to the frozen environment of Antarctica. Like Antarctica itself, the penguin was a mystery to the explorers who first saw it. Scientists originally classified it as a fish. After further study, however, they realized that penguins are actually feathered creatures that belong to the class *Aves*, or birds. **Ask:** Why is speed and agility in the water vital to the survival of Antarctic penguins? *(Since there is no food on the ice-covered land, penguins must be skilled swimmers to find food in the water; they also must be quick to escape from predators such as seals, sea lions, and orcas.)*
 EE2 Places and Regions: Standard 4

UNIT 11 REGIONAL ATLAS

1 FOCUS

These features and activities may be used as an introduction to the unit or as teaching tools throughout the course of the unit.

L1 Using Flash Cards Activity

Before beginning the study of this unit, use the **Countries of the World Flash Cards** to preview students' knowledge of Australia, Oceania, and Antarctica. Organize the students into two teams and test their knowledge. At the end of the game, ask students to summarize any physical or cultural similarities they noticed among countries in the region.

L2 Photo Research Activity

Have students research to find out more information about the subjects of the photos on pages 780–783. You may assign this as an individual or group activity. Students should report their findings to the rest of the class.

INTERDISCIPLINARY
c o n n e c t i o n

GEOLOGY Antarctic ice affects tropical waters. Each winter when Antarctica's coastal ice sheets form, they produce extremely cold salt water that sinks to the ocean floor. This cold water is picked up by ocean currents and carried to the tropics.

What Makes Australia, Oceania, and Antarctica a Region?

Both palm trees and polar ice lie within this diverse region that includes two continents—Australia and Antarctica—and some 25,000 islands scattered across vast expanses of the Pacific Ocean.

Australia is ancient and arid. Low mountains curve down its eastern coast, blocking rainfall to the flat interior where scrubland and deserts form what Australians call the "outback." Across the Tasman Sea lies New Zealand—lush, green, and mountainous. North of New Zealand's rugged shores lies the rest of Oceania, where groups of tropical islands dot the blue ocean waters like tiny jewels.

A different sort of jewel lies far to the south of New Zealand—Antarctica, a glittering kingdom of ice and snow that sits astride the bottom of the world.

1 Shouldering the day's catch, a spear fisher in the Cook Islands watches his companion take aim. The Cook Islands spread across 850,000 square miles (2.2 million sq. km) of ocean. Like people throughout Oceania, Cook Islanders depend on the sea for food.

BACKGROUND INFORMATION

Uluru Uluru (Ayers Rock) rises spectacularly above the relatively flat landscape of central Australia like a feature from another planet. Uluru is 1,141 feet high (348 m) and 5.6 miles (9.4 km) around at its base. Incredibly, it also is a monolith—a single stone or rock—the largest on Earth. Scientists believe it is about 500 million years old. Uluru's sandstone composition changes color depending on the time of day. It is most spectacular at sunset when it may appear deep red. One of Australia's most popular tourist attractions, Uluru is sacred to the Aborigines. It is adorned with paintings, and it figures prominently in Aboriginal legends. The Australian government recently returned ownership to the Aborigines.

🌐 **EE2 Places and Regions: Standards 4, 6;** 🌐 **EE6 The Uses of Geography: Standard 17**

② TEACH

L2 Place

Encourage students to discuss how geographic place may affect daily life. **Ask:** What would your life be like if you lived in a desert environment? How might life in a mild year-round climate differ from living in a place with significant seasonal change? How would your life be affected if you lived on a remote island? What activities and precautions would be part of your life in sub-zero temperatures? Have students make a list of the different ways that place can affect people's lives. Have them refer to this list as they read about the physical and cultural geography of this region.

GLENCOE *TECHNOLOGY*

NATIONAL GEOGRAPHIC
WORLD REGIONS
VIDEO PROGRAM

Unit 11, Australia, Oceania, and Antarctica
The following segments enhance the study of this unit:

- **Dream of a Lifetime**
- **Australia's Pioneers**
- **Haka Tradition**

Available in DVD and VHS

2 **A loaf-shaped mass** of sandstone, Uluru (also known as Ayers Rock) looms over the flat landscape of central Australia. Uluru is sacred to Aborigines, the country's native inhabitants. Aborigines share their homeland with Australia's other natives—kangaroos and other animals found nowhere else on Earth.

3 **Fringed with coral reefs,** the thickly forested islands of Palau seem to float on the surface of blue Pacific waters. Palau is a chain of about 200 islands a few hundred miles east of the Philippines. Its coral reefs are among the world's most biologically diverse.

4 **A sea of sheep** parts for two bicyclists on New Zealand's South Island. Sheep greatly outnumber people in New Zealand, where pastures thrive in a climate that is mild year-round. The nation ranks as one of the world's leading producers of lamb, mutton, and wool.

Unit 11   781

A TRAVELER'S LOG

Paul Theroux In this passage from *The Happy Isles of Oceania: Paddling the Pacific* (1992), author Theroux describes the view of Oceania from the air:

"After an hour of high clouds and blue ocean, the green islands shimmered into view. They were in the middle of nowhere: it was another experience of the Pacific being like the night sky, like outer space. . . . In the Solomon Sea below, there were about a dozen islands big and small; and they could not have been flatter. Only a few feet above sea level, without a single hump or mound, they appeared to be floating, like a thin layer of green weed . . . upon the sea."

EE1 The World in Spatial Terms: Standards 2, 3
EE2 Places and Regions: Standards 4, 6

UNIT 11 REGIONAL ATLAS

L2 Making Predictions

Remind students of the Age of Exploration in which Europeans sailed the globe in search of land, goods, and treasure. Ask how they think exploration may have influenced the cultures of the South Pacific region. If necessary, have students refer to the text and use prompts such as *New Zealand, Caroline Islands, and Gilbert Islands.*

Tasmanians Between 3,000 and 5,000 indigenous people once lived on Tasmania. Conflict begun by British settlers led to their relocation and extinction. The last indigenous Tasmanian died on nearby Flinders Island in 1876.

Polynesians Fewer than 20 percent of Polynesians are of pure Polynesian ancestry, and that percentage is shrinking. Islanders' ancestry may include French, English, German, or Chinese nationalities.

Lands Down Under

Europeans were latecomers to this region, much of which lies "down under" the Equator. Australia's original settlers were Aborigines; the first settlers of New Zealand were the Maori. During the 1800s, the British colonized both lands. Today, Australia and the islands of Oceania are a blend of European, traditional Pacific, and Asian cultures. Antarctica has no permanent human inhabitants.

Although huge livestock ranches spread across Australia and New Zealand, life in these two countries is largely urban, with most people living in coastal cities. For many Pacific Islanders, life is more traditional, and people support themselves mainly through fishing and subsistence farming.

1 A blend of cultures is reflected by an Aborigine wearing western-style clothing. Aborigines are thought to have arrived in Australia from Asia at least 40,000 years ago. Today, many Aborigines are striving to preserve their ancient traditions while living in a modern world.

BACKGROUND INFORMATION

Australian Slang Australian slang, a colorful English idiom, has adapted expressions from Aboriginal traditions. For example, when Aborigines took solitary journeys in search of spiritual guidance, the practice was called *go walkabout.* Now the term describes travel in general. Rhyming slang associated with the Cockneys, residents of London's East End district, has taken on an Aussie flavor. For example *"Captain Cook at,"* means "a look at." A third kind of slang relates to the unique Australian experience. The word *outback,* which compares the vast continental interior to a backyard, is an example.

🌐 **EE2 Places and Regions: Standard 4**
🌐 **EE4 Human Systems: Standard 10**

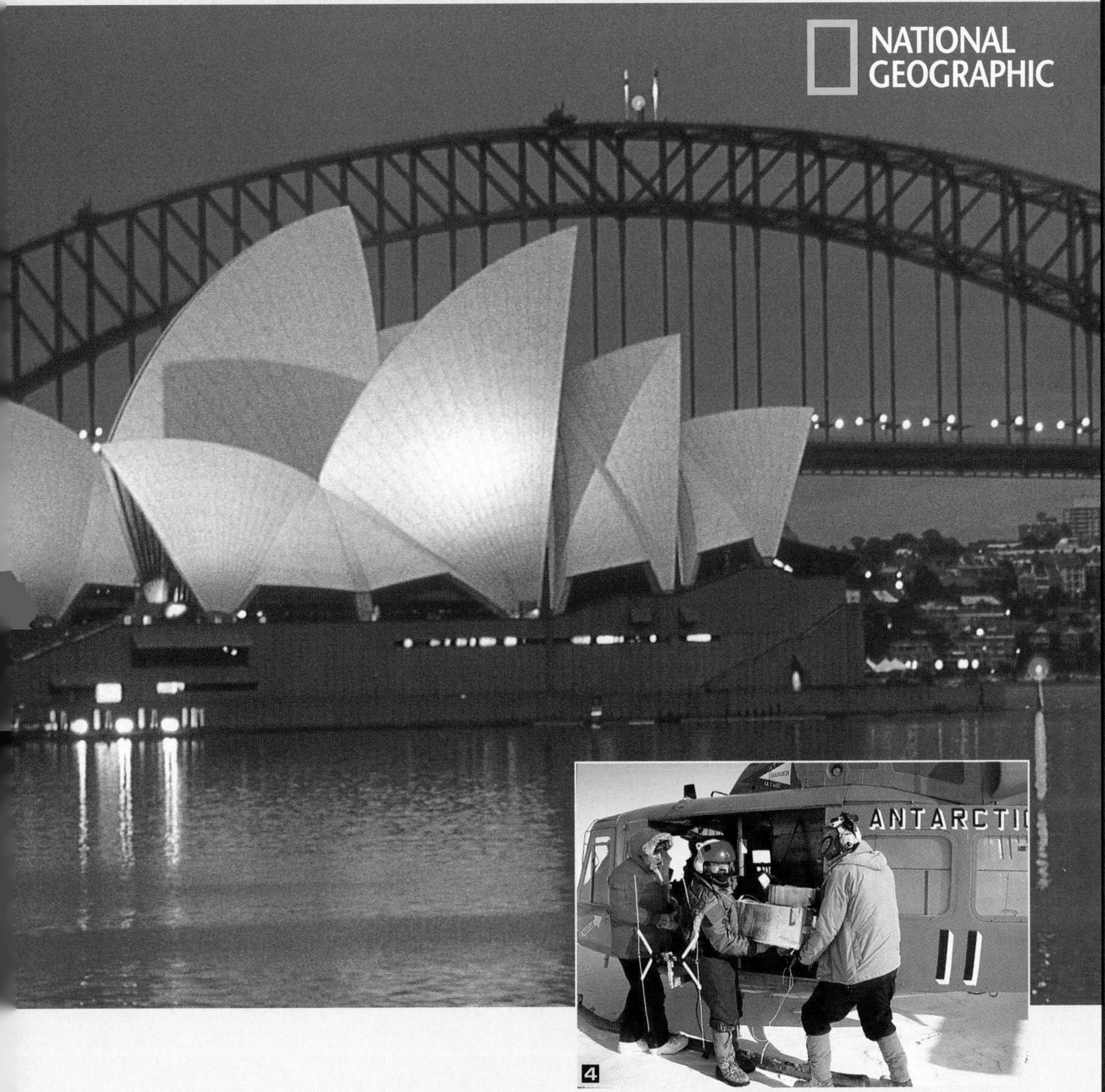

FYi

Oceania's Islands Opinions differ as to how many islands are in Oceania. Some estimates place the number at 20,000, but others believe there are more than 30,000.

**ASSESS**

Play a quick oral quiz game with students. Explain that you will call on a student and ask: Who? What? Where? or Why? Students will state a geographic fact that responds to the question. If students' answers are correct, they choose another student, who is then asked to respond to one of the questions. Continue until all students have responded. *(Facts should be accurate and relate to physical or cultural geography.)*

4 CLOSE

Have students state the most interesting fact they have learned thus far about this region. Then, have them ask a question about the region for which they would like to find an answer.

2 Thatched houses called *fale* sit beneath palm trees on an island in Samoa. Open sides allow cool ocean breezes to blow through the houses. Blinds made of palm leaves can be let down to keep out rain or glaring sun.

3 Mirrored in the waters of Sydney Harbor, the Sydney Opera House glows as evening falls. The white shells that form the building's roof resemble billowing sails—a fitting tribute to the city that is Australia's busiest seaport.

4 Bundled against the cold, scientists in Antarctica load equipment into a waiting helicopter. Antarctica is a continent reserved almost entirely for scientific research and exploration. The United States is one of many countries operating research stations here.

Unit 11 **783**

UNIT PROJECT

Regional Web Site Before students begin the study of this unit, tell them that they will be planning a Web site that could help interested persons learn about the physical and cultural geography of this region. Have students brainstorm and list on the board the types of information that would be useful to include about places in Australia, Oceania, and Antarctica. Examples might include physical features, natural resources, population characteristics, traditional and new economies, history, and languages. Have each student collect written information and illustrations that they can use in planning the Web site as they study the unit. **EE2 Places and Regions: Standards 4, 5**
EE4 Human Systems: Standards 9, 10, 12

These features and activities may be used as an introduction to the unit or as teaching tools throughout the course of the unit.

L1 Using Maps

Have groups of four study the maps on pages 784–787. Then have members take turns formulating sentences that tell about the region. Each member should create at least one sentence based on each map. *(Possible answers include: Tahiti is an island in Oceania, the southeastern coast is the most densely populated region of Australia, and sheep are raised in Australia and New Zealand.)*

L2 Comparing and Contrasting

Have students use information on one of the maps to formulate a sentence that compares or contrasts two places. *(Possible answers include: Australia and New Zealand are south of the Equator, but the Marshall Islands are north of the Equator.)*

Elevation Profile

The profile follows the Tropic of Capricorn ($23\frac{1}{2}°$S) from west to east across the surface of Australia.

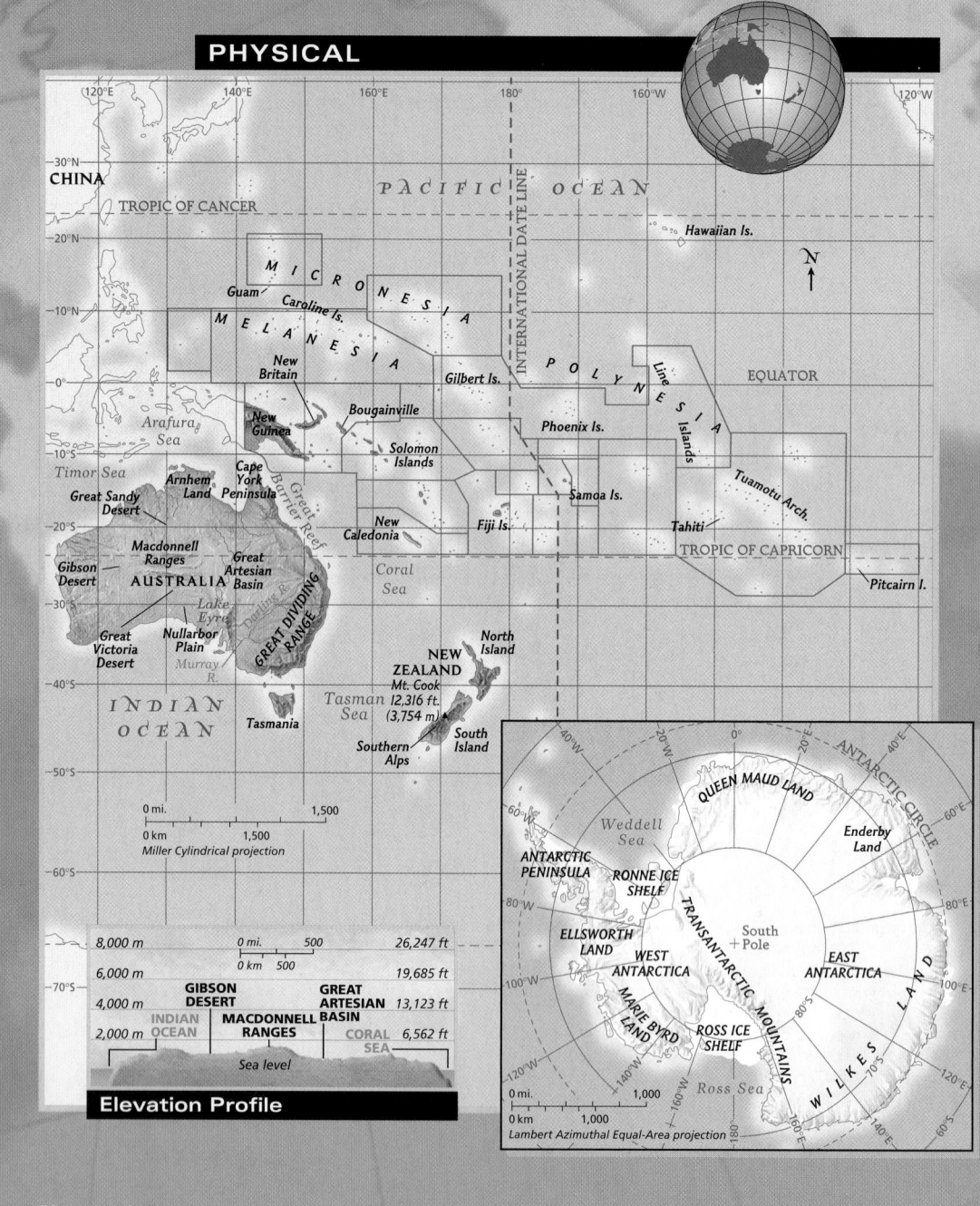

PHYSICAL

784   Unit 11

REGIONAL ATLAS ACTIVITY

Class Challenge Organize students into small groups and have them write at least six questions about the physical geography of this region. Explain that two questions should be about Australia, two about Oceania, and two about Antarctica. Each group will use its questions to challenge another group. Encourage students to use directions, map keys, scale, and physical characteristics to create the questions. Provide this example: In what direction would you travel going from Tasmania to South Island, New Zealand? *(east)* Allow time for groups to write questions and challenge one another. You may also want to repeat this activity at the end of the unit. **ELL** 📦 🌐 **EE1 The World in Spatial Terms: Standard 1**

POLITICAL

(120°E) 140°E 160°E 180° 160°W 140°W

PACIFIC OCEAN

30°N
CHINA
TROPIC OF CANCER
HAWAII
to U.S.

20°N

N

10°N
NORTHERN
MARIANA IS.
U.S.
PHILIPPINES
GUAM
U.S.
Koror
Palikir
MARSHALL
ISLANDS
Majuro
PALAU
FEDERATED STATES
OF MICRONESIA
Tarawa
EQUATOR

0°
INDONESIA
Yaren
NAURU
KIRIBATI
SAMOA
TOKELAU N.Z.
PAPUA
NEW GUINEA
Port
Moresby
Funafuti
TUVALU
SAMOA
AMERICAN
SAMOA
U.S.
FRENCH
POLYNESIA
Fr.

10°S
Timor
Sea
Arafura
Sea
Honiara
SOLOMON
ISLANDS
WALLIS &
FUTUNA Fr.
Apia
COOK
ISLANDS
N.Z.
VANUATU
Port-Vila
Suva
Great Sandy
Desert
Coral
Sea
NEW
CALEDONIA
Fr.
FIJI
ISLANDS
TONGA
PITCAIRN I.
U.K.

20°S
TROPIC OF CAPRICORN
NIUE N.Z.
Nuku'alofa

AUSTRALIA
Brisbane
Great Dividing Range

30°S
Perth
Sydney
Canberra
North
Island
0 mi.   1,500

Melbourne
NEW
ZEALAND
Auckland
0 km   1,500
Miller Cylindrical projection

INDIAN
OCEAN
Tasman
Sea
Tasmania
Christchurch
Wellington
South
Island

40°S

50°S
⊛ National capital
• Major city

60°S

ANTARCTICA map inset:
ATLANTIC OCEAN
NORWEGIAN CLAIM
ANTARCTIC CIRCLE
INDIAN OCEAN
BRITISH CLAIM
ARGENTINE CLAIM
AUSTRALIAN CLAIM
CHILEAN CLAIM
South Pole
ANTARCTICA
Unclaimed
PACIFIC OCEAN
NEW ZEALAND CLAIM
AUSTRALIAN CLAIM
FRENCH CLAIM
0 mi. 500
0 km 500
Azimuthal Equal-Area projection

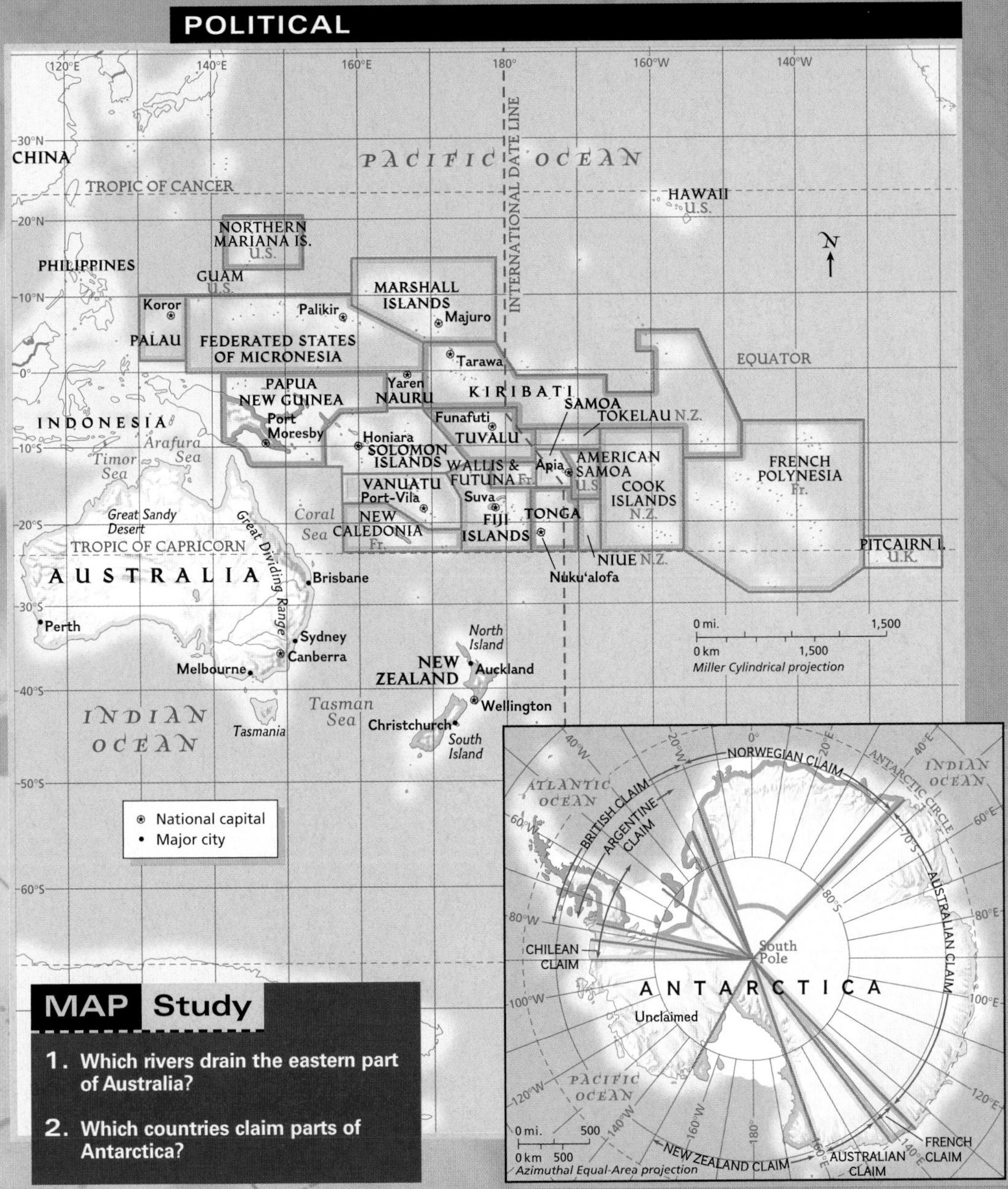

MAP Study

1. Which rivers drain the eastern part of Australia?

2. Which countries claim parts of Antarctica?

L2 Predicting Consequences

Have students study the political map on this page. Ask them to predict how the sizes of various islands and their locations may affect urbanization, housing, occupations, and leisure-time activities. Suggest that students write predictions in their GeoJournals and revise them if necessary as they progress through the unit.

MAP Study

Answers:

1. *Darling River, Murray River*

2. *Norway, Australia, France, New Zealand, Chile, Great Britain, Argentina*

Map Skills Practice
Place What is the national capital of Australia? *(Canberra)* New Zealand? *(Wellington)* Papua New Guinea? *(Port Moresby)*

Culture NOTE

New Zealand About 90 percent of all New Zealanders are descended from European settlers. The rest are Maori descendants of New Zealand's first settlers.

REGIONAL ATLAS ACTIVITY

Migration Explain that students are going to suggest routes to various countries that early migrants could have taken to settle this region. For ideas, have them use the maps on pages 784–785 and refer to the physical/political map of the world in the Reference Atlas at the front of the book. Tell students to speculate also on what kinds of technology early settlers would have needed to move from mainland areas to islands and from island to island. Have students research to find out whether their speculations are accurate.

▦ **EE4 Human Systems: Standard 9;** ▦ **EE5 Environment and Society: Standard 15**
▦ **EE6 The Uses of Geography: Standard 17**

L2 Interpreting a Map

Have partners use the statistical ranges under *Cities* on the population density map key to make a chart. Tell them to list each numerical range as column heads. They should find and list in each column cities in the region that fit within each range. Tell them to compare the sizes of these cities to those of cities in your state.

L2 Effects of Colonization

Explain that much of this region has been colonized at one time or another. Have students discuss how colonization may have affected the ethnic makeup of populations, population distribution, types of settlements, and economic development. Tell students to confirm or revise their speculations by consulting statistical data on the Internet.

□ NATIONAL GEOGRAPHIC **GEOFACT**

▶ **Antarctica's summer population includes tourists as well as scientists. Visitors can even swim in a natural hot pool on Deception Island. Volcanic activity, however, can turn the water from soothing to scalding without warning.**

UNIT 11 REGIONAL ATLAS

Australia, Oceania, and Antarctica

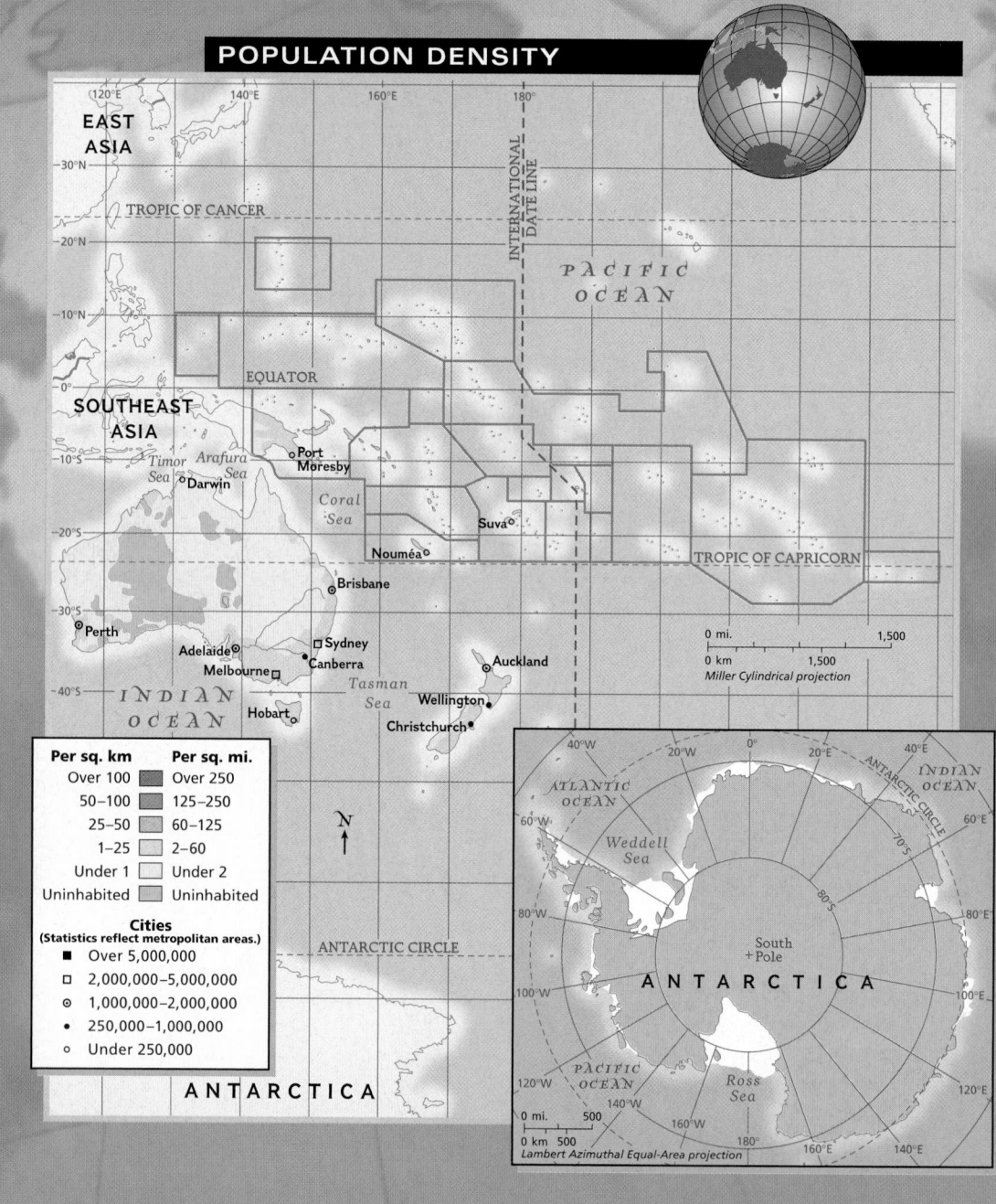

POPULATION DENSITY

Per sq. km	Per sq. mi.
Over 100	Over 250
50–100	125–250
25–50	60–125
1–25	2–60
Under 1	Under 2
Uninhabited	Uninhabited

Cities
(Statistics reflect metropolitan areas.)
■ Over 5,000,000
□ 2,000,000–5,000,000
◉ 1,000,000–2,000,000
• 250,000–1,000,000
○ Under 250,000

REGIONAL ATLAS ACTIVITY

Tourism Many South Pacific islands depend on tourism. Have partners choose one group of South Pacific islands and research reference materials to find data on the two major factors that draw visitors to these islands: the beauty of the environment and the presence of many traditional cultures. Have students find out how many tourists visit annually and what percentage of the islands' economies are based on tourism. Students should also analyze the effects, both positive and negative, that tourism may have on ecology and traditional cultures.

◉ **EE2 Places and Regions: Standard 6;** ◉ **EE4 Human Systems: Standard 11**
◉ **EE6 The Uses of Geography: Standard 18**

NATIONAL GEOGRAPHIC

ECONOMIC ACTIVITY

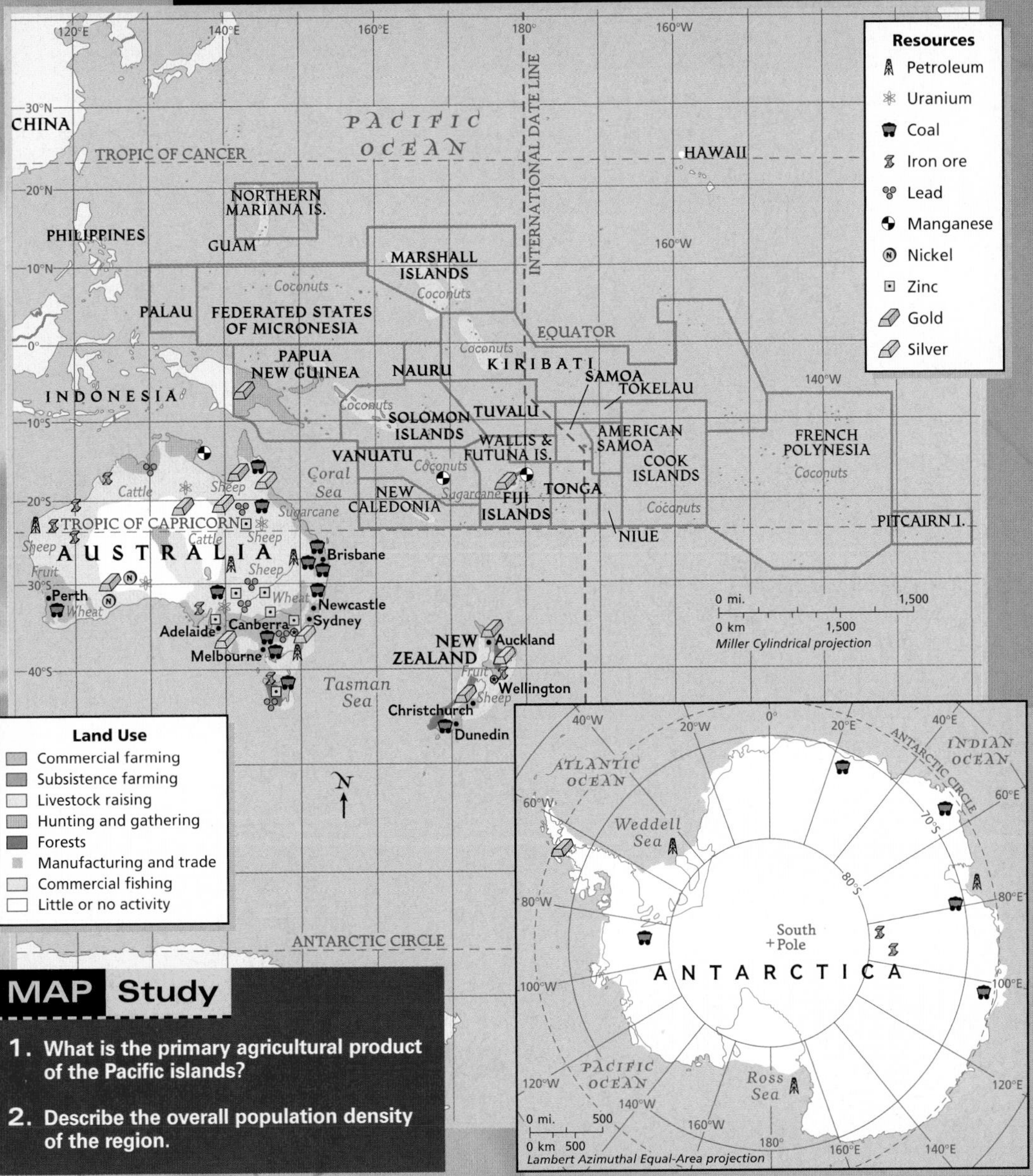
120°E
140°E
160°E
180°
160°W
30°N
CHINA
PACIFIC OCEAN
TROPIC OF CANCER
INTERNATIONAL DATE LINE
HAWAII
20°N
NORTHERN MARIANA IS.
PHILIPPINES
GUAM
MARSHALL ISLANDS
10°N
Coconuts
PALAU
FEDERATED STATES OF MICRONESIA
EQUATOR
0°
PAPUA NEW GUINEA
NAURU
KIRIBATI
SAMOA
TOKELAU
INDONESIA
SOLOMON ISLANDS
TUVALU
10°S
WALLIS & FUTUNA IS.
AMERICAN SAMOA
FRENCH POLYNESIA
VANUATU
Coral Sea
COOK ISLANDS
NEW CALEDONIA
FIJI ISLANDS
TONGA
20°S
Cattle
Sheep
Sugarcane
TROPIC OF CAPRICORN
PITCAIRN I.
NIUE
AUSTRALIA
Brisbane
Fruit
Wheat
30°S
Perth
Newcastle
Sydney
Adelaide
Canberra
Melbourne
NEW ZEALAND
Auckland
Wellington
40°S
Tasman Sea
Christchurch
Dunedin
140°W
0 mi. 1,500
0 km 1,500
Miller Cylindrical projection
Resources
Petroleum
Uranium
Coal
Iron ore
Lead
Manganese
Nickel
Zinc
Gold
Silver
Land Use
Commercial farming
Subsistence farming
Livestock raising
Hunting and gathering
Forests
Manufacturing and trade
Commercial fishing
Little or no activity
N
ANTARCTIC CIRCLE
40°W
20°W
0°
20°E
40°E
ATLANTIC OCEAN
INDIAN OCEAN
ANTARCTIC CIRCLE
60°W
60°E
Weddell Sea
70°S
80°S
80°W
80°E
South Pole
ANTARCTICA
100°W
100°E
PACIFIC OCEAN
Ross Sea
120°W
120°E
140°W
160°W
180°
160°E
140°E
0 mi. 500
0 km 500
Lambert Azimuthal Equal-Area projection

MAP Study

1. What is the primary agricultural product of the Pacific islands?
2. Describe the overall population density of the region.

L2 Human-Environment Interaction

Have students use the map and the key to identify five metals found in Australia. Encourage them to use the library and Internet resources to learn whether Australia is listed among world leaders in the production of any of these metals.

MAP Study

Answers

1. *coconuts*
2. *low population density; most areas less than 2 per sq. mi. (1 per sq. km)*

Map Skills Practice

Land Use Which country has the most diverse land use? *(Australia)*

FYI

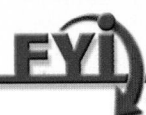

Freshwater Vast amounts of freshwater are trapped within the Antarctic ice cap. Scientists hope to find ways to use this untapped resource to supply the world's freshwater needs.

REGIONAL ATLAS ACTIVITY

Place Provide small groups of students with four to six index cards per group. Have members collaborate to write geographic questions about places whose answers can be determined from the map. For example, "In which two countries do many farmers raise sheep?" *(Australia and New Zealand)* Tell students to write the question on one side of the card and the answer on the other side. Have groups challenge one another by playing a question and answer game. If questions are unclear, have groups collaborate to reword the question. Collect the cards at the end of the game, and revisit the questions periodically.

EE1 The World in Spatial Terms: Standard 1

EE2 Place and Regions: Standard 4

Australia, Oceania, and Antarctica

These features and activities may be used as an introduction to the unit or as teaching tools throughout the course of the unit.

L1 Identify

Pair students and have them refer to the chart on pages 788–789 as they take turns completing the following activity. One partner should say the name of a country. The other should identify its capital, major export, major import, currency, and form of government. Have them continue the process until all the countries have been discussed.

Pacific Politeness Fijians usually smile and raise an eyebrow to greet each other. Dinner guests in New Zealand always take a gift, such as flowers or a box of chocolates. Houseguests also leave a gift with their host family.

COUNTRY PROFILES

COUNTRY * AND CAPITAL	FLAG AND LANGUAGE	POPULATION** AND DENSITY	LANDMASS	MAJOR EXPORT	MAJOR IMPORT	CURRENCY	GOVERNMENT
AUSTRALIA Canberra	English	19,900,000 7 per sq.mi. 3 per sq.km	2,988,888 sq.mi. 7,741,220 sq.km	Coal	Machinery	Australian Dollar	Parliamentary Democracy
FEDERATED STATES OF MICRONESIA Palikir	English, Local Languages	100,000 426 per sq.mi. 164 per sq.km	270 sq.mi. 699 sq.km	Fish	Foods	U.S. Dollar	Republic
FIJI Suva	English, Fijian, Hindi	900,000 123 per sq.mi. 47 per sq.km	7,054 sq.mi. 18,270 sq.km	Sugar	Machinery	Fiji Dollar	Republic
KIRIBATI Tarawa	English, Gilbertese	100,000 348 per sq.mi. 134 per sq.km	282 sq.mi. 730 sq. km	Coconut Products	Foods	Australian Dollar	Republic
MARSHALL ISLANDS Majuro	English, Local Languages	100,000 791 per sq.mi. 305 per sq.km	69 sq.mi. 179 sq.km	Coconut Products	Foods	U.S. Dollar	Republic
NAURU Yaren	Nauruan, English	10,000 1,412 per sq.mi. 545 per sq.km	9 sq.mi. 23 sq.km	Phosphates	Foods	Australian Dollar	Republic
NEW ZEALAND Wellington	English	4,000,000 38 per sq.mi. 15 per sq.km	104,452 sq.mi. 270,531 sq.km	Wool	Machinery	New Zealand Dollar	Parliamentary Democracy
PALAU Koror	English, Palauan	20,000 113 per sq.mi. 44 per sq.km	178 sq.mi. 461 sq.km	Fish	Machinery	U.S. Dollar	Republic
PAPUA NEW GUINEA Port Moresby	English, Local Languages	5,500,000 31 per sq.mi. 12 per sq.km	178,703 sq.mi. 462,841 sq.km	Gold	Machinery	Kina	Parliamentary Democracy
SAMOA Apia	Samoan, English	200,000 157 per sq.mi. 61 per sq.km	1,097 sq.mi. 2,841 sq.km	Coconut Products	Foods	Tala	Constitutional Monarchy

*COUNTRIES AND FLAGS NOT DRAWN TO SCALE   **POPULATIONS ARE ROUNDED, *SOURCE: 2003 WORLD POPULATION DATA SHEET*

FOR AN ONLINE UPDATE OF THIS INFORMATION, VISIT GEOGRAPHY.GLENCOE.COM AND CLICK ON "TEXTBOOK UPDATES."

COUNTRY PROFILE ACTIVITY

Making Generalizations Organize students into three groups. Assign each group a cluster of islands. Have each group member select a particular island to study. Students should use information from reference works such as encyclopedias and almanacs as well as the Internet to create political, cultural, and economic profiles of each island. Group members should then collaborate to chart generalizations—and exceptions—about their cluster of islands. Have each group present their charts to the class, noting exceptions if applicable. Display students' charts. Encourage them to refine their product as they gain new insights from this unit.   **EE2 Places and Regions: Standards 5, 6**

COUNTRY * AND CAPITAL	FLAG AND LANGUAGE	POPULATION** AND DENSITY	LANDMASS	MAJOR EXPORT	MAJOR IMPORT	CURRENCY	GOVERNMENT
SOLOMON ISLANDS Honiara	English, Local Languages	500,000 44 per sq.mi. 17 per sq.km	11,158 sq.mi. 28,899 sq.km	Cocoa	Machinery	Solomon Islands Dollar	Parliamentary Democracy
TONGA Nuku'alofa	Tongan, English	100,000 370 per sq.mi. 143 per sq.km	290 sq.mi. 751 sq.km	Squash	Foods	Pa'anga	Constitutional Monarchy
TUVALU Funafuti	Tuvaluan, English	10,000 1,000 per sq.mi. 385 per sq.km	10 sq.mi. 26 sq.km	Coconut Products	Foods	Tuvaluan Dollar	Parliamentary Democracy
VANUATU Port-Vila	Bislama, English, French	200,000 45 per sq.mi. 17 per sq.km	4,707 sq.mi. 12,191 sq.km	Coconut Products	Machinery	Vatu	Republic

*COUNTRIES AND FLAGS NOT DRAWN TO SCALE   **POPULATIONS ARE ROUNDED, SOURCE: 2003 WORLD POPULATION DATA SHEET

▲ Aerial view of harbor and city, Papeete, Tahiti

Fiji A *bure*, the traditional Fiji home, is one large room built of local hardwoods, a tightly thatched roof, and woven floor coverings. It contains four doors, one in each wall. These are usually kept open for air circulation.

L2 Distinguish Fact from Opinion

Remind students that life on a tropical island has advantages and disadvantages. Have partners summarize ways they have seen life in Oceania portrayed in the text, on TV, and in movies. Tell them to identify each idea as *fact* or *opinion*.

INTERDISCIPLINARY
connection

HISTORY AND ART In the early 1880s, Paul Gauguin left a career as a stockbroker in Paris, France, to become an artist. In 1891 he moved to Oceania where he spent the rest of his life. Gauguin's paintings of Pacific island life are important for artistic and cultural reasons. His style and brilliant colors influenced later artists. His paintings of life on Tahiti are a visual record of indigenous culture on that island.

COUNTRY PROFILE ACTIVITY

Culture and Art History Have small groups of students choose one indigenous culture of this region and research the kinds of art that culture has produced. Have students share what they learn with the class through an exhibition of pictures that illustrate characteristics typical of their chosen culture. Each picture should be accompanied by an informative caption. Groups can take turns explaining what they have learned about the art and its cultural meaning. Provide time for the class to examine the exhibit.

⊞ EE4 Human Systems: Standard 10
⊞ EE6 The Uses of Geography: Standard 17

① FOCUS

Write the word *eucalyptus* on the board. Ask students whether they or someone they know has used medicines containing eucalyptus. **Ask:** What kinds of medicines are these? *(cold remedies, cough drops, vapor rubs)* Explain that eucalyptus is native to Australia.

② TEACH

Cultural Exchange Point out that the eucalyptus tree is highly resistant to drought. Round, woody outgrowths that contain stored food develop on the trunk near the base of this tree. If the top of a young eucalyptus tree is damaged by fire or drought, new shoots emerge from the outgrowth, allowing the tree to continue growing. Have students study the physical map on page 784. **Ask:** Why would resistance to drought be essential to survival in central and western Australia? *(Much of that area has a very dry climate, and drought conditions are common.)*

Meeting National Standards

Geography for Life
The following standards are met in the Student Edition:

EE2 Places and Regions:
Standard 4
EE5 Environment and Society:
Standard 16

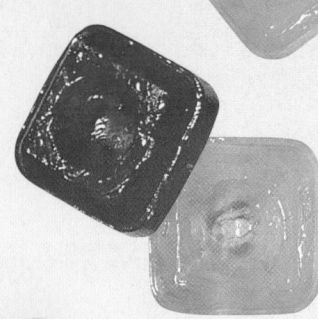

GLOBAL
CONNECTION

AUSTRALIA AND THE UNITED STATES

EUCALYPTUS

With their big noses, round faces, and cuddly teddy-bear appearance, koalas are among Australia's most famous native animals. If you wanted to see a koala in the wild, the best place to look would be in a eucalyptus tree. Koalas live in eucalyptus trees and eat almost nothing but eucalyptus leaves—about three pounds (1.4 kg) of leaves per day!

Like the koala, eucalyptus trees are native to Australia. More than 500 different kinds grow there. And for hundreds of years, they've been important not only to koalas, but to Australia's people as well.

Long before Europeans arrived in Australia, Aborigines used many different native plants to make medicines. They discovered that eucalyptus leaves contain a strong-smelling oil—eucalyptus oil—that has powerful antiseptic, or germ-fighting, properties. The Aborigines used the leaves to treat several common ailments, including infections, fevers, coughs, colds, and flu. They prepared the leaves in various ways so that the oil could be rubbed onto the skin, inhaled, or mixed with a liquid and swallowed.

When European colonists arrived in Australia, some were quick to recognize the value of Aboriginal remedies, especially those made from parts of eucalyptus trees. Eucalyptus preparations

▲ Koala nibbling eucalyptus leaf

BACKGROUND INFORMATION

Human-Environment Interaction The eucalyptus is one member of a large order of trees collectively known as myrtle. To geographers, eucalyptus is the most important myrtle because of the many uses people have found for it. Oil extracted from the leaves is used in medicines that relieve respiratory congestion and act as cough suppressants. The oil is also beneficial in reducing fevers and killing germs. Eucalyptus is a hardwood that is widely used in Australia for fuel and as a building material in home and fence construction.

◉ **EE2 Places and Regions: Standard 4**
◉ **EE5 Environment and Society: Standard 16**

▲ Eucalyptus tree in the Australian outback

became so popular that colonists tried them for just about every imaginable ailment, from headaches and rheumatism to hair loss and stomach ailments.

The popularity of eucalyptus quickly spread beyond Australia's shores. Eucalyptus oil was one of the first products to be exported from the young colony. By the nineteenth century, millions of the trees themselves were being shipped to the far corners of the world. You can find eucalyptus trees growing in southern California, Florida, and other parts of the southern United States.

Today, eucalyptus oil is an important ingredient in many common medicines, especially cough and cold remedies. The next time you pop a cough drop into your mouth or use a "vapor rub" to clear a stuffy nose, check the label. Chances are good the product contains eucalyptus oil.

▲ American cold sufferer who might benefit from eucalyptus oil

AT NIGHT

FYI

Koala Like the kangaroo, the koala is a marsupial, an animal that carries its young in a pouch. Young koalas and kangaroos are called *joeys*. The mother koala needs an abundant supply of eucalyptus to ensure the survival and proper growth of her joey.

3 ASSESS

Ask: Why would it be important for Australians to ensure the continued health of their eucalyptus trees? *(Possible answers: eucalyptus woods and oils are used in construction and medicine; they are a major Australian export; eucalyptus leaves are essential to the survival of the koala.)*

4 CLOSE

Have students summarize what European settlers in Australia learned from the Aborigines about the beneficial uses of the eucalyptus tree.

CONNECTION ACTIVITY

Medicine Have students use resources from the library, the Internet, or interviews with school or community health professionals to discover information about other trees and plants from Australia or Oceania that are the source of traditional remedies. Each student should write an article that identifies one tree or plant, tells where it is found, and describes its medicinal uses. Combine the individual articles into a collection titled "Plant Life and Modern Medicine," and display the collection.

🌐 **EE2 Places and Regions: Standard 4**
🌐 **EE5 Environment and Society: Standards 15, 16**
🌐 **EE6 The Uses of Geography: Standard 18**

PLANNING GUIDE

NOTE: The following materials may be used when teaching Chapter 32. Section-level support materials are shown at point-of-use in the margins of the Teacher Wraparound Edition.

TEACHING TRANSPARENCIES

L2 Unit 11 Map Overlay Transparencies

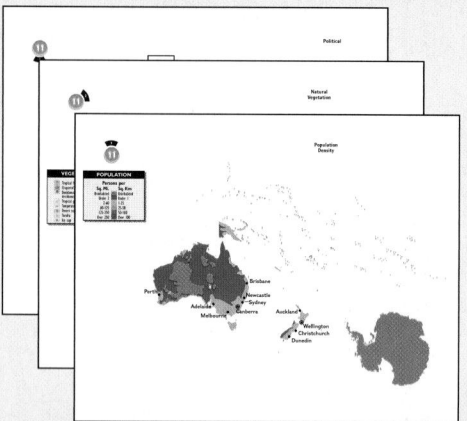

L2 Political Map Transparency 11

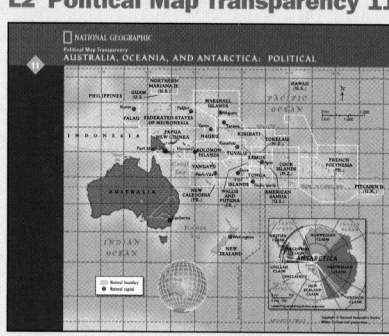

GEOGRAPHIC LITERACY

Focus on Geography Literacy

APPLICATION AND ENRICHMENT

L3 Enrichment Activity 32

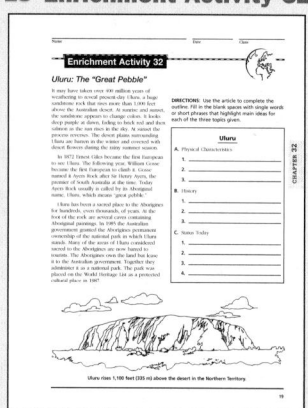

REVIEW AND REINFORCEMENT

L1 Vocabulary Activity 32 L1 Reinforcing L1 Reteaching Activity 32
Skills Activity 32

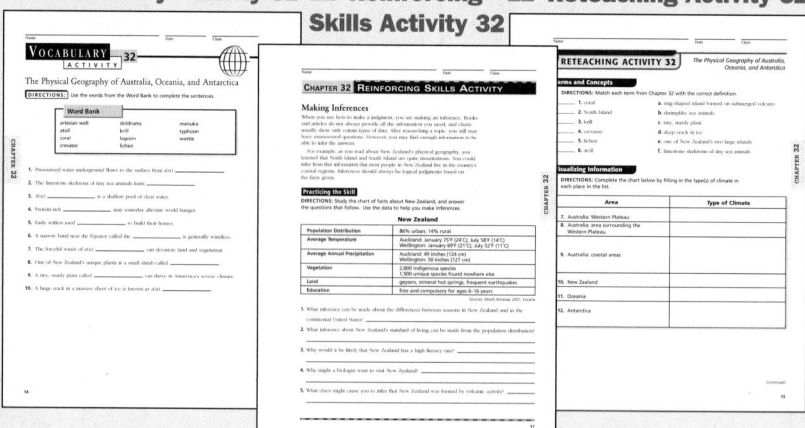

ASSESSMENT

L2 Chapter 32 Test Form A

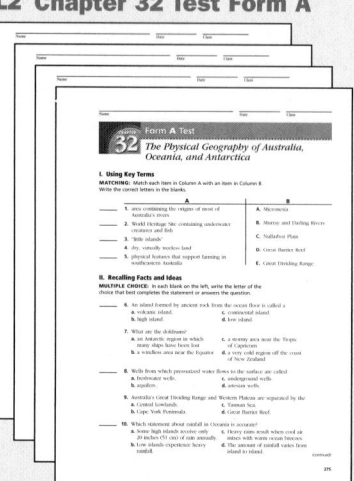

L2 Chapter 32 Test Form B

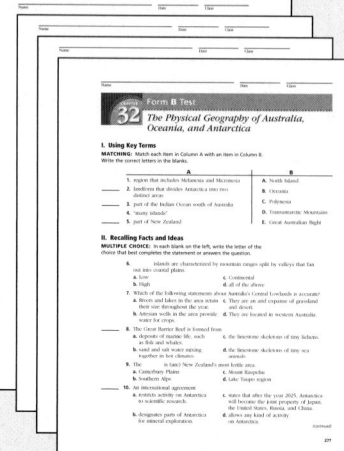

L1/ELL Performance Assessment Activity 32

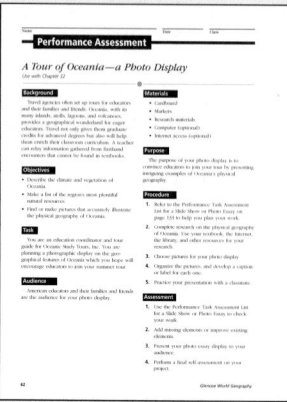

ExamView® Pro Testmaker

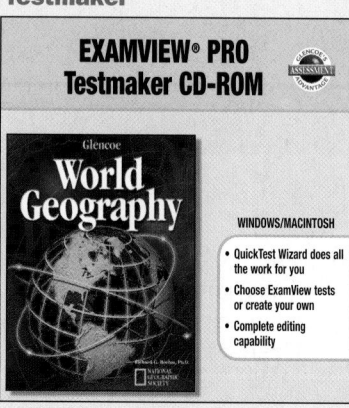

The following Spanish language materials are available in the Spanish Resources binder:

- Spanish Vocabulary Activities
- Spanish Guided Reading Activities
- Spanish Reteaching Activities
- Spanish Summaries
- Spanish Quizzes and Tests
- Spanish Reading Essentials and Study Guide

- World Regions Video
- MindJogger Videoquiz
- Vocabulary PuzzleMaker CD-ROM
- Interactive Tutor Self-Assessment CD-ROM
- ExamView® Pro Testmaker CD-ROM
- Audio Program
- TeacherWorks CD-ROM
- Interactive Student Edition CD-ROM
- Glencoe Skillbuilder Interactive Workbook CD-ROM, Level 2
- Presentation Plus! CD-ROM

Timesaving Tools

TeacherWorks™ — All-In-One Planner and Resource Center

- **Interactive Teacher Edition** Access your Teacher Wraparound Edition and your classroom resources with a few easy clicks.
- **Interactive Lesson Planner** Planning has never been easier! Organize your week, month, semester, or year with all the lesson helps you need to make teaching creative, timely, and relevant.

Use Glencoe's **Presentation Plus!** multimedia teacher tool to easily present dynamic lessons that visually excite your students. Using Microsoft PowerPoint® you can customize the presentations to create your own personalized lessons.

GEOGRAPHY Online

Use our Web site for additional resources. All essential content is covered in the Student Edition.

You and your students can visit geography.glencoe.com, the Web site companion to *Glencoe World Geography*. This innovative integration of electronic and print media offers your students a wealth of opportunities. The student text directs students to the Web site for the following options:

- Chapter Overviews
- Student Activities
- Self-Check Quizzes
- Textbook Updates

Answers are provided for you in the "Web Activity Lesson Plan." Additional Web resources and Interactive Tutor puzzles are also available.

Additional Glencoe Teacher Support

- **Teaching Strategies for the Geography Classroom** (including Block Scheduling Pacing Guides)
- **Graphic Organizer Transparencies Strategies and Activities**
- **Outline Map Resource Book**
- **Reading in the Content Area**

PLANNING GUIDE

SECTION RESOURCES

Daily Objectives	Reproducible Resources	Multimedia Resources

SECTION 1 The Land

1. Describe how mountains, plateaus, and lowlands differ in Australia and New Zealand.
2. Explain how volcanoes and continental shelves formed the islands of Oceania.
3. Discuss why the physical geography of Antarctica attracts scientists.

 Reproducible Lesson Plan 32-1
 Daily Lecture Notes 32-1
Guided Reading Activity 32-1*
Reading Essentials and Study Guide 32-1*
 Section Quiz 32-1*

 Daily Focus Skills Transparency 32-1
Political Map Transparency 11
Unit 11 Map Overlay Transparencies
Interactive Tutor Self-Assessment CD-ROM
ExamView® Pro Testmaker CD-ROM*
Presentation Plus! CD-ROM

SECTION 2 Climate and Vegetation

1. Examine how variations in rainfall affect Australia's climate and vegetation.
2. Consider how elevation affects climate patterns in New Zealand.
3. Identify what vegetation survives in the cold, dry Antarctic climate.

 Reproducible Lesson Plan 32-2
 Vocabulary Activity 32*
Daily Lecture Notes 32-2
Guided Reading Activity 32-2*
 Reading Essentials and Study Guide 32-2*
 Reteaching Activity 32*
Reinforcing Skills Activity 32
 Section Quiz 32-2*

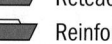 Daily Focus Skills Transparency 32-2
Political Map Transparency 11
Unit 11 Map Overlay Transparencies
Vocabulary PuzzleMaker CD-ROM
Interactive Tutor Self-Assessment CD-ROM
ExamView® Pro Testmaker CD-ROM*
Presentation Plus! CD-ROM

Blackline Master	💾 Software	📼 Videocassette	*Also available in Spanish*
🔖 Transparency	💿 CD-ROM	💿 DVD	

00:00 **OUT OF TIME?** Assign the Chapter 32 **Reading Essentials and Study Guide.**

Block Schedule

Activities that are particularly suited to use within the block scheduling framework are identified throughout this chapter by the following designation:

KEY TO ABILITY LEVELS

Teaching strategies have been coded for various learning styles and abilities.

L1 **BASIC** activities for all students

L2 **AVERAGE** activities for average to above-average students

L3 **CHALLENGING** activities for above-average students

ELL **ENGLISH LANGUAGE LEARNER** activities

Teacher to Teacher

Karen Brandt
Hermantown High School
Hermantown, MN

Presentations About Indigenous Peoples

Students work together in groups to prepare a presentation to the class about indigenous peoples of the region and their interrelationship with the physical geography.

Organize students into groups, and assign each group a specific indigenous people, such as the Aborigines of Australia. Tell students that they are to research and prepare a presentation lasting 20 to 30 minutes, allowing time for questions following the presentation. Explain that they should include a variety of media and props—computer-generated displays, maps, videos, artifacts, posters, food, dances, and models of homes. Students should explain how the people adapted to their physical environment, how the climate helped the people meet their needs, and how other elements of physical geography influenced various aspects of daily life.

You may wish to invite other classes to the presentations. Parents and community members may also be interested.

NATIONAL GEOGRAPHIC — TEACHER'S CORNER

Index to National Geographic Magazine:

The following articles may be used for research relating to this chapter:

- "Australia—A Harsh Awakening," by Michael Parfit, July 2000.
- "Australia By Bike: Closing the Circle," by Roff Smith, April 1998.
- "On the Edge of Antarctica: Queen Maud Land," by Jon Krakauer, February 1998.

National Geographic Society Products:

To order the following products for use with this chapter, call National Geographic Society at 1-800-368-2728.

- *Antarctica* (Video)
- *Australia* (Video)
- *Antarctica* (Map)
- *Australia* (Map)
- *Physical Earth* (Map)
- *National Geographic Desk Reference* (Book)
- *National Geographic Atlas of the World, Seventh Edition* (Book)

NGS ONLINE

Access National Geographic's Web site for current events, activities, links, interactive features, and archives.
www.nationalgeographic.com

Meeting National Standards

Geography For Life

The following standards are highlighted in Chapter 32:

Section 1 EE1 The World in Spatial Terms: Standards 1, 2
EE2 Places and Regions: Standards 4, 6
EE3 Physical Systems: Standard 7
EE4 Human Systems: Standard 11

Section 2 EE2 Places and Regions: Standards 4, 5
EE3 Physical Systems: Standard 8
EE5 Environment and Society: Standards 14, 15
EE6 The Uses of Geography: Standards 17, 18

Local Objectives

_____

_____

MEETING SPECIAL NEEDS

In addition to the Differentiated Instruction strategies found in each section, the following resources are also suitable for your special needs students:

- *ExamView® Pro Testmaker CD-ROM* allows teachers to tailor tests by reducing answer choices.
- The *Audio Program* includes the entire narrative of the student edition so that less-proficient readers can listen to the words as they read them.
- The *Reading Essentials and Study Guide* provides the same content as the student edition but is written two grade levels below the textbook.
- *Guided Reading Activities* give less-proficient readers point-by-point instructions to increase comprehension as they read each textbook section.
- *Enrichment Activities* include a stimulating collection of readings and activities for gifted and talented students.

Chapter Objectives

1. Describe the diverse landforms and natural resources of Australia, Oceania, and Antarctica.

2. Discuss the wide range of climates and vegetation throughout the region.

GLENCOE TECHNOLOGY

Use *MindJogger Videoquiz* to preview the Chapter 32 content.

GeoJournal

For access to additional photos, maps, and information on the geographic features of Australia, Oceania, and Antarctica, go to www.nationalgeographic.com (See Teacher pages in front for strategies for using journals in the geography classroom.

GEOGRAPHY Online

Introduce students to chapter content and key terms by having them access **Chapter Overview 32** at geography.glencoe.com

FOLDABLES
Study Organizer

Dinah Zike's Foldables are three-dimensional, interactive graphic organizers that help students practice basic writing skills, review key vocabulary terms, and identify main ideas. Have students complete the Foldable activity in the **Dinah Zike's Reading and Study Skills Foldables** booklet.

CHAPTER 32

The Physical Geography of Australia, Oceania, and Antarctica

GeoJournal

As you read this chapter, imagine that you are visiting interesting and beautiful locations in Australia, Oceania, and Antarctica. Write journal entries, using vivid details to explain why these places are appealing.

GEOGRAPHY Online

Chapter Overview Visit the **Glencoe World Geography** Web site at geography.glencoe.com and click on Chapter Overviews—Chapter 32 to preview information about the physical geography of the region.

ABOUT THE PHOTO

Visual Instruction The floating ice in this photo indicates that the summer season has arrived in Antarctica. In winter Antarctica's ice extends far out to sea. In fact, it grows by about 40,000 square miles (104,000 sq. km) per day and ultimately doubles the size of the continent. When chunks of ice break off the Antarctic ice sheet, the resulting icebergs threaten shipping. In November 1956, summertime in Antarctica, the *USS Glacier* sighted what is believed to be the world's largest iceberg. At 208 miles (335 km) long and 60 miles (97 km) wide, the iceberg was about the size of Belgium!

 **EE2 Places and Regions: Standard 4**

Guide to Reading

Consider What You Know

You may have seen photographs or movies showing the dry Australian outback or Antarctica's mountainous ice cap. What animals do you associate with these areas?

Reading Strategy

Categorizing Complete a graphic organizer similar to the one below by describing the three types of islands in Oceania.

Island	Description
Low Island	
High Island	
Continental Island	

Read to Find Out

- How do mountains, plateaus, and lowlands differ in Australia and New Zealand?
- How have volcanoes and continental shelves formed the islands of Oceania?
- Why does the physical geography of Antarctica attract scientists?

Terms to Know

- artesian well
- coral
- atoll
- lagoon
- krill

Places to Locate

- Australia
- Great Dividing Range
- Nullarbor Plain
- Murray River
- Darling River
- Oceania
- Melanesia
- Micronesia
- Polynesia
- New Zealand
- North Island
- South Island
- Antarctica

The Land

NATIONAL GEOGRAPHIC

A Geographic View

Australian Landscape

The land breathes magic. Not . . . colored scarves and playing cards, but real magic. Weepy eucalyptus trees with [curving sword]-shaped leaves. Dazzling-white ghost gums. Termite mounds: some red and bulbous as a Henry Moore sculpture; others, black and delicate as the spires of a Gothic cathedral. A glory of birds— sulfur-crested cockatoos that lift from trees in clouds, tiny bee-eaters, iridescent as opals.

—*Cathy Newman, "The Uneasy Magic of Australia's Cape York Peninsula,"* National Geographic, *June 1996*

Termite mound, Australia

On Australia's northeastern coast, the Cape York Peninsula displays a landscape of great contrasts. Rain forests, savannas, and wetlands form an exotic patchwork in this area. Australia, Oceania, and Antarctica together form the equally diverse South Pacific region, one that covers a huge portion of the globe. In this section you will explore the region's varied physical geography, including coastal lowlands bordering mountains and plateaus, islands rising from the sea, and a vast ice cap spanning a continent.

Australia: A Continent and a Country

As the only place on the earth that is both a continent and a country, **Australia** is unique. Although water surrounds Australia in the same way as an island, geographers classify it as a continent because of its tremendous size. Located in the Southern Hemisphere, its name comes from the Latin word *australis*, meaning "southern."

◀ *Evening in Antarctica*

1 FOCUS

Section Overview

This section discusses the landforms of Australia, Oceania, and Antarctica and the natural resources found there.

BELLRINGER
Skillbuilder Activity

Project transparency and have students answer questions.

Available as blackline master.

Daily Focus Skills Transparency 32-1

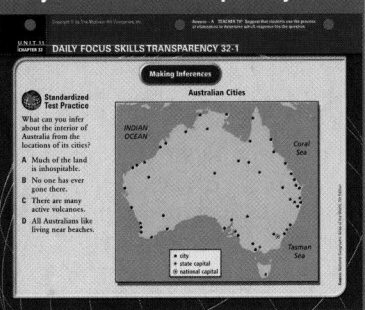

Guide to Reading

Consider What You Know
Answers: *Possible answers: Australia—kangaroos, koalas, duck-billed platypuses, wallabies; Antarctica—penguins, seals*

Reading Strategy
Answers low:*ring-shaped islands called atolls, formed by coral reef built up on rim of submerged volcano, little soil;* high: *some agriculture, mountain ranges split by valleys fanning out into plains;* continental: *rising and folding of ancient rock from the ocean floor, contain most of Oceania's mineral deposits*

Preteaching Vocabulary
Have students predict which term refers to a body of seawater *(lagoon)*, and which two terms refer to animal life *(coral, krill)*. Tell them to confirm their predictions as they read.

RESOURCE MANAGER

Reproducible Masters
- Reproducible Lesson Plan 32-1
- Daily Lecture Notes 32-1
- Guided Reading Activity 32-1
- Reading Essentials and Study Guide 32-1
- Section Quiz 32-1

Transparencies
- Daily Focus Skills Transparency 32-1
- Political Map Transparency 11
- Unit 11 Map Overlay Transparencies

Multimedia
- Interactive Tutor Self-Assessment CD-ROM
- ExamView® Pro Testmaker CD-ROM
- Presentation Plus! CD-ROM

NATIONAL GEOGRAPHIC World Explorer

Answer
The arid climate and the lack of freshwater do not support settlement or agriculture.

More About the Photo
Travel in the outback is often hazardous. Fires, flash floods, and vast, empty spaces can put travelers at risk.

2 TEACH

L1 Locate

Have students use the physical map on page 784 to locate these features or places and, if applicable, name the country with which they are associated: the Great Barrier Reef *(Australia)*; Polynesia *(Oceania)*; North Island *(New Zealand)*; South Pole *(Antarctica)*

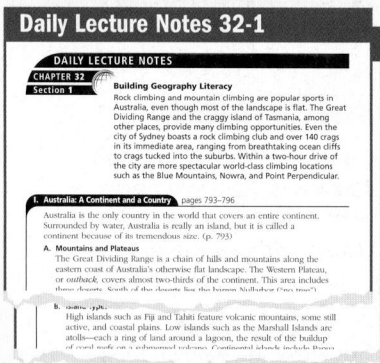

Daily Lecture Notes 32-1

DAILY LECTURE NOTES

CHAPTER 32
Section 1

Building Geography Literacy
Rock climbing and mountain climbing are popular sports in Australia, even though most of the landscape is flat. The Great Dividing Range and the craggy island of Tasmania, among other places, provide many climbing opportunities. Even the city of Sydney boasts a rock climbing club and over 140 crags in its immediate area, ranging from breathtaking ocean cliffs to crags tucked into the suburbs. Within a two-hour drive of the city are more spectacular world-class climbing locations such as the Blue Mountains, Nowra, and Point Perpendicular.

I. Australia: A Continent and a Country pages 793–796

Australia is the only country in the world that covers an entire continent. Surrounded by water, Australia is really an island, but it is called a continent because of its tremendous size. (p. 793)

A. Mountains and Plateaus
The Great Dividing Range is a chain of hills and mountains along the eastern coast of Australia's otherwise flat landscape. The Western Plateau, or *outback*, covers almost two-thirds of the continent. This area includes three deserts. South of the deserts lies the barren Nullarbor. (pp. 793–794)

B. Islands Types
High islands such as Fiji and Tahiti feature volcanic mountains, some still active, and coastal plains. Low islands such as the Marshall Islands are atolls—each a ring of land around a lagoon, the result of the buildup of coral reefs on a submerged volcano. Continental islands include Papua

---

NATIONAL GEOGRAPHIC GEOFACT

▶ Antarctica, the world's coldest and highest place, has mountains, valleys, and lowlands under its ice cap.

Mountains and Plateaus

A chain of hills and mountains known as the **Great Dividing Range** interrupts Australia's otherwise level landscape. The peaks stretch along Australia's eastern coast from the Cape York Peninsula to the island of Tasmania, separated from the mainland long ago by the sea. Most of Australia's rivers begin in the range, and they water the most fertile land in the country.

The Western Plateau, a low expanse of flat land in central and western Australia, covers almost two-thirds of the continent. Australians call this area where few people live the "outback." Across the plateau spread the hot sands of the Great Sandy, Great Victoria, and Gibson Deserts. Near the edges of the deserts, a few low mountain ranges and huge rock formations thrust up from the earth. When explorer Jean-Michel Cousteau visited the arid Western Plateau, he spoke of the land's effect on those few who inhabit it:

> *" For human or nonhuman, life in the vast dry sea, as we were soon to witness, demands extraordinary survival strategies, and those who endure do so with earthy ingenuity and tenacity. "*
> Jean-Michel Cousteau,
> *Cousteau's Australia Journey*, 1993

South of the Great Victoria Desert lies the **Nullarbor Plain**. The name comes from the Latin *nullus arbor*, meaning "no tree." This dry, virtually treeless land ends abruptly in giant cliffs. Hundreds of feet below the cliffs lies the churning Great Australian Bight, a part of the Indian Ocean.

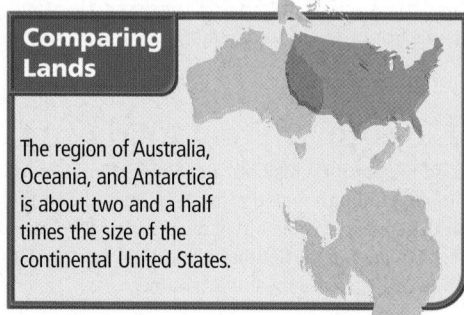

Comparing Lands

The region of Australia, Oceania, and Antarctica is about two and a half times the size of the continental United States.

NATIONAL GEOGRAPHIC **World Explorer**

Geography Skills for Life

Australian Outback The rugged Australian outback is sparsely populated.
Human-Environment Interaction Why do so few people live in the Western Plateau area?

Central Lowlands

The Great Dividing Range and Western Plateau are separated by the Central Lowlands. This arid expanse of grassland and desert stretches across the east central part of Australia. After heavy rainfall, rivers and lakes throughout the area fill with water, but because rains are infrequent, most rivers and lakes remain dry much of the year. In the southeast, however, the **Murray River** and the **Darling River** supply water that supports farming. A vast treasure of pressurized underground water, known as the Great Artesian Basin, lies underneath the lowlands. Although the water that gushes from artesian wells, or wells from which pressurized water flows to the surface, is too salty for humans or crops, ranchers use it to water livestock.

Great Barrier Reef

Along Australia's northeastern coast lies the Great Barrier Reef. This famous natural wonder is the world's largest coral reef, home to brilliantly

---

DIFFERENTIATED INSTRUCTION

Kinesthetic Have students with hands-on learning ability create a three-dimensional model of Australia to reinforce their understanding of its diverse physical features. Tell students to refer to the physical map and the physical profile of Australia on pages 784–785 to determine the elevations of various physical features. Remind them to decide on a scale that will enable their models to be easily moved. Suggest that they use clay or other modeling material to form Australia's mountains, lowlands, and coastal plains. Ask volunteers to share their finished models with the class. ⊕ **EE1 The World in Spatial Terms: Standard 1**
⊕ **EE2 Places and Regions: Standard 4**
▱ Refer to *Inclusion for the Social Studies Classroom Strategies and Activities.*

colored tropical fish and underwater creatures. Because of its unique beauty and the habitat it provides for multitudes of creatures, Australia has designated the reef a national park, and the United Nations has named it a World Heritage Site. Although its name suggests a single reef, the Great Barrier Reef is actually a string of more than 2,500 small reefs. Formed from coral, the limestone skeletons of a tiny sea animal, it extends 1,250 miles (2,012 km). This span equals the length of the coastline from New York City to Miami, Florida.

Economics
Natural Resources

Although only 10 percent of Australia's land can be farmed, agriculture is important to the country. Australian farmers make effective use of their land and water to grow wheat, barley, fruit,

---

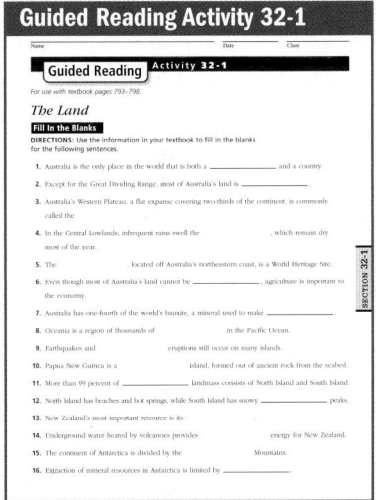

NATIONAL GEOGRAPHIC — MAP STUDY

Australia, Oceania, and Antarctica: Physical-Political

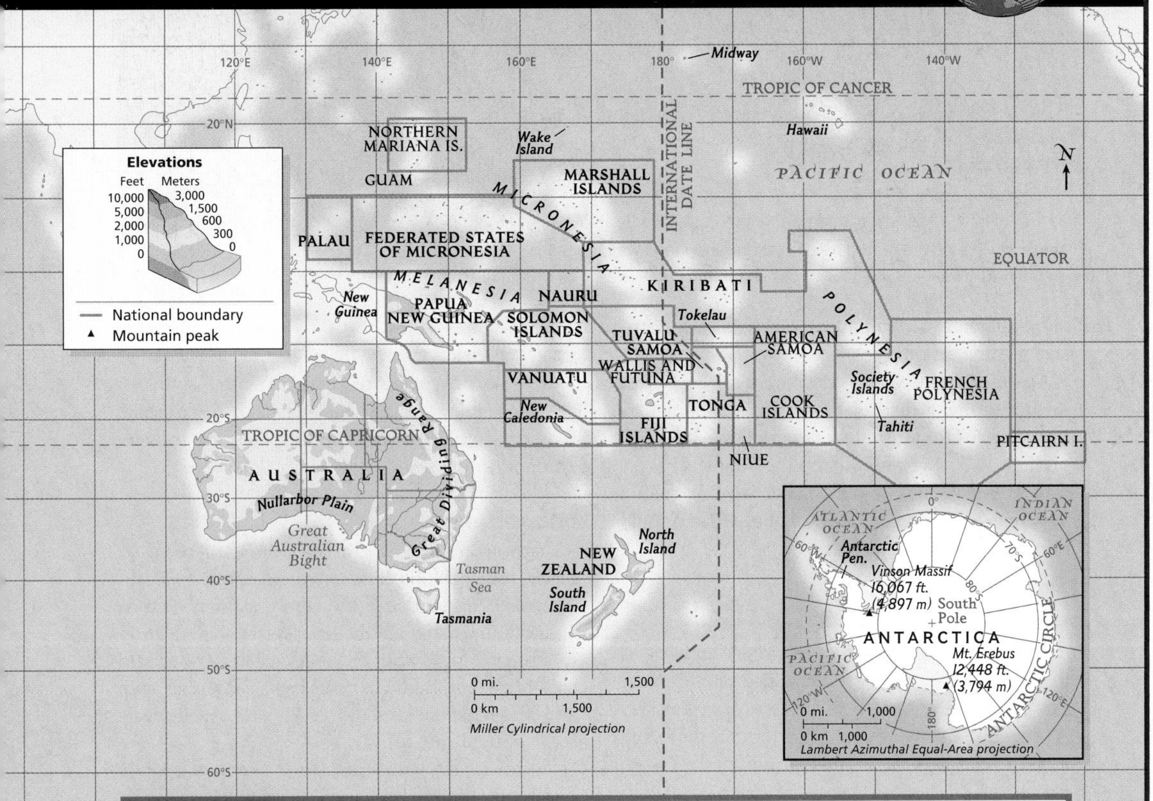

Geography Skills for Life

1. **Interpreting Maps** Which of New Zealand's two islands has higher elevations?

2. **Applying Geography Skills** In what part of Australia are most rivers found? How might their location affect population patterns?

Find NGS online map resources @ www.nationalgeographic.com/maps

---

L3 Math

Tell students that the majority of people in Australia, as in the U.S., are descendants of European immigrants. Have students find current statistics and create a pictograph comparing the total populations of the two countries. *(Ratio is about 9 [U.S.] to 1 [Australia]).* **Ask:** How might location be a factor in the population difference? *(distance from Europe, more complicated travel routes)*

L1/ELL

Guided Reading Activity 32-1

Guided Reading   Activity **32-1**

For use with textbook pages 793–798

The Land

Fill In the Blanks

DIRECTIONS: Use the information in your textbook to fill in the blanks for the following sentences.

1. Australia is the only place in the world that is both a _____ and a country.

2. Except for the Great Dividing Range, most of Australia's land is _____.

3. Australia's Western Plateau, a flat expanse covering two-thirds of the continent, is commonly called the _____.

4. In the Central Lowlands, infrequent rains swell the _____, which remain dry most of the year.

5. The _____, located off Australia's northeastern coast, is a World Heritage Site.

6. Even though most of Australia's land cannot be _____, agriculture is important to the economy.

7. Australia has one-fourth of the world's bauxite, a mineral used to make _____.

8. Oceania is a region of thousands of _____ in the Pacific Ocean.

9. Earthquakes and _____ eruptions still occur on many islands.

10. Papua New Guinea is a _____ island, formed out of ancient rock from the seabed.

11. More than 99 percent of _____ landmass consists of North Island and South Island.

12. South Island has beaches and hot springs, while South Island has snowy _____ peaks.

13. New Zealand's most important resource is its _____.

14. Underground water heated by volcanoes provides _____ energy for New Zealand.

15. The continent of Antarctica is divided by the _____ Mountains.

16. Extraction of mineral resources in Antarctica is limited by _____.

NATIONAL GEOGRAPHIC — MAP STUDY

Answers:

1. *South Island*

2. *in the southeast; that area has the highest population density on the continent*

Map Skills Practice

Location What mountains are found in Antarctica? *(Vinson Massif, Mt. Erebus)*

COOPERATIVE LEARNING ACTIVITY

Geography Quiz Game Organize students into teams. Have a player on the first team choose one of four areas—Australia, Oceania, New Zealand, or Antarctica. Ask that player to name one of the following features: a mountain range, a reef, a plateau, a desert, a basin, a plain, a water body, an island group, a continental island, or a peninsula, depending on the features the section describes for that area. If the player answers correctly, his or her team earns one point, and the first player on the next team takes a turn. If a player answers incorrectly, no points are awarded, and the next team answers. Continue play for a pre-set number of rounds. The team with the most points wins the game.

🌐 **EE3 Physical Systems: Standard 7**

NATIONAL GEOGRAPHIC World Explorer

Geography | **Skills for Life**
Pacific
Islands Volcanic peaks are found on high islands such as Tahiti (left), while low islands are known as atolls (right).
Region What is the third type of island found in the region?

NATIONAL GEOGRAPHIC World Explorer

Answer
continental island

More About the Photo
Many of the region's low islands would be threatened with submersion if global warming caused the icecaps in Antarctica to melt.

L1/ELL

Reading Essentials & Study Guide 32-1

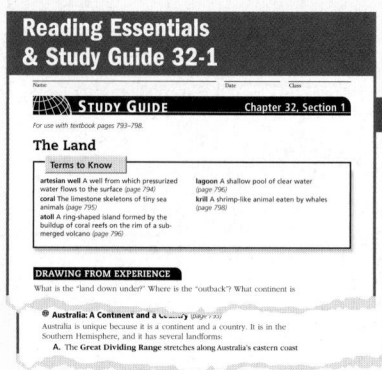

STUDY GUIDE Chapter 32, Section 1
For use with textbook pages 793–798.

The Land

Terms to Know

artesian well A well from which pressurized water flows to the surface *(page 794)*
coral The limestone skeletons of tiny sea animals *(page 795)*
atoll A ring-shaped island formed by the buildup of coral reefs on the rim of a submerged volcano *(page 796)*
lagoon A shallow pool of clear water *(page 796)*
krill A shrimp-like animal eaten by whales *(page 796)*

DRAWING FROM EXPERIENCE

What is the "land down under?" Where is the "outback"? What continent is

● **Australia: A Continent and a Country** *(page 793)*
Australia is unique because it is a continent and a country. It is in the Southern Hemisphere, and it has several landforms.
   A. The Great Dividing Range stretches along Australia's eastern coast

---

INTERDISCIPLINARY
connection

HISTORY In 1820 a Russian sea captain was the first person to record seeing Antarctica, and in 1898 Belgian sailors were the first people to spend a winter along Antarctica's coast. There is no daylight for months during an Antarctic winter. The ship's log tells how the prolonged darkness affected the sailors. "One seaman had fits. . . . Another went mad."

---

and sugarcane. In arid areas, ranchers raise cattle, sheep, and chickens.

Australia also yields rich mineral resources, including one-fourth of the world's bauxite—the raw material for aluminum production—and most of the world's high-quality opals. Deposits of coal, iron ore, lead, zinc, gold, nickel, and petroleum also make the country one of the world's major mining areas.

Oceania: Island Lands

Thousands of islands, differing in size and extending across millions of square miles of the Pacific Ocean, form the region called **Oceania** (OH•shee• A•nee•uh). Created by colliding tectonic plates millions of years ago, the islands are part of the Ring of Fire, named for its volcanic and earthquake activity.

Island Clusters

Oceania's islands are classified into three clusters, based on location, how the islands formed, and the inhabitants' cultures. **Melanesia**, meaning "black islands," lies north and east of Australia. The "little islands" of **Micronesia** extend north of Melanesia. **Polynesia**, or "many islands," spans an area larger than either Melanesia or Micronesia, ranging from Midway Island in the north to **New Zealand** in the south.

Island Types

Earthquakes and volcanic eruptions still occur on many high islands, one of three island types in Oceania. The landscapes of high islands, such as Tahiti and many of the islands of Fiji, feature mountain ranges split by valleys that fan out into coastal plains. Bodies of freshwater dot the land, and the volcanic soil on high islands supports some agriculture.

Volcanoes shaped Oceania's many low islands differently than they shaped the high islands. Low islands, such as many of the Marshall Islands in Micronesia, are ring-shaped islands, known as **atolls**, formed by the buildup of coral reefs on the rim of submerged volcanoes. Atolls encircle **lagoons**, shallow pools of clear water, and usually

---

CRITICAL THINKING ACTIVITY

Analyzing Information Project Political Map Transparency 11, and have students list the resources for each area of Australia, Oceania, and Antarctica as they read this section. Have them use these lists to decide which area on the map is least dependent on imported resources and explain why. *(Australia has more resources than any other area in the South Pacific region and thus would be least dependent on resources imported from other areas.)*

▣ **EE1 The World in Spatial Terms: Standard 1**
▣ **EE4 Human Systems: Standard 11**

rise only a few feet above sea level. Low islands have little soil and few natural resources.

Continental islands are the third type, formed by the rising and folding of ancient rock from the ocean floor. Most of Oceania's large islands, such as New Guinea and New Caledonia, fall into this category. Although volcanoes did not create these islands, many do have active volcanoes. Coastal areas consist of plains, swamps, and rivers. Beyond the coastal areas, the land rises into rugged interior mountains, plateaus, and steep valleys. Because of the variety of their rocks and soil, continental islands have most of Oceania's mineral deposits. Their mining industries produce oil, gold, nickel, and copper. Some larger forested islands support timber processing.

New Zealand: A Rugged Landscape

Located 1,200 miles (1,931 km) southeast of Australia, New Zealand's two largest islands make up 99 percent of the country's landmass. Both **North Island** and **South Island** display sandy beaches, emerald hillsides, and snow-tipped mountains.

North Island's northern region includes golden beaches, ancient forests, and rich soil that supports citrus orchards. A broad central plateau of volcanic stone features hot springs and several active volcanoes. Chief among them is Mount Ruapehu (ROO•uh•PAY•hoo), North Island's highest point. Mount Ruapehu often spews molten rock. Shining freshwater lakes—including Lake Taupo, New Zealand's largest lake—appear throughout the plateau. East of the plateau, a band of hills runs north and south. Here ranchers graze sheep and dairy cattle.

The towering, snowy peaks of the Southern Alps run along South Island's western edge. New Zealand's earliest inhabitants, the Maori, named the highest peak on South Island *Aorangi* (ow•RAHNG•ee), which means "cloud piercer." Today, Aorangi is known as Mount Cook and rises to 12,316 feet (3,754 m). This high country also features sparkling lakes, carved by glaciers, and tumbling rivers. Lowlands called the Canterbury Plains lie on the eastern coast. This land is New Zealand's flattest and most fertile area. Along the western coast, pounding surf meets rugged cliffs, deep fjords, and coastal caves.

NATIONAL GEOGRAPHIC World Explorer

Geography | **Skills for Life**

Canterbury Plains In addition to producing grain, New Zealand's Canterbury Plains are economically important for the livestock they support.
Place How does the eastern coast of South Island differ from the western coast?

NATIONAL GEOGRAPHIC World Explorer

Answer
South Island's eastern coast is flat and fertile; its western coast is rugged and rocky.

More About the Photo
New Zealanders often quip that theirs is the only country where sheep outnumber people.

NATIONAL GEOGRAPHIC GEOFACT

Scientists use satellites to learn about Antarctica. For example, satellite data confirm that the weight of Antarctica's ice flattens the earth at the South Pole. As a result, the earth is actually pear shaped rather than round.

3 ASSESS

Assign Section 1 Assessment as homework or as an in-class activity.

Have students use **Interactive Tutor Self-Assessment CD-ROM.**

L2

Section Quiz 32-1

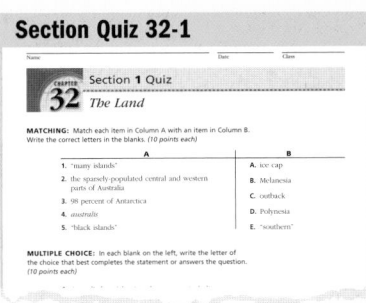

TEAM-TEACHING ACTIVITY: SCIENCE

The Southern Sky The constellation Ursa Major includes seven stars that people in the Northern Hemisphere call the Big Dipper. Two stars mark the outer edge of the cup, and always point to the North Star. Sailors use this information to find direction. In the Southern Hemisphere there is a similar astronomical guide. Give students this clue: The key is in a constellation called *Crux.* Have students work with a science teacher to find the following: the English translation of the name Crux *(the Cross)*, the name of this constellation *(the Southern Cross)*, its brightest star *(Alpha Crucis)*, and the point on Earth to which that star points *(the South Pole).* ● **EE1 The World in Spatial Terms: Standard 2**
● **EE2 Places and Regions: Standard 6**

Reteach

Have students answer the questions in "Read to Find Out" on page 793. Use their responses as the basis for a discussion of points that seem to need reinforcement or clarification.

Enrich

"The Wild Colonial Boy" is a popular ballad in Australia. It tells about Jim Doolan, a teenage immigrant from Ireland in the 1860s. In Australia he becomes an outlaw and eventually is killed by mounted police. Have interested students find a copy of the ballad and answer the following question: **How did Australian immigrants from Ireland feel about wealthy British ranchers?** *(Possible answer: the British government was an enemy that denied them justice.)*

 **CLOSE**

Have students discuss ways in which the different lands in this region are alike and ways in which they are different. Encourage them to be as specific as possible.

Objectives, goals, and answers to the student activity can be found in the Web Activity Lesson Plan feature at geography.glencoe.com

Natural Resources

New Zealand's fertile soil, perhaps its most important resource, greatly benefits the country's economy. About 55 percent of the land supports crops and livestock. New Zealand's sheep and wool products dominate exports, and its forests yield valuable timber. The country's rivers and dams produce abundant hydroelectric power, fulfilling about 75 percent of the country's needs. New Zealand also uses less typical means to generate power: geothermal energy is provided by water heated underground by volcanoes.

Warm and cold ocean currents meet in the waters off the New Zealand coasts, providing the country with a wide variety of fish. Tuna, marlin, and sharks are abundant in the warmer tropical currents, while cod and hake, a cod-like fish, thrive in the cold Antarctic currents.

Antarctica: A White Plateau

Antarctica, almost twice the size of Australia, lies at the southern extreme of the earth, beneath a massive ice cap. Antarctica's ice cap covers about 98 percent of the continent's landmass. The ice is as much as 2 miles (3.2 km) thick in places and holds 70 percent of the world's freshwater.

Like a jagged backbone, the Transantarctic Mountains extend northward across Antarctica and the Antarctic Peninsula to within 600 miles (966 km) of South America's Cape Horn. The mountains and the peninsula divide the continent into two areas. East of these mountains lies a high, ice-covered plateau. Coastal mountains and valleys near the plateau's edge form pathways for glaciers. To the west the landmass is largely below sea level, including underwater volcanoes.

Research Stations

Although Antarctica contains mineral resources, international agreements limit activity on Antarctica to scientific research. In year-round research stations, scientists from many countries gather fascinating information in this cold and barren land. They investigate weather patterns, measure environmental changes, and observe the sun and stars through an unpolluted atmosphere. The coastal sea also holds valuable resources. Fishing boats from several countries harvest **krill**, a shrimplike animal eaten by some whales. This plentiful, protein-rich food may someday help lessen world hunger.

Student Web Activity Visit the **Glencoe World Geography** Web site at geography.glencoe.com and click on Student Web Activities—Chapter 32 for an activity about the Ring of Fire.

SECTION 1 ASSESSMENT

Checking for Understanding

1. **Define** artesian well, coral, atoll, lagoon, krill.

2. **Main Ideas** Create a graphic organizer like the one below. List the features and resources for each region. Then choose two of the regions, and write a paragraph explaining how they differ.

Australia	Oceania	Antarctica
•	•	•
•	•	•
•	•	•

Critical Thinking

3. **Predicting Consequences** What group of people would be most affected if Australia's artesian wells dried up? Why?

4. **Comparing and Contrasting** Identify similarities and differences between New Zealand's two main islands and a high island such as Tahiti.

5. **Decision Making** Of the three types of islands found in Oceania, which type would you choose for a home? Explain why.

Analyzing Maps

6. **Location** Study the physical-political map on page 795. To which island region does Papua New Guinea belong?

Applying Geography

7. **Effects of Location** Consider the location of Oceania's islands in relation to other parts of the world. Write a paragraph explaining how this location might affect the development of natural resources.

SECTION 1 ASSESSMENT ANSWERS

1. All vocabulary terms are defined in the text.

2. Answers should include features and resources of Australia, Oceania, and Antarctica.

3. ranchers, because they use the salty water from the wells to water livestock

4. mountains, coastal plains, active volcanoes; New Zealand islands larger and support more people

5. Reasons should accurately identify characteristics of the island type chosen.

6. Melanesia

7. **Applying Geography** Students should explain that a remote location increases the expense of bringing in needed equipment, shipping goods to other regions, and attracting skilled workers.

Guide to Reading

Consider What You Know

Scientists who live and work at research stations in Antarctica's harsh climate make exciting discoveries about the earth. Why might this bleak and icy land be a good location for studying ecology, biology, climatology, or astronomy?

Reading Strategy

Organizing As you read about the climate and vegetation of Australia, Oceania, and Antarctica, complete a graphic organizer similar to the one below by describing each region.

Region	Climate	Vegetation
Australia		
Oceania		
New Zealand		
Antarctica		

Read to Find Out

- How do variations in rainfall affect Australia's climate and vegetation?
- How does elevation affect climate patterns in New Zealand?
- What vegetation survives in the cold, dry Antarctic climate?

Terms to Know

- wattle
- doldrums
- typhoon
- manuka
- lichen
- crevasse

Places to Locate

- Papua New Guinea
- Antarctic Peninsula

Climate and Vegetation

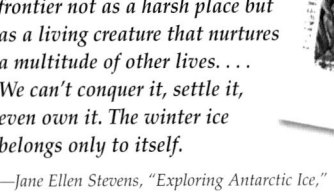
NATIONAL GEOGRAPHIC

A Geographic View

A Frozen Frontier

I have grown to love this cold, strange place.... Such a reaction may seem odd to those who have never heard the sigh of ice floes jostling on the swells.... Alighting here briefly, like a bird of passage, I have come to see this transient frontier not as a harsh place but as a living creature that nurtures a multitude of other lives.... We can't conquer it, settle it, even own it. The winter ice belongs only to itself.

—Jane Ellen Stevens, "Exploring Antarctic Ice," National Geographic, May 1996

Ice shelf, Antarctica

Just as there is a surprising variety of life in an area that appears to be a frozen desert, there are other startling geographic contrasts throughout Australia, Oceania, and Antarctica. In this section, you will learn about the climates and vegetation of one of the world's most geographically diverse regions.

Australia

In Australia, climate and vegetation vary greatly from area to area. The country's climate and vegetation regions include tropical rain forests in the northeast, dry desert expanses in the interior, and temperate areas of grasslands, scrub, and mixed forests along the eastern, southern, and southwestern coasts. Differences in rainfall cause these significant changes in climate and vegetation throughout Australia.

Subtropical high-pressure air masses block moisture-laden Pacific Ocean winds from reaching the Western Plateau, Australia's large

FOCUS

Section Overview

This section discusses climate and vegetation in Australia, Oceania, and Antarctica.

BELLRINGER
Skillbuilder Activity

- Project transparency and have students answer questions.
- Available as blackline master.

Daily Focus Skills Transparency 32-2

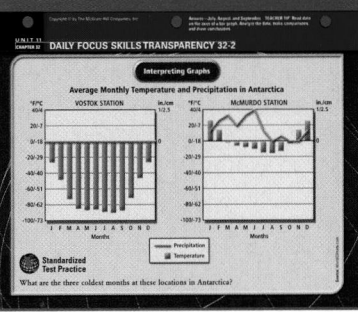

Guide to Reading

Consider What You Know
Answer *Possible answer: the remote location limits human-environment interaction; the cold and ice preserve specimens; and darkness enhances views of the night sky.*

Reading Strategy
Answers Students' answers should include adequate descriptions of the climate and vegetation of each country.

Preteaching Vocabulary
🔵 Use the **Vocabulary Puzzle-Maker CD-ROM** to create crossword and word-search puzzles.

RESOURCE MANAGER

📁 Reproducible Masters
- Reproducible Lesson Plan 32-2
- Vocabulary Activity 32
- Daily Lecture Notes 32-2
- Guided Reading Activity 32-2
- Reading Essentials and Study Guide 32-2
- Reteaching Activity 32
- Reinforcing Skills Activity 32
- Section Quiz 32-2

📽 Transparencies
- Daily Focus Skills Transparency 32-2
- Political Map Transparency 11
- Unit 11 Map Overlay Transparencies

Multimedia
- 💿 Vocabulary PuzzleMaker CD-ROM
- 💿 Interactive Tutor Self-Assessment CD-ROM
- 💿 ExamView® Pro Testmaker CD-ROM
- 💿 Presentation Plus! CD-ROM

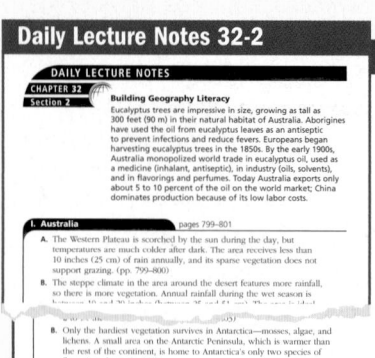

NATIONAL GEOGRAPHIC   MAP STUDY

Answers

1. *marine west coast and humid subtropical*

2. *Port Moresby is closer to the Equator.*

Map Skills Practice

Place On which island would you find a highlands climate between two areas of tropical rain forest climate? *(Papua New Guinea)*

② TEACH

L1 Locate

Have students refer to the physical map on page 784. **Ask: On which continent would you expect to find the greatest diversity in climate and vegetation? Why?** *(Australia; it has more climate zones than Antarctica.)* **Where would you expect to find only primitive plant life? Why?** *(Antarctica; harsh climate and frozen terrain)* **Do you think the islands of Oceania all have the same climate and vegetation? Why or why not?** *(No, they are widely scattered.)*

Daily Lecture Notes 32-2

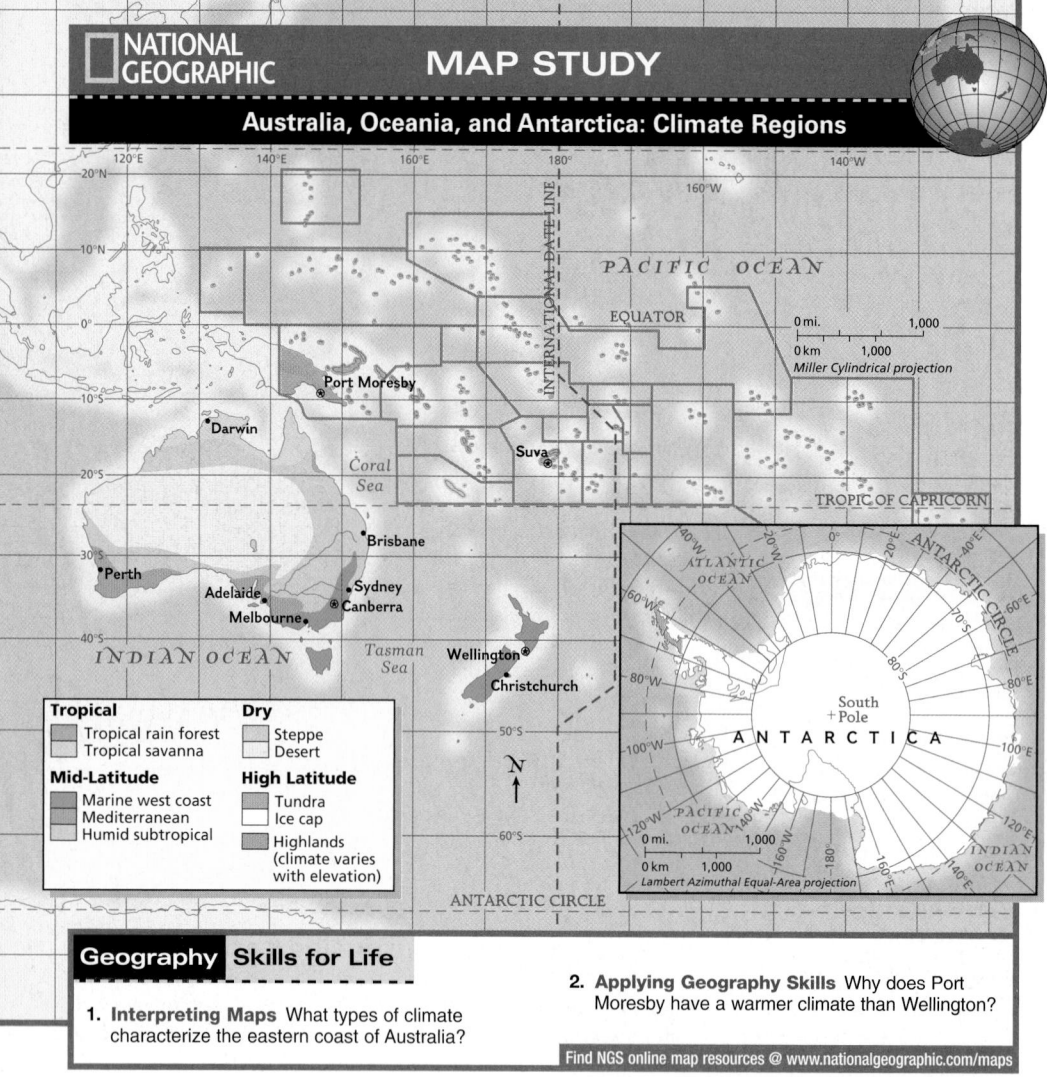

NATIONAL GEOGRAPHIC   MAP STUDY

Australia, Oceania, and Antarctica: Climate Regions

Tropical
- Tropical rain forest
- Tropical savanna

Mid-Latitude
- Marine west coast
- Mediterranean
- Humid subtropical

Dry
- Steppe
- Desert

High Latitude
- Tundra
- Ice cap
- Highlands (climate varies with elevation)

Geography Skills for Life

1. **Interpreting Maps** What types of climate characterize the eastern coast of Australia?

2. **Applying Geography Skills** Why does Port Moresby have a warmer climate than Wellington?

Find NGS online map resources @ www.nationalgeographic.com/maps

interior desert area. The sun scorches the land, but night temperatures drop dramatically. One traveler writes of the arid Western Plateau, as seen from a railroad car:

    ❝ . . . At twilight, the shrieking diesel horn scatters flights of long-beaked birds nesting in a sparse underbrush of burrs

and thistles. . . . Dawn purples a line of mesa-type, flat-topped hills outlined against a cloudless blue sky. ❞

    Hugh A. Mulligan, "The Ghan: Australia's Notoriously Lethargic Train to the Outback," *The Columbian,* November 11, 1999

With less than 10 inches (25 cm) of rain annually, there is not even enough vegetation for grazing.

DIFFERENTIATED INSTRUCTION

Visual/Spatial Students with strong visual/spatial skills might excel at creating a framework within which climate zone information can be classified. Have them write *temperature, precipitation,* and *vegetation* across the top of a sheet of paper and list *Australia, Oceania, New Zealand,* and *Antarctica* down the left side of the sheet. Tell students to look for information that fits each category as they read and enter it in the appropriate place on their charts. Ask them to make their work available to classmates as a study guide.

📖 **EE2 Places and Regions: Standard 5**

📁 Refer to *Inclusion for the Social Studies Classroom Strategies and Activities.*

NATIONAL GEOGRAPHIC — MAP STUDY

Australia, Oceania, and Antarctica: Natural Vegetation

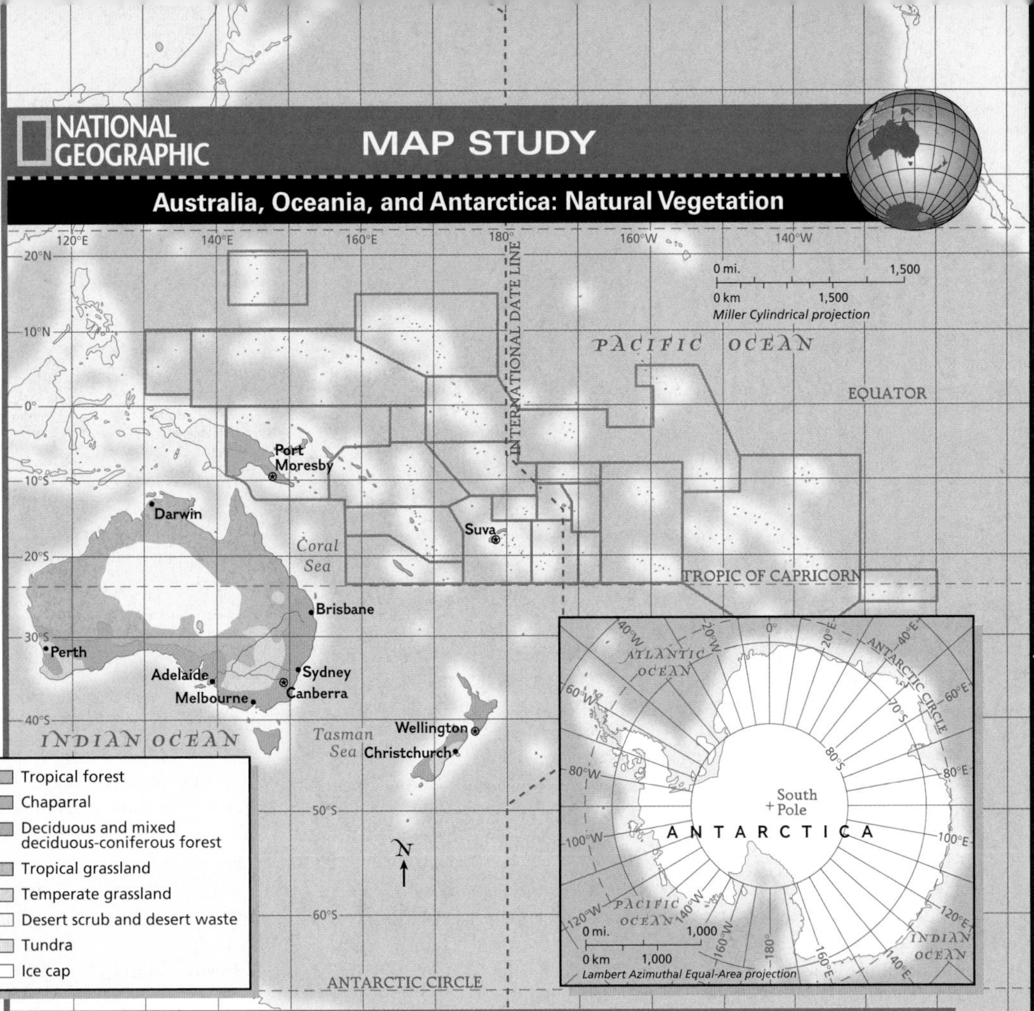

Legend:
- Tropical forest
- Chaparral
- Deciduous and mixed deciduous-coniferous forest
- Tropical grassland
- Temperate grassland
- Desert scrub and desert waste
- Tundra
- Ice cap

Geography Skills for Life

1. **Interpreting Maps** What type of vegetation is found in western Australia?

2. **Applying Geography Skills** What physical processes might affect patterns of economic conditions in southeastern Australia?

Find NGS online map resources @ www.nationalgeographic.com/maps

---

An area of milder steppe climate encircles Australia's desert region. Here more regular rainfall brings vegetation such as eucalyptus and acacia trees and small shrubs to life. Saplings of the acacia tree were used by early settlers to make wattle, a strong, interwoven wooden framework used for building homes. Rains fall only during the wet season, however, and the amount can vary greatly from year to year. Annual rainfall ranges from 10 to 20 inches (25 to 51 cm). Short grasses, ideal for grazing, also grow here, as do irrigated crops.

Australia's coastal areas have a variety of moister climates. The humid subtropical northeastern coast averages more than 20 inches (51 cm) of rain yearly. Less rain falls in the Mediterranean climate of the southern coasts and in the marine west coast climate along the southeastern coast. Coastal areas support most of Australia's agriculture.

Chapter 32 🌐 **801**

NATIONAL GEOGRAPHIC — MAP STUDY

Answers

1. deciduous and mixed deciduous-coniferous forest, chaparral, tropical grass-land, temperate grassland

2. A marine west coast climate favors settlement, agriculture, and industry.

Map Skills Practice

Place Where in the region is chaparral found? (along the southern coast of Australia)

L2 Identify

Surrounding Australia's interior deserts lies an area of steppe climate. **Ask:** What two native forms of vegetation are found in Australia's steppe climate region? (eucalyptus and acacia)

L1/ELL

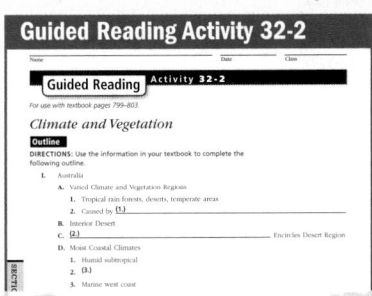

Guided Reading Activity 32-2

L1/ELL

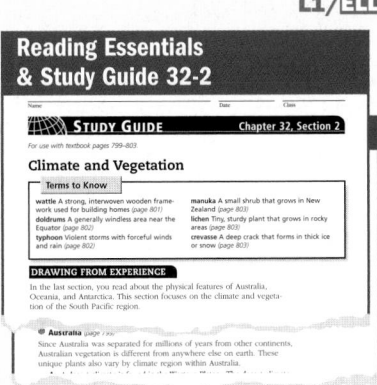

Reading Essentials & Study Guide 32-2

COOPERATIVE LEARNING ACTIVITY

Colder Than Outer Space Tell students that temperatures in Antarctica are colder than those on some parts of Mars. A visitor to Antarctica once wrote: "I raised my head to look around and found I couldn't move it back. My clothing had frozen solid as I stood." Allow time for groups of students to research the effects of cold on humans and human activities. Each group member should investigate one aspect of the effects of cold. Possible topics include physiological effects, psychological effects, and effects on housing, transportation, and communications. 🌐 **EE2 Places and Regions: Standard 4**
🌐 **EE5 Environment and Society: Standard 15**

NATIONAL GEOGRAPHIC **World Explorer**

Answer
marine west coast

More About the Photos
Water or the lack of water helps define many of this region's activities, including skiing, scuba diving, or desert expeditions.

□ NATIONAL GEOGRAPHIC **GEOFACT**

▶ **Lake Eyre is Australia's largest lake and the lowest point on the continent. It fills with water only every five to ten years. During wet periods, the lake becomes a habitat for creatures and birds for about two years before returning to its dry state.**

③ ASSESS

Assign Section 2 Assessment as homework or as an in-class activity.

⊙ Have students use **Interactive Tutor Self-Assessment CD-ROM**.

L2

Section Quiz 32-2

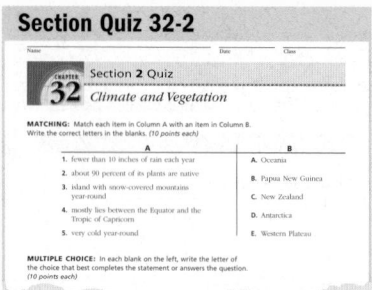

NATIONAL GEOGRAPHIC **World Explorer**

Geography **Skills for Life**
- - - - - - - - - - - - - - - - - **A Diverse Region** A ranching station in the Australian steppe (left), a tropical forest and island beach in Polynesia (middle), and a farm in the marine west coast climate of New Zealand (right) are just a sampling of the diverse landscapes of the region.
Place What kind of climate is found in most of New Zealand?

Oceania

Because much of Oceania lies between the Equator and the Tropic of Capricorn, most islands have a tropical rain forest climate. Most days are warm throughout the year, ranging from 70°F (21°C) to 80°F (27°C), though Pacific ocean winds cool atolls and the windward sides of higher islands. Some mountainous areas of **Papua New Guinea** even remain snow-covered year-round.

Seasons throughout most of Oceania alternate between wet and dry. The dry season features the cloudless blue skies often seen in travel advertisements, but the wet season brings constant rain and high humidity. The amount of rainfall varies from island to island. Low islands get little rainfall, but the larger landmasses of high islands give off warm, moisture-laden air. When this air rises and mixes with cool ocean breezes, heavy rains fall. Some high islands receive as much as 150 inches (381 cm) annually.

Only shrubs and grasses grow on dry, low islands, but coconut palms and other trees appear on islands with more rainfall. Hot, steamy rain forests thrive where heavy rains drench island interiors. A generally windless area called the **doldrums** occupies a narrow band near the Equator where opposing ocean currents meet. The eerie calm within the doldrums can change to violent storms called **typhoons**. Their forceful winds and heavy rain devastate land and vegetation and threaten lives.

New Zealand

A marine west coast climate is found in most of New Zealand. Ocean winds warm the land in winter and cool it in summer, preventing temperature extremes. Temperatures hover between 65°F (18°C) and 85°F (29°C) in summer and between 35°F (2°C) and 55°F (13°C) in winter. Abundant sunshine graces New Zealand's beaches and inland landscape, but clashing air masses may bring sudden clouds and rain.

Geographic differences also cause climatic variations. North Island's central plateau is warm and sunny during summer, but mountaintops may have snow year-round. Fierce winds or blizzards may strike these mountains at any time

---

CRITICAL THINKING ACTIVITY

Determining Cause and Effect Have partners study the map on page 801 and focus on Australia's natural vegetation. Tell them to choose one type of natural vegetation area. Have them draw a conclusion about the relationship between plant life and human ways of life in that part of Australia. *(Examples might include that grasslands are suitable for raising livestock and that people who live in grassland areas may work as ranchers.)* Combine pairs to form small groups. Have group members compare and contrast their conclusions.
⊛ **EE3 Physical Systems: Standard 8**
⊛ **EE5 Environment and Society: Standard 15**

of year. Mountainous areas exposed to western winds generally have more rainfall than do other areas. Although the country as a whole averages 25 to 60 inches (64 to 152 cm) of rain annually, the Southern Alps on South Island have an average annual rainfall of 315 inches (800 cm). Humidity levels in inland areas are about 10 percent lower than coastal areas. Maurice Shadbolt, a popular travel writer, describes New Zealand as a "long, lean land fated to fickle weather." In fact, he says, "At its most temperamental, New Zealand can offer the traveller all four seasons in one day."

New Zealand's geographic isolation gives rise to unique plant life. Almost 90 percent of the country's indigenous plants are native only to New Zealand. Manuka, a small shrub, carpets land where prehistoric volcanic eruptions destroyed ancient forests. Early settlers from Great Britain cut down almost all of the pinelike kauri trees, but some still grow among thriving evergreen forests. In an effort to repair severe erosion damage in deforested areas, New Zealand's forest service has imported several tree species from Europe and North America. A species of pine tree native to California in the United States, for example, now grows in large areas of the volcanic plateau of North Island. Willows and poplars from Europe also help keep soil on hillsides from eroding.

Antarctica

Antarctica is the earth's highest, driest, windiest, and coldest continent. Though very cold year-round, Antarctica's climate exhibits some variation. Air loses moisture as it rises over Antarctica's plateau, making the plateau drier than Australia's deserts, but much colder. Temperatures may plunge as low as −129°F (−89°C) in winter. The Antarctic Plateau descends to coastal areas that have a milder, moister climate. Annual snowfall averages no more than 2 inches (5 cm) inland, but along the coast it often measures 24 inches (61 cm).

Despite the severe climate, some species of mosses and algae have adapted well to life on Antarctica. In rocky areas along the coasts, tiny sturdy plants called lichens thrive. Of the approximately 800 plant species in Antarctica, about 350 are lichens. These plants survive by remaining dormant for long periods and almost instantly beginning to photosynthesize during brief periods of milder weather. The continent's only two flowering plants grow in a small area on the Antarctic Peninsula that lies in a tundra climate zone. Summer temperatures there may reach almost 60°F (16°C).

Although frozen, Antarctica's ice is not motionless. The cap's tremendous weight causes the frozen mass to spread toward the coasts. As it moves, the ice breaks into pieces, causing huge crevasses, or cracks, as much as 100 feet (30 m) wide.

Reteach

State the title of each section subhead in order. Ask individual students to restate the main idea or an important detail found in that subsection. Use the responses as a guide for reinforcement as needed.

Enrich

When people first arrived in New Zealand, the only native land mammals living there were bats. **Ask:** Why do you think this was so? *(Bats could fly over the water to New Zealand; other mammals could not.)* Have students conduct research to find what other kinds of wildlife are native to New Zealand.

④ CLOSE

Tell students to think of one original question and answer that they would add to the Section 2 Assessment. Use student ideas as the basis for a question and answer challenge.

SECTION 2 ASSESSMENT

Checking for Understanding

1. **Define** wattle, doldrums, typhoon, manuka, lichen, crevasse.

2. **Main Ideas** Create a Venn diagram like the one below. Fill in the climate factors for each location, putting those factors that both places have in common in the area where the circles overlap.

Comparing Climates
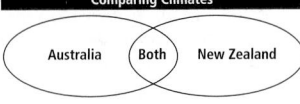

Australia — Both — New Zealand

Critical Thinking

3. **Making Inferences** What type of climate does most of New Zealand have? Why might it appeal to settlers?

4. **Problem Solving** What problems might researchers encounter in Antarctica, and how could these conditions be overcome?

5. **Identifying Cause and Effect** How do Pacific ocean currents and winds affect the climate of Oceania? How do they affect vegetation?

Analyzing Maps

6. **Human-Environment Interaction** Study the vegetation map on page 801. What type of vegetation is suitable for raising livestock, and where in Australia is it found?

Applying Geography

7. **Understanding Climate Maps** Note the climate regions on the map on page 800. Write a paragraph explaining how climate relates to the way farmers operate in New Zealand and Australia.

SECTION 2 ASSESSMENT ANSWERS

1. All vocabulary terms are defined in the text.

2. Answers should have factors specific to each country and those shared by both in the appropriate spaces on the diagram.

3. The marine west coast climate might appeal to settlers because of the cool summers and mild winters.

4. Answers should present well-reasoned ideas for overcoming the remote location, harsh climate, and barren landscape.

5. Pacific ocean winds cool atolls and the windward sides of higher islands. Also, when larger, higher islands give off moisture-laden air, it mixes with cool ocean breezes and causes heavy rainfall. Rain forests thrive where heavy rains fall.

6. grasslands circling the interior desert, and in the southeast

7. **Applying Geography** Dry climates in much of Australia make irrigation of crops or use of artesian water for watering livestock necessary; New Zealand's marine west coast climate, with its mild temperatures and greater rainfall, is more suitable to agriculture.

Teaching the Skill

Have students reread "A Geographic View" on page 799. Point out that writers *imply* certain points, or state them indirectly, by their choice of words or by the way they say things. Jane Ellen Stevens implies that permanent political communities will never be established in Antarctica. ("We can't conquer it, settle it, even own it.") Readers *infer* points that writers do not state directly by using their own knowledge or experience to draw probable conclusions from what they read.

Ask: What words and personal knowledge lead you to infer that Stevens probably prefers Antarctica this way? ("I . . . love this cold, strange place . . . I have come to see [it] as a living creature that nurtures a multitude of other lives. . . ." When someone enjoys something, they probably do not want to change it.)

Additional Practice
L1

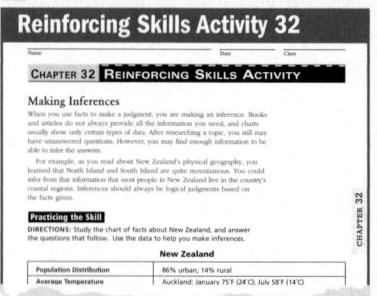

GLENCOE
TECHNOLOGY

Glencoe Skillbuilder Interactive Workbook, Level 2

CRITICAL THINKING
SkillBuilder

Making Inferences

You see a police car stopped behind another car by the roadside. The emergency lights are flashing on the police car. You infer, or conclude, that the driver was speeding based on the information you already have from similar circumstances. Making an inference means using information to draw a conclusion.

Learning the Skill

When you hear about a country or an event in news reports or read about it in magazines and books, you may still have questions afterward. Most sources do not contain all the information on a subject, but they may offer enough information for you to infer, or figure out, the answers to your questions.

Different sources present information in different forms. Statistical charts, for example, often compare information from which you might infer differences, similarities, or trends over time. These steps will help you make inferences from a chart:

- **Read the title and other labels to know what information the chart presents.**

- **Determine whether the chart provides detailed information about one topic, compares two or more topics, or shows changes over time.** Some charts may give several different types of information.

- **Make a list of the information that is not given in the chart, or the questions that arise from it.**

- **Infer answers to your questions.** Make logical inferences based on the facts given.

Solomon Islands	
Population	500,000
Government	Under British rule from 1893 to 1978, when it gained independence; member of the Commonwealth of Nations
Capital	Honiara
Languages	120 indigenous languages; English
Land	About 900 islands scattered over approximately 11,000 square miles (28,900 sq. km) of ocean
Geography	Mountainous volcanic islands and small atolls; coral reefs
Climate	Tropical
Rainfall	Ranges from 120 to 140 inches (305 to 356 cm) annually
Temperature	Ranges from 70° to 90°F (21° to 32°C)
Vegetation	Tropical forests on main islands
Exports	Fish, timber, cocoa
Life Expectancy	67 years

Sources: National Geographic Atlas of the World, 7th edition; 2001 World Population Data Sheet

Practicing the Skill

A tourist traveling to the Solomon Islands might use a chart to learn about the country. Answer the following questions by making inferences about the Solomon Islands from the information in the chart above.

1. Given the information in this chart, is it more likely that the form of government in the Solomon Islands is a parliamentary democracy or a communist state? Explain.

2. What can you infer about the health of the people in the Solomon Islands? Explain.

3. What can you infer about the animal life on the Solomon Islands? Explain.

4. What sorts of activities might a tourist enjoy in the Solomon Islands? Explain.

Applying the Skill

Locate a chart with information about another country in this region from a newspaper, magazine, or Web site. Use the steps to make inferences from the facts presented. Draft several questions based on your inferences. Exchange charts with another student, and complete each other's questions.

Go To The Glencoe Skillbuilder Interactive Workbook, Level 2 provides instruction and practice in key social studies skills.

ANSWERS TO PRACTICING THE SKILL

1. parliamentary democracy, because it was under British rule

2. Their health is generally good since life expectancy is a relatively high 67 years.

3. Animals would include species typical of a tropical rain forest environment.

4. Possible answers include swimming, boating, fishing, or nature walks.

CHAPTER 32 SUMMARY & STUDY GUIDE

SECTION 1 — The Land (pp. 793–798)

Terms to Know
- artesian well
- coral
- atoll
- lagoon
- krill

Key Points
- Australia, both a country and a continent, encompasses mountains, central lowlands, and expansive deserts. Rich mineral deposits and productive farms and ranches contribute to the Australian economy.
- Oceania's thousands of islands extend across the southern Pacific Ocean. The islands of Oceania were formed either directly or indirectly by volcanic activity.
- New Zealand's main features are two large islands with mountain ranges, rivers, and lakes. The country boasts rich soil and timberland.
- Antarctica is an ice-covered continent. While Antarctica may have important mineral resources, its key resource is the information it offers to scientists.

Organizing Your Notes
Use a chart like the one below to help you organize information about the physical features and resources of Australia, Oceania, and Antarctica.

	Geographic Features	Natural Resources
Australia		
Oceania		
New Zealand		
Antarctica		

SECTION 2 — Climate and Vegetation (pp. 799–803)

Terms to Know
- wattle
- doldrums
- typhoon
- manuka
- lichen
- crevasse

Key Points
- Australia generally has a hot, dry climate. Along the edges of the vast interior desert, the steppe receives sufficient rainfall for raising livestock. Only the coastal climates provide enough rainfall for growing crops without irrigation.
- Oceania enjoys a warm, moist tropical climate. Most islands have wet and dry seasons. The amount of rain during the wet season determines whether shrubs and grasses or dense rain forests will grow.
- New Zealand's marine west coast climate provides year-round rainfall, with temperatures that vary without being extreme.
- Antarctica's extremely cold and windy climate supports primarily lichens and mosses.

Organizing Your Notes
Use an outline like the one below to help you organize the information in this section about climate and vegetation.

Climate and Vegetation
I. Australia
  A. Mountains and Plateaus
  B. Central Lowlands
II. Oceania

CHAPTER CULMINATING ACTIVITY

Create a Mural Ask: If you were an artist visiting Australia, Oceania, and Antarctica, what images would you include in a portfolio? Have students review their notes and the text to create a portfolio of drawings or pictures that an artist might put together while traveling through the region. Suggest that they focus on unique landforms, vegetation, and animal life of the region. Encourage students to research images using library resources and the Internet as well as photos in the text. They should add a title and a brief caption for each illustration. ▣ EE2 Places and Regions: Standard 4

Using the Chapter 32 Summary & Study Guide

Use the Chapter 32 Summary & Study Guide to preview, review, condense, or reteach the chapter.

Preview/Review

🌐 **Vocabulary PuzzleMaker CD-ROM** reinforces "Terms to Know."

🌐 **Interactive Tutor Self-Assessment CD-ROM** provides a review of Chapter 32 content.

Condense

Have students read the Chapter 32 Summary & Study Guide.

🔊 Chapter 32 Audio Program

📁 Chapter 32 Guided Reading Activities

Reteach

📁 Chapter 32 Reteaching Activities (Spanish also available)

📁 Chapter 32 Reading Essentials and Study Guides

GLENCOE TECHNOLOGY

▢ NATIONAL GEOGRAPHIC
WORLD REGIONS
VIDEO PROGRAM

Unit 11, Australia, Oceania, and Antarctica
The following segments enhance the study of this unit:
- **Dream of a Lifetime**
- **Australia's Pioneers**
- **Haka Tradition**

805

CHAPTER
32
ASSESSMENT & ACTIVITIES

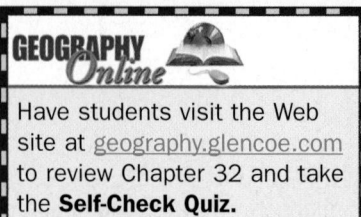
GLENCOE TECHNOLOGY

Use *MindJogger Videoquiz* to review the Chapter 32 content.

Reviewing Key Terms

1. b
2. f
3. e
4. i
5. a
6. j
7. h
8. d
9. g
10. c

Reviewing Facts

SECTION 1

1. the Great Barrier Reef
2. high islands, low islands, continental islands
3. land
4. Rivers and dams produce hydroelectric power; underground water heated by volcanoes produces geothermal energy.

SECTION 2

5. humid subtropical
6. Ocean winds warm the land in winter and cool it in summer.
7. the weight of the ice cap

Critical Thinking

1. Australia does not have an even distribution of population because of its mountains and deserts, where few people settle.

Reviewing Key Terms

Write the letter of the key term that best matches each definition below.

a. artesian well   f. doldrums
b. coral   g. typhoon
c. atoll   h. manuka
d. lagoon   i. lichen
e. krill   j. crevasse

1. limestone skeletons of a tiny sea animal

2. windless area near the Equator

3. shrimplike animal

4. small, sturdy plants

5. well from which pressurized water flows to the surface

6. huge crack in an ice cap

7. small shrub that grows in New Zealand

8. pool of water inside an atoll

9. violent Pacific Ocean storm

10. low, ring-shaped island

Reviewing Facts

SECTION 1

1. What formation lies just off Australia's northeastern coast?

2. Name the three types of islands that are found in Oceania.

3. What is New Zealand's main natural resource?

4. List the local resources that help to meet New Zealand's energy needs.

SECTION 2

5. What climate supports most of Australia's agricultural lands?

6. Describe the factor that prevents temperature extremes in New Zealand.

7. What causes the motion of the Antarctic ice cap?

Critical Thinking

1. Making Inferences Based on the information in Section 1, would you infer that Australia does or does not have an even distribution of population across the continent?

2. Comparing and Contrasting How are Oceania's islands similar? Different?

3. Identifying Cause and Effect Create a chart like the one below, and fill in the effects of different climates on vegetation. Then choose one effect, and write a paragraph describing its possible economic impact.

	Australia	Oceania	New Zealand	Antarctica
Climate				
Vegetation				

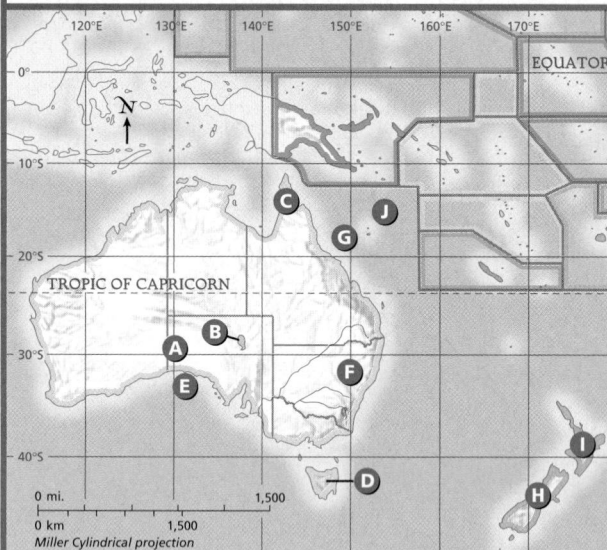

NATIONAL GEOGRAPHIC **Locating Places**
Australia and New Zealand: Physical-Political Geography
Match the letters on the map with the places and physical features of Australia and New Zealand. Write your answers on a sheet of paper.

1. Great Barrier Reef   4. Tasmania   7. Coral Sea
2. Great Victoria Desert   5. Cape York Peninsula   8. Lake Eyre
3. Great Dividing Range   6. Great Australian Bight   9. North Island
                                                        10. South Island

2. Similarities: many formed by volcanoes or have active volcanoes; Differences: size, origin (from volcanoes or rising ocean floor), landforms (mountainous, flat, or atolls)

3. Answers should include at least one example of vegetation and its economic impact for each climate type.

NATIONAL GEOGRAPHIC **Locating Places**

1. G	**3.** F	**5.** C	**7.** J	**9.** I
2. A	**4.** D	**6.** E	**8.** B	**10.** H

Using the Regional Atlas

1. Brisbane
2. along the northeastern, eastern, southeastern, and southwestern coasts

GEOGRAPHY Online

Self-Check Quiz Visit the **Glencoe World Geography** Web site at geography.glencoe.com and click on Self-Check Quizzes—Chapter 32 to prepare for the Chapter Test.

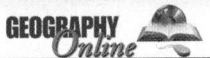

Using the Regional Atlas

Refer to the Regional Atlas on pages 784–787.

1. **Location** Which Australian city is located on the coast, just south of the Great Barrier Reef?
2. **Location** In which part of Australia are most of the coal deposits found?

Thinking Like a Geographer

Think about the activities of explorers, scientists, and tourists in Antarctica. What changes to Antarctica's physical geography might happen as a result? As a geographer, what safeguards would you suggest to preserve this unspoiled environment?

Problem-Solving Activity

Contemporary Issues Case Study Use print and nonprint resources to learn more about krill. Investigate how these tiny crustaceans fit into the food chain in the waters surrounding Antarctica. Find out about issues related to harvesting krill commercially as well as its potential for reducing world hunger. Write a brief report of your findings, and give recommendations for using krill responsibly.

GeoJournal

Travel Brochure Imagine that you are a travel writer, and draft a brochure about one location you wrote about in your GeoJournal. Include vivid details and information about the landforms, climate, and vegetation of the location you choose. Use your textbook and the Internet to make the brochure lively and interesting.

Technology Activity

Using the Internet for Research Search the Internet for photographs and information about plants mentioned in Section 2, such as acacia and manuka. Look for details about their habitats and their uses. Create a display of the information and images, and share the finished product with your class.

Standardized Test Practice

Use the chart below to choose the best answer for each of the following multiple-choice questions. If you have trouble answering the questions, use the process of elimination to narrow your choices.

Australian City	Average Yearly Precipitation (inches)	Average Temperature Range January (°F)	Average Temperature Range July (°F)
Alice Springs	10–20	75°–85°	45°–55°
Brisbane	over 30	75°–85°	55°–65°
Darwin	over 30	75°–85°	over 75°
Melbourne	20–30	65°–75°	45°–55°
Perth	over 30	75°–85°	45°–55°
Sydney	over 30	65°–75°	45°–55°

1. **If tourists were traveling to Australia in January and wanted to avoid both excessive heat and heavy rainfall, to which city should they travel?**

   A Melbourne
   B Brisbane
   C Darwin
   D Sydney

2. **What information in the chart shows that the Australian cities are in the Southern Hemisphere?**

   F July's temperatures are higher than January's.
   G January's temperatures are higher than July's.
   H The cities have abundant rain.
   J The cities have a dry season.

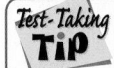

Test-Taking Tip Read the chart and become familiar with the information it contains before you answer the questions. Do not, however, study the chart in depth. The quickest way to answer both question 1 and question 2 is to read through each answer choice and use the process of elimination to get rid of those that you think are wrong.

Technology Activity

Displays should show evidence of thorough research.

Standardized Test Practice

1. A
2. G

Tested Objectives:
analyzing information
synthesizing information
making inferences

Additional Practice and Test-Taking Tips

Standardized Test Practice Workbook

CHAPTER BONUS TEST QUESTION

Are rabbits native to New Zealand, or were they brought there by people? How do you know? *(Before people arrived, the only land mammals that could reach New Zealand were those that could fly. Therefore, rabbits had to be brought by people.)*

Thinking Like a Geographer

Possible answers include that human activities may harm or destroy the ecosystem. Suggested safeguards should demonstrate ways to preserve the environment but allow research and responsible tourism to continue.

Problem-Solving Activity

Reports should include an explanation of the place of krill in the food chain, an analysis of harvesting methods, the potential for krill in alleviating world hunger, and recommendations for responsible use.

GeoJournal

Students' brochures should accurately present the landforms, climate, and vegetation of the chosen location in a manner that captures interest.

① FOCUS

Ask students to brainstorm the consequences to world exploration if no wind circulation existed on the earth. Relate this to the Viking, Spanish, Portuguese, and English explorers. Lead students to understand that without wind, travel by sailing ship would not have been possible. Therefore, ocean travel by ships (other than by oars) would not have occurred until motors were invented. **Ask: What is the term for the area where there usually is no wind circulation?** *(the doldrums)*

② TEACH

L2 Evaluating Information

Have pairs of students draw a map of the world showing the major ocean currents. (See page 61 for a map of ocean currents.) Have them use red to denote warm currents and blue to denote cold currents.

Direct students to tape a sheet of clear plastic over the map. Tell them to draw the major wind systems—warm air in pink and cold air in light blue. (See page 60 for a map of wind patterns.) Have students deduce the interrelationship between the air currents and the ocean currents.

Geography
Lab Activity

Air in Motion

▲ *Large tropical storms can be seen from space.*

Winds are horizontal air movements caused by temperature differences among air masses. Surface winds are usually strongest during the day, when the sun heats the ground. The increased ground temperature causes the air to spread out, become lighter, and rise. As thin air rises, cold air moves down to take its place. This movement of air is the wind blowing. Winds usually, but not always, become gentler at night. Wind patterns have a significant impact on an area's climate, and they are often themselves affected by local weather patterns and conditions. People generally identify winds based on the direction from which they blow.

Tropical storms are created when an area of low atmospheric pressure is surrounded by circulating winds. Twenty to twenty-five typhoons blast across the Pacific Ocean each year. The word *typhoon* comes from the Chinese word *tai-fung*, which means "great wind." These storms, which are called tropical cyclones or hurricanes in other parts of the world, have spiraling winds that reach 100 to 150 miles per hour (161 to 241 km per hour).

① ▶ Materials

- Drinking straw
- Scissors
- Thin, stiff plastic for the arrowhead and tail, 5⅞ in × 5⅞ in (15 cm × 15 cm)
- Clear tape
- Straight pin
- Wood block, 2 in × 2 in × 17¾ in (5 cm × 5 cm × 45 cm)
- Hammer
- Metal washer
- Photocopy of Figure 1—Compass
- Photocopy of Figure 2—Data chart

② ▶ Procedures

In this activity, you will build and use a wind vane to see how local changes in wind direction are related to local weather changes.

1. To construct the arrow, make two small slits in each end of the drinking straw. The slits at the arrow end should be 1⅛ inches (3 cm) long. The slits at the tail end should be 2 inches (5 cm) long. Make sure the slits align with each other.

2. Cut a small arrowhead and a large tail out of the plastic. Insert the arrowhead and the tail into the straw's slits, and secure them with a small amount of tape.

3. Balance the straw on your finger. NOTE: The balancing point may not be in the center of the straw. When you find this point, poke the straight pin through the straw. Enlarge the hole slightly.

GEOGRAPHY IN THE REAL WORLD

Harnessing Wind Power Historian Robert Temple, in his book *The Genius of China*, called the Chinese "the greatest sailors in history." By the A.D. 100s, the Chinese had developed sophisticated sails, masts, rudders, and other sailing equipment. Because of wind power, the Chinese became great explorers and traders more than 1,000 years before the Western "age of exploration." Point out that the state of California has experimented with the use of windmills to generate power for modern communities. Tell students to use reference materials or the Internet to research other attempts to harness the wind for contemporary uses.

🌐 **EE5 Environment and Society: Standard 14**
🌐 **EE6 The Uses of Geography: Standards 17, 18**

4. Photocopy Figure 1 (the compass), and tape it to the top of the wood block. Using the hammer, gently drive the pin through the metal washer and into the center of the compass.

5. Take the wind vane outside to an open area.

6. Hold the wind vane so that the *N* on the block points north. The wind vane's arrow will point into the wind. Use the compass to determine the direction from which the wind is blowing. This is the wind direction.

7. Photocopy or draw Figure 2 (the data chart), and record the wind direction three times a day, for five days.

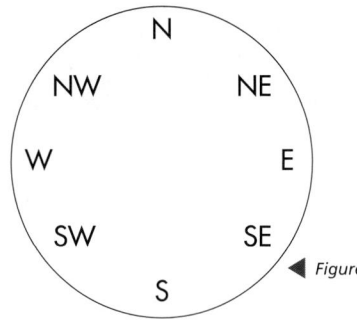

Figure 1

Date	Time	Wind Direction
	1. 2. 3.	
	1. 2. 3.	
	1. 2. 3.	
	1. 2. 3.	
	1. 2. 3.	

◀ *Figure 2*

3 ▶ Lab Report

1. Why do you think the arrow of a wind vane points into the wind?

2. In which direction did your arrow point most often?

3. According to your results, how often does the wind direction change in your area?

4. **Drawing Conclusions** Weather stations take wind direction readings from the tops of tall buildings or high poles. Why do you think this is so?

4 ▶ Find Out More

In addition to measuring wind direction, you can measure wind speed. Use nylon thread to attach a table tennis ball to the center of the straight edge on a protractor. In the windiest area of the school grounds, hold the protractor with the straight edge up and level. Now face the wind. The angle made by the nylon line on the protractor will be the wind speed in degrees. The degree of wind speed converts to the following wind speeds:

10 degrees = 8 mph (13 km/h)
20 degrees = 12 mph (19.2 km/h)
30 degrees = 15 mph (24 km/h)
40 degrees = 17.9 mph (28.8 km/h)
50 degrees = 20.9 mph (33.6 km/h)
60 degrees = 25.8 mph (41.6 km/h)
70 degrees = 32.8 mph (52.8 km/h)

Did You Know? Meteorologists use technology to monitor tropical storms and issue warnings that can save lives and property. Specialists scan satellite photographs for thunderstorm clusters. They reexamine cluster images hourly for signs of rotating winds. If these conditions develop, tropical storm warnings go out to people on ships, on aircraft, and along coastlines.

3 ASSESS

Have students answer the **Lab Report** questions on page 809.

4 CLOSE

Have students complete the **Find Out More** activity and summarize their findings. Remind them to hold the straight edge of the protractor up and level before facing the wind. Ask students to chart wind speed when they observe their wind vanes for wind direction. **Ask:** What was the highest wind speed during the week of observation? From which direction did the wind blow?

Record Winds The strongest winds measured on the earth's surface were recorded at Mount Washington, New Hampshire, on April 12, 1934. One gust reached 231 mph (372 kph)!

 **Meeting National Standards**

Geography for Life
The following standards are met in the Student Edition:

EE1 The World in Spatial Terms: Standards 1, 2, 3
EE6 The Uses of Geography: Standards 17, 18

ANSWERS TO LAB REPORT

1. The wind pushes on the wide tail, turning the arrow so that it points into the wind.

2. Answers will vary, depending on wind direction during the experiment.

3. Answers will vary. Local geography, such as mountains and bodies of water, will influence wind direction.

4. Weather direction is taken from the highest point because objects such as other buildings or high fences disturb the main air flow, resulting in inaccurate wind direction measurements.

NOTE: The following materials may be used when teaching Chapter 33. Section-level support materials are shown at point-of-use in the margins of the Teacher Wraparound Edition.

TEACHING TRANSPARENCIES

L2 Unit 11 Map Overlay Transparencies

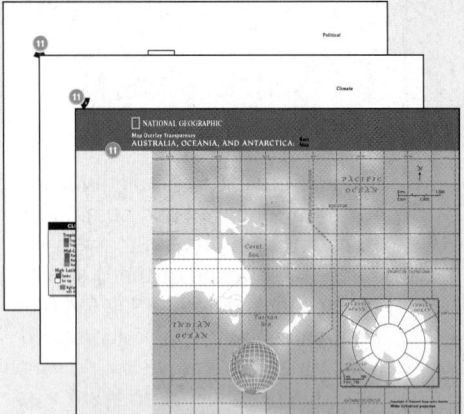

L2 Political Map Transparency 11

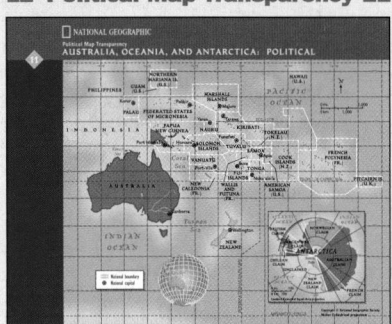

GEOGRAPHIC LITERACY

Focus on Geography Literacy

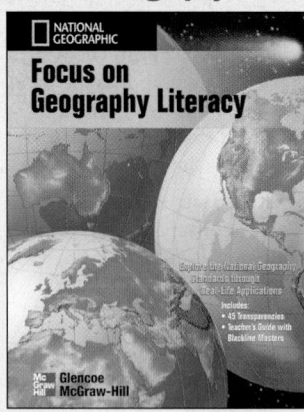

APPLICATION AND ENRICHMENT

L3 Enrichment Activity 33

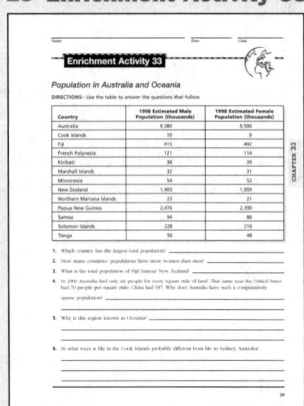

REVIEW AND REINFORCEMENT

L1 Vocabulary Activity 33   L1 Reinforcing   L1 Reteaching Activity 33
Skills Activity 33

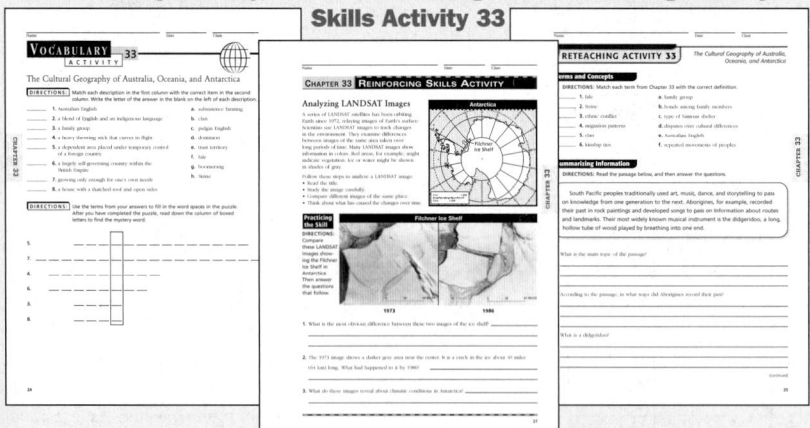

ASSESSMENT

L2 Chapter 33 Test Form A

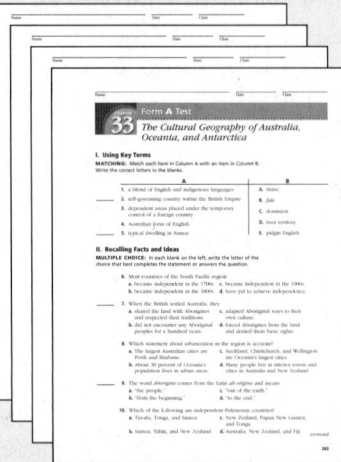

L2 Chapter 33 Test Form B

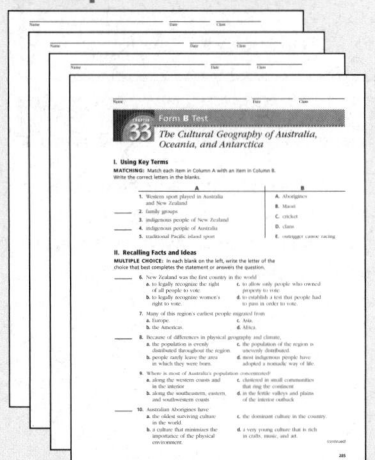

L1/ELL Performance Assessment Activity 33

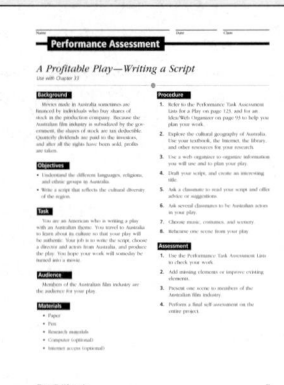

ExamView® Pro Testmaker

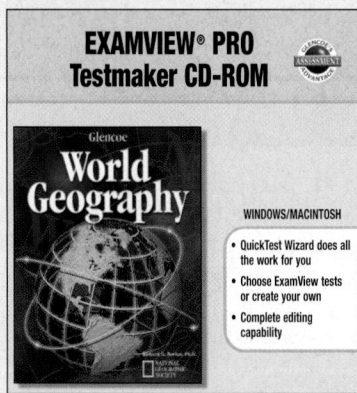

The following Spanish language materials are available in the Spanish Resources binder:

- Spanish Vocabulary Activities
- Spanish Guided Reading Activities
- Spanish Reteaching Activities
- Spanish Summaries
- Spanish Quizzes and Tests
- Spanish Reading Essentials and Study Guide

- World Regions Video
- MindJogger Videoquiz
- Vocabulary PuzzleMaker CD-ROM
- Interactive Tutor Self-Assessment CD-ROM
- ExamView® Pro Testmaker CD-ROM
- Audio Program
- TeacherWorks CD-ROM
- Interactive Student Edition CD-ROM
- Glencoe Skillbuilder Interactive Workbook CD-ROM, Level 2
- Presentation Plus! CD-ROM

Timesaving Tools

TeacherWorks™ All-In-One Planner and Resource Center

- **Interactive Teacher Edition** Access your Teacher Wraparound Edition and your classroom resources with a few easy clicks.
- **Interactive Lesson Planner** Planning has never been easier! Organize your week, month, semester, or year with all the lesson helps you need to make teaching creative, timely, and relevant.

Use Glencoe's **Presentation Plus!** multimedia teacher tool to easily present dynamic lessons that visually excite your students. Using Microsoft PowerPoint® you can customize the presentations to create your own personalized lessons.

GEOGRAPHY Online

Use our Web site for additional resources. All essential content is covered in the Student Edition.

You and your students can visit geography.glencoe.com, the Web site companion to *Glencoe World Geography*. This innovative integration of electronic and print media offers your students a wealth of opportunities. The student text directs students to the Web site for the following options:

- Chapter Overviews
- Student Activities
- Self-Check Quizzes
- Textbook Updates

Answers are provided for you in the "Web Activity Lesson Plan." Additional Web resources and Interactive Tutor puzzles are also available.

Additional Glencoe Teacher Support

- **Teaching Strategies for the Geography Classroom** (including Block Scheduling Pacing Guides)
- **Graphic Organizer Transparencies Strategies and Activities**
- **Outline Map Resource Book**
- **Reading in the Content Area**

PLANNING GUIDE

SECTION RESOURCES

Daily Objectives	Reproducible Resources	Multimedia Resources
SECTION 1 Population Patterns 1. Identify the peoples who settled Australia and Oceania. 2. Discuss how the region's geography affects population density, distribution, and growth. 3. Explain what factors account for settlement in urban and rural areas.	Reproducible Lesson Plan 33-1 Daily Lecture Notes 33-1 Guided Reading Activity 33-1* Reading Essentials and Study Guide 33-1* Section Quiz 33-1*	Daily Focus Skills Transparency 33-1 Political Map Transparency 11 Unit 11 Map Overlay Transparencies World Art Prints Interactive Tutor Self-Assessment CD-ROM ExamView® Pro Testmaker CD-ROM* Presentation Plus! CD-ROM
SECTION 2 History and Government 1. Describe the lifestyles of the region's indigenous peoples before colonization. 2. Summarize how colonial rule affected social, economic, and political structures. 3. Examine how today's governments reflect the region's history.	Reproducible Lesson Plan 33-2 Daily Lecture Notes 33-2 Guided Reading Activity 33-2* Reading Essentials and Study Guide 33-2* Section Quiz 33-2*	Daily Focus Skills Transparency 33-2 Political Map Transparency 11 Unit 11 Map Overlay Transparencies World Music: A Cultural Legacy Interactive Tutor Self-Assessment CD-ROM ExamView® Pro Testmaker CD-ROM* Presentation Plus! CD-ROM
SECTION 3 Cultures and Lifestyles 1. Discuss the role that religion plays in the region's culture. 2. Describe how the peoples of Australia and Oceania expressed their heritage through the arts. 3. Analyze how everyday life in the region reflects cultural diversity.	Reproducible Lesson Plan 33-3 Vocabulary Activity 33* Daily Lecture Notes 33-3 Guided Reading Activity 33-3* Reading Essentials and Study Guide 33-3* Reteaching Activity 33* Reinforcing Skills Activity 33 Section Quiz 33-3*	Daily Focus Skills Transparency 33-3 Political Map Transparency 11 Unit 11 Map Overlay Transparencies Vocabulary PuzzleMaker CD-ROM Interactive Tutor Self-Assessment CD-ROM ExamView® Pro Testmaker CD-ROM* Presentation Plus! CD-ROM

 Blackline Master   Software   Videocassette   *Also available in Spanish

 Transparency   CD-ROM   DVD

⏱ 00:00 OUT OF TIME?  Assign the Chapter 33 **Reading Essentials and Study Guide.**

Block Schedule

Activities that are particularly suited to use within the block scheduling framework are identified throughout this chapter by the following designation: 🔲

KEY TO ABILITY LEVELS

Teaching strategies have been coded for various learning styles and abilities.

L1 BASIC activities for all students

L2 AVERAGE activities for average to above-average students

L3 CHALLENGING activities for above-average students

ELL ENGLISH LANGUAGE LEARNER activities

Brian Lamoureux
Red Cloud Indian School
Pine Ridge, SD

Comparing Indigenous Peoples

This activity helps students learn about the similarities and differences of indigenous peoples of the United States and the Aborigines of Australia.

Direct students to the Internet to find data about the similarities and differences in terms of history, cultural values, economic activities, and relations with European settlers, for example.

Then ask students to make posters that demonstrate the similarities and differences. They also may write a short sketch or role-play a conversation between a Native American and an Aborigine, showing their understanding of the similarities and differences between the two cultures. Finally, have students give a short presentation on one aspect of their research. To conclude the activity, **Ask:** In what ways are the challenges faced by these groups similar? Different?

NATIONAL GEOGRAPHIC | TEACHER'S CORNER

Index to National Geographic Magazine:

The following articles may be used for research relating to this chapter:

- "Sydney," by Bill Bryson, August 2000.
- "Duck-Billed Platypus," by Melody Serena, April 2000.
- "Reclaiming a Lost Antarctic Base," by Michael Parfit, March 1993.

National Geographic Society Products:

To order the following products for use with this chapter, call National Geographic Society at 1-800-368-2728.

- *Antarctica* (Video)
- *Australia* (Video)
- *National Geographic Desk Reference* (Book)
- *National Geographic Atlas of the World, Seventh Edition* (Book)

NGS ONLINE

Access National Geographic's Web site for current events, activities, links, interactive features, and archives.
www.nationalgeographic.com

Meeting National Standards

Geography For Life

The following standards are highlighted in Chapter 33:

Section 1 EE1 The World in Spatial Terms: Standard 1
EE2 Places and Regions: Standards 4, 6
EE4 Human Systems: Standard 9
EE6 The Uses of Geography: Standard 18

Section 2 EE2 Places and Regions: Standard 6
EE4 Human Systems: Standard 13
EE5 Environment and Society: Standards 15, 16
EE6 The Uses Of Geography: Standard 17

Section 3 EE2 Places and Regions: Standard 4
EE4 Human Systems: Standards 9, 10, 12
EE6 The Uses of Geography: Standard 17

Local Objectives

_____

_____

MEETING SPECIAL NEEDS

In addition to the Differentiated Instruction strategies found in each section, the following resources are also suitable for your special needs students:

- *ExamView® Pro Testmaker CD-ROM* allows teachers to tailor tests by reducing answer choices.
- The *Audio Program* includes the entire narrative of the student edition so that less-proficient readers can listen to the words as they read them.
- The *Reading Essentials and Study Guide* provides the same content as the student edition but is written two grade levels below the textbook.
- *Guided Reading Activities* give less-proficient readers point-by-point instructions to increase comprehension as they read each textbook section.
- *Enrichment Activities* include a stimulating collection of readings and activities for gifted and talented students.

Chapter Objectives

1. Describe population patterns in Australia, Oceania, and Antarctica and how they have changed.
2. Discuss the forms of government that have developed in the region.

GLENCOE *TECHNOLOGY*

Use *MindJogger Videoquiz* to preview the Chapter 33 content.

GeoJournal

For access to additional photos, maps, and information on the cultural features of Australia, Oceania, and Antarctica, go to www.nationalgeographic.com (See Teacher pages in front for strategies for using journals in the geography classroom.)

GEOGRAPHY *Online*

Introduce students to chapter content and key terms by having them access **Chapter Overview 33** at geography.glencoe.com

FOLDABLES™
Study Organizer

Dinah Zike's Foldables are three-dimensional, interactive graphic organizers that help students practice basic writing skills, review key vocabulary terms, and identify main ideas. Have students complete the Foldable activity in the **Dinah Zike's Reading and Study Skills Foldables** booklet.

CHAPTER
33 The Cultural Geography of Australia, Oceania, and Antarctica

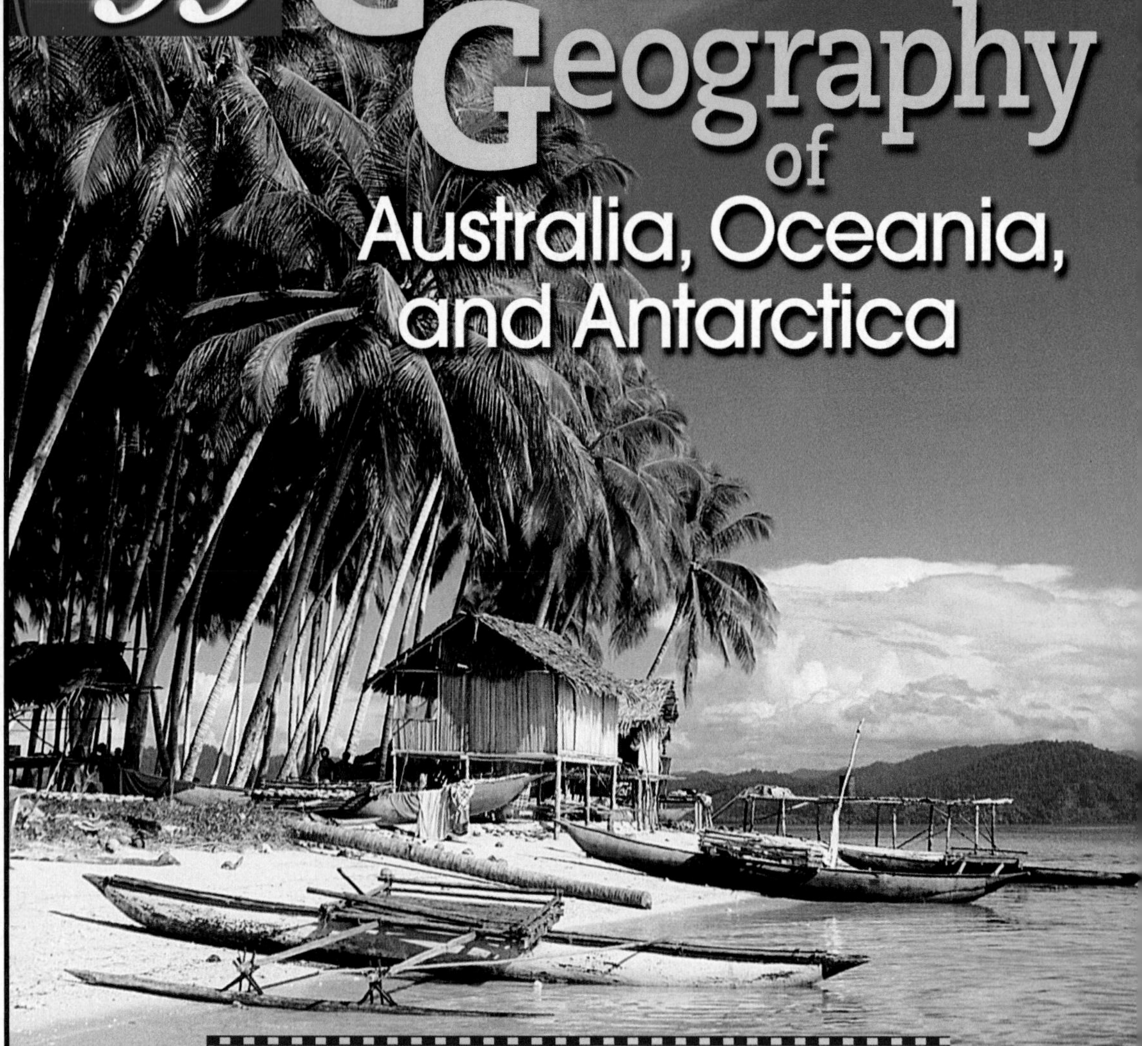

GeoJournal

As you read this chapter, use your journal to record similarities and differences in the ways people live in each of these three areas: Australia, Oceania, and Antarctica. Use clear and concise language to note interesting details about the region.

GEOGRAPHY *Online*

Chapter Overview Visit the **Glencoe World Geography** Web site at geography.glencoe.com and click on Chapter Overviews—Chapter 33 to preview information about the cultural geography of the region.

ABOUT THE PHOTO

Visual Instruction This peaceful scene along the coast of Papua New Guinea might look familiar to students as the stereotypical tropical paradise from movies and travel posters. Papua New Guinea's coasts have a darker side, however. Tsunamis sometimes cause massive destruction in this geologically active region. On July 17, 1998, a tsunami the U.S. Geological Survey called "the most devastating tsunami in this century" struck Papua New Guinea's coast. Scientists estimate that the average height of the wave was about 33 feet (about 10 m). Other tsunamis occurred there in 1873, 1935, and 1970, triggered by undersea earthquakes. **EE2: Places and Regions: Standard 6**

Guide to Reading

Consider What You Know

What images have you seen in the news or in films of the various peoples living in Australia, Oceania, and Antarctica? What geographic factors might account for the ways people live in each of these areas?

Reading Strategy

Taking Notes As you read about the population patterns of the region, use the major headings of the section to create an outline similar to the one below.

```
I.  Human Characteristics
    A.
    B.
    C.
II. Languages
```

Read to Find Out

• What peoples settled in Australia and Oceania?

• How does the region's geography affect population density, distribution, and growth?

• What factors account for settlement in urban and rural areas?

Terms to Know

• Strine

• pidgin English

Places to Locate

• Kiribati

• Sydney

• Melbourne

Population Patterns

NATIONAL GEOGRAPHIC

A Geographic View

Dream Journey

Lying back and looking at the night sky, I felt pulled upward into that shimmering immensity.... Laserlike, a shooting star cuts the sky ... and you suddenly understand how the Aborigines, who slept out here beneath these same stars for 50,000 years before the [Europeans] came, could devise their wonderful mythologies of the Sky Heroes who came down from the stars in that mystic Dreamtime and shaped the landscape.

Rock formations near Lake Argyle, Australia

—Harvey Arden, "Journey Into Dreamtime," National Geographic, *January 1991*

The Aborigines, Australia's earliest people, feel a direct relationship to the landscape that has shaped their movements throughout the island continent. Physical geography also has influenced migration and settlement patterns of other peoples in Australia and Oceania. In this section you will learn why Australia and Oceania have diverse cultures and what geographic factors influence where their populations live. You will also visit Antarctica, the cold, icy continent at the bottom of the world.

Human Characteristics

Australia and Oceania have populations with diverse ancestries—indigenous, European, and Asian. Both physical geography and the migration patterns of peoples have shaped the region's cultures.

◄ *Coastal scene, Papua New Guinea*

Chapter 33 🌐 811

① FOCUS

Section Overview

This section discusses the region's peoples and their languages, as well as population and settlement patterns.

BELLRINGER
Skillbuilder Activity

🔲 Project transparency and have students answer questions.

📁 Available as blackline master.

Daily Focus Skills Transparency 33-1

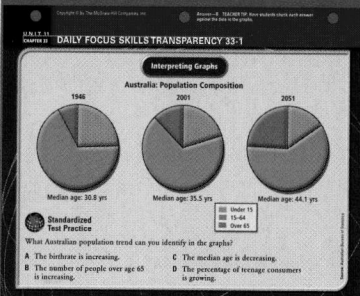

Guide to Reading

Consider What You Know
Answer *ranch life, seaside villages with palms, icebergs; vast distances and island locations*

Reading Strategy
Answer Students should complete the outline by including all heads in the section.

Preteaching Vocabulary
Have students find *pidgin* and *pidgin English* in a dictionary. **Ask:** Would the same kind of pidgin English be spoken in all parts of Oceania? *(No, there are different indigenous languages in Oceania.)*

RESOURCE MANAGER

📁 Reproducible Masters
• Reproducible Lesson Plan 33-1
• Daily Lecture Notes 33-1
• Guided Reading Activity 33-1
• Reading Essentials and Study Guide 33-1
• Section Quiz 33-1

📠 Transparencies
• Daily Focus Skills Transparency 33-1
• Political Map Transparency 11
• Unit 11 Map Overlay Transparencies

Multimedia
📀 World Art Prints
💿 Interactive Tutor Self-Assessment CD-ROM
💿 ExamView® Pro Testmaker CD-ROM
💿 Presentation Plus! CD-ROM

2 TEACH

Arts

Modern Aboriginal art is gaining worldwide recognition, but today's painters often work on canvas rather than rock. Clifford Possum Tjapaltjarri was one of the first to create paintings inspired by Aboriginal mythology. *The Art of Clifford Possum Tjapaltjarri* by Vivien Johnson shows examples of his art.

World Art Prints

Use these prints with accompanying strategies and activities to introduce students to other arts of this region.

L1 Locate

Have students examine the population density map on page 786.
Ask: Where do most Australians live? *(in the southeast)* Where do most New Zealanders live? *(North Island)*

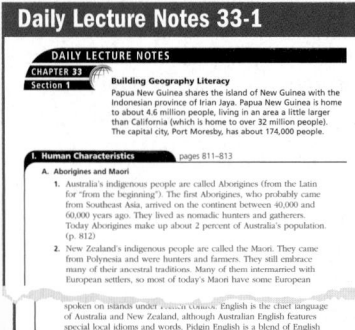

Daily Lecture Notes 33-1

DAILY LECTURE NOTES
CHAPTER 33
Section 1

Building Geography Literacy
Papua New Guinea shares the island of New Guinea with the Indonesian province of Irian Jaya. Papua New Guinea is home to about 4.6 million people, living in an area a little larger than California (which is home to over 32 million people). The capital city, Port Moresby, has about 174,000 people.

I. Human Characteristics pages 811–813

A. Aborigines and Maori

1. Australia's indigenous people are called Aborigines (from the Latin for "from the beginning"). The first Aborigines, who probably came from Southeast Asia, arrived on the continent between 40,000 and 60,000 years ago. They lived as nomadic hunters and gatherers. Today Aborigines make up about 2 percent of Australia's population. (p. 812)

2. New Zealand's indigenous people are called the Maori. They came from Polynesia and were hunters and farmers. They still embrace many of their ancestral traditions. Many of them intermarried with European settlers, so most of today's Maori have some European ...

spoken on islands under French control. English is the chief language of Australia and New Zealand, although Australian English features special local idioms and words. Pidgin English is a blend of English and an indigenous language. (p. 813)

the arts of AUSTRALIA

Rock Art The artistic tradition for which Australia's Aborigines are best known is rock art. Rock paintings and rock engravings, or petroglyphs, have diverse patterns and subject matter and may date from over 40,000 years ago. In addition to stylized shapes and symbols, petroglyphs showed human faces and bodies. Hunting scenes and animals also often appeared in rock art. The meanings of most of these paintings and petroglyphs, however, remain unknown.

Aborigines and Maori

Australia's Aborigines may have the oldest surviving culture in the world. The name given to them by European settlers is from the Latin *ab origine*, meaning "from the beginning." The first Aborigines probably arrived in Australia 40,000 to 60,000 years ago from Southeast Asia. They lived as nomadic hunters and gatherers in small kinship groups along the temperate coasts, in the northern rain forests, and across the vast interior deserts. Over the centuries, the Aborigines successfully learned to deal with the challenges posed by these environments. Today, Aborigines number about 315,000, making up about 2 percent of Australia's population.

New Zealand's indigenous peoples, known as the Maori (MOWR•ee), came from the Pacific islands of Polynesia. In New Zealand they hunted, fished, established villages, and raised crops. Many ancient Maori traditions still remain a part of Maori life. For example, Maori communities hold festive gatherings called *hui* in which important local events such

as weddings, funerals, and the dedication of new buildings are celebrated. As a result of intermarriage with European settlers over the years, most Maori people today have at least some European ancestry.

Pacific Islanders

The islands of Oceania were probably first settled by peoples from Asia more than 30,000 years ago. Waves of migrants from Asia continued to arrive over many centuries, while groups already living in the Pacific area moved from island to island. Today many different peoples speaking hundreds of languages live on Oceania's scattered islands. However, there are three major indigenous groups—Melanesians, Micronesians, and Polynesians—based on the island cluster on which each group lives. People on all three island clusters generally support themselves by fishing or farming.

The first cluster is Melanesia, located in the southwestern Pacific Ocean. It includes independent island countries, such as Papua New Guinea, Fiji, and the Solomon Islands, as well as French-ruled New Caledonia. Melanesian cultures differ greatly, even among groups living in different parts of the same island.

Next is Micronesia, situated in the western Pacific east of the Philippines. Among the independent countries of Micronesia are the Federated States of Micronesia, Nauru, and **Kiribati** (KIHR•uh•BAH•tee). The area also includes the United States island territories of Guam and the Marianas. Micronesians also have several different languages and cultures.

The last cluster is Polynesia, located in the central Pacific area. Three independent countries—Samoa, Tonga, and Tuvalu—are found in Polynesia. Other island groups, known as French Polynesia, are under French rule and include Tahiti, Polynesia's largest island. Most Polynesians share similar languages and cultures.

Europeans

From the 1500s to the late 1700s, Europeans sailed the waters around Australia, New Zealand, and Oceania. They set up trading settlements and eventually colonized the region. Europeans, mainly of British descent, still make up most of the populations of both Australia and New Zealand. Smaller numbers of European groups live on various Pacific

---

DIFFERENTIATED INSTRUCTION

English Learners Knowing the stories behind place names in the region may help students understand the extent of European influences. Note that *Tasmania* was named for Dutch explorer Abel Tasman. Tasman named New Zealand after Zeeland, a province in his native country, the Netherlands. Point out that many places in this region are named for Europeans. Have partners research to learn the origins of the place names *Victoria*, *Cook*, and *Wellington*. Note that the word *New* in a place name is almost always followed by the name of a place in Europe. (One exception is *New Guinea*.) **ELL**

EE2 Places and Regions: Standard 4

Refer to *Inclusion for the Social Studies Classroom Strategies and Activities.*

islands. For example, the French-ruled islands of Tahiti and New Caledonia are home to many people of European descent.

Asians

Asian communities also exist in the South Pacific area. Chinese traders and South Asian workers settled parts of Oceania during the 1800s, and today their descendants are included in the populations of places such as French Polynesia and Fiji. From the early 1900s to 1945, Japan ruled a number of Pacific islands, although few people of Japanese descent live there today. Australia and New Zealand once blocked non-European immigration, but the need for more workers finally led to more open immigration policies after the 1970s. Since then, increasing numbers of East Asians and Southeast Asians have migrated to Australia and New Zealand in search of economic opportunity.

Languages

Before the era of modern transportation and advanced communications, mountains, deserts, and ocean separated the peoples of the South Pacific area. As a result, isolated groups developed many different languages. Of the world's 3,000 languages, 1,200 are spoken today in Oceania alone, some by only a few hundred people.

European colonization brought European languages to the region. Today French is widely spoken in areas of Oceania that remain under French control. English is the major language of Australia and New Zealand. Australian English, called **Strine**, has a unique vocabulary made up of Aboriginal words, terms used by early settlers, and slang created by modern Australians. For example, Australians today call a barbecue a "barbie," and greet each other with the phrase "G'day." In many areas of Oceania, varieties of pidgin English, a blend of English and an indigenous language, developed to allow better communication among different groups.

Where People Live

Australia, Oceania, and Antarctica span a vast area; Australia and Oceania together cover about 5.7 percent of the earth's land surface. However, a high percentage of the region's land is unsuited for human habitation. Thus, the region has only one-half of one percent of the world's population.

Population Distribution

Because of uninhabitable land and vast differences in physical features and climates, population in Australia and Oceania is unevenly distributed. Australia is the region's most heavily populated country. About two-thirds of the South Pacific area's 31 million people live in Australia, which has almost 90 percent of the region's habitable land. Very few people, however, live in Australia's dry central plateaus and deserts. Most live along the southeastern, eastern, and southwestern coasts, which have a mild climate, fertile soil, and access to sea transportation. Most of New Zealand's people also live in coastal areas.

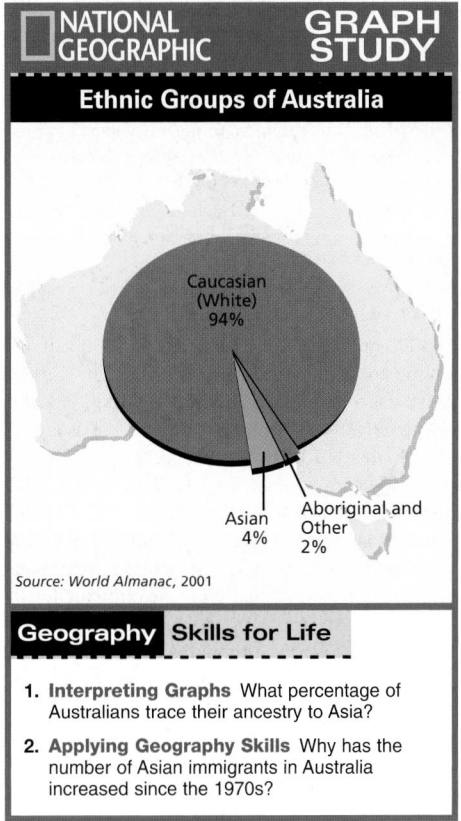

NATIONAL GEOGRAPHIC **GRAPH STUDY**

Ethnic Groups of Australia

Caucasian (White) 94%

Asian 4%

Aboriginal and Other 2%

Source: World Almanac, 2001

Geography | Skills for Life

1. **Interpreting Graphs** What percentage of Australians trace their ancestry to Asia?

2. **Applying Geography Skills** Why has the number of Asian immigrants in Australia increased since the 1970s?

L3 Math

Help students understand how the size of Antarctica compares with that of Australia. Have them use the "Country Profiles" in the Regional Atlas on page 788 to find the area of Australia's landmass. Have them subtract that figure from the area of Antarctica's landmass. *(5,400,000 – 2,988,888 = 2,411,112 square miles [6,268,891 sq. km]).* Note that Australia could fit into Antarctica and leave almost enough room for another continent of its size.

L1/ELL

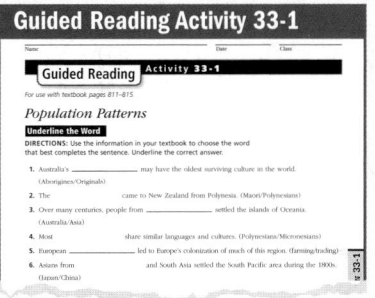

Guided Reading Activity 33-1

Guided Reading Activity 33-1

For use with textbook pages 811–815

Population Patterns

Underline the Word

DIRECTIONS: Use the information in your textbook to choose the word that best completes the sentence. Underline the correct answer.

1. Australia's _____ may have the oldest surviving culture in the world. (Aborigines/Originals)

2. The _____ came to New Zealand from Polynesia. (Maori/Polynesians)

3. Over many centuries, people from _____ settled the islands of Oceania. (Australia/Asia)

4. Most _____ share similar languages and cultures. (Polynesians/Micronesians)

5. European _____ led to Europe's colonization of much of this region. (farming/trading)

6. Asians from _____ and South Asia settled the South Pacific area during the 1800s. (Japan/China)

NATIONAL GEOGRAPHIC **GRAPH STUDY**

Answers

1. *4 percent*

2. *After the 1970s Australia no longer blocked non-European immigration, so Asian immigrants have come in search of economic opportunities.*

Skills Practice

Place To what extent do you think the interests of Aborigines are represented in the Australian government? *(traditionally, not much; recently their concerns have been given more attention)*

COOPERATIVE LEARNING ACTIVITY

Graphing the Region's Population

Copy the population data provided here on the board. Have small groups complete a circle graph reflecting the region's population distribution. Then have group members use an almanac to find the percentage of ethnic groups in each country and complete a circle graph using that information.

🌐 **EE1 The World in Spatial Terms: Standard 1**

🌐 **EE4 Human Systems: Standard 9**

COUNTRY	POPULATION
Australia	19.9 million
New Zealand	4 million
Papua New Guinea	5.5 million
Other	2.7 million

Answer
along the coasts of Australia and New Zealand

More About the Photo
In many societies young men wear certain decorations only after completing a rite of passage into adulthood.

L1/ELL

Reading Essentials & Study Guide 33-1

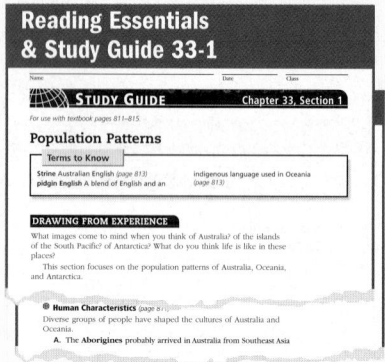

③ASSESS

Assign Section 1 Assessment as homework or as an in-class activity.

Ⓘ Have students use **Interactive Tutor Self-Assessment CD-ROM**.

L2

Section Quiz 33-1

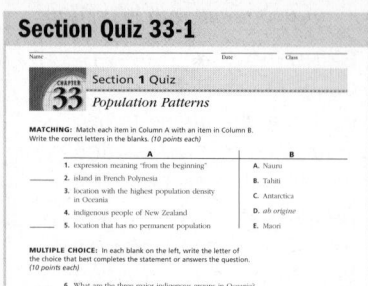

Geography Skills for Life
Diverse
Peoples The South Pacific region is home both to this indigenous man from Papua New Guinea (inset) and these children of European descent from Australia.
Place Where are the South Pacific's most urbanized areas located?

In Oceania, the population is divided unequally among the island countries. Papua New Guinea leads with about 5.5 million people, whereas Nauru—the world's smallest republic—has a population of only 10,000. Many more Pacific islanders live on their countries' coasts than in the often rugged interiors.

Antarctica's forbidding, icy terrain and merciless polar climate have never supported permanent human settlement. Conditions are difficult for all but short-term stays by research scientists and adventurous tourists. Although Antarctica measures about 5.5 million square miles (14.2 million sq. km), most research stations cluster along the Antarctic Peninsula, where summer temperatures may rise to a relatively mild 32°F (0°C). During this season the population of research stations reaches about 10,000, but only about 1,000 people remain during winter.

Population Density

Like population distribution, population density varies throughout the region. In Australia, for example, the population density averages only 7 people per square mile (3 per sq. km). In some interior rural areas, a person can travel 100 miles (161 km) without seeing another human being. In coastal urban areas, however, population density is much higher. Australia's urban areas are home to 85 percent of the country's total population. Like many developed countries, Australia has an aging population and a declining birthrate. Yet Australia's population probably will continue to increase because of immigration.

Oceania's population is growing at an average rate of 2.3 percent per year because it has a relatively young population. The land area of Oceania's 25,000 islands totals only 551,059 square miles (1,427,246 sq. km), and the population density varies greatly. Because Papua New Guinea has a large area, its population density is only 31 people per square mile (12 per sq. km). Tiny Nauru, measuring just 9 square miles (23 sq. km), has the highest population density in Oceania—about 1,412 people per square mile (545 per sq. km). In spite of its small area, mining of the island's rich phosphate deposits provides jobs and funding for economic development.

Urbanization

Most people in Australia and New Zealand live in cities or towns along the temperate coasts. The largest Australian cities are **Sydney** and **Melbourne**—each with more than 3 million residents. Sydney, located on the eastern coast, and Melbourne, on the southern coast, are port cities and commercial centers. Other coastal urban areas in Australia are Brisbane, Adelaide, and Perth. Few people, on the other hand, live in the hot, dry climate of Australia's interior.

New Zealand's ports of Auckland, Christchurch, and Wellington are Oceania's largest cities. These and other cities in the region offer newcomers opportunities for a high standard of living, quality health care, and excellent education.

Urban areas in Australia and Oceania draw people from within their own countries as well as from other countries. In Australia internal migration has

---

CRITICAL THINKING ACTIVITY

Predicting Consequences Direct students to review the information about population trends on page 814. Have each student choose one of the following trends: aging population and declining birthrate (Australia), population growth from immigration (Australia), or young population and steady growth (Oceania). Tell them to write a paragraph describing what they believe the trend's consequences will be for Australia or Oceania's economy, government services, culture, and daily life twenty years from now.
🌐 **EE4 Human Systems: Standard 9**
🌐 **EE6 The Uses of Geography: Standard 18**

led to shifts in population distribution. During the 1990s the population in rural areas declined while that of large cities and their suburbs grew rapidly. A similar pattern can be seen in Oceania, where 70 percent of the population lives in urban areas.

Government
Immigration

Rapid expansion of industry after World War II drew many immigrants to Australia. At first most immigrants came from European countries, such as the United Kingdom, Greece, Yugoslavia, and the Netherlands. In the 1980s Australia's industries still needed more workers, so the Australian government created programs to attract people from other regions. Today immigrants come from South Africa and various parts of Asia and Latin America. A number of them also come from Oceania. Population growth and uneven economic development in the various Pacific islands cause many young people and skilled workers to seek work elsewhere.

Student Web Activity Visit the **Glencoe World Geography** Web site at geography.glencoe.com and click on Student Web Activities—Chapter 33 for an activity about immigration and cultural diversity in Australia.

Publicly funded programs provide travel assistance to immigrants and help them adjust to Australian society. Most immigrant workers settle in major industrialized cities because of high-paying jobs. Today about 26 percent of Australia's population is foreign born. One worker from Lebanon describes his experience to a journalist:

> " *In this one factory you had people from maybe ten, twelve different countries, all speaking different languages. That's what Sydney was like. . . . It's a beautiful . . . country—beautiful. Great weather. Lovely lifestyle. Plenty of opportunity if you want to work hard.* "
>
> Bill Bryson, "Sydney," *National Geographic*, August 2000

Throughout Australia and Oceania, meeting the needs of a growing multiethnic population is a major concern. Diversity enriches the region's languages, arts, music, and lifestyles. At times, however, this same diversity may cause disagreements over issues such as immigration, health benefits, employment, and the effects of colonial rule. The next section highlights the legacy of the past and how it shapes life in Australia and Oceania today. Antarctica, with no permanent population, has a history that is unique to that icy continent.

SECTION ❶ ASSESSMENT

Checking for Understanding

1. **Define** Strine, pidgin English.

2. **Main Ideas** On a chart like the one below, fill in three main ideas from the section and then list important supporting details for each idea.

Main Ideas	Supporting Details

Critical Thinking

3. **Categorizing Information** From what areas have peoples migrated to Australia and Oceania?

4. **Identifying Cause and Effect** What geographic factors cause most of Australia's population to cluster in coastal urban areas?

5. **Predicting Consequences** What are possible positive and negative effects as modern technology and transportation attract more people to the South Pacific region?

Analyzing Maps

6. **Region** Study the population density map on page 786. What are the most sparsely populated areas of the South Pacific region?

Applying Geography

7. **Movement and Population** Create two maps, one of migration patterns during the last 100 years, and the other showing population distribution in the region today.

SECTION ❶ ASSESSMENT ANSWERS

1. All vocabulary terms are defined in the text.
2. Charts should include supporting details for the main ideas.
3. Asia, East Asia, Southeast Asia, Europe
4. mild climate, fertile soil, and access to sea transportation
5. positive: better economic opportunities and health care; negative: pollution, overcrowding, and loss of cultural traditions

6. Australia's central plateaus and deserts
7. **Applying Geography** Migration maps should show movement to urban areas in Australia and New Zealand from various world regions. Population distribution maps should show concentration of Australians and New Zealanders in coastal urban areas.

Reteach
Have students use the headings in this section to outline the material.

Enrich
Tell students that New Zealand's Kiri Te Kanawa is one of the world's most renowned opera singers. She lives in England, where she received her education, but remains a citizen of New Zealand. Kiri Te Kanawa's mother was of European descent. **Ask:** What can you infer from her name about the ethnicity of Ms. Kanawa's father? *(Ms. Kanawa's father was Maori.)*

Have students research the role of the outback in Australian life and culture. Ask them to provide examples of the ways different groups of Australians view this region differently.

Objectives, goals, and answers to the student activity can be found in the Web Activity Lesson Plan feature at geography.glencoe.com

FOCUS

Section Overview

This section discusses the history of the region, the lifestyles of its indigenous peoples, the era of colonial rule, and the rise of modern governments.

BELLRINGER
Skillbuilder Activity

 Project transparency and have students answer questions.

 Available as blackline master.

Daily Focus Skills Transparency 33-2

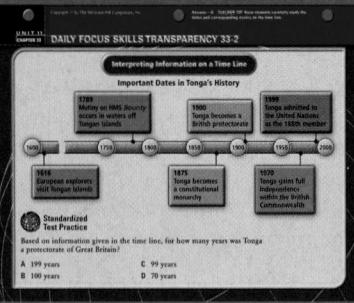

Guide to Reading

Consider What You Know
Answer *Possible answers may include South Pacific or Native American groups.*

Reading Strategy
Answers *died from new diseases; social structure weakened; treaty disputes resulted in loss of Maori lives and land*

Preteaching Vocabulary
Use each of the "Terms to Know" in a sentence, and have students infer the meaning from the context. Tell students to deduce meaning from the context when they encounter unfamiliar terms.

Guide to Reading

Consider What You Know
Various indigenous peoples lived in Australia and Oceania before the Europeans established colonies there. What indigenous groups in various parts of the world have you read about or seen in movies or on television?

Reading Strategy
Organizing Complete a web diagram similar to the one below by filling in the hardships the Maori faced after British settlement in New Zealand.

Maori Hardships

Read to Find Out
• What were the lifestyles of the region's indigenous peoples before colonization?

• How did colonial rule affect social, economic, and political structures?

• How do today's governments reflect the region's history?

Terms to Know
• clan
• boomerang
• trust territory
• dominion

Places to Locate
• Vanuatu
• Tonga

History and Government

NATIONAL GEOGRAPHIC

A Geographic View

Pacific Origins

Samoa itself is said to mean "sacred center".... [T]his is where the world began as the creator, Tagaloalagi, first called forth earth, sea, and sky from rock.... Language links and artifacts suggest that the first distinctly Polynesian culture may have developed here some 3,000 years ago. Over the centuries that followed, seafarers in double-hulled sailing vessels stocked with pigs, dogs, and fruits spread that culture across much of the Pacific.

—Douglas Chadwick, "The Samoan Way," National Geographic, July 2000

Samoan diver in Pacific waters

European and American influences in the past three centuries have profoundly changed the indigenous peoples and cultures of the South Pacific area. In this section you will learn about the early inhabitants of Australia and Oceania, the effects of Western settlement and rule in these areas, and the emergence of independent countries and new governments during the past 100 years.

Indigenous Peoples

Historians, anthropologists, archaeologists, and other scientists are continually uncovering new information about the history of early South Pacific peoples. At the same time, after years of Western dominance, indigenous peoples throughout the region are rediscovering their historical roots and are renewing their traditional cultures. All of these developments have heightened global interest in and appreciation of the South Pacific's pre-European past.

RESOURCE MANAGER

📁 Reproducible Masters
• Reproducible Lesson Plan 33-2
• Daily Lecture Notes 33-2
• Guided Reading Activity 33-2
• Reading Essentials and Study Guide 33-2
• Section Quiz 33-2

🖥 Transparencies
• Daily Focus Skills Transparency 33-2
• Political Map Transparency 11
• Unit 11 Map Overlay Transparencies

Multimedia
🎵 World Music: A Cultural Legacy
💿 Interactive Tutor Self-Assessment CD-ROM
💿 ExamView® Pro Testmaker CD-ROM
💿 Presentation Plus! CD-ROM

music of AUSTRALIA

The oldest music in Australia is that of the Aborigines. Music has always played a central role in both social and sacred life. Much of the traditional music in this region is based on vocals, though wind and percussion instruments are also very important.

Instrument Spotlight
In its traditional form, the **didgeridoo** (DIH•juh•ree•DOO) was made by nature when a eucalyptus branch fell to the ground and was hollowed out by termites. The Aborigines considered it sacred and continue to make it an important part of their spiritual ceremonies. Didgeridoos have become popular outside Australia and are manufactured and played all over the world. Through a combination of lip, tongue, and mouth movements, a wide variety of interesting sounds can be produced from this simple instrument.

Go To **World Music: A Cultural Legacy** Hear music of this region on Disc 2, Tracks 25–29.

Early Migrations

Various peoples from Asia settled the region of Australia and Oceania more than 40,000 years ago. Some may have migrated to Australia over land bridges during the Ice Age, when ocean levels were much lower than they are today. Others probably used canoes and rafts to reach the South Pacific region. The reason they came to these areas is a mystery. Because of their connection to the sea, some of these peoples, especially those who came to the South Pacific region, may have regarded exploration as a natural part of daily life. Author Peter Crawford, impressed with the daring of these early explorers, described the early Polynesians:

> ❝ *A tenacious, seafaring people had abandoned the shores of [S]outheast Asia and sailed into the Pacific. As their culture developed, they acquired new skills of survival, and new knowledge of the ocean world which became their home. . . . The vibrant Polynesian culture that grew and flourished . . . is testament to the invention and adaptability of its people.* ❞
> Peter Crawford, *Nomads of the Wind: A Natural History of Polynesia*, 1993

Economics
Indigenous Lifestyles

In the hot, dry Australian interior, the early Aborigines led a nomadic life. They used well-traveled routes to reach water and seasonal food sources. These same routes made trading and social exchanges possible. Clans, or family groups, traveled together within their ancestral territories, carrying only baskets, bowls, spears, and sticks for digging. To hunt animals, Aboriginal men used a heavy throwing stick, called a boomerang, that soars or curves in flight, and the women and children gathered plants and seeds.

In Oceania people settled in family groups along island coasts. For food they relied on fish, turtles,

---

② TEACH

Music Notes
The didgeridoo is usually played as part of an ensemble that includes a principal singer, who beats sticks together. Sometimes the singer may also beat a stick against the tube of the didgeridoo.

🎵 **World Music: A Cultural Legacy**
Use the accompanying Teacher Guide for background information, discussion questions, and worksheets about the music of this region.

L1 Locate
Have students refer to the map on page 818. Tell them to create a chart listing each country and the colonial power that once ruled it. Encourage students to suggest the effects of colonization on the South Pacific region.

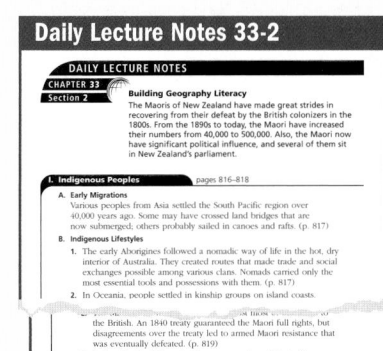

Daily Lecture Notes 33-2

> **DAILY LECTURE NOTES**
> **CHAPTER 33**
> **Section 2**
> **Building Geography Literacy**
> The Maoris of New Zealand have made great strides in recovering from their defeat by the British colonizers in the 1800s. From the 1890s to today, the Maori have increased their numbers from 40,000 to 500,000. Also, the Maori now have significant political influence, and several of them sit in New Zealand's parliament.
>
> **I. Indigenous Peoples** pages 816–818
> **A. Early Migrations**
> Various peoples from Asia settled the South Pacific region over 40,000 years ago. Some may have crossed land bridges that are now submerged; others probably sailed in canoes and rafts. (p. 817)
> **B. Indigenous Lifestyles**
> 1. The early Aborigines followed a nomadic way of life in the hot, dry interior of Australia. They created routes that made trade and social exchanges possible among various clans. Nomads carried only the most essential tools and possessions with them. (p. 817)
> 2. In Oceania, people settled in kinship groups on island coasts.
>
> the British. An 1840 treaty guaranteed the Maori full rights, but disagreements over the treaty led to armed Maori resistance that was eventually defeated. (p. 819)

DIFFERENTIATED INSTRUCTION

At-Risk Students Practice a focused reading exercise with students who have problems with reading comprehension. Have students read the subsection titled "Struggle for Power." Have them write down the information they recall and then reread the subsection to answer the following questions: How did World War I change colonial rule in Oceania? How did World War II affect the course of Oceania's history? What has happened since the 1970s? Have partners compare their answers to the questions.

⦿ EE4 Human Systems: Standard 13

📁 Refer to *Inclusion for the Social Studies Classroom Strategies and Activities.*

NATIONAL GEOGRAPHIC — MAP STUDY

Answers

1. *the United States and Germany*

2. *Possible answer: Guam provided a refueling station for U.S. ships.*

Map Skills Practice

Place Which island group included Tahiti? *(the Society Islands)* Which European country ruled those islands? *(France)*

L2 Interpretation

Ask: What non-European country acquired possessions in Oceania? *(Japan)* What historical event ended that country's rule in parts of Oceania? *(World War II)*

L1/ELL

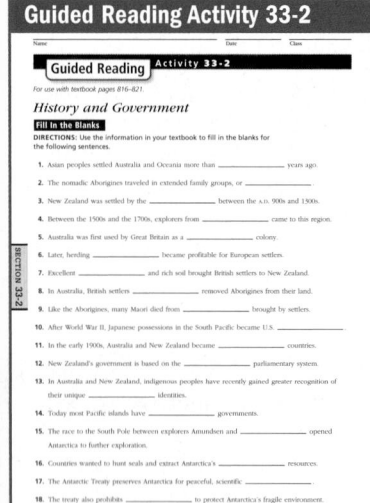

Guided Reading Activity 33-2

NATIONAL GEOGRAPHIC — MAP STUDY

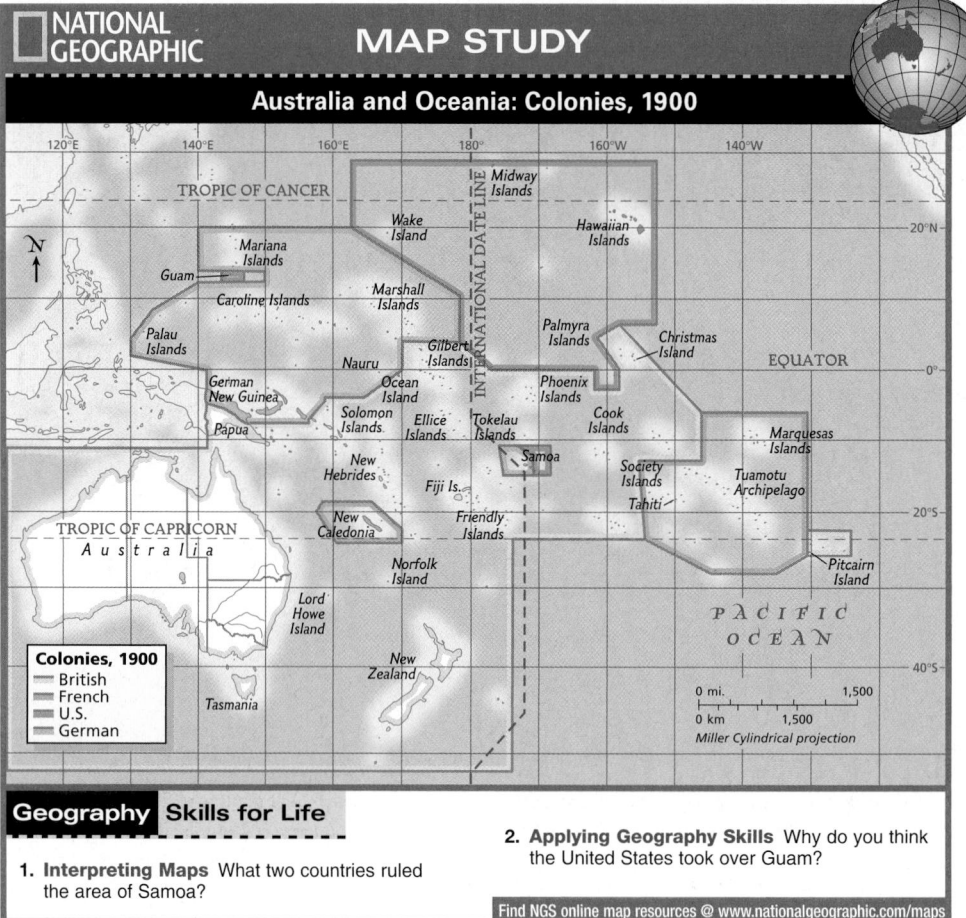

Australia and Oceania: Colonies, 1900

Colonies, 1900
- British
- French
- U.S.
- German

Geography | **Skills for Life**

1. **Interpreting Maps** What two countries ruled the area of Samoa?

2. **Applying Geography Skills** Why do you think the United States took over Guam?

Find NGS online map resources @ www.nationalgeographic.com/maps

---

and shrimp as well as breadfruit and coconuts. Pacific islanders also cultivated root crops, such as taro and yams, and raised smaller animals, such as chickens and pigs. Well-built canoes made lengthy voyages possible, and trade gradually developed among the islands. To make trading easier, people on some islands used long strings of shell pieces as money. Today in New Britain, an island off the northeast coast of Papua New Guinea, shell money still is exchanged for canned goods or vegetables at markets.

Increased trade was accompanied by migrations among the islands. Between the A.D. 900s and 1300s, the Maori people left eastern Polynesia and settled the islands of New Zealand. On New Zealand's North Island and South Island, Maori groups hunted, fished, established villages, and farmed the land. Maori farmers, like the Pacific islanders, grew root crops, such as taro and yams, which they had brought from their Polynesian homeland.

European Colonization

From the 1500s to the 1700s, Europeans of various nationalities explored vast stretches of the South Pacific region. Perhaps the most well-known explorer was the British sailor James Cook, who undertook three voyages to the region between 1768 and

---

COOPERATIVE LEARNING ACTIVITY

Comparing Government Systems Organize the class into small groups. Assign each group a country in the South Pacific region. Have members research the form and structure of the national government in that country. Have each group make a chart or other graphic that compares and contrasts their assigned country's government with the government of the United States. Tell students to focus on offices (governor general, president, prime minister), bodies (congress, parliament), and functions (makes laws, carries out laws). Use the completed graphics as the basis for a class discussion.

⊕ **EE4 Human Systems: Standard 13**

1779. Cook claimed eastern Australia for Great Britain, visited various South Pacific islands, circled Antarctica, and produced remarkably accurate records and maps of these places.

European Settlement

Great Britain at first used Australia as a colony for convicts sent out from overcrowded British prisons. The first shipload of prisoners arrived at Botany Bay, in what is today Sydney, in 1788. By the early 1850s, the imprisonment of British convicts in Australia had ended, and growing numbers of free British settlers were establishing coastal farms and settlements. Livestock, especially sheep, were introduced to the continent. As British textile manufacturers increased their demand for wool, Australian settlers profited greatly from exporting wool to the parent country. Another source of wealth for Australia was gold, which was discovered there in the early 1850s. The resulting gold rush nearly tripled Australia's population in 10 years and also promoted the mining of other mineral resources in the continent's interior.

Meanwhile, the British and other Europeans were also establishing settlements in Oceania. Attracted by excellent fishing waters and rich soil, British settlers arrived in New Zealand in the early 1800s. They brought with them sheep, cattle, and horses. By the end of the century, raising livestock had become a major part of New Zealand's economy. On some South Pacific islands, European businesspeople set up commercial plantations for growing sugarcane, pineapples, and other tropical products.

Indigenous Peoples

The arrival of Europeans in Australia and Oceania had a disastrous impact on indigenous peoples. As British migrants spread across Australia, they forcibly removed the Aborigines from the land and denied them basic rights. Many Aborigines resisted the European advance, but European diseases and weapons steadily reduced the Aboriginal population. In the mid-1800s, British-Australian authorities placed many Aborigines in reserves, or separate areas.

British settlement in New Zealand brought hardships to the Maori, who died from diseases carried by the newcomers. The Maori social structure also was weakened when the British colonists introduced new ways of farming and other aspects of European culture. As the number of European settlers increased, the British and some Maori chiefs signed a treaty in 1840 that guaranteed the Maori full rights under the British monarchy. Disagreements about the treaty, however, led to armed Maori resistance to British rule over the next 15 years. During these conflicts, many Maori were killed, and the Maori gradually lost most of their land to the British.

The Europeans also brought far-reaching changes to the other peoples of Oceania. Because European diseases had reduced indigenous island populations, the Europeans brought in workers from other Pacific islands and from more distant areas, such as South Asia. The resulting mix of cultures weakened indigenous societies and eventually led to ethnic conflicts. Meanwhile, Europeans sought to replace traditional ways of life with European beliefs and practices.

Struggle for Power

During the late 1800s and early 1900s, Britain, France, Germany, Spain, and the United States struggled for control of various Pacific islands. Many of these countries already had commercial interests in the area. The Europeans hoped to expand their influence and gain new sources of raw materials.

The two World Wars changed the course of Oceania's history. After World War I, many of Germany's Pacific colonies came under Japanese rule. Then in December 1941, Japanese airplanes bombed the United States Naval Base at Pearl Harbor in Hawaii. This attack brought the United States into World War II. During the conflict the United States and Japan fought a number of fierce battles on Pacific islands such as Guadalcanal and Iwo Jima.

Following Japan's defeat in World War II, Japan's South Pacific possessions, such as the islands of Micronesia, were turned over to the United States as trust territories. Trust territories were dependent areas that the United Nations placed under the temporary control of a foreign country. Since the 1970s most of these islands, including Palau, the Marshall Islands, and the Federated States of Micronesia, have become independent countries.

Independent Governments

Independence came to most of the South Pacific region during the 1900s. Australia and New Zealand

INTERDISCIPLINARY
connection

HISTORY In the late 1780s, British settlers began to colonize Australia. Among the first arrivals were 736 convicts exiled for crimes ranging from "minor theft" to violent robbery. At least 127 of them were women. Historians know of five who were under the age of 15.

L1/ELL

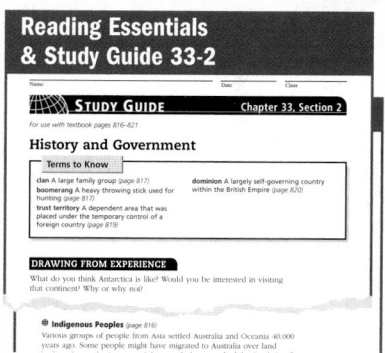

Reading Essentials & Study Guide 33-2

The Tasmanian Devil cartoon character is based on a real animal. This fierce-looking, toothy scavenger once roamed throughout Australia. Today it is found only in the island state of Tasmania.

CRITICAL THINKING ACTIVITY

Demonstrating Reasoned Judgment Tell students that British explorer Captain James Cook charted the New Zealand coast, survived a wreck on the Great Barrier Reef, and collected plant and animal specimens. Have students research to find additional information about Cook. Mention biographies such as *Captain James Cook* by Alan J. Villiers. Have students write an essay to answer the question: How did Cook's explorations positively and negatively affect the South Pacific region? 📦

🌐 **EE2 Places and Regions: Standard 6**
🌐 **EE4 Human Systems: Standard 13**
🌐 **EE6 The Uses Of Geography: Standard 17**

World Explorer

Answer
during the 1900s

More About the Photo
Traditional adornments worn by people in Papua New Guinea include boar's tusks, animal skins, animal teeth, claws, feathers, shells, bamboo, and paint.

ASSESS

Assign Section 2 Assessment as homework or as an in-class activity.

Have students use **Interactive Tutor Self-Assessment CD-ROM** to review Section 2.

L2

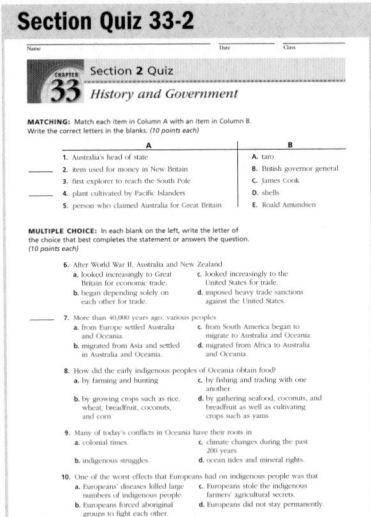

Section Quiz 33-2

became the region's first independent countries in the early 1900s. By the century's end, most of the Pacific islands had gained independence.

Australia and New Zealand

Australia and New Zealand both peacefully won their independence from British rule. In 1901 Britain's Australian colonies became states, united to form the Commonwealth of Australia. The new Australian country was a dominion, a largely self-governing country within the British Empire. Australia's form of government blended a United States-style federal system with a British-style parliamentary democracy. The British monarch—represented by a governor general—served as Australia's head of state, but a prime minister actually headed the national government.

In 1907 New Zealand became a self-governing dominion with a British parliamentary system. New Zealanders, however, contributed some political "firsts" of their own. In 1893 New Zealand became the first country in the world to legally recognize women's right to vote. New Zealand also was among the first countries to provide government assistance to the elderly, the sick, and the unemployed.

Until World War II, New Zealand and Australia maintained close economic, military, and political ties to Great Britain, now known as the United Kingdom. After 1945 British global influence declined, and the two Pacific countries looked increasingly to the United States for trade and military protection. In addition, Australia and New Zealand developed their own national characters based on increasingly diverse populations. The Aborigines and the Maori won greater recognition of their unique cultural identities, and many non-British immigrants settled in both countries. Many Australians now want to cut ties to the British monarchy and elect a president. In 2002, terrorist attacks on the Indonesian island of Bali shattered Australia's sense of security. More than a third of the nearly 200 people killed were Australians.

South Pacific Islands

Beginning in the 1960s, a number of the small islands in Oceania moved toward independence. Samoa—formerly Western Samoa—had been ruled by Germany until New Zealand assumed control after World War I. In 1962 Samoa became the first Pacific island territory to win its freedom. Today most of the South Pacific islands enjoy some form of independent government. For example, **Vanuatu**, once jointly governed by the United Kingdom and France, is a republic, and **Tonga**, formerly under British protection, is a constitutional monarchy. Some island countries, such as Fiji and the Solomon Islands, have been torn by ethnic conflict since independence. Many conflicts have roots in colonial times, when European rulers brought in foreign workers from other cultures, ignoring traditional ethnic and cultural patterns.

NATIONAL GEOGRAPHIC **World Explorer**

Geography Skills for Life

Promoting Culture An indigenous group in Papua New Guinea perform traditional ceremonial dances.
Place When did most countries in Oceania gain their independence?

TEAM-TEACHING ACTIVITY: SCIENCE

Preventing "the Sailor's Curse" In the 1700s it took months for a ship from England to reach Australia. On board a ship, the crew ate only dried foods, which lacked vitamin C. This nutritional deficiency led to *scurvy*, a disease that caused bleeding, pain in the joints, and even death. When a pioneer nutritionist, Dr. James Lind, discovered that citrus fruits, such as limes, prevented the disease, citrus fruits became a required provision on all British navy ships. Have students work with a science teacher to learn more about the benefits of vitamin C. Students should present their findings in a written report.
▦ EE5 Environment and Society: Standard 16
▦ EE6 The Uses of Geography: Standard 17

Antarctica

Europeans first sighted Antarctica during the early 1800s, but they believed that the icy continent had little, if any, commercial value. As a result, expeditions did not venture into Antarctica until much later. In the early 1900s, Norwegian explorer Roald Amundsen and British explorer Robert Scott, each with a team of four people, engaged in a dramatic race to be the first to reach the South Pole. Amundsen's team reached it on December 14, 1911; Scott's team arrived about a month later. Unfortunately, Scott and his team died on the return trip.

The race for the South Pole opened the rest of Antarctica for exploration. On their quests, Antarctic explorers looked for economic resources as well as adventure in the frozen landscape. The countries they represented hoped for new trading routes and seal-hunting areas as well as Antarctic mineral resources. Nonetheless, much of Antarctica remained unexplored until advances in radio communication and air travel made exploration easier and safer.

By the 1960s, scientists from 12 countries had established research centers in Antarctica. To preserve Antarctica as a peaceful scientific research site, the 12 countries signed the Antarctic Treaty in 1959. Since then, a number of other countries have

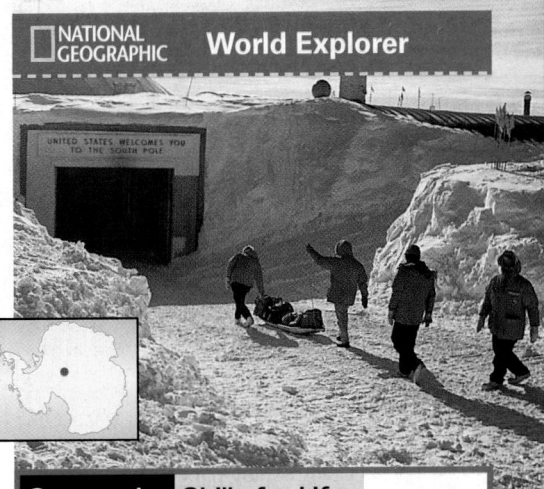

Geography | **Skills for Life**

Cold as Ice The Amundsen-Scott Station, managed by the United States, lies close to the South Pole on ice nearly 2 miles (3.2 km) deep.
Place What is the purpose of the Antarctic Treaty?

agreed to abide by the treaty. In 1991 the treaty countries made an additional agreement to prohibit mining and to protect the environment of this unique continent.

Answer
to preserve Antarctica as a peaceful site for research

More About the Photo The sign on this research facility reads: "The United States of America welcomes you to South Pole Station."

Reteach

Have students answer the questions in "Read to Find Out" on page 816. Use their responses as a basis for discussion of any points that need reinforcement.

Enrich

Share slang terms used by Australians, such as *Aussie*—an Australian; *bloke*—man or guy, *G'day*—hello. Encourage students to research other common Australian terms and share their findings with classmates.

CLOSE

Have students create art forms typical of South Pacific cultures.

SECTION 2 ASSESSMENT

Checking for Understanding

1. **Define** clan, boomerang, trust territory, dominion.

2. **Main Ideas** Use a chart like the one below to organize factors that contributed to the region's cultural diversity and forms of government.

Indigenous Peoples	European Colonization	Power Struggles

Critical Thinking

3. **Identifying Cause and Effect** What effects, both positive and negative, resulted from European colonization in this region?

4. **Comparing and Contrasting** Compare and contrast the views of South Pacific indigenous peoples and European settlers about the land—its value, ownership, and use.

5. **Making Generalizations** How has Antarctica benefited from international cooperation?

Analyzing Maps

6. **Place** Study the map on page 785. Identify an island or a group of islands that is today under the rule of the United States.

Applying Geography

7. **Physical Geography and Migration** Think about why and how people and goods moved throughout Oceania. Write a paragraph describing the reasons for this migration and how significant physical features influenced it.

SECTION 2 ASSESSMENT ANSWERS

1. All vocabulary terms are defined in the text.
2. Charts should identify indigenous and colonial peoples and accurately describe the power struggles that resulted in today's forms of government.
3. Positive effects may include introduction of livestock, development of agriculture and industry, profit from gold; disadvantages may include diseases, displacement of aboriginal

peoples, and the weakening of indigenous cultures because of imported workers.

4. Indigenous peoples believed the land was sacred and took from the land what they needed without altering it; Europeans wanted to individually own and develop the land to meet their economic needs.

5. International cooperation has led to a treaty that prevents damaging conflicts and exploitation

of natural resources.

6. Possible answers may include Northern Mariana Islands, Guam, or American Samoa.

7. **Applying Geography** Possible answers: individual islands lacked the resources necessary to be self-sufficient; separation of islands by the ocean led to trade by boat.

① FOCUS

Antarctica is a remote continent isolated by stormy seas. Temperatures there rarely rise above freezing, and winds sweeping the landscape often reach hurricane strength. Antarctica's physical geography and climate have prevented any permanent human settlement. The harsh Antarctic environment, however, is also the earth's most unspoiled. This relatively untouched area has proved to be an excellent site for scientific research.

② TEACH

Organize the class into small groups. Have each group list different kinds of experts that Byrd may have consulted before his first Antarctic expedition. *(geographers, meteorologists, physicians, aviation engineers)* Have them also list questions that Byrd may have asked and the advice that he may have received in response. Use group ideas as the basis for a class discussion.

GEOGRAPHY AND HISTORY

JOURNEY TO THE BOTTOM OF THE WORLD

AN EXPEDITION CARRYING TONS OF CANDY, 500 cases of eggs, and 60,000 sheets of writing paper? Where might such an expedition be headed? What conditions would warrant such provisions? These were a small portion of the supplies on a ship that left New York City in 1928, headed for Antarctica. Also aboard were United States Navy officer Richard E. Byrd and a crew of 53 scientists and other professionals.

Lure of the Unknown

The Byrd Antarctic Expedition set out to establish a foothold in one of the most ferocious climates on Earth. Antarctica is the world's coldest place, where winter temperatures can drop to –129°F (–89°C). Thick ice buries most of the continent. Violent winds lash the Polar Plateau, where the South Pole lies. Glaciers spill out between mountain peaks that rim the coast, creating vast ice shelves that limit access by sea.

In 1928 little was known about Antarctica. Whalers and sealers had hunted its coastal waters in the 1800s. In 1911 Antarctica was the site of the tragic race to the South Pole—Roald Amundsen of Norway made it back, while British explorer Robert Falcon Scott and his team perished. Other than these brave souls, few people had ventured inland. Admiral Byrd was determined to change that.

Admiral Byrd (at left) and companions visit Little America. An American stamp commemorates one of Byrd's expeditions to Antarctica. ▶

ANTARCTICA

Little America III: 1940–41
Little America V: 1956
Polar Plateau
South Pole
Little America I & II: 1929–30 and 1934–35
Little America IV: 1947
ROSS ICE SHELF
Ice front 1956

BYRD ANTARCTIC EXPEDITION II
U.S. POSTAGE 3 CENTS

BACKGROUND INFORMATION

Richard E. Byrd A graduate of the U.S. Naval Academy, Richard E. Byrd became a pilot in 1918. From a base on Greenland, Byrd commanded a military unit that flew exploratory missions in the Arctic. In 1926 he and fellow aviator Floyd Bennett flew above the Arctic Circle. In 1934 Byrd spent months alone in a makeshift weather station between Little America and the South Pole. He later described his harrowing exploits in a book titled *Alone*. The explorer's last trip to Antarctica was as commander of "Operation Deep Freeze," part of the United States government's participation in the International Geophysical Year of 1957–1958.

🌐 **EE5 Environment and Society: Standard 15**

🌐 **EE6 The Uses of Geography: Standard 17**

◀ Crunching through ice, the U.S.S. *Glacier* brings Admiral Byrd and crew back to Antarctica in 1955.

NATIONAL GEOGRAPHIC

Little America

Before leaving New York, Byrd spent three years preparing for the inhuman conditions in Antarctica. He worked with numerous experts to determine vital supplies. Clothing was especially important. Reindeer fur proved the warmest and was used for parkas, pants, and boots. Other animal skins, such as sealskin, also were used.

Stopping in New Zealand, the last outpost of civilization, the expedition still had to negotiate iceberg-filled waters to reach the Ross Ice Shelf, the thick expanse of Antarctic ice that would be home for 14 months. Arriving in late 1928, the crew and 80 sled dogs moved more than 650 tons (590 t) of material from ship to shore. The crew built the first scientific station on the frozen continent. A village complete with multiple weather-tight buildings, bunkhouses, and storerooms, the station was named Little America.

Once Little America was established, Byrd launched his assault on Antarctica. Using an airplane he had brought by ship, Byrd and his crew made numerous flights over vast areas never seen by humans. Byrd's expedition accomplished many firsts: a flight over the South Pole, the mapping of 150,000 square miles (388,000 sq. km) of new territory, the invention of specialized instruments, and more.

Byrd returned to Antarctica four more times to supervise the completion of Little America II through V. His expeditions laid the groundwork for future research and international cooperation. Today the United States and many other countries maintain scientific stations in Antarctica. Scientists work on a variety of projects there, from studying animal behavior to monitoring ozone depletion and global warming.

Looking Ahead

How did the hardships and dangers Byrd and his comrades endured benefit humankind? How might Antarctic research be important to the future of life on Earth?

1821 American seal hunters make first known landing on Antarctica

1901 British explorer Robert F. Scott begins first inland exploration

1911 Norwegian Roald Amundsen is first to reach South Pole

1928 Admiral Byrd (on medal, above) establishes Little America I (background photo)

1929 Byrd makes first flight over South Pole

1933–1955 Byrd establishes Little America II through V

1959 Twelve countries sign Antarctic Treaty, preserving Antarctica for peaceful endeavors

The Ross Ice Shelf is named for British explorer James Clark Ross, who discovered it while exploring Antarctica between 1839 and 1843. Ten years earlier Ross had located the position of the magnetic North Pole.

③ ASSESS

Have students answer the **Looking Ahead** question on this page.

④ CLOSE

Ask each student to choose one of Richard Byrd's accomplishments in the exploration of Antarctica. Have them write news bulletins that explain his achievements and their importance to scientific knowledge.

Meeting National Standards

Geography for Life
The following standards are met in the Student Edition:

EE1 The World in Spatial Terms: Standard 3

EE3 Physical Systems: Standard 7

EE5 Environment and Society: Standard 15

EE6 The Uses of Geography: Standard 18

ANSWERS TO LOOKING AHEAD

1. Possible answers: Byrd and his comrades contributed to the triumph of the human spirit, increased scientific knowledge of the Antarctic, developed practical ways to survive in extreme cold, and opened opportunities to study an unspoiled environment.

2. Possible answers: Antarctic research may help people better understand global climate change and discover ways to deal with it, learn how to preserve natural habitats, meet future freshwater needs, and endure extreme conditions.

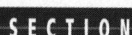

Section Overview

This section discusses the varied cultural influences and lifestyles of the South Pacific region.

BELLRINGER
Skillbuilder Activity

 Project transparency and have students answer questions.

 Available as blackline master.

Daily Focus Skills Transparency 33-3

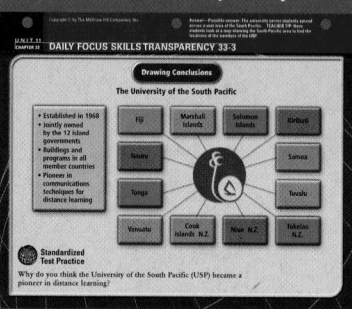

Guide to Reading

Consider What You Know
Answer *Possible answers will depend on student interests and recent trends in world music.*

Reading Strategy
Answer *Students should complete the outline by including all heads in the section.*

Preteaching Vocabulary
Use the **Vocabulary Puzzle-Maker CD-ROM** to create crossword and word-search puzzles.

Guide to Reading

Consider What You Know

World music, which includes musical expressions from many cultures, has become very popular in the United States. What instruments or types of music have you heard that come from other parts of the world?

Reading Strategy

Taking Notes As you read about the cultures and lifestyles of the region, use the major headings of the section to create an outline similar to the one below.

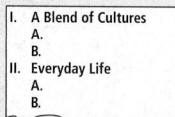

I. A Blend of Cultures
    A.
    B.
II. Everyday Life
    A.
    B.

Read to Find Out

- What role does religion play in the region's cultures?
- How have the peoples of Australia and Oceania expressed their heritages through the arts?
- How does everyday life in the region reflect cultural diversity?

Terms to Know

- subsistence farming
- *fale*

Places to Locate

- Papua New Guinea
- Samoa

Cultures and Lifestyles

NATIONAL GEOGRAPHIC

A Geographic View

Living in Australia

We're connected to Europe and North America culturally, but we're in an Asian time zone, which gives us an advantage. We have a highly educated workforce, . . . a first-rate international airport, good communications, and a stable and sophisticated financial system. We have a wonderful climate and attractive lifestyle— good restaurants, nice beaches, an optimistic way of looking at the world that I think outsiders find attractive. Once you develop a critical mass of those things, you find that more and more people want to come and be part of it.

—Sydney mayor Frank Sartor, quoted by Bill Bryson, "Sydney," National Geographic, August 2000

A girl visits Sydney, Australia

Australia, like other South Pacific countries, blends both European and indigenous elements in its culture. In recent years Asian influences also have increased in the region. In this section you will learn about the religions, arts, and lifestyles of the peoples of Australia and Oceania.

A Blend of Cultures

The movement of different peoples into the South Pacific region has contributed to the shaping of cultures there. Indigenous peoples developed lifestyles in harmony with their natural environment. Later, European immigrants brought their ways of life, using the environment to build Western-oriented societies.

RESOURCE MANAGER

Reproducible Masters

- Reproducible Lesson Plan 33-3
- Vocabulary Activity 33
- Daily Lecture Notes 33-3
- Guided Reading Activity 33-3
- Reading Essentials and Study Guide 33-3
- Reteaching Activity 33
- Reinforcing Skills Activity 33
- Section Quiz 33-3

Transparencies

- Daily Focus Skills Transparency 33-3
- Political Map Transparency 11
- Unit 11 Map Overlay Transparencies

Multimedia

- Vocabulary PuzzleMaker CD-ROM
- Interactive Tutor Self-Assessment CD-ROM
- ExamView® Pro Testmaker CD-ROM
- Presentation Plus! CD-ROM

GRAPH STUDY

Australia and Oceania: Religions

Religion	Number of Followers
Roman Catholic	8,097,000
Protestant	7,279,000
Anglican	5,386,000
Eastern Orthodox	691,000
Hindu	349,000
Other religions	1,232,000
Nonreligious	3,628,000

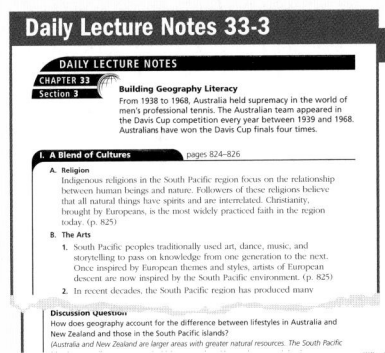

Roman Catholic 30%
Protestant 27.9%
Anglican 20%
Nonreligious 13.6%
Eastern Orthodox 2.6%
Hindu 1.3%
Other religions 4.6%

Sources: Britannica Book of the Year, 2000; World Almanac, 2001

Geography **Skills for Life**

1. Interpreting Graphs Which two religions have the largest number of followers in the region?

2. Applying Geography Skills Why do you think Christian religions are dominant in the region?

GRAPH STUDY

Answers

1. *Roman Catholic, Protestant*

2. *Many European settlers were Christians, as are their descendants.*

Skills Practice

Movement What religion is evidence of British colonization in the region? *(Anglican)*

 **TEACH**

L1 Place

Have students name specific examples of arts in Australia and Oceania that demonstrate the blending of traditional and modern lifestyles in this region today. *(wooden carvings on Maori meeting houses and films about historical events in the region)*

Daily Lecture Notes 33-3

DAILY LECTURE NOTES
CHAPTER 33
Section 3

Building Geography Literacy
From 1938 to 1968, Australia held supremacy in the world of men's professional tennis. The Australian team appeared in the Davis Cup competition every year between 1939 and 1968. Australians have won the Davis Cup finals four times.

I. A Blend of Cultures pages 824–826

A. Religion
Indigenous religions in the South Pacific region focus on the relationship between human beings and nature. Followers of these religions believe that all natural things have spirits and are interrelated. Christianity, brought by Europeans, is the most widely practiced faith in the region today. (p. 825)

B. The Arts
1. South Pacific peoples traditionally used art, dance, music, and storytelling to pass on knowledge from one generation to the next. Once inspired by European themes and styles, artists of European descent are now inspired by the South Pacific environment. (p. 825)
2. In recent decades, the South Pacific region has produced many

Discussion Question
How does geography account for the difference between lifestyles in Australia and New Zealand and those in the South Pacific islands? *(Australia and New Zealand are larger areas with greater natural resources. The South Pacific*

 GEOGRAPHY AND THE HUMANITIES

 World Music:
A Cultural Legacy

World Art and Architecture Transparencies

World Art Prints

Religion

The religious traditions of the region's indigenous peoples focus on the relationship of humans to nature. Australia's Aborigines, for example, believe in the idea of Dreamtime, the early time when they say wandering spirits created land features, plants, animals, and humans. They believe that all natural things—rocks, trees, plants, animals, and humans—have a spirit and are interrelated. Europeans later brought Christianity, which attracted many followers among the indigenous peoples. Christianity is the most widely practiced religion in Australia and Oceania today.

The Arts

South Pacific peoples traditionally used art, music, dance, and storytelling to pass on knowledge from generation to generation. Australian Aborigines, for example, recorded their past in rock paintings and developed songs to pass on information about routes and landmarks. In New Zealand, Maori artisans developed skills in canoe making, basketry, tattooing, and woodcarving. Today Maori meeting houses are decorated with elaborate wood carvings.

After a time of copying European themes and styles, European artists in the region began looking to the South Pacific environment for inspiration.

> *Strong emotional ties with the land ... are not the sole preserve of the Aborigines.... Australian writers and poets, ...composers and painters [have] come to realise that a tangle of eucalyptus trees, red gums in a dried-up steam bed, red rocks and dripping rain forest can have their own powerful visual appeal.*
>
> Roger Fenby, "Walkabout Oz," *BBC World Service* (online), August 4, 2000

MEETING SPECIAL NEEDS ACTIVITY

Learning Disabled Students with poor reading skills often benefit from having restating strategies modeled for them. Explain that you will model a restating strategy that will help them understand what they read. Have them turn to the Section 3 subhead "Traditional and Modern Lifestyles" and read the third sentence. Demonstrate restating by breaking that sentence into two simple sentences that each state one idea. *(Many Pacific islanders work at subsistence farming. Subsistence farmers grow only enough for their own needs.)* Have students use this strategy to restate compound and complex sentences in this section.

📂 Refer to *Inclusion for the Social Studies Classroom Strategies and Activities.*

Reading Essentials & Study Guide 33-3

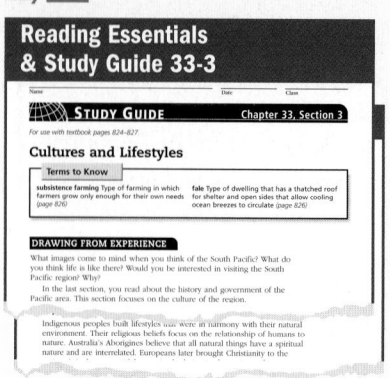

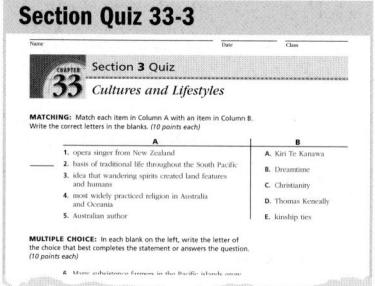

3 ASSESS

Assign Section 3 Assessment as homework or as an in-class activity.

🔵 Have students use **Interactive Tutor Self-Assessment CD-ROM**.

L2

Section Quiz 33-3

Answer
simple design, openness to allow cool air to circulate

More About the Photo Traditional houses in Papua New Guinea are being replaced by Western-style housing. At one time, villages had separate men's and women's houses.

In recent decades the South Pacific region has produced a number of outstanding musicians, writers, and artists. Australia's Joan Sutherland and New Zealand's Kiri Te Kanawa became famous opera performers. New Zealand author Sylvia Ashton-Warner wrote of her experiences as a schoolteacher in Maori communities. Australian writer Thomas Keneally wrote the novel *Schindler's List*, which was later made into an award-winning motion picture.

Australia and New Zealand also have contributed well-known movie stars such as Mel Gibson, Nicole Kidman, and Russell Crowe. Filmmakers in both countries have made popular motion pictures, such as *Gallipoli*, *Crocodile Dundee*, *Muriel's Wedding*, and *The Piano*.

Everyday Life

In many parts of Australia and Oceania, people have urban lifestyles that reflect modern influences. In other places in the region, people live in a more traditional way.

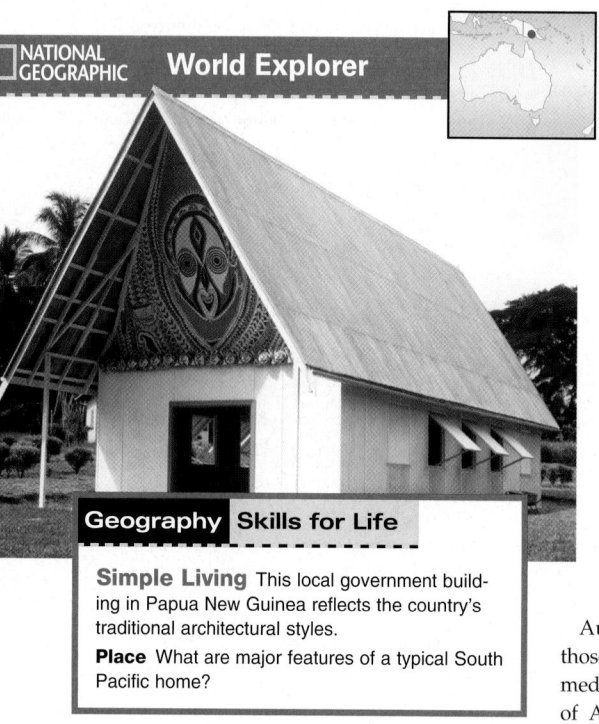

NATIONAL GEOGRAPHIC **World Explorer**

Geography **Skills for Life**

Simple Living This local government building in Papua New Guinea reflects the country's traditional architectural styles.

Place What are major features of a typical South Pacific home?

Economics
Traditional and Modern Lifestyles

Some Pacific island countries, such as **Papua New Guinea**, produce cash crops, including sugarcane, coffee, ginger, and copra—dried coconut meat. Others, such as Kiribati, have soil that is too poor for plantation agriculture. Many Pacific islanders work at subsistence farming, growing only enough for their own needs. These farmers grow bananas, coconuts, or sweet potatoes; raise chickens and pigs; or fish in ocean waters. Other islanders work in government offices, in the tourist trade, or in other service industries.

Kinship ties are the basis of traditional life throughout the region, but these bonds have weakened as young people find better job opportunities elsewhere. Even so, important events draw distant family members back home and help maintain the culture.

A typical traditional South Pacific home is very simple in design. On **Samoa**, this type of simple dwelling is called a *fale* and has a thatched roof for shelter and open sides that allow cooling ocean breezes to circulate. Blinds of coconut palm leaves can be lowered for privacy.

The simplicity of South Pacific island life contrasts greatly with the fast-paced, urbanized lifestyle in parts of Australia and New Zealand, where people are linked to the cities by roads and modern communications technology. A mild climate and nearness to the sea enable many people in the South Pacific region to enjoy outdoor activities.

Education and Health Care

The quality of education varies throughout the region. Both Australia and New Zealand provide free, compulsory education until age 15. Literacy rates are high in these two countries, and many students attend universities. Many students in Australia's remote outback receive and turn in assignments by mail or communicate with teachers by two-way radios.

Australians and New Zealanders, especially those in cities, generally have access to quality medical care and other social services. In some parts of Australia, rugged terrain and long distances

---

COOPERATIVE LEARNING ACTIVITY

Stories of Aboriginal Culture Organize students into small groups. Tell each group to research the culture of the Australian Aborigines. Members should collaborate to write an original story that communicates valuable information about one aspect of the culture. Have students adapt their original work for a recitation in the manner of storytelling. Each group member should recite one part of the story. Allow time for a question and answer session in which the storytellers can clarify the relationship between their work and Aboriginal culture. 📖 🌐 **EE2 Places and Regions: Standard 4**
🌐 **EE4 Human Systems: Standard 10**

make access to health care difficult. Modern technology, however, allows doctors to consult with patients through the use of two-way radios and through mobile clinics of the Flying Doctor Service.

Indigenous peoples, however, often do not receive these and other benefits. For example, many Aborigines suffer from poverty, malnutrition, and unemployment. In recent years the Australian government and private organizations have been trying to make up for past injustices, and the courts have recognized the claims of Aborigines to government assistance, land, and natural resources.

Many Pacific islanders also lack an adequate standard of living. On remote islands, fresh food, electricity, schools, and hospitals often are limited. Recently island countries, with international assistance, have begun to improve their quality of life.

Sports and Leisure

Sports and leisure activities reflect the region's diversity. Western-style resorts attract tourists to the beaches, where they and the local people enjoy the traditional Pacific island sport of surfing. Traditional sports, such as outrigger canoe racing or spearfishing, are popular, as are Western sports. For example, British settlers brought cricket and rugby to Australia and New Zealand.

In former American territories, islanders play baseball. The French introduced cycling and archery to islands they controlled. Even small communities often have facilities for these and

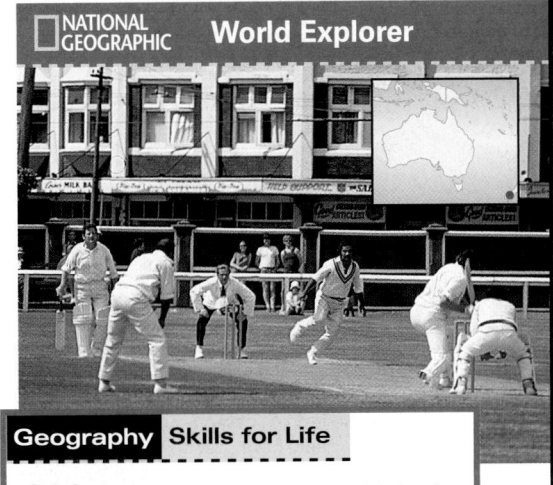

NATIONAL GEOGRAPHIC World Explorer

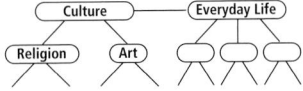

Cricket Cricket, first played in England during the late 1500s, today is a popular sport in New Zealand.
Place What other sports are played in Australia and Oceania?

other sports, such as soccer, volleyball, and tennis. In urban areas of Australia and New Zealand, where Western influence dominates, leisure activities include boating, fishing, waterskiing, and other water sports along the metropolitan beaches.

In the next chapter, you will learn how people in Australia and Oceania are meeting the challenges of their environment.

SECTION 3 ASSESSMENT

Checking for Understanding

1. **Define** subsistence farming, *fale*.

2. **Main Ideas** On a web like the one below, fill in important ideas and supporting details from each section to describe the culture and lifestyles of the region.

```
  Culture        Everyday Life
Religion   Art
```

Critical Thinking

3. **Drawing Conclusions** How does the art of the South Pacific reflect the artists' physical environment?

4. **Comparing and Contrasting** How does education in the South Pacific differ from education in your community?

5. **Predicting Consequences** How might the Internet and e-mail change education in Oceania?

Analyzing Maps

6. **Location** Examine the political map on page 785. Which Pacific islands are administered by New Zealand?

Applying Geography

7. **Forms of Government** Compare the political-physical maps on pages 117 and 795. How might Australia, Canada, and the United States be similar in the way they distribute governmental powers?

SECTION 3 ASSESSMENT ANSWERS

1. All vocabulary terms are defined in the text.

2. Webs should include supporting details for each of the main ideas.

3. Possible answers may include that Aborigines and Australian writers, poets, composers, and painters use the environment, such as eucalyptus trees, as subjects of their work.

4. Answers will depend on students' communities but should accurately describe education there and in the South Pacific.

5. They may make education accessible to people in remote areas.

6. Cook Islands, Tokelau, Niue

7. **Applying Geography** All three countries are large in land area and composed of many different regions with different needs and interests. As a result, they have federal systems of government in which power is distributed between a central government and state or provincial governments.

NATIONAL GEOGRAPHIC World Explorer

Answer
surfing, rugby, baseball, archery, soccer, volleyball, tennis

More About the Photo
The British/Australian sport of cricket reached New Zealand in the 1840s.

Reteach

Have students answer the questions in "Read to Find Out" on page 824. Use their responses as a basis for a discussion of points that need reinforcement.

Enrich

In Antarctica, about 45 research stations house scientists from 25 countries. Have students research experiments being conducted in Antarctica and the special challenges involved in working there.

4 CLOSE

Have students reread "A Geographic View" on page 824. Tell them to select one other country or island in the region and write a paragraph describing a lifestyle found there.

Teaching the Skill

Have students look at the LANDSAT images on page 828. **Ask:** How do the images differ from photographs of the rainforest you have seen? *(Photos show vegetation as seen up close. LANDSAT shows the forest as bands of color.)* **What do LANDSAT images show that photographs cannot?** *(LANDSAT can show vast areas in different colors as one image for comparison. It can take images of remote areas.)* **For what purposes might LANDSAT be valid and useful?** *(mapping land use, estimating crops and water quality)*

Additional Practice
L1

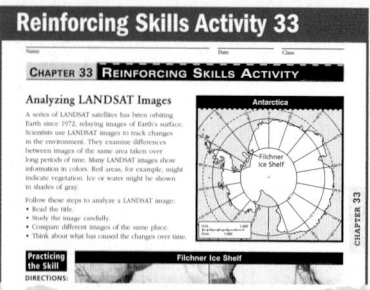

GLENCOE
TECHNOLOGY

Glencoe Skillbuilder Interactive Workbook, Level 2

This interactive CD-ROM reinforces student mastery of essential social studies skills.

Analyzing LANDSAT Images

Scientists and researchers who study the earth use satellites to help them gather data. Photographs taken by these satellites orbiting the earth provide a detailed record of conditions and changes on the earth's surface.

Learning the Skill

Scientists use LANDSAT images to receive a broad view of the surface of the earth. LANDSAT refers to a series of observation satellites that have been launched by the United States since 1972. The most recent satellite, LANDSAT 7, was launched on April 15, 1999. Orbiting at an altitude of about 500 miles (805 km), LANDSAT spacecraft have recorded millions of images of the earth.

The main purpose of LANDSAT is to map and monitor natural resources and changes to the environment. Farmers, government officials, environmentalists, and the military use LANDSAT data, which can be helpful in making decisions that affect the health of the planet. For example, these satellites can identify the locations of tropical forests and provide information about the rates and effects of deforestation.

One of LANDSAT's main benefits is its ability to capture images of every place on Earth. LANDSAT 7 completes a full orbit of the earth every 99 minutes, allowing over 14 orbits a day. LANDSAT 7 is able to provide photographic coverage of the entire earth in only 16 days.

Follow these steps to analyze a LANDSAT image:

- **Read the title.** This feature explains the data being collected, the location, and the time period.

Deforestation in Rondônia, Brazil

1975

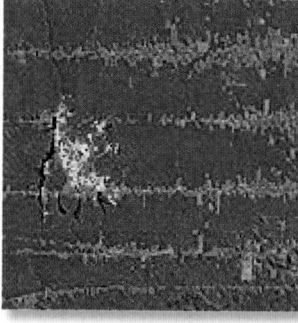

1992

- **Study the image carefully.** In the images on this page, red indicates healthy vegetation, light blue areas indicate deforested land, and light blue lines indicate roads.

- **Compare different images of the same place.** Notice changes that occur over time.

- **Think about what has caused the changes and how they may affect the area's physical and human geography.**

Practicing the Skill

The LANDSAT images on this page show an area of tropical forest in Brazil as it appeared in 1975 and in 1992. Use the images to answer the following questions.

1. Which image shows large areas of undisturbed tropical forest?

2. Compare the area in 1975 to the area in 1992.

3. How is the pattern of deforestation in the 1992 image connected to roadways?

4. How do you think these areas have changed in today's LANDSAT images? Explain your reasoning.

Locate LANDSAT images of Australia, Oceania, or Antarctica on the Internet. For each image, list its location and the kinds of data it includes. Choose one image, and write a paragraph describing two possible uses for the data.

ANSWERS TO PRACTICING THE SKILL

1. 1975 image
2. The amount of healthy vegetation has decreased, areas of deforestation have increased, and there are more roads.
3. Deforestation extends outward from the roads.

4. The areas of deforestation have probably increased farther along the existing roads. There are no indications that the trend is slowing.

SUMMARY & STUDY GUIDE

Using the Chapter 33 Summary & Study Guide

Use the Chapter 33 Summary & Study Guide to preview, review, condense, or reteach the chapter.

Preview/Review

⊕ **Vocabulary PuzzleMaker CD-ROM** reinforces "Terms to Know."

◉ **Interactive Tutor Self-Assessment CD-ROM** provides a review of Chapter 33 content.

Condense

Have students read the Chapter 33 Summary & Study Guide.

◉ Chapter 33 Audio Program

🗁 Chapter 33 Guided Reading Activities

Reteach

🗁 Chapter 33 Reteaching Activities (Spanish also available)

🗁 Chapter 33 Reading Essentials and Study Guides

SECTION 1 — Population Patterns (pp. 811–815)

Terms to Know
- Strine
- pidgin English

Key Points
- Many different peoples settled in the South Pacific, resulting in diverse cultures and lifestyles.
- The population of the South Pacific is unevenly distributed because both the physical geography and the climate differ dramatically from place to place and because many areas cannot support life.
- Migration between and within South Pacific countries has influenced population patterns and caused a blending of cultures.

Organizing Your Notes
Use a graphic organizer like the one below to help you organize your notes about the population patterns of the South Pacific.

Populations	Migration

SECTION 2 — History and Government (pp. 816–821)

Terms to Know
- clan
- boomerang
- trust territory
- dominion

Key Points
- Many of the area's earliest inhabitants came from Southeast Asia and survived by hunting, gathering, and, in some cases, farming.
- European countries were attracted to the area by its raw materials, rich fishing areas, and fertile coastal land.
- During the late 1800s and early 1900s, European countries, Japan, and the United States sought possessions in the region.
- Australia, New Zealand, and a number of Pacific islands are independent; a few island groups are still under foreign rule.

Organizing Your Notes
Create an outline using the format below to help you organize your notes for this section.

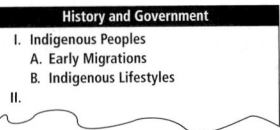

History and Government
I. Indigenous Peoples
    A. Early Migrations
    B. Indigenous Lifestyles
II.

SECTION 3 — Cultures and Lifestyles (pp. 824–827)

Terms to Know
- subsistence farming
- *fale*

Key Points
- The culture of the South Pacific is a mixture of Western and indigenous lifestyles.
- Some people in the area still live in traditional villages; others live in modern urban areas.
- Modern technology helps provide services to people in some remote areas.

Organizing Your Notes
Use a web like the one below to help you organize your notes for this section.

Cultures and Lifestyles

Traditional   Modern

Chapter 33 ⊕ 829

GLENCOE TECHNOLOGY

☐ NATIONAL GEOGRAPHIC
WORLD REGIONS VIDEO PROGRAM

Unit 11, Australia, Oceania, and Antarctica
The following segments enhance the study of this unit:
- **Dream of a Lifetime**
- **Australia's Pioneers**
- **Haka Tradition**

CHAPTER CULMINATING ACTIVITY

Drawing Conclusions **Ask:** What would we learn about South Pacific history if the region's early peoples had left a written record? Ask students to review their notes and Chapter 33. Then have them answer the question by taking the role of modern indigenous persons who are translating into English a historical chronicle written by an ancestor. The chronicle may include information about how and why the ancestors came to the South Pacific, what the area was like, how the people adapted to and interacted with the environment, and what daily life was like. Encourage students to review the chapter's photos and maps and any exercises they have completed in their study of this chapter. 🌐 **EE4 Human Systems: Standards 9, 12**

🌐 **EE6 The Uses of Geography: Standard 17**

CHAPTER 33 ASSESSMENT & ACTIVITIES

GLENCOE TECHNOLOGY

Use *MindJogger Videoquiz* to review the Chapter 33 content.

Reviewing Key Terms

1. trust territory
2. pidgin English
3. Strine
4. fale
5. dominion
6. subsistence farming
7. boomerang
8. clan

Reviewing Facts

SECTION 1

1. Maori, Aborigines, peoples from Asia
2. Because of uninhabitable land and differences in physical features, population is unevenly distributed and often concentrated in coastal areas.

SECTION 2

3. Aborigines were nomads; Pacific islanders settled in family groups.
4. European settlers established coastal farms; introduced livestock; started textile industries and mines; but disastrously impacted indigenous peoples through war, disease, and harsh governing.
5. to preserve Antarctica as a peaceful site for scientific research

SECTION 3

6. Indigenous peoples used the arts to pass on knowledge to younger generations or to create beautiful objects and

---

Reviewing Key Terms

Write the key term that best completes each of the following sentences. Refer to the Terms to Know in the Summary & Study Guide on page 829.

1. The Micronesian islands became a(n) _____ after World War II.
2. In some parts of Oceania, _____ is spoken.
3. Australians speak _____, a dialect of English.
4. A(n) _____ provides simple shelter on tropical islands.
5. In 1901 Australia became a(n) _____ of Great Britain.
6. Some islanders still make their livings by _____.
7. The _____ was originally a hunting tool.
8. Each aboriginal family group traveled as a(n) _____.

Reviewing Facts

SECTION 1

1. Who were the original settlers of Australia, New Zealand, and Oceania?
2. How has geography influenced settlement patterns in the region?

SECTION 2

3. What ways of life did Pacific indigenous peoples practice?
4. In what ways did European settlement influence the region?
5. Why was the Antarctic treaty established in 1959?

SECTION 3

6. How have the arts enriched life in the South Pacific region?
7. What are some characteristics of modern lifestyles in Australia, New Zealand, and Oceania?

Critical Thinking

1. **Identifying Cause and Effect** How did the South Pacific's physical geography contribute to its cultural diversity?
2. **Comparing and Contrasting** In what ways were European influences similar in Australia and in New Zealand? Different?
3. **Problem Solving** Use a Venn diagram to compare the lifestyles and living standards of indigenous and European peoples in the region.

European | Both | Indigenous People

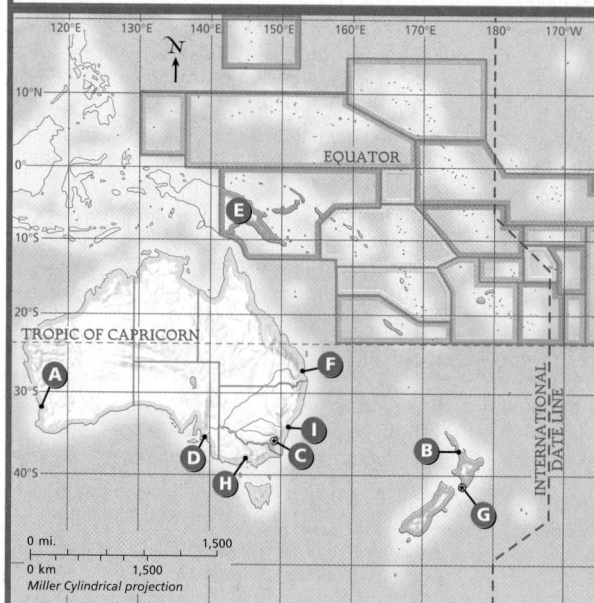

NATIONAL GEOGRAPHIC **Locating Places**
Australia and Oceania: Political Geography

Match the letters on the map with the places in Australia and Western Oceania. Write your answers on a sheet of paper.

1. Papua New Guinea
2. Sydney
3. Auckland
4. Melbourne
5. Canberra
6. Perth
7. Brisbane
8. Adelaide
9. Wellington

---

surroundings; today the region has outstanding musicians, writers, and artists.

7. Island life is simple and moves at a slow pace; in Australia and New Zealand, it is fast paced and revolves around urban areas. Throughout the region, people enjoy outdoor activities.

Critical Thinking

1. Because of the vast distances between parts of the region, different cultures developed and maintained their individuality.

2. Similarities include British colonization, introduction of farming and livestock, urbanization, similar governments, hardships and loss of culture for indigenous peoples. Differences for Australia include mining and industry, restricted immigration.

3. Diagrams should show details of everyday life for both groups.

Using the Regional Atlas

Refer to the Regional Atlas on pages 784–787.

1. **Region** What part of Australia has most of the country's coal deposits?

2. **Human-Environment Interaction** Which physical features limit economic activity in central Australia?

Thinking Like a Geographer

Analyze the effects of processes, such as migration and colonization, on the traditional cultures of the South Pacific's indigenous peoples.

Problem-Solving Activity

Contemporary Issues Case Study The issue of land rights in Australia and New Zealand involves cultural divergence, or separation, between indigenous peoples and those currently using the land. Use print resources and the Internet to research the opposing viewpoints on this issue. Then, write a paragraph stating a possible solution.

GeoJournal

Expository Writing Using the information you logged in your GeoJournal as you read this chapter, write a paragraph comparing and contrasting two cultures in the region. Use your textbook and the Internet as resources to make your information as clear and accurate as possible. Provide visuals to illustrate your ideas.

Technology Activity

Using the Internet for Research Use the Internet to research a specific cultural group in the region. Identify at least three Web sites you used in your research. After you have completed your research, create a poster to illustrate one aspect of the group's culture, such as homes, clothing, or the arts.

Standardized Test Practice

Choose the best answer for each of the following multiple-choice questions. If you have trouble answering the questions, use the process of elimination to narrow your choices.

1. **Which of the following has influenced population distribution in the South Pacific?**

   A Distance from North America

   B Location of rivers

   C Climate

   D Animal domestication

Test-Taking Tip Read the question carefully to determine what is being asked. For each answer choice, consider what factors may have the capacity to influence population distribution. Eliminate answer choices in which a direct correlation cannot be made. Do not forget to incorporate your knowledge of the region and cultures into your decision.

2. **When a group of people is described as *indigenous*, it means that they are**

   F highly dependent on the agriculture of a region.

   G the governing party of a region.

   H the earliest inhabitants of a land.

   J a culturally isolated group.

Test-Taking Tip Consider all of the times you may have heard this word used and in what context you heard it being used. Try to find elements with the structure of the word, such as suffixes, prefixes, and roots, that may reveal something about its meaning.

GeoJournal

Paragraphs should include appropriate information about each culture to compare and contrast them.

Technology Activity

Students should identify at least three Web sites. Their posters should use engaging and attractive visual media to present accurate information about one aspect of culture.

Standardized Test Practice
1. C
2. H

Tested Objectives: identifying cause-and-effect relationships making inferences

Additional Practice and Test-Taking Tips

 Standardized Test Practice Workbook

? CHAPTER BONUS TEST QUESTION

How might Australia be different today if gold had never been discovered there? *(Answers should point out that fewer immigrants would have resulted in a smaller and less-varied population.)*

NATIONAL GEOGRAPHIC Locating Places

1. E	**3.** B	**5.** C	**7.** F	**9.** G
2. I	**4.** H	**6.** A	**8.** D	

Using the Regional Atlas

1. the southeastern coast
2. vast deserts, mountains

Thinking Like a Geographer

Students' answers should demonstrate an understanding of the challenges brought to traditional cultures by European colonization and the influx of new settlers.

Problem-Solving Activity

Paragraphs should clearly explain a possible solution and use supporting details and persuasive techniques to convince the reader.

PLANNING GUIDE

NOTE: The following materials may be used when teaching Chapter 34. Section-level support materials are shown at point-of-use in the margins of the Teacher Wraparound Edition.

TEACHING TRANSPARENCIES

L2 Unit 11 Map Overlay Transparencies

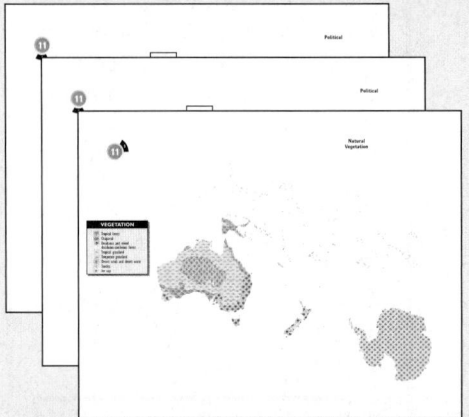

L2 Political Map Transparency 11

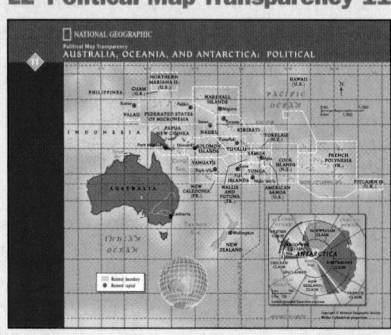

GEOGRAPHIC LITERACY

Focus on Geography Literacy

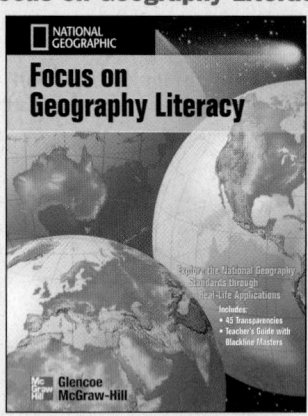

APPLICATION AND ENRICHMENT

L3 Enrichment Activity 34

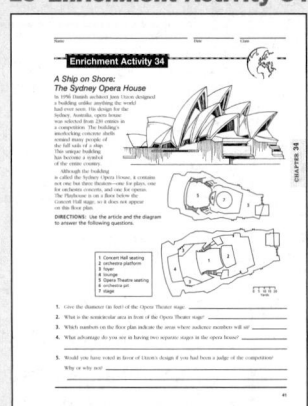

REVIEW AND REINFORCEMENT

L1 Vocabulary Activity 34 L1 Reinforcing L1 Reteaching Activity 34
Skills Activity 34

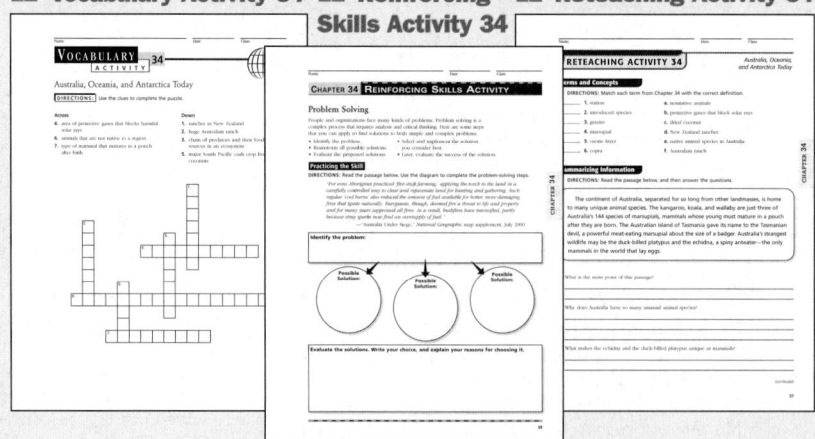

ASSESSMENT

L2 Chapter 34 Test Form A

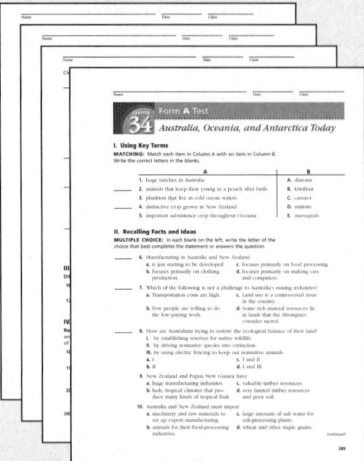

L2 Chapter 34 Test Form B

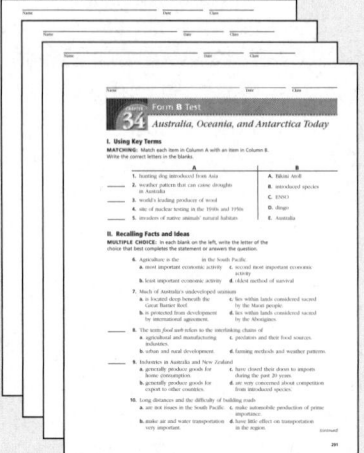

L1/ELL Performance Assessment Activity 34

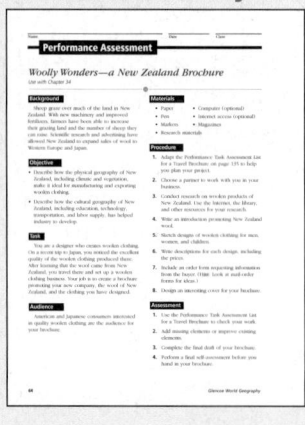

ExamView® Pro Testmaker

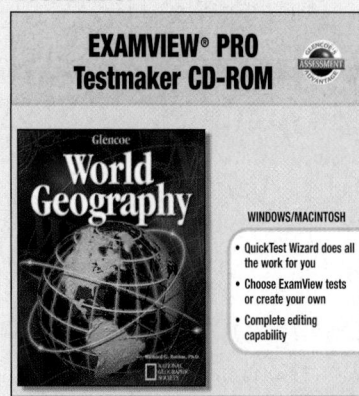

The following Spanish language materials are available in the Spanish Resources binder:

- 📁 **Spanish Vocabulary Activities**
- 📁 **Spanish Guided Reading Activities**
- 📁 **Spanish Reteaching Activities**
- 📁 **Spanish Summaries**
- 📁 **Spanish Quizzes and Tests**
- 📁 **Spanish Reading Essentials and Study Guide**

- 📼 ⦿ **World Regions Video**
- 📼 **MindJogger Videoquiz**
- 💿 **Vocabulary PuzzleMaker CD-ROM**
- 💿 **Interactive Tutor Self-Assessment CD-ROM**
- 💿 **ExamView® Pro Testmaker CD-ROM**
- 💿 **Audio Program**
- 💿 **TeacherWorks CD-ROM**
- 💿 **Interactive Student Edition CD-ROM**
- 💿 **Glencoe Skillbuilder Interactive Workbook CD-ROM, Level 2**
- 💿 **Presentation Plus! CD-ROM**

Timesaving Tools

TeacherWorks™ All-In-One Planner and Resource Center

- **Interactive Teacher Edition** Access your Teacher Wraparound Edition and your classroom resources with a few easy clicks.
- **Interactive Lesson Planner** Planning has never been easier! Organize your week, month, semester, or year with all the lesson helps you need to make teaching creative, timely, and relevant.

Use Glencoe's **Presentation Plus!** multimedia teacher tool to easily present dynamic lessons that visually excite your students. Using Microsoft PowerPoint® you can customize the presentations to create your own personalized lessons.

GEOGRAPHY Online

Use our Web site for additional resources. All essential content is covered in the Student Edition.

You and your students can visit geography.glencoe.com, the Web site companion to *Glencoe World Geography*. This innovative integration of electronic and print media offers your students a wealth of opportunities. The student text directs students to the Web site for the following options:

- Chapter Overviews
- Student Activities
- Self-Check Quizzes
- Textbook Updates

Answers are provided for you in the "Web Activity Lesson Plan." Additional Web resources and Interactive Tutor puzzles are also available.

▶ **Additional Glencoe Teacher Support**

- **Teaching Strategies for the Geography Classroom** (including Block Scheduling Pacing Guides)
- **Graphic Organizer Transparencies Strategies and Activities**
- **Outline Map Resource Book**
- **Reading in the Content Area**

PLANNING GUIDE

SECTION RESOURCES

Daily Objectives	Reproducible Resources	Multimedia Resources

SECTION 1 Living in Australia, Oceania, and Antarctica

1. Describe how people in Australia, New Zealand, and Oceania make their livings.
2. Discuss the role that trade plays in the economies of South Pacific countries.
3. Identify the means of transportation and communications that are used in the region.

Reproducible Resources

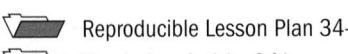
- Reproducible Lesson Plan 34-1
- Daily Lecture Notes 34-1
- Guided Reading Activity 34-1*
- Reading Essentials and Study Guide 34-1*
- Section Quiz 34-1*

Multimedia Resources
- Daily Focus Skills Transparency 34-1
- Political Map Transparency 11
- Unit 11 Map Overlay Transparencies
- Interactive Tutor Self-Assessment CD-ROM
- ExamView® Pro Testmaker CD-ROM*
- Presentation Plus! CD-ROM

SECTION 2 People and Their Environment

1. Specify why Australia, Oceania, and Antarctica face many environmental challenges.
2. Explain the effects that nuclear testing had on the region.
3. Discuss why global warming and the thinning of the ozone layer are special challenges for the region.

Reproducible Resources

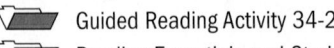
- Reproducible Lesson Plan 34-2
- Vocabulary Activity 34*
- Daily Lecture Notes 34-2
- Guided Reading Activity 34-2*
- Reading Essentials and Study Guide 34-2*
- Reteaching Activity 34*
- Reinforcing Skills Activity 34
- Section Quiz 34-2*

Multimedia Resources
- Daily Focus Skills Transparency 34-2
- Political Map Transparency 11
- Unit 11 Map Overlay Transparencies
- Vocabulary PuzzleMaker CD-ROM
- Interactive Tutor Self-Assessment CD-ROM
- ExamView® Pro Testmaker CD-ROM*
- Presentation Plus! CD-ROM

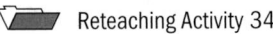 Blackline Master   💾 Software   📼 Videocassette   *Also available in Spanish*

🖋 Transparency   💿 CD-ROM   💿 DVD

 OUT OF TIME? Assign the Chapter 34 **Reading Essentials and Study Guide.**

 Block Schedule

Activities that are particularly suited to use within the block scheduling framework are identified throughout this chapter by the following designation: 🧊

KEY TO ABILITY LEVELS

Teaching strategies have been coded for various learning styles and abilities.

L1   **BASIC** activities for all students

L2   **AVERAGE** activities for average to above-average students

L3   **CHALLENGING** activities for above-average students

ELL   **ENGLISH LANGUAGE LEARNER** activities

Teacher to Teacher

Nancy Chambers
Forest High School
Forest, MS

South Pacific Game

Students work together to design a board game of contemporary features and challenges in the South Pacific.

Organize students into eight groups. Assign the game board to one group and one of the section subhead topics, such as agriculture, to each of the other seven groups. The game board group will create a path of about 40 squares against a background of a regional map or a collage of physical features. Topic groups should develop three "Good News" and three "Bad News" cards with a short news statement and an instruction to move from one to three spaces forward (Good News) or backward (Bad News). Examples: *"This year farms received ample rain. Move forward 3 spaces." "Saltwater rises on 100 acres. Move back 2 spaces."*

To play the game, prop the game board up so it is in clear view, and organize the class into two teams. Shuffle the cards into one stack, written side down. Teams take turns, with members drawing and reading cards aloud. Use self-adhesive notes to mark each team's place as play progresses. The first team that reaches the final square wins.

Meeting National Standards

Geography For Life

The following standards are highlighted in Chapter 34:

Section 1   EE2 Places and Regions:
Standard 6
EE4 Human Systems:
Standards 11, 12

Section 2   EE2 Places and Regions: Standard 4
EE3 Physical Systems:
Standards 7, 8
EE4 Human Systems:
Standards 11, 12
EE5 Environment and Society:
Standards 14, 15, 16
EE6 The Uses of Geography:
Standard 18

Local Objectives

_____

_____

NATIONAL GEOGRAPHIC   TEACHER'S CORNER

Index to National Geographic Magazine:

The following articles may be used for research relating to this chapter:

* "New Caledonia," by Thomas O'Neill, May 2000.
* *Biodiversity*, a National Geographic Special Edition, February 1999.

National Geographic Society Products:

To order the following products for use with this chapter, call National Geographic Society at 1-800-368-2728.

* *Antarctica* (Video)
* *Australia* (Video)
* *Technology's Price* (Video)

NGS ONLINE

Access National Geographic's Web site for current events, activities, links, interactive features, and archives.
www.nationalgeographic.com

MEETING SPECIAL NEEDS

In addition to the Differentiated Instruction strategies found in each section, the following resources are also suitable for your special needs students:

* **ExamView® Pro Testmaker CD-ROM** allows teachers to tailor tests by reducing answer choices.
* The **Audio Program** includes the entire narrative of the student edition so that less-proficient readers can listen to the words as they read them.
* The **Reading Essentials and Study Guide** provides the same content as the student edition but is written two grade levels below the textbook.
* **Guided Reading Activities** give less-proficient readers point-by-point instructions to increase comprehension as they read each textbook section.
* **Enrichment Activities** include a stimulating collection of readings and activities for gifted and talented students.

Chapter Objectives

1. Describe the various economic activities in Australia and Oceania.
2. Discuss the challenges to the region's environment.

GeoJournal

For access to additional photos, maps, and information on the contemporary issues of Australia, Oceania, and Antarctica, go to **www.nationalgeographic.com** (See Teacher pages in front for strategies for using journals in the geography classroom.)

Study Organizer

Dinah Zike's Foldables are three-dimensional, interactive graphic organizers that help students practice basic writing skills, review key vocabulary terms, and identify main ideas. Have students complete the Foldable activity in the **Dinah Zike's Reading and Study Skills Foldables** booklet.

CHAPTER 34 Australia, Oceania, and Antarctica Today

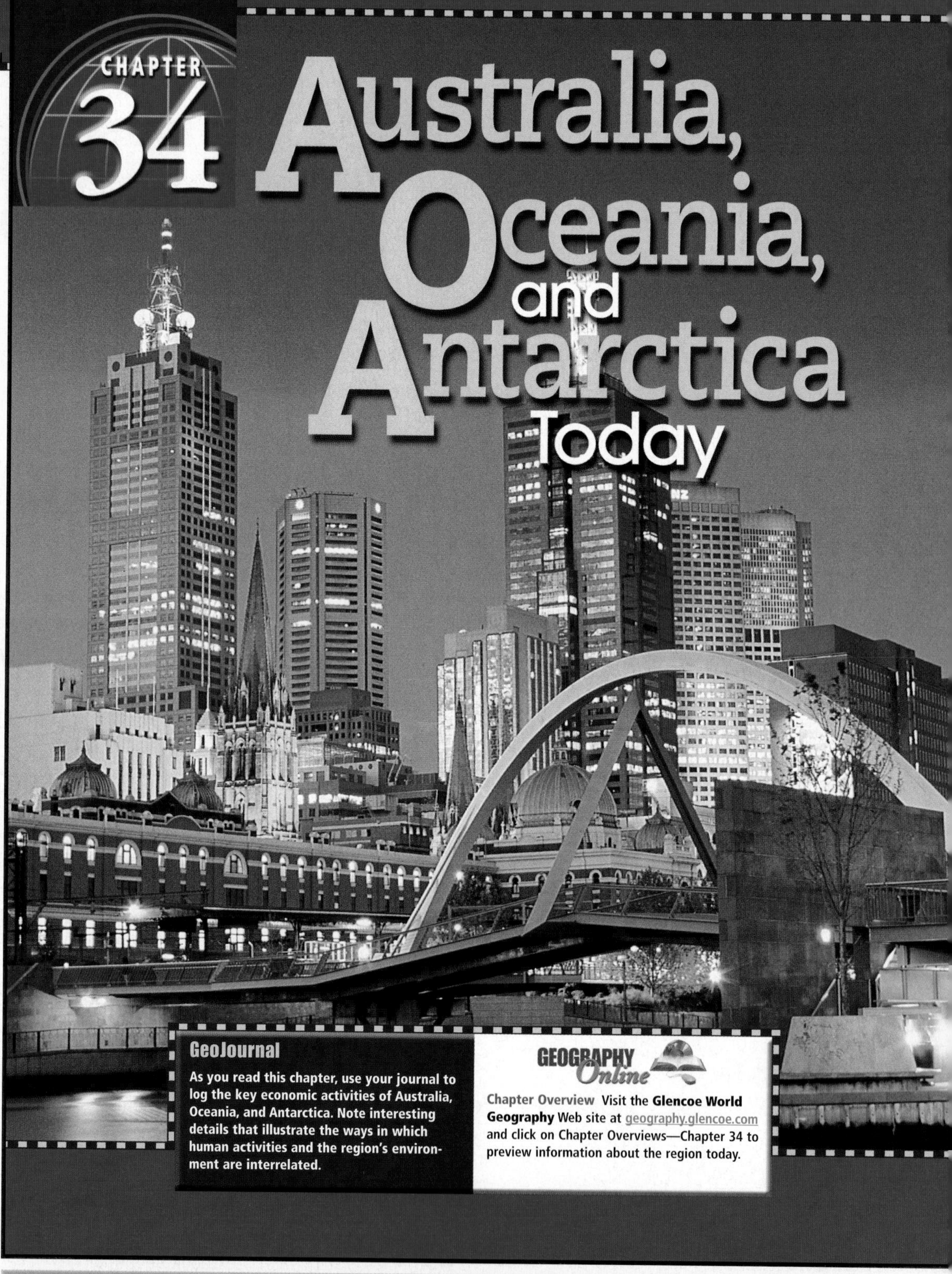

GeoJournal

As you read this chapter, use your journal to log the key economic activities of Australia, Oceania, and Antarctica. Note interesting details that illustrate the ways in which human activities and the region's environment are interrelated.

ABOUT THE PHOTO

Visual Instruction In the foreground of the photo, the bridge crosses the Yarra River, which flows through the center of Melbourne and the city's eastern suburbs. The focus of recreation in Melbourne, the river hosts a wide variety of wildlife species, including 200 species of birds and 15 species of fish, some of which migrate from the sea during their life cycles. Mammals, including platypus, koalas, echidnas, and kangaroos, thrive along the Yarra. 🌐 **EE2 Places and Regions: Standard 6**

Guide to Reading

Consider What You Know

Environments in Australia, Oceania, and Antarctica range from tropical rain forests to icy wastelands. What attractions or activities might draw people to visit or live in a region with such extreme differences in the physical environment?

Reading Strategy

Organizing Complete a web diagram similar to the one below by filling in the developing South Pacific countries that receive much-needed income from tourism.

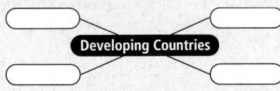

Developing Countries

Read to Find Out

• How do people in Australia, New Zealand, and Oceania make their livings?

• What role does trade play in the economies of South Pacific countries?

• What means of transportation and communications are used in the region?

Terms to Know

• station
• grazier
• copra

Places to Locate

• Fiji
• Papua New Guinea
• Nauru

◀ *Skyline of Melbourne, Australia, at night*

Living in Australia, Oceania, and Antarctica

NATIONAL GEOGRAPHIC

A Geographic View

Antarctic Diving

There's something special about peering beneath the bottom of the world. When Antarctica's summer diving season begins in September the sun has been largely absent for six months, and the water . . . has become as clear as any in the world. Visibility is measured not in feet but in football fields. . . . Only here can you orbit an electric-blue iceberg while being serenaded by the eerie trills of Weddell seals.

View from under Antarctic ice

—Norbert Wu, "Under Antarctic Ice," National Geographic, *February 1999*

The wonders hidden under Antarctic ice are among the many attractions of Australia, Oceania, and Antarctica. Tourism is a growing part of the region's economies. In this section you will learn how people in Australia and Oceania earn their livings despite remote geographic locations and challenging environments.

Agriculture

Agriculture is by far the most important economic activity in the South Pacific area. Australia and New Zealand—the region's major developed countries—export large quantities of farm products. Australia is the world's leading producer of wool, and New Zealand is known for the quality of its dairy products, lamb, beef, and wool.

Chapter 34 🌐 **833**

FOCUS

Section Overview

This section discusses the region's agricultural methods, industries, trade links, and transportation and communications challenges.

BELLRINGER
Skillbuilder Activity

📠 Project transparency and have students answer questions.

📁 Available as blackline master.

Daily Focus Skills Transparency 34-1

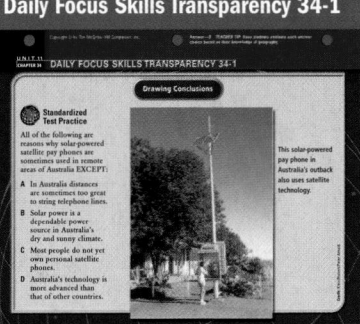

Guide to Reading

Consider What You Know
Answer *Possible answers include nearness to beaches and the ocean, mild climate, and the opportunity to see unique landscapes and interesting plant and animal life.*

Reading Strategy
Answer *Vanuatu, Marshall Islands, Solomon Islands, Federated States of Micronesia*

Preteaching Vocabulary
Tell students that the "Jackeroos" and "Jilleroos" they learned about in Chapter 33 work on *stations*. Have them infer the meaning of the term from the context.

RESOURCE MANAGER

📁 **Reproducible Masters**
• Reproducible Lesson Plan 34-1
• Daily Lecture Notes 34-1
• Guided Reading Activity 34-1
• Reading Essentials and Study Guide 34-1
• Section Quiz 34-1

📠 **Transparencies**
• Daily Focus Skills Transparency 34-1
• Political Map Transparency 11
• Unit 11 Map Overlay Transparencies

Multimedia
💿 Interactive Tutor Self-Assessment CD-ROM
💿 ExamView® Pro Testmaker CD-ROM
💿 Presentation Plus! CD-ROM

NATIONAL GEOGRAPHIC World Explorer

Answer
There is little vegetation because of the dry climate, so herds need large areas to find enough food.

More About the Photo Today there are about 27 million cattle in Australia. About 90 percent of the animals are raised for beef, most of which is exported.

② TEACH

L1 Locate

Have students make a three-column chart with the headings *Australia*, *New Zealand*, and *Oceania*. Have them list important livestock and agricultural products found in each part of the region. *(Australia: wool, sheep, cattle, wheat, sugarcane; New Zealand: dairy products, lamb, beef, wool, wheat, barley, potatoes, fruit; Oceania: fruit, sugarcane, coconuts, coffee, ginger, cacao)* **Ask:** Which part of the region has the most diversified agricultural economy? *(Australia)*

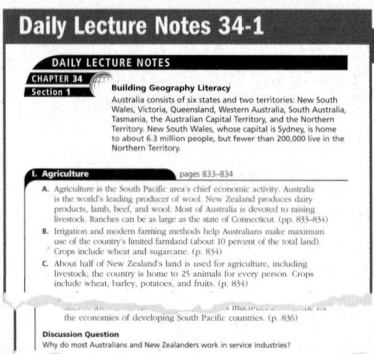

Daily Lecture Notes 34-1

DAILY LECTURE NOTES

CHAPTER 34
Section 1

Building Geography Literacy
Australia consists of six states and two territories: New South Wales, Victoria, Queensland, Western Australia, South Australia, Tasmania, the Australian Capital Territory, and the Northern Territory. New South Wales, whose capital is Sydney, is home to about 6.3 million people, but fewer than 200,000 live in the Northern Territory.

I. Agriculture   pages 833–834

A. Agriculture is the South Pacific area's chief economic activity. Australia is the world's leading producer of wool. New Zealand produces dairy products, lamb, beef, and wool. Most of Australia is devoted to raising livestock. Ranches can be as large as the state of Connecticut. (pp. 833–834)

B. Irrigation and modern farming methods help Australians make maximum use of the country's limited farmland (about 10 percent of the total land). Crops include wheat and sugarcane. (p. 834)

C. About half of New Zealand's land is used for agriculture, including livestock; the country is home to 25 animals for every person. Crops include wheat, barley, potatoes, and fruits. (p. 834)

the economies of developing South Pacific countries. (p. 836)

Discussion Question
Why do most Australians and New Zealanders work in service industries?

NATIONAL GEOGRAPHIC World Explorer

Geography Skills for Life
Cattle Station
A rancher rounds up cattle on a station in southern Australia.
Place Why are Australian ranches so large?

Although only 5 percent of Australians work in agriculture, much of their country's vast land area is devoted to raising livestock—primarily sheep and cattle. Because of the generally dry climate, ranchers must roam over large areas to find enough vegetation to feed their herds. As a result, some Australian ranches, called stations, are gigantic—as large as 6,000 square miles (15,540 sq. km), about the size of Connecticut or Hawaii.

In addition, because of Australia's dry climate, only about 10 percent of its land is suitable for growing crops. Irrigation, fertilizers, and modern technology help Australian farmers make the best use of their limited croplands. Wheat, for example, is grown in the dry Central Lowlands. By contrast, sugarcane thrives in the wetter climate and fertile soil of Australia's northeastern coast.

About half of New Zealand's land is used for agriculture. New Zealand ranchers, known as graziers, raise sheep, beef, dairy cattle, and red deer. Surprisingly, the country has 25 times more farm animals than people! New Zealand's soil, more fertile than that of Australia, allows farmers to grow wheat, barley, potatoes, and fruits. One of New Zealand's most distinctive fruits is the kiwifruit, a small, green-fleshed fruit named for its resemblance to the kiwi, the flightless bird that is the country's national symbol.

Throughout Oceania, the lack of arable soil limits commercial agriculture. As a result, most island farmers practice subsistence farming. They grow starchy roots and tubers—taro, cassava, and sweet potatoes—and raise pigs and chickens. Fishing adds to the diet of many South Pacific peoples.

Some South Pacific islands, however, have areas of rich soil—often volcanic—and ample rainfall. These islands produce a variety of crops, such as tropical fruits, sugarcane, coffee, and coconut products, for export. The major South Pacific cash crop, produced widely in the region, is copra (KOH•pruh), or dried coconut meat. Among the island countries that export are **Fiji**, a producer of sugarcane, copra, and ginger, and **Papua New Guinea**, a supplier of coffee, copra, and cacao.

Mining and Manufacturing

A variety of mineral deposits exist in some parts of the South Pacific region. Australia is a leading exporter of diamonds, gold, bauxite, opals, and iron ore. Extracting these minerals, however, is hampered by high transportation costs inside and outside the country. In addition, public debate about Aboriginal land rights limits where mining can occur. For example, Australia has the world's largest undeveloped supply of uranium ore, but much of it lies within ancestral lands sacred to the Aborigines.

With some exceptions, few significant mineral resources are found in other areas of the South Pacific region. New Zealand has a large aluminum smelting industry, and Papua New Guinea's rich deposits of gold and copper have only recently been exploited. Kiribati and Nauru, once dependent on phosphate mining, now face dwindling supplies. They are now encouraging foreign investment and seeking aid to develop new economic activities.

Government
Mining in Antarctica

Antarctica holds enormous untapped mineral resources, including petroleum, gold, iron ore, and coal. Scientists have used core sampling—drilling cylindrical sections through the Antarctic ice cap—to

DIFFERENTIATED INSTRUCTION

English Learners Specialized vocabulary of the region (especially Australia) may challenge students. Have them keep a glossary in which these terms are matched with referents used in the United States *(station = ranch)*. Pair English language learners with fluent English speakers, and have the pairs work together to find clues in the words that will help them remember meaning. *(Graz(e)* can be found in *grazier.)* **ELL**

📂 Refer to **Inclusion for the Social Studies Classroom Strategies and Activities.**

identify the presence of these and other key minerals. Although seven countries have made territorial claims to Antarctica, the voluntary 1991 Protocol on Environmental Protection, signed by 44 nations, prohibits mining on the continent.

Manufacturing

Australia and New Zealand are the South Pacific region's major producers of manufactured goods. Because agriculture is important in these two countries, food processing is their most important manufacturing activity. Relatively isolated geographically, Australia and New Zealand must import costly machinery and raw materials in order to set up major manufacturing industries capable of producing exports. As a result, industries in the two countries generally manufacture products for home consumption. Goods that cannot be produced domestically are imported.

The rest of the South Pacific region is less industrially developed than Australia and New Zealand. Manufacturing in the islands of Oceania is limited to small-scale enterprises, such as textile production, clothing assembly, and mass production of craft items.

Service Industries

Throughout Australia and Oceania, service industries have emerged as major contributors to national economies. As in other developed countries, most people in Australia and New Zealand make their living in service industries. In Oceania few countries are large enough to support extensive service industries other than tourism. **Nauru**, however, has begun to attract international banking and investment companies as a way of ending its traditional dependence on phosphate mining.

L3 Science

Have students choose a country that has established a scientific research station in Antarctica and learn more about the work being done there. Tell them to write a report describing their findings. Ask them to make a generalization about the value of the research to the South Pacific region.

L1/ELL

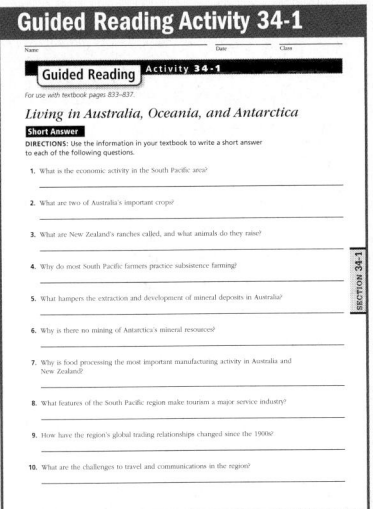

Guided Reading Activity 34-1

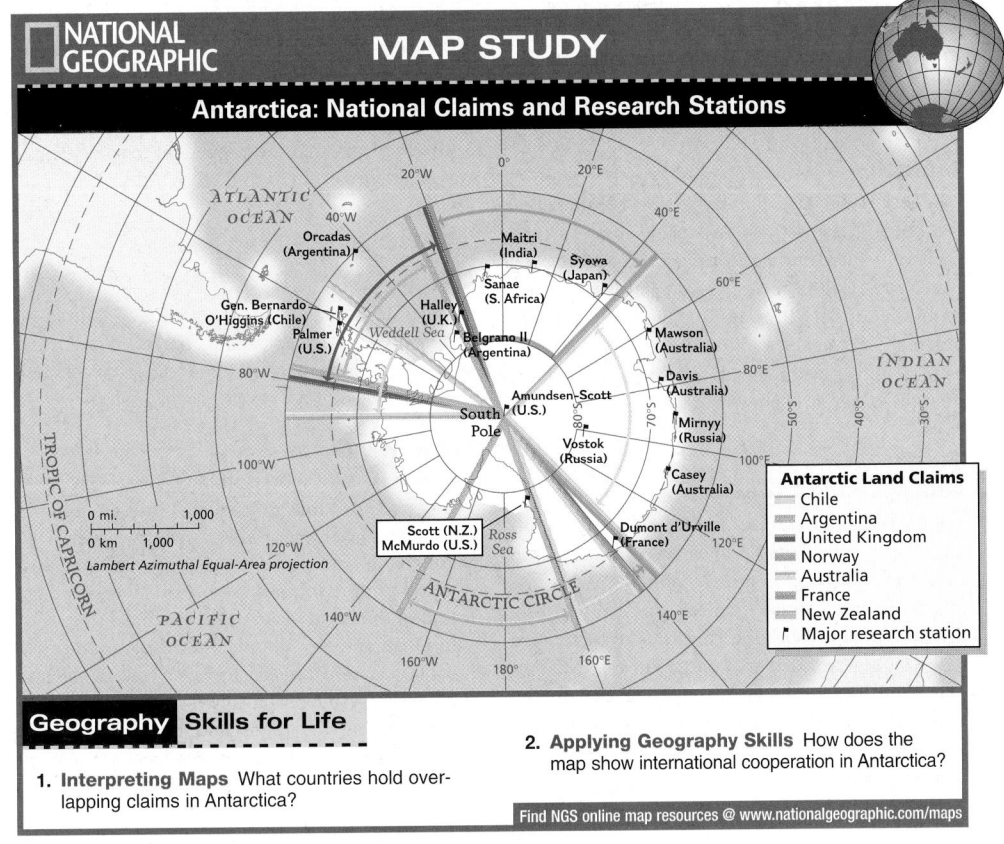

MAP STUDY

Antarctica: National Claims and Research Stations

Antarctic Land Claims
- Chile
- Argentina
- United Kingdom
- Norway
- Australia
- France
- New Zealand
- ⚑ Major research station

Geography Skills for Life

1. **Interpreting Maps** What countries hold overlapping claims in Antarctica?

2. **Applying Geography Skills** How does the map show international cooperation in Antarctica?

Find NGS online map resources @ www.nationalgeographic.com/maps

NATIONAL GEOGRAPHIC **MAP STUDY**

Answers
1. *Chile, Argentina, and the United Kingdom*
2. *Countries have established research stations in areas claimed by other countries.*

Map Skills Practice
Location What countries have allowed Russia to have research stations on land that they claim? *(Australia, Norway)*

COOPERATIVE LEARNING ACTIVITY

Urban Areas and Borders
Copy the outline at the right on the board. Organize students into small groups. Have members work together to complete the outline with information from the section as they read.
🌐 **EE4 Human Systems: Standard 11**

I. Australia
   A. Manufactured Products
   B. Transportation and Communications
II. New Zealand
   A. Manufactured Products
   B. Transportation and Communications
III. Oceania
   A. Manufactured Products
   B. Transportation and Communications

NATIONAL GEOGRAPHIC **World Explorer**

Answer
They attract tourists, which helps the countries' economies.

More About the Photo
Volcanic, largely forested Guadalcanal is the largest island in the Solomon Islands.

L1/ELL

Reading Essentials & Study Guide 34-1

ASSESS

Assign Section 1 Assessment as homework or as an in-class activity.

🌐 Have students use **Interactive Tutor Self-Assessment CD-ROM.**

L2

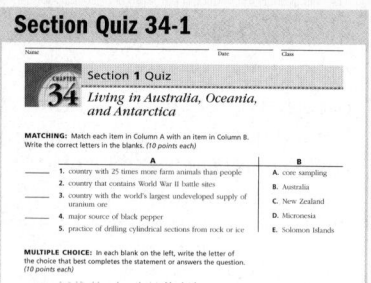

NATIONAL GEOGRAPHIC **World Explorer**

Geography **Skills for Life**

Battle Site Guadalcanal, one of the Solomon Islands, was the site of heavy fighting between the United States and Japan during World War II.
Place How do World War II battle sites benefit Pacific countries today?

Tourism

In recent decades the expansion of air travel has boosted tourism in Australia and Oceania. Each year thousands of tourists visit the region. Among the South Pacific region's attractions are its indigenous cultures, unique wildlife, and contrasting physical features—rock formations, tropical rain forests, geysers, mountain glaciers, sandy beaches, and coral reefs.

History
World War II in the Pacific

Today several countries in Oceania are promoting World War II battle sites on or near South Pacific islands as tourist destinations. Just as history buffs in the United States visit Civil War battlefields, people from the countries involved are now visiting World War II battle sites. For developing South Pacific countries, such as Vanuatu, the Marshall Islands, the Solomon Islands, and the Federated States of Micronesia, tourism provides a much-needed source of income.

Global Trade Links

In recent decades, improved transportation and communications links have increased trade between the once remote South Pacific region and other parts of the world. The South Pacific's agricultural and mining products are its greatest sources of export income. Countries in Oceania export copra, timber and wood products, fish, vegetables, and handicrafts. The spices of the vast South Pacific region are now found in kitchens around the world. For example, the islands of Micronesia are a major source of black pepper, and Tonga exports ginger and the costly vanilla beans used to flavor ice cream and baked goods. A number of South Pacific countries, however, must import food to supplement the subsistence crops.

During most of the 1900s, Australia and New Zealand traded exclusively with the United Kingdom and the United States. In recent years, however, these South Pacific countries have increased trade with their neighboring Asian countries of Japan, Taiwan, and China. In 1971 various island countries of Oceania set up the South Pacific Forum, an organization that promotes trade and economic growth. Because of few natural resources, some South Pacific islands are dependent to some degree on outside investment or foreign aid.

Transportation and Communications

Australia, Oceania, and Antarctica contain thousands of miles of coastland, barren desert, and solid ice. Physical barriers and long distances challenge travelers in the region.

Land Travel

Australia and New Zealand have the most developed road and rail systems in the region. In coastal areas of these countries, highways are well maintained, and subways provide public transportation in urban areas. Few roads, however, are found in the isolated Australian outback.

In Oceania many island countries are too small, too poor, or too rugged to have well-developed road or rail systems. Some governments, however, are improving the roads and bridges necessary for economic growth. Antarctica lacks permanent settlements and has no roads or rail systems.

CRITICAL THINKING ACTIVITY

Drawing Conclusions Point out to students that there are advantages and disadvantages to living in a place, such as a moderate climate or a lack of natural resources. Have students think of factors that would influence people's choices to settle in the South Pacific region. Write their responses on the board. Have them decide where in the South Pacific region each of the following people might choose to live: a farmer, a fisher, a millionaire, an actor, a miner, and a scientist. Tell them to list the geographic advantages that a particular place would offer to that person. 🌐 **EE2 Places and Regions: Standard 6**
🌐 **EE4 Human Systems: Standard 12**

Air and Water Travel

Long distances, harsh climates, or obstacles to land travel make air and water travel important to the region. Cargo ships and planes move imports and exports to and from far-flung Pacific territories. Commercial airlines and cruise ships bring travelers.

Water and air also provide important means of personal transportation. Pacific islanders began using outrigger canoes thousands of years ago, and many of Oceania's travelers continue to use boats today. Sailboats and motorized boats are common, and ferries link New Zealand's two major islands. Icebreakers—ships with reinforced bows—carry people and supplies to Antarctica as do small planes and helicopters, although winter blizzards often make transportation of any kind impossible. Severe winters isolate Antarctica:

> *Along about February the annual exodus [from the research stations] begins in earnest. Once the cold season takes hold, planes stop making regular flights to inland stations, and the ice layer spreads out to sea, making access by ship nearly impossible. Only a few hundred residents stay through the winter.*
>
> Michael D. Lemonick, "McMurdo Station," *Time*, January 15, 1990

Planes also provide transportation between islands in the South Pacific. In Australia's outback almost every station or farm has at least one plane. Ranchers often use helicopters to herd cattle over thousands of acres of rough terrain.

Communications

In the South Pacific area, the same geographic obstacles that hinder land travel also make communications difficult. The development of modern technology, however, has helped increase contacts within Australia, Oceania, and Antarctica and with the rest of the world. In the Australian outback, some cattle stations are large enough to maintain their own post offices and telephone exchanges. Others use two-way radios to communicate. Emerging technologies, such as cellular, digital, and satellite communications and the Internet, are becoming common in developed areas. A continuing challenge is to provide developing Pacific countries with access to these technologies.

Student Web Activity Visit the **Glencoe World Geography** Web site at geography.glencoe.com and click on Student Web Activities—Chapter 34 for an activity about research in Antarctica.

SECTION 1 ASSESSMENT

Checking for Understanding

1. **Define** station, grazier, copra.

2. **Main Ideas** On a table like the one below, fill in details about the key agricultural and mining products of countries in this region. Then describe the role the region plays in world trade.

Country	Agricultural Products	Mining Products

Critical Thinking

3. **Identifying Cause and Effect** How does importing more manufactured goods than it exports affect a country's economy?

4. **Predicting Consequences** What might be the consequences of opening Antarctica to mining?

5. **Drawing Conclusions** Why are Australia and Oceania trading more with East Asia and Southeast Asia than with the West?

Analyzing Maps

6. **Place** Study the map on page 835. Which Latin American countries hold claims in Antarctica? Which have research stations there?

Applying Geography

7. **Economic Activities** Create a table that shows major economic activities for six countries in the region. Then explain why the economies of some countries focus on one major product.

Objectives, goals, and answers to the student activity can be found in the Web Activity Lesson Plan feature at geography.glencoe.com

Reteach

Read aloud the title of each section subhead in order. Ask students to summarize the subsection's main idea. Use the responses as a guide for reinforcement.

Enrich

Invite a ham radio operator to show the class how a two-way radio works. **Ask:** Why would ham radios be important to people of the region before and after a tropical storm? *(to learn about the storm's path and severity and to call for help)*

4 CLOSE

Challenge students to create a quiz for Section 1, and exchange quizzes with a partner to answer the questions.

SECTION 1 ASSESSMENT ANSWERS

1. All vocabulary terms are defined in the text.

2. Tables should accurately identify agricultural and mining products of countries in the region.

3. Possible answers: A country must make money in ways other than manufacturing, such as tourism or service industries, to pay for imported goods. A country may earn less

from its exports than it spends on imports, resulting in a trade imbalance.

4. Possible answers: conflict among countries involved; harm to Antarctica's environment caused by irresponsible mining practices

5. Asia and Southeast Asia are nearer, and shipping costs are less.

6. Chile, Argentina; Chile, Argentina, Uruguay

7. **Applying Geography** Charts should show accurate facts, and explanations should be reasonable and well thought out.

Section Overview

This section discusses the environmental challenges facing Australia and Oceania and the role Antarctica plays in research on global climate changes.

BELLRINGER
Skillbuilder Activity

 Project transparency and have students answer questions.

 Available as blackline master.

Daily Focus Skills Transparency 34-2

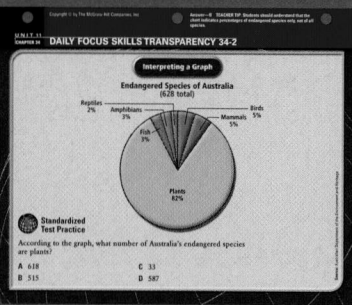

Guide to Reading

Consider What You Know
Answer *Possible answers may include kangaroo, koala, platypus, dingo, and eucalyptus.*

Reading Strategy
Answer Students should complete the outline by including all heads in the section.

Preteaching Vocabulary
🌐 Use the **Vocabulary Puzzle-Maker CD-ROM** to create crossword and word-search puzzles.

Guide to Reading

Consider What You Know

Australia's remarkable wildlife is recognizable around the world. What animals and plants unique to Australia can you name?

Reading Strategy

Taking Notes Use the major headings of the section to create an outline similar to the one below.

> I. Managing Resources
>   A.
>   B.
>   C.
> II. Atmosphere and Climate

Read to Find Out

- Why do Australia, Oceania, and Antarctica face many environmental challenges?
- What effects did nuclear testing have on the region?
- Why are the thinning of the ozone layer and global warming special challenges for this region?

Terms to Know

- marsupial
- introduced species
- food web
- ozone layer
- El Niño-Southern Oscillation (ENSO)
- diatom

Places to Locate

- Tasmania
- Murray-Darling River Basin
- Great Barrier Reef

People and Their Environment

NATIONAL GEOGRAPHIC

A Geographic View

From Leafy Grove to Salty Swamp

Behind us a forest of dead eucalyptus trees stood in a salty swamp, a graveyard of skeletons with gray arms raised in good-bye.... Once a leafy grove in Western Australia, this salt lake rose from the ground when nearby woodlands were cleared for farms. Thirsty trees had absorbed rainwater and kept the water table from rising, but when they were cut, the water surfaced and brought salt with it. The result: saline ponds and dead fields.

—Michael Parfit, "Australia: A Harsh Awakening," National Geographic, *July 2000*

Salty swamp, Australia

Beneath much of Australia's land surface there is a layer of salty subsoil or salty groundwater. Salts are carried to the surface as the water slowly evaporates. Scientists believe that 40 percent of Western Australia's productive wheat belt could be lost to salty swamps in the next fifty years. Today Australia, like other countries, is experiencing the environmental consequences of human activity. In this section you will learn about environmental challenges in Australia, Oceania, and Antarctica as well as the efforts under way to remedy environmental damage.

Managing Resources

Australia, Oceania, and Antarctica hold some of the planet's richest and most diverse natural resources. Unfortunately, these resources have not always been well managed, and today the region faces many environmental issues. Conservation efforts, however, are

---

RESOURCE MANAGER

📁 Reproducible Masters

- Reproducible Lesson Plan 34-2
- Vocabulary Activity 34
- Daily Lecture Notes 34-2
- Guided Reading Activity 34-2
- Reading Essentials and Study Guide 34-2
- Reteaching Activity 34
- Reinforcing Skills Activity 34
- Section Quiz 34-2

📖 Transparencies

- Daily Focus Skills Transparency 34-2
- Political Map Transparency 11
- Unit 11 Map Overlay Transparencies

Multimedia

- 💿 Vocabulary PuzzleMaker CD-ROM
- 💿 Interactive Tutor Self-Assessment CD-ROM
- 💿 ExamView® Pro Testmaker CD-ROM
- 💿 Presentation Plus! CD-ROM

gaining recognition in the region. Environmental issues concern voters and government leaders alike in Australia, New Zealand, and other South Pacific islands.

Australia's Unusual Animals

The continent of Australia, separated for so long from other landmasses, is home to many unique animal species. Kangaroos, koalas, and wallabies are just some of Australia's 144 species of marsupials—mammals whose young must mature in a pouch after they are born. The Australian island of **Tasmania** gave its name to the Tasmanian devil, a powerful meat-eating marsupial about the size of a badger. Australia's strangest wildlife may be the duck-billed platypus and the echidna, a spiny anteater—the only mammals in the world that lay eggs.

Australia's unusual wildlife species, however, have been seriously threatened by the human introduction of various nonnative animals. These introduced species include the hunting dogs called dingoes brought from Asia by migrating Aborigines. Sheep, cattle, foxes, cats, and rabbits were also brought by European settlers. In the absence of natural predators, these animals have multiplied and taken over the habitats of Australia's native species. Some of Australia's native species have become extinct, and at least 16 kinds of marsupials are now endangered. Efforts to restore Australia's ecological balance include the use of electric fencing to keep out nonnative animals, hunting and trapping programs, the introduction of natural predators, and the creation of native wildlife reserves.

Forest, Soil, and Water

The protection of forest, soil, and freshwater resources is a major concern throughout the South Pacific region. In Australia many sparse woodlands have been cleared for farms and grazing lands, leaving little protection against wind erosion. As in other parts of the world, soil conservation in the region is closely linked to reducing deforestation. Countries with valuable timber resources, such as New Zealand, Papua New Guinea, and Vanuatu, are developing plans to use forest resources without damaging the environment.

Drought, salt, irrigation, and agricultural runoff threaten Australia's freshwater sources. In the fertile

NATIONAL GEOGRAPHIC   World Explorer

Geography | Skills for Life

Wildlife The kangaroo and the Tasmanian devil (inset) are uniquely Australian mammals.
Place Why does Australia have such a variety of unusual animal species?

Murray-Darling River Basin, one of the world's largest drainage basins, the use of water for agriculture and growing city populations has dramatically reduced the rivers' flow.

Oceania also faces challenges in managing its freshwater resources. Many small coral atolls and volcanic islands hold only limited supplies of freshwater. Agricultural runoff and inadequate sanitation cause pollution that further threatens these supplies. The lack of clean drinking water keeps the standard of living low and poses barriers to economic growth in some countries of Oceania.

NATIONAL GEOGRAPHIC   World Explorer

Answer
because of Australia's separation from other landmasses for a very long time

More About the Photo
Kangaroos carry their young in pouches for up to 10 months; the Tasmanian devil, for about 5 months.

② TEACH

L2 Research Cause and Effect
Have students research the Aboriginal custom of "firestick farming," or thinning dry brush by setting "cool fires." Then have students write a paragraph on how removing undergrowth helps larger plants and trees grow.

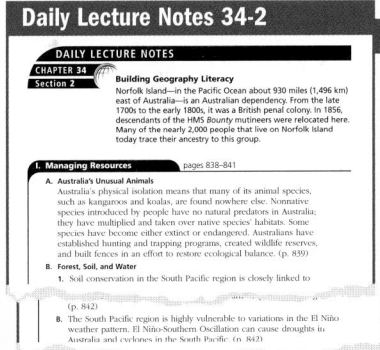

Daily Lecture Notes 34-2

DAILY LECTURE NOTES
CHAPTER 34
Section 2

Building Geography Literacy
Norfolk Island—in the Pacific Ocean about 930 miles (1,496 km) east of Australia—is an Australian dependency. From the late 1700s to the early 1800s, it was a British penal colony. In 1856, descendants of the HMS *Bounty* mutineers were relocated here. Many of the nearly 2,000 people that live on Norfolk Island today trace their ancestry to this group.

I. Managing Resources   pages 838–841

A. Australia's Unusual Animals
Australia's physical isolation means that many of its animal species, such as kangaroos and koalas, are found nowhere else. Nonnative species introduced by people have no natural predators in Australia; they have multiplied and taken over native species' habitats. Some species have become either extinct or endangered. Australians have established hunting and trapping programs, created wildlife reserves, and built fences in an effort to restore ecological balance. (p. 839)

B. Forest, Soil, and Water
1. Soil conservation in the South Pacific region is closely linked to _____ (p. 842)
2. The South Pacific region is highly vulnerable to variations in the El Niño weather pattern. El Niño-Southern Oscillation can cause droughts in Australia and cyclones in the South Pacific. (p. 842)

L1/ELL

Guided Reading Activity 34-2

Name _____ Date _____ Class _____

Guided Reading | Activity 34-2

For use with textbook pages 838–841

People and Their Environment

Underline the Word
DIRECTIONS: Use the information in your textbook to choose the word or phrase that best completes the sentence. Underline the correct answer.

1. Poor _____ of resources is causing environmental challenges in many parts of this region. (prices/management)
2. Because of Australia's long isolation, many _____ animals are found there. (common/unique)
3. _____ species of animals threaten the survival of many native Australian animals. (Mammalian/Introduced)
4. New Zealand and Papua New Guinea are trying to use their _____ resources in a way that prevents soil erosion. (forest/agricultural)

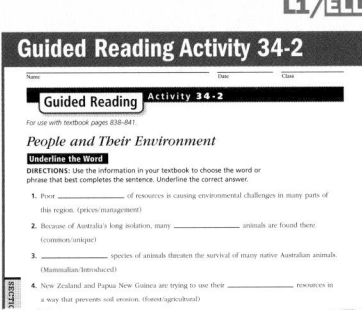

DIFFERENTIATED INSTRUCTION

Reading Support Paraphrasing can help students recall concepts and important details. However, paraphrasing requires the extensive use of synonyms to be effective. Ask students who have demonstrated verbal/linguistic skills to compile a "South Pacific Thesaurus." Students can identify key words that occur several times in this section. They should brainstorm or look up synonyms for these words and list them after the term. Encourage them to share their reference work with classmates.

☞ Refer to *Inclusion for the Social Studies Classroom Strategies and Activities.*

NATIONAL GEOGRAPHIC World Explorer

Answer
tourism, oil-shale mining, agriculture, toxic wastes

More About the Photo
Coral reefs consist of the skeletons of millions of tiny marine animals.

L1/ELL

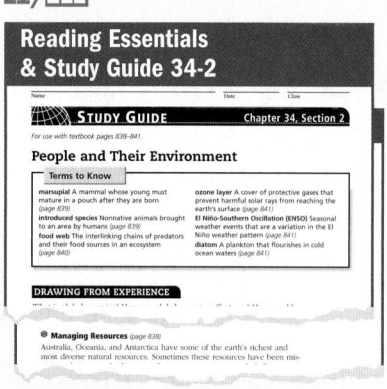

Reading Essentials
& Study Guide 34-2

ASSESS

Assign Section 2 Assessment as homework or as an in-class activity.

⊕ Have students use **Interactive Tutor Self-Assessment CD-ROM**.

L2

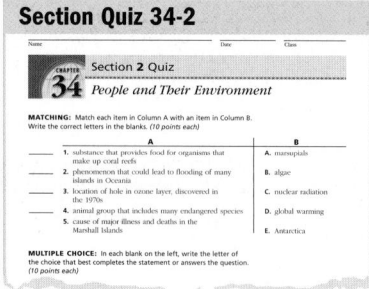

Section Quiz 34-2

NATIONAL GEOGRAPHIC World Explorer

Geography Skills for Life
Great Barrier Reef
The Great Barrier Reef (left) in Australia is home to hundreds of species of coral-forming organisms (right).
Human-Environment Interaction What human activities threaten the Great Barrier Reef?

Improvement will come with better management of runoff, construction of additional sanitation facilities, and development of less expensive ways of removing salt from ocean water.

Agricultural runoff, chemical fertilizers, and organic waste also threaten oceans in the South Pacific region. Toxic waste in particular endangers Australia's **Great Barrier Reef** and other Pacific coral reefs. Coral environments are increasingly stressed by tourists, boaters, and divers as well as oil-shale mining.

Pollution also affects all kinds of marine life, including the tiny organisms that make up coral reefs. Algae—on which these organisms thrive—and plankton are key parts of the ocean's food web, the interlinking chains of predators and their food sources in an ecosystem. As these tiny living things are destroyed, the larger plants and animals that rely on them for food also die off.

History
The Nuclear Legacy

The testing of nuclear weapons has had major effects on the region's environment. In the late 1940s and 1950s, the United States and other countries with nuclear capability carried out aboveground testing of nuclear weapons in the South Pacific. The dangers of such testing were gravely underestimated

at the time. In 1954 the United States exploded a nuclear device on Bikini Atoll, in the Marshall Islands. The people of Bikini Atoll had been moved to safety, but those living on Rongelap Atoll, downwind of the explosion, were exposed to massive doses of radiation that resulted in deaths, illnesses, and genetic abnormalities.

Although the American testing was stopped, the effects of radiation exposure and environmental damage have continued through several generations. Today the atolls affected by the testing remain off-limits to human settlement. Recent studies, however, offer hopeful signs of eventual environmental recovery. In the 1990s the United States government provided $90 million to help decontaminate Bikini Atoll and set up a $45 million trust fund for blast survivors and their offspring from Rongelap Atoll.

The nuclear legacy also has had political effects. Antinuclear activism is a major factor in regional politics. In 1986 New Zealand banned nuclear-powered ships and those with nuclear weapons from entering its waters. Because of this ban, the United States withdrew from a defense agreement with New Zealand. In the mid-1990s, French plans to conduct nuclear tests on an atoll in French

---

COOPERATIVE LEARNING ACTIVITY

South Pacific Wildlife Organize students into groups. Have each group member choose one unique animal found in this region. Tell students to collect pictures of their chosen animals and to write a caption for each. Captions should tell an interesting fact, such as "A newborn kangaroo joey could fit into a teaspoon." Have each group mount their pictures and typed captions on sheets of paper to form a book. Each group should work together to design a cover and title for their book. You might make color copies of the books and suggest that the class donate its books to the library of a nearby elementary school.

🌐 **EE3 Physical Systems: Standard 8**

Polynesia aroused antinuclear demonstrations. The international outcry led to an early halt to the tests.

Atmosphere and Climate

Like other world regions, Australia, Oceania, and Antarctica are threatened by global atmospheric and climate changes. In the 1970s scientists found a hole in the ozone layer over Antarctica:

> ❝ *The mysterious stuff called ozone, which until then was known to the public chiefly as an . . . element of smog in overcrowded cities, was being destroyed in the stratosphere by chemicals made and released in the 20th century by humans. . . . The hole was real; the ozone had dropped by 50 percent. . . .* ❞
>
> Samuel W. Matthews, "Is Our World Warming?" *National Geographic*, October 1990

The ozone layer's protective gases prevent harmful solar rays from reaching the earth's surface. The ozone hole over Antarctica grew dramatically between 1975 and 1993, when it covered more than 9 million square miles (23 million sq. km). In 1989 a similar ozone hole developed over the Arctic.

The loss of protective ozone may be behind the global rise in the rates of skin cancer and cataracts, conditions caused by overexposure to the sun's ultraviolet rays. Increased solar radiation that reaches the earth through ozone holes may also contribute to global warming, the gradual rise in Earth's temperatures over the last century.

Climate and weather in the South Pacific region are highly sensitive to changes in the El Niño weather pattern called El Niño-Southern Oscillation (ENSO). This seasonal weather event can cause droughts in Australia and powerful cyclonic storms in the South Pacific. These ENSO-related weather patterns are believed to be increasing in frequency and severity and may also be linked to global warming.

Some scientists claim that continued rises in Earth's temperatures could be devastating. If polar ice caps were to melt and thermal expansion of ocean waters occurred, many of Oceania's islands would be flooded by rising ocean levels. Rising ocean temperatures also affect certain types of plankton and algae that grow in warm waters, causing overgrowth and the choking out of other life-forms. Diatoms—plankton that flourish in cold ocean waters—would die if temperatures rose, affecting life-forms that feed on them. Scientists in the region, especially in Antarctica, are studying global warming and are hoping to discover causes, predict consequences, and provide solutions.

SECTION ② ASSESSMENT

Checking for Understanding

1. Define marsupial, introduced species, food web, ozone layer, El Niño-Southern Oscillation (ENSO), diatom.

2. Main Ideas On a chart like the one below, list resources and examples of their mismanagement in the region. Also list possible solutions.

Resource	Example of Mismanagement	Possible Solution

Critical Thinking

3. Comparing and Contrasting How are countries of the region similar and different in the challenges they face concerning water resources?

4. Decision Making Do you agree or disagree with New Zealand's nuclear ban? Explain your reasons.

5. Problem Solving What steps would you take to increase awareness about the risks of global warming? Explain.

Analyzing Maps

6. Location Study the physical-political map on page 796. Which countries are at the greatest risk from rising ocean levels as a result of continued global warming?

Applying Geography

7. Effects of Mining Study the map on page 787. Compare a mineral-rich area shown on the map to a mineral-rich area in another region. Explain the effects of mining on both environments.

◻ NATIONAL GEOGRAPHIC **GEOFACT**

▶ **Termites, pests in most urban areas of the world, serve an important agricultural function in Australia. By feeding on grass and plant litter, termites recycle the nutrients in the soil—vital in Australia, which has had little geologic activity to enrich the soil.**

Reteach

Have students answer the questions in "Read to Find Out" on page 838. Use their responses as a basis for a discussion of points that need reinforcement.

Enrich

Have students research French nuclear testing in Polynesia and its possible long-term effects on the population and the environment.

 **CLOSE**

Have students reread "A Geographic View" on page 838. Have them write a paragraph from the viewpoint of an Australian farmer to explain how the negative effects of clearing woodlands was not anticipated.

SECTION ② ASSESSMENT ANSWERS

1. All vocabulary terms are defined in the text.

2. Charts should include each type of resource, one example of mismanagement, and possible solutions.

3. Similar: agricultural runoff and toxic waste pollute water in Australia and Oceania; Different: Australia's freshwater supply has been reduced because of drought, salt, and irrigation, while Oceania's limited freshwater sources are polluted by inadequate sanitation, chemical fertilizers, and organic waste.

4. Answers should be supported by well-reasoned arguments.

5. public information campaigns, increased news coverage

6. Possible answers may include any low islands in Oceania and coastal areas of Australia and Antarctica.

7. Applying Geography Students should recognize that mining activities can destroy landforms and threaten habitats.

① FOCUS

Put the following categories on the board, and have students suggest how the melting of the Antarctic ice sheet could affect each:

- *sea levels*
- *coastal areas*
- *precipitation patterns*
- *human health*
- *crop yields*
- *animal life*

② TEACH

Tell students that some scientists believe that the melting of the Antarctic ice sheet is part of a natural geological cycle that has been going on for thousands of years. Other scientists, however, believe that global warming has dangerously accelerated this cycle. They say that human activities during the past century have led to increased heat-absorbing carbon dioxide in the atmosphere. If these activities continue unchecked, they could have serious global consequences.

L2 Debate
Have students identify as many pros and cons as they can to support the arguments of both those who think changes in Antarctica are part of a normal cycle and those who think rapid global warming presents risks.

Viewpoint
CASE STUDY on the Environment

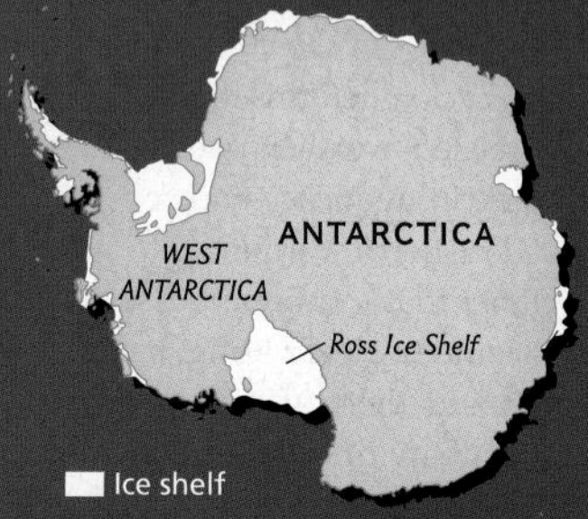

ANTARCTICA

WEST ANTARCTICA

Ross Ice Shelf

☐ Ice shelf

Antarctica's Melting Ice: Is Global Warming at Fault?

During the last century, Earth's average surface temperature crept steadily higher—a phenomenon called global warming. In the past few decades, vast expanses of Antarctic ice have started breaking up and large chunks have floated out to sea. Researchers speculate that if the huge West Antarctic ice sheet collapses and melts, sea levels could rise dramatically, causing flooding in coastal regions around the world. Is global warming responsible for Antarctica's melting ice?

LOOKING TO THE FUTURE

Global Warming Scientists expect that rising global temperatures could alter local climates and precipitation patterns, affecting natural vegetation, agricultural production, and freshwater resources.

In the United States, scientists expect an overall pattern of greater precipitation and evaporation, stronger rainstorms, and drier soils.

- ▣ **EE2 Places and Regions: Standard 4**
- ▣ **EE3 Physical Systems: Standard 7**
- ▣ **EE5 Environment and Society: Standard 15**
- ▣ **EE6 The Uses of Geography: Standard 18**

In March 2000 an iceberg twice the size of Delaware broke free from Antarctica's Ross Ice Shelf, part of the West Antarctic ice sheet. On the other side of the continent, an entire ice shelf disintegrated in 1995. Why is this happening? Antarctica is the coldest place on Earth. Nevertheless, the continent is a little warmer than it used to be. The average temperature in parts of West Antarctica has increased by almost 5°F (3°C) in the last 50 years. During the 1900s, the average temperature worldwide rose by 1°F (.5°C).

Most scientists believe that rising global temperatures are partly due to an increased amount of carbon dioxide (CO_2) in the atmosphere. Much of the carbon dioxide is caused by human activities such as burning gasoline, coal, and other fossil fuels. In the atmosphere, carbon dioxide is a powerful heat absorber, trapping heat that radiates from the sun-warmed ground. The trapped heat leads to global warming.

As global temperatures rise, ocean waters warm and then expand, and ice in places such as Antarctica begins to melt. The seas start creeping higher onto the edges of the continents. Sea levels in some parts of the world are already almost a foot (30 cm) higher than they were a century ago. However, this increase is trivial compared with the rise that could occur if the vast West Antarctic ice sheet melts. If this happens, sea levels could rise by 13 to 20 feet (4 to 6 m). Coastal communities worldwide would be flooded. Low-lying islands, such as Tuvalu and Kiribati in the Pacific, would disappear underwater.

Recent studies, however, indicate that the West Antarctic ice sheet has been receding for almost 8,000 years. Scientists have also uncovered evidence that the ice sheet may have collapsed about 400,000 years ago, before the last ice age. These findings have sparked a controversy.

Some scientists think that changes taking place in

◄ Cars spew carbon dioxide into the air, contributing to global warming.

Antarctic ice are part of a natural cycle that has nothing to do with recent global warming. They point out that the West Antarctic ice sheet began shrinking before people started burning large amounts of fossil fuels and adding carbon dioxide to the atmosphere.

Other scientists think that recent changes in Antarctic ice sheets are a direct result of human-caused global warming. While these scientists admit there might be a natural cycle at work in Antarctica, they argue that global warming is speeding up that cycle.

What's Your Point of View? Experts predict it will take 500 to 700 years for the West Antarctic ice sheet to melt completely, no matter what the cause. Should people today care about this issue? Why or why not?

Tavaerua Island (below) could disappear if sea level rises. Scientists (right) study Antarctic ice cores for clues to a changing climate. ▼

③ ASSESS

Have students answer the **What's Your Point of View?** questions on page 843.

④ CLOSE

Problem Solving Challenge students to work with a partner to formulate questions that they would want to ask experts on either side of the issue about their viewpoints.

global issues

Sea Levels Most experts concede that sea levels probably will rise in the next century. They anticipate a rise of about 2 feet (60 cm) along the eastern and southern coasts of the United States. Coastal areas at greatest risk would include Louisiana, Florida, Texas, North Carolina, and the eastern shore of Chesapeake Bay.

 Meeting National Standards

Geography for Life
The following standards are met in the Student Edition:

EE2 Places and Regions: Standard 4
EE3 Physical Systems: Standard 7
EE5 Environment and Society: Standard 15
EE6 The Uses of Geography: Standard 18

WHAT CAN YOU DO?

Plan and carry out an awareness campaign in your school or community about the potential dangers of global warming and the actions individuals can take to make a difference.

- Conserve energy in the home.
- Carpool or combine errands into one car trip.
- Help recycling efforts.

- Plant a tree; trees help cool the earth.
- Learn the latest facts about global warming, and post information in libraries or other public places.

▣ **EE5 Environment and Society: Standard 14**
▣ **EE6 The Uses of Geography: Standard 18**

Teaching the Skill

Guide students through this activity as practice. Have them reread the subsection: "Mining in Antarctica" on pages 834 and 835. Tell them to ask themselves these questions: "What is the problem?" *(Mining in Antarctica could harm the continent and have global consequences.)* "What practical solution to the problem was reached?" *(Forty-four nations voluntarily agreed to ban mining in Antarctica.)*

Additional Practice
L1

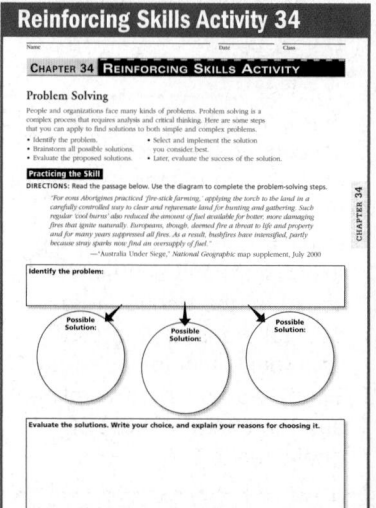

GLENCOE
TECHNOLOGY

Glencoe Skillbuilder Interactive Workbook, Level 2

This interactive CD-ROM reinforces student mastery of essential social studies skills.

CRITICAL THINKING

SkillBuilder

Problem Solving

Individuals and groups often face problems that require critical thinking to solve. Identifying problems and evaluating possible solutions are important skills used by individual citizens, local and national governments, and world organizations.

Learning the Skill

Whether a problem is simple or complex, local or global, the same problem-solving steps can be applied. You can practice these steps in your everyday life, just as governments and organizations do when addressing major conflicts.

Here are the steps involved in problem solving:

- **Identify the problem.** State clearly the issue at hand and the reasons the problem must be solved.

- **Brainstorm possible solutions to the problem.** Be open-minded and creative. Take notes on all the possibilities suggested.

- **Evaluate the proposed solutions.** Evaluate each proposed solution by listing its advantages and disadvantages and anticipating its possible consequences.

- **Choose and implement the best solution.** Choose the best possibility, understanding that it may have some drawbacks. Put your solution into practice.

- **At a later time, review the success of the solution.** If implementing your solution has not improved the situation or has resulted in further problems, begin the process again.

Environmentalists say the Great Barrier Reef will be under threat if the Australian government allows oil explorations in the area. After years of controversy, the government has started testing ways of tapping oil reserves around one of the world's most spectacular sites. Experts say there is more oil to be tapped in the reef's coastal rock next to the coral than has ever been found on the entire American continent.

Environmentalists say the processes involved could destroy the delicate coral. . . . "To do that [extract the oil] requires a lot of energy and the oil you get is very carbon intensive, making the whole process a very dirty kind of mining."

More than one million people visit the reef each year but oil pollution has the potential to ruin the tourist industry. . . . [The government] says the country cannot afford to ignore the reef's precious resources. . . . [S]uch is the sensitivity of the issue, the authorities have only given the go-ahead for one pilot area to be exploited for oil.

—*"World: Asia-Pacific Oil Threat to Great Barrier Reef,"* **BBC News** *(online), September 25, 1998*

Practicing the Skill

Read the excerpt above. Then use what you know about problem solving to answer these questions.

1. What is the problem?
2. What are the positions of environmental groups and the Australian government regarding the problem?
3. What are some possible solutions to the problem?
4. How has Australia tried to solve the problem?
5. How can the success of the solution be evaluated?

Applying the Skill

Work in a small group to find an environmental issue facing your community. As a group, apply the steps for problem solving to the issue you have chosen. Prepare a written report of your results. If possible, share your proposed solution with community authorities.

Go To ▶ The Glencoe Skillbuilder Interactive Workbook, Level 2 provides instruction and practice in key social studies skills.

ANSWERS TO PRACTICING THE SKILL

1. There are valuable oil reserves in the coastal rock of the Great Barrier Reef, but extraction and possible oil pollution could damage the reef and threaten the tourist industry.

2. Environmentalists: Oil exploration in the area could destroy coral and have serious local and global ecological consequences. Government: The vast oil reserves could have significant energy-related and economic benefits.

3. Prohibit oil extraction in the area; ban oil extraction for the present and fund research to find less harmful methods; test oil extraction in one place.

4. The government has decided to test the effects of oil extraction in one pilot area.

5. Success can be evaluated by studying the effects on the reef's ecology in the pilot area.

CHAPTER 34

SUMMARY & STUDY GUIDE

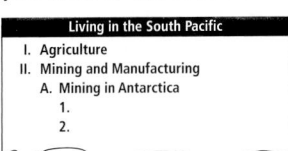

SECTION 1 — Living in Australia, Oceania, and Antarctica (pp. 833–837)

Terms to Know
- station
- grazier
- copra

Key Points
- Agriculture is the most important economic activity in the region, although mining is done in Australia and some island countries.
- Manufacturing in Australia and New Zealand centers on food processing, and the rest of the region engages in small-scale production of clothing and crafts.
- The importance of service industries, particularly tourism, is increasing in the economies of the region.
- Transportation and communications technologies, such as air travel, satellite communications, and the Internet, are helping people in the region to overcome geographic obstacles.

Organizing Your Notes
Create an outline using the format below to help you organize your notes for this section.

Living in the South Pacific
I. Agriculture
II. Mining and Manufacturing
A. Mining in Antarctica
1.
2.

SECTION 2 — People and Their Environment (pp. 838–841)

Terms to Know
- marsupial
- introduced species
- food web
- ozone layer
- El Niño-Southern Oscillation (ENSO)
- diatom

Key Points
- Australia, Oceania, and Antarctica have many natural resources, but the region's environment is threatened by human activity.
- Governments and individuals in the region are focusing on balanced management of water resources, forest, land, and wildlife.
- Nuclear testing conducted in Oceania during the 1940s and 1950s has had a lasting impact on people and the environment.
- Scientists are studying global warming and the thinning ozone layer to prevent potential risks.

Organizing Your Notes
Create a web diagram like the one below to help organize the notes you took for this section. Add other key ideas to the web, and draw lines to show connections between ideas.

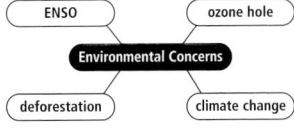

ENSO   ozone hole
Environmental Concerns
deforestation   climate change

◀ Thermal spring, Rotorua, New Zealand

Chapter 34 🌐 **845**

Using the Chapter 34 Summary & Study Guide

Use the Chapter 34 Summary & Study Guide to preview, review, condense, or reteach the chapter.

Preview/Review

🔘 **Vocabulary PuzzleMaker CD-ROM** reinforces "Terms to Know."

🔘 **Interactive Tutor Self-Assessment CD-ROM** provides a review of Chapter 34 content.

Condense

Have students read the Chapter 34 Summary & Study Guide.

🔘 Chapter 34 Audio Program

📁 Chapter 34 Guided Reading Activities

Reteach

📁 Chapter 34 Reteaching Activities (Spanish also available)

📁 Chapter 34 Reading Essentials and Study Guides

GLENCOE TECHNOLOGY

☐ NATIONAL GEOGRAPHIC

WORLD REGIONS VIDEO PROGRAM

Unit 11, Australia, Oceania, and Antarctica
The following segments enhance the study of this unit:

- **Dream of a Lifetime**
- **Australia's Pioneers**
- **Haka Tradition**

CHAPTER CULMINATING ACTIVITY

Predicting Consequences Ask: How do you think this region will change in the future? Have students create a magazine essay from the viewpoint of a photojournalist traveling through the region in the year 2010 to answer the question. The essay may discuss the state of agriculture, mining and manufacturing, transportation and communications, and resource management. Students should include pictures or original drawings that supplement the narrative. Encourage them to review the chapter's photos as well as the text.

📘 EE2 Places and Regions: Standard 4
📘 EE4 Human Systems: Standards 11, 12
📘 EE5 Environment and Society: Standard 16

Have students visit the Web site at geography.glencoe.com to review Chapter 34 and take the **Self-Check Quiz.**

GLENCOE TECHNOLOGY

Use *MindJogger Videoquiz* to review the Chapter 34 content.

Reviewing Key Terms

1. station; introduced species
2. marsupial
3. Diatoms; food web
4. El Niño-Southern Oscillation
5. grazier
6. copra
7. ozone layer

Reviewing Facts
SECTION 1

1. Agriculture is important to all countries in the region. Mining and manufacturing are important to some, such as Australia, but not to many others.
2. tourism, banking, investment companies
3. All countries in the region depend on air and ship travel for trade, while Australia and New Zealand also have extensive roads, which permit internal trade. The Internet provides efficient communications in many areas.

SECTION 2

4. Wildlife: non-native species and destruction of habitats; forests: clearing for farming, wind erosion; soil: deforestation, salination; water: drought, salt, agricultural runoff, pollution, toxic waste
5. death, illness, genetic abnormalities, and environmental damage

Reviewing Key Terms

Write the key term that best completes each of the following sentences. Refer to the Terms to Know in the Summary & Study Guide on page 845.

1. Ranchers on an Australian _____ will sometimes build fences to keep out _____.
2. The kangaroo, one type of _____, is native to Australia.
3. _____ are part of the _____ of larger life-forms.
4. Disruptions to weather patterns in the South Pacific caused by _____ may be increasing.
5. A New Zealand _____ makes a living by raising sheep, beef cattle, and dairy cattle.
6. Many countries in Oceania export _____.
7. Scientists discovered a reduction in the _____ in the 1970s.

Reviewing Facts

SECTION 1

1. How does the importance of agriculture, mining, and manufacturing vary among South Pacific countries?
2. What service industries are developing in Australia and Oceania?
3. How have changes in transportation and communications affected the location and patterns of economic activities in the South Pacific region?

SECTION 2

4. What are the major threats to the region's wildlife, forests, soil, and water?
5. What have been the effects of nuclear testing in Oceania?
6. What effects in the South Pacific have occurred because of atmospheric and climatic changes?

Critical Thinking

1. **Finding and Summarizing the Main Idea** What are three critical challenges to agriculture in Australia?
2. **Identifying Cause and Effect** In what ways could mining operations in Antarctica interfere with scientific research programs there?
3. **Problem Solving** Use a graphic organizer like the one below to describe three steps that countries in Oceania might take to reduce the impact of tourism on coral reefs.

Reduce tourist impact ▷

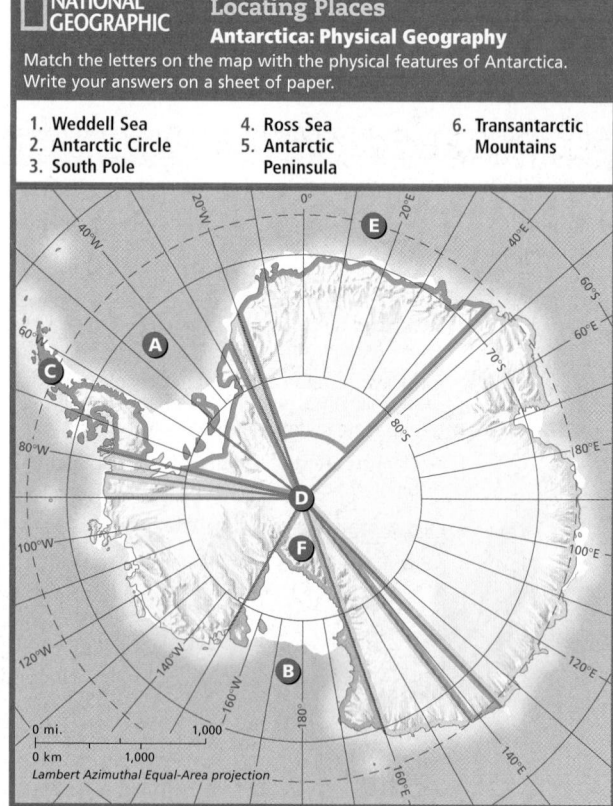

NATIONAL GEOGRAPHIC **Locating Places**
Antarctica: Physical Geography

Match the letters on the map with the physical features of Antarctica. Write your answers on a sheet of paper.

1. Weddell Sea
2. Antarctic Circle
3. South Pole
4. Ross Sea
5. Antarctic Peninsula
6. Transantarctic Mountains

Lambert Azimuthal Equal-Area projection

6. possibly a rise in rates of skin cancer and cataracts, droughts, cyclones, and global warming

Critical Thinking

1. little rainfall, need for vast grazing lands, limited land suitable for crops
2. Possible answers: Mining could cause scientific instruments to malfunction and alter the unpolluted conditions that benefit scientific research.
3. Accept all reasonable responses.

NATIONAL GEOGRAPHIC **Locating Places**

1. A 3. D 5. C
2. E 4. B 6. F

Using the Regional Atlas

1. southeastern Australia
2. rivers such as the Murray-Darling in Australia; oceans throughout the region from mining in coastal areas; forests

Using the Regional Atlas

Refer to the Regional Atlas on pages 784–787.

1. **Location** Where are most of the zinc deposits in the region?

2. **Human-Environment Interaction** Which physical features in the region are vulnerable to environmental damage from mining activities?

Thinking Like a Geographer

Using what you know about the physical geography of Oceania's islands, write a paragraph suggesting three ways these islands might address their lack of clean freshwater.

Problem-Solving Activity

Group Research Project With a small group of classmates, research one of the introduced species in Australia. Investigate the origins of the problem it has created, its effects on the environment, and suggested solutions. Brainstorm additional solutions, and evaluate each proposal. Prepare a report to the class on the solution you think is best.

GeoJournal

Descriptive Writing Using your GeoJournal data, select a human activity from each of the following areas: Australia, Oceania, and Antarctica. Then write a descriptive paragraph that compares how each of these activities has modified the physical environment.

Technology Activity

Using the Internet for Research Use the Internet to find information about global warming. List the sources you find on the Internet, and compare the different viewpoints on the issue of global warming. Then choose one solution that you support, and write an argument for adopting that solution.

Standardized Test Practice

Read the selection below. Then choose the best answer for the following multiple-choice question. If you have trouble answering the question, use the process of elimination to narrow your choices.

> *Rabbits are one of the more destructive wild animals that have been introduced into Australia. They damage the environment and reduce agricultural production. They compete with native wildlife for food and shelter, which reduces the populations of many native plants and animals. Because rabbits eat seedlings, there are fewer young plants to replace those that die naturally. Rabbits also compete with livestock for the same plants, eating them to below ground level. This loss of plant cover results in soil erosion.*

1. Based on the information in the paragraph, how do rabbits reduce agricultural production?

A They live in wheat-growing regions and eat the wheat seedlings.

B They compete with native wildlife for food.

C Dead plants are not replaced by enough new plants to prevent soil erosion.

D They eat the plants that provide food for livestock and cause soil erosion by eliminating plant cover.

 Look for the best answer choice for the question. The best answer choice is the one that offers *the most* correct information in response to the question.

 CHAPTER BONUS TEST QUESTION

How is air travel used in the South Pacific region? *(It is used to reach isolated places in the outback, to herd cattle, to carry tourists, to travel between small islands, and to bring supplies to Antarctica.)*

Thinking Like a Geographer

Possible answers may include water treatment plants, desalination, and improved sanitation methods.

Problem-Solving Activity

Proposed solutions will depend on the introduced species chosen. Students should follow the steps outlined in the "SkillBuilder" feature on page 844.

GeoJournal

Students might select an activity, such as transportation, mining, or tourism, and compare how it modifies the environment in each area.

Technology Activity

Students should list their Internet sources and provide clearly written summaries of at least two viewpoints. The chosen solution should be supported by well-reasoned arguments.

847

Appendix

CONTENTS

HONORING AMERICA

Flag Etiquette

Over the years, Americans have developed rules and customs concerning the use and display of the flag. One of the most important things every American should remember is to treat the flag with respect.

- The flag should be raised and lowered by hand and displayed only from sunrise to sunset. On special occasions, it may be displayed at night, but it should be illuminated.

- The flag may be displayed on all days, weather permitting, particularly on national and state holidays and on historic and special occasions.

- No flag may be flown above the American flag or to the right of it at the same height.

- The flag should never touch the ground or floor beneath it.

- The flag may be flown at half-staff by order of the president, usually to mourn the death of a public official.

- The flag may be flown upside down only to signal distress.

- When the flag becomes old and tattered, it should be destroyed by burning. According to an approved custom, the Union (stars on blue field) is first cut from the flag; then the two pieces, which no longer form a flag, are burned.

★ ★ ★ ★ ★ ★ ★

The Star-Spangled Banner

O! say can you see, by the dawn's early light,
What so proudly we hail'd at the twilight's last gleaming,
Whose broad stripes and bright stars through the perilous fight,
O'er the ramparts we watched, were so gallantly streaming?
And the Rockets' red glare, the Bombs bursting in air,
Gave proof through the night that our Flag was still there;
O! say, does that star-spangled banner yet wave
O'er the Land of the free and the home of the brave!

The Pledge of Allegiance

I pledge allegiance to the Flag of the United States of America and to the Republic for which it stands, one Nation under God, indivisible, with liberty and justice for all.

Glossary

A

aborigine an area's original inhabitants (p. 662)

absolute location the exact position of a place on the earth's surface (p. 20)

accretion a slow process in which a sea plate slides under a continental plate, creating debris that can cause continents to grow outward (p. 40)

acid deposition wet or dry airborne acids that fall to the earth (p. 321)

acid rain precipitation carrying large amounts of dissolved acids which damages buildings, forests, and crops, and kills wildlife (pp. 166, 321)

acupuncture an ancient practice that involves inserting fine needles into the body at specific points in order to cure disease and ease pain (p. 677)

alluvial plain floodplain, such as the Indo-Gangetic Plain in South Asia, on which flooding rivers have deposited rich soil (p. 572)

alluvial-soil deposits rich soil made up of sand and mud deposited by running water (p. 423)

altiplano Spanish for "high plain," a region in Peru and Bolivia encircled by the Andes peaks (p. 194)

amendment in U.S. history, official changes made to the Constitution (p. 144)

apartheid policy of strict separation of the races adopted in South Africa in the 1940s (p. 524)

aquaculture the cultivation of seafood (p. 695)

aquifer underground water-bearing layers of porous rock, sand, or gravel (pp. 49, 470)

arable suitable for growing crops (p. 464)

archipelago a group or chain of islands (pp. 646, 720)

artesian water underground water supply that is under enough pressure to rise into wells without being pumped (p. 794)

Asian Pacific Economic Cooperation Group (APEC) a trade group, whose members are Japan, China, South Korea, and Taiwan, that ensures that trade among the member countries is efficient and fair (p. 689)

Association of Southeast Asian Nations (ASEAN) organization formed in 1967 to promote regional development and trade in Southeast Asia (p. 763)

atheism the belief that there is no God (p. 376)

atmosphere a layer of gases that surrounds the earth (p. 35)

atoll ring-shaped island formed by coral building up along the rim of an underwater volcano (p. 796)

autocracy government in which a single individual possesses the power and authority to rule (p. 87)

avalanche mass of ice, snow, or rock that slides down a mountainside (p. 279)

axis an imaginary line that runs through the center of the earth between the North and South Poles (p. 56)

B

batik method of dyeing cloth to produce beautiful patterns, developed in Indonesia and Malaysia (p. 751)

bazaar a traditional marketplace ranging from a single street of stalls to an entire city district (p. 456)

bedouin member of the nomadic desert peoples of North Africa and Southwest Asia (p. 455)

bilingual speaking or using two languages (p. 148)

Bill of Rights the first 10 amendments to the United States Constitution (p. 144)

biologist scientist who studies plant and animal life (p. 324)

biomass plant and animal waste used especially as a source of fuel (p. 613)

biosphere the part of the earth where life exists (p. 35)

birthrate the number of births per year for every 1,000 people (p. 76)

black market any illegal market where scarce or illegal goods are sold, usually at high prices (p. 388)

blizzard a snowstorm with winds of more than 35 miles per hour, temperatures below freezing, and visibility of less than 500 feet for 3 hours or more (p. 125)

Bolsheviks a revolutionary group in Russia led by Vladimir Ilyich Lenin (p. 370)

boomerang curved throwing stick used by Aborigines for hunting in Australia (p. 817)

buffer state neutral territory between rival powers (p. 743)

C

cabinet heads of departments in the U.S. government who advise the president (p. 144)

calligraphy the art of beautiful handwriting (p. 679)

campesinos farm workers; generally, people who live and work in rural areas (p. 238)

canopy top layer of a rain forest, where the tops of tall trees form a continuous layer of leaves (p. 200)

cartography the science of mapmaking (p. 24)

cash crop farm crop grown to be sold or traded rather than used by the farm family (pp. 238, 538, 612, 760)

cataract a large waterfall (p. 500)

Glossary

caudillo a Latin American political leader from the late 1800s on, often a military dictator (p. 224)

cereal any grain, such as barley, oats, or wheat, grown for food (p. 431)

chaparral type of vegetation made up of dense forests of shrubs and short trees, common in Mediterranean climates (pp. 68, 281)

chernozem (cher•nuh•ZYAWM) rich, black topsoil found in the North European Plain, especially in Russia and Ukraine (p. 346)

chinampas floating farming islands made by the Aztec (p. 221)

chinook seasonal warm wind that blows down the Rockies in late winter and early spring (p. 124)

Chipko India's "tree-hugger" movement that protects forests through reforestation and by supporting limited timber production (p. 621)

chlorofluorocarbon chemical substance, found mainly in liquid coolants, that damages the earth's protective ozone layer (p. 695)

city-state in ancient Greece, independent community consisting of a city and the surrounding lands (p. 295)

clan tribal community or large group of people related to one another (pp. 529, 670, 817)

clear-cutting cutting down whole forests when removing timber (p. 165)

climate weather patterns typical for an area over a long period of time (p. 55)

Cold War power struggle between the Soviet Union and the United States after World War II (pp. 298, 371)

collective farm under communism, a large, state-owned farm on which farmers received wages plus a share of products and profits; also called a kolkhoz (p. 317)

command economy economic system in which economic decisions about production and distribution are made by some central authority (pp. 89, 388, 685)

commercial farming farming organized as a business (p. 538)

commodity goods produced for sale (pp. 158, 465)

commune a collective farming community whose members share work and products (p. 686)

communism society based on equality in which workers would control industrial production (pp. 298, 370)

condensation the process of excess water vapor changing into liquid water when warm air cools (p. 47)

coniferous trees that have cones and needle-shaped leaves, including many evergreens that keep their foliage throughout the winter (p. 68)

conquistador Spanish term for "conqueror," referring to soldiers who conquered Native Americans in Latin America (p. 222)

conservation farming a land-management technique that helps protect farmland (p. 539)

Constitution plan of government made for the United States in 1787 (p. 144)

consumer goods goods that directly satisfy human wants (p. 388)

continental drift the theory that the continents were once joined and then slowly drifted apart (p. 38)

continental shelf the part of a continent that extends underwater (p. 36)

cooperative a voluntary organization whose members work together and share expenses and profits (p. 686)

copra dried meat of a coconut (p. 834)

coral limestone deposits formed from the skeletons of tiny sea creatures (p. 795)

cordillera parallel chains or ranges of mountains (pp. 194, 719)

Coriolis effect an effect that causes the prevailing winds to blow diagonally rather than along strict north-south or east-west lines (p. 62)

cottage industry a business that employs workers in their homes (p. 615)

crevasse huge, deep crack that forms in thick ice or snow (p. 803)

Crusades series of religious wars (A.D. 1100–1300) in which European Christians tried to retake Palestine from Muslim rule (p. 296)

cultural diffusion the spread of new knowledge and skills from one culture to another (p. 84)

culture way of life of a group of people who share beliefs and similar customs (p. 80)

culture hearth a center where cultures developed and from which ideas and traditions spread outward (pp. 84, 447, 668)

culture region division of the earth based on a variety of factors, including government, social groups, economic systems, language, or religion (p. 83)

cuneiform Sumerian writing system using wedge-shaped symbols pressed into clay tablets (p. 447)

current cold or warm stream of seawater that flows in the oceans, generally in a circular pattern (p. 62)

cyclone storm with heavy rains and high winds that blow in a circular pattern around an area of low atmospheric pressure (pp. 579, 767)

czar ruler of Russia until the 1917 revolution (p. 369)

D

Dalits the "oppressed"; in India, people assigned to the lowest social class (p. 623)

death rate the number of deaths per year for every 1,000 people (p. 76)

deciduous trees, usually broad leaved such as oak and maple, that lose their leaves in autumn (p. 68)

deforestation the loss or destruction of forests, mainly for logging or farming (pp. 242, 507)

delta alluvial deposit at a river's mouth that looks like the Greek letter delta (Δ) (p. 503)

democracy any system of government in which leaders rule with consent of the citizens (p. 88)

desalination the removal of salt from seawater to make it usable for drinking and farming (pp. 48, 470)

desertification process in which arable land is turned into desert (pp. 508, 694)

developed country country that has a great deal of technology and manufacturing (p. 93)

developing country country in the process of becoming industrialized (pp. 93, 238)

dharma in Hinduism, a person's moral duty, based on class distinctions, which guides his or her life (p. 593)

dialect local form of a language used in a particular place or by a certain group (pp. 213, 302)

diatoms plankton that live in cold ocean water (p. 841)

dikes large banks of earth and stone that hold back water (p. 272)

dissident a citizen who speaks out against government policies (p. 689)

divide a high point or ridge that determines the direction rivers flow (p. 118)

doldrums a frequently windless area near the Equator (pp. 62, 802)

domesticate to adapt plants and animals from the wild to make them useful to people (pp. 446, 520)

dominion a partially self-governing country with close ties to another country (pp. 144, 820)

doubling time the number of years it takes a population to double in size (p. 76)

dry farming farming method used in dry regions in which land is plowed and planted deeply to hold water in the soil (pp. 143, 321)

dynasty a ruling house or continuing family of rulers, especially in China (p. 669)

dzong a fortified monastery of Bhutan, South Asia (p. 604)

E

e-commerce selling and buying on the Internet (p. 542)

economic sanctions trade restrictions (p. 689)

ecosystem the complex community of interdependent living things in a given environment (p. 22)

ecotourism tourism based on concern for the environment (pp. 546, 617)

El Niño a periodic reversal of the pattern of ocean currents and water temperatures in the mid-Pacific region (p. 63)

El Niño-Southern Oscillation (ENSO) a seasonal weather event that can cause droughts in Australia and powerful cyclones in the South Pacific (p. 841)

embargo a ban on trade (pp. 452, 468)

endemic native plant or animal species (p. 728)

Enlightenment a movement during the 1700s, emphasizing the importance of reason and questioning traditions and values (p. 297)

environmentalist person actively concerned with the quality and protection of the environment (p. 322)

equinox one of two days (about March 21 and September 23) on which the sun is directly above the Equator, making day and night equal in length (p. 56)

erosion wearing away of the earth's surface by wind, flowing water, or glaciers (p. 42)

escarpment steep cliff or slope between a higher and lower land surface (pp. 196, 500)

estuary an area where the tide meets a river current (pp. 197, 503)

ethnic cleansing the expelling from a country or killing of rival ethnic groups (p. 288)

ethnic diversity differences among groups of people based on their origins, languages, customs, or beliefs (p. 439)

ethnic group group of people who share common ancestry, language, religion, customs, or combination of such characteristics (pp. 82, 288, 363)

European Union an organization whose goal is to unite Europe so that goods, services, and workers can move freely among member countries (pp. 300, 313)

eutrophication process by which a body of water becomes too rich in dissolved nutrients, leading to plant growth that depletes oxygen (p. 168)

evaporation process of converting into vapor (p. 47)

exports commodities sent from one country to another for purposes of trade (p. 237)

extended family household made up of several generations of family members (pp. 229, 529)

extinction the disappearance or end of a species of animal or plant (p. 546)

F

fale traditional type of home in Samoa with open sides and thatched roof (p. 826)

fall line a boundary in the eastern United States where the higher land of the Piedmont drops to the lower Atlantic coastal plain (p. 118)

farm cooperative organization in which farmers share in growing and selling farm products (p. 317)

fault a crack or break in the earth's crust (pp. 40, 500)

fauna the animal life of a region (p. 724)

federal system form of government in which powers are divided between the national government and the state or provincial government (p. 87)

feudalism in medieval Europe and Japan, system of government in which powerful lords gave land to nobles in return for pledges of loyalty (p. 296)

fishery areas (freshwater or saltwater) in which fish or sea animals are caught (p. 120)

fjord (fee•YORD) long, steep-sided glacial valley now filled by seawater (p. 272)

flora the plant life of a region (p. 724)

foehn (FUHN) dry wind that blows from the leeward sides of mountains, sometimes melting snow and causing avalanches; term used mainly in Europe (p. 279)

fold a bend in layers of rock, sometimes caused by plate movement (p. 40)

food web the interlinking chains of predators and their food sources in an ecosystem (p. 840)

formal region a region defined by a common characteristic, such as production of a product (p. 21)

free port port city, such as Singapore, where goods can be unloaded, stored, and reshipped without the payment of import duties (p. 764)

free trade the removal of trade barriers so that goods can flow freely between countries (p. 94)

functional region a central point and the surrounding territory linked to it (p. 21)

futbol Spanish term for soccer (p. 230)

G

gauchos the cowhands of Argentina and Uruguay (p. 197)

genetically modified foods foods whose genes have been altered to make them grow bigger or faster or more resistant to pests (p. 317)

geographic information systems computer tools for processing and organizing details and satellite images with other pieces of information (p. 25)

glaciation the process whereby glaciers form and spread (p. 272)

glacier large body of ice that moves across the surface of the earth (p. 42)

glasnost Russian term for a new "openness," part of Mikhail Gorbachev's reform plans (p. 371)

global warming gradual warming of the earth and its atmosphere that may be caused in part by pollution and an increase in the greenhouse effect (pp. 58, 322)

glyph picture writing carved in stone (p. 221)

Good Friday Peace Agreement paved the way for Protestant and Roman Catholic communities to share political power in Northern Ireland (p. 304)

grazier person who raises sheep or cattle (p. 834)

greenhouse effect the capacity of certain gases in the atmosphere to trap heat, thereby warming the earth (pp. 58, 322)

green revolution program, begun in the 1960s, to produce higher-yielding, more productive strains of wheat, rice, and other food crops (p. 613)

grid system pattern formed as the lines of latitude and longitude cross one another (p. 20)

gross domestic product (GDP) the value of goods and services created within a country in a year (p. 465)

groundwater water within the earth that supplies wells and springs (pp. 49, 167)

guru a teacher or spiritual guide (p. 601)

H

habitat area with conditions suitable for certain plants or animals to live (p. 546)

haiku form of Japanese poetry originally consisting of 17 syllables and three lines, often about nature (p. 678)

hajj in Islam, the yearly pilgrimage to Makkah (p. 466)

headwaters the sources of river waters (p. 118)

heavy industry the manufacture of machinery and equipment needed for factories and mines (p. 317)

hemisphere half of a sphere or globe, as in the earth's Northern and Southern Hemispheres (p. 20)

hieroglyphics Egyptian writing system using pictures and symbols to represent words or sounds (p. 447)

Holocaust the mass killings of 6 million Jews by Germany's Nazi leaders during World War II (p. 298)

homogeneous of the same or similar kind or nature (p. 663)

human-environment interaction the study of the interrelationship between people and their physical environment (p. 22)

human geography also called cultural geography; the study of human activities and their relationship to the cultural and physical environments (p. 24)

hurricane a large, powerful windstorm that forms over warm ocean waters (p. 125)

hydroelectric power electrical energy generated by falling water (pp. 197, 348)

hydrosphere the watery areas of the earth, including oceans, lakes, rivers, and other bodies of water (p. 35)

hypothesis a scientific explanation for an event (p. 69)

icon religious image, usually including a picture of Jesus, Mary, or a saint, used mainly by Orthodox Christians (p. 377)

ideogram a pictorial character or symbol that represents a specific meaning or idea (p. 674)

immigration the movement of people into one country from another (p. 133)

impressionism artistic style that developed in Europe in the late 1800s and tried to show the natural appearance of objects with dabs or strokes of color (p. 305)

indigenous native to a place (p. 212)

industrial capitalism an economic system in which business leaders use profits to expand their companies (p. 297)

industrialization transition from an agricultural society to one based on industry (p. 93)

infrastructure the basic urban necessities like streets and utilities (pp. 443, 540)

insular constituting an island, as in Java (p. 720)

intelligentsia intellectual elite (p. 378)

interdependent relying on one another for goods, services, and ideas (p. 763)

introduced species plants and animals placed in areas other than their native habitat (p. 839)

jai alai (HY•LY) traditional handball-type game popular with Mexicans and Cubans (p. 231)

Japan Current a warm-water ocean current that adds moisture to the winter monsoons (p. 655)

jati in traditional Hindu society, a social group that defines a family's occupation and social standing (p. 588)

jazz musical form that developed in the United States in the early 1900s, blending African rhythms and European harmonies (p. 148)

jute plant fiber used to make string and cloth (p. 612)

karma in Hindu belief, the sum of good and bad actions in one's present and past lives (p. 593)

kolkhoz in the Soviet Union, a small farm worked by farmers who shared in the farm's production and profits (p. 390)

krill tiny shrimplike sea animals that live in cold Antarctic oceans (p. 798)

kums term for deserts in Central Asia (p. 425)

lagoon shallow pool of water at the center of an atoll (p. 796)

lama Buddhist religious leader (p. 675)

language family group of related languages that have all developed from one earlier language (pp. 81, 303)

latifundia in Latin America, large agricultural estates owned by families or corporations (p. 238)

leach to wash nutrients out of the soil (p. 506)

leeward facing away from the direction from which the wind is blowing (p. 64)

lichens sturdy small plants that grow like a crust on rocks or tree trunks (p. 803)

light industry manufacturing aimed at making consumer goods such as textiles or food processing rather than heavy machinery (p. 317)

lingua franca a common language used among people with different native languages (p. 526)

literacy rate the percentage of people in a given place who can read and write (p. 150)

lithosphere surface land areas of the earth's crust, including continents and ocean basins (p. 35)

llanos (LAH•nohs) fertile plains in inland areas of Colombia and Venezuela (p. 196)

location a specific place on the earth (p. 20)

lode deposit of minerals (p. 761)

loess (LEHS) fine, yellowish-brown topsoil made up of particles of silt and clay, usually carried by the wind (pp. 42, 275, 648)

longhouse in rural areas of Indonesia and Malaysia, a large, elevated building where people from several related families live (p. 752)

M

Maastricht Treaty a 1992 meeting of European governments in Maastricht, the Netherlands, that formed the European Union (p. 314)

magma molten rock that is pushed up from the earth's mantle (p. 38)

malnutrition faulty or inadequate nutrition (p. 230)

mantle thick middle layer of the earth's interior structure, consisting of dense, hot rock (p. 38)

mantra in Hinduism, a sacred word or phrase repeated in prayers and chants (p. 601)

manuka small shrubs that grow in plateau regions of New Zealand (p. 803)

maquiladoras in Mexico, manufacturing plants set up by foreign firms (p. 239)

maritime concerned with travel or shipping by sea (p. 741)

market economy an economic system based on free enterprise, in which businesses are privately owned, and production and prices are determined by supply and demand (pp. 89, 157, 388)

marsupial mammal whose offspring mature in a pouch on the mother's abdomen (p. 839)

mass culture popular culture spread by media such as radio and television (p. 525)

megacities cities with more than 10 million people (p. 217)

megalopolis a "super-city" that is made up of several large and small cities such as the area between Boston and Washington, D.C. (pp. 136, 591)

meltwater water formed by melting snow and ice (p. 321)

merchant marine a country's fleet of ships that engage in commerce or trade (p. 691)

meteorology the study of weather and weather forecasting (p. 24)

metropolitan area region that includes a central city and its surrounding suburbs (p. 135)

mica silicate mineral that readily splits into thin, shiny sheets (p. 574)

Middle Ages the period of European history from about A.D. 500 to about 1500 (p. 296)

migration the movement of people from place to place (p. 79)

minifundia in Latin America, small farms that produce food chiefly for family use (p. 238)

mistral strong northerly wind from the Alps that can bring cold air to southern France (p. 280)

mixed economy an economy in which the government supports and regulates enterprise through decisions that affect the marketplace (p. 89)

mixed farming raising several kinds of crops and live-stock on the same farm (p. 317)

mixed forest forest with both coniferous and deciduous trees (p. 68)

mobility able to move from place to place (p. 137)

monopoly total control of a type of industry by one person or one company (p. 162)

monotheism belief in one God (p. 448)

monsoon in Asia, seasonal wind that brings warm, moist air from the oceans in summer and cold, dry air from inland in winter (pp. 579, 654)

moraine piles of rocky debris left by melting glaciers (p. 42)

mosaic picture or design made with small pieces of colored stone, glass, shell, or tile (p. 228)

mosque in Islam, a house of public worship (p. 448)

movement ongoing movement of people, goods, and ideas (p. 22)

mural wall painting (p. 228)

N

nationalism belief in the right of each people to be an independent nation (p. 449)

nationalities large, distinct ethnic groups within a country (p. 364)

nationalize to place a company or industry under government control (p. 450)

Native American North America's first immigrant, who probably moved into the region from Asia thousands of years ago (p. 134)

natural increase the growth rate of a population; the difference between birthrate and death rate (p. 76)

natural resource substance from the earth that is not made by people but can be used by them (p. 91)

natural vegetation plant life that grows in a certain area if people have not changed the natural environment (p. 66)

nirvana in Buddhism, ultimate state of peace and insight toward which people strive (p. 594)

North American Free Trade Agreement (NAFTA) trade agreement made in 1994 by Canada, the United States, and Mexico (p. 240)

nuclear family family group made up of husband, wife, and children (p. 529)

nuclear proliferation the spreading development of nuclear arms (p. 623)

nuclear waste the by-product of producing nuclear power (p. 398)

O

oasis small area in a desert where water and vegetation are found (pp. 67, 429)

oligarchy system of government in which a small group holds power (p. 88)

oral tradition stories passed down from generation to generation by word of mouth (p. 528)

organic farming the use of natural substances rather than chemical fertilizers and pesticides to enrich the soil and grow crops (p. 318)

ozone layer atmospheric layer with protective gases that prevents solar rays from reaching the earth's surface (p. 841)

P

paddy flooded field in which rice is grown (p. 760)

pagoda a style of architecture most often found in traditional East Asian buildings, marked by gracefully curved tile roofs in the tower style (p. 679)

pampas grassy, treeless plains of southern South America (p. 196)

parliament in Canada, national legislature made up of the Senate and the House of Commons (p. 145)

pastoralism the raising of livestock (p. 430)

patois dialects that blend elements of indigenous, European, African, and Asian languages (p. 213)

patriarch the head of the Eastern Orthodox Church (p. 377)

patriotism love for or devotion to one's country (p. 151)

perceptual region a region defined by popular feelings and images rather than by objective data (p. 21)

perestroika (PEHR•uh•STROY•kuh) in Russian, "restructuring"; part of Gorbachev's plan for reforming Soviet government (p. 371)

permafrost permanently frozen layer of soil beneath the surface of the ground (pp. 68, 281, 349)

pesticide chemical used to kill insects, rodents, and other pests (p. 398)

petrochemical chemical product derived from petroleum or natural gas (p. 465)

phosphate natural mineral containing chemical compounds often used in fertilizers (p. 426)

physical geography the study of Earth's physical features (p. 24)

pidgin English a dialect mixing English and a local language (p. 813)

pipeline long network of underground or aboveground pipes (p. 162)

place a particular space with physical and human meaning (p. 21)

plate tectonics the term scientists use to describe the activities of continental drift and magma flow which create many of Earth's physical features (p. 38)

poaching illegal hunting of protected animals (pp. 546, 619)

pogrom in czarist Russia, an attack on Jews carried out by government troops or officials (p. 378)

polder low-lying area from which seawater has been drained to create new farmland (p. 272)

pollution the existence of impure, unclean, or poisonous substances in the air, water, or land (p. 94)

population density the average number of people in a square mile or square kilometer (p. 77)

population distribution the pattern of population in a country, a continent, or the world (p. 77)

post-industrial an economy with less emphasis on heavy industry and manufacturing and more emphasis on services and technology (p. 158)

prairie an inland grassland area (pp. 68, 124)

precipitation moisture that falls to the earth as rain, sleet, hail, or snow (p. 47)

prevailing wind wind in a region that blows in a fairly constant directional pattern (p. 62)

primate city a city that dominates a country's economy, culture, and government and in which population is concentrated; usually the capital (pp. 217, 738)

privatization a change to private ownership of state-owned companies and industries (p. 389)

prophet person believed to be a messenger from God (p. 448)

Q

qanat underground canal used in water systems of ancient Persians (p. 447)

quipu (KEE•poo) knotted cords of various lengths and colors used by the Inca to keep financial records (p. 222)

R

radioactive material material contaminated by residue from the generation of nuclear energy (p. 397)

rain shadow dry area found on the leeward side of a mountain range (p. 64)

raj Hindu word for empire (p. 595)

realism artistic style portraying everyday life that developed in Europe during the mid-1800s (p. 305)

reforestation replanting young trees or seeds on lands where trees have been cut or destroyed (p. 244)

Reformation religious movement that began in Germany in the 1400s, leading to the establishment of Protestant churches (p. 297)

refugee one who flees his or her home for safety (p. 288)

regions places united by specific characteristics (p. 21)

reincarnated in Hindu belief, being reborn repeatedly in different forms, until one has overcome earthly desires (p. 593)

relative location location in relation to other places (p. 20)

Renaissance in Europe, a 300-year period of renewed interest in classical learning and the arts, beginning in the 1300s (p. 296)

reparations a payment for damages (p. 298)

republic form of government without a monarch in which people elect their officials (p. 142)

retooling converting old factories for use in new industries (p. 161)

revolution in astronomy, the earth's yearly trip around the sun, taking 365¼ days (p. 56)

rift valley a crack in the earth's surface created by shifting (p. 500)

romanticism artistic style emphasizing individual emotions that developed in Europe in the late 1700s and early 1800s as a reaction to industrialization (p. 305)

Russification in nineteenth-century Russia, a government program that required everyone in the empire to speak Russian and to become a Christian (p. 370)

S

sadhu a Hindu hermit or holy man (p. 602)

samurai in medieval Japan, a class of professional soldiers who lived by a strict code of personal honor and loyalty to a noble (p. 670)

sanitation disposal of waste products (p. 516)

satellite a country controlled by another country, notably Eastern European countries controlled by the Soviet Union by the end of World War II (p. 371)

savanna a tropical grassland containing scattered trees (p. 507)

sedentary farming farming carried on at permanent settlements (p. 538)

serf laborer obliged to remain on the land where he or she works (p. 369)

service center convenient business location for rural dwellers (p. 518)

service industry business that provides a service instead of making goods (p. 238)

shamanism belief in a leader who can communicate with spirits (p. 675)

shantytowns makeshift communities on the edges of cities (p. 244)

shifting cultivation clearing forests to plant fields for a few years and then abandoning them (p. 770)

shifting farming method in which farmers move every few years to find better soil (p. 538)

shogun military ruler in medieval Japan (p. 670)

sickle large, curved knife with a handle, used to cut grass or tall grains (p. 760)

sirocco hot desert wind that can blow air and dust from North Africa to western Europe's Mediterranean coast (pp. 280–281)

slash-and-burn farming traditional farming method in which all trees and plants in an area are cut and burned to add nutrients to the soil (p. 244)

smog haze caused by the interaction of ultraviolet solar radiation with chemical fumes from automobile exhausts and other pollution sources (pp. 69, 167)

socialism political philosophy in which the government owns the means of production (p. 370)

socialist realism realistic style of art and literature that glorified Soviet ideals and goals (p. 380)

socioeconomic status level of income and education (p. 150)

solstice one of two days (about June 21 and December 22) on which the sun's rays strike directly on the Tropic of Cancer or Tropic of Capricorn, marking the beginning of summer or winter (p. 57)

sovereignty self-rule (p. 365)

sovkhoz in the Soviet Union, a large farm owned and run by the state (p. 390)

sphere of influence area of a country in which a foreign power has political or economic control (p. 743)

spreading a process by which new land is created when sea plates pull apart and magma wells up between the plates (p. 40)

state farm under communism, a state-owned farm managed by government officials (p. 317)

station Australian term for an outlying ranch or large farm (p. 834)

steppe wide, grassy plains of Eurasia; also, similar semiarid climate regions elsewhere (p. 355)

Strine colloquial English spoken in Australia (p. 813)

stupa a dome-shaped structure that serves as a Buddhist shrine (p. 604)

subcontinent large landmass that is part of a continent but still distinct from it, such as India (p. 569)

subduction a process by which mountains can form as sea plates dive beneath continental plates (p. 39)

subsistence crop a crop grown mainly to feed the farmer's family (p. 760)

subsistence farming producing just enough food for a family or a village to survive (pp. 538, 826)

suburbs outlying communities around a city (p. 135)

Sunbelt mild climate region, southern United States (p. 135)

supercells violent thunderstorms that can spawn tornadoes (p. 124)

sustainable development technological and economic growth that does not deplete the human and natural resources of a given area (pp. 242, 619)

syncretism a blending of beliefs and practices from different religions into one faith (p. 228)

taiga Russian term for the vast subarctic forest, mostly evergreens, that covers much of Russia and Siberia (p. 353)

tariff a tax on imports or exports (p. 163)

temperature degree of hotness or coldness measured on a set scale, such as Fahrenheit or Celsius (p. 56)

tierra caliente Spanish term for "hot land"; the lowest altitude zone of Latin American highlands climates (p. 203)

tierra fría Spanish term for "cold land"; the highest altitude zone of Latin American highlands climates (p. 203)

tierra templada Spanish term for "temperate land"; the middle altitude zone of Latin American highlands climates (p. 203)

timberline elevation above which it is too cold for trees to grow (pp. 124, 279)

trade deficit spending more money on imports than earning from exports (pp. 163, 689)

trade surplus earning more money from export sales than spending for imports (pp. 163, 689)

traditional economy a system in which tradition and custom control all economic activity; exists in only a few parts of the world today (p. 89)

tributary smaller river or stream that feeds into a larger river (p. 118)

trust territory region placed by United Nations under temporary political and economic control of another country after World War II (p. 819)

tsunami Japanese term used for a huge sea wave caused by an undersea earthquake (p. 646)

tundra vast, treeless plains in cold northern climates, characterized by permafrost and small, low plants, such as mosses and shrubs (p. 352)

typhoon a violent tropical storm that forms in the Pacific Ocean, usually in late summer (pp. 655, 768, 802)

Underground Railroad an informal network of safe-houses, in the United States, that helped thousands of enslaved people escape to freedom (p. 143)

unitary system a government in which all key powers are given to the national or central government (p. 87)

universal suffrage equal voting rights for all adult citizens of a nation (p. 524)

urbanization the movement of people from rural areas into cities (pp. 135, 216, 290, 517, 737)

viceroy representative of the Spanish monarch appointed to enforce laws in colonial Latin America (p. 222)

wadi in the desert, a streambed that is dry except during a heavy rain (p. 424)

wat in Southeast Asia, a temple (p. 750)

water cycle regular movement of water from ocean to air to ground and back to the ocean (p. 47)

wattle woven framework made from acacia saplings by early Australian settlers to build homes (p. 801)

weather condition of the atmosphere in one place during a short period of time (p. 55)

weathering chemical or physical processes, such as freezing, that break down rocks (p. 42)

welfare state nation in which the government assumes major responsibility for people's welfare in areas such as health and education (p. 306)

windward facing toward the direction from which the wind is blowing (p. 64)

World Trade Organization (WTO) an international body that oversees trade agreements and settles trade disputes among countries (p. 690)

ziggurat large step-like temple of mud brick built in ancient Mesopotamia (p. 454)

A Gazetteer (GA•zuh•TIHR) is a geographic index or dictionary. It shows latitude and longitude for cities and certain other places. This Gazetteer lists most of the world's largest independent countries, their capitals, and several important geographic features. The page numbers tell where each entry can be found on a map in this book. As an aid to pronunciation, many entries are spelled phonetically.

A

Abidjan (AH•bee•JAHN) Capital and port city of Côte d'Ivoire, Africa. 5°N 4°W (p. 487)

Abu Dhabi (AH•boo DAH•bee) Capital of the United Arab Emirates, on the Persian Gulf. 24°N 54°E (p. 411)

Abuja (ah•BOO•jah) Capital of Nigeria. 8°N 9°E (p. 487)

Accra (AH•kruh) Capital and port city of Ghana. 6°N 0° longitude (p. 487)

Aconcagua Highest peak of the Andes and of the Western Hemisphere, in western Argentina near the Chilean border. 32°S 76°W (p. 182)

Addis Ababa (AHD•dihs AH•bah•BAH) Capital of Ethiopia. 9°N 39°E (p. 487)

Adriatic (AY•dree•A•tihk) **Sea** Arm of the Mediterranean Sea between the Balkan Peninsula and Italy. (p. 260)

Aegean (ee•JEE•uhn) **Sea** Arm of the Mediterranean Sea between Greece and Turkey. (p. 260)

Afghanistan (af•GA•nuh•STAN) Country in Central Asia, west of Pakistan. (p. 411)

Ahaggar Mountains Highest plateau region in the central Sahara. (p. 410)

Albania (al•BAY•nee•uh) Country on the east coast of the Adriatic Sea, south of Yugoslavia. (p. 261)

Algeria Country in North Africa. (p. 411)

Algiers (al•JIHRZ) Capital of Algeria. 37°N 3°E (p. 411)

Alps Mountain system extending through central Europe. (p. 260)

Altay Mountains Mountain system between western Mongolia and China and between Kazakhstan and southern Russia. (p. 636)

Amazon River River flowing through Peru and Brazil in South America and into the Atlantic Ocean. (p. 182)

Amman Capital of Jordan. 32°N 36°E (p. 411)

Amsterdam (AM•stuhr•DAM) Capital of the Netherlands. 52°N 5°E (p. 261)

Amu Darya River in Turkmenistan in central and western Asia. (p. 410)

Amur River River in northeast Asia. (p. 338)

Andes (AN•deez) Mountain system along western South America. (p. 182)

Andorra (an•DAWR•uh) Country in southern Europe, between France and Spain. (p. 261)

Angola (ang•GOH•luh) Country in Africa, south of the Democratic Republic of the Congo. (p. 487)

Ankara Capital of Turkey. 40°N 33°E (p. 411)

Antananarivo (AHN•tah•NAH•nah•REE•voh) Capital of Madagascar. 19°S 48°E (p. 487)

Antigua Island in the West Indies, part of independent Antigua and Barbuda. 18°N 61°W (p. 183)

Apennines Mountain range in central Italy. (p. 260)

Appalachian Mountains Mountain system in eastern North America. (p. 117)

Arabian Sea Part of the Indian Ocean between India and the Arabian Peninsula. (p. 410)

Aral Sea Inland sea between Kazakhstan and Uzbekistan. (p. 410)

Argentina (AHR•juhn•TEE•nuh) Country in South America, east of Chile. (p. 183)

Arkansas River River in south-central United States, emptying into the Mississippi River. (p. 117)

Armenia (ahr•MEE•nee•uh) Southeastern European country between the Black and Caspian Seas. (p. 261)

Ashkhabad (ASH•kuh•BAD) Capital of Turkmenistan. 40°N 58°E (p. 411)

Asmara Capital of Eritrea. 16°N 39°E (p. 487)

Astana Capital of Kazakhstan. 52°N 72°E (p. 411)

Asunción (ah•SOON•SYOHN) Capital of Paraguay. 25°S 58°W (p. 183)

Athens Capital of Greece. 38°N 24°E (p. 261)

Atlas Mountains Mountain range on the northern edge of the Sahara. (p. 410)

Australia Country and continent southeast of Asia. (p. 785)

Austria (AWS•tree•uh) Country in central Europe, east of Switzerland. (p. 261)

Azerbaijan (A•zuhr•by•JAHN) European-Asian country on the Caspian Sea. (p. 411)

B

Baghdad (BAG•DAD) Capital of Iraq. 33°N 44°E (p. 411)

Bahamas Independent state comprising a chain of islands, cays, and reefs southeast of Florida and north of Cuba. 24°N 76°W (p. 183)

Bahrain (bah•RAYN) Independent state in the western Persian Gulf. (p. 411)

Baku Capital of Azerbaijan. 40°N 50°E (p. 411)

Balkan Mountains Mountain range extending across central Bulgaria to the Black Sea. (p. 260)

Balkan Peninsula Peninsula in southeastern Europe bordered on the west by the Adriatic Sea. (p. 261)

Baltic Sea Arm of the Atlantic Ocean in northern Europe that connects with the North Sea. (p. 260)

Bamako (BAH•mah•KOH) Capital of Mali. 13°N 8°W (p. 487)

Gazetteer

Bangkok Capital of Thailand. 14°N 100°E (p. 711)

Bangladesh (BAHNG•gluh•DESH) Country in South Asia, bordered by India and Myanmar. (p. 561)

Bangui (bahng•GEE) Capital of the Central African Republic. 4°N 19°E (p. 487)

Banjul Capital of Gambia. 13°N 17°W (p. 487)

Barbados Island country between the Atlantic Ocean and the Caribbean Sea. 14°N 59°W (p. 183)

Barbuda Island in the West Indies, part of independent Antigua and Barbuda. 18°N 62°W (p. 183)

Barents Sea Part of the Arctic Ocean, north of Norway and Russia. (p. 338)

Bay of Bengal Part of the Indian Ocean between eastern India and Southeast Asia. (p. 560)

Beijing Capital of China. 40°N 116°E (p. 637)

Beirut (bay•ROOT) Capital of Lebanon. 34°N 36°E (p. 411)

Belarus (BEE•luh•ROOS) Eastern European country west of Russia. (p. 261)

Belgium (BEHL•juhm) Country in northwestern Europe, south of the Netherlands. (p. 261)

Belgrade Capital of Serbia. 45°N 21°E (p. 261)

Belize (buh•LEEZ) Country in Central America. (p. 183)

Belmopan (BEHL•moh•PAHN) Capital of Belize. 17°N 89°W (p. 183)

Benin (buh•NEEN) Country in western Africa. (p. 487)

Ben Nevis Peak in the highlands region of the Grampian Mountains in Scotland. 54°N 5°W (p. 273)

Bering Sea Part of the north Pacific Ocean, extending between the United States and Russia. (p. 117)

Berlin Capital of Germany. 53°N 13°E (p. 261)

Bern Capital of Switzerland. 47°N 7°E (p. 261)

Bhutan (boo•TAHN) Country in the eastern Himalaya, northeast of India. 27°N 91°E (p. 561)

Bishkek (bihsh•KEHK) Capital and largest city of Kyrgyzstan. 43°N 75°E (p. 411)

Bissau (bih•SOW) Capital of Guinea-Bissau. 12°N 16°W (p. 487)

Black Sea Sea between Europe and Asia. (p. 260)

Bloemfontein (BLOOM•FAHN•TAYN) Judicial capital of the Republic of South Africa. 29°S 26°E (p. 487)

Bogotá (BOH•goh•TAH) Capital of Colombia. 5°N 74°W (p. 183)

Bolivia Republic in west central South America. (p. 183)

Bosnia-Herzegovina (BAHZ•nee•uh HERT•suh• goh•VEE•nuh) Southeastern European country between Yugoslavia and Croatia. (p. 261)

Bosporus Strait between European and Asian Turkey, connecting the Sea of Marmara with the Black Sea. (p. 410)

Botswana (baht•SWAH•nuh) Country in Africa, north of the Republic of South Africa. (p. 487)

Brahmaputra River River that begins in Tibet, flows through northeast India and Bangladesh, and empties into the Bay of Bengal. (p. 560)

Brasília (bruh•ZIHL•yuh) Capital of Brazil. 16°S 48°W (p. 183)

Bratislava (BRAH•tuh•SLAH•vuh) Capital and largest city of Slovakia. 48°N 17°E (p. 261)

Brazil (bruh•ZIHL) Largest country in South America, in east-central South America. (p. 183)

Brazzaville (BRA•zuh•VIHL) Capital of Congo. 4°S 15°E (p. 487)

Brunei (bru•NY) Country on the northern coast of the island of Borneo. (p. 711)

Brussels Capital of Belgium. 51°N 4°E (p. 261)

Bucharest (BOO•kuh•REHST) Capital of Romania. 44°N 26°E (p. 261)

Budapest Capital of Hungary. 48°N 19°E (p. 261)

Buenos Aires (BWAY•nuhs AR•eez) Capital of Argentina. 34°S 58°W (p. 183)

Bujumbura (BOO•juhm•BUR•uh) Capital of Burundi. 3°S 29°E (p. 487)

Bulgaria (BUHL•GAR•ee•uh) Country in southeastern Europe, south of Romania. (p. 261)

Burkina Faso (bur•KEE•nuh FAH•soh) Country in western Africa, south of Mali. (p. 487)

Burundi (bu•ROON•dee) Country in central Africa at the northern end of Lake Tanganyika. (p. 487)

C

Cairo (KY•roh) Capital of Egypt. 31°N 32°E (p. 411)

Cambodia (kam•BOH•dee•uh) Country in Southeast Asia, south of Thailand. (p. 711)

Cameroon (KA•muh•ROON) Country in west Africa, on the northeast shore of the Gulf of Guinea. (p. 487)

Canada Country in northern North America. (p. 117)

Canberra Capital of Australia. 35°S 149°E (p. 785)

Cape Town Legislative capital of the Republic of South Africa. 34°S 18°E (p. 487)

Cape Verde Republic consisting of a group of volcanic islands in the Atlantic Ocean. 15°N 26°W (p. 487)

Caracas (kah•RAH•kahs) Capital of Venezuela. 11°N 67°W (p. 183)

Caribbean (KAR•uh•BEE•uhn) **Sea** Part of the Atlantic Ocean, bounded by the West Indies, South America, and Central America. (p. 182)

Carpathian Mountains Mountain range in eastern Europe in Slovakia and Romania. (p. 260)

Caspian (KAS•pee•uhn) **Sea** Salt lake between Europe and Asia. (p. 260)

Caucasus Mountains Mountain range in southwestern Russia. (p. 410)

Central African Republic Country in central Africa, south of Chad. (p. 487)

Central Siberian Plateau Tableland area in Siberia. (p. 338)

Chad Country in north central Africa. (p. 487)

Chao Phraya (chow PRY•uh) River in Thailand, flowing south into the Gulf of Thailand. (p. 710)

Chile (CHIH•lee) Western South American country, along the Pacific Ocean. (p. 183)

China (People's Republic of China) Country in eastern and central Asia. (p. 637)

Chisinau (KEE•shee•NOW) Capital and largest city of Moldova. 47°N 29°E (p. 261)

Colombia Republic in northern South America. (p. 183)

Colombo Capital of Sri Lanka. 7°N 80°E (p. 561)

Colorado Plateau Highlands region in the western United States. (p. 117)

Colorado River River in the western United States that flows through the Grand Canyon. (p. 117)

Columbia Plateau Flat plains area primarily in western Washington State in the United States. (p. 117)

Comoros (KAH•muh•ROHZ) **Islands** Island country in the Indian Ocean between the island of Madagascar and Africa. 13°S 43°E (p. 487)

Conakry (KAH•nuh•kree) Capital of Guinea. 10°N 14°W (p. 487)

Congo Country in equatorial Africa. (p. 487)

Congo, Democratic Republic of the African country on the Equator, north of Zambia and Angola. (p. 487)

Congo River River that runs through the Democratic Republic of the Congo. (p. 486)

Copenhagen (KOH•puhn•HAY•guhn) Capital of Denmark. 56°N 12°E (p. 261)

Costa Rica (KAWS•tah REE•kuh) Central American country, south of Nicaragua. (p. 183)

Côte d'Ivoire (KOHT dee•VWAHR) West African country, south of Mali. (p. 487)

Croatia (kroh•AY•shuh) Southeastern European country on the Adriatic Sea. (p. 261)

Cuba Island country southeast of Florida. 21°N 80°W (p. 183)

Cyprus Island country in the eastern Mediterranean Sea, south of Turkey. 35°N 31°E (p. 261)

Czech (CHEHK) **Republic** Central European country south of Germany and Poland. (p. 261)

D

Dakar Capital of Senegal. 15°N 17°W (p. 487)

Damascus Capital of Syria. 34°N 36°E (p. 411)

Danube River River in Europe that begins in Germany and flows into the Black Sea. (p. 260)

Dardanelles Strait between European and Asian Turkey, connecting the Sea of Marmara with the Aegean Sea. (p. 260)

Dar es Salaam (DAHR EHS suh•LAHM) Capital of Tanzania. 7°S 39°E (p. 487)

Darling River River in southeast Australia. (p. 710)

Deccan Plateau The peninsula of India south of the Narmada River. (p. 560)

Denmark Country in northwestern Europe, between the Baltic and North Seas. (p. 261)

Dhaka Capital of Bangladesh. 24°N 90°E (p. 561)

Djibouti (juh•BOO•tee) Country in East Africa, on the Gulf of Aden. (p. 487)

Dnieper (NEE•puhr) **River** River that begins in Russia, flows through Belarus and Ukraine, and then drains into the Black Sea. (p. 260)

Dniester (NEE•stuhr) **River** River in south-central Europe that begins in Ukraine and flows southeast to the Black Sea. (p. 260)

Dodoma (doh•DOH•mah) Future capital of Tanzania. 7°S 36°E (p. 487)

Doha (DOH•hah) Capital of Qatar. 25°N 51°E (p. 411)

Dominica Island republic in the West Indies, lying in the center of the Lesser Antilles. 15°N 61°W (p. 183)

Dominican Republic Republic occupying the eastern two-thirds of Hispaniola Island in the West Indies. 19°N 70°W (p. 183)

Don River River in southwestern Russia. (p. 260)

Drakensberg (DRAH•kuhnz•BUHRG) **Range** Mountain range in South Africa. (p. 486)

Dublin Capital of Ireland. 53°N 6°W (p. 261)

Dushanbe (doo•SHAM•buh) Capital and largest city of Tajikistan. 39°N 69°E (p. 411)

E

East Timor Island country in the Indonesian archipelago, northwest of Australia. (p. 711)

Eastern Ghats Mountain range in India. (p. 560)

Ecuador (EH•kwuh•DAWR) Country in South America, south of Colombia. (p. 183)

Egypt (EE•jihpt) Country in northern Africa on the Mediterranean Sea. (p. 411)

Elbe River River in central Europe. (p. 260)

Elburz Mountains Mountain range in northern Iran parallel to the shore of the Caspian Sea. (p. 410)

El Salvador (ehl SAL•vuh•DAWR) Country in Central America, southwest of Honduras. (p. 183)

Equatorial Guinea (EE•kwuh•TOHR•ee•uhl GIH•nee) Country in western Africa, south of Cameroon. (p. 487)

Eritrea (EHR•uh•TREE•uh) Country in northeast Africa, north of Ethiopia. (p. 487)

Ertis River River in northeastern Kazakhstan and the western part of Russia. *See also* Irtysh River. (p. 410)

Estonia (eh•STOH•nee•uh) Northern European country on the Baltic Sea. (p. 261)

Ethiopia (EE•thee•OH•pee•uh) Country in eastern Africa, north of Somalia and Kenya. (p. 487)

Euphrates (yu•FRAY•teez) **River** River in southwestern Asia that flows through Syria and Iraq and joins the Tigris River. (p. 410)

F

Fiji (FEE•jee) Country comprising an island group in the southwest Pacific Ocean. 19°S 175°E (p. 785)

Finland Country in northern Europe, east of Sweden. (p. 261)

France Country in western Europe. (p. 261)

Freetown Capital and port city of Sierra Leone, in western Africa. 9°N 13°W (p. 487)

French Guiana Overseas department of France on the northeast coast of South America. (p. 183)

G

Gabon (ga•BOHN) Country in western Africa, on the Atlantic Ocean. (p. 487)

Gaborone (GAH•boh•ROH•nay) Capital of Botswana, in southern Africa. 24°S 26°E (p. 487)

Gambia Country in western Africa. (p. 487)

Ganges (GAN•JEEZ) **Plain** A fertile plains region in northern India traversed by the Ganges River. (p. 560)

Ganges River River in northern India and Bangladesh that flows into the Bay of Bengal. (p. 560)

Georgetown Capital of Guyana. 8°N 58°W (p. 487)

Georgia Asian/European country bordering the Black Sea, south of Russia. (p. 411)

Germany (Federal Republic of Germany) Country in north central Europe. (p. 261)

Ghana (GAH•nuh) Country in western Africa, on the Gulf of Guinea. (p. 487)

Gobi Desert in Central Asia. (p. 636)

Godavari River River in central India. (p. 560)

Gran Chaco Region in south-central South America located in Paraguay, Bolivia, and Argentina. (p. 182)

Great Britain Kingdom in western Europe comprising England, Scotland, and Wales. (p. 261)

Great Dividing Range Chain of hills and mountains, on Australia's eastern coast. (p. 784)

Great Indian Desert Region of sandy desert in northwest India and southeast Pakistan. (p. 560)

Great Plains Rolling treeless area of central North America. (p. 117)

Great Salt Lake Large saltwater lake in Utah in the United States that has no outlet. (p. 117)

Great Slave Lake A lake in the south-central mainland of the Northwest Territories in Canada. (p. 117)

Greece Country in southern Europe, on the Balkan Peninsula. (p. 261)

Greenland Island in the northwestern Atlantic Ocean. 74°N 40°W (p. 117)

Grenada Island in the self-governing West Indies. 17°N 61°W (p. 183)

Guam Island in the western Pacific. It is an unincorporated United States territory. 13°N 144°E (p. 785)

Guatemala (GWAH•tuh•MAH•luh) Country in Central America, south of Mexico. (p. 183)

Guatemala City Capital of Guatemala and the largest city in Central America. 15°N 91°W (p. 183)

Guinea (GIH•nee) West African country on the Atlantic coast. 11°N 12°W (p. 487)

Guinea-Bissau (GIH•nee bih•SOW) West African country on the Atlantic coast. 12°N 20°W (p. 487)

Gulf of Aden Arm of the Indian Ocean between the Arabian Peninsula and Africa. (p. 410)

Gulf of Mexico Gulf on the southern coast of North America. (p. 182)

Gulf of Thailand Inlet of the South China Sea. (p. 710)

Guyana Republic in northern South America. (p. 183)

H

Hainan (HY•NAHN) Island province of China in the South China Sea. 19°N 109°E (p. 637)

Haiti (HAY•tee) Republic occupying the western third of Hispaniola Island in the West Indies. 19°N 72.25°W (p. 183)

Hanoi Capital of Vietnam. 21°N 106°E (p. 711)

Harare (huh•RAH•ray) Capital of Zimbabwe. 18°S 23°E (p. 487)

Havana Capital of Cuba. 23°N 82°W (p. 183)

Helsinki Capital of Finland. 60°N 24°E (p. 261)

Himalaya (HIH•muh•LAY•uh) Mountain range in South Asia, bordering the Indian subcontinent on the north. (p. 560)

Hindu Kush Mountain range in Central Asia. (p. 560)

Honduras (hahn•DUR•uhs) Central American republic. (p. 183)

Hong Kong Administrative district and port in southern China. 22°N 115°E (p. 637)

Hudson Bay Inland sea in east-central Canada. (p. 117)

Hungary (HUHNG•guh•ree) Central European country, south of Slovakia. (p. 261)

I

Iberian (eye•BIHR•ee•uhn) **Peninsula** Peninsula in southwestern Europe. (p. 260)

Iceland Island country between the north Atlantic and Arctic Oceans. 65°N 20°W (p. 261)

India South Asian country south of China. (p. 561)

Indochina Southeast peninsula of Asia. (p. 710)

Indonesia (IHN•duh•NEE•zhuh) Group of islands that forms the Southeast Asian country of the Republic of Indonesia. 5°S 119°E (p. 711)

Indus River River in Asia that rises in Tibet and flows through Pakistan to the Arabian Sea. (p. 560)

Iran (ih•RAHN) Southwest Asian country, formerly called Persia. (p. 411)

Iraq (ih•RAHK) Southwest Asian country, south of Turkey. (p. 411)

Ireland (EYER•luhnd) Island west of England, occupied by the Republic of Ireland and by Northern Ireland. 54°N 8°W (p. 261)

Irrawaddy River River in central Myanmar formed by the confluence of the Mali and Nmai Rivers. (p. 710)

Gazetteer

Irtysh River River in northeast Kazakhstan and the western part of Russia, in Asia. (p. 410)

Islamabad (ihs•LAH•muh•BAHD) Capital of Pakistan. 34°N 73°E (p. 561)

Israel (IHZ•ree•uhl) Country in Southwest Asia, south of Lebanon. (p. 561)

Isthmus of Panama Narrow strip of land that forms the link in Central America between North America and South America. (p. 182)

Italy (IH•tuhl•ee) Southern European country, south of Switzerland and east of France. (p. 261)

J

Jakarta Capital of Indonesia. 6°S 107°E (p. 711)

Jamaica (juh•MAY•kuh) Island country in the West Indies. 18°N 78°W (p. 183)

Japan Country in East Asia, consisting of four main islands of Hokkaido, Honshu, Shikoku, and Kyushu, plus thousands of small islands. 37°N 134°E (p. 637)

Jerusalem (juh•ROO•suh•luhm) Capital of Israel and a holy city for Christians, Jews, and Muslims. 32°N 35°E (p. 411)

Jordan Country in Southwest Asia. (p. 411)

Jutland Peninsula extending north from Germany. (p. 260)

K

K2 (Godwin Austen) Himalayan mountain in Jammu and Kashmir. 35°N 76°E (p. 560)

Kabul Capital of Afghanistan. 35°N 69°E (p. 411)

Kalahari Desert Plateau and part desert located in the southern part of Africa. (p. 486)

Kamchatka Peninsula Peninsula in northeast Russia, in Asia. (p. 338)

Kampala (kahm•PAH•lah) Capital of Uganda. 0° latitude 32°E (p. 487)

Kara Sea Arm of the Arctic Ocean north of Russia. (p. 338)

Kathmandu (KAT•MAN•DOO) Capital of Nepal. 28°N 85°E (p. 561)

Kazakhstan (KA•zak•STAN) Large Asian country south of Russia, bordering the Caspian Sea. (p. 411)

Kenya (KEH•nyuh) Country in eastern Africa, south of Ethiopia. (p. 487)

Khartoum Capital of Sudan. 16°N 33°E (p. 487)

Khyber Pass Mountain pass between Afghanistan and Pakistan. 34°N 71°E (p. 560)

Kiev (KEE•EHF) Capital of Ukraine. 50°N 31°E (p. 261)

Kigali (kee•GAH•lee) Capital of Rwanda, in central Africa. 2°S 30°E (p. 487)

Kilimanjaro Highest mountain in Africa, located in Tanzania. 3°S 37°E (p. 486)

Kingston Capital of Jamaica. 18°N 77°W (p. 183)

Kinshasa (kihn•SHAH•suh) Capital of the Democratic Republic of the Congo. 4°S 15°E (p. 487)

Kiribati (KIHR•uh•BAS) One of the two Federated States of Micronesia. 5°S 170°W (p. 785)

Korean Peninsula Peninsula on which both North and South Korea are located. (p. 636)

Krishna River River of the Deccan Plateau in south India. (p. 560)

Kuala Lumpur (KWAH•luh LUM•PUR) Capital of Malaysia. 3°N 102°E (p. 711)

Kunlun Shan Mountain ranges in western China on the north edge of the Plateau of Tibet. (p. 636)

Kuwait (ku•WAYT) Country between Saudi Arabia and Iraq, on the Persian Gulf. (p. 411)

Kyrgyzstan (KIHR•gih•STAN) Small Central Asian country on China's western border. (p. 411)

L

Labrador Sea Part of the Atlantic Ocean south of Baffin Bay off the coast of Newfoundland. (p. 117)

Lagos Port city of Nigeria. 6°N 3°E (p. 487)

Lake Baikal Lake in southern Siberia, Russia. It is the largest freshwater lake in Eurasia. (p. 338)

Lake Chad Reservoir located in Chad. (p. 486)

Lake Erie One of the Great Lakes of the United States and Canada. (p. 117)

Lake Huron One of the Great Lakes of the United States and Canada. (p. 117)

Lake Malawi Lake in southeast Africa. (p. 486)

Lake Michigan One of the Great Lakes of the United States and Canada. (p. 117)

Lake Ontario The easternmost and smallest of the Great Lakes of the United States and Canada. (p. 117)

Lake Superior One of the Great Lakes of the United States and Canada. (p. 117)

Lake Tanganyika Lake in east-central Africa. (p. 486)

Lake Titicaca Lake on the border between Peru and Bolivia. Highest navigable lake in the world. (p. 182)

Lake Victoria Freshwater lake in Tanzania and Uganda. (p. 486)

Lake Volta Reservoir located in Ghana. (p. 486)

Lake Winnipeg Lake in south-central Manitoba, Canada. (p. 117)

Laos (LOWS) Southeast Asian country, south of China and west of Vietnam. (p. 711)

La Paz (lah PAHZ) Administrative capital of Bolivia, and the highest capital in the world. 17°S 68°W (p. 183)

Latvia (LAT•vee•uh) Northeastern European country on the Baltic Sea, west of Russia. (p. 261)

Lebanon (LEH•buh•nuhn) Country on the Mediterranean Sea, south of Syria. (p. 411)

Lena River River in east-central Russia. (p. 338)

Lesotho (luh•SOH•toh) Country in southern Africa. (p. 487)

Liberia (ly•BIHR•ee•uh) West African country, south of Guinea. 7°N 10°W (p. 487)

Libreville (LEE•bruh•VIHL) Capital and port city of Gabon. 1°N 9°E (p. 487)

Libya (LIH•bee•uh) North African country on the Mediterranean Sea, west of Egypt. (p. 411)

Liechtenstein (LIHK•tuhn•STYN) Small country in central Europe. (p. 261)

Lilongwe (lih•LAWNG•gway) Capital of Malawi. 14°S 34°E (p. 487)

Lima (LEE•muh) Capital of Peru. 12°S 77°W (p. 183)

Lisbon Capital of Portugal. 39°N 9°W (p. 261)

Lithuania (LIH•thuh•WAY•nee•uh) European country on the Baltic Sea, west of Belarus. (p. 261)

Ljubljana (lee•OO•blee•AH•nuh) Capital of Slovenia. 46°N 14°E (p. 261)

Llanos Vast plains in northern South America. (p. 182)

Loire River River in Europe that rises in southeastern France and empties into the Bay of Biscay. (p. 260)

Lomé (loh•MAY) Capital and port city of Togo in Africa. 6°N 1°E (p. 487)

London Capital of the United Kingdom, on the Thames River. 52°N 0° longitude (p. 261)

Luanda Capital of Angola. 9°S 13°E (p. 487)

Lusaka Capital of Zambia. 15°S 28°E (p. 487)

Luxembourg (LUHK•suhm•BUHRG) European country between France, Germany, and Belgium. (p. 261)

M

Macau (muh•KOW) Administrative district and port in southern China. (p. 638)

Macedonia (MA•suh•DOH•nee•uh) Republic in southeastern Europe, north of Greece. Macedonia also refers to a geographic region in the Balkan Peninsula. (p. 261)

Mackenzie River River in the western portion of the Northwest Territories in Canada. (p. 117)

Madagascar (MA•duh•GAS•kuhr) Island in the Indian Ocean, southeast of Africa. (p. 487)

Madrid Capital of Spain. 40°N 4°W (p. 261)

Malabo (mah•LAH•boh) Capital of Equatorial Guinea. 4°N 9°E (p. 487)

Malawi (muh•LAH•wee) Southeastern African country, south of Tanzania and east of Zambia. (p. 487)

Malaysia (muh•LAY•zhuh) Federation of states in Southeast Asia on the Malay Peninsula and the island of Borneo. (p. 711)

Maldives (MAWL•DEEVZ) Island country in the Indian Ocean near South Asia. 5°N 42°E (p. 561)

Mali (MAH•lee) Country in western Africa, south of Algeria. (p. 487)

Malta An independent state consisting of three islands in the Mediterranean Sea. 36°N 15°E (p. 261)

Managua (mah•NAH•gwah) Capital of Nicaragua. 12°N 86°W (p. 183)

Manila (muh•NIH•luh) Capital and port city of the Republic of the Philippines. 15°N 121°E (p. 711)

Marshall Islands Independent group of atolls and reefs in the western Pacific Ocean. 11°N 108°E (p. 785)

Maseru (MA•suh•ROO) Capital of Lesotho, in southern Africa. 29°S 27°E (p. 487)

Mauritania (MAWR•uh•TAY•nee•uh) West African country, north of Senegal. (p. 487)

Mauritius (maw•RIH•shuhs) Island country in the Indian Ocean east of Madagascar. 21°S 58°E (p. 487)

Mato Grosso Plateau Highlands area in southwest Brazil. (p. 182)

Mbabane (EHM•bah•BAH•nay) Capital of Swaziland, in southeastern Africa. 26°S 31°E (p. 487)

Mediterranean Sea Inland sea enclosed by Europe, Asia, and Africa. (p. 260)

Mekong River River in Southeast Asia that flows south through Laos, Cambodia, and Vietnam. (p. 710)

Meseta The plains of central Spain. (p. 260)

Mexico Country in North America, south of the United States. (p. 183)

Mexico City Capital and most populous city of Mexico. 19°N 99°W (p. 183)

Minsk (MIHNTSK) Capital of Belarus. 54°N 28°E (p. 261)

Mississippi River River in the central United States that rises in Minnesota and flows southeast into the Gulf of Mexico. (p. 117)

Missouri River River in the central United States that joins the Mississippi River. (p. 117)

Mogadishu (MAH•guh•DIH•shoo) Capital and major seaport of Somalia, in eastern Africa. 2°N 45°E (p. 487)

Moldova (mahl•DOH•vuh) European country between Ukraine and Romania. (p. 261)

Monaco (MAH•nuh•KOH) Independent principality in southern Europe, on the Mediterranean. (p. 261)

Mongolia (mahn•GOHL•yuh) Country in Asia between Russia and China. (p. 637)

Monrovia (muhn•ROH•vee•uh) Capital and major seaport of Liberia, in western Africa. 6°N 11°W (p. 411)

Mont Blanc The highest mountain of the Alps, in southeastern France. 46°N 7°E (p. 260)

Monte Carlo Capital of Monaco. 44°N 8°E (p. 261)

Montevideo (MAHN•tuh•vuh•DAY•oh) Capital of Uruguay. 35°S 56°W (p. 183)

Morocco (muh•RAH•koh) Country in northwestern Africa on the Mediterranean Sea and the Atlantic Ocean. (p. 411)

Moscow Capital of Russia. 56°N 38°E (p. 339)

Mount Ararat Mountain in eastern Turkey. 39°N 44°3 (p. 410)

Mount Elbrus Highest point in the Caucasus Mountains. 43°N 42°E (p. 410)

Mount Everest (EHV•ruhst) Highest mountain in the world, in the Himalaya mountain ranges between Nepal and Tibet. 28°N 87°E (p. 560)

Mount Fuji Peak in south-central Honshu, Japan. It is the highest peak in Japan. 35°N 138°E (p. 636)

Mount Logan Peak in northwest Arizona in the United States. 60°N 140°W (p. 117)

Mount McKinley Highest peak in North America, located in Denali National Park in Alaska. 63°N 151°W (p. 117)

Mount Pinatubo Active volcanic mountain in the Philippines. 15°N 170°E (p. 710)

Mount Whitney Peak in the Sierra Nevada range in central California. 36°N 118°W (p. 117)

Mozambique (MOH•zuhm•BEEK) Country in south-eastern Africa, south of Tanzania. (p. 487)

Murray River River in Australia. (p. 784)

Muscat Capital of Oman. 23°N 59°E (p. 411)

Myanmar (MYAHN•MAHR) Country in Southeast Asia, south of China, formerly called Burma. (p. 711)

N

Nairobi Capital of Kenya. 1°S 37°E (p. 487)

Namib Desert Arid region along the coast of Namibia in southwestern Africa. (p. 486)

Namibia (nuh•MIH•bee•uh) Country in southwestern Africa, on the Atlantic Ocean. (p. 487)

Narmada River River in central India that flows into the Gulf of Khambat in the Arabian Sea. (p. 560)

Nassau (NA•SAW) Capital of the Bahamas. 25°N 77°W (p. 183)

Nauru (nah•OO•roo) One of the two Federated States of Micronesia. 32°S 166°E (p. 785)

N'Djamena (uhn•jah•MAY•nah) Capital of Chad. 12°N 15°E (p. 487)

Nepal (nuh•PAWL) Mountain country between India and China. (p. 561)

Netherlands Western European country on the North Sea. (p. 261)

New Delhi Capital of India. 29°N 77°E (p. 561)

New Zealand Major island country in the south Pacific, southeast of Australia. 42°S 175°E (p. 785)

Niamey (nee•AH•may) Capital and commercial center of Niger, in western Africa. 14°N 2°E (p. 487)

Nicaragua (NIH•kuh•RAH•gwuh) Republic in Central America. (p. 183)

Nicosia (NIH•kuh•SEE•uh) Capital of Cyprus. 35°N 33°E (p. 261)

Niger (NY•juhr) Landlocked country in western Africa, north of Nigeria. (p. 487)

Nigeria (ny•JIHR•ee•uh) Country in western Africa, south of Niger. (p. 487)

Niger River River in western Africa. (p. 486)

Nile River Longest river in the world, flowing north and east through eastern Africa. (p. 410)

North European Plain Plain that sweeps across western and central Europe into Russia and includes most of European Russia. (p. 260)

North Korea (kuh•REE•uh) Asian country in the northernmost part of the Korean Peninsula. (p. 637)

North Sea Arm of the Atlantic Ocean extending between the European continent on the south and east and Great Britain on the west. (p. 260)

Norway Country on the Scandinavian Peninsula. (p. 261)

Nouakchott (nu•AHK•SHAHT) Capital of Mauritania. 18°N 16°W (p. 487)

Nullarbor Plain Dry, treeless area that lies south of the Great Victorian Desert in Australia. (p. 784)

O

Ob River A river in western Russia. (p. 338)

Ohio River Major river in the midwestern United States, emptying into the Mississippi River. (p. 117)

Oman (oh•MAHN) Country on the Arabian Sea and the Gulf of Oman. (p. 411)

Orinoco River River in Venezuela. (p. 182)

Oslo Capital of Norway. 60°N 11°E (p. 261)

Ottawa Capital of Canada. 45°N 76°W (p. 107)

Ouagadougou (WAH•gah•DOO•goo) Capital of Burkina Faso, in western Africa. 12°N 2°W (p. 487)

P

Pakistan South Asian country on the Arabian Sea, northwest of India. (p. 561)

Palau (puh•LOW) Island country in the western Pacific Ocean. 7°N 135°E (p. 785)

Pamirs Mountainous region of Central Asia. (p. 410)

Pampas Plains area of South America. (p. 182)

Panama (PA•nuh•MAH) Republic in south Central America, on the Isthmus of Panama. (p. 183)

Panama City Capital of Panama. 9°N 79°W (p. 183)

Papua New Guinea (PA•pyuh•wuh noo GIH•nee) Independent island country in the south Pacific Ocean. 7°S 142°E (p. 785)

Paraguay (PAR•uh•GWY) Country in South America, north of Argentina. (p. 183)

Paraguay River River in south central South America. (p. 182)

Paramaribo (PAR•uh•MAR•uh•BOH) Capital and port city of Suriname. 6°N 55°W (p. 183)

Paraná River River in southeast central South America. (p. 182)

Paris Capital and river port of France. 49°N 2°E (p. 261)

Patagonia Plateau region of South America primarily in Argentina. (p. 182)

Peace River River in western Alberta, Canada. (p. 117)

Persian Gulf Arm of the Arabian Sea between Iran and Saudi Arabia. (p. 410)

Peru (puh•ROO) Country in South America, south of Ecuador and Colombia. (p. 183)

Philippines (FIH•luh•PEENZ) Country in the Pacific Ocean, southeast of China. (p. 711)

Phnom Penh (NAHM PEHN) Capital of Cambodia. 12°N 106°E (p. 711)

Poland Country on the Baltic Sea in eastern Europe. 52°N 18°E (p. 261)

Po River River in northern Italy that flows to the Adriatic Sea. (p. 260)

Port-au-Prince (POHRT•oh•PRIHNTS) Capital of Haiti. 19°N 72°W (p. 183)

Port Moresby (MOHRZ•bee) Capital of Papua New Guinea. 10°S 147°E (p. 785)

Porto-Novo (POHR•toh•NOH•voh) Capital and port city of Benin, in western Africa. 7°N 3°E (p. 487)

Portugal (POHR•chih•guhl) Country on the Iberian Peninsula, south and west of Spain. (p. 261)

Prague (PRAHG) Capital of the Czech Republic. 50°N 15°E (p. 261)

Pretoria (prih•TOHR•ee•uh) Administrative capital of the Republic of South Africa. 26°S 28°E (p. 487)

Puerto Rico Island in the West Indies. It is a self-governing commonwealth in union with the United States. 18°N 66°W (p. 183)

Pyongyang (PYAWNG•YAHNG) Capital of North Korea. 39°N 126°E (p. 637)

Pyrenees Mountains Mountain range extending along the border of France and Spain. (p. 260)

Q

Qatar (KAH•tuhr) Country on the southwestern shore of the Persian Gulf. (p. 411)

Qin Ling Mountain range in northern China. (p. 636)

Quito Capital of Ecuador. 0° latitude 79°W (p. 183)

R

Rabat Capital of Morocco. 34°N 7°W (p. 411)

Red River River in the south-central United States, emptying into the Mississippi River. (p. 117)

Red (Hong) River River in Vietnam that empties into the South China Sea. (p. 710)

Red Sea Inland sea between the Arabian Peninsula and northeast Africa. (p. 410)

Reykjavík (RAY•kyuh•VIHK) Capital of Iceland. 64°N 22°W (p. 261)

Rhine River in western Europe that flows to the North Sea. (p. 260)

Rhône River in Switzerland and France. (p. 260)

Riga Capital of Latvia. 57°N 24°E (p. 261)

Río de la Plata Estuary of the Paraná and Uruguay Rivers between Uruguay and Argentina. (p. 182)

Rio Grande River in the United States forming part of the boundary between the United States and Mexico. (p. 117)

Riyadh (ree•YAHD) Capital of Saudi Arabia. 25°N 47°E (p. 411)

Rocky Mountains An extensive mountain system in western North America. (p. 117)

Romania (ru•MAY•nee•uh) Country in eastern Europe, south of Ukraine. (p. 261)

Rome Capital of Italy. 42°N 13°E (p. 261)

Rub' al Khali Desert region in the southern Arabian Peninsula, also called the Empty Quarter. (p. 410)

Russia Largest country in the world, covering parts of Europe and Asia. (p. 339)

Rwanda (roo•AHN•dah) Country in Africa, south of Uganda. (p. 487)

S

Sahara Vast region of deserts and oases in North Africa. (p. 410)

St. Lawrence River River in southern Quebec and southeast Ontario, Canada. (p. 117)

St. Lucia Independent island state in the Caribbean Sea. 13°N 60°W (p. 183)

St. Vincent Principal island of St. Vincent and the Grenadines, south of St. Lucia. 13°N 61°W (p. 183)

Samoa Group of independent islands in the southwest Pacific Ocean. 13°S 172°W (p. 785)

Sanaa (sa•NAH) Capital of Yemen. 15°N 44°E (p. 411)

San José Capital of Costa Rica. 10°N 84°W (p. 183)

San Marino (SAN muh•REE•noh) Small European country, located on the Italian peninsula. (p. 261)

San Salvador (san SAL•vuh•DAWR) Capital of El Salvador. 14°N 89°W (p. 183)

Santiago Capital of Chile. 33°S 71°W (p. 183)

Santo Domingo (SAN•tuh duh•MIHNG•goh) Capital of the Dominican Republic. 19°N 70°W (p. 183)

São Francisco River River in eastern Brazil flowing into the Atlantic Ocean. (p. 182)

Sao Tome and Principe (SOWN•tuh MAY PRIHN•sih•pee) Small island country in the Gulf of Guinea off the coast of central Africa. 1°N 7°E (p. 487)

Sarajevo (SAR•uh•YAY•voh) Capital of Bosnia and Herzegovina. 43°N 18°E (p. 261)

Saskatchewan River River in south-central Canada that flows into Lake Winnipeg. (p. 117)

Saudi Arabia (SOW•dee uh•RAY•bee•uh) Country on the Arabian Peninsula. (p. 411)

Scandinavia A peninsula in northern Europe. (p. 261)

Sea of Japan (East Sea) Branch of the Pacific Ocean between Japan and the Korean Peninsula. (p. 636)

Sea of Okhotsk An inlet of the Pacific Ocean on the eastern coast of Russia. (p. 338)

Seine (SAYN) **River** French river that flows through Paris and into the English Channel. (p. 260)

Senegal (SEH•nih•GAWL) Country on the coast of western Africa, on the Atlantic Ocean. (p. 487)

Seoul (SOHL) Capital of South Korea. 38°N 127°E (p. 637)

Serbia and Montenegro (SUHR•bee•uh) (mahn•tuh•NEH•groh) European country south of Hungary. (p. 261)

Seychelles (say•SHEHLZ) Small island country in the Indian Ocean near East Africa. 6°S 56°E (p. 487)

Siberia An area in the region of north-central Asia, primarily in Russia. (p. 338)

Sierra Leone (see•EHR•uh lee•OHN) Country in western Africa, south of Guinea. (p. 487)

Sierra Madre del Sur Mountain range along the coast of southern Mexico. (p. 182)

Sierra Madre Occidental Mountain range running parallel to the Pacific Ocean coast in Mexico. (p. 182)

Sierra Madre Oriental Mountain range running parallel to the Gulf of Mexico coast in Mexico. (p. 182)

Sierra Nevada Mountain range in eastern California in the United States. (p. 117)

Sinai Peninsula Peninsula in northeast Egypt between the Gulf of Suez and the Gulf of Aqaba. (p. 410)

Singapore Multi-island country in Southeast Asia near the tip of the Malay Peninsula. 2°N 104°E (p. 711)

Skopje (SKAW•pyeh) Capital of the Republic of Macedonia. 42°N 21°E (p. 261)

Slave River River in west-central Canada between Lake Athabaska and Great Slave Lake. (p. 117)

Slovakia (sloh•VAH•kee•uh) Central European country south of Poland. (p. 261)

Slovenia (sloh•VEE•nee•uh) Small central European country on the Adriatic Sea, south of Austria. (p. 261)

Sofia Capital of Bulgaria. 43°N 23°E (p. 261)

Solomon Islands Independent island group in the west Pacific Ocean. 8°S 159°E (p. 784)

Somalia (soh•MAH•lee•uh) Country in east Africa, on the Gulf of Aden and the Indian Ocean. (p. 487)

South Africa Country at the southern tip of Africa. (p. 487)

South China Sea Part of the Pacific Ocean extending from Japan to the tip of the Malay Peninsula. (p. 636)

South Korea Country in Asia on the Korean Peninsula between the Yellow Sea and the Sea of Japan. (p. 637)

Spain Country on the Iberian Peninsula. (p. 261)

Sri Lanka (sree LAHNG•kuh) Island country in the Indian Ocean south of India. 9°N 83°E (p. 561)

Stockholm Capital of Sweden. 59°N 18°E (p. 261)

Strait of Gibraltar Passage connecting Mediterranean Sea to the Atlantic Ocean. (p. 260)

Strait of Hormuz Strait between the northern tip of Oman, the southeastern Arabian Peninsula, and the southern coast of Iran. (p. 410)

Strait of Malacca Ocean trade route running between Indonesia and Malaysia, near Singapore. (p. 710)

Sucre (SOO•kray) Constitutional capital of Bolivia. 19°S 65°W (p. 183)

Sudan Northeast African country on the Red Sea. (p. 487)

Suriname Republic in South America. (p. 183)

Suva Capital of Fiji. 18°S 177°E (p. 785)

Swaziland (SWAH•zee•LAND) South African country west of Mozambique. (p. 487)

Sweden Northern European country on the eastern side of the Scandinavian Peninsula. (p. 261)

Switzerland (SWIHT•suhr•luhnd) European country in the Alps, south of Germany. (p. 261)

Syr Darya River in west-central Asia in Kyrgyzstan, Uzbekistan, and Kazakhstan. (p. 410)

Syria (SIHR•ee•uh) Country in Asia on the eastern side of the Mediterranean Sea. (p. 411)

T

Taipei (TY•PAY) Capital of Taiwan. 25°N 122°E (p. 637)

Taiwan (TY•WAHN) Island country off the southeast coast of China, claimed by China. 24°N 122°E (p. 637)

Tajikistan (tah•JIH•kih•STAN) Central Asian country north of Afghanistan. (p. 411)

Taklimakan Desert Desert in western China. (p. 636)

Tallinn (TA•luhn) Capital and largest city of Estonia. 59°N 25°E (p. 261)

Tanzania (TAN•zuh•NEE•uh) East African country on the coast of the Indian Ocean. (p. 487)

Tashkent Capital of Uzbekistan. 41°N 69°E (p. 411)

Tasman Sea Part of the south Pacific Ocean between Australia and New Zealand. (p. 784)

Taurus Mountains Mountain range in southern Turkey. (p. 410)

Tbilisi (tuh•BEE•luh•see) Capital of the Republic of Georgia. 42°N 45°E (p. 411)

Tegucigalpa (tuh•GOO•suh•GAL•puh) Capital of Honduras. 14°N 87°W (p. 183)

Tehran (TAY•RAN) Capital of Iran. 36°N 52°E (p. 411)

Thailand (TY•LAND) Southeast Asian country south of Myanmar. (p. 711)

Thames (TEHMZ) **River** River in southern England that flows into the North Sea. (p. 260)

Thimphu (thihm•POO) Capital of Bhutan. 28°N 90°E (p. 561)

Tian Shan Mountain range in western China. (p. 636)

Tierra del Fuego Archipelago off southern South America. 54°N 68°W (p. 182)

Tirana (tih•RAH•nuh) Capital of Albania. 42°N 20°E (p. 261)

Togo (TOH•goh) West African country between Benin and Ghana, on the Gulf of Guinea. (p. 487)

Tokyo Capital of Japan. 36°N 140°E (p. 637)

Tonga South Pacific island country. 20°S 175°W (p. 785)

Trinidad and Tobago (TRIH•nih•DAD tuh•BAY•goh) Independent republic comprising the islands of Trinidad and Tobago, located in the Atlantic Ocean off the northeast coast of Venezuela. 11°N 61°W (p. 183)

Tripoli Capital of Libya. 33°N 13°E (p. 411)

Tunis Capital of Tunisia. 37°N 10°E (p. 411)

Tunisia (too•NEE•zhuh) North African country on the Mediterranean Sea between Libya and Algeria. (p. 411)

Turkey Country in southeastern Europe and western Asia. (p. 411)

Turkmenistan (tuhrk•MEH•nuh•STAN) Central Asian country on the Caspian Sea. (p. 411)

Tuvalu Independent island group in the western Pacific Ocean. 8°S 178°E (p. 785)

Uganda (oo•GAHN•duh) East African country south of Sudan. (p. 487)

Ukraine (yoo•KRAYN) Large eastern European country west of Russia, on the Black Sea. (p. 261)

Ulaanbaatar (OO•LAHN•BAH•TAWR) Capital of Mongolia. 48°N 107°E (p. 637)

United Arab Emirates Country of seven states on the eastern side of the Arabian Peninsula. (p. 411)

United Kingdom Country in western Europe made up of England, Scotland, Wales, and Northern Ireland. (p. 261)

United States Country in North America located between Canada and Mexico. (p. 117)

Ural Mountains Mountain range in Russia which marks the traditional boundary between European Russia and Asian Russia. (p. 338)

Ural River River in eastern Europe and western Asia, originating in the Ural Mountains. (p. 338)

Uruguay (UR•uh•GWY) South American country, south of Brazil on the Atlantic Ocean. (p. 183)

Uzbekistan (uz•BEH•kih•STAN) Central Asian country south of Kazakhstan. (p. 411)

Vanuatu (vahn•wah•TOO) Country made up of islands in the Pacific Ocean, east of Australia. 17°S 170°W (p. 785)

Vatican (VA•tih•kuhn) **City** Headquarters of the Roman Catholic Church, located in the city of Rome, Italy. 42°N 13°E (p. 261)

Venezuela Republic in northern South America. (p. 183)

Verkhoyansk Range Mountain range in northeastern Russia, just east of the Lena River. (p. 338)

Vesuvius Volcano on the east side of the Bay of Naples in Italy. 41°N 14°E (p. 261)

Vienna Capital of Austria. 48°N 16°E (p. 261)

Vientiane (vyehn•TYAHN) Capital of Laos. 18°N 103°E (p. 711)

Vietnam (vee•ET•NAHM) Southeast Asian country, east of Laos and Cambodia. (p. 711)

Vindhya Range Mountain range in central India. (p. 560)

Vistula River River in southwestern Poland that flows north into the Baltic Sea. (p. 260)

Volga River River in western Russia that flows south into the Caspian Sea. (p. 338)

W

Warsaw Capital of Poland. 52°N 21°E (p. 261)

Washington, D.C. Capital of the United States, near the Atlantic coast. 39°N 77°W (p. 107)

Wellington Capital of New Zealand. 41°S 175°E (p. 785)

Western Ghats Mountain range in southern India. (p. 560)

Western Sahara Territory in Northwest Africa. (p. 410)

West Siberian Plain Area of flat land that stretches from the Arctic Ocean to the grasslands of Central Asia. (p. 338)

Windhoek (VIHNT•HUK) Capital of Namibia, in southwestern Africa. 22°S 17°E (p. 487)

Xi (SHEE) **River** River in southeast China, known in its upper course as the Hongshui. (p. 636)

Yablonovyy Range Mountain range in southern Russia. (p. 338)

Yamoussoukro (YAH•muh•SOO•kroh) Second capital of Côte d'Ivoire, in western Africa. 7°N 6°W (p. 487)

Yangon Capital of Myanmar. 17°N 96°E (p. 711)

Yangtze River Major river in central China. (p. 636)

Yaoundé (yown•DAY) Capital of Cameroon, in western Africa. 4°N 12°E (p. 487)

Yellow River River in north-central and eastern China, also known as the Huang He. (p. 636)

Yellow Sea Large inlet of the Pacific Ocean between northeast China and the Korean Peninsula. (p. 636)

Yemen (YEH•muhn) Country on the Arabian Peninsula, south of Saudi Arabia. (p. 411)

Yenisey River A river in western Russia that flows north into the Kara Sea. (p. 338)

Yerevan (YEHR•uh•VAHN) Capital and largest city of Armenia. 40°N 44°E (p. 411)

Yucatán Peninsula Peninsula including parts of southeastern Mexico, Belize, and Guatemala in Central America. (p. 182)

Yukon River River in the Yukon Territory, Canada. (p. 117)

Z

Zagreb (ZAH•grehb) Capital and largest city of Croatia. 46°N 16°E (p. 261)

Zagros Mountains Mountain system in southern and southwestern Iran. (p. 410)

Zambezi River River in south-central Africa. (p. 486)

Zambia (ZAM•bee•uh) Country in south-central Africa, east of Angola. (p. 487)

Zimbabwe (zim•BAH•bwee) Country in south-central Africa, southeast of Zambia. (p. 487)

Gazetteer

A

aborigine/aborigen Habitante originario de un área (pág. 662)

absolute location/ubicación absoluta La posición exacta de un lugar en la superficie de la tierra (pág. 20)

accretion/acrecentamiento Un proceso lento en el cuál una plataforma marina se desliza por debajo de una plataforma continental, creando restos que pueden causar que los continentes crezcan hacia fuera (pág. 40)

acid deposition/deposición ácida Ácidos secos o húmedos que lleva el viento y que caen a la tierra (pág. 321)

acid rain/lluvia ácida Precipitación que lleva grandes cantidades de ácidos disueltos, los cuales dañan los edificios, los bosques y las cosechas y matan la fauna (págs. 166, 321)

acupuncture/acupuntura Una práctica antigua que involucra la inserción de agujas finas dentro del cuerpo en puntos específicos para curar enfermedades y aliviar el dolor (pág 677)

alluvial plain/llanura aluvial Llanura en la que los ríos inundados han depositado tierra rica, como la Llanura Indogangéctica en el Asia del Sur (pág. 572)

alluvial-soil deposits/depósitos de tierra aluvial Tierra rica compuesta de arena y lodo depositados por aguas corrientes (pág. 423)

altiplano Una región en Perú y Bolivia rodeada por la cordillera de los andes (pág. 194)

amendment/enmienda En la historia de los Estados Unidos, cambios oficiales que se le hacen a la Constitución (pág. 144)

apartheid/segregación racial Política de estricta separación de las razas adoptada en Sudáfrica en los años 40 (pág. 524)

aquaculture/acuacultura El cultivo de los mariscos (pág. 695)

aquifer/acuífero/aguas freáticas Capas subterráneas de roca porosa, arena o grava que acumulan agua (págs. 49, 470)

arable /arable Tierra idónea para cultivo (pág. 464)

archipelago/archipiélago Un grupo o cadena de islas (págs. 646, 720)

artesian water/agua artesiana Abastecimiento de agua subterránea que está bajo suficiente presión para subir a los pozos sin tener que ser bombeada (pág. 794)

Asian Pacific Economic Cooperation Group (APEC)/(APEC) Grupo de cooperación económica del Pacífico Asiático Un grupo de comercio, cuyos miembros son Japón, China, Corea del Sur y Taiwan, que asegura que el comercio entre los países miembros es eficiente y justo (pág. 689)

Association of Southeast Asian Nations (ASEAN)/ Asociación de Naciones del Asia del Sudeste (ANSEA) Organización formada en 1967 para promover el desarrollo y el comercio regional en el Asia del Sudeste (pág. 763)

atheism/ateísmo La creencia de que no hay Dios (pág. 376)

atmosphere/atmósfera Una capa de gases que rodea la Tierra (pág. 35)

atoll/atolón Isla en forma de aro formada por coral que se acumula por todo el borde de un volcán submarino (pág. 796)

autocracy/autocracia Gobierno en el cual un solo individuo posee el poder y la autoridad para gobernar (pág. 87)

avalanche/avalancha Masa de hielo, nieve o roca que se desliza por el lado de una montaña (pág. 279)

axis/eje Referente a la Tierra, una línea imaginaria que le atraviesa por el centro entre el Polo Norte y el Polo Sur (pág. 56)

B

batik/batik Método de teñir tela para producir bellos estampados, desarrollado en Indonesia y Malasia (pág. 751)

bazaar/bazar Un mercado tradicional con puestos. Puede estar en una sola calle o extenderse hasta un distrito completo (pág. 456)

bedouin/beduino Miembro de los pueblos nómadas del desierto del África del Norte y Asia del Sudoeste (pág. 455)

bilingual/bilingüe Que habla o usa dos idiomas (pág. 148)

Bill of Rights Las diez primeras enmiendas de la constitución estadounidense (pág. 144)

biologist/biólogo Científico que estudia la vida vegetal y animal (pág. 324)

biomass/biomasa Desperdicio vegetal y animal usado especialmente como fuente de combustible (pág. 613)

biosphere/biosfera La parte de la Tierra donde existe la vida (pág. 35)

birthrate/índice de natalidad El número de nacimientos por año por cada 1000 personas (pág. 76)

black market/mercado negro Cualquier mercado ilegal donde se venden productos escasos o ilegales, por lo general a precios altos (pág. 388)

blizzard/ventisca Una tormenta de nieve con vientos de más de 35 millas por hora, temperaturas abajo del punto de congelación y visibilidad de menos de 500 pies que dura 3 horas o más (pág. 125)

Bolsheviks/Bolcheviques Un grupo revolucionario en Rusia dirigido por Vladimir Ilyich Lenin (pág. 370)

boomerang/bumerang Palo curvo que se tira utilizado por los aborígenes de Australia para cazar (pág. 817)

buffer state/estado neutral Territorio neutral entre poderes rivales (pág. 743)

C

cabinet/gabinete Directores de departamentos en la rama ejecutiva del gobierno de EE.UU. quienes aconsejan al Presidente (pág. 144)

calligraphy/caligrafía El arte de escribir a mano de forma bella (pág. 679)

campesinos Trabajadores agrícolas; generalmente gente que vive y trabaja en áreas rurales (pág. 238)

canopy/follaje o copa Capa superior del bosque de lluvia, donde se juntan las puntas de los árboles altos formando una capa continua de hojas (pág. 200)

cartography/cartografía La ciencia de hacer mapas (pág. 24)

cash crop/cosecha comercial Cosecha agrícola cultivada para venderse o trocarse en lugar de usarse para la familia del agricultor (págs. 238, 538, 612, 760)

cataract/catarata Un gran salto de agua (pág. 500)

caudillo Término para un líder político de Latinoamérica desde los últimos años de los 1800 en adelante, con frecuencia un dictador militar (pág. 224)

cereal/cereal Cualquier grano, como la cebada, la avena o el trigo, que se cultiva para alimento (pág. 431)

chaparral/chaparral Tipo de vegetación compuesta de densos bosques de matorrales y arbustos, común en los climas mediterráneos (págs. 68, 281)

chernozem Capa vegetal de tierra negra y rica que se halla en la planicie del norte de Europa, especialmente en Rusia y Ucrania (pág. 346)

chinampas Islas flotantes de agricultura hechas por los aztecas (pág. 221)

chinook/chinuco Viento cálido estacional que sopla por las Montañas Rocosas al final del invierno y al principio de la primavera (pág. 124)

Chipko/**Chipko** Movimiento en India en que la gente abraza árboles para proteger los bosques, reforestándolos y limitando la tala (pág. 621)

cholorofluorocarbons/clorofluorocarbonos También llamados CFCs; sustancias químicas que se hallan principalmente en líquidos refrigerantes que dañan la capa de ozono que protege a la Tierra (pág. 695)

city-state/ciudad-estado En la antigua Grecia, comunidad independiente que consistía de una ciudad y las tierras circundantes (pág. 295)

clan/clan Comunidad tribal o grupo grande de gente relacionada entre sí (págs. 529, 670, 817)

clear-cutting/deforestación Cortar todos los árboles de un bosque para utilizar la madera (pág. 165)

climate/clima Patrones del tiempo típicos de un área durante un largo período de tiempo (pág. 55)

Cold War/Guerra Fría Se refiere a la lucha por el poder entre la Unión Soviética y los Estados Unidos después de la Segunda Guerra Mundial (págs. 298, 371)

collective farm/granja colectiva Bajo el comunismo, una granja enorme, propiedad del estado, en la cual los agricultores recibían sueldos más una parte de los productos y ganancias; también denominada kolkhoz (pág. 317)

command economy/economía controlada Sistema económico en el que las decisiones económicas acerca de la producción y la distribución las toma alguna autoridad central (págs. 89, 388, 685)

commercial farming/agricultura comercial Agricultura organizada como un negocio (pág. 538)

commodity/mercancía Bienes producidos para su venta (págs. 158, 465)

commune/comuna En la China, una comunidad agrícola colectiva cuyos miembros compartían el trabajo y los productos (pág. 686)

communism/comunismo Sociedad basada en la igualdad en la que los trabajadores controlarían la producción industrial (págs. 298, 370)

condensation/condensación El proceso del cambio de vapor de agua a agua líquida cuando el aire caliente se enfría (pág. 47)

coniferous/coníferas Árboles que tienen conos y hojas con forma de agujas, la mayoría de los cuales mantienen su follaje durante el invierno (pág. 68)

conquistador Término español para referirse a los soldados que conquistaron a los indios de Latinoamérica (pág. 222)

conservation farming/agricultura de conservación Técnica de administración de la tierra que ayuda a proteger la tierra agrícola (pág. 539)

Constitution/Constitución Plan que hizo el gobierno para los Estados Unidos en 1787 (pág. 144)

consumer goods/bienes de consumo Bienes que satisfacen directamente los deseos humanos (pág. 388)

continental drift/movimiento continental La teoría que dice que los continentes estaban juntos y se fueron separando lentamente (pág. 38)

continental shelf/plataforma continental La parte de un continente que se extiende bajo el agua (pág. 36)

cooperative/cooperativa Una organización voluntaria cuyos miembros trabajan juntos y comparten los gastos y las ganancias (pág. 686)

copra/copra La carne seca del coco (pág. 834)

coral/coral Depósitos de piedra caliza formados por los esqueletos de animales marinos (pág. 795)

cordillera/cordillera Cadenas paralelas de montañas (págs. 194, 719)

Coriolis effect/efecto Coriolis Un efecto que causa que los vientos soplen diagonalmente en vez de sus líneas normales norte/sur o este/oeste (pág. 62)

cottage industry/industria casera Un negocio que emplea trabajadores en sus casas (pág. 615)

crevasse/grieta Una brecha enorme y honda que se forma en la nieve o en el hielo grueso (pág. 803)

Crusades/Cruzadas Serie de guerras religiosas (1100–1300 D.C.) en las que los cristianos europeos trataron de recuperar Palestina del control musulmán (pág. 296)

cultural diffusion/difusión cultural La difusión de conocimientos y costumbres de una cultura a otra (pág. 84)

culture/cultura Modo de vida de un grupo de gente que comparte creencias y costumbres similares (pág. 80)

culture hearth/hogar de la cultura Un centro donde las culturas se desarrollan y desde el cual las ideas y las tradiciones se difunden (págs. 84, 447, 668)

culture region/región cultural División de la tierra basada en una variedad de factores que incluyen el gobierno, los grupos sociales, los sistemas económicos, el lenguaje o la religión (pág. 83)

cuneiform/cuneiforme Sistema de escritura Sumeria que usa símbolos en forma de cuñas hundidas en tabletas de arcilla (pág. 447)

current/corriente Corriente de agua de mar fría o cálida que fluye en los océanos, por lo general en forma circular (pág. 62)

cyclone/ciclón Tormenta con lluvias y vientos fuertes que sopla en círculo alrededor de un área de baja presión atmosférica (págs. 579, 767)

czar/zar El emperador de Rusia hasta la revolución de 1917 (pág. 369)

D

Dalits/**Dalit** Los oprimidos; clase social más baja de la India (pág. 623)

death rate/tasa de mortalidad El número de muertes por año por cada 1000 personas (pág. 76)

deciduous/deciduo Describe árboles, usualmente de follaje ancho como los robles y arces, que pierden las hojas en el otoño (pág. 68)

deforestation/deforestación La pérdida o destrucción de los bosques, debido principalmente a la tala de árboles para explotación forestal o agricultura (págs. 242, 507)

delta/delta Sección triangular de tierra que se forma en la boca de un río y que se parece a la letra griega delta (Δ) (pág. 503)

democracy/democracia Un sistema de gobierno en el cual los líderes gobiernan con el consentimiento de los ciudadanos (pág. 88)

desalination/desalinización La eliminación de la sal del agua de mar para que se pueda usar para beber y en la agricultura (págs. 48, 470)

desertification/desertificación Proceso en el cual la tierra arable se vuelve desierto, (págs. 508, 694)

developed country/país desarrollado País que tiene un gran avance en tecnología y manufactura (pág. 93)

developing country/país en vías de desarrollo País en el proceso de industrialización (págs. 93, 238)

dharma En hinduismo, el deber moral que guía la vida de una persona, de acuerdo a las diferencias de clase (pág. 593)

dialect/dialecto Variedad local de un lenguaje usado en un lugar en particular o por cierto grupo (págs. 213, 302)

diatoms/diátomo Plancton que vive en agua fría en los océanos (pág. 841)

dikes/diques Bancos grandes de tierra y piedras que detienen el agua (pág. 272)

dissident/disidente Un ciudadano que habla en contra de las políticas del gobierno (pág. 689)

divide/bifurcación Un punto alto o cresta que determina la dirección en la que fluyen los ríos (pág. 118)

doldrums/zona de calmas ecuatoriales Un área cerca del Ecuador frecuentemente sin viento (págs. 62, 802)

domesticate/domesticar El tomar plantas y animales silvestres para adaptarlos y hacerlos útiles para la gente (págs. 446, 520)

dominion/dominio Un país con gobierno propio parcial y con ligas cercanas a otro país (pág. 820)

doubling time/tiempo de duplicación El número de años que le toma a una población duplicar su tamaño (pág. 76)

dry farming/agricultura seca Método de agricultura que se usa en regiones secas en el que la tierra se ara y se siembra profundo para retener el agua en la tierra (págs. 143, 321)

dynasty/dinastía Una casa gobernante o la continuación de una familia de gobernantes, especialmente en China (pág. 669)

dzong Un monasterio fortificado de Bhutan, Asia del sur (pág. 604)

E

e-commerce/comercio electrónico Comprar y vender en el Internet (pág. 542)

economic sanctions/sanciones económicas Restricciones de comercio (pág. 689)

ecosystem/ecosistema La compleja comunidad de seres vivientes que, en cierto medio ambiente, dependen los unos de los otros (pág. 22)

ecotourism/ecoturismo Turismo basado en preocupación por el medio ambiente (págs. 546, 617)

El Niño Un cambio total periódico del patrón de las corrientes del océano y las temperaturas del agua en la región del Pacífico medio (pág. 63)

El Niño-Southern Oscillation (ENSO)/ El Niño oscilación del sur Un cambio en el clima de temporada que puede causar sequías en Australia y ciclones poderosos en el Pacífico del sur (pág. 841)

embargo/embargo Una prohibición en el comercio (págs. 452, 468)

endemic/endémico Que describe especies de plantas o animales nativos de un área particular (pág. 728)

Enlightenment/Iluminación Un movimiento durante principios de los 1700 que enfatizaba la importancia de la razón y cuestionaba las tradiciones y valores (pág. 297)

environmentalist/ambientalista Persona activamente preocupada con la calidad y la protección del medio ambiente (pág. 322)

equinox/equinoccio Uno de dos días (el 21 marzo y el 23 de septiembre) cuando el Sol está directamente encima del ecuador, haciendo que el día y la noche sean de igual duración (pág. 56)

erosion/erosión El desgaste de la superficie de la Tierra por el viento, el fluir del agua o los glaciares (pág. 42)

escarpment/escarpa Risco o escarpadura entre una superficie de tierra alta y otra más baja (págs. 196, 500)

estuary/estuario Área en donde la marea se encuentra con la corriente de un río (págs. 197, 503)

ethnic cleansing/purificación de raza Cuando se saca de un país a personas de cierta raza o una matanza entre grupos étnicos rivales (pág. 288)

ethnic diversity/diversidad étnica Diferencias entre grupos o gente basadas en sus orígenes, lenguajes, costumbres o creencias (pág. 439)

ethnic group/grupo étnico Grupo de personas quienes comparten los mismos antepasados, lenguaje, religión, costumbres o una combinación de estas características (págs. 82, 288, 363)

European Union/Unión Europea Una organización cuya meta es unir a Europa para que los bienes, servicios y trabajadores puedan moverse libremente en todos los países miembros (págs. 300, 313)

eutrophication/eutroficación Proceso por el cual un cuerpo de agua se hace demasiado rico en nutrientes disueltos, haciendo que la abundancia de plantas agote el oxígeno (pág. 168)

evaporation/evaporación El cambio a vapor (pág. 47)

exports/exportaciones Recursos o bienes que se envían desde un país a otro para comercio (pág. 237)

extended family/parentela Una familia compuesta de varias generaciones de parientes; (págs. 229, 529)

extinction/extinción La desaparición o fin de una especie de animal o planta (pág. 546)

F

fale Tipo de casa tradicional en Samoa, con los lados abiertos y el techo de paja (pág. 826)

fall line/línea de caída Una frontera en el este de Estados Unidos donde la tierra más alta de Piamonte cae a la planicie más baja de la costa atlántica (pág. 118)

farm cooperative/cooperativa agrícola Organización en la que los agricultores comparten en el cultivo y la venta de los productos agrícolas (pág. 317)

fault/falla Una grieta o hendidura en la corteza terrestre (págs. 40, 500)

fauna/fauna La vida animal de una región (pág. 724)

federal system/sistema federal Divide los poderes de gobierno entre el gobierno nacional y el estatal o local (pág. 87)

feudalism/feudalismo Sistema de gobierno durante la época medieval en Europa y Japón, en el cual los poderosos señores feudales daban tierras a los nobles a cambio de su lealtad (pág. 296)

fishery/pesquería Zonas (de agua fresca o salada) donde se pescan peces u otros animales marinos (pág. 120)

fjord/fiordo Valle glacial con largos acantilados llenos de agua de mar (pág. 272)

Spanish Glossary

flora/flora La vida de las plantas de una región (pág. 724)

foehn/fohn Viento seco y cálido que sopla del lado sotavento de las montañas, a veces derrite la nieve y provoca avalanchas; el término se usa predominantemente en Europa (pág. 279)

fold/pliegue Un doblez en las capas de roca, a veces causado por el movimiento de las plataformas (pág. 40)

food web/red alimenticia Los enlaces entre los depredadores y sus fuentes de comida en un ecosistema (pág. 840)

formal region/región formal Una región definida por características comunes, tales como la fabricación de un producto (pág. 21)

free port/zona libre Ciudad portuaria, como Singapur, donde los bienes se desembarcan, se almacenan y se vuelven a embarcar sin pago de impuestos portuarios (pág. 764)

free trade/libre comercio La eliminación de barreras comerciales para que los bienes puedan circular libremente entre países (pág. 94)

functional region/región funcional Un punto central y el territorio que lo rodea que está relacionado con ese punto central (pág. 230)

fútbol Se conoce en Norteamérica como el "soccer" (pág. 230)

G

gauchos Los vaqueros de Argentina y Uruguay (pág. 197)

genetically modified foods/alimentos modificados genéticamente Alimentos cuyos genes han sido alterados para hacerlos más grandes, crecer más rápido o ser más resistentes a las plagas (pág. 317)

geographic information systems/sistemas de información geográfica Herramientas de computadora para procesar y organizar los detalles y las imágenes de satélite junto con otras piezas de información (pág. 25)

glaciation/formación de glaciares El proceso por el cual se forman y se extienden los glaciares (pág. 272)

glacier/glaciar Grandes cuerpos de hielo que se mueven a través de la superficie de la Tierra (pág. 42)

glasnost/glasnost Término ruso para una nueva "apertura"; parte de los planes de reforma de Gorbachev (pág. 371)

global warming/calentamiento global Calentamiento gradual de la Tierra y su atmósfera que puede ser causado en parte por la contaminación y un aumento del efecto de invernadero (págs. 58, 322)

glyph/glifo Escritura a base de dibujos esculpida en piedra (pág. 221)

Good Friday Peace Agreement/Acuerdo de paz de Viernes Santo Por medio de este acuerdo, las comunidades Protestantes y Católicas Romanas comparten poder político en Irlanda del Norte (pág. 304)

grazier/ganadero Persona que cría ganado ovejuno y vacuno (pág. 834)

greenhouse effect/efecto invernadero La capacidad de ciertos gases en la atmósfera de atrapar el calor y hacer que la Tierra se caliente (págs. 58, 322)

green revolution/revolución verde Programa comenzado en los años 60 para producir cepas de mayor rendimiento de trigo, arroz y otras cosechas de alimento (pág. 613)

grid system/sistema de cuadrícula Patrón formado a medida que las líneas de latitud y longitud se intersectan (pág. 20)

gross domestic product (GDP)/producto interno bruto (PIB) El valor de los bienes y los servicios creados dentro de un país en un año (pág. 465)

groundwater/agua subterránea Agua que yace debajo de la superficie de la Tierra, que abastece pozos y manantiales (págs. 49, 167)

guru/gurú Maestro o guía espiritual (pág. 601)

H

habitat/hábitat Area con condiciones idóneas para que vivan ciertas plantas o animales (pág. 546)

haiku Forma de poesía japonesa que consiste de 17 sílabas y tres líneas, con frecuencia trata de la naturaleza (pág. 678)

hajj En el Islam, el peregrinaje anual a la Meca (pag. 466)

headwaters/cabeceras Las fuentes de aguas de río (pág. 118)

heavy industry/industria pesada La manufactura de maquinaria y equipo necesario para fábricas y minas (pág. 317)

hemisphere/hemisferio Mitad de una esfera o globo, como en los Hemisferios Norte y Sur de la Tierra (pág. 20)

hieroglyphics/jeroglíficos Sistema de escritura egipcia que usa dibujos y símbolos para representar palabras o sonidos (pág. 447)

Holocaust/Holocausto El asesinato masivo de 6 millones de judíos por los líderes Nazi de Alemania durante la Segunda Guerra Mundial (pág. 298)

homogeneous/homogéneo De la misma clase o naturaleza (pág. 663)

human-environment interaction/interacción humana-ambiental El estudio de las interrelaciones de la gente con sus ambientes físicos (pág. 22)

human geography/geografía humana También llamada geografía cultural; es el estudio de las actividades humanas y sus relaciones con los ambientes culturales y físicos (pág. 24)

hurricane/huracán Una gran tormenta de vientos fuertes que se forma sobre las aguas cálidas del océano (pág. 125)

hydroelectric power/energía hidroeléctrica Energía eléctrica generada por la caída del agua (págs. 197, 348)

hydrosphere/hidrosfera Las zonas acuosas de la Tierra que incluyen los océanos, lagos, ríos y otros cuerpos de agua (pág. 35)

hypothesis/hipótesis Una explicación científica para un evento (pág. 69)

icon/icono Imagen religiosa, usualmente incluye un cuadro de Jesús, María o un santo, usado principalmente por los cristianos ortodoxos (pág. 377)

ideogram/ideograma Un carácter pictórico o un símbolo que representa un significado específico o una idea (pág. 674)

immigration/inmigración El movimiento de gente saliendo de un país y entrando a otro (pág. 133)

impressionism/impresionismo Estilo artístico que se desarrolló en Europa en los últimos años de los 1800 y que trató de mostrar la apariencia natural de los objetos con toques o pinceladas de color (pág. 305)

indigenous/indígena Nativo de un lugar (pág. 212)

industrial capitalism/capitalismo industrial Un sistema económico en el cual los líderes de negocios usan sus utilidades para expandir sus compañías (pág. 297)

industrialization/industrialización Transición de una sociedad agrícola a una industrial (pág. 93)

infrastructure/infraestructura Las necesidades urbanas básicas como calles y servicios (págs. 443, 540)

insular/insular Constituye una isla, como en Java (pág. 270)

intelligentsia/intelectualidad Círculo intelectual (pág. 378)

interdependent/interdependiente Depender los unos de los otros para bienes, servicios e ideas (pág. 763)

introduced species/especies introducidas Plantas y animales colocadas en áreas diferentes a su hábitat natural (pág. 839)

jai alai/jai alai Juego de mano tradicional popular en México y Cuba (pág. 231)

Japan Current/Corriente de Japón Corriente oceánica de agua templada que le proporciona humedad a los monzones de invierno (pág. 655)

jati En la sociedad tradicional Hindú, un grupo social que define la ocupación de la familia y su posición social (pág. 588)

jazz/jazz Forma musical que se desarrolló en los Estados Unidos a principios de los 1900, mezcla ritmos africanos con harmonías europeas (pág. 148)

jute/yute Fibra vegetal que se usa para hacer cordón y tela (pág. 612)

karma/karma En la creencia Hindú, la suma de las acciones buenas y malas en la vida presente y las vidas pasadas de una persona (pág. 593)

kolkhoz En la Unión Soviética, una granja pequeña trabajada por granjeros que comparten la producción y las utilidades (pág. 390)

krill Diminutos animales marinos parecidos a los camarones que viven en los frígidos océanos de la Antártica (pág. 798)

kums Término regional para los desiertos de Asia central (pág. 425)

lagoon/laguna Estanque de poca profundidad en el centro de un atolón (pág. 796)

lama/lama Líder religioso budista (pág. 675)

language family/familia de lenguajes Grupo de lenguajes relacionados que se desarrollaron de un lenguaje anterior (págs. 81, 303)

latifundia/**latifundios** En la moderna Latinoamérica, extensas propiedades de cultivo que pertenecen a familias o corporaciones (pág. 238)

leach/lixiviar Lavar la tierra para sacarle los nutrientes (pág. 506)

leeward/sotavento Con cara en contra de la dirección de donde sopla el viento (pág. 64)

lichens/líquenes Plantas diminutas y fuertes que crecen como una corteza sobre las rocas y los troncos de los árboles (pág. 803)

light industry/industria ligera Manufactura con fines de producir bienes como textiles o alimentos para el consumidor en vez de maquinaria pesada (pág. 317)

lingua franca/lengua franca Un lenguaje común usado entre la gente con diferentes lenguas nativas (pág. 526)

literacy rate/índice de alfabetización El porcentaje de personas en un lugar dado que puede leer y escribir (pág. 150)

lithosphere/litosfera Áreas de superficie terrestre de la corteza de la Tierra, incluye los continentes y las cuencas de los océanos (pág. 35)

llanos Llanuras fértiles tierra adentro en áreas de Colombia y Venezuela (pág. 196)

location/ubicación Un lugar específico en la Tierra (pág. 20)

lode/veta Depósito de minerales (pág. 761)

loess/loes Capa superficial del suelo, fina, amarillenta y marrón compuesta de partículas de limo y arcilla, usualmente arrastrada por el viento (págs. 42, 275, 648)

longhouse/casa larga En zonas rurales de Indonesia y Malasia, un edificio alto donde viven miembros de varias familias que están relacionadas entre sí (pág. 752)

Maastricht Treaty/Tratado de Maastricht Una reunión en 1992 de los gobiernos europeos en Maastricht, Holanda, en la que se formó la Unión Europea (pág. 314)

magma/magma Roca fundida que es enviada hacia arriba desde el manto de la Tierra (pág. 38)

malnutrition/malnutrición Nutrición pobre o inadecuada (pág. 230)

mantle/manto Gruesa capa mediana de la estructura interior de la Tierra, consiste de densa piedra caliente (pág. 38)

mantra/mantra En Hinduismo, una palabra o frase sagrada que se repite en los rezos y cantos (pág. 601)

manuka Pequeños arbustos que crecen en las mesetas de Nueva Zelanda (pág. 803)

maquiladoras En México, plantas de manufactura montadas por firmas extranjeras (pág. 239)

maritime/marítimo Relacionado a los viajes o la transportación por mar (pág. 741)

market economy/economía de mercado Un sistema económico basado en la libre empresa, en el que los negocios son de propiedad privada y la producción y los precios se determinan por la oferta y la demanda (págs. 89, 157, 388)

marsupial/marsupial Tipo de mamífero que da a luz a crías que maduran en una bolsa en el abdomen de la madre (pág. 839)

mass culture/cultura popular Cultura de las masas extendida por los medios de comunicación como la radio y la televisión (pág. 525)

megacities/megaciudad Una ciudad con más de 10 millones de habitantes (pág. 217)

megalopolis/megalópolis Una "super-ciudad" compuesta por varias ciudades grandes y pequeñas, como el área entre Boston y Washington, D.C. (págs. 136, 591)

meltwater/aguanieve Agua formada al derretirse la nieve y el hielo (pág. 321)

merchant marine/marina mercante La flota de barcos de un país que participa en el intercambio comercial (pág. 691)

meteorology/meteorlogía El estudio del clima y el pronóstico del tiempo (pág. 24)

metropolitan area/área metropolitana Región que incluye una ciudad central y sus suburbios circundantes (pág. 135)

mica/mica Mineral de silicato que típicamente se parte en delgadas láminas brillantes (pág. 574)

Middle Ages/Edad Media El período de la historia europea que va aproximadamente desde 500 D.C. hasta 1500 D.C. (pág. 296)

migration/migración El movimiento de gente de un lugar a otro (pág. 79)

minifundia/**minifundios** En Latinoamérica, pequeñas granjas que producen alimento principalmente para el uso de la familia (pág. 238)

mistral/mistral Viento fuerte del norte que sopla desde los Alpes y que trae aire frío al sur de Francia (pág. 280)

mixed economy/economía mixta Una economía en la cual el gobierno apoya y regula la empresa tomando decisiones que afectan el mercado (pág. 89)

mixed farming/agricultura mixta Cultivo de varias clases de cosechas y ganado en la misma granja (pág. 317)

mixed forest/bosque mixto Tierras forestales con árboles de coníferas y deciduos (pág. 68)

mobility/mobilidad Poder moverse de un lugar a otro (pág. 137)

monopoly/monopolio Control total de un tipo de industria por una persona o una compañía (pág. 162)

monotheism/monoteísmo Creencia en un solo Dios (pág. 448)

monsoon/monzón En Asia, viento veraniego que trae aires cálidos y húmedos desde los océanos, aire seco y frío desde las tierras interiores en el invierno (págs. 579, 654)

moraine/morena Montones de deshechos rocosos que dejaron los glaciares al fundirse (pág. 42)

mosaic/mosaico Dibujo o diseño hecho con pequeños pedazos de piedra, vidrio, concha o azulejo de colores (pág. 228)

mosque/mezquita En Islam, una casa de oración pública (pág. 448)

movement/movimiento Movimiento actual de gente, bienes e ideas (pág. 22)

mural/mural Pintura en las paredes (pág. 228)

N

nationalism/nacionalismo Creencia en el derecho de cada persona a ser una nación independiente (pág. 449)

nationalities/nacionalidades Grandes y diversos grupos étnicos distintos dentro de un país (pág. 364)

nationalize/nacionalizar Colocar una compañía o industria bajo el control del gobierno (pág. 450)

Native American/Nativo Americano Los primeros inmigrantes de Norte América, quienes vinieron a la región probablemente de Asia hace cientos de años (pág. 134)

natural increase/incremento natural La tasa de crecimiento de una población; la diferencia entre la tasa ce crecimiento y la de mortalidad (pág. 76)

natural resource/recurso natural Sustancia de la tierra que no está hecha por la gente pero que ellos la pueden usar (pág. 91)

natural vegetation/vegetación natural Vida vegetal que crece en ciertas zonas si la gente no cambia el medio ambiente (pág. 66)

nirvana En Budismo, el máximo estado de paz y entendimiento que la gente trata de alcanzar (pág. 594)

North American Free Trade Agreement (NAFTA)/Tratado de Libre Comercio de Norteamérica (TLCNA) Tratado comercial hecho en 1994 entre Canadá, los Estados Unidos y México (pág. 240)

nuclear family/familia Grupo familiar constituido de esposo, esposa e hijos (pág. 529)

nuclear proliferation/proliferación nuclear El desarrollo expansivo de armas nucleares (pág. 623)

nuclear waste/desperdicio nuclear El producto secundario de producir energía nuclear (pág. 398)

O

oasis Pequeña área en el desierto donde hay agua y vegetación (págs. 67, 429)

oligarchy/oligarquía Sistema de gobierno en el cual un grupo pequeño tiene el poder (pág. 88)

oral tradition/tradición hablada Historias pasadas de generación en generación por palabra de boca en boca (pág. 528)

organic farming/agricultura orgánica El uso de sustancias naturales en lugar de fertilizantes y pesticidas para enriquecer la tierra y cultivar las cosechas (pág. 318)

ozone layer/capa de ozono Capa atmosférica con gases protectores que evitan que los rayos solares alcancen la superficie de la tierra (pág. 841)

P

paddy/arrozal Campos inundados en los que se cultiva el arroz (pág. 760)

pagoda/pagoda Un estilo de arquitectura encontrado más a menudo en los edificios tradicionales de Asia del este, marcados por techos de azulejo graciosamente curvados en estilo de torres (pág. 679)

pampas/pampa Llanos con pasto, sin árboles en América del Sur (pág. 196)

Parliament/parlamento En Canadá, la legislatura nacional conformada por el Senado y la Casa de los Comunes (pág. 145)

pastoralism/pastoreo críar y pastorear ganado (pág. 430)

patois/dialecto Dialectos que mezclan elementos de los lenguajes indígenas, europeos, africanos y asiáticos (pág. 213)

patriarch/patriarca El dirigente de una Iglesia Ortodoxa del Este (pág. 377)

patriotism/patriotismo Amor o devoción de una persona por su país (pág. 151)

perceptual region/región perceptual Una región definida por sentimientos e imágenes populares en vez de datos objetivos (pág. 21)

perestroika En Rusia, "reestructuración"; parte del plan de Gorbachev para reformar el gobierno soviético (pág. 371)

permafrost Capa de tierra por debajo de la superficie del suelo que está permanentemente congelada (págs. 68, 281, 349)

pesticide/pesticida Sustancia química que se usa para matar insectos, roedores y otras plagas (pág. 398)

petrochemical/petroquímico Producto químico derivado del petróleo o del gas natural (pág. 465)

phosphate/fosfato Mineral natural que contiene compuestos químicos que a menudo se usan en fertilizantes (pág. 426)

physical geography/geografía física El estudio de las características físicas de la Tierra (pág. 24)

pidgin English/Inglés corrompido Un dialecto que mezcla el inglés con los idiomas locales (pág. 813)

pipeline/tubería Una red grande de tuberías que pueden estar bajo tierra o sobre la tierra (pág. 162)

place/lugar Un espacio particular con significado físico y humano (pág. 21)

plate tectonics/placa tectónica Es el término científico que se usa para describir las actividades del movimiento continental y del flujo del magma, los cuales crean muchas de las características físicas de la Tierra (pág. 38)

poaching/cazar o pescar en veda La caza o pesca prohibida de animales protegidos (págs. 546, 619)

pogrom En la Rusia zarista, un ataque contra los judíos llevado a cabo por las tropas o los oficiales del gobierno (pág. 378)

polder/pólder Zona en Holanda, bajo el nivel del mar, de la cual se ha drenado el agua del mar para crear nuevas tierras de agricultura (pág. 272)

pollution/polución La existencia de sustancias sucias, impuras o venenosas en el aire, el agua o la tierra (pág. 94)

population density/densidad de población Número promedio de personas en una milla o kilómetro cuadrado (pág. 77)

population distribution/distribución demográfica El patrón de población en un país, un continente o en el mundo (pág. 77)

post-industrial/postindustrial Una economía con menos énfasis en la industria pesada y de manufactura y más énfasis en servicios y tecnología (pág. 158)

prairie/pradera Pastizal tierra adentro (págs. 68, 124)

precipitation/precipitación Humedad que cae a la tierra, como lluvia, nevisca, granizo o nieve (pág. 47)

prevailing wind/viento dominante Viento en una región que sopla en una dirección casi constantemente (pág. 62)

primate city/ciudad prócer Ciudad que domina la economía, cultura y el gobierno de un país y en la que la población está concentrada; usualmente la capital (págs. 217, 738)

privatization/privatización El cambio de propiedad de las compañías e industrias, pasando de ser propiedad del estado a ser propiedad privada (pág. 389)

prophet/profeta Persona de quien se cree que es un mensajero de Dios (pág. 448)

qanat Canales subterráneos que se usaban en los sistemas de acueductos en la antigua Persia (pág. 447)

quipu Cuerda con cordones anudados de varios largos y colores que usaban los incas para llevar sus registros financieros (pág. 222)

R

radioactive material/material radioactivo Material contaminado por residuos que provienen de la generación de energía nuclear (pág. 397)

rain shadow/sombra de lluvia Zona seca que se halla del lado sotavento de una cordillera (pág. 64)

raj Palabra hindú para imperio (pág. 595)

realism/realismo Estilo artístico que capta la vida cotidiana que se desarrolló en Europa a mediados de los años 1800 (pág. 305)

reforestation/reforestación La siembra de árboles jóvenes o semillas en terrenos donde los árboles han sido talados o destruidos (pág. 244)

Reformation/Reforma Movimiento religioso que comenzó en Alemania en los 1400 y que condujo al establecimiento de Iglesias Protestantes (pág. 297)

refugee/refugiado Persona que tiene que dejar su hogar y huir a otro lugar para estar a salvo (pág. 288)

regions/regiones Lugares unidos por características específicas (pág. 21)

reincarnated/reencarnado En la creencia Hindú, el renacer repetidas veces en distintas formas, hasta que uno ha vencido todos los deseos terrenales (pág. 593)

relative location/ubicación relativa La posición de un lugar en relación a otros lugares (pág. 20)

Renaissance/Renacimiento En Europa, un período de renovado interés por las enseñanzas y artes clásicas que comenzó cerca del 1300 y duró 300 años (pág. 296)

reparations/reparaciones Un pago por daños (pág. 298)

republic/república Forma de gobierno sin monarca, en el cual la gente elige a sus oficiales (pág. 142)

retooling/modificación Cambiar las fábricas antiguas para usarlas en industrias nuevas (pág. 161)

revolution/revolución En astronomía, el viaje de la Tierra alrededor del Sol que toma 365$\frac{1}{4}$ días (pág. 56)

rift valley/valle hundido Una grieta en la superficie terrestre creada por los movimientos de tierra (pág. 500)

romanticism/romanticismo Estilo artístico que enfati-zaba las emociones individuales. Se desarrolló en Europa en los últimos años de los 1700 y principios de los 1800 como una reacción a la industrialización (pág. 305)

Russification/Rusificación En la Rusia del siglo XIX, programa de gobierno que requería que todo el mundo en el imperio hablara ruso y se convirtiera al Cristianismo (pág. 370)

S

sadhu Un ermitaño hindú o un hombre santo (pág. 602)

samurai/samurai En el Japón medieval, una clase de soldados profesionales quienes se regían por un código estricto de honor personal y lealtad a un noble (pág. 670)

sanitation/sanidad Eliminación de productos de desperdicio (pág. 516)

satellite/satélite Un país controlado por otro, como los países de Europa del este controlados por la Unión Soviética a finales de la Segunda Guerra Mundial (pág. 371)

savanna/sabana Un pastizal tropical que contiene árboles dispersos (pág. 507)

sedentary farming/agricultura sedentaria Agricultura que toma lugar en asentamientos permanentes (pág. 538)

serf/siervo Obrero de la propiedad de un noble y obligado a permanecer en la tierra donde trabajaba (pág. 369)

service center/centro de servicio Ubicación de negocios conveniente para los habitantes del campo (pág. 518)

service industry/industria de servicios Negocios que proveen servicios, en vez de producir bienes (pág. 238)

shamanism/shamanismo Creencia en un líder que se puede comunicar con los espíritus (pág. 675)

shantytowns/barrios Comunidades improvisadas a las orillas de las ciudades (pág. 244)

shifting cultivation/rotación de cultivos Deforestar para plantar campos por unos cuantos años y abandonarlos (pág. 770)

shifting farming/cultivo migratorio Método en el cual los agricultores se mudan después de unos cuantos años para hallar mejor tierra (pág. 538)

shogun/shogún En el Japón medieval, un gobernante militar del país (pág. 670)

sickle/hoz Cuchillo grande y curvo con un mango, usado para cortar pasto o granos altos (pág. 760)

sirocco/siroco Viento caliente del desierto que sopla aire y polvo desde el África del Norte hasta la costa mediterránea de Europa (págs. 280-281)

slash-and-burn farming/agricultura de corte y quema Método tradicional de cultivo en el que todos los árboles y plantas en el área se cortan y se queman para añadir nutrientes al suelo (pág. 244)

smog/smog Neblina irritante causada por la interacción de la radiación solar ultravioleta con humos químicos del escape de los automóviles y otras fuentes de contaminación (págs. 69, 167)

socialism/socialismo Filosofía política en la que el gobierno era propietario de los medios de producción (págs. 370)

socialist realism/realismo socialista En la Unión Soviética, estilo realista de arte y literatura que glorificaba los ideales y las metas soviéticas (pág. 380)

socioeconomic status/posición socioeconómica Nivel de ingresos y educación (pág. 150)

solstice/solsticio Uno de dos días (el 21 de junio y el 22 de diciembre) en que los rayos del Sol dan directamente en el Trópico de Cáncer o el Trópico de Capricornio, para marcar el principio del verano o el invierno (pág. 57)

sovereignty/soberanía Autogobierno (pág. 365)

sovkhoz En la Unión Soviética, una enorme granja del estado y que el estado mismo opera (pág. 390)

sphere of influence/esfera de influencia Zona del país en la que una potencia extranjera tiene control político o económico (pág. 743)

spreading/extensión Un proceso por el cual se crea nueva tierra cuando las plataformas marinas se separan y el magma fluye hacia arriba entre las plataformas (pág. 40)

state farm/granja estatal Bajo el comunismo, una granja de propiedad del estado dirigida por oficiales del gobierno (pág. 317)

station/estación Término australiano para un rancho o granja grande en áreas remotas (pág. 834)

steppe/estepa Vastas llanuras de pastizales de Eurasia; también regiones en otros lugares con climas semiáridos similares (pág. 355)

Strine Inglés coloquial que se habla en Australia (pág. 813)

stupa/stupa Estructura en forma de cúpula que sirve de santuario budista (pág. 604)

subcontinent/subcontinente Gran área de tierra que forma parte de un continente pero es diferente, como la India (pág. 569)

subduction/subducción Proceso por el que la corteza oceánica se hunde bajo la continental (pág. 39)

subsistence crop/cultivo de subsistencia Un cultivo que sirve principalmente para alimentar a la familia del agricultor (pág. 760)

subsistence farming/agricultura de subsistencia Agricultura tradicional cuya meta es producir lo suficiente para que una familia o una aldea coma y sobreviva (págs. 538, 826)

suburbs/suburbios Comunidades en las afueras y que circundan una ciudad central (pág. 135)

Sunbelt/Franja del Sol Parte sur de los Estados Unidos, denominada así debido a su clima (pág. 135)

supercells/superceldas Tormenta de rayos y truenos violenta que puede producir tornados (pág. 124)

sustainable development/desarrollo sostenido
Crecimiento tecnológico y económico que no agota los recursos humanos y naturales de un área dada (págs. 242, 619)

syncretism/sincretismo Una mezcla de creencias y prácticas de diferentes religiones en una fe (pág. 228)

taiga Término ruso para un vasto bosque que cubre gran parte de Rusia y Siberia (pág. 353)

tariff/tarifa Un impuesto sobre bienes importados o exportados (pág. 163)

temperature/temperatura Una medida de cuán caliente o cuán frío está algo, generalmente se mide en grados con una escala fija, como Fahrenheit o Centígrados (pág. 56)

tierra caliente La zona más baja de los climas de montaña de Latinoamérica (pág. 203)

tierra fría La zona de altitud más alta de los climas de montaña de Latinoamérica (pág. 203)

tierra templada La zona de altitud media de los climas de montaña de Latinoamérica (pág. 203)

timberline/límite de la vegetación selvática Elevación por encima de la cual hace demasiado frío para que crezcan los árboles (págs. 124, 279)

trade deficit/déficit comercial Gastar más dinero en importaciones que lo que se gana en exportaciones (págs. 163, 689)

trade surplus/superávit comercial Ganar más dinero por exportaciones que lo que se gasta en importaciones (págs. 163, 689)

traditional economy/economía tradicional Sistema en que las costumbres determinan las actividades económicas; existe en pocos lugares (pág. 89)

tributary/afluente Pequeños ríos y arroyos que se alimentan de los ríos más grandes (pág. 118)

trust territory/territorio en fideicomiso Región, que después de la Segunda Guerra Mundial fue colocada temporáneamente por las Naciones Unidas bajo el control político y económico de otra nación (pág. 819)

tsunami Término japonés usado para una ola de mar enorme causada por un maremoto (pág. 646)

tundra Vastas llanuras sin árboles en climas fríos del norte, caracterizadas por la capa del subsuelo conge-lada y pequeñas plantas como musgos y arbustos (pág. 352)

typhoon/tifón Un ciclón que se forma en el Océano Pacífico, usualmente al final del verano (págs. 655, 768, 802)

Underground Railroad/Ferrocarril subterráneo Una red informal de refugios, en los Estados Unidos, que ayudó a miles de esclavos a escapar hacia la libertad (pág. 143)

unitary system/sistema unitario Le da todos los poderes clave al gobierno nacional o central (pág. 87)

universal suffrage/sufragio universal Derechos de igualdad de votación para todos los adultos residentes de una nación (pág. 524)

urbanization/urbanización El movimiento de personas de las áreas rurales a las ciudades (págs. 135, 216, 290, 517, 737)

viceroy/virrey Representante del monarca español asignado para hacer cumplir las leyes en las colonias americanas (pág. 222)

W

wadi En el desierto, cauce seco excepto durante las lluvias fuertes (pág. 424)

wat En el Asia del Sudeste, un templo (pág. 750)

water cycle/ciclo de agua Movimiento regular del agua desde el océano hasta el aire y el suelo y de vuelta al océano (pág. 47)

wattle/zarzo Árboles de acacia; los primeros colonos de Australia entretejían los zarzos jóvenes para construir sus casas (pág. 801)

weather/tiempo Condición de la atmósfera en un lugar durante un período de tiempo corto (pág. 55)

weathering/erosión Procesos químicos o físicos, como congelación, que desbaratan las rocas (pág. 42)

welfare state/estado benefactor Nación en la que el gobierno asume la responsabilidad principal por el bienestar de la gente en cuanto a salud y educación (pág. 306)

windward/barlovento Con la cara hacia la dirección desde donde el viento está soplando (pág. 64)

World Trade Organization/Organización Mundial del Comercio Organismo internacional que supervisa acuerdos comerciales y resuelve disputas comerciales entre países (pág. 690)

Z

ziggurat/zigurat En la antigua Mesopotamia, gran templo escalonado hecho de ladrillos de arcilla (pág. 454)

Index

c = chart
d = diagram
g = graph

m = map
p = photo
ptg = painting

A

Aberdeen, Scotland, *p 258*
Abidjan, Côte d'Ivoire, *p 480–81*, 518
Aboh, Nigeria, 503
Aborigines: Ainu, 663; in Australia, 781, *p 782*, 811–12, 817–19, 825; in Taiwan, 662–63; Uluru and, *p 781*; use of eucalyptus by, 790
absolute location, 3, 9, 14, 20
Accra, Ghana, 518
accretion, 40, *d 40*
acid deposition, 321
acid rain, 95, 166–67, *m 166*, 321, 326–27, 398, 694
Addis Ababa, Ethiopia, 518
Adriatic Sea, 274, 292
Aegean Sea, 274, 422, 447
Afar people, *p 484*
Afghanistan, *c 414, m451;* agriculture in, 464; government in, 452; Hindu Kush mountains, *p 407;* in Islamic Women's Games, 457; Khyber Pass and, 570; population of, 441, 443; standard of living in, 456; war against terrorism in , 164, 451–52
Africa: birthrate in, 76; as developing country, 93; early kingdoms in, *m 520;* ethnic groups, colonial rule, and conflict, *m 523;* hunger in, *m 544;* independent countries in, *m 522;* Sinai Peninsula and, 36; slave trade in, 521–22, *m 521;* tropical savannas in, 67. *See also* Africa south of the Sahara; North Africa, Central Asia, Southwest Asia
Africa south of the Sahara, *m 486, m 487, m 501;* agriculture in, 537–39, *g 538;* arts in, 527–29; climate regions in, 505–13, *m 506;* communications in, 541–42; conflict in, 544–45; country profiles, *c 490–94;* culture in, 525–29; desertification in, 544; economic activity, *m 489;* ecotourism in, 546–47; education in, 527; endangered animals in, 546; European colonization in, 521–23; fishing in, 539–40; Great Rift Valley, 500; highlands in, 500; history of, 519–24; industrialization in, 540–41; ivory trade in, 548–49; lakes in, 502; landforms in, 499–01; land use in, 545–47; languages in, 525–26; lifestyles in, 529; logging in, 539; mining resources in, 540; mountains in, 500; natural resources in, 504; physical barriers in, 503; plateaus in, 500; population density, *m 488;* population patterns in, 515–18; rain forests in, 545–46; religions in, 526–27, *g 526;* river basins in, 503; hunger in, 543–45; transportation in, 541; urbanization in, 517; vegetation in, 505–13, *m 507;* water systems in, 500, 502–03
Agra, India, *p 558–59*, 604
Agricultural Revolution, 84
agriculture: campesinos, 238; canal irrigation, 447; cash crops, 238, 538, 612–13, 760; cereals, 431; collective farms in, 317; commercial farming, 538; communes, 686;

conservation farming, 539; cooperatives, 317, 686; desertification and, 539; domestication, 446; dry farming, 321; genetically modified food, 317; graziers, 834; green revolution, 613, 624–25; high-yield variety (HYV) seeds, 625; kolkhozes, 390; livestock, 238; mixed farming, 317; organic farming, 318; overgrazing and, 539; rice and soy, 654, 760; Russian, *p 391;* sedentary farming, 538; shifting cultivation, 770; shifting farming, 538; slash-and-burn farming, 244, 538, 620, 770; soil erosion and, 539; sovkhozes, 390; state farms in, 317; stations, 834; subsistence crop, 760; subsistence farming, 538, 611–12, 826, 834; subtropical, 464; in tropical rain forest, 506. *See also specific regions*
AIDS (acquired immunodeficiency syndrome), 516, 605
Ainu, 663
air pollution, 95, 322, 398; in Indonesia, *p 770*
Alaska: Inuit village in, 105; purchase from Russia, 142; severe earthquake in, 40
Alaska Range, 116
Albania, *c 264*
Alexander II (Czar), 370
Alexander III (Czar), 374
Alexandria, Egypt, *p 453*
Algeria, *c 414, 442, 466, 468;* desert art in, *p 427*
Algerian Sahara, *p 406–07*
alluvial plain, 572
alluvial soil, 423
Alps: climate in, 279; earthquakes in, 320; location of, 275; Rhine River through, 276; southern European climate and, 280
al-Qaeda, 164
Altay Mountains, 647
altiplano, 194
Amazon Basin, 66, 197, 241
Amazon rain forest, 200–01, 242–44; clearing field in, *p 249*
Amazon River, *p 193*, 197, 241
Amnok River, 649
Amritsar, India, 604
Amu Darya River, 447, 470
Amur River, 349, 375
Anatolian Peninsula, 422
Anatolian Plateau, 425
Andes, 194, 196, *p 241;* peaks of, *p 179*
Andorra, *c 264*
Angkor Wat, *p 741*
Angola, *c 490,* 503, 504, 540
animals: African elephants, 548–49; endangered species, 546, 549; endemic species, 728; in farming, 612; giant panda, 652; introduced species, 839; marsupials, 839; poaching of, 546, 619; rain forest, 201; wolves, 324
Annam Cordillera, 722
Annapurna Range, *p 573, p 618*
Antarctica, 35, 42, *m 784, m 785, m 795;* Byrd Expedition to, 822–23, *p 822–23;* climate regions in, *m 800,* 803; communications in, 837; economic activity in, *m 787;* expeditions to, 821–23; human settlement in, 814; ice cap in, 48; melting ice in, 842–43; mining in, 834–35; national claims in, *m 835;* natural resources in, 838–41; ozone layer over, 841; penguins in, *p 778–79;* population density in, *m 786;*

research stations in, 798, *m 835;* Ross Ice Shelf in, 843; scientific research in, *p 783;* vegetation in, *m 801,* 803; view from under ice in, *p 833;* as white plateau, 798; winter ice in, *p 799*
Antarctic Circle, 60
Antarctic Peninsula, 798, 814
Antarctic Plateau, 803
Antarctic Treaty, 821
anthrax, 164
Antigua, *c 186*
Anti-Taurus Mountains, 475
Antwerp, Belgium, 318
Aorangi, 797
apartheid, 524
Apennine Mountains, 320
Apennine Peninsula, 272, 274
Appalachian Mountains, 116
aquaculture, 695–96
aquifer, 49, 470
Arabian Desert, 428
Arabian Peninsula, 421–22, 424, 440
Arabian Sea, 556, 569, 573
Arabic language, 440
Arabs, 440, 441, 450–51
Arafat, Yasir, *p 450*
Arakan Yoma Range, 722
Aral Sea, 422, 473; shrinking, *m 473*
archipelago, 646, 720
architecture: Angkor Wat, *p 741;* Badshahi Mosque, *p 592;* Eiffel Tower, *p 318;* European influences, 268–69, *p 268–69;* Gothic style, 268; Islamic, 455; Notre Dame de Paris, 296; pagoda, 679; Queen Anne style, 269; in Southeast Asia, 750–51; stupas, 603–04; Taj Mahal, 604
Arctic Circle, 60, 68, 278, 352
Arctic Ocean, *p 46,* 47, 349, 350
Argentina, *c 186;* climate regions in, 201, *g 202;* hydroelectric power in, 197; livestock in, 238; lowlands and plains in, 196; population density in, 214
Arizona: desert climate in, 56; lightning in, *p 56*
Armenia, *c 414;* Christianity in, 408, 454; ethnic groups in, 441; leisure time in, 457
Armenians, 441
art: East Asian, 648, 678–79; Latin American, 228–29; mosaics, 228; murals, 228; Southeast Asian, 750–52. *See also entries for culture regions*
Aryans, 593
Asia: birthrate in, 76; as continent, 35; developing countries in, 93; tropical savannas in, 67. *See also* East Asia; South Asia; Southeast Asia
Asian Development Bank (ADB), 763
Asia-Pacific Economic Cooperation Group (APEC), 393, 689
Asir Mountains, 424
Asmara, Eritrea, *p 518*
Assam, India, 572
Association of Southeast Asian Nations (ASEAN), 763
asteroids, 35
Aswan High Dam, 27, 409, 423, 472, *p 472*
Atacama Desert, *p 201,* 202
Atatürk Dam, 474–75
atheism, 376
Athens, Greece, 295; Acropolis in, 321; Parthenon in, 305

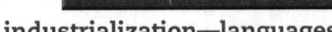

N